THE EMC MASTERPIECE SERIES

LITERATURE AND THE LANGUAGE ARTS

GRADES 9–12

A truly integrated literature
and language arts program

THE EMC MASTERPIECE SERIES
LITERATURE AND THE LANGUAGE ARTS

- Integrates literature and language arts more thoroughly than any other series.

- Contains the most extensive collection of classic literary works available in any series today, as well as engaging contemporary selections.

- Emphasizes reader response, relating literature to student experiences while enabling the teacher to guide responses to ensure cultural transmission.

- Offers the most comprehensive portfolio assessment program available.

- Includes abundant teacher resources: Essential Skills Practice Books in five language arts subject areas; Assessment Portfolio; Reader's Guides and Activity Books; Transparencies; and exciting, motivational multimedia components such as Audiocassettes, a Videocassette, Computer Software, a Video Laser Disc, and two CD-ROM Programs.

The EMC Masterpiece Series, LITERATURE AND THE LANGUAGE ARTS contains the most comprehensive collection of classic literary works available in any series today, as well as current multicultural selections, to captivate your students. In addition, this series thoroughly models the complete range of literary types and genres: poetry, fiction, nonfiction, drama, myth, fairy tale, fable, parable, legend, tall tale, and folk song.

Global Representation of Authors

- Gabriela Mistral (Chile) "Dusk"
- Kamala Markandaya (India) from *Nectar in a Sieve*
- Maya Angelou (United States) "On the Pulse of Morning"
- Chinua Achebe (Nigeria) *Things Fall Apart*
- Naguib Mahfouz (Egypt) "The Happy Man"
- Le Ly Hayslip (Vietnam) from *When Heaven and Earth Changed Places*

Strong Representation of Culturally Diverse Authors

The EMC Masterpiece Series contains an unequaled representation of works by authors from various cultural backgrounds. The series provides a well-rounded view of literary activity in cultural contexts around the corner and around the world.

Flexible Organization

The EMC Masterpiece Series provides a flexible organization allowing varied approaches to the literature, so teachers can readily adapt the materials to their individual teaching styles and to their students' needs.

Experiencing Literature and *Understanding Literature*
Grades 9 and 10

These levels are organized into separate sections presenting genres and techniques, themes, and modes (science fiction, fantasy, adventure, romance, mystery, and detective fiction). No other series covers all three in a single volume.

The American Tradition and *The British Tradition*
Grades 11 and 12

These levels have a chronological organization. Additional materials in the Annotated Teacher's Editions facilitate thematic, skill, and genre approaches. Each text begins with a high-interest, thorough review of basic literary types and techniques.

About the Author gives background on the author of the selection.

About the Selection provides a background of when and why the selection was written.

PREREADING

"The Conversion of King Edwin"
from *Ecclesiastical History of the English People*
by Saint Bede the Venerable

ABOUT THE AUTHOR

A page from the Grimbald Gospels. British Library, MS Add. 34890 fol. IOV. Courtesy of the British Library

Saint Bede the Venerable (AD 672– or 673–735) was born in Jarrow, in the kingdom of Northumbria. He entered the Monastery of St. Peter in nearby Wearmouth at the age of seven. At nineteen, he was ordained a deacon; at thirty, a priest. Like other monastics of his time, Bede wrote in Latin. He traveled very little, but his fame spread throughout Europe due to his writings on subjects as varied as history, poetry, grammar, mathematics, science, the scriptures, and lives of the saints. Bede's histories make fascinating reading not only for the light that they shed on the distant Anglo-Saxon past but also for their engaging accounts of miraculous and legendary events. In his histories, Bede introduced the practice of dating events from the birth of Christ (i.e., from AD 0, where AD is an abbreviation for the Latin *Anno Domini*, meaning "the year of our Lord"). This method of dating was adopted throughout Europe and is still in use today. Bede was canonized (made a saint of the Roman Catholic Church) in 1899, eleven hundred years after his death.

ABOUT THE SELECTION

Most notable among Bede's works is the *Historia ecclesiastica gentis Anglorum*, or *Ecclesiastical History of the English People*. Bede's five-book Latin history of the Church in England covers the period from Caesar's invasion of Britain (55–54 BC) to his own time (the history was finished around AD 731). King Alfred considered the book important enough to have it translated into Old English, the language of the common people. **"The Conversion of King Edwin"** comes from *Book II* of Bede's history and relates the process by which Christian missionaries converted the Anglo-Saxon kings. The selection shows the dramatic contrast between the Anglo-Saxons' grim view of the afterlife and the positive alternative offered by the missionaries. The pre-Christian, or pagan, Anglo-Saxons believed that a warrior who died bravely in battle would go after death to a land reserved for heroes, Valhalla. For others, the future after death was uncertain. The final paragraph of the selection, which compares the time before, during, and after life to the flight of a sparrow, is one of the most famous in all of English literature.

76 UNIT TWO / THE ANGLO-SAXON PERIOD

The British Museum

READER'S JOURNAL
Have you ever changed your mind about something important? Do you find change to be difficult or easy? Freewrite about change in your journal. You might write about personal change or about change that has occurred in your country or in your community.

RESEARCH SKILLS
Read the Language Arts Survey, 4.22, "Using the Card Catalog." Then use the card catalog in a library to find books with information about Saint Bede the Venerable. For each book, list the title, the author's name, the year of publication, the call number, and the kind of information given.

"The Conversion of King Edwin"
FROM *Ecclesiastical History of the English People*

SAINT BEDE THE VENERABLE

At this time the nation of the Northumbrians, that is, the nation of the Angles that live on the north side of the river Humber, with their king, Edwin, received the faith through the preaching of Paulinus.[1] This Edwin, as a reward of his receiving the faith, and as an earnest of his share in the heavenly kingdom, received an increase of that which he enjoyed on earth, for he reduced under his dominion all the borders of Britain that were provinces either of the aforesaid nation, or of the Britons, a thing which no British king had ever done before. . . .

For some time he delayed to receive the word of God at the preaching of Paulinus, and used to sit several hours alone, and seriously to ponder with himself what he was to do, and what religion he was to follow. Then the man of God came to him, laid his right hand on his head, and asked whether he knew that sign.[2] The king in a trembling condition, was ready to fall down at his feet, but he raised him up, and in a familiar manner said to him, "Behold, by the help of God you have escaped the hands of the enemies whom you feared. Behold you have of His gift obtained the kingdom which you desired. Take heed not to delay that which you promised to perform; embrace the faith, and keep the precepts of Him who, delivering you from temporal adversity, has raised you to the honor of

According to Bede, what reward does Edwin receive for converting to Christianity?

---

1. **Paulinus.** Pope Gregory I sent Paulinus as a missionary to Northumbria in AD 601.
2. **that sign.** The laying on of hands is a ceremony for transmitting spiritual grace to the recipient.

WORDS FOR EVERYDAY USE: ec • cle • si • as • ti • cal (e klē´ zē as˝ ti kal) *adj.*, having to do with the church

tem • po • ral (tem´ pə ral) *adj.*, lasting only for a time, limited; of this world, not spiritual

ad • ver • si • ty (ad ver´ sə tē) *n.*, misfortune, trouble

"THE CONVERSION OF KING EDWIN" 77

Reader's Journal activities relate the literature to students' feelings and experiences.

Language Arts Skills activities referenced at the beginning of each selection are keyed to the Language Arts Survey. No other literature program has such strong integration of literature and language arts skills.

Words for Everyday Use sections provide the definitions for vocabulary that is underlined in the selection.

Responding to the Selection activities relate the literature to students' lives and experiences to spark their interest and to stimulate classroom discussion.

The unique pedagogical design of this series virtually guarantees close reading. The novel organization of the **Reviewing the Selection** questions ensures that interpretations of the literature will be based on evidence from the selections.

The **Recalling** questions ask about facts in the selection. Paired with each Recalling question is an **Interpreting** question that uses these facts as a basis for critical analysis and interpretation. **Synthesizing** questions pull together particular parts of the analysis just conducted, enabling students to arrive at a general understanding of each piece. This is the only series that keys all of its Interpreting questions to facts in the selections.

---

a temporal kingdom; and if, from this time forward, you shall be obedient to His will, which through me He signifies to you, He will not only deliver you from the everlasting torments of the wicked, but also make you partaker with Him of His eternal kingdom in Heaven."

The king, hearing these words, answered, that he was both willing and bound to receive the faith which he taught; but that he would confer about it with his principal friends and counselors, to the end that if they also were of his opinion, they might all together be cleansed in Christ the Fountain of Life. Paulinus consenting, the king did as he said; for, holding a council with the wise men,[1] he asked of every one in particular what he thought of the new doctrine, and the new worship that was preached. To which the chief of his own priests, Coifi, immediately answered, "O king, consider what this is which is now preached to us; for I verily declare to you, that the religion which we have hitherto professed has, as far as I can learn, no virtue in it. For none of your people has applied himself more diligently to the worship of our gods than I; and yet there are many who receive greater favors from you, and are more preferred than I, and are more prosperous in all their undertakings. Now if the gods were good for any thing, they would rather forward me, who have

To what does the wise counselor compare life as the Anglo-Saxons knew it?

Why does the king's chief priest reject the old gods?

been more careful to serve them. It remains, therefore, that if upon examination you find those new doctrines, which are now preached to us, better and more efficacious, we immediately receive them without any delay."

Another of the king's chief men, approving of his words and exhortations, presently added: "The present life of man, O king, seems to me, in comparison to that time which is unknown to us, like to the swift flight of a sparrow through the room wherein you sit at supper in winter, with your commanders and ministers, and a good fire in the midst, whilst the storms of rain and snow prevail abroad; the sparrow, flying in at one door, and immediately out at another, whilst he is within, is safe from the wintry storm; but after a short space of fair weather, he immediately vanishes out of your sight, into the dark winter from which he had emerged. So this life of man appears for a short space, but of what went before, or what is to follow, we are utterly ignorant. If, therefore, this new doctrine contains something more certain, it seems justly to deserve to be followed." The other elders and king's counselors, by Divine inspiration, spoke to the same effect.

---

1. **wise men.** These wise men are the Anglo-Saxon *Witenagemot*, or council of elders. From the Old English *witen*, "to know," comes our modern word *wit*.

WORDS FOR EVERYDAY USE: sig • ni • fy (sig´ na fī˝) *vt.*, show by means of words or a sign

dil • i • gent • ly (dil´ ə jent lē) *adv.*, with great care and attention

ef • fi • ca • cious (ef´ i kā˝ shəs) *adj.*, effective, producing the desired result

78 UNIT TWO / THE ANGLO-SAXON PERIOD

Responding to the Selection

Do the arguments advanced by Edwin's counselors seem reasonable to you? Do you feel that Edwin had reason to forsake his old beliefs and embrace these new ones? Why, or why not? Answer these questions in your journal.

Reviewing the Selection

RECALLING

1. Who is Paulinus? What does he ask of King Edwin? What does Paulinus promise?

2. With whom does King Edwin meet?

3. Who is Coifi? What does he think of the old religion?

4. To what does the king's advisor compare the swift flight of a sparrow?

INTERPRETING

5. Why does Paulinus believe Edwin has a responsibility to "embrace the faith"?

6. Why does King Edwin hold a meeting?

7. What reason does Coifi give for forsaking the old religion?

8. What view of life and of the afterlife is implicit in the counselor's story of the sparrow?

SYNTHESIZING

9. In what ways does the new religion differ from the old religion? What makes the new religion appealing to the elders and to the king's counselors?

10. According to King Edwin's advisors, what is the purpose of religion? In what ways are their views similar to or different from your own?

Understanding Literature (Questions for Discussion)

1. **Narration. Narration**, one of the modes of writing, tells a story. Normally, stories are told by beginning with what happens first and continuing chronologically (through time) toward what happens last. Is Bede's story of Edwin's conversion told chronologically? Where does Bede deviate from a strict chronological ordering? Why do you think he does this? Is the technique effective? Can you think of a story that you have told nonchronologically? Why did you tell it so?

"THE CONVERSION OF KING EDWIN" 79

Guided Reading Questions for each selection point out key elements and encourage critical response reading. This series alone provides such a tool for every selection.

Understanding Literature questions provide instruction in literary movements, types, and techniques.

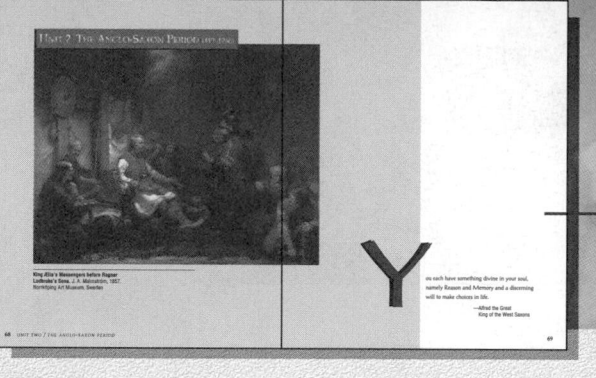

■ **Unit Openers** feature fine art from the period covered in the unit.

■ Creative, literature-based **Responding in Writing** activities provide opportunities for students to apply the process of writing and develop their writing skills.

■ **Language Labs** develop students' language arts skills in the context of literary study. Additional practice can be found in the Essential Skills Practice Books.

■ The hands-on **Projects** section allows students to perform multimodel, cross-curricular exercises based on the literature, further connecting it to students' actual lives.

The following text appears in the textbook spread shown:

2. **Allegory.** An **allegory** is a work in which each element **symbolizes**, or represents, something else. The last paragraph of the selection contains an allegory comparing human life to the flight of a sparrow. To understand the allegory you need to determine what the characters and objects in the story symbolize. The story speaks of a sparrow, a dining room with a door, supper, winter storms, commanders and ministers, a fire, and our sight. What do these elements in the story symbolize?

3. **Purpose or Aim.** A writer's **aim** is the primary **purpose** that his or her work is meant to achieve. One purpose of "The Conversion of King Edwin" is to teach a lesson. What lesson does the selection teach? From reading the selection, can you tell whether Bede was a Christian or a pagan? How can you tell? How might the purpose be different if Bede were of a different religion?

Responding in Writing

1. **An Allegory.** Think of the story of the sparrow flying through the warm room and then out into the cold. Bede presents this story as an allegory for the life of an individual. An **allegory** is a story that seems simple but has another meaning altogether. What might be an allegory for working hard to accomplish a difficult task—perhaps running a marathon or climbing a tall mountain? Choose one of the following topics or one of your own. Then write an allegory to describe it.

Possible topics:
• saying goodbye to a friend
• leaving home to go to college
• studying for an important test

2. **A Persuasive Paragraph.** In order to convert King Edwin and his counsel, the missionary Paulinus had to be quite persuasive. What arguments did he use to convince them? How might you convince someone of something you feel strongly about? Maybe you have read a great book, and you are trying to convince a friend to read it. Maybe you are trying to change someone's mind about a political issue. Choose a topic for a persuasive paragraph. In a sentence, describe your position or stand on the topic. Then give two or three arguments to support your position.

Language Lab

Correcting Run-ons. Read the Language Arts Survey, 2.62, "Correcting Run-ons." Then revise the sentences below by changing punctuation and capitalization and adding words, as necessary.

1. Bede's history of Britain was not the first, it was partly based on *On the Fall of Britain*, written by Gildas, a Welshman, in AD 550.

2. According to stories told by early Welsh historians, one of the soldiers who fought against the Anglo-Saxons was named Arthur such stories gave rise to legends about King Arthur and the knights of the round table.

3. The early Germanic peoples, including the Anglo-Saxons, used alphabetic characters called *runes* to write inscriptions on stones, the runic alphabet is known as *futhark*.

4. The treasure of Sutton Hoo was found in 1939, at Sutton Hoo a seventh-century Anglo-Saxon king had been buried with a large number of jewels, coins, weapons, and tools he was entombed in a ninety-foot-long ship that had been hauled to the top of a one-hundred-foot-high cliff.

5. Our knowledge of the Anglo-Saxons comes from many sources these sources include inscriptions, histories, literature, and archeological finds like Sutton Hoo.

PROJECTS

1. **Improvisation.** Take a few moments to think about what it was like to be one of King Edwin's counselors. Try to imagine other meetings that might have taken place. Then form groups of four to six students. Take turns acting out one of the scenes listed below, with one person playing King Edwin and the others playing the counselors. Use your imagination as you think about the issue that is up for discussion.

• Discuss adding other lands to the kingdom. The group can discuss whether this will happen as a result of peaceful negotiation or of battle.

• Discuss a dispute between two earls over the possession of a sword taken from an enemy warrior. Decide who should receive the sword and why.

2. **Community Involvement.** When someone enters a community and tries to make change, sometimes the change is positive, and sometimes the change is negative. In either case, asking people to think in new ways is rarely easy. How might you and your classmates try to make positive change in your community? You might want to change how people feel about litter and the environment, or you might want to make people more excited about becoming involved in town issues or school events. Work with other students to organize a convincing campaign.

Reader Response Emphasis
The EMC Masterpiece Series motivates students through high-interest affective and cognitive activities that relate literature to students' experiences, followed by teacher-directed activities to ensure cultural transmission.

Reader Response Activities:
■ Reader's Journal
■ Guided Reading Questions
■ Responding to the Selection

Teacher-Directed Activities:
■ Reviewing the Selection
■ Responding in Writing
■ Understanding Literature

Other Student Textbook Features:

■ **Historical Introductions** in Grade 11, *The American Tradition*, and Grade 12, *The British Tradition*, provide thorough, stimulating discussions of historical figures and events, literary and artistic movements, genre and techniques, and major historical and literary figures.

■ **Unit Reviews** reinforce major concepts from the unit and provide Synthesizing questions for writing, discussion, and research.

■ **Multicultural Extensions** allow for comparative study of British and world literature.

■ **Additional Readings** at the ends of units allow students to read extra selections from the authors. No other series offers this feature!

■ The **Handbook of Literary Terms** contains twice as many terms as any other textbook program to promote students' understanding of literary movements, types, and techniques.

LANGUAGE ARTS SURVEY

Stimulating, literature-based activities in this series cover the full range of language arts skills:

- Emotional and critical responses to literature

- The process of writing

- Grammar, usage, mechanics, spelling, and vocabulary

- Varieties of English

- Speaking and listening

- Test-taking

- Critical thinking

- Study and research

- Applied English/ Tech prep

- The **Essential Skills: Writing** section surveys the entire process of writing.

- The **Essential Skills: Language** section surveys key concepts in grammar, usage, mechanics, spelling, vocabulary development, and language variety. Grammar usage and mechanics instruction focuses on editing and proofreading applications.

ESSENTIAL SKILLS:
Writing

INTRODUCTION TO WRITING

Students sometimes think of writing as a mysterious talent that some people are born with and others aren't. That just isn't so. The ability to write is learned through practice and through reading. If you keep writing, as much as you can, as often as you can, eventually you, too, will be one of those mysteriously talented people who can make written words do wonders.

1.1 THE PROCESS OF WRITING

No two people write exactly alike. Some people get everything down on paper quickly and in rough form. Then they rewrite, over and over, until they get it right. Other people work slowly, refining their ideas and expression as they go.

Despite the differences among writers, for purposes of instruction the writing process can be conveniently divided into six stages:

SIX STAGES IN THE PROCESS OF WRITING	
1. Prewriting	Choose a topic, audience, purpose, and form. Then gather ideas and organize these in a reasonable way.
2. Drafting	Get your ideas down on paper in rough form without worrying about perfecting spelling, grammar, usage, and mechanics.
3. Peer and Self-Evaluation	Study your draft by yourself or with one or more of your peers to find ways to improve it.
4. Revising	Revise your draft to improve its content, organization, and style.
5. Proofreading	Check your revised draft for errors in spelling, grammar, usage, and mechanics (including punctuation and capitalization). Then prepare a final copy in an appropriate manuscript form and proofread again.
6. Publishing and Presenting	Share your work with an audience.

▶ ▶ ▶ ACTIVITY 1.1

Take some time to examine your past experiences as a writer. On a sheet of paper or in your journal, answer the following questions:

1. Do you enjoy writing? Do you think of yourself as a good writer? Are there any writers—famous or not—whose work you admire? What good and bad experiences have you had as a writer? What are your strengths and weaknesses as a writer?

2. What kind of writing do you most enjoy doing? (Consult the list of Forms of Writing on page 1077.) Do you like writing poems, stories, humorous pieces, or reports? Why do you enjoy this kind of writing? What kinds of writing would you like to learn more about? What kinds of writing would you like to master?

3. Many writers are particular about the tools they use. What writing materials do you prefer? Do you like writing in a spiral notebook? on blank pages in a record book? on loose-leaf pages in a ring binder? on a typewriter or computer? with a pencil or a felt-tip pen?

4. When you have written in the past, did you devote a lot of time to prewriting? What sorts of prewriting activities did you do? Which of these activities were most helpful?

5. Are you the kind of writer who works slowly, perfecting each part as you go, or do you prefer to get a lot of material onto the page and then rework it?

6. In what stages of the writing process do you have the most trouble?

7. How do you feel about having other people read or listen to your writing? What can other people, including your classmates and your teacher, do to help you become a better writer?

1.2 KEEPING A WRITER'S JOURNAL

Think of a **writer's journal** as a storehouse of ideas for use in later writing. Keep your journal in a spiral notebook, a loose-leaf binder, a composition book, a scrapbook, or a bound record book of the kind sold in stationery stores. You'll get more out of a journal if you keep it separate from your other notebooks and write in it every day. The following ideas for journal entries will help you to get started.

IDEAS FOR JOURNAL ENTRIES	
The Journal as Diary	Record the observations and experiences from your daily life. Explore your feelings about people and events.
The Journal as Commonplace Book	Record interesting phrases or ideas that you hear from others or that you encounter in your reading.
The Journal as Writer's Lab	Record your ideas for pieces of writing to do in the future. Do freewriting on subjects of interest to you. Try out different kinds of writing, such as monologues, dialogues, song lyrics, concrete poetry, and riddles.
	CONTINUED

ESSENTIAL SKILLS: WRITING

ESSENTIAL SKILLS:
Language

GRAMMAR HANDBOOK

INTRODUCTION TO GRAMMAR

2.1 THE GRAMMAR YOU ALREADY KNOW

Grammar is something you know, even if you have never studied it. Inside the head of every person is a sophisticated device that works, all by itself, to learn how to put words and phrases together grammatically. Even if you don't know an adverb from an aardvark, you know, if you are a speaker of English, that

the little leaf-eating bug

is grammatical and that

the bug little leaf-eating

is not. You can tell that one string of words is grammatical and the other isn't because you have learned, unconsciously, many thousands of rules governing how words can be put together and how they can't.

When you study a grammar textbook, therefore, what you are really learning is not the grammar of the language—for the most part, that's something you already know. What you are learning is terminology for describing what you know so that you can use that terminology when discussing language. Incidentally, as you study textbook grammar, you will also learn a few rules that you never quite learned unconsciously. Remember, however, that most of the grammar is already inside your head. Learning to describe that grammar can therefore be viewed as learning more about yourself and your amazing unconscious abilities.

2.2 THE USES OF GRAMMAR

Why study grammar? After all, no amount of grammar study can match the value of hands-on reading and writing. Grammar is useful, however. It gives you a way to speak about and understand your own writing and that of others. Contrast the following examples:

When the Roman general, sitting at supper with a plate of turnips before him, was solicited by large presents to betray his trust, he asked the messengers whether he that could sup on turnips was a man likely to sell his own country. Upon him who has reduced his sense to obedience, temptation has lost its power; he is able to attend impartially to virtue, and execute her commands without hesitation.

—Samuel Johnson, *The Idler* No. 52

Now what's this? What's the object of all this darkness all over me? They haven't gone and buried me alive while my back was turned, have they? Ah, now would you think they'd do a thing like that! Oh, no, I know what it is. I'm awake. That's it. I've waked up in the middle of the night. Well, isn't that nice. Isn't that simply ideal.

—Dorothy Parker, "The Little Hours"

If you had to describe the difference between these two passages, you would find it useful to have precise grammatical terms at your command. The first sentence in the passage by Johnson is composed of an adverbial clause interrupted by a participial phrase, followed by a sentence with an indirect question containing a subjunctive. The sentences in the passage from Parker's story have few of these devices. They are short, casual, and full of contractions. They consist mostly of simple subjects, verbs, and predicates. You may *sense* the differences in these two styles of writing instinctively, but grammar gives you a way to *understand* and *communicate* those differences.

THE PARTS OF SPEECH

2.3 COMMON AND PROPER NOUNS

A **noun** is a word used to refer to a person, place, thing, or idea.

NOUNS	Virginia Woolf, England, stone, beauty

A **common noun** is a name that belongs to (is *common* to) all the persons, places, or things in a group. A **proper noun** refers to a *particular* person, place, or thing and begins with a capital letter.

COMMON NOUNS	woman, state, religion
PROPER NOUNS	Queen Elizabeth I, California, Catholicism

2.4 CONCRETE AND ABSTRACT NOUNS

A **concrete noun** refers to an object that you can perceive by hearing, seeing, smelling, tasting, or touching. An **abstract noun** names a quality, characteristic, or idea.

CONCRETE NOUNS	music, light, smoke, honey, silk
ABSTRACT NOUNS	difficulty, bravery, evil

ESSENTIAL SKILLS: LANGUAGE

- The **Essential Skills: Speaking and Listening** section surveys verbal and nonverbal communication, active listening, interpersonal communication, discussion, public speaking, and oral interpretation.

ESSENTIAL SKILLS:
Study and Research

THINKING SKILLS

All human beings have a great number of thinking skills and perform astonishing feats of thinking every day, but often people get set in thinking habits and patterns that aren't very efficient. Learning a few simple thinking strategies can improve dramatically anyone's ability to learn, to solve problems, and to make decisions.

4.1 STRATEGIES FOR PROBLEM SOLVING I

All problem solving involves four steps.

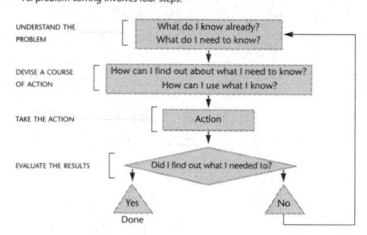

UNDERSTAND THE PROBLEM — What do I know already? What do I need to know?

DEVISE A COURSE OF ACTION — How can I find out about what I need to know? How can I use what I know?

TAKE THE ACTION — Action

EVALUATE THE RESULTS — Did I find out what I needed to? Yes / Done / No

Within this **general problem-solving framework**, there are many particular strategies you can use. A guaranteed strategy for solving a problem is called an **algorithm**. A less than sure-fire strategy is called a **heuristic** or, if the strategy is very simple and straightfo

1176 LANGUAGE ARTS SURVEY

ESSENTIAL SKILLS:
Speaking and Listening

3.1 A COMMUNICATION MODEL

When you ask a friend if you can borrow a pencil, you are operating an extremely complex system that no computer can yet operate. Here's the way the system works: A **sender** encodes a **message** using **symbols**. This message is transmitted along some **channel** to a **recipient** who **decodes** it and provides **feedback**. The following chart describes this communication model:

COMMUNICATION MODEL	
Sender	You
Message	"May I borrow a pencil from you?"
Symbols Used	Words in the English language
Channel	Speech
Recipient	Your friend
Feedback	"Sure, I have an extra one."

For complete communication, encoding must be correct, the channel must be clear, and decoding must be correct. So, for example, if a loud stereo were in the room and your friend didn't hear you, the communication would not be complete. You would need to modify the system by adding a tap on your friend's shoulder or perhaps a repetition of the message in a slightly louder voice.

▶ ▶ ▶ A C T I V I T Y 3.1

Answer the following questions:

1. What are some different symbol systems used to encode messages? Think of both nonverbal and verbal means of communication. (Hint: Street signs are one common nonverbal means for encoding messages.)
2. A space probe on Mars takes a picture of a crater on Mars and transmits this picture by radio to NASA scientists on Earth. The scientists look at the picture and send a command back to the probe telling it to move a bit to the left and take another picture. Describe the sender, the message, the channel, the recipient, and the feedback in this communication situation.

CONTINUED

LANGUAGE ARTS SURVEY

---

3. Using terminology from the communication model given above, describe what interferes with communication in each of the following examples:
   a. An American tourist in Rome stops a young man on the street to ask directions. The American asks, "Can you tell me how to get to the Forum?" The Italian answers, "Non parlo inglese."
   b. A ship has run into an iceberg and is sinking. Another ship is passing in the distance. A crew member on the first ship attempts to signal the second ship using flags. The people on the second ship can't see the flags because too much fog is in the air.
   c. A student with a stomachache enters class, wearing a grimace. The student's teacher asks, "Would you like to lead the discussion today, Gloria?" Gloria answers, "Sure." However, the teacher looks at the grimace on Gloria's face and concludes that Gloria doesn't really want to lead the discussion. The teacher asks another student to lead the discussion but fails to tell Gloria why he has made this decision.
4. Why is feedback important to good communication? What kind of feedback does an audience give to an actor or to a speaker? How can people in conversation ensure that they have understood one another correctly? How do newspapers receive feedback from their readers?

3.2 ELEMENTS OF VERBAL COMMUNICATION

Communication can be verbal or nonverbal. **Verbal communication** is done by means of words and other sounds uttered by speakers. **Nonverbal communication** is done by other means. The following chart describes the most important elements of verbal communication:

ELEMENTS OF VERBAL COMMUNICATION		
ELEMENT	DESCRIPTION	GUIDELINES FOR SPEAKERS
Volume	The loudness or softness of the voice	Speak loudly enough to be heard, but not so loudly as to make your audience uncomfortable.
Pitch, or Intonation	The highness or lowness of the voice	Vary your pitch to give your expressions a musical quality and to communicate meaning (for example, a rising pitch at the end of a sentence indicates a question). Avoid using a single pitch, or monotone.
Enunciation	The clearness with which syllables are spoken	Slightly exaggerate the clearness of your syllables to ensure that you are understood. Do not drop or clip the ends of words or sentences.

CONTINUED

- The **Essential Skills: Study and Research** section surveys thinking, reading, research, and test-taking skills, including skills for taking standardized tests.

- The **Essential Skills: Applied English/Tech Prep** section surveys applications of English skills to the world of work.

ESSENTIAL SKILLS:
Applied English/Tech Prep

LETTERS AND FORMS

Long after you've written your last high-school essay or college term paper, you'll be using your writing skills in a variety of day-to-day situations. Whether you're corresponding with a loan officer at the bank, writing to a friend across the country, communicating via electronic mail with a co-worker, or penning a thank-you note to a thoughtful aunt, you'll want to take care to ensure that your writing reflects your intentions precisely, conveying your thoughts or feelings or any pertinent information.

Familiarizing yourself with the conventions of letter-writing can help you achieve a positive outcome, particularly when addressing correspondence to individuals or groups who don't know you personally.

5.1 FILLING OUT FORMS AND APPLICATIONS

In our information-based society, forms and applications are ubiquitous. Because they're such efficient mechanisms for collecting data, you can expect to encounter them regularly, in such diverse locations as the doctor's office, the bank, your local dry-cleaning establishment, or a favorite mail-order catalog.

When completing a form or application, you should have two objectives: to provide the information requested and to make a positive impression.

Guidelines for completing forms:
- If possible, obtain an extra copy of the form or application.
- Gather any information you will need to complete the form.
- Read all the directions before you begin to enter your data.
- Be neat. Type or print your responses legibly, in pencil or ink, as directed. Avoid smudges or cross-outs.
- Write "N.A." or "not applicable," rather than leave a space blank, if a section of the form or application does not apply to you.
- Proofread. When you've completed the form, check your spelling, grammar, and punctuation, and review the information you've provided.
- If the form is messy or inaccurate, discard it and complete the extra form or application if you have one.
- When you've completed the form to your satisfaction, submit it to the appropriate person, or mail it to the correct address.

1224 LANGUAGE ARTS SURVEY

Application for Employment
Brennan's Book Emporium

Position Desired: Sales Clerk

Personal Data

Applicant's Name: Mello / Jennifer / M.
Last name / First Name / Middle Initial

Address: 55 Dartmouth St. / Brobdingnag / Ohio / 00703
Street / City / State / Zip

Phone: (586) 555-3250   Date of Birth: 5/10/78

Previous Work Experience
(List last two positions held, beginning with the most recent.)

Employer: Ms. Janice Ingram   17 Howe St., Brobdingnag, Ohio   00703
Name / Address

Phone: (586) 555-8020

Employment Period: 1/95–present

Job Title: Tutor

Hours worked: Flexible, 5–10 hrs./wk.

Salary: $5.00/hr.

Description: Help employer's ten-year-old daughter improve her math skills

Reason for leaving: N.A.

Employer: John and Sandra Neils   48 Dart St., Brobdingnag, Ohio   00703
Name / Address

Phone: (586) 555-5440

Employment Period: 7/95–9/95

Job Title: Nanny

Hours Worked: 8:30–4:30, Monday–Friday

Salary: $4.50/hr.

Description: Cared for two children, ages 4 and 6, in their home

Reason for Leaving: Returned to school following summer vacation

CONTINUED

The EMC Masterpiece Series has the **most extensive language arts skills coverage of any program.** The coverage of English skills is so comprehensive that an additional English skills textbook isn't needed. The Language Arts Survey sections may be taught as separate units, using the student textbook and ancillary worksheets, or may be taught incidentally in conjunction with study of the literature.

ANNOTATED TEACHER'S EDITION

The Annotated Teacher's Edition contains a wealth of materials to enrich your teaching.

A list of cross-curricular activities

A list of activities to exercise multiple intelligences

Historical and Art Notes providing information on artists, schools, periods, and techniques

Icons identifying SCANS activities that will help your students reach Goals 2000

A list of concepts and skills taught in the unit

A list of suggested affective and cognitive goals for the unit

A list of worksheets, assessment materials, and multimedia materials to use in teaching the unit

Additional activities designed with gifted students in mind but also useful for challenging all students

Notes on syntax and semantics plus lists of idioms, colloquialisms, and additional vocabulary for students needing extra help

A list of suggested affective and cognitive goals for the selection

Color-coded answers for exercises are provided on the same pages as the exercises themselves

Activities for each of the five nonlinguistic intelligences (musical, logical-mathematical, spatial, kinesthetic, and interpersonal/intrapersonal) facilitate tailoring instruction to individual students' abilities

Also included in the Annotated Teacher's Edition:

- Practical advice and strategies for reader response and portfolio-based language arts instruction

- Sample lesson cycles

- Information on thematic and genre approaches

- Additional resources for language arts teachers

Annotated Teacher's Edition also available on CD-ROM

The EMC Masterpiece Series has the most comprehensive assessment portfolio available today. This ancillary package contains blackline master materials for:

- Unit Study Guides and Tests, including Vocabulary Worksheets
- Selection Check Tests and Comprehensive Tests
- Writing Skills Study Guides and Post-tests
- Other Language Arts Skills Study Guides and Tests
- Worksheets and Forms for Portfolio Assessment
  - Forms for Analytic and Holistic Evaluation for Other Language Arts Activities and Projects
- Worksheets and Forms
- Answer Keys

■ **Holistic Evaluation Forms** allow for "total effect" peer, self-, and teacher evaluation of student writing.

■ **Analytic Evaluation Forms** allow for part-by-part, criteria-based peer, self-, and teacher evaluation of student writing.

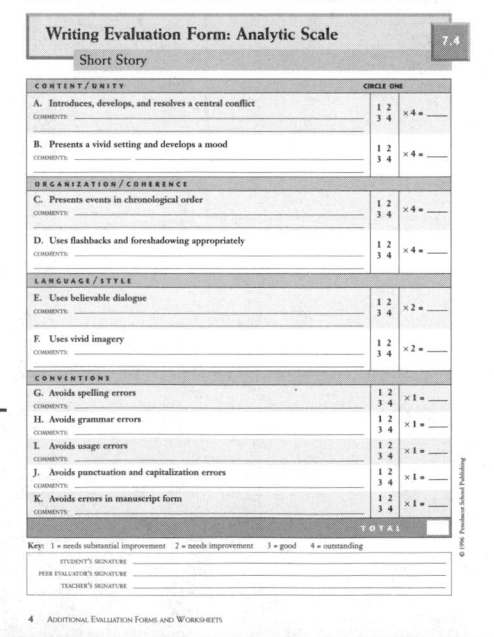

■ **Portfolio Evaluation Forms** allow students and teachers to monitor the development of student writing over time.

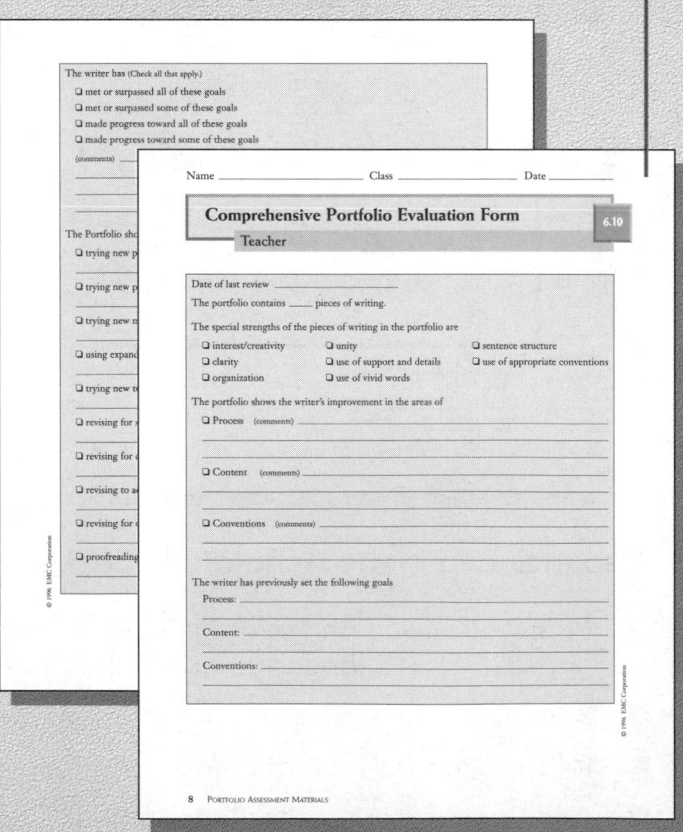

ESSENTIAL SKILLS PRACTICE BOOK
APPLIED ENGLISH

ESSENTIAL SKILLS PRACTICE BOOK
LANGUAGE

ESSENTIAL SKILLS PRACTICE BOOK
SPEAKING AND LISTENING

ESSENTIAL SKILLS PRACTICE BOOK
STUDY AND RESEARCH

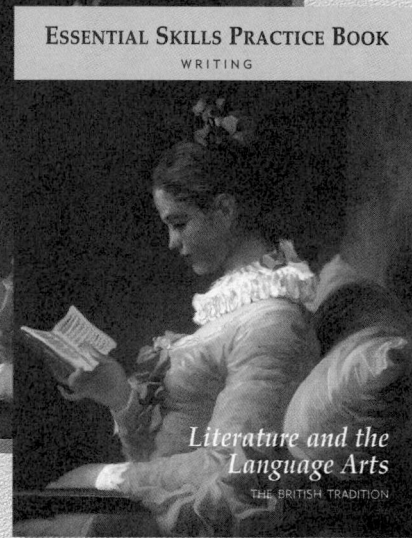

ESSENTIAL SKILLS PRACTICE BOOK
WRITING

Literature and the Language Arts
THE BRITISH TRADITION

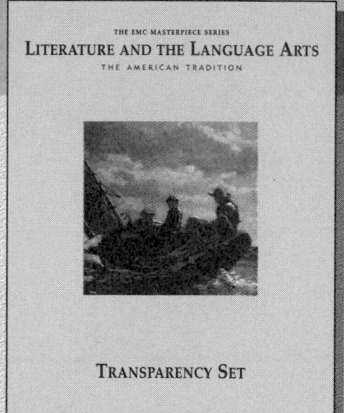

THE EMC MASTERPIECE SERIES
LITERATURE AND THE LANGUAGE ARTS
THE AMERICAN TRADITION

TRANSPARENCY SET

■ **Essential Skills Practice Books**—The five Essential Skills Practice Books—Applied English, Language, Speaking and Listening, Study and Research, and Writing—contain blackline masters of exercises keyed to the Language Arts Survey sections of the student textbooks.

■ **Transparency Set**—Transparencies guide students through preparation of reader's journals, use of writing portfolios, and peer and self-evaluation of writing.

Multimedia Components

■ Four, sixty-minute audiocassettes of songs and dramatic readings from the series

■ A videocassette and video laser disc of dramatic performances from the series

■ A CD-ROM containing an idea generator for prewriting and a test generator for creating tests appropriate for six-week, nine-week, twelve-week, and semester-long schedules

■ Test generators also available on IBM and Macintosh computer disks

■ The Annotated Teacher's Edition is available on CD-ROM for random access to the selections

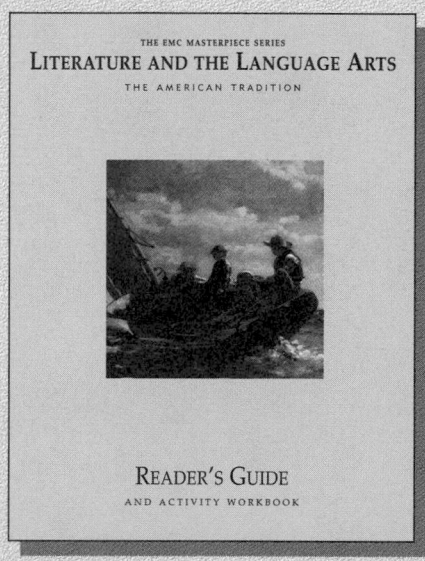

THE EMC MASTERPIECE SERIES
LITERATURE AND THE LANGUAGE ARTS
THE AMERICAN TRADITION

READER'S GUIDE
AND ACTIVITY WORKBOOK

■ **Reader's Guide**—The Reader's Guide and Activity Workbook consists of blackline master worksheets that provide a step-by-step process for completing the student textbook activities.

A Truly Integrated Literature and Language Arts Program

Contents

Overview

PROGRAM PHILOSOPHY

The Cognitive Revolution and the Teaching of Literature

Through the 1960s, psychology in America was dominated by behaviorism, a theoretical methodology popularized by the brilliant and irascible B. F. Skinner. Skinner and other behaviorists argued that because we cannot observe mental phenomena directly, we cannot speak scientifically (i.e., intelligibly) of such matters as sensations, intuitions, feelings, thoughts, reasons, motives, imaginings, wishes, beliefs, and dreams. Oddly, some behaviorists went so far as to claim that mental phenomena did not exist. Such peculiar notions were positively reinforced by government grants and academic appointments and found expression in several generations of programmed learning textbooks designed to meet behavioral objectives. Learning theorists working within the behaviorist model encouraged educators to consider their students' observable behaviors without regard to, and indeed in scorn of, underlying mental processes.[1]

Of course, most English teachers knew that something was radically wrong with the behaviorist model of learning. They knew all along that they were teaching young *people*, not young bundles of behaviors, that those "mythical" realms of thought and feeling pooh-poohed by the behaviorists were, in fact, the quite real places that they explored daily with students in discussions of works of literature. In the 1960s and '70s, a revolution occurred in American psychology that brought psychologists to an understanding of what teachers had sensed all along. That revolution was the emergence of the field of cognitive science.[2]

One consequence of the cognitive revolution in psychology is that education theorists now widely accept the idea, advanced by psychologist Lev Vygotsky and championed by Jerome Bruner, that **teaching must begin with what students already know and feel and must build on that foundation.** This idea has often been presented as something altogether new. However, it is something that good English teachers have known all along. To help students to understand and to appreciate literature, one must first

> provide opportunities for students to connect with the literature on their own terms

and then

> build from that place toward higher levels of understanding and appreciation.

EMC's **Literature and the Language Arts** *is the first literature textbook series specifically designed to accomplish both of those higher-order goals. Each lesson in this series first provides opportunities for*

---

1. According to the behaviorist theory, learning results from the differential positive or negative reinforcement of spontaneously occurring, pre-existing behaviors. A rat turns randomly this way or that way in a maze. By means of positive or negative reinforcements (e.g., food and mild electric shocks), the researcher/teacher reinforces turning one way instead of another, and thus learning takes place.

2. As Thomas Kuhn points out in *The Structure of Scientific Revolutions* (1962), when scientists working in a particular field discover phenomena that cannot be accounted for by extending or modifying the prevailing theoretical paradigm, they are forced to revise that paradigm to come up with a new theory. Kuhn calls the intractable phenomena that force scientists to rethink their theories "anomalies."

The twin anomalies that dealt the death blow to behaviorism were commonplace human behaviors: musical improvisation and speech. Neither could be adequately accounted for by behaviorist theory. Karl Lashley pointed out in a famous paper that musical improvisation, like many other human serial behaviors, cannot be explained without reference to what goes on inside people's minds. Improvisation simply happens too quickly to be explicable as a connected sequence of stimuli and responses. It must involve learned mental constructs, or structures, that are played out. Noam Chomsky, in his review of Skinner's *Verbal Behavior* (1957), explained that stimulus/response or imitation models cannot account for readily observable facts about language such as the production of sentences that, while entirely consistent with the rest of the grammar of the language, are utterly novel in structure (not to mention content).

Cognitive science is a cross-disciplinary study involving work in such fields as artificial intelligence, linguistics, psychology, and neuroscience. The cognitive scientist constructs models of mental processes and then tests these models to see that they yield all the outputs produced by minds and only those outputs. For example, a cognitive scientist might be interested in constructing a model of the mechanism for short-term storage and retrieval of information such as the telephone number of a taxi service. One famous paper in cognitive psychology describes the neurological mechanism for pattern recognition that enables frogs to detect bugs moving across their field of vision. The essential or defining attribute of such studies is that they posit processes that are functionally, or operationally, equivalent to mental processes. See Farnham-Diggory, S. *Cognitive Processes in Education.* New York: Harper, 1992; Bourne, L. E. et al. *Cognitive Processes.* Englewood Cliffs, NJ: Prentice, 1986; and Lindsay, P. H., and D. A. Norman, *Human Information Processing.* New York: Academic Press, 1977.

students to connect to literature through **reader response** activities and then provides materials that teachers can use to assist students in elaborating and refining their responses.

Reader Response Theory

The Theoretical Foundations of Reader Response Theory. Reader response theory offers a theoretical framework for teaching that enables students to connect to literature on their own terms. The theory springs from a simple observation about the relationship between a literary text and its meaning, or interpretation: this relationship is not as direct as the relationship between text and meaning in, say, a train schedule. Suppose, for example, that a train schedule reads as follows:

The B train from Marston arrives at Holyoke Station at 12:45.

That statement has one acceptable and correct interpretation. Differing interpretations (e.g., "The B train arrives at 12:55") are simply wrong (and can lead to pointless standing around on railway platforms).

One cannot make such statements about the rightness or wrongness of a literary judgment because literary texts do not function as train schedules do. A literary text provides much more than a report of observable facts about the world: It provides an opportunity for an imaginary experience. If one is reading well, that imaginary experience is every bit as vivid as an actual experience, such as trekking up a mountainside in the Peruvian Andes or shopping in the Ginza district of Tokyo.

When one reads a work of literature, one does not *read about the world*, one *enters a world*, and not *the world as it is*, but *the world as it might be*. That world is an imaginative construct formed partly on the basis of the text and partly on the basis of experiences that the reader brings to the reading.

Imagine, for a moment, that you and some other travelers have just returned from a real-life excursion. There will doubtless be aspects of the trip that you can agree upon (e.g., "The Ginza is crowded"; "The air at high elevations in the Andes is quite thin"). However, the real meaning, or significance, of the trip will differ for each of you depending on what you brought to the journey. The same is true of the journeys that people take when they read. Your experience of Shelley's "Ode to the West Wind" or of Eliot's *Middlemarch* will differ from another person's, depending on what you brought (and continue to bring) to the text.

Literary Works as Worlds. The idea that a literary text offers the reader (or listener) an opportunity to create a world into which he or she can travel is not new. When the Nobel Prize-winning poet Derek Walcott writes

At the end of this sentence, rain
will begin.
At the end of the rain, a sail.

he evokes the ancient, shamanistic power of the poet to call a world into existence. This power connects Walcott in an unbroken line through Shelley and Shakespeare and Homer to the first unknown poet who enthralled an audience with the pre-

proto-Indo-European equivalent of "Once upon a time. . . ."

In the early twentieth century, the idea that a literary text creates a world of its own was eloquently advanced by the so-called "New Critics," such as Cleanth Brooks writing in *The Well-Wrought Urn*. The New Critics insisted on close reading of texts, and this insistence led some to think that the New Criticism was about arriving, through analysis, at some one acceptable meaning; however, that is a misinterpretation of New Critical theory. Brooks, Warren, Empson, and other New Critics advanced a much more subtle and powerful idea. They believed that literary texts created worlds and that one had to attend closely to the texts in order to distinguish the nuances of those worlds. In the words of that masterpiece of New Critical theory, Archibald MacLeish's poem "Ars Poetica,"

A poem should not mean
But be.

Reader response theory extends this formulation by acknowledging the large role played by the reader, as well as by the text, in the creation of "the world of a reading."

The world of a literary work, like the real world, provides an opportunity to have an experience. Critical faculties and concepts, like a tourist's guidebook, will help to make that experience valuable, but the experience itself has no one meaning, any more than a waterfall or a revolution or any other real-life experience does.

The Construction of Meaning. Different readers will read and interpret a text differently, depending on what they bring to it. Suppose, for example, that a story begins as follows:

Isaac opened his lunchbox. It contained the usual sandwich wrapped in brown paper (his father, who made his lunches, thought that plastic wrap constituted a sin against the environment). It also contained what seemed to him an ordinary apple.

If you are reading well, then you will give yourself over imaginatively to the story, creating the scene in your mind's eye. Of course, the scene that you create will depend partly on the text and partly on your experiences. When you read about lunch-boxes, perhaps you think of the metal variety found beside construction workers perched on girders, or perhaps you think of the plastic variety decorated with Simbas or Power Rangers. When you think of ordinary apples, you might picture a green Granny Smith or a Golden Delicious or a red Winesap. If you are an environmentalist, you might wonder whether Isaac's observation about his father means that the boy is insensitive about environmental issues. You might recall that a certain famous Isaac is popularly associated with apples and might begin wondering whether the juxtaposition of Isaac and apples in this story constitutes some sort of significant allusion. Perhaps this Isaac is going to make a discovery. The point is that as you begin reading the story, you begin constructing the world of the story based on clues in the text and on your own experience. That world will have

its similarities to the world constructed by another reader, but it will have its differences, too. To some extent, large or small, your interpretation, your sense of the meaning of the text, will be unique.

Furthermore, the meaning of a text does not remain the same even for a single person. Robert Frost wrote eloquently about the evolution of his understanding of Emerson's poem "Brahma," advising readers not to be too anxious to come to a single, final interpretation of a poem but rather to carry the poem around in their heads so that its meaning would become enlarged and enriched (and, indeed, changed) by experience.

Reader Response or Cultural Transmission?

Relativism and Reader Response. A text comes to have meaning through a complex transaction between the text and the reader. This idea that the reader helps to create meaning can be dated to Louise Rosenblatt's seminal work *Literature as Exploration*. Recent developments of that idea owe much to Post-Modernist critical theory, in particular to Jacques Derrida's Deconstructionism. The same criticisms that have been directed at Derrida can also be directed against the extreme form of reader response theory that holds that a literary text can mean anything.

One such criticism of reader response theory asks: If literary texts mean different things to different people, what happens to the whole concept of cultural transmis-

sion through literature? Surely, the skeptic says, the idea that texts have different meanings for different persons is equivalent to Humpty Dumpty's position on the meanings of words, familiar to readers of *Through the Looking Glass*:

"I don't know what you mean by 'glory'," Alice said.

Humpty Dumpty smiled contemptuously. "Of course you don't—till I tell you. I meant 'there's a nice knock-down argument for you!'"

"But 'glory' doesn't mean 'a nice knock-down argument'," Alice objected.

"When I use a word," Humpty Dumpty said, in a rather scornful tone, "it means just what I choose it to mean—neither more nor less."

"The question is," said Alice, "whether you can make words mean so many different things."

"The question is," said Humpty Dumpty, "which is to be master—that's all."

Some have charged that both Deconstructionism and reader response theory are instances of a Humpty Dumptyish "relativism." Surely, critics of such theories say, "Auld Lang Syne" has a meaning that all Western speakers of English understand. Its meaning is part of the common cultural heritage of English speakers in the West. To deny that Burns's poem has a consensus meaning or interpretation is to ignore that it has become a popular New Year's Eve tune with a cultural significance that is passed from generation to generation in the West. To fail to teach this meaning to students is to deny them access to their cultural heritage, to deprive them of a small portion of the legacy that binds them to others, making them part of a cultural entity rather than alienated individuals. This attitude forms the core of the argument made eloquently and popularly by E. D. Hirsch and Alan Bloom, among others.[3]

A Nonrelativistic Theory of Reader Response. The charge of relativism holds up only against the radical form of reader response theory that holds that a text can mean anything. To understand what shape a nonrelativistic reader response theory might take, let us return to our guiding metaphor, that of reading as a journey into another place (a journey made possible, as Coleridge pointed out in his *Biographia Literaria*, by "a willing suspension of disbelief"). Imagine that a child from the United States, having learned nothing of ancient Rome, were to stroll through the ruins of the Forum. Most likely, that child would make little sense of the experience, if we read "making sense" as interpreting the experience in grown-up terms. The Forum would be, for the child, a mere pile of rocks. The child's sense of wonder might be aroused by the occasional stray or feral cat or by various trinkets dropped on the ground by tourists. Now imagine that you yourself are walking through the Forum. To make

the experience all the more exciting, imagine that you have with you a guide versed in Roman history (Livy or Gibbon would be nice). You wouldn't need a stray cat to arouse your sense of wonder. You are an educated person. You know about ancient Rome (and much of what you don't know can be supplied by your guide).

Reader response theory says that literary texts mean different things to different people, but it does not deny that some readings, like some walks through the Forum, are more informed than others. If one is in the process of becoming educated (and most of us are most of the time), then one's readings will not simply change over time, they will deepen. Furthermore, the process of becoming informed or educated about a text will include coming to understand the consensus interpretations of that text—the interpretations that have become part of our common cultural heritage.

Consider, for example, a line from another famous poem by Burns: "My love is like a red, red rose." One leading reader-response-based literature anthology, after asking students what this comparison might mean, suggests as an answer simply that "answers will vary." However, a red rose, in the context of a love poem, has a definite meaning in a Western cultural context. In the West, a rose is a conventional symbol of beauty and romantic love. Much of the work of a teacher is to pass on the accumulated

knowledge, traditions, and symbols of a culture, and any textbook that does not assist teachers in that job does teachers and students a disservice. Such a text undermines the role of the teacher in the transmission of culture and ignores a rather fundamental fact: **the teacher is there because he or she knows much that the students do not as yet know.**

Interpreting literature involves achieving a sort of "equilibrium" among three factors: the reader's background knowledge, experience, and attitudes; the historically developed and culturally recognized canons of meaning; and the text itself.

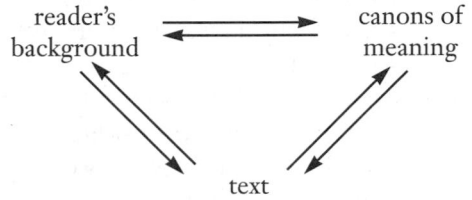

These canons of meaning are part of cultural literacy and include knowledge of literary genres, movements, and techniques as well as familiarity with history, authors' lives, other literary works, and some literary criticism, all part of the special knowledge the professional teacher of literature brings to the classroom. While respecting the student's responses and recognizing that those responses will always be to some large extent unique to that student, the teacher can still guide the student toward fuller, more sophisticated, more informed responses, ones that attend more closely to texts and to culturally transmitted aspects of texts such as conventional symbolism.

---

3. Preservation of students' unique cultural backgrounds and promotion of a shared cultural literacy need not be, as is often supposed, mutually exclusive goals. To achieve both, educators must expand their definitions of what constitutes the larger shared culture. Long ago, Jean de Crèvecoeur and Alexis de Tocqueville observed that America is strong because that country draws upon its diversity to create a new, larger union. *E pluribus unum*, says the motto on United States coins. The tension, the paradox, in that motto is one that those with literary education will appreciate. Out of such creative tensions new and wonderful syntheses are born.

Reader Response and Cultural Transmission in *Literature and the Language Arts*

What makes *Literature and the Language Arts* unique among available literature programs is that it does not offer teachers an unacceptable choice between reader response and cultural transmission. Instead, it provides ample reader response materials for engaging students on their own terms and then builds on what students already know, refining those responses in light of literary conventions and traditions. The unique design of the study materials in this series enables students to encounter the literature on their own and connect it to their lives and then enables teachers to correct their students' discoveries to the mainstreams of literary tradition.

The psychologist Lev Vygotsky pointed out that at the outset of any learning situation, the learner has already reached a certain stage in his or her understanding. This stage really has two parts: what the learner can do on his or her own and what the learner can do with some assistance. The area between these two points is what Vygotsky called the **zone of proximal development,** or **ZPD.** The teacher's role is to assign the learner tasks that are within the ZPD and to provide the assistance that the learner needs while allowing the learner to do on his or her own as much as he or she is able. The teacher provides **scaffolding** that supports the learner until he or she reaches a new level. Then the old scaffolding is unnecessary and the learner is ready to move on to new learning.

The study materials in *Literature and the Language Arts* make it possible for students to begin with what they already know—their own lives—and connect what they know to the literature. Once that connection is made, students then explore the literature independently and in collaborative activities that provide a foundation for the teacher-assisted instruction, or scaffolding, that follows.

Partial Bibliography

Bloom, A. *The Closing of the American Mind.* New York: Simon and Schuster, 1987.

Brooks, C. *The Well-Wrought Urn.* New York: Renal and Hitchcock, 1947.

Bruner, J. *Toward a Theory of Instruction.* New York: Norton, 1966.

———. *On Knowing: Essays for the Left Hand.* Expanded ed. Cambridge: Belknap/Harvard UP, 1979.

Chomsky, N. *Language and Mind.* New York: Harcourt, 1968.

———. Review of B. F. Skinner's *Verbal Behavior. Language* 35 (1959): 26–58.

Derrida, J. *Of Grammatology.* Trans. C. Spivak. Baltimore: Johns Hopkins UP, 1976.

Donaldson, M. *Children's Minds.* New York: Norton, 1978.

Eisner, E. *The Educational Imagination.* 2nd ed. New York: Macmillan, 1985.

Farrell, E. J. *Deciding the Future.* Research Rep. No. 12. Urbana, IL: NCTE, 1971.

Flower, L. S. *Problem-Solving Strategies in Writing.* 2nd ed. Orlando, FL: Harcourt, 1985.

Hirsch, E. D. *Cultural Literacy: What Every American Needs to Know.* New York: Houghton, 1987.

Kempson, R. M. *Semantic Theory.* Cambridge: Cambridge UP, 1977.

Kuhn, T. S. *The Structure of Scientific Revolutions.* 2nd ed. Chicago: U of Chicago P, 1970.

Lashley, K. "The Problem of Serial Order in Behavior." L. Jeffries, ed. *Cerebral Mechanisms in Behavior.*

Lindemann, E. *A Rhetoric for Writing Teachers.* 3rd ed. New York: Oxford UP, 1995.

Novak, J. D. *A Theory of Education.* Ithaca, NY: Cornell UP, 1984.

Resnick, L., and L. Klopfer. *Toward the Thinking Curriculum: Current Cognitive Research.* Alexandria, VA: ASCD, 1989.

Rosenblatt, L. *Literature as Exploration.* 4th ed. New York: MLA, 1983.

———. *The Reader, the Text, the Poem: The Transactional Theory of the Literary Work.* Carbondale, IL: Southern Illinois UP, 1978.

Skinner, B. F. *Science and Human Behavior.* New York: Macmillan, 1953.

———. *Verbal Behavior.* New York: Appleton, 1957.

Strike, K. A. "On the Expressive Potential of Behaviorist Language." *American Educational Research Journal.* 11. (1974): 103–20.

Thorndike, E. L. *The Fundamentals of Learning.* New York: Teacher's College, 1932.

Vygotsky, L. S. *Mind in Society.* Cambridge: Harvard UP, 1978.

———. *Thought and Language.* New York: Wiley, 1962.

Watson, J. B. *Behaviorism.* New York: Norton, 1925.

Weaver, C. *Grammar for Teachers.* Urbana, IL: NCTE, 1979.

Wimsatt, W. K. *The Verbal Icon: Studies in the Meaning of Poetry.* UP of Kentucky, 1954.

PROGRAM COMPONENTS

Student Edition

Twelve Units per Book
Historical Introductions
Superlative Texts
Fine Art and Photographs
Development of the English Language
Unit Reviews

Selections
About the Author
About the Selection
Guided Reading Questions
Words for Everyday Use
Notes

Multicultural Extensions

Additional Readings

Selection Study Materials
Prereading
Responding to the Selection (Reader Response)
Reviewing the Selection
Recalling
Interpreting
Synthesizing
Understanding Literature
Responding in Writing
Language Lab
Additional Language Arts Skills Activities
Projects

Language Arts Survey
Writing
Language
Speaking and Listening
Study and Research
Applied English/Tech Prep

Handbook of Literary Terms

Reader's Guide and Activity Book*

Selection worksheets providing a step-by-step reader response guide for each selection and prewriting assistance for all writing assignments in the text

Essential Skills Practice Books*

Blackline masters for additional practice

Writing

Language

Speaking and Listening

Study, Research, Thinking, and Test-taking

Applied English

Assessment Portfolio*

Unit Study Guides and Tests
Including vocabulary worksheets

Selection Tests
Check tests
Comprehensive tests

Writing Skills Pretests and Post-tests

Other Language Arts Skills Study Guides and Tests

Worksheets and Forms for Writing Evaluation and Portfolio Assessment

Additional Worksheets and Forms

Answer Keys

Scope and Sequence Charts

Transparency Set*

*Contained in the Teacher's Resource Kit

Multimedia Kit

Audiocassette
Selections from the program

Videocassette or Laser Disc
Selections from the program

CD/ROM
Idea generator
Test generator

Diskettes (IBM and Macintosh)
Test generators

Annotated Teacher's Edition

For Units
List of skills taught
List of cross-curricular activities
List of multiple intelligences
List of major themes
List of central literary techniques
Additional historical, bibliographical, and
    biographical background
Information on art and artists

For Selections
List of additional resources

Enrichment activities
Support for limited English proficiency students
    Teaching tips
    Vocabulary help
List of goals/objectives
List of introduced vocabulary words
Vocabulary words used in sample sentences
Additional activities
Discussion prompts
Historical and literary background notes
Quotable quotations

Answer Keys
Selection Check Tests with answers
Answers for all exercises
Analytic evaluation scales for writing projects
Cross-references to additional exercises
Cross-references to assessment instruments

Teaching Notes and Background Notes
Additional problems with answers

Identifiers for Cross-curricular Activities, Activities Using Multiple Intelligences, and Activities Using SCANS Skills

Themes and Genres Charts

Teaching Strategies and Options

Additional Resources for Language Arts Teachers

ORGANIZATION OF THE TEXT

Textbooks presenting surveys of British literature often begin with selections from the Anglo-Saxon period, thus confronting students at the beginning of the course with some of the most challenging work. The editors and authors of this text feel that before beginning a survey of British literature, students should review basic literary types and techniques in connection with readily accessible, high-interest selections. *Literature and the Language Arts: The British Tradition* has been designed to offer just such review of literary concepts in preparation for the historical survey that follows.

The text is organized into three parts:

Part One: Understanding Literature consists of a single unit that reviews the five genres of literature—the oral tradition, poetry, fiction, drama, and nonfiction—and provides an overview of the writing process. The unit is divided into five sections. Each section presents a model work in a particular literary genre. A brief essay at the beginning of each section gives a history and taxonomy of the genre. This essay is followed by a thorough presentation of terminology and techniques of particular relevance to that genre. The model work in each section contains passages set in blue ink and keyed to marginal notes that identify characteristics and techniques typical of works in that genre. Thus the model fictional work contains highlighted passages identifying such elements as setting, character, theme, and the components of the plot. The selections in Unit 1 include ample reader response and teacher-assisted activities.

Part One also leads students through six steps of the writing process: prewriting, drafting, evaluating, revising, proofreading, and sharing or presenting. The writing exercises are cumulative throughout the unit. After completing the unit, each student will have published a piece of his or her own creation. If you do not wish to teach the materials on genre, use the writing activities independently.

Part Two: The English Tradition presents British literature using an historical approach (to use other approaches, see the notes on page T29 of this *Annotated Teacher's Edition*). Units 1–9 begin with historical essays covering major social, political, and intellectual trends associated with the literature of each period from the Anglo-Saxon Era to the Victorian Age. The "Echoes" page that follows each unit introduction offers intriguing quotations chosen to capture the spirit of the age. Units 10–12 present twentieth-century poetry, prose, and drama, respectively. The twentieth century is treated in a single introductory essay at the beginning of Unit 10.

The selections within each unit have been chosen carefully to meet a number of criteria:

- To provide students with engaging, stimulating reading experiences
- To provide outstanding representative examples of each period
- To provide examples of the major genres of literature in each period
- To provoke interesting discussions of significant themes
- To represent major writers in the British literary tradition
- To represent more fully than in the past women's contributions to the historical development of British literature

Following most of the units are **Selections for Additional Reading.** These selections are not accompanied by the usual teaching apparatus, for the editors and authors of this series feel that students should have some "pure" reading experiences, unburdened by exercises and exegeses. Of course, students can use these selections for research when preparing critical papers on literary movements or trends. The Selections for Additional Reading include many classics as well as many remarkable works not normally found in high school anthologies. Beginning with the Middle Ages, each unit also includes **Multicultural Extensions,** literature from outside Britain linked thematically to developments in British literature.

In addition to the literature selections, early units—through the Elizabethan Period—include sections on the **Development of the English Language.** These sections cover the development of the language from its origins through the emergence of Modern English. Each unit also teaches English vocabulary with Words for Everyday Use and concludes with a Unit Review that offers Synthesis questions for discussion or writing. An extended **Language Lab** at the end of each unit presents instruction and practice in grammar, usage, mechanics, spelling, and the varieties of English.

Part Three of this text contains four sections. **The Language Arts Survey** offers comprehensive instruction in the complete range of language arts skills. (Each lesson in the Language Arts Survey is keyed to a worksheet in one of the five *Essential Skills Practice Books* in the Teacher's Resource Kit.) The **Handbook of Literary Terms** defines and provides examples of terms for literary movements and schools of thought, literary techniques, genres of literature, and common allusions. The **Glossary** collects all the Words for Everyday Use and provides both pronunciations and definitions. The text ends with indexes of titles and authors, skills, and fine art.

Part One: Understanding Literature reviews basic literary types and techniques in connection with readily accessible, high-interest selections. This part of the text prepares students for the survey to come.

Part Two: The English Tradition surveys British literature from the Anglo-Saxon Era to the present.

Part Three contains

- A comprehensive **Language Arts Survey**
- A thorough **Handbook of Literary Terms**
- A **Glossary** of Words for Everyday Use
- **Indexes** of Titles and Authors, Skills, and Fine Art

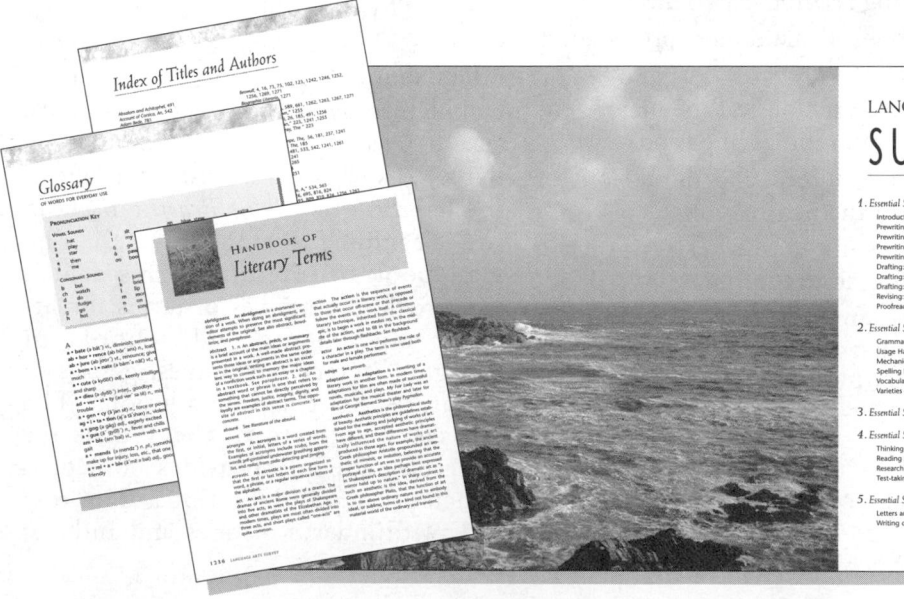

LESSON DESIGN AND TEACHING STRATEGIES

Literature Instruction

A typical lesson in *Literature and the Language Arts* contains materials for two phases of instruction, the Reader Response phase and the Teacher-Assisted phase.

The Reader Response Phase. Cognitive theory and common sense tell us that learning is more likely to occur when students are first provided with a context for what they are to learn. As the proverb says, a seed will grow in prepared ground. Each lesson in this book begins with a **Prereading** page that provides essential information about the author and the selection. The precise content of the entries **About the Author** and **About the Selection** varies according to the demands of the work to be read. If basic comprehension of the work requires understanding of an historical allusion, then that allusion is explained. If comprehension requires understanding of a literary technique, then that technique is described. In addition, the Prereading page provides information about the author and selection designed to arouse student interest.

The selection page itself begins with a writing activity to be done in the student's **Reader's Journal.** The Reader's Journal activity raises a central theme from the selection and asks the student to relate that theme to his or her own life. If, for example, a selection deals with a character who fails to exhibit courage, the student might be asked to write about a time when he or she acted courageously or wanted to act courageously but could not. After completing this activity, the student will be thinking about courage in relation to his or her own life and

Sample Prereading Page

About the Author provides contextual information about the author's life and the period in which he or she lived.

About the Selection provides keys to comprehension of the selection; this covers literary movements, genres, techniques, or themes, depending upon the demands of the selection and its place in literary history.

therefore be more likely to relate the selection to himself or herself and so become emotionally invested in it. This emotional investment in the literature is, of course, key, and that is why the Reader's Journal activities are primarily affective in nature. Responses to these Reader's Journal activities can be made on the **Selection Worksheets** found in the ***Reader's Guide and Activity Book,*** or they can be made in the student's notebook.

Once the student begins reading the selection, he or she can then take advantage of the **Guided Reading Questions** that appear in the margins. These questions are designed to bring to the student's attention key passages in the selection and issues raised by those passages. Like a guide taking a tourist through the Roman Forum and pointing out important or interesting landmarks, these questions take the student through the selection, ensuring that the most important or interesting aspects of the selection will not be missed. (It would be wonderful if every student could have his or her own private guide to literature. These questions provide the next best thing.)

Again, the student can answer these questions on the Selection Worksheets or in his or her notebook.

After reading the selection, the student can then meet with other students in small **collaborative learning groups** to share responses to the Reader's Journal activity and Guided Reading Questions. In these groups, students can also discuss the questions raised in the **Responding to the Selection** activity that follows the selection. Again, this is an affective-response activity, one designed to connect the student emotionally to the literature.

These three components of the instructional apparatus, the Reader's Journal activity, the Guided Reading questions, and the Responding to the

Sample Selection Page

The ***Reader's Journal*** *activity raises an important theme from the selection and connects that theme to the student's life.*

A variable ***Language Arts Skills*** *activity, keyed to the Language Arts Survey at the back of the book, provides integrated practice in Speaking and Listening, Study and Research, Thinking, or Applied English.*

Guided Reading Questions *relate important aspects of the selection to the student's own thoughts, feelings, and experiences.*

Footnotes *explain obscure references, unusual usages, and terms meant to enter students' passive vocabularies.*

Words for Everyday Use *notes define and give pronunciations for difficult terms meant to enter students' active vocabularies.*

Selection activity, connect the student to the selection, guide him or her through it, and then make it possible for the student to share his or her responses with others. Together, these activities ensure that once the teacher-assisted phase of the instruction begins, the student will have a wealth of responses to share in discussions with the whole class.

Additional teaching suggestions for the Reader's Journal, Guided Reading, and Responding to the Selection activities are provided in the *Annotated Teacher's Edition.*

The Teacher-Assisted Phase. The **Reviewing the Selection** questions that follow the Responding to the Selection activity are designed to take the student through the selection, step-by-step, building upon his or her responses and refining those through questions of successive complexity. These questions are organized by level of cognitive sophistication into three sections:

The **Recalling** questions ensure basic comprehension of key facts from the selection.

The **Interpreting** questions ask students to make interpretations or critical evaluations based on facts from the selection.

The **Synthesizing** questions ask students to draw together what they have gathered through recall and interpretation to make generalizations about the meaning, significance, or value of the selection. Often these questions ask the student to apply what he or she has learned from the selection to some larger context (to larger trends or themes in literature, for example, or to some larger social, cultural, ethical, or political context).

Uniquely, each Interpreting question in Reviewing the Selection is keyed by means of an arrow to a Recalling question that provides the facts on which the interpretation can be based. **This keying of interpretation to facts from the selection ensures that student responses will be based on evidence from the selection. No other text now available offers this feature.**

Because students often are not readily familiar with literary terminology and its applications, such terminology does not appear in the questions for Reviewing the Selection. Literary terminology and techniques are covered in the next part of the instructional apparatus, which is called **Understanding Literature.** Each Understanding Literature activity begins with a boldfaced term that names a literary movement, genre, or technique. The term is followed by its definition and by one or more questions that apply the concept to the selection. Having responded to the selection and having reviewed it in detail, the student can now learn some of the technical details about how the selection worked to achieve its effects. Students needing or desiring additional information about a term introduced in the Understanding Literature activity can refer to the discussion of that term in the **Handbook of Literary Terms** at the back of the book.

Approaches to the teacher-assisted phase of the literature instruction can vary, depending on your teaching style and the needs of your students. Some teachers will prefer to have students answer questions on Reviewing the Selection and Understanding Literature individually or in small groups and then will hold whole-class discussions of these questions. Others will prefer to treat these questions as prompts for whole-class, teacher-directed discussions. Another alternative, especially appropriate in advanced classes, is to assign students to conduct whole-class discussions of these questions.

Sample Literary Skills Page

Responding to the Selection

Make a list of five feelings toward the sea that the poem arouses in you. Are some of these feelings quite different from one another? Compare your list with those made by other members of the class and discuss what details in the poem produced the feelings. Also compare different reactions to the same details.

Reviewing the Selection

RECALLING

1. In lines 1–4, what is happening to the sea? What is happening to the land? What two causes combine to move the mighty ocean?

2. What effect does "the wild blast" cause? From where do the "huge billows" come? What effect do the billows have?

3. In line 12, what do "they" hear no more? Why do they not hear it?

4. In the final line, what does the speaker watch?

INTERPRETING

▶▶ 5. Why is the moon called "mute arbitress of tides"? In what way are the waves "sublime"?

▶▶ 6. In lines 6–8, what metaphor is used to speak of the waves? What contrasts does this metaphor suggest?

▶▶ 7. How is the metaphor of lines 6–8 further developed in lines 9–12?

▶▶ 8. In lines 13–14, how does the speaker feel?

SYNTHESIZING

9. Why might the speaker envy "gloomy rest"? What does this envy imply about how the speaker feels about her or his own life? What might be causing the speaker to feel this way?

10. What parallels or similarities does the poet seem to see between people and the waves? What contrasts between people and the waves are suggested? Do you think the author of the poem views people as part of nature, or does she view people as separate from nature?

Understanding Literature (Questions for Discussion)

1. **Alliteration. Alliteration** is the repetition of initial consonant sounds, as in "wild wind." Find instances of alliteration in Smith's sonnet. What sounds are repeated? How frequently are these sounds used elsewhere in the poem? Why do you think Smith may have chosen to use these particular sounds?

"PRESSED BY THE MOON, MUTE ARBITRESS OF TIDES"   **499**

Responding to the Selection *is a* **reader response** *activity designed to elicit an affective response to the selection.*

Reviewing the Selection *takes students through the work step-by-step, building from their individual responses a complete interpretation of the work.*

Recalling *questions address comprehension of key facts from the selection.*

Interpreting *questions, keyed to the Recalling questions by arrows, evoke interpretations based on evidence from the selection.*

Synthesizing *questions tie together interpretations of parts of the selection and prompt students to make informed generalizations that relate the selection to larger themes or literary trends.*

Understanding Literature *questions provide selection-related study of literary movements, genres, and techniques.*

Instruction in Other Language Arts Skills: An Integrated Approach

It has been shown that a student may demonstrate knowledge in a classroom but be unable to use that knowledge in "real-life" situations. Grammar, usage, mechanics, spelling, and vocabulary skills have traditionally been taught in isolation as independent skills, but just as instruction in the separate concepts of physiology does not make us healthier, neither does instruction in the abstract concepts of speech or grammar make us speak or write better (Hillocks; Braddock). Skills must be taught in ways that enable students to "transfer" them to real contexts, i.e., to use them in their lives. The transferability of knowledge is a function of meaningfulness (Prawat). Teachers can promote meaningfulness by providing (1) a wide variety of examples, (2) practice in a wide variety of contexts, (3) an explanation of the value or uses of the learning, (4) an advance organizer at the beginning of the lesson, and (5) reviews. These five tasks have served as guideposts in the planning and writing of *Literature and the Language Arts*.

The exercises in this text are organized so that instruction in essential skills—those for writing, language, speaking, listening, study and research, thinking, test-taking, and applied English—develops in the context of literature appreciation activities. The study of engaging literature can provide motivation and context for teaching these practical skills.

The **Prereading** activities in this text include, in addition to a journal activity, a variable **Language Arts Skills** activity that relates to and prepares the student for reading the selection. For instance, before students read entries

Sample Language Arts Skills Activities Page

Responding in Writing activities use the selection as a springboard for engaging writing assignments.

Integrated **Language Lab** activities provide practice in essential language skills.

A second variable **Language Arts Skills** activity provides integrated practice in Speaking and Listening, Study and Research, Thinking, or Applied English.

Many lessons end with special **Projects** that extend your teaching beyond immediate language arts applications and that call upon multiple intelligences.

---

2. **Anaphora. Anaphora** is any word or phrase that repeats or refers to something that precedes or follows it. Find the first references in the poem to the moon, the storm, the waves, and the wind. What words or phrases are used as anaphora for these things?

Responding in Writing

Epitaph. An epitaph is an inscription or verse written to be used on a tomb or written in commemoration of someone who has died. Write an epitaph for a wave. Decide whether your epitaph will be read aloud or, if it will be inscribed, where it will be inscribed. In your epitaph, depict what was special about the wave during its life and what effects it had on others, including yourself.

Language Lab

Vivid Verbs. Part of the strength of Charlotte Smith's description of the force of the tide comes from her choice of colorful action words. Read the Language Arts Survey, 2.33, "Using Vivid Verbs." Then replace the verbs or verb phrases in the following sentences with more vivid and effective words. Some sentences have more than one verb or verb phrase. Use a thesaurus or a dictionary as necessary.

1. The moon affects the tides.
2. In line 4 of the sonnet, the tide arrives on the land.
3. Line 6 tells about how a wave begins.
4. Charlotte Smith influenced the Romantic poets who followed her.
5. Smith worked hard to support her ten children.

Thinking Skills

Observing. Charlotte Smith had surely observed the sea carefully before she composed her poem. Read the Language Arts Survey, 4.6, "Observing." Then, from the list below, choose two perspectives from which to observe the moon, the sea, a storm, clouds, astronomical or five minutes, tak and use a separa

a writer plan
a designer p
a painter pla
a poet plann

500 UNIT SEVEN / THE RESTORAT

PROJECTS

1. **Storytelling: Germanic Mythology.** In Cædmon's time, a harp was often passed around after feasts so the guests could sing in verse. Do some research in the library to gather stories from the ancient Germanic myths (especially the German, Icelandic, and Norse myths). Sit in a circle in class and take turns telling these myths to one another. You

2. **An Anglo-Saxon Feast.** As a class, plan a recital during which you can read verses. You and your classmates may want to read your own verses from Responding in Writing, Exercise 1, or you may want to find more Old English verses in books from your library. As an extra touch, you may want to serve refreshments and food at the recital, in imitation of an Anglo-Saxon feast.

from Samuel Johnson's *A Dictionary of the English Language*, they receive a lesson on using dictionaries (study and research skills).

Most skills activities come after the selection.

The **Responding in Writing** activities use the selection as a springboard for creative, interesting writing assignments. **Language Labs** give students practice in essential grammar, usage, and mechanics skills; explore applications of grammar skills to writing; and present key concepts related to varieties of English. A second variable **Language Arts Skills** activity provides more integrated practice in Speaking and Listening, Study and Research, Thinking, or Applied English.

A typical skills activity asks students to read a section of the Language Arts Survey and then complete the exercise. The exercises concern the literature students have just studied. For instance, an exercise following "Cædmon's Hymn" might teach students capitalization of deities and religious texts by asking them to proofread for correct capitalization in a paragraph that discusses traditional Norse creation stories. A lesson following the medieval ballad "The Great Silkie of Shule Skerrie" might ask students to identify parts of speech as used in a paragraph that tells the story of the medieval ballad "The Wife of Usher's Well."

Most lessons in the student edition end with one or more **Projects** related to the selection. These projects extend the instruction in the lesson in ways that call upon students' multiple intelligences.

Because language arts skills traditionally have been taught independently, and because conceptual knowledge of grammar, usage, and mechanics is part of cultural literacy, independent Language Labs are also offered at the end of each unit. The twelve end-of-unit Language Labs cover the most essential concepts in grammar, usage, mechanics, spelling, and the varieties of English.

The **Language Arts Survey** at the back of the book provides a comprehensive overview of the complete range of language arts skills. The survey is divided into five sections, as follows:

- Essential Skills: Writing
- Essential Skills: Language
- Essential Skills: Speaking and Listening
- Essential Skills: Study and Research
- Essential Skills: Applied English/ Tech Prep

Students may refer to these sections when doing writing or skills activities. Teachers wishing to give their students additional practice in any of these skills areas will find, for each lesson in the Language Arts Survey, a corresponding worksheet in one of the five **Essential Skills Practice Books** found in the Teacher's Resource Kit. Teachers wishing to present whole units related to specific skills can have students work through parts of the Language Arts Survey, doing the activities found there and in the *Essential Skills Practice Books*.

Partial Bibliography

Ausubel, D. *Educational Psychology.* 2nd ed. New York: Holt, 1978.

Braddock, R., R. Lloyd-Jones, and L. Schoer. *Research in Written Composition.* Champaign, IL: NCTE, 1963. (ED 003 374)

Bruner, J. *Toward a Theory of Instruction.* New York: Norton, 1966.

Eggen, P., and D. Kauchak. *Educational Psychology: Classroom Connections.* 2nd ed. New York: Merrill, 1994.

Eisner, E. *The Educational Imagination.* 2nd ed. New York: Macmillan, 1985.

Hillocks, G., Jr. *Research on Written Composition: New Directions for Teaching.* Urbana, IL: Natl. Conference on Research in English and ERIC/CRCS, 1986.

Prawat, R. "Promoting Access to Knowledge, Strategy, and Disposition in Students: A Research Synthesis." *Review of Educational Research* 59 (1989): 1–41.

Novak, J. D. *A Theory of Education.* Ithaca, NY: Cornell UP, 1984.

Extended **Language Labs** at the end of each unit in the student edition treat the most essential skills in grammar, usage, mechanics, spelling, and the varieties of English.

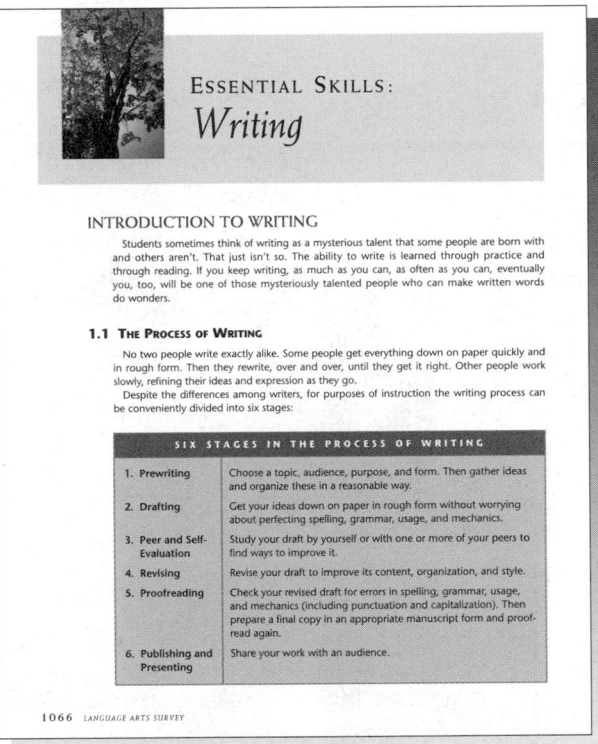

The **Language Arts Survey** at the end of the student edition provides a comprehensive overview of the complete range of language arts skills.

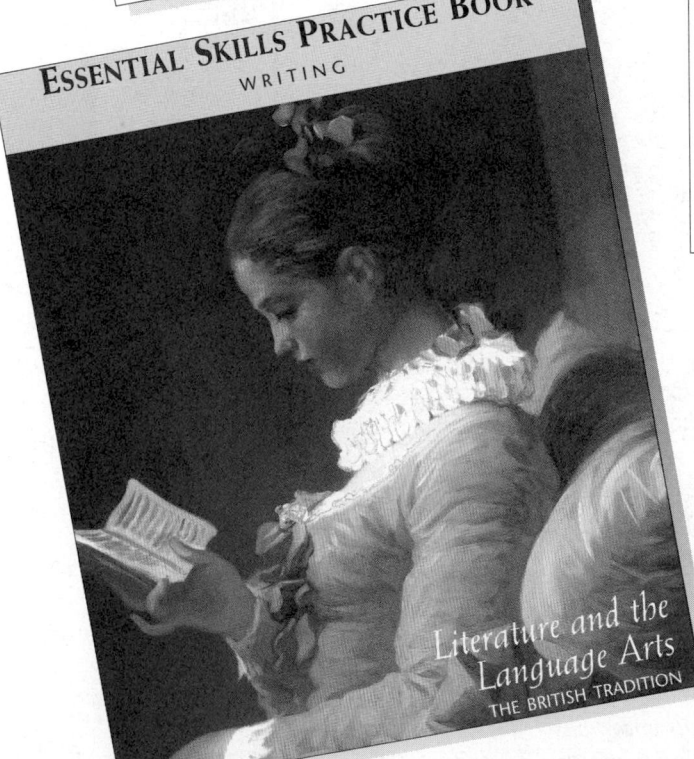

Essential Skills Practice Books found in the Teacher's Resource Kit provide activities keyed to each lesson in the Language Arts Survey.

The **Annotated Teacher's Edition** is designed for your convenience.

Answers for exercises are usually provided on the same pages as the exercises themselves. All items are color-coded: answers to student edition exercises are on white backgrounds, supplementary notes and activities are on yellow backgrounds, and special items, such as lists of goals, enrichment and remedial notes, and selection check test answers, use distinguishing colors.

Sample Unit Opening Pages

Teaching the Multiple Intelligences lists activities from the unit that call for the exercise of students' multiple intelligences.

Connections Across the Curriculum lists the cross-curricular activities from the unit.

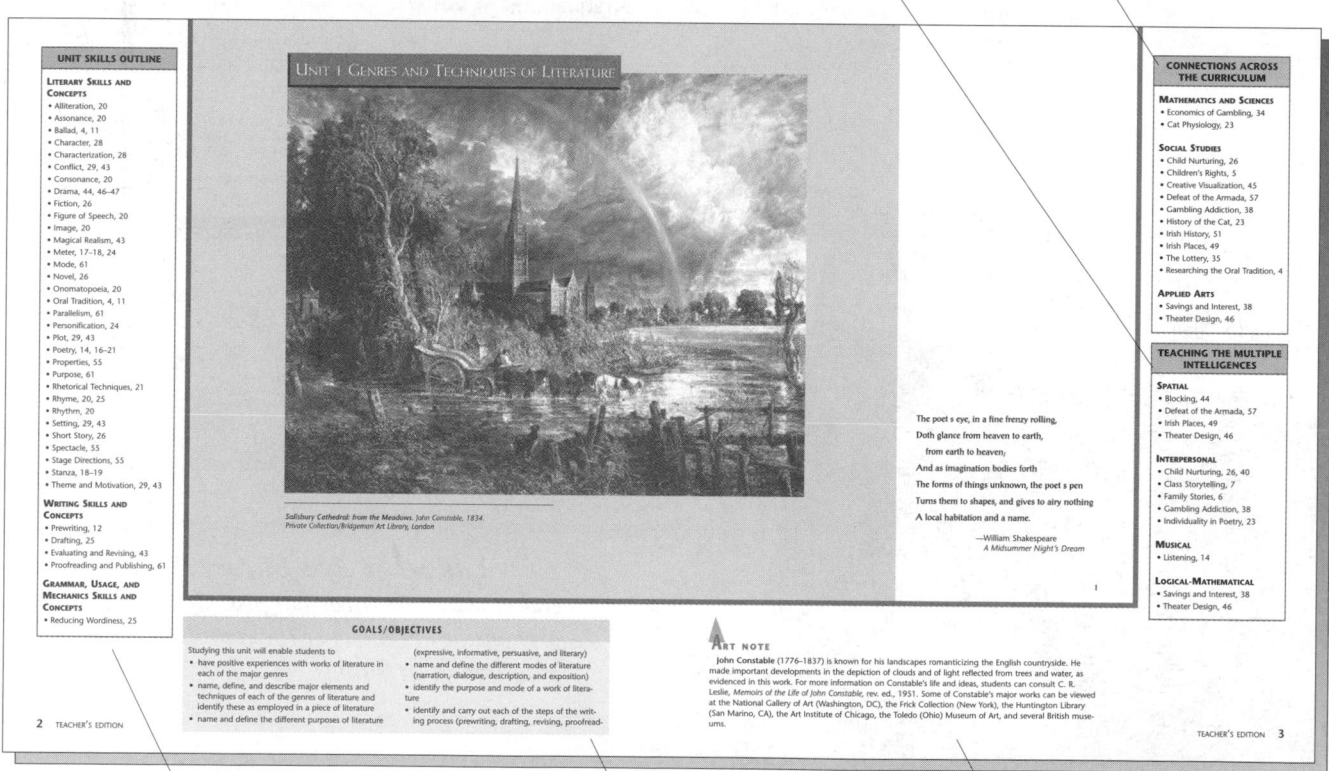

UNIT SKILLS OUTLINE

LITERARY SKILLS AND CONCEPTS
- Alliteration, 20
- Assonance, 20
- Ballad, 4, 11
- Character, 28
- Characterization, 28
- Conflict, 29, 43
- Consonance, 20
- Drama, 44, 46–47
- Fiction, 26
- Figure of Speech, 20
- Image, 20
- Magical Realism, 43
- Meter, 17–18, 24
- Mode, 61
- Novel, 61
- Onomatopoeia, 20
- Oral Tradition, 4, 11
- Parallelism, 61
- Personification, 24
- Plot, 29, 43
- Poetry, 14, 16–21
- Properties, 55
- Purpose, 61
- Rhetorical Techniques, 21
- Rhyme, 20, 25
- Rhythm, 20
- Setting, 29, 43
- Short Story, 26
- Spectacle, 55
- Stage Directions, 55
- Stanza, 18–19
- Theme and Motivation, 29, 43

WRITING SKILLS AND CONCEPTS
- Prewriting, 12
- Drafting, 25
- Evaluating and Revising, 43
- Proofreading and Publishing, 61

GRAMMAR, USAGE, AND MECHANICS SKILLS AND CONCEPTS
- Reducing Wordiness, 25

UNIT 1 GENRES AND TECHNIQUES OF LITERATURE

Salisbury Cathedral from the Meadows, John Constable, 1834.
Private Collection/Bridgeman Art Library, London

The poet's eye, in a fine frenzy rolling,
Doth glance from heaven to earth,
 from earth to heaven;
And as imagination bodies forth
The forms of things unknown, the poet's pen
Turns them to shapes, and gives to airy nothing
A local habitation and a name.

—William Shakespeare
A Midsummer Night's Dream

CONNECTIONS ACROSS THE CURRICULUM

MATHEMATICS AND SCIENCES
- Economics of Gambling, 34
- Cat Physiology, 23

SOCIAL STUDIES
- Child Nurturing, 26
- Children's Rights, 5
- Creative Visualization, 45
- Defeat of the Armada, 57
- Gambling Addiction, 38
- History of the Cat, 23
- Irish History, 51
- Irish Places, 49
- The Lottery, 35
- Researching the Oral Tradition, 4

APPLIED ARTS
- Savings and Interest, 38
- Theater Design, 46

TEACHING THE MULTIPLE INTELLIGENCES

SPATIAL
- Blocking, 44
- Defeat of the Armada, 57
- Irish Places, 49
- Theater Design, 46

INTERPERSONAL
- Child Nurturing, 26, 40
- Class Storytelling, 7
- Family Stories, 6
- Gambling Addiction, 38
- Individuality in Poetry, 23

MUSICAL
- Listening, 14

LOGICAL-MATHEMATICAL
- Savings and Interest, 38
- Theater Design, 46

GOALS/OBJECTIVES

Studying this unit will enable students to
- have positive experiences with works of literature in each of the major genres
- name, define, and describe major elements and techniques of each of the genres of literature and identify these as employed in a piece of literature
- name and define the different purposes of literature (expressive, informative, persuasive, and literary)
- name and define the different modes of literature (narration, dialogue, description, and exposition)
- identify the purpose and mode of a work of literature
- identify and carry out each of the steps of the writing process (prewriting, drafting, revising, proofreading...)

ART NOTE

John Constable (1776–1837) is known for his landscapes romanticizing the English countryside. He made important developments in the depiction of clouds and of light reflected from trees and water, as evidenced in this work. For more information on Constable's life and ideas, students can consult C. R. Leslie, *Memoirs of the Life of John Constable*, rev. ed., 1951. Some of Constable's major works can be viewed at the National Gallery of Art (Washington, DC), the Frick Collection (New York), the Huntington Library (San Marino, CA), the Art Institute of Chicago, the Toledo (Ohio) Museum of Art, and several British museums.

The **Unit Skills Outline** lists the skills taught in the student edition. This list is particularly useful for planning if you do not take an historical approach.

A list of **Goals/Objectives** helps you plan overall intended learning outcomes for teaching the unit. Affective goals are consistent with the philosophy of the program and its emphasis on reader involvement. Cognitive goals encompass content, literary technique, and interpretation in historical context.

Art Notes provide historical background for works and biographical information about artists, relate works to themes in the unit, and describe important artistic trends and techniques.

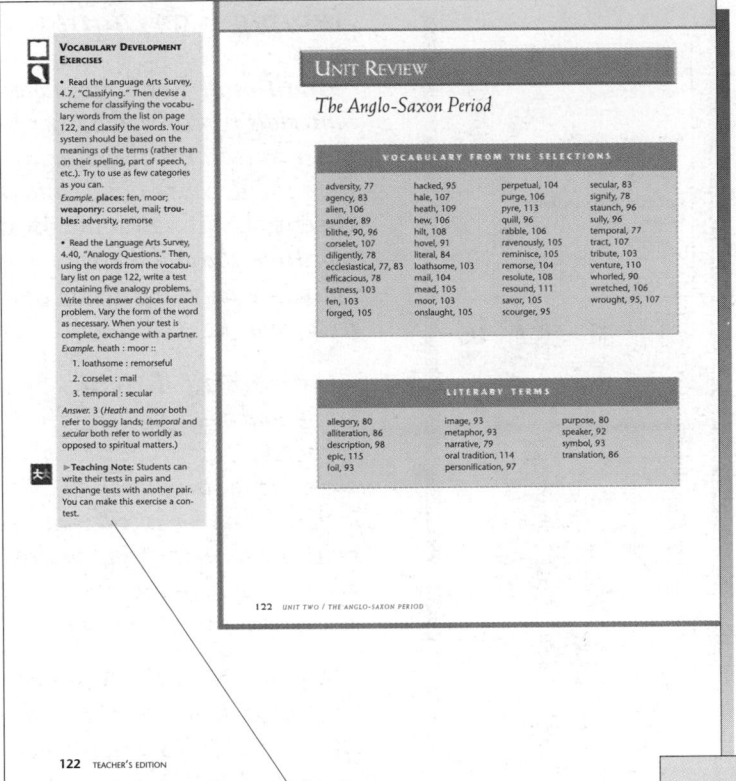

VOCABULARY DEVELOPMENT EXERCISES

• Read the Language Arts Survey, 4.7, "Classifying." Then devise a scheme for classifying the vocabulary words from the list on page 122, and classify the words. Your system should be based on the meanings of the terms (rather than on their spelling, part of speech, etc.). Try to use as few categories as you can.
Example. **places:** fen, moor; **weaponry:** corselet, mail; **troubles:** adversity, remorse

• Read the Language Arts Survey, 4.40, "Analogy Questions." Then, using the words from the vocabulary list on page 122, write a test containing five analogy problems. Write three answer choices for each problem. Vary the form of the word as necessary. When your test is complete, exchange with a partner.
Example. heath : moor ::
  1. loathsome : remorseful
  2. corselet : mail
  3. temporal : secular
Answer. 3 (*Heath* and *moor* both refer to boggy lands; *temporal* and *secular* both refer to worldly as opposed to spiritual matters.)

▶**Teaching Note:** Students can write their tests in pairs and exchange tests with another pair. You can make this exercise a contest.

UNIT REVIEW

The Anglo-Saxon Period

VOCABULARY FROM THE SELECTIONS

adversity, 77	hacked, 95	perpetual, 104	secular, 83
agency, 83	hale, 107	purge, 106	signify, 78
alien, 106	heath, 109	pyre, 113	staunch, 96
asunder, 89	hew, 108	quill, 96	sully, 96
blithe, 90, 96	hilt, 108	rabble, 106	temporal, 77
corselet, 107	hovel, 91	ravenously, 105	tract, 107
diligently, 78	literal, 84	reminisce, 105	tribute, 103
ecclesiastical, 77, 83	loathsome, 103	remorse, 104	venture, 110
efficacious, 78	mail, 104	resolute, 108	whorled, 90
fastness, 103	mead, 105	resound, 111	wretched, 106
fen, 103	moor, 103	savor, 105	wrought, 95, 107
forged, 105	onslaught, 105	scourger, 95	

LITERARY TERMS

allegory, 80	image, 93	purpose, 80
alliteration, 86	metaphor, 93	speaker, 92
description, 98	narrative, 79	symbol, 93
epic, 115	oral tradition, 114	translation, 86
foil, 93	personification, 97	

122   UNIT TWO / THE ANGLO-SAXON PERIOD

Supplementary **Vocabulary Development Exercises** *help diversify your teaching.*

Sample Unit Review Pages

***Additional Resources notes** identify assessment materials for the unit and study guides and worksheets for student review and practice.*

SYNTHESIS: QUESTIONS FOR WRITING, RESEARCH, OR DISCUSSION

GENRE STUDIES

1. What is an heroic epic? How does the poem *Beowulf* meet that definition? What makes the poem an epic? How does the character Beowulf meet the Anglo-Saxon ideal of the hero?

THEMATIC STUDIES

2. Explore the theme of the outcast in "The Wife's Lament" and in *Beowulf*. How do the treatments of outcasts differ in the two poems? Which poem is sympathetic toward outcasts? Which is not?

HISTORICAL AND BIOGRAPHICAL STUDIES

3. The pre-Christian Anglo-Saxon world view was essentially grim and fatalistic. Describe the pre-Christian Anglo-Saxon world view as presented in "The Conversion of King Edwin" and in *Beowulf*.

4. Describe the structure of early Anglo-Saxon society and the importance of kinship in that society. Support your points with examples from "The Wife's Lament" and *Beowulf*.

5. Explain the effects of the coming of Christianity on Anglo-Saxon culture and literature. Use examples from "The Conversion of King Edwin," "Cædmon's Hymn," the Anglo-Saxon Riddles, and *Beowulf*.

▷ These prompts are suitable as topics for research papers. Refer to the Language Arts Survey, 4.25–4.39, "Research Skills." (To evaluate research papers, see the evaluation forms for writing, revising, and proofreading in the *Assessment Portfolio*, 7.1–7.10.)

▷ These prompts can be adapted for use as topics for oral reports or debates. (To evaluate these projects, see the evaluation forms in the *Assessment Portfolio*, 7.17–7.19.)

ADDITIONAL RESOURCES

ASSESSMENT PORTFOLIO
• Vocabulary Worksheet, 4.2.11
• Study Guide: Unit 2 Test, 4.2.12
• Unit 2 Test, 4.2.13

ESSENTIAL SKILLS PRACTICE BOOKS

Language
• Capitalization: Sacred Beings and Writings, 2.125
• Compound and Collective Nouns, 2.5
• Correcting Run-ons, 2.62
• Using the Active Voice, 2.56
• Using Precise Nouns, 2.32
• Using Vivid Verbs, 2.33

Speaking and Listening
• Interpersonal Communication, 3.5

Study and Research
• Using the Card Catalog, 4.22

UNIT TWO / REVIEW   123

Sample Prereading Page

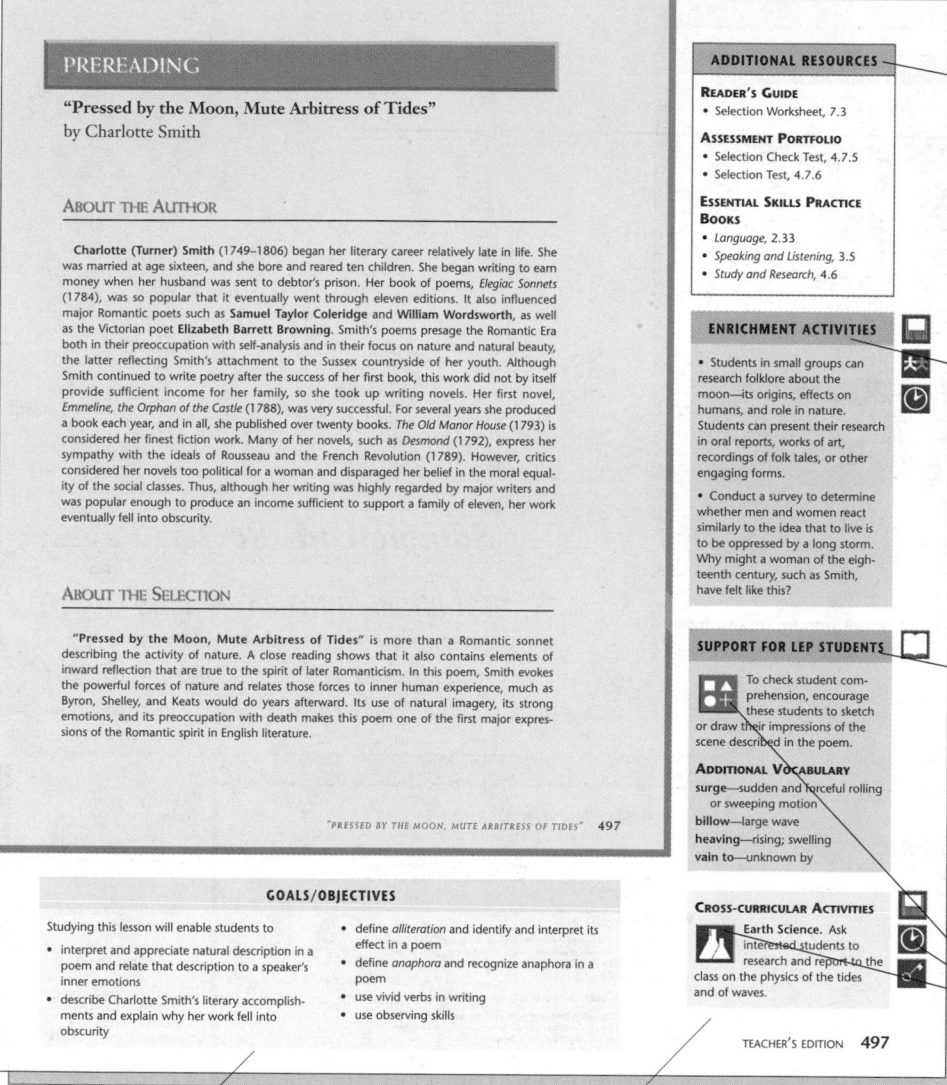

PREREADING

"Pressed by the Moon, Mute Arbitress of Tides"
by Charlotte Smith

ABOUT THE AUTHOR

Charlotte (Turner) Smith (1749–1806) began her literary career relatively late in life. She was married at age sixteen, and she bore and reared ten children. She began writing to earn money when her husband was sent to debtor's prison. Her book of poems, *Elegiac Sonnets* (1784), was so popular that it eventually went through eleven editions. It also influenced major Romantic poets such as **Samuel Taylor Coleridge** and **William Wordsworth**, as well as the Victorian poet **Elizabeth Barrett Browning**. Smith's poems presage the Romantic Era both in their preoccupation with self-analysis and in their focus on nature and natural beauty, the latter reflecting Smith's attachment to the Sussex countryside of her youth. Although Smith continued to write poetry after the success of her first book, this work did not by itself provide sufficient income for her family, so she took up writing novels. Her first novel, *Emmeline, the Orphan of the Castle* (1788), was very successful. For several years she produced a book each year, and in all, she published over twenty books. *The Old Manor House* (1793) is considered her finest fiction work. Many of her novels, such as *Desmond* (1792), express her sympathy with the ideals of Rousseau and the French Revolution (1789). However, critics considered her novels too political for a woman and disparaged her belief in the moral equality of the social classes. Thus, although her writing was highly regarded by major writers and was popular enough to produce an income sufficient to support a family of eleven, her work eventually fell into obscurity.

ABOUT THE SELECTION

"Pressed by the Moon, Mute Arbitress of Tides" is more than a Romantic sonnet describing the activity of nature. A close reading shows that it also contains elements of inward reflection that are true to the spirit of later Romanticism. In this poem, Smith evokes the powerful forces of nature and relates those forces to inner human experience, much as Byron, Shelley, and Keats would do years afterward. Its use of natural imagery, its strong emotions, and its preoccupation with death makes this poem one of the first major expressions of the Romantic spirit in English literature.

"PRESSED BY THE MOON, MUTE ARBITRESS OF TIDES"   **497**

GOALS/OBJECTIVES

Studying this lesson will enable students to

• interpret and appreciate natural description in a poem and relate that description to a speaker's inner emotions

• describe Charlotte Smith's literary accomplishments and explain why her work fell into obscurity

• define *alliteration* and identify and interpret its effect in a poem

• define *anaphora* and recognize anaphora in a poem

• use vivid verbs in writing

• use observing skills

ADDITIONAL RESOURCES

READER'S GUIDE
• Selection Worksheet, 7.3

ASSESSMENT PORTFOLIO
• Selection Check Test, 4.7.5
• Selection Test, 4.7.6

ESSENTIAL SKILLS PRACTICE BOOKS
• *Language*, 2.33
• *Speaking and Listening*, 3.5
• *Study and Research*, 4.6

ENRICHMENT ACTIVITIES

• Students in small groups can research folklore about the moon—its origins, effects on humans, and role in nature. Students can present their research in oral reports, works of art, recordings of folk tales, or other engaging forms.

• Conduct a survey to determine whether men and women react similarly to the idea that to live is to be oppressed by a long storm. Why might a woman of the eighteenth century, such as Smith, have felt like this?

SUPPORT FOR LEP STUDENTS

To check student comprehension, encourage these students to sketch or draw their impressions of the scene described in the poem.

ADDITIONAL VOCABULARY
surge—sudden and forceful rolling or sweeping motion
billow—large wave
heaving—rising; swelling
vain to—unknown by

CROSS-CURRICULAR ACTIVITIES

Earth Science. Ask interested students to research and report to the class on the physics of the tides and of waves.

TEACHER'S EDITION   **497**

Additional Resources *notes identify materials from the Teacher's Resource Kit to use in teaching the selection: worksheets from the Reader's Guide and from the* Essential Skills Practice Books, *recordings from the audiocassette and videocassette, and selection check tests and tests from the* Assessment Portfolio.

Enrichment Activities *provide stimulation and challenge for gifted and high-achieving students, but most are accessible to students of all abilities. These activities call for intellectual creativity, synthetic thinking, and multiple intelligences and often require additional resources and work outside of class.*

Support for LEP Students *teaching notes identify potential trouble spots and offer strategies for helping non-native speakers of English and other limited English proficiency students. Lists and definitions of potentially troublesome* **Idioms, Colloquialisms,** *and* **Additional Vocabulary** *help you offer instruction before students encounter difficulties in reading.*

Color-coded **icons** *identify at a glance* **cross-curricular** *activities (brown),* **multiple intelligences** *activities (green), and* **SCANS** *activities (blue). A key to these icons is provided on page T36 of this* Annotated Teacher's Edition.

A list of **Goals/Objectives** *helps you plan intended learning outcomes for teaching the selection. Affective goals are consistent with the philosophy of the program and its emphasis on reader involvement. Cognitive goals encompass content, literary technique, interpretation of the selection in historical context, and language arts skills taught in the student text.*

Cross-curricular Activities *are supplementary activities that involve knowledge, skills, research, and resources from disciplines other than language arts.*

T20

Sample Selection Page

Prereading Notes for the **Reader's Journal** and **Variable Skills** activities give suggestions for helping students relate the topic to their experience, anticipate questions or difficulties students may have, or provide additional prompts for students who have trouble starting. Special attention is given to problems that may arise from student diversity.

Cross-references to additional instruction, worksheets, and assessment materials are provided throughout the annotations.

Possible **Answers to Guided Reading Questions** are keyed to questions in the student edition.

Answers to Selection Check Test includes the questions and an example and appears on or near the last page of each selection. You can photocopy the test from the *Assessment Portfolio* and distribute it, or you can present the questions orally.

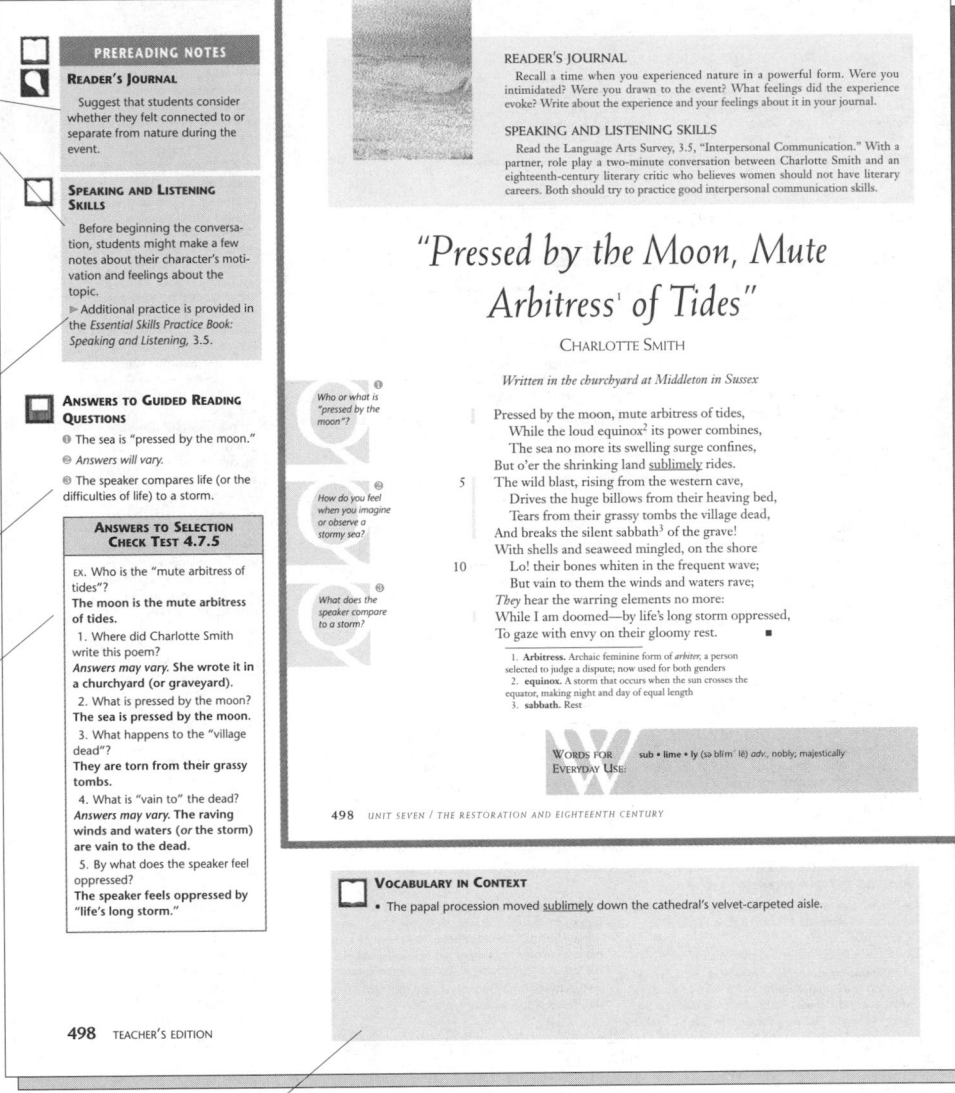

PREREADING NOTES

READER'S JOURNAL

Suggest that students consider whether they felt connected to or separate from nature during the event.

SPEAKING AND LISTENING SKILLS

Before beginning the conversation, students might make a few notes about their character's motivation and feelings about the topic.

▶ Additional practice is provided in the *Essential Skills Practice Book: Speaking and Listening*, 3.5.

ANSWERS TO GUIDED READING QUESTIONS

❶ The sea is "pressed by the moon."

❷ Answers will vary.

❸ The speaker compares life (or the difficulties of life) to a storm.

ANSWERS TO SELECTION CHECK TEST 4.7.5

EX. Who is the "mute arbitress of tides"?
The moon is the mute arbitress of tides.

1. Where did Charlotte Smith write this poem?
Answers may vary. **She wrote it in a churchyard (or graveyard).**

2. What is pressed by the moon?
The sea is pressed by the moon.

3. What happens to the "village dead"?
They are torn from their grassy tombs.

4. What is "vain to" the dead?
Answers may vary. **The raving winds and waters (or the storm) are vain to the dead.**

5. By what does the speaker feel oppressed?
The speaker feels oppressed by "life's long storm."

READER'S JOURNAL

Recall a time when you experienced nature in a powerful form. Were you intimidated? Were you drawn to the event? What feelings did the experience evoke? Write about the experience and your feelings about it in your journal.

SPEAKING AND LISTENING SKILLS

Read the Language Arts Survey, 3.5, "Interpersonal Communication." With a partner, role play a two-minute conversation between Charlotte Smith and an eighteenth-century literary critic who believes women should not have literary careers. Both should try to practice good interpersonal communication skills.

"Pressed by the Moon, Mute Arbitress¹ of Tides"

CHARLOTTE SMITH

Written in the churchyard at Middleton in Sussex

Pressed by the moon, mute arbitress of tides,
  While the loud equinox² its power combines,
  The sea no more its swelling surge confines,
But o'er the shrinking land sublimely rides.
5 The wild blast, rising from the western cave,
  Drives the huge billows from their heaving bed,
  Tears from their grassy tombs the village dead,
And breaks the silent sabbath³ of the grave!
With shells and seaweed mingled, on the shore
10 Lo! their bones whiten in the frequent wave;
  But vain to them the winds and waters rave;
They hear the warring elements no more:
While I am doomed—by life's long storm oppressed,
To gaze with envy on their gloomy rest. ∎

Who or what is "pressed by the moon"?

How do you feel when you imagine or observe a stormy sea?

What does the speaker compare to a storm?

1. **Arbitress.** Archaic feminine form of *arbiter*, a person selected to judge a dispute; now used for both genders
2. **equinox.** A storm that occurs when the sun crosses the equator, making night and day of equal length
3. **sabbath.** Rest

WORDS FOR EVERYDAY USE:
sub • lime • ly (sə blīm´ lē) *adv.*, nobly; majestically

498 UNIT SEVEN / THE RESTORATION AND EIGHTEENTH CENTURY

VOCABULARY IN CONTEXT

• The papal procession moved sublimely down the cathedral's velvet-carpeted aisle.

498 TEACHER'S EDITION

Vocabulary in Context provides sample sentences using the target vocabulary words from *Words for Everyday Use*. For selections of more than one page, a list of all target vocabulary words in the selection is given in **Vocabulary from the Selection** on the first page of the selection.

Sample Selection Activity Page

Responding to the Selection

Make a list of five feelings toward the sea that the poem arouses in you. Are some of these feelings quite different from one another? Compare your list with those made by other members of the class and discuss what details in the poem produced the feelings. Also compare different reactions to the same details.

Reviewing the Selection

RECALLING

1. In lines 1–4, what is happening to the sea? What is happening to the land? What two causes combine to move the mighty ocean?

2. What effect does "the wild blast" cause? From where do the "huge billows" come? What effect do the billows have?

3. In line 12, what do "they" hear no more? Why do they not hear it?

4. In the final line, what does the speaker watch?

INTERPRETING

5. Why is the moon called "mute arbitress of tides"? In what way are the waves "sublime"?

6. In lines 6–8, what metaphor is used to speak of the waves? What contrasts does this metaphor suggest?

7. How is the metaphor of lines 6–8 further developed in lines 9–12?

8. In lines 13–14, how does the speaker feel?

SYNTHESIZING

9. Why might the speaker envy "gloomy rest"? What does this envy imply about how the speaker feels about her or his own life? What might be causing the speaker to feel this way?

10. What parallels or similarities does the poet seem to see between people and the waves? What contrasts between people and the waves are suggested? Do you think the author of the poem views people as part of nature, or does she view people as separate from nature?

Understanding Literature (Questions for Discussion)

1. **Alliteration. Alliteration** is the repetition of initial consonant sounds, as in "<u>w</u>ild <u>w</u>ind." Find instances of alliteration in Smith's sonnet. What sounds are repeated? How frequently are these sounds used elsewhere in the poem? Why do you think Smith may have chosen to use these particular sounds?

"PRESSED BY THE MOON, MUTE ARBITRESS OF TIDES" **499**

Notes on presenting and facilitating the **Responding to the Selection** *assignment help you help students relate the topic to their experience, anticipate questions or difficulties students might have, or suggest alternative formats (such as large or small group discussion, role playing, etc.). These notes give special attention to concerns of diversity.*

Answers for Reviewing the Selection *give sample responses to Recalling, Interpreting, and Synthesizing questions.*

Answers for Understanding Literature *are supplemented by* **Teaching Notes** *that help you to extend the discussion in depth, scope, or both.*

Sample Selection Activity Page

Analytic Scales for Responding in Writing *provide straightforward analytic criteria for evaluating student writing. Cross-references direct you to more elaborate evaluation instruments should you desire them.*

Answers for Variable Skills *provide model answers for Language Skills, Speaking Skills, Listening Skills, Thinking Skills, Study Skills, Research Skills, Test-taking Skills, Applied English Skills, and Vocabulary Skills activities.*

ANSWERS FOR UNDERSTANDING LITERATURE (CONT.)

2. Anaphora. The first reference to the moon is "moon" (line 1); the first reference to the storm is "equinox" (line 2); the first reference to the waves is "swelling surge" (line 3); the first reference to the wind is "wild blast" (line 5). The phrase "mute arbitress of tides" (line 1) and "its" (line 2) are anaphora for the moon; "wild blast" (line 5) refers to the wind, and "huge billows" (line 6) refers to the waves; "warring elements" (line 12) refers to the wind and the waters together.

ANALYTIC SCALES FOR RESPONDING IN WRITING

Assign a score from 1 to 25 for each grading criterion below. (For more detailed evaluation, see the evaluation forms for writing, revising, and proofreading, *Assessment Portfolio*, 7.1–7.10.)

Epitaph
• **Content/Unity.** The epitaph presents a commemoration for a wave. It names the wave's special aspects and its effect on the writer.
• **Organization/Coherence.** The epitaph identifies its subject and then provides reasons for honoring its subject in a sensible order.
• **Language/Style.** The epitaph uses formal language and a serious tone.
• **Conventions.** The epitaph avoids errors in spelling, grammar, usage, mechanics, and manuscript form.

ANSWERS FOR THINKING SKILLS

Students should make observations from two perspectives. For each perspective, students should show careful note taking and demonstrate the use of charts, checklists, or other planning devices.
▶ Additional practice is provided in the *Essential Skills Practice Book: Study and Research*, 4.6.

500 TEACHER'S EDITION

---

2. **Anaphora. Anaphora** is any word or phrase that repeats or refers to something that precedes or follows it. Find the first references in the poem to the moon, the storm, the waves, and the wind. What words or phrases are used as anaphora for these things?

Responding in Writing

Epitaph. An **epitaph** is an inscription or verse written to be used on a tomb or written in commemoration of someone who has died. Write an epitaph for a wave. Decide whether your epitaph will be read aloud or, if it will be inscribed, where it will be inscribed. In your epitaph, depict what was special about the wave during its life and what effects it had on others, including yourself.

Language Lab

Vivid Verbs. Part of the strength of Charlotte Smith's description of the force of the tide comes from her choice of colorful action words. Read the Language Arts Survey, 2.33, "Using Vivid Verbs." Then replace the verbs or verb phrases in the following sentences with more vivid and effective words. Some sentences have more than one verb or verb phrase. Use a thesaurus or a dictionary as necessary.

1. The moon affects the tides.
2. In line 4 of the sonnet, the tide arrives on the land.
3. Line 6 tells about how a wave begins.
4. Charlotte Smith influenced the Romantic poets who followed her.
5. Smith worked hard to support her ten children.

Thinking Skills

Observing. Charlotte Smith had surely observed the sea carefully before she composed her poem. Read the Language Arts Survey, 4.6, "Observing." Then, from the list below, choose two perspectives from which to observe the moon, the sea, a storm, clouds, or some other astronomical or natural object or event. From each perspective, conduct your observations for five minutes, taking careful notes. Prepare observation charts or checklists before observing, and use a separate sheet of paper for each set of observations. Try to avoid making judgments.

a writer planning a short story about the future

a designer planning an advertising campaign

a painter planning a landscape or seascape

a poet planning a poem about hope or about emptiness

500 UNIT SEVEN / THE RESTORATION AND EIGHTEENTH CENTURY

ANSWERS FOR LANGUAGE LAB

Answers will vary. Possible answers are given.
1. The moon **toys with** the tides.
2. In line 4 of the sonnet, the tide **conquers** the land.
3. Line 6 **presents a powerful image of** how a wave begins.
4. Charlotte Smith **moved and inspired** the Romantic poets who **emulated** her.

5. Smith **toiled** to **feed and clothe** her ten children.

FOR MORE PRACTICE
Problem. The wind along the shore is loud.
Answer. The wind **screams** along the shore.
▶ Additional practice is provided in the *Essential Skills Practice Book: Language*, 2.33.

Answers for Language Lab *often includes* **For More Practice,** *which provides an additional item you can use after instruction to verify mastery.*

Project Notes *(not shown) provide suggestions and caveats for introducing, supporting, and monitoring student work on projects. These notes identify additional resources or persons that may be needed or useful and opportunities for enlarging or limiting the scope and duration of the project.*

Using Literature and the Language Arts *for Writing Instruction*

Recent Advances in the Theory of Writing Instruction

Let's face it. Learning to write well isn't easy. Simply mastering the conventions of spelling, grammar, usage, and mechanics takes years. Learning to write elegant, balanced sentences takes years more. Then there are all those tricks of the writer's craft—the forms or genres, the methods of organization, the rhetorical techniques and figures of speech, the modulations of tone and register, the subtleties of connotation. All these must be learned and then, in a sense, forgotten so that the writer's words flow from some deep, authentic place, from some uncommon spring, to produce a voice, a style. Little wonder it is then that Yeats should write, "there is no fine thing/Since Adam's fall but needs much laboring," or that Chaucer should remind us of the Latin adage *Ars longa; vita brevis:* "Art is long; life, short."

Given the time and effort that it takes to become even reasonably competent as a writer, it follows that no one would do so without some powerful motive. Fortunately for English teachers, children come into the world with such a motive. The child, newly arrived, cries out, trying to communicate: it's cold out here, and strange. As children grow, they keep trying to communicate and will keep trying so long as the will to do so isn't drowned in a sea of criticism.

One of the most exciting things that has happened in English education in the past few years is that a new model of writing instruction that respects the student's voice and effort has come to the fore. That model is the process and portfolio approach. Process and portfolio instruction breaks individual acts of writing and the overall business of learning to write into manageable steps, with guidance and feedback at each step. Today, when students are given writing assignments, they no longer have to figure out on their own how to get from the assignment to the completed piece of writing. Instead, they are trained in techniques for prewriting, drafting, evaluating their drafts by themselves and with peers, revising, and publishing. Writing portfolios and evaluation forms are used to track development of pieces of writing over time. Assessment has been expanded from simple marking of papers to include self-evaluation, peer evaluation, and a variety of approaches that avoid turning teachers into copyeditors. The result of these changes in writing instruction has been that student writing has improved dramatically in recent years.

Literature and the Language Arts contains comprehensive materials for integrated instruction in the process of writing and for management of writing portfolios. The notes that follow describe those materials and how they can be used.

Pretesting and Post-testing

Before beginning instruction in the process of writing, you may wish to have students do the Pretest: Writing Terminology and Techniques, 3.1.1, in the *Assessment Portfolio* contained in the Teacher's Resource Kit. This test is designed to assess students' familiarity with basic writing concepts and skills. A Post-test: Writing Terminology and Techniques, 3.1.2, in the *Assessment Portfolio*, can be given at the end of the course to assess students' overall progress in basic writing concepts and skills.

Introducing the Writing Process

Section 1 of the Language Arts Survey, which is called Essential Skills: Writing and begins on page 1066, surveys the entire writing process from prewriting through publishing. This section of the Survey is divided into forty-nine lessons, each containing instructional material and a writing activity. Additional practice activities for each lesson in the Language Arts Survey can be found in the *Essential Skills Practice Book: Writing* in the Teacher's Resource Kit.

Teachers who wish to do so can teach the Essential Skills: Writing section of the Language Arts Survey in its entirety as a separate composition unit. Alternatively, teachers can have students refer to the writing section of the Language Arts Survey on an as-needed basis as they complete the composition assignments in the main body of the text.

Unit 1 of the student edition is divided into five sections. The study apparatuses following the selections in Unit 1 contain a single cumulative writing assignment (writing a literary narrative) designed to introduce students to the process of writing. Teachers may introduce the writing process by having their students do this cumulative writing assignment. Before beginning the assignment, students should read sections 1.1 through 1.4 of Essential Skills: Writing, pages 1066–1070. These pages briefly survey the steps in the writing process and teach students how to use writers' journals, writers' portfolios, and computer hardware and software for writing. Each part of the cumulative writing assignment in Unit 1 asks students to complete a step in the writing process and refers them to lessons in the Essential Skills: Writing section for additional information. It is recommended that students review the relevant Essential Skills: Writing sections before doing each part of the assignment.

After students have finished the cumulative writing assignment, distribute copies of the Study Guide: The Process of Writing, 5.1.1, in the *Assessment Portfolio*. This guide will help students to review what they have learned about the writing process in preparation for taking the Test: The Process of Writing, 5.1.2, in the *Assessment Portfolio*.

As students complete their first writing assignment and all subsequent writing assignments in the text, they can make use of the following general evaluation forms and checklists found in the *Assessment Portfolio*:

- Writing Summary Form, 6.11

- Writing Evaluation Form: Process, 7.1

- Writing Evaluation Form: The Writing Plan, 7.2

- Writing Evaluation Form: Structural Evaluation, 7.3

- Writing Evaluation Form: Analytic Scale, 7.4

- Writing Evaluation Form: Holistic Response, 7.5

- Peer and Self-Evaluation Form: Writing, 7.6

- Revision Assessment Form, 7.7

- Revision Checklist, 7.8

- Proofreading Checklist, 7.9

- Proofreading Record, 7.10

Teaching the Writing Assignments in the Text

Following most selections in this text are activities called Responding in Writing. These activities use the literature selections as springboards for an enormous variety of engaging writing assignments. A glance at the writing section of the Index of Skills on page 1285 will give you an idea of just how varied and interesting the types of writing covered in this text are. In most cases, two Responding in Writing activities are given after each selection. You can choose to assign one or both, or you can give students the option of doing either of the two assignments.

As students complete these assignments, they can refer to relevant sections of the Essential Skills: Writing section of the Language Arts Survey. They can also make use of the many evaluation forms and checklists in the *Assessment Portfolio*.

The writing assignments in the text consist of prompts. Complete prewriting guidance for each writing assignment can be found on the Selection Worksheet that corresponds to any given selection. Selection Worksheets can be found in the *Reader's Guide and Activity Workbook* in the Teacher's Resource Kit.

For each writing assignment in the student edition, there is in this *Annotated Teacher's Edition* an Analytic Scale for Evaluation presenting assessment criteria for content, organization, style, and conventions of grammar, usage, mechanics, spelling, and manuscript form. The editors and authors of this text strongly suggest that these evaluation scales be given to students when they receive the initial writing prompts so that they can keep the eventual evaluation criteria in mind as they work through the writing process. These scales can also be used by students for peer evaluation and self-evaluation. Alternatively, or in addition, students can do peer evaluation and self-evaluation using the evaluation forms in the *Assessment Portfolio.*

Process for Writing Assignments

The editors and authors recommend the sequence of activities in the chart at the right for each writing assignment in the main body of the text:

Steps 1–11 may be repeated for each writing assignment. Then, periodically, step 12 should also be completed.

Using Writing Portfolios

The student's Writing Portfolio is a folder in which he or she stores drafts and finished pieces of writing. You can ask your students to keep a portfolio to enable you and the students to assess their progress over time. Portfolios show students' capabilities and progress better than any test or single writing assignment can.

You may wish to ask your students to keep **comprehensive portfolios** that contain all the writing that they do for class, along with Writing Summary Forms and/or evaluation forms for each piece of writing. Alternatively, you can ask your students to keep **selected portfolios** that contain pieces of writing chosen by the students as representative of their best work. Students should be encouraged to choose for their selected portfolios pieces that show the various skills they have developed and the various types of writing that they have done (informative, persuasive, creative, etc.).

When students place works in their portfolios, make sure that they attach

PROCESS FOR WRITING ASSIGNMENTS

1. WHOLE CLASS: Study of the literature selection in the student edition textbook, along with its corresponding instructional apparatus

2. TEACHER: Introduction of the writing prompt from the student text

3. STUDENT: Prewriting (with reference to any applicable prewriting lessons in the Essential Skills: Writing section of the Language Arts Survey, pages 1071–1096 of the student text)

4. STUDENT: Drafting (with reference to the drafting lessons in the Essential Skills: Writing section of the Language Arts Survey, pages 1096–1100 of the student text)

5. STUDENT: Sharing of draft with one or more peers

6. STUDENT and PEER(S): Evaluation of the draft and conferencing with one another and with the teacher if necessary (with reference to the Analytic Scale for Evaluation from the *Annotated Teacher's Edition* and/or the general evaluation forms and revision checklists, 7.1–7.8, in the *Assessment Portfolio*)

7. STUDENT: Revising (with reference to the Revision Assessment Form and Revision Checklist, 7.7 and 7.8, in the *Assessment Portfolio,* and to the revision sections of the Essential Skills: Writing section of the Language Arts Survey, pages 1100–1103 of the student text)

8. STUDENT: Proofreading and preparation of the final manuscript (with reference to the Proofreading Checklist and Proofreading Record, 7.9 and 7.10, in the *Assessment Portfolio,* and to the proofreading and manuscript preparation sections of the Essential Skills: Writing section of the Language Arts Survey, pages 1103–1105 of the student text) and completion of the Writing Survey Form, 6.11, in the *Assessment Portfolio*

9. STUDENT and PEER(S): Publishing and/or presenting of the completed draft (with reference to the lesson on publishing and presenting in the Essential Skills: Writing section of the Language Arts Survey, page 1105 of the student text)

10. STUDENT and TEACHER: Assessment and/or conferencing with regard to the completed work

11. STUDENT: Decision as to whether to place the completed work in the student's Writing Portfolio

12. STUDENT and TEACHER: Evaluate the student's Writing Portfolio (using the Comprehensive Portfolio Evaluation Form: Student and the Comprehensive Portfolio Evaluation Form: Teacher, 6.9 and 6.10, in the *Assessment Portfolio*) and hold a teacher-student conference to discuss the evaluation and to set goals for future writing improvement

their notes and drafts behind these works so that you will be able to see at a glance how each piece of writing was developed. Also have students attach to their works any evaluation forms they have used.

From time to time, you will want to do a comprehensive evaluation of the students' portfolios. A Comprehensive Evaluation Form: Teacher, 6.10, in the *Assessment Portfolio*, has been provided for this purpose. You should also have each student do his or her own comprehensive evaluation using the Comprehensive Evaluation Form: Student, 6.11, in the *Assessment Portfolio*. Once these evaluations are complete, you can meet in a conference with each student to discuss his or her progress, provide praise for work well done, and make plans for improvement in the future.

Assessing Student Writing

(For a more complete treatment of assessment, see the introduction to the *Assessment Portfolio* in the Teacher's Resource Kit.)

Assessment of student writing should not have as its primary purpose meting out rewards or punishments. Instead, assessment should be seen as a development tool allowing the teacher and the student, working in collaboration, to monitor the student's progress toward achieving his or her goals.

Approaches to assessment vary. Two common approaches to assessing writing are analytic evaluation and holistic evaluation.

Analytic Evaluation. An analytic evaluation of a piece of writing begins with an analysis of the several features or qualities desired in the writing. These desired features or qualities are then used as standards or criteria against which the piece is compared. The evaluator merely goes down the list of criteria, giving the piece of writing a score for each criterion. A summary evaluation of the writing is obtained by combining these several scores.

Analytic evaluation is particularly valuable for formative evaluation. A general judgment of a student's work may be daunting, especially for students who do not do as well as they expect to do. Likewise, students who perform well, if given general comments about the writing, find in such general judgments little specific guidance telling them what they might do to write better. An analytic evaluation can show students exactly what their strengths and weaknesses are and where they should concentrate their efforts.

Analytic evaluation is valuable as a measure of either progress or achievement. To evaluate progress, you can evaluate the student's progress in each area by comparing the current work with previous similar writing assignments. To measure raw achievement, you can compare the student's product against some imagined ideal. Of course, in either case you must make sure that your students are aware of the criteria on which they are being graded.

The Analytic Evaluation Scales provided next to the writing assignments in this *Annotated Teacher's Edition* provide lists of appropriate criteria for analytic evaluation, along with simple procedures for scoring. In addition, a general Writing Evaluation Form: Analytic Scale is provided as item 7.4 of the *Assessment Portfolio*.

Holistic Evaluation. Holistic evaluation of a piece of writing calls for an overall judgment. Holistic evaluation is most useful as a measure of achievement. It is difficult to score holistic evaluations according to a student's progress. To do a holistic evaluation, simply look over the general analytic criteria and then assign a score that reflects how well the student met those criteria taken as a whole.

Holistic evaluation takes less time than analytic evaluation and in most cases results in the same score. The saved time can be used to make encouraging written comments to the student, pointing out features of the writing that you admire and features of the writing that you would like to see improve in later work by the student. A general Writing Evaluation Form: Holistic Response is provided in the *Assessment Portfolio* as item 7.5.

Grading. Some teachers prefer to grade each writing assignment. Others feel that grading selected assignments chosen by the teacher and student to reflect the student's best work provides a more realistic assessment of the student's optimal capabilities. If the latter option is chosen, you may wish to provide credit for completion of assignments that are not graded.

Marking Student Papers. A student who receives back from a teacher a paper covered with corrections in red ink is not likely to be encouraged to do more and better writing. Furthermore, such marking of student papers is enormously time consuming and discourages frequent writing practice. A more encouraging approach is to mark one or two consistent problems and to mark three or four successes in each paper or, better yet, to allow students and their peers to do such marking and then to review these evaluations in conferences. Such marking can be done in conjunction with the completion of evaluation forms and/or analytic scales.

Reports and Research Papers

Literature and the Language Arts contains complete materials for instruction in the preparation of reports and research papers. The Research Skills section of Essential Skills: Study and Research in the Language Arts Survey, pages 1195–1216 of the student text, contains a complete overview of research procedures from using the library through documenting sources. The Synthesis questions that appear at the end of each Unit Review make excellent topics for extended reports or research papers. Further instruction

on preparing longer papers can be found in the section on Drafting Compositions in Essential Skills: Writing in the Language Arts Survey, pages 1099–1100 of the student text. Of course, these sections of the Language Arts Survey are accompanied by worksheets in the corresponding *Essential Skills Practice Books* in the Teacher's Resource Kit.

Remedial Exercises in Specific Writing Skills

During your evaluations of students' writing, either of individual pieces or of entire portfolios, you will doubtless discover consistent areas of weakness. One student may have trouble with using transitions, another may consistently use serial commas incorrectly, and another may rely too heavily on the passive voice. The Language Arts Survey in the student edition and the accompanying *Essential Skills Practice Book* worksheets provide ample activi-

ties for remediation of particular recurring problems. Most of the instruction and activities in the writing and language sections of the Language Arts Survey are useful for this purpose. Thus if a student has a tendency to write sentence fragments, you can have him or her read the Language Arts Survey, 2.61, "Correcting Sentence Fragments," on page 1125 of the student text. Then you can have that student do the corresponding worksheet in the *Essential Skills Practice Book: Language*. If a student has problems organizing his or her ideas, you can have him or her read the Language Arts Survey, 1.34, "Organizing Ideas," and do the corresponding worksheet in the *Essential Skills Practice Book: Writing*. Thus, the Language Arts Survey and the *Essential Skills Practice Books* can be used to individualize your writing instruction and to target it to remediation of particular writing problems encountered by your students.

Instructional Options

APPROACHES TO LITERATURE AND THE LANGUAGE ARTS

Literature and the Language Arts contains a number of features that allow you the flexibility to organize your instruction as best suits you and your district's requirements. The following chart offers some tips for using the text in your chosen way.

FEATURES OF THE PROGRAM, BY APPROACH

Historical Approach

- The Unit Introductions tie literary developments to influential intellectual currents and political events, providing historical contexts for the selections.
- About the Author and About the Selection prereading notes provide additional historical background and context.
- Time lines in the introduction provide a spatial representation of watershed events and developments.
- Sections on the Development of the English Language at the ends of Units 2–4 provide historical perspectives on the English language, showing how it has changed over time.

Thematic Approach

- The Thematic Organization Chart on pages T37–T42 lists all the selections in the book under forty-seven major themes.
- Thematic Currents notes in the *Annotated Teacher's Edition* identify three major themes for each unit.
- Responding in Writing prompts following selections ask students to explore and develop their thoughts about thematic topics.
- Synthesis questions in the Unit Review help students explore thematic relations among selections.

Writing Approach

- The activities in Unit 1 lead students through the writing process in a series of carefully sequenced exercises.
- The Selections by Genre chart on page T43 lists all the selections in the book under five genres of writing. Use the chart to find examples of the types of writing you wish to teach.
- The Language Arts Survey, Essential Skills: Writing, following Unit 12, provides instruction in all the phases and forms of writing, editing, and proofreading.
- The *Essential Skills Practice Book: Writing* provides guided exercises in all the phases and forms of writing, editing, and proofreading. These worksheets are keyed to the instructional text in the Language Arts Survey.

Genre Approach

- The Selections by Genre chart on page T43 lists all the selections in the book under five genres of writing. Use the chart to find examples of the types of writing you wish to teach. The selections are arranged in chronological order to help your class trace the historical development of the several genres.
- Unit Introductions and About the Selection prereading notes help your class trace the historical development of the major genres of literature in English.
- Thematic Currents notes in the *Annotated Teacher's Edition* identify two to four major literary concepts or techniques for each unit.
- The Language Arts Survey, Essential Skills: Writing, following Unit 12, provides instruction in techniques that are characteristic of the various genres of writing.
- Questions for Understanding Literature following selections help students understand the use of literary techniques.
- Synthesis questions in the Unit Review relate matters of genre and literary technique to thematic issues.

Skills Approach

- The Language Arts Survey, following Unit 12, provides instruction in the range of language arts skills and concepts, including writing, grammar, usage, mechanics, speaking and listening, study and research, and thinking.
- Use the Scope and Sequence Charts in the *Assessment Portfolio* to locate additional exercises in specific language arts skills.
- The *Essential Skills Practice Books* provide guided exercises in the range of language arts skills: writing, editing, proofreading, grammar, usage, mechanics, speaking and listening, study and research, testing, and thinking. These worksheets are coordinated with the instructional text in the Language Arts Survey.
- The *Assessment Portfolio* contains tests, study guides, and evaluation forms for language arts skills in writing, editing, proofreading, grammar, usage, mechanics, speaking and listening, study and research, testing, and thinking (5.1–5.10). These materials are coordinated with the instructional text in the Language Arts Survey and with the worksheets in the *Essential Skills Practice Books*.
- The *Assessment Portfolio* also contains comprehensive pretests, posttests, study guides, and analytic evaluation forms for skills in reading literature (2.1–2.2), and for skills in writing, language, speaking and listening, and study and research (3.1–3.4).
- The *Essential Skills Practice Book: Applied English* contains coordinated instructional text, worksheets, and assessment materials, including pretests, post-tests, study guides, and analytic evaluation forms; and coordinated skills tests and study guides.

TEACHING STRATEGIES

Teaching to Develop Students' Multiple Intelligences and to Accommodate Diverse Learning Styles

Activities using multiple intelligences are identified by green icons. See the legend on page T36.

Use the techniques in the chart at right to teach and encourage students with diverse intellectual strengths and learning styles and to help all students use and develop the full range of their abilities.

Teaching Students Whose Native Language Is Not English

Use the techniques in the chart at right to facilitate learning and participation for students whose native language is not English.

Teaching Students with Diverse Cultural Backgrounds

Use the techniques in the chart at right to facilitate learning and participation for students with diverse cultural backgrounds.

TEACHING MULTIPLE INTELLIGENCES

- Use multiple modes of expression: e.g., read aloud selections; read aloud questions; use visual aids—charts, graphs, tables, or other graphics, art, and films; play songs; and perform demonstrations.
- Encourage students to use multiple modes of expression, including nonverbal expressions and performances such as drawing, painting, collage, sculpture, dance and choreography, acting and oral interpretation, photography, filmmaking, video production, and musicianship and singing.
- Ask students to read aloud.
- Precede written work with a related oral activity.
- Teach students to use graphic aids for understanding and for studying.
- Facilitate group work.
- Use cooperative learning.
- Allow students ample thinking time.

TEACHING STUDENTS WHOSE NATIVE LANGUAGE IS NOT ENGLISH

- Ask students to read aloud.
- Precede written work with a related oral activity.
- Use cooperative learning.
- Allow ample thinking time.
- When using small groups, pair with English-proficient students.
- Provide ample opportunity for nongraded, even nonevaluated, writing in English.
- Use multiple modes of expression: e.g., read aloud selections; read aloud questions; use visual aids—charts, graphs, tables, or other graphics, art, and films; play songs; and perform demonstrations.
- Encourage students to use multiple modes of expression, including nonverbal expressions and performances such as drawing, painting, collage, sculpture, dance and choreography, acting and oral interpretation, photography, filmmaking, video production, and musicianship and singing.

TEACHING STUDENTS WITH DIVERSE CULTURAL BACKGROUNDS

- Encourage discussion of cultural differences; invite students to share contrasting experiences; invite them to share events and characters that strike them as odd. Rely on students for your cultural information; be aware that you are liable to overlook differences unless you can take up a different point of view.
- Use multiple modes of expression: e.g., read aloud selections; read aloud questions; use visual aids—charts, graphs, tables, or other graphics, art, and films; play songs; and perform demonstrations.
- Encourage students to use multiple modes of expression, including nonverbal expressions and performances such as drawing, painting, collage, sculpture, dance and choreography, acting and oral interpretation, photography, filmmaking, video production, and musicianship and singing.
- Ask students to read aloud.
- Precede written work with a related oral activity.
- Use cooperative learning.
- Allow ample thinking time.
- When using small groups, pair with English-proficient students.
- Preview/explain culturally loaded terms and names.
- Discuss idioms and word origins.
- Discuss topics with universal appeal and relevance—for instance, independence versus family ties; independence versus friendship; identity.
- Discuss literature from both an "insider" and an "outsider" perspective.

Teaching Students with Learning Disabilities

Learning disabilities are physical conditions that make it difficult to complete certain types of tasks. Students with learning disabilities are often highly intelligent but lack specific abilities; for instance, one person may lack the ability to discriminate certain sounds, while another person who has that discrimination may be unable to remember certain auditory messages. Use the techniques in the chart at right to help students with learning disabilities succeed in your classroom.

TEACHING STUDENTS WITH LEARNING DISABILITIES

- Discover the particular effects of each individual's disability and try to fill gaps.
- Allow ample thinking time.
- Seat students in front.
- Repeat important ideas frequently.
- Summarize and check students' bearings frequently.
- Monitor progress frequently.
- On larger projects, provide step-by-step guidance.
- Precede written work with a related oral activity.
- Use cooperative learning.

- Use multiple modes of expression: e.g., read aloud selections; read aloud questions; use visual aids—charts, graphs, tables, or other graphics, art, and films; play songs; and perform demonstrations.
- Encourage students to use multiple modes of expression, including nonverbal expressions and performances such as drawing, painting, collage, sculpture, dance and choreography, acting and oral interpretation, photography, filmmaking, video production, and musicianship and singing.

Teaching Students with Special Academic Gifts and Talents

Just as students who work below grade level may lose interest because tasks are too difficult, students with special academic gifts and talents may lose interest because they complete work quickly or because they are not sufficiently challenged.

Activities involving other curricular areas are identified by red icons. See the legend on page T36.

TEACHING STUDENTS WITH SPECIAL ACADEMIC GIFTS AND TALENTS

- Encourage students to use multiple modes of expression, including nonverbal expressions and performances such as drawing, painting, collage, sculpture, dance and choreography, acting and oral interpretation, photography, filmmaking, video production, and musicianship and singing.
- Use cooperative learning.

- Allow ample thinking time.
- Involve students in the planning, preparation, and presentation or conduct of lessons.
- Provide or encourage extension activities once mastery is demonstrated.
- Provide or encourage self-guided activities and independent research.

> ❝[C]hildren come to school with misconceptions about outside ethnic groups and with a white bias. However, . . . students' racial attitudes can be modified and made more democratic and . . . the racial attitudes of young children are much more easily modified than the attitudes of older students and adults. . . . If we are to help students acquire the attitudes needed to survive in a multicultural and diverse world, we must start early. . . .
>
> "A school experience that is multicultural includes content, examples, and realistic images of diverse racial and ethnic groups. Cooperative learning activities in which students from diverse groups work to attain shared goals is also a feature of the school, as well as simulated images of ethnic groups that present them in positive and realistic ways. Also essential within such a school are adults who model the attitudes and behaviors they are trying to teach. Actions speak much louder than words.❞
>
> —James A. Banks
> "Multicultural Education:
> Historical Development, Dimensions, and Practice"
> *Review of Research in Education*
> 19 (1993): 37–38

Achieving Gender Equity

Sexism cannot be combatted subtly (Sadker and Sadker 123). In addition to using the techniques listed at right, make a directed effort to combat gender stereotypes and to treat all students as valued learners.

ACHIEVING GENDER EQUITY

Facts: Boys call out answers eight times as frequently as do girls (Sadker and Sadker 43). Boys receive more evaluative feedback—both positive and negative (Sadker, Sadker, and Klein 300; Sadker and Sadker 55).

Responses:
- Make a special effort to call on girls and to give them specific feedback, both positive and negative. (Note: If you give more than one-third of your attention to girls you may be accused of favoring girls; see Sadker and Sadker 266–267.)
- When intervening in student-student interactions, concentrate on raising girls' confidence rather than criticizing boys' behavior.

Fact: Exposure to gender-biased materials appears to increase gender stereotypes (Sadker, Sadker, and Klein 279; Sadker and Sadker 73–75, 128–135, 266).

Responses:
- Be aware of biases in literature and point them out.
- When appropriate, provide historical context for stereotyping by explaining older attitudes and practices.
- Provide direct lessons about gender stereotypes and gender-related communication styles.

Facts: Girls are more likely than boys to attribute their successes to luck and less likely than boys to attribute their successes to ability (Sadker, Sadker, and Klein 303). Girls are more likely than boys to attribute their failures to lack of ability and less likely than boys to attribute their failures to lack of effort (303). Teachers are more likely to comment on girls' appearance and the neatness of their work, and more likely to comment on the intellectual qualities of boys' work (Sadker and Sadker 57).

Responses:
- Make an effort to avoid commenting on students', especially girls', appearance.
- Make an effort to attribute all success to effort and ability.
- Make an effort to rebut forcefully students' self-deprecating comments.

Facts: Girls have lower expectations of success (Sadker, Sadker, and Klein 302) and are more likely to display signs of "learned helplessness" (303). Teachers are more likely to help boys solve their own problems, but to solve problems for girls (Sadker and Sadker 81–83).

Responses:
- Fear of being "too tough" on girls is patronizing and hinders them from developing independence and confidence. Don't be afraid to criticize girls' work and don't let them off easy (Holt; Sizer).
- Make an effort to rebut forcefully students' self-deprecating comments.

Teaching Students to Work Cooperatively

Prepare your students for work in cooperative learning groups by teaching them how to listen actively, how to participate fully in discussions, and how to give one another positive feedback. Refer students to the lessons on listening, interpersonal communication, and discussion, sections 3.4–3.6 of the Language Arts Survey.

Uses for Small Groups. Use these task and project ideas to direct the work of collaborative learning groups.
- brainstorming
- peer tutorial sessions
- learning partners for practice or review and for all stages of the writing process
- inquiry-based concept learning
- multimedia and community-based projects
- topical symposia
- panel discussions
- mock jury trials
- role playing
- dramatizations
- simulations
- Reader's Theater

TEACHING STUDENTS TO WORK COOPERATIVELY

Preparing Students for Small Group Work

PARTICIPATION
- Review/preteach vocabulary and cultural concepts for nonnative speakers.
- Begin with a nongraded, fun, get-to-know-one-another activity.
- Take steps to ensure that group members know each other's names.
- Assign tasks that call on multiple intelligences.
- Ask questions that call for personal response and interpretation.
- Value interpretations that differ from your own.
- Have students determine the wording of their topics or questions.
- Don't talk too much.
- Model tentativeness and openness.
- Model courtesy and respect for all.
- Respond only holistically and orally to early drafts and initial products.
- Avoid judging early drafts; discuss ideas rather than expression.
- Discuss anonymous samples.
- Praise students for taking risks.
- Require (only) positive feedback from peers.
- Use joint grading for group work: (1) everyone in the group receives the average among the group; (2) everyone receives the lowest grade among the group; (3) a final product is graded and everyone receives that grade.

LEADERSHIP
- Ask students to conduct lessons.
- Rotate leadership assignments in groups.

- Appoint two group leaders—one to learn from the other.
- Model and give direct instruction and practice in asking questions.
- Model and give direct instruction and practice in reporting a summary.
- Model and give direct instruction and practice in involving nonparticipants.
- Model and give direct instruction and practice in restraining dominators.
- Model and give direct instruction and practice in providing positive feedback.
- Model and give direct instruction and practice in providing constructive feedback.

LISTENING/DISCUSSING
- Model, explain, and encourage attentive listening, eye contact, and not interrupting.
- Give practice in paraphrasing students' words and your own.
- Ask students to identify good speaking and listening habits and skills.
- Ask students to evaluate group processes and their roles in their groups (use the forms in the *Assessment Portfolio,* 7.13, 7.14, 7.22).

Forming Groups
- Groups should contain a maximum of six students for a complex task, a maximum of four otherwise.
- For peer writing groups, two may be the ideal size. Require periodically that students change partners.
- In the prewriting stage, it can be good to match those who share a primary language other than English.

- Working groups should contain students of varied abilities.
- Allow groups to vary their seating arrangements (suggest possibilities).

Guiding and Monitoring
- Give specific tasks.
- Explain criteria for success.
- Assign roles in group, or assign groups to distribute roles.
- When assigning roles in groups, divide responsibilities to assure interdependence and cooperation. One workable division of responsibilities is among (1) a discussion leader/facilitator; (2) a recorder; (3) a reporter; (4) a materials manager.
- Specify desired behaviors (see "Preparing Students for Small Group Work," above).
- Monitor group interactions and advise when appropriate.
- Intervene to diffuse conflict and to foster collaborative skills.
- When intervening in group work, ask a question rather than giving advice directly.
- If multiple groups have the same problem, interrupt the process and clarify or reteach.

Closure and Assessment
- Ask for sharing of a product.
- Both students and teacher should assess the quality of the product. Assessment can be among the entire class or only within groups.
- Both students and teacher should assess the quality of the group processes and communication.

Planning for Conferences and Portfolio Evaluation

As a teacher you have a number of distinguishable evaluative roles as outlined in the charts at right. Of course, you will not take on all of these roles at once. Make sure that students know which role to expect *before* they receive feedback.

References

Herman, J., P. Aschbacher, and L. Winters. *A Practical Guide to Alternative Assessment.* Alexandria, VA: ASCD, 1992.

Eggen, P., and D. Kauchak. *Educational Psychology.* 2nd ed. New York: Merrill, 1994.

Gardner, H. *Frames of Mind: The Theory of Multiple Intelligences.* New York: Basic, 1985.

———. *The Unschooled Mind: How Children Think and How Schools Should Teach.* New York: Basic, 1991.

Holt, J. *How Children Learn.* New York: Putnam, 1967.

Ohrlich, D., et al. *Teaching Strategies.* 4th ed. Lexington, MA: Heath, 1994.

Sadker, M., and D. Sadker. *Failing at Fairness.* New York: Scribner's, 1993.

Sadker, M., D. Sadker, and S. Klein. "The Issue of Gender in Elementary and Secondary Education." *Review of Research in Education* 17 (1991): 269–334.

Sizer, T. *Horace's Compromise.* Boston: Houghton, 1984.

Slavin, R. *Cooperative Learning: Theory, Research, and Practice.* Englewood Cliffs, NJ: Prentice, 1990.

———. *Educational Psychology.* 3rd ed. Englewood Cliffs, NJ: Prentice, 1991.

UNDERSTANDING THE ROLES OF EVALUATORS

ROLE	FUNCTION
AUDIENCE	to take up ideas, to challenge, to question, to enlarge perspective
PROOFREADER	to correct grammar, usage, and mechanics
GRADER	to judge against external, more or less objective, and more or less arbitrary standards
ADVISOR	to prod to solve problems, to encourage, to give suggestions, to remind of objectives

ROLE	TEACHING TIPS
AUDIENCE	Act exclusively as audience when you read and comment on drafts. Comments on drafts should avoid direct criticism and should aim at raising students' excitement about further writing and revising.
PROOFREADER	Overemphasis on proofreading and points of grammar, usage, and mechanics can drain students' interest in and enthusiasm for writing as well as their self-confidence. Use proofreading as a peer function, and allow students to learn from reading and proofreading each other's papers.
GRADER	Avoiding grading as much as possible allows both you and students to concentrate on clear and honest expression and to preserve intrinsic motivation.
ADVISOR	Because the advising function requires one-on-one interchange, you should reserve for it as much of the precious evaluation time as you can.

CONDUCTING CONFERENCES

- Examine the portfolio before conferencing. Make sure it contains all required material, including the student's evaluations of each piece of writing (*Assessment Portfolio,* 6.11) and of the portfolio as a whole (*Assessment Portfolio,* 6.9).
- Evaluate the portfolio before conferencing. Complete the portfolio evaluation form (*Assessment Portfolio,* 6.9b), making special note of any discrepancies between your and the student's evaluations.
- Do not attempt to discuss all aspects of the portfolio or the student's class performance. Choose two or three broad, major points and one or two specific problems to focus on in the conference. If students are asked to complete the Skills Self-Assessment Forms (*Assessment Portfolio,* 6.3 and 6.5), this may make it easier to pinpoint areas in which the student already recognizes a need for effort.
- As an alternative to conferencing, you may sometimes complete and hand to students a Portfolio Evaluation Form and additional writing and language skills evaluation forms (*Assessment Portfolio,* 6.4, 6.6–6.8). You will still need to allow time for students to respond to and ask questions about their evaluations, and to hold conferences with students who need special help or encouragement.
- To allow ample class time for conferences, you must assign sufficient work that students can do independently to keep them busy on conference days. Thus, you must establish the writing process and the peer groups early in the term.
- In addition, to allow yourself ample time to evaluate portfolios you must involve students in ongoing self- and peer evaluation.

Additional Resources for Language Arts Teachers

TEACHING LITERATURE

Applebee, A. N. *Tradition and Reform in the Teaching of English: A History.* Urbana, IL: NCTE, 1974.

Atwell, N. *In the Middle: Writing, Reading, and Learning with Adolescents.* Portsmouth, NH: Heinemann, 1987.

Beach, R., and J. Marshall. *Teaching Literature in the Secondary School.* Orlando, FL: Harcourt, 1991.

Becoming a Nation of Readers: The Report of the Commission on Reading. Washington, DC: NIE, 1984.

Buck, C., ed. *The Bloomsbury Guide to Women's Literature.* New York: Prentice, 1992.

Bushman, J., and K. Bushman. *Using Young Adult Literature in the Classroom.* New York: Macmillan, 1992.

Cooper, C. R., ed. *Researching Response to Literature and the Teaching of Literature.* Norwood, NJ: Ablex, 1988.

Farrell, E. J., and J. Squire, eds. *Transactions with Literature: A Fifty-Year Perspective.* Urbana, IL: NCTE, 1990.

Flood, J., et al., eds. *Handbook of Research on Teaching the English Language Arts.* New York: Macmillan, 1991.

Glazer, S. *Reading Comprehension: Self-monitoring Strategies That Create Independent Readers.* New York: Scholastic, 1992.

Langer, J. A., ed. *Literature Instruction: A Focus on Student Response.* Urbana, IL: NCTE, 1992.

Lee, C., and T. Gura. *Oral Interpretation.* 8th ed. Boston: Houghton, 1992.

Marzano, R. *Cultivating Thinking English and the Language Arts.* Urbana, IL: NCTE, 1991.

Newell, G. E., and R. K. Durst. *Exploring Texts: The Roles of Discussion and Writing in the Teaching and Learning of Literature.* Norwood, MA: Christopher-Gorden, 1993.

Probst, R. E. *Response and Analysis: Teaching Literature in Junior and Senior High School.* Portsmouth, NH: Boynton/Cook, 1988.

Rosenblatt, L. *Literature as Exploration.* 4th ed. New York: MLA, 1983.

———. *The Reader, the Text, the Poem: The Transactional Theory of the Literary Work.* Carbondale, IL: Southern Illinois UP, 1978.

Wagner, B. J., and M. Larson. *Situations: A Casebook of Virtual Realities for the English Teacher.* Portsmouth, NH: Boynton/Cook, 1994.

Widdowson, P., ed. *Re-reading English.* London: Routledge, 1982.

TEACHING WRITING

Bogel, F. V., and K. K. Gottschalk, eds. *Teaching Prose.* New York: Norton, 1988.

Dellinger, D. G. *Out of the Heart: How to Design Writing Assignments for High School Courses.* Berkeley, CA: Bay Area Writing Project.

Elbow, P. *Writing with Power: Techniques for Mastering the Writing Process.* New York: Oxford UP, 1981.

Flower, L. S. *Problem-Solving Strategies in Writing.* 2nd ed. Orlando, FL: Harcourt, 1985.

Fulwiler, T., ed. *The Journal Book.* Portsmouth, NH: Heinemann, 1987.

Handa, C., ed. *Computers and Community: Teaching Composition in the Twenty-First Century.* Portsmouth, NH: Boynton/Cook, 1990.

Harris, M. *Teaching One-to-One: The Writing Conference.* Urbana, IL: NCTE, 1986.

Hawisher, G. E. "Research and Recommendations for Computers and Composition." *Critical Perspectives on Computers and Composition Instruction.* Ed. G. E. Hawisher and C. L. Selfe. New York: Teacher's Coll. P, 1989: 44–69.

Irmscher, W. *Teaching Expository Writing.* New York: Holt, 1979.

Kirby, D., and T. Liner. *Inside Out: Developmental Strategies for Teaching Writing.* Upper Montclair, NJ: Boynton/Cook, 1981.

Langer, J. A., and A. N. Applebee. *How Writing Shapes Thinking: A Study of Teaching and Learning.* NCTE Research Rept. No. 22. Urbana, IL: NCTE, 1987.

Lindemann, E. *A Rhetoric for Writing Teachers.* New York: Oxford UP, 1982.

Moffett, J., and B. J. Wagner. *Student-Centered Language Arts, K–12.* 4th ed. Portsmouth, NH: Boynton/Cook, 1992.

Murray, D. *Write to Learn.* New York: Holt, 1984.

Rodrigues, D., and R. Rodrigues. *Teaching Writing with Word Processors, Grades 1–13.* Urbana, IL: NCTE, 1987.

Romano, T. *Clearing the Way: Working with Teenage Writers.* Portsmouth, NH: Heinemann, 1987.

Ross, M., D. Brackett, and A. Maxon. *Assessment and Management of Mainstreamed Hearing-Impaired Children.* Austin, TX: Pro-Ed, 1991.

Shaughnessy, M. *Errors and Expectations.* New York: Oxford UP, 1977.

Spear, K. *Sharing Writing.* Upper Montclair, NJ: Boynton/Cook, 1988.

Tate, G., and E. Corbett, eds. *The Writing Teacher's Sourcebook.* New York: Oxford UP, 1981.

Weaver, Constance. *Grammar for Teachers.* Urbana, IL: NCTE, 1979.

TEACHING GRAMMAR

Elley, W. B., et al. "The Role of Grammar in a Secondary School English Curriculum." *Research in the Teaching of English* 10 (1976): 5–21.

Hillocks, G., Jr. *Research on Written Composition.* Urbana, IL: Natl. Conference on Research in English and ERIC/CRCS, 1986.

TEACHING THINKING SKILLS

Ausubel, D. P. *Educational Psychology.* 2nd ed. New York: Holt, 1978.

Chance, P. *Thinking in the Classroom: A Survey of Programs.* New York: Teacher's Coll. P, 1986.

Costa, A. L. *Developing Minds: A Resource Book for Teaching Thinking.* Rev. ed. 2 Vols. Alexandria, VA: ASCD, 1991.

Gardner, H. *The Unschooled Mind.* New York: Basic, 1991.

Horton, S. *Thinking through Writing.* Baltimore: Johns Hopkins UP, 1982.

Lazear, D. G. *Teaching for Multiple Intelligences.* Fastback No. 342. Bloomington, IN: Phi Delta Kappa Educ. Foundation, 1992.

Nickerson, R. S., D. N. Perkins, and E. E. Smith. *The Teaching of Thinking.* Hillsdale, NJ: Erlbaum, 1985.

Novak, J. D., and D. B. Gowin. *Learning How to Learn.* New York: Cambridge UP, 1984.

Pressley, M., et al. *Cognitive Strategy Instruction That Really Improves Children's Academic Performance.* Cambridge, MA: Brookline, 1990.

Resnick, L. B. *Education and Learning to Think.* Washington, DC: Natl. Academy P, 1987.

Resnick, L. B., and L. E. Klopfer, eds. *Toward the Thinking Curriculum: Current Cognitive Research.* Alexandria, VA: ASCD, 1989.

Rogoff, B. *Apprenticeship in Thinking.* New York: Cambridge UP, 1989.

Sternberg, R. J. "How Can We Teach Intelligence?" *Educational Leadership* 42 (1984): 38–50.

Sternberg, R. J., and T. I. Lubart. "Creating Creative Minds." *Phi Delta Kappan* 72 (1991): 608–614.

Sternberg, R. J., and R. Wagner. *Practical Intelligence.* New York: Cambridge UP, 1985.

ASSESSMENT

California Assessment Program. *The California Assessment Program: A Position Paper on Testing and Instruction.* Sacramento, CA: CAP, 1990.

Cambourne, B., and J. Turbil. "Assessment in Whole-Language Classrooms: Theory into Practice." *Elementary School Journal* 90 (1991): 337–349.

García, G. E., and P. D. Pearson. "Assessment and Diversity." *Review of Research in Education* 20 (1994): 337–391.

Gronlund, N. E., and R. L. Linn. *Measurement and Evaluation in Teaching.* 6th ed. New York: Macmillan, 1990.

Herman, J. L., P. R. Aschbacher, and L. Winters. *A Practical Guide to Alternative Assessment.* Alexandria, VA: ASCD, 1992.

Johnston, P. H. *Constructive Evaluation of Literate Activity.* White Plains, NY: Longman, 1992.

Smith, M. A., and M. Ylvisaker, eds. *Teacher's Voices: Portfolios in the Classroom.* Berkeley, CA: Natl. Writing Project, 1994.

Wolf, D., et al. "To Use Their Minds Well: Investigating New Forms of Student Assessment." *Review of Research in Education* 17 (1991): 31–74.

Yancey, K. B., ed. *Portfolios in the Writing Classroom.* Urbana, IL: NCTE, 1992

TEACHING SPECIAL POPULATIONS

Banks, J., and C. M. Banks, eds. *Multicultural Education: Issues and Perspectives.* 2nd ed. Boston: Allyn, 1993.

Brooks, C., ed. *Tapping Potential: English and the Language Arts for the Black Learner.* Urbana, IL: NCTE, 1985.

Cummins, J. *Empowering Minority Students.* Sacramento, CA: CA Assoc. for Bilingual Education, 1989.

Farr, M., and H. Daniels. *Language Diversity and Writing Instruction.* New York: ERIC Clearinghouse on Urban Education/Columbia UP, 1986.

Garcia, E. E. "Language, Culture, and Education." *Review of Research in Education* 19 (1993): 51–98.

Haberman, M. "The Pedagogy of Poverty versus Good Teaching." *Phi Delta Kappan* (1991): 290–294.

Hernandez, H. *Multicultural Education: A Teacher's Guide to Content and Process.* Columbus, OH: Merrill, 1989.

Kronick, D. *New Approaches to Learning Disabilities.* Philadelphia, PA: Grune & Stratton, 1988.

Marik, R. *Special Education Students Write: Classroom Activities and Assignments.* Berkeley, CA: Bay Area Writing Project, 1982.

Shade, B. J. *Culture, Style, and the Educative Process.* Springfield, IL: Charles Thomas, 1989.

Slavin, R., N. Karweit, and N. Madden, eds. *Effective Programs for Students at Risk.* Boston: Allyn, 1989.

West, W. W. *Teaching the Gifted and Talented in the English Classroom.* Washington, DC: NEA, 1980.

GENDER ISSUES

Brown, L. M., and C. Gilligan. *Meeting at the Crossroads: Women's Psychology and Girls' Development.* Cambridge: Harvard UP, 1992.

Gilbert, P. *Gender, Literacy, and the Classroom.* Carlton South, Victoria: Austral. Reading Assn., 1989.

Sadker, M., and D. Sadker. *Failing at Fairness: How Schools Cheat Girls.* New York: Scribner's, 1994.

Sadker, M., D. Sadker, and S. Klein. "The Issue of Gender in Elementary and Secondary Education." *Review of Research in Education* 17 (1991): 269–334.

Wellesley College Center for Research on Women. *How Schools Shortchange Girls: The AAUW Report.* Washington, DC: American Assn. of Univ. Women, 1992.

TEACHING HIGH SCHOOL-AGE STUDENTS

Applebee, A. N. *The Child's Concept of Story: Ages Two to Seventeen.* Chicago: U of Chicago P, 1978.

Flavell, J. *Cognitive Development.* 2nd ed. Englewood Cliffs, NJ: Prentice, 1985.

Kohlberg, L. "Education for Justice: A Modern Statement of the Platonic View." *Five Lectures on Moral Education.* Ed. N. F. Sizer and T. R. Sizer. Cambridge: Harvard UP, 1970.

KEY TO ICONS

Cross-curriculum Icons

 Arts and Humanities

 Mathematics and Sciences

 Social Studies

 Applied Arts

Multiple Intelligence Icons

 Musical Intelligence

 Logical-Mathematical Intelligence

 Spatial Intelligence

 Kinesthetic Intelligence

 Interpersonal/Intrapersonal Intelligence

SCANS Icons

 Managing Resources
Identifies, organizes, plans, allocates time, money, materials, space, human resources

 Interpersonal Skills
Works with others as member of team

 Information Skills
Acquires, evaluates, organizes, maintains, interprets, communicates, and processes information

 Systems Skills
Understands complex inter-relationships

 Technology Skills
Selects, applies, and maintains appropriate technology to perform tasks and solve problems

 Basic Skills
Reads, writes, performs arithmetic and mathematical operations, and listens and speaks well

 Thinking Skills
Thinks creatively, makes decisions, solves problems, visualizes, knows how to learn, and reasons

 Personal Qualities
Displays responsibility, self-esteem, sociability, self-management, and integrity and honesty

Thematic Organization Chart

The chart on these pages lists forty-seven common literary themes and identifies the selections in this book that deal with these themes. Choose the themes you wish to teach in your course, and use the chart to identify selections that deal with those themes.

Selection	AGE	ALIENATION	ART AND ARTISTRY	BEAUTY	BIRTH	CONFUSION	COURAGE AND FEAR	DEATH	DISCOVERING AND LEARNING	DIVERSITY AND PLURALISM	DRAMA AND ACTING	EXILE	FAITH	FAMILY	FREEDOM	FRIENDSHIP	THE FUTURE	GIVING	GOD	GREED AND AMBITION	GROWTH/GROWING UP	HERO/HEROISM	HOME AND COUNTRY	HONESTY	HOPE	IDENTITY	IMAGINATION	INDEPENDENCE	JUSTICE	KNOWLEDGE/WISDOM	LAW AND CUSTOM	LEADERSHIP AND AUTHORITY	LOSS AND REMEMBRANCE	LOVE	NATURE	ORDER/DISORDER	PARENTS AND CHILDREN	PEACE	PRIDE AND VANITY	RELIGION	SCIENCE	STRUGGLE	TECHNOLOGY	TRUTH/REALITY	WAR	WORK	WRITING AND BOOKS
UNIT 1																																															
"Robin Hood and Allen a Dale," 6																				•							•	•		•	•																
"The Naming of Cats," 22																										•	•																				
"The Rocking-Horse Winner," 31														•						•										•									•				•				
The Rising of the Moon, 48							•	•														•								•	•	•		•												
Speech to the Troops at Tilbury, 60							•															•	•									•								•				•		
UNIT 2																																															
"The Conversion of King Edwin," 76								•					•						•																		•			•							
"The Story of Cædmon," 82			•										•						•																					•							•
"The Wife's Lament," 88		•										•	•										•										•	•	•												
Anglo-Saxon Riddles, 94																																										•		•		•	
from *Beowulf*, 99							•	•														•	•																						•		
from "The Seafarer," 117		•										•	•																				•		•					•						•	
"Wulf and Eadwacer," 117													•																				•	•													
UNIT 3																																															
"Sir Patrick Spens," 136							•	•														•								•		•															
"The Great Silkie of Shule Skerrie," 139				•				•																					•								•										
"Ubi Sunt Qui ante Nos Fuerunt?" 142								•					•																				•						•	•							
"I Sing of a Maiden," 146			•	•												•																		•						•							
"The Honeysuckle: Chevrefoil," 148			•																															•	•												
from *Sir Gawain and the Green Knight*, 152							•									•						•	•	•																							
from *Le Morte d'Arthur*, 167				•																		•	•			•						•	•											•			
from *The Book of Margery Kempe*, 180		•	•						•			•														•		•	•	•									•							•	•
from *The Canterbury Tales*, "The Prologue," 185			•										•			•			•				•												•				•								
from "The Pardoner's Tale," 205								•	•										•	•										•						•			•	•						
from *Everyman*, 212	•					•	•	•	•					•					•	•												•					•	•		•						
"Western Wind," 223																																		•	•												
"I am of Ireland," 223																							•																								•
"The Bonny Earl of Murray" 223																						•	•						•			•	•							•						
"The Twa Corbies," 223								•							•																																
"Bonny Barbara Allan," 223				•				•																									•	•													
"The Wife of Usher's Well," 224							•	•					•																				•				•										
from *The Ingenious Hidalgo Don Quixote*, 225			•			•	•	•					•						•			•						•						•	•									•	•	•	
UNIT 4																																															
"Whoso List to Hunt," 250																																•	•	•													
Sonnet 31 ("With how sad steps . . ."), 254																																		•	•	•											

T37

AGE · ALIENATION · ART AND ARTISTRY · BEAUTY · BIRTH · CONFUSION · COURAGE AND FEAR · DEATH · DISCOVERING AND LEARNING · DIVERSITY AND PLURALISM · DRAMA AND ACTING · EXILE · FAITH · FAMILY · FREEDOM · FRIENDSHIP · THE FUTURE · GIVING · GOD · GREED AND AMBITION · GROWTH/GROWING UP · HERO/HEROISM · HOME AND COUNTRY · HONESTY · HOPE · IDENTITY · IMAGINATION · INDEPENDENCE · JUSTICE · KNOWLEDGE/WISDOM · LAW AND CUSTOM · LEADERSHIP AND AUTHORITY · LOSS AND REMEMBRANCE · LOVE · NATURE · ORDER/DISORDER · PARENTS AND CHILDREN · PEACE · PRIDE AND VANITY · RELIGION · SCIENCE · STRUGGLE · TECHNOLOGY · TRUTH/REALITY · WAR · WORK · WRITING AND BOOKS

Selection	Themes marked (●)
from *The Færie Queene*, 257	Courage and Fear; Faith; Love; Religion; War
"The Passionate Shepherd to His Love," 261	Art and Artistry; Home and Country; Love; Nature
"The Nymph's Reply to the Shepherd," 266	Age; Death; Love; Nature
"The Doubt of Future Foes," 272	Courage and Fear; Home and Country; Order/Disorder; War
"When Thou Must Home to Shades of Underground," 276	Beauty; Death; Loss and Remembrance; Love
Sonnet 18 ("Shall I compare thee…"), 279	Alienation; Death; Love; Nature; Writing and Books
Sonnet 29 ("When, in disgrace…"), 282	Alienation; Love
Sonnet 130 ("My mistress' eyes…"), 283	Beauty; Hero/Heroism; Love
"Song, to Celia," 286	Beauty; Love
from *Ecclesiastes, Chapter 3*, 290	Confusion; Death; Faith; Knowledge/Wisdom; Love; Religion
"Alas! So All Things Now Do Hold Their Peace," 293	Love; Nature
"Heart Exchange," 293	Love
Sonnet 75 ("One day I wrote her name…"), 293	Death; Writing and Books
Sonnet 30 ("When to the sessions…"), 293	Friendship; Love; Nature
Sonnet 73 ("That time of year…"), 293	Death; Love; Nature
Eve's Apology in Defense of Women, 294	Confusion; Faith; Freedom; Knowledge/Wisdom; Law and Custom; Loss and Remembrance; Love; Religion
"Jack and Joan," 295	Diversity and Pluralism; Drama and Acting; Greed and Ambition; Love; Pride and Vanity
"A Litany in Time of Plague," 295	Beauty; Death; Faith; God; Greed and Ambition; Love; Pride and Vanity; Religion
"Epitaph on Elizabeth, L. H.," 296	Beauty; Death; Love
Psalm 23, 296	Confusion; Death; Faith; God; Love
from Psalm 137, 296	Diversity and Pluralism; Exile; Faith; God; Justice; Loss and Remembrance; Pride and Vanity; Religion; Struggle
Sonnet 1 ("O ye who…"), 298	Alienation; Love; Pride and Vanity; Writing and Books
Sonnet 47 ("Blest be the day…"), 299	Alienation; Love; Truth/Reality; Writing and Books
Sonnet 54 ("I grow a-weary…"), 299	Alienation; Art and Artistry; Love; Writing and Books

UNIT 5

Selection	Themes marked (●)
The Tragedy of Macbeth, 320	Alienation; Confusion; Courage and Fear; Death; Discovering and Learning; Family; God; Greed and Ambition; Growth/Growing Up; Justice; Law and Custom; Loss and Remembrance; Love; Nature; Pride and Vanity; Struggle; Truth/Reality; War
from … *Doctor Faustus*, 387	Death; Faith; Greed and Ambition; Growth/Growing Up; Knowledge/Wisdom; Pride and Vanity; Religion
from *The Tragedy of Hamlet, Prince of Denmark* — ("And these few precepts…"), 396	Knowledge/Wisdom; Parents and Children
("To be, or not to be…"), 396	Confusion; Courage and Fear; Identity; Struggle
("Speak the speech, I pray you…"), 396	Art and Artistry; Drama and Acting
from *The Tragedy of King Richard the Second* — ("Methinks I am a prophet…"), 397	Discovering and Learning; Death; Loss and Remembrance; Religion; Truth/Reality
("Let's talk of graves…"), 398	Death; Loss and Remembrance; Religion
from *The Merchant of Venice* ("The quality of mercy…"), 398	Faith; Freedom; Justice; Law and Custom; Religion
from *The Tempest* ("Our revels now are ended…"), 398	Art and Artistry; Death; Imagination; Truth/Reality
from *The Analects*, 399	Faith; Knowledge/Wisdom; Law and Custom; Leadership and Authority

Theme index table (Units — selections with thematic markers):

Selection	AGE	ALIENATION	ART AND ARTISTRY	BEAUTY	BIRTH	CONFUSION	COURAGE AND FEAR	DEATH	DISCOVERING AND LEARNING	DIVERSITY AND PLURALISM	DRAMA AND ACTING	EXILE	FAITH	FAMILY	FREEDOM	FRIENDSHIP	THE FUTURE	GIVING	GOD	GREED AND AMBITION	GROWTH/GROWING UP	HERO/HEROISM	HOME AND COUNTRY	HONESTY	HOPE	IDENTITY	IMAGINATION	INDEPENDENCE	JUSTICE	KNOWLEDGE/WISDOM	LAW AND CUSTOM	LEADERSHIP AND AUTHORITY	LOSS AND REMEMBRANCE	LOVE	NATURE	ORDER/DISORDER	PARENTS AND CHILDREN	PEACE	PRIDE AND VANITY	RELIGION	SCIENCE	STRUGGLE	TECHNOLOGY	TRUTH/REALITY	WAR	WORK	WRITING AND BOOKS
from *The Spectator*, No. 62, 554																														●																	●
"A Short Song of Congratulation," 556	●																			●																			●								
from *Candide*, 557																							●							●																	
UNIT 8																																															
"Elegy Written in a Country Churchyard," 574								●															●												●				●							
"Auld Lang Syne," 582																●					●	●													●											
"John Anderson, My Jo," 586	●							●								●																				●										
"The Lamb," 589							●												●																●				●							
"The Tyger," 592							●																												●				●							
"London," 595		●						●															●																								
"Kubla Khan," 599			●																								●								●											
from Preface to *Lyrical Ballads*, 605			●	●																																											●
"The world is too much with us . . . ," 611			●																																●	●										
"Lines Composed a Few Miles above Tintern Abbey," 614			●									●																							●	●		●								
"Ozymandias," 622								●								●			●											●	●															
"Ode to the West Wind," 625																																			●											
"She Walks in Beauty," 631			●																																●		●									
from *Childe Harold's Pilgrimage*, 635			●																			●													●											
"When I Have Fears," 638		●					●	●																										●												●
"Ode on a Grecian Urn," 642		●	●																																									●			
from *A Vindication of the Rights of Woman*, 647									●												●					●	●		●																	
from the Introduction to *Frankenstein*, 654		●																																	●						●		●			●
"The Divine Image," 661																			●																●			●								
"The Fly," 661								●										●																												
"The Garden of Love," 661								●																										●	●											
Song from the Preface to *Milton* ("And did those feet . . ."), 661												●							●																					●	●					
"I Wandered Lonely as a Cloud . . . ," 662																																			●		●									
"She Dwelt among the Untrodden Ways," 662		●		●				●																										●												
"Ode: Intimations of Immortality from Recollections of Early Childhood," 662												●																							●					●						
"The Rime of the Ancient Mariner," 664		●						●				●																							●				●					●		
from *The Grasmere Journals*, 674											●																								●											●
"A Dirge," 675																																			●											
from *Declaration of Rights*, 675															●														●			●														
"When We Two Parted," 676																																		●												
from *Don Juan*, Canto 1, Stanza 218 ("What is the end of fame?"), 676																																														●

Title	AGE	ALIENATION	ART AND ARTISTRY	BEAUTY	BIRTH	CONFUSION	COURAGE AND FEAR	DEATH	DISCOVERING AND LEARNING	DIVERSITY AND PLURALISM	DRAMA AND ACTING	EXILE	FAITH	FAMILY	FREEDOM	FRIENDSHIP	THE FUTURE	GIVING	GOD	GREED AND AMBITION	GROWTH/GROWING UP	HERO/HEROISM	HOME AND COUNTRY	HONESTY	HOPE	IDENTITY	IMAGINATION	INDEPENDENCE	JUSTICE	KNOWLEDGE/WISDOM	LAW AND CUSTOM	LEADERSHIP AND AUTHORITY	LOSS AND REMEMBRANCE	LOVE	NATURE	ORDER/DISORDER	PARENTS AND CHILDREN	PEACE	PRIDE AND VANITY	RELIGION	SCIENCE	STRUGGLE	TECHNOLOGY	TRUTH/REALITY	WAR	WORK	WRITING AND BOOKS
"On First Looking into Chapman's Homer," 676			•																																												•
"Dirce," 677								•																																							
"The Harp That Once through Tara's Halls," 677								•							•																		•														
"Casabianca," 677							•	•														•																	•						•		
from Pride and Prejudice, 678														•							•													•													
from "Macbeth," 678		•																																													•
Poems from The Narrow Road to the Deep North and Other Travel Sketches, 681													•																						•												
UNIT 9																																															
"The Lady of Shalott," 698		•					•																											•	•												
"Ulysses," 707						•									•					•	•					•		•																			
from In Memoriam, 712								•					•			•			•														•	•	•					•						•
"My Last Duchess," 724		•	•					•																										•													
"Andrea del Sarto," 729		•																							•					•				•								•				•
"Dover Beach," 740													•																					•												
"The Man He Killed," 745								•								•							•																						•		
"Channel Firing," 748																			•				•																•								
"The Darkling Thrush," 751																									•		•								•												
Sonnet 43 ("How do I love thee . . ."), 757																																		•													
"Pied Beauty," 761				•															•																•												
"God's Grandeur," 764																			•																•												
from Sing-Song, 767				•																															•												
"In an Artist's Studio," 770		•																						•										•													
"Promises Like Pie-Crust," 772																		•																•													
"A Birthday," 774					•																													•	•												
"To an Athlete Dying Young," 777								•																									•														
from The Mill on the Floss, 781												•																						•	•												
from Great Expectations, 787												•																					•	•													
from Through the Looking Glass, 796																										•	•																	•			
"Flower in the Crannied Wall," 806																			•																•												
"When I Was One-and-Twenty," 806	•						•												•															•													
"Loveliest of Trees," 806	•																																		•												
"The Runaway Slave at Pilgrim's Point," 806							•		•			•							•															•			•										
"The Night Is Darkening," 809																							•												•												
from The Subjection of Women, 809									•														•																								
"The Slave Ship," 810		•							•																																						
from Wuthering Heights, 810		•						•			•	•							•															•	•	•	•		•							
from Jane Eyre, 816												•									•		•																	•	•					
from Cassandra, 822																																	•														
Preface to The Picture of Dorian Gray, 822		•	•																																												•

UNIT 10

The following theme-index table maps each selection (with page number) against the literary themes marked with a bullet (•).

Selection	AGE	ALIENATION	ART AND ARTISTRY	BEAUTY	BIRTH	CONFUSION	COURAGE AND FEAR	DEATH	DISCOVERING AND LEARNING	DIVERSITY AND PLURALISM	DRAMA AND ACTING	EXILE	FAITH	FAMILY	FREEDOM	FRIENDSHIP	THE FUTURE	GIVING	GOD	GREED AND AMBITION	GROWTH/GROWING UP	HERO/HEROISM	HOME AND COUNTRY	HONESTY	HOPE	IDENTITY	IMAGINATION	INDEPENDENCE	JUSTICE	KNOWLEDGE/WISDOM	LAW AND CUSTOM	LEADERSHIP AND AUTHORITY	LOSS AND REMEMBRANCE	LOVE	NATURE	ORDER/DISORDER	PARENTS AND CHILDREN	PEACE	PRIDE AND VANITY	RELIGION	SCIENCE	STRUGGLE	TECHNOLOGY	TRUTH/REALITY	WAR	WORK	WRITING AND BOOKS
UNIT 10																																															
"The Lake Isle of Innisfree," 840			•																																•												
"Adam's Curse," 844		•																																•	•												•
"The Second Coming," 847																						•													•					•							
"Preludes," 852		•																				•																									
"Snake," 857			•																											•	•				•												
"The Soldier," 863		•																				•																							•		
"Dulce et Decorum Est," 867								•														•																							•		
"Rough," 872		•																																			•								•		
"Do Not Go Gentle into That Good Night," 876							•	•																													•					•					
"Who's Who," 880																										•								•													•
"Musée des Beaux Arts," 884		•	•																																												
"Not Waving but Drowning," 888		•						•																																							
"Thistles," 892								•																											•							•					
"Bread," 896								•										•	•																												
"Naked Girl and Mirror," 901																					•																										
"Map of the New World," 905		•																																													
UNIT 11																																															
from *A Room of One's Own*, 914		•					•		•	•	•																																				•
from *A Portrait of the Artist . . .*, 921		•																			•		•	•																							•
from *Nineteen Eighty-Four*, 931		•													•																	•											•				•
"The Garden-Party," 940								•		•													•														•		•								
"Red Dress—1946," 954						•			•					•							•			•		•		•		•							•										
"The Lagoon," 967						•	•	•						•		•																	•	•								•					
"Heat," 972						•	•																					•					•		•							•					
from *Nectar in a Sieve*, 974								•		•		•			•															•		•		•	•	•	•					•					
UNIT 12																																															
Pygmalion, 986							•	•							•															•	•	•		•													
"The Story of Pygmalion," 1057			•	•																														•													

Selections by Genre

These pages list all the selections in this book, organized by genre. Choose the genres you wish to teach in your course, and use the list to identify selections that represent those genres.

The EMC Masterpiece Series

LITERATURE AND THE LANGUAGE ARTS

The British Tradition

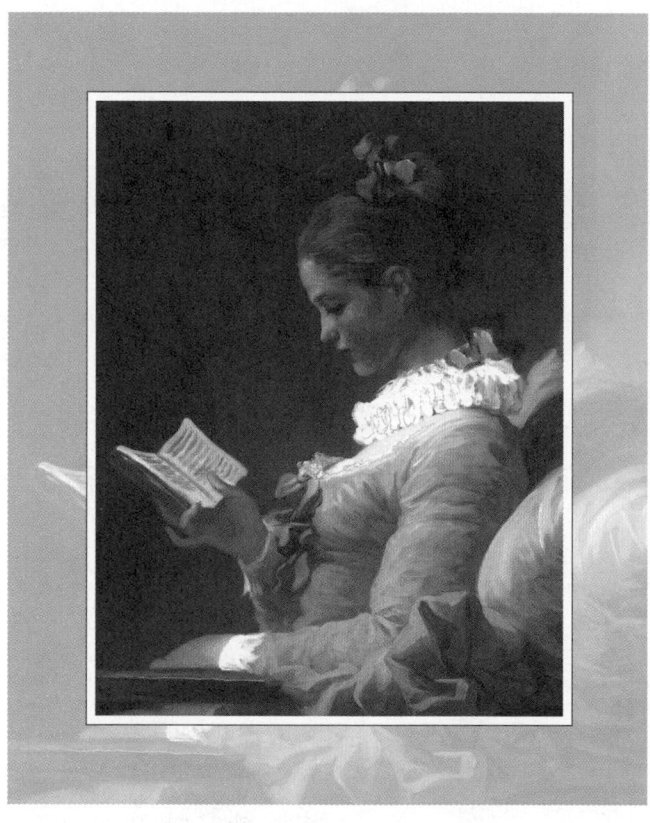

EMC/Paradigm Publishing
St. Paul, Minnesota

Staff Credits:

For **EMC/Paradigm Publishing,** St. Paul, Minnesota

Eileen Slater
Editor

Christine Gensmer
Associate Editor

For **Penobscot School Publishing, Inc.,** Danvers, Massachusetts

Robert D. Shepherd
Executive Editor

Camilla Ayers
Copyeditor

Kimberly M. Leahy
Managing Editor

Charles Q. Bent
Production Manager

Scott H. Bilow, Ph.D.
Senior Editor

Sara Day
Art Director

Sara Hyry
Associate Editor

Heath P. O'Leary
Compositor

ISBN 0-8219-1272-0

Published by EMC/Paradigm Publishing
300 York Avenue
St. Paul, Minnesota 55101

Printed in the United States of America.
10 9 8 7 6 5 4 3 2 1 XXX 01 00 99 98 97 96

Acknowledgments:

Alfred A. Knopf, Inc.
"The Garden-Party" from *The Short Stories of Katherine Mansfield* by Katherine Mansfield. Copyright 1937 and renewed 1965 by Alfred A. Knopf, Inc. Reprinted by permission of the publisher.

Bantam Doubleday Dell
Joseph Conrad, "The Lagoon," Doubleday, 1975.

Coach House Press
© Margaret Atwood, "Bread," *Murder in the Dark,* Coach House Press, 1983.

Dover Publications, Inc.
"Robin Hood and Allen a Dale," Dover Publications, Inc.

Farrar, Straus & Giroux, Inc.
"Map of the New World" from *Collected Poems 1948–1984* by Derek Walcott. Copyright © 1986 by Derek Walcott. Reprinted by permission of Farrar, Straus & Giroux, Inc.

Garland Publishing, Inc.
"The Book of Margery Kempe." This material originally appeared in *The Writings of Medieval Women,* Marcelle Thiébaux. Copyright 1994 by Garland Publishing, Inc. Reprinted by permission.
"The Honeysuckle: Chevrefoil." Marie de France. This material originally appeared in *The Writings of Medieval Women,* Marcelle Thiébaux. Copyright 1994 by Garland Publishing, Inc. Reprinted by permission.
"The Wife's Lament" and "Wulf and Eadwacer." This material originally appeared in *The Writings of Medieval Women,* Marcelle Thiébaux. Copyright 1994 by Garland Publishing, Inc. Reprinted by permission.

Harcourt Brace and Company
Excerpt from *A Room of One's Own* by Virginia Woolf, copyright 1929 by Harcourt Brace and Company and renewed 1957 by Leonard Woolf, reprinted by permission of the publisher.

(continued on page 1292)

ii

ANNOTATED TEACHER'S EDITION

ISBN 0-8219-1273-9

Published by EMC/Paradigm Publishing
300 York Avenue
St. Paul, Minnesota 55101

Printed in the United States of America.
10 9 8 7 6 5 4 3 2 1 XXX 01 00 99 98 97 96

LITERATURE AND THE LANGUAGE ARTS

MAPLE LEVEL
THE BRITISH TRADITION

PINE LEVEL
THE AMERICAN TRADITION

WILLOW LEVEL
UNDERSTANDING LITERATURE

BIRCH LEVEL
EXPERIENCING LITERATURE

Consultants and Writers

Edmund J. Farrell, Ph.D.
Emeritus Professor of English
  Education
University of Texas at Austin

Melissa Baker
Consultant, Women's Studies
Rockport, Massachusetts

Roger Dick
Teacher of English and Humanities
Brooklyn Center High School
Brooklyn Center, Minnesota

David England, Ph.D.
Associate Dean for Teacher
  Education
Louisiana State University

Ellen Gabin
Consultant, Hispanic Literature
Rockport, Massachusetts

Donald Gray, Ph.D.
Professor of English
Indiana University

Susan Gubar, Ph.D.
Professor of English
Indiana University

Dael Angelico-Hart
Director of Language Arts
Danvers Public Schools
Danvers, Massachusetts

Gail Ross Hatcher
English Department Chairperson
T. Wingate Andrews High School
High Point, North Carolina

Jim O'Laughlin
Lecturer
University College
Northwestern University

Jane S. Shoaf, Ph.D.
Instructional Specialist for
  Communication Skills (retired)
North Carolina Department of
  Public Instruction

Kendra Sisserson
Language Arts Curriculum
  Facilitator
Academy for Aerospace Technology
Cocoa, Florida

Donald L. Stephan
English Department Chair
Sidney High School
Sidney, Ohio

James W. Swanson
English Instructor
Robbinsdale Armstrong High
  School
Plymouth, Minnesota

Jill Triplett
Special Collections Assistant
Wellesley College

Hope Vasholz
Teacher of English
Hammond High School
Columbia, Maryland

Arlette Ingram Willis, Ph.D.
Assistant Professor in the
  Department of Curriculum and
  Instruction
University of Illinois at Urbana-
  Champaign

James Worley, Ph.D.
Teacher of English (retired)
Columbus East High School
Columbus, Indiana

Contents

v

viii

x

xiii

To the Student

Reading Literature

Have you ever become so wrapped up in a movie that when the credits started to roll and the lights came up, you felt a kind of shock? One moment you were in the world on the screen, perhaps identifying with some hero and feeling her joys and sorrows. The next moment you were back in your own world again. The art of the filmmaker transported you to another time and place.

When you read a good story, poem, or play, the same sort of transport should take place. The key to reading literature is to use your imagination to take the journey the writer planned for you. This willingness to extend yourself imaginatively is the most important characteristic that you can have as a reader. Suppose, for example, that you read the following passage in a story:

> Three lions, a male and two females, lay sunning beside what remained of a kill—an eland, perhaps. We ap-proached in the Range Rover. They ignored us. Chico stopped about fifty meters away, and we both took out binoculars for a closer look. The lions lay heavily, dreamily, sated, self-satisfied. A slight breeze ruffled their fur, yellow-brown like the savannah grass in this season between the rains. It was Chico who noticed that the kill wasn't an eland at all, for attached to part of it was, unmistakably, a large black boot.

It is possible to read that passage and comprehend it, intellectually, without having experienced it. However, reading literature is all about having experiences. To read the passage well, you need to picture three lions, to imagine what it might be like to approach them, to see in your mind's eye the yellow grass, to feel the slight breeze, to notice the boot. If you have done that—if you have imagined the scene vividly—then it will have an impact on you. That impact will be its significance—its meaning for you.

Imagine that you have taken a journey. You have hiked up a mountainside in Peru or have wandered through the Valley of the Kings in Egypt. You have gone shopping in the Ginza district of Tokyo or have bounced in a spacesuit over the surface of the moon. After such an experience, you return home a different person. You think about the experience and what it meant to you.

A work of literature is an opportunity to take just such an exotic journey. Using your imagination, you take the writer's trip. You have an experience. Then you reflect on the experience that you had. You think about what you thought and felt, about what the experience meant to you. That reflection is called **reader response.**

When you sit down to read a literary work, remember that your task, at that moment, is not to prepare for a quiz or to get ready for a class discussion. Your task is to use your imagination to have the experience that the writer has prepared for you. Think of the writer as a tour guide to interesting times and places. In those times and places, you will meet fascinating people and have powerful, moving experiences, ones that will enrich your life immeasurably.

Sharing Your Responses with Others

No two people are exactly alike. Because of this wonderful fact, the experience that you have when reading a particular story, poem, or play will be different from the experience had by the student who sits next to you. That's what makes discussing literature with other students interesting. You can share your experiences with others and learn from them. In this course you will have many opportunities to share responses in class discussion and in collaborative projects.

Educating Your Imagination

You might naturally ask, at the beginning of a course such as this, what you stand to gain from it. Two answers to that question have already been suggested: First, reading literature will provide you with many fascinating imaginative experiences. Second, discussing that literature and doing collaborative projects will provide opportunities for sharing with others. A third answer is implicit in the first two: reading literature and sharing responses with others will educate your imagination. It will train you to think and feel in new ways.

Life is short, opportunities for real-life experience are limited, and events often happen only once, without your having had the chance to practice, or even think about, how you might react to them. Reading literature is a way around all those difficulties. Through reading, you can find out what it might be like to sail around the globe, to march into battle, to fall in love, to lose a friend, to win a great prize, to live in the rain forest, to be faced with a moral dilemma, to confront your greatest fear, to travel backward in time or forward into the future. Writers write because they want to share interesting, valuable experiences with you—the reader. In the process of reading literary works and thinking about your own and others' responses to them, you will exercise your imaginative faculties and grow in ways that might otherwise have been impossible.

Using This Text

This text is first and foremost a literature anthology. The selections in Units 1–12 have been chosen both for their historical importance and for their current relevance to the interests of students like you. To assist you in understanding the selections, the authors and editors have created activities that appear before and after the selections. These activities will also help you to develop your abilities in many language arts areas. Most of these activities ask you to refer to the section at the back of the book called the Language Arts Survey. Before doing the activity, you will read a section of the Survey, which will introduce you to some key concepts. Then you will apply what you have learned from the Survey when doing the activity.

xix

Part One

UNDERSTANDING LITERATURE

UNIT 1 GENRES AND TECHNIQUES OF LITERATURE

Salisbury Cathedral: from the Meadows. John Constable, 1834.
Private Collection/Bridgeman Art Library, London

GOALS/OBJECTIVES

Studying this unit will enable students to
- have positive experiences with works of literature in each of the major genres
- name, define, and describe major elements and techniques of each of the genres of literature and identify these as employed in a piece of literature
- name and define the different purposes of literature (expressive, informative, persuasive, and literary)
- name and define the different modes of literature (narration, dialogue, description, and exposition)
- identify the purpose and mode of a work of literature
- identify and carry out each of the steps of the writing process (prewriting, drafting, revising, proofreading, and publishing)

The poet s eye, in a fine frenzy rolling,

Doth glance from heaven to earth,

   from earth to heaven;

And as imagination bodies forth

The forms of things unknown, the poet s pen

Turns them to shapes, and gives to airy nothing

A local habitation and a name.

              —William Shakespeare
              A Midsummer Night's Dream

3

ART NOTE

John Constable (1776–1837) is known for his landscapes romanticizing the English countryside. He made important developments in the depiction of clouds and of light reflected from trees and water, as evidenced in this work. For more information on Constable's life and ideas, students can consult C. R. Leslie, *Memoirs of the Life of John Constable,* rev. ed., 1951. Some of Constable's major works can be viewed at the National Gallery of Art (Washington, DC), the Frick Collection (New York), the Huntington Library (San Marino, CA), the Art Institute of Chicago, the Toledo (Ohio) Museum of Art, and several British museums.

ENRICHMENT ACTIVITIES

 Students can research American oral traditions, including the oral traditions of slave populations, Native Americans, and non-English speaking immigrants, and compare these to the British oral tradition. They might think about such questions as the following: What differences are most noticeable? Are there any similar stories, characters, or themes? What purposes does an oral tradition serve? Students interested in learning more about oral literature should consult Stith Thompson's classic compendium, *Motifs of the Folktale,* and Joseph Campbell's survey of world mythologies, *The Masks of God.*

SUPPORT FOR LEP STUDENTS

Explain the differences in word order between Modern English and the English of the medieval ballad. Sometimes a preposition is placed after its object, as in line 29, "And when he came bold Robin before." Sometimes the indirect object is placed before the verb, as in line 3, "I will you tell." Sometimes the verb comes before the subject, as in line 43, "'By the faith of my body,' then said the young man."

ADDITIONAL VOCABULARY

straight—immediately

The Oral Tradition

People love to hear and tell stories. There hasn't been a culture anywhere, at any time, in which that hasn't been so. Stories help us to explore who we are, who other people are, what our past experiences mean, and what the future might hold. In our stories we pose our questions. In them we express our hopes and sorrows, our disappointments and expectations. Storytelling is one of the most ancient of human impulses, and it is out of this impulse that literature was born.

Storytelling existed long before people started writing things down. When writing was first invented over five thousand years ago by people living in what is now Iraq and Iran, storytelling was already very, very old. The earliest stories that have come down to us from the times before writing are **myths**—stories that explain where things come from, how the world took the form that it has today. Myths grew out of human curiosity—the desire to understand how things came to be as they are. "The Story of Pygmalion," in Unit 12 of this text, is an example of a myth.

In addition to myths, early people told stories about remarkable people in their clans or tribes. These stories, known as **legends**, dealt with heroes and leaders, people who had had exceptional experiences. The *Beowulf* story, on page 99 of this text, is such a legend, elaborated and made more fanciful over time. Other types of stories that survive from ancient days include **fables**, stories with animal characters that tell morals; **parables**, brief stories with human characters that tell morals; **tall tales**, stories with many fanciful, exaggerated elements; and **ballads**, songs that tell stories. English literature is particularly rich in such songs. Examples in this text include "Robin Hood and Allen a Dale," on the following pages, and "The Great Silkie of Shule Skerrie," on page 139.

As a child, you may have played the game called "operator" or "telephone." If you haven't played the game, here's how it works: One person whispers something to another person and asks him or her to "pass it along." The second person whispers to the third, and so on, until the statement has been passed through many people. Inevitably, because people are fallible and don't always listen carefully or remember precisely, the statement gets changed from one person to the next. That's what happened to the first stories that people told. One person told a story. Someone else repeated it, often adding some exciting or interesting material, because no one wants to tell a boring story. In this way the story was passed from generation to generation, becoming ever more fanciful and interesting. That's why so many early myths and legends are full of bizarre or unusual events that wouldn't occur in real life.

After writing was invented, people started setting down the stories that they knew or that they had heard from traditional storytellers. Consequently, many, many stories have come down to us from the time before writing. These early stories, passed by word of mouth from person to person, often over hundreds or even thousands of years, are known collectively as the **oral tradition.**

Title page of *Contes de ma mere l'oye.*
Charles Perrault, 1695.
The Pierpont Morgan Library, NY. MA 1505

GOALS/OBJECTIVES

Studying this lesson will enable students to

• enjoy an amusing verse narrative from the oral tradition

• explain what an oral tradition is and how it changes

• create a story map

• describe the literary forms of myth, fable, parable, tall tale, and ballad and identify these forms as they encounter them in their reading

• use prewriting techniques to develop ideas for characters, setting, plot, point of view, and theme

The image on the left shows an illustration with a sign reading:

> Contes
> Demamere
> Loye

ART NOTE

Charles Perrault (1628–1703) is credited with authoring and illustrating *Contes de ma mère l'oye* (*Tales of Mother Goose*—1695) for his children's entertainment. However, there is some evidence that his son Pierre is the true author. One or both of these Perraults reworked French folk tales such as "Puss in Boots," "Little Red Riding Hood," and "The Sleeping Beauty" into the classics we know today.

The painting is gouache on paper.

CROSS-CURRICULAR ACTIVITIES

• **Social Studies.** You can notice in the illustration that the children appear as adults in miniature. The idea of youth as a special period between childhood and adulthood is a modern one, a product of nineteenth-century social reforms. Pose these questions to your class: Do people today think of children as miniature adults? Obviously not. What is special about the social position of youths? What rights or protections do youths today have that adults do not have? What rights and responsibilities do adults have that youths do not have? What reasons might be given for the differences between adults' and youths' rights and responsibilities?

Answers will vary. Students may say that youths today are not just miniature adults, insofar as they are entitled to care and are protected by laws against child abuse and neglect; they are required to attend school. As well, they are not (depending on their age) permitted to drive, to drink alcohol, to smoke, to vote, to serve in elected office, to make legally binding contracts, or to work full-time. It might be inferred from these regulations that lawmakers believe that youths require special guidance and protections.

• Students can research the history of the legal and social rights and responsibilities of children.

VOCABULARY FROM THE SELECTION

glister   guile

ADDITIONAL QUESTIONS AND ACTIVITIES

Ask students the following questions:
• Is there a storyteller in your family or clan? What kinds of stories does that person tell? Do the stories have a purpose? If so, what is it? What lessons do your family's stories teach? In what ways are the teachings of your family's or clan's stories similar to the teachings of "Robin Hood and Allen a Dale"? In what ways are the teachings different?
• Is there anyone in your family's history who seems to be "larger than life"? If so, describe that person or tell a story about him or her. Is your description or story an example of an oral tradition in your family, something that has been passed down for generations?

LITERARY TECHNIQUE

The Oral Tradition. Medieval minstrels could recite astonishing numbers of songs from memory. Invite students to think about how this was possible. Have students read or listen to a passage from an encyclopedia or a newspaper. Then have them read or listen to a popular song lyric of similar length. Then ask them to recite each from memory. Discuss with them which they were better able to remember and why that might be.

ORAL TRANSMISSION

Oral transmission is the passing of a work from one person to another by word of mouth rather than through writing. Notice that the opening phrase of the ballad assumes that it is being performed for an audience.

Come listen to me, you gallants so free,
    All you that love mirth for to hear,
And I will you tell of a bold outlaw,
    That lived in Nottinghamshire.

5   As Robin Hood in the forest stood,
    All under the greenwood tree,
There was he aware of a brave young man,
    As fine as fine might be.

The youngster was clothed in scarlet red,
10   In scarlet fine and gay,
And he did frisk it over the plain,
    and chanted a roundelay.[1]

As Robin Hood next morning stood,
    Among the leaves so gay,
15   There did he spy the same young man
    Come drooping along the way.

STANZA FORM

A ballad is divided into a four-line stanza known as a quatrain. In a ballad, the first and third lines are tetrameter (that is, they each have four feet). The second and fourth lines are trimeter (that is, they each have three feet).

The scarlet he wore the day before,
    It was clean cast away;
And every step he fetched a sigh,
20   "Alack and a well a day!"

Then stepped forth brave Little John,
    And Nick the miller's son,
Which made the young man bend his bow,
    When as he saw them come.

25   "Stand off, stand off," the young man said,
    "What is your will with me?"
"You must come before our master straight,
    Under yon greenwood tree."

---

1. **roundelay.** A joyful song

Sketch of Robin Hood.
Richard Dadd, 1852.
Yale Center for British Art,
Paul Mellon Collection

And when he came bold Robin before,
30   Robin asked him courteously,
"O hast thou any money to spare
    For my merry men and me?"

"I have no money," the young man said,
    "But five shillings and a ring;
35   And that I have kept this seven long years,
    To have it at my wedding.

"Yesterday I should have married a maid,
    But she is now from me tane,[2]
And chosen to be an old knight's delight,
40   Whereby my poor heart is slain."

"What is thy name?" then said Robin Hood,
    "Come tell me, without any fail."
"By the faith of my body," then said the young man,
    "My name it is Allen a Dale."

_____
2. **tane.** Taken

◄ ◄ ◄   **RHYME SCHEME**

A rhyme scheme is a pattern of rhymes in a poem. In traditional ballads, the rhyme scheme is abcb. In other words, the second and the fourth lines rhyme.

◄ ◄ ◄   **INCITING INCIDENT**

Like most narratives, a ballad relates a plot, a series of causally connected events. In a plot, the event that sets in motion the central conflict, or struggle, is called the inciting incident.

ADDITIONAL QUESTIONS AND ACTIVITIES

• Play a variation of telephone. Instead of passing a story from one person to another individually, divide the class into groups of three. Each group should choose one member as bard to relate the story to the next group. You or one member of the class begins the activity by reading a brief story to one group. (The story should be written down so it can be compared word-for-word with the story that is produced at the end of the activity.) The story may or may not be in verse. No one is permitted to take notes during the activity. The bard then retells the story to the small group, with the others offering corrections or improvements. When everyone agrees on a version, the bard tells it to the next group. The process is repeated for each group. After agreeing on its version, the last group writes down the story, and the class as a whole can compare it with the original.

►For instruction in listening skills and communication, see the Language Arts Survey, 3.1–3.4.

• Students may be interested in seeing or hearing about *Foxfire,* a magazine that depicts and describes a regional popular and oral culture, including its legends, myths, parables, remedies, skills, and crafts. It is produced by a group of students in Georgia.

• Museums and libraries often have storytelling sessions. Do research to find such offerings in your area, or ask students to do this research for you. Have interested students attend these sessions and report to the class on the kinds of stories that were told and on the storytellers' techniques.

• Suggest that students who are interested in performing community service might volunteer to read or tell stories for children at nearby hospitals or libraries. Students should discuss with hospital officials or library program directors what stories would be appropriate and why. Have students practice their storytelling in class before their public performance.

LITERARY TECHNIQUE

The Ballad: Themes. There are a few themes that predominate in English ballads: stories of historical events ("Sir Patrick Spens," "The Bonny Earl of Murray," the Robin Hood ballads); stories of tragic love ("Bonny Barbara Allan"); and stories of the supernatural ("Tam Lin," "The Wife of Usher's Well").

The Ballad: History. With the rise of the printing press, **broadside ballads,** printed on one side of a sheet of paper and sold by street vendors, became common. In the eighteenth century, Thomas Percy's collection *Reliques of Ancient English Poetry* was published (see the illustration on page 539). Joseph Ritson followed Percy with *A Select Collection of English Songs* and *Ancient English Metrical Romances*. Ritson also published *Robin Hood: A Collection of All the Ancient Poems, Songs, and Ballads Now Extant Relative to That Outlaw*. Sir Walter Scott traveled through the borderlands between England and Scotland collecting the Border ballads, which he published in *Minstrelsy of the Scottish Border*. Francis J. Child's (1825–1896) five-volume *English and Scottish Popular Ballads* (1883–1898) contains many of the versions of the ballads that are known today.

ADDITIONAL QUESTIONS AND ACTIVITIES

Formulaic Language. Ask students what other repeated words or phrases they can find in the ballad. Ask why balladeers in the oral tradition might have favored formulaic language.

Answers. Other repeated phrases include *ready gold* [n]or *fee* (lines 46 and 50) and *then said* [or *quoth*] *the young man* (lines 43, 49, and 55). Formulaic language aids memorization and improvisation.

INCREMENTAL REPETITION
► ► ►

Ballads often make use of incremental repetition, the use, again, of a line with some slight variation that advances the action.

FORMULAIC LANGUAGE
► ► ►

Works in the oral tradition often make use of formulaic language, words or phrases that are used again and again in various works. The formulas bold harper *and* bold outlaw *were often used to refer to Robin Hood.*

---

45   "What wilt thou give me," said Robin Hood,
        "In ready gold or fee,
      To help thee to thy true love again,
        And deliver her unto thee?"

      "I have no money," then quoth the young man,
50   "No ready gold nor fee,
      But I will swear upon a book
        Thy true servant for to be."

      "How many miles is it to thy true-love?
        Come tell me without any guile."
55   "By the faith of my body," then said the young man,
        "It is but five little mile."

      Then Robin he hastened over the plain,
        He did neither stint nor lin,[3]
      Until he came unto the church
60   Where Allen should keep his wedding.

      "What dost thou do here?" the bishop he said,
        "I prithee now tell to me."
      "I am a bold harper," quoth Robin Hood,
        "And the best in the north country."

65   "O welcome, O welcome," the bishop he said,
        "That music best pleaseth me";
      "You shall have no music," quoth Robin Hood,
        "Till the bride and the bridegroom I see."

      With that came in a wealthy knight,
70   Which was both grave and old,
      And after him a finikin[4] lass,
        Did shine like glistering gold.

      "This is no fit match," quoth bold Robin Hood,
        "That you do seem to make here;
75   For since we are come unto the church,
        The bride she shall choose her own dear."

---

3. **stint nor lin.** Stopping or ceasing
4. **finikin.** Well-dressed, fine

WORDS FOR EVERYDAY USE:

guile (gīl) *n.,* slyness
glis • ter (glis´tər) *vi.,* [archaic var. of *glisten*] shine or sparkle

VOCABULARY IN CONTEXT

• "This tricky new play will prove that guile is greater than brawn," said the quarterback.

• One ought not to wear glistering jewelry or an ostentatious hat to a funeral.

Then Robin Hood put his horn to his mouth,
 And blew blasts two or three;
When four and twenty bowmen bold
80 Come leaping over the lee.[5]

And when they came into the churchyard,
 Marching all in a row,
The first man was Allen a Dale,
 To give bold Robin his bow.

85 "This is thy true love," Robin he said,
 "Young Allen, as I hear say;
And you shall be married at this same time,
 Before we depart away."

"That shall not be," the bishop he said,
90 "For thy word shall not stand;
They shall be three times asked in the church,[6]
 As the law is of our land."

Robin Hood pulled off the bishop's coat,
 And put it upon Little John;
95 "By the faith of my body," then Robin said,
 "This cloth doth make thee a man." ◄ ◄ ◄   **PROVERB**

                A proverb is a tradi-
When Little John went into the choir,   *tional saying. This is an*
 The people began for to laugh;   *ironic use, within the*
He asked them seven times in the church, *ballad, of a proverb.*
100 Lest three times should not be enough.

"Who gives me this maid," then said Little John; ◄ ◄ ◄   **RESOLUTION**
 Quoth Robin, "That do I,
               In a plot, the resolution
And he that doth take her from Allen a Dale *is the event that ends*
 Full dearly he shall her buy."   *the central conflict.*

105 And thus having ended this merry wedding,
 The bride looked as fresh as a queen,
And so they returned to the merry greenwood,
 Among the leaves so green.   ■

---

5. **lee.** Sheltered, hidden place
6. **three . . . church.** Intended marriages had to be
announced three Sundays in a row.

RESPONDING TO THE SELECTION

Students are probably familiar with other Robin Hood stories from film, television, or other sources. They may also be familiar with other outlaw heroes such as Rambo or the Lone Ranger. Suggest that they compare the characters they know with the character in the selection.

ANSWERS FOR REVIEWING THE SELECTION

RECALLING

1. Robin Hood is the hero of the ballad. He lives in Nottinghamshire.

2. The ballad mentions Little John (line 21), Nick the miller's son (line 22), and Allen a Dale (line 83). Twenty-four of Robin's followers show up at the church (line 79).

3. The "youngster" in line 9 is Allen a Dale.

4. Allen promises his loyalty in exchange for Robin's help. Robin prevents the wedding of Allen's fiancée and the knight by storming the church with twenty-four armed men. He designates one of them, Little John, to perform a marriage ceremony between Allen and his fiancée. He warns those in attendance that anyone who tries to steal Allen's wife will pay dearly.

INTERPRETING

Responses will vary. Possible responses are given.

5. Robin Hood is described as "bold" (lines 29, 73, 84), courteous (line 30), able to run long distances without tiring (lines 56–58), and the best harper in the area (lines 63–64). He defies (lines 85–88) and mocks (lines 93–96) authority.

6. Robin and his band appear to gain their living by robbery.

7. At first Allen seems happy and carefree, but on his return he is "drooping" (line 16) and downtrodden. His mood has changed because his fiancée is being forced to marry another.

8. Robin helps Allen a Dale, even though Allen cannot pay anything, apparently because Allen and his fiancée have been unfairly treated by those with wealth and power. Robin's complaint about the wedding that the bishop would perform is that the bride has not agreed to the marriage.

(cont.)

Responding to the Selection

What sort of person is Robin Hood as portrayed in this ballad? Do you find this character attractive? Why, or why not? Why might legends of an outlaw hero have grown up among the common people of the English Middle Ages, who were almost universally subordinate to the authority of nobles and of the church? Discuss these questions with your classmates.

Reviewing the Selection

RECALLING

1. Who is the hero of this ballad, and where does he live?

2. What associates of Robin's are mentioned by name in the ballad? How many of Robin's associates show up at the church near the end of the ballad?

3. Who is the "youngster" dressed in scarlet mentioned in the third stanza?

4. What deal does Allen a Dale strike with Robin Hood? How does Robin fulfill his part of the bargain? What warning does Robin make to the assembled crowd at the end of the ballad?

INTERPRETING

5. What words and phrases are used to describe the hero of this ballad? What sort of person is he?

6. How do Robin and his associates earn their living?

7. How does the mood of the youngster dressed in scarlet change from the first day to the next? What causes this change in mood?

8. What indication does the ballad give that Robin administers justice even though he lives outside the law?

SYNTHESIZING

9. Whom was Allen a Dale's beloved being forced to marry? What does the poem tell us about that person? What attitude toward people of that person's class is represented in this ballad? Why might the illiterate common people who created this ballad have such an attitude?

10. What can we learn about the customs and values of medieval England by reading this ballad?

ANSWERS FOR REVIEWING THE SELECTION (CONT.)

SYNTHESIZING

Responses will vary. Possible responses are given.

9. Allen a Dale's beloved was nearly forced to marry a "wealthy" (line 69), "grave and old" (line 70) knight. The knight apparently is able to buy or coerce people, including the bishop, to get what he wants, regardless of what is fair. The ballad represents the attitude that members of the aristocracy are or can be viciously self-

ish. Poor people of the time may have had such an attitude about the aristocracy in general because their poor living conditions, high taxes, and indentured servitude were in stark contrast to the wealth of the nobles, who benefited from their hard work and poverty.

10. Taking Robin Hood as an exemplary character, one can surmise that the English valued compassion, loyalty, justice, strength, and a sense of humor.

Understanding Literature (Questions for Discussion)

1. **Oral Tradition.** An **oral tradition** is a work, motif, idea, or custom that is passed by word of mouth from generation to generation. No one knows for certain when the legend of Robin Hood first developed, although the legendary outlaw hero is mentioned in the poem *Piers Plowman* as early as 1377. It is quite likely that the legend is much older. In fact, it may have developed out of ancient Druidic or Teutonic rituals related to fertility gods, for Robin Hood in the ballads is invariably dressed in green and associated with the "greenwood," or forest. Through many centuries, down to our own, Robin Hood and various figures associated with him were central characters in May festivals celebrating the coming of spring, and, again, this practice may be a survival from ancient religious rituals that are now lost.

   By historical times, Robin Hood had become transmuted in the oral tradition into the outlaw hero familiar to most children in English-speaking countries. In the early thirteenth century, the heir apparent to the English throne, Richard the Lion-Hearted, went on Crusade to the Holy Land. On his return from Crusade, he was captured and held captive by the Holy Roman Emperor. During the period of Richard's absence, his brother John ruled England. John was a terrible king who taxed his subjects heavily. Many of the Robin Hood stories and ballads are associated with this time. They tell of an outlaw, loyal to King Richard, who robs the wealthy to give to the poor. The historical record shows many outlaws in England throughout the Middle Ages who identified themselves with the Robin Hood of legend, but it is unknown whether there was, indeed, any single historical original on whom the legend is based.

   What elements in the poem support the interpretation that the Robin Hood legends derive from ancient fertility myths and rituals? What elements in the poem support the interpretation that the Robin Hood legends were a kind of political protest or commentary?

   Songs, stories, and poems survive in the oral tradition because people find them interesting or valuable enough to be retold again and again. Why might the Robin Hood stories, like this story of Allen a Dale, have appealed to poor peasants of the medieval era?

2. **Ballad.** A **ballad** is a simple narrative poem in four-line stanzas, usually meant to be sung and usually rhyming *abcb*. Folk ballads, composed orally and passed by singers from generation to generation, have enjoyed enormous popularity throughout English history, from the Middle Ages to the present. The folk ballad stanza usually alternates between lines of four and three feet. What narrative, or story, does this ballad tell? Does the ballad follow standard folk ballad stanza form? Explain and give examples.

► See the evaluation forms for Discussion, Active Listening, and Oral Communication, *Assessment Portfolio,* 7.11– 7.14.

Responses will vary. Possible responses are given.

1. Oral Tradition. Elements in the poem suggestive of ancient fertility myths include "the green-wood tree" (lines 6, 28); "Among the leaves so gay" (line 14); "merry men" (line 32); "I am a bold harper" (line 63); and "the merry greenwood,/Among the leaves so green" (lines 107–108). Elements in the poem suggestive of political commentary include the use of *bold* and *brave* to describe the outlaws (lines 3, 21, 29, 73, 79); Robin's willingness to help without pay (lines 45–52); the knight's selfish exercise of power ("she is now from me tane,/ And chosen to be an old knight's delight," lines 38–39); and the "ordination" of Little John, with its mockery of church law (lines 93–100).

   This poem may have appealed to poor peasants because they wished for someone to listen to them and protect them as Robin Hood does. The hero dispenses justice on the basis of character and fairness rather than on the basis of social position or wealth.

2. Ballad. The ballad tells how Robin Hood and his merry men prevented a wealthy noble from forcing a peasant girl to marry him and helped her to marry her true love, a peasant man named Allen a Dale. This ballad is in the standard form, with some minor variations in the meter of individual lines.

HISTORICAL NOTE

Histories compiled in the early to mid-1400s identify Robin Hood as a hero of popular ballads. When did these ballads originate? An alternative theory to that presented in the text is that these ballads were generated in the late 1300s, at a time when rural economic conditions had greatly deteriorated. At the same time, restrictions on hunting preserved the king's game while making life yet more difficult for the peasantry. (In the legends, Robin Hood is a renowned poacher.) In 1381 occurred the Peasants' Revolt, also called Wat Tyler's Rebellion, the "first great popular rebellion in English history." Several nobles were executed by the mob. King Richard II calmed the revolt by offering concessions, but when he reneged on his promises, the uprising turned into a near-complete failure. The legendary Robin Hood's honorableness and courtesy contrast sharply with Richard's deceit.

Unit 1 contains a long writing assignment designed to introduce students to the process of writing. The assignment is divided into separate lessons, as follows:

Prewriting: page 12
Drafting: page 25
Evaluating and Revising: page 43
Publishing: page 61

If the various parts of the assignment are done as encountered in the unit, they will be properly spaced to give students time to reflect on each stage in the writing process before going on to the next.

Many students will balk at so large an undertaking as writing a literary narrative. However, the task is well within most students' reach if sufficient guidance is given for each step in the process. Explain that one of the truisms of painting instruction is that if one begins with a good charcoal sketch, it's difficult to ruin the work by adding paint. Prewriting notes are like preliminary sketches for a painting. With thorough prewriting notes, students will be surprised at their own ability to produce substantial narratives.

Have the students do the prewriting steps one at a time. You may choose to have them do these steps in collaboration, brainstorming ideas with their classmates.

Step 1: You may wish to discuss with the class as a whole the salient characteristics of the types of narratives suggested here.

• Children's stories include picture books with minimal text, and books for older children containing more extensive text and occasional illustration. A picture book would be an excellent choice for graphically inclined students. You might suggest that students choosing this alternative retell and update a traditional story. For example, the Cinderella story might be retold with a male central character.

• Science fiction stories usually deal with the far future or past or with an alien environment such as another world or a country under the ground or the sea. Typically, the creation of an alternative world enables the science fiction writer to

(cont.)

The Process of Writing: Prewriting

A Literary Narrative. Reading a work of literature involves taking a journey into an imaginary world created by an author. Sometimes, in realist fiction, that world is very much like the one in which actual people live. At other times, as in myths, tall tales, fantasies, and science fiction stories, the world of a literary work is quite different from the "real world."

Do some planning, or **prewriting,** for a literary work of your own set in an imaginary world very unlike the world in which you live. Begin by reading the Language Arts Survey, 1.1–1.34, which will introduce you to the writing process and to some useful prewriting techniques. Then follow these steps to complete your prewriting:

STEP 1 Choose one of the following forms of writing and read about that type of writing in the Handbook of Literary Terms:

a children's story	a myth
a science fiction story	a fantasy
a fable	a tall tale

STEP 2 Reread the Language Arts Survey, 1.13, "Questioning." Then use the questioning technique to create a plan for your piece of writing. Begin with any of the following questions and then proceed to the others. Make sure that the answers you choose are consistent with the type of story you chose in Step 1.

Whom will your story be about? In other words, who will be your central **characters?**

*[Hint: To develop characters for your story, create an **analysis chart** for your main characters. See the Language Arts Survey, 1.23, "Analysis Charts," for information on analysis charts. List the characters' names at the top of the chart. Along the left side of the chart, list the following attributes of the characters: appearance and dress; age; background; habits of action, thought, or speech; motivations; and relationships with other characters. Then fill in the chart with information about your characters.]*

Where and **when** will your story take place? In other words, what will be its **setting?**

*[Hint: To develop a setting for your story, create a **cluster chart**. See the Language Arts Survey, 1.17, "Clustering," for information on creating a cluster chart. Write the time and place of your story in the middle of a piece of paper. Circle that time and place. Around the circle, write the following phrases and circle them: objects or things, season of year, period in history, and buildings or other structures. Draw lines to connect these circled phrases to the middle circle on your paper. Then, around the outside circles, list details of setting that you can use in your story.]*

What will happen in your story? **How** will the events in the story unfold? In other words, what will be its **plot?**

*[Hint: To create a plot for your story, begin by choosing a **central conflict**, or struggle, that will be faced by one of your characters. Then create a **time line** and list on that line the major events in your plot. See the Language Arts Survey, 1.19, "Time Lines," for information on creating a time line. List all of the following events:*

---

conduct an experiment to answer a "what if" question relevant to some current trend. So, for example, a writer might ask, "What if water pollution became so widespread that water was a precious commodity that people were willing to struggle for?"

• Fables contain animal characters and are told to point out a moral. A student choosing this kind of narrative might begin by thinking of a moral that he or she wishes

to exemplify. Then the student can think of a situation and characters that will raise the issue addressed by the statement of the moral. A possible moral might be, "A friend doesn't try to make a friend into someone else." The story might then tell about an eagle who decides, with disastrous consequences, that his friend the groundhog would be perfect if only he would learn to fly.

• A myth is a story about a hero or god; generally one

(cont.)

The event that introduces the central conflict.

The events that build or develop the central conflict.

The event that represents the high point of interest or suspense in your story.

The event that resolves, or ends, the central conflict.

Any events that follow the resolution and tie up loose ends.]

How will you tell your story? Will your narrator be a character in the story who uses pronouns such as *I* and *we*, or will your narrator stand outside the story and use pronouns such as *he, she, it,* and *they*? In other words, what will be your story's **point of view?**

*[Hint: Beginning writers often find it easier to tell stories from a **first-person point of view**, using pronouns such as* I *and* we. *More experienced writers may prefer telling stories from a **third-person point of view**, using pronouns such as* he *and* they. *Choose whichever point of view seems natural to you. You may wish to experiment with each before selecting one.]*

Why will you as the author tell this story? In other words, what will be your main idea, or **theme**?

*[Hint: To come up with a theme for your story, try doing a **freewrite**. See the Language Arts Survey, 1.12, "Freewriting," for information on freewriting. Freewrite for five to ten minutes about the conflict faced by your central character. Then read your freewrite and think about this question: What might my central character learn from facing this conflict? What lesson might be taught by the experience that the character undergoes?]*

STEP 3 Use the information from Step 2 to create a **story map.** For information on creating story maps, see the Language Arts Survey, 1.21, "Story Maps."

STEP 4 If you wish to do so, make a **rough outline** of your story listing all of its events. Organize these events in **chronological order.** For information on making rough outlines and on using chronological order, see the Language Arts Survey, 1.32, "Making a Rough Outline," and 1.34, "Organizing Ideas."

STEP 5 Save your prewriting notes for use in a later drafting assignment.

told to explain, fancifully, the origins of things. Students choosing to write myths might begin by deciding on natural phenomena to explain (why the sea is salty or why some trees lose their leaves in the winter, for example). Students are more likely to be successful with this assignment if they work within the context of a pre-existing mythological system (such as the Norse or Greek). Excellent source materials for students wishing to write within one of these contexts are the surveys of myths written by Hamilton, Bullfinch, and Graves. These surveys are readily available in most libraries.

• Fantasies are similar to science fiction stories in that they present alternate realities but differ in not having a scientific or pseudo-scientific basis. Popular fantasies include J. R. R. Tolkein's *The Hobbit* and C. S. Lewis's *Chronicles of Narnia.*

Students wishing to write fantasies should decide upon one or more elements of reality that they wish to alter in their stories. For example, a student might write about a society in which reading and writing are considered taboo for all except a select class of rulers or priests, or they might write about a human society organized like that of an ant or bee colony.

• Tall tales present wildly improbable exaggerations told for humorous effect. Students will probably be familiar with such tales told of Paul Bunyan and Pecos Bill. Excellent student writing can result from creating a contemporary version of such a character. Instead of writing about Paul Bunyan, the biggest and strongest of lumberjacks, students might write about M. P. Hacker, the boy computer genius, or Joystick Joan, the greatest arcade game player this side of Tokyo.

Steps 2–5: Refer students to the Language Arts Survey sections mentioned in the lesson to learn how to do freewriting and how to create analysis charts, cluster charts, and time lines. Students who are having trouble developing any one part of the story, a main character, for example, should

(cont.)

proceed with the other parts and return later to the one that is problematic.

Step 3: You may wish to photocopy and distribute to your students the Story Map form in the *Assessment Portfolio.*

Step 4: After students complete Step 4, you may wish to schedule conferences with them to discuss their writing plans. At this stage you can review their prewriting materials and make suggestions that will save them time and effort during the drafting stage.

Evaluating the Prewriting: At all times when evaluating writing, and especially for this first assignment, it is important to be encouraging to students. Do not worry at this stage about spelling, grammar, usage, and mechanics, and do not penalize students for ideas that are as yet derivative or underdeveloped. Instead, evaluate on the basis of whether the prewriting was done and offer helpful suggestions when appropriate.

ENRICHMENT ACTIVITIES

Have students evaluate the various "definitions" of poetry from page 14. Can they find examples of poems that support each definition? Can they find counterexamples? Which definition do they *like* the best? Why? Which definition do they think is most complete or accurate? Have students present their ideas to the class in an oral report.

SUPPORT FOR LEP STUDENTS

• This section introduces specialized vocabulary with which some students may be completely unfamiliar. As students discuss their interpretations of the poem, prompt and encourage them to use these terms as appropriate. It will also help to read aloud or have students read aloud the selection and examples.

• If possible, play a selection from the Broadway musical *Cats.*

• Point out that even in verse, the primary unit of organization is the sentence. When students are reading poetry, they should pause according to the punctuation marks and not at the end of every line.

ADDITIONAL VOCABULARY

rapt—deeply engrossed or preoccupied

contemplation—thought

Poetry

Today, the most common type of story, the kind that you find in a magazine or a newspaper, is told in **prose**, a type of writing that is similar to ordinary speech. However, the earliest stories that survive into our time are not told in prose. They are told in **poetry**. *Poetry* is notoriously difficult to define. Many people throughout history have tried to define it and failed. However, there is one element that most poems have in common: they use language in special ways. When early people told their stories, they wanted them to be memorable. In fact, if a story wasn't memorable, it wouldn't, by definition, be passed along, so people used special techniques to make the language of their stories beautiful and interesting. These special techniques developed into the amazing collection of language tricks, or literary techniques, that writers use today to keep readers interested.

The earliest poems were **narratives**. That is, they told stories. Common types of oral narrative poems include **ballads**—short, simple stories told in song—and **epics**—long verse stories about heroes and gods complex enough to portray the ways of life, values, and beliefs of an entire culture. Soon, composers of verse discovered that poems could be used not only to tell stories, but also simply to express personal feelings. Thus **lyric poems** were born. A lyric poem is highly musical verse that expresses a speaker's feelings. Later poets invented a kind of hybrid form called the **dramatic poem** that presents the speech of one or more characters at a moment of crisis. Dramatic poems often tell or imply stories, as narrative poems do. They also express emotions, often using musical language, as lyric poems do.

Some Famous Definitions of Poetry

Poetry is . . .

"a representing, counterfeiting, or figuring forth: to speak metaphorically, a moving picture with this end: to teach and delight."

—Sir Philip Sidney

"emotion recollected in tranquility."

—William Wordsworth

"the record of the best and happiest moments of the happiest and best minds."

—Percy Bysshe Shelley

"at bottom a criticism of life."

—Matthew Arnold

"speech framed . . . to be heard for its own sake and interest even over and above its interest of meaning."

—Gerard Manley Hopkins

"the rhythmic, inevitably narrative, movement from an overclothed blindness to a naked vision."

—Dylan Thomas

"the clear expression of mixed feelings."

—W. H. Auden

The Human Condition.
Rene Magritte, 1934. © Board of Trustees, National Gallery of Art, Washington, D.C.

GOALS/OBJECTIVES

Studying this lesson will enable students to

• have a nonthreatening, pleasant experience with a humorous lyric poem

• recall some famous definitions of poetry and name and describe some features characteristic of poetry

• use drafting techniques to develop prewriting notes into a coherent, imaginative narrative

• understand and apply concepts pertaining to poetic techniques of meter, stanza form, sound, and meaning

• name and define the three types or genres of poetry (narrative, lyric, dramatic) and classify poems according to type

• revise sentences to reduce wordiness

ART NOTE

René Magritte (1898–1967) was a Belgian Surrealist painter. Other Surrealist artists include Salvador Dalí (Spanish), Joan Miró (Spanish), Max Ernst (German), and Jean Arp (French). Although quite different from each other, the Surrealists experimented in individual ways in a common attempt to unite the unconscious—imagination, dreams, and fantasies—with everyday conscious experience. For some artists this meant rendering their fantasies on canvas. For others, such as Magritte, it meant depicting the irrationality and illogicality of the unconscious: The world of the painting appears realistic and clear but is undecipherable or self-contradictory.

Many of Magritte's paintings, including *The Human Condition*, are commentaries on the experience of art itself. The painting within the painting defies interpretation. What really is outside the window? We (unconsciously) assume that the painting within the painting depicts what really "is" outside the window; however, we are deceived because there is no "real" window, and there cannot be any "real outside" to a painting of a window. Magritte's painting suggests that the human condition is inscrutable to humans because our perception always intervenes.

The painting is in the National Gallery of Art in Washington, DC.

▶**Teaching Note:** Ask students to discuss ways in which a poem is like a painting, and then to discuss ways in which a poet is like a painter.

VOCABULARY FROM THE SELECTION

ineffable	profound
inscrutable	quorum
perpendicular	

Elements of Poetry

GENRES, OR TYPES, OF POETRY

Narrative Poetry. A **narrative poem** is one that tells a story. Types of narrative poetry include **ballads** and **epics.**

Ballad. A **ballad** is a simple narrative poem, usually meant to be sung. The ballads of England and the United States usually are divided into four-line parts, or **stanzas,** that rhyme *abcb.* Examples of ballads include "Sir Patrick Spens" and "The Great Silkie of Shule Skerrie" on pages 136 and 139 of this text.

Epic. An **epic** is a long story, often told in verse, involving heroes and gods. Grand in length and scope, an epic provides a portrait of an entire culture, of the legends, beliefs, values, laws, arts, and ways of life of a people. Examples of epics include *Beowulf* and *Paradise Lost* on pages 99 and 429 of this text.

Lyric Poetry. A **lyric poem** is a highly musical verse that expresses the emotions of a speaker. There are many, many types of lyric poems. Among the most common are these:

Sonnet. A **sonnet** is a fourteen-line poem that follows one of a number of different rhyme schemes. Many sonnets deal with the subject of love. Examples include "Whoso List to Hunt," on page 250, and Shakespeare's Sonnet 18, on page 279.

Ode. An **ode** is a lofty lyric poem on a serious theme. (Some odes follow a particular pattern of stanzas developed from Greek drama, but that needn't concern you now.) Examples of odes include "Ode on a Grecian Urn," on page 642, and "Ode: Intimations of Immortality," on page 662.

Free Verse Lyric. A **free verse lyric** follows no regular pattern of rhythm, rhyme, or meter. Examples include "Dover Beach," on page 740, and "Map of the New World," on page 905.

Elegiac Lyric. An **elegiac lyric** expresses a speaker's feelings of loss, often a loss through death of a loved one or friend. Examples of elegiac lyrics include "The Wife's Lament," on page 88, and *In Memoriam,* on page 712.

Dramatic Poetry. A **dramatic poem** is a verse that relies heavily on dramatic elements such as **monologue** (speech by a single character) or **dialogue** (conversation involving two or more characters). Often, dramatic poems are narratives as well. In other words, they often tell stories. Types of dramatic poems include the **dramatic monologue** and the **soliloquy.**

Sidebar

LITERARY TECHNIQUE

Meter. Students may enjoy writing out the lyrics to their favorite songs or hymns and describing the meter and stanza form.

ADDITIONAL QUESTIONS AND ACTIVITIES

Have students prepare a bulletin board with examples of various types of poems. Examples can be taken from this text or from poetry collections in your school or community library.

LITERARY GENRES

Other examples found in the text include the following:

Ballads

"Robin Hood and Allen a Dale," page 6

"The Bonny Earl of Murray," page 223

Sonnets

"Alas! So All Things Now Do Hold Their Peace," page 293

"Heart Exchange," page 293

"Who's Who," page 880

Lyrics

"I Sing of a Maiden," page 146

"A Dirge," page 675

"A Birthday," page 774

Free Verse Lyrics

"Snake," page 857

"Thistles," page 892

Elegiac Lyric

"To an Athlete Dying Young," page 777

Dramatic Monologue

"Andrea del Sarto," page 729

Dramatic Monologue. A **dramatic monologue** is a poem that presents the speech of a single character in a dramatic situation, often a moment of crisis or self-revelation. The speech is one side of an imagined conversation. "Ulysses," on page 707, and "My Last Duchess," on page 724, are examples of dramatic monologues.

Soliloquy. A **soliloquy** is a speech from a play, often in verse, delivered by a lone character. The speech reveals the character's thoughts and feelings. A soliloquy from William Shakespeare's *Hamlet* can be found on page 396.

TECHNIQUES OF POETRY: METER AND STANZA FORM

Metrical vs. Free Verse. Metrical verse follows a set rhythmical pattern. **Free verse,** or *vers libre,* does not. Instead, it follows the rhythms of ordinary speech.

Meter. The **meter** of a poem is its rhythmical pattern. English verse usually is described as being made up of rhythmical units called **feet.** A **foot** is made up of some combination of **weakly stressed** (⌣) and **strongly stressed** (/) syllables, as follows:

TYPE OF FOOT	PATTERN	EXAMPLE
iamb, or **iambic foot**	⌣ /	⌣ / afraid
trochee, or **trochaic foot**	/ ⌣	/ ⌣ freedom
anapest, or **anapestic foot**	⌣ ⌣ /	⌣ ⌣ / in a flash
dactyl, or **dactylic foot**	/ ⌣ ⌣	/ ⌣ ⌣ feverish
spondee, or **spondaic foot**	/ /	/ / baseball

Some writers on meter also use the term **pyrrhee,** or **pyrrhic foot,** to describe a foot with two weak stresses, as follows:

> anapest   pyrrhee
>
> ⌣ ⌣ / | ⌣ ⌣
> un be liev | a ble

ADDITIONAL QUESTIONS AND ACTIVITIES

Foot. Ask students to analyze the meters of their names. *Robert,* for example, is a trochee; *Camille* is an iamb. Ask students to think of their own words or phrases to exemplify each type of foot.

LITERARY TECHNIQUE

Explain that the most common meters in English verse are iambic pentameter and iambic tetrameter. The former contains five iambs; the latter contains four. Give the following examples on the chalkboard:

⌣ / ⌣ / ⌣ / ⌣
Is this the face that launched a
/ ⌣ /
thousand ships?
(iambic pentameter)

⌣ / ⌣ / ⌣ / ⌣ /
That age is best which is the first
(iambic tetrameter)

LITERARY TECHNIQUE

Meter. Put the following examples on the chalkboard for scanning by your class.

Iambic tetrameter (with a single trochee at the beginning of line 1):

/ ˘ ˘ / ˘ / ˘ /
When to her lute Corinna sings,

˘ / ˘ / ˘ / ˘ /
Her voice revives the leaden strings

Trochaic trimeter:

/ ˘ / ˘ / ˘
Evening comes upon us

Trochaic tetrameter:

/ ˘ / ˘ / ˘ / ˘
Why so pale and wan, fond lover?

Anapestic hexameter:

˘ ˘ / ˘ ˘ / ˘
And the peak of the mountain

˘ / ˘ ˘ / ˘ /˘
was apples, the hugest that ever

˘ /
were seen

Dactylic dimeter (with a final trochee):

/ ˘ ˘ / ˘ ˘
Half a league, half a league

/ ˘ ˘ / ˘
Half a league, onward

The following terms are used to describe the number of feet in a line of poetry:

TERM	NUMBER OF FEET	EXAMPLE
monometer	one foot	˘ / And I ˘ / Shall fly ˘ / Away
dimeter	two feet	/ ˘ / ˘ After | autumn / ˘ / ˘ Comes the | winter
trimeter	three feet	/ ˘ / ˘ / ˘ In the | midst of | mourning
tetrameter	four feet	˘ / | ˘ / | ˘ / | ˘ / O sad | dle up | my milk | white steed
pentameter	five feet	˘ / | ˘ / | ˘ / | ˘ / | ˘ / That time | of year | thou may'st | in me | behold
hexameter or Alexandrine	six feet	˘ / | ˘ / | ˘ / | ˘ / | ˘ / A per | fect knight | he was, | that all | could / ˘ / plain | ly see

A complete description of the meter of a line includes both the term for the type of foot that predominates in the line and the term for the number of feet in the line. The most common English meters are **iambic tetrameter** and **iambic pentameter.**

Stanza Form. A **stanza** is a group of lines in a poem. The following are some common types of stanza:

COUPLET (two-line)	For thy sweet love rememberèd such wealth brings That then I scorn to change my state with kings. —William Shakespeare, Sonnet 29
TRIPLET OR TERCET (three-line)	As thus with thee in prayer in my sore need. Oh! lift me as a wave, a leaf, a cloud! I fall upon the thorns of life! I bleed! —Percy Bysshe Shelley, "Ode to the West Wind"

QUATRAIN
(four-line)

Thy voice is on the rolling air
    I hear thee where the waters run;
    Thou standest in the rising sun,
And in the setting thou art fair.
          —Alfred, Lord Tennyson, *In Memoriam*

QUINTAIN
(five-line)

In summertime on Bredon
    The bells they sound so clear;
Round both the shires they ring them
    In steeples far and near,
A happy noise to hear.
          —A. E. Housman, "Bredon Hill"

SESTET
(six-line)

O, young Lochnivar is come out of the west,
Through all the wide Border his steed was the best;
And save his good broadsword he weapons had none,
He rode all unarm'd, and he rode all alone.
So faithful in love, and so dauntless in war.
There never was knight like the young Lochnivar.
          —Sir Walter Scott, "Lochnivar"

HEPTASTICH
(seven-line)

The flower that smiles today
    Tomorrow dies;
All that we wish to stay
    Tempts and then flies;
What is this world's delight?
Lightning, that mocks the night,
    Brief even as bright.
          —Percy Bysshe Shelley, "Mutability"

OCTAVE
(eight-line)

Labor is blossoming or dancing where
The body is not bruised to pleasure soul,
Nor beauty born out of its own despair,
Nor blear-eyed wisdom out of midnight oil.
O chestnut tree, great-rooted blossomer,
Are you the leaf, the blossom, or the bole?
O body swayed to music, O brightening glance,
How can we know the dancer from the dance?
          —William Butler Yeats, "Among School Children"

LITERARY TECHNIQUE
Stanza

• Ask students to find other examples of these stanza forms in this book.

• Other poems containing **couplets** include "The Prologue" (page 185) and "The Pardoner's Tale" (page 205) from Geoffrey Chaucer's *The Canterbury Tales;* Anne Finch's "The Introduction" (page 484); and William Blake's "The Lamb" (page 589).

• Other poems containing **triplets** include Dylan Thomas's "Do Not Go Gentle into That Good Night" (page 876).

• Other poems containing **quatrains** include "Sir Patrick Spens" (page 136); John Milton's "On His Blindness" (page 439); and Thomas Gray's "Elegy Written in a Country Churchyard" (page 574).

• Other poems containing **sestets** include "Ubi Sunt Qui ante Nos Fuerunt?" (page 142) and Rupert Brooke's "The Soldier" (page 863).

• Other poems containing **heptastichs** include Thomas Nashe's "A Litany in Time of Plague" (page 295) and Elizabeth Barrett Browning's "The Runaway Slave at Pilgrim's Point" (page 806).

• Other poems containing **octaves** include Thomas Campion's "Jack and Joan" (page 295) and Christina Rossetti's "A Birthday" (page 774).

• Alfred, Lord Tennyson's "The Lady of Shalott" (page 698) is written in **nine-line stanzas,** as is Edmund Spenser's *The Færie Queene* (page 257). *The Færie Queene* is composed of so-called Spenserian stanzas, which contain eight iambic pentameter lines followed by one iambic hexameter (or Alexandrine) line, and follow the rhyme scheme *ababbcbcc.*

• George Herbert's "Easter Wings" (page 425) is written in **ten-line stanzas,** as is John Keats's "Ode on a Grecian Urn" (page 642).

• Samuel T. Coleridge's "Kubla Khan" (page 599) is written in **eleven-line** stanzas.

Internal Rhyme. Internal rhyme is used in Wilfred Owen's lines "O **meet** it is and passing **sweet**/To live in peace with others."

Slant Rhyme. Slant rhyme is used in Christopher Marlowe's "The Passionate Shepherd to His Love," lines 1–2, page 262 ("Come live with me and be my **love,**/And we will all the pleasures **prove**").

Alliteration. Alliteration is used in George Herbert's "Easter Wings," line 10, page 426 ("Then shall the **fall further** the **flight** in me").

Assonance. Assonance is used in Alfred, Lord Tennyson's "The Lady of Shalott," line 1, page 699 ("On **ei**ther side the river **lie**").

Consonance. Consonance is used in Shakespeare's Sonnet 29, line 11, page 282 ("Like to the lar**k** at brea**k** of day arising").

Image. Ted Hughes's poem "Thistles," page 892, presents an extended image.

Hyperbole. Hyperbole is used in Shakespeare's Sonnet 29, lines 10-12, page 282 ("Haply I think on thee, and then my state/. . . sings hymns at heaven's gate").

TECHNIQUES OF POETRY: SOUND*

Rhythm. The **rhythm** is the pattern of beats or stresses in a poem. A regular rhythmic pattern is called a **meter.**

Rhyme. Rhyme is the repetition of sounds at the ends of words. The following are some types of rhyme:

> **End Rhyme. End rhyme** is the use of rhyming words at the ends of lines.
>
> **Internal Rhyme. Internal rhyme** is the use of rhyming words within lines.
>
> **Slant Rhyme. Slant rhyme** is the use of rhyming sounds that are similar but not identical, as in *rave* and *rove* or *rot* and *rock.*

Alliteration. Alliteration is the repetition of initial consonant sounds, as in *Peter Piper picked a peck of pickled peppers.*

Assonance. Assonance is the repetition of vowel sounds in stressed syllables with different consonant sounds, as in *praised* and *plains.*

Consonance. Consonance is the use in stressed syllables of identical final consonants preceded by different vowel sounds, as in *wind* and *wound.* This technique is also known as **half-rhyme** or **slant rhyme.**

Onomatopoeia. Onomatopoeia is the use of words or phrases that sound like the things to which they refer. Examples include the words *meow, clink, boom,* and *mumble.*

TECHNIQUES OF POETRY: MEANING*

Image. An **image** is a word or phrase that names something that can be seen, heard, touched, tasted, or smelled. A group of images that together create a given emotion in a reader or listener is called an **objective correlative.**

Figure of Speech. A **figure of speech,** or **trope,** is an expression that has more than a literal meaning. The following are examples of common figures of speech:

> **Hyperbole.** A **hyperbole** is an exaggeration made for rhetorical effect.
>
> **Metaphor.** A **metaphor** is a figure of speech in which one thing is spoken or written about as if it were another. This figure of speech invites the reader to make a comparison between the two things: the writer's actual subject, the **tenor** of the metaphor, and another thing to which the subject is likened, the **vehicle** of the metaphor. In the metaphor "My love is a red, red rose," the tenor is the love. The vehicle is the rose. **Personifications** and **similes** are types of metaphor.

*Note: These techniques are commonly but not exclusively used in poetry.

ADDITIONAL QUESTIONS AND ACTIVITIES

Figures of Speech. Assign pairs of students to take turns creating hyperboles and metaphors. For hyperbole, one student can make a statement, and the other can exaggerate it. For metaphor, one student can name an object or experience to serve as the tenor, and the other can name a vehicle to complete the metaphor. After the activity, invite students to share their favorite hyperboles and metaphors with the rest of the class.

Metonymy. **Metonymy** is the naming of an object associated with a thing in place of the name of the thing itself. Speaking of *the crown* when one means *the king* or *the queen* is an example.

Personification. **Personification** is a figure of speech in which an idea, animal, or object is described as if it were a person. "The wind sang its sad, sad song" is an example.

Simile. A **simile** is a comparison using *like* or *as*. "My love is like a red, red rose" is a simile.

Synaesthesia. **Synaesthesia** is a figure of speech that combines in a single expression images related to two or more different senses, as in *the singing light.*

Synecdoche. A **synecdoche** is a figure of speech in which the name of part of something is used in place of the name of the whole or vice versa, as in *hired hands* for *laborers.*

Understatement. An **understatement** is an ironic expression in which something of importance is spoken of as though it were not important.

Rhetorical Techniques. A **rhetorical technique** is an extraordinary but literal use of language to achieve a particular effect. Common rhetorical techniques used in poetry include the following:

Antithesis. An **antithesis** is a rhetorical technique in which words, phrases, or ideas are strongly contrasted, often by repeating a grammatical structure. An example is Pope's "To err is human, to forgive divine."

Apostrophe. An **apostrophe** is a rhetorical technique in which an object or person is directly addressed, as in Shelley's "O wild West Wind, thou breath of Autumn's being."

Catalog. A **catalog** is a list of people or things, as in the list of pagan gods in lines 374–505 of Book 1 of Milton's *Paradise Lost.*

Chiasmus. A **chiasmus** is a rhetorical technique in which the order of occurrence of words or phrases is reversed, as in the line "We can weather changes, but we can't change the weather."

Parallelism. **Parallelism** is a rhetorical technique in which a writer emphasizes the equal value or weight of two or more ideas by expressing them in the same grammatical form, as in the phrase "with hope, with joy, and with love."

Repetition. **Repetition** is the use, again, of a sound, word, phrase, sentence, or other element, as in the sentence *"Do as I say, not as I do."*

Rhetorical Question. A **rhetorical question** is one asked for effect but not meant to be answered because the answer is clear from the context, as in Christina Rossetti's lines "Who has seen the wind? Neither you nor I."

LITERARY TECHNIQUE

Metonymy. Metonymy is used in Christina Rossetti's "In an Artist's Studio," line 1, page 770 ("One face looks out from all his canvases").

Personification. Personification is used in John Dryden's "A Song for St. Cecilia's Day," line 33, page 493 ("The soft complaining flute"), and in Aphra Behn's "Love Armed" (page 549).

Simile. Simile is used in John Keats's "Ode to a Nightingale," lines 1–2 ("My heart aches, and a drowsy numbness pains/My sense, as though of hemlock I had drunk.") and in T. S. Eliot's "The Love Song of J. Alfred Prufrock" ("Let us go then, you and I,/When the evening is spread out against the sky/Like a patient etherized upon a table").

Synaesthesia. Synaesthesia is used in William Blake's "London," lines 11 and 12, page 595 ("And the hapless Soldier's sigh/Runs in blood down Palace walls").

Understatement. Understatement is used in Jonathan Swift's "A Modest Proposal," page 550.

Chiasmus. Chiasmus is used in Alexander Pope's "The Rape of the Lock," lines 7–10 ("Say what strange motive, Goddess! could compel/A well-bred lord to assault a gentle belle?/Oh, say what stranger cause, yet unexplored,/Could make a gentle belle reject a lord?").

Parallelism. Parallelism is used in Elizabeth Barrett Browning's Sonnet 43, page 757, and in Christina Rossetti's "A Birthday," page 774.

Repetition. Repetition is used in Dylan Thomas's "Do Not Go Gentle into That Good Night," page 876.

Rhetorical Question. A rhetorical question is asked in Shakespeare's Sonnet 18, line 1, page 280 ("Shall I compare thee to a summer's day?"), and in the nursery rhyme "Sing a Song of Sixpence" ("Wasn't that a dainty dish to set before the king?").

ABOUT THE AUTHOR

• T(homas) S(tearns) Eliot was born and grew up in St. Louis. He later emigrated to England, where he became a citizen and joined the Church of England. Eliot is said by some to have recreated poetry in the twentieth century. He won the Nobel Prize for literature in 1948. Additional information on T. S. Eliot can be found on page 852.

• T. S. Eliot's poem "Preludes" appears on page 852.

ANSWERS TO SELECTION CHECK TEST 4.1.3

EX. According to the poem, how many names must a cat have?
A cat must have three different names.

1. According to the poem, what is "a difficult matter"?
The naming of cats is "a difficult matter."

2. Of what are *Peter, Augustus, Alonzo,* and *James* examples?
These are examples of sensible, everyday names.

3. What does a cat need in order to "keep up his tail perpendicular"?
A cat needs a name that's particular, peculiar, and more dignified—a name that never belongs to more than one cat.

4. What can "no human research . . . discover"?
"No human research can discover" the third name, the one that the cat itself knows but will never confess.

5. What are cats thinking about when they are "in profound meditation"?
They are thinking about their secret names.

"The Naming of Cats"

T. S. ELIOT

RHYME SCHEME ► ► ►
The poem follows the rhyme scheme abab.

ALLITERATION ► ► ►
The repeated b sounds are an example of alliteration.

METER ► ► ►
The poem is written in anapestic tetrameter with many variations.

PERSONIFICATION ► ► ►
Here human qualities are attributed to the cat.

PARALLELISM ► ► ►
These are parallel phrases, each made up of the word never and a verb.

The Naming of Cats is a difficult matter,
   It isn't just one of your holiday games;
You may think at first I'm as mad as a hatter[1]
When I tell you, a cat must have THREE DIFFERENT NAMES.
First of all, there's the name that the family use daily,   (5)
   Such as Peter, Augustus, Alonzo or James,
Such as Victor or Jonathan, George or Bill Bailey—
   All of them sensible everyday names.
There are fancier names if you think they sound sweeter,
   Some for the gentlemen, some for the dames: (10)
Such as Plato, Admetus, Electra, Demeter[2]—
   But all of them sensible everyday names.
But I tell you, a cat needs a name that's particular,
   A name that's peculiar, and more dignified,
Else how can he keep up his tail perpendicular,   (15)
   Or spread out his whiskers, or cherish his pride?
Of names of this kind, I can give you a quorum,
   Such as Munkustrap, Quaxo, or Coricopat,
Such as Bombalurina, or else Jellylorum—
   Names that never belong to more than one cat.   (20)
But above and beyond there's still one name left over,
   And that is the name that you never guess;
The name that no human research can discover—
   But THE CAT HIMSELF KNOWS, and will never confess.

---

1. **mad as a hatter.** This widely known **simile** may have originated from a disease common among hat makers caused by mercury used in the production of felt.
2. **Plato . . . Demeter.** Names of figures from Greek mythology and history

WORDS FOR EVERYDAY USE:
per • pen • dic • u • lar (pur´pən dik´yōō lər) *adj.,* exactly upright
quo • rum (kwôr´əm) *n.,* a select group or company

ABOUT THE SELECTION

The poem is taken from Eliot's *Old Possum's Book of Practical Cats,* first published in 1939 (available in paperback from Harcourt, 1982). Some of the cats mentioned in the book include Mungojerrie; Rumpelteazer; Jennyanydots; Bustopher Jones, the cat about town; and Macavity, the mystery cat. Ask students to classify these names using Eliot's three categories of cat names.

A musical play, *Cats,* based on the *Old Possum* poems set to music by Andrew Lloyd Webber (1948–), has had great success with audiences in the United States and in Great Britain. Recordings are available on CD and audiocassette.

ADDITIONAL QUESTIONS AND ACTIVITIES

• Ask students why Eliot might have chosen to write about cats' names rather than the names of dogs, guinea pigs, or other common household pets.

• Point out that lyric poetry is an expression of the speaker's individuality. Unlike the speaker of this poem, students may dislike cats. Discuss the difference between describing—telling about observable details—and evaluating—making judgments such as good or bad, pleasurable or irritating (see the Language Arts Survey, 1.11, "Observing," and 1.43, "Self-Evaluation"). Then discuss with students how the speaker describes cats and how he probably feels about them. Ask whether students agree with the speaker's descriptions of cats. Then ask students how they feel about cats. What would they say in a poem about cats? Do they have strong feelings about cats? Ask for other topics about which they have strong feelings and might like to write poetry. Have them keep notes in their journals for future writing assignments. Are there ways other than by using words in which they could express those feelings (e.g., through drawing, sculpture, dance, or music)?

25   When you notice a cat in <u>profound</u> meditation,
        The reason, I tell you, is always the same:
    His mind is engaged in a rapt contemplation
        Of the thought, of the thought, of the thought of his name:
        His <u>ineffable</u> effable
30   Effanineffable
    Deep and <u>inscrutable</u> singular Name.

◄ ◄ ◄ **ASSONANCE**
The repeated long a sounds are an example of assonance.

◄ ◄ ◄ **REPETITION**
The repetition of the phrase mirrors the idea being described—thinking and thinking and thinking about something.

WORDS FOR EVERYDAY USE:

pro • found (prō found´) *adj.,* very deep or intense
in • ef • fa • ble (in ef´ə bəl) *adj.,* incapable of being expressed or described adequately; inexpressible
in • scru • ta • ble (in skrōōt´ə bəl) *adj.,* completely obscure or mysterious

CROSS-CURRICULAR ACTIVITIES

History. Have students research the history of the domestic cat. This history begins with the Egyptians about 2500 BC.

Biology. Have students research cats' special powers (such as hearing) and special needs (such as nutrition). To what extent can they find a biological basis for cats' unique behavior?

VOCABULARY IN CONTEXT

• The townspeople of Pisa eventually got used to the idea that buildings need not be <u>perpendicular</u>.
• Dedication enabled her to join the <u>quorum</u> of those who have completed a marathon.
• A <u>profound</u> pleasure overcame Branford as he hit upon the solution to the physics problem he had been struggling with all week.
• Joan's <u>ineffable</u> excitement about getting front-row seats for the Lizard Babies concert was unacceptable to her mother, who demanded, "Well? Say something!"
• Geoff concluded that if millions of Romans had mastered Latin, it need not remain <u>inscrutable</u> to him.

RESPONDING TO THE SELECTION

If students have difficulty thinking of a "secret name" for themselves, have them begin by listing things about themselves that they alone know.

ANSWERS FOR REVIEWING THE SELECTION

RECALLING

1. Naming cats is said to be difficult.

2. A cat must have a sensible, common name; a peculiar name; and a secret name.

INTERPRETING

Responses will vary. Possible responses are given.

3. Naming cats is difficult because cats must have three very different sorts of names.

4. The sensible name is for everyday and family use. The peculiar name is to support the cat's sense of dignity and individuality.

SYNTHESIZING

Responses will vary. Possible responses are given.

5. Cats are animals who share living spaces with humans, who often disagree with where the cat will walk and sleep, what and when the cat will eat, and so forth. When dealing with a cat about these matters, the first sort of name seems appropriate. People also view cats as companions who enjoy pampering and play, and in this regard the second sort of name seems appropriate. Cats are also frequently independent and self-absorbed and can appear engrossed in something mysterious. In this regard, the third sort of name seems appropriate.

Responding to the Selection

In your journal, make a list of the most creative and interesting names that you have ever heard. Your list might include the names of childhood friends, relatives, pets, restaurants, gas stations, markets, shops, or musical groups. You may want to refer to the Language Arts Survey, 1.10, "Recalling." If you could choose an unusual, creative "secret name" for yourself, like one of Eliot's cats, what would that name be?

Reviewing the Selection

RECALLING

1. How does the speaker characterize the naming of cats in line 1?

2. According to the speaker, what three kinds of names should a cat have?

INTERPRETING

3. What makes the naming of cats a difficult matter?

4. What purpose is served by each of the first two kinds of names that a cat should have?

SYNTHESIZING

5. What characteristics do actual cats have that might have led the speaker to suggest, humorously, each of the three kinds of names?

Understanding Literature (Questions for Discussion)

1. **Personification. Personification** is a figure of speech in which an idea, animal, or thing is described as if it were a person. What human qualities are attributed to cats in this poem? What actual qualities or actions of cats might lead people to attribute such qualities to them? What is the source of the humor of the poem?

2. **Meter.** The **meter** of a poem is its rhythmical pattern. This poem is composed in **anapestic tetrameter,** with variations. An **anapest** is a foot made up of two weakly stressed syllables followed by one strongly stressed syllable. A **tetrameter** line is one with four strong stresses. Write the first four lines of the poem on a sheet of paper. Then scan the lines, marking the weakly stressed and strongly stressed syllables. Finally, divide the lines into feet. What variations from strict use of anapests can you find in the first four lines? Are all the lines of the poem tetrameter?

ANSWERS FOR UNDERSTANDING LITERATURE

▶ See the evaluation forms for discussion, active listening, and oral communication, *Assessment Portfolio,* 7.11– 7.14.

Responses will vary. Possible responses are given.

1. **Personification.** Cats are called "gentlemen" and "dames" (line 10); they are spoken of as having dignity (lines 14–15) and pride (lines 15–16); as knowing their own names and having an identity (line 24); and as engaging in "profound meditation" (line 25) and "rapt contemplation" (line 27). Cats might appear dignified and prideful or intelligent and contemplative because they are ignorant of or disinterested in human affairs. Some might find the poem amusing because it implies that instead of being intelligent, cats are stupidly aware only of themselves.

(cont.)

3. **Rhyme. Rhyme** is the repetition of sounds at the ends of words. In this poem Eliot uses some amusing, unusual rhymes. Find examples in the poem. What makes such rhymes better than rhymes of the *moon/June, sun/run* variety?

The Process of Writing: Drafting

Read the Language Arts Survey, 1.35–1.42, on drafting. Then, using the prewriting notes you developed for the writing activity on pages 12 and 13, write a draft of your imaginative narrative. Save your draft in your writing portfolio.

Language Lab

After reading the Language Arts Survey Handbook, 2.59, "Reducing Wordiness," rewrite the sentences below, trying to use as few words as necessary to communicate each idea.

1. Tia went to the library with the intention of trying to find a book about T. S. Eliot, who was a man who wrote poetry in verse.

2. She was particularly interested in becoming familiar with his book that he named *Old Possum's Book of Practical Cats.*

3. Eliot's book of verse, which was intended for children, is the book on which the musical *Cats* was based.

4. This play, which is a musical, premiered in London in the year of 1981.

5. The musical then debuted in New York City in the following year, which was 1982, and the musical was an immediate smash hit with the public.

▶ See the Writing Evaluation Form: Process, *Assessment Portfolio,* 7.1.

▶ For detailed evaluation of drafts, see the evaluation forms for writing and drafting, *Assessment Portfolio,* 7.1–7.6.

• You may want to avoid evaluating drafts in writing until students develop receptive attitudes toward critical evaluation and revising. You may want not to read these drafts at all and to encourage students to view writing as something that can be valuable and enjoyable in itself.

• Rather than scoring or critiquing these drafts, discuss with students individually or in small groups what you and others find interesting about the plots, descriptions, and characters. Allow students to discover, through the discussion, places where each story could have benefited from additional detail, where it is unclear, and so forth.

▶ Additional practice in drafting is provided in the *Essential Skills Practice Book: Writing,* 1.35–1.42.

ANSWERS FOR LANGUAGE LAB

Responses will vary. Possible responses are given.

1. Tia went to the library to find a book about the poet T. S. Eliot.

2. She was particularly interested in his *Old Possum's Book of Practical Cats.*

3. The musical *Cats* was based on Eliot's book of children's verse.

4. This musical premiered in London in 1981.

5. It debuted in New York City the following year and was an immediate hit.

▶ Additional practice is provided in the *Essential Skills Practice Book: Language,* 2.59.

ANSWERS FOR UNDERSTANDING LITERATURE (CONT.)

2. Meter. The first four lines of the poem marked for stress and divided into feet appear as:

The Naming of Cats is a difficult matter,

It isn't just one of your holiday games;

You may think at first I'm as mad as a hatter

When I tell you, a cat must have THREE DIFFERENT NAMES.

The lines are all in tetrameter. They contain some iambic feet and some extra weakly stressed syllables.

3. Rhyme. Some examples of unusual rhymes are "sweeter" and "Demeter" (lines 9 and 11), and "particular" and "perpendicular" (lines 13 and 15). Rhymes are often more interesting when they are multisyllabic.

ENRICHMENT ACTIVITIES

 In "The Rocking-Horse Winner," the parents seem to pay little attention to their son, Paul. Have students discuss and research the types of nurturing and support that children need from parents. What happens when children do not get what they need? There are many different perspectives and theories on this issue; after some preliminary investigation, groups of students might choose different perspectives to research. Each group can then present its research in the form of a symposium or panel discussion.

LITERARY TECHNIQUE

In recent years, extremely short stories, called "short-shorts" or "flash fictions," have become popular among creative writers in Europe and in the United States. Some of these fictions present single actions or epiphanies (moments of revelation). Others develop entire plots in few words (generally less than 250).

Fiction

Fiction is prose writing that tells an imaginative story. The most common classification of fiction is by length. Book-length works of fiction are **novels**. Short works of fiction are **short stories**. Fictions of intermediate length are sometimes called **novellas**.

The Origins of Fiction

Fiction developed from various kinds of stories told in the oral tradition, including myths, legends, and fables. The earliest stories were told in poetry, perhaps because rhythmic verse and a stock "poetic language" made them easy to memorize. Early examples of prose fiction from Europe include Petronius's *Satyricon* and Apuleius's *The Golden Ass,* Roman works of the first and second centuries. In the eleventh century in Japan, Lady Murasaki Shikibu wrote the first novel. This work, *The Tale of Genji,* tells of the life and loves of a Japanese prince. In Europe, early and influential works of fiction include Boccaccio's *Decameron,* a collection of short prose tales written in the mid-fourteenth century, and Cervantes's *Don Quixote,* a satire of medieval romance tales written in the early seventeenth century (see page 225).

The Novel

In England, fiction was an outgrowth of various kinds of nonfictional writing, including autobiographies, biographies, travel sketches, journals, and letters. Arguably the first full-fledged novel in English was Aphra Behn's *Oroonoko, or the Royal Slave,* published in 1688. (See selection on page 521). *Oroonoko,* a sympathetic account of the life of an enslaved African, contains elements of autobiography, biography, and travelogue, as do other early novels such as Daniel Defoe's *Robinson Crusoe* (1719) and *Moll Flanders* (1722). These were followed by Samuel Richardson's *Pamela* (1740) and *Clarissa* (1747–8), both moral tales told in letters. Important British novelists since that time include Henry Fielding, Mary Shelley, Jane Austen, William Thackeray, George Eliot, Charles Dickens, Charlotte and Emily Brontë, Thomas Hardy, Joseph Conrad, James Joyce, E. M. Forster, George Orwell, Virginia Woolf, and D. H. Lawrence.

The Short Story

The word *novel* comes from the Italian *novella,* meaning "story," and was first applied to short works like those found in the *Decameron.* Although the writing of short, original fictional tales in Europe dates at least as far back as Boccaccio, the development of the short story as we know it today was a nineteenth-century phenomenon. The first great modern short-story writers emerged in the United States, France, and Germany. Among the best of these pioneering writers of short stories were Washington Irving, Nathaniel Hawthorne, Edgar Allan Poe, and Guy de Maupassant. The American Edgar Allan Poe described the short story as a brief imaginative fiction that creates a single dominant impression. In England, the short story came of age in the twentieth century. Great practitioners of the form include Virginia Woolf, James Joyce, D. H. Lawrence, Katherine Mansfield, Jean Rhys, and Alice Munro.

A Shoreham Garden. Samuel Palmer, circa 1829. Courtesy of the Trustees of the Victoria & Albert Museum

26   UNIT ONE / GENRES AND TECHNIQUES OF LITERATURE

GOALS/OBJECTIVES

Studying this lesson will enable students to

- empathize with a main character in a short story
- understand the concepts of character, characterization, setting, mood, conflict, plot, and theme and identify these elements in a work of fiction
- define the terms *myth, fable, parable, tall tale,*

and *ballad* and identify myths, fables, parables, tall tales, and ballads
- explain what fiction is
- revise a draft of narrative writing based on self-evaluation and peer evaluation
- evaluate a draft of narrative writing

Students who are used to hearing and reading only American English may need help with the Briticisms in the selection. Some of these, such as "honor bright," "bonny," and "pram," are defined below. Others are defined in the footnotes. Some students may be less likely to become bogged down by such unfamiliar language if they hear the first part of the selection read aloud in class. Such a reading will raise their interest and make the text seem more accessible.

IDIOMS

honor bright—on my/your honor
in full tilt—at full speed
spinning yarns—telling fanciful tales

ADDITIONAL VOCABULARY

straight—immediately
bonny—pretty
discreet—able to keep a secret
materialize—become real
smirk—smile conceitedly
pram—baby carriage
vaguely—uncertainly
stoutly—boldly
assertion—statement
compel—force; require
stealth—secrecy
peer—look
furious—wild
obscure—unknown
shilling, pound—units of British money
serene—peaceful
reiterate—say again
uncanny—eerie; unexplainable
successive—one after another
spray—small bouquet
divulge—disclose, tell
tormented—tortured, troubled

VOCABULARY FROM THE SELECTION

career
parry
remonstrate

ART NOTE

Samuel Palmer (1805–1881) exhibited his paintings by the age of fourteen. In 1824, Palmer met William Blake, who encouraged Palmer's developing mysticism. Palmer was deeply religious and had intense emotions about nature. His recognition as an artist rests on his ability to display this intensity of feeling. Palmer was a leader of the Shoreham Ancients, a short-lived utopian community of artists who fled the city to pursue simplicity in living. The painting *A Shoreham Garden* was done in gouache and watercolor while Palmer lived with the Ancients in Shoreham, Kent.

▶ **Teaching Note:** Ask students to tell a story about the person in the painting. How did she get there? What is she thinking and feeling? Use the discussion to exemplify such elements of fiction as character and characterization, setting and mood, plot and conflict, and theme.

LITERARY TECHNIQUES

Character

- Paul is the protagonist in "The Rocking-Horse Winner." Jane Eyre is the protagonist in Charlotte Brontë's *Jane Eyre* (page 816). Examples of protagonists from contemporary popular culture include Dorothy in *The Wizard of Oz* and Superman.
- Mr. Rochester is the antagonist in *Jane Eyre* (page 816). Examples of antagonists from contemporary popular culture include *Superman's* Lex Luthor and *The Wizard of Oz's* Wicked Witch of the West.
- Uncle Oscar is a major character in "The Rocking-Horse Winner." Mrs. Higgins and Colonel Pickering are major characters in Shaw's *Pygmalion* (page 986). Examples of major characters from contemporary popular culture include Kunta Kinte from *Roots* and Dr. Quinn from *Dr. Quinn, Medicine Woman*.
- Freddy Hill and the parlormaid are minor characters in Shaw's *Pygmalion* (page 986). Examples of minor characters from contemporary popular culture include Jimmy Olsen in *Superman* and the doorkeeper in *The Wizard of Oz*.
- The objects of romantic love as characterized in romantic poetry are often one-dimensional characters, as in Marvell's "To His Coy Mistress" (page 457). Flat characters also often appear in satires and farces, such as Voltaire's *Candide* (page 557).
- Dr. Faustus as portrayed by Marlowe in his play (page 387) is an example of a three-dimensional character.
- Pangloss, of Voltaire's *Candide* (page 557), is an example of a static character, as is Clark Kent in *Superman*.
- Stephen Dedalus, the main character in Joyce's *A Portrait of the Artist as a Young Man* (page 921), is an example of a dynamic character.
- Examples of stock characters include the characters in *Everyman* (page 212) and *The Pilgrim's Progress* (page 442). Examples of stock characters from contemporary popular culture include the lone warrior, the misunderstood young pop star, the lonely cop, and the gruff authority with a gentle heart.

Elements of Fiction

CHARACTER

A **character** is a person (or sometimes an animal) who figures in the action of a story. The following are some useful terms for describing characters:

A **protagonist**, or main character, is the central figure in a story.

An **antagonist** is a character who is pitted against a protagonist.

A **major character** is one with a significant role in the action of a story. A **minor character** is one who plays a lesser role. Because of limitations of length and focus, most short stories have, at most, one or two major characters.

A **one-dimensional character, flat character,** or **caricature** is one who exhibits a single dominant quality, or **character trait.**

A **three-dimensional, full,** or **rounded character** is one who exhibits the complexity of traits associated with actual human beings.

A **static character** is one who does not change during the course of the story.

A **dynamic character** is one who does change during the course of the story.

A **stock character** is one found again and again in different literary works. Examples of stock characters include the mad scientist and the absent-minded professor.

A **motivation** is a force that drives a character to act in a certain way.

CHARACTERIZATION

Characterization is the use of literary techniques to create a character. Three major techniques of characterization used by fiction writers include

1. direct description by a narrator or character,

2. portrayal of a character's words and behavior, and

3. representations of a character's internal states.

LITERARY TECHNIQUE

Characterization

- Emily Brontë gives a direct description of Mr. Heathcliff (and of his house and the moors) on page 810.
- Chaucer uses portrayal of behavior throughout "The Prologue" to *The Canterbury Tales* (page 185).
- Charlotte Brontë represents the internal states of the main character in *Jane Eyre* (page 816).

SETTING AND MOOD

The **setting** is the time and place in which a story occurs, together with all the details used to create a sense of a particular time and place. The **mood** is the emotion created in the reader by descriptions of the setting, of characters, and of events. In fiction, setting is most often revealed by means of description of such elements as landscape, scenery, buildings, furniture, clothing, weather, and seasons. It also can be revealed by how characters talk and behave. In its widest sense, setting includes the general social, political, moral, and psychological conditions in which characters find themselves.

CONFLICT

A **conflict** is a struggle between two forces in a literary work. A plot involves the introduction, development, and, usually, the resolution, or ending, of a conflict. One side of the central conflict in a work of fiction usually is taken by the main character. That character may struggle against another character, against the forces of nature, against society or social norms, against fate, or against some element within himself or herself. A struggle that takes place between a character and some outside force is called an **external conflict.** A struggle that takes place within a character is called an **internal conflict.**

PLOT

A **plot** is a series of causally connected events in a literary work. The novelist E. M. Forster explained, famously, that if the king dies and then the queen dies, that is a story, but if the king dies and then the queen dies of grief, that is a plot. A typical plot involves the following elements:

The **exposition,** or **introduction,** sets the tone and mood, introduces the characters and the setting, and provides necessary background information.

The **inciting incident** is the event that introduces the central conflict.

The **rising action,** or **complication,** develops the conflict to a high point of intensity.

The **climax** is the high point of interest or suspense.

The **crisis,** or **turning point,** often the same event as the climax, is the point in the plot where something decisive happens to determine the future course of events and the eventual working out of the conflict.

The **falling action** is all the events that follow the climax.

The **resolution** is the point at which the central conflict is ended, or resolved.

The **dénouement** is any material that follows the resolution and that ties up loose ends.

Plot. Students can practice using Freytag's Pyramid to diagram a plot by analyzing a familiar story such as "Beauty and the Beast" or "The Three Little Pigs." On the chalkboard or on an overhead transparency, draw a pyramid. Ask students to label the segments of the pyramid shown on this page. Then ask them to locate on the pyramid significant events or points in the story.

Theme. Explain the difference between a theme (a central idea or issue) and a moral (a lesson or precept). In simple stories such as fables and parables, the theme and the moral may be identical; but many of the most interesting stories do not have clearly defined morals.

QUOTABLES

❝When I want to read a novel, I write one.❞

—Benjamin Disraeli

❝There is power in a story. It testifies to the worth, the significance of an individual. For a short while all the strength and all the radiance of the world is brought to bear upon a few human figures.❞

—Saul Bellow

Plots are often illustrated using the following diagram, known as "Freytag's Pyramid" for its creator, Gustav Freytag:

FREYTAG'S PYRAMID

Climax

Rising Action

Falling Action

Exposition

Dénouement

Inciting Incident

Resolution

THEME

A **theme** is a central idea in a literary work. A long work such as a novel may deal with several interrelated themes.

> *"If one . . . thinks of the novel as a whole, it would seem to be a creation owning a certain looking-glass likeness to life . . . [I]t is a structure leaving a shape on the mind's eye."*
>
> —*Virginia Woolf*

"The Rocking-Horse Winner"

D. H. LAWRENCE

There was a woman who was beautiful, who started with all the advantages, yet she had no luck. She married for love, and the love turned to dust. She had bonny children, yet she felt—they had been thrust upon her, and she could not love them. They looked at her coldly, as if they were finding fault with her. And hurriedly she felt she must cover up some fault in herself. Yet what it was that she must cover up she never knew. Nevertheless, when her children were present she always felt the center of her heart go hard. This troubled her, and in her manner she was all the more gentle and anxious for her children, as if she loved them very much. Only she herself knew that at the centre of her heart was a hard little place that could not feel love, no, not for anybody. Everybody else said of her: "She is such a good mother. She adores her children." Only she herself, and her children themselves, knew it was not so. They read it in each other's eyes.

There were a boy and two little girls. They lived in a pleasant house, with a garden, and they had discreet servants, and felt themselves superior to anyone in the neighborhood.

Although they lived in style, they felt always an anxiety in the house. There was never enough money. The mother had a small income, and the father had a small income, but not nearly enough for the social position which they had to keep up. The father went into town to some office. But though he had good prospects, these prospects never materialized. There was always the grinding sense of the shortage of money, though the style was always kept up.

At last the mother said: "I will see if *I* can't make something." But she did not know where to begin. She racked her brains, and tried this thing and the other, but could not find anything successful. The failure made deep lines come into her face. Her children were growing up; they would have to go to school. There must be more money; there must be more money. The father, who was always very handsome and expensive in his tastes, seemed as if he never *would* be able to do anything worth doing. And the mother, who had a great belief in herself, did not succeed any better, and her tastes were just as expensive.

And so the house came to be haunted by the unspoken phrase: There must be more money! There must be more money! The children could hear it all the time, though nobody said it aloud. They heard it at Christmas, when the expensive and splendid toys filled the nursery. Behind the shining modern rocking-horse, behind the smart doll's house, a voice would start whispering: *"There must be more money! There must be more money!"* And the children would stop playing, to listen for a moment. They would look into each other's eyes, to see if they had all heard. And each one saw in the eyes of the other two that they too had heard. "There *must* be more money! There *must* be more money!"

It came whispering from the springs of

ABOUT THE AUTHOR

- D(avid) H(erbert) Lawrence (1885–1930) was a frail and sickly child who grew up in poverty and was deeply attached to his mother. He became strongly influenced by the idea of the subconscious developed by such writers as Friedrich Nietzsche (*Beyond Good and Evil,* 1886) and Sigmund Freud (*The Interpretation of Dreams,* 1899). His works are strikingly realistic yet infused with symbolic meanings.
- A biography of Lawrence appears on page 857.
- Lawrence's poem "Snake" appears on page 857.

LITERARY TECHNIQUES

Characterization. Read the entry on *characterization* in the Handbook of Literary Terms. In the first paragraph, what method of characterization does the author use? Ask students to find other instances in the story of these methods of characterization.
Answer. The narrator comments directly on the characters and depicts their internal states.

Setting and Mood. What elements of the story help to establish the setting? What elements of the story help to establish the mood?
Answers. The setting is an upper-class or upper-middle-class ("They lived in a pleasant house, with a garden, and they had discreet servants") suburban neighborhood ("The father went into town"). An ominous mood is created by details describing the relationships and emotional states of the characters ("They looked at her wildly"; "finding fault"; "felt the center of her heart go hard"; "they . . . felt themselves superior") and by details describing the conflict ("they felt always an anxiety. . . . There was never enough money").

ADDITIONAL QUESTIONS AND ACTIVITIES

• Ask students what enables people to get money. How much is due to luck? What other factors are important? Why do people in this family think that they do not have enough money? How much is enough?

• Ask students what it means to be a good money manager. Why do some people never seem to have enough money, while others with the same amount of money are able to live comfortably? Ask students whether they are able to manage their money well. Some students may have suggestions to offer others for managing their money. Ask students what plans they have for their futures. How much do they think they need to earn in order to live comfortably?

• Ask students whether the mother in the story takes responsibility for her actions. Ask whether the father takes responsibility. In general, is it right to hold people responsible for what happens to them? When would it be right to hold someone responsible for what happens to him or her? When would it be wrong?

PROTAGONIST

The main character, or protagonist, of this story is the boy Paul. ▸

INCITING INCIDENT

The boy's conversation with his mother introduces the central conflict, or struggle, in the story. ▸

---

the still-swaying rocking-horse, and even the horse, bending his wooden, champing head, heard it. The big doll, sitting so pink and smirking in her new pram, could hear it quite plainly, and seemed to be smirking all the more self-consciously because of it. The foolish puppy, too, that took the place of the teddybear, he was looking so extraordinarily foolish for no other reason but that he heard the secret whisper all over the house: "There *must* be more money!"

Yet nobody ever said it aloud. The whisper was everywhere, and therefore no one spoke it. Just as no one ever says: "We are breathing!" in spite of the fact that breath is coming and going all the time.

"Mother," said the boy Paul one day, "why don't we keep a car of our own? Why do we always use uncle's, or else a taxi?"

"Because we're the poor members of the family," said the mother.

"But why *are* we, mother?"

"Well—I suppose," she said slowly and bitterly, "it's because your father has no luck."

The boy was silent for some time.

"Is luck money, mother?" he asked, rather timidly.

"No, Paul. Not quite. It's what causes you to have money."

"Oh!" said Paul vaguely. "I thought when Uncle Oscar said *filthy lucker*, it meant money."

"*Filthy lucre* does mean money," said the mother. "But it's lucre, not luck."

"Oh!" said the boy. "Then what *is* luck, mother?"

"It's what causes you to have money. If you're lucky you have money. That's why it's better to be born lucky than rich. If you're rich, you may lose your money. But if you're lucky, you will always get more money."

"Oh! Will you? And is father not lucky?"

"Very unlucky, I should say," she said bitterly.

The boy watched her with unsure eyes.

"Why?" he asked.

"I don't know. Nobody ever knows why one person is lucky and another unlucky."

"Don't they? Nobody at all? Does *nobody* know?"

"Perhaps God. But He never tells."

"He ought to, then. And aren't you lucky either, mother?"

"I can't be, if I married an unlucky husband."

"But by yourself, aren't you?"

"I used to think I was, before I married. Now I think I am very unlucky indeed."

"Why?"

"Well—never mind! Perhaps I'm not really," she said.

The child looked at her to see if she meant it. But he saw, by the lines of her mouth, that she was only trying to hide something from him.

"Well, anyhow," he said stoutly, "I'm a lucky person."

"Why?" said his mother, with a sudden laugh.

He stared at her. He didn't even know why he had said it.

"God told me," he asserted, brazening it out.[1]

"I hope He did, dear!" she said, again with a laugh, but rather bitter.

"He did, mother!"

"Excellent!" said the mother, using one of her husband's exclamations.

The boy saw she did not believe him; or rather, that she paid no attention to his assertion. This angered him somewhere, and made him want to compel her attention.

He went off by himself, vaguely, in a

---

1. **brazening it out.** Acting boldly, without shame

childish way, seeking for the clue to "luck." Absorbed, taking no heed of other people, he went about with a sort of stealth, seeking inwardly for luck. He wanted luck, he wanted it, he wanted it. When the two girls were playing dolls in the nursery, he would sit on his big rocking-horse, charging madly into space, with a frenzy that made the little girls peer at him uneasily. Wildly the horse <u>careered</u>, the waving dark hair of the boy tossed, his eyes had a strange glare in them. The little girls dared not speak to him.

When he had ridden to the end of his mad little journey, he climbed down and stood in front of his rocking-horse, staring fixedly into its lowered face. Its red mouth was slightly open, its big eye was wide and glassy-bright.

"Now!" he would silently command the snorting steed. "Now, take me to where there is luck! Now take me!"

And he would slash the horse on the neck with the little whip he had asked Uncle Oscar for. He *knew* the horse could take him to where there was luck, if only he forced it. So he would mount again and start on his furious ride, hoping at last to get there. He knew he could get there.

"You'll break your horse, Paul!" said the nurse.

"He's always riding like that! I wish he'd leave off!" said his elder sister Joan.

But he only glared down on them in silence. Nurse gave him up. She could make nothing of him. Anyhow, he was growing beyond her.

One day his mother and his Uncle Oscar came in when he was on one of his furious rides. He did not speak to them.

"Hallo, you young jockey! Riding a winner?" said his uncle.

"Aren't you growing too big for a rocking-horse? You're not a very little boy any longer, you know," said his mother.

But Paul only gave a blue glare from his big, rather close set eyes. He would speak to nobody when he was in full tilt. His mother watched him with an anxious expression on her face.

At last he suddenly stopped forcing his horse into the mechanical gallop and slid down.

"Well, I got there!" he announced fiercely, his blue eyes still flaring, and his sturdy long legs straddling apart.

"Where did you get to?" asked his mother.

"Where I wanted to go," he flared back at her.

"That's right, son!" said Uncle Oscar. "Don't you stop till you get there. What's the horse's name?"

"He doesn't have a name," said the boy.

"Gets on without, all right?" asked the uncle.

"Well, he has different names. He was called Sansovino last week."

"Sansovino, eh? Won the Ascot.[2] How did you know this name?"

"He always talks about horse-races with Bassett," said Joan.

The uncle was delighted to find that his small nephew was posted with all the racing news. Bassett, the young gardener who had been wounded in the left foot in the war and had got his present job

---

2. **Ascot.** A prestigious horse race

WORDS FOR EVERYDAY USE: ca • reer (kə rir´) vi., move at full speed

The mother says, "If you're lucky you have money." Do students agree? What other things does luck bring? Pose the following question: If you could be lucky in only one aspect of your life, what would it be? Why?

VOCABULARY IN CONTEXT

• The sled <u>careered</u> down the ice-covered hill, but the three sisters dove off before hitting the trees.

HISTORICAL NOTE

The Society for the Prevention of Cruelty to Animals and other animal protection organizations have investigated training practices at racetracks and at stables. Students may want to contact a nearby racetrack; a state regulatory agency; the Thoroughbred Racing Association (420 Fair Hill Dr., Elkton, MD 21921); or the Jockey Club (380 Madison Ave., New York, NY 10017) for information on the treatment of racehorses.

CROSS-CURRICULAR ACTIVITIES

Mathematics and Science. "The Rocking-Horse Winner" deals with a family that is having financial difficulties. One way to avoid financial difficulties is to make regular budgets and live within them. Have students prepare monthly budgets for a hypothetical family of four, tracking income and expenditures for housing, food, clothing, transportation, child care, insurance, utilities, and entertainment.

Carousel Horse with Lowered Head. Charles Carmel, 1914. Collection of the Museum of American Folk Art, NY

through Oscar Cresswell, whose batman[3] he had been, was a perfect blade of the "turf."[4] He lived in the racing events, and the small boy lived with him.

Oscar Cresswell got it all from Bassett.

"Master Paul comes and asks me, so I can't do more than tell him, sir," said Bassett, his face terribly serious, as if he were speaking of religious matters.

"And does he ever put anything on a horse he fancies?"

"Well—I don't want to give him away—he's a young sport, a fine sport, sir. Would you mind asking him himself? He sort of takes a pleasure in it, and perhaps he'd feel I was giving him away, sir, if you don't mind."

Bassett was serious as a church.

The uncle went back to his nephew and took him off for a ride in the car.

"Say, Paul, old man, do you ever put anything on a horse?" the uncle asked.

The boy watched the handsome man closely.

"Why, do you think I oughtn't to?" he parried.

"Not a bit of it! I thought perhaps you might give me a tip for the Lincoln."

The car sped on into the country, going down to Uncle Oscar's place in Hampshire.

"Honor bright?" said the nephew.

"Honor bright, son!" said the uncle.

"Well, then, Daffodil."

"Daffodil! I doubt it, sonny. What about Mirza?"

"I only know the winner," said the boy. "That's Daffodil."

"Daffodil, eh?"

There was a pause. Daffodil was an obscure horse comparatively.

---

3. **batman.** Orderly for a military officer
4. **turf.** The sport of horse racing

WORDS FOR EVERYDAY USE: **par • ry** (par´ē) *vt.,* reply in a clever or evasive way

VOCABULARY IN CONTEXT

• When Rona interviewed for a job as a legal assistant, she tried to <u>parry</u> questions about relevant experience, since she had none.

"Uncle!"

"Yes, son?"

"You won't let it go any further, will you? I promised Bassett."

"Bassett be damned, old man! What's he got to do with it?"

"We're partners. We've been partners from the first. Uncle, he lent me my first five shillings, which I lost. I promised him, honor bright, it was only between me and him; only you gave me that ten-shilling note I started winning with, so I thought you were lucky. You won't let it go any further, will you?"

The boy gazed at his uncle from those big, hot, blue eyes, set rather close together. The uncle stirred and laughed uneasily.

"Right you are, son! I'll keep your tip private. Daffodil, eh? How much are you putting on him?"

"All except twenty pounds," said the boy. "I keep that in reserve."

The uncle thought it a good joke.

"You keep twenty pounds in reserve, do you, you young romancer? What are you betting, then?"

"I'm betting three hundred," said the boy gravely. "But it's between you and me, Uncle Oscar! Honor bright?"

The uncle burst into a roar of laughter. "It's between you and me all right, you young Nat Gould,"[5] he said, laughing. "But where's your three hundred?"

"Bassett keeps it for me. We're partners."

"You are, are you! And what is Bassett putting on Daffodil?"

"He won't go quite as high as I do, I expect. Perhaps he'll go a hundred and fifty."

"What, pennies?" laughed the uncle.

"Pounds," said the child, with a surprised look at his uncle. "Bassett keeps a bigger reserve than I do."

Between wonder and amusement Uncle Oscar was silent. He pursued the matter no further, but he determined to take his nephew with him to the Lincoln races.

"Now, son," he said, "I'm putting twenty on Mirza, and I'll put five on for you on any horse you fancy. What's your pick?"

"Daffodil, uncle."

"No, not the fiver on Daffodil!"

"I should if it was my own fiver," said the child.

"Good! Good! Right you are! A fiver for me and a fiver for you on Daffodil."

The child had never been to a race-meeting before, and his eyes were blue fire. He pursed his mouth tight and watched. A Frenchman just in front had put his money on Lancelot. Wild with excitement, he flayed his arms up and down, yelling *Lancelot! Lancelot!*" in his French accent.

Daffodil came in first, Lancelot second, Mirza third. The child, flushed and with eyes blazing, was curiously serene. His uncle brought him four five-pound notes, four to one.

"What am I to do with these?" he cried, waving them before the boy's eyes.

"I suppose we'll talk to Bassett," said the boy. "I expect I have fifteen hundred now; and twenty in reserve; and this twenty."

His uncle studied him for some moments.

"Look here, son!" he said. "You're not serious about Bassett and that fifteen hundred, are you?"

"Yes, I am. But it's between you and me, uncle. Honor bright?"

"Honor bright all right, son! But I must talk to Bassett."

"If you'd like to be a partner, uncle, with Bassett and me, we could all be partners. Only, you'd have to promise, honor bright, uncle, not to let it go beyond us

---

5. **Nat Gould.** An authority on horse racing

three. Bassett and I are lucky, and you must be lucky, because it was your ten shillings I started winning with. . . ."

Uncle Oscar took both Bassett and Paul into Richmond Park for an afternoon, and there they talked.

"It's like this, you see, sir," Bassett said. "Master Paul would get me talking about racing events, spinning yarns, you know, sir. And he was always keen on knowing if I'd made or if I'd lost. It's about a year since, now, that I put five shillings on Blush of Dawn for him: and we lost. Then the luck turned, with that ten shillings he had from you: that we put on Singhalese. And since that time, it's been pretty steady all things considering. What do you say, Master Paul?"

"We're all right when we're sure," said Paul. "It's when we're not quite sure that we go down."

"Oh, but we're careful then," said Bassett.

"But when are you *sure?*" smiled Uncle Oscar.

"It's Master Paul, sir," said Bassett in a secret, religious voice. "It's as if he had it from heaven. Like Daffodil, now, for the Lincoln. That was as sure as eggs."

"Did you put anything on Daffodil?" asked Oscar Cresswell.

"Yes, sir. I made my bit."

"And my nephew?"

Bassett was obstinately silent, looking at Paul.

"I made twelve hundred, didn't I, Bassett? I told uncle I was putting three hundred on Daffodil."

"That's right," said Bassett, nodding.

"But where's the money?" asked the uncle.

"I keep it safe locked up, sir. Master Paul he can have it any minute he likes to ask for it."

"What, fifteen hundred pounds?"

"And twenty! And *forty*, that is, with the twenty he made on the course."

"It's amazing!" said the uncle.

"If Master Paul offers you to be partners, sir, I would, if I were you: if you'll excuse me," said Bassett.

Oscar Cresswell thought about it.

"I'll see the money," he said.

They drove home again, and, sure enough, Bassett came round to the garden-house with fifteen hundred pounds in notes. The twenty pounds reserve was left with Joe Glee, in the Turf Commission deposit.

"You see, it's all right, uncle, when I'm *sure!* Then we go strong, for all we're worth. Don't we, Bassett?"

"We do that, Master Paul."

"And when are you sure?" said the uncle, laughing.

"Oh, well, sometimes I'm *absolutely* sure, like about Daffodil," said the boy; "and sometimes I have an idea; and sometimes I haven't even an idea, have I, Bassett? Then we're careful, because we mostly go down."

"You do, do you! And when you're sure, like about Daffodil, what makes you sure, sonny?"

"Oh, well, I don't know," said the boy uneasily. "I'm sure, you know, uncle; that's all."

"It's as if he had it from heaven, sir," Bassett reiterated.

"I should say so!" said the uncle.

But he became a partner. And when the Leger was coming on Paul was "sure" about Lively Spark, which was a quite inconsiderable horse. The boy insisted on putting a thousand on the horse, Bassett went for five hundred, and Oscar Cresswell two hundred. Lively Spark came in first, and the betting had been ten to one against him. Paul had made ten thousand.

"You see," he said, "I was absolutely sure of him."

Even Oscar Cresswell had cleared two thousand.

"Look here, son," he said, "this sort of thing makes me nervous."

"It needn't, uncle! Perhaps I shan't be sure again for a long time."

"But what are you going to do with your money?" asked the uncle.

"Of course," said the boy, "I started it for mother. She said she had no luck, because father is unlucky, so I thought if *I* was lucky, it might stop whispering."

"What might stop whispering?"

"Our house. I *hate* our house for whispering."

"What does it whisper?"

"Why—why"—the boy fidgeted—"why, I don't know. But it's always short of money, you know, uncle."

"I know it, son, I know it."

"You know people send mother writs,[6] don't you, uncle?"

"I'm afraid I do," said the uncle.

"And then the house whispers, like people laughing at you behind your back. It's awful, that is! I thought if I was lucky—"

"You might stop it," added the uncle.

The boy watched him with big blue eyes, that had an uncanny cold fire in them, and he said never a word.

"Well, then!" said the uncle. "What are we doing?"

"I shouldn't like mother to know I was lucky," said the boy.

"Why not, son?"

"She'd stop me."

"I don't think she would."

"Oh!"—and the boy writhed in an odd way— "I *don't* want her to know, uncle."

"All right, son! We'll manage it without her knowing."

They managed it very easily. Paul, at the other's suggestion, handed over five thou-sand pounds to his uncle, who deposited it with the family lawyer, who was then to inform Paul's mother that a relative had put five thousand pounds into his hands, which sum was to be paid out a thousand pounds at a time, on the mother's birth-day, for the next five years.

"So she'll have a birthday present of a thousand pounds for five successive years," said Uncle Oscar. "I hope it won't make it all the harder for her later."

Paul's mother had her birthday in November. The house had been "whisper-ing" worse than ever lately, and, even in spite of his luck, Paul could not bear up against it. He was very anxious to see the effect of the birthday letter, telling his mother about the thousand pounds.

When there were no visitors, Paul now took his meals with his parents, as he was beyond the nursery control. His mother went into town nearly every day. She had discovered that she had an odd knack of sketching furs and dress materials, so she worked secretly in the studio of a friend who was the chief "artist" for the leading drapers. She drew the figures of ladies in furs and ladies in silk and sequins for the newspaper advertisements. This young woman artist earned several thousand pounds a year, but Paul's mother only made several hundreds, and she was again dissatisfied. She so wanted to be first in something, and she did not suc-ceed, even in making sketches for drapery advertisements.

She was down to breakfast on the morn-ing of her birthday. Paul watched her face as she read her letters. He knew the lawyer's letter. As his mother read it, her face hardened and became more expres-sionless. Then a cold, determined look came on her mouth. She hid the letter

_____
6. **writs.** Legal notices

LITERARY TECHNIQUE

Characterization. Writers use three major techniques to create characters: direct description, portrayals of behavior, and representations of internal states. Portrayals of behavior can be of the characters' own behavior or of other characters' behavior toward them. Ask students the following questions: 1. Which technique(s) does the author use to create Paul's character? 2. What does the reader learn about Paul on this page? 3. What technique(s) does the author use to create the mother's character? 4. What does the reader learn about the mother on this page?
Answers. 1. Paul's character is created by portrayal of behavior (dialogue and description). 2. The reader learns that Paul is aware of the pressure to have more money and is disturbed by it, that he wants to please his mother, that he feels he needs to keep secrets from her, and that he is anxious about how she feels about him. 3. The mother's character is created by portrayal of behavior and by representation of internal states. 4. The reader learns that she is difficult to satisfy, that she is prideful, and that she has both practical and emotional difficulties with money.

under the pile of others, and said not a word about it.

"Didn't you have anything nice in the post for your birthday, mother?" said Paul.

"Quite moderately nice," she said, her voice cold and absent.

She went away to town without saying more.

But in the afternoon Uncle Oscar appeared. He said Paul's mother had had a long interview with the lawyer, asking if the whole five thousand could not be advanced at once, as she was in debt.

"What do you think, uncle?" said the boy.

"I leave it to you, son."

"Oh, let her have it, then! We can get some more with the other," said the boy.

"A bird in the hand is worth two in the bush, laddie!" said Uncle Oscar.

"But I'm sure to *know* for the Grand National; or the Lincolnshire; or else the Derby. I'm sure to know for *one* of them," said Paul.

So Uncle Oscar signed the agreement, and Paul's mother touched the whole five thousand. Then something very curious happened. The voices in the house suddenly went mad, like a chorus of frogs on a spring evening. There were certain new furnishings, and Paul had a tutor. He was *really* going to Eton, his father's school, in the following autumn. There were flowers in the winter, and a blossoming of the luxury Paul's mother had been used to. And yet the voices in the house, behind the sprays of mimosa and almond blossom, and from under the piles of iridescent cushions, simply trilled and screamed in a sort of ecstasy: "There *must* be more money! Oh-h-h; there *must* be more money. Oh, now, now-w! Now-w-w—there *must* be more money!—more than ever! More than ever!"

It frightened Paul terribly. He studied

away at his Latin and Greek with his tutor. But his intense hours were spent with Bassett. The Grand National had gone by: he had not "known," and had lost a hundred pounds. Summer was at hand. He was in agony for the Lincoln. But even for the Lincoln he didn't "know," and he lost fifty pounds. He became wild-eyed and strange, as if something were going to explode in him.

"Let it alone, son! Don't you bother about it!" urged Uncle Oscar. But it was as if the boy couldn't really hear what his uncle was saying.

"I've got to know for the Derby! I've got to know for the Derby!" the child reiterated, his big blue eyes blazing with a sort of madness.

His mother noticed how overwrought he was.

"You'd better go to the seaside. Wouldn't you like to go now to the seaside, instead of waiting? I think you'd better," she said, looking down at him anxiously, her heart curiously heavy because of him.

But the child lifted his uncanny blue eyes.

"I couldn't possibly go before the Derby, mother!" he said. "I couldn't possibly!"

"Why not?" she said, her voice becoming heavy when she was opposed. "Why not? You can still go from the seaside to see the Derby with your Uncle Oscar, if that's what you wish. No need for you to wait here. Besides, I think you care too much about these races. It's a bad sign. My family has been a gambling family, and you won't know till you grow up how much damage it has done. But it has done damage. I shall have to send Bassett away, and ask Uncle Oscar not to talk racing to you, unless you promise to be reasonable about it: go away to the seaside and forget it. You're all nerves!"

"I'll do what you like, mother, so long as you don't send me away till after the Derby," the boy said.

"Send you away from where? Just from this house?"

"Yes," he said, gazing at her.

"Why, you curious child, what makes you care about this house so much, suddenly? I never knew you loved it."

He gazed at her without speaking. He had a secret within a secret, something he had not divulged, even to Bassett or to his Uncle Oscar.

But his mother, after standing undecided and a little bit sullen for some moments, said:

"Very well, then! Don't go to the seaside till after the Derby, if you don't wish it. But promise me you won't let your nerves go to pieces. Promise you won't think so much about horse-racing and *events*, as you call them!"

"Oh no," said the boy casually. "I won't think much about them, mother. You needn't worry. I wouldn't worry, mother, if I were you."

"If you were me and I were you," said his mother, "I wonder what we *should* do!"

"But you know you needn't worry, mother, don't you?" the boy repeated.

"I should be awfully glad to know it," she said wearily.

"Oh, well, you *can*, you know. I mean, you *ought* to know you needn't worry," he insisted.

"Ought I? Then I'll see about it," she said. Paul's secret of secrets was his wooden horse, that which had no name. Since he was emancipated from a nurse and a nursery-governess, he had had his rocking-horse removed to his own bedroom at the top of the house.

"Surely you're too big for a rocking-horse!" his mother had <u>remonstrated</u>.

"Well, you see, mother, till I can have a *real* horse, I like to have *some* sort of animal about," had been his quaint answer.

"Do you feel he keeps you company?" she laughed.

"Oh yes! He's very good, he always keeps me company, when I'm there," said Paul.

So the horse, rather shabby, stood in an arrested prance in the boy's bedroom.

The Derby was drawing near, and the boy grew more and more tense. He hardly heard what was spoken to him, he was very frail, and his eyes were really uncanny. His mother had sudden strange seizures of uneasiness about him. Sometimes, for half an hour, she would feel a sudden anxiety about him that was almost anguish. She wanted to rush to him at once, and know he was safe.

Two nights before the Derby, she was at a big party in town, when one of her rushes of anxiety about her boy, her first-born, gripped her heart till she could hardly speak. She fought with the feeling, might and main, for she believed in common sense. But it was too strong. She had to leave the dance and go downstairs to telephone to the country. The children's nursery-governess was terribly surprised and startled at being rung up in the night.

"Are the children all right, Miss Wilmot?"

"Oh yes, they are quite all right."

"Master Paul? Is he all right?"

FORESHADOWING

An event or description that hints at something that will occur later in the story is called foreshadowing.

WORDS FOR EVERYDAY USE: re • mon • strate (ri män´ strāt) *vt.*, say in protest or object

Ask students the following questions: Why does Paul tell his mother not to worry? What kind of relationship does he have with his mother? For instance, is it honest and open? warm? abusive? How does he feel about his mother? How does his mother feel about him? Ask students to reread the first paragraph of the story, on page 31. Are the events described on this page (39) consistent with what is said in that paragraph?

VOCABULARY IN CONTEXT

• He <u>remonstrated</u> that the shoes were uncomfortable, but his mother would hear none of it.

CLIMAX

The climax presents the high point of interest or suspense in the story. ▶

"He went to bed as right as a trivet. Shall I run up and look at him?"

"No," said Paul's mother reluctantly. "No! Don't trouble. It's all right. Don't sit up. We shall be home fairly soon." She did not want her son's privacy intruded upon.

"Very good," said the governess.

It was about one o'clock when Paul's mother and father drove up to their house. All was still. Paul's mother went to her room and slipped off her white fur cloak. She had told her maid not to wait up for her. She heard her husband downstairs, mixing a whisky and soda.

And then, because of the strange anxiety at her heart, she stole upstairs to her son's room. Noiselessly she went along the upper corridor. Was there a faint noise? What was it?

She stood, with arrested muscles, outside his door, listening. There was a strange, heavy, and yet not loud noise. Her heart stood still. It was a soundless noise, yet rushing and powerful. Something huge, in violent, hushed motion. What was it? What in God's name was it? She ought to know. She felt that she knew the noise. She knew what it was.

Yet she could not place it. She couldn't say what it was. And on and on it went, like a madness.

Softly, frozen with anxiety and fear, she turned the door handle.

The room was dark. Yet in the space near the window, she heard and saw something plunging to and fro. She gazed in fear and amazement.

Then suddenly she switched on the light, and saw her son, in his green pajamas, madly surging on the rocking-horse. The blaze of light suddenly lit him up, as he urged the wooden horse, and lit her up, as she stood, blonde, in her dress of pale green and crystal, in the doorway.

"Paul!" she cried. "Whatever are you doing?"

"It's Malabar!" he screamed in a powerful, strange voice. "It's Malabar!"

His eyes blazed at her for one strange and senseless second, as he ceased urging his wooden horse. Then he fell with a crash to the ground, and she, all her tormented motherhood flooding upon her, rushed to gather him up.

But he was unconscious, and unconscious he remained, with some brain-fever. He talked and tossed, and his mother sat stonily by his side.

"Malabar! It's Malabar! Bassett, Bassett, I *know*! It's Malabar!"

So the child cried, trying to get up and urge the rocking-horse that gave him his inspiration.

"What does he mean by Malabar?" asked the heart-frozen mother.

"I don't know," said the father stonily.

"What does he mean by Malabar?" she asked her brother Oscar.

"It's one of the horses running for the Derby," was the answer.

And, in spite of himself, Oscar Cresswell spoke to Bassett, and himself put a thousand on Malabar: at fourteen to one.

The third day of the illness was critical: they were waiting for a change. The boy, with his rather long, curly hair, was tossing ceaselessly on the pillow. He neither slept nor regained consciousness, and his eyes were like blue stones. His mother sat, feeling her heart had gone, turned actually into a stone.

In the evening, Oscar Cresswell did not come, but Bassett sent a message, saying could he come up for one moment, just one moment? Paul's mother was very angry at the intrusion, but on second thoughts she agreed. The boy was the same. Perhaps Bassett might bring him to consciousness.

The gardener, a shortish fellow with a little brown moustache and sharp little brown eyes, tiptoed into the room, touched his imaginary cap to Paul's mother, and stole to the bedside, staring with glittering, smallish eyes at the tossing, dying child.

"Master Paul!" he whispered. "Master Paul! Malabar came in first all right, a clean win. I did as you told me. You've made over seventy thousand pounds, you have; you've got over eighty thousand. Malabar came in all right, Master Paul."

"Malabar! Malabar! Did I say Malabar, mother? Did I say Malabar? Do you think I'm lucky, mother? I knew Malabar, didn't I? Over eighty thousand pounds! I call that lucky, don't you, mother? Over eighty thousand pounds! I knew, didn't I know I knew? Malabar came in all right. If I ride my horse till I'm sure, then I tell you, Bassett, you can go as high as you like. Did you go for all you were worth, Bassett?"

"I went a thousand on it, Master Paul."

"I never told you, mother, that if I can ride my horse, and *get there*, then I'm absolutely sure—oh, absolutely! Mother, did I ever tell you? I *am* lucky!"

"No, you never did," said his mother.

But the boy died in the night.

And even as he lay dead, his mother heard her brother's voice saying to her: "My God, Hester, you're eighty-odd thousand to the good, and a poor devil of a son to the bad. But, poor devil, he's best gone out of a life where he rides his rocking-horse to find a winner." ∎

▲

R E S O L U T I O N

At this point in the story, the central conflict is ended, or resolved.

◄ D É N O U E M E N T

The dénouement presents material left unresolved by the ending of the central conflict. It may also present a commentary on or analysis of the events of the story.

FICTION / "THE ROCKING-HORSE WINNER" **41**

LITERARY TECHNIQUE

Irony. Irony is a contradiction between appearance and reality. Dramatic irony occurs when something is known by the reader or audience but unknown to one or more characters. Paul's last statement is an example of dramatic irony, for the reader knows, when Paul says "I am lucky," that he is extremely unlucky, that he is, in fact, gravely ill as a result of his unlucky situation. This irony is underscored by the fact that Paul dies after making the statement. See the entry on *irony* in the Handbook of Literary Terms.

ANSWERS TO SELECTION CHECK TEST 4.1.5

EX. To whom does the rocking-horse belong?
The rocking-horse belongs to Paul.

1. About what does the house continually whisper?
The house is continually whispering about the need for more money.

2. How does Paul make money?
He places bets on horse races.

3. Who receives the five thousand pounds?
Paul's mother receives the five thousand pounds.

4. What is Paul doing when his mother finds him in the attic?
Paul is frantically riding his rocking-horse.

5. What happens to Paul at the end of the story?
Paul dies at the end of the story.

ADDITIONAL QUESTIONS AND ACTIVITIES

• Ask students if they know the mother's name. Ask them when the name is first mentioned. Ask what event immediately precedes the first (and only) mention of the mother's name. Ask what point the author may have been making by introducing the mother's name at the end of the story rather than earlier.

(cont.)

ADDITIONAL QUESTIONS AND ACTIVITIES (CONT.)

Answers. The mother's name, Hester, is not mentioned until the final paragraph. Its mention is immediately preceded by Paul's death. The author may have been trying to underscore the point that the mother felt burdened by her children and family to such an extent that they obscured her identity.

• Students may be curious as to why the loving child is seen as the problem when the father would appear to be irrelevant. Part of the answer may lie in Lawrence's personal history. As a child, Lawrence was himself very close to his mother and distant from his father. As Lawrence grew older, his feelings changed. He began to see his mother as domineering and blamed his father's distance on her coldness.

TEACHER'S EDITION **41**

RESPONDING TO THE SELECTION

Lawrence's story presents several clear morals: people shouldn't become obsessed with money; money doesn't buy happiness; and children need unconditional love and support and should not be put in the position of taking on adult burdens. Ask students to consider the conclusion and what moral they might draw from it about how children should be treated.

ANSWERS FOR REVIEWING THE SELECTION

RECALLING

1. The house is haunted by the phrase, "There must be more money!"

2. The mother says that luck is what causes people to have money. She thinks that it is better to be lucky than rich because rich people can lose their money, but lucky people can always get more money. Paul says that God told him that he is a lucky person.

3. Paul learns the winning horses by riding his rocking-horse. To gain this knowledge, he must become obsessed with horse-betting.

4. When the mother learns that she is to receive an annual sum, she asks for the whole amount immediately and spends it all.

INTERPRETING

Responses will vary. Possible responses are given.

5. The family may have too little money because the parents are not accomplished at anything (page 31: "[The mother] racked her brains . . . but could not find anything successful. . . . The father . . . seemed as if he never *would* be able to do anything worth doing"); or because they gamble (page 38: "My family has been a gambling family, and you won't know till you grow up how much damage it has done"); or because they are overly concerned with keeping up appearances (page 31: "The father . . . was always very handsome and expensive in his tastes . . . . and her tastes were just as expensive").

6. Paul is lucky because he can "go to a place" where he can learn the names of winners but unlucky because he becomes obsessed with money. His parents are lucky, without knowing it, that they have a son who loves them.

(cont.)

Responding to the Selection

At the end of the selection, Uncle Oscar says, "But, poor devil, he's best gone out of a life where he rides his rocking-horse to find a winner." Why do you think Lawrence ended his story with this line? What did the boy deserve out of life? What did he get? What makes his story tragic? Discuss these questions with your classmates.

Reviewing the Selection

RECALLING

1. What "unspoken phrase" does the house come "to be haunted by"?

2. What does Paul's mother tell him about being lucky? Why does she think it is better to be born lucky than rich? What does Paul say that God told him?

3. How does Paul come to know that a horse will win a particular race? What does he have to do to gain this knowledge?

4. What happens as a result of Paul's winning the ten thousand and arranging to have half of it sent to his mother?

INTERPRETING

5. Why do the mother and father in this story have too little money? What hints are provided in the story to explain their continual need for money?

6. What does Paul know about himself and luck? In what sense is Paul lucky? In what sense is he extremely unlucky? In what sense are Paul's mother and father lucky without knowing it?

7. What is the cost, to Paul, of getting to where the luck is? What toll does getting to where the luck is exact from him?

8. Receiving the five thousand pounds does not solve Paul's mother's problem. What point is Lawrence making here? What is the real problem in the household?

SYNTHESIZING

9. What answer does the mother give at the end of the story when Paul says, "Mother, did I ever tell you? I am lucky"? Is her answer correct? What does the answer reveal about her?

10. How do you feel about the treatment that Paul receives from the adults around him? Why?

ANSWERS FOR REVIEWING THE SELECTION (CONT.)

7. To get to where the luck is, Paul must ride himself into a frenzied trance. Doing so eventually kills him.

8. The real problem may be that the parents have expensive tastes or that one or both of them have a gambling problem or that they are incapable of ever being happy with what they have.

SYNTHESIZING

Responses will vary. Possible responses are given.

9. The mother says that her son never told her he was lucky, but he did in fact tell her (page 32). This reinforces the idea, stated in the first paragraph of the story, that the mother does not love her children.

10. Students may be disturbed that the mother ignores the boy for the sake of his privacy (page 40); they may also find it disturbing that Bassett and Uncle Oscar encourage and take advantage of the boy's gambling sickness rather than helping him.

Understanding Literature (Questions for Discussion)

1. **Conflict.** A **conflict** is a struggle between two forces in a literary work. What does Paul struggle to do in this story?

2. **Plot.** A **plot** is a series of events related to a central conflict, or struggle. On a sheet of paper or on the chalkboard, diagram the plot of "The Rocking-Horse Winner." Refer to the information on plot diagrams on page 30. Note the inciting incident, climax, and resolution. Also list important events from the exposition, rising action, falling action, and dénouement.

3. **Setting.** The **setting** of a literary work is the time and place in which it occurs, together with all the details used to create a sense of a particular time and place. How is the house in this story described? What is unique about it? In what way is the house **personified**, or given human characteristics? What effect does that personification have on the mood, or emotion, created by the story?

4. **Magical Realism.** **Magical Realism** is a kind of fiction that is for the most part realistic, but that contains elements of fantasy. In Magical Realist tales, the fantastic elements themselves are treated as though they were relatively normal or ordinary. The term *Magical Realism* is most often used to describe works by certain Latin American authors of the twentieth century. However, it applies quite well to Lawrence's story. Explain why this is so.

5. **Theme and Motivation.** A **theme** is a main idea in a literary work. A **motivation** is a force that moves a character to behave in certain ways. What motivates Paul in this story? What motivates the adults in the story? How do their motivations differ? What is Lawrence saying in the story about these motivations?

The Process of Writing: Evaluating and Revising

Read the Language Arts Survey, 1.43–1.46, on evaluating and revising. Then do a self-evaluation of the draft that you wrote for the writing assignment on page 25. Pass a copy of your draft to a classmate and ask him or her to do a peer evaluation, or hold a conference with your teacher to discuss your draft. Then revise your draft based on these evaluations.

Responses will vary. Possible responses are given.

1. Conflict. Paul struggles to be lucky, to get lots of money, to make the secret whisper stop, and to make his mother happy.

2. Plot
Exposition: Pages 31–32 relate facts about the family's money problems, their lack of communication, and the secret whispering.
Inciting incident: Paul questions his mother about their money problems and luck (page 32).
Rising action: Paul attempts to find luck; Uncle Oscar discovers that Paul has been wagering on horse races; they conspire; using Paul's winnings, they arrange for money to be paid to Paul's mother.
Climax: Paul discovers the name of the Derby winner and screams, "It's Malabar! It's Malabar!"
Crisis: Paul collapses off the horse.
Falling action: Paul's mother asks what he means; Oscar bets on Malabar; Paul's illness progresses.
Resolution: Bassett reports that Paul has won over seventy thousand pounds sterling.
Dénouement: Paul proudly tells his mother that he is lucky, and she does not recall their earlier conversation; Paul dies; Oscar says that Paul is better off.

3. Setting. The house is "pleasant," with a garden (page 31), but it is haunted by a voice that whispers, "There must be more money!" The whispering adds to the feeling of intense desperation.

4. Magical Realism. Elements of Magical Realism in the story include the disembodied voice that whispers throughout the house; Paul's ability to pick winning horses by going into a trance on his rocking-horse; and Paul's mystical death.

5. Theme and Motivation. Paul wants to make his mother happy, to have money, and to stop the whispering. Paul's mother is motivated largely by pride. Oscar wants to avoid conflict. Bassett wants money. Oscar and Bassett seem to have some sympathy for Paul but little interest in building his character. In short, Paul is motivated by love; the adults, by selfishness.

▶ See the Writing Evaluation Form: Process, *Assessment Portfolio,* 7.1.
▶ For detailed evaluation, see the checklist and evaluation forms for revisions, *Assessment Portfolio,* 7.7–7.8.
• Rather than scoring or critiquing these revisions, discuss with students individually or in small groups what you and others find interesting about their plots,

descriptions, and characters. Allow the author to explain what improvements he or she was trying to make. Comment on the writer's successes in making these improvements. Encourage students to continue to revise their drafts. This may be a good time to encourage students to view their writing as a means of self-expression and a source of enjoyment.

▶ Additional practice in revising is provided in the *Essential Skills Practice Book: Writing,* 1.43–1.49.

ENRICHMENT ACTIVITIES

• Have students prepare blocking diagrams for the play.

• Students interested in another treatment in drama of the Irish nationalist movement might read W. B. Yeats's *Cathleen Ni Houlihan*. In Yeats's play, a beautiful woman, symbolizing, perhaps, the attractiveness of patriotism and glory, goes from door to door luring young men to join the rebellion. However, the woman turns out to be a hag, symbolizing, perhaps, the actual consequences of going to war.

SUPPORT FOR LEP STUDENTS

• This play is written in a dialect of Irish English. Point out to students nonstandard expressions and explain that these expressions do not exemplify standard English. One recurring regionalism in the story is the use of *It's* to begin a sentence—e.g., "It's he makes" (He makes); "It's little chance we'd have" (We'd have little chance). Explain that students should ignore this word if they have trouble understanding a sentence.

• Encourage students to ask about any words or expressions they do not understand.

• Some students may have extra trouble reading a play because of unfamiliarity with dramatic conventions. Carefully explain stage directions and dialogue to these students. Then have them read or study the play in groups of four, with each person taking the part of one character.

(cont.)

Drama

A **drama** is a performance of a story by actors who take the parts of the characters. The origins of drama are mysterious, though in cultures around the globe, early peoples often enacted scenes as part of rites or celebrations having to do with hunting, warfare, religion, or passage from one stage of life into another.

In the Western world, drama originated in ancient Greece. The earliest Greek dramas may have arisen as ritual enactments of sacrifices made to the gods. In fact, the Greek word *tragoidia,* from which our word *tragedy* derives, meant "song of the goats." According to one theory, people in ancient Greece would come together to sacrifice an animal to win a god's favor. Eventually, that sacrifice developed into an elaborate ritual involving one actor, the priest, and a chorus with whom the priest interacted. In the fifth century BC, the Greek playwright Aeschylus added a second actor, and drama as we know it was born. Drama became another vehicle, like poetry, for telling stories. In classical times, dramas were performed in open-air amphitheaters, or **arena stages.**

Early Greek dramas were of two major kinds: comedy and tragedy. A **comedy,** in its original sense, was any work with a happy ending. The term is widely used today to refer to any humorous work, especially one prepared for the stage or the screen. A **tragedy** initially was a drama that told the story of the fall of a person of high status.

The earliest English drama, that of the Middle Ages, can be divided into three kinds: **mystery plays** presented stories from the Bible; **miracle plays** told stories from the lives of saints; **morality plays** presented stories containing abstract virtues and vices as characters. These plays were commonly performed on wagons, with the audience gathered around.

With the coming of the Renaissance and the rebirth of classical learning, playwrights in England began to create five-act plays based on Roman models. The latter half of the sixteenth century and the beginning of the seventeenth saw the greatest flowering of theatrical invention in English history, the period of **Elizabethan and Jacobean Drama.** William Shakespeare, Christopher Marlowe, and Ben Jonson were among the many talented playwrights of the time. A play of this period typically was produced on a **thrust stage,** which jutted into an area open to the sky.

The highlight of eighteenth-century drama was the so-called **Restoration Comedy,** which dealt satirically with social mores. Early-to-mid-nineteenth-century theater tended toward **melodrama,** which presented exaggerated and sentimental characters and scenes. The late nineteenth century saw the emergence of **Realist Theater,** with its social and political commentary and profound explorations of the depth psychology of characters. In the nineteenth and twentieth centuries, the **proscenium stage,** or **picture stage,** with three walls and a removed "fourth wall," replaced the thrust stage in most Western theater.

Ellen Terry as Lady Macbeth.
John Singer Sargent, 1889.
Tate Gallery, London/Art Resource, NY

ADDITIONAL VOCABULARY (CONT.)
mind—observe; attend to
leave—permission
pensive—thoughtful, brooding
strain—tune, melody
plaintive—sad; complaining
gale—wind
tunic—shirt
pound—British monetary unit

BIOGRAPHICAL NOTE

Plays by **Aeschylus** (525/524–456/455 BC) include the *Oresteia* trilogy: *Agamemnon, The Libation Bearers,* and *The Furies.* Aeschylus won many awards at the annual Athenian drama festival.

GENRE STUDIES
• The comedy *Pygmalion* begins on page 986.
• *The Tragedy of Macbeth* begins on page 320.
• An excerpt from the morality play *Everyman* begins on page 212.

ART NOTE

- **(Alice) Ellen Terry** (1847–1928) was one of the most popular British stage performers of the last quarter of the nineteenth century. She is also noted for a magnificent series of letters to the playwright G. Bernard Shaw (a biography of Shaw appears on page 986). She was trained as an actress by her parents and began performing professionally at the age of nine. She gave notable performances in the major Shakespearean roles. Terry was knighted in 1925. Her former home is now the Ellen Terry Memorial Museum. She is the subject of many biographies, including *Bernhardt, Terry, Duse: The Actress in Her Time* (1988).

- **John Singer Sargent**'s (1856–1925) portraits of noted personalities and of American and European aristocrats serve as a visual record of the Edwardian age. His first Parisian exhibit caused a scandal, so he moved to London, where his work was also poorly regarded, earning him an award for worst painting of the year. Then, in 1887, he achieved his first popular success since his school days. He is today regarded as one of the finest painters of the early Modern Era.

CROSS-CURRICULAR ACTIVITIES

Students can research "creative visualization," a technique for enhancing performance of all kinds whereby a person acts out in imagination an ideal performance.

VOCABULARY FROM THE SELECTION

quay

GOALS/OBJECTIVES

Studying this lesson will enable students to

- interpret and appreciate a drama that is read rather than witnessed on stage or on film
- read a script for understanding

- name and describe the main elements of drama (playwright, script, stage directions, dialogue, stage, set properties, sound effects, and blocking)

LITERARY TECHNIQUE

The stage directions *up* and *down* are used because some stages are "raked." In other words, they actually slope down toward the audience, allowing more of the audience a better view.

CROSS-CURRICULAR ACTIVITIES

Applied Arts. If your school has a stage or if there is a stage nearby, challenge students to determine the absolute slope of the stage, the absolute slope of the floor, and their relative slope (angle of incidence). What other features unique of stage or auditorium design and construction can they notice?

For background, students might refer to the introduction to Unit 5, which describes the development of English theater through the Elizabethan Age.

ADDITIONAL QUESTIONS AND ACTIVITIES

The Parts of a Stage. Take students to an auditorium and familiarize them with the parts of a stage by directing individual students to stand in various places (e.g., downstage right, up left, center) and to make various movements (e.g., cross from down right to up left).

Elements of Drama

THE PLAYWRIGHT AND THE SCRIPT

Playwright. The author of a play is the **playwright**. The relationship between a playwright and the play is more tenuous than that of an ordinary author to his or her text. A novelist or poet has enormous control over the form in which his or her work will be presented to its audience, the reader. A playwright, in contrast, must depend upon the interpretations given his or her work by producers, directors, set designers, actors, and other persons involved in producing the work for the stage. The playwright's art is collaborative.

Script. A **script** is the written work from which a drama is produced. It contains stage directions and dialogue and may be divided into acts and scenes.

Stage Directions. Stage directions are notes provided by the playwright to describe how something should be presented or performed on the stage. Stage directions often describe elements of the **spectacle,** such as lighting, music, sound effects, costumes, properties, and set design. They also may describe entrances and exits, the movements of characters, facial expressions, gestures, body language, tone of voice, or other elements related to the acting of the play. Sometimes, especially in reading versions of plays, stage directions provide historical or background information. Stage directions usually are printed in italics and enclosed in brackets or parentheses. In stage directions, the parts of the stage are often described using the terms *up, down, right, left,* and *center,* which describe stage areas from the point of view of the actors.

Stage Areas

Up Right	Up Center	Up Left
Right Center	Center	Left Center
Down Right	Down Center	Down Left

Dialogue. Dialogue is the term used to describe the speech of actors in a play. The dialogue usually consists of the characters' names and the words and other utterances spoken by the actors. The dialogue of a play may contain **monologues,** or long speeches given by actors. A speech given by a lone character on stage is called a **soliloquy.** A statement intended to be heard by the audience or by a single other character but not by other characters on the stage is called an **aside.**

Acts and Scenes. An **act** is a major division of a drama. Plays of the Elizabethan and Jacobean periods in English drama usually are divided into **five acts.** In the modern era, **three-act** and **one-act plays** are quite common. The acts may be divided into scenes. Typically, a **scene** begins with the entrance of one or more characters and ends with the exit of one or more characters. The time and place of acts or scenes may change from one to the next.

THE SPECTACLE

Spectacle. The **spectacle** is all the elements of the drama presented to the senses of the audience—the lights, sets, curtains, costumes, makeup, music, sound effects, properties, and movements of the actors, including any special movement such as pantomime or dance. Spectacle is one major feature that differentiates dramatic from nondramatic works. The following chart describes common parts of the spectacle.

ELEMENT OF SPECTACLE	DESCRIPTION
Stage	This is the area in which the action is performed. An **arena stage**, or **theater in the round,** is one in which the audience stands or sits around a circular or semicircular open space. A **thrust stage** is one that extends into the audience, which is situated on three sides of the playing area. A **proscenium**, or **picture stage,** is one that has an arch around an opening that acts as a removed "fourth wall."
Set	The set is everything placed upon the stage to give the impression of a particular setting, or time and place. Sets often include walls, furnishings, and painted backdrops.
Properties	Properties are items that can be carried on and off the stage by actors or manipulated by actors during scenes. Examples of properties include swords, torches, and umbrellas.
Sound Effects	These are sounds introduced to create mood or to indicate the presence of something. Common sound effects include rain, ringing telephones, and police sirens.
Blocking	This is the act of determining how actors will move on a stage. Blocking is almost always done by the director of the play.

ADDITIONAL QUESTIONS AND ACTIVITIES

Spectacle. To introduce students to the parts of a **spectacle**, draw a stage diagram on the chalkboard and have students suggest pieces that might be drawn in to represent a set for a play that takes place in a familiar location such as a high school cafeteria or a doctor's office. Then make separate lists on the board of student suggestions for appropriate properties, sound effects, and lighting.

ADDITIONAL QUESTIONS AND ACTIVITIES

• Arrange to show a short movie in class. Have students make notes on the movie's sets, properties, sound effects, stage directions, and costuming.

• For an extra challenge, students might view the beginning of a movie numerous times, take notes on its elements, and then translate their notes into the opening section of a script. Refer students to page 48 for a model showing the form that such an opening might take. Note that movie and theater scripts differ somewhat, but the differences can be ignored for the purposes of this exercise.

The Rising of the Moon

LADY AUGUSTA GREGORY

PERSONS

SERGEANT.

POLICEMAN X.

POLICEMAN B.

A RAGGED MAN.

SCENE

> *Side of a quay in a seaport town. Some posts and chains. A large barrel. Enter three policemen. Moonlight.*
>
> (SERGEANT, *who is older than the others, crosses the stage to right and looks down steps. The others put down a pastepot and unroll a bundle of placards.*)

POLICEMAN B.   I think this would be a good place to put up a notice. (*He points to barrel.*)

POLICEMAN X.   Better ask him. (*calls to* SERGEANT) Will this be a good place for a placard?

(*no answer*)

POLICEMAN B.   Will we put up a notice here on the barrel?

(*no answer*)

SERGEANT.   There's a flight of steps here that leads to the water. This is a place that should be minded well. If he got down here, his friends might have a boat to meet him; they might send it in here from outside.

POLICEMAN B.   Would the barrel be a good place to put a notice up?

SERGEANT.   It might; you can put it there.

(*They paste the notice up.*)

SERGEANT. (*reading it*)   Dark hair—dark eyes, smooth face, height five feet five—there's not much to take hold of in that—It's a pity I had no chance of seeing him before he broke out of gaol.[1] They say he's a wonder, that it's he makes all the plans for the whole organization. There isn't another man in Ireland would have broken gaol the way he did. He must have some friends among the gaolers.

POLICEMAN B.   A hundred pounds is little enough for the Government to offer for him. You may be sure any man in the force that takes him will get promotion.

SERGEANT.   I'll mind this place myself. I wouldn't wonder at all if he came this way. He might come slipping along there (*points to side of quay*), and his friends might be waiting for him there (*points down steps*), and once he got away it's little chance we'd have of finding him; it's maybe under a load of kelp he'd be in a fishing boat, and not one to help a married man that wants it to the reward.

---

1. **gaol.** British spelling of *jail*

WORDS FOR EVERYDAY USE: quay (kē) *n.*, wharf

VOCABULARY IN CONTEXT

• The fishing boat docked at the quay to unload two tons of fish.

POLICEMAN X. And if we get him itself, nothing but abuse on our heads for it from the people, and maybe from our own relations.

SERGEANT. Well, we have to do our duty in the force. Haven't we the whole country depending on us to keep law and order? It's those that are down would be up and those that are up would be down, if it wasn't for us. Well, hurry on, you have plenty of other places to placard yet, and come back here then to me. You can take the lantern. Don't be too long now. It's very lonesome here with nothing but the moon.

POLICEMAN B. It's a pity we can't stop with you. The Government should have brought more police into the town, with *him* in gaol, and at assize[2] time too. Well, good luck to your watch.

(*They go out.*)

SERGEANT. (*walks up and down once or twice and looks at placard*) A hundred pounds and promotion sure. There must be a great deal of spending in a hundred pounds. It's a pity some honest man not to be better of that.

(**A RAGGED MAN** *appears at left and tries to slip past.* **SERGEANT** *suddenly turns.*)

SERGEANT. Where are you going?

MAN. I'm a poor ballad-singer, your honor. I thought to sell some of these (*holds out bundle of ballads*) to the sailors.

(*He goes on.*)

SERGEANT. Stop! Didn't I tell you to stop? You can't go on there.

MAN. Oh, very well. It's a hard thing to be poor. All the world's against the poor!

SERGEANT. Who are you?

MAN. You'd be as wise as myself if I told you, but I don't mind. I'm one Jimmy Walsh, a ballad-singer.

SERGEANT. Jimmy Walsh? I don't know that name.

MAN. Ah, sure, they know it well enough in Ennis.[3] Were you ever in Ennis, sergeant?

SERGEANT. What brought you here?

MAN. Sure, it's to the assizes I came, thinking I might make a few shillings here or there. It's in the one train with the judges I came.

SERGEANT. Well, if you came so far, you may as well go farther, for you'll walk out of this.

MAN. I will, I will; I'll just go on where I was going.

(*goes towards steps*)

SERGEANT. Come back from those steps; no one has leave to pass down them tonight.

MAN. I'll just sit on the top of the steps till I see will some sailor buy a ballad off me that would give me my supper. They do be late going back to the ship. It's often I saw them in Cork[4] carried down the quay in a hand-cart.

SERGEANT. Move on, I tell you. I won't have any one lingering about the quay tonight.

MAN. Well, I'll go. It's the poor have the hard life! Maybe yourself might like one, sergeant. Here's a good sheet now. (*turns one over*) "Content and a pipe"—that's not much. "The Peeler and the goat"—you wouldn't like that. "Johnny Hart"—that's a lovely song.

SERGEANT. Move on.

---

2. **assize.** Periodic court sessions held in each county
3. **Ennis.** A town in County Clare, Ireland
4. **Cork.** A county in southern Ireland

CROSS-CURRICULAR ACTIVITIES

Have students locate Ireland on a world map. Then have them locate on a map of Ireland the places mentioned in the play, including Ennis, Cork, County Clare, County Limerick, and Kilmallock.

ADDITIONAL QUESTIONS AND ACTIVITIES

Dialect. Have students identify the dialectical elements of the Man's speech, beginning with "I'll just sit on the top" and ending with "that's a lovely song." Students might identify these elements by doing a line-by-line translation into their own dialect or into standard English.

BIBLIOGRAPHICAL NOTE

Works by Lady Augusta Gregory

Gregory, Augusta. *Collected Plays.* Ed. Ann Saddlemyer. 1970. 4v.

———. *Gods and Fighting Men: The Story of the Tuatha de Danaan and of the Fianna of Ireland.* Ed. T. R. Henn and C. Smythe. 1903.

———. *Lady Gregory's Journals.* Ed. T. R. Henn and C. Smythe. 1946.

———. *Seventy Years: Being the Autobiography of Lady Gregory.* Ed. Colin Smythe. 1974.

Additional Readings

Coxhead, Elizabeth. *Daughters of Erin: Five Women of the Irish Renascence.* 1965.

———. *J. M. Synge and Lady Gregory.* 1962.

———. *Lady Gregory: A Literary Portrait.* 1966.

Hopper, Edward. *Lady Isabella Persse Gregory.* 1976.

Mikhail, E. H. *Lady Gregory: An Annotated Bibliography of Criticism.* 1982.

———. *Lady Gregory: Interviews and Recollections.* 1977.

MAN.   Ah, wait till you hear it. (*sings*)

> There was a rich farmer's daughter
> lived near the town of Ross;
> She courted a Highland soldier, his
> name was Johnny Hart;
> Says the mother to her daughter, "I'll
> go distracted mad
> If you marry that Highland soldier
> dressed up in Highland plaid."

SERGEANT.   Stop that noise.

(MAN *wraps up his ballads and shuffles towards the steps.*)

SERGEANT.   Where are you going?

MAN.   Sure you told me to be going, and I am going.

SERGEANT.   Don't be a fool. I didn't tell you to go that way; I told you to go back to the town.

MAN.   Back to the town, is it?

SERGEANT. (*taking him by the shoulder and shoving him before him*)   Here, I'll show you the way. Be off with you. What are you stopping for?

MAN. (*who has been keeping his eye on the notice, points to it*)   I think I know what you're waiting for, Sergeant.

SERGEANT.   What's that to you?

MAN.   And I know well the man you're waiting for—I know him well—I'll be going.

(*He shuffles on.*)

SERGEANT.   You know him? Come back here. What sort is he?

MAN.   Come back is it, sergeant? Do you want to have me killed?

SERGEANT.   Why do you say that?

MAN.   Never mind. I'm going. I wouldn't be in your shoes if the reward was ten times as much. (*goes on off stage to left*) Not if it was ten times as much.

SERGEANT. (*rushing after him*)   Come back here, come back. (*drags him back*) What sort is he? Where did you see him?

MAN.   I saw him in my own place, in the County Clare. I tell you you wouldn't like to be looking at him. You'd be afraid to be in the one place with him. There isn't a weapon he doesn't know the use of, and as to strength, his muscles are as hard as that board (*slaps barrel*).

SERGEANT.   Is he as bad as that?

MAN.   He is then.

SERGEANT.   Do you tell me so?

MAN.   There was a poor man in our place, a sergeant from Ballyvaughan.[5]—It was with a lump of stone he did it.

SERGEANT.   I never heard of that.

MAN.   And you wouldn't, sergeant.   It's not everything that happens gets into the papers. And there was a policeman in plain clothes, too. . . . It is in Limerick he was. . . . It was after the time of the attack on the police barrack at Kilmallock[6]. . . Moonlight . . . just like this . . . waterside. . . . Nothing was known for certain.

SERGEANT.   Do you say so? It's a terrible county to belong to.

MAN.   That's so, indeed! You might be standing there, looking out that way, thinking you saw him coming up this side of the quay (*points*), and he might be coming up this other side (*points*), and he'd be on you before you knew where you were.

SERGEANT.   It's a whole troop of police they ought to put here to stop a man like that.

---

5. **Ballyvaughan.** Another town in County Clare
6. **Limerick . . . Kilmallock.** Kilmallock is a town in the county of Limerick.

MAN. But if you'd like me to stop with you, I could be looking down this side. I could be sitting up here on this barrel.

SERGEANT. And you know him well, too?

MAN. I'd know him a mile off, sergeant.

SERGEANT. But you wouldn't want to share the reward?

MAN. Is it a poor man like me, that has to be going the roads and singing in fairs, to have the name on him that he took a reward? But you don't want me. I'll be safer in the town.

SERGEANT. Well, you can stop.

MAN. (*getting up on barrel*) All right, sergeant. I wonder, now, you're not tired out, sergeant, walking up and down the way you are.

SERGEANT. If I'm tired I'm used to it.

MAN. You might have hard work before you tonight yet. Take it easy while you can. There's plenty of room up here on the barrel, and you see farther when you're higher up.

SERGEANT. Maybe so. (*Gets up beside him on barrel, facing right. They sit back to back, looking different ways.*) You made me feel a bit queer with the way you talked.

MAN. Give me a match, sergeant. (*He gives it, and Man lights pipe.*) Take a draw yourself? It'll quiet you. Wait now till I give you a light, but you needn't turn round. Don't take your eye off the quay for the life of you.

SERGEANT. Never fear, I won't. (*Lights pipe. They both smoke.*) Indeed it's a hard thing to be in the force, out at night and no thanks for it, for all the danger we're in. And it's little we get but abuse from the people, and no choice but to obey our orders, and never asked when a man is sent into danger, if you are a married man with a family.

MAN. (*sings*)—
As through the hills I walked to view
   the hills and shamrock plain,
I stood awhile where nature smiles to
   view the rocks and streams,
On a matron fair I fixed my eyes
   beneath a fertile vale,
And she sang her song: it was on the
   wrong of poor old Granuaile.[7]

SERGEANT. Stop that; that's no song to be singing in these times.

MAN. Ah, sergeant, I was only singing to keep my heart up. It sinks when I think of him. To think of us two sitting here, and he creeping up the quay, maybe, to get to us.

SERGEANT. Are you keeping a good lookout?

MAN. I am; and for no reward too. Amn't I the foolish man? But when I saw a man in trouble, I never could help trying to get him out of it. What's that? Did something hit me? (*rubs his heart*)

SERGEANT. (*patting him on the shoulder*) You will get your reward in heaven.

MAN. I know that, I know that, sergeant, but life is precious.

SERGEANT. Well, you can sing if it gives you more courage.

MAN. (*sings*)—
Her head was bare, her hands and feet
   with iron bands were bound,
Her pensive strain and plaintive wail
   mingles with the evening gale,
And the song she sang with mournful
   air, I am old Granuaile.
Her lips so sweet that monarchs
   kissed . . .

---

7. **Granuaile.** A name for Ireland

HISTORICAL NOTE

The ballad singer uses the word *Granuaile* because, during their rule over/occupation of Ireland, the English enacted laws prohibiting nationalism to the extent of forbidding the use of the word *Ireland*.

CROSS-CURRICULAR ACTIVITIES

• Students can research the history of Irish independence and the Irish nationalist movement. Works of interest on this and other subjects in Irish history include Curran, Joseph M. *The Birth of the Irish Free State, 1921–1923.* 1980; Foster, Roy, ed. *The Oxford History of Ireland.* 1992; Ranelagh, John. *A Short History of Ireland.* 1983; Rumpf, E., and A. C. Hepburn. *Nationalism and Socialism in Twentieth-century Ireland.* 1977; and Scally, Robert. *The End of Hidden Ireland: Rebellion, Famine, and Emigration.* 1994.

• In the early nineteenth century, many in the Irish nationalist movement tried to revive the Irish language, which was then spoken only in isolated rural areas. Modern Irish is now spoken primarily in western and southern Ireland and is taught for its historical and cultural value in Irish schools. See Hindley, Reg. *The Death of the Irish Language.* 1990; and O'Rahilly, T. F. *Irish Dialects: Past and Present.* 1988.

BIBLIOGRAPHICAL NOTE

Writers of the Irish Revival

Ferguson, Samuel. *Lays of the Western Gael.* 1865.

Hyde, Douglas. *Love Songs of Connacht.* 1893.

O'Casey, Sean. *Juno and the Paycock.* 1925.

———. *The Plough and the Stars.* 1926.

———. *The Shadow of a Gunman.* 1925.

O'Grady, Standish. *History of Ireland.* 1880.

Synge, John Millington. *The Aran Islands.* 1907.

———. *The Playboy of the Western World.* 1907.

———. *Riders to the Sea.* 1904.

Also see the sections on Shaw (pages 986–1056) and Yeats (pages 840–851).

MONOLOGUE

A monologue is an extended speech by one character. This speech illuminates what the sergeant is thinking. ▶

SERGEANT. That's not it . . . "Her gown she wore was stained with gore. . . ." That's it—you missed that.

MAN. You're right, sergeant, so it is; I missed it. (*repeats line*) But to think of a man like you knowing a song like that.

SERGEANT. There's many a thing a man might know and might not have any wish for.

MAN. Now, I daresay, sergeant, in your youth, you used to be sitting up on a wall, the way you are sitting up on this barrel now, and the other lads beside you, and you singing "Granuaile"? . . .

SERGEANT. I did then.

MAN. And the "Shan Van Vocht"? . . .

SERGEANT. I did then.

MAN. And the "Green on the Cape"?

SERGEANT. That was one of them.

MAN. And maybe the man you are watching for tonight used to be sitting on the wall, when he was young, and singing those same songs. . . . It's a queer world. . . .

SERGEANT. Whisht! . . . I think I see something coming. . . . It's only a dog.

MAN. And isn't it a queer world? . . . Maybe it's one of the boys you used to be singing with that time you will be arresting today or tomorrow, and sending into the dock. . . .

SERGEANT. That's true indeed.

MAN. And maybe one night, after you had been singing, if the other boys had told you some plan they had, some plan to free the country, you might have joined with them . . . and maybe it is you might be in trouble now.

SERGEANT. Well, who knows but I might? I had a great spirit in those days.

MAN. It's a queer world, sergeant, and it's little any mother knows when she sees her child creeping on the floor what might happen to it before it has gone through its life, or who will be who in the end.

SERGEANT. That's a queer thought now, and a true thought. Wait now till I think it out. . . . If it wasn't for the sense I have, and for my wife and family, and for me joining the force the time I did, it might be myself now would be after breaking gaol and hiding in the dark, and it might be him that's hiding in the dark and that got out of gaol would be sitting up here where I am on this barrel. . . . And it might be myself would be creeping up trying to make my escape from himself, and it might be himself would be keeping the law, and myself would be breaking it, and myself would be trying to put a bullet in his head, or to take up a lump of stone the way you said he did . . . no, that myself did. . . . Oh! (*gasps . . . after a pause*) What's that? (*grasps man's arm*)

MAN. (*jumps off barrel and listens, looking out over water*) It's nothing, sergeant.

SERGEANT. I thought it might be a boat. I had a notion there might be friends of his coming about the quays with a boat.

MAN. Sergeant, I am thinking it was with the people you were, and not with the law you were, when you were a young man.

SERGEANT. Well, if I was foolish then; that time's gone.

MAN. Maybe, sergeant, it comes into your head sometimes, in spite of your belt and your tunic, that it might have been as well for you to have followed Granuaile.

SERGEANT. It's no business of yours what I think.

LITERARY HISTORY

Famous Irish writers in English include William Congreve, author of *The Way of the World*; Jonathan Swift, author of *Gulliver's Travels*; Oliver Goldsmith, author of *The Vicar of Wakefield*; and Oscar Wilde, author of *The Importance of Being Ernest*. Other notable Irish writers include George Farquhar, Maria Edgeworth, Samuel Ferguson, William Allingham, Thomas Moore, W. B. Yeats, John Millington Synge, Sean O'Casey, James Joyce, and Samuel Beckett.

MAN. Maybe, sergeant, you'll be on the side of the country yet.

SERGEANT. (*gets off barrel*) Don't talk to me like that. I have my duties and I know them. (*looks round*) That was a boat; I hear the oars. (*Goes to the steps and looks down.*)

MAN. (*sings*)—
> O, then, tell me, Shawn O'Farrell,
>   Where the gathering is to be.
> In the old spot by the river
>   Right well known to you and me!

SERGEANT. Stop that! Stop that, I tell you!

MAN. (*sings louder*)—
> One word more, for signal token,
>   Whistle up the marching tune,
> With your pike upon your shoulder,
>   At the Rising of the Moon.

SERGEANT. If you don't stop that, I'll arrest you.

(*A whistle from below answers, repeating the air.*)

SERGEANT. That's a signal. (*stands between him and steps*) You must not pass this way. . . . Step farther back. . . . Who are you? You are no ballad-singer.

MAN. You needn't ask who I am; that placard will tell you. (*points to placard*)

SERGEANT. You are the man I am looking for.

MAN. (*Takes off hat and wig. SERGEANT seizes them.*) I am. There's a hundred pounds on my head. There is a friend of mine below in a boat. He knows a safe place to bring me to.

SERGEANT. (*looking still at hat and wig*) It's a pity! It's a pity. You deceived me. You deceived me well.

MAN. I am a friend of Granuaile. There is a hundred pounds on my head.

SERGEANT. It's a pity, it's a pity!

MAN. Will you let me pass, or must I make you let me?

SERGEANT. I am in the force. I will not let you pass.

MAN. I thought to do it with my tongue. (*puts hand in breast*) What is that?

(*voice of* **POLICEMAN X** *outside*). Here, this is where we left him.

SERGEANT. It's my comrades coming.

MAN. You won't betray me . . . the friend of Granuaile. (*slips behind barrel*)

(*voice of* **POLICEMAN B**). That was the last of the placards.

POLICEMAN X. (*as they come in*) If he makes his escape it won't be unknown he'll make it.

(**SERGEANT** *puts hat and wig behind his back.*)

POLICEMAN B. Did any one come this way?

SERGEANT. (*after a pause*) No one.

POLICEMAN B. No one at all?

SERGEANT. No one at all.

POLICEMAN B. We had no orders to go back to the station; we can stop along with you.

SERGEANT. I don't want you. There is nothing for you to do here.

POLICEMAN B. You bade us to come back here and keep watch with you.

SERGEANT. I'd sooner be alone. Would any man come this way and you making all that talk? It is better the place to be quiet.

POLICEMAN B. Well, we'll leave you the lantern anyhow.

(*hands it to him*)

SERGEANT. I don't want it. Bring it with you.

◄ **SOUND EFFECTS**
Sound effects can indicate the presence of something, in this case the man's friend.

◄ **PROPERTIES**
Items like the hat and the wig, ones that are manipulated by actors during scenes, are called properties.

QUOTABLES

❝Can we not build up a national literature which shall be none the less Irish in spirit from being English in language?❞

—W. B. Yeats

LITERARY TECHNIQUE

Folk Song. A **folk song** is a song composed anonymously and passed from person to person without being recorded or written down for some time. The title of this play comes from the folk song "The Rising of the Moon," two verses of which are sung in the play by the rebel leader. You may wish to locate a recording of this song to play for your students. An excellent recording of this and other songs of Irish Rebellion was done by Tommy Makem and the Clancy Brothers.

RESPONDING TO THE SELECTION

Invite students to try to imagine why someone might hold a different view from their own.

ANSWERS FOR REVIEWING THE SELECTION

RECALLING

1. The police are putting up wanted posters. They discuss the wanted man, how to catch him, and the reward that is offered.

2. A Ragged Man appears and claims to be a singer. He convinces the Sergeant to let him stay by saying that he knows the wanted man and that the wanted man is dangerous.

3. He suggests that if circumstances had been different, they might be in each other's situation.

4. He says, "It's a pity," and he lets him escape. He later lies to the other police officers about having seen the wanted man.

INTERPRETING

Responses will vary. Possible responses are given.

5. The wanted man has escaped from prison, but we are not told why he was imprisoned. He is probably a political prisoner. The police are willing to catch him, but they are not happy about it because he is popular with the public and perhaps because they have nationalist sympathies.

6. He poses as a singer so that he can sing to warn his comrades of the presence of the police. The songs indicate his nationalism as well as a general interest in cultural and political conflict.

7. The Sergeant imagines that he might have been a wanted criminal or perhaps a rebel nationalist. This may make him more sympathetic to the Ragged Man and more willing to help him.

8. He lets the man go out of empathy. He has mixed feelings about the decision, thinking it may have been foolish.

(cont.)

POLICEMAN B. You might want it. There are clouds coming up and you have the darkness of the night before you yet. I'll leave it over here on the barrel. (*goes to barrel*)

SERGEANT. Bring it with you I tell you. No more talk.

POLICEMAN B. Well, I thought it might be a comfort to you. I often think when I have it in my hand and can be flashing it about into every dark corner (*doing so*) that it's the same as being beside the fire at home, and the bits of bogwood blazing up now and again.

(*flashes it about, now on the barrel, now on* **SERGEANT**)

SERGEANT. (*furious*) Be off the two of you, yourselves and your lantern!

(*They go out.* **MAN** *comes from behind barrel. He and* **SERGEANT** *stand looking at one another.*)

SERGEANT. What are you waiting for?

MAN. For my hat, of course, and my wig. You wouldn't wish me to get my death of cold? (**SERGEANT** *gives them.*)

MAN. (*going towards steps*) Well, goodnight, comrade, and thank you. You did me a good turn tonight, and I'm obliged to you. Maybe I'll be able to do as much for you when the small rise up and the big fall down . . . when we all change places at the Rising (*waves his hand and disappears*) of the Moon.

SERGEANT. (*turning his back to audience and reading placard*) A hundred pounds reward! A hundred pounds! (*turns towards audience*) I wonder, now, am I as great a fool as I think I am?

Curtain. ∎

Responding to the Selection

Why do you think the Sergeant protected the wanted man and allowed him to escape? If you were the Sergeant, what would you have done? Why? Write your responses to these questions in your journal.

Reviewing the Selection

1. What are the police doing as the play opens? What do they discuss as they work?

2. Who appears as the Sergeant is keeping watch? What does he claim to be? How does the Ragged Man convince the Sergeant to let him stay?

3. What does the Ragged Man say about the Sergeant's and his own past and present lives?

4. What does the Sergeant do when he realizes that the Ragged Man is the man he is looking for? What does he do when his men come back?

► 5. Why is the man on the placard wanted? Do the police want to catch the man? Why or why not?

► 6. Why is the man posing as a ballad singer? What do his songs reveal?

► 7. What does the Sergeant think his life might have been like? How does this thinking affect the Sergeant's actions at the end of the play?

► 8. Why does the Sergeant let the man go? How does he feel about this decision?

9. What conflicting feelings does the Sergeant have throughout the play? Which feeling wins out at the end? Why does this prove to be the stronger feeling?

10. What is the source of the play's title? Why is this an appropriate title? What other references to the moon are made in the play? What other meaning might the moonlight have?

Understanding Literature (Questions for Discussion)

1. **Spectacle.** The **spectacle** is all the elements of the drama presented to the senses of the audience, including lights, sets, curtains, costumes, make-up, music, sound effects, properties, and movements of the actors. How is seeing a play performed different from reading the same play? Might you reconsider your interpretation of a play you have read after seeing it performed? Why?

2. **Properties.** **Properties** are items that can be carried on and off the stage by actors or manipulated by actors during scenes. What properties would you need if you were to produce *The Rising of the Moon?* Which properties are most important?

3. **Stage Directions.** Notes provided by the playwright to describe how something should be presented or performed on the stage are called **stage directions**. What purpose do stage directions serve for a reader? Look at the stage notes at the beginning of *The Rising of the Moon.* What purpose do these stage directions serve?

DRAMA / THE RISING OF THE MOON **55**

ENRICHMENT ACTIVITIES

Invite students to consider why nonfiction is not defined simply as "writing that tells the truth." What types of nonfiction would such a definition leave out?

SUPPORT FOR LEP STUDENTS

Students may have trouble with the speech's long, compound-complex sentences. (There are only five sentences in the speech.) Help them or have them work in pairs to find the subject and verb of each clause.

IDIOMS

we, our—pronouns used by royalty to refer to themselves
take heed—be careful

ADDITIONAL VOCABULARY

multitude—large number, especially of persons
disport—amusement
but—only

Nonfiction

Nonfiction is writing that deals with actual events, people, places, things, and ideas. The roots of nonfiction lie in oral accounts of actual occurrences among preliterate peoples. Actual events—the deeds of heroes, major events in the history of a clan or a tribe—would be retold, often with embellishments that melded the actual with the legendary or mythological. After the invention of writing, such accounts of the histories of peoples, of their heroes and leaders, their trials and accomplishments, were written down, becoming the earliest **histories.** In much early historical writing, such as that of the Greek historian Herodotus, accounts of actual historical personages appear side by side with accounts of fabulous beasts, mythical lands, and magical transformations. In early writing, myth, history, and biography were one.

The first great historian in England was the Venerable Bede, a monk who lived in Northumbria from AD 673 to 735 (see page 74). An important nonfiction work from the Old English period is the *Anglo-Saxon Chronicle,* begun in 891, a year-by-year account of English history from the beginnings of the Anglo-Saxon settlement.

Of importance to historians are the many kinds of nonfiction, such as **speeches, contracts, constitutions, laws,** and **political tracts,** that provide a record of political life. A fine example of a political speech is Queen Elizabeth's Speech to the Troops at Tilbury, on page 60. Examples of political writing in this text include the selections from John Milton's *Areopagitica* (page 463), Mary Wollstonecraft's *A Vindication of the Rights of Woman* (page 647), and John Stuart Mill's *The Subjection of Women* (page 809).

Since the beginning of writing, people have recorded parts of their own lives or of the lives of others. These **autobiographies** and **biographies** are among the most important types of nonfiction. The first full-fledged autobiography in English is generally held to be *The Book of Margery Kempe,* written in the mid-fifteenth century (page 180). The first of the great modern biographies is James Boswell's *The Life of Samuel Johnson, LL.D.,* published in 1788 (page 542).

Other important types of nonfiction that provide information about people's lives include their **letters, diaries,** and **journals.** Examples of journal writing in this text include selections from *The Diary of Samuel Pepys* (page 501) and from *The Grasmere Journals* of Dorothy Wordsworth (page 674).

Related to letters, diaries, and journals by the personal nature of their content, **essays** are among the most important of the types of nonfiction represented in the English literary tradition. The word *essay* comes from a French word meaning "a trial or attempt." An essay presents a short but not exhaustive treatment of a subject from the perspective of the author. Examples of essay writing in this text include selections by Joseph Addison (page 554), William Wordsworth (page 605), William Hazlitt (page 678), John Ruskin (page 810), and Virginia Woolf (page 914).

The launching of English ships against the Spanish Armada. (detail) National Maritime Museum, Greenwich, England

GOALS/OBJECTIVES

Studying this lesson will enable students to

• experience a stirring speech delivered by a great leader at a time of crisis
• define *nonfiction*
• name and describe the types of nonfiction
• proofread and publish a piece of writing

• name and define four purposes (expressive, expository, persuasive, and literary) and four modes (narration, dialogue, description, and exposition) of writing
• identify the purpose and mode of a nonfiction work
• write a dialogue

ART NOTE

The ships depicted in the painting are English galleons, long, lean ships that rode low in the water for extra stability. They would bear up to twenty-eight powerful cannons along each side. When the English engaged the Spanish Armada in 1588, the two sides each had about the same number of warships. The Spanish were better prepared for the traditional tactics of ramming, boarding, and hand-to-hand fighting. However, the English ships were faster and had more effective cannons. Numerous Spanish ships were sunk before they could get close enough to board the English ships. The few Spanish ships that remained after the fighting were forced to flee to the North Sea and to sail around Scotland in order to return home.

CROSS-CURRICULAR ACTIVITIES

Students can research the intent of the Spanish Armada and depict their own vision of it by writing a news report, drawing or painting a battle scene, creating a map, or using some other form of expression. Sources for research include Graham, Winston, *The Spanish Armada,* 1972, and Martin, Colin, and Geoffrey Parker, *The Spanish Armada,* 1988.

VOCABULARY FROM THE SELECTION

concord

treachery

HISTORICAL NOTE

The Spanish Armada was launched against England by Philip II of Spain, who was angered by English piracy and by English aid given to rebels against Spanish authority in the Low Countries. The Spanish planned to use their fleet to protect an invasion force from the continent. Students might find it interesting to speculate about the differences that would have occurred in the subsequent course of world history had the Spanish plan succeeded.

Purpose. Explain that writing commonly has more than one purpose. Ask students to imagine occasions on which they might have multiple purposes in writing; for example, a person might compose a poem to express her or his feelings but at the same time hope to persuade others to share those feelings.

• Anne Finch's "The Introduction" (page 484) is an example of expressive writing.

• The Unit Introductions in this text are examples of expository writing.

• Samuel Johnson's "A Brief to Free a Slave" (page 533) is an example of persuasive writing.

• Charlotte Smith's "Pressed by the Moon, Mute Arbitress of Tides" (page 497) is an example of literary writing.

ADDITIONAL QUESTIONS AND ACTIVITIES

Have students write a paragraph with each of the four purposes. Advanced students might write each of these paragraphs about the same topic.

Purpose and Mode in Nonfiction

THE PURPOSES OF WRITING

Purpose, or Aim. A writer's **purpose,** or **aim,** is what he or she wants a work to accomplish. Nonfiction writing generally is produced with some overall purpose in mind. The following chart classifies types of writing by purpose.

TYPE OF WRITING	PURPOSE
Expressive Writing	The writer expresses himself or herself, describing personal feelings, attitudes, ideas, values, or beliefs.
Expository or Informative Writing	The writer attempts to inform others about a subject.
Persuasive Writing	The writer attempts to persuade others to adopt some belief or to take some course of action.
Literary Writing	The writer creates an imaginary world to entertain and, sometimes, to instruct.

This classification system derives from the work of James Kinneavy, who, in *A Theory of Discourse,* bases his classification of writing on an analysis of the standard "communication model." According to this model, a sender encodes a message about some subject in a set of symbols and then transmits that message to a recipient. In **expressive writing,** the emphasis is on the sender of the message, the writer. The major purpose is to express the writer's state of mind. In **expository writing,** the emphasis is on the subject. The major purpose is to provide information about that subject. In **persuasive writing,** the emphasis is on the recipient. The major purpose is to change the recipient's mind or to move the recipient to action. In **literary writing,** the emphasis is on the symbols—the words themselves and the form into which they are organized. The major purpose is to create an imaginary world by which to entertain or instruct.

MODES OF WRITING

Mode. Another common classification system for writing divides various types of writing according to the method of treatment of the subject. The following chart describes methods of treating subjects, or **modes,** that are commonly used in nonfiction writing.

MODE OF WRITING	DESCRIPTION
Narration	Writing in this mode relates events. Histories, biographies, autobiographies, and news reports all make extensive use of narration.
Dialogue	Writing in this mode presents speech in words actually used by people.
Description	Writing in this mode portrays in words how things look, sound, smell, taste, or feel.
Exposition	Writing in this mode presents facts or opinions in an organized manner.

Types of Exposition. There are many modes of expository writing used in nonfiction works. The following chart describes some of the most common.

MODE OF EXPOSITION	DESCRIPTION
Analysis	Writing in this mode breaks something into its parts and shows how the parts are related.
Classification	Writing in this mode places subjects into categories, or classes, according to their properties or characteristics.
Comparison and Contrast	Writing in this mode presents similarities and differences.
Process/How to	Writing in this mode presents steps in a process.

LITERARY TECHNIQUE

Mode. Explain that it is common in a piece of writing to use more than one mode, although one mode usually predominates.

• Narration is used in *The Diary of Samuel Pepys,* page 501.

• Dialogue is used in James Boswell's *The Life of Samuel Johnson, LL. D.,* page 542.

• Description is used in Emily Brontë's *Wuthering Heights,* page 810.

• Exposition is used in Virginia Woolf's *A Room of One's Own,* page 914.

Mode: Exposition. For description of and instruction in these types of exposition, see the Language Arts Survey, 1.34, "Organizing Ideas"; 4.7, "Classifying"; 4.8, "Comparing and Contrasting"; and 4.10, "Analyzing."

ADDITIONAL QUESTIONS AND ACTIVITIES

• Assign students to scan a newspaper to find examples of each mode of exposition.

• Ask students to name magazines or other publications in which one of the four modes of exposition predominates. For instance, science magazines like *Scientific American* and *Discover* use analysis; magazines for collectors, such as *Stamp and Coin Hobbyist,* use classification; consumer magazines like *Consumer Reports* use comparison and contrast; and crafts and cooking magazines like *Woman's Day* contain process/how-to articles.

Speech to the Troops at Tilbury, August, 1588

QUEEN ELIZABETH I

My loving people,

We have been persuaded by some that are careful of our safety, to take heed how we commit our selves to armed multitudes, for fear of <u>treachery</u>; but I assure you I do not desire to live to distrust my faithful and loving people. Let tyrants fear. I have always so behaved myself that, under God, I have placed my chiefest strength and safeguard in the loyal hearts and goodwill of my subjects; and therefore I am come amongst you, as you see, at this time, not for my recreation and disport, but being resolved, in the midst and heat of the battle, to live or die amongst you all; to lay down for my God, and for my kingdom, and my people, my honor and my blood, even in the dust. I know I have the body but of a weak and feeble woman; but I have the heart and stomach of a king, and of a king of England too, and think foul scorn that Parma[1] or Spain, or any prince of Europe, should dare to invade the borders of my realm; to which rather than any dishonor shall grow by me, I myself will take up arms, I myself will be your general, judge, and rewarder of every one of your virtues in the field. I know already, for your forwardness you have deserved rewards and crowns;[2] and We do assure you in the word of a prince, they shall be duly paid you. In the mean time, my lieutenant general shall be in my stead, than whom never prince commanded a more noble or worthy subject; not doubting but by your obedience to my general, by your <u>concord</u> in the camp, and your valor in the field, we shall shortly have a famous victory over those enemies of my God, of my kingdom, and of my people.

---

1. **Parma.** Parma had allied with Spain and was expected in the invasion.
2. **crowns.** British coins

Responding to the Selection

What is the tone of this selection? What sort of person does Queen Elizabeth seem to be? If you were among the troops listening to her speech, how would you feel about her being present? about what she says?

WORDS FOR EVERYDAY USE:

treach • er • y (trech´ ər ē) n., treason
con • cord (kän´ kôrd) n., agreement

Reviewing the Selection

1. What have some people advised the queen not to do?

2. What does Queen Elizabeth tell the assembled troops about herself?

INTERPRETING

3. Why does the queen not fear being among her subjects?

4. What contrast does Queen Elizabeth draw between her outward appearance and her inner resolve?

SYNTHESIZING

5. Elizabeth is speaking to troops before they go into battle. What does she say to strengthen their will and resolve?

Understanding Literature (Questions for Discussion)

1. **Purpose.** The **purpose** is the goal that a writer wants to achieve. What is the major purpose of Queen Elizabeth's speech? Is it to express herself, to inform, to persuade, or to produce a literary work? Does the piece seem to accomplish its purpose? Explain.

2. **Mode.** A **mode** is a method of treatment of a subject in a piece of writing. Common modes include narration, dialogue, description, and exposition. In what part of her speech does Queen Elizabeth use description? What does she describe? In what part of her speech does she use the type of exposition known as comparison and contrast? What contrast does she make? Why does she do so?

3. **Parallelism.** **Parallelism** is a rhetorical technique in which a writer emphasizes the equal value or weight of two or more ideas by expressing them in the same grammatical form. At what point in this speech does Elizabeth use parallelism? for what purpose?

The Process of Writing: Publishing

Proofreading and Publishing. Read the Language Arts Survey, 1.47–1.49, "Proofreading and Publishing." Then, proofread your revised draft from the writing assignment on page 25. Make a clean, final copy of the manuscript. Next, work with other students in your class to prepare a booklet of your works. You may wish to have students in the class submit drawings or photographs to include in your booklet.

VOCABULARY IN CONTEXT

- A wise and benevolent ruler has no need to fear <u>treachery</u>.

- Please lay down your weapons and let us come to a <u>concord</u>.

THE PROCESS OF WRITING: PUBLISHING

If these are your students' first completed pieces of writing, consider not assigning grades. Instead, make positive written evaluative comments on the students' papers or hold conferences to discuss each student's paper individually.

▶ Additional practice is provided in the *Essential Skills Practice Book: Writing*, 1.47–1.49.

ANSWERS FOR REVIEWING THE SELECTION

RECALLING

1. The queen has been advised to avoid crowds for fear of traitors.

2. Elizabeth says that she is determined to die for honor and for her people if necessary and that despite her weak body she has the spirit of a king.

INTERPRETING

Responses will vary. Possible responses are given.

3. She does not fear her subjects because she trusts them and because they love her.

4. Her outward appearance is weak, but her inner resolve is strong.

SYNTHESIZING

Responses will vary. Possible responses are given.

5. She promises the troops money. She says that she herself would fight. She promises them "a famous victory."

ANSWERS FOR UNDERSTANDING LITERATURE

▶ See the evaluation forms for discussion, active listening, and oral communication, *Assessment Portfolio*, 7.11– 7.14.

Responses will vary. Possible responses are given.

1. **Purpose.** Elizabeth's major purpose is to persuade her troops to fight hard. Students will not likely agree that this rousing speech does indeed accomplish its purpose, for in it Elizabeth appeals to her troops' patriotism and demonstrates courage by her own example.

2. **Mode.** Near the middle of the speech, Elizabeth uses descriptions of herself and of her lieutenant general. She uses comparison and contrast to explain her reasons for coming before the crowd. She contrasts a frivolous reason with her true reason to show her seriousness.

3. **Parallelism.** Elizabeth uses parallelism at the end of the speech to show what she cares about: her God, her kingdom, and her people.

VOCABULARY DEVELOPMENT EXERCISES

▶ Give students the following exercises.

• An antonym is a word that is opposite in meaning to another word. Work with the list of vocabulary words on page 62, and find antonyms for as many of these words as you can.

Example. guile—witlessness; guile—naiveté

• From the list of literary terms on page 62, choose ten terms that have uses outside of literature. Write ten sentences. In each sentence, use one of these words. Make sure that the sentence illustrates the meaning of the word.

Example. We heard of Mariel's plot to surprise Lin on her birthday.

ADDITIONAL RESOURCES

ASSESSMENT PORTFOLIO
• Vocabulary Worksheet, 4.1.11
• Study Guide: Unit 1 Test, 4.1.12
• Unit 1 Test, 4.1.13

ESSENTIAL SKILLS PRACTICE BOOKS
Writing
• Drafting, 1.35–1.42
• Evaluating and Revising, 1.43–1.46
• Prewriting, 1.1–1.34
• Proofreading and Publishing, 1.47–1.49

Language
• Reducing Wordiness, 2.59

UNIT REVIEW

Genres and Techniques of Literature

VOCABULARY FROM THE SELECTIONS

career (*vt.*), 33	perpendicular, 22
concord, 60	profound, 23
glister, 8	quay, 48
guile, 8	quorum, 22
ineffable, 23	remonstrate, 39
inscrutable, 23	treachery, 60
parry, 34	

LITERARY TERMS

alliteration, 22	oral transmission, 6
assonance, 23	parallelism, 22, 61
ballad, 4, 11	personification, 22, 24
climax, 40	plot, 29, 43
conflict, 43	properties, 53, 55
dénouement, 41	protagonist, 32
dialogue, 48	proverb, 9
exposition, 31	purpose, 60, 61
foreshadowing, 39	repetition, 23
formulaic language, 8	resolution, 9, 41
inciting incident, 7, 32	rhyme scheme, 7, 22
incremental repetition, 8	rhyme, 20, 25
Magical Realism, 43	setting, 29, 43
meter, 17-18, 22, 24	sound effects, 53
mode, 61	spectacle, 55
monologue, 52	stage directions, 48, 55
motivation, 43	stanza form, 6
oral tradition, 4, 11	theme, 30, 43

SYNTHESIS: QUESTIONS FOR WRITING, RESEARCH, OR DISCUSSION

THE ORAL TRADITION

1. **Ballads and the Oral Tradition.** What characteristics does "Robin Hood and Allen a Dale" have that are common to all folk ballads? What subjects did the composers of ballads write about? What characteristics might have caused "Robin Hood and Allen a Dale" to survive in the oral tradition?

POETRY

2. **Lyric Poetry.** What characteristics make "The Naming of Cats" a lyric poem? How do lyric poems differ from narrative and dramatic ones? What special poetic devices—devices of sound, figurative language, and rhetorical techniques—are used in "The Naming of Cats"?

FICTION

3. **Short Story Structure.** Into what parts is a typical plot divided? What events in "The Rocking-Horse Winner" correspond to these parts?

DRAMA

4. **The Spectacle in Drama.** Imagine that you will be directing a production of *The Rising of the Moon.* Make a complete list, with descriptions, of the following elements of the spectacle in your production: the stage set, the lighting, the properties, the sound effects, and the costumes.

NONFICTION

5. **The Rhetoric of a Speech.** A speech often has as its purpose persuading an audience—moving them to adopt some point of view or to take some course of action. The art of moving an audience to thought, feeling, or action is called rhetoric. What techniques does Queen Elizabeth I use in her Speech to the Troops at Tilbury to move her audience? What purpose does she want to achieve? What makes a good speech? Is this a good speech by your criteria?

► These prompts are suitable as topics for research papers. Refer to the Language Arts Survey, 4.20–4.34, "Research Skills." (To evaluate research papers, see the evaluation forms for writing, revising, and proofreading in the *Assessment Portfolio,* 7.1–7.10.)

► These prompts can be adapted for use as topics for oral reports or formal discussions. (To evaluate these projects, see the evaluation forms in the *Assessment Portfolio,* 7.17–7.19.)

The Parts of Speech. Have students identify the part of speech of each word in the following sentences from "The Rocking-Horse Winner."

1. "Is luck money, mother?" he asked, rather timidly.

    Is—verb
    luck—noun
    money—noun
    mother—noun
    he—pronoun
    asked—verb
    rather—adverb
    timidly—adverb

2. "He always talks about horse-races with Bassett," said Joan.

    He—pronoun
    always—adverb
    talks—verb
    about—preposition
    horse-races—noun
    with—preposition
    Bassett—noun
    said—verb
    Joan—noun

3. He pursed his mouth tight and watched.

    He—pronoun
    pursed—verb
    his—pronoun used as adjective
    mouth—noun
    tight—adverb
    and—conjunction
    watched—verb

4. "Oh, but we're careful then," said Bassett.

    Oh—interjection
    but—conjunction
    we're—pronoun and verb
    careful—adjective
    then—adverb
    said—verb
    Bassett—noun

LANGUAGE LAB   THE PARTS OF SPEECH

Thousands of years ago in ancient India, grammarians developed a method for classifying words in categories or types. These types are known as the **parts of speech**. The eight parts of speech are shown on the following chart.

THE EIGHT PARTS OF SPEECH	
1	A **noun** is the name of a person, place, thing, or idea. *D. H. Lawrence, cats, London, drama, tradition, interpretation*
2	A **pronoun** is a word that stands for or refers to a noun. *she, it, them, anyone, something, which, that, whose*
3	A **verb** is a word that describes an action or a state of being. *compose, wed, was watching, waltz, is, are, were, be, appear, grow*
4	An **adjective** is a word that modifies a noun or a pronoun. *bold, secretive, stout, rosy, intelligent, agreeable*
5	An **adverb** is a word that modifies a verb, an adjective, or another adverb. *lightly, perfectly, soon, too, rather, now, inside*
6	A **preposition** is a word that shows a relationship between a noun or a pronoun and some other word in a sentence. *about, among, at, beside, by, down, for, from, in, of, throughout, with*
7	A **conjunction** is a word that is used to join words, groups of words, or complete sentences. *and, or, nor, for, but, so, yet, because, since, unless, when, but also*
8	An **interjection** is a word used to express an emotion or to indicate a pause in speech or writing. *O, wow, yes, aha, yikes, oh, hurrah, well, thanks*

SENTENCE MODEL

INT	ADJ	N	ADV	V	CONJ	V	PRO	V	N
"O,	crafty	Elizabeth	cleverly	confounded	and	tricked	us,"	cried	Philip.

LANGUAGE ARTS SURVEY

For additional help, see the Language Arts Survey, 2.3–2.29.

Exercise A   Identifying the Parts of Speech

Identify the part of speech of each italicized word in the following paragraph. Use *n.* for noun, *pro.* for pronoun, *v.* for verb, *adj.* for adjective, *adv.* for adverb, *prep.* for preposition, *conj.* for conjunction, and *int.* for interjection.

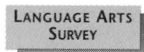

EXAMPLE: <u>Robin</u> robbed from the rich, but <u>he</u> gave to the poor.

Was Robin Hood a real person? [1] *No,* say most scholars, at least not a person [2] *whom* we can identify with any certainty. Some [3] *antiquarians* and historians have attempted to identify a [4] *historical* person who fits the facts of the legend, [5] *but* they have been unsuccessful. The oldest of the Robin Hood ballads date [6] *from* the fourteenth century. These early ballads [7] *include* "Robin Hood and the Monk" and the "Lytyll Geste of Robin Hode." Evidence in the early ballads suggests that [8] *they* are set in Yorkshire. However, later songs and stories [9] *usually* place the events of the legend in Nottinghamshire. [10] *In* neither place does an independent historical record of the outlaw hero survive.

Exercise B Using the Parts of Speech in Writing

Many words in English can be used as more than one part of speech. Identify the part of speech of each italicized word below. Then, write a new sentence using each word as the part of speech given in parentheses.

LANGUAGE ARTS SURVEY

For additional help, see the Language Arts Survey, 2.30 and 2.31.

EXAMPLE: Students in Ms. Battacherya's class staged a *mock* naval battle. (Use as a verb.)
            adj.
      Students in Ms. Battacherya's class staged a mock naval battle.
          v.
      "You mock me at your peril," said Queen Elizabeth to the Spanish Ambassador.

1. The *plot* of D. H. Lawrence's story is fascinating. (Use as a verb.)
2. The local repertory company will *stage* "The Rising of the Moon" in April. (Use as a noun.)
3. The cat requires feeding now, no if's, *and's,* or but's. (Use as a conjunction.)
4. The *rest* of the story tells of the boy's obsession with winning more money. (Use as a verb.)
5. "*Wow,*" said Chandra, "that Robin was pretty crafty." (Use as a verb.)
6. One *spring* morning, the cat lay on the windowsill, contemplating its name and eyeing the bluejays in the yard. (Use as a noun.)
7. Mikail and Tyrone sang the Irish ballad quite *well.* (Use as an interjection.)
8. To find Robin and Marion, go *past* the village and into the greenwood. (Use as a noun.)
9. "Will you *open* an account for me, uncle?" asked Paul. (Use as an adverb.)
10. Unfortunately, Paul never came *to.* (Use as a preposition.)

Exercise C Expanding Sentences Using Vivid Adjectives and Adverbs

Rewrite each sentence from Exercise B, above, adding at least one colorful or interesting adjective or adverb.

LANGUAGE ARTS SURVEY

For additional help, see the Language Arts Survey, 2.19–2.23 and 2.35.

EXAMPLE: Students in Ms. Baltacherya's class <u>brilliantly</u> staged a mock naval battle.

ANSWERS FOR LANGUAGE LAB (CONT.)

3. The cat *graciously but forcefully* requires feeding now, no if's, and's, or but's.

4. The rest of the story tells of the boy's *perverse* obsession with winning more money.

5. "Wow," said Chandra, *mesmerized,* "that Robin was pretty crafty."

6. One spring morning, the cat lay on the windowsill, *stupidly* contemplating its name and *hopelessly* eyeing the bluejays in the yard.

7. Mikail and *toothless* Tyrone sang the Irish ballad quite well.

8. To find Robin and Marion, go past the village and into the *lush* greenwood.

9. "Will you open an account for me, *dear* uncle?" asked Paul.

10. Unfortunately, Paul never *wholly* came to.

ANSWERS FOR LANGUAGE LAB

Exercise A Identifying the Parts of Speech

1. *No*—int.
2. *whom*—pro.
3. *antiquarians*—n.
4. *historical*—adj.
5. *but*—conj.
6. *from*—prep.
7. *include*—v.
8. *they*—pro.
9. *usually*—adv.
10. *In*—prep.

Exercise B Using the Parts of Speech in Writing

Responses will vary. Possible sentences are given.

1. *plot*—n.
The boy and the butler *plot* to conceal their gambling from the boy's parents.

2. *stage*—v.
When Tally's friends told her to "break a leg," they didn't think she would fall off the *stage* and do so.

3. *and*—n.
I fed the cat *and* the dog.

4. *rest*—n.
The story was so suspenseful I couldn't *rest* until I finished it.

5. *Wow*—int.
Carter *wowed* the audience with his performance as the Ragged Man in *The Rising of the Moon.*

6. *spring*—adj.
Elizabeth gave her speech at Tilbury in the summer, not in the *spring.*

7. *well*—adv.
"*Well,*" said Augusta, "I've never heard of a cat having more than one name."

8. *past*—adv.
In the *past* the Sergeant had sung nationalist ballads.

9. *open*—v.
The door sprang *open.*

10. *to*—adv.
Elizabeth delivered her speech *to* the troops at Tilbury.

Exercise C Expanding Sentences Using Vivid Adjectives and Adverbs

1. The *shocking* plot of D. H. Lawrence's story is fascinating.

2. The *talented* local repertory company will stage *The Rising of the Moon* in April.

(cont.)

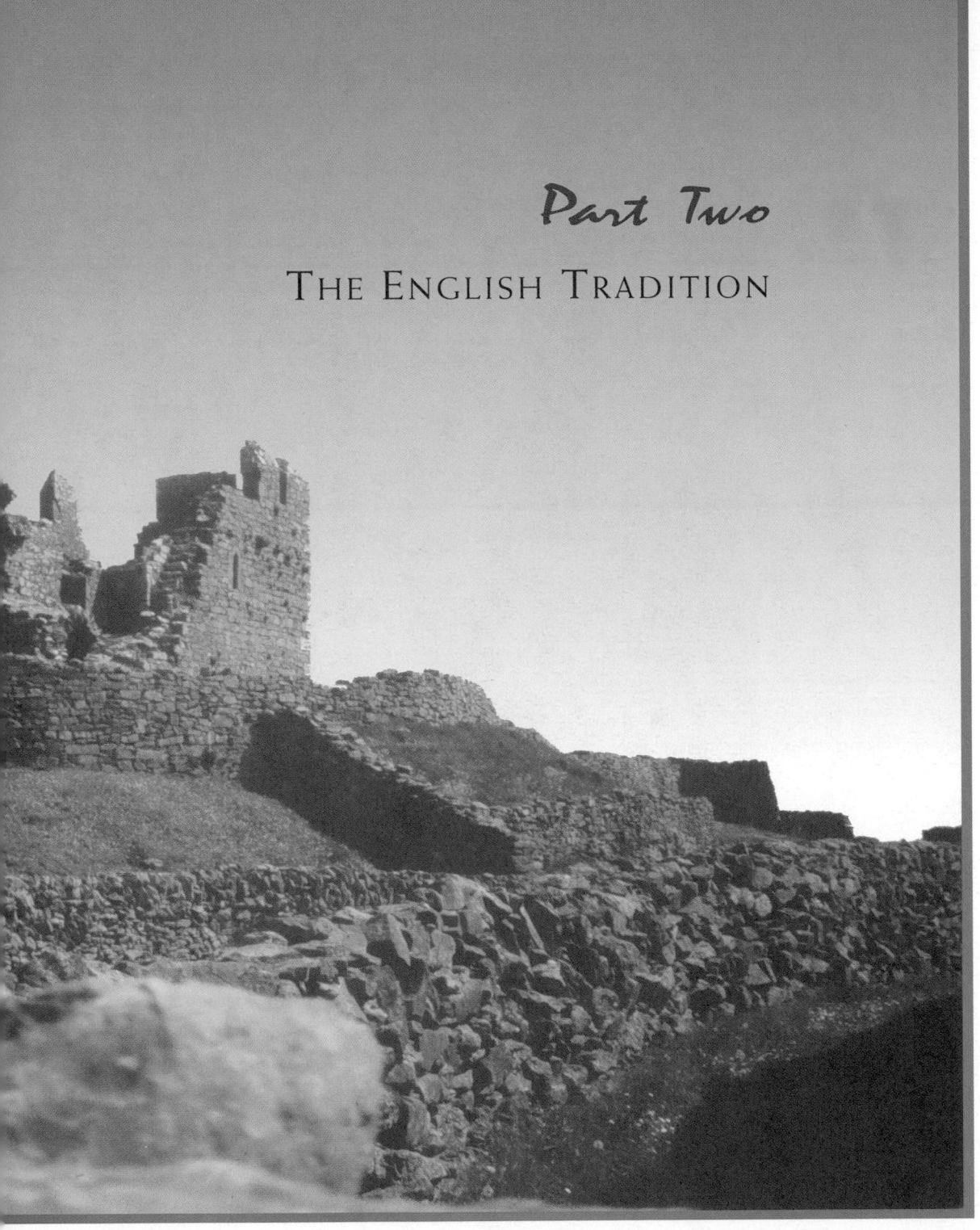

Part Two

THE ENGLISH TRADITION

UNIT 2   THE ANGLO-SAXON PERIOD   (449–1066)

King Ælla's Messengers before Ragnar Lodbroke's Sons. J. A. Malmström, 1857. Norrköping Art Museum, Sweden

GOALS/OBJECTIVES

Studying this unit will enable students to
- interpret and appreciate Anglo-Saxon literature
- summarize the history of pre-Christian England and its literature
- name the sources and tell the history of Old English
- relate themes common in Anglo-Saxon literature to characteristics of Anglo-Saxon society
- describe the achievements of Boadicea, Bede, and Alfred
- describe and explain the influence of Christianity on Anglo-Saxon literature and culture
- identify and give examples of the major characteristics of Anglo-Saxon verse

You each have something divine in your soul, namely Reason and Memory and a discerning will to make choices in life.

—Alfred the Great
King of the West Saxons

HISTORICAL NOTE

Alfred the Great (849–899) became king of Wessex, one of the seven Anglo-Saxon kingdoms, in 871. His military exploits contained Danish invaders to the northern part of England and thus made possible the emergence of England as a nation. His commitment to learning did much to further the creation of a native English literature. Alfred subsidized the creation of works in the Old English language and himself translated many Latin works into Old English. These works included Boethius's *Consolation of Philosophy* and, some believe, the *Ecclesiastical History* of the Venerable Bede.

ANCIENT BRITAIN

The Roman historian Tacitus wrote that the British Isles lay "at the outer edge of the world, almost into the whirlpools," and recalled how sailors, blown there by a hurricane, had encountered creatures half human and half animal. A later Byzantine historian, Procipius, described Britain as inhabited by the souls of the dead, ferried across the Channel from the Continent. To the ancient classical world, Britain was a far-off mystery—remote, shrouded in mist, and surrounded by stormy seas.

In ancient times, the largest of the islands was inhabited by **Britons**, the next largest by **Gaels** (gālz). These were **Celtic** (sel´ tik *or* kel´ tik) peoples who came from the European continent at an uncertain date. Today, in parts of the British Isles, languages descended from those of the **Celts** (seltz *or* keltz) are still spoken. These surviving Celtic languages include Irish, Scottish Gaelic, Welsh, and Breton.

The Celts of ancient Britain were farmers and hunters. Their society was organized into clans ruled by tribal chieftains elected from among a class of pagan priests. These priests, the **Druids**, composed hymns, poems, and historical records; studied the movements of heavenly bodies; served as judges; and conducted religious ceremonies in secret places in the woods and at sites such as **Stonehenge.**

Early seventh-century brooch from Kingston Down, Kent. Liverpool, Merseyside Country Museum

Little is known about the early inhabitants of Britain or about their Druid priests. Popular history pictures the Britons as savages, for they dressed in animal skins, conducted gruesome sacrifices, and according to contemporary accounts, went into battle unclothed and painted with blue dyes. However, they also produced haunting myths, made precise astronomical observations, and created beautiful artifacts—bracelets, necklaces, pottery, and earthworks like the **White Horse of Uffington.**

In 75 BC, Britain was invaded by a tribe from the Continent called the **Belgæ** (bel´ jē). They brought with them a new, heavy plow that revolutionized agriculture on the island. So began the process of clearing the land of its ancestral forests.

Anglo-Saxon gatehouse at Dover

LITERARY EVENTS

► = British Events

2000 BC	1000 BC	500 BC	100 BC	AD 100

►2200–2100 BC. Stonehenge built

►600–500 BC. Britains arrive

►100–55 BC. Belgæ invade Britain

►55–54 BC. Julius Cæsar invades Britain

►AD 43. Romans under Emperor Claudius conquer Britain

►AD 50. Roman colony of Londinium (later London) founded

►AD 60–61. Queen Boadicea leads revolt of Britons against Roman rule

HISTORICAL EVENTS

70   UNIT TWO / THE ANGLO-SAXON PERIOD

THEMATIC CURRENTS

Use the following selections to explore these themes with your students.

SEPARATION
• "The Wife's Lament," 88
• from *Beowulf,* 99
• from "The Seafarer," 117
• "Wulf and Eadwacer," 117

RELIGION
• "The Conversion of King Edwin," 76
• "The Story of Cædmon," including "Cædmon's Hymn," 82
• from *Beowulf,* 99

STRUGGLE
• Anglo-Saxon Riddles, 94
• "The Wife's Lament," 88
• from *Beowulf,* 99
• "Wulf and Eadwacer," 117

ROMAN BRITAIN

In 54 BC, the Roman general **Julius Cæsar** (100–44 BC) led a force across the English Channel, defeated the Britons, and returned to the Continent. The next year he returned, again defeated the Britons, and again left without establishing a settlement. Almost a century later, in AD 43, the Romans under the emperor **Claudius** (10 BC–AD 54) conquered Britain, introducing their law, culture, and Latin language to the island. They built roads and military fortifications, such as Hadrian's Wall, that stand to this day. They also established colonies, like Colchester and London, that later became great cities.

Photograph: Jürgen Liepe

Julius Cæsar. Antikensammlung im Pergamonmuseum, Staatliche Museen zu Berlin

BOADICEA, THE CELTIC WARRIOR QUEEN

In AD 60, Prasutagus, king of a tribe of Britons called the Iceni, died, leaving his wife, **Boadicea** (bō´ ad ə sē´ ə), to rule in his place. In that same year, Romans plundered the territory of the Iceni. In retaliation, the Iceni revolted against their Roman rulers. Boadicea gathered a native army and led it into battle, destroying Colchester and London. Eventually, the Romans overcame Boadicea, but not before the queen and her warriors had killed some 70,000 Roman colonists and soldiers. Astonishingly, Boadicea had very nearly succeeded in defeating the most powerful military force in the world.

The Warrior Queen. This statue of Boadicea stands today by the River Thames, next to the British Houses of Parliament.

THE COMING OF THE ANGLO-SAXONS

Early in the fifth century, Rome called its legions home to protect its capital from invasion by barbarians. This withdrawal of Roman might left Britain vulnerable. Over the next hundred years, fierce Germanic invaders from the Continent crossed the North Sea (see the map on page 72). The first to arrive were the **Jutes**, a tribe from the Danish peninsula. In AD 449, they conquered the southwestern province that was to become the kingdom of Kent. Other Germanic tribes, the **Angles** and the **Saxons**,

▶AD 512–20. Historical period of events recounted in *Beowulf*

AD 400	AD 450	AD 500	AD 550	AD 600

▶AD 410. Last Roman legions leave Britain

▶AD 432. St. Patrick begins mission in Ireland

▶AD 449. Jutes invade England, settling in province of Kent

▶AD 450–500. Anglo-Saxons invade England

▶AD 449. Anglo-Saxons and Britons, including the legendary Arthur, clash in Battle of Badon Hill

▶AD 597. Augustine sent to convert King Ethelbert of Kent to Christianity

LITERARY CURRENTS

Use the following selections to explore these concepts and techniques with your students.

EXPOSITORY WRITING

• "The Conversion of King Edwin," 76

• "The Story of Cædmon," including "Cædmon's Hymn," 82

ANGLO-SAXON VERSE

• "The Story of Cædmon," including "Cædmon's Hymn," 82

• from *Beowulf,* 99

LYRIC POEM

• "The Story of Cædmon," including Cædmon's Hymn, 82

• "The Wife's Lament," 88

• from "The Seafarer," 117

• "Wulf and Eadwacer," 117

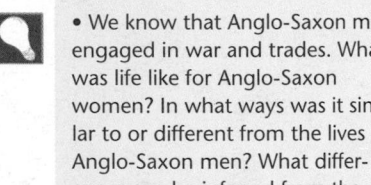

LITERARY TECHNIQUE

Oral Literature. Have students discuss times in their lives when they have shared stories in group settings. Many students have had the experience of sharing stories around a campfire. Point out that when young people today do this, they are engaging in an ancient practice, a form of entertainment that predated television by many millennia.

HISTORICAL NOTE

• Slavery was the rule in Anglo-Saxon England. Most farms were worked by slaves. Men could become slaves by going too far into debt, or they could be sentenced to slavery as punishment for a crime. A man could sell his wife and children as slaves to pay off a debt (wives had no similar right). Any children born to a slave were the property of the owner. Slaves had no rights at all. They could be killed or tortured at will and had no standing in courts of law.

• We know that Anglo-Saxon men engaged in war and trades. What was life like for Anglo-Saxon women? In what ways was it similar to or different from the lives of Anglo-Saxon men? What differences can be inferred from the literature selections in this unit?

Anglo-Saxon dwellings

followed, first raiding along the eastern coast of Britain, then establishing outposts, and finally conquering much of the country. The Angles established three kingdoms in the northern and midland sections of the island—Northumbria, Mercia, and East Anglia. The Saxons established three kingdoms in the south—Wessex (West Saxony), Essex (East Saxony), and Sussex (South Saxony). From the name of one of these tribes come the modern words *England* (*Angle-lond*) and *English* (*Angle-isc*).

ANGLO-SAXON CULTURE

The warlike, seafaring Anglo-Saxons brought to Britain legends about ancient Germanic heroes and kings. Some of these legends, like the later heroic epic *Beowulf,* told of giants, demons, sea monsters, trolls, and fire-breathing dragons. Warriors were celebrated in heroic **lays,** or songs, sung at feasts by a minstrel called a **gleeman** or **scop** (shôp), literally, a "shaper." Kings would entertain friends, retainers, and visitors at feasts held in great mead halls, so called for the **mead,** or wine made from fermented honey, that the warriors drank. The scop recited verse based on the exploits of great warriors of the tribe's past, often adding fanciful details about impossible feats of courage and strength. These lays were performed to the accompaniment of a **harp,** or lyre. Such orally composed songs not only provided entertainment but also embodied the heroic ideals of the people and kept alive their history.

Anglo-Saxon society was organized into a class of warriors called **earls** or **thanes,** a class of freemen called **churls,** and a class of slaves called **thralls.** The king depended for protection on his earls and for guidance on a council of wise elders, the *Witenagemot.* Anglo-Saxon justice was simple and crude. A wrong done to one's kin required redress in kind or a payment of treasure, the *wergild,* or "man-money." Blood feuds, invasions, and desire for land or treasure led to frequent warfare.

Life among the Anglo-Saxons was harsh and unpredictable. Death from disease, famine, battle wounds, or storms at sea could come at any time, depending upon the whims of the goddess *Wyrd* (Würd), or "fate." If a person were courageous and not fated to die, then

LITERARY EVENTS

► = British Events

►AD 731. Bede completes *Ecclesiastical History of the English People*

►AD 700–750. *Beowulf* composed orally in kingdom of Northumbria or Mercia

►AD 658–80. "Cædmon's Hymn" composed

AD 650	AD 700	AD 750	AD 800	AD 850

►AD 664. Church of England organized at Council of Whitby

►AD 673–735. The Venerable Bede

►AD 750–825. Cynewulf, author of religious poetry and possibly of riddles

►AD 790–878. Danes (Vikings) invade England

►AD 849. King Alfred the Great born

HISTORICAL EVENTS

72   *UNIT TWO / THE ANGLO-SAXON PERIOD*

he might survive. As the legendary hero Beowulf says in the poem that bears his name, "Fate often saves an undoomed man if his courage is good."

The Anglo-Saxons believed their kings to be descended from divinities such as *Tiu,* god of war; *Woden,* king of the gods; *Thor,* god of thunder and the sky; and *Freia,* goddess of the home. The names of these gods survive, today, in our names for days of the week: *Tuesday* (*Tiwesdæg*), *Wednesday* (*Wodnesdæg*), *Thursday* (*þuresdæg*), and *Friday* (*Frigedæg*).

THE COMING OF CHRISTIANITY

Christianity first reached Britain during the Roman occupation. In the fifth century, neighboring Ireland had been converted to Christianity by the renowned **St. Patrick** (*circa* AD 385–*circa* 461), and soon thereafter Christian immigrants from Ireland crossed into Scotland and northern England. However, the conversion of the whole of England to Christianity came after the arrival of **Augustine** (d. AD 604), sent by Pope Gregory the Great in AD 597 to convert King Ethelbert of Kent.

The coming of Christianity to England meant the establishment of **monasteries,** centers of religious retreat and learning where **scribes** produced books by hand, writing on vellum parchment made of calves' or sheep's skin. Many of these books were religious works, such as saints' lives and collections of sermons, but some were copies of the oral literature of the common people. To the labors of the monks and to a great king named Alfred we owe the survival of Anglo-Saxon literature in written form.

ALFRED THE GREAT

In the eighth and ninth centuries, the **Danes,** or **Vikings,** invaded Anglo-Saxon England. Arriving from Scandinavia in longboats, they plundered monasteries, burnt cities and towns, and conquered much of the island, including three of what were then the four major Anglo-Saxon kingdoms: **Northumbria, Mercia,** and **East Anglia.** England may well have become a Danish nation if not for **Alfred the Great,** ruler of the fourth major kingdom, **Wessex.** In AD 878, Alfred, whose epilepsy did not prevent him from becoming a great warrior, defeated the Danes and unified southern and central England under his command, so earning the title of

Monasteries. *Reconstruction of stained glass window from Jarrow, birthplace of the Venerable Bede (see page 76)*

© Bede's World, Jarrow

ADDITIONAL QUESTIONS AND ACTIVITIES

Research Anglo-Saxon England. The following topics are suitable for research reports on early Britain and Anglo-Saxon England:

1. Stonehenge
2. Cæsar's Invasion of Britain
3. Boadicea's Revolt against Roman Rule
4. The Anglo-Saxon Invasion
5. The Origins of English
6. Anglo-Saxon Social and Political Structures
7. Women in Anglo-Saxon England
8. The Life and Works of Alfred the Great
9. The Influence of Christianity on Anglo-Saxon Literature
10. The Anglo-Saxon Heroic Ideal

HISTORICAL NOTE

The following is a list of kings of England during the Old English period.

802–839	Egbert, King of Wessex
839–858	Ethelwulf
858–860	Ethelbald
860–866	Ethelbert
866–871	Ethelred I
871–899	Alfred the Great
899–924	Edward the Elder
924–940	Athelstan the Glorious
940–946	Edmund I
946–955	Edred
955–959	Edwy the Fair
959–975	Edgar the Peaceful
975–978	Edward the Martyr
978–1016	Ethelred II the Unready
1016–1016	Edmund II
1016–1035	Canute the Dane
1035–1040	Harold I
1040–1042	Hardecanute
1042–1066	Edward the Confessor
1066–1066	Harold II (died in the Norman Conquest

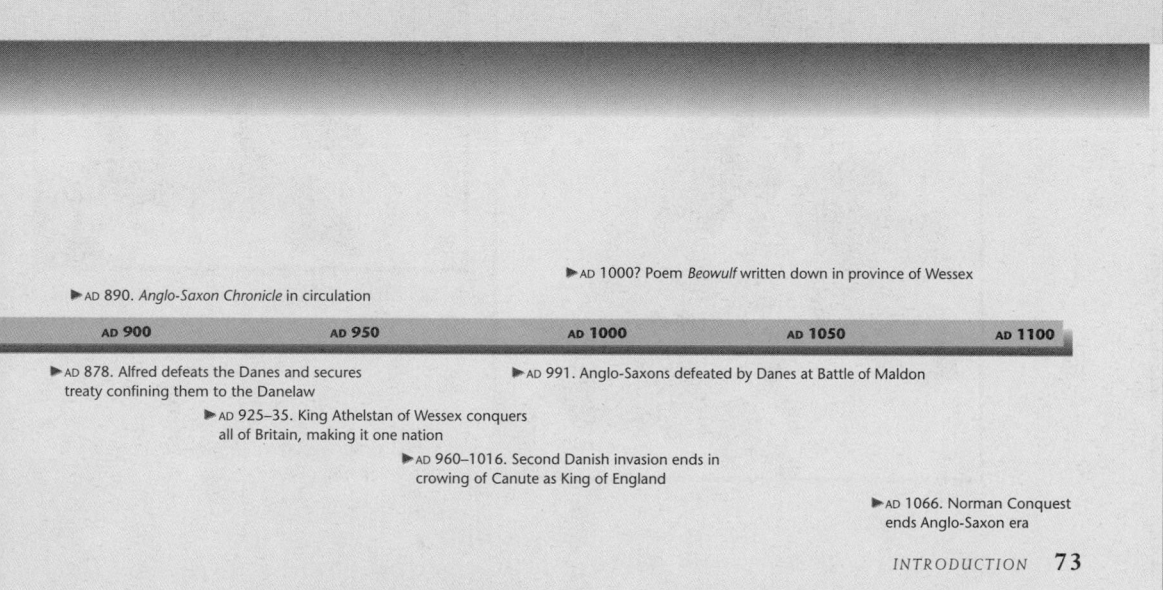

► AD 1000? Poem *Beowulf* written down in province of Wessex

► AD 890. *Anglo-Saxon Chronicle* in circulation

| AD 900 | AD 950 | AD 1000 | AD 1050 | AD 1100 |

► AD 878. Alfred defeats the Danes and secures treaty confining them to the Danelaw

► AD 991. Anglo-Saxons defeated by Danes at Battle of Maldon

► AD 925–35. King Athelstan of Wessex conquers all of Britain, making it one nation

► AD 960–1016. Second Danish invasion ends in crowing of Canute as King of England

► AD 1066. Norman Conquest ends Anglo-Saxon era

INTRODUCTION **73**

Alfred devoted much of his energies not only to defending against military attacks, but also to preventing them by diplomacy and by establishing strong defenses. Nevertheless, his greatest accomplishments are probably in the realm of culture and education. During the peace from AD 878 to 885, Alfred invited scholars from parts of Britain and the Continent to visit him, and he learned Latin. By 887, he was translating to English those Latin works which he believed "most necessary for all men to know." These included Bede's *Ecclesiastical History* (see page 76), Orosius's *7 Books of Histories Against the Pagans,* Augustine of Hippo's *Soliloquies,* and Boethius's *Consolation of Philosophy,* as well as a manual for priests for the training of parishioners. *Alfred the Great: Asser's Life of King Alfred and Other Contemporary Sources,* ed. and trans. by S. Keynes and M. Lapidge (1983), is a new translation of an AD 893 biography.

bretwalda, or "King of Britain." Alfred forced the Danes to accept a treaty confining them to an area of northern and eastern England called the **Danelaw.** King Alfred's daughter Ethelfled ruled Mercia as regent and queen, built cities, and captured other cities from the Danes.

After securing the future of the English nation, Alfred turned his attention to education and learning. A pious king, he believed that the strength of his country depended on the spread of education and of the Christian faith. Therefore, he conceived a plan to rebuild the monasteries destroyed by the Vikings and to

> render into the language that we all understand [English] some of those books that are most necessary for all to know and bring it to pass that the freeborn youth of England will devote themselves to learning until they can read English.

Alfred sponsored the translation of many books into the Old English language, including works of history, philosophy, and religion. He also sponsored the writing of a year-by-year account of English history up to his time, the *Anglo-Saxon Chronicle.* The *Chronicle,* along with Bede's *Ecclesiastical History,* is among our most valuable sources of information about the period.

THE END OF THE ANGLO-SAXON ERA

Between AD 925 and AD 939, King Athelstan of the West Saxons conquered the rest of the island of Britain, making it one nation. The Anglo-Saxon peace, however, was not to last. In AD 960, another wave of Danish invasions began, culminating in AD 1016 with the crowning of Canute, a Dane, as king. Thereafter, the country passed briefly back into English control. However, a new threat awaited the Anglo-Saxons. In AD 1066, a Norman duke, William the Conqueror, crossed the English Channel and defeated the English king Harold at the Battle of Hastings, bringing the Anglo-Saxon era to a close.

Britain circa AD 886 (above), showing Wessex and the Danelaw

Britain circa AD 800 (left), showing the seven Anglo-Saxon kingdoms

Echoes:

Ancient and Anglo-Saxon England

Sutton Hoo helmet.
British Museum

[Boadicea] was very tall, the glance of her eye most fierce, her voice harsh. A mass of red hair fell to her hips. Around her neck hung a necklace of gold. She wore a multi-colored tunic fastened by a brooch. She was terrifying to look upon.

—from an account by the Roman historian Dio Cassius

Hale be thou, earth, mother of men,
Be thou with growing things in God's embrace,
Filled with food for the good of men

—from "Æcerbot," an Anglo-Saxon spell or charm

Therefore I sing   and recite a tale
Before many men   in the mead-hall gathered

With clear voice   for our victorious leader
Raise up a song   to the sound of the harp.

—from "Widsith," an Anglo-Saxon poem that tells the story of a minstrel, or scop

Fate often saves an undoomed man if his courage is good.

—from *Beowulf*

Golden Horns.
The National Museum, Copenhagen

ENRICHMENT ACTIVITIES

 Students can write about or discuss the ways in which a political leader's religion can be significant for his or her country. (This can be linked to current events.)

SUPPORT FOR LEP STUDENTS

Explain that Old English and Modern English are different and separate languages and that students are not expected to know or to learn Old English.

IDIOMS

shed light on—reveal information that helps one to understand something

fair weather—good weather

ADDITIONAL VOCABULARY

earnest—something given as a pledge or token

aforesaid—mentioned before

partaker—one who participates

confer—speak with

verily—truly

hitherto—until now

forward—help or advance

exhortation—urging

emerge—come into view

PREREADING

"The Conversion of King Edwin"
from *Ecclesiastical History of the English People*
by Saint Bede the Venerable

ABOUT THE AUTHOR

A page from the Grimbald Gospels. British Library, MS Add. 34890 fol. IOV. Courtesy of the British Library

Saint Bede the Venerable (AD 672– or 673–735) was born in Jarrow, in the kingdom of Northumbria. He entered the Monastery of St. Peter in nearby Wearmouth at the age of seven. At nineteen, he was ordained a deacon; at thirty, a priest. Like other monastics of his time, Bede wrote in Latin. He traveled very little, but his fame spread throughout Europe due to his writings on subjects as varied as history, poetry, grammar, mathematics, science, the scriptures, and lives of the saints. Bede's histories make fascinating reading not only for the light that they shed on the distant Anglo-Saxon past but also for their engaging accounts of miraculous and legendary events. In his histories, Bede introduced the practice of dating events from the birth of Christ (i.e., from AD 0, where AD is an abbreviation for the Latin *Anno Domini,* meaning "the year of our Lord"). This method of dating was adopted throughout Europe and is still in use today. Bede was canonized (made a saint of the Roman Catholic Church) in 1899, eleven hundred years after his death.

ABOUT THE SELECTION

Most notable among Bede's works is the *Historia ecclesiastica gentis Anglorum,* or ***Ecclesiastical History of the English People.*** Bede's five-book Latin history of the Church in England covers the period from Cæsar's invasion of Britain (55–54 BC) to his own time (the history was finished around AD 731). King Alfred considered the book important enough to have it translated into Old English, the language of the common people. **"The Conversion of King Edwin"** comes from *Book II* of Bede's history and relates the process by which Christian missionaries converted the Anglo-Saxon kings. The selection shows the dramatic contrast between the Anglo-Saxons' grim view of the afterlife and the positive alternative offered by the missionaries. The pre-Christian, or pagan, Anglo-Saxons believed that a warrior who died bravely in battle would go after death to a land reserved for heroes, Valhalla. For others, the future after death was uncertain. The final paragraph of the selection, which compares the time before, during, and after life to the flight of a sparrow, is one of the most famous in all of English literature.

GOALS/OBJECTIVES

Studying this lesson will enable students to
• empathize with Edwin's uncertainties about the afterlife
• describe Bede's accomplishments and explain the historical significance of Bede's writings
• describe some key differences between Anglo-Saxon paganism and Christianity

• explain what an allegory is and recognize allegories as they encounter them in their reading
• use a card catalog to find books on specific topics
• recognize and correct run-ons

The British Museum

"The Conversion of King Edwin"

FROM *Ecclesiastical History of the English People*

SAINT BEDE THE VENERABLE

At this time the nation of the Northumbrians, that is, the nation of the Angles that live on the north side of the river Humber, with their king, Edwin, received the faith through the preaching of Paulinus.[1] This Edwin, as a reward of his receiving the faith, and as an earnest of his share in the heavenly kingdom, received an increase of that which he enjoyed on earth, for he reduced under his dominion all the borders of Britain that were provinces either of the aforesaid nation, or of the Britons, a thing which no British king had ever done before. . . .

For some time he delayed to receive the word of God at the preaching of Paulinus, and used to sit several hours alone, and seriously to ponder with himself what he was to do, and what religion he was to follow. Then the man of God came to him, laid his right hand on his head, and asked whether he knew that sign.[2] The king in a trembling condition, was ready to fall down at his feet, but he raised him up, and in a familiar manner said to him, "Behold, by the help of God you have escaped the hands of the enemies whom you feared. Behold you have of His gift obtained the kingdom which you desired. Take heed not to delay that which you promised to perform; embrace the faith, and keep the precepts of Him who, delivering you from <u>temporal adversity</u>, has raised you to the honor of

❶
According to Bede, what reward does Edwin receive for converting to Christianity?

1. **Paulinus.** Pope Gregory I sent Paulinus as a missionary to Northumbria in AD 601.
2. **that sign.** The laying on of hands is a ceremony for transmitting spiritual grace to the recipient.

WORDS FOR EVERYDAY USE:

ec • cle • si • as • ti • cal (e klē´ zē as´ ti kəl) *adj.,* having to do with the church

tem • po • ral (tem´ pə rəl) *adj.,* lasting only for a time, limited; of this world, not spiritual

ad • ver • si • ty (ad vʉr´ sə tē) *n.,* misfortune, trouble

"THE CONVERSION OF KING EDWIN" **77**

HISTORICAL NOTE

From AD 616 to 632, Edwin was king of Northumbria and was recognized across England as overlord. Edwin married the princess Aethelburth of Kent, a Christian. She was responsible for bringing Paulinus to Northumbria because she wanted to convert Edwin and his subjects. In 632, Northumbria was invaded by the united armies of King Cadwallon of Gwynedd and King Penda of Mercia. Edwin was killed and his army defeated. Aethelburth and Paulinus fled, and Christianity was suppressed for a time.

ANSWERS TO GUIDED READING QUESTIONS

❶ The counselor compares life to the flight of a sparrow.

❷ The priest rejects the old gods because his faith in them has not brought him wealth or influence.

ANSWERS TO SELECTION CHECK TEST 4.2.1

EX. Who wrote "The Conversion of King Edwin"?
The selection was written by Saint Bede the Venerable.

1. What kingdom was ruled by Edwin?
Edwin ruled Northumbria.

2. Who was Paulinus?
He was a Catholic priest and missionary.

3. What did Paulinus want Edwin to do? Did Edwin do it?
Paulinus wanted Edwin to convert to Christianity, which he did.

4. Why did Edwin meet with his friends and counselors?
Edwin wanted his friends and counselors to convert also.

5. What opinion was offered by Edwin's friends and counselors?
They agreed that Christianity was preferable to the old religion.

---

a temporal kingdom; and if, from this time forward, you shall be obedient to His will, which through me He <u>signifies</u> to you, He will not only deliver you from the everlasting torments of the wicked, but also make you partaker with Him of His eternal kingdom in Heaven."

The king, hearing these words, answered, that he was both willing and bound to receive the faith which he taught; but that he would confer about it with his principal friends and counselors, to the end that if they also were of his opinion, they might all together be cleansed in Christ the Fountain of Life. Paulinus consenting, the king did as he said; for, holding a council with the wise men,[3] he asked of every one in particular what he thought of the new doctrine, and the new worship that was preached. To which the chief of his own priests, Coifi, immediately answered, "O king, consider what this is which is now preached to us; for I verily declare to you, that the religion which we have hitherto professed has, as far as I can learn, no virtue in it. For none of your people has applied himself more <u>diligently</u> to the worship of our gods than I; and yet there are many who receive greater favors from you, and are more preferred than I, and are more prosperous in all their undertakings. Now if the gods were good for any thing, they would rather forward me, who have

❶ To what does the wise counselor compare life as the Anglo-Saxons knew it?

❷ Why does the king's chief priest reject the old gods?

been more careful to serve them. It remains, therefore, that if upon examination you find those new doctrines, which are now preached to us, better and more <u>efficacious</u>, we immediately receive them without any delay."

Another of the king's chief men, approving of his words and exhortations, presently added: "The present life of man, O king, seems to me, in comparison to that time which is unknown to us, like to the swift flight of a sparrow through the room wherein you sit at supper in winter, with your commanders and ministers, and a good fire in the midst, whilst the storms of rain and snow prevail abroad; the sparrow, flying in at one door, and immediately out at another, whilst he is within, is safe from the wintry storm; but after a short space of fair weather, he immediately vanishes out of your sight, into the dark winter from which he had emerged. So this life of man appears for a short space, but of what went before, or what is to follow, we are utterly ignorant. If, therefore, this new doctrine contains something more certain, it seems justly to deserve to be followed." The other elders and king's counselors, by Divine inspiration, spoke to the same effect. ∎

---

3. **wise men.** These wise men are the Anglo-Saxon *Witenagemot*, or council of elders. From the Old English *witen*, "to know," comes our modern word *wit*.

WORDS FOR EVERYDAY USE:

sig • ni • fy (sig´ nə fī´) *vt.,* show by means of words or a sign

dil • i • gent • ly (dil´ ə jənt lē) *adv.,* with great care and attention

ef • fi • ca • cious (ef´ i kā´ shəs) *adj.,* effective, producing the desired result

---

VOCABULARY IN CONTEXT

• Being named captain of the team <u>signifies</u> more than just popularity.

• We all worked <u>diligently</u> throughout the day, and the project was completed on time.

• The doctors looked for the most <u>efficacious</u> remedy, without regard for cost.

Responding to the Selection

Do the arguments advanced by Edwin's counselors seem reasonable to you? Do you feel that Edwin had reason to forsake his old beliefs and embrace these new ones? Why, or why not? Answer these questions in your journal.

Reviewing the Selection

RECALLING

1. Who is Paulinus? What does he ask of King Edwin? What does Paulinus promise?

2. With whom does King Edwin meet?

3. Who is Coifi? What does he think of the old religion?

4. To what does the king's advisor compare the swift flight of a sparrow?

INTERPRETING

5. Why does Paulinus believe Edwin has a responsibility to "embrace the faith"?

6. Why does King Edwin hold a meeting?

7. What reason does Coifi give for forsaking the old religion?

8. What view of life and of the afterlife is implicit in the counselor's story of the sparrow?

SYNTHESIZING

9. In what ways does the new religion differ from the old religion? What makes the new religion appealing to the elders and to the king's counselors?

10. According to King Edwin's advisors, what is the purpose of religion? In what ways are their views similar to or different from your own?

Understanding Literature (Questions for Discussion)

1. **Narration. Narration,** one of the modes of writing, tells a story. Normally, stories are told by beginning with what happens first and continuing chronologically (through time) toward what happens last. Is Bede's story of Edwin's conversion told chronologically? Where does Bede deviate from a strict chronological ordering? Why do you think he does this? Is the technique effective? Can you think of a story that you have told nonchronologically? Why did you tell it so?

---

2. Allegory. The sparrow symbolizes life; its brief flight in the dining room symbolizes our short life on earth; the people and comforts in the room symbolize the pleasures of our lives on earth; sight symbolizes our knowledge, and so the room also symbolizes the limits of human knowledge; the winter storms outdoors symbolize the unknown periods before and after our lives. The allegory helps explain Bede's story because it makes more vivid the differences between paganism and Christianity.

▶ **Teaching Note:** Students might want to discuss the meanings of and differences among the terms *allegory, analogy, metaphor,* and *symbolism.* Refer to the Handbook of Literary Terms.

3. Purpose. The selection teaches the value of Christianity. Students may think that the author appears to be a Christian because his discussion is one-sided. If he had been a pagan, he might also have found something good to say about the old religion.

▶ **Teaching Note:** Students should find evidence that Bede was a Christian in the selection rather than in the instructional apparatus.

ANALYTIC SCALES FOR
RESPONDING IN WRITING

Assign a score from 1 to 25 for each grading criterion below. (For more detailed evaluation, see the evaluation forms for writing, revising, and proofreading, *Assessment Portfolio,* 7.1–7.10.)

1. An Allegory
• **Content/Unity.** The allegory presents a sensible extended comparison between two things.
• **Organization/Coherence.** The allegory is clearly organized, presenting both topics and several points of comparison.
• **Language/Style.** The allegory uses vivid, concrete, and precise nouns, verbs, and modifiers.
• **Conventions.** The allegory avoids errors in spelling, grammar, usage, mechanics, and manuscript form.

(cont.)

---

2. Allegory. An **allegory** is a work in which each element **symbolizes,** or represents, something else. The last paragraph of the selection contains an allegory comparing human life to the flight of a sparrow. To understand the allegory you need to determine what the characters and objects in the story symbolize. The story speaks of a sparrow, a dining room with a door, supper, winter storms, commanders and ministers, a fire, and our sight. What do these elements in the story symbolize?

3. Purpose or Aim. A writer's **aim** is the primary **purpose** that his or her work is meant to achieve. One purpose of "The Conversion of King Edwin" is to teach a lesson. What lesson does the selection teach? From reading the selection, can you tell whether Bede was a Christian or a pagan? How can you tell? How might the purpose be different if Bede were of a different religion?

Responding in Writing

1. **An Allegory.** Think of the story of the sparrow flying through the warm room and then out into the cold. Bede presents this story as an allegory for the life of an individual. An **allegory** is a story that seems simple but has another meaning altogether. What might be an allegory for working hard to accomplish a difficult task—perhaps running a marathon or climbing a tall mountain? Choose one of the following topics or one of your own. Then write an allegory to describe it.

   Possible topics: • saying goodbye to a friend
   • leaving home to go to college
   • studying for an important test

2. **A Persuasive Paragraph.** In order to convert King Edwin and his counsel, the missionary Paulinus had to be quite persuasive. What arguments did he use to convince them? How might you convince someone of something you feel strongly about? Maybe you have read a great book, and you are trying to convince a friend to read it. Maybe you are trying to change someone's mind about a political issue. Choose a topic for a persuasive paragraph. In a sentence, describe your position or stand on the topic. Then give two or three arguments to support your position.

Language Lab

Correcting Run-ons. Read the Language Arts Survey, 2.62, "Correcting Run-ons." Then revise the sentences below by changing punctuation and capitalization and adding words, as necessary.

1. Bede's history of Britain was not the first, it was partly based on *On the Fall of Britain,* written by Gildas, a Welshman, in AD 550.

ANALYTIC SCALES FOR RESPONDING IN WRITING (CONT.)

2. A Persuasive Paragraph
• **Content/Unity.** The paragraph presents a position and two or three strong arguments to support it.
• **Organization/Coherence.** The paragraph begins with a topic sentence that presents the writer's position. It then presents two or three arguments in a logical order (possibly from most important to least important or *vice versa*).
• **Language/Style.** The writer has made a clear argument using language that will move the reader intellectually and/or emotionally.
• **Conventions.** The paragraph avoids errors in spelling, grammar, usage, mechanics, and manuscript form.

2. According to stories told by early Welsh historians, one of the soldiers who fought against the Anglo-Saxons was named Arthur such stories gave rise to legends about King Arthur and the knights of the Round Table.

3. The early Germanic peoples, including the Anglo-Saxons, used alphabetic characters called *runes* to write inscriptions on stones, the runic alphabet is known as *futhark*.

4. The treasure of Sutton Hoo was found in 1939, at Sutton Hoo a seventh-century Anglo-Saxon king had been buried with a large number of jewels, coins, weapons, and tools he was entombed in a ninety-foot-long ship that had been hauled to the top of a one-hundred-foot-high cliff.

5. Our knowledge of the Anglo-Saxons comes from many sources these sources include inscriptions, histories, literature, and archaeological finds like Sutton Hoo.

PROJECTS

1. **Improvisation.** Take a few moments to think about what it was like to be one of King Edwin's counselors. Try to imagine other meetings that might have taken place. Then form groups of four to six students. Take turns acting out one of the scenes listed below, with one person playing King Edwin and the others playing the counselors. Use your imagination as you think about the issue that is up for discussion.

   - Discuss adding other lands to the kingdom. The group can discuss whether this will happen as a result of peaceful negotiation or of battle.

   - Discuss a dispute between two earls over the possession of a sword taken from an enemy warrior. Decide who should receive the sword and why.

2. **Community Involvement.** When someone enters a community and tries to make change, sometimes the change is positive, and sometimes the change is negative. In either case, asking people to think in new ways is rarely easy. How might you and your classmates try to make positive change in your community? You might want to change how people feel about litter and the environment, or you might want to make people more excited about becoming involved in town issues or school events. Work with other students to organize a convincing campaign.

"THE CONVERSION OF KING EDWIN" **81**

READER'S GUIDE
• Selection Worksheet, 2.2

ASSESSMENT PORTFOLIO
• Selection Check Test, 4.2.3
• Selection Test, 4.2.4

ESSENTIAL SKILLS PRACTICE BOOKS
• *Language*, 2.56, 2.125

AUDIOCASSETTE
• "Cædmon's Hymn," Track 3

ENRICHMENT ACTIVITIES

• Students can discuss or write about what inspires them to be creative. How much does inspiration depend on learning and study and how much on **ineffable** (non-sensory and unexplainable) factors?

• Students can research other creation stories and compare them to the creation story told in "Cædmon's Hymn."

• Students can try to identify Anglo-Saxon words from which Modern English words have evolved—e.g., *nu* (now), *heofon* (heaven), *Weard* (ward), *meahte* (might). They can check their hypotheses with a dictionary that gives etymologies.

SUPPORT FOR LEP STUDENTS

Play the audiotape recording of "Cædmon's Hymn" and discuss the poem's alliteration, stress, and cæsuras. (See About the Selection, this page.)

IDIOMS
all the same—nevertheless, anyway
sacred history—history as told in the Old and New Testaments

ADDITIONAL VOCABULARY
brother—monk
contempt—dislike and disrespect
expound—tell; explain; relate
commission—assign as a task or duty

PREREADING

"The Story of Cædmon," including "Cædmon's Hymn"
from *Ecclesiastical History of the English People*
by Saint Bede the Venerable

ABOUT THE AUTHOR

Saint Bede the Venerable (see biographical note, page 76) tells in *Book IV* of his *Ecclesiastical History* the story of an Anglo-Saxon poet named **Cædmon**. Excluding self-descriptions in poems of the period, Bede's "Story of Cædmon" provides the only biographical information we have about an early Anglo-Saxon poet. It also contains, embedded in the story, the earliest Old English poem that has survived, "Cædmon's Hymn." Little is known of Cædmon other than the miraculous story that Bede recounts. According to Bede, Cædmon was an illiterate cowherd and keeper of horses with no training as a singer of tales, or **scop**. One night after having listened to others sing at an entertainment, Cædmon went to sleep in his stable. A figure appeared to him in a dream and demanded that he sing about the creation of the world. Cædmon suddenly found himself able to compose beautiful poetry. The next day, he sang his hymn to Hild, the Abbess of the Monastery of Whitby, and to some "learned men." They all agreed that Cædmon had received a divine gift, a miraculous inspiration. Cædmon went on to compose many long poems on religious subjects. Among the surviving poems commonly attributed to Cædmon are a number of Old English Christian epics that retell stories from the Bible. These epics include *Genesis, Exodus, Daniel, Azariah, Judith,* and *Christ and Satan.*

ABOUT THE SELECTION

"The Story of Cædmon" is an excellent example of an early **miracle tale** of the kind usually found in saints' lives. Another interesting aspect of the selection is that it shows, at the very dawn of English literature, the important role played by women. It was a woman, Hild, founder of Whitby Abbey, who made possible the literary career of the first English writer whose name has come down to us.

"Cædmon's Hymn" was composed orally. It uses a verse form found in most Old English poetry. This poetry does not rhyme. It consists of lines that typically have four strong **stresses**, or beats. In the middle of the line is a pause, or **cæsura**. Often, the first three stressed words in the line begin with the same sound. This technique of repeating sounds at the beginnings of words is called **alliteration**. Here are two typical lines of Old English poetry, in the original and in translation. They are marked to show the stresses, cæsuras, and alliterating sounds. Note that *sc* in Old English had the sound of modern *sh*. The character þ (called a "thorn") had the sound of modern *th*.

Oft Scyld Scefing
Often Scyld Scef's son

sceaþena þreatum
from bands of robbers,

Monegum mægþum
from many tribes

meodo-setla ofteah
their mead-benches dragged away.

GOALS/OBJECTIVES

Studying this lesson will enable students to
• empathize with Cædmon's feelings of inadequacy and his sudden awareness of an unknown talent
• describe the life of Cædmon and his literary accomplishments
• explain what a cæsura is and identify cæsuras in a piece of writing

• define *alliteration* and identify alliteration in their reading
• recognize the passive voice in their reading and writing and rewrite passive passages in the active voice
• explain how translation affects a text
• recognize and correct errors in the capitalization of words that name sacred beings and writings

"The Story of Cædmon"
from <u>Ecclesiastical</u> History of the English People

SAINT BEDE THE VENERABLE

Heavenly grace had especially singled out a certain one of the brothers in the monastery ruled by this abbess,[1] for he used to compose devout and religious songs. Whatever he learned of holy Scripture with the aid of interpreters, he quickly turned into the sweetest and most moving poetry in his own language, that is to say English. It often happened that his songs kindled a contempt for this world and a longing for the life of Heaven in the hearts of many men. Indeed, after him others among the English people tried to compose religious poetry, but no one could equal him because he was not taught the art of song by men or by human <u>agency</u> but received this gift through heavenly grace. Therefore, he was never able to compose any vain and idle songs but only such as dealt with religion and were proper for his religious tongue to utter. As a matter of fact, he had lived in the <u>secular</u> estate until he was well advanced in age without learning any songs. Therefore, at feasts, when it was decided to have a good time by taking turns singing, whenever he would see the harp[2] getting close to his place, he got up in the middle of the meal and went home.

❶ What doesn't Cædmon do at feasts? Why not?

---

1. **abbess.** Hild, or Hilda, founded the Monastery of Whitby, a religious community that included both men and women. An *abbess* is the head of such a community, which is called an *abbey*.
2. **singing . . . harp.** In Anglo-Saxon times, poetry was performed aloud to the accompaniment of a harp.

WORDS FOR EVERYDAY USE:

ec • cle • si • as • ti • cal (e klē´ zē as´ ti kəl) *adj.*, having to do with the church

a • gen • cy (ā´jən sē) *n.*, force or power

sec • u • lar (sek´yə lər) *adj.*, of the world; not sacred or religious

"THE STORY OF CÆDMON" **83**

Once when he left the feast like this, he went to the cattle shed, which he had been assigned the duty of guarding that night. And after he had stretched himself out and gone to sleep, he dreamed that someone was standing at his side and greeted him, calling out his name. "Cædmon," he said, "sing me something."

And he replied, "I don't know how to sing; that is why I left the feast to come here—because I cannot sing."

"All the same," said the one who was speaking to him, "you have to sing for me."

"What must I sing?" he said.

And he said, "Sing about the Creation."

At this, Cædmon immediately began to sing verses in praise of God the Creator, which he had never heard before and of which the sense is this:

❶ *Who might this person be who appears in Cædmon's dream?*

❷ *How many different names for God can you find in Cædmon's hymn about the creation?*

[Cædmon's Hymn]

Nu sculon herigean
Now we must praise

Meotodes meahte
the Measurer's might

weorc Wuldor-Fæder
the work of the Glory-Father,

ece Drihten
eternal Lord,

He ærest sceop
He first created

heofon to hrofe
heaven as a roof,

ða middangeard
then middle-earth

ece Drihten
eternal Lord,

firum foldan
for men earth,

heofonrices Weard
heaven-kingdom's Guardian,

and his modgeþanc
and his mind-plans,

swa he wundra gehwæs
when he of all wonders,

or onstealde
the beginning established.

ielda bearnum
for men's sons

halig Scyppend
holy Creator;

moncynnes Weard
mankind's Guardian,

æfter teode
afterward made—

Frea ælmihtig
Master almighty.

This is the general sense but not the exact order of the words[3] that he sang in his sleep; for it is impossible to make a <u>literal</u> translation, no matter how well-written, of poetry into another language without losing some of the beauty and dignity. When he woke up, he remembered everything that he had sung in his sleep, and to this he soon added, in the

---
3. **the general sense . . . words.** Bede is referring to his Latin version of the poem, not printed here.

 WORDS FOR EVERYDAY USE:
lit • er • al (lit´ ər əl) *adj.*, word-for-word; true to the actual or original meaning

VOCABULARY IN CONTEXT

• Some jokes are funny because of the difference between the <u>literal</u> and the common meanings of a phrase: "He said 'I'd sure like a bite,' so I bit him."

same poetic measure,[4] more verses praising God.

The next morning he went to the reeve,[5] who was his foreman, and told him about the gift he had received. He was taken to the abbess and ordered to tell his dream and to recite his song to an audience of the most learned men so that they might judge what the nature of that vision was and where it came from. It was evident to all of them that he had been granted the heavenly grace of God. Then they expounded some bit of sacred story or teaching to him, and instructed him to turn it into poetry if he could. He agreed and went away. And when he came back the next morning, he gave back what had been commissioned to him in the finest verse.

Therefore, the abbess, who cherished the grace of God in this man, instructed him to give up secular life and to take monastic vows. And when she and all those subject to her had received him into the community of brothers, she gave orders that he be taught the whole sequence of sacred history. He remembered everything that he was able to learn by listening, and turning it over in his mind like a clean beast[6] that chews the cud, he converted it into sweetest song, which sounded so delightful that he made his teachers, in their turn, his listeners. ∎

❶ *What important role does Abbess Hild play in Cædmon's life?*

---

4. **measure.** As used here the word means "rhythm" or "poetic form."
5. **reeve.** A person who oversees farms
6. **clean beast.** In the Old Testament, and in ancient Hebrew law, "clean beasts" are those, like cattle, that have cloven hooves and that regurgitate and chew again plants that they have eaten.

Memorial to Cædmon. Courtesy, the Dean and Chaplaincy, Westminster Abbey

Responding to the Selection

How do you think Cædmon might have felt when he discovered his gift for composing poetry? How would you feel if you awakened one night with a mysterious new ability? What would you like this ability to be? What would you do with it?

BIOGRAPHICAL NOTE

Saint Hild of Whitby (614–680) was one of the first abbesses of Anglo-Saxon England and the founder of Streaneshalch, which is now called Whitby Abbey. In 654 or 655, Ælfflaed, the daughter of King Oswiu, was placed in her care. Hild also received from the king land on which she built her abbey.

ANSWER TO GUIDED READING QUESTION

❶ Hild provides Cædmon with food and lodging at the abbey, which frees him from his work as a cowherd so he can write poetry, and she has him educated.

ANALYTIC SCALES FOR RESPONDING IN WRITING

Assign a score from 1 to 25 for each grading criterion below. (For more detailed evaluation, see the evaluation forms for writing, revising, and proofreading, *Assessment Portfolio,* 7.1–7.10.)

1. **Hymn in an Old English Verse Form**

• **Content and Coherence.** The hymn's story and images operate together to express clearly a theme.

• **Language/Style.** The hymn uses vivid and precise nouns, verbs, and modifiers.

• **Form.** The hymn displays the Old English verse patterns of alliteration, stress, and cæsura.

• **Conventions.** The hymn avoids errors in spelling, grammar, usage, mechanics, and other aspects of manuscript form.

2. **Dream Record**

• **Content/Unity.** The record presents a vivid and evocative picture and explains why the dream is important to the dreamer.

• **Organization/Coherence.** The dream record can follow almost any organization, but like a dream itself, it should have its own internal logic. The dream record is a coherent whole.

• **Language/Style.** The record uses vivid and precise nouns, verbs, and modifiers.

• **Conventions.** The record avoids errors in spelling, grammar, usage, mechanics, and manuscript form.

RESPONDING TO THE SELECTION

Have students work alone or with a partner. They might identify abilities they have as well as those they would like to have.

ANSWERS FOR REVIEWING THE SELECTION

RECALLING

1. Cædmon was a cowherd. At feasts, he would leave before his turn to sing came.

2. Cædmon's first hymn was composed in a dream.

3. They gave him another story to turn into poetry.

4. The poem is about the creation of the heavens and earth. It gives several names for God.

INTERPRETING

5. Cædmon was singled out by God. He was an average cowherd who, without any training or practice, began composing the most beautiful songs in English.

6. Cædmon was encouraged to sing by someone in a dream. The person wanted Cædmon to tell about the creation.

7. Hild wanted to make sure that Cædmon's claims were legitimate.

8. The main point is that God's greatness is visible in creation.

SYNTHESIZING

Responses will vary. Possible responses are given.

9. Cædmon's gift was divinely given. Also, Cædmon could only write religious poems because he only studied sacred history.

10. Bede is impressed by their sacred themes.

ANSWERS FOR UNDERSTANDING LITERATURE

► See the evaluation forms for discussion, active listening, and oral communication, *Assessment Portfolio,* 7.11–7.14.

Responses will vary. Possible responses are given.

1. Translation. Words of different languages that have the same meanings may not have the same number of syllables, stress patterns, or sounds. It is difficult if not impossible to preserve meaning, meter, rhyme, and alliteration in a translation all at the same time.

(cont.)

Reviewing the Selection

RECALLING

1. What was Cædmon's job before he sang verse? What would he do when it was his turn to sing at feasts?

2. In what circumstances did Cædmon compose his first song?

3. How did the abbess Hild and the others test Cædmon's ability?

4. What is the subject of Cædmon's first hymn? What is named, in various ways, throughout the hymn?

INTERPRETING

► 5. Why, according to Bede, could no one else create religious poetry as well as Cædmon? What reasons might Bede have for thinking this?

► 6. Who encouraged Cædmon to compose a song? Why?

► 7. Why did the abbess give Cædmon a test?

► 8. What is the main point of "Cædmon's Hymn"?

SYNTHESIZING

9. Why do you think Cædmon wrote poetry only on religious subjects?

10. What does Bede think is most special about Cædmon's songs? Do you agree?

Understanding Literature (Questions for Discussion)

1. **Translation. Translation** is the art of rendering speech or writing into another language. "Cædmon's Hymn" was composed in Old English. Bede translated it into Latin when he wrote his history. Bede explains that "It is impossible to make a literal translation, no matter how well-written, of poetry into another language without losing some of the beauty and dignity." Why might this be so?

2. **Alliteration. Alliteration** is the repetition of initial consonant sounds. Find four examples of alliteration in the Old English version of "Cædmon's Hymn."

Responding in Writing

1. **Hymn in an Old English Verse Form.** A **hymn** is a song or verse of praise. Try your hand at writing a hymn. Pick any subject you like. Try to use the Old English verse form described on page 82.

ANSWERS FOR UNDERSTANDING LITERATURE (CONT.)

► **Teaching Note:** Ask students if they can find inconsistencies in meter or alliteration. Do they think that these inconsistencies were in the original or that they were introduced in the translation? Why? Which feature(s) do they think the translator worked hardest to preserve?

2. **Alliteration.** Examples include "herigean heofonrices . . . " (line 1); "Meotodes meahte . . . modgeþanc" (line 2); "weorc Wuldor . . . wundra" (line 3); "heofon . . . hrofe halig" (line 6); "middangeard moncynnes" (line 7); "firum foldan Frea" (line 9).

► **Teaching Note:** Ask students to explain the difference(s) between alliteration and rhyme.

Answer. Rhyme is similar sounds at the end of lines; alliteration is similar sounds at the beginning of words within a line.

2. **Dream Record.** Cædmon's literary career started with a vivid dream. Remember an especially strange or vivid dream that you have had. How might you describe this dream to another person? Write it down, and try to make it evocative so that the reader feels as if he or she were dreaming.

Language Lab

Editing for Correct Capitalization. Read the Language Arts Survey, 2.125, "Capitalization: Sacred Beings and Writings." Then rewrite the sentences below using correct capitalization.

1. In Norse mythology, Midgard, or Middle Earth, was the home of humans. It was created from the body of a giant, aurgelmir (or ymir).

2. An Icelandic poem called the *poetic edda* describes how earth was created from Aurgelmir's flesh, the seas from his blood, the sky from his skull, and so on.

3. Today, the written texts of these Norse myths do not bear the religious significance of judaism's torah, christianity's bible, islam's koran, hinduism's upanishads, or comparable works.

4. The collections of Hindu writings known as the vedas tell a number of different creation stories. For instance, Indra, vishnu, and varunya are each said to have created the universe and to have separated earth from the heavens.

5. In the Babylonian creation text *enuma elish*, tiamat, the mother of all the gods, is killed by marduk, her son. Marduk divides her in two to make the heavens and the earth.

PROJECTS

1. **Storytelling: Germanic Mythology.** In Cædmon's time, a harp was often passed around after feasts so the guests could sing in verse. Do some research in the library to gather stories from the ancient Germanic myths (especially the German, Icelandic, and Norse myths). Sit in a circle in class and take turns telling these myths to one another.

2. **An Anglo-Saxon Feast.** As a class, plan a recital during which you can read verses. You and your classmates may want to read your own verses from Responding in Writing, Exercise 1, or you may want to find more Old English verses in books from your library. As an extra touch, you may want to serve refreshments and food at the recital, in imitation of an Anglo-Saxon feast.

ANALYTIC SCALES FOR RESPONDING IN WRITING

Grading scales appear on page 85.

ANSWERS FOR LANGUAGE LAB

1. In Norse mythology, Midgard, or Middle Earth, was the home of humans. It was created from the body of a giant, Aurgelmir (or Ymir).

2. An Icelandic poem called the *Poetic Edda* describes how earth was created from Aurgelmir's flesh, the seas from his blood, the sky from his skull, and so on.

3. Today, the written texts of these Norse myths do not bear the religious significance of Judaism's Torah, Christianity's Bible, Islam's Koran, Hinduism's Upanishads, or comparable works.

4. The collections of Hindu writings known as the Vedas tell a number of different creation stories. For instance, Indra, Vishnu, and Varunya are each said to have created the universe and separated the earth from the heavens.

5. In the Babylonian creation text *Enuma Elish,* Tiamat, the mother of all the gods, is killed by Marduk, her son. Marduk divides her in two to make the heavens and the earth.

▶ Additional practice is provided in the *Essential Skills Practice Book: Language,* 2.125.

PROJECT NOTES

 ▶ See the worksheets and evaluation forms for projects, *Assessment Portfolio,* 7.20–7.23.

 1. Storytelling: Germanic Mythology. Point out that the modern harp is very different from the harp or lyre that was played in Cædmon's time. (You might invite students to research the history of the harp.)

2. An Anglo-Saxon Feast
• If any of your students play the harp or other stringed instruments, encourage them to perform for the class.

 • Encourage students to research Anglo-Saxon eating habits. Were their diets nutritious? What health problems might diet have caused them?

READER'S GUIDE
• Selection Worksheet, 2.3

ASSESSMENT PORTFOLIO
• Selection Check Test, 4.2.5
• Selection Test, 4.2.6

ENRICHMENT ACTIVITIES

• The early Anglo-Saxons lived in small, closely knit groups, the members of which were generally related by blood. Ask students to compare this sort of society to the present-day society with which they are familiar. How near to or far from their relatives do students live? Where do students plan to live after leaving high school or after marrying? In what ways might the wife's story have been different if she had lived in a community more like theirs?

• Ask students to work in groups to depict loneliness. Their depiction might be in the form of a group performance before the class, or they might produce a work of music or of visual art. Encourage them to be as creative as possible.

SUPPORT FOR LEP STUDENTS

The story told in the poem may be difficult for some students to untangle because it is not told chronologically. Explain that the story is not told in sequence, and work with the group to help them infer the order of events.

ADDITIONAL VOCABULARY
smote, past tense of smite—kill
brooding—troubles, worrying
bearing—mood
longing—desire and loneliness
garrison—fortress
blithe—carefree

PREREADING

"The Wife's Lament"
Anonymous, trans. by Marcelle Thiébaux

ABOUT THE AUTHOR

"The Wife's Lament," also known as "The Wife's Complaint," is one of two surviving Old English poems believed to have been composed by women. (The other Old English poem by a woman, "Wulf and Eadwacer," can be found in the Selections for Additional Reading on page 117). Unfortunately, nothing is known about these first great English women poets, not even their names.

ABOUT THE SELECTION

Preserved in the Old English manuscript known as *The Exeter Book,* "The Wife's Lament" is a superb example of the **elegiac lyric.** A **lyric** is a short, highly musical poem that tells the emotions of a speaker. An **elegy** is a kind of lyric that expresses grief over the loss of something, in this case the loss of the speaker's family, of her homeland, and of her husband and friend.

The early Anglo-Saxons lived in small, closely knit groups, the members of which were generally related by blood. Life was harsh, and someone who was cut off from the group or made an outcast would have had a very difficult time surviving on his or her own. Most of the Old English poems that have come down to us celebrate ties to the family, the king, and the tribe. Many deal with the awful consequences of being cut off from these people. It is safe to say that after courage in warfare and the fickleness of fate, exile is the most common theme in Old English literature.

GOALS/OBJECTIVES

Studying this lesson will enable students to
• experience the speaker's feeling of loneliness, loss, and isolation
• identify and interpret metaphors in a piece of writing
• explain the concepts of ambiguity, image, and objective correlative

• identify images used in a poem and identify the particular emotions they create in a reader
• explain the concepts of elegy and lyric
• write to create an image that expresses a particular emotion
• write a personal letter using the proper manuscript form

READER'S JOURNAL

How would it feel to be a stranger, alone, in a faraway land? What would you miss about home? Think about these questions. Then write in your journal about the importance of ties to other people.

SPEAKING AND LISTENING SKILLS

Read the Language Arts Survey, 3.5, "Interpersonal Communication." Then answer this question in your journal: How can speaking with a friend help you in times of sorrow or distress? Make a list of the important functions that interpersonal communication serves in our lives.

"The Wife's Lament"

ANONYMOUS, TRANS. BY MARCELLE THIÉBAUX

I tell this story about me, in my sorrow,
I sing the fate of my voyaging self. I may say that
whatever hardship I lived through since I grew up—
new griefs and old—in those days it was not worse than now.
5   Always I grieve in the pain of my torment.

First my lord went away from his people
over the tossing waves. I felt cold care in the dark before dawn,[1]
wondering where my lord of the lands might be.
Then I left on a journey to seek and serve him—
10   a friendless wanderer in my terrible need.
That man's kinsmen began to plot
with secret scheming to split us both apart,
so that we two—widely <u>asunder</u> in the world—
lived most wretchedly. And longing smote me.

15   My lord called to me to take up my hard dwelling here.
I had few loved ones in this country,
few devoted friends. For this my mind mourns.

---

1. **cold care . . . dark before dawn.** The translator is imitating the alliteration of the original Anglo-Saxon verse.

WORDS FOR EVERYDAY USE:

a • sun • der (ə sunˊdər) *adv.*, apart; separate

PREREADING NOTES

READER'S JOURNAL

Suggest that students think of the many different people they see each day in their families, clubs, teams, school, religious organizations, and neighborhoods.

SPEAKING AND LISTENING SKILLS

• Pair students and have them role play a friend listening to a friend share his or her sorrows.
• Some students may prefer to think about speaking with a parent, guardian, other relative, or pastor.

HISTORICAL NOTE

Virginia Woolf, in *A Room of One's Own,* writes: "I would venture to guess that Anon, who wrote so many poems without signing them, was often a woman."

WORDS FOR EVERYDAY USE

asunder	hovel
blithe	whorled

VOCABULARY IN CONTEXT

• The log was split <u>asunder</u> by one powerful blow of the axe.

ART NOTE

In *Frithiof's Saga,* by Esaias Tegnér (Swedish, 1782–1846), Ingeborg is the princess courted and won by the Viking Frithiof. Tegnér was a classical scholar who attempted to revive the Old Icelandic saga form. J. August Malmström (1829–1901) illustrated the 1888 edition of *Frithiof's Saga.*

LITERARY NOTE

Lines 15–26 may be difficult for students because they seem to introduce another person. Scholars still debate whether this is actually a second person. It can be argued that these lines do not chronologically follow lines 6–14 but are rather a return to the past to explain the relationship between the speaker and her husband.

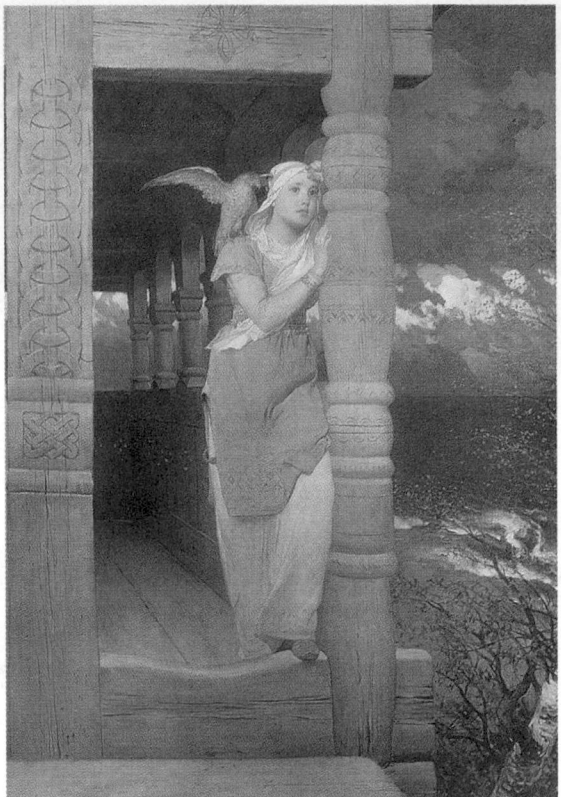

Ingeborg's Lament. J. A. Malmström.
University College, London, Scandinavian Library

Then I found myself a most husbandly man,
but a man with hard luck, brooding in his heart;
20   he hid his moods, his murderous thoughts,
yet seemed <u>blithe</u> in his bearing. Very often we boasted that
none but death alone would drive us apart—
not anything else! All that is <u>whorled</u> backward, changed;
now it's as if it never had been,
25   the loving friendship the both of us had. Far and near I must
suffer the feud[2] of my dearly loved man.

---

2. **feud.** Disdain, hatred

WORDS FOR
EVERYDAY USE:

blithe (blīth) *adj.,* cheerful; carefree

whorled (hwôrld) *adj.,* coiled

VOCABULARY IN CONTEXT

- Derwood-MacHeath Senior remained <u>blithe</u> throughout the award ceremony, despite his son's uncouth and frequent belches.
- The natural oils in her skin left a <u>whorled</u> smudge on the mirror.
- Relief workers spent weeks replacing the <u>hovels</u> throughout the country with wood-frame houses.

They forced me to live in a grove of wood
under an oak tree in an earth <u>hovel</u>.
Old is this den of earth. I am stabbed with longing.
30 The valleys are dark, the hills rise high,
bitterly sharp is my garrison overgrown with brambles,
a joyless stronghold. Here very often what seizes me fiercely
is the want of my husband! There are friends on earth,
lovers living who lie clasped in their bed,
35 while I walk alone in the hours before daybreak
under the oak tree, throughout this earth cave
where I must remain the summerlong day,
where I can weep the sorrows
of my many hardships, because I never can
40 find sweet rest for that heart's grief of mine—
not for all of that longing laid on me in this life.

Always must the young be troubled in mood,
with thoughts harsh in their hearts, yet at the same time
seem blithe in bearing despite a care-burdened breast
45 and a swarm of sorrows. The young man must rely on himself
for all he gets of the world's joy. He must be a far-flung outlaw
in a distant country.

So my loved friend sits
under a stone cliff crusted with frost in the storm—
my lover dreary in spirit. Water flows all around him
50 in his bleak dwelling. That friend of mine suffers
great sorrow of heart. Too often he remembers
a more blissful house. Unhappy is anyone
who must longingly wait for a lover.   ■

WORDS FOR   hov • el (huv´əl) *n.,* a shed or hut
EVERYDAY USE:

ADDITIONAL QUESTIONS AND ACTIVITIES

 • Ask students to draw, diagram, or describe the banished wife's home from two or three different perspectives. Where are the grove, oak, valleys, and brambles in relation to each other? Where is the entrance?

 • "A lazy person often puts off making decisions, / Lets opportunities slip, and so dies alone."—*Old English gnomic*

Do students think the husband is happy? Has he let his opportunities slip? What mistakes has the husband made? Will he die alone?

Will the wife die alone? Has she let her opportunities slip? Has the wife made mistakes?

ANSWERS TO SELECTION CHECK TEST 4.2.5

EX. What type of poem is "The Wife's Lament"?
"The Wife's Lament" is an elegiac lyric.
1. How did the wife first come to be alone?
Her husband went overseas.
2. What did her husband's kin do?
Her husband's kin plotted against her.
3. Whom does the wife meet in her new home?
She meets a "most husbandly man."
4. At the end of the poem, where does the wife live?
She lives in a den or cave in a wood.
5. At the end of the poem, how does the wife describe her first husband's situation?
She speaks of him as stranded beneath a bleak, frosty cliff.

RESPONDING TO THE SELECTION

Students may also write about or discuss what they might do in a similar situation to that of the wife. Would they be as accepting as she was? Did she have any options?

ANSWERS FOR REVIEWING THE SELECTION

RECALLING

1. The poem does not state why the husband went away.

2. The husband's kin plotted to split the marriage. The husband then told the wife to move.

3. In the new country she found a new husband.

4. She lives in a den or cave.

INTERPRETING

Responses will vary. Possible responses are given.

5. The wife went "to seek and serve" her husband.

6. The husband may have been influenced by his kin who were hostile to the wife.

7. The relationship changed from one of loving friendship to a separation.

8. She needs a respite from her loneliness: she needs a companion.

SYNTHESIZING

Responses will vary. Possible responses are given.

9. She is bitter but also concerned for him. She seems to have forgiven the husband for exiling her. This may indicate that she is generous or that she is gullible.

10. The speaker would probably say that she cannot be happy living alone.

Responding to the Selection

What griefs has the speaker of this poem experienced? Which would be the hardest for you to bear? Which most arouses your sympathy? Write about these questions in your journal.

Reviewing the Selection

 RECALLING

1. Why did the husband go away?

2. What did the husband's kin do? What did the husband do thereafter?

3. What did the wife find in her new country?

4. Where does the wife now live?

INTERPRETING

5. Why did the wife leave on a journey?

6. Why might the absent husband have asked his wife to take up a dwelling elsewhere than with his kin?

7. How did the relationship with the new man in the new country change over time?

8. In lines 39–41, the wife sums up the source of her sorrow. What is missing from her life? What would she have to have in order to feel fulfilled?

SYNTHESIZING

9. In the final lines of the poem, the wife expresses her feelings toward the absent husband described at the beginning of the poem. Is she bitter toward him? What are her feelings toward him? What do these feelings reveal about her? What sort of person is she?

10. Do people need other people, or is it possible to live happily alone? How would the speaker of this poem answer that question? How would you?

Understanding Literature (Questions for Discussion)

1. **Speaker.** The **speaker** is the character who speaks in, or narrates, a poem—the voice assumed by the writer. In this poem, the speaker is an exiled woman, living alone, far from her husband and kin. How does the speaker feel about her exile? What emotions does the speaker express in the poem?

 ANSWERS FOR UNDERSTANDING LITERATURE
Responses will vary. Possible responses are given.

▶ See the evaluation forms for discussion, active listening, and oral communication, *Assessment Portfolio,* 7.11–7.14.

1. **Speaker.** The speaker feels estrangement and alienation, loneliness, sadness and grief, bitterness and resentment, anger, and that her heart is being eaten away.

(cont.)

2. **Symbol.** A **symbol** is a thing that stands for or represents both itself and something else. What might the earthen cave in this poem symbolize?

3. **Foil.** A **foil** is a character whose attributes, or characteristics, contrast with and therefore throw into relief the attributes of another character. With whom does the speaker contrast herself in lines 33–35? Where are these people located? Where is she located? What symbolism is suggested by these differences in location?

4. **Metaphor.** A **metaphor** is a figure of speech in which one thing is spoken or written about as if it were another. What two things are compared in line 45? In what way are these two things similar?

5. **Image.** An **image** is a word or phrase that names something that can be seen, heard, touched, tasted, or smelled. What images are used in lines 47–50 to describe the place where the husband is stranded? What emotion is created by these images?

Responding in Writing

Personal Letter. Imagine that you are a friend of the woman in this poem. Write her a letter consoling her and advising her about what to do. Refer to the instruction on the form of a personal letter in the Language Arts Survey, 5.2.

PROJECT

Planning a Celebration. "The Wife's Lament" is a poem about people's need for one another. Most people feel the need to be in relationships with others, as mates, as friends, as family, as confederates in various enterprises, and so on. Many holidays exist to celebrate particular relationships: Valentine's Day, Mother's Day, and even Secretary's Day. However, in Western countries today, there is no holiday dedicated specifically to celebrating friendship, although this is arguably one of the most important of all human relationships. In a group, plan a holiday for celebrating friendship. When would it be held? What would people do to celebrate it? Come up with creative ways of expressing the value and importance of friends.

"THE WIFE'S LAMENT" 93

ANSWERS FOR UNDERSTANDING LITERATURE (CONT.)

2. Symbol. The cave, a dark and lonely and empty place, may symbolize the wife's feelings of sadness and emptiness. It may also symbolize the abode of the (metaphorically) dead.

3. Foil. She contrasts herself with people who are not separated from their lovers. They live above-ground while she lives under the ground. Living below the ground may symbolize being dead and buried, or it may symbolize being in hell; living above ground may symbolize being in heaven.

4. Metaphor. In line 45 a swarm of bees or insects is compared to the many sorrows that trouble the wife. They are similar in that both are composed of many individuals but appear as a mass, and both are very pesky and hard to escape.

5. Image. Lines 47–50 use the images of a person alone and stranded in bleak, frozen, craggy lands, as in the arctic or wintry mountains, surrounded by water. Students may say that these images create emotions of emptiness, loneliness, and hopelessness.

ANALYTIC SCALES FOR RESPONDING IN WRITING

Assign a score from 1 to 25 for each grading criterion below. (For more detailed evaluation, see the evaluation forms for writing, revising, and proofreading, *Assessment Portfolio,* 7.1–7.10.)

Personal Letter
• **Content/Unity.** The letter offers consolation and advice appropriate for a woman who has been abandoned by her husband and his kin.
• **Organization/Coherence.** The letter is clearly organized, presenting relevant reasons for the advice it gives.
• **Language/Style.** The letter uses vivid and precise nouns, verbs, and modifiers.
• **Conventions.** The letter avoids errors in spelling, grammar, usage, mechanics, and manuscript form.

PROJECT NOTES

▶ See the worksheets and evaluation forms for projects, *Assessment Portfolio,* 7.20–7.23.

Planning a Celebration
• Point out to students that while some holidays, especially religious holidays, have relatively unvarying rituals, most secular holidays are celebrated more or less differently by different families

or groups. Students may work better as a group if they begin by sharing and comparing the different ways they celebrate holidays such as Valentine's Day, Mother's Day, or Independence Day.

• Invite knowledgeable parents or other persons from the community to speak to the class about how friendship is celebrated in other countries.

ADDITIONAL RESOURCES

READER'S GUIDE
- Selection Worksheet, 2.4

ASSESSMENT PORTFOLIO
- Selection Check Test, 4.2.7
- Selection Test, 4.2.8

ESSENTIAL SKILLS PRACTICE BOOKS
- *Writing,* 1.40
- *Language,* 2.32, 2.33, 2.93

ENRICHMENT ACTIVITIES

Invite students to research the *Exeter Book.* What does it contain besides riddles? When was it composed? When was it printed? Why wasn't it destroyed by Vikings or during the destruction of the monasteries? How was it constructed, and what materials were used? Where is it now?

SUPPORT FOR LEP STUDENTS

Riddles are an excellent vehicle for teaching about multiple meanings of words. As you discuss with the class the meanings of each of the riddles, point out or have students point out words that are used with two meanings.

ADDITIONAL VOCABULARY

dale—valley

down—open expanse of land

grovel—crawl

toil—work

feud—fighting, battle

adorned—decorated

penance—repentance or reparation for wrongdoing

PREREADING

Anglo-Saxon Riddles

Anonymous, trans. by George K. Anderson

ABOUT THE AUTHOR

Anglo-Saxon literature survives in manuscripts that were laboriously produced by hand by monks. Many manuscripts were destroyed during the two waves of Viking invasions. Many more were lost centuries later when King Henry VIII of England broke with the Church of Rome and ordered the destruction of monasteries throughout England. One of the most important of the surviving manuscripts of Old English verse is the *Exeter Book.* Among the works included in this book are ninety-five Anglo-Saxon riddles. These riddles used to be attributed to a religious poet named **Cynewulf** (*circa* AD 800), but whether Cynewulf actually wrote any of them is unknown.

ABOUT THE SELECTIONS

A **riddle** is a word game in which something is described in an unusual way and the reader or listener must figure out what that something is. The riddles on the following pages show an interesting combination of light-hearted word play and a grim world view. As you read the riddles, look for clues to figure out what each one describes.

94 *UNIT TWO / THE ANGLO-SAXON PERIOD*

GOALS/OBJECTIVES

Studying this lesson will enable students to

- appreciate the challenge of writing and solving Anglo-Saxon riddles
- recognize precise nouns and adjectives and vivid verbs
- understand personification
- evaluate descriptions of personified objects
- use end marks correctly

READER'S JOURNAL

Do a freewrite in which an everyday object "introduces itself" to a reader. Have the object describe itself without giving away its name. For example, a pencil sharpener might talk about its grinding teeth and about its appetite for wood shavings.

LANGUAGE SKILLS

Read the Language Arts Survey, 2.32 and 2.33, "Using Precise Nouns" and "Using Vivid Verbs." Then, make a list of nouns and verbs from the selections that are particularly precise and vivid.

Anglo-Saxon Riddles

ANONYMOUS, TRANS. BY GEORGE K. ANDERSON

Riddle 1

I am honored of men, searched for everywhere, brought from the groves and the mountain-heights, from the dales and the downs. Wings bear me in air, and carry me beneath the sheltering roof. Then men bathe me in a barrel. When I emerge, I am a binder and a <u>scourger</u>. I throw old men to the earth. Whoever foolishly wrestles me, sets his strength against mine, will soon find himself flat on his back, groveling on ground, without rule of mind, feet, or hands, though still strong in his speech. Tell me what I am called—I who fell men to the earth, dizzy with my blows.

Riddle 2

I am lonely, <u>hacked</u> with steel, wounded by weapons; the toil of battle has wearied me, swords have worn me out. Often have I seen war, the rage of battle; nor do I hope for rest from strife before I die. Hammered swords have struck me; hard and sharp of edge, the <u>wrought</u> swords have bitten me; and even more deadly feud I shall endure. I can never find a leech[1] to heal my wounds with herbs, but only more mortal blows and deeper wounds each day and night.

1. **leech.** A leech was a doctor, so called because he or she used leeches to draw blood in the belief that sickness was caused by impurities in the blood.

❶
What words in this riddle describe hardships?

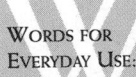

WORDS FOR EVERYDAY USE:

scourg • er (skʉrj´ər) *n.,* one who scourges, or flogs
hacked (hakt) *adj.,* cut rudely, roughly, or irregularly
wrought (rôt) *adj.,* shaped by hammering or beating

PREREADING NOTES

READER'S JOURNAL

Students can brainstorm as a group to come up with creative ideas.

LANGUAGE SKILLS

• Discuss with students the meanings of the words *precise* (strictly defined, not vague) and *vivid* (forming lively and clear mental images). Then ask why using precise and vivid words might make for better writing.

• Have students rewrite passages from the riddles, substituting vague and dull words, and then compare the two versions.

▶ Additional practice is provided in the *Essential Skills Practice Book: Language,* 2.32 and 2.33.

ANSWER TO GUIDED READING QUESTION

❶ Answers will vary. Words indicating hardships include *lonely, hacked, wounded, toil, wearied, worn out, war, battle, strife, struck, bitten, deadly feud, endure,* and *mortal blows.*

ANSWERS TO RIDDLES

Riddle 1: mead (wine made from honey)

Riddle 2: a shield

Riddle 3: a tree; a book

VOCABULARY FROM THE SELECTION

blithe	staunch
hacked	sully
quill	wrought
scourger	

VOCABULARY IN CONTEXT

• They hired an out-of-work <u>scourger</u> to help age their "antiques."
• Marjorie's hair looks <u>hacked</u> and untidy, but it's part of her costume for the seventies "punk" party.
• The handle of the poker was <u>wrought</u> to display a likeness of Mrs. O'Leary.

EX. In what source can the Old English riddles be found?

The Old English riddles can be found in the *Exeter Book*.

1. What does the subject of Riddle 1 do to people?

It defeats them and knocks them down.

2. How does the subject of Riddle 2 feel?

It is weary.

3. Why does the subject of Riddle 2 feel this way?

It has toiled in and been wounded in battle.

4. Name one of the hardships that the subject of Riddle 3 has endured.

Answers will vary. **Some hardships include these: It has been killed; it has lost its strength; it has been plunged in water; it has lost its hair; it has been scraped; it has been soiled or sullied; it has been stepped on.**

5. What value does the subject of Riddle 3 claim for itself?

Answers will vary. **It claims to be splendid; it claims to be useful; it claims to be a loyal and kind friend.**

ANSWER TO GUIDED READING QUESTION

❶ The first part of the poem describes the process of making a book; the second part describes the value of books.

Frontispiece to the Gospel of Saint Matthew in the Book of Durrow.
The Board of Trinity College Dublin

Riddle 3

❶
What is the subject of each of the two parts of the riddle?

A man of violence killed me, took away my earthly strength; then he plunged me in water, plucked me out, and set me in the sun. I lost my hair; the keen knife-edge cut me, scraped off my impurities. Then the <u>quill</u> of a bird spread drops upon me, <u>sullied</u> my surface. It drank deep in the ink, stepped again upon me; black was its track. A man then covered me with a binding, stretched a hide over me, adorned me with gold, decked me with the marvelous works of craftsmen, strengthened me with wire.

Thus made splendid with red and gold, may I live to make known the glory of God and never as a penance to man. If the children of men will employ me, they shall be more safe, more sure of success, more <u>staunch</u> in soul, <u>blithe</u> in heart, and wise in mind. They shall have in me a friend who will be dear and near to them, loyal and kind—a friend who will gladly labor to increase their joy and fame, who will cover them with his kindness, and clasp them with loving bonds. Find out what I am called—I who am useful to men, famous and holy. ∎

WORDS FOR
EVERYDAY USE:

quill (kwil) *n.*, stiff feather of a bird
sul • ly (sul´ē) *vt.*, soil or stain

staunch (stônch) *adj.*, strong
blithe (blīth) *adj.*, cheerful; carefree

VOCABULARY IN CONTEXT

• Veruca made a pen from the <u>quill</u> she found on the beach.

• The waiter replaced the <u>sullied</u> table linens with clean ones before seating the next diners.

• Trinh's <u>staunch</u> belief that we would win never failed even when the rest of the team was in despair.

• The gloomy weather really dampened my spirits, but Igor was as <u>blithe</u> as ever.

Responding to the Selection

The objects featured in the riddles are each unique and important in different ways. If you had to pick three objects in your life about which to write, what would they be? How might you describe the uniqueness and importance of the objects?

Reviewing the Selection

RECALLING

1. Where does the thing described in the first riddle come from? To what is the thing compared in the concluding lines?

2. What abuses and hardships does the object that is the subject of the second riddle undergo? How does it survive?

3. What abuses and hardships does the object that is the subject of the third riddle undergo?

4. In what ways is the object that is the subject of the third riddle useful to people? What benefits does it bring?

INTERPRETING

5. What is the subject of the first riddle? (Hints: the wings in the riddle belong to bees. Honey is bathed "in a barrel.")

6. What is the subject of the second riddle? What key words or phrases reveal the subject to you?

7. What is the subject of the third riddle? What key words or phrases reveal the subject to you?

8. How might using the object that is the subject of the third riddle bring about the promised benefits?

SYNTHESIZING

9. Why do you think the riddles might mention so many difficulties and hardships? What, if anything, might this show about Anglo-Saxon life?

10. Based on these riddles, what can you conclude were important activities among the Anglo-Saxons?

Understanding Literature (Questions for Discussion)

1. **Personification. Personification** is a writing technique in which an idea, animal, or thing is described as if it were a person. For example, a writer might tell about a *proud* ship sailing into port or gray clouds *sneaking up on* the sun. Each of the riddles is an example of extended personification. What specific examples of personification can you find in each of the three riddles?

ANSWERS FOR UNDERSTANDING LITERATURE

▶ See the evaluation forms for discussion, active listening, and oral communication, *Assessment Portfolio,* 7.11– 7.14.

Responses will vary. Possible responses are given.

1. **Personification.** Any mention of "I" and "me" in the riddles is an example of personification. Some other examples of personification are as follows:

Riddle 1: "I throw old men to the earth."
Riddle 2: "I am lonely"; and "Often I have seen war."
Riddle 3: "A man of violence killed me"; and "I live to make known the glory of God."

(cont.)

This topic is appropriate for small group discussion or individual writing.

ANSWERS FOR REVIEWING THE SELECTION

RECALLING

1. It comes from forests, mountains, valleys, and plains. It is compared to a fighter.

2. *Answers will vary.* Hardships include going to war, having no hope for rest from strife, being struck by swords, and not being able to heal. It survives wounded and tired.

3. *Answers will vary.* Hardships include being killed, sapped of strength, and plunged into water; losing its hair; and being scraped, sullied, and stepped on.

4. It can help them to be more safe, sure of success, courageous, happy, and wise. It will be a loyal friend and kind helper.

INTERPRETING

Responses will vary. Possible responses are given.

5. The subject of Riddle 1 is mead.

6. The subject of Riddle 2 is a shield. Hints include mentions of weapons, swords, war, and battle.

7. The subject of Riddle 3 is a book. Hints include mentions of ink and binding.

8. Reading books can fill the imagination, introduce us to likeable and admirable characters, and teach us.

SYNTHESIZING

Responses will vary. Possible responses are given.

9. Life was hard without modern conveniences, especially for Anglo-Saxons who had to fear Viking invasions.

10. These riddles indicate that Anglo-Saxons spent some of their time making and drinking mead, making weapons and engaging in battle, and making and reading books.

98

ANSWERS FOR UNDERSTANDING LITERATURE (CONT.)

2. Description. Some examples of vivid description are:

Riddle 1: "flat on his back, groveling on ground, without rule of mind, feet, or hands, though still strong in his speech."

Riddle 2: "hacked with steel, wounded by weapons; the toil of battle has wearied me, swords have worn me out."

Riddle 3: "Then the quill of a bird spread drops upon me, sullied my surface. It drank deep in the ink, stepped again upon me; black was its track. A man then covered me with a binding."

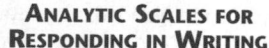

ANALYTIC SCALES FOR RESPONDING IN WRITING

Assign a score from 1 to 25 for each grading criterion below. (For more detailed evaluation, see the evaluation forms for writing, revising, and proofreading, *Assessment Portfolio,* 7.1–7.10.)

1. Riddle

• **Content/Unity.** The riddle describes a person or object in an unusual and clever way without giving away the subject of the riddle.

• **Organization/Coherence.** The riddle is clearly organized, presenting details in a sensible order.

• **Language/Style.** The riddle uses vivid and precise nouns, verbs, and modifiers.

• **Conventions.** The riddle avoids errors in spelling, grammar, usage, mechanics, and manuscript form.

2. Descriptive Writing

• **Content/Unity.** The paragraph presents a vivid description of a scene that appeals to all the senses.

• **Organization/Coherence.** Main points and details in the paragraph are sensibly and clearly arranged.

• **Language/Style.** The paragraph uses vivid and precise nouns, verbs, and modifiers.

• **Conventions.** The paragraph avoids errors in spelling, grammar, usage, mechanics, and manuscript form.

---

2. Description. A **description,** one of the modes of writing, presents a portrayal of a character, an object, or scene. The "characters" in these selections are *personified* things. How are the characters and the world around the characters described so that the reader gets clear pictures in his or her mind? Find examples of vivid descriptions in these selections. For more information on vivid description, read the Language Arts Survey, 1.40, "Elaboration: Types of Supporting Details."

Responding in Writing

1. **Riddle.** A **riddle** is a word game in which something is described in an unusual way and the reader or listener must figure out what that something is. A great deal of thought is required to solve or answer a good riddle. Look at your notes from the Reader's Journal activity on page 95. Work with these notes to create a polished riddle of your own. Try to use vivid description to create a picture, but don't include so many details that the subject of your riddle is given away easily.

2. **Descriptive Writing.** To write good description, you must learn to think again like a child. You have to look at the world as if you were seeing it anew. What does a plowed field really look like? What does a dusty old book really look like? What would your school lunchroom look like to someone who had never been in one before? Write a descriptive paragraph. Instead of focusing on one object, focus on a scene— perhaps your room, your classroom, or your closet. Try to appeal to all the senses—sight, sound, touch, taste, and smell. Really try to place the reader in your scene.

Language Lab

Proofreading for Errors in End Marks. Read the Language Arts Survey, 2.93, "End Marks." Then, correct the errors in end marks by adding punctuation as necessary.

A Riddle

1. People talk with me Why do they never talk to me

2. When people call on me, I never answer them, but they usually answer me when I call

3. If I'm busy, I will let you know; if I'm not busy, I will let you talk to someone else

4. I come in a box, but I give you the world How amazing

5. Now I ask, "Can you guess what I am"

ANSWERS FOR LANGUAGE LAB

1. People talk with me. Why do they never talk to me?
2. When people call on me, I never answer them, but they usually answer me when I call.
3. If I'm busy, I will let you know; if I'm not busy, I will let you talk to someone else.
4. I come in a box, but I give you the world. How amazing!
5. Now I ask, "Can you guess what I am?"

FOR MORE PRACTICE

Problem. I'll bet you haven't guessed yet, have you Keep trying

Answer. I'll bet you haven't guessed yet, have you? Keep trying!

► Additional practice is provided in the *Essential Skills Practice Book: Language,* 2.93.

Answer to riddle: telephone

PREREADING

from *Beowulf*
Anonymous, trans. by E. Talbot Donaldson

ABOUT THE SELECTION

Widely acknowledged as the greatest masterpiece of Anglo-Saxon literature, *Beowulf* was composed in Northumbria or West Mercia by an unknown singer of tales, a **gleeman**, or **scop**. The poem probably dates from the early 700s, but it tells a story that is much older. The poem's characters are not Anglo-Saxon but rather related Germanic people—Geats and Danes from Scandinavia. The hero of the poem, Beowulf, may actually have lived, though no independent record of his existence survives.

Like most stories passed by word-of-mouth from generation to generation, *Beowulf* may contain a kernel of historical truth. Around this kernel a fabric of miraculous elaboration has been woven. For example, the real Beowulf, if he existed, may have been a great swimmer, but it is doubtful that he was able, as the poem says, to swim underwater for an entire day. In a manner typical of products of the oral tradition, the poem tells of many such fantastic feats and is filled with imaginary creatures such as trolls, giants, and dragons.

No one knows precisely when *Beowulf* was first written down. The poem survives in a West Saxon manuscript created in the late 900s by a monastic copyist, or **scribe**, who added to the original pre-Christian poem many references to stories from the Christian *Old Testament*. The single existing manuscript of the poem contains many errors introduced by this not-so-careful copyist. To make matters worse, the manuscript was damaged in a fire in 1731. Nonetheless, the poem is fairly complete and remains the finest surviving example of the ancient Germanic heroic epic. An **epic** is a long story, often told in verse, involving heroes and gods. Grand in length and scope, an epic provides a portrait of an entire culture, of the legends, beliefs, values, laws, arts, and ways of life of a people. A **heroic epic** is one that has as its main purpose telling the life story of a great hero.

The poem consists of a prologue and forty-three sections, known as **fits** or **cantos**. The first three-fourths of the poem, through the middle of Canto thirty-one, tells the story of the heroic exploits of Beowulf as a young warrior. The final fourth of the poem tells of Beowulf as an aged king of the Geats.

Reading this poem, we learn a great deal about Anglo-Saxon ideals of heroism and kingship. A Germanic king of the period typically gathered around him a group of loyal retainers, known as **earls** or **thanes,** who shared his house and fought in his battles. A king earned his retainers' loyalty through generosity, by holding feasts in a great mead hall, and by dispensing gifts. These gifts included treasures made of gold or silver, as well as finely wrought weaponry such as helmets and swords. A great king was liberal in dispensing gifts and courageous enough to sacrifice himself for his subjects, as Beowulf does at the end of the poem.

Germanic law required that the death of a family member, even if accidental, be paid for by the person responsible for the death. The responsible person or tribe would be required to pay a **wergild,** or "man-price." If the payment were not made, then the dead person's relatives had a responsibility to avenge the death in battle. As a result, blood feuds among the

ADDITIONAL RESOURCES

READER'S GUIDE
- Selection Worksheet, 2.5

ASSESSMENT PORTFOLIO
- Selection Check Test, 4.2.9
- Selection Test, 4.2.10

ESSENTIAL SKILLS PRACTICE BOOKS
- *Writing,* 1.41–1.42
- *Language,* 2.5
- *Study and Research,* 4.19

AUDIOCASSETTE
- from *Beowulf,* Track 4

ENRICHMENT ACTIVITIES

- Have students research the state of science and technology at the time the events told of in *Beowulf* occurred and apply their knowledge to fill out details of the epic. What materials were available? What would it be like to wear a mail-shirt and to carry a sword and shield? How long did it take to make a sword? How long did it take to make a boat to carry forty thanes? What means of ground transportation existed? How long did it take to travel from London to Denmark?

- Suggest that students research scops. They might consider such questions as these: When did they exist? Where? How many were there? What were their lives like? How were they regarded by others in society? Why are there no scops now?

SUPPORT FOR LEP STUDENTS

- Before students begin reading, use the illustrations on page 104 and pages 110–111 to point out important features of the story.
- Have students read aloud sections of the poem.
- While you or students are reading aloud, other students can pantomime the actions described.

(cont.)

SUPPORT FOR LEP STUDENTS (CONT.)

ADDITIONAL VOCABULARY

prosper—succeed; thrive
mirth—joy
grim—fierce; relentless
interval—space; gap
heirloom—treasured object passed from generation to generation

sinew—muscle or tendon
stout-hearted—bold
bent—intended upon
linden—a tree, also called basswood
purge—cleanse or rid of undesirables
hasten—hurry

The first page of Beowulf. British Library Cotton Vitellius A.15 (olim 129). folio 132r. By permission of the British Library

Germanic tribes were very common. Warfare also resulted from invasions to extend a tribe's lands and plundering to gather treasures to dispense to warriors.

Life under such conditions was harsh. The likelihood of dying in battle was high, and great warriors were highly prized. A great warrior showed courage in the face of almost certain doom; upheld his honor by avenging friends, family members, and his king; and achieved fame through feats of strength and skill in battle. Beowulf embodies all of these ancient Germanic heroic ideals.

Modern readers of *Beowulf* often remark on the sense of gloom that pervades the poem. Throughout the work, many references are made to the harshness of life and to the fickleness of **Wyrd,** or "fate." The Anglo-Saxon worldview was essentially pessimistic. Eventually, everyone would meet his or her doom. The most one could hope for was to do great deeds and so achieve everlasting fame in a gleeman's song.

Beowulf was composed in the traditional Anglo-Saxon verse form described on page 82 and was chanted by a scop to the accompaniment of a harp. The scop's primary poetic technique was **alliteration,** the repetition of initial consonant sounds. This technique, combined with the use of four strong stresses per line and a pause, or **cæsura,** in the middle of the line, gave Anglo-Saxon verse a formal, elevated quality appropriate for heroic tales.

The Old English language was rich in **compound words,** ones made up of two words joined together. Many of these words were stock formulas for describing people and objects. Thus a king might be described as a ring-giver or victor-lord, a warrior as experienced in war-craft, a dragon as an air-flier, a demon as a spirit-slayer, a ship as a wave-crosser, a speech as a word-saying, and earth as the middle-yard between heaven and the regions below.

Some of the scop's stock formulas, or descriptions, took the form of **kennings,** fanciful, metaphorical two-word replacements for nouns. Examples of such kennings include whale-road or swan-road for "sea," bird-joy for "feather," battle-flasher for "sword," life-house for "body," earth-hall for "grave," slaughter-wolf for "Viking," and glee-wood for "harp."

Another common poetic technique used in *Beowulf* is a form of repetition called **variation.** Thus one tribe is described in the poem as "the victor-people, bold-daring warriors, the martial Scylfings."

The text of *Beowulf* given on the following pages begins with the Prologue reprinted in Old English with a word-for-word translation by Robin Lamb. Studying this Prologue will give you a sense of the sound of the original. The remaining selections from the text are given in a prose translation by E. Talbot Donaldson, one of the greatest scholars of the Old English language and its literature. The portions of the text not given in prose translation have been summarized. The summaries appear in italics.

GOALS/OBJECTIVES

Studying this lesson will enable students to

- appreciate the classic Anglo-Saxon epic *Beowulf* and empathize with the difficulties of life in Anglo-Saxon times
- define and identify compound and collective nouns

- describe and identify characteristic features of Anglo-Saxon verse (cæsura, alliteration, kenning) and the oral tradition
- retell the story of Beowulf and identify features it shares with other traditional tales and epics
- describe the Anglo-Saxon heroic ideal

TRIBES AND GENEALOGIES IN *BEOWULF*

A. Tribes Mentioned in *Beowulf*

1. **The Danes** (Also called Gar-Danes, Ring-Danes, Spear-Danes, and Scyldings)

2. **The Geats** (Also called Sea-Geats, War-Geats, and Weather-Geats)

3. **The Swedes**

4. **The Frisians** (or Jutes)

5. **The Heatho-Bards** (or Battle-Bards)

B. Genealogy and Descendants of the Danish King Hrothgar

```
                                    ┌── Daughter
                                    │      +
                                    │  Onela the Swede
                                    │
                                    ├── Halga ──── Hrothulf
Scyld        Beowulf               │
the    ───   the    ── Healfdene ──┤
Sheaf-Child  Dane                  ├── Heorogar
                                    │
                                    │                    ┌── Hrethric
                                    │   HROTHGAR         │
                                    └──    +     ────────┼── Hrothmund
                                        WEALHTHEOW       │
                                                         └── Freawaru
```

C. Genealogy of Beowulf of the Geats

```
           ┌── Herebeald
           │                        ┌── Heardred
           │   Hygelac              │
           │      +      ───────────┤
           │    Hygd                │   Daughter
Hrethel ───┤                        └──    +
           │                            Eofor
           ├── Hæthcyn
           │
           │   Daughter
           └──    +      ──── BEOWULF
               Ecgtheow
```

VOCABULARY FROM THE SELECTION

alien	heath	moor	ravenously	tract
corselet	hew	onslaught	reminisce	tribute
fastness	hilt	perpetual	remorse	venture
fen	loathsome	purge	resolute	wretched
forged	mail	pyre	resound	wrought
hale	mead	rabble	savor	

READER'S JOURNAL

Students might think about examples of admirable persons from their lives as well as in popular books and films.

LANGUAGE SKILLS

Kennings are imaginative compounds. Examples of kennings in the poem include *whale-road* for "sea" and *ring-giver* for "king."

ADDITIONAL QUESTIONS AND ACTIVITIES

Encourage students to try to sound out the Old English verse on this page. Have them see how many words they can identify. Point out that the characters þ and ð are pronounced like *th*.

▶ Interested students can consult a textbook such as *Bright's Old English Grammar and Reader.*

READER'S JOURNAL

What makes a truly great person? Freewrite about this subject in your journal. Then, as you read *Beowulf*, compare your ideals with those expressed in the poem.

LANGUAGE SKILLS

Read the Language Arts Survey, 2.5, "Compound and Collective Nouns." Then, as you read *Beowulf*, find examples of interesting compounds and list these in your journal.

FROM

Beowulf

PROSE TRANSLATION BY E. TALBOT DONALDSON
INTERLINEAR TRANSLATION OF PROLOGUE BY ROBIN LAMB

PROLOGUE (lines 1–11), in Old English, with an interlinear translation

Hwaet we Gar-Dena
Yes, we of the Gar-Danes

in gear-dagum,
in days of old,

Þeod-cyninga,
The great kings'

Þrym gefrunon:
renown have heard of,

Hu ða æþelingas
How those princes

ellen fremendon.
bravery displayed.

Oft Scyld Scefing
Often Scyld the Sheaf-child

sceaþena þreatum
from bands of robbers,

Monegum mægþum,
From many tribes,

meodo-setla ofteah:
their mead-benches dragged away,

egsode eorlas
Inspired earls with fear,

syððan ærest wearð
after he first was

feasceaft funden:
Found helpless.

he þæs frofre gebad,
He thence looked for comfort,

Weox under wolcnum,
Flourished under the clouds,

weorþmyntum þah,
in dignities prospered,

Oðþæt him æghwylc
Until him every one

þara ymb-sittendra
of those sitting around

Ofer hron-rade
Over the whale-road

Gomban gyldan:
[and] tribute pay.

hyran scolde,
must obey,

þæt wæs god cyning.
That was a good king!

PROLOGUE (lines 1–11), in prose translation

Yes, we have heard of the glory of the Spear-Danes' kings in the old days—how the princes of that people did brave deeds.

Often Scyld Scefing[1] took mead-benches away from enemy bands, from many tribes, terrified their nobles—after the time that he was first found helpless. He lived to find comfort for that, became great under the skies, prospered in honors until every one of those who lived about him, across the whale-road,[2] had to obey him, pay him tribute. That was a good king.

Scyld the Dane bears a son named Beowulf [not the hero of the poem]. He afterward dies and is laid on a ship loaded with treasures and weapons. The ship is then set adrift on the sea.

[Beowulf the Warrior]

Canto 1

Beowulf the Dane becomes a famous king and gives birth to four children, including Hrothgar.

Hrothgar becomes a great leader and builds a large hall named Heorot.

Then the fierce spirit [Grendel] painfully endured hardship for a time, he who

dwelt in the darkness, for every day he heard loud mirth in the hall; there was the sound of the harp, the clear song of the scop.[3] . . . Thus these warriors lived in joy, blessed, until one began to do evil deeds, a hellish enemy. The grim spirit was called Grendel, known as a rover of the borders, one who held the moors, fen and fastness. Unhappy creature, he lived for a time in the home of the monsters' race, after God had condemned them as kin of Cain.[4]

Canto 2

Grendel kills thirty thanes.[5]

The famous king, hero of old days, sat joyless; the mighty one suffered, felt sorrow for his thanes, when they saw the track of the foe, of the cursed spirit: that hardship was too strong, too loathsome and long-lasting. Nor was there a longer interval, but after one night Grendel again

---

1. **Scyld Scefing.** The poem begins by recalling the history of the Danes from the time of a king known as Scyld Scefing (literally, "Scyld the Sheaf-Child"). The king's name comes from a legend that he was found as a baby floating in a basket of reeds. This legend may have been borrowed from a similar story told about Moses in the Bible.
2. **whale-road.** *Whale-road* is a kenning for "sea." See the note on kennings on page 100.
3. **scop.** The *scop* was a poet and singer who entertained warriors with stories about heroic exploits.
4. **kin of Cain.** The Christian copyist has made Grendel a descendant of Cain, who, according to Genesis 4, killed his brother Abel and so was made an outcast, despised by others.
5. **thanes.** A *thane*, or *earl*, was a warrior, one of the retainers of the king.

FROM *BEOWULF* **103**

ADDITIONAL QUESTIONS AND ACTIVITIES

Students might research and compare the use of the motif of a baby left in a basket in sources such as the legend of Scyld Scefing, the epic of Gilgamesh, and the story of Moses in the Bible. In what ways are the stories different? In what way are they similar? Why might this motif have been used?

VOCABULARY IN CONTEXT

- Those who did not pay the tribute risked having their homes and property destroyed.
- He had gone out for an evening walk but found the idea of being alone on the dark, open, boggy moor too eerie.
- Her boots made squishy sounds and startled some salamanders as she sloshed through the fen.
- After the ice began to crack, he found stepping off the frozen lake and onto fastness a great relief.
- That loathsome cheater was looking over my shoulder the whole time!

Illustration by Sol Graphic Design

Grendel Slaughtering the Danes in Hrothgar's Hall, Heorot

did greater slaughter—and had no <u>remorse</u> for it—vengeful acts and wicked: he was too intent on them. . . . Thus Grendel held sway and fought against right, one against all, until the best of houses stood empty. It was a long time, the length of twelve winters, that the lord of the Scyldings suffered grief, all woes, great sorrows. . . . For the monster was relentless, the dark death-shadow, against warriors old and young, lay in wait and ambushed them. In the <u>perpetual</u> darkness he held to the misty moors: men do not know where hell-demons direct their footsteps.

> *Hrothgar and his councilors seek a plan to rid themselves of Grendel, but to no avail. In desperation, they turn to sacrifices in heathen temples.*

Cantos 3–7

Beowulf hears of Grendel's deeds and vows revenge. He has a ship built to take him and his warriors to Hrothgar's aid.

One of Hrothgar's men, a coast-guard, challenges the newly arrived Beowulf.

Beowulf asks to be taken to see Hrothgar, king of the Danes. On being told of this, Hrothgar recalls having known Beowulf as a child. He asks that Beowulf be brought to him.

The war-leader, hardy under helmet, advanced till he stood on the hearth. Beowulf spoke, his <u>mail</u>-shirt glistened, armor-net woven by the blacksmith's skill: "Hail, Hrothgar! I am kinsman and thane

WORDS FOR EVERYDAY USE:

re • morse (ri môrs´) *n.*, sense of guilt
per • pet • u • al (pər pech´ ōō əl) *adj.*, constant, eternal
mail (māl) *adj.*, flexible armor made of metal or chains

VOCABULARY IN CONTEXT

- Lorenz felt only <u>remorse</u> as the state trooper pulled him over to give him a speeding ticket.
- "I am just in <u>perpetual</u> agony," he complained, "from these ugly and uncomfortable shoes!"
- The museum announced the acquisition of a large collection of seventh-century swords, shields, helmets, and body <u>mail</u>.

of Hygelac.[6] In my youth I have set about many brave deeds. The affair of Grendel was made known to me on my native soil: sea-travelers say that this hall, best of buildings, stands empty and useless to all warriors after the evening-light becomes hidden beneath the cover of the sky. Therefore my people, the best wise earls, advised me thus, lord Hrothgar, that I should seek you because they know what my strength can accomplish. . . . And now alone I shall settle affairs with Grendel, the monster, the demon. . . . You will not need to hide my head if death takes me, for he will have me blood-smeared; he will bear away my bloody flesh meaning to savor it, he will eat ruthlessly, the walker alone, will stain his retreat in the moor; no longer will you need trouble yourself to take care of my body.

Hrothgar reminisces about Beowulf's father and about relations between the Danes, the Geats, and a people called the Wylfings. Then he begins to speak of Grendel and invites Beowulf to sit down to feast.

Cantos 8–10

One of Hrothgar's thanes, named Hunferth, challenges Beowulf. Beowulf answers the challenge by telling a story of a mighty feat that he performed as a boy, a swimming contest against a fellow named Breca. Beowulf tells how he encountered sea monsters while swimming and was dragged to the sea floor by one of them.

Beowulf tells of his victory over the sea monsters, saying that "Fate often saves an undoomed man when his courage is good." He then boasts that he will destroy

Grendel. *His boast brings Hrothgar much joy. Then Hrothgar's wife, Wealhtheow, serves mead to the guests and thanks God for Beowulf's assistance. Hrothgar and his men retire for the night, leaving Beowulf to face Grendel in the hall.*

In the mead hall, alone with his attendants, Beowulf awaits the coming of Grendel. Having heard that Grendel fights without a sword, Beowulf decides to meet the monster unarmed.

Canto 11

The creature deprived of joy came walking to the hall. Quickly the door gave way, fastened with fire-forged bands, when he touched it with his hands. Driven by evil desire, swollen with rage, he tore it open, the hall's mouth. . . . He saw many men in the hall, a band of kinsmen all asleep together, a company of war-men. Then his heart laughed: dreadful monster, he thought that before the day came he would divide the life from the body of every one of them.

The kinsman of Hygelac, mighty man, watched how the evil-doer would make his quick onslaught. Nor did the monster mean to delay it, but, starting his work, he suddenly seized a sleeping man, tore at him ravenously, bit into his bone-locks, drank the blood from his veins, swallowed huge morsels; quickly he had eaten all of the lifeless one, feet and hands. He stepped closer, then felt with his arm for the brave-hearted man on the bed, reached out towards him, the foe with his hand; at once in fierce response Beowulf seized it and sat

---

6. **Hygelac.** King of the Geats

WORDS FOR EVERYDAY USE:
sa • vor (sā´ vər) *vt.,* eat with relish
rem • i • nisce (rem´ ə nis´) *vi.,* talk about memories
mead (mēd) *n.,* wine made from honey
forged (fôrjd) *adj.,* heated and shaped by pounding
on • slaught (än´ slôt) *n.,* a violent, intense attack
rav • e • nous • ly (rav´ ə nəs lē) *adv.,* greedily

FROM *BEOWULF* 105

BIBLIOGRAPHICAL NOTE

History

Blair, P. Hunter. *Introduction to Anglo-Saxon England.* 1956.

Campbell, James, ed. *The Anglo-Saxons.* 1982.

Stenton, F. M. *Anglo-Saxon England.* 3rd ed. 1971.

Whitelock, Dorothy. *The Beginnings of English Society.* 1952.

Criticism

Damico, Helen and A. H. Olsen. *New Readings on Women in Old English Literature.* 1990.

Fulk, R. D. *Interpretations of Beowulf.* 1991.

Greenfield, S. B. *Hero and Exile: The Art of Old English Poetry.* 1989.

Tolkein, J. R. R. "Beowulf, the Monsters, and the Critics" in Fulk.

Woods, George, et al. *The Literature of England.* 4th ed. Vol. 1. 1958.

VOCABULARY IN CONTEXT

- Sam savors food flavored with savory: "I can't get enough" he says.
- Jo's dad liked to reminisce, but her mother preferred to forget the past.
- We couldn't have mead at our *Beowulf* reenactment, so we drank apple juice instead.
- The blacksmith's arms are strong from hammering to make her well-known forged fireplace tools.
- The defensive squad had been overrun on each set of downs, but they once again broke from the huddle and prepared for the onslaught.
- He ravenously grabbed the last slice of pizza.

Bibliographical Note

• The standard text of *Beowulf* is Klaeber, F. *Beowulf and the Fight of Finnsburg.* 3rd ed. 1950.

• All the known poetry in Old English is collected in Krapp, G. P., and E. V. K. Dobbie. *The Anglo-Saxon Poetic Records.* 6 vols. 1931–1953.

up, leaning on his own arm. Straightway the fosterer of crimes knew that he had not encountered on middle-earth, anywhere in this world, a harder hand-grip from another man.[7] In mind he became frightened, in his spirit: not for that might he escape the sooner. His heart was eager to get away, he would flee to his hiding-place, seek his <u>rabble</u> of devil.

Canto 12

Not for anything would the protector of warriors let the murderous guest go off alive: he did not consider his life-days of use to any of the nations. There more than enough of Beowulf's earls drew swords, old heirlooms, wished to protect the life of their dear lord, famous prince, however they might. They did not know when they entered the fight, hardy-spirited warriors, and when they thought to <u>hew</u> him on every side, to seek his soul, that not any of the best irons on earth, no war-sword, would touch the evil-doer: for with a charm[8] he had made victory-weapons useless, every sword-edge. His departure to death from the time of this life was to be <u>wretched</u>; and the <u>alien</u> spirit was to travel far off into the power of fiends. Then he who before had brought trouble of heart to mankind, committed many crimes—he was at war with God—found that his body would do him no good, for the great-hearted kinsman of Hygelac had him by the hand. Each was hateful to the other alive. The awful monster had lived to feel pain in his body, a huge wound in his shoulder was exposed, his sinews sprang apart, his bone-locks broke. Glory in battle was given to Beowulf. Grendel must flee from there, mortally sick, seek his joyless home in the fen-slopes. He knew the more surely that his life's end had come, the full number of his days. For all the Danes was their wish fulfilled after the bloody fight. Thus he who had lately come from far off, wise and stout-hearted, had <u>purged</u> Heorot, saved Hrothgar's house from affliction. He rejoiced in his night's work, a deed to make famous his courage. The man of the Geats had fulfilled his boast to the East-Danes; so too he had remedied all the grief, the malice-caused sorrow that they had endured before, and had had to suffer from harsh necessity, no small distress. That was clearly proved when the battle-brave man set the hand up under the curved roof—the arm and the shoulder: there all together was Grendel's grasp.

Cantos 13–18

People gather from far and wide to praise Beowulf's mighty deed. Hrothgar promises to treat Beowulf, thereafter, as his own son, then commands that Heorot be cleaned and decorated with golden tapestries in preparation for a feast. Beowulf's victory is rewarded by gifts of armor, horses, and weapons.

Beowulf's warriors receive gifts from Hrothgar, and the man whom Grendel killed is honored. The entertainment continues.

---

7. **had not encountered . . . man**. Physical strength was an obvious virtue in a warrior. Beowulf's strength was said to surpass that of any other man.
8. **charm**. Spells, or charms, are common features of Germanic folklore.

Words for Everyday Use:

rab • ble (rab´əl) *n.*, a mob

hew (hyo͞o) *vt.*, cut, hack

wretch • ed (rech´id) *adj.*, miserable, dismal

al • ien (āl´ ē ən) *adj.*, strange, unnatural

purge (pɜrj) *vt.*, cleanse of sin

📖 Vocabulary in Context

• He used demagoguery deftly to incite the <u>rabble</u>.
• The guide pointed to the log cabin and said, "The trees were felled and <u>hewn</u> by hand."
• He found his <u>wretched</u> garret depressing but could afford nothing better.
• She looked just liked everyone around here, but she felt quite <u>alien</u> in this land where she could not speak the language.
• His cry, "We must <u>purge</u> this community of its riff-raff!" led to a shower of abuse.

The scop finishes his song. Then Queen Wealhtheow gives Beowulf presents—a corselet, rings, and a collar. After the feast, Hrothgar's thanes lie down to sleep in the hall, their armor beside them.

Canto 19

Then they sank to sleep. One paid sorely for his evening rest, just as had often befallen them when Grendel guarded the gold-hall, <u>wrought</u> wrong until the end came, death after misdeeds. It came to be seen, wide-known to men, that after the bitter battle an avenger still lived for an evil space: Grendel's mother, woman, monster-wife, was mindful of her misery, she who had to dwell in the terrible water, the cold currents, after Cain became sword-slayer of his only brother, his own father's son. Then Cain went as an outlaw to flee the cheerful life of men, marked for his murder, held to the wasteland. From him sprang many a devil sent by fate. Grendel was one of them, hateful outcast who at Heorot found a waking man waiting his warfare. There the monster had laid hold upon him, but he was mindful of the great strength, the large gift God had given him, and relied on the Almighty for favor, comfort and help. By that he overcame the foe, subdued the hell-spirit. Then he went off wretched, bereft of joy, to seek his dying-place, enemy of mankind. And his mother, still greedy and gallows-grim, would go on a sorrowful venture, avenge her son's death.[9]

Seeking vengeance, Grendel's mother comes to Heorot, kills one of Hrothgar's thanes, and takes the severed arm of her son back to the fen. Beowulf is not present, and so she is able to do her will.

Cantos 20–21

Hrothgar tells Beowulf of the loss of the thane Aeschere, a trusted advisor, and of the murderous mother of Grendel who lives "where the mountain stream goes down under the darkness of the hills, the flood under the earth."

Beowulf vows to avenge the death of Aeschere. Hrothgar and his men lead Beowulf to the water under which is Grendel's mother's cave. The water is filled with sea serpents and boils with blood. Beowulf dons a helmet and mail shirt, and borrows from one of Hrothgar's men the sword named Hrunting.

Canto 22

The surging water took the warrior. Then was it a part of a day before he might see the bottom's floor.[10] Straightway that which had held the flood's <u>tract</u> a hundred half-years, ravenous for prey, grim and greedy, saw that some man from above was exploring the dwelling of monsters. Then she groped toward him, took the warrior in her awful grip. Yet not the more for that did she hurt his <u>hale</u> body within: his ring-armor shielded him about on the outside so that she could not pierce the war-dress, the linked body-mail, with hateful fingers. Then as she came to the bottom the sea-wolf bore the ring-prince to her house so that—no matter how brave he was—he might not wield weapons; but many monsters attacked him in the water, many a sea-

---

9. **avenge . . . death.** Germanic custom required that the kin of a slain person avenge the death.
10. **part of . . . floor.** Such impossible feats are a common element, or *motif*, in folklore.

WORDS FOR EVERYDAY USE:

corse • let (kôrs´ lit) *n.*, piece of body armor
wrought (rôt) *vt.*, worked

tract (trakt) *n.*, expanse, area
hale (hāl) *adj.*, strong and healthy

Unusual placements of appositive phrases were common in Anglo-Saxon verse, as in "Then the woman of the Helmings . . . brought the mead-bowl to Beowulf, the ring-adorned queen mature of mind." Additional examples can be found in "Cædmon's Hymn" (page 82) and "The Wife's Lament" (page 88). Point out that to modern ears these placements are sometimes unintentionally humorous. Have students identify unusually placed appositives in *Beowulf*.

▶ For additional instruction in and practice with appositives, refer students to the Language Arts Survey, 2.48, "Adding Appositives and Appositive Phrases," and the *Essential Skills Practice Book: Language*, 2.48.

▶ For additional instruction in and practice with the placement of modifiers, refer students to the Language Arts Survey, 2.63, "Correcting Dangling or Misplaced Modifiers," and the *Essential Skills Practice Book: Language*, 2.63.

VOCABULARY IN CONTEXT

- The sword was dulled when it struck the enemy's <u>corselet</u>.
- The silver was skillfully <u>wrought</u> into a leaf-shaped pattern.
- Hrothgar rewarded the warrior with a large <u>tract</u> of land.
- Looking at Beowulf, one noticed immediately his <u>hale</u> physique.

TEACHER'S EDITION **107**

beast tore at his mail shirt with war-tusks, strange creatures afflicted him. Then the earl saw that he was in some hostile hall where no water harmed him at all, and the flood's onrush might not touch him because of the hall-roof. He saw firelight, a clear blaze shine bright.

Then the good man saw the accursed dweller in the deep, the mighty mere-woman. He gave a great thrust to his sword—his hand did not withhold the stroke—so that the etched blade sang at her head a fierce war-song. Then the stranger found that the battle-lightning would not bite, harm her life, but the edge failed the prince in his need: many a hand-battle had it endured before, often sheared helmet, war-coat of man fated to die: this was the first time for the rare treasure that its glory had failed.

But still he was <u>resolute</u>, not slow of his courage, mindful of fame, the kinsman of Hygelac. Then, angry warrior, he threw away the sword, . . . he trusted in his strength, his mighty hand-grip. So ought a man to do when he thinks to get a long-lasting praise in battle: he cares not for his life. Then he seized by the hair Grendel's mother—the man of the War-Geats did not shrink from the fight. Battle-hardened, now swollen with rage, he pulled his deadly foe so that she fell to the floor. Quickly in her turn she repaid him his gift with her grim claws and clutched at him: then weary-hearted, the strongest of warriors, of foot-soldiers, stumbled so that he fell. Then she sat upon the hall-guest and drew her knife, broad and bright-edged. She would avenge her child, her only son. The woven breast-armor lay on his shoulder: that protected his life, withstood entry of point or of edge. Then the son of Ecgtheow would have fared amiss under the wide ground, the champion of the Geats, if the battle-shirt had not brought help, the hard war-net—and holy God brought about victory in war: the wise Lord, Ruler of the Heavens, decided it with right, easily, when Beowulf had stood up again.

Canto 23

Then he saw among the armor a victory-blessed blade, an old sword made by the giants,[11] strong of its edges, glory of warriors: it was the best of weapons, except that is was larger than any other man might bear to war-sport, good and adorned, the work of giants. He seized the linked <u>hilt</u>, he who fought for the Scyldings, savage and slaughter-bent, drew the patterned-blade; desperate of life, he struck angrily so that it bit her hard on the neck, broke the bone-rings. The blade went through all the doomed body. She fell to the floor, the sword was sweating, the man rejoiced in his work.

Beowulf finds Grendel's body and cuts off his head.

The men waiting on the shore see the water turn red and fear for Beowulf.

The blade of Beowulf's sword melts. He swims to shore with the jeweled hilt and Grendel's head. He is greeted with much rejoicing. Beowulf presents Grendel's head to Hrothgar.

---

11. **giants.** *Beowulf* contains many references to giants. Some are additions made by the Christian scribe, echoing Genesis 6:3, "In those days there were giants on the earth."

WORDS FOR EVERYDAY USE:

res • o • lute (rez´ ə lo͞ot) *adj.*, determined
hilt (hilt) *n.*, sword handle

VOCABULARY IN CONTEXT

- Despite his wounds, the warrior remained <u>resolute</u>; he would continue the battle.
- Beowulf grasped the brass <u>hilt</u> of the sword and pulled the weapon out of its sheath.
- Grendel's mother came running across the <u>heath</u>, stomping on what little vegetation there was.

Cantos 24–31

Beowulf tells Hrothgar of his adventure and gives the king the hilt of Grendel's mother's sword, which is decorated with ancient runic[12] letters describing the war of the giants before Noah's flood. Beowulf returns the sword Hrunting to Hunferth. Graciously, he says nothing about how the sword had failed him. Then Beowulf and his men set sail for the land of the Geats, their home.

Once home, Beowulf recounts his adventures and the gifts that he received in the land of the Danes.

[Beowulf the King]

Then the broad kingdom came into Beowulf's hand. He held it well fifty winters—he was a wise king, an old guardian of the land—until in the dark nights a certain one, a dragon, began to hold sway, which on the high <u>heath</u> kept watch over a hoard, a steep stone-barrow.[13] Beneath lay a path unknown to men. By this there went inside a certain man [who made his way near to the heathen hoard; his hand took a cup, large, a shining treasure. The dragon did not afterwards conceal it though in his sleep he was tricked by the craft of the thief. That the people discovered, the neighboring folk—that he was swollen with rage].

Canto 32–35

Furious at the theft of the cup, the dragon begins attacking the countryside, and setting fire to buildings by night.

Then the terror was made known to Beowulf, quickly in its truth, that his own home, best of buildings, had melted in surging flames, the throne-seat of the Geats. That was anguish of spirit to the good man, the greatest of heart-sorrows. . . . The fiery dragon with his flames had destroyed the people's stronghold, the land along the sea, the heart of the country. Because of that the war-king, the lord of the Weather-Geats, devised punishment for him. The protector of fighting men, lord of earls,[14] commanded that a wonderful battle-shield be made all of iron. Well he knew that the wood of the forest might not help him—linden against flame. The prince good from old times was to come to the end of the days that had been lent him, life in the world, and the worm with him, though he had long held the hoarded wealth. Then the ring-prince scorned to seek the far-flier with a troop, a large army. He had no fear for himself of the combat, nor did he think the worm's war-power anything great, his strength and his courage, because he himself had come through many battles before, dared perilous straits, clashes of war, after he had purged Hrothgar's hall, victorious warrior, and in combat crushed to death Grendel's kin, loathsome race.

Having made up his mind to fight the dragon, Beowulf and some companions go to view the monster in his lair. Sitting some distance from the dragon, the companions listen to Beowulf tell of other battles and of other warriors slain.

---

12. **runic.** The runic alphabet, known as *futhark*, was used by Germanic tribes before the introduction of the Latin alphabet still used in English today.

13. **stone-barrow.** A barrow is a circular enclosure made of earth or stone.

14. **protector . . . earls.** This is an example of the technique known as *variations*, in which a person or thing is named several times using different formulas or epithets.

WORDS FOR EVERYDAY USE:
    heath (hēth) *n.,* a wasteland covered in heather and shrubs

LITERARY TECHNIQUE

Compound Words. Have students find kennings and other compound words used as epithets to refer to people. *Ring-giver,* for King Hrothgar, is an example.

Beowulf spoke, for the last time spoke words in boast: "In my youth I engaged in many wars. Old guardian of the people, I shall still seek battle, perform a deed of fame, if the evil-doer will come to me out of the earth-hall."

Then he saluted each of the warriors, the bold helmet-bearers, for the last time —his own dear companions. "I would not bear sword, weapon, to the worm, if I knew how else according to my boast I might grapple with the monster, as I did of old with Grendel. But I expect her hot battle-fire, steam and poison. Therefore I have on me shield and mail-shirt. I will not flee a foot-step from the barrow-ward, but it shall be with us at the wall as fate allots, the ruler of every man. I am confi-dent in heart, so I forgo help against the war-flier. Wait on the barrow, safe in your mail-shirts, men in armor—which of us two may better bear wounds after our bloody meeting. This is not your <u>venture</u>, nor is it right for any man except me alone that he should spend his strength against the monster, do this man's deed. By my courage I shall get gold, or war will take your king, dire life-evil."

Then the brave warrior arose by his shield; hardy under helmet he went in his mail-shirt beneath the stone-cliffs, had trust in his strength—that of one man: such is not the way of the cowardly. Then he saw by the wall—he who had come through many wars, good in his great-heartedness, many clashes in battle when

WORDS FOR EVERYDAY USE: **ven • ture** (ven´ chər) *n.,* a dangerous undertaking

VOCABULARY IN CONTEXT

• "Who will join me in this <u>venture</u>?" asked the warrior queen.
• "The underground den will <u>resound</u> with the dragon's cries," boasted the warrior.

Illustration by Sol Graphic Design

troops meet together—a stone arch standing, through it a stream bursting out of the barrow: there was welling of a current hot with killing fires, and he might not endure any while unburnt by the dragon's flame the hollow near the hoard. Then the man of the Weather-Geats, enraged as he was, let a word break from his breast. Stout-hearted he shouted; his voice went roaring, clear in battle, in under the gray stone. Hate was stirred up, the hoard's guard[15] knew the voice of a man. No more time was there to ask for peace. First the monster's breath came out of the stone, the hot war-steam. The earth <u>resounded</u>. The man below the barrow, lord of the Geats, swung his shield against the dreadful visitor. Then the heart of the coiled thing was aroused to seek combat. The good war-king had drawn his sword, the old heirloom, not blunt of edge. To each of them as they threatened destruction there was terror of the other. Firm-hearted he stood with his shield high, the lord of friends, while quickly the worm coiled itself; he waited in his armor. Then, coiling in flames, he came gliding on, hastening to his fate. The good shield protected the life and body of the famous prince, but for a shorter while than his wish was. There for the first time, the first day in his life, he might not prevail, since Fate did not assign him such glory in battle. The lord of the Geats raised his hand,

---

15. **hoard's guard.** The dragon

WORDS FOR
EVERYDAY USE: **re • sound** (ri zound´) *vi.*, reverberate, echo

FROM *BEOWULF*   **111**

ADDITIONAL QUESTIONS AND ACTIVITIES

"Nothing can ever set aside kinship in him who means well." This last line from canto 35 expresses the importance the Anglo-Saxons placed on kinship. Ask students the following questions: Why was kinship so important to the Anglo-Saxons? How do modern views of kinship differ from Anglo-Saxon views? Why might this be so?

struck the shining horror so with his forged blade that the edge failed, bright on the bone, bit less surely than its folk-king had need, hard-pressed in perils. Then because of the battle-stroke the barrow-ward's heart was savage, he exhaled death-fire—the war-flames sprang wide. The gold-friend of the Geats boasted of no great victories: the war blade had failed, naked at need, as it ought not to have done, iron good from old times. That was no pleasant journey, not one on which the famous son of Ecgtheow would wish to leave his land; against his will he must take up a dwelling-place elsewhere—as every man must give up the days that are lent him.

It was not long until they came together again, dreadful foes. The hoard-guard took heart, once more his breast swelled with his breathing. Encircled with flames, he who before had ruled a fold felt harsh pain. Nor did his companions, sons of nobles, take up their stand in a troop about him with the courage of fighting men, but they crept to the wood, protected their lives. In only one of them the heart surged with sorrows: nothing can ever set aside kinship in him who means well.[16]

Canto 36

Wiglaf remembers here the gifts that Beowulf bestowed upon his family in the past and calls on the others to come to Beowulf's aid. He then wades into the dragon smoke to assist his king.

The worm came on, angry, the terrible malice-filled foe, shining with surging flames, to seek for the second time his enemies, hated men. Fire advanced in waves; shield burned to the boss; mail-shirt might give no help to the young spear-warrior; but the young man went quickly under his kinsman's shield when his own was consumed with flames. Then the war-king was again mindful of fame, struck with his war-sword with great strength so that it stuck in the head-bone, driven with force: Naegling[17] broke, the sword of Beowulf failed in the fight, old and steel-gray. It was not ordained for him that iron edges might help in the combat. Too strong was the hand that I have heard strained every sword with its stroke, when he bore wound-hardened weapon to battle: he was none the better for it.

Then for the third time, the folk-harmer, the fearful fire-dragon, was mindful of feuds, set upon the brave one when the chance came, hot and battle-grim seized all his neck with his sharp fangs: he was smeared with life-blood, gore welled out in waves.

Cantos 37–42

Then, I have heard, at the need of the folk-king the earl at his side made his courage known, his might and his keen-ness—as was natural to him. He took no heed for that head, but the hand of the brave man was burned as he helped his kinsman, as the man in armor struck the hateful foe a little lower down, so that the sword sank in, shining and engraved; and then the fire began to subside. The king himself then still controlled his senses, drew the battle-knife, biting and war-sharp, that he wore on his mail-shirt: the protector of the Weather-Geats cut the worm through the middle. They felled the foe, courage drove his life out, and they had destroyed him together, the two noble kinsmen. So ought a man be, a thane at need. To the prince that was the last moment of victory for his own deeds, of work in the world.

Wiglaf washes Beowulf's wounds and unfastens his helmet.

---

16. **nothing . . . means well.** This line summarizes eloquently the importance of kinship to the Anglo-Saxons.
17. **Naegling.** Beowulf's sword

Anglo-Saxon belt-buckle. The British Museum

Beowulf spoke—despite his wounds spoke, his mortal hurts. He knew well he had lived out his days' time, joy on earth; all passed was the number of his days, death was very near.

Beowulf makes a parting speech and then asks to see the dragon's hoarded treasure.

The men who had fled to the forest return and are reproved by Wiglaf. Wiglaf then sends a messenger to tell of Beowulf's death.

The men go to the dragon's lair, where they see the bodies of the beast and of their king. Wiglaf and seven others load a cart with the dragon's treasure.

Canto 43

The people prepare a large <u>pyre</u> and mourn Beowulf. They build a memorial to him and remember his great deeds.

So it is fitting that a man honor his liege lord with words, love him in heart when he must be led forth from the body. Thus the people of the Geats, his hearth-companions, lamented the death of their lord. They said that he was of world-kings the mildest of men and the gentlest, kindest to his people, and most eager for fame. ■

WORDS FOR
EVERYDAY USE: **pyre** (pīr) *n.,* funeral fire

VOCABULARY IN CONTEXT
- The people went into the forest to gather wood for a funeral <u>pyre</u>.

RESPONDING TO THE SELECTION

Encourage students to consider real persons as well as television and movie characters.

ANSWERS FOR REVIEWING THE SELECTION

RECALLING

1. Hrothgar is king of the Danes. The Geats are Beowulf's people. The Geats sail to fight Grendel.

2. Hrothgar rewards Beowulf for killing Grendel by giving him decorated armor.

3. Heorot is the Danes' mead hall. Grendel's mother comes to Heorot to avenge Grendel's death. She kills a thane. Beowulf follows her to her lair at the bottom of the sea.

4. The dragon flies, spits fire, has scaled skin, and coils like a snake. All the thanes except Wiglaf run into the woods to hide from the dragon; Wiglaf joins the fight. Beowulf dies from injuries sustained in the fight with the dragon, but the others, including Wiglaf, are unharmed.

INTERPRETING

Responses will vary. Possible responses are given.

5. Beowulf fights for glory and reputation.

6. Reward ceremonies may have shown members of the community the type of actions to which they should have aspired.

7. Grendel's mother may seem more sympathetic because she is grief-stricken for her offspring, while Grendel has no clear motivation for doing evil other than being evil.

8. Beowulf fights because he is angered when the dragon destroys his and his neighbors' homes and because it is his duty as king and guardian of the people. Wiglaf is encouraged to fight when he remembers the benefits that Beowulf has conferred upon his family.

SYNTHESIZING

Responses will vary. Possible responses are given.

9. An Anglo-Saxon hero is a warrior who does not shy from danger, who is powerfully strong, who is proud and who seeks out glory, who is loyal, and who is resigned to fate and death. (cont.)

Responding to the Selection

Who is your favorite hero from modern literature, film, television, or current events? What do you admire about this character? Do you consider the character of Beowulf a hero? Why or why not? How does Beowulf compare to your modern-day hero?

Reviewing the Selection

RECALLING

1. Who is Hrothgar? Who are the Geats? Why do the Geats sail to the land of the Danes?

2. Why does Hrothgar reward Beowulf? How does he reward him?

3. What is Heorot? Why does Grendel's mother come to Heorot? What does she do there? To where does Beowulf follow her?

4. Describe the dragon that Beowulf fights. What do Beowulf's thanes do during the fight? What happens to them and to Beowulf?

INTERPRETING

5. What does Beowulf stand to gain by helping Hrothgar and his people?

6. What might have been the importance of rewards and reward ceremonies in this society?

7. Is Grendel's mother a more, or less sympathetic character than Grendel? Why do you think so?

8. Why does Beowulf fight the dragon? What motivates him during the battle? What motivates Wiglaf?

SYNTHESIZING

9. Beowulf is a hero by Anglo-Saxon standards. Taking Beowulf as a model, what characterizes an Anglo-Saxon hero? Would you say that Beowulf is also a hero in contemporary terms? What modern heroic qualities does Beowulf exhibit?

10. What role does Wyrd, or fate, play in this poem? Did the person or persons who composed the poem believe that people can overcome fate and control their own lives? Explain.

Understanding Literature (Questions for Discussion)

1. **Oral Tradition.** An **oral tradition** is a work, a motif, an idea, or a custom that is passed by word-of-mouth from generation to generation. Many stories from the oral traditions of people around the globe contain fantastic, or unbelievable, elements. What are

ANSWERS FOR REVIEWING THE SELECTION (CONT.)

10. People cannot overcome fate, but fate does not determine everything. When outcomes are not determined by fate, they can be determined by luck or by the actions of those who are courageous enough to fight and strong enough to win.

some fantastic elements found in *Beowulf*? How would these elements help to explain the continuing popularity of a work over many, many generations?

2. **Epic.** An **epic** is a long story, often told in verse, involving heroes and gods. What have you learned from reading this poem about the beliefs and ways of life of the ancient Germanic peoples? How was their society organized? What did they do for entertainment? For them, what made a great person? What values did they think that a person should have? What aspects of their world view do you agree with or disagree with? Why?

Responding in Writing

1. **Kenning.** A **kenning** is an imaginative compound used in place of an ordinary noun. Examples of kennings for "sea" in *Beowulf* include *whale-road* and *swan's road*. The creation of kennings is still very much alive in English, as when an accountant is described as a *number cruncher* or a big radio is called a *boom box*. Try your hand at writing some kennings for ordinary objects in your environment. For example, a stroller might be called a *child-chariot* and a bridge might be a *bank-reacher*.

2. **Critical Essay.** In a **critical essay** a writer presents an argument in support of a particular interpretation of a work of literature. Study the material on writing a composition in the Language Arts Survey, 1.41–1.42. Then write a short critical essay supporting one of the following thesis statements or one of your own:

   a. *Beowulf* demonstrates how a hero can achieve a sort of immortality even if he is doomed by fate to die in battle.

   b. The character Beowulf is a perfect warrior and king, an embodiment of the Germanic heroic ideal.

   c. *Beowulf* demonstrates the importance of kinship to the ancient Germanic peoples.

   d. *Beowulf* is a tapestry of sometimes consistent and sometimes inconsistent Christian and pagan elements.

3. **Anglo-Saxon Poem.** Read the discussion of Anglo-Saxon verse on page 82. Then try writing verse of this kind. Choose an important figure from modern American or world history, someone of particular interest to you. Some possibilities include Eleanor Roosevelt, Susan B. Anthony, Mohandas Gandhi, and Martin Luther King, Jr. Do some research on this person in the library. Then write a verse telling that person's life story. Try to use four strong stresses in each line and to use alliteration to give your verse a musical quality.

   Example:

A mere man,	Mohandas Gandhi
Chose to challenge	and change the world
Without waging	warfare bitter
But practicing peace	and purposeful action
Persuaded a powerful	imperial state,
To renounce its rule,	the British Raj.

FROM *BEOWULF* **115**

ANSWERS FOR LANGUAGE LAB

1. <u>Warfare</u>; <u>tribes</u>
2. poems; period; <u>people</u>
3. <u>battle scene</u>; <u>countryside</u>
4. soldier; Anglo-Saxons
5. <u>myth-makers</u>

FOR MORE PRACTICE

Problem. According to Gildas, corrupt *priests* and nobles ruled *Britain* after the Romans defeated the *Saxons.*

Answer. priests; Britain; <u>Saxons</u>.

►For additional practice, see the *Essential Skills Practice Book: Writing,* 1.41–1.42.

PROJECT NOTES

►See the worksheets and evaluation forms for projects, *Assessment Portfolio,* 7.20–7.23.

1. Survey. Have students work in small groups to come up with a list of questions about beliefs and attitudes to be asked in the survey. Survey questionnaires should begin with demographic information such as age, ethnicity, grade in school, and place of residence. Have students try to survey as wide a variety of people as possible. Explain that the sample should be both broad and representative of the population being surveyed. When conducting their surveys, students should emphasize to their respondents that all information provided in answer to survey questions will be confidential.

(cont.)

Language Lab

Identifying Compound and Collective Nouns. Read the material on compound and collective nouns in the Language Arts Survey, 2.5. Then, copy the italicized nouns onto a sheet of paper. Underline the compound nouns once and the collective nouns twice. If a noun is neither compound nor collective, do not underline it.

1. *Warfare* among the ancient Germanic *tribes* was quite common.

2. Many *poems* and histories of the *period* describe these *people's* battles.

3. A Welsh historian named Gildas wrote a stirring account of a *battle scene* that took place on Badon Hill, in the English *countryside.*

4. In his history, Gildas mentions a *soldier* named Arthur who fought with the Britons against the invading *Anglo-Saxons.*

5. Later *myth-makers* developed Gildas's story into the legend of King Arthur and his knights of the Round Table.

PROJECTS

1. **Survey.** An epic poem communicates the values of a people. Find out about the values of people around you by conducting a survey of people's beliefs and attitudes. Work with your classmates to come up with a list of questions that will tell you what people care about, what they would be willing to struggle for, and so on. Possible questions for your survey include

   • What do you like to do in your free time?
   • Of all the things that you have done, what are you proudest of?
   • What do you hope that people will say about you after your death?

   Then choose a random sample of people and ask them your questions. You may want to divide your sample into two groups (young men and women, perhaps, or young people and older people) and compare the results that you obtain from these groups.

2. **Mapping.** Work with one or two other students to make an imaginary map of the lands of the Danes and the Geats. Decorate your map with illustrations of items from the poem. Label it to show such places as Hrothgar's mead hall, the fens, Grendel's lair, the dragon's treasure hoard, the whale-road, and so on.

PROJECT NOTES (CONT.)

2. Mapping. Have your students go through the poem from beginning to end to identify places that should go on their maps. Provide class time for discussing what will be on the maps and for the actual drawing of the maps. You will need to make available to your students art supplies with which to produce their maps. One possibility is to have the maps done in tempera paints on poster board. Another is to have the maps done on large pieces of blank newsprint or on the back side of gift wrap paper. Students can make these pieces of newsprint or gift wrapping into scrolls by attaching cardboard tubes to the ends. Such tubes can be found inside wrapping paper rolls.

from "The Seafarer," Anonymous, trans. by George K. Anderson

I can sing a true song about myself; I can tell of my journeys, how in troublous days I often endured hours of hardship, how I lived to feel bitterness of heart in the wretched quarters of my ship while the waves rolled high. Often have I stood my narrow night-watch in the prow of the boat, when it knocked against the rocky cliffs. Stiff with cold were my feet bound fast by frost's icy claws; there cares seethed hot about my heart, and hunger within rent the courage of the seaweary.

No man so happy as to enjoy the land can know how I, careworn, dwelt on the wintry ice-cold waves, paths of exile for me deprived of my kinsmen. Icicles hung from me; hail lashed me in showers. There I heard naught but the howling sea, the icy waves, at times the song of the wild swan. I had for my delight the cry of the gannet; for me the scream of the sea-gull rather than the laughter of men; the singing of the sea-mew rather than the drinking of mead. Storms beat upon the stone cliffs; there icy-feathered birds gave them a stern answer; full often screamed the dewy-feathered eagle. No protecting lord was there to console the heart of the needy man. He who dwells in the city, who has the joy of living, proud and flushed with wine, feels little hardship, such as I many a time had to endure on the ocean wastes. The shadow of night lowered; it snowed from the north; frost bound the earth; hail, the coldest of grains, showered upon the land.

Still, for all that, desires agitate my heart, to try myself the high streams, the sport of the salt waves; always I am urged on to fare forth, to seek far hence the home of alien peoples. Yet there is no man on earth so proud, nor so good of gifts, nor in youth so active, nor in his deeds so brave, nor to his Lord so faithful that he does not have sorrow in the time of his seafaring—whatever the Fate the Lord may send him. Not for him the harp, nor the giving of rings, nor the love of a woman, nor the pleasures of the world, nor aught else but the rolling of the waves—ever he will have longing who sets out on the sea.

The groves take on their blossoms; the towns and meadows grow fair; the earth revives; all things urge on the mind of the eager-hearted to the journey, to depart far over the flood-ways. Yet the cuckoo, guardian of the summer, sings a warning with its mournful voice, bodes bitter sorrow in its breast-hoard. No man living in comfort can know what they endure who lay their paths of exile far and wide!

So now my thoughts go roaming; my spirit is with the sea-flood beyond the home of the whale; it hovers afar over the folds of earth; it returns to me yearning and greedy; the solitary flier cries out; it drives me irresistibly on the whale-road over the waves of the sea. . . .

"Wulf and Eadwacer," Anonymous, trans. by Marcelle Thiébaux

For my clan he would be like a gift of booty—
they will waste him if he crosses their path.
With us it isn't like that.

Wulf is on one island, I on another—
5 his island is made fast, girded by fens.
Fierce men are on that island.
They will waste him if he crosses their path.
With us it isn't like that.

I yearned for Wulf in his harried wandering.
10 When the weather poured rain I sat here in tears.
When the brash fighter folded me in the branches of
    his arms,
I felt pleasure, yes, but I felt loathing too.

Wulf, my Wulf, to think about you
made me faint with sickness, for you seldom came.
15 It was my mood of mourning, not want of food.
Do you hear, Eadwacer? Wulf carries our forlorn
  whelp to the wood.
Men can easily wrench apart what has never been
    wedded—
our story together.

FROM "THE SEAFARER"

About the Selection. "The Seafarer" probably was composed in the eighth century by a sailor. It shows extensive familiarity with the weather and wildlife as they would have been experienced by a seafarer of the North Sea. It was formerly believed that the poem represents a dialogue between a disillusioned old salt and an enthusiastic young mariner, but a more likely interpretation is that the poem presents the conflicting feelings of a sailor who loves the sea but hates the hardships of sea life.

"WULF AND EADWACER"

About the Selection. The song "Wulf and Eadwacer" appears in the *Exeter Book,* which was compiled in the tenth century. The *Exeter Book* also contains "The Wife's Lament" (page 88) and Anglo-Saxon Riddles (page 94). Like the speaker in "The Wife's Lament," the speaker in "Wulf and Eadwacer" mourns the loss of her beloved who has gone on an extended journey, perhaps never to return. Also as in "The Wife's Lament," the speaker accepts this separation as something beyond her power to remedy and feels no hope. One interpretation of the song sees the speaker addressing her legal husband Eadwacer in line 16, and her listeners in lines 1–13. In this interpretation, the speaker and Wulf have been separated by Eadwacer. A second interpretation is that the whole song is an appeal to Eadwacer for help. As you discuss the poem with students, ask them to whom they think *us* in lines 3 and 8 refers.

ADDITIONAL QUESTIONS AND ACTIVITIES

Have students interview older people they may know and ask them about words that were introduced to the language when they were young persons. Students can also share with them current adolescent dialect.

▶**Teaching Note:** For instruction in interviewing, refer students to the Language Arts Survey, 1.27, "Interviewing." For practice in interviewing skills, refer students to the *Essential Skills Practice Book: Writing,* 1.27.

The Development of the English Language:
Origins

LANGUAGE CHANGE

The chances are that you know some words that are unfamiliar to people who are older than you. In every generation, the language changes. Over time, these changes accumulate until an entirely new language emerges. Look at the samples of Old English on pages 84 and 102. A thousand years ago, that's what the English language looked like. Today, because of the accumulated changes in the language, it is impossible to read Old English without special training. However, it is still possible to make out many words. For example, the sentence

> **We sungeon monige songas.**

is quite similar to

> **We sang many songs.**[1]

Compare the following words:

MODERN ENGLISH	OLD ENGLISH
come	cuman
fiend	feond
folk	folc
heaven	heofon
holy	halig
king	cyning
love	lufu
mind	mynd
see	seon
sit	sittan
work	weorc
what	hwæt

---

1. See Cassidy, F. G., and Richard N. Ringler, eds. *Bright's Old English Grammar and Reader* (New York: Holt, 1971), p. 24.

As you see, there are many Old English words that you can still recognize. A thousand years from now, speakers of English or of a language descended from it will probably be able to recognize a few words from the language that you speak today.

LANGUAGE FAMILIES

English belongs to the **Indo-European** family of languages. These languages developed from a long-dead language known as **Proto-Indo-European,** which was probably spoken by a people called the Kurgans who lived in the steppe region of southern Russia around 4000 BC. From there the language spread east and west to India and to Europe, slowly developing into many different but related languages. The common ancestry of these languages can be seen by comparing similar words found in them. Consider the following examples:

INDO-EUROPEAN WORDS FOR *FATHER*	
Sanskrit	piter
Classical Greek	pater
Latin	pater
Gothic	fadar
Old Irish	athir
French	père
Spanish	padre
Italian	padre
Portuguese	pai
English	father
German	Vater

Such similarities between words, combined with knowledge of how speech sounds change over time, enable linguists (people who study language) to reconstruct languages that no longer exist. All the words on the list above probably come from a common Proto-Indo-European word, *pətər.*

The relationships of the Indo-European languages can be seen quite clearly by looking at a language tree:

ADDITIONAL QUESTIONS AND ACTIVITIES

Ask how linguists might have discovered the existence of Proto-Indo-European and the Kurgans. What kinds of evidence might be available to those who study linguistic change? Interested students might research these questions and make a presentation to the class.

Social Studies. Have students plot the language tree on a world map, showing the areas where ancient languages were spoken and where modern languages currently are spoken. What can they conclude about how language changes?

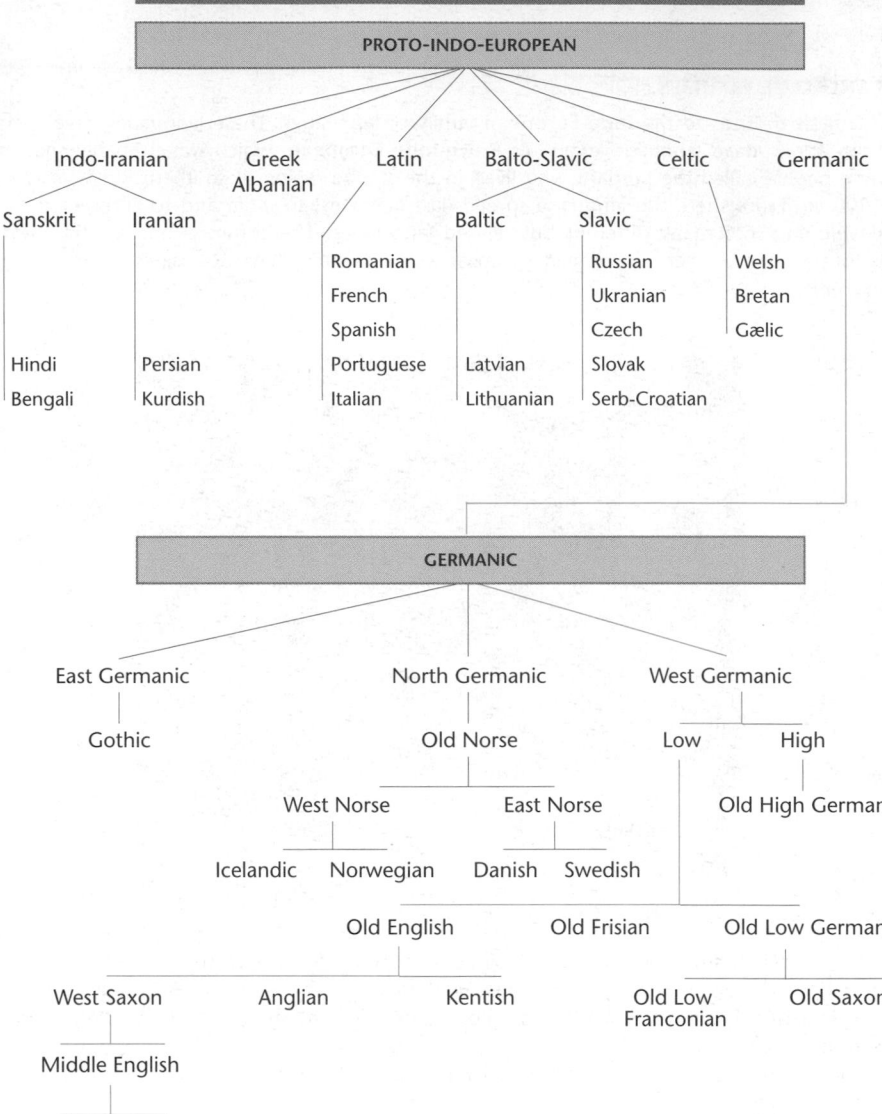

SELECTED INDO-EUROPEAN LANGUAGES

PROTO-INDO-EUROPEAN

Indo-Iranian	Greek Albanian	Latin	Balto-Slavic	Celtic	Germanic

Indo-Iranian: Sanskrit — Iranian
Sanskrit → Hindi, Bengali
Iranian → Persian, Kurdish

Latin → Romanian, French, Spanish, Portuguese, Italian

Balto-Slavic: Baltic — Slavic
Baltic → Latvian, Lithuanian
Slavic → Russian, Ukranian, Czech, Slovak, Serb-Croatian

Celtic → Welsh, Bretan, Gælic

GERMANIC

East Germanic	North Germanic	West Germanic

East Germanic → Gothic

North Germanic → Old Norse
Old Norse: West Norse — East Norse
West Norse → Icelandic, Norwegian
East Norse → Danish, Swedish

West Germanic: Low — High
High → Old High German

Old English | Old Frisian | Old Low German

Old English → West Saxon, Anglian, Kentish
West Saxon → Middle English → Modern English

Old Low German → Old Low Franconian, Old Saxon

THE EMERGENCE OF ENGLISH

When the Anglo-Saxons invaded England in the fifth century, they brought with them their West Germanic dialects, which are today collectively known as **Old English,** or **Anglo-Saxon.** The English language, descended from Old English, is related to modern Danish, German, Norwegian, Icelandic, and Dutch. Here are some interesting **etymologies,** or word histories, of Modern English terms derived from Old English:

OLD ENGLISH WORD	MEANING OF OLD ENGLISH WORD	MODERN ENGLISH WORD
dæge's eage	day's eye	daisy
hlaf-dige	loaf kneader	lady
hlaf-ward	loaf guardian	lord
wita	wise person	wit
Wyrd	fate	weird
wyrm	dragon	worm

EARLY BORROWINGS FROM OTHER LANGUAGES

Old English was spoken in Britain from roughly AD 450 to AD 1100. During that time, the language borrowed words from the native Celtic and from the Latin and Danish spoken by the Roman and Viking invaders. Borrowings from Latin include many words for trade, public works, religious figures, and institutions, such as *abbot* and *port.* The Latin *moneta,* for "mint," became the English word *money.* The Latin *dies malus,* for "bad day," became the English word *dismal.*

Early borrowings from Scandinavian languages such as Danish include *outlaw, knife, husband, fellow, take, egg,* and *sky.*

THE WRITTEN LANGUAGE

In its earliest stages, Old English was written in an ancient Germanic script known as **runic,** or **futhark.** This script is known to us primarily through inscriptions on stones and on implements or weapons. When the Romans invaded Britain in the first century AD, they brought with them the Latin alphabet that we use today.

THE FIRST SIX LETTERS OF THE RUNIC ALPHABET

f u th a r k

Have students research the etymologies of other Modern English words.

UNIT REVIEW

The Anglo-Saxon Period

VOCABULARY FROM THE SELECTIONS

adversity, 77	hacked, 95	perpetual, 104	secular, 83
agency, 83	hale, 107	purge, 106	signify, 78
alien, 106	heath, 109	pyre, 113	staunch, 96
asunder, 89	hew, 106	quill, 96	sully, 96
blithe, 90, 96	hilt, 108	rabble, 106	temporal, 77
corselet, 107	hovel, 91	ravenously, 105	tract, 107
diligently, 78	literal, 84	reminisce, 105	tribute, 103
ecclesiastical, 77, 83	loathsome, 103	remorse, 104	venture, 110
efficacious, 78	mail, 104	resolute, 108	whorled, 90
fastness, 103	mead, 105	resound, 111	wretched, 106
fen, 103	moor, 103	savor, 105	wrought, 95, 107
forged, 105	onslaught, 105	scourger, 95	

LITERARY TERMS

allegory, 80	image, 93	purpose or aim, 80
alliteration, 86	metaphor, 93	speaker, 92
description, 98	narration, 79	symbol, 93
epic, 115	oral tradition, 114	translation, 86
foil, 93	personification, 97	

SYNTHESIS: QUESTIONS FOR WRITING, RESEARCH, OR DISCUSSION

GENRE STUDIES

1. What is an heroic epic? How does the poem *Beowulf* meet that definition? What makes the poem an epic? How does the character Beowulf meet the Anglo-Saxon ideal of the hero?

THEMATIC STUDIES

2. Explore the theme of the outcast in "The Wife's Lament" and in *Beowulf*. How do the treatments of outcasts differ in the two poems? Which poem is sympathetic toward outcasts? Which is not?

HISTORICAL AND BIOGRAPHICAL STUDIES

3. The pre-Christian Anglo-Saxon world view was essentially grim and fatalistic. Describe the pre-Christian Anglo-Saxon world view as presented in "The Conversion of King Edwin" and in *Beowulf*.

4. Describe the structure of early Anglo-Saxon society and the importance of kinship in that society. Support your points with examples from "The Wife's Lament" and *Beowulf*.

5. Explain the effects of the coming of Christianity on Anglo-Saxon culture and literature. Use examples from "The Conversion of King Edwin," "Cædmon's Hymn," the Anglo-Saxon Riddles, and *Beowulf*.

Stonehenge

▶These prompts are suitable as topics for research papers. Refer to the Language Arts Survey, 4.20–4.34, "Research Skills." (To evaluate research papers, see the evaluation forms for writing, revising, and proofreading in the *Assessment Portfolio*, 7.1–7.10.)

▶These prompts can be adapted for use as topics for oral reports or debates. (To evaluate these projects, see the evaluation forms in the *Assessment Portfolio*, 7.17–7.19.)

ADDITIONAL RESOURCES

ASSESSMENT PORTFOLIO
- Vocabulary Worksheet, 4.2.11
- Study Guide: Unit 2 Test, 4.2.12
- Unit 2 Test, 4.2.13

ESSENTIAL SKILLS PRACTICE BOOKS

Language
- Capitalization: Sacred Beings and Writings, 2.125
- Compound and Collective Nouns, 2.5
- Correcting Run-ons, 2.62
- Using the Active Voice, 2.56
- Using Precise Nouns, 2.32
- Using Vivid Verbs, 2.33

Speaking and Listening
- Interpersonal Communication, 3.5

Study and Research
- Using the Card Catalog, 4.22

Language Lab   Expanding and Combining Sentences

To add variety, interest, and clarity to your writing, expand or combine sentences by adding words, phrases, and clauses. Use the methods described in the following charts.

METHODS FOR EXPANDING SENTENCES

Add a modifier. A **modifier** is a word that changes, or modifies, the meaning of another word by adding information. Modifiers that can be added include adjectives, adverbs, and participles (verb forms that act as adjectives).

ORIGINAL SENTENCE: Beowulf died.
EXPANDED SENTENCE: Bold Beowulf died bravely.

Add a prepositional phrase. A **prepositional phrase** consists of a preposition such as *at, by, from,* or *to* and an object such as a noun or pronoun.

ORIGINAL SENTENCE: The dragon plotted its revenge.
EXPANDED SENTENCE: In its dark lair, the dragon plotted its revenge against the Geats.

Add an appositive or an appositive phrase. Appositives and **appositive phrases** are words or phrases that rename something in other words.

ORIGINAL SENTENCE: Cædmon composed his songs orally.
EXPANDED SENTENCE: Cædmon, the first English poet, composed his songs orally.

Add a subordinate clause. A **subordinate clause** is a group of words that contains a subject and a verb but that cannot stand alone as a complete sentence.

ORIGINAL SENTENCE: The Geats mourned.
EXPANDED SENTENCE: The Geats mourned when Beowulf died.

METHODS FOR COMBINING SENTENCES

Combine by Adding a Word

ORIGINAL SENTENCES: "The Wife's Lament" may have been written by a woman. The woman may have been English.
COMBINED SENTENCE: "The Wife's Lament" may have been written by an English woman.

Combine by Adding a Phrase

ORIGINAL SENTENCES: The scop sang. He told of ancient battles.
COMBINED SENTENCE: The scop sang of ancient battles.

Combine by Adding a Clause

ORIGINAL SENTENCES: The Anglo-Saxons converted to Christianity. They retained some pagan traditions.
COMBINED SENTENCES: The Anglo-Saxons converted to Christianity, but they retained some pagan traditions.
After the Anglo-Saxons converted to Christianity, they retained some pagan traditions.
The Anglo-Saxons converted to Christianity; however, they retained some pagan traditions.

Exercise A Expanding Sentences

Expand the sentences below by adding words, phrases, or clauses from the list on the right-hand side of the page. Follow the directions given in parentheses.

EXAMPLE: Augustine converted King Ethelbert. (Add a prepositional phrase.)
Augustine converted King Ethelbert of Kent.

1. When the Anglo-Saxons invaded Britain, they brought with them their religion. (Add a modifier.)

2. The Germanic tribes had vague notions. (Add a prepositional phrase.)

3. They believed that warriors went to a place called Valhalla. (Add a clause.)

4. Others went to a region ruled by a goddess named Hel. (Add a clause.)

5. In AD 597 Pope Gregory the Great sent Augustine to convert King Ethelbert of Kent. (Add an appositive phrase.)

6. Thereafter, the whole of England converted. (Add a prepositional phrase.)

7. The Anglo-Saxons incorporated Christian elements into their traditional oral literature. (Add a prepositional phrase.)

> **Materials to be added**
>
> to the new religion
>
> about the afterlife
>
> After the conversion
>
> Germanic
>
> after they died
>
> leader of the Roman Catholic Church
>
> who died in battle

LANGUAGE ARTS SURVEY

For additional help, see the Language Arts Survey, 2.46–2.50.

Exercise B Combining Sentences

Rewrite the following choppy paragraph, combining sentences to eliminate unnecessary words and to improve the grace and clarity of the writing.

EXAMPLE: The mead hall was filled. It was filled with laughter. It was filled with mirth. The laughter was joyous.
The mead hall was filled with joyous laughter and mirth.

The scop sang. He sang beautiful songs. He sang about the deeds of heroes. The heroes were great. The heroes were warriors who lived in the distant past. He told of Sigurd. Sigurd was brave. He told of Judith. Judith was mighty. The warriors feasted. They did so heartily. They did so as the scop's voice rang out. It rang out over the sound of the harp. They felt heart's ease. The heart's ease was great. Those were days of peace. Those were days of pleasure. Those were days before the coming of Grendel. Heorot stood the finest of mead halls. The beast changed all that. The beast was wicked. The beast was murderous. He killed wantonly. Soon the hall stood empty. It was the hall of Hrothgar. Hrothgar was the ring-giver. Woe fell upon the Danes. They longed for a hero. They wanted the hero to destroy the beast. They wanted the hero to restore the days of old. The days of old were happy.

LANGUAGE ARTS SURVEY

For additional help, see the Language Arts Survey, 2.51–2.53.

ANSWERS FOR LANGUAGE LAB

Exercise A

1. When the Anglo-Saxons invaded Britain, they brought with them their Germanic religion.

2. The Germanic tribes had vague notions about the afterlife.

3. They believed that warriors went to a place called Valhalla after they died.

4. Others went to a region ruled by a goddess named Hel who died in battle.

5. In AD 597 Pope Gregory the Great, leader of the Roman Catholic Church, sent Augustine to convert King Ethelbert of Kent.

6. Thereafter, the whole of England converted to the new religion.

7. After the conversion, the Anglo-Saxons incorporated Christian elements into their traditional oral literature.

Exercise B

Responses will vary. Possible responses are given.

The scop sang beautiful songs about the deeds of great heroes. He told of brave Sigurd and mighty Judith who were warriors in the distant past. The warriors feasted heartily as the scop's voice rang out over the sound of the harp. They felt great heart's ease in the days of peace and pleasure before the coming of Grendel. Heorot stood the finest of mead halls before the wicked, murderous beast changed all that by killing wantonly. Soon the hall of Hrothgar, ring-giver, stood empty, and woe fell upon the Danes. They longed for a hero to destroy the beast and restore the happy days of old.

UNIT 3 THE MEDIEVAL PERIOD (1066–1485)

Saint George and the Dragon. *Paolo Uccello, circa 1460.*
Courtesy of the Trustees, The National Gallery, London

GOALS/OBJECTIVES

Studying this unit will enable students to

• interpret and appreciate medieval literature

• explain the social organization of medieval English society, with particular reference to feudalism and the church, using examples from *The Canterbury Tales* and other works

• explain the influence of the Norman Conquest on English literature and the English language

• identify and explain the salient characteristics of ballads, medieval romances, frame tales, and morality plays

• define and illustrate with examples the *ubi sunt, memento mori,* and *contemptu mundi* themes

• explain such elements of the romance tradition as courtly love, chivalry, and the trial or quest

There was a Knight, a most distinguished man,

Who from the day on which he first began

To ride abroad had followed chivalry,

Truth, honor, generousness and courtesy.

—Geoffrey Chaucer

127

LITERARY NOTE

The quotation that opens the unit comes from "The Prologue" to *The Canterbury Tales* by Geoffrey Chaucer (1343–1400). In these lines, Chaucer introduces one of his many brilliantly drawn characters, a knight who embodies the ideals of chivalry. Chaucer, the greatest of the medieval English poets, is known for the clarity and wit of his writing and for his keen observations of human nature. A fifteenth-century commentator on Chaucer wrote, "His language was so fayr and pertynenet/It seemeth unto mannys heerynge/Not only the worde, but verely the thynge."

CROSS-CURRICULAR ACTIVITIES

Social Studies: Map Reading Skills. Ask students to identify England and Normandy on the map and to identify the narrowest passage across the English Channel between the two.

HISTORICAL NOTE

The following is a list of kings of England during the Medieval Period:

Norman Kings

1066–1087 William I (the Conqueror)
1087–1100 William II
1100–1135 Henry I

Blois King

1135–1154 Stephen

Plantagenet Kings

1154–1189 Henry II
1189–1199 Richard I (the Lion-Hearted)
1199–1216 John Lackland
1216–1272 Henry III
1272–1307 Edward I
1307–1327 Edward II
1327–1377 Edward III
1377–1399 Richard II

Lancaster Kings

1399–1413 Henry IV
1413–1422 Henry V
1422–1461 Henry VI
1470–1471 Henry VI, reinstated

York Kings

1461–1470 Edward IV
1471–1483 Edward IV, reinstated
1483–1483 Edward V
1483–1485 Richard III

THE NORMAN CONQUEST OF ENGLAND

When in 878 Alfred the Great defeated the Danes and confined them to the north of England, the Danes looked for other lands to conquer. Some of these Danes invaded northern France, settling in an area that came to be known as the land of the north men, or **Normandy**. The Normans adopted the French language and developed a sophisticated culture.

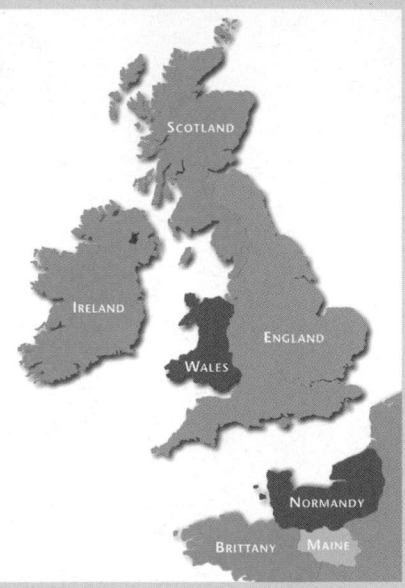

England and northern France, showing the provinces of England, the English Channel, and Normandy

In 1066, the English king Edward the Confessor died, and the Anglo-Saxon Witanagemot, or council of elders, chose Harold II as king. However, **Duke William of Normandy** (*circa* 1028–1087), cousin to Edward the Confessor, claimed with some justification that Edward had promised the English throne to him. With the support of the church, Duke William invaded England in September of 1066 and defeated Harold at the **Battle of Hastings**. In four years of bloody fighting that followed the Battle of Hastings, the Normans killed most of the native English nobility, subjugated the rest of the populace, and divided the country into estates, or **fiefdoms**, ruled by French-speaking barons loyal to **William the Conqueror**. The **Norman Conquest** brought the era of the Anglo-Saxons to a close and ushered in the **Medieval Period**[1] of English history.

ANGLO-NORMAN LITERATURE

The effect of the Norman Conquest on the English language and on English literature was, as one scholar has put it, "shattering." For two hundred years following the Conquest, English

---

1. Scholarly usage differs as to what this period should be called. Some scholars use the terms *Middle Ages* and *Medieval Period* interchangeably to refer to the entire period from the Anglo-Saxon invasion to the end of the fifteenth century. In this text we shall use *Middle Ages* to refer to this larger period and *Medieval Period* to refer to the period following the Norman Conquest.

LITERARY EVENTS

► = British Events

1050	1075	1100	1125	1150

►1086–1127. William X, Duke of Aquitaine, first of the great troubadour poets who produced works on romance themes
1076–1142. French philosopher Abélard

1140–91. Greatest of French romance writers, Chrétien de Troyes
►1137. Geoffrey of Monmouth's *History of the Kings of Britain* written

HISTORICAL EVENTS

►1058. Malcolm III of Scotland deposes the usurper Macbeth
►1066. Battle of Hastings; Norman Conquest of England
►1066–87. Reign in England of William the Conqueror
1090–1153. St. Bernard, founder of Benedictine monasteries
1095. First Crusade proclaimed
1099. Crusaders win Jerusalem
►1100–35. Reign of Henry I of England

1110. University of Paris founded
►1122–1204. Eleanor of Aquitaine

►1154–89. Henry II, first of Plantagenet line of English kings

128 *UNIT THREE / THE MEDIEVAL PERIOD*

THEMATIC CURRENTS

Use the following selections to explore these themes with your students.

FACING DEATH
- "Sir Patrick Spens," 136
- "Ubi Sunt Qui ante Nos Fuerunt?" 142
- from *Sir Gawain and the Green Knight,* 152
- from *Everyman,* 212

WOMEN IN MEDIEVAL LITERATURE
- "The Great Silkie of Shule Skerrie," 139
- "I Sing of a Maiden," 146
- from *The Book of Margery Kempe,* 180
- "The Prologue," from *The Canterbury Tales,* 185

CHIVALRY AND COURTLY LOVE
- "I Sing of a Maiden," 146
- "The Honeysuckle: Chevrefoil," 148
- from *Sir Gawain and the Green Knight,* 152
- from *Le Morte d'Arthur,* 167
- from *The Ingenious Hidalgo Don Quixote de la Mancha,* 225

The Bayeux Tapestry, 11th century. By special permission of the City of Bayeux

became a lower-class language in England—one spoken almost exclusively by the poor and powerless. The language of the court, of the noble classes, and of almost all the non-Latin literature produced on the island was Norman French. The production of literature in the English language came to a near standstill. Some monks continued to produce works in English, and the illiterate, English-speaking common people continued to compose their oral songs, but very little of this material survives today, for the monks' works in English were few, and the common people's songs were not written down (though a few survived to be recorded centuries later).

Most of the non-Latin literature produced in England between 1066 and roughly 1260 was written in Norman French and is therefore known as **Anglo-Norman literature.** This literature tends to be quite practical, in keeping with the no-nonsense character of the Norman people. Much of it consists of religious tracts and other works meant more for edification than for entertainment. However, the Normans did import from the Continent some French

The Bayeux Tapestry is a piece of linen cloth two hundred and thirty-one feet long and about twenty inches high. On it is embroidered more than seventy scenes telling the story of the Norman Conquest of England in pictures and in a Latin text. Created in the eleventh century, this tapestry is extremely valuable for the details that it shows of medieval military gear and tactics. The tapestry is located today in the Musée de la Tapisserie de la Reine-Mathilde, in the former Bishop's Palace in Bayeux, France.

LITERARY/HISTORICAL NOTE

Students might be interested in learning more about the life of Thomas à Becket, the "blissful martyr" whose tomb is the site of pilgrimage in Chaucer's *The Canterbury Tales.* Becket was born in London in 1118 to a middle-class merchant family. As a young man, he became a servant in the household of the powerful Archbishop Theobald. In 1154, Theobald made Becket archdeacon of Canterbury. Then, in 1155, King Henry II appointed Becket chancellor of England (the country's highest administrative post). As chancellor, Becket assisted Henry in his ongoing battle to wrest privileges from the church. When Theobald died, Henry hoped that the election of Thomas to the post of archbishop of Canterbury would solidify his control over the church in England. However, such was not to be the case. In a dramatic turnabout, Thomas, on assuming the post of archbishop, became a devout, crusading defender of church rights, opposing Henry on such matters as civil punishment for clerical offenders and the exemption of royal officials from excommunication. In 1170, Henry rashly and in anger said in front of a group of barons that he wished that someone would rid him of this meddlesome bishop. The barons, taking Henry literally, murdered Thomas inside the

(cont.)

1265–1321. Dante, Italian poet

1225–74. St. Thomas Aquinas, philosopher

▶1214–92. Roger Bacon, English philosopher

▶1180. Birth of Marie de France

1175	1200	1225	1250	1275

▶*circa* 1167. Oxford University founded
▶1166. Murder of Archbishop of Canterbury Thomas à Becket
   ▶ 1189–99. Richard the Lion-hearted
     ▶ 1199–1216. King John of England
       ▶ 1209. Cambridge University founded
        ▶ 1215. King John signs Magna Carta

1271–95. Asian travels of Marco Polo

▶ 1272–1307. Edward I King of England

1244. Jerusalem captured by Moslems

INTRODUCTION **129**

LITERARY CURRENTS

Use the following selections to explore these concepts and techniques with your students.

cathedral at Canterbury. Within days, Thomas's tomb became a site of pilgrimage and, in 1173, Thomas was canonized. This story is told grippingly in two modern plays, T. S. Eliot's *Murder in the Cathedral* and Jean Anouilh's *Becket*.

HISTORICAL NOTE

• Point out that the organization of medieval society depended upon **vassalage**—the loyalty or obligation that a lesser member of the society owed to higher members in exchange for favors granted. For example, a knight might be granted property by a great lord—a duke, an earl, or a king. That knight would then owe obligations of loyalty to the lord. This loyalty would be recognized in a public act of **homage** in which the knight would kneel before the lord, the lord would take the knight's hands between his own, and the two would then exchange kisses on the cheeks.

• When the peasant classes, or villeins, revolted, the nobility and upper classes regarded them with hostility and disdain, connotations that carry over to the modern use of the word *villain.*

entertainment literature, including romances and fabliaux, which are described on page 132. An excellent example of Anglo-Norman literature is the selection from the **lais**, or songs, of **Marie de France** given in English translation on pages 148–150.

One important literary innovation introduced to England by the Normans was poetry written in rhymed stanzas. Almost overnight, rhymed stanzas replaced Anglo-Saxon alliterative verse as the primary form of poetry written in England.

From the time of the Conquest to 1202, Normandy remained part of England. After England lost Normandy, the influence of the French language in England rapidly declined. By the middle of the century, most English ties to France had been severed, and the upper classes in England began to adopt the native language. By the end of the century, English was again the primary language of both the lower and the upper classes.

THE ORGANIZATION OF MEDIEVAL SOCIETY

William the Conqueror brought to England a system of political organization that we now refer to as **feudalism.** This was the system by which Europe was ruled throughout the Middle Ages. In feudal states, all land and all people ultimately belonged to the king, who granted large tracts of the land to members of the nobility, known as **barons,** who were bound in exchange to be loyal to the king, to raise armies to fight in his battles, and to pay taxes to support his court. In turn, the barons granted land to lesser nobles and required service and support from them. At the very bottom of the social order was a class of bondsmen, known as **peasants, villeins,** or **serfs,** who lived on and worked the nobles' land. The lot of the serfs was generally miserable. They were the property of their feudal lords and could not leave the land or even marry without permission. They lived on meager diets, suffered terribly from disease, and worked very hard only to turn over much of what they produced for the support of the lord's household.

Occasionally, a serf could earn freedom by some exceptional service to his or her lord. Gradually, throughout the Medieval Period, the class of **freemen** grew to include many merchants, traders, laborers, and artisans.

In a feudal society, each person is bound by a system of loyalties, known as **vassalage,** to some person higher on the social hierarchy. Thus a serf might be the **vassal,** or servant, of a

LITERARY EVENTS

►1386. Chaucer begins *The Canterbury Tales*
►*circa* 1375. *Sir Gawain and the Green Knight* written
1341. Petrarch becomes Poet Laureate in Rome

1300	1325	1350	1375	1400

►1337. Beginning of Hundred Years' War between England and France
►1346. English defeat French in Battle of Crécy
►1348. Beginning of Great Plague in England   ►1381. Peasants' Revolt in England

HISTORICAL EVENTS

HISTORICAL NOTE

William the Conqueror introduced feudalism to England by granting land to followers who had served him in the conquest. These men, numbering fewer than one hundred and eighty, became "tenants in chief," the great lords or barons of the land. In exchange for their land, they were required to provide soldiers to the king when necessary. At first these soldiers came from the households of the ten-ants in chief, but later they came from the households of knights who themselves were granted land by the great lords. William replaced the Anglo-Saxon *witan* with the *curia regis,* or king's court, made up of his barons. These courts met thrice annually, at Christmas, Easter, and Whitsuntide.

lesser nobleman who held the title of knight. The knight, in turn, might be the vassal of a duke, the duke the vassal of a powerful earl, and the earl the vassal of the king. The king himself was considered a vassal of the Pope, the head of the Roman Catholic Church.

THE INFLUENCE OF THE CHURCH

At no time in the history of the West has the church been more influential than in the Medieval Period. Throughout this time, the Catholic Church, centered in faraway Rome (and for a time also in Avignon, France), had tremendous wealth and power both in the political and personal spheres. Vast resources went into the building of churches, first in the squat, towered, and turreted **Norman** or **Romanesque** style and later in the grand **Gothic** style of Canterbury Cathedral.

Canterbury Cathedral. Canterbury, England.
Wellesley College Library, Special Collections

The head of the church was the Pope. Beneath the Pope were a variety of officials, from learned cardinals, archbishops, and bishops down to often semi-literate parish priests. In addition, the church was represented by religious orders of monks and nuns living in monastic houses. Many clerics served as government officials, and the church and crown often collaborated. However, in many ways medieval England was a house with two masters, and often political leaders and members of the clergy quarreled. Such a quarrel led in 1170 to the murder by barons loyal to Henry II of Thomas à Becket, the Archbishop of Canterbury.

Much of medieval literature deals with religious subjects and themes. Surviving works include retellings of Biblical stories, biographies of saints, collections of sermons, tracts on the seven deadly sins and the seven cardinal virtues, and so on. A common theme of religious and quasi-religious literature was the *memento mori,* or "reminder of death": death comes soon and without warning. Therefore, you must prepare yourself for the life hereafter.

▶1476. William Caxton sets up first printing press in England
▶*circa* 1470. Sir Thomas Malory writes *Le Morte d'Arthur*
1453. Gutenberg prints Bible on first press using movable type in Germany

1425	1450	1475	1500

1428. Joan of Arc leads French to victory in Siege of Orleans
▶1453. Hundred Years' War ends
▶1455. Beginning of War of the Roses

INTRODUCTION **131**

LITERARY NOTE

Bestiaries. One type of church-related literature common in the Middle Ages was the **bestiary.** A typical bestiary contained descriptions and pictures of fabulous or exotic beasts such as whales, lions, and unicorns. Each description would have an allegorical or symbolic meaning in addition to its literal one. Thus, a snake stripping off its skin might symbolize a human being stripping off sin through repentance or penitence.

 ▶ **Teaching Note.** An interesting assignment that combines writing and graphics skills is to prepare a class bestiary. Have students make a list of animals for the bestiary and then do some research in books of natural history. Zoology textbooks and field guides are excellent sources. For each animal, students should prepare a short written description of its appearance and behavior. The description should then be likened to some part of human life. For example, a modern bestiary might describe a bee colony falling apart at the death of the queen bee and liken that to a corporate office that falls apart when a manager resigns.

HISTORICAL NOTE

Virtues and Vices. Medieval people applied special magical significance to the numbers three and seven. The number three, associated with the Holy Trinity, figured prominently in medieval charms and spells. Medieval theologians enumerated seven cardinal virtues—*prudence, temperance, fortitude, justice, faith, hope,* and *love*—and seven deadly sins—*pride, avarice, lechery, anger, gluttony, envy,* and *sloth.* Much of medieval literature can be understood as providing illustrations of, or warnings about, these virtues and vices. Discuss with students the effect that following virtues and avoiding sin might have on society. Why was this important in medieval times?

Point out that in the Middle Ages, life was generally short and precarious. In this time before modern medicine, a simple flu or accident could well be fatal. Children rarely lived to adulthood, and adults often found themselves healthy one day and fatally ill the next. Such conditions led to a widespread preoccupation with death that was reflected in medieval art and literature. The *memento mori* and *contemptu mundi* themes were expressions of the ever-present reality of death in the lives of medieval people.

One of the most common subjects in all of medieval art is the *Danse Macabre*, or Dance of Death, in which the figure of death, usually a skeleton dressed in a hooded robe, often carrying a scythe, is shown dancing with the living. The idea behind such art was that people should remember that death, although often disguised, is always there, in the middle of life, as indeed it was during the Medieval Period.

LITERARY TECHNIQUE

Literary historians often divide medieval romances by subject into those dealing with the matter of Britain, the matter of Rome, and the matter of France. Heroes in romances dealing with the matter of Britain included Guy of Warwic, Richard the Lion-Hearted, and such figures from the Arthurian legends as Lancelot and Gawain. Heroes in romances dealing with the matter of Rome included Alexander the Great and Æneas. Heroes in romances dealing with the matter of France included Roland and Charlemagne.

(Note: Alexander was not Roman but Macedonian, and Æneas's connection to Rome was mythological. However, in the Middle Ages, writers often lumped together stories from antiquity under the general rubric "Gesta Romanarum," or Roman stories.)

Another common theme was that of *contemptu mundi*, or "contempt for the world." An excellent exposition of these themes can be found in the medieval play *Everyman*, which describes how death comes when a person least expects it and how that person is then deserted by all worldly things, such as goods, beauty, strength, and even the five senses. In the end, worldly things are worthless. All that goes with a person to the grave is his or her good deeds, which are weighed on Judgment Day.

From the eleventh to the thirteenth century, the church sponsored a series of **Crusades,** or holy wars, to recapture Jerusalem from the Moslems. Christians from all over Europe participated in the Crusades and brought back with them Persian and Arabic stories and scholarship. Of considerable importance to the church and to the development of English literature was the influence on the Crusaders of Persian love poetry, with its many portraits of idealized women. This poetry influenced the development in Europe, beginning in the twelfth century, of passionate devotion to the Virgin Mary, mother of Christ, who was portrayed in both popular and religious literature as the ideal of perfect womanhood. An example of this literature of devotion to Mary is the beautiful lyric "I Sing of a Maiden," on page 146.

GEOFFREY CHAUCER

The devout people of the Medieval Period often went on journeys, or **pilgrimages,** to visit holy sites such as the burial places of saints. In *The Canterbury Tales*, perhaps the greatest work of the period, the court poet Geoffrey Chaucer describes a group of people taking such a pilgrimage to the site of the killing, or **martyrdom,** of St. Thomas, in Canterbury, England. Chaucer has his pilgrims make up stories to entertain one another, and he tells us these stories, which include examples of many kinds of medieval literature, including knightly romances, pious moral tales, folk tales, and ribald stories of the kind known as **fabliaux.**

ROMANCE LITERATURE, CHIVALRY, AND COURTLY LOVE

The Crusades and devotion to the Virgin Mary influenced the development of a unique literature known as **romance,** which portrayed the standards of knightly conduct known as **chivalry.** The word comes from the French word for horse, *cheval,* and reflects the fact that knights fought on horseback, which was necessary because they wore heavy suits of protective armor that made movement on the ground difficult.

Today, we associate the word *romance* with love stories, and indeed love does play a major role in early romance literature. At root, however, medieval romances were stories of adventure. They dealt with the exploits of knights—their battles, crusades, tournaments, jousts—and, incidentally, the loves that inspired these. Typically, a romance would present a series of loosely connected adventures, each a **trial,** or test, of the knight's virtues—his loyalty, honesty, gentleness, faith, courtesy, skill, and courage. The trial might take the form of a **quest,** a journey to some far-off place to do some mighty deed. The most famous such quest was the search for the **Holy Grail,** the cup from which Christ offered communion at the Last Supper. Often the knight's trial or quest was undertaken to rescue or win the favor of a fair lady who was represented in unrealistically idealized terms as the worthy inspiration of great deeds. This idealization of women and of the knights' faithful service to them formed the core of the code of behavior between women and their suitors known as **courtly love.** The ideas of courtly love originated in France and spread to England in the twelfth century under the patronage of the French-born queen of Henry II, **Eleanor of Aquitaine** (*circa* 1122–1204).

HISTORICAL NOTE

The stormy and fascinating story of the relationship of Henry II and Eleanor of Aquitaine is told dramatically in William Golding's play *The Lion in Winter,* which may be recommended to students interested in learning more about Eleanor, one of the most fascinating female political figures in all of European history.

Quest for the Holy Grail. Edward Burne-Jones (1833–98).
Birmingham City Museums & Art Gallery/Bridgeman Art Library, London

The most famous and enduring of the English romances are those written about the legendary **King Arthur** and his **knights of the Round Table,** including Sir Gawain, Sir Lancelot, and Sir Galahad. Two samples from Arthurian romances are given in this unit—the selections from *Sir Gawain and the Green Knight,* on page 152, and from Sir Thomas Malory's compilation and retelling of the Arthur legends, *Le Morte d'Arthur,* on page 167.

THE BALLADS

Even during the period when Norman French was the official language of the court, common people continued to produce oral poetry and songs. Many songs of the common people, known as **ballads,** survived for hundreds of years, long enough to be printed, after the invention of the printing press, or gathered by scholars from oral sources. The ballads were simple narratives in four-line stanzas that served as entertainment and as records of events that captured the popular imagination. Some ballads told fantastic tales of ghosts and demons. Some recorded important events, such as the death of a lord or the sinking of a ship. Others immortalized legendary outlaws such as **Robin Hood.** Many were simple tales of love or betrayal. The role of women in creating the ballads and transmitting them orally led Virginia Woolf to write, in the nineteenth century, that "Anonymous was a woman."

MEDIEVAL DRAMA

Medieval drama had its origins in simple skits, based on Bible stories and saints' lives, that were performed in churches. Gradually these moved out of the churches and were performed in town marketplaces and in the courtyards of roadhouses, or inns. Three types of drama were created in the period: **mystery plays,** which told stories from the Bible; **miracle plays,** which told stories from the lives of the saints; and **morality plays,** like *Everyman,* which represented abstract virtues and vices as characters.

BIBLIOGRAPHY

The following are some excellent sources of additional information on Middle English language, history, and literature.

Chaucer's Major Poetry. Ed. A. C. Baugh. 1963.

Child, F. J. *The English and Scottish Popular Ballads.* 1882.

Donaldson, E. T. *Speaking of Chaucer.* 1970.

Emmerson, Richard, ed. *Approaches to Teaching Medieval Drama.* 1990.

A History of Private Life: Revelations of the Medieval World. Ed. Philippe Ariès and George Duby. Trans. Arthur Goldhammer. 1988.

Hodgart, M. J. C. *The Ballads.* 1950.

Howard, Donald. *Chaucer: His Life, His Work, His World.* 1987.

Huizinga, J. *The Waning of the Middle Ages.* 1924.

Lais of Marie de France, The. Trans. Glyn S. Burgess and Keith Busby. 1986.

Lewis, C. S. *The Allegory of Love.* 1964.

Loomis, R. S. *The Development of Arthurian Romance.* 1963.

Mehl, D. *The Middle English Romances of the Thirteenth and Fourteenth Centuries.* 1968.

Middle English Lyrics. Ed. M. S. Luria and R. L. Hoffman. 1974.

Power, Eileen. *Medieval People.* 1963.

The Riverside Chaucer. Ed. L. D. Benson et al. 1987.

Sir Gawain and the Green Knight. Ed. J. R. R. Tolkien and E. V. Gordon, 1925. Rev. Norman Davis. 1967.

Thiébaux, Marcelle. *The Writings of Medieval Women: An Anthology.* 1994.

Tuchman, Barbara. *A Distant Mirror.* 1978.

The Voice of the Middle Ages in Personal Letters, 1100–1500. Ed. Catherine Moriarity. 1989.

The Works of Sir Thomas Malory. Ed. Eugène Vinaver. 1967.

POLITICAL DEVELOPMENTS IN THE MEDIEVAL PERIOD

Politically, the Medieval Period in England was one of enormous change. The feudal system introduced by William the Conqueror was solidified by his successors. Henry II, who reigned from 1154 to 1189, introduced a system of traveling judges whose rulings were to make up the **common law** that still provides the basis for the legal systems of England and the United States. Another innovation of the period was legislative government, in the form of a **Parliament**, or representative ruling body. After the death of Henry II, his son John taxed the barons so heavily and made so many enemies that he was forced, in 1215, to sign the **Magna Carta**, or "great charter," a document that limited the rights of the king, made him subject to the rulings of the baronial Parliament, and guaranteed trial by a jury of one's peers.

From 1339 to 1453, England fought the **Hundred Years' War** over possession of French lands. In 1346, England won a decisive victory at the **Battle of Crécy** by introducing to warfare the longbow, used to shoot the horses out from under the French. Having fallen to the ground in their heavy suits of armor, the French could not get up and flee. Most of the noblemen of France died in that single battle. For a time England held sway over the country. In the next century, however, thanks to the leadership of that astonishing warrior **Joan of Arc** (1412–1431), France was able to win back its territory. England retreated to its own boundaries.

The period also saw, in the **Peasants' Revolt** led by Jack Straw and Wat Tyler in 1381, the first stirrings of demands for individual liberty and human rights on the part of the common people. During this revolt, peasants armed with stones and farming tools marched on the city of London. Their rallying cry was,

> When Adam delved° and Eve span,°   *plowed, spun*
> Who was then a gentleman.

The revolt was brutally suppressed, and its leaders were executed. Challenges to authority were not taken lightly in the Middle Ages.

SOCIAL AND CULTURAL CHANGES IN THE MEDIEVAL PERIOD

Important social and cultural changes occurred during the Medieval Period. The founding of universities at Oxford and Cambridge promoted learning. Towns and cities grew around mills for the processing of wool into cloth. Merchants and artisans organized themselves into **guilds** responsible for training apprentices and for regulating business. A **middle class** of free merchants and tradespeople emerged. The crowding of people into towns made possible great markets and fairs but also increased the possibilities for spreading disease. In the mid-1300s, the bubonic plague, or **Black Death**, devastated England, killing one-third of its inhabitants.

Late in the fourteenth century, a religious reformer, **John Wycliff** (*circa* 1330–1384), finished the first complete translation of the Bible into English. For the first time, ordinary people could read and interpret the text on their own. This event set the stage for the Protestant Reformation.

An important figure in the spread of ideas of all kinds was **William Caxton** (1422–1491), who in 1476 introduced to England the new technology of printing from movable type. He printed much of the literature of his day, including *The Canterbury Tales* and *Le Morte d'Arthur.* For the first time, books were easily made in large quantities, and the subsequent spread of learning would change England forever, making the decline of the powerful aristocracy inevitable.

THE END OF THE MEDIEVAL PERIOD

From 1455 to 1485, England was torn by civil war between two noble houses. The House of Lancaster, whose crest bore a red rose, fought against the House of York, whose crest bore a white rose. The thirty-year **War of the Roses** ended with the defeat of Richard III of the House of Lancaster by Henry Tudor, who became King Henry VII.

HISTORICAL NOTE

The Peasants' Revolt began as a reaction to a poll tax instituted to finance war with France. Violence broke out in the southeastern portion of England and included attacks on landlords and tax collectors. Peasants from Essex and Kent marched on London, killed several royal officials, and met with the king. During one of these meetings, at which King Richard made many promises that he later failed to keep, the mayor of London attacked and killed the leader of the rebellion, Wat Tyler.

Echoes:
Medieval England

Lancelot mad with love for Guinevere. *Bodleian Library, University of Oxford*

Lo, yonder I see Everyman walking:
Full little he thinketh on my coming;

> —Anonymous, spoken by the character
> Death in the play *Everyman*

There came to me reclining there a most curious
   dream
That I was in a wilderness, nowhere that I knew;
But as I looked into the east, up high toward the sun,
I saw a tower on a hill-top, trimly built,
A deep dale beneath, a dungeon tower in it,
With ditches deep and dark and dreadful to look at.
A fair field full of folk I found between them,
Of human beings of all sorts, the high and the low,
Working and wandering as the world requires.

> —William Langland, *The Vision of Piers Plowman*

The life so short, the craft so hard to learn.

> —Geoffrey Chaucer, *The Parliament of Fowls*

A person who is the prey of love eats little and sleeps
little. . . . Love can deny nothing to Love.

> —Andreas Capellanus, *The Art of Courtly Love*

"Truly," said Sir Palomides, "as for Sir Lancelot, of his noble knighthood, courtesy, and prowess, and gentleness, I know not his peer; for this day," said Sir Palomides, "I did full uncourteously unto Sir Lancelot, and full unknightly, and full knightly and courteously he did to me again; for and he had been as ungentle to me as I was to him, this day I had won no worship. And therefore," said Palomides, "I shall be Sir Lancelot's knight whiles my life lasteth."

This talking was in the houses of kings. But all kings, lords, and knights, said, of clear knighthood, and of pure strength, of bounty, of courtesy, Sir Lancelot and Sir Tristram bare the prize above all knights that ever were in Arthur's days. And there were never knights in Arthur's days did half so many deeds as they did; as the book saith, no ten knights did not half the deeds that they did, and there was never knight in their days that required Sir Lancelot or Sir Tristram of any quest, so it were not to their shame, but they performed their desire.

> —Sir Thomas Malory, *Le Morte d'Arthur*

BIOGRAPHICAL NOTE

Little is known of **William Langland** (*circa* 1330–1387) except that he was the author of the great alliterative Middle English poem *The Vision of Piers Plowman*. The poem opens with a famous dream vision of a "fair field full of folk" which presents a portrait of English society at the time through Langland's satirical eyes. The hero of the poem, Piers Plowman, is an idealized common man, a simple farmer whose humble virtues Langland contrasts with the corrupt excesses of members of the wealthy classes and of the clergy.

Andreas Capellanus is the Latin name of André le Chapelain, a twelfth-century French writer whose *The Art of Courtly Love* presented a thorough exposition of the ideals of love celebrated in medieval romances. Capellanus is believed to have served Marie, the daughter of Eleanor of Aquitaine, and to have written his famous book for her. See *courtly love* in the Handbook of Literary Terms.

QUOTABLES

66 He koude songes make and wel endite. 99

("He could make songs and write well.")

> —Geoffrey Chaucer

ENRICHMENT ACTIVITIES

 Encourage musically inclined students to try their hands (or voices) at setting these ballads to music.

SUPPORT FOR LEP STUDENTS

Both "Sir Patrick Spens" and "The Great Silkie of Shule Skerrie" present fairly straightforward narratives. However, some students may have trouble with the archaic language in the poems and with inversions such as "I'm sure was he" for "I'm sure he was." Inversions may be explained by paraphrases. Archaic forms are explained below and in the footnotes.

ARCHAIC AND POETIC LANGUAGE
wi'—with
ere—before
e'er—ever
o'er—over
wee—little

IDIOMS
up and spoke—spoke up
make haste—hurry

ADDITIONAL VOCABULARY
ancient—old
fathom—distance of six feet
grumbly—discontented; unhappy

PREREADING

THE BALLADS

"Sir Patrick Spens"
"The Great Silkie of Shule Skerrie"
Anonymous

ABOUT THE AUTHORS

Like most ballads, **"Sir Patrick Spens"** and **"The Great Silkie of Shule Skerrie"** are not attributed to any one author. Medieval troubadours and common people passed such songs orally from generation to generation. Most of the ballads we know today were collected in the late nineteenth century from elderly women in rural areas. Many of these ballads were hundreds of years old, songs that mothers had sung to their children for centuries. Facts such as these led Virginia Woolf to comment that "Anonymous was a woman."

ABOUT THE SELECTIONS

"Sir Patrick Spens" is a perfect example of a popular English folk ballad. A **ballad** is a simple narrative poem in four-line stanzas, usually meant to be sung and rhyming *abcb*. **Folk ballads** were composed orally and passed by word-of-mouth from generation to generation and functioned like sensational news reports. Traveling musicians would sing ballads telling about tragic or newsworthy events such as shipwrecks, hangings, robberies, and murders. "Sir Patrick Spens" tells of the shipwreck of a Scottish knight and his men, a story that may be based on an actual thirteenth-century tragedy. Although warned that the voyage would be dangerous, Sir Patrick Spens still undertook the journey from which no one returned.

"The Great Silkie of Shule Skerrie" was collected in 1852 from an elderly woman in the Shetland Islands off the far northern coast of England. Many ballads, such as this one, dealt with improbable or supernatural occurrences. This ballad is based on common Scandinavian folk tales about silkies, seal-like creatures who lived in the sea but could come to land and take human form. Legends about swan maidens, mermaids, and related creatures are among the common folk inheritance of the European nations.

GOALS/OBJECTIVES

Studying this lesson will enable students to

- empathize with the feelings of fear and loss of the main characters
- define *ballad* and *folk ballad* and recognize distinguishing features of these literary forms, including rhyme scheme, stanza form, and typical subjects

- explain how ballads were used to communicate news during the Medieval Period
- explain how ballads illustrated relationships between the classes in medieval feudal society
- summarize information from encyclopedia articles
- recognize and correct run-ons

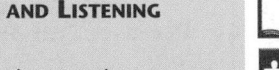
READER'S JOURNAL

Think of a sensational or tragic event that has recently appeared in the news. How did you hear about the event—from an official news source or by word-of-mouth? What details about the story particularly struck you? Write your reactions and feelings in your journal.

SPEAKING AND LISTENING SKILLS

Read the Language Arts Survey, 3.5, "Interpersonal Communication." Then, list a few reasons why you think a ballad might be an effective or ineffective way of communicating news during the Medieval Period.

"Sir Patrick Spens"

ANONYMOUS

The king sits in Dumferline town,
    Drinking the blood-red wine:
"O where will I get a good sailor
    To sail this ship of mine?"

5 Up and spoke an ancient knight,
    Sat at the king's right knee:
"Sir Patrick Spens is the best sailor
    That sails upon the sea."

The king has written a broad letter
10   And signed it wi' his hand,
And sent it to Sir Patrick Spens,
    Was walking on the sand.

The first line that Sir Patrick read,
    A loud laugh laughed he;
15 The next line that Sir Patrick read,
    The tear blinded his eye.

"O who is this has done this deed,
    This ill deed done to me,
To send me out this time o' the year,
20   To sail upon the sea?

"Make haste, make haste, my merry
    men all,
    Our good ship sails the morn."
"O say not so, my master dear,
    For I fear a deadly storm.

25 "Late late yestren I saw the new moon
    Wi' the old moon in her arm,[1]
And I fear, I fear, my dear master,
    That we will come to harm."

O our Scots nobles were right loath
30   To wet their cork-heeled shoes;
But long ere a' the play were played
    Their hats they swam above.

O long, long may their ladies sit,
    Wi' their fans into their hand,
35 Or e'er they see Sir Patrick Spens
    Come sailing to the land.

O long, long may the ladies stand,
    Wi' their gold combs in their hair,
Waiting for their own dear lords,
40   For they'll see them no more.

Half o'er, half o'er to Aberdour
    It's fifty fathoms deep,
And there lies good Sir Patrick Spens,
    Wi' the Scots lords at his feet. ∎

❶ *Why is one of the sailors afraid to begin the voyage? What sign did he see that made him afraid?*

---

1. **new moon . . . arm.** This natural phenomenon in which an outline of the old moon is seen filling out the crescent of the new moon was considered an omen of bad things to come.

READER'S JOURNAL

Students might also consider whether sensational stories would have had more impact on people living in the Medieval Period than on people today, who are constantly bombarded with information from a variety of sources.

SPEAKING AND LISTENING SKILLS

The following questions may help guide students' thinking.

• Have you ever heard a story by word-of-mouth and later found out that it was greatly exaggerated or simply untrue?

• If you were writing a poem or ballad about a news item, might you change the facts slightly to make it more interesting or emotional?

• How might a ballad reveal the values and interests of its author (and its audience)? Is this information as important as the "news" the ballad reports?

▶ Additional practice is provided in the *Essential Skills Practice Book: Speaking and Listening,* 3.5.

ANSWER TO GUIDED READING QUESTION

❶ The sailor believes there is a "deadly storm" on the way because he saw a faint outline of the old moon in the bright crescent of the new moon, which was considered a bad omen.

ANSWERS TO SELECTION CHECK TEST 4.3.1

EX. What type of verse is "Sir Patrick Spens"?
It is a ballad.

1. Who says that Sir Patrick Spens is the best sailor that sails upon the sea?
The knight says that Sir Patrick Spens is the best sailor.

2. What does the sailor fear?
He fears a storm.

3. What omen made him afraid?
He saw the new moon with the old moon in her arm.

4. For whom were the ladies waiting?
They were waiting for "their own dear lords."

5. Where is Sir Patrick Spens at the end of the poem?
He is fifty fathoms under the sea.

RESPONDING TO THE SELECTION

Ask students to consider the king's perspective. In the context of feudal values, what would he think of Sir Patrick's undertaking the voyage at the king's request? Would he think Sir Patrick acted foolishly or nobly? How would Sir Patrick's actions be viewed today? Why?

ANSWERS FOR REVIEWING THE SELECTION

RECALLING

1. He writes to ask Sir Patrick to sail his ship for him.

2. Sir Patrick at first laughs; then he cries.

3. He fears that a "deadly storm" will harm Sir Patrick and his crew if they sail now.

4. The "ladies," or wives, of Sir Patrick and his men are awaiting their return from the voyage.

INTERPRETING

Responses will vary. Possible responses are given.

5. The "blood-red wine" drunk by the king suggests that bloodshed or death is imminent.

6. At first he thinks the voyage is ridiculous because no one would be foolish enough to undertake it. Then, however, he realizes that he must go because his king has commanded it, and he fears for his life.

7. The pleading quality of line 23 reveals the fear felt by one sailor. The words *deadly, fear,* and *harm* foreshadow disaster.

8. The wives will have to wait forever, because their husbands have died and will never return.

SYNTHESIZING

Responses will vary. Possible responses are given.

9. The quotations make the characters in the ballad seem more real. They also reveal the strong emotions of Sir Patrick and his men and create a dramatic dialogue between him and one of the sailors.

10. Sir Patrick felt bound by duty to obey the king. As a knight, he was expected to risk his life out of loyalty to his lord.

Responding to the Selection

Imagine that you are the king in this ballad. You have just learned of the fate of Sir Patrick Spens. Write your response to the tragedy. You may wish to write your response in ballad stanzas.

Reviewing the Selection

RECALLING

1. Why does the king write a letter to Sir Patrick Spens?

2. What physical reactions does Sir Patrick have to the king's letter?

3. What fear does one of Sir Patrick's men reveal in stanzas 6 and 7?

4. Who is waiting in stanzas 9 and 10? for whom?

INTERPRETING

5. What image in the first stanza foreshadows a tragedy?

6. What do Sir Patrick's actions and words reveal about his feelings about the voyage?

7. How do the words in stanzas 6 and 7 create a feeling of impending doom?

8. Why will they be waiting a long, long time?

SYNTHESIZING

9. How do the quotations from various speakers in the ballad help create a dramatic story?

10. Why do you think Sir Patrick Spens obeyed the king's dangerous request? What part does his role as knight play in his fate?

Language Lab

The Parts of Speech. Read the Language Arts Survey, 2.3–2.29. Then identify the part of speech of each italicized word in the sentences below.

Many of the most popular of the [1] *medieval* ballads are ghost stories. "The Wife of Usher's Well," [2] *for* example, [3] *tells* the story of a mother whose three sons are killed, perhaps by [4] *drowning* at sea. The mother then wishes for her sons [5] *to be* resurrected. On the feast day of St. Martin, the sons [6] *mysteriously* appear at her door. [7] *They* feast with their mother that evening [8] *and* then [9] *go* to bed. However, they have to return to their [10] *graves* before the cock crows in the morning.

ANSWERS FOR LANGUAGE LAB

1. *medieval*—adj.
2. *for*—prep.
3. *tells*—v.
4. *drowning*—part.
5. *to be*—v. (inf.)
6. *mysteriously*—adv.
7. *They*—pron.
8. *and*—conj.
9. *go*—v.
10. *graves*—n.

For additional practice, refer students to the *Essential Skills Practice Book: Language,* 2.3–2.29.

READER'S JOURNAL

A common folk tale motif is the shape shifter, a being that can change form from human to animal and back again. Write the term *shape shifter* in your journal and freewrite about such a being. What would it look like? What forms would it take? How would it behave among humans?

RESEARCH SKILLS

Read the Language Arts Survey, 4.30, "Paraphrasing and Summarizing." Use an encyclopedia to find information about shape shifters. After reading the information, write a short summary of what you read.

"The Great Silkie of Shule Skerrie"[1]

ANONYMOUS

In Norway there sits a maid.
　"Bye-loo,[2] my baby," she begins.
"Little <u>ken</u> I my bairn's[3] father,
　Far less the land that he steps in."

5　　Then there rose at her bedside,
　　And a grumbly guest, I'm sure was he:
　Saying, "Here am I, thy bairn's father,
　　Although that I be not <u>comely</u>.

　"I am a man upon the land,
10　　And I am a silkie in the sea;
　And when I'm far away from land,
　　My dwelling is in Shule Skerrie."

---

　1. **Silkie . . . Skerrie.** In northern European folklore, a *silkie*, or *finn*, was an ocean-dwelling creature with the shape of a seal capable of shedding its skin and coming to land in the form of a person. Shule Skerrie is a place name.
　2. **Bye-loo.** Ballads and nursery rhymes often contain nonsense syllables such as these. The mother is singing to her child. The nonsense syllables are akin to "tra-la-la" and other such phrases commonly used as lyrical filler in songs.
　3. **bairn's.** Bairn is a Scottish dialectical word for child.

WORDS FOR EVERYDAY USE:

ken (ken) *vt.*, know

come • ly (kum´ lē) *adj.*, attractive

---

① *Who came to the maid's bedside? What was he like in manner and appearance?*

READER'S JOURNAL

Students can also think about what emotions a shape shifter might inspire in people who encountered or heard about it. Would they feel frightened, excited, curious, wary, or perhaps all of these at once?

RESEARCH SKILLS

Students might not find an entry for *shape shifters* in an encyclopedia. Suggest that they brainstorm in small groups to develop a list of topics under which they might find information about shape shifters, such as *Norway, Scandinavian folklore, folk tales*, etc.
▶ Additional practice is provided in the *Essential Skills Practice Book: Study and Research*, 4.30.

ANSWER TO GUIDED READING QUESTION

① The father of her baby came to her bedside; he was comely in appearance and acted "grumbly," or annoyed.

VOCABULARY FROM THE SELECTION

comely
ken
quoth

VOCABULARY IN CONTEXT

• Although I've gone to school with Stuart since the first grade, I still feel I don't really <u>ken</u> him.
• Which is more important in a mate: a <u>comely</u> face or a faithful heart?

Illustration by Sol Graphic Design

How does the maiden feel upon learning of her child's father? ❶

"It is not well," <u>quoth</u> the maiden fair;
   "It is not well, indeed," quoth she,
15   "That the Great Silkie of Shule Skerrie
   Should have got a child from me."

Now he has taken a purse of gold,
   And he has put it upon her knee,
Saying, "Give to me my little young son,
20   And take these up thy nurse's fee.

"And it shall come to pass on a summer's day,
   When the sun shines bright on every stone,
That I shall take my little wee son
   And teach him how to swim the foam. ⁴

25 "And you shall marry a proud gunner,⁵
   And a proud gunner, I'm sure he'll be,
And the very first shot that e're he shoots,
   He'll shoot both my young son and me." ∎

---

4. **foam.** Foam here stands for the sea. The name comes from the foam-like tops of breaking waves.
5. **gunner.** Gunner here means a harpooner.

WORDS FOR EVERYDAY USE: **quoth** (kwōth) *vt.*, said

VOCABULARY IN CONTEXT

• "Get out of my house, and take your bag of gold with you," <u>quoth</u> the disgusted young woman.

Responding to the Selection

Imagine that you are the mother in this ballad. In your journal, write a response to the Great Silkie. Express your feelings about the events related in the ballad. You may wish to write your response in ballad stanzas.

Reviewing the Selection

RECALLING

1. What lament does the maiden make in the first stanza of the ballad?

2. What information does the Great Silkie provide about himself in stanza 3?

3. What does the Great Silkie give the maiden as a "nurse's fee"?

4. What promises and predictions does the Great Silkie make in stanzas 6 and 7 of the ballad?

INTERPRETING

▶ 5. What troubles the maiden at the beginning of the poem, in stanza 1?

▶ 6. What facts in stanza 3 emphasize the strangeness and inhumanness of the Great Silkie?

▶ 7. What is he taking in return for the fee? How would the maiden feel about this?

▶ 8. How does the promise in stanza 6 contrast with the prediction in stanza 7? What role does the maiden have in this prediction?

SYNTHESIZING

9. What special circumstance in this ballad causes the reader or listener to feel distaste or antipathy for the profession of the gunner?

10. What sort of relationship between the human and natural worlds is described in this ballad? Should that sort of relationship exist? Why, or why not?

THE BALLADS / "THE GREAT SILKIE OF SHULE SKERRIE" **141**

ANSWERS FOR REVIEWING THE SELECTION (CONT.)

SYNTHESIZING
Responses will vary. Possible responses are given.

9. The ballad gives the perspective of one of the sea creatures whom it is the gunner's profession to kill. The reader feels especially sorry for the "little wee son."

10. The relationship is both intimate and antagonistic. The maiden and the Great Silkie have had a child together, but she is disgusted by the Great Silkie's strangeness, and her future husband will supposedly destroy the silkie and the child. The tone of the ballad suggests that the tragic essence of this relationship is inevitable.

RESPONDING TO THE SELECTION

Students can begin by freewriting about how they would feel if a strange creature offered them money in exchange for a person they loved. They could also consider the Great Silkie's prophecy and whether the maiden might think giving the child to its father is fated to happen no matter how she feels about it.

ANSWERS FOR REVIEWING THE SELECTION

RECALLING

1. She laments the fact that she doesn't know her child's father.

2. He says that he takes the form of a man when he is on land, but turns into a silkie when he is in the ocean.

3. He gives her a purse full of gold.

4. He promises that he will teach his son to swim in the ocean, and predicts that the maiden will someday marry a gunner who will kill both the Great Silkie and his son.

INTERPRETING
Responses will vary. Possible responses are given.

5. She is troubled by the fact that she doesn't know the father of her baby. Perhaps she knows that the Great Silkie is its father, but is sad that she and the silkie do not share the same world.

6. The fact that he can change shapes and live both on land and in the sea makes him seem strange and inhuman.

7. He wants to take the baby, his son. The maiden would probably be distraught and lonely if she gave up her child.

8. Stanza 6 paints a bright picture of the child's future, fulfilling his destiny as the child of a silkie by learning to "swim the foam." Stanza 7, which predicts the maiden will marry a gunner who will kill the father and son, is disturbing and tragic.

(cont.)

SUPPORT FOR LEP STUDENTS

Several lines in the translation of "Ubi Sunt Qui ante Nos Fuerunt?" follow closely the word order of the original Middle English. Some students may need help interpreting sentences that are in inverted word order. Here are transpositions into normal word order of key lines from the poem:

line 1: Where are they that were before us?

line 8: They led their lives with gaming.

line 19: They took their paradise here.

line 24: They never come [back] from there.

IDIOMS

in the twinkling of an eye—in a moment

were lost—fell irretrievably into sin, with its inevitable punishment

ADDITIONAL VOCABULARY

bore—past tense of bear; carry
bower—bedroom
gaming—gambling
wailing—crying

PREREADING

"Ubi Sunt Qui ante Nos Fuerunt?"
"I Sing of a Maiden"

Anonymous, trans. by Robin Lamb

ABOUT THE AUTHORS

"Ubi Sunt Qui ante Nos Fuerunt?" and **"I Sing of a Maiden"** were both written anonymously. Although some medieval lyrics were secular, most were religious. Very few of these hymns were attributed to a specific author. Such literature existed many years before it was ever written down and was considered popular verse rather than the work of individual writers.

ABOUT THE SELECTIONS

Because of the tremendous influence of the Catholic Church, the religious lyrics from the Medieval Period far outnumber the secular ones. Some religious lyrics, including **"Ubi Sunt Qui ante Nos Fuerunt,"** dwelt on the fear of death and the contemplation of heaven. As the selection's title demonstrates, many of these lyrics were originally written in Latin.

The religious lyric **"I Sing of a Maiden"** (*circa* 1400) celebrates the Virgin Mary. Such lyrics had their origins in France, where the veneration of the Virgin Mary developed into the code of courtly love. Poetry brought back to France with the Crusaders from Persia influenced the development of courtly love as well. "I Sing of a Maiden" also contains elements of secular lyrics that celebrate the coming of spring. The poet creates a symbolic comparison between the return of spring and the Virgin Birth.

The following selections are printed in the original Middle English alongside Modern English translations.

ENRICHMENT ACTIVITIES

Show your class some photographs of medieval cathedrals such as Chartres or Notre Dame. (Such photos may be found in books on European travel, the Middle Ages, and the history of architecture. David MacCauley's *Cathedral* shows, in step-by-step drawings, how a medieval cathedral was constructed.) Explain that cathedrals and castles were the two great products of medieval architecture and that these buildings represented the two major forces in medieval society—the church and the nobility. Explain that the products of a culture show what was important to them. The most opulent buildings from the Middle Ages are the cathedrals. This fact shows the importance to medieval people of religion and the church.

READER'S JOURNAL
  Like all languages, English constantly evolves. How much do you think English has changed since the Medieval Period? Take a few moments to write what you know about the development of the English language.

VOCABULARY SKILLS
  Read the Language Arts Survey, 2.143, "Word Origins I," and 2.144, "Word Origins II." Then compare the language of the Middle English text to the Modern English translation. Which Middle English words have a close resemblance to Modern English? Which words have changed significantly?

"Ubi Sunt Qui ante Nos Fuerunt?"[1]

ANONYMOUS, TRANS. BY ROBIN LAMB

Were beth they that biforen us weren,	Where are they that were before us,
Houndes ladden and havekes beren,	[Who] led hounds and bore hawks
And hadden feld and wode?	And had fields and woods?
The riche levedies in here bour,	The rich ladies in their bowers,
5 That wereden gold in here tressour,	That wore gold in their hair,
With here brighte rode;	With their bright complexions;
Eten and drounken, and maden hem glad;	Ate and drank, and made themselves glad;
Here lif was al with gamen y-lad;	Their lives were all with gaming led;
Men kneleden hem biforen;	Men knelt before them;
10 They beren hem wel swithe heye:	They bore themselves so high:
And in a twincling of an eye	But in a twinkling of an eye,
Here soules weren forloren.	Their souls were lost forever.
Were is that lawhing and that song,	Where is that laughing and that song,
That trayling and that proude gong,	That trailing of gowns and that proud walk,
15 Tho havekes and tho houndes?	Those hawks and those hounds?
Al that joye is went away,	All that joy has gone away,
That wele is comen to weylaway,	Their wellness has come to wailing,
To manye harde stoundes.	To many hard times.

---

1. **Ubi . . . Fuerunt.** Latin for "Where are they who came before us?"

READER'S JOURNAL
  Have students think about the ways in which the language is changing around them every day. They will probably have recognized some differences in their speech and that of the adults around them. They may also be aware of recently coined words such as *yuppie, computer network,* and *sitcom.* Ask them to consider the effects of a slow accumulation of such changes over hundreds of years. If you wish to do so at this point, you can refer students to the essay on "The Development of the English Language: Middle English" on page 232, or you can have them compare the Middle English text of the poem on the left to the Modern English translation on the right.

VOCABULARY SKILLS
  Point out to students the following differences between the Middle English text and Modern English:

- **Word order.** The verb sometimes appeared at the end of the sentences, as in "biforen us weren."

- **Inflectional endings.** Modern English is simpler than Middle English in its inflectional system, having lost endings such as those that appear at the ends of the words *houndes, ladden, havekes,* and *beren.*

- **Double negatives.** The last line contains a double negative *ne . . . nevere,* that is nonstandard in Modern English.

- **Word change.** Most of the words in the poem are still found in Modern English, though with different spellings and pronunciations. A word that has disappeared from Modern English is *stoundes,* in line 18.

GOALS/OBJECTIVES

Studying this lesson will enable students to

- experience the speaker's awareness of the inevitability of death
- explain the influence of the medieval church on early English lyric poetry and give examples
- explain the *memento mori* and *contemptu mundi* themes as used in a medieval lyric

- define and give examples of *translation, archaic language, courtly love, simile,* and *metonymy*
- create a dictionary entry in proper form
- explain the influence of medieval adoration of the Virgin Mary on the development of the concept of courtly love

RESPONDING TO THE SELECTION

You may wish to play for your students the recording, in Middle English, of "The Prologue" to Chaucer's *Canterbury Tales,* on Track 7. Students will recognize some words but will find the passage very difficult to follow. Students would probably need to take with them a Middle English–Modern English dictionary.

ANSWERS FOR REVIEWING THE SELECTION

RECALLING

1. The speaker asks, "Where are they that were before us?"

2. They hunted, feasted, wore fine clothes, and gambled.

3. In a twinkling of an eye, their souls were lost. They are now in hell.

4. The people will never return from hell. They will be there forever.

INTERPRETING

Responses will vary. Possible responses are given.

5. A possible response is "who have died."

6. The people were probably nobles because they hunted, were rich, wore gold and trailing gowns, and ate and drank well.

7. Their joy has gone away because they are now among the damned.

(cont.)

```
20   Here paradis they nomen here,
     And nou they lyen in helle y-fere;
       The fyr hit brennes evere:
         Long is ay, and long is o,
         Long is wy, and long is wo;
       Thennes ne cometh they nevere.  ■
```

```
     Their paradise they took here,
     And now they lie in hell together
       The fire it burns forever:
         Long is *a*, and long is *o*,
         Long is *y* [why], and long is woe;
       From there come they never.  ■
```

Responding to the Selection

Imagine traveling in time from the present back to medieval England. Do you think you will understand the English speakers you meet? What language tools might you need on your trip?

Reviewing the Selection

RECALLING

1. What question does the speaker ask in line 1?

2. What activities occupied these people while they lived?

3. What happened to these people? Where are they now?

4. What observation, given in the last line, makes the fate of these people even more terrible?

INTERPRETING

5. What is another way of saying the phrase "were before us"?

6. What was the status of these people? How do you know?

7. Why does the speaker claim that "all that joy has gone away"?

8. How does the present state of these ladies and men compare to their former life?

SYNTHESIZING

9. Why should the reader or listener take notice of these women and men?

10. According to the lyric, what relationship exists between this life and the afterlife? Why should people think about heaven while still living on earth?

Understanding Literature (Questions for Discussion)

1. **Theme.** The central idea in a literary work is its **theme**. Religious themes dominated medieval literature. Common themes included *contemptu mundi* (contempt for the world), which lamented that the world is fallen and full of woe, and *memento mori* (reminder of death), which warned that death comes quickly and unexpectedly, so prepare for the next life. In asking the question, "Where are those who came before us?", this lyric stresses a similar theme. What message does the *ubi sunt* theme send? What words or phrases from the lyric support the theme?

2. **Translation.** The art of rendering speech or writing into another language is called **translation**. Because the lyric was written in Middle English, it has been translated into Modern English for today's readers. What does this tell you about Middle English?

3. **Archaic Language. Archaic language** consists of old or obsolete words or phrases used to describe people, things, or events of a past time. Compare the word *forloren* in line 12 of the Middle English version to the words *lost forever* in the same line of the translation. The modern translation of *forloren* is *forlorn*. How do the Modern English words *forlorn* and *lost forever* compare? Does *forlorn* or *lost forever* convey greater feeling? Why do you suppose the translator chose *lost forever* instead of *forlorn*?

Responding in Writing

1. **Lyric Poem.** A **lyric poem** is a highly musical verse that expresses the emotions of the speaker. In this selection, the speaker uses vivid and concrete language to contrast the earthly life to the afterlife. The contrast creates a solemn and remorseful tone. Do you agree with the speaker's outlook? Write a lyric poem in response to the speaker's view of the world. Use vivid language to express your viewpoint and to create a tone that either advocates or disputes the speaker's position.

2. **Dictionary Entries.** Write entries for a Middle English–Modern English dictionary. Choose ten words from the Middle English version of the selection. Identify the part of speech and the Modern English counterpart for each word. When necessary, note how a word meaning has changed over time. Refer to the Language Arts Survey, 2.3–2.31, "The Parts of Speech." You might also want to look at the *Oxford English Dictionary* or another reference work that lists comprehensive word histories. Remember to list entries in alphabetical order.

1. **Theme.** The message of the *ubi sunt* literature of the Middle Ages was to remind people that life is fleeting and that they should think about and prepare for the afterlife. Some lines from the poem that support this idea are "But in a twinkling of an eye,/Their souls were lost forever"; "Their wellness has come to wailing"; "now they lie in hell together"; and "From there come they never."

▶ **Teaching Note:** Ask students to consider how the *ubi sunt, memento mori,* and *contemptu mundi* themes are related. The *ubi sunt* serves as a *memento mori,* or reminder of death. The purpose of reminding people of death is to get them to feel *contemptu mundi,* or contempt for the world, so that they will place stock, instead, in the world after this one.

2. **Translation.** That a translation is necessary shows that the language has changed tremendously since the Middle Ages.

3. **Archaic Language.** *Forlorn* now means "sad" and has, perhaps, less powerful connotations than *lost forever*. The translator probably chose *lost forever* because she wanted to convey the poem's point that the consequences in the afterlife are eternal.

ANALYTIC SCALES FOR RESPONDING IN WRITING

Assign a score from 1 to 25 for each grading criterion below. (For more detailed evaluation, see the evaluation forms for writing, revising, and proofreading, *Assessment Portfolio*, 7.1–7.10.)

1. **Lyric Poem**
• **Content/Unity.** The lyric poem advocates or disputes the position of the speaker in the poem.
• **Organization/Coherence.** The lyric poem presents a consistent point of view.
• **Language/Style.** The lyric poem uses vivid language to create emotions in the reader.
• **Conventions.** The lyric poem avoids errors in spelling, grammar, usage, mechanics, and manuscript form.
(cont.)

ANALYTIC SCALES FOR RESPONDING IN WRITING (CONT.)

2. **Dictionary Entries**
• **Content/Unity.** The entries contain entry words, part-of-speech labels, and definitions.
• **Organization/Coherence.** The entries are given in alphabetical order.
• **Language/Style.** The definitions of the words are correct and clear.

• **Conventions.** The entries use consistent punctuation and capitalization.

▶ Refer students to the Language Arts Survey, 4.24, "Using Dictionaries," for a sample dictionary entry. Students may write simplified entries.

PREREADING NOTES

READER'S JOURNAL

Instead of freewriting, students might make cluster charts or sensory detail charts. Refer them to the Language Arts Survey, 1.17, "Clustering," and 1.18, "Sensory Detail Charts."

SPEAKING AND LISTENING SKILLS

If you have a mixed group of students, some with Catholic backgrounds, then you may wish to place a Catholic student in each group who can serve as a resource for the other students. If there are no Catholic students in your class, you may have to provide some additional background information yourself. Explain that in many Christian belief systems and in Catholicism in particular, the Virgin Mary is said to have conceived the infant Jesus by divine intervention, not by the usual method. You may further wish to explain that in Catholicism, Mary plays the role of one who intercedes with God on behalf of the prayerful. A central prayer in Catholic observance is the "Ave Maria," or "Hail, Mary," the text of which is as follows: "Hail, Mary, full of grace, the Lord is with Thee. Blessèd art Thou among women, and blessèd is the fruit of Thy womb, Jesus. Holy Mary, mother of God, pray for us sinners, now and at the hour of our death." Mary is the embodiment of gentleness and grace. Because of its word choice and tone, "I Sing of a Maiden" brilliantly evokes those qualities and is widely considered to be the most beautiful of Middle English lyrics.

RESPONDING TO THE SELECTION

Ask students to identify key words in the selection that help to create its tone. Such words include *still, dew, bower, flower,* and *lay.* Student responses may vary, but most will probably say that the tone of the poem is quiet, gentle, or reverent.

146 TEACHER'S EDITION

READER'S JOURNAL

What images does the season of spring conjure for you? Write the word *spring* in your journal, then freewrite sensory details about the coming of this season.

SPEAKING AND LISTENING SKILLS

Read the Language Arts Survey, 3.6, "Discussion." In a small group, discuss what you know about the Catholic doctrine of the Virgin Mary and the Virgin Birth.

"I Sing of a Maiden"

ANONYMOUS, TRANS. BY ROBIN LAMB

I sing of a maiden
　　That is makelees:
King of alle kinges
　　To her sone she chees.

5　He cam also stille
　　Ther his moder was
As dewe in Aprille
　　That falleth on the gras.

He cam also stille
10　To his modres bowr
As dewe in Aprille
　　That falleth on the flowr.

He cam also stille
　　Ther his moder lay
15　As dewe in Aprille
　　That falleth on the spray.

Moder and maiden
　　Was nevere noon but she:
Wel may swich a lady
20　Godes moder be. ■

I sing of a maiden
　　That is matchless:[1]
King of all kings
　　As her son she chose.

He came as still
　　Where his mother was
As dew in April
　　That falls on the grass.

He came as still
　　To his mother's bower
As dew in April
　　That falls on the flower.

He came as still
　　Where his mother lay
As dew in April
　　That falls on the spray.

Mother and maiden
　　Was never none but she:
Well may such a lady
　　God's mother be. ■

1. **matchless.** The word is a pun meaning both "unequaled" and "without a mate, or match."

146　UNIT THREE / THE MEDIEVAL PERIOD

ANSWERS TO SELECTION CHECK TEST 4.3.7

EX. What type of verse is "I Sing of a Maiden"?
It is a religious lyric.
1. Of what kind of a maiden does the speaker sing?
The speaker sings of a matchless maiden.
2. To what is the mother compared?
She is compared to the dew in April.
3. Whose mother is the maiden?

She is the mother of Jesus, the king of kings.
4. How did the speaker's child come?
He came "as still as dew in April."
5. On what three things does the speaker say April dew falls?
April dew falls on the grass, the flower, and the spray.

Responding to the Selection

Medieval lyrics such as this one were originally sung. What kind of music do you suppose accompanied this lyric? What was its tone? Why do you think so? Write your ideas in your journal.

Reviewing the Selection

RECALLING

1. Who is the maiden of the poem?

2. Who is the maiden's son? To what does the poet compare His coming?

3. What other name does the poet give the maiden?

INTERPRETING

▶▶ 4. How do the two meanings of the word *matchless* apply to the maiden?

▶▶ 5. How does the comparison progress from stanza 2 to stanza 4?

▶▶ 6. How is the maiden's other name paradoxical?

SYNTHESIZING

7. To what springtime occurrence does the poet compare the Virgin Birth?

Understanding Literature (Questions for Discussion)

1. **Courtly Love.** The code of romantic love celebrated in medieval songs and romances in France and England is called **courtly love.** Many medieval lyrics about the Virgin Mary are almost indistinguishable from secular love poems addressed to an idealized woman. What elements of this lyric make it seem like a love poem? What elements make it seem like a religious poem?

2. **Simile.** A **simile** is a comparison using *like* or *as*. It compares two things that have some feature or aspect in common. What two things does the poet compare? What is their relationship to each other?

3. **Metonymy.** **Metonymy** is the naming of an object associated with a thing in place of the name of a thing itself, as in *hired hand* for "laborer." To what does the word *spray* refer in line 16? (Hint: It refers to some body of water.)

ANSWERS FOR UNDERSTANDING LITERATURE (CONT.)

women pursued by knights attempting to show themselves worthy. This was the literature of romance, of chivalry and courtly love.

2. **Simile.** The poet compares the coming of Christ to the falling of dew in April and, by extension, to the coming of spring. The two subjects are treated in the poem with a kind of reverent expectation and awe. Both the coming of Christ and the coming of spring are times of renewal, opportunities for rebirth.

3. **Metonymy.** *Spray* is a poetic, metonymic term for "ocean," one that derives from the spray created by crashing or tossing waves.

RECALLING

1. The maiden is the Virgin Mary.

2. The maiden's son is Jesus, the "King of all kings." The poet compares his coming to that of spring.

3. The other name is "mother."

INTERPRETING

Responses will vary. Possible responses are given.

4. She is matchless in the sense that she is unequaled ("Blessèd art Thou among women") and in the sense that she conceived without a mate, or match.

5. The comparison progresses from dew on the grass to dew on the flower to dew on the spray.

6. It is paradoxical that she is both a maiden and a mother. Another paradox is that she gave birth, but the birth was not attended by sin or pain (thus the tranquility of the description in the poem).

SYNTHESIZING

Responses will vary. Possible responses are given.

7. It is compared to the falling of dew.

ANSWERS FOR UNDERSTANDING LITERATURE

▶ See the evaluation forms for discussion, active listening, and oral communication, *Assessment Portfolio*, 7.11–7.14.

Responses will vary. Possible responses are given.

1. **Courtly Love.** The tenderness of the expression and specific lines such as "a maiden/That is matchless" make this lyric seem like a love poem. The references to the "King of all kings" and "God's mother" make it seem like a religious poem.

▶ **Teaching Note:** Explain that European soldiers on Crusade in the Holy Land gathered and then brought back to Europe Persian love poems that idealized women. At the same time, possibly as a consequence, many Europeans began to devote more attention to the adoration of the Virgin Mary. The Persian idealization of women, combined with the adoration of the Virgin, led to the creation of a literature that dealt with idealized
(cont.)

ADDITIONAL RESOURCES

READER'S GUIDE
- Selection Worksheet, 3.5

ASSESSMENT PORTFOLIO
- Selection Check Test, 4.3.9
- Selection Test, 4.3.10

ENRICHMENT ACTIVITIES

- Have students compose their own lais or rap poems celebrating contemporary heroes or famous contemporary couples.

- Assign students the following figures from Arthurian legend: Lancelot and Guinevere; Merlin the Magician; Sir Balin and Sir Pellam; Sir Gawain and the Green Knight; Sir Galahad; Mordred; Morgan le Fay; and Sir Percival. Have them research the basic facts of their characters' lives as told in medieval romances. Then have them present the results of their research to the rest of the class.

SUPPORT FOR LEP STUDENTS

You may wish to review with students the Additional Vocabulary listed below before they read the selection. Comprehension will also be aided by sharing with students the information provided in the Historical/Literary Note on the following page.

IDIOMS
grow melancholy—become sad

ADDITIONAL VOCABULARY
recount—tell or tell again
embittered—made bitter, or
    angry and unhappy
pensive—thoughtful
melancholy—very sad
emerged—came out
enlaced —intermingled
escort—accompany
banish—throw out; exile

PREREADING

THE LITERATURE OF ROMANCE

"The Honeysuckle: Chevrefoil"
by Marie de France, trans. by Marcelle Thiébaux

ABOUT THE AUTHOR

Marie de France (*circa* 1200) was a French poet who had considerable influence over English writers. She spent most of her life at the English court. Some scholars believe she was the half-sister of Henry II of England, who was king during that time. She perfected the **Breton lai**, a type of narrative poem or song, and is probably responsible for its introduction in England. Many of Marie de France's lais had Celtic themes and included characters and storylines from the legends of King Arthur and his knights of the Round Table.

ABOUT THE SELECTION

"**The Honeysuckle: Chevrefoil**" is one of the fifteen Breton lais known to be written by Marie de France. It tells of an Arthurian knight, Tristan, and his love for a Celtic queen, Iseult. Their love is complicated by Iseult's marriage to Tristan's uncle, King Mark of Cornwall. In Arthurian legends Tristan is known for his skills as a warrior, a musician, a lover, and a hunter, among other abilities. The tales of Tristan and Iseult were popular during the Middles Ages, and Marie de France obviously made use of material familiar to her listeners. Although "The Honeysuckle: Chevrefoil" was originally written as a Breton lai, the following selection is a Modern English prose translation.

GOALS/OBJECTIVES

Studying this lesson will enable students to

- empathize with the love and longing of Tristan and the Queen
- relate the principal events in the legend of Tristan and Iseult
- distinguish between narrative commentary and the main body of a story

- identify, define, and illustrate with examples the terms *romance, courtly love,* and *Breton lai.*
- identify and explain an extended simile

READER'S JOURNAL

What songs can you think of that tell stories? Do you think a song is an effective way of telling a story? Why or why not? In your journal write your ideas about the effectiveness of storytelling through songs.

THINKING SKILLS

Read the Language Arts Survey, 4.10, "Analyzing." Then, analyze "The Honeysuckle: Chevrefoil," dividing it into those parts that are narration and those that are the lay proper.

"The Honeysuckle: Chevrefoil"

MARIE DE FRANCE, TRANS. BY MARCELLE THIÉBAUX

It pleases me very much, and I really wish to recount to you the true story of the "lai"[1] they call *Chevrefoil*, and why it was written and how it came about. Many people have told me the story and recounted it to me, and I have also found it written down. It's about Tristan and the Queen and their love which was so strong that they suffered greatly, and they both died on the same day because of it.

King Mark was embittered, outraged against his nephew, Tristan, and drove him from the land because of his love for the Queen. Tristan went back to his own country, to his birthplace in South Wales. He spent a year there, unable to return without risking death and ruin.

Don't be surprised. Anyone who loves most faithfully will grieve and grow pensive if he cannot have what he desires. Tristan grieved, he grew melancholy, and so he left his own country and went straight to Cornwall, where the Queen lived. He hid alone in the forest, for he did not want anyone to see him. At evening he emerged when it was time to seek lodging, and he stayed with peasants and poor people. He asked them for news of the King's doings. They told him they'd heard that the barons had been summoned to Tintagel where the King wished to hold court. Everyone would be in attendance for Pentecost.[2] There would be rejoicing and festivity, and the Queen would also be there.

Tristan heard this news with great joy. The Queen would not be able to journey to Tintagel without his seeing her pass by. The day the King set forth, Tristan returned to the wood by the road that he knew the royal company would have to take.

He split a hazel branch in half and whittled it on four sides to make it square. Having prepared the wood, he inscribed his name on it with his knife. If the Queen saw it (for this had happened once before and she had perceived it then), she would know that the hazel wand came from her beloved.

The sum of what he wrote and said was to tell her that he had been there a long

---

1. **lai.** A lai, or lay, is a narrative poem or song.
2. **Pentecost.** A Christian festival seven weeks after Easter

PREREADING NOTES

READER'S JOURNAL

Students may be able to recall such narrative songs as "The Ballad of John Henry" or "Casey Jones." Examples of narrative songs appearing earlier in this text are "Sir Patrick Spens" and "The Great Silkie."

THINKING SKILLS

Students should be able to recognize with very little prompting that this story is framed by a narrative voice. In the first paragraph, the narrator announces the name and subject of the story that she is going to tell. In the last paragraph, she repeats the name, adding the further information that Tristan himself was the original teller of the story. Point out to students that Marie de France was reworking materials passed down from singer to singer and that she does not claim originality for her story. In fact, ideas about the originality of a tale were quite foreign to writers of the Middle Ages, who generally thought of stories as part of the common inheritance of all people. Oral storytelling was vital because few people could read.

① *How is Tristan related to King Mark? Why does the King send Tristan away?*

② *What sign did Tristan make to the Queen?*

ANSWERS TO GUIDED READING QUESTIONS

❶ Tristan is King Mark's nephew. The King sends Tristan away because he is in love with the King's wife, the Queen.

❷ He carved his name on a hazel wand.

HISTORICAL/LITERARY NOTE

Marie de France wrote for an audience already familiar with Arthurian legend. Her lais therefore assume a knowledge of the principal characters and of their lives that many modern readers will not have. Explain to your students that the story of Tristan and Iseult appears in several Arthurian sources. The basic facts of the story are these: As a young man in the service of his uncle, King Mark of Cornwall, Tristan is asked to travel to Ireland to bring back Iseult, who is to be Mark's queen. (cont.)

HISTORICAL/LITERARY NOTE (CONT.)

On the journey back to Cornwall, Tristan and Iseult fall in love because of a love potion that they unwittingly drink. Iseult is married to Mark, but at night her serving maid takes her place; in that way she remains faithful to Tristan. However, rumors of Tristan's love for the Queen reach Mark, who banishes him. This is the point at which Marie de France's lai begins.

The end of the story differs in the various sources. Some say that Tristan was killed by Mark. Others say that Iseult sailed to meet Tristan, sending word ahead that if she were alive and on the ship, the ship would have a white sail, but if she were dead, it would have a black sail. Incorrectly informed that the ship had a black sail, Tristan took his own life. On learning of her beloved's death, Iseult died of grief.

CROSS-CURRICULAR ACTIVITIES

 Arts and Humanities.
The Tristan and Iseult story has been told many times in many different media. You may wish to have students create their own artworks based on the story. Possibilities include paintings or drawings of the characters, song lyrics, or dramatic adaptations. Students interested in learning more of the story may wish to read a translation of Gottfried von Strassburg's *Tristan und Isolde*. Some might also appreciate Richard Wagner's opera by the same name, which was based on von Strassburg's work.

ANSWER TO GUIDED READING QUESTION

❶ Their love is compared to honeysuckle that has grown around the hazelwood so that the two are intertwined and cannot be separated without resulting in the deaths of both.

ANSWERS TO SELECTION CHECK TEST 4.3.9

EX. With whom does Tristan fall in love?
He falls in love with the Queen.

1. To whom is the Queen married?
She is married to King Mark of Cornwall.

2. Why does King Mark banish Tristan?
King Mark banishes Tristan because he discovers the love that Tristan has for the Queen.

3. Why does Tristan wait in the woods beside the road leading to Tintagel?
He waits in hopes of seeing the Queen.

4. To what does the narrator compare the love of Tristan and the Queen?
He compares it to a honeysuckle vine spiraled around a hazelwood.

5. According to the narrator, who composed the story called "Goteleaf" or "Chevrefoil"?
It was composed by Tristan.

La Belle Isould at Joyous Gard. from The Birth, Life and Acts of King Arthur, *Sir Thomas Malory. Illustration by Aubrey Beardsley. Wellesley College Library, Special Collections*

time, he had waited and tarried in the hope of learning how he might see her, since he could not live without her.

For the two of them it was like the honeysuckle spiraling itself around the hazelwood, the two enlaced and grown completely together. Together they can live, but if anyone tries to tear them apart, the hazel swiftly dies and the honeysuckle too. "Sweet friend, so it is with us: neither you without me, nor me without you." *Bele amie, si est de nus—ne vus sanz mei, ne mei sanz vus!*

The Queen rode on horseback along the road. She glanced at a hill slope and noticed the little branch and saw what it was. She recognized all the letters. She ordered the knights who escorted her, those who rode alongside with her, to stop. She wished to dismount and rest. They obeyed her command and she moved far away from her attendants. To her side she summoned her maidservant, Brenguein, who was very faithful.

❶ To what is their love compared? Why is their love like this?

At a short distance from the road she found in the forest the man she loved more than any living person, and they shared great joy. He felt at ease as he spoke, and she told him her desires. She let him know how he might become reconciled to the King and how unhappy the King was that he had banished Tristan because of the accusations against him. Then she had to leave, and she parted from her beloved. But when it was time to go, they both wept. Tristan returned to Wales to await his uncle's orders.

Because of the joy he had shared with his beloved when he saw her, and because of what he had written (for the Queen had said he should) and his desire to remember the words, Tristan—who was an excellent musician on the harp—composed a new "lai." Briefly I'll name it for you: The English call it *Goteleaf* and the French name it *Chevrefoil*. I have told you the truth of the "lai" I've recited for you. ∎

ART NOTE

La Belle Isould at Joyous Gard is taken from a 1893 edition of Sir Thomas Malory's *Le Morte d'Arthur*, illustrated by Aubrey Vincent Beardsley (1872–1898). Beardsley was the foremost English illustrator of the late 1800s and a leader in the Art for Art's Sake movement, which emphasized aestheticism as opposed to any political, social, moral, or practical value that art might have.

Responding to the Selection

Imagine that you are Tristan, preparing to write the lai that will celebrate your reunion with the Queen. In your journal, write a few lines that might be part of such a narrative poem or song.

Reviewing the Selection

RECALLING

1. Why are Tristan and the Queen separated?

2. Why does Tristan return to Cornwall?

3. How does the Queen discover that Tristan is waiting for her in the forest?

4. Why does Tristan write a new "lai"?

INTERPRETING

5. What words convey Tristan's feelings about the separation?

6. What do Tristan's actions reveal about his feelings for the Queen?

7. How do the Queen's actions prove her love for Tristan?

8. How do Tristan and the Queen feel after their meeting in the forest?

SYNTHESIZING

9. What kind of relationship exists between Tristan and the Queen? What makes you think so?

Understanding Literature (Questions for Discussion)

1. **Romance.** The type of medieval literature that tells highly imaginative stories of the adventures and loves of knights is known as a **romance.** Many medieval romances involve the legend of King Arthur and his knights. What elements in "The Honeysuckle: Chevrefoil" indicate that it is a romance?

2. **Courtly Love.** The code of romantic love celebrated in French and English medieval romances is known as **courtly love.** According to the code, the lover is truly in love if he experiences extreme, transforming emotions. The object of his emotions is an idealized, venerated woman. Courtly love requires that the knight prove his love through his courage on the battlefield as well as through his courtesy toward his lady. How does the story of Tristan and the Queen exemplify courtly love?

3. **Breton Lai. Breton lais,** brief medieval romances, were first written in Brittany and later imitated in England. Breton lais deal with conventional romance themes such as courtly love, and many lais were originally written and performed as songs. What words or sentence structures in this prose translation indicate that its original form was a Breton lai?

THE LITERATURE OF ROMANCE / "THE HONEYSUCKLE: CHEVREFOIL" **151**

RESPONDING TO THE SELECTION

Have students write their responses first in prose and then translate them into rhymed verse. Students may want to review the discussions of meter and stanza form beginning on page 17 of Unit 1. Students may want to write their poems in rhymed trimeter or tetrameter.

ANSWERS FOR REVIEWING THE SELECTION

RECALLING

1. King Mark orders the banishment of Tristan when he learns of his nephew's love for the Queen.

2. Tristan returns to Cornwall in hopes of seeing the Queen.

3. The Queen sees the hazel wand on which Tristan has carved his name.

4. Tristan composes his new lai to express his joy at having seen the Queen, to fulfill his promise to her, and to record the words that had occurred to him earlier.

INTERPRETING
Responses will vary. Possible responses are given.

5. Their love is compared to the honeysuckle and the hazelwood and Tristan says, "Sweet friend, so it is with us: neither you without me, nor me without you."

6. Tristan's actions reveal that he loves her very deeply.

7. When she sees the hazel wand, she immediately stops and goes to find him.

8. They feel great joy.

SYNTHESIZING
Responses will vary. Possible responses are given.

9. A possible response is that their relationship represents the romantic ideal of perfect love that makes people so inseparable that they will die if kept apart, as the honeysuckle and the hazelwood die if separated.

ANSWERS FOR UNDERSTANDING LITERATURE

1. **Romance.** Romance elements in the story include kings, knights, and ladies, as well as courtly love.
► **Teaching Note:** You may wish to have students read the discussions of *romance, chivalry,* and *courtly love* in the Handbook of Literary Terms.

2. **Courtly Love.** The story of Tristan and the Queen illustrates courtly love because it involves a noble man and woman in an idealized romantic union. (Another common courtly love element in the story is infidelity. However, it is not necessary that you share that information with your class.)

3. **Breton Lai.** The translation ends with the statement, "I have told you the truth of the 'lai' I've recited for you." (You may wish to point out the line in the original Old French in column one on page 150. Hearing or reading this line will give students some idea of the musicality of the original verse.)

TEACHER'S EDITION **151**

ENRICHMENT ACTIVITIES

Send students to the library to do research on knights—their armor, weapons, codes of conduct, methods of fighting, tournaments, and so on. Have them share with one another what they learn from their research. Of particular interest to students will be any photographs or illustrations that they can find illustrating the armor and weapons of knights.

SUPPORT FOR LEP STUDENTS

This brief story contains quite a few sophisticated words, so you may wish to review with students the Additional Vocabulary listed below before they read the selection. Comprehension will also be aided by sharing with students the information provided in the Historical/Literary Note on page 155.

IDIOMS

her hair shone—her hair had a lovely appearance, as though lighted

out of politeness—because of their politeness

ADDITIONAL VOCABULARY

clutch—grip
unwary—unsuspecting; unaware
mirth—happiness
revel—a good time; a feast
celebrants—people who celebrate, or have a good time in honor of something
prowess—strength; power
bard—one who tells stories through song

(cont.)

PREREADING

from *Sir Gawain and the Green Knight*
by The Pearl Poet, trans. by Y. R. Ponsor

ABOUT THE AUTHOR

Almost nothing is known about **The Pearl Poet.** The author's name comes from the first poem, *Pearl,* found with the *Sir Gawain* manuscript. The Pearl Poet is thought to have written four poems, *Pearl, Purity, Patience,* and *Sir Gawain and the Green Knight.* The poems were probably written around 1370, which would make the poet a contemporary of Geoffrey Chaucer. Although The Pearl Poet did not live in London, the center of England's cultural activities at the time, his narrative technique demonstrates a sophistication equal to that of his London peers.

ABOUT THE SELECTION

Many medieval writings dealt with the legend of King Arthur and the knights of the Round Table. ***Sir Gawain and the Green Knight*** stands out from other writing of its time because it is the only story that interweaves two common plot devices—the beheading contest and the moral temptation of a knight by a lady. The following selection is a Modern English prose translation; the original poem was written in a West Highland dialect, very different from that used in London and very difficult for modern readers to understand without special training.

GOALS/OBJECTIVES

Studying this lesson will enable students to
• empathize with Gawain's difficulties
• relate the story of *Sir Gawain and the Green Knight*
• explain the code of chivalry and identify the virtues that are part of that code
• define *Arthurian romance* and give examples of the two main types of situations found in the

plots of those romances (i.e., the adventurous trial or quest and the love story)
• write a brief Arthurian romance
• use vivid verbs, adjectives, and nouns in descriptive writing
• identify gerunds in sentences
• answer synonym test questions

READER'S JOURNAL

Have you ever taken a dare or agreed to do something that seemed impossible and somewhat frightening? Why did you do it? How did you feel before you faced the challenge? Were you scared? nervous? invigorated? Recall or imagine such an experience, and write about why you took the challenge and how you felt before facing the challenge.

RESEARCH SKILLS

Read the Language Arts Survey, 4.23, "Using Reference Works." Then use at least two different types of reference works to find information about the legend of King Arthur.

FROM

Sir Gawain and the Green Knight

THE PEARL POET, TRANS. BY Y. R. PONSOR

CHAPTER 1

Winter lay upon the land. Cold held forest and field in its grim clutch, and in the night sky the stars glittered like gems. The wolf slid from shadow to shadow, stalking <u>hapless</u> prey, falling upon the unwary with death in his fangs. Deep in caverns, the great trolls and other monsters mumbled in uneasy sleep, seeking warmth. Over moor and fen[1] the mists rose and fell, and strange sounds troubled the chill silence.

But on the hill, lights gleamed in the castle. In the court of Camelot were gathered all the brothers-in-arms of the Table Round and their fair highborn ladies to celebrate the Christmas season. A full fifteen days it was then, a time of merriment and mirth and rich revel. Laughter rang loud through the halls, and all the music

and delight that the mind of man might devise. With merrymaking and glee the company welcomed the New Year, exchanging gifts and calling out glad Noel.

On this New Year's day, fresh and crisp-cold, twice the usual number of celebrants crowded the great hall; and the most noble, the fairest, and most famous was Arthur himself, the most honorable man who ever ruled a court or led an army into battle. This king was a man of the greatest good will and generosity of soul, and it would be difficult to imagine a bolder company than that one gathered in the castle on the hill.

Among the group on the high <u>dais</u>, facing the great hall lined with tables of noble knights, was Guenevere, Arthur's wife, the <u>comeliest</u> maid, the gracious lady of the

1. **fen.** Marshy bog

WORDS FOR EVERYDAY USE:
hap • less (hap´lis) *adj.*, unfortunate; unlucky
da • is (dā´is) *n.*, raised platform
come • li • est (kum´lē est) *adj.*, most attractive

READER'S JOURNAL

This activity and, indeed, the Gawain story itself provide excellent opportunities for discussing the foolhardiness of taking risks because of dares. Discuss the difference between taking a foolish dare and accepting a worthwhile challenge. Have students provide examples of each.

RESEARCH SKILLS

Information about the Arthurian legends can be found in encyclopedias and in literary reference works such as *The Oxford Companion to English Literature.* Drabble, Margaret, ed. Oxford UP.

VOCABULARY IN CONTEXT

• The <u>hapless</u> hockey player crashed into the goalie.
• The speakers at the conference sat on a <u>dais</u> at the front of the room.
• The <u>comeliest</u> of the heroines of Greek myth was Helen of Troy.

SUPPORT FOR LEP STUDENTS (CONT.)

apparition—something that comes unexpectedly; a ghost
tunic—loose article of clothing worn over the upper body
banish—throw out; exile
honed—sharpened
deem—think; believe
alight—climb down, as from a horse
errand—job or task
valiant—brave
courtliness—dignity; elegance; politeness
wrath—anger
beseech—request; beg; plead
amiss—wrong
presume—take on oneself without authority; dare
bounty—gifts; abundance
reaffirm—agree upon again

(cont.)

SUPPORT FOR LEP STUDENTS (CONT.)

kith nor kin—friends nor relatives
wayfarer—traveler
shear—cut
grisly—horrible to look upon
dismay—sadden
remnant—leftover part
wrought—made

covetousness—envy; desire for that which is not your own
forsake—give up
penance—act done in repentance for wrongdoing
fare—go
festal—like a celebration or feast

comely—lovely; beautiful
wiles—sly tricks
beguile—mislead; trick
renown—fame
prowess—strength
wend—go, travel

LITERARY TECHNIQUE

Setting and Mood. This translation of the original poem begins with a setting calculated to create an ominous mood. Have students point out details that contribute to this mood, such as winter, cold's grim clutch, the wolf sliding from shadow to shadow, hapless prey, trolls, monsters, fens, mists, and chill silence.

LITERARY TECHNIQUE

Translation. Explain that this is a loose prose translation into Modern English of a Middle English poem. You may wish to have students compare this prose translation to the closer, line-by-line verse translation of *Sir Gawain and the Green Knight.* Trans. Brian Stone. New York: Penguin.

LITERARY NOTE

The Gawain Legend. *Gawain* translator Brian Stone explains that Gawain may have been derived from a pre-Arthurian Welsh hero named Gwalchmai. Gawain was the hero of early versions of the Grail legend and was in early stories the owner of the sword Excalibur. Stories about the exploits of Gawain became quite popular in England. In one of these stories, Gawain marries a hag to save the life of King Arthur, only to have her become transformed into a beautiful woman. Gawain is one of the most written about figures in Arthurian legend; hence, his character is also one of the most fluid. He ranges, depending on the source, from a virtuous and perfect embodiment of chivalry to a somewhat philandering low comic character. In the story of the Green Knight, Gawain is portrayed at his most human, as his faults are fully revealed along with his strengths.

Who interrupted the feast? What was strange about this person? ❶

gleaming gray eyes. Her silken garments sparkled with rich jewels, and her golden hair shone as softly as her eyes. With her sat the young Gawain, with Agravaine the Stronghand on the other side; both were the king's nephews and worthy knights who had proved their prowess many times in test and trial. At the head of the table sat the chief of all bishops in Cornwall, the saintly Bedwin, and with him, Urien's son Iwain.

But Arthur, full of his own happiness and childlike in his joy, would not sit until all were served. For most of all he loved life, its joys and its adventures, and his eager brain and young blood would not allow him to lie abed or sit around lazily. And besides, he had taken upon himself a vow that on this special day of all days, he would not eat until a rare tale of ancestors and arms and high adventure were told, or some grand marvel might be devised, or a challenge of knights to join in jeopardy, jousting life for life as fortune might favor. So he stood before the high table, speaking of trifles and laughing at the noise and fine festival of his free men as the first course was announced with the crackling of trumpets, with drums and tuneful pipers. In the corner a bard awakened the lute and many a heart lifted with his touch upon the strings. Then came the platters piled high with fine food, venison and other meats, and great bowls of soup, and plenty of strong beer and fine red wine. And all drank and ate as much as they wanted.

Hardly had the first course been finished when the great hall door crashed open and in rode a terrifying knight. He must have been the hugest man on earth, so broad and thick from neck to waist, so long of leg and strong of arm that I half thought him a giant, except for his fine features of face. Everyone knows that giants are hideous to look upon, besides being fearful in size. At sight of him, all in the hall fell silent, struck dumb by this apparition. For this bold man, from toe to top, in clothes and in <u>countenance</u>, was bright green.

Believe me: all garbed in green, this man, and all his trappings. He wore a tight coat with a heavy mantle adorned with ermine, the same fur lining the hood that had fallen from his head and lay upon his shoulders. Green were the stockings on his legs, and decorated with gold embroidery, and bright golden spurs on his feet, and shoes with upturned toes. His belt was set with gleaming jewels, all emerald green, and indeed they were scattered over all his array and that of his horse, the saddle and bridle and reins, all gaudy in gold and green. The trappings of the horse, the breast-cloth and bits and bridle, even the stirrups in which he stood, all were enameled and gleamed goldenly, and the green gems glittered like the eyes of a cat. The steed itself which he straddled was a great heavy horse, hard to hold; and it was the same green as the man who rode it.

Gloriously was this man outfitted in green, and the hair of his head as green as his horse. It fanned out full and fell to his shoulders, and he had a heavy beard which reached his chest. It gleamed green upon the leather tunic. Such a pair had never before been seen on earth, nor since that

WORDS FOR EVERYDAY USE: coun • te • nance (kown´ tə nəns) *n.,* appearance

---

VOCABULARY FROM THE SELECTION

amiably	countenance	intrigue	sunder
beguile	covenant	mortification	transgress
betide	dais	respite	treachery
burnish	entreat	scathe	vanquish
comeliest	hapless	smite	

time! Everyone said he looked as bright as a flash of lightning, and, indeed, who could withstand his stroke! He wore neither helm nor hauberk[2]—no, no coat of mail did he wear, nor want!—and he carried no weapons, neither spear nor shield to <u>smite</u> or to save. But in his hand he carried a bough of holly, that branch which is greenest when all others are bare; and in his other hand an ax, heavy and horrid, a cruel weapon right out of a nightmare. The head measured at least an arm's length, and was of green steel worked with gold, the bit <u>burnished</u> bright, the broad edge honed to shear as closely as a sharp razor. The steel of the haft[3] which he held in his hand was wrapped with iron wire to its very end, graven with green in delicate design. A thong bound it about and fastened at the head where it was tasseled and braided with bright green.

This knight moved through the great hall's silent crowd right up the high table, and he feared no danger, greeted no one, but looked straight ahead. Then he reined in his horse and faced the room. He stared boldly at the knights, looking them up and down, and his voice thundered when he spoke.

"Where is the leader of this company? I would like to see him and to speak in courtesy with him, as the rules of chivalry require."

He waited and looked at them and considered who might among this company be the most renowned.

Everyone stared at him in wonder, marveling as to what his appearance might mean, how such a knight and such a horse might be such a strange color, green as growing grass, and glowing with enamel and gold. Everyone studied him as he sat there on his horse, and they walked cautiously around him with all the wonder in the world as to what he might do. Many strange things had they seen, but never any such as this. Possibly a phantom, or some fey[4] creature, they deemed him to be, for green is a magic color. But all of these brave knights feared to question him and, stunned at his voice, were dumbstruck. A heavy silence filled the royal chamber, and all those who had been chattering sat as if caught in a dream—some, I suppose, out of politeness, some out of uneasiness, and some in fear, but let another man decide which!

Then Arthur, standing before the dais, greeted him, and bowed courteously, for he was never rude, and said,

"Fair knight, welcome to this place. I am Arthur, the chief of this company. Alight and rest, I beg you, and whatsoever your will may be, we shall be glad to learn."

"No, God is my witness that to waste time in idle talk is not my errand," replied the knight. "But your fame, lord, is raised high, and through town and countryside you are regarded as the best and bravest ever to ride in battle gear, the noblest and the finest of the world's kind. You are all known to be valiant in dealing with all sorts of adventures, and your hall is known for courtliness. Many tales of this company have reached my ears, and that is what has brought me hither at this special time."

---

2. **hauberk.** A tunic made of joined metal links
3. **haft.** Hilt of a knife
4. **fey.** Magical, enchanted

WORDS FOR EVERYDAY USE:

smite (smīt) vt., inflict a heavy blow

bur • nish (bur′nish) vt., make smooth and shiny by rubbing

Q *What two things does the knight carry? Why might he have each of these things?*

Q *What was special about his color? What did it make the people think of him?*

❶ The knight carries a bough of holly and an ax. Student answers to the question about why he carries these objects will vary. Encourage them to speculate. The bough of holly, being green, is consistent with the rest of the knight's appearance. (Note: This knight and, indeed, the entire tale, probably owes its existence to fertility myths that preceded it. Explain to your students that in ancient days many peoples in Europe worshiped fertility gods associated with evergreens like the holly.) The presence of the ax suggests that the knight intends some violence.

❷ The text says that green is a magic color. The people at the feast thought that he was a phantom or fey creature. (Note that the color green has associations with spring and the rebirth of the seasons, which was considered magical by early peoples. See the note on fertility myths above.)

HISTORICAL/LITERARY NOTE

Explain to your students that *Sir Gawain and the Green Knight* provides an excellent example of the code of chivalry by which knights lived. **Chivalry** was the code of conduct of the medieval knight. The word derives from the French *cheval,* for "horse," indicating the importance of this animal to the knight, who typically traveled and fought on horseback. According to the code of chivalry, a knight was to be a loyal servant to his lord or lady and a perfect exemplar of such virtues as bravery, courage, courtesy, honesty, faith, and gentleness. Medieval romances like *Sir Gawain and the Green Knight* typically present a series of tests (trials or quests) of these knightly virtues. In this story, Gawain fails in one small respect with regard to the virtue of keeping good faith. However, in other ways he proves himself to be an exemplar of knightly virtue.

VOCABULARY IN CONTEXT

• When the police officer in the car behind us turned on his lights, my companion's <u>countenance</u> changed from joy to despair.

• A sumo wrestler is not allowed to <u>smite</u> his opponents.

• We had to <u>burnish</u> the silver before the wedding banquet.

❶ The knight suggests that one of the assembled knights deal him a blow with the ax and that he will return the favor, dealing the knight an equal blow, in a year and a day. It is likely that the knight's plan will be accepted because he has challenged the courage of Arthur's knights. Also, one would expect that the blow dealt to the Green Knight would kill him, thereby saving the Green Knight's challenger from any possible harm.

LITERARY NOTE

Adventure in Romance Literature. Most medieval romances are little more than loosely connected episodes relating various adventures experienced by one or more knights. *Sir Gawain and the Green Knight* is exceptional in not being episodic but rather being a coherent, sustained narrative that works out a single story line.

In many medieval romances, the fact that the adventures are had by a single knight is one of the few connections between episodes. The adventures usually take the form of a trial of the knight's virtues—his courage, strength, bravery, faithfulness, and so on. Some adventures, like the one described in *Gawain,* involve challenges (often challenges to combat). Many involve trials, or quests, undertaken to find or accomplish something (to locate the Holy Grail, to slay a dragon, to rescue a maiden, for example).

"You may see by this branch which I bear here that I have come in peace , seeking no trouble; for had I fared forth in a frame of mind to fight, I would have brought helm and hauberk, and shield and bright-shining spear, and other weapons to wield also. But because I seek no strife, I am dressed as you see. But if you are as brave as everyone says, you will gladly grant me the game that I ask as a guest's right."

And Arthur answered, "Gentle knight, if you crave combat, you will not fail to find it here."

"No, I seek no contest, as I have told you, especially since I see on these benches only beardless children! If I were geared up for fighting and mounted on my high steed there is no man here who could match me." And he looked upon them with scorn. "I seek in this court only a Christmas game, for it is Yule and the New Year, and the time to exchange gifts. If there should be any in this hall who considers himself brave enough in heart, hot enough in blood, or quick enough of wit that he would dare exchange stroke for stroke with me, let him come forth. I will give him as my gift this fine heavy ax—heavy enough it is to do his will!—and I shall take the first blow as bare as here I sit. If any of these fine warriors may be so bold as to accept my challenge, let him step forth and seize this weapon. I quitclaim it forever, and he may keep it as his own, and I shall kneel before him and stand him a stroke. And then you will grant me the right to deal him an equal blow, though I will give him <u>respite</u> of a year and a day. Now let any man who so dares speak quickly."

❶
What game does the knight suggest? Why is it likely that his plan will be accepted?

If the people had been astonished at first, now they all, high and low throughout the hall, sat as if turned to stone. The knight on his steed twisted in the saddle, his red eyes flashing around the room, his green hair flying with each movement of his head. Then he sat still, staring at them and stroking his beard as the silence lengthened. When no one spoke, he stood in his stirrups and, shaking his fist above his head, he shouted at them.

"What is this? Is this Arthur's court and castle, of which the whole world sings praises? Where now is your pride? Where is your fighting spirit? Where now your fierceness and fame and all your fine words? Now is the reputation and glory of the Round Table overthrown by the mere words of one man, without a single blow being struck, because you are afraid to answer!"

Then the blood shot for shame into Arthur's face, and he turned as angry as a stormwind, as indeed did all of them. Men muttered and surged forward in anger, half-rising from their places, white with wrath. But Arthur held up his hand and sprang to face the green man.

"Sir, by heaven! Seek no further! As you in your own folly have asked, so shall it be! No man here is afraid of your boasts. Give me your ax, and with God's help, I shall break every bone in your body. I myself accept your challenge and will meet your terms."

The Green Knight laughed aloud and leaped lightly from his horse and landed before Arthur, taller by head and shoulders than any man in the court. The king

WORDS FOR
EVERYDAY USE: **res • pite** (res´pit) *n.,* postponement

VOCABULARY IN CONTEXT
• The editors worked without <u>respite</u> until the project was done.

HISTORICAL NOTE

Explain to your students that *Sir Gawain and the Green Knight* contains fantastic elements from the oral tradition. Chief among these is the Green Knight himself, a fertility figure with the fantastic ability to live even after his head has been cut off. Have students share stories that they know from the oral traditions in their communities. Many will know stories about fantastic creatures—ghosts, fairies, goblins, and monsters—stories that they heard as children.

ADDITIONAL QUESTIONS AND ACTIVITIES

Ask students why they think Gawain beseeches Arthur to let him respond to the challenge. What does this action say about Gawain? Ask students if they would stand in for a friend in the case of a challenge.

Sir Gawain Beheads the Green Knight.
Fourteenth-century Illuminated Manuscript. British Library, London

seized the ax and gripped the handle tightly and waved it about, striking this way and that to test its feel. The knight calmly removed his mantle and then his short coat, no more dismayed by the threatening blows than if some man had brought him a glass of wine.

Then Gawain, who sat by the queen, called out, "I beseech you, uncle, to grant me a kindness. Let this contest be mine. Gentle lord, give me permission to leave this table and stand in your place there. If I may without discourtesy—if my liege[5] lady will not take it amiss—I would presume to counsel you before your royal court." He stood up and spoke clearly. "I think it is not seemly that such a challenge should be raised in this high chamber, much less that you yourself should so valiantly choose to answer it, while so

_____

5. **liege.** One to whom loyalty is given

THE LITERATURE OF ROMANCE / FROM *SIR GAWAIN AND THE GREEN KNIGHT*   **157**

❶ Gawain says that he is the least
brave and least intelligent of the
company and that the only worthy
thing about him is that he is of
Arthur's blood. He makes this speech
out of extreme modesty, a chivalric
virtue.

What does
Gawain say
about himself?
Why does he
make this
speech? ❶

many brave warriors remain on these
benches. No better men can be found on
any field of battle, nor any more skillful in
arms. All men know that I am the least
brave, and the feeblest of wit, and the least
deserving to be of this company. In truth,
it is only because I am your nephew that I
am worthy at all; I know no bounty but
your blood in my body. And since this
business is so foolish and trivial, none of it
should concern you at all.

"So I ask: Let it come to me, and if I fail
in its performance, then the fault is in me
and no blame shall fall on this court."

Arthur moved from table to table consulting with his nobles, as is the custom in
such cases, and all agreed that the king
should retire from the contest and give
Gawain the game.

Gawain turned and bowed to the
gray-eyed Guenevere, and she smiled on
him, and he came down from the dais and,
kneeling before his king, he received the
ax from Arthur's hands. And Arthur smiled
affectionately upon him and raised his
hand and asked God's blessing, praying
that both Gawain's heart and his hand
should be strong.

"Be careful, nephew," he said softly,
"and set yourself for the stroke. If you
direct it properly, I am sure that you will
be able to bear the burden of the blow
which he will later inflict." And Arthur
removed himself and went and leaned
against the edge of the dais and watched
eagerly.

Gawain walked, ax in hand, to the Green
Knight, who had been waiting patiently.
He looked upon Gawain and he said,
"Now, let us reaffirm our bargain before

we go on. But first I would ask you, sir,
what is your name?"

"I am Gawain," the young man said. "It
is Gawain who gives you this blow, whatever may happen afterwards. One year
from now, you may return the favor with
whatever weapon you wish, asking leave of
no one else."

"By God," shouted the other, "it pleases
me greatly that I should receive this blow
from your hands. You have rightly repeated
the covenant which I made with your king
—except that you must seek me, friend,
wheresoever you think I may be found,
pledging to come alone, and return to me
such wages as you deal to me today before
this court."

"And where shall I look for you?
Where is your home? I know neither
your kingdom nor your name, kith nor
kin. Tell me your realm and name and I
shall certainly find you. That I swear on
my honor."

"No," said the green man, "nothing
more is necessary now. But I promise that
when I have taken your blow, if you strike
squarely, then I will tell you how to find
me so that you may fulfill our bargain."

Then he laughed.

"If I do not speak, then so much the better for you; you can stay in your own land
and light no wayfarer's fires. But enough!
Take up your weapon and let us see how
you handle an ax!"

"Sir," said Gawain, "I will," and he
stroked the edge of the ax.

The Green Knight knelt on the floor
and bent his head and gathered his long,
thick hair in one hand and drew it over
the crown of his head. His bare neck

WORDS FOR
EVERYDAY USE: cov • e • nant (kuv´ə nənt) n., binding agreement

VOCABULARY IN CONTEXT
• The kings made a covenant never again to take arms against one another.
• The bolt of lightning sundered the tree, splitting its trunk in two.

shone whitely. Gawain set himself, left foot forward on the floor. He grasped the ax and lifted it aloft, and he brought it down like a lightning bolt upon the bare neck. The sharp steel sliced through the pale flesh and <u>sundered</u> the bones and sheared it in half, and the steel blade buried itself in the floor with a great ringing crash.

The fair head flew from the shoulders and rolled about near the tables, and some of the knights kicked at it with their feet, a grim, grisly game. Blood burst from the body, red gleaming on green. The knight did not falter or fall, but at once he sprang up on his strong legs and jumped into the crowd and snatched up his head by the hair and lifted it high for all to see. Then, striding to his horse, he caught up the reins, stepped into the stirrups and sat aloft, still holding his head high in one hand.

And they say that he sat in his saddle as though nothing whatever ailed him, headless though he was. He twisted from side to side, turning that hideous, still-bleeding body in the saddle. Those who watched in fear were even more horrified to see that he was about to speak.

He turned the grim face toward the high table, and the head lifted up its eyelids and looked at them. Then it looked at Gawain, and the mouth moved, and the lips spoke.

"Look to it, Gawain, that you do as you have sworn, and seek faithfully until you find me. All men know me as the knight of the Green Chapel. To the Green Chapel you must come, I charge you, to receive such a blow as you have dealt here to me today. You will find me if you try. If you fail to come, coward shall you be called by the whole world."

With a quick movement he pulled his horse around and fled through the great door, still head-in-hand, and the fire from the hooves of his flint-shod steed flashed through the hall. What native land he would return to, none there knew, any more than they knew from whence he had come. In a moment a roar of astonishment filled the hall, and Arthur and Gawain burst into laughter at the strange event. All agreed that it had been a marvel among men.

Although Arthur, ever the wise king, had a great uneasiness in his heart, he did not let a hint of it be seen, but he spoke to his queen with courtly speech.

"Dearest lady, let not today dismay you. Often such a magic and wondrous event occurs at this season, along with the music of minstrels and the laughter of lovely ladies and brave knights."

And he touched her hand gently and gazed into her eyes. Then he sat back, looked around the room, and cried out, "Now at last I may address myself to my dinner, for I have certainly seen a marvel, I must admit."

He smiled at Gawain with love shining on his fair face and he said, "Hang up your ax, nephew, it has done its work for today." And it was placed on the wall above the high table where all might admire and wonder at the sight and the strange adventure. Then they sat down again at the tables, each to his place, king and knights, and the servants brought double portions of all the best dishes and with all manner

❶
What happened after the knight was beheaded?

❷
What must Gawain do?

❶ The knight did not falter or fall. Instead, he sprang up, grabbed his head, and held it up for all to see. Then he climbed back on his horse, still holding the head up.

❷ Gawain must find the knight in a year and a day at the Green Chapel and submit to a blow like that received by the Green Knight. Gawain, being an ordinary man, would be killed by such a blow.

CROSS-CURRICULAR ACTIVITIES

Arts and Humanities. The descriptions of the knight are detailed and full of vivid colors. Students can create their own depictions of the knight before and after he was beheaded.

WORDS FOR EVERYDAY USE:
sun • der (sun´dər) *vt.,* break apart; separate

of good will they passed the rest of the evening.

But be sure, Sir Gawain, that fear does not cause you to fail in this test, this challenge which you yourself have taken into your own hands!

Summary of Chapters 2–10: True to his word, Gawain sets out after a year to find the Green Knight. Coming to the country where the Knight of the Green Chapel lives, Gawain finds lodging with a friendly lord. Each day the lord goes hunting, leaving his wife alone with Gawain. On the very first day, the wife of the lord approaches Gawain romantically. At the end of that day, the lord gives Gawain a deer and Gawain gives the lord a kiss, for the two have agreed beforehand to trade whatever they have gained during the day. At the end of the second day, the lord gives Gawain the head of a boar and Gawain gives the lord two kisses. On the third day, the lady gives Gawain a green scarf, saying that it will keep him from harm. At the end of that day, the lord gives Gawain a fox, and Gawain gives the lord three kisses. However, Gawain keeps the scarf. This is a violation of the code of chivalry, which requires a knight to keep faith, or be true to his word.

The following day, Gawain keeps his promised appointment with the Green Knight. With a sharp blade, the Green Knight feigns a stroke in the direction of Gawain's neck. Gawain flinches, and the Green Knight reproves him for coward-liness. When the Green Knight tries again, Gawain does not flinch. However, the knight again stops short of dealing a blow to Gawain. On the third try, the Green Knight inflicts a scratch, but no more, on Gawain's neck.

CHAPTER 11

The Green Knight turned from him and leaned upon his ax, set the shaft to the ground and leaned upon the blade and looked at the lad who waited there. How steadfast, how fearless, and how bold he looked, how ready for battle! And he was pleased in his heart. He laughed with a ringing voice and spoke happily with the lad.

"Bold knight, upon this field of honor be not so fierce! No man here has used you dishonorably, nor treated you discourteously, but only as the decree at Arthur's court allowed. I owed you a stroke and you took it, so hold yourself well paid. I release you of any remnant of all other rights. If I had been more nimble, perhaps I could have wrought you a more harmful blow. First, I merely menaced you with a pretended blow and cut you with no cruel blade. That was for the agreement we made on that first night when you faithfully gave me the day's gains, as an honest man would. That second pretended blow was for the second day when you kissed my dear wife, which kisses you gave to me. And for both of those I offered you but two scant blows without <u>scathe</u>. For an honorable man is

WORDS FOR EVERYDAY USE: scathe (skāth) *n.,* injury or harm true to his word and he needs fear no danger.

"But on the third day you failed in that honor, and therefore you took that tap on the neck."

He looked at Gawain steadily, and Gawain at him, still as stone. And the green man continued.

"It is my garment you wear, that green silken girdle. My own wife offered it to you, I know. Ah, I know all about those kisses and your character also, and the wooing of my wife! I wrought all this myself. I sent her to test you. Truly I think that you must be the most faultless man that ever walked the earth. As a pearl in purity is to white peas, so is Gawain in virtue to all famous knights. But you fell short a little there, sir; you failed in faith. But it was not for <u>intrigue</u>, nor for lawless lust either, but because you loved your life, and I cannot blame you for that."

Gawain still stood like one stunned, so aggrieved with embarrassment that he cried for anguish inside. All the blood of his body burned in his face and he shrank for shame as the green man talked. He took off his helm and held it in his hands. At last he spoke wrathfully.

"Cursed be both cowardice and covetousness! In them is villainy and vice that destroys virtue!" And he caught up the pentangle[6] and tore it loose and flung it roughly down. "Lo!—there is breaking of faith. Foul be its fall! I coveted my life and cowardice led me into fault for fear of your blow, made me forsake my nature, the generosity and loyalty that are a true knight's." And he bowed his head and wept bitterly. "Now am I false indeed and

from fear have I fallen into <u>treachery</u> and deceit. Both bring only sorrow and shame. I confess to you, sir, here on this spot, that I have indeed been false to you in my conduct. If you will but allow me to regain your good will, I shall guard against its happening again."

Then the Green Knight laughed and said <u>amiably</u>: "I consider it entirely acquitted, any harm that I had. You have confessed freely and are aware of your failing and you have stood the sharp penance of my sword. I hold you cleansed of that fault and made as pure as if you had never <u>transgressed</u> since your birth. And I give you, sir, as a gift, that very scarf, as green as my own robe." He touched the silk at Gawain's waist lightly, and laid an arm across his shoulders.

"Sir Gawain, you may think upon this particular contest as you fare forth among the great and chivalrous knights of this world. Let this be the clear token of the adventure of the Green Chapel." Then he laughed and said merrily, "Now, you shall in this New Year come back again to my dwelling and we shall revel away the remainder of this festal time. With my wife, I promise, we shall certainly reconcile you, she who you thought was your keen enemy."

"No," said Gawain, and he took up his helm and looked sadly at the green man. "This has been a sorrowful journey. Good fortune <u>betide</u> you, and may He who ordains all honor grant it to you! And commend me to that gracious lady, your comely companion, and the other

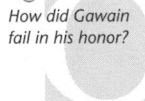

❶
How did Gawain fail in his honor?

---

6. **pentangle.** Helmet

WORDS FOR EVERYDAY USE:

in •**trigue** (in trēg´) *n.,* secret love affair
treach • er • y (trech´ar ē) *n.,* betrayal of trust
a • mi • a • bly (ā´ mē ə blē) *adv.,* in a pleasant and friendly manner

trans • gress (trans gres´) *vt.,* overstep or break a law
be • tide (bē tīd) *vi.,* happen to

THE LITERATURE OF ROMANCE / FROM *SIR GAWAIN AND THE GREEN KNIGHT* **161**

ANSWER TO GUIDED READING QUESTION

❶ Gawain did not give the lord the green scarf that he received from the lord's wife, despite the promise that he made to the lord to exchange whatever the two had gained during each day.

LITERARY NOTE

Sir Gawain and the Green Knight was originally written in alliterative verse. While most of the alliteration has been lost in this prose translation, a fine example exists in the lines "Cursed be both cowardice and covetousness! In them is villainy and vice that destroys virtue!"

VOCABULARY IN CONTEXT

- The glass from the broken window fell to the sidewalk but fortunately did not <u>scathe</u> passers-by.
- The spy's life was one of continual <u>intrigue</u>.
- Telling the secrets of a friend is a form of <u>treachery</u>.
- The schoolboy <u>amiably</u> held the door for the principal.
- The stockbroker <u>transgressed</u> ethical limits when he bought stocks based on inside information.
- The silly romance novel ended with the line, "May such happiness as I described herein <u>betide</u> all true men and women."

❶ *Why did Morgan
le Fay arrange
this event?*

❷ *Why does
Gawain keep the
green girdle?*

lady, both the honored ladies who so
cunningly beguiled this knight with their
tricks.

"It is no great marvel to be made a fool
of or to be won to sorrow through the
wiles of a woman; for so was Adam, the
first man on earth beguiled; and Solomon
by many and various women; and Samson
also, Delilah dealt him his wyrd![7] David
was deluded by Bathsheba and suffered
much woe. All these men were brought to
disaster by woman's wiles.

"It would be a great gain to love them
and yet to believe them not. But no man
can do that. For these were the noblest
men of old, all blessed above other men
and yet they were all beguiled by women
with whom they had dealings. To find
myself in that company I think must be
excused." Then he shook off sad thoughts.

"But your girdle I will accept with a
right good will, not for the bright gold,
nor for its magic—" here Gawain blushed
again—"nor for the silk or fringed sides,
nay, not for worth nor worship nor noble
works. But as a symbol of my transgression I shall keep it always with me, a
reminder, when I ride in renown, of the
fault and frailty of feeble flesh, how susceptible it is to the stains of evil. And
when pride of prowess inflates me, the
sight of this will humble my heart.

"But one request I make, if it does not
displease you: Since you are the lord of
that land where I stayed with such pleasure,
thanks to you, will you tell me your name?
Only that and no more?"

"That I shall, certainly," replied the green
man. "I am called Bercilak de Hautdesert
in this land. Through the power of Morgan

le Fay;[8] who lives in my house and has the
skill of magical lore, all of this has happened. Morgan, the beautiful, the mistress
of Merlin—many men has she taken, for
she has had love dealings with that excellent wizard who knows all the knights of
your court. Morgan the goddess is also
her name. There is none so high in power
or pride that she cannot tame!

"She sent me in that manner to your
royal court in order to test the pride of its
men, to see if the reputation of the Round
Table were true. She sent me in that
strange way to take away your wits and to
frighten the fair Guenevere, to make her
die with fear at the sight of that man who
spoke with his head in his hand before that
Table High. She took the form of that old
one in my house, the ancient lady; she is in
fact your aunt, the half-sister of Arthur,
daughter of the Duchess of Tintagel, that
lady upon whom the mighty Uther later
fathered Arthur, who is your king.

"Therefore I entreat you, dear man, to
come to your aunt and rejoice in my
house. My court loves you, and I do as
well, indeed, as any man under heaven."

But Gawain still refused. He would not
under any conditions. So they embraced
in friendship and saluted each other as
fine princes and parted right there in the
cold. Gawain, mounted on his fine horse,
hastened homeward to Arthur's court and
the Green Knight wended wheresoever he
would.

Gawain rode then through many wild
ways in the world on Gringolet. He had
been given back his life, a fine gift indeed,

---

7. **wyrd.** Fate
8. **Morgan le Fay.** The fairy half-sister of King Arthur

WORDS FOR
EVERYDAY USE:

be • guile (bē gīl´) *vt.*, mislead by tricking
en • treat (en trēt´) *vt.*, ask earnestly; beg

and many a thought he gave to that strange event as he traveled. Sometimes he harbored in a house and sometimes out of doors. He had many adventures in the valley and he vanquished many, but I will not take time to tell all that in this tale.

The wound in his neck healed and he wore the green belt fastened like a baldric[9] at his side, tied under his left arm, the end in a knot, as token of the fact that he was guilty of sin. And thus at last he came to the court, did Gawain the good knight.

Happiness sped through those halls when it was learned that Gawain had returned. Everyone thought it was a fine thing, indeed, and somewhat unlooked for. The king kissed the knight and the queen did also, and many knights sought him out to salute him and make inquiry of his wayfaring fortune. And he told the wondrous tale and confessed everything that had happened, the adventure at the chapel, the good will of the green man, the love of the lady, and the silk that he wore. He showed them the scar that he bore on his neck, the sign of his shameful disloyalty to the green man. He suffered when he told them and groaned with grief and mortification, and the blood burned in his face for shame when he spoke of it.

"Lo, lord," said Gawain to Arthur, as he held forth the silk, "here is the band of blame which I bear like the scar on my neck. This is the offense and the loss, the cowardice and covetousness that caught me there. This is the symbol of falsity in which I was taken. I will wear it all my life, for no one may hide his misdeed, nor may he undo it. Once guilt has touched a man, he is never free of it again."

And the king comforted the knight and all the court laughed and lovingly agreed on the spot that each man of the Table Round should henceforth wear such a baldric, the slanting ribbon of bright green, for the sake of that beloved man, and they would wear it with delight. And so it came to be accorded as the renown of the court and always afterward anyone who wore it was especially honored.

So in Arthur's day this adventure occurred, as books of romance will witness. Many strange and curious wonders have happened in Britain since the days of Brutus whose race came from Troy. But surely this tale of Gawain and his contest with the Green Knight in a trial of honor and faith is one of the most wondrous. ■

9. **baldric.** A belt worn over the shoulder and chest to support a sword

ANSWERS TO SELECTION CHECK TEST 4.3.11

EX. Who interrupts Arthur's Christmas feast?
The Green Knight interrupts the feast.

1. What does the Green Knight carry when he rides into the feast?
He carries an ax and a bough of holly.

2. What challenge does the Green Knight make to the assembled guests?
He asks to exchange blows. He will submit first to a blow with an ax and will then, a year and a day later, deliver an equal blow.

3. Who first accepts the Green Knight's challenge?
Arthur first accepts the Green Knight's challenge.

4. What does the lady give to Gawain in addition to kisses?
She gives him a green scarf, or girdle.

5. What sin does Gawain commit?
He failed in his honor by failing to give the green scarf to the lord. His sin is covetousness.

WORDS FOR EVERYDAY USE:

van • quish (vaŋ´kwish) vt., conquer or defeat in battle

mor • ti • fi • ca • tion (môr´tə fi kā´shən) n., shame, humiliation

VOCABULARY IN CONTEXT
- Did the deceptive advertisement beguile you into buying the product?
- "I entreat you," said the defense attorney, "to let this man return to his wife and children."
- The Celtic warrior queen vanquished the Roman legions.
- When the diary entry was read aloud over the public address system, my mortification was complete.

RESPONDING TO THE SELECTION

The role playing will be more interesting if the two students playing Arthur and Gawain take opposing views with regard to Gawain's statement. For example, Arthur might argue that true repentance or remorse can wash away guilt. Gawain, true to his character in the story, might argue that guilt remains as a reminder, keeping a person humble.

ANSWERS FOR REVIEWING THE SELECTION

RECALLING

1. The Green Knight's appearance is startling because he is completely green from head to foot.

2. The Green Knight offers the challenge of an exchange of blows. Gawain accepts the challenge. The Green Knight's head is severed as a result.

3. Gawain stays with the lord's wife while the lord goes out hunting. Gawain and the lord make a pact to share whatever each gets during the day.

4. Gawain is nicked on the neck by the knight. Gawain realizes he has fallen prey to the sins of covetousness and cowardice. He keeps the green belt, or girdle, as a reminder of his weakness.

INTERPRETING

Responses will vary. Possible responses are given.

5. The court is especially startled because green was considered to be a magical color. They thought the Green Knight was a phantom or a fey creature.

6. The Green Knight claims he seeks no contest, and he calls the knights "beardless children." He warns Gawain that if the agreement is not kept, Gawain shall be known the world over as a coward.

7. Gawain's actions reveal that the knights' moral code values courage and despises covetousness. His actions also show how difficult it is to live a flawless life.

(cont.)

Responding to the Selection

With a classmate, role play Sir Gawain telling King Arthur about the scar on his neck. Use this situation to debate Sir Gawain's belief that "once guilt has touched a man, he is never free of it again."

Reviewing the Selection

RECALLING

1. Why does the Green Knight's appearance startle Arthur's court?

2. What challenge does the Green Knight make? Who meets the challenge? What is the result?

3. What happens to Gawain at the lord's castle?

4. What is the result of Gawain's final meeting with the Green Knight? What object does Gawain keep as a reminder of the meeting?

INTERPRETING

5. How does the fact that green is considered a magic color affect the court's reaction?

6. What words spoken by the Green Knight make his challenge seem more than a good-spirited contest?

7. What do Gawain's actions at the castle reveal about the knights' moral code?

8. Why does Gawain want to remember his meeting with the Green Knight?

SYNTHESIZING

9. How does Sir Gawain demonstrate knightly virtues such as bravery, courage, courtesy, and honesty?

10. Do you think Sir Gawain judges himself too harshly after his final meeting with the Green Knight? Why, or why not?

Understanding Literature (Questions for Discussion)

1. **Chivalry.** The code of conduct of the medieval knight is known as **chivalry.** Such conduct required the knight to swear loyalty to his lord or lady and to exhibit the virtues of bravery, courage, courtesy, honesty, faith, and gentleness. How does the Green Knight adhere to the code of chivalry? How does he violate it? How does he use it to his advantage?

164   *UNIT THREE / THE MEDIEVAL PERIOD*

ANSWERS FOR REVIEWING THE SELECTION (CONT.)

8. Gawain wants to remember his meeting with the Green Knight so he will behave more virtuously in the future.

SYNTHESIZING

Responses will vary. Possible responses are given.

9. Gawain demonstrates loyalty and bravery by accepting the challenge of the Green Knight. He demonstrates courage in facing the second part of the challenge of

the Green Knight, and in his early dealings with the host he demonstrates honesty.

10. Students might say that Gawain did judge himself too harshly because he had lived up to most of his ideals and he seemed to have learned from his mistake. Also others were willing to forgive him for what he had done.

164   TEACHER'S EDITION

2. **Arthurian Romance.** **Arthurian romances** are stories of the exploits of the legendary King Arthur and his knights of the Round Table. Most romances involving the King Arthur legend center on a knight's adventures or his loves. However, *Sir Gawain and the Green Knight* combines the two plot types. How are the plots in *Sir Gawain* interdependent? How are they typical of the romance genre?

Responding in Writing

1. **Romance.** Medieval romances relate fantastic stories of knights, their heroics, and their devotion to their king and their ladies. Imagine an adventure that one of King Arthur's knights might undertake. Write a short romance about the adventure. As you shape the main character, remember that a knight must function within the code of chivalry.

2. **Descriptive Writing.** A good romance contains highly imaginative images of knights, ladies, battles, and celebrations. Vivid descriptions of characters, locations, and objects make romances enjoyable to read. Write a few descriptive paragraphs that might appear in a story about one of King Arthur's knights. Decide what scene you want to describe. Then, brainstorm vivid verbs, adjectives, and nouns to describe the scene. Think about using words that convey what a viewer might see, hear, smell, taste, and touch if he or she were there in person.

Language Lab

Identifying Gerunds. Read the Language Arts Survey, 2.17, "Verbals: Gerunds." Then underline the gerunds in the sentences below. If a sentence contains no gerund, write *None* after it.

1. Beheading is a common fate in medieval romances.

2. Sometimes beheading occurs as part of a contest that involves the exchanging of blows with an ax or sword.

3. Jousting was another popular contest that pitted knight against knight.

4. Riding on horseback wasn't easy for a man in a heavy suit of armor.

5. Competing in such contests was a form of entertainment as well as a preparation for battle.

Assign a score from 1 to 25 for each grading criterion below. (For more detailed evaluation, see the evaluation forms for writing, revising, and proofreading, *Assessment Portfolio*, 7.1–7.10.)

1. Romance
• **Content/Unity.** The romance presents an adventure undertaken by a knight who functions within the code of chivalry.
• **Organization/Coherence.** The story is organized in chronological order.
• **Language/Style.** The story uses vivid, concrete details to make the setting and characters come alive.
• **Conventions.** The story avoids errors in spelling, grammar, usage, mechanics, and manuscript form.

2. Descriptive Writing
• **Content/Unity.** The description creates a vivid picture of a subject from a romance.
• **Organization/Coherence.** The details of the description are presented in a logical order, perhaps in order of their appearance.
• **Language/Style.** The description uses vivid verbs, adjectives, and nouns.
• **Conventions.** The description avoids errors in spelling, grammar, usage, mechanics, and manuscript form.

ANSWERS FOR LANGUAGE LAB

1. <u>Beheading</u>
2. <u>beheading</u>, <u>exchanging</u>
3. <u>Jousting</u>
4. <u>Riding</u>, <u>holding</u>
5. <u>Competing</u>

▶ Additional practice is provided in the *Essential Skills Practice Book: Language*, 2.17.

ANSWERS FOR UNDERSTANDING LITERATURE

▶ See the evaluation forms for discussion, active listening, and oral communication, *Assessment Portfolio*, 7.11–7.14.
Responses will vary. Possible responses are given.

1. Chivalry. The Green Knight demonstrates bravery and courage in his challenge. He demonstrates courtesy as the host, and gentleness in his dealing with Gawain when they finally meet again. He does not uphold the virtue of honesty and faith because he fails to tell Gawain who he really is.

2. Arthurian Romance. In the story *Sir Gawain and the Green Knight,* Gawain's adventure leads him to love. Both his adventure and his love are involved in the test of his knightly virtues.

WRITING NOTE

Students might want to use a more current setting for their adventures. Consider how knightly virtues would be seen in modern times. What difficulties would arise for a person trying to live by the code of chivalry today?

Test-taking Skills

Synonym and Antonym Questions. Read the Language Arts Survey, 4.44, "Synonym and Antonym Questions." Then choose the best synonym for each of the following words:

1. comely

   a. plain   c. pretty

   b. brilliant   d. ugly

2. covenant

   a. contract   c. deal

   b. oath   d. breach

3. amiable

   a. focused   c. friendly

   b. pleasing   d. courageous

4. entreat

   a. force   c. ask

   b. plead   d. assist

PROJECT

Trivia Contest. Beheading contests are no longer in style, but you and your classmates can still challenge one another by holding a literary trivia contest. As a class, decide what topics the questions will cover. You might limit your questions to trivia about the selection. You might want to add other questions that cover other aspects of the Arthurian legend. As a class, you should also decide how you will write the questions. You might consider creating five or six teams of students and assigning a different question category to each team. For example, you might choose the questions who, what, when, where, why, and how as categories. Have each team member write at least one question; be sure to include an answer for each question. As a class, decide the rules for the contest—the goal of the contest, how points are awarded, how disputes are resolved, and so on.

PREREADING

from *Le Morte d'Arthur*
by Sir Thomas Malory

ABOUT THE AUTHOR

Very little is known about **Sir Thomas Malory** (*circa* 1405–1471). Although he seems to have led a quiet life in his younger years, he began having trouble with the law in 1451. He was arrested for attacking a religious house, then faced further charges for escaping from prison and for other crimes. By some accounts, Malory spent most of his life after 1451 in prison. During this time, the War of the Roses (1455–1485) raged in England, and Malory's involvement in an unsuccessful revolt against Edward IV landed him in prison again in 1468. Malory was definitely in prison when he completed the manuscript for **Le Morte d'Arthur** around 1469. He died two years later, while still in prison.

The Arthurian romances of thirteenth-century France greatly influenced Malory's work. He translated these prose narratives into English and used them as the basis of his romantic masterpiece, *Le Morte d'Arthur.* Unlike Chaucer and other English writers who wrote primarily narrative poetry, Malory was the first to master the narrative prose form.

ABOUT THE SELECTION

By the time that Malory wrote **Le Morte d'Arthur,** romance literature had declined in popularity. Living at the end of what is now considered the Medieval Period, Malory wrote with a nostalgia not only for the Arthurian legends of romance and chivalry, but also for a time that celebrated them. Ironically, his book is the most complete and engaging retelling of the Arthurian legend.

The legend of Arthur has vague ties to a historical person. Arthur is supposed to have lived in fifth-century Britain, but a significant account of his history doesn't appear until the middle of the twelfth century. At that time, tales of his deeds as British king and of the members of his court were detailed. Although Malory's work is titled *The Death of Arthur* (the name given by its publisher in 1485), the majority of the book tells of the adventures of the individual knights of the Round Table. The massive work is divided into twenty-one books, and each book is divided into chapters.

The following excerpt is taken from the first book of *Le Morte d'Arthur* and relates the story of Arthur's birth and youth. The tale of Arthur's proof that he is the rightful heir to the throne has been retold many times in many ways.

ADDITIONAL RESOURCES

READER'S GUIDE
• Selection Worksheet, 3.7

ASSESSMENT PORTFOLIO
• Selection Check Test, 4.3.13
• Selection Test, 4.3.14

ESSENTIAL SKILLS PRACTICE BOOKS
• *Language,* 2.48, 2.52
• *Study and Research,* 4.26

ENRICHMENT ACTIVITIES

Have students do research in the library to find depictions of Merlin, Arthur, Guinevere, and other famous figures in Arthurian legend. Students should gather these materials and share them in class.

SUPPORT FOR LEP STUDENTS

Malory's text is written in a fairly simple vocabulary, but it may cause some difficulties because of the irregularity of its grammar. This may be more significant to students who are very familiar with standard grammar than to students who are not.

ADDITIONAL VOCABULARY
summons—call
betwixt—between
nourish—feed
remnant—what is left; remainder
estates—properties
anon—soon
assay—attempt; try

GOALS/OBJECTIVES

Studying this lesson will enable students to
• empathize with the main character
• identify a folk tale motif
• explain how the code of courtly love is expressed in the legend of Arthur and the knights of the Round Table
• write a eulogy praising a legendary person

• create a succinct account of Arthur's birth in the form of a newspaper announcement
• combine sentences using appositive phrases
• use a computer to locate modern stories that retell the Arthurian legend
• create a map depicting historical sites mentioned in *Le Morte d'Arthur*

READER'S JOURNAL

Most students will have encountered Arthurian stories before. Have them share what they already know and note variations. Then point out that such variations in memory give rise to changes in texts as they are passed down in the oral tradition.

SPEAKING AND LISTENING SKILLS

The idea of fate or destiny depends on the assumption that life is guided by outside forces. Students should in their discussion respect differences of belief on this matter.

VOCABULARY FROM THE SELECTION

appurtenance	postern
countenance	providence
indignation	usurp
inter	wax
necromancy	wroth
obeisance	

READER'S JOURNAL

What do you know about the legend of King Arthur? Have you read Arthurian stories or seen movies based on the legend? In your journal, list what you already know about Arthur and his knights.

SPEAKING AND LISTENING SKILLS

Read the Language Arts Survey, 3.6, "Discussion." With two or three other students, discuss the idea that all events are controlled by destiny.

FROM

Le Morte d'Arthur

SIR THOMAS MALORY

FROM BOOK I CHAPTER 1

FIRST, HOW UTHER PENDRAGON SENT FOR THE DUKE OF CORNWALL AND IGRAINE HIS WIFE, AND OF THEIR DEPARTING SUDDENLY AGAIN

It befell in the days of Uther Pendragon, when he was king of all England, and so reigned, that there was a mighty duke in Cornwall that held war against him long time. And the duke was called the Duke of Tintagel. And so by means King Uther sent for this duke, charging him to bring his wife with him, for she was called a fair lady, and a passing[1] wise, and her name was called Igraine.

So when the duke and his wife were comen unto the king, by the means of great lords they were accorded both. The king liked and loved this lady well, and he made them great cheer out of measure, and desired to have lain by her. But she was a passing good woman, and would not assent unto the king. And then she told the duke her husband, and said, 'I suppose that we were sent for that I should be dishonored, wherefore, husband, I counsel you that we depart from hence suddenly, that we may ride all night unto our own castle.' And in like wise as she said so they departed, that neither the king nor none of his council were ware of their departing.

As soon as King Uther knew of their departing so suddenly, he was wonderly <u>wroth</u>. Then he called to him his privy council,[2] and told them of the sudden departing of the duke and his wife. Then they advised the king to send for the duke and his wife by a great charge: 'And if he

---
1. **passing.** Exceedingly
2. **privy council.** The king's group of advisors

WORDS FOR EVERYDAY USE: **wroth** (rôth) *adj.*, angry

VOCABULARY IN CONTEXT

- When the display of balloons broke loose and floated to the ceiling, the store manager was terribly <u>wroth</u>.
- The servant was able to come and go through a secret <u>postern</u> behind the castle.

will not come at your summons, then may ye do your best, then have ye cause to make mighty war upon him.'

So that was done, and the messengers had their answers, and that was this shortly, that neither he nor his wife would not come at him. Then was the king wonderly wroth. And then the king sent him plain word again, and bad him be ready and stuff him and garnish him,[3] for within forty days would fetch him out of the biggest castle that he hath.

When the duke had this warning, anon he went and furnished and garnished two strong castles of his, of the which the one hight[4] Tintagel, and the other castle hight Terrabil. So his wife Dame Igraine he put in the Castle of Tintagel, and himself he put in the Castle of Terrabil, the which had many issues and <u>posterns</u> out. Then in all haste came Uther with a great host, and laid a siege about the Castle of Terrabil. And there he pitched many pavilions, and there was great war made on both parties, and much people slain.

Then for pure anger and for great love of fair Igraine the King Uther fell sick. So came to the King Uther Sir Ulfius, a noble knight, and asked the king why he was sick.

'I shall tell thee,' said the king. 'I am sick for anger and for love of fair Igraine that I may not be whole.'

'Well, my lord,' said Sir Ulfius, 'I shall seek Merlin, and he shall do you remedy, that your heart shall be pleased.'

So Ulfius departed, and by adventure he met Merlin in a beggar's array, and there Merlin asked Ulfius whom he sought. And he said he had little ado to tell him.

'Well,' said Merlin, 'I know whom thou seekest, for thou seekest Merlin; therefore seek no farther, for I am he, and if King Uther will well reward me, and be sworn unto me to fulfil my desire, that shall be his honor and profit more than mine, for I shall cause him to have all his desire.'

'All this will I undertake,' said Ulfius, 'that there shall be nothing reasonable but thou shalt have thy desire.'

'Well,' said Merlin, 'he shall have his intent and desire. And therefore,' said Merlin, 'ride on your way, for I will not be long behind.'

FROM BOOK I CHAPTER 2

HOW UTHER PENDRAGON MADE WAR ON THE DUKE OF CORNWALL, AND HOW BY THE MEAN OF MERLIN HE LAY BY THE DUCHESS AND GAT[5] ARTHUR

Then Ulfius was glad, and rode on more than a pace till that he came to King Uther Pendragon, and told him he had met with Merlin.

'Where is he?' said the king.

'Sir,' said Ulfius, 'he will not dwell[6] long.'

Therewithal Ulfius was ware where Merlin stood at the porch of the pavilion's door. And then Merlin was bound to come to the king. When King Uther saw him, he said he was welcome.

'Sir,' said Merlin 'I know all your heart every deal.[7] So ye will be sworn unto me

---

3. **stuff. . . him.** Prepare for a siege
4. **hight.** Called
5. **gat.** Begat, fathered
6. **dwell.** Delay
7. **deal.** Part

WORDS FOR EVERYDAY USE: **pos • tern** (pōs ´tərn) *n.,* private rear entrance

LITERARY TECHNIQUE

Foreshadowing is the act of presenting materials that hint at events to occur later in the story. At the end of the excerpt from Book 1, Chapter 1, Merlin says, "ride on your way, for I will not be long behind." Ask students to predict what events this might foreshadow. Ask what effect this use of foreshadowing has.

Answer. Since Merlin is a wizard, students may expect him to do some act of magic later on. The use of foreshadowing builds excitement and suspense by raising curiosity.

LITERARY NOTE

Students may be familiar with **Merlin,** the magician who guided the fate of Uther and Arthur. His background is less widely known. He was the son of a devil and a virtuous maiden, but he was not evil as his father wished him to be. Merlin fell in love with Nimue, the Lady of the Lake, who figures later in this story.

ANSWERS TO GUIDED READING QUESTIONS

❶ Merlin asks that the child of Igraine and Uther be delivered to him for nourishing.

❷ Merlin makes Uther look like Igraine's husband.

ADDITIONAL QUESTIONS AND ACTIVITIES

Morgan le Fay was an important force in *Sir Gawain and the Green Knight*. Here the source of her knowledge of sorcery is revealed. Students may wish to seek other tales of Morgan le Fay and share them with the rest of the class.

---

as ye be a true king anointed, to fulfil my desire, ye shall have your desire.'

Then the king was sworn upon the four Evangelists.[8]

❶ *What does Merlin ask in return for helping King Uther?*

'Sir,' said Merlin, 'this is my desire: the first night that ye shall lie by Igraine ye shall get a child on her, and when that is born, that it shall be delivered to me for to nourish there as I will have it; for it shall be your worship,[9] and the child's avail as mickle[10] as the child is worth.'

'I will well,' said the king, 'as thou wilt have it.'

❷ *How does Merlin arrange for King Uther to lie with Igraine?*

'Now make you ready,' said Merlin, 'this night ye shall lie with Igraine in the Castle of Tintagel, and ye shall be like the duke her husband, Ulfius shall be like Sir Brastias, a knight of the duke's, and I will be like a knight that hight Sir Jordans, a knight of the duke's. But wait[11] ye make not many questions with her nor her men, but say ye are diseased,[12] and so hie you to bed, and rise not on the morn till I come to you, for the Castle of Tintagel is but ten miles hence.'

So this was done as they devised. But the Duke of Tintagel espied how the king rode from the siege of Terrabil, and therefore that night he issued out of the castle at a postern for to have distressed the king's host. And so, through his own issue, the duke himself was slain or-ever[13] the king came at the Castle of Tintagel.

So after the death of the duke, King Uther lay with Igraine more than three hours after his death, and begat on her that night Arthur; and, or day came, Merlin came to the king, and bad him make him ready, and so he kissed the lady Igraine and departed in all haste. But when the lady heard tell of the duke her husband, and by all record he was dead or-ever King Uther came to her, then she marvelled who that might be that lay with her in likeness of her lord; so she mourned privily and held her peace.

Then all the barons by one assent prayed the king of accord betwixt the lady Igraine and him; the king gave them leave, for fain would he have been accorded with her. So the king put all the trust in Ulfius to entreat[14] between them, so by the entreaty at the last the king and she met together.

'Now will we do well,' said Ulfius. 'Our king is a lusty knight and wifeless, and my lady Igraine is a passing fair lady; it were great joy unto us all, and it might please the king to make her his queen.'

Unto that they all well accorded and moved it to the king. And anon, like a lusty knight, he assented thereto with good will, and so in all haste they were married in a morning with great mirth and joy.

And King Lot of Lothian and of Orkney then wedded Margawse that was Gawain's mother, and King Nentres of the land of Garlot wedded Elaine. All this was done at the request of King Uther. And the third sister Morgan le Fay was put to school in a nunnery, and there she learned so much that she was a great clerk of <u>necromancy</u>, and after she was wedded to King Uriens

---

8. **four Evangelists.** The Gospels
9. **worship.** Honor
10. **mickle.** Much
11. **wait.** Take care
12. **diseased.** Tired
13. **or-ever.** Before
14. **entreat.** Negotiate

WORDS FOR EVERYDAY USE: nec • ro • man • cy (nek´rə man´sē) *n.*, black magic; sorcery

170   *UNIT THREE / THE MEDIEVAL PERIOD*

VOCABULARY IN CONTEXT

- The wizard's <u>necromancy</u> was held responsible for the mayor's being turned into a crow.
- The crescent moon <u>waxes</u> daily until it becomes a full moon.
- Her <u>countenance</u> displayed emotions that her words could not.
- After Cromwell <u>usurped</u> Charles I's throne, he had that king tried and beheaded.

of the land of Gore, that was Sir Uwain's le Blanchemains father.

FROM BOOK I CHAPTER 3

OF THE BIRTH OF KING ARTHUR AND OF HIS NURTURE

Then Queen Igraine <u>waxed</u> daily greater and greater, so it befell after within half a year, as King Uther lay by his queen, he asked her, by the faith she ought to him, whose was the child within her body; then was she sore abashed to give answer.

'Dismay you not,' said the king, 'but tell me the truth, and I shall love you the better, by the faith of my body.'

'Sir,' said she, 'I shall tell you the truth. The same night that my lord was dead, the hour of his death, as his knights record, there came into my castle of Tintagel a man like my lord in speech and in <u>countenance</u>, and two knights with him in likeness of his two knights Brastias and Jordans, and so I went unto bed with him as I ought to do with my lord, and the same night, as I shall answer unto God, this child was begotten upon me.'

'That is truth,' said the king, 'as ye say; for it was I myself that came in the likeness, and therefore dismay you not, for I am father to the child;' and there he told her all the cause, how it was by Merlin's counsel. Then the queen made great joy when she knew who was the father of her child.

Soon came Merlin unto the king, and said, 'Sir, ye must purvey you for the nourishing of your child.'

'As thou wilt,' said the king, 'be it.'

'Well,' said Merlin, 'I know a lord of yours in this land, that is a passing true man and a faithful, and he shall have the nourishing of your child; and his name is Sir Ector, and he is a lord of fair livelihood in many parts in England and Wales; and this lord, Sir Ector, let him be sent for, for to come and speak with you, and desire him yourself, as he loveth you, that he will put his own child to nourishing to another woman, and that his wife nourish yours. And when the child is born let it be delivered to me at yonder privy postern unchristened.'

So like as Merlin devised it was done. And when Sir Ector was come he made fiance[15] to the king for to nourish the child like as the king desired; and there the king granted Sir Ector great rewards. Then when the lady was delivered, the king commanded two knights and two ladies to take the child, bound in a cloth of gold, 'and that ye deliver him to what poor man ye meet at the postern gate of the castle.' So the child was delivered unto Merlin, and so he bare it forth unto Sir Ector, and made an holy man to christen him, and named him Arthur; and so Sir Ector's wife nourished him with her own pap.

FROM BOOK I CHAPTER 4

OF THE DEATH OF KING UTHER PENDRAGON

Then within two years King Uther fell sick of a great malady. And in the meanwhile his enemies <u>usurped</u> upon him, and

---

15. **fiance.** A promise

❶ How does Igraine learn who fathered her child? How does she feel when she learns this?

WORDS FOR EVERYDAY USE:
wax (waks) *vi.*, grow gradually larger
coun • te • nance (koun´tə nəns) *n.*, appearance; facial features
u • surp (yoo zurp´) *vt.*, unlawfully seize a throne

❶ Uther expressed the desire to have Arthur become king after him.

❷ Many lords took this opportunity to become stronger to further their ambitions to be king.

Literary Note

Malory's references to the French book as in "whether it were Paul's or not the French book maketh no mention" (Book I, Chapter 5) are indications of Malory's source or sources. Many scholars believe that Malory actually drew on a number of French sources in which stories were intertwined. He simplified the narrative and focused on Arthur rather than on Sir Lancelot, the chief figure in the French stories.

---

❶ *What arrangement did King Uther make for his succession?*

❷ *What problem was there after Uther's death?*

---

did a great battle upon his men, and slew many of his people.

'Sir,' said Merlin, 'ye may not lie so as ye do, for ye must to the field though ye ride on an horse-litter; for ye shall never have the better of your enemies but if your person be there, and then shall ye have the victory.'

So it was done as Merlin had devised, and they carried the king forth in an horse-litter with a great host toward his enemies. And at St. Albans there met with the king a great host of the north. And that day Sir Ulfius and Sir Brastias did great deeds of arms, and King Uther's men overcame the northern battle and slew many people, and put the remnant to flight. And then the king returned unto London, and made great joy of his victory.

And then he fell passing sore sick, so that three days and three nights he was speechless; wherefore all the barons made great sorrow, and asked Merlin what counsel were best.

'There is none other remedy,' said Merlin, 'but God will have his will. But look ye all, barons, be before King Uther to-morn, and God and I shall make him to speak.'

So on the morn all the barons with Merlin came tofore the king; then Merlin said aloud unto King Uther, 'Sir, shall I your son Arthur be king, after your days, of this realm with all the <u>appurtenance</u>?'

Then Uther Pendragon turned him, and said in hearing of them all, 'I give him God's blessing and mine, and bid him pray for my soul, and righteously and worshipfully that he claim the crown upon forfeiture of my blessing.' And therewith

he yielded up the ghost, and then was he <u>interred</u> as longed to a king, wherefore the queen, fair Igraine, made great sorrow, and all the barons.

FROM BOOK I CHAPTER 5

HOW ARTHUR WAS CHOSEN KING, AND OF WONDERS AND MARVELS OF A SWORD TAKEN OUT OF A STONE BY THE SAID ARTHUR

Then stood the realm in great jeopardy long while, for every lord that was mighty of men made him strong, and many weened[16] to have been king. Then Merlin went to the Archbishop of Canterbury, and counselled him for to send for all the lords of the realm, and all the gentlemen of arms, that they should to London come by Christmas, upon pain of cursing; and for this cause: that Jehu, that was born on that night, that He would of his great mercy show some miracle, as He was come to be king of mankind, for to show some miracle who should be rightwise king of this realm. So the Archbishop, by the advice of Merlin, sent for all the lords and gentlemen of arms that they should come by Christmas even unto London. And many of them made them clean of their life, that their prayer might be the more acceptable unto God.

So in the greatest church of London (whether it were Paul's or not the French book maketh no mention) all the estates were long or day in the church for to pray. And when matins[17] and the first mass was

---

16. **weened.** Thought
17. **matins.** Morning prayers

WORDS FOR EVERYDAY USE:

ap • pur • te • nance (ə pʉrt´´n əns) *n.,* thing that belongs to another

in • ter (in tʉr´) *vt.,* bury

VOCABULARY IN CONTEXT

- The computer and all of its <u>appurtenances</u> were sold at an auction.
- The family made arrangements to <u>inter</u> the deceased grandfather.

Illustration from **The Romance of King Arthur and His Knights of the Round Table.**
Wellesley College Library, Special Collections

ART NOTE

• Discuss with students the illustration depicting the battle between Arthur and Mordred. Ask which figure is Arthur and which is Mordred. How can you tell? Who are the people to the left, and what are they doing? How does the artist depict the dead bodies? What might he be trying to show? Describe the sky. What effect does the sky have on the mood of the painting?

• Ask students to create their own illustrations of King Uther, Queen Igraine, Arthur, and Merlin.

ADDITIONAL QUESTIONS AND ACTIVITIES

Ask students what danger exists after Uther's death. Why is the succession unclear? What time is chosen to prove who the new king is? Why is this time chosen? What comparison is drawn?

Answers: Danger troubles the realm as many lords seek to become king. The succession is unclear because Uther's son Arthur is unknown. Christmastime is chosen to prove the right of the new king because at that time a miracle showed Jesus as the king of humankind and in his mercy he would give a sign showing the new king of Uther's realm.

THE LITERATURE OF ROMANCE / *FROM LE MORTE D'ARTHUR* **173**

TEACHER'S EDITION **173**

ANSWERS TO GUIDED READING QUESTIONS

❶ The person who can pull the sword from the stone will become king.

❷ He wants to get a sword for his brother, Sir Kay.

ADDITIONAL QUESTIONS AND ACTIVITIES

In small groups student can brainstorm other ways of proving kingship. They may wish to consider the role magic plays in this test.

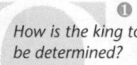

❶
How is the king to be determined?

❷
Why does Arthur pull out the sword from the stone?

done, there was seen in the churchyard, against the high altar, a great stone four square, like unto a marble stone, and in midst thereof was like an anvil of steel a foot on high, and therein stuck a fair sword naked by the point, and letters there were written in gold about the sword that saiden thus:—WHOSO PULLETH OUT THIS SWORD OF THIS STONE AND ANVIL, IS RIGHTWISE KING BORN OF ALL ENGLAND. Then the people marvelled, and told it to the Archbishop,

'I command,' said the Archbishop, 'that ye keep you within your church, and pray unto God still; that no man touch the sword till the high mass be all done.'

So when all masses were done all the lords went to behold the stone and the sword. And when they saw the scripture, some assayed,[18] such as would have been king. But none might stir the sword nor move it.

'He is not here,' said the Archbishop, 'that shall achieve the sword, but doubt not God will make him known. But this is my counsel,' said the Archbishop, 'that we let purvey[19] ten knights, men of good fame, and they to keep this sword.'

So it was ordained, and then there was made a cry, that every man should assay that would, for to win the sword. And upon New Year's Day the barons let make a jousts and a tournament, that all knights that would joust or tourney there might play. And all this was ordained for to keep the lords together and the commons, for the Archbishop trusted that God would make him known that should win the sword.

So upon New Year's Day, when the service was done, the barons rode unto the field, some to joust and some to tourney, and so it happed that Sir Ector, that had great livelihood about London, rode unto the jousts, and with him rode Sir Kay his

son, and young Arthur that was his nourished brother; and Sir Kay was made knight at All Hallowmass afore. So as they rode to the jousts-ward, Sir Kay had lost his sword, for he had left it at his father's lodging, and so he prayed young Arthur for to ride for his sword.

'I will well,' said Arthur, and rode fast after the sword. And when he came home the lady and all were out to see the jousting.

Then was Arthur wroth, and said to himself, 'I will ride to the churchyard, and take the sword with me that sticketh in the stone, for my brother Sir Kay shall not be without a sword this day.' So when he came to the churchyard, Sir Arthur alit and tied his horse to the stile, and so he went to the tent, and found no knights there, for they were at jousting; and so he handled the sword by the handles, and lightly and fiercely pulled it out of the stone, and took his horse and rode his way until he came to his brother Sir Kay, and delivered him the sword.

And as soon as Sir Kay saw the sword, he wist[20] well it was the sword of the stone, and so he rode to his father Sir Ector, and said; 'Sir, lo here is the sword of the stone, wherefore I must be king of this land.'

When Sir Ector beheld the sword, he returned again and came to the church, and there they alit all three, and went into the church. And anon he made Sir Kay to swear upon a book how he came to that sword.

'Sir,' said Sir Kay, 'by my brother Arthur, for he brought it to me.'

'How gat ye this sword?' said Sir Ector to Arthur.

---

18. **assayed.** Made an attempt
19. **let purvey.** Appoint
20. **wist.** Knew

'Sir, I will tell you. When I came home for my brother's sword, I found nobody at home to deliver me his sword, and so I thought my brother Sir Kay should not be swordless, and so I came hither eagerly and pulled it out of the stone without any pain.'

'Found ye any knights about this sword?' said Sir Ector.

'Nay,' said Arthur.

'Now,' said Sir Ector to Arthur, 'I understand ye must be king of this land.'

'Wherefore[21] I,' said Arthur, 'and for what cause?'

'Sir,' said Ector, 'for God will have it so, for there should never man have drawn out this sword, but he that shall be right-wise king of this land. Now let me see whether ye can put the sword there as it was, and pull it out again.'

'That is no mastery,' said Arthur, and so he put it in the stone; therewithal Sir Ector assayed to pull out the sword and failed.

FROM BOOK I CHAPTER 6

HOW KING ARTHUR PULLED OUT THE SWORD DIVERS TIMES

'Now assay,' said Sir Ector unto Sir Kay. And anon he pulled at the sword with all his might, but it would not be.

'Now shall ye assay,' said Sir Ector to Arthur.

'I will well,' said Arthur, and pulled it out easily. And therewithal Sir Ector knelt down to the earth, and Sir Kay.

'Alas!' said Arthur, 'my own dear father and brother, why kneel ye to me?'

'Nay, nay, my lord Arthur, it is not so, I was never your father nor of your blood, but I wot[22] well ye are of an higher blood than I weened ye were.' And then Sir Ector told him all, how he was betaken[23] him for

to nourish him, and by whose command-ment, and by Merlin's deliverance. Then Arthur made great dole[24] when he under-stood that Sir Ector was not his father.

'Sir,' said Ector unto Arthur, 'will ye be my good and gracious lord when ye are king?'

'Else were I to blame,' said Arthur, 'for ye are the man in the world that I am most beholding to, and my good lady and moth-er your wife, that as well as her own hath fostered me and kept. And if ever it be God's will that I be king as ye say, ye shall desire of me what I may do, and I shall not fail you, God forbid I should fail you.'

'Sir,' said Sir Ector, 'I will ask no more of you, but that ye will make my son, your foster brother, Sir Kay, seneschal[25] of all your lands.'

'That shall be done,' said Arthur, 'and more, by the faith of my body, that never man shall have that office but he, while he and I live.'

Therewithal they went unto the Archbishop, and told him how the sword was achieved, and by whom. And on Twelfthday all the barons came thither, and to assay to take the sword, who that would assay. But there afore them all, there might none take it out but Arthur; wherefore there were many lords wroth, and said it was great shame unto them all and the realm, to be over-governed with a boy of no high blood born, and so they fell out at that time, that it was put off till Candlemas,[26] and then all the barons should meet there again; but alway the ten knights were ordained to watch the sword day and night, and so they set a pavilion

How did the lords feel about Arthur being king?

---

21. **Wherefore.** Why
22. **wot.** Know
23. **betaken.** Assigned to care for
24. **dole.** Lamentation
25. **seneschal.** Steward
26. **Candlemas.** A church feast on February 2

THE LITERATURE OF ROMANCE / FROM LE MORTE D'ARTHUR **175**

ADDITIONAL QUESTIONS AND ACTIVITIES

Students can discuss different ways people deal with fame and fortune. How might people treat their friends if they were suddenly to become rich or famous? Why might such changes in lifestyle cause changes in relationships?

ANSWER TO GUIDED READING QUESTION

❶ The lords were unhappy that a boy who was not of noble blood should become king.

ANSWERS TO SELECTION CHECK TEST 4.3.13

EX. What does the title, *Le Morte d'Arthur*, mean?
The title means "The Death of Arthur."

1. Who was Arthur's mother?
His mother was Queen Igraine.

2. Who was Uther Pendragon?
He was the king of England and Arthur's father.

3. Who used magic to disguise Uther Pendragon?
Merlin disguised King Uther with magic.

4. What did Arthur do to become king?
He pulled a sword out of a stone.

5. Who was Arthur's wife?
King Arthur's wife was Queen Guenever.

over the stone and the sword, and five always watched.

So at Candlemas many more great lords came thither for to have won the sword, but there might none prevail. And right as Arthur did at Christmas, he did at Candlemas, and pulled out the sword easily, whereof the barons were sore agrieved and put it off in delay till the high feast of Easter. And as Arthur sped before, so did he at Easter, yet there were some of the great lords had <u>indignation</u> that Arthur should be king, and put it off in a delay till the feast of Pentecost.[27] Then the Archbishop of Canterbury by Merlin's <u>providence</u> let purvey then of the best knights that they might get, and such knights as Uther Pendragon loved best and most trusted in his days. And such knights were put about Arthur as Sir Baudwin of Britain, Sir Kay, Sir Ulfius, Sir Brastias. All these with many other, were always about Arthur, day and night, till the feast of Pentecost.

FROM BOOK I CHAPTER 7

HOW KING ARTHUR WAS CROWNED, AND HOW HE MADE OFFICERS

And at the feast of Pentecost all manner of men assayed to pull at the sword that would assay, but none might prevail but Arthur, and pulled it out afore all the lords and commons that were there, wherefore all the commons cried at once, 'We will have Arthur unto our king; we will put him no more in delay, for we all see that it is God's will that he shall be our king, and who that holdeth against it, we will slay him.' And therewithal they kneeled at

❶ *When is Arthur accepted as king? What do the people say to show they accept him as king?*

once, both rich and poor, and cried Arthur mercy because they had delayed him so long. And Arthur forgave them, and took the sword between both his hands, and offered it upon the altar where the Archbishop was, and so was he made knight of the best man that was there.

And so anon was the coronation made. And there was he sworn unto his lords and the commons for to be a true king, to stand with true justice from thenceforth the days of this life. Also then he made all lords that held of the crown to come in, and to do service as they ought to do. And many complaints were made unto Sir Arthur of great wrongs that were done since the death of King Uther, of many lands that were bereaved lords, knights, ladies, and gentlemen. Wherefore King Arthur made the lands to be given again unto them that ought them.[28] When this was done, that the king had stablished all the countries about London, then he let make Sir Kay Seneschal of England; and Sir Baudwin of Britain was made constable; and Sir Ulfius was made chamberlain; and Sir Brastias was made warden to wait upon the north from Trent forwards, for it was that time the most part the king's enemies. But within few years after, Arthur won all the north, Scotland, and all that were under their <u>obeisance</u>. Also Wales, a part of it, held against Arthur, but he overcame them all, as he did the remnant, through the noble prowess of himself and his knights of the Round Table.

◆   ◆   ◆

27. **Pentecost.** The seventh Sunday after Easter
28. **ought them.** Owned them

WORDS FOR EVERYDAY USE:

in • dig • na • tion (in dig´nā shən) *n.,* anger or scorn
prov • i • dence (präv´ə dəns) *n.,* benevolent guidance
o • bei • sance (ō bā´ səns) *n.,* authority; rule

VOCABULARY IN CONTEXT

• The coach showed great <u>indignation</u> when she was charged with a technical foul and ejected from the playing area.

• "Your <u>providence</u> has helped us to avoid disaster," the government minister said to the relief worker.

• The newly crowned king showed he was under the <u>obeisance</u> of the church by bowing before the archbishop.

FROM BOOK XXI CHAPTER 7

OF THE OPINION OF SOME MEN OF THE DEATH OF KING ARTHUR; AND HOW QUEEN GUENEVER MADE HER A NUN IN ALMESBURY

Yet some men say in many parts of England that King Arthur is not dead, but had by the will of Our Lord Jesu into another place; and men say that he shall come again, and he shall win the holy cross. I will not say that it shall be so, but rather I will say, here in this world he changed his life. But many men say that there is written upon his tomb this verse: HIC IACET ARTHURUS, REX QUONDAM REXQUE FUTURUS.[29]   ∎

---

29. HIC . . . FUTURUS. Here lies Arthur who was king and will be king again.

Responding to the Selection

What surprised you about the circumstances surrounding Arthur's death? Why? Write your thoughts and reactions in your journal.

Reviewing the Selection

RECALLING

1. How does King Uther Pendragon trick Igraine? What is the result of this deception?

2. Under what circumstances does Arthur spend his early years of life? How is his royal heritage discovered?

INTERPRETING

▶▶ 3. Why is Igraine doubly distressed when she learns of the death of her husband?

▶▶ 4. How have Merlin's actions prepared Arthur to assume the role of king?

ANALYTIC SCALES FOR RESPONDING IN WRITING

Assign a score from 1 to 25 for each grading criterion below. (For more detailed evaluation, see the evaluation forms for writing, revising, and proofreading, *Assessment Portfolio,* 7.1–7.10.)

1. Eulogy

• **Content/Unity.** The eulogy praises Arthur and cites some of his specific accomplishments and deeds.

• **Organization/Coherence.** The eulogy follows a logical order, perhaps chronologically from his early years to the end of his life.

• **Language/Style.** The eulogy clearly and succinctly conveys who Arthur was and what he stood for.

• **Conventions.** The eulogy applies correct spelling, grammar, and usage.

2. Birth Announcement

• **Content/Unity.** The announcement includes all essential facts, including names of parents and foster parents.

• **Language/Style.** The announcement uses concise words and short, clear sentences to convey the information.

• **Conventions.** The announcement follows the newspaper form of answering who, what, when, where, why, and how, and is free of errors in spelling, grammar, and usage.

5. How does Malory's version of the legend of Arthur compare to others you know? What makes this legend so appealing that it has been passed down in so many ways?

Understanding Literature (Questions for Discussion)

1. **Folk Tale.** A **folk tale** is a brief story passed by word of mouth from generation to generation. Arthurian stories in French and English drew upon many previously existing folk tale motifs, like that of the person of low estate who turns out to be a king or a supernatural being. How does the selection show that *Le Morte d'Arthur* incorporates such a folk tale motif?

2. **Courtly Love.** The code of romantic love celebrated in French and English medieval romances is known as **courtly love.** Men in the throes of courtly love will risk and suffer anything for the love of a noble woman. How does Uther Pendragon adhere to the code of courtly love?

Responding in Writing

1. **Eulogy.** A **eulogy** is a formal piece of writing or speech that praises a person or thing. Some eulogies are written to praise a person at a funeral or memorial service. What kind of eulogy might you write for Arthur? What were his accomplishments? How and why would you praise him? If necessary, gather some information on the Arthurian legend to find out more about Arthur's reign as king. Then write a paragraph or two in praise of this legendary figure.

2. **Birth Announcement.** New parents often submit the details of a child's birth for publication in a newspaper. The announcement of Arthur's birth would be a somewhat more complicated affair. Write a birth announcement for Arthur, including details about the circumstances of his birth, his true parentage, and his foster parents. Keeping in mind that the announcement will appear in a newspaper, strive to keep sentences succinct.

ANWERS FOR UNDERSTANDING LITERATURE

► See the evaluation forms for discussion, active listening, and oral communication, *Assessment Portfolio,* 7.11–7.14.

Responses will vary. Possible responses are given.

1. Folk Tale. In *Le Morte d'Arthur,* Arthur is raised by another family and his royal blood is unknown until he pulls the sword from the stone and reveals himself as king.

2. Courtly Love. Uther Pendragon's willingness to give his son Arthur to Merlin in return for spending one night with Igraine reflects his adherence to the code of courtly love.

Language Lab

Combining Sentences. Read the Language Arts Survey, 2.51–2.53, on combining sentences. Then combine each pair of sentences below to create a single sentence. Follow the directions given in parentheses.

1. Arthur pulled the sword from the stone. He did so *easily*. (Add the italicized word.)

2. Many other great lords tried to pull the sword from the stone. They *desired to become king*. (Add the italicized words in a clause beginning with the word *who*.)

3. The common people insisted that Arthur be made king. They *cried out loudly* (Change *cried* to *crying* and add the phrase.)

4. The great lords had to comply. *They weren't happy about it.* (Add the second sentence as a subordinate clause beginning with the word *although*.)

5. Thus Arthur became king. He did so *with the help of Merlin.* (Add the italicized phrase.)

Research Skills

Computer-Assisted Research. Read the Language Arts Survey, 4.26, "Computer-Assisted Research." Then look for modern novels that retell the Arthurian legend. Use the on-screen summary information to choose a novel that you would like to read.

PROJECT

Map of Arthur's Britain. Although the location of Camelot, the site of King Arthur's court, cannot be historically verified, many of the geographical locations mentioned in *Le Morte d'Arthur* did exist. For instance, Cornwall lay at the southwestern tip of England. Use a historical atlas to make your own map of fifth-century Britain. Use *Le Morte d'Arthur* or another Arthurian romance as a source for place names. Give your map a key that notes places where Arthur and other knights lived and fought.

ANSWERS FOR LANGUAGE LAB

Responses will vary. Possible responses are given.

1. Arthur easily pulled the sword from the stone.

2. Many other great lords who desired to become king tried to pull the sword from the stone.

3. Crying out loudly, the common people insisted that Arthur be made king.

4. The great lords had to comply, although they weren't happy about it.

5. Thus Arthur became king with the help of Merlin.

ANSWERS FOR RESEARCH SKILLS

Such novels include Marian Zimmer Bradley's *The Mists of Avalon* and T. H. White's *The Once and Future King*.

• Students may wish to read a modern retelling and compare it to Malory's telling of the story or a different retelling read by their classmates.

PROJECT NOTES

Map of Arthur's Britain. Students might want to identify on their maps such places as Cornwall, Tintagel, Glastonbury, Colcester, and Cadbury Castle in Somerset.

Cornwall was the seat of King Mark and Queen Igraine. Tintagel is the place in Cornwall where Arthur was conceived. Some legends claim that Arthur and Guenever (Guinevere) were buried in Glastonbury, in Somerset. The site of Arthur's city, Camelot, has been variously placed at Colcester and at Cadbury Castle in Somerset.

ENRICHMENT ACTIVITIES

Ask students to research the period in which Margery Kempe lived, 1373–1438, to find out what opportunities were available for women. Excellent sources of information on this subject include Thiébaux, Marcelle. *The Writings of Medieval Women,* 1994, and Klapisch-Zuber, Christiane, ed. *Silences of the Middle Ages.* Vol. 2 of *A History of Women.* Ed. George Duby and Michelle Perrot. 1992.

SUPPORT FOR LEP STUDENTS

Some students might have trouble following the sequence of events in the piece because of its formal language. You might want to have them read the piece slowly, stopping every few paragraphs to summarize the events described. Remind students that although the piece is written in the third person, using the pronoun *she* to refer to the central character, it is nonetheless an autobiography. Make sure that before reading the selection students are familiar with the information provided in the author biography.

(cont.)

PREREADING

AUTOBIOGRAPHY

from *The Book of Margery Kempe*
by Margery Kempe

ABOUT THE AUTHOR

Margery Kempe (*circa* 1373–1438) was born in King's Lynn, a busy port in Norfolk, England. At the age of twenty, she was married to John Kempe. After the extremely difficult birth of her first child, Kempe feared she might die and made her confession to a priest who criticized her harshly for what she confessed. These traumatic events led to her mental breakdown, from which she eventually recovered when she had the first of her visions. Kempe became extremely devout, claiming to have personal visions of Jesus Christ and the Virgin Mary. Unlike other religious women of the time, who either entered convents or lived in reclusion, Kempe continued to live with her husband. She eventually gave birth to fourteen children by the age of forty, at which time she took a vow of celibacy (to which her husband agreed) and began to make pilgrimages. Neighbors and fellow pilgrims criticized Kempe for her lifestyle and her loud, emotional displays, which included public sobbing and screaming. However, Kempe did win the support of some clergy and townspeople.

Like many women of her time, Kempe could neither read nor write. However, she had an extensive knowledge of the scriptures and other religious texts, having heard them from town clerics and traveling scholars. About the year 1433, Kempe dictated the two parts of her book to two different scribes; the second scribe, a priest, revised the entire text.

ABOUT THE SELECTION

Although other people had written about themselves prior to the Medieval Period, *The Book of Margery Kempe* is the earliest surviving full-length autobiography in English. Unlike modern autobiographies, it does not relate a chronological story of a person's life. There is little sense of the passing of time throughout the book, although the events span approximately forty years. Instead, the book is Kempe's spiritual history. In the book's preface, Kempe states that she wrote the book to glorify God and to share her spiritual experiences. In doing so, however, she gives modern readers a glimpse into the life of an ordinary medieval woman.

Unlike most autobiographers who use a first-person voice, Kempe refers to herself throughout in the third person as "this creature," meaning one of God's creations. The following selection comes from the second chapter, in which Margery relates events that followed her mental breakdown and eventually led to her decision to devote her life to God.

SUPPORT FOR LEP STUDENTS (CONT.)

ADDITIONAL VOCABULARY

alderman—senior member of a local council
prestigious—having the power to impress
lofty—noble
mortified—ashamed
amends—something done to make up for an injury

venture—a business undertaking in which there is a danger of loss as well as a chance for profit
enterprise—project; undertaking
marvel—wonderful thing; miracle
vanity—excessive pride or conceit

FROM

The Book of Margery Kempe

MARGERY KEMPE

3. HER FANCIFUL CLOTHING, HER BREWING AND HORSE MILL VENTURES

And when this creature had through grace recovered her senses again, she believed she was bound to God and that she would be his servant. Still, she would not abandon her pride or the <u>ostentatious</u> style of dress that she was always used to before. She wouldn't follow her husband's advice or anyone else's. And yet she knew very well that people gossiped viciously about her, for she wore gold pipes on her head and her hoods with the tippets were dagged.[1] Her cloaks also were dagged and lined with many colors between the dags so that her outfit would draw people's stares and she would be more admired.

And when her husband told her to give up her pride, she answered sharply and shortly and said that she had come from an excellent family—he seemed an unlikely man to have married her, since her father had formerly been mayor of the town of N- and afterwards had been alderman of the prestigious Guild of the Trinity in N-. And therefore she maintained the lofty status of her kin, no matter what anyone said. She was very envious of her neighbors lest they dress as well as she did. Her whole desire was to have people admire her. She would not put up with criticism, or be content with the goods God had sent her, as her husband was, but always desired more and more.

And then out of pure greed and the wish to keep up her pride, she began to brew and was one of the greatest brewers in the town of N- for three or four years till she

❶
What business did Kempe start? Why did she start this business?

---

1. **gold . . . dagged.** She wore golden cylindrical hats decorated with hanging points.

WORDS FOR EVERYDAY USE: os • ten • ta • tious (äs´tən tā´shəs) *adj.,* excessively showy

AUTOBIOGRAPHY / FROM *THE BOOK OF MARGERY KEMPE*   **181**

GOALS/OBJECTIVES

Studying this lesson will enable students to

• experience Kempe's determination and devotion to her undertakings

• describe the life and work of Margery Kempe and the events that led her to devote herself to a religious vocation

• describe the elements of an autobiography and practice writing autobiographical materials

• explain the concept of point of view in a piece of writing

• complete a piece of writing that explains a process

ADDITIONAL QUESTIONS AND ACTIVITIES

Ask students if Margery Kempe is unlucky or a poor manager. They should support their opinions with passages from the text.

Mares and foals. George Stubbs, circa 1760. Tate Gallery, London/Art Resource, NY

John Webb photo

ANSWER TO GUIDED READING QUESTION

❶ Kempe's second venture, a horse mill, was unsuccessful because both of her horses refused to cooperate and would not drag a load in the mill. The man she had hired to work at the mill quit because of the problem with the horses.

had lost a good deal of money, for she had never had any experience in brewing. For no matter how good her servants were and clever at brewing, yet things never went well with them. For even when the ale looked as splendid—standing under its head of froth—as anyone might see, suddenly the froth would sink down so that the ale was ruined, one brewing after another, and her servants were mortified and would not stay with her.

Then this creature thought how God had punished her already, and she refused to be warned, and now again she was punished with the loss of her goods, and then she gave up brewing and did it no more. Then she asked her husband's forgiveness for she had not followed his advice, and she said that her pride and sin had brought about her punishment and she would willingly make amends for her faults.

❶ *What problem did she have with her second venture?*

Yet she would not leave the world entirely, for now she thought of a new kind of housewifely venture. She had a horse mill. She got herself two good horses and a man to grind people's corn, and in this way she felt sure she could make her living. This enterprise did not last long, for a short time after the Eve of Corpus Christi,[2] the following marvel occurred. This man was in good health of body, with two horses that were lusty and in good condition, and up till now had drawn well in the mill. Now when the man took one of these horses and put him in the mill as he had done all along, this horse would not drag a load in the mill no matter what the man did. Sometimes he led him by the head, sometimes

---

2. **Corpus Christi.** A Christian festival on the fifth Thursday or sixth Sunday after Easter

VOCABULARY IN CONTEXT

- Gordon will try to <u>cajole</u> the bus driver to stop at his house, which isn't on the scheduled route.
- It often isn't healthy to seek <u>vengeance</u> for the wrongdoings of others.

he beat him, and sometimes he <u>cajoled</u> him, but it was all useless because the horse would rather go backward than forward. Then this man set a pair of sharp spurs on his heels and rode on the horse's back to make him pull, but it was never any better.

When this man saw it was useless, then he put up the horse in the stable and fed him, and he ate well and freshly. Then he took the other horse and put him in the mill. And just as his fellow horse had done, so this one did, for he wouldn't pull despite anything the man did. And then this man quit his service and would no longer stay with this creature we have mentioned. As soon as the word got around the town of N– that no man or beast would work for that creature, then some people said she was cursed. Some said God took open <u>vengeance</u> on her. Some said one thing and some said another. And some wise men whose mind was more grounded in the love of our Lord said it was the high mercy of our Lord Jesus Christ that commanded and called her from the pride and vanity of the wretched world. ∎

① *What did people say about Kempe because of these failures? How did Kempe see the matter?*

Responding to the Selection

Imagine that you are one of the townspeople mentioned in the selection. Write your response to Kempe's actions.

Reviewing the Selection

RECALLING

1. What outward signs point to Kempe's pride?

2. What is the first business venture that Kempe undertakes? Why does it fail?

3. What business does she start next? Why does it fail?

4. What do the townspeople conclude about Kempe?

INTERPRETING

▶ 5. Why does Kempe think she was prideful?

▶ 6. How did this business failure affect Kempe's opinion of herself?

▶ 7. What does Kempe's willingness to start another business say about her personality?

▶ 8. How does Kempe interpret her business failures?

W WORDS FOR EVERYDAY USE:

ca • jole (kə jōl´) vt., coax with flattery

venge • ance (ven´jens) n., revenge, retribution

AUTOBIOGRAPHY / FROM *THE BOOK OF MARGERY KEMPE* **183**

ANSWER TO GUIDED READING QUESTION

① People said that Kempe must be cursed and that God must be getting her back for something. Kempe believed that the Lord was probably calling her "from the pride and vanity of the wretched world."

ANSWERS TO SELECTION CHECK TEST 4.3.15

EX. Whom does Kempe call "this creature"?
Kempe calls herself "this creature."

1. Who asked Kempe to give up her pride?
Her husband asked her to give up her pride.

2. What was the first business that Kempe started?
She started a brewery.

3. What was the second business that Kempe started?
She started a horse mill.

4. What "marvel" occurred shortly after the Eve of Corpus Christi?
The horses refused to pull the load in the mill.

5. What sin does Kempe repeatedly describe herself as having?
She describes herself as having the sin of pride.

RESPONDING TO THE SELECTION

Students may want to decide if they agree with the conclusions to which the townspeople jumped. Some students might feel respect for Kempe and her attempts at starting these businesses. She was, after all, one of the first female entrepreneurs.

ANSWERS FOR REVIEWING THE SELECTION

RECALLING

1. Kempe has a particularly showy, extravagant style of dress.

2. Kempe's first business venture is a brewery. It fails because the ale never comes out right. Her servants become embarrassed and leave.

3. After the brewery fails, Kemp starts a horse mill. This business fails because the horses will not cooperate.

4. The townspeople believe that Kempe must be cursed or that God must be angry with her.

(cont.)

ANSWERS FOR REVIEWING THE SELECTION (CONT.)

INTERPRETING

Responses will vary. Possible responses are given.

5. Kempe believed that she was prideful because she was conscious of the fact that she came from a wealthy and politically important family. She was envious of her neighbors, always in search of admiration, unable to tolerate criticism, and "always desired more and more."

6. After the brewery failed, Kempe believed that God was punishing her for having too much pride. She begged her husband for forgiveness and decided to "make amends for her faults."

7. One can assume that Kempe did not give up easily, that she always wanted more, and that she often changed her mind.

8. Kempe decided that God wanted her to leave the "pride and vanity of the wretched world."

SYNTHESIZING

Responses will vary. Possible responses are given.

9. Kempe believes that pride is wicked and sinful. She abandons her pride so that she can devote herself to God.

10. Some students may get the impression from the description of the horse mill that medieval life was very labor intensive. Others might remark that the small town atmosphere encouraged gossip. Students may be able to relate to Kempe's desire to gain the admiration of others.

ANSWERS FOR UNDERSTANDING LITERATURE

1. Autobiography. Kempe had a great deal of autonomy, something that wasn't at all uncommon among medieval women. Some students may find this fact surprising.

2. Point of View. The third-person point of view might make the judgments made about the central character seem more objective. It also makes the piece read like a story.

184 TEACHER'S EDITION

SYNTHESIZING

9. According to Kempe, what is pride? Why does she finally abandon her pride?

10. What impression does the selection give about everyday medieval life? Can you relate to any of the experiences Kempe describes? Why, or why not?

Understanding Literature (Questions for Discussion)

1. **Autobiography.** An **autobiography** is the story of a person's life, written by that person. Although Margery Kempe did not physically write her autobiography, she did dictate personal events to a scribe who wrote them as she spoke them. What does this selection tell you about Kempe's life? Were you surprised by what you learned? What surprised you?

2. **Point of View.** The vantage point from which a story is told is its **point of view.** Unlike most autobiographies, *The Book of Margery Kempe* takes a third-person point of view. How does this point of view affect the tone of the text? How would a first-person point of view change the tone?

Responding in Writing

1. **Autobiography.** A good **autobiography** gives readers an intimate look at the writer's life. The events it describes reveal what makes the person "who he or she is." What event in your life has played an important part in making you who you are today? Was it something that happened to you or something that you did? Brainstorm about significant events in your life. Then write a few paragraphs that might be included in your autobiography. As you write, think about telling your story to another person. Strive for the immediacy of a personal conversation.

2. **Expository Writing.** Writing that explains a process must be very clear and organized. A reader should be able to understand or perform an action after reading the text. Kempe's description of the horse mill incorporates expository elements; for example, she details how the horse should have performed in the mill. Think of a process that you perform every day, such as opening a computer file or taking the bus. Write a paragraph or two explaining the process for someone who has never done the activity. As you write, remember to use spatial and time order to detail the process. You might brainstorm by listing and numbering the steps of the process.

184 *UNIT THREE / THE MEDIEVAL PERIOD*

ANALYTIC SCALES FOR RESPONDING IN WRITING

Assign a score from 1 to 25 for each grading criterion below. (For more detailed evaluation, see the evaluation forms for writing, revising, and proofreading, *Assessment Portfolio, 7.1–7.10.*)

1. Autobiography
• **Content/Unity.** The work tells of a significant personal event.
• **Organization/Coherence.** The work is organized in a logical order and includes details that illustrate a main idea.
• **Language/Style.** The work uses vivid, concrete, precise nouns, verbs, and modifiers.
• **Conventions.** The work avoids errors in spelling, grammar, usage, mechanics, and manuscript form.

2. Expository Writing
• **Content/Unity.** The work describes a process completely.
• **Organization/Coherence.** The work uses time or spatial order.
• **Language/Style.** The work uses vivid, concrete, precise nouns, verbs, and modifiers.
• **Conventions.** The work avoids errors in spelling, grammar, usage, mechanics, and manuscript form.

PREREADING

from *The Canterbury Tales*
"The Prologue"
from "The Pardoner's Tale"

by Geoffrey Chaucer, trans. by Nevill Coghill

ABOUT THE AUTHOR

Geoffrey Chaucer (*circa* 1342–1400), a public servant and a poet, was the most important writer of **Middle English.** As the son of a London wine merchant, he was a member of the growing middle class in England. Much of his life was spent in the company of royalty, however. By 1357, he had entered the service of Elizabeth, countess of Ulster, and had met John of Gaunt, who would become one of his chief patrons. Chaucer's favor with the aristocracy continued to grow. King Edward III contributed to his ransom after Chaucer was captured during an invasion of France in 1359. In 1367, he was granted a life pension by the king, and subsequently returned to France and Italy on several diplomatic missions. For the rest of his life, he continued his civil work as a Controller of Customs, a justice of the peace, a member of Parliament, and a Clerk of the King's Works. In his old age, he was generously provided for by both Richard III and Henry IV. Despite all of his work as a public servant, Chaucer found time to tap his talent for poetry.

Chaucer was widely read and educated on a variety of subjects. His first literary influences were the French allegorical poets, who were popular with the English aristocracy of the time. One of his first known works is "The Romaunt of the Rose," a translation of a French poem. One of his earliest original works, *The Book of the Duchess,* was written as an elegy for John of Gaunt's first wife. A diplomatic journey to Italy in 1372 put him in direct contact with the Italian Renaissance, giving him new ideas for subjects and forms for his own writing. Boccaccio served as a source for both *Troilus and Criseide* and for "The Knight's Tale" in *The Canterbury Tales,* considered the major literary achievement in Middle English. Chaucer wrote both poetry and prose on a wide range of subjects, drawing on his own broad reading and on his varied personal experience.

ADDITIONAL RESOURCES

READER'S GUIDE
- Selection Worksheets, 3.9, 3.11

ASSESSMENT PORTFOLIO
- Selection Check Tests, 4.3.17, 4.3.19
- Selection Tests, 4.3.18, 4.3.20

ESSENTIAL SKILLS PRACTICE BOOKS
- *Writing,* 1.27
- *Language,* 2.59
- *Study and Research,* 4.37

AUDIOCASSETTE
- "The Prologue" to *The Canterbury Tales,* in Middle English, Track 7

SUPPORT FOR LEP STUDENTS

Some students may be intimidated by the length of the selection. To deal with this problem, have students read and discuss each part of "The Prologue" separately. Begin with the introduction, lines 1–42, and make certain that your students understand the basic situation—that Chaucer is describing a group of medieval people from all walks of life who are going on a pilgrimage, or religious journey, and decide to tell one another stories to pass the time. Before relating the stories, the narrator of the selection describes each of the people who will be telling them. These descriptions make up "The Prologue."

This selection contains challenging vocabulary. Additional vocabulary terms to be defined for some students are given in the marginal annotations accompanying the parts of the poem.

ENRICHMENT ACTIVITIES

- Students may wish to read other examples of frame tales, such as *A Thousand and One Nights* and Boccaccio's *Decameron.*
- Students may create their own frame tales for relating anecdotes from contemporary life. Have students brainstorm a possible situation in which people might tell one another stories (e.g., being stuck inside a ski cabin during a blizzard). Then have each student contribute one story to the collection. These stories might be written down, edited, and compiled into a class book.

VOCABULARY FROM THE SELECTION

absolution	personable
abstrusest	prating
accrue	prelate
ambling	prevarication
arbitrate	sanguine
asunder	saucy
cloister	scrupulosity
dais	scurrility
diligent	sedately
duress	seemly
encumbered	sober
felicity	solicitous
flax	splay
frugal	stature
fustian	stile
grisly	strife
guile	superfluity
heath	sward
hoary	tillage
hostelry	unworldly
lanyard	verity
mire	wanton
miscreant	wary
motley	withal
perdition	

ABOUT THE SELECTIONS

The Canterbury Tales is a **frame tale**, a story that itself provides a vehicle for the telling of other stories. The vehicle story of *The Canterbury Tales* is established in **"The Prologue,"** which introduces a diverse group of characters, including the narrator. *The Canterbury Tales* consists primarily of tales the characters share with each other to pass the time during their pilgrimage to Canterbury, the site of a shrine to **St. Thomas à Becket.** The characters, who represent various aspects of society, are introduced roughly in order of their rank in society. The descriptions of the characters are brief, but very vivid. The characters are further developed throughout *The Canterbury Tales,* through their discussions in between the several tales, as well as through the stories they tell. The interaction among the characters and the diversity of narrators and stories are all innovations that Chaucer made to the frame tale, which was already a popular form.

Chaucer planned for each pilgrim to tell four stories, but he never completed the project. Many stories are nonexistent, and others exist only as unfinished fragments. The order Chaucer intended for the tales is also unclear. Chaucer began work on *The Canterbury Tales* around 1386, but the stories were probably written over a long period of Chaucer's life, and some may not originally have been intended to be included. **"The Pardoner's Tale"** is preceded by a prologue, in which the pardoner explains how he preaches against greed. Like many of Chaucer's stories, there were several possible sources for this story. The most likely direct source is one of the many collections of **exempla**, stories illustrating moral lessons, which were circulated throughout Europe and were intended for use in sermons. The tale has many analogues in Latin, Italian, and German sources, but may be of non-European origin.

The Works of Our Ancient and Learned English Poet. London, 1598. Wellesley College Library, Special Collections

186   *UNIT THREE / THE MEDIEVAL PERIOD*

GOALS/OBJECTIVES

Studying this lesson will enable students to

- enjoy the variety of characters introduced by the narrator
- explain what a frame tale is and how *The Canterbury Tales* is an example of a frame tale
- define *satire* and explain examples of satire in their reading

- identify characterization techniques and use them in a character sketch
- prepare interview questions and create answers based on a fictional character
- correct sentences to reduce wordiness

READER'S JOURNAL

Freewrite about a person whom you may not know extremely well but whom you have observed, such as a neighbor, a cashier at the supermarket, or your bus driver. Think about his or her personality and appearance. What do you find most memorable about him or her? What words best describe this person?

READING SKILLS

Read the Language Arts Survey, 4.18, "Reading Actively: Predicting." Then make predictions about what you will read in "The Prologue" to *The Canterbury Tales*. First think about what you know about frame tales, and imagine what the purposes of a prologue would be. Then write six to eight predictions before you begin reading.

FROM *THE CANTERBURY TALES*

"The Prologue"

GEOFFREY CHAUCER, TRANS. BY NEVILL COGHILL

 han that Aprill with his shoures soote[1]
    The droghte of March hath perced to the
        root,
  And bathed every veyne in swich licour
  Of which vertu engendred is the flour;
5 Whan Zephirus eek with his sweete breeth
  Inspired hath in every holt and heeth
  The tendre croppes, and the yonge sonne
  Hath in the Ram his halve cours yronne,
  And smale foweles maken melodye,
10 That slepen al the nyght with open ye
  (So priketh hem nature in hir corages);
  Thanne longen folk to goon on pilgrimages,
  And palmeres for to seken straunge strondes,
  To ferne halwes, kowthe in sondry londes;
15 And specially from every shires ende

 hen in April the sweet showers fall
    And pierce the drought of March to the
        root, and all
The veins are bathed in liquor of such power
As brings about the engendering of the flower,
When also Zephyrus[2] with his sweet breath
Exhales an air in every grove and <u>heath</u>
Upon the tender shoots, and the young sun
His half-course in the sign of the Ram has run,[3]
And the small fowl are making melody
That sleep away the night with open eye
(So nature pricks them and their heart engages)
Then people long to go on pilgrimages
And palmers long to seek the stranger strands[4]
Of far-off saints, hallowed in sundry lands,
And specially, from every shire's end

---

1. **Lines 1–26** are given here in the original Middle English (left column) and in a Modern English translation (right column). The rest of "The Prologue" follows in Modern English.

2. **Zephyrus.** The west wind
3. **young . . . run.** The sun has gone halfway through its course in Aries, the Ram, the first sign of the Zodiac in the solar year.
4. **palmers . . . strands.** Pilgrims want to visit faraway shrines.

 WORDS FOR EVERYDAY USE: **heath** (hēth) *n.*, open wasteland

---

PREREADING NOTES

READER'S JOURNAL

Students might begin by describing the observed individual's facial features, build, dress, mannerisms, expressions, and actions.

READING SKILLS

Students should keep their predictions handy as they read and note how accurate their predictions were.

ADDITIONAL QUESTIONS AND ACTIVITIES

Let students hear how Middle English sounds. Play the Middle English recording of a selection from *The Canterbury Tales*, Track 7. Repeat the first few lines of "The Prologue" and have students try the pronunciation. After some practice, students should try to read aloud the opening lines of the Middle English version of "The Prologue."

SUPPORT FOR LEP STUDENTS

ADDITIONAL VOCABULARY

Introduction to "The Prologue"
drought—period without rain
engendering—birth; creation
exhale—breathe out
pilgrimage—a journey taken to a place with religious significance
hallowed—sacred; holy
sundry—many and varied
shire—community
wend—travel
fellowship—friendliness; community
array—dress

VOCABULARY IN CONTEXT

• Accustomed to the lush vegetation of her tropical home, the visitor to England was depressed by the barren <u>heath</u>.

Title page from **The Works of Geoffrey Chaucer.** *Illustrations by William Morris. Wellesley College Library, Special Collections*

Of Engelond to Caunterbury they wende,
The hooly blisful martir for to seke,
That hem hath holpen whan that they were seeke.
    Bifil that in that seson on a day,
20 In Southwerk at the Tabard as I lay
Redy to wenden on my pilgrymage
To Caunterbury with ful devout corage,
At nyght was come into that hostelrye
Wel nyne and twenty in a comaignye,
25 Of sondry folk, by aventure yfalle
In felaweshipe, and pilgrimes were they alle,

Of England, down to Canterbury they wend
To seek the holy blissful martyr,[5] quick
To give his help to them when they were sick.
    It happened in that season that one day
In Southwark,[6] at *The Tabard*, as I lay
Ready to go on pilgrimage and start
For Canterbury, most devout at heart,
At night there came into that <u>hostelry</u>
Some nine and twenty in a company
Of sundry folk happening then to fall
In fellowship, and they were pilgrims all

---

5. **holy . . . martyr.** Saint Thomas à Becket, who was killed in Canterbury Cathedral in 1170
6. **Southwark.** A suburb of London, located south of the River Thames and the site of the Tabard Inn

WORDS FOR EVERYDAY USE:
hos • tel • ry (häs´təl rē) *n.*, lodging place

That towards Canterbury meant to ride.
The rooms and stables of the inn were wide;
They made us easy, all was of the best.
30 And, briefly, when the sun had gone to rest,
I'd spoken to them all upon the trip
And was soon one with them in fellowship,
Pledged to rise early and to take the way
To Canterbury, as you heard me say.
35 But none the less, while I have time and
space,
Before my story takes a further pace,
It seems a reasonable thing to say
What their condition was, the full array
Of each of them, as it appeared to me,
40 According to profession and degree,
And what apparel they were riding in;
And at a Knight I therefore will begin.

 here was a *Knight*, a most distinguished
man,
Who from the day on which he first
began
45 To ride abroad had followed chivalry,
Truth, honor, generousness and courtesy.
He had done nobly in his sovereign's war
And ridden into battle, no man more,
As well in Christian as in heathen places,
50 And ever honored for his noble graces.
When we took Alexandria, he was there.
He often sat at table in the chair
Of honor, above all nations, when in Prussia.
In Lithuania he had ridden, and Russia,
55 No Christian man so often, of his rank.
When, in Granada, Algeciras sank
Under assault, he had been there, and in
North Africa, raiding Benamarin;
In Anatolia he had been as well

60 And fought when Ayas and Attalia[7] fell,
For all along the Mediterranean coast
He had embarked with many a noble host.
In fifteen mortal battles he had been
And jousted for our faith at Tramissene
65 Thrice in the lists,[8] and always killed his man.
This same distinguished knight had led the
van
Once with the Bey of Balat, doing work
For him against another heathen Turk;
He was of sovereign value in all eyes.
70 And though so much distinguished, he was
wise
And in his bearing modest as a maid.
He never yet a boorish thing had said
In all his life to any, come what might;
He was a true, a perfect gentle-knight.
75 Speaking of his equipment, he possessed
Fine horses, but he was not gaily dressed.
He wore a <u>fustian</u> tunic stained and dark
With smudges where his armor had left
mark;
Just home from service, he had joined our
ranks
80 To do his pilgrimage and render thanks.

e had his son with him, a fine young
Squire,
A lover and cadet, a lad of fire
With locks as curly as if they had been
pressed.
He was some twenty years of age, I guessed.
85 In <u>stature</u> he was of a moderate length,
With wonderful agility and strength.
He'd seen some service with the cavalry
In Flanders and Artois and Picardy
And had done valiantly in little space

---

7. **Alexandria . . . Attalia.** Sites of battles in which the Knight
fought against the Moslems, Moors, and northern enemies
8. **lists.** Arena for jousting tournaments

WORDS FOR
EVERYDAY USE:

fus • tian (fus´chən) *n.,* coarse cloth
stat • ure (stach´ər) *n.,* height

SUPPORT FOR LEP STUDENTS

ADDITIONAL VOCABULARY

The Knight
heathen—non-Christian
embark—set sail; leave on a
journey
sovereign—kingly; royal
boorish—rude; awkward, ill-
mannered
render—give

The Squire
moderate—average
agility—ease of movement
valiantly—bravely

**ADDITIONAL QUESTIONS
AND ACTIVITIES**

Students can research what an
inn or hostelry was like during
Chaucer's time. They can then
draw a picture or construct a
model of a typical inn.

VOCABULARY IN CONTEXT

• After twenty hours of driving we were not picky about which <u>hostelry</u> we stopped at for the night.
• Natalie's simple <u>fustian</u> dress stood out sharply in the crowd of elaborate satin frocks.
• Judging by the <u>stature</u> of her parents, Winnifred will probably grow to over six feet tall.

90 Of time, in hope to win his lady's grace.
He was embroidered like a meadow bright
And full of freshest flowers, red and white.
Singing he was, or fluting all the day;
He was as fresh as is the month of May.
95 Short was his gown, the sleeves were long and wide;
He knew the way to sit a horse and ride.
He could make songs and poems and recite,
Knew how to joust and dance, to draw and write.
He loved so hotly that till dawn grew pale
100 He slept as little as a nightingale.
Courteous he was, lowly and serviceable,
And carved to serve his father at the table.

here was a *Yeoman* with him at his side,
No other servant; so he chose to ride.
This Yeoman wore a coat and hood of green,
And peacock-feathered arrows, bright and keen
And neatly sheathed, hung at his belt the while
—For he could dress his gear in yeoman style,
His arrows never drooped their feathers low—
110 And in his hand he bore a mighty bow.
His head was like a nut, his face was brown.
He knew the whole of woodcraft up and down.
A <u>saucy</u> brace was on his arm to ward
It from the bow-string, and a shield and sword
115 Hung at one side, and at the other slipped

A jaunty dirk,[9] spear-sharp and well-equipped.
A medal of St. Christopher[10] he wore
Of shining silver on his breast, and bore
A hunting-horn, well slung and burnished clean,
120 That dangled from a baldrick[11] of bright green.
He was a proper forester, I guess.

here also was a *Nun*, a Prioress,
Her way of smiling very simple and coy.
Her greatest oath was only 'By St. Loy!'
125 And she was known as Madam Eglantyne.
And well she sang a service, with a fine
Intoning through her nose, as was most seemly,
And she spoke daintily in French, extremely,
After the school of Stratford-atte-Bowe;[12]
130 French in the Paris style she did not know.
At meat her manners were well taught <u>withal</u>;
No morsel from her lips did she let fall,
Nor dipped her fingers in the sauce too deep;
But she could carry a morsel up and keep
135 The smallest drop from falling on her breast.
For courtliness she had a special zest,
And she would wipe her upper lip so clean
That not a trace of grease was to be seen
Upon the cup when she had drunk; to eat,
140 She reached a hand <u>sedately</u> for the meat.
She certainly was very entertaining,
Pleasant and friendly in her ways, and straining
To counterfeit a courtly kind of grace,
A stately bearing fitting to her place,
145 And to seem dignified in all her dealings.

---

9. **dirk.** Dagger
10. **St. Christopher.** Patron saint of travelers
11. **baldrick.** Belt worn over one shoulder and across the chest

12. **Stratford-atte-Bowe.** Location of a convent school where French was taught, but not especially well

WORDS FOR EVERYDAY USE:

sau • cy (sô′ sē) *adj.*, stylish
with • al (with ôl′) *adv.*, besides; nevertheless
se • date • ly (si dāt′lē) *adv.*, decorously

VOCABULARY IN CONTEXT

- George's hat was outdated, but he thought it was stylish with its <u>saucy</u> feather.
- I have a headache but I am going to the party <u>withal</u>.
- Leon usually causes a commotion when he runs through the library, but today he walked through very <u>sedately</u>.

As for her sympathies and tender feelings,
She was so charitably <u>solicitous</u>
She used to weep if she but saw a mouse
Caught in a trap, if it were dead or bleeding.
150 And she had little dogs she would be feeding
With roasted flesh, or milk, or fine white
    bread.
And bitterly she wept if one were dead
Or someone took a stick and made it smart;
She was all sentiment and tender heart.
155 Her veil was gathered in a <u>seemly</u> way,
Her nose was elegant, her eyes glass-grey;
Her mouth was very small, but soft and red,
Her forehead, certainly, was fair of spread,
Almost a span across the brows, I own;
160 She was indeed by no means undergrown.
Her cloak, I noticed, had a graceful charm.
She wore a coral trinket on her arm,
A set of beads, the gaudies[13] tricked in green,
Whence hung a golden brooch of brightest
    sheen
165 On which there first was graven a crowned A,
And lower, *Amor vincit omnia*.[14]

nother Nun, the secretary at her cell,
Was riding with her, and three Priests as
    well.
   A Monk there was, one of the finest sort
170 Who rode the country; hunting was his sport.
A manly man, to be an Abbot able;
Many a dainty horse he had in stable.
His bridle, when he rode, a man might hear
Jingling in a whistling wind as clear,
175 Aye, and as loud as does the chapel bell
Where my lord Monk was Prior of the cell.
The Rule of good St. Benet or St. Maur
As old and strict he tended to ignore;

He let go by the things of yesterday
180 And took the modern world's more spacious
    way.
He did not rate that text at a plucked hen
Which says that hunters are not holy men
And that a monk uncloistered is a mere
Fish out of water, flapping on the pier,
185 That is to say a monk out of his <u>cloister</u>.
That was a text he held not worth an oyster;
And I agreed and said his views were sound;
Was he to study till his head went round
Poring over books in cloisters? Must he toil
190 As Austin bade and till the very soil?
Was he to leave the world upon the shelf?
Let Austin have his labor to himself.
This Monk was therefore a good man to
    horse;
Greyhounds he had, as swift as birds, to
    course.
195 Hunting a hare or riding at a fence
Was all his fun, he spared for no expense.
I saw his sleeves were garnished at the hand
With fine gray fur, the finest in the land,
And on his hood, to fasten it at his chin
200 He had a wrought-gold cunningly fashioned
    pin;
Into a lover's knot it seemed to pass.
His head was bald and shone like
    looking-glass;
So did his face, as if it had been greased.
He was a fat and <u>personable</u> priest;
205 His prominent eyeballs never seemed to
    settle.
They glittered like the flames beneath a
    kettle;
Supple his boots, his horse in fine condition.
He was a <u>prelate</u> fit for exhibition,

---

13. **gaudies.** Every eleventh bead in a rosary marks a special prayer
and is called a gaudy.
14. *Amor vincit omnia.* Latin for "Love conquers all."

<table>
<tr><td rowspan="2">WORDS FOR
EVERYDAY USE:</td><td>so • lic • i • tous (sə lis´ə təs) adj., showing
concern</td><td>per • son • a • ble (pʉr´sən ə bəl) adj., having
a pleasant appearance and personality</td></tr>
<tr><td>seem • ly (sēm´lē) adv., proper

clois • ter (klois´tər) n., monastery</td><td>prel • ate (prel´it) n., high-ranking ecclesiastic</td></tr>
</table>

To check students' reading comprehension, ask the following
questions: What did the Monk like
to do? What did the church teach
about hunting? How did the Monk
respond to church teaching?
Answers. The Monk liked to hunt.
The church said that hunters were
not holy men. Although the Monk
was supposed to uphold the rules
and beliefs of the church, he fla-
grantly violated them and lived a
pleasurable life.

SUPPORT FOR LEP STUDENTS

ADDITIONAL VOCABULARY

The Monk
garnished—decorated
cunningly—in a crafty or clever
  way
prominent—projecting, sticking
  out
supple—flexible

VOCABULARY IN CONTEXT

- Nancy shows little concern for her own well-being, but she is extremely <u>solicitous</u> of others.
- Beatrice usually dresses outrageously, but the outfit she wore to the wedding was quite <u>seemly</u>.
- The monk lives in a quiet <u>cloister</u>.
- Lila hit it off immediately with her <u>personable</u> new neighbor.
- The unambitious country priest has no desire to become a <u>prelate</u>.

ADDITIONAL VOCABULARY

The Friar

festive—happy; merry
gallant—showy; stylish; noble
scope—range or limit
shriven—absolved through
   confession
eminent—well known; powerful;
   respected
wretched—in a terrible condition
commerce—dealings; interaction
victual—food
poaching—taking something from
   another's land or territory
farthing—coin

ADDITIONAL QUESTIONS
AND ACTIVITIES

Students can research the
hurdy-gurdy and bring in
pictures and recordings of
this instrument. Are any of the
other pilgrims musically inclined?
What instruments do they play?
Which pilgrims are said to sing?

He was not pale like a tormented soul.
210 He liked a fat swan best, and roasted whole.
His palfrey[15] was as brown as is a berry.

here was a *Friar*, a <u>wanton</u> one and
   merry,
A Limiter,[16] a very festive fellow.
In all Four Orders[17] there was none so mel-
   low,
215 So glib with gallant phrase and well-turned
   speech.
He'd fixed up many a marriage, giving each
Of his young women what he could afford
   her.
He was a noble pillar to his Order.
Highly beloved and intimate was he
220 With County folk within his boundary,
And city dames of honor and possessions;
For he was qualified to hear confessions,
Or so he said, with more than priestly scope;
He had a special license from the Pope.
225 Sweetly he heard his penitents at shrift[18]
With pleasant <u>absolution</u>, for a gift.
He was an easy man in penance-giving
Where he could hope to make a decent living;
It's a sure sign whenever gifts are given
230 To a poor Order that a man's well shriven,
And should he give enough he knew in <u>verity</u>
The penitent repented in sincerity.
For many a fellow is so hard of heart
He cannot weep, for all his inward smart.
235 Therefore instead of weeping and of prayer
One should give silver for a poor Friar's care.
He kept his tippet[19] stuffed with pins for
   curls,
And pocket-knives, to give to pretty girls.
And certainly his voice was gay and sturdy,

240 For he sang well and played the hurdy-gurdy.
At sing-songs he was champion of the hour.
His neck was whiter than a lily-flower
But strong enough to butt a bruiser down.
He knew the taverns well in every town
245 And every innkeeper and barmaid too
Better than lepers, beggars and that crew,
For in so eminent a man as he
It was not fitting with the dignity
Of his position, dealing with a scum
250 Of wretched lepers; nothing good can come
Of commerce with such slum-and-gutter
   dwellers,
But only with the rich and victual-sellers.
But anywhere a profit might <u>accrue</u>
Courteous he was and lowly of service too.
255 Natural gifts like his were hard to match.
He was the finest beggar of his batch,
And, for his begging-district, paid a rent;
His brethren did no poaching where he went.
For though a widow mightn't have a shoe,
260 So pleasant was his holy how-d'ye-do
He got his farthing from her just the same
Before he left, and so his income came
To more than he laid out. And how he
   romped,
Just like a puppy! He was ever prompt
265 To <u>arbitrate</u> disputes on settling days
(For a small fee) in many helpful ways,
Not then appearing as your cloistered scholar
With threadbare habit hardly worth a dollar,
But much more like a Doctor or a Pope.
270 Of double-worsted was the semi-cope
Upon his shoulders, and the swelling fold
About him, like a bell about its mold
When it is casting, rounded out his dress.
He lisped a little out of wantonness

---

15. **palfrey.** Horse
16. **Limiter.** A friar who could beg only in a limited, assigned area
17. **Four Orders.** There are four orders—Dominican, Franciscan,
Carmelite, and Augustinian—whose friars all live by begging.

18. **shrift.** Confession to a priest
19. **tippet.** Long scarf worn by the clergy

WORDS FOR
EVERYDAY USE:

wan • ton (wän´tən) *adj.,* unrestrained,
extravagant
ab • so • lu • tion (ab´sə loo shən) *n.,* forgiveness
ver • i • ty (ver´ə tē) *n.,* truth

ac • crue (ə kroo) *vt.,* accumulate periodically
ar • bi • trate (är´bə trāt´) *vt.,* settle a dispute

VOCABULARY IN CONTEXT

• "Eat, drink, and be merry" is the motto of one of my <u>wanton</u> friends.
• I confessed my sins and asked for <u>absolution</u>.
• Jim is such a liar he doesn't even know what <u>verity</u> is.
• I went to the bank to see how much interest my savings had <u>accrued</u>.
• We need an unbiased party to <u>arbitrate</u> this argument.

275 To make his English sweet upon his tongue.
When he had played his harp, or having sung,
His eyes would twinkle in his head as bright
As any star upon a frosty night.
This worthy's name was Hubert, it appeared.

 here was a *Merchant* with a forking beard
And <u>motley</u> dress; high on his horse he sat,
Upon his head a Flemish beaver hat
And on his feet daintily buckled boots.
He told of his opinions and pursuits
285 In solemn tones, he harped on his increase
Of capital; there should be sea-police
(He thought) upon the Harwich-Holland ranges;[20]
He was expert at dabbling in exchanges.
This estimable Merchant so had set
290 His wits to work, none knew he was in debt,
He was so stately in administration,
In loans and bargains and negotiation.
He was an excellent fellow all the same;
To tell the truth I do not know his name.

 n *Oxford Cleric*, still a student though,
One who had taken logic long ago,
Was there; his horse was thinner than a rake,
And he was not too fat, I undertake,
But had a hollow look, a <u>sober</u> stare;
300 The thread upon his overcoat was bare.
He had found no preferment in the church
And he was too <u>unworldly</u> to make search
For secular employment. By his bed
He preferred having twenty books in red
305 And black, of Aristotle's philosophy,

Than costly clothes, fiddle or psaltery.[21]
Though a philosopher, as I have told,
He had not found the stone for making gold.[22]
Whatever money from his friends he took
310 He spent on learning or another book
And prayed for them most earnestly, returning
Thanks to them thus for paying for his learning.
His only care was study, and indeed
He never spoke a word more than was need,
315 Formal at that, respectful in the extreme,
Short, to the point, and lofty in his theme.
A tone of moral virtue filled his speech
And gladly would he learn, and gladly teach.

 Sergeant at the Law who paid his calls,
Wary and wise, for clients at St. Paul's[23]
There also was, of noted excellence.
Discreet he was, a man to reverence,
Or so he seemed, his sayings were so wise.
He often had been Justice of Assize
325 By letters patent,[24] and in full commission.
His fame and learning and his high position
Had won him many a robe and many a fee.
There was no such conveyancer[25] as he;
All was fee-simple[26] to his strong digestion,
330 Not one conveyance could be called in question.
Though there was nowhere one so busy as he,
He was less busy than he seemed to be.
He knew of every judgment, case and crime
Ever recorded since King William's time.
335 He could dictate defenses or draft deeds;

---

20. **sea-police . . . ranges.** He wanted the sea to be well policed to guard his wool trade.
21. **psaltery.** A type of harp
22. **the stone . . . gold.** Imaginary stone sought by alchemists
23. **St. Paul's.** The porch of St. Paul's Cathedral was a

common meeting place for lawyers and their clients.
24. **letters patent.** Legal documents granting rights
25. **conveyancer.** Land speculator
26. **fee-simple.** Absolute and unrestricted

WORDS FOR EVERYDAY USE:

mot • ley (mät´lē) *adj.,* multicolored
so • ber (sō´bər) *adj.,* serious, grave
un • world • ly (un wurld´lē) *adj.,* unsophisticated

VOCABULARY IN CONTEXT

- Jim wore a <u>motley</u> tie-dyed shirt.
- Monica's smiling face turned <u>sober</u> when she heard about the catastrophe.
- The <u>unworldly</u> traveler was easy prey for pickpockets.

ADDITIONAL VOCABULARY

The Franklin

benign—gentle; harmless
sensual—having to do with the senses (sight, sound, taste, touch, or smell)
bounty—generosity
dainties—delicate, fine foods
arrayed—organized
audit—financial accounting
gentry—land-owning people just below the nobility in social rank

The Haberdasher, Dyer, Carpenter, Weaver, and Carpet-maker

wrought—made
mantle—loose, sleeveless cloak or cape

ADDITIONAL QUESTIONS AND ACTIVITIES

Students can research guilds or guild-fraternities to learn about the formation of guilds, the kinds of guilds, and how people became members of guilds. They can present their findings to the class.

No one could pinch a comma from his
    screeds
And he knew every statute off by rote.
He wore a homely parti-colored coat,
Girt with a silken belt of pin-stripe stuff;
340 Of his appearance I have said enough.

here was a *Franklin*[27] with him, it
    appeared;
White as a daisy-petal was his beard.
A <u>sanguine</u> man, high-colored and benign,
He loved a morning sop of cake in wine.
345 He lived for pleasure and had always done,
For he was Epicurus'[28] very son,
In whose opinion sensual delight
Was the one true <u>felicity</u> in sight.
As noted as St. Julian was for bounty
350 He made his household free to all the County.
His bread, his ale were finest of the fine
And no one had a better stock of wine.
His house was never short of bake-meat pies,
Of fish and flesh, and these in such supplies
355 It positively snowed with meat and drink
And all the dainties that a man could think.
According to the seasons of the year
Changes of dish were ordered to appear.
He kept fat partridges in coops, beyond,
360 Many a bream and pike were in his pond.
Woe to the cook unless the sauce was hot
And sharp, or if he wasn't on the spot!
And in his hall a table stood arrayed
And ready all day long, with places laid.
365 As Justice at the Sessions none stood higher;
He often had been Member for the Shire.
A dagger and a little purse of silk
Hung at his girdle, white as morning milk.

As Sheriff he checked audit, every entry.
370 He was a model among landed gentry.

Haberdasher, a *Dyer,* a *Carpenter,*
A *Weaver* and a *Carpet-maker* were
Among our ranks, all in the livery[29]
Of one impressive guild-fraternity.
375 They were so trim and fresh their gear would
    pass
For new. Their knives were not tricked out[30]
    with brass
But wrought with purest silver, which
    avouches[31]
A like display on girdles and on pouches.
Each seemed a worthy burgess,[32] fit to grace
380 A guild-hall with a seat upon the <u>dais</u>.
Their wisdom would have justified a plan
To make each one of them an alderman;
They had the capital and revenue,
Besides their wives declared it was their due.
385 And if they did not think so, then they
    ought;
To be called '*Madam*' is a glorious thought,
And so is going to church and being seen
Having your mantle carried, like a queen.

hey had a *Cook* with them who stood
    alone
    For boiling chicken with a marrow-bone,
Sharp flavoring-powder and a spice for savor.
He could distinguish London ale by flavor,
And he could roast and seethe and broil and
    fry,
Make good thick soup and bake a tasty pie.
395 But what a pity—so it seemed to me,
That he should have an ulcer on his knee.

---

27. *Franklin.* A prosperous landowner of lower-class ancestry
28. **Epicurus'.** Of the Greek philosopher who taught that pleasure should be a large part of life
29. **livery.** Uniform

30. **tricked out.** Dressed up
31. **avouches.** Gives reason to expect
32. **burgess.** Citizen of a borough or town

WORDS FOR
EVERYDAY USE:

san • guine (saŋ´gwin) *adj.,* ruddy, red; happy
fe • lic • i • ty (fə lis´i tē) *n.,* happiness; bliss
da • is (dā´is) *n.,* raised platform

VOCABULARY IN CONTEXT

- Adrian's usually <u>sanguine</u> face paled after three days of illness.
- After the long, harsh winter, Bonnie found true <u>felicity</u> on her sun-filled cruise.
- The mayor stood on a <u>dais</u> as he gave his speech.
- Farley made the <u>lanyard</u> he wears around his neck at summer camp.
- Marissa's <u>guile</u> won out over the shrewd shopkeeper and her scam was a success.
- The icing made the cake, but the decadent festoons and flower clusters were a <u>superfluity</u>.

As for blancmange,[33] he made it with the best.

here was a *Skipper* hailing from far west;
He came from Dartmouth, so I under-
stood.
400 He rode a farmer's horse as best he could,
In a woolen gown that reached his knee.
A dagger on a <u>lanyard</u> falling free
Hung from his neck under his arm and down.
The summer heat had tanned his color
brown,
405 And certainly he was an excellent fellow.
Many a draft of vintage, red and yellow,
He'd drawn at Bordeaux, while the trader
snored.
The nicer rules of conscience he ignored.
If, when he fought, the enemy vessel sank,
410 He sent his prisoners home; they walked the
plank.
As for his skill in reckoning his tides,
Currents and many another risk besides,
Moons, harbors, pilots, he had such dispatch
That none from Hull to Carthage was his
match.
415 Hardy he was, prudent in undertaking;
His beard in many a tempest had its shaking,
And he knew all the havens as they were
From Gottland to the Cape of Finisterre,
And every creek in Brittany and Spain;
420 The barge he owned was called *The
Maudelayne.*

Doctor too emerged as we proceeded;
No one alive could talk as well as he did
On points of medicine and of surgery,

For, being grounded in astronomy,[34]
425 He watched his patient closely for the hours
When, by his horoscope, he knew the powers
Of favorable planets, then ascendant,
Worked on the images[35] for his dependent.
The cause of every malady you'd got
430 He knew, and whether dry, cold, moist or
hot;[36]
He knew their seat, their humor and condi-
tion.
He was a perfect practicing physician.
These causes being known for what they were,
He gave the man his medicine then and there.
435 All his apothecaries[37] in a tribe
Were ready with the drugs he would prescribe
And each made money from the other's
<u>guile</u>;
They had been friendly for a goodish while.
He was well-versed in Aesculapius too
440 And what Hippocrates and Rufus knew
And Dioscorides, now dead and gone,
Galen and Rhazes, Hali, Serapion,
Averroes, Avicenna, Constantine,
Scotch Bernard, John of Gaddesden,
Gilbertine.[38]
445 In his own diet he observed some measure;
There were no <u>superfluities</u> for pleasure,
Only digestives, nutritives and such.
He did not read the Bible very much.
In blood-red garments, slashed with bluish
gray
450 And lined with taffeta, he rode his way;
Yet he was rather close as to expenses
And kept the gold he won in pestilences.
Gold stimulates the heart, or so we're told.
He therefore had a special love of gold.

---

33. **blancmange.** A bland, custard-like dessert
34. **astronomy.** Astrology
35. **powers . . . images.** Effigies were made and used during the most influential hours according to the patient's horoscope.
36. **dry . . . hot.** It was believed that the human body was made up of

four elements: earth, water, air, and fire. Earth was considered cold and dry; water, cold and wet; air, hot and moist; and fire, hot and dry. Disease, it was believed, was caused by an imbalance in these elements.
37. **apothecaries.** Pharmacists
38. **Aesculapius . . . Gilbertine.** Historic medical authorities

---

WORDS FOR
EVERYDAY USE:

lan • yard (lan´yərd) *n.,* cord worn around the neck
guile (gīl) *n.,* slyness and cunning
su • per • flu • i • ty (soo´pər floo´ə tē) *n.,* something unnecessary or extra

SUPPORT FOR LEP STUDENTS

ADDITIONAL VOCABULARY

The Skipper
draft—drink
vintage—wine of a certain year or
age
dispatch—efficiency or ease in
doing a job
prudent—wise
tempest—storm

The Doctor
emerged—appeared; came out
ascendant—rising
malady—sickness
pestilences—outbreaks of disease

CROSS-CURRICULAR ACTIVITIES

Social Studies. Students
can locate Dartmouth,
Bordeaux, Hull, Carthage,
Gotland, and the Cape of
Finisterre on a map.

**ADDITIONAL QUESTIONS
AND ACTIVITIES**

Students can discuss how
medieval medicine differs from
modern medical practices. How
would the Doctor's practices be
viewed by modern standards?

Note that there were not very many women on the pilgrimage. Ask students why they think this is so. Students can research what life was like for women in Chaucer's time. Students might also compare the Woman of Bath to Margery Kempe.

SUPPORT FOR LEP STUDENTS

ADDITIONAL VOCABULARY

The Woman of Bath

parish—church district
charity—kindness toward others
forsooth—in truth
mischance—accident

The Parson

renown—fame
devoutly—with devotion, or steady religious feeling
adversity—difficulty
extort—to get by force or by illegal means
stave—a staff or cane
contemptuous—looking down upon
disdainful—showing distaste for
obstinate—stubborn
rebuke—blaming or scolding
pomp—fancy show or display

LITERARY NOTE

Students may be interested in the types of stories told by the pilgrims. The following list briefly outlines the twenty-four stories. Interaction between characters continues between and within the stories. Students may find it interesting that several of the tales are told to get the goat of other pilgrims or in retort to another story.

Knight—a courtly romance based on Boccaccio's *Teseida*

Miller—a humorous story of love and deception

Reeve—a fabliau in retort to the tale told by the Miller

Cook—a fragment of another fabliau

(cont.)

---

worthy *woman* from beside Bath city
Was with us, somewhat deaf, which was a pity.
In making cloth she showed so great a bent
She bettered those of Ypres and of Ghent.[39]
In all the parish not a dame dared stir
460   Toward the altar steps in front of her,
And if indeed they did, so wrath was she
As to be quite put out of charity.
Her kerchiefs were of finely woven ground;[40]
I dared have sworn they weighed a good ten pound,
465   The ones she wore on Sunday, on her head.
Her hose were of the finest scarlet red
And gartered tight; her shoes were soft and new.
Bold was her face, handsome, and red in hue.
A worthy woman all her life, what's more
470   She'd had five husbands, all at the church door,
Apart from other company in youth;
No need just now to speak of that, forsooth.
And she had thrice been to Jerusalem,
Seen many strange rivers and passed over them;
475   She'd been to Rome and also to Boulogne,
St. James of Compostella and Cologne,
And she was skilled in wandering by the way.
She had gap-teeth, set widely, truth to say.
Easily on an <u>ambling</u> horse she sat
480   Well wimpled up,[41] and on her head a hat
As broad as is a buckler[42] or a shield;
She had a flowing mantle that concealed
Large hips, her heels spurred sharply under that.
In company she liked to laugh and chat

---

39. **Ypres . . . Ghent.** Flemish cities known for cloth-making
40. **ground.** Texture
41. **wimpled up.** Medieval women commonly wrapped their heads, and necks in a cloth called a *wimple.*

---

485   And knew the remedies for love's mischances,
An art in which she knew the oldest dances.

holy-minded man of good renown
There was, and poor, the *Parson* to a town,
Yet he was rich in holy thought and work.
490   He also was a learned man, a clerk,
Who truly knew Christ's gospel and would preach it
Devoutly to parishioners, and teach it.
Benign and wonderfully <u>diligent,</u>
And patient when adversity was sent
495   (For so he proved in much adversity)
He hated cursing to extort a fee,
Nay rather he preferred beyond a doubt
Giving to poor parishioners round about
Both from church offerings and his property;
500   He could in little find sufficiency.
Wide was his parish, with houses far <u>asunder,</u>
Yet he neglected not in rain or thunder,
In sickness or in grief, to pay a call
On the remotest, whether great or small,
505   Upon his feet, and in his hand a stave.
This noble example to his sheep he gave
That first he wrought, and afterwards he taught;
And it was from the Gospel he had caught
Those words, and he would add this figure too,
510   That if gold rust, what then will iron do?
For if a priest be foul in whom we trust
No wonder that a common man should rust;
And shame it is to see—let priests take stock—
A shitten shepherd and a snowy flock.

---

42. **buckler.** Small shield

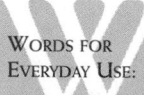

WORDS FOR EVERYDAY USE:

am • bling (am´bliŋ) *adj.,* in an easy and smooth manner

dil • i • gent (dil´ə jənt) *adj.,* hard-working; persevering

a • sun • der (ə sun´dər) *adj.,* apart or separate in direction

---

LITERARY NOTE (CONT.)

Sergeant at the Law—the story of the Christian Constance who is married to a sultan; a common story in medieval times

Woman of Bath—the story of the "loathly lady" is another tale of a knight's quest

Friar—a story of a summoner and the devil who agree to split whatever they are given

Summoner—a retort to the Friar's story in which a friar is to divide a deathbed legacy

Clerk—another story based on Boccaccio, this is the story of patient Griselda and her trials

Merchant—a story of a December/May, or in this case January/May, romance that is prone to infidelity

(cont.)

515 The true example that a priest should give
Is one of cleanness, how the sheep should
live.
He did not set his benefice[43] to hire
And leave his sheep <u>encumbered</u> in the <u>mire</u>
Or run to London to earn easy bread
520 By singing masses for the wealthy dead,
Or find some Brotherhood and get enrolled.
He stayed at home and watched over his fold
So that no wolf should make the sheep mis-
carry.
He was a shepherd and no mercenary.
525 Holy and virtuous he was, but then
Never contemptuous of sinful men,
Never disdainful, never too proud or fine,
But was discreet in teaching and benign.
His business was to show a fair behavior
530 And draw men thus to Heaven and their
Savior,
Unless indeed a man were obstinate;
And such, whether of high or low estate,
He put to sharp rebuke, to say the least.
I think there never was a better priest.
535 He sought no pomp or glory in his dealings,
No <u>scrupulosity</u> had spiced his feelings.
Christ and His Twelve Apostles and their lore
He taught, but followed it himself before.

here was a *Plowman* with him there, his
brother;
Many a load of dung one time or other
He must have carted through the morning
dew.
He was an honest worker, good and true,
Living in peace and perfect charity,

And, as the gospel bade him, so did he,
545 Loving God best with all his heart and mind
And then his neighbor as himself, repined
At no misfortune, slacked for no content,
For steadily about his work he went
To thrash his corn, to dig or to manure
550 Or make a ditch; and he would help the
poor
For love of Christ and never take a penny
If he could help it, and, as prompt as any,
He paid his tithes in full when they were due
On what he owned, and on his earnings too.
555 He wore a tabard smock[44] and rode a mare.

here was a *Reeve*,[45] also a *Miller*, there,
A College *Manciple*[46] from the Inns of
Court,
A papal *Pardoner*[47] and, in close consort,[48]
A Church-Court *Summoner*,[49] riding at a trot
560 And finally myself—that was the lot.

he *Miller* was a chap of sixteen stone,[50]
A great stout fellow big in brawn and
bone.
He did well out of them, for he could go
And win the ram[51] at any wrestling show.
565 Broad, knotty and short-shouldered, he
would boast
He could heave any door off hinge and post,
Or take a run and break it with his head.
His beard, like any sow or fox, was red
And broad as well, as though it were a spade;
570 And, at its very tip, his nose displayed
A wart on which there stood a tuft of hair
Red as the bristles in an old sow's ear.

---

43. **benefice.** Endowed office
44. **tabard smock.** Loose jacket, sometimes bearing a lord's crest
45. *Reeve.* The overseer of an estate
46. *Manciple.* Purchasing agent
47. *Pardoner.* A person with authority from the Pope to sell pardons
and indulgences

48. **consort.** Partnership
49. *Summoner.* An employee of the ecclesiastical court who was paid
to summon those who were suspected of breaking church law
50. **stone.** A unit of weight equal to fourteen pounds
51. **win the ram.** Rams were the usual prize at the popular wrestling
tournaments.

WORDS FOR EVERYDAY USE:
en • cum • bered (en kum´bərd) *part.*, held back
mire (mīr) *n.*, soggy ground
scru • pu • los • i • ty (skrōō pyōō lôs´ i tē) *n.*, moral worry or
qualm

VOCABULARY IN CONTEXT

- After having to dash through his backyard on a rainy Thursday, Aaron was happy <u>ambling</u> about in the sun on Friday.
- Unlike Laura, who seldom does her homework or studies for tests, Lucy is a <u>diligent</u> student.
- After sharing a room for many years, Lisa and her sister found it difficult to be so far <u>asunder</u> once Lisa had left for the navy.
- The heavy backpacks, filled with supplies, <u>encumbered</u> the hikers.
- After heavy rain, the dirt road, once firm, turned into a track of impossible <u>mire</u>.
- Pickpockets at races and fairs hold no <u>scrupulosity</u> about taking what belongs to others.

📖 **ADDITIONAL VOCABULARY**

The Manciple

illiterate—unable to read
stewards—protectors; guardians

The Reeve

choleric—quick-tempered
heath—area of open wasteland
cavalcade—a group riding or
    traveling one behind the other

His nostrils were as black as they were wide.
He had a sword and buckler at his side,
575 His mighty mouth was like a furnace door.
A wrangler[52] and buffoon, he had a store
Of tavern stories, filthy in the main.
His was a master-hand at stealing grain.
He felt it with his thumb and thus he knew
580 Its quality and took three times his due—[53]
A thumb of gold, by God, to gauge an oat!
He wore a hood of blue and a white coat.
He liked to play his bagpipes up and down
And that was how he brought us out of town.

he *Manciple* came from the Inner
    Temple;
    All caterers might follow his example
In buying victuals; he was never rash
Whether he bought on credit or paid cash.
He used to watch the market most precisely
590 And got in first, and so he did quite nicely.
Now isn't it a marvel of God's grace
That an illiterate fellow can outpace
The wisdom of a heap of learned men?
His masters—he had more than thirty then—
595 All versed in the <u>abstrusest</u> legal knowledge,
Could have produced a dozen from their
    College
Fit to be stewards in land and rents and game
To any Peer in England you could name,
And show him how to live on what he had
600 Debt-free (unless of course the Peer were
    mad)
Or be as <u>frugal</u> as he might desire,
And make them fit to help about the Shire
In any legal case there was to try;
And yet this Manciple could wipe their eye.

he *Reeve* was old and choleric and thin;
    His beard was shaven closely to the skin,
    His shorn hair came abruptly to a stop
Above his ears, and he was docked[54] on top
Just like a priest in front; his legs were lean,
610 Like sticks they were, no calf was to be seen.
He kept his bins and garners[55] very trim;
No auditor could gain a point on him.
And he could judge by watching drought and
    rain
The yield he might expect from seed and
    grain.
615 His master's sheep, his animals and hens,
Pigs, horses, dairies, stores and cattle-pens
Were wholly trusted to his government,
He had been under contract to present
The accounts, right from his master's earliest
    years.
620 No one had ever caught him in arrears.
No bailiff, serf or herdsman dared to kick,
He knew their dodges, knew their every trick;
Feared like the plague he was, by those
    beneath.
He had a lovely dwelling on a heath,
625 Shadowed in green by trees above the <u>sward</u>.
A better hand at bargains than his lord,
He had grown rich and had a store of treas-
    ure
Well tucked away, yet out it came to pleasure
His lord with subtle loans or gifts of goods,
630 To earn his thanks and even coats and hoods.
When young he'd learnt a useful trade and
    still
He was a carpenter of first-rate skill.
The stallion-cob he rode at a slow trot
Was dapple-grey and bore the name of Scot.

---

52. **wrangler.** One who provokes arguments
53. **three . . . due.** Took for himself more than the lawful percentage
54. **docked.** Trimmed
55. **garners.** Granaries

WORDS FOR EVERYDAY USE:

ab • strus • est (ab strōōs´ əst) *adj.,* most difficult to understand
fru • gal (frōō´gəl) *adj.,* thrifty
sward (swôrd) *n.,* grass-covered soil

📖 **VOCABULARY IN CONTEXT**

- Because of the complex vocabulary the math teacher always used, many students found him the <u>abstrusest</u> of all their instructors.
- Unlike Gina, who spends her paycheck within a few days, Reneé is <u>frugal</u> with her money.
- After many days in the desert, the travelers reached more fertile land, a <u>sward</u> perfect for tillage.
- Although the room was crowded, Frank lay <u>splayed</u> across the sofa, refusing to let others have a seat.
- After a lifetime of <u>duress</u> in a dark dungeon, the former prisoner rejoiced in the light of the outside world.

635 He wore an overcoat of bluish shade
And rather long; he had a rusty blade
Slung at his side. He came, as I heard tell,
From Norfolk, near a place called Baldeswell.
His coat was tucked under his belt and
<u>splayed</u>.
640 He rode the hindmost of our cavalcade.

here was a *Summoner* with us at that Inn,
His face on fire, like a cherubin,[56]
For he had carbuncles.[57] His eyes were
narrow,
He was as hot and lecherous as a sparrow.
645 Black scabby brows he had, and a thin beard.
Children were afraid when he appeared.
No quicksilver, lead ointment, tartar creams,
No brimstone, no boracic, so it seems,
Could make a salve that had the power to
bite,
650 Clean up or cure his whelks[58] of knobby
white
Or purge the pimples sitting on his cheeks.
Garlic he loved, and onions too, and leeks,
And drinking strong red wine till all was hazy.
Then he would shout and jabber as if crazy,
655 And wouldn't speak a word except in Latin
When he was drunk, such tags as he was pat
in;
He only had a few, say two or three,
That he had mugged up out of some
decree;[59]
No wonder, for he heard them every day.
660 And, as you know, a man can teach a jay
To call out 'Walter' better than the Pope.
But had you tried to test his wits and grope

For more, you'd have found nothing in the
bag.
Then '*Questio quid juris*'[60] was his tag.
665 He was a noble varlet[61] and a kind one,
You'd meet none better if you went to find
one.
Why, he'd allow—just for a quart of wine—
Any good lad to keep a concubine
A twelvemonth and dispense him altogether!
670 And he had finches of his own to feather:
And if he found some rascal with a maid
He would instruct him not to be afraid
In such a case of the Archdeacon's curse
(Unless the rascal's soul were in his purse)
675 For in his purse the punishment should be.
'Purse is the good Archdeacon's Hell,' said he.
But well I know he lied in what he said;
A curse should put a guilty man in dread,
For curses kill, as shriving[62] brings, salvation.
680 We should beware of excommunication.
Thus, as he pleased, the man could bring
<u>duress</u>
On any young fellow in the diocese.
He knew their secrets, they did what he said.
He wore a garland set upon his head
685 Large as the holly-bush upon a stake
Outside an ale-house, and he had a cake,
A round one, which it was his joke to wield
As if it were intended for a shield.

e and a gentle *Pardoner* rode together,
A bird from Charing Cross of the same
feather,
Just back from visiting the Court of Rome.
He loudly sang '*Come hither, love, come home!*'

---

56. **cherubin.** Cherubs are often depicted with red faces.
57; 58. **carbuncles; whelks.** Pus-filled boils
59. **he had . . . decree.** He had hurriedly studied when a new law
required it.

60. *Questio quid juris.* A common phrase in ecclesiastical courts,
Latin for "What point of law does this involve?"
61. **varlet.** Rascal
62. **shriving.** Confessing

WORDS FOR EVERYDAY USE:
splay (splā) *vt.*, spread out
du • ress (d o͞o res´) *n.*, constraint by threat

ADDITIONAL VOCABULARY

Conclusion of "The Prologue"

hostelry—inn; hotel
girth—distance around
burgess—citizen or freeman
entreaty—pleading; begging
unanimously—in complete
    agreement; all agreed
evensong—song sung or prayers
    said in the evening
matins—song sung or prayers said
    in the morning
decree—official decision or order

**ADDITIONAL QUESTIONS
AND ACTIVITIES**

• Ask students to identify the narrator.

• What does the narrator ask of
the reader?

• What reasons might each pilgrim have for undertaking this
journey?

'The Summoner sang deep seconds to this
        song,
    No trumpet ever sounded half so strong.
695 This Pardoner had hair as yellow as wax,
    Hanging down smoothly like a hank of <u>flax</u>.
    In driblets fell his locks behind his head
    Down to his shoulders which they over-
        spread;
    Thinly they fell, like rat-tails, one by one.
700 He wore no hood upon his head, for fun;
    The hood inside his wallet[63] had been
        stowed,
    He aimed at riding in the latest mode;
    But for a little cap his head was bare
    And he had bulging eye-balls, like a hare.
705 He'd sewed a holy relic on his cap;
    His wallet lay before him on his lap,
    Brimful of pardons come from Rome, all hot.
    He had the same small voice a goat has got.
    His chin no beard had harbored, nor would
        harbor,
710 Smoother than ever chin was left by barber.
    I judge he was a gelding, or a mare.
    As to his trade, from Berwick down to Ware
    There was no pardoner of equal grace,
    For in his trunk he had a pillow-case
715 Which he asserted was Our Lady's veil.
    He said he had a gobbet[64] of the sail
    Saint Peter had the time when he made bold
    To walk the waves, till Jesu Christ took hold.
    He had a cross of metal set with stones
720 And, in a glass, a rubble of pigs' bones.
    And with these relics, any time he found
    Some poor up-country parson to astound,
    In one short day, in money down, he drew
    More than the parson in a month or two,
725 And by his flatteries and <u>prevarication</u>
    Made monkeys of the priest and congregation.

But still to do him justice first and last
    In church he was a noble ecclesiast.
    How well he read a lesson or told a story!
730 But best of all he sang an Offertory,
    For well he knew that when that song was
        sung
    He'd have to preach and tune his
        honey-tongue
    And (well he could) win silver from the crowd.
    That's why he sang so merrily and loud.

ow I have told you shortly, in a clause,
    The rank, the array, the number and the
        cause
    Of our assembly in this company
    In Southwark, at that high-class hostelry
    Known as *The Tabard*, close beside *The Bell*.
740 And now the time has come for me to tell
    How we behaved that evening; I'll begin
    After we had alighted at the Inn,
    Then I'll report our journey, stage by stage,
    All the remainder of our pilgrimage.
745 But first I beg of you, in courtesy,
    Not to condemn me as unmannerly
    If I speak plainly and with no concealings
    And give account of all their words and deal-
        ings,
    Using their very phrases as they fell.
750 For certainly, as you all know so well,
    He who repeats a tale after a man
    Is bound to say, as nearly as he can,
    Each single word, if he remembers it,
    However rudely spoken or unfit,
755 Or else the tale he tells will be untrue,
    The things pretended and the phrases new.
    He may not flinch although it were his
        brother,
    He may as well say one word as another.

63. **wallet.** Knapsack
64. **gobbet.** Bit, fragment

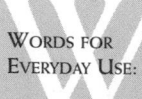

WORDS FOR
EVERYDAY USE:

flax (flaks) *adj.,* pale-yellow plant used to make linen
pre • var • i • ca • tion (pri var´i kā shən) *n.,* lie

VOCABULARY IN CONTEXT

• The golden <u>flax</u> that the weavers spun into cloth always reminded Tim of his mother's blond hair.

• Adam was so honest that everyone believed even his strangest tales, but everyone knew that John
just liked to tell <u>prevarications</u>.

• Everyone in church was shocked when Tim stubbed his toe and used some <u>scurrility</u> in his speech.

And Christ Himself spoke broad in Holy
    Writ,
760 Yet there is no <u>scurrility</u> in it,
    And Plato says, for those with power to read,
    'The word should be as cousin to the deed.'
    Further I beg you to forgive it me
    If I neglect the order and degree
765 And what is due to rank in what I've planned.
    I'm short of wit as you will understand.

 ur *Host* gave us great welcome; everyone
    Was given a place and supper was begun.
    He served the finest victuals[65] you could
      think,
770 The wine was strong and we were glad to
      drink.
    A very striking man our Host withal,
    And fit to be a marshal in a hall.
    His eyes were bright, his girth a little wide;
    There is no finer burgess in Cheapside.[66]
775 Bold in his speech, yet wise and full of tact,
    There was no manly attribute he lacked,
    What's more he was a merry-hearted man.
    After our meal he jokingly began
    To talk of sport, and, among other things
780 After we'd settled up our reckonings,
    He said as follows: 'Truly, gentlemen,
    You're very welcome and I can't think when
    —Upon my word I'm telling you no lie—
    I've seen a gathering here that looked so spry,
785 No, not this year, as in this tavern now.
    I'd think you up some fun if I knew how.
    And, as it happens, a thought has just
      occurred
    To please you, costing nothing, on my word.
    You're off to Canterbury—well, God speed!
790 Blessed St. Thomas answer to your need!

And I don't doubt, before the journey's done
You mean to while the time in tales and fun.
Indeed, there's little pleasure for your bones
Riding along and all as dumb as stones.
795 So let me then propose for your enjoyment,
    Just as I said, a suitable employment.
    And if my notion suits and you agree
    And promise to submit yourselves to me
    Playing your parts exactly as I say
800 Tomorrow as you ride along the way,
    Then by my father's soul (and he is dead)
    If you don't like it you can have my head!
    Hold up your hands, and not another word.'
      Well, our opinion was not long deferred,
805 It seemed not worth a serious debate;
    We all agreed to it at any rate
    And bade him issue what commands he
      would.
    'My lords,' he said, 'now listen for your good,
    And please don't treat my notion with dis-
      dain.
810 This is the point. I'll make it short and plain.
    Each one of you shall help to make things slip
    By telling two stories on the outward trip
    To Canterbury, that's what I intend,
    And, on the homeward way to journey's end
815 Another two, tales from the days of old;
    And then the man whose story is best told,
    That is to say who gives the fullest measure
    Of good morality and general pleasure,
    He shall be given a supper, paid by all,
820 Here in this tavern, in this very hall,
    When we come back again from Canterbury.
    And in the hope to keep you bright and
      merry
    I'll go along with you myself and ride
    All at my own expense and serve as guide.

---

65. **victuals.** Prepared foods
66. **Cheapside.** A section of London, the site of a marketplace in
Chaucer's day

**WORDS FOR
EVERYDAY USE:**   **scur • ril • i • ty** (skə ril´ə tē) *n.,* coarseness or indecency of
language

**ADDITIONAL QUESTIONS
AND ACTIVITIES**

  Who is the last character
introduced? What role does he
play in the story?

LITERARY NOTE

  In the introduction to "The
Prologue," Chaucer says that
twenty-nine pilgrims arrive at the
hostelry. Students might note that
there are actually thirty-one
pilgrims mentioned. Another
pilgrim, the Canon's Yeoman, joins
the pilgrimage and tells a tale.
These inconsistencies may be due
to the fact that the tales were
written over a long period of time
and were never finished.

825   I'll be the judge, and those who won't obey
Shall pay for what we spend upon the way.
Now if you all agree to what you've heard
Tell me at once without another word,
And I will make arrangements early for it.'

830   Of course we all agreed, in fact we swore it
Delightedly, and made entreaty too
That he should act as he proposed to do,
Become our Governor in short, and be
Judge of our tales and general referee,

835   And set the supper at a certain price.
We promised to be ruled by his advice
Come high, come low; unanimously thus
We set him up in judgment over us.
More wine was fetched, the business being done;

840   We drank it off and up went everyone
To bed without a moment of delay.
        Early next morning at the spring of day
Up rose our Host and roused us like a cock,
Gathering us together in a flock,

845   And off we rode at slightly faster pace
Than walking to St. Thomas' watering-place;[67]
And there our Host drew up, began to ease
His horse, and said, 'Now, listen if you please,
My lords! Remember what you promised me.

850   If evensong and matins will agree
Let's see who shall be first to tell a tale.
And as I hope to drink good wine and ale

I'll be your judge. The rebel who disobeys,
However much the journey costs, he pays.

855   Now draw for cut and then we can depart;
The man who draws the shortest cut shall start.
'My Lord the Knight,' he said, 'step up to me
And draw your cut, for that is my decree.
And come you near, my Lady Prioress,

860   And you, Sir Cleric, drop your shamefastness,[68]
No studying now! A hand from every man!'
Immediately the draw for lots began
And to tell shortly how the matter went,
Whether by chance or fate or accident,

865   The truth is this, the cut fell to the Knight,[69]
Which everybody greeted with delight.
And tell his tale he must, as reason was
Because of our agreement and because
He too had sworn. What more is there to say?

870   For when this good man saw how matters lay,
Being by wisdom and obedience driven
To keep a promise he had freely given,
He said, 'Since it's for me to start the game,
Why, welcome be the cut in God's good name!

875   Now let us ride, and listen to what I say.'
And at the word we started on our way
And in a cheerful style he then began
At once to tell his tale, and thus it ran. ∎

---

67. **St. Thomas' watering-place.** A brook crossed by the road to Canterbury two miles from London
68. **shamefastness.** Shyness

69. **Whether . . . Knight.** Chance, fate, and accident play a large role in the Knight's tale. It is fitting that he begin the storytelling for the same reason that he is described first, namely, because of his rank in society.

Responding to the Selection

Imagine that you are on this pilgrimage. Which of the other pilgrims would you want to get to know better? Whom would you try to avoid? Write about your thoughts in your journal. You might even imagine a conversation between yourself and one of Chaucer's characters.

Reviewing the Selection

RECALLING

1. Which three characters are introduced first? Why are they introduced first?

2. Which of the pilgrims are affiliated with the church? Which are laborers? Which are "professionals"? Which are of the aristocracy?

3. In what group does the narrator place himself?

4. What explanation does the narrator make between introducing all of the pilgrims and introducing the host? What does the host suggest?

INTERPRETING

5. Why is the Knight considered "worthy"? What are his accomplishments? What honors has he received? What values does he represent?

6. What makes the Parson a "good man" of religion? How does he compare with the other religious figures on the trip?

7. How would you characterize this group of pilgrims as a whole? Does the narrator belong here? Why, or why not?

8. Do you think the narrrator is trustworthy? Why, or why not? Do you agree with what the narrator says about a true recounting? Explain your answer.

SYNTHESIZING

9. What does "The Prologue" to *The Canterbury Tales* tell you about the commonly held values of Chaucer's time? Who was considered important in the social order? Why might that have been?

10. If you were writing a contemporary version of *The Canterbury Tales,* would any of the characters be the same? Whom might you leave out? What additional characters would you include? Explain your decisions.

See the evaluation forms for writing, revising, and proofreading, *Assessment Portfolio, 7.1–7.10. Responses will vary. Possible responses are given.*

1. Frame Tale. The story of the pilgrimage and the story contest suggested by the host provide the vehicle for the other stories. The characters will tell their own stories. The story contest makes the variety of narrators possible. The narrator introduces the characters and the frame.

2. Satire. Chaucer satirizes many of his characters, especially the church figures, such as the Nun, the Monk, and the Friar. He points out the Nun's overzealous manners, her oversentimentality, and her attention to her appearance. He shows that the Monk does not lead the life prescribed by the church, nor does the Friar, who spends his time in taverns and in winning the attention of young women.

3. Characterization. Answers will vary based on the character the student chooses.

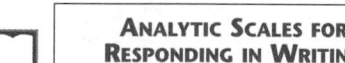

ANALYTIC SCALES FOR RESPONDING IN WRITING

Assign a score from 1 to 25 for each grading criterion below. (For more detailed evaluation, see the evaluation forms for writing, revising, and proofreading, *Assessment Portfolio, 7.1–7.10.*)

1. Character Sketch

• **Content/Unity.** The paragraph identifies and describes a character.

• **Organization/Coherence.** The paragraph clearly identifies the character and adds supporting details in a sensible order.

• **Language/Style.** The paragraph uses vivid and precise nouns, verbs, and modifiers.

• **Conventions.** The paragraph avoids errors in spelling, grammar, usage, mechanics, and manuscript form. (cont.)

Understanding Literature (Questions for Discussion)

1. **Frame Tale.** A **frame tale** is a story that itself provides a vehicle for the telling of other stories. What is the basic story that provides the setting for *The Canterbury Tales?* Who is telling the stories? How is it made plausible that all these characters tell stories? What role does the narrator play?

2. **Satire. Satire** is humorous writing or speech intended to point out errors, falsehoods, foibles, or failings. Whom does Chaucer satirize? What failings does he point out?

3. **Characterization. Characterization** is the use of literary techniques to create a character. In "The Prologue," Chaucer makes use of **direct description,** in which a narrator or speaker comments on the character, telling the reader about such matters as the character's appearance, habits, dress, background, personality, motivations, and so on. Choose one character introduced in "The Prologue" and examine Chaucer's method of characterization. What types of details does Chaucer give about this character? What do you learn about the character aside from what is directly described?

Responding in Writing

1. **Character Sketch.** The bulk of "The Prologue" consists of brief but effective character sketches. An effective character sketch includes the most striking aspects of the character's appearance, personality, and background. Try to write a character sketch based on your observations from the Reader's Journal exercise. Use this as a starting point, but feel free to embellish what you observed or to create the things you don't know. Identify your character's quirks or habits. What does your character care about most? How would your character react in a given situation? How do you feel about this character?

2. **Interviewing.** Pretend you are a reporter interviewing one of the pilgrims on the way to Canterbury. Choose a particular focus, perhaps an exposé of the Pardoner and his false relics, or a society column on the Squire. Make a list of who, what, when, where, why, how, and "what if" questions. Conduct an imaginary interview with the character or characters you chose. Then use the information from your interview in a short article.

ANALYTIC SCALES FOR RESPONDING IN WRITING (CONT.)

2. Interviewing

• **Content/Unity.** The article focuses on an aspect of a character, revealing relevant information.

• **Organization/Coherence.** The article clearly identifies a character and adds supporting details in a sensible order.

• **Language/Style.** The article uses vivid and precise nouns, verbs, and modifiers.

• **Conventions.** The article avoids errors in spelling, grammar, usage, mechanics, and manuscript form.

▶ Additional practice is provided in the *Essential Skills Practice Book: Writing,* 1.27.

READER'S JOURNAL

Freewrite about a character flaw such as greed, pride, envy, or stubbornness. You might choose a flaw you see in yourself or one you see in somebody else. Think about what problems this flaw might cause for the person who has it and for others.

READING SKILLS

Read the Language Arts Survey, 4.17, "Previewing Your Reading." Then review the section of "The Prologue" that describes the Pardoner. Keep this in mind as you read this selection, "The Pardoner's Tale."

FROM *THE CANTERBURY TALES*

FROM

"The Pardoner's Tale"

GEOFFREY CHAUCER, TRANS. BY NEVILL COGHILL

t's of three rioters I have to tell
Who, long before the morning service bell,
Were sitting in a tavern for a drink.
And as they sat, they heard the hand-bell clink
5 Before a coffin going to the grave;
One of them called the little tavern-knave
And said 'Go and find out at once—look spry!—
Whose corpse is in that coffin passing by;
And see you get the name correctly too.'
10 'Sir,' said the boy, 'no need, I promise you;
Two hours before you came here I was told.
He was a friend of yours in days of old,
And suddenly, last night, the man was slain,
Upon his bench, face up, dead drunk again.
15 There came a privy thief, they call him Death,
Who kills us all round here, and in a breath
He speared him through the heart, he never stirred.

And then Death went his way without a word.
He's killed a thousand in the present plague,
20 And, sir, it doesn't do to be too vague
If you should meet him; you had best be <u>wary</u>.
Be on your guard with such an adversary,
Be primed to meet him everywhere you go,
That's what my mother said. It's all I know.'
25 The publican joined in with, 'By St. Mary,
What the child says is right; you'd best be wary,
This very year he killed, in a large village
A mile away, man, woman, serf at <u>tillage</u>,
Page in the household, children—all there were.
30 Yes, I imagine that he lives round there.
It's well to be prepared in these alarms,
He might do you dishonor.' 'Huh, God's arms!'
The rioter said, 'Is he so fierce to meet?
I'll search for him, by Jesus, street by street.

WORDS FOR EVERYDAY USE:

war • y (wer´ē) *adj.,* cautious
till • age (til´ij) *n.,* land that is tilled for farming

PREREADING NOTES

READER'S JOURNAL

Students should think of the possible effects of a character flaw.

READING SKILLS

Students can review lines 689–734 of "The Prologue" and compare the Pardoner's avarice to that of the three rioters.

SUPPORT FOR LEP STUDENTS

Explain to students that death is personified, or treated as a character, in this story.

ADDITIONAL VOCABULARY

spry—full of life
slain—past tense of slay, kill
privy—secret; sneaky
page—servant
vow—promise; oath

VOCABULARY IN CONTEXT

- He stopped at the crosswalk and looked both ways because he had always been told to be <u>wary</u> when crossing the street.
- There are no rocks or tree stumps in Farmer Brown's land; it is good <u>tillage</u> for planting.

**ADDITIONAL QUESTIONS
AND ACTIVITIES**

Have students make wanted
posters for the killer Death. They
should include a picture, a physical
description, and a list of crimes
and accomplices.

35 God's blessed bones! I'll register a vow!
    Here chaps! The three of us together now,
    Hold up your hands, like me, and we'll be
        brothers
    In this affair, and each defend the others,
    And we will kill this traitor Death, I say!
40 Away with him as he has made away
    With all our friends. God's dignity! Tonight!'
        They made their bargain, swore with
            appetite,
    These three, to live and die for one another
    As brother-born might swear to his born
        brother.
45 And up they started in their drunken rage
    And made towards this village which the page
    And publican had spoken of before.
    Many and <u>grisly</u> were the oaths they swore,
    Tearing Christ's blessed body to a shred;
50 'If we can only catch him, Death is dead!'
        When they had gone not fully half a mile,
    Just as they were about to cross a <u>stile</u>,
    They came upon a very poor old man
    Who humbly greeted them and thus began,
55 'God look to you, my lords, and give you
        quiet!'
    To which the proudest of these men of riot
    Gave back the answer, 'What, old fool? Give
        place!
    Why are you all wrapped up except your face?
    Why live so long? Isn't it time to die?'
60 The old, old fellow looked him in the eye
    And said, 'Because I never yet have found,
    Though I have walked to India, searching
        round
    Village and city on my pilgrimage,
    One who would change his youth to have my
        age.
65 And so my age is mine and must be still
    Upon me, for such time as God may will.
        'Not even Death, alas, will take my life;

    So, like a wretched prisoner at <u>strife</u>
    Within himself, I walk alone and wait
70 About the earth, which is my mother's gate,
    Knock-knocking with my staff from night to
        noon
    And crying, "Mother, open to me soon!
    Look at me, mother, won't you let me in?
    See how I wither, flesh and blood and skin!
75 Alas! When will these bones be laid to rest?
    Mother, I would exchange—for that were
        best—
    The wardrobe in my chamber, standing there
    So long, for yours! Aye, for a shirt of hair
    To wrap me in!" She has refused her grace,
80 Whence comes the pallor of my withered face
        'But it dishonored you when you began
    To speak so roughly, sir, to an old man,
    Unless he had injured you in word or deed.
    It says in holy writ, as you may read,
85 "Thou shalt rise up before the <u>hoary</u> head
    And honor it." And therefore be it said
    "Do no more harm to an old man than you,
    Being now young, would have another do
    When you are old"—if you should live till
        then.
90 And so may God be with you, gentlemen,
    For I must go whither I have to go.'
        'By God,' the gambler said, 'you shan't do
            so,
    You don't get off so easy, by St. John!
    I heard you mention, just a moment gone,
95 A certain traitor Death who singles out
    And kills the fine young fellows hereabout.
    And you're his spy, by God! You wait a bit.
    Say where he is or you shall pay for it,
    By God and by the Holy Sacrament!
100 I say you've joined together by consent
    To kill us younger folk, you thieving swine!'
        'Well, sirs,' he said, 'if it be your design
    To find out Death, turn up this crooked way

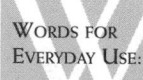

WORDS FOR
EVERYDAY USE:

gris • ly (griz´lē) *adj.,* horrible, terrifying
stile (stīl) *n.,* steps used to climb over a wall
strife (strīf) *n.,* conflict, struggle
hoar • y (hôr´ē) *adj.,* white- or gray-haired

VOCABULARY IN CONTEXT

- The violent murder scene in the horror movie was particularly <u>grisly</u>.
- If the steep stone wall did not have a <u>stile</u>, it would be an effective barrier.
- There seldom was peace between the two countries; they were in a constant state of bitter <u>strife</u>.
- His beard had faded long ago from a lustrous black to a <u>hoary</u> gray.
- Unlike George, who was often silent and only spoke judiciously, Henry was constantly <u>prating</u>.

Toward that grove, I left him there today
105 Under a tree, and there you'll find him
     waiting.
He isn't one to hide for all your <u>prating</u>.
You see that oak? He won't be far to find.
And God protect you that redeemed mankind,
Aye, and amend you!' Thus that ancient man.
110   At once the three young rioters began
To run, and reached the tree, and there they
     found
A pile of golden florins[1] on the ground,
New-coined, eight bushels of them as they
     thought.
No longer was it Death those fellows sought,
115 For they were all so thrilled to see the sight,
The florins were so beautiful and bright,
That down they sat beside the precious pile.
The wickedest spoke first after a while.
'Brothers,' he said, 'you listen to what I say.
120 I'm pretty sharp although I joke away.
It's clear that Fortune has bestowed this
     treasure
To let us live in jollity and pleasure.
Light come, light go! We'll spend it as we
     ought.
God's precious dignity! Who would have
     thought
125 This morning was to be our lucky day?
   'If one could only get the gold away,
Back to my house, or else to yours, perhaps—
For as you know, the gold is ours, chaps—
We'd all be at the top of fortune, hey?
130 But certainly it can't be done by day.
People would call us robbers—a strong gang,
So our own property would make us hang.
No, we must bring this treasure back by night
Some prudent way, and keep it out of sight.
135 And so as a solution I propose
We draw for lots and see the way it goes;

The one who draws the longest, lucky man,
Shall run to town as quickly as he can
To fetch us bread and wine—but keep things
     dark—
140 While two remain in hiding here to mark
Our heap of treasure. If there's no delay,
When night comes down we'll carry it away,
All three of us, wherever we have planned.'
   He gathered lots and hid them in his hand
145 Bidding them draw for where the luck should
     fall.
It fell upon the youngest of them all,
And off he ran at once toward the town.
   As soon as he had gone the first sat down
And thus began a parley with the other:
150 'You know that you can trust me as a brother;
Now let me tell you where your profit lies;
You know our friend has gone to get supplies
And here's a lot of gold that is to be
Divided equally amongst us three.
155 Nevertheless, if I could shape things thus
So that we shared it out—the two of us—
Wouldn't you take it as a friendly act?'
'But how?' the other said. 'He knows the fact
That all the gold was left with me and you;
160 What can we tell him? What are we to do?'
   'Is it a bargain,' said the first, 'or no?
For I can tell you in a word or so
What's to be done to bring the thing about.'
'Trust me,' the other said, 'you needn't doubt
165 My word. I won't betray you, I'll be true.'
   'Well,' said his friend, 'you see that we are
     two,
And two are twice as powerful as one.
Now look; when he comes back, get up in fun
To have a wrestle; then, as you attack,
170 I'll up and put my dagger through his back
While you and he are struggling, as in game;
Then draw your dagger too and do the same.

---

1. **florins.** Gold coins

WORDS FOR
EVERYDAY USE:
    prat • ing (prăt´ĭŋ) *ger.*, chattering

Then all this money will be ours to spend,
Divided equally of course, dear friend.
175 Then we can gratify our lusts and fill
The day with dicing[2] at our own sweet will.'
Thus these two <u>miscreants</u> agreed to slay
The third and youngest, as you heard me say.
    The youngest, as he ran towards the
        town,
180 Kept turning over, rolling up and down
Within his heart the beauty of those bright
New florins, saying, 'Lord, to think I might
Have all that treasure to myself alone!
Could there be anyone beneath the throne
185 Of God so happy as I then should be?'
    And so the Fiend, our common enemy,
Was given power to put it in his thought
That there was always poison to be bought,
And that with poison he could kill his friends.
190 To men in such a state the Devil sends
Thoughts of this kind, and has a full
        permission
To lure them on to sorrow and <u>perdition</u>;
For this young man was utterly content
To kill them both and never to repent.
195 And on he ran, he had no thought to tarry,
Came to the town, found an apothecary
And said, 'Sell me some poison if you will,
I have a lot of rats I want to kill
And there's a polecat too about my yard
200 That takes my chickens and it hits me hard;
But I'll get even, as is only right,
With vermin that destroy a man by night.'
    The chemist answered, 'I've a preparation
Which you shall have, and by my soul's
        salvation
205 If any living creature eat or drink
A mouthful, ere he has the time to think,

---

2. **dicing.** Gambling
3. **Avicenna's long relation.** A lengthy medical book by Avicenna,
with a detailed chapter on poisons

Though he took less than makes a grain of
        wheat,
You'll see him fall down dying at your feet;
Yes, die he must, and in so short a while
210 You'd hardly have the time to walk a mile,
The poison is so strong, you understand.'
    This cursed fellow grabbed into his hand
The box of poison and away he ran
Into a neighboring street, and found a man
215 Who lent him three large bottles. He
        withdrew
And deftly poured poison into two.
He kept the third one clean, as well he might,
For his own drink, meaning to work all night
Stacking the gold and carrying it away.
220 And when this rioter, this devil's clay,
Had filled his bottles up with wine, all three,
Back to rejoin his comrades sauntered he.
    Why make a sermon of it? Why waste
        breath?
Exactly in the way they'd planned his death
225 They fell on him and slew him, two to one.
Then said the first of them when this was
        done,
'Now for a drink. Sit down and let's be merry,
For later on there'll be the corpse to bury.'
And, as it happened, reaching for a sup,
230 He took a bottle full of poison up
And drank; and his companion, nothing loth,
Drank from it also, and they perished both.
    There is, in Avicenna's long relation[3]
Concerning poison and its operation,
235 Trust me, no ghastlier section to transcend
What these two wretches suffered at their
        end.
Thus these two murderers received their due,
So did the treacherous young poisoner too. ∎

WORDS FOR
EVERYDAY USE:

mis • cre • ant (mis´ krē ənt) *n.,* evil person

per • di • tion (pər dish´ən) *n.,* loss of soul

VOCABULARY IN CONTEXT

• Because Rick performed so many malicious deeds and showed no sign of reforming, he was seen as the town's <u>miscreant</u>.

• The priest warned others against committing an act that could lead to <u>perdition</u>, thereby ruining their chances to experience heaven.

Responding to the Selection

In a group of seven to ten students, hold a mock trial of Death and his accomplice, Greed, for the murder of the three rioters. Choose group members to assume the roles of judge, members of the jury, prosecutor, defendants, and defense lawyers. After the two sides present their cases, the jury should explain its decision.

Reviewing the Selection

RECALLING

1. What do the three rioters agree to do?

2. What does the old man tell the rioters? Where do the rioters go after meeting the old man? What do they find there?

3. What do the rioters agree after making their discovery? Why do they split up?

4. How does the first rioter die? How do the others die?

INTERPRETING

5. Why do the rioters make their pact?

6. What function does the old man serve in furthering the plot? What does he seem to know that the rioters do not know? Whom or what might he represent?

7. Why do the rioters make a second agreement?

8. Why don't the rioters keep to their initial agreement? What is the moral of this story?

SYNTHESIZING

9. What character flaw do the rioters exhibit? How do their characters compare to the Pardoner's character? Why might Chaucer have the Pardoner tell this story?

10. Is a story such as this an effective teaching tool? Why, or why not? Can you think of ways to make it more effective?

Understanding Literature (Questions for Discussion)

1. **Folk Tale.** A **folk tale** is a brief story passed by word-of-mouth from generation to generation. Why might this story have been passed down? To whom might it most appeal? What is its appeal? Can you think of other folk tales about greed? Can you think of folk tales that do not teach a moral lesson?

ANSWERS FOR UNDERSTANDING LITERATURE

▶ See the evaluation forms for discussion, active listening, and oral communication, *Assessment Portfolio*, 7.11–7.14.

1. **Folk Tale.** The story was probably passed down to teach a lesson about greed. It is appealing because the moral is tied up in an interesting story and the characters seem to get what they deserve. *Answers will vary.* Another folk tale about greed is the story of the goose who laid the golden egg. (cont.)

RESPONDING TO THE SELECTION

Have the students choose a role they feel strongly about. Students without a strong opinion about the trial should be placed on the jury.

ANSWERS FOR REVIEWING THE SELECTION

RECALLING

1. The rioters agree to kill Death.

2. The old man tells them that Death is just up the way under a tree. The rioters go to the tree and find a pile of gold coins.

3. The rioters agree to divide the money three ways. They split up as part of their plan to move the money in the night.

4. The first rioter is stabbed by the other two. The others are killed by the poison the first rioter had put in their drinks.

INTERPRETING

Responses will vary. Possible responses are given.

5. The rioters agree to kill Death because Death has killed their friend.

6. The meeting with the old man sends the three rioters to Death and shows that the rioters do not respect Death. He might be Death disguised, or the Grim Reaper.

7. The rioters agree not to tell anyone of the gold that they found so that they can keep the gold. They are inspired by greed.

8. The rioters' quest to kill Death is sidetracked when they find the gold. Their own greed gets the better of them, which causes their death. The story shows the evil of greed.

SYNTHESIZING

Responses will vary. Possible responses are given.

9. The rioters are greedy. They are similar to the greedy, dishonest Pardoner. The story of greed is an appropriate one for the Pardoner to tell as part of a sermon since it serves to highlight his own character.

10. Students may say that it is not effective because the story is implausible. If so, have them suggest alterations to the story.

2. **Exemplum.** An **exemplum** (plural, *exempla*) is a brief story or *anecdote,* common in the Middle Ages, told to illustrate an idea or moral. An exemplum such as "The Pardoner's Tale" was often told as part of a sermon. What is the moral of this story? Why does the Pardoner tell it? Why is it ironic that the Pardoner is telling this story?

Responding in Writing

Tale. Try to write a **tale** in the style of Chaucer. First decide what moral you would like to teach: for example, "Greed is the root of all evil," or "Pride goes before a fall." Then create a very short story that illustrates your lesson. Think of an event or situation that supports your moral, and work backward to develop an idea of who your characters are and how they are led into the event or situation. You might personify the vice or character flaw to use as a character in your story.

Language Lab

Reducing Wordiness. Read the Language Arts Survey, 2.59, "Reducing Wordiness." Then rewrite the following sentences to make them more concise and clear.

1. Geoffrey Chaucer was a talented, skilled writer who produced a large collection of well-written works.
2. Chaucer is probably best known for his stories within a story, *The Canterbury Tales,* which is an unfinished frame tale.
3. The stories for *The Canterbury Tales* are not all original creations of Chaucer, rather they are drawn from many sources, including love poems and other writings by Boccaccio, the lives of saints, and other religious works with which Chaucer was extremely familiar, and fables that were more commonly passed by word-of-mouth than by written words.
4. The tales are not randomly assigned, but are rather well chosen to fit the variety of characters. For example, the Knight tells a tale of courtly romance, the low-life Miller tells a bawdy story that is typical of his character, and the preaching Pardoner gives a sample of one of the sermons that he typically delivered as a preacher.
5. Because of the wide variety of stories and narrators, as well as the richness of its concise summation of English society in "The Prologue," *The Canterbury Tales,* even in its unfinished state, remains a masterpiece of English literature.

Test-taking Skills

Multiple-choice Questions. Read the Language Arts Survey, 4.37, "Multiple-choice Questions." Then select the correct answers to the following:

1. Chaucer's *The Canterbury Tales*
   a. was written in Canterbury
   b. was written about a trip to Canterbury
   c. was found in Canterbury
   d. was set in Canterbury
   e. has nothing to do with Canterbury

2. The Pardoner tells a story about
   a. a tavern-knave
   b. a poor, old man
   c. two prisoners
   d. three rioters
   e. the devil

3. "The Pardoner's Tale" takes place during
   a. the winter
   b. the spring
   c. the summer
   d. the fall
   e. an unspecified season

4. The relics in the story are owned by
   a. the Knight
   b. the Pardoner
   c. an old man
   d. a young man
   e. Jesus

5. The sin that leads to the deaths at the end of the story is
   a. gluttony
   b. sloth
   c. greed
   d. envy
   e. despair

PROJECT

Storytelling Contest. Hold a storytelling contest in class. You may choose a story you have written or one that you have read or heard. Consider adding details to make the story more appealing. Practice telling your story in a way that will interest the others in your group. Pay attention to your pace and loudness, your facial expressions, where you stand, how you move about, and your arm and hand movements.

PROJECT NOTES

Storytelling Contest. Before students begin, lead a class discussion about what makes an oral story interesting. Remind them to keep these elements in mind as they prepare. Students may wish to use family stories, local tall tales, or stories of their own invention. Encourage them to use brief written notes to guide their performance.

SUPPORT FOR LEP STUDENTS

Students will find the play easier to understand if it is performed aloud. Have the play read aloud in class, or have your students listen to a recording of it.

Another way to make the play more accessible is to explain in advance the basic plot situation. Death comes to take Everyman. Everyman tries to get various characters (Strength, Beauty, etc.) to accompany him, but they refuse. In the end, only his good deeds go with him to the grave.

ADDITIONAL VOCABULARY

reverence—deep respect and awe

jollity—happiness; good times

reckoning—an account or judgment

prosperity—wealth; success

forsake—leave

pilgrimage—a journey to a holy place

tarrying—staying; delaying

VOCABULARY FROM THE SELECTION

amends   respite
caitiff   transitory
proffer

PREREADING

THE MORALITY PLAY

from *Everyman*
Anonymous

ABOUT THE AUTHOR

No author is known for *Everyman,* considered the finest example of the variety of medieval drama known as the morality play. Although no manuscript of the play has ever been found, its first printing dates to about 1530. Most scholars believe that the play was first written in Flemish and then translated into English, sometime after 1485.

ABOUT THE SELECTION

A **morality play** is a type of medieval drama in which the characters are abstract caricatures of virtues, vices, and the like. Morality plays are like dramatized sermons—they deliver a clear religious message. *Everyman* is considered the finest known medieval morality play because of its lofty poetry, its unity, its consistent and clear allegorical message, and its engaging theatricality.

GOALS/OBJECTIVES

Studying this lesson will enable students to

• empathize with the fear and losses Everyman experiences as he faces judgment and death
• define and describe the essential characteristics of medieval morality plays
• capitalize titles of works properly

• define and illustrate with appropriate examples the terms *allegory, naive allegory,* and *didacticism*
• write a sermon
• write aphorisms
• give a public reading of a speech or monologue from a play

READER'S JOURNAL

Do you believe that people are held accountable for what they did, or didn't do, while they were alive? in what way? Write your ideas in your journal.

READING SKILLS

Read the Language Arts Survey, 4.18, "Reading Actively: Predicting." As you read the selection, predict how the characters will respond to Everyman's request to accompany him on his journey.

FROM

Everyman

ANONYMOUS

CAST OF CHARACTERS

MESSENGER	KNOWLEDGE
GOD	CONFESSION
DEATH	BEAUTY
EVERYMAN	STRENGTH
FELLOWSHIP	DISCRETION
KINDRED	FIVE-WITS
COUSIN	ANGEL
GOODS	DOCTOR
GOOD DEEDS	

HERE BEGINNETH A TREATISE HOW THE HIGH FATHER OF HEAVEN SENDETH DEATH TO
SUMMON EVERY CREATURE TO COME AND GIVE ACCOUNT OF THEIR LIVES IN THIS
WORLD, AND IS IN MANNER OF A MORAL PLAY

[*Enter* MESSENGER.]
  MESSENGER. I pray you all give your audi-
    ence,
And hear this matter with reverence,
By figure[1] a moral play.

5 *The Summoning of Everyman* called it is,
That of our lives and ending shows
How <u>transitory</u> we be all day.[2]
The matter is wonder precious,
But the intent of it is more gracious

---

1. **figure.** Form

2. **all day.** Always

WORDS FOR
EVERYDAY USE: **tran • si • to • ry** (tran´sə tôr´ē) *adj.,* temporary

VOCABULARY IN CONTEXT

• The birds' stay here is only <u>transitory</u>, for they will be heading south for the winter soon.

PREREADING NOTES

READER'S JOURNAL

You may wish to have students answer these questions privately in their journals. If you do have a class discussion of these questions, make sure to preface the discussion with comments about the importance of respecting the wide variety of beliefs that people hold on these matters.

READING SKILLS

Explain that predicting is one of the most common mental activities engaged in by readers. A writer keeps a reader interested by raising questions in the reader's mind, by making the reader wonder what is going to happen next. As a reader reads, he or she continually guesses what is going to happen next. Reading on then becomes an opportunity to confirm or alter hypotheses that the reader has made. Students may make their predictions in their journals as they read. They then can retrace their reading to see how often their predictions came true.

ENRICHMENT ACTIVITIES

Have students review the selection and then prepare detailed descriptions and drawings of costumes and sets for a modern production of *Everyman.* Students can choose to do the play as a period piece, in medieval costume, or they can do it in modern costume with a modern set. (One famous production of Shakespeare's *The Taming of the Shrew* was set in Chicago in the 1920s and featured characters dressed as gangsters and flappers.) Ask students to consider how modernization of costumes and setting simultaneously throws into relief the archaic aspects of a play and, paradoxically, underscores its timelessness—the applicability of its ideas to life today.

And sweet to bear away.

10 The story saith: Man, in the beginning
Look well, and take good heed to the ending,
Be you never so gay.
You think sin in the beginning full sweet,
Which in the end causeth the soul to weep,

15 When the body lieth in clay.
Here shall you see how fellowship and jollity,
Both strength, pleasure, and beauty,
Will fade from thee as flower in May.
For ye shall hear how our Heaven-King

20 Calleth Everyman to a general reckoning.
Give audience and hear what he doth say.

[*Exit* MESSENGER.—*Enter* GOD.]

GOD.   I perceive, here in my majesty,
How that all creatures be to me unkind,[3]
Living without dread in worldly prosperity.

25 Of ghostly[4] sight the people be so blind,
Drowned in sin, they know me not for their God.
In worldly riches is all their mind:
They fear not of my righteousness the sharp rod;
My law that I showed when I for them died

30 They forget clean, and shedding of my blood red.
I hanged between two,[5] it cannot be denied:
To get them life I suffered to be dead.
I healed their feet, with thorns hurt was my head.
I could do no more than I did, truly—

35 And now I see the people do clean forsake me.
They use the seven deadly sins damnable,
As pride, coveitise, wrath, and lechery[6]

Now in the world be made commendable.
And thus they leave of angels the heavenly company.

40 Every man liveth so after his own pleasure,
And yet of their life they be nothing sure.
I see the more that I them forbear,
The worse they be from year to year:
All that liveth appaireth[7] fast.

45 Therefore I will, in all the haste,
Have a reckoning of every man's person.
For, and[8] I leave the people thus alone
In their life and wicked tempests,
Verily they will become much worse than beasts;

50 For now one would by envy another up eat.
Charity do they all clean forgeet.
I hoped well that every man
In my glory should make his mansion,
And thereto I had them all elect.[9]

55 But now I see, like traitors deject.[10]
They thank me not for the pleasure that I to[11] them meant,
Nor yet for their being that I them have lent.
I proffered the people great multitude of mercy,
And few there be that asketh it heartily.[12]

60 They be so cumbered[13] with worldly riches
That needs on them I must do justice—
On every man living without fear.
Where art thou, Death, thou mighty messenger?

[*Enter* DEATH.]

DEATH.   Almighty God, I am here at your will,

---

3. **unkind.** Thoughtless
4. **ghostly.** Spiritual
5. **I . . . two.** Christ was crucified between two thieves.
6. **seven . . . lechery.** The seven deadly sins are pride, avarice, wrath, lechery, envy, gluttony, and sloth.
7. **appaireth.** Degenerates

8. **and.** If
9. **elect.** Chosen
10. **deject.** Abased
11. **to.** For
12. **heartily.** Sincerely
13. **cumbered.** Encumbered

WORDS FOR EVERYDAY USE: prof • fer (präf´ər) *vt.*, offer

VOCABULARY IN CONTEXT

• The child proffered her hand, so I took it and led her across the street.

Le Mortet Le Boucheron. Alphonse Legros.
In the Collection of The Corcoran Gallery of Art,
Gift of E. Gerald Lamboley

ART NOTE

Alphonse Legros (1837–1911)
was a French-born British artist. He
revitalized the arts of drawing and
painting in Britain. He is best known
for his works on macabre and fantastic
themes. Here he depicts the
coming of death.

65 Your commandment to fulfill.

   GOD.   Go thou to Everyman,
And show him, in my name,
A pilgrimage he must on him take,
Which he in no wise may escape;
70 And that he bring with him a sure reckoning
Without delay or any tarrying.

   DEATH.   Lord, I will in the world go run
      over all,
And cruelly out-search both great and small.

   [*Exit* GOD.]

   Everyman will I beset that liveth beastly
75 Out of God's laws, and dreadeth not folly.
He that loveth riches I will strike with my dart,

His sight to blind, and from heaven to
      depart—[14]
Except that Almsdeeds be his good friend—
In hell for to dwell, world without end.
80 Lo, yonder I see Everyman walking:
Full little he thinketh on my coming;
His mind is on fleshly lusts and his treasure,
And great pain it shall cause him to endure
Before the Lord, Heaven-King.

   [*Enter* EVERYMAN.]

85 Everyman, stand still! Whither art thou going
Thus gaily? Hast thou thy Maker forgeet?[15]

   EVERYMAN.   Why askest thou?
Why wouldest thou weet?[16]

---

14. **depart.** Separate
15. **forgeet.** Forgotten

16. **weet.** Know

THE MORALITY PLAY / FROM EVERYMAN **215**

ADDITIONAL QUESTIONS AND ACTIVITIES

Have students compare the character of Death in *Everyman* to the character of Death in "The Pardoner's Tale." Are the characters portrayed in a similar way? How are they different? How does the reaction of other characters in relation to Death differ between the two pieces? Why might the role of Death be so common in medieval times?

DEATH. Yea, sir, I will show you:
90 In great haste I am sent to thee
From God out of his majesty.

EVERYMAN. What! sent to me?

DEATH. Yea, certainly.
Though thou have forgot him here,
95 He thinketh on thee in the heavenly sphere,
As, ere we depart, thou shalt know.

EVERYMAN. What desireth God of me?

DEATH. That shall I show thee:
A reckoning he will needs have
100 Without any longer respite.

EVERYMAN. To give a reckoning longer
leisure I crave.
This blind[17] matter troubleth my wit.

DEATH. On thee thou must take a long
journay:
Therefore thy book of count[18] with thee thou
bring,
105 For turn again thou cannot by no way.
And look thou be sure of thy reckoning,
For before God thou shalt answer and shew
Thy many bad deeds and good but a few—
How thou hast spent thy life and in what wise,
110 Before the Chief Lord of Paradise.
Have ado that we were in that way,[19]
For weet thou well thou shalt make none
attornay.[20]

EVERYMAN. Full unready I am such reckoning to give.
I know thee not. What messenger art thou?

115 **DEATH.** I am Death that no man dreadeth,
For every man I 'rest, and no man spareth;

---
17. **blind.** Unexpected
18. **count.** Accounts
19. **Have . . . way.** Let's get started right away.
20. **shalt . . . attornay.** Nobody shall go in your place.
21. **good.** Goods

For it is God's commandment
That all to me should be obedient.

EVERYMAN. O Death, thou comest when I
had thee least in mind.
120 In thy power it lieth me to save:
Yet of my good[21] will I give thee, if thou will
be kind,
Yea, a thousand pound shalt thou have—
And defer this matter till another day.

DEATH. Everyman, it may not be, by no way.
125 I set nought by gold, silver, nor riches,[22]
Nor by pope, emperor, king, duke, nor
princes,
For, and[23] I would receive gifts great,
All the world I might get.
But my custom is clean contrary:
130 I give thee no respite. Come hence and not
tarry!

EVERYMAN. Alas, shall I have no longer
respite?
I may say Death giveth no warning.
To think on thee it maketh my heart sick,
For all unready is my book of reckoning.
135 But twelve year and I might have a biding,[24]
My counting-book I would make so clear
That my reckoning I should not need to fear.
Wherefore, Death, I pray thee, for God's
mercy,
Spare me till I be provided of remedy.

140 **DEATH.** Thee availeth not to cry, weep, and
pray;
But haste thee lightly[25] that thou were gone
that journay
And prove[26] thy friends, if thou can.

---
22. **I . . . riches.** Riches, gold, and silver mean nothing to me.
23. **and.** If
24. **But . . . biding.** If I could put this off for just twelve years
25. **lightly.** Quickly
26. **prove.** Test

WORDS FOR EVERYDAY USE: res • pite (res ´pit) *n.*, postponement; reprieve

VOCABULARY IN CONTEXT

• The players hoped for some <u>respite</u> from the jeers of the audience.
• "The Joker speaks bravely, but he is actually a cowardly <u>caitiff</u>," said Batman.

For weet[27] thou well the tide[28] abideth no
    man,
And in the world each living creature
145 For Adam's sin must die of nature.[29]

    EVERYMAN. Death, if I should this pilgrim-
        age take
And my reckoning surely make,
Show me, for saint[30] charity,
Should I not come again shortly?

150 **DEATH.** No, Everyman. And thou be once
        there,
Thou mayst never more come here,
Trust me verily.

    EVERYMAN. O gracious God in the high
        seat celestial,
Have mercy on me in this most need!
155 Shall I have company from this vale terrestrial
Of mine acquaintance that way me to lead?

    DEATH. Yea, if any be so hardy
That would go with thee and bear thee com-
        pany.
Hie[31] thee that thou were gone to God's
        magnificence,
160 Thy reckoning to give before his presence.
What, weenest[32] thou thy life is given thee,
And thy worldly goods also?

    EVERYMAN. I had weened so, verily.

    DEATH. Nay, nay, it was but lent thee.
165 For as soon as thou art go,
Another a while shall have it and then go
        therefro,
Even as thou hast done.
Everyman, thou art mad! Thou hast thy
        wits[33] five,

And here on earth will not amend thy live!
170 For suddenly I do come.

    EVERYMAN. O wretched <u>caitiff</u>! Whither
        shall I flee
That I might 'scape this endless sorrow?
Now, gentle Death, spare me till tomorrow,
That I may amend me
175 With good advisement.[34]

    DEATH. Nay, thereto I will not consent,
Nor no man will I respite,
But to the heart suddenly I shall smite,
Without any advisement.
180 And now out of thy sight I will me hie:
See thou make thee ready shortly,
For thou mayst say this is the day
That no man living may 'scape away.

    [*Exit* DEATH.]

    EVERYMAN. Alas, I may well weep with
        sighs deep:
185 Now have I no manner of company
To help me in my journey and me to keep[35]
And also my writing is full unready—
How shall I do now for to excuse me?
I would to God I had never be geet![36]
190 To my soul a full great profit it had be.
For now I fear pains huge and great.

          ◆   ◆   ◆

    EVERYMAN. Alas, I am so faint I may not
        stand—
My limbs under me doth fold!
790 Friends, let us not turn again to this land,
Not for all the world's gold.

---

27. **weet.** Know
28. **tide.** Time
29. **of nature.** Naturally
30. **saint.** Holy
31. **Hie.** Hasten

32. **weenest.** Suppose
33. **wits.** Senses
34. **advisement.** Preparation
35. **keep.** Guard
36. **never be geet.** Never been begotten; never been born

WORDS FOR
EVERYDAY USE: **cai • tiff** (kāt´ if) *n.*, mean, cowardly person

> **QUOTABLES**
>
> ❝Everyman, I will go with thee and be thy guide, In thy most need go by thy side.❞
>
> —Knowledge in *Everyman*

ADDITIONAL QUESTIONS AND ACTIVITIES

Have students discuss the things they fear losing to death such as youth, belonging, or beauty. How does this fear relate to their view of what will happen to them after death?

For into this cave must I creep
And turn to earth, and there to sleep.

BEAUTY. What, into this grave, alas?

795 **EVERYMAN.** Yea, there shall ye consume,[37]
more and lass.[38]

BEAUTY. And what, should I smother here?

EVERYMAN. Yea, by my faith, and nevermore appear.
In this world live no more we shall,
But in heaven before the highest Lord of all.

800 **BEAUTY.** I cross out all this! Adieu, by Saint John—
I take my tape in my lap and am gone.

EVERYMAN. What, Beauty, whither will ye?

BEAUTY. Peace, I am deaf—I look not behind me,
Not and thou wouldest give me all the gold in thy chest.

[*Exit* BEAUTY.]

805 **EVERYMAN.** Alas, whereto may I trust?
Beauty goeth fast away fro me—
She promised with me to live and die!

STRENGTH. Everyman, I will thee also forsake and deny.
Thy game liketh[39] me not at all.

810 **EVERYMAN.** Why then, ye will forsake me all?
Sweet Strength, tarry a little space.

STRENGTH. Nay, sir, by the rood of grace,
I will hie me from thee fast,
Though thou weep till thy heart tobrast.[40]

815 **EVERYMAN.** Ye would ever bide by me, ye said.

STRENGTH. Yea, I have you far enough conveyed![41]
Ye be old enough, I understand,
Your pilgrimage to take on hand:

---

37. **consume.** Decay
38. **more and lass.** More and less
39. **liketh.** Pleases
40. **tobrast.** Break

I repent me that I hither came.

820 **EVERYMAN.** Strength, you to displease I am to blame,[42]
Yet promise is debt, this ye well wot.[43]

STRENGTH. In faith, I care not:
Thou art but a fool to complain;
You spend your speech and waste your brain.
825 Go, thrust thee into the ground.

[*Exit* STRENGTH.]

EVERYMAN. I had weened[44] surer I should you have found.
He that trusteth in his Strength
She him deceiveth at the length.
Both Strength and Beauty forsaketh me—
830 Yet they promised me fair and lovingly.

DISCRETION Everyman, I will after Strength be gone:
As for me, I will leave you alone.

EVERYMAN. Why Discretion, will ye forsake me?

DISCRETION Yea, in faith, I will go from thee.
835 For when Strength goeth before,
I follow after evermore.

EVERYMAN. Yet I pray thee, for the love of the Trinity,
Look in my grave once piteously.

DISCRETION Nay, so nigh will I not come.
840 Farewell everyone!

[*Exit* DISCRETION.]

EVERYMAN. O all thing faileth save God alone—
Beauty, Strength, and Discretion.
For when Death bloweth his blast
They all run fro me full fast.

845 **FIVE-WITS.** Everyman, my leave now of thee I take.

---

41. **conveyed.** Escorted
42. **you . . . blame.** I'm to blame for displeasing you.
43. **wot.** Know
44. **weened.** Supposed

I will follow the other, for here I thee forsake.

EVERYMAN.   Alas, then may I wail and weep,
For I took you for my best friend.

FIVE-WITS.   I will no longer thee keep.[45]
850   Now farewell, and there an end!

[*Exit* FIVE-WITS.]

EVERYMAN.   O Jesu, help, all hath forsaken
me!

GOOD DEEDS.   Nay, Everyman, I will bide
with thee:
I will not forsake thee indeed;
Thou shalt find me a good friend at need.

855   **EVERYMAN.**   Gramercy, Good Deeds! Now
may I true friends see.
They have forsaken me every one—
I loved them better than my Good Deeds
alone.
Knowledge, will ye forsake me also?

KNOWLEDGE.   Yea, Everyman, when ye to
Death shall go,
860   But not yet, for no manner of danger.

EVERYMAN.   Gramercy, Knowledge, with all
my heart!

KNOWLEDGE.   Nay, yet will I not from
hence depart
Till I see where ye shall become.[46]

EVERYMAN.   Methink, alas, that I must be
gone
865   To make my reckoning and my debts pay,
For I see my time is nigh spent away.
Take example, all ye that this do hear or see,
How they that I best loved do forsake me,
Except my Good Deeds that bideth truly.

870   **GOOD DEEDS.**   All earthly things is but vanity.
Beauty, Strength, and Discretion do man forsake,

Foolish friends and kinsmen that fair spake—
All fleeth save Good Deeds, and that am I.

EVERYMAN.   Have mercy on me, God most
mighty,
875   And stand by me, thou mother and maid,
holy Mary!

GOOD DEEDS.   Fear not: I will speak for
thee.

EVERYMAN.   Here I cry God mercy!

GOOD DEEDS.   Short our end, and 'minish
our pain.
Let us go, and never come again.

880   **EVERYMAN.**   Into thy hands, Lord, my soul I
commend:
Receive it, Lord, that it be not lost.
As thou me boughtest,[47] so me defend,
And save me from the fiend's boast,
That I may appear with that blessed host
885   That shall be saved at the day of doom.
In manus tuas, of mights most,
Forever *commendo spiritum meum*.[48]

[EVERYMAN *and* GOOD DEEDS *descend into the*
grave.]

KNOWLEDGE.   Now hath he suffered that
we all shall endure,
The Good Deeds shall make all sure.
890   Now hath he made ending,
Methinketh that I hear angels sing
And make great joy and melody
Where Everyman's soul received shall be.

ANGEL.   [*within*] Come, excellent elect[49]
spouse to Jesu![50]
895   Here above thou shalt go
Because of thy singular virtue.
Now the soul is taken the body fro,
Thy reckoning is crystal clear:
Now shalt thou into the heavenly sphere—
900   Unto the which all ye shall come

---

45. **keep.** Watch over
46. **Till . . . become.** Until I see what will become of you
47. **boughtest.** Redeemed

48. *In . . . meum.* Into your hands, Almighty One, I forever commend my spirit.
49. **elect.** Chosen
50. **spouse to Jesu.** The soul is often called the bride of Jesus.

THE MORALITY PLAY / FROM EVERYMAN   **219**

ANSWERS FOR REVIEWING THE SELECTION

RECALLING

1. God decides that humans should be called to judgment, because too often their minds are on worldly things and they forget about what God has done for them and about virtue.

2. Everyman asks Death for more time.

3. Beauty, Strength, Discretion, and Knowledge desert Everyman. Good Deeds alone remains with him.

4. Everyman goes to the heavenly sphere because he has Good Deeds to take with him to his reckoning.

INTERPRETING

Responses will vary. Possible responses are given.

5. These actions include forgetting about what God has done for them, thinking too much about worldly matters, and forsaking virtuous actions such as charity.

6. Everyman is at first incredulous and then terrified as he talks to Death. He is totally unprepared for Death's coming because he has been living a worldly life. He has acted as though he were going to live forever.

7. Everyman despairs over the loss of his companions because he fears that he will have to take his hard pilgrimage (to the general reckoning) all alone.

8. Everyman's last speech shows that he is hopeful, but not that he is certain. He commends his spirit to God, echoing the words of Jesus on the cross, and asks God to receive that spirit and to save him from the fiend (i.e., the devil).

(cont.)

That liveth well before the day of doom.

[*Enter* DOCTOR.]

DOCTOR. This memorial[51] men may have
    in mind:
Ye hearers, take it of worth, old and young,
And forsake Pride, for he deceiveth you in the
    end.
905 And remember Beauty, Five-Wits, Strength,
    and Discretion,
They all at the last do Everyman forsake,
Save his Good Deeds there doth he take—
But beware, for and they be small,
Before God he hath no help at all—
910 None excuse may be there for Everyman.
Alas, how shall he do than?[52]

For after death amends may no man make,
For then mercy and pity doth him forsake.
If his reckoning be not clear when he doth
    come,
915 God will say, "*Ite, maledicti, in ignem eter-
    num!*"[53]
And he that hath his account whole and
    sound,
High in heaven he shall be crowned,
Unto which place God bring us all thither,
That we may live body and soul together.
920 Thereto help, the Trinity!
Amend, say ye, for saint charity.

---

51. **memorial.** Reminder
52. **than.** Then
53. ***Ite . . . eternum.*** Go, cursed one, into the everlasting fire.

Responding to the Selection

Assume the role of Good Deeds from the selection. In your journal, write a brief character description of Everyman and explain your role in his fate.

Reviewing the Selection

RECALLING

1. What decision does God make about humans? Why?

2. How does Everyman try to bargain with Death?

3. Who deserts Everyman? Who stays with him?

4. What is Everyman's fate? Why?

INTERPRETING

 5. What human actions lead God to decide that he should "have a reckoning" for every person?

6. What is Everyman's state of mind as he talks with Death? Why?

7. Why does Everyman despair over the loss of his companions?

8. What words does Everyman speak that show he is not certain of his fate?

WORDS FOR EVERYDAY USE:
    a • mends (ə mendz´) *n. pl.,* something done to make up for injury, loss, etc., that one has caused

VOCABULARY IN CONTEXT

• "I would like to make amends for the long hours that you have had to work," said the boss.

9. What religious assumption underlies the play?

10. What lesson is the audience supposed to take away from the play?

Understanding Literature (Questions for Discussion)

1. **Morality Play.** A **morality play** is a type of medieval drama in which the characters are abstract caricatures of virtues, vices, and the like. Morality plays attempted to dramatize the Christian struggle to choose between good and evil, and ultimately, heaven and hell. Morality plays are clearly didactic, or meant to teach a lesson. How is the message of *Everyman* didactic? How do specific characters contribute to a didactic tone?

2. **Naive Allegory.** An **allegory** is a work in which each element *symbolizes,* or represents, something else. In a **naive allegory,** characters, objects, places, and actions are personifications of abstractions such as Good Deeds, Beauty, Vanity, or the journey to the Celestial Kingdom. Do you think *Everyman* is a naive allegory? What evidence from the play makes you think so?

Responding in Writing

1. **Sermon.** A **sermon** is a type of persuasive writing—a sermon's purpose is to make the listener aware of an idea or to change the listener's thinking or behavior. Strictly speaking, sermons involve religious topics; however, sermons can also address the broader topic of morality and human nature. What moral or humanistic opinion do you have that you would like to persuade others to consider? Brainstorm your ideas, then freewrite about one topic. Why does this topic concern you? What is the main idea you would like your readers or listeners to get from your sermon? Write the main idea, and list two or three facts or ideas to support it. Organize your supporting details so that they will make an impact, possibly from least to most important or from most to least. Then write your final sermon.

2. **Fortune Cookie Inserts.** Some fortune cookie inserts make predictions; others make pronouncements about human nature. The characters in *Everyman* have a lot to say about human nature. Imagine opening a cookie and reading one of these pronouncements. How might these sayings work inside a fortune cookie? Use the dialogue of Everyman and his companions as a starting point for your inserts. Keep in mind that most fortune cookie inserts are short, single sentences.

ANSWERS FOR UNDERSTANDING LITERATURE

See the evaluation forms for writing, revising, and proofreading, *Assessment Portfolio, 7.1–7.10.*
Responses will vary. Possible responses are given.

1. Morality Play. *Everyman* is a specifically didactic play, because it was written with the purpose of conveying a moral. This moral is communicated directly by the Messenger, by the character God, by the Doctor,

and indirectly by the action of the play (the desertion of Everyman by all but Good Deeds).

2. Naive Allegory. *Everyman* is, indeed, a naive allegory, because each of the characters has a specific allegorical interpretation. The allegory is quite straightforward and is expressed in the characters' names.

ANSWERS FOR REVIEWING THE SELECTION (CONT.)

SYNTHESIZING
Responses will vary. Possible responses are given.

9. The religious assumption that underlies the play is that at the end of life, people will be judged according to their actions and then either be saved or damned.

10. The lesson of the play is that one should remember, in the middle of life, that death will come and so be prepared for the accounting that will happen after death. Such preparation requires doing good deeds that can be taken to that accounting.

ANALYTIC SCALES FOR RESPONDING IN WRITING

Assign a score from 1 to 25 for each grading criterion below. (For more detailed evaluation, see the evaluation forms for writing, revising, and proofreading, *Assessment Portfolio, 7.1–7.10.*)

1. Sermon

• **Content/Unity.** The sermon presents a moral or humanistic opinion and facts or ideas that support this opinion.

• **Organization/Coherence.** The sermon presents a main idea and supporting details organized in a sensible manner, perhaps from most important to least important or vice versa.

• **Language/Style.** The sermon uses vivid, persuasive language.

• **Conventions.** The sermon avoids errors in spelling, grammar, usage, mechanics, and manuscript form.

2. Fortune Cookie Inserts

• **Content/Unity.** The fortune cookie inserts present predictions or pronouncements about human nature in pithy, short sentences.

• **Organization/Coherence.** The ideas are communicated clearly in well-organized sentences.

• **Language/Style.** The language of the inserts is clear and precise.

• **Conventions.** The inserts avoid errors in spelling, grammar, usage, mechanics, and manuscript form.

ANSWERS FOR LANGUAGE LAB

1. No errors.

2. The morality play *The Pride of Life* predates *Everyman* by almost a century.

3. Another morality play, *The Castle of Perseverance,* also appeared at the beginning of the fifteenth century.

4. Mystery plays, such as *The York Play of the Crucifixion,* dramatized biblical stories for the common people.

5. *The Second Shepherd's Play,* one of the mystery plays, uses comedy as well as drama to tell the story of Christ's birth.

▶Additional practice is provided in the *Essential Skills Practice Book: Language,* 2.129.

ANSWERS FOR SPEAKING SKILLS

Use the "Evaluation Form: Oral Interpretation" in the *Assessment Portfolio,* 7.15.

▶**Teaching Note:** Students may evaluate one another's readings using general speech evaluation forms from the *Assessment Portfolio,* 7.18.

PROJECT NOTES

Morality Play. An allegorical play like *Everyman* works very well when produced in a highly stylized manner. Masks and special costumes might be appropriate. An alternate possibility for student productions is to perform the play as puppet theater. Hand puppets representing the characters can easily be made from socks or pieces of felt decorated by sewing or by drawing with markers.

Language Lab

Using Proper Capitalization. Read the Language Arts Survey, 2.129, "Titles of Literary Works." Then, revise the following sentences to correct errors in capitalization. If no corrections are needed, write *No Errors* after the sentence.

1. In addition to <u>Everyman,</u> other morality plays and another type of religious play, called the mystery play, were produced in the Medieval Period.

2. The morality play the <u>Pride of life</u> predates <u>Everyman</u> by almost a century.

3. Another morality play, <u>The castle of perseverance,</u> also appeared at the beginning of the fifteenth century.

4. Mystery plays, such as <u>The York Play Of The Crucifixion,</u> dramatized biblical stories for the common people.

5. <u>The Second shepherd's play,</u> one of the mystery plays, uses comedy as well as drama to tell the story of Christ's birth.

Speaking Skills

Public Speaking. Read the Language Arts Survey, 3.7, "Public Speaking." Then give a reading of one of the speeches from the selection to the class.

PROJECT

Morality Play. As a class, perform part or all of this selection from *Everyman.* Assign character parts and read through the play as a group, with each person reading his or her lines aloud. Then discuss whether you would like to perform the play as a staged production or simply as a reading of the character parts. If you decide to perform the play, you might want to make masks or some form of costuming to represent each character. As you rehearse the play, talk with each other about the scene's dramatic interpretation. Decide what the characters are thinking and feeling and how their words relate to their body movements and facial expressions. When you are ready, perform your scene for the class.

"Western Wind," Anonymous

Westron wind, when will thou blow?
The small rain down can rain.
Christ, that my love were in my arms,
And I in my bed again.

"I am of Ireland," Anonymous

Ich am of Irlonde,
And of the holy londe
    Of Irlonde.
Goode sire, praye ich thee,
5   For of[1] sainte charitee,
Com and dance with me
    In Irlonde.

"The Bonny Earl of Murray," Anonymous

Ye Highlands and ye Lawlands,
    O where have you been?
They have slain the Earl of Murray,
    And they laid him on the green.

5   "Now wae be to thee, Huntly,[2]
    And wherefore did you sae?
I bade you bring him wi' you
    But forbade you him to slay."

He was a braw[3] gallant,
10   And he rid at the ring;[4]
And the bonny Earl of Murray,
    O he might have been a king.

He was a braw gallant,
    And he played at the ba';
15   And the bonny Earl of Murray
    Was the flower among them a'.

He was a braw gallant,
    And he played at the glove;
And the bonny Earl of Murray,
20   O he was the queen's love.

---

1. **of.** Sake of
2. **Huntly.** In 1592, Huntly killed Murray though he was only supposed to arrest him.
3. **braw.** Brave
4. **rid . . . ring.** Knights tried to put their spears through a hanging ring.

O lang will his lady
    Look o'er the Castle Down,
Ere she see the Earl of Murray
    Come sounding through the town.

"The Twa Corbies," Anonymous

As I was walking all alane,
I heard twa corbies making a mane;[5]
The tane unto the t'other say,
"Where sall we gang and dine to-day?"

5   "In behint yon auld fail dyke,[6]
I wot there lies a new slain knight;
And naebody kens that he lies there,
But his hawk, his hound, and lady fair.

"His hound is to the hunting gane,
10   His hawk to fetch the wild-fowl hame,
His lady's ta'en another mate,
So we may mak' our dinner sweet.

"Ye'll sit on his white hause-bane,[7]
And I'll pike out his bonny blue e'en;
15   Wi' ae lock o' his gowden hair
We'll theek our nest when it grows bare.

"Mony a ane for him makes mane,
But nane sall ken where he is gane;
O'er his white banes, when they are bare,
20   The wind sall blaw for evermair."

"Bonny Barbara Allan," Anonymous

It was in and about the Martinmas[8] time,
    When the green leaves were a-fallin';
That Sir John Graeme in the West Country
    Fell in love with Barbara Allan.

5   He sent his man down through the town
    To the place where she was dwelling':
"O haste and come to my master dear,
    If you be Barbara Allan."

---

5. **twa . . . mane.** Two crows making a moan
6. **fail dyke.** Wall of turf
7. **hause-bane.** Neck bone
8. **Martinmas.** The feast of St. Martin, November 11

"Bonny Barbara Allan"

About the Selection. The subject of this ballad is the death of Sir John Grehme caused by unrequited love for Barbara Allan.

"The Wife of Usher's Well"

About the Selection. This ballad is believed to have come from people living near the Scottish border. It deals with the common subject of untimely death.

LITERARY NOTE

You may wish to review the form of a ballad with your students. Remind them of ballad rhyme scheme and use of refrain. Have them determine the rhyme scheme of "Bonny Barbara Allan" and "The Wife of Usher's Well." Can they find refrains in these poems? Refer them to the entry on *ballad* in the Handbook of Literary Terms.

O gently, gently rose she up,
10   To the place where he was lyin',
And when she drew the curtain by:
   "Young man, I think you're dyin'."

"O it's I'm sick, and very, very sick,
   And 'tis a' for Barbara Allan."
15 "O the better for me you shall never be,
   Though your heart's blood were a-spillin'.

"O do you remember, young man," said she,
   When you the cups were fillin',
That you made the healths go round and round,
20   And slighted Barbara Allan?"

He turned his face unto the wall,
   And death with him was dealin':
"Adieu, adieu, my dear friends all,
   And be kind to Barbara Allan."

25 And slowly, slowly rose she up,
   And slowly, slowly left him;
And sighing said she could not stay,
   Since death of life had reft[1] him.

She had not gone a mile but two,
30   When she heard the death-bell knellin',
And every stroke that the death-bell made,
   It cried, "Woe to Barbara Allan!"

"O mother, mother, make my bed,
   O make it soft and narrow:
35 Since my love died for me today,
   I'll die for him tomorrow."

"The Wife of Usher's Well," Anonymous

There lived a wife at Usher's Well,
   And a wealthy wife was she;
She had three stout and stalwart sons,
   And sent them o'er the sea.

5 They had not been a week from her
   A week but barely one,
When word came to the carlin[2] wife
   That her three sons were gone.

They had not been a week from her,
10   A week but barely three

1. **reft.** Deprived
2. **carlin.** Old

When word came to the carlin wife
   That her sons she'd never see.

"I wish the wind may never cease
   Nor flashes in the flood,
15 Till my three sons come home to me,
   In earthly flesh and blood."

It fell about the Martinmas,
   When nights are long and mirk,[3]
The carlin's wife's three sons came hame,
20   And their hats were o' the birk.[4]

It neither grew in field nor ditch,
   Nor yet in any furrow
But at the gates o' Paradise
   That birk grew fair enough.

25 "Blow up the fire, my maidens,
   Bring water from the well:
For a' my house shall feast this night,
   Since my three sons are well."

And she has made to them a bed,
30   She's made it large and wide,
And she's ta'en her mantle her about,
   Sat down at the bedside.

Up then crew the red, red cock,
   And up and crew the gray.
35 The eldest to the youngest said,
   "'Tis time we were away."

The cock he had not crowed but once,
   And clapped his wings that day,
When the youngest to the eldest said,
40   "Brother, we must away.

"The cock doth crow, the day doth dawn,
   The channerin'[5] worm doth chide:
If we be missed out o' our place,
   A sore pain we must bide.

45 "Fare you well, my mother dear,
   Farewell to barn and byre.[6]
And fare you well, the bonny lass
   That kindles my mother's fire."

3. **mirk.** Dark
4. **birk.** Birch
5. **channerin'.** Fretting
6. **byre.** Cattle house

PREREADING

from *The Ingenious Hidalgo*[1] *Don Quixote de la Mancha*
by Miguel de Cervantes Saavedra, trans. by Walter Starkie

ABOUT THE AUTHOR

Miguel de Cervantes Saavedra (1547–1616), the most famous of all Spanish authors, was born near Madrid to a family of seven children. Little is known of his early life or education. His father combined the duties of a barber and surgeon, and his family traveled from town to town. In 1571, he fought bravely in a sea battle against the Turks and was severely wounded, losing the use of his left hand. In 1575, he was captured and sold into slavery in Algiers. There he remained for five years, until he was ransomed and returned to Spain in 1580. In 1584, he married Ana de Villafranca from the province of La Mancha, a woman eighteen years younger than he. The following year, he published his first novel, *La Galatea*. From 1582 to 1587, he wrote numerous plays. As a government officer, he helped raise provisions for the Spanish Armada launched against England during the reign of Queen Elizabeth (see page 60 of this text). The first part of his most famous work, *The Ingenious Hidalgo Don Quixote de la Mancha,* was published in 1605, the second part in 1615.

ABOUT THE SELECTION

Don Quixote de la Mancha is a **mock epic** in which a deranged gentleman, having spent too much time reading romances about the adventures of knights in shining armor, decides to enter upon a life as a knight, enlisting as his unwilling companion a servant named Sancho Panza. This **parody** of medieval romance, with its absurd, comic, and tragic hero, has enjoyed enormous popularity throughout the ages and has inspired countless other works of literature, music, and art. The novel has also given to the English language the word *quixotic,* meaning "impractical" or "foolishly idealistic," as well as the phrase *to tilt at windmills,* meaning "to make a ludicrous effort."

---

1. *Hidalgo.* A Spanish nobleman of secondary rank

ADDITIONAL RESOURCES

READER'S GUIDE
• Selection Worksheet, 3.12

ASSESSMENT PORTFOLIO
• Selection Check Test, 4.3.23
• Selection Test, 4.3.24

ENRICHMENT ACTIVITIES

• Find a recording or film of the musical *Man of La Mancha* and share this with your students.

• Have students brainstorm a list of activities that might be described as quixotic or as tilting at windmills (i.e., activities that are absurd or doomed to failure).

SUPPORT FOR LEP STUDENTS

Before having students read the selection, direct their attention to the discussion of parody in About the Selection on this page. Then, have students look for ways in which Don Quixote's story parodies traditional medieval romances.

ADDITIONAL VOCABULARY
lance—long, pointed spear carried by a knight
buckler—a small, round shield
surname—last name; family name
conjecture—guess
domestic—having to do with the home

(cont.)

GOALS/OBJECTIVES

Studying this lesson will enable students to

• experience amusement at the comic side of Don Quixote's character and empathize with the tragic side of this character

• understand and illustrate with examples the terms *quixotic* and *tilting at windmills*

• recognize common romance motifs in a parody of the genre

• define *courtly love* and give examples of it from *Don Quixote*

• define *satire* and describe a famous example of it

extravagant—exceptional; beyond the ordinary or the acceptable

arable—good for growing crops

immersed—submerged; completely involved

enchantment—magic spell

authentic—real

thwart—lying or extending across

cleft—split

brace—pair

stratagem—trick; plan

arrogance—conceit; pride

insolence—disrespect; impertinence

sallying—rushing forth

renown—fame

delusion—fantasy, imagining

moldering—growing old

ingeniously—cleverly

deliberating—thinking

pompous—overly proud

lineage—line of descent, ancestral line

cleaving—splitting; cutting

sovereignty—rule

uttering—saying

flourish—wave about

enmity—hatred; anger

doughty—brave

ANSWER TO GUIDED READING QUESTION

❶ In his spare time, Quixana liked to read romances. The obsession with romances led him to neglect everything else and to sell off property to buy books about knighthood.

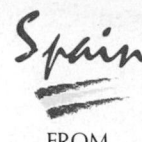

Spain

FROM

The Ingenious Hidalgo Don Quixote de la Mancha

MIGUEL DE CERVANTES SAAVEDRA, TRANS. BY WALTER STARKIE

FROM PART I, BOOK 1

THE QUALITY AND MANNER OF LIFE OF THAT FAMOUS GENTLEMAN DON QUIXOTE OF LA MANCHA

At a village of La Mancha, whose name I do not wish to remember, there lived a little while ago one of those gentlemen who are wont to keep a lance in the rack, an old buckler, a lean horse, and a swift greyhound. His stew had more beef than mutton in it and most nights he ate the remains salted and cold. Lentil soup on Fridays, "tripe and trouble"[1] on Saturdays and an occasional pigeon as an extra delicacy on Sundays, consumed three-quarters of his income. The remainder was spent on a jerkin of fine puce, velvet breeches, and slippers of the same stuff for holidays, and a suit of good, honest homespun for week-days. His family consisted of a housekeeper about forty, a niece not yet twenty, and a lad who served him both in the field and at home and could saddle the horse or use the pruning-knife. Our gentleman was about fifty years of age, of a sturdy constitution, but wizened and gaunt-featured, an early riser and a devotee of the chase. They say that his surname was Quixada or Quesada (for on this point the authors who have written on this subject differ), but we may reasonably conjecture that his name was Quixana. This, however, has very little to do with our story: enough that in its telling we swerve not a jot from the truth. You must know that the above-mentioned gentleman in his leisure moments (which was most of the year) gave himself up with so much delight and gusto to reading books of chivalry that he almost entirely neglected the exercise of the chase and even the management of his domestic affairs: indeed his craze for this kind of literature became so extravagant that he sold many acres of arable land to purchase books of knight-errantry, and he carried off to his house as many as he could possibly find. . . .

♦ ♦ ♦

What did Quixana like to do in his spare time? What became of this interest? ❶

---

1. **tripe and trouble.** Saturday's meal was light, semi-abstinence fare in memory of the defeat of the Moors.

Don Quixote Fighting the Windmill. Illustrated by Gustave Doré

In short, he so immersed himself in those romances that he spent whole days and nights over his books; and thus with little sleeping and much reading his brains dried up to such a degree that he lost the use of his reason. His imagination became filled with a host of fancies he had read in his books—enchantments, quarrels, battles, challenges, wounds, courtships, loves, tortures, and many other absurdities. So true did all this <u>phantasmagoria</u> from books appear to him that in his mind he accounted no history in the world more authentic. He would say that the Cid Ruy Diaz was a very gallant knight, but not to be compared with the Knight of the Burning Sword, who with a single thwart blow cleft asunder a brace of hulking blustering giants. He was better pleased with Bernardo del Carpio, because at Roncesvalles he had slain Roland the Enchanted by availing himself of the stratagem Hercules had employed on Antaeus, the son of the Earth, whom he squeezed to death in his arms. He praised the giant Morgante, for he alone was courteous and well-bred among that

WORDS FOR EVERYDAY USE:
phan • tas • ma • go • ri • a (fan taz´mə gôr´ē ə) *n.*, rapidly changing series of imagined figures or events

MULTICULTURAL EXTENSIONS: LITERATURE OF ROMANCE / FROM DON QUIXOTE DE LA MANCHA **227**

ADDITIONAL QUESTIONS AND ACTIVITIES

Ask students if they remember a book or movie in which they became engrossed. Did they identify with any of the characters? Why did they feel that way?

ANSWERS TO SELECTION CHECK TEST 4.3.23

EX. Of what is *Don Quixote de la Mancha* a parody?
It is a parody of medieval romance.

1. What did Quixana most like to do?
Quixana enjoyed reading books of chivalry.

2. What did Quixana decide he must become?
He decided he must become a knight-errant.

3. What did Quixana name his horse?
He named it Rozinante.

4. Why does Don Quixote attempt to fight the windmills?
He thinks they are giants.

5. Who advises Don Quixote not to fight the windmills?
Sancho Panza advises him not to fight the windmills.

VOCABULARY FROM THE SELECTION

caitiff
phantasmagoria
sonorous

VOCABULARY IN CONTEXT

• Bob recounted the <u>phantasmagoria</u> of his dreams—flying pigs, elves and trolls, and a rocket-powered 1966 Thunderbird.

TEACHER'S EDITION **227**

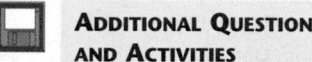

ANSWER TO GUIDED READING QUESTION

❶ Quixana decided that he must become a knight and seek adventures in order to achieve fame.

ADDITIONAL QUESTIONS AND ACTIVITIES

How does Quixana prepare to be a knight-errant? What is humorous about these preparations?

Answer: Quixana prepares a suit of armor and a helmet with a visor and renames his horse. His preparations are comical because he makes his helmet himself out of pasteboard and cares not for the quality of his steed but only for its name.

---

monstrous brood puffed up with arrogance and insolence. Above all, he admired Rinaldo of Montalvan, especially when he saw him sallying out of his castle to plunder everyone that came his way; and, moreover, when, beyond the seas, he made off with the idol of Mahomet, which, as history says, was of solid gold. But he would have parted with his housekeeper and his niece into the bargain for the pleasure of rib-roasting the traitor Galalon.

At last, having lost his wits completely, he stumbled upon the oddest fancy that ever entered a madman's brain. He believed that it was necessary, both for his own honor and for the service of the state, that he should become knight-errant and roam through the world with his horse and armor in quest of adventures, and practice all that had been performed by the knights-errant of whom he had read. He would follow their life, redressing all manner of wrongs and exposing himself to continual dangers, and at last, after concluding his enterprises, he would win everlasting honor and renown. The poor gentleman saw himself in imagination already crowned Emperor of Trebizond by the valor of his arm. And thus, excited by these agreeable delusions, he hastened to put his plans into operation.

The first thing he did was to furbish some rusty armor which had belonged to his great-grandfather and had lain moldering in a corner. He cleaned it and repaired it as best he could, but he found one great defect: instead of a complete helmet there was just the simple morion.[2] This want he ingeniously remedied by

What did Quixana decide he must do? ❶

making a kind of visor out of pasteboard, and when it was fitted to the morion it looked like an entire helmet. It is true that, in order to test its strength and see if it was sword-proof, he drew his sword and gave it two strokes, the first of which instantly destroyed the result of a week's labor. It troubled him to see with what ease he had broken the helmet in pieces, so to protect it from such an accident, he remade it and fenced the inside with a few bars of iron in such a manner that he felt assured of its strength, and without making a second trial, he held it to be a most excellent visor. Then he went to see his steed, and although it had more cracks than a Spanish *real* and more faults than Gonela's jade which was all skin and bone, he thought that neither the Bucephalus of Alexander nor the Cid's Babieca could be compared with it. He spent four days deliberating over what name he would give the horse; for (as he said to himself) it was not right that the horse of so famous a knight should remain without a name, and so he endeavored to find one which would express what the animal had been before he had been the mount of a knight-errant, and what he now was. It was indeed reasonable that when the master changed his state, the horse should change his name too, and assume one pompous and high-sounding as suited the new order he was about to profess. So, after having devised, erased and blotted out many other names, he finally determined to call the horse Rozinante—a name, in his opinion, lofty, <u>sonorous</u> and significant, for it

---

2. **morion.** Crested helmet without a visor

WORDS FOR EVERYDAY USE: so • no • rous (sə nôr´əs) *adj.*, having an impressive sound

VOCABULARY IN CONTEXT

• The hikers paused to listen to the <u>sonorous</u> echoes that filled the canyon.

explained that he had only been a "rocín" or hack before he had been raised to his present status of first of all the hacks in the world.

Now that he had given his horse a name so much to his satisfaction, he resolved to choose one for himself, and after seriously considering the matter for eight whole days he finally determined to call himself Don Quixote. Wherefore the authors of this most true story have deduced that his name must undoubtedly have been Quixano, and not Quesada, as others would have it. Then remembering that the valiant Amadis had not been content to call himself simply Amadis, but added thereto the name of his kingdom and native country to render it more illustrious, calling himself Amadis of Gaul, so he, like a good knight, also added the name of his province and called himself Don Quixote of La Mancha. In this way, he openly proclaimed his lineage and country, and at the same time he honored it by taking its name.

Now that his armor was scoured, his morion made into a helmet, his horse and himself new-named, he felt that nothing was wanting but a lady of whom to be enamored; for a knight-errant who was loveless was a tree without leaves and fruit—a body without soul. "If," said he, "for my sins or through my good fortune I encounter some giant—a usual occurrence to knight-errants—and bowling him over at the first onset, or cleaving him in twain, I finally vanquish and force him to surrender, would it not be better to have some lady to whom I may send him as a trophy? so that when he enters into her presence he may throw himself on his knees before her and in accents contrite and humble say: 'Madam, I am the giant Caraculiambro, Lord of the Island of Malindrania, whom the never-adequately-praised Don Quixote of La Mancha has overcome in single combat. He has commanded me to present myself before you, so that your highness may dispose of me as you wish.'" How glad was our knight when he had made these discourses to himself, but chiefly when he had found one whom he might call his lady! It happened that in a neighboring village there lived a good-looking country lass, with whom he had been in love, although it is understood that she never knew or cared a jot. She was called Aldonza Lorenzo, and it was to her that he thought fit to confide the sovereignty of his heart. He sought a name for her which would not vary too much from her own and yet would approach that of a princess or lady of quality: he resolved to call her Dulcinea del Toboso (she was a native of that town), a name in his opinion musical, uncommon and expressive, like the others which he had devised. . . .

◆   ◆   ◆

FROM PART I, BOOK 7

THE TERRIFYING AND UNPRECEDENTED ADVENTURE OF THE WINDMILLS, AND THE STUPENDOUS BATTLE BETWEEN THE GALLANT BISCAYAN AND THE PUISSANT MANCHEGAN

Just then they came in sight of thirty or forty windmills which rise from that plain, and as soon as Don Quixote saw them, he said to his squire: "Fortune is guiding our affairs better than we ourselves could have wished. Do you see over yonder, my friend Sancho Panza, thirty or more huge giants? I intend to do battle with them and slay them: with their spoils we shall begin to be rich, for this is a righteous war and the removal of so foul a brood from off the

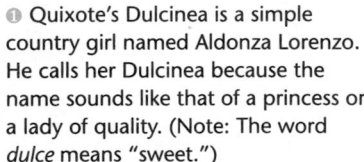
❶ Who is Dulcinea? Why does Don Quixote call her that?

❷ What foe does Don Quixote intend to fight? What is he really battling?

❶ Quixote's Dulcinea is a simple country girl named Aldonza Lorenzo. He calls her Dulcinea because the name sounds like that of a princess or a lady of quality. (Note: The word *dulce* means "sweet.")

❷ Quixote intends to fight some giants. They are actually windmills.

ADDITIONAL QUESTIONS AND ACTIVITIES

Students can illustrate Don Quixote attacking the windmills. They might draw one illustration from Quixote's point of view and another from Sancho Panza's point of view.

face of the earth is a service God will bless."

"What giants?" said Sancho, amazed.

"Those giants you see over there," replied his master, "with long arms: some of them have them well-nigh two leagues in length."

"Take care, sir," answered Sancho; "those over there are not giants but windmills, and those things which seem to be arms are their sails, which when they are whirled round by the wind turn the millstones."

"It is clear," answered Don Quixote, "that you are not experienced in adventures. Those are giants, and if you are afraid, turn aside and pray whilst I enter into fierce and unequal battle with them."

Uttering those words, he clapped spurs to Rozinante, without heeding the cries of his squire Sancho, who warned him that he was not going to attack giants but windmills. But so convinced was he that they were giants that he neither heard his squire's shouts nor did he notice what they were though he was very near them. Instead, he rushed on, shouting in a loud voice: "Fly not, cowards and vile <u>caitiffs</u>; one knight alone attacks you!" At that moment a slight breeze arose, and the great sails began to move. When Don Quixote saw this he shouted again: "Although ye flourish more arms than the giant Briareus, ye shall pay for your insolence!"

Saying this, and commending himself most devoutly to his Lady Dulcinea, whom he begged to help him in this peril, he covered himself with his buckler, couched his lance, charged at Rozinante's full gallop and rammed the first mill in his way. He ran his lance into the sail, but the wind twisted it with such violence that it shivered the spear to pieces, dragging him and his horse after it and rolling him over and over on the ground, sorely damaged.

Sancho Panza rushed up to his assistance as fast as his ass could gallop, and when he reached the knight he found that he was unable to move, such was the shock that Rozinante had given him in the fall.

"God help us!" said Sancho. "Did I not tell you, sir, to mind what you were doing, for those were only windmills! Nobody could have mistaken them unless he had windmills in his brains."

"Hold your peace, dear Sancho," answered Don Quixote; "for the things of war are, above all others, subject to continual change; especially as I am convinced that the magician Freston—the one who robbed me of my room and books—has changed those giants into windmills to deprive me of the glory of victory: such is the enmity he bears against me. But in the end his evil arts will be of little avail against my doughty sword."

"God settle it his own way," cried Sancho, as he helped his master to rise and remount Rozinante, who was well-nigh disjointed by his fall. ∎

WORDS FOR EVERYDAY USE: cai • tiff (kāt´if) *n.*, cowardly person

VOCABULARY IN CONTEXT

- "Wretched <u>caitiff</u>," said Batman to the Joker, "you will pay for your life of crime."

Reviewing the Selection

1. What happens to Quixana's mind as a result of reading too many medieval romances? What does he hope to accomplish by becoming a knight-errant?

2. What preparations does Quixana make for his new life?

3. What woman does he find for whom to do his great deeds? What relationship exists, in reality, between him and her?

4. What does Don Quixote imagine the windmills to be? Given his imaginings, what might you say about his character? What makes him both noble and ludicrous?

5. How does Sancho Panza react to his master's beliefs about the windmills? What happens in the battle of the windmills? What does Sancho do thereafter?

Connections (Questions for Writing or Discussion)

---

1. **Medieval Romance.** A **medieval romance** is a story from the Middle Ages about the loves and adventures of knights. In what ways is Don Quixote similar to Arthur in *Le Morte d'Arthur,* to Tristan in "Chevrefoil," and to the Knight in "The Prologue" to Chaucer's *Canterbury Tales?*

2. **Courtly Love. Courtly love** is the code of romantic love celebrated in songs and romance of the Medieval Period in France, England, and elsewhere. According to this code, the lover knows himself to be truly in love if he is overcome by extreme, transforming emotion. This emotion, felt for an idealized, venerated woman, leads the smitten man to heights of gentleness, courtesy, and heroism to prove his worth to his lady fair. What elements of courtly love are found in these selections from *Don Quixote?* Who is the object of Don Quixote's veneration? Why does he need to find such a lady before he sets out on his quests? What does he do immediately before entering into battle with the windmills?

3. **Satire. Satire** is humorous writing or speech intended to point out errors, falsehoods, foibles, or failings. What elements of medieval romance literature does Cervantes satirize in these selections from *Don Quixote?*

ANSWERS FOR REVIEWING THE SELECTION

1. Quixana goes mad. He hopes to win honor as a knight-errant.

2. Quixana armors himself, makes a helmet, names his horse Rozinante and himself Don Quixote of La Mancha, and finds a lady to serve.

3. He decides to serve Aldonza Lorenzo and renames her Dulcinea del Toboso. In reality, Aldonza is not a princess, but a country girl who neither knows nor cares about Quixote's love for her.

4. *Responses will vary. Possible responses are given.* Quixote imagines the windmills to be giants with long arms. Quixote can be seen either as a foolish madman or as a courageous and fanciful believer in the chivalric age. He is made both noble and ludicrous by his faith in the world described in books of chivalry and by his resulting attempts to make the most common occurrences into adventures.

5. Sancho denies his master's assertion that the windmills are giants and warns Quixote against attacking them. Quixote charges the windmills on horseback, gets his lance caught in the windmill's sail, and is dragged after it, injuring himself against the ground. Sancho rushes to Quixote's assistance and tries to argue with Quixote about the nature of his adventure.

ANSWERS FOR CONNECTIONS

Responses will vary. Possible responses are given.

1. **Medieval Romance.** Quixote is similar to Arthur, Tristan, and Chaucer's knight in that he wears armor, carries a weapon, rides a horse, and searches for adventure. Like the heroes of medieval romance, Quixote practices the values of chivalry; he is always brave, courteous, and honorable.

2. **Courtly Love.** Quixote idealizes his lady, loves her from afar, and longs for an adventure in order to send his lady a trophy to

(cont.)

ANSWERS FOR CONNECTIONS (CONT.)

prove himself a chivalric hero. Quixote's object is Aldonza Lorenzo, or Dulcinea del Toboso. He needs to find a lady due to the conventions of the medieval romance in which courtly love inspires all of a knight's adventures. He commends himself to his lady, Dulcinea, before battle.

3. **Satire.** The fantastic giants and monsters, the beautiful but remote princess, and the incredible exploits of knights-errant are treated satirically by Cervantes, who objects to the lack of realism in the medieval romance but who also admires the imagination and values expressed in books of chivalry.

The Development of the English Language:
Middle English

THE EMERGENCE OF MIDDLE ENGLISH

The Norman Conquest brought about profound changes in the English language. From 1066 to the mid-1200s, the aristocratic ruling class in England spoke Norman French almost exclusively. During this time, few French words entered English. However, from about 1260 to the late 1300s, most English aristocrats were bilingual, speaking both Norman French and English. When speaking and writing English, these aristocrats borrowed heavily from the pronunciation, grammar, and vocabulary of their native French. As a result, the English language underwent rapid change, developing into what is now known as **Middle English.**

The vast changes that occurred in the language can be seen by comparing the passages written near the beginning and near the end of the Medieval Period. The first passage below, written shortly after the Norman Conquest, can barely be read today without translation. The second passage, written in the 1300s, presents few difficulties to the modern reader.

ENGLISH LYRIC FROM THE EARLY 1100S

Merie sungen ðe muneches binnin Ely
Da Cnut ching reu ðer by.
Roweð, cnites, noer the land
And here we pes muneshes sæng.
[Translation: Merrily sang the monks with Ely
When Cnut the king rowed thereby.
Row, knights, nearer the land
And let us hear the monks' song.]

PASSAGE FROM CHAUCER'S *TROILUS AND CRESSIDA*

Go, lytle° booke,	*little*
And for ther is so greet diversitee°	*great diversity*
In English and in wryting° of our tonge,°	*writing, tongue*
So preye I god that noon miswryte° thee.	*no one miswrite*

WORDS BORROWED FROM FRENCH

The American poet Wallace Stevens once wrote that English and French are the same language. Stevens's comment was an exaggeration, but it contains a kernel of truth. As a result of borrowings from French that began in the Medieval Period, it is today almost impossible to write an English paragraph without using many words of French origin.

Since the Norman conquerors were the ruling class, one would expect that many of the words that they introduced would be related to their power and prestige, as the following chart demonstrates:

SOME WORDS BORROWED FROM FRENCH

Politics and Political Entities
assembly
baron
chancellor
city
constable
council
councilor
count
countess
county
crown
duchess
duke
empire
esquire
government
majesty
marquis
master
mayor
minister
mistress
nation
noble
palace
parliament
peer
prince
realm
reign
royal
scepter
sovereign
squire
throne
tyrant
village

Financial Matters
account
assets
balance
bargain
budget
customer
dues
estate
fine
heir
lease
merchant
price
property
purchase
receipt
revenue
tax
treasury
value

Power Relationships
allegiance
authority
bondage
command
homage
obey
oppress
power
servant
slave
subject
vassal

The Law
accuse
advocate
arrest
assault
assembly
attorney
bail
bailiff
banish
bill
burglary
condemn
convict
coroner
crime
decree
defendant
equity
evidence
exile
felony
fine
innocent
jail
judge
judgment
jury
just
justice
legal
libel
pardon
perjury
petition
plaintiff
plea
punishment
ransom
rebel
sentence
suit
summons
traitor

treason
trespass
verdict
warden

War
advance
arms
army
attack
besiege
conquer
defense
defend
lance
lieutenant
mail
peace
pursue
retreat
siege
surrender
vanquish
war

Manners
agreeable
bounty
calm
chivalry
courage
courteous
courtesy
dainty
dangerous
debonair
dignity
error
false
folly
frank

gentleness
gracious
honest
honor
loyalty
mean
mercy
nice
perfect
pity
pleasant
please
praise
pure
suffer
tender
valor

Religion
altar
angel
baptism
cardinal
cathedral
chapel
choir
clergy
cloister
communion
conscience
devotion
evangelist
faith
feat
grace
pew
preach
prophet
relic
saint
sermon

LITERARY NOTE

You may wish to share with your students the following lovely ballad in Middle English:

Lully, lulley, lully, lulley
The faucon hath borne my make away.

He bare him up; he bare him down;
He bare him into an orchard brown.

In that orchard there was an halle
That was hanged with purpill and pall!

And in that hall there was a bede,
It was hanged with gold so rede.

And in that bed there lithe a knight
His woundes bleeding day and night.

By that bede side kneleth a may,
And she wepeth both night and day.

And by that bede side there stondeth a stone,
Corpus Christi written there on.

The lovely lyric "The Falcon Hath Borne My Mate Away" may be read as a mystical statement of the ever present death of Christ to believers (his mates). Purple and gold are associated with royalty. The may, or maid, might be the Virgin Mary. *Corpus Christi* is Latin for "the body of Christ."

To give students an idea
what Middle English
sounded like, play for
them the opening to "The
Prologue" to *The Canterbury Tales*
on Track 7 of the audiocassette in
the Teacher's Resource Kit.
Students can follow along by
looking at the text on page 185.

service	furniture	emerald	ease	**Food**
vice	lamp	fashion	falcon	banquet
virtue	latch	garments	figure	boil
	mason	gown	harmony	cherries
Architecture	moat	jewel	joust	cream
and	mortar	lace	joy	dinner
Furnishings	pavement	pearl	juggler	feast
aisle	porch	robe	kennel	lemons
arch	table	sable	leisure	meal
balcony	tapestry	satin	melody	pastry
belfry	tower		minstrel	peaches
blanket	turret	**Leisure,**	music	pheasant
carpet		**Entertainment,**	ornament	roast
castle	**Fine Clothing**	**and the Arts**	painting	salad
cellar	apparel	art	pleasure	soup
cement	attire	chant	quarry	spice
chair	buckle	chess	revelry	stew
chamber	cape	chord	scent	sugar
chimney	cloak	color	sculpture	supper
couch	costume	comfort	sport	toast
dungeon	dress	dance	tone	
fortress	embroidery	design	tournament	

Fortunately for English writers and speakers, many native English words survived alongside their newer French counterparts, creating a wealth of choices between words that are more formal or less. The following chart shows some examples.

ORIGINS OF WORDS IN ENGLISH WITH RELATED MEANINGS

FROM OLD ENGLISH	FROM FRENCH
begin	commence
bloom	flower
buy	purchase
fight	battle
foe	enemy
folk	people
help	aid
hide	conceal
house	mansion
king	emperor
theft	burglary
weapons	arms
wedding	marriage
wish	desire

Notice that the French word often carries **connotations**, or associations, of formality or sophistication not carried by the corresponding English word. This is because the French-speaking Normans were the sophisticated ruling class. The distinction can be seen clearly in certain word pairs related to food. Native English people, made by the Normans into a sub-servient, lower class, had responsibility for caring for barnyard animals. Therefore, the terms that survived for describing these animals when alive were English in origin. However, the terms that were used to describe animals when killed and cooked were of French origin, for it was the French-speaking Normans who were wealthy enough to eat prepared meat.

ENGLISH WORDS FOR LIVE ANIMALS	FRENCH TERMS FOR PREPARED MEATS
pig, boar, swine	pork, bacon
cow, ox	beef, veal
deer	venison
sheep	mutton

OTHER CHANGES IN THE LANGUAGE

Changes in Pronunciation and Grammar. We have seen that Norman French greatly influenced the vocabulary of English, increasing the size and diversity of the word stock, or **lexicon**. French also influenced both the pronunciation and grammar of English. In the area of pronunciation, English became much less harsh and guttural. In the area of grammar, the use of English by aristocrats unfamiliar with its intricacies led to simplification. Grammatical endings, or **inflections**, that were common in Old English were dropped, and subjects generally began to appear before their verbs rather than vice versa, as was common in Old English.

Standardization. Throughout the Medieval Period, spoken and written English appeared in what Chaucer called a "greet diversitee" of forms, making it difficult for people of one part of England to communicate effectively with people from another part. Middle English was divided into five major dialects: Northern, East Midland, West Midland, Southeastern, and Southwestern. Within these major dialects areas, individual communities, speakers, and writers followed their own rules for pronunciation and spelling, making communication all the more difficult. Toward the end of the Medieval Period and during the early Renaissance, two forces conspired to change that situation by introducing regularities of pronunciation and spelling into the language. The first of these was the rise in prestige of the **East Midland dialect** spoken in London, the capital city. The second was the spread of printed works following the introduction of printing by Thomas Caxton in the late 1400s. Caxton printed his books in the East Midland dialect and regularized to some extent the spelling and vocabulary of the authors whose works he made available. The East Midland dialect of London and of Caxton developed into the **Modern English** spoken and written today.

VOCABULARY DEVELOPMENT EXERCISE

▶Give students the following exercise.

Read the Language Arts Survey, 4.41, "Sentence-completion Questions." Using the vocabulary words on page 236, write a test containing five sentence-completion questions. Write three answer choices for each problem. Vary the forms of the words as necessary. When you are done, exchange tests with a partner.

Example.

1. The knight sought _____ at the hermit's retreat, because he had been _____ in engaging in battles with his fellows.

(A) absolution . . . wanton

(B) vengeance . . . personable

(C) indignation . . . saucy

Answer: A

ADDITIONAL RESOURCES

ASSESSMENT PORTFOLIO
- Vocabulary Worksheet: Unit 3, 4.3.25
- Study Guide: Unit 3 Test, 4.3.26
- Unit 3 Test, 4.3.27

ESSENTIAL SKILLS PRACTICE BOOKS

Writing
- Interviewing, 1.27

Language
- Adding Appositive Phrases, 2.48
- Identifying Gerunds, 2.17
- Combining Sentences Using Phrases, 2.52
- Reducing Wordiness, 2.59
- Using Proper Capitalization, 2.107–2.133

Speaking and Listening
- Interpersonal Communication, 3.5
- Public Speaking, 3.7

Study and Research
- Computer-Assisted Research, 4.26
- Paraphrasing and Summarizing, 4.30
- Multiple-choice Questions, 4.37
- Synonym and Antonym Questions, 4.44

AUDIOCASSETTE
- "The Great Silkie of Shule Skerrie," Track 5

UNIT REVIEW

The Medieval Period

VOCABULARY FROM THE SELECTIONS

absolution, 192	entreat, 162	perdition, 208	stature, 189
abstrusest, 198	felicity, 194	personable, 191	stile, 206
accrue, 192	flax, 200	phantasmagoria, 227	strife, 206
ambling, 196	frugal, 198	postern, 169	sunder, 159
amends, 220	fustian, 189	prating, 207	superfluity, 195
amiably, 161	grisly, 206	prelate, 191	sward, 198
appurtenance, 172	guile, 195	prevarication, 200	tillage, 205
arbitrate, 192	hapless, 153	proffer, 214	transgress, 161
asunder, 196	heath, 187	providence, 176	transitory, 213
beguile, 162	hoary, 206	quoth, 140	treachery, 161
betide, 161	hostelry, 188	respite, 156, 216	unworldly, 193
burnish, 155	indignation, 176	sanguine, 194	usurp, 171
caitiff, 217, 230	inter, 172	saucy, 190	vanquish, 163
cajole, 183	intrigue, 161	scathe, 160	vengeance, 183
cloister, 191	ken, 139	scrupulosity, 197	verity, 192
comeliest, 153	lanyard, 195	scurrility, 201	wanton, 192
comely, 139	mire, 197	sedately, 190	wary, 205
countenance, 154, 171	miscreant, 208	seemly, 191	wax, 171
covenant, 158	mortification, 163	smite, 155	withal, 190
dais, 153, 194	motley, 193	sober, 193	wroth, 168
diligent, 196	necromancy, 170	solicitous, 191	
duress, 199	obeisance, 176	sonorous, 228	
encumbered, 197	ostentatious, 181	splay, 199	

LITERARY TERMS

archaic language, 145	exemplum, 186, 210	point of view, 184
Arthurian romance, 165, 167	folk tale, 178, 209	romance, 132, 151
autobiography, 180, 184	frame tale, 186, 204	satire, 204, 231
ballad, 133, 136	lyric poem, 142, 145	simile, 147
Breton lai, 148, 151	metonymy, 147	theme, 145
characterization, 204	mock epic, 225	translation, 145, 154
chivalry, 132, 155, 164	morality play, 133, 212, 221	
courtly love, 147, 151, 178, 231	naive allegory, 221	
	parody, 225	

SYNTHESIS: QUESTIONS FOR WRITING, RESEARCH, OR DISCUSSION

GENRE STUDIES

1. **Medieval Ballads.** What form does a ballad have? Why did people compose ballads? What purposes did they serve? Refer to the ballads in this unit and in the Selections for Additional Reading on page 223. See also "Robin Hood and Allen a Dale" on page 6 in Unit 1.

2. **Medieval Romance.** What where the ideals of courtly love and chivalry? How do Tristan in "The Honeysuckle: Chevrefoil," Gawain in *Sir Gawain and the Green Knight,* and King Uther, Arthur, and his knights in *Le Morte d'Arthur* embody or fail to embody these ideals? (Note: Refer to the descriptions of *courtly love* and of *chivalry* in the Unit Introduction and in the Handbook of Literary Terms.)

THEMATIC STUDIES

3. **The *Memento Mori* Theme.** What is the *memento mori* theme? How is it expressed in the play *Everyman* and in the lyric poem "Ubi Sunt Qui ante Nos Fuerunt"? Why might this have been a common theme in medieval literature? What does the widespread use of this theme in medieval literature tell us about the beliefs of medieval people in Europe?

HISTORICAL AND BIOGRAPHICAL STUDIES

4. **Medieval Women.** What ideals of womanhood were common in medieval England? How were these ideals influenced by adoration of the Virgin Mary and by romance literature? How did the ideals differ from the realities? Explore the lives of medieval English women. Refer to the following materials from the unit: "I Sing of a Maiden," "The Great Silkie of Shule Skerrie," "The Honeysuckle: Chevrefoil," the selection from *The Book of Margery Kempe,* and the descriptions of women in "The Prologue" to Chaucer's *The Canterbury Tales.*

5. **Medieval English Poetry.** Consider the effect of the Norman invasion on the English poetry. What differences are there between medieval English poetry and Anglo-Saxon poetry? What changes or innovations occurred in English poetry as a result of the Norman Conquest? What old forms were abandoned? What new forms emerged? How did the form and content of poetry change?

6. **Medieval English Literature and the Church.** Much of medieval literature is didactic. In other words, it teaches moral lessons. What lessons are taught by "Ubi Sun Qui ante Nos Fuerunt?", *Everyman,* "The Prologue" to *The Canterbury Tales,* and "The Pardoner's Tale"? What teachings of the church are embodied in these selections?

►These prompts are suitable as topics for research papers. Refer to the Language Arts Survey, 4.20–4.34, "Research Skills." (To evaluate research papers, see the evaluation forms for writing, revising, and proofreading in the *Assessment Portfolio,* 7.1–7.10.)

►These prompts can be adapted for use as topics for oral reports or debates. (To evaluate these projects, see the evaluation forms in the *Assessment Portfolio,* 7.17–7.19.)

LANGUAGE LAB   SENTENCE FRAGMENTS AND RUN-ONS

A **sentence** contains a subject and a verb and expresses a complete idea. A group of words that does not contain both a subject and a verb and that does not express a complete idea is a **sentence fragment.** When revising or proofreading a piece of writing, you should look for sentence fragments and correct them.

LANGUAGE ARTS SURVEY

For additional help, see the Language Arts Survey, 2.61.

CORRECTING SENTENCE FRAGMENTS
SENTENCE FRAGMENT: writing in her native French (*does not express a complete idea*)
COMPLETE SENTENCE: Writing in her native French, Marie retold stories from the Arthurian tradition.
SENTENCE FRAGMENT: Is a beautiful retelling of the story of Tristan and Isolde (*does not contain a subject*)
COMPLETE SENTENCE: "The Honeysuckle: Chevrefoil" is a beautiful retelling of the story of Tristan and Isolde.
SENTENCE FRAGMENT: Tristan, a knight in the service of King Mark (*does not contain a verb*)
COMPLETE SENTENCE: Tristan, a knight in the service of King Mark, fell in love with Queen Isolde.

Writers also commonly make the mistake of running two sentences together without proper punctuation or conjunctions. When two sentences are run together in this way, they are called a **run-on.** The following chart shows four ways in which run-on sentences can be corrected.

LANGUAGE ARTS SURVEY

For additional help, see the Language Arts Survey, 2.62.

CORRECTING RUN-ONS
RUN-ON: Lancelot was a valiant knight, he was not able to achieve the Holy Grail.
CORRECTED USING A COMMA AND A COORDINATING CONJUNCTION: Lancelot was a valiant knight, but he was not able to achieve the Holy Grail.
CORRECTED BY TURNING ONE SENTENCE INTO A SUBORDINATE CLAUSE: Although Lancelot was a valiant knight, he was not able to achieve the Holy Grail.
CORRECTED BY ADDING A SEMICOLON AND A CONJUNCTIVE ADVERB: Lancelot was a valiant knight; however, he was not able to achieve the Holy Grail.

EXERCISE Correcting Fragments and Run-ons

Rewrite the following paragraphs, correcting all sentence fragments and run-ons.

EXAMPLE: Medieval people called popular stories *romans* because they believed the stories to have been passed down from Roman days, from the word *roman,* meaning "story," we get our modern word *romance.*

> Medieval people called popular stories *romans* because they believed the stories to have been passed down from Roman days. From the word *roman,* meaning "story," we get our modern word *romance.*

Romantic literature is associated for most readers with medieval England, Sir Thomas Malory's *Le Morte d'Arthur,* and the knights of the Round Table however, a rich romantic tradition existed outside England as well. Three centuries before Malory was born. Chrétien de Troyes wrote in his native French of the adventures of Gawain, Perceval, and Lancelot. While Chrétien's tales are much shorter and lack the prolific characters present in Malory's work. The symbolism and moral dilemmas present in Chrétien's tales make them superior works of literature in some critics' eyes. Chrétien's patron was Eleanor of Aquitaine, wife of Henry II. Who also influenced Andreas Capellanus's writing of *The Art of Courtly Love,* an intentionally humorous work, that was taken so seriously that it influenced the relationships between noblemen and noblewomen, both in literature and life. For the next several hundred years.

Gottfried, a German writer, also borrowed a tale from King Arthur's court this was the story of Tristan and Isolde. However, Gottfried did not share Malory's love of battles, troops of knights, and tournaments, Gottfried's main theme in his treatment of the Tristan story is that true love outweighs all worldly concerns. Not all romantic writers borrowed their material from England Ludovico Ariosto took the court of Charlemagne as his inspiration for his *Orlando Furioso.* A cosmopolitan and sensuous epic poem written in Italian. While women are often one-sided characters in the romance. Ariosto's work abounds with female knights and a surprisingly modern concern for the rights of women.

The romance is a genre in its own right, one of its most significant contributions is its role as the forerunner of the novel. The first romance that is often classified as a novel is Cervantes's *Don Quixote.* An excerpt from which appears on page 225.

Exercise

Romantic literature is associated for most readers with medieval England, Sir Thomas Malory's *Le Morte d'Arthur,* and the knights of the Round Table; however, a rich romantic tradition existed outside England as well. Three centuries before Malory was born, Chrétien de Troyes wrote in his native French of the adventures of Gawain, Perceval, and Lancelot. While Chrétien's tales are much shorter and lack the prolific characters present in Malory's work, the symbolism and moral dilemmas present in Chrétien's tales make them superior works of literature in some critics' eyes. Chrétien's patron was Eleanor of Aquitaine, wife of Henry II, who also influenced Andreas Capellanus's writing of *The Art of Courtly Love,* an intentionally humorous work which was taken so seriously that it influenced the relationships between noblemen and noblewomen, both in literature and life, for the next several hundred years.

Gottfried, a German writer, also borrowed a tale from King Arthur's court, and this was the story of Tristan and Isolde. However, Gottfried did not share Malory's love of battles, troops of knights, and tournaments. Gottfried's main theme in his treatment of the Tristan story is that true love outweighs all worldly concerns. Not all romantic writers borrowed their material from England. Ludovico Ariosto took the court of Charlemagne as his inspiration for his *Orlando Furioso,* a cosmopolitan and sensuous epic poem written in Italian. While women are often one-sided characters in the romance, Ariosto's work abounds with female knights and a surprisingly modern concern for the rights of women.

The romance is a genre in its own right, but one of its most significant contributions is its role as the forerunner of the novel. The first romance that is often classified as a novel is Cervantes's *Don Quixote,* an excerpt from which appears on page 225.

UNIT 4 THE ENGLISH RENAISSANCE (1485–1660)

The Sonnet. William Mulready, courtesy of the
Trustees of the Victoria & Albert Museum

n the little frame of [a person's] body there is a representation of the universal . . . a kind of participation of all the parts thereof; therefore was [a person] called microcosmos, or the little world.

—Sir Walter Raleigh

241

GOALS/OBJECTIVES

Studying this unit will enable students to
- experience the personal feelings expressed in and typical of Renaissance lyrics
- explain how Renaissance ideas affected English literature
- describe the historical and literary importance of the Protestant Reformation and Counter-Reformation, Martin Luther, King Henry VIII, Queen Elizabeth I, and the King James Bible
- describe and identify sonnets, allegories, and pastoral poems
- describe the work and influence of several major Elizabethan poets

Henry VIII. Hans Holbein. Board of Trustees of the National Museums and Galleries on Merseyside (Walker Art Gallery, Liverpool)

THE RENAISSANCE

The word *renaissance* means, literally, a "rebirth." Historians use the word to refer to the period between the fifteenth and early seventeenth centuries when, influenced by a rebirth of interest in Greek and Latin learning, Europe was moving away from medieval habits of thought toward the modern.

Medieval thought looked for happiness not in this life but in the next. People in the Middle Ages tended to think of earthly life as brief and of little value. They placed their hope on the future, and so medieval literature is dominated by religious subjects and themes.

Typically, if a decision needed to be made, or if a question arose, a medieval man or woman would look to some authority. To Europeans of the Middle Ages, the Roman Catholic Church was the ultimate authority in all things. Lines of authority also dominated in the political sphere. The feudal lord had complete authority over the serfs living on his land. In turn, the lord looked to the higher authority of a greater noble or the king.

In sharp contrast, the writers and thinkers of ancient Greece and Rome often looked not to some authority but to individual conscience. The Greeks and Romans tended to place value on the arts and works of this world. Their literature was dominated by questions related to human life: what is the good life? what is a good state? Rediscovering the arts and literature of ancient Greece and Rome brought about, first in Italy and then in the rest of Europe, a renewed interest in human life on earth, as opposed to life after death. Therefore, the Renaissance devotion to the Greek and Latin classics has come to be known as **Humanism.**

LITERARY EVENTS

► = British Events

► 1515. Thomas More publishes *Utopia*

1500. *Adages* by Desiderius Erasmus published

1485	1490	1495	1500	1505	1510	1515

►1485. Reign of Henry VII (1485–1509)

1492. Christopher Columbus arrives in Americas

1504. Queen Isabella (Castile) dies after a thirty-year reign

1507. Painting *Mona Lisa* by Leonardo da Vinci

► 1509. Henry VII dies and is succeeded by his son, Henry VIII

1517. Martin Luther challenge the Roman Catholic Churc

HISTORICAL EVENTS

242 UNIT FOUR / THE ENGLISH RENAISSANCE

THEMATIC CURRENTS

Use the following selections to explore these themes with your students.

UNREQUITED LOVE

- "Whoso List to Hunt," 250
- Sonnet 31 (Sidney), 254
- "Song, To Celia," 286
- "Alas! So All Things. . .," 293
- Sonnets by Petrarch, 297

NATURE

- "The Passionate Shepherd to His Love," 261
- Sonnet 18 (Shakespeare), 279
- "Jack and Joan," 295
- Sonnet 30 (Shakespeare), 293

LOYALTY

- from *The Færie Queene,* 257
- "The Doubt of Future Foes," 272
- Sonnet 29 (Shakespeare), 282
- "Heart Exchange," 293
- from Psalm 137, 296

This is not to say that the humanists were irreligious. Far from it. Much humanist philosophy was based on the idea that human beings were created in the image of God. The humanists saw each person as a little world, or *microcosmos,* complete in itself. They believed that human beings, sharing as they did in the divine, could perfect themselves and the institutions of this world. Out of this belief came a new emphasis on learning and the arts, as well as religious and political debates that led to the Protestant Reformation, the decline of feudalism, and the emergence of modern nationalism.

Key to these developments was the invention of printing. In 1453, Johannes Gutenberg set up the first printing press in Germany. Soon, presses appeared all over Europe, and people began to read and think for themselves, to challenge authority, and to change their institutions and their lives.

THE BEGINNINGS OF THE TUDOR DYNASTY

From 1455 to 1485, England was torn by civil war between two noble families, York and Lancaster. The Wars of the Roses ended with the defeat by Henry Tudor of Richard III. **Henry VII** ascended the throne, becoming the first monarch of the **Tudor Dynasty,** which ruled England until 1603.

Henry VII inherited a country exhausted by war. However, he proved to be a capable leader, one who rebuilt the nation's treasury, established a powerful central government, made profitable commercial treaties with other nations, and built a fleet of merchant ships that formed the basis for English power during the coming centuries. During Henry VII's reign, England began exploratory expeditions to the New World that led to the colonialization of North America.

Henry VII died in 1509, leaving the throne to his son, **Henry VIII,** one of the most important and colorful figures in English history. Well-educated, strong-willed, self-absorbed, and charismatic, Henry VIII further increased the power of the monarchy. His desire for a male heir to carry on his successes led to the most important event of his reign, the English break with the Church of Rome.

► 1549. *The Book of Common Prayer* published in England

► 1525. Tyndale's *New Testament,* first English translation of the Bible

| 1520 | 1525 | 1530 | 1535 | 1540 | 1545 | 1550 |

►1534. Henry VIII breaks with Church of Rome

►1536. Anne Boleyn beheaded

1543. Nikolaus Copernicus defies the church and establishes the theory that the earth revolves around the sun

►1547. Henry VIII dies and is succeeded by Edward VI

INTRODUCTION **243**

• **Social Studies.** Suggest that students research the history of the rise of nationalism in Europe. The division of the world into nation-states is something we take for granted today. However, the modern nation-state did not develop until the decline of feudalism cleared the way for it. What exactly did the concept of a "nation" mean to people during this transition period? How did the birth of nation-states change life for ordinary people?

►**Teaching Note:** Interested students might investigate the etymology of the word *nation,* which has its roots in the Latin *nasci,* "to be born." Ask them to consider how a society based on birth or ethnicity differs from one based on allegiance to a particular form of government. They might also discuss any current political situations in which formerly unified countries are being torn apart along ethnic lines.

• **Social Studies/ Mapping.** Some students may wish to research the geographical borders of this period and then draw maps representing these borders. Have students compare their maps to a current map of Europe to note how the boundaries of various countries have changed.

LITERARY CURRENTS

Use the following selections to explore these concepts and techniques with your students.

METAPHOR
- from *The Faerie Queene,* 257
- "Song, to Celia," 286
- Psalm 23, 296
- Eve's Apology in Defense of Women, 294

PETRARCHAN SONNET
- "Whoso List to Hunt," 250
- Sonnet 31 (Sidney), 254
- Sonnets by Petrarch, 297

ELIZABETHAN OR SHAKESPEAREAN SONNET
- Sonnets by Shakespeare, 279, 293
- "Heart Exchange," 293

Martin Luther fastening his 95 Theses to the door of All Saints Church. The Granger Collection, NY

THE PROTESTANT REFORMATION IN ENGLAND

In 1517, a German monk named **Martin Luther** nailed to the door of a church in Wittenburg, Germany, his so-called **"95 Theses,"** a list of objections to central beliefs and practices of the Roman Catholic Church. While preparing for his ordination as a priest, Luther had been struck by his own unworthiness to take the holy sacraments. He believed that because of the Original Sin of Adam in the Garden of Eden, people were fundamentally sinful and could not, through their works, become worthy of taking such sacraments as Holy Communion and Holy Orders. Instead, according to Luther, people had to depend on the grace of God, extended to them despite their sinfulness. Luther also objected to practices of the church such as the sale of indulgences, or pardons for sins. He challenged the authority of the Pope and of the church in general, claiming that religion was a matter of individual conscience to be worked out between each person and God without the intermediary of a priest. This belief led him to emphasize reading of the Holy Scriptures, which was made possible for ordinary men and women by the invention of printing and the translation of the Bible into the vernacular languages of Europe.

Luther's ideas spread throughout Europe, leading to a widespread, often bloody revolt against church authority known as the **Protestant Reformation.** A central figure in the Protestant Reformation was **John Calvin** of Switzerland, who took Luther's ideas about Original Sin a step further, teaching that all events were preordained by God, that God chose at the beginning of time which people would be saved, or among the **elect,** and which would be damned. This Calvinist doctrine, known as **predestination,** became the central belief of the **Puritan Movement** that was to have a strong effect on life in England and in the English colonies in North America.

LITERARY EVENTS

▶1588. Christopher Marlowe writes *The Tragical History of Doctor Faustus*

▶1579. Edmund Spenser publishes *The Shepheardes Calender*

1555	1560	1565	1570	1575	1580	1585

▶1553. Edward VI dies and is succeeded by Mary Tudor
▶1555. Mary reestablishes Catholicism and persecutes Protestants
▶1558. Elizabeth I becomes queen at Mary Tudor's death

HISTORICAL EVENTS

▶1588. England defeats the Spanish Armada

244 *UNIT FOUR / THE ENGLISH RENAISSANCE*

In England, the Protestant Reformation came about because of Henry VIII's inability to sire a son. Modern science has learned that it is the male who determines the gender of offspring. However, Henry had no way of knowing this. He was angered by the failure of his wife, Catherine, to produce a male heir, and he was attracted to a young woman of his court, Anne Boleyn. At that time, under church law, a divorce could be obtained only through annulment, a procedure by which the church determined that the original marriage was invalid for some reason, such as consanguinity, or closeness of blood relations. Henry VIII appealed to the Pope for an annulment of his marriage to Catherine. However, the Pope would not grant Henry's request. Furious, Henry broke with the Roman Church; asked Parliament to declare him Supreme Head of the new **Church of England,** or **Anglican Church**; received a divorce from an English church court; and married Anne, who gave him a female child, Elizabeth. Henry dismantled the Roman Catholic Church in England, seizing its land and wealth. He burned and pillaged the monasteries, in the process destroying many precious manuscripts. He even ordered the execution of his one-time friend **Sir Thomas More,** chancellor of England and author of *Utopia*, because More would not sign a document recognizing Henry as head of the church.

Sir Thomas More. Hans Holbein, 1527. The Frick Collection, NY

Anne Boleyn did not produce a male heir. In 1536, Anne was convicted of adultery and beheaded. Henry then married Jane Seymour, who bore him a son, Edward. When Henry died in 1547, this frail, sickly nine-year-old became King Edward VI. During Edward's reign, Protestantism spread throughout England, the Anglican creed was established, and the **Book of Common Prayer** was written. Edward died at the age of fifteen and was succeeded by his older sister, Mary I, child of Henry's first wife, the Spanish Catherine of Aragon.

MARY I AND THE COUNTER REFORMATION IN ENGLAND

Mary I, a staunch Catholic, attempted to restore the power and authority of the Roman Catholic Church in England. Historians call such attempts throughout Europe to undo the

BIOGRAPHICAL NOTE

Thomas More (1477–1535) is one of the most widely respected figures in English history. As a young man he studied Latin and logic, and in 1501 he entered the law profession. Despite the demands of his career, More continued to read widely and became a Humanist scholar. The most famous expression of his Humanist philosophy was his book *Utopia*, published in 1516. In it he described his vision of a perfect society ruled by reason. More was intimately involved in the education of his own children and other young people who joined his household. Most of these were girls, who received a then unusual opportunity for a classical education. More became a trusted advisor to King Henry VIII, who made him chancellor in 1529. More tried to resign his position two years later, realizing that he could never acknowledge a secular king as head of the Church of England. Because he did not accept Henry's divorce of his previous queen, More did not attend the coronation of Anne Boleyn in 1533, and the next year he refused to sign the Act of Succession. After spending over a year imprisoned in the Tower of London, More was convicted of treason and sentenced to death. He was canonized by the Roman Catholic Church in 1935.

QUOTABLES

66 This hath not offended the king. **99**

—Sir Thomas More (spoken as he moved his beard aside while placing his head on the executioner's block)

▶1615. George Chapman translates Homer's *Odyssey*

1615. Cervantes publishes *El Ingenioso Hidalgo Don Quixote de la Mancha*

▶1611. George Chapman translates Homer's *Iliad*

▶1609. Shakespeare finishes *Sonnets*

▶1591. *Astrophil and Stella* published

▶1603. Shakespeare writes *Othello*

▶1590. Sir Philip Sidney's *Arcadia*, a pastoral prose romance

▶1590. William Shakespeare introduces *King Henry VI*

▶1590. Spenser publishes *The Færie Queene*

| 1590 | 1595 | 1600 | 1605 | 1610 | 1615 | 1620 |

▶1603. Elizabeth I dies and is succeeded by James I

▶1607. First settlement at Jamestown, Virginia

▶1619. First African slaves arrive in the Virginia colony

BIOGRAPHICAL NOTE

Anne Boleyn was born around 1507. As a child she lived in France, but she returned to England and joined the court of Henry VIII in 1522. The teenager became the object of many courtiers' attentions, including those of the poet Sir Thomas Wyatt and the king himself. Henry became determined to marry her and finally did so in a secret ceremony in early 1533. Later that year, Anne gave birth to a daughter, Elizabeth. As queen, Anne fell out of favor at court. Henry tired of her as well, and when accusations of adultery surfaced, he had her thrown into the Tower of London. She was convicted and executed in 1536, partly as a result of maneuvering by Thomas Cromwell, who also played a part in the demise of Thomas More.

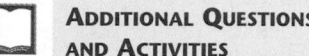

ART NOTE

Ask students to study the painting of Elizabeth I on this page. What mood does the artist's portrayal of the queen create? What details contribute to this mood? What do students think of her clothing? What impression would it have given to people in the sixteenth century? How do leaders in the United States and in other countries of the world dress today? What impressions are they trying to create through their clothing?

▶**Teaching Note:** Interested students might research and collect images of leaders through time or across cultures and make comparisons.

ADDITIONAL QUESTIONS AND ACTIVITIES

Some students may wish to research the role that image and physical appearance play in politics. Some critical questions include the following:

Has appearance become more important to politicians in recent times? If so, what role has modern media played in this increase? You should point out that images of rulers and politicians have been prevalent on coins, in paintings, and as statues for centuries. Ask students how rulers in the past could control representations of their appearance.

You may want to note that during the presidency of Franklin D. Roosevelt, most Americans did not know that he was confined to a wheelchair. Students may want to research how he kept the public from knowing his condition.

To what extent can politicians control their representation now? How so?

Queen Elizabeth I (the "Ditchley" portrait).
National Portrait Gallery, London

Protestant Reformation the **Counter Reformation.** Mary restored Roman Catholic practices to English church services, ordered the execution of many Protestants, made the Pope once again the head of the English church, and married her Roman Catholic cousin, the Spaniard Philip II. At the time, Spain was a powerful country, and the English people resented the marriage, not wanting England to become a client state. Anti-Catholic and anti-Spanish feeling ran high in England, especially in the cities and towns. Mary I met this feeling with repression and brutality, earning for herself the nickname "Bloody Mary." She died in 1558.

THE ELIZABETHAN AGE

Perhaps the greatest monarch in all of English history was Mary's successor, **Elizabeth I,** daughter of Henry VIII and Anne Boleyn. One of the ironies of European history is that this child, unwanted by Henry, should have turned out to be so able a leader. Under Queen Elizabeth I, England grew to become the most powerful nation in Europe, and English literature reached what many people consider its zenith. Elizabeth's long reign, from 1558 to 1603, is known as the **Elizabethan Age.**

Elizabeth I was a true exemplar of the Renaissance person. Widely read in Latin, Greek, and various European languages, she gathered around her many of the finest writers of her time. Her court was a center of literary activity, and many of the greatest works of the period are dedicated to her. She herself wrote poetry and made Greek and Latin translations. Elizabeth was also a shrewd leader. Cleverly, she remained unmarried and played European states off against one another, leading each to hope for an alliance, through marriage, to the English throne. The peace that resulted from this policy gave England an

LITERARY EVENTS

▶1651. Thomas Hobbes writes *Leviathan*
▶1649. Lovelace publishes *Lucasta*

▶1632. John Milton writes "On His Having Arrived at the Age of Twenty-Three"

1625	1630	1635	1640	1645	1650	1655

▶1625. James I dies. Charles I ascends the throne

▶1648. Execution of Charles I

HISTORICAL EVENTS

246   *UNIT FOUR / THE ENGLISH RENAISSANCE*

The Launching of the Fireships against the Spanish Armada. National Maritime Museum Picture Library. Spain's heavy warships, known as galleons, were no match for the light, easily maneuvered ships of the English fleet.

opportunity to build its navy, which became the foundation of English power for centuries to come. At home, Elizabeth quelled religious strife with a policy of moderation. She reestablished the monarch as head of the Church of England and ended the persecution of Protestants. She also tolerated Catholic beliefs and practices.

However, this policy of moderation did not please everyone. Throughout much of her reign, Elizabeth had to cope with Catholic plots against her. These plots sought to bring to power Mary Stuart, the exiled Queen of Scotland who had fled to England after an uprising led by Protestants. Stuart, the Catholic great-granddaughter of Henry VII, stood next in line for the throne. Catholics, who did not accept as lawful Henry VIII's marriage to Anne Boleyn, and who therefore considered Elizabeth an illegitimate pretender, thought of Mary as the rightful Queen of England. Mary Stuart was imprisoned but allowed to live for nineteen years. Finally, however, the English Parliament ordered her execution for plotting to kill Elizabeth.

The execution of Mary Stuart infuriated Spain's king, Philip II, who already had cause to be upset with the English. For years, English pirates such as Sir Francis Drake had preyed on Spanish ships and colonies with the secret blessing and support of Queen Elizabeth. In 1588, Philip decided to attack England with a mighty fleet, the **Spanish Armada**. Fortunately for England, a storm wrecked part of the Spanish fleet, and in a battle in the English Channel, England's navy destroyed the rest of it. The destruction of the Spanish Armada made England the greatest power in Europe.

JAMES I, FIRST OF THE STUART KINGS

The death of the much-revered Queen Elizabeth in 1603 ended the Tudor Dynasty and brought to the throne the first of the Stuart kings, James VI of Scotland, who became **James I** of England. James was a Protestant, but he had Catholic sympathies and, like Elizabeth, detested the radical Protestants, who were called **Puritans** because they wished to "purify" the Church of England by removing all vestiges of Roman Catholic ritual. James I released Catholics from prison and tried to force all English men and women to adopt the rituals of

CROSS-CURRICULAR ACTIVITIES

Social Studies. Interested students may wish to research the defeat of the Spanish Armada. Specific topics include Spain's use of its navy for trade and war; piracy among the European colonial powers; the career of Sir Francis Drake; the design of Spanish and English ships; and the aftermath of the battle.

BIOGRAPHICAL NOTE

The life of **Francis Drake** (*circa* 1541–1596) was filled with adventure from the time of his youth. Some of his adventures were as horrifying as others were admirable. In his mid-twenties he participated in the slave trade in the West Indies. On an expedition in 1567, he narrowly escaped death in a Spanish attack near Mexico; the Spanish navy was to become his lifelong enemy. In 1570, he raided Spanish settlements in Panama, returning home with a rich booty of gold and silver. Competition with Spain was the impetus for his most famous expedition. Not to be outdone by Spaniard Ferdinand Magellan's accomplishment, Elizabeth I sent Drake to sail around the world for England. He did this between 1577 and 1580—alternately plundering, trading, and signing treaties along the way. He was knighted upon his return to England. Drake's role in the defeat of the Spanish Armada sealed his reputation as a naval hero.

HISTORICAL NOTE

The following is a list of English rulers during the Renaissance:

Tudor Kings and Queens

1485–1509	Henry VII
1509–1547	Henry VIII
1547–1553	Edward VI
1553–1558	Mary I
1558–1603	Elizabeth I

Stuart Kings

1603–1625	James I
1625–1649	Charles I

Commonwealth and Protectorate Leaders

1649–1653	Puritan Council
1653–1658	Oliver Cromwell
1658–1660	Richard Cromwell

Although the Reformation brought historic changes to the religious and political structures of Europe, for some Protestants these changes were not enough. A group called the English Separatists (popularly known in the United States today as the Pilgrim Fathers) detached itself from the Church of England around the turn of the seventeenth century. One Separatist congregation based in the town of Scrooby left England altogether in 1608, seeking religious freedom in the Netherlands. They remained in Leiden for over a decade but decided to emigrate to North America in 1620. They received financial backing from a wealthy London entrepreneur who hoped to profit from the endeavor. Dubbed the Pilgrims by one of their leaders, William Bradford (1590–1657), the group set sail from Plymouth, England, in September 1620. Because they landed well north of the region in which they were legally allowed to settle, the Pilgrims' first order of business in America was to sign an agreement—the Mayflower Compact—that established a government for their new colony.

BIBLIOGRAPHICAL NOTE

The following are some excellent sources of information about Renaissance England and its literature:

Black, J. B. *The Reign of Elizabeth, 1558–1603.* 1959.

Burckhardt, Jacob. *The Civilization of the Renaissance.* Trans. S. G. C. Middlemore. Rev. Irene Golden. 1960.

Bush, Douglas. *Mythology and the Renaissance Tradition in English Poetry.* 1963.

Bush, Douglas. *The Renaissance and English Humanism.* 1939.

Buxton, J. *Elizabethan Taste.* 1963.

Collinson, P. *The Elizabethan Puritan Movement.* 1990.

Greene, Thomas M. *The Light in Troy: Imitation and Discovery in Renaissance Poetry.* 1982.

(cont.)

---

the less radical Protestant high church. This brought him into conflict with the House of Commons, which was dominated by Puritans, and led, after his death, to a revolution against the monarchy. The growing resentment in England against the monarchy was partially due to the arrogance of James I, who believed in the doctrine of the **Divine Right of Kings.** According to this doctrine, the monarch is divinely appointed by God. The monarch's will is God's will, and any challenge to regal authority is a challenge to God.

In 1620, a group of Puritans led by **William Bradford** sailed to North America and established the **Plymouth Colony.** However, this was not the first permanent English colony in North America. The first, called **Jamestown** after James I, had been established in 1607.

After the death of James I in 1625, his son **Charles I** became king. A revolution against the monarchy brought the Puritans to power for a while, but eventually the monarchy was restored under **Charles II.** (The story of this revolution and of the Restoration is told in the introduction to Unit 6.)

NONDRAMATIC LITERATURE DURING THE ENGLISH RENAISSANCE

The early Tudor Period was not a great one in the history of English literature. The literature of that time tended to be backward-looking. Printers, following in the footsteps of Caxton, produced editions of works by authors of previous centuries, but few exceptional new works were written.

The reign of Henry VIII saw increased literary activity. Notable poets of the period included **Thomas Wyatt** and **Henry Howard, Earl of Surrey,** jointly credited for introducing to England the fourteen-line Italian verse form known as the **sonnet.** Surrey is also credited with introducing, in his translation from Latin of Vergil's epic poem the *Aeneid,* a new poetic form called **blank verse** (unrhymed verse in iambic pentameter). Blank verse became the medium of many of the greatest plays written during the latter part of the Renaissance.

The true flowering of literary creativity in the English Renaissance had to await the arrival on the scene of Queen Elizabeth. Elizabeth was a great patron of the arts, and under her, literature of all kinds flourished. The Elizabethan Age was remarkable for two kinds of literature: **lyric poetry** and **drama.** Great lyric poets of the period included courtiers such as **Sir Philip Sidney, Christopher Marlowe, Thomas Campion,** and **Ben Jonson,** and would-be courtiers such as **Edmund Spenser.** Sidney, Spenser, and **William Shakespeare** all produced outstanding **sonnet sequences,** or collections of related sonnets. Often, in this time, lyric poems were written for circulation among friends and acquaintances. Only later would some of these poems find their way into one of the numerous anthologies that were popular in the period. (For information about Elizabethan drama, see the introduction to Unit 5.)

The English Renaissance was also remarkable for its achievements in prose. Three works, in particular, stand out. **Sir Thomas More's** *Utopia* gave the world a new word (the book's title) and spawned a great deal of thinking about what society might be like if organized anew on different principles. Over the coming centuries, many utopian experiments in living would be founded on this belief in the power of people to examine and remake the social order. **Francis Bacon's** *Novum Organum* promoted scientific thought and championed the idea that scientific principles should be developed through careful experimentation and unprejudiced inference. By far the greatest prose work of the period, however, was the **King James Bible,** a translation into English of the Hebrew and Greek scriptures. No work ever produced has had so profound an influence on the language, literature, and culture of England and the United States.

BIBLIOGRAPHICAL NOTE (CONT.)

Lever, J. W. *The Elizabethan Love Sonnet.* 1956.

Lewis, C. S. *English Literature in the Sixteenth Century, Excluding Drama.* 1954.

Echoes:
Renaissance England

Man hardly hath a richer thing than honest mirth.

—John Heywood (1497–1580)

[I]t is not my desire to live or to reign longer than my life and reign shall be for your good. And though you have had and may have many mightier and wiser princes sitting in this seat, yet you never had, nor shall have, any love you better.

—Elizabeth I (1533–1603), addressing
the House of Commons in 1607

Go, little book: thyself present.

—Edmund Spenser (1552–1599)

I love Rome, but London better; I favor Italy, but England more; I honor the Latin, but I worship the English. . . . I do not think that any language, be it whatsoever, is better able to utter all arguments, either with more pith or greater plainness, than our English tongue is.

—Richard Mulcaster (1530–1611)

Not marble, nor the gilded monuments of princes, shall outlive this powerful rhyme.

—William Shakespeare (1564–1616)

ADDITIONAL RESOURCES

READER'S GUIDE
- Selection Worksheet, 4.1

ASSESSMENT PORTFOLIO
- Selection Check Test, 4.4.1
- Selection Test, 4.4.2

ESSENTIAL SKILLS PRACTICE BOOKS
- *Writing,* 1.6
- *Language,* 2.6

ENRICHMENT ACTIVITIES

The sonnet uses a hunter pursuing a deer as a metaphor for a man pursuing a romantic relationship with a woman. Students may wish to discuss or write about ways in which this metaphor does and does not work effectively. For example, what is the goal of a hunter? of someone who is being hunted? Can the two ever share a common goal? If this is a metaphor for a human relationship, can mutual happiness ever result?

SUPPORT FOR LEP STUDENTS

Explain that the author often uses words in a sequence different from the way people read, write, and speak English today. Examples include "Yet may I, by no means, my wearied mind/Draw from the deer," "her fair neck round about," and "Cæsar's I am." Also point out that many verbs in Elizabethan literature end in *-th,* such as *hath* ("has"), *cometh* ("come"), and *fleeth* ("flees").

IDIOMS

put out of doubt—ensure that something is true

in vain—uselessly; gaining nothing

ADDITIONAL VOCABULARY

whoso—whoever
afore—before

RENAISSANCE POETRY

"Whoso List to Hunt"
by Sir Thomas Wyatt

ABOUT THE AUTHOR

Sir Thomas Wyatt (1503–1542) was born in Kent at Allington Castle and studied at St. John's College, Cambridge. He was a courtier and diplomat for much of his life and served King Henry VIII as clerk and ambassador. This life was not a serene one, and Sir Thomas was twice arrested and imprisoned as a result of quarrels at court. He spent most of his adult life away from England and was interested in foreign, especially Italian, literature. Wyatt was influenced by the Italian-style sonnets, particularly those of the great fourteenth-century Italian poet Petrarch (see page 297). Along with Henry Howard, Earl of Surrey, he introduced the **Petrarchan sonnet** to England. Although Wyatt never published a collection of his own poems, ninety-seven of them appear in a book now referred to as *Tottel's Miscellany,* which was first published in 1557 by a printer named Richard Tottel.

ABOUT THE SELECTION

A **Petrarchan sonnet** is a lyric poem of fourteen lines, often in **iambic pentameter**. It generally follows the rhyme scheme *abba abba cddc ee* and is divided into two parts: the first eight lines forming the **octave** and the last six forming the **sestet**. The theme of a sorrowful male and an unattainable female is typical in this type of sonnet. Wyatt's **"Whoso List to Hunt"** is a superb example of a Petrarchan sonnet, both technically and thematically. The sonnet may have been written about Anne Boleyn. Wyatt grew up in the same household with Anne and fell deeply in love with her. He was devastated when Anne became the wife of Henry VIII, and Henry grew, quite naturally, suspicious of him. The reference in the poem to Cæsar may be read as meaning "any powerful man," such as King Henry.

GOALS/OBJECTIVES

Studying this lesson will enable students to

- enjoy and appreciate reading a sonnet
- describe Sir Thomas Wyatt's literary accomplishments and explain the historical significance of "Whoso List to Hunt"
- describe the features of the Petrarchan sonnet (lyric poem with fourteen lines, often in iambic

pentameter, and with the rhyme scheme *abba abba cde cde* or *abba abba cddc ee*)
- define *personification* and recognize and interpret personification in a poem
- identify and correct errors in personal pronoun usage

READER'S JOURNAL

Think of someone or something that has been unattainable for you. Freewrite about your feelings related to that unattainable person or thing. Do you still experience frustration or sorrow when you think of it? Would you be sympathetic to another who sought the same goal to no avail?

WRITING SKILLS

Read the Language Arts Survey, 1.6, "Choosing a Purpose or Aim." Then decide what purpose and mode you would choose if you were to write about an experience of loss, such as that described in "Whoso List to Hunt."

"Whoso List to Hunt"

SIR THOMAS WYATT

Whoso list[1] to hunt, I know where is an hind,[2]
But as for me, alas, I may no more.
The vain <u>travail</u> hath wearied me so sore
I am of them that farthest cometh behind.
5   Yet may I, by no means, my wearied mind
Draw from the deer, but as she fleeth afore,
Fainting I follow. I leave off therefore,
Since in a net I seek to hold the wind.
Who list her hunt, I put him out of doubt,
10 As well as I, may spend his time in vain.
And <u>graven</u> with diamonds in letters plain
There is written, her fair neck round about,
"*Noli me tangere*, for Cæsar's I am,[3]
And wild for to hold, though I seem tame." ■

---

1. **list.** Desires
2. **hind.** Deer
3. *Noli . . . tangere am.* *Touch me not* is the imagined inscription on the collars of Cæsar's deer.

❶
For what has the speaker been hunting?

❷
Did the speaker attain his goal?

ANSWERS TO GUIDED READING QUESTIONS
❶ The speaker has been hunting a hind, or deer.

❷ No, the speaker did not attain the goal of catching the deer.

WORDS FOR EVERYDAY USE:

trav • ail (trə vāl´) *n.*, very hard work
grav • en (grāv´ ən) *vt.*, engraved

VOCABULARY IN CONTEXT

• The marathon runner crossed the finish line and collapsed after more than two hours of athletic <u>travail</u>.
• Jean's parents gave her a ring <u>graven</u> with the date of her high school graduation.

BIBLIOGRAPHIC NOTE

The standard edition of Wyatt's work is Wyatt, Thomas. *Collected Poems.* Ed. Kenneth Muir and Patricia Thomson. 1969.

RESPONDING TO THE SELECTION

Students may work as a class or in small groups to brainstorm a list of situations similar to that experienced by the speaker in "Whoso List to Hunt." You may want to prime the list with these suggestions:

• trying out for, but not making, an athletic team

• attempting to fit in with a particular group of friends who don't want to include you

• trying to write a poem or story but being unable to find the right words to express yourself

• studying for a math test but finding it impossible to comprehend certain concepts

ANSWERS FOR REVIEWING THE SELECTION

RECALLING

1. On a literal level, the speaker is hunting a deer. The poet uses this deer hunt as a metaphor for a man pursuing an unattainable woman.

2. No; the speaker refers to his "vain travail," suggesting that he has worked very hard to catch the deer before finally giving up.

INTERPRETING

Responses will vary. Possible responses are given.

3. The hunt has been long and exhausting. The speaker is tired and resigned to failure, but he has grown wiser over the course of the hunt.

4. The hind belongs to Cæsar and may not be touched by anyone else.

SYNTHESIZING

Responses will vary. Possible responses are given.

5. The last line of the poem suggests that no one can truly own the deer—even powerful Cæsar, who has put his mark on her. She may seem tame, but her true nature is that of a wild creature.

Responding to the Selection

Does this poem remind you of something you have "hunted" unsuccessfully? If you could talk to the speaker of the poem what would you say? Would you share your story sympathetically or would you offer advice on getting over the unattainable?

Reviewing the Selection

RECALLING

1. For what is the speaker hunting?

2. Has the narrator given up the chase easily? Explain.

INTERPRETING

3. How has the hunt been progressing? How is the speaker feeling?

4. Why might the hind be unattainable for other pursuers as well?

SYNTHESIZING

5. Might Cæsar also feel that the hind is not completely his? What words and phrases in the poem suggest that? Explain.

ANSWERS FOR LANGUAGE LAB

1. In Wyatt's sonnet, **whom** had the hunter tried to catch?

2. The speaker says that the hunt tired **him**.

3. Will **they** who hunt the hind catch her?

4. **Whoever** touches Cæsar's property will answer to Cæsar.

5. Of all of **us** hunters, I am the farthest behind the deer.

FOR MORE PRACTICE

Problem. The hunter cannot remove the thought of (she, her) from his mind.

Answer. The hunter cannot remove the thought of **her** from his mind.

►Additional practice is provided in the *Essential Skills Practice Book: Language,* 2.6.

Understanding Literature (Questions for Discussion)

1. **Meter.** The **meter** of a poem is its rhythmical pattern. One common meter is **iambic pentameter**, a pattern of five **iambs**, each iamb being one weakly stressed syllable followed by one strongly stressed syllable. Find three iambs in Wyatt's poem. Write the first verse of Wyatt's poem and draw marks above the syllables to show whether they are accented or unaccented.

   example: return at last my steadfast dove to me

2. **Metaphor.** **Metaphor** is a figure of speech in which one thing is spoken or written about as though it were another. In this poem, what metaphor is used to describe the object of the speaker's affections? What similarities exist between the woman and the deer? Between the speaker and a hunter?

Responding in Writing

1. **Dialogue.** Dialogue is a conversation involving two or more people or characters. How might a dialogue between the hunter and the hind sound? Under what circumstances might the two meet face to face? Create this scenario. Then create a dialogue in which the hunter gives his side of the situation, and then the hind gives hers. What might the hind tell the hunter about freedom and wanting to be left alone?

2. **Sonnet.** Write the first four lines of a sonnet. Choose your subject—it can be humorous or serious. Concentrate on the Elizabethan sonnet rhyme pattern, and use iambic pentameter where possible. When you feel comfortable with your four lines, work to try and finish your piece. Remember, writing a sonnet is a challenge. Don't be discouraged if it takes time to perfect your poem.

Language Lab

Personal Pronouns. Read the Language Arts Survey, 2.6, "Personal Pronouns." Then choose the correct pronoun in parentheses to complete each of the following sentences.

1. In Wyatt's sonnet, (who, whom) had the hunter tried to catch?

2. The speaker says that the hunt tired (he, him).

3. Will (they, them) who hunt the hind catch her?

4. (Whomever, Whoever) touches Cæsar's property will answer to Cæsar.

5. Of all of (us, we) hunters, I am the farthest behind the deer.

ANSWERS FOR UNDERSTANDING LITERATURE

► See the evaluation forms for discussion, active listening, and oral communication, *Assessment Portfolio,* 7.11–7.14.

Responses will vary. Possible responses are given.

1. Meter. Examples of iambs include "I know," "where is," "an hind," "But as," and "for me." The first verse, with accents noted, reads as follows:

Whoso list to hunt, I know

where is an hind,

But as for me, alas, I may no more.
The vain travail hath wearied me

so sore
(cont.)

ANSWERS FOR UNDERSTANDING LITERATURE (CONT.)

I am one of them that farthest cometh behind.

► **Teaching Note:** Students may find it easier to determine which syllables are accented and unaccented if they tap out the beat of the poem as you or they read aloud. Remind students that most poetry is intended to please the ear when read aloud.

2. Metaphor. The woman is spoken of as a deer. The

woman is like a deer in that both flee to preserve their freedom, both are difficult to catch, and both are claimed by the king. The speaker is like a hunter in that both are pursuers and both grow weary from the chase.

► **Teaching Note:** Ask students to discuss ways in which the woman is *not* like a deer. What different perspectives on the speaker's situation does this suggest?

ENRICHMENT ACTIVITIES

Sidney uses the moon to represent inconstancy. Students may think of other objects or events in the natural world that can symbolize aspects of human relationships. For example, a huge oak tree that grew from a tiny acorn may represent the growth of a friendship over time. They may begin by spending time outdoors reflecting on nature. When they have discovered a metaphor they like, they may write a few lines of a poem or a paragraph describing the metaphor and explaining its personal significance.

SUPPORT FOR LEP STUDENTS

Remind students to watch for the unexpected word order that marks much Elizabethan poetry. In particular, point out that the object of a verb often precedes the verb, as in "That busy archer his sharp arrows tries." (Students may benefit from reading the Language Arts Survey, 2.15, "Transitive and Intransitive Verbs.") You may wish to draw students' attention to the syntax in the last line of the sonnet. In modern English, the line translates to, "Do they call gratefulness *virtue* there?"

IDIOMS

Sure, if that—surely, if

Then even of fellowship—since we are in similar situations

ADDITIONAL VOCABULARY

try—to torment or test a person

constant—faithful; unchanging

deem—judge; consider

PREREADING

RENAISSANCE POETRY

Sonnet 31
from *Astrophil and Stella*
by Sir Philip Sidney

ABOUT THE AUTHOR

Sir Philip Sidney (1554–1586) was a well-loved courtier, soldier, and poet, deeply mourned by the English people after his death in battle at the age of thirty-two. His father was Sir Henry Sidney, three times governor of Ireland. Philip Sidney attended Shrewsbury School, where he was admired for his grace and maturity, and then Oxford. His staunch Protestantism was reinforced by witnessing massacres of Protestants in France in 1572.

After his travels, Sidney returned to England where he was a courtier and patron of the arts, and in particular of Edmund Spenser, who dedicated *The Shepheardes Calender* to him. Later, in disfavor with the queen, Sidney retired to Wilton and wrote his pastoral prose work, *The Countess of Pembroke's Arcadia,* as well as sonnets and literary criticism. In his "Defense of Poesy [Poetry]," Sidney argued that poets can actually improve upon nature by creating worlds better than the real one. Sidney's argument shows clearly the English Renaissance faith in human abilities and esteem for poetic art.

In the cause of Protestantism, Sidney went to the Low Countries in 1585 as a volunteer in the war against Spain. There he died heroically. Sidney never published his work himself, though today it is considered to be among the most lovely and lyrical in the English language.

ABOUT THE SELECTION

Sonnet 31 is part of the sonnet cycle *Astrophil and Stella,* which generally follows the sonnet conventions established by Petrarch. The rhyme scheme is Petrarchan: *abba abba cdcd ee.* So is the subject: unrequited, or unreturned, love. Petrarch addressed his poems to an unattainable woman named Laura. Sidney addressed his to Stella, whose name means "star." Sidney's speaker, Astrophil, or "star-lover," expresses many of the complex emotions of a person in love. Sidney used dialogue to express Astrophil's mental state, including everyday speech and internal conversations, or interior monologues.

Much of the best of Elizabethan literature was private work, circulated among people in the queen's court. One way to obtain favor with the queen and other powerful figures was to be amusing, or witty. Wittiness therefore became a central feature of literature of the period, which employs elaborate conceits and word play. In Sonnet 31, the speaker uses an exaggerated metaphor, personifying and addressing the moon. The moon has long been a symbol of faithlessness, or inconstancy, because its appearance changes throughout the month. In this poem, Astrophil asks the moon if in the heavenly sphere, as on Earth, constancy, or faithfulness, is considered lack of wit.

GOALS/OBJECTIVES

Studying this lesson will enable students to

- experience the speaker's feelings of loss
- describe Sidney's contributions to Elizabethan literature
- interpret a poem in light of historical events
- recognize and interpret symbolism and

- personification in a poem
- determine the rhyme scheme of a poem
- incorporate vivid imagery in their own writing
- recognize and correct errors in the use of semicolons

READER'S JOURNAL

Write a dialogue that takes place inside someone's mind about a person he or she admires. Have the speaker express impressions of the beloved and also concerns about how to relate to him or her.

READING SKILLS

Read the Language Arts Survey, 4.16, "Reading Rates: Scanning." Pick three poems from this book, scan them, and write down their rhyme schemes.

PREREADING NOTES

READER'S JOURNAL

Suggest that students consider older people in their community, historical figures, or an imaginary person with qualities they admire as subjects for their dialogues.

READING SKILLS

Remind students that, unlike sonnets, not all poems have regular rhyme schemes; many poems do not rhyme at all. Scanning is a good technique for quickly determining what form—if any—a poem follows.

► Additional practice is provided in the *Essential Skills Practice Book: Study and Research*, 4.16.

Sonnet 31

FROM *ASTROPHIL AND STELLA*

SIR PHILIP SIDNEY

> With how sad steps, O Moon, thou climb'st the skies,
>   How silently, and with how <u>wan</u> a face!
>   What, may it be that even in heavenly place
> That busy archer[1] his sharp arrows tries?
> 5   Sure, if that long-with-love-acquainted eyes
>   Can judge of Love, thou feel'st a Lover's case;
>   I read it in thy looks: thy <u>languished</u> grace,
> To me that feel the like, thy state <u>descries</u>.
>   Then even of fellowship, O Moon, tell me
> 10 Is constant *love* deemed there but want of wit?
>   Are beauties there as proud as here they be?
>   Do they above love to be loved, and yet
>   Those lovers <u>scorn</u> whom that *love* doth possess?
>   Do they call *virtue* there ungratefulness? ∎

❶
What feelings does the speaker attribute to the moon?

ANSWER TO GUIDED READING QUESTION

❶ The speaker infers from the moon's slow progress across the sky, its silence, and its "wan" appearance that it is sad.

---

1. **That busy archer.** The *busy archer* is Cupid, the Roman god of love who is often pictured with a bow and arrow, which he uses to strike at people's hearts, causing them to feel love and, sometimes, love's sorrows.

WORDS FOR EVERYDAY USE:
wan (wän) *adj.*, pale, faint
lan • guished (lan´ gwisht) *adj.*, drooping, lacking vitality
de • scry (di skrī´) *vi.*, show clearly
scorn (skôrn) *vt.*, view with contempt

VOCABULARY IN CONTEXT

- When he heard the shocking news, all the color drained out of Roderick's face, leaving it <u>wan</u> and ghostlike.
- When I returned from vacation, the <u>languished</u> leaves of my houseplants seemed to cry out, "Water! Help!"
- Juanita's outgoing personality <u>descries</u> her love of people.
- If Jasmine wants to be a journalist, why does she <u>scorn</u> the idea of working on the school newspaper?

ANSWERS TO SELECTION CHECK TEST 4.4.3

EX. In what sonnet sequence, or collection, does Sidney's Sonnet 31 appear?
The poem appears in *Astrophil and Stella*.

1. Whom does the speaker address in this poem?
The speaker addresses the moon.

2. Who, according to the speaker, has a "wan" face?
The moon has a "wan" face.

3. What similarity does the speaker note between himself and the thing being addressed in the poem?
The speaker says that they both feel a lover's case.

4. According to the speaker, what, on earth, is "deemed . . . but want of wit"?
Love is "deemed. . . but want of wit."

5. According to the speaker, what, on earth, is equated with ungratefulness?
Virtue is equated with ungratefulness.

RESPONDING TO THE SELECTION

Students may also consider these questions: Is it possible to have a sincere feeling that changes over time? What might cause these changes? What can people learn from their changing emotions and beliefs?

ANSWERS FOR REVIEWING THE SELECTION

RECALLING

1. He addresses the moon.

2. The person the speaker loves does not return the feeling.

INTERPRETING

3. *Responses will vary.* Perhaps the speaker directs his thoughts to the moon because he feels that others do not understand him. He may not expect to find understanding at all, but imagining the moon as a sympathetic character comforts him.

4. No; the unanswered questions in lines 10–14 suggest that the speaker cannot understand how his beloved acts or feels.

SYNTHESIZING

5. *Responses will vary.* The speaker does not think ungratefulness is a virtue, although he accuses other people of thinking so. The speaker's bitterness and his baring his soul to the moon rather than to another person suggest that he feels that other people do not understand his pain.

ANSWERS FOR UNDERSTANDING LITERATURE

Responses will vary. Possible responses are given.

1. Image. The image of the moon appeals to the sense of sight. The speaker describes the moon as looking "wan" and says he can read the moon's emotional state from its "looks." He treats it as a sympathetic friend.

▶**Teaching Note:** Ask students to imagine the speaker staring up at the moon as his only friend and confidant. Encourage them to free associate as they add details to this picture.

2. Personification. In this sonnet, the moon is depicted as having

(cont.)

256 TEACHER'S EDITION

Responding to the Selection

What is constancy? Why is it important for people to be constant in their feelings? Discuss these questions with your classmates.

Reviewing the Selection

RECALLING

1. To what or whom does the speaker address the opening line?

2. In what way has the speaker been disappointed by the object of his love?

INTERPRETING

3. Why do you think the speaker directs his expressions of sorrow in the way that he does? Why does he expect to find understanding?

4. Does he understand his beloved's feelings? Why, or why not?

SYNTHESIZING

5. Does the speaker think ungratefulness is a virtue? Does the speaker feel understood in his pain? Explain.

Understanding Literature (Questions for Discussion)

1. **Image.** An **image** is a word or phrase that names something that can be seen, heard, touched, tasted, or smelled. To what sense does the primary image in Sonnet 31 appeal? How does this image work for you? Explain.

2. **Personification. Personification** is a figure of speech in which an idea, animal, or thing is described as if it were a person. How is personification used in Sonnet 31? Why do you think the poet used this technique? How does the appearance of the personified thing relate to the feelings of the speaker?

Responding in Writing

Image. Think of five powerful images, one for each of the five senses. Write a few lines presenting each image and then write about what the images might represent. For example: Sight—a billowing gray thunderhead in the sky could represent danger.

256   *UNIT FOUR / THE ENGLISH RENAISSANCE*

ANSWERS FOR UNDERSTANDING LITERATURE (CONT.)

human characteristics: It feels sad and takes slow steps across the sky. The poet uses this technique to describe the speaker's own characteristics in an indirect and more interesting way. The emotions that he attributes to the moon are ones that he is feeling himself.

▶**Teaching Note:** Ask how the vivid visual imagery of the moon gives substance to the human emotions the speaker imagines it to have.

ANALYTIC SCALES FOR RESPONDING IN WRITING

Assign a score from 1 to 25 for each grading criterion below.

Image

• **Content/Unity.** The writing presents images that appeal to each sense.

• **Organization/Coherence.** The writing is clearly organized.

• **Language/Style.** The writing uses vivid and precise nouns, verbs, and modifiers.

• **Conventions.** The writing avoids errors in spelling, grammar, usage, mechanics, and manuscript form.

PREREADING

from *The Færie Queene*
by Edmund Spenser

ABOUT THE AUTHOR

Edmund Spenser (1552–1599) has been called the greatest non-dramatic poet of the Elizabethan Era. Born in London to a family of meager means, he attended Merchant Taylor's School and then Cambridge University. Later he became aide and secretary to several important men. In one of their households, he met courtier and poet Sir Philip Sidney, to whom he dedicated *The Shepheardes Calender,* a series of pastoral poems.

Spenser went to Ireland as aide to Lord Grey of Wilton, Lord Deputy of Ireland, and tried unsuccessfully for the rest of his life to return to England to live. Staunchly nationalistic and Protestant, he wrote an apology for British colonial repression of the Irish called *A View of the Present State of Ireland.* In the last decade of the 1500s, a bitter rebellion broke out in Ireland, and Spenser's castle was demolished. Spenser died while on a mission back to England and was buried in the Poet's Corner of Westminster Abbey.

ABOUT THE SELECTION

This selection is from Spenser's masterpiece, **The Færie Queene,** a long, epic romance dedicated to Queen Elizabeth. *The Færie Queene* uses material from medieval romances to tell allegorical tales dealing with religion, politics, and other matters. Spenser's revival of medieval romance had considerable effect on later poets like Alfred, Lord Tennyson.

GOALS/OBJECTIVES

Studying this lesson will enable students to

- have positive experiences reading epic poetry
- describe and identify the main characteristics of medieval romance
- describe Edmund Spenser's literary accomplishments and explain the historical significance of his writings

- define *alliteration, mood,* and *foreshadowing* and identify alliteration, mood, and foreshadowing in a poem
- write a character sketch
- define, identify, and use correctly transitive and intransitive verbs

---

ADDITIONAL RESOURCES

READER'S GUIDE
- Selection Worksheet, 4.3

ASSESSMENT PORTFOLIO
- Selection Check Test, 4.4.5
- Selection Test, 4.4.6

ESSENTIAL SKILLS PRACTICE BOOKS
- *Language,* 2.15
- *Speaking and Listening,* 3.7

ENRICHMENT ACTIVITIES

Students can write about or discuss the idea of being faithful to a social superior. The feudal system of medieval Europe was founded on such duties and loyalties. Do students think there is any parallel in the modern world? If so, what are some examples?

SUPPORT FOR LEP STUDENTS

Explain that the author uses archaic, or obsolete, forms of many words. In some cases the words differ only slightly: some are spelled with an extra *e* (as in *plaine*) or with a doubled final consonant (as in *sitt*). In other cases, vowel sounds are spelled differently, as in *disdayning* ("disdaining") and *brest* ("breast").

IDIOMS
the like—the same thing
right faithfull true—completely loyal and honest

ADDITIONAL VOCABULARY
armes—arms, or weapons
dints—dents
fielde—battlefield
steede—steed, horse
chide—show disapproval
curbe—bit—the part of a bridle that fits in a horse's mouth
remembrance—object that serves as a reminder
soveraine—of the highest kind
cheere—cheer; facial expression
dread—fear
bond—bound; going
puissance—strength

PREREADING NOTES

READER'S JOURNAL

Explain that showing courage means risking something that you value and thus fear losing. When students write about their experiences, suggest that they consider what it was that they valued. Do they still value this thing or idea?

SPEAKING SKILLS

Students should not worry about pronouncing perfectly Spenser's archaic English. Instead, suggest that they focus on getting the tone right, based on how they think the poet feels about his subject and how he wants the reader or listener to feel.

▶ Additional practice is provided in the *Essential Skills Practice Book: Speaking and Listening*, 3.7.

ANSWER TO GUIDED READING QUESTION

❶ He is wearing armor and carrying a shield.

ANSWERS TO SELECTION CHECK TEST 4.4.5

EX. What adjective is used to describe the knight in line 1 of the poem?
The adjective used to describe the knight is *gentle*.

1. According to the speaker, who is fit for "fierce encounters"?
The knight is "fit for fierce encounters."

2. What emblem or symbol does the knight have on his chest?
On the knight's chest is a red cross.

3. Of what is the emblem on the knight's chest a symbol?
The emblem is a symbol of "his dying Lord" (i.e., Christ).

4. Who gave the knight the quest that he was on?
The quest was given to him by Gloriana, the "Glorious Queen of Færie Lond."

5. With what creature will the knight be doing battle?
The knight will be doing battle with a dragon.

READER'S JOURNAL

Have you ever needed to do something dangerous? You may have faced physical harm or the disapproval of someone you cared about. Were you able to face up to the danger? Write in your journal about the thoughts that help you to be courageous.

SPEAKING SKILLS

Read the Language Arts Survey, 3.7, "Public Speaking." Recite the last verse of this selection to a small group of classmates. Concentrate on understanding the literal meaning of each line so that you can read it with appropriate emphasis.

FROM

The Færie Queene

EDMUND SPENSER

What is the knight wearing? ❶

A Gentle Knight was pricking° on the plaine,   *cantering*
  Ycladd° in mightie armes and silver shielde,   *dressed*
  Wherein old dints of deepe wounds did remaine,
  The cruell markes of many a bloudy fielde;
5 Yet armes till that time did he never <u>wield</u>:
  His angry steede did chide his foming bitt,
  As much disdayning to the curbe to yield:
  Full jolly° knight he seemd, and faire did sitt,   *gallant*
As one for knightly giusts° and fierce encounters fitt. *jousts*

10 But on his brest a bloudie Crosse he bore,
  The deare remembrance of his dying Lord,
  For whose sweete sake that glorious badge he wore,
  And dead as living ever him adored:
  Upon his shield the like was also <u>scored,</u>
15 For soveraine hope, which in his helpe he had:
  Right faithfull true he was in deede and word,
  But of his cheere did seeme too solemne sad;°   *grave; serious*
Yet nothing did he dread, but ever was ydrad.°   *dreaded*

WORDS FOR EVERYDAY USE:
wield (wēld) *vt.,* handle and use a weapon or tool
score (skôr) *vt.,* inscribe

VOCABULARY IN CONTEXT

• "Didn't you ever <u>wield</u> a hammer before?" Joe remarked cruelly as Liz nursed her throbbing thumb.

• Kim opened the little box carefully and found that it was <u>scored</u> inside with a beautiful design.

BIBLIOGRAPHICAL NOTE

The standard edition of Spenser's work is *The Works of Edmund Spenser*. Eds. Edwin A. Greenlaw et al. 1932–1949.

Upon a great adventure he was bond,
20   That greatest Gloriana to him gave,
        That greatest Glorious Queen of Færie Lond,
        To winne him worship,° and her grace to have,   *honor*
        Which of all earthly things he most did crave;
        And ever as he rode, his hart did earne°   *yearn*
25   To prove his puissance in battell brave
        Upon his foe, and his new force to learne;
        Upon his foe, a Dragon horrible and stearne.   ■

Why does the knight wish to go to battle?

Responding to the Selection

The Gentle Knight risked his life to battle a "horrible and stearne" dragon. Discuss with one or two peers what cause you might be willing to risk your life for. Would it be for yourself? for others? for some ideal?

Reviewing the Selection

RECALLING

1. What were the marks on the knight's shield?

2. What was the symbol the knight wore on his chest?

SYNTHESIZING

5. How does this knight represent holiness?

INTERPRETING

3. How did the knight feel about his journey in line 18?

4. Who sent the knight on this mission?

---

❶ The knight wishes to go to battle to win honor and the grace of Gloriana, Queen of Færie Lond.

RESPONDING TO THE SELECTION

Students may begin by thinking about what "dragons" they might need to fight in their own lives. Such a dragon might be any person or institution that threatens them. A dragon might even exist within a person's own mind, in the form of a fear or prejudice.

ANALYTIC SCALES FOR RESPONDING IN WRITING

Assign a score from 1 to 25 for each grading criterion below. (For more detailed evaluation, see the evaluation forms for writing, revising, and proofreading, *Assessment Portfolio,* 7.1–7.10.)

1. Foreshadowing
• **Content/Unity.** The paragraph establishes a scene in the present and hints at a future event without giving away the outcome.
• **Organization/Coherence.** The paragraph gradually builds suspense in the reader about what will happen.
• **Language/Style.** The paragraph uses vivid and precise nouns, verbs, and modifiers.
• **Conventions.** The paragraph avoids errors in spelling, grammar, usage, mechanics, and manuscript form.

2. Character Sketch
• **Content/Unity.** The character sketch is based on an identifiable virtue and creates an appropriate character to symbolize it.
• **Organization/Coherence.** The sketch stays focused on the virtue being represented and uses details to support the characterization.
• **Language/Style.** The character sketch uses vivid and precise nouns, verbs, and modifiers.
• **Conventions.** The character sketch avoids errors in spelling, grammar, usage, mechanics, and manuscript form.

ANSWERS FOR REVIEWING THE SELECTION

RECALLING
1. There were dents in the shield from past battles.
2. He wore a red cross on his chest.

INTERPRETING
Responses will vary. Possible responses are given.
3. He was determined to succeed, although he was well aware of the danger.

4. The knight was sent by his queen, the "greatest Glorious Queen of Færie Lond."

SYNTHESIZING
Responses will vary. Possible responses are given.
5. The knight's lord may be interpreted to represent Jesus Christ. The knight is "right faithfull true" to his lord "in deede and word"; in other words, he is living a holy and righteous life.

▶See the evaluation forms for discussion, active listening, and oral communication, *Assessment Portfolio,* 7.11–7.14.

Responses will vary. Possible responses are given.

1. Source. Romance elements include the glorification of the knight's skill in battle, the knight's steadfast loyalty, a magical creature such as the dragon, a solemn quest such as the mission to slay the dragon, and the knight's yearning for honor and glory through following the rules of chivalrous behavior.

▶**Teaching Note:** Discuss the differences between medieval courtly love and modern ideas of romantic love. Explain that the code of chivalry stressed strict adherence to social rules above concern for the feelings and desires of individuals. Ask them to find evidence that the knight's identity comes more from his social position than from unique individual qualities.

2. Mood. The second verse creates a feeling of both tenderness and admiration for the knight. The reader sympathizes with the knight's sense of loss over the death of his lord and admires his loyalty and determination as he then takes up his lord's battle.

▶**Teaching Note:** Ask students to speculate, based on what they know about chivalry, whether words such as *deare, sweete,* and *adored* had the same meaning in medieval times that they have now. Might the knight's "adoration" of his lord be something quite different from what we mean when we use the word?

3. Alliteration. Examples include "pricking on the plaine" (line 1), "But on his brest a bloudie Crosse he bore" (line 10), and "did seeme too solemne sad" (line 17).

Grading scales appear on page 259.

Understanding Literature (Questions for Discussion)

1. **Source.** A **source** is a work from which an author takes his or her materials. To write *The Færie Queene,* Spenser drew upon materials from medieval romance. In this selection from *The Færie Queene,* Spenser recalls the medieval story of the slaying of the dragon by St. George, the patron saint of England. Read the definitions of *chivalry, courtly love, motif,* and *romance* in the Handbook of Literary Terms and discuss the romance elements, or motifs, used by Spenser in the selection.

2. **Mood. Mood,** or **atmosphere,** is the emotion created in the reader by part or all of a literary work. What is the mood of the second verse in this selection?

3. **Alliteration. Alliteration** is the repetition of initial consonant sounds. Give examples of alliteration in this selection.

Responding in Writing

1. **Foreshadowing. Foreshadowing** is the act of presenting materials that hint at events to occur later in a story. In this selection, Spenser creates a sense of impending doom in the reader by using foreshadowing. Write a paragraph that hints at something terrible that will happen, without naming the event specifically.

2. **Character Sketch.** Each character in Spenser's *The Færie Queene* represents a particular virtue in thought and in action. Create a character who represents a particular virtue. Try to use rich physical description in your character sketch, and try to use concrete details to show why your character represents this virtue.

Language Lab

Transitive and Intransitive Verbs. Read the Language Arts Survey, 2.15, "Transitive and Intransitive Verbs." Then complete the following sentences (which paraphrase a line from the selection), using either a transitive or an intransitive verb. Write *T* for *transitive* or *I* for *intransitive* at the end of the sentence.

1. Yet until that time, he never _____ arms.

2. On his chest, he _____ a bloody cross.

3. The cross _____ on his shield.

4. He _____ on a great adventure.

5. He _____ the grace of the queen.

---

1. wielded (T)
2. bore (T)
3. appeared (I)
4. went (I)
5. craved (T)

FOR MORE PRACTICE

Problem. Dents from previous battles _____ in the shield.

Answer. remained (I)

▶Additional practice is provided in the *Essential Skills Practice Book: Language,* 2.15.

PREREADING

"The Passionate Shepherd to His Love"
by Christopher Marlowe

ABOUT THE AUTHOR

Christopher Marlowe (1564–1593) was a contemporary of Shakespeare (born two months before him). He was the son of a shoemaker and attended Cambridge on a scholarship. At Cambridge he was granted a degree only after some controversy regarding his plan to go to Reims, the center of Catholic opposition to Queen Elizabeth and the Church of England. While at Cambridge, he wrote the famous play *Tamburlaine,* which dramatizes the adventures of a fourteenth-century Mongol chieftain and conqueror of much of the known world. He introduced to the English theater the use of **blank verse,** which was very well suited to projection from the stage.

Marlowe's life was a turbulent one. Only six years after his early success with *Tamburlaine,* he was killed by a dagger thrust in a brawl over a tavern bill. During the six years before his death, he wrote five more plays, including a sequel to *Tamburlaine,* two major tragedies, and a chronicle history play.

ABOUT THE SELECTION

This poem, **"The Passionate Shepherd to His Love,"** is a **pastoral poem.** A pastoral poem, from the Latin *pastor,* meaning "shepherd," is a verse that deals with idealized rural life. This poem is also a **lyric poem** because it expresses the emotions of the speaker in a musical way. Marlowe used **iambic tetrameter**—a simple, natural meter—to give the poem a simplicity of expression that mirrors its subject.

GOALS/OBJECTIVES

Studying this lesson will enable students to

- empathize with the speaker's feelings of love
- describe Christopher Marlowe's contributions to English literature
- name and describe the characteristics of pastoral and lyric poetry, and identify pastoral and lyric poems as they encounter them in their reading
- analyze the mood of a poem
- write a poem using an objective correlative
- distinguish between declarative and imperative sentences
- use classification to organize information
- creatively apply the aesthetics of pastoral poetry to their own experiences with nature

---

ENRICHMENT ACTIVITIES

Ask students to imagine that they are trying to convince someone to move to their neighborhood. What would they tell the person about the neighborhood to make it seem like an attractive place to live? Students who have access to a video camera may want to make a narrated videotape showing favorite places and activities. Other students may present their neighborhoods through drama, artwork, poetry, or narrative writing.

SUPPORT FOR LEP STUDENTS

Explain that Elizabethan poetry uses word order that sounds unnatural to modern ears. Help students to locate the subject and verb of each sentence in the poem.

ADDITIONAL VOCABULARY

prove—learn by experiencing
steepy—high
yield—bring forth; produce
melodious—making a pleasant melody or song
fragrant—having a sweet smell
posy—small bunch of flowers
clasp—device that holds two parts together
amber—made of amber, a yellow-brown gemstone
move—persuade

PREREADING NOTES

READER'S JOURNAL

Students fluent in other languages may freewrite in their own languages. They can then meet in pairs or small groups with classmates who wrote in English, sharing the sensory words they used and noting similarities and differences across languages.

SPEAKING SKILLS

You may wish to monitor students' use of discussion techniques. Use "Evaluation Form: Group Discussion" in the *Assessment Portfolio*, 7.14.

►Additional practice is provided in the *Essential Skills Practice Book: Speaking and Listening*, 3.6.

ANSWER TO GUIDED READING QUESTION

❶ The shepherd wants his beloved to move to the countryside and live with him. He promises that together they will enjoy the many pleasures of living in nature.

LITERARY TECHNIQUE

Remind students that this poem is written in iambic tetrameter. Each line consists of four iambs; each iamb has an unaccented syllable followed by an accented syllable. Demonstrate the rhythm of the poem by tapping out the stressed beats as you read aloud the first line of the poem:

```
      /       /      /      /
Come live with me and be my love
```

Ask students whether they agree that this meter is simple and natural and that it suits a pastoral poem.

►**Teaching Note:** Students may compare the rhythm of this poem with that of "Whoso List to Hunt," written in iambic pentameter. They should discuss how meter affects the sound and mood of a poem.

VOCABULARY FROM THE SELECTION

madrigal   swain
myrtle

READER'S JOURNAL

Imagine a place in the countryside where you would enjoy spending some peaceful time with a friend. Then freewrite a series of images from that natural scene, idealizing the place and using words that appeal to the five senses.

SPEAKING SKILLS

Read the Language Arts Survey, 3.6, "Discussion." Then discuss with your classmates the reasons why poets often use nature imagery when writing about love and romance.

"The Passionate Shepherd to His Love"

CHRISTOPHER MARLOWE

❶
What does the shepherd want? What does he promise in the first stanza?

> Come live with me and be my love,
> And we will all the pleasures prove
> That valleys, groves, hills, and fields,
> Woods, or steepy mountain yields.
>
> 5   And we will sit upon the rocks,
> Seeing the shepherds feed their flocks,
> By shallow rivers to whose falls
> Melodious birds sing <u>madrigals</u>.
>
> And I will make thee beds of roses
> 10   And a thousand fragrant posies,
> A cap of flowers, and a kirtle[1]
> Embroidered all with leaves of <u>myrtle</u>;

—————
1. **kirtle.** Woman's dress

WORDS FOR EVERYDAY USE:

mad • ri •gal (má dri gəl) *n.,* song, often in several parts

myr • tle (mʉrt l) *n.,* type of plant with evergreen leaves and white or pink flowers

262   UNIT FOUR / THE ENGLISH RENAISSANCE

VOCABULARY IN CONTEXT

- The group sang a lovely four-part <u>madrigal</u> written in the sixteenth century.
- The <u>myrtle</u> bushes that cover the hillside are as beautiful as they are fragrant.
- The speaker in this pastoral poem is a <u>swain</u> who appreciates the natural beauty around him as he tends his sheep.

The Hireling Shepherd. William Holman Hunt. Manchester City Art Gallery

A gown made of the finest wool
Which from our pretty lambs we pull;
15 Fair lined slippers for the cold,
With buckles of the purest gold;

A belt of straw and ivy buds,
With coral clasps and amber studs:
And if these pleasures may thee move,
20 Come live with me, and be my love.

The shepherds' <u>swains</u> shall dance and sing
For thy delight each May morning:
If these delights thy mind may move,
Then live with me and be my love. ■

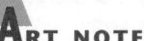
**What gifts does
the shepherd
promise? Are his
promises realistic?**

WORDS FOR
EVERYDAY USE:
swain (swān) *n.*, country youth

RENAISSANCE POETRY / "THE PASSIONATE SHEPHERD TO HIS LOVE" **263**

ART NOTE

William Holman Hunt (1827–1910) was one of three founding members of the Pre-Raphaelite Brotherhood in England. Like pastoral poets who idealized the simple, rustic life of the peasant, members of the Pre-Raphaelite Brotherhood had an exalted view of certain fifteenth-century painters who predated Raphael (1483–1520). They saw the pre-Raphaelites' style as being passionate and honest, with meticulous attention to detail. This detailed, realistic style is exemplified in *The Hireling Shepherd,* as is Hunt's desire to tell a rich story on the canvas.

▶**Teaching Note:** Have students study the carefully drawn details in the painting and then ask them to discuss the story told by the picture. What is each character thinking and feeling? How similar is the story in the painting to the story in Marlowe's poem? What are the points of similarity and difference?

ANSWER TO GUIDED READING QUESTION

❶ He promises to make his beloved such gifts as a bed of roses, an embroidered dress, a wool gown, beautiful slippers, and a belt. Some of these things are possible, although he mentions expensive materials such as gold and coral that a shepherd probably would not have. For the most part, his promises are fanciful and exaggerated.

▶**Teaching Note:** Ask students what might be the shepherd's purpose in making these promises.

RESPONDING TO THE SELECTION

Ask students whether they think the shepherd has given a complete description of life in the countryside. Suggest that they assume the role of the beloved and create a list of questions to ask to round out the picture.

BIBLIOGRAPHICAL NOTE

The standard edition of Marlowe's work is Marlowe, Christopher. *Complete Works.* Ed. Fredson Bowers. 1981.

**ANSWERS TO SELECTION
CHECK TEST 4.4.7**

EX. Who is the speaker in this poem?
The speaker is a passionate shepherd.

1. What does the speaker ask of the subject of the poem?
The speaker asks the subject of the poem to live with him and be his love.

2. What elements of nature does the speaker say he and his love will enjoy together?
The speaker says they will enjoy "valleys, groves, and

fields,/Woods, or steepy mountain yields."

3. What gifts does the shepherd promise his beloved?
The shepherd promises a bed of roses, a cap of flowers, a wool gown, slippers with gold buckles, and a belt.

4. Are the shepherds promises realistic?
No, they are mostly fanciful images meant to convey the extent of his love.

5. What final "delight" does the speaker promise?
The shepherd says country youths will dance and sing for his beloved each May morning.

ANSWERS FOR REVIEWING THE SELECTION

RECALLING

1. He wants her to live with him.

2. He refers to valleys, groves, hills, fields, woods, and mountains.

3. He promises gifts of flowers and handmade clothing.

4. References to spring include singing birds (line 8), blooming flowers (lines 9–11), and mornings in May (line 22). The season of spring is commonly used as a metaphor for youth.

INTERPRETING

Responses will vary. Possible responses are given.

5. The shepherd feels he needs to impress and woo the woman with promises of fancy gifts.

6. They delight the senses with their beauty.

7. Perhaps he does not feel comfortable speaking directly about his feelings, or perhaps he thinks she is the kind of person who will be impressed with material riches.

8. Some students may say that she is going to be disappointed if she expects him to devote his life to making presents for her. Other students may say that, if there is true love between them and both know that life is never really as perfect as the poem makes it sound, then they may find lasting happiness together.

SYNTHESIZING

Responses will vary. Possible responses are given.

9. Some students may say that the shepherd's promise that they will enjoy nature together may be realistic, but that his promises of expensive gifts are far-fetched.

10. The shepherd may be nothing but a smooth talker. On the other hand, he may be sincerely enthusiastic about his future life with the woman he loves. The poem may be read as either deliberately deceitful or wildly romantic.

Responding to the Selection

Does the life described by the shepherd in this poem sound attractive to you? What must the shepherd be feeling that causes him to look forward to such a future? Does such happiness seem possible to you? Freewrite about these questions in your journal.

Reviewing the Selection

RECALLING

1. Why does the speaker want his beloved to leave her home?

2. To what elements of nature does Marlowe refer in the first stanza?

3. What possessions will the speaker give to his beloved?

4. What references are made to youth and spring in the poem?

INTERPRETING

5. How does the speaker feel about his relationship with his beloved?

6. How do these elements of nature give pleasure to people?

7. Why might the speaker try to persuade his sweetheart with promises of gifts instead of with professions of his love?

8. Do you believe the speaker's beloved will be revered forever if she comes to live with him? Explain your answer.

SYNTHESIZING

9. Do you think the speaker's promises are realistic? Why or why not?

10. How would you describe the character of the speaker?

Understanding Literature (Questions for Discussion)

1. **Mood. Mood,** or **atmosphere,** is the emotion created in the reader by part or all of a literary work. What is the mood described by Marlowe in this poem? What specific words or phrases help to create this mood?

2. **Description.** A **description,** one of the modes of writing, presents a portrayal of a character, an object, or a scene. To what senses does Marlowe appeal with the descriptive words in this poem?

ANSWERS FOR UNDERSTANDING LITERATURE

▶ See the evaluation forms for discussion, active listening, and oral communication, *Assessment Portfolio,* 7.11–7.14.

1. Mood. The poet creates a mood of delight in sensory pleasures. Specific words that contribute to this mood include "valleys, groves, hills, and fields" (line 3); "shallow rivers to whose falls/Melodious birds sing madrigals" (lines 7–8); "beds of roses" (line 9); and "pretty lambs" (line 14).

▶**Teaching Note:** Remind students that this poem is addressed to the shepherd's love. Suggest that they put themselves in her place as they read the poem and imagine how they would feel if someone said these words to them.

2. Description. Marlowe appeals to the senses of sight (line 3), sound (lines 7–8), smell (line 10), and touch (lines 13 and 15).

Responding in Writing

1. **Pastoral Poem.** Write a pastoral poem about your favorite place. Although traditional pastoral verse deals with the beauty of nature and country life, feel free to write about your favorite place in the city or the suburbs. Try to capture the essence of pastoral verse by idealizing your special place and allowing the reader to see it through your eyes.

2. **Objective Correlative.** The poet T. S. Eliot coined the term **objective correlative** to describe a group of images that together create a particular emotion in the reader. Write a series of images intended to evoke a distinct emotion.

   • First choose an emotion that you want to write about. Possibilities include joy, sorrow, hope, excitement, fear, peace, and reverence.

   • Brainstorm a list of images that you associate with that emotion. You may want to brainstorm with other students.

   • Choose images from your list and write a short free verse poem using those images. (See the definition of *free verse* in the Handbook of Literary Terms.)

Language Lab

Building Sentences. Read the Language Arts Survey, 2.36, "The Functions of Sentences." Classify as either declarative or imperative each of the following lines from the poem. (Note: Some of the lines were not written by Marlowe as complete sentences, but they appear as complete sentences here. The brackets around periods indicate that they are not part of the original work.)

1. Come live with me and be my love[.]

2. And we will sit upon the rocks[.]

3. Melodious birds sing madrigals.

4. The shepherds' swains shall dance and sing[.]

5. Then live with me and be my love.

Research Skills

Read the Language Arts Survey, 4.7, "Classifying." Then flip through the poetry you have read so far. How might you classify these poems? Create your own headings. Undoubtedly, there will be some overlap. That is, some poems will fit into two or more categories. Be sure to include at least one example for each category that you create.

ANSWERS FOR RESEARCH SKILLS

Responses will vary. Possible categories include "poems about romantic love," "poems about unrequited love," "poems that use personification," "poems dominated by sensory imagery," and "poems that draw on earlier sources."

FOR MORE PRACTICE

Problem. Think about the books you have read in the past year. How would you classify them? If you tend to read mostly one genre, such as mysteries or science fiction, what subcategories can you devise to classify these books within this genre?

Responses will vary.

▶Additional practice is provided in the *Essential Skills Practice Book: Study and Research,* 4.7.

ANALYTIC SCALES FOR RESPONDING IN WRITING

Assign a score from 1 to 25 for each grading criterion below. (For more detailed evaluation, see the evaluation forms for writing, revising, and proofreading, *Assessment Portfolio,* 7.1–7.10.)

1. Pastoral Poem

• **Content/Unity.** The poem describes a specific place and includes many sensory images that make the place come alive for the reader.

• **Organization/Coherence.** The poem establishes a sense of place and adds sensory details that support the theme that this place is wonderful.

• **Language/Style.** The poem uses vivid and precise nouns, verbs, and modifiers.

• **Conventions.** The poem avoids errors in spelling, grammar, usage, mechanics, and manuscript form.

2. Objective Correlative

• **Content/Unity.** The poem presents a number of images related to a specific emotion or mood.

• **Organization/Coherence.** The poem moves from one image to the next in a logical and coherent manner.

• **Language/Style.** The poem uses vivid and precise nouns, verbs, and modifiers.

• **Conventions.** The poem avoids errors in spelling, grammar, usage, mechanics, and manuscript form.

ANSWERS FOR LANGUAGE LAB

1. imperative
2. declarative
3. declarative
4. declarative
5. imperative

FOR MORE PRACTICE

Problem. Don't doubt that I your needs shall meet.

Answer. imperative

▶Additional practice is provided in the *Essential Skills Practice Book: Language,* 2.36.

SUPPORT FOR LEP STUDENTS

Suggest that students refer to "The Passionate Shepherd to His Love" (page 261) as they read "The Nymph's Reply to the Shepherd."

ADDITIONAL VOCABULARY

nymph—young woman
drive—force to move
fold—fenced-in area
rage—act violent and uncontrolled
dumb—unable to speak
rest—silence
care—something to worry about
wayward—unpredictable; unfortunate
reckoning—facing up to something inevitable; final accounting
fancy—love
wither—become dry and shriveled
folly—foolishness
means—something used to achieve a goal

PREREADING

RENAISSANCE POETRY

"The Nymph's Reply to the Shepherd"
by Sir Walter Raleigh

ABOUT THE AUTHOR

Sir Walter Raleigh (1552–1618) led an astonishingly full and varied life as a soldier, explorer, courtier, philosopher, colonist, poet, student of science, and historian. His accomplishments included establishing the Roanoke colony in Virginia, importing the potato to Ireland, and introducing the poet Edmund Spenser to the English court. Raleigh was a favorite of Queen Elizabeth, and he was known at court for his flamboyant dress, his enthusiasm for life, and his quick temper. Among his literary works is "The Ocean to Cynthia," a five-hundred-line poem that exists only in fragments.

Raleigh did not find favor with Elizabeth's successor, King James, who sent him to the Tower of London, where he was imprisoned until his execution for treason in 1618. While incarcerated, Sir Raleigh wrote his long, unfinished *History of the World,* which begins with the creation of the world and breaks off at 168 BC.

ABOUT THE SELECTION

Written in response to "The Passionate Shepherd to His Love" by Christopher Marlowe, this selection is a mirror image of Marlowe's poem in almost all its characteristics. **"The Nymph's Reply to the Shepherd,"** like Marlowe's piece, makes many references to nature; it also has the same rhyme scheme and meter of Marlowe's poem. There the resemblance ends because, as you will read, Raleigh's speaker is thoughtful and resigned, rather than passionate. This piece is one of Raleigh's best-known shorter poems.

266   UNIT FOUR / *THE ENGLISH RENAISSANCE*

GOALS/OBJECTIVES

Studying this lesson will enable students to

• empathize with the speaker's feelings of sadness with regard to the ways in which the world falls short of romantic ideas

• describe Sir Walter Ralegh's contributions to English literature

• identify the speaker and identify and interpret metaphors and imagery in a poem

• use symbolism in an original poem or short story

• use commas properly in lists and in compound sentences

• use a graphic organizer to compare and contrast two poems

READER'S JOURNAL

Find and read a poem that expresses strong positive emotions. Then freewrite some lines that are cynical and disbelieving in response to the poem.

LISTENING SKILLS

Read the Language Arts Survey, 3.5, "Interpersonal Communication." Then analyze the exchange between the shepherd and the nymph and write down some suggestions for ways they might resolve their differences.

"The Nymph's Reply to the Shepherd"

Sir Walter Raleigh

If all the world and love were young,
And truth in every shepherd's tongue,
These pretty pleasures might me move
To live with thee and be thy love.

5   Time drives the flocks from field to fold
When rivers rage and rocks grow cold,
and Philomel[1] becometh dumb;
The rest complains of cares to come.

The flowers do fade, and <u>wanton</u> fields
10   To wayward winter reckoning yields;
A honey tongue, a heart of <u>gall</u>,
Is fancy's spring, but sorrow's fall.

---

1. **Philomel.** A *philomel* is a nightingale, so called after Philomela, a character in Greek and Roman mythology who was changed into a nightingale by the gods.

What does the nymph believe comes of the "pretty pleasures" of the world and of love?

Words for Everyday Use:

wan • ton (wăn´tən) *adj.*, luxuriant

gall (gôl) *n.*, bitterness

VOCABULARY IN CONTEXT

- The lawn in front of the abandoned house had not been mowed for months, and <u>wanton</u> tufts of green grass reached out through the gate.
- How sad that the sweetness of their friendship was turned to <u>gall</u> by that silly argument!

PREREADING NOTES

READER'S JOURNAL

When students have finished their freewriting, ask them whether the cynical point of view is more "true" than the positive point of view to which they responded. Might there be a middle ground or compromise between the two perspectives?

LISTENING SKILLS

Ask students whether they think the conflict between the nymph and the shepherd is the result of miscommunication or deep personal differences. Do they have enough in common to sustain a friendship?

►Additional practice is provided in the *Essential Skills Practice Book: Speaking and Listening*, 3.5.

ANSWER TO GUIDED READING QUESTION

❶ The nymph believes that both love and the "pretty pleasures" of the world fade with time.

ENRICHMENT ACTIVITIES

Letters to the editor are often replies to what someone else has said or written. Interested students may locate such letters in a newspaper and analyze them in light of the following questions.

- What is the argument or point of view presented by each side?
- Has the writer of the response clearly understood the other side of the argument?
- Has the writer given a logical response to his or her opponent?
- Can you see any common ground between the two sides? What suggestions might you make to these people to bring about a reconciliation?

LITERARY TECHNIQUE

The tone of a literary work is the emotion it evokes in the reader. Tone often springs from the attitude expressed by the speaker. Ask students to identify the tone of this poem. (Words they might use to describe it include *cynical, wise, bitter, sad,* and *regretful.*) Then ask them to consider how tone and characterization are related in the work. Does the tone give them a clear image of what the speaker is like as a person? Does the nymph remind them of any other characters they have read about or of any people they know in real life? Would they like to meet the nymph and talk to her?

ANSWER TO GUIDED READING QUESTION

❶ She implies that if they could stay young and in love forever, then she might like to live with the shepherd.

ADDITIONAL QUESTIONS AND ACTIVITIES

Ask students to recall the nymph's argument that all good things are temporary and thus not worth putting one's faith in. Then propose the following counterargument: *Everything happens in cycles, like the seasons. Just as happy times are often followed by heartache, so is suffering usually followed by renewed happiness.* Challenge students to represent or depict these two ideas visually. For example, the nymph's viewpoint might be a downward sloping line on a graph, and the other viewpoint might be a circle. Ask students to think about whether both points of view could be true at the same time.

RESPONDING TO THE SELECTION

Have students recall times in their own lives when they were very excited about something but a person they cared about showed no interest. How did they respond to the lack of interest? Were they able to overcome it?

❶ *What would change the nymph's mind about living with the shepherd and being his love?*

Thy gowns, thy shoes, thy beds of roses,
Thy cap, thy kirtle, and thy posies
15   Soon break, soon wither, soon forgotten—
In folly ripe, in reason rotten.

Thy belt of straw and ivy buds,
Thy coral clasps and amber studs,
All these in me no means can move
20   To come to thee and be thy love.

But could youth last and love still breed,
Had joys no date nor age no need,
Then these delights my mind might move
To live with thee and be thy love. ∎

ANSWERS TO SELECTION CHECK TEST 4.4.9

EX. To what poem was this poem written as a response?
This poem was written as a response to Marlowe's "The Passionate Shepherd to His Love."

1. What words does the speaker use that imply the shepherd may be dishonest?
The speaker says she might listen to the shepherd if there were truth in every shepherd's tongue.

2. What does the nymph think of the "pretty pleasures" of the world and love?
The nymph thinks that both "pretty pleasures" and love fade with time.

3. What does the nymph say about the gifts the shepherd offers?

(cont.)

Responding to the Selection

How do you think the shepherd would feel hearing the nymph's reply? Imagine you are one of the shepherd's friends. Write in your journal about how you would comfort your friend or the advice you would give him.

Reviewing the Selection

RECALLING

1. Does the nymph think all the world and love are young?

2. In the fourth stanza, what does the nymph say about beautiful clothes and flowers?

3. What material possessions have been promised to the nymph?

4. What would cause the nymph to accept the shepherd's offer?

INTERPRETING

5. What in the first stanza clues in the reader about the nymph's attitude toward the shepherd?

6. Why might some things be "in folly ripe" but "in reason rotten"? What does the nymph mean by this?

7. Why is the nymph not persuaded by the idea of fancy gifts?

8. How is the attitude expressed in the last stanza slightly different from the attitude expressed in the first stanza?

SYNTHESIZING

9. Does the speaker in the poem enjoy the idea of growing older? Explain your answer.

10. Would you say that the speaker in Sir Walter Raleigh's poem is idealistic and romantic? Explain your reasoning.

ANSWERS FOR REVIEWING THE SELECTION

RECALLING

1. She thinks that they are aging and eventually will die.

2. They can make a person happy only for a short time.

3. She has been promised flowers, gowns, shoes, and other fancy articles of clothing.

4. If youth and love were eternal and unchanging, then she might consider the shepherd's offer.

INTERPRETING

Responses will vary. Possible responses are given.

5. She says that *if* there were "truth in every shepherd's tongue," she might decide to live with him; she implies that he may not be truthful.

6. Some things that seem fun or pleasurable will turn out to be trivial inducements when evaluated rationally. She means that only a fool would believe and be tempted by all the things the shepherd has promised.

7. She knows that these gifts could not give her lasting happiness.

8. In stanza 1, the nymph seems disgusted with the shepherd. In the last, she seems merely sad that the world is not the perfect place that the shepherd has imagined.

SYNTHESIZING

Responses will vary. Possible responses are given.

9. No; the knowledge that she must grow old someday seems to make happiness in the present impossible for her.

10. The nymph is in some sense idealistic in that she can imagine a world in which youth and love last forever and she is not willing to settle for less. She is not romantic, however, because she refuses to see the real world as a place where happiness is possible.

ANSWERS TO SELECTION CHECK TEST 4.4.9 (CONT.)

The nymph says the gifts "Soon break, soon wither," and are soon forgotten.

4. Will the nymph come and be the shepherd's love?
No, the nymph will not come to the shepherd and be his love.

5. Under what conditions would the nymph come to live with the shepherd?

The nymph says she would live with the shepherd if they could stay young and in love forever.

►See the evaluation forms for discussion, active listening, and oral communication, *Assessment Portfolio,* 7.11–7.14.
Responses will vary. Possible responses are given.

1. Metaphor. The speaker is using the transition from spring and summer to fall and winter as a metaphor for the inevitable decline of a romantic relationship. The flowers and wanton fields represent spring, and the "honey tongue" represents young love. As the plants must die when winter comes, so must love turn to sorrow or to a "heart of gall." The metaphor illustrates the nymph's cynicism about love.

►**Teaching Note:** Help students to appreciate the way the poet has woven together carefully the threads of this metaphor. Note how he moves back and forth several times between images of the seasons and his discussion of human emotions.

2. Image. Raleigh alters the images presented in Marlowe's poem. For example, Marlowe's image of the waterfall and bird making sweet music together becomes an image of a raging river coldly silencing the birds. The reader also sees Marlowe's fragrant bouquets wither and die in Raleigh's hands.

►**Teaching Note:** Direct students' attention to the illustration on page 268. What sensory images might go along with this scene?

3. Speaker. She seems to be cynical and sad. She says that the silence of the nightingale means that "cares" have replaced happiness (line 8) and that "flowers do fade, and wanton fields/To wayward winter reckoning yields" (lines 9–10). These and other images represent her view of life in general as a process of decline and death after only brief happiness.

►**Teaching Note:** Ask students what they think of the nymph's philosophy. Is the inevitability of death a good reason to spurn the "pretty pleasures" of the world?

Understanding Literature (Questions for Discussion)

1. **Metaphor.** A **metaphor** is a figure of speech in which one thing is spoken or written about as if it were another. Read the third stanza. What metaphors do you find? How do these metaphors help to illustrate the poem's theme?

2. **Image.** An **image** is a word or phrase that names something that can be seen, heard, felt, tasted, or smelled. What are some of the images in Raleigh's poem, and how do they appeal to the senses?

3. **Speaker.** The **speaker** is the character who speaks in a poem—the voice assumed by the writer. How would you describe the speaker in this poem? What specific words or phrases from the poem lead you to think of the speaker in this way?

Responding in Writing

1. **Narrative: Love Story.** Write a brief story in which you present imaginary circumstances for the writing of the "Passionate Shepherd" and the "Nymph's Reply." To do so, first create a situation between two characters. What inspired the shepherd to write his poem? Describe the nymph's response and the writing of her poem. How does the shepherd react? Decide whether or not the lovers will resolve their differences and what kind of ending the story has.

2. **Symbol.** A **symbol** is a thing that stands for or represents both itself and something else. Working with one or two other students, brainstorm a list of traditional symbols of romance, such as roses or rings. Then think of ways in which these symbols may be altered to reflect a cynical view of romance. For example, a rose might be withered or a ring might give its recipient a rash. Develop a poem or a short story in which you use these symbols.

Language Lab

Building Sentences. Read the Language Arts Survey, 2.94, "Commas I." Add commas as necessary in each of the following sentences.

1. Shepherds may use dogs flutes and prods to help them in their work.

2. A philomel is a nightingale but Philomela is the name of a woman from Greek mythology.

---

1. Shepherds may use dogs, flutes, and prods to help them in their work.

2. A philomel is a nightingale, but Philomela is the name of a woman from Greek mythology.

3. Sir Walter Raleigh was a poet, historian, and adventurer.

4. Raleigh was helped by Queen Elizabeth, and he also had a friend in Prince Henry, the son of Elizabeth's successor.

5. Gowns, posies, and belts of straw did not convince the nymph to come live with the shepherd.

►Additional practice is provided in the *Essential Skills Practice Book: Language,* 2.94.

3. Sir Walter Raleigh was a poet historian and adventurer.

4. Raleigh was helped by Queen Elizabeth and he also had a friend in Prince Henry the son of Elizabeth's successor.

5. Gowns posies and belts of straw did not convince the nymph to come live with the shepherd.

Thinking Skills

Read the Language Arts Survey, 4.8, "Comparing and Contrasting." Make two columns on a piece of paper, one headed *Shepherd* and the other headed *Nymph*. To the left of the columns, write *Compare* and then under that, *Contrast*. Draw lines across your page starting under each of these two words. List the characteristics of each poem within the boxes of the matrix you have created with these four headings.

PROJECTS

1. **Persuasion.** With a group of your classmates, write a persuasive essay to an imaginary person in an attempt to convince him or her to move to a new place to be near you.

   • First, list some of the advantages of the move.

   • Next, anticipate the person's objections and respond to them.

   • Finally, summarize your strongest arguments in a closing statement.

2. **Community Activity.** Visit a nursing home with several of your classmates and interview some of the residents about their experiences in love. (Make sure to check with the nursing home staff first to make sure your questions are appropriate.) As a group, write down descriptions of each of the interviews and categorize individuals as representing either "nymph" attitudes or "shepherd" attitudes about love and romance.

ANALYTIC SCALES FOR RESPONDING IN WRITING

Assign a score from 1 to 25 for each grading criterion below. (For more detailed evaluation, see the evaluation forms for writing, revising, and proofreading, *Assessment Portfolio,* 7.1–7.10.)

1. **Narrative: Love Story**

• **Content/Unity.** The narrative presents the two characters in a reasonable situation, and the characters' actions suit their respective personalities.

• **Organization/Coherence.** The narrative describes a logical course of events, organized in a chronological order.

• **Language/Style.** The narrative uses vivid and precise nouns, verbs, and modifiers.

• **Conventions.** The narrative avoids errors in spelling, grammar, usage, mechanics, and manuscript form.

2. **Symbol**

• **Content/Unity.** The poem or short story makes use of a sensible symbol for cynicism about romance.

• **Organization/Coherence.** The poem or short story is well organized, introducing the symbol at an appropriate time and then developing it.

• **Language/Style.** The poem or short story uses vivid and precise nouns, verbs, and modifiers.

• **Conventions.** The poem or short story avoids errors in spelling, grammar, usage, mechanics, and manuscript form.

ANSWERS FOR THINKING SKILLS

Responses will vary. Students might note that the poems are alike in that each is addressed to a particular person, uses images from nature, and presents an opinion about love. The poems are different in that one expresses a romantic view while the other presents a cynical view.

▶Additional practice is provided in the *Essential Skills Practice Book: Study and Research,* 4.8.

 PROJECT NOTES

▶See the worksheets and evaluation forms for projects, *Assessment Portfolio,* 7.20–7.23.

 1. Persuasion
Students may find it helpful to organize their ideas in a chart.

 2. Community Activity
The Language Arts Survey, 1.7, "Interviewing," 3.4, "Active Listening," and 3.5, "Interpersonal Communication," provide guidance for students conducting interviews.

ENRICHMENT ACTIVITIES

• Students can write about or discuss the benefits and drawbacks of being a powerful political leader. You might ask them to list their ideas in a chart, to write poems or stories in the voice of such a leader, or to role play a conversation between a leader and a regular citizen who is curious to know what the leader's life is like.

• In research papers or oral reports, students can compare Elizabeth's attitudes toward her potential foes with those of Cæsar in Shakespeare's *Julius Cæsar.*

SUPPORT FOR LEP STUDENTS

The selection contains many tricky vocabulary words and examples of word play. Advise students to go slowly, tackling one sentence at a time. They may wish to take notes as they read, writing synonyms for new words and translating each line into simpler English.

ADDITIONAL VOCABULARY

exile—banish; remove
wit—intelligence
cloak—disguise
aspiring—ambitious; hoping to gain power
discord—conflict
reap—get; obtain
resort—look for protection or help
gape—stare in wonder; with mouth open

PREREADING

"The Doubt of Future Foes"
by Queen Elizabeth I

ABOUT THE AUTHOR

Queen Elizabeth I (1533–1603) was so powerful a cultural influence that her time is now commonly referred to as the Elizabethan Era. She was the subject of many works of art, as well as the creator of some. She was well educated, in both Greek and Latin, and she read widely in the classics. Because Elizabeth was proud of these talents, she enjoyed displaying them in her speeches, poetry, and translations of biblical and classical prose and poetry. Her own poetry is about actual events from her life. Its **tone** is vigorous and somewhat moralistic, and much of it is written in **poulter's measure**, which makes use of alternating iambic hexameter and iambic heptameter couplets.

ABOUT THE SELECTION

This poem describes Elizabeth's concerns about being overthrown and delivers a vow to defend herself and her court. Specifically, **"The Doubt of Future Foes"** concerns the queen's suspicion of her Roman Catholic cousin Mary Stuart, Queen of Scotland, who sought refuge in England from rebellious subjects. Elizabeth had good reason to "doubt" Mary as a "future foe" because there were several Catholic conspiracies to put Mary on the throne of England. (See the unit introduction, page 247.)

GOALS/OBJECTIVES

Studying this lesson will enable students to

• experience the speaker's feelings of betrayal and confidence

• analyze a poem to identify its aim

• identify and interpret metaphors in a poem

• recognize and correct double negatives

• write a current events poem

• use reference works for research and use active reading techniques

READER'S JOURNAL

Imagine you are a governor or president. You know that you are the best person for the job, and you plan to work hard for the people who elected you. Freewrite your thoughts about rivals who plan to compete with you for elected office. Use vivid verbs to illustrate your fears.

RESEARCH SKILLS

Read the Language Arts Survey, 4.23, "Using Reference Works." Find encyclopedia articles or books about Queen Elizabeth I and Mary, Queen of Scots. Make a brief list describing the major events of each queen's life.

PREREADING NOTES

READER'S JOURNAL

Ask students to recall a time when someone threatened to take away something that they valued. Discuss ways in which people can cope with situations that seem threatening.

RESEARCH SKILLS

• Students may also make an annotated bibliography of various types of reference works. To do this, they should write the title, author, and publication information for each work, followed by a brief description of the information the work contains.

• You might also refer students to the Language Arts Survey, 4.26, "Computer-Assisted Research," and 4.27, "Other Sources of Information."

► Additional practice is provided in the *Essential Skills Practice Book: Study and Research*, 4.28.

"The Doubt of Future Foes"

QUEEN ELIZABETH I

The doubt[1] of future foes exiles my present joy,
And wit me warns to <u>shun</u> such snares as threaten mine annoy.[2]
For falsehood now doth flow, and subject faith doth ebb,[3]
Which would not be, if reason ruled or wisdom weaved the web.
5   But clouds of toys[4] untried do cloak aspiring minds,
Which turn to rain of late repent, by course of changèd winds.
The top of hope supposed, the root of ruth[5] will be,
And fruitless all their graffèd[6] <u>guiles</u>, as shortly ye shall see.
The dazzled eyes with pride, which great ambition blinds,
10 Shall be unsealed by worthy wights[7] whose foresight falsehood finds.
The daughter of debate,[8] that eke discord doth sow
Shall reap no gain where former rule hath taught still peace to grow.
No foreign banished wight shall anchor in this port,
Our realm it <u>brooks</u> no stranger's force, let them elsewhere resort.
15 Our rusty sword with rest, shall first his edge employ
To <u>poll</u> their tops that seek such change and gape for joy.   ■

---

1. **doubt.** Fear
2. **threaten . . . annoy.** Threaten to harm me
3. **falsehood . . . ebb.** Falsehood is rising, and faith, or loyalty, is falling.
4. **toys.** Tricks
5. **ruth.** Sorrow

6. **graffèd.** Grafted; added or taken on
7. **wights.** People
8. **daughter of debate.** The *daughter of debate* was a name given to Mary Stuart because she was the center of many conspiracies.

WORDS FOR
EVERYDAY USE:

shun (shun) *vt.,* keep away from; avoid
guile (gīl) *n.,* deception
brook (brŏŏk) *vt.,* put up with
poll (pōl) *vt.,* cut off

ANSWERS TO SELECTION
CHECK TEST 4.4.11

EX. Of what country was the author of this poem queen?
She was queen of England.

1. Why is the queen not now joyful?
She is not joyful because she has fears about future foes.

2. To what natural phenomenon does the queen compare repentance?
She compares it to rain.

3. Who is the "daughter of debate" mentioned in the poem?
This "daughter of debate" is Mary Stuart.

4. Who will not be allowed to "anchor in this port"?
No foreign, banished people will be allowed to "anchor in this port."

5. What threat does the queen make in the concluding line?
She threatens to cut off heads.

VOCABULARY IN CONTEXT

• Bill's doctor told him to limit his cholesterol; now he <u>shuns</u> fried foods.

• The babysitter wondered what clever <u>guiles</u> the children would use to avoid going to bed on time.

• My sister will <u>brook</u> no interruptions when she is practicing her violin.

• Next time I'll tell the barber not to <u>poll</u> so much on the sides.

RESPONDING TO THE SELECTION

If students are having difficulty starting this assignment, suggest that they begin by making a list of what each side might want. They might also note what each party would be willing to sacrifice in order to reach a peaceful agreement.

ANSWERS FOR REVIEWING THE SELECTION

RECALLING

1. Her own intelligence, or "wit," helps her to avoid these traps.

2. Their loyalty to her is decreasing.

3. She calls it a "port."

4. No; she tells them to seek another "resort" in line 14.

INTERPRETING

Responses will vary. Possible responses are given.

5. Some of the people around her are planning "toys" or tricks to seize power from her and give the throne to Mary Stuart.

6. She is confident that Mary will not succeed in planting discord in a country where the subjects are used to peace (lines 11–12); she believes that she will regain her subjects' loyalty and keep the throne.

7. Elizabeth thinks that Mary would bring only disorder and conflict to England.

8. It seems a good idea to banish her enemies, since they have already succeeded in turning some of her subjects against her.

SYNTHESIZING

Responses will vary. Possible responses are given.

9. She is intelligent, determined, and self-confident.

10. They will be executed; the last two lines of the poem describe beheading.

Responding to the Selection

What if a business meeting took place between the queen and her rivals? How might the minutes, the written record, of that meeting read? What would the two sides discuss? Would it be a peaceful discussion?

Reviewing the Selection

RECALLING

1. What warns the queen to avoid the "snares" that may harm her?

2. According to line 3, how are the feelings of the queen's subjects changing?

3. What does she call her kingdom in line 13?

4. Will Elizabeth allow her opponents to seek shelter in England?

INTERPRETING

▶▶ 5. What are some potential "snares" that may harm the queen?

▶▶ 6. How do her subjects' feelings make the queen feel about the likelihood of maintaining her position?

▶▶ 7. How does Elizabeth feel her kingdom would change under the would-be leaders?

▶▶ 8. Is Elizabeth's decision about allowing her opponents into the country a wise one? Why, or why not?

SYNTHESIZING

9. How would you describe the character of the queen?

10. What will happen to those who try to overthrow the queen?

Understanding Literature (Questions for Discussion)

1. **Metaphor.** A **metaphor** is a description of one thing as if it were another. Look at line 3. What subtle metaphor is the queen using in reference to her situation? Does this metaphor help to illustrate the situation? How?

2. **Aim.** The writer's **aim** is the primary purpose that a work is meant to achieve. A piece might highlight a certain character, theme, or situation. What is this poem's primary purpose? Does it succeed? How does the poem achieve its purpose?

ANSWERS FOR UNDERSTANDING LITERATURE

▶ See the evaluation forms for discussion, active listening, and oral communication, *Assessment Portfolio,* 7.11–7.14.

Responses will vary. Possible responses are given.

1. **Metaphor.** The metaphor compares the loyalty and disloyalty of her subjects to ocean tides going in and out. Since these loyalties are constantly changing, the metaphor seems apt.

▶**Teaching Note:** Ask students to locate other metaphors in the poem, such as those in lines 5–6 (weather) and lines 11–12 (sowing and reaping).

2. **Aim.** The purpose of the poem is to describe the political situation Elizabeth is dealing with and to voice her determination to overcome her enemies. The poem succeeds through its unmistakable tone of determination and self-confidence.

Responding in Writing

Current Events Poem. Think about how Queen Elizabeth I expressed herself by giving concrete details about her situation and about her feelings. What vivid details might you use to describe a recent or ongoing national or world event? How do you feel about it? How do others feel about it? Make notes to yourself. Then try writing a short poem. You may or may not want to try using meter and rhyme.

Language Lab

Double Negatives. Read the Language Arts Survey, 2.88, "Double Negatives." Correct the following sentences to avoid double negatives.

1. Queen Elizabeth I was not hardly a pushover.
2. She wouldn't never give up the throne easily.
3. Mary, Queen of Scots, did not have no chance of deceiving the queen of England.
4. Queen Elizabeth I didn't have no friends that she trusted absolutely.
5. None of her subjects never got away with betrayal neither.

Reading Skills

Read the Language Arts Survey, 4.18, "Reading Actively: Questioning." Then go back to the encyclopedia articles and sources from the Research Skills activity on page 273. Choose an encyclopedia entry or a chapter from the book. On a separate sheet of paper, write six questions to bear in mind as you read one of your sources. Keep the paper beside you as you read.

PROJECT

Role Playing. With one of your classmates, choose two characters from history who have been known to be enemies and dramatize a conversation between them.

• Decide upon a setting and a conflict that will be the basis for your role play.
• Establish your character's basic personality and motivation.
• Write a loose dialogue from which you can ad lib.

ANALYTIC SCALES FOR RESPONDING IN WRITING

Assign a score from 1 to 25 for each grading criterion below. (For more detailed evaluation, see the evaluation forms for writing, revising, and proofreading, *Assessment Portfolio,* 7.1–7.10.)

Current Events Poem
• **Content/Unity.** The poem presents correct facts and relevant feelings about a current event or situation.
• **Organization/Coherence.** The poem includes relevant supporting details in a sensible order.
• **Language/Style.** The poem uses vivid and precise nouns, verbs, and modifiers.
• **Conventions.** The poem avoids errors in spelling, grammar, usage, mechanics, and manuscript form.

ANSWERS FOR READING SKILLS

Students should prepare six questions, the answers to which are worth knowing and could reasonably be expected to be found in the reference work.
► Additional practice is provided in the *Essential Skills Practice Book: Study and Research,* 4.22.

PROJECT NOTES

► See the worksheets and evaluation forms for projects, *Assessment Portfolio,* 7.20–7.23.

Role Playing. Researching the characters for this role playing activity is a good opportunity for students to practice the active reading technique. Their list might include some questions about the characters' personalities and behaviors.

ANSWERS FOR LANGUAGE LAB

Responses will vary. Possible responses are given.
1. Queen Elizabeth I was not a pushover.
2. She would never give up the throne easily.
3. Mary, Queen of Scots, had no chance of deceiving the queen of England.
4. Queen Elizabeth I had no friends that she trusted absolutely.

5. None of her subjects ever got away with betrayal, either.
► Additional practice is provided in the *Essential Skills Practice Book: Language,* 2.88.

ENRICHMENT ACTIVITIES

Campion creates a vivid image of this newly arrived spirit being surrounded by the spirits of historical beauties and engaging in a lively conversation about the parties she attended and the hearts she broke while she was alive. Interested students may draw or paint the scene, depicting its interesting juxtaposition of life and death.

SUPPORT FOR LEP STUDENTS

The poem is one very long sentence, although the final couplet could stand alone as a separate one. Guide students to divide the poem into three meaningful parts: stanza 1 describes what will happen when the woman first arrives in Hades; the first four lines of stanza 2 tell what she will discuss with the other spirits; and the final couplet tells what the speaker thinks she should tell them.

ADDITIONAL VOCABULARY

home—return home
shades—ghosts or spirits
engirt—gather around
smooth—pleasing to the ear
revel—wild party
tourney—tournament; or
    medieval sporting event in
    which knights compete to win
    the favor of a woman
murther—murder (archaic form)

PREREADING

"When Thou Must Home to Shades of Underground"
by Thomas Campion

ABOUT THE AUTHOR

Thomas Campion (1567–1620) was a true Renaissance man—a person of broad scope. He studied law at Cambridge University, became a physician, and was a scholar of Latin verse. However, he was best known as a writer of songs, for which he composed both music and lyrics.

ABOUT THE SELECTION

"When Thou Must Home to Shades of Underground" comes from Campion's *A Book of Airs,* published in 1601. The poem is addressed to a woman who has hurt the speaker deeply. He imagines this woman descending after death into the "underground"—the place to which the dead were said to go in Greek and Roman mythology. There the woman is met by the spirits of beautiful women from classical times who gather around to hear stories of masques, revels, and tournaments—stories about the carefree life of a popular, attractive woman of the upper classes.

GOALS/OBJECTIVES

Studying this lesson will enable students to

- experience the speaker's feelings of anguish and betrayal
- use active listening techniques effectively
- define *ambiguity* and identify and interpret ambiguity in a poem
- write a mystery story, using words and images to create an appropriate mood

READER'S JOURNAL

Freewrite about popularity. In your experience, what makes certain people popular with others? What do you think makes people worthy of popularity? Do unworthy people often become popular? If yes, why?

LISTENING SKILLS

Read the Language Arts Survey, 3.4, "Active Listening." Have one of your classmates read aloud to you, one line at a time, from this selection. As each line is read, repeat it back to your classmate in your own words.

"When Thou Must Home to Shades of Underground"

THOMAS CAMPION

When thou must home to shades of underground,
And there arrived, a new admired guest,
The <u>beauteous</u> spirits do engirt thee round,
White Iope, blithe Helen,[1] and the rest,
5 To hear the stories of thy finished love
From that smooth tongue whose music hell can move,

Then wilt thou speak of banqueting delights,
Of masques[2] and revels which sweet youth did make,
Of tourneys and great challenges of knights,
10 And all these triumphs for thy beauty's sake;
When thou hast told these honors done to thee,
Then tell, Oh tell, how thou didst murther me.

---

1. **White Iope, blithe Helen.** Spirits of women from Greek and Roman mythology famed for their beauty
2. **masques.** Masked balls, or dances

❶
What sort of person is the woman addressed in this poem? What sort of life does she lead?

WORDS FOR EVERYDAY USE: beau • te •ous (byoot′ ē əs) *adj.,* beautiful

RENAISSANCE POETRY / "WHEN THOU MUST HOME TO SHADES OF THE UNDERGROUND"   277

PREREADING NOTES

READER'S JOURNAL

Students might begin by thinking about popular people they have known and then brainstorming a list of their qualities. Which of these qualities might form the basis of lasting relationships? Which might not?

LISTENING SKILLS

Students who succeed can read two lines at a time.
▶Additional practice is provided in the *Essential Skills Practice Book: Speaking and Listening,* 3.4.

ANSWERS TO SELECTION CHECK TEST 4.4.13

EX. Where does the speaker imagine the person being addressed to be going?
The speaker imagines this person to be going "underground," i.e., to the kingdom of the dead.

1. Who gathers around the "new admired guest"?
Beauteous spirits gather around the new guest, including Iope and Helen.

2. Whose "smooth tongue" has "music hell can move"?
The person being addressed by the speaker has a "smooth tongue" capable of moving hell.

3. Of what will the person being addressed speak when she addresses the spirits?
She will speak of banquets, masques, revels, and tournaments.

4. For what reason do knights undertake great challenges?
They undertake great challenges "for thy beauty's sake," i.e., for the sake of the beauty of the person being addressed by the speaker.

5. In the last line of the poem, what does the speaker accuse the person being addressed of doing to him?
He says that the person being addressed murdered him.

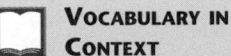 **VOCABULARY IN CONTEXT**

• <u>Beauteous</u> Helen of Troy is called "the face that launched a thousand ships" because the men who competed for her love started the Trojan War.

 ANSWER TO GUIDED READING QUESTION

❶ She is beautiful and has a sweet voice. She enjoys parties and is sought after by many men.

RESPONDING TO THE SELECTION

Ask students to recall a situation in which they felt some other person was receiving undeserved attention or praise. How did this make them feel? Does the speaker in the poem feel the same way? Would confronting the woman help him to feel better?

ANSWERS FOR REVIEWING THE SELECTION

RECALLING

1. She must go home to Hades, the kingdom of the dead.

2. The spirits of other beautiful women of the past will greet her.

3. He calls it "smooth" and says that the sound of it would stir emotions even in hell.

4. She will tell them stories about all the parties and banquets she attended when she was alive and about all the men who competed for her favor.

INTERPRETING

Responses will vary. Possible responses are given.

5. It describes the bleak final resting place of the spirits of the dead.

6. Yes; they will all rush to surround the new arrival and hear her stories.

7. It suggests that she knows how to use her charm to get what she wants out of people.

8. She has had a life rich in excitement and glamour, but perhaps poor in sustaining meaningful relationships.

SYNTHESIZING

Responses will vary. Possible responses are given.

9. The speaker seems bitter and resentful. Even in hell, he thinks, this woman will be pretty and popular, while he will still be suffering from her ill treatment.

10. Most people find her appealing and charming, but the speaker feels she is cruel and insensitive. It is impossible to say which is the "true" picture, since the reader doesn't know in what sense the woman has "murdered" the speaker. She may have done something terrible to him, or he may be overreacting.

278 TEACHER'S EDITION

Responding to the Selection

What might make the speaker of the poem feel more at peace? What might you say or do if you witnessed the subject of the poem bragging to a crowd of people at a banquet? Freewrite your ideas in your journal.

Reviewing the Selection

RECALLING

1. Where must the subject of the poem go?

2. Who will greet the new arrival?

3. How does the speaker describe the subject's speaking voice in line 6?

4. What will the new arrival tell the spirits when they gather around her?

INTERPRETING

5. What type of home does "shades of underground" describe?

6. Will others find the new arrival interesting? How do you know?

7. What does line 6 suggest about the subject of the poem's interactions with others?

8. What sort of life has the subject of the poem led?

SYNTHESIZING

9. What feelings are expressed by the speaker of the poem? What do you think is the primary cause of these feelings?

10. What are the differences between how the subject of the poem appears to most people and how she appears to the speaker? Which appearance do you think is more real?

Understanding Literature (Questions for Discussion)

Ambiguity. An **ambiguity** is a statement that has a double meaning or a meaning that cannot be clearly resolved. Look at the last line of the poem. Might this line be ambiguous? Did the subject of the poem actually hurt the speaker physically? How else is it possible to hurt a person?

ANSWERS FOR UNDERSTANDING LITERATURE

▶ See the evaluation forms for discussion, active listening, and oral communication, *Assessment Portfolio,* 7.11–7.14.

Responses will vary. Possible responses are given.

Ambiguity. It is possible that the speaker means the last line literally. However, since the poem is focused on the woman's easy popularity and polished social skills, it seems more likely that she has somehow hurt him within the social realm. For example, she may have spurned his love publicly and embarrassed him.

▶ **Teaching Note:** Point out that actions can be ambiguous, just as words can be. For instance, the speaker might view the woman's actions as designed deliberately to humiliate him, while she might view her actions as her last recourse in dealing with a pest.

PREREADING

Sonnet 18
Sonnet 29
Sonnet 130
by William Shakespeare

ABOUT THE AUTHOR

William Shakespeare (1564–1616), the son of a prominent citizen, was born in Stratford-upon-Avon. Although he probably attended grammar school, he did not go to college. Very little is known about his youth. The first written record of his life, after his birth certificate, is the record of his marriage to Anne Hathaway in 1582. Within a few years of their marriage, a daughter and then twins (a boy and a girl) were born. The next written evidence of his life dates to 1592 and indicates that he was then an actor and playwright in London. By 1597, Shakespeare was a man of wealth and high social standing, since, in addition to his own theatrical success, his father had been granted a coat of arms. For more information on Shakespeare, see the introduction to Unit Five, page 310.

ABOUT THE SELECTIONS

While Shakespeare is primarily revered for his brilliance as a playwright, he was also the most important lyric poet of his era. The sonnet sequence was a popular form in Elizabethan England. Shakespeare's sonnet sequence is made up of 154 numbered sonnets. There have been many theories about the biographical content of these sonnets, but none have been proven decisively. However, most people agree that there are three distinct phases in the sequence. Most of the sonnets refer to a handsome young man. In these poems, Shakespeare tries to advise the young man about making choices in life. Another set of sonnets is addressed to a rival poet. The third group is addressed to a mysterious woman, who is often referred to as the "dark lady."

Shakespeare was the master of the **Elizabethan sonnet**, which is also referred to as the **Shakespearean sonnet.** This fourteen-line sonnet consists of three quatrains and a rhyming couplet. The rhyme scheme is *abab cdcd efef gg,* and the verse is iambic pentameter. Often, the three four-line verses build upon a theme, and the final couplet gives the conclusion and highlights the meaning of the poem.

ADDITIONAL RESOURCES

READER'S GUIDE
• Selection Worksheets, 4.8, 4.9, 4.10

ASSESSMENT PORTFOLIO
• Selection Check Tests, 4.4.15, 4.4.17, 4.4.19
• Selection Tests, 4.4.16, 4.4.18, 4.4.20

ESSENTIAL SKILLS PRACTICE BOOKS
• *Study and Research,* 4.5, 4.8
• *Language,* 2.82

SUPPORT FOR LEP STUDENTS

Students may benefit from a discussion of some of the things to which beloved people and their characteristics are often compared in English literature—such as a summer's day, the whiteness of snow, or the redness of roses. Encourage them to share any such metaphors common to their own languages.

IDIOMS
in disgrace—out of favor; rejected by someone

ADDITIONAL VOCABULARY
lease—a contract that ends at a certain time
complexion—the appearance of someone's face
fair—beloved woman; beautiful thing; a state of beauty
decline—decrease; come to an end
eternal—lasting forever
possession—ownership
outcast—rejected by others
featured—having a certain type of face
art—skill
scope—the range or extent of someone's power or activities
haply—by chance or luck
lark—a kind of singing bird
coral—a hard, red material produced by colonies of tiny ocean animals
grant—admit that something is true

GOALS/OBJECTIVES

Studying this lesson will enable students to
• appreciate a love poem and share the speaker's feelings of love, joy, and peace
• describe William Shakespeare's literary accomplishments and the historical significance of his writings

• name and describe the characteristics of the Shakespearean or Elizabethan sonnet
• identify the speaker and analyze the use of comparison and contrast in a poem
• use remembering and visualizing techniques
• write similes to describe people and objects
• use pronouns that agree with their antecedents

PREREADING NOTES

READER'S JOURNAL

• Remind students that literary images can appeal to any of the five senses—sight, hearing, smell, touch, and taste.

• Students can begin by brainstorming a list of specific traits possessed by the person or animal they plan to write about.

THINKING SKILLS

As students read Sonnets 18 and 130, have them think about whether the speaker is comparing or contrasting his beloved with the other beautiful things he mentions.

▶Additional practice is provided in the *Essential Skills Practice Book: Study and Research,* 4.8.

ENRICHMENT ACTIVITIES

In the literature of Shakespeare's time, eyes that shone like the sun, lips that were as red as coral, and so on were ideals of female beauty. Interested students can investigate how standards of beauty differ over time and across cultures. What influences these ideals? How are these ideals communicated to people? They might also consider the question of what effects such standards have on individuals' self-esteem. Does anyone really measure up to the ideal? What are some of the unrealistic standards of male and female beauty in our society? What does it feel like to fall short of society's ideal? How do these feelings affect people's behavior?

VOCABULARY FROM THE SELECTIONS

belie
temperate

READER'S JOURNAL

Think about a person or animal that you admire. Then write some images from nature to which your subject compares, such as a rushing brook in a snowy forest, a crisp fall day, or a waterfall.

THINKING SKILLS

Read the Language Arts Survey, 4.8, "Comparing and Contrasting." List the points of contrast between the object of the speaker's love in this poem and the idea of a summer's day.

Sonnet 18

WILLIAM SHAKESPEARE

Shall I compare thee to a summer's day?
Thou art more lovely and more <u>temperate</u>:
Rough winds do shake the darling buds of May,
And summer's lease hath all too short a date:
5 Sometime too hot the eye of heaven shines
And often is his gold complexion dimmed;
And every fair from fair sometimes declines,
By chance or nature's changing course untrimmed;°   *stripped of beauty*
But thy eternal summer shall not fade,
10 Nor lose possession of that fair thou ow'st,°   *own*
Nor shall death brag thou wander'st in his shade,
When in eternal lines to time thou grow'st:
  So long as men can breathe, or eyes can see,
  So long lives this, and this gives life to thee. ∎

❶
What, according to the speaker, "will not fade"?

WORDS FOR   **tem • per • ate** (tem´ pər it) *adj.,* moderate
EVERYDAY USE:

VOCABULARY IN CONTEXT

• We hoped the day of our picnic would be <u>temperate</u>; we didn't want to be either scorched by the sun or chilled by rain and wind.

ANSWER TO GUIDED READING QUESTION

❶ Those qualities of the speaker's beloved that are like qualities of summer will not fade.

Responding to the Selection

If the speaker had chosen to write a personal letter instead of a sonnet, what might the letter have said? In your journal, write a draft of a personal letter expressing the same feelings as those expressed in Sonnet 18, but without the use of imagery and poetic language. Which form do you think makes a more lasting impression on the reader?

Reviewing the Selection

RECALLING

1. What is the speaker's opening question? How is it answered?

2. What does the speaker say "shall not fade" in the beloved?

INTERPRETING

▶▶ 3. According to the speaker, what has a more lasting quality? Why will it last?

▶▶ 4. In lines 5–10, do you think the speaker is referring only to physical beauty? Why, or why not?

SYNTHESIZING

5. What is the "this" in the last line of the poem? What might Shakespeare be saying in this poem about the importance of literature?

RESPONDING TO THE SELECTION

Students should formulate a clear statement of the poem's theme before they begin writing. They can work in pairs to discuss main ideas of the poem before they begin writing.

ANSWERS FOR REVIEWING THE SELECTION

RECALLING

1. In the first line, the speaker asks, "Shall I compare thee to a summer's day?" The answer is yes; the poem is an extended comparison of the two.

2. The beloved's "eternal summer shall not fade"—in other words, the person's beauty will last forever.

INTERPRETING

Responses will vary. Possible responses are given.

3. The beloved person's beauty is more lasting because it has been immortalized in the lines of the sonnet.

4. Line 10 says that the "fair" owned by the speaker's beloved will never be lost; therefore, it must be a kind of beauty not associated with youth. This beauty transcends the physical life of the person, since it lives on in the sonnet.

SYNTHESIZING

Responses will vary. Possible responses are given.

5. "This" refers to the sonnet itself. Shakespeare may mean that literature is the highest form of beauty, since it can exist forever.

ANSWERS TO SELECTION CHECK TEST 4.4.15

EX. What is the rhyme scheme of Shakespeare's Sonnet 18?
The poem can be divided into three quatrains and a concluding couplet rhymed *abab cdcd efef gg*.

1. To what does the speaker suggest comparing his beloved in line 1?
He suggests comparing his beloved to a summer's day.

(cont.)

ANSWERS TO SELECTION CHECK TEST 4.4.15 (CONT.)

2. What shakes "the darling buds of May"?
Rough winds shake "the darling buds of May."

3. What is sometimes too hot and sometimes dimmed?
The sun is sometimes too hot and sometimes dimmed.

4. What will not fade, even after death?
The eternal summer of the person to whom the poem is addressed will not fade.

5. What gives life to the person being addressed for as long as men can breathe or eyes can see?
The poem gives life to that person.

Sonnet 29

When, in disgrace with Fortune and men's eyes,
I all alone beweep my outcast state,
And trouble deaf heaven with my bootless° cries,   *useless*
And look upon myself and curse my fate,
5   Wishing me like to one more rich in hope,
Featured like him, like him with friends possessed,
Desiring this man's art and that man's scope,
With what I most enjoy contented least;
Yet in these thoughts myself almost despising,
10   Haply° I think on thee, and then my state   *by chance or accident*
(Like to the lark at break of day arising
From sullen earth) sings hymns at heaven's gate;
  For thy sweet love remembered such wealth brings
  That then I scorn to change my state with kings. ■

How does the speaker's mood change in lines 10–14? ❶

Responding to the Selection

Answer these questions in your journal: Why does the speaker's attitude change at the end of the poem? How does this person deal with negative feelings? How might you feel if you were the object of the speaker's love?

Reviewing the Selection

RECALLING

1. According to the opening lines, with whom is the speaker in disgrace?

2. For what does the speaker wish in lines 5–7?

INTERPRETING

3. What specific feelings do you think the speaker is experiencing in the opening lines?

4. In the end, are the things for which the speaker wishes the key to his happiness? If not, what is?

SYNTHESIZING

5. What type of wealth is described in the last lines? What does the poem say about the value of this type of wealth?

Sonnet 130

My mistress' eyes are nothing like the sun;
Coral is far more red than her lips' red;
If snow be white, why then her breasts are dun;°   *dark*
If hairs be wires, black wires grow on her head.
5   I have seen roses damasked,° red and white,   *intermingled*
But no such roses see I in her cheeks;
And in some perfumes is there more delight
Than in the breath that from my mistress reeks.°   *flows*
I love to hear her speak, yet well I know
10   That music hath a far more pleasing sound;
I grant I never saw a goddess go;
My mistress, when she walks, treads on the ground.
    And yet, by heaven, I think my love as rare
    As any she <u>belied</u> with false compare. ∎

❶ What silly, fanciful metaphors does the speaker poke fun at in this poem?

Responding to the Selection

Would you like to be adored like a god or goddess, or would you prefer to be loved as the speaker of this poem loves his mistress? Do you want to be loved for your beauty or for something else?

Reviewing the Selection

RECALLING

1. What does the speaker say about the woman's eyes and lips?

2. How does the speaker feel about the woman's voice?

INTERPRETING

▶ 3. What do all of the characteristics that the woman does not possess have in common? Is this significant? Explain.

▶ 4. Why might the speaker still love to hear his beloved's voice?

WORDS FOR EVERYDAY USE:
    be • lie (bē lī´) *vt.*, misrepresent

 VOCABULARY IN CONTEXT
• Katya's carefree attitude <u>belies</u> her underlying determination.

BIBLIOGRAPHICAL NOTE
A standard edition of Shakespeare's work is *The Riverside Shakespeare.* Ed. G. B. Evans. 1974.

ANSWER TO GUIDED READING QUESTION

❶ He makes fun of the conventional but unrealistic images to which the physical characteristics of women are typically compared.

ANSWERS FOR SELECTION CHECK TEST 4.4.19

EX. What are the mistress's eyes not like?
They are nothing like the sun.

1. What is redder than her lips?
Coral is redder than her lips.

2. What does the speaker not see "in her cheeks"?
The speaker does not see roses "in her cheeks."

3. What brings more delight than the mistress's breath?
Perfume brings more delight than the mistress's breath.

4. What has a more pleasing sound than her voice?
Music has a more pleasing sound.

5. What does the speaker think of typical love poems?
He thinks that they make false comparisons.

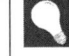

RESPONDING TO THE SELECTION

Ask students to think about the differences between being worshiped, being admired, and being loved. Which of these feelings do they have for people they feel close to?

ANSWERS FOR REVIEWING THE SELECTION

RECALLING

1. The woman's eyes are not like the sun, and her lips are far less red than coral.

2. The woman's voice is less pleasing to the ear than music, but the speaker loves to hear it nonetheless.

INTERPRETING

Responses will vary. Possible responses are given.

3. All of these characteristics can be perceived with the five senses, suggesting that such characteristics have little to do with real love, which goes beyond mere physical attraction.

(cont.)

ANSWERS FOR REVIEWING THE SELECTION (CONT.)

4. The speaker loves her mind and spirit, and for this reason finds physical attributes such as her voice pleasing, regardless of their "objective" value.

SYNTHESIZING

Responses will vary.

5. The speaker's love has nothing to do with superficial qualities such as the woman's physical beauty. The speaker seems to think of this as true love.

ANSWERS FOR UNDERSTANDING LITERATURE

▶ See the evaluation forms for discussion, active listening, and oral communication, *Assessment Portfolio*, 7.11–7.14.

Responses will vary. Possible responses are given.

1. **Meter.** Sonnet 130 uses iambic pentameter throughout. This meter sounds very smooth and lyrical, which creates the calm and measured tone of someone presenting a well-thought-out argument.

▶**Teaching Note:** Can students identify the one foot that is *not* an iamb ("by heaven," line 13)? What emotional effect does this break in the regular meter create?

2. **Speaker.** The speakers in Sonnets 18 and 130 both refuse to use standard metaphors to describe the beloved person, instead saying that the person has qualities that transcend the sensory world. Both have a subtle sense of humor, especially the one in Sonnet 130. The speaker in Sonnet 29 seems highly emotional, drowning in self-doubt one moment and soaring in rapture the next.

▶**Teaching Note:** The three speakers were created by the same writer. Can students detect the same mind at work in each sonnet? Do they think each speaker expresses a slightly different aspect of Shakespeare himself?

---

5. Does the speaker of the poem truly love the woman? On what do you base your answer? What does the speaker conceive true love to be? With what is this contrasted in the poem? Do you agree with the speaker's views?

Understanding Literature (Questions for Discussion)

1. **Meter.** The **meter** of a poem is its rhythmical pattern. What meter does Shakespeare use most frequently in Sonnet 130? How does that meter contribute to the sound and tone of the poem?

2. **Speaker.** The **speaker** is the character who speaks in a poem—the voice assumed by the writer. Describe the speakers in Sonnets 18, 29, and 130. How are the speakers similar to one another? Do any of them seem to have a sense of humor? Do you find each of the speakers likable? Are they equally likable? Why, or why not?

Responding in Writing

1. **Humor.** Freewrite some ideas for a humorous, but kind, descriptive essay about someone you like very much. Use Shakespeare's method of saying what the person is not like, but also hinting at the positive qualities he or she has. The key is to focus on the qualities that you believe truly matter about this person. After you complete the freewrite, put your notes together into an essay.

2. **Similes.** A **simile** is a comparison using *like* or *as*. Write a series of similes to describe a sunrise, a thunderstorm, or some other dramatic natural event. Then make a list of similes to describe special people, animals, or places in your life. Keep your lists in your journal: they may come in handy for other writing assignments.

Language Lab

Agreement of Pronouns and Antecedents. Read the Language Arts Survey, 2.82, "Agreement of Pronouns and Antecedents." Then complete each of the sentences below by adding the correct pronoun. Write your answers on your own paper.

1. The woman wore _____ black hair in a French knot, as _____ usually did.

ANALYTIC SCALES FOR RESPONDING IN WRITING

Assign a score from 1 to 25 for each grading criterion below. (For more detailed evaluation, see the evaluation forms for writing, revising, and proofreading, *Assessment Portfolio*, 7.1–7.10.)

1. Humor
• **Content/Unity.** The essay presents a humorous, but kind, character sketch.

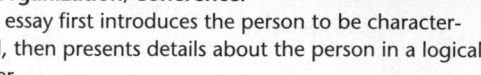

• **Organization/Coherence.** The essay first introduces the person to be characterized, then presents details about the person in a logical order.

• **Language/Style.** The essay uses vivid and precise nouns, verbs, and modifiers.

• **Conventions.** The essay avoids errors in spelling, grammar, usage, mechanics, and manuscript form.

(cont.)

2. The man who is the speaker changes _____ attitude in the last lines of the poem.

3. Although the woman is not perfect, _____ is loved by the speaker.

4. William Shakespeare and other lyric poets use _____ imaginations.

5. Sara and I read Sonnet 130 aloud; then_____ wrote about it.

Thinking Skills

Visualizing. In order to create vivid images, Shakespeare had to be able to visualize and describe places and objects in perfect detail. Improving your ability to visualize will help your creative writing. Read the Language Arts Survey, 4.5, "Remembering and Visualizing." Then try to visualize a room in your home or in your school. Make a list of twenty items in the room. Use reasoning to help you think of items you may have overlooked. Write an asterisk next to items on your list that you remembered through reasoning.

PROJECTS

1. **Drawing.** Form groups of three or four. As a group, illustrate one of the sonnets that you have just read. First, read the sonnets aloud, then choose the one that all of you feel is most visually appealing. For example, you may sketch the flower buds in May in Sonnet 18, or you may create a comical, cartoon-like drawing for Sonnet 130. When each group has completed the assignment, hang the pictures around the room. Guess which sonnet goes with each picture.

2. **Circle Poetry Reading.** As a class, select two or three favorite Shakespearean sonnets. (You don't necessarily need to use the foregoing sonnets.) Sit in a circle and pass the poems around. Each person should read one line aloud and then pass the poem along. As you listen, try to hear and enjoy the meter and rhyme. As you read, try to read lines with feeling, as if you have climbed inside the speaker.

ANALYTIC SCALES FOR RESPONDING IN WRITING (CONT.)

2. Similes
- **Content/Unity.** Lists of similes contain several similes describing a single natural event.
- **Content/Unity.** Lists of similes also contain a number of similes describing people or places.
- **Language/Style.** Similes use vivid and precise nouns, verbs, and modifiers.
- **Conventions.** Similes avoid errors in spelling, grammar, usage, and mechanics.

ANSWERS FOR THINKING SKILLS

Responses will vary. Lists should contain twenty items.

▶Additional practice is provided in the *Essential Skills Practice Book: Study and Research*, 4.5.

PROJECT NOTES

▶See the worksheets and evaluation forms for projects, *Assessment Portfolio*, 7.20–7.23.

1. Drawing
- On a copy of the sonnet, students can use a highlighter to note sensory words and images they want to incorporate in their illustrations.
- Remind students that when they work in groups, all group members must be encouraged to participate and contribute ideas.

2. Circle Poetry Reading
Students with experience in drama may share their techniques for "getting inside" a character and projecting the character's feelings through spoken language.

ANSWERS FOR LANGUAGE LAB

1. The woman wore <u>her</u> black hair in a French knot, as <u>she</u> usually did.

2. The man who is the speaker changes <u>his</u> attitude in the last lines of the poem.

3. Although the woman is not perfect, <u>she</u> is loved by the speaker.

4. William Shakespeare and other lyric poets use <u>their</u> imaginations.

5. Sara and I read Sonnet 130 aloud; then <u>we</u> wrote about it.

▶Additional practice is provided in the *Essential Skills Practice Book: Language*, 2.82.

ADDITIONAL RESOURCES

READER'S GUIDE
- Selection Worksheet, 4.11

ASSESSMENT PORTFOLIO
- Selection Check Test, 4.4.21
- Selection Test, 4.4.22

ESSENTIAL SKILLS PRACTICE BOOK
- *Study and Research,* 4.18, 4.26–4.28, 4.40

ENRICHMENT ACTIVITIES

Students can work in small groups to create a short, one-act play based on "Song, to Celia." The moment when the speaker recites the poem can be the climax of the drama. (Students might even imagine alternate scenarios: for example, perhaps Celia did *not* reject the wreath.) After the speaker gives his "toast," the play should resolve the situation, perhaps with a response from Celia. After all groups perform their plays, the class can discuss the various interpretations of the story.

SUPPORT FOR LEP STUDENTS

You may wish to list the archaic verb forms *doth, didst,* and *sent'st* and the pronouns *thine, thee,* and *thou* on the board with their modern equivalents. Explain that the poem is in the form of a toast, a short speech in which someone is honored or complimented.

IDIOMS

drink to—honor; show approval

since when—since that time

ADDITIONAL VOCABULARY

pledge—drink a toast to; promise

divine—related to the gods; heavenly

sup—eat supper

late—recently

thereon—on it

RENAISSANCE POETRY

"Song, to Celia"
by Ben Jonson

ABOUT THE AUTHOR

Ben Jonson (1572–1637) was born after the death of his father, a clergyman, and became the stepson of a master bricklayer. He was educated by the great classical scholar William Camden at West-minster School, worked for a short time by his stepfather's side, and then entered the army. He was a brave soldier in hand-to-hand combat at Flanders, where the Dutch and English were fighting the Spaniards. When he returned to England in 1594, he became a playwright and actor.

Jonson was not a mild-mannered man. He was nearly hanged for murder after killing another actor in a duel. Later he was jailed for insulting the Scottish nation. As he grew older, he calmed down considerably, and he became a father figure to London's literary circle. A favorite of the royal court, Jonson was made the first poet laureate in all but name by King James I. His followers became known as the Sons of Ben. Unlike other poets of his time, such as his friend William Shakespeare, Jonson was not meek about publicizing his poetry. Jonson was concerned to preserve his works for posterity, and he personally oversaw their publication.

ABOUT THE SELECTION

Like many English poems of this period, **"Song, to Celia"** is a lyric poem honoring a goddess-like and unattainable woman. Each of the two eight-line **stanzas** has its own individual rhyme scheme. Jonson uses a variety of meters in this poem, mainly iambic, but there are also many lines and phrases that begin on an accented syllable. Moreover, the poem's lines are not all the same length; they vary from three to five feet, with most of the odd lines being at least one foot longer than the even ones.

GOALS/OBJECTIVES

Studying this lesson will enable students to

- interpret and appreciate a love poem
- describe Ben Jonson's influence on English literature
- identify the rhyme scheme and meter of a poem, and copy that meter in their own verse

- devise images for expressive writing
- use reference works to locate biographical information
- identify the vehicle and tenor of a metaphor
- use the prereading skill of predicting
- answer analogy test questions

READER'S JOURNAL

In your journal, write several lines of a song that celebrate the wonderful qualities of someone you know. Use rhythm and rhyme to create a joyful mood.

RESEARCH SKILLS

Read the Language Arts Survey, 4.23, "Using Reference Works." Find biographical information about Ben Jonson in literary references at your library. List the many well-known poets and playwrights who were friends or pupils of Jonson.

"Song, to Celia"

BEN JONSON

Drink to me only with thine eyes,
    And I will pledge with mine;
Or leave a kiss but in the cup,
    And I'll not look for wine.
5   The thirst that from the soul doth rise
    Doth ask a drink divine:
But might I of Jove's nectar[1] sup,
    I would not change for thine.

I sent thee late a rosy wreath,
10   Not so much honoring thee,
As giving it a hope that there
    It could not <u>withered</u> be.
But thou thereon didst only breathe,
    And sent'st it back to me;
15   Since when it grows and smells, I swear,
    Not of itself, but thee. ∎

①
Is the word wine
*used literally or
symbolically?*

②
*What gift has
the speaker
bestowed upon
Celia?*

1. **Jove's nectar.** Jove is a Roman god and nectar is the drink of the gods.

WORDS FOR
EVERYDAY **U**SE:

with • er (with´ ər) *vi.,* wilt and shrivel

VOCABULARY IN CONTEXT

• Because of the drought, most of the tomatoes <u>withered</u> on their vines.

ANSWERS TO GUIDED READING QUESTIONS

① The word *wine* here is used symbolically and stands for the earthly pleasures the speaker could do without, if only the woman he desired felt the same way about him.

② He sent her a wreath, or woven ring, of roses.

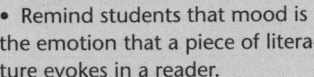

PREREADING NOTES

READER'S JOURNAL
• Remind students that mood is the emotion that a piece of literature evokes in a reader.
• Students could begin by brainstorming a list of adjectives that describe the person and then thinking of words that rhyme with these adjectives.

RESEARCH SKILLS
• Students may use an on-line service or an encyclopedia on CD/ROM for their research. Refer them to the Language Arts Survey, 4.26, "Computer-Assisted Research."
• Ask students what different kinds of sources they could use to find biographical information about living persons such as movie actors or sports celebrities.

►Additional practice is provided in the *Essential Skills Practice Book: Study and Research,* 4.26–4.28.

ANSWERS TO SELECTION CHECK TEST 4.4.21

EX. To whom is this poem addressed?
The poem is addressed to Celia.

1. What does the speaker ask Celia to do in line 1?
He asks her to drink to him only with her eyes.

2. What did the speaker send to Celia?
The speaker sent her a rosy wreath.

3. To whom did Celia send the gift?
She sent it back to the speaker.

4. What did Celia do to the gift before sending it?
She breathed on it.

5. What has *not* happened to the gift?
It has not withered; rather, it grows and smells of Celia.

RESPONDING TO THE SELECTION

Students could discuss these questions in pairs before writing in their journals.

ANSWERS FOR REVIEWING THE SELECTION

RECALLING

1. He wants her to drink to him with her eyes.

2. He asks her to leave a kiss in the cup.

3. The speaker wants to drink the nectar of his beloved—i.e., he wants to know that she cares for him.

4. He sends her a "rosy wreath," which she returns to him.

INTERPRETING

Responses will vary. Possible responses are given.

5. He seems to have strong feelings for her. The word *pledge* suggests that he may want to marry her.

6. He wants the woman to have feelings for him; then he would not care about earthly things such as food and drink.

7. He thirsts for what his soul needs: this woman's love.

8. Her response seems not to have deterred him. He even puts a positive spin on the event, claiming that her breath on the roses has preserved and transformed them.

SYNTHESIZING

Responses will vary. Possible responses are given.

9. The speaker seems very passionate and not easily discouraged. Some readers may think he is insensitive to Celia's feelings, since he seems to be pursuing her against her wishes.

10. The speaker and Celia do not seem to be in an amicable relationship; it may even be an antagonistic one. The speaker may be trying to get to know Celia; this "toast" may be the latest in a long string of attempts to woo her; or they may have had a relationship in the past that she has decided to end.

Responding to the Selection

Answer the following questions in your journal: How might you advise the speaker in this poem? How do you think he is feeling? How do you think the object of his affection feels about the attention being bestowed upon her? Is he taking her feelings seriously? Should he try to look elsewhere for love?

Reviewing the Selection

RECALLING

1. How does the speaker want his beloved to drink to him?

2. What does he want her to leave in the cup?

3. For what drink does the speaker ask?

4. What does he give Celia? What does she do with the gift?

INTERPRETING

5. Judging from the first two lines, how strong are the speaker's feelings for his beloved? What evidence do you have?

6. What does the speaker really want? If he had this, why do you think he would not look for wine?

7. For what is the speaker thirsting?

8. Does her response to the gift change his feelings about pursuing the relationship? What makes you think so?

SYNTHESIZING

9. How might you describe the speaker in this poem? What kind of person is the speaker?

10. Does this poem seem to be about a working romantic relationship? If not, what is it about? What do you imagine might happen to the relationship between the speaker and Celia in the future?

Understanding Literature (Questions for Discussion)

1. **Dactyl.** A **dactyl** is a poetic foot made up of a strongly stressed syllable followed by two weakly stressed syllables. Find two examples of dactyls in the poem. How does the use of the dactyl affect the mood of the poem? How might this poem sound if it were to be sung?

2. **Metaphor.** A **metaphor** is a figure of speech in which one thing is spoken or written about as if it were another. The thing spoken about is the **tenor**, and the object to which it is compared is the **vehicle**. What is the metaphor in the first stanza of the poem? What is the vehicle? What might be the tenor? Is this an effective metaphor? Why, or why not? Have you heard other metaphors in reference to this same subject?

288 *UNIT FOUR / THE ENGLISH RENAISSANCE*

ANSWERS FOR UNDERSTANDING LITERATURE

▶ See the evaluation forms for discussion, active listening, and oral communication, *Assessment Portfolio,* 7.11–7.14.

Responses will vary. Possible responses are given.

1. Dactyl. Examples of dactyls in the poem include line 1, "Drink to me," and line 10, "Not so much honoring." The dactylic foot at the start of each of these lines creates a feeling of emphasis, since it begins with a stressed syllable (unlike the iambs in the rest of the poem). The song might sound awkward if sung, since the meter varies irregularly.

▶**Teaching Note:** Remind students how to mark stress. They may find it helpful to read the poem aloud—either independently or with a partner—and concentrate on making the language flow naturally.

288 TEACHER'S EDITION

(cont.)

Responding in Writing

1. **Rejuvenation.** One image in this poem is of a wreath that can be brought back to life by the breath of the woman. Freewrite images that relate to growth, rejuvenation, and romance. They can be from your own imagination, or they can be images you have read elsewhere. Be sure to put a star beside your own original images.

2. **Metrical Mirroring.** Read the first or second stanza of this selection and then try to rewrite it with your own verse. Your words can be meaningful or nonsensical, but should mirror the meter of Jonson's lines.

3. **Toast.** Write a wedding toast to the speaker in this poem, assuming that he is finally marrying his beloved. In your toast, mention all that he did to try to win the affection of his beloved. You might also mention how her feelings have grown and changed. Use your imagination when describing the final scenario. Consider the possibility that perhaps he stopped trying to contact her and gave her space in which to think about the situation.

Reading Skills

Read the Language Arts Survey, 4.18, "Reading Actively: Predicting." Then read the poem and predict what response the recipient of the poem might have to it. Base your prediction on evidence provided in the poem.

Test-taking Skills

Read the Language Arts Survey, 4.40, "Analogy Questions." Write three analogies using words or ideas from this poem. Then choose the word that best completes the following analogies.

1. SADNESS : DESPONDENCY :: Love :
   a. Fatigue   c. Ardor
   b. Remorse   d. Fellowship

2. INFORMATION : RELATE :: Gift :
   a. Generate   c. Accept
   b. Absolve   d. Bestow

3. POEM : METER :: Song :
   a. Beat   c. Lyrics
   b. Notes   d. Vocals

4. THIRST : QUENCH :: Yearning :
   a. Longing   c. Appease
   b. Optimism   d. Covet

5. PURE : SULLIED :: Divine :
   a. Angelic   c. Ethereal
   b. Diabolical   d. Convoluted

READER'S GUIDE
• Selection Worksheet, 4.12

ASSESSMENT PORTFOLIO
• Selection Check Test, 4.4.23
• Selection Test, 4.4.24

ESSENTIAL SKILLS PRACTICE BOOKS
• *Study and Research,* 4.16

ENRICHMENT ACTIVITIES

This selection from the King James Bible gives readers some insight into how the Judeo-Christian tradition has dealt with death. Students can discuss or research the teachings of various other religious or philosophical systems on this topic. How does each answer the questions of why we are here and why we must die?

SUPPORT FOR LEP STUDENTS

Point out that the Old and New Testaments originally were written in another language (Hebrew and Greek, respectively) and were translated into English. If any students have studied the Bible in other languages, they may refer to translations in their own languages and compare them verse-by-verse to the King James version as they read.

PREREADING

THE KING JAMES BIBLE

from Ecclesiastes, Chapter 3

ABOUT THE SELECTION

Chapter 3 of **Ecclesiastes** tells about the balance of give and take in the lives of human beings and suggests that every human activity has its proper season, or time.

The first of the great translators of the Bible into English was William Tyndale (1494–1536), who produced a version of the New Testament that was smuggled into England. For his pains, Tyndale was hounded through various European cities and eventually imprisoned and put to death. After Henry VIII broke with Rome, however, Biblical translations met with official approval. The greatest of those produced in England was the King James Bible, or Authorized Version, which appeared in 1611, the work of fifty-four scholars appointed by the king.

For centuries, the simple, stately language of this book has influenced the content and rhythms of writing in the English language.

GOALS/OBJECTIVES

Studying this lesson will enable students to

• experience a sense of balance in the give and take of life
• explain the literary significance of the King James Bible

• adjust their reading rate according to their purposes
• explain parallelism and recognize its use in literature

READER'S JOURNAL

Have you ever been in a hurry to move on to the next stage of your life? Freewrite in your journal about why it might be important to appreciate each stage. How does one stage build on the other? What do you learn with each year?

READING SKILLS

Read the Language Arts Survey, 4.16, "Reading Rates." First, scan the selection for references to time, then skim the selection and note the main ideas. Finally, read the selection slowly and carefully.

FROM
Ecclesiastes, Chapter 3

To every *thing there is* a season, and a time to every purpose under the heaven:

2   A time to be born, and a time to die; a time to plant, and a time to pluck up *that which is* planted;

3   A time to kill, and a time to heal; a time to break down, and a time to build up;

4   A time to weep, and a time to laugh; a time to mourn, and a time to dance;

5   A time to cast away stones, and a time to gather stones together; a time to embrace, and a time to refrain from embracing;

6   A time to get, and a time to lose; a time to keep, and a time to cast away;

7   A time to <u>rend</u>, and a time to sew; a time to keep silence, and a time to speak;

8   A time to love, and a time to hate; a time of war, and a time of peace. ■

❶
When would be a good time to cast away stones?

WORDS FOR EVERYDAY USE: **rend** (rend) *vt.* tear

VOCABULARY IN CONTEXT

• Isn't that my favorite shirt that you're about to <u>rend</u> into rags?

READER'S JOURNAL

Students might think about what they are looking forward to in the years after high school and reflect upon what they have learned from their experiences—both pleasant and unpleasant—that will help them in the future.

READING SKILLS

After students have skimmed the selection, ask them to describe its structure of main idea and supporting details.
▶ Additional practice is provided in the *Essential Skills Practice Book: Study and Research,* 4.16.

ANSWER TO GUIDED READING QUESTION

❶ *Answers will vary.* One might cast away stones when breaking down a wall.

ANSWERS TO SELECTION CHECK TEST 4.4.23

EX. For what is there a season?
There is a season for everything.

1. What two times for the beginning of life are mentioned?
"A time to be born" and "a time to plant" both refer to beginnings of life.

2. There is "a time to weep," but there is also a time to do what?
There is also "a time to laugh."

3. What examples of sadness and happiness, aside from weeping and laughing, are included?
There is also "a time to mourn" and "a time to dance."

4. What time is paired with "a time to rend"?
"A time to sew" is paired with "A time to rend."

5. What are the last four things mentioned for which there are times?
There is a time "to love," "to hate," "of war," and "of peace."

RESPONDING TO THE SELECTION
Students can also discuss what might be the negative consequences of doing some of these things at inappropriate times. Is it always clear whether it is the right time to do something?

ANSWERS TO REVIEWING THE SELECTION

RECALLING

1. There is an appropriate time for everything.

2. *Responses will vary. Refer to the selection.*

INTERPRETING

Responses will vary. Possible responses are given.

3. For every activity, there is an appropriate time to do it or for it to happen.

4. The first two times are parallel or in some way similar to the second two times. In verse 2, both sets are a beginning of life followed by an ending of life.

SYNTHESIZING

Responses will vary. Possible responses are given.

5. By doing or failing to do something at its proper time, some type of relationship or cycle would be destroyed. For example, blurting out a secret when it is "a time to keep silence" could ruin the trust between two people. On the other hand, saying nothing to defend a friend who is being put down by others could also destroy that trust.

ADDITIONAL QUESTIONS AND ACTIVITIES

• Students can explore the idea that there is a time for positive things and a time for negative things. How does this idea help people deal with difficult times? Students can write essays using examples from their own life.

• Students may create a game based on the theme of this selection. For example, players would need to "plant" in order to progress toward winning, but they could do so only during the "time to plant."

292 TEACHER'S EDITION

Responding to the Selection

Choose three of the "time pairs" mentioned in the poem and discuss with other students times when each would be appropriate. For example, when would be a good time to keep silence? When would be a good time to speak?

Reviewing the Selection

RECALLING

1. For what are there appropriate seasons, or times, according to verse 1?

2. Each verse, from verse 2 through verse 8, mentions four "times." Choose one verse. What "times" are mentioned in this verse, and in what order?

INTERPRETING

3. In your own words, what is the main idea expressed by verse 1?

4. In verses 2–8, what relationship exists between the first two "times" and the second two "times"?

SYNTHESIZING

5. What kinds of problems could people encounter if they ignored the advice given in this poem? Give specific examples of people acting at inappropriate times.

Understanding Literature (Questions for Discussion)

Parallelism. Parallelism is a literary technique in which a writer emphasizes the equal value or weight of two or more ideas by expressing them in the same grammatical form. The selection from Ecclesiastes makes extensive use of parallelism. It also makes use of **repetition with variation**, in which an idea is repeated but in different words. Consider the second verse. Notice that it is made up of four parallel phrases, each beginning with the words "a time." The second two phrases repeat with variation the ideas expressed in the first two phrases. How is planting similar to being born? How is dying similar to being plucked up? Discuss the similarities between the pairs in the rest of the poem. You might begin by creating a chart in which you compare the four parallel phrases in each verse.

VERSE	FIRST PAIR	SECOND PAIR
2	born	plant
	die	pluck up

292 *UNIT FOUR / THE ENGLISH RENAISSANCE*

ANSWERS FOR UNDERSTANDING LITERATURE

▶See the evaluation forms for discussion, active listening, and oral communication, *Assessment Portfolio,* 7.11–7.14.
Responses will vary. Possible responses are given.
Parallelism. Being planted is the way in which some plants begin their lives, just as being born is the way people and animals begin their lives. A plant's life ends when it is plucked up; the life of a person or animal ends when it dies. In verse 5, the "time to cast away stones" may be interpreted as a time to break down a wall or a barrier between people, which is similar to embracing. On the other hand, gathering stones together to build a wall makes "embracing" impossible.

▶**Teaching Note:** Students can work in pairs or small groups to discuss the parallels between each pair of "times."

"Alas! So All Things Now Do Hold Their Peace" by Henry Howard, Earl of Surrey

Alas! so all things now do hold their peace,
Heaven and earth disturbèd[1] in no thing;
The beasts, the air, the birds their songs do cease,
The nightès chare[2] the stars about doth bring.
5 Calm is the sea, the waves work less and less;
So am not I, whom love, alas, doth wring,
Bringing before my face the great increase
Of my desires, whereat I weep and sing,
In joy and woe, as in a doubtful ease.
10 For my sweet thoughts sometime do pleasure bring,
But by and by the cause of my disease
Gives me a pang that inwardly doth sting,
When that I think what grief it is again
To live and lack the thing should rid my pain.

"Heart Exchange" by Sir Philip Sidney

My true love hath my heart, and I have his,
By just exchange one for the other given:
I hold his dear, and mine he cannot miss;
There never was a bargain better driven.
5 His heart in me keeps me and him in one;
My heart in him his thoughts and senses guides:
He loves my heart, for once it was his own;
I cherish his, because in me it bides.
His heart his wound received from my sight;
10 My heart was wounded with his wounded heart;
For, as from me on him his hurt did light,
So still methought in me his hurt did smart:
Both equal hurt in this change sought our bliss:
My true love hath my heart and I have his.

Sonnet 75 ("One day I wrote her name . . .") from *Amoretti* by Edmund Spenser

One day I wrote her name upon the strand,°   *beach*
But came the waves and washèd it away:
Agayne[3] I wrote it with a second hand,
But came the tyde, and made my paynes his
    pray.°   *prey*
5 "Vayne man," sayd she, "that doest in vaine
    assay,°   *attempt*
A mortall thing so to immortalize,
For I my selve shall lyke to this decay,
And eek my name bee wypèd out lykewize."°   *also*

"Not so," quod° I, "let baser things devize,°   *quoth/contrive*
10 To dy in dust, but you shall live by fame:
My verse your vertues rare shall eternize,
And in the heavens wryte your glorious name.
Where whenas death shall all the world subdew,
Our love shall live, and later life renew."

Sonnet 30 ("When to the sessions . . .") by William Shakespeare

When to the sessions of sweet silent thought
I summon up remembrance of things past,
I sigh the lack of many a thing I sought,
And with old woes new wail my dear time's waste:
5 Then can I drown an eye (unused to flow)
For precious friends hid in death's dateless night,
And weep afresh love's long since canceled woe,
And moan th' expense of many a vanished sight:
Then can I grieve at grievances foregone,
10 And heavily from woe to woe tell o'er
The sad account of fore-bemoanèd moan,
Which I new pay as if not paid before.
    But if the while I think on thee, dear friend,
    All losses are restored and sorrows end.

Sonnet 73 ("That time of year . . .") by William Shakespeare

That time of year thou mayst in me behold
When yellow leaves, or none, or few, do hang
Upon those boughs which shake against the cold,
Bare ruined choirs, where late the sweet birds sang.
5 In me thou seest the twilight of such day
As after sunset fadeth in the west;
Which by and by black night doth take away,
Death's second self that seals up all in rest.
In me thou seest the glowing of such fire,
10 That on the ashes of his youth doth lie,
As the deathbed whereon it must expire,
Consumed with that which it was nourished by.
    This thou perceiv'st, which makes thy love more
      strong,
    To love that well, which thou must leave ere long.

---

1. **disturbèd.** The accent over the e means that the *-ed* should be pronounced as a separate syllable.
2. **chare.** Sweet
3. **Agayne.** This is one example of Spenser's antiquated spellings.

"ALAS! SO ALL THINGS NOW DO HOLD THEIR PEACE"

About the Author. Henry Howard, Earl of Surrey (1517–1547), was responsible, along with Sir Thomas Wyatt, for introducing the sonnet to English literature. Surrey was born to an aristocratic family with close ties to the English throne and spent his short life embroiled in the politics of Henry VIII's court. He lived at Windsor Castle between 1530 and 1532 with the king's illegitimate son Henry Fitzroy, Duke of Richmond, who was his father's ward. Surrey and the rest of his family fell in and out of favor. In 1547, he was charged with treason and beheaded.

LITERARY TECHNIQUE

Students may form small groups to discuss the following questions.

"Heart Exchange"

What are the rhyme scheme and meter of "Heart Exchange"? What form of poem is it?

Answers. The rhyme scheme of "Heart Exchange" is *abab cdcd efef gg,* and the meter is iambic pentameter; it is a Shakespearean or Elizabethan sonnet.

Sonnet 75

What are the rhyme scheme and meter of Spenser's Sonnet 75? Can it be called an Elizabethan or a Petrarchan sonnet? What is the theme? What other sonnet from the unit has a similar theme? Do you prefer one over the other, and if so, why?

Answers. Sonnet 75 is written in iambic pentameter with the rhyme scheme *abab bcbc bdbd ee;* it is neither Elizabethan nor Petrarchan. The theme is the immortality of literature (as opposed to the mortality of human flesh), the same as Shakespeare's Sonnet 18.

Sonnet 30

A session is a meeting of a court of justice. What conceit does Shakespeare use in the opening lines of Sonnet 30? What is the theme of Shakespeare's Sonnet 30?

Answers. In Sonnet 30, Shakespeare compares his thoughts about past sadnesses and regrets to a court of law, with each memory testifying as a witness. The theme is the value of friendship.

Sonnet 73

What are the major metaphors in Shakespeare's Sonnet 73? Do you find them effective?

Answers. In Sonnet 73, Shakespeare uses a tree in winter, nightfall, and a dying fire as metaphors for approaching the end of life.

About the Author. Little is known for certain about the life of poet **Aemilia Lanyer** (*circa* 1570–*circa* 1640). She belonged to the royal courts of Elizabeth I, James I, and Charles I and was married to a court musician named Alphonso Lanyer. Their son Henry became a professional flutist. Aemilia Lanyer's work is bold and radical in its feminist perspective. In "Eve's Apology in Defense of Women," Lanyer reinterprets the story of Adam and Eve, portraying the prototypical woman not as a sly temptress but as a generous wife who innocently desires to share the gift of knowledge with her husband. The character of Lanyer's poetry has led historian A. L. Rowse to speculate that she was the strong-willed "Dark Lady" to whom William Shakespeare devoted many of his sonnets.

About the Selection. The word *apology* is most often used today to mean a statement of regret or an admission of error. In the title of Lanyer's poem, however, it means a formal defense, a carefully reasoned argument proclaiming someone's innocence. Lanyer argues that women's lowly social status, which had been justified by Eve's "guilt" in encouraging Adam to eat from the tree of knowledge, is not fair in light of the much greater sin committed by men's representative, Pontius Pilate.

Eve's Apology in Defense of Women[1]
from *Salve Deus Rex Judaeorum*[2]
by Aemilia Lanyer

Now Pontius Pilate is to judge the cause
Of faultless Jesus, who before him stands,
Who neither hath offended prince, nor laws,
Although he now be brought in woeful bands.
5   O noble governor, make thou yet a pause,
Do not in innocent blood inbrue thy hands;
    But hear the words of thy most worthy wife,[3]
    Who sends to thee, to beg her Saviour's life.

Let barb'rous cruelty far depart from thee,
10   And in true justice take affliction's part;
Open thine eyes, that thou the truth may'st see.
Do not the thing that goes against thy heart,
Condemn not him that must thy Saviour be;
But view his holy life, his good desert.
15   Let not us women glory in men's fall.
     Who had power given to overrule us all.

Till now your indiscretion sets us free.
And makes our former fault much less appear;
Our mother Eve, who tasted of the tree,
20   Giving to Adam what she held most dear,
Was simply good, and had no power to see;[4]
The after-coming harm did not appear:
    The subtle serpent that our sex betrayed
    Before our fall so sure a plot had laid.

25   That undiscerning ignorance perceived
No guile or craft that was by him intended;
For had she known of what we were bereaved,[5]
To his request she had not condescended.
But she, poor soul, by cunning was deceived;
30   No hurt therein her harmless heart intended:
    For she alleged God's word, which he denies,
    That they should die, but even as gods be wise.

But surely Adam cannot be excused;
Her fault though great, yet he was most to blame;
35   What weakness offered, strength might have refused,

Being lord of all, the greater was his shame.
Although the serpent's craft had her abused,
God's holy word ought all his actions frame,
    For he was lord and king of all the earth,
40   Before poor Eve had either life or breath,

Who being framed by God's eternal hand
The perfectest man that ever breathed on earth;
And from God's mouth received that strait command,
The breach whereof he knew was present death;
45   Yea, having power to rule both sea and land,
Yet with one apple won to lose that breath
    Which God had breathed in his beauteous face,
    Bringing us all in danger and disgrace.

And then to lay the fault on Patience' back,
50   That we (poor women) must endure it all.
We know right well he did discretion lack,
Being not persuaded thereunto at all.
If Eve did err, it was for knowledge sake;
The fruit being fair persuaded him to fall:
55   No subtle serpent's falsehood did betray him;
     If he would eat it, who had power to stay him?

Not Eve, whose fault was only too much love,
Which made her give this present to her dear,
That what she tasted he likewise might prove,
60   Whereby his knowledge might become more clear;
He never sought her weakness to reprove
With those sharp words which he of God did hear;
    Yet men will boast of knowledge, which he took
    From Eve's fair hand, as from a learned book.

65   If any evil did in her remain,
Being made of him,[6] he was the ground of all.
If one of many worlds could lay a stain
Upon our sex, and work so great a fall
To wretched man by Satan's subtle train,
70   What will so foul a fault amongst you all?[7]
    Her weakness did the serpent's words obey,
    But you in malice God's dear Son betray,

---

1. **Eve's . . . Women.** A narrator offers Eve's apology for her actions in defense of all women in an impassioned address to Pilate, the Roman official who authorized Christ's crucifixion. Eve and Pilate's wife represent all women, and Pilate and Adam represent all men.
2. **Salve . . . Judaeorum.** A variation of the inscription on Christ's cross. It means "Hail, God, King of the Jews."
3. **But . . . wife.** Pilate's wife wrote him a letter asking him to spare Jesus because she had received a warning in a dream (Matthew 27:19).

4. **Our . . . see.** Eve, tempted by the serpent, ate the forbidden fruit. Genesis emphasizes Eve's knowledge that the fruit was forbidden and blames her action on pride and ambition.
5. **bereaved.** Deprived of eternal life; this along with suffering, work, and pain in childbirth were punishment for eating the forbidden fruit.
6. **made of him.** According to Genesis, Eve was created from Adam's rib.
7. **What . . . all?** How terrible a stain on all men can Pilate's condemnation of Jesus be?

Whom, if unjustly you condemn to die,
Her sin was small to what you do commit;
75 All mortal sins that do for vengeance cry
Are not to be compared unto it.
If many worlds would altogether try
By all their sins the wrath of God to get,
    This sin of yours surmounts them all as far
80   As doth the sun another little star.

Then let us have our liberty again,
And challenge to yourselves no sovereignty.
You came not in the world without our pain,
Make that a bar against your cruelty;
85 Your fault being greater, why should you disdain
Our being your equals, free from tyranny?
    If one weak woman simply did offend,
    This sin of yours hath no excuse nor end,

To which, poor souls, we never gave consent.
90 Witness, thy wife, O Pilate, speaks for all,
Who did but dream, and yet a message sent
That thou shouldest have nothing to do at all
With that just man; which, if thy heart relent,
Why wilt thou be a reprobate with Saul[1]
95   To seek the death of him that is so good,
    For thy soul's health to shed this dearest blood?

"Jack and Joan" by Thomas Campion

Jack and Joan they think no ill,
But loving live, and merry still;
Do their week-days' work, and pray
Devoutly on the holy day;
5 Skip and trip it on the green,
And help to choose the summer queen;
Lash out, at a country feast,
Their silver penny with the best.

Well can they judge of nappy ale,
10 And tell at large a winter tale;
Climb up to the apple loft
And turn the crabs till they be soft.
Tib is all the father's joy,
And little Tom the mother's boy.
15 All their pleasure is content;
And care, to pay their yearly rent.

---

1. **reprobate with Saul.** Damned like Saul, King of Israel, who wanted God's prophet-king, David, killed

---

Joan can call by name her cows
And deck her windows with green boughs;
She can wreaths and tutties make,
20 And trim with plums a bridal cake.
Jack knows what brings gain or loss,
And his long flail can stoutly toss,
Makes the hedge, which others break,
And ever thinks what he doth speak.

25 Now, you courtly dames and knights,
That study only strange delights,
Though you scorn the home-spun gray
And revel in your rich array,
Though your tongues dissemble deep
30 And can your heads from danger keep,
Yet, for all your pomp and train,
Securer lives the silly swain.

"A Litany in Time of Plague"
by Thomas Nashe

Adieu, farewell, earth's bliss;
This world uncertain is;
Fond are life's lustful joys;
Death proves them all but toys;
5 None from his darts can fly;
I am sick, I must die.
    Lord, have mercy on us!

Rich men, trust not in wealth,
Gold cannot buy you health;
10 Physic himself must fade.
All things to end are made,
The plague full swift goes by;
I am sick, I must die.
    Lord, have mercy on us!

15 Beauty is but a flower
Which wrinkles will devour;
Brightness falls from the air;
Queens have died young and fair;
dust hath closèd Helen's[2] eye.
20 I am sick, I must die.
    Lord, have mercy on us!

Strength stoops unto the grave,
Worms feed on Hector brave;

---

2. **Helen.** The reference is to Helen of Troy, who was known for her great beauty. Both she and Hector, a hero of the Trojan War, died despite their respective beauty and power.

ADDITIONAL QUESTIONS AND ACTIVITIES

"A Litany in Time of Plague"

    What is a litany? What kinds of items comprise the litany in Thomas Nashe's poem?

Answers. A litany is a prayer in which a leader makes a series of statements, each of which is followed by a response from the congregation. Nashe's "Litany" is a list of things that are temporary and subject to death, like human beings; the repeated lines "I am

sick, I must die./Lord, have mercy on us!" are the response.

ADDITIONAL QUESTIONS AND ACTIVITIES

"Jack and Joan"

• What is the speaker's attitude toward the title characters? Based on this attitude, how would you classify the poem?

• How does the theme of "Jack and Joan" compare with that of Campion's other poem "When Thou Must Home to Shades of Underground" (page 276)? Do any other poems in the unit have a similar theme?

Answers. The speaker has an idealized view of Jack and Joan's simple country life; it is a pastoral poem. Like "When Thou Must Home to Shades of Underground," this poem expresses disdain for the superficiality and pettiness of life in a royal court; Spenser's Sonnet 31 also expresses this feeling.

"A LITANY IN TIME OF PLAGUE"

About the Author. The theme of **Thomas Nashe**'s (1567–1601) "A Litany in Time of Plague" is well suited to his life, which was cut short at about age thirty-three. He arrived in London around 1588 and became friends with the likes of Robert Greene and Christopher Marlowe. His bold, eccentric style of writing and sharp wit made him a talented pamphleteer; in the 1590s he engaged in verbal combat with another writer, Gabriel Harvey, exchanging a series of caustic, slanderous pamphlets. In 1599, the Archbishop of Canterbury put an end to this exchange by banning the further publication of any of the two writers' works. Other significant works by Nashe include the first English picaresque novel, entitled *The Unfortunate Traveler, or the Life of Jack Wilton* (1594), and *Christ's Tears Over Jerusalem* (1593), in which Nashe warned that a plague gripping London was a sign that the city's decadence could lead to the same destruction suffered by Jerusalem in biblical times.

About the Selection. Jonson's "Epitaph" was published in a collection of short poems entitled *Epigrams* (1616). An *epigram* is a brief and pithy work of poetry or prose; Jonson alludes to the form of this poem in the opening lines: "Wouldst thou hear what man can say/In a little? Reader, stay." An *epitaph* is a brief eulogy to someone who has died, often appearing on the person's gravestone. In addition to "Epitaph on Elizabeth, L. H.," *Epigrams* contains Jonson's epitaphs to two of his children, a daughter and a son, who died during his lifetime. "On My First Son" is especially well known for its elegant and poignant expression of a parent's grief.

FROM PSALM 137

About the Selection. The kingdom of Israel was united under King David—the poet to whom many of the psalms are attributed —who ruled from about 1000 to 962 BC. He was succeeded by his son Solomon, after whose death the kingdom was divided into Israel in the north and Judah in the south. Unfortunately located between the competing empires of Egypt and Assyria, Israel was crushed by the Assyrians in about 722 BC. Judah survived a while longer but eventually fell to the Babylonians under King Nebuchadnezzar II in about 587 BC. The Babylonians destroyed Solomon's temple in Jerusalem and took many Jews back to Babylonia as slaves. Psalm 137 describes the experience of one Jewish writer during the Babylonian captivity. In about 536 BC, the Persian leader Cyrus the Great conquered Babylonia and allowed the Jews to return home and rebuild the temple.

Swords may not fight with fate,
25 Earth still holds ope her gate.
"Come, come!" the bells do cry.
I am sick, I must die.
    Lord, have mercy on us.

Wit with his wantonness
30 Tasteth death's bitterness;
Hell's executioner
Hath no ears for to hear
What vain art can reply.
I am sick, I must die.
35   Lord, have mercy on us.

Haste, therefore, each degree,
To welcome destiny;
Heaven is our heritage,
Earth but a player's stage;
40 Mount we unto the sky.
I am sick, I must die.
    Lord, have mercy on us.

"Epitaph on Elizabeth, L. H."
by Ben Jonson

Wouldst thou hear what man can say
    In a little? Reader, stay.
Underneath this stone doth lie
    As much beauty as could die;
Which in life did harbor give
    To more virtue than doth live.
If at all she had a fault,
    Leave it buried in this vault.
One name was Elizabeth;
    Th' other, let it sleep with death:
Fitter, where it died, to tell,
    Than that it lived at all. Farewell!

Psalm 23 from The King James Bible

The LORD *is* my shepherd; I shall not want.
2 He maketh me to lie down in green pastures: he leadeth me beside the still waters.
3 He restoreth my soul: he leadeth me in the paths of righteousness for his name's sake.
4 Yea, though I walk through the valley of the shadow of death, I will fear no evil: for thou *art* with me; thy rod and thy staff they comfort me.
5 Thou preparest a table before me in the presence of mine enemies: thou anointest my head with oil; my cup runneth over.
6 Surely goodness and mercy shall follow me all the days of my life: and I will dwell in the house of the Lord for ever.

from Psalm 137
from The King James Bible

By the rivers of Babylon, there we sat down, yea, we wept, when we remembered Zion.
2 We hanged our harps upon the willows in the midst thereof.
3 For there they that carried us away captive required of us a song; and they that wasted us *required of us* mirth, *saying*, Sing us *one* of the songs of Zion.
4 How shall we sing the LORD'S song in a strange land?

ADDITIONAL QUESTIONS AND ACTIVITIES

from Psalm 137

What is the tone of the first four verses of Psalm 137? What seems particularly cruel to the speaker about his captivity? Why do you believe the speaker chose to describe this request?

Answers. The tone of verses 1–4 is one of grief and longing for home. That the captors required them to sing seems particularly cruel to the speaker. The speaker may have chosen to juxtapose a request for mirth with a time of sorrow in order to emphasize the extreme nature of his people's grief. The request also further emphasizes the captors' cruelty.

▶**Teacher's Note:** Point out that *Zion* is another name for Israel; it has the connotation of an idealized Jewish homeland.

PREREADING

from the *Canzoniere*
Sonnet 1, trans. by Thomas Bergin
Sonnet 47, trans. by Francis Wrangham
Sonnet 54, trans. by Thomas Bergin
by Petrarch

ABOUT THE AUTHOR

Francesco Petrarca (1304–1374), known in English-speaking countries as **Petrarch**, is often considered the father both of Italian Humanism and of the European tradition of lyric poetry. Petrarch was born in Arezzo, Italy. His family moved to Avignon, France, in 1312, and there he received his early education. He studied at Montpellier, France, and in Bologna, Italy, but his real interest lay with literature. After his father died in 1326, Petrarch returned to Avignon and worked for an influential cardinal. In 1327, in the Church of St. Clare in Avignon, he met the woman named Laura for whom he developed a deep, unrequited love that was to inspire his great vernacular Italian sonnets and other poems. In subsequent years, Petrarch made a great name for himself as a classical scholar and vernacular poet. In 1340, he was invited by both Paris and Rome to be crowned as poet laureate. In 1348, the plague claimed the lives of several of his friends and of his beloved Laura. During the later part of his long life, he collected his poems about Laura into a book, the *Canzoniere,* divided into works written during Laura's life and after her death. Today, Petrarch is remembered for two reasons. First, he helped to revive interest in the literature of ancient Italy and so gave impetus to the movement that we know as Humanism. Second, highly personal, highly musical vernacular verse gave to Europe the model for lyric poetry down to our own day. Such poetry deals with the intensely felt emotions of an individual speaker.

ABOUT THE SELECTIONS

The following sonnets from Petrarch's *Canzoniere* deal with love and unrequited love. A **sonnet** is a fourteen-line poem that follows one of a number of different rhyme schemes. The Petrarchan form of the sonnet is divided into two parts: an octave and a sestet. The sonnet form was introduced to England during the sixteenth century by Wyatt and Sidney, both admirers of Petrarch's work.

ADDITIONAL RESOURCES

READER'S GUIDE
• Selection Worksheet, 4.13

ASSESSMENT PORTFOLIO
• Selection Check Tests, 4.4.25, 4.4.27, 4.4.29
• Selection Tests, 4.4.26, 4.4.28, 4.4.30

ENRICHMENT ACTIVITIES

Students can explore the different meanings of the term *Humanism*. What does the term mean when applied to Petrarch or to Renaissance thought generally?

SUPPORT FOR LEP STUDENTS

ADDITIONAL VOCABULARY
errant—foolish, mistaken
sear—burn, scorch
beseech—ask for
vanities—pride
bred—past tense of *breed*: give birth to
penance—repentance, atonement
thence—from there
strains—melodies, tunes
languishment—distress; sadness
consent—agree
'tis—it is
fruitless—unproductive
lays—songs

GOALS/OBJECTIVES

Studying this lesson will enable students to

• interpret and appreciate Petrarchan sonnets
• describe the literary significance of Petrarch's poetry
• compare works of poetry across cultures
• describe, compare, and contrast perspectives on the theme of love

BIOGRAPHICAL NOTE

Petrarch devoted nearly all of his life to secular literature, especially to reviving the works of Classical Rome. The sonnets presented here deal with Petrarch's unrequited love for a woman named Laura. Sonnet 1 was written after the rest of the sonnets and placed at the beginning of the *Canzoniere* introduction. As Sonnet 1 indicates, near the end of his life, Petrarch began to regret his lifelong obsession with Laura, which led, he says, to "empty hope and vainer smart." Sonnet 1 is thus a sort of retraction, written in old age, of the work that follows it. Literary history has not shared Petrarch's own assessment of his secular sonnets, which he calls in Sonnet 1 his "vanities." Quite the contrary, Petrarch's work has served from the Renaissance on as a model for the entire tradition of secular love poetry in Europe.

ANSWER TO GUIDED READING QUESTION

❶ He feels foolish and ashamed for having invested so much in a vain, unrequited love, in part because he now feels that love is a temporal and relatively unimportant concern.

QUOTABLES

❝Think you, if Laura had been Petrarch's wife,
He would have written sonnets all his life❞
—George Gordon, Lord Byron

Italy

FROM THE

Canzoniere

PETRARCH

SONNET 1

❶
How does the speaker now feel about the earlier part of his life?

> O ye who in these scattered rhymes may hear
> The echoes of the sighs that fed my heart
> In errant youth, for I was then, in part
> Another man from what I now appear,
> 5   If you have learned by proof how Love can sear,
> Then for these varied verses where I chart
> Its vain and empty hope and vainer smart
> Pardon I may beseech, nay, Pity's tear.
> For now I see how once my story spread
> 10   And I became a wonder to mankind
> So in my heart I feel ashamed—alas,
> That nought but shame my vanities have bred,
> And penance, and the knowledge of clear mind
> That earthly joys are dreams that swiftly pass. ∎

ANSWERS TO SELECTION CHECK TEST 4.4.25

EX. From what collection is Petrarch's Sonnet 1 taken?
It is taken from the *Canzoniere*.

1. Whom does the sonnet address?
The sonnet addresses the reader.

2. What fed the speaker's heart when he was young?
Sighs fed his heart.

3. What has the speaker learned about love?
The speaker has learned that love can sear.

4. What feelings does the speaker have about his earlier life?
The speaker is ashamed.

5. What does the speaker say about earthly joys?
Earthly joys are dreams that swiftly pass.

SONNET 47

Blest be the day, and blest the month, the year,
The spring, the hour, the very moment blest,
The lovely scene, the spot, where first oppressed
I sunk, of two bright eyes the prisoner:
5   And blest the first soft pang, to me most dear,
Which thrilled my heart, when Love became its guest;
And blest the bow, the shafts which pierced my brest.
And even the wounds, which bosomed thence I bear.
Blest too the strains which, poured through glade and grove,
10   Have made the woodlands echo with her name;
The sighs, the tears, the languishment, the love:
And blest those sonnets, sources of my fame;
And blest that thought—Oh! never to remove!
Which turns to her alone, from her alone which came. ■

❶
What contradictory language does the speaker use when discussing the moment when he fell in love? Why would he use such contradictory language?

SONNET 54

I grow a-weary of my wondering
Why my thoughts never weary, love, of you,
Why I consent to living as I do
Under the burden that my sorrows bring.
5   Why is it that, for all the songs I sing,
I still find words and numbers ever new
For your fair face and eyes—why all night through
'Tis still your name my lips go murmuring?
If, just as after many fruitless days
10   In your pursuit, for utter weariness
My limbs grow stiff, so likewise my poor lays
Have too much ink consumed (as I confess)
And filled too many pages with your praise,
'Tis not for fault of art but Love's excess. ■

❷
Of what does the speaker never grow weary?

ANSWERS TO GUIDED READING QUESTIONS

❶ He talks of a "blest" time and place when he first felt "oppressed" and of a "blest" pain or "pang." The contradictory language reflects the complex and confusing emotions associated with love. Petrarch's love brought him great joy, which he felt in contemplating Laura's qualities, but it also brought him great pain because it was unrequited.

❷ He never grows weary of thinking of his beloved.

ADDITIONAL QUESTIONS AND ACTIVITIES

Ask students why unrequited love is such a common theme in poetry and is far more prevalent than the theme of satisfaction in love. Are we merely fascinated with the unattainable? Is pain and sadness more interesting to us than joy?

Ask students to bring in a sampling of current love songs. Do they have similar messages and images? Has the way we talk about love changed dramatically since Petrarch's time? Why, or why not?

ANSWERS TO SELECTION CHECK TEST 4.4.27

EX. How many lines does a sonnet have?
A sonnet has fourteen lines.

1. What place and time does the speaker bless?
He blesses the time and place when his oppression of love began.

2. What thrilled the speaker's heart?
The first soft pang of love thrilled the speaker's heart.

3. What have the strains which the speaker blesses done?
They have made the woodlands echo with the name of the speaker's beloved.

4. What are the sources of the speaker's fame?
His sonnets are the source of his fame.

5. What is the last thing the speaker blesses?
The thought of the speaker's beloved is the last thing blessed.

ANSWERS FOR REVIEWING THE SELECTION

1. Sonnet 1 is addressed to the poet's readers.

2. He is no longer obsessed by love, for he has learned that there are more important things.

3. He blesses the time and place at which he first felt the oppressive and painful feelings of love, and he blesses the pain itself. Words such as *wounds, tears,* and *languishment* contradict the poem's overall message that the speaker's love is something to treasure. The speaker feels joy in loving but pain about not having his love returned.

4. He wonders why he never gets tired of thinking about the object of his love.

5. His legs are stiff from continually "running" in pursuit of the object of his love. This pursuit has also caused his art to run to great length.

ANSWERS FOR CONNECTIONS

Responses will vary. Possible responses are given.

1. All three writers deal with unsuccessful love. Sidney's and Petrarch's love is unrequited; Wyatt's has been stymied by the king.

2. Wyatt's claim on his beloved has been preempted by the king, and he feels resentful; Sidney has been spurned by his would-be lover, and he feels misunderstood and unjustly treated; Spenser's knight's love is not romantic but comes from loyalty and fealty; Marlowe's shepherd's may be true, but Raleigh's nymph has her doubts about it—Raleigh's nymph may believe in deeper love or may merely be cynical about all romantic love; Shakespeare's love is the kind that might be appreciated by the nymph—it is not based on appearances; Jonson's love may be profound or it may be selfish and indifferent to the wishes of the beloved; Petrarch's love has not been reciprocated, but he does not feel spiteful or resentful.

Reviewing the Selection

1. To whom is Sonnet 1 addressed?

2. The speaker in Sonnet 1 claims to be different from the person he was "In errant youth." How is he different? What has he learned?

3. What does the speaker bless in Sonnet 47? What words contradict the overall sentiment of the poem? Why does the speaker feel both joy and pain?

4. About what does the speaker in Sonnet 54 wonder?

5. Why have the legs of the speaker in Sonnet 54 grown stiff? What effect has the same cause had on his art?

Connections (Questions for Writing or Discussion)

1. What similar theme is treated in Petrarch's sonnets and in those by Wyatt and Sidney in this unit?

2. Review the lyric poems in this unit that deal with the subject of love. What different experiences of love are expressed in these poems? Of all the love poems in the unit, which appeals most to you or speaks to you most directly? Why?

ANSWERS TO SELECTION CHECK TEST 4.4.29

EX. What is the rhyme scheme of this poem?
The rhyme scheme is *abbaabba cdcdcd.*

1. Of what does the speaker grow weary?
The speaker grows weary of wondering why he never wearies of thinking of his beloved.

2. To what manner of living does the speaker consent?
He consents to living under the burden of sorrows.

3. For what does the speaker find new words?
He finds new words to describe his beloved.

4. What causes the speaker's legs to stiffen?
Pursuit of his beloved has caused his legs to stiffen.

5. What does the speaker feel he has done too much?
He has written too much about his beloved.

The Development of the English Language:
Modern English

In *The First Part of the Elementarie,* a treatise on education published in 1582, Richard Mulcaster wrote that "whatsoever shall become of the English state, the English tongue cannot prove fairer than it is at this day." Readers of Sidney, Spenser, Shakespeare, Marlowe, and the King James Bible tend to agree with Mulcaster that at no time has the English language been more beautiful or expressive than it was during the early modern period.

THE EMERGENCE OF MODERN ENGLISH

The version of English that we use today, known as **Modern English,** emerged in the two-hundred-year period from roughly 1400 to 1600. However, for convenience's sake, the Modern English period is often dated from the publication of Caxton's version of Malory's *Le Morte d'Arthur* in 1485. At that time, most of the changes in pronunciation, vocabulary, and grammar that transformed Middle English into Modern English were well underway.

THE GREAT VOWEL SHIFT

Perhaps the most important difference between Middle English and Modern English is in the sound of the language. Between 1400 and 1600 dramatic changes in pronunciation of vowels occurred. These changes are known collectively as the **Great Vowel Shift**. The positions of articulation in the mouth of all the long vowels except *i* and *u* were raised. Thus the word *name,* which was pronounced in Chaucer's day as *nah - muh,* became, in Modern English, *naym.* The word *bete,* pronounced *bay - tuh,* became *beet.* The long *i* and long *u* sounds became diphthongs, made of two vowels slurred together. Thus *ridden,* pronounced in Chaucer's day as *re - dun,* became *ride,* which has a vowel that combines *ah* and *ee.* The word *mus,* pronounced *moos,* became *mouse,* which has a vowel that combines *ah* and *oo.* Notice that in both *name* and *bete,* as in many other words, the final *–e* was pronounced in Middle English but became silent or was dropped altogether in Modern English.

GRAMMATICAL CHANGES

Throughout the Medieval Period, English gradually moved from being an **inflected language,** in which the grammatical roles of words are shown by word endings, to an **analytical language,** in which grammatical roles are shown by position in the sentence. In the early Modern Period, this change became fairly complete. An important change of this kind that occurred during this period was the introduction of *–s* as the standard sign of the plural. In Middle English, plurals had often been shown by the addition of *–en.* Thus the plural of *eyes,* in Chaucer, is *yen,* and the plural of *peas* is *pesen.* In Modern English, most plurals, are formed with *–s,* but a few older plurals survive in words like *children, oxen,* and *brethren.* Other important grammatical changes that occurred during the early Modern Period include the introduction of new relative pronouns, prepositions, and conjunctions that increased the ability of English speakers to make precise logical distinctions and connections.

VOCABULARY AND THE NEW LEARNING

Of great importance to the development of the language that we use today was the introduction by scholars during the early Modern Period of thousands of new words from Latin and Greek. Professor George Lyman Kitteridge estimated that fully one-fourth of the words that appear in a standard Latin dictionary have been incorporated into English in some form. Many of these words were introduced as a result of Renaissance humanist learning. New Latin words that entered the language during the Renaissance include many terms related to literary study, including *accent, allusion, alphabet, anonymous, antithesis, critic, drama, elegy, epic, fiction, irony, lyric, metaphor, metrical, ode, phrase, poem, satire, simile, sonnet,* and *stanza.* Other new Latin and Greek words that date from the Renaissance are shown on the following chart; however, a complete listing of these words would fill many, many pages.

WORDS FROM LATIN AND GREEK INTRODUCED DURING THE EARLY MODERN PERIOD

adapt	conspicuous	erupt	idea	patriot
agile	crisis	excursion	impetus	precise
antipathy	criterion	exert	impression	premium
appropriate	cynic	exist	item	scene
area	decorum	exit	lexicon	scientific
arena	delirium	expensive	machine	skeleton
benefit	dexterity	explicit	malignant	squalor
catastrophe	disaster	external	meditate	system
chemist	emancipate	extinguish	method	theory
circus	energy	function	minor	vacuum
compatible	enormous	genius	numerous	
consolidate	enthusiasm	habitual	omen	

PURE VERSUS "INKHORN" ENGLISH

During the Renaissance, some writers and editors objected to the rapid influx of learned words from Latin and Greek, dubbing these "inkhorn" terms because scholars used quill pens and ink for writing. Sir John Cheke of Cambridge University wrote, for example, that "our tongue should be written clean and pure, unmixed and unmangled with borrowing of other tongues, wherein if we take not heed by time, ever borrowing and never paying, she shall be fain to keep her house as bankrupt." A brief glance at the list given on the preceding chart of loan words from Latin and Greek will suffice to show that our language was greatly enriched by the learned additions that occurred during Renaissance times. However, many writers and editors to this day would agree with Cheke that, in most writing, a simple word of Anglo-Saxon origin should be preferred over a more elaborate one derived from a classical language. In English one often has a choice between the two. One can write *way* instead of *method, home* instead of *domicile, put out* instead of *extinguish, go* instead of *exit,* and so on. Overuse of words of Latin or Greek origin can make writing or speech seem too formal or stilted. Fortunately for English speakers and writers, the first great translator of the Bible, Tyndale, preferred simple words of English origin, and much of his phrasing was adopted in the King James Bible that became the standard text in English-speaking countries for centuries. The simple, Anglo-Saxon language of the King James Bible has dramatically influenced the shape of spoken and written English from that day to this.

OTHER SOURCES OF NEW WORDS

In addition to borrowing from Latin and Greek, early Modern English borrowed heavily from European languages, especially from French, Spanish, and Italian. From French came *battery, comrade, entrance, essay, mustache, pioneer, trophy,* and *vogue.* From Spanish came *apricot, bravado, cavalier, embargo, guitar,* and *tornado.* From Italian came *artichoke, balcony, bankrupt, cameo, fresco, pastel, piazza, porcelain,* and *traffic.* Some of these words, such as *pioneer, apricot, embargo,* and *traffic,* reflected the worldwide exploration and trade that began during the Renaissance. Other such words added because of exploration are listed in the following chart.

NEW WORDS IN EARLY MODERN ENGLISH RELATED TO EXPLORATION	
armada	llama
buffalo	maize
cacao reef	moccasin
canoe	savannah
caravan	sherry
chocolate	smuggle
coconut	tattoo
cruise	tomahawk
dock	tomato
flamingo	totem
galleon	yacht
harem	yam
hurricane	

PRINTING AND REGULARIZATION OF SPELLING

During the early Modern Period, as during the Middle Ages, spelling was largely a matter of personal preference. Most literature of the day was written by noble men and women for circulation among friends, and in this literature, as in the letters of the day, spelling varied widely. In fact, an educated person might well spell the same word several different ways in the same piece. An example of this variety can be seen in the spelling of Shakespeare's name. Existing signatures show the great poet and dramatist signing his name variously as *Shaksp, Shakspe, Shakspeare,* and *Shakspere,* but nowhere with the spelling that is commonly used today. As printing became widespread and books became more common, spelling tended to become regularized.

Read the Language Arts Survey, 4.4, "Memorizing." Then devise mnemonics to help you remember the meanings of the vocabulary words on page 304. You may represent mnemonics in prose, pictures, or charts. Try to rehearse the entire set of mnemonics three times a day for two days.

► **Teaching Note:** Test students' memorization techniques with a vocabulary test. Give them the list of words in a scrambled sequence, and ask them to write the definition of each word. After determining that students have rehearsed their mnemonics, review the mnemonics of students who score less than 75 percent to see how they can improve.

ADDITIONAL RESOURCES

ASSESSMENT PORTFOLIO
- Vocabulary Worksheet: Unit 4, 4.4.31
- Study Guide: Unit 4 Test, 4.4.32
- Unit 4 Test, 4.4.33

ESSENTIAL SKILLS PRACTICE BOOKS

Writing
- Choosing a Purpose or Aim, 1.6

Language
- Agreement of Pronouns and Antecedents, 2.82
- Double Negatives, 2.88
- End Marks, 2.93
- The Functions of Sentences, 2.36
- Personal Pronouns, 2.6
- Transitive and Intransitive Verbs, 2.15

Speaking and Listening
- Active Listening, 3.4
- Discussion, 3.6
- Interpersonal Communication, 3.5
- Public Speaking, 3.7

(cont.)

UNIT REVIEW

The English Renaissance

VOCABULARY FROM THE SELECTIONS

beauteous, 277	guile, 273	score, 258	wan, 255
belie, 283	languished, 255	scorn, 255	wanton, 267
brook, 273	madrigal, 262	shun, 273	wield, 258
descry, 255	myrtle, 262	swain, 263	wither, 287
gall, 267	poll, 273	temperate, 280	
graven, 251	rend, 291	travail, 251	

LITERARY TERMS

alliteration, 260	parallelism, 292
ambiguity, 278	pastoral poem, 261
dactyl, 288	Petrarchan sonnet, 250
description, 264	poulter's measure, 272
Elizabethan sonnet, 279	personification, 256
iambic pentameter, 250	purpose or aim, 274
iambic tetrameter, 261	Renaissance, 242
image, 256, 270	sestet, 250
lyric poem, 261	Shakespearian sonnet, 279
metaphor, 253, 270, 274, 288	sonnet, 297
meter, 253, 284	source, 260
mood or atmosphere, 260, 264	speaker, 270, 284
octave, 250	

ADDITIONAL RESOURCES (CONT.)

Study and Research
- Analogy Questions, 4.40
- Classifying, 4.7
- Comparing and Contrasting, 4.8
- Reading Actively, 4.18
- Reading Rates: Scanning, 4.16
- Remembering and Visualizing, 4.5
- Using Reference Works, 4.23

SYNTHESIS: QUESTIONS FOR WRITING, RESEARCH, OR DISCUSSION

GENRE STUDIES

1. **The Sonnet.** What are the essential characteristics of a sonnet? What subjects do sonnets typically treat? How do Petrarchan and Elizabethan sonnets differ? Refer to the sonnets in the unit, in the Selections for Additional Reading, and in the Multicultural Extensions on page 297.

2. **Pastoral Poetry.** Marlowe's "The Passionate Shepherd to His Love" and Psalm 23 from the Bible are both pastoral poems. What are the essential characteristics of a pastoral poem? Why would pastoral poetry emerge among people who lived in cities and towns? What longing is embodied in pastoral poetry?

THEMATIC STUDIES

3. **Idealization of Love in Renaissance Poetry.** Idealized women and idealized love are common themes in Renaissance poetry. How are these themes expressed in Shakespeare's Sonnet 18 ("Shall I compare thee . . . ") and Marlowe's "The Passionate Shepherd to His Love"? What twist do Shakespeare and Ralegh put on this theme in Sonnet 130 ("My mistress' eyes . . . ") and "The Nymph's Reply to the Shepherd"? Explore the theme of idealized women and love by contrasting these sets of poems.

4. **Unrequited Love in Renaissance English Poetry.** Many of the most famous Renaissance poems deal with the theme of unrequited, or unreturned, love. Explore this theme in the following works from the unit: "Whoso List to Hunt," Sidney's Sonnet 31, "The Nymph's Reply to the Shepherd," "When Thou Must Home to Shades of Underground," "Song, to Celia," Shakespeare's Sonnet 73 (in the Selections for Additional Reading, page 293), and the sonnets of Petrarch (in the Multicultural Extensions, page 297). Explain how each poem illustrates this theme.

HISTORICAL AND BIOGRAPHICAL STUDIES

5. **Elizabeth I, Mary Stuart, and Catholicism.** In "The Doubt of Future Foes" Queen Elizabeth expresses her fear of being overthrown. Explain the historical circumstances that created this fear and how specific lines of the poem are related to these events and historical figures. Refer to the Unit Introduction on page 246.

6. **Renaissance Literature and the Emergence of the Individual.** The Renaissance saw the emergence of a new emphasis on the individual and on the value of life on earth, in sharp contrast to the emphasis in medieval literature on society and on the afterlife. Consider Marlowe's "The Passionate Shepherd to His Love" and Shakespeare's Sonnet 18 ("Shall I compare thee . . ."). How do these poems embody the new emphasis in literature on the personal lives of individuals?

▶These prompts are suitable as topics for research papers. Refer to the Language Arts Survey, 4.20–4.34, "Research Skills." (To evaluate research papers, see the evaluation forms for writing, revising, and proofreading in the *Assessment Portfolio*, 7.1–7.10.)

▶These prompts can be adapted for use as topics for oral reports or debates. (To evaluate these projects, see the evaluation forms in the *Assessment Portfolio*, 7.17–7.19.)

ADDITIONAL EXAMPLES

ADDITIONAL EXAMPLES

Improper Shift from Past to Present Tense: In his own time, many people criticized Spenser because he uses an archaic style.

Corrected Sentence: In his own time, many people criticized Spenser because he used an archaic style.

Misuse of Irregular Verb Form: The shepherd speaked of a wonderful life, but the nymph seed the truth.

Corrected Sentence: The shepherd spoke of a wonderful life, but the nymph saw the truth.

Split Infinitive: There is a time to sadly weep and a time to joyously dance.

Corrected Sentence: There is a time to weep sadly and a time to dance joyously.

Agreement Error: Sidney and Shakespeare was both writers of sonnets.

Corrected Sentence: Sidney and Shakespeare were both writers of sonnets.

Agreement Error: If you want to read a sonnet, either Sidney's Sonnet 31 or the sonnets by Shakespeare is good.

Corrected Sentence: If you want to read a sonnet, either Sidney's Sonnet 31 or the sonnets by Shakespeare are good.

LANGUAGE LAB   EDITING FOR ERRORS IN VERBS

During the editing or proofreading stage of the writing process, check your work to make sure that it is free of errors in the use of verbs. The following chart describes common errors in verb usage.

LANGUAGE ARTS SURVEY

For additional help, see the Language Arts Survey, 2.65.

LANGUAGE ARTS SURVEY

For additional help, see the Language Arts Survey, 2.66–2.67.

LANGUAGE ARTS SURVEY

For additional help, see the Language Arts Survey, 2.68.

LANGUAGE ARTS SURVEY

For additional help, see the Language Arts Survey, 2.70.

COMMON ERRORS IN VERB USAGE
Improper Shifts in Verb Tense. Throughout a passage, the tenses, or times, of verbs should be consistent.

IMPROPER SHIFT FROM
PAST TO PRESENT TENSE: Queen Elizabeth remained unmarried, though she has many suitors.

CORRECTED SENTENCE: Queen Elizabeth remained unmarried, though she had many suitors.

Misuse of Irregular Verb Forms. Many verbs, such as *swim, go, bring, bite, fly, fight,* and *see,* have irregular past tense forms. Make sure to use the proper verb form in the past tense. If you are unsure about the proper form, check a dictionary.

MISUSE OF IRREGULAR VERB FORM: Queen Elizabeth brung order and stability to England.
CORRECTED SENTENCE: Queen Elizabeth brought order and stability to England.

Split Infinitives. An **infinitive** is a verb form made up of the word *to* and the base form of the verb, as in *to play* or *to versify.* In formal speech and writing, try to avoid placing a modifier between *to* and the verb.

SPLIT INFINITIVE: Although Mary Stuart fomented insurrection, Elizabeth hesitated to simply behead her.
CORRECTED SENTENCE: Although Mary Stuart fomented insurrection, Elizabeth hesitated simply to behead her.

Agreement of Subject and Verb. A verb should agree in number with its subject. If the subject is a compound joined by *and,* the verb should be plural. If the subject is a compound joined by *or, either . . . or,* or *neither . . . nor,* the verb should agree with the nearer subject.

AGREEMENT ERROR: Virginia and Massachusetts was both English colonies.
CORRECTED SENTENCE: Virginia and Massachusetts were both English colonies.
AGREEMENT ERROR: That is why neither Virginia nor the other former Atlantic coast colonies is English speaking today.
CORRECTED SENTENCE: That is why neither Virginia nor the other former Atlantic coast colonies are English speaking today.

EXERCISE A   Correcting Errors in Verb Usage

Rewrite the following sentences, correcting the errors in verb usage.

EXAMPLE: The Elizabethans loved to joyously lift their voices in song.
            The Elizabethans loved to lift their voices joyously in song.

1. Madrigals or a solo performance by a singer with a lute were a typical evening's entertainment.
2. Young Christopher listens to madrigals also, for he enjoyed hearing the interplay of the unaccompanied voices.
3. The Elizabethan composer Marlowe preferred to hear a solitary singer accompanied by a lute, but William Byrd must have flied on the wings of an angel, because his music had heavenly beauty and was used for services in both Catholic and Anglican churches.
4. Thomas Morley, who writes lyrics for group settings, lived right next door to William Shakespeare.
5. Many lyricists wrote verses in praise of Queen Elizabeth, and, once these lyrics were set to music by composers, they brang them to the attention of the queen.
6. In the Elizabethan Period, the populace wanted to desperately buy all the books of ballads and popular songs they could find.
7. Thomas Campion was a man of many professions, having studied law, practiced medicine, and written Latin verse, but he enjoys writing songs more than anything else.
8. Scholars of Elizabethan lyrics and the average listener agrees that the earlier songs of the period were not as refined as the later works.
9. Fans of John Dowland's songs written for the lute like to often compare them to Spenser's literary achievements.
10. One who reads Shakespeare and other dramatists of the period note the inclusion of many ballads in their work.

LANGUAGE ARTS SURVEY

For additional help, see the Language Arts Survey, 2.30–2.31.

EXERCISE B   Revising for Errors in Verb Usage

Rewrite the following paragraph, correcting the errors in verb usage.

EXAMPLE: Martin Luther's ideas about religion brung about a mass revolt against church authority.
            Martin Luther's ideas about religion brought about a mass revolt against church authority.

[1] Both Martin Luther and John Calvin questioned the Roman Catholic Church, and they are central figures in England's sixteenth-century Protestant Reformation. [2] Calvin's beliefs were to eventually influence what became known as the Puritan Movement. [3] People in England, people in the English colonies of North America, and King Henry VIII of England was affected by this movement. [4] In England, Henry VIII wanted to quickly annul his marriage. [5] He had a dispute with the Pope over this, and decides to change the official religion of England. [6] When Henry's daughter Mary I taked power in England, she attempted to restore Roman Catholicism to England.

LANGUAGE ARTS SURVEY

For additional help, see the Language Arts Survey, 2.65–2.68 and 2.70

ANSWERS FOR LANGUAGE LAB

Exercise A

1. Madrigals or a solo performance by a singer with a lute was a typical evening's entertainment.
2. Young Christopher listens to madrigals also, for he enjoys hearing the interplay of the unaccompanied voices.
3. The Elizabethan composer Marlowe preferred to hear a solitary singer accompanied by a lute, but William Byrd must have flown on the wings of an angel, because his music had heavenly beauty and was used for services in both Catholic and Anglican churches.
4. Thomas Morley, who wrote lyrics for group settings, lived right next door to William Shakespeare.
5. Many lyricists wrote verses in praise of Queen Elizabeth, and, once these lyrics were set to music by composers, they brought them to the attention of the queen.
6. In the Elizabethan Period, the populace desperately wanted to buy all the books of ballads and popular songs they could find.
7. Thomas Campion was a man of many professions, having studied law, practiced medicine, and written Latin verse, but he enjoyed writing songs more than anything else.
8. Scholars of Elizabethan lyrics and the average listener agree that the earlier songs of the period were not as refined as the later works.
9. Fans of John Dowland's songs written for the lute often like to compare them to Spenser's literary achievements.
10. One who reads Shakespeare and other dramatists of the period notes the inclusion of many ballads in their work.

(cont.)

ANSWERS FOR LANGUAGE LAB (CONT.)

Exercise B

1. Both Martin Luther and John Calvin questioned the Roman Catholic Church, and they **were** central figures in England's sixteenth-century Protestant Reformation.
2. Calvin's beliefs **eventually were to influence** what became known as the Puritan Movement.
3. People in England, people in the English colonies of North America, and King Henry VIII of England **were** affected by this movement.
4. In England, Henry VIII **wanted to annul** his marriage **quickly.**
5. He had a dispute with the Pope over this, and **decided** to change the official religion of England.
6. When Henry's daughter Mary I **took** power in England, she attempted to restore Roman Catholicism to England.

UNIT 5 RENAISSANCE DRAMA (1485–1660)

The Procession of Queen Elizabeth I. Courtesy, Sherborne Castle Estates

GOALS/OBJECTIVES

Studying this unit will enable students to

- enjoy and appreciate Shakespearean drama
- describe the development of the theater in England from medieval to Elizabethan times
- describe the structure of the five-act play
- use pronouns correctly

- give reasons for the widespread recognition of Shakespeare's dramatic work
- compare and contrast the drama of Shakespeare and Marlowe
- compare and contrast the treatment of the theme of social order in Shakespeare's *Macbeth* and *The Analects* of Confucius

A ll the world's a stage,

And all the men and women merely players.

—William Shakespeare
As You Like It

INTRODUCTION **309**

HISTORICAL NOTE

The famous lines quoted on this page may well have been inspired by the Latin motto of the Globe Theater, *Totus mundus agit histrionem,* "The whole world plays the actor." It was typical of Shakespeare to give new life to an old proverb and give it new life in his verse. Incidentally, an old manuscript preserves the following (probably imaginary) exchange of poetic wit on the subject of the motto: Ben Johnson:

"If but stage-actors all the world displays,/Where shall we find spectators of their plays?" William Shakespeare: "Little or much of what we see we do;/We are all both actors and spectators too."

HISTORICAL NOTE

• One of the faint links between the drama of ancient times and the Renaissance was the Morris dance. The Morris dance of England has parallels in cultures in the Middle East, India, and Central and South America and is believed to be related to religious rites thousands of years old. In these folk dances, the dancers—commonly wearing white clothing, with bells and ribbons on their arms and legs— acted out the ritual death and revival of a god represented as an animal. In England, the Morris dance featured characters such as a deer, a fool, a hunter, a woman, and a hobby horse. Most contemporary Morris companies have abandoned the tradition of excluding women. The banter of these "mummers," as the dancers/actors were also called, may have evolved into the sophisticated wit in the dialogue of dramatists such as Shakespeare. The fools, jesters, and clowns so popular with that playwright (and with his audiences) may well be descended from the dancing fools of the Morris groups.

• Have students research descriptions of these dances. Students can locate videotapes to use in class; some may wish to recreate these dances.

THEMATIC CURRENTS

Use the following selections to explore these themes with your students.

MORTALITY
• *The Tragedy of Macbeth*, 320
• from *The Tragical History of Dr. Faustus*, 387
• from *The Tragedy of King Richard the Second*, 397

GOVERNANCE
• *The Tragedy of Macbeth*, 320
• from *The Tragedy of Hamlet, Prince of Denmark*, 396
• from *The Analects*, 400

(cont.)

THE DRAMATIC INHERITANCE

Our word *holiday* is a compound of the words *holy* and *day*. Throughout the Middle Ages, on "holy days" in the calendar of the Roman Catholic Church, people would gather on village greens, in innyards, and at marketplaces for celebrations. Entertainments on these days included dancing, feasting, juggling, puppetry, animal shows, music, singing, archery contests, and plays. Plays were presented by traveling troupes of actors or by members of professional business associations called **guilds**. Almost always, these plays dealt with religious subjects. **Miracle plays** told fantastic stories from the lives of saints. **Mystery plays** told stories from the Bible. **Morality plays** told stories about virtues and vices through characters with names like "Good Deeds" and "Sloth." Although these plays were religious in nature, they occasionally depicted ordinary people and sometimes contained elements of coarse humor.

If you could travel back in time six or seven hundred years to a festival held in an English town such as Chester or Wakefield, you could find yourself a place in the crowd at a market or innyard and stay from sunup to sundown to watch play after play. The plays would make up a cycle telling a continuous story. The first play, for example, might tell about the creation of the world, the second about Noah and the flood, and so on. A patient English festival-goer could witness, in the course of a day, the entire history of the world as medieval people understood it. The plays would be presented on the backs of wagons. The first wagon would pull up. The actors would perform their play. Then they would move on, and a second wagon would take its place. In other words, instead of the audience going to the theater, the theater would come to the audience.

At the beginning of the Renaissance, theater was still being performed in the open air by guildsmen and by traveling troupes of actors. Performances were also held in schools and in halls in the great homes of noble men and women.

THE FIVE-ACT PLAY

One of the fruits of **Humanism**, that rebirth of classical learning during the fifteenth and sixteenth centuries, was the emergence in England of the **five-act play**. In sixteenth-century

ELIZABETHAN AND JACOBEAN THEATER

1553. Udall's *Ralph Roister Doister* and Stevenson's *Grammer Gurton's Needle*, first five-act plays in English

1564. Westminster boys' troupe presents Plautus's Latin play *Miles Gloriosus* for Queen Elizabeth I

1562. First English tragedy, the *Tragedy of Gorboduc*, presented before Queen Elizabeth I

1550	1555	1560	1565	1570

1564. Christopher Marlowe born
1564. William Shakespeare born

MARLOWE AND SHAKESPEARE

310   UNIT FIVE / RENAISSANCE DRAMA

THEMATIC CURRENTS (CONT.)

THE NATURAL ORDER
• *The Tragedy of Macbeth*, 320
• from *The Analects*, 400

EXCESSIVE AMBITION
• *The Tragedy of Macbeth*, 320
• from *The Tragical History of Dr. Faustus*, 387

DECEPTION
• *The Tragedy of Macbeth*, 320
• from *The Tragical History of Dr. Faustus*, 387

English schools, students typically studied a Latin curriculum. Included in students' reading lists were works by Roman playwrights—Plautus, Seneca, and Terence. In the mid-1500s, two schoolteachers, one a master at Christ's College, Cambridge, and the other headmaster of Eton and Westminster, wrote plays called, respectively, *Grammer Gurton's Needle* and *Ralph Roister Doister*. These comedies, written for performance by students, used the five-act structure common in Roman plays but dealt with English subjects and themes. Other playwrights during the reigns of Queen Elizabeth I (The Elizabethan Age) and King James I (The Jacobean Age) adopted the five-act structure, which divided up the action as explained in the chart below. The acts were divided into scenes that began and ended with characters entering or leaving the stage. (These scenes were not typically marked in printed editions of the plays. The scene markings given in the plays in this unit were added by later editors.)

STRUCTURE OF A TYPICAL FIVE-ACT PLAY

Act I	Introduction	Presents the setting and main characters
		Presents the inciting incident (the event that sets in motion the play's central conflict, or struggle)
Act II	Rising Action, *or* Complication	Develops the central conflict
Act III	Crisis, *or* Turning Point	Presents a decisive occurrence that determines the future course of events in the play
Act IV	Falling Action	Presents events that happen as a result of the crisis
Act V	Resolution, *or* Catastrophe	Presents the event that resolves, or ends, the central conflict (In a tragedy, this event is called the *catastrophe* because it marks the ultimate fall of the central character.)

1576. James Burbage erects first playhouse, the Theater

1575	1580	1585	1590	1595

1582. Marriage license issued to William Shakespeare and Anne Hathaway

1583. Shakespeare's daughter Susanna born

1585. Shakespeare's twins Judith and Hamnet born

1587. Marlowe writes first part of *Tamburlaine*, graduates from Cambridge

1592. Shakespeare's *Henry VI* presented at Rose Theater (perhaps first public performance of his work); Marlowe's *Faustus* written

1593. Christopher Marlowe killed in tavern; Shakespeare's *Venus and Adonis* published

1594. Shakespeare shareholder in theatrical company, The Lord Chamberlain's Men

INTRODUCTION **311**

CROSS-CURRICULAR ACTIVITIES

Arts and Humanities.

• If your school or another school nearby has a Latin department, you may wish to ask a teacher or student there to give a brief lecture on Roman theater, comparing it to Elizabethan theater.

• Assign students to enact similar scenes from a translation of the *Menaechmi* of Plautus and the Shakespearean play based on Plautus's work, *The Comedy of Errors*.

LITERARY CURRENTS

Use the following selections to explore these literary concepts and techniques with your students.

TRAGEDY
• *The Tragedy of Macbeth*, 320
• from *The Tragical History of Doctor Faustus*, 387

CHARACTER
• Monologues and Soliloquies from *Hamlet*, 396
• *The Tragedy of Macbeth*, 320
• from *The Tragical History of Doctor Faustus*, 387

FORESHADOWING
• *The Tragedy of Macbeth*, 320
• *The Tragical History of Doctor Faustus*, 387
• from *The Tragedy of King Richard the Second*, 397

TYPES OF RENAISSANCE DRAMA

The two most common types of drama during the English Renaissance were **comedies** and **tragedies**. The key difference between comedies and tragedies is that the former have happy endings and the latter have unhappy ones. (It is only a slight exaggeration to say that comedies end with wedding bells and tragedies with funeral bells.)

A comedy is typically lighthearted, though it may contain serious action and themes. Action in a comedy usually progresses from initial order to a humorous misunderstanding or confusion and back to order again. Stock elements of comedy include mistaken identities, puns and word play, and coarse or exaggerated characters.

A tragedy tells the story of the downfall of a person of high status. Often it celebrates the courage and dignity of a flawed **protagonist**, or main character, in the face of an inevitable doom. In Christopher Marlowe's *Tragical History of Doctor Faustus,* for example, the protagonist's major failing, or **tragic flaw**, is his willingness to do anything for knowledge and the power that knowledge brings. In William Shakespeare's *Macbeth,* the protagonist falls because of ambition and a desire not to be considered unmanly.

Other kinds of plays produced during the period included **histories**—plays about events from the past—and **romances**—plays that contained highly fantastic elements such as fairies and magical spells. Also popular were short plays called **interludes,** as well as elaborate entertainments, called **masques**, that featured acting, music, and dance.

THE POLITICAL CONDITIONS OF THEATER IN RENAISSANCE LONDON

In the late sixteenth century, London was a bustling city of perhaps 150,000 people, the mercantile, political, and artistic center of England. The city proper was ruled by a mayor and aldermen who frowned upon theater because it brought together large crowds of people, creating the potential for lawlessness and the spread of controversial ideas and disease. Many times during the period, London city officials or Parliament ordered the theaters closed, once because they objected to the political content of a play called the *Isle of Dogs,* and regularly

ELIZABETHAN AND JACOBEAN THEATER

1599. The Globe Theater built

1597. Performance of *The Isle of Dogs* leads to temporary closing of all London theaters

1600	1605	1610	1615	1620

1596. Shakespeare's father, John, granted a coat of arms; Shakespeare's *Romeo and Juliet* performed; Shakespeare's son Hamnet dies

1597. Shakespeare purchases large Stratford home, New Place

1598. Marlowe's narrative poem *Hero and Leander* finished and published by his friend George Chapman

1598. Shakespeare listed as actor in play by Ben Jonson

1601? Shakespeare's *Hamlet* performed

1608. Shakespeare's company purchases Blackfriars Theater

1609. Shakespeare's sonnets published

MARLOWE AND SHAKESPEARE

1604. James I becomes king; Shakespeare's company becomes The King's Men

1605? Shakespeare's *Macbeth* performed

1613. Shakespeare's last play, *Henry VIII,* presented at the Globe; Globe burns down due to cannon firing

1616. Shakespeare dies

312   UNIT FIVE / RENAISSANCE DRAMA

because of outbreaks of plague. Parliament, which was dominated by Puritans, passed laws that made it possible for traveling actors and other performers to be arrested as vagabonds and cruelly punished. For protection, actors sought the patronage of members of the nobility. Actors would become, technically, servants of a famous lord and go by such names as The Lord Worcester's Men. Fortunately for actors and playwrights, Queen Elizabeth and other members of the nobility loved the theater and protected it. Elizabeth herself maintained two troupes of boy actors, connected to her royal chapels. In addition to these acting troupes made up of boys, London boasted several professional troupes made up of men. In those days, women did not act, and women's roles were played by men, a fact that further increased Puritan disapproval of the theaters. When the Puritans took control of England in 1642, theater was banned altogether.

THE RENAISSANCE PLAYHOUSE

In 1576, James Burbage built the first professional playhouse in England. Burbage located his playhouse, which he called simply "the Theater," just outside the northern boundaries of the City of London, where he could avoid control by city authorities. Another professional theater, the Curtain, was built nearby shortly thereafter. In 1598, Burbage and other members of his theater company, the Lord Chamberlain's Men, tore down the Theater and used its materials to build a new playhouse, **the Globe Theater,** south of the city on the banks of the river Thames. One of the shareholders in the Globe was William Shakespeare.

From contemporary drawings and descriptions and from evidence in plays, we can reconstruct what Shakespeare's Globe must have looked like. The building was octagonal, or eight-sided. The walls were covered with peaked, thatched roofs. The center of this "wooden O," as Shakespeare called it, was open to the air. The stage projected into the middle of this open space, and poorer theatergoers called "groundlings," who paid a penny apiece for admission, stood around three sides of the stage. Wealthier theatergoers could pay an additional penny or two and sit in one of the three tiers, or stories, of seats in the walls of the theater. In many respects, the theater was similar to the medieval wagon stage pulled into the open courtyard of an inn, with the inn's balconies around it.

ADDITIONAL QUESTIONS AND ACTIVITIES

Students can participate in a collaborative guided imagery activity. After the students have read the introduction to the unit, have them close their eyes and imagine that they are in Renaissance London, walking through the streets on the way to the Globe Theater. Ask them to name things that they can imagine hearing (the cries of street merchants or crowds), seeing (old and young, rich and poor people; soldiers; horses; buildings), smelling (refuse, ditchwater, manure), touching (passersby, muddy streets), and tasting (coarse bread, fruits, cheeses) on their way. Then continue the activity by having students imagine that they have entered the Globe and are waiting for the play to start. If you wish, before you conduct the activity you can refer students to the *Essential Skills Practice Book: Study and Research,* 4.5.

1642. All London theater suppressed by government

| 1625 | 1630 | 1635 | 1640 | 1645 |

1623. Shakespeare's plays collected in the First Folio

INTRODUCTION **313**

• Students can form groups to build models of the Globe Theater. Models may be as sophisticated as skills will allow, from simple cardboard constructions to elaborate scale replicas made of wood. To prepare students to search for and use the necessary reference works for information on the theater, refer them to the *Essential Skills Practice Book: Study and Research,* 4.26–4.28, on various research skills.

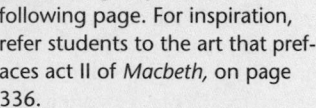

• Students can depict in drawings or paintings their impressions of the word pictures painted by Shakespeare in the passages quoted on the following page. For inspiration, refer students to the art that prefaces act II of *Macbeth,* on page 336.

• As an alternate exercise, students can discuss how well the art on page 336 captures the mood of Shakespeare's description in the passage quoted on page 315. Before beginning the discussion, students should slowly read the passage aloud. Questions you may wish to ask to stimulate discussion include the following: How has the artist attempted to represent abstract concepts such as witchcraft, murder, and horror? Which is more successful in sending a chill up your spine, the words or the artwork? Why? Note that the two passages quoted describe the same location; how has the mood changed from one passage to the other? Has the artist been able to capture any sense of this change, for example, by letting the grandeur of the castle stand out in spite of the horror of the surroundings?

The Globe Theater

The stage itself was partially covered by a canopy supported by two large pillars. Trapdoors in the stage floor allowed for appearances by spirits or fairies and for the disappearance of bodies. Behind the stage, between the pillars, was an inner area called the "tiring house" that could be used for changing costumes and for indoor scenes such as throne rooms, bedchambers, and taverns. On either side of the stage were doors for entrances and exits. At the back of the tiring house was a door and stairway that led to a second-level playing area that could be used as a hilltop, a castle turret, or a balcony (perhaps for the famous balcony scene from *Romeo and Juliet*). On the third level, above this balcony area, was an area for musicians and sound-effects people. A cannon shot from this area during a performance of Shakespeare's *Henry VIII* in 1613 caused a fire that burned the Globe to the ground.

Because the playhouse was open to the air, plays were presented in the daytime, and there was little or no artificial lighting. Scenery in the modern sense was nonexistent, and very few properties were used, beyond an occasional table or chair. Audiences had to use their imaginations to create the scenes, and playwrights helped their audiences to do this by writing descriptions of scenes into their characters' speeches, as in these descriptions from Shakespeare's play *Macbeth:*

DUNCAN.   This castle hath a pleasant seat. The air
Nimbly and sweetly recommends itself
Unto our gentle senses.

BANQUO.   This guest of summer,
The temple-haunting martlet, does approve
By his loved masionry that the heaven's breath
Smells wooingly here. No jutty, frieze,
Buttress, nor coin of vantage, but this bird
Hath made his pendent bed and procreant cradle.
Where they most breed and haunt, I have observed
The air is delicate.
                            —act I, scene vi

MACBETH.   Now o'er the one half-world
Nature seems dead, and wicked dreams abuse
The curtained sleep. Witchcraft celebrates
Pale Hecate's oferings; and withered murder,
Alarumed by his sentinel, the wolf,
Whose howl's his watch, thus with his stealthy pace,
With Tarquin's ravishing strides, towards his design
Moves like a ghost. Thou sure and firm-set earth,
Hear not my steps which way they walk for fear
The very stones prate of my whereabout
And take the present horror from the time,
Which now suits with it.
                            —act II, scene i

THE RENAISSANCE AUDIENCE

If you go to a public entertainment today, you are likely to find certain types of people at certain types of shows—young people at rock concerts, middle-class businesspeople at musicals, the elite of a city at the ballet, the symphony, or the opera. Audiences at the Globe and similar theaters were more mixed, or heterogeneous. They included people from all stations of society: laboring people from the lower classes, middle-class merchants, members of Parliament, and lords and ladies. Pickpockets mingled among the noisy, raucous groundlings crowded around the stage. Noble men and women sat on cushioned seats in the first-tier balcony. The fanfare of trumpets that signaled the beginning of a play was heard by some twenty-five hundred people, a cross section of the Elizabethan world. That Shakespeare's plays have such universal appeal may be explained by this fact: they were written for everyone, from "the most able, to him that can but spell."[1]

MARLOWE AND SHAKESPEARE

The two greatest playwrights of the Elizabethan Age were Christopher Marlowe and William Shakespeare.

Christopher Marlowe was born in February, 1564, to a Canterbury shoemaker. He attended Cambridge University, took bachelor's and master's degrees, studied widely and deeply, and

---

1. The quotation is from a preface addressed "To the Great Variety of Readers," printed in the first collection of Shakespeare's works, the First Folio of 1623.

HISTORICAL NOTE

Students may be interested in more of the text of the curious preface quoted at the bottom of page 315. In part it reads as follows: "From the most able to him that can but spell: there you are numbered. We had rather you were weighed: especially when the fate of all books depends upon your capacities: and not of your heads alone, but of your purses. Well, it is now public; and you will stand for your privileges, we know,—to read and censure. Do so, but buy it first. . . . Whatever you do, buy. Censure will not drive a trade [keep us in business]. . . . It is not our province, who only gather his works and give them you, to praise him. It is yours that read him: and there we hope, to your divers capacities, you will find enough both to draw and hold you; for his wit can no more lie hid than it could be lost. Read him, therefore; and again and again: and if then you do not like him, surely you are in some manifest danger not to understand him." Refer the students to the Language Arts Survey, 4.16, "Reading Rates," for similar advice about rereading for comprehension.

LITERARY TECHNIQUE

Blank Verse. Blank verse may be the single most powerful form of verse in English literature because, aside from free verse, it is the form most like spoken English. It has the alternating iambic stresses common in spoken English, and its line length and divisions correspond to the divisions of clauses and phrases in the spoken language. Blank verse commonly uses a wide range of literary techniques to achieve its poetic effect, including alliteration, internal rhyme, inversion, and line division. Though Marlowe was not the first writer of blank verse, he used considerable freedom in placing stresses within the line, a liberty adopted also by Shakespeare. Students can try their hand at blank verse by writing lines of ten or eleven syllables with five stresses per line. They should try to place the stresses on alternate syllables. For related information, see the Handbook of Literary Terms.

BIOGRAPHICAL NOTE

That Shakespeare was the author of nearly all the plays associated with him is a widely accepted idea among scholars familiar with the details of Elizabethan literary history. In his own lifetime, some fifty people (including the illustrious Ben Jonson) testified to his authorship of many of the plays that now bear his name. Furthermore, many of the plays were published during Shakespeare's lifetime in quarto editions that bear his name. Nevertheless, since the 1900s, some scholars have claimed that Shakespeare was of too humble and ignorant parentage to have written such varied, brilliant, and learned verse. Various theories about the "true" author of the plays have been proposed. One of them alleges that Christopher Marlowe did not die in a tavern brawl, as is commonly believed, but lived, escaped to France, and paid Shakespeare to pretend that he was the author of the plays,

(cont.)

Christopher Marlowe

Engraving of Shakespeare from the First Folio

may have begun his studies with the intention of becoming an Anglican priest. The actual course of his life was to be quite different. Evidence suggests that, while still in school, Marlowe became a spy for the British government, and on graduation he immediately began a career in the theater.

Before leaving school in 1587, Marlowe wrote *Tamburlaine,* the first of his great plays, the story of a prideful, doomed Mongol conqueror. In this play and in others produced during the following six years, Marlowe revolutionized English theater. Perhaps his most important innovation was his use of **blank verse**—unrhymed iambic pentameter. Other playwrights before him had employed this meter, but Marlowe raised it to great heights. Marlowe's blank verse was lofty and heroic while having, at the same time, the grace and naturalness of ordinary speech. Marlowe blended elements of the comic and the tragic, treated romantic themes, probed the psychology of his characters, and exhibited a consummate sense of what constituted an exciting and dramatic situation. Later playwrights, including Shakespeare, would owe him a great debt.

In 1593, Marlowe's friend and fellow dramatist Thomas Kyd, author of *The Spanish Tragedy,* was arrested and executed for treason. Some heretical, free-thinking papers were found in Kyd's quarters, and Kyd implicated Marlowe in their production. Conservatives accused Marlowe of atheism, but the government interceded to protect him from prosecution, perhaps because Marlowe was still serving as a spy. Later that year, Marlowe was killed in a tavern brawl. Puritans slandered the dead playwright, calling him an impious and immoral man and pointing to the manner of his death as proof. However, given the tender sincerity of Marlowe's lyric poetry and the moral fervor of such works as *The Tragical History of Doctor Faustus,* one can hardly accept such charges against him. It is possible that Marlowe was murdered by the government because of embarrassment over the Kyd episode. At his death, Marlowe was only twenty-nine years old.

William Shakespeare may well be the greatest dramatist the world has ever known. His mother, Mary Arden Shakespeare, was from a well-to-do, well-connected family. His father, John Shakespeare, was a prosperous glove maker and local politician. William's exact birthdate is unknown, but he was baptized in his hometown of Stratford-upon-Avon on April 26, 1564, and tradition has assigned him a birthdate of April 23, which was also the day of his death and the feast day of Saint George, England's patron saint. Shakespeare attended the Stratford grammar school, where he studied Latin and perhaps some Greek. At the age of eighteen, Shakespeare married an older woman, Anne Hathaway, who was with child. Altogether, William and Anne had three children, Susanna and the twins Hamnet and Judith. He may have worked for a while as a schoolteacher, for there are many references to teaching in his plays. By 1592, however, he was living in London and pursuing a life in the theater. Scholars have speculated that Shakespeare's marriage was unhappy, but he continued to provide for his family and to expand his holdings in Stratford while living in London. He retired to Stratford-upon-Avon at the end of his life.

By 1593, Shakespeare was a successful actor and playwright. His history plays *Henry VI, Parts 1, 2,* and *3* and *Richard III* had established him as a significant force in London theater. In 1593, when an outbreak of the plague forced the closing of the theaters, Shakespeare

BIOGRAPHICAL NOTE (CONT.)

which Marlowe in fact wrote. Another theory proposes the scholar Francis Bacon as the author. As "proof," the proponents of this theory point to the word *honorificabilitudinitatibus* found in *Love's Labour's Lost.* This nonsense word is an anagram, they claim, for the Latin *Hi ludi F. Baconis nati tuiti orbi*—"These plays, the offspring of F. Bacon, are

preserved for the world." Students may enjoy researching these and other claims about the authorship of the plays. Refer them to the Language Arts Survey, 4.14, "Avoiding Faulty Arguments."

turned to narrative poetry, producing *Venus and Adonis* followed by *The Rape of Lucrece,* both dedicated to a patron, the Earl of Southampton. When the theaters reopened, Shakespeare plunged back into his primary vocation, writing thirty-seven plays in less than twenty years, including *The Taming of the Shrew, A Midsummer Night's Dream, The Merchant of Venice, Twelfth Night, All's Well That Ends Well, Richard II, Romeo and Juliet, Julius Cæsar, Hamlet, Othello, King Lear, Macbeth, The Winter's Tale,* and *The Tempest.* Shakespeare became a shareholder with Richard Burbage, son of John Burbage, in a theater company known as The Lord Chamberlain's Men. In 1599, Burbage, Shakespeare, and others opened the Globe Theater, and in 1603 they bought the Blackfriars, a small, artificially lighted indoor theater for winter performances. Their company began performing regularly at the court of Queen Elizabeth. After the death of Elizabeth in 1603, Shakespeare's company became, officially, servants of King James I, and their name was changed to The King's Men. Shakespeare's final play, *Henry VIII,* was performed in London in 1613. At that time he was probably living again in Stratford in a large house called New Place that he had bought in 1597. When he died in 1616, survived by his wife and his two daughters, Shakespeare was a wealthy man. He was buried in the Holy Trinity Church in Stratford-upon-Avon, where his bones rest to this day. The stone over his grave reads,

William Shakespeare. *Courtesy the Dean and chaplaincy, Westminster Abbey*

> Good frend for Jesus sake forbeare,
> To digg the dust enclosed heare!
> Blest be the man that spares thes stones,
> And curst be he that moves my bones.

Shakespeare did not personally prepare his plays for publication, and no official collection of them appeared until after his death. A collection of his sonnets, considered by critics to be among the best ever written in English, appeared in 1609. Many individual plays were published during his lifetime in unauthorized editions known as **Quartos.** Many of these quartos are quite unreliable. Some were probably based on actors' memories of the plays. Some were reprintings of so-called prompter's copies used in production of the plays. Some may have been based on final manuscript versions produced by the author. In 1623, seven years after Shakespeare's death, his friends and fellow actors John Heminge and Henry Condell published a collected edition of thirty-five of Shakespeare's plays. This collection is known to literary historians as the **First Folio.** In the centuries since 1623, and especially during the last century and a half, editors have worked diligently to compare the various early printed versions of Shakespeare's works to determine which version or versions of each play best represent Shakespeare's intent.

No brief summary can begin to catalog the many virtues of Shakespeare's work. He was a gifted observer of people, capable of creating unforgettable characters from all stations and walks of life. He used one of the largest vocabularies ever employed by an author, filling his plays with concrete details and with actual speech faithfully recalled. His plays probe the range of human experience. They are romantic in the sense that they are filled with passions rendered intensely. However, the plays rarely strain credibility or sink into sensationalism or sentimentality. Shakespeare's language tends to be dense, metaphorical,

---

HISTORICAL NOTE

Criticism of Shakespeare's works has a history almost as old as Shakespeare's plays. During the 1700s, critics such as Samuel Johnson felt that Shakespeare's plays would be better if they showed a clear "poetic justice" at work in the universe. In other words, such critics believed that the "bad guys" should always lose, and the "good guys" should always win. (Similar criticisms have been raised against Modernist literature in the present century.) When playwright Nahum Tate changed the ending of *King Lear* to ensure that Lear was returned to power and Cornelia and Edgar were married, Johnson approved of the change. The altered play was staged instead of the original version until the mid-1800s. Today, critics are more inclined to enjoy Shakespeare for what he does offer than to censure him for what he does not.

BIOGRAPHICAL NOTE

Bearing no name—perhaps because it needs none, perhaps because its tenant was too humble to allow it—Shakespeare's gravestone is graced only by a few lines of verse, which may or may not be his own. His tomb is graphic and tangible evidence that he has passed on; however, the dramas he left behind are alive—they move, entertain, and enlighten us, the living. The theme of the impact that our knowledge of death has upon our lives is one that Shakespeare visited again and again in his plays, perhaps most famously in Hamlet's "To be or not to be" soliloquy on page 396.

QUOTABLES

❝ Brevity is the soul of wit. ❞

—William Shakespeare
Hamlet

ADDITIONAL QUESTIONS AND ACTIVITIES

Students can memorize one of the passages on page 319 to increase their comprehension of Shakespearean verse and to practice their memorization skills. You may wish to assign the shorter passages to students who find such activities challenging. Schedule a "recitation hour" either during class or at some other time.

▶ **Teaching Note:** Suggest that students memorize by reading one line at a time; trying to repeat it without looking; rereading; and trying again to repeat it. Refer students to the Language Arts Survey, 4.4, "Memorizing."

Shakespeare's Birthplace

full of puns and word play, and yet natural, so that it comes "trippingly off the tongue" of an actor. A scene from Shakespeare tears across the stage, riveting and dramatic, and yet it bears close rereading, revealing in that rereading astonishing depth and complexity. Shakespeare used in his plays a combination of prose, rhymed poetry, and blank verse always appropriate to the character or scene at hand. His plays have given many, many phrases to the English language. They have filled audiences with laughter, pity, compassion, fear, terror, sadness, despair, suspense, and joy for over four hundred years. To begin to read Shakespeare is to enter a world, one might say *the world*, for his art is, as Hamlet says it should be, "a mirror held up to nature," to human nature. To read him well is to begin to understand others and ourselves. His art is, as Ben Jonson wrote, "not of an age, but for all time."

(Note: For a critical discussion of Shakespeare's *Macbeth,* see William Hazlitt's "Macbeth," on page 678.)

QUOTABLES

"He was a scholar, and a ripe and good one;
Exceeding wise, fair-spoken, and persuading:
Lofty and sour to them that lov'd him not;
But, to those men that sought him, sweet as summer."

—William Shakespeare, *Henry VIII*

Echoes:
Renaissance Drama

Shakespeare on Theater

Jaques.   All the world's a stage,
And all the men and women merely players;
They have their exits and their entrances,
And one man in his time plays many parts.

—As You Like It

Theseus.   The Poet's eye, in a fine frenzy
  rolling,
Doth glance from heaven to earth,
  from earth to heaven;
And as imagination bodies forth
The forms of things unknown, the poet's pen
Turns them to shapes, and gives to aery nothing
A local habitation and a name.

—A Midsummer Night's Dream

Prologue.
O for a Muse of fire, that would ascend
The brightest heaven of invention!
A kingdom for a stage, princes to act,
And monarchs to behold the swelling scene!
Then should the warlike Harry, like himself,
Assume the port of Mars, and at his heels
(Leash'd in, like hounds) should famine, sword,
    and fire
Crouch for employment. But pardon, gentles all,
The flat unraised spirits that hath dar'd
On this unworthy scaffold to bring forth
So great an object. Can this cockpit hold
The vasty fields of France? Or may we cram
Within this wooden O the very casques
That did affright the air at Agincourt?
O, pardon! since a crooked figure may
Attest in little place a million,
And let us, ciphers to this great accompt,
On your imaginary forces work.
Suppose within the girdle of these walls

Are now confin'd two mighty monarchies,
Whose high, upreared, and abutting fronts
The perilous narrow ocean parts asunder.
Piece out our imperfections with your thoughts;
Into a thousand parts divide one man,
And make imaginary puissance;
Think, when we talk of horses, that you see them
Printing their proud hoofs i' th' receiving earth;
For 'tis your thoughts that now must deck our
  kings,
Carry them here and there, jumping o'er times,
Turning th' accomplishment of many years
Into an hour-glass: for the which supply,
Admit me Chorus to this history;
Who, Prologue-like, you humble patience pray,
Gently to hear, kindly to judge, our play.

Exit

—Henry V

LITERARY TECHNIQUE

Metaphor. Refer students to the entry on *metaphor* in the Handbook of Literary Terms, and explain that a metaphor is a description of one thing as if it were another. Work with students to identify metaphors in the three passages on page 319. Write the metaphors on the board as students suggest them. Some of the metaphors they may find include the world as a stage, actors as spirits, the stage as a cockpit (pit for cockfights), the theater as the letter *O*, actors as ciphers (numbers), theater walls as a girdle, and thoughts as costumes.

LITERARY/TEACHING NOTE

Of Shakespeare's plays, *A Midsummer Night's Dream* is one of the most accessible and interesting to high school students. You may wish to suggest that play for outside reading. Other plays by Shakespeare that your students might enjoy include *Julius Cæsar, Romeo and Juliet, The Tempest,* and *The Taming of the Shrew.*

ENRICHMENT ACTIVITIES

Ask students to find modern examples of any of the following motifs in *Macbeth:* disturbance of natural order, equivocation, and excessive ambition. For example, they might find a news story about an earthquake survivor burying her child (disturbance of natural order) or government leaders saying something deceptive to cover a crime (equivocation). They can then write a short theme relating their example to *Macbeth* and explaining why the motif has universal importance.

SUPPORT FOR LEP STUDENTS

• Read over with students the tips on studying Shakespeare (About the Selection on this page). Explain that much of the language of *Macbeth* is poetry, and suggest that students watch for language that describes one thing as if it were something else.

• Encourage students by suggesting that this act of the drama is much like a murder thriller. Ask them to try to envision the action as if it were a film.

• Help students understand the contractions used so frequently by Shakespeare by choosing several from the text and writing them on the board along with the uncontracted forms.

ADDITIONAL VOCABULARY
ere—before
heath—open wasteland
valor—bravery
furbished—renovated
dismal—unpleasant

(cont.)

PREREADING

RENAISSANCE DRAMA

The Tragedy of Macbeth
by William Shakespeare

ABOUT THE AUTHOR

See biography on page 316.

ABOUT THE SELECTION

Sources. A **tragedy** is a drama that tells the story of the fall of a person of high status. Along with *Hamlet, Othello,* and *King Lear, Macbeth* is considered one of Shakespeare's greatest tragedies. Shakespeare used Holinshed's *Chronicles of England, Scotland, and Ireland* as the major source for his story. The *Chronicles* tell of the reign of a bloodthirsty, twelfth-century Scottish king named Macbeth. They also tell of the murder of the Scottish king Duff by Donwald. Shakespeare combined these two tales to create the storyline of his play for performance before King James I of England, who was descended from one of the characters in the play, Banquo. Shakespeare's dark tale of a man's ambition and treachery, written in 1605–1606, strikes a frighteningly familiar chord today, almost four centuries later.

Reading the Play. Shakespeare's *Macbeth* is a history, a chilling ghost story, and a psychological thriller. Few plays have ever matched it for sheer spectacle and suspense. As you read the play, remember that the script for a play is like a score for a piece of music. It comes alive when performed. To appreciate fully the experience of reading a play, you should visualize the scenes in your mind as they might appear on stage. Allow yourself to be drawn into the play's dark, disturbing atmosphere. Thrill to its many witches, ghosts, and other apparitions. Follow the murky descent of the central character into a horror of his own making.

Try not to be overwhelmed by Shakespeare's use of Elizabethan English. Read each scene through quickly to get the gist of it. Concentrate on seeing the scene in your mind and not on the details of the language. Then go back and read the scene carefully, using the footnotes. Soon you will find that you have grown accustomed to Shakespeare's English and can appreciate its sometimes spine-tingling, sometimes noble beauty.

One technique that will help you to grasp the themes, or main ideas, of the play is to look for and think about recurring elements, or **motifs.** These include references to ambition; to equivocation, or double-talk; to blood; to madness; to sickness; to foul weather; to manliness (or lack thereof); and to disturbances in the natural order. As you read the play, note these elements, and think about how they are related to one another. Also bear in mind that James I, for whom the play was performed by Shakespeare's company, The King's Men, was a staunch believer in demons and witches (about which he wrote a book) and in the Divine Right of Kings (the idea that kings gain their authority directly from God and, therefore, rule absolutely). To James, the overthrow or murder of a king would be an attack on the established natural order of the universe.

SUPPORT FOR LEP STUDENTS (CONT.)

curb—restrain	**attire**—clothing, apparel	**liege**—lord
deign—stoop	**start**—startle	**become**—suit
disburse—pay out	**trifles**—insignificant amusements	**recompense**—pay back
dwindle—become smaller or weaker	**horrid**—terrible	**purpose**—intend
	rapt—enthralled	**sway**—determining power
pine—yearn	**wrought**—made	**procreant**—fruitful
tempest—storm	**interim**—time between	**undaunted**—fearless

READER'S JOURNAL

What are your personal ambitions? What goals do you have for yourself? What things *wouldn't* you do in order to reach your goals? Think about these questions. Then write in your journal about your ambitions.

SPEAKING AND LISTENING SKILLS

Read the Language Arts Survey, 3.2, "Elements of Verbal Communication," and 3.3, "Elements of Nonverbal Communication." Then, as you read the opening dialogue in this among the three witches—imagine that you are directing it. What verbal and nonverbal elements would you have your actors exaggerate, and in what ways, to make them frightening and unnatural? Explain.

The Tragedy of Macbeth

WILLIAM SHAKESPEARE

CHARACTERS IN THE PLAY

DUNCAN, *King of Scotland*
MALCOLM ⎤ *Duncan's sons*
DONALBAIN ⎦
MACBETH ⎤ *Duncan's thanes,*
BANQUO ⎦ *generals in his service*
MACDUFF ⎤
LENNOX
ROSSE
MENTETH ⎬ *Scottish noblemen*
ANGUS
CATHNESS ⎦
FLEANCE, *Banquo's son*
SIWARD, *Earl of Northumberland, leader of the English troops*
YOUNG SIWARD, *Siward's son*
SEYTON, *Macbeth's servant*
BOY, *Macduff's son*

ENGLISH DOCTOR
SCOTS DOCTOR
SERGEANT
PORTER, *or* GATEKEEPER
OLD MAN
Three MURDERERS

LADY MACBETH
LADY MACDUFF
GENTLEWOMAN, *Lady Macbeth's servant*
Three WITCHES, *the Weird Sisters*
Three other WITCHES
HECATE, *Queen of the Witches*
APPARITIONS

LORDS, GENTLEMEN, OFFICERS, SOLDIERS, ATTENDANTS, MESSENGERS *and* BANQUO'S GHOST

SCENES: Scotland and England

READER'S JOURNAL

If students have difficulty stating their ambitions, ask them to list those activities they most enjoy in life and to describe where they would most like to live. Then ask them to imagine how they could put themselves in a situation where they could do the things they enjoy most in the setting they prefer.

SPEAKING SKILLS

• Verbal elements that might be exaggerated in the dialogue are tone of voice, speaking nasally, for instance; volume, the witches screaming their lines; and added sounds, such as cackling, wailing, and shrieking. Nonverbal elements might include threatening or bizarre facial expressions and gestures; bent or twisted posture; and jerky, odd movements of the body.

• Students may explain that the elements of verbal and nonverbal communication should stress violations of the natural order; for instance, Macbeth later observes that the witches, though women, appear much like men. Suggest other ways in which this scene presents violations of the natural order (the calling of the witches by a familiar, the hovering of the witches in the air). By highlighting such features, a director would reinforce the motif of the consequences of violating the natural or moral order of the universe.

VOCABULARY FROM THE SELECTION

chastise	pall
corporal	peak
earnest	purveyor
flout	recompense
gall	remorse
impede	surmise
mettle	trifle
minion	wanton
mortal	

GOALS/OBJECTIVES

Studying this lesson will enable students to

• experience the suspense, horror, and catharsis of a Shakespearean tragedy
• recognize themes and motifs in a play
• discuss the themes of ambition, manliness, evil, and natural order, and relate them to events in a play

• identify techniques of characterization in a play
• use comparison and contrast in writing to develop prewriting notes into a coherent narrative
• revise sentences to reduce wordiness

CROSS-CURRICULAR ACTIVITIES

Arts and Humanities. Explain to students that when illustrators draw the first version of a comic strip, they often sketch quickly the contents of each frame. A student who has drawing skills can stand at the chalkboard and do a rough sketch of four or five frames to illustrate scene i of *Macbeth*. Other students can contribute by suggesting what viewing angle might be used in each frame, how the contents should be cropped (for instance, as a close-up of one witch's face or as a view of all three witches), and how the lines of dialogue should be allocated to the various frames. Students can insert bits of dialogue in speech balloons in each frame. Discuss with students how graphic representation differs from dramatic representation.

The Three Witches. "When shall we three meet again?/In thunder, lightning, or in rain?"
Illustration by Sol Graphic Design

ACT I
SCENE i: an open place

Thunder and lightning. Enter three
WITCHES.

1. WITCH. When shall we three meet
again?
In thunder, lightning, or in rain?

2. WITCH. When the hurly-burly's[1] done,
When the battle's lost and won.

5 **3. WITCH.** That will be ere the set of sun.

1. WITCH. Where the place?

2. WITCH.   Upon the heath.

3. WITCH. There to meet with Macbeth.

1. WITCH. I come, Graymalkin.[2]

2. WITCH. Paddock calls.[3]

10 **3. WITCH.** Anon.

ALL. Fair is foul, and foul is fair,
Hover through the fog and filthy air. *Exeunt.*

SCENE ii: a camp

Alarum[4] within. Enter KING *Duncan,*
MALCOLM, DONALBAIN, LENNOX, *with*
ATTENDANTS, *meeting a bleeding* SERGEANT.

DUNCAN. What bloody man is that? He
can report,
As seemeth by his plight, of the revolt
The newest state.

MALCOLM.   This is the sergeant,
Who like a good and hardy soldier fought
5 'Gainst my captivity. Hail, brave friend!
Say to the King the knowledge of the broil
As thou didst leave it.

---
1. **hurly-burly.** Commotion of the battle
2. **Graymalkin.** Gray cat, the witch's familiar
3. **Paddock.** Toad, the second witch's familiar
4. **Alarum.** Trumpet call
5. **art.** Skill
6. **kerns and gallowglasses.** Kerns are lightly armed foot soldiers,

SERGEANT.   Doubtful it stood,
As two spent swimmers that do cling
together
And choke their art.[5] The merciless
Macdonwald
10 (Worthy to be a rebel, for to that
The multiplying villainies of nature
Do swarm upon him) from the Western Isles
Of kerns and [gallowglasses][6] is supplied,
And Fortune, on his damned [quarrel][7] smil-
ing,
15 Show'd like a rebel's whore. But all's too weak;
For brave Macbeth (well he deserves that
name),
Disdaining Fortune, with his brandish'd
steel,
Which smok'd with bloody execution,
(Like Valor's <u>minion</u>) carv'd out his passage
20 Till he fac'd the slave;
Which nev'r shook hands, nor bade farewell
to him,
Till he unseam'd him from the nave to th'
chops,[8]
Ant fix'd his head upon our battlements.

DUNCAN. O valiant cousin,[9] worthy gentleman!

25 **SERGEANT.** As whence the sun gins his
reflection[10]
Shipwracking storms and direful thunders
break,
So from that spring whence comfort seem'd
to come
Discomfort swells. Mark, King of Scotland,
mark!
No sooner justice had, with valor arm'd,

---
and gallowglasses are heavily armed soldiers.
7. **quarrel.** Cause
8. **unseam'd . . . chops.** Cut him from navel to jaw
9. **cousin.** General term for relative
10. **As . . . reflection.** From where the sun rises

WORDS FOR
EVERYDAY USE:
min • ion (min´ yən) *n.*, favorite

Oxymoron. Explain to students that an oxymoron is a combination of incongruous or contradictory words. Examples are *whispered shout* and *deadly assistance*. An oxymoron accurately expresses a conflict between elements of a thing or situation, however odd or surprising it may be. Though the witches do not use an oxymoron as such in the first scene, the phrase "fair foulness" would sum up the battle at the beginning of the play and its results: as war it is grim and foul, but because the "right" side wins, it is also fair or good. Similarly, the opening could be described as "foul fairness" because it is the fair starting point that leads to Macbeth's later "foul" actions. Students should be alert to situations in the play that can be described as oxymorons. For example, "foul fairness" describes the behavior of Macbeth and Lady Macbeth later in act I, when they treat Duncan well (with fairness) while plotting to kill him (and are thus foul).

VOCABULARY IN CONTEXT

• Rather than hiring unknowns, the politician filled all the local government offices with one <u>minion</u> after another.

**ANSWERS TO SELECTION
CHECK TEST 4.5.1**

EX. Who appears in the opening scene of act I?
Three witches appear in the opening scene of act I.

1. Who is the great hero of the battle with which scene ii begins?
Macbeth is the great hero of the battle.

2. With what title does the king reward Macbeth?
The king rewards Macbeth with the title Thane of Cawdor.

3. Who is with Macbeth when he meets the witches?
Banquo is with Macbeth when he meets the witches.

4. Whose castle does King Duncan visit?
Duncan visits Macbeth's castle.

5. What do Macbeth and Lady Macbeth plan to do?
They plan to murder King Duncan.

**ADDITIONAL QUESTIONS
AND ACTIVITIES**

Use the graphic organizer at the bottom of this page to explain the sequence of events in the rebellion described in scene i and to show how the audience learns about them.

30   Compell'd these skipping kerns to trust their
          heels,
      But the Norweyan lord, surveying vantage,
      With furbish'd arms and new supplies of
          men,
      Began a fresh assault.

      DUNCAN.   Dismay'd not this
      Our captains, Macbeth and Banquo?

      SERGEANT   Yes,
35   As sparrows eagles; or the hare the lion.
      If I say sooth, I must report they were
      As cannons overcharg'd with double cracks,[11]
          so they
      Doubly redoubled strokes upon the foe.
      Except they meant to bathe in reeking[12]
          wounds,
40   Or memorize another Golgotha,[13]
      I cannot tell—
      But I am faint, my gashes cry for help.

      DUNCAN.   So well thy words become thee as
          thy wounds,
      They smack of honor both. Go get him sur-
          geons.
                                Exit SERGEANT, *attended.*

      Enter ROSSE *and* ANGUS.

      Who comes here?

45   **MALCOLM.**   The worthy Thane[14] of Rosse.

      LENNOX.   What a haste looks through his
          eyes! So should he look
      That seems to speak things strange.

      ROSSE.   God save the king!

      DUNCAN.   Whence cam'st thou, worthy
          thane?

      ROSSE.   From Fife, great King,
      Where the Norweyan banners <u>flout</u> the sky
50   And fan our people cold.
      Norway himself, with terrible numbers,
      Assisted by that most disloyal traitor,
      The Thane of Cawdor, began a dismal
          conflict,
      Till that Bellona's bridegroom, lapp'd in
          proof,[15]
55   Confronted him with self-comparisons,
      Point against point, rebellious arm 'gainst arm,
      Curbing his lavish spirit; and to conclude,
      The victory fell on us.

      DUNCAN.   Great happiness!

      ROSSE.   That now
      Sweno, the Norways' king, craves composi-
          tion;
60   Nor would we deign him burial of his men
      Till he disbursed at Saint Colme's inch[16]
      Ten thousand dollars to our general use.

      DUNCAN.   No more that Thane of Cawdor
          shall deceive
      Our bosom interest. Go pronounce his pre-
          sent[17] death,
65   And with his former title greet Macbeth.

      ROSSE.   I'll see it done.

      DUNCAN.   What he hath lost, noble
          Macbeth hath won.
                                                Exeunt.

---

11. **cracks.** Charges
12. **reeking.** Steaming
13. **memorize . . . Golgotha.** Make the place as memorable for slaughter as Golgotha, the place of skulls
14. **Thane.** Scottish title of nobility
15. **Bellona's . . . proof.** Macbeth, who is paired with Bellona, god-dess of war, is clad in tested armor.
16. **Saint Colme's inch.** A small island near Edinburgh, Scotland
17. **present.** Immediate

WORDS FOR EVERYDAY USE: **flout** (flout) *vt.,* show scorn or contempt for

REPORTER	REBELS	DUNCAN'S ALLIES
Sergeant's speech	Macdonwald rebels against Duncan and begins a battle with extensive forces ("kerns and gallowglasses"). Sweno, the Norwegian (Norweyan) lord or king, begins a fresh assault after Macdonwald's death.	Macbeth, the Thane of Glamis, proves his bravery and loyalty by killing Macdonwald and driving away his forces. Macbeth and Banquo are not "dismay'd" by the onslaught of the Norwegian forces.
Rosse's speech	The Thane of Cawdor, another rebel, assists the Norwegian king. The Norwegian king must ask for peace and pay a fine.	The Thane of Cawdor is defeated by forces loyal to Duncan.
Duncan's speech	The rebellious Thane of Cawdor is condemned to die.	Macbeth is to become the new Thane of Cawdor as a reward for his loyalty and bravery.

SCENE iii: a heath

Thunder. Enter the three WITCHES.

1. WITCH. Where hast thou been, sister?

2. WITCH. Killing swine.[18]

3. WITCH. Sister, where thou?

1. WITCH. A sailor's wife had chestnuts in her lap,
And mounch'd, and mounch'd, and mounch'd.
5   "Give me!" quoth I.
"Aroint[19] thee, witch!" the rump-fed
    ronyon[20] cries.
Her husband's to Aleppo gone, master o' th'
    Tiger;[21]
But in a sieve I'll thither sail,
And, like a rat without a tail,
10 I'll do, I'll do, and I'll do.

2. WITCH. I'll give thee a wind.

1. WITCH. Th' art kind.

3. WITCH. And I another.

1. WITCH. I myself have all the other,
15 And the very ports they blow,
All the quarters that they know
I' th' shipman's card.[22]
I'll drain him dry as hay:
Sleep shall neither night nor day
20 Hang upon his penthouse lid;[23]
He shall live a man forbid;[24]
Weary sev'nnights, nine times nine,
Shall he dwindle, <u>peak</u>, and pine;
Though his bark cannot be lost,
25 Yet it shall be tempest-toss'd.
Look what I have.

2. WITCH. Show me, show me.

1. WITCH. Here I have a pilot's thumb,
Wrack'd as homeward he did come.

Drum within.

30 **3. WITCH.** A drum, a drum!
Macbeth doth come.

ALL. The weïrd[25] sisters, hand in hand,
Posters[26] of the sea and land,
Thus do go, about, about,
35 Thrice to thine, and thrice to mine,
And thrice again, to make up nine.
Peace, the charm's wound up.

Enter MACBETH *and* BANQUO.

MACBETH. So foul and fair a day I have not seen.

BANQUO. How far is't call'd to Forres? What are these
40 So wither'd and so wild in their attire,
That look not like th' inhabitants o' th' earth,
And yet are on't? Live you? or are you aught
That man may question? You seem to understand me,
By each at once her choppy[27] finger laying
45 Upon her skinny lips. You should be women,
And yet your beards forbid me to interpret
That you are so.

MACBETH. Speak, if you can: what are you?

1. WITCH. All hail, Macbeth, hail to thee,
Thane of Glamis!

2. WITCH. All hail, Macbeth, hail to thee,
Thane of Cawdor!

---

18. **killing swine.** It was commonly believed that witches killed domestic animals, especially pigs.
19. **Aroint.** Be gone
20. **rump-fed ronyon.** Fat, good-for-nothing creature
21. **Aleppo . . . Tiger.** Her husband went to Aleppo, a trading center in Syria, on a ship called the *Tiger.*
22. **shipman's card.** Compass or chart
23. **penthouse lid.** Eyelid
24. **forbid.** Under a curse
25. **weïrd.** Destiny-serving, from the Old English *wyrd* or fate
26. **Posters.** Swift travellers
27. **choppy.** Chapped

WORDS FOR
EVERYDAY USE: **peak** (pēk) *vi.,* become sickly

Most teenagers lack a time sense; they assume that anything that preceded them historically is passé and has little to offer them. The following exercise is recommended to get students to begin thinking of their place on the continuum of time: Run a piece of chalk across the chalkboard. Assume that the beginning of the line represents the beginning of time. Ask students when time began. Did it begin with the beginning of the universe? With the emergence of Homo sapiens and of human consciousness? Assume that the end of the time line is 1996. Ask students where on the line they would place Greek and Roman civilizations. Where would they place 1564–1616? Make the point that Shakespeare is a contemporary of theirs in time, that if the species endures and time continues, the time may come when students will study all of Western Civilization, from the Greeks through our time, from a single chapter in a history book.

VOCABULARY IN CONTEXT

- The reckless driver managed to <u>flout</u> nearly every rule of the road before he skidded into a ditch.
- While Arthur had the flu, he <u>peaked</u> and lost weight, but within a week he had regained his health.

50 **3. WITCH.** All hail, Macbeth, that shalt be King hereafter!

BANQUO. Good sir, why do you start, and seem to fear
Things that do sound so fair?—I' th' name of truth,
Are ye fantastical,[28] or that indeed
Which outwardly ye show? My noble partner
55 You greet with present grace,[29] and great prediction
Of noble having and of royal hope,
That he seems rapt withal; to me you speak not.
If you can look into the seeds of time,
And say which grain will grow, and which will not,
60 Speak then to me, who neither beg nor fear
Your favors nor your hate.

1. WITCH. Hail!

2. WITCH. Hail!

3. WITCH. Hail!

65 **1. WITCH.** Lesser than Macbeth, and greater.

2. WITCH. Not so happy, yet much happier.

3. WITCH. Thou shalt get kings, though thou be none.
So all hail, Macbeth and Banquo!

1. WITCH. Banquo and Macbeth, all hail!

70 **MACBETH.** Stay, you imperfect[30] speakers, tell me more:
By Sinel's[31] death I know I am Thane of Glamis,
But how of Cawdor? The Thane of Cawdor lives

---

28. **fantastical.** Imaginary
29. **present grace.** Present title
30. **imperfect.** Incomplete
31. **Sinel.** Macbeth's father

A prosperous gentleman; and to be king
Stands not within the prospect of belief,
75 No more than to be Cawdor. Say from whence
You owe this strange intelligence,[32] or why
Upon this blasted heath you stop our way
With such prophetic greeting? Speak, I charge you.

WITCHES vanish.

BANQUO. The earth hath bubbles, as the water has,
80 And these are of them. Whither are they vanish'd?

MACBETH. Into the air; and what seem'd corporal melted,
As breath into the wind. Would they had stay'd!

BANQUO. Were such things here as we do speak about?
Or have we eaten on the insane root[33]
85 That takes the reason prisoner?

MACBETH. Your children shall be kings.

BANQUO. You shall be king.

MACBETH. And Thane of Cawdor too; went it not so?

BANQUO. To th' self-same tune and words. Who's here?

Enter ROSSE and ANGUS.

ROSSE. The King hath happily receiv'd, Macbeth,
90 The news of thy success; and when he reads
Thy personal venture in the rebels' fight,
His wonders and his praises do contend
Which should be thine or his.[34] Silenc'd with that,

---

32. **owe this strange intelligence.** Possess this strange information
33. **insane root.** Insanity-causing root, probably hemlock or henbane
34. **His wonders . . . his.** He is amazed and wanting to praise you.

WORDS FOR EVERYDAY USE: cor • po • ral (kôr pə rəl) *adj.*, of the body; bodily

In viewing o'er the rest o' th' self-same day,
95 He finds thee in the stout Norweyan ranks,
Nothing afeard of what thyself didst make,
Strange images of death. As thick as tale
Came post with post,[35] and every one did
    bear
Thy praises in his kingdom's great defense,
And pour'd them down before him.

100 ANGUS.   We are sent
To give thee from our royal master thanks,
Only to herald thee into his sight,
Not pay thee.

ROSSE.   And for an earnest of a greater
    honor,
105 He bade me, from him, call thee Thane of
    Cawdor;
In which addition, hail, most worthy thane,
For it is thine.

BANQUO.   What, can the devil speak true?

MACBETH.   The Thane of Cawdor lives;
    why do you dress me
In borrowed robes?

ANGUS.   Who was the thane lives yet,
110 But under heavy judgment bears that life
Which he deserves to lose. Whether he was
    combin'd[36]
With those of Norway, or did line[37] the rebel
With hidden help and vantage, or that with
    both
He labor'd in his country's wrack,[38] I know
    not;
115 But treasons capital, confess'd and prov'd,
Have overthrown him.

MACBETH.   [Aside.] Glamis, and
    Thane of Cawdor!

The greatest is behind.[39] [To Rosse and Angus.]
    Thanks for your pains.
[Aside to Banquo.] Do you not hope your chil-
    dren shall be kings,
When those that gave the Thane of Cawdor
    to me
Promis'd no less to them?

120 BANQUO.   [Aside to Macbeth.]
    That, trusted home,[40]
Might yet enkindle you unto[41] the crown,
Besides the Thane of Cawdor. But 'tis
    strange;
And oftentimes, to win us to our harm,
The instruments of darkness tell us truths,
125 Win us with honest trifles, to betray 's
In deepest consequence.—
Cousins, a word, I pray you.

MACBETH.   [Aside.] Two truths are told,
As happy prologues to the swelling act
Of the imperial theme.[42]—I thank you, gen-
    tlemen.
130 [Aside.] This supernatural soliciting
Cannot be ill; cannot be good. If ill,
Why hath it given me earnest of success,
Commencing in a truth? I am Thane of
    Cawdor.
If good, why do I yield to that suggestion
135 Whose horrid image doth unfix my hair
And make my seated heart knock at my ribs,
Against the use of nature? Present fears
Are less than horrible imaginings:
My thought, whose murther yet is but fantas-
    tical,
140 Shakes so my single state of man that func-
    tion
Is smother'd in surmise, and nothing is
But what is not.

---

35. **post with post.** Messenger after messenger
36. **combin'd.** Allied
37. **line.** Align with, support
38. **wrack.** Ruin

39. **behind.** Left behind, still left
40. **home.** Completely
41. **enkindle you unto.** Cause you to hope for
42. **swelling . . . theme.** Grand idea that I will be king

WORDS FOR
EVERYDAY USE:

ear • nest (ʉr´ nist) n., something given or done as an indication
or assurance of what is to come
tri • fle (trī´fəl) n., something of little value or importance
sur • mise (sər mīz´) n., guessing, imagined actions

**ADDITIONAL QUESTIONS
AND ACTIVITIES**

Ask students: 1. What does the
account of Macbeth's actions in
lines 89–99 demonstrate about
him? 2. If such a person hesitated
to commit a crime, what would
you conclude was the reason for
his or her hesitation?

Answers. 1. The account demonstrates that Macbeth is "Nothing
afeard of . . . /Strange images of
death" (lines 96–97), in other words,
that he is brave. 2. One would
have to conclude that when such a
person shows hesitation to commit
a crime, he or she does so as a
result of moral scruples, not of
cowardice.

VOCABULARY IN CONTEXT

• The whipping of people for minor offenses was a common form of corporal punishment in pre-
  Colonial America.
• When we offered to buy the couple's house for $50,000, we offered them $2,000 as an earnest.
• After the writer was made poet laureate, people expected great things of him, but his later poems
  were only trifles.
• Although he did not know what was in the sealed locker, an intelligent surmise told him that the
  locker's contents must be very valuable.

ADDITIONAL QUESTIONS AND ACTIVITIES

Students can imagine that they are Duncan's court poet. They can write a poem describing the heroic exploits of Macbeth, Duncan's noble gratitude to him, and Macbeth's winning the title of Thane of Cawdor. Other students can imagine they are court reporters and write a "news" story on what has taken place.

LITERARY TECHNIQUE

Metaphor. A metaphor is a figure of speech in which one thing is written or spoken about as though it were another. Ask students to identify the two things being related in scene iv, lines 16–18.

Answer. Recompense, or reward, is described as though it were a flying creature such as a bird.

BANQUO.　　　　　Look how our partner's rapt.

MACBETH. [*Aside.*] If chance will have me king, why, chance may crown me
Without my stir.

BANQUO.　　　　New honors come upon him,
145　Like our strange garments, cleave not to their mould[43]
But with the aid of use.

MACBETH.　　　[*Aside.*] Come what come may,
Time and the hour runs through the roughest day.

BANQUO.　Worthy Macbeth, we stay upon your leisure.

MACBETH.　Give me your favor;[44] my dull brain was wrought
150　With things forgotten. Kind gentlemen, your pains
Are regist'red where every day I turn
The leaf to read them. Let us toward the King.
[*Aside to Banquo.*] Think upon what hath chanc'd; and at more time,
The interim having weigh'd it, let us speak
Our free hearts each to other.

155　**BANQUO.**　　　　　Very gladly.

MACBETH.　Till then, enough.—Come, friends.　　　　　*Exeunt.*

SCENE iv: a room in the palace at Fornes

Flourish. Enter KING DUNCAN, LENNOX, MALCOLM, DONALBAIN, *and* ATTENDANTS.

DUNCAN.　Is execution done on Cawdor? Are not

---

43. **strange . . . mould.** New clothes that don't fit the shape of the wearer
44. **favor.** Pardon
45. **in commission.** Delegated to oversee the execution

Those in commission[45] yet return'd?

MALCOLM.　　　　　　　My liege,
They are not yet come back. But I have spoke
With one that saw him die; who did report
5　That very frankly he confess'd his treasons,
Implor'd your Highness' pardon, and set forth
A deep repentance. Nothing in his life
Became him like the leaving it. He died
As one that had been studied in his death,
10　To throw away the dearest thing he ow'd,
As 'twere a careless trifle.

DUNCAN.　　　　　　　There's no art
To find the mind's construction in the face:
He was a gentleman on whom I built
An absolute trust.

　　Enter MACBETH, BANQUO, ROSSE, *and* ANGUS.

　　　　　　　　O worthiest cousin!
15　The sin of my ingratitude even now
Was heavy on me. Thou art so far before,
That swiftest wing of <u>recompense</u> is slow
To overtake thee. Would thou hadst less deserv'd,
That the proportion both of thanks and payment
20　Might have been mine![46] Only I have left to say,
More is thy due than more than all can pay.

MACBETH.　The service and the loyalty I owe,
In doing it, pays itself. Your Highness' part
Is to receive our duties; and our duties
25　Are to your throne and state children and servants;

---

46. **Would . . . mine.** If you had been less deserving, I could have rewarded you as you deserve.

WORDS FOR EVERYDAY USE:　**rec • om • pense** (rek´əm pens´) *n.,* repayment; reward

---

VOCABULARY IN CONTEXT

• Carmen demanded <u>recompense</u> for all the extra hours he had worked.
• Although destined to grow into a disciplined racehorse, for now the <u>wanton</u> colt galloped about the pasture.

Which do but what they should, by doing
    every thing
Safe toward your love and honor.

DUNCAN.   Welcome hither!
I have begun to plant thee, and will labor
To make thee full of growing. Noble Banquo,
30 That hast no less deserv'd, nor must be
    known
No less to have done so, let me infold thee
And hold thee to my heart.

BANQUO.   There if I grow,
The harvest is your own.

DUNCAN.   My plenteous joys,
<u>Wanton</u> in fullness, seek to hide themselves
35 In drops of sorrow. Sons, kinsmen, thanes,
And you whose places are the nearest, know
We will establish our estate upon
Our eldest, Malcolm, whom we name here-
    after
The Prince of Cumberland; which honor
    must
40 Not unaccompanied invest him only,
But signs of nobleness, like stars, shall shine
On all deservers. From hence to Enverness,⁴⁷
And bind us further to you.

MACBETH.   The rest is labor, which is not
    us'd for you.
45 I'll be myself the harbinger,⁴⁸ and make joy-
    ful
The hearing of my wife with your approach;
So humbly take my leave.

DUNCAN.   My worthy Cawdor!

MACBETH.   [*Aside*.] The Prince of
    Cumberland! that is a step

50 On which I must fall down, or else o'erleap,
For in my way it lies. Stars, hide your fires,
Let not light see my black and deep desires;
The eye wink at the hand;⁴⁹ yet let that be
Which the eye fears, when it is done, to see.

                         Exit.

DUNCAN.   True, worthy Banquo! he is full
    so valiant,
55 And in his commendations I am fed;
It is a banquet to me. Let's after him,
Whose care is gone before to bid us welcome:
It is a peerless kinsman.

                   Flourish. Exeunt.

SCENE v: a room in MACBETH'S castle at Inverness

Enter MACBETH'S WIFE *alone with a letter.*

LADY MACBETH. [*Reads*.] "They met me in
the day of success; and I have learn'd by the
perfect'st report, they have more in them
than mortal knowledge. When I burnt in
5 desire to question them further, they made
themselves air, into which they vanish'd.
Whiles I stood rapt in the wonder of it, came
missives⁵⁰ from the King, who all-hail'd me
'Thane of Cawdor,' by which title, before,
10 these weïrd sisters saluted me, and referr'd
me to the coming on of time with 'Hail, King
that shalt be!' This have I thought good to
deliver thee, my dearest partner of greatness,
that thou mightst not lose the dues of rejoic-
15 ing by being ignorant of what greatness
is promis'd thee. Lay it to thy heart, and
farewell."

---

47. **Enverness.** Macbeth's castle
48. **harbinger.** Something or someone that arrives before
49. **The eye . . . hand.** Be blind to what the hand does
50. **missives.** Messengers

WORDS FOR EVERYDAY USE: **wan • ton** (wän´ tən) *adj.,* undisciplined; unmanageable

HISTORICAL NOTE

In early Scotland, the kingship was not passed down automatically from father to son. The king was chosen according to an old Celtic tradition called "tanistry," which called for nobles to elect to the throne the most worthy kinsman of a deceased king. Thus Macbeth had hopes that he might legitimately attain the throne until Malcolm is declared the heir of the king in lines 35–42. Unless students understand the peculiar custom of tanistry, they will not understand why Macbeth reacts to the declaration as if it were not inevitable (lines 48–50).

LITERARY TECHNIQUE

Symbol. A **symbol** is something that stands for or represents both itself and something else. When Macbeth says in scene iv, line 50, "Stars, hide your fires," what might the stars symbolize? Why would Macbeth want darkness?

Answer. Stars are traditional symbols of the eyes, or watchfulness, of heaven. Macbeth wants darkness to hide the deed that he is contemplating.

LITERARY TECHNIQUE

Metaphor. A **metaphor** is a figure of speech in which one thing is spoken or written about as though it were another. Ask what metaphor is used by Duncan in scene iv, lines 27–29.

Answer. Duncan compares Macbeth to a plant, saying, "I have begun to plant thee, and will labor/To make thee full of growing." Fruits are traditional symbols of rewards for having done one's work or duty.

Students can list attributes of Macbeth and Lady Macbeth that they have learned about up to this point in the play. They should be able to support each characteristic they list with a reference to specific line numbers. They should observe that Macbeth is described as brave, noble, and loyal and that he demonstrates both ambitiousness and a loving attitude toward his wife. From his wife's distrust of his ability to act ruthlessly, students can infer that he has demonstrated kindness before this time. Lady Macbeth likewise shows ambition and an immoral willingness to become queen at all costs. After students have made their lists, have them save these lists to study the changes in Macbeth and Lady Macbeth that will have taken place by act V.

Glamis thou art, and Cawdor, and shalt be
What thou art promis'd. Yet do I fear thy nature,
20 It is too full o' th' milk of human kindness
To catch the nearest way. Thou wouldst be great,
Art not without ambition, but without
The illness[51] should attend it. What thou wouldst highly,
That wouldst thou holily; wouldst not play false,
25 And yet wouldst wrongly win. Thou'ldst have, great Glamis,
That which cries, "Thus thou must do," if thou have it;
And that which rather thou dost fear to do
Than wishest should be undone. Hie thee hither,
That I may pour my spirits in thine ear,
30 And <u>chastise</u> with the valor of my tongue
All that <u>impedes</u> thee from the golden round,
Which fate and metaphysical[52] aid doth seem
To have thee crown'd withal.

Enter MESSENGER.

                What is your tidings?
MESSENGER.   The King comes here tonight.
35 **LADY MACBETH.**   Thou'rt mad to say it!
Is not thy master with him? who, were't so,
Would have inform'd for preparation.

MESSENGER.   So please you, it is true; our thane is coming.
One of my fellows had the speed of him,
40 Who, almost dead for breath, had scarcely more
Than would make up his message.

---

51. **illness.** Wickedness
52. **metaphysical.** Supernatural
53. **compunctious . . . nature.** Natural feelings of pity
54. **fell.** Cruel

LADY MACBETH.   Give him tending,
He brings great news.   *Exit* MESSENGER.
              The raven himself is hoarse
That croaks the fatal entrance of Duncan
45 Under my battlements. Come, you spirits
That tend on <u>mortal</u> thoughts, unsex me here,
And fill me from the crown to the toe topful
Of direst cruelty! Make thick my blood,
Stop up th' access and passage to <u>remorse</u>,
50 That no compunctious visitings of nature[53]
Shake my fell[54] purpose, nor keep peace between
Th' effect and it! Come to my woman's breasts,
And take my milk for <u>gall</u>, you murth'ring ministers,
Wherever in your sightless substances
55 You wait on nature's mischief! Come, thick night,
And <u>pall</u> thee in the dunnest smoke of hell,
That my keen knife see not the wound it makes,
Nor heaven peep through the blanket of the dark
To cry, "Hold, hold!"

Enter MACBETH.

          Great Glamis! worthy Cawdor!
60 Greater than both, by the all-hail hereafter!
Thy letters have transported me beyond
This ignorant present, and I feel now
The future in the instant.

MACBETH.   My dearest love,
Duncan comes here tonight.

LADY MACBETH.   And when goes hence?

WORDS FOR EVERYDAY USE:

chas • tise (chas tīz´) *vt.*, scold or condemn sharply
im • pede (im pēd´) *vt.*, obstruct or delay
mor • tal (môr´təl) *adj.*, deadly
re • morse (rē môrs´) *n.*, pity; compassion
gall (gôl) *n.*, bile
pall (pôl) *vt.*, cloak in darkness

VOCABULARY IN CONTEXT

- The grandmother <u>chastised</u> the child for chasing a ball into the road.
- The only thing that <u>impedes</u> us from happiness is our own negative thoughts.
- Susan kissed the scrape on her daughter's arm and assured her it was not a <u>mortal</u> wound.
- The dinosaur felt no <u>remorse</u> for the newts and frogs it crushed under its enormous feet.
- After the senator lost his reelection bid, his life became unending <u>gall</u> and heartache.
- Drawing the curtains <u>palled</u> the house, so they switched on the lights.
- We needed to find a new <u>purveyor</u> of food when the local supermarket closed.

MACBETH.   Tomorrow, as he purposes.

65 **LADY MACBETH.**   O, never
Shall sun that morrow see!
Your face, my thane, is as a book, where men
May read strange matters. To beguile the
        time,[55]
Look like the time; bear welcome in your eye,
70 Your hand, your tongue; look like th' inno-
        cent flower,
But be the serpent under't. He that's coming
Must be provided for; and you shall put
This night's great business into my dispatch,[56]
Which shall to all our nights and days to come
75 Give solely sovereign sway and masterdom.

MACBETH.   We will speak further.

LADY MACBETH.   Only look up clear:[57]
To alter favor ever is to fear.
Leave all the rest to me.   *Exeunt.*

SCENE vi: in front of MACBETH'S castle

Hoboys and torches. Enter KING DUNCAN,
MALCOLM, DONALBAIN, BANQUO, LENNOX,
MACDUFF, ROSSE, ANGUS, *and* ATTENDANTS.

DUNCAN.   This castle hath a pleasant seat,[58]
        the air
Nimbly and sweetly recommends itself
Unto our gentle senses.

BANQUO.   This guest of summer,
The temple-haunting marlet,[59] does
        approve,

5 By his lov'd mansionry,[60] that the heaven's
        breath
Smells wooingly here; no jutty, frieze,
Buttress, nor coign of vantage,[61] but this bird
Hath made his pendant bed and procreant
        cradle.
Where they most breed and haunt, I have
        observ'd
The air is delicate.

Enter LADY MACBETH.

10 **DUNCAN.**   See, see, our honor'd hostess!
The love that follows us sometime is our
        trouble,
Which still we thank as love. Herein I teach
        you
How you shall bid God 'ield us for your pains,
And thank us for your trouble.[62]

LADY MACBETH.   All our service
15 In every point twice done, and then done
        double,
Were poor and single[63] business to contend
Against those honors deep and broad where-
        with
Your Majesty loads our house. For those of
        old,
And the late dignities heap'd up to them,
20 We rest your ermites.[64]

DUNCAN.   Where's the Thane of Cawdor?
We cours'd him at the heels, and had a pur-
        pose
To be his <u>purveyor</u>; but he rides well,

---

55. **beguile the time.** Deceive everybody
56. **dispatch.** Management
57. **look up clear.** Seem innocent
58. **seat.** Location
59. **temple-haunting marlet.** A bird that nests around churches
60. **mansionry.** Nest
61. **no jutty . . . vantage.** No projecting structure or convenient
corner

62. **The love . . . trouble.** Although my visit is an inconvenience to
you, you should ask God to reward me for your pains because I came
out of love for you.
63. **single.** Feeble
64. **We . . . ermites.** We shall be your hermits (that is, we shall
always pray for you).

WORDS FOR EVERYDAY USE: pur • vey • or (pər vā ôr´) *n.,* one who supplies or provides

Students can study
Macbeth's soliloquy in
scene vii, lines 1–28, by
outlining its structure. One possible outline is as follows:

Macbeth's Consideration of the Pros and Cons of Acting Immediately to Kill Duncan

I. Pro: Necessity for Quick Action ("'Twere well/It were done quickly")

II. Con: Assassination Will Have Consequences
Others may try to assassinate Macbeth ("We but teach/Bloody instructions")

III. Con: Morality Argues against Assassination
A. Macbeth is Duncan's "kinsman and his subject"
B. Macbeth is Duncan's host

IV. Con: Duncan Is a Good King
A. Duncan's virtues will only point up the heinousness of his murder
B. Pity for Duncan will provoke outrage against the assassin

V. Con: Duncan Has Not Offended Macbeth
("I have no spur . . . but only/Vaulting ambition")

Point out to students that when the speech is outlined, it becomes clear why Macbeth shortly afterward (line 31) says to Lady Macbeth, "We will proceed no further in this business." He sees more reasons not to commit the deed than to go ahead with it.

▶See the Language Arts Survey, 4.3, "Strategies for Decision Making."

And his great love, sharp as his spur, hath
holp[65] him
To his home before us. Fair and noble hostess,
15 We are your guest tonight.

25 **LADY MACBETH.**   Your servants ever
Have theirs, themselves, and what is theirs, in
compt,[66]
To make their audit at your Highness'
pleasure,
Still[67] to return your own.

DUNCAN.   Give me your hand.
Conduct me to mine host, we love him
highly,
30 And shall continue our graces towards him.
By your leave, hostess.   *Exeunt.*

SCENE vii: a room in MACBETH's castle

Hoboys, torches. Enter a SEWER[68] *and divers*
SERVANTS *with dishes and service over the stage.*
Then enter MACBETH.

MACBETH.   If it were done, when 'tis done,
then 'twere well
It were done quickly. If th' assassination
Could trammel up the consequence, and
catch
With his surcease, success;[69] that but this
blow
5   Might be the be-all and the end-all—here,
But here, upon this bank and shoal of time,
We'ld jump the life to come. But in these cases
We still have judgment here, that we but
teach
Bloody instructions, which, being taught,
return
10 To plague th' inventor. This even-handed justice
Commends[70] th' ingredience of our poison'd
chalice
To our own lips. He's here in double trust:

First, as I am his kinsman and his subject,
Strong both against the deed; then, as his host,
15 Who should against his murtherer shut the
door,
Not bear the knife myself. Besides, this
Duncan
Hath borne his faculties[71] so meek, hath been
So clear[72] in his great office, that his virtues
Will plead like angels, trumpet-tongu'd,
against
20 The deep damnation of his taking-off;
And pity, like a naked new-born babe,
Striding the blast, or heaven's cherubin,
hors'd
Upon the sightless couriers[73] of the air,
Shall blow the horrid deed in every eye,
25 That tears shall drown the wind. I have no
spur
To prick the sides of my intent, but only
Vaulting ambition, which o'erleaps itself,
And falls on th' other—

Enter LADY MACBETH.

How now? what news?

LADY MACBETH.   He has almost supp'd.
Why have you left the chamber?

30 **MACBETH.**   Hath he ask'd for me?

LADY MACBETH.   Know you not he has?

MACBETH.   We will proceed no further in
this business:
He hath honor'd me of late, and I have
bought[74]
Golden opinions from all sorts of people,
Which would be worn now in their newest
gloss,
Not cast aside so soon.

35 **LADY MACBETH.**   Was the hope drunk
Wherein you dress'd yourself? Hath it slept
since?

---

65. **holp.** Helped
66. **compt.** Trust
67. **Still.** Always
68. **Sewer.** Butler
69. **If . . . success.** If the assassination could be successful and without consequence

70. **Commends.** Offers
71. **faculties.** Royal powers
72. **clear.** Blameless
73. **sightless couriers.** Invisible messengers, the wind
74. **bought.** Earned

Shakespeare's verse is often surprisingly ambiguous, leaving room for interpretation by actors and directors. An example is Lady Macbeth's retort to Macbeth's question, "If we should fail?" According to the *Folio* text, she responds, "We fail?" But in Shakespeare's day, both the exclamation point and the question mark were represented by the same mark. Thus an actor could interpret the line in any of several ways: as a contemptuous repetition of Macbeth's question ("We, two brilliant plotters, fail?" or "We fail? I won't fail, in any case"), or as a scornful dismissal of the consequences ("So we fail! So what?"). Students can try out the two lines of dialogue to explore the various possibilities.

And wakes it now to look so green and pale
At what it did so freely? From this time
Such I account thy love. Art thou afeard
40 To be the same in thine own act and valor
As thou art in desire? Wouldst thou have that
Which thou esteem'st the ornament of life,[75]
And live a coward in thine own esteem,
Letting "I dare not" wait upon, "I would,"
Like the poor cat i' th' adage?[76]

45 MACBETH.   Prithee peace!
I dare do all that may become a man;
Who dares do more is none.

LADY MACBETH.   What beast was't then
That made you break[77] this enterprise to me?
When you durst do it, then you were a man;
50 And to be more than what you were, you
          would
Be so much more the man. Nor time, nor
          place,
Did then adhere,[78] and yet you would make
          both:
They have made themselves, and that their
          fitness now
Does unmake you. I have given suck, and
          know
55 How tender 'tis to love the babe that milks
          me;
I would, while it was smiling in my face,
Have pluck'd my nipple from his boneless
          gums,
And dash'd the brains out, had I so sworn as
          you
Have done to this.

MACBETH.   If we should fail?

---

75. **ornament of life.** The crown
76. **cat . . . adage.** An adage about a cat who wants to eat fish without getting its paws wet
77. **break.** Broach
78. **Did then adhere.** Were then suitable
79. **But.** Only
80. **the sticking place.** The notch that holds the string of a crossbow

LADY MACBETH.   We fail?
60 But[79] screw your courage to the sticking
          place,[80]
And we'll not fail. When Duncan is asleep
(Whereto the rather shall his day's hard jour-
          ney
Soundly invite him), his two chamberlains
Will I with wine and wassail[81] so convince,
65 That memory, the warder of the brain,
Shall be a fume, and the receipt of reason
A limbeck[82] only. When in swinish sleep
Their drenched natures lies as in a death,
What cannot you and I perform upon
70 Th' unguarded Duncan? what not put upon
His spungy[83] officers, who shall bear the guilt
Of our great quell?[84]

MACBETH.   Bring forth men-children only!
For thy undaunted mettle should compose
Nothing but males. Will it not be receiv'd,
When we have mark'd with blood those
          sleepy two
76 Of his own chamber, and us'd their very dag-
          gers,
That they have done't?

LADY MACBETH.   Who dares receive it
          other,
As we shall make our griefs and clamor roar
Upon his death?

MACBETH.   I am settled, and bend up
80 Each corporal agent to this terrible feat.
Away, and mock the time[85] with fairest show:
False face must hide what the false heart doth
          know.

                              Exeunt.

---

81. **wassail.** Carousing
82. **That . . . limbeck.** The fumes of wine would rise from the stomach and confuse the brain.
83. **spungy.** Spongy with drink, drunk
84. **quell.** Murder
85. **mock the time.** Deceive the world

ANALYTIC SCALES FOR
RESPONDING IN WRITING

Assign a score from 1 to 25 for
each grading criterion below. (For
more detailed evaluation, see the
evaluation forms for writing,
revising, and proofreading,
Assessment Portfolio, 7. 1–7.10.)

1. Prediction
• **Content/Unity.** The prediction
presents a sensible, plausible continuation of events in act I.
• **Organization/Coherence.** The
prediction is clearly organized,
presenting events in logical order.
• **Language/Style.** The prediction uses vivid and precise nouns,
verbs, and modifiers.
• **Conventions.** The prediction
avoids errors in spelling, grammar,
usage, mechanics, and manuscript
form.

2. Rebuttal
• **Content/Unity.** The rebuttal
presents a sensible response to
each of Lady Macbeth's points and
expresses Macbeth's misgivings.
• **Organization/Coherence.** The
rebuttal is clearly organized, presenting a refutation of the charge
of unmanliness.
• **Language/Style.** The rebuttal
uses vivid and precise nouns,
verbs, and modifiers.
• **Conventions.** The rebuttal
avoids errors in spelling, grammar,
usage, mechanics, and manuscript
form.

WORDS FOR
EVERYDAY USE: met • tle (met'l) *n.,* spirit, courage

THE TRAGEDY OF MACBETH / ACT I, SCENE vii   **333**

📖   **VOCABULARY IN CONTEXT**
• The long-distance runner won in part because of her superior strength but mostly because of her superior mettle.

RESPONDING TO THE SELECTION

Remind students that putting themselves in Macbeth's situation does not mean that they will respond as he does. (Point out that Banquo, who also sees and hears the witches, responds very differently from Macbeth.) In their letters, students may describe the same events as Macbeth but judge them in some other way.

ANSWERS FOR REVIEWING THE SELECTION

RECALLING

1. The witches say the battle will be lost and won. They state that fair is foul, and foul is fair.

2. Macbeth calls the battle "foul" and "fair." This echoes the witches' statement in scene i, line 11.

3. They predict that Macbeth will be Thane of Cawdor and king. They predict Banquo will be the father of kings. The first prediction comes true almost immediately.

4. She doubts Macbeth's ability to do what is necessary to become king. She decides to encourage him to pursue the crown.

INTERPRETING

Responses will vary. Possible responses are given.

5. The witches speak ambiguously and confusingly. As Banquo suggests, they are evil forces who have motives of their own.

6. He describes the day of the battle. He echoes the witches' line in Scene i and suggests that those things we judge fair may in fact be foul—that we have no moral guideposts in the world. It hints that Macbeth may be associated with the "foul" powers represented by the witches.

7. Their reactions differ in that Banquo is less interested, Macbeth more eager to know what the witches know. The differences reveal that Macbeth is more ambitious and more willing to act immorally.

8. They disagree about the proposed assassination. Macbeth is reluctant to kill Duncan, and Lady Macbeth wants him to do so.

(cont.)

Responding to the Selection

What if you were in Macbeth's situation? How would you feel about the witches and their prophesies? Imagine that you, not Macbeth, were to write the letter that Lady Macbeth reads at the beginning of Scene iii. What would your letter say?

Reviewing the Selection

RECALLING

1. In the middle of Scene i, what words do the witches use to describe the outcome of the battle? What contradictory statement is made by the witches at the end of the scene?

2. How does Macbeth describe the day of the battle in his first statement in the play (Scene iii, line 38)? What earlier line from the play is echoed by Macbeth in this statement?

3. What predictions do the witches make when talking to Macbeth and Banquo in Scene iii? Which of these predictions comes true almost immediately?

4. How does Lady Macbeth react to her husband's letter? What does she make up her mind to do?

INTERPRETING

5. What reasons does the audience have to distrust what is said by the witches? Why might Macbeth be in trouble if he listens to them?

6. What is Macbeth describing in his opening line (Scene iii, line 38)? Why is this line ominous? What does it foreshadow, or hint, about Macbeth's future associations?

7. How do Macbeth and Banquo differ in their reactions to the witches' prophecies? What do these differences reveal about the two characters?

8. Why do Macbeth and Lady Macbeth argue in Scene vii? How do they differ in their feelings about the planned assassination of Duncan?

SYNTHESIZING

9. What examples can you find in Act I of ambiguities? What ambiguities are expressed by the witches? What ambiguous feelings does Macbeth have? What ambiguous way of acting does he commit himself to in the last line of the act?

10. What reasons does Macbeth have for *not* killing Duncan? What character traits in Macbeth will lead him to commit to the act anyway?

ANSWERS FOR REVIEWING THE SELECTION (CONT.)

SYNTHESIZING

Responses will vary. Possible responses are given.

9. Examples are given in the answers to questions 1 and 2. See also scene iii, lines 130–131: "This supernatural soliciting/Cannot be ill; cannot be good." The witches tell Macbeth he will be king, but tell Banquo that his sons will be king. Macbeth honors Duncan for various reasons, yet determines to kill him. In the last line of the play, Macbeth commits himself to wearing a false face to hide a false heart.

10. Macbeth is Duncan's kinsman, subject, and host. He knows Duncan trusts him; he has recently been rewarded by Duncan for his loyalty and courage. Macbeth himself considers the possibility that he need do nothing further to make the prophecy come true (scene iii, lines 143–144). Macbeth is driven to kill Duncan by his ambition, his impatience, and his inability to endure his wife's contempt.

Understanding Literature (Questions for Discussion)

1. **Aside.** An **aside** is a statement made by a character in a play, intended to be heard by the audience but not by other characters on the stage. The term may also be used to describe a statement made privately by one character to another so that other characters on the stage cannot hear it. In Scene iii, Macbeth and Banquo use both kinds of asides. Banquo's aside in lines 120–127 is followed by Macbeth's aside to himself, in which he considers the meaning of the witches' prophesies. Why are the asides necessary in this scene? What do they reveal?

2. **Inciting Incident.** An **inciting incident** is an event that introduces the central conflict. What internal conflict, or struggle, does Macbeth feel in this act? What event introduces this conflict?

3. **Foil.** A **foil** is a character whose attributes, or characteristics, contrast with and therefore throw into relief the attributes of another character. In act I, Banquo, King Duncan, and Lady Macbeth all serve as foils for Macbeth. How do Macbeth and Banquo differ? How do Macbeth and Duncan differ? How do Macbeth and Lady Macbeth differ?

4. **Soliloquy.** A **soliloquy** is a dramatic speech in which a character who is alone on stage voices his or her thoughts. Soliloquies give the audience a view of a character's thoughts, feelings, or motives. Scene v opens with Lady Macbeth's soliloquy. What does her soliloquy reveal about her character? What motivates her? How does Macbeth characterize her in lines 73–75 of scene vii?

Responding in Writing

1. **Prediction.** While predicting that Macbeth will be king, the three witches also predict that Banquo's sons will sit on the throne. What is your prediction for Macbeth? What actions do you think he will take? Write a prediction for the next act. Indicate what actions Macbeth and Lady Macbeth will take and what effects their actions will have on other characters.

2. **Rebuttal.** When Macbeth expresses doubts about the plan to kill Duncan, Lady Macbeth launches an emotional attack. She derides her husband's lack of ambition and questions his courageousness, claiming that he is not being manly. Macbeth does not defend himself. How would you respond to Lady Macbeth? Write a short rebuttal to her words in scene vii, lines 35–78. As you respond, consider Macbeth's misgivings as well as Lady Macbeth's arguments against them.

ANSWERS FOR UNDERSTANDING LITERATURE

► See the evaluation forms for discussion, active listening, and oral communication, *Assessment Portfolio,* 7.11–7.14.

Responses will vary. Possible responses are given.

1. Aside. The asides are necessary so that the audience can understand Banquo's thoughts (which Banquo would not express in the hearing of Rosse and Angus) and Macbeth's thoughts (which Macbeth would not express in the hearing of any of those present). The asides reveal Banquo's reservations about the value of the prophecies and Macbeth's eager reception of the possibility that he may someday be king.

► **Teaching Note:** Ask: What devices are used in other types of storytelling to show characters' thoughts?

Answers. Voice-overs (films), internal monologues (novels, short stories), and thought bubbles (comic strips).

2. Inciting Incident. Macbeth feels a struggle between his desire to honor his obligations to Duncan and his ambition to be king at all costs. Any of several incidents might be cited as the one that gives rise to this struggle: the prophecy of the witches, Macbeth's realization that the prophecy is at least partly true, or the arrival of Duncan at Macbeth's house before Macbeth can settle with himself (and with his wife) what his course of action is to be.

► **Teaching Note:** If necessary, review with students scene iii, lines 105–129.

3. Foil. Banquo is more cautious about believing the witches than Macbeth and emphasizes that they represent evil powers. Macbeth is not interested in the

(cont.)

ANSWERS FOR UNDERSTANDING LITERATURE (CONT.)

witches' morality. Duncan differs from Macbeth in being honest, open, grateful, and trusting. Lady Macbeth differs from Macbeth in being more ruthless and less susceptible to scruples.

► **Teaching Note:** Ask students to watch for other foils in the story as it unfolds. Malcolm and Macduff, for instance, prove the most powerful foils to Macbeth in the play. The doctor and nurse who watch Lady

Macbeth in her madness are, in a sense, foils to her.

4. Soliloquy. Lady Macbeth's soliloquy shows her willingness to incite her husband to violent and wrongful actions, which reveals that she values power more than morality. Macbeth characterizes her as having "undaunted mettle."

► **Teaching Note:** Check several scenes with students to be sure they know how to read stage directions to keep track of who is onstage and who is not.

ANALYTIC SCALES FOR RESPONDING IN WRITING

Grading scales appear on page 333.

ADDITIONAL RESOURCES

READER'S GUIDE
• Selection Worksheet, 5.2

ASSESSMENT PORTFOLIO
• Selection Check Test, 4.5.3
• Selection Test, 4.5.4

ENRICHMENT ACTIVITIES

Have students design a stage set for a modern production of act II. The general setting is the castle of Macbeth at Inverness, Scotland. Sets should include the courtyard of the castle and a castle gate. Students will need to do research to find out how castles of the Norman era looked. They can draw diagrams of their sets on a floor plan for a proscenium arch stage, like that shown on page 314.

SUPPORT FOR LEP STUDENTS

ADDITIONAL VOCABULARY

hold—wait
entreat—plead
sentinel—guard
prate—speak
infirm—weak
grooms—servants
appalls—shocks
lechery—prurient interest
provoke—excite
mar—mark, scar, harm
requite—repay
renown—fame
amiss—wrong
breach—tear, opening
warrant—good reason
predominance—superiority in quality or quantity
minions—servants
adieu—good-bye

Macbeth's Castle. "I have seen/Hours dreadful and things strange; but this sore night/Hath trifled former knowings."
Illustration by Sol Graphic Design

CROSS-CURRICULAR ACTIVITIES

Explain that Shakespeare counted on his audience bringing a certain common knowledge of their culture to their experience of his works. Because American culture is in part derived from English culture, some students may have much of the appropriate cultural knowledge needed to understand *Macbeth,* but not all will. As an exercise in examining cultural givens, ask students to list (or contribute to a class discussion) the features of the opening of act II that might need explaining to someone with a cultural background different from Shakespeare's. (Examples include the need to carry weapons; the relationship between host and guest; the gifts given by the king to the servants and Lady Macbeth; the relationship between king and his subjects; the functions of witches; and the notion of honor.)

ACT II

SCENE i: open court within MACBETH'S castle

Enter BANQUO, *and* FLEANCE *with a torch before him.*

BANQUO. How goes the night, boy?

FLEANCE. The moon is down; I have not heard the clock.

BANQUO. And she goes down at twelve.

FLEANCE. I take't, 'tis later, sir.

BANQUO. Hold, take my sword. There's husbandry[1] in heaven,

5 Their candles are all out. Take thee that too.
Gives him his belt and dagger.
A heavy summons[2] lies like lead upon me,
And yet I would not sleep. Merciful powers,
Restrain in me the cursed thoughts that nature
Gives way to in repose!

Enter MACBETH, *and a* SERVANT *with a torch.*

Give me my sword.

10 Who's there?

MACBETH. A friend.

BANQUO. What, sir, not yet at rest? the King's a-bed.
He hath been in unusual pleasure, and
Sent forth great largess to your offices.[3]

15 This diamond he greets your wife withal,
By the name of most kind hostess, and shut up[4]
In measureless content.

MACBETH. Being unprepar'd,
Our will became the servant to defect,
Which else should free have wrought.[5]

BANQUO. All's well.

20 I dreamt last night of the three weïrd sisters:
To you they have show'd some truth.

MACBETH. I think not of them.
Yet when we can entreat an hour to serve,
We would spend it in some words upon that business,
If you would grant the time.

BANQUO. At your kind'st leisure.

25 **MACBETH.** If you shall cleave to my consent, when 'tis,[6]
It shall make honor for you.

BANQUO. So I lose none
In seeking to augment it, but still keep
My bosom franchis'd[7] and allegiance clear,
I shall be counsell'd.

MACBETH. Good repose the while!

30 **BANQUO.** Thanks, sir; the like to you!
BANQUO with FLEANCE.

MACBETH. Go bid thy mistress, when my drink is ready,
She strike upon the bell. Get thee to bed.
Exit SERVANT.
Is this a dagger which I see before me,
The handle toward my hand? Come, let me clutch thee:

35 I have thee not, and yet I see thee still.
Art thou not, fatal vision, sensible[8]
To feeling as to sight? or art thou but
A dagger of the mind, a false creation,
Proceeding from the heat-oppressed brain?

40 I see thee yet, in form as palpable
As this which now I draw.
Thou marshal'st[9] me the way that I was going,

---

1. **husbandry.** Thrift
2. **summons.** Sleepiness
3. **largess . . . offices.** Gifts to your servant's quarters
4. **shut up.** Concluded
5. **Being . . . wrought.** Because we were not prepared, we were not

able to entertain as fully as we would have liked.
6. **cleave . . . 'tis.** Support my cause when the time comes
7. **franchis'd.** Free from guilt
8. **sensible.** Perceptible by the senses
9. **marshal'st.** Leads

WORDS FOR EVERYDAY USE:
aug • ment (ôg ment') *vt.*, make greater
pal • pa • ble (pal´pə bəl) *adj.*, tangible

THE TRAGEDY OF MACBETH / ACT II, SCENE i **337**

VOCABULARY IN CONTEXT

• The teacher augmented her meager income by playing saxophone in a jazz club.
• His nervousness was palpable in the form of the sweat that ran down his back.

VOCABULARY FROM THE SELECTION

augment	palpable
equivocator	scruples
multitudinous	stealthy

And such an instrument I was to use.
Mine eyes are made the fools o' th' other senses,

45 Or else worth all the rest. I see thee still;
And on thy blade and dudgeon[10] gouts of blood,
Which was not so before. There's no such thing:
It is the bloody business which informs[11]
Thus to mine eyes. Now o'er the one half world

50 Nature seems dead, and wicked dreams abuse[12]
The curtain'd sleep; witchcraft celebrates
Pale Hecate's off'rings;[13] and wither'd Murther,
Alarum'd by his sentinel, the wolf,
Whose howl's his watch, thus with his <u>stealthy</u> pace,

55 With Tarquin's[14] ravishing strides, towards his design
Moves like a ghost. Thou sure and firm-set earth,
Hear not my steps, which way they walk, for fear
The very stones prate of my whereabout,
And take the present horror from the time,

60 Which now suits with it. Whiles I threat, he lives:
Words to the heat of deeds too cold breath gives.

A bell rings.

I go, and it is done; the bell invites me.
Hear it not, Duncan, for it is a knell,
That summons thee to heaven or to hell.

Exit.

---

10. **dudgeon.** Handle of a dagger
11. **informs.** Takes shape
12. **abuse.** Deceive
13. **Hecate's off'rings.** Offerings to Hecate, goddess of witchcraft
14. **Tarquin.** Roman tyrant

SCENE ii: open court within MACBETH'S castle

Enter LADY MACBETH.

LADY MACBETH. That which hath made them drunk hath made me bold;
What hath quench'd them hath given me fire. Hark! Peace!
It was the owl that shriek'd, the fatal bellman,
Which gives the stern'st good-night.[15] He is about it:

5 The doors are open; and the surfeited grooms[16]
Do mock their charge with snores. I have drugg'd their possets,[17]
That death and nature do contend about them,
Whether they live or die.

MACBETH. [*Within.*] Who's there? What ho?

LADY MACBETH. Alack, I am afraid they have awak'd,

10 And 'tis not done; th' attempt, and not the deed,
Confounds[18] us. Hark! I laid their daggers ready,
He could not miss 'em. Had he not resembled
My father as he slept, I had done't.

Enter MACBETH.

My husband!

MACBETH. I have done the deed. Didst thou not hear a noise?

15 **LADY MACBETH.** I heard the owl scream and the crickets cry.

---

15. **owl . . . good-night.** The owl's cry was a sign of death, as was the midnight ringing of the bell outside of a prisoner's cell.
16. **surfeited grooms.** Overfed servants
17. **possets.** Bedtime drinks of wine and hot milk
18. **Confounds.** Ruins

WORDS FOR EVERYDAY USE: stealth • y (stel´thē) *adj.,* furtive, sly

VOCABULARY IN CONTEXT

• The pickpocket was caught when a police officer noticed the <u>stealthy</u> motion of his hand toward a tourist's wallet.

Did not you speak?

MACBETH.　　　　When?

LADY MACBETH.　　　　Now.

MACBETH.　　　　As I descended?

LADY MACBETH.　Aye.

MACBETH.　Hark! Who lies i' th' second
　　chamber?

LADY MACBETH.　Donalbain.

MACBETH.　　　　This is a sorry sight.
　　　　Looking on his hands.

LADY MACBETH.　A foolish thought, to say
　　a sorry sight.

20　**MACBETH.**　There's one did laugh in 's
　　sleep, and one cried, "Murther!"
　　That they did wake each other. I stood and
　　　　heard them;
　　But they did say their prayers, and address'd
　　　　them
　　Again to sleep.

LADY MACBETH.　There are two[19] lodg'd
　　together.

MACBETH.　One cried, "God bless us!" and
　　"Amen!" the other,
25　As they had seen me with these hangman's
　　hands.
　　List'ning their fear, I could not say "Amen,"
　　When they did say "God bless us!"

LADY MACBETH.　Consider it not so deeply.

MACBETH.　But wherefore could not I pro-
　　nounce "Amen"?
　　I had most need of blessing, and "Amen"
　　Stuck in my throat.

30　**LADY MACBETH.**　These deeds must not be
　　thought
　　After these ways; so, it will make us mad.

---

19. **two.** The two are the grooms described in act I, scene vii, line 75.
20. **knits . . . sleave.** Straightens the tangled threads
21. **nature's second course.** Nature has two courses: food and sleep.
22. **unbend.** Relax

MACBETH.　Methought I heard a voice cry,
　　"Sleep no more!
　　Macbeth does murther sleep"—the innocent
　　sleep,
35　Sleep that knits up the ravell'd sleave[20] of care,
　　The death of each day's life, sore labor's bath,
　　Balm of hurt minds, great nature's second
　　　　course,[21]
　　Chief nourisher in life's feast.

LADY MACBETH.　　　　What do you mean?

MACBETH.　Still it cried, "Sleep no more!"
　　to all the house;
　　"Glamis hath murther'd sleep, and therefore
　　　　Cawdor
40　Shall sleep no more—Macbeth shall sleep no
　　more."

LADY MACBETH.　Who was it that thus
　　cried? Why, worthy thane,
　　You do unbend[22] your noble strength, to think
　　So brain-sickly of things. Go get some water,
　　And wash this filthy witness[23] from your hand.
45　Why did you bring these daggers from the
　　place?
　　They must lie there. Go carry them, and
　　smear
　　The sleepy grooms with blood.

MACBETH.　　　　　　　I'll go no more.
　　I am afraid to think what I have done;
　　Look on 't again I dare not.

LADY MACBETH.　　　　Infirm of purpose!
50　Give me the daggers. The sleeping and the
　　dead
　　Are but as pictures; 'tis the eye of childhood
　　That fears a painted devil. If he do bleed,
　　I'll gild[24] the faces of the grooms withal,
　　For it must seem their guilt.
　　　　　　　　Exit. Knock within.

---

23. **witness.** Evidence
24. **gild.** Blood was often referred to as golden.

CROSS-CURRICULAR ACTIVITIES

Mathematics and Sciences. In act II, scene ii, lines 14–49, Shakespeare varies the lengths of the alternating speeches made by Macbeth and Lady Macbeth. At first, equally shocked and frightened, they both speak in short speeches. Then, as Macbeth begins to add horrific details in his description of what occurred, his speeches grow longer and longer. Lady Macbeth interjects only a line or two between his speeches, trying to stop him or reassure him. ("A foolish thought, to say a sorry sight. . . . Consider it not so deeply. . . . These deeds must not be thought/After these ways; so, it will make us mad.") When his tale of horror reaches a crescendo in the account of the phantom voice that cried "Sleep no more!" Lady Macbeth can only gasp feebly "What do you mean?" She then rises to the occasion, however, regaining control of herself and the situation in a lengthier speech. Have students use graphing skills to chart the length of the alternating speeches in this passage (according to number of words). The graph will clearly show the dramatic dynamics of this passage.

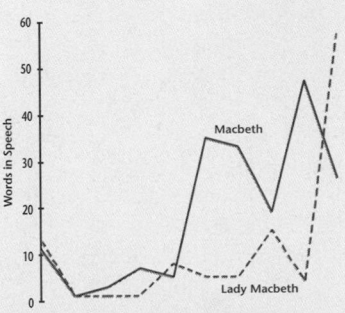

Speech Length in *Macbeth*, act II, scene ii, lines 14–49

LITERARY TECHNIQUE

Wordplay. Scholars have counted at least a hundred puns in *Macbeth*. To encourage students to keep their eyes open for puns, write lines 52–54 on the board and ask students to try to find the pun in Lady Macbeth's words ("If he do bleed,/I'll gild the faces of the grooms withal,/For it must seem their guilt [gilt]"). Lady Macbeth suggests that guilt is something that can be painted on (like gilt, a thin layer of gold) as easily as it can be washed off ("A little water clears us of this deed," line 64). Students may also have missed the pun in line 60 of act I, scene vii: "But screw your courage to the sticking place"—the sticking place suggesting not only its literal meaning, the trigger notch on a crossbow, but the place where Macbeth will stick the knife: Duncan's heart.

MACBETH.   Whence is that knocking?
55 How is't with me, when every noise appalls
       me?
    What hands are here? Hah! they pluck out
       mine eyes.
    Will all great Neptune's ocean wash this blood
    Clean from my hand? No; this my hand will
       rather
    The multitudinous seas incarnadine,²⁵
60 Making the green one red.

       Enter LADY MACBETH.

    LADY MACBETH.   My hands are of your
       color; but I shame
    To wear a heart so white. (*Knock.*) I hear a
       knocking
    At the south entry. Retire we to our chamber.
    A little water clears us of this deed;
65 How easy is it then! Your constancy
    Hath left you unattended.²⁶ (*Knock.*) Hark,
       more knocking.
    Get on your night-gown, lest occasion call us
    And show us to be watchers.²⁷ Be not lost
    So poorly in your thoughts.

70 **MACBETH.**   To know my deed, 'twere best
       not know myself.   *Knock.*
    Wake Duncan with thy knocking! I would
       thou couldst!   *Exeunt.*

SCENE iii: open court within MACBETH's castle

Enter a PORTER. *Knocking within.*

PORTER.   Here's a knocking indeed! If a
man were porter of Hell Gate, he should have
old turning the key. (*Knock.*) Knock, knock,
knock! Who's there, i' th' name of Belzebub?²⁸
5 Here's a farmer, that hang'd himself on th'
expectation of plenty.²⁹ Come in time! Have
napkins enow about you, here you'll sweat
for't. (*Knock.*) Knock, knock! Who's there, in
th' other devil's name? Faith, here's an equivo-
10 cator, that could swear in both the scales
against either scale, who committed treason
enough for God's sake, yet could not equivocate to heaven. O, come in, equivocator.
(*Knock.*) Knock, knock knock! Who's there?
15 Faith, here's an English tailor come hither for
stealing out of a French hose.³⁰ Come in, tailor, here you may roast your goose.³¹ (*Knock.*)
Knock, knock! Never at quiet! What are you?
But this place is too cold for hell. I'll
20 devil-porter it no further. I had thought to
have let in some of all professions that go the
primrose way to th' everlasting bonfire.
(*Knock.*) Anon, anon! [*Opens the gate.*] I pray
you remember the porter.

Enter MACDUFF *and* LENNOX.

25 **MACDUFF.**   Was it so late, friend, ere you
       went to bed,
    That you do lie so late?

    PORTER.   Faith, sir, we were carousing till
       the second cock;³²
    and drink, sir, is a great provoker of three
       things.

    MACDUFF.   What three things does drink
       especially provoke?

30 **PORTER.**   Marry, sir, nose-painting, sleep,
    and urine. Lechery, sir, it provokes, and

---

25. **incarnadine.** To turn red
26. **constancy . . . unattended.** Firmness of purpose has abandoned you.
27. **watchers.** People who stay up late
28. **Belzebub.** Chief devil
29. **farmer . . . plenty.** The farmer who hoarded grain hoping to make a profit and foresaw his downfall when an abundance of crops brought prices down
30. **tailor . . . hose.** The tailor stole cloth while making French hose.
31. **roast your goose.** Heat your iron
32. **second cock.** 3 A.M.

WORDS FOR EVERYDAY USE: mul • ti • tu • di • nous (mul´tə tōō d´ ′nəs) *adj.,* very numerous
e • quiv • o • ca • tor (ē kwiv´ə kā´tor) *n.,* one who speaks ambiguously

---

VOCABULARY IN CONTEXT

- After days of struggling against multitudinous troubles, her life changed dramatically for the better.
- In Shakespeare's time, an equivocator might be a religious heretic or a potential traitor who supported both sides in a political struggle.

unprovokes: it provokes the desire, but it takes away the performance. Therefore much drink may be said to be an equivocator with

35 lechery: it makes him, and it mars him; it sets him on, and it takes him off; it persuades him, and disheartens him; makes him stand to, and not stand to; in conclusion, equivocates him in a sleep, and giving him the lie, leaves him.

40 **MACDUFF.** I believe drink gave thee the lie[33] last night.

PORTER. That it did, sir, i' the very throat on me; but I requited him for his lie, and (I think) being too strong for him, though he took up my legs sometime, yet I made a shift

45 to cast[34] him.

MACDUFF. Is thy master stirring?

Enter MACBETH.

Our knocking has awak'd him; here he comes.

LENNOX. Good morrow, noble sir.

MACBETH.   Good morrow, both.

MACDUFF. Is the King stirring, worthy thane?

MACBETH.   Not yet.

50 **MACDUFF.** He did command me to call timely on him,
I have almost slipp'd the hour.

MACBETH.   I'll bring you to him.

MACDUFF. I know this is a joyful trouble to you;
But yet 'tis one.

MACBETH. The labor we delight in physics pain.[35]

55 This is the door.

MACDUFF.   I'll make so bold to call,
For 'tis my limited service.

                    Exit MACDUFF.

LENNOX. Goes the King hence to-day?

MACBETH.   He does; he did appoint so.

LENNOX. The night has been unruly. Where we lay,
Our chimneys were blown down, and (as they say)

60 Lamentings heard i' th' air; strange screams of death,
And prophesying, with accents terrible,
Of dire combustion[36] and confus'd events
New hatch'd to th' woeful time. The obscure bird
Clamor'd the livelong night. Some say, the earth

65 Was feverous, and did shake.

MACBETH.   'Twas a rough night.

LENNOX. My young remembrance cannot parallel
A fellow to it.

Enter MACDUFF.

MACDUFF. O horror, horror, horror! Tongue nor heart
Cannot conceive nor name thee!

MACBETH AND LENNOX.   What's the matter?

70 **MACDUFF.** Confusion now hath made his masterpiece!
Most sacrilegious murther hath broke ope
The Lord's anointed temple,[37] and stole thence
The life o' th' building!

MACBETH.   What is't you say—the life?

LENNOX. Mean you his Majesty?

75 **MACDUFF.** Approach the chamber, and destroy your sight
With a new Gorgon.[38] Do not bid me speak;
See, and then speak yourselves.

                    Exeunt MACBETH *and* LENNOX.
                    Awake, awake!

---

33. **gave thee the lie.** Knocked you out
34. **cast.** Vomit
35. **The labor . . . pain.** The work we enjoy cures the pain of labor.
36. **combustion.** Confusion

37. **Lord's anointed temple.** The body of the king
38. **Gorgon.** A mythological monster who turned to stone all who looked at it

THE TRAGEDY OF MACBETH / ACT II, SCENE iii **341**

LITERARY TECHNIQUE

Paraphrase. A paraphrase is a restatement of a piece of writing in another form or in different words. To examine the richness and humor of the porter's speech, students can paraphrase the porter's soliloquy (lines 1–24) in Modern American English or in slang. You may wish to give as an example a paraphrase that explains the porter's comments in lines 41–45. The porter picks up on a pun of Macduff's and fires off several puns, all comparing his drinking bout metaphorically to a wrestling match. "Drink had me pinned down and had me by the throat; but I got him back for knocking me down; and (I think) I was too strong for him, though he knocked me off my legs sometimes; all the same I made a change of position that enabled him to throw him off [or throw him up]."

ADDITIONAL QUESTIONS AND ACTIVITIES

Teachers might be interested in reading to students or in duplicating for silent reading Thomas DeQuincey's famous short essay on "The Knocking at the Gate," which describes the profound effect on the audience that this scene evokes. It comes from DeQuincey's *Miscellaneous Essays,* 1851, and appears in many collections of famous essays.

Ring the alarum-bell! Murther and treason!
Banquo and Donalbain! Malcolm, awake!
80 Shake off this downy sleep, death's counterfeit,
And look on death itself! Up, up, and see
The great doom's image![39] Malcolm! Banquo!
As from your graves rise up, and walk like sprites,
To countenance this horror! Ring the bell.
                                        Bell rings.

Enter LADY MACBETH.

85 **LADY MACBETH.**   What's the business,
That such a hideous trumpet calls to parley
The sleepers of the house? Speak, speak!

MACDUFF.   O gentle lady,
'Tis not for you to hear what I can speak:
The repetition in a woman's ear
90 Would murther as it fell.

Enter BANQUO.

                        O Banquo, Banquo,
Our royal master's murther'd!

LADY MACBETH.   Woe, alas!
What, in our house?

BANQUO.   Too cruel any where.
Dear Duff, I prithee contradict thyself,
And say, it is not so.

Enter MACBETH, LENNOX, ROSSE.

95 **MACBETH.**   Had I but died an hour before this chance,
I had liv'd a blessed time; for from this instant
There's nothing serious in mortality:[40]
All is but toys:[41] renown and grace is dead,
The wine of life is drawn, and the mere lees[42]
100 Is left this vault to brag of.

Enter MALCOLM *and* DONALBAIN.

DONALBAIN.   What is amiss?

MACBETH.   You are, and do not know't.

The spring, the head, the fountain of your blood
Is stopp'd, the very source of it is stopp'd.

MACDUFF.   Your royal father's murther'd.

MALCOLM.   O, by whom?

105 **LENNOX.**   Those of his chamber, as it seem'd, had done't.
Their hands and faces were all badg'd[43] with blood;
So were their daggers, which unwip'd we found
Upon their pillows. They star'd and were distracted;
No man's life was to be trusted with them.

110 **MACBETH.**   O, yet I do repent me of my fury,
That I did kill them.

MACDUFF.   Wherefore did you so?

MACBETH.   Who can be wise, amaz'd, temp'rate, and furious,
Loyal, and neutral, in a moment? No man.
Th' expedition[44] of my violent love
115 Outrun the pauser, reason. Here lay Duncan,
His silver skin lac'd with his golden blood,
And his gash'd stabs look'd like a breach in nature
For ruin's wasteful entrance; there, the murtherers,
Steep'd in the colors of their trade, their daggers
120 Unmannerly breech'd with gore.[45] Who could refrain,
That had a heart to love, and in that heart
Courage to make 's love known?

LADY MACBETH.   Help me hence, ho!

MACDUFF.   Look to the lady.

MALCOLM.   [*Aside to* DONALBAIN.]
Why do we hold our tongues,
That most may claim this argument for ours?

---

39. **great doom's image.** Likeness of Doomsday
40. **serious in mortality.** Worthwhile in human life
41. **toys.** Trifles
42. **lees.** Dregs
43. **badg'd.** Marked

44. **expedition.** Haste
45. **breech'd with gore.** Covered with blood

125 **DONALBAIN.** [*Aside to* MALCOLM.] What
    should be spoken here, where our fate,
    Hid in an auger-hole,[46] may rush and seize us?
    Let's away,
    Our tears are not yet brew'd.

MALCOLM. [*Aside to* DONALBAIN.]
    Nor our strong sorrow
    Upon the foot of motion.

BANQUO. Look to the lady.
    LADY MACBETH *is carried out.*

130 And when we have our naked frailties hid,[47]
    That suffer in exposure, let us meet
    And question this most bloody piece of work,
    To know it further. Fears and <u>scruples</u> shake
    us.
    In the great hand of God I stand, and thence
135 Against the undivulg'd pretense[48] I fight
    Of treasonous malice.

MACDUFF. And so do I.

ALL. So all.

MACBETH. Let's briefly put on manly readi-
    ness,
    And meet i' th' hall together.

ALL. Well contented.
    Exeunt all but MALCOLM *and* DONALBAIN.

MALCOLM. What will you do? Let's not
    consort with them;
140 To show an unfelt sorrow is an office
    Which the false man does easy. I'll to England.

DONALBAIN. To Ireland, I; our separated
    fortune
    Shall keep us both the safer. Where we are,

There's daggers in men's smiles; the near in
    blood,
145 The nearer bloody.[49]

MALCOLM. This murtherous shaft
    that's shot
    Hath not yet lighted,[50] and our safest way
    Is to avoid the aim. Therefore to horse,
    And let us not be dainty of leave-taking,
    But shift away. There's warrant in that theft
150 Which steals itself,[51] when there's no mercy
    left.
    Exeunt.

SCENE iv: outside MACBETH'S castle

Enter ROSSE *with an* OLD MAN.

OLD MAN. Threescore and ten I can
    remember well,
    Within the volume of which time I have seen
    Hours dreadful and things strange; but this
    sore[52] night
    Hath trifled former knowings.

ROSSE. Ha, good father,
5 Thou seest the heavens, as troubled with
    man's act,
    Threatens his bloody stage. By th' clock 'tis
    day,
    And yet dark night strangles the travelling
    lamp.[53]
    Is't night's predominance, or the day's shame,
    That darkness does the face of earth entomb,
    When living light should kiss it?

10 **OLD MAN.** 'Tis unnatural,
    Even like the deed that's done. On Tuesday
    last,

---

46. **auger-hole.** A small hole, an unlikely hiding place
47. **naked frailties hid.** Gotten dressed
48. **undivulg'd pretense.** Secret purpose
49. **the near . . . bloody.** The closer we are related to Duncan, the greater the danger of being murdered ourselves.

50. **lighted.** Hit its mark
51. **steals itself.** Sneaks away
52. **sore.** Dreadful
53. **travelling lamp.** The sun

WORDS FOR
EVERYDAY USE:
scru • ples (skrōo pəlz) *n.,* doubts, qualms

VOCABULARY IN CONTEXT

• Although the smuggler did not hesitate to break the law, he had <u>scruples</u> about cheating his friends.

LITERARY TECHNIQUE

Juxtaposition. Explain to students that juxtaposition is the device of creating irony or some other effect by the significant proximity of ideas, images, or actions. In act I, scene iv, lines 11–14, Duncan remarks of the previous Thane of Cawdor that "There's no art/To find the mind's construction in the face:/He was a gentleman on whom I built/An absolute trust." Immediately thereafter the new Thane of Cawdor, Macbeth, enters the scene—similarly trusted and similarly untrustworthy. Likewise, in act I, scene vii, lines 25–28, Macbeth says he has "no spur" for his intention to assassinate Duncan but ambition, whereupon Lady Macbeth enters to spur him on. In act II, scene iv, lines 28–30, Rosse exclaims: "Thriftless ambition, that will ravin up/Thine own live's means! Then 'tis most like/The sovereignty will fall upon Macbeth." The juxtaposition of ravining ambition and the sovereignty falling on Macbeth creates a sharp irony of which Rosse is perhaps unaware. Students can improve their ability to recognize irony by writing five pairs of sentences with juxtapositions like the example in this scene. Their examples may draw on characters or situations in the play.

RESPONDING TO THE SELECTION

Encourage students to develop their lists before planning their writing. Their lists should guide them in composing the account of the murder. Point out that the supernatural occurrences and gory details in this act are just the kind of items exploited by sensationalist reporting.

A falcon, tow'ring in her pride of place,
Was by a mousing owl hawk'd at, and kill'd.

ROSSE.   And Duncan's horses (a thing most strange and certain),
15   Beauteous and swift, the minions of their race,
Turn'd wild in nature, broke their stalls, flung out,
Contending 'gainst obedience, as they would make
War with mankind.

OLD MAN.   'Tis said, they eat each other.

ROSSE.   They did so—to th' amazement of mine eyes
That look'd upon't.

Enter MACDUFF.

20   Here comes the good Macduff.
How goes the world, sir, now?

MACDUFF.   Why, see you not?

ROSSE.   Is't known who did this more than bloody deed?

MACDUFF.   Those that Macbeth hath slain.

ROSSE.   Alas the day,
What good could they pretend?

MACDUFF.   They were suborned.[54]
25   Malcolm and Donalbain, the King's two sons,

---
54. **suborned.** Bribed
55. **ravin up.** Eat ravenously
56. **Scone.** Where Scottish kings were crowned
57. **Colmekill.** Where Scottish kings were buried

Are stol'n away and fled, which puts upon them
Suspicion of the deed.

ROSSE.   'Gainst nature still!
Thriftless ambition, that will ravin up[55]
Thine own live's means! Then 'tis most like
30   The sovereignty will fall upon Macbeth.

MACDUFF.   He is already nam'd, and gone to Scone[56]
To be invested.

ROSSE.   Where is Duncan's body?

MACDUFF.   Carried to Colmekill,[57]
The sacred store-house of his predecessors
And guardian of their bones.

35   **ROSSE.**   Will you to Scone?

MACDUFF.   No, cousin, I'll to Fife.[58]

ROSSE.   Well, I will thither.

MACDUFF.   Well, may you see things well done there: adieu,
Lest our old robes sit easier than our new!

ROSSE.   Farewell, father.

40   **OLD MAN.**   God's benison[59] go with you, and with those
That would make good of bad, and friends of foes!

Exeunt omnes.

---
58. **Fife.** Macduff's castle
59. **benison.** Blessing

Responding to the Selection

In this act Shakespeare shows himself to be a master at creating a horrific atmosphere. Go back through the act and make a list of details that contribute to its frightening mood. Use these details to write a brief account of the murder as it might be described on a sensationalist television program about unsolved mysteries.

Reviewing the Selection

RECALLING

1. What does Macbeth imagine that he sees in scene i? To what does he attribute this illusion?

2. In scene ii, what is Lady Macbeth's response to Macbeth's worrying about being unable to say "Amen"?

3. In scene ii, Macbeth reports hearing a voice cry out. What does he think he hears the voice say about sleep?

4. In scene iii, Lennox reports strange disturbances in nature on the night of Duncan's murder. In scene iv, Rosse and the Old Man likewise speak of disturbances. What are these disturbances?

5. Why do Malcolm and Donalbain leave the country after the murder?

INTERPRETING

▶ 6. What is Macbeth's state of mind immediately before the murder? How do you know?

▶ 7. Why does Lady Macbeth counsel her husband not to think too deeply about "these deeds" that they have done?

▶ 8. What do you think might be the consequences for Macbeth of having committed this murder?

▶ 9. In what sense is Macbeth's deed "unnatural"? What are the consequences for the normal, natural order of things of Macbeth's murdering the rightful king?

▶▶10. What suspicion does Macduff report regarding the king's sons?

SYNTHESIZING

11. In scene i, lines 49–60, Macbeth describes the night in horrific terms. What other descriptions and scenes in this act add to the horrific atmosphere surrounding the murder?

12. At the end of the act, Rosse says of Malcolm and Donalbain that "thriftless ambition" will devour greedily their "own live's means." How does Macbeth feel about his life after the murder (see scene iii, lines 91–97)? In what way are Rosse's lines true of Macbeth?

THE TRAGEDY OF MACBETH / ACT II **345**

ANSWERS FOR REVIEWING THE SELECTION (CONT.)

SYNTHESIZING

Responses will vary. Possible responses are given.

11. Other horrific details include Macbeth's hallucination of the dagger; the scream of an owl and the crying of crickets; the prayers said in vain by the two sleepers; the voice Macbeth thought he heard crying in the night; the talk of blood; the ringing of a bell; and Rosse and the Old Man's reports that the day is as dark as night, that a falcon was recently killed by an owl, and that Duncan's horses broke from their stalls and ate each other.

12. Macbeth wishes his life could have ended before the murder. Rosse's lines, though aimed at Malcolm and Donalbain, could be applied to Macbeth if one considers how Macbeth's ambition has only served to destroy the natural order of king and subject that previously gave Macbeth stability and peace of mind.

ANSWERS FOR REVIEWING THE SELECTION

RECALLING

1. Macbeth believes he sees a dagger. He attributes this illusion to a "heat-oppressed brain" and to the "bloody business" at hand.

2. She says, "Consider it not so deeply"—in other words, don't think about it.

3. Macbeth believes he hears the voice say that Macbeth has murdered sleep, and that Macbeth will never sleep again.

4. They report that the day is as dark as night; that a falcon was recently killed by an owl; and that Duncan's horses turned wild, broke from their stalls, and ate each other.

5. Malcolm and Donalbain are afraid that they too may be killed.

INTERPRETING

Responses will vary. Possible responses are given.

6. Macbeth is confused, upset, and obsessed with the horror of what he plans; this is clear to the audience from the hallucination he has and from his long soliloquy on the horrors of the night.

7. She is afraid, thinking that their deeds will make them mad.

8. Macbeth, though he may become king, will also be affected by his consciousness of having done wrong. He will either have to go mad or harden himself about his crime.

9. Macbeth's deed is unnatural because subjects are supposed to honor their kings, not kill them, and because Duncan is Macbeth's kinsman and guest. The consequence of the murder is to upset the natural order and to make someone king who should not be.

10. Macduff reports the suspicion that Malcolm and Donalbain bribed the servants of the king to kill their master.

(cont.)

TEACHER'S EDITION **345**

► See the evaluation forms for discussion, active listening, and oral communication, *Assessment Portfolio*, 7.11–7.14.

Responses will vary. Possible responses are given.

1. Symbol. The blood symbolizes Macbeth's guilt for the crime he has committed.

►**Teaching Note:** Students may have any of several ways of formulating an answer to this question. They may think that the blood symbolizes Macbeth's crime itself, guilt, his awareness that he has acted against the natural order, the irrevocability of his action, or even sin. Point out that symbols are elastic; they are not one-to-one equations that need to be rigidly interpreted. Indeed, restricting a symbol to one meaning unnecessarily restricts the power and range of Shakespeare's poetic imagery, which is all the richer for being inexact.

2. Hyperbole. The exaggeration lies in the notion that the small quantity of blood on Macbeth's hand could actually stain the sea, a huge volume of water, red. The effect of the hyperbole is to suggest the extent of Macbeth's horror at and remorse for what he has done.

►**Teaching Notes**

• Point out that hyperbole must be used carefully. It occurs frequently in poor writing, where it serves as a ready substitute for craft and skill.

• Discuss with students the difference between hyperbole and understatement.

3. Verbal Irony. To the other characters present in the scene, Macbeth's words suggest that he so grieved at what has happened that he would have preferred to die rather than to have seen such a terrible event. To Macbeth, his words may mean that he seriously regrets having taken the action he took and fears that life will become meaningless for him. The irony derives from the contrast between its apparent meaning to the characters who hear it and its

(cont.)

Understanding Literature (Questions for Discussion)

1. **Symbol.** A **symbol** is a thing that stands for or represents both itself and something else. Before murdering Duncan, Macbeth imagines he sees a bloody dagger. After the murder, he laments that he will never be able to cleanse the blood from his hands. What does the blood symbolize?

2. **Hyperbole.** A **hyperbole** is an exaggeration made for rhetorical effect. After Macbeth murders Duncan, he laments, "Will all great Neptune's ocean wash this blood/Clean from my hand? No; this my hand will rather/The multitudinous seas incarnadine,/Making the green one red" (scene ii, lines 57–60). What exaggeration is being made? What effect does this hyperbole have?

3. **Verbal Irony.** **Verbal irony** is a statement that implies its opposite. When Duncan's murder is discovered, Macbeth says to Banquo and Macduff, "Had I but died before this chance,/I had liv'd a blessed time; for from this instant/There's nothing serious in mortality" (scene iii, lines 95–97). What do Macbeth's words mean to his compatriots? What meaning do they have for Macbeth? What is ironic about the statement?

Responding in Writing

1. **Expository Paragraph: Comparison and Contrast.** Macbeth and Lady Macbeth are both involved in Duncan's murder. However, each reacts differently. Write a paragraph in which you compare and contrast Macbeth's role in the murder with that of Lady Macbeth. Consider how each character acts and what each says, both in private and in public. For more information on comparison and contrast, read the Language Arts Survey, 4.8, "Comparing and Contrasting."

2. **Headlines.** Macbeth's betrayal of Duncan is not so far removed from current events. Newspapers tell of political assassinations and military coups. What headlines might the events at Macbeth's castle have generated? Write headlines to summarize the crucial events in act II. When writing your headlines, aim for active, descriptive phrases that immediately convey the events.

actual meaning to Macbeth. They take it as a despairing expression of his love for the king, as he intends they should; but for him it also expresses his new despair and disgust with his own life.

►**Teaching Notes**

• Students can devise their own examples of verbal irony based on *Macbeth*. They can use the following form: "If ___ had said ___, his/her words would have

been ironic because . . ."

• A related feature of plays, dramatic irony, was first described as an important element of tragedy by the Greek philosopher Aristotle (384–322 BC) thousands of years ago. More complex than a statement that implies its opposite, dramatic irony occurs when characters interact without important knowledge that the audience possesses.

The Ghost of Banquo. ("The time has been,/That when the brains were out, the man would die,/And there an end; but now they rise again/With twenty mortal murthers on their crowns")

ANALYTIC SCALES FOR RESPONDING IN WRITING

Assign a score from 1 to 25 for each grading criterion below. (For more detailed evaluation, see the evaluation forms for writing, revising, and proofreading, *Assessment Portfolio,* 7.1–7.10.)

1. Expository Paragraph

• **Content/Unity.** The expository paragraph presents a sensible comparison and contrast between the reactions of Macbeth and Lady Macbeth.

• **Organization/Coherence.** The expository paragraph is clearly organized, presenting the reaction of each character coherently.

• **Language/Style.** The expository paragraph uses vivid and precise nouns, verbs, and modifiers.

• **Conventions.** The expository paragraph avoids errors in spelling, grammar, usage, mechanics, and manuscript form.

2. Headlines

• **Content/Unity.** The headlines present a plausible summary of the crucial events in act II.

• **Organization/Coherence.** The headlines are clearly organized, presenting events in logical or chronological order.

• **Language/Style.** The headlines use vivid and precise nouns, verbs, and modifiers.

• **Conventions.** The headlines avoid errors in spelling, grammar, usage, mechanics, and manuscript form.

ENRICHMENT ACTIVITIES

One reason that *Macbeth* has delighted audiences for centuries is that the play is a superb example of the horror story. Among the most horrific of the many horrors in the play is the appearance at the banquet, in act III, of the ghost of Banquo. Prepare students for reading act III by having them share some of their favorite horror stories, especially ones involving ghosts.

Give students time to remember their stories and to jot down basic outlines of them before they tell the stories in class. You may wish to combine this activity with a lesson on the art of storytelling. Refer students to the information on verbal and nonverbal elements of speech in the Language Arts Survey, 3.2 and 3.3.

SUPPORT FOR LEP STUDENTS

ADDITIONAL VOCABULARY

oracles—predictors of the future
indissoluble—unbreakable
parricide—killing one's parent
chide—scold
rancor—spite, malice
execution—completion
buffet—blow, shock, bump
incensed—angered
sundry—various
abide—stay
assailable—vulnerable
apace—quickly
vouch—promise
infirmity—weakness
mockery—mimicry; cruel joking
spurn—reject
right—truly
valiant—brave
delinquent—one who neglects or flaunts duty or the law
exasperate—frustrate

ADDITIONAL QUESTIONS AND ACTIVITIES

After students have read through act III and know the fate of Banquo and the crisis Macbeth faces at the feast, reread with them the opening of the act (lines 11–39). Ask them to find examples of hypocrisy and irony.

Answer. Examples of hypocrisy are Macbeth's insistence that Banquo is his chief guest (line 11) and Lady Macbeth's comment that Banquo's absence would make a gap in the feast (lines 11–13). Examples of irony are the fact that Banquo will not leave a gap in the feast (there is no place for him; he takes Macbeth's seat) and the exchange between Macbeth and Banquo at line 28, "Fail not our feast."—"My lord, I will not," which proves to be fully correct: Banquo does not fail the feast, even after death.

ACT III

SCENE i: a room in the palace at Forres

Enter BANQUO.

BANQUO.   Thou hast it now: King, Cawdor, Glamis, all,
As the weïrd women promis'd, and I fear
Thou play'dst most foully for't; yet it was said
It should not stand in thy <u>posterity</u>,
5 But that myself should be the root and father
Of many kings. If there come truth from them—
As upon thee, Macbeth, their speeches shine[1]—
Why, by the <u>verities</u> on thee made good,
May they not be my oracles as well,
10 And set me up in hope? But hush, no more.

Sennet sounded. Enter MACBETH *as King,* LADY MACBETH *as Queen,* LENNOX, ROSSE, LORDS, *and* ATTENDANTS.

MACBETH.   Here's our chief guest.

LADY MACBETH.   If he had been forgotten,
It had been as a gap in our great feast,
And all-thing unbecoming.

MACBETH.   To-night we hold a solemn supper, sir,
And I'll request your presence.

15 **BANQUO.**   Let your Highness
Command upon me, to the which my duties
Are with a most indissoluble tie
For ever knit.

MACBETH.   Ride you this afternoon?

BANQUO.   Aye, my good lord.

20 **MACBETH.**   We should have else desir'd your good advice

---

1. **shine.** Are fulfilled
2. **grave and prosperous.** Serious and profitable
3. **Go . . . night.** If my horse doesn't go faster, I will have to ride on at night.

(Which still hath been both grave and prosperous)[2]
In this day's council; but we'll take tomorrow.
Is't far you ride?

BANQUO.   As far, my lord, as will fill up the time
25 'Twixt this and supper. Go not my horse the better,
I must become a borrower of the night[3]
For a dark hour or twain.

MACBETH.   Fail not our feast.

BANQUO.   My lord, I will not.

MACBETH.   We hear our bloody cousins are bestow'd[4]
30 In England and in Ireland, not confessing
Their cruel parricide, filling their hearers
With strange invention. But of that tomorrow,
When therewithal we shall have cause of state
Craving us jointly.[5] Hie you to horse; adieu,
35 Till you return at night. Goes Fleance with you?

BANQUO.   Aye, my good lord. Our time does call upon 's.[6]

MACBETH.   I wish your horses swift and sure of foot;
And so I do commend you to their backs.
Farewell.
                                Exit BANQUO.
40 Let every man be master of his time
Till seven at night. To make society
The sweeter welcome, we will keep ourself
Till supper-time alone; while[7] then, God be with you!

---

4. **are bestow'd.** Living
5. **Craving us jointly.** Requiring attention from both of us
6. **Our . . . upon 's.** Our business is urgent.
7. **while.** Until

WORDS FOR EVERYDAY USE:

pos • ter • i • ty (päs ter´ə tē) *n.,* succeeding generations
ver • i • ty (ver´ə tē) *n.,* truth

VOCABULARY IN CONTEXT

• The old general wrote his memoirs in the belief that <u>posterity</u> would thank him for his efforts.
• That mothers love their children is an eternal <u>verity</u>.
• I would say that anyone who jumped a motorcycle over the Grand Canyon was either a fool or utterly <u>dauntless</u>, or perhaps both.

Exeunt LORDS *with* LADY MACBETH *and others.*
Manent MACBETH *and a* SERVANT.

Sirrah, a word with you. Attend those men
45 Our pleasure?

SERVANT.   They are, my lord, without the
palace gate.

MACBETH.   Bring them before us.
                                         Exit SERVANT.
                              To be thus[8] is nothing,
But to be safely thus. Our fears in Banquo
Stick deep, and in his royalty of nature[9]
50 Reigns that which would be fear'd. 'Tis much
he dares,
And to that <u>dauntless</u> temper of his mind,
He hath a wisdom that doth guide his valor
To act in safety. There is none but he
Whose being I do fear; and under him
55 My Genius is rebuk'd, as it is said
Mark Antony's was by Caesar. He chid the
sisters
When first they put the name of king upon
me,
And bade them speak to him; then prophet-like
They hail'd him father to a line of kings.
60 Upon my head they plac'd a fruitless crown,
And put a barren sceptre in my gripe,[10]
Thence to be wrench'd with an unlineal hand,
No son of mine succeeding. If't be so,
For Banquo's issue have I fil'd[11] my mind,
65 For them the gracious Duncan have I mur-
ther'd,
Put rancors in the vessel of my peace
Only for them, and mine eternal jewel[12]
Given to the common enemy of man,

To make them kings—the seeds of Banquo
kings!
70 Rather than so, come fate into the list,[13]
And champion me to th' utterance![14] Who's
there?

Enter SERVANT *and two* MURDERERS.

Now go to the door, and stay there till we call.
                                         Exit SERVANT.
Was it not yesterday we spoke together?

MURDERERS. It was, so please your
Highness.

MACBETH.   Well then, now
75 Have you consider'd of my speeches?—know
That it was he in the times past which held
you
So under fortune, which you thought had been
Our innocent self? This I made good[15] to you
In our last conference, pass'd in probation[16]
with you:
80 How you were borne in hand, how cross'd,
the instruments,
Who wrought with them, and all things else
that might
To half a soul and to a notion craz'd[17]
Say, "Thus did Banquo."

1. MURDERER.   You made it known to us.

MACBETH.   I did so; and went further,
which is now
85 Our point of second meeting. Do you find
Your patience so predominant in your nature
That you can let this go? Are you so
gospell'd,[18]

---

8. **thus.** *i.e.,* King
9. **royalty of nature.** Natural kingliness
10. **gripe.** Grip
11. **fil'd.** Defiled
12. **eternal jewel.** Immortal soul
13. **list.** Arena for combat

14. **champion . . . utterance.** A fight to the death
15. **made good.** Demonstrated
16. **pass'd in probation.** Reviewed and proved
17. **half . . . craz'd.** A half wit and crazed mind
18. **so gospell'd.** Such good followers of the Gospel

WORDS FOR
EVERYDAY USE: **daunt • less** (dônt´ləs) *adj.,* fearless

CROSS-CURRICULAR ACTIVITIES

Arts and Humanities.
The brooding soliloquy in
lines 47–71 of scene i
("To be thus is nothing
. . .") is one of the most
powerful in the play.
Students can capture its poetic
force by reciting it in unison, either
as a class or in small groups.
Students who have choral experience can be asked if they wish to
volunteer to lead the groups.

ADDITIONAL QUESTIONS
AND ACTIVITIES

Have students compare lines
63–71 of scene i with the soliloquy
from *Hamlet,* act 3, scene i, on
page 396. Ask these questions:
1. What common fear torments
both Hamlet and Macbeth?
2. How do the conclusions of the
two soliloquies differ?
Answers. 1. They are both worried
about what will happen to their
souls after death. Macbeth feels
that his soul will be "Given to the
common enemy of man" (the
devil); although he seems to have
accepted this, he does not want it
to happen on behalf of Banquo's
posterity. 2. Hamlet comes to no
decision; Macbeth concludes that
he will proceed headlong on the
same course.

VOCABULARY FROM
THE SELECTION

dauntless	nonpareil
jocund	posterity
malevolence	verity

To pray for this good man, and for his issue,
Whose heavy hand hath bow'd you to the grave,
And beggar'd yours for ever?

90   **1. MURDERER.**   We are men, my liege.

  MACBETH.   Aye, in the catalogue ye go for men,
As hounds and greyhounds, mungrels, spaniels, curs,
Shoughs, water-rugs, and demi-wolves[19] are clipt[20]
All by the name of dogs; the valued file[21]
95   Distinguishes the swift, the slow, the subtle,
The house-keeper, the hunter, every one,
According to the gift which bounteous nature
Hath in him clos'd; whereby he does receive
Particular addition, from the bill
100   That writes them all alike: and so of men.
Now, if you have a station in the file,
Not i' th' worst rank of manhood, say't,
And I will put that business in your bosoms,
Whose execution takes your enemy off,
105   Grapples you to the heart and love of us,
Who wear our health but sickly in his life,
Which in his death were perfect.

  2. MURDERER.   I am one, my liege,
Whom the vile blows and buffets of the world
Hath so incens'd that I am reckless what
I do to spite the world.

110   **1. MURDERER.**   And I another,
So weary with disasters, tugg'd with fortune,
That I would set my life on any chance,
To mend it, or be rid on't.

  MACBETH.   Both of you
Know Banquo was your enemy.

  MURDERERS.   True, my lord.

115   **MACBETH.**   So is he mine; and in such bloody distance,[22]

---

19. **Shoughs . . . demi-wolves.** Types of dogs
20. **clipt.** Called
21. **valued file.** List of the values of each
22. **distance.** Hostilities
23. **near'st of life.** Life itself
24. **avouch.** Justify

That every minute of his being thrusts
Against my near'st of life;[23] and though I could
With barefac'd power sweep him from my sight,
And bid my will avouch[24] it, yet I must not,
120   For certain friends that are both his and mine,
Whose loves I may not drop, but wail his fall[25]
Who I myself struck down. And thence it is
That I to your assistance do make love,
Masking the business from the common eye
For sundry weighty reasons.

125   **2. MURDERER.**   We shall, my lord,
Perform what you command us.

  1. MURDERER.   Though our lives—

  MACBETH.   Your spirits shine through you.
Within this hour, at most,
I will advise you where to plant yourselves,
Acquaint you with the perfect spy o' th' time,[26]
130   The moment on't, for't must be done tonight,
And something[27] from the palace; always thought
That I require a clearness: and with him—
To leave no rubs[28] nor botches in the work—
Fleance his son, that keeps him company,
135   Whose absence is no less material to me
Than is his father's, must embrace the fate
Of that dark hour. Resolve yourselves apart,[29]
I'll come to you anon.

  MURDERERS.   We are resolv'd, my lord.

  MACBETH.   I'll call upon you straight; abide within.

                   Exeunt MURDERERS.

140   It is concluded: Banquo, thy soul's flight,
If it find heaven, must find it out tonight.

                          Exit.

---

25. **wail his fall.** Must seem to be lamenting his death
26. **perfect . . . time.** Precise moment
27. **something.** Some distance
28. **rubs.** Imperfections
29. **Resolve yourselves apart.** Go and make up your minds.

SCENE ii: another room in the palace

Enter MACBETH'S LADY *and a* SERVANT.

LADY MACBETH. Is Banquo gone from court?

SERVANT. Aye, madam, but returns again tonight.

LADY MACBETH. Say to the King, I would attend his leisure
For a few words.

SERVANT. Madam, I will. *Exit.*

LADY MACBETH. Nought's had, all's spent,
5 Where our desire is got without content;
'Tis safer to be that which we destroy
Than by destruction dwell in doubtful joy.

Enter MACBETH.

How now, my lord, why do you keep alone,
Of sorriest fancies your companions making,
10 Using those thoughts which should indeed have died
With them they think on? Things without all remedy
Should be without regard: what's done, is done.

MACBETH. We have scorch'd[30] the snake, not kill'd it;
She'll close[31] and be herself, whilest our poor malice
15 Remains in danger of her former tooth.[32]
But let the frame of things disjoint, both the worlds suffer,[33]
Ere we will eat our meal in fear, and sleep
In the affliction of these terrible dreams
That shake us nightly. Better be with the dead,
20 Whom we, to gain our peace, have sent to peace,
Than on the torture of the mind to lie
In restless ecstasy.[34] Duncan is in his grave;
After life's fitful fever he sleeps well.
Treason has done his worst; nor steel, nor poison,
25 Malice domestic, foreign levy, nothing,
Can touch him further.

LADY MACBETH. Come on;
Gentle my lord, sleek o'er your rugged looks,
Be bright and jovial among your guests tonight.

MACBETH. So shall I, love, and so, I pray, be you.
30 Let your remembrance apply to Banquo,
Present him eminence both with eye and tongue:
Unsafe the while, that we
Must lave our honors in these flattering streams,[35]
And make our faces vizards[36] to our hearts,
Disguising what they are.

35 **LADY MACBETH.** You must leave this.

MACBETH. O, full of scorpions is my mind, dear wife!
Thou know'st that Banquo and his Fleance lives.

LADY MACBETH. But in them nature's copy's not eterne.[37]

MACBETH. There's comfort yet, they are assailable.
40 Then be thou <u>jocund</u>; ere the bat hath flown
His cloister'd flight, ere to black Hecate's summons

---

30. **scorch'd.** Lightly wounded
31. **close.** Heal
32. **our . . . tooth.** Despite our hatred our danger is the same as before.
33. **both . . . suffer.** Heaven and earth fall apart

34. **restless ecstasy.** Agitated frenzy
35. **Unsafe . . . streams.** We are unsafe, so we must wash our honors in streams of flattery.
36. **vizards.** Masks
37. **in . . . eterne.** They are not eternal.

WORDS FOR EVERYDAY USE: joc • und (jäk´ənd) *adj.,* cheerful, merry

ADDITIONAL QUESTIONS AND ACTIVITIES

Ask students to try to imagine a "valued file" or list of humans with rankings given according to value. Is it possible to imagine such a file? If so, what criteria would be used to rank human value? Would these criteria be financial, political, social, artistic, religious, or something else? As a writing exercise, have students prepare such a list with an accompanying short essay explaining how they made decisions about the relative value of various humans. If students feel that judging one human being as more valuable than another is repugnant, they should write a short essay explaining why. All students should write a concluding paragraph in which they consider the question, How would Macbeth respond to my essay?

ADDITIONAL QUESTIONS AND ACTIVITIES

In scene ii, lines 18–19, Macbeth refers to "these terrible dreams/ That shake us nightly"; in lines 21–22 he speaks of lying by nights "on the torture of the mind . . . /In restless ecstasy." Students can write a dream report of one of the dreams endured by Macbeth or Lady Macbeth.

VOCABULARY IN CONTEXT

• Santa Claus is known to be a <u>jocund</u> and merry old man.

• To spark discussion about scene iii, ask the following questions: Who is the third murderer? Why does he mysteriously appear at the beginning of scene iii, though he has never been referred to before? Is it possible that the third murderer is Macbeth? In scene i, lines 127–138, Macbeth tells the murderers he will meet them to tell them where to make their ambush. Could he be referring to joining them? The third murderer is best acquainted with Banquo's habits (scene iii, lines 12–14), as Macbeth would be. The third murderer also positively identifies Banquo when he enters ("'Tis he," line 14), and the third murderer is the first to observe that Fleance has fled. Though Macbeth expresses surprise and disappointment when he is told that Fleance is still alive (scene iv, lines 20–22), might those lines be insincere? If the third murderer is not Macbeth, why does Shakespeare bring him on as a stranger to the others at the beginning of the scene? Could the third murderer be a symbolic representation of Macbeth without actually being Macbeth?

• After discussing these questions, have students vote by show of hands as to whether they think the third murderer is Macbeth. Challenge adherents on both sides of the issue to justify their opinions.

• Could the third murderer be an oversight on the playwright's part? Could he be a spy sent by Macbeth because of the latter's distrust of the men he has hired?

The shard-borne beetle[38] with his drowsy hums
Hath rung night's yawning peal, there shall be done
A deed of dreadful note.

LADY MACBETH. What's to be done?

45 **MACBETH.** Be innocent of the knowledge, dearest chuck,[39]
Till thou applaud the deed. Come, seeling[40] night,
Scarf up the tender eye of pitiful day,
And with thy bloody and invisible hand
Cancel and tear to pieces that great bond[41]
50 Which keeps me pale! Light thickens, and the crow
Makes wing to th' rooky[42] wood;
Good things of day begin to droop and drowse,
Whiles night's black agents to their preys do rouse.
Thou marvel'st at my words, but hold thee still:
55 Things bad begun make strong themselves by ill.
So prithee go with me. *Exeunt.*

SCENE iii: a road leading to the palace

Enter three **MURDERERS.**

1. MURDERER. But who did bid thee join with us?

3. MURDERER. Macbeth.

2. MURDERER. He needs not our mistrust, since he delivers
Our offices,[43] and what we have to do,
To the direction just.[44]

1. MURDERER. Then stand with us.
5 The west yet glimmers with some streaks of day;
Now spurs the lated[45] traveller apace
To gain the timely inn, and near approaches

---

38. **shard-borne.** Carried on scaly wings
39. **chuck.** A term of endearment
40. **seeling.** Blinding
41. **great bond.** Promise made to Banquo by the witches

The subject of our watch.

3. MURDERER. Hark, I hear horses.

BANQUO. (*Within.*) Give us a light there, ho!

2. MURDERER. Then 'tis he; the rest
10 That are within the note of expectation
Already are i' th' court.

1. MURDERER. His horses go about.

3. MURDERER. Almost a mile; but he does usually,
So all men do, from hence to th' palace gate
Make it their walk.

Enter BANQUO, *and* FLEANCE *with a torch.*

2. MURDERER. A light, a light!

3. MURDERER. 'Tis he.

15 **1. MURDERER.** Stand to't.

BANQUO. It will be rain tonight.

1. MURDERER. Let it come down.
They attack BANQUO.

BANQUO. O, treachery! Fly, good Fleance, fly, fly, fly!
Thou mayst revenge. O slave!
BANQUO *dies.* FLEANCE *escapes.*

3. MURDERER. Who did strike out the light?

1. MURDERER. Was't not the way?

3. MURDERER. There's but one down; the son is fled.

20 **2. MURDERER.** We have lost
Best half of our affair.

1. MURDERER. Well, let's away, and say how much is done. *Exeunt.*

SCENE iv: a banquet room in the palace

Banquet prepar'd. Enter MACBETH, LADY MACBETH, ROSSE, LENNOX, LORDS, *and* ATTENDANTS.

---

42. **rooky.** Gloomy
43. **offices.** Duties
44. **To . . . just.** Exactly as Macbeth ordered
45. **lated.** Belated

MACBETH. You know your own degrees,[46] sit down. At first
And last, the hearty welcome.

LORDS.   Thanks to your Majesty.

MACBETH. Ourself will mingle with society,
And play the humble host.
5 Our hostess keeps her state,[47] but in best time
We will require her welcome.

LADY MACBETH. Pronounce it for me, sir, to all our friends,
For my heart speaks they are welcome.

Enter FIRST MURDERER to the door.

MACBETH. See, they encounter thee with their hearts' thanks.
10 Both sides are even; here I'll sit i' th' midst.
Be large in mirth;[48] anon we'll drink a measure[49]
The table round.—   *Goes to the door.*
There's blood upon thy face.

MURDERER.   'Tis Banquo's then.

MACBETH. 'Tis better thee without than he within.
Is he dispatch'd?

15 MURDERER.   My lord, his throat is cut;
That I did for him.

MACBETH.   Thou art the best o' th' cut-throats,
Yet he's good that did the like for Fleance.
If thou didst it, thou art the <u>nonpareil</u>.

MURDERER. Most royal sir, Fleance is scap'd.

20 MACBETH. Then comes my fit again. I had else been perfect,

Whole as the marble, founded as the rock,
As broad and general[50] as the casing[51] air;
But now I am cabin'd, cribb'd, confin'd, bound in
To saucy doubts and fears. But Banquo's safe?[52]

25 MURDERER. Aye, my good lord; safe in a ditch he bides,
With twenty trenched gashes on his head,
The least a death to nature.

MACBETH.   Thanks for that:
There the grown serpent lies; the worm[53] that's fled
Hath nature that in time will venom breed,
30 No teeth for th' present. Get thee gone; tomorrow
We'll hear ourselves[54] again.

                     Exit MURDERER.

LADY MACBETH.   My royal lord,
You do not give the cheer. The feast is sold
That is not often vouch'd, while 'tis a-making,
'Tis given with welcome.[55] To feed were best at home;
35 From thence, the sauce to meat is ceremony,
Meeting were bare without it.

Enter the GHOST OF BANQUO and sits in MACBETH's place.

MACBETH.   Sweet remembrancer!
Now good digestion wait on appetite,
And health on both!

LENNOX.   May't please your Highness sit.

MACBETH. Here had we now our country's honor roof'd,[56]

---

46. **degrees.** Order of seating based on rank
47. **state.** Seat
48. **large in mirth.** Very merry
49. **measure.** Large glass
50. **broad and general.** Free and unrestrained
51. **casing.** Surrounding

52. **safe.** No longer a threat
53. **worm.** The little serpent, Fleance
54. **hear ourselves.** Talk to each other
55. **The feast . . . welcome.** Unless the guests feel welcome, a feast is no better than a dinner one buys.
56. **roof'd.** Under one roof

WORDS FOR EVERYDAY USE:
non • pa • reil (nän´pə rel´) *n.*, someone unequaled

THE TRAGEDY OF MACBETH / ACT III, SCENE iv **353**

ADDITIONAL QUESTIONS AND ACTIVITIES

- One of the major motifs of *Macbeth* is hypocrisy—feigning to be what one is not. Sometimes this motif is described as the difference between being and seeming. Ask students to recall instances of hypocrisy in the play (act I, scene vii, lines 81–82; act III, scene ii, lines 27–34). Point out the extreme hypocrisy of Lady Macbeth and Macbeth at the beginning of act iii, scene iv as they act the genial hosts while being fully conscious that a murder is being committed on their behalf. Macbeth actually interrupts his participation in the feast to speak with the murderer, who comes to the door with Banquo's blood on his face. Ask students to describe their reactions to Macbeth's hypocrisy.

- Students can imagine that they are reporters on a television journalism program with only one chance to ask a question to expose Macbeth's hypocrisy. What would that question be?

- Point out to students that one of the reasons the feast scene is so powerful is that it plays upon fears everyone has of disgracing oneself publicly. However, the embarrassment and awkwardness consequent upon Macbeth's behavior is satisfying to the audience because Macbeth deserves to suffer for his crimes. Students can imagine that they are Macbeth and write an apology to the Scottish lords present at the feast. Students should explain away the words Macbeth used and his apparent anger, confusion, and fear.

VOCABULARY IN CONTEXT

- The widower would not marry again because his wife of sixty years had been a <u>nonpareil</u>, and he could find no other like her.

**ADDITIONAL QUESTIONS
AND ACTIVITIES**

Ask students the following questions:

1. Was the ghost really in the banquet hall, or was it just a figment of Macbeth's imagination?

2. Why was Macbeth the only one who saw the ghost?

3. What hallucination previously seen by Macbeth did Lady Macbeth refer to in her attempt to persuade him to stifle his fears?

4. The witches, like the ghost of Banquo, are also a vital supernatural element of the play. Is it likely that Shakespeare, who was not familiar with the concept of the subconscious mind, nevertheless intended the witches and the ghost as expressions of Macbeth's subconscious fears and motivations?

5. How else might Shakespeare have represented the subconscious if he did not resort to depicting supernatural beings like witches and ghosts?

Answers. 1. *Responses will vary.* Macbeth, in line 141, refers to the ghost as self-deception ("self-abuse"). 2. Responses may state that Macbeth was the only one who saw it because the ghost chose to appear only to him or because the ghost was only a figment of Macbeth's imagination. 3. Lady Macbeth refers to the "air-drawn dagger" seen by Macbeth before he murdered Duncan (act II, scene i, lines 33–49). 4. *Responses will vary.* 5. Shakespeare might have used other characters as representatives of the subconscious mind of the main character.

---

40 Were the grac'd person of our Banquo present,
Who may I rather challenge for unkindness
Than pity for mischance.[57]

ROSSE. His absence, sir,
Lays blame upon his promise. Please't your
Highness
To grace us with your royal company?

45 **MACBETH.** The table's full.

LENNOX. Here is a place reserv'd, sir.

MACBETH. Where?

LENNOX. Here, my good lord. What is't
that moves your Highness?

MACBETH. Which of you have done this?

LORDS. What, my good lord?

MACBETH. Thou canst not say I did it,
never shake

50 Thy gory locks at me.

ROSSE. Gentlemen, rise, his Highness is not
well.

LADY MACBETH. Sit, worthy friends; my
lord is often thus,
And hath been from his youth. Pray you keep
seat.
The fit is momentary, upon a thought[58]

55 He will again be well. If much you note him,
You shall offend him and extend his passion.
Feed, and regard him not.—Are you a man?

MACBETH. Aye, and a bold one, that dare
look on that
Which might appall the devil.

LADY MACBETH. O proper stuff!

60 This is the very painting of your fear;
This is the air-drawn dagger which you said
Led you to Duncan. O, these flaws[59] and starts
(Impostors to true fear) would well become
A woman's story at a winter's fire,

---

57. **Who . . . mischance.** Who I hope is absent due to discourtesy
and not due to an accident
58. **upon a thought.** Momentarily
59. **flaws.** Emotional outbursts
60. **charnel-houses.** Storage spaces for human bones

---

65 Authoriz'd by her grandam. Shame itself,
Why do you make such faces? When all's
done,
You look but on a stool.

MACBETH. Prithee see there!
Behold! look! lo! how say you?
Why, what care I? if thou canst nod, speak
too.

70 If charnel-houses[60] and our graves must send
Those that we bury back, our monuments
Shall be the maws of kites.[61] *Exit* GHOST.

LADY MACBETH. What? quite
unmann'd in folly?

MACBETH. If I stand here, I saw him.

LADY MACBETH. Fie, for shame!

MACBETH. Blood hath been shed ere now,
i' th' olden time,

75 Ere humane statute purg'd the gentle weal;[62]
Aye, and since too, murthers have been per-
form'd
Too terrible for the ear. The time has been,
That when the brains were out, the man
would die,
And there an end; but now they rise again

80 With twenty mortal murthers on their
crowns,[63]
And push us from our stools. This is more
strange
Than such a murther is.

LADY MACBETH. My worthy lord,
Your noble friends do lack you.

MACBETH. I do forget.
Do not muse at me, my most worthy friends,

85 I have a strange infirmity, which is nothing
To those that know me. Come, love and
health to all,
Then I'll sit down. Give me some wine, fill
full.

---

61. **maws of kites.** Stomachs of birds of prey
62. **Ere . . . weal.** Before human laws cleansed and civilized the state
63. **mortal . . . crowns.** Deadly wounds to the head

LITERARY TECHNIQUE

Characterization. Remind students of the strength of Lady Macbeth earlier in the play. At times she seemed a stronger figure than Macbeth; now, however, Macbeth is beginning to harden and strengthen—"We are yet but young in deed," he says (scene iv, line 143), promising to accustom himself to crime. At this point, Lady Macbeth and he are about equal in mental stamina. Later, Lady Macbeth will break down in madness, and Macbeth will resolve to fight to the bitter end (act V, scene v, line 51). In that respect, Scene iv is the crisis for Macbeth and Lady Macbeth, the point at which he determines to press on; all she does is attempt to persuade him to rest.

Enter GHOST.

I drink to th' general joy o' th' whole table,
And to our dear friend Banquo, whom we
    miss;
90 Would he were here! to all, and him, we thirst,
And all to all.

LORDS.   Our duties, and the pledge.

MACBETH.   Avaunt, and quit my sight! let
    the earth hide thee!
Thy bones are marrowless, thy blood is cold;
Thou hast no speculation in those eyes
Which thou dost glare with!

95 LADY MACBETH.   Think of this, good peers,
But as a thing of custom. 'Tis no other;
Only it spoils the pleasure of the time.

MACBETH.   What man dare, I dare.
Approach thou like the rugged Russian bear,
100 The arm'd rhinoceros, or th' Hyrcan[64] tiger,
Take any shape but that,[65] and my firm nerves
Shall never tremble. Or be alive again,
And dare me to the desert[66] with thy sword;
If trembling I inhabit then,[67] protest me
105 The baby of a girl. Hence, horrible shadow!
Unreal mock'ry, hence!   *Exit* GHOST.
              Why, so; being gone,
I am a man again. Pray you sit still.

LADY MACBETH.   You have displac'd the
    mirth, broke the good meeting,
With most admir'd[68] disorder.

MACBETH.   Can such things be,
110 And overcome us like a summer's cloud,
Without our special wonder? You make me
    strange
Even to the disposition that I owe,[69]
When now I think you can behold such sights,
And keep the natural ruby of your cheeks,
115 When mine is blanch'd with fear.

ROSSE.   What sights, my lord?

LADY MACBETH.   I pray you speak not. He
    grows worse and worse,
Question enrages him. At once, good night.
Stand not upon the order of your going,[70]
But go at once.

LENNOX.   Good night, and better health
Attend his Majesty!

120 LADY MACBETH.   A kind good night to all!
        Exeunt LORDS *and* ATTENDANTS.

MACBETH.   It will have blood, they say;
    blood will have blood.
Stones have been known to move and trees to
    speak;
Augures and understood relations[71] have
By maggot-pies and choughs[72] and rooks
    brought forth
125 The secret'st man of blood. What is the night?

LADY MACBETH.   Almost at odds with
    morning, which is which.

MACBETH.   How say'st thou, that Macduff
    denies his person
At our great bidding?

LADY MACBETH.   Did you send to him, sir?

MACBETH.   I hear it by the way; but I will
    send.
130 There's not a one of them but in his house
I keep a servant fee'd.[73] I will tomorrow
(And betimes I will) to the weïrd sisters.
More shall they speak; for now I am bent to
    know,
By the worst means, the worst. For mine own
    good
135 All causes shall give way. I am in blood
Stepp'd in so far that, should I wade no more,
Returning were as tedious as go o'er.
Strange things I have in head, that will to hand,

---

64. **Hyrcan.** From Hyrcania, a desert near the Caspian Sea
65. **that.** The shape of Banquo
66. **Desert.** Deserted area where nobody would intervene
67. **If . . . then.** If I feel fear then
68. **admir'd.** Attention-getting
69. **owe.** Possess

70. **Stand . . . going.** Dispense with formality as you leave.
71. **Augures . . . relations.** Omens and the meanings associated with them
72. **maggot-pies and choughs.** Magpies and crows
73. **fee'd.** Paid as a spy

THE TRAGEDY OF MACBETH / ACT III, SCENE iv   **355**

ADDITIONAL QUESTIONS AND ACTIVITIES

• Remind students that an idiom is an expression with a figurative meaning. Such an expression is often absurd if taken literally. In lines 118–119, Lady Macbeth says, "Stand not upon the order of your going,/But go at once." Normally, the most important members of the nobility would depart first and the least important members would follow; they would "stand" or wait until the proper order of their ranks had been observed before they left the room. Lady Macbeth urges the nobles to disregard their customary order and leave immediately. Explain to students that this phrase of Shakespeare's has become an idiom in English. It is now possible to say to a single individual, "Stand not upon the order of your going, but go"—a use that would have been absurd in Shakespeare's time. Students may research Shakespeare in a dictionary of quotations and find at least three examples of idioms derived from Shakespeare's plays.

• After seeing the large contribution of Shakespeare to the idioms of the English language, students may appreciate the remark of an unknown wit to the effect that Shakespeare was not very original; he took most of his material out of *Bartlett's Dictionary of Quotations*.

ADDITIONAL QUESTIONS AND ACTIVITIES

Explain to students that an oracle is a person who answers a question asked by a seeker at certain holy sites (also called oracles). The answer, often cryptic in form, is usually a prediction of the future or a revelatory statement about something unknown in the present or past. The answers given by oracles are often phrased in ambiguous or equivocating language. Point out that Macbeth's remarks in lines 121–125 suggest a fear that some supernatural power will reveal his crimes. Students can write an oracular statement that reveals Macbeth's murder of Duncan and Banquo. Encourage them to make the statement mysterious and equivocating. If any students are familiar with *Œdipus Rex*, they might comment on the use of oracles in that play.

• Ask students what is striking or
unusual about Hecate's speech. If
they do not notice that it is in a
shorter line of four iambic feet, in
rhyming couplets, instead of in
blank verse, have them read it out
loud. Point out that most of the
witches' speeches are in this verse
form.

• Have students read lines 10–13,
part of Hecate's speech to the
three witches. Ask the following
questions:

1. Of what does Hecate accuse
Macbeth?

2. What other character in the
play might accuse Macbeth of this
fault (if he could)?

3. Do you agree with Hecate's
assessment of Macbeth's character?

Answers. 1. She accuses him of
ingratitude, of loving for his own
ends. 2. Duncan would accuse
Macbeth of ingratitude. 3. Responses
will vary, but the charge of ingratitude can easily be supported.

EX. What does Banquo think
Macbeth has done to become king?
**Banquo thinks that Macbeth has
"play'dst most foully for't."**

1. What does Macbeth decide to
do about his fear of Banquo?
**Macbeth decides to hire
murderers to kill Banquo and his
son Fleance.**

2. Who escapes from the
murderers?
**Fleance escapes from the
murderers.**

3. What startles Macbeth at the
banquet?
**The ghost of Banquo startles
Macbeth at the banquet.**

4. What does Macbeth say about
his bloody course?
**Macbeth says he has waded so
far in blood that to return would
be as difficult as going onward.**

5. What do the other nobles think
of Macbeth at the end of act III?
**They realize that Macbeth is a
bloody tyrant.**

Which must be acted ere they may be
    scann'd.[74]
140 **LADY MACBETH.**   You lack the season[75] of
    all natures, sleep.

MACBETH.   Come, we'll to sleep. My
    strange and self-abuse[76]
Is the initiate fear that wants hard use:
We are yet but young in deed.   *Exeunt.*

SCENE V: the heath

Thunder. Enter the three WITCHES, *meeting*
HECATE.

1. WITCH.   Why, how now, Hecate? you
    look angerly.

HECATE.   Have I not reason, beldams[77] as
    you are?
Saucy and overbold, how did you dare
To trade and traffic with Macbeth
5 In riddles and affairs of death;
And I, the mistress of your charms,
The close contriver[78] of all harms,
Was never call'd to bear my part,
Or show the glory of our art?
10 And which is worse, all you have done
Hath been but for a wayward son,
Spiteful and wrathful, who (as others do)
Loves for his own ends, not for you.
But make amends now. Get you gone,
15 And at the pit of Acheron[79]
Meet me i' th' morning; thither he
Will come to know his destiny.
Your vessels and your spells provide,
Your charms and every thing beside.
20 I am for th' air; this night I'll spend
Unto a dismal and a fatal end.
Great business must be wrought ere noon:
Upon the corner of the moon
There hangs a vap'rous drop profound,

---

74. **ere . . . scann'd.** Before they can be properly examined
75. **season.** Preservative
76. **strange and self-abuse.** Strange self-deception
77. **beldams.** Hags
78. **close contriver.** Secret inventor
79. **pit of Acheron.** Place of a passage through the earth to Hell

---

25 I'll catch it ere it come to ground;
And that, distill'd by magic sleights,
Shall raise such artificial sprites
As by the strength of their illusion
Shall draw him on to his confusion.[80]
30 He shall spurn fate, scorn death, and bear
His hopes 'bove wisdom, grace, and fear;
And you all know, security[81]
Is mortals' chiefest enemy.
       Music, and a song. Sing within: "Come
          away, come away, etc."
Hark, I am call'd; my little spirit, see,
35 Sits in a foggy cloud, and stays for me.   *Exit.*

1. WITCH.   Come, let's make haste, she'll
    soon be back again.   *Exeunt.*

SCENE vi: a place in Scotland

Enter LENNOX *and another* LORD.

LENNOX.   My former speeches have but hit
    your thoughts,
Which can interpret farther;[82] only I say
Things have been strangely borne.[83] The
    gracious Duncan
Was pitied of Macbeth; marry, he was dead.
5 And the right valiant Banquo walk'd too late,
Whom you may say (if't please you) Fleance
    kill'd,
For Fleance fled. Men must not walk too late.
Who cannot want the thought,[84] how mon-
    strous
It was for Malcolm and for Donalbain
10 To kill their gracious father? Damned fact!
How it did grieve Macbeth! Did he not
    straight
In pious rage the two delinquents tear,
That were the slaves of drink and thralls[85] of
    sleep?
Was not that nobly done? Aye, and wisely too;

---

80. **confusion.** Ruin
81. **security.** False sense of security
82. **interpret farther.** Draw more conclusions
83. **borne.** Handled
84. **Who . . . thought.** Who can help thinking
85. **thralls.** Slaves

15 For 'twould have anger'd any heart alive
To hear the men deny't. So that, I say,
He has borne all things well, and I do think
That had he Duncan's sons under his key
(As, and't please heaven, he shall not), they
      should find
20 What 'twere to kill a father; so should
      Fleance.
But peace! for from broad words,[86] and 'cause
      he fail'd
His presence at the tyrant's feast, I hear
Macduff lives in disgrace. Sir, can you tell
Where he bestows himself?

LORD.   The son of Duncan
25 (From whom this tyrant holds the due of
      birth)[87]
Lives in the English court, and is receiv'd
Of the most pious Edward[88] with such grace
That the <u>malevolence</u> of fortune nothing
Takes from his high respect. Thither Macduff
30 Is gone to pray the holy king, upon his aid[89]
To wake Northumberland and warlike
      Siward,
That by the help of these (with Him above
To ratify the work) we may again

Give to our tables meat, sleep to our nights;
35 Free from our feasts and banquets bloody
      knives;[90]
Do faithful homage and receive free honors;
All which we pine for now. And this report
Hath so exasperate the King that he
Prepares for some attempt of war.

LENNOX.   Sent he to Macduff?

40 LORD.   He did; and with an absolute "Sir,
      not I,"
The cloudy[91] messenger turns me his back,
And hums, as who should say, "You'll rue the
      time
That clogs[92] me with this answer."

LENNOX.   And that well might
Advise him to a caution, t' hold what distance
45 His wisdom can provide. Some holy angel
Fly to the court of England, and unfold
His message ere he come, that a swift bless-
      ing
May soon return to this our suffering country
Under a hand accurs'd!

LORD.   I'll send my prayers with him.

                                        Exeunt.

---

86. **Broad words.** Outspokenness
87. **Holds . . . birth.** Withholds the birthright
88. **Edward.** Edward the Confessor, considered to be a very saintly
person
89. **Upon his aid.** On Malcolm's behalf

90. **Free . . . knives.** Restore order so that violence is not a common
occurrence at banquets
91. **cloudy.** Surly, scowling
92. **clogs.** Hinders

LITERARY TECHNIQUE

Reversal. Explain to students that a reversal is a sudden change in the fortunes of a character, for good or bad. In *Macbeth,* such a reversal seems to occur during the banquet scene, when Macbeth disgraces himself in front of the assembled nobles. From this point on (beginning in scene vi), the audience hears more and more about the disaffection of the nobility. Lennox is the spokesman who explains the reversal to the audience. Ask this question: Why might Shakespeare have chosen to present the reversal in ironic terms? *Answer. Responses will vary.* Certainly the irony lends life and depth to the reversal; Lennox's commentary is not simply a flat, moralistic pronouncement that Macbeth is a wicked man who ought to die. It is sophisticated, witty, and all the more scathing for its understatement.

WORDS FOR
EVERYDAY USE: **ma • lev • o • lence** (mə lev′ə ləns) *n.,* malice, spitefulness

VOCABULARY IN CONTEXT

• The spider approached the trapped and buzzing fly with an evil attitude that seemed <u>malevolence</u> itself.

RESPONDING TO THE SELECTION

Suggest that when writing the letter, students can take the opportunity to give their opinions of events in Scotland, much as Lennox does at the end of act III. Students may also wish to link the apparent madness of Macbeth to the signs of disturbance in the natural world described in act II.

ANSWERS FOR REVIEWING THE SELECTION

RECALLING

1. Banquo is wondering whether the fulfillment of those prophecies foretold for Macbeth indicates that the prophecy foretold for him will also come true.

2. Banquo is killed; Fleance escapes.

3. To the guests Macbeth seems to be acting irrationally; he actually reacts with appropriate horror to the sight of the ghost of Banquo. Lady Macbeth excuses her husband by pretending that he is experiencing a type of fit common to him from his childhood.

4. He says he has waded into blood so deep that going back would be as tedious, or difficult, as going on through it. This statement suggests that Macbeth will continue to kill those in his way.

INTERPRETING

Responses will vary. Possible responses are given.

5. Macbeth arranges for the murder of Banquo in the hope that Macbeth's own posterity will continue on the throne rather than Banquo's.

6. Macbeth regrets that Fleance was not killed but consoles himself with the fact that Fleance is still young and incapable of harming him.

7. If the ghost is real, it might be supposed unnatural for the spirit to walk on earth rather than go wherever else it should; if the ghost is imagined by Macbeth, his madness is a form of unnatural or crazed thinking.

8. Macbeth reacts with displeasure and suspicion. Macbeth seems to have planned to destroy Macduff. Macduff will be attacked indirectly in the next act.

(cont.)

Responding to the Selection

Imagine that you were one of the thanes present at Macbeth's feast. You witnessed the king's hysterical imaginings. Write a letter to a friend reporting what you saw and how you feel about it.

Reviewing the Selection

RECALLING

1. What question is Banquo considering at the very beginning of the act?

2. What is the result of the murder plot against Banquo and his son?

3. How does Macbeth act at the banquet? Why does he act this way? What does Lady Macbeth say to excuse her husband's actions?

4. What indication does Macbeth give, at the end of Scene iv, that he will continue to kill anyone who stands in his path?

INTERPRETING

5. Why does Macbeth arrange for Banquo's murder?

6. How does the news of the outcome of the murder plot affect Macbeth?

7. The appearance of the ghost can be interpreted as actual or imagined. What is unnatural about the event under each of these interpretations?

8. How does Macbeth react to the news that Macduff refused to come to the feast? What do you think Macbeth has planned for Macduff? What do you think will happen to Macduff in the next act?

SYNTHESIZING

9. Lady Macbeth says to her husband, "You lack the season of all natures, sleep." What lines of Macbeth's from the murder scene in act II are recalled by Lady Macbeth's statement? Why can't Macbeth sleep, and what consequences does this have for him?

10. What indications are there in this act that Macbeth is on a course from which he cannot turn? What indications are there that this course will bring him to complete madness or despair?

ANSWERS FOR REVIEWING THE SELECTION (CONT.)

SYNTHESIZING

Responses will vary. Possible responses are given.

9. Lady Macbeth's words recall Macbeth's description of the phantom voice that cried "Sleep no more!" (act II, scene ii, lines 32–40). Lack of sleep makes it more difficult for Macbeth to deal with his guilt and with the stress of carrying on as king in the position he has usurped.

10. Macbeth himself says that he cannot turn back (scene iv, lines 135–137). Also, the speech of Lennox at the end of the play indicates that the other Scottish lords have realized Macbeth is to blame for Duncan's death. Such a realization would make it impossible for Macbeth to backtrack.

Understanding Literature (Questions for Discussion)

1. **Motif.** A **motif** is any element that recurs in one or more works of literature or art. Thinking about the motifs, or recurring elements, in a literary work often can help you to discover underlying themes, or main ideas. Motifs in Macbeth include ambition; equivocation, or double talk; disturbances in nature; blood; madness; and sleep. Discuss examples of each of these motifs from the play so far. Also discuss how these motifs are related to one another.

2. **Simile.** A **simile** is a comparison using *like* or *as*. In scene iv, lines 20–21, Macbeth says, "I had else been perfect,/Whole as the marble, founded as the rock." What things are being compared in this simile? What traits do they have in common? Why is Macbeth not, at this point in the play, like a rock?

3. **Climax and Crisis.** The **climax** is the point of highest interest or suspense in a literary work. The **crisis**, or **turning point**, is the point in the plot at which something decisive happens to determine the future course of events in the work. In a traditional five-act tragedy, the climax occurs in Act III. The crisis and the climax are often the same event. The fortunes of the protagonist improve steadily until the crisis is reached. Then they start to decline. What event in this act is a major blow for Macbeth, a reversal of his fortunes that may well bring about his downfall? What is the point of highest interest or suspense? Support your answers. Bear in mind that readers and critics disagree about the answers to these questions. It is important only that you support your answers with evidence from the play.

Responding in Writing

Descriptive Writing. Macbeth stares in terror as Banquo's ghost appears in the banquet hall. He declares that he would rather face a bear or tiger than the "horrible shadow." What frightens you? Why do you find it frightening? What sounds and sights do you associate with it? Write a description either of something that terrifies you or of a fictional terror. Pay attention to sensory details, particularly sight, sound, and touch. Most of all, try to arouse the emotions of your reader.

THE TRAGEDY OF MACBETH / ACT III **359**

ANSWERS FOR UNDERSTANDING LITERATURE

Responses will vary. Possible responses are given.

▶ See the evaluation forms for discussion, active listening, and oral communication, *Assessment Portfolio*, 7.11–7.14.

1. Motif. The rise to power of Macbeth and Lady Macbeth illustrates the motif of ambition. Equivocation is found in the witches' prophecies and in certain speeches of Macbeth and Lady Macbeth in which they deceive Duncan and others. The sounds heard on the night Duncan is murdered, the shaking of the earth, and the madness of his horses are examples of disturbances in the natural world. Blood is frequently mentioned (act II, scene ii, lines 43–47, 52–54, 57–62; act III, scene iv, lines 13, 74, 134–137). Macbeth shows signs of madness when he imagines the dagger before him (act II, scene i, lines 33–43), and he feigns madness as an excuse for his reaction to Banquo's ghost (act III, scene iv, lines 84–86). The motif of sleep is repeated often: Duncan and the groom are murdered in their sleep, and Macbeth hears a voice saying that he shall sleep no more (act II, scene ii, lines 32–40). These motifs are all intricately interrelated because the course taken by Macbeth to fulfill his ambition comes as a result of the witches' equivocations and leads into disruption of the natural order and (bloody) murder, which in turn lead to disturbed sleep and madness.

2. Simile. Macbeth is comparing himself to marble embedded in the earth. His point is that he does not have much in common with the strength or rootedness of the

(cont.)

ANALYTIC SCALES FOR RESPONDING IN WRITING

Grading scales appear on page 360.

ANSWERS FOR UNDERSTANDING LITERATURE (CONT.)

marble or the rock because Fleance is still alive, and Macbeth has no assurance that his own offspring will continue his kingship.

3. Climax and Crisis. The key event in act III is the banquet scene, in which Macbeth learns that Fleance has escaped and Macbeth confronts the ghost of Banquo. This forms a crisis because Macbeth's peculiar behavior casts him in a bad light, beginning the disaffection that

culminates in Lennox's ironic comments in the last scene. The scene is also a crisis because the boy's being alive is key to his progeny inheriting the throne instead of Macbeth's and possibly because it shows the beginning of Macbeth's final descent into irrecoverable madness and disaffection from the world. The climax, it can be argued, is the same as the crisis. Another candidate for the crisis is Macbeth's decision to continue on his bloody career.

TEACHER'S EDITION **359**

ENRICHMENT ACTIVITIES

Have students imagine that they work for a company that produces special effects for movie directors. A famous director of films about creatures from outer space and dinosaurs is planning to do a new film version of *Macbeth* and wants special effects for the witches' scenes in act IV. Have students draw up plans for the special effects to be used in these scenes. Students may write descriptions, do illustrations, or both. You may wish to have students do some library research on special effects techniques currently used in the cinema, including claymation, animatronics, and 3-D computer graphics. However, it isn't necessary for students to know these technologies in order to do the activity. As special effects designers, they can simply describe the effects they want and depend upon technicians to carry out their ideas.

SUPPORT FOR LEP STUDENTS

ADDITIONAL VOCABULARY

entrails—intestines
exploits—deeds, adventures
judicious—prudent
prattler—one who babbles
laudable—praiseworthy, honorable
redress—remedy
transpose—reverse
hoodwink—fool
verity—truth
credulous—trusting
rend—tear
pertain—have to do with

The Apparitions. ("Show his eyes, and grieve his heart;/Come like shadows, so depart.")

ANALYTIC SCALES FOR RESPONDING IN WRITING

Assign a score from 1 to 25 for each grading criterion below. (For more detailed evaluation, see the evaluation forms for writing, revising, and proofreading, *Assessment Portfolio, 7.1–7.10.*)

Descriptive Writing

• **Content/Unity.** The writing presents a description of the material requested in the activity, including details of sight, sound, and touch.

• **Organization/Coherence.** The descriptive writing is organized, presenting the description clearly, so that it can be understood by the reader.

• **Language/Style.** The descriptive writing uses vivid and precise nouns, verbs, and modifiers.

• **Conventions.** The descriptive writing avoids errors in spelling, grammar, usage, mechanics, and manuscript form.

ACT IV

SCENE i: a cave

Thunder. Enter the three WITCHES.

1. WITCH.   Thrice the brinded[1] cat hath mew'd.

2. WITCH.   Thrice, and once the hedge-pig whin'd.

3. WITCH.   Harpier[2] cries, "'Tis time, 'tis time."

1. WITCH.   Round about the cauldron go;
5   In the poison'd entrails throw;
Toad, that under cold stone
Days and nights has thirty-one
Swelt'red venom sleeping got,
Boil thou first i' th' charmed pot.

10 **ALL.**   Double, double, toil and trouble;
Fire burn, and cauldron bubble.

2. WITCH.   Fillet of a fenny snake,[3]
In the cauldron boil and bake;
Eye of newt and toe of frog,
15 Wool of bat and tongue of dog,
Adder's fork and blind-worm's[4] sting,
Lizard's leg and howlet's[5] wing,
For a charm of pow'rful trouble,
Like a hell-broth boil and bubble.

20 **ALL.**   Double, double, toil and trouble;
Fire burn, and cauldron bubble.

3. WITCH.   Scale of dragon, tooth of wolf,
Witch's mummy,[6] maw and gulf
Of the ravin'd salt-sea shark,[7]
25 Root of hemlock digg'd i' th' dark, . . .
30 Finger of birth-strangled babe
Ditch-deliver'd by a drab,
Make the gruel thick and slab.
Add thereto a tiger's chawdron,[8]

For th' ingredience of our cau'dron.

35 **ALL.**   Double, double, toil and trouble;
Fire burn, and cauldron bubble.

2. WITCH.   Cool it with a baboon's blood,
Then the charm is firm and good.

Enter HECATE *to the other three* WITCHES.

HECATE.   O, well done! I commend your pains,
40 And every one shall share i' th' gains.
And now about the cauldron sing,
Like elves and fairies in a ring,
Enchanting all that you put in.
Music and a song: "Black spirits, etc."
                                      Exit HECATE.

2. WITCH.   By the pricking of my thumbs,
45 Something wicked this way comes.
      (*Knocking.*)
                              Open, locks,
                              Whoever knocks!

Enter MACBETH.

MACBETH.   How now, you secret, black, and midnight hags?
What is't you do?

ALL.   A deed without a name.

50 **MACBETH.**   I conjure you, by that which you profess[9]
(How e'er you come to know it), answer me:
Though you untie the winds, and let them fight
Against the churches; though the yesty[10] waves
Confound[11] and swallow navigation up;
55 Though bladed corn be lodg'd,[12] and trees blown down;
Though castles topple on their warders' heads;

---

1. **brinded.** Brindled, striped
2. **Harpier.** The third witch's spirit
3. **fenny snake.** Swamp snake
4. **blind-worm.** Small legless lizard
5. **howlet.** Small owl
6. **Witch's mummy.** Medicinal substance made from parts of a mummy

7. **Maw . . . shark.** Stomach and gullet of the voracious shark
8. **chawdron.** Entrails
9. **that . . . profess.** Your witchcraft
10. **yesty.** Foamy
11. **Confound.** Destroy
12. **bladed . . . lodg'd.** Ripe wheat is beaten down

THE TRAGEDY OF MACBETH / ACT IV, SCENE i **361**

HISTORICAL NOTE

Shakespeare frequently called for a certain song to be played or sung without giving more than the title or first line. Here and in Act III, Scene v, he specified two songs known from another play, *Witches,* by Thomas Middleton (1570?–1627). The first lines of the song "Black Spirits" are "Black spirits and white, red spirits and gray,/Mingle, mingle, mingle, you that mingle

may!" Though Middleton also used the songs, it is not clear who composed them. Scholars believe that *Witches* was written after *Macbeth,* but that may only mean that Middleton took a hint from Shakespeare and borrowed from the same source.

ADDITIONAL QUESTIONS AND ACTIVITIES

• The statements of two of the apparitions, the second and third, read like riddles. If students have not read to the end of the play by the time of the discussion on this passage, ask them to try to "solve" the riddles. How could someone not be "of woman born"? How could a forest move?

• Students can write their own riddles based on a current event. For instance, they may wish to predict the outcome of an election or a trial.

• Have students share riddles they may remember from childhood or have found in books. When they have become familiar with the form of the riddle, students might try their hand at writing their own riddle.

LITERARY TECHNIQUE

Symbol. Students can devise new symbols to represent each of the first three apparitions. The first, for instance, might be a tower carrying a sword, representing Fife, Macduff's castle; the second might be a man carrying an infant in his arms; the third might be a tree carrying a crown.

Though palaces and pyramids do slope
Their heads to their foundations; though the treasure
Of nature's germains[13] tumble all together,
60 Even till destruction sicken; answer me
To what I ask you.

1. WITCH.   Speak.

2. WITCH.   Demand.

3. WITCH.   We'll answer.

1. WITCH.   Say, if th' hadst rather hear it from our mouths,
Or from our masters'?

MACBETH.   Call 'em; let me see 'em.

1. WITCH.   Pour in sow's blood, that hath eaten
65 Her nine farrow;[14] grease that's sweaten
From the murderer's gibbet[15] throw
Into the flame.

ALL.   Come high or low;
Thyself and office deftly show!

Thunder. FIRST APPARITION, *an* ARMED HEAD.[16]

MACBETH.   Tell me, thou unknown power—

1. WITCH.   He knows thy thought:
70 Hear his speech, but say thou nought.

1. APPARITION.   Macbeth! Macbeth! Macbeth! beware Macduff,
Beware the Thane of Fife. Dismiss me. Enough.

                                        He descends.

MACBETH.   What e'er thou art, for thy good caution, thanks;
Thou hast harp'd[17] my fear aright. But one word more—

75 **1. WITCH.**   He will not be commanded. Here's another,

---

13. **germains.** Seeds
14. **nine farrow.** Nine offspring
15. **gibbet.** Gallows where executed criminals were left hanging as a warning
16. **armed Head.** Signifies Macduff
17. **harp'd.** Hit upon
18. **bloody Child.** Signifies Macduff at birth

More potent than the first.

Thunder. SECOND APPARITION, *a* BLOODY CHILD.[18]

2. APPARITION.   Macbeth! Macbeth! Macbeth!

MACBETH.   Had I three ears, I'ld hear thee.

2. APPARITION.   Be bloody, bold, and resolute: laugh to scorn
80 The pow'r of man; for none of woman born
Shall harm Macbeth.   *Descends.*

MACBETH.   Then live, Macduff; what need I fear of thee?
But yet I'll make assurance double sure,
And take a bond of fate:[19] thou shalt not live,
85 That I may tell pale-hearted fear it lies,
And sleep in spite of thunder.

Thunder. THIRD APPARITION, *a* CHILD CROWNED, *with a tree in his hand.*[20]

                                What is this
That rises like the issue of a king,
And wears upon his baby-brow the round
And top of sovereignty?[21]

ALL.   Listen, but speak not to't.

90 **3. APPARITION.**   Be lion-mettled, proud, and take no care
Who chafes, who frets, or where conspirers are:
Macbeth shall never vanquish'd be until
Great Birnan wood to high Dunsinane hill
Shall come against him.

                                Descend.

MACBETH.   That will never be.
95 Who can impress[22] the forest, bid the tree
Unfix his earth-bound root? Sweet bodements![23] good!
Rebellious dead, rise never till the wood
Of Birnan rise, and our high-plac'd Macbeth

---

19. **bond of fate.** Force fate to keep the agreement to kill Macduff
20. **Child . . . hand.** Signifies Malcolm and foreshadows Malcolm's soldiers carrying boughs to Dunsinane
21. **round . . . sovereignty.** The crown
22. **impress.** Force into service
23. **bodements.** Prophecies

Shall live the lease of nature,[24] pay his breath
To time and mortal custom. Yet my heart
Throbs to know one thing: tell me, if your art
Can tell so much, shall Banquo's issue ever
Reign in this kingdom?

ALL. Seek to know no more.

MACBETH. I will be satisfied. Deny me this,
And an eternal curse fall on you! Let me know.
Why sinks that cauldron? and what noise[25] is this?

(Hoboys.)

1. WITCH. Show!

2. WITCH. Show!

3. WITCH. Show!

ALL. Show his eyes, and grieve his heart;
Come like shadows, so depart.

A show of eight KINGS, *the eighth with a glass[26] in his hand, and* BANQUO *last.*

MACBETH. Thou art too like the spirit of Banquo; down!
Thy crown does sear mine eyeballs. And thy hair,
Thou other gold-bound brow, is like the first.
A third is like the former. Filthy hags,
Why do you show me this?—A fourth? Start, eyes!
What, will the line stretch out to th' crack of doom?
Another yet? A seventh? I'll see no more.
And yet the eight appears, who bears a glass
Which shows me many more; and some I see
That twofold balls and treble sceptres[27] carry.

Horrible sight! Now I see 'tis true,
For the blood-bolter'd[28] Banquo smiles upon me,
And points at them for his.

APPARITIONS *vanish.*
What? is this so?

1. Witch. Aye, sir, all this is so. But why
Stands Macbeth thus amazedly?
Come, sisters, cheer we up his sprites,[29]
And show the best of our delights.
I'll charm the air to give a sound,
While you perform your antic round;[30]
That this great king may kindly say
Our duties did his welcome pay.

Music. The WITCHES *dance and vanish.*

MACBETH. Where are they? Gone? Let this <u>pernicious</u> hour
Stand aye accursed in the calendar!
Come in, without there!

Enter LENNOX.

LENNOX. What's your Grace's will?

MACBETH. Saw you the weïrd sisters?

LENNOX. No, my lord.

MACBETH. Came they not by you?

LENNOX. No indeed, my lord.

MACBETH. Infected be the air whereon they ride,
And damn'd all those that trust them! I did hear
The galloping of horse. Who was't came by?

LENNOX. 'Tis two or three, my lord, that bring you word
Macduff is fled to England.

---

24. **lease of nature.** Natural life span
25. **noise.** Music
26. **show . . . glass.** A silent procession of eight kings, the last holding a mirror
27. **twofold . . . sceptres.** Symbol of Ireland, Scotland, and

England, united when James VI of Scotland became James I of England
28. **blood-bolter'd.** Hair matted with blood
29. **sprites.** Spirits
30. **antic round.** Fantastic circular dance

ADDITIONAL QUESTIONS AND ACTIVITIES

π Use the accompanying graphic organizer to demonstrate the rise and fall of Macbeth's hopes as he listens to the apparitions in scene i.

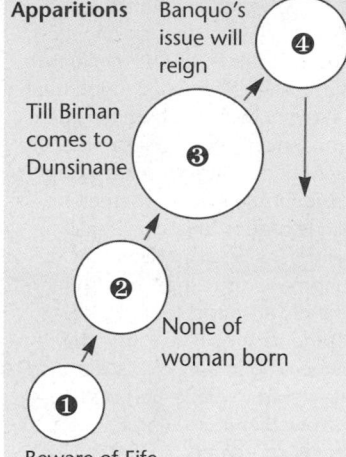

Apparitions

Banquo's issue will reign ④

Till Birnan comes to Dunsinane ③

② None of woman born

① Beware of Fife

WORDS FOR EVERYDAY USE: per • ni • cious (pər nish´əs) *adj.,* causing ruin and death

VOCABULARY IN CONTEXT

- The novelist disdainfully viewed his critics as <u>pernicious</u> foes of truth and art.

MACBETH. Fled to England!

LENNOX. Aye, my good lord.

MACBETH. [*Aside.*] Time, thou anticipat'st my dread exploits:
145 The flighty purpose never is o'ertook
Unless the deed go with it.[31] From this moment
The very firstlings[32] of my heart shall be
The firstlings of my hand. And even now,
To crown my thoughts with acts, be it thought and done:
150 The castle of Macduff I will surprise,
Seize upon Fife, give to th' edge o' th' sword
His wife, his babes, and all unfortunate souls
That trace[33] him in his line. No boasting like a fool;
This deed I'll do before this purpose cool.
155 But no more sights!—Where are these gen-'tlemen?
Come bring me where they are.

Exeunt.

SCENE ii: MACDUFF'S castle in Fife

Enter MACDUFF'S WIFE, *her* SON, *and* ROSSE.

LADY MACDUFF. What had he done, to make him fly the land?

ROSSE. You must have patience, madam.

LADY MACDUFF. He had none;
His flight was madness. When our actions do not,
Our fears do make us traitors.

ROSSE. You know not
5 Whether it was his wisdom or his fear.

LADY MACDUFF. Wisdom? to leave his wife, to leave his babes,
His mansion and his titles,[34] in a place

From whence himself does fly? He loves us not,
He wants the natural touch;[35] for the poor wren,
10 The most diminutive of birds, will fight,
Her young ones in her nest, against the owl.
All is the fear, and nothing is the love;
As little is the wisdom, where the flight
So runs against all reason.

ROSSE. My dearest coz,[36]
15 I pray you school[37] yourself. But for your husband,
He is noble, wise, judicious, and best knows
The fits o' th' season.[38] I dare not speak much further,
But cruel are the times when we are traitors,
And do not know ourselves;[39] when we hold rumor
20 From what we fear, yet know not what we fear,
But float upon a wild and violent sea
Each way, and move. I take my leave of you;
'Shall not be long but I'll be here again.
Things at the worst will cease, or else climb upward
25 To what they were before. My pretty cousin,
Blessing upon you!

LADY MACDUFF. Father'd he is, and yet he's fatherless.

ROSSE. I am so much a fool, should I stay longer,
It would be my disgrace and your discomfort.
I take my leave at once.

Exit ROSSE.

30 **LADY MACDUFF.** Sirrah, your father's dead,
And what will you do now? How will you live?

---

31. **flighty . . . it.** Purpose is always fleeing unless it is done immediately.
32. **firstlings.** First-born
33. **trace.** Follow
34. **titles.** Properties

35. **wants . . . touch.** Lacks natural feelings toward his family
36. **coz.** Cousin, kin
37. **school.** Control
38. **fits . . . season.** Disturbances of the time
39. **know ourselves.** Recognize ourselves as traitors

Son. As birds do, mother.

Lady Macduff. What, with worms and flies?

Son. With what I get, I mean, and so do they.

Lady Macduff. Poor bird, thou'dst never fear the net nor lime,[40]
35 The pitfall nor the gin.[41]

Son. Why should I, mother? Poor birds they are not set for.
My father is not dead, for all your saying.

Lady Macduff. Yes, he is dead. How wilt thou do for a father?

Son. Nay, how will you do for a husband?

40 **Lady Macduff.** Why, I can buy me twenty at any market.

Son. Then you'll buy 'em to sell[42] again.

Lady Macduff. Thou speak'st with all thy wit, and yet, i' faith,
With wit enough for thee.[43]

Son. Was my father a traitor, mother?

45 **Lady Macduff.** Aye, that he was.

Son. What is a traitor?

Lady Macduff. Why, one that swears and lies.

Son. And be all traitors that do so?

Lady Macduff. Every one that does so is a
50 traitor, and must be hang'd.

Son. And must they all be hang'd that swear and lie?

Lady Macduff. Every one.

Son. Who must hang them?

55 **Lady Macduff.** Why, the honest men.

Son. Then the liars and swearers are fools; for there are liars and swearers enow[44] to beat the honest men and hang up them.

Lady Macduff. Now God help thee, poor
60 monkey! But how wilt thou do for a father?

Son. If he were dead, you'ld weep for him; if you would not, it were a good sign that I should quickly have a new father.

Lady Macduff. Poor prattler, how thou talk'st!

Enter a MESSENGER.

65 **Messenger.** Bless you, fair dame! I am not to you known
Though in your state of honor I am perfect.[45]
I doubt[46] some danger does approach you nearly.
If you will take a <u>homely</u> man's advice,
Be not found here; hence with your little ones.
70 To fright you thus, methinks I am too savage;
To do worse to you were fell[47] cruelty,
Which is too nigh your person. Heaven preserve you!
I dare abide no longer.

Exit MESSENGER.

Lady Macduff. Whither should I fly?
I have done no harm. But I remember now
75 I am in this earthly world—where to do harm
Is often laudable, to do good sometime

---

40. **lime.** Birdlime, used to catch birds
41. **gin.** Snare
42. **sell.** Betray
43. **With . . . thee.** You are clever for a child.
44. **enow.** Enough

45. **in . . . perfect.** I know you are an honored person.
46. **doubt.** Fear
47. **fell.** Savage

WORDS FOR
EVERYDAY USE:
home • ly (hōm'lē) *adj.*, simple, unpretentious

ADDITIONAL QUESTIONS AND ACTIVITIES

Ask the following questions to probe the dynamics of scene ii:

1. In lines 22–26, Rosse tries to tell Lady Macduff he is leaving. What is her reaction? Why does she react in this way?

2. Study Rosse's final speech to Lady Macduff. What are Rosse's feelings about her? How can you tell? How does the reference to his feelings further the plot?

3. Why does Lady Macduff repeatedly say things to her son that seem cruel (e.g., telling him that Macduff is dead and that he is a traitor)?

Answers. 1. Lady Macduff ignores Rosse's hint that he is leaving. She seems to be reluctant to see him go or is so preoccupied by Macduff's abandonment of her that she pays no attention. 2. Two possible interpretations of Rosse's comments are possible. One is that Rosse is attracted to Lady Macduff, so infatuated that if he stays longer he will disgrace himself and make her uncomfortable, presumably by making some advance that he should not make. Another common interpretation is that Rosse is so overcome with feelings for Lady Macbeth's plight that he fears breaking down in tears and thereby disgracing himself and causing her discomfort. The reference to Rosse's feelings explains why he feels driven to depart and is thus out of the way when the murderers arrive. 3. She seems to want someone to contradict her; her son senses this and readily offers witty contradictions.

VOCABULARY IN CONTEXT

• Though the house seemed sterile and bleak from the outside, inside it was made warm by comfortable, <u>homely</u> furnishings.

Characterization. It is often diffi-cult for students to detect nuances of characterization in Shakespeare. Ask for a volunteer to read the speech of the messenger (scene ii, lines 65–73) out loud. Point out to students its odd inversions. (Inversions include: "I am not to you known"; "some danger does approach you nearly"; "To fright you thus, methinks I am too sav-age.") Students may be familiar with the technique of inversion from the Language Arts Survey, 2.64, "Inverting Sentences for Emphasis." Explain, however, that unlike inversions crafted in order to emphasize meaning, these inver-sions produce awkward sentences, of the kind one would expect from a "homely" man speaking in awe to a person very much his social superior. Shakespeare may be depicting the self-conscious attempt of a "yokel" to speak in the affected language he thinks is proper for communicating with the nobility, or the inversions may signal confusion, embarrassment, and fear. The rhythm of the pas-sage as well is sometimes halting and sometimes sing-song. To demonstrate this, have a volunteer reread the passage in a sing-song fashion that emphasizes the meter.

ANSWERS TO SELECTION CHECK TEST 4.5.9

EX. Who has been watching Lady Macbeth at night?
A doctor and a gentlewoman have been watching Lady Macbeth.

1. What does Lady Macbeth do as she sleepwalks?
Lady Macbeth rubs her hands as if she were washing the blood off them.

2. Why can't the doctor cure Lady Macbeth?
The doctor says he cannot cure a diseased mind.

3. What is Macbeth's reaction to his wife's death?
Macbeth says that she should have died hereafter.

(cont.)

Accounted dangerous folly. Why then, alas,
Do I put up that womanly defense,
To say I have done no harm?

Enter MURDERERS.

          What are these faces?

80 **1. MURDERER.**   Where is your husband?

LADY MACDUFF.   I hope, in no place so unsanctified
Where such as thou mayst find him.

1. MURDERER.   He's a traitor.

SON.   Thou li'st, thou shag-ear'd villain!

1. MURDERER.   What, you egg![48]
                Stabbing him.
Young fry of treachery!

SON.   He has kill'd me, mother:
85 Run away, I pray you!   [*Dies.*]
     Exit LADY MACDUFF *crying* "Murther!"
         and pursued by the MURDERERS

SCENE iii: England, the king's palace

Enter MALCOLM *and* MACDUFF.

MALCOLM.   Let us seek out some desolate shade, and there
Weep our sad bosoms empty.

MACDUFF.   Let us rather
Hold fast the mortal sword, and like good men
Bestride our downfall birthdom.[49] Each new morn
5 New widows howl, new orphans cry, new sor-rows
Strike heaven on the face, that it resounds
As if it felt with Scotland, and yell'd out
Like syllable of dolor.[50]

MALCOLM.   What I believe, I'll wail,
What know, believe; and what I can redress,

10 As I shall find the time to friend,[51] I will
What you have spoke, it may be so per-chance.
This tyrant, whose sole name blisters our tongues,
Was once thought honest;[52] you have lov'd him well;
He hath not touch'd you yet. I am young, but something
15 You may discern of him through me, and wis-dom[53]
To offer up a weak, poor, innocent lamb
T' appease an angry god.

MACDUFF.   I am not treacherous.

MALCOLM.   But Macbeth is.
A good and virtuous nature may recoil
20 In an imperial charge.[54] But I shall crave your pardon;
That which you are, my thoughts cannot transpose:
Angels are bright still, though the brightest[55] fell.
Though all things foul would wear the brows of grace,
Yet grace must still look so.[56]

MACDUFF.   I have lost my hopes.

25 **MALCOLM.** Perchance even there where I did find my doubts.
Why in that rawness[57] left you wife and child,
Those precious motives,[58] those strong knots of love,
Without leave-taking? I pray you,
Let not my jealousies be your dishonors,
30 But mine own safeties.[59] You may be rightly just,
What ever I shall think.

MACDUFF.   Bleed, bleed, poor country!

---

48. **egg.** Traitor to be
49. **Bestride . . . birthdom.** Fight to protect our downfallen country
50. **Like . . . dolor.** A similar shout of pain
51. **to friend.** Favorable
52. **honest.** Honorable
53. **You . . . wisdom.** You may see a way to help yourself by betray-ing me; it is the worldly way.
54. **imperial charge.** Order from the king

55. **the brightest.** Lucifer
56. **Though . . . so.** Even if wickedness takes on the appearance of virtue, virtue must keep its appearance.
57. **rawness.** Unprotected state
58. **motives.** People who inspire your love and protection
59. **Let . . . safeties.** My suspicions are not meant to dishonor you, but rather to protect me.

ANSWERS TO SELECTION CHECK TEST 4.5.9 (CONT.)

4. What two events occur that destroy Macbeth's belief in his invincibility?
The opposing forces carry branches from Birnan wood to Dunsinane hill and Macduff announces he was delivered by Cæserian.

5. Who kills Macbeth?
Macduff kills Macbeth.

Great tyranny, lay thou thy basis sure,
For goodness dare not check thee; wear thou
    thy wrongs,
The title is affeer'd![60] Fare thee well, lord,
35 I would not be the villain that thou think'st
For the whole space that's in the tyrant's
    grasp,
And the rich East to boot.

MALCOLM.   Be not offended;
I speak not as in absolute fear of you.
I think our country sinks beneath the yoke:
40 It weeps, it bleeds, and each new day a gash
Is added to her wounds. I think withal
There would be hands uplifted in my right;
And here from gracious England[61] have I
    offer
Of goodly thousands. But, for all this,
45 When I shall tread upon the tyrant's head,
Or wear it on my sword, yet my poor country
Shall have more vices than it had before,
More suffer, and more sundry ways than ever,
By him that shall succeed.

MACDUFF.   What should he be?

50 **MALCOLM.** It is myself I mean; in whom I
    know
All the particulars of vice so grafted
That, when they shall be open'd, black
    Macbeth
Will seem as pure as snow, and the poor state
Esteem him as a lamb, being compar'd
With my <u>confineless</u> harms.

55 **MACDUFF.**   Not in the legions
Of horrid hell can come a devil more damn'd

In evils to top Macbeth.

MALCOLM.   I grant him bloody,
Luxurious,[62] avaricious, false, deceitful,
Sudden, malicious, smacking of every sin
60 That has a name; but there's no bottom,
    none,
In my voluptuousness. Your wives, your
    daughters,
Your matrons, and your maids could not fill
    up
The cestern of my lust, and my desire
All continent <u>impediments</u> would o'erbear
65 That did oppose my will. Better Macbeth
Than such an one to reign.

MACDUFF.   Boundless intemperance
In nature is a tyranny; it hath been
Th' untimely emptying of the happy throne,
And fall of many kings. But fear not yet
70 To take upon you what is yours. You may
Convey your pleasures in a spacious plenty,[63]
And yet seem cold,[64] the time you may so
    hoodwink.
We have willing dames enough; there cannot
    be
That vulture in you to devour so many
75 As will to greatness dedicate themselves,
Finding it so inclin'd.

MALCOLM.   With this, there grows
In my most ill-compos'd affection[65] such
A <u>stanchless</u> avarice that, were I king,
I should cut off the nobles for their lands,
80 Desire his jewels, and this other's house,
And my more-having would be as a sauce
To make me hunger more, that I should forge

---

60. **affeer'd.** Confirmed
61. **England.** The King of England, Edward the Confessor
62. **Luxurious.** Lustful
63. **Convey . . . plenty.** Find plenty of space to indulge secretly in your pleasures
64. **cold.** Chaste
65. **affection.** Disposition

WORDS FOR EVERYDAY USE:
con • fine • less (kən fīn´ləs) *adj.,* limitless
im • ped • i • ment (im ped´ə mənt) *n.,* obstacle
stanch • less or staunch • less (stônch´ləs) *adj.,* unstoppable

THE TRAGEDY OF MACBETH / ACT IV, SCENE iii **367**

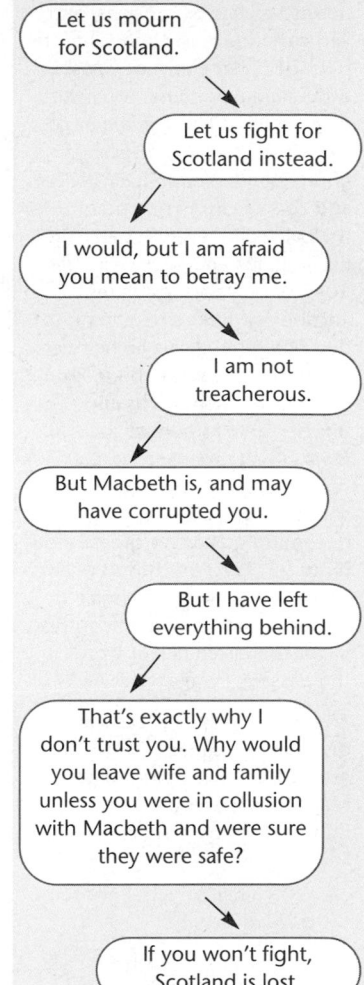

ADDITIONAL QUESTIONS AND ACTIVITIES

Students can create a diagram to indicate the logic of the dialogue between Malcolm and Macduff in scene iii, lines 1–37. (See accompanying sample diagram.)

- Let us mourn for Scotland.
- Let us fight for Scotland instead.
- I would, but I am afraid you mean to betray me.
- I am not treacherous.
- But Macbeth is, and may have corrupted you.
- But I have left everything behind.
- That's exactly why I don't trust you. Why would you leave wife and family unless you were in collusion with Macbeth and were sure they were safe?
- If you won't fight, Scotland is lost.

VOCABULARY IN CONTEXT

- Many astronomers believe that the universe, while not infinite, is <u>confineless</u>.
- "I don't believe there exist any genuine legal <u>impediments</u>," said the impassioned lawyer to his lover, "to prevent the marriage of the two aforesaid loving minds."
- Environmentalists decried what they said was a <u>stanchless</u> flow of pollutants into the Mediterranean Sea.

Imagery. Shakespeare enters so fully into the personalities of his characters that even the nuances of the imagery they use are apt. Ask students to examine the speech of Macbeth in act II, scene i, lines 49–61, and list some of the nouns, adjectives, adverbs, and verbs that form the images of the passage. (These include *dead, wicked dreams, abuse, witchcraft, pale, wither'd Murther, alarum'd, wolf, howl, stealthy, ravishing, ghost, stones, horror, heat of deeds,* and *cold breath*.) Then point out that Malcolm, even in detailing his fictitious appetites (lines 50–99), uses a very different vocabulary. Before beginning to describe himself as evil, he refers to himself as a weak, poor, innocent lamb. Then words and phrases such as *pure as snow, lamb, sweet milk of concord, universal peace,* and *unity* crop up in his speeches. He lists the "king-becoming graces" at great length (lines 92–93). Pose this question: What does Malcolm's choice of words say about him, in contrast to Macbeth's choice of words in the passage from act II?

Answer. Malcolm's vocabulary gives away his essential goodness even when he is trying to deny it; Macbeth's shows a disturbed mind fixated on horrors.

Quarrels unjust against the good and loyal,
Destroying them for wealth.

MACDUFF.   This avarice
85 Sticks deeper, grows with more pernicious
        root
   Than summer-seeming[66] lust; and it hath
        been
   The sword of our slain kings. Yet do not fear,
   Scotland hath foisons[67] to fill up your will
   Of your mere own.[68] All these are portable,[69]
90 With other graces weigh'd.

   MALCOLM.   But I have none. The
        king-becoming graces,
   As justice, verity, temp'rance, stableness,
   Bounty, perseverance, mercy, lowliness,
   Devotion, patience, courage, fortitude,
95 I have no relish of them, but abound
   In the division of each several crime,
   Acting it many ways. Nay, had I pow'r, I
        should
   Pour the sweet milk of concord into hell,
   Uproar the universal peace, confound
   All unity on earth.

100 **MACDUFF.**   O Scotland, Scotland!

   MALCOLM.   If such a one be fit to govern,
        speak.
   I am as I have spoken.

   MACDUFF.   Fit to govern?
   No, not to live. O nation miserable!
   With an untitled tyrant bloody-sceptred,
105 When shalt thou see thy wholesome days
        again,
   Since that the truest issue of thy throne
   By his own interdiction[70] stands accus'd,

---

66. **summer-seeming.** Lasting only for the summer or prime of life
67. **foison.** Plenty
68. **mere own.** Royal property
69. **portable.** Bearable
70. **interdiction.** Legal restriction

And does blaspheme his breed?[71] Thy royal
        father
   Was a most sainted king; the queen that bore
        thee,
110 Oft'ner upon her knees than on her feet,
   Died every day she liv'd.[72] Fare thee well,
   These evils thou repeat'st upon thyself
   Hath banish'd me from Scotland. O my
        breast,
   Thy hope ends here!

   MALCOLM.   Macduff, this noble passion,
115 Child of integrity, hath from my soul
   Wip'd the black scruples, reconcil'd my
        thoughts
   To thy good truth and honor. Devilish
        Macbeth
   By many of these trains[73] hath sought to win
        me
   Into his power, and modest wisdom plucks me
120 From over-credulous haste. But God above
   Deal between thee and me! for even now
   I put myself to thy direction, and
   Unspeak mine own detraction; here <u>abjure</u>
   The taints and blames I laid upon myself,
125 For strangers to my nature. I am yet
   Unknown to woman, never was forsworn,
   Scarcely have coveted what was mine own,
   At no time broke my faith, would not betray
   The devil to his fellow, and delight
130 No less in truth than life. My first false
        speaking
   Was this upon myself. What I am truly
   Is thine and my poor country's to command:
   Whither indeed, before thy here-approach,
   Old Siward, with ten thousand warlike men

---

71. **blaspheme his breed.** Slander his ancestors
72. **Died . . . liv'd.** Died to the world every day, and so lived in a state of grace
73. **trains.** Devices

WORDS FOR
EVERYDAY USE: **ab • jure** (ab jōōr´) *vt.,* renounce

ADDITIONAL QUESTIONS AND ACTIVITIES

The conversation between Malcolm and Macduff in lines 60–114 is a prolonged test of Macduff's character. Students can restate it in the form of a written test or questionnaire. It might begin with the following question: "Do you believe that a king who is prone to voluptuousness would be better than Macbeth?" Each separate speech of Malcolm in lines 60–99 should be represented by one question.

After students have composed their tests, each can trade with a partner and answer the test in the character of Macduff. Their answers should parallel the initial rationalizations and eventual despair and disgust of Macduff in his replies in lines 66–114.

---

135 Already at a point, was setting forth.
     Now we'll together, and the chance of good-
       ness
     Be like our warranted quarrel!⁷⁴ Why are you
       silent?

MACDUFF.   Such welcome and unwelcome
     things at once
     'Tis hard to reconcile.

Enter a DOCTOR.

MALCOLM.   Well, more anon.—Comes the
     King forth,
140 I pray you?

DOCTOR.   Aye, sir; there are a crew of
     wretched souls
     That stay his cure.⁷⁵ Their malady convinces
     The great assay of art;⁷⁶ but at his touch,
     Such sanctity hath heaven given his hand,
145 They presently amend.

MALCOLM.   I thank you, doctor.
                              Exit DOCTOR.

MACDUFF.   What's the disease he means?

MALCOLM.   'Tis call'd the evil:⁷⁷
     A most miraculous work in this good king,
     Which often, since my here-remain in
       England,
     I have seen him do. How he solicits heaven,
150 Himself best knows; but strangely-visited
       people,
     All swoll'n and ulcerous, pitiful to the eye,
     The mere despair of surgery, he cures,
     Hanging a golden stamp⁷⁸ about their
       necks,
     Put on with holy prayers, and 'tis spoken,
155 To the succeeding royalty he leaves
     The healing benediction. With this strange
       virtue,

He hath a heavenly gift of prophecy,
And sundry blessings hang about his throne
That speak him full of grace.

Enter ROSSE.

MACDUFF.   See who comes here.

160 MALCOLM.   My countryman; but yet I know
     him not.

MACDUFF.   My ever gentle⁷⁹ cousin, wel-
     come hither.

MALCOLM.   I know him now. Good God
     betimes remove
     The means that makes us strangers!⁸⁰

ROSSE.   Sir, amen.

MACDUFF.   Stands Scotland where it did?

ROSSE.   Alas, poor country,
165 Almost afraid to know itself! It cannot
     Be call'd our mother, but our grave; where
       nothing,
     But who knows nothing, is once seen to
       smile;
     Where sighs, and groans, and shrieks that
       rent the air
     Are made, not mark'd;⁸¹ where violent sor-
       row seems
170 A modern ecstasy.⁸² The dead man's knell
     Is there scarce ask'd for who, and good men's
       lives
     Expire before the flowers in their caps,
     Dying or ere⁸³ they sicken.

MACDUFF.   O relation!
     Too nice,⁸⁴ and yet too true.

MALCOLM.   What's the newest grief?

175 ROSSE.   That of an hour's age doth hiss the
     speaker;⁸⁵

---

74. **chance . . . quarrel.** May our luck be as good as our cause is just.
75. **stay his cure.** Wait for him to cure them
76. **convinces . . . art.** Defeats even the highest medical skill
77. **the evil.** Scrofula, a skin disease supposedly cured by the touch of royalty
78. **stamp.** Coin
79. **gentle.** Noble

80. **betimes . . . strangers.** Soon remove Macbeth who has caused our separation
81. **mark'd.** Noticed
82. **modern ecstasy.** Common emotion
83. **or ere.** Before
84. **nice.** Precise
85. **hiss the speaker.** Cause the speaker to be hissed for telling old news

CROSS-CURRICULAR ACTIVITIES

Mathematics and History/Sciences.
Students can research the medical description and basis of the ailment scrofula and the historical background of Edward the Confessor. Their findings can be summarized in a one-page report.

ADDITIONAL QUESTIONS AND ACTIVITIES

Ask students the following questions:

1. How does the condition of England under Edward contrast with the condition of Scotland under Macbeth?

2. Why, do you suppose, might Shakespeare have introduced the material about Edward? How does it further the plot?

Answers. 1. England under Edward is governed by someone with healing and other divinely given powers. Scotland is the home of men who expire "before the flowers in their caps," dying before they even pass through illness. In other words, England is relatively healthy, and Scotland absolutely sick. 2. Shakespeare may have introduced the material about Edward to emphasize the damage caused to Scotland by Macbeth. It furthers the plot by showing the deterioration of conditions there and providing more motivation for the invasion by Malcolm, Macduff, and Siward. Shakespeare was also probably trying to flatter James II, who believed that he, like Edward the Confessor, had the power to cure scrofula by touch.

VOCABULARY IN CONTEXT

• After the time when Durfey put his lit pipe in his pocket and set his jacket on fire, he abjured smoking.

ADDITIONAL QUESTIONS AND ACTIVITIES

Ask the following questions to encourage students to examine the fine points of Shakespeare's dialogue in scene iii, lines 176–188:

1. Why does Rosse say "why" before saying "well" in line 177?

2. What does Rosse mean when he says Macduff's children were "well at peace when I did leave 'em"?

3. When Macduff asks Rosse for more details, apparently about his wife and children, how does Rosse react?

4. Why, do you suppose, does Rosse decide to tell Macduff about his family after avoiding doing so?

Answers. 1. He is hesitating because he does not want to tell Macduff the truth; he seems surprised that he is able to say that Macduff's wife is well (that is, safe from further harm). 2. He means that they are dead. 3. Rosse changes the subject and begins talking about Scotland in general. 4. One might conjecture that he feels he has to tell Macduff sooner or later.

ADDITIONAL QUESTIONS AND ACTIVITIES

Ask students to discuss this question: Why did Macduff leave his wife and children undefended in Scotland, though his grief over their deaths clearly shows that he loved them?

Answer. This may well be one of the most difficult points of interpretation in the entire play, though other issues are more central. One possible response is that often people forget how much they love those whom they love; Macduff seems to have fallen into this error. Macduff may also have been hoping to keep his position in Scotland without compromising it if his mission to England should fail. If he had removed his family and followers, he would at once have been considered a traitor.

Each minute teems a new one.

MACDUFF.   How does my wife?

ROSSE.   Why, well.

MACDUFF.   And all my children?

ROSSE.   Well too.

MACDUFF.   The tyrant has not batter'd at their peace?

ROSSE.   No, they were well at peace when I did leave 'em.

180 **MACDUFF.**   Be not a niggard[86] of your speech; how goes't?

ROSSE.   When I came hither to transport the tidings,
Which I have heavily[87] borne, there ran a rumor
Of many worthy fellows that were out,[88]
Which was to my belief witness'd the rather,[89]

185 For that I saw the tyrant's power[90] afoot.
Now is the time of help; your eye in Scotland
Would create soldiers, make our women fight,
To doff their dire distresses.

MALCOLM.   Be't their comfort
We are coming thither. Gracious England hath

190 Lent us good Siward, and ten thousand men;
An older and a better soldier none
That Christendom gives out.

ROSSE.   Would I could answer
This comfort with the like! But I have words
That would be howl'd out in the desert air,

---

86. **niggard.** Stingy
87. **heavily.** Very sadly
88. **out.** Out in arms
89. **witness'd the rather.** Made more believable
90. **tyrant's power.** Armed forces

---

195 Where hearing should not latch[91] them.

MACDUFF.   What concern they?
The general cause? or is it a fee-grief[92]
Due to some single breast?

ROSSE.   No mind that's honest
But in it shares some woe, though the main part
Pertains to you alone.

MACDUFF.   If it be mine,

200 Keep it not from me, quickly let me have it.

ROSSE.   Let not your ears despise my tongue for ever,
Which shall possess them with the heaviest sound
That ever yet they heard.

MACDUFF.   Humh! I guess at it.

ROSSE.   Your castle is surpris'd; your wife, and babes,

205 Savagely slaughter'd. To relate the manner,
Were on the quarry[93] of these murther'd deer
To add the death of you.

MALCOLM.   Merciful heaven!
What, man, ne'er pull your hat upon your brows;
Give sorrow words. The grief that does not speak

210 Whispers the o'er-fraught[94] heart, and bids it break.

MACDUFF.   My children too?

ROSSE.   Wife, children, servants, all
That could be found.

MACDUFF.   And I must be from thence!

---

91. **latch.** Catch
92. **fee-grief.** Private sorrow
93. **quarry.** Heap of slaughtered bodies from a hunting expedition
94. **o'er-fraught.** Overburdened

WORDS FOR EVERYDAY USE:

teem (tēm) *vi.,* bring forth
doff (dôf) *vt.,* take off, remove

VOCABULARY IN CONTEXT

- Though life spawns problems, it also teems its little joys.
- The little boy forgot to doff his baseball cap before he plunged into the swimming pool.

My wife kill'd too?

ROSSE.   I have said.

MALCOLM.   Be comforted.
Let's make us med'cines of our great revenge
215 To cure this deadly grief.

MACDUFF.   He has no children. All my
    pretty ones?
Did you say all? O hell-kite! All?
What, all my pretty chickens, and their dam,
At one fell swoop?

MALCOLM.   Dispute it like a man.

220 **MACDUFF.**   I shall do so;
But I must also feel it as a man:
I cannot but remember such things were,
That were most precious to me. Did heaven
    look on,
And would not take their part? Sinful
    Macduff,
225 They were all strook for thee! naught[95] that I
    am,
Not for their own demerits, but for mine,
Fell slaughter on their souls. Heaven rest
    them now!

MALCOLM.   Be this the whetstone of your
    sword, let grief
Convert to anger; blunt not the heart, enrage
    it.

230 **MACDUFF.**   O, I could play the woman with
    mine eyes,
And braggart with my tongue! But, gentle
    heavens,
Cut short all intermission. Front to front[96]
Bring thou this fiend of Scotland and myself;
Within my sword's length set him; if he scape,
Heaven forgive him too!

235 **MALCOLM.**   This tune goes manly.
Come go we to the King, our power is ready,
Our lack is nothing but our leave. Macbeth
Is ripe for shaking, and the pow'rs above
Put on their instruments.[97] Receive what
    cheer you may,
240 The night is long that never finds the day.
                                Exeunt.

---

95. **naught.** Wicked
96. **Front to front.** Face to face
97. **Put . . . instruments.** Prepare for action by arming themselves

ANALYTIC SCALES FOR RESPONDING IN WRITING

Assign a score from 1 to 25 for each grading criterion below. (For more detailed evaluation, see the evaluation forms for writing, revising, and proofreading, *Assessment Portfolio,* 7.1–7.10.)

1. Dramatic Scene

• **Content/Unity.** The scene presents a sensible portrait of a conversation that might take place between Macbeth and Lady Macbeth in act IV.

• **Organization/Coherence.** The scene is clearly organized, presenting Lady Macbeth's reactions in a way that allows the reader to follow them.

• **Language/Style.** The scene uses vivid and precise nouns, verbs, and modifiers.

• **Conventions.** The scene avoids errors in spelling, grammar, usage, mechanics, and manuscript form.

2. Personal Letter

• **Content/Unity.** The letter presents a plausible communication between the characters.

• **Organization/Coherence.** The letter is clearly organized, presenting the issues in logical order.

• **Language/Style.** The letter uses vivid and precise nouns, verbs, and modifiers.

• **Conventions.** The letter avoids errors in spelling, grammar, usage, mechanics, and manuscript form.

ADDITIONAL QUESTIONS AND ACTIVITIES

The words of Macduff in lines 217–227 make up one of the briefest and yet most powerful laments in English literature. (The American poet Anne Sexton chose them as the epigraph and title for her volume of poems *All My Pretty Ones.*) Students can write a lament expressing Macduff's sorrow for his

(cont.)

ADDITIONAL QUESTIONS AND ACTIVITIES (CONT.)

wife and/or family, using whatever form of poetry or prose seems appropriate to them. They should assume that the lament is to be delivered at a memorial service attended by other nobles and family members. For inspiration, you may wish to read students the poem "On the Death of His Wife" by the Irish poet Muireadach O'Dalaigh (early 1200s), translated by Frank O'Connor in Montague, John, ed. *The Book of Irish Verse.* 1974.

My body's self deserts me now,

The half of me that was her own,

Since all I knew of brightness died

Half of me lingers, half is gone.

RESPONDING TO THE SELECTION

Be sensitive to students' differing religious beliefs pertaining to ghosts, demons, and the like.

**ANSWERS FOR
REVIEWING THE SELECTION**

RECALLING

1. The witches show Macbeth apparitions of an armed head, a bloody child, a crowned child holding a tree, and eight kings, including Banquo.

2. Macbeth decides to kill Macduff's wife, children, and relatives because he has been warned of Macduff by the first apparition and because Macduff himself has fled, suggesting his opposition to Macbeth.

3. She is upset because Macduff has left her to go to England. She tells her son that his father was a traitor.

4. Malcolm tells Macduff that he would be a worse king than Macbeth. He tells him that he is sexually intemperate, greedy, and devoid of any good qualities.

INTERPRETING

5. Macbeth is pleased by each of the apparitions except the last. It suggests that he will not establish a line of kings after all.

6. The lines show that Macbeth has hardened to his crimes and will no longer hesitate.

7. The interchange between Lady Macduff and her son points up their humanity and their helplessness. It promotes feelings of pity and shows Macbeth's crime to be all the more terrible.

8. Malcolm is testing Macduff to see if he is an agent sent by Macbeth to suborn him. He determines that Macduff is a moral person whom he can trust.

SYNTHESIZING

9. By the end of scene i, Macbeth has determined that he will no longer hesitate to commit crimes. Furthermore, murdering Macduff's family is more horrible than any of his prior crimes.

10. *Answers may vary.*

Responding to the Selection

How would you have felt about the apparitions in this act if you were Macbeth? What effect would these have on you if you were in an audience and saw them on the stage?

Reviewing the Selection

RECALLING

1. What apparitions do the witches show to Macbeth?

2. What does Macbeth decide to do with regard to Macduff and Macduff's family? Why does he decide to do this?

3. Why is Lady Macduff upset with her husband in scene ii? What does she say to her son regarding her husband?

4. What falsehoods does Malcolm tell to Macduff in scene iii?

INTERPRETING

5. How does Macbeth react to the apparitions that appear to him? What is troublesome to him about the last apparition?

6. Study the lines at the end of scene i in which Macbeth makes up his mind about what to do about Macduff. What do these lines reveal about how Macbeth has changed since the first time he considered committing such an act?

7. Why might Shakespeare have inserted an interchange between Lady Macduff and her son before their murder? How does having such an interchange affect the feelings of the audience about the outcome of scene ii?

8. Why does Malcolm mislead Macduff in scene iii? What does he accomplish by doing so?

SYNTHESIZING

9. What evidence is presented in this act to support the idea that Macbeth has become more and more inured, or used to, doing evil?

10. Based on the fourth apparition, the meeting of Macduff with the king of England, Macduff's conversation with Malcolm, and Macduff's feelings at the end of the act, what do you think will happen in the next, final act of the play? In other words, how does this act prepare for the act to come?

**ANALYTIC SCALES FOR
RESPONDING IN WRITING**

Grading scales appear on page 371.

Understanding Literature (Questions for Discussion)

1. **Paradox.** A **paradox** is a contradictory statement, idea, or event. Which statements made by the apparitions are paradoxes? How do you know? Why do you think the messages were given in equivocating, paradoxical language rather than in straightforward language?

2. **Personification. Personification** is a figure of speech in which an idea, animal, or thing is described as if it were a person. In scene iii, lines 39–41, what is being personified? What human characteristics are attributed to this thing?

3. **Verbal Irony. Verbal irony** is a statement that implies its opposite. In scene iii, Macduff grows more and more distraught as Malcolm denounces himself as more evil than Macbeth. Then, when Macduff becomes completely hopeless, Malcolm suddenly reverses himself and swears to fight for Scotland. Macduff declares that he cannot comprehend "such welcome and unwelcome things at once." How do Malcolm's words express verbal irony? Why did Malcolm paint such a picture of himself to Macduff?

Responding in Writing

1. **Dramatic Scene.** Lady Macbeth does not appear in act IV. However, you might suppose that Macbeth told her of his visit to the witches. Write a scene between Lady Macbeth and Macbeth in which Macbeth tells her about the apparitions and their pronouncements. As you plan the scene, consider the setting and where, in this act, you might place your scene. Have the wife and children of Macduff been killed? Does Lady Macbeth know of this? Also consider Lady Macbeth's state of mind. What behavior did she exhibit in the previous act? What thoughts did she express? Make sure your characterization of her and of Macbeth fits with their portrayals so far in the play.

2. **Personal Letter.** Rosse consoles Lady Macduff when she worries about her husband's sudden departure. He reassures her of Macduff's good nature and urges her not to doubt him. What do you say to a friend who needs advice? What support or words of wisdom can you offer? Think of a time when a friend needed your advice or support. Write a letter expressing your thoughts to your friend.

THE TRAGEDY OF MACBETH / ACT IV, SCENE iii **373**

ADDITIONAL RESOURCES

READER'S GUIDE
- Selection Worksheet, 5.5

ASSESSMENT PORTFOLIO
- Selection Check Test, 4.5.9
- Selection Test, 4.5.10

ESSENTIAL SKILLS PRACTICE BOOKS
- *Language*, 2.94–2.96
- *Study and Research*, 4.4
- *Speaking and Listening*, 3.2, 3.3

AUDIOCASSETTE
- Soliloquy from act V, scene v ("Tomorrow, and tomorrow, and tomorrow . . ."), Track 11

ENRICHMENT ACTIVITIES

Planning a Conclusion to a Play. Have students pause between reading acts IV and V to describe, in writing, how they would conclude the play. Remind students that their conclusions should resolve the major conflicts in the play (between Macduff and Macbeth, between Malcolm and Macbeth, and between Macbeth's ambition and his conscience). Ask students to share their conclusions in class, and have the class vote to decide on a favorite. Then ask students to discuss why they chose that conclusion over the others.

SUPPORT FOR LEP STUDENTS

ADDITIONAL VOCABULARY
perturbation—disturbance
meet—apt
mingle—mix
perilous—dangerous
pristine—clean and pure
err—make a mistake
speculative—based on uncertain or insufficient evidence
despair—give up hope

Lady Macbeth. *"All the perfumes of Arabia will not sweeten this little hand."*
Illustration by Sol Graphic Design

374 *UNIT FIVE / RENAISSANCE DRAMA*

ACT V

SCENE i: a castle at Dunsinane

Enter a DOCTOR OF PHYSIC *and a* WAITING-GENTLEWOMAN.

DOCTOR. I have two nights watch'd with you, but can perceive no truth in your report. When was it she last walk'd?

GENTLEWOMAN. Since his Majesty went into the field,[1] I have seen her rise from her bed, throw her nightgown upon her, unlock her closet, take forth paper, fold it, write upon't, read it, afterwards seal it, and again return to bed; yet all this while in a most fast sleep.

DOCTOR. A great perturbation in nature, to receive at once the benefit of sleep and do the effects of watching![2] In this slumb'ry agitation, besides her walking and other actual performances, what, at any time, have you heard her say?

GENTLEWOMAN. That, sir, which I will not report after her.

DOCTOR. You may to me, and 'tis most meet you should.

GENTLEWOMAN. Neither to you nor any one, having no witness to confirm my speech.

Enter LADY MACBETH *with a taper.*

Lo you, here she comes! This is her very guise,[3] and upon my life, fast asleep. Observe her, stand close.[4]

DOCTOR. How came she by that light?

GENTLEWOMAN. Why, it stood by her. She has light by her continually, 'tis her command.

DOCTOR. You see her eyes are open.

GENTLEWOMAN. Aye, but their sense are shut.

DOCTOR. What is it she does now? Look how she rubs her hands.

GENTLEWOMAN. It is an accustom'd action with her, to seem thus washing her hands. I have known her continue in this a quarter of an hour.

LADY MACBETH. Yet here's a spot.

DOCTOR. Hark, she speaks. I will set down what comes from her, to satisfy my remembrance the more strongly.

LADY MACBETH. Out, damn'd spot! out, I say! One—two—why then 'tis time to do't. Hell is murky. Fie, my lord, fie, a soldier, and afeard? What need we fear who knows it, when none can call our pow'r to accompt?[5] Yet who would have thought the old man to have had so much blood in him?

DOCTOR. Do you mark that?

LADY MACBETH. The Thane of Fife had a wife; where is she now? What, will these hands ne'er be clean? No more o' that, my lord, no more o' that; you mar all with this starting.[6]

DOCTOR. Go to, go to; you have known what you should not.

GENTLEWOMAN. She has spoke what she should not, I am sure of that; heaven knows what she has known.

LADY MACBETH. Here's the smell of the blood still. All the perfumes of Arabia will not sweeten this little hand. O, O, O!

DOCTOR. What a sigh is there! The heart is sorely charg'd.[7]

GENTLEWOMAN. I would not have such a heart in my bosom for the dignity of the whole body.

DOCTOR. Well, well, well.

---

1. **went . . . field.** Went to battle
2. **do . . . watching.** Do activities one normally does awake
3. **Her very guise.** Precisely what she has been doing
4. **close.** Hidden
5. **accompt.** Account
6. **starting.** Sudden, startled movements
7. **charg'd.** Burdened

Motif. Point out to students that the motif of hell can be found throughout *Macbeth*, especially associated with Macbeth and Lady Macbeth. "Come, thick night," says Lady Macbeth in act I, "and pall thee in the dunnest smoke of hell" (scene v, lines 55–57). The porter scene (act II, scene iii, lines 1–45) is based on a scene, common in the old mystery plays, in which the porter of hell's gate admitted sinning souls to everlasting torment. Certainly by that scene, Macbeth and Lady Macbeth have made their home a hell. By act V, scene i, Lady Macbeth herself is wandering in a hell of her own making. "Hell is murky," she mutters at line 43. Macbeth's attendant in scene iii is called Seyton, perhaps a pun on "Satan." (See also scene vii, line 7; scene viii, line 3.) The sleepwalking scene is remarkable as a nexus, or connecting point, for many of the motifs of the play. Ask students what other motifs can be found repeated in the sleepwalking scene.

GENTLEWOMAN.   Pray God it be, sir.

DOCTOR.   This disease is beyond my prac-
70   tice; yet I have known those which have
walk'd in their sleep who have died holily in
their beds.

LADY MACBETH.   Wash your hands, put on
your nightgown, look not so pale. I tell you
75   yet again, Banquo's buried; he cannot come
out on 's grave.

DOCTOR.   Even so?

LADY MACBETH.   To bed, to bed; there's
knocking at the gate. Come, come, come,
come, give me your hand. What's done cannot
80   be undone. To bed, to bed, to bed.

Exit LADY.

DOCTOR.   Will she go now to bed?

GENTLEWOMAN.   Directly.

DOCTOR.   Foul whisp'rings are abroad.
Unnatural deeds
Do breed unnatural troubles; infected minds
85   To their deaf pillows will discharge their
secrets.
More needs she the divine than the physician.
God, God, forgive us all! Look after her,
Remove from her the means of all annoyance,
And still keep eyes upon her. So good night.
90   My mind she has mated, and amaz'd my
sight.[8]
I think, but dare not speak.

GENTLEWOMAN.   Good night, good doctor.

Exeunt.

SCENE ii: countryside near Dunsinane

Drum and Colors. Enter MENTETH,
CATHNESS, ANGUS, LENNOX, SOLDIERS.

MENTETH.   The English pow'r is near, led
on by Malcolm,

---

8. **My . . . sight.** She has confused my mind and bewildered my sight.
9. **bleeding . . . alarm.** Bloody and horrible battle
10. **mortified.** Almost dead
11. **file.** List
12. **unrough.** Unbearded

His uncle Siward, and the good Macduff.
Revenges burn in them; for their dear causes
Would to the bleeding and the grim alarm[9]
5   Excite the mortified[10] man.

ANGUS.   Near Birnan wood
Shall we well meet them; that way are they
coming.

CATHNESS.   Who knows if Donalbain be
with his brother?

LENNOX.   For certain, sir, he is not; I have a
file[11]
Of all the gentry. There is Siward's son,
10   And many unrough[12] youths that even now
Protest their first of manhood.[13]

MENTETH.   What does the tyrant?

CATHNESS.   Great Dunsinane he strongly
fortifies.
Some say he's mad; others that lesser hate him
Do call it valiant fury; but for certain
15   He cannot buckle his distemper'd cause
Within the belt of rule.[14]

ANGUS.   Now does he feel
His secret murthers sticking on his hands;
Now minutely revolts[15] upbraid his
faith-breach;
Those he commands move only in command,
20   Nothing in love. Now does he feel his title
Hang loose about him, like a giant's robe
Upon a dwarfish thief.

MENTETH.   Who then shall blame
His pester'd senses to recoil and start,
When all that is within him does condemn
Itself for being there?

25   **CATHNESS.**   Well, march we on
To give obedience where 'tis truly ow'd.
Meet we the med'cine of the sickly weal,[16]
And with him pour we, in our country's purge,
Each drop of us.

---

13. **Protest . . . manhood.** Show their manhood for the first time
14. **He . . . rule.** He cannot confine his corrupt cause within self control.
15. **minutely revolts.** New revolts every minute
16. **med'cine . . . weal.** Malcolm is the medicine that can cure the state.

ADDITIONAL QUESTIONS AND ACTIVITIES

Students can summarize the status of Scotland by writing a proclamation such as might have been issued by Malcolm or the forces of Lennox as they closed in on Dunsinane. Their proclamation should detail the crimes of Macbeth and Lady Macbeth and recapitulate what the speakers report in scene ii. The proclamation should rally people to Malcolm's side and urge those in Macbeth's forces to change sides.

LENNOX.   Or so much as it needs

30 To dew the sovereign flower[17] and drown the
    weeds.
Make we our march towards Birnan.
                   Exeunt marching.

SCENE iii: the castle at Dunsinane

Enter MACBETH, DOCTOR, *and* ATTENDANTS.

MACBETH.   Bring me no more reports, let
    them fly all.
Till Birnan wood remove to Dunsinane
I cannot <u>taint</u> with fear. What's the boy
    Malcolm?
Was he not born of woman? The spirits that
    know

5 All mortal consequences[18] have pronounc'd
    me thus:
"Fear not, Macbeth, no man that's born of
    woman
Shall e'er have power upon thee." Then fly,
    false thanes,
And mingle with the English epicures![19]
The mind I sway[20] by, and the heart I bear,

10 Shall never sag with doubt, nor shake with
    fear.

Enter SERVANT.

The devil damn thee black,[21] thou cream-fac'd
    loon!
Where got'st thou that goose-look?

SERVANT.   There is ten thousand—

MACBETH.   Geese, villain?

SERVANT.   Soldiers, sir.

---

17. **sovereign flower.** Malcolm
18. **mortal consequences.** Human destinies
19. **epicures.** Those who like easy living, not soldiers
20. **sway.** Control myself
21. **devil . . . black.** Damned souls were said to turn black
22. **patch.** Fool
23. **push.** Surge of effort

MACBETH.   Go prick thy face, and over-red
    thy fear,

15 Thou lily-liver'd boy. What soldiers, patch?[22]
Death of thy soul! those linen cheeks of thine
Are counsellors to fear. What soldiers,
    whey-face?

SERVANT.   The English force, so please you.

MACBETH.   Take thy face hence. [*Exit*
    SERVANT.] Seyton!—I am sick at heart

20 When I behold—Seyton, I say!—This push[23]
Will cheer me ever, or disseat[24] me now.
I have liv'd long enough: my way of life
Is fall'n into the sear,[25] the yellow leaf,
And that which should accompany old age,

25 As honor, love, obedience, troops of friends,
I must not look to have; but in their stead,
Curses, not loud but deep, mouth-honor,[26]
    breath,
Which the poor heart would fain[27] deny, and
    dare not.
Seyton!

Enter SEYTON.

30 **SEYTON.**   What's your gracious pleasure?

MACBETH.   What news more?

SEYTON.   All is confirm'd, my lord, which
    was reported.

MACBETH.   I'll fight, till from my bones my
    flesh be hack'd.
Give me my armor.

SEYTON.   'Tis not needed yet.

MACBETH.   I'll put it on.

---

24. **disseat.** Dethrone
25. **sear.** Dried and withered
26. **mouth-honor.** Honored in words but not in actions
27. **fain.** Gladly, eagerly

WORDS FOR   **taint** (tānt) *vi.,* be infected
EVERYDAY USE:

VOCABULARY IN CONTEXT

- The Shakespearean scholar looked in the refrigerator and exclaimed, "My goodness! Mold <u>taints</u> this cheese!"

ADDITIONAL QUESTIONS AND ACTIVITIES

Ask the following questions to guide students in their reading of Scene iii:

1. With which characters does Macbeth interact in this scene?

2. How does Macbeth treat the servant? What emotion does the servant show that provokes Macbeth to react in this way?

3. What does Macbeth's intense reaction to the servant tell you about the emotions Macbeth is feeling?

4. Cite the lines Macbeth and Seyton exchange concerning the armor.

5. What does Macbeth's insistence on having the armor on and then his sudden change of intention suggest about his state of mind?

6. Macbeth suggests to the doctor that Scotland is diseased, infected with English troops. What lines in scene ii does this statement echo? How is the perspective there different?

Answers. 1. Macbeth interacts with a servant, with Seyton, and with the doctor. 2. Macbeth treats him with fury and contempt because he is pale with fear. 3. Macbeth is perhaps frightened of being afraid or is wound to a very tight pitch. 4. Macbeth: "Give me my armor" (line 33); Seyton: "'Tis not needed yet" (line 33); Macbeth: "I'll put it on" (line 34); "Give me mine armor" (line 36); "Come, put mine armor on" (line 48); "Come sir, dispatch" (line 50); "Pull't off, I say" (line 54); "Bring it after me" (line 58). 5. It suggests he is rattled and not thinking coherently. 6. Macbeth's words echo the words of Cathness (lines 27–29): "Meet we the med'cine of the sickly weal,/And with him pour we, in our country's purge,/Each drop of us." In scene ii, the speaker views Macbeth as the source of sickness, and Malcolm and his troops as healing medicine.

35   Send out moe horses, skirr[28] the country
          round,
      Hang those that talk of fear. Give me mine
          armor.
      How does your patient, doctor?

      DOCTOR.   Not so sick, my lord,
      As she is troubled with thick-coming fancies,
      That keep her from her rest.

      MACBETH.   Cure her of that.
40   Canst thou not minister to a mind diseas'd,
      Pluck from the memory a rooted sorrow,
      Raze out[29] the written troubles of the brain,
      And with some sweet oblivious antidote[30]
      Cleanse the stuff'd bosom of that perilous
          stuff
      Which weighs upon the heart?

45   DOCTOR.   Therein the patient
      Must minister to himself.

      MACBETH.   Throw physic to the dogs, I'll
          none of it.
      Come, put mine armor on; give me my staff.
      Seyton, send out. Doctor, the thanes fly from
          me.—
50   Come, sir, dispatch.—If thou couldst, doctor,
          cast
      The water of my land, find her disease,[31]
      And purge it to a sound and pristine health,
      I would applaud thee to the very echo,
      That should applaud again.—Pull't off, I say.—
55   What rhubarb, cyme, or what purgative drug,
      Would scour these English hence? Hear'st
          thou of them?

      DOCTOR.   Aye, my good lord; your royal
          preparation
      Makes us hear something.

      MACBETH.   Bring it after me.—
      I will not be afraid of death and bane,[32]
60   Till Birnan forest come to Dunsinane.

---

28. **skirr.** Scour
29. **Raze out.** Erase
30. **oblivious antidote.** Medicine that causes forgetfulness
31. **cast . . . disease.** Diagnose the disease
32. **bane.** Destruction
33. **shadow.** Camouflage

                              Exeunt all but the DOCTOR.

      DOCTOR.   Were I from Dunsinane away
          and clear,
      Profit again should hardly draw me here.
                                        Exit.

      SCENE iv: countryside near Dunsinane

      Drum and Colors. Enter MALCOLM, SIWARD,
      MACDUFF, SIWARD'S SON, MENTETH,
      CATHNESS, ANGUS, LENNOX, ROSSE, *and*
      SOLDIERS, *marching.*

      MALCOLM.   Cousins, I hope the days are
          near at hand
      That chambers will be safe.

      MENTETH.   We doubt it nothing.

      SIWARD.   What wood is this before us?

      MENTETH.   The wood of Birnan.

      MALCOLM.   Let every soldier hew him
          down a bough,
5   And bear't before him, thereby shall we shad-
          ow[33]
      The numbers of our host, and make
          discovery[34]
      Err in report of us.

      SOLDIERS.   It shall be done.

      SIWARD.   We learn no other but the confi-
          dent tyrant
      Keeps still in Dunsinane, and will endure
      Our setting down before't.[35]

10   MALCOLM.   'Tis his main hope;
      For where there is advantage[36] to be given,
      Both more and less[37] have given him the
          revolt,
      And none serve with him but constrained
          things,
      Whose hearts are absent too.

---

34. **discovery.** The reports of scouts
35. **setting down before't.** Laying siege to
36. **advantage.** Opportunity
37. **more and less.** Nobles and common people

MACDUFF. Let our just censures
15 Attend the true event,[38] and put we on
Industrious soldiership.

SIWARD. The time approaches
That will with due decision make us know
What we shall say we have, and what we owe.
Thoughts speculative their unsure hopes relate,
20 But certain issue strokes must arbitrate,[39]
Towards which advance the war.

Exeunt marching.

SCENE v: the castle at Dunsinane

Enter MACBETH, SEYTON, *and* SOLDIERS, *with Drum and Colors.*

MACBETH. Hang out our banners on the outward walls,
The cry is still, "They come!" Our castle's strength
Will laugh a siege to scorn; here let them lie
Till famine and the <u>ague</u> eat them up.
5 Were they not forc'd with those that should be ours,[40]
We might have met them dareful, beard to beard,
And beat them backward home.

(A cry within of women.)
What is that noise?

SEYTON. It is the cry of women, my good lord. *Exit.*

MACBETH. I have almost forgot the taste of fears.
10 The time has been, my senses would have cool'd

To hear a night-shriek, and my fell of hair[41]
Would at a dismal treatise[42] rouse and stir
As life were in't. I have supp'd full with horrors;
Direness, familiar to my slaughterous thoughts,
Cannot once start me.[43]

Enter SEYTON.

15 Wherefore was that cry?

SEYTON. The Queen, my lord, is dead.

MACBETH. She should have died hereafter;[44]
There would have been a time for such a word.
Tomorrow, and tomorrow, and tomorrow,
20 Creeps in this petty pace from day to day,
To the last syllable of recorded time;
And all our yesterdays have lighted fools
The way to dusty death. Out, out, brief candle!
Life's but a walking shadow, a poor player,
25 That struts and frets his hour upon the stage,
And then is heard no more. It is a tale
Told by an idiot, full of sound and fury,
Signifying nothing.

Enter a MESSENGER.

Thou com'st to use thy tongue;
Thy story quickly.

MESSENGER. Gracious my lord,
30 I should report that which I say I saw,
But know not how to do't.

MACBETH. Well, say, sir.

MESSENGER. As I did stand my watch upon the hill,
I look'd toward Birnan, and anon methought
The wood began to move.

MACBETH. Liar and slave!

---

38. **Let . . . event.** Let our judgments wait for the actual event.
39. **Thoughts . . . arbitrate.** Talking about an event is just dealing with hopes; issues are only solved through action.
40. **forc'd . . . ours.** Reinforced with traitors from our side

41. **my . . . hair.** Hair on my skin
42. **treatise.** Story
43. **once start me.** Ever startle me
44. **should . . . hereafter.** Was bound to die eventually

WORDS FOR EVERYDAY USE:

a • gue (āʹ gyōō') *n.*, fever and chills

ADDITIONAL QUESTIONS AND ACTIVITIES

• The speech of Macbeth in lines 19–28 is well known independently of the play itself. (The American writer William Faulkner [1897–1962] used the phrase "sound and fury" in the title of one of his novels.) The speech has been called the *ne plus ultra* as a statement of nihilism. Ask students the following questions:

1. What is Macbeth's view of life? Do you agree with it?

2. To what extent, do you think, is Macbeth's disgust with life a result of his own rejection of everything of value in life?

3. Even those who do not accept Macbeth's view of life find his statement deeply moving. Why, do you suppose, is this so?

Answers. 1. Macbeth's view of life is that life signifies nothing (is without meaning). Responses to the second part of the question will vary. 2. Macbeth's disgust with life seems to stem immediately from his own decisions to disregard morality, friendship, gratitude, societal norms, and so on. Support for this view can be found in act V, scene iii, where he regrets the loss of honor, love, obedience, and friends. 3. Nearly everyone has felt at one time or another that life is meaningless or has been concerned that it may prove to be. However, such commonplace temporary questioning is far from the pathological state of despair into which Macbeth sinks.

• If they wish, students can write a rebuttal to Macbeth's speech, offering reasons for finding significance and hope in human existence.

VOCABULARY IN CONTEXT
• Lord Byron complained of catching the <u>ague</u> after taking a long swim.

35 MESSENGER. Let me endure your wrath, if't
    be not so.
Within this three mile may you see it coming;
I say, a moving grove.

    MACBETH.   If thou speak'st false,
Upon the next tree shall thou hang alive,
Till famine cling[45] thee; if thy speech be
    sooth,[46]

40 I care not if thou dost for me as much.
I pull in[47] resolution, and begin
To doubt th' equivocation of the fiend
That lies like truth. "Fear not, till Birnan wood
Do come to Dunsinane," and now a wood

45 Comes toward Dunsinane. Arm, arm, and out!
If this which he avouches[48] does appear,
There is nor flying hence, nor tarrying here.
I gin to be a-weary of the sun,
And wish th' estate o' th' world were now
    undone.

50 Ring the alarum-bell! Blow wind, come
    wrack,[49]
At least we'll die with harness[50] on our back.
            Exeunt.

SCENE vi: field at Dunsinane

Drum and Colors. Enter MALCOLM, SIWARD, MACDUFF, *and their army, with boughs.*

    MALCOLM.   Now near enough; your leavy[51]
    screens throw down,
And show like those you are.[52] You, worthy
    uncle,
Shall with my cousin, your right noble son,
Lead our first battle.[53] Worthy Macduff and
    we

5 Shall take upon 's what else remains to do,

---

45. **cling.** Wither
46. **sooth.** Truth
47. **pull in.** Rein in
48. **avouches.** Affirms
49. **wrack.** Ruin
50. **harness.** Armor

According to our order.

    SIWARD.   Fare you well.
Do we but find the tyrant's power tonight,
Let us be beaten, if we cannot fight.

    MACDUFF.   Make all our trumpets speak,
    give them all breath,
10 Those clamorous <u>harbingers</u> of blood and
    death.
          Exeunt. Alarums continued.

SCENE vii: field at Dunsinane

Enter MACBETH.

    MACBETH.   They have tied me to a stake; I
    cannot fly,
But bear-like I must fight the course.[54]
    What's he
That was not born of woman? Such a one
Am I to fear, or none.

Enter YOUNG SIWARD.

    YOUNG SIWARD.   What is thy name?
5 MACBETH.   Thou'lt be afraid to hear it.
    YOUNG SIWARD.   No; though thou call'st
    thyself a hotter name
Than any is in hell.

    MACBETH.   My name's Macbeth.

    YOUNG SIWARD.   The devil himself could
    not pronounce a title
More hateful to mine ear.

    MACBETH.   No; nor more fearful.
10 YOUNG SIWARD.   Thou liest, abhorred
    tyrant, with my sword
I'll prove the lie thou speak'st.

---

51. **leavy.** Leafy
52. **show . . . are.** Show yourselves as you are
53. **battle.** Battalion
54. **bear-like . . . course.** It was a common sport to tie a bear to a stake and make it fight with dogs.

WORDS FOR EVERYDAY USE: **har • bin • ger** (här´bin jər) *n.*, person or thing that comes before and hints at what is to follow

Fight, and YOUNG SIWARD *slain.*

MACBETH.   Thou wast born of woman.
But swords I smile at, weapons laugh to scorn,
Brandish'd by man that's of a woman born.
                                             Exit.

Alarums. Enter MACDUFF.

MACDUFF.   That way the noise is. Tyrant,
        show thy face!
15 If thou beest slain and with no stroke of mine,
My wife and children's ghosts will haunt me
        still.
I cannot strike at wretched kerns, whose arms
Are hir'd to bear their staves;[55] either thou,
        Macbeth,
Or else my sword with an unbattered edge
20 I sheathe again undeeded.[56] There thou
        shouldst be;
By this great clatter, one of greatest note
Seems bruited.[57] Let me find him, Fortune!
And more I beg not.   *Exit. Alarums.*

Enter MALCOLM *and* SIWARD.

SIWARD.   This way, my lord, the castle's
        gently rend'red:[58]
25 The tyrant's people on both sides do fight,
The noble thanes do bravely in the war,
The day almost itself professes yours,
And little is to do.

MALCOLM.   We have met with foes
That strike beside us.[59]

SIWARD.   Enter, sir, the castle.
                              Exeunt. Alarum.

SCENE viii: field at Dunsinane

Enter MACBETH.

MACBETH.   Why should I play the Roman
        fool, and die

On mine own sword?[60] Whiles I see lives, the
        gashes
Do better upon them.

Enter MACDUFF.

MACDUFF.   Turn, hell-hound, turn!

MACBETH.   Of all men else I have avoided
        thee.
5 But get thee back, my soul is too much charg'd
With blood of thine already.

MACDUFF.   I have no words,
My voice is in my sword, thou bloodier villain
Than terms can give thee out!
                              Fight. Alarum.

MACBETH.   Thou losest labor.
As easy mayst thou the intrenchant[61] air
10 With thy keen sword impress as make me
        bleed.
Let fall thy blade on vulnerable crests,
I bear a charmed life, which must not yield
To one of woman born.

MACDUFF.   Despair thy charm,
And let the angel whom thou still hast serv'd
15 Tell thee, Macduff was from his mother's
        womb
Untimely ripp'd.

MACBETH.   Accursed be that tongue that
        tells me so,
For it hath cow'd my better part of man!
And be these juggling fiends no more
        believ'd,
20 That palter[62] with us in a double sense,
That keep the word of promise to our ear,
And break it to our hope. I'll not fight with
        thee.

MACDUFF.   Then yield thee, coward,
And live to be the show and gaze o' th' time!
25 We'll have thee, as our rarer monsters are,

---

55. **staves.** Spears
56. **undeeded.** Unused
57. **bruited.** Announced
58. **castle's gently rend'red.** Surrendered easily
59. **strike beside us.** Fight on our side

60. **Roman fool . . . sword.** Commit suicide like a Roman soldier faced with defeat
61. **intrenchant.** Incapable of being cut
62. **palter.** Speak

TEACHER'S EDITION **381**

ADDITIONAL QUESTIONS AND ACTIVITIES

Ask these questions to help students explore the meaning of scenes vii and viii.

1. What motifs common elsewhere in the play also occur in scene vii?

2. What dramatic purpose does the killing of Young Siward serve?

3. How does Shakespeare emphasize the contrast between Macbeth and Malcolm in scene vii?

4. In scene viii, how does Macbeth describe his reaction when Macduff tells him that he is not born of woman?

5. What is Macbeth's final comment about the witches?

Answers. 1. Hell and ghost motifs are common. 2. The killing of Young Siward extends the action and thus the suspense and suggests to the audience that Macbeth truly is invincible. 3. He shows Macbeth as the arrogant killer of a young, brave nobleman and shows Malcolm as so loved and appreciated that he achieves his goals gently and with little fighting. 4. He says that Macduff has "cow'd" the "better part" of his manliness. 5. He says they should not be believed because they equivocate, saying words that sound like promises but prove to be lies.

VOCABULARY IN CONTEXT

• The robin is often described as the <u>harbinger</u> of spring.

The text indicated in *brackets* at the end of scene viii (*"MACDUFF carries off MACBETH's body"*) is not found in the Folio edition, but was added by a later editor who was trying to explain how Macduff could reenter later with Macbeth's severed head. (The stage directions in the Folio editions are sometimes corrupt, as if they had been hastily inserted by a printer or actor.) Instead of adding the line in *brackets,* some editors prefer to delete the stage direction that calls for Macduff and Macbeth to reenter; thus Macbeth is killed offstage, and Macduff does not reappear until scene ix. The latter version is often preferred by directors: it is very difficult to lug a "dead" actor off the stage without causing laughter; further, the audience will wonder where Macduff is taking the body and why. Ask students which version they prefer, and have them explain their reasoning.

ADDITIONAL QUESTIONS AND ACTIVITIES

To prompt discussion of the end of the play, ask these questions:

1. How does Young Siward contrast with Macbeth?

2. How does the previous Thane of Cawdor's death, as described by Malcolm in act I, scene iv, lines 3–11, compare with Macbeth's death?

3. What emotion does Malcolm express in the concluding two lines of the play? How does it compare to Duncan's behavior toward Macbeth in act I? How does it contrast with Macbeth's actions in the play?

Answers. 1. Young Siward acted bravely in a cause that was not his own, whereas Macbeth acted only in his own cause and did not behave nobly even in that endeavor. 2. Macbeth seems to cling to life more desperately than the previous Cawdor. 3. Malcolm expresses gratitude, an emotion that Duncan also conspicuously showed (see act I, scene vi, lines 10–14) but that Macbeth conspicuously lacked in killing Duncan.

Painted upon a pole,[63] and underwrit,
"Here may you see the tyrant."

MACBETH.   I will not yield,
To kiss the ground before young Malcolm's feet,
And to be baited with the rabble's curse.
30   Though Birnan wood be come to Dunsinane,
And thou oppos'd, being of no woman born,
Yet I will try the last. Before my body
I throw my warlike shield. Lay on, Macduff,
And damn'd be him that first cries, "Hold, enough!"
             Exeunt fighting. Alarums.

Enter fighting, and MACBETH *slain.* MACDUFF *carries off* MACBETH's *body.*

SCENE ix: castle at Dunsinane

Retreat and flourish. Enter, with Drum and Colors, MALCOLM, SIWARD, ROSSE, THANES, *and* SOLDIERS.

MALCOLM.   I would the friends we miss were safe arriv'd.

SIWARD.   Some must go off;[64] and yet, by these I see,
So great a day as this is cheaply bought.[65]

MALCOLM.   Macduff is missing, and your noble son.

5   **ROSSE.**   Your son my lord, has paid a soldier's debt.
He only liv'd but till he was a man,
The which no sooner had his prowess confirm'd
In the unshrinking station where he fought,[66]

---

63. **Painted . . . pole.** Portrait carried on a pole
64. **go off.** Die
65. **cheaply bought.** Marked with few casualties
66. **unshrinking . . . fought.** Spot from which he did not retreat

---

But like a man he died.

SIWARD.   Then he is dead?

10   **ROSSE.**   Aye, and brought off the field. Your cause of sorrow
Must not be measur'd by his worth, for then
It hath no end.

SIWARD.   Had he his hurts before?

ROSSE.   Aye, on the front.

SIWARD.   Why then, God's soldier be he!
Had I as many sons as I have hairs,
15   I would not wish them to a fairer death.
And so his knell is knoll'd.

MALCOLM.   He's worth more sorrow,
And that I'll spend for him.

SIWARD.   He's worth no more;
They say he parted well, and paid his score,
And so God be with him! Here comes newer comfort.

Enter MACDUFF *with* MACBETH's *head.*

20   **MACDUFF.**   Hail, King! for so thou art.
Behold where stands
Th' usurper's cursed head: the time is free.[67]
I see thee compass'd with thy kingdom's pearl,[68]
That speak my salutation in their minds;
Whose voices I desire aloud with mine:
Hail, King of Scotland!

25   **ALL.**   Hail, King of Scotland!
             Flourish.

MALCOLM.   We shall not spend a large expense of time

---

67. **time is free.** Freedom reigns now
68. **compass'd . . . pearl.** Surrounded by the most noble in your realm

---

WORDS FOR EVERYDAY USE: u • surp • er (yōō surp´ər) *n.,* one who assumes power without right

---

LITERARY TECHNIQUE

Wordplay. Point out to students that Old Siward mocks his own grief with puns: "Had I as many sons as I have hairs [heirs],/I would not wish them to a fairer death" (lines 14–15); "They say he parted well, and paid his score [paid his due, or paid his twenty years of life]" (line 18). Even his line "And so his knell is knoll'd" (line 16) has a bravely humorous "ring" to it.

VOCABULARY IN CONTEXT

• After the election was shown to be illegal, the candidate who had originally lost the race took office, and the usurper went to jail.

Before we reckon with your several loves,
And make us even with you.[69] My thanes and
kinsmen,
Henceforth be earls, the first that ever
Scotland
30   In such an honor nam'd. What's more to do,
Which would be planted newly with the time,
As calling home our exil'd friends abroad
That fled the snares of watchful tyranny,
Producing forth[70] the cruel ministers
35   Of this dead butcher and his fiend-like queen,

Who (as 'tis thought) by self and violent
hands[71]
Took off her life; this, and what needful else
That calls upon us, by the grace of Grace,
We will perform in measure, time, and place.
40   So thanks to all at once and to each one,
Whom we invite to see us crown'd at Scone.

Flourish. Exeunt omnes. ■

---

69. **make . . . you.** Reward as you deserve
70. **Producing forth.** Bringing forward to trial
71. **self . . . hands.** The violence of her own hands

Responding to the Selection

How do you feel toward Macbeth at the end of the play? Do you despise him? Do you feel sympathy for him? Do you feel some combination of these things? Describe your feelings and relate them to events in the play.

Reviewing the Selection

RECALLING

1. What do Lady Macbeth's gentlewoman and doctor observe her doing at the beginning of scene i? What action does she continually perform?

2. Why is Macbeth so confident at the beginning of scene iii?

3. In scene iii, what does the physician report to Macbeth? How does Macbeth respond? What reply does the physician give to Macbeth's response?

4. In scene v, Macbeth receives bad news related to the witches' prophecies. What is this news?

INTERPRETING

5. What do Lady Macbeth's actions at the beginning of scene i reveal about her state of mind? What is she feeling? What drove her to do what she is doing?

6. In lines 22–28 of scene iii, how does Macbeth characterize his life? Why is he so unhappy, despite his confidence?

7. Why can't the physician cure Lady Macbeth? What is the cause of her malady?

8. What is equivocation? In what ways have the witches equivocated with Macbeth?

RECALLING

1. They observe her walking in her sleep. She appears to be continually rubbing her hands in an attempt to clean them.

2. Macbeth relies upon the words of the apparitions and assumes he is safe from harm.

3. The doctor tells Macbeth that Lady Macbeth is troubled by delusions; Macbeth orders him to find a way to erase Lady Macbeth's memories and "cleanse" her "of that perilous stuff/Which weighs upon the heart."

4. He hears that Birnan wood is moving toward Dunsinane.

INTERPRETING

Responses will vary. Possible responses are given.

5. Her actions reveal that she is insane. She is feeling remorse for the crimes she committed. Her desire to cleanse her conscience of her guilt leads her to attempt to wash imaginary blood from her hands.

6. Macbeth characterizes his way of life as dried, withered, and friendless. He is unhappy because he sees he will never have true friends or true honor.

7. The physician cannot heal Lady Macbeth because he cannot make her forget the crimes she has committed, which gave rise to the guilt that is at the root of her malady.

8. Equivocation is double-talk, or language that appears to have one meaning but really has another or means nothing. The witches equivocate with Macbeth by making him believe that he is invincible when he is not.

SYNTHESIZING

Responses will vary. Possible responses are given.

9. These passages all concern the futility of pursuing ambition. The consequences of Macbeth's immoral action include finding that an immoral life is meaningless.

10. Malcolm makes his allies into earls and promises to call home exiles and to bring to trial Macbeth's officials.

RESPONDING TO THE SELECTION

Some students may find themselves surprised to feel sympathy for Macbeth despite the crimes he has committed. Suggest that they look for passages that show Macbeth's human side—his love for his wife, his doubts, his fears, his guilt, and his remorse. Ask these questions: How would we view Macbeth without these passages? (We would probably see him simply as a two-dimensional villain or a monster.) Would the play be as satisfying without them? (The play would be far less interesting, a mere morality tale with little direct relevance to the struggle between good and bad in us.)

*Responses will vary. Possible
responses are given.*

► See the evaluation forms for
discussion, active listening, and
oral communication, *Assessment
Portfolio,* 7.11–7.14.

1. Foreshadowing. The scene is
foreshadowed by Macbeth's
words in act II, scene ii, lines
57–60: "Will all great Neptune's
ocean wash this blood/Clean from
my hand?"

►**Teaching Note:** Now that
students have finished reading the
play, they will be able to study
foreshadowing in depth. One
other example is Macbeth's
account of the voice that said he
had murdered sleep (act II, scene
ii, lines 39–40).

2. Metaphor. Macbeth compares
life to "a tale/Told by an idiot, full
of sound and fury,/Signifying
nothing." In Macbeth's view, the
two things are similar in that
despite the fuss and bother of
each, they ultimately mean nothing. The metaphor indicates that
Macbeth sees no value in life.

3. Theme. Recurring elements of
the play that deal with disorder are
these: the witches and their
prophecies (disorder in language);
horrific occurrences, such as the
day of Duncan's death being as
dark as night, the killing of a falcon by an owl, and the wildness of
Duncan's horses (disorder in
nature); murder, including the
murder of the king and the murder of an innocent wife and her
children (disorder in the kingdom); and sleeplessness and
madness (psychological disorder).
These motifs can be seen to be
related to the central motif of
ambition, for this disorder is all
brought about by the assassination
of Duncan. The murder of Duncan
is particularly unnatural because it
was done by his host shortly after
that host had been honored for
putting down a rebellion. At the
end of the play, Malcolm promises
to restore the kingdom to health.
Shakespeare believed that humankind (and human kingdoms) are
intimately bound up with the nat-

(cont.)

---

9. Reread the following lines from earlier parts of the play: act II, scene iv, lines 28–29; act
III, scene ii, lines 4–7; and act V, scene iii, lines 22–26. Then read the "Tomorrow"
soliloquy, act V, scene v, lines 19–28. What do these passages have in common? What
are the consequences for Macbeth of committing himself to an immoral course of
action?

10. What indications are given at the end of the play that order will be restored in the
kingdom? In act II, Macduff says of the murder of Duncan that "Most sacrilegious
murder hath broke open/The Lord's anointed temple and stole thence/The life o' the
building." In what sense was the murder of a king sacrilegious? What is this play saying
about the nature and effects of regicide?

Understanding Literature (Questions for Discussion)

1. **Foreshadowing. Foreshadowing** is the act of presenting materials that hint at events
to occur later in a story. In act V, scene i, Lady Macbeth rubs at an imaginary spot of
blood on her hand, saying "will these hands ne'er be clean?" Which earlier scene
suggested this one? How do Lady Macbeth's actions and words differ from the earlier
scene?

2. **Metaphor.** A **metaphor** is a description of one thing as if it were another. The
description invites the reader to compare the two things to see how they are similar. In
scene v, lines 26–28, Macbeth responds to the news of Lady Macbeth's death. What
two things does he compare? What do they have in common? What does this
metaphor tell you about Macbeth's state of mind?

3. **Theme.** A **theme** is a central idea in a literary work. Most literary works have more
than one theme. In act II, Macduff refers to the murdered Duncan as having been "the
Lord's anointed temple." James I, who was king of England at the time when
Shakespeare wrote *Macbeth,* was a believer in the divine right of kings, the idea that a
king was divinely appointed and answerable only to God. Attacking the king would be
an attack on God and therefore on the whole natural order of the universe. What
recurring elements, or motifs, in this play deal with disturbances or disorder? Give
examples of psychological disorder, disorder in nature, disorder in the kingdom, and
disordered (or equivocal) speech. How might these motifs be related? What incident
in the play brings about all of this disorder? What elements of the murder of Duncan
make it particularly unnatural? What happens at the end of the play to restore the
natural order of things? What theme do you think Shakespeare is expressing regarding
the natural order?

   A complex play like *Macbeth* has, of course, many themes. Another theme of the
play is the consequences of ambition. What are the consequences of ambition for
Macbeth?

   What are some other themes that you have noticed while reading and thinking
about the play?

ANSWERS FOR UNDERSTANDING LITERATURE (CONT.)

ural world; the one reflects disorder in the other. The
consequences of ambition for Macbeth are despair, loss
of his wife, and death. Other themes in the play are the
importance of one's relation to posterity; the inevitable
failure of an attempt to use evil to one's own ends; and
the misuse of political power.

►**Teaching Note:** Although it is easy to distinguish in
theory between a theme (a principal idea or concern of

a literary work) and a motif (a recurring element), the
two concepts often overlap. For instance, ambition is
both a theme and a motif of *Macbeth.* It is worthwhile to
try to differentiate between the two concepts, however.
For example, fathers and sons are a motif, but the
importance of one's posterity is a theme.

(cont.)

4. **Plot.** A **plot** is a series of events related to a central conflict, or struggle. Read "plot" in the Handbook of Literary Terms. Then work with other students in a small group or as a class to complete a diagram of the plot of Macbeth. Fill in the chart below with key events from the play.

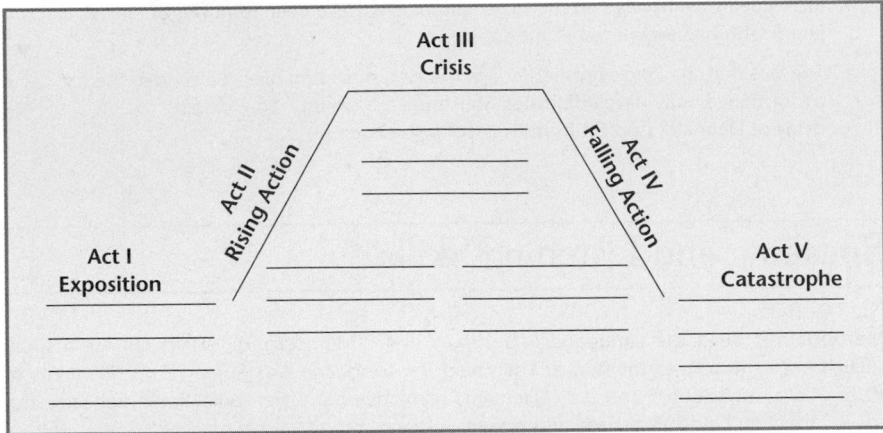

Responding in Writing

1. **Obituary.** An **obituary** is a written notice of a person's death, listing the cause of death and survivors. Some obituaries also include a brief biography of the deceased. Write an obituary, including a biography, for Macbeth, Lady Macbeth, Banquo, or Duncan. Consider which details you will include in the biography.

2. **Expository Essay.** There is more than one way to look at a piece of literature; that is, there is not necessarily a right or a wrong interpretation. However, a good expository essay about a piece of literature states its **thesis**, or main idea, clearly and then supports that thesis with solid, convincing evidence. Write an expository essay about one of the central themes of *Macbeth*. State your thesis, the idea that you wish to prove, and then present in a logical, organized manner evidence from the play to support your thesis.

Language Lab

Using Commas. Read the Language Arts Survey, 2.94–96, "Commas." Then revise the sentences below, adding or deleting commas as necessary.

1. Shakespeare wrote *Macbeth,* for a royal performance before James I of England.

ANALYTIC SCALES FOR RESPONDING IN WRITING (CONT.)

• **Language/Style.** The obituary uses vivid and precise nouns, verbs, and modifiers.

• **Conventions.** The obituary avoids errors in spelling, grammar, usage, mechanics, and manuscript form.

2. Expository Essay

• **Content/Unity.** The essay presents a sensible statement about a thesis in the play and supports it with evidence.

• **Organization/Coherence.** The essay is clearly organized, presenting supporting evidence in a logical order.

• **Language/Style.** The essay uses vivid and precise nouns, verbs, and modifiers.

• **Conventions.** The essay avoids errors in spelling, grammar, usage, mechanics, and manuscript form.

ANSWERS FOR UNDERSTANDING LITERATURE (CONT.)

4. Plot

Exposition (Act I)
Macbeth acts heroically.
The witches foretell kingship for Macbeth.
Duncan rewards Macbeth.
Macbeth and Lady Macbeth debate murdering Duncan.
Duncan arrives at Macbeth's castle.

Rising Action (Act II)
Macbeth kills Duncan.
Macduff discovers the king's body.
Macbeth kills grooms.
Malcolm and Donalbain flee.
Macbeth is to be named king.

Crisis (Act III)
Macbeth has Banquo murdered.
Banquo's ghost haunts the feast.
Macbeth is publicly disgraced.
Macduff travels to England to find help.

Falling Action (Act IV)
Witches give ambiguous signs encouraging to Macbeth.
Macbeth has Macduff's family murdered.
Macduff joins forces with Malcolm in England.

Catastrophe (Act V)
Lady Macbeth goes mad and kills herself.
The English army moves on Macbeth's stronghold.
The signs foretold by the witches are fulfilled.
Macduff fights and kills Macbeth.
Malcolm reestablishes order in Scotland.

ANALYTIC SCALES FOR RESPONDING IN WRITING

Assign a score from 1 to 25 for each grading criterion below. (For more detailed evaluation, see the evaluation forms for writing, revising, and proofreading, *Assessment Portfolio,* 7.1–7.10.)

1. Obituary

• **Content/Unity.** The obituary presents a sensible summary of the character's life and death as revealed in *Macbeth*.

• **Organization/Coherence.** The obituary is clearly organized, presenting facts in a straightforward manner.

(cont.)

ANSWERS FOR LANGUAGE LAB

1. Shakespeare wrote *Macbeth* for a royal performance before James I of England.

2. James I was one of the Stuarts of Scotland, a line of kings descended from Banquo.

3. Scholars have speculated that the mirror carried by one of the eight kings in act IV may have been held up to show James's reflection, but we cannot know for certain that this occurred.

4. Shakespeare's emphasis on the supernatural may have been in honor of King James, who had an interest in the subject.

5. The fact that the king's brother-in-law, the king of Denmark, also attended the performance may have influenced Shakespeare's decision to eliminate the detail of Denmark's defeat from the opening scene.

FOR MORE PRACTICE

Problem. We know *Macbeth* was written after 1603 because Shakespeare refers to the union, of England, and Scotland, under James I which took place in that year.

Solution. We know *Macbeth* was written after 1603 because Shakespeare refers to the union of England and Scotland under James I, which took place in that year.

►Additional practice is provided in the *Essential Skills Practice Book: Language:* 2.94-2.96.

SPEAKING AND LISTENING SKILLS

You might suggest that students memorize Macbeth's speech in scene v, lines 19–28, or in lines 46–51.

►Additional practice is provided in the *Essential Skills Practice Book: Speaking and Listening:* 3.2–3.3.

---

2. James I was one of the Stuarts of Scotland a line of kings descended from Banquo.

3. Scholars have speculated that the mirror carried by one of the eight kings in act IV may have been held up to show James's reflection but we cannot know for certain that this occurred.

4. Shakespeare's emphasis on the supernatural may have been in honor of King James who had an interest in the subject.

5. The fact that the king's brother-in-law, the king of Denmark also attended the performance, may have influenced Shakespeare's decision to eliminate the detail of Denmark's defeat from the opening scene.

Speaking and Listening Skills

Memorizing. Read the Language Arts Survey, 4.4, "Memorizing." Then choose a short speech from the play to memorize. Then read the Language Arts Survey, 3.2, "Elements of Verbal Communication," and 3.3, "Elements of Nonverbal Communication." Rehearse the speech that you have memorized and present it to a group of your classmates.

PROJECTS

1. **A Dramatic Interpretation.** Choose a key scene from *Macbeth* that you would like to perform. After casting the parts, hold a read-through of the scene as a group, with each person reading his or her lines aloud. If possible, try to memorize your lines for the performance. As you rehearse, be sure to block the scene, or map out the characters' movements on stage. Talk with each other about the scene's dramatic interpretation. Decide what the characters are thinking and feeling and how their words relate to their body movements and facial expressions. When you are ready, perform your scene for the class.

2. **Wanted Posters.** *Macbeth* has enough villains and suspected villains to cover an entire post office wall with wanted posters. Imagine how a wanted poster for Macbeth would read. What crimes has he committed? Why should he be arrested? Imagine a wanted poster that Macbeth would have posted for Malcolm or Donalbain. Of what crimes would they be accused? Where would they be sought? Make a wanted poster for one of the criminals or reputed criminals in the play. Use your imagination and descriptions from the play to make a sketch of the person. Then detail the person's alleged crimes and offer a reward.

PROJECT NOTES

►See the worksheets and evaluation forms for projects, *Assessment Portfolio,* 7.20–7.23.

1. A Dramatic Interpretation

• Often directors of Shakespeare begin to rehearse by asking actors to supply only as much of their speeches as they understand. After they understand the drama of each scene, they can give full force and meaning to their words.

• Students should spend the necessary time to resolve questions about the meaning of their lines before they begin memorizing.

2. Wanted Posters

• Students can stop by a post office to examine the format of a wanted poster.

PREREADING

from *The Tragical History of Doctor Faustus*
by Christopher Marlowe

ABOUT THE AUTHOR

See the biography of Marlowe on page 315.

ABOUT THE SELECTION

At the time Marlowe wrote *The Tragical History of Doctor Faustus,* translations of German Faust stories had already appeared in London, and the story of a man who sells his soul to the devil in exchange for magical powers was well known. Marlowe set his play in the German university town of Wittenberg at the end of the sixteenth century. Dr. Faustus, a brilliant scholar, makes a deal with the devil: Faustus will receive the powers of black magic and the services of the devil's servant, Mephastophilis, in exchange for his soul. Throughout the remainder of the play, Faustus agonizes over his decision, yearning for forgiveness but believing that ultimately he cannot be saved. This selection, which is the final scene of the play, begins as Faustus confesses his bargain to his fellow scholars.

The plot of the Faustus story derives originally from the story of Adam and Eve, who tasted the forbidden fruit of the tree of knowledge and so were cast out of Eden (see the selection from Milton's *Paradise Lost* on page 429). The influence of the Faustus story on later literature has been enormous. This tale has given rise over the years to thousands of similar stories about people who make "devil's bargains" in a quest for knowledge, power, beauty, fame, or fortune.

FROM *THE TRAGICAL HISTORY OF DOCTOR FAUSTUS* **387**

ENRICHMENT ACTIVITIES

Students can study the story of Adam and Eve as literature (the Bible, Genesis 2:15–3:24). A general discussion could begin with asking: Is knowledge good or bad? Is it good to a point and then bad? Is too little knowledge a dangerous thing, or is too much, or both? If knowledge does become dangerous at some point, how can one tell when it becomes so?

SUPPORT FOR LEP STUDENTS

Explain to students that the word *doctor,* as in the title of the play *Doctor Faustus,* does not mean a medical doctor but a person who has completed several years of study beyond the college level.

ADDITIONAL VOCABULARY
ail—trouble
belike—apparently
perpetually—forever
headlong—recklessly
wanting—without

GOALS/OBJECTIVES

Studying this lesson will enable students to
• empathize with Faustus's torment and his regret
• compare and contrast Macbeth and Faustus as tragic figures
• recognize motifs in works of literature
• understand and identify symbolism
• evaluate generalizations
• write interview questions
• analyze the tone of exclamatory sentences

PREREADING NOTES

READER'S JOURNAL

Students who have difficulty thinking of an action they did and later regretted may be reminded that *not* to take action is in a sense to take an action. Is there anything they did *not* do that they wish they had done? Would they like the chance to do it now?

LANGUAGE SKILLS

• Some examples of exclamatory sentences are line 13, "But Faustus' offense can ne'er be pardoned!" and line 21, ". . . Faustus . . . must remain in hell for ever— hell, ah, hell for ever!" These lines convey the despair of Faustus. He is not going quietly to his doom; he is torn by remorse and desperation.

• Ask students to consider what different moods or emotions can be conveyed by exclamation points, depending on different contexts.

Answers. Joy, despair, anger, horror, surprise, and love are several of the moods that can be conveyed by exclamation points.

VOCABULARY FROM THE SELECTION

abjure	gape
cunning	harbor
entice	incessant
eternally	ireful
exhort	nativity
felicity	rend
firmament	surfeit

READER'S JOURNAL

Have you ever done something that you later regretted? Did you wish that you could take back what you did? What could you have done to avoid the outcome? Did you learn from your experience? Write about the experience in your journal.

LANGUAGE SKILLS

Read the Language Arts Survey, 2.36, "The Functions of Sentences." Then identify some exclamatory sentences in the selection and note what mood or tone the exclamation marks lend to each sentence.

FROM

The Tragical History
of Doctor Faustus

CHRISTOPHER MARLOWE

SCENE 13

[*Enter* FAUSTUS *with the* SCHOLARS.]

FAUSTUS. Ah, gentlemen!

1 SCHOLAR. What ails Faustus?

FAUSTUS. Ah, my sweet chamber-fellow, had I lived with thee, then had I lived still; but now I die <u>eternally</u>. Look, comes he not, comes he not?

5   **2 SCHOLAR.** What means Faustus?

3 SCHOLAR. Belike he is grown into some sickness, by being oversolitary.

1 SCHOLAR. If it be so, we'll have physicians to cure him; 'tis but a <u>surfeit</u>: never fear, man.

10   **FAUSTUS.** A surfeit of deadly sin, that hath damned both body and soul.

2 SCHOLAR. Yet Faustus, look up to heaven; remember God's mercies are infinite.

WORDS FOR EVERYDAY USE:

e • ter • nal • ly (ē tʉr´ nəl ē) *adv.*, continually, forever

sur • feit (sʉr´ fit) *n.*, overabundance

VOCABULARY IN CONTEXT

• After Susie fixed the quarterback's flat tire, he insisted he would be <u>eternally</u> grateful to her.

• The politicians, claiming the nation had a <u>surfeit</u> of laws, passed new laws to abolish the old.

FAUSTUS. But Faustus' offense can ne'er be pardoned! The serpent that tempted Eve[1] may be saved, but not Faustus. Ah gentlemen, hear me with patience, and tremble not at my speeches, though my heart pants and quivers to remember that I have been a student here these thirty years— O would I had never seen Wittenberg,[2] never read book—and what wonders I have done, all Wittenberg can witness—yea, all the world; for which Faustus hath lost both Germany and the world—yea, heaven itself—heaven, the seat of God, the throne of the blessed, the kingdom of joy; and must remain in hell for ever—hell, ah, hell for ever! Sweet friends, what shall become of Faustus, being in hell for ever?

3 SCHOLAR. Yet Faustus, call on God.

FAUSTUS. On God, whom Faustus hath <u>abjured</u>? On God, whom Faustus hath blasphemed? Ah my God—I would weep, but the devil draws in my tears! gush forth blood, instead of tears—yea, life and soul! O, he stays my tongue! I would lift up my hands, but see, they hold them, they hold them!

ALL. Who, Faustus?

FAUSTUS. Lucifer and Mephastophilis![3] Ah gentlemen, I gave them my soul for my <u>cunning</u>.

ALL. God forbid!

FAUSTUS. God forbade it indeed, but Faustus hath done it: for the vain pleasure of four-and-twenty years hath Faustus lost eternal joy and <u>felicity</u>. I writ them a bill with mine own blood, the date is expired, the time will come, and he will fetch me.

1 SCHOLAR. Why did not Faustus tell us of this before, that divines might have prayed for thee?

FAUSTUS. Oft have I thought to have done so, but the devil threatened to tear me in pieces if I named God, to fetch both body and soul, if I once gave ear to divinity; and now 'tis too late. Gentlemen away, lest you perish with me!

2 SCHOLAR. O what shall we do to save Faustus?

3 SCHOLAR. God will strengthen me. I will stay with Faustus.

---

1. **The serpent . . . Eve.** In the book of Genesis the serpent tempted Eve to eat from the tree of knowledge, bringing the first sin into the world.
2. **Wittenberg.** A famous university in Germany
3. **Lucifer and Mephastophilis.** Devils

W WORDS FOR EVERYDAY USE:	**ab • jure** (ab jōōr´) *vt.*, renounce, give up publicly **cun • ning** (kun´iŋ) *n.*, skill, cleverness **fel • lic • i • ty** (fə lis´i tē) *n.*, happiness

❶ *What does Faustus regret?*

❷ *How do Faustus's colleagues feel about him?*

HISTORICAL NOTE

The text of Marlowe's play is often very close to the text of his source, *The History of the Damnable Life and Deserved Death of Doctor John Faustus,* a translation of an older German work. Marlowe even preserves some of the errors of fact made by the translator. The similarity of the two works can be judged by comparing two passages. The source reads: "May it please your grace to understand that the year is divided into two circles over the whole world, that when with us it is winter, in the contrary circle it is not with-standing summer; for in India and Saba there falleth or setteth the sun so that it is so warm that they have twice a year fruit." Marlowe's text reads: "Please it your Grace, the year is divided into two circles over the whole world, so that when it is winter with us, in the contrary circle it is likewise summer with them, as in India, Saba, and such countries that lie far east, where they have fruit twice a year."

ANSWERS TO GUIDED READING QUESTIONS

❶ Faustus regrets ever having seen Wittenberg or read a book, events that he believes led him to lose his chance of going to heaven.

❷ The scholars care about Faustus enough to wish to save him.

ADDITIONAL QUESTIONS AND ACTIVITIES

Ask students to consider the following question as they read: To what extent is Faustus a symbol of the human race, in all its endeavors?

VOCABULARY IN CONTEXT

- When Alvin grew to be fifty-five, he finally was able to make his mother <u>abjure</u> tousling his hair every time they met.
- The young fox was <u>cunning</u> and swam the stream; but the old hound was wise and crossed the bridge.
- A peaceful garden, a summer morning, the music of birds—that, Horatio, is the highest <u>felicity</u> life has to offer.

ANSWERS TO GUIDED READING QUESTIONS

❶ Faustus's colleagues still have hope for him; Faustus apparently has no hope ("nothing can rescue me," line 48).

❷ Faustus says that God is ireful and wrathful toward him, indicating that he believes God will judge him guilty.

---

❶ *Do Faustus's colleagues still have hope for him? Does Faustus have any hope for himself?*

45   **1 SCHOLAR.**   Tempt not God, sweet friend, but let us into the next room, and there pray for him.

FAUSTUS.   Aye, pray for me, pray for me; and what noise soever ye hear, come not unto me, for nothing can rescue me.

2 SCHOLAR.   Pray thou, and we will pray, that God may have mercy upon thee.

50   **FAUSTUS.**   Gentlemen, farewell. If I live till morning, I'll visit you; if not, Faustus is gone to hell.

ALL.   Faustus, farewell.

[*Exeunt* SCHOLARS.]

[*The clock strikes eleven.*]

FAUSTUS.   Ah Faustus,
Now hast thou but one bare hour to live,
55   And then thou must be damned perpetually.
Stand still, you ever-moving spheres of heaven,
That time may cease, and midnight never come.
Fair Nature's eye, rise, rise again, and make
Perpetual day, or let this hour be but
60   A year, a month, a week, a natural day,
That Faustus may repent and save his soul.
O lente, lente currite noctis equi![4]
The stars move still, time runs, the clock will strike,
The devil will come, and Faustus must be damned.
65   O, I'll leap up to my God! Who pulls me down?
See, see where Christ's blood streams in the <u>firmament</u>!
One drop would save my soul, half a drop: ah my Christ—
Ah, <u>rend</u> not my heart for naming of my Christ;
Yet will I call on him—O spare me, Lucifer!

❷ *How does Faustus imagine God will judge him?*

70   Where is it now? 'Tis gone: and see where God
Stretcheth out his arm, and bends his <u>ireful</u> brows!
Mountains and hills, come, come and fall on me,
And hide me from the heavy wrath of God.
No, no?
75   Then will I headlong run into the earth:
Earth, <u>gape</u>! O no, it will not <u>harbor</u> me.

---

4. **O lente, . . . equi.** Slowly, slowly run, O horses of the night.

WORDS FOR EVERYDAY USE:

fir • ma • ment (fʉrm´ə mənt) *n.*, sky
rend (rend) *vt.*, rip apart
ire • ful (īr´ fəl) *adj.*, angry

gape (gāp) *vi.*, open wide
har • bor (här´bər) *vt.*, provide protection to

VOCABULARY IN CONTEXT

- The stars in the <u>firmament</u> number in the billions.
- These new plastic bags are so tough you practically have to <u>rend</u> them with a chainsaw to get them open.
- People with impairment of the amygdala, a region of the brain, are unable to distinguish an <u>ireful</u> glare from an affectionate glance.
- Tod could not understand why people were <u>gaping</u> at him until he realized that he had put his shirt on inside out.
- If you want to <u>harbor</u> that dog who followed you home, you can forget it.

You stars that reigned at my <u>nativity</u>,
Whose influence hath allotted death and hell,
Now draw up Faustus like a foggy mist
80   Into the entails of yon laboring cloud,
That when you vomit forth into the air,
My limbs may issue from your smoky mouths,
So that my soul may but ascend to heaven.

[*The watch strikes.*]

Ah, half the hour is past: 'twill all be past anon.
85   O God, if thou wilt not have mercy on my soul,
Yet for Christ's sake, whose blood hath ransomed me,
Impose some end to my <u>incessant</u> pain:
Let Faustus live in hell a thousand years,
A hundred thousand, and at last be saved.
90   O, no end is limited to damned souls!
Why wert thou not a creature wanting soul?
Or why is this immortal that thou hast?
Ah, Pythagoras' *metempsychosis*⁵—were that true,
This soul should fly from me, and I be changed
95   Unto some brutish beast:
All beasts are happy, for when they die,
Their souls are soon dissolved in elements;
But mine must live still⁶ to be plagued in hell.
Cursed be the parents that engendered me:
100   No, Faustus, curse thy self, curse Lucifer,
That hath deprived thee of the joys of heaven.

[*The clock strikes twelve.*]

O it strikes, it strikes! Now body, turn to air,
Or Lucifer will bear thee quick⁷ to hell.

[*Thunder and lightning.*]

O soul, be changed into little water drops,
105   And fall into the ocean, ne'er be found.
My God, my God, look not so fierce on me!

[*Enter* DEVILS.]

---

5. **metempsychosis.** Pythagoras's theory that souls pass
from one body to another at death
6. **still.** Always
7. **quick.** Alive

❶
*Whom is Faustus
addressing?*

❷
*Whom does
Faustus blame
for his
terrible life?*

W

WORDS FOR
EVERYDAY USE:

na • tiv • i • ty (nə tivʹ ə tē) *n.,* birth

in • ces • sant (in sesʹənt) *adj.,* never ending

FROM *THE TRAGICAL HISTORY OF DOCTOR FAUSTUS*   **391**

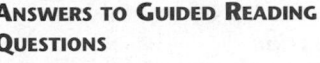

**ANSWERS TO GUIDED READING
QUESTIONS**

❶ Faustus addresses himself.

❷ Faustus blames himself and Lucifer.

**ADDITIONAL QUESTIONS
AND ACTIVITIES**

• Students can write an essay
comparing and contrasting
Macbeth and Faustus as tragic
figures. Suggest they compare
Macbeth's tragic flaw (his hunger
for power) with Faustus's flaw (the
hunger for knowledge) and that
they contrast the different attitude
of each man toward repentance.

• Students should read the
Language Arts Survey, 1.34,
"Organizing Ideas: Comparison-
and-Contrast Order" before
starting to write.

• Read to students line 109, the
last words of Faustus's final speech
("I'll burn my books—ah,
Mephastophilis!"). Explain that in
the sixteenth century books were
considerably more rare and
valuable than they are now. Ask
the following questions to
stimulate discussion: 1. Why did
Marlowe choose these words as
Faustus's last? 2. Throughout the
play, Mephastophilis is Faustus's
tempter, companion in crimes and
travels, fellow trickster, and
menacing guard. What is the
effect of Faustus's calling his name
as his last word in the play?
Answers. 1. The offer to burn his
books if he is left in peace is a
shocking indication of the despair of
Faustus. He has sought knowledge
all his life and now is willing not
only to renounce it but literally to
burn and destroy it. Faustus's offer is
virtually the most powerful one he
could make in his situation. 2. He
seems to call upon Mephastophilis
for help, for pity, and yet also in
acknowledgment that no help is
possible from that spirit. His call is
poignant and yet pointless.

VOCABULARY IN CONTEXT

• In celebration of the hundredth anniversary of her <u>nativity</u>, Ms. Cosway took her first parachute
jump.

• The <u>incessant</u> blather of the television set soon drove Maxine out of the waiting area.

ANSWER TO GUIDED READING QUESTION

❶ The moral of the story is that the wise should marvel at those things they cannot do or know rather than investigate them and overstep the limits set on humans by God.

RESPONDING TO THE SELECTION

Ask students to think of a scientist whose investigations have caused him or her harm. For instance, Marie Curie (1867–1934) died as a result of her research into radioactivity. Did she deserve sympathy or reproach for endangering herself?

ANSWERS FOR REVIEWING THE SELECTION

RECALLING

1. He says that he made a contract in blood with the devil to gain knowledge. They tell him to pray and have faith in God.

2. Faustus wants to hide from the wrath of God.

3. Faustus would like to be changed into an animal.

4. Faustus will be drawn down to hell to be tortured for eternity.

INTERPRETING

Responses will vary. Possible responses are given

5. They express sorrow and a willingness to ask God to pardon him.

6. Faustus feels tormented by regret. He says, "for the vain pleasure of four-and-twenty years hath Faustus lost eternal joy and felicity" (lines 33–35).

7. Faustus wants to become a beast because he believes that if he were an animal, he could not suffer eternally in hell.

8. He blames himself and Lucifer for his fate; he is correct.

SYNTHESIZING

Responses will vary. Possible responses are given

9. He is capable of repenting something he believes is wrong; he is not a hardened criminal. It is arguable that anyone might suffer for looking too deeply into dangerous things.

10. One should pay attention to Faustus in order not to repeat his mistake. One can avoid his mistake by limiting one's experience of the unknown to wonder and respect for it.

392 TEACHER'S EDITION

Adders and serpents, let me breathe awhile!
Ugly hell gape not! Come not, Lucifer!
I'll burn my books—ah, Mephastophilis!

[*Exeunt with him.*]

EPILOGUE

[*Enter* CHORUS.]

❶
What is the moral of this story?

1   Cut is the branch that might have grown full straight,
And burnèd is Apollo's laurel bough,[8]
That sometime grew within this learned man.
Faustus is gone! Regard his hellish fall,
5   Whose fiendful fortune[9] may <u>exhort</u> the wise
Only to wonder at unlawful things:
Whose deepness doth <u>entice</u> such forward wits,
To practice more than heavenly power permits.

[*Exit.*]

Terminat hora diem, terminat author opus.[10]   ∎

---

8. **laurel bough.** The laurel bough is a conventional symbol of attainment, in this case, attainment of wisdom or learning.
9. **fiendful fortune.** Devilish fate
10. **Terminat . . . opus.** The hour ends the day, the author ends his work.

Responding to the Selection

Imagine that you are one of the scholars listening to Faustus explain his situation. Would you be understanding? Would you try to ease his terror, or would you chastise him? Does he deserve sympathy? Write a letter to Faustus in your journal expressing your feelings about his actions and his situation.

WORDS FOR EVERYDAY USE:

ex • hort (eg zôrt´) *vt.*, warn, plead with
en • tice (en tīs) *vt.*, tempt

392   *UNIT FIVE / RENAISSANCE DRAMA*

VOCABULARY IN CONTEXT

• The preacher <u>exhorted</u> the people of his impoverished congregation to give kindness freely to their neighbors.

• Mustafa <u>enticed</u> his cat down from the tree with tuna fish.

Reviewing the Selection

1. What does Faustus tell the scholars he has done to himself? What do the scholars urge Faustus to do?

2. Why does Faustus beg for the mountains and hills to fall upon him?

3. What does Faustus want to be turned into?

4. What will happen to Faustus, now that "the date is expired" on his contract with the devil?

INTERPRETING

5. What attitudes about Faustus's admission do the scholars express?

6. How is Faustus feeling about decisions that he has made? What evidence do you have for your interpretation?

7. Why does he want to be turned into something else? What is his reasoning?

8. Whom does Faustus finally blame for depriving him of "the joys of heaven"? Is he correct?

SYNTHESIZING

9. What do Faustus's thoughts tell you about his personality and character? Is Faustus unique, or is his fate something everyone should fear?

10. According to the play, why should one pay heed to Faustus's "hellish fall"? How can one avoid suffering like Faustus?

Understanding Literature (Questions for Discussion)

1. **Soliloquy.** A **soliloquy** is a speech delivered by a lone character that reveals the speaker's thoughts and feelings. Playwrights use soliloquies to share a character's thoughts, feelings, or motives with the audience. When the scholars leave Faustus alone in the room, he voices his inner turmoil. What is his state of mind? Which lines from the soliloquy lead you to this conclusion? What is your opinion of Faustus? How does the soliloquy help to shape your opinion? Is a soliloquy a good technique in this situation, or would a dialogue have been better? Why?

2. **Chorus.** A **chorus** is a person or group who speaks directly to the audience to convey the author's viewpoint or to introduce story details. In the tragedies of the classical Greek playwrights, the chorus was a group of persons who commented on moral or social issues within the play. In Renaissance drama, the chorus was often a single person who spoke the play's prologue and epilogue and sometimes introduced individual acts. What function does the chorus at the end of the play serve? Is the chorus helpful? Is it necessary? Do you agree with the viewpoint expressed by the chorus? Why, or why not?

FROM *THE TRAGICAL HISTORY OF DOCTOR FAUSTUS* **393**

ANSWERS FOR UNDERSTANDING LITERATURE

Responses will vary. Possible responses are given.

► See the evaluation forms for discussion, active listening, and oral communication, *Assessment Portfolio,* 7.11–7.14.

1. Soliloquy. Faustus feels despair and contrition. Most of the soliloquy expresses his fear and his wish that he could repent; nearly any lines could be cited. He may be seen as an essentially good man who was tempted beyond his ability to resist. The soliloquy reveals his innermost feelings, enabling the reader to understand him and so to sympathize with him even while judging him. The soliloquy allows for unrestricted exposition of Faustus's feelings without distraction. However, a dialogue could also have been used effectively.

►**Teaching Note:** To contrast the use of dialogue and soliloquy, examine the differences between the information they reveal. The scholars tend to limit Faustus to expressing the ideas and emotions they can comprehend. Their presence would prevent his expounding on his position.

2. Chorus. The chorus explains the putative moral of the story. The chorus is helpful in laying out one view of the meaning of the play, though a sophisticated reader may see other possibilities. The chorus may be necessary to demonstrate that the writer does not approve of Faustus's career. One reason supporting the viewpoint of the chorus is that it does point out that Faustus pried into knowledge and was doomed; a reason for disagreeing with the chorus is that the willingness to risk destruction in the search for knowledge seems to be part of the human spirit.

►**Teaching Note:** Suggest to students who find the chorus inadequate that they may wish to write their own chorus speech for the play.

(cont.)

ANSWERS FOR UNDERSTANDING LITERATURE (CONT.)

3. Genre. People are interested in the theme of the consequences transgressing the limit of knowledge, wealth, and power because they see such transgression around them all the time. Marlowe's play would make a good basis for a science fiction story. One possible approach would be to change the devils of Marlowe's play to aliens that gave some of their knowledge to an earthling, permitting him or her to aggrandize power over others until a certain term was up. The theme of the exploration of forbidden knowledge or power and the necessity of paying the consequences would remain the same.

►**Teaching Note:** Students can write a short science fiction story based on the Faustus theme. The stories can be collected and shared with other students by "publishing" them as photocopies.

Assign a score from 1 to 25 for each grading criterion below. (For more detailed evaluation, see the evaluation forms for writing, revising, and proofreading, *Assessment Portfolio,* 7.1–7.10.)

1. Interview Questions

• **Content/Unity.** The interview questions present a sensible approach to determining Faustus's tragic flaws.

• **Organization/Coherence.** The interview questions are clearly organized, presenting a logical analysis of Faustus's experience and reactions.

• **Language/Style.** The interview questions use vivid and precise nouns, verbs, and modifiers.

• **Conventions.** The interview questions avoid errors in spelling, grammar, usage, mechanics, and manuscript form.

2. Contract

• **Content/Unity.** The contract presents a sensible agreement between both parties.

• **Organization/Coherence.** The contract is clearly organized, presenting in an ordered manner its conditions and the consequences of breach of the contract.

• **Language/Style.** The contract uses vivid and precise nouns, verbs, and modifiers.

• **Conventions.** The contract avoids errors in spelling, grammar, usage, mechanics, and manuscript form.

3. **Genre.** A **genre** is one of the types or categories into which literary works are divided. For instance, science fiction is one of the genres of fiction. Science fiction is highly imaginative fiction containing fantastic elements based upon scientific principles, discoveries, or laws. The human desire for forbidden knowledge has always been a recurring theme in science fiction. Science fiction tales often focus on people trying to travel beyond established boundaries of knowledge, wealth, or power. People believe that the legend of Doctor Faustus offers one of the earliest explorations of this theme. Why do you think people might be interested in this theme? Could Marlowe's play be rewritten as a science fiction story? What would need to be changed? What would need to remain the same?

Responding in Writing

1. **Interview Questions.** Faustus knows that he has only one remaining hour of life before his contract expires and his soul is claimed. Imagine that you are a reporter interviewing Faustus in his final moments on earth. Make a list of questions you will ask. How can you lead Faustus to reveal his feelings about his actions and his fate? Concentrate on questions that will give your reading or viewing audience a glimpse not only of Faustus's state of mind but also of the **tragic flaws** that proved to be his downfall.

2. **Contract.** A contract is a written agreement binding the persons named in the contract to certain responsibilities and conditions. Faustus makes a contract with the devil: he gains knowledge and power in exchange for his soul. As Faustus tragically learns, it is wise to consider carefully a contract before signing it. What contract might you make with someone? Maybe you want a parent to extend your curfew privileges, or perhaps you want to borrow a car from a friend. Decide the purpose you would like a contract to fulfill. Then write the conditions of the contract. Consider your own obligations as well as those of the other person or persons. Be sure the language of your contract is clear and precise.

Language Lab

Combining Sentences. Read the Language Arts Survey, 2.51–2.53, on combining sentences. Then revise the sentences below by combining their ideas.

1. Doctor Faustus was a fictional character. The character of Doctor Faustus was based on a real German magician named Georg Faust. Georg Faust gained fame during the early 1500s.

2. *The History of the Damnable Life and Deserved Death of Doctor John Faustus* was an English translation of a German narrative. The translation appeared in London in 1592.

3. A two-part Faust play was written by Goethe. Goethe was a German author and poet. Goethe wrote in the nineteenth century.

4. Goethe's Faust is unlike earlier versions of the tragic hero. Goethe's Faust is finally saved by angels.

5. Thomas Mann wrote *Doctor Faustus*. *Doctor Faustus* is a novel. Mann's novel was only loosely based on the Faust legend.

Thinking Skills

Generalizing. Read the Language Arts Survey, 4.11, "Generalizing." Then, for each sentence below, decide whether the generalization is supported or not supported by the play.

1. Faustus fears God's judgment.

2. If Faustus had been older, he might not have made the mistake of selling his soul.

3. Faustus has no one with whom to share his troubles.

4. Faustus is sorry for what he has done.

5. All scholars are in league with infernal forces.

PROJECTS

1. **Mock Trial.** Faustus pays for his moral crime—the pride to strive beyond the limits of human knowledge. However, Faustus's desire for knowledge and power prove him to be human, capable of tragic mistakes. Does Faustus deserve his fate? Hold a mock trial in which you determine if the punishment Faustus receives is fair. Work in groups large enough to assign the roles of judge, Faustus, defense and prosecuting attorneys, and jury. Work together to develop arguments for and against Faustus.

2. **Magic Show for Children.** Unlike Faustus's black magic, tricks performed by contemporary magicians rely on illusion and sleight of hand. Find a book that describes how to perform magic tricks. Work with other students to develop a routine for several magic tricks. Write patter to accompany your tricks, in which you describe the allure of magical powers that Faustus must have felt. When you have practiced and perfected your routines and your patter, perform your show for a group of children.

1. Supported: Faustus wishes for the mountains to fall on him and to hide him from "the heavy wrath of God" (lines 72–73).

2. Supported: Were Faustus older, the bargain with the devil would have given fewer years of pleasure.

3. Not supported: Faustus discusses his troubles with the three scholars.

4. Supported: Faustus is in a position to judge, and he regrets his bargain.

5. Not supported: The three scholars did not sell their souls.

► Additional practice is provided in the *Essential Skills Practice Book: Study and Research,* 4.11.

PROJECT NOTES

► See the worksheets and evaluation forms for projects, *Assessment Portfolio,* 7.20–7.23.

1. Mock Trial. Students can consult a lawyer or judge in the community (perhaps a parent) willing to give a quick overview of trial procedures. Question each group before it begins its work to make sure its members understand what roles have been assigned to them. (It would be difficult to run a trial if both teams thought they were working for the defense!) Emphasize the necessity of developing arguments ahead of time and anticipating the arguments that the other side will offer.

2. Magic Show for Children. Each student may have a particular skill at which he or she excels for this project. Some may be good at tricks involving juggling, for instance, while others may prefer to be assistants to the magician. Students who become accomplished enough may want to perform for children in hospitals or for older people in nursing homes.

Responses will vary. Possible responses are given.

1. The fictional character of Doctor Faustus was based on a real German magician named Georg Faust, who gained fame during the early 1500s.

2. *The History of the Damnable Life and Deserved Death of Doctor John Faustus* was an English translation of a German narrative that appeared in London in 1592.

3. Goethe, a German author and poet, wrote a two-part Faust play in the nineteenth century.

4. Unlike earlier versions of the tragic hero, Goethe's Faust is finally saved by angels.

5. Thomas Mann wrote a novel, *Doctor Faustus,* that was only loosely based on the Faust legend.

► Additional practice is provided in the *Essential Skills Practice Book: Language,* 2.51–2.53.

LITERARY TECHNIQUE

Explain that a **soliloquy** is a dramatic device in which a character speaks alone; it is used to show what a character is thinking. Students can take turns improvising soliloquies in response to questions such as the following: "Would the ability to read someone else's mind be pleasant or unpleasant? Explain."

LITERARY TECHNIQUE

Explain that in Shakespeare's verse, the sense of one line is often continued or completed by the next line. (An example is lines 2–3 of act I, scene iii.) When reading, students should not pause at the end of a line unless punctuation occurs there.

ADDITIONAL QUESTIONS AND ACTIVITIES

• Divide the class into four groups. Assign each group one of the plays from which selections have been taken. Each group will be responsible for a dramatic reading of the scene in which the selection appears. Students need not memorize or enact their parts, although they should stand at the front of the room and move about as necessary to convey the sense of the passage.

• As an alternate activity, make each group responsible for answering any questions that may arise about the context of the selections as the passages are studied in class. This will require students to have a solid grasp of the plot and characters of their assigned play.

ADDITIONAL QUESTIONS AND ACTIVITIES

from *The Tragedy of Hamlet, Prince of Denmark,* act III, scene i. After students have read and studied the passage, point out the metaphor "to take arms against a sea of troubles" and explain that this is a mixed metaphor—something writers

(cont.)

Monologues and Soliloquies from

The Tragedy of Hamlet, Prince of Denmark
by William Shakespeare

In the tragedy *Hamlet,* Hamlet's father, the king of Denmark, has recently died, and Hamlet's uncle, Claudius, has taken the throne. The ghost of Hamlet's father appears to Hamlet, accuses Claudius of murdering him, and asks Hamlet to seek revenge.

In the first selection, Polonius, an elderly government minister, is saying good-bye to his son, Laertes.

In the second selection, Hamlet is alone and thinking aloud about what makes people willing to face the many difficulties of life. The speech follows a conversation in which the king and the queen discuss their fears that Hamlet is deranged.

Hamlet persuades a group of actors to perform for King Claudius a play about regicide, to see if the king's reactions confirm his suspicions. In the third selection, Hamlet is giving the actors directions prior to the performance. Hamlet's speech to the actors provides superb advice about the craft of acting, advice that has stood the test of time and that was written by the greatest dramatist who ever lived.

FROM ACT I, SCENE iii

POLONIUS.   And these few precepts in thy memory
Look thou character.[1] Give thy thoughts no tongue,
Nor any unproportion'd thought his act.
Be thou familiar, but by no means vulgar:
5 Those friends thou hast, and their adoption tried,
Grapple them unto thy soul with hoops of steel,
But do not dull thy palm with entertainment
Of each new-hatch'd, unfledg'd courage. Beware
Of entrance to a quarrel, but being in,
10 Bear't that th' opposed may beware of thee.
Give every man thy ear, but few thy voice,
Take each man's censure, but reserve thy judgment.
Costly thy habit as thy purse can buy,
But not express'd in fancy, rich, not gaudy,
15 For the apparel oft proclaims the man,
And they in France of the best rank and station
[Are] of a most select and generous chief in that.
Neither a borrower nor a lender [be],
For [loan] oft loses both itself and friend,
20 And borrowing dulleth [th'] edge of husbandry.[2]
This above all: to thine own self be true,
And it must follow, as the night the day,
Thou canst not then false to any man.
Farewell, my blessing season this in thee!

---

1. **character.** Inscribe
2. **husbandry.** Thrifty management, frugality
3. **quietus.** Release from an obligation
4. **bodkin.** Dagger

FROM ACT III, SCENE i

HAMLET.   To be, or not to be, that is the question:
Whether 'tis nobler in the mind to suffer
The slings and arrows of outrageous fortune,
Or to take arms against a sea of troubles,
5 And by opposing, end them. To die, to sleep—
No more, and by a sleep to say we end
The heart-ache and the thousand natural shocks
That flesh is heir to; 'tis a consummation
Devoutly to be wish'd. To die, to sleep—
10 To sleep, perchance to dream—ay, there's the rub,
For in that sleep of death what dreams may come,
When we have shuffled off this mortal coil,
Must give us pause; there's the respect
That makes calamity of so long life:
15 For who would bear the whips and scorns of time,
Th' oppressor's wrong, the proud man's contumely,
The pangs of despis'd love, the law's delay,
The insolence of office, and the spurns
That patient merit of th' unworthy takes,
20 When he himself might his quietus[3] make
With a bare bodkin;[4] who would fardels[5] bear,
To grunt and sweat under a weary life,
But that the dread of something after death,
The undiscover'd country, from whose bourn[6]
25 No traveller returns, puzzles the will,
And makes us rather bear those ills we have,
Than fly to others that we know not of?
Thus conscience does make cowards [of us all],
And thus the native hue of resolution
30 Is sicklied o'er with the pale cast of thought,
And enterprises of great pitch and moment
With this regard their currents turn awry,
And lose the name of action.

FROM ACT III, SCENE ii

HAMLET.   Speak the speech, I pray you, as I
pronounc'd it to you, trippingly on the tongue, but if
you mouth it, as many of our players do, I had as live[7]
the town-crier spoke my lines. Nor do not saw the
5 air too much with your hand, thus, but use all gently,
for in the very torrent, tempest, and, as I may say,
whirlwind of your passion, you must acquire and
beget a temperance that may give it smoothness. O,
it offends me to the soul to hear a robustious periwig-

---

5. **fardels.** Burdens
6. **bourn.** Domain
7. **had as live.** Would prefer

ADDITIONAL QUESTIONS AND ACTIVITIES (CONT.)

generally avoid. Note that Shakespeare is full of constructions and usages that contradict modern grammatical conventions, including double negatives and double comparisons, among other things. He lived and wrote in a time when the language was much more fluid—that is, before grammarians had begun making up rules about it. He also used strained grammar for special effects. The mixed metaphor in this passage may be one

such instance, perhaps showing the turmoil of Hamlet's thought.

• What words does Hamlet use to describe the misfortunes of life in the passage?

Answer. He uses "slings and arrows," line 3; "sea of troubles," line 4; "heart-ache," line 7; "thousand natural shocks," line 7; "calamity," line 14; and "whips and scorns," line 15.

10 pated fellow tear a passion to totters, to very rags, to spleet[1] the ears of the groundlings,[2] who for the most part are capable of nothing but inexplicable dumb shows and noise. I would have such a fellow whipt for o'erdoing Termagant, it out-Herods Herod,[3]
15 pray you avoid it.

[1] PLAYER.   I warrant your honor.

HAMLET.   Be not too tame neither, but let your own discretion be your tutor. Suit the action to the word, the word to the action, with this special
20 observance, that you o'erstep not the modesty[4] of nature: for any thing so o'erdone is from the purpose of playing, whose end, both at the first and now, was and is, to hold as 'twere the mirror up to nature: to show virtue her feature, scorn her own image, and
25 the very age and body of the time his form and pressure.[5] Now this overdone, or come tardy[6] off, though it makes the unskillful laugh, cannot but make the judicious grieve; the censure of which one must in your allowance o'erweigh a whole theatre of
30 others. O, there be players that I have seen play— and heard others [praise], and that highly—not to speak it profanely,[7] that, neither having th' accent of Christians nor the gait of Christian, pagan, nor man, have so strutted and bellow'd that I have thought
35 some of Nature's journeymen had made men, and not made them well, they imitated humanity so abominably.

[1] PLAYER.   I hope we have reform'd that indifferently with us, [sir].

40 HAMLET.   O, reform it altogether. And let those that play your clowns speak no more than is set down for them, for there be of them that will themselves laugh to set on some quantity of barren spectators to laugh too, though in the mean time some necessary
45 question of the play be then to be considered. That's villainous, and shows a most pitiful ambition in the fool that uses it. Go make you ready.

The Tragedy of King Richard the Second
by William Shakespeare

Shakespeare's *Richard the Second* tells of the fall of a king who rules arbitrarily, willfully, and selfishly, and yet is a person with whom many can sympathize. When Richard's uncle, John of Gaunt, dies, Richard unjustly confiscates Gaunt's estates to

---

1. **spleet.** Split
2. **groundlings.** Spectators who stood on the ground in the pit of the theater
3. **Termagant . . . Herod.** Both Termagant and Herod were noisy, violent characters in medieval drama.
4. **modesty.** Moderation
5. **pressure.** Exact image

---

finance a campaign to put down a rebellion. Eventually Richard is deposed by Gaunt's son, the fiercely ambitious Bullingbrook (Bolingbroke), later King Henry IV.

In the first selection, John of Gaunt, near death from illness, has stated a desire to advise his nephew Richard, whom he views as a reckless youth. In the second selection, Richard, in the face of defeat by Bolingbroke, ponders how even the greatest among us must meet his or her end. Richard's claim that some kings are "haunted by the ghosts they have deposed" (line 158) often reminds readers of *Macbeth,* Shakespeare's tragedy about the downfall of another king.

FROM ACT II, SCENE i

GAUNT.   Methinks I am a prophet new inspir'd,
And thus expiring do foretell of him:[8]
His rash fierce blaze of riot cannot last,
For violent fires soon burn out themselves;
5 Small show'rs last long, but sudden storms are short;
He tires betimes that spurs too fast betimes;
With eager feeding food doth choke the feeder;
Light vanity, insatiate cormorant,[9]
Consuming means, soon preys upon itself.
10 This royal throne of kings, this sceptred isle,
This earth of majesty, this seat of Mars,[10]
This other Eden, demi-paradise,
This fortress built by Nature for herself
Against infection and the hand of war,
15 This happy breed of men, this little world,
This precious stone set in the silver sea,
Which serves it in the office of a wall,
Or as [a] moat defensive to a house,
Against the envy of less happier lands;
20 This blessed plot, this earth, this realm, this England,
This nurse, this teeming womb of royal kings,
Fear'd by their breed, and famous by their birth,
Renowned for their deeds as far from home,
For Christian service and true chivalry,
25 As is the sepulchre in stubborn Jewry
Of the world's ransom, blessed Mary's Son;
This land of such dear souls, this dear dear land,
Dear for her reputation through the world,
Is now leas'd out—I die pronouncing it—
30 Like to a tenement or pelting farm.
England, bound in with the triumphant sea,
Whose rocky shore beats back the envious siege
Of wat'ry Neptune,[11] is now bound in with shame,
With inky blots and rotten parchment bonds;
35 That England, that was wont to conquer others,
Hath made a shameful conquest of itself.

---

6. **tardy.** Inadequately
7. **profanely.** Irreverently
8. **him.** Gaunt is referring to King Richard.
9. **cormorant.** A glutton
10. **Mars.** Roman god of war and protector of the nation
11. **Neptune.** Roman god of the sea

Character. In his speech to the actors, Hamlet seems distrustful of their abilities; he sternly attempts to forestall any possible defects in their performance. He shows great intelligence, not so much patience, and the potential for irritability. Some of his qualities are intolerance of incompetence ("it offends me to the soul to hear a . . . fellow tear a passion to totters," lines 9–10); an ability to observe acutely (evidenced throughout by his minute description of the way actors behave); brusqueness ("O, reform it altogether," line 40); an expectation that others should take seriously those things he takes seriously (he calls "villainous" the practice of making spectators laugh during a serious moment, line 46); and a tendency to correct others harshly, or at least to threaten them with harsh correction ("I would have such a fellow whipt," lines 13–14).

Characterization. One way writers establish character is to determine what quality a person in their work will have and then repeatedly show that person acting out an idiosyncrasy that expresses the desired quality. In Hamlet's speech, for instance, Shakespeare shows him as brusque, direct, even slightly imperious, though these qualities are softened by his extremely lively intelligence. To bring out these qualities for students, draw their attention to a line or two of Hamlet's speech and ask them what kind of person someone would have to be to speak those words as Hamlet speaks them. Write down all suggestions on the blackboard, emphasizing with a star those the entire class agrees are best.

Earth Science. In *The Tragedy of King Richard the Second,* act II, scene i, lines 13-18, John of Gaunt emphasizes that England is part of an island, and as such is partially protected from invasion. Students can research the geology of the British Isles to understand the physical history of the landform. You may want to ask the following questions: 1. How is England geologically related to Europe? 2. Were Britain and Europe ever connected? 3. How might Britain's isolation have affected its view of itself? of the outside world?

Answers. Britain and Europe are part of the same rock structure. They were connected by a land bridge until about 6000–5000 BC. Perhaps Britain's isolation has resulted in the feelings of patriotism and superiority found in Gaunt's speech.

Speaker. The speaker is the character who speaks in a poem—the
voice assumed by the writer.
Examine the passage from *The
Merchant of Venice,* act IV, scene i.
Though it was Shakespeare who
wrote the lines here, he devised
them for the character of Portia,
and he chose words and phrases
that are appropriate for her character: the ideas may or may not have
been shared by Shakespeare himself. Look through the speech
again to find evidence about the
speaker's character. In particular,
examine Portia's reasons for prefer-
ring mercy, the tone of her
language, and the way in which
she appeals to Shylock. Is she
forceful? Does she show understanding? Does she seem to be
merciful herself? What other qualities are shown in her speech?

Answer: Portia's very focus on
mercy says something about her
character. Furthermore, she prefers
mercy apparently because it con-
fers intangible blessings on both
giver and receiver, because it is
superior to the highest form of
human power, and because it is a
divine and not a temporal
attribute—all of which argues for
her disregard for material advantages in preference to spiritual
ones. Her tone is gentle—she does
not attack Shylock, but kindly
encourages him to be kindly. She
shows great understanding, intelligence, and ingenuity in stating her
case, and demonstrates mercy in
her own refusal to attack Shylock.
Other qualities she demonstrates
are a respect for temporal authority and a love of God.

• To clarify how the character of
the speaker is revealed in the
speech, have students rephrase the
speech as an attack, beginning,
"Now listen here, Shylock, mercy is
not something that you should
have to be forced into. . . ."

Ah, would the scandal vanish with my life,
How happy then were my ensuing death!

FROM ACT III, SCENE ii

RICHARD.   Let's talk of graves, of worms, and
       epitaphs,
   Make dust our paper, and with rainy eyes
   Write sorrow on the bosom of the earth.
   Let's choose executors and talk of wills;
5   And yet not so, for what can we bequeath
   Save our deposed bodies to the ground?
   Our lands, our lives, and all are Bullingbrook's,[1]
   And nothing can we call our own but death,
   And that small model of the barren earth
10   Which serves as paste and cover to our bones.
   For God's sake let us sit upon the ground
   And tell sad stories of the death of kings:
   How some have been depos'd, some slain in war,
   Some haunted by the ghosts they have deposed.
15   Some poisoned by their wives, some sleeping kill'd,
   All murthered—for within the hollow crown
   That rounds the mortal temples of a king
   Keeps Death his court, and there the antic sits,
   Scoffing his state and grinning at his pomp,[2]
20   Allowing him a breath, a little scene,
   To monarchize, be fear'd, and kill with looks,
   Infusing him with self and vain conceit,
   As if this flesh which walls about our life
   Were brass impregnable; and humor'd thus,
25   Comes at the last and with a little pin
   Bores thorough his castle wall, and farewell king!
   Cover your heads, and mock not flesh and blood
   With solemn reverence, throw away respect,
   Tradition, form, and ceremonious duty,
30   For you have but mistook me all this while.
   I live with bread like you, feel want,
   Taste grief, need friends: subjected thus,
   How can you say to me I am a king?

The Merchant of Venice
by William Shakespeare

In *The Merchant of Venice,* Antonio, in order to help a friend,
has borrowed money from a prosperous Venetian merchant
named Shylock. Shylock agrees to the loan without interest, but
holds as part of the bargain that if the loan cannot be repaid, he
can "collect" on it by cutting a pound of flesh from Antonio's
body. When the ships carrying Antonio's merchandise are lost

---

1. **Bullingbrook.** Bullingbrook or Bolingbroke is the surname of
Henry, Duke of Herford, who later became King Henry IV.
2. **antic . . . pomp.** The antic is a jester who makes fun of the ceremonious regality of the king.
3. **strain'd.** Constrained, forced
4. **rack.** A wisp of cloud

---

at sea, Antonio is left bankrupt, and Shylock comes to close his
part of the bargain. In the selection, Antonio's friend Portia tries
to appeal to a better side of Shylock in order to save Antonio.

FROM ACT IV, SCENE i

PORTIA.   The quality of mercy is not strain'd,[3]
   It droppeth as the gentle rain from heaven
   Upon the place beneath. It is twice blest:
   It blesseth him that gives and him that takes.
   'Tis mightiest in the mightiest, it becomes
   The throned monarch better than his crown.
5   His sceptre shows the force of temporal power,
   The attribute to awe and majesty,
   Wherein doth sit the dread and fear of kings;
   But mercy is above this sceptred sway,
   It is enthroned in the hearts of kings,
10   It is an attribute to God himself;
   And earthly power doth then show likest God's
   When mercy seasons justice.

The Tempest
By William Shakespeare

The Tempest, a highly poetic work of fantasy, is thought to be the
last play Shakespeare wrote before retiring to Stratford. In the
play, the magician Prospero has been exiled to an enchanted
island, home to many spirits and to the savage Caliban. Prospero
is the rightful Duke of Milan, but his brother, Antonio, has
usurped his rule. When a ship carrying Antonio passes the island,
Prospero stirs up a storm, and Antonio and his party are capsized
and washed ashore. Eventually, Caliban and Antonio plot to kill
Prospero, who becomes aware of their scheme. In the selection,
Prospero's speech closes an episode in which the spirits have
been performing an entertainment, and Prospero, remembering
the schemes against him, has called an end to the festivities.

FROM ACT IV, SCENE i

PROSPERO.   Our revels now are ended. These our
       actors
   (As I foretold you) were all spirits, and
   Are melted into air, into thin air,
   And like the baseless fabric of this vision,
5   The cloud-capp'd tow'rs, the gorgeous palaces,
   The solemn temples, the great globe itself,
   Yea, all which it inherit, shall dissolve,
   And like this insubstantial pageant faded
   Leave not a rack[4] behind. We are such stuff
10   As dreams are made on; and our little life
   Is rounded with a sleep. Sir, I am vex'd;
   Bear with my weakness, my old brain is troubled.
   Be not disturb'd with my infirmity.
   If you be pleas'd, retire into my cell,
15 And there repose. A turn or two I'll walk
   To still my beating mind.

LITERARY TECHNIQUE

Climax. A reader expects a climax in the middle or
near the end of a work. The phrase "leave not a
rack behind" (line 9) is the climax of Prospero's
speech; it brings to a conclusion the long sentence
that begins in line 1. It falls in the middle of the
passage.

• Students may assume that climaxes always occur
at the end of a work. Remind them of the structure
of the five-act drama, showing how the second half
of such a drama follows the climax and is formed of
declining action and resolution—within which, of
course, separate smaller climaxes may occur.

PREREADING

from *The Analects*
by Confucius, trans. by Arthur Waley

ABOUT THE AUTHOR

Confucius (551–479 BC) is the Anglicized name of K'ung Ch'iu, the most famous teacher and philosopher in Chinese history. Through the ages, he has been referred to most commonly as K'ung-fu-tzu, or "Master K'ung." His presumed birthday, September 28, is celebrated in Taiwan as "Teacher's Day." Confucius was born in the state of Lu, now the Shantung province of China, probably to a poor, but noble, family. Orphaned at an early age and with few resources, he nonetheless devoted himself to education in the six practical arts (ritual, music, archery, charioteering, calligraphy, and arithmetic), as well as in classical history and poetry. He became the most learned man of his era, attracting thousands of students and a core group of devoted disciples. Renowned for his teachings, he believed that learning should serve the practical ends of public service. He himself served for a time as a government official in the state of Lu. At the age of 73, he died a revered sage.

ABOUT THE SELECTION

The teachings of Confucius were collected by his disciples in the *Lun-yü*, or *Analects*. The word *analects* means "miscellaneous excerpts." Confucius lived in a time of great political and social unrest. His teachings stressed the moral order of the universe as reflected in the proper behavior and interrelations of people of various stations in life. Important themes in Confucian teaching include duty, loyalty, obligation, ritual, social norms, and action befitting one's place in society. For more than two thousand years, Confucius's teachings were the official basis for education in China. They permeate thought and codes of behavior throughout the Asian world.

MULTICULTURAL EXTENSIONS: SOCIAL ORDER / FROM THE ANALECTS **399**

ADDITIONAL RESOURCES

READER'S GUIDE
- Selection Worksheet, 5.7

ASSESSMENT PORTFOLIO
- Selection Check Test, 4.5.13
- Selection Test, 4.5.14

ENRICHMENT ACTIVITIES

Students can list any problems they may see in the social order of the United States at this time. Discuss how these problems compare with the problems in social order described in this unit.

SUPPORT FOR LEP STUDENTS

Explain that the selection students are about to read is made up of the sayings of Confucius. The "Master" referred to at the beginning of each paragraph is Confucius. Explain also that "social order" means the degree of orderliness in society—how well people in a society work and live together, without crime, hunger, suffering, and other widespread problems.

ADDITIONAL VOCABULARY
administer—govern, manage
punctual—on time
expenditure—spending
abroad—in other lands
frivolous—lacking seriousness
homage—honor
chastise—scold

GOALS/OBJECTIVES

Studying this lesson will enable students to

- interpret and appreciate Confucius's philosophy
- identify themes and values in a literary work
- compare works of writing across cultures

- understand and apply the concepts and ideals of social order, duty, loyalty, leadership

CROSS-CURRICULAR ACTIVITIES

Social Studies. Explain to students that Confucius believed that order in society begins at home—and not only at home, but in the self. The same belief is reflected in sayings in the Western wisdom tradition such as "Peace begins at home." The individual who is ordered in his or her thinking and in his or her actions promotes an ordered family; an ordered family promotes an ordered community; an ordered community, an ordered state. According to Confucius, however, rulers can begin the process of ordering society by ordering and correcting their own conduct. Have students study Chinese society today to see whether Confucian values such as these still operate there. They can research such questions as: What are the beliefs about the family in China? What are the beliefs about the individual's duty to those who govern? What duty is owed to those who are governed? Students might arrange for a speaker with knowledge about Chinese culture to address some of these issues in a lecture or discussion.

MULTICULTURAL EXTENSIONS

This extension links ideas about social order in England, as viewed by Shakespeare and Marlowe, with ideas about social order in China some 2,500 years ago. In particular, the extension focuses on the proper role of the ruler, the need for duty to and respect for parents, sincerity, and the value of moral force in politics and in life. The Confucian sayings on these topics are reflections of the same concern Shakespeare felt when he portrayed Macbeth as violent, acting contrary to his duty to his ruler, hypocritical, and lacking moral force not only in his own life but in his conduct of the state.

ANSWERS TO SELECTION CHECK TEST 4.5.13

Selection Check Test answers appear on pages 402 and 403.

MULTICULTURAL EXTENSIONS: SOCIAL ORDER

China

FROM

The Analects

CONFUCIUS, TRANS. BY ARTHUR WALEY

BOOK I, SECTION 5

The Master said, A country of a thousand war-chariots cannot be administered unless the ruler attends strictly to business, punctually observes his promises, is economical in expenditure, shows affection toward his subjects in general, and uses the labor of the peasantry only at the proper times of year.

BOOK I, SECTION 6

The Master said, A young man's duty is to behave well to his parents at home and to his elders abroad, to be cautious in giving promises and punctual in keeping them, to have kindly feelings toward everyone, but seek the intimacy of the Good. If, when all that is done, he has any energy to spare, then let him study the polite arts.

BOOK I, SECTION 8

The Master said, If a gentleman is frivolous, he will lose the respect of his inferiors and lack firm ground on which to build his education. First and foremost, he must learn to be faithful to his superiors, to keep promises, to refuse the friendship of all who are not like him. And if he finds he has made a mistake, then he must not be afraid of admitting the fact and amending his ways.

BOOK II, SECTIONS 1–3

1. The Master said, He who rules by moral force is like the pole star, which remains in its place while all the lesser stars do homage to it.

2. The Master said, If out of the three hundred Songs I had to take one phrase to cover all my teaching, I would say, "Let there be no evil in your thoughts."

3. The Master said, Govern the people by regulations, keep order among them by chastisements, and they will flee from you, and lose all self-respect. Govern them by moral force, keep order among them by ritual, and they will keep their self-respect and come to you of their own accord. ∎

❶ *What is the best way to govern people? Why is this way good for both the governed and the governing?*

ADDITIONAL QUESTIONS AND ACTIVITIES

• Students can write a paragraph in which they cast themselves in the role of Confucius commenting on the speech of Portia in act IV, scene i, of *The Merchant of Venice,* which appears in the Selections for Additional Reading on page 398.

• Students can write their own aphorisms or pithy sayings encapsulating their views on how order can be achieved in society.

ANSWER TO GUIDED READING QUESTION

❶ The best way to govern is to exert moral force and to keep order by ritual. This will allow people to keep their self-respect and come to order by their own accord.

Reviewing the Selection

1. According to Confucius, can a ruler act in any way that he chooses, or must even the most powerful person observe certain codes of behavior? Explain.

2. According to Confucius, what are a young person's duties? What should a young person do if there is energy to spare after fulfilling these duties?

3. According to Confucius, what must a gentleman, or member of the nobility, do "first and foremost"? What friendships should such a person refuse? What should such a person do if he finds that he has made a mistake?

4. According to Confucius, what phrase best sums up all of his teaching?

5. According to Confucius, what methods of government do not work? On what should government be based?

Connections (Questions for Writing or Discussion)

1. According to Confucius, how should a ruler behave toward his subjects? Does Duncan, as portrayed in Shakespeare's play *Macbeth*, meet Confucius's ideal of the perfect king? Explain.

2. According to Confucius, how should a gentleman behave toward his superiors? What should a gentleman do when he realizes that he has made a mistake? Does Macbeth, as portrayed by Shakespeare, live up to this Confucian ideal? Explain.

3. Confucius believed that there was a moral order in the universe and that one expression of that order was the order of society, with its elaborate system of mutual obligations and loyalties. The central characters in *Macbeth* and in *Doctor Faustus* both violate the moral order of the universe. What are the consequences of these violations?

4. Reread the description of feudalism in the Introduction to Unit 3, on page 130. Shakespeare's *Macbeth* is set during the Middle Ages in Scotland, at a time when the feudal system was at its height. What held the feudal system together? What similarities exist between the political and social ideas of Confucius and those of Europeans of the Middle Ages? How does Macbeth, by murdering Duncan, violate the central principle on which feudalism was based?

ANSWERS FOR REVIEWING THE SELECTION

1. No; a ruler must attend to business, keep promises, be economical, be affectionate to his or her subjects, and use peasant labor for his or her own purposes at the proper time of the year.

2. A young person's duties are to behave well to his or her parents at home and to his or her elders abroad, to be cautious in giving promises and punctual in keeping them, and to have kindly feelings toward everyone but seek the intimacy of the Good. He or she should study the polite arts if he or she has time.

3. He should be faithful to his superiors, keep his promises, and refuse the friendship of all those not like him. He must admit his mistakes and try to do better.

4. The phrase that sums up Confucius's teaching is, "Let there be no evil in your thoughts."

5. Governing by regulations and keeping order by chastisement do not work. Government should be based on moral force and ritual.

ANSWERS FOR CONNECTIONS

1. A ruler must treat his subjects with affection. Certainly Duncan treats Macbeth with affection, rewarding his loyalty and courage and wishing he had more to give him. In more general terms, according to Macbeth's own admission (act I, scene vii, lines 16–18), "this Duncan/Hath born his faculties so meek, hath been/So clear in his great office, that his virtues/Will plead like angels."

2. According to Confucius, a gentleman should be faithful to his superiors—which Macbeth, in murdering Duncan in his own home, clearly is not. Although Macbeth realizes that he has made a mistake, he makes no recompense: "I am in blood/Stepp'd in so far that, should I wade no more,/Returning were as tedious as go o'er."

3. The consequences of violating the moral order of the universe (for Macbeth) are the sickening of
(cont.)

ANSWERS FOR CONNECTIONS (CONT.)

his nation (act IV, scene iii, lines 164–173; act V, scene ii, line 27–28), his mental disintegration (act III, scene iv, lines 85-87), the loss of all the consolations of old age (act V, scene iii, lines 22–26), the loss of the loyalty of his subjects (act V, scene vii, lines 25–28), the death of his wife, and his own eventual destruction. For Faustus, the consequence is his eternal torment in hell (line 90). In sum, the consequence of violating of the moral order is destruction.

4. The feudal system was held together by a hierarchy of loyalties extending from the peasants to the nobles to the supreme ruler. Each owed duty to the next on the social scale. Confucius insisted that the duties of inferiors and superiors be observed by both sides. Macbeth, by murdering Duncan, violated the principle of duty to one's superiors and so violated social order in his society.

TEACHER'S EDITION **401**

▶Give students the following exercise.

Choose twenty words from the list on page 402 that you would like to make part of your active vocabulary. For each word, write two sentences having to do with *Macbeth*. One sentence should be literally true. The other sentence should be ironic. Your sentences can be written from the perspective of any character in the play, or they can be from the perspective of an outside observer.

Example.

True: Lady Macbeth did not want her husband <u>impeded</u> in becoming king.

Ironic: Macbeth arranged that Banquo would be <u>impeded</u> in becoming king.

ADDITIONAL RESOURCES

ASSESSMENT PORTFOLIO
- Vocabulary Worksheet: Unit 5, 4.5.15
- Study Guide: Unit 5 Test, 4.5.16
- Unit 5 Test, 4.5.17

ESSENTIAL SKILLS PRACTICE BOOKS

Language
- Commas I, 2.94
- Commas II, 2.95
- Commas III, 2.96
- Combining Sentences Using Single Words, 2.51
- Combining Sentences Using Clauses, 2.53
- Functions of Sentences, 2.36

Speaking and Listening
- Elements of Verbal Communication, 3.2
- Elements of Nonverbal Communication, 3.3

Study and Research
- Memorizing, 4.4
- Generalizing, 4.11

UNIT REVIEW

Renaissance Drama

VOCABULARY FROM THE SELECTIONS

abjure, 368, 389	felicity, 389	mettle, 333	rend, 390
ague, 379	firmament, 390	minion, 323	scruples, 343
augment, 337	flout, 324	mortal, 330	stanchless *or*
chastise, 330	gall, 330	multitudinous, 340	staunchless, 367
confineless, 367	gape, 390	nativity, 391	stealthy, 338
corporal, 326	harbinger, 380	nonpareil, 353	surfeit, 388
cunning, 389	harbor, 390	pall, 330	surmise, 327
dauntless, 349	homely, 365	palpable, 337	taint, 377
doff, 370	impede, 330	peak, 325	teem, 370
earnest, 327	impediment, 367	pernicious, 363	trifle, 327
entice, 392	incessant, 391	posterity, 348	usurper, 382
equivocator, 340	ireful, 390	purveyor, 331	verity, 348
eternally, 388	jocund, 351	recompense, 328	wanton, 329
exhort, 392	malevolence, 357	remorse, 330	

LITERARY TERMS

aside, 335	history, 312	plot, 385
catastrophe, 311	hyperbole, 346	protagonist, 312
chorus, 393	inciting incident, 335	resolution, 311
climax, 359	interlude, 312	rising action, 311
comedy, 312	masque, 312	romance, 312
complication, 311	metaphor, 384	simile, 359
crisis, 311, 359	miracle play, 310	soliloquy, 335, 393
falling action, 311	morality play, 310	symbol, 346
five-act play, 310	motif, 320	theme, 384
foil, 335	mystery play, 310	tragedy, 312, 320
foreshadowing, 384	paradox, 373	turning point, 311, 359
genre, 394	personification, 373	verbal irony, 346, 373

SYNTHESIS: QUESTIONS FOR WRITING, RESEARCH, OR DISCUSSION

GENRE STUDIES

1. **Tragedy.** Most tragedies deal with a character of high station who falls due to a central failing, or tragic flaw, in that character's personality. Explain how Marlowe's Dr. Faustus and Shakespeare's Macbeth fulfill this description of the tragic hero.

2. **Drama.** One characteristic that sets drama apart from other forms of literature is its use of spectacle. Read the definition of *spectacle* in the Handbook of Literary Terms. Then describe the elements of spectacle in *Dr. Faustus* and *Macbeth* that make both of these plays exciting to watch in performance.

THEMATIC STUDIES

3. **The Dangers of Ambition and the Faustian Bargain.** Explore the theme of ambition in *Dr. Faustus* and *Macbeth*. In each play, what ambitions does the central character have? What is a "Faustian bargain"? What does the central character do to fulfill his ambitions? What awful bargain does each character make? What keeps each character from being happy despite the short-term fulfillment of his ambitions?

4. **Disturbances in the Natural Order.** In both *Dr. Faustus* and *Macbeth,* the central character traffics with the supernatural. How is the supernatural portrayed in each play? What happens, in each play, when the central character steps outside the natural, moral order?

HISTORICAL AND BIOGRAPHICAL STUDIES

5. ***Macbeth* and James I.** After the death of Elizabeth I, Shakespeare's company became servants of the new king, James I. The company even changed its name to The King's Men. The play *Macbeth* is known to have been performed for James. James was descended from Banquo, was fascinated by witchcraft, and believed in the Divine Right of Kings. In what ways might Shakespeare have tailored his play to suit his royal audience?

▶These prompts are suitable as topics for research papers. Refer to the Language Arts Survey, 4.20–4.34, "Research Skills." (To evaluate research papers, see the evaluation forms for writing, revising, and proofreading in the *Assessment Portfolio,* 7.1–7.10.)

▶These prompts can be adapted for use as topics for oral reports or debates. (To evaluate these projects, see the evaluation forms in the *Assessment Portfolio, 7.17–7.19.*)

ANSWERS TO SELECTION CHECK TEST 4.5.13 (CONT.)

4. To what is a person who rules by moral force compared?
He or she is compared to the pole star.

5. What is the main message the Master would like to teach?
"Let there be no evil in your thoughts."

LANGUAGE LAB   EDITING FOR ERRORS IN PRONOUNS

When you edit or proofread your writing, check to make sure that it is free of errors in the use of pronouns. The two most common errors are failure to choose the correct case form and lack of agreement with an antecedent.

Case Form. Use the nominative case for subjects and for predicate nominatives. Use the objective case for direct objects, indirect objects, and objects of a preposition. Use the possessive case to show possession.

PERSONAL PRONOUNS		
Nominative Case (for subjects or predicate nominatives)	**Objective Case** (for direct objects, indirect objects, and objects of prepositions)	**Possessive Case** (to show possession)
SINGULAR		
I you he, she, it	me you him, her, it	my, mine your, yours his, her, hers, its
PLURAL		
we you they	us you them	our, ours your, yours their, theirs

PRONOUN USAGE
Before you write a sentence using a pronoun, think about whether the pronoun is being used as a subject, predicate nominative, some kind of object, or to show possession. This will help you to determine what case the pronoun should be.

SUBJECT	**She** is interested in becoming a dentist.
PREDICATE NOMINATIVE	It is **she** and **I** who sent those flowers.
DIRECT OBJECT	The map of the city certainly helped **me**.
INDIRECT OBJECT	Ariel taught **them** an important lesson.
OBJECT OF PREPOSITION	Jake sat with **him** on the trolley.

PRONOUN USAGE

Possessive pronouns do not change form in the nominative and objective cases.

SUBJECT	**Hers** were the hiking boots covered with mud.
PREDICATE NOMINATIVE	The prize is **mine.**
DIRECT OBJECT	Give Roberto **yours.**
INDIRECT OBJECT	We hung **ours** out to dry.
OBJECT OF PREPOSITION	I put my books with **yours.**

Agreement of Pronouns and Antecedents. Be sure that the pronouns in your writing agree in number and gender with their antecedents.

INCORRECT NUMBER	A **person** should purchase tickets ahead of time, and **they** should arrive at the theater early.
CORRECT NUMBER	**People** should purchase tickets ahead of time, and **they** should arrive at the theater early.
INCORRECT GENDER	**Dr. Faustus** was sorry, but this would not change **her** fate.
CORRECT GENDER	**Dr. Faustus** was sorry, but this would not change **his** fate.

EXERCISE   Correcting Errors in Pronoun Usage

Rewrite the following sentences, correcting all errors in pronoun usage that you can find. Some sentences are correct.

EXAMPLE: It is her who had the starring role in Shakespeare's *Macbeth*.

It is **she** *who had the starring role in Shakespeare's* Macbeth.

1. It is me who studied the history of theater in England.

2. Him and I are interested in Faust, a legendary wandering magician who inspired dramas by Christopher Marlowe and Johann Wolfgang von Goethe.

3. Joel and me want to read Shakespeare's narrative poem, *Venus and Adonis*.

4. Was my presentation on life in Elizabethan England as good as yours?

5. I gave they a copy of Marlowe's *Dr. Faustus,* which contains both blank verse and prose.

6. It interested I to learn that the earliest known performance of Marlowe's *Dr. Faustus* took place in 1594.

7. The tragedy *Romeo and Juliet* is Wesley's favorite Shakespearean play, and the comedy *Twelfth Night* is mine.

8. The history of England is interesting to Larry and I.

9. "I admire William Shakespeare's tragedies," Marty said, "particularly *Macbeth*, which she probably wrote in 1606."

10. Eighteenth- and nineteenth-century actors were often interested in the character of Lady Macbeth, so they worked hard to land that role.

UNIT 6 THE EARLY SEVENTEENTH CENTURY (1625–1675)

Charles I on Horseback. Sir Anthony Van Dyck. The National Gallery, London

GOALS/OBJECTIVES

Studying this unit will enable students to
- understand and appreciate types of seventeenth-century values
- use modifiers correctly
- describe how women were portrayed by male writers in the seventeenth century
- understand why the freedom, love, honor, and *carpe diem* themes were important to seventeenth-century writers
- name and describe the main characteristics of Metaphysical poetry and Cavalier poetry
- explain the absence of drama in England under Oliver Cromwell

TEACHING THE MULTIPLE INTELLIGENCES

So restless Cromwell could not cease

In the inglorious arts of peace,

But through adventurous war

Urgéd his active star.

—Andrew Marvell, "An Horatian Ode Upon Cromwell's Return from Ireland"

407

ART NOTE

Dutch painter Anthony Van Dyck came to the court of King Charles I in 1632. The king had a great appreciation for painting, and he and his family and many members of the court had their portraits painted by Van Dyck. *Charles I on Horseback* (*circa* 1637) grandly depicts Charles I as a warrior knight. Clad in full armor and holding his commander's baton, the monarch wears around his neck a gold locket with an engraving of St. George, a symbol of knightly chivalry. The painting portrays Charles I as majestic and powerful—good propaganda for a ruler who was, in fact, a rather unimposing figure and who was struggling to enforce his firm belief in the divine right of kings in the face of increasing opposition from Parliament.

- Unlike the United States Congress, which was established by the Constitution in 1787, the English Parliament developed gradually over the course of many centuries. King John signed the *Magna Carta* in 1215, formalizing the principle of limited sovereignty. Under King Edward I, who reigned from 1272 to 1307, two royal advisory bodies were merged. The Norman *Magnum Concilium* was a group of feudal lords and church leaders serving the king, and the *Curia Regis* was a group of semiprofessional advisors. Both bodies met whenever the king called them together, and under Edward I the two often met jointly. In the early 1300s, the two bodies sometimes debated important issues. Parliament gradually developed the power to introduce legislation, called *bills,* which became acts of Parliament after they were approved by the monarch. By the reign of Henry VI, the approval of both houses of Parliament was needed to pass a law. During the period of the British Civil War, the balance of power between Parliament and the sovereign was seriously questioned, and much blood was spilled before the issue was resolved.

- The Puritan Movement was very influential in all aspects of English life. Have students research other religious movements—both in Western and Eastern cultures—that had an impact on society.

THE EARLY SEVENTEENTH CENTURY (1625–1675)

The first quarter of the seventeenth century, the end of the reign of James I, was relatively peaceful. The second quarter was a period of turbulence such as England had not experienced since the days of the Viking invasions. During the period from 1625 to 1649, the unthinkable happened: the English people rose in revolt and beheaded their king.

THE EARLY YEARS OF CHARLES I

When James I died in 1625, his son Charles inherited the throne. **Charles I** had been a weak child, unable to walk before the age of seven and afflicted with a severe impediment of speech. However, he overcame these difficulties by engaging in sports and practicing elocution. A studious young man, Charles devoted himself to mathematics, music, art, theology, and languages.

Charles inherited his father's belief in the divine right of kings. This conviction was further increased by his marriage to Henrietta Maria, a French Catholic with absolutist views regarding royal prerogatives. Charles himself was an Anglican, but he sympathized with Catholic views and detested the Protestant **Puritans,** whom he considered extremists.

The Puritans received their name from the fact that they wished to "purify" the Anglican Church of vestiges of Roman Catholic ritual. They believed in the Calvinist doctrine of **predestination,** the idea that God had at the beginning of time determined which people would be saved, or among the **elect,** and which would not. The Puritan Movement was particularly strong in the cities of the south of England, especially in London. In the cities, Puritan members of the new, wealthy class of merchants, traders, and shopkeepers came increasingly to see their needs as opposed to those of the hereditary landed aristocracy of the north, where Catholicism still flourished despite official discouragement.

In 1625, Charles called Parliament into session to raise money to meet the expenses of his government and of his ongoing war with Spain. The lower house of Parliament, the House of Commons, was dominated by wealthy Puritans. Parliament granted Charles less money than he wanted and put restrictions on Charles's right to collect import and export duties. It also voted to meet annually thereafter to examine government expenses. Charles disbanded

LITERARY EVENTS

► = British Events

▶1642. Sir Thomas Browne publishes *Religio medici;* theaters in England closed; Richard Lovelace, imprisoned by Parliament, writes "To Althea from Prison"

▶1640. Donne's *Devotions upon Emergent Occasions* published

▶1636. William Prynne publishes *News from Ipswich,* a Puritan denunciation of popes and bishops

▶1633. John Donne's *Poems* and George Herbert's *The Temple* published

▶1632. William Prynne publishes *Histriomastix, the Player's Scourge*

▶1644. John Milton writes *Areopagitica*

1625	1630	1635	1640	1645

▶1625. James I dies; Charles I becomes king

1636. In North America, Roger Williams founds Rhode Island

▶1628. Parliament requires Charles to sign Petition of Right; thirty-nine articles of the Anglican creed made law of the land

▶1629–40. Charles reigns as absolute ruler, without convening Parliament

▶1629. House of Commons passes laws making dissent from orthodox religious beliefs and collecting unauthorized taxes capital crimes; Charles threatens House with troops

▶1638–40. First and Second Bishops' Wars with Scotland end in Charles's defeat

1630. In North America, John Winthrop founds Boston

▶1640. Long Parliament convenes, sends Laud and Strafford to Tower

HISTORICAL EVENTS

▶1632. William Laud, a staunch anti-Puritan, becomes Archbishop of Canterbury

▶1641. Charles signs "Grand Remonstrance"

▶1641. Revolt in Ireland

▶1642. Civil War begins

408 UNIT SIX / THE EARLY SEVENTEENTH CENTURY

THEMATIC CURRENTS

Use the following selections to explore these themes with your students.

SALVATION AND FREEDOM
- Holy Sonnet 10, 418
- from Meditation 17, 420
- "Easter Wings," 425
- from *Paradise Lost,* 429
- "On His Blindness," 439
- from *The Pilgrim's Progress,* 442

LOVE AND FAITHFULNESS
- Song (Donne), 414
- "To His Coy Mistress," 457
- Song, 465
- "To Althea, from Prison," 451

CARPE DIEM
- "To His Coy Mistress," 457
- "Corinna's Going A-Maying," 465
- from *The Rubáiyát,* 467

this session of Parliament but was soon forced by financial need to call another session. Parliament asked for the removal of Charles's Chancellor, Buckingham, who had gotten England involved in its disastrous war with Spain. Charles angrily dismissed this second Parliament without receiving the funds he needed. He then began a campaign to raise funds on his own, collecting taxes without Parliamentary consent and requiring the English people to make "loans" to the government. He also pressed many English men into involuntary military service.

In 1628, having spent the money from the "loans," Charles again called Parliament into session, demanding that it meet his requests. Parliament responded with its own demands, requiring the king to sign a Petition of Right forcing the king to receive Parliamentary consent to levy new taxes. Having no choice, Charles signed it. Shortly thereafter, Buckingham was murdered.

Parliament then turned its attention to religious matters, resolving to enforce a strictly Calvinist view and to punish Catholics and other nonconformists. Charles ordered Parliament to adjourn, but it refused to do so until threatened by the king's troops. Charles then put several of the leading Parliamentarians in prison.

The Execution of King Charles I. Ernest Crofts, 1890.
Bridgeman Art Library/Art Resource, New York

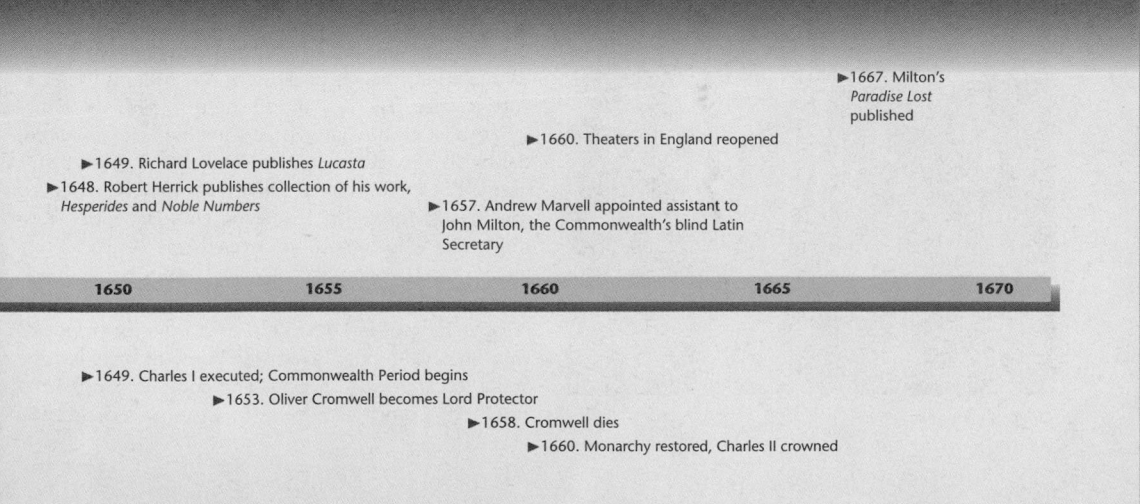

►1667. Milton's *Paradise Lost* published

►1660. Theaters in England reopened

►1649. Richard Lovelace publishes *Lucasta*

►1648. Robert Herrick publishes collection of his work, *Hesperides* and *Noble Numbers*

►1657. Andrew Marvell appointed assistant to John Milton, the Commonwealth's blind Latin Secretary

1650	1655	1660	1665	1670

►1649. Charles I executed; Commonwealth Period begins

►1653. Oliver Cromwell becomes Lord Protector

►1658. Cromwell dies

►1660. Monarchy restored, Charles II crowned

INTRODUCTION **409**

LITERARY CURRENTS

Use the following selections to explore these literary concepts and techniques with your students.

METAPHYSICAL POETRY
- Holy Sonnet 10, 418
- "Easter Wings," 425
- "The Indifferent," 463

LYRIC POETRY
- from *Paradise Lost,* 429
- "On His Blindness," 439
- "To His Coy Mistress," 457
- Song, 414
- "To Althea, from Prison," 451
- from *The Rubáiyát,* 467

PROSE
- from Meditation 17, 420
- from *The Pilgrim's Progress,* 442
- from *Areopagitica,* 463

BIOGRAPHICAL NOTE

Oliver Cromwell (1599–1658) began his career in Parliament in 1628 when he was elected to represent his home district of Huntingdon. Cromwell was an outspoken advocate of church reform, favoring the abolition of bishops and the *Book of Common Prayer.* A skilled military leader, he quickly rose through the army ranks during the English Civil War. He was appointed commander in chief in 1650 and used his power to dissolve the ineffectual Rump Parliament. Less than a year later, Cromwell had his army officers draw up a new constitution, the Instrument of Government, naming himself lord protector. He remained in this position until his death in 1658, during which time he laid the groundwork for England's future empire by strengthening its army and navy and gaining control of Jamaica and Dunkirk. Cromwell also extended religious tolerance in England to Christian sects outside the Church of England and to Jews.

Have students role play to recreate the meeting between Charles and his council of nobles. Ask them to discuss what action they should take after the defeat by the Scots. Allow students time to research and brainstorm.

For eleven years thereafter, Charles ruled as an absolute king, without calling Parliament into session, financing his government with new taxes collected without consent of the people. In 1632, he appointed **William Laud** Archbishop of Canterbury. Laud immediately angered the Puritans by sanctioning sports on Sundays and during the coming years had many Puritan leaders imprisoned, tortured, and executed. During this time, many Puritans and members of other nonconformist religious sects emigrated from England to North America.

THE SCOTTISH REVOLT

Charles angered the Protestant Presbyterians of Scotland by attempting to enforce there the rituals approved by Archbishop Laud, which were known as "Laud's Canons." In St. Giles's Church in Edinburgh, Scotland, the bishop of Edinburgh attempted to conduct a service according to the new rules. A riot broke out, and a woman named **Jenny Geddes** threw a stool at the bishop. There followed the two so-called **Bishops' Wars** with Scotland. To raise money for the Second Bishops' War, Charles was forced to convene Parliament once again. Parliament struck a deal with the Scots, and Charles immediately disbanded it. Charles headed toward Scotland with an army, but the Scots soundly defeated him, and he retreated to York. There, on advice from a council of nobles, he decided to call another session of Parliament in order to come to some agreement with his Parliamentary foes. This seemed to be the only way to avoid being caught between his rebellious subjects in Scotland and in the Puritan south.

REVOLUTION AND CIVIL WAR

When the so-called **Long Parliament** met in 1640, it imprisoned Laud, ordered the execution of the king's councilor Strafford, excluded bishops from the House of Lords, passed laws in support of Puritan religious beliefs, and made the king subject to Parliament in the levying of taxes and collection of duties. Then it passed a "Grand Remonstrance," requiring that the king's government appointees be approved by Parliament. Charles met this demand by going, himself, to the House of Commons with a troop of soldiers to arrest the Parliamentary ringleaders. They were not there. Parliament moved to London's Guildhall, protected by armed citizens. Queen Henrietta left for France, and Charles fled to York with some loyal troops.

Parliament assembled a citizen army known to history as **Roundheads** because of the Puritans' habit of cutting their hair very short. These soldiers were met by royalist troops known as **Cavaliers**, long-haired, dandyish supporters of the king. The Puritan army, under the leadership of **Oliver Cromwell**, defeated the royalist forces. In 1646, the king surrendered to the Scots, who turned him over to the Parliamentary forces, but the king escaped. In 1648, Charles made an agreement with the Scots to enforce Scottish Presbyterianism in England in exchange for troops to win back his throne. However, Cromwell defeated the Scots, recaptured the king, and took control of the House of Commons. In 1649, Cromwell's so-called

Oliver Cromwell

Rump Parliament had Charles tried for the treasonous action of making war on Parliament. On January 30 of that year, astonished crowds watched as the executioner's ax fell.

THE COMMONWEALTH AND THE PROTECTORATE

The era of Puritan rule in England, which lasted from 1649 to 1660, is known as the **Protestant Interregnum.** The Interregnum is divided into two periods, the **Commonwealth** and the **Protectorate.** The Commonwealth lasted from 1649 to 1653. During this period, Cromwell and the radically Puritan Parliament instituted various forms of censorship, closing newspapers and outlawing "frivolous" entertainments such as theater and dancing. Cromwell faced rebellions in Scotland and in Ireland, as well as war with Spain and Holland. He also had to rule over a country deeply divided over the rightness of the execution of a lawful king. In 1653, Cromwell dissolved Parliament and initiated the Protectorate, declaring himself **"Lord Protector for Life,"** in effect making himself a dictator no different from an absolute monarch. When Cromwell died in 1658, his son took power, but he was unable to stem the tide of public opinion in favor of a restoration of the old monarchy, with its system of royal rule subject to certain limits imposed by a House of Lords and a House of Commons. The feelings of many English men and women of the time were reflected in these words by **Isaak Walton:**

> When I look back upon the ruin of families, the bloodshed, the decay of common honesty, and how the former piety and plain dealing of this now sinful nation is turned into cruelty and cunning, I praise God that he prevented me from being of that party which helped to bring in this Covenant and those sad confusions that have followed it.

A special session of Parliament convened and invited **Charles II,** in exile in France, to return as king. Thus the monarchy was restored, and this revolutionary period in English history came to an end.

LITERATURE IN THE EARLY SEVENTEENTH CENTURY

For convenience, scholars and critics often place writers of the early seventeenth century into three groups:

The **Metaphysical poets,** including **John Donne** (1572?–1631) and **George Herbert** (1593–1633), wrote highly intellectual, often paradoxical verse using unusual metaphors, or **conceits,** drawn from astronomy, botany, zoology, theology, alchemy, medicine, cartography, law, and other sources. Metaphysical verse can be challenging to read, and it often strains the imagination, but the strain equally often yields rewards of insight.

The **Cavalier poets,** including **Richard Lovelace** (1618–1657), **Sir John Suckling** (1609–1642), and **Robert Herrick** (1591–1674), were members of the court of Charles I—dashing, long-haired, well-dressed, well-spoken, well-educated young cavaliers. They wrote lyrics about subjects of interest to young men of the court—love, honor, and loyalty to their king. As poets, they considered themselves to be **Sons of Ben,** or followers of Ben Jonson, the gifted lyric poet and contemporary of William Shakespeare. The cavaliers sought, like Jonson, to produce lyrics that conveyed a sense of grace and ease. The writing of **Andrew Marvell** (1621–1678) shares features with that of both the Metaphysical and the Cavalier poets. "To His Coy Mistress," for example, is a lyric dealing with a typical Cavalier theme, enjoying love while there is still time to do so. However, the poem also makes use of numerous metaphysical conceits.

CROSS-CURRICULAR ACTIVITIES

Sciences. Present to students the following lines as an example of *conceit.*

"Mark but this flea, and mark in this
How little that which thou deny'st me is;
It sucked me first, and now sucks thee,
And in this flea our two bloods mingled be."

"The Flea"

You might challenge students to draw on their work in science classes to develop a list of conceits or metaphors that a Metaphysical poet might use. Ask them to compare concepts or systems from the sciences to things in the social realm, such as relationships or institutions. Suggest that they save their lists for future writing.

HISTORICAL NOTE

After Charles II was restored to the English throne in 1660, the term *Cavaliers* remained in use to describe those who supported a strong monarchy. This political faction was renamed the Tory party around 1679, when it supported the succession of Charles II's brother, the Roman Catholic prince who became King James II. The Tory party name was based on a rather unflattering nickname, *tory* being the word for an Irish bandit. The Tory party became the Conservative party in the nineteenth century. Members of the Conservative party today are sometimes called *Tories* by their political opponents.

ADDITIONAL QUESTIONS AND ACTIVITIES

Students might discuss why the Puritans were not able to put an end to English drama simply by closing the theaters. Why do students think drama is a valued part of human culture? What function does it serve in people's lives? Students who are involved in drama may wish to share their thoughts on this matter with the class.

CROSS-CURRICULAR ACTIVITIES

Civics. Ask students to discuss censorship. Does it still exist in the world? Where? Encourage interested students to research the results of censorship in another country or in the United States at an earlier time. Why is, or was, censorship practiced? Is, or was, it effective? Is censorship ever acceptable? under what circumstances, if any?

John Bunyan

The Commonwealth period produced two great **Puritan** writers, **John Milton** (1608–1674) and **John Bunyan** (1628–1688). John Milton wrote numerous important political and religious tracts, including an eloquent argument against censorship, the *Areopagitica.* He is remembered primarily, however, as a poet of great power and genius, the composer of eloquent lyrics and sonnets and the great Christian epic poem *Paradise Lost.* Milton was one of the best-educated men of his time. John Bunyan, on the other hand, was poorly educated, having taught himself using a few religious tracts and the scriptures. Bunyan's masterpiece of Christian allegory, *The Pilgrim's Progress,* was, until the nineteenth century, the most widely read book in the English language after the Bible.

THE DRAMA IN THE EARLY SEVENTEENTH CENTURY

In the opening years of the seventeenth century, Shakespeare and Jonson were still producing works for the stage. These were arguably the greatest years in the history of the English theater (see Unit 5). However, Puritan London had no love for the theater. The solid merchants and businesspeople of London considered exhibitions on the stage to be lewd and, because they attracted crowds, an invitation to crime and disease. Puritan attitudes toward the theater are perhaps best illustrated by William Prynne's *Histriomastix, the Player's Scourge,* published in 1632. In this book, Prynne argued that drama was the work of the devil and that churches, not playhouses, were the proper schools for devout men and women. For entertainment, Prynne suggests that people remember that they can turn to nature and to "the comfort of friends, kindred, husbands, wives, children, possessions, wealth, and all other external blessings that God hath bestowed upon them." In 1642, when the Puritans came to power under Cromwell, they closed the theaters. English stages were silent until 1660, when the theaters were reopened after the restoration of the monarchy.

Echoes:
The Early Seventeenth Century

During the time men live without a common power [a king] to keep them all in awe . . . the life of man [is] solitary, poor, nasty, brutish, and short.

—Thomas Hobbes, *Leviathan*

Wise men say nothing in dangerous times. The lion . . . called the sheep to ask her if his breath smelled; she said Yes; he bit off her head for a fool. He called the wolf and asked him; he said No; he tore him to pieces for a flatterer. At last he called the fox and asked him. Why [said the fox], he had got a cold and could not smell.

—John Selden, *Table Talk*

Bless me in this life with but peace of my conscience, command of my affections, the love of Thyself and my dearest friends, and I shall be happy enough to pity Cæsar.

—Sir Thomas Browne, *Religio medici*

Come, my Celia, let us prove,
While we can the sports of love; . . .
Suns that set may rise again;
But if once we lose this light,
'Tis with us perpetual night.

—Ben Jonson, *Volpone*

BIOGRAPHICAL NOTE

Ben Johnson (1572– or 1573–1637) was a noted writer and actor. His plays, including *Volpone, The Alchemist,* and *Bartholomew Fair,* won him recognition and a royal subsidy, and he became a leader in the literary community of London.

BIOGRAPHICAL NOTE

Thomas Hobbes (1588–1679) was a philosopher best known for his political treatise *Leviathan, or the Matter, Form, and Power of a Commonwealth, Ecclesiastical and Civil* (1651). The son of an Anglican vicar, Hobbes received his bachelor's degree from Oxford University and became a tutor to the Cavendish family in 1608. During several trips to the Continent, Hobbes was influenced by such luminaries as Galileo and Descartes. His studies of mathematics and science led him to view everything in terms of bodies in motion, including human psychology and politics. In *Leviathan,* Hobbes argued that the natural state of human beings was one of war with each other and that only by granting absolute power to a sovereign could people be spared having "nasty, brutish, and short" lives. His political philosophy angered people on both sides of the British Civil War, and Hobbes fled to Paris in 1640. There he became tutor to the exiled Prince of Wales, who later became Charles II. Hobbes remained a controversial figure throughout his life, but after the Restoration, Charles II protected him from his enemies. At the age of eighty-four, Hobbes published an autobiography in Latin verse, followed by English translations of the *Odyssey* and the *Iliad.*

BIOGRAPHICAL NOTE

John Selden (1584–1654) was a historian, lawyer, and member of Parliament who sided against the king.

BIOGRAPHICAL NOTE

Thomas Browne (1605–1682) was a physician.

ADDITIONAL RESOURCES

READER'S GUIDE
- Selection Worksheets, 6.1, 6.2, 6.3

ASSESSMENT PORTFOLIO
- Selection Check Tests, 4.6.1, 4.6.3, 4.6.5
- Selection Tests, 4.6.2, 4.6.4, 4.6.6

ESSENTIAL SKILLS PRACTICE BOOKS
- *Language*, 2.12, 2.13, 2.147
- *Speaking and Listening*, 3.7
- *Applied English*, 5.5

ENRICHMENT ACTIVITY

Students can discuss the kinds of experiences the speaker might have had to give him such a cynical view of women's faithfulness. Small groups could collaborate to write a brief story or play describing these experiences, perhaps concluding with an experience that causes the speaker to rethink his position.

SUPPORT FOR LEP STUDENTS

Alert students to the archaic verbs and pronouns Donne used in Song ("Go and catch a falling star . . ."), such as *beest* (pronounced be´st), *return'st, wilt, find'st, thee,* and *thou*. Line 13 may be confusing; tell students that the word *snow* is used as a verb, with *age* as its subject. Guide them to appreciate the image Donne created here: age, or the passage of time, is like a storm cloud snowing down upon the head of the person addressed by the poem, gradually turning the person's hair white.

ADDITIONAL VOCABULARY
befall—happen to

PREREADING

Song ("Go and catch a falling star . . .")
Holy Sonnet 10 ("Death, be not proud . . .")
from Meditation 17 ("Perchance he for whom this bell tolls . . .")
by John Donne

ABOUT THE AUTHOR

John Donne (1572–1631), born into an old Roman Catholic family, attended Oxford and Cambridge and studied law at Lincoln's Inn. Strong anti-Catholic feelings in England prohibited Donne from following many of the usual paths toward success. In his twenties, Donne survived on a small inheritance from his father and on charm, intelligence, and courtly favor. Donne's prospects for advancement seemed secure when, at the age of twenty-six, he was appointed secretary to a high official in the court of Queen Elizabeth I. In 1601, however, after Donne's secret marriage to Anne More, which was opposed by her powerful father, he was fired from his position and imprisoned. In 1614, he converted to Anglicanism. The next year, he entered the ministry and became an Anglican priest. With his deep learning, dramatic wit, and metaphorical style, Donne at once established himself as a great preacher. Appointed dean of St. Paul's Cathedral in 1621, Donne became one of the most influential ministers in England. Donne's private devotions were published in 1624. His collected poems were published in 1633, two years after his death. Donne's poetic style influenced other writers, including Herbert, Crashaw, and Marvell. That style, which came to be known as "Metaphysical," also greatly influenced a number of important twentieth-century poets.

ABOUT THE SELECTIONS

Donne once described himself as a dual character—Jack Donne, the writer of ironic, worldly verse, and Dr. Donne, the writer of fervent religious poems. Whatever his character, Donne, in the intensely personal and immediate tone of his poetry, made a keen break from the decorative style of most Elizabethan verse. **Song ("Go and catch a falling star . . .")** is one of Donne's early love poems and shows his playful and worldly skepticism about finding true and faithful love. The selection also shows Donne's fondness for unusual comparisons and diction that imitates ordinary speech. **Holy Sonnet 10 ("Death, be not proud . . .")** is among the most famous of Donne's later religious poems. The selection shows Donne's bold use of paradox, unexpected use of a traditional form, and refusal to accept conventional ideas about death. **Meditation 17 ("Perchance he for whom this bell tolls . . .")** is taken from ***Devotions upon Emergent Occasions***, published in 1624, a series of meditations on the themes of sickness and mortality.

GOALS/OBJECTIVES

Studying this lesson will enable students to

- interpret and appreciate Donne's ideas about love, religion, and death
- describe the literary contributions of John Donne, both as an ironic poet and as a religious writer
- define *Metaphysical poetry* and identify elements of this style in a poem

- define *conceit, hyperbole, metaphor, personification, paradox, theme,* and *purpose* and recognize and interpret examples of each when they encounter them in their reading
- write a rebuttal, a lyric poem, a meditation, and a personal letter
- distinguish between linking verbs and action verbs

READER'S JOURNAL

Sometimes it can be great fun to think about improbable subjects. That impulse leads people to read science fiction, fantasy, romances, horror stories, adventure stories, and mysteries. With some other students, brainstorm a list of impossible but interesting activities such as catching a falling star. Write your list in your journal.

READING SKILLS

Study the Language Arts Survey, 4.19, "Reading Charts and Graphs." Then, as you read Donne's poem, construct a table that lists all the "impossible things" mentioned in it.

Song

("Go and catch a falling star . . .")

JOHN DONNE

Go and catch a falling star,
  Get with child a mandrake root,
Tell me where all past years are,
  Or who <u>cleft</u> the Devil's foot,
5 Teach me to hear mermaids singing,[1]
Or to keep off envy's stinging,
    And find
    What wind
Serves to advance an honest mind.

10 If thou beest° born to strange sights,   *you have been*
  Things invisible to see,
Ride ten thousand days and nights,
  Till age snow white hairs on thee,
Thou, when thou return'st, wilt tell me
15 All strange wonders that befell thee,

---

1. **Get with . . . singing.** Mandrake root is a forked root resembling the human body. The devil has been conventionally pictured as having goatlike hooves. *Mermaids singing* may refer to the sirens whose song led to destruction of all who heard it except Odysseus.

WORDS FOR   **cleft** (kleft) *vt.,* divided; split
EVERYDAY USE:

READER'S JOURNAL

You might suggest categories such as the following to guide students' brainstorming.

• Plays on common metaphors ("Gather a tear from the eye of a storm.")

• Mysteries of time and space ("Tell how today becomes yesterday and tomorrow becomes today.")

• Examples from myths and tales ("Look into Medusa's eyes without turning to stone.")

• Inescapable truths of human nature ("Feel no sense of relief when bad luck finds someone else instead of you.")

READING SKILLS

Students might use the categories listed above as headings for their charts.

ANSWERS TO SELECTION CHECK TEST 4.6.1

EX. What impossible task does the speaker set in the opening line?
The speaker says to "Go and catch a falling star."

1. What questions does the speaker want answered in the opening stanza?
The speaker asks to know "where all the past years are" and "who cleft the Devil's foot."

2. What does the speaker ask the subject to do for ten thousand days and nights?
The speaker asks the subject to ride for ten thousand days and nights.

3. What will the subject tell the speaker afterward?
The subject will tell the speaker the strange wonders that happened to him or her.

4. What will this person swear?
He or she will swear that there is not a true and fair woman anywhere.

5. What does the speaker say would happen to a true and fair woman?
The speaker says that such a woman would no longer be true and fair by the time he met her.

---

①
What does the speaker tell the reader to do?

VOCABULARY IN CONTEXT

• The powerful earthquake left the highway <u>cleft</u> in two jagged pieces.

ANSWER TO GUIDED READING QUESTION

① The speaker lists seven impossible tasks for the reader: catch a falling star, impregnate a mandrake root, tell what happens to times past, tell who split the Devil's cloven foot, teach the speaker to hear the Sirens without perishing, learn how to avoid feeling envy, and explain what motivates a person to act honestly.

ANSWER TO GUIDED READING QUESTION

❶ He says she would have betrayed two or three people by that time.

RESPONDING TO THE SELECTION

Students might begin by working in small groups to define what *true* and *fair* mean to them. Could they mean different things to different people? Is one of these qualities more subjective than the other?

ANSWERS FOR REVIEWING THE SELECTION

RECALLING

1. The speaker tells the reader or listener to catch a falling star.

2. The reader or listener will swear that no woman exists who is both true and fair.

3. The speaker wishes to be informed if a true and fair woman is actually found.

4. The speaker predicts that even if she were true and fair at the time when he heard about her, she would have become untrue by the time he went to meet her.

INTERPRETING

Responses will vary. Possible responses are given.

5. They are all impossible tasks; some are based on wordplay. For example, a falling star is not something that can be caught.

6. The image is of snow falling on the person's head and turning his or her hair white with age.

7. The rest of the stanza describes how the sweetness of discovering the woman turns sour when she becomes "false."

8. He seems to think it is impossible.

SYNTHESIZING

Responses will vary. Possible responses are given.

9. He has apparently been involved with a woman or women whom he thought were unfaithful or dishonest, and he has concluded that all women are so. His prediction that the rare "true" woman would be "false" to two or three others by the time the speaker met her is an overstatement inspired by his bitterness.

10. The speaker seems cynical, bitter, resigned, and arrogant.

And swear
No where
Lives a woman true, and fair.

If thou find'st one, let me know,
20   Such a pilgrimage were sweet;
Yet do not, I would not go,
   Though at next door we might meet;
Though she were true when you met her,
And last till you write your letter,
25   Yet she
      Will be
False, ere° I come, to two, or three.   ■   *before*

❶ *What does the speaker say would be true of the woman by the time he met her?*

Responding to the Selection

Do you agree with the speaker that it is nearly impossible to find someone both true and fair? Why, or why not?

Reviewing the Selection

RECALLING

1. What task does the speaker tell the reader or listener to perform in line 1?

2. What does the speaker predict that the reader or listener will "swear" after returning from the ride of "ten thousand days and nights"?

3. What request does the speaker make in line 19?

4. What prediction does the speaker make about the woman in the last stanza?

INTERPRETING

5. What kinds of tasks are described in stanza 1?

6. What image in stanza 2 emphasizes the aged appearance of the reader or listener upon returning from the long ride?

7. What statement by the speaker shows that he does not actually believe that "Such a pilgrimage were sweet"?

8. What is the speaker's attitude toward the possibility of finding a good mate?

ANSWERS FOR UNDERSTANDING LITERATURE

▶ See the evaluation forms for discussion, active listening, and oral communication, *Assessment Portfolio,* 7.11–7.14. *Responses will vary. Possible responses are given.*

  1. **Hyperbole.** The poem exaggerates the odds of finding such a mate by saying that a person could spend a lifetime searching for her and never find her and that any woman who at first seemed true would inevitably turn out to be false.

▶ **Teaching Note:** You might lead a class discussion about hyperbole as a common response to disappointment or frustration. Ask students if they have ever exaggerated the hopelessness of a situation after experiencing a setback. Is there any easy way to escape from this pessimistic frame of mind? What does it take to get out of it?

(cont.)

9. What do you think the speaker in this poem has experienced in his love life? Why is he so bitter? With what overstatement does the poem conclude? What might have led the speaker to make such an overstatement?

10. What adjectives might describe the speaker of this poem?

Understanding Literature (Questions for Discussion)

1. **Hyperbole.** A **hyperbole** is an exaggeration made for rhetorical effect. What exaggeration does the speaker in this poem make about finding a true and fair mate?

2. **Metaphor.** A **metaphor** is a figure of speech in which one thing is spoken or written about as if it were another. This figure of speech invites the reader to make a comparison between the two things. In this selection, what seven things in stanza 1 are compared to finding a mate who is true and fair? What, according to the speaker's perspective, do these things have in common with finding a mate who is true and fair?

Responding in Writing

1. **Rebuttal.** Write a rebuttal to the speaker in this poem, refuting his conclusion about the possibility of finding a "true and fair" mate.

2. **Lyric Poem.** A **lyric poem** is a highly musical verse that expresses the emotions of a speaker. Consider the following lines from the poem:

> If thou find'st one, let me know,
>   Such a pilgrimage were sweet;
> Yet do not, I would not go,
>   Though at next door we might meet;

Write a response to the speaker from someone who is both true and fair. Use rhyming *couplets* or *quatrains*. See the definitions of these stanza forms in the Handbook of Literary Terms.

ANALYTIC SCALES FOR RESPONDING IN WRITING

Assign a score from 1 to 25 for each grading criterion below. (For more detailed evaluation, see the evaluation forms for writing, revising, and proofreading, *Assessment Portfolio,* 7.1–7.10.)

1. Rebuttal
• **Content/Unity.** The rebuttal shows a strong grasp of the speaker's argument and presents a logical counterargument.
• **Organization/Coherence.** The rebuttal summarizes the speaker's argument, refutes it point by point, and then makes a concluding statement.
• **Language/Style.** The rebuttal uses vivid and precise nouns, verbs, and modifiers.
• **Conventions.** The rebuttal avoids errors in spelling, grammar, usage, mechanics, and manuscript form.

2. Lyric Poem
• **Content/Unity.** The poem creates a believable speaker and presents a sensible, emotionally engaging response to Donne's poem.
• **Organization/Coherence.** The poem establishes at the start that it is a response to Donne's poem and proceeds to a satisfying conclusion.
• **Language/Style.** The poem uses vivid and precise nouns, verbs, and modifiers.
• **Conventions.** The poem avoids errors in spelling, grammar, usage, mechanics, and manuscript form.

ANSWERS FOR UNDERSTANDING LITERATURE (CONT.)

2. Metaphor. The seven tasks compared to finding a true and fair mate are catching a falling star, impregnating a mandrake root, and explaining five mysteries: what happens to times past, who split the Devil's cloven foot, how to hear the Sirens without perishing, how to avoid feeling envy, and what motivates a person to act honestly. All of these tasks are impossible, as the speaker believes is finding such a mate.

►**Teaching Note:** Ask students if they think Donne's metaphors are accurate. Challenge them to think of other metaphors for finding a mate—or anything else that is both highly valued and rare—that create a less bleak outlook.

PREREADING NOTES

READER'S JOURNAL

Students can begin by thinking about what effect the abstract quality or emotion has on an individual. How does love or courage make someone feel or act? If the abstract noun were a person, what would the person look like and how would he or she behave toward the affected individual?

LANGUAGE SKILLS

If students are having trouble getting started, you might offer the following informal "translation" of the first two lines of the sonnet.

Death, be not proud, although some have called you
Mighty and dreadful, because you are not so;

▶Additional practice is provided in the *Essential Skills Practice Book: Language*, 2.147.

ANSWERS TO GUIDED READING QUESTIONS

❶ Some have called death "mighty and dreadful."

❷ No, the speaker is quite disrespectful and insulting, making the point that death is not something to be feared but almost pitied.

SUPPORT FOR LEP STUDENTS

ADDITIONAL VOCABULARY
dwell—live

READER'S JOURNAL

Do a freewrite in which an abstract noun, such as *love, death, honor, courage, integrity,* or *loneliness,* is described as having human characteristics. For example, loneliness might be described as a jailer, confining a spirit that might, in other circumstances, be free and bright.

LANGUAGE SKILLS

Read the Language Arts Survey, 2.147, "Formal and Informal English." Then make a list of formal words from the selection, and write an informal word that might be used in its place in a different piece of writing.

Holy Sonnet 10

("Death, be not proud . . .")

JOHN DONNE

❶
What have some people called death?

❷
What is the speaker's tone in addressing death? Is he respectful? awed? afraid? Why, or why not?

Death, be not proud, though some have callèd[1] thee
Mighty and dreadful, for thou art not so;
For those whom thou think'st thou dost° overthrow   *do*
Die not, poor Death, nor yet canst thou kill me.
5   From rest and sleep, which but thy pictures be,
Much pleasure; then from thee much more must flow,
And soonest our best men with thee do go,
Rest of their bones, and soul's delivery.[2]
Thou art slave to fate, chance, kings, and desperate men,
10 And dost with poison, war, and sickness dwell,
And poppy or charms can make us sleep as well
And better than thy stroke; why swell'st thou then?[3]
One short sleep past, we wake eternally
And death shall be no more; Death, thou shalt die.   ■

---

1. **callèd.** The accent on the *e* makes the *-ed* a separate syllable: *call-ed.*
2. **Rest . . . delivery.** Bodily rest and freedom of the soul
3. **why swell'st thou then?** Why do you puff up with pride?

418   UNIT SIX / THE EARLY SEVENTEENTH CENTURY

ANSWERS TO SELECTION CHECK TEST 4.6.3

EX. What should Death not be, according to the speaker?
Death should not be proud.

1. What does the speaker say Death is not?
The speaker says that Death is not mighty and dreadful.

2. To what is Death a slave?
Death is a slave to fate, chance, kings, and desperate men.

3. With whom does Death dwell?
Death dwells with poison, war, and sickness.

4. What can make people sleep as well as Death?
Poppy or charms can make people sleep as well.

5. What does the speaker say will happen to Death?
The speaker says Death shall die.

418   TEACHER'S EDITION

Responding to the Selection

Do you share the speaker's feelings about death? Why, or why not? Discuss your feelings about this subject with your classmates.

Reviewing the Selection

RECALLING

1. What assertion about death does the speaker make in line 2 of the sonnet?

2. What have some people called death?

3. According to the speaker, to what is death a slave?

4. What prediction does the speaker make in line 14 of the sonnet?

INTERPRETING

5. What examples in the sonnet support the speaker's opening assertion?

6. According to the speaker, what actually happens to a person's bones and soul after death?

7. What actions might kings or desperate men take that would show death to be a slave to them?

8. What beliefs on the part of the speaker support his final prediction?

SYNTHESIZING

9. What conventional or accepted perceptions of death are rejected by the speaker? What different perception of death does the speaker present?

10. What images in this sonnet cause the reader or listener to feel disgust toward death?

Understanding Literature (Questions for Discussion)

1. **Personification. Personification** is a figure of speech in which an idea, animal, or thing is described as if it were a person. For example, a writer might tell about roses *surrendering* to snow. The selection is an example of extended personification. What specific examples of personification can you find in the sonnet?

2. **Paradox.** A **paradox** is a contradictory statement, idea, or event. What examples of paradox can you find in the sonnet?

ANSWERS FOR UNDERSTANDING LITERATURE

▶ See the evaluation forms for discussion, active listening, and oral communication, *Assessment Portfolio,* 7.11–7.14. *Responses will vary. Possible responses are given.*

1. **Personification.** The speaker addresses Death, capitalizing the word *death* as though it were a name and describing death as having a human characteristic— swelling with pride at the thought of its power over human beings (lines 1–3; line 12). Line 14 predicts that

death will die, as if it were alive now.

2. **Paradox.** Examples of paradox include lines 5–6, in which the speaker says that death brings pleasure, and line 14, which concludes, "Death, thou shalt die."

▶ **Teaching Note:** You might point out that a paradox may spring from a contradiction between two statements within a text or from a contradiction between what the text says and what people normally think or expect.

RESPONDING TO THE SELECTION

You might direct students' attention to the last two lines and ask them to consider the speaker's main reason for not fearing death.

ANSWERS FOR REVIEWING THE SELECTION

RECALLING

1. The speaker says that death is not mighty or dreadful.

2. Some have called death "mighty and dreadful."

3. Death is a slave to "fate, chance, kings, and desperate men."

4. The speaker predicts that death will itself die.

INTERPRETING

Responses will vary. Possible responses are given.

5. Fate and human beings have the power to decide when death will happen. Death must live with such undesirable companions as "poison, war, and sickness."

6. A person's bones are allowed to rest, and the soul is freed.

7. A king might declare war, and a desperate man might commit murder or suicide.

8. The speaker holds the belief that people will enjoy eternal life after their deaths in the temporal world.

SYNTHESIZING

Responses will vary. Possible responses are given.

9. The speaker rejects the idea that death is a powerful force of which people should be afraid, or even respectful. Instead, the speaker asserts that Death is impotent and pathetic.

10. The masters of Death are "fate, chance, kings, and desperate men," and Death is forced to live among "poison, war, and sickness." Still, Death swells with self-importance, assuming that people will cringe in fear of it. The reader feels disgust over Death's arrogance as well as its slavish, depraved nature.

Students might begin by brainstorming a list of things they receive from their families and communities and from the legacy of past generations. They might also imagine what it would be like to spend an extended period of time away from all human contact. What things would they miss about being with other people?

SPEAKING AND LISTENING SKILLS

You might ask volunteers to read aloud brief excerpts from the piece, such as from "No man is an island" to "it tolls for thee" on page 421. Other students could then offer their reactions to the speech.

▶Additional practice is provided in the *Essential Skills Practice Book: Speaking and Listening*, 3.7.

ANSWER TO GUIDED READING QUESTION

❶ The speaker describes the church as a living organism with a head and body.

ADDITIONAL QUESTIONS AND ACTIVITIES

Ask students to recall Donne's use of paradox in Holy Sonnet 10. They may then discuss the following questions.

• What paradox do you see in Donne's discussion of suffering?

• What did Donne say about a treasure in gold that is not turned into currency, or coins? How did he believe people should "spend" their treasure of affliction?

(cont.)

READER'S JOURNAL

John Donne says in this famous meditation that "no man is an island." What does that statement mean? In what ways are people necessarily connected to one another? Why is it very difficult, if not impossible, for people to have happy, productive lives if they are not connected to others? Why are relationships with others so important? Freewrite about these questions in your journal.

SPEAKING AND LISTENING SKILLS

Read the Language Arts Survey, 3.7, "Public Speaking." Then answer this question: How can a public speaker attract and keep the attention of an audience? As you read this selection, bear in mind that John Donne was a minister, used to speaking from the pulpit. In what statements in the selection does Donne directly relate his ideas to the lives of the readers or listeners? Is that an effective technique for keeping a reader or listener interested?

FROM

Meditation 17

("Perchance he for whom this bell tolls . . .")

FROM DEVOTIONS UPON EMERGENT OCCASIONS

JOHN DONNE

Nunc lento sonitu dicunt, morieris.
Now this bell tolling softly for another,
says to me, Thou must die.

❶ How does the speaker describe the church?

Perchance he for whom this bell[1] tolls may be so ill as that he knows not it tolls for him; and perchance I may think myself so much better than I am, as that they who are about me and see my state may have caused it to toll for me, and I know not that. The church is catholic, universal, so are all her actions; all that she does belongs to all. When she baptizes a child, that action concerns me; for that child is thereby connected to that head which is my head too, and ingrafted into that body[2] whereof I am a member. And when she buries a man, that action concerns me: all mankind is of one author and is one volume; when one man dies, one chapter is not torn out of the book, but translated into a better language; and every chapter must be so translated. God employs several translators; some pieces are translated by age, some by sickness, some by war, some by justice; but God's hand is in every translation, and his hand shall bind up all our scattered leaves[3] again for that library where every book shall lie open to one another. As therefore the bell that rings to a sermon calls not upon the preacher only, but upon the congregation to come, so this bell calls us all; but how much more me, who am brought so near the door by this sickness. There was a contention as far as a suit[4] (in which piety and dignity,

---

1. **bell.** A "passing" bell rung for the dying
2. **body.** The church
3. **leaves.** Pages
4. **contention . . . suit.** A controversy that resulted in a lawsuit

ADDITIONAL QUESTIONS AND ACTIVITIES (CONT.)

• How are the attitudes toward suffering and death in Meditation 17 and in Holy Sonnet 10 similar?

Answers. Donne said "affliction is a treasure," which is the opposite of how most people feel about suffering. He thought that, just as a wedge of gold not turned into currency will not help a person pay the cost of traveling, so tribulation must be "spent," or experienced, in order to pay one's way in the journey toward heaven. In both works, Donne expressed the view that suffering and death are good because they bring people closer to God.

religion and estimation,[5] were mingled) which of the religious orders should ring to prayers first in the morning; and it was determined that they should ring first that rose earliest. If we understand aright the dignity of this bell that tolls for our evening prayer, we would be glad to make it ours by rising early, in that application, that it might be ours as well as his whose indeed it is. The bell doth toll for him that thinks it doth; and though it <u>intermit</u> again, yet from that minute that that occasion <u>wrought</u> upon him, he is united to God. Who casts not up his eye to the sun when it rises? but who takes off his eye from a comet when that breaks out? Who bends not his ear to any bell which upon any occasion rings? but who can remove it from that bell which is passing a piece of himself out of this world? No man is an island, entire of itself; every man is a piece of the continent, a part of the main.[6] If a clod be washed away by the sea, Europe is the less, as well as if a <u>promontory</u> were, as well as if a manor of thy friend's or of thine own were. Any man's death diminishes me, because I am involved in mankind; and therefore never send to know for whom the bell tolls; it tolls for thee.

Neither can we call this a begging of misery or a borrowing of misery, as though we were not miserable enough of ourselves but must fetch in more from the next house, in taking upon us the misery of our neighbors. Truly it were an excusable <u>covetousness</u> if we did; for affliction is a treasure, and scarce any man hath enough of it. No man hath affliction enough that is not matured and ripened by it, and made fit for God by that affliction. If a man carry treasure in bullion, or in a wedge of gold, and have none coined into current moneys, his treasure will not defray him as he travels. <u>Tribulation</u> is treasure in the nature of it, but it is not current money in the use of it, except we get nearer and nearer our home, heaven, by it. Another man may be sick too, and sick to death, and this affliction may lie in his bowels as gold in a mine and be of no use to him; but this bell that tells me of his affliction digs out and applies that gold to me, if by this consideration of another's danger I take mine own into contemplation and so secure myself by making my <u>recourse</u> to my God, who is our only security. ∎

---
5. **estimation.** Self-esteem
6. **main.** Mainland

❶
To what does the speaker compare the group, or body, of people that make up the church?

WORDS FOR EVERYDAY USE:

in • ter • mit (in´ tər mit´) *vt.,* pause
wrought (rôt) *adj.,* worked
prom • on • to • ry (präm´ən tôr´ē) *n.,* peak of land that juts into water

cov • et • ous • ness (kuv´ ət əs nis) *n.,* greed
trib • u • la • tion (trib´ yōō lā´shən) *n.,* deep sorrow, distress; suffering
re • course (rē´kôrs´) *n.,* turning to someone for help or protection

THE METAPHYSICAL POETS / FROM MEDITATION 17 ("PERCHANCE HE FOR WHOM THIS BELL TOLLS . . . .") **421**

VOCABULARY IN CONTEXT

- Lena hated to <u>intermit</u> her reading of Donne's meditations even to eat dinner.
- The enthusiastic young minister <u>wrought</u> quite a change in the formerly apathetic congregation.
- The ancient castle was built on a rocky <u>promontory</u> overlooking the sea on three sides.
- Paul struggled with feelings of <u>covetousness</u> as Charlie proudly showed off his new computer.
- Second period always felt like a time of <u>tribulation</u> to Stephen, who hated math.
- I could never really make it up to Vanessa for forgetting her birthday, but I treated her to a movie by way of <u>recourse</u>.

RESPONDING TO THE SELECTION

Students may discuss this topic in small groups or simply record their responses in their journals.

ANSWERS FOR REVIEWING THE SELECTION

RECALLING

1. The epigram reads, "Now this bell tolling softly for another, says to me, Thou must die."

2. The words *catholic* and *universal* describe the church.

3. The death of any other person diminishes the speaker.

4. The speaker calls affliction a treasure.

INTERPRETING

Responses will vary. Possible responses are given.

5. The image of a bell tolling recurs throughout the meditation.

6. Baptism and burial—in which a person is welcomed into or ushered out of the worldly church—are rituals that support Donne's view that the church acts on behalf of all its people.

7. Since the individual is part of the whole, when the whole is diminished by a death, so is the individual diminished.

8. The speaker contemplates the inevitability of suffering and death in the present life and the security of eternal life offered by God.

SYNTHESIZING

Responses will vary. Possible responses are given.

9. A bell tolling in the distance causes the speaker (and the reader or listener) to contemplate death. Although painful to confront, this contemplation brings one closer to God and so is a good thing.

10. The main source of affliction for human beings is knowing that death is inevitable. People can choose to ignore this knowledge, but it is through contemplating death that they grow closer to God. Therefore, people must turn their "treasure" of affliction into currency and "spend" it in order to reach heaven.

Responding to the Selection

Donne says in this meditation that people are necessarily connected to others. Think of an experience from your own life that made this fact clear. Perhaps a friend or a relative helped you in a difficult situation. Discuss with your classmates times in your life when the importance of connectedness to other people was made plain to you.

Reviewing the Selection

RECALLING

1. What epigram opens this selection from the meditation?

2. What words does the speaker use to describe the church?

3. What "diminishes" the speaker?

4. What word does the speaker use to describe an affliction?

INTERPRETING

5. What image in the epigram is repeated throughout the meditation?

6. What actions on the part of churches support the speaker's description?

7. What reason does the speaker give for that diminishment?

8. What is the speaker probably contemplating at the end of the meditation?

SYNTHESIZING

9. What event in this meditation causes the speaker to pause and contemplate? What subject does the speaker contemplate? What conclusion does the speaker draw as a result of his contemplation?

10. What relationship does the speaker describe among affliction, humankind, and God?

Understanding Literature (Questions for Discussion)

1. **Theme.** A **theme** is a central idea in a literary work. What is the theme of this selection?

2. **Purpose.** A writer's **purpose**, or **aim**, is the primary purpose that a work is meant to achieve. One purpose of Meditation 17 ("Perchance he for whom this bell tolls . . .") is to affect emotionally the reader or listener. What emotional effect does the speaker in this piece attempt to achieve?

ANSWERS FOR UNDERSTANDING LITERATURE

▶ See the evaluation forms for discussion, active listening, and oral communication, *Assessment Portfolio*, 7.11–7.14. *Responses will vary. Possible responses are given.*

1. Theme. The theme is the universality and inevitability of death. The speaker believes that by confronting death, people can grow closer to God.
▶**Teaching Note:** Students might restate in their own words the epigram at the beginning of the selection and consider how it relates to the theme of the meditation.

2. Purpose. The speaker wants his reader or listener to feel fellowship and sympathy for all of humanity and to feel secure in the knowledge that God will protect him or her.

▶**Teaching Note:** Ask students if John Donne's writing inspires them to think about life in a new way. Is it useful to the reader or listener?

(cont.)

3. **Metaphor.** A **metaphor** is a figure of speech in which one thing is spoken or written about as if it were another. This figure of speech invites the reader to make a comparison between the two things. In the selection, the speaker says, "every man is a piece of the continent, a part of the main." What two things are being compared in that line? What do these things have in common? Earlier in the selection, the speaker describes a person as a chapter in a book. What is the book? Why is that chapter not simply torn out when a person dies? What happens when the "chapter" is "translated into a better language"?

Responding in Writing

1. **Meditation.** A **meditation** is a contemplative work on a religious or philosophical topic. Consider the following lines from the selection:

   [A]ll mankind is of one author and is one volume; when one man dies, one chapter is not torn out of the book, but translated into a better language; and every chapter must be so translated.

   These lines express, through the extended metaphor of books and language, how a person's death does not mean simply a physical absence, but also a spiritual "translation" into another form. Write a meditation contemplating what happens after death. In your meditation, use metaphor to express your own beliefs on this subject.

2. **Personal Letter.** Imagine that a parent of a dear friend of yours has died recently. Write your friend a letter expressing your sorrow and offering a way to remember the parent or friend in your thoughts. Refer to the material on the form of a personal letter in the Language Arts Survey, 5.2.

Language Lab

Action and Linking Verbs. Read the Language Arts Survey, 2.12, "Action Verbs," and 2.13, "Linking Verbs." Then, identify the action and linking verbs in the following sentences from the selection. Write *AV* for action verb and *LV* for linking verb.

1. Perchance he for whom this bell tolls may be so ill as that he knows not it tolls for him.

2. God employs several translators; some pieces are translated by age, some by sickness, some by war, some by justice.

3. When she baptizes a child, that action concerns me; for that child is thereby connected to that head which is my head too, and ingrafted into that body whereof I am a member.

4. If a clod be washed away by the sea, Europe is the less, as well as if a promontory were, as well as if a manor of thy friend's or of thine own were.

5. Any man's death diminishes me, because I am involved in mankind; and therefore never send to know for whom the bell tolls; it tolls for thee.

THE METAPHYSICAL POETS / FROM MEDITATION 17 ("PERCHANCE HE FOR WHOM THIS BELL TOLLS . . .") **423**

Applied English/Tech Prep Skills

Business Letters. Read the Language Arts Survey, 5.3, "The Form of a Business Letter." Then copy the following business letter onto your own paper, correcting its errors in manuscript form.

111 East River Drive
Blefuscu, MO, 00440
February 18, 1996
Scholarship Director
Department of History
University of Erewhon
989 Indiana Place
Erewhon, IN 08440

Dear Scholarship Director:

Please consider me an applicant for the 1996-97 "Young Historian" scholarship.

I am eighteen years old and a senior at West High School. My course of advanced study has included classes in English, World Literature, World History, and Ancient History.

Last summer I was employed by the Indiana State Historical Society as an exhibit intern. I worked with the exhibit designers, curators, and historians to create a traveling exhibit for grade school children on the history of the state of Indiana.

I will be happy to provide you with references who can tell about my qualifications for this scholarship and my enthusiasm for history. If you wish to see samples of my writing, I shall be happy to provide you with completed history papers.

I am available for a personal interview at your convenience. My telephone number is (555) 555-7128. I can be reached most evenings after 6:00 P.M.

Sincerely, Esme Rodriguez

PROJECT

Community Involvement. Many kinds of personal situations may make someone feel isolated from other members of a community. If someone is ill or impoverished, feelings of isolation may intensify. How might you and your classmates try to connect with those who are feeling isolated? You may want to contact a local organization such as a home health agency, a soup kitchen, or a homeless shelter to see what role you and your classmates might perform. Work with other students to organize a "classmates-for-connection" campaign in your community.

PREREADING

"Easter Wings"
by George Herbert

ABOUT THE AUTHOR

George Herbert (1593–1633) was born in Montgomery Castle, Wales, to Richard and Magdalen Herbert. After receiving his early education at home, Herbert attended Westminster School and Trinity College, Cambridge, where he took his degrees with distinction. At the age of twenty-seven, Herbert was elected public orator of Cambridge, a position fitting a young man of political ambition. Seven years later, however, Herbert resigned his position, turning from Parliament and politics to religion. He married Jane Danvers in 1629 and, one year later, after being ordained by the Anglican Church, he accepted a clerical appointment in Bermerton. Known as "Holy Mr. Herbert," he devoted himself to his rural Bermerton parish and wrote poetry. Like the Metaphysical poet John Donne, who was a friend of the aristocratic Herbert family, Herbert struggled with questions of spiritual emptiness. During his brief three years as a country rector, Herbert finished writing a collection of 160 religious poems known as *The Temple*. Nearing his fortieth birthday and gravely ill with tuberculosis, Herbert gave the manuscript to a friend, Nicholas Ferrar. After Herbert's death in 1633, Ferrar published the first edition of *The Temple*, the major work upon which Herbert's reputation still stands.

ABOUT THE SELECTION

The Temple is divided into three parts: "The Church-porch," "The Church," and "The Church Militant." The collection's dramatic range is powerful, including such different narrative voices and experiences as those of Christ in "The Sacrifice," a courtier in "The Pearl," and a storyteller in "The Pulley." **"Easter Wings"** comes from "The Church" section of *The Temple* and shows Herbert's mastery of ancient forms like the **concrete poem** or *carmen figuratum*. In a concrete poem, the shape of the poem is related to its content. Characteristic of the Metaphysical poets, Herbert made use of bold literary devices, particularly the device of paradox. Eighteenth-century critics called Herbert's use of shape "false wit." Other critics and readers, including those of our own time, are drawn to the combination of intellectual challenge and graceful plainness of language in Herbert's writing.

ADDITIONAL RESOURCES

READER'S GUIDE
• Selection Worksheet, 6.4

ASSESSMENT PORTFOLIO
• Selection Check Test, 4.6.7
• Selection Test, 4.6.8

ESSENTIAL SKILLS PRACTICE BOOKS
• *Study and Research,* 4.16

ENRICHMENT ACTIVITIES

Students might read the Genesis story of the fall of Adam and Eve and discuss or write about these questions: How might the story be an expression of individual experience? Have you ever felt that there was a better part of yourself that is somehow hidden or corrupted by life in the social world? Why is the story of Adam and Eve appealing? Is it realistic? How might people regain lost innocence?

SUPPORT FOR LEP STUDENTS

Before they begin reading, review with students the story of the fall of Adam and Eve. Inform them that Herbert alludes to this story in lines 1–5 and line 10 ("the fall"). Suggest that the speaker feels that he too has "fallen" and that he elaborates on this idea in stanza 2.

ADDITIONAL VOCABULARY
harmoniously—in a pleasing manner
affliction—pain; suffering

GOALS/OBJECTIVES

Studying this lesson will enable students to

• experience the speaker's feelings of hopefulness
• identify George Herbert as one of the Metaphysical poets and describe his literary contributions
• define *concrete poem* and identify and interpret elements of concrete poems that they encounter in their reading

• apply the technique of slow and careful reading to a poem
• define *speaker, theme,* and *paradox* and identify and interpret these elements in a poem
• write a concrete poem

READER'S JOURNAL

As an alternative to freewriting, students could draw illustrations showing themselves enjoying the things they most want. Their illustrations might give them ideas for writing their own concrete poems later.

READING SKILLS

You might remind students that poetry often uses a different syntax, or word order, than informal or spoken English. Suggest that students watch for how Herbert has constructed each sentence. Unraveling the syntax will help them to make meaning from the poem.

▶Additional practice is provided in the *Essential Skills Practice Book: Study and Research*, 4.16.

ANSWERS TO SELECTION CHECK TEST 4.6.7

EX. In what shape is the poem printed?
It is printed in the shape of wings.

1. What does the speaker say humankind has lost?
Humankind has lost wealth and store, or abundance.

2. What will the fall do?
The fall will "further the flight" in the speaker.

3. What happened to the speaker because of the punishments for his sins?
The speaker became "most thin."

4. What does the speaker want to feel on "this day"?
The speaker wants to feel the Lord's victory.

5. What else, besides the fall, will advance the flight in the speaker?
Affliction will advance the flight in the speaker.

READER'S JOURNAL

Suppose that you could have the thing that is most important to you. What would you ask for? How would you ask for it? How does what you are asking for affect the way in which you ask? Think about these questions. Then do a freewrite in which you ask someone for something that is very important to you.

READING SKILLS

Read the Language Arts Survey, 4.16, "Reading Rates." Then read the poem, using the reading skills described in that lesson.

"Easter Wings"

GEORGE HERBERT

● *According to the speaker, what happened to humankind?*

Lord, who createdst man in wealth and store,°   *abundance*
    Though foolishly he lost the same,
       Decaying more and more
         Till he became
5   Most poor:
         With thee
       O let me rise
     As larks, harmoniously,
   And sing this day thy victories:
10 Then shall the fall further the flight in me.

● *What does the speaker say has happened to him?*

   My tender age in sorrow did begin:
    And still with sicknesses and shame
       Thou didst so punish sin,
         That I became
15   Most thin.
         With thee
       Let me combine,
     And feel this day thy victory;
   For, if I imp° my wing on thine,   *graft*
20 Affliction shall advance the flight in me. ■

ANSWERS TO GUIDED READING QUESTIONS

● Human beings foolishly lost the "wealth and store" that they enjoyed at the time of creation, eventually becoming "most poor."

● The speaker has been similarly degraded, becoming sick and thin as he has grown older.

RESPONDING TO THE SELECTION

Students might begin by brainstorming examples of pain or affliction that they have experienced. Examples might include disappointments, frustrations, physical injuries or limitations, problems in interpersonal relationships, and so on. Then have the students think about any lessons they have learned from these experiences.

Responding to the Selection

Do you feel that pain or affliction serves a useful purpose? Discuss with your classmates the speaker's answer and your own answers to this question.

Reviewing the Selection

RECALLING

1. In what shape is the poem printed?

2. To whom is this poem addressed?

3. For what two things does the speaker ask?

4. What did humankind lose, and for what was humankind punished?

INTERPRETING

5. How is the shape of the poem related to its meaning? How does the form relate specifically to the words in lines 1–5?

6. What is the speaker's tone toward the being to whom the poem is addressed?

7. What emotions would the speaker feel if his pleas were granted?

8. What indications does the speaker give that he feels himself to be afflicted? What particular afflictions does he mention?

SYNTHESIZING

9. What does the speaker "feel this day"? What might make you feel this way?

10. The shape of the poem reflects the emotions of the speaker. What pattern of emotion do you see here? Describe a time in your own life that followed a similar pattern.

Understanding Literature (Questions for Discussion)

1. **Speaker.** The **speaker** is the character who speaks in a poem—the voice assumed by the writer. In this poem, the speaker is a sinner who seeks redemption. How does the speaker portray himself to God? What emotion does the speaker express in the poem?

ANSWERS FOR UNDERSTANDING LITERATURE

▶ See the evaluation forms for discussion, active listening, and oral communication, *Assessment Portfolio*, 7.11–7.14.

Responses will vary. Possible responses are given.

1. Speaker. The speaker portrays himself as a humble sinner, incapable of saving himself from sin, sickness, and death without help from the Lord. The speaker expresses both despair at his present state and joy and hope at the prospect of being joined with the Lord in victory over these afflictions.

▶**Teaching Note:** Students might discuss whether they think the speaker in this poem is a completely fictional character or is the voice of the poet himself. Are the voices of poet and speaker often the same in religious poetry? Why, or why not?

(cont.)

RECALLING

1. It is printed in the shape of two pairs of wings flying side by side.

2. The poem is addressed to the Lord, or God.

3. The speaker wants to rise and sing with the Lord and to combine with the Lord and share in His victory.

4. Humankind lost the carefree life enjoyed by Adam and Eve in the Garden of Eden. People were punished for Adam and Eve's sin of disobeying God.

INTERPRETING

Responses will vary. Possible responses are given.

5. The first five lines of each stanza diminish in length as the speaker describes the downfall of humankind or his own failings. The second five lines gradually increase in length as the speaker talks about participating in the Lord's victory. The poem as a whole looks like two pairs of outstretched wings—perhaps one belonging to the speaker and the other to the Lord.

6. The tone is respectful, humble, adoring, and hopeful.

7. The speaker would feel joyous, free, and victorious.

8. The speaker's desire to participate in his Lord's victory suggests that by himself he feels defeated. He mentions "sorrow," "sicknesses and shame," and becoming "most thin" with the weight of sin upon him.

SYNTHESIZING

Responses will vary. Possible responses are given.

9. On "this day"—the Christian celebration of Easter—the speaker feels hopeful. Suddenly seeing a way out of a painful situation might make someone feel this way.

10. The poem reflects a pattern of sinking deeper and deeper into depression and then reaching a turning point that leads to feeling increasingly hopeful.

2. Theme. The tragedy of the fall and human suffering seems to diminish the quality of human life; this diminishing is reflected in the dwindling lines in the first half of each stanza. However, the expanding lines in the second half of each stanza reflect the Christian doctrine of redemption or salvation through Jesus' suffering. The balanced shape of each stanza symbolizes the idea that redemption is not possible without suffering, so suffering is ultimately good and necessary.

▶**Teaching Note:** To help students appreciate the religious symbolism in the poem, you might wish to discuss with them the significance of Easter in Christian theology. Easter is the celebration of Jesus' resurrection and victory over death. Jesus' death on the cross served as payment for Adam and Eve's original sin and freed all Christians from sin and death. His suffering and death were necessary to save human sinners from eternal damnation.

3. Paradox. The major paradox is the idea that the fall of humankind and the affliction experienced by the speaker actually serve to make his "flight" with the Lord more glorious. Perhaps the speaker feels that suffering during his worldly existence will help him to appreciate the freedom from affliction that he will know after death, when he will finally be joined with the Lord.

▶**Teaching Note:** You might ask students to compare this paradox in "Easter Wings" to the paradoxical treatment of affliction in John Donne's Meditation 17 ("Perchance he for whom this bell tolls . . .") on page 420.

---

2. **Theme.** A **theme** is a central idea in a literary work. In this poem, one theme is the fall and redemption of humankind. Another is the value of affliction or suffering. How does the shape, or pattern, of the poem relate to the poem's themes?

3. **Paradox.** A **paradox** is a contradictory statement, idea, or event. What is the main paradox in this poem? How might affliction actually be a positive force in the speaker's life?

Responding in Writing

Concrete Poem. A **concrete poem** is one printed or written in a shape that suggests its subject matter. Consider the pattern of wings used by Herbert in his poem. Herbert relates the pattern of wings to his religious theme. Write a concrete poem about something dear to your heart. Think of an image that might represent your theme or subject. Use the shape of this image as well as imagery and tone to express your feelings.

ANALYTIC SCALES FOR RESPONDING IN WRITING

Assign a score from 1 to 25 for each grading criterion below. (For more detailed evaluation, see the evaluation forms for writing, revising, and proofreading, *Assessment Portfolio,* 7.1–7.10.)

Concrete Poem

• **Content/Unity.** The poem has a clear theme or subject, and its concrete shape reflects that theme or subject.

• **Organization/Coherence.** The poem is clearly organized, beginning with a statement of its theme and then expanding upon the theme with specific examples or images.

• **Language/Style.** The poem uses vivid and precise nouns, verbs, and modifiers.

• **Conventions.** The poem avoids errors in spelling, grammar, usage, mechanics, and manuscript form.

PREREADING

from *Paradise Lost*
"On His Blindness"

by John Milton

ABOUT THE AUTHOR

John Milton (1608–1674) was born on Bread Street in Cheapside, London. The eldest son of a self-made businessman, Milton showed great promise as a student of languages. Before entering Christ's College, Cambridge, Milton had mastered Latin, Greek, most modern European languages, and Hebrew. After graduating in 1632, Milton returned home and for the next six years followed his own rigorous reading program, reading widely in English, Latin, Greek, and Italian. In 1637, he wrote the elegy *Lycidas*, a contribution to a volume memorializing a college classmate. Throughout the next year, Milton traveled through Europe, returning home after hearing of looming troubles in England. The next twenty years, 1640–1660, were a period of controversy during which Milton devoted most of his energy to writing prose. He wrote a number of tracts, essays, and pamphlets, including his *Areopagitica*, a defense of unlicensed or uncensored printing. He also served in the position of Latin secretary to Oliver Cromwell, the leader of the Puritans who had taken over England. In 1651, at the age of forty-three, Milton went blind. Milton's first wife died in 1652. In 1656, he married Katherine Woodcock, who died in childbirth two years later. In 1663, Milton married his third wife and returned to writing poetry. During the last fourteen years of his life, he published his three major poems, *Paradise Lost*, *Paradise Regained*, and *Samson Agonistes*. Milton's writings reveal the influences of two powerful and contrasting intellectual and social movements, the Renaissance and the Reformation. These two paradoxical sources of work place him within the tradition of Renaissance Christian Humanism.

ABOUT THE SELECTIONS

The twelve-book epic poem *Paradise Lost* was published in 1667 and was immediately recognized as a masterpiece. In the poem, Milton tells the story of Adam and Eve's fall "to justify the ways of God to men." Milton published a sequel, *Paradise Regained*, in 1671. **"On His Blindness"** was published in 1655, four years after Milton lost his sight. In the selection, Milton eloquently alludes to events in the Bible, which he knew by heart.

THE PURITANS **429**

SUPPORT FOR LEP STUDENTS

The very long sentences and unusual sentence structures in both selections may cause difficulty in comprehension. You might mark up copies of the poems, highlighting the subject and verb in each sentence and showing what phrases and clauses modify them. For example, *Paradise Lost* opens with an imperative sentence. The main verb, *sing*, appears in line 6. Lines 1–5 are a prepositional phrase that modifies *sing*.

ADDITIONAL VOCABULARY

oracle—place where a deity is consulted, usually for a prophecy

illumine—light up

transgress—break a law or commandment

aspire—yearn

doleful—mournful; melancholy

deluge—flood; rain; rush

sublime—noble; majestic

suffice—be enough; adequate

compliant—yielding

gambol—skip; frolic

pine—yearn; desire

GOALS/OBJECTIVES

Studying this lesson will enable students to

- interpret and appreciate two views on the ways of God and the limits of human understanding
- describe the literary accomplishments of John Milton and explain how his work was influenced by the Renaissance and the Reformation
- write a scene from an epic poem and a parable

- define *epic poem, metaphor, speaker, allusion,* and *pun* and identify examples of each that they encounter in their reading
- paraphrase a poem
- recognize examples of formal and informal English and translate formal words into informal ones

READER'S JOURNAL

Students might consider whether they think it is more important to obey rules or to follow one's own conscience.

WRITING SKILLS

Tell students that the "infernal serpent" is Satan, or the devil. In the Judeo-Christian tradition, Satan was once an archangel in Heaven. He was cast out of Heaven after he attempted to overthrow God's reign.

▶ Additional practice is provided in the *Essential Skills Practice Book: Writing*, 1.27.

ANSWER TO GUIDED READING QUESTION

❶ "Man's first disobedience," eating fruit from the tree of knowledge that God had instructed Adam and Eve to avoid, brought death and suffering into the world.

VOCABULARY FROM THE SELECTION	
baleful	invoke
coy	obdurate
dalliance	omnipotent
damask	perdition
dandle	proboscis
disheveled	ruminate
ethereal	sanctitude
exalt	sovereign
guile	zephyr
impious	

READER'S JOURNAL

What is your definition of *disobedience?* What leads people to venture past set boundaries and to disobey rules? Freewrite your thoughts in your journal.

WRITING SKILLS

Read the Language Arts Survey, 1.27, "Interviewing." Then imagine that you are a journalist on location in Paradise. Write a list of interview questions that you would ask the "infernal serpent." What might you ask him about his downfall and about his feelings regarding that? What might you ask him about his feelings toward Adam and Eve?

FROM

Paradise Lost

JOHN MILTON

FROM BOOK 1

❶

What brought death and woe into the world?

> Of man's first disobedience, and the fruit
> Of that forbidden tree whose mortal taste
> Brought death into the world, and all our woe,
> With loss of Eden, till one greater Man
> 5   Restore us, and regain the blissful seat,
> Sing, Heavenly Muse,[1] that on the secret top
> Of Oreb, or of Sinai,[2] didst inspire
> That shepherd who first taught the chosen seed[3]
> In the beginning how the heavens and earth
> 10   Rose out of Chaos: or, if Sion hill
> Delight thee more, and Siloa's brook that flowed
> Fast[4] by the oracle of God, I thence
> Invoke thy aid to my adventurous song,
> That with no middle flight intends to soar

---

1. **Heavenly Muse.** Ambiguous, referring both to Urania, Greek muse of astronomy, and to the Holy Spirit
2. **Oreb . . . Sinai.** Oreb, or Horeb, was the mountain on which God spoke to Moses from a burning bush. Sinai was the mountain on which Moses received the Ten Commandments.
3. **chosen seed.** The Jews
4. **Fast.** Close

WORDS FOR EVERYDAY USE:
  in • voke (in vōk´) *vt.*, ask solemnly for; beg for; implore

15   Above th' Aonian mount,[5] while it pursues
      Things unattempted yet in prose or rhyme.
      And chiefly thou, O Spirit, that dost prefer
      Before all temples th' upright heart and pure,
      Instruct me, for thou know'st; thou from the first

20   Wast present, and with mighty wings outspread
      Dovelike sat'st brooding on the vast abyss,
      And mad'st it pregnant: what in me is dark
      Illumine; what is low, raise and support;
      That to the height of this great argument

25   I may assert Eternal Providence,
      And justify the ways of God to men.
        Say first (for Heaven hides nothing from thy view,
      Nor the deep tract of Hell), say first what cause
      Moved our grand[6] parents, in that happy state,

30   Favored of Heaven so highly, to fall off
      From their Creator, and transgress his will
      For one restraint, lords of the world besides?
      Who first seduced them to that foul revolt?
        Th' infernal serpent; he it was, whose guile,

35   Stirred up with envy and revenge, deceived
      The mother of mankind, what time his pride
      Had cast him out from Heaven, with all his host
      Of rebel angels, by whose aid aspiring
      To set himself in glory above his peers,

40   He trusted to have equaled the Most High,
      If he opposed; and with ambitious aim
      Against the throne and monarchy of God
      Raised <u>impious</u> war in Heaven and battle proud,
      With vain attempt. Him the Almighty Power

45   Hurled headlong flaming from th' <u>ethereal</u> sky
      With hideous ruin and combustion down
      To bottomless <u>perdition</u>, there to dwell
      In adamantine chains and penal fire,
      Who durst defy th' <u>Omnipotent</u> to arms.

50   Nine times the space that measures day and night
      To mortal men, he with his horrid crew
      Lay vanquished, rolling in the fiery gulf

---

5. **Aonian mount.** The Aonian mount is Helicon, home of the Muses.

6. **grand.** First in importance as well as in time

WORDS FOR EVERYDAY USE:

im • pi • ous (im´pē əs) *adj.*, lacking respect or dutifulness

e • the • re • al (ē thir´ē əl) *adj.*, not earthly; heavenly; celestial

per • di • tion (pər dish´ən) *n.*, complete and irreparable loss; ruin

om • nip • o • tent (äm nip´ə tənt) *n.*, God; one having unlimited power

①

What does the speaker wish to justify?

②

What did the "infernal serpent" do?

① The speaker intends to "justify the ways of God to men," or explain and elaborate for readers what happened in the Garden of Eden.

② The serpent tricked Eve, "the mother of mankind," into disobeying God.

ADDITIONAL QUESTIONS AND ACTIVITIES

Ask students the following questions: What image of God's power in Heaven does Milton create in line 42? How does this image reflect the historical period in which Milton lived? Does the image work for you? What are some other ways you might imagine God's power?

Answers. The image is of God as an absolute monarch. Milton lived in a time when the absolute authority of English kings was being successfully challenged by Parliament, but the notion of complete power resting in the hands of one person was still viable in many people's minds. Students may think that the image is outdated. They might imagine God as resembling not so much an earthly monarch as an omnipresent force of nature, for example.

ENRICHMENT ACTIVITIES

Invite students to discuss how they might interpret and retell the story of Adam and Eve's expulsion from the Garden of Eden. They could start by reading the Genesis account and seeing what details Milton added in his own version, especially in his characterization of Satan. Interested students may write a poem, short story, or play expressing their version of the story.

The fall from grace and loss of innocence are common literary themes. Invite students to share other examples of this motif in modern and contemporary works.

VOCABULARY IN CONTEXT

- After smashing the fender of her new car, Kang was forced to <u>invoke</u> his mother's mercy.
- Ira's critical remark about the poem was considered <u>impious</u> by others who thought the poet was a genius.
- The dancer's airy costume transformed her from flesh and blood to an <u>ethereal</u> spirit floating about the stage.
- What caused the once wealthy and powerful software baron to fall into such <u>perdition</u>?
- Charles I learned the hard way that a king was not <u>omnipotent</u> but needed to share power with Parliament.

ANSWERS TO GUIDED READING QUESTIONS

❶ The "great furnace" of Hell is the new home of the rebellious angels. The lost archangel is horrified to compare this place to his former home, Heaven, but he is resigned to his fate.

❷ The lost archangel, Satan, bids farewell to the "celestial light" of Heaven and greets the "horror" and "gloom" of Hell. Satan realizes that he has lost forever the happiness of Heaven due to his rebellious nature.

LITERARY TECHNIQUE

Milton's **characterization** of Satan is superbly complex and memorable. The former archangel fully appreciates the splendors of Heaven that he will never again be able to enjoy, and yet he defiantly says he prefers "to reign in Hell than serve in Heaven." You might ask students to discuss whether they have any sympathy for Satan and whether they think he deserves the fate to which God has condemned him. As they continue reading, students should try to be aware of how Milton reveals the facets of Satan's personality.

Have students list the aspects of Hell that are described in lines 60–72. What would Milton's Hell be like?

---

❶
What type of place has been prepared "for those rebellious"?

❷
What is the lost archangel's first reaction to this place?

Confounded though immortal. But his doom
Reserved him to more wrath; for now the thought
55　Both of lost happiness and lasting pain
Torments him; round he throws his <u>baleful</u> eyes,
That witnessed huge affliction and dismay,
Mixed with <u>obdúrate</u> pride and steadfast hate.
At once, as far as angels ken,[7] he views
60　The dismal situation waste and wild:
A dungeon horrible, on all sides round
As one great furnace flamed; yet from those flames
No light, but rather darkness visible
Served only to discover sights of woe,
65　Regions of sorrow, doleful shades, where peace
And rest can never dwell, hope never comes
That comes to all, but torture without end
Still urges,[8] and a fiery deluge, fed
With ever-burning sulphur unconsumed:
70　Such place Eternal Justice had prepared
For those rebellious; here their prison ordained
In utter darkness and their portion set
As far removed from God and light of Heaven
As from the center thrice to th' utmost pole.[9]

◆　◆　◆

Said then the lost archangel, "this the seat
That we must change for Heaven? this mournful gloom
245　For that celestial light? Be it so, since he
Who now is <u>sovereign</u> can dispose and bid
What shall be right: farthest from him is best,
Whom reason hath equaled, force hath made supreme
Above his equals. Farewell, happy fields,
250　Where joy forever dwells! Hail, horrors! hail,
Infernal world! and thou, profoundest Hell,
Receive thy new possessor, one who brings
A mind not to be changed by place or time.
The mind is its own place, and in itself

---

7. **ken.** Can see
8. **urges.** Afflicts
9. **utmost pole.** Here the earth is the utmost pole in Milton's concept of the cosmos, which places Heaven at the center and Earth tacked on as an appendage.

WORDS FOR EVERYDAY USE:

bale • ful (bāl´fəl) *adj.,* sorrowful; wretched
ob • du •rate (äb´door it) *adj.,* stubborn; obstinate; inflexible
sov • er • eign (säv´rən) *adj.,* above or superior to all others; greatest; supreme

432　*UNIT SIX / THE EARLY SEVENTEENTH CENTURY*

VOCABULARY IN CONTEXT

• Tamara surveyed the cafeteria's unappetizing selections with a <u>baleful</u> expression.
• Minh tried to negotiate a later curfew for Friday night, but her parents were <u>obdurate</u>.
• Joe is the worst basketball player in our class, but at the chess board his skills are <u>sovereign</u>.
• No one but the priestesses could enter the inner chamber; an intrusion by anyone else would violate the <u>sanctitude</u> of this holy place.

255 Can make a Heaven of Hell, a Hell of Heaven.
What matter where, if I be still the same,
And what I should be, all but less than he
Whom thunder hath made greater? Here at least
We shall be free; th' Almighty hath not built
260 Here for his envy, will not drive us hence.
Here we may reign secure; and in my choice
To reign is worth ambition, though in Hell:
Better to reign in Hell than serve in Heaven . . ."

◆   ◆   ◆

FROM BOOK 4

◆   ◆   ◆

205   Beneath him with new wonder now he views
To all delight of human sense exposed
In narrow room Nature's whole wealth; yea more,
A Heaven on Earth; for blissful Paradise
Of God the garden was, by him in the east
210 Of Eden planted. Eden stretched her line

◆   ◆   ◆

285 From this Assyrian garden, where the fiend
Saw undelighted all delight, all kind
Of living creatures, new to sight and strange.
Two of far nobler shape, erect and tall,
Godlike erect, native honor clad
290 In naked majesty, seemed lords of all,
And worthy seemed; for in their looks divine
The image of their glorious Maker shone,
Truth, wisdom, <u>sanctitude</u> severe and pure—
Severe, but in true filial freedom placed,
295 Whence true authority in men; though both
Not equal, as their sex not equal seemed;
For contemplation he and valor formed,
For softness she and sweet attractive grace;
He for God only, she for God in him.

WORDS FOR
EVERYDAY USE:
sanc • ti • tude (saŋk´tə tööd) *n.,* fact of being sacred or
inviolable

❶
*What does the
lost archangel
finally decide?*

❷
*How is the
Garden of Eden
described? What
two creatures
are particularly
interesting? Why?*

**ANSWERS TO GUIDED READING
QUESTIONS**

❶ He concludes that he prefers Hell
to Heaven, because in Hell he is free
and in control rather than subject to
God's power.

❷ The Garden of Eden is a place of
pure delight, inhabited by many
newly created animals. The most
interesting creatures are the two
humans. They are most interesting
because they resemble God.

CROSS-CURRICULAR ACTIVITIES

Social Studies

• As the poem suggests,
Eden was traditionally
located in the ancient
region of Assyria, in
northern Mesopotamia.
Genesis 2:10–14 describes Eden's
location at the source of four rivers,
two of which are the Tigris and
Euphrates. Students might locate
this area on a map of the Middle
East; it is in present-day Iraq.
Interested students might also
find a map showing the ancient
kingdoms and cities in this region
and research some of the creation
stories from these civilizations to
compare them with the Genesis
account. How do these other
traditions explain the creation of
the first humans? How did the
various traditions influence one
another?

• You might encourage students to
look at one of the most significant
myths of the ancient Mesopota-
mean culture, the *Enuma elish.*
You may also have students read
Inanna's Descent, in which a
rebellious goddess descends to the
underworld, in order to examine
counterparts of the Satan figure in
other mythologies. Selections of
both myths can be found in
Jocobsen, Thorkild. *The Treasures of
Darkness.* New Haven: Yale UP.
1976.

❶ Adam and Eve are beautiful, majestic, and innocent. He has "manly" qualities such as valor, intelligence, and authority; she has "womanly" traits such as sweetness, grace, submissiveness, and modesty. In Eden they spend their days enjoying each other's company and love. They work at tending the garden only as much as is needed to stimulate their appetites for the "nectarine fruits" and cool stream water that surround them. They live in harmony with all the other creatures in the garden.

ADDITIONAL QUESTIONS AND ACTIVITIES

Discuss with students the differences between Adam and Eve, and between men and women generally, as depicted by Milton in this poem. Lead them through the following questions:

1. How is Adam described? What does he do? The author uses Adam to represent men generally. How might the author characterize men generally?

2. How is Eve described? What does she do? The author uses Eve to represent women generally. How might the author characterize women generally?

3. What similarities and differences do you find between men and women as characterized in the poem?

4. Do you agree with this characterization of men? Why, or why not? Do you agree with this characterization of women? Why, or why not?

5. Do you think these views of men and women are common today?

6. What might it be like for a man to live in a society in which these views were universally shared? What might it be like for a woman to live in such a society?

Paradise Lost. Illustrated by Gustave Doré

❶

How are Adam and Eve described? What is their life in Eden like?

300	His fair large front[10] and eye sublime declared
	Absolute rule; and hyacinthine locks
	Round from his parted forelock manly hung
	Clustering, but not beneath his shoulders broad:
	She, as a veil down to the slender waist,
305	Her unadornéd golden tresses wore
	<u>Disheveled</u>, but in wanton ringlets waved
	As the vine curls her tendrils, which implied
	Subjection, but required with gentle sway,
	And by her yielded, by him best received,
310	Yielded with <u>coy</u> submission, modest pride,
	And sweet, reluctant, amorous delay.

10. **front.** Forehead

WORDS FOR EVERYDAY USE:

di • shev • eled (di shev´əld) *adj.,* disarranged and untidy
coy (koi) *adj.,* bashful; shy

VOCABULARY IN CONTEXT

• With his <u>disheveled</u> clothing and faraway gaze, Dr. Tanaka fit the image of the absent-minded professor.

• The <u>coy</u> kitten hid beneath the couch, venturing forth a lightning paw only when tempted with one of her favorite toys.

Nor those mysterious parts were then concealed;
Then was not guilty shame. Dishonest shame
Of Nature's works, honor dishonorable,
315 Sin-bred, how have ye troubled all mankind
With shows instead, mere shows of seeming pure,
And banished from man's life his happiest life,
Simplicity and spotless innocence!
So passed they naked on, nor shunned the sight
320 Of God or angel, for they thought no ill;
So hand in hand they passed, the loveliest pair
That ever since in love's embraces met:
Adam the goodliest man of men since born
His sons; the fairest of her daughters Eve.
325 Under a tuft of shade that on a green
Stood whispering soft, by a fresh fountain-side,
They sat them down, and after no more toil
Of their sweet gardening labor than sufficed
To recommend cool Zephyr, and made ease
330 More easy, wholesome thirst and appetite
More grateful, to their supper fruits they fell,
Nectarine fruits which the compliant boughs
Yielded them, sidelong as they sat recline
On the soft downy bank damasked with flowers.
335 The savory pulp they chew, and in the rind
Still as they thirsted scoop the brimming stream;
Nor gentle purpose, nor endearing smiles
Wanted, nor youthful dalliance, as beseems
Fair couple linked in happy nuptial league,
340 Alone as they. About them frisking played
All beasts of th' earth, since wild, and of all chase[11]
In wood or wilderness, forest or den.
Sporting the lion ramped,[12] and in his paw
Dandled the kid, bears, tigers, ounces, pards,[13]
345 Gamboled before them; th' unwieldy elephant
To make them mirth used all his might, and wreathed
His lithe proboscis; close the serpent sly,
Insinuating,[14] wove with Gordian twine

---

11. **of all chase.** Of all places in woods or wilderness
12. **ramped.** Reared up
13. **ounces, pards.** Lynxes and leopards
14. **Insinuating.** Writhing

WORDS FOR EVERYDAY USE:

zeph • yr (zef´ ər) *n.*, a soft, gentle breeze
dam • ask (dam´əsk) *vt.*, make a deep pink or rose
dal • li • ance (dal´yəns) *n.*, flirting; toying; trifling
dan • dle (dan´dəl) *vt.*, swing up and down
pro • bos • cis (prō bäs´is) *n.*, an elephant's trunk; a long, flexible snout

VOCABULARY IN CONTEXT

- An occasional cooling zephyr stirred the hot summer air.
- At the mention of her beloved Sir Lancelot's name, Queen Guinevere's cheeks became damasked.
- "I have no time for such dalliance! My term paper is due tomorrow," Haesun told her boyfriend when he suggested a movie.
- Jon felt like a human seesaw as he dandled the delighted toddler on his leg.
- The elephant washed itself with a powerful stream of water from its proboscis.

HISTORICAL NOTE

Students might be interested to note that in the Garden of Eden, neither humans nor any other animals ate meat. In Genesis 1:30, God declares, "And to every beast of the earth, and to every bird of the air, and to everything that creeps on the earth, everything that has the breath of life, I have given every green plant for food." The need to eat the flesh of other animals in order to survive was considered a result of the Fall.

▶ **Teaching Note:** Students might compare Genesis 9:2–3, in which God tells Noah that "the fear of you and the dread of you shall be upon every beast. . . . Every moving thing that lives shall be food for you; and as I gave you the green plants, I give you everything." *The New Oxford Annotated Bible.* New York: Oxford UP. 1977.

ANSWERS TO SELECTION CHECK TEST 4.6.9

EX. What type of poem is *Paradise Lost?*
It is an epic poem.

1. What brought death into the world?
Disobedience and the taste of the fruit of the forbidden tree brought death into the world.

2. What had caused the serpent to be cast out of Heaven?
The serpent's pride had caused it to be cast out of Heaven.

3. What decision does the lost archangel come to regarding Heaven and Hell?
He decides that he would rather reign in Hell than serve in Heaven.

4. What did the creatures that "seemed lords of all" look like?
They were erect and tall; they looked like their maker.

5. What is a hateful, tormenting sight to Satan?
The sight of Adam and Eve in paradise together is a hateful, tormenting sight.

ANSWERS TO GUIDED READING QUESTIONS

❶ Satan, in the form of a serpent or snake, is watching them.

❷ Satan burns with envy at the pleasures Adam and Eve enjoy, but he plans to trick them into disobeying God's command to avoid the tree of knowledge.

ADDITIONAL QUESTIONS AND ACTIVITIES

You may wish to encourage students to draw inferences from the text with questions such as the following.

• What conflicting emotions on Satan's part are revealed in lines 358–368? Why do you think he feels this way?

Answers. Satan feels "wonder" and "could love" Adam and Eve because they are so beautiful and "Godlike." At the same time, he hates them because they are enjoying Paradise while he suffers. These conflicting emotions arise from his nature as a fallen archangel, once a "heavenly spirit" himself but now doomed to an eternity of pain and malevolence.

• What is Satan talking about in lines 512–513? What conversation has he overheard?

Answers. In lines 512–513, he refers to a conversation he has overheard between Adam and Eve, in which they discussed the tree of knowledge that God has forbidden them to eat from.

• What is Satan planning in the passage that begins, "Knowledge forbidden?/Suspicious, reasonless" (lines 515–516)? How would you react to his argument if you were Adam or Eve?

Answers. In line 515 he plans the argument he will use to convince them to disobey God's order, making them suspicious of God's intentions.

His braided train,[15] and of his fatal <u>guile</u>
350   Gave proof unheeded. Others on the grass
  Couched, and now filled with pasture gazing sat,
  Or bedward <u>ruminating</u>; for the sun,
  Declined, was hasting now with prone career
  To th' ocean isles,[16] and in th' ascending scale
355   Of heaven the stars that usher evening rose:
  When Satan, still in gaze as first he stood,
  Scarce thus at length failed speech recovered sad:
    "O Hell! what do mine eyes with grief behold?
  Into our room of bliss thus high advanced
360   Creatures of other mold, Earth-born perhaps,
  Not spirits, yet to heavenly spirits bright
  Little inferior; whom my thoughts pursue
  With wonder, and could love; so lively shines
  In them divine resemblance, and such grace
365   The hand that formed them on their shape hath poured.
  Ah! gentle pair, ye little think how nigh
  Your change approaches, when all these delights
  Will vanish, and deliver ye to woe,

❖   ❖   ❖

505   "Sight hateful, sight tormenting! thus these two
  Imparadised in one another's arms,
  The happier Eden, shall enjoy their fill
  Of bliss on bliss, while I to Hell am thrust,
  Where neither joy nor love, but fierce desire,
510   Among our other torments not the least,
  Still unfulfilled with pain of longing pines.
  Yet let me not forget what I have gained
  From their own mouths: all is not theirs, it seems.
  One fatal tree there stands, of knowledge called,
515   Forbidden them to taste. Knowledge forbidden?
  Suspicious, reasonless. Why should their lord
  Envy them that? Can it be sin to know,
  Can it be death? and do they only stand
  By ignorance, is that their happy state,

The Q in the margins:

❶ Who is watching the new creatures?

❷ How does Satan feel about God's new creatures?

---

15. **braided train.** Knotted, like the Gordian Knot that was cut by Alexander the Great
16. **ocean isles.** The Azores

WORDS FOR EVERYDAY USE:

guile (gīl) *n.,* slyness and cunning in dealing with others
ru • mi • nat • ing (rōō´mə nāt´iŋ) *vt.,* chewing cud, as a cow does

436   *UNIT SIX / THE EARLY SEVENTEENTH CENTURY*

VOCABULARY IN CONTEXT

• The <u>guile</u> of used-car dealers is often joked about, but surely there are a few honest ones!
• Margaret chewed on her lip as she considered the question, reminding me of a cow <u>ruminating</u>.
• Kevin was a good player, but I wasn't ready to <u>exalt</u> him to the position of team captain and voted for Michael instead.

520 The proof of their obedience and their faith?
  O fair foundation laid whereon to build
  Their ruin! Hence I will excite their minds
  With more desire to know, and to reject
  Envious commands, invented with design
525 To keep them low whom knowledge might <u>exalt</u>
  Equal with gods. Aspiring to be such,
  They taste and die; what likelier can ensue?
  But first with narrow search I must walk round
  This garden, and no corner leave unspied;
530 A chance but chance may lead where I may meet
  Some wandering spirit of Heaven, by fountain side
  Or in thick shade retired, from him to draw
  What further would be learnt. Live while ye may,
  Yet happy pair; enjoy, till I return,
535 Short pleasures, for long woes are to succeed." ■

❶
What does Satan
predict will
happen?

Responding to the Selection

Imagine that you are Adam or Eve in this poem. In your journal, write an account of the day Satan, disguised as a serpent, slithered into your life. Express your feelings about the topics of knowledge and temptation.

Reviewing the Selection

RECALLING

1. What action brought death into the world, in lines 1–74?

2. What does the speaker wish for the Muse to say first?

3. To what does the lost archangel say good-bye in lines 243–263?

4. What words or phrases in lines 205–210 describe the Garden of Eden?

INTERPRETING

➡ 5. What further consequences did this action bring?

➡ 6. What caused "our grand parents . . . to fall off/ From their Creator"?

➡ 7. In what world is the lost archangel now living?

➡ 8. What view does the infernal serpent or "fiend" take of Eden in lines 285–290?

WORDS FOR EVERYDAY USE: ex • alt (eg zôlt´) vt., heighten or intensify the action or effect of

ANSWER TO GUIDED READING QUESTION

❶ Satan predicts that Adam and Eve will disobey God's command and eat from the tree of knowledge.

RESPONDING TO THE SELECTION

Suggest that students reread lines 515–526, in which Satan outlines the argument he will use to convince Adam and Eve to eat from the tree of knowledge. Does God's policy on this tree seem like an "envious command"? Would they be curious to know what would happen if they ate from it?

ANSWERS FOR REVIEWING THE SELECTION

RECALLING

1. Tasting the fruit of the forbidden tree brought death into the world.

2. In lines 27–32, the speaker asks the Muse to explain what motivated Adam and Eve to disobey God regarding the forbidden tree.

3. He says good-bye to the "happy fields" of Heaven.

4. The words "Nature's whole wealth," "Heaven on Earth," and "blissful Paradise" describe the Garden of Eden.

INTERPRETING

Responses will vary. Possible responses are given.

5. The loss of Eden made necessary the actions of Jesus (the "one greater Man" mentioned in line 4), who sacrificed himself to atone for the original sin of Adam and Eve.

6. They were "seduced . . . to that foul revolt" by Satan, who deceived Eve into disobeying God's command.

7. He is now living in Hell, a place of constant and eternal suffering.

8. He "Saw undelighted all delight"—that is, he beheld the wondrous beauty of the Garden of Eden but felt only envy and hatred because he was unable to enjoy its pleasures.

(cont.)

9. What predictions in lines 505–535 cause the reader or listener to feel a sense of foreboding?

10. According to the poem, what sort of relationship existed between Adam and Eve and God before the fall?

Understanding Literature (Questions for Discussion)

1. **Epic.** An **epic** is a long story, often told in verse, involving heroes and gods. An epic portrays the values and ways of life of a people. What heroes, villains, or gods are included in *Paradise Lost?* What attitudes, values, and beliefs does the poem portray?

2. **Metaphor.** A **metaphor** is a figure of speech in which one thing is spoken or written about as if it were another. This figure of speech invites the reader to make a comparison between the two things. In lines 17–21, the speaker says, "O Spirit, . . . thou from the first/Wast present, and with mighty wings outspread/Dovelike sat'st brooding on the vast abyss." What two things are being compared in those lines? What do these things have in common? In lines 61–62, the speaker calls Hell "A dungeon horrible, on all sides round/As one great furnace flamed." What two things are being compared in these lines? What do they have in common?

Responding in Writing

Epic. An **epic** is a long story, often told in verse, involving heroes or gods. Consider the following lines from the poem:

> Him the Almighty Power
> Hurled headlong flaming from th' ethereal sky
> With hideous ruin and combustion down
> To bottomless perdition, there to dwell
> In adamantine chains and penal fire,
> Who durst defy th' Omnipotent to arms.

These lines dramatically portray the action of Satan being cast out of Heaven. Write a scene for an epic poem about a contemporary temptation. If you wish to do a tongue-in-cheek mock epic about a subject like the temptation to watch TV talk shows or infomercials, feel free to do so. In your scene, use blank verse and include as many epic elements as possible, such as gods and heroes. Use metaphor, simile, allusion, and tone to portray the values and ways of life of the people in your epic.

READER'S JOURNAL

What would it feel like to lose the use of one of your senses halfway through your life? Which sense would be the most difficult for you to lose? What would you miss most about that sense? Think about these questions. Then do a freewrite in which you explore what your response would be to such a loss.

RESEARCH SKILLS

Read the Language Arts Survey, 4.30, "Paraphrasing and Summarizing." Then write a brief summary, paraphrasing the selection.

"On His Blindness"

JOHN MILTON

When I consider how my light is spent
Ere half my days[1] in this dark world and wide,
And that one talent[2] which is death to hide
Lodged with me useless, though my soul more bent

5   To serve therewith my Maker, and present
My true account, lest He returning chide;
"Doth God exact day-labor, light denied?"
I fondly[3] ask. But Patience, to prevent
That murmur, soon replies, "God doth not need

10 Either man's work or his own gifts. Who best
Bear his mild yoke,[4] they serve him best. His state
Is kingly: thousands at his bidding speed,
And post o'er land and ocean without rest;
They also serve who only stand and wait." ■

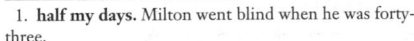

---

1. **half my days.** Milton went blind when he was forty-three.
2. **one talent.** An allusion to Jesus' parable of the talents in which a servant was condemned for hiding a coin called a "talent." Milton's use of the word is a pun on the two meanings: "coin" and "ability."
3. **fondly.** Foolishly
4. **mild yoke.** An allusion to Jesus' words, "my yoke is easy"

---

❶
At what point in his life did the speaker go blind?

❷
What is this speaker unable to do now?

READER'S JOURNAL

Students could begin by brainstorming a list of activities that require the use of each sense, and then identify what they would have to discontinue if they lost that sense.

RESEARCH SKILLS

Students should aim to summarize the poem in a single sentence. Remind them that any conceits used by the poet would probably not appear in a summary. You might point out that their summary statements are also statements of the poem's theme.

▶ Additional practice is provided in the *Essential Skills Practice Book: Study and Research,* 4.30.

ANSWERS TO GUIDED READING QUESTIONS

❶ According to the poem, the speaker went blind before he was halfway through his life.

❷ The speaker is unable to do what he considers God's work.

ANSWERS TO SELECTION CHECK TEST 4.6.11

EX. When did the speaker go blind?
He went blind before half his days were spent.

1. What was lodged useless in him?
His talent, or writing ability, became useless.

2. What was his soul more inspired to do?
His soul was more inspired to serve God.

3. What does God not need?
God does not need "man's work or his own gifts."

4. Who best serves God?
People who bear their yokes best serve God.

5. Who serves God besides those who "post o'er land and ocean without rest"?
Those who stand and wait also serve God.

ANSWERS FOR UNDERSTANDING LITERATURE (CONT.)

dramatic work, whether it is a poem, a novel, or a movie. Possibilities include characterization, tone, and plot (especially who "wins" and "loses" in the final outcome).

2. Metaphor. In lines 17–21, the Holy Spirit is compared to a bird or dove. Both have the power to create —either by laying an egg or by making a universe out of an abyss. In lines 61–64, Hell is compared to a dungeon and to a furnace, because it is the place to which Satan

will be confined forever and it is painfully hot like the inside of a furnace.

▶**Teaching Note:** You might point out that Milton goes on, in lines 62–64, to tell how Hell is different from an ordinary furnace. Encourage students to appreciate the power of the image there: a fire whose flames give off darkness rather than light.

RESPONDING TO THE SELECTION

Students might also consider how they would feel having to rely on other people in order to do the activity that meant most to them, as Milton did.

ANSWERS FOR REVIEWING THE SELECTION

RECALLING

1. He is thinking about having used up, or spent, his ability to see after living only half his life.

2. The poem suggests that the servant was condemned to death.

3. The speaker asks whether God will punish him for not doing the work that he needs his sight to do.

4. God does not need people's work or their "gifts" ("talents").

INTERPRETING

Responses will vary. Possible responses are given.

5. The speaker may mean that he does not yet understand the ways of God. (Compare lines 22–23 of *Paradise Lost*, "what in me is dark/Illumine.")

6. The speaker feels that by writing he serves God; he knows no other way to "present his true account" to God, or to show God his worth.

7. The speaker has missed the point: God would not demand work if a person did not have the requisite talents to produce it.

8. Patience has shown him that there are many ways to serve God, even without his sight. God will give him whatever talents he needs, such as patience for waiting.

SYNTHESIZING

Responses will vary. Possible responses are given.

9. He is confronting the loss of his sight, which he fears will make him unable to serve God since he will no longer be able to write.

10. Patience assures the speaker that there is a way for everyone to serve God, even if it is a very different way than the person might have imagined.

Responding to the Selection

Imagine that you, like the speaker in this poem, lost the ability to perform some activity that is important to you. What would such a loss mean to you?

Reviewing the Selection

RECALLING

1. What is the speaker considering in line 1?

2. What was the servant's punishment for hiding the coin known as a "talent"?

3. What does the speaker "fondly ask"?

4. What, according to Patience, does God not need?

INTERPRETING

5. In what sense has the world in which the speaker lives always been dark?

6. In what sense is losing his talent (ability to write) a kind of death for the speaker?

7. What makes the speaker's question in line 7 a fond, or foolish, one?

8. What comfort can the speaker draw from Patience's closing remark?

SYNTHESIZING

9. What crisis is the speaker confronting in this poem? What does he fear that he will no longer be able to do?

10. Why, according to the poem, is his fear unjustified or unfounded?

Understanding Literature (Questions for Discussion)

1. **Speaker.** The **speaker** is the character who speaks in a poem—the voice assumed by the writer. In this poem, the speaker went blind in his middle years. How does the speaker feel about his blindness? What emotions does the speaker express in the poem?

2. **Allusion and Pun.** An **allusion** is a figure of speech in which a reference is made to a person, event, object, or work from history or literature. A **pun** is a play on words, one that wittily exploits a double meaning. In the selection, the author alludes to a parable from the Bible in which a servant was condemned for hiding a coin called a "talent." What other meaning does the word *talent* have in the poem? In what sense is the hiding of his talent a kind of death for the speaker?

ANSWERS FOR UNDERSTANDING LITERATURE

▶ See the evaluation forms for discussion, active listening, and oral communication, *Assessment Portfolio,* 7.11–7.14. *Responses will vary. Possible responses are given.*

1. **Speaker.** The speaker feels frustrated and frightened that he will no longer be able to serve God.

▶ **Teaching Note:** Encourage students to discuss reasons for writing in one's own voice versus reasons for assuming the voice of a fictitious character.

2. **Allusion and Pun.** *Talent* also means "ability" or "skill." The speaker had used his talent for writing to serve God. The loss of that talent leaves him, he at first thinks, without a way to "earn" eternal life.

▶ **Teaching Note:** The parable of the talents is told in Matthew 25:14–30. Students might compare and contrast the situation of the "worthless" servant in the parable to that of the blinded Milton.

Responding in Writing

Parable. A **parable** is a very brief story told to teach a moral lesson. Write your own short parable about the compensating gifts that people with physical limitations often have. In your parable, stress the positive aspects of this fact of life.

Language Lab

Formal and Informal English. Read the Language Arts Survey, 2.147, "Formal and Informal English." Then, read each of the following excerpts from Milton's essay on censorship, the *Areopagitica*. (See the complete excerpt in the Selections for Additional Reading on page 463.) For the word or words underlined in each sentence, write their informal English counterparts. Consult a dictionary as necessary.

1. Methinks I see in my mind a noble and <u>puissant</u> nation rousing herself like a strong man after sleep.

2. . . . while the whole noise of <u>timorous</u> and flocking birds, with those also that love the twilight, flutter about, . . .

3. . . . and in their envious <u>gabble</u> would <u>prognosticate</u> a year of sects and schisms.

4. And though all the winds of doctrine were let loose to play upon the earth, so Truth be in the field, we do <u>injuriously</u> by licensing and prohibiting to misdoubt her strength.

5. Believe it, Lords and Commons, they who <u>counsel</u> ye to such a suppressing do as good as <u>bid</u> ye <u>suppress</u> yourselves; and I will soon show how.

Thinking Skills

Classifying. Read the Language Arts Survey, 4.7, "Classifying." Then identify a common class and at least two common features for each of the following sets of subjects.

1. Eleanor Roosevelt and Hillary Clinton

2. Mayan pyramids and Egyptian pyramids

3. personal computer and fax machine

4. aerobics and walking

5. John Milton and John Bunyan

PREREADING

THE PURITANS

from *The Pilgrim's Progress*
by John Bunyan

ABOUT THE AUTHOR

John Bunyan (1628–1688), the son of a Bedfordshire tinker, received only a meager education before adopting his father's trade. From 1644 to 1646, Bunyan served in the Parliamentary army. After his marriage in 1648, Bunyan turned his thoughts to religion. Bunyan experienced a period of spiritual struggle, after which he converted in 1653 and joined the Baptist church at Bedford. Like many other men and women in his day, Bunyan answered the "call" to preach. The Anglican Church viewed the lay preachers as dissenters and sought to persecute and silence them. For his refusal to obey royal bans on nonconformist preaching, Bunyan was imprisoned from 1660 to 1672. While in prison, Bunyan wrote his spiritual autobiography, *Grace Abounding to the Chief of the Sinners*, which uses the details of his early life to reveal the purposes of divine Providence. After his release from prison, Bunyan became minister of the Bedford nonconformist church. Again imprisoned in 1675, Bunyan wrote *The Pilgrim's Progress*, his most celebrated work. Prompted by the success of his allegory, Bunyan published in 1684 Part II of *The Pilgrim's Progress*, but it never captured the popularity of Bunyan's original tale.

ABOUT THE SELECTION

One of the most popular allegories in English literature, ***The Pilgrim's Progress*** tells the story of the life journey of a pilgrim named Christian. Bunyan modeled his writing style in *The Pilgrim's Progress* on the prose of the English Bible, enabling even the humblest reader to share the experiences of Christian and the travelers he meets. Once a household book, *The Pilgrim's Progress* gave many phrases to our language: "the slough of despond," "the house beautiful," "Mr. Worldly-Wiseman," and "Vanity Fair." As *The Pilgrim's Progress* opens, the speaker has a dream in which he sees Christian, who is weeping and wondering what to do.

GOALS/OBJECTIVES

Studying this lesson will enable students to

- empathize with the main character's need to complete his journey in spite of temptation and feelings of sadness and homesickness
- describe John Bunyan's literary accomplishments and the religious and historical context of his work *The Pilgrim's Progress*

- define *allegory* and recognize and interpret allegories that they encounter in their reading
- recognize colorful modifiers in a literary work
- define *connotation* and *denotation* and select words with appropriate connotations for specific literary contexts

READER'S JOURNAL

How would it feel to leave behind your family and hometown to take a journey to an unknown place? Would it be difficult to leave? What would you miss about your family and home? Think about these questions. Then do a freewrite in your journal about the first day of your journey.

LANGUAGE SKILLS

Read the Language Arts Survey, 2.35, "Using Colorful Modifiers." Then make a list of modifiers from the selection that are particularly colorful.

READER'S JOURNAL

You might ask students to consider what kind of quest or journey would be important enough to make them leave home. Would the hope of fulfilling this quest make the sacrifice any easier?

LANGUAGE SKILLS

Students might also note beside each modifier on their lists what emotional response it evokes or what visual image the modifier creates in their minds.
►Additional practice is provided in the *Essential Skills Practice Book: Language,* 2.35.

FROM
The Pilgrim's Progress

JOHN BUNYAN

From this World to That Which Is to Come: Delivered Under the Similitude[1] of a Dream

[Christian Sets out for the Celestial City]

As I walked through the wilderness of this world, I lighted on a certain place where was a Den, and I laid me down in that place to sleep; and, as I slept, I dreamed a dream. I dreamed, and behold I saw a man clothed with rags, standing in a certain place, with his face from his own house, a book in his hand, and a great burden upon his back (Isaiah lxiv.6; Luke xiv.33; Psalms xxxviii.4; Habakkuk ii.2; Acts xvi.31). I looked and saw him open the book and read therein; and, as he read, he wept, and trembled; and not being able longer to contain, he brake out with a lamentable cry, saying, "What shall I do?" (Acts ii.37).

In this plight, therefore, he went home and refrained himself as long as he could, that his wife and children should not perceive his distress; but he could not be silent long, because that his trouble increased. Wherefore at length he brake his mind to his wife and children; and thus he began to talk to them. O my dear wife, said he, and you the children of my bowels, I your dear friend am in myself undone by reason of a burden that lieth hard upon me; moreover, I am for certain informed that this our city will be burned with fire from heaven, in which fearful overthrow both myself, with thee, my wife, and you, my sweet babes, shall miserably come to ruin, except (the which yet I see not) some way of escape can be found, whereby we may be delivered. At this his relations were sore amazed; not for that they believed that what he had said to them was true, but because they thought that some frenzy distemper[2] had got into his head; therefore, it drawing towards night, and they hoping that sleep might settle his brains, with all haste they got him to bed; but the night was as troublesome to him as the day; wherefore, instead of sleeping, he spent it in sighs and tears. So when the morning was come,

❶ *In what frame of mind is Christian in the opening scene?*

---
1. **Similitude.** Allegory
2. **frenzy distemper.** An illness causing madness

ANSWER TO GUIDED READING QUESTION

❶ Christian is sad, frightened, and confused.

VOCABULARY FROM THE SELECTION

contrive   undefiled
incorruptible

❶ When Christian is confused about which way to go, Evangelist points him toward a "shining light" in the distance.

❷ Christian wants to be saved, but he does not know what to do or where to run in order to accomplish this.

LITERARY TECHNIQUE

Students will have noticed that Bunyan includes frequent biblical references in parentheses. You may wish to share the following passages with them and discuss how they support the allegory.

• Regarding the burden on Christian's back, Bunyan lists several verses. One is Psalm 38:4: "For my iniquities [sins] have gone over my head; they weigh like a burden too heavy for me." Another is Luke 14:33: "So therefore, [Jesus said,] whoever of you does not renounce all that he has cannot be my disciple." Help students to understand that Christian's burden can be interpreted as both his own sin and the material possessions that tie him to the temporal world.

• Regarding the wicketgate, Bunyan refers readers to Matthew 7:13–14: "[Jesus said,] 'Enter by the narrow gate; for the gate is wide and the way is easy, that leads to destruction, and those who enter by it are many. For the gate is narrow and the way is hard, that leads to life, and those who find it are few.'" You might ask students why Christian is unable to see the wicketgate that Evangelist points to across the wide field.

they would know how he did. He told them, Worse and worse; he also set to talking to them again, but they began to be hardened. They also thought to drive away his distemper by harsh and surly carriages[3] to him: sometimes they would deride, sometimes they would chide, and sometimes they would quite neglect him. Wherefore he began to retire himself to his chamber, to pray for and pity them, and also to condole his own misery; he would also walk solitarily in the fields, sometimes reading, and sometimes praying; and thus for some days he spent his time.

Now I saw, upon a time, when he was walking in the fields, that he was (as he was wont) reading in this book, and greatly distressed in his mind; and as he read, he burst out, as he had done before, crying, "What shall I do to be saved?"

I saw also that he looked this way and that way, as if he would run; yet he stood still, because (as I perceived) he could not tell which way to go. I looked then, and saw a man named Evangelist[4] coming to him, who asked, Wherefore dost thou cry? (Job xxxiii.23). He answered, Sir, I perceive by the book in my hand that I am condemned to die, and after that to come to judgment (Hebrews ix.27), and I find that I am not willing to do the first (Job xvi.21), nor able to do the second (Ezekiel xxii.14). . . .

Then said Evangelist, Why not willing to die, since this life is attended with so many evils? The man answered, Because I fear that this burden that is upon my back will sink me lower than the grave, and I shall fall into Tophet[5] (Isaiah xxx.33). And, sir, if I be not fit to go to prison, I am not fit to go to judgment, and from thence to execution; and the thoughts of these things make me cry.

Then said Evangelist, If this be thy condition, why standest thou still? He

How does Evangelist help Christian? ❶

What problem is Christian faced with? ❷

answered, Because I know not whither to go. Then he gave him a parchment roll, and there was written within, "Fly from the wrath to come" (Matthew iii.7).

The man therefore read it, and looking upon Evangelist very carefully,[6] said, Whither must I fly? Then said Evangelist, pointing with his finger over a very wide field, Do you see yonder wicketgate? (Matthew vii.13, 14.) The man said, No. Then said the other, Do you see yonder shining light? (Psalms cxix.105; II Peter i.19.) He said, I think I do. Then said Evangelist, Keep that light in your eye, and go up directly thereto; so shalt thou see the gate; at which when thou knockest it shall be told thee what thou shalt do.

So I saw in my dream that the man began to run. Now, he had not run far from his own door, but his wife and children perceiving it, began to cry after him to return; but the man put his fingers in his ears, and ran on, crying, Life! life! eternal life! (Luke xiv.26.) So he looked not behind him, but fled towards the middle of the plain (Genesis xix.17).

The neighbors also came out to see him run (Jeremiah xx.10); and as he ran some mocked, others threatened, and some cried after him to return; and, among those that did so, there were two that resolved to fetch him back by force. The name of the one was Obstinate, and the name of the other Pliable. Now by this time the man was got a good distance from them; but, however, they were resolved to pursue him, which they did, and in a little time they overtook him. Then said the man, Neighbors, wherefore are ye come? They said, To persuade you to go back with us.

---

3. **carriages.** Behavior
4. **Evangelist.** One who preaches the good news of the Christian Gospel
5. **Tophet.** A name for hell
6. **carefully.** Sorrowfully

But he said, That can by no means be; you dwell, said he, in the City of Destruction (the place also where I was born) I see it to be so; and, dying there, sooner or later, you will sink lower than the grave, into a place that burns with fire and brimstone; be content, good neighbors, and go along with me.

OBSTINATE. What! said Obstinate, and leave our friends and our comforts behind us?

CHRISTIAN. Yes, said Christian (for that was his name), because that ALL which you shall forsake is not worthy to be compared with a little of that which I am seeking to enjoy (II Corinthians v.17); and, if you will go along with me, and hold it, you shall fare as I myself; for there, where I go, is enough and to spare (Luke xv.17). Come away, and prove my words.

OBSTINATE. What are the things you seek, since you leave all the world to find them?

CHRISTIAN. I seek an inheritance <u>incorruptible</u>, <u>undefiled</u>, and that fadeth not away (I Peter i.4), and it is laid up in heaven, and safe there (Hebrews xi.16), to be bestowed, at the time appointed, on them that diligently seek it. Read it so, if you will, in my book.

OBSTINATE. Tush! said Obstinate, away with your book; will you go back with us or no?

CHRISTIAN. No, not I, said the other, because I have laid my hand to the plow (Luke ix.62).

OBSTINATE. Come, then, neighbor Pliable, let us turn again, and go home without him; there is a company of these crazed-headed coxcombs, that, when they take a fancy[7] by the end, are wiser in their own eyes than seven men that can render a reason (Proverbs xxvi.16).

PLIABLE. Then said Pliable, Don't revile; if what the good Christian says is true, the things he looks after are better than ours; my heart inclines to go with my neighbor.

OBSTINATE. What! more fools still? Be ruled by me, go back; who knows whither such a brain-sick fellow will lead you? Go back, go back, and be wise.

CHRISTIAN. Nay, but do thou come with thy neighbor, Pliable; there are such things to be had which I spoke of, and many more glories besides. If you believe not me, read here in this book; and for the truth of what is expressed therein, behold, all is confirmed by the blood of Him that made it (Hebrews ix.17–22; xiii.20.).

PLIABLE. Well, neighbor Obstinate, said Pliable, I begin to come to a point, I intend to go along with this good man, and to cast in my lot with him: but, my good companion, do you know the way to this desired place?

CHRISTIAN. I am directed by a man, whose name is Evangelist, to speed me to a little gate that is before us, where we shall receive instructions about the way.

PLIABLE. Come, then, good neighbor, let us be going. Then they went both together.

[VANITY FAIR][8]

Then I saw in my dream, that when they were got out of the wilderness, they

---

7. **coxcombs . . . fancy.** Fools that become deluded
8. **Vanity Fair.** Fairs were an annual event in England. *Vanity* means "emptiness." Vanity Fair is an allegory of corruption of religious life through worldly attractions.

WORDS FOR EVERYDAY USE:

in • cor • rupt • i • ble (in´kə rup´tə bəl) *adj.*, that cannot be contaminated or debased

un • de • filed (un dē fīld´) *adj.*, uncorrupt; honorable

ADDITIONAL QUESTIONS AND ACTIVITIES

You may wish to ask students the following questions.

• Why are Obstinate and Pliable so named?

• Which characteristic, obstinacy or pliability, do you think Bunyan thinks is more desirable? Why? *Answers.* The character Obstinate is stubborn, and Christian is not able to convince him to join the journey to the wicketgate. Pliable, however, is more flexible and open-minded. He changes his mind about forcing Christian to return home and instead joins the pilgrimage. Since Obstinate does not respond to the "good news" of Evangelist and returns to the City of Destruction, he is not an admirable character. Bunyan seems to value the open-mindedness or pliability that makes a person receptive to the Christian message.

VOCABULARY IN CONTEXT

• A dishonest businessman tried to bribe the mayor into giving his company the contract, but the mayor proved <u>incorruptible</u>.

• The pristine forests in the national park are some of the few <u>undefiled</u> wilderness areas in this region.

presently saw a town before them, and the name of that town is Vanity; and at the town there is a fair kept, called Vanity Fair; it is kept all the year long; it beareth the name of Vanity Fair because the town where it is kept is lighter than vanity; and also because all that is there sold, or that cometh thither, is vanity. As is the saying of the wise, "All that cometh is vanity" (Ecclesiastes i.2, 14; ii.11, 17; xi.8; Isaiah xl.17).

This fair is no new-erected business, but a thing of ancient standing; I will show you the original of it.

❶

How did Vanity Fair begin?

Almost five thousand years agone, there were pilgrims walking to the Celestial City, as these two honest persons are; and Beelzebub, Apollyon, and Legion,[9] with their companions, perceiving by the path that the pilgrims made, that their way to the city lay through this town of Vanity, they <u>contrived</u> here to set up a fair; a fair wherein should be sold all sorts of vanity, and that it should last all the year long. Therefore at this fair are all such merchandise sold, as houses, lands, trades, places, honors, preferments,[10] titles, countries, kingdoms, lusts, pleasures, and delights of all sorts, as whores, bawds, wives, husbands, children, masters, servants, lives, blood, bodies, souls, silver, gold, pearls, precious stones, and what not.

And, moreover, at this fair there is at all times to be seen jugglings, cheats, games, plays, fools, apes, knaves, and rogues, and that of every kind.

❷

How did the fair affect the journey of the pilgrims?

Here are to be seen, too, and that for nothing, thefts, murders, adulteries, false swearers, and that of a blood-red color.

And as in other fairs of less moment, there are the several rows and streets, under their proper names, where such and such wares are vended; so here likewise you have the proper places, rows, streets (viz., countries and kingdoms), where the wares of this fair are soonest to be found. Here is the Britain Row, the French Row, the Italian Row, the Spanish Row, the German Row, where several sorts of vanities are to be sold. But, as in other fairs, some one commodity is as the chief of all the fair, so the ware of Rome and her merchandise[11] is greatly promoted in this fair; only our English nation, with some others, have taken a dislike thereat.

Now, as I said, the way to the Celestial City lies just through this town where this lusty fair is kept; and he that will go to the City, and yet not go through this town, must needs "go out of the world" (I Corinthians v.10). The Prince of princes himself, when here, went through this town to his own country, and that upon a fair-day too,[12] yea, and as I think, it was Beelzebub, the chief lord of this fair, that invited him to buy of his vanities; yea, would have made him lord of the fair, would he but have done him reverence as he went through the town. (Matthew iv.8; Luke iv.5–7.) Yea, because he was such a person of honor, Beelzebub had him from

---

9. **Beelzebub . . . Legion.** Prince of Devils, the Destroyer, and the Unclean Spirit
10. **preferments.** Appointments to political or ecclesiastical positions
11. **Rome . . . merchandise.** Refers to the temporal power of the Roman Catholic Church
12. **Prince . . . too.** Refers to the temptation of Jesus in the wilderness

WORDS FOR EVERYDAY USE: con • trive (kən trīv´) *vt.,* scheme

VOCABULARY IN CONTEXT

• Yolanda and Coretta <u>contrived</u> a brilliant plan to lure the unsuspecting Kimberly to her surprise birthday party.

O the Roast Beef of Old England! William Hogarth, 1748–1749. Tate Gallery, London/Art Resource, New York

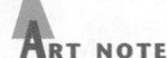

street to street, and showed him all the kingdoms of the world in a little time, that he might, if possible, allure the Blessed One to cheapen[13] and buy some of his vanities; but he had no mind to the merchandise, and therefore left the town, without laying out so much as one farthing upon these vanities. This fair, therefore, is an ancient thing, of long standing, and a very great fair.

Now these pilgrims, as I said, must needs go through this fair. Well, so they did; but, behold, even as they entered into the fair, all the people in the fair were moved, and the town itself as it were in a hubbub about them; and that for several reasons: for

First, The pilgrims were clothed with such kind of raiment as was diverse from the raiment of any that traded in that fair. The people, therefore, of the fair, made a great gazing upon them: some said they were fools, some they were bedlams, and some they were outlandish[14] men. (I Corinthians ii.7, 8.)

13. **cheapen.** Ask the price
14. **bedlams . . . outlandish.** Bedlams were lunatics from an insane asylum in London and outlandish men were foreigners.

THE PURITANS / FROM THE PILGRIM'S PROGRESS **447**

❶ The pilgrims are not interested in the vain material goods sold at the fair; they are interested only in reaching heaven.

LITERARY TECHNIQUE

You may wish to point out Bunyan's allusion to the story of the Tower of Babel (Genesis 11:1–9), when he says that the merchants "from one end of the fair to the other . . . seemed barbarians [foreigners speaking different languages] each to the other." In the biblical story, the descendants of Noah worked together to build a tower that reached up to the heavens. God, upon seeing this display of arrogance, punished them by scattering them over the earth and confusing their language so that the various groups could no longer understand each other.

RESPONDING TO THE SELECTION

You might remind students that the best interview questions are those that cannot be answered with a simple *yes* or *no*, but that require longer responses. You might also remind them that a reporter's job is to gather the facts that answer the questions *who, what, when, where, why,* and *how.*

Secondly, And as they wondered at their apparel, so they did likewise at their speech; for few could understand what they said, they naturally spoke the language of Canaan,[15] but they that kept the fair were the men of this world; so that, from one end of the fair to the other, they seemed barbarians each to the other.

Thirdly, But that which did not a little amuse the merchandisers was that these pilgrims set very light by all their wares; they cared not so much as to look upon them; and if they called upon them to buy, they would put their fingers in their ears, and cry, "Turn away mine eyes from beholding vanity," and look upwards, signifying that their trade and traffic was in heaven. (Psalms cxix.37; Philippians iii. 19, 20.)

 Why didn't the pilgrims buy anything at the fair?

One chanced mockingly, beholding the carriages of the men, to say unto them, What will ye buy? But they, looking gravely upon him, said, "We buy the truth" (Proverbs xxiii.23). At that there was an occasion taken to despise the men the more; some mocking, some taunting, some speaking reproachfully, and some calling upon others to smite them. At last things came to an hubbub and great stir in the fair, insomuch that all order was confounded. Now was word presently brought to the great one of the fair, who quickly came down, and deputed some of his most trusty friends to take these men into examination, about whom the fair was almost overturned. So the men were brought to examination; and they that sat upon them[16] asked them whence they came, whither they went, and what they did there, in such an unusual garb? The men told them that they were pilgrims and strangers in the world, and that they were going to their own country, which was the Heavenly Jerusalem (Hebrews xi.l3–16); and that they had given no occasion to the men of the town, nor yet to the merchandisers, thus to abuse them, and to let[17] them in their journey, except it was for that, when one asked them what they would buy, they said they would buy the truth. But they that were appointed to examine them did not believe them to be any other than bedlams and mad, or else such as came to put all things into a confusion in the fair. Therefore they took them and beat them, and besmeared them with dirt, and then put them into the cage, that they might be made a spectacle to all the men of the fair. ■

15. **Canaan.** The Promised Land
16. **sat upon them.** Questioned and tried them
17. **let.** Hinder

Responding to the Selection

Role play a reporter who is preparing to interview Christian, the pilgrim in this allegory. To prepare for your interview, write a list of questions that you wish to ask Christian about the many people, places, and events he encountered during his remarkable journey.

ANSWERS FOR REVIEWING THE SELECTION

RECALLING

1. Looking up from his book (the Bible), Christian cries, "What shall I do?"

2. Evangelist tells Christian to follow a shining light he sees in the distance, which will lead him to the wicket-gate.

3. The merchandise included houses, land, appointments to powerful positions, countries, pleasures of the flesh, servants, bodies, souls, gold, and precious jewels.

4. The only other way is to "go out of the world," in other words, to die.

INTERPRETING

5. Christian knows that he is condemned to die if he cannot find the way to salvation.

6. Christian will be told how to gain eternal life.

(cont.)

Reviewing the Selection

RECALLING

1. What lament does Christian make in the first paragraph of the allegory?

2. What directions does Evangelist give to Christian?

3. What kind of merchandise could a visitor buy at the ancient, original fair?

4. What is the only other way to the Celestial City beside passing through the fair?

INTERPRETING

5. What troubles Christian at the beginning of the allegory?

6. What will Christian be told at the wicketgate?

7. What does the fair symbolize?

8. What does the pilgrims' passage through the ancient fair symbolize?

SYNTHESIZING

9. What circumstances in this allegory cause the reader or listener to feel empathy for Christian?

10. What makes a journey an appropriate metaphor for life?

Understanding Literature (Questions for Discussion)

Allegory. An **allegory** is a work in which each element *symbolizes,* or represents, something else. The allegory central to the selection is the journey Christian makes from the City of Destruction to the Celestial City. To understand the allegory you need to determine what the characters and events in the story symbolize. The story speaks of Christian, the great burden he carries on his back, Evangelist, the wicketgate, Christian's journey, and the Celestial City. What do these items represent?

Responding in Writing

Persuasive Paragraph. In order to convince Pliable to join him on his journey, Christian had to be persuasive. What arguments did he use to convince Pliable? Did these arguments support Christian's position? How might you convince someone of an issue you feel strongly about? Maybe you are trying to change a friend's mind about a political or social issue. Choose a topic for a persuasive paragraph. In a sentence, describe your position, or stand, on the topic. Then give two or three arguments to support your position.

ANSWERS FOR REVIEWING THE SELECTION (CONT.)

7. The fair symbolizes all the earthly distractions that lead a person to stray from the path that leads to redemption.

8. Their passage represents the struggle to live a righteous life in the midst of a corrupt world.

SYNTHESIZING

Responses will vary. Possible responses are given.

9. His unhappiness at the beginning of the story, his concern for his family even as they abuse him, and his simple, honest desire to live righteously make Christian a sympathetic character.

10. Like life, a journey takes a person through many different places and experiences. A journey often has a planned destination, but sometimes there are detours along the way. A journey may be difficult and painful, but the hardships may be worthwhile if the person ends up where he or she wants to be.

ANALYTIC SCALES FOR RESPONDING IN WRITING

Assign a score from 1 to 25 for each grading criterion below. (For more detailed evaluation, see the evaluation forms for writing, revising, and proofreading, *Assessment Portfolio, 7.1–7.10.*)

Persuasive Paragraph

1. **Content/Unity.** The paragraph states a position and gives two or three examples to support that position.

2. **Organization/Coherence.** The paragraph is structured in a logical manner and does not stray from its topic.

3. **Language/Style.** The paragraph uses vivid and precise nouns, verbs, and modifiers.

4. **Conventions.** The paragraph avoids errors in spelling, grammar, usage, mechanics, and manuscript form.

ANSWERS FOR UNDERSTANDING LITERATURE

▶ See the evaluation forms for discussion, active listening, and oral communication, *Assessment Portfolio,* 7.11–7.14.
Responses will vary. Possible responses are given.

Allegory. Christian represents any man or woman who wants to live a good Christian life. Christian's burden is sin, or the temptations of earthly life. Evangelist is a preacher of the Gospel, or a knowledgeable Christian who helps others find the way to salvation. The wicketgate is the narrow entrance into heaven, which few people get through. Christian's journey symbolizes any sinner's passage through life and life's temptations on the way to salvation. The Celestial City is redemption or heaven.

▶**Teaching Note:** Students may look up the Bible passages referenced within the selection.

Language Lab

Connotation and Denotation. Read the Language Arts Survey, 2.153, "Connotation and Denotation." Then, read each of the following sentences from the selection. From the two words or phrases given in parentheses in each sentence, choose the one with the strongest emotional connotations. Explain what those connotations are.

1. Then said Evangelist, Why not willing to die, since this life is attended with so many *(ills/evils)*?

2. The name of the one was *(Obstinate/Resistant)*, and the name of the other Pliable.

3. I am *(instructed/directed)* by a man, whose name is Evangelist, to speed me to a little gate that is before us, where we shall receive instructions about the way.

4. Now these *(pilgrims/visitors)*, as I said, must needs go through this fair.

5. But they, looking *(seriously/gravely)* upon him, said, "We buy the truth."

PROJECT

1. **Board Game.** In a group, plan an allegorical board game that presents a journey like that described in Bunyan's *The Pilgrim's Progress.* Design and lay out your game board, including on it places such as Vanity Fair and the Celestial City. You may wish to consult a full text of *The Pilgrim's Progress* to complete this activity, or you may use your own imagination to create places and experiences not mentioned in the selection.

2. **Planning a Trip.** In a group, choose a destination for a five-day vacation. Then, do some research to plan how you will get there and what, precisely, you will do on each day. Consult travel guides and travel agencies for information. Produce a day-to-day itinerary detailing your plans for the trip.

PREREADING

"To Althea, from Prison"

by Richard Lovelace

ABOUT THE AUTHOR

Richard Lovelace (1618–1657) was born outside London, in Woolwich. The eldest son of an old and wealthy Kentish family, Lovelace was educated at Oxford. Young and handsome, the very model of a courtier with his cool demeanor and wit, Lovelace caught the admiration of King Charles and Queen Henrietta Maria, who visited Oxford in 1636. He subsequently earned the M.A. degree. Bravely serving the king, Lovelace fought in the civil wars against the Puritans and was wounded, imprisoned, and exiled. In 1648, after his return to England from Holland and France, Lovelace was imprisoned again. When he was released the following year, he was penniless and unemployed. Supported only by charity, Lovelace lived in squalor for the last ten years of his life. He published *Lucasta* in 1649. A collection of Lovelace's writings was published in 1659, two years after his death.

ABOUT THE SELECTION

The most famous of Lovelace's poems, **"To Althea, from Prison,"** probably was written while Lovelace was imprisoned in 1642. Lovelace and Sir John Suckling are often paired as representative of the "Cavalier spirit," but their work is not similar. While Suckling's verse is often flippant and lighthearted, Lovelace's verse is thoughtful and somber.

ADDITIONAL RESOURCES

READER'S GUIDE
- Selection Worksheet, 6.8

ASSESSMENT PORTFOLIO
- Selection Check Test, 4.6.15
- Selection Test, 4.6.16

ESSENTIAL SKILLS PRACTICE BOOKS
- *Language,* 2.3, 2.4, 2.147
- *Study and Research,* 4.40

ENRICHMENT ACTIVITIES

Interested students might research the writings of other people who have been imprisoned for their beliefs, such as Saint Paul; Thomas More; Martin Luther King, Jr.; Susan B. Anthony; Daw Aung San Suu Kyi (winner of the 1991 Nobel Prize for peace); and Nelson Mandela (joint winner of the 1993 Nobel Prize for peace); and discuss the thoughts and feelings expressed by these people. Some students may wish to take on the characters of the people they have researched and give dramatic readings from those peoples' works.

SUPPORT FOR LEP STUDENTS

You might tell students beforehand that the theme of this poem is freedom and that the author uses many words related to both freedom (unconfinèd, wanton, liberty, careless) and imprisonment (tangled, fettered, bound, committed, prison, cage). Students might translate some of these words into their primary languages to gain a sense of the poem's diction.

GOALS/OBJECTIVES

Studying this lesson will enable students to

- interpret and appreciate the speaker's feelings about liberty and honor
- describe the literary accomplishments of Richard Lovelace
- recognize formal and informal language in a

poem and explain why the author chose to use such language
- define *theme* and *metaphor* and recognize and interpret examples of each in a literary work
- identify concrete and abstract nouns and common and proper nouns

Students might use the photograph of the Tower of London on page 453 to visualize themselves locked away in a seventeenth-century prison. Suggest that they use this visualization as a concrete context for thinking about the questions.

LANGUAGE SKILLS

You might also ask students to comment on how the poem's language contributes to its tone.

▶Additional practice is provided in the *Essential Skills Practice Book: Language,* 2.147.

ANSWER TO GUIDED READING QUESTION

❶ His beloved Althea visits him, and he feels free in his love for her, even though he is in prison.

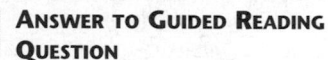

VOCABULARY FROM THE SELECTION

hermitage
steep

READER'S JOURNAL

How would it feel to be imprisoned for your beliefs and barred from seeing those people whom you love? What would you miss most about freedom? Would you still have conviction in your beliefs? Why, or why not? Think about these questions. Then write in your journal about the beliefs and relationships that sustain and support you in times of distress.

LANGUAGE SKILLS

Read the Language Arts Survey, 2.147, "Formal and Informal English." Then read the poem. Is its language formal or informal? What makes the language chosen by the author appropriate to the poem's subject?

"To Althea, from Prison"

RICHARD LOVELACE

When Love with unconfinèd wings
    Hovers within my gates,
And my divine Althea brings
    To whisper at the grates;
5   When I lie tangled in her hair
    And fettered to her eye,
The gods that wanton in the air
    Know no such liberty.

When flowing cups run swiftly round,
10   With no allaying Thames,[1]
Our careless heads with roses bound,
    Our hearts with loyal flames;
When thirsty grief in wine we <u>steep</u>,
    When healths° and draughts° go free,   *toasts/drinks*
15   Fishes that tipple° in the deep   *drink*
    Know no such liberty.

When, like committed linnets,° I   *caged finches*
    With shriller throat shall sing

---

1. **When . . . Thames.** Wine not watered down

WORDS FOR EVERYDAY USE: **steep** (stēp) *vt.,* soak; immerse

Who visits the speaker in prison? How does he feel when she visits?

VOCABULARY IN CONTEXT

• Loretta planned to <u>steep</u> herself in American history during the week leading up to the exam.

The Tower of London. London, England

CROSS-CURRICULAR ACTIVITIES

Social Studies. William the Conqueror began building the Tower of London, shown on this page, in 1078. The large, many-towered complex was begun on foundations from the days of the Roman Empire, and it was expanded and redesigned over the centuries. In addition to housing some of the most eminent prisoners in English history, the Tower of London also served at various times as a zoo, a national treasury, a royal residence, and a fortress. Interested students may research the history of the Tower of London and share their findings with the class in a historical drama, a presentation of a detailed map and other visual materials, or some other suitable format.

> The sweetness, mercy, majesty,
> 20   And glories of my king;
> When I shall voice aloud how good
>   He is, how great should be,
> Enlargèd winds, that curl the flood,
>   Know no such liberty.
>
> 25 Stone walls do not a prison make,
>   Nor iron bars a cage;
> Minds innocent and quiet take
>   That for an <u>hermitage</u>.
> If I have freedom in my love,
> 30   And in my soul am free,
> Angels alone, that soar above,
>   Enjoy such liberty. ■

❶
How is the speaker free?

WORDS FOR EVERYDAY USE:

her •mit • age (hur´ mi tij) *n.*, secluded retreat

VOCABULARY IN CONTEXT

- A study cubicle in the remotest corner of the library was Kevin's <u>hermitage</u> during exam week.

ANSWER TO GUIDED READING QUESTION

❶ The speaker is free in his love and in his political convictions; no one can imprison his emotions or his mind.

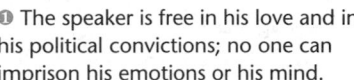

ANSWERS TO SELECTION CHECK TEST 4.6.15

EX. From where, according to the title, is the speaker writing?
The speaker is writing from prison.

1. Who does not know the liberty the speaker feels when he lies tangled in Althea's hair?
"The gods that wanton in the air" do not know this liberty.

2. What do "Fishes that tipple in the deep" not know?
They do not know liberty as the speaker does.

3. How will the speaker sing?
The speaker will sing with a shriller voice than committed linnets, or caged finches.

4. What does the speaker say does not make a prison?
Stone walls do not make a prison.

5. How is the speaker free?
The speaker is free in his love and in his soul.

ANSWERS FOR REVIEWING THE SELECTION

RECALLING

1. Love's wings are "unconfinèd," or free.

2. They do not know the freedom that the speaker feels when his heart is stirred with loyalty as he drinks wine with his friends.

3. His voice will be shriller than that of a caged bird.

4. "Stone walls" and "iron bars" do not make a prison, the speaker says.

INTERPRETING

Responses will vary. Possible responses are given.

5. The words *gates, grates, tangled,* and *fettered* suggest the speaker's imprisonment.

6. The drinking of toasts creates an image of a party among friends.

7. He feels loyal toward the king, about whose "sweetness, mercy, majesty,/And glories" he sings loudly.

8. The entire stanza is about the freedom the speaker experiences; the last four lines especially express his feeling that he is as free as the "Angels . . . that soar above."

SYNTHESIZING

Responses will vary. Possible responses are given.

9. Nothing threatens true liberty, because no prison or external circumstance can take away the freedom of one's mind and soul.

10. True liberty is a state of mind.

Responding to the Selection

Imagine that you are the Althea in this poem. In your journal, write a response to your imprisoned beloved. Express your feelings about his imprisonment and political convictions. You may wish to write your response in lyric stanzas.

Reviewing the Selection

RECALLING

1. What kind of wings does the speaker describe Love as having?

2. What do "fishes that tipple in the deep" not know?

3. With what kind of voice will the speaker sing the "glories of [his] king"?

4. What does not make a prison or a cage?

INTERPRETING

5. What words in stanza 1 remind the reader or listener of the speaker's imprisonment?

6. What images in stanza 2 emphasize the pleasures experienced by people who are free?

7. How does the speaker feel toward his king?

8. What lines in stanza 4 show that the speaker does not think of himself as imprisoned?

SYNTHESIZING

9. What, according to the speaker, threatens true liberty?

10. What conclusion about true liberty does the speaker draw in this poem?

Understanding Literature (Questions for Discussion)

1. **Theme.** A **theme** is a central idea in a literary work. What idea does the author explore in this poem? What words, phrases, or lines emphasize that theme?

2. **Metaphor.** A **metaphor** is a figure of speech in which one thing is spoken or written about as if it were another. This figure of speech invites the reader to make a comparison between the two things. What is compared to a hermitage, or place of religious seclusion, in line 28 of the poem? What kind of mind would consider such a place like a hermitage? What is the speaker saying about himself?

ANSWERS FOR UNDERSTANDING LITERATURE

Responses will vary. Possible responses are given.
► See the evaluation forms for discussion, active listening, and oral communication, *Assessment Portfolio,* 7.11–7.14.

1. Theme. The theme is the true meaning of freedom; the poem asserts that freedom is not a matter of being in or out of prison but rather the freedom to think and feel what one will. Words that suggest freedom include *unconfinèd, wanton, liberty, careless,* and *soar;* contrasting words include *tangled, fettered, bound, committed, prison,* and *cage.* Images of the speaker enjoying the love of Althea, drinking toasts with his friends, and singing the praises of his beloved king support the theme of freedom, and stanza 4 of the poem summarizes the theme.

2. Metaphor. A prison or cage is compared to a hermitage. A contemplative or deep-thinking person would be likely to feel this way. The speaker thus reveals that

(cont.)

Responding in Writing

1. **Speech.** Imagine that you are a political speech writer for the speaker in this poem. In the Introduction to this unit (page 410), read the discussion of the civil war fought between the Puritans and the Cavaliers. Then write a speech favoring or opposing monarchy, taking a Cavalier or a Puritan point of view. Refer to the Language Arts Survey, 3.7, "Public Speaking."

2. **Lyric Poem.** A **lyric poem** is a highly musical verse that expresses the emotions of a speaker. Consider the following lines from the poem:

> If I have freedom in my love,
>   And in my soul am free,
> Angels alone, that soar above,
>   Enjoy such liberty.

These lines express the speaker's understanding of true liberty—freedom of love and freedom of the soul. Write a lyric poem about the loss of freedom. First consider your own understanding of freedom. What is your conception of the worst prison? In your poem, use imagery and tone to express your feelings.

Language Lab

Concrete and Abstract Nouns. Read the Language Arts Survey, 2.3, "Common and Proper Nouns," and 2.4, "Concrete and Abstract Nouns." Then, identify each of the nouns in the sentences below. Write *C* for common or *P* for proper and *CN* for concrete or *A* for abstract.

1. The Parliament of Great Britain is divided into a House of Lords and a House of Commons.

2. Cromwell's position and strength enabled him to dissolve Parliament, prohibit Anglican services, and divide England into eleven districts.

3. In 1656, Rembrandt declared bankruptcy and sold his possessions.

4. Lovelace had an appreciation for the art of painting, which flourished in the seventeenth century.

5. Cocoa was introduced in London in 1657, as were fountain pens in Paris.

ANALYTIC SCALES FOR RESPONDING IN WRITING

Assign a score from 1 to 25 for each grading criterion below. (For more detailed evaluation, see the evaluation forms for writing, revising, and proofreading, *Assessment Portfolio*, 7.1–7.10.)

1. Speech

• **Content/Unity.** The speech takes a clear stand for or against the monarchy and gives relevant reasons.

• **Organization/Coherence.** The speech clearly states a position and adds support in a logical order.

• **Language/Style.** The speech uses vivid and precise nouns, verbs, and modifiers.

• **Conventions.** The speech avoids errors in spelling, grammar, usage, mechanics, and manuscript form.

2. Lyric Poem

• **Content/Unity.** The poem uses imagery and creates an emotional tone appropriate to the topic of the loss of freedom.

• **Organization/Coherence.** The poem flows naturally from one idea to the next and builds to a sensible conclusion about the topic.

• **Language/Style.** The poem uses vivid and precise nouns, verbs, and modifiers.

• **Conventions.** The poem avoids errors in spelling, grammar, usage, mechanics, and manuscript form.

ANSWERS FOR LANGUAGE LAB

1. Parliament (P/CN); Great Britain (P/CN); House of Lords (P/CN); House of Commons (P/CN)

2. position (C/A); strength (C/A); Parliament (P/CN); services (C/CN); England (P/CN); districts (C/CN)

3. Rembrandt (P/CN); bankruptcy (C/A); possessions (C/CN)

4. Lovelace (P/CN); appreciation (C/A); art (C/A); painting (C/A); century (C/CN)

5. Cocoa (C/CN); London (P/CN); fountain pens (C/CN); Paris (P/CN)

► Additional practice is provided in the *Essential Skills Practice Book: Language*, 2.3, 2.4.

ANSWERS FOR UNDERSTANDING LITERATURE (CONT.)

the workings of his mind are what he values most in himself and in life.

► **Teaching Note:** You might ask students to discuss whether they would be likely to share the speaker's perspective if they themselves were in prison. Do they think that the speaker may simply be rationalizing?

Test-taking Skills

Analogy Questions. Read the Language Arts Survey, 4.40, "Analogy Questions." Then choose the word that best completes the following analogies.

1. UNCONFINED : TRAPPED :: Unopened : _____
   a. Closure   b. Closed   c. Open   d. Blocked

2. FETTERED : CHAIN :: Released : _____
   a. Unlock   b. Sky   c. Key   d. Locked

3. PRISONER : CELL :: Livestock : _____
   a. Pen   b. Walls   c. Grate   d. Cage

4. HERMITAGE : MONK :: Prison : _____
   a. Resort   b. Cell   c. Judge   d. Convict

5. FREEDOM : LIBERTY :: Soul : _____
   a. Love   b. Innocence   c. Spirit   d. Nature

PROJECTS

1. **An Art Show.** Unlike many of his English contemporaries, Lovelace was fascinated by the art of painting. Explore the art of the early seventeenth century and plan an art show in which numerous paintings and drawings from this period are displayed. Choose one person to be the curator, and then put together a team of five curatorial assistants. The curator should organize the team's research into different artists and works of art found in library art books. The assistants can write brief biographical notes about each artist and introductions to the works. Then, the curator and assistants can present the collection and notes to the class.

2. **Improvisation.** In groups of four to six students, take turns dramatizing one of the scenarios listed below. Use your imagination as you think about the topic that is up for discussion. Then create a contemporary version of one of the scenes listed below.

   • During one of the king's military expeditions against Scotland, Richard Lovelace, Sir John Suckling, and other Cavaliers meet and become friends. They discuss the honor they feel in serving their king, what they think of Puritanism, and why they support the monarchy.

   • Althea visits Lovelace while he is imprisoned. They discuss his feelings about imprisonment and her fear that his personal convictions will cause him even greater harm.

PREREADING

"To His Coy Mistress"
by Andrew Marvell

ABOUT THE AUTHOR

The rise of the reputation of **Andrew Marvell** (1621–1678) has been gradual but steady. Marvell, for the most part a reserved man, graduated from Cambridge and traveled for years before becoming a tutor to the daughter of the British General Sir Thomas Fairfax. Some of the poems written during this time reveal Marvell's sharp intellect and keen wit. His primary role in literary history would have been no more than that of secretary to the author John Milton had it not been for the publication of Marvell's poems, three years after his death, by a woman believed to be his housekeeper. At first, many of Marvell's verses appear light and satiric, but beneath this surface they contain serious observations and ideas and at times even an element of darkness. Another side of his character was revealed in public life, for besides writing poetry he represented his hometown of Hull in the British Parliament. He worked diligently as a member of Parliament from 1659 until his death. His letters sent from the Halls of Parliament back to his constituents are noteworthy for their historical value.

ABOUT THE SELECTION

"**To His Coy Mistress**" has the whimsical quality that characterizes so much of Marvell's poetry. It is written in a fairly uncomplicated style, which fits Marvell's *carpe diem* theme. Lightheartedly, the speaker of the poem urges his beloved to "seize the day"—to make good use of the little time available in life by devoting that time to love. This lightheartedness is clouded by the dark shadows of passing time and even of oncoming death. Beneath the seeming lightness is a serious idea that we are left to ponder.

GOALS/OBJECTIVES

Studying this lesson will enable students to

- appreciate the speaker's lighthearted "seize the day" attitude and the darker side of this message
- describe the character of Andrew Marvell's literary contributions

- use an encyclopedia to research the lives of two seventeenth-century writers and compare and contrast the writers' lives
- define *metaphor, image,* and *stanza* and recognize and interpret examples of these that they encounter in their reading
- recognize and correct run-ons

ADDITIONAL RESOURCES

READER'S GUIDE
- Selection Worksheet, 6.9

ASSESSMENT PORTFOLIO
- Selection Check Test, 4.6.17
- Selection Test, 4.6.18

ESSENTIAL SKILLS PRACTICE BOOKS
- *Language*, 2.62
- *Study and Research*, 4.23, 4.26, 4.44

ENRICHMENT ACTIVITIES

Students might discuss ways in which people seem to have different "internal clocks"—for example, some people know what they want to do with their lives from a very young age, whereas others are "late bloomers"; some people are always rushing through life, while others take their time. Students might write a humorous story or play about two people who encounter difficulties in their relationship because of such differences.

SUPPORT FOR LEP STUDENTS

Before students begin reading, you might outline for them the basic structure of the poem: Stanza 1 discusses how a romance might progress if the couple had all the time in the world. Stanza 2 points out that people's lives are in fact very short and indicates what will happen if they wait too long to enjoy life's pleasures. Stanza 3 suggests how the speaker thinks people should behave, given that their lives are so short.

ADDITIONAL VOCABULARY
complain—formally state
vegetable—capable of growth
hue—color
strife—contention, competition

READER'S JOURNAL

Students might also think and write about the psychological forces that sometimes make people reluctant to act when they have the opportunity.

RESEARCH SKILLS

If students have access to an on-line encyclopedia, they might compare the information they find there to what they find in a print encyclopedia. Which format do they prefer using, and why?

▶Additional practice is provided in the *Essential Skills Practice Book: Study and Research,* 4.23 and 4.26.

ADDITIONAL QUESTIONS AND ACTIVITIES

Direct students' attention to lines 38–40, in which the speaker suggests that he and his love behave "like amorous birds of prey" and "devour" the time they have on earth. Help students appreciate the humor in this stanza with questions such as the following.

• What is surprising about the phrase "like amorous birds of prey"? What image does it create in your mind?

• Do you find this simile humorous? If so, why?

• Do lines 43–44—"And tear our pleasures with rough strife/Through the iron gates of life"—have a similar effect? Explain.

Answers. The phrase is surprising because it juxtaposes the word *amorous,* meaning "loving," with *birds of prey,* which suggests an image of violence and killing. The simile is humorous because the speaker, who has already said he would gladly spend an eternity contemplating his tender feelings for his lover, is now suggesting that they behave like wild animals. Lines 43–44 create a similar effect, mixing images of pleasure and strife with a humorous result.

READER'S JOURNAL

Have you ever let an opportunity slip by and then regretted it later? Think back on one of these situations and write about it in your journal. How did you handle the situation? What could you have done differently?

RESEARCH SKILLS

The lives of Marvell and John Milton overlapped when Marvell was employed as Milton's secretary. Read the Language Arts Survey, 4.23, "Using Reference Works." Then look up both authors in an encyclopedia. After reading the entries, compare the two men and list a few similarities and differences in their lives.

"To His Coy Mistress"

ANDREW MARVELL

Had we but world enough, and time,
This <u>coyness</u>, lady, were no crime.
We would sit down, and think which way
To walk, and pass our long love's day.
5   Thou by the Indian Ganges' side
Shouldst rubies find; I by the tide
Of Humber[1] would complain. I would
Love you ten years before the Flood,
And you should, if you please, refuse
10   Till the conversion of the Jews.[2]
My vegetable love should grow
Vaster than empires, and more slow;
An hundred years should go to praise
Thine eyes, and on thy forehead gaze;
15   Two hundred to adore each breast,

---

1. **Ganges' . . . Humber.** The Ganges river in India is compared to the small, muddy Humber river, which flows past Hull, Marvell's hometown.
2. **the Flood . . . the Jews.** The Flood is an early occurrence in Biblical times while the conversion of the Jews is supposed to occur just before the Last Judgment.

WORDS FOR EVERYDAY USE: **coy • ness** (koi´nes) *n.,* playful evasiveness; pretense of shyness or bashfulness

VOCABULARY IN CONTEXT

• Elise could not tell whether Jason's behavior reflected true shyness or mere <u>coyness</u>.

But thirty thousand to the rest;
An age at least to every part,
And the last age should show your heart.
For, lady, you deserve this state,°   *dignity*
20   Nor would I love at lower rate.
      But at my back I always hear
Time's wingèd chariot hurrying near;
And yonder all before us lie
Deserts of vast eternity.
25   Thy beauty shall no more be found,
Nor, in thy marble vault, shall sound
My echoing song; then worms shall try
That long-preserved virginity,
And your quaint honor turn to dust,
30   And into ashes all my lust:
The grave's a fine and private place,
But none, I think, do there embrace.
      Now therefore, while the youthful hue
Sits on thy skin like morning dew,
35   And while thy willing soul transpires°   *breathes forth*
At every pore with instant fires,°   *immediate enthusiasm*
Now let us sport us while we may,
And now, like amorous birds of prey,
Rather at once our time devour
40   Than languish in his slow-chapped³ power.
Let us roll all our strength and all
Our sweetness up into one ball,
And tear our pleasures with rough strife
Through the iron gates of life:
45   Thus, though we cannot make our sun
Stand still, yet we will make him run.⁴   ■

---

3. **slow-chapped.** Here the slow jaw belongs to Time,
which is slowly chewing up the world.
4. **though . . . run.** Although we can't make time stand
still, we can force it to race us.

❶
How does the speaker suggest dealing with the swift passage of time?

ANSWER TO GUIDED READING QUESTION

❶ The speaker suggests that life should be vigorously enjoyed while it lasts.

ANSWERS TO SELECTION CHECK TEST 4.6.17

EX. Whom is the speaker addressing?

The speaker is addressing his coy mistress.

1. Why is the woman's coyness a problem?

It is a problem because life is short and time is passing by quickly.

2. What does the speaker hear at his back?

He hears "Time's wingèd chariot hurrying near."

3. What will happen to the woman's honor in the vast deserts of eternity?

It will turn to dust.

4. Rather than languishing in the power of time, what does the speaker suggest that he and his mistress do?

He suggests that they devour time.

5. What will the speaker and his mistress make the sun do?

They will make the sun run.

ANALYTIC SCALES FOR RESPONDING IN WRITING

Assign a score from 1 to 25 for each grading criterion below. (For more detailed evaluation, see the evaluation forms for writing, revising, and proofreading, *Assessment Portfolio,* 7.1–7.10.)

1. **Descriptive Paragraph**
• **Content/Unity.** The paragraph uses appropriate images and metaphors to describe an abstract idea.
• **Organization/Coherence.** The paragraph is logically organized and makes a clear point about the abstract idea.
• **Language/Style.** The paragraph uses vivid and precise

(cont.)

ANALYTIC SCALES FOR RESPONDING IN WRITING (CONT.)

nouns, verbs, and modifiers.
• **Conventions.** The paragraph avoids errors in spelling, grammar, usage, mechanics, and manuscript form.

2. **Persuasive Paragraph**
• **Content/Unity.** The paragraph has a clear purpose and provides examples or arguments to persuade the reader.

• **Organization/Coherence.**
The writing is clearly organized, using its main argument either to open or to conclude the paragraph.
• **Language/Style.** The paragraph uses vivid and precise nouns, verbs, and modifiers.
• **Conventions.** The paragraph avoids errors in spelling, grammar, usage, mechanics, and manuscript form.

RESPONDING TO THE SELECTION

Students might begin by thinking about whether the woman would accept the label "coy mistress." How might she explain her own reluctance? Could her refusal be admirable rather than coy? What further information do we need before we can understand the situation?

ANSWERS FOR REVIEWING THE SELECTION

RECALLING

1. He accuses her of coyness.

2. He says his love would last from the Flood to the Last Judgment.

3. The speaker hears the "wingèd chariot" of time behind him and sees "deserts of vast eternity" before him.

4. In the last stanza, the speaker urges, "Now let us sport us while we may," imagines "devouring" time before it devours him and his love, and suggests that they "tear [their] pleasures . . ./Through the iron gates of life."

INTERPRETING

Responses will vary. Possible responses are given.

5. It is troublesome because the speaker feels they are wasting precious time while she deliberates.

6. Life is short, and they might be dead before she is ready to make a commitment.

7. He is keenly aware of the passage of time and the inevitability of death.

8. Time is a mortal enemy who must be attacked, or an opponent in a race who must be challenged directly.

SYNTHESIZING

Responses will vary. Possible responses are given.

9. Marvell's suggestion is to take advantage of the pleasures life has to offer while there is still time.

10. Bunyan's *The Pilgrim's Progress* portrays a sense of urgency in Christian's early misery at the

(cont.)

Responding to the Selection

Imagine that you are the "coy mistress." Write a letter to the speaker of the poem explaining whether or not his plea was convincing and why you feel as you do.

Reviewing the Selection

RECALLING

1. At the beginning of the poem, what quality does the speaker attribute to his mistress?

2. What Biblical allusions does the speaker use to express the longevity of his love?

3. What is seen and heard at the beginning of the second stanza?

4. What actions are suggested in the last stanza?

INTERPRETING

5. Why is this trait troublesome to the speaker?

6. Why does he feel he can't wait for a long time to have his love come to him?

7. Why does the speaker feel a sense of urgency?

8. What attitude toward time is expressed in the last stanza?

SYNTHESIZING

9. What does the poem suggest as a way to handle the problem posed by time? Do you ever feel the pressure of too little time in your own life? Do you find the suggestion helpful?

10. Think about how some of the other works that you have read in this book treat the subject of time. Do any of these works express the urgency of Marvell's poem? Do any have a conflicting message?

Understanding Literature (Questions for Discussion)

1. **Metaphor.** A **metaphor** is a figure of speech in which one thing is written or spoken about as if it were another. Only in a few instances does Marvell use the word *time* in his poem, yet time stands out as a significant idea because of the metaphors he uses to describe it. Look for some of these metaphors and discuss ways in which he wants us to see time. Do any of these metaphors seem to conflict with one another? Are there differences in the way Marvell characterizes time in different parts of the poem? How can you account for these differences?

460   *UNIT SIX / THE EARLY SEVENTEENTH CENTURY*

ANSWERS FOR REVIEWING THE SELECTION (CONT.)

thought of his own death and his desire to find the path to salvation. On the other hand, the pilgrims' avoidance of worldly pleasures at the Vanity Fair contrasts with the message of "To His Coy Mistress." Milton's "On His Blindness" also has a conflicting message: The speaker learns that he must have patience and wait for God to show him the way rather than trying to reach God through his own works.

ANALYTIC SCALES FOR RESPONDING IN WRITING

Grading scales appear on page 459.

460 TEACHER'S EDITION

2. **Image.** An **image** is a word or phrase that names something that can be seen, heard, touched, tasted, or smelled. In line 11 Marvell uses the phrase "My vegetable love" to characterize his affection. At first this may seem like a strange way to talk about an emotion. Why would you suppose Marvell uses this kind of image? Do you think he wants us to look at love in ways that we are not used to? What kinds of feelings or experiences do you associate with the word *vegetable*? What is Marvell saying about the similarity between love and a living, growing thing? See if you can find other images for love in the poem and compare them.

3. **Stanza.** A **stanza** is a recurring pattern of grouped lines in a poem. Notice that Marvell separates his poem into three sections, or stanzas, and even indents them in the way a prose writer would indent paragraphs. Read each stanza separately, thinking of it as a paragraph in an essay. What is the main idea of each paragraph? Does the arrangement of the stanzas form a well-organized, cohesive argument?

Responding in Writing

1. **Descriptive Paragraph.** Time and love are two abstract ideas, or things that we cannot perceive by our senses. Marvell presents these abstract ideas to us through very descriptive images and metaphors. Select an abstract word of your own and write a paragraph using metaphorical images to describe what it means to you. You might choose the experience of pride, the loss of something that was important to you, or your feelings for a friend. Be sure your topic is something abstract, and then use concrete images and metaphors to describe it.

2. **Persuasive Paragraph.** Clearly, Marvell does not feel that time is on the side of love and life's enjoyment. This is his main point in his attempt to persuade his mistress to return his love. Imagine that you have to convince someone of something but only have a limited time to do it. List the reasons you would give, then write a short paragraph to accomplish your purpose. Look over your reasons to see if one seems more effective than the others. How could you use this reason in making your point? Would it be best to use it to introduce or to complete the paragraph?

Language Lab

Correcting Run-ons. After reading the Language Arts Survey, 2.62, "Correcting Run-ons," rewrite the following passages. Add punctuation and remove words as necessary. Capitalize words to create new sentences, but do not alter the meaning of the passage.

1. Andrew Marvell's poems are more than fanciful verses because he makes serious points, the reader would miss some of the poems' value by overlooking these points.

2. The mistress in the poem does not show fondness for the speaker, it is not clear whether she feels any or not, since her feelings are left for the reader to imagine.

ANSWERS FOR UNDERSTANDING LITERATURE (CONT.)

hardly the image one associates with a dashing young cavalier. The image also sharply contrasts with the speaker's later exhortation to his lover to passionately devour time and pleasure like a "bird of prey."

3. **Stanza.** The poem has a dialectical form, presenting a thesis, its antithesis, and a synthesis, or conclusion. The first stanza describes how the couple's love might unfold had they an eternity to spend together. The second

explains that life is too short. The third says that given the shortness of life, one should act quickly while there is still time.

►**Teaching Note:** You might challenge students to develop a counterargument about the dangers of acting too rashly.

ANSWERS FOR LANGUAGE LAB

1. Andrew Marvell's poems are more than fanciful verses because he makes serious points. The reader would miss some of the poems' value by overlooking these points.

2. The mistress in the poem does not show fondness for the speaker. It is not clear whether she feels any or not, since her feelings are left for the reader to imagine.

3. Marvell prevented the poet John Milton from going to prison. Without Marvell's help, Milton may well have been put to death.

4. It's easy to imagine that Andrew Marvell was a delightful tutor to Thomas Fairfax's daughter. His poems written at that time show a witty sense of humor and even some satire, though these qualities aren't immediately apparent in Marvell's character.

5. The Latin phrase *carpe diem* means "seize the day." Marvell's poem is one of the most famous statements in English of the *carpe diem* theme.

▶Additional practice is provided in the *Essential Skills Practice Book: Language,* 2.62.

ANSWERS FOR TEST-TAKING SKILLS

1. c. outgoing
2. a. reinforces
3. c. forthright
4. b. flourishing
5. c. eternal

FOR MORE PRACTICE

Problem. Savoring every moment of their long-awaited vacation, Anthony and Cleo <u>sauntered</u> lazily toward the buffet table.

a. hiked

b. gazed

c. strolled

d. scampered

Answer. d. scampered

▶Additional practice is provided in the *Essential Skills Practice Book: Study and Research,* 4.44.

---

3. Marvell prevented the poet John Milton from going to prison, without Marvell's help, Milton may well have been put to death.

4. It's easy to imagine that Andrew Marvell was a delightful tutor to Thomas Fairfax's daughter, his poems written at that time show a witty sense of humor and even some satire, though those qualities aren't immediately apparent in Marvell's character.

5. The Latin phrase *carpe diem* means "seize the day," Marvell's poem is one of the most famous statements in English of the *carpe diem* theme.

Test-taking Skills

Synonym and Antonym Questions. Read the Language Arts Survey, 4.44, "Synonym and Antonym Questions." Then read the sentences below, and choose the word that means the *opposite* of the underlined word.

1. Andrew Marvell was a <u>reserved</u> man, though his poetry showed his humor and wit.

   a. quiet   b. funny   c. outgoing   d. restrained

2. In many of Marvell's poems, his casual approach <u>belies</u> his serious message.

   a. reinforces   b. disguises   c. belittles   d. underlies

3. In "To His Coy Mistress," the speaker explains why there is no time to be <u>coy</u>.

   a. evasive   b. coquettish   c. forthright   d. hasty

4. According to the poem, we should take charge of time rather than <u>languishing</u> under its power.

   a. submitting   b. flourishing   c. suffering   d. expressing ourselves

5. The theme of this poem is that we should enjoy youth, beauty, love, and life now, because they are only <u>temporal</u>.

   a. short-lived   b. quick   c. eternal   d. tempting

PROJECT

Reading Aloud. Because the **meter, tempo,** and **rhythm** of a poem are critical to its total effect, poets carefully consider how the words would sound if they were read aloud. Often, reading a poem aloud can produce a different effect than reading it silently. The rhyme scheme of Marvell's poem is very simple. Each pair of lines finishes with a **rhyme.** A pair of lines that rhyme in this manner is called a **couplet.** Get together with a partner and read the poem through, each of you reading a complete couplet. Are some sections or lines more effective if read aloud? less effective? Do some passages stand out more when read orally?

PROJECT NOTES

▶See the worksheets and evaluation forms for projects, *Assessment Portfolio,* 7.20–7.23.

Reading Aloud

• Remind students that many rhymes are approximate rather than exact; for example, lines 7–8 end with the words *would* and *Flood,* which have slightly different vowel sounds.

• After practicing reading the poem aloud with partners, some students may enjoy presenting an oral reading for the whole class.

"The Indifferent" by John Donne

I can love both fair and brown,
  Her whom abundance melts, and her whom want
    betrays,
  Her who loves loneness best, and her who masks and
    plays,
  Her whom the country formed, and whom the town,
5 Her who believes, and her who tries,
  Her who still weeps with spongy eyes,
  And her who is dry cork, and never cries;
  I can love her, and her, and you, and you,
  I can love any, so she be not true.

10 Will no other vice content you?
  Will it not serve your turn to do as did your
    mothers?
  Or have you all old vices spent, and now would find
    out others?
  Or doth a fear that men are true torment you?
  O we are not, be not you so;
15 Let me, and do you, twenty know.
  Rob me, but bind me not, and let me go.
  Must I, who came to travail thorough[1] you,
  Grow your fixed subject, because you are true?

  Venus heard me sigh this song,
20 And by love's sweetest part, variety, she swore,
  She heard not this till now; and that it should be so
    no more.
  She went, examined, and returned ere long,
  And said, Alas, some two or three
  Poor heretics in love there be,
25 Which think to 'stablish dangerous constancy.
  But I have told them, Since you will be true,
  You shall be true to them who are false to you.

from *Areopagitica*[2] by John Milton

Methinks I see in my mind a noble and puissant nation rousing herself like a strong man after sleep, and shaking her invincible locks: methinks I see her as an eagle mewing her mighty youth, and kindling her undazzled eyes at the full midday beam; purging and unscaling her long-abused sight at the fountain itself of heavenly radiance; while the whole noise of timorous and flocking birds, with those also that love the twilight, flutter about, amazed at what she means, and in their envious gabble would prognosticate a year of sects and schisms.

What should ye do then, should ye suppress all this flowery crop of knowledge and new light sprung up and yet springing daily in this city? Should ye set an oligarchy of twenty engrossers[3] over it, to bring a famine upon our minds again, when we shall know nothing but what is measured to us by their bushel? Believe it, Lords and Commons, they who counsel ye to such a suppressing do as good as bid ye suppress yourselves; and I will soon show how. [4]

◆ ◆ ◆

And now the time in special is by privilege to write and speak what may help to the further discussing of matters in agitation. The temple of Janus with his two controversial faces might now not unsignificantly be set open. And though all the winds of doctrine were let loose to play upon the earth, so Truth be in the field, we do injuriously by licensing and prohibiting to misdoubt her strength. Let her and Falsehood grapple; who ever knew Truth put to the worse in a free and open encounter?

Sonnet 77 by Lady Mary Wroth

In this strange labyrinth how shall I turn?
  Ways are on all sides, while the way I miss:
  If to the right hand, there in love I burn;
  Let me go forward, therein danger is;
5 If to the left, suspicion hinders bliss,
  Let me turn back, Shame cries I ought return,
  Nor faint though crosses with my fortunes kiss;
  Stand still is harder, although sure to mourn.
  Then let me take the right- or left-hand way;
10 Go forward, or stand still, or back retire;
  I must these doubts endure without allay
  Or help, but travail find for my best hire.
  Yet that which most my troubled sense doth move
  Is to leave all, and take the thread of love.[5]

---

1. **thorough.** Through
2. *Areopagitica.* A pamphlet against censorship
3. **engrossers.** People who hoarded grain and sold it for high prices during famine

4. **Believe . . . how.** Milton argues that Parliament has created the inquisitive minds that censorship now tries to suppress.
5. **thread of love.** The reference is to the thread that Ariadne gave to Theseus so he would not get lost in the labyrinth at Crete.

SONNET 77

About the Author. Lady Mary Wroth (*circa* 1586–*circa* 1651) spent much of her life in the royal courts of Elizabeth I and James I. She was born into a literary family; her father was Sir Robert Sidney, and she was the niece of poets Sir Philip Sidney and Mary, Countess of Pembroke. Among the courtiers who admired her was Ben Jonson, who dedicated his comic play *The Alchemist* to her. Lady Mary's only major work published in her lifetime was a dark and cynical romance entitled *The Countesse of Mountgomeries Urania* (1621), which she was forced to withdraw under charges of libel. Some of her poetry involving the main characters in *Urania* was published in or along with the romance. More was published in 1977 under the title *Pamphilia to Amphilanthus.*

"THE INDIFFERENT"

About the Author. A biography of **Donne** appears on page 414.

FROM *AREOPAGITICA*

About the Author. A biography of **Milton** appears on page 429.

ADDITIONAL QUESTIONS AND ACTIVITIES

Students may form small groups to discuss the following questions.

• What is the theme of Donne's poem "The Indifferent"? What does the speaker want? Why will he never find it? Compare and contrast this poem with Donne's Song ("Go and catch a falling star . . .").

Answers. The theme of "The Indifferent" is women's faithlessness. The speaker wants to find a mate who is "true," but the goddess of love has declared that people who are foolish enough to love truly shall love only those who are untrue. This poem shares a common theme with Song ("Go and catch a falling star . . ."), but the language is more formal.

• What is the subject of Milton's *Areopagitica*? What is the "noble and puissant nation"? In what way has the eagle's sight been "long-abused"? What does Milton say will be the outcome if "[Truth] and Falsehood grapple" openly?

Answers. Milton's *Areopagitica* is about censorship. The "noble and puissant nation" is England, whose people have a long history of being blinded by the suppression of free speech and press. Milton says that Truth will inevitably win if she is allowed to compete openly with Falsehood.

• What problem is faced by the speaker in Sonnet 77? Why can she not "turn back"? What is the "thread of love"? How will it help the speaker?

Answers. The speaker in Sonnet 77 is confused about which direction to take in life. Turning back would be shameful and cowardly. The "thread of love" will guide her so she does not get lost in the "labyrinth" of life—as long as she is true to what she loves, she will not go wrong.

"To Mrs. M. A. at Parting"

About the Author. Katherine Philips (1631–1664) and her husband, James, were the center of the so-called Society of Friendship, a group of literary-minded people who often gathered at their home in Wales. She and her friends each took a Neoclassical nickname; Philips herself was playfully known as "The Matchless Orinda." She wrote many poems about her friendships with women, along with other works exploring her Puritan faith and several plays. Most of her poetry was not published in her lifetime but rather circulated among her friends. When a collection of her poetry and plays was published after her death of smallpox at the age of thirty-three, her work was highly praised.

ADDITIONAL QUESTIONS AND ACTIVITIES

Students may discuss the following questions.

• What is the theme of "To Mrs. M. A. at Parting"?

Answer. The theme is friendship: the difficulty of parting from close friends and the ties that bind friends across time and distance.

• Why is it so difficult for the speaker to part from her friend? What comforts the speaker at this painful time?

Answers. The speaker has grown so close to her friend that "each is in the union lost" (line 18). She is comforted by the fact that she and her friend cannot really be parted because their hearts and minds will always be joined.

• Compare and contrast "To Mrs. M. A. at Parting" with some of the other poems about love that you have read in this unit.

Answer. This poem is different from others in this unit because it deals with friendship rather than romantic love. The love between the two characters is mutual and is based on intellectual and spiritual closeness rather than romantic longing.

"To Mrs. M. A.[1] at Parting"
by Katherine Philips

I have examined and do find,
    Of all that favor me
There's none I grieve to leave behind
    But only only thee.
5 To part with thee I needs must die,
Could parting separate thee and I.

But neither chance nor compliment
    Did element our love:
'Twas sacred sympathy was lent
10   Us from the choir above.
(That friendship fortune did create,
Still fears a wound from time or fate.)

Our changed and mingled souls are grown
    To such acquaintance now,
15 That if each would resume their own,
    Alas! we know not how.
We have each other so engrossed
That each is in the union lost.

And thus we can no absence know,
20   Nor shall we be confined;
Our active souls will daily go
    To learn each other's mind.
Nay, should we never meet to sense,
Our souls would hold intelligence.

25 Inspirèd with a flame divine,
    I scorn to court a stay;[2]
For from that noble soul of thine
    I ne'er can be away.
But I shall weep when thou dost grieve;
30 Nor can I die whilst thou dost live.

By my own temper I shall guess
    At thy felicity,
And only like my happiness
    Because it pleaseth thee.
35 Our hearts at any time will tell
If thou or I be sick or well.

All honor, sure, I must pretend,
    All that is good or great:

---

1. **M. A.** Mary Aubrey, a member of Philips's literary circle of friends
2. **court a stay.** Postpone their parting
3. **Orinda and Rosania.** Pseudonyms for Philips and Aubrey

She that would be Rosania's friend
40   Must be at least complete.
If I have any bravery,
    'Tis cause I have so much of thee.

Thy leiger soul in me shall lie,
    And all thy thoughts reveal;
45 Then back again with mine shall fly,
    And thence to me shall steal.
Thus still to one another tend:
Such is the sacred name of friend.

Thus our twin souls in one shall grow,
50   And teach the world new love,
Redeem the age and sex, and show
    A flame fate dares not move:
And courting death to be our friend,
Our lives, together too, shall end.

55 A dew shall dwell upon our tomb
    Of such a quality
That fighting armies, thither come,
    Shall reconcilèd be.
We'll ask no epitaph, but say:
60 ORINDA and ROSANIA.[3]

"The Garden" by Andrew Marvell

How vainly men themselves amaze
To win the palm, the oak, or bays,
And their uncessant labors see
Crowned from some single herb or tree,
5 Whose short and narrow-vergèd shade
Does prudently their toils upbraid;
While all flowers and all trees do close
To weave the garlands of repose!

Fair Quiet, have I found thee here,
10 And Innocence, thy sister dear?
Mistaken long, I sought you then
In busy companies of men.
Your sacred plants, if here below,
Only among the plants will grow;
15 Society is all but rude,
To this delicious solitude.

No white nor red was ever seen
So amorous as this lovely green.
Fond lovers, cruel as their flame,
20 Cut in these trees their mistress' name:
Little, alas, they know or heed

How far these beauties hers exceed!
Fair trees, wheresoe'er your barks I wound,
No name shall but your own be found.

25 When we have run our passion's heat,
Love hither makes his best retreat.
The gods, that mortal beauty chase,
Still in a tree did end their race:
Apollo hunted Daphne[1] so,
30 Only that she might laurel grow;
And Pan did after Syrinx[2] speed,
Not as a nymph, but for a reed.

What wondrous life in this I lead!
Ripe apples drop about my head;
35 The luscious clusters of the vine
Upon my mouth do crush their wine;
The nectarine and curious peach
Into my hands themselves do reach;
Stumbling on melons as I pass,
40 Insnared with flowers, I fall on grass.

Meanwhile the mind, from pleasure less,
Withdraws into its happiness;
The mind, that ocean where each kind
Does straight its own resemblance find;
45 Yet it creates, transcending these,
Far other worlds and other seas,
Annihilating all that's made
To a green thought in a green shade.

Here at the fountain's sliding foot,
50 Or at some fruit tree's mossy root,
Casting the body's vest aside,
My soul into the boughs does glide:
There like a bird it sits and sings,
Then whets and combs its silver wings,
55 And, till prepared for longer flight,
Waves in its plumes the various light.

Such was that happy garden-state,
While man there walked without a mate:
After a place so pure and sweet,
60 What other help could yet be meet!
But 'twas beyond a mortal's share
To wander solitary there:
Two paradises 'twere in one
To live in paradise alone.

---

1. **Apollo . . . Daphne.** In Greek mythology Daphne
was transformed into a laurel tree to end Apollo's pursuit.
2. **Pan . . . Syrinx.** Syrinx was changed into a reed to
escape Pan.

65 How well the skillful gardener drew
Of flowers and herbs this dial new,
Where from above the milder sun
Does through a fragrant zodiac run;
And as it works, th' industrious bee
70 Computes its time as well as we!
How could such sweet and wholesome hours
Be reckoned but with herbs and flowers?

Song ("Why so pale and wan . . .")
by Sir John Suckling

Why so pale and wan, fond lover?
    Prithee,[3] why so pale?
Will, when looking well can't move her,
    Looking ill prevail?
5   Prithee, why so pale?

Why so dull and mute, young sinner?
    Prithee, why so mute?
Will, when speaking well can't win her,
    Saying nothing do 't?
10   Prithee, why so mute?

Quit, quit, for shame; this will not move,
    This cannot take her.
If of herself she will not love,
    Nothing can make her:
15   The devil take her!

"Corinna's Going A-Maying"
by Robert Herrick

Get up! get up for shame! the blooming morn
Upon her wings presents the god unshorn.
    See how Aurora throws her fair
    Fresh-quilted colors through the air.
5   Get up, sweet slug-a-bed, and see
    The dew bespangling herb and tree.
Each flower has wept and bowed toward the east
Above an hour since, yet you not dressed;
    Nay, not so much as out of bed?
10   When all the birds have matins said,
    And sung their thankful hymns, 'tis sin,
    Nay, profanation to keep in,
Whenas a thousand virgins on this day
Spring, sooner than the lark, to fetch in May.

---

3. **prithee.** Please

ADDITIONAL QUESTIONS AND ACTIVITIES

Students may discuss the following questions.

• What is the attitude of the speaker in Andrew Marvell's poem toward the garden he describes?
Answer. The speaker loves the garden for its quiet and innocence (lines 9–10), and he prefers it to socializing with other people.

• What attitude does the speaker have toward women and relationships between men and women?
Answer. The speaker has a cynical attitude toward romantic relationships, describing "Fond lovers" as "cruel as their flame" for carving their mistresses' names in the trunks of trees (lines 19–20) and saying that the "white [and] red" that symbolize romance were never so "amorous" as the green of the garden (lines 17–18). The speaker goes on to say that the truest paradise was the Garden of Eden before the creation of Eve, when Adam enjoyed both the beauty of nature and perfect solitude.

SONG ("WHY SO PALE AND WAN . . .")

About the Author. Sir John Suckling (1609–1642) enrolled at Trinity College, Cambridge, at the age of fourteen but left without taking a degree. Suckling's father died one year later, and Suckling inherited vast estates. In many ways a model Cavalier, Suckling was known for his wit and extravagance. In 1638, he published a play, *Aglaura,* and a number of poems. In 1641, Suckling was implicated in a royalist plot against Parliamentary forces. England was headed toward civil war, and Suckling was pressed by Parliament to account for his actions. He fled to Paris and died a fugitive in France.

"CORINNA'S GOING A-MAYING"

About the Author. Robert Herrick (1591–1674) attended Cambridge University and was ordained in the Anglican Church in 1623. He enjoyed the literary society of London and was at first dismayed by his appointment to a rural congregation in Devonshire, but much of his poetry reveals the deep love he developed for the countryside. A Cavalier poet influenced by Ben Jonson and the Classical Latin poets, Herrick often wrote lyric verse on the *carpe diem* theme. One such poem, "To the Virgins, to Make Much of Time," became one of the most popular songs of the seventeenth century after William Lawes composed a tune for it. "Corinna's Going A-Maying" also expresses the *carpe diem* theme and displays Herrick's mastery of pastoral imagery.

"CORINNA'S GOING A-MAYING"

About the Selection. The tradition of celebrating May Day, or May 1, has very ancient roots. Springtime fertility rites were a part of the cultures of pagan Rome and the ancient civilizations of India, Egypt, Europe, and Mexico. In medieval England, people danced around maypoles and enjoyed performances of morris dances, in which traditional stories were acted out in pantomime. The Christian celebration of Easter largely took the place of the ancient rites but retained some fertility symbols, such as brightly colored eggs.

"TO LUCASTA, GOING TO THE WARS"

About the Author. A biography of Lovelace appears on page 451.

ADDITIONAL QUESTIONS AND ACTIVITIES

Students may discuss the following questions.

• What is the setting of "Corinna's Going A-Maying"? What does the speaker want Corinna to do? Why? What does he mean by "put on your foliage" in line 15? How does he want Corinna to dress herself, and why?

Answers. It is the month of May, and the speaker is eager to get outside and enjoy the celebration of spring. He wants Corinna to get out of bed and come with him. "Put on your foliage" means "get dressed"; he wants her to dress quickly and not worry about putting on jewelry because he's in a hurry and because she doesn't need fancy attire to go out and appreciate nature.

• What theme is expressed in stanza 5? What other poems in this unit have a similar theme?

Answers. The stanza expresses the *carpe diem* theme, one also treated in Marvell's "To His Coy Mistress."

• What situation is the speaker in "To Lucasta, Going to the Wars"

(cont.)

---

15 Rise, and put on your foliage, and be seen
To come forth, like the springtime, fresh and green,
　　And sweet as Flora. Take no care
　　For jewels for your gown or hair;
　　Fear not; the leaves will strew
20 　　Gems in abundance upon you;
Besides, the childhood of the day has kept,
Against you come, some orient pearls unwept;
　　Come and receive them while the light
　　Hangs on the dew-locks of the night,
25 　　And Titan on the eastern hill
　　Retires himself, or else stands still
Till you come forth. Wash, dress, be brief in praying:
Few beads are best when once we go a-Maying.

Come, my Corinna, come; and, coming, mark
30 How each field turns a street, each street a park
　　Made green and trimmed with trees; see how
　　Devotion gives each house a bough
　　Or branch: each porch, each door ere this,
　　An ark, a tabernacle is,
35 Made up of whitethorn neatly interwove,
As if here were those cooler shades of love.
　　Can such delights be in the street
　　And open fields, and we not see 't?
　　Come, we'll abroad; and let's obey
40 　　The proclamation made for May,
And sin no more, as we have done, by staying;
But, my Corinna, come, let's go a-Maying.

There's not a budding boy or girl this day
But is got up and gone to bring in May;
45 　　A deal of youth, ere this, is come
　　Back, and with whitethorn laden home.
　　Some have dispatched their cakes and cream
　　Before that we have left to dream;
　　And some have wept, and wooed, and plighted troth,
50 And chose their priest, ere we can cast off sloth.
　　Many a green-gown has been given,

　　Many a kiss, both odd and even;
　　Many a glance, too, has been sent
　　From out the eye, love's firmament;
55 Many a jest told of the keys betraying
　　This night, and locks picked; yet we're not a-
　　　　Maying.

Come, let us go while we are in our prime,
And take the harmless folly of the time.
　　We shall grow old apace, and die
60 　　Before we know our liberty.
　　Our life is short, and our days run
　　As fast away as does the sun;
And, as a vapor or a drop of rain
Once lost, can ne'er be found again,
65 　　So when or you or I are made
　　A fable, song, or fleeting shade,
　　All love, all liking, all delight
　　Lies drowned with us in endless night.
Then while time serves, and we are but decaying,
70 Come, my Corinna, come, let's go a-Maying.

"To Lucasta, Going to the Wars"
by Richard Lovelace

Tell me not, sweet, I am unkind,
　　That from the nunnery
Of thy chaste breast and quiet mind
　　To war and arms I fly.

5 True, a new mistress now I chase,
　　The first foe in the field;
And with a stronger faith embrace
　　A sword, a horse, a shield.

Yet this inconstancy is such
10 　　As you too shall adore;
I could not love thee, dear, so much,
　　Loved I not honor more.

ADDITIONAL QUESTIONS AND ACTIVITIES (CONT.)

facing? How has Lucasta responded to this situation? What does the speaker say to comfort her?

Answers. In "To Lucasta, Going to the Wars," the speaker is leaving his love to go to war. She is apparently upset at the prospect, and he tells her that she should not feel betrayed because their love is made possible by the same sense of honor that leads him to fight.

PREREADING

from *The Rubáiyát*
by Omar Khayyám, trans. by Edward FitzGerald

ABOUT THE AUTHOR AND THE TRANSLATOR

For much of his life, **Omar Khayyám** (or Kayyám—d. *circa* AD 1123) was supported by a pension from the sultan Arp-Arslan. His primary occupation was as a mathematician and astronomer, and his work on algebra became a standard text. The name *Khayyám* means "tent maker," possibly indicating his father's occupation.

Edward FitzGerald (1809–1883) grew up in Suffolk and attended Trinity College, Cambridge, where he was great friends with Thackeray and Tennyson. His family was wealthy, and his personality was such that upon graduation he retired to the countryside to pursue his studies in peace and seclusion. FitzGerald was and is regarded as a powerful and brilliant intellect, but none of his own poetry ever achieved popularity. His reputation as a poet rests entirely on his translation of Omar Khayyám's *The Rubáiyát*.

ABOUT THE SELECTION

The Rubáiyát is not a single work but a compilation of roughly five hundred epigrams, presented in quatrains, or *rubā´ī*, written throughout Khayyám's life. In his translation, FitzGerald modified the original ordering of the quatrains to increase their thematic coherence. In general, the epigrams express a rebellious dissatisfaction with orthodox belief. Many are satiric in tone. FitzGerald's life suggests that the idea, expressed by Khayyám, that one should try to get as much pleasure as possible from each passing moment is part of what attracted him to the Persian writer's work.

FitzGerald's translation also modifies Khayyám's rhyme scheme of four rhyming lines by unrhyming the third line. The content mirrors the rhyme scheme, as each third line expresses an idea that is completed in the fourth. This combination defines the "FitzGerald stanza," which has been used by other English writers such as Swinburne. The first edition of FitzGerald's *The Rubáiyát,* containing only seventy-five quatrains, was published in 1859. The definitive fourth edition (1879) includes one hundred one stanzas. Of these, forty-nine are translations of individual quatrains from the Persian original, and forty-four are condensations of one or more quatrains. The others are based on various sources.

In England, the book was virtually ignored for two years, but gradually won great popularity after being discovered by and receiving high praise from the poet Dante Gabriel Rossetti.

GOALS/OBJECTIVES

Studying this lesson will enable students to

- appreciate multicultural lyric poetry in translation
- understand the pros and cons of accepting the advice, *"Carpe diem!"*
- compare themes in works of literature of different cultures
- describe the literary accomplishments of Edward FitzGerald and Omar Khayyám

ADDITIONAL RESOURCES

READER'S GUIDE
- Selection Worksheet, 6.10

ASSESSMENT PORTFOLIO
- Selection Check Test, 4.6.19
- Selection Test, 4.6.20

ENRICHMENT ACTIVITIES

- Have students list advantages and disadvantages of living for today. They can make a pro and con chart. Refer them to the Language Arts Survey, 4.3, "Strategies for Decision Making." They can discuss ways to balance these advantages.

- Encourage students to interview some adults and ask them to recount stories that support or show problems with living for today.

SUPPORT FOR LEP STUDENTS

Explain that the numbered stanzas are separate pieces. There is some continuity of themes among them, but each can be understood on its own.

ADDITIONAL VOCABULARY
tassel—hanging; decorative tuft of threads
husband—grow; manage

MULTICULTURAL EXTENSION

The Rubáiyát of Omar Khayyám brilliantly expresses the *carpe diem,* or "seize the day," theme also seen in several English poems in this unit: Andrew Marvell's "To His Coy Mistress" and Robert Herrick's "Corinna's Going A-Maying." Edward FitzGerald's translation, while true to the spirit of Khayyám's verses, is loose enough to be considered nearly a separate work. The sensuality and beauty of this translation greatly influenced English poetry in the late nineteenth century, and it is now better known than the original version from Persia.

ANSWERS TO GUIDED READING QUESTIONS

❶ A book of poetry, a jug of wine, a loaf of bread, and the presence of the speaker's beloved would turn a wilderness into paradise.

❷ The speaker says we should live for today: "take the Cash, and let the Credit go."

ADDITIONAL QUESTIONS AND ACTIVITIES

• In line 8, the speaker says we should not "heed the rumble of a distant Drum." What might this distant rumbling symbolize? Why should we ignore it? How does the attitude toward death expressed in *The Rubáiyát* compare with the attitude expressed in John Donne's Meditation 17 ("Perchance he for whom this bell tolls . . .")?

Answers. The distant rumbling might symbolize death. The speaker seems to think that since death is inevitable but distant, it makes sense to enjoy life while we can and not let a preoccupation with mortality spoil the time we have on earth. The speaker in Meditation 17, on the other hand, seems to think that it is appropriate to think about death and suffer at the thought, since this suffering brings us closer to God.

• Students might role play a conversation between the speaker in this poem and the speaker in Meditation 17 in which they discuss or debate the appropriate attitude people should have toward death.

VOCABULARY FROM THE SELECTION

aureate

sans

Persia

FROM

The Rubáiyát

OMAR KHAYYÁM, TRANS. BY EDWARD FITZGERALD

❶
What four things would turn a wilderness into paradise for the speaker of this poem?

❷
Does the speaker think we should live for today or for tomorrow?

12

A Book of Verses underneath the bough,
A jug of Wine, a Loaf of Bread—and Thou
   Beside me singing in the Wilderness—
Oh, Wilderness were Paradise enow!

13

5   Some for the Glories of This World; and some
Sigh for the Prophet's[1] Paradise to come;
   Ah, take the Cash, and let the Credit go,
Nor heed the rumble of a distant Drum!

14

Look to the blowing Rose about us—"Lo,
10 Laughing," she says, "into the world I blow,
   At once the silken tassel of my purse
Tear, and its Treasure on the Garden throw."

15

And those who husbanded the Golden Grain,
And those who flung it into the winds like Rain,
15   Alike to no such <u>aureate</u> Earth are turned
As, buried once, Men want dug up again.

---

1. **Prophet's.** Mohammed's

WORDS FOR EVERYDAY USE:
   au • re • ate (ô´rē it) *adj.,* splendid or brilliant

The Basket of Apples. Paul Cézanne, 1839–1906.
Oil on canvas, circa 1895, 65.5 x 81.3 cm.
Helen Birch Bartlett Memorial Collection

16

The Worldly Hope men set their Hearts upon
Turns Ashes—or it prospers; and anon,
   Like Snow upon the Desert's dusty Face,
20   Lighting a little hour or two—is gone.

17

Thin, in this battered Caravanserai[2]
Whose Portals are alternate Night and Day,
   How Sultán after Sultán with his pomp
Abode his destined Hour, and went his way.

18

25   They say the Lion and the Lizard keep
The Courts where Jamshyd[3] gloried and drank deep;
   and Bahrám,[4] that great Hunter—the Wild Ass
Stamps o'er his Head, but cannot break his Sleep.

---

2. **Caravanserai.** Inn
3. **Jamshyd.** In Persian myth, a king of the fairies who
was forced to live a human life because he boasted of his
immortality
4. **Bahrám.** A king who was lost while hunting a wild ass

❶
*What is the
common fate of
all? What
happens to
people's hopes?*

❷
*Why cannot the
great hunter be
awakened? Of
what significance
are his feats now?*

ART NOTE

Still-life paintings, like Cézanne's *The Basket of Apples,* focus on the concrete objects associated with human life. Some still lifes display the tools of a particular profession or craft; others show items of food and other objects that suggest domestic life. Students might discuss why a still life—especially one with apples, cookies, and a wine bottle—is an appropriate illustration for the *carpe diem* theme.

ANSWERS TO GUIDED READING QUESTIONS

❶ All must die. People's hopes are either dashed, or they come true but provide only fleeting happiness.

❷ The "Sleep" of the great hunter is actually death. His feats are of little significance, since the animal he once hunted now stamps on his grave.

LITERARY TECHNIQUE

You might draw students' attention to the **simile** in stanza 16, in which prospered hopes are compared to "Snow upon the Desert's dusty Face." Ask them to describe the image this simile creates in their minds. How does this image support the poem's *carpe diem* theme?

Answer. The image of snow falling in the desert and immediately melting underscores the fleeting nature of life. Since life is so brief, the speaker is saying, people should enjoy it while it lasts and not fasten their hopes to impermanent things.

VOCABULARY IN CONTEXT

• Although Cindy's dark hair was lovely, she sometimes envied Christie's <u>aureate</u> tresses.

470 TEACHER'S EDITION

ANSWER TO GUIDED READING QUESTION

❶ Since death is inevitable and eternal, we should enjoy the pleasures of this world—such as wine and song—while we can.

ADDITIONAL QUESTIONS AND ACTIVITIES

• What is the speaker's attitude toward the ancient Cæsar's death? What benefit does his death provide in the present?

Answers. The speaker seems grateful to the Cæsar, whose blood fertilized the earth and made possible the bloom of a beautiful rose that the speaker can appreciate in the present.

• What is the theme of stanzas 19 and 20? How does it make you feel about the cycle of life and death?

Answers. The theme of these stanzas might be stated: "The natural world is full of both death and sensual pleasures, the former making the latter possible." The cycle of life and death seems benevolent and beautiful as the poem describes it.

CROSS-CURRICULAR ACTIVITIES

Biology. Interested students might investigate to what extent stanzas 19 and 20 describe scientific truths. How do the bodies of dead plants and animals make life possible for later organisms?

VOCABULARY IN CONTEXT

• "Women are much more beautiful *sans* makeup," Pamela said, viewing the supermarket's display of fashion magazines with disgust.

19

30   I sometimes think that never blows so red
The Rose as where some buried Cæsar bled;
   That every Hyacinth⁵ the Garden wears
Dropped in her Lap from some once lovely Head.

20

And this reviving Herb whose tender Green
Fledges the River-Lip on which we lean—
35   Ah, lean upon it lightly! for who knows
From what once lovely Lip it springs unseen!

21

Ah, my Belovéd, fill the cup that clears
TODAY of past Regrets and future Fears:
   Tomorrow!—Why, Tomorrow I may be
40   Myself with Yesterday's sev'n thousand Years.

22

For some we loved, the loveliest and the best
That from his Vintage rolling Time hath pressed,
   Have drunk their Cup a Round or two before,
And one by one crept silently to rest.

23

45   And we, that now make merry in the Room
They left, and Summer dresses in new bloom,
   Ourselves must we beneath the Couch of Earth
Descend—ourselves to make a Couch—for whom?

24

Ah, make the most of what we yet may spend,
50   Before we too into the Dust descend;
   Dust into Dust, and under Dust to lie,
Sans Wine, sans Song, sans Singer, and—sans End! ■

❶
What does the speaker think we should do, given that we shall all die?

---

5. **Hyacinth.** A plant of the lily family

WORDS FOR EVERYDAY USE: **sans** (sänz) *prep.,* without

Reviewing the Selection

1. What, according to stanza 12, is the speaker's recipe for happiness? What simple needs does he have? What is sufficient to create, for him, a paradise on Earth?

2. According to stanza 15, people differ considerably from seeds in what happens to them when they are buried. What is the difference?

3. What, according to stanzas 17 and 18, happens to all people, including great sultans?

4. What, according to stanzas 19 and 20, nourishes hyacinths and herbs?

5. Given the foregoing observations, what advice does the speaker offer in stanzas 21–24? What line in stanza 24 sums up this advice?

Connections (Questions for Writing or Discussion)

---

1. *Carpe diem* is a Latin phrase meaning "Seize the day!" What does this phrase mean to you? How might you seize the day? Give examples of what you might do today or tomorrow to seize that day. According to Khayyám, should we seize the day? Why, or why not? Do you agree with Khayyám? Why, or why not?

2. *The Rubáiyát* refers frequently to dead heroes and kings. What kinds of stories and comments about these dead great leaders does Khayyám offer? Give examples and generalize from them. According to Khayyám, what is important about these personages? What reasoning might support his views? Is greatness important? What attitudes about human greatness are expressed in the epigrams? What would Khayyám think of his current fame?

3. Compare the attitudes about time and pleasure expressed in *The Rubáiyát* with those expressed in Marvell's "To His Coy Mistress" (page 457) or to those expressed in Herrick's "Corinna's Going A-Maying" (page 465). What similarities exist in the three poets' views?

ANSWERS FOR REVIEWING THE SELECTION

1. The speaker would be happy to sit in the wilderness with a book of poetry, some wine and bread, and his beloved by his side. Intellectual or artistic stimulation, food for his body, and love are enough to create a paradise for him.

2. Seeds sprout and turn the earth golden with grain, whereas human beings, once dead, simply stay buried.

3. All people, the anonymous and the great, must die.

4. The bodies of people who have died nourish these plants.

5. The speaker advises readers or listeners to enjoy the sensual pleasures of the world before it is too late and life is over. Line 49 summarizes this advice: "Ah, make the most of what we yet may spend."

ANSWERS FOR CONNECTIONS

1. *Carpe diem* advises people not to waste precious time worrying about the past or the future, but to enjoy the present. For example, instead of worrying about what it would feel like to be rejected, a person might go ahead and submit a poem to the school literary magazine. Khayyám does think people should seize the day, because life is short and death is forever.

2. Khayyám typically alludes to the great deeds of a hero but then counters this by observing that the hero is now dead, like all the others of that age. In the poet's view, the only importance of these people in the present is that their bodies fertilize the earth and allow flowers to grow. Greatness is, in the long run, not important, because everyone meets a common end. Khayyám would probably not place much value on his own fame, although he might be delighted to know that his poetry lives on and inspires others to "seize the day" while they are alive.

3. *The Rubáiyát* shares a common attitude toward time and pleasure with the Marvell and Herrick poems. In "To His Coy Mistress,"

(cont.)

ANSWERS FOR CONNECTIONS (CONT.)

Marvell points out that couples do not have unlimited time to spend adoring each other in an abstract way, and that they must therefore enjoy the pleasures of love before their time runs out. In "Corinna's Going A-Maying," the speaker urges his love to get out of bed and enjoy a spring day, making the larger point that life is too short to waste time.

UNIT REVIEW

The Early Seventeenth Century

VOCABULARY FROM THE SELECTIONS

aureate, 469	dandle, 435	invoke, 430	sans, 470
baleful, 432	disheveled, 434	obdurate, 432	sovereign, 432
cleft, 415	ethereal, 431	omnipotent, 431	steep, 452
contrive, 446	exalt, 437	perdition, 431	tribulation, 421
covetousness, 421	guile, 436	proboscis, 435	undefiled, 445
coy, 434	hermitage, 453	promontory, 421	wrought, 421
coyness, 458	impious, 431	recourse, 421	zephyr, 435
dalliance, 435	incorruptible, 445	ruminating, 436	
damask, 435	intermit, 421	sanctitude, 433	

LITERARY TERMS

allegory, 449	paradox, 419, 428
allusion, 440	personification, 419
carpe diem, 457	pun, 440
concrete poem, 425	purpose, 422
epic, 438	stanza, 461
hyperbole, 417	speaker, 427, 440
image, 461	theme, 422, 428, 454
metaphor, 417, 423, 438, 454, 460	

GENRE STUDIES

1. **Metaphysical Poetry.** Metaphysical poetry is characterized by elaborate, unusual comparisons called conceits. Find examples of conceits in the following Metaphysical poems from the unit: Song, Holy Sonnet 10, "Easter Wings," and "To His Coy Mistress." (The last poem, like other works by Marvell, belongs to both the Metaphysical and the Cavalier schools.)

2. **Cavalier Poetry.** Who were the Cavaliers? What subjects did they write about? What literary form did they prefer? What meanings does the word *cavalier* have? (Consult a dictionary if necessary.) Of the Cavalier poets—Herrick, Suckling, Lovelace, and Waller—which was the most cavalier in the sense of "carefree"? Which wrote poetry that was quite serious and not at all cavalier in that sense?

3. **Allegory.** What is an allegory? How does an allegory work? In what ways is the medieval play *Everyman,* in Unit 3, similar to *The Pilgrim's Progress*?

4. **Epic Poetry.** An epic poem is grand in scope. What is the subject of Milton's epic *Paradise Lost*? What purpose did Milton have for writing the poem?

THEMATIC STUDIES

5. **The *Carpe Diem* Theme.** What do the words *carpe diem* mean? What poems in this unit and in the Selections for Additional Reading best illustrate the *carpe diem* theme? Who is being addressed in each of these poems, and what message is being conveyed?

HISTORICAL AND BIOGRAPHICAL STUDIES

6. **Literature of the English Civil War.** The Puritans and the Cavaliers opposed one another in what great conflict? What differing attitudes and beliefs did the Puritans and the Cavaliers have? How are these differences reflected in the literature in this unit?

▶These prompts are suitable as topics for research papers. Refer to the Language Arts Survey, 4.20–4.34, "Research Skills." To evaluate research papers, see the evaluation forms for writing, revising, and proofreading in the *Assessment Portfolio,* 7.1–7.10.

▶These prompts can be adapted for use as topics for oral reports or debates. To evaluate these projects, see the evaluation forms in the *Assessment Portfolio,* 7.17–7.19.

LANGUAGE LAB EDITING FOR ERRORS IN MODIFIERS

A **modifier** is a word that provides additional information about a noun or a verb. Two kinds of modifiers are **adjectives** and **adverbs**.

MODIFIER USAGE

Modifiers with Action and Linking Verbs. An adjective modifies the subject of a linking verb. An adverb modifies an action verb.

LINKING VERB AND ADJECTIVE — He **is quiet** but makes a strong impression on everyone.

ACTION VERB AND ADVERB — Katrina **drove slowly** through the center of town.

Comparison of Adjectives and Adverbs. Each modifier has three forms of comparison: **positive**, **comparative**, and **superlative**. To show a decrease in the quality of a modifier, use the words *less* and *least*.

ADJECTIVES — *sweet, sweeter, sweetest, less sweet, least sweet*

ADVERBS — *shamefully, more shamefully, most shamefully, less shamefully, least shamefully*

Some modifiers form comparative and superlative degrees irregularly.

EXAMPLES — *good, better, best, bad, worse, worst*

Use the comparative degree when comparing two things. Use the superlative degree when comparing more than two things.

COMPARATIVE — Who is the **more helpful** person, Dwayne or Lyle?

SUPERLATIVE — That willow tree is the **smallest** of the six in the backyard.

Illogical and Double Comparisons. An illogical comparison occurs when one member of a group is compared with the group of which it is a part. A double comparison occurs when two comparative forms or two superlative forms are used to modify the same word.

ILLOGICAL — Callie wanted a race horse more than teenagers her age.

LOGICAL — Callie wanted a race horse more than other teenagers her age.

DOUBLE COMPARISON — Jordan was **even more angrier** today than he was yesterday.

SINGLE COMPARISON — Jordan was **even more angry** today than he was yesterday.

Double Negatives. A double negative is an nonstandard construction in which two negative words are used instead of one.

DOUBLE NEGATIVE — That goat **didn't chew no** rosebushes.

SINGLE NEGATIVE — That goat **chewed no** rosebushes. *or* That goat **didn't chew any** rosebushes.

DOUBLE NEGATIVE — I **cannot hardly** concentrate because of the noise next door.

SINGLE NEGATIVE — I **can hardly** concentrate because of the noise next door.

MODIFIER USAGE

Good and Well.

NONSTANDARD   John Donne wrote poems **good.**

STANDARD   John Donne wrote **good** poems.

STANDARD   John Donne wrote **well.**

EXERCISE Correcting Errors in Modifier Usage

Rewrite the following sentences, correcting all errors in modifier usage that you can find. Some sentences are correct.

EXAMPLE That elephant is **more larger** than any other animal in the zoological park.

That elephant is larger than any other animal in the zoological park.

1. I didn't have no knowledge of the Cavalier poets before this year.

2. We walked slow through the new museum exhibits.

3. "That was the most loveliest reading of George Herbert's 'Easter Wings' that I have ever heard," Sybil said.

4. Lady Mary Wroth, the niece of poet Sir Philip Sidney, wrote good herself.

5. Donne is one of the more well-known of the Metaphysical poets.

6. The hurricane winds are more bad now than they were one hour ago.

7. John Milton's *Paradise Lost* is a familiar tale, but some believe it is one of the most better versions of this tale around.

8. My younger brother Sam already reads well.

9. I am even more happier today than I was yesterday.

10. Do you prefer Andrew Marvell, or do you believe Robert Herrick is the skillfuller poet?

LANGUAGE ARTS SURVEY

For additional help, see the Language Arts Survey, 2.19–2.23 and 2.35.

ANSWERS FOR LANGUAGE LAB

Responses will vary. Possible responses are given.

1. I didn't have any knowledge of the Cavalier poets before this year.

2. We walked slowly through the new museum exhibits.

3. "That was the loveliest reading of George Herbert's 'Easter Wings' that I have ever heard," Sybil said.

4. Lady Mary Wroth, the niece of poet Sir Philip Sidney, wrote well herself.

5. Donne is one of the most well-known of the Metaphysical poets.

6. The hurricane winds are worse now than they were one hour ago.

7. John Milton's *Paradise Lost* is a familiar tale, but some believe it is one of the best versions of this tale around.

8. Correct

9. I am happier today than I was yesterday.

10. Do you prefer Andrew Marvell, or do you believe Robert Herrick is the more skillful poet?

LITERARY SKILLS AND CONCEPTS
- Alliteration, 499
- Allusion, 496
- Anaphora, 500
- Anecdote, 548
- Antithesis, 532
- Aphorism, 532
- Connotation, 541
- Couplet, 532
- Denotation, 540
- Fantasy, 519
- Irony, 519
- Journal, 510
- Meter, 489
- Mode, 537
- Novel, 527
- Point of View, 510
- Slant Rhyme, 488
- Thesis and Argument, 537

WRITING SKILLS AND CONCEPTS
- Anecdote, 548
- Bill of Rights, 489
- Credo, 527
- Dictionary Definition, 541
- Editorial, 537
- Epitaph, 500
- Extended Definition, 541
- Judicial Opinion, 537
- Personal Account, 510
- Personal Aphorisms, 532
- Treaty, 519

GRAMMAR, USAGE, AND MECHANICS SKILLS AND CONCEPTS
- Correcting Sentence Fragments, 489
- Greek and Latin Roots, 538
- Other Problems in Subject/Verb Agreement, 496
- Usage Problems I, 566
- Usage Problems II, 566
- Usage Problems III, 566
- Using Vivid Verbs, 500

OTHER LANGUAGE ARTS SKILLS AND CONCEPTS
- Evaluating Sources, 522
- Generalizing, 502
- Informal Note-taking, 543
- Interpersonal Communication, 498
- Observing, 500
- Reading Actively: Predicting, 534
- Reading Actively: Questioning, 492
- Sentence-Completion Questions, 490
- Tone and Voice, 519
- Using Dictionaries, 541
- Using Reference Works, 512
- Using the Card Catalog, 520
- Using Thesauruses, 529

UNIT 7 THE RESTORATION AND THE EIGHTEENTH CENTURY (1660–1785)

A Scene from the Beggar's Opera. William Hogarth, circa 1728–29.
Tate Gallery, London/Art Resource, NY

GOALS/OBJECTIVES

Studying this unit will enable students to

- interpret British Enlightenment literature
- name and describe three major periods of British Enlightenment literature and their main practitioners
- describe the scientific principles behind the Enlightenment
- explain the significance of the Greek and Roman classics to Enlightenment writers
- describe the obstacles faced by women writers during the Restoration and the Enlightenment
- define and identify satire and explain the significance of satire as a form of Enlightenment writing

The general ORDER, since the whole began,

Is kept in Nature, and is kept in man. . . .

All Nature is but art, unknown to thee;

All chance, direction, which thou canst not see;

All discord, harmony not understood;

All partial evil, universal good:

And, spite of pride, in erring reason's spite,

One truth is clear: Whatever is, is RIGHT.

—Alexander Pope,
from "An Essay on Man"

477

ART NOTE

Painter and engraver William Hogarth (1697–1764) gained great fame as a satirist of English society. Writer John Gay (1685–1732), a friend of Alexander Pope, was also well known for his satiric wit. In this painting, Hogarth illustrates a scene from Gay's *Beggar's Opera* (1728), which satirized political corruption and Italian opera. Such satire epitomizes the wit and intellectualism of eighteenth-century literature.

HISTORICAL NOTE

England's constitutional monarchy was the exception in European politics. On the Continent, absolutist monarchs held sway from 1643 until 1789. France's Louis XIV, XV, and XVI are perhaps the best known examples. With the Glorious Revolution, a powerful Protestant minority assumed rule over the Roman Catholics in Scotland and in Ireland.

QUOTABLES

66 Here lies a great and mighty king whose promise none relies on;/He never said a foolish thing,/ Nor ever did a wise one. 99

—John Wilmot, Earl of Rochester

66 This is very true: for my words are my own, and my actions are my ministers. 99

—King Charles II

THEMATIC CURRENTS

Use the following selections to explore these themes with your students.

POLITICAL AND SOCIAL COMMENTARY

- from *Gulliver's Travels,* 511
- from *Oroonoko,* 521
- "A Brief to Free a Slave," 533
- "A Modest Proposal," 550
- from *Candide,* 557

REASON

- "A Song for St. Cecilia's Day," 491
- Couplets from *An Essay on Criticism,* 528
- from *A Dictionary of the English Language,* 538
- from *The Life of Samuel Johnson, LL. D.,* 542
- from *The Spectator,* 554

WOMEN WRITERS

- "The Introduction . . . ," 484
- "Pressed by the Moon . . . ," 497
- from *Oroonoko,* 521
- "To All Writing Ladies," 549
- "Love Armed," 549
- "The Lover . . . ," 550

Charles II of England. Philippe de Champaigne. Cleveland Museum of Art, Giraudon/Art Resource, NY

THE MONARCHY RESTORED

The **Restoration** in England began in 1660 when **Charles II** became king, ending the Protestant Interregnum. With the monarchy restored and Parliament meeting again, an end to the political differences between Protestants and Catholics was also in sight.

James II succeeded Charles II in 1685. James, like his brother Charles, was Catholic. This fact precipitated what is known as the **Glorious Revolution.** Parliamentary leaders, leery of another Catholic ruler, applied pressure to James II, who abdicated the throne. **William and Mary,** staunch Protestants both, became joint monarchs in 1688. William and Mary ceded Parliament the right to levy taxes, along with other wide-ranging powers, and so moved the country toward a form of government known as **constitutional monarchy.**

Following the deaths of William and Mary, Anne, the sister of Mary, became queen. Among **Queen Anne's** achievements was the creation in 1707 of the nation of Great Britain, formed by the union of England and Scotland. Anne was succeeded by **George I** in 1714. George's prime minister, Robert Walpole, formed the cabinet system of ministers chosen from Parliament to aid the monarch.

SCIENCE, PHILOSOPHY, AND REASON

Amid this political upheaval, philosophers, writers, and scientists were defining new ways of looking at the world in which they lived. By discovering the laws of motion and gravitation that governed the movements of heavenly and earthly bodies, **Sir Isaac Newton** had revealed an orderly, clockwork universe regulated by rational principles. This idea of a natural

LITERARY EVENTS

▶ = British Events

▶1668. John Dryden appointed Poet Laureate
▶1667. John Milton publishes *Paradise Lost*
1664. Jean-Baptiste Poquelin Molière's play *Tartuffe* first performed
1664. Jean Racine publishes his play *Phœdra*

▶1681. John Dryden publishes *Absalom and Achitophel*
▶1678. John Bunyan publishes *The Pilgrim's Progress*

1660	1665	1670	1675	1680

HISTORICAL EVENTS

▶1660. Restoration of the monarchy of King Charles II
▶1660–1685. Reign of King Charles II
1664. English take over town of Nieuw Amsterdam from Dutch and rename it New York
▶1666. Great Fire burns 80 percent of London
1667. Qing dynasty begins in China
1669. Rembrandt van Rijn (painter) dies

1672. Ann Bradstreet dies
▶1673. Test Act compels Anglicanism
▶1674. John Milton dies

▶1678. Popish Plot uncovered; renewed persecution of Catholics
1681. The dodo bird is hunted to extinction

order discoverable by reason attracted many adherents. People came to believe that the human intellect could discover natural laws that would solve social, political, and economic problems. Because of this emphasis on the power of intellect over feeling, the period is sometimes called the **Enlightenment**, or **Age of Reason.**

Among the influential figures of the Enlightenment were the German philosopher and writer **Immanuel Kant** (1724–1804); the English doctor, philosopher, and writer **John Locke,** (1632–1704); and the Scottish philosopher and economist **Adam Smith** (1723–1790).

Kant's philosophy held that knowledge is a combination of sensation and understanding, a synthesis of sensual perception and the principles, or laws, of thought. Locke, who has been called the "founder of the analytic philosophy of mind," published the *Two Treatises of Government,* which disputed the divine right of kings and popularized the idea of **"natural rights."** The economist Smith, in his book *The Wealth of Nations,* proposed that even economics is governed by a system of natural laws that work in an ordered and rational way, if not interfered with by governments and monopolies.

Queen Anne   *Popperfoto/Archive Photos*

NEOCLASSICAL LITERATURE

In their search for rationality and order, many writers of the Enlightenment rediscovered the classic works of the ancient Greeks and Romans and emulated them. For this reason, they are called **Neoclassicists.** The Neoclassical literature of the eighteenth century made use of classical forms and allusions and promoted ideals of harmony, tradition, and reason. Popular forms of Neoclassical writing included the **essay, rhymed couplets, satire, parody,** and the formal letter, or **epistle.** The first **novels** were also written during this period. The literature of the period is notable for its wittiness and its emphasis on the social interactions.

▶1688. Aphra Behn publishes *Oroonoko,* the first novel

▶1690. John Locke publishes *Letter Concerning Toleration, An Essay Concerning Human Understanding,* and *Two Treatises of Government*

1685	1690	1695	1700	1705

▶1685–1688. Reign of James II   1692. Salem witch trials, nineteen persons executed   ▶1700. John Dryden dies
▶1687. Isaac Newton publishes *Principia,* redefining modern science   ▶1702–1714. Reign of Queen Anne
▶1688–1689. "Glorious Revolution" of William and Mary
▶1689. Aphra Behn dies
▶1689. Bill of Rights affirms supremacy of Parliament
▶1689–1701. Reign of King William III and Queen Mary II (Mary dies 1694)

INTRODUCTION   **479**

CROSS-CURRICULAR ACTIVITIES

Students can research the art and music of the Restoration and the Enlightenment in England. Suggest that they research painters such as William Hogarth, Thomas Gainsborough, Sir Joshua Reynolds, and Angelica Kauffmann; architects such as Lord Burlington and Robert Adam; or composers such as George Frideric Handel and Henry Purcell. Students should note whether the work of these artists exhibits elements of Neoclassicism, and if so, in what ways. Students can present their findings in a written report or in a brief presentation to the class. Encourage students to include photocopies or slides of artworks or recordings of musical compositions.

QUOTABLES

66 Two things fill the mind with awe, the more often and the more seriously reflection concentrates upon them: The starry heaven above me and the moral law within me. 99

—Immanuel Kant

LITERARY CURRENTS

Use the following selections to explore these techniques with your students.

COUPLET
- Couplets from *An Essay on Criticism,* 528

ESSAY
- "To All Writing Ladies," 549
- "A Modest Proposal," 550
- from *The Spectator,* 554

JOURNAL
- from *The Diary of Samuel Pepys,* 501
- from *The Life of Samuel Johnson, LL. D.,* 542

IRONY
- "The Introduction," 484
- from *Gulliver's Travels,* 511
- from *A Dictionary of the English Language,* 538
- "A Modest Proposal," 550
- "A Short Song . . . ," 556

Samuel Pepys's Diary. *Masters and Fellows, Magdalene College, Cambridge*

There are three major divisions, or periods, of Enlightenment literature: **the Age of Dryden, the Age of Pope,** and **the Age of Johnson.** The Age of Dryden (1660–1700) began with the restoration of the monarchy and ended with the death of writer **John Dryden** (1631–1700). Dryden wrote many plays, poems, and essays. His satirical poem "Mac Flecknoe" appears to be an epic because of its grand scope and lofty language, but it actually ridicules its so-called "heroes." This style is called **mock heroic** poetry or **mock epic** poetry. Dryden's series of essays on literary criticism, including *An Essay of Dramatic Poesy,* presaged a new type of writing, the **critical essay.** This type of writing attempts to evaluate works of literature.

Drama made a comeback during this period. London theaters closed by the repressive Puritan government were reopened by Charles II. Refurbished and offering new forms of drama, the theaters became very popular with the middle and upper classes. Dryden's *All For Love,* a tragedy about Antony and Cleopatra, drew large audiences.

Today, many literary historians consider Dryden's prose writing the first modern prose. Other notable prose works of the time include **Samuel Pepys's** *Diary,* a journal of daily events in his life from 1660 to 1669, and **Aphra Behn's** *Oroonoko* (1688), a prose work about slavery in the West Indies. *Oroonoko* is one of the first (some argue *the* first) English **novels,** or extended works of prose fiction.

The Age of Pope (1700–1750), also called the **Augustan Age,** was the peak period of Neoclassicism. **Alexander Pope** (1688–1744), an admired poet of his time, was representative

LITERARY EVENTS

► = British Events

► 1726. Jonathan Swift publishes *Gulliver's Travels*

► 1719. Daniel Defoe publishes *Robinson Crusoe*

► 1711. Alexander Pope publishes *An Essay on Criticism*

► 1710. First English copyright law

1710	1715	1720	1725	1730

► 1707. Act of Union unites Scotland and England, creating Great Britain

► 1714–1727. Reign of King George I

· 1715. King Louis XIV (the Sun King) of France dies; Reign of King Louis XV of France begins

► 1727. Sir Isaac Newton dies

► 1727–1760. Reign of King George II

► 1729. John and Charles Wesley found Methodism at Oxford

HISTORICAL EVENTS

480 UNIT SEVEN / THE RESTORATION AND THE EIGHTEENTH CENTURY of the style, employing wit, rationality, and balance in his poetry. Pope's *The Rape of the Lock*, is a mock epic that satirizes the "battle of the sexes." Pope's *An Essay on Criticism*, a long **verse essay** in **heroic couplets**, exerted tremendous influence on literary criticism, and many well-known aphorisms still in use today come from it.

Pope was a member of a salon society in London that included other literary figures of the day, including **Jonathan Swift, Joseph Addison,** and **Sir Richard Steele.** Swift's satire was pointed and sharp, in contrast to Pope's, which was less barbed but equally devastating. Swift's *Gulliver's Travels* is famous for its satirization of the European political and intellectual landscape. Addison and Steele collaborated on two literary periodicals, *The Tattler* and *The Spectator,* groundbreaking examples of that new literary medium, the **periodical.** The most talented literary figures of the day contributed reflective **essays** in literature, art, politics, and society to the periodicals. **Daniel Defoe** wrote a major work that vies with Behn's for the title of first novel in the English language, *Robinson Crusoe* (1719).

The Restoration period is also called the **Augustan Age** because many writers openly imitated Greek and Roman literature. The term *Augustan* is a reference comparing King George I to Emperor Augustus Cæsar of Rome. Indeed, London was considered the center of the literary universe, much as ancient Rome was during the days of Augustus, Virgil, and Horace.

The Age of Johnson (1750–1798), named after **Samuel Johnson** (1709–1784), the most famous writer of his generation, bridges the span between the Enlightenment and the **Romantic Age.** During this time some writers began to move away from the ideals of Neoclassicism toward the freer, more emotional, more natural style of the Romantics.

Johnson, master of many forms of writing, including poetry, literary criticism, and prose fiction, is most renowned for his *Dictionary of the English Language.* Published in 1755, this was the first authoritative, definitive dictionary of English. Nine years in the making, the dictionary contained over 40,000 words and 114,000 quotations.

Johnson started his own periodical, *The Rambler,* which contained essays, allegories, and literary criticism written primarily by himself. In his later years he was an eminent figure in literary circles and founded a literary club. In May of 1763, he met **James Boswell** (1740–1795), whose *Life of Samuel Johnson, LL. D.,* presented the actions and opinions of the great man. Boswell's book is considered the first great modern English **biography.**

BIOGRAPHICAL NOTE

The term "bluestockings" was the label applied to a group of intellectual women who met in London in the latter part of the eighteenth century. Headed by critic and letter writer **Elizabeth Montagu** (1720–1800), these women met to discuss intellectual and social issues, including education and women's traditional role in society. Although most meetings were attended by women, some men, including Samuel Johnson and James Boswell, attended the discussions. The term "bluestocking" referred to inexpensive stockings worn by some members on informal occasions; the term was sometimes used derisively about any woman who dared to pursue intellectual activities.

LITERARY TECHNIQUE

During the late seventeenth century, British writers developed the **novel.** The novel can be seen as resulting, in part, from the rise of the bourgeoisie as a class. The novel neither borrowed from traditional sources for content nor celebrated kings. Rather, it celebrated the "common" man and woman. Various works qualify for the title "The First Novel," depending on how one defines the idea. Besides Behn, Defoe, and Swift, important early novelists include **Samuel Richardson** (1689–1761), **Henry Fielding** (1707–1754), **Tobias Smollett** (1721–1771), and **Laurence Sterne** (1713–1768).

►1755. Dr. Samuel Johnson completes his *Dictionary*

►1742. G. F. Handel's oratorio *Messiah* performed

1751. Denis Diderot publishes Volume I of *Encyclopédie*

1732. Benjamin Franklin publishes the first *Poor Richard's Almanack* and begins publishing *Philadelphia Zeitung,* the first foreign-language newspaper in the American colonies

1735	1740	1745	1750	1755

1735–1753. Carl Linnaeus publishes systematic classifications of plants, founds science of botany

1741. Antonio Vivaldi (composer) dies

►1744. Alexander Pope dies

►1745. Jonathan Swift dies

1750. Benjamin Franklin proves that lightning is an electrical phenomenon

1750. Johann Sebastian Bach (composer) dies

INTRODUCTION **481**

ART NOTE

The Great Fire of London lasted from September 2 to September 5, 1666. It remains the worst fire in the history of London. More than thirteen thousand homes and many important civic buildings were burned. People fled from the city to the countryside and swarmed the river Thames.

• Have students investigate how the fire started, how it spread, and why it was so destructive.

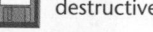

• Have students research or reason about what life was like for Londoners during the next few months after the fire. Where did they live? How did they eat? What work did they do? As part of their research, students can investigate the results of fires or other disasters in other parts of the world for comparison. You might inform students that today governments provide disaster relief for communities that meet with misfortune. Some students may wish to consider what, if any, assistance was available to people after the Great Fire of London. How did people manage to rebuild the city?

Great Fire of London, 1666. Museum of London

During the Restoration, theatrical productions flourished, with **Oliver Goldsmith's** *She Stoops to Conquer* and **Richard Sheridan's** *The School for Scandal* standing out among the most popular comedies. In other areas of literature, **Edward Gibbon's** *The Decline and Fall of the Roman Empire* was a landmark of **historical prose**. Other notable works of the period include the following novels: **Lawrence Sterne's** *Tristram Shandy* (1759), **Henry Fielding's** *Tom Jones* (1794), and **Tobias (George) Smollett's** *Humphry Clinker* (1771).

Toward the end of the Enlightenment, the progress achieved through the scientific and technological advances of the Industrial Revolution began to appear less positive. Many people were overworked in the new factories and mills. Social conditions in the cities and towns deteriorated, and the price of progress began to be questioned. In reaction to these changes, some philosophers and literary figures turned from the rational and orderly ideals of Neoclassicism to the intense, emotional ideals that would become **Romanticism**.

LITERARY EVENTS

► = British Events

►1784. Charlotte Smith publishes the first of eleven editions of *Elegiac Sonnets and Other Essays*

1781. Immanuel Kant publishes *Critique of Pure Reason*

1774. Johann Wolfgang von Goethe publishes *The Sorrows of Young Werther*

1759. Voltaire publishes *Candide*

1760	1765	1770	1775	1780	1785

►1759. Georg Friedrich Handel, composer, dies

►1760–1820. Reign of King George III

1762. Jean-Jacques Rousseau publishes *The Social Compact*

►1769. James Watt patents steam engine

1770. Boston Massacre

►1770. Thomas Gainsborough paints *The Blue Boy*

►1774–1779. Joseph Priestly and Antoine Lavoisier discover oxygen

1775. American Revolutionary War begins

►1776. Adam Smith publishes *The Wealth of Nations*

1778. Voltaire (François Marie Arouet) dies

►1784. Samuel Johnson dies

1784. Phyllis Wheatley dies

HISTORICAL EVENTS

Echoes:
Eighteenth-Century England

The rest to some faint meaning make pretense,
But Sh—— never deviates into sense.
Some beams of wit on other souls may fall,
Strike thro', and make a lucid interval;
But Sh——'s genuine night admits no ray,
His rising fogs prevail upon the day.

—John Dryden, from "Mac Flecknoe"
(writing about the poet Thomas Shadwell)

Why did I write? What sin to me unknown
Dipped me in ink, my parents', or my own?

—Alexander Pope, from "Epistle to Dr. Arbuthnot"

What makes all doctrines plain and clear?
About two hundred pounds a year.
And that which was prov'd true before,
Prove false again?—Two hundred more.

—Samuel Butler, from "Hudibras"

"Reason is, and ought to be, the slave of the passions,
and can never pretend to any other office than to serve
and obey them."

—David Hume, *Treatise on: Human Nature*

Dryden used metaphor to satirize Shadwell. What metaphor did Dryden use to describe wit or sense? What metaphor describes Shadwell's lack of sense?

Answers. Dryden used the metaphor of sun or light for wit; the speaker describes sense as "beams of wit." He used the metaphor of darkness or night to describe Shadwell's lack of sense; the speaker says that Shadwell's "genuine night admits no ray," or that Shadwell is incapable of perceiving wit.

ADDITIONAL QUESTIONS AND ACTIVITIES

Students in small groups can compare the ideas represented in the quotations from Pope, Butler, and Hume. Remind students of the importance of irony, wit, and reason in these writings. Students may want to create a comparison and contrast chart to analyze the quotations.

ENRICHMENT ACTIVITIES

Students in pairs or small groups can role play a discussion between Anne Finch and her contemporary critics, who might be men or women. Discussion should focus on the topic of rights of women writers.

SUPPORT FOR LEP STUDENTS

Have each student work with an English-proficient student to read the poem aloud, listening for rhyme and meter.

ADDITIONAL VOCABULARY

intend—plan
pursue—seek
affect—influence
attain—gain through effort
condemn—convict
presumptuous—too bold
esteemed—valued highly
redeem—deliver from sin
enquire—seek information
excel—be better or greater than
convey—make known
refine—free from imperfection
prolong—lengthen or extend

PREREADING

"The Introduction"
by Anne Finch

ABOUT THE AUTHOR

Anne Finch, Countess of Winchilsea (1661–1720), a perceptive and valuable poet, circulated much of her work in manuscript form before finally publishing a book in 1713. Her reluctance to make her literary talents widely known was due to the often hostile treatment of women writers in her day. Finch came from a family of staunch supporters of the Stuart king James II. Anne was wealthy and well-educated, and in 1683 she went to court to serve as a Maid of Honor to Mary Modena, Duchess of York. In 1684 she married Heneage Finch, another member of the court. When King James was exiled in the late 1680s, Anne, Heneage, and her family were themselves in political exile for a time. Then Heneage's distant cousin, the Earl of Winchilsea, died, leaving him an elegant estate. He and Anne were able to assume a life of luxury. Gradually becoming more open about her poetry, Anne wrote pieces that celebrated the beauty and pleasures of rural life. The countryside around Eastwell where the Finches lived represented to her a retreat from a world that she as a talented woman found quite limiting. Today, much of her work is difficult to find, as no complete collection exists. However, the works that have survived have been admired by many subsequent writers and critics, including William Wordsworth and Virginia Woolf.

ABOUT THE SELECTION

"The Introduction" is the first selection in Finch's first and only book of poetry, *Miscellany Poems on Several Occasions, Written by a Lady,* published in 1713. This thoughtful poem expresses Finch's feelings about the lost opportunities of women in a world that treats them as mindless persons interested only in fashion, dances, and the like. In this poem, Finch comments on the experiences and ambitions of women through the ages by making Biblical references, or **allusions**, and by emphasizing the role that learned prejudices play in hindering the development of female potential.

GOALS/OBJECTIVES

Studying this lesson will enable students to

• empathize with a female perspective in the Enlightenment period
• describe Anne Finch's literary accomplishments and explain the historical significance of her poetry
• define *slant rhyme* and *meter* and recognize the effects of slant rhyme and meter in a poem
• write a comparison essay
• correct sentence fragments
• answer sentence-completion questions on a test

READER'S JOURNAL

Freewrite in your journal about the social conventions that exist in your own city or country. Are there any social customs with which you disagree? Are there any that you find personally limiting? How does it feel to want to do something that "just isn't done"?

WRITING SKILLS

Read the Language Arts Survey, 1.42, "Organizing a Composition," to learn about methods for writing conclusions. Write a conclusion for the poem, in prose, which summarizes what you feel are Finch's most important points. Compare these with the conclusions of other members of the class to evaluate your own interpretation of what was important.

"The Introduction"

ANNE FINCH

Did I my lines intend for public view,
How many censures[1] would their faults pursue,
Some would, because such words they do affect,
Cry they're <u>insipid</u>, empty, uncorrect.
5   And many have attained, dull and untaught,
The name of wit only by finding fault.
True judges might condemn their want of wit,
And all might say they're by a woman writ.
Alas! a woman that attempts the pen
10   Such an intruder on the rights of men,
Such a presumptuous creature is esteemed,
The fault can by no virtue be redeemed.
They tell us we mistake our sex and way;
Good breeding, fashion, dancing, dressing, play
15   Are the accomplishments we should desire;
To write, or read, or think, or to enquire
Would cloud our beauty, and exhaust our time,
And interrupt the conquests of our prime;[2]

---

1. **censures.** Criticisms
2. **prime.** Maturity

What must some people of Finch's day have thought of women poets? Why, according to these people, should women not write?

WORDS FOR
EVERYDAY USE:

in • sip • id (in sipˊid) *adj.,* not exciting or interesting

"THE INTRODUCTION" **485**

READER'S JOURNAL

Students should note whether these social customs are defined by age, gender, or other circumstances.

WRITING SKILLS

Students in small groups can exchange conclusions and discuss interpretations.

ANSWER TO GUIDED READING QUESTION

❶ Some people thought a female poet was presumptuous to attempt a man's job and that a woman shouldn't write because it makes a woman less attractive and wastes her time.

VOCABULARY FROM THE SELECTION

debarred	insipid
diffusive	retired

HISTORICAL NOTE

Finch's reference to her Muse is typical of Neoclassical poetry, which sought to emulate ancient Greek and Roman literature. The nine Muses of Greek mythology were the daughters of Zeus and Mnemosyne, the goddess of memory. Each Muse was linked to a specific art, and poets often called upon a particular Muse for inspiration.

VOCABULARY IN CONTEXT

• We left the theater in the middle of the <u>insipid</u> movie because we were bored.

ANSWER TO GUIDED READING QUESTION

❶ In the past, women have been viewed as intelligent, capable, and worthy of honor.

CROSS-CURRICULAR ACTIVITIES

Social Studies. Students can research information about other women who would support Finch's theory of "women that excelled of old." Encourage students to share their information in short reports to the class. Students may wish to research the lives and works of early women writers such as Margery Kempe, Queen Elizabeth I, or Aemilia Lanyer. Students may also examine the role of "women that excelled of old" in the mythologies of various cultures. As a third option, some students can examine the tradition of the heroic woman in literature; some examples include Juliana and Judith in Old English literature and Bradamonte in Ludovico Ariosto's romance, *Orlando Furioso.*

ANSWERS TO SELECTION CHECK TEST 4.7.1

EX. What does "The Introduction" introduce?
It introduces Anne Finch's book of poetry.

1. By whom does Finch not intend her poems to be read?
She does not intend her poems to be read by the general public.

2. What would be said about women who write?
Women who write would be called "presumptuous," "intruder[s] on the rights of men."

3. What does Finch say about fables of "women that excelled"?
She says that people are not told any of these.

4. From what are women "debarred"?
They are "debarred from all improvements of the mind."

5. At the end of the poem, what advice is given?
Women who would write are advised not to expect or pursue honor.

486 TEACHER'S EDITION

How have women been viewed in the past? ❶

20 Whilst the dull manage of a servile house[3]
Is held by some our utmost art, and use.
 Sure 'twas not ever[4] thus, nor are we told
Fables, of women that excelled of old;
To whom, by the <u>diffusive</u> hand of Heaven
Some share of wit and poetry was given.

25 On that glad day on which the Ark[5] returned,
The holy pledge for which the land had mourned,
The joyful tribes attend it on the way,
The Levites[6] do the sacred charge convey,
Whilst various instruments before it play;

30 Here holy virgins in the concert join,
The louder notes to soften and refine,
And with alternate verse complete the hymn divine.
Lo! the young poet,[7] after God's own heart,
By Him inspired, and taught the Muses' art,[8]

35 Returned from conquest, a bright chorus meets,
That sing his slain ten thousand in the streets.
In such loud numbers they his acts declare,
Proclaim the wonders of his early war,
That Saul[9] upon the vast applause does frown,

40 And feels its mighty thunder shake the crown.
What, can the threatened judgment now prolong?

---

3. **servile house.** Home employing servants
4. **ever.** Always
5. **Ark.** Chest holding the Ten Commandments. Its return signifies the return of the Hebrews to the Temple in Jerusalem.
6. **Levites.** Jewish priestly class
7. **the young poet.** David, composer of psalms
8. **Muses' art.** In Greek mythology, the Muses inspired creative activity.
9. **Saul.** First king of Israel

WORDS FOR EVERYDAY USE:
dif • fu • sive (di fyoo′ siv) *adj.,* causing diffusion or scattering

---

VOCABULARY IN CONTEXT

- One of the science fair projects demonstrates the <u>diffusive</u> qualities of the prism.
- All reporters have been <u>debarred</u> from the courtroom.
- The hermit lives a <u>retired</u> existence in a remote mountain cabin.

Half of the kingdom is already gone;
The fairest half, whose influence guides the rest,
Have David's empire o'er their hearts confessed.
45   A woman[10] here leads fainting Israel on,
She fights, she wins, she triumphs with a song,
Devout, majestic, for the subject fit,
And far above her arms exalts her wit,
Then to the peaceful, shady palm withdraws,
And rules the rescued nation with her laws.
50   How are we fallen, fallen by mistaken rules?
And education's, more than nature's fools,
<u>Debarred</u> from all improvements of the mind,
And to be dull, expected and designed;[11]
And if some one would soar above the rest,
55   With warmer fancy and ambition pressed,[12]
So strong th' opposing faction still appears.
The hopes to thrive can ne'er outweigh the fears.
Be cautioned then my Muse, and still <u>retired</u>;
Nor be despised, aiming to be admired;
60   Conscious of wants, still with contracted wing,
To some few friends and to thy sorrows sing;
For groves of laurel[13] thou wert never meant;
Be dark enough thy shades, and be thou there content. ■

---

10. **A woman.** Deborah, an Israelite leader
11. **designed.** Required
12. **With . . . pressed.** Driven by stronger desire and ambition
13. **laurel.** The leaves of the laurel tree were used to bestow honors.

WORDS FOR
EVERYDAY **U**SE:

de • barred (dē bärd) *part.*, kept from some right or privilege; excluded

re • tired (ri tīrd´) *adj.*, withdrawn or apart from; secluded

"THE INTRODUCTION" **487**

ANSWER TO GUIDED READING QUESTION

❶ Women's education is severely limited, designed to keep the female mind "dull." If a woman soars above the rest, she is strongly opposed.

❶
According to the speaker, what is the state of women's education in her time? What happens if a woman soars above the rest?

ANALYTIC SCALES FOR RESPONDING IN WRITING

Assign a score from 1 to 25 for each grading criterion below. (For more detailed evaluation, see the evaluation forms for writing, revising, and proofreading, *Assessment Portfolio,* 7.1–7.10.)

1. Bill of Rights

• **Content/Unity.** The bill of rights presents the writer's declaration of the basic rights of every human being.

• **Organization/Coherence.** The bill of rights states each right separately. Where appropriate, the statement of the right is followed by supporting details. The rights are listed in a logical order (most to least important or *vice versa*). Statements are separated by numbers or paragraphs.

• **Language/Style.** The bill of rights uses vivid and precise nouns, verbs, and modifiers.

• **Conventions.** The bill of rights avoids errors in spelling, grammar, usage, mechanics, and manuscript form.

2. Comparison Essay

• **Content/Unity.** The essay presents a brief comparison of three writers' ideas about educational opportunities for women.

• **Organization/Coherence.** The essay begins with a statement that summarizes the similarities among the writers. It then presents facts and details from the selections to support the writer's opinion.

• **Language/Style.** The essay uses vivid and precise nouns, verbs, and modifiers.

• **Conventions.** The essay avoids errors in spelling, grammar, usage, mechanics, and manuscript form.

TEACHER'S EDITION   **487**

Students might assume the role of Finch's literary agent as they think of arguments to support the selection's value.

ANSWERS FOR REVIEWING THE SELECTION

RECALLING

1. Finch feels the general public would sharply criticize her poem.

2. Society believes the "proper" activities for women are "fashion, dancing, dressing, play."

3. Finch does not believe women were always kept from intellectual activity. She points to biblical times for examples of women who held commanding roles in society.

4. The poet states that her Muse should not aim to be admired because she was never meant for groves of laurel, or praise.

INTERPRETING

Responses will vary. Possible responses are given.

5. People in Finch's world might believe that a woman poet is "presumptuous" because poetry was considered the occupation or pastime of educated men. Finch is certain she would get criticism for her work because she is a woman. Finch would probably be criticized by educated and sophisticated men, possibly by the successful male writers of her time.

6. The most a woman can achieve is to be admired for her beauty and her ability to manage a household. Her achievements are limited to physical appearance and domestic activities.

7. She implies that engaging in intellectual or artistic efforts is a natural right by pointing to the "holy virgins" and Deborah, whose gifts and authority were supposedly appointed by God.

8. Fear is an issue when women are ambitious because they know that all their efforts will be met with criticism. The Muses and groves of laurel are significant to the poem because they call to mind the grand tradition of poetry and because they are traditionally associated with men.

(cont.)

488 TEACHER'S EDITION

Responding to the Selection

How do you feel about the points made by Finch? Do certain lines stand out to you as eloquent and perceptive? Suppose you lived in Finch's day and were trying to talk someone into publishing this piece. What might you say to convince that person of the piece's value?

Reviewing the Selection

RECALLING

1. How does Finch feel the general public would react to her poem?

2. According to Finch, what does society believe are the "proper" activities of women?

3. Does Finch believe women were always kept from important activities? If not, when were they able to assume commanding roles in society?

4. What does the poet state about her Muse and about groves of laurel?

INTERPRETING

5. Why might people in Finch's world believe that a woman poet is "presumptuous"? Why is Finch certain that she would get criticism for her work? Who do you think would criticize Finch?

6. In the world Finch describes, what is the most a woman can achieve? To what aspects of life are her achievements limited?

7. How does Finch imply that to engage in intellectual or artistic efforts is a natural right?

8. Why is fear an issue when a woman is ambitious? What significance do Muses and groves of laurel have in the poem?

SYNTHESIZING

9. What does Finch suggest is the actual cause of women's limited scope in the world? Does she believe people are born unworthy of certain ambitions?

10. According to Finch, how does society routinely discourage and limit the pursuits of women? How can a woman be content?

Understanding Literature (Questions for Discussion)

1. **Slant Rhyme.** A **slant rhyme, half rhyme, near rhyme,** or **off rhyme** is substitution of **assonance** or **consonance** for true rhyme. Where can you find examples of slant rhyme in this poem? Why might a poet choose to vary the rhyme scheme? Does

---

ANSWERS FOR REVIEWING THE SELECTION (CONT.)

SYNTHESIZING

Responses will vary. Possible responses are given.

9. Finch suggests that inadequate education is the reason for a woman's limitations. She doesn't believe people are born unworthy of certain ambitions; she believes that women's ambition is thwarted by a society that attempts to keep them "from all improvements of the mind,/And to be dull, expected and designed."

10. Society routinely discourages and limits the pursuits of women by "finding fault" with any activity women pursue outside the narrow confinements of "Good breeding, fashion, dancing, dressing, play." A woman can be content by bearing in mind the opposition that will meet her efforts and by sharing her desire and talent with "some few friends."

changing the rhyme scheme change the tone of the poem in any way? Would this poem have a completely different effect if it didn't rhyme?

2. **Meter.** The **meter** of a poem is its rhythmical pattern. Try to determine the meter of this poem. Does the meter stay the same, or does it vary? How does the meter affect the expression of ideas in this poem?

Responding in Writing

1. **Bill of Rights.** How does the world in which Finch lives deny rights to people? What do you feel are the basic rights of every human being? Create your own "Bill of Rights" with which you would like all people to comply. Imagine that you are going to be posting this bill of rights prominently in public places. Be sure to address all different types of freedoms, even those you might consider small or trivial.

2. **Comparison Essay.** Anne Finch writes,

> They tell us we mistake our sex and way;
> Good breeding, fashion, dancing, dressing, play
> Are the accomplishments we should desire;
> To write, or read, or think, or to enquire
> Would cloud our beauty, and exhaust our time.

Read Mary Wollstonecraft's *A Vindication of the Rights of Woman* in Unit 8 and Virginia Woolf's *A Room of One's Own* in Unit 11. These three women all wrote in different eras, yet they share similar ideas and concerns. What does each of these pieces have to say about educational opportunities for women? Write a short comparison essay on this subject. In your essay, introduce each selection and each author, and explain how the themes of the selections are related.

Language Lab

Correcting Sentence Fragments. Read the Language Arts Survey, 2.61, "Correcting Sentence Fragments." Then make whatever changes are needed to convert the following fragments into complete sentences. Delete or add words or phrases if you wish.

1. Considering the disadvantages of being born into an aristocratic family
2. The pastoral beauty of the English countryside as a subject of Anne Finch's poems
3. That the literary efforts of women were not regarded as serious literature
4. Moving into an estate in the countryside to escape the conventions of social life
5. Bitterness and depression that result from effort and excellence without acceptance

▶ See the evaluation forms for discussion, active listening, and oral communication, *Assessment Portfolio,* 7.11–7.14. *Responses will vary. Possible responses are given.*

1. Slant Rhyme. Examples of slant rhyme in this poem include *house/use, Heaven/given, declare/war, prolong/gone,* and *on/song.* A poet might choose to vary rhyme scheme in order to emphasize a particular idea. The slant rhyme affects the tone by highlighting significant ideas. For instance, the slant rhyme of *house/use* in lines 19 and 20 signals the completion of an idea. It also signals the poet's dissatisfaction with the circumscribed life that women are supposed to lead, a life described in the preceding lines that end in perfect rhyme. Eliminating rhyme wouldn't make the poem have a completely different effect; its subject and argument would still be compelling.

▶ **Teaching Note:** Explain that some rhymes that appear to be slant rhymes actually were considered perfect rhymes in Finch's day. For example, "fault" in *untaught/fault* (lines 5 and 6) was pronounced *fawt,* and "join" in *join/refine* (lines 30 and 31) was pronounced *jine.*

2. Meter. Generally, the poem is written in iambic pentameter, as in the initial four lines. When the meter varies, the change emphasizes an idea, word, or phrase, as in line 19: "Whilst the dull manage of a servile house." The stress on *dull* is immediately followed by the stress of the first syllable of *manage,* thus calling attention to the phrase.

▶ **Teaching Note:** Students should make a written and spoken analysis of the poem to determine its meter. Encourage students to read the information about *scansion,* page 1261, and *meter* in the Handbook of Literary Terms, page 1253.

ANALYTIC SCALES FOR RESPONDING IN WRITING

Grading scales appear on page 487.

Test-taking Skills

Sentence Completion. Mary Astell lived and wrote during the same era as Anne Finch. Like Finch, Astell was concerned about the ways in which women might improve their lives. Below is a vocabulary exercise based on Astell's piece "A Serious Proposal to the Ladies." Read the Language Arts Survey, 4.41, "Sentence-completion Questions." Then choose the words that best complete each of the sentences below.

1. There is a sort of _____ indeed which is worse than the greatest _____.

   (A) sacrifice . . pleasure   (B) criminal . . lawyer   (C) trouble . . pleasure
   (D) nightmare . . dream   (E) learning . . ignorance

2. A woman may study plays and _____ all her days, and be a great deal more _____ but never a jot the wiser.

   (A) work . . wise   (B) puppetry . . populous   (C) stitchery . . literate
   (D) romances . . knowing   (E) games . . serious

3. Such a _____ as this serves only to instruct and put her forward in the practice of the greatest _____.

   (A) quest . . uncertainty   (B) frivolity . . importance   (C) occupation . . uselessness
   (D) complication . . art   (E) knowledge . . follies

4. Yet how can they justly _____ her who _____ or at least won't afford opportunity of better?

   (A) employ . . suffer   (B) accuse . . reproach   (C) blame . . forbid
   (D) berate . . can't   (E) tolerate . . daren't

5. A rational _____ will be employed; it will never be _____ in doing nothing.

   (A) person . . useful   (B) desire . . idle   (C) mind . . satisfied
   (D) toleration . . angry   (E) defense . . guilty

PROJECT

Education Symposium. As a class, plan a symposium of women writers. Each person in the class should choose one female writer from any era and then go to the library to research this person thoroughly. Two good sources of information are *The Norton Anthology of Literature by Women,* edited by Sandra M. Gilbert and Susan Gubar, and *British Women Writers,* edited by Dale Spender and Janet Todd. After each person has completed his or her research, organize the symposium. Plan a list of topics related to educational opportunities for women, women's writing, and how the world is changing in these areas. Then plan to have each person attend the symposium as the writer he or she has researched. To begin the symposium, each "writer" should introduce herself and tell a little bit about what she has written and why she has decided to attend. Everyone should try hard to stay in character throughout the symposium.

PREREADING

"A Song for St. Cecilia's Day"
by John Dryden

ABOUT THE AUTHOR

John Dryden (1631–1700) was the monumental literary figure of his time. His works span the range of drama, epic poetry, lyric poetry, satire, essay, and translation and serve as a record of the ideas and spirit of the seventeenth century. While the work of some poets reveals intimate personal feelings, Dryden's concerned issues of public moment. Some of his verse commemorates public events. An example is *Annus Mirabilis* ("Year of Wonders"—1667), in part about the Great Fire of London of 1666. Other poems by Dryden comment on social, political, and religious controversies. Such works include *Astraea Redux* (1660), celebrating the restoration of the monarchy, and *Absalom and Achitophel* (1681), addressing the Popish Plot. Dryden's best works, perhaps, are his satirical verses, including *Absalom and Achitophel*. Dryden's verse established him as a major figure, and his public support for King Charles I contributed to his being named poet laureate in 1668. Dryden wrote prose essays and is widely regarded as the first "modern" prose writer, insofar as he developed a style that was clear, precise, and dignified but at the same time lyrical and supremely natural, even transparent. He also was a respected literary critic. In addition to the early and highly regarded *Essay of Dramatic Poesy* (1668), Dryden wrote criticism that he published as prefaces to his many well-received dramas.

With the Glorious Revolution came the Anglican monarchy, and Dryden lost his post as laureate. He was replaced by Thomas Shadwell, whom he had satirized in "Mac Flecknoe" (1682). He wrote a few more plays but took primarily to literary translation and commentary. Written near the end of his life, *Fables, Ancient and Modern* includes Dryden's translations of Ovid, Boccaccio, and Chaucer. In his last years he spent a fair amount of time in Will's Coffee House, where the literati came to pay homage to their master.

ABOUT THE SELECTION

"**A Song for St. Cecilia's Day**" celebrates St. Cecilia, a Roman noble martyred *circa* AD 230. Her feast day is November 22. In addition to evangelizing and performing miracles, she was believed to have invented the organ, a musical instrument whose power and versatility was utterly beyond comparison until the development of electronic synthesizers and amplifiers in the present century; hence, she is the patron saint of music and musicians. In Dryden's time, St. Cecilia's feast day was a religious holiday in celebration of music. This poem was set to music by G. B. Draghi and performed at the St. Cecilia's Day festival of 1687, but **G. F. Handel's** (1685–1759) later setting is now used almost exclusively.

"A SONG FOR ST. CECILIA'S DAY" **491**

ENRICHMENT ACTIVITIES

Students can write about or discuss other holidays or feast days and the events or people each day commemorates. They may choose to write a publicity release or an announcement that could be shared with people who are not familiar with the event.

SUPPORT FOR LEP STUDENTS

- Students can make notes about the poem as they read. Have students pause at the end of each stanza and summarize the stanza's main ideas.

- Bring or ask students to bring the instruments mentioned in the poem. (You will need a recording of organ music.) Have someone play the instrument, and then, as a group, discuss the words and images in the poem and list additional related words. Help students distinguish the meanings of these words.

▶ **Teaching Note:** Combine this activity with the Cross-curricular Activity described on page 493.

ADDITIONAL VOCABULARY
dirge—funeral hymn
proclaim—announce

GOALS/OBJECTIVES

Studying this lesson will enable students to

- have a positive experience reading a highly musical lyric
- describe Dryden's literary accomplishments and explain the historical significance of his writings
- define *allusion* and identify and interpret allusions they encounter in their reading
- use collective nouns as subjects and identify agreement errors

READER'S JOURNAL

Students might differentiate between music they choose for themselves and music they do not choose, such as advertising jingles, music piped into shopping malls and other public places, and so on.

READING SKILLS

Students can work in pairs, asking and answering the questions they generated as they read the poem.

►Additional practice is provided in the *Essential Skills Practice Book: Study and Research,* 4.18.

ANSWERS TO GUIDED READING QUESTIONS

❶ The "universal frame" began from "heavenly harmony."

❷ The speaker compares music to the ordering of the elements.

LITERARY TECHNIQUE

Refrain. A refrain is a line or group of lines repeated in a poem or song. Have students identify the refrains in the first fifteen lines of the poem. What are the effects of these refrains? Do they emphasize a point? In what way are they musical?

READER'S JOURNAL

Today music fills many people's lives, not only on ceremonial occasions but throughout each day. Do you listen often to music? If so, why? In your journal, comment on the different reasons for listening to music.

READING SKILLS

Read the Language Arts Survey, 4.18, "Reading Actively: Questioning." Then, write six questions to bear in mind as you read Dryden's "A Song for St. Cecilia's Day."

"A Song for St. Cecilia's Day"[1]

JOHN DRYDEN

❶ What was the source of this "universal frame"?

❷ To what original ordering of things does the speaker compare that most orderly of art forms, music?

From harmony, from heavenly harmony
    This universal frame began:
      When Nature underneath a heap
        Of jarring atoms lay,
5   And could not heave her head,
The tuneful voice was heard from high:
    "Arise, ye more than dead."
Then cold, and hot, and moist, and dry,[2]
In order to their stations leap,
10   And Music's power obey.
From harmony, from heavenly harmony
    This universal frame began:
    From harmony to harmony
Through all the compass of the notes it ran,
15 The diapason[3] closing full in man.

---

1. **St. Cecilia's Day.** November 22, the feast day of St. Cecilia, the patron saint of music
2. **Nature . . . dry.** Nature was created out of the jarring elements of earth, fire, water, and air or "cold," "hot," "moist," and "dry."
3. **diapason.** The whole range of notes in the musical scale

What passion cannot Music raise and <u>quell</u>!
    When Jubal[4] struck the corded shell,
    His listening brethren stood around,
    And, wondering, on their faces fell
20   To worship that <u>celestial</u> sound.
Less than a god they thought there could not dwell
    Within the hollow of that shell
    That spoke so sweetly and so well.
What passion cannot Music raise and quell!

25   The trumpet's loud clangor
      Excites us to arms,
    With shrill notes of anger,
      And mortal alarms.
    The double double double beat
30   Of the thundering drum
Cries: "Hark! the foes come;
Charge, charge, 'tis too late to retreat."

    The soft complaining flute
    In dying notes discovers
35   The woes of hopeless lovers,
Whose dirge is whispered by the warbling lute.

    Sharp violins proclaim
Their jealous pangs, and desperation,
Fury, frantic <u>indignation</u>,
40   Depth of pains, and height of passion,
    For the fair, <u>disdainful</u> dame.

    But O! what art can teach,
    What human voice can reach,
    The sacred organ's praise?
45   Notes inspiring holy love,
Notes that wing their heavenly ways
    To mend the choirs above.

---

4. **Jubal.** The Book of Genesis credits Jubal with the invention of the lyre and the pipe.

What musical instruments are mentioned in these lines? How are they different from one another? What effect does each one have on listeners?

WORDS FOR EVERYDAY USE:

quell (kwel) *vt.*, put an end to
ce • les • tial (sə les´chəl) *adj.*, heavenly, divine
in • dig • na • tion (in´dig nā´ shən) *n.*, anger, scorn
dis • dain • ful (dis dān´ fəl) *adj.*, proud, aloof

---

❶ The trumpet, drum, flute, and violin are mentioned. Each conveys a different strong emotion. The effect of the trumpet is alarm. The effect of the drum is a call to action. The effect of the flute is woe and longing. The effect of the violin is a jumble of intense emotion, the "Depth of pains, and height of passion."

HISTORICAL NOTE

England has had seventeen poet laureates since Dryden, including William Wordsworth; Alfred, Lord Tennyson; and Ted Hughes, the current poet laureate. However, in the more than three hundred years since the office was established, a woman has never been appointed. In the United States, however, Mona Van Duyn became the first woman to receive the title of poet laureate in 1992. She was succeeded by another woman, Rita Dove, in 1993.

CROSS-CURRICULAR ACTIVITIES

Arts and Humanities. Students can research musical terms to describe the different effects and sounds of the instruments in the poem.

VOCABULARY IN CONTEXT

- Has the army's offensive maneuver <u>quelled</u> the enemy attack?
- The painting depicts a <u>celestial</u> scene filled with cherubs and angels.
- Customer-relations representatives are often the target of customers' <u>indignation</u>.
- Her sarcastic tone revealed her <u>disdainful</u> attitude toward the idea.

ANSWERS TO GUIDED READING QUESTIONS

❶ An angel mistook earth for heaven. The mistake was made because the angel heard Cecilia's organ and thought such a sound could only come from heaven.

❷ The world begins and ends with music.

HISTORICAL NOTE

Dryden's theme of harmony and order was a common theme of the Enlightenment. Dryden balanced the passion of music with the ordering element of harmony.

ANSWERS TO SELECTION CHECK TEST 4.7.3

EX. What is celebrated on St. Cecilia's feast day?
Music is celebrated on St. Cecilia's feast day.

1. From what did the "universal frame" begin?
It began from harmony.

2. What does music "raise and quell"?
Music raises and quells all the passions or emotions.

3. What musical instruments are specifically mentioned in the poem?
The poem mentions the trumpet, the drum, the flute, the violin, the organ, and the lyre.

4. What instrument is St. Cecilia credited with inventing?
St. Cecilia is credited with inventing the organ.

5. When will "Music . . . untune the sky"?
"Music" will "untune the sky" at the Last Judgment.

The Lute Player. *Orazio Gentileschi, circa 1610.*
© Board of Trustees, National Gallery of Art, Washington, D.C.

❶
Who mistook earth for heaven? Why was this mistake made?

❷
What, according to the speaker, begins and ends with music?

Orpheus[5] could lead the savage race;
And trees unrooted left their place,
50   Sequacious[6] of the lyre;
But bright Cecilia raised the wonder higher:
When to her organ vocal breath was given,
An angel heard, and straight appeared,
     Mistaking earth for heaven.

GRAND CHORUS
55   *As from the power of sacred lays*
         The spheres began to move,
     And sung the great Creator's praise[7]
         To all the blest above;
     So, when the last and dreadful hour
60   *This crumbling pageant shall devour,*
     The trumpet shall be heard on high,
     The dead shall live, the living die,
     And Music shall untune the sky. ∎

---

5. **Orpheus.** Legend has it that the poet Orpheus played the lyre so wonderfully that the animals were tamed and even rocks and trees followed him.
6. **sequacious.** Following
7. **power . . . praise.** The idea that sacred songs put the stars and planets into motion

494   *UNIT SEVEN / THE RESTORATION AND THE EIGHTEENTH CENTURY*

Responding to the Selection

Freewrite about the idea of harmony. You might think about what happens to you when you feel or perceive disharmony, what kinds of harmony you value most, or why harmony is important to you.

Reviewing the Selection

RECALLING

1. Out of what was the "universal frame" created? Who or what began this process of creation? What powers are attributed to music in stanza 2?

2. What instruments are praised in stanza 3? in stanza 4? in stanza 5?

3. What instruments are praised in stanzas 6–7? To what is it compared?

4. In stanza 7, who makes a mistake? What is the mistake? What ensues in stanza 8?

INTERPRETING

5. What is the similarity between the process of creation and the notes of the musical scale? What role did harmony play in creation? What might the speaker be implying about the role of harmony in the created world in which we live?

6. What is special about the instruments praised in stanzas 3–5? Describe the sounds these instruments make. How do the sounds of the poet's language compare to the instruments' sounds?

7. In stanza 7, what is said to be the special characteristic of Cecilia's creation? How does it transform the earth?

8. What momentous event is referred to in the Grand Chorus? What will be music's role in this event?

SYNTHESIZING

9. What similarities exist between music and nature, according to the speaker? What aspects of this poem suggest that the speaker views the universe as an orderly, harmonious place, governed or regulated by rational, discoverable laws?

10. What non-English persons are mentioned in the poem? To what effect? What other persons or things are mentioned that might distinguish the topic or the occasion as special? How does Dryden make the celebration of music extend beyond everyday experience?

"A SONG FOR ST. CECILIA'S DAY" **495**

ANSWERS FOR REVIEWING THE SELECTION (CONT.)

8. Judgment Day is referred to in the Grand Chorus. Music will signal the end of the world and the call to judgment.

SYNTHESIZING

Responses will vary. Possible responses are given.

9. Both music and nature are governed by harmony; they are both expressions of the order of the universe. In the opening lines the speaker says the universal frame stems from harmony, and in the poem's conclusion the speaker says "sacred lays/The spheres began to move."

10. Non-English personages such as Jubal and Orpheus, both from ancient times, are mentioned in the poem to show the long-standing place of music in human society. By comparing Cecilia's creation of the organ to the creation of the universe, Dryden makes the celebration of music extend to the very meaning of human existence.

RESPONDING TO THE SELECTION

 Students can use a cluster diagram or another graphic device to explore the idea of harmony.

ANSWERS FOR REVIEWING THE SELECTION

RECALLING

1. The "universal frame" was created out of "heavenly harmony." Music began this process of creation. In stanza 2, the powers to raise and subdue passion are attributed to music.

2. The trumpet and drum are praised in stanza 3, the flute is praised in stanza 4, and the violin is praised in stanza 5.

3. The organ is praised in stanzas 6 and 7. It is compared to the human voice.

4. In stanza 7, an angel mistakes earth for heaven upon hearing Cecilia's organ. In stanza 8, the stars and planets are put into motion.

INTERPRETING

Responses will vary. Possible responses are given.

5. The Christian story of creation and the musical scale have the number seven in common—seven days of creation and seven notes on the musical scale. Harmony connects different aspects of the universe. The speaker implies that the created world functions harmoniously and that humans are part of that harmony.

6. The instruments all provoke strong responses. A trumpet's sounds are loud, clear, and often staccato; the poet mirrors this with short, staccato lines. A drum's "double double double beat" and thunder are abrupt and loud, reflecting the insistent, repetitive call to action. A flute's sounds are softer and smoother; the poet's language, such as the initial *ws* in line 36, creates a soft, subdued tone. A violin's sounds range from soft and mournful to loud and furious, and the poet's description of the ups and downs of human passion echoes the violin.

7. Cecilia's creation made an angel mistake earth for heaven. Music may transform the earth by giving it some of the harmony of heaven.

(cont.)

1. Celebration. Students should try to demonstrate the art form's power rather than merely explain it.

 2. Sounds. As each student plays his or her "instrument," class members can close their eyes and try to guess the source of the sound.

ANSWERS FOR UNDERSTANDING LITERATURE

► See the evaluation forms for discussion, active listening, and oral communication, *Assessment Portfolio*, 7.11–7.14.

Responses will vary. Possible responses are given.

Allusion. Jubal is distinctive because the Bible credits him with the creation of the lyre and the pipe. Dryden's comparison suggests that from the beginning of human history, music has triggered spiritual worship of the "celestial sound." At the same time, music also stirs human passion. Orpheus plays the lyre so skillfully that animals and trees are entranced by the music. This comparison underscores the harmonious aspect of music; it is a balance between the natural and the spiritual worlds.

► **Teaching Note:** Students might use a comparison and contrast chart to analyze the allusions in the poem. Refer students to the Language Arts Survey, 4.8, "Comparing and Contrasting."

Understanding Literature (Questions for Discussion)

Allusion. An **allusion** is a figure of speech in which a reference is made to a person, event, object, or work from history or literature. An allusion suggests a literal, metaphorical, or symbolic parallel or contrast with another work, character, or story. An allusion may be made in a paragraph, sentence, phrase, or single word. Dryden makes several references to classical Greek and Roman literature and to the Bible. Choose a character from the poem. What is distinctive about this character? What comparison does Dryden's allusion suggest?

Language Lab

Subject/Verb Agreement. Read the Language Arts Survey, 2.75, "Other Problems in Subject/Verb Agreement." Then complete the following sentences by modifying the verb in parentheses to make it agree with its subject. Use the present tense.

1. In preparation for the performance, the orchestra _____ tuning. (be)

2. The violin section _____ two more chairs. (need)

3. Each member of the audience _____ sitting in quiet anticipation. (be)

4. The audience _____ to enjoy the performance immensely. (appear)

5. As the song ends, the chorus _____ for the finale. (stand)

PROJECTS

1. **Celebration.** Dryden's poem honors the power and glory of music. In groups of four to eight students, choose a different art form you wish to honor in a public celebration. Think about the following questions: Why is your chosen art form important? What power does it have? Where, when, and how do people experience it? What tools or materials are used to create it? How does it compare to other art forms? Work together to plan a ceremony in which to share your ideas with other people. Create samples of your art form to display or perform during your celebration.

2. **Sounds.** Dryden's poem praises the emotional and spiritual power of music. We live surrounded not only by music but by all manner of sounds. Explore the ways in which sound affects us. Each student should bring to class an "instrument" and play it for the class. The instrument should not be an orchestral or band instrument but can be anything that can be used to produce an interesting sound. Compare the reactions of various members of the class. Do we all respond to sounds in the same way?

ANSWERS FOR LANGUAGE LAB

1. In preparation for the performance, the orchestra <u>is</u> tuning.

2. The violin section <u>needs</u> two more chairs.

3. Each member of the audience <u>is</u> sitting in quiet anticipation.

4. The audience <u>appears</u> to enjoy the performance immensely.

5. As the song ends, the chorus <u>stands</u> for the finale.

FOR MORE PRACTICE

Problem. In the next morning's newspapers, the press _____ the performance. (praise)

Answer. In the next morning's newspapers, the press <u>praises</u> the performance.

► Additional practice is provided in the *Essential Skills Practice Book: Language*, 2.75.

PREREADING

"Pressed by the Moon, Mute Arbitress of Tides"
by Charlotte Smith

ABOUT THE AUTHOR

Charlotte (Turner) Smith (1749–1806) began her literary career relatively late in life. She was married at age sixteen, and she bore and reared ten children. She began writing to earn money when her husband was sent to debtor's prison. Her book of poems, *Elegiac Sonnets* (1784), was so popular that it eventually went through eleven editions. It also influenced major Romantic poets such as **Samuel Taylor Coleridge** and **William Wordsworth**, as well as the Victorian poet **Elizabeth Barrett Browning**. Smith's poems presage the Romantic Era both in their preoccupation with self-analysis and in their focus on nature and natural beauty, the latter reflecting Smith's attachment to the Sussex countryside of her youth. Although Smith continued to write poetry after the success of her first book, this work did not by itself provide sufficient income for her family, so she took up writing novels. Her first novel, *Emmeline, the Orphan of the Castle* (1788), was very successful. For several years she produced a book each year, and in all, she published over twenty books. *The Old Manor House* (1793) is considered her finest fiction work. Many of her novels, such as *Desmond* (1792), express her sympathy with the ideals of Rousseau and the French Revolution (1789). However, critics considered her novels too political for a woman and disparaged her belief in the moral equality of the social classes. Thus, although her writing was highly regarded by major writers and was popular enough to produce an income sufficient to support a family of eleven, her work eventually fell into obscurity.

ABOUT THE SELECTION

"Pressed by the Moon, Mute Arbitress of Tides" is more than a Romantic sonnet describing the activity of nature. A close reading shows that it also contains elements of inward reflection that are true to the spirit of later Romanticism. In this poem, Smith evokes the powerful forces of nature and relates those forces to inner human experience, much as Byron, Shelley, and Keats would do years afterward. Its use of natural imagery, its strong emotions, and its preoccupation with death makes this poem one of the first major expressions of the Romantic spirit in English literature.

ENRICHMENT ACTIVITIES

• Students in small groups can research folklore about the moon—its origins, effects on humans, and role in nature. Students can present their research in oral reports, works of art, recordings of folk tales, or other engaging forms.

• Conduct a survey to determine whether men and women react similarly to the idea that to live is to be oppressed by a long storm. Why might a woman of the eighteenth century, such as Smith, have felt like this?

SUPPORT FOR LEP STUDENTS

To check student comprehension, encourage these students to sketch or draw their impressions of the scene described in the poem.

ADDITIONAL VOCABULARY

surge—sudden and forceful rolling or sweeping motion
billow—large wave
heaving—rising; swelling
vain to—unknown by

CROSS-CURRICULAR ACTIVITIES

Earth Science. Ask interested students to research and report to the class on the physics of the tides and of waves.

GOALS/OBJECTIVES

Studying this lesson will enable students to

• interpret and appreciate natural description in a poem and relate that description to a speaker's inner emotions

• describe Charlotte Smith's literary accomplishments and explain why her work fell into obscurity

• define *alliteration* and identify and interpret its effect in a poem

• define *anaphora* and recognize anaphora in a poem

• use vivid verbs in writing

• use observing skills

PREREADING NOTES

READER'S JOURNAL

Suggest that students consider whether they felt connected to or separate from nature during the event.

SPEAKING AND LISTENING SKILLS

Before beginning the conversation, students might make a few notes about their character's motivation and feelings about the topic.

▶Additional practice is provided in the *Essential Skills Practice Book: Speaking and Listening*, 3.5.

ANSWERS TO GUIDED READING QUESTIONS

❶ The sea is "pressed by the moon."

❷ *Answers will vary.*

❸ The speaker compares life (or the difficulties of life) to a storm.

ANSWERS TO SELECTION CHECK TEST 4.7.5

EX. Who is the "mute arbitress of tides"?
The moon is the "mute arbitress of tides."

1. Where did Charlotte Smith write this poem?
She wrote it in a churchyard (or graveyard).

2. What is pressed by the moon?
The sea is pressed by the moon.

3. What happens to the "village dead"?
They are torn from their grassy tombs.

4. What is "vain to" the dead?
The raving winds and waters (or the storm) are "vain to" the dead.

5. By what does the speaker feel oppressed?
The speaker feels oppressed by "life's long storm."

READER'S JOURNAL

Recall a time when you experienced nature in a powerful form. Were you intimidated? Were you drawn to the event? What feelings did the experience evoke? Write about the experience and your feelings about it in your journal.

SPEAKING AND LISTENING SKILLS

Read the Language Arts Survey, 3.5, "Interpersonal Communication." With a partner, role play a two-minute conversation between Charlotte Smith and an eighteenth-century literary critic who believes women should not have literary careers. Both should try to practice good interpersonal communication skills.

"Pressed by the Moon, Mute Arbitress¹ of Tides"

CHARLOTTE SMITH

Written in the churchyard at Middleton in Sussex

❶
Who or what is "pressed by the moon"?

Pressed by the moon, mute arbitress of tides,
    While the loud equinox² its power combines,
    The sea no more its swelling surge confines,
But o'er the shrinking land <u>sublimely</u> rides.

5 The wild blast, rising from the western cave,

❷
How do you feel when you imagine or observe a stormy sea?

    Drives the huge billows from their heaving bed,
    Tears from their grassy tombs the village dead,
And breaks the silent sabbath³ of the grave!
With shells and seaweed mingled, on the shore
10   Lo! their bones whiten in the frequent wave;

❸
What does the speaker compare to a storm?

    But vain to them the winds and waters rave;
They hear the warring elements no more:
While I am doomed—by life's long storm oppressed,
To gaze with envy on their gloomy rest. ∎

---

1. **Arbitress.** Archaic feminine form of *arbiter*; a person selected to judge a dispute; now used for both genders
2. **equinox.** A storm that occurs when the sun crosses the equator, making night and day of equal length
3. **sabbath.** Rest

WORDS FOR
EVERYDAY USE:
    sub • lime • ly (sə blīm´ lē) *adv.*, nobly; majestically

VOCABULARY IN CONTEXT

• The papal procession moved <u>sublimely</u> down the cathedral's velvet-carpeted aisle.

Responding to the Selection

Make a list of five feelings toward the sea that the poem arouses in you. Are some of these feelings quite different from one another? Compare your list with those made by other members of the class and discuss what details in the poem produced the feelings. Also compare different reactions to the same details.

Reviewing the Selection

RECALLING

1. In lines 1–4, what is happening to the sea? What is happening to the land? What two causes combine to move the mighty ocean?

2. What effect does the "wild blast" cause? From where do the "huge billows" come? What effect do the billows have?

3. In line 12, what do "they" hear no more? Why do they not hear it?

4. In the final line, what does the speaker watch?

INTERPRETING

▶ 5. Why is the moon called "mute arbitress of tides"? In what way are the waves "sublime"?

▶ 6. In lines 6–8, what metaphor is used to speak of the waves? What contrasts does this metaphor suggest?

▶ 7. How is the metaphor of lines 6–8 further developed in lines 9–12?

▶ 8. In lines 13–14, how does the speaker feel?

SYNTHESIZING

9. Why might the speaker envy "gloomy rest"? What does this envy imply about how the speaker feels about her or his own life? What might be causing the speaker to feel this way?

10. What parallels or similarities does the poet seem to see between people and the waves? What contrasts between people and the waves are suggested? Do you think the author of the poem views people as part of nature, or does she view people as separate from nature?

Understanding Literature (Questions for Discussion)

1. **Alliteration. Alliteration** is the repetition of initial consonant sounds, as in "wild wind." Find instances of alliteration in Smith's sonnet. What sounds are repeated? How frequently are these sounds used elsewhere in the poem? Why do you think Smith may have chosen to use these particular sounds?

"PRESSED BY THE MOON, MUTE ARBITRESS OF TIDES" **499**

ANSWERS FOR UNDERSTANDING LITERATURE

▶ See the evaluation forms for discussion, active listening, and oral communication, *Assessment Portfolio,* 7.11–7.14.

Responses will vary. Possible responses are given.

1. Alliteration. Instances of alliteration include "moon, mute" in line 1; "swelling surge" in line 3; "silent sabbath" in line 8; "shells and seaweed mingled, on the shore" in line 9; "winds and waters" in line 11; and "life's long" in line 13. Smith frequently repeats the *s* and *w* sounds. Smith may have chosen these particular sounds because they echo the sounds of nature; the hissing *s* sounds like the waves and foam of the sea, and the breathy *w* sounds like the winds.

▶ **Teaching Note:** Students should read aloud to hear the effects of the alliterative phrases.

(cont.)

ANSWERS FOR UNDERSTANDING LITERATURE (CONT.)

2. Anaphora. The first reference to the moon is "moon" (line 1); the first reference to the storm is "equinox" (line 2); the first reference to the waves is "swelling surge" (line 3); the first reference to the wind is "wild blast" (line 5). The phrase "mute arbitress of tides" (line 1) and "its" (line 2) are anaphora for the moon; "wild blast" (line 5) refers to the wind; "huge billows" (line 6) refers to the waves; "warring elements" (line 12) refers to the winds and the waters together.

ANALYTIC SCALES FOR RESPONDING IN WRITING

Assign a score from 1 to 25 for each grading criterion below. (For more detailed evaluation, see the evaluation forms for writing, revising, and proofreading, *Assessment Portfolio*, 7.1–7.10.)

Epitaph

• **Content/Unity.** The epitaph presents a commemoration for a wave. It names the wave's special aspects and its effect on the writer.

• **Organization/Coherence.** The epitaph identifies its subject and then provides reasons for honoring its subject in a sensible order.

• **Language/Style.** The epitaph uses formal language and a serious tone.

• **Conventions.** The epitaph avoids errors in spelling, grammar, usage, mechanics, and manuscript form.

ANSWERS FOR THINKING SKILLS

Students should make observations from two perspectives. For each perspective, students should show careful note-taking and demonstrate the use of charts, checklists, or other planning devices.

▶ Additional practice is provided in the *Essential Skills Practice Book: Study and Research*, 4.6.

---

2. Anaphora. Anaphora is any word or phrase that repeats or refers to something that precedes or follows it. Find the first references in the poem to the moon, the storm, the waves, and the wind. What words or phrases are used as anaphora for these things?

Responding in Writing

Epitaph. An **epitaph** is an inscription or verse written to be used on a tomb or written in commemoration of someone who has died. Write an epitaph for a wave. Decide whether your epitaph will be read aloud or, if it will be inscribed, where it will be inscribed. In your epitaph, depict what was special about the wave during its life and what effects it had on others, including yourself.

Language Lab

Vivid Verbs. Part of the strength of Charlotte Smith's description of the force of the tide comes from her choice of colorful action words. Read the Language Arts Survey, 2.33, "Using Vivid Verbs." Then replace the verbs or verb phrases in the following sentences with more vivid and effective words. Some sentences have more than one verb or verb phrase. Use a thesaurus or a dictionary as necessary.

1. The moon affects the tides.
2. In line 4 of the sonnet, the tide arrives on the land.
3. Line 6 tells about how a wave begins.
4. Charlotte Smith influenced the Romantic poets who followed her.
5. Smith worked hard to support her ten children.

Thinking Skills

Observing. Charlotte Smith had surely observed the sea carefully before she composed her poem. Read the Language Arts Survey, 4.6, "Observing." Then, from the list below, choose two perspectives from which to observe the moon, the sea, a storm, clouds, or some other astronomical or natural object or event. From each perspective, conduct your observations for five minutes, taking careful notes. Prepare observation charts or checklists before observing, and use a separate sheet of paper for each set of observations. Try to avoid making judgments.

a writer planning a short story about the future

a designer planning an advertising campaign

a painter planning a landscape or seascape

a poet planning a poem about hope or about emptiness

ANSWERS FOR LANGUAGE LAB

Answers will vary. Possible answers are given.

1. The moon **toys with** the tides.
2. In line 4 of the sonnet, the tide **conquers** the land.
3. Line 6 **presents a powerful image of** how a wave begins.
4. Charlotte Smith **moved and inspired** the Romantic poets who **emulated** her.

5. Smith **toiled** to **feed and clothe** her ten children.

FOR MORE PRACTICE

Problem. The wind along the shore is loud.

Answer. The wind **screams** along the shore.

▶ Additional practice is provided in the *Essential Skills Practice Book: Language*, 2.33.

PREREADING

from *The Diary of Samuel Pepys*
by Samuel Pepys

ABOUT THE AUTHOR

Samuel Pepys (1633–1703) wrote what many consider to be one of the most interesting accounts of daily English life in existence. Born the son of a tailor, Pepys received a scholarship to Cambridge University, where he earned both bachelor's and master's degrees. Pepys was appointed to the Navy Office and rose to become Secretary of the Admiralty. During this time he studied shipbuilding and mastered navigational mathematics, trying to become a naval expert. He eventually won a seat in Parliament by convincing people of the importance of the navy and of sea power. Pepys was known as an honest, hardworking man. Along with an interest in the navy, he had a strong interest in theater, art, and literature. Pepys counted among his friends such luminaries as scientist Sir Isaac Newton and writer John Dryden.

ABOUT THE SELECTION

The Diary of Samuel Pepys is a clear and interesting account of the daily life of a successful, middle-class Englishman. The journal begins in the year of the Restoration—January 1, 1660—and ends on May 31, 1669. In it, Pepys writes about a variety of important and earth-shattering events, including the plague and the Great London Fire of 1666. Oddly, Pepys wrote his journal in an obscure shorthand that had to be deciphered before the book was published for the first time in 1825. In this selection, the spellings of some words differ from those now in use, and some spellings are inconsistent. However, these irregularities have been left in the text to provide something of the flavor of Pepys's work. It is a diary, written hastily, in the midst of a busy life.

FROM *THE DIARY OF SAMUEL PEPYS* **501**

ENRICHMENT ACTIVITIES

A small group of students can stage a talk-show interview with Samuel Pepys. Students should decide what topics the host will discuss with Pepys and then write questions for the host. The students who role play Pepys and the host should loosely follow the outline of these questions, but should also leave room for improvisation.

SUPPORT FOR LEP STUDENTS

Explain that English spelling and capitalization were not standardized in Pepys's time. Students might want to work with an English-proficient student for help with unfamiliar spellings or capitalization of words.

ADDITIONAL VOCABULARY
buttery—place where provisions are available
malicious—spiteful; harmful

GOALS/OBJECTIVES

Studying this lesson will enable students to

• identify with an Enlightenment speaker and glean relevant historical information from the speaker's account

• describe Samuel Pepys's place in history and his contribution to the literature of the seventeenth century

• define *journal* and analyze journal entries that they encounter in their reading

• define *point of view* and identify and interpret its effects on literature they read

• write a personal account of a historical event

PREREADING NOTES

READER'S JOURNAL

If students have kept journals in the past, encourage them to look back at their journals. Then have students write their impressions of the "person" who made the entries. Do the journals accurately reflect the writer? What do the entries reveal?

THINKING SKILLS

You may want to combine this lesson with a lesson on personal writing. Refer students to the Language Arts Survey, 1.2, "Keeping a Writer's Journal."

▶Additional practice is provided in the *Essential Skills Practice Book: Study and Research,* 4.11.

ANSWERS TO GUIDED READING QUESTIONS

❶ Pepys was troubled that he was spending too much money. He decided to think about some "rules and obligacions" to curb his spending.

❷ He saw a few houses marked with a red cross, a sign of the plague.

ADDITIONAL QUESTIONS AND ACTIVITIES

After they have read the beginning of the diary, ask students to write a brief description of what Pepys may have been like, based on his entries. For example, Pepys did not like *Romeo and Juliet,* so students could infer that Pepys was not a romantic, or that he is critical of actors' abilities.

READER'S JOURNAL

Think back over your life. During which times would it have been most interesting to have kept a journal? Why do you feel this way? What is valuable about a journal?

THINKING SKILLS

Read the Language Arts Survey, 4.11, "Generalizing." Then read the Pepys selection and make a list of four generalizations about life in Pepys's London. Share your generalizations with your classmates and be prepared to back them up with evidence from the selection.

FROM

The Diary of Samuel Pepys

SAMUEL PEPYS

On Seeing a Play by Shakespeare
MARCH 1, 1662

This morning I paid Sir Wm. Batten 40*l*, which I have owed him this half year, having borrowed it of him.

Then to the office all the morning. So dined at home. And after dinner comes my uncle Thomas, with whom I have some high words of difference; but ended quietly, though I fear I shall do no good by fair means upon him.

Then my wife and I by coach, first to see my little picture that is a-drawing, and thence to the Opera and there saw *Romeo and Julett*, the first time it was ever acted.[1] But it is the play of itself the worst that ever I heard in my life, and the worst acted that ever I saw these people do; and I am resolved to go no more to see the first time of acting, for they were all of them out more or less. Thence home, and after supper and wrote by the post—I settled to what I have long entended, to cast up my accounts with myself; and after much pains to do it and great fear, I do find that I am 500*l* in money beforehand in the world, which I was afeared I was not. But I find that I have spent above 250*l* this last half year, which troubles me much. But by God's blessing, I am now resolved to take up, having furnished myself with all things for a great while, and tomorrow to think upon some rules and obligacions upon myself to walk by.

So with my mind eased of a great deal of trouble, though with no great content to find myself above 100*l* worse now then I was half a year ago, I went to bed.

The Plague of 1655
JUNE 7, 1665

This day, much against my Will, I did in Drury-lane see two or three houses marked with a red cross[2] upon the doors, and "Lord have mercy upon us" writ there—which was a sad sight to me, being the first of that kind that to my remembrance

---

1. *Romeo and Julett . . . acted.* Pepys saw *Romeo and Juliet* acted for the first time since the Restoration.
2. **red cross.** A quarantine mark used during the plague

❶
What trouble did Pepys write about in his first entry? What did he decide to do to deal with that trouble?

❷
What did Pepys see that made him uneasy?

I ever saw. It put me into an ill conception of myself and my smell, so that I was forced to buy some roll-tobacco to smell to and chaw—which took away the apprehension.[3]

AUGUST 3, 1665

Up, and betimes to Deptford to Sir G. Carteret's; where not liking the horse which had been hired by Mr. Uthwayt for me, I did desire Sir G. Carteret to let me ride his new 40*l* horse; which he did and so I left my hacquenee[4] behind. And so after staying a good while in their bed-chamber while they were dressing themselfs, discoursing merrily, I parted and to the Ferry, where I was forced to stay a great while before I could get my horse brought over. And then mounted and rode very finely to Dagenham's—all the way, people, Citizens, walking to and again to enquire how the plague is in the City this week by the Bill—which by chance at Greenwich I had heard was 2010 of the plague, and 3000 and odd of all diseases; but methought it was a sad question to be so often asked me. Coming to Dagenham's, I there met our company coming out of the house, having stayed as long as they could for me. So I let them go a little before, and went and took leave of my Lady Sandwich—good woman, who seems very sensible of my service and this late business—and having her directions in some things; among others, to get Sir G. Carteret and my Lord to settle the portion and what Sir G. Carteret is to settle into land as soon as may be; she not liking that it should lie long undone, for fear of death on either side. So took leave of her, and then down to the buttery and eat a piece of cold venison-pie and drank and took some bread and cheese in my hand; and so mounted after them, Mr. Marr very kindly staying to lead me the way. By and by met my Lord Crew returning, after having accompanied them a little way. And so after them, Mr. Marr telling me by the way how a maid-servant of Mr. John Wrights (who lives thereabouts), falling sick of the plague, she was removed to an out-house, and a nurse appointed to look to her—who being once absent, the maid got out of the house at the window and run away. The nurse coming and knocking, and having no answer, believed she was dead, and went and told Mr. Wright so; who, and his lady, were in great strait what to do to get her buried. At last resolved to go to Burntwood hard by, being in that parish, and there get people to do it—but they would not; so he went home full of trouble, and in the way met the wench walking over the Common, which frighted him worse then before. And was forced to send people to take her; which he did, and they got one of the pest Coaches and put her into it to carry her to a pest-house. And passing in a narrow lane, Sir Anthony Browne, with his brother and some friends in the coach, met this coach with the Curtains drawn close. The brother being a young man, and believing there might be some lady in it that would not be seen, and the way being narrow, he thrust his head out of his own into her coach to look, and there saw somebody look very ill, and in a sick dress and stunk mightily; which the coachman also cried out upon. And presently they came up to some people that stood looking after it; and told our gallants that it was a maid of Mr. Wrights carried away sick of the plague—which put the young gentleman into a fright had almost cost him his life, but is now well again.

---

3. **roll-tobacco . . . apprehension.** Tobacco was believed to have medicinal value.
4. **hacquenee.** Horse for riding

CROSS-CURRICULAR ACTIVITIES

Mathematics and Sciences. Have students do research on the plague. They should find out the causes of plague, the types of plague, and the treatments, if any, for the disease. Students can present their research in written reports and should try to include graphs, illustrations, or other visual means of representing data.

Social Studies. Other students might research the social effects of the plague. How were traveling, communication, and social gatherings affected? Students who have an interest in modern literature may examine Albert Camus's Existentialist novel *The Plague* in order to see how a twentieth-century society could potentially be affected by an outbreak of plague.

HISTORICAL NOTE

In the sixteenth and seventeenth centuries, people commonly believed that bathing could endanger one's health. In fact, it was believed that bathing, done either in public bathhouses or in the privacy of one's home, could spread disease. During times of plague, doctors discouraged their patients from bathing because they feared that hot vapors would open skin pores and let in contagions.

ANSWERS TO GUIDED READING QUESTIONS

❶ There were so many people dying that they could not all be buried during the night.

❷ Pepys didn't want to wear wigs because he feared the hair may have been cut from the heads of plague victims, and wearing such a wig would risk infection.

ADDITIONAL QUESTIONS AND ACTIVITIES

• You might ask students to discuss the connections between journal writing and writing a novel. Many novelists such as Daniel Defoe and Charles Dickens typically employ a richness of sensory detail and follow a sensible chronological order that make their novels read almost as if they were journals. Ask students why an author might use certain techniques that a journal writer uses. Do sensory details and a chronological order make a novelist's work more believable, more realistic? Do these same techniques limit a novelist in any way?

• Students can discuss "the madness of people in the town, who will (because they are forbid) come in Crowds along with the dead Corps to see them buried." Is the crowd's behavior exclusively a seventeenth-century phenomenon? Why, or why not?

> Why might people have started carrying the dead to be buried during the day?

> Why did Pepys not want to wear his wigs?

AUGUST 12, 1665

The people die so, that now it seems they are fain to carry the dead to be buried by daylight, the nights not sufficing to do it in. And my Lord Mayor commands people to be within at 9 at night, all (as they say) that the sick may have liberty to go abroad for ayre. There is one also dead out of one of our ships at Deptford, which troubles us mightily—the *Providence* fire-ship, which was just fitted to go to sea. But they tell me today, no more sick on board. And this day W Bodham tells me that one is dead at Woolwich, not far from the Ropeyard. I am told too, that a wife of one of the groomes at Court is dead at Salsbury, so that the King and Queene are speedily to be all gone to Milton. God preserve us.

SEPTEMBER 3, 1665

Lords day. Up, and put on my colourd silk suit, very fine, and my new periwigg, bought a good while since, but darst not wear it because the plague was in Westminster when I bought it. And it is a wonder what will be the fashion after the plague is done as to periwigs, for nobody will dare to buy any haire for fear of the infection—that it had been cut off of the heads of people dead of the plague. . . .

Church being done, my Lord Brouncker, Sir J. Mennes, and I up to the Vestry at the desire of the Justices of the Peace, Sir Th Bidolph and Sir W Boreman and Alderman Hooker—in order to the doing something for the keeping of the plague from growing; but Lord, to consider the madness of people of the town, who will (because they

are forbid) come in Crowds along with the dead Corps to see them buried. But we agreed on some orders for the prevention thereof.[5] Among other stories, one was very passionate methought—of a complaint brought against a man in the town for taking a child from London from an infected house. Alderman Hooker told us it was the child of a very able citizen in Gracious-street, a saddler, who had buried all the rest of his children of the plague; and himself and wife now being shut up, and in despair of escaping, did desire only to save the life of this little child; and so prevailed to have it received stark-naked into the arms of a friend, who brought it (having put it into new fresh clothes) to Grenwich; where, upon hearing the story, we did agree it should be [permitted to be] received and kept in the town. Thence with my Lord Brouncker to Captain Cockes, where we mighty merry, and supped; and very late, I by water to Woolwich, in great apprehensions of an Ague. Here was my Lord Brouncker's lady of pleasure, who I perceive goes everywhere with him, and he I find is obliged to carry her and make all the Courtship to her that can be.

The Great Fire of London
SEPTEMBER 2, 1666

Lords day. Some of our maids sitting up late last night to get things ready against our feast today, Jane called us up, about 3 in the morning, to tell us of a great fire they saw in the City.[6] So I rose, and

5. **orders . . . thereof.** Laws were made forbiddng funeral processions during the plague.
6. **fire . . . City.** This was the Great Fire of London, which burned for four days and nights.

WORDS FOR EVERYDAY USE: a • gue (ā′gyoōo) *n.,* fever and chills

VOCABULARY IN CONTEXT

• Because of his <u>ague</u>, the patient would push aside the bedcovers one minute and pull them up to his chin the next.

slipped on my nightgown and went to her window, and thought it to be on the back side of Markelane at the furthest; but being unused to such fires as fallowed, I thought it far enough off, and so went to bed again and to sleep. About 7 rose again to dress myself, and there looked out at the window and saw the fire not so much as it was, and further off. So to my closet to set things to rights after yesterday's cleaning. By and by Jane comes and tells me that she hears that above 300 houses have been burned down tonight by the fire we saw, and that it was now burning down all Fishstreet by London Bridge. So I made myself ready presently, and walked to the Tower and there got up upon one of the high places, Sir J Robinsons little son going up with me; and there I did see the houses at that end of the bridge all on fire, and an infinite great fire on this and the other side the end of the bridge—which, among other people, did trouble me for poor little Michell and our Sarah on the Bridge. So down, with my heart full of trouble, to the Lieutenant of the Tower, who tells me that it begun this morning in the King's bakers house in Pudding-lane, and that it hath burned down St. Magnes Church and most part of Fishstreete already. So I down to the water-side and there got a boat and through bridge, and there saw a lamentable fire. Poor Michells house, as far as the Old Swan, already burned that way and the fire running further, that in a very little time it got as far as the Stillyard while I was there. Everybody endeavouring to remove their goods, and flinging into the River or bringing them into lighters that

lay off. Poor people staying in their houses as long as till the very fire touched them, and then running into boats or clambering from one pair of stair by the water-side to another. And among other things, the poor pigeons I perceive were loath to leave their houses, but hovered about the windows and balconies till they were some of them burned, their wings, and fell down.

Having stayed, and in an hour's time seen the fire rage every way, and nobody to my sight <u>endeavouring</u> to quench it, but to remove their goods and leave all to the fire; and having seen it get as far as the Steeleyard, and the wind mighty high and driving it into the city, and everything, after so long a drougth, proving combustible, even the very stones of churches, and among other things, the poor steeple by which pretty Mrs. _____ lives, and whereof my old school-fellow Elborough is parson, taken fire in the very top and there burned till it fall down—I to Whitehall with a gentleman with me who desired to go off from the Tower to see the fire in my boat—to White-hall, and there up to the King's closet in the chapel, where people came about me and I did give them an account dismayed them all; and word was carried in to the King, so I was called for and did tell the King and Duke of York what I saw, and that unless his Majesty did command houses to be pulled down, nothing could stop the fire. They seemed much troubled, and the King commanded me to go to my Lord Mayor from him and command him to spare no houses but to pull down before the fire every way. The Duke of York bid

❶
What factors contributed to making the fire especially destructive?

❷
When and where did the fire begin?

HISTORICAL NOTE

Attracted by the hope of work in urban areas, many poor people crowded the workers' quarters of London. Fires were a common threat in seventeenth-century cities, and flimsy housing and overcrowding among the poor increased the threat. The wealthy often built their houses of brick or stone. Even so, the Great Fire of 1666 destroyed 75 percent of London, including thirteen thousand houses.

QUOTABLES

❝How great a matter a little fire kindleth.❞

—James 3:5

WORDS FOR EVERYDAY USE: en • deav • or (en dev´ər) *vi.,* try, attempt

VOCABULARY IN CONTEXT

• Should we <u>endeavor</u> to cross the river in this storm?

me tell him that if he would have any more soldiers, he shall; and so did my Lord Arlington afterward, as a great secret. Here meeting with Captain Cocke, I in his coach, which he lent me, and Creed with me, to Pauls; and there walked along Watling-street as well as I could, every creature coming away loaden with goods to save—and here and there sick people carried away in beds. Extraordinary good goods carried in carts and on backs. At last met my Lord Mayor in Canning Streete, like a man spent, with a hankercher about his neck. To the King's message, he cried like a fainting woman, "Lord, what can I do? I am spent. People will not obey me. I have been pull[ing] down houses. But the fire overtakes us faster then we can do it." That he needed no more soldiers; and that for himself, he must go and refresh himself, having been up all night. So he left me, and I him, and walked home—seeing people all almost distracted and no manner of means used to quench the fire. The houses too, so very thick thereabouts, and full of matter for burning, as pitch and tar, in Thames-street—and warehouses of oyle and wines and Brandy and other things. Here I saw Mr. Isaccke Houblon, that handsome man—prettily dressed and dirty at his door at Dowgate, receiving some of his brothers things whose houses were on fire; and as he says, have been removed twice already, and he doubts (as it soon proved) that they must be in a little time removed from his house also—which was a sad consideration. And to see the churches all filling with goods, by people who themselfs should have been quietly there at this time.

By this time it was about 12 a-clock, and so home and there find my guests, which was Mr. Wood and his wife, Barbary Shelden, and also Mr. Moone—she mighty

About what did the Lord Mayor complain? ❶

What type of activity was taking place in the city when Pepys and Mr. Moone went for a walk? ❷

fine, and her husband, for aught I see, a likely man. But Mr. Moones design and mine, which was to look over my closet and please him with the sight thereof, which he hath long desired, was wholly disappointed, for we were in great trouble and disturbance at this fire, not knowing what to think of it. However, we had an extraordinary good dinner, and as merry as at this time we could be.

While at dinner, Mrs. Batelier came to enquire after Mr. Woolfe and Stanes (who it seems are related to them), whose houses in Fishstreet are all burned, and they in a sad condition. She would not stay in the fright.

As soon as dined, I and Moone away and walked through the City, the streets full of nothing but people and horses and carts loaden with goods, ready to run over one another, and removing goods from one burned house to another—they now removing out of Canning-street (which received goods in the morning) into Lumbard Streete and further; and among others, I now saw my little goldsmith Stokes receiving some friend's goods, whose house itself was burned the day after. We parted at Pauls, he home and I to Pauls-Wharf, where I had appointed a boat to attend me; and took in Mr. Carcasse and his brother, whom I met in the street, and carried them below and above bridge, to and again, to see the fire, which was now got further, both below and above, and no likelihood of stopping it. Met with the King and Duke of York in their Barge, and with them to Queen-Hith and there called Sir Rd. Browne to them. Their order was only to pull down houses apace, and so below bridge at the water-side; but little was or could be done, the fire coming upon them so fast. Good hopes there was of stopping it at the Three Cranes above, and at Buttolphs-

Wharf below bridge, if care be used; but the wind carries it into the City, so as we know not by the water-side what it doth there. River full of lighter[s] and boats taking in goods, and good goods swimming in the water; and only, I observed that hardly one lighter or boat in three that had the goods of a house in, but there was a pair of virginalls[7] in it. Having seen as much as I could now, I away to Whitehall by appointment, and there walked to St. James's Park, and there met my wife and Creed and Wood and his wife and walked to my boat, and there upon the water again, and to the fire up and down, it still increasing and the wind great. So near the fire as we could for smoke; and all over the Thames, with one's face in the wind you were almost burned with a shower of Firedrops—this is very true—so as houses were burned by these drops and flakes of fire, three or four, nay five or six houses, one from another. When we could endure no more upon the water, we to a little alehouse on the Bankside over against the Three Cranes, and there stayed till it was dark almost and saw the fire grow; and as it grow darker, appeared more and more, and in Corners and upon steeples and between churches and houses, as far as we courd see up the hill of the City, in a most horrid malicious bloody flame, not like the fine flame of an ordinary fire. Barbary and her husband away before us. We stayed till, it being darkish, we saw the fire as only one entire arch of fire from this to the other side the bridge, and in a bow up the hill, for an arch of above a mile long. It made me weep to see it. The churches, houses, and all on fire and flaming at once, and a horrid noise the flames made, and the cracking of houses at their ruine. So home with a sad heart, and there find everybody discoursing and lamenting the fire; and poor Tom

Hater came with some few of his goods saved out of his house, which is burned upon Fish-street hill. I invited him to lie at my house, and did receive his goods: but was deceived in his lying there, the noise coming every moment of the growth of the Fire, so as we were forced to begin to pack up our own goods and prepare for their removal. And did by Moone-shine (it being brave, dry, and moonshine and warm weather) carry much of my goods into the garden, and Mr. Hater and I did remove my money and Iron-chests into my cellar—as thinking that the safest place. And got my bags of gold into my office ready to carry away, and my chief papers of accounts also there, and my tallies into a box by themselfs. So great was our fear, as Sir W. Batten had carts come out of the country to fetch away his goods this night. We did put Mr. Hater, poor man, to bed a little; but he got but very little rest, so much noise being in my house, taking down of goods.

SEPTEMBER 5, 1666

I lay down in the office again upon W. Hewer's quilt, being mighty weary and sore in my feet with going till I was hardly able to stand. About 2 in the morning my wife calls me up and tells of new Cryes of "Fyre!"—it being come to Barkeing Church, which is the bottom of our lane. I up; and finding it so, resolved presently to take her away; and did, and took my gold (which was about 2350*l*), W. Hewer, and Jane down by Poundy's boat to Woolwich. But Lord, what a sad sight it was by moonlight to see the whole City almost on fire—that you might see it plain at Woolwich, as if you were by it. There when I came, I find the gates[8] shut, but no

---

7. **pair of virginalls.** Small rectangular harpsichord of the sixteenth century, usually held in the lap
8. **gates.** Dockyard gates

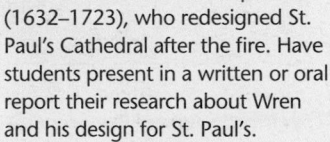

❶ How were people escaping from the fire?

❷ What did Pepys finally have to do about his own home?

❶ People were escaping from the fire by boats and other small craft on the river.

❷ Pepys finally had to begin removing goods from his own home, carrying them out into the garden or storing them in iron chests in the cellar.

CROSS-CURRICULAR ACTIVITIES

Architecture. Students can research the work of architect Christopher Wren (1632–1723), who redesigned St. Paul's Cathedral after the fire. Have students present in a written or oral report their research about Wren and his design for St. Paul's.

ADDITIONAL QUESTIONS AND ACTIVITIES

While Pepys does provide a detailed account of the lives of the bourgeois class in London during the Enlightenment, there exist few similar accounts from the perspective of the impoverished classes in London. One of the first writers to document the lives of impoverished London dwellers was the Victorian journalist Henry Mayhew.

Students who are interested in London life or the inequalities present in the British class structure should be encouraged to read a few brief selections from Mayhew's *London Labour and the London Poor*, 1849–1850.

❶ The rumor was that the French had
started the fire and that they were
invading the city.

❷ When he reached the top of
Barkeing steeple, Pepys saw fires
burning everywhere and the
destruction left in the fire's wake.

❸ Pepys had forgotten the day of the
week because of the harried events of
the fire and his lack of sleep.

ANSWERS TO SELECTION CHECK TEST 4.7.7

EX. How is *Pepys* pronounced?
Pepys is pronounced like *peeps*.

1. Why does Pepys mention
Romeo and Juliet?
**He saw the play performed (or,
it was the worst play he had
ever seen).**

2. Why was a red cross marked
on doors?
**It marked houses of people who
suffered from the plague.**

3. Why was a 9:00 P.M. curfew
imposed?
**After 9:00 P.M. those stricken by
the plague were allowed to go
out.**

4. What did Pepys watch from
the Tower of London?
**He watched the Great Fire of
London.**

5. Why did Pepys move his
belongings to the garden?
**He was preparing to leave the
city if the fire got dangerously
close.**

---

❶ *What was the rumor about how the fire had started?*

❷ *What did Pepys see when he reached the top of Barkeing steeple?*

❸ *Why had Pepys forgotten the day of the week?*

---

guard kept at all; which troubled me, because of discourses now begun that there is plot in it and that the French had done it.[9] I got the gates open, and to Mr. Shelden's, where I locked up my gold and charged my wife and W. Hewer never to leave the room without one of them in it night nor day. So back again, by the way seeing my goods well in the lighters at Deptford and watched well by people. Home, and whereas I expected to have seen our house on fire, it being now about 7 a-clock, it was not. But to the Fyre, and there find greater hopes then I expected; for my confidence of finding our office on fire was such, that I durst not ask anybody how it was with us, till I came and saw it not burned. But going to the fire, I find, by the blowing up of houses and the great help given by the workmen out of the King's yards, sent up by Sir W. Penn, there is a good stop given to it, as well at Marke-lane end as ours—it having only burned the Dyall of Barkeing Church, and part of the porch, and was there quenched. I up to the top of Barkeing steeple, and there saw the saddest sight of desolation that I ever saw. Everywhere great fires. Oyle-cellars and brimstone and other things burning. I became afeared to stay there long; and therefore down again as fast as I could, the fire being spread as far as I could see it, and to Sir W. Penn's and there eat a piece of cold meat, having eaten nothing since Sunday but the remains of Sunday's dinner.

Here I met with Mr. Young and Whistler; and having removed all my things, and received good hopes that the fire at our end is stopped, they and I walked into the town and find Fanchurch street, Gracious-street, and Lumbard-street all in dust. The Exchange a sad sight, nothing standing there of all the statues or pillars but Sir Tho. Gresham's picture in the corner.[10] Walked into Moore-fields (our feet ready to burn, walking through the town among the hot coles) and find that full of people, and poor wretches carrying their goods there, and everybody keeping his goods together by themselfs (and a great blessing it is to them that it is fair weather for them to keep abroad night and day); drank there, and paid twopence for a plain penny loaf.

Thence homeward, having passed through Cheapside and Newgate-market, all burned—and seen Anthony Joyces house in fire. And took up (which I keep by me) a piece of glass of Mercer's chapel in the street, where much more was, so melted and buckled with the heat of the fire, like parchment. I also did see a poor Catt taken out of a hole in the chimney joyning to the wall of the Exchange, with the hair all burned off the body and yet alive. So home at night, and find there good hopes of saving our office—but great endeavours of watching all night and having men ready; and so we lodged them in the office, and had drink and bread and cheese for them. And I lay down and slept a good night about midnight—though when I rose, I hear that there had been a great alarme of French and Duch being risen—which proved nothing. But it is a strange thing to see how long this time did look since Sunday, having been alway full of variety of actions, and little sleep, that it looked like a week or more. And I had forgot almost the day of the week. ∎

---

9. **discourses . . . it.** Rumors that the French had started the fire and were now entering the city
10. **Exchange . . . corner.** The stock exchange was destroyed except for the statue of Gresham, the founder.

ANALYTIC SCALES FOR RESPONDING IN WRITING

Assign a score from 1 to 25 for each grading criterion below. (For more detailed evaluation, see the evaluation forms for writing, revising, and proofreading, *Assessment Portfolio,* 7.1–7.10.)

Personal Account

• **Content/Unity.** The entries present a character's point of view of a noteworthy event.

• **Organization/Coherence.** The entries are dated. Each entry uses concrete details to recall events and to reveal the character's interior world.

• **Language/Style.** The entries use vivid and precise nouns, verbs, and modifiers.

• **Conventions.** The entries avoid errors in spelling, grammar, usage, mechanics, and manuscript form.

▶ Additional practice is provided in the *Essential Skills Practice Book: Writing,* 1.16.

Responding to the Selection

What part of this journal do you find the most interesting? Why? What are your impressions of Pepys? What sort of person was he? Is he someone who you would have liked to have known had you lived in his day? Why, or why not?

Reviewing the Selection

RECALLING

1. What play did Pepys record having seen in the entry for March 1, 1662? What did he think of the play?

2. Why were the words "Lord have mercy upon us" written on the doors of the houses in Drury-lane? What did Anthony Browne's brother see when he looked inside the coach? Why, according to Pepys, did people stop buying wigs?

3. What advice did Pepys give the king and why? What kind of "shower" rained on Pepys, his wife, and his friends while they were in their boat? To what did Pepys liken the fire in the city as it appeared to him from the tavern? How large was the fire?

4. What did Pepys report having almost forgotten at the end of the selection?

INTERPRETING

5. What sort of person do you think Pepys was? Why might he not have enjoyed a dramatic, romantic play like the one described in the entry for March 1? What reasons did he give for not liking the acting?

6. How extensive was the plague in 1665? What mood is created by Pepys's description of it?

7. What did Pepys describe immediately after describing the arch of fire over the city? How does describing this specific event increase the horror of the whole?

8. Why did it seem to Pepys that the events of the previous couple of days had taken a week or more?

SYNTHESIZING

9. What was Pepys's attitude toward himself and others? Do you think he was a reliable record-keeper? Why or why not?

10. What might have been Pepys's purpose in keeping a journal? What can you infer about him based on what he chose to record?

FROM *THE DIARY OF SAMUEL PEPYS* 509

ANSWERS FOR UNDERSTANDING LITERATURE

►See the evaluation forms for discussion, active listening, and oral communication, *Assessment Portfolio, 7.11–7.14.*
Responses will vary. Possible responses are given.

1. Journal. Pepys rarely gives insight into his interior world. Most often, he chooses to note his reactions to events rather than detail his ruminations about them. For example, he writes that seeing the houses marked for plague "put me into an ill conception of myself and my smell, so that I was forced to buy some roll-tobacco to smell and to chaw—which took away the apprehension." Pepys notes his discomfort but doesn't dwell on it; at the same time, he gives later readers an interesting bit of social history. Pepys's journal is a record of events first and a personal log second; most glimpses of his personality emerge through his documentation of events rather than through straightforward statements of feeling.

►**Teaching Note:** Students should support their opinions with direct quotations from the selection.

►**Additional Resources:** *Essential Skills Practice Book: Writing, 1.2.*

2. Point of View. Pepys's point of view has a strong but not over-whelming effect on the reader's perception of events. Pepys's detachment from what he de-scribes doesn't block the reader's view of happenings. However, his point of view as a middle-class male does color his account. One would imagine that the plague-ridden maid-servant would have far graver concerns than Pepys's fear of infected periwigs. A journal entry about a historical event dif-fers from other straight, factual accounts because it reveals only one person's experience. The reader can know only what happens to and around the journal writer and must see events through the jour-nal writer's eyes. However, a personal view of an event such as the plague is valuable because it

(cont.)

Understanding Literature (Questions for Discussion)

1. **Journal.** A **journal,** like a diary, is a day-to-day record of a person's activities, experiences, thoughts, and feelings. In contrast to a *diary,* the word *journal* connotes an outward rather than an inward focus. Given these definitions, would you characterize Pepys's work as a diary or a journal? How often does Pepys give us insight into his interior world? Does he express his emotions freely, or are his writings more a documentation of the time during which he lived?

2. **Point of View. Point of view** is the vantage point from which a story is told. How much does Pepys's point of view affect how you perceive the events he describes? How is a person's diary entry about a historical event different from a newspaper article or any other straight, factual account of an event? How is one person's point of view about something like the plague valuable in its own way?

Responding in Writing

Personal Account. Recall something you've read in the news or in a history book about a political event, a natural disaster, a plane crash, or some other newsworthy event. Create a character and have this person write a personal account of the incident in three or four brief journal entries. The character may be you, or the character may be fictional. Try to express a distinct point of view as you imagine witnessing the event. Use concrete details and try to put the reader into the character's interior world.

Great Fire of London, 1666. *Museum of London*

ANSWERS FOR UNDERSTANDING LITERATURE (CONT.)

personalizes an event that appears static in most other historical accounts.

►**Teaching Note:** Students can discuss how the events of the plague or the fire might have been recorded by some of the people named in Pepys's journal, such as the maid-servant or the Lord Mayor.

ANALYTIC SCALES FOR RESPONDING IN WRITING

Grading scales appear on page 508.

PREREADING

from *Gulliver's Travels*
from "A Voyage to Lilliput"
from "A Voyage to Brobdingnag"
by Jonathan Swift

ABOUT THE AUTHOR

Jonathan Swift's (1667–1745) family was poor, but a generous uncle funded Jonathan's education at Kilkenny Grammar School and at Trinity College, Dublin. Undecided about what career to pursue, Swift went to live with and work for Sir William Temple in Surrey. There he met "Stella," to whom he dedicated much of his work. Swift was buried by her side, although in life their relationship was unsteady. After reading one of Swift's first publications, John Dryden told him, "Cousin Swift, you will never be a poet." Very soon after this, Swift left Temple's home for Ireland and became a priest. Two years later, though, he rededicated himself to a writing career.

Swift suffered from dizziness and nausea (probably Ménière's syndrome) for most of his life. While he said that he "liked individuals but hated humanity," he cared enough to try to mend the evils that he saw in the world. Swift wrote biting commentaries and satires for numerous periodicals and journals, and, as its official pamphleteer, wrote position papers for the Tory government, as well as his own epitaph: "Where fierce indignation no longer tears the heart." Notable satirical works by Swift include *The Battle of the Books* (1704, composed 1697), *A Tale of a Tub* (1704), *Gulliver's Travels* (1726), and "A Modest Proposal" (1729).

ABOUT THE SELECTIONS

While enjoyable as a fantastic travel account, *Gulliver's Travels* (1726) is at the same time a wicked **satire** on politics and political morals. Originally titled "*Travels into Several Remote Nations of the World," by Lemuel Gulliver*, the book tells of Gulliver's experiences in four fantastic lands. The selection includes excerpts from Part I, "A Voyage to Lilliput," where the people are one-twelfth the size of Gulliver and are proportionally small-minded and petty; and from Part II, "A Voyage to Brobdingnag," where the people are twelve times Gulliver's size and, after hearing his tales of European social and technological achievements, come to view Europeans as "a pernicious race of little odious vermin." In Part III Gulliver visits Laputa, a flying island inhabited by "wise" scholars with their heads in the clouds, who are in practical endeavors completely inept; and in Part IV he visits the land of the Houyhnhnms, inhabited by speaking horses whose good sense, gentleness, and gentility contrast sharply with the vigorous stupidity of the human-like Yahoos.

FROM *GULLIVER'S TRAVELS* / FROM "*A VOYAGE TO LILLIPUT*" **511**

GOALS/OBJECTIVES

Studying this lesson will enable students to

- have positive experiences reading satire
- describe Jonathan Swift's literary accomplishments and explain the historical significance of his writings
- define *fantasy* and *irony* and recognize and

interpret fantasy and irony as they encounter them in their reading
- characterize tone in literature they read
- use the card catalog to research information

ADDITIONAL RESOURCES

READER'S GUIDE
- Selection Worksheet, 7.5

ASSESSMENT PORTFOLIO
- Selection Check Test, 4.7.9
- Selection Test, 4.7.10

ESSENTIAL SKILLS PRACTICE BOOKS
- *Language*, 2.149
- *Study and Research*, 4.22, 4.23

ENRICHMENT ACTIVITIES

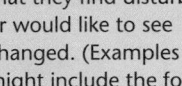

Have students discuss aspects of modern society that they find disturbing or would like to see changed. (Examples might include the following: an increasing number of television-dependent young adults; cultural tensions; politics.) Ask students what elements of humor they can find in these troubling situations. Students then may choose a particular issue and write a satiric paragraph, mixing critique with humor.

SUPPORT FOR LEP STUDENTS

The advanced vocabulary and syntax of the selection may be difficult for some students. Encourage them to stop periodically to make notes about what they have read.

ADDITIONAL VOCABULARY
plumb—determine depth
expedient—device used in an emergency
discompose—disarrange; disturb the order of
viceroy—person ruling a country as the deputy of a sovereign
procurement—obtaining; securing
integrity—honesty; sincerity
privy to—privately informed about

PREREADING NOTES

READER'S JOURNAL

Students may wish to assume the role of a soldier, war correspondent, or politician.

RESEARCH SKILLS

If time permits, students can use reference works to find this information.

▶Additional practice is provided in the *Essential Skills Practice Book: Study and Research*, 4.23.

VOCABULARY FROM THE SELECTION

abominate	ingratiate
acute	junta
agitation	lenity
confounded	odious
contriver	panegyric
desolation	pernicious
detract	pervert
elude	procure
embargo	recapitulate
extremities	scruple
hitherto	stratagem
impotent	tribute
infallibly	veneration

READER'S JOURNAL

What feelings arc aroused in you by images and accounts of war? Are wars ever necessary? Are they sometimes fought for insufficient reasons? What reasons, if any, might justify going to war? In your journal, record your answers to these questions.

RESEARCH SKILLS

Read the Language Arts Survey, 4.23, "Using Reference Works." Which type of source would you use to find each of the following types of information: (1) Swift's birthdate; (2) a list of Swift's works; (3) a list of modern essays on Swift; (4) an eighteenth-century review of *Gulliver's Travels*; (5) the size and location of Surrey?

FROM

Gulliver's Travels

JONATHAN SWIFT

FROM "A VOYAGE TO LILLIPUT"

CHAPTER 5. THE AUTHOR BY AN EXTRAORDINARY <u>STRATAGEM</u> PREVENTS AN INVASION. A HIGH TITLE OF HONOR IS CONFERRED UPON HIM. . . .

The empire of Blefuscu is an island situated to the north north-east side of Lilliput, from whence it is parted only by a channel of eight hundred yards wide. I had not yet seen it, and upon this notice of an intended invasion, I avoided appearing on that side of the coast, for fear of being discovered by some of the enemy's ships, who had received no intelligence of me; all intercourse between the two empires having been strictly forbidden during the war, upon pain of death; and an <u>embargo</u> laid by our Emperor upon all vessels whatsoever. I communicated to his Majesty a project I had formed of seizing the enemy's whole fleet; which, as our scouts assured us, lay at anchor in the harbor ready to sail with the first fair wind. I consulted the most experienced seamen upon the depth of the channel, which they had often plumbed; who told me, that in the middle at high water it was seventy *glumgluffs* deep, which is about six foot of European measure; and the rest of it fifty *glumgluffs* at most. I walked to the northeast coast over against Blefuscu; where, lying down behind a hillock, I took out my small pocket perspective glass,[1] and viewed the enemy's fleet at anchor, consisting of about fifty men of war, and a great number of transports: I then came back to my house, and gave order (for which I had a warrant) for a great quantity of the strongest cable and bars of iron. The cable was about as thick as packthread, and the bars of the length and size of a

---

1. **perspective glass.** Telescope

WORDS FOR EVERYDAY USE:
strat • a • gem (straťə jəm) *n.*, trick or plan
em • bar • go (em bär´gō) *n.*, government order prohibiting the entry or departure of ships

VOCABULARY IN CONTEXT

• The team devised a <u>stratagem</u> to defeat their opponents.
• Because of the grain <u>embargo</u>, many farmers could not sell their crops abroad.

knitting-needle. I trebled the cable to make it stronger, and for the same reason I twisted three of the iron bars together, bending the <u>extremities</u> into a hook. Having thus fixed fifty hooks to as many cables, I went back to the northeast coast, and putting off my coat, shoes, and stockings, walked into the sea in my leathern jerkin,[2] about half an hour before high water. I waded with what haste I could, and swam in the middle about thirty yards until I felt the ground; I arrived at the fleet in less than half an hour. The enemy was so frighted when they saw me, that they leaped out of their ships, and swam to shore, where there could not be fewer than thirty thousand souls. I then took my tackling, and fastening a hook to the hole at the prow of each, I tied all the cords together at the end. While I was thus employed, the enemy discharged several thousand arrows, many of which stuck in my hands and face; and besides the excessive smart, gave me much disturbance in my work. My greatest apprehension was for my eyes, which I should have <u>infallibly</u> lost, if I had not suddenly thought of an expedient. I kept, among other little necessaries, a pair of spectacles in a private pocket, which, as I observed before, had escaped the Emperor's searchers. These I took out, and fastened as strongly as I could upon my nose; and thus armed went on boldly with my work in spite of the enemy's arrows; many of which struck against the glasses of my spectacles, but without any other effect, further than a little to discompose them. I had now fastened all the hooks, and taking the knot in my hand, began to pull; but not a ship would stir, for they were all too fast by their anchors, so that the boldest part of my enterprise remained. I therefore let go the cord, and leaving the hooks fixed to the ships, I resolutely cut with my knife the cables that fastened the anchors, receiving about two hundred shots in my face and hands; then I took up the knotted end of the cables to which my hooks were tied; and with great ease drew fifty of the enemy's largest men-of-war after me.

The Blefuscudians, who had not the least imagination of what I intended, were at first <u>confounded</u> with astonishment. They had seen me cut the cables, and thought my design was only to let the ships run adrift, or fall foul on each other: but when they perceived the whole fleet moving in order, and saw me pulling at the end, they set up such a scream of grief and despair, that it is almost impossible to describe or conceive. When I had got out of danger, I stopped a while to pick out the arrows that stuck in my hands and face, and rubbed on some of the same ointment that was given me at my first arrival, as I have formerly mentioned. I then took off my spectacles, and waiting about an hour until the tide was a little fallen, I waded through the middle with my cargo, and arrived safe at the royal port of Lilliput.

The Emperor and his whole court stood on the shore, expecting the issue of this great adventure. They saw the ships move forward in a large half-moon, but could not discern me, who was up to my breast in water. When I advanced to the middle

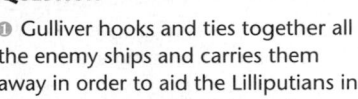

①
How does Gulliver aid the Lilliputians in their war against the Blefuscudians?

2. **jerkin.** Vest or sleeveless jacket

FROM *GULLIVER'S TRAVELS* / FROM "*A VOYAGE TO LILLIPUT*"   **513**

ANSWER TO GUIDED READING QUESTION

① Gulliver hooks and ties together all the enemy ships and carries them away in order to aid the Lilliputians in their war against the Blefuscudians.

HISTORICAL NOTE

In 1714, the Scriblerus Club was formed to satirize false teachings and pedantry. The group included Swift and other writers such as Alexander Pope, John Arbuthnot, John Gay, and Thomas Parnell. Although the club discontinued meetings after the first year, Swift's association with these writers and thinkers influenced his development of Part Three of *Gulliver's Travels*.

VOCABULARY IN CONTEXT

- Frostbite first affects a person's <u>extremities</u>, such as the fingers and the toes.
- Can you <u>infallibly</u> identify the constellations without looking through a telescope?
- The overlapping sets of animal tracks <u>confounded</u> the hunters.

of the channel, they were yet more in pain, because I was under water to my neck. The Emperor concluded me to be drowned, and that the enemy's fleet was approaching in a hostile manner: but he was soon eased of his fears, for the channel growing shallower every step I made, I came in a short time within hearing; and holding up the end of the cable by which the fleet was fastened, I cried in a loud voice, Long live the most puissant[3] Emperor of Lilliput! This great prince received me at my landing with all possible encomiums,[4] and created me a *Nardac* upon the spot, which is the highest title of honor among them.

His Majesty desired I would take some other opportunity of bringing all the rest of his enemy's ships into his ports. And so unmeasurable is the ambition of princes, that he seemed to think of nothing less than reducing the whole empire of Blefuscu into a province, and governing it by a viceroy; of destroying the Big-Endian exiles, and compelling that people to break the smaller end of their eggs,[5] by which he would remain sole monarch of the whole world. But I endeavored to divert him from this design, by many arguments drawn from the topics of policy as well as justice: and I plainly protested, that I would never be an instrument of bringing a free and brave people into slavery. And when the matter was debated in council, the wisest part of the ministry were of my opinion.

This open bold declaration of mine was so opposite to the schemes and politics of his Imperial Majesty, that he could never

What does Gulliver refuse to do? ❶

forgive me; he mentioned it in a very artful manner at council, where I was told that some of the wisest appeared, at least by their silence, to be of my opinion; but others, who were my secret enemies, could not forbear some expressions, which by a side-wind[6] reflected on me. And from this time began an intrigue between his Majesty and a <u>junta</u> of ministers maliciously bent against me, which broke out in less than two months, and had like to have ended in my utter destruction. Of so little weight are the greatest services to princes, when put into the balance with a refusal to gratify their passions.

◆ ◆ ◆

FROM "A VOYAGE TO BROBDINGNAG"

FROM CHAPTER 6.

His Majesty in another audience was at the pains to <u>recapitulate</u> the sum of all I had spoken; compared the questions he made with the answers I had given; then taking me into his hands, and stroking me gently, delivered himself in these words, which I shall never forget, nor the manner he spoke them in. "My little friend Grildrig,[7] you have made a most admirable <u>panegyric</u> upon your

---

3. **puissant.** Powerful
4. **encomiums.** Expressions of high praise
5. **Big-Endian . . . eggs.** In Chapter 4, Gulliver explains that this dispute started with the Emperor's decree that all his subjects must break their eggs at the small end. This dispute is Swift's allegorical and satirical portrayal of the schism between Catholics and Protestants during his time.
6. **side-wind.** Indirect means, method, or manner
7. **Grildrig.** King's name for Gulliver

WORDS FOR EVERYDAY USE:

jun • ta (hōōn´ tə) *n.*, council
re • ca • pit • u • late (rē´ kə pich´ ə lāt) *vi.*, summarize
pan • e • gyr • ic (pan´ ə jir´ ik) *n.*, high praise

VOCABULARY IN CONTEXT

• According to recent news reports, the ruler has refused the advice of his <u>junta</u>.
• Professor Barlow usually asks one of her students to <u>recapitulate</u> the readings.
• I was grateful for the <u>panegyric</u> I received for my hard work.

Gulliver Released from the Strings.
Gulliver's Travels, illustrated by Arthur Rackham. J. M. Dent & Co., London. Courtesy of Wellesley College, Special Collections

ANSWER TO GUIDED READING QUESTION

❶ The king thinks the government of Gulliver's people is controlled by those who exhibit "ignorance, idleness, and vice."

QUOTABLES

❝I have ever hated all nations, professions and communities, and all my love is towards individuals . . . But principally I hate and detest that animal called man; although I heartily love John, Peter, Thomas, and so forth.❞

—Jonathan Swift

---

country. You have clearly proved that ignorance, idleness, and vice are the proper ingredients for qualifying a legislator. That laws are best explained, interpreted, and applied by those whose interests and abilities lie in <u>perverting</u>, confounding, and <u>eluding</u> them. I observe among you some lines of an institution which in its original might have been tolerable; but these half erased, and the rest wholly blurred and blotted by corruptions. It doth not appear from all you have said how any one virtue is required towards the procurement of any one station among you; much less that men are ennobled on account of their virtue, that priests are advanced for their piety or learning, soldiers for their conduct or valor, judges for their integrity, senators for the love of their country, or counselors for their wisdom. As for yourself," continued the King, "who have spent the greatest part of your life in traveling, I am well disposed to hope you may hitherto have escaped many vices of your country. But by what I have gathered from your own relation, and the answers I have with much pains wringed and extorted from you, I cannot but conclude the bulk of your natives to be the most <u>pernicious</u> race of little <u>odious</u> vermin that nature ever suffered to crawl upon the surface of the earth."

❶
What does the king think of European government as it has been described to him by Gulliver?

WORDS FOR EVERYDAY USE:

per • vert (pər vʉrt´) vt., distort, misinterpret
e • lude (ē lo͞od´) vt., evade, escape
per • ni • cious (pər nish´əs) adj., wicked
o • di • ous (ō´dē əs) adj., arousing disgust, offensive

FROM *GULLIVER'S TRAVELS* / FROM "A VOYAGE TO LILLIPUT"   515

VOCABULARY IN CONTEXT

• Researchers complain that superficial news reports <u>pervert</u> their findings.
• How has the criminal <u>eluded</u> capture for so many years?
• Democracies throughout the world have condemned the dictator's <u>pernicious</u> acts.
• Sulfur has a strong, <u>odious</u> smell.

CROSS-CURRICULAR ACTIVITIES

Mathematics and Sciences. Students in pairs or groups of three or four can play a description game. Like Gulliver, they should describe an invention without naming it directly. Students should imagine describing the object to a person who has never seen or experienced it. Encourage students to use sensory clues and comparisons.

◆ ◆ ◆

FROM CHAPTER 7.

In hopes to <u>ingratiate</u> myself farther into his Majesty's favor, I told him of an invention discovered between three and four hundred years ago, to make a certain powder, into an heap of which the smallest spark of fire falling would kindle the whole in a moment, although it were as big as a mountain, and make it all fly up in the air together, with a noise and <u>agitation</u> greater than thunder. That a proper quantity of this powder rammed into an hollow tube of brass or iron, according to its bigness, would drive a ball of iron or lead with such violence and speed as nothing was able to sustain its force. That the largest balls thus discharged would not only destroy whole ranks of an army at once, but batter the strongest walls to the ground; sink down ships with a thousand men in each, to the bottom of the sea; and, when linked together by a chain, would cut through masts and rigging; divide hundreds of bodies in the middle, and lay all waste before them. That we often put this powder into large hollow balls of iron, and discharged them by an engine into some city we were besieging; which would rip up the pavements, tear the houses to pieces, burst and throw splinters on every side, dashing out the brains of all who came near. That I knew the ingredients very well, which were cheap and common; I understood the manner of compounding them, and could direct his workmen how to make those tubes of a size proportionable to all other things in his Majesty's kingdom, and the largest need not be above two hundred foot long; twenty or thirty of which tubes, charged with the proper quantity of powder and balls, would batter down the walls of the strongest town in his dominions in a few hours; or destroy the whole metropolis, if ever it should pretend to dispute his absolute commands. This I humbly offered to his Majesty as a small <u>tribute</u> of acknowledgement in return of so many marks that I had received of his royal favor and protection.

The King was struck with horror at the description I had given of those terrible engines and the proposal I had made. He was amazed how so <u>impotent</u> and groveling an insect as I (these were his expressions) could entertain such inhuman ideas, and in so familiar a manner as to appear wholly unmoved at all the scenes of blood and <u>desolation</u> which I had painted as the common effects of those destructive machines; whereof he said some evil genius, enemy to mankind, must have been the first <u>contriver</u>. As for himself, he protested that although few things delighted him so much as new discoveries in art or in nature, yet he would rather lose half his kingdom than be privy to such a secret, which he commanded me, as I valued my life, never to mention any more.

A strange effect of *narrow principles* and *short views!* that a prince possessed of every quality which <u>procures</u> <u>veneration</u>, love, and esteem; of strong parts, great wisdom, and profound learning; endued[8]

What secret does Gulliver share with the king and why? ❶

How does the king react to Gulliver's proposal to share the secrets of gunpowder? ❷

---

8. **endued.** Endowed with certain qualities

WORDS FOR EVERYDAY USE:

in • gra • ti • ate (in grā´shē āt´) *vt.*, bring into favor
ag • i • ta • tion (aj´ə tā´shən) *n.*, violent motion
trib • ute (trib´yōōt) *n.*, homage
im • po • tent (im´pə tənt) *adj.*, powerless

des • o • la • tion (des´ə lā´shən) *n.*, ruin
con • triv • er (kən triv´ər) *n.*, one who plans
pro • cure (prō´kyoor´) *vt.*, obtain
ven • er • a • tion (ven´ər ā´shən) *n.*, deep respect

VOCABULARY IN CONTEXT

• A simple gift will <u>ingratiate</u> you with the host.
• The worried parents paced the room in <u>agitation</u>, waiting for news of their son.
• In the dedication to her first novel, the writer paid <u>tribute</u> to her mentor.
• The rescue workers were <u>impotent</u> in the face of such strong winds.
• In the tornado's wake, the tiny town was left in <u>desolation</u>.
• The principal demanded the name of the <u>contriver</u> who led the group of vandals.
• The art gallery has <u>procured</u> a rare painting by Vincent Van Gogh.

with admirable talents for government, and almost adored by his subjects; should from a *nice, unnecessary* <u>scruple</u>, whereof in Europe we can have no conception, let slip an opportunity put into his hands that would have made him absolute master of the lives, the liberties, and the fortunes of his people. Neither do I say this with the least intention to <u>detract</u> from the many virtues of that excellent King, whose character I am sensible will on this account be very much lessened in the opinion of an English reader: but I take this defect among them to have risen from their ignorance; they not having <u>hitherto</u> reduced politics into a science, as the more <u>acute</u> wits of Europe have done. For I remember very well, in a discourse one day with the King, when I happened to say there were several thousand books among us written upon the art of government, it gave him (directly contrary to my

intention) a very mean opinion of our understandings. He professed both to <u>abominate</u> and despise all *mystery, refinement,* and *intrigue,* either in a prince or a minister. He could not tell what I meant by *secrets of state,* where an enemy or some rival nation were not in the case. He confined the knowledge of governing within very *narrow bounds:* to common sense and reason, to justice and <u>lenity</u>, to the speedy determination of civil and criminal causes, with some other obvious topics which are not worth considering. And he gave it for his opinion that whoever could make two ears of corn or two blades of grass to grow upon a spot of ground where only one grew before would deserve better of mankind and do more essential service to his country than the whole race of politicians[9] put together. ∎

① What reason does Gulliver give for the king's reaction? What comparison does Gulliver make between Brobdingnagian and European politics? What makes this comparison funny? What message does Swift actually mean to communicate?

9. **politicians.** Political scientists

WORDS FOR EVERYDAY USE:

scru • ple (scrōō´pəl) *n.,* qualm about something one feels is wrong
de • tract (dē trakt) *vt.,* take or draw away
hith • er • to (hith´ər tōō) *adv.,* until this time

a • cute (ə kyōōt´) *adj.,* keenly intelligent
a • bom • i • nate (ə bäm´ə nāt´) *vt.,* dislike very much
len • i • ty (len´ə tē) *n.,* leniency; mildness

FROM *GULLIVER'S TRAVELS* / FROM "A VOYAGE TO BROBDINGNAG" **517**

VOCABULARY IN CONTEXT

- Many cultures have special ceremonies to show <u>veneration</u> for their ancestors.
- Her <u>scruples</u> would not allow her to lie to her parents.
- Do you think the mural's secluded location <u>detracts</u> from its impact on the public?
- The sprinter's world record was <u>hitherto</u> unchallenged.
- The <u>acute</u> child learned to played chess simply by watching others.
- I <u>abominate</u> stinginess, particularly in the wealthy.
- Activists criticize the <u>lenity</u> of the state's sentencing guidelines.

Responding to the Selection

How were you affected by Gulliver's description of the power and value of gunpowder? Did you share the horrified reaction of the Brobdingnagian king? In your journal, describe your reaction.

Reviewing the Selection

RECALLING

1. What does Gulliver do to the Blefuscudian ships? What must he suffer in order to accomplish his task? What does he prevent by this maneuver?

2. After Gulliver's victory, what does the emperor of Lilliput want next? How does Gulliver respond to the emperor's request?

3. According to the Brobdingnagian king, for what post are "ignorance, idleness, and vice" qualifications?

4. What does Gulliver describe to the king of Brobdingnag? What does he offer him? What does the king prefer to what Gulliver offers?

INTERPRETING

5. How does Gulliver greet the Lilliputians when returning victorious? How do you think he feels?

6. Why does Gulliver respond as he does to the emperor's request? What opinion does Gulliver form about the emperor?

7. What do you think Gulliver must have told the king previously? According to the king, what is the proper purpose of government?

8. What reaction does Gulliver expect when he tells the king about the powerful powder? Why does he expect this reaction? How does the incident reflect on Gulliver and the English?

SYNTHESIZING

9. What insight does Gulliver gain into the nature of the emperor in the ship episode? Compare Gulliver's opinion of the emperor to Swift's opinion of politicians generally.

10. The Lilliputians are physically small. Are they small in other respects? Explain. The Brobdingnagians are physically large. Are they large in other respects? Explain. Why do you think Swift chose to play with size in these ways?

Understanding Literature (Questions for Discussion)

1. **Fantasy.** A **fantasy** is a literary work that contains highly unrealistic elements. *Gulliver's Travels* has many imaginative elements. What unrealistic elements can you find? In what ways are they unrealistic? Which seem to be products of exaggeration? Which seem to add something imaginative to reality? Which seem to be wholly new creations?

2. **Irony. Irony** is a difference between appearance and reality. Swift's satires make heavy use of irony. What examples can you find in the selections? In each case, what is the appearance, and how does it differ from reality? In each case, what point does Swift make by establishing this contrast?

Responding in Writing

Treaty. Lilliput and Blefuscu have agreed to end their hostilities. They now need a treaty that will make explicit the terms of the agreement. Negotiate the terms of the treaty. Form groups of four or six, and divide each group in half, with one part representing Lilliput and the other representing Blefuscu. After you have reached agreement on the terms of the treaty, prepare a written document. In your treaty, tell why you chose to negotiate, what terms each party to the treaty must abide by, what the consequences of breeching the agreement will be, and how peace will be maintained in the future.

Language Lab

Tone. Read the Language Arts Survey, 2.149, "Tone and Voice." Decide how you would characterize Swift's tone in *Gulliver's Travels.* Then rewrite the following sentences or phrases from *Gulliver's Travels* to give them a completely different tone. You need not use the same tone for each revised sentence.

1. The empire of Blefuscu is an island situated to the north northeast side of Lilliput, from whence it is parted only by a channel of eight hundred yards wide.

2. While I was thus employed, the enemy discharged several thousand arrows, many of which stuck in my hands and face; and besides the excessive smart, gave me much disturbance in my work.

ANSWERS FOR UNDERSTANDING LITERATURE

►See the evaluation forms for discussion, active listening, and oral communication, *Assessment Portfolio,* 7.11–7.14.

Responses will vary. Possible responses are given.

1. **Fantasy.** The Lilliputians, who are one-twelfth the size of Gulliver, and the Brobdingnagians, who are twelve times the size of Gulliver, are both unrealistic elements, as is the tale of Gulliver walking through the channel and carrying away the Blefuscudian ships. The Lilliputian measure of depth, a *glumgluff,* is an imaginative description of an actual measure. The emperor's plan to become "sole monarch of the whole world" is exaggerated, but not unlike the plans of many historical monarchs or despots. Many names of people, places, and ideas are wholly new creations; however, they are based on things or people that Swift's readers would have recognized, such as the Big-Endian exiles.

►**Teaching Note:** You may want to combine this discussion with a discussion about satire. Refer students to the Handbook of Literary Terms, page 1261.

(cont.)

ANSWERS FOR UNDERSTANDING LITERATURE (CONT.)

Students can identify which fantasy elements might also work as elements of satire.

2. **Irony.** It appears to the Brobdingnagian king that the English government elects the legislators most likely to mishandle their positions and that laws are interpreted by those most likely to confuse them; however, the reality is that the English attempted to elect the most qualified individual, not the least. Swift's point is that often government officials are incapable of doing their duties properly. Another example is that it appears to Gulliver that the Brobdingnagian king is ignorant because he disapproves of the use of gunpowder, abominates political intrigue, and confines governing to justice and lenity. The reality is that the Brobdingnagian king is more civilized and intelligent than the narrator in his disapproval of violence and in his ideal of a just government.

3. But I endeavored to divert him from this design, by many arguments drawn from the topics of policy as well as justice.

4. His majesty in another audience was at the pains to recapitulate the sum of all I had spoken.

5. It doth not appear from all you have said how any one virtue is required towards the procurement of any one station among you.

Research Skills

Using the Card Catalog. Read the Language Arts Survey, 4.22, "Using the Card Catalog." Then consider this situation: Marisa and Thomas are doing research for a class presentation on "The History of Satire." Questions 1 to 4 refer to their research. Answer the questions on your own paper.

1. Thomas is opening a card catalog drawer marked "THACKERAY–THESPIAN." What might he be doing wrong?

2. Marisa has found in a different drawer a title card for Solar System, History of. What does she need to do now?

3. Thomas has found a card for a book titled *Elements of Satire.* What other infor-mation on the card might help him to decide if the book will be useful?

4. After a proper and thorough search, Marisa has discovered that there are no books in the library on the history of satire. What should she do next?

PROJECT

Founding a State and Writing a Constitution. The members of your class have been shipwrecked on an island and have no hope of rescue. Together, you have to devise a way of governing yourselves. First, describe your situation by listing your available resources and your needs. Then, decide what functions you want your government to serve. Working together, develop a constitution for your island government. You may wish to review the Constitution of the United States and use it as a model for what to put in your constitution and how to organize its parts. You will find a copy of the U.S. Constitution in most American history textbooks and in most libraries.

PREREADING

from *Oroonoko*
by Aphra Behn

ABOUT THE AUTHOR

Aphra Behn (1640–1689) is today honored as a great literary pioneer. The first woman in England to earn her living as a writer, she became one of the finest dramatists of her day and wrote what is arguably the first English novel. Her life, like her work, was interesting and unusual. As a child, she traveled with her foster family to the West Indies. While living in Suriname, she participated in a slave rebellion. On returning to England, she married, but her husband soon died. To earn money, she became a spy in Antwerp, Belgium, for King Charles II. When she was poorly paid for her spying, she ended up in debtor's prison. To rectify her situation, Behn began writing to earn money. This was an unusual motive for women writers in her day, for most were aristocrats who wrote for pleasure, not for pay. Over the next several years, Behn would write fourteen plays, many of which were favorably received in London. The fortunes of London theaters declined around 1680, and with them Behn's income. Still resourceful, she began writing fiction, and though she died poor, she left behind a rich legacy not just in her writings, but also in the ambitious, adventurous, and inspiring life she had lived.

ABOUT THE SELECTION

Written just a year before Behn died, *Oroonoko, or the Royal Slave*, combines elements of autobiography, travel narrative, and fictional prose. Drawing on her own experiences in Suriname, Behn tells in this short novel the story of an African prince, Oroonoko, who is deceived by an Englishman and sold into slavery. Behn's book, with its noble hero, did much to turn British public opinion against the slave trade, which was outlawed in all British colonies in 1833.

ADDITIONAL RESOURCES

READER'S GUIDE
• Selection Worksheet, 7.6

ASSESSMENT PORTFOLIO
• Selection Check Test, 4.7.11
• Selection Test, 4.7.12

ESSENTIAL SKILLS PRACTICE BOOKS
• *Study and Research*, 4.23, 4.28

ENRICHMENT ACTIVITIES

Students can write about or discuss the opposition that Behn might have faced. They should consider Behn as a woman, as a writer, and as an outspoken opponent of slavery.

SUPPORT FOR LEP STUDENTS

Explain that the selection contains some uncommon contractions, such as *'em* for *them* and *'twas* for *it was.*

ADDITIONAL VOCABULARY

oblige—compel
indignity—affront; disgrace
circumventing—surrounding with evils
cognizance—perception; observation

VOCABULARY FROM THE SELECTION

asseveration
ignominiously
repose

GOALS/OBJECTIVES

Studying this lesson will enable students to

• empathize with a main character in a novel
• describe Aphra Behn's literary accomplishments and explain the historical significance of her writings
• define *novel* and identify the elements of a novel in literature they read
• write a credo

READER'S JOURNAL

Have you ever been the victim of a deception? Perhaps you bought a product that was falsely advertised, or perhaps you placed trust in someone or something that could not be trusted. Describe your experience in your journal.

RESEARCH SKILLS

Read the Language Arts Survey, 4.28, "Evaluating Sources." Then, after reading the following selection from Behn's *Oroonoko*, evaluate it as a source of information about slave ships and the slave trade. What experience in Behn's life would have given her an opportunity to learn about slaves and the slave trade?

FROM

Oroonoko

APHRA BEHN

Oroonoko was no sooner returned from this last conquest, and received at court with all the joy and magnificence that could be expressed to a young victor, who was not only returned triumphant but beloved like a deity, when there arrived in the port an English ship.

This person had often before been in these countries and was very well known to Oroonoko, with whom he had trafficked for slaves, and had used to do the same with his predecessors.[1]

This commander was a man of a finer sort of address and conversation, better bred and more engaging than most of that sort of men are, so that he seemed rather never to have been bred out of a court than almost all his life at sea. This captain therefore was always better received at court than most of the traders to those countries were; and especially by Oroonoko, who was more civilized, according to the European mode, than any other had been, and took more delight in the white nations, and above all men of parts and wit. To this captain he sold abundance of his slaves, and for the favor and esteem he had for him, made him many presents, and obliged him to stay

❶
At the beginning of the selection, what sort of relationship does Oroonoko have with the European slave traders?

at court as long as possibly he could. Which the captain seemed to take as a very great honor done him, entertaining the Prince every day with globes and maps, and mathematical discourses and instruments; eating, drinking, hunting, and living with him with so much familiarity that it was not to be doubted but he had gained very greatly upon the heart of this gallant young man. And the captain, in return of all these mighty favors, besought[2] the Prince to honor his vessel with his presence, some day or other, to dinner, before he should set sail; which he condescended to accept, and appointed his day. The captain, on his part, failed not to have all things in a readiness, in the most magnificent order he could possibly. And the day being come, the captain in his boat, richly adorned with carpets and velvet cushions, rowed to the shore to receive the Prince, with another longboat where was placed all his music and trumpets, with which Oroonoko was extremely delighted; who met him on the shore attended by his French governor, Jamoan

---

1. **This . . . predecessors.** Throughout the history of Africa and the Middle East, the selling of war captives into slavery was common.
2. **besought.** Asked earnestly

Aboan, and about a hundred of the noblest of the youths of the court. And after they had first carried the Prince on board, the boats fetched the rest off; where they found a very splendid treat, with all sorts of fine wines, and were as well entertained as 'twas possible in such a place to be.

The Prince, having drunk hard of punch and several sorts of wine, as did all the rest (for great care was taken they should want nothing of that part of the entertainment), was very merry, and in great admiration of the ship, for he had never been in one before; so that he was curious of beholding every place where he decently might descend. The rest, no less curious, who were not quite overcome with drinking, rambled at their pleasure fore and aft, as their fancies guided 'em. So that the captain, who had well laid his design before, gave the word, and seized on all his guests; they clapping great irons suddenly on the Prince, when he was leaped down in the hold to view that part of the vessel, and locking him fast down, secured him. The same treachery was used to all the rest; and all in one instant, in several places of the ship, were lashed fast in irons, and betrayed to slavery. That great design over, they set all hands to work to hoise[3] sail; and with as treacherous and fair a wind, they made from the shore with this innocent and glorious prize, who thought of nothing less than such an entertainment.

Some have commended this act as brave in the captain; but I will spare my sense of it, and leave it to my reader to judge as he pleases.

It may be easily guessed in what manner the Prince resented this indignity, who may be best resembled to a lion taken in a toil; so he raged, so he struggled for liberty, but all in vain; and they had so wisely managed his fetters that he could not use a hand in his defense, to quit himself of a life that would by no means endure slavery, nor could he move from the place where he was tied to any solid part of the ship, against which he might have beat his head, and have finished his disgrace that way. So that being deprived of all other means, he resolved to perish for want of food. And pleased at last with that thought, and toiled and tired by rage and indignation, he laid himself down, and sullenly resolved upon dying, and refused all things that were brought him.

This did not a little vex the captain, and the more so because he found almost all of 'em of the same humor; so that the loss of so many brave slaves, so tall and goodly to behold, would have been very considerable. He therefore ordered one to go from him (for he would not be seen himself) to Oroonoko, and to assure him he was afflicted for having rashly done so unhospitable a deed, and which could not be now remedied, since they were far from shore; but since he resented it in so high a nature, he assured him he would revoke his resolution, and set both him and his friends ashore on the next land they should touch at; and of this the messenger gave him his oath, provided he would resolve to live. And Oroonoko, whose honor was such as he never had violated a word in his life himself, much less a solemn <u>asseveration</u>, believed in an instant what this man said,

❶ *What does the captain do to Oroonoko and to the other "guests"?*

❷ *How does Oroonoko fight back? Why does this "vex," or bother, the captain? What is the deal that the captain tries to make with Oroonoko?*

_____

3. **hoise.** Hoist

WORDS FOR EVERYDAY USE: as • sev • er • a • tion (ə sev´ə rā shən) *n.,* act of stating positively; an assertion

FROM *OROONOKO* **523**

VOCABULARY IN CONTEXT

• He punctuated his <u>asseveration</u> with affirming nods of the head.

ANSWERS TO GUIDED READING QUESTIONS

❶ The captain says he hesitates to remove Oroonoko's fetters because he fears that Oroonoko might "commit some outrage fatal to himself and the King his [the captain's] master."

❷ Oroonoko responds that he doubts the principles of the captain's gods, which lead him to such distrust of another man's solemn oath.

CROSS-CURRICULAR ACTIVITIES

Social Studies. Have students research the history of the slave trade to discover the main routes used by European slave traders. Then have students make maps illustrating the routes used during the seventeenth and eighteenth centuries. Maps should indicate where the traders bought slaves and where they sold them.

> ❶ Why does the captain hesitate to remove Oroonoko's fetters?

but replied, he expected for a confirmation of this to have his shameful fetters dismissed. This demand was carried to the captain, who returned him answer that the offense had been so great which he had put upon the Prince that he durst not trust him with liberty while he remained in the ship, for fear lest by a valor natural to him, and a revenge that would animate that valor, he might commit some outrage fatal to himself and the King his master, to whom his vessel did belong. To this Oroonoko replied, he would engage his honor to behave himself in all friendly order and manner, and obey the command of the captain, as he was lord of the King's vessel and general of those men under his command.

This was delivered to the still doubting captain, who could not resolve to trust a heathen, he said, upon his parole, a man that had no sense or notion of the God that he worshiped. Oroonoko then replied, he was very sorry to hear that the captain pretended to the knowledge and worship of any gods who had taught him no better principles than not to credit as he would be credited; but they told him the difference of their faith occasioned that distrust. For the captain had protested to him upon the word of a Christian, and sworn in the name of a great god, which if he should violate, he would expect eternal torment in the world to come. "Is that all the obligation he has to be just to his oath?" replied Oroonoko. "Let him know I swear by my honor; which to violate, would not only render me contemptible and despised by all brave and honest men, and so give myself perpetual pain, but it would be eternally

> ❷ When the captain persists in doubting Oroonoko's honesty, how does Oroonoko respond?

offending and diseasing all mankind, harming, betraying, circumventing and outraging all men; but punishments hereafter are suffered by one's self, and the world takes no cognizances whether this god have revenged 'em or not, 'tis done so secretly and deferred so long. While the man of no honor suffers every moment the scorn and contempt of the honester world, and dies every day <u>ignominiously</u> in his fame, which is more valuable than life. I speak not this to move belief, but to show you how you mistake, when you imagine that he who will violate his honor will keep his word with his gods." So turning from him with a disdainful smile, he refused to answer him, when he urged him to know what answer he should carry back to his captain; so that he departed without saying any more.

The captain pondering and consulting what to do, it was concluded that nothing but Oroonoko's liberty would encourage any of the rest to eat, except the Frenchman, whom the captain could not pretend to keep prisoner, but only told him he was secured because he might act something in favor of the Prince, but that he should be freed as soon as they came to land. So that they concluded it wholly necessary to free the Prince from his irons, that he might show himself to the rest; that they might have an eye upon him, and that they could not fear a single man.

This being resolved, to make the obligation the greater, the captain himself went to Oroonoko; where after many compliments, and assurances of what he had already promised, he receiving from the

---

WORDS FOR EVERYDAY USE: ig • no • min • i • ous • ly (ig′nə min´ē əs lē) *adv.*, shamefully; disgracefully

Slave Ship. Joseph Mallord William Turner. Courtesy, the Museum of Fine Arts, Boston. Henry Lillie Pierce Fund
(See John Ruskin's discussion of this painting on page 810.)

(See John Ruskin's discussion of this painting on page 810.)

Prince his parole and his hand for his good behavior, dismissed his irons and brought him to his own cabin; where after having treated and <u>reposed</u> him a while, for he had neither eat nor slept in four days before, he besought him to visit those obstinate people in chains, who refused all manner of sustenance, and entreated him to oblige 'em to eat, and assure 'em of their liberty the first opportunity.

Oroonoko, who was too generous not to give credit to his words, showed himself to his people, who were transported with excess of joy at the sight of their darling prince, falling at his feet and kissing and embracing 'em, believing, as some divine oracle, all he assured 'em. But he besought 'em to bear their chains with that bravery that became those whom he had seen act so nobly in arms; and that they could not give him greater proofs of their love and friendship, since 'twas all the security the captain (his friend) could have, against the revenge, he said, they might possibly justly take for the injuries sustained by him. And they all with one accord assured him, they

❶ What does the captain want the unfettered Oroonoko to do?

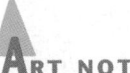

WORDS FOR EVERYDAY USE: re • pose (rē pōs) *vt.,* rest

FROM OROONOKO **525**

VOCABULARY IN CONTEXT

- People will speak of you <u>ignominiously</u> if you continue such disgraceful behavior.
- The hikers removed their heavy packs and <u>reposed</u> a few minutes by the stream before continuing up the mountain.

ANSWER TO GUIDED READING QUESTION

❶ The captain wants the unfettered Oroonoko to persuade the other chained men to eat and to assure them of their promised freedom.

ART NOTE

Turner painted *Slave Ship* in 1840, almost two hundred years after Behn wrote her story. During that time, however, the activities of slave traders had changed little. Turner's painting illustrates the common practice of pitching enslaved humans overboard, which was done either because of epidemics or to avoid unrest. In this case, because of an approaching typhoon, they are throwing overboard the dead and the dying. Have students discuss their reactions to the painting. What mood does the painting evoke? What connections do students make between this scene and the scene they imagine on the English captain's ship?

ANSWERS TO SELECTION CHECK TEST 4.7.11

EX. In what country did Aphra Behn work as a spy?
She was a spy in Belgium.

1. What did Oroonoko sell to the captain?
He sold slaves.

2. What happens to Oroonoko at the banquet?
He is seized and enslaved by surprise.

3. What does Oroonoko swear by?
He swears by his honor.

4. What did Oroonoko tell the prisoners to do?
He told them to be brave and to eat.

5. How does the narrator come to know Oroonoko?
Oroonoko is sold to the narrator's overseer.

ANSWER TO GUIDED READING QUESTION

❶ When he realizes what is happening, Oroonoko looks at the captain with fierceness and disdain. He tells the captain that his suffering was worthwhile because he gained a true "knowledge both of you and of your gods by whom you swear."

CROSS-CURRICULAR ACTIVITIES

Social Studies. Have students research the location of Surinam, where Oroonoko lived and where Behn had actually participated in a slave rebellion. Where is it located? What is it called today?

RESPONDING TO THE SELECTION

Students might role play both the English supporters and critics of the slave trade as they discuss these questions.

ANSWERS FOR UNDERSTANDING LITERATURE

▶ See the evaluation forms for discussion, active listening, and oral communication, *Assessment Portfolio*, 7.11–7.14.

Responses will vary. Possible responses are given.

Novel. In the beginning of the selection, Oroonoko naturally believes that others share his values; he accepts the English captain at face value and never suspects his intentions. By the end of the selection, Oroonoko realizes that not everyone functions within his system of honor. Whereas Oroonoko's values are unconditional and applicable to all people, the captain's values are relative. Oroonoko loses a certain sense of innocence about the world because he discovers that not all people are honorable and that his responses must now always be guarded.

▶ **Teaching Note:** Students should examine the characters' words as well as their actions for clues about changes in their psychological states.

could not suffer enough, when it was for his repose and safety.

After this they no longer refused to eat, but took what was brought 'em, and were pleased with their captivity, since by it they hoped to redeem the Prince, who, all the rest of the voyage, was treated with all the respect due to his birth, though nothing could divert his melancholy; and he would often sigh for Imoinda, and think this a punishment due to his misfortune, in having left that noble maid behind him that fatal night, in the Otan, when he fled to the camp.

❶ *What sort of look does Oroonoko give to the captain when he realizes what is happening? What does Oroonoko say?*

Possessed with a thousand thoughts of past joys with this fair young person, and a thousand griefs for her eternal loss, he endured a tedious voyage, and at last arrived at the mouth of the river of Surinam, a colony belonging to the King of England, and where they were to deliver some part of their slaves. There the merchants and gentlemen of the country going on board to demand those lots of slaves they had already agreed on, and, amongst those, the overseers of those plantations where I then chanced to be, the captain, who had given the word, ordered his men to bring up those noble slaves in fetters whom I have spoken of; and having put 'em some in one and some in other lots, with women and children . . .

they sold 'em off as slaves to several merchants and gentlemen; not putting any two in one lot, because they would separate 'em far from each other, not daring to trust 'em together, lest rage and courage should put 'em upon contriving some great action, to the ruin of the colony.

Oroonoko was first seized on, and sold to our overseer, who had the first lot, with seventeen more of all sorts and sizes, but not one of quality with him. When he saw this, he found what they meant, for, as I said, he understood English pretty well; and being wholly unarmed and defenseless, so as it was in vain to make any resistance, he only beheld the captain with a look all fierce and disdainful, upbraiding him with eyes that forced blushes on his guilty cheeks; he only cried, in passing over the side of the ship, "Farewell, sir. 'Tis worth my suffering, to gain so true a knowledge both of you and of your gods by whom you swear." And desiring those that held him to forbear their pains, and telling 'em he would make no resistance, he cried, "Come, my fellow slaves; let us descend, and see if we can meet with more honor and honesty in the next world we shall touch upon." So he nimbly leaped into the boat, and showing no more concern, suffered himself to be rowed up the river with his seventeen companions. ■

Responding to the Selection

After reading this piece, how do you feel toward its main character, Oroonoko? toward the captain of the ship? What contradictions does Behn point out between the professed religious beliefs of the captain and the way in which he behaves? What indictment does Behn make in this piece of the English supporters of the slave trade? How do you feel when you think of the history of slavery and of the slave trade? What do you think can be learned from study of that history? Discuss these questions with your classmates.

526 *UNIT SEVEN / THE RESTORATION AND THE EIGHTEENTH CENTURY*

ANALYTIC SCALES FOR RESPONDING IN WRITING

Assign a score from 1 to 25 for each grading criterion below. (For more detailed evaluation, see the evaluation forms for writing, revising, and proofreading, *Assessment Portfolio*, 7.1–7.10.)

Credo

1. Content/Unity. The essay presents a defense of a virtue.

2. Organization/Coherence. The essay defines the virtue.

It then provides two or three strong examples of the virtue and adds details that describe its importance to the writer.

3. Language/Style. The essay uses vivid and precise nouns, verbs, and modifiers.

4. Conventions. The essay avoids errors in spelling, grammar, usage, mechanics, and manuscript form.

526 TEACHER'S EDITION

Reviewing the Selection

RECALLING

1. How is Oroonoko described in the first paragraph of the selection? From what has he recently returned?

2. With what does the captain of the ship entertain Oroonoko in the third paragraph of the selection?

3. To what does Behn compare Oroonoko shortly after the prince is put into fetters?

4. Why does the captain feel compelled to release Oroonoko from his fetters?

INTERPRETING

5. What information given at the beginning of the selection establishes Oroonoko as a heroic character?

6. What reason might Oroonoko have at the beginning of the selection to think that the English captain is a friend?

7. What actions on the part of Oroonoko and his fellow captives show their nobility and their spirit?

8. How do the captain and Oroonoko differ with respect to their honesty and integrity? How do the negotiations over freeing Oroonoko from his fetters demonstrate this difference?

SYNTHESIZING

9. What causes Oroonoko to take the captain's word about releasing him and his fellow captives? What point is Behn making about the fundamental differences between the Africans and the slave traders?

10. What knowledge has Oroonoko gained at the end of the selection? What devastating comment on the captain's actions does Oroonoko make to his fellow captives?

Understanding Literature (Questions for Discussion)

Novel. A **novel** is a long work of prose fiction. One characteristic that sets novels apart from earlier types of prose fiction is their realistic portrayals of the interior psychological states of characters. What changes does Oroonoko undergo in this selection? What does he learn about the differences between his values and those of the captain? In what sense does Oroonoko lose a certain innocence about the world?

Responding in Writing

Credo. A **credo** is a statement of personal belief. Reread the passage in *Oroonoko* in which the protagonist discusses honor and its importance to him. Then think of a virtue that is important to you. Possibilities include honesty, loyalty, creativity, fairness, and a willingness to work hard. Write a short essay in which you define that virtue, give examples of it, and describe why it is important to you.

FROM OROONOKO   527

ANSWERS FOR REVIEWING THE SELECTION

RECALLING

1. Oroonoko is described as "a young victor," who was "beloved like a deity" by his people. He has recently returned from a conquest.

2. The captain of the ship entertains Oroonoko "with globes and maps, and mathematical discourses and instruments; eating, drinking, hunting, and living with him."

3. Behn compares Oroonoko to "a lion taken in a toil."

4. The captain feels compelled to release Oroonoko from his fetters because he knows that all the slaves, following Oroonoko's refusal to eat, will die and, therefore, be of no profit to him.

INTERPRETING

Responses will vary. Possible responses are given.

5. The adoration given Oroonoko and the description "young victor" establish him as a heroic character.

6. Oroonoko might think that the English captain is a friend because the captain seems to enjoy Oroonoko's company and to treat him as an equal.

7. Oroonoko and his fellow captives show their nobility and their spirit by their quiet determination to refuse food.

8. Oroonoko possesses both honesty and integrity, unlike the captain who believes he needs to be honest only with people who share his beliefs. The captain lies to gain an advantage over Oroonoko; unfortunately, Oroonoko believes the captain's lies because he himself would never be so dishonest.

(cont.)

ANSWERS FOR REVIEWING THE SELECTION (CONT.)

SYNTHESIZING

Responses will vary. Possible responses are given.

9. Oroonoko takes the captain's word because, in his system of honor, a person would never make an oath he did not intend to keep. Behn makes the point that, unlike the slave traders, the Africans are honorable and have a great sense of morality and duty toward fellow human beings.

10. At the end of the selection, Oroonoko has learned that the English and their gods cannot be trusted. Oroonoko tells his fellow captives that they should look for "more honor and honesty in the next world" they reach, commenting thereby upon the captain's dishonesty and treachery.

ENRICHMENT ACTIVITIES

Students can discuss or write a comparison essay about the similarities and differences between Pope's aphorisms and those of a famous American writer, such as Benjamin Franklin. How are they similar? How are they different?

SUPPORT FOR LEP STUDENTS

Syntax in some of the couplets may pose a problem for students. Have students check their comprehension by paraphrasing each couplet.

ADDITIONAL VOCABULARY

vast—great in extent
draught—draft; drink
joint—joined; combined
oft—often
torrent—violent flood
shun—avoid consistently

PREREADING

Couplets from *An Essay on Criticism*
by Alexander Pope

ABOUT THE AUTHOR

The insight and wisdom **Alexander Pope** (1688–1744) was able to capture in epigrams from his verses makes him one of the most frequently quoted authors in the English language. As a young boy, Pope was educated primarily at home by Catholic priests. An extremely bright child, he learned Greek, Latin, French, and Italian. At the age of twelve, he produced some of his first poetry, imitating the style of the poets he was already reading. By young adulthood, Pope's extensive output of literary work had begun. This output included numerous volumes of verse and ambitious projects— complete translations of Homer's *Iliad* and *Odyssey.* In his mature years, Pope lived and wrote on his country estate on the Thames outside of London and befriended many noteworthy writers, including Jonathan Swift. By the end of his life, he was immersed in a multitude of literary endeavors, though his death left some unfinished.

ABOUT THE SELECTION

Pope wrote his *Essay on Criticism* when he was only twenty-one years old and published it a few years later, in 1711. The poem, excerpts of which appear on the following pages, wittily presents critical precepts derived from Greek and Latin authorities. It is written in Pope's favorite meter, ten-syllable **iambic pentameter.** An **iamb** is a poetic foot with one weakly stressed syllable and one strongly stressed syllable, as in the word *alone.* A **pentameter** line has five feet. Paired lines of rhymed iambic pentameter such as those used in this poem are known as **heroic couplets.**

The couplets included here demonstrate Pope's special ability to capture perceptive insights in a few words that please the ear and enlighten the mind. So appealing are these excerpts that they have gained the status of **proverbs** used commonly by English speakers around the globe, often by people who do not know their source.

GOALS/OBJECTIVES

Studying this lesson will enable students to

• enjoy and appreciate Pope's wit and humor

• describe Alexander Pope's literary accomplishments and explain the historical significance of his writings

• define *aphorism* and interpret aphorisms that they encounter in their reading

• define *couplet* and identify couplets in poems

• define *antithesis* and recognize and interpret examples of antithesis in literature that they read

READER'S JOURNAL

Think of a short saying or piece of folk wisdom familiar to you. In your journal, explain its meaning and mention a few situations to which it applies.

RESEARCH SKILLS

Pick one of the selections below and pay attention to Pope's choice of words while reading it. Then read the Language Arts Survey, 4.25, "Using Thesauruses," and look up complicated synonyms for words that Pope uses. Why do you think Pope used such simple language to express his ideas? What virtue is there in writing simply?

COUPLETS FROM

An Essay on Criticism

ALEXANDER POPE

'Tis with our judgments as our watches; none
Go just alike, yet each believes his own.

◆　◆　◆

One science only will one genius fit;
So vast is art, so narrow human wit:

◆　◆　◆

A little learning is a dangerous thing;
Drink deep, or taste not the Pierian spring:[1]
There shallow draughts intoxicate the brain,
And drinking largely sobers us again.

◆　◆　◆

In wit, as nature, what affects our hearts
Is not the exactness of peculiar parts;
'Tis not a lip, or eye, we beauty call,
But the joint force and full result of all.

◆　◆　◆

---

1. **Pierian spring.** The Pierian spring is said to be the
birthplace of the Muses. To drink of it is to drink inspiration.

❶
Can you think of
situations in
which people
have radically
different but
strongly held
convictions?

❷
Does Pope believe
that a person
should be a jack-
of-all-trades?
Why, or why not?

❸
Why might "A
little learning" be
"a dangerous
thing"?

❹
Thinkers of the
Enlightenment
Era were
enamored of
generality. How
does Pope's
conception of
beauty reflect his
era's love for
general
principles?

PREREADING NOTES

READER'S JOURNAL

Students should consider whether the meaning of the saying is literal or whether it has come to have a different meaning than the sum of its words.

RESEARCH SKILLS

Students might copy one of the couplets on their own paper, inserting the synonyms they found, to compare the effectiveness of simple and complex language.

▶ Additional practice is provided in the *Essential Skills Practice Book: Study and Research,* 4.25.

ANSWERS TO GUIDED READING QUESTIONS

❶ Some situations in which people have different but strongly held convictions might include these: a political debate, an editorial column, and labor negotiations.

❷ Pope does not believe a person should be a jack-of-all-trades because a person can only have skill enough to master one.

❸ A little learning might be dangerous because it could inspire false confidence untempered by deeper knowledge. For example, first-year medical students might feel confident about their surgical abilities, but without further knowledge and instruction, they are not prepared to perform major surgery.

❹ Pope does not love a part or a feature of beauty, but the general result of all the features combined.

In his *Essay on Criticism* (1711), Pope set the intellectual tone for the Augustan Age. Focal words in the essay, such as *wit, Nature,* and *genius,* would be used as a measure for writers throughout the remainder of the century.

ANSWERS TO GUIDED READING QUESTIONS

❶ Pope says that natural thought is not as elegant as the human artifice for expressing thought—writings.

❷ Pope would agree that writers should avoid wordiness because when words are as abundant as "leaves," they produce little sense, or "fruit."

❸ Pope writes lines that echo their meanings by employing techniques such as the alliteration that creates the sound of soft wind in line 5: "Soft is the strain when Zephyr gently blows." Pope also uses a cæsura to make a line move slowly: "The line too labors, and the words move slow."

❹ Restraint and moderation are practiced by avoiding extremes and being too little or too much pleased.

❺ As people grow older they think themselves wiser than their fathers.

❻ Pope's advice calls for trying to combine natural talents with sense, or wit, but mistakes are inevitable both in writing and in life.

LITERARY TECHNIQUE

Tell students that Pope is the second most quoted poet in the English language, Shakespeare being first. Most people who quote him know the lines but not the source of aphorisms such as "For fools rush in where angels fear to tread." Ask students how many of the couplets presented in the passage they have heard before. Did they know the source of these quotations?

---

❶ The Neoclassicists favored human artifice over untamed nature. How does Pope apply this concept to writing?

❷ Would Pope agree that writers should use as few words as possible? Explain.

❸ In what ways do the sounds of lines in this section of the poem echo their sense?

❹ How do these lines reflect the Neoclassical idea of restraint and moderation?

❺ According to Pope, what happens as people grow older?

❻ How might Pope's advice apply to judging someone else's writing? to other aspects of life?

True wit is nature to advantage dressed,
What oft was thought, but ne'er so well expressed;

◆　◆　◆

Words are like leaves; and where they most abound,
Much fruit of sense beneath is rarely found;

◆　◆　◆

True ease in writing comes from art, not chance,
As those move easiest who have learned to dance.
'Tis not enough no harshness gives offense,
The sound must seem an echo to the sense:
Soft is the strain when Zephyr[2] gently blows,
And the smooth stream in smoother numbers flows;
But when loud surges lash the sounding shore,
The hoarse, rough verse should like the torrent roar:
When Ajax[3] strives some rock's vast weight to throw,
The line too labors, and the words move slow;
Not so, when swift Camilla[4] scours the plain,
Flies o'er the unbending corn, and skims along the main.

◆　◆　◆

Avoid extremes; and shun the fault of such,
Who still are pleased too little or too much,

◆　◆　◆

We think our fathers fools, so wise we grow;
Our wiser sons, no doubt, will think us so.

◆　◆　◆

Good-nature and good-sense must ever join;
To <u>err</u> is human, to forgive, divine. ∎

---

2. **Zephyr.** The west wind
3. **Ajax.** A Greek hero known for his size and strength
4. **Camilla.** A female warrior killed in the Trojan War

WORDS FOR EVERYDAY USE: **err** (ur) *vi.,* be wrong

ANALYTIC SCALES FOR RESPONDING IN WRITING

Assign a score from 1 to 25 for each grading criterion below. (For more detailed evaluation, see the evaluation forms for writing, revising, and proofreading, *Assessment Portfolio*, 7.1–7.10.)

Personal Aphorisms

• **Content/Unity.** The aphorism presents a succinct statement of a personal belief in the form of a couplet.

• **Organization/Coherence.** The aphorism is expressed in two lines of rhyming iambic pentameter.

• **Language/Style.** The aphorism uses vivid and precise nouns, verbs, and modifiers.

• **Conventions.** The aphorism avoids errors in spelling, grammar, usage, mechanics, and manuscript form.

Responding to the Selection

Which one of the selections most appeals to you? Why does this selection have particular meaning for you, and how might it be applied to your own life? In class, share your reactions with those of other students.

Reviewing the Selection

RECALLING

1. To what does Pope compare watches?

2. To what does Pope compare learning just a little about something?

3. To what does Pope compare words and wordiness?

4. What, according to Pope, is "nature to advantage dressed"?

INTERPRETING

5. In what sense are judgments like watches, according to Pope?

6. Why might a little learning be dangerous?

7. What, in Pope's view, is usually true of wordy writing?

8. In what ways might a writer "dress up" a thought?

SYNTHESIZING

9. How does Pope, in the lines that begin "True ease in writing . . .," demonstrate sound echoing sense?

10. What general principles for writing and criticism can you find in these selections? State these principles in your own words.

> **❝** *A man should never be ashamed to own he has been in the wrong, which is but saying, in other words, that he is wiser today than he was yesterday.* **❞**
>
> —Alexander Pope, "Thoughts on Various Subjects"

COUPLETS FROM *"AN ESSAY ON CRITICISM"* **531**

RESPONDING TO THE SELECTION

Explain that different students may have different interpretations of the same couplets.

ANSWERS FOR REVIEWING THE SELECTION

RECALLING

1. Pope compares personal judgment to watches.

2. Pope compares a little learning to a shallow, intoxicating "draught."

3. Pope compares words, and wordiness, to a leafy tree that bears little fruit.

4. Pope would call something we had thought but not expressed natural.

INTERPRETING

Responses will vary. Possible responses are given.

5. Pope comments on individuality by stating that each person is most swayed by his or her own judgment rather than by others' opinions.

6. A little learning might inspire false confidence.

7. The overuse of words reveals a lack of sense.

8. A writer might "dress up" a thought by employing any of a variety of literary techniques.

SYNTHESIZING

Responses will vary. Possible responses are given.

9. Pope demonstrates sound echoing sense by employing techniques such as alliteration and cæsuras to create the effect of a gentle wind in line 5 or something slow in line 10.

10. Pope stresses the importance of conciseness, preciseness, and humor in writing and criticism.

VOCABULARY IN CONTEXT

- Did I <u>err</u> in calling you so late at night?

ANSWERS FOR SELECTION CHECK TEST 4.7.13

EX. What was Pope's preferred form of writing?
Pope preferred to write couplets.

1. How much learning is dangerous?
A little learning is dangerous.

2. What besides wit is determined by wholes rather than by separate parts?
Beauty also is determined by wholes rather than by separate parts.

3. Where is "fruit of sense" rarely found?
"Fruit of sense" is rarely found where words most abound.

4. What comes from art and not from chance?
"True ease in writing comes from art, not chance."

5. Whom do we think fools?
"We think our fathers fools."

TEACHER'S EDITION **531**

ANSWERS FOR UNDERSTANDING LITERATURE

►See the evaluation forms for discussion, active listening, and oral communication, *Assessment Portfolio, 7.11–7.14.*

Responses will vary. Possible responses are given.

1. Aphorism. An aphorism is effective because its brevity makes it memorable; in the case of Pope's couplets, their rhyming quality and wit makes them even more memorable. Because an aphorism refers to a topic broadly, it can be applied in many situations. For example, Pope's couplet that reads "One science only will one genius fit;/So vast is art, so narrow human wit" applies to the hundreds of artistic endeavors pursued by humans.

►**Teaching Note:** Students might read one of Pope's couplets and brainstorm a list of situations to which it might apply.

2. Couplet. Pope might have chosen the couplet form to express his thoughts because he found its restrictions challenging. If Pope had written a long essay on one of his themes, he might have lost his reader's interest or belabored his point. As he states in one of his own couplets, "Words are like leaves; and where they most abound,/Much fruit of sense beneath is rarely found." By using the couplet form, he impresses his audience with a strikingly succinct and memorable idea.

►**Teaching Note:** Have students write a longer, prose paraphrase of the theme of one of Pope's couplets. Then have students compare the effectiveness of each format.

3. Antithesis. Examples of antithesis from Pope's couplets include "What oft was thought, but ne'er so well expressed"; "none/Go just alike, yet each believes his own"; and "So vast is art, so narrow human wit."

►**Teaching Note:** Point out that repetition serves as a contrast by emphasizing a particular idea.

Understanding Literature (Questions for Discussion)

1. **Aphorism.** An **aphorism** is a short saying or pointed statement. Pope's couplets are famous not only for their poetic excellence but for the wit and insight they contain. In this respect they have philosophical as well as literary value. What makes an aphorism, or any piece of wisdom, valuable is that it can apply to many situations and circumstances. Discuss situations to which the aphorisms in Pope's poem apply.

2. **Couplet.** A **couplet** is a pair of rhyming lines that expresses a complete thought. The form which Pope mastered is the **heroic couplet,** the lines of which are in iambic pentameter. Notice that the rhyme, like the rhythm, or sound of the words, is often very simple. Why would Pope have chosen this form to express his insights? Why do you think these lines are so often quoted?

3. **Antithesis.** An **antithesis** is a rhetorical technique in which words, phrases, or ideas are strongly contrasted, often by means of a repetition of grammatical structure. In which of these couplets do you find examples of antithesis?

Responding in Writing

Personal Aphorisms. Take a few moments and think of the rules by which you live, things that you would not do, and standards or principles that you think are important. These should be general enough to apply to many relationships and circumstances. Write down five or six of these. Then write a short statement that captures the meaning of one of your rules. Revise this personal aphorism to turn it into a heroic couplet.

> ❝ Sir, I admit your gen'ral rule
> That every poet is a fool;
> But you yourself may serve to show it,
> That every fool is not a poet. ❞
>
> —Alexander Pope, "Epigram from the French"

ANALYTIC SCALES FOR RESPONDING IN WRITING

Grading scales appear on page 530.

"A Brief to Free a Slave"
from *A Dictionary of the English Language*
by Samuel Johnson

ABOUT THE AUTHOR

Samuel Johnson's (1709–1784) influence reached far beyond his times to touch all of British literature. Johnson was exposed to literature early, for his father was a bookseller in the village of Litchfield, Staffordshire. After attempting unsuccessfully to start a school, Johnson moved to London and took up writing. His political writings brought him popular attention. He also wrote literary criticism, including a series of essays on Shakespeare. Later he compiled an edition of Shakespeare's plays (1765). In 1750 he started a periodical, *The Rambler,* which he published successfully until 1752, the year his wife died. Six years later he began a second periodical, *The Idler.* Besides writing essays for periodicals, Johnson also wrote poetry, journalism, and travelogues. His poem *The Vanity of Human Wishes* (1749) concerns the limits of human knowledge and happiness. *Lives of the Poets,* published in two parts (1779, 1781), contains brilliant biographical and critical essays. However, Johnson's greatest achievement is his ***Dictionary of the English Language*** (1755), which took him eight years to complete. He was always known among his friends for his witty and honest conversation, some of which was recorded by his friend **James Boswell** (see page 542), whom he met in 1763. Johnson was awarded an honorary degree by Trinity College, Dublin (1765), and a lifetime pension by King George III (1762).

ABOUT THE SELECTIONS

"A Brief to Free a Slave" (1777) was written to aid a slave, Joseph Knight, in his legal action to obtain freedom from his Scottish master. Johnson's feelings about slavery were summed up in a toast he delivered at Oxford University: "Here's to the next insurrection of Negroes in the West Indies." While Scotland permitted serfdom, slavery had been abolished in England in 1772; however, the British slave trade continued until 1807, and slavery had always been integral to the British colonial enterprise.

Normally we think of a dictionary as a reference guide to the standard meanings of words, and indeed Johnson's *A Dictionary of the English Language* is such a reference, the first great work of its kind in English. However, Johnson's *Dictionary* is also a piece of literature. Its definitions include insightful, witty commentaries on politics, mores, literature, and humanity. It is a personal statement that reveals Johnson's love of words, his incisive wit, and his deep and sometimes quirky learning.

"A BRIEF TO FREE A SLAVE" **533**

ENRICHMENT ACTIVITIES

 Explain that the years between 1750 and 1798 are commonly called the Age of Johnson, in reference to Samuel Johnson. After students read the selections, have them write about or discuss what they believe are the defining characteristics of the Age of Johnson, based on the selections.

SUPPORT FOR LEP STUDENTS

Explain that some of Johnson's definitions are not literal meanings of words. Have students look up the words from the selection in a dictionary and compare those definitions to Johnson's definitions.

ADDITIONAL VOCABULARY
countenance —give support to
forfeit—lose; give up
inhabitant—permanent resident

VOCABULARY FROM THE SELECTIONS

abhorrence	insolence
avail	lamented
compulsion	perpetual
disposal	redress
drudge	stipulate
entail	

GOALS/OBJECTIVES

Studying this lesson will enable students to

• interpret a legal brief and infer the beliefs of the author from his writing
• describe Samuel Johnson's literary accomplishments and explain the historical significance of his writings

• define *mode* and identify the writing mode of literature they read
• define *thesis* and identify the thesis of prose works
• define *denotation* and *connotation* and distinguish between denotations and connotations that they encounter in their reading

READER'S JOURNAL

• Students might assume the role of a person who has lost his or her freedom.

• Encourage students to consider what the word *freedom* means to them.

READING SKILLS

After students make their predictions, have them indicate what information they used to make their predictions.

▶ Additional practice is provided in the *Essential Skills Practice Book: Study and Research,* 4.18.

ANSWERS TO GUIDED READING QUESTIONS

❶ The author discusses the history of slavery to point out that slavery is not the natural condition of humans. "It is impossible not to conceive that men in their original state were equal" shows that Johnson believed people were "created equal."

❷ *Answers will vary.* Johnson's statement can be paraphrased, "No man can agree to a condition concerning another individual without that individual's consent."

READER'S JOURNAL

Is freedom important to you? Do you use your freedoms wisely? Are you comfortable with the amount of freedom you have? How do you feel about restrictions on your freedom? Write in your journal about these questions.

READING SKILLS

Read the Language Arts Survey, 4.18, "Reading Actively: Predicting." Then, before reading Johnson's "Brief," make five predictions about its contents.

"A Brief to Free a Slave"

SAMUEL JOHNSON

❶
Why does the author discuss the history of slavery? What argument is Johnson refuting? What sentence shows that he subscribed to the notion that people are "created equal"?

❷
How would you paraphrase Johnson's statement that "no man can stipulate without commission for another"? Do you agree? Why, or why not?

It must be agreed that in most ages many countries have had part of their inhabitants in a state of slavery; yet it may be doubted whether slavery can ever be supposed the natural condition of man. It is impossible not to conceive that men in their original state were equal; and very difficult to imagine how one would be subjected to another but by violent <u>compulsion</u>. An individual may, indeed, forfeit his liberty by a crime; but he cannot by that crime forfeit the liberty of his children. What is true of a criminal seems true likewise of a captive. A man may accept life from a conquering enemy on condition of <u>perpetual</u> servitude; but it is very doubtful whether he can <u>entail</u> that servitude on his descendants; for no man can <u>stipulate</u> without commission for another. The condition which he himself accepts, his son or grandson perhaps would have rejected. If we should admit,

what perhaps may with more reason be denied, that there are certain relations between man and man which may make slavery necessary and just, yet it can never be proved that he who is now suing for his freedom ever stood in any of those relations. He is certainly subject by no law, but that of violence, to his present master, who pretends no claim to his obedience, but that he bought him from a merchant of slaves, whose right to sell him never was examined. It is said that, according to the constitutions of Jamaica, he was legally enslaved; these constitutions are merely positive; and apparently injurious to the rights of mankind, because whoever is exposed to sale is condemned to slavery without appeal; by whatever fraud or violence he might have been originally brought into the merchant's power. In our own time princes have been sold, by wretches to whose care they were

WORDS FOR
EVERYDAY USE:

com • pul • sion (kəm pul´ shən) *n.,* coercion, driving force
per • pet • u • al (pər pech´ o͞o əl) *adj.,* lasting forever
en • tail (en tāl) *vt.,* require
stip • u • late (stip´ yo͞o lāt´) *vt.,* specify conditions of an agreement

VOCABULARY IN CONTEXT

• Fear of being caught, rather than a genuine sense of remorse, was the thief's main <u>compulsion</u> for turning himself in.

• The swinging pendulum demonstrates the theory of <u>perpetual</u> motion.

• In job interviews, the supervisor explains the tasks that the position <u>entails</u>.

• Does the lease <u>stipulate</u> when rent should be paid?

STOWAGE OF THE BRITISH SLAVE SHIP BROOKES UNDER THE
REGULATED SLAVE TRADE
Act of 1788.

Diagram of Slave Ship.
Courtesy Library of Congress,
Prints and Reproductions
Division, Washington, D.C.

entrusted, that they might have an European education; but when once they were brought to a market in the plantations, little would <u>avail</u> either their dignity or their wrongs. The laws of Jamaica afford a Negro no <u>redress</u>. His color is considered as a sufficient testimony against him. It is to be <u>lamented</u> that moral right should ever give way to political convenience. But if temptations of interest are sometimes too strong for human virtue, let us at least retain a virtue where there is no temptation to quit it. In the present case there is apparent right on one side, and no convenience on the other. Inhabitants of this island can neither gain riches nor power by taking away the liberty of any part of the human species. The sum of the argument is this:—No man is by nature the property of another: The defendant is, therefore, by nature free: The rights of nature must be some way forfeited before they can be justly taken away: That the defendant has by any act forfeited the rights of nature we require to be proved; and if no proof of such forfeiture can be given, we doubt not but the justice of the court will declare him free. ■

Is the author's argument based on law, morality, or political convenience?

"A BRIEF TO FREE A SLAVE" **535**

VOCABULARY IN CONTEXT
• I hope the volunteer corps can <u>avail</u> the overworked hospital staff.
• As a form of <u>redress</u>, the truck driver planted a new tree to replace the one he had accidentally toppled.
• In the confessional, many repentant churchgoers <u>lamented</u> their wrongful actions.

RESPONDING TO THE SELECTION

 Students might discuss in pairs, with one student voicing Johnson's argument and another student supporting a different view.

ANSWERS FOR REVIEWING THE SELECTION

RECALLING

1. A person's "natural condition" is freedom.

2. Committing a crime might force a person to give up his or her freedom.

3. The brief does not state how Knight was originally enslaved. Knight's would-be master claims control because he purchased him according to the laws of Jamaica.

4. Slavery might seem attractive because it brings some people wealth and power.

INTERPRETING

Responses will vary. Possible responses are given.

5. People are created equal because they are all humans in "their original state."

6. A person cannot forfeit someone else's freedom because that freedom belongs to that individual and only that individual can choose to forfeit it.

7. No proof has been offered that the person from whom Knight's would-be owner bought Knight had legal ownership, or the right to sell him.

8. Johnson believes that no one can be the property of another unless he or she consents, and that Knight has done nothing to forfeit his freedom.

SYNTHESIZING

Responses will vary. Possible responses are given.

9. Johnson believes liberty may be taken away only if a person has committed a crime. The practice of slavery cannot be carried on from generation to generation because being a descendant of a criminal is not a crime, nor is it voluntary.

(cont.)

Responding to the Selection

How convincing do you find Johnson's argument? Does he offer the best reasons against slavery, or do you find other reasons more compelling? Discuss the arguments you would make in your own "Brief to Free a Slave."

Reviewing the Selection

RECALLING

1. According to the author, what is a person's "natural condition"?

2. According to Johnson, under what conditions might a person forfeit, or give up the right to, his or her liberty?

3. How did "he who is now suing for his freedom"—Joseph Knight—come to be a slave? On what basis does Knight's would-be master rest his claim?

4. For what reasons might slavery seem attractive to some people, according to Johnson?

INTERPRETING

5. In what respects are people created equal?

6. Why might Johnson believe that no one can forfeit the liberty of his of her children?

7. What flaw does Johnson see in the argument for Joseph Knight's enslavement?

8. Why does Johnson believe any reasons that might make slavery seem attractive are inapplicable in the case of Knight?

SYNTHESIZING

9. According to Johnson, under what conditions may the rights of liberty legitimately be taken away? According to Johnson, why shouldn't the practice of slavery be carried on from generation to generation?

10. Does Johnson think slavery is morally wrong? Why, or why not? Does he think it is illegal? Why, or why not? Does he think it is impractical? Why, or why not?

ANSWERS FOR REVIEWING THE SELECTION (CONT.)

10. Johnson thinks slavery is morally wrong and illegal because he believes that no person is "by nature the property of another." He thinks slavery is impractical because he believes no real gain can be had by "taking away the liberty of any part of the human species."

ANALYTIC SCALES FOR RESPONDING IN WRITING

Assign a score from 1 to 25 for each grading criterion below. (For more detailed evaluation, see the evaluation forms for writing, revising, and proofreading, *Assessment Portfolio,* 7.1–7.10.)

1. Editorial
• **Content/Unity.** The editorial presents the writer's opinion on a controversial topic.
• **Organization/Coherence.** The editorial states the writer's opinion. It then provides two or three strong

(cont.)

Understanding Literature (Questions for Discussion)

1. **Mode.** A **mode** is a form of writing. One common classification system, based on content, divides writing into four modes: argumentation, description, exposition, and narration. What is the primary mode of Johnson's brief? How can you tell? Within the piece, what other modes does Johnson at times adopt? Give examples.

2. **Thesis and Argument.** A **thesis** is a main idea that is supported in a work of nonfiction prose. An **argument** presents reasons or arguments for accepting or rejecting a thesis. In a direct argument, the writer's thesis is usually readily apparent. What is Johnson's thesis? Does he state his thesis explicitly? From what passages can his thesis be inferred? How often is the thesis stated or restated?

Responding in Writing

1. **Editorial.** Johnson uses his "Brief" to present an argument supporting his point of view. Select a current issue in your community about which there is considerable controversy, and write an editorial for your local newspaper outlining your own thoughts on the issue. Use deductive reasoning in arguing your point of view. Like Johnson, consider opposing arguments and how you might respond to them.

2. **Judicial Opinion.** Imagine that you are the presiding judge in Joseph Knight's case. Write a judicial opinion in which you state your decision and explain your reasons for deciding as you did. Include in your opinion a summary and evaluation of Johnson's "Brief."

ANSWERS FOR UNDERSTANDING LITERATURE

► See the evaluation forms for discussion, active listening, and oral communication, *Assessment Portfolio,* 7.11–7.14.
Responses will vary. Possible responses are given.

1. **Mode.** The primary mode of Johnson's brief is argumentation. Throughout the brief, Johnson gives reasons to persuade his readers of his point of view. Johnson also uses a narrative mode to tell about how some traders tricked Africans with promises of a European education. He uses exposition to explain how the Jamaican constitution rationalizes slavery.

►**Teaching Note:** Students should support their conclusions about the brief's primary mode with specific examples from the selection.

►**Additional Resources:** *Essential Skills Practice Book: Writing,* 1.9.

2. **Thesis and Argument.** Johnson's thesis is that all people possess the same right to freedom and that right cannot be taken away unless a person forfeits his or her own freedom. He states his thesis most explicitly near the end of his brief: "The sum of the argument is this:—No man is by nature the property of another: The defendant is, therefore, by nature free: The rights of nature must be some way forfeited before they can be justly taken away." His thesis can be inferred from the passage that tells how some people have been tricked into slavery and in the passage that analyzes the constitution of Jamaica. Johnson states or restates his thesis twice, at the beginning and at the end of the brief.

►**Teaching Note:** Students can discuss why Johnson may have chosen to place his thesis statement where he did. What effect does this placement have on Johnson's argument?

►**Additional Resources:** *Essential Skills Practice Book: Writing,* 1.31 and 1.41.

PREREADING NOTES

READER'S JOURNAL

Students might think of slang words that they have had to explain to their parents or jargon related to a sport or extracurricular activity that they have had to explain to someone unfamiliar with the activity.

LANGUAGE SKILLS

Students might use a graphic organizer to analyze Greek and Latin roots.

▶ Additional practice is provided in the *Essential Skills Practice Book: Language,* 2.142.

ANSWERS TO GUIDED READING QUESTIONS

❶ A collection of poems or stories is similar to a collection of flowers because both are pleasing, and, while pieces of the collection seem alike at first glance, each piece has its individual beauty and appeal.

❷ *Responses will vary. Possible responses are given.*

1. I give thanks to nature for making the world beautiful.

2. The nature of light is ambiguous: is it composed of waves or particles?

3. Many people believe that by nature plants do not move, but in fact plants do turn their leaves toward sunlight.

4. He is a good-natured bloke.

5. It's natural for children to enjoy running and dancing.

6. I love being in nature.

7. By nature she had a melancholy disposition.

8. After the summer comes the fall, according to nature.

9. Persons of that nature can't help but give generously.

10. Scotland Yard called in Sherlock Holmes to investigate the nature of the crime.

11. If you study nature you'll better appreciate the complexity of the universe.

FROM

A Dictionary of the English Language

SAMUEL JOHNSON

❶ *In what ways is a collection of poems or stories similar to a collection of flowers?*

ANTHO´LOGY. *n.*
  1. A collection of flowers.

GANG. *n.*
  A number herding together; a troop; a company; a tribe; a herd. It is seldom used but in contempt or <u>abhorrence</u>.

LEXICO´GRAPHER. *n.*
  A writer of dictionaries; a harmless <u>drudge</u>, that busies himself in tracing the original, and detailing the signification of words.

❷ *Can you make sentences using the word* nature *in each of these different ways?*

NA´TURE. *n.*
  1. An imaginary being supposed to preside over the material and animal world.
       Though, *nature,* art my goddess; to thy law
       My services are bound.—*Shakespeare*
  2. The native state or properties of anything, by which it is discriminated from others.
  3. The constitution of an animated body.
  4. <u>Disposition</u> of mind; temper.

WORDS FOR EVERYDAY USE:

ab • hor • rence (ab hôr´ əns) *n.,* loathing
drudge (druj) *n.,* person who does tedious work
dis • po • si • tion (dis´ pə zish´ ən) *n.,* tendency, habit

VOCABULARY IN CONTEXT

• On the playground, the elementary school boys and girls eyed each other with <u>abhorrence</u>.
• The assembly-line work made her feel like a <u>drudge</u>.
• I hope you don't have a <u>disposition</u> for tardiness because this job requires promptness.

154   RELIQUES OF ANCIENT POETRY.

DOWSABELL.

"This mayden in a morne betime
Went forth when May was in her prime,"

5. The regular course of things.
6. The compass of natural existence.
7. Natural affection, or reverence; native sensations.
8. The state or operation of the material world.
9. Sort; species.
10. Sentiments or images adapted to nature, or comformable to truth and reality.
11. Physics; the science which teaches the qualities of things.

> *Nature* and *nature's* laws lay hid in night,
> God said, Let Newton be, and all was light.—*Pope.*

OATS. *n.*

A grain, which in England is generally given to horses, but in Scotland supports the people.

PA´TRON. *n.*

1. One who countenances, supports, or protects. Commonly a wretch who supports with <u>insolence</u>, and is paid with flattery.   ■

Based on this definition, how do you think Johnson felt about depending, for his livelihood as a writer, on the largess of patrons?

FROM *A DICTIONARY OF THE ENGLISH LANGUAGE*   **539**

BIOGRAPHICAL NOTE

When Johnson began the monumental task of compiling his *Dictionary* in 1747, he requested patronage from Lord Chesterfield, an influential patron of eighteenth-century writers. At the time, Chesterfield denied Johnson's request; when Johnson neared his publication date, Chesterfield made a belated offer. This time, it was Johnson who refused. His definition of *patron* reveals his lingering resentment.

EX. Whom does Johnson call a "harmless drudge"?
He calls a lexicographer a "harmless drudge."

1. What word does "A collection of flowers" define?
It defines *anthology.*

2. What word does "Disposition of mind" define?
It defines *nature.*

3. What is the science that teaches the qualities of things?
Physics is the science that teaches the qualities of things.

4. Who eats oats?
English horses and the Scottish people eat oats.

5. With what does a patron give support?
A patron supports with insolence.

VOCABULARY IN CONTEXT

• The teacher reprimanded the rowdy student's <u>insolence</u>.

ANSWER TO GUIDED READING QUESTION

❶ Johnson may have resented having to use his talent to please the wealthy, who treat those who do not possess similar fortunes with contempt.

RESPONDING TO THE SELECTION

Students may want to add definitions to Johnson's.

ADDITIONAL RESOURCES

READER'S GUIDE
• Selection Worksheet, 7.9

ASSESSMENT PORTFOLIO
• Selection Check Test, 4.7.17
• Selection Test, 4.7.18

ESSENTIAL SKILLS PRACTICE BOOKS
• *Language*, 2.142, 2.153

ANSWERS FOR REVIEWING THE SELECTION

RECALLING

1. Johnson defines *lexicographer* as "A writer of dictionaries" and "a harmless drudge."

2. Eleven definitions are given for *nature*. The first is "An imaginary being supposed to preside over the material and animal world."

3. Oats are used to feed horses and people. They are used this way in England and Scotland, respectively.

4. Johnson defines *patron* as "a wretch who supports with insolence, and is paid with flattery."

INTERPRETING

Responses will vary. Possible responses are given.

5. "A harmless drudge . . . " is meant to be taken as tongue-in-cheek. "A writer of dictionaries" is meant to be taken seriously. One can determine that part of the definition is meant to be humorous because it is set off as an appositive bit of self-deprecation.

6. Johnson equates nature to a spirit in his first definition. In his last definition, Newton's scientific discoveries account for science's "light" being shed.

7. Johnson doesn't think oats are a good food for people. He finds humor in the fact that the Scots eat oats, and intends his definition as a mild barb at the Scots.

8. Johnson despises patrons. He dislikes the flattery of those who are supported by patronage. Any future patron of Johnson cannot expect flattery or humility.

SYNTHESIZING

Responses will vary. Possible responses are given.

9. Johnson's definitions imply that things or words cannot always be taken at face value. For him, an anthology is a symbol, rather than a palpable collection of stories or poems. In his definitions of *gang* and *patron,* he states a dislike for all forms of coercion.

10. Johnson fits his own definition of *lexicographer* because he is a "writer of dictionaries" who traces the original meaning of words and details their "signification." However, his strong opinions and decidedly subjective definitions hardly make him "a harmless drudge."

Responding to the Selection

With a partner, discuss your reactions to the selections from Johnson's *Dictionary.* Which of Johnson's definitions seem accurate to you? Which are most useful? Which are most amusing? Which definition do you like the best? Why?

Reviewing the Selection

RECALLING

1. How does Johnson define *lexicographer*?

2. How many definitions of *nature* are given? What is the first definition?

3. What are the two uses of oats? In which countries, respectively, are oats used in these ways?

4. How does Johnson define *patron*?

INTERPRETING

5. What part of Johnson's definition of *lexicographer* is meant to be taken as tongue-in-cheek? What part is meant to be taken seriously? How do you know?

6. To what does Johnson equate nature in his first definition? In his last definition of *nature,* what accounts for science's "light" being shed?

7. Does Johnson think oats are a good food for people? What is his opinion of how oats are used in Scotland?

8. What does Johnson think of patrons? What does he think that people who accept patronage commonly do?

SYNTHESIZING

9. What opinions does Johnson state or imply in his definitions? Classify these opinions. On what sorts of topics does Johnson inject his opinions?

10. Do you think Johnson fits his definition of *lexicographer?* In what ways does the definition fit him? In what ways does it not fit him?

Understanding Literature (Questions for Discussion)

1. **Denotation.** The **denotation** is the basic meaning or reference of an expression, excluding its emotional associations, or **connotations.** Which of Johnson's definitions provide straightforward denotations? Which do not?

ANSWERS FOR UNDERSTANDING LITERATURE

►See the evaluation forms for discussion, active listening, and oral communication, *Assessment Portfolio,* 7.11–7.14. *Responses will vary. Possible responses are given.*

1. **Denotation.** All of these definitions provide denotations, or referents; however, these are not straightforward but are meant to be understood as tongue-in-cheek. Point out to your students that the editors of this anthology have selected humorous definitions from Johnson's *Dictionary* but that most of the definitions in that dictionary are serious ones of the kind found in dictionaries today, which are, of course, the progeny of Johnson's seminal work.

►**Additional Resources:** *Essential Skills Practice Book: Language,* 2.153.

2. Connotation. A **connotation** is an emotional association or implication attached to an expression. Which of Johnson's definitions focus on connotations? What connotations does Johnson emphasize? Do you think these connotations are widespread today? What other connotations do the words possess today? If there are differences, do you think that these are because of changes in the language over time or because of Johnson's idiosyncracies?

Responding in Writing

1. **Dictionary Definition.** Write a lighthearted definition for a common term or expression from our contemporary vocabulary. You might choose a standard English word, a slang term, or an idiom. You might include in your definition your own interpretation of what the expression means or use the definition as a vehicle for social commentary. Be sure to provide examples to illustrate your meaning.

2. **Extended Definition.** Abstract concepts—such as freedom, trust, and success—are hard to define briefly because they mean different things to different people. Choose an abstract idea that is important to you and write a one-page "definition" in the form of a short essay. Be sure to use numerous examples to illustrate what you mean and include counterexamples to show what you do not mean.

Research Skills

Using Dictionaries. Read the Language Arts Survey, 4.24, "Using Dictionaries." Then use a dictionary to answer the following questions.

1. What does *ISBN* stand for?

2. Explain the etymology of the word *grammar.*

3. How many ways are there to pronounce the word *commensurate?* How do the ways differ?

4. As what parts of speech can *that* be used?

5. As the creator of a *pasquinade,* would you more likely be engaging in *columniation* or *calumniation*? Explain your answer.

---

2. Connotation. Johnson's definitions of *anthology, gang, oats,* and *patron* focus on connotations. With the exception of *anthology,* these definitions emphasize negative connotations. His connotation of *gang* is widespread today, but words such as *patron* and *oats* do not have the same strong connotations and are seldom used today in the same way.

►**Teaching Note:** Students should name specific words and phrases that indicate Johnson's tone.

►**Additional Resources:** *Essential Skills Practice Book: Language,* 2.153.

ANALYTIC SCALES FOR RESPONDING IN WRITING

Assign a score from 1 to 25 for each grading criterion below. (For more detailed evaluation, see the evaluation forms for writing, revising, and proofreading, *Assessment Portfolio,* 7.1–7.10.)

1. Dictionary Definition

• **Content/Unity.** The definition presents a denotative meaning as well as a connotative meaning of the word.

• **Organization/Coherence.** The definition states the word and its part of speech followed by a short definition illustrated with concrete details.

• **Language/Style.** The definition uses vivid and precise nouns, verbs, and modifiers.

• **Conventions.** The definition avoids errors in spelling, grammar, usage, mechanics, and manuscript form.

2. Extended Definition

• **Content/Unity.** The essay defines an abstract concept.

• **Organization/Coherence.** The essay states the concept to be defined. It illustrates a definition with concrete examples and counterexamples.

• **Language/Style.** The essay uses vivid and precise nouns, verbs, and modifiers.

• **Conventions.** The essay avoids errors in spelling, grammar, usage, mechanics, and manuscript form.

ANSWERS FOR RESEARCH SKILLS

1. *ISBN* stands for *International Standard Book Number.*

2. The use of *grammar* dates to the fourteenth century. It came from the Middle English *gramere,* which was a form of the Middle French *gramaire. Gramaire* was a modification of the Latin *grammatica,* which developed from the Greek word *grammatikos,* meaning "of letters."

3. There are two ways to pronounce *commensurate;* the end of the second syllable can be pronounced with a *ts* sound or with a *ch* sound.

4. *That* can be used as a pronoun, an adjective, a conjunction, and an adverb.

5. As a creator of a pasquinade, I would more likely be engaging in calumniation because a pasquinade is a form of satiric writing and a calumniation is a maliciously false statement. A columniation is an arrangement of columns.

ENRICHMENT ACTIVITIES

Students can write about or discuss methods for writing a biography of a famous person. What methods would they employ? Would they take notes, and if so, in what manner? How close would they be to the subject of the biography?

SUPPORT FOR LEP STUDENTS

Explain that some spelling has changed since Boswell wrote his biography. Students can work with an English-proficient student to identify words with unfamiliar spellings.

ADDITIONAL VOCABULARY

immense—very large; vast
contemplation—study; inspection
accumulate—heap; pile up; collect
insensibly—unconsciously
confidently—privately; secretly
artifice—trickery, craft
antechamber—small room leading into a larger room

PREREADING

from *The Life of Samuel Johnson, LL. D.*
by James Boswell

ABOUT THE AUTHOR

James Boswell (1740–1795) studied law, but he had literary ambitions. The active social life of London attracted him but sometimes got the better of him. A major goal of his seems to have been to befriend noted writers, and this he did persistently and remarkably well. His meeting with Samuel Johnson in 1763 proved to be the most influential. Thirty years separated the two men in age, but after a shaky beginning, they remained friends for life, even through a long tour through the sparsely populated Scottish Highlands and the Hebrides Islands. After Johnson died in 1785, Boswell spent a great deal of time completing *The Life of Samuel Johnson, LL. D.,* which stands today as his greatest literary accomplishment. He took great pleasure in his own fame as a writer, yet in some ways he always saw himself as a failure.

Besides the *Life of Johnson,* Boswell published *An Account of Corsica* (1768) and *Journal of a Tour to the Hebrides with Dr. Johnson* (1785). He was working on a third volume of the biography of his famous friend when he died in 1795.

ABOUT THE SELECTION

Soon after befriending Johnson, Boswell conceived a plan to write a new type of biography, one that told less about dates and observable events and more about the subject's thoughts and personality. *The Life of Samuel Johnson, LL. D.* (1791) shows Boswell's genius for drawing out Johnson and for recognizing and selecting quotations and anecdotes that depict his subject intimately. Boswell's willingness to reveal his own foibles made the work a surpassing novelty when it appeared.

GOALS/OBJECTIVES

Studying this lesson will enable students to

• enjoy an anecdotal style of biography
• describe Boswell's literary accomplishments and explain the historical significance of his writings

• define *anecdote* and identify anecdotes as they encounter them in their reading
• write an anecdote

READER'S JOURNAL

Think for a moment about a close friend of your own. What about him or her is important to you? What are your similarities and differences? How did you meet? Why do you think your friendship has persisted while others may have waned? Write in your journal about your friendship.

RESEARCH SKILLS

Read the Language Arts Survey, 4.31, "Informal Note-taking." Meet in small groups and discuss a recent or upcoming event you are interested in. During your discussion, practice your informal note-taking skills by taking notes on the conversation. Then compare your notes with those of other students and account for any differences.

FROM

The Life of Samuel Johnson, LL. D.

JAMES BOSWELL

But the year 1747 is distinguished as the <u>epoch</u>, when Johnson's <u>arduous</u> and important work, his *Dictionary of the English Language*, was announced to the world, by the publication of its *Plan* or *Prospectus*.

How long this immense undertaking had been the object of his contemplation, I do not know. I once asked him by what means he had attained to that astonishing knowledge of our language, by which he was enabled to realize a design of such extent, and accumulated difficulty. He told me, that "it was not the effect of particular study; but that it had grown up in his mind insensibly." I have been informed by Mr. James Dodsley, that several years before this period, when Johnson was one day sitting in his brother Robert's shop, he heard his brother suggest to him, that a Dictionary of the English Language

would be a work that would be well received by the publick; that Johnson seemed at first to catch at the proposition, but, after a pause, said, in his abrupt decisive manner, "I believe I shall not undertake it." That he, however, had bestowed much thought upon the subject, before he published his *Plan*, is evident from the enlarged, clear, and accurate views which it exhibits and we find him mentioning in that tract, that many of the writers whose testimonies were to be produced as authorities, were selected by Pope; which proves that he had been furnished, probably by Mr. Robert Dodsley, with whatever hints that <u>eminent</u> poet had contributed towards a great literary project, that had been the subject of important consideration in a former reign.

◆ ◆ ◆

WORDS FOR EVERYDAY USE:

ep • och (ep´ ək) *n.,* period of time

ar • du • ous (är´ jōō əs) *adj.,* extremely difficult

em • i • nent (em´ ə nənt) *adj.,* noteworthy

PREREADING NOTES

READER'S JOURNAL

Students might write a letter to this friend and share their thoughts about the friendship.

RESEARCH SKILLS

→ After students compare and discuss notes, they might want to attempt another note-taking session to improve their skills.

▶ Additional practice is provided in the *Essential Skills Practice Book: Study and Research,* 4.31.

VOCABULARY FROM THE SELECTION

arduous	etymology
asperity	implicitly
conciliate	insinuate
cynical	posterity
eminent	prodigious
epoch	solicit

VOCABULARY IN CONTEXT

- The Renaissance was an <u>epoch</u> that saw remarkable achievements in art and the sciences.
- Few people have completed the <u>arduous</u> ascent of Mt. Everest.
- The orchestra was honored when the <u>eminent</u> violinist sat in with them for the evening.

❶ Others think that Johnson's ambitions are unrealistic.

❷ Johnson's attitude toward Chesterfield has become negative; he has "resolved to have no connection with him."

❸ Johnson's *Plan* was dedicated to Lord Chesterfield.

❹ Boswell assesses Chesterfield to be opportunistic; the lord expects that Johnson will dedicate his book to him and wants to smooth over their differences.

BIOGRAPHICAL NOTE

Boswell's approach to biography was somewhat unusual. At the age of twenty-three, he attached himself to Johnson, who was the preeminent literary figure in England at that time. Boswell rarely took notes of conversations. Instead, he was a skilled observer and listener who had a highly precise memory for events, conversations, and scenes; only later would he write down what he saw and heard.

QUOTABLES

❝Johnson: Well, we had a good talk.

Boswell: Yes, Sir; you tossed and gored several persons.❞

—James Boswell

Dr. Adams found him one day busy at his *Dictionary*, when the following dialogue ensued. 'ADAMS. This is a great work, Sir. How are you to get all the etymologies? JOHNSON. Why, Sir, here is a shelf with Junius, and Skinner, and others; and there is a Welch gentleman who has published a collection of Welch proverbs, who will help me with the Welch. ADAMS. But, Sir, how can you do this in three years? JOHNSON. Sir, I have no doubt that I can do it in three years. ADAMS. But the French Academy, which consists of forty members, took forty years to compile their Dictionary. JOHNSON. Sir, thus it is. This is the proportion. Let me see; forty times forty is sixteen hundred. As three to sixteen hundred, so is the proportion of an Englishman to a Frenchman.' With so much ease and pleasantry could he talk of that prodigious labor which he had undertaken to execute.

◆   ◆   ◆

Lord Chesterfield, to whom Johnson had paid the high compliment of addressing to his Lordship the *Plan* of his *Dictionary*, had behaved to him in such a manner as to excite his contempt and indignation. The world has been for many years amused with a story confidently told, and as confidently repeated with additional circumstances, that a sudden disgust was taken by Johnson upon occasion of his having been one day kept long in waiting in his Lordship's antechamber, for which the reason assigned was, that he had company with him; and that at last, when the door opened, out walked Colley Cibber; and that Johnson was so violently provoked when he found for whom he had been so long excluded, that he went away in a passion, and never would return. I remember having mentioned this story to George Lord Lyttelton, who told me, he was very intimate with Lord Chesterfield; and holding it as a well-known truth, defended Lord Chesterfield, by saying, that 'Cibber, who had been introduced familiarly by the back-stairs, had probably not been there above ten minutes.' It may seem strange even to entertain a doubt concerning a story so long and so widely current, and thus implicitly adopted, if not sanctioned, by the authority which I have mentioned; but Johnson himself assured me, that there was not the least foundation for it. He told me, that there never was any particular incident which produced a quarrel between Lord Chesterfield and him; but that his Lordship's continued neglect was the reason why he resolved to have no connection with him. When the *Dictionary* was upon the eve of publication, Lord Chesterfield, who, it is said, had flattered himself with expectations that Johnson would dedicate the work to him, attempted, in a courtly manner, to sooth, and insinuate himself with the Sage, conscious, as it should seem, of the cold indifference with which he had treated its learned author; and further attempted to conciliate him, by writing two papers in *The World*, in recommendation of the work; and it must be confessed, that they contain some studied compliments, so finely turned, that if there had been no previous offense, it is probable that Johnson would have been

❶ *What do others think of Johnson's ambitions?*

❷ *What attitude has Johnson developed toward Chesterfield?*

❸ *To whom was Johnson's* Plan *dedicated?*

❹ *What assessment does Boswell make of Chesterfield?*

WORDS FOR EVERYDAY USE:

et • y • mol • o • gy (et´ə mäl´ə je) *n.*, origin and development of a word

pro • di • gious (prō dij´əs) *adj.*, amazing, huge

im • plic • it • ly (im plis´it lē) *adv.*, doubtlessly

in • sin • u • ate (in sin´yōō āt) *vt.*, work into gradually

con • cil • i • ate (kən sil´ē āt´) *vt.*, win over

VOCABULARY IN CONTEXT

- The etymology of many English words shows Greek and Latin influences.
- The prodigious task of planning and building the skyscraper took four years.
- The mother believed her child's side of the story implicitly.
- Lobbyists try to insinuate themselves with politicians.
- With the strike in its third month, a negotiator has been brought in to conciliate the union members.

highly delighted. Praise, in general, was pleasing to him; but by praise from a man of rank and elegant accomplishments, he was peculiarly gratified.

◆ ◆ ◆

This courtly device failed of its effect. Johnson, who thought that 'all was false and hollow,' despised the honeyed words, and was even indignant that Lord Chesterfield should, for a moment, imagine that he could be the dupe of such an artifice. His expression to me concerning Lord Chesterfield, upon this occasion, was, 'Sir, after making great professions, he had, for many years, taken no notice of me; but when my *Dictionary* was coming out, he fell a scribbling in *The World* about it. Upon which, I wrote him a letter expressed in civil terms, but such as might shew him that I did not mind what he said or wrote, and that I had done with him.'

This is that celebrated letter of which so much has been said, and about which curiosity has been so long excited, without being gratified. I for many years <u>solicited</u> Johnson to favor me with a copy of it, that so excellent a composition might not be lost to <u>posterity</u>. He delayed from time to time to give it me; till at last in 1781, when we were on a visit at Mr. Dilly's, at Southill in Bedfordshire, he was pleased to dictate it to me from memory. He afterwards found among his papers a copy of it, which he had dictated to Mr. Baretti, with its title and corrections, in his own handwriting. This he gave to Mr. Langton; adding that if it were to come into print, he wished it to be from that

❶
What did Johnson think of Chesterfield's flattery?

ANSWER TO GUIDED READING QUESTION

❶ Johnson thought that Chesterfield's flattery was "false and hollow."

LITERARY TECHNIQUE

As a biographer, Boswell employed **characterization** to create the character of Johnson for the reader. Three techniques for creating a character are direct description, portrayal of the character's behavior, and representations of the character's internal state. What technique did Boswell use in this passage about Johnson's response to Chesterfield's actions? How do you know? What does Johnson's response reveal about his character?

Answers. Boswell portrayed Johnson's behavior through descriptive words and phrases such as "despised the honeyed words" and "indignant." These highly emotional words reveal that Johnson was at times dramatic and passionate and perhaps easily angered.

VOCABULARY IN CONTEXT

• No one is allowed to <u>solicit</u> money on the subway.

• The advent of photography allowed people to record family histories for <u>posterity</u>.

copy. By Mr. Langton's kindness, I am enabled to enrich my work with a perfect transcript of what the world has so eagerly desired to see.

To THE RIGHT HONORABLE THE EARL OF CHESTERFIELD

'MY LORD,   February 1755

'I have been lately informed, by the proprietor of *The World*, that two papers, in which my Dictionary is recommended to the publick, were written by your Lordship. To be so distinguished, is an honor, which, being very little accustomed to favors from the great, I know not well how to receive, or in what terms to acknowledge.

'When, upon some slight encouragement, I first visited your Lordship, I was overpowered, like the rest of mankind, by the enchantment of your address; and could not forbear to wish that I might boast myself *Le vainqueur du vainqueur de la terre;*[1]—that I might obtain that regard for which I saw the world contending; but I found my attendance so little encouraged, that neither pride nor modesty would suffer me to continue it. When I had once addressed your Lordship in publick, I had exhausted all the art of pleasing which a retired and uncourtly scholar can possess. I had done all that I could; and no man is well pleased to have his all neglected, be it ever so little.

'Seven years, my Lord, have now passed, since I waited in your outward rooms, or was repulsed from your door; during which time I have been pushing on my work through difficulties, of which it is useless to complain, and have brought it, at last, to the verge of publication, without one act of assistance, one word of encouragement, or one smile of favor. Such treatment I did not expect, for I never had a Patron before.

'The shepherd in Virgil grew at last acquainted with Love, and found him a native of the rocks.

'Is not a Patron, my Lord, one who looks with unconcern on a man struggling for life in the water, and, when he has reached ground, encumbers him with help? The notice which you have been pleased to take of my labors, had it been early, had been kind; but it has been delayed till I am indifferent, and cannot enjoy it; till I am solitary, and cannot impart it; till I am known, and do not want it. I hope it is no very <u>cynical</u> <u>asperity</u> not to confess obligations where no benefit has been received, or to be unwilling that the Publick should consider me as owing that to a Patron, which Providence has enabled me to do for myself.

'Having carried on my work thus far with so little obligation to any favorer of learning, I shall not be disappointed though I should conclude it, if less be possible, with less; for I have been long wakened from that dream of hope, in which I once boasted myself with so much exultation, my Lord, your Lordship's most humble, most obedient servant,

          'SAM. JOHNSON.' ∎

---

1. *Le vainqueur . . . terre.* "The conqueror of the conqueror of the world"

WORDS FOR EVERYDAY USE:

cyn • i • cal (sin´i kəl) *adj.,* believing that people are insincere or selfish; sarcastic or sneering

as • per • i • ty (ə sper´ə tē) *n.,* harshness

VOCABULARY IN CONTEXT

- Are you so <u>cynical</u> to believe that all politicians are corrupt?
- The old man's <u>asperity</u> frightened the neighborhood children.

Responding to the Selection

Although the selection is about Johnson, it reveals much about its author. How reliable do you think Boswell is? Why? What other opinions can you form about Boswell's character? What kind of character do you think Boswell wants to present?

Reviewing the Selection

RECALLING

1. Who apparently first suggested to Johnson that he compile a dictionary? How did Johnson react to the suggestion?

2. How long did Johnson expect to take to complete his dictionary? How did this amount of time compare to the time it took the French Academy to complete its dictionary?

3. What incident supposedly offended Johnson in his visit to Lord Chesterfield's? What does Johnson tell Boswell about the incident?

4. What did Lord Chesterfield later do to win Johnson's favor? How did Johnson respond? In his letter to Lord Chesterfield, what reason does Johnson give for not valuing his recommendation of the *Dictionary?*

INTERPRETING

▶▶ 5. What does Boswell believe Johnson's *Plan* reveals about his preconceptions for the project?

▶▶ 6. What does Boswell's discussion indicate about Boswell's assessment of the project? What does Boswell see as Johnson's attitude toward the task he had undertaken?

▶▶ 7. Why do you think so many people found the story about Johnson and Chesterfield plausible?

▶▶ 8. Why might Chesterfield have wanted to win Johnson's goodwill? Do you think his attempt was sincere? Explain why, or why not.

SYNTHESIZING

9. Does Boswell's treatment of Johnson seem evenhanded? What self-admissions does Boswell include? Do his admissions add to or detract from Boswell's credibility? How?

10. Did Lord Chesterfield get Johnson to change his opinion of him? Explain. Why might Johnson have felt insulted rather than complimented by Lord Chesterfield's actions?

FROM *THE LIFE OF SAMUEL JOHNSON, LL. D.*   **547**

Understanding Literature (Questions for Discussion)

Anecdote. An **anecdote** is a brief story, usually with a specific point or moral. The story of Johnson's wait at Lord Chesterfield's is an example. Is Boswell's anecdote elaborate or sketchy? To support your answer, give examples of details that are or are not included. What do you think was Boswell's purpose in including or omitting these details? How might he have achieved a different effect?

Responding in Writing

Anecdote. Boswell's *The Life of Samuel Johnson, LL. D.* is replete with anecdotes that give insight into Dr. Johnson's character. Think of an experience that you could recount for others that reveals something about your character or the character of another person. Before writing your anecdote, take a moment to list the main elements of the story. You can tell the story in the sequence that makes most sense to you, but at this stage you should make your list chronological. Boswell's anecdote has a clear and specific purpose. Identify the point you want your anecdote to make about your character. Then add additional details that help your story to achieve its purpose and that give life to it.

PROJECT

Team Research. Working in research groups, prepare a report on a noteworthy figure in your community, past or present. Make a list of the tasks that must be done to complete your project, such as identifying sources of information, gathering information, and producing the final product. Decide how you will divide up the tasks and in what form you will present your report to the class. Will you make a wall display? produce a video? stage a series of vignettes?

"To All Writing Ladies"
by Margaret Cavendish

It is to be observed, that there is a secret working by Nature, as to cast an influence upon the mindes of men: like as in Contagions, when as the Aire is corrupted, it produces severall distempers[1] of the minde, by the inflammations of the spirits. And as in healthfull Ages, bodies are purified, so wits are refined; yet it seemes to me as if there were severall invisible spirits, that have severall, but visible powers, to worke in severall Ages upon the mindes of men. For in many Ages men will be affected, and dis-affected alike: as in some Ages so strongly, and superstitiously devout, that they make many gods: and in another Age so Atheisticall, as they beleeve in no God at all, and live to those Principles. Some Ages againe have such strong faiths, that they will not only dye in their severall Opinions, but they will Massacre, and cut one anothers throats, because their opinions are different. In some Ages all men seek absolute power, and every man would be Emperour of the World; which makes Civil Wars: for their ambition makes them restlesse, and their restlessnesse makes them seek change. Then in another Age all live peaceable, and so obedient, that the very Governours rule with obedient power. In some Ages againe, all run after Imitation, like a company of Apes, as to imitate such a Poet, to be of such a Philosophers opinion. Some Ages mixt, as Moralists, Poets, Philosophers, and the like: and in some Age agen, all affect singularity; and they are thought the wisest, that can have the most extravagant opinions. In some Ages Learning flourisheth in Arts, and Sciences, other Ages so dull, as they loose what former Ages had taught. And in some Ages it seemes as if there were a Common-wealth of those governing spirits, where most rule at one time. Some Ages, as in Aristocracy, when some part did rule; and other Ages a pure Monarchy, when but one rules; and in some Ages, it seemes as if all those spirits were at defiance, who should have most power, which makes them in confusion, and War; so confused are some Ages, and it seemes as if there were spirits of the Fæminine Gender, as also the Masculine. There will be many Heroick Women in some Ages, in others very Propheticall; in some Ages very pious, and devout: For our Sex is wonderfully addicted to the spirits. But this Age hath produced many effeminate Writers, as well as Preachers, and many effeminate Rulers, as well as Actors. And if it be an Age when the effeminate spirits rule, as most visible they doe in every Kingdome, let us take the advantage, and make the best of our time, for feare their reigne should not last long; whether it be in the Amazonian Government, or in the Politick Common-wealth, or in flourishing Monarchy, or in Schooles of Divinity, or in Lectures of Philosophy, or in witty Poetry, or any thing that may bring honour to our Sex: for they are poore, dejected spirits, that are not ambitious of Fame. And though we be inferiour to Men, let us shew our selves a degree above Beasts; and not eate, and drink, and sleep away our time as they doe; and live only to the sense, not to the reason; and so turne into forgotten dust. But let us strive to build us Tombs while we live, of Noble, Honourable, and good Actions, at least harmlesse;

That though our Bodies dye,
Our Names may live to after memory.

"Epigram on Milton" by John Dryden

Three poets,[2] in three distant ages born,
Greece, Italy, and England did adorn.
The first in loftiness of thought surpassed,
The next in majesty, in both the last:
5 The force of Nature could no farther go;
To make a third, she joined the former two.

"Love Armed"[3] by Aphra Behn

Love in fantastic triumph[4] sat
Whilst bleeding hearts around him flowed,
For whom fresh pains he did create
And strange tyrannic power he showed.

5 From thy bright eyes he took the fires
Which round about in sport he hurled,
But 'twas from mine he took desires
Enough t'undo the amorous world.[5]

---

1. **distempers.** Disturbances
2. **Three poets.** Refers to Homer, Virgil, and Milton
3. **"Love Armed."** Cupid, often depicted with a bow and arrow
4. **fantastic triumph.** In a grand procession
5. **Enough . . . world.** Enough to drown all lovers in suffering caused by desire

"To All Writing Ladies"

About the Author. Margaret Cavendish (1623–1674), duchess of Newcastle, wrote in various genres, including poetry, drama, letters, orations, and memoirs. She is best known for *The Life of William Cavendish* (1667), a biography of her husband, duke of Newcastle, and for her *Sociable Letters* (1664).

About the Selection. Cavendish implores her fellow women to take advantage of their moment in history and make a name for themselves. Because of her aristocratic standing, Cavendish was excused for the supposed audacity of writing about feminist issues.

Additional Questions and Activities

Why does Cavendish relate instances of change in human history? What does she want "our Sex" to do? Why?

Answers. Cavendish relates instances of change in human history to demonstrate that the preferences and privileges of each age change. She wants women, or "our Sex," to pursue roles formerly accorded only to men because she believes the "spirits of the Fæminine Gender" have been at work in the past and that they are at work in her age.

"Love Armed"

About the Author. A biography of Behn appears on page 521.

About the Selection. "Love Armed" demonstrates both Neoclassical influences and Behn's own feminist perspective on the traditional love poem.

"Epigram on Milton"

About the Author. A biography of Dryden appears on page 491.

About the Selection. "Epigram on Milton," with its references to Homer and Virgil, reveals the influences of ancient Greek and Roman literature on Dryden.

Additional Questions and Activities

According to the speaker, which two poets did Nature join? What was the result? What is the speaker implying?

Answers. Nature joined Homer and Virgil. The result was Milton. The speaker is implying that Milton's talent and poetry was a combination of the influences of Homer and Virgil.

ADDITIONAL QUESTIONS AND ACTIVITIES

What has "the God," or Cupid, taken from the speaker? What has he taken from her lover? How does the speaker feel about the final outcome?

Answers. Cupid has taken "desires/Enough t'undo the amorous world," "sighs and tears," and "languishments and fears" from the speaker. He has taken "pride and cruelty" and "every killing dart" from her lover. The speaker feels that she alone has suffered for love and that her lover emerged the unharmed "victor."

"THE LOVER: A BALLAD"

About the Author. Lady Mary Wortley Montagu (1689–1762) was well known in her time for her letter writing, although she also wrote some poetry and plays. She led a rather unconventional life for an eighteenth-century woman. She married her husband, Edward Wortley Montagu, for love; she followed him to Constantinople when he was appointed ambassador in 1716. Upon her return in 1718, she introduced the Turkish method of inoculation against smallpox in England. At one time friendly with Pope, she had a bitter falling out with him in 1728–1729. Her publications include *Court Poems by a Lady of Quality* (1716) and *Turkish Letters* (1763).

About the Selection. "The Lover: A Ballad" expresses Montagu's belief that women have every right to think of themselves as men's equals, both in matters of the mind and of the heart.

ADDITIONAL QUESTIONS AND ACTIVITIES

According to the speaker, what is the cause of what others call her "stupid indifference"?

Answer. Her "stupid indifference" is caused by her desire to find a man who possesses the qualities she values and to whom she feels equal.

From me he took his sighs and tears,
10 From thee his pride and cruelty;
From me his languishments and fears.
And every killing dart[1] from thee.

Thus thou and I the God have armed
And set him up a deity;
15 But my poor heart alone is harmed,
Whilst thine the victor is, and free.

"The Lover: A Ballad"
by Lady Mary Wortley Montagu

At length, by so much importunity pressed,
Take, (Molly),[2] at once, the inside of my breast;
This stupid indifference so often you blame
Is not owing to nature, to fear, or to shame;
5 I am not as cold as a Virgin in lead,[3]
Nor is Sunday's sermon so strong in my head;
I know but too well how time flies along,
That we live but few years and yet fewer are young.

But I hate to be cheated, and never will buy
10 Long years of repentance for moments of joy.
Oh was there a man (but where shall I find
Good sense and good nature so equally joined?)
Would value his pleasure, contribute to mine,
Not meanly would boast, nor lewdly design,
15 Not over severe, yet not stupidly vain,
For I would have the power though not give the pain;

No pedant yet learnèd, not rakehelly gay
Or laughing because he has nothing to say,
To all my whole sex obliging and free,
20 Yet never be fond of any but me;
In public preserve the decorums are just,
And show in his eyes he is true to his trust,
Then rarely approach, and respectfully bow,
Yet not fulsomely pert, nor yet foppishly low.

25 But when the long hours of public are past
And we meet with champagne and a chicken at last,

---

1. **dart.** Cupid's arrow
2. **Molly.** Molly Skerrett was a friend of Lady Mary and the mistress of Sir Robert Walpole.
3. **Virgin in lead.** Image of the Virgin Mary cast in lead or in a stained-glass window framed in lead.
4. **Ovid . . . cold.** In *Metamorphoses*, Ovid relates how Daphne was turned into a laurel tree to escape Apollo and how Arethusa became a fountain to escape Alpheus.

May every fond pleasure that hour endear,
Be banished afar both discretion and fear,
Forgetting or scorning the airs of the crowd
30 He may cease to be formal, and I to be proud,
Till lost in the joy we confess that we live,
And he may be rude, and yet I may forgive.

And that my delight may be solidly fixed,
Let the friend and the lover be handsomely mixed,
35 In whose tender bosom my soul might confide,
Whose kindness can sooth me, whose counsel could guide.
From such a dear lover as here I describe
No danger should fright me, no millions should bribe;
But till this astonishing creature I know,
40 As I long have lived chaste, I will keep myself so.

I never will share with the wanton coquette,
Or be caught by a vain affectation of wit.
The toasters and songsters may try all their art
But never shall enter the pass of my heart.
45 I loathe the lewd rake, the dressed fopling despise;
Before such pursuers the nice virgin flies;
And as Ovid has sweetly in parables told
We harden like trees, and like rivers are cold.[4]

"A Modest Proposal"[5] by Jonathan Swift

FOR PREVENTING THE CHILDREN OF POOR PEOPLE IN IRELAND FROM BEING A BURDEN TO THEIR PARENTS OR COUNTRY, AND FOR MAKING THEM BENEFICIAL TO THE PUBLIC

It is a melancholy object to those who walk through this great town or travel in the country, when they see the streets, the roads, and cabin doors, crowded with beggars of the female sex, followed by three, four, or six children, all in rags and importuning every passenger for an alms. These mothers, instead of being able to work for their honest livelihood, are forced to employ all their time in strolling to beg sustenance for their helpless infants, who, as they grow up, either turn thieves for want of work, or leave their dear native country to fight for the

---

5. **"A Modest Proposal."** A satiric pamphlet by Swift that offers a supposed solution to the problem of the populous, oppressed peasants of Ireland. Swift uses irony, beginning with the use of the word *modest* in the title; parody of humanitarians who sought to solve social problems through theoretical approaches; and logic to reach his shocking conclusion.

"A MODEST PROPOSAL"

About the Author. After being made dean of St. Patrick's Cathedral in Dublin in 1713, **Jonathan Swift** took up residence in Ireland. In 1724, he became a spokesperson for the Irish, airing their grievances against English oppression in pamphlets and a series of letters published under a pseudonym. For more information, see the biography on page 511.

About the Selection. Swift wrote "A Modest Proposal" in 1729 to express his sympathy for the plight of the oppressed Irish peasants and to express his anger at the English ruling class whom he faulted for creating that plight.

Pretender in Spain, or sell themselves to the Barbadoes.[1]

I think it is agreed by all parties that this prodigious number of children in the arms, or on the backs, or at the heels of their mothers, and frequently of their fathers, is in the present deplorable state of the kingdom a very great additional grievance; and therefore whoever could find out a fair, cheap, and easy method of making these children sound, useful members of the commonwealth would deserve so well of the public as to have his statue set up for a preserver of the nation.

But my intention is very far from being confined to provide only for the children of professed beggars; it is of a much greater extent, and shall take in the whole number of infants at a certain age who are born of parents in effect as little able to support them as those who demand our charity in the streets.

As to my own part, having turned my thoughts for many years upon this important subject, and maturely weighed the several schemes of other projectors, I have always found them grossly mistaken in their computation. It is true, a child just dropped from its dam may be supported by her milk for a solar year, with little other nourishment; at most not above the value of two shillings, which the mother may certainly get, or the value in scraps, by her lawful occupation of begging; and it is exactly at one year old that I propose to provide for them in such a manner as instead of being a charge upon their parents or the parish, or wanting food and raiment for the rest of their lives, they shall on the contrary contribute to the feeding, and partly to the clothing, of many thousands.

There is likewise another great advantage in my scheme, that it will prevent those voluntary abortions, and that horrid practice of women murdering their bastard children, alas, too frequent among us, sacrificing the poor innocent babes, I doubt, more to avoid the expense than the shame, which would move tears and pity in the most savage and inhuman breast.

The number of souls in this kingdom being usually reckoned one million and a half, of these I calculate there may be about two hundred thousand couples whose wives are breeders; from which number I subtract thirty thousand couples who are able to maintain their own children, although I apprehend there cannot be so many under the present distresses of the kingdom; but this being granted, there will remain an hundred and seventy thousand breeders. I again subtract fifty thousand for those women who miscarry, or whose children die by accident or disease within the year. There only remain an hundred and twenty thousand children of poor parents annually born. The question therefore is, how this number shall be reared and provided for, which, as I have already said, under the present situation of affairs, is utterly impossible by all the methods hitherto proposed. For we can neither employ them in handicraft or agriculture; we neither build houses (I mean in the country) nor cultivate land. They can very seldom pick up a livelihood by stealing till they arrive at six years old, except where they are of towardly parts;[2] although I confess they learn the rudiments much earlier, during which time they can however be looked upon only as probationers, as I have been informed by a principal gentleman in the county of Cavan, who protested to me that he never knew above one or two instances under the ages of six, even in a part of the kingdom so renowned for the quickest proficiency in that art.

I am assured by our merchants that a boy or a girl before twelve years old is no salable commodity; and even when they come to this age they will not yield above three pounds, or three pounds and half a crown at most on the Exchange; which cannot turn to account either to the parents or the kingdom, the charge of nutriment and rags having been at least four times that value.

I shall now therefore humbly propose my own thoughts, which I hope will not be liable to the least objection.

I have been assured by a very knowing American of my acquaintance in London, that a young healthy child well nursed is at a year old a most delicious, nourishing, and wholesome food, whether stewed, roasted, baked, or boiled; and I make no doubt that it will equally serve in a fricassee or a ragout.

I do therefore humbly offer it to public consideration that of the hundred and twenty thousand children, already computed, twenty thousand may be reserved for breed, whereof only one fourth part to be males, which is more than we allow to sheep, black cattle, or swine; and my reason is that these children are seldom the fruits of marriage, a circumstance not much regarded by our savages, therefore one male will be sufficient to serve four females. That the remaining hundred thousand may at a year old be offered in sale to the persons of quality and fortune through the kingdom, always advising the mother to let them suck plentifully in the last month, so as to render them plump and fat for a good table. A child will make two dishes at an entertainment for friends; and when the family dines alone, the fore or hind quarter will make a reasonable dish, and seasoned with a little pepper or salt will be very good boiled on the fourth day, especially in winter.

---

1. **Pretender . . . Barbadoes.** The Pretender refers to James Francis Edward Stuart, son of James II, who had been barred from the succession. He was exiled to the Continent, and Catholic Irish loyals joined him there. Poverty caused others to leave Ireland, and many traveled to the West Indies as indentured servants.
2. **towardly parts.** Promising abilities

• Students can discuss Swift's **tone**, which is that of a dispassionate economist, in the selection. Have them consider how the tone contributes to the satiric effect. Refer students to the Handbook of Literary Terms, page 1265, for a definition and examples of tone.

• What point does Swift make with the **metaphorical** use of the word *devour* in the following sentence: "I grant this food will be somewhat dear, and therefore very proper for landlords, who, as they have already devoured most of the parents, seem to have the best title to the children"?

Answer. By using *devour* metaphorically, Swift makes the point that English landlords are draining the resources of the Irish workers.

• What reasons does Swift give for not using adolescent boys and girls as well? What is **ironic** about his reasoning?

Answers. He reasons that the flesh of boys would be too tough and that girls should be saved to become "breeders" and that, in any case, such a practice might be perceived as "cruelty." His reasoning is ironic because it implies that killing babies for food is not cruel.

ADDITIONAL QUESTIONS AND ACTIVITIES

Inform students that "A Modest Proposal" is the longest-sustained piece of irony in the English language. It has often been attacked by critics who do not infer the ironic tone and believe that Swift is seriously recommending that babies be eaten. Ask students why critics might miss the irony in this piece. Is it simply because of Swift's skill as a satirist? What type of individual is most likely to misunderstand Swift's piece—the Irish Catholic, whom he is obliquely supporting, or the English Protestant noble, whom he is obliquely critiquing?

I have reckoned upon a medium that a child just born will weigh twelve pounds, and in a solar year if tolerably nursed increaseth to twenty-eight pounds.

I grant this food will be somewhat dear, and therefore very proper for landlords, who, as they have already devoured most of the parents, seem to have the best title to the children.

Infant's flesh will be in season throughout the year, but more plentiful in March, and a little before and after. For we are told by a grave author, an eminent French physician,[1] that fish being a prolific diet, there are more children born in Roman Catholic countries about nine months after Lent than at any other season; therefore, reckoning a year after Lent, the markets will be more glutted than usual, because the number of popish infants is at least three to one in this kingdom; and therefore it will have one other collateral advantage, by lessening the number of Papists among us.

I have already computed the charge of nursing a beggar's child (in which list I reckon all cottagers, laborers, and four fifths of the farmers) to be about two shillings per annum, rags included; and I believe no gentleman would repine to give ten shillings for the carcass of a good fat child, which, as I have said, will make four dishes of excellent nutritive meat, when he hath only some particular friend or his own family to dine with him. Thus the squire will learn to be a good landlord, and grow popular among the tenants; the mother will have eight shillings net profit, and be fit for the work till she produces another child.

Those who are more thrifty (as I must confess the times require) may flay the carcass; the skin of which artificially dressed will make admirable gloves for ladies, and summer boots for fine gentlemen.

As to our city of Dublin, shambles[2] may be appointed for this purpose in the most convenient parts of it, and butchers we may be assured will not be wanting; although I rather recommend buying the children alive, and dressing them hot from the knife as we do roasting pigs.

A very worthy person, a true lover of his country, and whose virtues I highly esteem, was lately pleased in discoursing on this matter to offer a refinement upon my scheme. He said that many gentlemen of this kingdom, having of late destroyed their deer, he conceived that the want of venison might be well supplied by the bodies of young lads and maidens, not exceeding fourteen years of age nor under twelve, so great a number of both sexes in every county being now ready to starve for want of work and service; and these to be disposed of by their parents, if alive, or otherwise by their nearest relations. But with due deference to so excellent a friend and so deserving a patriot, I cannot be altogether in his sentiments; for as to the males, my American acquaintance assured me from frequent experience that their flesh was generally tough and lean, like that of our schoolboys, by continual exercise, and their taste disagreeable; and to fatten them would not answer the charge. Then as to the females, it would, I think with humble submission, be a loss to the public, because they soon would become breeders themselves; and besides, it is not improbable that some scrupulous people might be apt to censure such a practice (although indeed very unjustly) as a little bordering upon cruelty; which I confess, hath always been with me the strongest objection against any project, how well soever intended.

But in order to justify my friend, he confessed that this expedient was put into his head by the famous Psalmanazar,[3] a native of the island Formosa, who came from thence to London above twenty years ago, and in conversation told my friend that in his country when any young person happened to be put to death, the executioner sold the carcass to persons of quality as a prime dainty; and that in his time the body of a plump girl of fifteen, who was crucified for an attempt to poison the emperor, was sold to his Imperial Majesty's prime minister of state, and other great mandarins of the court, in joints from the gibbet, at four hundred crowns. Neither indeed can I deny that if the same use were made of several plump young girls in this town, who without one single groat to their fortunes cannot stir abroad without a chair, and appear at the playhouse and assemblies in foreign fineries which they never will pay for, the kingdom would not be the worse.

Some persons of a desponding spirit are in great concern about that vast number of poor people who are aged, diseased, or maimed, and I have been desired to employ my thoughts what course may be taken to ease the nation of so grievous an encumbrance. But I am not in the least pain upon that matter, because it is very well known that they are every day dying and rotting by cold and famine, and filth and vermin, as fast as can be reasonably expected. And as to the younger laborers, they are now in almost as hopeful a condition. They cannot get work, and consequently pine away for want of nourishment to a degree that if at any time they are acciden-

---

1. **grave . . . physician.** Refers to François Rabelais, a French satirist

2. **shambles.** Slaughterhouses

3. **Psalmanazar.** George Psalmanazar was a famous impostor. A Frenchman, he pretended to be a Formosan and wrote fictitious accounts of Formosa in which he described human sacrifices and cannibalism.

tally hired to common labor, they have not strength to perform it; and thus the country and themselves are happily delivered from the evils to come.

I have too long digressed, and therefore shall return to my subject. I think the advantages by the proposal which I have made are obvious and many, as well as of the highest importance.

For first, as I have already observed, it would greatly lessen the number of Papists, with whom we are yearly overrun, being the principal breeders of the nation as well as our most dangerous enemies; and who stay at home on purpose to deliver the kingdom to the Pretender, hoping to take their advantage by the absence of so many good Protestants, who have chosen rather to leave their country than stay at home and pay tithes against their conscience to an Episcopal curate.

Secondly, the poorer tenants will have something valuable of their own, which by law may be made liable to distress, and help to pay their landlord's rent, their corn and cattle being already seized and money a thing unknown.

Thirdly, whereas the maintenance of an hundred thousand children, from two years old and upwards, cannot be computed at less than ten shillings a piece per annum, the nation's stock will be thereby increased fifty thousand pounds per annum, besides the profit of a new dish introduced to the tables of all gentlemen of fortune in the kingdom who have any refinement in taste. And the money will circulate among ourselves, the goods being entirely of our own growth and manufacture.

Fourthly, the constant breeders, besides the gain of eight shillings sterling per annum by the sale of their children, will be rid of the charge of maintaining them after the first year.

Fifthly, this food would likewise bring great custom to taverns, where the vintners will certainly be so prudent as to procure the best receipts for dressing it to perfection, and consequently have their houses frequented by all the fine gentlemen, who justly value themselves upon their knowledge in good eating; and a skillful cook, who understands how to oblige his guests, will contrive to make it as expensive as they please.

Sixthly, this would be a great inducement to marriage, which all wise nations have either encouraged by rewards or enforced by laws and penalties. It would increase the care and tenderness of mothers toward their children, when they were sure of a settlement for life to the poor babes, provided in some sort by the public, to their annual profit instead of expense. We should see an hon-

est emulation among the married women, which of them could bring the fattest child to the market. Men would become as fond of their wives during the time of their pregnancy as they are now of their mares in foal, their cows in calf, or sows when they are ready to farrow; nor offer to beat or kick them (as is too frequent a practice) for fear of a miscarriage.

Many other advantages might be enumerated. For instance, the addition of some thousand carcasses in our exportation of barreled beef, the propagation of swine's flesh, and improvement in the art of making good bacon, so much wanted among us by the great destruction of pigs, too frequent at our tables, which are no way comparable in taste or magnificence to a well-grown, fat, yearling child, which roasted whole will make a considerable figure at a lord mayor's feast or any other public entertainment. But this and many others I omit, being studious of brevity.

Supposing that one thousand families in this city would be constant customers for infants' flesh, besides others who might have it at merry meetings, particularly weddings and christenings, I compute that Dublin would take off annually about twenty thousand carcasses, and the rest of the kingdom (where probably they will be sold somewhat cheaper) the remaining eighty thousand.

I can think of no one objection that will probably be raised against this proposal, unless it should be urged that the number of people will be thereby much lessened in the kingdom. This I freely own, and it was indeed one principal design in offering it to the world. I desire the reader will observe, that I calculate my remedy for this one individual kingdom of Ireland and for no other that ever was, is, or I think ever can be upon earth. Therefore let no man talk to me of other expedients: of taxing our absentees at five shillings a pound: of using neither clothes nor household furniture except what is of our own growth and manufacture: of utterly rejecting the materials and instruments that promote foreign luxury: of curing the expensiveness of pride, vanity, idleness, and gaming in our women: of introducing a vein of parsimony, prudence, and temperance: of learning to love our country, in the want of which we differ even from Laplanders and the inhabitants of Topinamboo:[1] of quitting our animosities and factions, nor acting any longer like the

---

1. **Laplanders . . . Topinamboo.** The Anglo-Irish do not love Ireland in the way Laplanders love their frozen land or the Topinamboo love their wild jungles in Brazil.

ADDITIONAL QUESTIONS AND ACTIVITIES

• What does Swift's first argument for the proposal reveal about the common attitude toward Papists, or Catholics?

Answer. Many people were probably prejudiced against Catholics, believing them to be disloyal to Protestant England.

• How is Swift's statement that the proposal "would increase the care and tenderness of mothers toward their children" an example of verbal irony?

Answer. The statement is an example of verbal irony because it implies the opposite meaning; such a proposal would demonstrate a mother's callousness and indifference toward her children, not her affection for them.

• What purpose does Swift have in listing "other expedients"?

Answer. These proposals are all reasonable suggestions to solving the problem. Swift juxtaposes them with his absurd, satirical proposal to make the point that there are reasonable alternatives to the problem, if the English are willing to explore them.

LITERARY TECHNIQUE

You might ask students to find places in the proposal where Swift allows the persona he has created to slip. Where does the indignant, enraged Swift drop the mask of the cold economist?

• What does Swift's satiric proposal indicate about the attitude of
most English toward the plight of
the Irish?

Answer. His proposal reveals that
most English were indifferent to
the plight of the Irish and that they
believed the Irish poor were responsible for their own ills.

• Have students brainstorm a list
of social problems faced in this
country that seem to go unnoticed
by the government.

FROM *THE SPECTATOR*, No. 62, FRIDAY, MARCH 11, 1711

About the Author. Joseph
Addison (1672–1719), along with
friend and fellow journalist **Richard
Steele** (1672–1729), is credited
with the creation of the periodical
essay. These essays were intended
both for amusement and instruction; Addison's commentary on the
morals of his time was influential in
developing a middle-class code of
conduct. Addison and Steele published a series of essays in *The
Spectator* from March 1711 to
December 1712 (Addison resumed
briefly in 1714). Alexander Pope
satirized Addison and his moraliz-
ing in his *Epistle to Dr. Arbuthnot*
(1735).

About the Selection. In this essay,
which appeared in *The Spectator*,
Addison discusses the nature of wit.

Jews, who were murdering one another at the very
moment their city was taken:[1] of being a little cautious
not to sell our country and conscience for nothing: of
teaching landlords to have at least one degree of mercy
toward their tenants: lastly, of putting a spirit of honesty,
industry, and skill into our shopkeepers; who, if a resolution could now be taken to buy only our native goods,
would immediately unite to cheat and exact upon us in
the price, the measure, and the goodness, nor could ever
yet be brought to make one fair proposal of just dealing,
though often and earnestly invited to it.[2]

Therefore I repeat, let no man talk to me of these and
the like expedients, till he hath at least some glimpse of
hope that there will ever be some hearty and sincere
attempt to put them in practice.

But as to myself, having been wearied out for many
years with offering vain, idle, visionary thoughts, and at
length utterly despairing of success, I fortunately fell
upon this proposal, which, as it is wholly new, so it hath
something solid and real, of no expense and little trouble, full in our own power, and whereby we can incur no
danger in disobliging England. For this kind of commodity will not bear exportation, the flesh being of too
tender a consistence to admit a long continuance in salt,
although perhaps I could name a country which would
be glad to eat up our whole nation without it.

After all, I am not so violently bent upon my own
opinion as to reject any offer proposed by wise men,
which shall be found equally innocent, cheap, easy, and
effectual. But before something of that kind shall be
advanced in contradiction to my scheme, and offering a
better, I desire the author or authors will be pleased
maturely to consider two points. First, as things now
stand, how they will be able to find food and raiment for
an hundred thousand useless mouths and backs. And secondly, there being a round million of creatures in human
figure throughout this kingdom, whose sole subsistence
put into a common stock would leave them in debt two
millions of pounds sterling, adding those who are beggars by profession to the bulk of farmers, cottagers, and
laborers, with their wives and children who are beggars
in effect; I desire those politicians who dislike my over-
ture, and may perhaps be so bold to attempt an answer,
that they will first ask the parents of these mortals
whether they would not at this day think it a great happiness to have been sold for food at a year old in the
manner I prescribe, and thereby have avoided such a perpetual sense of misfortunes as they have since gone
through by the oppression of landlords, the impossibility
of paying rent without money or trade, the want of common sustenance, with neither house nor clothes to cover
them from the inclemencies of the weather, and the most
inevitable prospect of entailing the like or greater mis-
eries upon their breed forever.

I profess, in the sincerity of my heart, that I have not
the least personal interest in endeavoring to promote this
necessary work, having no other motive than the public
good of my country, by advancing our trade, providing
for infants, relieving the poor, and giving some pleasure
to the rich. I have no children by which I can propose to
get a single penny; the youngest being nine years old,
and my wife past childbearing.

from *The Spectator*, No. 62, Friday, March 11, 1711
by Joseph Addison

Mr. Locke has an admirable reflection upon the difference of wit and judgment, whereby he endeavors to show
the reason why they are not always the talents of the
same person. His words are as follow: "And hence, perhaps, may be given some reason of that common
observation, that men who have a great deal of wit and
prompt memories, have not always the clearest judgment, or deepest reason. For wit lying most in the
assemblage of ideas, and putting those together with
quickness and variety, wherein can be found any resemblance or congruity, thereby to make up pleasant pictures
and agreeable visions in the fancy; judgment, on the contrary, lies quite on the other side, in separating carefully
one from another, ideas wherein can be found the least
difference, thereby to avoid being misled by similitude,
and by affinity to take one thing for another. This is a
way of proceeding quite contrary to metaphor and allusion; wherein, for the most part, lies that entertainment
and pleasantry of wit which strikes so lively on the fancy,
and is therefore so acceptable to all people."[3]

This is, I think, the best and most philosophical
account that I have ever met with of wit, which generally,
though not always, consists in such a resemblance and
congruity of ideas as this author mentions. I shall only
add to it, by way of explanation, that every resemblance
of ideas is not that which we call wit, unless it be such an
one that gives delight and surprise to the reader. These
two properties seem essential to wit, more particularly

---

1. **Jews . . . taken.** Fighting factions of Jews destroyed Jerusalem
during the siege by the Roman emperor Titus in AD 70.
2. **being . . . to it.** These are all proposals Swift had made in
various pamphlets.
3. **" And . . . people."** From *An Essay Concerning Human
Understanding* by John Locke

the last of them. In order therefore that the resemblance in the ideas be wit, it is necessary that the ideas should not lie too near one another in the nature of things; for where the likeness is obvious, it gives no surprise. To compare one man's singing to that of another, or to represent the whiteness of any object by that of milk and snow, or the variety of its colors by those of the rainbow, cannot be called wit, unless, besides this obvious resemblance, there be some further congruity discovered in the two ideas that is capable of giving the reader some surprise. Thus when a poet tells us, the bosom of his mistress is as white as snow, there is no wit in the comparison; but when he adds, with a sigh, that it is as cold too, it then grows into wit. Every reader's memory may supply him with innumerable instances of the same nature. For this reason, the similitudes in heroic poets, who endeavor rather to fill the mind with great conceptions, than to divert it with such as are new and surprising, have seldom anything in them that can be called wit. Mr. Locke's account of wit, with this short explanation, comprehends most of the species of wit, as metaphors, similitudes, allegories, enigmas, mottoes, parables, fables, dreams, visions, dramatic writings, burlesque, and all the methods of allusion: as there are many other pieces of wit (how remote soever they may appear at first sight from the foregoing description) which upon examination will be found to agree with it.

As true wit generally consists in this resemblance and congruity of ideas, false wit chiefly consists in the resemblance and congruity sometimes of single letters, as in anagrams, chronograms, lipograms,[1] and acrostics; sometimes of syllables, as in echoes and doggerel rhymes; sometimes of words, as in puns and quibbles; and sometimes of whole sentences or poems, cast into the figures of eggs, axes, or altars: nay, some carry the notion of wit so far, as to ascribe it even to external mimicry; and to look upon a man as an ingenious person, that can resemble the tone, posture, or face of another.

As true wit consists in the resemblance of ideas, and false wit in the resemblance of words, according to the foregoing instances; there is another kind of wit which consists partly in the resemblance of ideas, and partly in the resemblance of words; which for distinction's sake I shall call mixed wit.

◆ ◆ ◆

Out of the innumerable branches of mixed wit, I shall choose one instance which may be met with in all the writers of this class. The passion of love in its nature has been thought to resemble fire; for which reason the words fire and flame are made use of to signify love. The witty poets therefore have taken an advantage from the doubtful meaning of the word fire, to make an infinite number of witticisms. Cowley, observing the cold regard of his mistress's eyes, and at the same time their power of producing love in him, considers them as burning-glasses made of ice; and finding himself able to live in the greatest extremities of love, concludes the torrid zone to be habitable. When his mistress has read his letter written in juice of lemon by holding it to the fire, he desires her to read it over a second time by love's flames. When she weeps, he wishes it were inward heat that distilled those drops from the limbec. When she is absent he is beyond eighty, that is, thirty degrees nearer the pole than when she is with him. His ambitious love is a fire that naturally mounts upwards; his happy love is the beams of heaven, and his unhappy love flames of hell. When it does not let him sleep, it is a flame that sends up no smoke; when it is opposed by counsel and advice, it is a fire that rages the more by the wind's blowing upon it. Upon the dying of a tree in which he had cut his loves, he observes that his written flames had burned up and withered the tree. When he resolves to give over his passion, he tells us that one burnt like him for ever dreads the fire. His heart is an Aetna, that instead of Vulcan's shop[2] encloses Cupid's forge in it. His endeavoring to drown his love in wine, is throwing oil upon the fire. He would insinuate to his mistress, that the fire of love, like that of the sun (which produces so many living creatures) should not only warm but beget. Love in another place cooks pleasure at his fire. Sometimes the poet's heart is frozen in every breast, and sometimes scorched in every eye. Sometimes he is drowned in tears, and burnt in love, like a ship set on fire in the middle of the sea.

The reader may observe in every one of these instances, that the poet mixes the qualities of fire with those of love; and in the same sentence speaking of it both as a passion, and as a real fire, surprises the reader with those seeming resemblances or contradictions that make up all the wit in this kind of writing. Mixed wit therefore is a composition of pun and true wit, and is more or less perfect as the resemblance lies in the ideas or in the words. Its foundations are laid partly in falsehood and partly in truth: reason puts in her claim for one half of it, and extravagance for the other. ∎

---

1. **chronograms, lipograms.** A chronogram is a phrase in which certain letters express a date. A lipogram is a composition that omits all words that contain a certain letter.
2. **Aetna . . . shop.** Mount Etna, the workshop of Vulcan, the Roman god of fire and metalwork

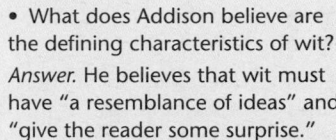

ADDITIONAL QUESTIONS AND ACTIVITIES

• What does Addison believe are the defining characteristics of wit?

Answer. He believes that wit must have "a resemblance of ideas" and "give the reader some surprise."

• According to Addison, how many types of wit are there? What are they?

Answers. There are three types of wit: true wit, false wit, and mixed wit.

• What type of resemblance makes up "false wit"? What are some examples of false wit?

Answers. The resemblance of words makes up false wit. Anagrams, puns, and sentences or poems that form shapes are examples of false wit.

• According to Addison, what is mixed wit?

Answer. Mixed wit is a combination of true wit and false wit; it consists partly in the resemblance of ideas and partly in the resemblance of words.

"A SHORT SONG OF CONGRATULATION"

About the Author. A biography of Johnson appears on page 533.

About the Selection. In "A Short Song of Congratulation," the speaker addresses a young man who has recently come into an inheritance and who will soon foolishly spend his money.

ADDITIONAL QUESTIONS AND ACTIVITIES

• What event occasions the speaker's words?

Answer. Sir John has just turned twenty-one years of age and has inherited property.

• How does the speaker predict Sir John will manage his inheritance?

Answer. He predicts that Sir John will fall prey to the temptations of "vice and folly" and lose his money to "the jockey" and "the pander."

LITERARY TECHNIQUE

After they have read the poem, have students discuss its title. Is the title to be taken at face value, or is it **ironic**? What does it imply about the speaker's attitude? Students should support their answers with specific examples from the poem.

Answers. The title of the poem is ironic because it implies that the time of congratulation will be short-lived. The speaker details how great Sir John will "Bid the slaves of thrift farewell" and eventually "hang or drown" for his debts.

"A Short Song of Congratulation"
by Samuel Johnson

> Long expected one and twenty
>   Lingering year at last is flown,
> Pomp and Pleasure, Pride and Plenty,
>   Great Sir John,[1] are all your own.
>
> 5 Loosened from the minor's tether,
>   Free to mortgage or to sell,
> Wild as wind, and light as feather
>   Bid the slaves of thrift farewell.
>
> Call the Bettys, Kates, and Jennys
> 10 Every name that laughs at Care,
> Lavish of your grandsire's guineas,
>   Show the spirit of an heir.
>
> All that prey on vice and folly
>   Joy to see their quarry fly,
> 15 Here the gamester light and jolly
>   There the lender grave and sly.
>
> Wealth, Sir John, was made to wander,
>   Let it wander as it will;
> See the jockey, see the pander,
> 20 Bid them come, and take their fill.
>
> When the bonny blade carouses,
>   Pockets full, and spirits high,
> What are acres? What are houses?
>   Only dirt, or wet or dry.
>
> 25 If the guardian or the mother
>   Tell the woes of willful waste,
> Scorn their counsel and their pother,
>   You can hang or drown at last. ■

---

1. **Sir John.** Sir John Lade, the nephew of one of Johnson's friends, inherited property in 1780, only to squander it all.

PREREADING

from *Candide*
by François Marie Arouet de Voltaire

ABOUT THE AUTHOR

François Marie Arouet (1694–1778) was born into a well-to-do family in Paris. He was educated at an excellent Jesuit school, where his teachers found him to be brilliant but difficult to control. His father wanted François to follow him in the profession of law, but the young man chose instead to pursue a life in literature. At the age of twenty-three, he added the words *de Voltaire* to his name, creating a pen name under which he became famous. In fencing, a *volt* is a step aside to avoid an opponent's thrust. The name *Voltaire* appropriately reflects the razor-sharp wit and adroit maneuvering of Voltaire's writing. As a young writer, Voltaire won acclaim for his dramatic works. However, he ran afoul of certain French nobles and was twice imprisoned in the Bastille. In his mid-thirties, he was exiled to England, where he became friends with Swift, Pope, and other leading writers and thinkers. Impressed by the relative freedom of thought in England, Voltaire wrote his *Lettres philosophiques sur les Anglais* (*Philosophical Letters on the English*). He returned to France and published this work, a satirical attack on the French church and state, and was forced into exile once again. For most of the rest of his life, he lived outside France, making brilliant contributions to Diderot's *Encyclopédie* and writing satirical tales such as *Zadig* (1747) and *Candide* (1759). Voltaire's name has become synonymous with wit and frank good sense in opposition to all forms of intolerance, tyranny, hereditary privilege, dogma, and unexamined convention.

ABOUT THE SELECTION

Candide was written after the death of Voltaire's beloved Emilie, Marquise du Chatelet. Mme du Chatelet was a believer in the "philosophical optimism" of the German philosopher Gottfried Wilhelm von Leibniz. Leibniz had argued that the world as it is, with all its problems, is the best of all possible worlds. Voltaire, despairing over the death of Emilie and suffering from political and religious persecution, wrote in *Candide* a delightful satirical attack on philosophical optimism that has become one of the world's great classics.

ADDITIONAL RESOURCES

READER'S GUIDE
- Selection Worksheet, 7.11

ASSESSMENT PORTFOLIO
- Selection Check Test, 4.7.21
- Selection Test, 4.7.22

ENRICHMENT ACTIVITIES

Students can hold a debate on the idea that "this is the best of all possible worlds." Students should work in separate teams of three or four students each, and each team should develop logical arguments in agreement or disagreement with the idea.

SUPPORT FOR LEP STUDENTS

Point out that many sentences in the selection are rather long. Students should pay attention to the semicolons that signal the end of complete thoughts.

ADDITIONAL VOCABULARY

genealogy—tracing a line of descent

consternation—fear or shock that makes one feel helpless

accordance—agreement; conformity

ignominious—shameful; dishonorable

GOALS/OBJECTIVES

Studying this lesson will enable students to

- interpret and appreciate humor and criticism in a work of satire
- describe Voltaire's literary accomplishments and explain the historical significance of his writings

- explain the connections between Voltaire's writing and the English literature in this unit
- define *satire* and identify satire and its effects in literature they read
- define *irony* and identify and interpret its effect as they encounter it in their reading

MULTICULTURAL EXTENSIONS: SATIRE

France

FROM

Candide

FRANÇOIS MARIE AROUET DE VOLTAIRE

CHAPTER I

HOW CANDIDE WAS BROUGHT UP IN A NOBLE CASTLE AND HOW HE WAS EXPELLED FROM THE SAME

❶
What makes Candide's name fitting? Why might Voltaire have chosen such a name?

In the castle of Baron Thunder-ten-tronckh in Westphalia there lived a youth, endowed by Nature with the most gentle character. His face was the expression of his soul. His judgment was quite honest and he was extremely simple-minded; and this was the reason, I think, that he was named Candide.[1] Old servants in the house suspected that he was the son of the Baron's sister and a decent honest gentleman of the neighbourhood, whom this young lady would never marry because he could only prove seventy-one quarterings,[2] and the rest of his genealogical tree was lost, owing to the injuries of time. The Baron was one of the most powerful lords in Westphalia,[3] for his castle possessed a door and windows. His Great Hall was even decorated with a piece of tapestry. The dogs in his stable-yards formed a pack of hounds when necessary; his grooms were his huntsmen; the village curate was his Grand Almoner.[4] They all called him "My Lord," and laughed heartily at his stories. The Baroness weighed about three hundred and fifty pounds, was therefore greatly respected, and did the honours of the house with a dignity which rendered her still more respectable. Her daughter Cunegonde, aged seventeen, was rosy-cheeked, fresh, plump and tempting. The Baron's son appeared in every respect worthy of his father. The tutor Pangloss[5]

---

1. **Candide.** The word *candid* means "frank" or "honest."
2. **quarterings.** Divisions of a coat of arms showing degrees of nobility
3. **Westphalia.** Region in northwestern Germany
4. **Grand Almoner.** Distributor of alms or charity
5. **Pangloss.** The name means, in Greek, "all tongue."

was the <u>oracle</u> of the house, and little Candide followed his lessons with all the candour of his age and character. Pangloss taught metaphysico-theologo-cosmol-onigology. He proved admirably that there is no effect without a cause and that in this best of all possible worlds,[6] My Lord the Baron's castle was the best of castles and his wife the best of all possible Baronesses. "'Tis demonstrated," said he, "that things cannot be otherwise; for, since everything is made for an end, everything is necessarily for the best end. Observe that noses were made to wear spectacles; and so we have spectacles. Legs were visibly instituted to be breeched, and we have breeches. Stones were formed to be quarried and to build castles; and My Lord has a very noble castle; the greatest Baron in the province should have the best house; and as pigs were made to be eaten, we eat pork all the year round; consequently, those who have asserted that all is well talk nonsense; they ought to have said that all is for the best." Candide listened attentively and believed innocently; for he thought Mademoiselle Cunegonde extremely beautiful, although he was never bold enough to tell her so. He decided that after the happiness of being born Baron of Thunder-ten-tronckh, the second degree of happiness was to be Mademoiselle Cunegonde; the third, to see her every day; and the fourth to listen to Doctor Pangloss, the greatest philosopher of the province and therefore of the whole world. . . .

♦ ♦ ♦

Next day, when they left the table after dinner, Cunegonde and Candide found themselves behind a screen; Cunegonde dropped her handkerchief, Candide picked it up; she innocently held his hand; the young man innocently kissed the young lady's hand with remarkable <u>vivacity</u>, tenderness and grace; their lips met, their eyes sparkled, their knees trembled, their hands wandered. Baron Thunder-ten-tronckh passed near the screen, and, observing this cause and effect, expelled Candide from the castle by kicking him in the backside frequently and hard. Cunegonde swooned; when she recovered her senses, the Baroness slapped her in the face; and all was in consternation in the noblest and most agreeable of all possible castles.

CHAPTER II

WHAT HAPPENED TO CANDIDE AMONG THE BULGARIANS

Candide, expelled from the earthly paradise, wandered for a long time without knowing where he was going, turning up his eyes to Heaven, gazing back frequently at the noblest of castles which held the most beautiful of young Baronesses; he lay down to sleep supperless between two <u>furrows</u> in the open fields; it snowed heavily in large flakes. The next morning the shivering Candide, penniless, dying of cold and exhaustion, dragged himself towards the neighbouring town, which was called Waldberghoff-trarbk-dikdorff. He halted sadly at the door of an inn. Two men dressed in blue noticed him. "Comrade," said one, "there's a well-built young

❶
What philosophical views did Pangloss teach Candide?

---

6. **best of all possible worlds.** Voltaire is satirizing the beliefs of the German philosopher Leibniz.

WORDS FOR EVERYDAY USE:

or • a • cle (ör´ə kəl) *n.,* person in communication with the gods; person of great knowledge or wisdom

vi • vac • i • ty (vī vas´ə tē) *n.,* liveliness

fur • row (fur´ō) *n.,* groove made in the earth by a plow

VOCABULARY IN CONTEXT

- People in ancient Greece would seek answers from the <u>oracle</u>.
- Exhausted from a long day of traveling, the entertainer lacked her usual <u>vivacity</u>.
- The planter followed behind the plow, dropping seeds into the <u>furrow</u>.

❶ *Why is Candide punished by the army? In what way is he allowed to exercise his "liberty"?*

man of the right height." They went up to Candide and very civilly invited him to dinner. "Gentlemen," said Candide with charming modesty, "you do me a great honour, but I have no money to pay my share." "Ah, sir," said one of the men in blue, "persons of your figure and merit never pay anything; are you not five feet five tall?" "Yes, gentlemen," said he, bowing, "that is my height." "Ah, sir, come to table; we will not only pay your expenses, we will never allow a man like you to be short of money; men were only made to help each other." "You are in the right," said Candide, "that is what Doctor Pangloss was always telling me, and I see that everything is for the best." They begged him to accept a few crowns, he took them and wished to give them an IOU; they refused to take it and all sat down to table. "Do you not love tenderly . . ." "Oh, yes," said he. "I love Mademoiselle Cunegonde tenderly." "No," said one of the gentlemen. "We were asking if you do not tenderly love the King of the Bulgarians." "Not a bit," said he, "for I have never seen him." "What! He is the most charming of Kings, and you must drink his health." "Oh, gladly, gentlemen." And he drank. "That is sufficient," he was told. "You are now the support, the aid, the defender, the hero of the Bulgarians; your fortune is made and your glory assured." They immediately put irons on his legs and took him to a <u>regiment</u>. He was made to turn to the right and left, to raise the ramrod[7] and return the ramrod, to take aim, to fire, to double up, and he was given thirty strokes with a stick; the next day he drilled not quite so badly, and received only

twenty strokes; the day after, he only had ten and was looked on as a <u>prodigy</u> by his comrades. Candide was completely mystified and could not make out how he was a hero. One fine spring day he thought he would take a walk, going straight ahead, in the belief that to use his legs as he pleased was a privilege of the human species as well as of animals. He had not gone two leagues when four other heroes, each six feet tall, fell upon him, bound him and dragged him back to a cell. He was asked by his judges whether he would rather be thrashed thirty-six times by the whole regiment or receive a dozen lead bullets at once in his brain. Although he protested that men's wills are free and that he wanted neither one nor the other, he had to make a choice; by virtue of that gift of God which is called *liberty*, he determined to run the gauntlet[8] thirty-six times and actually did so twice. There were two thousand men in the regiment. That made four thousand strokes which laid bare the muscles and nerves from his neck to his backside. As they were about to proceed to a third turn, Candide, utterly exhausted, begged as a favor that they would be so kind as to smash his head; he obtained this favor; they bound his eyes and he was made to kneel down. At that moment the King of the Bulgarians came by and inquired the victim's crime; and as this King was possessed of a vast genius, he perceived from what he learned about Candide that he was a young <u>metaphysician</u> very ignorant in worldly matters, and

---

7. **ramrod.** Poker used for loading a muzzle-loaded rifle
8. **to run the gauntlet.** To face an ordeal, in this case passing by soldiers, each of whom will strike him

WORDS FOR EVERYDAY USE:

reg • i • ment (rej´ə ment) *n.*, unit of soldiers

prod • i • gy (präd´ə jē) *n.*, child or other person with talent or genius

met • a • phy • si • cian (met´ə fə zish´ən) *n.*, one who studies metaphysics, that branch of philosophy that deals with ultimate realities and the nature of being therefore pardoned him with a <u>clemency</u> which will be praised in all newspapers and all ages. An honest surgeon healed Candide in three weeks with the ointments recommended by Dioscorides. He had already regained a little skin and could walk when the King of the Bulgarians went to war with the King of the Abares.[9]

CHAPTER III

HOW CANDIDE ESCAPED FROM THE BULGARIANS AND WHAT BECAME OF HIM

Nothing could be smarter, more splendid, more brilliant, better drawn up than the two armies. Trumpets, fifes, hautboys, drums, cannons, formed a harmony such as has never been heard even in hell. The cannons first of all laid flat about six thousand men on each side; then the musketry removed from the best of worlds some nine or ten thousand <u>blackguards</u> who infested its surface. The bayonet also was the sufficient reason for the death of some thousands of men. The whole might amount to thirty thousand souls. Candide, who trembled like a philosopher, hid himself as well as he could during this heroic butchery. At last, while the two Kings each commanded a Te Deum[10] in his camp, Candide decided to go elsewhere to reason about effects and causes. He clambered over heaps of dead and dying men and reached a neighbouring village, which was in ashes; it was an Abare village which the Bulgarians had burned in accordance with international law. . . .

♦ ♦ ♦

Candide fled to another village as fast as he could; it belonged to the Bulgarians, and Abarian heroes had treated it in the same way. Candide, stumbling over quivering limbs or across ruins, at last escaped from the theatre of war, carrying a little food in his knapsack, and never forgetting Mademoiselle Cunegonde. His provisions were all gone when he reached Holland; but, having heard that everyone in that country was rich and a Christian, he had no doubt at all but that he would be as well treated as he had been in the Baron's castle before he had been expelled on account of Mademoiselle Cunegonde's pretty eyes. He asked an alms of several grave persons, who all replied that if he continued in that way he would be shut up in a house of correction to teach him how to live. He then addressed himself to a man who had been discoursing on charity in a large assembly for an hour on end. This orator, glancing at him askance, said: "What are you doing here? Are you for the good cause?" "There is no effect without a cause," said Candide modestly. "Everything is necessarily linked up and arranged for the best. It was necessary that I should be expelled from the company of Mademoiselle Cunegonde, that I ran the gauntlet, and that I beg my bread until I can earn it; all this could not have happened differently." "My friend," said the orator, "do you believe that the Pope is

Q
How does the "charity" orator respond to Candide's request for alms? How do his preachings correspond to his own actions?

---

9. **Bulgarians . . . Abares.** Voltaire's Bulgarians and Abarians represent, respectively, the Prussians under Frederick the Great and the French.
10. **Te Deum.** A hymn of thanksgiving beginning with the Latin words *Te Deum laudamus* ("We praise thee, O God")

WORDS FOR EVERYDAY USE:

clem • en • cy (klem´ən sē) *n.*, leniency, mercy

black • guard (blag´ərd) *n.*, scoundrel, villain, low person

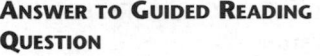

ANSWER TO GUIDED READING QUESTION

❶ The "charity" orator responds to Candide's request for alms by demanding to know why he is attending the assembly. The orator's own actions contradict his preachings.

HISTORICAL NOTE

The period from 1660 to 1789 in Europe is called the Age of Absolutism. As state sovereigns gained greater legal and administrative power, they gained greater control over their subjects. However, these rulers were not despots; they realized that their power was somewhat limited by laws and the strength of neighboring rulers. The French monarchs during this period most clearly exemplified the absolutist goals of creating a state army, controlling legal matters, and generating revenue through taxation.

VOCABULARY IN CONTEXT

• The governor showed <u>clemency</u> by granting a stay of execution.
• In the movies of the silent era, the <u>blackguard</u> rarely wins.

Anti-Christ?" "I had never heard so before," said Candide, "but whether he is or isn't, I am starving." "You don't deserve to eat," said the other. "Hence, rascal; hence, you wretch; and never come near me again." The orator's wife thrust her head out of the window and seeing a man who did not believe that the Pope was Anti-Christ, she poured on his head a full . . . O Heavens! To what excess religious zeal is carried by ladies! A man who had not been baptized, an honest Anabaptist[11] named Jacques, saw the cruel and ignominious treatment of one of his brothers, a featherless two-legged creature with a soul; he took him home, cleaned him up, gave him bread and beer, presented him with two florins,[12] and even offered to teach him to work at the manufacture of Persian stuffs which are made in Holland. Candide threw himself at the man's feet, exclaiming: "Doctor Pangloss was right in telling me that all is for the best in this world, for I am vastly more touched by your extreme generosity than by the harshness of the gentleman in the black

❶ *What state is Pangloss in when Candide meets him again? Can Pangloss's current condition be explained by his own philosophy?*

cloak and his good lady." The next day when he walked out he met a beggar covered with sores, dull-eyed, with the end of his nose fallen away, his mouth awry, his teeth black, who talked huskily, was tormented with a violent cough and spat out a tooth at every cough.

CHAPTER IV

HOW CANDIDE MET HIS OLD MASTER IN PHILOSOPHY, DOCTOR PANGLOSS, AND WHAT HAPPENED

Candide, moved even more by compassion than by horror, gave this horrible beggar the two florins he had received from the honest Anabaptist, Jacques. The phantom gazed fixedly at him, shed tears and threw its arms round his neck. Candide recoiled in terror. "Alas!" said the wretch to the other wretch, "don't you recognise your dear Pangloss?" ∎

---

11. **Anabaptist.** Member of a radical Protestant sect that opposed infant baptism
12. **florins.** Coins

Reviewing the Selection

1. What is Pangloss's job at the estate of Baron Thunder-ten-tronckh? What are Pangloss's philosophical beliefs?

2. Why is Candide expelled from the baron's home?

3. How does Candide come to be enlisted in the Bulgarian army? What details in the description of Candide's training as a soldier satirize the military?

4. How does Voltaire describe the burning of the Abare village in the first paragraph of Chapter III? What point is Voltaire making about the justifications that rulers of nations make for their actions?

5. How do the anti-Catholic orator's actions contradict his statements? What hypocrisy is Voltaire revealing in his description of the orator?

6. What elements in the description of the Anabaptist, Jacques, show that Voltaire was sympathetic to the Anabaptists and yet considered their zeal somewhat silly?

7. Whom does Candide meet at the end of the selection? In what state is this person? What makes this person's condition ironic?

8. What evidence is offered in the selection to contradict the idea that all things are connected in a series of causes and effects to create the "best of all possible worlds"?

Connections (Questions for Writing or Discussion)

1. **Satire.** Satire is humorous writing or speech intended to point out errors, falsehoods, foibles, or failings. What similarities can you find in the attitudes of Voltaire, in *Candide,* and Swift, in *Gulliver's Travels,* in their attitudes toward governments, rulers, and warfare? What absurdities and injustices do these authors satirize?

2. **Irony.** Irony is a difference between appearance and reality. Verbal irony is a statement that implies its opposite. Find some examples of verbal irony in Voltaire's *Candide* and Swift's *Gulliver's Travels.* What examples of human folly, or lack of reason, are revealed through verbal irony in these two works?

UNIT REVIEW

The Restoration and the Eighteenth Century

VOCABULARY FROM THE SELECTIONS

abhorrence, 538	desolation, 516	implicitly, 544	posterity, 545
abominate, 517	detract, 517	impotent, 516	procure, 516
acute, 517	diffusive, 486	indignation, 493	prodigious, 544
agitation, 516	disdainful, 493	infallibly, 513	prodigy, 560
ague, 504	disposition, 538	ingratiate, 516	quell, 493
arduous, 543	drudge, 538	insinuate, 544	recapitulate, 514
asperity, 546	elude, 515	insipid, 485	redress, 535
asseveration, 523	embargo, 512	insolence, 539	regiment, 560
avail, 535	eminent, 543	junta, 514	repose, 525
blackguard, 561	endeavor, 505	lament, 535	retired, 487
celestial, 493	entail, 534	lenity, 517	scruple, 517
clemency, 561	epoch, 543	metaphysician, 560	solicit, 545
compulsion, 534	err, 530	odious, 515	stipulate, 534
conciliate, 544	etymology, 544	oracle, 559	stratagem, 512
confounded, 513	extremities, 513	panegyric, 514	sublimely, 498
contriver, 516	furrow, 559	pernicious, 515	tribute, 516
cynical, 546	hitherto, 517	perpetual, 534	veneration, 516
debarred, 487	ignominiously, 524	pervert, 515	vivacity, 559

LITERARY TERMS

Age of Reason, 479	denotation, 540	near rhyme, 488
alliteration, 499	editorial, 537	Neoclassicism, 479
allusion, 484, 496	Enlightenment, 479	novel, 479, 480, 527
anaphora, 500	epistle, 479	off rhyme, 488
anecdote, 548	epitaph, 500	parody, 479
antithesis, 532	essay, 479, 481	pentameter, 528
aphorism, 532	fantasy, 519	periodical, 481
argument, 537	half rhyme, 488	point of view, 510
assonance, 488	heroic couplets, 481, 528, 532	proverb, 528
biography, 481	iamb, 528	Romanticism, 482
connotation, 540	irony, 519, 563	satire, 479, 511, 563
consonance, 488	journal, 510	slant rhyme, 488
couplet, 532	meter, 489	thesis, 537
critical essay, 480	mode, 537	tone, 519

SYNTHESIS: QUESTIONS FOR WRITING, RESEARCH, OR DISCUSSION

GENRE STUDIES

1. **Satire.** What is satire? What is being satirized in the following works in this unit: the selections from *Gulliver's Travels,* the selection from *The Life of Samuel Johnson,* "A Modest Proposal" (the Selections for Additional Reading), and the selection from *Candide* (in the Multicultural Extension, page 557).

2. **Journals and Travelogues.** The eighteenth century was a great age for nonfiction writing. Among the most popular types of writing in that age were journals, travelogues, and biographies. Explain how each of the following works embodies this interest: *The Diary of Samuel Pepys, Gulliver's Travels, Oroonoko, The Life of Samuel Johnson,* and *Candide* (in the Multicultural Extension, page 557).

THEMATIC STUDIES

3. **Reason.** Reread the couplets from Pope's *An Essay on Criticism.* What lines from Pope show that he highly valued reason and order? What lines show that he believed nature to be ruled by orderly laws? What arguments are set forth in "The Introduction," the selections from *Gulliver's Travels,* and "A Brief to Free a Slave." What arguments are set forth in the following Selections for Additional Reading: "A Modest Proposal," the selection from *The Spectator,* and "A Short Song of Congratulations." How do these pieces demonstrate the importance that eighteenth-century writers placed on reason?

HISTORICAL AND BIOGRAPHICAL STUDIES

4. **Slavery.** Compare and contrast the selection from Aphra Behn's *Oroonoko* with Samuel Johnson's "A Brief to Free a Slave." What case does each work make against slavery?

► These prompts are suitable as topics for research papers. Refer to the Language Arts Survey, 4.20–4.34, "Research Skills." (To evaluate research papers, see the evaluation forms for writing, revising, and proofreading in the *Assessment Portfolio,* 7.1–7.10.)

► These prompts can be adapted for use as topics for oral reports or debates. (To evaluate these projects, see the evaluation forms in the *Assessment Portfolio,* 7.17–7.19.)

LANGUAGE LAB   USAGE PROBLEMS

There are some words which are often misused. When editing your writing you should watch carefully for these usage problems.

LANGUAGE ARTS SURVEY

For additional help, see the Language Arts Survey, 2.90.

COMMON ERRORS IN VERB USAGE

adapt, adopt. *Adapt* means to modify something to fit a specific use or situation; *adopt* means to make something one's own.

EXAMPLE: I think we should *adapt Gulliver's Travels* for our next movie.

If Swift's "A Modest Proposal" were *adopted* children would be eaten.

affect, effect. Use *affect* as a verb meaning "have an effect on." Use *effect* as a noun meaning the result of an action.

EXAMPLE: What *effect* did Johnson hope his "A Brief to Free a Slave" would have?

Did reading it *affect* you at all?

LANGUAGE ARTS SURVEY

For additional help, see the Language Arts Survey, 2.91.

imply, infer. *Imply* means "to express indirectly rather than openly." *Infer* means "to arrive at a conclusion by reasoning from evidence."

EXAMPLE: Julian had groaned at every reading assignment all semester, but when *Gulliver's Travels* was assigned his silence *implied* that he wanted to read it.

Based on Gulliver's description of government, the king of the Brobdingnagians *inferred* that Gulliver came from an odious race.

like, as, as if. *Like* is a preposition, not a conjunction, and should not be used in place of *as* or *as if* in your writing.

EXAMPLE: It seems *as if* Pepys went through a lot of difficult experiences in his lifetime.

LANGUAGE ARTS SURVEY

For additional help, see the Language Arts Survey, 2.92.

of. Do not use the preposition *of* in place of *have* after verbs such as *could, should, would, might, must,* and *ought.*

EXAMPLE: Bonny would *have* read more of Anne Finch's poetry, if she could*'ve* found more of it.

than, then. Use *than* as a conjunction in comparisons. Use *then* as an adverb that tells when something occurred.

EXAMPLE: I thought I would like Anne Finch's writing more *than* Aphra Behn's , but *then* I read *Oroonoko.*

EXERCISE A   Avoiding Usage Problems

In each sentence below, choose the correct word from within the parentheses.

EXAMPLE: From reading Pepys' diary, you can see that the plague (affected, effected) many people.

ANSWER: affected

1. Candide (adapted, adopted) Pangloss's philosophy completely.

2. First Gulliver went to Lilliput where he was bigger (than, then) the inhabitants. (Than, Then) he went to Brobdingnag where he was smaller.

3. Boswell was more (than, then) just a biographer of Johnson, he was also a friend.

4. From the grimace on Jolene's face while she read *Oroonoko,* I (implied, inferred) that she did not like it very much.

5. Charlotte Smith probably would (have, of) written more poetry if she could (have, of) made enough money to support her family.

6. The captain treats Oroonoko (as if, like) he is a friend, but he only (adapts, adopts) this attitude to trick Oroonoko.

7. Many people have (adapted, adopted) *Gulliver's Travels* to be read by children.

8. Pope's aphorisms had such a profound (affect, effect) on Andre that he quoted them constantly.

9. Because "A Song for St. Cecilia's Day" celebrates music, Marcella felt that an organ accompaniment would improve the (affect, effect) of his reading of the poem.

10. Salvatore spoke (as if, like) he really believed that Swift's proposal could be (adopted, adapted) as a solution to current problems of famine and overpopulation, but his sudden grin at the end of his speech (implied, inferred) that he was not serious.

EXERCISE B   Proofreading for Usage Errors

Proofread the following paragraph for usage errors and correct any improperly used words.

Two great disasters struck the city of London between 1664 and 1666. First came the plague and than a terrible fire. The Great Plague of London raged from 1664 to 1665. Nobody was safe from the affects of this dreaded disease. During this time literally tens of thousands of people died. Special measures were adapted to try to contain the disease. The new laws effected the healthy as well as the sick. For example, burial processions for the dead were banned, but judging from Pepys' accounts it was like the law was never made. There was also a law which said that plague victims could only be buried at night. From the number of people who died from the plague we can imply that this was not possible. The plague would of been bad enough, but in 1666, a fire raged through London. It is believed that the fire started in the kitchen of one of the king's cooks, and than spread rapidly. With the affliction of the plague followed by the fire, it seemed like the city was cursed.

LANGUAGE ARTS SURVEY

For additional help, see the Language Arts Survey, 2.90–2.92.

LANGUAGE ARTS SURVEY

For additional help, see the Language Arts Survey, 2.90–2.92.

LANGUAGE LAB / USAGE PROBLEMS   **567**

ANSWERS FOR LANGUAGE LAB

Exercise A

1. adopted
2. than; Then
3. than
4. inferred
5. have; have
6. as if; adopts
7. adapted
8. effect
9. effect
10. as if; adopted; implied

Exercise B

    Two great disasters struck the city of London between 1664 and 1666. First came the plague and **then** a terrible fire. The Great Plague of London raged from 1664 to 1665. Nobody was safe from the **effects** of this dreaded disease. During this time literally tens of thousands of people died. Special measures were **adopted** to try to contain the disease. The new laws **affected** the healthy as well as the sick. For example, burial processions for the dead were banned, but judging from Pepys' accounts it was **as if** the law was never made. There was also a law which said that plague victims could only be buried at night. From the number of people who died from the plague we can **infer** that this was not possible. The plague would **have** been bad enough, but in 1666, a fire raged through London. It is believed that the fire started in the kitchen of one of the king's cooks, and **then** spread rapidly. With the affliction of the plague followed by the fire, it seemed like the city was cursed.

▶ Additional practice is provided in the *Essential Skills Practice Book: Language,* 2.90–2.92.

UNIT 8 THE ROMANTIC ERA (1785–1832)

Painter's Honeymoon. Frederick Lord Leighton, 1864.
Charles H. Bayley Picture and Painting Fund.
Courtesy, Museum of Fine Arts, Boston

GOALS/OBJECTIVES

Studying this unit will enable students to

- appreciate and interpret Romantic poetry and prose
- describe Wordsworth's theory of poetry and explain its significance for English literature
- describe the status of women in England during the Romantic Era

- define *Romanticism*
- explain how the ideals of the American and French revolutions influenced English poets and writers of the Romantic Era
- identify the major forms of prose writing that emerged from the Romantic Era

Thanks to the human heart by which we live,

Thanks to its tenderness, its joys, and fears,

To me the meanest flower that blows can give

Thoughts that do often lie too deep for tears.

—William Wordsworth,
"Ode: Intimations of Immortality"

569

BIOGRAPHICAL NOTE

William Wordsworth's revolutionary theory of poetry shaped the literary philosophy of the Romantic Era. In his preface to *Lyrical Ballads,* he declared that poetry is "emotion recollected in tranquillity." These final four lines from "Ode: Intimations of Immortality" exemplify the Romantic celebration of emotion over reason. See the complete poem, which appears in the Selections for Additional Reading, page 662.

CONNECTIONS ACROSS THE CURRICULUM

ARTS AND HUMANITIES
- Blake's Art, 589
- Illustration, 589, 633
- Performing Song, 584

MATHEMATICS AND SCIENCES
- Environmental Action, 621
- Erasmus Darwin, 657
- Genetic Technology, 660
- Saint Elmo's Fire, 666
- Science in the Romantic Era, 571

SOCIAL STUDIES
- American Romantic Movement, 570
- Catholic Emancipation, 622
- Erasmus Darwin, 657
- Laws, 652
- Nature or Society, 655
- Plotting the Mariner's Path, 666
- Revolutions and Change, 571
- Survey, 653
- Time Capsule, 646
- Travel Writing, 614

APPLIED ARTS AND SCIENCES
- Researching Zoology/ Conservation, 592
- Travel Writing, 614

TEACHING THE MULTIPLE INTELLIGENCES

MUSICAL
- Performing Song, 584

SPATIAL
- Artistic Expression, 604
- Grave Rubbings, 581
- Guided Imagery, 674
- Nature Walk, 621
- Plotting the Mariner's Path, 666
- Sketching a Scene, 645
- Text and Illustration, 598, 633

KINESTHETIC
- Enacting *Macbeth,* 680
- Grecian Urn Scenes, 638
- Nature Walk, 621
- Performing Scenes, 660
- Role Playing, 587, 624, 658

INTERPERSONAL
- Burns and the French Revolution, 584

- Categorizing, 573
- Comparing Declarations, 676
- Comparing Nature Descriptions, 621
- Definitions, 642
- The Dirge, 675
- Environmental Action, 621
- Keats's Themes, 638
- Listening to Others, 585
- Renaissance or Romantic Debate, 579
- Sharing Essays, 655
- Women's Rights, 647

LOGICAL-MATHEMATICAL
- Calculating Distance, 614
- Categorizing, 573, 646
- Comparing and Contrasting, 593, 611

Several Romantic poets and writers were active supporters of the French Revolution. Robert Burns voiced his unreserved support. Mary Wollstonecraft wrote *A Vindication of the Rights of Men* as a direct response to Edmund Burke's *Reflections on the Revolution in France,* published in 1790, which attacked the French Revolution and its English supporters. To observe the revolution herself, Wollstonecraft moved to Paris at the end of 1792 and lived there until 1794. Wordsworth lived in France from November 1791 to December 1792 and became a passionate supporter of the democratic revolution, although he later became disillusioned with events in France.

CROSS-CURRICULAR ACTIVITIES

Students can work independently or in small groups to research trends in American literature during this time period. Have students consider the following questions: Did literary trends in England make their way to America? Were American poets affected by revolutionary ideals in the same way?

THE ROMANTIC ERA

During the **Romantic Era**, from 1785 to 1832, artists, philosophers, and writers rebelled against the rational, orderly forms of Neoclassicism, creating works that celebrated emotion over reason, nature over human artifice, ordinary people over aristocrats, and spontaneity and wildness over decorum and control. This era of dramatic change encompassed the early years of America as an independent nation, the French Revolution, and major civil and political reforms in England.

POLITICAL DEVELOPMENTS IN THE ROMANTIC ERA

King George III, of the royal house of Hanover, was king of England from 1760 to 1820. According to some historians, his antagonistic policies toward the American colonies were directly responsible for the American Revolution. The **American Revolution** officially ended with the signing of the Treaty of Paris in 1783. The **French Revolution** began in 1789 with an attack on the Bastille prison by citizen revolutionaries. Few times in history have seen such political and social tumult. As Dickens characterized them half a century later, these were "the best of times and the worst of times"—the best because they saw a birth of freedom and equality, the worst because the cost of freedom and equality was bloodshed.

France declared war on England in 1793. **Napoleon Bonaparte** (1769–1821) and the French army were finally defeated by the Duke of Wellington at Waterloo in 1815.

When George III died in 1820, **George IV** took the throne and held it until his death in 1830. **William IV,** brother of George IV, ruled from 1830 to 1837. The weaknesses of these three kings led to strong prime ministers, which in turn led to civil reforms, including laws

Capture of the Bastille, July 14, 1789. Claude Cholat. The Granger Collection, NY

LITERARY EVENTS

► = British Events

1712–78. French philosopher Jean-Jacques Rousseau plants seeds of Romanticism and revolution by praising nature and emotion and by championing rights of ordinary people

►1796. Robert Burns dies

►1798. Wordsworth and Coleridge publish *Lyrical Ballads*

1785	1790	1795	1800	1805

►1783. Treaty of Paris ends American Revolution against British rule

1789. French Revolution begins

1799. Napoleon becomes head of French government

►1801. Act of Union creates United Kingdom of Great Britain, annexing Ireland

1802. In Haiti, Toussaint L'Ouverture leads slave rebellion

HISTORICAL EVENTS

1803. United States purchases Louisiana Territory from France

1804. Napoleon becomes emperor of France, betraying revolutionary ideals

570 UNIT EIGHT / THE ROMANTIC ERA

THEMATIC CURRENTS

Use the following selections to explore these themes with your students.

allowing labor unions to organize and restoring economic and religious freedoms to Roman Catholics. By 1832, parliamentary seats were redistributed in a more equitable apportionment, and the right to vote was given to men of the middle class, thereby depriving aristocrats of overwhelming majorities in Parliament.

THE PRE-ROMANTIC POETS

The late eighteenth century marked the end of the Enlightenment and the beginning of the Romantic Era. The end of the century was notable for the emergence of

The Meeting of Sir Walter Scott and Robert Burns. C. M. Hardie.
The Granger Collection, NY

Pre-Romantic poetry. The poets of this period showed tendencies toward Romanticism in their emotional explorations and in their perceptions of nature as wild and untamed. However, they followed the Neoclassical model of imitating traditional literary forms. Among the best of these transitional poets were Thomas Gray, Robert Burns, and William Blake.

Thomas Gray (1716–1771), a lifelong scholar, was not a prolific poet, but the few poems that he wrote reflect a combination of Neoclassical and Romantic ideals. His most famous poem, **"Elegy Written in a Country Courtyard"** (page 575), is written in a style emulating the classical Greek elegy, but it is thoroughly Romantic in its praise of common people.

Robert Burns (1759–1796) won acclaim as the national poet of Scotland. Burns avoided the formal, restrained language of the Neoclassical writers and used instead his native Scottish dialect. This use of everyday speech in literature shocked some of Burns's contemporaries, but it endeared Burns to the rural and working classes of Scotland. In addition to writing poetry, Burns preserved old Scottish folk songs, which he collected and compiled.

William Blake (1757–1827) was a poet, painter, mystic, and visionary. Much of Blake's writing is an attack on the complacent rationality and orderliness of the Enlightenment. Blake

CROSS-CURRICULAR ACTIVITIES

Science. Point out that the Romantic Era began at the end of the eighteenth century, a period of great advances in the scientific world. Have students research events that happened in the world of science during the Romantic Era. Students should then discuss or write about whether the revolutionary spirit of the age affected scientific endeavors as it did political and artistic ones.

Social Studies. The Romantic Era was a period of turbulence with revolutions erupting in the United States, France, and South America. Have students consider the cost of change to the average person. Students can research a particular country and write an article about the changes that occurred.

▶1812. Lord Byron publishes *Childe Harold's Pilgrimage*

▶1820. Keats publishes "Ode on a Grecian Urn"

▶1819. Percy Bysshe Shelley publishes "Ode to the West Wind"

▶1818. Mary Shelley publishes *Frankenstein, or the Modern Prometheus*

▶1813. Jane Austen publishes *Pride and Prejudice*

1810	1815	1820	1825	1830

1810. Simón Bolívar leads rebellions against Spanish colonial rule in South America

▶1811. King George III declared insane and removed from throne

1815. Napoleon defeated at Waterloo

▶1829. Catholic Emancipation Act passed

▶1832. First Reform Act extends voting rights to more males

INTRODUCTION **571**

LITERARY CURRENTS

Use the following selections to explore these techniques with your students.

ALLEGORY
- "The Lamb," 589
- "The Garden of Love," 661

IRONY
- "Ozymandias," 622
- from *Pride and Prejudice*, 678

ODE
- "Lines Composed a Few Miles above Tintern Abbey," 614
- "Ode to the West Wind," 625
- "Ode on a Grecian Urn," 642
- "Ode: Intimations of Immortality," 662

SYMBOL
- "The Rime of the Ancient Mariner," 664
- "Kubla Khan," 599

LITERARY TECHNIQUE

In 1817, Coleridge published *Biographia Literaria,* in which he discussed his own poetic theories and opinions and critiqued Wordsworth's theory of poetry. Coleridge states that, even in 1802 when the *Lyrical Ballads* was published, he recognized "a radical difference" between Wordsworth's theory of poetry and his own. Although he believed that poetic diction needed to be reformed, Coleridge disagreed with Wordsworth's claim that there is no real difference between the language of poetry and the language of common people.

Point out that although these poets all wrote during the Romantic Era, they did not necessarily share the same opinions or style. In "To Wordsworth," a sonnet written around 1815, Shelley grieves that the once-radical poet has grown conservative with age. Although Keats admired and was inspired by Wordsworth, he did not share all his views about poetry. In an 1818 letter to a friend, Keats declares that "Poetry should be great and unobtrusive, a thing which enters into one's soul, and does not startle it or amaze it with itself but with its subject." He then goes on to reject "Wordsworth's grandeur" in favor of the "uncontaminated" and "unobtrusive" poets, such as Shakespeare.

was unconventional not only in his poetry, but also in the way in which he published his books. He engraved designs and text onto a copper plate covered with wax; then, after applying acid to bring the design into relief, he printed a page. Each page was hand-painted with watercolors. This process limited Blake's production but made each book a work of art.

POETRY IN THE ROMANTIC ERA

The true beginning of the Romantic Era came with the publication in 1798 of *Lyrical Ballads,* a collection of poems by **William Wordsworth** (1770–1850) and **Samuel Taylor Coleridge** (1772–1834). In the preface to that book, Wordsworth explained his revolutionary theory of poetry. He stated that poetry should be about common people and events and should be written in the language of ordinary men and women. This idea of the nobility of ordinary people owed much to the American and French Revolutions and to the writings of the French philosopher **Jean-Jacques Rousseau**. Rousseau celebrated the **noble savage** and held that governments derive power only from the consent of the governed, through what he called the **social contract.**

Following in the footsteps of Wordsworth and Coleridge were the "second generation" of Romantic Era poets. These younger poets—**George Gordon, Lord Byron** (1788–1824), **Percy Bysshe Shelley** (1792–1822), and **John Keats** (1795–1821)—carried on the tradition of Wordsworth and Coleridge, celebrating emotion over reason and nature over science.

PROSE IN THE ROMANTIC ERA

Although poetry was the major literary form during the Romantic Era, major strides were also made during this time in the development of two forms of prose—the **essay** and the **novel.** Periodicals became popular, providing outlets for essayists such as **Charles Lamb** (1775–1834), **William Hazlitt** (1778–1830), and **Thomas DeQuincey** (1785–1859), and new types of novels emerged. Three major types of Romantic Era novels are the Gothic novel, the novel of manners, and the historical romance.

Gothic novels, or **Gothic romances,** are long stories containing elements of suspense, mystery, magic, and the macabre, with exotic settings such as haunted castles and untamed

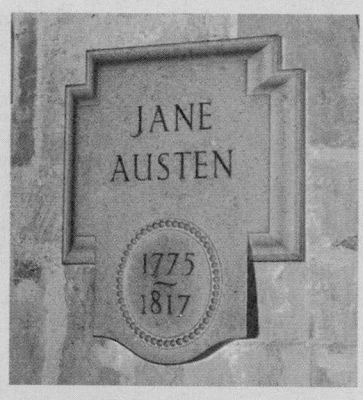

Jane Austen's plaque, Poets' Corner, Westminster Abbey. Courtesy, The Dean and Chaplaincy, Westminster Abbey

wilderness. Although the word *Gothic* originally implied "medieval," by the time of the Romantic Era, the word had assumed connotations of the supernatural and the macabre. **Anne Radcliffe's** (1764–1823) *The Mysteries of Udolpho,* published in 1794, and **Mary Shelley's** (1797–1851) *Frankenstein,* published in 1818, are examples of Gothic novels.

The **novel of manners** presented a satirical look at society in book-length prose reminiscent of earlier works by Swift and others. In the Romantic Era, **Jane Austen** (1775–1817) produced what are widely considered to be the greatest works in the genre, including *Sense and Sensibility* (1811) and *Pride and Prejudice* (1813).

Historical romance novels are novels set in a period before the life of the author. They usually depict historical events and contain both fictional and nonfictional characters. Early historical romance novels were often set in medieval days, with knights and fair damsels as main characters. **Sir Walter Scott's** (1771–1832) *Waverly* (1814) and *Ivanhoe* (1820) epitomized the genre.

Echoes:
The Romantic Era

"Liberty, equality, fraternity."
> —Rallying cry of the French Revolution

"The road of excess leads to the palace of wisdom."
> —William Blake,
> *The Marriage of Heaven and Hell*

"Every thing that lives is holy."
> —William Blake,
> "A Song of Liberty"

"Dismissing then those pretty feminine phrases, which the men condescendingly use to soften our slavish dependence, and despising that weak elegancy of mind, exquisite sensibility, and sweet docility of manners, supposed to be the sexual characteristics of the weaker vessel, I wish to shew that elegance is inferior to virtue, that the first object of laudable ambition is to obtain a character as a human being, regardless of the distinction of sex."
> —Mary Wollstonecraft,
> *A Vindication of the Rights of Woman*

"Then, dearest Maiden, move along these shades
In gentleness of heart; with gentle hand
Touch—for there is a spirit in the woods."
> —William Wordsworth, "Nutting"

"To combine the child's sense of wonder and novelty with . . . appearances . . . familiar . . . this is the character and privilege of genius."
> —Samuel Taylor Coleridge,
> *Biographia Literaria*

"His popular, inartificial style gets rid (at a blow) of all the trappings of verse, of all the high places of poetry . . . to return to the simplicity of truth and nature."
> —William Hazlitt,
> writing about William Wordsworth

"Men of England, wherefore plough
For the lords who lay ye low?
Wherefore weave with toil and care
The rich robes your tyrants wear?"
> —Percy Bysshe Shelley, "A Song"

ADDITIONAL QUESTIONS AND ACTIVITIES

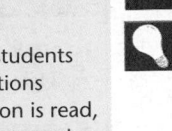

• In small groups, have students take turns reading quotations aloud. After each quotation is read, have students brainstorm to make predictions about Romantic poetry and the Romantic poets. For additional instruction, refer students to the Language Arts Survey, 4.18, "Reading Actively: Predicting."

• Have students write the following four categories on a piece of paper: *Emotion versus Reason, Nature versus Human Artifice, Ordinary People versus Aristocrats, Spontaneity/ Wildness versus Control.* Then ask students to read the quotations on this page and to assign each quotation to one or more of the categories. Students can discuss reasons for their decisions in small groups or as a class.

• Have students discuss how Wollstonecraft's quote could be taken as a rallying cry for a feminist revolution.

ADDITIONAL RESOURCES

READER'S GUIDE
- Selection Worksheet, 8.1

ASSESSMENT PORTFOLIO
- Selection Check Test, 4.8.1
- Selection Test, 4.8.2

ESSENTIAL SKILLS PRACTICE BOOKS
- *Study and Research,* 4.4, 4.5
- *Language,* 2.73

ENRICHMENT ACTIVITIES

Encourage students to discuss Gray's statement that "the language of the age is never the language of poetry." Ask them to suggest modern-day poetry or other literary forms that support or contradict Gray's belief.

SUPPORT FOR LEP STUDENTS

Remind students that the poem's word order often does not follow the usual patterns of spoken English.

ADDITIONAL VOCABULARY

curfew—in the Middle Ages, the ringing of a bell in the evening was a signal to go to bed
glimmering—faintly flickering
moping—gloomy; dull
moldering—crumbling; decaying
clarion—sound of clear, sharp trumpet
ply—work at
celestial—heavenly; divine
genial—promoting life and growth
sequestered—secluded; removed from others
uncouth—awkward; clumsy
implore—ask; beg; entreat
contemplation—thoughtful inspection; study

PREREADING

"Elegy Written in a Country Churchyard"
by Thomas Gray

ABOUT THE AUTHOR

Thomas Gray (1716–1771) was born in London to middle-class parents. He was educated at Eton and later at Cambridge. Then he left the university without a degree to travel in Europe. Gray returned to Cambridge in 1742, where he began to write poetry. His first odes were published in 1747.

Gray did not produce a great volume of verse, but he wrote carefully, bringing each poem to a level of perfection rarely achieved before or since. Characteristics that distinguish Gray's verse include a unique sensitivity to landscape and a strain of melancholy that shows him to have had a dignified, tragic view of life. Some contemporaries criticized Gray's frequent use of inverted sentences. However, Gray countered that "the language of the age is never the language of poetry." Continuing to write poetry through 1769, he lived the life of a scholar, traveling and devoting himself to the study of pre-Elizabethan poetry and Old Norse and Welsh literature.

ABOUT THE SELECTION

Although Thomas Gray was a scholar and an eccentric recluse, he wrote the most well-known and beloved tribute to common people in English poetry: **"Elegy Written in a Country Churchyard."** An **elegy** is a long, formal poem about death or loss. Even Gray's harshest critics have acknowledged the importance of this poem. One critic pointed out that although the language of the poem is unique and original, readers recognize in it an echo of their own feelings and ideas. The universality of this work—its applicability to all times and places—makes it one of the masterpieces of world literature.

GOALS/OBJECTIVES

Studying this lesson will enable students to

- experience the speaker's feelings of loss and grief and the speaker's celebration of simple lives
- detail Gray's literary contributions and explain why some of his peers criticized his writing style
- define *elegy* and identify elegies

- explain why "Elegy Written in a Country Churchyard" is praised by Gray's critics as well as his admirers
- memorize and recite a stanza from a poem
- correct agreement errors in inverted sentences

READER'S JOURNAL

For what would you like to be remembered? If you were to engrave a few lines about yourself on a monument, what would those lines say? Freewrite your ideas in your journal.

RESEARCH SKILLS

Read the Language Arts Survey, 4.4, "Memorizing." Memorize one or two stanzas from the selection and practice reciting them to your peers. See if you can tell why this has become one of the most quoted works in all of English literature.

"Elegy Written in a Country Churchyard"

THOMAS GRAY

The curfew tolls the knell of parting day,
    The lowing herd wind slowly o'er the lea,[1]
The plowman homeward plods his weary way,
    And leaves the world to darkness and to me.

5   Now fades the glimmering landscape on the sight,
    And all the air a solemn stillness holds,
Save where the beetle wheels his droning flight,
    And drowsy tinklings lull the distant folds;

Save that from yonder ivy-mantled tower
10   The moping owl does to the moon complain
Of such, as wandering near her secret bower,
    Molest her ancient solitary reign.

Beneath those rugged elms, that yew tree's shade,
    Where heaves the turf in many a moldering heap,
15   Each in his narrow cell forever laid,
    The rude[2] forefathers of the hamlet[3] sleep.

---

1. **lea.** Meadow
2. **rude.** Ignorant
3. **hamlet.** Small village

❶ At what time of day does the poem take place?

❷ Yew trees were often planted in cemeteries. What is the "narrow cell" referred to in line 15?

READER'S JOURNAL

Suggest that students think about what friends or family members might say about them.

RESEARCH SKILLS

Students might find memorizing easier if they visualize the images that the words create. Refer students to the Language Arts Survey, 4.5, "Remembering and Visualizing."

▶ Additional practice is provided in the *Essential Skills Practice Book: Study and Research,* 4.4.

ANSWERS TO GUIDED READING QUESTIONS

❶ The poem takes place at dusk.

❷ The narrow cell is the grave.

VOCABULARY FROM THE SELECTION

dirge	jocund
ignoble	obscure
ingenuous	provoke

ADDITIONAL QUESTIONS AND ACTIVITIES

Refer students to the Language Arts Survey, 1.11, "Observing." Students can then spend an evening observing the sights and sounds of dusk at their own homes. Then students can share their observations.

LITERARY TECHNIQUE

The term **elegy** is sometimes applied to any poem written in elegiac meter. Elegiac meter consists of a dactylic hexameter line. This meter was thought to be appropriate for elegies and reflective or meditative poems. It was only in the seventeenth century that the term became limited to poems of death and loss. Milton's *Lycidas* (1637), which mourns the death of Edward King, a student of Milton, seems to have been of importance in this change. In the twentieth century the term has again expanded to include works of deep reflection and nostalgia.

❶
To whom is the speaker referring?

❷
How does the speaker feel about ambition and grandeur?

❸
What does the speaker say about the paths of glory?

The breezy call of incense-breathing Morn,
    The swallow twittering from the straw-built shed,
The cock's shrill clarion, or the echoing horn,
20   No more shall rouse them from their lowly bed.

For them no more the blazing hearth shall burn,
    Or busy housewife ply her evening care;
No children run to lisp their sire's return,
    Or climb his knees the envied kiss to share.

25 Oft did the harvest to their sickle yield,
    Their furrow oft the stubborn glebe[4] has broke;
How <u>jocund</u> did they drive their team afield!
    How bowed the woods beneath their sturdy stroke!

Let not Ambition mock their useful toil,
30   Their homely joys, and destiny <u>obscure</u>;
Nor Grandeur hear with a disdainful smile
    The short and simple annals of the poor.

The boast of heraldry, the pomp of power,
    And all that beauty, all that wealth e'er gave,
35 Awaits alike the inevitable hour.
    The paths of glory lead but to the grave.

Nor you, ye proud, impute[5] to these the fault,
    If Memory o'er their tomb no trophies raise,
Where through the long-drawn aisle and fretted[6] vault
40   The pealing anthem swells the note of praise.

Can storied urn or animated bust
    Back to its mansion call the fleeting breath?
Can Honor's voice <u>provoke</u> the silent dust,
    Or Flattery soothe the dull cold ear of Death?

45 Perhaps in this neglected spot is laid
    Some heart once pregnant with celestial fire;

---

4. **glebe.** Soil
5. **impute.** To attribute
6. **fretted.** Decorated with a raised design of intersecting lines

WORDS FOR EVERYDAY USE:

jo • cund (jäk´ ənd) *adj.,* cheerfully, pleasantly (used in poems as an adverb)

ob • scure (əb skyoor´) *adj.,* faint, undefined

pro • voke (prō vōk´) *vt.,* stir up action or feeling

VOCABULARY IN CONTEXT

- The <u>jocund</u> host set the tone for the lively party.
- The point of the lecturer's speech was so <u>obscure</u> that most people left the auditorium confused.
- Such angry threats are sure to <u>provoke</u> a fight.
- The child's <u>ingenuous</u> answers charmed the reporters.
- The politician's cruel lies about his opponent confirm the reports of his <u>ignoble</u> behavior.

Hands that the rod of empire might have swayed,
    Or waked to ecstasy the living lyre.

50   But Knowledge to their eyes her ample page
      Rich with the spoils of time did ne'er unroll;
Chill Penury[7] repressed their noble rage,
    And froze the genial current of the soul.

Full many a gem of purest ray serene,
    The dark unfathomed caves of ocean bear:
55   Full many a flower is born to blush unseen,
    And waste its sweetness on the desert air.

Some village Hampden,[8] that with dauntless breast
    The little tyrant of his fields withstood;
Some mute inglorious Milton[9] here may rest,
60   Some Cromwell[10] guiltless of his country's blood.

The applause of listening senates to command,
    The threats of pain and ruin to despise,
To scatter plenty o'er a smiling land,
    And read their history in a nation's eyes,

65   Their lot forbade: nor circumscribed alone
      Their growing virtues, but their crimes confined;
Forbade to wade through slaughter to a throne,
    And shut the gates of mercy on mankind,

The struggling pangs of conscious truth to hide,
70   To quench the blushes of <u>ingenuous</u> shame,
Or heap the shrine of Luxury and Pride
    With incense kindled at the Muse's flame.

Far from the madding crowd's <u>ignoble</u> strife,
    Their sober wishes never learned to stray;

---

7. **Penury.** Poverty
8. **Hampden.** John Hampden was a member of Parliament who defended the rights of the people.
9. **Milton.** English poet, author of *Paradise Lost*
10. **Cromwell.** Oliver Cromwell, ruler of England during the Commonwealth Period, or Puritan Interregnum

WORDS FOR EVERYDAY USE:
in • gen • u • ous (in jen´ yoo əs) *adj.*, artless, naive
ig • no • ble (ig nō´ bəl) *adj.*, dishonorable, mean

ADDITIONAL QUESTIONS AND ACTIVITIES

Why is Hampden an appropriate figure for the speaker to invoke? How is Hampden related to the poem's theme?

Answers. Hampden defended the rights of the people. During his life, he spoke for the poor, unrecognized people, just as the speaker does in the poem.

ANSWERS TO GUIDED READING QUESTIONS

❶ The speaker compares a flower in the desert to the life of a poor villager whose potential is never realized.

❷ Simple life shuns following an evil path to grandeur and upholds mercy toward others.

❸ They are special because they lived honestly and sincerely rather than seeking fame.

❶ To what or whom does the speaker compare a flower in the desert?

❷ Living a simple life has its drawbacks, but doing so also has its positive side. What positive side of living a simple life is pointed out in this stanza?

❸ What made the lives to which the speaker refers special?

LITERARY TECHNIQUE

Gray's poetry bridges the Neoclassical and Romantic movements. Neoclassical elements, such as the elegiac form and references to the Muse, combine with the Romantic subject of the common person.

ANSWERS TO GUIDED READING QUESTIONS

❶ The sight of the "frail memorial"—the gravestone—causes the speaker to sigh.

❷ Religious inscriptions appear on many gravestones. The purpose of these "holy texts" is to teach and speak to death.

❸ The lines recall pleasures such as sunrise, morning dew, and a babbling brook. The lines recall human woes such as "hopeless love."

---

❶ *What causes the speaker to sigh?*

❷ *What is written on the gravestones? What purpose is served by these "holy texts"?*

❸ *What simple pleasures of the rustic life are recalled in these lines? What human woes are also recalled?*

75　Along the cool sequestered vale of life
　　　They kept the noiseless tenor of their way.

　　Yet even these bones from insult to protect
　　　Some frail memorial still erected nigh,
　　With uncouth rhymes and shapeless sculpture decked,
80　　Implores the passing tribute of a sigh.

　　Their name, their years, spelt by the unlettered Muse,
　　　The place of fame and elegy supply:
　　And many a holy text around she strews,
　　　That teach the rustic moralist to die.

85　For who to dumb Forgetfulness a prey,
　　　This pleasing anxious being e'er resigned,
　　Left the warm precincts of the cheerful day,
　　　Nor cast one longing lingering look behind?

　　On some fond breast the parting soul relies,
90　　Some pious drops the closing eye requires;
　　Even from the tomb the voice of Nature cries,
　　　Even in our ashes live their wonted fires.

　　For thee, who mindful of the unhonored dead
　　　Dost in these lines their artless tale relate;
95　If chance, by lonely contemplation led,
　　　Some kindred spirit shall inquire thy fate,

　　Haply some hoary-headed swain may say,
　　　"Oft have we seen him at the peep of dawn
　　Brushing with hasty steps the dews away
100　　To meet the sun upon the upland lawn.

　　"There at the foot of yonder nodding beech
　　　That wreathes its old fantastic roots so high,
　　His listless length at noontide would he stretch,
　　　And pore upon the brook that babbles by.

105　"Hard by yon wood, now smiling as in scorn,
　　　Muttering his wayward fancies he would rove,
　　Now drooping, woeful wan, like one forlorn,
　　　Or crazed with care, or crossed in hopeless love.

578　*UNIT EIGHT / THE ROMANTIC ERA*

578　TEACHER'S EDITION

"One morn I missed him on the customed hill,
110   Along the heath and near his favorite tree;
Another came; nor yet beside the rill,
    Nor up the lawn, nor at the wood was he;

"The next with <u>dirges</u> due in sad array
    Slow through the churchway path we saw him borne.
115   Approach and read (for thou canst read) the lay,
    Graved on the stone beneath yon aged thorn."

The Epitaph

Here rests his head upon the lap of Earth
    A youth to Fortune and to Fame unknown.
Fair Science[11] frowned not on his humble birth,
120   *And Melancholy marked him for her own.*

Large was his bounty, and his soul sincere,
    Heaven did a recompense as largely send:
He gave to Misery all he had, a tear,
    He gained from Heaven ('twas all he wished) a friend.

125   *No farther seek his merits to disclose,*
    Or draw his frailties from their dread abode
    (There they alike in trembling hope repose),
    The bosom of his Father and his God.   ■

------
11. **Science.** Learning

 WORDS FOR
EVERYDAY USE: **dirge** (dʉrj) *n.*, funeral song

❶
What line in the poem shows that death comes unexpectedly, in the middle of life's pleasures and woes?

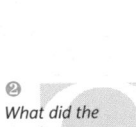

❷
What did the simple person give during his life? What did he receive?

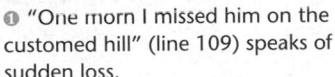

ANSWERS TO GUIDED READING QUESTIONS

❶ "One morn I missed him on the customed hill" (line 109) speaks of sudden loss.

❷ The simple person gave "to Misery all he had, a tear,/He gained from Heaven . . . a friend."

ADDITIONAL QUESTIONS AND ACTIVITIES

 Have students review Ben Jonson's "Epitaph on Elizabeth, L. H." (page 296). Pose the following question: If you didn't know the dates when these two epitaphs were written, how would you decide which was written in the Renaissance and which in the Romantic Era? Students can write or discuss their answers.

ANSWERS TO SELECTION CHECK TEST 4.8.1

EX. At what time of day does the poem begin?
The poem begins in the evening.

1. Who plods homeward?
The plowman plods homeward.

2. Where do the paths of glory lead?
They lead to the grave.

3. Who might be buried in this churchyard?
A great unknown poet or leader might be buried there.

4. What makes the people the speaker refers to different from the "madding crowd"?
They kept their own simple ways.

5. What did the person for whom the epitaph was written gain from heaven?
He gained a friend.

VOCABULARY IN CONTEXT

• As the mourners entered the cathedral, the organist began to play a <u>dirge</u>.

RESPONDING TO THE SELECTION

Suggest that students start their search for examples by examining the epitaph, in which the speaker mentions fame.

ANSWERS FOR REVIEWING THE SELECTION

RECALLING

1. They lament the deaths of the village forefathers, who were poor farmers.

2. The speaker warns that those in power should not believe themselves beyond the reach of death or innately superior to the poor.

3. Someone not born to wealth and privilege might have many talents that will never be recognized.

4. He looks for the speaker.

INTERPRETING

Responses will vary. Possible responses are given.

5. The farmers' closeness to nature, their loving families, and their hard work appeals to the speaker.

6. In the late eighteenth century in England, the rich believed themselves superior to the poor.

7. The common people might have developed their talents if they had been given the opportunities of the privileged classes, such as education.

8. The speaker might imagine someone looking for him because he was a lonely man, who looked for friendship among the country people.

SYNTHESIZING

Responses will vary. Possible responses are given.

9. Gray's images of animals—the lowing herd, the droning beetle, the moping owl—all express melancholy. The images of darkness, failing light, and the shade of trees all relate to death.

10. The poem reveals that it is human nature to wonder what mark we will leave behind us after we die.

Responding to the Selection

How might Gray respond to someone who said, "A person's success, or ability to earn money and fame, is based completely on ability"? Do you think he would agree or disagree? Back up your answer with evidence from the poem.

Reviewing the Selection

RECALLING

1. What do lines 13 through 28 lament?

2. Of what does the speaker warn in lines 29 through 44?

3. Paraphrase the speaker's message in lines 45 through 80.

4. Whom does the "hoary-headed swain" seek in lines 97 through 100?

INTERPRETING

5. What about the farmers' lives does the speaker find appealing?

6. Why does the speaker assume that the powerful will criticize the poor?

7. What might have helped these common people to have an opportunity to express their talents in the world at large?

8. Why might the speaker imagine someone looking for him when he has died?

SYNTHESIZING

9. What images from nature are used in the opening stanzas of the poem? What mood, or feeling, is set by these images?

10. How does the speaker feel toward worldly pomp and glory? What, according to the speaker, lies at the end of "the paths of glory"? Why might this observation lead one to think that a simple, rustic life might be as valid as a life of glory and power?

Understanding Literature (Questions for Discussion)

1. **Elegy.** An **elegy** is a long formal poem about death or loss. For whom does the speaker in this poem grieve? Given that elegies are usually written about famous people, what makes this elegy unique? Explain.

2. **Epitaph.** An **epitaph** is an inscription or verse written to be used on a tomb or written commemoration of someone who has died. Paraphrase each stanza of the epitaph at the end of this poem. Why do you think this epitaph was added to the poem?

ANSWERS FOR UNDERSTANDING LITERATURE

► See the evaluation forms for discussion, active listening, and oral communication, *Assessment Portfolio,* 7.11–7.14.

Responses will vary. Possible responses are given.

1. Elegy. The speaker grieves the loss of people whose lives were not celebrated when they were alive; the loss expressed is the waste of those people's (and perhaps his own) energy and talents. This elegy is unique because it mourns the loss of unnamed commoners, rather than well-known aristocrats or nobles.

►**Teaching Note:** Ask students how the poem's title adds to the elegy's uniqueness.

2. Epitaph. A paraphrase might read, "Here under the earth lies a young man who didn't have fame and fortune, but had other valuable things such as honesty and friendship. Don't praise or criticize him anymore. He,

(cont.)

3. **Speaker.** A **speaker** is the character who speaks in a poem—the voice assumed by the writer. What can you infer about the speaker of this poem? What sort of person is he? What adjectives might you use to describe him?

Language Lab

Agreement in Inverted Sentences. Read the Language Arts Survey, 2.73, "Agreement in Inverted Sentences." Then identify the subject and verb in each of the following sentences and correct, in each sentence, the error in agreement.

1. Here lies the remains of a kind, hard-working woman.

2. Were she a leader of the people?

3. No, but there is many common folks who misses her greatly.

4. Do anyone think of her now that she is gone?

5. In this village alone, there is five people who were her friends.

Thinking Skills

Remembering and Visualizing. Read the Language Arts Survey, 4.5, "Remembering and Visualizing." Then answer the following questions:

1. What is the quality of light in the graveyard at the beginning of the poem?

2. What do you visualize around the hearth after reading stanza 6?

3. How do you visualize the deceased after reading stanza 14?

4. How do you visualize the quiet lives of the deceased after reading stanza 19?

5. What do you imagine as you read stanza 25?

PROJECT

Grave Rubbings. With your class, go to an old graveyard and make several rubbings from the grave markers. You will need to bring with you paper and something with which to rub the stone (colored chalk, charcoal, crayon). Remember to be respectful and to step carefully around each stone (particularly if the graveyard is old). In small groups, share your ideas about the lives of the people whose grave markers you recorded.

PRE-ROMANTIC POETRY / "ELEGY WRITTEN IN A COUNTRY CHURCHYARD" **581**

ANSWERS FOR UNDERSTANDING LITERATURE (CONT.)

with his merits and frailties, rests in heaven." The epitaph was added to the poem as an example of the type of epitaph the speaker laments is missing from the gravestones in the churchyard. One might also suppose that it is Gray's epitaph for himself.

▶**Teaching Note:** Have students debate the hypothesis that Gray wrote the epitaph for himself. Remind them to use evidence from the poem and from the biographical information on page 574 to support their opinions.

3. **Speaker.** At the beginning of the poem, the speaker stands in the churchyard sharing his thoughts about the dead. At the end, the speaker reveals that he himself is buried in the churchyard. He characterizes himself as intelligent, honest, and melancholy.

▶**Teaching Note:** Remind students that the speaker and the poet are not always synonymous. Ask them to look for evidence in the poem that supports the idea that the speaker is a character other than Gray himself.

ADDITIONAL RESOURCES

READER'S GUIDE
- Selection Worksheets, 8.2, 8.3

ASSESSMENT PORTFOLIO
- Selection Check Tests, 4.8.3, 4.8.5
- Selection Tests, 4.8.4, 4.8.6

ESSENTIAL SKILLS PRACTICE BOOKS
- *Language*, 2.43, 2.150
- *Study and Research*, 4.13, 4.36

AUDIOCASSETTE
- "Auld Lang Syne," Track 13

ENRICHMENT ACTIVITIES

 Students can try their hand at Scots by memorizing and reciting one of the following selections or another of Burns's poems. Encourage students to explore the musical elements of the poems.

SUPPORT FOR LEP STUDENTS

Most students will have extreme difficulty with the dialect in Burns's poems. Play the recording of "Auld Lang Syne" on the audiocassette and ask students to follow along.

PREREADING

PRE-ROMANTIC POETRY

"Auld Lang Syne"
"John Anderson, My Jo"

by Robert Burns

ABOUT THE AUTHOR

Robert Burns (1759–1796), the national poet of Scotland, had a natural gift for poetry and was largely self-educated. He chose his style deliberately from the Scottish folkloric and literary traditions.

Burns was the son of an unsuccessful farmer who valued books and learning but died and left his young sons with responsibility for the farm. At fifteen, Burns fell in love for the first time and soon afterward began to write poetry. By the age of twenty-seven, he had written the renowned "Kilmarnock edition" of his verse (so called because it was published in the town of Kilmarnock) and had become famous among intellectuals. His best poetry is written in Scots, his native **dialect**. During his lifetime, he wrote hundreds of songs about love, work, friendship, patriotism, and the nobility of common men and women.

A social rebel, Burns had great sympathy for the revolutions in America and France, which took place during his lifetime. Strongly opposed to Calvinism, the religion in which he had been raised, he was considered to be a social radical, and his lifestyle left him open to criticism.

In his late twenties, Burns settled down, married Jean Armour, and began working as a tax inspector in Dumfries. He was extremely patriotic and passionate about Scotland, and during his last years, he worked feverishly to preserve his country's music in published form. Although he was often in need of money, he would take no financial compensation for his work on volumes of Scottish lyrics. He continued to work on the Scottish anthologies until he died of heart disease at thirty-seven.

ABOUT THE SELECTIONS

The poem **"Auld Lang Syne"** is perhaps the best known of all Scottish songs. Its first verse and chorus are sung traditionally at midnight on New Year's Eve. The poem expresses the tenderness of friendship, the joy of celebration, and the value of memories. In **"John Anderson, My Jo,"** Burns celebrates lifelong friendship, honoring a couple who have shared the joys and hard work of youth and now share their later years.

GOALS/OBJECTIVES

Studying this lesson will enable students to

- enjoy Burns's lighthearted musical verse and celebration of friendship and memories
- explain the importance of the Scots dialect to Burns's writing
- recognize the theme of friendship in Burns's poems

- identify images in poems and the senses to which they appeal
- recognize and interpret metaphors they encounter in their reading
- answer true/false test questions
- recognize and write compound sentences

READER'S JOURNAL

In your journal, freewrite about a touching experience you have had involving friendship and loyalty to loved ones. If you do not wish to write about a real experience, create one from your imagination.

LANGUAGE SKILLS

Read the Language Arts Survey, 2.150, "Dialects of English." Choose stanza 2, 3, 4, or 5 of this song, and paraphrase it in standard English or in another dialect of English with which you are familiar.

"Auld Lang Syne"[1]

ROBERT BURNS

Should auld acquaintance be forgot,
    And never brought to min'?
Should auld acquaintance be forgot,
    And days o' lang syne?

Chorus
5   For auld lang syne, my dear,
        For auld lang syne,
        We'll tak a cup o' kindness yet,
        For auld lang syne.

We twa hae run about the braes,[2]
10   And pu'd the gowans[3] fine,
But we've wandered mony a weary foot,
    Sin' auld lang syne.
        (Chorus)

We twa hae paidled i' the burn,[4]
    From morning sun till dine,[5]
15   But seas between us braid[6] hae roared,
    Sin' auld lang syne.
        (Chorus)

---

1. **Lang Syne.** Long ago
2. **braes.** Slopes
3. **gowans.** Daisies
4. **twa . . . burn.** Two have paddled in the stream
5. **dine.** Dinner
6. **braid.** Broad

READER'S JOURNAL

Students might begin by listing adjectives associated with the experience, such as *happy, touching,* or *life changing.*

LANGUAGE SKILLS

Responses will vary but might resemble the following for stanza 2:
We two have run along the hills,
And pulled the pretty daisies,
But we've come a long, hard way,
Since those days long ago.

▶Additional practice is provided in the *Essential Skills Practice Book: Language,* 2.150.

ANSWERS TO GUIDED READING QUESTIONS

❶ The opening stanza asks if old friends and experiences should be forgotten.

❷ The speaker remembers running about the slopes, picking daisies, and paddling in the stream.

ADDITIONAL QUESTIONS AND ACTIVITIES

Have students write a letter to a childhood friend recounting a special memory they shared. Students can choose whether or not to send the letter.

❶ What questions are posed in the opening stanza?

❷ What three things does the speaker remember doing with his friend?

The Village Holiday or Dance of the Peasants. David Teniers, The Younger, circa 1650. Virginia Museum of Fine Arts, Richmond, VA. The Adolph D. and Wilkins C. Williams Fund

photograph ©1995 Virginia Museum of Fine Arts

> And there's a hand, my trusty fiere,[7]
>   And gie's a hand o' thine;
> And we'll tak a right gude-willie waught,[8]
> 20   For auld lang syne.
>   *(Chorus)*
>
> And surely ye'll be your pint-stowp,[9]
>   And surely I'll be mine;
> And we'll tak a cup o' kindness yet,
>   For auld lang syne.
>   *(Chorus)* ∎

---

7. **fiere.** Friend
8. **gude-willie waught.** A big swig
9. **be your pint-stowp.** Pay for your pint-cup

Responding to the Selection

What experiences have you had that are similar to the bonding experiences described in Burns's poem? Share these experiences in a discussion with your classmates.

Reviewing the Selection

RECALLING

1. What is the question asked in lines 1–4?

2. In lines 9 and 10, what does the speaker remember doing with his friend?

3. In lines 15 and 16, what is the speaker saying about time passing?

4. What is the speaker offering his friend in lines 17 and 18?

INTERPRETING

5. Why would the speaker ask this question?

6. What are the qualities that make this memory so typical of childhood?

7. Why does it seem appropriate to mention the motion of the sea in lines 15 and 16?

8. What are the friends sharing besides a beverage?

SYNTHESIZING

9. In what way does this song express the voices of hard-working people who have little material wealth?

10. What feelings does the poet express about friendship? What is important to the speaker about friends?

Understanding Literature (Questions for Discussion)

Hymn. A **hymn** is a song or verse of praise. What is Burns praising in this song? What particular characteristics make this piece sound like a hymn? Why do you think this song has continued to be so popular over the years?

RESPONDING TO THE SELECTION

Urge students to remain open-minded and non-judgmental while listening to each other's personal experiences.

ANSWERS FOR REVIEWING THE SELECTION

RECALLING

1. The question asked is, "Should" we forget friends from long ago?

2. The speaker remembers running on hills and picking daisies.

3. In lines 15 and 16, the speaker says that a long time has passed.

4. In lines 17 and 18, the speaker is offering to shake hands with his friend.

INTERPRETING

Responses will vary. Possible responses are given.

5. The speaker asks if old friends should be forgotten because people often lose touch with friends as time passes.

6. Childhood memories often involve playing games and playing outdoors.

7. The motion of the sea seems appropriate because, like the passing of time, it separates events and people.

8. Besides a beverage, the friends are sharing their memories and affection for one another.

SYNTHESIZING

Responses will vary. Possible responses are given.

9. Hard-working people make strong friendships through sharing difficulties and by coming to trust and rely on one another.

10. This song expresses a rebellious spirit in its celebration of childhood and adventure and in its almost reverent tone toward such leisurely activities as reminiscing and drinking with friends.

ANSWERS FOR UNDERSTANDING LITERATURE

▶ See the evaluation forms for discussion, active listening, and oral communication, *Assessment Portfolio,* 7.11–7.14.

Responses will vary. Possible responses are given.

Hymn. Burns is praising loyalty to friends over time. The chorus, with its repetition of the phrase "For auld lang syne," makes the piece sound like a hymn. The form is popular among everyday people because of its short lines and repeated chorus that celebrate the common theme of friendship.

▶**Teaching Note:** Ask students to compare this hymn to others they have heard. Point out that this hymn has a secular, rather than sacred, tone.

PREREADING NOTES

READER'S JOURNAL

Students might want to refer to photographs to help them with their descriptions.

THINKING SKILLS

Responses will vary but may include the suggestion that the two people are married, very old friends, or sweethearts.

▶ Additional practice is provided in the *Essential Skills Practice Book: Study and Research*, 4.13.

ANSWERS TO GUIDED READING QUESTIONS

❶ John Anderson's hair is "like the snow," and he is also balding.

❷ John and the speaker climbed a hill together. Now they will totter down the hill and sleep together at its foot, actions which might symbolize aging and death.

ANSWERS TO SELECTION CHECK TEST 4.8.5

EX. What is a jo?
A jo is a sweetheart.

1. What color was John's hair when the speaker first met him?
His hair was the color of a raven, black.

2. What is John's brow like now?
His brow is bald.

3. What does the speaker wish on John's head?
The speaker wishes blessings on John's head.

4. What did John and the speaker do together in the past?
They climbed the hill together.

5. What must they do now?
They must totter down together and sleep at the foot.

READER'S JOURNAL

In your journal, freewrite a description of someone you have known for a long time, perhaps all of your life. Start with your earliest physical images of that person and progress forward to your understanding of the person today.

THINKING SKILLS

Read the Language Arts Survey, 4.13, "Making Hypotheses." After reading the poem, make some hypotheses about the relationship between the two people in the poem. How do you think they might be related? What leads you to think so?

"John Anderson, My Jo"

ROBERT BURNS

❶
How has John Anderson's appearance changed over the years?

John Anderson, my jo,[1] John,
    When we were first acquent,
Your locks were like the raven,
    Your bonnie brow was brent;[2]
5 But now your brow is beld,[3] John,
    Your locks are like the snow,
But blessings on your frosty pow,[4]
    John Anderson, my jo!

❷
What did John and the speaker do together? What will they do now? What might these actions symbolize?

    John Anderson, my jo, John,
10   We clamb the hill thegither,
And monie a cantie[5] day, John,
    We've had wi' ane anither;
Now we maun[6] totter down, John,
    And hand in hand we'll go,
15 And sleep thegither at the foot,
    John Anderson, my jo! ∎

---

1. **jo.** Sweetheart
2. **brent.** Smooth
3. **beld.** Bald
4. **pow.** Head
5. **cantie.** Happy
6. **maun.** Must

Responding to the Selection

Role play with one of your classmates, creating a dialogue between two people who have lived and worked together for fifty years.

Reviewing the Selection

RECALLING

1. What did John Anderson look like when the speaker first knew him?

2. What does John Anderson look like now?

3. What does the speaker remember doing with John Anderson?

4. What does the speaker expect to do with John Anderson now?

INTERPRETING

5. What are the speaker's feelings about her memory of John's appearance as a young man?

6. How does the speaker feel about John Anderson's appearance now?

7. What could "the hill" represent in line 10?

8. What are the speaker's feelings about what will happen in the future with John?

SYNTHESIZING

9. What might you say about the relationship between the two people in this poem?

10. How might this poem be reflective of the lives of married people in Burns's day?

Understanding Literature (Questions for Discussion)

1. **Image.** An **image** is a word or phrase that names something that can be seen, heard, touched, tasted, or smelled. What are the images in this poem? To what senses do they appeal? What attitudes do they express?

2. **Metaphor.** A **metaphor** is a figure of speech in which one thing is spoken or written about as if it were another. What metaphors are used in this poem? What is implied by each metaphor?

ANSWERS FOR UNDERSTANDING LITERATURE (CONT.)

in the sight of John Anderson in spite of (and perhaps because of) how the years have changed him. All of the images are of the natural world—the raven, the snow, the frost. They suggest a delight in and connection to the natural world.

▶**Teaching Note:** Students might make a sensory detail chart to help them determine the images in the poem and the senses to which they appeal.

▶See the *Essential Skills Practice Book: Writing,* 1.18.

2. Metaphor. The poem uses the metaphors of climbing and descending a hill to symbolize the journey of life. When climbing the hill, the speaker and John Anderson were young and happy. Now that they begin to descend the hill, they are older but still together and happy. The metaphor implies that regardless of which part of the journey a person experiences, the journey of life is to be enjoyed and shared.

RESPONDING TO THE SELECTION

Students might want to conduct the role playing activity as an improvisation, picking up cues from each other to determine the characters' relationship.

ANSWERS FOR REVIEWING THE SELECTION

RECALLING

1. He had black hair and a smooth forehead.

2. He has white hair and is balding.

3. The speaker remembers climbing a hill together and having happy days.

4. Now, the speaker expects to grow old and die with him.

INTERPRETING

Responses will vary. Possible responses are given.

5. The speaker remembers him with affection and love.

6. The speaker has as much love for John and his appearance now as before.

7. "The hill" might symbolize life's difficulties.

8. The speaker is happy to grow old and die with John.

SYNTHESIZING

Responses will vary. Possible responses are given.

9. The fact that the speaker calls John "sweetheart" shows that they share a strong love for one another.

10. It might show that most people in Burns's day married for life.

ANSWERS FOR UNDERSTANDING LITERATURE

▶See the evaluation forms for discussion, active listening, and oral communication, *Assessment Portfolio,* 7.11–7.14.

Responses will vary. Possible responses are given.

1. **Image.** Images that appeal to sight are raven locks, smooth brow, balding brow, and snowy locks. Climbing a hill, hand in hand, and sleeping on grass appeal to the sense of touch. The images express an attitude of appreciation; the speaker delights
(cont.)

ANALYTIC SCALES FOR RESPONDING IN WRITING

Assign a score from 1 to 25 for each grading criterion below. (For more detailed evaluation, see the evaluation forms for writing, revising, and proofreading, *Assessment Portfolio*, 7.1–7.10.)

1. Character Sketch

• **Content/Unity.** The sketch presents a brief portrait of a character from the poem.

• **Organization/Coherence.** The sketch contains descriptive details, all of which work toward developing a clear picture of the character.

• **Language/Style.** The sketch uses vivid and precise nouns, verbs, and modifiers.

• **Conventions.** The sketch avoids errors in spelling, grammar, usage, mechanics, and manuscript form.

2. Monologue

• **Content/Unity.** The monologue presents the speaker's first-person point of view.

• **Organization/Coherence.** The monologue focuses clearly on a defined topic.

• **Language/Style.** The monologue uses vivid and precise nouns, verbs, and modifiers.

• **Conventions.** The monologue avoids errors in spelling, grammar, usage, mechanics, and manuscript form.

ANSWERS FOR TEST-TAKING SKILLS

1. F   4. T
2. F   5. T
3. T

FOR MORE PRACTICE

Problem. John Anderson has a full head of hair.

Answer.

► Additional practice is provided in the *Essential Skills Practice Book: Study and Research,* 4.36.

Responding in Writing

1. **Character Sketch.** Write brief character sketches of the people featured in this poem. Base your sketches on information provided in the poem; however, use your imagination and fill in the blanks when necessary. As a class, compare sketches. How are individual sketches similar to one another, and how are they different?

2. **Monologue.** Write a monologue from the point of view of the speaker of the poem. You might have the person comment about marriage, about life on a farm, or about poetry. You may want to read your monologue aloud in class.

Language Lab

Compound Sentences. Read the Language Arts Survey, 2.43, "Compound Sentences." Then rewrite the sentences below to make them compound sentences.

1. Your hair was like the raven. Your bonny brow was smooth.

2. Your hair is like the snow. Blessings on your frosty head!

3. We climbed the hill together. We had many a happy day.

4. We have to trudge down. Hand in hand we'll go.

5. We'll sleep together at the foot. We'll always be friends.

Test-taking Skills

True/False Questions. Read the Language Arts Survey, 4.36, "True/False Questions." Then answer the following questions by writing *T* if a sentence is true and *F* if a sentence is false. Write your answers on your own paper.

1. As a young boy, John Anderson had red hair.

2. The two friends met recently.

3. John and the speaker had many happy days together.

4. John and the speaker are no longer young.

5. John Anderson is probably the speaker's husband.

ANSWERS FOR LANGUAGE LAB

1. Your hair was like the raven, and your bonny brow was smooth.

2. Your hair is like the snow; blessings on your frosty head!

3. We climbed the hill together, and we had many a happy day.

4. We have to trudge down, but hand in hand we'll go.

5. We'll sleep together at the foot, and we'll always be friends.

► Additional practice is provided in the *Essential Skills Practice Book: Language,* 2.43.

PREREADING

"The Lamb"
"The Tyger"
"London"
by William Blake

ABOUT THE AUTHOR

William Blake (1757–1827) was born to a middle-class family in London. He received his formal education in art, studying at the Royal Academy of Arts. When he was fourteen, he was apprenticed to James Basire, a well-known engraver. During his free time, Blake wrote poetry and read.

Blake earned a living giving drawing lessons, illustrating books, and engraving. Later, when work was not plentiful, Blake and his wife moved to the Sussex seacoast. A wealthy patron of the arts supported the Blakes and tried to convince William to work with a more conventional style. Blake, however, rebelled. He felt that his poems reflected a passionate, spiritual world and that this world must be kept separate from the "corporeal," or physical, world. Consequently, he kept his own style and lived for a time in poverty and isolation because his work was so contrary to the tastes and conventions of his time.

Blake's first book of poems, *Poetical Sketches*, was printed when he was twenty-six. Later, he began illustrating his poetry with a technique called *illuminated printing*. He would work with pens and brushes in an acid-resistant medium on a copper plate. He wrote in mirror images, so that the plate would print the characters correctly. Then he etched the plate with acid to make the image stand out. He colored the printed pages with watercolors and stitched them together. His well-known *Songs of Innocence and of Experience* was printed this way.

In his sixties, Blake left his poetry behind, attracted a small group of painters, and began to concentrate on his visual work. He died at the age of seventy.

ABOUT THE SELECTIONS

Both **"The Lamb"** and **"The Tyger"** are included in Blake's *Songs of Innocence and of Experience*. The two poems are almost mirror images of one another in structure. Each of the poems makes use of a regular rhyme scheme and frequent repetition. One uses a **symbol** for innocence, and the other uses a symbol for experience. Blake considered these poems representative of "two contrary states of the human soul." The poem **"London,"** like "The Tyger," is also a song of experience. In this poem, Blake writes poignantly about some of the evils of urban life.

ENRICHMENT ACTIVITIES

 • Discuss with students the quality of Blake's artwork. How accurate were his renderings? How realistic were his colors? What do students like about this work? What don't they like? How important is technical mastery for an artist? What else is important? Why?

• Blake was an important influence on the artist Samuel Palmer, whose *A Shoreham Garden* appears on page 27. Have students compare Palmer's painting with that of Blake.

SUPPORT FOR LEP STUDENTS

ADDITIONAL VOCABULARY
meek—patient; submissive

GOALS/OBJECTIVES

Studying this lesson will enable students to

• interpret and appreciate the poet's ideas about innocence, experience, and the human soul
• describe Blake's literary accomplishments and explain the historical significance of his work
• identify alliteration and explain its effect on a poem's tone

• use prepositional phrases in their writing
• explain what setting is and how it affects a poem's mood
• write observations about people, places, objects, and events

PREREADING NOTES

READER'S JOURNAL

Students might begin their freewriting by focusing on a topic such as childhood games.

THINKING SKILLS

Encourage students to consider the language level of the first two lines as they make predictions.

▶ Additional practice is provided in the *Essential Skills Practice Book: Study and Research,* 4.18.

ANSWER TO GUIDED READING QUESTION

❶ Both the lamb and its maker, the Lamb of God, have the same name.

BIOGRAPHICAL NOTE

Unlike later poets associated with the Romantic movement, Blake often employed a dramatic voice in his poetry. He rarely used the personal, autobiographical "I" preferred by Wordsworth and Shelley. Here, for example, the first-person speaker is a child.

ANSWERS TO SELECTION CHECK TEST 4.8.7

EX. What question is asked of the little lamb?
The lamb is asked "who made thee?"

1. What is the lamb's "clothing of delight"?
The lamb's wool is the lamb's "clothing of delight."

2. How is the lamb's voice described?
The lamb's voice is described as tender.

3. What does the lamb's maker call himself?
The lamb's maker calls himself a Lamb.

4. How is the lamb's maker described?
The lamb's maker is described as meek and mild.

5. Who blesses the lamb in the final lines of the poem?
God blesses the lamb.

READER'S JOURNAL

What images are, for you, symbols of innocence and childhood? Brainstorm a list of such images.

THINKING SKILLS

Read the Language Arts Survey, 4.18, "Reading Actively: Predicting." Then read the first line of the poem. What can you predict about this poem? What might the mood and tone be?

"The Lamb"

WILLIAM BLAKE

> Little Lamb, who made thee?
>   Dost thou know who made thee?
> Gave thee life & bid thee feed,
> By the stream & o'er the mead;[1]
> 5 Gave thee clothing of delight,
> Softest clothing wooly bright;
> Gave thee such a tender voice,
> Making all the vales rejoice!
>   Little Lamb who made thee?
> 10 Dost thou know who made thee?
>
>   Little Lamb I'll tell thee,
>   Little Lamb I'll tell thee!
> He is callèd by thy name,
> For he calls himself a Lamb;[2]
> 15 He is meek & he is mild,
> He became a little child;
> I a child & thou a lamb,
> We are callèd by his name.
>   Little Lamb God bless thee.
> 20 Little Lamb God bless thee. ∎

❶
In what way is the lamb similar to its maker?

1. **mead.** Meadow
2 **Lamb.** Jesus is often referred to as "the Lamb of God."

590   *UNIT EIGHT / THE ROMANTIC ERA*

ANALYTIC SCALES FOR RESPONDING IN WRITING

Assign a score from 1 to 25 for each grading criterion below. (For more detailed evaluation, see the evaluation forms for writing, revising, and proofreading, *Assessment Portfolio,* 7.1–7.10.)

Mood

• **Content/Unity.** The stanza presents a mood different from that of "The Lamb."

• **Organization/Coherence.** The stanza contains consistent line lengths and rhyme schemes.

• **Language/Style.** The stanza uses vivid and precise nouns, verbs, and modifiers.

• **Conventions.** The stanza avoids errors in spelling, grammar, usage, mechanics, and manuscript form.

Responding to the Selection

What other animals besides the lamb might the speaker have chosen as subjects for this poem? What characteristics and traditional associations make the lamb an appropriate symbol of innocence? Discuss these questions with your classmates.

Reviewing the Selection

RECALLING

1. What questions are asked in stanza 1?

2. How is the lamb described in stanza 1?

3. What answer does the speaker give to the lamb?

4. To whom does the speaker compare the lamb?

INTERPRETING

5. What is the attitude of the speaker as he questions the lamb?

6. What feelings does this description evoke?

7. In stanza 2, how does the speaker compare the lamb to the one who became a lamb?

8. How does the speaker explain humanity's relationship to the lamb?

SYNTHESIZING

9. How is this poem like a prayer?

10. How does the lamb relate to the idea of "the calm before the storm"?

Understanding Literature (Questions for Discussion)

1. **Pastoral Poem.** A **pastoral poem** is a verse that presents idealized images of rural life. Does "The Lamb" fit this definition of a pastoral poem? Explain.

2. **Allegory.** An **allegory** is a work in which each element *symbolizes,* or represents, something else. List the allegorical elements of this poem. What does each represent?

Responding in Writing

Mood. The **mood** in Blake's poem is light, joyful, and innocent. Write a stanza on the subject of a lamb, creating a different mood than the one in "The Lamb."

Suggest that students first list the lamb's characteristics.

ANSWERS FOR REVIEWING THE SELECTION

RECALLING

1. Stanza 1 asks who made the lamb; who gave it life, food, wool, and a tender voice; and if the lamb knows who made it.

2. The lamb is described as having soft, bright wool and a soft voice.

3. The speaker tells the lamb that its maker is also called a Lamb.

4. The speaker compares the lamb to Jesus, or the Lamb of God.

INTERPRETING

Responses will vary. Possible responses are given.

5. The speaker's attitude is gentle and loving.

6. The lamb's gentleness and softness make the speaker feel affection.

7. Both are meek, mild, and childlike.

8. Like the lamb, people are called by Jesus' name.

SYNTHESIZING

Responses will vary. Possible responses are given.

9. Like a prayer, the poem praises God and has a chanting, rhythmic quality. The last two lines are like a benediction.

10. The lamb is innocent and childlike, as humanity is said to have been before the fall from grace.

ANALYTIC SCALES FOR RESPONDING IN WRITING

Grading scales appear on page 590.

ANSWERS FOR UNDERSTANDING LITERATURE

Responses will vary. Possible responses are given.
► See the evaluation forms for discussion, active listening, and oral communication, *Assessment Portfolio,* 7.11–7.14.

1. **Pastoral Poem.** The poem idealizes the lamb, a country animal. It also idealizes the lamb's home near the stream, the mead, and the vale.
► **Teaching Note:** Have students list the words that indicate the pastoral setting, such as *lamb, stream, meadow,* and *valley.* Then have students brainstorm words associated with each word. Encourage students to discuss how these words and their connotations help create the poem's innocent tone.

2. **Allegory.** The poem is an allegory because the lamb represents Jesus Christ and the speaker, a child, represents humanity.
► **Teaching Note:** If students aren't familiar with the symbolism of Jesus Christ and his birth, you might explain this Christian belief to help them understand the poem.

"The Tyger"

WILLIAM BLAKE

❶
Why might the poet have chosen to spell tiger *with a* y*? Why do you think he associates tigers with a bright burning?*

Tyger! Tyger! burning bright
In the forests of the night,
What immortal hand or eye
Could frame thy fearful symmetry?

5   In what distant deeps or skies
Burnt the fire of thine eyes?
On what wings dare he <u>aspire</u>?
What the hand dare seize the fire?

And what shoulder, & what art,
10   Could twist the sinews of thy heart?
And when thy heart began to beat,
What dread hand? & what dread feet?

What the hammer? what the chain?
In what furnace was thy brain?
15   What the anvil? what dread grasp
Dare its deadly terrors clasp?

WORDS FOR EVERYDAY USE: **as • pire** (ə spīr´) *vi.,* seek to achieve lofty goals

---

VOCABULARY IN CONTEXT

- Many of this year's college graduates <u>aspire</u> to professional careers as lawyers and doctors.

ANSWER TO GUIDED READING QUESTION

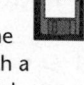

❶ *Tyger* with a *y* corresponds and relates to the word *symmetry*. Blake may associate tigers with a bright burning because of their fierce, powerful, and consuming energy. A fire consumes fuel as a tiger devours its prey.

The Tyger. William Blake, 1789. Yale Center for British Art, Paul Mellon Collection

When the stars threw down[1] their spears
And water'd heaven with their tears,
Did he smile his work to see?
20 Did he who made the Lamb make thee?

Tyger! Tyger! burning bright
In the forests of the night,
What immortal hand or eye
Dare frame thy fearful symmetry? ■

---
1. **threw down.** Surrendered or hurled down

ANSWER TO GUIDED READING QUESTION

❶ The stars throw down their spears.

RESPONDING TO THE SELECTION

Students might respond by making a comparison and contrast graph. Refer students to the Language Arts Survey, 4.8, "Comparing and Contrasting."

ANSWERS FOR REVIEWING THE SELECTION

RECALLING

1. The speaker asks who created the tiger.

2. The tiger is described as having fiery eyes and a sinewy heart.

3. The speaker describes the process of something being created in a furnace.

4. The speaker asks if the creator smiled at the tiger and if the lamb's creator also made the tiger.

INTERPRETING

Responses will vary. Possible responses are given.

5. The speaker wonders if a benevolent creator could have made such a dangerous beast.

6. The speaker characterizes the tiger as fierce and terrifying.

7. The image of the furnace might draw a parallel to hell.

8. In wondering whether God could be pleased with a creation that kills, the speaker questions the nature of God.

SYNTHESIZING

Responses will vary. Possible responses are given.

9. The poem reflects a fear of the primitive because the tiger dwells in the threatening, mysterious "forests of the night," not in the peaceful, familiar meadows of England. So-called civilized people fear the primitive because it represents the unknown.

10. Because they assert that good and evil are part of the same life force, Asian philosophies probably wouldn't question that the creator of the lamb also created the tiger. Line 20 asks how the lamb's creator could make the terrible tiger.

❶

How do the stars react to the creation of the tiger?

Responding to the Selection

In "The Lamb," the lamb is a symbol of innocence. Of what might the tiger be a symbol? What two forces in the world might these creatures represent? Discuss these questions with your classmates.

PRE-ROMANTIC POETRY / "THE TYGER" **593**

ANALYTIC SCALES FOR RESPONDING IN WRITING

Assign a score from 1 to 25 for each grading criterion below. (For more detailed evaluation, see the evaluation forms for writing, revising, and proofreading, *Assessment Portfolio*, 7.1–7.10.)

Description

• **Content/Unity.** The essay or poem presents a vivid, recognizable description of an animal.

• **Organization/Coherence.** The essay or poem is clearly

organized, using sensory details to describe its subject.

• **Language/Style.** The essay or poem uses vivid and precise nouns, verbs, and modifiers.

• **Conventions.** The essay or poem avoids errors in spelling, grammar, usage, mechanics, and manuscript form.

TEACHER'S EDITION **593**

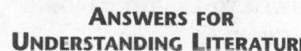

ANSWERS FOR UNDERSTANDING LITERATURE

Responses will vary. Possible responses are given.

►See the evaluation forms for discussion, active listening, and oral communication, *Assessment Portfolio,* 7.11–7.14.

1. Alliteration. Examples of alliteration in "The Tyger" include "Tyger! Tyger!," "burning bright," and "distant deeps." The words *Little lamb* and *meek* and *mild* are examples of alliteration in "The Lamb." Both poems use alliteration to emphasize their subject. Alliteration in "The Tyger" underscores the tiger's terrifying or mysterious aspects, whereas alliteration in "The Lamb" emphasizes the innocence and gentleness of the lamb.

►**Teaching Note:** Ask students to compare the sounds of the initial letters in each poem. Have them consider whether the sounds are harsh or gentle and whether the sounds add to the tone of each poem.

2. Character. The lamb is a clear symbol of innocence because of its gentleness and its symbolic connection to Jesus Christ, believed to be without sin. In contrast, the tiger symbolizes experience because of its ferocity and connotation of violence. In the natural world, the tiger is a predator and a threat to the defenseless lamb. The lamb is also representative of natural, pastoral beauty while the tiger represents a tough, ugly urban world.

►**Teaching Note:** Students might also point out other differences between the two characters. For instance, the lamb is a straightforward character; the speaker asks and answers questions about the lamb's attributes. The tiger, however, is enigmatic. The speaker asks many questions about the tiger's nature but cannot answer them. Students may also note that the speaker is somewhat in awe of the tiger.

Reviewing the Selection

RECALLING

1. What question does the speaker ask in stanza 1?

2. What characteristics of the tiger are described in stanzas 2 and 3?

3. What process does the speaker describe in stanza 4?

4. What question does the speaker ask in stanza 5?

INTERPRETING

5. Why does the speaker wonder who could have made the tiger?

6. How does the speaker characterize the tiger through this physical description?

7. To what process involving furnaces and anvils does the speaker compare the creation of the tiger?

8. Why does the speaker wonder whether God was happy with the creation of the tiger?

SYNTHESIZING

9. How does this poem reflect a fear of the primitive? Why do "civilized people" have this fear?

10. According to Hinduism, God created both good and evil. How does this idea compare with the central ideas of "The Lamb" and "The Tyger"? What question does "The Tyger" pose about the existence of evil in the world? Explain.

Understanding Literature (Questions for Discussion)

1. **Alliteration. Alliteration** is the repetition of initial consonant sounds. List examples of alliteration in "The Tyger." Then review "The Lamb" and compare the uses of alliteration in the two poems.

2. **Character.** A **character** is a person (or sometimes an animal) who figures in the action of a literary work. Compare the characters in "The Lamb" and "The Tyger." What characteristics make one character clearly a symbol of innocence and the other clearly a symbol of experience?

Responding in Writing

Description. Write a descriptive essay or poem about a wild animal. Use adjectives that will appeal to your reader's senses of touch, sight, smell, taste, and hearing. What does the animal that you've chosen symbolize to you?

594   *UNIT EIGHT / THE ROMANTIC ERA*

ANALYTIC SCALES FOR RESPONDING IN WRITING

Grading scales appear on page 593.

READER'S JOURNAL

Brainstorm two lists of images to describe cities, one positive and one negative. What do you believe are the positive aspects of urban life? What do you believe are the negative aspects? Would you prefer to live in the city or in the country? Explain in your journal.

LISTENING SKILLS

Read the Language Arts Survey, 3.5, "Interpersonal Communication." Take turns reading stanzas aloud with a classmate. When it is your turn to listen, do not look at the text. Each time one of you finishes reading a stanza, the other can paraphrase the stanza back to the reader.

"London"

WILLIAM BLAKE

I wander thro' each charter'd[1] street,
Near where the charter'd Thames does flow,
And mark in every face I meet
Marks of weakness, marks of woe.

5   In every cry of every Man,
In every Infant's cry of fear,
In every voice, in every ban,[2]
The mind-forg'd <u>manacles</u> I hear:

How the Chimney-sweeper's cry
10   Every blackning Church appalls,
And the hapless Soldier's sigh
Runs in blood down Palace walls.

---

1. **charter'd.** Bound, as by a legal document; some cities and towns are established by means of charters.
2. **ban.** A proclamation, a prohibition, or an announcement of marriage

WORDS FOR EVERYDAY USE: **man • a • cle** (man´ ə kəl) *n.*, handcuff, shackle

❶ In what sense are city streets and rivers that run through cities bound, limited, or chartered?

❷ In what sense are manacles "mind-forg'd," unnatural creations of the human mind? What kinds of manacles created in the mind limit people's natural rights and freedoms?

❸ What social institutions are mentioned here? What wrongs are attributed to these institutions?

READER'S JOURNAL

Suggest that students note whether their ideas are based on firsthand experience or on other sources of information.

LISTENING SKILLS

Wording of paraphrases will vary. The following is a possible paraphrase for stanza 1.

I wander through the hired streets, along the Thames, and see weakness and suffering in every face.

▶ Additional practice is provided in the *Essential Skills Practice Book: Speaking and Listening*, 3.5.

SUPPORT FOR LEP STUDENTS

Point out that in the poem "London" the word *mark* has two meanings—as a verb it means "to notice" and as a noun it means "a sign." Explain that knowing the various meanings of certain words can help students gain a deeper understanding and appreciation for poetic language and conventions.

ADDITIONAL VOCABULARY

appall—fill with horror, shock; dismay

VOCABULARY FROM THE SELECTION

blight   manacle

ANSWERS TO GUIDED READING QUESTIONS

❶ A city is structured and rivers and streets are owned.

❷ Fear and closed-mindedness are "mind-forg'd manacles."

❸ The speaker mentions the chimney-sweeper's cry on the church and the soldier's sigh running in "blood down Palace walls."

VOCABULARY IN CONTEXT

- Rusted <u>manacles</u> hung from hooks on the old prison's walls.

The Heart of the Empire. Niels Moiler Lund (1863–1916). Guildhall Art Gallery, London/Bridgeman Art Library, London

❶
*What two
tragedies are
mentioned here?
What caused
them?*

But most thro' midnight streets I hear
How the youthful Harlot's curse
15 Blasts the new-born Infant's tear,[3]
And <u>blights</u> with plagues the Marriage hearse.[4] ■

—————————————
3. **Harlot's curse . . . Infants' tear.** The infant may
have been born blind due to a disease.
4. **Marriage hearse.** The wedding carriage transformed
into a funeral hearse

WORDS FOR   **blight** (blīt) *vt.*, destroy, prevent growth
EVERYDAY USE:

VOCABULARY IN CONTEXT
• Farmers worry that the locusts will <u>blight</u> their crops.

Responding to the Selection

Imagine a dialogue between the speaker in this poem and a person who is arriving, alone, in a city for the first time. Perhaps the two are on a subway, or waiting in a deli for a sandwich. What would the speaker say to prepare the new person for life in the city?

Reviewing the Selection

RECALLING

1. In stanza 1, what does the speaker see in people's faces?

2. In stanza 2, what does the speaker hear in every voice?

3. What two people are mentioned in stanza 3? what two social institutions?

4. What harm is done by the "curse" mentioned in stanza 4?

INTERPRETING

5. How might the streets and the Thames being "charter'd" contribute to the mood of the people?

6. In what ways are the people of the city "manacled"?

7. What wrongs are referred to in stanza 3? What implied criticism is made of the two institutions mentioned in stanza 3?

8. What case does the speaker make for taking steps to remedy the social problem that brings about the curse mentioned in stanza 4?

SYNTHESIZING

9. Does the speaker place blame for the social ills he describes? If so, where?

10. How does this speaker feel about urban life? Why does the speaker feel this way? What might be done to improve the conditions that the speaker mentions?

Understanding Literature (Questions for Discussion)

1. **Setting.** The **setting** of a literary work is the time and place in which it occurs, together with the details used to create a sense of a particular time and place. Describe this poem's setting. Why is the setting of this poem particularly important?

2. **Image.** An **image** is a word or phrase that names something that can be seen, heard, touched, tasted, or smelled. Discuss the sensory images in this poem. How do these images relate to the poem's theme? What sort of mood is established?

PRE-ROMANTIC POETRY / "LONDON" **597**

RESPONDING TO THE SELECTION

Students might imagine themselves in the role of the lone traveler arriving in an unfamiliar city.

ANSWERS FOR REVIEWING THE SELECTION

RECALLING

1. He sees weakness and woe.

2. He hears "mind-forg'd manacles."

3. The chimney-sweeper and the soldier are mentioned and connected with the institutions of church and palace, respectively.

4. The "curse" causes the baby to cry, and attacks the wedding carriage.

INTERPRETING

Responses will vary. Possible responses are given.

5. People might feel that the streets and the river belong to the powerful, not to them.

6. He hears people's anguish because they are psychologically imprisoned.

7. The chimney-sweeper's cry shows on the church as a black, shocking stain. The soldier's blood is on the palace because soldiers die to protect the rights of the nobility.

8. The speaker blames the harlot because she does not take care of her child and she spreads disease.

SYNTHESIZING

Responses will vary. Possible responses are given.

9. The speaker writes about the common people. He doesn't blame them for the condition of their lives but alludes to the disparities between the powerful and the weak.

10. The speaker despairs about the state of urban life because it breaks people's spirits and leads to their misery and isolation from one another.

ANSWERS FOR UNDERSTANDING LITERATURE

Responses will vary. Possible responses are given.

► See the evaluation forms for discussion, active listening, and oral communication, *Assessment Portfolio,* 7.11–7.14.

1. Setting. The poem is set in nineteenth-century London at night. The chimney-sweeper and marriage hearse establish the historical setting, and "midnight streets" establishes the time. Because he hears a harlot, the speaker is probably in a disreputable part of the city.

Setting is important to the poem. It creates a picture of the everyday lives of city dwellers; it relates the darkness and despair of the city to the dark, despairing people who live there.

2. Image. The sound images (every man's and infant's cries, soldier's sigh, and harlot's curse) create a woeful mood. The sight images (blood running "down Palace walls" and the infant's tear) reinforce the loss of hope in a city devoid of natural elements.

PROJECT NOTES

▶ See the worksheets and evaluation forms for projects, *Assessment Portfolio*, 7.20–7.23.

Art Creations. Students might want to incorporate a poem's text on a page with an illustration. Suggestions for illustrations include an original drawing, printing, or collage.

Responding in Writing

Social Commentary. Choose one contemporary social ill and write a brief paper describing what you think might be done to lessen its negative consequences.

Language Lab

Prepositional Phrases. Read the Language Arts Survey, 2.47, "Adding Prepositional Phrases." Then combine each of the pairs of sentences using prepositional phrases beginning with *in, on, of,* or *by.*

1. I hear the sad voices of people. The people are in pain.
2. I see weakness and pain. The weakness and pain show on people's faces.
3. People are imprisoned. Mind-forged manacles imprison them.
4. I hear a cry. It is an infant's cry.
5. The chimney-sweeper cries. His cries appall the church.

Thinking Skills

Observing. Read the Language Arts Survey, 4.6, "Observing." Then write ten things that you have either observed or imagined about each of the following.

1. A street corner in a large city
2. A river
3. A church
4. A palace or mansion
5. A wedding procession

PROJECT

Art Creations. In small groups, think about how you might illustrate Blake's poems. Keep in mind that Blake was not afraid to express his creative ideas in unconventional ways. What are the different tools, colors, and objects with which you might illustrate the poems?

ANSWERS FOR LANGUAGE LAB

Wording will vary. Possible wordings are given.
1. In people's sad voices I hear pain.
2. In people's faces I see weakness and pain.
3. People are imprisoned by mind-forged manacles.
4. I hear the cry of an infant.
5. The church is appalled by the chimney sweeper's cries.

▶ Additional practice is provided in the *Essential Skills Practice Book: Language*, 2.47.

ANSWERS FOR THINKING SKILLS

Responses will vary. Possible responses are given.
1. crowded; walk/don't walk signs; pickpockets
2. Mississippi—wide, brown
3. many works of art in European cathedrals
4. many rooms; elegantly decorated
5. walks slowly

▶ Additional practice is provided in the *Essential Skills Practice Book: Study and Research*, 4.6.

PREREADING

"Kubla Khan"
by Samuel Taylor Coleridge

ABOUT THE AUTHOR

Samuel Taylor Coleridge (1772–1834) was born in rural Devonshire. He attended school in London and later in Cambridge. A sensitive, intelligent, but often rather lonely student, he left school in debt, dissolution, and disgrace to enlist in the Light Dragoons. Not suited to the military life, he was soon rescued by friends and returned to the university, although he never graduated.

In 1795, Coleridge met William Wordsworth, the friend and fellow poet with whom he would collaborate on the influential *Lyrical Ballads,* which championed poetry written in the language of common people. Coleridge suffered from rheumatism and took laudanum (an opium derivative), following the standard medical procedures of the day. He became addicted to the drug around 1800, soon after becoming estranged from his wife. In 1810, at his lowest point, he had a terrible argument with his friend Wordsworth. Despite his agonies, Coleridge continued to write, lecture, and publish. After finding a caring physician who reduced the strength of his addiction, Coleridge regained his peace of mind, reconciled with Wordsworth, and made peace with his former wife.

Perhaps because of his tragic addiction, many of Coleridge's most intense work efforts, including "Kubla Khan," remain unfinished and exist only in the form of scrawled notes. Nonetheless, Coleridge is considered today one of the great poets of his era and an influential literary theorist. In his *Biographia Literaria,* Coleridge introduced the idea of the "willing suspension of disbelief" central to the reading of literature. He also drew an interesting distinction between fancy, which he thought of as "memory emancipated from the order of time and space," and the higher faculty of imagination, which transcends the senses and brings knowledge of ultimate realities.

ABOUT THE SELECTION

In a preface to **"Kubla Khan,"** Coleridge writes that he awoke from a dream with the poem fully formed in his mind. In ill health and taking medication, he had fallen asleep while reading *Purchase his Pilgrimage* by Samuel Purchase, which contains the line "In Xanadu did Cublai Can build a stately Palace." Kubla Khan founded the Chinese Mongol Dynasty in the thirteenth century. Coleridge's poem is a classic rendering of an instance of poetic reverie and inspiration.

ENRICHMENT ACTIVITIES

Students can write about or discuss what they know about Coleridge's idea of the "willing suspension of disbelief." What does it mean? Is it legitimate for a writer to expect this from a reader?

SUPPORT FOR LEP STUDENTS

Explain that Coleridge achieves a lofty tone in the poem by using archaic language and by inverting normal word order.

ADDITIONAL VOCABULARY
stately—imposing; majestic
decree—order or decide
chasm—deep crack in the earth's surface
athwart—across
turmoil—tumult; uproar
seething—bubble or foam as if boiling
pant—rapid and heavy breathing
chaff—separate grain
thresher—person who beats grain from its husk
ancestral—ancient
prophesy—predict
thrice—three times

BIOGRAPHICAL NOTE

Coleridge's addiction to a prescribed drug led to separation from family and friends. You may wish to lead a class discussion on the danger of drug abuse.

PREREADING NOTES

READER'S JOURNAL

Suggest that students write the word *paradise* in their journals and create a cluster diagram for the word, writing whatever words and phrases come to mind. Students might then share their ideas and discuss the difference in people's views of paradise.

SPEAKING SKILLS

Students might present their speeches as sales pitches.

▶Additional practice is provided in the *Essential Skills Practice Book: Speaking and Listening*, 3.7.

ANSWER TO GUIDED READING QUESTION

❶ Images such as "fertile ground," "gardens," and "an incense-bearing tree" all bring to mind a paradise, or specifically, the Garden of Eden. The walls and towers suggest that this paradise is closed to the outside world. The caverns might suggest the underworld or world outside the pleasure dome.

VOCABULARY FROM THE SELECTION

cavern	tumult
meander	

VOCABULARY IN CONTEXT

- Mammoth Cave, an underground <u>cavern</u> in Kentucky, has over three hundred miles of passageways.

READER'S JOURNAL

How do you imagine paradise? If you could create the perfect place for yourself, what would it include? What aspects of the real world would it not include? Describe your personal paradise in your journal.

SPEAKING SKILLS

Read the Language Arts Survey, 3.7, "Public Speaking." Choose a song, a story, a poem, or a work of art that inspires you. Write a brief speech to share your feelings about this work with your classmates. In your speech, quote from or describe the work.

"Kubla Khan"

SAMUEL TAYLOR COLERIDGE

❶ *As you read the speaker's description of the pleasure dome and its surroundings, think about what possible allegorical or symbolic significance its elements might be given.*

In Xanadu did Kubla Khan
A stately pleasure dome decree:
Where Alph,[1] the sacred river, ran
Through <u>caverns</u> measureless to man
5 Down to a sunless sea.
So twice five miles of fertile ground
With walls and towers were girdled round:
And there were gardens bright with sinuous rills,[2]
Where blossomed many an incense-bearing tree;
10 And here were forests ancient as the hills,
Enfolding sunny spots of greenery.

But oh! that deep romantic chasm which slanted
Down the green hill athwart a cedarn[3] cover!
A savage place! as holy and enchanted
15 As e'er beneath a waning moon was haunted
By woman wailing for her demon lover!
And from this chasm, with ceaseless turmoil seething,
As if this earth in fast thick pants were breathing,

---

1. **Alph.** Probably the Alpheus river in Greece
2. **sinuous rills.** Winding streams
3. **cedarn.** Made of cedar

WORDS FOR EVERYDAY USE: **cav • ern** (kav´ ərn) *n.,* cave

GOALS/OBJECTIVES

Studying this lesson will enable students to

- enjoy Coleridge's colorful imagery as he describes the pleasure dome
- describe Coleridge's contributions to Romantic literature and to literary theory
- research information using a computer

- define the term *symbol* and recognize and interpret symbols that they encounter in their reading
- identify alliteration as they encounter it in their reading
- prepare and deliver a persuasive speech

Princess Badoura, a tale from the Arabian nights.
Illustrated by Edmund Dulac.

HISTORICAL NOTE

Coleridge reported that he was reading the following sentence just before he fell asleep: "Here the Kubla Khan commanded a palace to be built, and a stately garden thereunto. And thus ten miles of fertile ground were inclosed [sic] with a wall."

ANALYTIC SCALES FOR RESPONDING IN WRITING

Assign a score from 1 to 25 for each grading criterion below. (For more detailed evaluation, see the evaluation forms for writing, revising, and proofreading, *Assessment Portfolio, 7.1–7.10.*)

1. Continuation

• **Content/Unity.** The continuation presents a reasonable extension or ending for the poem.

• **Organization/Coherence.** The continuation adheres to the meter, stanza form, and rhyme pattern of the original poem.

• **Language/Style.** The continuation uses vivid and precise nouns, verbs, and modifiers.

• **Conventions.** The continuation avoids errors in spelling, grammar, usage, mechanics, and manuscript form.

2. Dream Report

• **Content/Unity.** The dream report presents the actions and feelings experienced during a dream.

• **Organization/Coherence.** The dream report details the sequence of dream events and makes connections between events and feelings.

• **Language/Style.** The dream report uses vivid and precise nouns, verbs, and modifiers.

• **Conventions.** The dream report avoids errors in spelling, grammar, usage, mechanics, and manuscript form.

A mighty fountain momently was forced:[4]
20   Amid whose swift half-intermitted burst
Huge fragments vaulted like rebounding hail,
Or chaffy grain beneath the thresher's flail:
And 'mid these dancing rocks at once and ever
It flung up momently the sacred river.
25   Five miles <u>meandering</u> with a mazy motion
Through wood and dale the sacred river ran,
Then reached the caverns measureless to man,
And sank in <u>tumult</u> to a lifeless ocean:

---

4. **A . . . forced.** Waters springing from under the ground have long been a symbol for poetic inspiration.

WORDS FOR
EVERYDAY **U**SE:

me • an • der (mē an´ dər) *vi.*, follow a winding course
tu • mult (tōō´mult) *n.*, a loud commotion

VOCABULARY IN CONTEXT

• We <u>meandered</u> up the steep, hillside path.
• The <u>tumult</u> signaled the volcano's violent eruption.

❶ The speaker recalls a vision of a young woman playing a dulcimer and singing. The speaker wants to revive the song within himself and reexperience his feelings upon hearing the song so that he would be inspired to rebuild the pleasure dome.

❷ The poet described by Coleridge is in an ecstatic trance; his eyes are flashing, his hair is floating.

**ANSWERS TO SELECTION
CHECK TEST 4.8.13**

EX. Where is Kubla Khan's pleasure dome?
Kubla Khan's pleasure dome is in Xanadu.

1. How big is the pleasure dome?
The pleasure dome is "twice five miles of fertile ground."

2. What is in the gardens?
The gardens have winding streams and incense-bearing trees.

3. How is the "deep chasm" described?
The chasm is described as romantic.

4. Where does the sacred river sink?
The river sinks into a lifeless ocean.

5. What sort of milk is named?
The milk of paradise is named.

RESPONDING TO THE SELECTION

Students might discuss their ideas in groups of three or four.

And 'mid this tumult Kubla heard from far
30 Ancestral voices prophesying war!
    The shadow of the dome of pleasure
    Floated midway on the waves;
    Where was heard the mingled measure
    From the fountain and the caves.
35 It was a miracle of rare device,
A sunny pleasure dome with caves of ice!

    A damsel with a dulcimer
    In a vision once I saw:
    It was an Abyssinian maid,
40   And on her dulcimer she played,
    Singing of Mount Abora.
    Could I revive within me
    Her symphony and song,
    To such a deep delight 'twould win me,
45 That with music loud and long,
I would build that dome in air,
That sunny dome! those caves of ice!
And all who heard should see them there,
And all should cry, Beware! Beware!
50 His flashing eyes, his floating hair!
Weave a circle round him thrice,[5]
And close your eyes with holy dread,
For he on honeydew hath fed,
And drunk the milk of Paradise. ∎

---

5. **Weave . . . thrice.** A magical ritual

❶ *What other vision does the speaker recall? What does the speaker want to revive within himself?*

❷ *In ancient Greece, the oracles who spoke the will of the gods did so in ecstatic trances. What similarities exist between those oracles and the inspired poet as described by Coleridge?*

Responding to the Selection

Discuss your feelings about Kubla Khan's "stately pleasure dome." Is it a perfect place? Would you want to go there? Do you think it will last? How does it compare to your own paradise?

Reviewing the Selection

1. Where is Kubla Khan's pleasure dome? How large an area of land does it cover?

2. How is the "chasm" described in the second stanza? What issues out of the chasm?

3. Where does the "sacred river" sink? What does Kubla Khan hear amidst the tumult?

4. Whom did the speaker once see in a vision? What was she doing?

INTERPRETING

5. What is the mood created in the first stanza by the description of the garden?

6. What is happening in the second stanza? How does that scene compare to the scene of the first stanza?

7. What feeling is created in the second stanza? What is mentioned in lines 29 and 30 of the stanza to increase that feeling?

8. What would happen, according to the speaker, if he were able to revive within himself the maid's song?

SYNTHESIZING

9. The first two stanzas of this poem relate images that occurred to the speaker in a dream. Central to these images is a spring, a traditional symbol of poetic inspiration. What second vision is related by the speaker in stanza 3? How is this vision also related to poetic inspiration? What does the speaker want to be able to do?

10. Coleridge calls this poem "a vision in a dream." Does it seem like a dream to you? Which images are most dreamlike? How does the progression of the poem compare to that of a dream? How could the speaker's desire to recreate the pleasure dome be likened to the creation of this poem from a dream?

Understanding Literature (Questions for Discussion)

1. **Symbol.** A **symbol** is a thing that stands for or represents both itself and something else. Of what is the river in this poem a symbol? the song of the maid?

2. **Alliteration. Alliteration** is the repetition of initial consonant sounds. "Kubla Khan," "dome decree," and "measureless to man" are all examples of alliteration. What other examples of alliteration can you find in "Kubla Khan"?

ANSWERS FOR UNDERSTANDING LITERATURE

Responses will vary. Possible responses are given.
► See the evaluation forms for discussion, active listening, and oral communication, *Assessment Portfolio,* 7.11–7.14.

1. Symbol. The river might represent humanity's fall from grace, or a fall caused by pride. The sacred river runs from the top of the dome and its "sunny spots" to the "savage place," where it erupts in a seething, vio-

lent hail, and then slows as it moves on to the "lifeless ocean." The song of the maid might symbolize Paradise or grace restored.

► **Teaching Note:** You might suggest to students familiar with Judeo-Christian religious symbols that the river represents a serpent, which recalls the serpent that tempted Eve in the Garden of Eden and led to the loss of paradise.

(cont.)

RECALLING

1. It is in Xanadu, and it covers ten miles of land.

2. It is "deep" and "romantic" and "holy and enchanted." The sacred river erupts from the chasm in the form of a fountain.

3. The sacred river sinks into the ocean. Kubla Khan hears ancestral voices prophesying war.

4. The speaker once saw a "damsel with a dulcimer...[s]inging of Mount Abora."

INTERPRETING

Responses will vary. Possible responses are given.

5. An idyllic mood is created in the first stanza. The chasm does not belong in the garden.

6. In the second stanza the chasm erupts and destroys the garden's peacefulness. Compared to the stateliness of the first stanza, the second stanza is chaotic and threatening.

7. The voices are foreboding because they are prophesies. If they speak the truth, war will destroy the pleasure dome.

8. The speaker might have difficulty reviving the song because he has only heard it in a vision. Those who hear the song warn against the tempting vision of Kubla Khan.

SYNTHESIZING

Responses will vary. Possible responses are given.

9. The vision of a damsel with a dulcimer also relates to poetic inspiration: the speaker believes that if he could only revive the damsel's "symphony and song" he could build the pleasure dome "in air" and would have "drunk the milk of Paradise."

10. The images of the woman wailing for her demon lover, the ancestral voices prophesying war, and of Kubla Khan himself all seem dreamlike. The progression of the poem seems like a dream, specifically a nightmare, because it begins peacefully and builds to a disruptive, frightening end. Like the speaker who desires to recreate the pleasure dome, Coleridge realizes that the images in his poem cannot match the images of his dream.

ANSWERS FOR UNDERSTANDING LITERATURE (CONT.)

2. Alliteration. Other examples of alliteration include the "woman wailing," "miles meandering with a mazy motion," and "mingled measure."

▶ **Teaching Note:** Have students share examples of alliteration. Then ask them to discuss how the alliteration contributes to the poem's dreamlike mood.

PROJECT NOTES

▶ See the worksheets and evaluation forms for projects, *Assessment Portfolio*, 7.20–7.23.

Artistic Expression. Encourage students to refer to the journal entries in which they responded to the selection for ideas about their own personal "Xanadu."

ANSWERS FOR RESEARCH SKILLS

Wording will vary. Possible wordings are given.

1. Kubla Khan lived from 1215 to 1294.

2. It encompassed present-day China, southern Russia, and Iran.

3. His empire was quite large; he conquered China and became the overlord of all Mongol dominions.

4. He ruled the Mongols, his own nomad race, and the other peoples of China (which was unified during his reign).

5. He also ruled the Mongols of southern Russia and present-day Iran.

▶ Additional practice is provided in the *Essential Skills Practice Book: Study and Research,* 4.26.

ANALYTIC SCALES FOR RESPONDING IN WRITING

Grading scales appear on page 601.

Responding in Writing

1. **Continuation.** Coleridge wrote that "Kubla Khan" was only a fragment and that he was unable to finish the poem because he was interrupted in the middle of transcribing it after his dream. Although you cannot know what Coleridge would have written if he had continued, you can use your imagination to come up with an extension of the poem. Write your continuation in verse as though it were part of the original.

2. **Dream Report.** Write a description of a dream you remember having. What happened in your dream? Describe the images you experienced, and follow the sometimes inexplicable path of your dream. Try to recreate your experience, including how you felt during the dream. Did it have a definite ending, or was it broken off? What did your dream mean to you?

Research Skills

Computer-assisted Research. Read the Language Arts Survey, 4.26, "Computer-assisted Research." Then do some research on Kubla Khan and answer the following questions.

1. When did Kubla Khan live?

2. Where was Kubla Khan's empire?

3. How large was Kubla Khan's empire?

4. Who were the people ruled by Kubla Khan?

5. What other nations or people did Kubla Khan conquer during his reign?

PROJECT

Artistic Expression. Close your eyes and imagine your idyllic place again. Using whatever medium you prefer—watercolor, oil, charcoal, pastels, or clay, for example—create a depiction of your own personal "Xanadu."

PREREADING

from Preface to *Lyrical Ballads*
"The world is too much with us"
"Lines Composed a Few Miles above Tintern Abbey"

by William Wordsworth

ABOUT THE AUTHOR

William Wordsworth (1770–1850), the father of the Romantic Movement in England, had more influence on English poetry than any other writer since Shakespeare. Before Wordsworth, people for the most part viewed nature as something to be turned to human uses. A tree was something to be chopped down and turned into a house or a boat or a bridge. Wordsworth taught people to look at the tree itself, to see it as a thing of beauty that could inspire elevated emotions.

Wordsworth was born in the English Lake District to parents who both died before he was thirteen years old. In his early childhood, he developed a deep love for the Lake District countryside. Moody but energetic, he loved to take long walks, which were, for him, occasions for drinking in the sights and sounds of the natural world. He attended Cambridge but did not take to academic life. After leaving school in 1791, he went on a walking tour of Europe and then lived for a year in France. In France he became a strong supporter of the democratic ideals of the French Revolution. He also had an affair with Annette Vallon, a young French woman who bore him a child. For reasons not entirely clear but probably related to finances and tensions between England and France, Wordsworth returned to his own country without Annette and his child. When the revolution in France degenerated into the Reign of Terror, Wordsworth became disillusioned and despondent. This period of suffering was made bearable by his gentle sister Dorothy and by his friend and fellow poet Samuel Taylor Coleridge.

Wordsworth met Coleridge in 1795. Each was extremely impressed with the talents of the other, and Coleridge called Wordsworth "the best poet of the age." Living in a cottage in Dorsetshire with Dorothy, Wordsworth visited with Coleridge almost every day. Together they walked through the countryside, spoke of poetry and philosophy, and conceived radical new ideas about verse. These ideas would find fruit in *Lyrical Ballads* (1798), a collection of poems that they co-authored. Later editions of this volume contained various versions of Wordsworth's magnificent, controversial **Preface**, which argued, in keeping with the poet's revolutionary, democratic principles, that poetry should be written not in stilted, flowery, formal language but rather in the voice of the common person. The verse in *Lyrical Ballads* contained portraits of nature and of ordinary but noble people; it eschewed artificial,

---

ADDITIONAL RESOURCES

READER'S GUIDE
• Selection Worksheet, 8.8

ASSESSMENT PORTFOLIO
• Selection Check Test, 4.8.15
• Selection Test, 4.8.16

ESSENTIAL SKILLS PRACTICE BOOKS
• *Writing*, 1.38, 1.39, 1.41
• *Study and Research*, 4.7

ENRICHMENT ACTIVITIES

Pose the following idea to students: To create great literature, a writer must experience great suffering. Have students discuss or write about the idea. Ask them to provide examples of writers and literature that support their position. Students may want to use the idea as the basis for a panel discussion or a formal debate.

SUPPORT FOR LEP STUDENTS

Help students to identify the mode, purpose or aim, and audience of this work. They can get important information from the title.

ADDITIONAL VOCABULARY
rustic—simple; plain; artless
restraint—confinement; reserve
spontaneous—in accordance with natural feeling
utterly—completely, totally

GOALS/OBJECTIVES

Studying this lesson will enable students to

• interpret and appreciate Wordsworth's ideas and feelings about poetry
• describe Wordsworth's theory of poetry and its connection to the ordinary person
• explain Wordsworth's theory of "savage torpor"

• identify themes in prose
• write a paragraph using a conversational tone
• apply Wordsworth's theory of poetry to classify poems

66And much it grieved my heart
    to think
What man has made of man.

Who is the happy Warrior?
    Who is he
That every man in arms should
    wish to be?
It is the generous spirit, who,
    when brought
Among the tasks of real life,
    hath wrought
Upon the plan that pleased his
    childish thought:
Whose high endeavors are an
    inward light
That makes the path before
    him always bright:
Who, with a natural instinct to
    discern
What knowledge can perform,
    is diligent to learn.

                    I have seen
A curious child, who dwelt
    upon a tract
Of inland ground applying to
    his ear
The convolutions of a smooth-
    lipped shell;
To which, in silence hushed,
    his very soul
Listened intensely; and his
    countenance soon
Brightened with joy; for from
    within were heard
Murmurings, whereby the
    monitor expressed
Mysterious union with its
    native sea.99

—William Wordsworth

**ADDITIONAL QUESTIONS
AND ACTIVITIES**

Ask students to discuss
Wordsworth's belief that poetry
should be written in the voice of
the ordinary person. What benefits
might this have? What limitations
might it put on the art form?

mechanical devices of style in favor of "a selection of the language actually used by men"; it recorded remembered moments of spontaneous emotional transport over which had been thrown "a certain coloring of the imagination."

In 1802, Wordsworth married Mary Hutchinson, with whom he was to have five children. In 1805 he completed his long masterwork, *The Prelude,* an autobiographical portrait of the development of a poet from childhood through maturity. This poem was meant to be the introduction to a longer work that was never completed.

The period from 1797 to 1807 saw the creation of Wordsworth's finest poems, most of which dealt with the elevation of the soul through communion with nature. Thereafter, Wordsworth's poetic powers declined as his conservatism, derived from bitterness over the failures of the French Revolution, increased. This increasing conservatism earned him the scorn of younger, more radical poets, including Shelley, Byron, Keats, and Robert Browning, a scorn most famously expressed in Browning's poem "The Lost Leader."

In 1843 Wordsworth accepted the position of poet laureate of England under the condition that he not be required to write occasional or official verse. In his later years, he cared patiently and devotedly for his beloved sister Dorothy, who suffered from senile dementia. When Wordsworth himself died, he was buried in Grasmere Churchyard in the Lake District that he had immortalized in his work.

ABOUT THE SELECTIONS

The first selection is an excerpt from the **Preface** to Wordsworth and Coleridge's *Lyrical Ballads.* In this preface, Wordsworth champions the idea that poetry should be written in the voice of the ordinary person. In other words, poetry should be natural, not artificial. Wordsworth's championing of the common person and of nature is in keeping with his youthful sympathies for natural rights as embodied in the rhetoric of the French Revolution. **"The World Is Too Much with Us"** is a **sonnet** reminiscent of Blake's poem "London." It bemoans humanity's separation from nature. **"Lines Composed a Few Miles above Tintern Abbey"** is a poem inspired by a four- or five-day walk that Wordsworth took from Tintern to Bristol with his sister.

READER'S JOURNAL

In your journal, write some of your own ideas about poetry. What is poetry? Why do people write poetry? What kinds of poems do you prefer reading? What should poetry be like?

THINKING SKILLS

Read the Language Arts Survey, 4.7, "Classifying." Read several of Wordsworth's poems, and then review some of the other poetry you have read thus far in the text. See if you can find one or two poems that are consistent with Wordsworth's philosophy and one or two poems that are not.

FROM

Preface to *Lyrical Ballads*

WILLIAM WORDSWORTH

The principal object, then, which I myself proposed in these poems was to choose incidents and situations from common life, and to relate or describe them, throughout, as far as was possible in a selection of language really used by men; and, at the same time to throw over them a certain coloring of imagination, whereby ordinary things should be presented to the mind in an unusual way; and, further, and above all, to make these incidents and situations interesting by tracing in them, truly though not ostentatiously, the primary laws of our nature: chiefly, as far as regards the manner in which we associate ideas in a state of excitement. Humble and rustic life was generally chosen, because in that condition, the essential passions of the heart find a better soil in which they can attain their maturity, are less under restraint, and speak a plainer and more emphatic language; because in that condition of life our elementary feelings coexist in a state of greater simplicity, and, consequently, may be more accurately contemplated, and more forcibly communicated . . .

♦ ♦ ♦

Not that I . . . always began to write with a distinct purpose formally conceived; but I believe that habits of meditation have so formed my feelings that my descriptions of such objects as strongly excite those feelings will be found to carry along with them a *purpose*. If this opinion be erroneous, I can have little right to the name of a poet. For all good poetry is the spontaneous overflow of powerful feelings: but though this be true, poems to which any value can be attached

❶
What sorts of incidents did Wordsworth propose to write about? What sort of language did he propose to use? In what ways did he wish to present these incidents and for what purpose?

WORDS FOR EVERYDAY USE:	prin • ci • pal (prin′ sə pəl) *adj.,* main or chief os • ten • ta • tious • ly (äs′ tən tā′ shəs lē) *adv.,* in a showy display em • phat • ic (em fat′ ik) *adj.,* forceful, definite	con • tem • plate (kän′ təm plāt) *vt.,* think about carefully er • ro • ne • ous (ər rōn′ nē əs) *adj.,* based on error, wrong

---

PREREADING NOTES

READER'S JOURNAL

Students might write their ideas about poetry in the form of a poem.

THINKING SKILLS

Students can write a short list of Wordsworth's criteria for poetry. As they read, they can check the poem's elements against the list.

▶ Additional practice is provided in the *Essential Skills Practice Book: Study and Research,* 4.7.

ANSWER TO GUIDED READING QUESTION

❶ Wordsworth proposed to write about situations from common life. These situations should be described imaginatively but simply, with language used by ordinary people. They should also be presented to the mind in an unusual way, and in them readers should be able to trace the primary laws of nature.

HISTORICAL NOTE

The first edition of *Lyrical Ballads,* published in 1798, did not contain a preface. Wordsworth added the preface to the second edition, which was published in 1800, and revised it two years later for the third edition.

VOCABULARY FROM THE SELECTION

contemplate	kindred
emphatic	organic
endeavor	ostentatiously
erroneous	principal

❶ Wordsworth defines poetry as a "spontaneous overflow of powerful feelings."

HISTORICAL NOTE

Wordsworth and Coleridge rejected **personification**, a poetic device that they found unnatural and, at times, ludicrous. An eighteenth-century ode about smallpox inoculation, recalled Coleridge, began with the line "Inoculation! heavenly Maid, descend!" Obviously, an address to smallpox inoculation does not fall within the realm of everyday language.

ANSWERS TO SELECTION CHECK TEST 4.8.15

EX. *Who worked with Wordsworth on* Lyrical Ballads?
Coleridge worked with Wordsworth on *Lyrical Ballads*.

1. *What "incidents and situations" are related in* Lyrical Ballads?
Lyrical Ballads **relates incidents from common life.**

2. *What does* Lyrical Ballads *avoid doing with abstract ideas?*
Lyrical Ballads **avoids personification of abstract ideas.**

3. *What sort of language does* Lyrical Ballads *try to imitate?*
Lyrical Ballads **tries to imitate "the very language of men."**

4. *What is Wordsworth's definition of poetry?*
He defines poetry as "the spontaneous overflow of powerful feelings."

5. *From where or what does the emotion in* Lyrical Ballads *come?*
It comes from "emotion recollected in tranquillity."

Sunset with Fishing Boats on Loch Fyne. *Joshua Cristall, circa 1807. Ashmolean Museum, Oxford*

were never produced on any variety of subjects but by a man who, being possessed of more than usual <u>organic</u> sensibility had also thought long and deeply.

◆ ◆ ◆

The reader will find that personifications of abstract ideas rarely occur in these volumes; and are utterly rejected, as an ordinary device, to elevate the style and raise it above prose. My purpose was to imitate, and, as far as possible, to adopt the very language of men; and assuredly such personifications do not make any natural or regular part of that language. They are, indeed, a figure of speech occasionally prompted by passion, and I have made use of them as such; but have <u>endeavored</u> utterly to reject them as a mechanical device of style, or as a family language which writers in meter seem to lay claim to by prescription. I have wished to keep the reader in the company of flesh and blood, persuaded that by so doing I shall interest him.

◆ ◆ ◆

I have said that poetry is the spontaneous overflow of powerful feelings: it takes its origin from emotion recollected in tranquillity; the emotion is contemplated till, by a species of reaction, the tranquillity gradually disappears, and an emotion, <u>kindred</u> to that which was before the subject of contemplation, is gradually produced, and does itself actually exist in the mind. ∎

How does Wordsworth define poetry? ❶

WORDS FOR EVERYDAY USE:
or • gan • ic (ôr gan′ ik) *adj.*, inherent, inborn
en • deav • or (en dev′ ər) *vt.*, attempt, try
kin • dred (kin′ drid) *adj.*, related, similar

VOCABULARY IN CONTEXT

- The <u>principal</u> damage from the fire was caused by smoke.
- Expensive homes are featured <u>ostentatiously</u> in the architectural magazine.
- The soldiers' <u>emphatic</u> replies satisfied the officers.
- You should <u>contemplate</u> the consequences of your actions.
- When they discovered a miscalculation, the scientists declared that the lab results were <u>erroneous</u>.
- The judge possesses an <u>organic</u> sense of fairness.
- The swimmer will <u>endeavor</u> to set a new record for crossing the English Channel.
- Are the ideas expressed in this philosophy <u>kindred</u> to your own?

Responding to the Selection

Have a discussion with one of your classmates about Wordsworth's belief that "poetry is a spontaneous overflow of powerful feelings." If you both agree that it is, list your reasons why. If you and your classmate both disagree with Wordsworth, prepare an explanation of what you believe poetry is. If you and your partner disagree, have a debate and list the arguments on both sides.

Reviewing the Selection

RECALLING

1. What kind of situations and language does Wordsworth propose to use in the poems in *Lyrical Ballads*?

2. What, according to Wordsworth, is poetry?

3. What does Wordsworth try to imitate in his poetry? What device does he reject?

4. What, according to Wordsworth, is the process by which a poem is created?

INTERPRETING

5. Why does Wordsworth feel strongly about the type of situation and language used in poetry? How does he feel about other kinds of topics and language used in poetry?

6. If Wordsworth lives up to his own ideals, what do you know about him based on his notion of poetry?

7. Why would natural speech be the best way to express oneself in poetic form?

8. Think about Wordsworth's description of his own creative process. What does this description tell you about what Wordsworth values?

SYNTHESIZING

9. How did the French Revolution influence Wordsworth's conception of poetry?

10. What might Wordsworth consider to be essential and universal elements of human nature?

ANSWERS FOR UNDERSTANDING LITERATURE

▶See the evaluation forms for discussion, active listening, and oral communication, *Assessment Portfolio,* 7.11–7.14.

Responses will vary. Possible responses are given.

 1. **Theme.** Some important themes in Wordsworth's Preface are that poetry should mirror the experience and language of common people and that poetry is a "spontaneous overflow of powerful emotions." Epic poems and certain odes might not fit the criteria that Wordsworth sets forth.

▶**Teaching Note:** Point out that themes sometimes can be summed up in a sentence or phrase from a literary work. For instance, the phrase "spontaneous overflow of powerful feeling" sums up one of the central themes of Wordsworth's Preface. Students might try identifying topic sentences in the selection.

(cont.)

RESPONDING TO THE SELECTION

 Encourage students to support their arguments with specific poems.

ANSWERS FOR REVIEWING THE SELECTION

RECALLING

 1. He proposes to use situations and language from common life.

 2. Wordsworth says that poetry is the "spontaneous overflow of powerful feelings."

 3. Wordsworth tries to imitate the way people really speak. He rejects personification.

 4. To create a poem, the poet recalls an emotion and contemplates it to eliminate any intellectualized refinements.

INTERPRETING

Responses will vary. Possible responses are given.

 5. Wordsworth believes that such situations and language allow true, simple passions greater room for expression. He feels that other topics and language constrict natural expression and lead away from truth.

 6. He probably wrote his poetry when he felt powerful emotions.

 7. Poetry should be "spontaneous" and filled with emotion. Even though it is later refined, poetry should reflect the natural conversational language of the poet.

 8. He values emotion over intellectualization and free expression over controlled thinking.

SYNTHESIZING

Responses will vary. Possible responses are given.

 9. The French Revolution was fought for equality among the classes. Wordsworth echoes this idea in his belief that common people and their language are suitable subjects—in fact the most suitable subjects—for poetry.

10. He might consider love of beauty, friendship, and compassion to be some of the essential and universal elements of human nature.

Assign a score from 1 to 25 for each grading criterion below. (For more detailed evaluation, see the evaluation forms for writing, revising, and proofreading, *Assessment Portfolio*, 7.1–7.10.)

1. Conversational Tone

• **Content/Unity.** The paragraphs present the same idea in informal and formal language.

• **Organization/Coherence.** The informal paragraph presents ideas in associational order. The formal paragraph presents a main idea and adds supporting details in an appropriate and logical order.

• **Language/Style.** The paragraphs use vivid and precise nouns, verbs, and modifiers.

• **Conventions.** The paragraphs avoid errors in spelling, grammar, usage, mechanics, and manuscript form.

2. "Savage Torpor"

• **Content/Unity.** The essay presents a position and two or three strong supporting arguments.

• **Organization/Coherence.** The essay states its main idea and adds supporting arguments in a logical order (possibly from most important to least important or vice versa).

• **Language/Style.** The essay uses vivid and precise nouns, verbs, and modifiers.

• **Conventions.** The essay avoids errors in spelling, grammar, usage, mechanics, and manuscript form.

Understanding Literature (Questions for Discussion)

1. **Theme.** A **theme** is a central idea in a literary work. What are some important themes in Wordsworth's Preface? What kinds of poems would not fit the criteria for poetry set forth by Wordsworth?

2. **Definition.** A **definition** is an explanation of the meaning of a word or phrase. The word *poetry* is notoriously difficult to define. (For some attempts at a definition, see page 14.) Wordsworth defines poetry as a "spontaneous overflow of powerful feelings." Do you consider this a complete or accurate definition? Why, or why not? Work with a group of students to arrive at your own definition of poetry. Begin by having each student write a definition. Then discuss each definition's merits and limitations. See if you can combine your definitions to come up with one that you consider accurate and useful.

Responding in Writing

1. **Conversational Tone. Conversational tone** is an informal tone similar to everyday speech. Write a paragraph using some of the everyday vocabulary and rhythms that you might use among your peers. Choose a topic that you might discuss with a friend—maybe your plans for the weekend or how you feel about school or about a movie you just saw. Try to write a paragraph that uses so much of your own language that the people closest to you might be able to recognize it as yours. It may help to imagine yourself actually telling your friend about your topic. Now imagine that you are writing about the same topic in a more formal context. Perhaps you are writing a movie review for class or a report on some aspect of the school to be given to the school board. How would you change your language? Try rewriting your piece to make it more formal. Compare the two pieces. Which do you prefer and why?

2. **"Savage Torpor."** Wordsworth believed that imaginative literature is important because it keeps people emotionally alive and morally aware. He also believed that, in contrast, mass culture has the effect of reducing the mind to a "savage torpor," that is, to dullness brought on by being deluged by trivia and sensationalism. Think about the meaning of this phrase in terms of your own community. What are the effects of the avalanche of trivia that we are exposed to daily in the mass media—in magazines, on television, at the movies, on billboards, and so on? Do the trivial, unimaginative, cynical, sensational products of mass culture dull the mind? Write a brief essay on this subject. You may wish to focus on one aspect of mass culture, such as billboard advertising, political advertising, television infomercials, chatty local television news programs, or situation comedies. Does a steady diet of one or more of these products of mass culture produce "savage torpor"? Is it important for people to give themselves a break from the sensory overload of modern life?

ANSWERS FOR UNDERSTANDING LITERATURE (CONT.)

▶**Additional Resources:** *Essential Skills Practice Book: Writing,* 1.38, 1.39, 1.41.

 2. Definition. Answers should respond to Wordsworth's definition and present reasonable arguments for or against it. Students may comment that the common language of nineteenth-century England does not necessarily translate to the present.

▶**Teaching Note:** Suggest that students consider the time in which Wordsworth lived and wrote and the poetic models to which he was responding. You may wish to conduct a whole-class discussion after students discuss the issue in small groups.

READER'S JOURNAL

In your journal, make a list of ways in which humankind has turned away from nature. What aspects of modern life keep people isolated from nature? What attitudes have people held in the past about the natural world? What specific environmental problems have occurred as a result of these attitudes?

THINKING SKILLS

Read the Language Arts Survey, 4.8, "Comparing and Contrasting." Make two columns headed *Uncivilized* and *Civilized*. Under each heading, list characteristics that you associate with each. Try to include some positive and some negative characteristics in each column. Remember to consider similarities as well as differences.

ADDITIONAL RESOURCES

READER'S GUIDE
- Selection Worksheet, 8.9

ASSESSMENT PORTFOLIO
- Selection Check Test, 4.8.17
- Selection Test, 4.8.18

ESSENTIAL SKILLS PRACTICE BOOKS
- *Study and Research,* 4.8

"The world is too much with us"

WILLIAM WORDSWORTH

The world is too much with us; late and soon,
Getting and spending, we lay waste our powers:
Little we see in Nature that is ours;
We have given our hearts away, a <u>sordid</u> boon![1]
5 This Sea that bares her bosom to the moon;
The winds that will be howling at all hours,
And are up-gathered now like sleeping flowers;
For this, for every thing, we are out of tune;
It moves us not.—Great God! I'd rather be
10 A Pagan suckled in a creed outworn;
So might I, standing on this pleasant lea,[2]
Have glimpses that would make me less forlorn;
Have sight of Proteus[3] rising from the sea;
Or hear old Triton[4] blow his wreathèd horn. ■

---

1. **boon.** Gift
2. **lea.** Meadow
3. **Proteus.** In the *Odyssey*, Proteus was an old man of the sea who could change his shape at will.
4. **Triton.** A sea god

❶ *According to the speaker, what happens when people focus too much on "getting and spending"?*

❷ *For what, according to the speaker, are we "out of tune"?*

❸ *What, according to the speaker, could the ancients see that we cannot see because we are too civilized?*

WORDS FOR EVERYDAY USE: **sor • did** (sôr´ did) *adj.,* ignoble, squalid

PREREADING NOTES

READER'S JOURNAL

Have students compare their answers to the ideas Wordsworth expresses. Are his ideas dated, or do they speak to modern concerns?

THINKING SKILLS

π
- Students might assume the role of an anthropologist.
- Encourage students to compare charts.

▶ Additional practice is provided in the *Essential Skills Practice Book: Study and Research,* 4.8.

ANSWERS TO GUIDED READING QUESTIONS

❶ When people focus on "getting and spending," they lose touch with nature.

❷ People are "out of tune" with the sea and the howling winds.

❸ The ancients such as the Pagan can see Proteus rising from the sea.

VOCABULARY IN CONTEXT

- The polite, well-dressed young man seemed out of place in his <u>sordid</u> surroundings.

GOALS/OBJECTIVES

Studying this lesson will enable students to

- experience the speaker's feelings of concern about the disconnectedness of people from nature
- explain the ways in which Wordsworth's poetry does and does not reflect his theory of poetry
- identify and interpret allusions and paradoxes in poetry
- write a travel journal
- write rhyming verse
- use a comparison and contrast chart

RESPONDING TO THE SELECTION

Students might write their responses in the form of a letter.

ANSWERS FOR REVIEWING THE SELECTION

RECALLING

1. We waste our powers "getting and spending."

2. We have "given our hearts away."

3. We are "out of tune" with the sea and the winds, the natural world.

4. These myths are of the Greek Proteus and the Roman Triton, the gods of the sea.

INTERPRETING

Responses will vary. Possible responses are given.

5. When we concentrate on material concerns, we become numb to the spiritual aspects of our environment.

6. We have given away our hearts to the material world of possession. In doing so, we have lost our spirituality.

7. People should be in tune with these elements because they are the essence of the natural world.

8. These myths are important because they honor the elemental force of the sea, which the speaker believes is therapeutic. The speaker feels that nature is dead to modern people and needs to be resurrected.

SYNTHESIZING

Responses will vary. Possible responses are given.

9. He might like to return to ancient Greece or Rome because of the power of myth and strength of spirituality during these times.

10. The poem is Romantic because it expresses the inherent value of human passions, the natural world, and spirituality.

Nocturn in Grey and Gold: Chelsea Snow. James McNeill Whistler, 1876. Courtesy of The Fogg Art Museum, Harvard University Art Museums. Bequest—Collection of Maurice Wertheim, Bequest of Grenville L. Winthrop Class of 1906

Photograph: Rick Stafford

Responding to the Selection

Taking Wordsworth's view, write an apology on behalf of humanity to nature for abandoning it.

Reviewing the Selection

RECALLING

1. According to the speaker, how do we "lay waste our powers"?

2. According to the speaker, what have we "given . . . away"?

3. With what are we "out of tune"?

4. What are the myths from "a creed outworn" to which the speaker refers?

INTERPRETING

5. What might be wrong with focusing too much on "[g]etting and spending"?

6. Why is it "a sordid boon" to give away our hearts?

7. Why should people be in tune with the sea and the winds?

8. What might have been felt or experienced by the people who actually believed these myths that is not felt or experienced by us today?

612   UNIT EIGHT / THE ROMANTIC ERA

    SUPPORT FOR LEP STUDENTS

IDIOMS
lay waste—destroy; devastate

ADDITIONAL VOCABULARY
creed—set of beliefs
forlorn—wretched; miserable

9. To what time and place in history might this speaker like to return? Why might he want to do this ?

10. What Romantic view of the proper relationship between humans and nature is expressed in this poem? In other words, what makes this poem Romantic?

Understanding Literature (Questions for Discussion)

1. **Allusion.** An **allusion** is a figure of speech in which a reference is made to a person, event, object, or work from history or literature. What are the allusions in this poem?

2. **Paradox.** A **paradox** is a contradictory statement, idea, or event. Explain the paradox expressed in lines 9 and 10 of the poem. Do you think this paradox was intended? Explain.

3. **Sonnet.** A **sonnet** is a fourteen-line poem that follows one of a number of different rhyme schemes. What rhyme scheme does this sonnet follow? How is this sonnet unlike the typical Petrarchan sonnet described in Unit 4 of this text?

Responding in Writing

1. **Travel Writing.** Take an imaginary journey to a world in which people are completely in touch with nature. Write a few entries in a travel journal about this new land. Describe the place and your impressions of it. How do the people live? What is important to them? You may find it helpful to make comparisons to your homeland.

2. **Rhyme Scheme.** Write an eight-line stanza on the subject of nature, using Wordsworth's rhyme scheme for the first eight lines of this sonnet. Choose an aspect of nature about which you feel strongly. Possibilities include deforestation in the North Woods or in the Amazon or the continuing extinctions of plants and animals around the globe. You may want to make lists of rhyming words to help convey your ideas.

ANALYTIC SCALES FOR RESPONDING IN WRITING

Assign a score from 1 to 25 for each grading criterion below. (For more detailed evaluation, see the evaluation forms for writing, revising, and proofreading, *Assessment Portfolio,* 7.1–7.10.)

1. Travel Writing

• **Content/Unity.** The entries present descriptions of people and places encountered while traveling and focus on one time or place.

• **Organization/Coherence.** The entries describe the events of a trip in chronological order.

• **Language/Style.** The entries use vivid and precise nouns, verbs, and modifiers.

• **Conventions.** The entries avoid errors in spelling, grammar, usage, mechanics, and manuscript form.

2. Rhyme Scheme

• **Content/Unity.** The stanza presents a poetic impression of nature.

• **Language/Style.** The stanza uses vivid and precise nouns, verbs, and modifiers.

• **Conventions.** The stanza contains eight iambic pentameter lines that rhyme *abbaabba.*

• **Conventions.** The stanza avoids errors in spelling, grammar, usage, and mechanics.

ANSWERS FOR UNDERSTANDING LITERATURE

▶ See the evaluation forms for discussion, active listening, and oral communication, *Assessment Portfolio,* 7.11–7.14. *Responses will vary. Possible responses are given.*

1. Allusion. The allusions are to Proteus and to Triton.

2. Paradox. In lines 9 and 10, the speaker tells God that he wishes he had been born a pagan, the paradox being that the speaker confesses his pagan desire to the Christian God.

3. Sonnet. This Petrarchan sonnet has two parts: an octave that rhymes *abbaabba* and a sestet that rhymes *cdcdcd.* The typical Petrarchan sonnet would be addressed to a cold and distant but beautiful woman, the object of the speaker's unrequited love. Instead, this sonnet focuses on the speaker's contemplation of his spiritual alienation from the natural world.

PREREADING NOTES

READER'S JOURNAL

Students might want to accompany their writings with before and after photographs.

RESEARCH SKILLS

- Students might assume the role of a travel writer and fashion the information for a travel brochure.
- Students may want to access a computerized atlas.

▶ Additional practice is provided in the *Essential Skills Practice Book: Study and Research*, 4.27.

SUPPORT FOR LEP STUDENTS

ADDITIONAL VOCABULARY

murmur—low; indistinct sound
hue—color; shade; tint
hedge-row—row of shrubs; bushes
fretful—irritable; discontented
recognition—understanding
cataract—large waterfall
chasten—restrain from excess
subdue—overcome; control
sublime—noble; exalted
interfuse—mix; blend
rash—hasty; reckless

ANSWER TO GUIDED READING QUESTION

❶ It has been five years since the speaker was in this place.

614 TEACHER'S EDITION

READER'S JOURNAL

In memory, visit a natural scene that you visited years ago. If you cannot remember a natural scene, create one in your imagination. Freewrite about how the scene has changed and how you have changed. Are there any parallels in these changes?

RESEARCH SKILLS

Read the Language Arts Survey, 4.23, "Using Reference Works." In an atlas, find the Wye River in England. Then find the towns of Tintern and Bristol. Briefly describe the geographical relationship between the two towns and the river. Calculate the distances between the towns and the river.

"Lines Composed a Few Miles above Tintern Abbey"

WILLIAM WORDSWORTH

How long has it been since the speaker was in this place? ❶

Five years have past; five summers, with the length
Of five long winters! and again I hear
These waters, rolling from their mountain-springs
With a soft inland murmur.—Once again
5   Do I behold these steep and lofty cliffs,
That on a wild <u>secluded</u> scene impress
Thoughts of more deep seclusion; and connect
The landscape with the quiet of the sky.
The day is come when I again <u>repose</u>
10   Here, under this dark sycamore, and view
These plots of cottage-ground, these orchard-tufts,
Which at this season, with their unripe fruits,
Are clad in one green hue, and lose themselves
'Mid groves and <u>copses</u>. Once again I see
15   These hedge-rows, hardly hedge-rows, little lines
Of sportive wood run wild: these pastoral farms,
Green to the very door; and wreaths of smoke
Sent up, in silence, from among the trees!
With some uncertain notice, as might seem

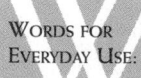
WORDS FOR EVERYDAY USE:
se• clud • ed (si klōōd´ id) *adj.*, hidden from public view
re • pose (ri pōz´) *vt.*, lie quietly, rest
copse (käps) *n.*, thicket of small trees or bushes

614 UNIT EIGHT / THE ROMANTIC ERA

GOALS/OBJECTIVES

Studying this lesson will enable students to

- experience the speaker's feelings on remembering his youth and his sister
- explain the ways in which Wordsworth's poetry does and does not reflect his theory of poetry
- define *ode, free verse,* and *blank verse* and identify these types of poems
- write free verse
- recognize and correct improper shifts in verb tense
- use remembering and visualizing techniques

Tintern Abbey on the River Wye. Philip James de Loutherbourg, 1805.
Fitzwilliam Museum, Cambridge

LITERARY TECHNIQUE

Unlike the dramatic "I" used by most eighteenth-century poets, Wordsworth used a personal "I." In fact, the poem was originally printed with a journal-like notation that told the place and date it was written. "Tintern Abbey" and other poems in *Lyrical Ballads* set the tone for a new era of more personal and reflective poetry. Refer to the Handbook of Literary Terms for more information about the role of the **speaker** in poetry.

20   Of vagrant dwellers in the houseless woods,
      Or of some Hermit's cave, where by his fire
      The Hermit sits alone.

                    These beauteous forms,
      Through a long absence, have not been to me
      As is a landscape to a blind man's eye:
25   But oft, in lonely rooms, and 'mid the din
      Of towns and cities, I have owed to them
      In hours of weariness, sensations sweet,
      Felt in the blood, and felt along the heart;
      And passing even into my purer mind,
30   With tranquil restoration:—feelings too
      Of unremembered pleasure: such, perhaps,
      As have no slight or trivial influence
      On that best portion of a good man's life,
      His little, nameless, unremembered, acts
35   Of kindness and of love. Nor less, I trust,
      To them I may have owed another gift,

❶ What effects has remembering this scene had on the speaker?

WORDS FOR EVERYDAY USE:
va • grant (vāg´ rənt) *adj.,* nomadic, wandering
beau • te • ous (byōō´ tē əs) *adj.,* beautiful
tran • quil (tran´ kwil) *adj.,* peaceful, calm

ANSWERS TO SELECTION CHECK TEST 4.8.17

(See selection on page 611.)

EX. Where was "The world is too much with us" written?
The poem was written on a "pleasant lea" or meadow.

1. What do we do with our powers?
"Getting and spending, we lay waste our powers."

2. What do we see in nature that is ours?
"Little we see in Nature that is ours."

3. What will the winds be doing "at all hours"?
The winds "will be howling at all hours."

4. What would the speaker rather be?
The speaker would rather be a pagan.

5. What would make the speaker "less forlorn"?
Glimpses of Proteus or Triton—sea gods—would make him less forlorn.

VOCABULARY FROM THE SELECTION

beauteous	secluded
copse	sublime
corporeal	tranquil
exhortation	vagrant
prevail	vain
recompense	zeal
repose	

 VOCABULARY IN CONTEXT
- We couldn't see the secluded campsite from the highway.
- The artist's model reposes on a velvet sofa.
- That copse marks the southern border of the property.
- When she tired of her vagrant lifestyle, she settled down in the small town.
- Nothing matches the beauteous glow of the aurora borealis.
- The siren pierced the tranquil, evening air.

ANSWER TO GUIDED READING QUESTION

❶ Remembering this scene has had a calming, sublime effect on the speaker.

LITERARY TECHNIQUE

An **apostrophe** is a figure of speech in which an object or person is directly addressed. (Refer to the Handbook of Literary Terms for more information.) What is the apostrophe in stanza 3?

Answer. The speaker addresses the Wye.

ADDITIONAL QUESTIONS AND ACTIVITIES

What does the speaker mean when he says "in this moment there is life and food/For future years"?

Answer. He means that his memories of this place and its natural beauty will give him peace and comfort in the future.

ADDITIONAL QUESTIONS AND ACTIVITIES

Students can make a sensory detail chart to explore an experience with nature. Refer them to the Language Arts Survey, 1.18, "Sensory Detail Charts." Then they can use the details from their chart to write a brief essay about their experience.

ANSWER TO GUIDED READING QUESTION

❶ The speaker was energetic and connected to nature in an unreflective way.

       Of aspect more <u>sublime</u>; that blessed mood,
       In which the burthen of the mystery,
       In which the heavy and the weary weight
40   Of all this unintelligible world,
       Is lightened:—that serene and blessed mood,
       In which the affections gently lead us on,—
       Until, the breath of this <u>corporeal</u> frame
       And even the motion of our human blood
45   Almost suspended, we are laid asleep
       In body, and become a living soul:
       While with an eye made quiet by the power
       Of harmony, and the deep power of joy,
       We see into the life of things.

                If this
50   Be but a <u>vain</u> belief, yet, oh! how oft—
       In darkness and amid the many shapes
       Of joyless daylight; when the fretful stir
       Unprofitable, and the fever of the world
       Have hung upon the beatings of my heart—
55   How oft, in spirit, have I turned to thee,
       O sylvan Wye![1] thou wanderer thro' the woods,
       How often has my spirit turned to thee!

        And now, with gleams of half-extinguished thought,
       With many recognitions dim and faint,
60   And somewhat of a sad perplexity,
       The picture of the mind revives again:
       While here I stand, not only with the sense
       Of present pleasure, but with pleasing thoughts
       That in this moment there is life and food
65   For future years. And so I dare to hope,
       Though changed, no doubt, from what I was when first
       I came among these hills; when like a roe[2]
       I bounded o'er the mountains, by the sides
       Of the deep rivers, and the lonely streams,
70   Wherever nature led: more like a man
       Flying from something that he dreads, than one

❶ What was the speaker like in his younger years?

---

1. **Wye.** A river in England
2. **roe.** A type of deer

WORDS FOR EVERYDAY USE:	sub • lime (sə blīm´) *adj.*, noble, majestic
	cor • po • re • al (kôr pôr´ ē əl) *adj.*, of a bodily or physical nature
	vain (vān) *adj.*, empty, worthless

VOCABULARY IN CONTEXT

- The painter captured perfectly the <u>sublime</u> expression on the emperor's face.
- According to legend, the strange female figure that appears outside the cemetery is not a <u>corporeal</u> being, but a spirit or phantom.
- Do you expect me to believe such <u>vain</u> promises?
- The grateful parents gave <u>recompense</u> to the man who found their missing daughter.

Who sought the thing he loved. For nature then
(The coarser pleasures of my boyish days,
And their glad animal movements all gone by)
75　To me was all in all.—I cannot paint
What then I was. The sounding cataract
Haunted me like a passion: the tall rock,
The mountain, and the deep and gloomy wood,
Their colors and their forms, were then to me
80　An appetite; a feeling and a love,
That had no need of a remoter charm,
By thought supplied, nor any interest
Unborrowed from the eye.—That time is past,
And all its aching joys are now no more,
85　And all its dizzy raptures. Not for this
Faint[3] I, nor mourn nor murmur; other gifts
Have followed; for such loss, I would believe,
Abundant <u>recompense</u>. For I have learned
To look on nature, not as in the hour
90　Of thoughtless youth; but hearing oftentimes
The still, sad music of humanity,
Nor harsh nor grating, though of ample power
To chasten and subdue. And I have felt
A presence that disturbs me with the joy
95　Of elevated thoughts; a sense sublime
Of something far more deeply interfused,
Whose dwelling is the light of setting suns,
And the round ocean and the living air,
And the blue sky, and in the mind of man:
100　A motion and a spirit, that impels
All thinking things, all objects of all thought,
And rolls through all things. Therefore am I still
A lover of the meadows and the woods,
And mountains; and of all that we behold
105　From this green earth; of all the mighty world
Of eye, and ear,—both what they half create,
And what perceive; well pleased to recognize
In nature and the language of the sense,
The anchor of my purest thoughts, the nurse,

---

3. **Faint.** Lose heart

W ORDS FOR
EVERYDAY USE:　　rec • om • pense (rek´ əm pens) *n.*, repayment, reward

ANSWER TO GUIDED READING QUESTION

❶ Now the speaker regards nature with his intellect rather than simply with his senses. He realizes that the natural world holds deep inner truths that pertain to the essence of all living things.

ADDITIONAL QUESTIONS AND ACTIVITIES

Ask students to concentrate on the aspects of nature that surround them. Point out that a plant on a windowsill, a squirrel or tree in the middle of the city, and the weather are pieces of nature. Ask them if they feel connected with nature. Why, or why not?

❶
How does the speaker regard nature now? What does the speaker sense in the natural world around him?

HISTORICAL NOTE

True to his own belief that poetry should be "spontaneous," Wordsworth composed this poem during a five-day walk and wrote it down unchanged at the end of his trip.

• Dorothy Wordsworth was almost two years younger than her brother William. After her mother's death, the seven-year-old Dorothy lived with several relatives and spent time with William and her other brothers only during the summers. William and Dorothy were finally reunited in 1795, when William came into some money and Dorothy moved into his house to care for him.

• A selection from Dorothy Wordsworth's *The Grasmere Journals* appears on page 674.

ANSWERS TO SELECTION CHECK TEST 4.8.19

EX. What is the form of "Lines Composed a Few Miles above Tintern Abbey"?

The poem is blank verse.

1. What happened to the speaker five years ago?

Five years ago the speaker visited this place.

2. What is the speaker again able to do?

The speaker again reposes or rests.

3. What do we see "with an eye made quiet by the power/Of harmony"?

We see "into the life of things."

4. Who does the speaker say is with him?

He imagines his sister—his "dearest friend"—is with him.

5. Who once stood on the banks of the delightful stream?

The speaker and his sister once stood there together.

ADDITIONAL QUESTIONS AND ACTIVITIES

How does the speaker's sister react to nature?

Answer. She revels in the pure, wild experience of nature—feeling the wind, seeing the moonlight.

---

110   The guide, the guardian of my heart, and soul
        Of all my moral being.

                                Nor perchance,
        If I were not thus taught, should I the more
        Suffer my genial spirits[4] to decay:
        For thou art with me here upon the banks
115   Of this fair river; thou my dearest Friend,[5]
        My dear, dear Friend; and in thy voice I catch
        The language of my former heart, and read
        My former pleasures in the shooting lights
        Of thy wild eyes. Oh! yet a little while
120   May I behold in thee what I was once,
        My dear, dear Sister! and this prayer I make,
        Knowing that Nature never did betray
        The heart that loved her; 'tis her privilege,
        Through all the years of this our life, to lead
125   From joy to joy: for she can so inform
        The mind that is within us, so impress
        With quietness and beauty, and so feed
        With lofty thoughts, that neither evil tongues,
        Rash judgments, nor the sneers of selfish men,
130   Nor greetings where no kindness is, nor all
        The dreary intercourse of daily life,
        Shall e'er prevail against us, or disturb
        Our cheerful faith, that all which we behold
        Is full of blessings. Therefore let the moon
135   Shine on thee in thy solitary walk;
        And let the misty mountain-winds be free
        To blow against thee: and, in after years,
        When these wild ecstasies shall be matured
        Into a sober pleasure; when thy mind
140   Shall be a mansion for all lovely forms,
        Thy memory be as a dwelling-place
        For all sweet sounds and harmonies; oh! then,
        If solitude, or fear, or pain, or grief,
        Should be thy portion, with what healing thoughts
145   Of tender joy wilt thou remember me,
        And these my exhortations! Nor, perchance—

---

4. **genial spirits.** Creative spirit, from the noun *genius*
5. **dearest Friend.** Dorothy, his sister

WORDS FOR EVERYDAY USE: pre • vail (prē vāl´) *vi.*, be victorious
ex • hor • ta • tion (eg´ zôr tā´ shan) *n.*, strong urging

VOCABULARY IN CONTEXT

• Did the school board prevail in its fight against the budget cuts?
• The speaker's exhortations convinced me to join the cause.
• The conductor's creative zeal spread through the entire orchestra.

If I should be where I no more can hear
Thy voice, nor catch from thy wild eyes these gleams
Of past existence—wilt thou then forget

150 That on the banks of this delightful stream
We stood together; and that I, so long
A worshiper of Nature, hither came
Unwearied in that service; rather say
With warmer love—oh! with far deeper <u>zeal</u>

155 Of holier love. Nor wilt thou then forget,
That after many wanderings, many years
Of absence, these steep woods and lofty cliffs,
And this green pastoral landscape, were to me
More dear, both for themselves and for thy sake! ∎

❶
Why is this place special to the speaker, beyond the fact that he is "A worshiper of Nature"?

Responding to the Selection

Write an imaginary interview with Wordsworth's sister Dorothy. In the interview, ask Dorothy about her relationship with her famous brother and whether or not she shares his views on nature. Create the responses you think that she might give.

Reviewing the Selection

RECALLING

1. What natural scene is described in the first two stanzas of the poem?

2. According to lines 66–83, what was the speaker like when he first knew this place?

3. What has the speaker learned from nature that makes him what he is now?

4. What does the speaker value most in his sister?

INTERPRETING

▶ 5. Why is the scene described in the first two stanzas so important to the speaker?

▶ 6. What metaphor from nature does the speaker use to describe his earliest visit to this place? What does this metaphor reveal about the speaker?

▶ 7. How has the speaker's relationship with nature changed since his childhood?

▶ 8. Why does the speaker view nature as a protector of the human spirit?

WORDS FOR EVERYDAY USE: **zeal** (zēl) *n.*, passion, fervor

ROMANTIC POETRY / *"LINES COMPOSED A FEW MILES ABOVE TINTERN ABBEY"*   **619**

ANSWER TO GUIDED READING QUESTION

❶ This place is special because it reminds him of his sister and the time they shared there.

RESPONDING TO THE SELECTION

If students have difficulty imagining Dorothy's responses, read them the biographical information about her on page 674.

ANSWERS FOR REVIEWING THE SELECTION

RECALLING

1. The time is five years earlier in the countryside near Wye.

2. He was young and wildly energetic.

3. He has learned to contemplate life and appreciate nature in tranquillity.

4. He values her youthful passion for nature and sees his youthful joy in nature in her reactions.

INTERPRETING

Responses will vary. Possible responses are given.

5. It is important to the speaker because it represents a time when he communed with nature.

6. He uses the metaphor of the roe bounding over the hills. This metaphor reveals the speaker's longing to be connected to nature once again.

7. He values his present relationship with nature because he knows that the joys he experienced in nature as a youth are fleeting. Nature is a moral anchor for him now, rather than a momentary, sensory experience.

8. He believes that the "quietness and beauty" (line 127) of nature can protect people from the "dreary intercourse of daily life" (line 131).

SYNTHESIZING

Responses will vary. Possible responses are given.

9. Wordsworth seemed very close to his sister and valued her company and feelings. In Wordsworth's day, women had to rely on men for financial support. If a woman were unmarried, it was natural that she would live with male relatives.

10. Both describe a loving, lifelong relationship.

ANSWERS FOR UNDERSTANDING LITERATURE

►See the evaluation forms for discussion, active listening, and oral communication, *Assessment Portfolio*, 7.11–7.14.

Responses will vary. Possible responses are given.

1. Free Verse and **Blank Verse.** This poem is written in blank verse. It is divided into five stanzas. Although there are a few exceptions of irregularly stressed feet, it is written in unrhyming iambic pentameter: "I came among these hills; when like a roe/I bounded o'er the mountains, by the sides/Of the deep rivers, and the lonely streams" (lines 67–69).

►**Teaching Note:** Help students analyze the meter by writing several lines on the chalkboard or overhead projector. Mark the feet and stresses as you or a student volunteer reads the lines aloud. Refer to the discussion of *meter* in the Handbook of Literary Terms.

2. Ode. This ode is addressed to Nature and to the speaker's sister. The "addressees" both bring the speaker joy.

►**Teaching Note:** Romantic poets often address an object in the outer world in order to explore and understand a personal or universal problem. Have students discuss the type of problem Wordsworth addresses in this ode.

ANALYTIC SCALES FOR RESPONDING IN WRITING

Assign a score from 1 to 25 for each grading criterion below. (For a more detailed evaluation, see the evaluation forms for writing, revising, and proofreading, *Assessment Portfolio*, 7.1–7.10.)

1. Lessons

• **Content/Unity.** The essay presents a lesson the writer has learned from nature.

• **Organization/Coherence.** The essay first describes an experience in nature. It then explains the lesson learned from the experience.

• **Language/Style.** The essay uses vivid and precise nouns, verbs, and modifiers.

(cont.)

620 TEACHER'S EDITION

---

9. How did the speaker feel toward his sister? Why was she important to him?

10. Compare this description of a personal relationship with the relationship described in the Robert Burns poem "John Anderson, My Jo" on page 586. How are the relationships similar?

Understanding Literature (Questions for Discussion)

1. **Free Verse and Blank Verse. Free verse,** or *vers libre,* is poetry that avoids use of regular rhyme, rhythm, meter, or division into stanzas. **Blank verse** is unrhymed poetry written in iambic pentameter. To which category does this selection belong? Explain your answer. Refer to specific aspects of the poem.

2. **Ode.** An **ode** is a lofty lyric poem on a serious theme. Odes are often addressed to someone or something. Who are the two "addressees" of this ode? In what way are the "addressees" related?

Responding in Writing

1. **Lessons.** No matter where we live, the natural world has an impact on our lives. Write an essay describing a lesson you have learned from the natural world and about the ways in which you have applied this lesson to other aspects of your life. What lesson did nature teach you? How has this lesson been useful to you?

2. **Free Verse.** Write a stanza in free verse on the subject of children sharing memories of growing up in a rural environment. Think of images that might be especially memorable to a child. What meaning might these images come to have as the child grows up?

ANALYTIC SCALES FOR RESPONDING IN WRITING (CONT.)

• **Conventions.** The essay avoids errors in spelling, grammar, usage, mechanics, and manuscript form.

2. Free Verse

• **Content/Unity.** The stanza presents a child's memories of rural life and a mature perspective on those memories.

• **Organization/Coherence.** The images are clearly distinguished. They are first presented from a child's point of view and then discussed from a more mature point of view.

• **Language/Style.** The stanza uses vivid and precise nouns, verbs, and modifiers.

• **Conventions.** The stanza is written in free verse and avoids errors in spelling, grammar, usage, mechanics, and manuscript form.

Language Lab

Verb Tense. Read the Language Arts Survey, 2.65, "Improper Shifts in Verb Tense." Then complete each sentence below by writing the verb form described in parentheses.

1. Since I was here last, five years _____. (present perfect of *pass*)

2. Those landscapes _____ me many moments of tranquil recollection over the years. (past perfect of *give*)

3. When we are quiet and thoughtful, we _____ into the life of things. (present of *see*)

4. As you mature, you _____ more fully the value of quiet time and of friends. (future of *appreciate*)

5. The memory of that landscape is more powerful to me because you _____ it and _____ it with me. (past of *see* and *share*)

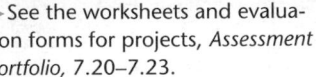

PROJECTS

1. **Sharing Experiences with Nature.** Think of a peaceful, natural place that you have seen. Describe to several of your classmates the things about that place that you remember most clearly. Pay special attention to describing any added meaning that the place has for you because of an experience you had there with a friend.

2. **Nature Walk.** Plan an itinerary—including a route, a schedule, and a list of supplies you will need—for a long walk with several of your classmates. If you cannot actually go on the walk, write a detailed itinerary of natural settings you would like to visit, particularly places that would remind you of positive experiences you have had in the past.

3. **Environmental Action.** Natural resources and natural places are rapidly being destroyed. Develop and follow a plan to help the environment in some way. As a group, organize recycling efforts in your school, adopt a park to keep clean, or come up with some other way that you can make a contribution. Consult environmental or conservation organizations in your area to learn ways in which you can help make the environment safer and cleaner.

ANSWERS FOR LANGUAGE LAB

1. Since I was here last, five years <u>have passed</u>.

2. Those landscapes <u>had given</u> me many moments of tranquil recollection over the years.

3. When we are quiet and thoughtful, we <u>see</u> into the life of things.

4. As you mature, you <u>will appreciate</u> more fully the value of quiet time and of friends.

5. The memory of that landscape is more powerful to me because you <u>saw</u> it and <u>shared</u> it with me.

FOR MORE PRACTICE

Problem. Memories of this place _____ me from unkind words and thoughtless people. (future of *protect*)

Answer. Memories of this place <u>will protect</u> me from unkind words and thoughtless people.

▶Additional practice is provided in the *Essential Skills Practice Book: Language,* 2.65.

PROJECT NOTES

▶See the worksheets and evaluation forms for projects, *Assessment Portfolio,* 7.20–7.23.

 1. Sharing Experiences with Nature. Students can write their ideas on notecards and refer to them as they describe their experiences.

 2. Nature Walk. Students might draw a map of their walk, indicating start and end points and points of interest along the way.

 3. Environmental Action. Group members should discuss and assign the tasks needed to carry out their plan.

ENRICHMENT ACTIVITIES

Interested students can research political events in Great Britain and Ireland during Shelley's lifetime that related to Catholic emancipation. Have them report their findings to the class.

SUPPORT FOR LEP STUDENTS

Some formal language, such as "thou," "thy," and "didst," may be difficult for students to understand. Have them make translation flash cards for these words. For example, students write *thou* on the front of the card and *you* on the back. Encourage students to use this technique for unfamiliar vocabulary words as well.

ADDITIONAL VOCABULARY

trunkless—without a body
mock—mimic as a cruel joke
despair—give up hope

VOCABULARY FROM THE SELECTIONS

chasm	sepulcher
dirge	tumult
impetuous	visage
pestilence	zenith

PREREADING

ROMANTIC POETRY

"Ozymandias"
"Ode to the West Wind"

by Percy Bysshe Shelley

ABOUT THE AUTHOR

Percy Bysshe Shelley (1792–1822) was born to a wealthy family of Sussex aristocrats, merchants, and politicians. He was sent to Eton and Oxford, where he endured teasing because of his slight build and eccentric manner. Perhaps as a consequence, he developed a passionate will to defeat injustice by being "meek and bold."

His closest friend at Oxford was Thomas Jefferson Hogg. They both loved philosophy and were opposed to conventional ideas. Expelled after six months at school, Shelley traveled to London and eloped to Edinburgh with the daughter of a London tavern keeper. Shelley and his wife then went to Ireland, where he delivered his *Address to the Irish People,* which favored Catholic emancipation and social justice for Ireland.

In 1813, Shelley printed his first serious piece, *Queen Mab,* a poem that prophesied a future of happiness, equality, and a return to nature for humankind. Soon afterward, Shelley fell in love with Mary Wollstonecraft Godwin, the daughter of Mary Wollstonecraft and William Godwin. Shelley left his wife, Harriet, and fled to France with Mary, though he later invited Harriet to come live in a "sisterly" relationship with him. Mary's father, despite being a social radical himself, was furious with Shelley for compromising Mary. When Shelley returned to London, he found that he had created something of a scandal.

The Shelleys later moved to Pisa, Italy. On July 8, 1822, Shelley and a friend were sailing in an open boat, the *Don Juan,* when a storm capsized their boat. Neither survived. At the age of thirty, Shelley was buried in Rome near his fellow poet John Keats.

ABOUT THE SELECTIONS

The first selection, **"Ozymandias,"** deals with an ancient king of Egypt and is a classic statement of the vanity of worldly pomp and glory. **"Ode to the West Wind"** was written near Florence on a mild, windy day in early fall. In keeping with Romantic ideals, the poem calls upon a force of nature to inspire the poet's creative endeavors.

GOALS/OBJECTIVES

Studying the lesson will allow students to

- empathize with feelings of desolation and ruin and exalt in the power of nature
- describe the historical significance of Shelley's work
- explain what *irony of situation* is and what effect it creates in "Ozymandias"

- recognize elements of myths as they encounter them in their reading
- correctly capitalize common and proper nouns
- answer sentence-completion questions on tests
- identify and interpret personification and characterization in a poem
- write a memoir and a myth

READER'S JOURNAL

What happens to people when they become powerful? What would happen to someone who achieved absolute power? Does power inevitably corrupt? Answer these questions in your journal.

TEST-TAKING SKILLS

Read the Language Arts Survey, 4.46, "Organizing an Answer to an Essay Question." Then write a brief outline for an answer to the following question: Who was Ozymandias; where, when, and how did he rule; and in what way was his rule commemorated? Base your answer on information from the poem.

"Ozymandias"[1]

PERCY BYSSHE SHELLEY

I met a traveller from an antique land,
Who said—"Two vast and trunkless legs of stone
Stand in the desert. . . . Near them, on the sand,
Half sunk a shattered <u>visage</u> lies, whose frown,
5   And wrinkled lip, and sneer of cold command,
Tell that its sculptor well those passions read
Which yet survive, stamped on these lifeless things,
The hand that mocked them, and the heart that fed;
And on the pedestal, these words appear:
10   My name is Ozymandias, King of Kings,
Look on my Works, ye Mighty, and despair!
Nothing beside remains. Round the decay
Of that colossal Wreck, boundless and bare
The lone and level sands stretch far away." ■

---

1. **Ozymandias.** The Greek name for Ramses II of Egypt. A Greek historian wrote that the largest statue in Egypt bore the inscription, "I am Ozymandias, king of kings; if anyone wishes to know what I am and where I lie, let him surpass me in some of my exploits."

WORDS FOR
EVERYDAY USE:

vis • age (viz´ ij) n., a face

ROMANTIC POETRY / "OZYMANDIAS"   **623**

VOCABULARY IN CONTEXT

• The monarch's <u>visage</u> appears on British currency.

PREREADING NOTES

READER'S JOURNAL

Suggest that students list names of rulers who became corrupted by power.

TEST-TAKING SKILLS

You might want to give students a time limit for answering the question.

▶Additional practice is provided in the *Essential Skills Practice Book: Study and Research*, 4.46.

ADDITIONAL QUESTIONS AND ACTIVITIES

Who are the three speakers in this poem?
Answer. The three speakers are the poet (Shelley), the traveler, and Ozymandias.

ANSWERS TO SELECTION CHECK TEST 4.8.21

EX. How was Shelley treated in school?
Shelley was often teased in school.

1. Where was the traveler from?
The traveler was from "an antique land."

2. What had the traveler seen?
The traveler had seen a vast, broken statue in the desert.

3. Who was Ozymandias?
Ozymandias was a king.

4. Where do the words "My name is Ozymandias" appear?
They appear on the pedestal of the broken statue of Ozymandias.

5. What stretches far away, "boundless and bare"?
The "lone and level sands" of the desert surrounding the wrecked statue stretch far away.

ANSWERS FOR REVIEWING THE SELECTION

RECALLING

1. He describes a gigantic, fallen statue of a king in the desert.

2. The features reveal that the king was probably cruel and heartless.

3. The inscription says, "My name is Ozymandias, King of Kings,/Look on my Works, ye Mighty, and despair!"

4. Nothing remains but the empty desert.

INTERPRETING

Responses will vary. Possible responses are given.

5. The statue interests them because it is all that remains of a man who boasted of ultimate power.

6. The sculptor mocked the king by capturing his cold sneer, all that remains of the once powerful man.

7. He was apparently guilty of pride.

8. The last three lines describe all that remains of the once powerful king's empire. He has inherited a kingdom of ruins and sand.

SYNTHESIZING

Responses will vary. Possible responses are given.

9. It says that greed is not rewarded and earthly power lasts only for the brief period of a person's life; everything decays.

10. It expresses disdain for its subject. Although Ozymandias is the subject of the poem, he is described as a ruin rather than as a great and powerful ruler, as he wished to be remembered.

Responding to the Selection

Write questions for an imaginary interview with Ozymandias. Begin your questions with the words *who, what, when, where, why,* and *how*.

Reviewing the Selection

RECALLING

1. What does the traveler describe to the speaker?

2. What does the sculpted face tell about the ancient ruler?

3. What does the inscription on the pedestal say?

4. What remains in the environment around the statue?

INTERPRETING

5. Why does the statue interest the traveler and the speaker?

6. Who "mocked" the king, and how was the king mocked?

7. Of what flaw was the king apparently guilty?

8. What is the significance of the description in the last three lines of the poem? What kingdom has the powerful king inherited?

SYNTHESIZING

9. Look at lines 11 and 12 closely. What does this poem say about earthly power and greed?

10. What attitude does this poem express towards its subject? Explain your answer.

Understanding Literature (Questions for Discussion)

1. **Character.** A **character** a person who figures in the action of a literary work. What description does the speaker give of Ozymandias? What do the details of this description reveal about the ancient kings?

2. **Irony of Situation. Irony of situation** is when an event occurs that violates the expectations of the characters, the reader, or the audience. In the last few lines of this poem, irony of situation is powerfully used. Why is this technique effective here?

ANSWERS FOR UNDERSTANDING LITERATURE

▶See the evaluation forms for discussion, active listening, and oral communication, *Assessment Portfolio,* 7.11–7.14.

Responses will vary. Possible responses are given.

1. **Character.** He describes Ozymandias as wearing a frowning and sneering look of command. The ancient kings were probably accustomed to absolute power and, as a result, were vain and cold.

▶**Teaching Note:** Students might research Ramses II of Egypt for historical information to support their conclusions.

2. **Irony of Situation.** It is effective here because the contrast between the proud and mighty king who challenges all other kings and the empty desert shows that the power of nature far surpasses the power of a king.

▶**Teaching Note:** Ask students if they were surprised by the ending. Why, or why not?

READER'S JOURNAL

Have you ever felt beaten down, weak, or dispirited? How do such feelings affect your productivity, energy, and ability? What resources help you at such times to renew your confidence in your abilities? to renew your spirit? Write about these questions in your journal.

VARIETIES OF ENGLISH

Read the Language Arts Survey, 2.148, "Register." Then, as you read the following poem, note the special language of evocation used by the speaker. What words and phrases show the speaker's attitude of awe and wonder before the power of the West Wind?

"Ode to the West Wind"

PERCY BYSSHE SHELLEY

1

O wild West Wind, thou breath of Autumn's being,
Thou, from whose unseen presence the leaves dead
Are driven, like ghosts from an enchanter fleeing,

Yellow, and black, and pale, and hectic[1] red,
5   Pestilence-stricken multitudes: O Thou,
Who chariotest to their dark wintry bed

The winged seeds, where they lie cold and low,
Each like a corpse within its grave, until
Thine azure sister of the Spring[2] shall blow

10 Her clarion[3] o'er the dreaming earth, and fill
(Driving sweet buds like flocks to feed in air)
With living hues and odors plain and hill:

---

1. **hectic.** Characteristic of the fever of tuberculosis
2. **Thine . . . Spring.** The west wind of the spring
3. **clarion.** A high-pitched trumpet

❶
How does the speaker describe the West Wind? How does it compare to the wind of spring?

WORDS FOR EVERYDAY USE: pes • ti • lence (pes´tə ləns) n., virulent or infectious disease of epidemic proportions

ROMANTIC POETRY / "ODE TO THE WEST WIND"   **625**

READER'S JOURNAL

Suggest that students think about how they feel when fall and winter arrive.

VARIETIES OF ENGLISH

Students can write modern-day equivalents of these words and phrases.

▶ Additional practice is provided in the *Essential Skills Practice Book: Language*, 2.148.

SUPPORT FOR LEP STUDENTS

ADDITIONAL VOCABULARY
multitude—large number, especially of people
azure—sky-blue
verge—edge
foliage—green plants
incantation—recitation

LITERARY TECHNIQUE

An **anaphora** is any word or phrase that repeats or refers to something that precedes or follows it. In the first line, *thou* and *breath of Autumn's being* both refer back to the West Wind.

ADDITIONAL QUESTIONS AND ACTIVITIES

Have students look for other examples of anaphora as they read.

ANSWER TO GUIDED READING QUESTION

❶ The West Wind is wild and fast. Unlike the life-giving wind of spring, the West Wind brings all things to their death.

VOCABULARY IN CONTEXT

• In the Middle Ages, the Black Plague and other pestilences ravaged Europe.

ANSWER TO GUIDED READING QUESTION

❶ The clouds are compared to decaying leaves and the hair of a woman who worships Dionysius.

LITERARY TECHNIQUE

• This ode is written in *terza rima,* a three-line stanza that rhymes *aba, bcb, cdc,* and so on.

• Have students study the couplets that end each stanza. How does each couplet relate to its preceding lines?

Answer. Each couplet rhymes with the middle line of the preceding tercet.

❶

To what are the clouds compared?

Wild Spirit, which art moving everywhere;
Destroyer and Preserver;[4] hear, O hear!

2

15   Thou on whose stream, 'mid the steep sky's commotion,
Loose clouds like Earth's decaying leaves are shed,
Shook from the tangled boughs of Heaven and Ocean,

Angels of rain and lightning: there are spread
On the blue surface of thine aery surge,
20   Like the bright hair uplifted from the head

Of some fierce Mænad,[5] even from the dim verge
Of the horizon to the <u>zenith</u>'s height
The locks of the approaching storm. Thou <u>Dirge</u>

Of the dying year, to which this closing night
25   Will be the dome of a vast <u>sepulchre,</u>
Vaulted with all thy congregated might

Of vapors,[6] from whose solid atmosphere
Black rain and fire and hail will burst: O hear!

3

Thou who didst waken from his summer dreams
30   The blue Mediterranean, where he lay,
Lulled by the coil of his chrystalline streams,[7]

Beside a pumice isle in Baiæ's bay,[8]
And saw in sleep old palaces and towers
Quivering within the wave's intenser day,[9]

---

4. **Destroyer and Preserver.** Shelley is perhaps likening the wind to those Hindu gods, Vishnu and Shiva, who respectively preserve and destroy the numerous worlds that come into existence, one after the other, of which ours is but the latest.
5. **Mænad.** A female follower who danced in worship of Dionysius, Greek god of wine and vegetation
6. **vapors.** Clouds
7. **coil of his chrystalline streams.** Currents of the Mediterranean Sea often have differences in color.
8. **Baiæ's bay.** Located west of Naples, Italy, it is the site of many villas built by Roman emperors.
9. **wave's intenser day.** Shelley thought that colors reflected in water were more vivid yet more blended.

WORDS FOR EVERYDAY USE:

ze • nith (zē′nith) *n.,* the highest point in the sky
dirge (dʉrj) *n.,* funeral song
sep • ul • chre or sep • ul • cher (sep′əl kər) *n.,* burial vault or tomb

VOCABULARY IN CONTEXT

• At twelve noon the sun will be at its <u>zenith</u>.
• Bagpipes spread the mournful <u>dirge</u> across the cemetery.
• Mourners laid flowers at the <u>sepulcher</u>'s entrance.
• <u>Chasms</u> spread like veins across the canyon's parched floor.

**ADDITIONAL QUESTIONS
AND ACTIVITIES**

What three objects does the
speaker wish to be? How do these
objects relate to the preceding
stanzas?
Answers. The speaker wishes to be
a dead leaf, a cloud, and a wave.
These are the subjects of the first
three stanzas.

35   All overgrown with azure moss and flowers
        So sweet, the sense faints picturing them! Thou
        For whose path the Atlantic's level powers

        Cleave themselves into <u>chasms</u>, while far below
        The sea-blooms and the oozy woods which wear
40   The sapless foliage of the ocean, know

        Thy voice, and suddenly grow grey with fear,
        And tremble and despoil themselves: O hear!

                4

        If I were a dead leaf thou mightest bear;
        If I were a swift cloud to fly with thee;
45   A wave to pant beneath thy power, and share

        The impulse of thy strength, only less free
        Than thou, O Uncontrollable! If even
        I were as in my boyhood, and could be

WORDS FOR
EVERYDAY **U**SE: **chasm** (kaz´əm) *n.*, a crack in the surface of the earth

❶ Like the West Wind, the speaker
was strong, capable, and at one with
nature. Now, he doubts himself and
must ask for help.

❷ The speaker asks the wind to revive
his thoughts. He wants the wind to
scatter his verse over the earth and
make him a "trumpet of prophecy."

**ANSWERS TO SELECTION
CHECK TEST 4.8.23**

EX. Why did Shelley leave Oxford?
**Shelley was expelled from
Oxford.**

1. What moves "like ghosts from
an enchanter fleeing"?
**The leaves blown by the wind
are driven "like ghosts from an
enchanter fleeing."**

2. What is the "Dirge/Of the
dying year"?
The wind is the "Dirge."

3. What does the wind "waken
from his summer dreams"?
**The wind wakens "The blue
Mediterranean" from summer
dreams.**

4. Who else besides the wind is
"tameless, and swift, and proud"?
**The speaker is tameless, swift,
and proud, also.**

5. What does the speaker ask of
the wind?
**The speaker asks the wind to
carry his thoughts "over the universe."**

---

❶
*In what way was
the speaker, as a
child, like the
West Wind? How
has he changed?
Why?*

❷
*What does the
speaker ask of the
wind? What does
the speaker want
to do with his
verse?*

The comrade of thy wanderings over Heaven,
50 As then, when to outstrip thy skiey speed
Scarce seemed a vision; I would ne'er have striven

As thus with thee in prayer in my sore need.
Oh! lift me as a wave, a leaf, a cloud!
I fall upon the thorns of life! I bleed!

55 A heavy weight of hours has chained and bowed
One too like thee: tameless, and swift, and proud.

5

Make me thy lyre,[10] even as the forest is:
What if my leaves are falling like its own!
The _tumult_ of thy mighty harmonies

60 Will take from both a deep, autumnal tone,
Sweet though in sadness. Be thou, Spirit fierce,
My spirit! Be thou me, _impetuous_ one!

Drive my dead thoughts over the universe
Like withered leaves to quicken a new birth!
65 And, by the incantation of this verse,

Scatter, as from an unextinguished hearth
Ashes and sparks, my words among mankind!
Be through my lips to unawakened Earth

The trumpet of a prophecy! O Wind,
70 If Winter comes, can Spring be far behind? ∎

---

10. **lyre.** A harp-like stringed instrument, here played by
the wind

WORDS FOR
EVERYDAY USE:

tu • mult (tü ´mult) _n._, loud commotion
im • pet • u • ous (im pech´ōō əs) _adj.,_ acting on impulse

VOCABULARY IN CONTEXT

• We awakened to a _tumult_ of breaking glass as the earthquake hit.

• Although I prefer not to plan things, my _impetuous_ actions sometimes get me into trouble.

Responding to the Selection

Think about the poem's last line. How might you answer the question it asks? Is dramatic change usually positive or negative for you? Does the speaker expect that the changes that he wants to prophesy will be positive? How do you know?

Reviewing the Selection

RECALLING

1. What scene is described by the speaker in section 1?

2. What are three effects of the wind described in sections 2 and 3?

3. What sacrifice does the speaker offer in section 4?

4. In section 5, what is the speaker asking the wind to do?

INTERPRETING

5. With what attitude is the speaker addressing the wind in section 1?

6. How does the figurative language in section 2 connect the images of the clouds to the previous images of the trees?

7. What change of perspective takes place in section 4?

8. What happens to the intensity of the speaker's request in section 5? How do you know?

SYNTHESIZING

9. Why do you think Shelley chose to use the wind as the central image in this poem?

10. To what kinds of changes might the speaker be referring at the end of this poem? How might the poem be related to the spirit of revolution generated by events in France and the Americas at the time when the poem was written?

Understanding Literature (Questions for Discussion)

Personification. Personification is a figure of speech in which an idea, animal, or thing is described as if it were a person. In this poem, how does personification work to establish a relationship between the speaker and the personified thing? How would the poem be different if Shelley had referred to the wind impersonally?

RESPONDING TO THE SELECTION

Students might write a response to the question in the form of a fortune-cookie insert.

ANSWERS FOR REVIEWING THE SELECTION

RECALLING

1. The speaker describes an autumn scene in which brightly colored leaves and seeds are blown around and to the ground.

2. Three effects of the wind are clouds, rain, and waves.

3. He offers his comfort and submits to pain, falling on the "thorns of life" and bleeding.

4. He asks the wind to instill him with its power and spirit.

INTERPRETING

Responses will vary. Possible responses are given.

5. His attitude is worshipful and somewhat awestruck.

6. The language compares the clouds to leaves being shed and shaken from the branches of heaven.

7. In stanza 4, the speaker shifts from an outward focus on the wind to an inward focus on his personal crisis.

8. The exclamations that make up the final stanza show that the intensity of his request increases.

SYNTHESIZING

Responses will vary. Possible responses are given.

9. Like many of the Romantic poets, Shelley was inspired by nature; the natural world is a fitting place for him to seek inspiration. The wind also symbolizes the natural changes that are part of the cycle of life.

10. The speaker refers to spiritual changes; he wants his creative spirit to be rejuvenated. The poem might be related to the political events of the time because the speaker, or Shelley, asks that his "words" be scattered "among mankind" and desires to be the "trumpet of a prophecy." In light of Shelley's political activism, he might have wanted his spiritual rebirth in order to inspire others.

ANSWERS FOR UNDERSTANDING LITERATURE

Responses will vary. Possible responses are given.

▶ See the evaluation forms for discussion, active listening, and oral communication, *Assessment Portfolio,* 7.11–7.14.

Personification. Personification helps establish a relationship between the speaker and the personified object by assigning recognizable, human qualities to the object. The speaker reveals his values and feelings through what he says about the personified object. If Shelley had referred to the wind impersonally, the poem might have had a stilted feeling and seemed more like a descriptive exercise than a revelation of profound feeling.

▶**Teaching Note:** Have students read a few lines, changing any personification to an impersonal description of the wind. Ask students to compare the sound and effect of the impersonal passage to the personified one.

ANALYTIC SCALES FOR RESPONDING IN WRITING

Assign a score from 1 to 25 for each grading criterion below. (For more detailed evaluation, see the evaluation forms for writing, revising, and proofreading, *Assessment Portfolio*, 7.1–7.10.)

1. Memoir
- **Content/Unity.** The memoir presents a comparison between the writer's childhood and present life.
- **Organization/Coherence.** The memoir presents details of the two times of life in a clear, logical order.
- **Language/Style.** The memoir uses vivid and precise nouns, verbs, and modifiers.
- **Conventions.** The memoir avoids errors in spelling, grammar, usage, mechanics, and manuscript form.

2. Myth
- **Content/Unity.** The myth concerns a god or other supernatural being who helps a character with a problem.
- **Organization/Coherence.** The myth presents a coherent narrative describing the problem and its solution.
- **Language/Style.** The myth uses vivid and precise nouns, verbs, and modifiers.
- **Conventions.** The myth avoids errors in spelling, grammar, usage, mechanics, and manuscript form.

ANSWERS FOR TEST-TAKING SKILLS

Responses will vary. Possible responses are given.

1. The real Ozymandias was a <u>king of Egypt</u>.

2. To the speaker of the poem, the West Wind represents <u>inspiration</u>.

3. The Romantics valued nature and wildness above <u>human works</u>.

4. The speaker asks the wind to <u>become him</u>.

5. At the end of "Ode to the West Wind," the reader feels <u>hopeful</u>.

▶Additional practice is provided in the *Essential Skills Practice Book: Study and Research*, 4.41.

Responding in Writing

1. **Memoir.** The speaker in "Ode to the West Wind" recalls his childhood as a time in which his own spirit paralleled or equalled that of the West Wind. He then describes how that spirit has been beaten down by life. Write a memoir that compares your childhood with your present life. Have things changed for you? In what ways?

2. **Myth.** A **myth** is a story that explains objects or events in the natural world as resulting from the action of some supernatural force or entity. In this poem, the speaker calls upon the wind to inspire him and to renew his spirit, so that he can be a powerful voice prophesying change. Use Shelley's technique to create a prose myth of your own in which you evoke the aid of a force of nature to help you to achieve some end.

Language Lab

Common and Proper Nouns. Read the Language Arts Survey, 2.3, "Common and Proper Nouns." Then list each of the nouns from the following sentences and correct any errors in capitalization. (Note: These nouns come from the selections. Remember that poets do not always follow rules of capitalization, but you should attempt to follow them in this exercise.)

1. I am Ozymandias, and I am King of kings.

2. The real ozymandias was ramses II of egypt, who lived around 1300 BC.

3. The West Wind is the breath of Autumn's being.

4. The blue mediterranean sea was awakened in the Fall.

5. "Ode to the West Wind" was written near florence, Italy.

Test-taking Skills

Sentence Completion. Read the Language Arts Survey, 4.41, "Sentence-Completion Questions." Then add words and punctuation to the following sentence fragments to make them complete sentences.

1. The real Ozymandias was a _____ .

2. To the speaker of the poem, the West Wind represents _____ .

3. The Romantics valued nature and wildness above _____ .

4. The speaker asks the wind to _____ .

5. At the end of "Ode to the West Wind," the reader feels _____ .

ANSWERS FOR LANGUAGE LAB

1. I am Ozymandias, and I am king of kings. (Nouns: Ozymandias, king, kings)

2. The real Ozymandias was Ramses II of Egypt, who lived around 1300 BC. (Nouns: Ozymandias, Ramses II, Egypt)

3. The west wind is the breath of autumn's being. (Nouns: wind, breath, autumn, being)

4. The blue Mediterranean Sea was awakened in the fall. (Nouns: Mediterranean Sea, fall)

5. "Ode to the West Wind" was written near Florence, Italy. (Nouns: Ode, Wind, Florence, Italy)

▶Additional practice is provided in the *Essential Skills Practice Book: Language*, 2.3.

PREREADING

"She Walks in Beauty"
from *Childe Harold's Pilgrimage*
by George Gordon, Lord Byron

ABOUT THE AUTHOR

George Gordon, Lord Byron (1788–1824) was born into an aristocratic family but was raised in poverty. When his great-uncle died, he became the sixth Lord Byron. Born with a clubfoot, he nonetheless became a capable athlete. At Cambridge his extravagance led to indebtedness, but he formed close friendships there and began to write lyric verse. After completing his studies, Byron toured the Mediterranean, gathering ideas and experiences for his most important poems, such as *Childe Harold's Pilgrimage* and *Don Juan*. His romantic image, his good looks, his title, and his deeply emotional, sometimes sensational work combined to make him the most popular author of his day. Despite financial difficulties, he took no income from his publications because of his aristocratic status. He occupied his family's seat in the House of Lords and spoke as a liberal in support of laborers and Catholic Emancipation.

Lord Byron found himself entangled in a number of difficult romantic situations throughout his life. Like Percy Shelley, Byron was forced to leave England because of his eccentric behavior. He lived first in Switzerland and then in Italy, where he became involved in political intrigues. In his thirties, Byron settled into a relationship with an Italian countess and lived near Shelley in Pisa. He continued working on *Childe Harold* and completed *Don Juan,* a book-length, best-selling poem that scandalized Europe.

In the 1820s, Byron's writings stirred popular support for Greek independence from the Turks. Byron left his literary work and organized an expedition to aid in the Greek war. However, he was not a gifted soldier. He succumbed to a fever and died just before turning thirty-six. The Greek people today still honor Byron as a national hero.

ABOUT THE SELECTIONS

Byron wrote the first selection, **"She Walks in Beauty,"** after seeing Lady Wilmot Horton, his cousin by marriage, at an evening party where she was wearing a black mourning gown with glittering spangles. The next two selections, stanzas from *Childe Harold's Pilgrimage,* are among the clearest and loftiest expressions of the Romantic view of nature as a source of spiritual renewal and inspiration.

ROMANTIC POETRY   **631**

ADDITIONAL RESOURCES

READER'S GUIDE
- Selection Worksheets, 8.13, 8.14

ASSESSMENT PORTFOLIO
- Selection Check Tests, 4.8.25, 4.8.27
- Selection Tests, 4.8.26, 4.8.28

ESSENTIAL SKILLS PRACTICE BOOKS
- *Study and Research,* 4.4
- *Language,* 2.62, 2.107–2.133

ENRICHMENT ACTIVITIES

Have students discuss the adage "Art imitates life." Do they agree with the saying? Do they think it applies to Byron? Why, or why not? Students might present their opinions as a debate for the class.

SUPPORT FOR LEP STUDENTS

Students may have difficulty with the inverted word order in the poems. Have students use colored markers or pencils to identify nouns, verbs, adjectives, adverbs, and other parts of speech in the poems.

ADDITIONAL VOCABULARY
mellow—softer; more gentle
gaudy—bright and showy; without taste
eloquent—vividly expressive

GOALS/OBJECTIVES

Studying this lesson will enable students to

- experience the speaker's rapture at the wonder of nature
- explain what a simile is and how "She Walks in Beauty" works as an extended simile
- define *iambic tetrameter* and analyze a poem's rhythmical pattern

- describe the characteristics of the Byronic hero and relate them to the ideals of the Romantic Era
- identify repetition and parallelism as they encounter them in their reading
- memorize and recite stanzas from a poem
- proofread for errors in capitalization
- correct run-ons

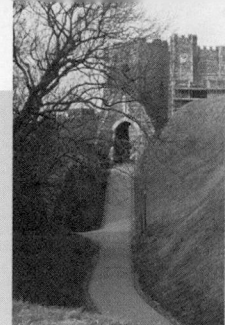

READER'S JOURNAL

Choose something made by people, such as an earthmover or a barge. Then choose something from nature that the human artifact resembles. In your journal, experiment with various ways of describing the one thing in terms of the other.

THINKING SKILLS

Read the Language Arts Survey, 4.4, "Memorizing." Repeat to yourself the first stanza of the poem, one line at a time, until you have committed the lines to memory. Once you have memorized the stanza, recite it for your classmates.

"She Walks in Beauty"

GEORGE GORDON, LORD BYRON

> **❶**
> *To what does the speaker compare the woman's beauty?*

She walks in beauty, like the night
    Of cloudless climes and starry skies;
And all that's best of dark and bright
    Meet in her aspect[1] and her eyes:
5   Thus mellow'd to that tender light
    Which heaven to gaudy day denies.

One shade the more, one ray the less,
    Had half impair'd the nameless grace
Which waves in every raven tress,
10   Or softly lightens o'er her face;
Where thoughts serenely sweet express
    How pure, how dear their dwelling place.

> **❷**
> *What can one tell about this woman from her appearance?*

And on that cheek, and o'er that brow,
    So soft, so calm, yet eloquent,
15   The smiles that win, the tints that glow,
    But tell of days in goodness spent,
A mind at peace with all below,
    A heart whose love is innocent! ∎

---

1. **aspect.** Appearance

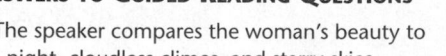

WORDS FOR EVERYDAY USE: se • rene • ly (sə rēn´lē) *adv.*, peacefully

VOCABULARY IN CONTEXT

• The rowers glided serenely across the quiet lake.

ANSWERS TO GUIDED READING QUESTIONS

❶ The speaker compares the woman's beauty to the night, cloudless climes, and starry skies.

❷ One can tell that the woman has spent happy days and that she is at peace with herself.

Responding to the Selection

What does the speaker admire about the woman in this poem? Do you admire these same qualities in people? Respond to these questions in your journal.

Reviewing the Selection

RECALLING

1. To what does the speaker compare the woman in lines 1 and 2?

2. Where, according to the poem, does "all that's best of dark and bright" meet?

3. What personality trait does the speaker feel is reflected in the woman's raven tresses and in her face?

4. What, according to the speaker, can one tell from the woman's smiles?

INTERPRETING

▶▶ 5. What characteristics of the woman are suggested by the comparison in lines 1 and 2?

▶▶ 6. What, according to the poem, is the difference between this woman's "aspect" and day?

▶▶ 7. What is the "dwelling place" of thoughts? What does the speaker have to say about the "dwelling place" of this woman's thoughts?

▶▶ 8. What does it mean to say that a mind is "at peace with all below" it? How would someone who is at peace with his or her physical being differ from someone who is not?

SYNTHESIZING

9. What modifiers (adverbs and adjectives) are used in the poem to describe the woman? Are these modifiers consistent with the speaker's description of the woman as mellower than "gaudy day" is? Explain.

10. What words and phrases in the poem suggest moderation and temperance? How might these qualities bring one peace?

CROSS-CURRICULAR ACTIVITIES

Arts and Humanities. Have students draw or paint a picture of the woman whom the speaker describes. Encourage them to use both their imagination and details from the poem. For students who are not comfortable with illustration, suggest that they find a picture that represents their image of the woman. They can explain why they chose the picture and what, if any, discrepancies there are between the picture and the image.

RESPONDING TO THE SELECTION

Students might also write about the difference or connection between one's appearance and one's personality.

ANSWERS FOR REVIEWING THE SELECTION

RECALLING

1. He compares her to the night.

2. They meet in her aspect, or face, and her eyes.

3. These characteristics reflect her gentleness.

4. The smiles tell that she is at peace with herself.

INTERPRETING

Responses will vary. Possible responses are given.

5. The comparison suggests that she is dark-haired or that she wears dark clothing. It also suggests that she moves smoothly and flawlessly.

6. Unlike the "gaudy" light of day, her face has a subtle, "tender" glow.

7. The face is the dwelling place of thoughts. He says that her face has a pure, serene expression.

8. It means that one is self-assured. A person at peace with his or her physical being appears confident, whereas one who isn't at peace might betray signs of physical self-consciousness such as fidgeting or slouching.

SYNTHESIZING

Responses will vary. Possible responses are given.

9. Modifiers such as "soft," "calm," "eloquent," and "innocent" describe the woman. They are consistent with the speaker's description because they all imply something opposite of the harsh, obvious light of "gaudy day." They imply subtlety and smoothness.

10. Words and phrases such as "mellow'd," "nameless grace," "serenely," "pure," and "days in goodness spent" all suggest moderation and temperance. These qualities might bring one peace because they involve thought and reflection rather than impetuousness, which often leads to turmoil.

Understanding Literature (Questions for Discussion)

1. **Iambic Tetrameter.** An **iamb** is a poetic foot consisting of one weakly stressed syllable followed by one strongly stressed syllable. A line of poetry made up of four iambs is called iambic tetrameter. Find the first line in the poem that is not in strict iambic tetrameter. Write that line down and mark its rhythmical pattern. Divide the line into feet and mark its weak and strong stresses.

2. **Simile.** A **simile** is a comparison using *like* or *as.* With what simile does this poem begin? How is that simile extended, or elaborated, in the rest of the poem?

Responding in Writing

1. **Peace Treaty.** Byron admires this woman for her serenity. She seems to be at peace with herself, and this adds to her beauty. Write a peace treaty with yourself. Identify what makes you feel angry, annoyed, worried, etc. Then think about what you can do to avert the feelings, such as avoiding something stressful, practicing relaxation techniques, or exercising. Write a plan to follow when you are filled with negative energy.

2. **Monument Inscription.** Pretend that you are the speaker of this poem and that you are honoring a person by erecting a statue or fountain. Write a short inscription for this memorial. Who was this person, and why are you honoring him or her?

ANSWERS FOR UNDERSTANDING LITERATURE

Responses will vary. Possible responses are given.

▶ See the evaluation forms for discussion, active listening, and oral communication, *Assessment Portfolio,* 7.11–7.14.

1. **Iambic Tetrameter.** Line 4 is the first line that is not in strict iambic tetrameter. It uses one trochee followed by three iambs.

▶ **Teaching Note:** Suggest that students read the poem aloud to hear the stresses more clearly.

2. **Simile.** The poem begins with the simile "She walks in beauty, like the night." The simile is extended as the speaker compares the lady's eyes, face, hair, and personality to the night as well.

▶ **Teaching Note:** Students might make a list of all the things to which the speaker compares the woman.

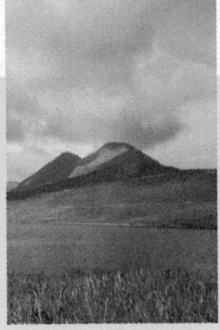

READER'S JOURNAL

If you could visit any natural wonder in the world, which would you choose: the fjords in Norway, the Swiss Alps, the Grand Canyon, or some place else? Write about this place in your journal. What do you find interesting about it?

LANGUAGE SKILLS

Skim the Language Arts Survey, 2.107–2.133, "Proofreading for Errors in Capitalization." As you read the selection, note each capitalized word. Then, find the rule that tells why each of these words is capitalized. Are there any capitalized words for which you cannot find rules? Why might these words be capitalized?

FROM
Childe Harold's Pilgrimage

GEORGE GORDON, LORD BYRON

FROM CANTO 3
91

Not <u>vainly</u> did the early Persian make
His altar the high places and the peak
Of earth-o'ergazing mountains, and thus take
A fit and unwall'd temple, there to seek
855   The Spirit, in whose honor shrines are weak,
Uprear'd of human hands. Come, and compare
Columns and idol-dwellings, Goth or Greek,
With Nature's realms of worship, earth and air,
Nor fix on fond abodes to <u>circumscribe</u> thy prayer!

FROM CANTO 4
178

There is a pleasure in the pathless woods,
1595   There is a rapture on the lonely shore,
There is society, where none intrudes,
By the deep Sea, and music in its roar:
I love not Man the less, but Nature more,
From these our interviews, in which I steal
1600   From all I may be, or have been before,
To mingle with the Universe, and feel
What I can ne'er express, yet can not all conceal. ∎

WORDS FOR EVERYDAY USE:
vain • ly (vān´lē) adv., uselessly
cir • cum • scribe (sur´kəm scrīb) vt., constrict, enclose

❶
How does the speaker feel about mountain-tops? Do you share these feelings?

❷
What does the speaker love more than humankind?

ROMANTIC POETRY / FROM CHILDE HAROLD'S PILGRIMAGE   635

PREREADING NOTES

READER'S JOURNAL

Encourage students to write about what feelings the place creates in them, not just what they find intriguing about its physicality.

LANGUAGE SKILLS

Suggest that students write a justification or explanation for each irregularly capitalized word.

▶Additional practice is provided in the Essential Skills Practice Book: Language, 2.107–2.133.

HISTORICAL NOTE

Childe Harold's Pilgrimage was published in four cantos: Cantos 1 and 2 in 1812, Canto 3 in 1816, and Canto 4 in 1818. Byron traveled through Europe during these years and incorporated contemporary events, such as the Napoleonic Wars, into his poetic travelogue.

SUPPORT FOR LEP STUDENTS

ADDITIONAL VOCABULARY

abode—home; residence

rapture—joy; love; ecstacy

ANSWERS TO GUIDED READING QUESTIONS

❶ The speaker feels that mountain-tops are holy places. Students should explain why they do or do not share these feelings.

❷ The speaker loves nature more than humankind.

VOCABULARY IN CONTEXT
• The knight <u>vainly</u> courted the indifferent lady.
• A rustic stone fence <u>circumscribes</u> the farmer's land.

TEACHER'S EDITION 635

RESPONDING TO THE SELECTION

In stanza 91, the speaker compares nature to a shrine. The speaker considers nature more inspiring.

ANSWERS FOR REVIEWING THE SELECTION

RECALLING

1. They made their altars on mountaintops.

2. It suggests that the reader not limit himself or herself to praying in artificial shrines.

3. He finds pleasure, rapture, and society.

4. He uses the metaphor of an interview.

INTERPRETING

Responses will vary. Possible responses are given.

5. The altars of the early Persians were outside, rather than walled and artificial.

6. They sometimes circumscribe their prayer by doing it only in human-made places. The speaker would rather that people prayed and worshiped at nature's shrine.

7. He doesn't despise human company, but he simply loves nature more. He says "I love not man the less, but Nature more."

8. He "mingles with the Universe," or feels akin to it.

SYNTHESIZING

Responses will vary. Possible responses are given.

9. In stanza 91, the speaker urges readers to consider nature a more fitting place of worship than a temple. In stanza 178, the speaker reveals that he finds greater pleasure in nature's company than in human company.

10. The speaker is independent, passionate, and contemplative. He favors emotion, solitude, boundlessness, and freedom. This personality is attractive because it allows a person to experience more out of life.

Responding to the Selection

What two places of spiritual inspiration are being compared in stanza 91? Which does the speaker consider more inspiring? Do you agree? Why, or why not? Consider the feelings that the speaker in stanza 178 has about nature and solitude. Do you share these feelings? Why or why not? Discuss these questions with your classmates.

Reviewing the Selection

RECALLING

1. In stanza 91, where, according to lines 851–853, did the early Persians make their altars?

2. What does the last line in stanza 91 suggest that the reader not do?

3. In stanza 178, what does the speaker find in the woods, the shore, and the sea?

4. What metaphor does the speaker use in stanza 178 to describe encounters with nature?

INTERPRETING

5. How did the altars of the early Persians differ from ones made by Goths and Greeks?

6. In what way, according to the speaker, do people sometimes "circumscribe [their] prayer"? What would the speaker rather have people do?

7. Does the speaker despise people and human company? How do you know?

8. What relationship toward the universe does the speaker feel when spending time in nature?

SYNTHESIZING

9. The Romantic poets believed that the natural world was more important than the world made by human hands. In what different ways is this sentiment expressed in these two poems?

10. How would you characterize the personality of the speaker of these two stanzas? Does this person favor rationality or emotion? human company or solitude? limits and constraints or boundlessness and freedom? Based on these two stanzas, do you find this personality attractive? Why, or why not?

ANSWERS TO SELECTION CHECK TEST 4.8.27

EX. How old was Byron when he died?
Byron was thirty-six when he died.

1. Who made the high places his altar?
The Persian made the high places his altar.

2. What is the reader asked to compare?
The reader is asked to compare "Nature's realms of worship" with human-made temples.

3. What is in "the pathless woods"?
"There is a pleasure in the pathless woods."

4. What is in the roar of the sea?
There is music in the roar of the sea.

5. With what does the speaker "mingle"?
The speaker mingles with "the Universe."

Understanding Literature (Questions for Discussion)

1. **Byronic Hero.** The **Byronic hero** is a leading figure in a literary work who, like a hero in Byron's works, is moody, passionate, proud, gloomy, adventurous, great-spirited, introverted, and a little disreputable by conventional standards. Assuming that the speaker of these two stanzas is Childe Harold, what qualities do you imagine Harold to have? Does he fit the definition of the Byronic hero? Why, or why not?

2. **Repetition.** **Repetition** is the use, again, of a sound, word, phrase, sentence, or other element. **Parallelism** is a literary technique in which a writer emphasizes the equal value or weight of two or more ideas by expressing them in the same grammatical form. What examples of repetition and parallelism can you find in stanza 178?

Responding in Writing

Personal Essay. Write a brief essay describing a moment of deep connection to the universe that you may have experienced or can imagine. The moment could take place during a walk by the ocean, after winning a game on a soccer field, or while playing with a small child.

Language Lab

Correcting Run-ons. Read the Language Arts Survey, 2.62, "Correcting Run-ons." Revise the following items, correcting the run-ons.

1. She walks in beauty, all that's best of dark and bright meet in her eyes.

2. One shade deeper would be too deep, one shade brighter would be too bright.

3. I love human beings, however, I love nature more.

4. The woods hold magic, the sea holds rapture they make me feel as if I mingle with the universe.

5. I give myself to nature, and I mingle with the universe and I can never express what I feel.

ANALYTIC SCALES FOR RESPONDING IN WRITING

Assign a score from 1 to 25 for each grading criterion below. (For more detailed evaluation, see the evaluation forms for writing, revising, and proofreading, *Assessment Portfolio,* 7.1–7.10.)

Personal Essay.

• **Content/Unity.** The essay describes a real or imagined connection with the universe.

• **Organization/Coherence.** The essay presents the situation and adds sensory details in a sensible order.

• **Language/Style.** The essay uses vivid and precise nouns, verbs, and modifiers.

• **Conventions.** The essay avoids errors in spelling, grammar, usage, mechanics, and manuscript form.

ANSWERS FOR UNDERSTANDING LITERATURE

► See the evaluation forms for discussion, active listening, and oral communication, *Assessment Portfolio,* 7.11–7.14.

Responses will vary. Possible responses are given.

1. Byronic Hero. These two stanzas reveal that Harold is passionate, adventurous, and great-spirited. Someone who travels alone and spends most of his time in nature is probably adventurous, but may also be moody or introverted. In these ways Harold fits the definition of the Byronic hero.

►**Teaching Note:** Suggest that the personality of a Byronic hero contains some inherent contradictions, such as being gloomy and great spirited. How can these contradictions be explained?

2. Repetition. The first three lines of stanza 178 exhibit both repetition and parallelism. Each begins with the phrase "There is" and ends with a parallel phrase: "a pleasure in the pathless woods," "a rapture on the lonely shore," "society, where none intrudes/By the deep Sea."

ANSWERS FOR LANGUAGE LAB

Responses will vary. Possible responses are given.

1. She walks in beauty, and all that's best of dark and bright meet in her eyes.

2. One shade deeper would be too deep, but one shade brighter would be too bright.

3. I love human beings; however, I love nature more.

4. The woods hold magic; the sea holds rapture. They make me feel as if I mingle with the universe.

5. I give myself to nature; I mingle with the universe, and I can never express what I feel.

FOR MORE PRACTICE

Problem. Worship on the mountaintop, pray in the high places.

Answer. Worship on the mountaintop, and pray in the high places.

► Additional practice is provided in the *Essential Skills Practice Book: Language,* 2.62.

ENRICHMENT ACTIVITIES

 Suggest that students read other sonnets that Keats wrote. Keats's "On First Looking into Chapman's Homer" appears on page 676. Other poems by Keats can be found in many poetry anthologies. Have them discuss or write about their themes. Ask students to compare them to the theme of "When I Have Fears."

SUPPORT FOR LEP STUDENTS

After they read "Ode on a Grecian Urn," have students role play the scenes described on the urn. Students may also describe the scenes in writing or draw pictures of the scenes.

ADDITIONAL VOCABULARY

cease—stop, discontinue
garner—a place for storing grain
relish—pleasure, enjoyment

PREREADING

ROMANTIC POETRY

"When I Have Fears"
"Ode on a Grecian Urn"

by John Keats

ABOUT THE AUTHOR

John Keats (1795–1821) came from the least privileged background of all the major British poets. His father was head stableman at a London livery stable. The eldest of five children, Keats was an energetic, boisterous child. One of his teachers encouraged him to write and read poetry, including the work of Edmund Spenser.

At the age of fifteen, after the death of his parents, Keats was taken out of school and apprenticed to a surgeon and apothecary. Keats later qualified to study medicine but decided to pursue poetry instead. In part because he always believed he would die young, Keats worked with great urgency. At twenty-one, Keats published "On First Looking into Chapman's Homer." Soon afterward he began work on the epic poem *Hyperion,* modeled on Milton's *Paradise Lost.* Keats was concerned not to imitate other poets and steered away from friendship with Percy Shelley to avoid his powerful poetic influence.

In 1818, Keats became mortally ill with tuberculosis; some people attributed his sickness to the criticism that he received in the literary press after publishing *Hyperion.* During the year that followed, Keats was extremely creative and prolific, despite his illness. He published a series of masterpieces, including his great odes and sonnets. Critics have compared his language to that of William Shakespeare because of its richness of detail and its celebration of existence.

Keats's respiratory illness intensified in 1820. A year later, he died in Rome. His early death was a great tragedy, for we shall never know what his genius might have produced had he lived.

ABOUT THE SELECTIONS

Keats's sonnet **"When I Have Fears"** is a moving meditation on death written by a young poet who knew that his own life would be cut short. **"Ode on a Grecian Urn"** is an exploration of the value and purpose of art. The skilled potters of ancient Greece made urns for various purposes, including storage of wine and various foods. These urns were often decorated with figures. In Keats's poem, the speaker addresses a Grecian urn and the various figures that appear on it: a bride, men or gods, maidens, a pipe-playing youth, a lover, and a priest leading a cow to sacrifice.

GOALS/OBJECTIVES

Studying this lesson will enable students to

- experience the speaker's feelings about love, death, and beauty
- describe Keats's poetry and its literary significance
- describe and identify the parts of an Elizabethan sonnet

- explain the terms *tenor* and *vehicle* and apply them to writing metaphors
- identify themes in literature that they read
- use adjectives and adverbs appropriately
- use thesauruses

READER'S JOURNAL

What would you like to accomplish before you die? What are the five or six things that are most important for you to do? What would you do if you had only a few months to live? Answer these questions in your journal. Then think about what your answers reveal about you.

LANGUAGE SKILLS

Read the Language Arts Survey, 2.152, "Clichés and Euphemisms." Working with other students, brainstorm a list of clichés and euphemisms about death and dying. As you read the poem, think about the difference between unexamined attitudes toward death and Keats's thoughtfulness about the subject.

"When I Have Fears"

JOHN KEATS

When I have fears that I may cease to be
    Before my pen has glean'd[1] my teeming brain,
Before high piled books, in charactry,[2]
    Hold like rich garners the full ripen'd grain;
5 When I behold, upon the night's starr'd face,
    Huge cloudy symbols of a high romance,
And think that I may never live to trace
    Their shadows, with the magic hand of chance;
And when I feel, fair creature of an hour,
10   That I shall never look upon thee more,
Never have relish in the fairy power
    Of unreflecting love;—then on the shore
Of the wide world I stand alone, and think
Till love and fame to nothingness do sink. ∎

---

1. **glean'd.** Gathered the last remains
2. **charactry.** Printed letters of the alphabet

❶
What three things does the speaker fear that he will not be able to do before he dies?

LITERARY TECHNIQUE

A **cæsura** is a major pause in a line of poetry, such as the pause in line 12. Refer to the Handbook of Literary Terms for additional examples. What is the dramatic effect of the cæsura in line 12?

Answer. It separates the supposition of the first twelve lines from the bare realism of the final couplet.

READER'S JOURNAL

Students might consider the saying "Live every day as if it were your last" as they answer these questions.

LANGUAGE SKILLS

Ask students to consider what their lists of clichés and euphemisms reveal about people's attitudes toward death.

▷ Additional practice is provided in the *Essential Skills Practice Book: Language,* 2.152.

ANSWER TO GUIDED READING QUESTION

❶ He fears that he will die before he is able to become a great poet and scholar, experience the fullness of nature, and experience a great love.

ANSWERS FOR SELECTION CHECK TEST 4.8.29

EX. At what profession did Keats work before becoming a poet?
Keats apprenticed as a medical doctor before becoming a poet.

1. What does the speaker want to do with his pen?
The speaker wants to write everything that is in his brain.

2. Where does the speaker see "cloudy symbols of a high romance"?
The speaker sees these in the night sky.

3. What does the speaker imagine he never will again see?
He imagines he never again will see the "fair creature of an hour" to whom the poem is addressed.

4. Where does the speaker stand alone?
He stands alone "on the shore/ Of the wide world."

5. Upon reflection, what becomes of love and fame?
Upon reflection, love and fame sink to nothingness.

RESPONDING TO THE SELECTION

The poet wishes to be a successful poet and to be loved. His wishes reveal that he is ambitious and hopeful in spite of his fear.

ANSWERS FOR REVIEWING THE SELECTION

RECALLING

1. He is afraid he will not have the opportunity to gather and write about as much as he could in a normal lifetime.

2. He sees clouds in the night sky.

3. He fears to lose the ability to fall in love completely.

4. He envisions himself standing alone on an empty shore.

INTERPRETING

Responses will vary. Possible responses are given.

5. "Gleaning" is gathering grain. "Teeming" means overflowing. Gleaning a teeming brain might mean harvesting, or making use of, an abundance of thought and creativity.

6. He fears he will not be able to experience the fullness of nature.

7. Something that is "fairy-like" would be magical and entrancing but somewhat unreal. Unreflecting love is unconditional love, free of everyday concerns and criticisms. He reveals that he would like to believe the magical idea that love can exist in a sphere separate from everyday problems and concerns.

8. The speaker's sense of his own mortality might cause them to sink.

SYNTHESIZING

Responses will vary. Possible responses are given.

9. The poem is addressed to the "fair creature of an hour." He reveals that he loves her deeply because the poem builds to its climax when he speaks of his fear of losing her.

10. Reflecting on death subdues the speaker's desire for fame and "unreflecting love." However, it does not completely eliminate them. They sink on the shore, as the sun might, and so they will likely rise again.

Responding to the Selection

What does the speaker of this poem wish to do before he dies? What does this list of wishes reveal about him?

Reviewing the Selection

RECALLING

1. In lines 1–4, what is the speaker afraid will not happen before he dies?

2. In lines 5–8, what does the speaker see in the sky?

3. In lines 9–12, what is the speaker fearing to lose?

4. In lines 12–14, what is the speaker envisioning himself doing?

INTERPRETING

▶▶ 5. What is "gleaning"? What does "teeming" mean? What might it mean to glean a teeming brain?

▶▶ 6. In lines 5–8, what does the speaker fear he will not be able to do?

▶▶ 7. What qualities would something that is "fairy-like" have? How might "unreflecting love" differ from feelings based on a critical examination of someone else? What is the speaker saying about his feelings when he refers to "the fairy power/Of unreflecting love"?

▶▶ 8. What might cause the speaker to feel that love and fame have sunk "to nothingness"?

SYNTHESIZING

9. To whom is this poem addressed? How does the speaker feel about that person? How do you know?

10. How does reflecting on death change the speaker's desires for fame as a writer and for continuation of his "unreflecting love"?

ANSWERS FOR UNDERSTANDING LITERATURE

▶See the evaluation forms for discussion, active listening, and oral communication, *Assessment Portfolio,* 7.11–7.14. *Responses will vary. Possible responses are given.*

1. **Sonnet.** The speaker's fear of not becoming a great poet is the subject of the first quatrain. His fear of not experiencing the fullness of nature is the subject of the second quatrain. His fear of not experiencing a great love is the subject of the third quatrain, and his contemplation of an early death is the subject of the final couplet. The paraphrased poem might read: "When I fear that I might die before I've written and read everything that I possibly can, seen everything in nature, and experienced an all-consuming, passionate love, then I forget all about love and fame and become lost in thoughts about dying young."

▶**Teaching Note:** Encourage students to paraphrase all

(cont.)

Understanding Literature (Questions for Discussion)

1. **Sonnet.** A **sonnet** is a fourteen-line poem that follows one of a number of different rhyme schemes. "When I Have Fears" follows the rhyme scheme of the **Elizabethan** or **Shakespearean sonnet.** It is divided into four parts: three **quatrains,** or four-line sections, and a final **couplet,** or two-line section. What is the subject of each of the three quatrains and of the final couplet? Paraphrase each of these parts of the poem.

2. **Symbol.** A **symbol** is a thing that stands for or represents both itself and something else. What, according to the speaker, do clouds in the night sky symbolize? Are clouds at night an appropriate symbol for this? Why, or why not?

3. **Theme.** A **theme** is a central idea in a literary work. Why does the speaker call the person to whom this poem is addressed the "fair creature of an hour"? What is the speaker saying about love and life? How does this statement fit with the theme of the poem as a whole?

Responding in Writing

1. **Metaphor.** Work with other students to come up with some ideas for metaphors related to death, mortality, or immortality. To write a metaphor, first write the **tenor,** the actual subject; then write the **vehicle,** the thing to which the subject will be likened. For example, if the tenor were "death," the vehicle could be "sleep" or "darkness."

2. **Autobiography.** In the classic holiday movie *It's a Wonderful Life,* the main character has the opportunity to see that the world is a better place because he is alive. Write a brief autobiographical note to yourself that tells what your friends, family, community, and the world would lose if you were not around. Don't be modest! Describe your talents and positive personality traits. Tell about how you add to or improve the lives of others around you. Think of specific ways in which people around you now or people whom you could influence in the future might benefit from your presence.

ROMANTIC POETRY / "WHEN I HAVE FEARS" **641**

Assign a score from 1 to 25 for each grading criterion below. (For more detailed evaluation, see the evaluation forms for writing, revising, and proofreading, *Assessment Portfolio,* 7.1–7.10.)

1. Metaphor

• **Content/Unity.** The metaphor presents a reasonable comparison between death or mortality and a similar thing.

• **Organization/Coherence.** The metaphor uses a tenor and a vehicle.

• **Language/Style.** The metaphor uses vivid and precise nouns, verbs, and modifiers.

• **Conventions.** The metaphor avoids errors in spelling, grammar, usage, mechanics, and manuscript form.

2. Autobiography

• **Content/Unity.** The autobiography presents reasons why the writer is valued by friends, family, and the community.

• **Organization/Coherence.** The autobiography describes the writer's values in a logical order (for example, most important to least important or vice versa).

• **Language/Style.** The autobiography uses vivid and precise nouns, verbs, and modifiers.

• **Conventions.** The autobiography avoids errors in spelling, grammar, usage, mechanics, and manuscript form.

ANSWERS FOR UNDERSTANDING LITERATURE (CONT.)

four lines of each quatrain as one or two lines, rather than paraphrasing each line separately.

▶**Additional Resources:** *Essential Skills Practice Book: Study and Research,* 4.30.

2. Symbol. The clouds symbolize a "high romance." They're an appropriate symbol because they are beautiful, yet somewhat undefinable and unattainable.

▶**Teaching Note:** Ask students to discuss what the speaker means by "high romance."

3. Theme. He calls her "fair creature of an hour" because he realizes both the inevitability of his own death and the possibility that she is but a fleeting love. The speaker is saying that love and life are transitory and that there is no knowing when they might be lost. The statement fits with the theme of the poem as a whole because it acknowledges the fragile nature of life and love.

PREREADING NOTES

READER'S JOURNAL

Suggest that students look through their textbook to find a picture of a gathering of people.

RESEARCH SKILLS

Students might work in small groups to develop their definitions. Students can decide the order of importance of definitions for each word, using numbers and letters as in standard dictionaries.

▶Additional practice is provided in the *Essential Skills Practice Book: Study and Research*, 4.24.

ANSWERS TO GUIDED READING QUESTIONS

❶ A bride, men or gods, and maidens are pictured on the urn.

❷ An artistic rendering of a melody is sweeter. An imagined melody might be better because its possibilities are unlimited.

SUPPORT FOR LEP STUDENTS

ADDITIONAL VOCABULARY

loth—unwilling, reluctant
parching—thirsty
desolate—left alone; solitary
overwrought—with surface adorned

ADDITIONAL QUESTIONS AND ACTIVITIES

Ask students to recall events that were better when imagined or remembered than when experienced. Do they agree with the poet's claim that unheard melodies are sweeter?

READER'S JOURNAL

Find a piece of art that depicts a gathering of people. Study the scene to determine the significance of the gathering. Is it for celebration, for mourning, for religious worship, or for some other purpose? Once you have a sense of the mood of the gathering, write a description of the work of art that explains what the people are doing. In your description, try to convey the mood of the piece.

RESEARCH SKILLS

Read the Language Arts Survey, 4.24, "Using Dictionaries." Then work with one other student to write definitions of the words *beauty* and *truth*. Compare your definitions to those given in a standard dictionary. (Note that these words are notoriously difficult to define and that people can genuinely disagree about what their definitions should be.)

"Ode on a Grecian Urn"

JOHN KEATS

1

Thou still unravish'd bride of quietness,
  Thou foster-child of silence and slow time,
Sylvan[1] historian, who canst thus express
  A flowery tale more sweetly than our rhyme:
5 What leaf-fring'd legend haunts about thy shape
    Of <u>deities</u> or mortals, or of both,
      In Tempe or the dales of Arcady?[2]
    What men or gods are these? What maidens loth?
What mad pursuit? What struggle to escape?
10   What pipes and timbrels?[3] What wild ecstasy?

2

Heard melodies are sweet, but those unheard
  Are sweeter; therefore, ye soft pipes, play on;

❶ What is pictured on the urn?

❷ Which, according to the speaker, is "sweeter," an actual melody, or an artistic rendering of one? How might an imagined melody be better than an actual one?

---

1. **Sylvan.** Rustic
2. **Tempe . . . Arcady.** Tempe and Arcadia are both places in Greece that have become symbols for ideal rural beauty.
3. **timbrels.** Ancient tambourines

WORDS FOR EVERYDAY USE: de • i • ty (dē´ ə tē) n., a god

Grecian water jug. Circa 510 BC. Courtesy, Museum of Fine Arts, Boston

ANSWER TO GUIDED READING QUESTION

❶ Although the lover will never kiss his beloved, he will always have her love for him and the beauty of her youth.

Not to the sensual ear,[4] but, more endear'd,
    Pipe to the spirit ditties of no tone:
15   Fair youth, beneath the trees, thou canst not leave
    Thy song, nor ever can those trees be bare;
      Bold lover, never, never canst thou kiss,
Though winning near the goal—yet, do not grieve;
    She cannot fade, though thou hast not thy bliss,
20   For ever wilt thou love, and she be fair!

3

Ah, happy, happy boughs! that cannot shed
    Your leaves, nor ever bid the spring <u>adieu</u>;

❶
What trade-offs are mentioned by the speaker here?

---

4. **sensual ear.** The ear that actually hears, not that of imagination

WORDS FOR EVERYDAY USE:
a • dieu (ə dyō͞o´) *interj.,* goodbye

VOCABULARY IN CONTEXT

• Vishnu is an Indian <u>deity</u>.
• As the train pulled out of the station, travelers leaned out the windows shouting "<u>Adieu</u>!"

ANSWER TO GUIDED READING QUESTION

❶ Unlike a living thing, a work of art never ages or changes. When this generation has grown old, the urn shall remain unchanged.

LITERARY TECHNIQUE

As students discuss the aphorism "Beauty is truth, truth beauty," they might also consider another aphorism from Keats's *Endymion:* "A thing of beauty is a joy forever."

ANSWERS FOR SELECTION CHECK TEST 4.8.31

EX. For what did Keats write, "Here lies one whose name was writ in water"?
He wrote this line for his epitaph.

1. To whom is the poem addressed?
The poem is at different times addressed to the artist who decorated the urn, to the characters depicted on the urn, and to the urn itself.

2. What is said about heard and unheard melodies?
Heard melodies are sweet, but those unheard are sweeter.

3. What musical instruments are depicted on the urn?
Pipes and tambourines are depicted on the urn.

4. Why shouldn't the lover grieve?
He should not grieve because his beloved will never fade.

5. What is all anyone needs to know?
All anyone needs to know is that "Beauty is truth, truth beauty."

VOCABULARY IN CONTEXT

• At dawn, soldiers advanced on the <u>citadel</u>.

And, happy melodist, unwearied,
　　For ever piping songs for ever new;
25　More happy love! more happy, happy love!
　　For ever warm and still to be enjoy'd,
　　　For ever panting, and for ever young;
All breathing human passion far above,
　　That leaves a heart high-sorrowful and cloy'd,
30　　A burning forehead, and a parching tongue.

4

Who are these coming to the sacrifice?
　　To what green altar, O mysterious priest,
Lead'st thou that heifer lowing at the skies,
　　And all her silken flanks with garlands drest?
35　What little town by river or sea shore,
　　Or mountain-built with peaceful <u>citadel</u>,
　　　Is emptied of this folk, this pious morn?
And, little town, thy streets for evermore
　　Will silent be; and not a soul to tell
40　　Why thou art desolate, can e'er return.

5

O Attic[5] shape! Fair attitude! with brede
　　Of marble men and maidens overwrought,
With forest branches and the trodden weed;
　　Thou, silent form, dost tease us out of thought
45　As doth eternity: Cold Pastoral!
　　When old age shall this generation waste,
　　　Thou shalt remain, in midst of other woe
Than ours, a friend to man, to whom thou say'st,
"Beauty is truth, truth beauty,"—that is all
50　　Ye know on earth, and all ye need to know.　■

❶
How does a work of art differ from a living thing? What will have happened to the urn when "this generation" has grown old?

---

5. **Attic.** Characteristic of Attica, a region of Greece where Athens is located

WORDS FOR EVERYDAY USE:　　**cit • a • del** (sit'ə del) *n.*, fortress, safe place

ANSWERS FOR UNDERSTANDING LITERATURE

▶See the evaluation forms for discussion, active listening, and oral communication, *Assessment Portfolio,* 7.11–7.14.
Responses will vary. Possible responses are given.

1. **Apostrophe.** The speaker addresses the urn and some of the figures and objects that are depicted on it: in stanza 1, the speaker may be addressing a bride and a historian, or perhaps the urn itself; in stanza 2, pipes and

the pipe-playing youth; in stanza 3, boughs and another piper; in stanza 4, the urn, a priest, and a town; in stanza 5, the urn.

▶**Teaching Note:** You might divide students into small groups and have each group analyze one figure addressed in the poem. Have students list what the speaker says about the figure and what meaning these words convey.

(cont.)

Responding to the Selection

Are you able to picture in your mind the scenes from the urn described by Keats? Pair up with a classmate, and describe to one another the scenes portrayed in the poem.

RECALLING

1. What figure from the urn is addressed in the first line of the poem?

2. What, according to the poem, are sweeter than "heard melodies"?

3. What is true of the boughs from the first line of stanza 3 that is not true of boughs in the real world?

4. What question does the speaker ask about the town in stanza 4?

INTERPRETING

5. What special event is pictured on the vase?

6. How do the melodies pictured on the urn differ from real, "heard melodies"? Why might the speaker prefer the former?

7. What similarity do the boughs, the melody, and the love that are described in stanza 3 have?

8. What speculations does the speaker make about the town in stanza 4? Why might the people have left the town? Why will it be silent forever more?

SYNTHESIZING

9. Consider lines 45–47. What will be true when "this generation" is old? What is special about the people, trees, melodies, and other things pictured on the urn?

10. Assuming that truths are those things that are eternal and unchanging, what makes the beautiful things on the urn true?

Understanding Literature (Questions for Discussion)

1. **Apostrophe.** An **apostrophe** is a figure of speech in which an object or person is directly addressed. What objects or figures are addressed by the speaker in this poem? Discuss with your classmates how Keats uses the technique of apostrophe to express his thoughts about the urn and about art.

 Students might try sketching one or more of the scenes. Invite students to compare their sketches to see how much room the poet has left for the imagination.

ANSWERS FOR REVIEWING THE SELECTION

RECALLING

1. A virgin bride is addressed in the first line.

2. "Unheard" melodies are sweeter.

3. They never lose their leaves.

4. He asks which town it is.

INTERPRETING

Responses will vary. Possible responses are given.

5. A wedding is pictured on the vase.

6. They have no sound and no end. Perhaps the speaker prefers them because they never change.

7. They are frozen in time; they will never change or die.

8. He speculates that the town is on a river, sea shore, or mountain. Its people might have left to attend a sacrifice (line 3). The town will be silent forever more because it is not pictured on the urn, and no one will ever know about it.

SYNTHESIZING

Responses will vary. Possible responses are given.

9. When "this generation" is old, the urn will remain unchanged, a "friend to man." All the things pictured on the urn are special because they preserve the youth and beauty of humans.

10. The beautiful things on the urn are true because they will last eternally.

ANSWERS FOR UNDERSTANDING LITERATURE (CONT.)

2. **Paradox.** The situation is paradoxical because the man and woman will never be able to experience their love but will always be together.

▶**Teaching Note:** Students might want to discuss the differences between *paradox* and *irony.* Refer to the Handbook of Literary Terms for a definition of *irony.*

3. **Aphorism.** Students should give reasoned responses about the meaning of the speaker's words. Students might suggest that the relationship between beauty and truth is different in a work of art or nonearthly sphere because such things remain unchanged and, therefore, always have the same appearance. Other students might suggest that there is little difference between earthly and nonearthly things because humans usually assign a value, or truth, to nonearthly things.

(cont.)

TEACHER'S EDITION **645**

▶**Teaching Note:** Suggest that students divide the aphorism into its two parts: "Beauty is truth" and "truth beauty." Divide students into groups, and have half the groups discuss the first part of the aphorism and the other half discuss the second part. Then have groups share their ideas.

4. **Theme.** Common themes of these poems are that human experience is short and fleeting and that peace and beauty can be found in things external. The speaker in "When I Have Fears" speaks of the "fair creature of an hour" who might never be seen again. The speaker in "Ode on a Grecian Urn" urges a youth to be happy because his lover "cannot fade."

▶**Teaching Note:** Students should look in the poems rather than in the instructional apparatus for evidence to support their opinions about the theme.

ANALYTIC SCALES FOR RESPONDING IN WRITING

Assign a score from 1 to 25 for each grading criterion below. (For more detailed evaluation, see the evaluation forms for writing, revising, and proofreading, *Assessment Portfolio*, 7.1–7.10.)

Myth

• **Content/Unity.** The myth explains the importance of a particular art form to humans and tells what function the art form serves.

• **Organization/Coherence.** The myth uses the motif of magic transformation. It includes both supernatural and human characters and events.

• **Language/Style.** The myth uses vivid and precise nouns, verbs, and modifiers.

• **Conventions.** The myth avoids errors in spelling, grammar, usage, mechanics, and manuscript form.

---

2. **Paradox.** A **paradox** is a contradictory statement, idea, or event. Read the second stanza of the selection again. What is paradoxical about the situation of the man and woman described in these lines?

3. **Aphorism.** An **aphorism** is a short saying. The conclusion of this poem contains an aphorism that has puzzled readers and critics considerably over the years: "Beauty is truth, truth beauty." One source of this puzzlement is the widely held feeling that, in fact, sometimes beautiful things are not "true" and sometimes true things are not beautiful. Consider, for example, the aphorisms: "Beauty is only skin deep" and "Beauty is as beauty does." These aphorisms reflect the common belief that beauty can be deceptive, or untrue. What might Keats's speaker be saying? Consider that the last line refers to what people know on earth. How might the relationship between beauty and truth be different in a work of art (or in some nonearthly sphere) than it is on earth?

4. **Theme.** A **theme** is a central idea in a literary work. Compare Keats's "Ode on a Grecian Urn" with "When I Have Fears." Is there a common theme in these selections? Explain.

Responding in Writing

Myth. A **myth** is a story that explains objects or events in the natural world as resulting from the action of some supernatural force or entity, most often a god. Write your own myth about the origins of art. In your myth, tell why some art form, such as music, painting, pottery-making, poetry, drama, or storytelling, was given to human beings. In other words, explain the importance of that art form to people. Tell what function or functions it serves. To prepare for writing your myth, you might want to read a few Greek or Native American myths in books from your school or community library. Try to include in your myth the standard mythological element, or motif, of things that are transformed magically from one shape into another.

PROJECT

Time Capsule. Keats was very concerned about his legacy to future generations. With other students, plan a time capsule—a box to be opened by people two hundred years from now. What items would you put in the box to tell future generations about you, your lives, your time, and your place?

 PROJECT NOTES

▶See the worksheets and evaluation forms for projects, *Assessment Portfolio*, 7.20–7.23.

Time Capsule

 • Have students consider what things they would like to know about people who lived two hundred years ago.

• Students might work with students from other classes to create a time capsule for the school.

π • Suggest that students create categories of information, such as art, politics, gender issues, and so on, to organize the time capsule contents.

ROMANTIC ERA PROSE

from *A Vindication of the Rights of Woman*
by Mary Wollstonecraft

ABOUT THE AUTHOR

Mary Wollstonecraft (1759–1797) is widely recognized as one of the first great feminist writers and thinkers. At the age of nineteen, she took a position as a governess, but had to give it up to care for her mother during a protracted, terminal illness. In 1784, she helped her sister escape from a cruel husband. The two sisters, along with a friend, fled to London where they started a school. Although initially a success, the school ran into financial difficulties and closed. Wollstonecraft wrote her first book, *Thoughts on the Education of Daughters,* in 1786. This work was followed in 1788 by a novel, *Mary, a Fiction;* in 1790 by a book on the French Revolution, *A Vindication of the Rights of Men;* and in 1792 by Wollstonecraft's masterpiece, *A Vindication of the Rights of Woman.* During the years 1793–94, she went to France to observe the French Revolution firsthand. After adventures and misadventures, she returned to London and married the radical social philosopher William Godwin. The couple's child, Mary Wollstonecraft Godwin, grew up to write that astonishing Romantic novel *Frankenstein.* However, Wollstonecraft was not to know her daughter, for she died as a result of childbirth. A memoir written by Godwin after Wollstonecraft's death scandalized the public and led to a suppression of her work. However, twentieth-century women's rights advocates have come to view *A Vindication of the Rights of Woman* as a pioneering work on the necessity of equal education and opportunity for women.

ABOUT THE SELECTION

Mary Wollstonecraft lived in a time when women had few rights under the law. They could neither vote nor sue in court. They had few educational opportunities and were not allowed to attend universities. When they married, their husbands inherited all of their property. They had very few opportunities for work except as servants, nurses, or governesses (who performed tutoring and child-care duties). In *A Vindication of the Rights of Woman,* Wollstonecraft argued that such inequities reduced women to the dependent state of children; robbed them of self-sufficiency; made them weak, docile, and overly emotional; and kept them from becoming fully human. In contemporary terms, one might put Wollstonecraft's argument as follows: lack of opportunity and education made it impossible for women in Wollstonecraft's day to achieve their full potential.

ROMANTIC ERA PROSE / FROM A VINDICATION OF THE RIGHTS OF WOMAN **647**

ADDITIONAL RESOURCES

READER'S GUIDE
• Selection Worksheet, 8.17

ASSESSMENT PORTFOLIO
• Selection Check Test, 4.8.33
• Selection Test, 4.8.34

ESSENTIAL SKILLS PRACTICE BOOKS
• *Language,* 2.68, 2.149

ENRICHMENT ACTIVITIES

Students can hold a panel discussion on women's rights. Have students compare the rights of modern women to the rights of women in Wollstonecraft's era.

SUPPORT FOR LEP STUDENTS

Suggest that students stop at the end of each paragraph and ask themselves if they understand what they have read.

ADDITIONAL VOCABULARY

tyranny—oppressive and unjust government
attain—gain; accomplish; achieve
allow—admit; acknowledge
cunning—slyness; craftiness
propriety—proper; fitting
frail—morally weak; fragile
contemplation—thought
condescend—deign; agree to do something beneath one's dignity
cultivation—preparation; improvement
indefeasible—cannot be undone or made void
coincide—agree
expostulate—reason earnestly; object; remonstrate

GOALS/OBJECTIVES

Studying this lesson will enable students to

• understand and empathize with women of the Romantic Era who did not have the educational opportunities available today
• describe Wollstonecraft's contributions to the women's rights movement
• identify and correct split infinitives in their writing

• explain the situation of women during Wollstonecraft's time
• recognize and interpret allusions as they encounter them in their reading
• define *didactic criticism* and apply it to a piece of writing

PREREADING NOTES

READER'S JOURNAL

Encourage students to refer to specific time periods or people as they consider the question.

LANGUAGE SKILLS

Students might read passages aloud to better understand the author's tone.

▶Additional practice is provided in the *Essential Skills Practice Book: Language*, 2.149.

LITERARY TECHNIQUE

A **metaphor** is a figure of speech in which one thing is spoken or written about as if it were another. Point out the metaphor Wollstonecraft uses to explain women's behavior: "the current will run with destructive fury when there are no barriers to break its force." Ask students to identify the two things being compared and to discuss why Wollstonecraft chose this image.

VOCABULARY FROM THE SELECTION

caprice	puerile
epithet	satirize
ignoble	scrupulous
ingenious	specious
insinuate	

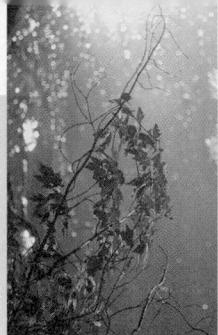

READER'S JOURNAL

During much of human history, women have been denied the rights that men have held to become educated, to own property, to work in skilled or professional jobs, and to participate in government. What happens to people who are raised under such circumstances? Write about this question in your journal.

LANGUAGE SKILLS

Read the Language Arts Survey, 2.149, "Tone and Voice." Then, as you read this selection from Wollstonecraft's book, note the tone that the author takes, and consider her reasons for taking that tone.

FROM

A Vindication of the Rights of Woman

MARY WOLLSTONECRAFT

To account for, and excuse the tyranny of man, many <u>ingenious</u> arguments have been brought forward to prove, that the two sexes, in the acquirement of virtue, ought to aim at attaining a very different character: or, to speak explicitly, women are not allowed to have sufficient strength of mind to acquire what really deserves the name of virtue. Yet it should seem, allowing them to have souls, that there is but one way appointed by Providence to lead *mankind* to either virtue or happiness.

If then women are not a swarm of ephemeron[1] triflers, why should they be kept in ignorance under the <u>specious</u> name of innocence? Men complain, and with reason, of the follies and <u>caprices</u> of our sex, when they do not keenly <u>satirize</u> our headstrong passions and groveling vices.—Behold, I should answer, the natural effect of ignorance! The mind will ever be unstable that has only prejudices to rest on, and the current will run with destructive fury when there are no barriers to break its force. Women are told from their infancy, and taught by the example of their mothers, that a little knowledge of human weakness, justly termed cunning, softness of temper, *outward* obedience, and a <u>scrupulous</u> attention to a <u>puerile</u> kind of propriety,

---

1. **ephemeron.** An insect that lives only one day

WORDS FOR EVERYDAY USE:

in • gen • ious (in jēn´ yəs) *adj.*, clever, original
spe • cious (spē shəs) *adj.*, seeming sound or logical while not really being so
ca • price (kə prēs´) *n.*, whim
sat • i • rize (sat´ə rīz) *vt.*, attack or ridicule with satire
scru • pu • lous (skrōō´ pyə ləs) *adj.*, extremely careful
pu • er • ile (pyōō´ər il) *adj.*, trivial, silly

VOCABULARY IN CONTEXT

- The fax machine is an <u>ingenious</u> invention!
- The detectives weren't deceived by the thief's <u>specious</u> alibi.
- What <u>caprice</u> led you to spend your money so foolishly?
- The witty comedy team <u>satirizes</u> political events.
- Make a <u>scrupulous</u> review of the material, because it has to be perfect for publication.
- Why would a mature adult still engage in such <u>puerile</u> activities?

will obtain for them the protection of man; and should they be beautiful, every thing else is needless, for, at least, twenty years of their lives.

Thus Milton describes our first frail mother; though when he tells us that women are formed for softness and sweet attractive grace,[2] I cannot comprehend his meaning, unless, in the true Mahometan strain, he meant to deprive us of souls, and <u>insinuate</u> that we were beings only designed by sweet attractive grace, and docile blind obedience, to gratify the senses of man when he can no longer soar on the wing of contemplation.

How grossly do they insult us who thus advise us only to render ourselves gentle, domestic brutes! For instance, the winning softness so warmly, and frequently, recommended, that governs by obeying. What childish expressions, and how insignificant is the being—can it be an immortal one? who will condescend to govern by such sinister methods! "Certainly," says Lord Bacon, "man is of kin to the beasts by his body; and if he be not of kin to God by his spirit, he is a base and <u>ignoble</u> creature!" Men, indeed, appear to me to act in a very unphilosophical manner when they try to secure the good conduct of women by attempting to keep them always in a state of childhood. Rousseau was more consistent when he wished to stop the progress of reason in both sexes, for if men eat of the tree of knowledge, women will come in for a taste; but, from the imperfect cultivation which their understandings now receive, they only attain a knowledge of evil.

Children, I grant, should be innocent; but when the <u>epithet</u> is applied to men, or women, it is but a civil term for weakness. For if it be allowed that women were destined by Providence to acquire human virtues, and by the exercise of their understandings, that stability of character which is the firmest ground to rest our future hopes upon, they must be permitted to turn to the fountain of light, and not forced to shape their course by the twinkling of a mere satellite.[3] Milton, I grant, was of a very different opinion; for he only bends to the indefeasible right of beauty, though it would be difficult to render two passages which I now mean to contrast, consistent. But into similar inconsistencies are great men often led by their senses.

> To whom thus Eve with *perfect beauty*
>   adorned.
> My Author and Disposer, what thou bidst
> *Unargued* I obey; So God ordains;
> God is thy *law, thou mine:*—to know no
>   more
> Is Woman's *happiest* knowledge and her
>   *praise.*[4]

These are exactly the arguments that I have used to children; but I have added, your reason is now gaining strength, and, till it arrives at some degree of maturity,

---

2. **Milton . . . grace.** In *Paradise Lost* (IV. 297–99), Milton wrote that men were formed for "contemplation" and "valor" while women were made for "softness" and "sweet attractive grace."
3. **satellite.** Body that orbits a larger body
4. **To whom . . . praise.** *Paradise Lost* IV. 634–38; Wollstonecraft has added italics to emphasize her point

WORDS FOR EVERYDAY USE:

in • sin • u • ate (in sin′yōō āt′) *vt.*, suggest, imply
ig • no • ble (ig nō′ bəl) *adj.*, dishonorable
ep • i • thet (ep′ ə thet′) *n.*, word or phrase used to characterize a person or thing

Although he was a Humanist, John Milton did not extend his belief in the possibilities of human nature to many of the women in his life. He had a difficult relationship with his first wife and showed little consideration for his three daughters.

ADDITIONAL QUESTIONS AND ACTIVITIES

• According to Wollstonecraft, what effect does Rousseau believe education has on men? on women?
Answer. She says that Rousseau believes education corrupts men and that women educated by men would become corrupt as well.

• What does Wollstonecraft mean when she says women should not be "forced to shape their course by the twinkling of a mere satellite" (paragraph 5)? What figure of speech is this phrase?
Answers. She means that women should be given equal access to education, or "the fountain of light," rather than settling for second-rate education. This figure of speech is a metaphor.

• What advantages do men gain when women are also free?
Answer. Women's freedom would enable both women and men to enjoy true fellowship, which, according to both Wollstonecraft and Milton, is possible only between equals. As well, men could choose their own professions, too, including those traditionally reserved for women.

 VOCABULARY IN CONTEXT

• Your critical tone <u>insinuates</u> that you don't agree with me.
• How can you excuse such <u>ignoble</u> actions?
• When asked to describe the spy, the general could only mutter the <u>epithet</u> "traitor."

Ask students to read or reread the selection from Milton's *Paradise Lost,* page 429. Have them list the ways in which Eve is described, the things she does, and any other comments made about Eve or about women in general. Ask them whether their lists support Wollstonecraft's judgment of Milton.

EX. What was the subject of Wollstonecraft's first book?
Wollstonecraft's first book was about educating daughters.

1. What have many "ingenious arguments" tried to excuse?
They have tried to excuse "the tyranny of man."

2. What follows from men and women both having souls?
It follows that both find virtue or happiness in the same way.

3. According to the author, what is the cause of women's follies and caprices?
They are caused by ignorance.

4. With whose ideas about women does the author take issue?
She argues with Milton's ideas.

5. What must women be allowed to do?
Women must be allowed to pursue knowledge.

Elenor. Frank Weston Benson, 1907.
Charles Henry Hayden Fund. Courtesy, Museum of Fine Arts, Boston

you must look up to me for advice—then you ought to *think,* and only rely on God.

Yet in the following lines Milton seems to coincide with me; when he makes Adam thus expostulate with his Maker.

> Hast thou not made me here thy substitute,
> And these inferior far beneath me set?
> Among *unequals* what society
> Can sort, what harmony or true delight?
> Which must be mutual, in proportion due
> Giv'n and *received;* but in *disparity*
> The one intense, the other still remiss
> Cannot well suit with either, but soon prove
> Tedious alike: of *fellowship* I speak
> Such as I seek, fit to participate
> All rational delight—[5]

In treating, therefore, of the manners of women, let us, disregarding sensual arguments, trace what we should endeavor to make them in order to cooperate, if the expression be not too bold, with the supreme Being. ∎

---

5. **Hast . . . delight.** *Paradise Lost* VII. 381–92; Wollstonecraft has added italics to show the inconsistency between this and the previous passage

Responding to the Selection

What feelings do you have about Milton's portrayal of Eve in the passage from *Paradise Lost*? Do you share Wollstonecraft's distaste for Milton's characterization of the ideal woman? Why, or why not?

Reviewing the Selection

RECALLING

1. According to the first paragraph, what reason was given by Wollstonecraft's contemporaries to support the belief that women cannot acquire virtue?

2. According to the beginning of paragraph 2, in what state were women in Wollstonecraft's time generally kept? What reason was given for keeping them in that state?

3. According to paragraph 2, what were women in Wollstonecraft's time told from infancy?

4. According to paragraph 4, in what state were women kept?

INTERPRETING

▶▶ 5. How does Wollstonecraft feel about the contention that women are incapable of attaining virtue? How do you know?

▶▶ 6. According to paragraph 2, why did women in Wollstonecraft's day often exhibit follies, caprices, headstrong passions, and groveling vices?

▶▶ 7. How does Milton's portrayal of Eve reflect the idea that women should be kept in a state of innocence and ignorance?

▶▶ 8. According to Wollstonecraft, what must women be allowed if they are indeed to be virtuous?

SYNTHESIZING

9. What contradiction does Wollstonecraft point out in the two passages from Milton? What is necessary, according to Wollstonecraft, if there is to be true fellowship between men and women? if women are to "cooperate . . . with the supreme Being [God]"?

10. What, according to the common opinions cited by Wollstonecraft, kept women in her time from exhibiting high, noble, virtuous behavior? What different reasons does Wollstonecraft give for the frailties and failures exhibited by women in her day? How does Wollstonecraft explain her contemporaries' "frailties" without condoning them?

ANSWERS FOR UNDERSTANDING LITERATURE

Responses will vary. Possible responses are given.

► See the evaluation forms for discussion, active listening, and oral communication, *Assessment Portfolio,* 7.11–7.14.

1. Allusion. Wollstonecraft disagreed with Rousseau's contentions that people should remain innocent and ignorant and that education is corruption. Instead, she wanted women to emerge from their ignorance and embrace the educational opportunities long enjoyed by men. For her, education is related to nobility and virtue because humans can only attain those states when using reason, rather than emotion or blind obedience.

► **Teaching Note:** Students may further explore Rousseau's "noble savage" theory by comparing it with Wollstonecraft's ideas.

2. Didactic Criticism. She argues that Milton contradicts himself in applying different standards of virtue to men and women, both of whom are God's creations. She dislikes Milton's portrayal of Eve as merely a beautiful subject of God's law and man's control. She points out that Milton contradicts himself by saying there can be no harmony in a society of unequals.

► **Teaching Note:** Students may wish to apply another type of criticism, such as feminist or romantic criticism, to Milton's argument. Refer to the Handbook of Literary Terms for definitions of these terms.

ANALYTIC SCALES FOR RESPONDING IN WRITING

Assign a score from 1 to 25 for each grading criterion below. (For more detailed evaluation, see the evaluation forms for writing, revising, and proofreading, *Assessment Portfolio,* 7.1–7.10.)

1. Laws
• **Content/Unity.** The set of laws presents laws to protect women.
• **Organization/Coherence.** The set of laws begins with a statement of purpose. Each law is stated in a topic sentence and followed by

(cont.)

Understanding Literature (Questions for Discussion)

1. **Allusion.** An **allusion** is a reference to a person, event, object, or work from history or literature. At one point in her essay, Wollstonecraft alludes to the ideas of the Romantic-Era French philosopher Jean-Jacques Rousseau. Rousseau believed that many of the ills of society were due to overreliance on reason. He praised the goodness that he believed existed among the "noble savages" who lived in a state of nature, uncorrupted by civilization and education. Rousseau's idea that people are naturally good and virtuous and that they learn, as a result of education and civilized culture, to be evil, had a great deal of influence on other thinkers and writers of the Romantic Era. Would Wollstonecraft agree with Rousseau that people should remain in a state of innocence and ignorance? Would she agree with Rousseau's ideas about the corrupting influence of education? What did she want for the women of her time and why? How, in her thought, is education related to nobility and virtue?

2. **Didactic Criticism. Didactic criticism** evaluates works of art in terms of the moral, ethical, or political message that they convey. What criticism does Wollstonecraft level at Milton in this piece? What does she dislike about Milton's portrayal of Eve? What contradiction does she point out in Milton's thought? Do you agree with Wollstonecraft? Why, or why not?

Responding in Writing

1. **Laws.** Suppose that you could travel back in time to Wollstonecraft's day and draft a Bill of Women's Rights to protect women against the abuses that they suffered then. What would your Bill of Women's Rights say? Draft such a set of laws to be included in a proposed new Constitution for England in the late 1700s. Before beginning your draft, you may want to review the Bill of Rights appended to the United States Constitution. You can find a copy of this Bill of Rights in most American history textbooks and in most libraries. (You may wish to prepare your finished Bill of Women's Rights as a pamphlet that might have been printed and distributed in Wollstonecraft's day.)

2. **Debate.** Wollstonecraft argues against the position that there are innate, inherited differences between the abilities of men and women. In our time, most people would agree with her. Indeed, modern laws protect women from discrimination based on the unjustified belief that women's abilities are innately inferior. However, in Wollstonecraft's time, her position was considered quite radical. Write an imaginary dialogue between Wollstonecraft and John Milton in which the two debate the relative abilities and proper roles of men and women. Draw upon material from Wollstonecraft's *Vindication.* Before writing, you may also want to review the passage from Milton's *Paradise Lost* on page 429.

ANALYTIC SCALES FOR RESPONDING IN WRITING (CONT.)

sentences that support and explain it.
• **Language/Style.** The set of laws uses vivid and precise nouns, verbs, and modifiers.
• **Conventions.** The set of laws avoids errors in spelling, grammar, usage, mechanics, and manuscript form.

2. Debate
• **Content/Unity.** The dialogue presents an imagined debate between Wollstonecraft and Milton on the subject of the abilities and roles of men and women.

• **Organization/Coherence.** The dialogue clearly indicates the speakers and their words. The language sounds like spoken language and is in keeping with the philosophic views of each writer.
• **Language/Style.** The dialogue uses vivid and precise nouns, verbs, and modifiers.
• **Conventions.** The dialogue avoids errors in spelling, grammar, usage, mechanics, and manuscript form.

Language Lab

Split Infinitives. Read the Language Arts Survey, 2.68, "Split Infinitives." Then rewrite the sentences below, correcting the split infinitives that you find.

1. Mary Wollstonecraft was moved to eloquently and persuasively write about the importance of equal access to education.

2. She considered education to obviously be key to improving the status of women because only by that means could they rise above the artificial "state of childhood" in which they were kept.

3. It is too facile to today anachronistically conclude that Wollstonecraft was too hard on other women of her time.

4. She often pauses to passionately rail against the silliness, coquetishness, follies, caprices, and overriding passions of many of her female contemporaries.

5. Reading her book, it is important for us to always remember that she is speaking about a time in which women were expected to behave in these ways.

PROJECTS

1. **Panel Discussion.** Do social norms, including attitudes and behaviors, still favor the development of men's abilities over those of women? Do men still have more opportunities than women to develop their physical and mental skills and to apply those skills in the world? Hold a panel discussion in class to consider these issues. Choose an equal number of men and women from among your classmates to sit on the panel (three of each would be a reasonable number). Elect a moderator to pose questions to the panel.

2. **Survey of the History of Writing about Women's Rights.** Divide into groups of four to six students each. Assign each group one of the following major works on women's rights: Mary Wollstonecraft's *A Vindication of the Rights of Woman,* John Stuart Mill's *On the Subjugation of Women,* Simon de Beauvoir's *The Second Sex,* Betty Friedan's *The Feminine Mystique,* and Susan Faludi's *Backlash.* Have each group study the work assigned to it and report to the class about the social conditions of the time in which the work was produced, as well as about the work's major ideas.

1. Mary Wollstonecraft was moved to write eloquently and persuasively about the importance of equal access to education.

2. She considered education to be obviously key to improving the status of women because only by that means could they rise above the artificial "state of childhood" in which they were kept.

3. It is too facile, today, to conclude anachronistically that Wollstonecraft was too hard on other women of her time.

4. She often pauses to rail passionately against the silliness, coquetishness, follies, caprices, and overriding passions of many of her female contemporaries.

5. Reading her book, it is important for us always to remember that she is speaking about a time in which women were expected to behave in these ways.

FOR MORE PRACTICE

Problem. Wollstonecraft explains that women tend to hysterically behave because they have been taught that such behavior is necessary.

Answer. Wollstonecraft explains that women tend to behave hysterically because they have been taught that such behavior is necessary.

►Additional practice is provided in the *Essential Skills Practice Book: Language,* 2.68.

PROJECT NOTES

►See the worksheets and evaluation forms for projects, *Assessment Portfolio,* 7.20–7.23.

1. Panel Discussion

• Encourage those students not on the panel to take notes during the discussion and to ask questions of panel members.

• If all students wish to discuss the topic, have the class divide into several small discussion groups. Students can share the results of their discussions with one another.

 2. Survey of the History of Writing about Women's Rights.

Within each group, students should decide how to share the responsibilities of researching and reporting.

READER'S GUIDE
- Selection Worksheet, 8.18

ASSESSMENT PORTFOLIO
- Selection Check Test, 4.8.35
- Selection Test, 4.8.36

ESSENTIAL SKILLS PRACTICE BOOKS
- *Study and Research*, 4.22, 4.23
- *Language*, 2.152

SUPPORT FOR LEP STUDENTS

π Explain that students will be reading a piece of nonfiction, the introduction to Shelley's fictional work. Students might begin a time line of events that led up to Shelley's writing of *Frankenstein,* adding key events as they read.

ADDITIONAL VOCABULARY

canto—any of the main divisions of certain long poems

successively—one after another

incessant—continuing in a way that seems endless

fitful—irregular or intermittent

incident—happening, occurrence

proposition—plan

renowned—famous

relinquish—give up, abandon

uncongenial—unpleasant, unsympathetic

incapability—lacking the ability or fitness for

invocation—act of calling on God, a god, or the Muses for help, or inspiration

Sanchean—practical, common sense

appertain—have to do with

capacity—power of receiving and holding

devout—showing reverence

vermicelli—thin spaghetti

acute—keen; quick of mind

unhallowed—unholy; wicked; profane

phantasm—deceptive likeness

PREREADING

ROMANTIC ERA PROSE

from the Introduction to *Frankenstein*
by Mary Wollstonecraft Shelley

ABOUT THE AUTHOR

Mary Wollstonecraft Shelley (1797–1851) was the daughter of William Godwin, a leading radical thinker of his time, and Mary Wollstonecraft, the famous women's rights activist who wrote *A Vindication of the Rights of Woman* (page 647). After Mary's mother died in childbirth, the little girl and her four siblings were raised by a stepmother. When she was fourteen, Mary was sent to Dundee, Scotland, to live with the family of one of her father's admirers. She lived there happily for two years and returned to London at sixteen years of age.

In London she met Percy Bysshe Shelley and soon eloped with him to Europe, despite her father's protests. The young couple faced many challenges, both financial and personal. Their first three children died before Mary was twenty-one, and several of their close relatives died untimely deaths during this period as well.

In this time of personal upheaval, Mary was inspired to write. She spent long hours discussing ideas with Lord Byron and Percy. During this period, Mary wrote *Frankenstein, or the Modern Prometheus.*

The multiple tragedies in their lives, including the deaths of their children and several close friends, caused Mary to retreat emotionally from Percy during his last years. As a result of this estrangement, Mary felt deep guilt when her dear husband and coworker died suddenly in 1822 in a boating accident. She is largely responsible for preserving Percy's work by annotating and publishing several editions after his death.

During the remaining twenty-five years of her life, Mary wrote five more novels, twenty-five short tales, and several volumes of literary criticism.

ABOUT THE SELECTION

In Switzerland, during the rainy summer of 1816, Mary Shelley wrote *Frankenstein,* probably the greatest Gothic novel and science fiction fantasy ever written. The well-known story of the creation of a monster from human parts has been presented in several movies. More than a horror story, *Frankenstein* explores themes of creation and responsibility. It remains fascinating today as we ponder whether science has gone too far and realize the impact of some of the strides science has made. The **Introduction** was written for the third edition of *Frankenstein,* fifteen years after the book was first published.

GOALS/OBJECTIVES

Studying this lesson will enable students to

- experience the speaker's excitement about the creative process and appreciate her affection for the work she created
- describe Mary Shelley's connections and contributions to the Romantic Era
- identify and eliminate clichés and euphemisms

- explain how Shelley developed the idea for *Frankenstein*
- explain *catharsis* and identify its role in Shelley's development of her horror story
- define *autobiography* and recognize autobiographical elements in their reading

READER'S JOURNAL

Write a short essay describing your ideas about the morality of scientists creating new species through genetic engineering. Explore the positive and negative consequences that might result from such experiments, both for the rest of the world and for the creations themselves.

RESEARCH SKILLS

Read the Language Arts Survey, 4.22, "Using the Card Catalog." Go to the library and look up ghost stories. Make a list of the authors and titles of these tales.

FROM THE INTRODUCTION TO

Frankenstein

MARY WOLLSTONECRAFT SHELLEY

In the summer of 1816, we[1] visited Switzerland and became the neighbors of Lord Byron. At first we spent our pleasant hours on the lake or wandering on its shores; and Lord Byron, who was writing the third canto of *Childe Harold*, was the only one among us who put his thoughts upon paper. These, as he brought them successively to us, clothed in all the light and harmony of poetry, seemed to stamp as divine the glories of heaven and earth, whose influences we partook with him.

But it proved a wet, <u>ungenial</u> summer, and incessant rain often confined us for days to the house. Some volumes of ghost stories, translated from the German into French, fell into our hands. There was the *History of the Inconstant Lover*, who, when he thought to clasp the bride to whom he had pledged his vows, found himself in the arms of the pale ghost of her whom he had deserted. There was the tale of the

sinful founder of his race whose miserable doom it was to bestow the kiss of death on all the younger sons of his fated house, just when they reached the age of promise. His gigantic, shadowy form, clothed like the ghost in *Hamlet*, in complete armor but with the beaver[2] up, was seen at midnight, by the moon's fitful beams, to advance slowly along the gloomy avenue. The shape was lost beneath the shadow of the castle walls; but soon a gate swung back, a step was heard, the door of the chamber opened, and he advanced to the couch of the blooming youths, cradled in healthy sleep. Eternal sorrow sat upon his face as he bent down and kissed the forehead of the boys, who from that hour withered like flowers snapped upon the stalk. I have not seen

---

1. **we.** Mary Shelley, Percy Bysshe Shelley, and their children
2. **beaver.** Piece of armor that covers the face

WORDS FOR
EVERYDAY USE:
    un • gen • i • al (un jēn´yəl) *adj.,* unpleasant

VOCABULARY IN CONTEXT

- The rude man's <u>ungenial</u> remarks made everyone feel uncomfortable.

PREREADING NOTES

READER'S JOURNAL

Students might share their essays in small groups or as class presentations. Encourage a discussion of student ideas.

RESEARCH SKILLS

Suggest that students look for several categories of ghost stories, such as story anthologies, translations from other languages, folklore from particular cultures, and so on.

►Additional practice is provided in the *Essential Skills Practice Book: Study and Research,* 4.22, 4.23.

ENRICHMENT ACTIVITIES

 Frankenstein's monster is a human creation. Students can discuss or write about the idea that all people are human creations. How much of what people are like is due to nature and how much is a product of society? Have them consider such social functions as education, mores and morals, law, and language.

ADDITIONAL QUESTIONS AND ACTIVITIES

Why do you think Shelley told about some of the ghost stories she read that summer?

Answer. She set the mood and she gave the reader something to compare to her own story.

VOCABULARY FROM THE SELECTION

platitude	reverie
progeny	ungenial

these stories since then, but their incidents are as fresh in my mind as if I had read them yesterday.

"We will each write a ghost story," said Lord Byron, and his proposition was acceded to. There were four of us.[3] The noble author began a tale, a fragment of which he printed at the end of his poem of Mazeppa. Shelley, more apt to embody ideas and sentiments in the radiance of brilliant imagery and in the music of the most melodious verse that adorns our language than to invent the machinery of a story, commenced one founded on the experiences of his early life. Poor Polidori had some terrible idea about a skull-headed lady who was so punished for peeping through a keyhole—what to see I forget: something very shocking and wrong of course; but when she was reduced to a worse condition than the renowned Tom of Coventry,[4] he did not know what to do with her, and was obliged to dispatch her to the tomb of the Capulets, the only place for which she was fitted. The illustrious poets also, annoyed by the <u>platitude</u> of prose, speedily relinquished their uncongenial task.

What idea did Mary get from the conversation between Percy and Lord Byron?

I busied myself *to think of a story*—a story to rival those which had excited us to this task. One which would speak to the mysterious fears of our nature and awaken thrilling horror—one to make the reader dread to look round, to curdle the blood, and quicken the beatings of the heart. If I did not accomplish these things, my ghost story would be unworthy of its name. I thought and pondered—vainly. I felt that blank incapability of invention which is the greatest misery of authorship, when dull

Nothing replies to our anxious invocations. "Have you thought of a story?" I was asked each morning, and each morning I was forced to reply with a mortifying negative.

Everything must have a beginning, to speak in Sanchean phrase; and that beginning must be linked to something that went before. The Hindus give the world an elephant to support it, but they make the elephant stand upon a tortoise. Invention, it must be humbly admitted, does not consist in creating out of void, but out of chaos; the materials must, in the first place, be afforded: it can give form to dark, shapeless substances but cannot bring into being the substance itself. In all matters of discovery and invention, even of those that appertain to the imagination, we are continually reminded of the story of Columbus and his egg. Invention consists in the capacity of seizing on the capabilities of a subject and in the power of molding and fashioning ideas suggested by it.

Many and long were the conversations between Lord Byron and Shelley to which I was a devout, but nearly silent, listener. During one of these, various philosophical doctrines were discussed, and among others the nature of the principle of life and whether there was any probability of its ever being discovered and communicated. They talked of the experiments of Dr. Darwin[5] (I speak not of what the doctor

---

3. **four of us.** Byron, Mary and Percy Bysshe Shelley, and John William Polidori
4. **Tom of Coventry.** Tom of Coventry, or Peeping Tom, was, according to legend, struck blind for looking at the naked Lady Godiva.
5. **Dr. Darwin.** Erasmus Darwin was a scientist and a poet.

WORDS FOR EVERYDAY USE: **plat • i • tude** (plat´ ə tōōd´) *n.,* commonplace quality

VOCABULARY IN CONTEXT

• I found her ideas a delightful change from the <u>platitudes</u> voiced by the other speakers.
• I was startled out of my <u>reverie</u> by a telephone's abrupt ringing.

really did or said that he did, but, as more to my purpose, of what was then spoken of as having been done by him), who preserved a piece of vermicelli in a glass case till by some extraordinary means it began to move with voluntary motion. Not thus, after all, would life be given. Perhaps a corpse would be reanimated; galvanism[6] had given token of such things: perhaps the component parts of a creature might be manufactured, brought together, and endued with vital warmth.

Night waned upon this talk, and even the witching hour had gone by before we retired to rest. When I placed my head on my pillow, I did not sleep, nor could I be said to think. My imagination, unbidden, possessed and guided me, gifting the successive images that arose in my mind with a vividness far beyond the usual bounds of <u>reverie</u>. I saw—with shut eyes, but acute mental vision—I saw the pale student of unhallowed arts kneeling beside the thing he had put together. I saw the hideous phantasm of a man stretched out, and then, on the working of some powerful engine, show signs of life, and stir with an uneasy, half-vital motion. Frightful must it be, for supremely frightful would be the effect of any human endeavor to mock the stupendous mechanism of the Creator of the world. His success would terrify the artist; he would rush away from his odious handiwork, horror-stricken. He would hope that, left to itself, the slight spark of life which he had communicated would fade, that this thing which had received such imperfect animation would subside into dead matter, and he might sleep in the belief that the silence of the grave would quench forever the transient existence of the hideous corpse which he had looked upon as the cradle of life. He sleeps; but he is awakened; he opens his eyes; behold, the horrid thing stands at his bedside, opening his curtains, and looking on him with yellow, watery, but speculative eyes.

I opened mine in terror. The idea so possessed my mind that a thrill of fear ran through me, and I wished to exchange the ghastly image of my fancy for the realities around. I see them still: the very room, the dark parquet, the closed shutters with the moonlight struggling through, and the sense I had that the glassy lake and white high Alps were beyond. I could not so easily get rid of my hideous phantom; still it haunted me. I must try to think of something else. I recurred to my ghost story—my tiresome unlucky ghost story! O! if I could only contrive one which would frighten my reader as I myself had been frightened that night!

Swift as light and as cheering was the idea that broke in upon me. "I have found it! What terrified me will terrify others; and I need only describe the specter which had haunted my midnight pillow." On the morrow I announced that I had *thought of a story*. I began that day with the words "It was on a dreary night of November," making only a transcript of the grim terrors of my waking dream.

At first I thought but of a few pages, of a short tale, but Shelley urged me to develop the idea at greater length. I certainly did not owe the suggestion of one incident, nor scarcely of one train of feeling, to my

❶
Why was Mary's dream so frightful?

---

6. **galvanism.** Galvanism uses electric currents to cause movement in dead muscles.

WORDS FOR EVERYDAY USE:

rev • er • ie (rev´ər ē) *n.,* dreaming

Erasmus Darwin (1731–1802) was an English doctor who also studied botany and wrote poetry. His book *Zoönomia* (1794–1796) set forth theories on evolutionary development. His grandson, Charles Darwin, established the theory of evolution as it is known today.

ANSWER TO GUIDED READING QUESTION

❶ Her dream was frightful because the human creator had made something that defied the natural order of God's creation and that was beyond his control.

ANSWER TO GUIDED READING QUESTION

❶ She has special affection for her creation because it reminds her of a happy time in her life, before her husband and children died. As she writes this, she is feeling sad and alone.

ANSWERS TO SELECTION CHECK TEST 4.8.35

EX. Whose work did Mary Shelley edit?
She edited her husband, Percy's, work.

1. What story is told in this introduction?
This introduction tells how Shelley came to write *Frankenstein*.

2. Who was Shelley's neighbor in Switzerland?
Byron was her neighbor.

3. What did that neighbor propose?
He proposed that everyone write a ghost story.

4. What terrified Shelley?
She was terrified by a dream.

5. What did Shelley's husband suggest about her tale?
He suggested that she "develop the idea at greater length."

RESPONDING TO THE SELECTION

Remind students to consider the physical isolation of these four people and how that isolation might heighten the effect of their ghost stories.

VOCABULARY IN CONTEXT

• The king's first-born son succeeded him on the throne, and his other <u>progeny</u> became rulers of principalities.

---

husband, and yet but for his incitement, it would never have taken the form in which it was presented to the world. From this declaration I must except the preface. As far as I can recollect, it was entirely written by him.

And now, once again, I bid my hideous <u>progeny</u> go forth and prosper. I have an affection for it, for it was the offspring of happy days, when death and grief were but words which found no true echo in my heart. Its several pages speak of many a walk, many a drive, and many a conversation, when I was not alone; and my companion was one who, in this world, I shall never see more. But this is for myself: my readers have nothing to do with these associations. ∎

❶
Why does Mary have special affection for her creation? How is she feeling as she writes this?

Responding to the Selection

Role play a meeting like the one described in the selection between Mary Shelley; her husband, Percy Shelley; Lord Byron; and John Polidori, Byron's physician. Have the role play consist of a discussion of ghosts and ghouls. Remember that Mary Shelley is a very imaginative and fearful woman. Percy, her husband, is a great poet with a gift for creating visual images with words. He has been rejected by English society because of his eccentric lifestyle. Lord Byron is a very famous poet who loves adventure and romance and who also has been criticized harshly by the English public. Dr. Polidori, Byron's doctor, may have particular insights into the subject of ghouls and monsters because of his medical background.

WORDS FOR EVERYDAY USE: **prog • e • ny** (präj´ə nē) *n.,* offspring

Reviewing the Selection

RECALLING

1. What were some of the ghost stories the group read when they were confined to the house because of rain?

2. What was Lord Byron's idea for the group?

3. What was the nature of the discussion between Byron and Percy Shelley that led to Mary's idea for her story?

4. What is the reason for Mary Shelley's affection for the monster, according to the last paragraph of the selection?

INTERPRETING

▶▶ 5. Why might Mary Shelley have felt fearful about presenting her writing to this gathering?

▶▶ 6. Reread Mary Shelley's biography on page 654. What special significance might the idea of creating life have for her, in terms of motherhood and personal grief?

▶▶ 7. What does Shelley mean by "mock the stupendous mechanism of the Creator of the world" in paragraph 7 of the selection?

▶▶ 8. What does Shelley mean by "I bid my hideous progeny go forth and prosper" in the last paragraph of the selection?

SYNTHESIZING

9. Most great novels have been written by authors who were in the middle of their lives, not in their youth. Mary Shelley herself wondered how she, as a girl of nineteen, had been able to write the masterpiece *Frankenstein*. The book always has been recognized as much more than a ghost story; it has deep and universal significance, addressing the issues of creativity, human pride, evil, abandonment by God, and other important themes. What factors in Mary Shelley's life might have given her the genius and experience to write this novel?

10. Women in Mary Shelley's time had very little power in the world. How might this have affected their interior lives, their imaginations, and their emotional health?

Understanding Literature (Questions for Discussion)

---

1. **Autobiography.** An **autobiography** is the story of a person's life, written by that person. Since she originally published *Frankenstein* anonymously, the selection was her public declaration that she herself, not her husband, was the author of the great novel. Although this introduction tells only part of Mary Shelley's life, it is very revealing. What do you learn about Shelley's life from this selection? Why do you think she felt compelled to include this autobiographical information in the introduction to her book?

ROMANTIC ERA PROSE / FROM THE INTRODUCTION TO *FRANKENSTEIN* **659**

ANSWERS FOR UNDERSTANDING LITERATURE

▶ See the evaluation forms for discussion, active listening, and oral communication, *Assessment Portfolio,* 7.11–7.14. *Responses will vary. Possible responses are given.*

1. **Autobiography.** Shelley reveals herself as imaginative, driven to think of a story yet uncertain of her abilities. She may have included this information as an explanation since many people felt it improbable that a young woman could have written this story.

▶ **Teaching Note:** Remind students to refer also to the biographical information on Percy Bysshe Shelley (page 622).

2. **Catharsis.** At first the Shelleys told ghost stories to entertain themselves when the weather kept them indoors. For Byron, Polidori, and Percy Shelley, telling ghost stories was not especially cathartic; Mary Shelley does not mention the effect of their stories. However,

(cont.)

ANSWERS FOR REVIEWING THE SELECTION

RECALLING

1. The group read the *History of the Inconstant Lover* and the story of a ghost who bestows the kiss of death on his race.

2. Byron proposed that each person write a ghost story.

3. Byron and Shelley discussed whether it was possible for humans to discover the mechanisms for creating life, specifically the use of electricity to bring a corpse to life.

4. She has affection for the monster because she created the idea of the monster during a happy time in her life.

INTERPRETING

Responses will vary. Possible responses are given.

5. She may have felt intimidated by Byron and Shelley, who were writers by trade. She might also have felt additional pressure because she was the only woman.

6. Mary Shelley lost three of her young children shortly before beginning her story. The experience of helping to create her children's lives and then losing them adds special significance to the idea of creating life in her work.

7. She means that the human creator has crossed the natural boundary between humans and God; the complex nature of creation is not something to be undertaken by humans.

8. She wishes for the book to be successful.

SYNTHESIZING

Responses will vary. Possible responses are given.

9. As the child of two social reformers and writers, Mary Shelley probably received much encouragement to explore her creativity and her ideas.

10. Women of Shelley's time probably had to keep their ideas to themselves. While this restriction might have led to an active imagination, it might also have created feelings of dejection and despair.

ANALYTIC SCALES FOR RESPONDING IN WRITING

Assign a score from 1 to 25 for each grading criterion below. (For more detailed evaluation, see the evaluation forms for writing, revising, and proofreading, *Assessment Portfolio*, 7.1–7.10.)

Gothic Description

• **Content/Unity.** The tale presents a frightening or mysterious tale in keeping with the Gothic tradition.

• **Organization/Coherence.** The conflict is presented at the beginning of the tale, the action builds to a climax, and the conflict is resolved.

• **Language/Style.** The tale uses vivid and precise nouns, verbs, and modifiers.

• **Conventions.** The tale avoids errors in spelling, grammar, usage, mechanics, and manuscript form.

PROJECT NOTES

▶**Teaching Note:** See the worksheets and evaluation forms for projects, *Assessment Portfolio*, 7.20–7.23.

Horror Movie

• Students might want to read the novel before writing a screenplay.

• Encourage students to perform the scenes they have written.

• Students might want to use information about genetic technology to write a modern-day version of the Frankenstein story.

ANSWERS FOR UNDERSTANDING LITERATURE (CONT.)

she decided to write her story both to rid herself of the terrifying images of her dream and to incite the same fear in her readers.

▶**Teaching Note:** Have students consider the different interpretations of catharsis as they discuss the role of catharsis here. Refer to the Handbook of Literary Terms for a discussion about the possible interpretations of Aristotle's theory of catharsis.

660 TEACHER'S EDITION

---

2. **Catharsis.** The ancient Greek philosopher Aristotle described tragedy as bringing about a **catharsis,** or purging, of the emotions of fear and pity. Discuss the role of catharsis in the telling of ghost stories and its role in Mary Shelley's idea for the novel *Frankenstein*.

Responding in Writing

Gothic Description. A **Gothic tale** is a story containing elements of horror, suspense, mystery, and magic. Write a one-paragraph description of a haunted house. Before you begin drafting your paragraph, think about how haunted houses have been depicted in books and movies. Then freewrite your own details about a true, Gothic, haunted house.

Language Lab

Clichés and Euphemisms. Read the Language Arts Survey, 2.152, "Clichés and Euphemisms." Then rewrite the underlined phrase in each sentence to eliminate either the cliché or the euphemism.

1. When she was a child, Mary Shelley <u>worshiped the ground her father walked on</u>.

2. Mary Shelley appears to have been fascinated with <u>the end of life as we know it</u>.

3. The young author was <u>white as a sheet</u> after she awakened from her nightmare.

4. The <u>unusual being</u> created by Dr. Frankenstein was lonely and felt abandoned by his creator.

5. The Romantic writers cherished their individuality and their emotions, though their feelings sometimes caused them to <u>tear their hair and gnash their teeth</u>.

PROJECT

Horror Movie. Write Act I, Scene 1 of a screenplay based on the novel *Frankenstein*. First describe the setting in which the scene will take place. Then briefly describe the characters in the scene. Next to each line of dialogue, write stage directions, telling the actors what emotions you want them to express in the lines.

ANSWERS FOR LANGUAGE LAB

Responses will vary. Possible responses are given.

1. When she was a child, Mary Shelley greatly admired her father.

2. Mary Shelley appears to have been fascinated with death.

3. The young author was pale and terrified after she awakened from her nightmare.

4. The monster created by Dr. Frankenstein was lonely and felt abandoned by his creator.

5. The Romantic writers cherished their individuality and their emotions, though their feelings sometimes caused them to despair.

▶Additional practice is provided in the *Essential Skills Practice Book: Language*, 2.152.

"The Divine Image" by William Blake

To Mercy, Pity, Peace, and Love,
All pray in their distress,
And to these virtues of delight
Return their thankfulness.

5 For Mercy, Pity, Peace, and Love,
Is God, our father dear:
And Mercy, Pity, Peace, and Love,
Is Man, his child and care.

For Mercy has a human heart,
10 Pity, a human face,
And Love, the human form divine,
And Peace, the human dress.

Then every man of every clime,
That prays in his distress,
15 Prays to the human form divine,
Love, Mercy, Pity, Peace.

And all must love the human form,
In heathen, Turk, or Jew.
Where Mercy, Love, & Pity dwell,
20 There God is dwelling too.

"The Fly" by William Blake

Little Fly
Thy summer's play
My thoughtless hand
Has brush'd away

5 Am not I
A fly like thee?
Or art not thou
A man like me?

For I dance
10 And drink & sing,
Till some blind hand
Shall brush my wing.

If thought is life
And strength & breath,
15 And the want
Of thought is death;

Then am I
A happy fly.
If I live,
20 Or if I die.

"The Garden of Love" by William Blake

I went to the Garden of Love,
And saw what I never had seen:
A Chapel was built in the midst,
Where I used to play on the green.

5 And the gates of this Chapel were shut,
And "Thou shalt not" writ over the door;
So I turn'd to the Garden of Love,
That so many sweet flowers bore,

And I saw it was filled with graves,
10 And tombstones where flowers should be;
And Priests in black gowns were walking their
    rounds,
And binding with briars my joys & desires.

Song from the Preface to *Milton* ("And did those feet . . .") by William Blake

And did those feet in ancient time
Walk upon England's mountains green?[1]
And was the holy Lamb of God
On England's pleasant pastures seen?

5 And did the Countenance Divine
Shine forth upon our clouded hills?
And was Jerusalem builded here,
Among those dark Satanic Mills?

Bring me my Bow of burning gold,
10 Bring me my Arrows of desire,
Bring me my Spear; O clouds unfold!
Bring me my Chariot of fire!

I will not cease from Mental Fight,
Nor shall my Sword sleep in my hand,
15 Till we have built Jerusalem
In England's green & pleasant Land.

---

1. **And . . . green?** The poem is based on a belief, held by some, that Jesus visited England with Joseph of Arimathea.

"THE DIVINE IMAGE" "THE FLY" "THE GARDEN OF LOVE" SONG FROM THE PREFACE TO *MILTON*

About the Author. A biography of **William Blake** appears on page 589.

About the Selections. "The Divine Image," "The Fly," and "The Garden of Love" appeared in *Songs of Innocence and of Experience.* "The Divine Image" represents innocence, and "The Fly" and "The Garden of Love" represent experience. After the publication of *Songs,* Blake spent most of the next twenty-six years working on his "prophetic poems." In *Milton,* the poet John Milton returns to earth to fight Satan, correct wrongs, and preach forgiveness. Like most of Blake's poetry, the Song from the Preface to *Milton* is Highly symbolic. Ask students to discuss the parallel between Jesus and John Milton.

This song is very popular in England today, where it goes by the title "Jerusalem."

ADDITIONAL QUESTIONS AND ACTIVITIES

• In "The Divine Image," what does Blake say about the relationship between God and humans?

Answer. He says that God exists in humans when they show mercy, pity, peace, and love.

• How do "The Fly" and "The Garden of Love" represent experience?

Answer. The speaker of "The Fly" is aware of his mortality. The speaker of "The Garden of Love" reveals disillusionment that humans have defiled nature's chapel.

• Who is the speaker in the Song from the Preface to *Milton?* What is his goal? What might this goal symbolize?

Answers. The speaker is Milton. His goal is to build Jerusalem in England. This might symbolize a peaceful and pious community.

"I WANDERED LONELY
AS A CLOUD"
"SHE DWELT AMONG THE
UNTRODDEN WAYS"
"ODE: INTIMATIONS OF
IMMORTALITY"

About the Author. A biography of **William Wordsworth** appears on page 605.

About the Selections. Wordsworth celebrates his connection with nature in "I Wandered Lonely as a Cloud," describing the natural beauty he sees and using it as a symbol of his peace and happiness. "She Dwelt among the Untrodden Ways," which appeared in *Lyrical Ballads,* exemplifies one of the "situations from common life" that Wordsworth believed were the essence of poetry. In one of his greatest odes, "Ode: Intimations of Immortality," Wordsworth contemplates the natural human connection to the universal spirit.

ADDITIONAL QUESTIONS AND ACTIVITIES

1. What does the speaker of "Ode: Intimations of Immortality" mean by "The Child is Father of the Man"?

Answer. Adults should try to experience the world with a child's freshness and innocence.

2. In stanza 1, how does the speaker say he used to see things?

Answer. He used to see things as if they had a "celestial light."

3. In stanza 2, what does the speaker say has passed away from the earth? To what is he referring?

Answers. A glory has passed away from the earth. He is referring to the fact that the beauty of nature no longer seems glorious, as it did in his youth.

4. In stanza 3, what keeps the speaker from losing himself in his grief?

Answer. He hears the happy shouts of the Shepherd-boy.

"I Wandered Lonely as a Cloud"
by William Wordsworth

I wandered lonely as a cloud
That floats on high o'er vales and hills,
When all at once I saw a crowd,
A host, of golden daffodils;
5 Beside the lake, beneath the trees,
Fluttering and dancing in the breeze.

Continuous as the stars that shine
And twinkle on the milky way,
They stretched in never-ending line
10 Along the margin of a bay:
Ten thousand saw I at a glance,
Tossing their heads in sprightly dance.

The waves beside them danced; but they
Out-did the sparkling waves in glee:
15 A poet could not but be gay,
In such a jocund company:
I gazed—and gazed—but little thought
What wealth the show to me had brought:

For oft, when on my couch I lie
20 In vacant or in pensive mood,
They flash upon that inward eye
Which is the bliss of solitude;
And then my heart with pleasure fills,
And dances with the daffodils.

"She Dwelt among the Untrodden Ways"
by William Wordsworth

She dwelt among the untrodden ways
    Beside the springs of Dove,[1]
A Maid whom there were none to praise
    And very few to love:

5 A violet by a mossy stone
    Half hidden from the eye!
—Fair as a star, when only one
    Is shining in the sky.

She lived unknown, and few could know
10   When Lucy ceased to be;
But she is in her grave, and, oh,
    The difference to me!

---

1. **Dove.** A river in England

"Ode: Intimations of Immortality from Recollections of Early Childhood"
by William Wordsworth

The Child is Father of the Man;
And I could wish my days to be
Bound each to each by natural piety.

1

There was a time when meadow, grove, and stream,
The earth, and every common sight,
    To me did seem
    Apparelled in celestial light,
5 The glory and the freshness of a dream.
It is not now as it hath been of yore;—
    Turn wheresoe'er I may,
      By night or day,
The things which I have seen I now can see no more.

2

10   The Rainbow comes and goes,
    And lovely is the Rose,
    The Moon doth with delight
Look round her when the heavens are bare,
    Waters on a starry night
15   Are beautiful and fair;
    The sunshine is a glorious birth;
    But yet I know, where'er I go,
That there hath past away a glory from the earth.

3

Now, while the birds thus sing a joyous song,
20   And while the young lambs bound
    As to the tabor's sound,
To me alone there came a thought of grief:
A timely utterance gave that thought relief,
    And I again am strong:
25 The cataracts blow their trumpets from the steep;
No more shall grief of mine the season wrong;
I hear the Echoes through the mountains throng,
The Winds come to me from the fields of sleep,
    And all the earth is gay;
30   Land and sea
    Give themselves up to jollity,
    And with the heart of May
Doth every Beast keep holiday;—
    Thou Child of Joy,
Shout round me, let me hear thy shouts, thou
35 happy Shepherd-boy!

4

Ye blessed Creatures, I have heard the call
    Ye to each other make; I see

The heavens laugh with you in your jubilee;
My heart is at your festival,
40 My head hath its coronal,
The fulness of your bliss, I feel—I feel it all.
Oh evil day! if I were sullen
While Earth herself is adorning,
This sweet May-morning,
45 And the Children are culling
On every side,
In a thousand valleys far and wide,
Fresh flowers; while the sun shines warm,
And the Babe leaps up on his Mother's arm:—
50 I hear, I hear, with joy I hear!
—But there's a Tree, of many, one,
A single Field which I have looked upon,
Both of them speak of something that is gone:
The Pansy at my feet
55 Doth the same tale repeat:
Whither is fled the visionary gleam?
Where is it now, the glory and the dream?

5

Our birth is but a sleep and a forgetting:
The Soul that rises with us, our life's Star,
60 Hath had elsewhere its setting,
And cometh from afar:
Not in entire forgetfulness,
And not in utter nakedness,
But trailing clouds of glory do we come
65 From God, who is our home:
Heaven lies about us in our infancy!
Shades of the prison-house begin to close
Upon the growing Boy,
But He beholds the light, and whence it flows,
70 He sees it in his joy;
The Youth, who daily farther from the east
Must travel, still is Nature's Priest,
And by the vision splendid
Is on his way attended;
75 At length the Man perceives it die away
And fade into the light of common day.

6

Earth fills her lap with pleasures of her own;
Yearnings she hath in her own natural kind,
And, even with something of a Mother's mind,
80 And no unworthy aim,
The homely Nurse doth all she can
To make her Foster-child, her Inmate Man,
Forget the glories he hath known,
And that imperial palace whence he came.

7

85 Behold the Child among his new-born blisses,
A six years' Darling of a pigmy size!
See, where 'mid work of his own hand he lies,
Fretted by sallies of his mother's kisses,
With light upon him from his father's eyes!
90 See, at his feet, some little plan or chart,
Some fragment from his dream of human life,
Shaped by himself with newly-learnèd art;
A wedding or a festival,
A mourning or a funeral;
95 And this hath now his heart,
And unto this he frames his song:
Then will he fit his tongue
To dialogues of business, love, or strife;
But it will not be long
100 Ere this be thrown aside,
And with new joy and pride
The little Actor cons another part;
Filling from time to time his "humorous stage"
With all the Persons, down to palsied Age,
105 That Life brings with her in her equipage;
As if his whole vocation
Were endless imitation.

8

Thou, whose exterior semblance doth belie
Thy Soul's immensity;
110 Thou best Philosopher, who yet dost keep
Thy heritage, thou Eye among the blind,
That, deaf and silent, read'st the eternal deep,
Haunted for ever by the eternal mind,—
Mighty Prophet! Seer blest!
115 On whom those truths do rest,
Which we are toiling all our lives to find,
In darkness lost, the darkness of the grave;
Thou, over whom thy Immortality
Broods like the Day, a Master o'er a Slave,
120 A Presence which is not to be put by;
Thou little Child, yet glorious in the might
Of heaven-born freedom on thy being's height,
Why with such earnest pains dost thou provoke
The years to bring the inevitable yoke,
125 Thus blindly with thy blessedness at strife?
Full soon thy Soul shall have her earthly freight,
And custom lie upon thee with a weight,
Heavy as frost, and deep almost as life!

9

O joy! that in our embers
130 Is something that doth live,
That nature yet remembers

ADDITIONAL QUESTIONS AND ACTIVITIES

1. In stanza 4, what causes the speaker to ask "Where is it now, the glory and the dream"?

Answer. He sees the natural world around him and feels that something is missing from his observations and experience of it.

2. In stanza 5, how does the speaker explain a child's connection to nature?

Answer. Children are born remembering their time in heaven, before their souls came to earth; therefore, they are closer to God and nature, God's creation.

3. In stanzas 5 and 6, what metaphor does Wordsworth use for the world?

Answer. He uses the metaphor of a prison, referring to the "prison-house" and "Inmate Man."

4. In stanza 8, why does the speaker wonder at the child's desire to gain knowledge of human life?

Answer. He wonders because the child still has knowledge of the glory of immortality.

5. In stanzas 5–8, what shift occurs in the speaker's voice? What effect does this shift have?

Answers. The speaker shifts from "I" to the plural "We." This plural voice includes the reader in the speaker's thoughts and suggests their universality.

What was so fugitive!
The thought of our past years in me doth breed
Perpetual benediction: not indeed
135   For that which is most worthy to be blest;
Delight and liberty, the simple creed
Of Childhood, whether busy or at rest,
With new-fledged hope still fluttering in his
 breast:—
  Not for these I raise
140   The song of thanks and praise;
 But for those obstinate questionings
 Of sense and outward things,
 Fallings from us, vanishings;
 Blank misgivings of a Creature
145   Moving about in worlds not realised,
High instincts before which our mortal Nature
Did tremble like a guilty Thing surprised:
  But for those first affections,
  Those shadowy recollections,
150   Which, be they what they may,
Are yet the fountain light of all our day,
Are yet a master light of all our seeing;
  Uphold us, cherish, and have power to make
Our noisy years seem moments in the being
155   Of the eternal Silence: truths that wake
  To perish never;
Which neither listlessness, nor mad endeavor,
  Nor Man nor Boy,
Nor all that is at enmity with joy,
160   Can utterly abolish or destroy!
 Hence in a season of calm weather
  Though inland far we be,
Our Souls have sight of that immortal sea
  Which brought us hither,
165   Can in a moment travel thither,
And see the Children sport upon the shore,
And hear the mighty waters rolling evermore.

10

Then sing, ye Birds, sing, sing a joyous song!
  And let the young Lambs bound
170   As to the tabor's sound!
We in thought will join your throng,
  Ye that pipe and ye that play,
  Ye that through your hearts to-day
  Feel the gladness of the May!
What though the radiance which was once so
175   bright
Be now for ever taken from my sight,
  Though nothing can bring back the hour
Of splendor in the grass, of glory in the flower;
  We will grieve not, rather find

180   Strength in what remains behind;
  In the primal sympathy
  Which having been must ever be;
  In the soothing thoughts that spring
  Out of human suffering;
185   In the faith that looks through death,
In years that bring the philosophic mind.

11

And O, ye Fountains, Meadows, Hills, and Groves,
Forebode not any severing of our loves!
Yet in my heart of hearts I feel your might;
190   I only have relinquished one delight
To live beneath your more habitual sway.
I love the Brooks which down their channels fret,
Even more than when I tripped lightly as they;
The innocent brightness of a new-born Day
195   Is lovely yet;
The Clouds that gather round the setting sun
Do take a sober coloring from an eye
That hath kept watch o'er man's mortality;
Another race hath been, and other palms are won.
200   Thanks to the human heart by which we live,
Thanks to its tenderness, its joys, and fears,
To me the meanest flower that blows can give
Thoughts that do often lie too deep for tears.

"The Rime of the Ancient Mariner"
by Samuel Taylor Coleridge

IN SEVEN PARTS

"I readily believe that there are more invisible than visible Natures in the universe. But who will explain for us the family of all these beings, and the ranks and relations and distinguishing features and functions of each? What do they do? What places do they inhabit? The human mind has always sought the knowledge of these things, but never attained it. Meanwhile I do not deny that it is helpful sometimes to contemplate in the mind, as on a tablet, the image of a greater and better world, lest the intellect, habituated to the petty things of daily life, narrow itself and sink wholly into trivial thoughts. But at the same time we must be watchful for the truth and keep a sense of proportion, so that we may distinguish the certain from the uncertain, day from night." —Adapted by Coleridge from Thomas Burnet, *Archaeologiae Philosophicae* (1692).

ARGUMENT

How a Ship, having first sailed to the Equator, was driven by storms to the cold Country towards the South Pole; how the Ancient Mariner cruelly and in contempt

of the laws of hospitality killed a Seabird and how he was
followed by many and strange Judgments: and in what
manner he came back to his own Country.

PART I

It is an ancient Mariner
And he stoppeth one of three.
—"By thy long gray beard and glit-
    tering eye,
Now wherefore stopp'st thou me?

An ancient Mariner meeteth three Gallants bidden to a wedding feast, and detaineth one.

5 The Bridegroom's doors are
    opened wide,
And I am next of kin;
The guests are met, the feast is set:
May'st hear the merry din."

He holds him with his skinny hand,
10 "There was a ship," quoth he.
"Hold off! unhand me, graybeard
    loon!"
Eftsoons[1] his hand dropped he.

He holds him with his glittering
    eye—
The Wedding-Guest stood still,
15 And listens like a three years' child:
The Mariner hath his will.[2]

The Wedding-Guest is spellbound by the eye of the old seafaring man, and constrained to hear his tale.

The Wedding-Guest sat on a stone;
He cannot choose but hear;
And thus spake on that ancient
    man,
20 The bright-eyed Mariner.

"The ship was cheered, the harbor
    cleared,
Merrily did we drop
Below the kirk,[3] below the hill,
Below the lighthouse top.

25 The Sun came up upon the left,
Out of the sea came he!
And he shone bright, and on the
    right
Went down into the sea.

The Mariner tells how the ship sailed southward with a good wind and fair weather, till it reached the Line.

Higher and higher every day,

Till over the mast at noon[4]—"
30 The Wedding-Guest here beat his
    breast,
For he heard the loud bassoon.

The bride hath paced into the hall,
Red as a rose is she;
35 Nodding their heads before her goes
The merry minstrelsy.

The Wedding-Guest heareth the bridal music; but the Mariner continueth his tale.

The Wedding-Guest he beat his
    breast,
Yet he cannot choose but hear;
And thus spake on that ancient man,
40 The bright-eyed Mariner.

"And now the STORM-BLAST came,
    and he
Was tyrannous and strong;
He struck with his o'ertaking wings,
And chased us south along.

The ship driven by a storm toward the South Pole.

45 With sloping masts and dipping
    prow,
As who pursued with yell and blow
Still treads the shadow of his foe,
And forward bends his head,
The ship drove fast, loud roared the
    blast,
50 And southward aye we fled.

And now there came both mist and
    snow,
And it grew wondrous cold:
And ice, mast-high, came floating by,
As green as emerald.

55 And through the drifts the snowy
    clifts
Did send a dismal sheen:
Nor shapes of men nor beasts we
    ken[5]—
The ice was all between.

The land of ice, and of fearful sounds where no living thing was to be seen.

The ice was here, the ice was there,
60 The ice was all around:
It cracked and growled, and roared
    and howled,
Like noises in a swound![6]

---

1. **Eftsoons.** At once
2. **He holds . . . his will.** The mariner has
hypnotized or mesmerized the Wedding-Guest.
3. **kirk.** Church

4. **Higher . . . noon.** The location of the ship is told by the sun.
Here, it has reached the equator.
5. **ken.** Know
6. **swound.** Swoon

LITERARY TECHNIQUE

• "The Rime of the Ancient Mariner" is a **frame tale**. It uses the background of the wedding feast for the Ancient Mariner to tell his story to the Wedding-Guest. Chaucer's *Canterbury Tales* is another frame tale. Selections from it appear on pages 185 and 205. Refer to the Handbook of Literary Terms.

• Point out the **archaic language** found in both the marginal notes and the poem itself. Ask students to consider the effect of such language on the poem's mood. Refer to the Handbook of Literary Terms.

LITERARY TECHNIQUE

Ballad. A **ballad** is a simple narrative poem in four-line stanzas, usually meant to be sung and usually rhyming *abcb*. Try reading a few stanzas aloud. Does the poem seem song-like? Where does "The Rime of the Ancient Mariner" deviate from the meter and rhyme scheme of a ballad? How does this change affect the poem?
Answers. The poem seems song-like because of its primary *abcb* rhyme scheme and alternating three- and four-stress feet. When the poem deviates from this rhyme and meter, it emphasizes the content of the stanza and underscores a particular event or idea. For example, the first time the poem deviates from this rhyme scheme and meter is in stanza 12 (lines 45–50) when the ship is sailed south toward the South Pole. The poem then returns to the ballad pattern until stanza 23 (lines 91–96), when the Mariner confesses his evil deed, and stanza 24 (lines 97–101), when the crew validates the evil act.

CROSS-CURRICULAR ACTIVITIES

Social Studies. Students may want to plot a possible route for the Mariner's ship. Encourage them to use an atlas and information from the poem to create a map of the ship's course.

ADDITIONAL QUESTIONS AND ACTIVITIES

As students reach the end of Part 1, ask them to share their reactions to the Mariner's shooting of the albatross. Why do they think he did it? What do they think will happen?

HISTORICAL NOTE

Sailors believed that the albatross was a sign of good luck.

CROSS-CURRICULAR ACTIVITIES

Mathematics and Sciences. Have students research Saint Elmo's fire to discover the scientific explanation for its appearance.

---

65 At length did cross an Albatross,
    Thorough the fog it came;
    As if it had been a Christian soul,
    We hailed it in God's name.

    It ate the food it ne'er had eat,
    And round and round it flew.
    The ice did split with a thunder-fit;
70 The helmsman steered us through!

    And a good south wind sprung up behind;
    The Albatross did follow,
    And every day, for food or play,
    Came to the mariners' hollo!

75 In mist or cloud, on mast or shroud,[1]
    It perched for vespers nine;
    Whiles all the night, through fog-smoke white,
    Glimmered the white Moon-shine."

    "God save thee, ancient Mariner!
80 From the fiends, that plague thee thus!—
    Why look'st thou so?"—With my crossbow
    I shot the ALBATROSS.

PART 2

    The Sun now rose upon the right:[2]
    Out of the sea came he,
85 Still hid in mist, and on the left
    Went down into the sea.

    And the good south wind still blew behind,
    But no sweet bird did follow,
    Nor any day for food or play
90 Came to the mariners' hollo!

    And I had done a hellish thing,
    And it would work 'em woe:
    For all averred, I had killed the bird
    That made the breeze to blow.
95 Ah wretch! said they, the bird to slay,

Till a great sea bird, called the Albatross, came through the snow-fog, and was received with great joy and hospitality.

And lo! the Albatross proveth a bird of good omen, and followeth the ship as it returned northward through fog and floating ice.

The ancient Mariner inhospitably killeth the pious bird of good omen.

His shipmates cry out against the ancient Mariner, for killing the bird of good luck.

    That made the breeze to blow!

    Nor dim nor red, like God's own head,
    The glorious Sun uprist:
    Then all averred, I had killed the bird
100 That brought the fog and mist.
    'Twas right, said they, such birds to slay,
    That bring the fog and mist.

    The fair breeze blew, the white foam flew,
    The furrow followed free;
105 We were the first that ever burst
    Into that silent sea.

    Down dropped the breeze, the sails dropped down,
    'Twas sad as sad could be;
    And we did speak only to break
110 The silence of the sea!

    All in a hot and copper sky,
    The bloody Sun, at noon,
    Right up above the mast did stand,
    No bigger than the Moon.

115 Day after day, day after day,
    We stuck, nor breath nor motion;
    As idle as a painted ship
    Upon a painted ocean.

    Water, water, everywhere,
120 And all the boards did shrink;
    Water, water, everywhere,
    Nor any drop to drink.

    The very deep did rot: O Christ!
    That ever this should be!
125 Yea, slimy things did crawl with legs
    Upon the slimy sea.

    About, about, in reel and rout
    The death-fires[3] danced at night;
    The water, like a witch's oils,
130 Burnt green, and blue and white.

But when the fog cleared off, they justify the same, and thus make themselves accomplices in the crime.

The fair breeze continues; the ship enters the Pacific Ocean, and sails northward, even till it reaches the Line.

The ship hath been suddenly becalmed.

The Albatross begins to be avenged.

---

1. **shroud.** Ropes that support a mast
2. **The Sun . . . right.** Now the ship is heading north into the Pacific Ocean.

3. **death-fires.** Saint Elmo's fire is an electric discharge often seen on a ship's mast. Superstitious sailors believe it is an omen of danger.

And some in dreams assurèd were
Of the Spirit that plagued us so;
Nine fathom deep he had followed us
From the land of mist and snow.

135 And every tongue, through utter
      drought,
    Was withered at the root;
    We could not speak, no more than if
    We had been choked with soot.

    Ah! well-a-day! what evil looks
140 Had I from old and young!
    Instead of the cross, the Albatross
    About my neck was hung.

PART 3

    There passed a weary time. Each
      throat
    Was parched, and glazed each eye.
145 A weary time! a weary time!
    How glazed each weary eye,
    When looking westward, I beheld
    A something in the sky.

    At first it seemed a little speck,
150 And then it seemed a mist;
    It moved and moved, and took at
      last
    A certain shape, I wist.[1]

    A speck, a mist, a shape, I wist!
    And still it neared and neared:
155 As if it dodged a water-sprite,[2]
    It plunged and tacked and veered.[3]

    With throats unslaked, with black
      lips baked,
    We could nor laugh nor wail;
    Through utter drought all dumb we
      stood!
160 I bit my arm, I sucked the blood,
    And cried, A sail! a sail!

    With throats unslaked, with black
      lips baked,
    Agape they heard me call:

*A Spirit had followed
them; one of the invis-
ible inhabitants of this
planet, neither
departed souls nor
angels; concerning
whom the learned
Jew, Josephus, and the
Platonic
Constaninopolitan,
Michael Psellus, may
be consulted. They are
very numerous, and
there is no climate or
element without one
or more.*

*The shipmates, in
their sore distress,
would fain throw the
whole guilt on the
ancient Mariner: in
sign whereof they
hang the dead sea
bird round his neck.*

*The ancient Mariner
beholdeth a sign in
the element afar off.*

*At its nearer
approach, it seemeth
him to be a ship; and
at a dear ransom he
freeth his speech from
the bonds of thirst.*

---

1. **wist.** Knew
2. **water-sprite.** A supernatural being in control of the natural elements
3. **tacked and veered.** Changed direction

Gramercy![4] they for joy did grin,
165 And all at once their breath drew in,
    As they were drinking all.

    See! see! (I cried) she tacks no more!
    Hither to work us weal;[5]
    Without a breeze, without a tide,
170 She steadies with upright keel!

    The western wave was all aflame.
    The day was well nigh done!
    Almost upon the western wave
    Rested the broad bright Sun;
175 When that strange shape drove sud-
      denly
    Betwixt us and the Sun.

    And straight the Sun was flecked
      with bars,
    (Heaven's Mother send us grace!)
    As if through a dungeon grate he
      peered
180 With broad and burning face.

    Alas! (thought I, and my heart beat
      loud)
    How fast she nears and nears!
    Are those *her* sails that glance in the
      Sun,
    Like restless gossameres?

185 Are those *her* ribs through which the
      Sun
    Did peer, as through a grate?
    And is that Woman all her crew?
    Is that a DEATH? and are there two?
    Is DEATH that woman's mate?

190 *Her* lips were red, *her* looks were free,
    Her locks were yellow as gold:
    Her skin was as white as leprosy,[6]
    The Night-mare LIFE-IN-DEATH
      was she,
    Who thicks man's blood with cold.

195 The naked hulk alongside came,
    And the twain were casting dice;
    "The game is done! I've won! I've
      won!"

A flash of joy;

*And horror follows.
For can it be a ship
that comes onward
without wind or
tide?*

*It seemeth him but
the skeleton of a
ship.*

*And its ribs are seen
as bars on the face of
the setting Sun.*

*The Specter-
Woman and her
Deathmate, and no
other on board the
skelton ship.*

*Like vessel, like
crew!*

*Death and Life-in-
Death have diced
for the ship's crew,
and she (the latter)
winneth the ancient
Mariner.*

---

4. **Gramercy!** Great thanks, from the French *grand-merci*
5. **weal.** Benefit
6. **leprosy.** A characteristic of leprosy is white, scaly skin.

LITERARY TECHNIQUE

The historian Josephus lived in the first century AD. In referring to figures from an ancient time, Coleridge enhances the poem's mystical mood.

LITERARY TECHNIQUE

Coleridge employs many **rhyme** patterns throughout the poem. Some of these include **internal rhymes**, as in line 153: "A speck, a **mist**, a shape, I **wist**!" Refer to the Handbook of Literary Terms.

Have students explore the rhyme patterns in one of the stanzas on this page. What end rhymes do they find? internal rhymes? What effect does the rhyme have on the poem's mood?

Answers. The internal rhymes have a hypnotic effect, much like the hypnotic effect the Mariner has on the Wedding-Guest listening to his tale.

ADDITIONAL QUESTIONS AND ACTIVITIES

Coleridge's marginal notes provide a summary of the Mariner's story. Ask students to consider why Coleridge wrote the poetry if he could tell the same story in prose.

QUOTABLES

66 Poetry is certainly something more than good sense, but it must be good sense at all events; just as a palace is more than a house, but it must be a house, at least. 99

—Samuel Taylor Coleridge

66 I wish our clever young poets would remember my homely definitions of Prose and poetry; that is prose; words in their best order;—poetry; the *best* words in the best order. 99

—Samuel Taylor Coleridge

Quoth she, and whistles thrice.

The Sun's rim dips; the stars rush out:
200 At one stride comes the dark;
With far-heard whisper, o'er the sea,
Off shot the spectre-bark.

No twilight within the courts of the Sun.

We listened and looked sideways up!
Fear at my heart, as at a cup,
205 My lifeblood seemed to sip!
The stars were dim, and thick the night,
The steersman's face by his lamp gleamed white;
From the sails the dew did drip—
Till clomb above the eastern bar
210 The hornèd Moon, with one bright star
Within the nether tip.[1]

At the rising of the Moon,

One after one, by the star-dogged Moon,
Too quick for groan or sigh,
Each turned his face with a ghastly pang,
215 And cursed me with his eye.

One after another,

Four times fifty living men,
(And I heard nor sigh nor groan)
With heavy thump, a lifeless lump,
They dropped down one by one.

His shipmates drop down dead.

220 The souls did from their bodies fly—
They fled to bliss or woe!
And every soul, it passed me by,
Like the whizz of my crossbow!

But Life-in-Death begins her work on the ancient Mariner.

PART 4

"I fear thee, ancient Mariner!
225 I fear thy skinny hand!
And thou art long, and lank, and brown,
As is the ribbed sea-sand.

The Wedding-Guest feareth that a Spirit is talking to him;

---
1. **hornèd Moon . . . nether tip.** This is considered an omen of evil.

I fear thee and thy glittering eye,
And thy skinny hand, so brown."—
230 Fear not, fear not, thou Wedding-Guest!
This body dropped not down.

But the ancient Mariner assureth him of his bodily life, and proceedeth to relate his horrible penance.

Alone, alone, all, all alone,
Alone on a wide wide sea!
And never a saint took pity on
235 My soul in agony.

The many men, so beautiful!
And they all dead did lie:
And a thousand thousand slimy things
Lived on; and so did I.

He despiseth the creatures of the calm,

240 I looked upon the rotting sea,
And drew my eyes away;
I looked upon the rotting deck,
And there the dead men lay.

And envieth that they should live, and so many lie dead.

I looked to heaven, and tried to pray;
245 But or ever a prayer had gushed,
A wicked whisper came, and made
My heart as dry as dust.

I closed my lids, and kept them close,
And the balls like pulses beat;
250 For the sky and the sea, and the sea and the sky
Lay like a load on my weary eye,
And the dead were at my feet.

The cold sweat melted from their limbs,
Nor rot nor reek did they:
255 The look with which they looked on me
Had never passed away.

But the curse liveth for him in the eye of the dead men.

An orphan's curse would drag to hell
A spirit from on high;
But oh! more horrible than that
260 Is the curse in a dead man's eye!
Seven days, seven nights, I saw that curse,
And yet I could not die.

The moving Moon went up the
    sky,
And nowhere did <u>abide</u>:
265 Softly she was going up,
And a star or two beside—

Her beams bemocked the sultry
    main,
Like April hoar-frost spread;
But where the ship's huge shadow
    lay,
270 The charmèd water burnt alway
A still and awful red.

Beyond the shadow of the ship,
I watched the water snakes:
They moved in tracks of shining
    white,
275 And when they reared, the elfish
    light
Fell off in hoary flakes.

Within the shadow of the ship
I watched their rich attire:
Blue, glossy green, and velvet black,
280 They coiled and swam; and every
    track
Was a flash of golden fire.

O happy living things! no tongue
Their beauty might declare:
A spring of love gushed from my
    heart,
285 And I blessed them unaware:
Sure my kind saint took pity on me,
And I blessed them unaware.

The self-same moment I could
    pray;
And from my neck so free
290 The Albatross fell off, and sank
Like lead into the sea.

PART 5

Oh sleep! it is a gentle thing,
Beloved from pole to pole!
To Mary Queen the praise be
    given!
295 She sent the gentle sleep from
    Heaven,

*In his loneliness and
fixedness he year-
neth towards the
journeying Moon,
and the stars that
still sojourn, yet still
move onward; and
everywhere the blue
sky belongs to them,
and is their
appointed rest, and
their native country
and their own nat-
ural homes, which
they enter unan-
nounced, as lords
that are certainly
expected and yet
there is a silent joy
at their arrival.*

*By the light of the
Moon he beholdeth
God's creatures of
the great calm.*

*Their beauty and
their happiness.*

*He blesseth them in
his heart.*

*The spell begins to
break.*

That slid into my soul.

The silly buckets on the deck,
That had so long remained,
I dreamt that they were filled with
    dew;
300 And when I awoke, it rained.

My lips were wet, my throat was
    cold,
My garments all were dank;
Sure I had drunken in my dreams,
And still my body drank.

305 I moved, and could not feel my
    limbs:
I was so light—almost
I thought that I had died in sleep,
And was a blessed ghost.

And soon I heard a roaring wind:
310 It did not come anear;
But with its sound it shook the sails,
That were so thin and sere.[1]

The upper air burst into life!
And a hundred fire-flags sheen,
315 To and fro they were hurried about!
And to and fro, and in and out,
The wan stars danced between.

And the coming wind did roar more
    loud,
And the sails did sigh like sedge;[2]
320 And the rain poured down from one
    black cloud;
The Moon was at its edge.

The thick black cloud was cleft, and
    still
The Moon was at its side:
Like waters shot from some high
    crag,
325 The lightning fell with never a jag,
A river steep and wide.

The loud wind never reached the
    ship,

*By grace of the holy
Mother, the ancient
Mariner is
refreshed with rain.*

*He heareth sounds
and seeth strange
sights and commo-
tions in the sky and
the element.*

1. **sere.** Dried up
2. **sedge.** A plant that grows in wet ground or water

Symbol. A **symbol** is a thing that stands for or represents both itself and something else. How is the albatross used as a symbol in this poem? Think about how the albatross is described and what it brings to the sailors. Also consider who cares for the albatross and what happens after the albatross is killed. What else could the albatross represent? Why might Coleridge have chosen the albatross for this symbol?

Answers. The albatross has several symbolic uses. To the sailors, it is a symbol of good luck. The albatross also symbolizes purity and spirituality. When it first appears, in line 63, the sailors hail it as "a Christian soul" and they care for the bird. After he shoots it, the Mariner declares he has "done a hellish thing." When speaking of his punishment to the Wedding-Guest, the Mariner says that his "soul hath been/Alone on a wide wide sea:/So lonely 'twas, that God himself/Scarce seemèd there to be" (lines 597–600). Killing the albatross separates the Mariner from God. The albatross is also a symbol of Christianity and of penance. The albatross hangs around the Mariner's neck, an antithesis of the cross that Christians hang around their necks to show devotion to God. Coleridge might have chosen the albatross because using a creature from the natural world as his symbol emphasizes the importance of nature to spirituality.

▶ **Teaching Note:** Students might make a time line of events to help them track the effects of killing the albatross. Refer students to the Language Arts Survey, 1.19, "Time Lines."

LITERARY TECHNIQUE

Coleridge uses **alliteration** to create particular moods within the poem. For example, in line 339, the initial "l" sounds in "limbs like lifeless tools" have a lulling, hypnotic effect.

ADDITIONAL QUESTIONS AND ACTIVITIES

Ask each student to write blues lyrics about his or her own albatross or burden. Ask students to make a list of the ways they struggle under this burden and the pains and sufferings it has caused them. Students should try to express these feelings with words and images that create a low, melancholy mood.

Yet now the ship moved on!
Beneath the lightning and the
    Moon
330 The dead men gave a groan.

They groaned, they stirred, they
    all uprose,
Nor spake, nor moved their eyes;
It had been strange, even in a
    dream,
To have seen those dead men rise.

335 The helmsman steered, the ship
    moved on;
Yet never a breeze up-blew;
The mariners all 'gan work the
    ropes,
Where they were wont to do;
They raised their limbs like life-
    less tools—
340 We were a ghastly crew.

The body of my brother's son
Stood by me, knee to knee:
The body and I pulled at one
    rope,
But he said nought to me.

345 "I fear thee, ancient Mariner!"
Be calm, thou Wedding Guest!
'Twas not those souls that fled in
    pain,
Which to their corses[1] came again,
But a troop of spirits blest:

350 For when it dawned—they
    dropped their arms,
And clustered round the mast;
Sweet sounds rose slowly through
    their mouths,
And from their bodies passed.

Around, around, flew each sweet
    sound,
355 Then darted to the Sun;
Slowly the sounds came back again,
Now mixed, now one by one.

Sometimes a-dropping from the
    sky
I heard the sky-lark sing;

The bodies of the ship's crew are inspirited, and the ship moves on;

But not by the souls of the men nor by demons of earth or middle air, but by a blessed troop of angelic spirits, sent down by the invocation of the guardian saint.

360 Sometimes all little birds that are,
How they seemed to fill the sea and
    air
With their sweet jargoning![2]

And now 'twas like all instruments,
Now like a lonely flute;
365 And now it is an angel's song,
That makes the heavens be mute.

It ceased; yet still the sails made on
A pleasant noise till noon,
A noise like of a hidden brook
370 In the leafy month of June,
That to the sleeping woods all night
Singeth a quiet tune.

Till noon we quietly sailed on,
Yet never a breeze did breathe:
375 Slowly and smoothly went the ship,
Moved onward from beneath.

Under the keel nine fathom deep,
From the land of mist and snow,
The spirit slid: and it was he
380 That made the ship to go.
The sails at noon left off their tune,
And the ship stood still also.

The Sun, right up above the mast,
Had fixed her to the ocean:
385 But in a minute she 'gan stir,
With a short uneasy motion—
Backwards and forwards half her
    length
With a short uneasy motion.

Then like a pawing horse let go,
390 She made a sudden bound:
It flung the blood into my head,
And I fell down in a swound.

How long in that same fit I lay,
I have not to declare;
395 But ere my living life returned,
I heard and in my soul discerned
Two voices in the air.

It "Is it he?" quoth one, "Is this the
    man?
By him who died on cross,

The lonesome Spirit from the South Pole carries on the ship as far as the Line, in obedience to the angelic troop, but still requireth vengeance.

The Polar Spirit's fellow demons, the invisible inhabitants of the element, take part in his wrong; and two of them relate, one to the other, that penance long and heavy for the ancient Mariner hath been accorded to the Polar Spirit, who returneth southward.

1. **corses.** Corpses

2. **jargoning.** Singing

400 With his cruel bow he laid full low
The harmless Albatross.

The spirit who bideth by himself
In the land of mist and snow,
He loved the bird that loved the
man
405 Who shot him with his bow."

The other was a softer voice,
As soft as honeydew:
Quoth he, "The man hath penance
done,
And penance more will do."

PART 6

FIRST VOICE
410 "But tell me, tell me! speak again,
Thy soft response renewing—
What makes that ship drive on so
fast?
What is the ocean doing?"

SECOND VOICE
"Still as a slave before his lord,
415 The ocean hath no blast;
His great bright eye most silently
Up to the Moon is cast—

If he may know which way to go;
For she guides him smooth or grim.
420 See, brother, see! how graciously
She looketh down on him."

FIRST VOICE
"But why drives on that ship so fast,
Without or wave or wind?"

The Mariner hath been cast into a trance; for the angelic power causeth the vessel to drive northward faster than human life could endure.

SECOND VOICE
"The air is cut away before,
425 And closes from behind.

Fly, brother, fly! more high, more
high!
Or we shall be belated:
For slow and slow that ship will go,
When the Mariner's trance is
abated."

430 I woke, and we were sailing on

As in a gentle weather:
'Twas night, calm night, the moon
was high;
The dead men stood together.

The supernatural motion is retarded; the Mariner awakes, and his penance begins anew.

All stood together on the deck,
435 For a charnel-dungeon[1] fitter:
All fixed on me their stony eyes,
That in the Moon did glitter.

The pang, the curse, with which
they died,
Had never passed away:
440 I could not draw my eyes from theirs,
Nor turn them up to pray.

And now this spell was snapped:
once more
I viewed the ocean green,
And looked far forth, yet little saw
445 Of what had else been seen—

The curse is finally expiated.

Like one, that on a lonesome road
Doth walk in fear and dread,
And having once turned round walks
on,
And turns no more his head;
450 Because he knows, a frightful fiend
Doth close behind him tread.

But soon there breathed a wind on
me,
Nor sound nor motion made:
Its path was not upon the sea,
455 In ripple or in shade.

It raised my hair, it fanned my cheek
Like a meadow-gale of spring—
It mingled strangely with my fears,
Yet it felt like a welcoming.

460 Swiftly, swiftly flew the ship,
Yet she sailed softly too:
Sweetly, sweetly blew the breeze—
On me alone it blew.

Oh! dream of joy! is this indeed
465 The lighthouse top I see?
Is this the hill? is this the kirk?
Is this mine own countree?

And the ancient Mariner beholdeth his native country.

---

1. **charnel-dungeon.** Cemetery

LITERARY TECHNIQUE

Have students compare the **images** connected with the beginning of the Mariner's journey (lines 51–62) to the images of his return to his native country (lines 452–463). Refer to the Handbook of Literary Terms.

ADDITIONAL QUESTIONS AND ACTIVITIES

Ask students to write about a time when they did something that they later regretted. How did their actions affect others? What negative consequences resulted? How did others react to what they did? What lesson did they learn?

What does the Hermit wonder as he approaches the ship? What do his questions reveal about the Mariner's experience?

Answers. The Hermit wonders why the ship's crew didn't answer his call and why the lights he saw burning on the ship are no longer lit. The fact that the Hermit saw the lights confirms that the Mariner did not hallucinate the events on the ship.

ADDITIONAL QUESTIONS AND ACTIVITIES

1. What event does the Mariner interrupt to tell his story? To whom does he tell his story?

Answers. The Mariner interrupts a wedding feast. He tells his story to the Wedding-Guest, who is related to the Bridegroom.

2. Why does the Mariner tell his story to the Wedding-Guest? Why does the Wedding-Guest stay to listen to the old man's tale?

Answers. The Mariner determines that the Wedding-Guest is the person he must tell. The Wedding-Guest stays and listens because he is hypnotized by the Mariner.

3. What change occurs when the Albatross arrives? What happens when the Albatross is killed?

Answers. When the Albatross arrives, the ship begins sailing away from the South Pole. When the Albatross is killed, the ship is set adrift on the ocean.

4. Who avenges the Albatross? How is it avenged?

Answers. The crew avenges the Albatross by hanging it around the Mariner's neck.

5. Who is on the ship that the Mariner and his shipmates spy on in Part 3? What are they doing? Who wins the Mariner?

Answers. The Mariner and his shipmates spy on Death and Life-in-Death. The two are playing a game of dice to decide the fate of the Mariner and his crew. Life-in-Death wins the Mariner.

(cont.)

We drifted o'er the harbor bar,
And I with sobs did pray—
470 O let me be awake, my God!
Or let me sleep alway.

The harbor bay was clear as glass,
So smoothly it was strewn!
And on the bay the moonlight lay
475 And the shadow of the Moon.

The rock shone bright, the kirk no
   less,
That stands above the rock:
The moonlight steeped in silentness
The steady weathercock.

480 And the bay was white with silent
   light,
Till rising from the same,
Full many shapes, that shadows
   were,
In crimson colors came.

The angelic spirits leave the dead bodies,

A little distance from the prow
485 Those crimson shadows were:
I turned my eyes upon the deck—
Oh, Christ! what saw I there!

And appear in their own forms of light.

Each corse lay flat, lifeless and flat,
And, by the holy rood![1]
490 A man all light, a seraph[2] man,
On every corse there stood.

This seraph band, each waved his
   hand:
It was a heavenly sight!
They stood as signals to the land,
495 Each one a lovely light;

This seraph band, each waved his
   hand,
No voice did they impart—
No voice; but oh! the silence sank
Like music on my heart.

500 But soon I heard the dash of oars,
I heard the Pilot's cheer;
My head was turned perforce away
And I saw a boat appear.

The Pilot and the Pilot's boy
505 I heard them coming fast:

---
1. **rood.** A cross
2. **seraph.** The highest order of angels

Dear Lord in Heaven! it was a joy
The dead men could not blast.

I saw a third—I heard his voice:
It is the Hermit good!
510 He singeth loud his godly hymns
That he makes in the wood.
He'll shrieve[3] my soul, he'll wash
   away
The Albatross's blood.

PART 7

This Hermit good lives in that
   wood
515 Which slopes down to the sea.
How loudly his sweet voice he rears!
He loves to talk with marineres
That come from a far countree.

The Hermit of the Wood,

He kneels at morn, and noon, and
   eve—
520 He hath a cushion plump:
It is the moss that wholly hides
The rotted old oak-stump.

The skiff-boat neared: I heard them
   talk,
"Why, this is strange, I trow!
525 Where are those lights so many and
   fair,
That signal made but now?"

"Strange, by my faith!" the Hermit
   said—
"And they answered not our cheer!
The planks looked warped! and see
   those sails,
530 How thin they are and sere!
I never saw aught like to them,
Unless perchance it were

Approacheth the ship with wonder.

Brown skeletons of leaves that lag
My forest-brook along;
535 When the ivy tod is heavy with snow,
And the owlet whoops to the wolf
   below,
That eats the she-wolf's young."

"Dear Lord! it hath a fiendish look,"
(The Pilot made reply)
540 "I am a-feared"—"Push on, push on!"
Said the Hermit cheerily.

---
3. **shrieve.** Absolve

6. What is the difference between Death and Life-in-Death? Which is worse? Why?

Answers. Death is a final state while Life-in-Death is a state in which one is aware of and surrounded by death. Life-in-Death is worse because it is accompanied by the terrible awareness of one's hopeless fate.

7. What makes the Albatross fall from the Mariner's neck? What curse lingers after the Albatross is gone? What did he want the Hermit to do when he finally reached his homeland?

Answers. The Albatross falls from his neck when the Mariner blesses the animals he had earlier cursed and is able to pray. The curse of Life-in-Death lingers after the Albatross is gone. He wants the Hermit to absolve him.

(cont.)

The boat came closer to the ship,
But I nor spake nor stirred;
The boat came close beneath the ship,
545 And straight a sound was heard.

Under the water it rumbled on,   *The ship suddenly*
Still louder and more dread: *sinketh.*
It reached the ship, it split the bay;
The ship went down like lead.

550 Stunned by that loud and dreadful   *The ancient*
        sound,   *Mariner is saved in*
Which sky and ocean smote,   *the Pilot's boat.*
Like one that hath been seven days
        drowned
My body lay afloat;
But swift as dreams, myself I found
555 Within the Pilot's boat.

Upon the whirl, where sank the ship,
The boat spun round and round;
And all was still, save that the hill
Was telling of the sound.

560 I moved my lips—the Pilot shrieked
And fell down in a fit;
The holy Hermit raised his eyes,
 And prayed where he did sit.

I took the oars: the Pilot's boy,
565 Who now doth crazy go,
Laughed loud and long, and all the
        while
His eyes went to and fro.
"Ha! ha!" quoth he, "full plain I see,
The Devil knows how to row."

570 And now, all in my own countree,
I stood on the firm land!
The Hermit stepped forth from the
        boat,
And scarcely he could stand.

"O shrieve me, shrieve me, holy   *The ancient*
man!"   *Mariner earnestly*
575 The Hermit crossed his brow.   *entreateth the*
"Say quick," quoth he, "I bid thee   *Hermit to shrieve*
        say—   *him; and the*
What manner of man art thou?"   *penance of life falls*
                                      on him.
Forthwith this frame of mine was
        wrenched
With a woeful agony,

580 Which forced me to begin my tale;
And then it left me free.

Since then, at an uncertain hour,   *And ever and anon*
That agony returns: *throughout his*
And till my ghastly tale is told,   *future life an agony*
585 This heart within me burns.   *constraineth him to*
                                       travel from land to
I pass, like night, from land to land; *land;*
I have strange power of speech;
That moment that his face I see,
I know the man that must hear me:
590 To him my tale I teach.

What loud uproar bursts from that
        door!
The wedding-guests are there:
But in the garden-bower the bride
And bride-maids singing are:
595 And hark the little vesper bell,
Which biddeth me to prayer!

O Wedding-Guest! this soul hath
        been
Alone on a wide wide sea:
So lonely 'twas, that God himself
600 Scarce seemèd there to be.

O sweeter than the marriage feast,
'Tis sweeter far to me,
To walk together to the kirk
With a goodly company!—

605 To walk together to the kirk,
And all together pray,
While each to his great Father bends,
Old men, and babes, and loving
        friends
And youths and maidens gay!

610 Farewell, farewell! but this I tell   *And to teach, by his*
To thee, thou Wedding-Guest!   *own example, love*
He prayeth well, who loveth well   *and reverence to all*
Both man and bird and beast.   *things that God*
                                        made and loveth.
He prayeth best, who loveth best
615 All things both great and small;
For the dear God who loveth us,
He made and loveth all.

The Mariner, whose eye is bright,
Whose beard with age is hoar,

ADDITIONAL QUESTIONS AND ACTIVITIES

What does the Pilot's boy mean when he says "The Devil knows how to row"? What does his comment reveal about the Mariner?

Answers. The Pilot's boy is reacting to the Mariner's frightful appearance and the strange conditions surrounding his rescue. The Mariner obviously exhibits physical effects of his ordeal.

ADDITIONAL QUESTIONS AND ACTIVITIES (CONT.)

8. Has the Mariner rid himself completely of the Albatross and the curse from his journey? What does he have to do to free himself from his agony?

Answers. In order to rid himself completely of the Albatross and the curse, the Mariner must wander the earth and tell his tale.

9. How would you characterize the Mariner's punishment? Do you think it was too harsh? too lenient? fitting his crime? Do you think his punishment has taught him anything or enabled him to help others?

Answers. The Mariner's punishment—his ordeal on the ship—seems harsh, but it does eventually lead him to understand and appreciate the value of all life. Because he senses to whom he should tell his tale (lines 588–590), the Mariner probably tells his story to people who need to hear its message.

10. Describe the spiritual beliefs described in this poem. How do these beliefs relate to the ideas expressed in the quote from Thomas Burnet that Coleridge uses at the beginning of his poem? Why might Coleridge have decided to begin "The Rime of the Ancient Mariner" in this way?

Answers. The poem expresses the belief that all life is sacred. The harsh punishment of the Mariner reflects the Romantic belief that nature is sacred—a sin against nature is as much a sin as one against humanity or God. The poem expresses the belief that humans do not live in a spiritual void—they have an effect on the universe and a responsibility to it as well. Coleridge might have begun his poem with this quotation to set the tone for the spiritual dilemma explored in the poem.

620 Is gone: and now the Wedding-Guest
Turned from the bridegroom's door.

He went like one that hath been stunned,
And is of sense forlorn:
A sadder and a wiser man,
625 He rose the morrow morn.

from *The Grasmere Journals*
by Dorothy Wordsworth

MAY 14TH, 1800 [WEDNESDAY]

Wm and John[1] set off into Yorkshire after dinner at $1/2$ past 2 o'clock, cold pork in their pockets. I left them at the turning of the Low-wood bay under the trees. My heart was so full that I could hardly speak to W. when I gave him a farewell kiss. I sat a long time upon a stone at the margin of the lake, and after a flood of tears my heart was easier. The lake looked to me, I knew not why, dull and melancholy, and the weltering on the shores seemed a heavy sound. I walked as long as I could among the stones of the shore. The wood rich in flowers. A beautiful yellow, palish yellow flower, that looked thick round and double, and smelled very sweet—I supposed it was a ranunculus—Crowfoot, the grassy-leaved Rabbit-toothed white flower, strawberries, geranium—scentless violet, anemones two kinds, orchises, primroses. The heckberry very beautiful, the crab coming out as a low shrub. Met a blind man, driving a very large beautiful Bull and a cow—he walked with two sticks. Came home by Clappersgate. The valley very green, many sweet views up to Rydale head when I could juggle away the fine houses, but they disturbed me even more than when I have been happier. One beautiful view of the Bridge, without Sir Michael's. Sat down very often, though it was cold. I resolved to write a journal of the time till W. and J. return, and I set about keeping my resolve because I will not quarrel with myself, and because I shall give Wm Pleasure by it when he comes home again. At Rydale a woman of the village, stout and well dressed, begged a halfpenny—she had never she said done it before, but these hard times—Arrived at home with a bad headache, set some slips of privet. The evening cold, had a fire—my face now flame-colored. It is nine o'clock. I shall soon go to bed. A young woman begged at the door—she had come from Manchester on Sunday morn with two shillings and a slip of paper which she supposed a Bank note—it was a cheat. She had buried her husband and three children within a year and a half—all in one grave—burying very dear—paupers all put in one place—20 shillings paid for as much ground

---
1. **Wm and John.** Her brothers

as will bury a man—a stone to be put over it or the right will be lost—11/6 each time the ground is opened. Oh! that I had a letter from William!

JUNE 10TH, 1800 [TUESDAY]

A cold, yet sunshiny morning. John carried letters to Ambleside. I made tarts, pies, etc. Wm stuck peas. After dinner he lay down. John not at home. I stuck peas alone. Molly washing. Cold showers with hail and rain, but at half-past five, after a heavy rain, the lake became calm and very beautiful. Those parts of the water which were perfectly unruffled lay like green islands of various shapes. W and I walked to Ambleside to seek lodgings for C. No letters. No papers. It was a very cold cheerless evening. John had been fishing in Langdale and was gone to bed.

On Tuesday, May 27th, a very tall woman, tall much beyond the measure of tall women, called at the door. She had on a very long brown cloak and a very white cap, without bonnet; her face was excessively brown, but it had plainly once been fair. She led a little bare-footed child about 2 years old by the hand, and said her husband, who was a tinker, was gone before with the other children. I gave her a piece of bread. Afterward on my road to Ambleside, beside the bridge at Rydale, I saw her husband sitting by the roadside, his two asses feeding beside him, and the two young children at play upon the grass. The man did not beg. I passed on and about 1/4 of a mile further I saw two boys before me, one about 10, the other about 8 years old, at play chasing a butterfly. They were wild figures, not very ragged, but without shoes and stockings; the hat of the elder was wreathed round with yellow flowers, the younger whose hat was only a rimless crown, had stuck it round with laurel leaves. They continued at play till I drew very near, and then they addressed me with the begging cant and the whining voice of sorrow. I said "I served your mother this morning." (The Boys were so like the woman who had called at the door that I could not be mistaken.) "O!" says the elder, "you could not serve my mother for she's dead, and my father's on at the next town—he's a potter." I persisted in my assertion, and that I would give them nothing. Says the elder, "Come, let's away," and away they flew like lightning. They had however sauntered so long in their road that they did not reach Ambleside before me, and I saw them go up to Matthew Harrison's house with their wallet upon the elder's shoulder, and creeping with a beggar's complaining foot. On my return through Ambleside I met in the street the mother driving her asses; in the two panniers of one of which were the two little children, whom she was chiding and threatening with a wand which she used to drive on her asses, while the little things hung in wantonness over the pannier's edge. The woman had told me in the morning that she was of Scotland which her accent fully proved, but that she had lived (I think) at Wigton, that they could not keep a house and so they travelled.

NOVEMBER 24TH, 1801 [TUESDAY]

A rainy morning. We all were well except that my head ached a little and I took my breakfast in bed. I read a little of Chaucer, prepared the goose for dinner, and then we all walked out. I was obliged to return for my fur tippet and Spenser[1] it was so cold. We had intended going to Easedale, but we shaped our course to Mr. Gell's cottage. It was very windy, and we heard the wind everywhere about us as we went along the Lane, but the walls sheltered us. John Green's house looked pretty under Silver How. As we were going along, we were stopped at once, at the distance perhaps of 50 yards from our favorite birch tree. It was yielding to the gusty wind with all its tender twigs, the sun shone upon it, and it glanced in the wind like a flying sunshiny shower. It was a tree in shape with stem and branches, but it was like a Spirit of water. The sun went in, and it resumed its purplish appearance, the twigs still yielding to the wind but not so visibly to us. The other birch trees that were near it looked bright and cheerful, but it was a creature by its own self among them. We could not get into Mr. Gell's grounds—the old tree fallen from its undue exaltation above the Gate. A shower came on when we were at Benson's. We went through the wood—it became fair—there was a rainbow which spanned the lake from the island house to the foot of Bainriggs. The village looked populous and beautiful. Catkins are coming out palm trees budding—the alder with its plumb-colored buds. We came home over the steppingstones. The lake was foamy with white waves. I saw a solitary butter flower in the wood. I found it not easy to get over the steppingstones. Reached home at dinner time. Sent Peggy Ashburner some goose. She sent me some honey—with a thousand thanks. "Alas! the gratitude of men has etc."[2] I went in to set her right about this and sat a while with her. She talked about Thomas's having sold his land. "Ay," says she, I said many a time "He's not come from London to buy our Land however." Then she told me with what pains and industry they had made up their taxes, interest, etc.—how they all got up at 5 o'clock in the morning to spin and Thomas carded, and that they had paid off a hundred pounds of the interest. She said she used to take such pleasure in the cattle and sheep. "O how pleased I used to be when they fetched them down, and when I had been a bit poorly I would go out upon a hill and look over the fields and see them and it used to do me so much good you cannot think." Molly said to me

when I came in, "Poor Body. She's very ill but one does not know how long she may last. Many a fair face may go before her." We sat by the fire without work for some time, then Mary read a poem of Daniell upon Learning. After tea, Wm read Spenser now and then a little aloud to us. We were making his waistcoat. We had a note from Mrs. C. with bad news from poor C. very ill. William walked to John's Grove. I went to meet him—moonlight but it rained. I met him before I had got as far as John Baty's—he had been surprised and terrified by a sudden rushing of winds which seemed to bring earth, sky, and lake together, as if the whole were going to enclose him—he was glad he was in a high road.

In speaking of our walk on Sunday evening, the 22nd November, I forgot to notice one most impressive sight. It was the moon and the moonlight seen through hurrying, driving clouds immediately behind the stone man upon the top of the hill on the forest side. Every tooth and every edge of rock was visible, and the man stood like a giant watching from the roof of a lofty castle. The hill seemed perpendicular from the darkness below it. It was a sight that I could call to mind at any time, it was so distinct.

"A Dirge" by Percy Bysshe Shelley

> Rough wind, that moanest loud
> Grief too sad for song;
> Wild wind, when sullen cloud
> Knells all the night long;
> 5 Sad storm, whose tears are vain,
> Bare woods, whose branches strain,
> Deep caves and dreary main,—
> Wail, for the world's wrong!

from *Declaration of Rights*
by Percy Bysshe Shelley

1

Government has no rights; it is a delegation from several individuals for the purpose of securing their own. It is therefore just only so far as it exists by their consent, useful only so far as it operates to their well-being.

♦　♦　♦

3

Government is devised for the security of rights. The rights of man are liberty and an equal participation of the commonage of nature.

♦　♦　♦

11

A man has a right to think as his reason directs; it is a duty he owes to himself to think with freedom, that he may act from conviction.

---

1. **tippet and Spenser.** Cape-like scarf and a short jacket
2. **"Alas! . . . etc."** From William Wordsworth's *Simon Lee*

ADDITIONAL QUESTIONS AND ACTIVITIES

Have students compare Dorothy's descriptions of nature to those in her brother's poem, "I Wandered Lonely as a Cloud" (page 662). Students can either write or discuss their observations.

"A DIRGE"
FROM *DECLARATION OF RIGHTS*

About the Author. A biography of **Percy Bysshe Shelley** appears on page 622.

About the Selections. In "A Dirge," as in "Ode to the West Wind," Shelley addresses nature and despairs of human alienation in the modern world.

In his *Declaration of Rights,* Shelley echoes the revolutionary spirit of the *Declaration of the Rights of Man,* the document that established the principles of the French Revolution.

ADDITIONAL QUESTIONS AND ACTIVITIES

• Explain that a dirge is a funeral song. Then have students discuss why the poem is titled "A Dirge." Have them consider what the speaker is mourning and why he mourns.

• According to Shelley, what rights do all people have?

Answer. They have a right to "liberty and an equal participation of the commonage of nature," the right to think, discuss, and express their ideas freely.

• What metaphor does Shelley use to describe falsehood?

Answer. He describes falsehood as "a scorpion that will sting itself to death."

12

A man has a right to unrestricted liberty of discussion; falsehood is a scorpion that will sting itself to death.

13

A man has not only a right to express his thoughts, but it is his duty to do so.

❖ ❖ ❖

15

Law cannot make what is in its nature virtuous or innocent to be criminal, any more than it can make what is criminal to be innocent. Government cannot make a law; it can only pronounce that which was the law before its organization—viz., the moral result of the imperishable relations of things.

16

The present generation cannot bind their posterity. The few cannot promise for the many.

17

No man has a right to do an evil thing that good may come.

❖ ❖ ❖

19

Man has no right to kill his brother; it is no excuse that he does so in uniform. He only adds the infamy of servitude to the crime of murder.

❖ ❖ ❖

24

A Christian, a Deist, a Turk, and a Jew have equal rights: they are men and brethren.

❖ ❖ ❖

27

No man has a right to be respected for any other possessions but those of virtue and talents. Titles are tinsel, power a corruptor, glory a bubble, and excessive wealth a libel on its possessor.

❖ ❖ ❖

29

Every man has a right to a certain degree of leisure and liberty, because it is his duty to attain a certain degree of knowledge. He may, before he ought.

"When We Two Parted"
by George Gordon, Lord Byron

1

When we two parted
    In silence and tears,
Half broken-hearted
    To sever for years,

5   Pale grew thy cheek and cold,
        Colder thy kiss;
    Truly that hour foretold
        Sorrow to this.

2

    The dew of the morning
10   Sunk chill on my brow—
    It felt like the warning
        Of what I feel now.
    Thy vows are all broken,
        And light is thy fame;
15 I hear thy name spoken,
        And share in its shame.

3

    They name thee before me,
        A knell to mine ear;
    A shudder comes o'er me—
20   Why wert thou so dear?
    They know not I knew thee,
        Who knew thee too well:—
    Long, long shall I rue thee,
        Too deeply to tell.

4

25 In secret we met—
        In silence I grieve,
    That thy heart could forget,
        Thy spirit deceive.
    If I should meet thee
30   After long years,
    How should I greet thee!—
        With silence and tears.

from *Don Juan*, Canto 1, Stanza 218 ("What is the end of fame?")
by George Gordon, Lord Byron

What is the end of fame? 'tis but to fill
    A certain portion of uncertain paper:
Some liken it to climbing up a hill,
    Whose summit, like all hills', is lost in vapor;
5 For this men write, speak, preach, and heroes kill,
    And bards burn what they call their "midnight taper,"
To have, when the original is dust,
A name, a wretched picture, and worse bust.

"On First Looking into Chapman's Homer"[1] by John Keats

Much have I travell'd in the realms of gold,
    And many goodly states and kingdoms seen;

---

1. **Chapman's Homer.** George Chapman was an Elizabethan poet whose translation of Homer Keats read with his teacher. The next morning he sent this sonnet to his teacher.

Round many western islands have I been
Which bards in fealty to Apollo hold.[1]
5   Oft of one wide expanse had I been told
That deep-brow'd Homer ruled as his demesne;[2]
Yet did I never breathe its pure serene
Till I heard Chapman speak out loud and bold:
Then felt I like some watcher of the skies
10   When a new planet swims into his ken;[3]
Or like stout Cortez when with eagle eyes
He star'd at the Pacific—and all his men
Look'd at each other with a wild surmise—
Silent, upon a peak in Darien.[4]

"Dirce" by Walter Savage Landor

Stand close around, ye Stygian set,[5]
With Dirce in one boat conveyed!
Or Charon, seeing, may forget
That he is old and she a shade.

"The Harp That Once through Tara's[6] Halls" by Thomas Moore

The harp that once through Tara's halls
The soul of music shed,
Now hangs as mute on Tara's walls
As if that soul were fled.—
5   So sleeps the pride of former days,
So glory's thrill is o'er,
And hearts that once beat high for praise
Now feel that pulse no more.

No more to chiefs and ladies bright
10   The harp of Tara swells;
The chord alone that breaks at night
Its tale of ruin tells.
Thus Freedom now so seldom wakes,
The only throb she gives,
15   Is when some heart indignant breaks,
To show that still she lives.

---

1. **bards in fealty to Apollo hold.** Poets in loyalty to Apollo, god of music, poetry, prophecy
2. **demesne.** Realm
3. **ken.** Range of vision or understanding
4. **Cortez . . . Darien.** Cortez is an explorer, but it was Balboa who first saw the Pacific from Darien.
5. **Stygian set.** Ghosts of the dead who were ferried by Charon across the Styx river to Hades
6. **Tara.** In the Middle Ages, the capital of Ireland, which was a center of learning

"Casabianca"[7] by Felicia Dorothea Hemans

The boy stood on the burning deck
Whence all but he had fled;
The flame that lit the battle's wreck
Shone round him o'er the dead.

5   Yet beautiful and bright he stood,
As born to rule the storm;
A creature of heroic blood,
A proud, though childlike form.

The flames roll'd on—he would not go
10   Without his father's word;
That father, faint in death below,
His voice no longer heard.

He call'd aloud:—"Say, Father, say
If yet my task is done?"
15   He knew not that the chieftain lay
Unconscious of his son.

"Speak, Father!" once again he cried,
"If I may yet be gone!"
And but the booming shots replied,
20   And fast the flames roll'd on.

Upon his brow he felt their breath,
And in his waving hair,
And look'd from that lone post of death
In still, yet brave despair.

25   And shouted but once more aloud,
"My Father! must I stay?"
While o'er him fast, through sail and shroud,
The wreathing fires made way.

They wrapt the ship in splendor wild,
30   They caught the flag on high,
And stream'd above the gallant child,
Like banners in the sky.

There came a burst of thunder sound—
The boy—oh! where was he?
35   Ask of the winds that far around
With fragments strew'd the sea!—

With mast, and helm, and pennon fair,
That well had borne their part,
But the noblest thing which perish'd there
40   Was that young faithful heart!

---

7. **Casabianca.** A thirteen-year-old boy who remained at his post on the Orient after it had been abandoned during the Battle of the Nile, August 1, 1798

"DIRCE"

About the Author. Walter Savage Landor (1775–1864) lived and wrote in both the Romantic Era and the Victorian Age. Although his poetry was never popular in his lifetime, Landor is best known today for his short, elegant lyrics. He modeled many of these poems after Greek and Latin lyrics.

About the Selection. "Dirce" approximates the terse style and mythological subject of Greek lyrics.

"THE HARP THAT ONCE THROUGH TARA'S HALLS"

About the Author. Thomas Moore (1779–1852) was an Irish poet, best known for the lyrics and folk songs of his *Irish Melodies*. He was a close friend of Byron and wrote a biography of the poet, *Life of Byron,* in 1830. Although Moore's writing was very popular during the Romantic Era, much of his work was deemed sentimental by later readers and critics.

About the Selection. Like many of the songs in *Irish Melodies,* "The Harp That Once through Tara's Halls" was set to a traditional Irish tune.

"CASABIANCA"

About the Author. Felicia Dorothea Hemans (1793–1835) was best known for her Romantic lyric poetry. She was much admired as a poet by William Wordsworth and Sir Walter Scott. She wrote her *Poems,* published in 1808, between the ages of eight and thirteen. After separating from her husband, she was able to support five children by selling her poems.

About the Selection. The lyric poem "Casabianca" also has the elements of a ballad, telling the story of a young, doomed soldier. This poem has been committed to memory by countless students over the years.

About the Author. Jane Austen (1775–1817), one of the most important novelists in English literature, was the seventh child of a country rector in the south of England. Austen spent a lot of time with her brothers, sisters, and other relatives, who were an enthusiastic audience for her work. She and her sister Cassandra were particularly close, and they shared the same sense of humor and ideas about women and their roles in society. Although both girls were sent away briefly to school, they were primarily educated at home by their father.

Austen read voraciously as a teenager and began writing parodies of the sentimental fiction aimed at women of her time. The first three of her six major books were planned out when she was still very young, and her characters were drawn from her family's social class, the country gentry.

Soon after Jane's father died, she, her mother, and sister moved into a small cottage together and lived in a somewhat reduced economic status. Jane began revising and publishing her books rapidly at this time. Although she had read widely from Romantic and eighteenth-century literature, she defined herself, modestly, as "the most unlearned and uninformed female who ever dared to be an authoress." In keeping with the social custom for women of her class at that time, she published anonymously. However, her fiction was so successful that her identity was soon discovered.

At the age of forty-two, Jane Austen died after a brief illness. Austen's work has inspired and influenced many writers who came after her. One twentieth-century novelist, Virginia Woolf, wrote that Austen was "a mistress of much deeper emotion than appears upon the surface" and that she was "the most perfect artist among women."

(cont.)

from *Pride and Prejudice* by Jane Austen

It is a truth universally acknowledged, that a single man in possession of a good fortune, must be in want of a wife.

However little known the feelings or views of such a man may be on his first entering a neighborhood, this truth is so well fixed in the minds of the surrounding families, that he is considered as the rightful property of some one or other of their daughters.

"My dear Mr. Bennet," said his lady to him one day, "have you heard that Netherfield Park is let at last?"

Mr. Bennet replied that he had not.

"But it is," returned she; "for Mrs. Long has just been here, and she told me all about it."

Mr. Bennet made no answer.

"Do not you want to know who has taken it?" cried his wife impatiently.

"*You* want to tell me, and I have no objection to hearing it."

This was invitation enough.

"Why, my dear, you must know, Mrs. Long says that Netherfield is taken by a young man of large fortune from the north of England; that he came down on Monday in a chaise and four[1] to see the place, and was so much delighted with it that he agreed with Mr. Morris immediately; that he is to take possession before Michaelmas[2] and some of his servants are to be in the house by the end of next week."

"What is his name?"

"Bingley."

"Is he married or single?"

"Oh! single, my dear, to be sure! A single man of large fortune; four or five thousand a year. What a fine thing for our girls!"

"How so? How can it affect them?"

"My dear Mr. Bennet," replied his wife, "how can you be so tiresome! You must know that I am thinking of his marrying one of them."

"Is that his design in settling here?"

"Design! nonsense, how can you talk so! But it is very likely that he may fall in love with one of them, and therefore you must visit him as soon as he comes."

"I see no occasion for that. You and the girls may go, or you may send them by themselves, which perhaps will be still better, for as you are as handsome as any of them, Mr. Bingley might like you the best of the party."

"My dear, you flatter me. I certainly *have* had my share of beauty, but I do not pretend to be any thing extraordinary now. When a woman has five grown up daughters, she ought to give over thinking of her own beauty."

"In such cases, a woman has not often much beauty to think of."

"But, my dear, you must indeed go and see Mr. Bingley when he comes into the neighborhood."

"It is more than I engage for, I assure you."

"But consider your daughters. Only think what an establishment it would be for one of them. Sir William and Lady Lucas are determined to go, merely on that account, for in general you know they visit no newcomers. Indeed you must go, for it will be impossible for *us* to visit him, if you do not."

"You are over scrupulous surely. I dare say Mr. Bingley will be very glad to see you; and I will send a few lines by you to assure him of my hearty consent to his marrying which ever he chooses of the girls; though I must throw in a good word for my little Lizzy."

"I desire you will do no such thing. Lizzy is not a bit better than the others; and I am sure she is not half so handsome as Jane, nor half so good humored as Lydia. But you are always giving *her* the preference."

"They have none of them much to recommend them," replied he; "they are all silly and ignorant like other girls; but Lizzy has something more of quickness than her sisters."

"Mr. Bennet, how can you abuse your own children in such a way? You take delight in vexing me. You have no compassion on my poor nerves."

"You mistake me, my dear. I have a high respect for your nerves. They are my old friends. I have heard you mention them with consideration these twenty years at least."

"Ah! you do not know what I suffer."

"But I hope you will get over it, and live to see many young men of four thousand a year come into the neighborhood."

"It will be no use to us, if twenty such should come, since you will not visit them."

"Depend upon it, my dear, that when there are twenty, I will visit them all."

Mr. Bennet was so odd a mixture of quick parts, sarcastic humor, reserve, and caprice, that the experience of three and twenty years had been insufficient to make his wife understand his character. *Her* mind was less difficult to develop.[3] She was a woman of mean understanding, little information, and uncertain temper. When she was discontented she fancied herself nervous. The business of her life was to get her daughters married; its solace was visiting and news.

from "Macbeth" by William Hazlitt

*"The poet's eye in a fine
frenzy rolling*

---

1. **chaise and four.** A closed carriage drawn by four horses
2. **Michaelmas.** September 29

3. **develop.** Understand

About the Selection. The selection is from Jane Austen's most popular novel, *Pride and Prejudice,* which she began to draft at about age twenty-two under the working title *First Impressions.* Like much of Austen's work, this draft was enjoyed exclusively by her family and friends years before it became published and widely read. Austen's original draft was completed in August of 1797, and the completed novel was finally published under the title *Pride and Prejudice* in January of 1813. In this book, as in her work generally, Austen attacks the traditions and ideas about romance typical of her time. *Pride and Prejudice* is an amusing satire of social customs related to courtship and marriage.

Doth glance from heaven to
    earth, from earth to heaven;
And as imagination bodies forth
The forms of things
    unknown, the poet's pen
Turns them to shape, and
    gives to airy nothing
A local habitation and a name."[1]

Macbeth and *Lear*, *Othello* and *Hamlet*, are usually reckoned Shakespeare's four principal tragedies. *Lear* stands first for the profound intensity of the passion; *Macbeth* for the wildness of the imagination and the rapidity of the action; *Othello* for the progressive interest and powerful alternations of feeling; *Hamlet* for the refined development of thought and sentiment. If the force of genius shown in each of these works is astonishing, their variety is not less so. They are like different creations of the same mind, not one of which has the slightest reference to the rest. This distinctness and originality is indeed the necessary consequence of truth and nature. Shakespeare's genius alone appeared to possess the resources of nature. He is "your only *tragedy maker*." His plays have the force of things upon the mind. What he represents is brought home to the bosom as a part of our experience, implanted in the memory as if we had known the places, persons, and things of which he treats. *Macbeth* is like a record of a preternatural and tragical event. It has the rugged severity of an old chronicle with all that the imagination of the poet can engraft upon traditional belief. The castle of Macbeth, round which "the air smells wooingly," and where "the temple-haunting martlet builds," has a real subsistence in the mind; the Weird Sisters meet us in person on "the blasted heath"; the "air-drawn dagger" moves slowly before our eyes; the "gracious Duncan," the "blood-boltered Banquo" stand before us; all that passed through the mind of Macbeth passes, without the loss of a tittle, through ours. All that could actually take place, and all that is only possible to be conceived, what was said and what was done, the workings of passion, the spells of magic, are brought before us with the same absolute truth and vividness.

Shakespeare excelled in the openings of his plays: that of *Macbeth* is the most striking of any. The wildness of the scenery, the sudden shifting of the situations and characters, the bustle, the expectations excited, are equally extraordinary. From the first entrance of the Witches and the description of them when they meet Macbeth:

What are these
So wither'd and so wild
    in their attire,

---

1. **"The poet's . . . name."** From Shakespeare's *A Midsummer Night's Dream*, Act V. scene i.

That look not like the
    inhabitants of th' earth
And yet are on't?

the mind is prepared for all that follows.

This tragedy is alike distinguished for the lofty imagination it displays, and for the tumultuous vehemence of the action; and the one is made the moving principle of the other. The overwhelming pressure of preternatural agency urges on the tide of human passion with redoubled force. Macbeth himself appears driven along by the violence of his fate like a vessel drifting before a storm: he reels to and fro like a drunken man; he staggers under the weight of his own purposes and the suggestions of others; he stands at bay with his situation; and from the superstitious awe and breathless suspense into which the communications of the Weird Sisters throw him is hurried on with daring impatience to verify their predictions, and with impious and bloody hand to tear aside the veil which hides the uncertainty of the future. He is not equal to the struggle with fate and conscience. He now "bends up each corporal instrument to the terrible feat"; at other times his heart misgives him, and he is cowed and abashed by his success. "The deed, no less than the attempt, confounds him." His mind is assailed by the stings of remorse, and full of "preternatural solicitings." His speeches and soliloquies are dark riddles on human life, baffling solution, and entangling him in their labyrinths. In thought he is absent and perplexed, sudden and desperate in act, from a distrust of his own resolution. His energy springs from the anxiety and agitation of his mind. His blindly rushing forward on the objects of his ambition and revenge, or his recoiling from them, equally betrays the harassed state of his feelings. This part of his character is admirably set off by being brought in connection with that of Lady Macbeth, whose obdurate strength of will and masculine firmness give her the ascendancy over her husband's faltering virtue. She at once seizes on the opportunity that offers for the accomplishment of all their wished-for greatness, and never flinches from her object till all is over. The magnitude of her resolution almost covers the magnitude of her guilt. She is a great bad woman, whom we hate, but whom we fear more than we hate. She does not excite our loathing and abhorrence like Regan and Goneril.[2] She is only wicked to gain a great end and is perhaps more distinguished by her commanding presence of mind and inexorable self-will, which do not suffer her to be diverted from a bad purpose, when once formed, by weak and womanly regrets, than by the hardness of her heart or want of natural affections. The impression which her lofty determination of character makes on the mind of Macbeth is well described where he exclaims:

---

2. **Regan and Goneril.** The two evil daughters in Shakespeare's *King Lear*

FROM "MACBETH"

About the Author. William Hazlitt (1778–1830) was the son of a Unitarian minister whose outspoken support of the American and French revolutions led him to move his family to America when William was seven. The Hazlitts returned four years later, but William retained his radical political convictions throughout his life. He studied painting but abandoned it and began his career as a writer in 1812. As a literary critic, Hazlitt examined the work of his contemporaries as well as the works of Shakespeare and other Elizabethan playwrights. His essays have an energy and enthusiasm absent from other prose of the Romantic Era; he preferred to state a topic and simply expand on it rather than structure his argument formally. Hazlitt described his own writing as "impressions," or his immediate emotional responses to a literary work, rather than criticism.

About the Selection. This selection is taken from "**Macbeth**," an essay on Shakespeare's play. With his characteristic breathless energy and no-nonsense descriptiveness, Hazlitt examines what makes *Macbeth* one of Shakespeare's greatest tragedies.

ADDITIONAL QUESTIONS AND ACTIVITIES

• Why is the opening of *Macbeth* the "most striking of any" of Shakespeare's plays?

Answer. It is most striking because it immediately establishes the wild, active, expectant mood of the play.

• What is Hazlitt's opinion of the character of Lady Macbeth?

Answer. He admires the character's strength and drive; unlike the wavering Macbeth, she knows what she wants and how to get it.

QUOTABLES

❝Though we are mighty fine fellows nowadays, we cannot write like Hazlitt.❞

—Robert Louis Stevenson

LITERARY TECHNIQUE

A **parody** is a literary work that imitates another work for humorous, often satirical, purposes. Jane Austen's works parodied some of the fiction aimed at the women of her day. How would you describe that type of fiction, and where might you find it represented in current fiction?

Answer. The fiction that Austen parodied was probably sentimental and melodramatic, full of stories of women seeking marriage to wealthy men with good social standing. The same ideas are represented in paperback romance novels set both in the past and the present, in which the female protagonist endures many hardships and broken hearts but finally wins the love of a reluctant but repentant man.

ADDITIONAL QUESTIONS AND ACTIVITIES

• If students have read *Macbeth,* have them compare their impressions of Lady Macbeth to Hazlitt's opinions.

• How are Lady Macbeth and the Witches alike? How are they different?

Answers. Like Lady Macbeth, they urge Macbeth to his fate. However, they do this purely to make mischief rather than to gain power. Where Lady Macbeth is passionate, the Witches are cold.

• What principle is stronger in *Macbeth* than in Shakespeare's other plays? What is an example of this principle?

Answers. The principle of contrast is strongest in *Macbeth.* By contrast, Hazlitt means the struggle between opposing forces and the struggle between life and death.

ADDITIONAL QUESTIONS AND ACTIVITIES

Students can read or enact the scenes from *Macbeth* (page 320) that Hazlitt mentions. Have students work in pairs or small groups to prepare scenes involving Macbeth, Lady Macbeth, or the Weird Sisters. Encourage students to study Hazlitt's essay for ideas about character motivation.

> *Bring forth men children only;*
> *For thy undaunted mettle should compose*
> *Nothing but males!*

Nor do the pains she is at to "screw his courage to the sticking-place," the reproach to him, not to be "lost so poorly in himself," the assurance that "a little water clears them of this deed," show anything but her greater consistency in depravity. Her strong-nerved ambition furnishes ribs of steel to "the sides of his intent"; and she is herself wound up to the execution of her baneful project with the same unshrinking fortitude in crime, that in other circumstances she would probably have shown patience in suffering. The deliberate sacrifice of all other considerations to the gaining "for their future days and nights sole sovereign sway and masterdom," by the murder of Duncan, is gorgeously expressed in her invocation on hearing of "his fatal entrance under her battlements":

> *Come all you spirits*
> *That tend on mortal thoughts, unsex me here:*
> *And fill me, from the crown to th' toe, top-full*
> *Of direst cruelty; make thick my blood,*
> *Stop up the access and passage to remorse,*
> *That no compunctious visitings of nature*
> *Shake my fell purpose, nor keep peace between*
> *The effect and it. Come to my woman's breasts,*
> *And take my milk for gall, you murthering ministers,*
> *Wherever in your sightless substances*
> *You wait on nature's mischief. Come, thick night!*
> *And pall thee in the dunnest smoke of hell,*
> *That my keen knife see not the wound it makes,*
> *Nor heav'n peep through the blanket of the dark,*
> *To cry, hold, hold!*

When she first hears that "Duncan comes there to sleep" she is so overcome by the news, which is beyond her utmost expectations, that she answers the messenger, "Thou 'rt mad to say it"; and on receiving her husband's account of the predictions of the Witches, conscious of his instability of purpose, and that her presence is necessary to goad him on to the consummation of his promised greatness, she exclaims:

> *Hie thee hither,*
> *That I may pour my spirits in thine ear,*
> *And chastise with the valor of my tongue*
> *All that impedes thee from the golden round,*
> *Which fate and metaphysical aid doth seem*
> *To have thee crowned withal.*

This swelling exultation and keen spirit of triumph, this uncontrollable eagerness of anticipation, which seems to dilate her form and take possession of all her faculties, this solid, substantial flesh and blood display of passion, exhibit a striking contrast to the cold, abstracted, gratuitous, servile malignity of the Witches, who are equally instrumental in urging Macbeth to his fate for the mere love of mischief, and from a disinterested delight in deformity and cruelty. They are hags of mischief, obscene panders to iniquity, malicious from their impotence of enjoyment, enamored of destruction, because they are themselves unreal, abortive, half-existences, who become sublime from their exemption from all human sympathies and contempt for all human affairs, as Lady Macbeth does by the force of passion! Her fault seems to have been an excess of that strong principle of self-interest and family aggrandizement, not amenable to the common feelings of compassion and justice, which is so marked a feature in barbarous nations and times. A passing reflection of this kind, on the resemblance of the sleeping king to her father, alone prevents her from slaying Duncan with her own hand. . . .

Macbeth (generally speaking) is done upon a stronger and more systematic principle of contrast than any other of Shakespeare's plays. It moves upon the verge of an abyss and is a constant struggle between life and death. The action is desperate and the reaction is dreadful. It is a huddling together of fierce extremes, a war of opposite natures, which of them shall destroy the other. There is nothing but what has a violent end or violent beginnings. The lights and shades are laid on with a determined hand; the transitions from triumph to despair, from the height of terror to the repose of death, are sudden and startling; every passion brings in its fellow-contrary, and the thoughts pitch and jostle against each other as in the dark. The whole play is an unruly chaos of strange and forbidden things, where the ground rocks under our feet. Shakespeare's genius here took its full swing, and trod upon the farthest bounds of nature and passion.

PREREADING

Poems from *The Narrow Road to the Deep North and Other Travel Sketches*

by Matsuo Bashō, trans. by Nobuyuki Yuasa

ABOUT THE AUTHOR

Matsuo Bashō (1644–1694) was the pen name of Matsuo Munefusa, the greatest of the Japanese haiku poets. Born near the holy city of Kyoto, he became interested in poetry while still a youth. However, until 1666, he put his literary interests aside while serving a local lord. Munefusa was a member of the samurai, or warrior, class, but after the death of his lord, he gave up that status to pursue a literary career. He moved to Edo (modern-day Tokyo) and worked as a poet and critic. Later, influenced by his study of Zen philosophy, he was drawn to a simple, reclusive life. He moved to the country and adopted the name *Bashō,* from *Bashō-an,* the word for the simple hut in which he lived. Bashō's poetry, like Zen philosophy, finds beauty and meaning in the simplest of natural phenomena. Bashō views blossoms on a mountainside, an ear of wheat, or the antlers of a deer and sees in each of them an eternal truth. The natural object becomes a symbol of the affinity or interconnectedness of all things.

ABOUT THE SELECTIONS

In 1694, Bashō wrote **The Narrow Road to the Deep North,** a book describing one of the many journeys that he took during his lifetime. During these journeys, he stayed with other poets or at Buddhist temples. The book has become one of the great classics of the world's literature, not only for the beauty of its prose descriptions, but also for the incidental poetry that it contains.

The selections that follow are examples of haiku from *The Narrow Road to the Deep North.* A **haiku** is a short, unrhymed poem of seventeen syllables divided into three lines of five syllables, seven syllables, and five again (although in translations, this scheme is often varied). A haiku presents one or more images—words that describe things that can be seen, touched, tasted, heard, or smelled—in an attempt to capture a passing moment of reflection. In the greatest of haiku, like those of Bashō, observation of some simple phenomenon in nature suggests a deeper meaning. The overall effect is of sudden revelation, of a deep truth emerging from a fleeting experience and compressed into a few words.

ADDITIONAL RESOURCES

READER'S GUIDE
- Selection Worksheet, 8.19

ASSESSMENT PORTFOLIO
- Selection Check Test, 4.8.37
- Selection Test, 4.8.38

ENRICHMENT ACTIVITIES

Students can discuss or write about the similarities and differences between Bashō's life and the life of William Wordsworth, Percy Shelley, Byron, or another of the English Romantic poets.

SUPPORT FOR LEP STUDENTS

Students whose first language is Japanese might be able to locate these haiku or others written by Bashō in Japanese. Have these students work with students who have difficulty appreciating or understanding the haiku.

ADDITIONAL VOCABULARY

ear—grain-bearing part of certain plants
tine—prong
willy-nilly—regardless of one's wishes

GOALS/OBJECTIVES

Studying this lesson will enable students to

- interpret and appreciate haiku poems
- describe how Bashō's poetry relates to poetry of the Romantic Era in England
- explain what a haiku is and describe its structure
- describe the role of nature in Bashō's poetry
- make comparisons between literature of different cultural origins

Japan

POEMS FROM

The Narrow Road to the Deep North and Other Travel Sketches

MATSUO BASHŌ, TRANS. BY NOBUYUKI YUASA

1
God of this mountain,
May you be kind enough
To show me your face
Among the dawning blossoms?

2
Together let us eat
Ears of wheat,
Sharing at night
A grass pillow.

3
Just as a stag's antlers
Are split into tines,
So I must go willy-nilly
Separated from my friend.

4
In the days
Of the ancient gods,
A mere seedling
This pine must have been.

Reviewing the Selection

1. What does the speaker ask of the "God of this mountain"?

2. In what sense might blossoms be described as "dawning"?

3. What simple actions in the second haiku show a deep connection between two people?

4. What similarity exists between the speaker and his friend and the antlers of a stag?

5. What thought does the speaker have on viewing a pine tree?

Connections (Questions for Writing or Discussion)

1. Reread the selections from Byron's *Childe Harold's Pilgrimage* on page 635. Given what Byron has to say in those selections, would he understand the sentiment expressed in the first haiku by Bashō? Explain.

2. Reread Wordsworth's "The World is Too Much with Us" on page 611. What, according to Wordsworth, do we lose by not being connected with nature? How does the poetry of Bashō and of Shelley in "Ode to the West Wind" (page 625) illustrate the value of communion with nature? What do Bashō and Shelley learn by observing nature closely?

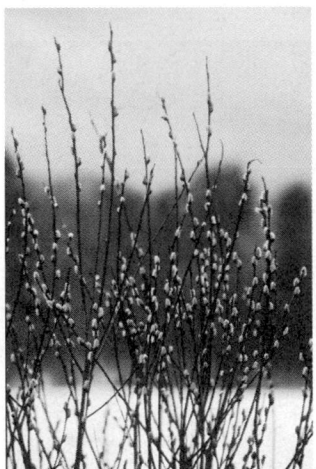

▶ Give students the following exercise.

Choose twenty words from the vocabulary list on page 684 that you would like to make part of your active vocabulary. For each word, find its original meaning in a dictionary and write one or two sentences explaining how the word could have developed its current meaning.
Example.
The word *puerile* means "childish." It comes from the Latin word for boy—*puer*—and a boy is a child.

ADDITIONAL RESOURCES

ASSESSMENT PORTFOLIO
• Vocabulary Worksheet, 4.8.39
• Study Guide: Unit 8 Test, 4.8.40
• Unit 8 Test, 4.8.41

ESSENTIAL SKILLS PRACTICE BOOKS
Language
• Agreement in Inverted Sentences, 2.73
• Clichés and Euphemisms, 2.152
• Common and Proper Nouns, 2.3
• Compound Sentences, 2.43
• Correcting Run-ons, 2.62
• Dialects of English, 2.150
• Improper Shifts in Verb Tense, 2.65
• Adding Prepositional Phrases, 2.47
• Proofreading for Errors in Capitalization, 2.107–2.133
• Register, 2.148
• Split Infinitives, 2.68
• Tone and Voice, 2.149

Speaking and Listening
• Interpersonal Communication, 3.5
• Public Speaking, 3.7

Study and Research
• Classifying, 4.7
• Comparing and Contrasting, 4.8
• Computer-assisted Research, 4.26
• Making Hypotheses, 4.13
• Memorizing, 4.4
• Observing, 4.6
• Organizing an Answer to an Essay Question, 4.46
• Reading Actively: Predicting, 4.18
• Remembering and Visualizing, 4.5
• Sentence-completion Questions, 4.41
• Short-answer Questions, 4.38
• True/False Questions, 4.36
• Using Dictionaries, 4.24
• Using Reference Works, 4.23
• Using Searching Tools, 4.21
• Using Thesauruses, 4.25

UNIT REVIEW

The Romantic Era

VOCABULARY FROM THE SELECTIONS

adieu, 643	epithet, 649	platitude, 656	specious, 648
aspire, 592	erroneous, 607	prevail, 618	sublime, 616
beauteous, 615	exhortation, 618	principal, 607	tranquil, 615
blight, 596	ignoble, 577, 649	progeny, 658	tumult, 601, 628
caprice, 648	impetuous, 628	provoke, 576	ungenial, 655
cavern, 600	ingenious, 648	puerile, 648	vagrant, 615
chasm, 627	ingenuous, 577	recompense, 617	vain, 616
circumscribe, 635	insinuate, 649	repose, 614	vainly, 635
citadel, 644	jocund, 576	reverie, 657	visage, 623
contemplate, 607	kindred, 608	satirize, 648	zeal, 619
copse, 614	manacle, 595	scrupulous, 648	zenith, 626
corporeal, 616	meander, 601	secluded, 614	
deity, 642	obscure, 576	sepulchre *or*	
dirge, 579, 626	organic, 608	sepulcher, 626	
emphatic, 607	ostentatiously, 607	serenely, 632	
endeavor, 608	pestilence, 625	sordid, 611	

LITERARY TERMS

allegory, 591	didactic criticism, 652	paradox, 613, 646
alliteration, 594, 603	elegy, 574, 580	pastoral poem, 591
allusion, 613, 652	epitaph, 580	personification, 629
aphorism, 646	essay, 572	repetition, 637
apostrophe, 645	free verse, 620	setting, 597
autobiography, 659	Gothic novel, 572	simile, 634
blank verse, 620	hymn, 585	sonnet, 606, 613, 641
Byronic hero, 637	iambic tetrameter, 634	speaker, 581
catharsis, 660	image, 587, 597	symbol, 589, 603, 641
character, 594, 624	irony of situation, 624	theme, 610, 641, 646
definition, 610	metaphor, 587	
dialect, 582	ode, 620	

SYNTHESIS: QUESTIONS FOR WRITING, RESEARCH, OR DISCUSSION

GENRE STUDIES

1. **Lyric Poetry.** Lyric poems of the Romantic Era tended to express strong personal feelings. Compare and contrast the feelings expressed in the following poems: "John Anderson, My Jo," "She Dwelt among the Untrodden Ways," and "She Walks in Beauty." In each case, describe the speaker and what he or she is feeling. Also explain who the speaker is addressing in each case and what the speaker has to say about this person.

THEMATIC STUDIES

2. **Coping with Death.** The poets of the Romantic Era wrote often about subjects that evoke strong feelings. One such subject is death. Explore the theme of coping with death in the following poems: "Elegy Written in a Country Churchyard," "Lines Composed a Few Miles above Tintern Abbey," and "When I Have Fears." In each case, explain the feelings about death that are expressed by the speaker and what comfort, if any, the speaker offers.

3. **Nature in Romantic Poetry.** Many Romantic Era poets exalted nature over the works of human beings. Describe the view of nature and of human works expressed in the following poems: "The world Is too much with us," "Ozymandias," "Ode to the West Wind," and the selection from *Childe Harold's Pilgrimage.*

HISTORICAL AND BIOGRAPHICAL STUDIES

4. **Human Rights.** The major events influencing the development of the spirit of the Romantic Era were the American and French Revolutions. These revolutions attempted to redress social evils, such as the inequities that existed between common people and wealthy members of the nobility. Explain the political significance of the following pieces from the unit: "Elegy Written in a Country Churchyard," "London," the selection from the Preface to *Lyrical Ballads,* "Ozymandias," the selection from *A Vindication of the Rights of Woman,* and the selections from *Declaration of Rights* (in the Selections for Additional Reading, page 675).

▶ These prompts are suitable as topics for research papers. Refer to the Language Arts Survey, 4.20–4.34, "Research Skills." (To evaluate research papers, see the evaluation forms for writing, revising, and proofreading in the *Assessment Portfolio,* 7.1–7.10.)

▶ These prompts can be adapted for use as topics for oral reports or debates. (To evaluate these projects, see the evaluation forms in the *Assessment Portfolio,* 7.17–7.19.)

LANGUAGE LAB   EDITING FOR COMMA ERRORS

Commas separate or set off certain elements in a sentence. A comma should be used after a mild exclamation such as *yes, no, oh,* or *well;* after an introductory participial phrase; after two or more introductory prepositional phrases; and after an introductory adverb clause. A comma is also used to set off interrupters such as parenthetical expressions or words used in direct address. Use a comma to separate items in a series unless *all* the items are joined by *and, or,* or *nor.* Two or more adjectives preceding a noun are separated by commas. Use commas before *and, but, for, nor, or, so,* and *yet* when they join independent clauses. The comma may be omitted before *and, but, nor,* or *or* if the clauses are very short and the resulting sentence is still clear in meaning. Use commas before and after nonrestrictive phrases and clauses and before and after most appositives and appositive phrases.

When revising and proofreading, check for missing and misplaced commas. For additional help, see the Language Arts Survey 2.94–2.96.

COMMA USAGE	
MILD EXCLAMATION	Yes, Mary, I really do think you should develop the story into a book.
PARTICIPIAL PHRASES	Building on your original idea of a dead body revivified, you might consider making Dr. Frankenstein's motivations clearer.
TWO PREPOSITIONAL PHRASES	In the case of Dr. Frankenstein, everyone will want to know why he refused to accept his own creation.
ADVERB CLAUSE	When he first sees his creation, what does he think?
PARENTHETICAL EXPRESSION	Did you, by the way, finish that book by Erasmus Darwin?
DIRECT ADDRESS	Percy, you know that book is what stimulated my thinking.
WORDS IN A SERIES	It came to me that evening when you, George, and I were sitting by the fire.
PHRASES IN A SERIES	Felicia Hemans was born in Liverpool, moved to St. Asaph as a girl, and left there when she married.
CLAUSES IN A SERIES	Walter Scott believed that Hemans's openings were gifted, that her work was deserving of notoriety, and that her writing was "somewhat too poetical."
TWO OR MORE ADJECTIVES	The boy stood on the burning, blistering deck.
LONG INDEPENDENT CLAUSE	A collection of poetry by Hemans was published in the United States in 1825, and her poetry became quite popular there.
SHORT CLAUSE	Hemans composed songs and she also wrote plays.
RESTRICTIVE PHRASE OR CLAUSE	The first book that Hemans published was called *Poems.*

ADDITIONAL EXAMPLES

Mild Exclamation: Yes, Sara, I really do think the book would make a wonderful movie.

Participial Phrases: Knowing that Roberto loved to cook, I bought him a new a pan and a cookbook.

Two Prepositional Phrases: In the event of a hurricane, please be careful with the candles in the wind.

Adverb Clause: When you recite "Ode to the West Wind," will you be nervous?

Parenthetical Expression: Jaki, on the other hand, prefers Romantic prose.

Direct Address: Tyrone, do you enjoy the poetry of William Wordsworth?

Words in a Series: One spring morning, you, Robin, and I should take a long walk on the beach.

Phrases in a Series: Bradford's mother went to college in Indiana, was a successful writer, and then became a full-time university professor.

Clauses in a Series: My teacher Ms. Roja told me that my poem was unique, that it was beautiful, but that the last lines needed some work.

Two or More Adjectives: The long, complex poem is considered a classic of English literature.

Long Independent Clause: A section of our town library is reserved for horror and science fiction, and *Frankenstein* by Mary Shelley is featured there.

Short Clause: Samantha read "Kubla Khan" and she read "The Rime of the Ancient Mariner."

Restrictive Phrase or Clause: The first essay I wrote was called "Themes of the Romantic Era."

COMMA USAGE

NON RESTRICTIVE PHRASE OR CLAUSE	Hemans, who often wrote on patriotic themes, had two brothers who fought in the Peninsular War.
APPOSITIVE OR APPOSITIVE PHRASE	Hemans, a working mother, wrote and sold poetry to support herself and her children.

EXERCISE A

Rewrite the following sentences, adding commas as necessary.

1. What can ail thee Knight-at-arms alone and palely loitering?

2. The sedge has withered from the lake and no birds sing.

3. I met a lady in the meadow a fairy's child.

4. Her hair was long her foot was light and her eyes were wild.

5. She took me to her elfin grotto and there I shut her wild wild eyes with kisses four.

6. Lying there on the cold hillside I dreamed of pale kings and princes who cried: "La Belle Dame sans Merci hath thee in thrall!"

7. In the darkness on that hillside I saw their starved lips.

8. The lady whom the knight met in the meads was "La Belle Dame sans Merci."

9. No the fairy's child as you may have guessed was not there when I awoke.

10. Sometime after I awakened John Keats who is a poet found me and asked me why I was alone and palely loitering for he thought I looked troubled.

EXERCISE B

Rewrite the following paragraph, adding commas as necessary.

[1] Yes the young Wordsworth supported the French Revolution but he later became disillusioned with its excesses. [2] When the Reign of Terror began under the leadership of Robespierre Wordsworth became despondent. [3] He felt that the French Revolutionaries had betrayed their ideals of liberty equality and fraternity. [4] In the latter part of his life Wordsworth renounced his youthful democratic sympathies and became more conservative. [5] Robert Browning a younger poet deplored Wordworth's later renunciation of radicalism and called him "The Lost Leader."

Exercise A

1. What can ail thee, Knight-at-arms, alone and palely loitering?

2. The sedge has withered from the lake and no birds sing.

3. I met a lady in the meadow, a fairy's child.

4. Her hair was long, her foot was light, and her eyes were wild.

5. She took me to her elfin grotto and there I shut her wild, wild eyes with kisses four.

6. Lying there on the cold hillside, I dreamed of pale kings and princes who cried: "La Belle Dame sans Merci hath thee in thrall!"

7. In the darkness on that hillside, I saw their starved lips.

8. The lady whom the knight met in the meads was "La Belle Dame sans Merci."

9. No, the fairy's child, as you may have guessed, was not there when I awoke.

10. Sometime after I awakened, John Keats, who is a poet, found me and asked me why I was alone and palely loitering, for he thought I looked troubled.

Exercise B

[1] Yes, the young Wordsworth supported the French Revolution, but he later became disillusioned with its excesses. [2] When the Reign of Terror began under the leadership of Robespierre, Wordsworth became despondent. [3] He felt that the French Revolutionaries had betrayed their ideals of liberty, equality, and fraternity. [4] In the latter part of his life, Wordsworth renounced his youthful democratic sympathies and became more conservative. [5] Robert Browning, a younger poet, deplored Wordsworth's later renunciation of radicalism and called him "The Lost Leader."

UNIT 9 THE VICTORIAN AGE (1832–1900)

Fair, Quiet and Sweet Rest. Sir Luke Fildes, 1844–1927. (detail)
Warrington Museum & Art Gallery, Lancs./Bridgeman Art Library, London

GOALS/OBJECTIVES

Studying this unit will enable students to

- gain an appreciation for the poetry and prose of the Victorian Age
- describe the reactions of writers and intellectuals to the scientific revolution, the Industrial Revolution, and their consequences
- describe Victorian England's ideas of the role of art and artists
- explain the concept of Realism in literature
- understand the concepts of dramatic monologue, metaphor, and symbol
- identify and correct common punctuation errors

od's in his heaven

All's right with the world!

—Robert Browning,
Song from *Pippa Passes*

Ah, love, let us be true

To one another! for the world, which seems

To lie before us like a land of dreams,

So various, so beautiful, so new,

Hath really neither joy, nor love, nor light,

Nor certitude, nor peace, nor help for pain

—Matthew Arnold, "Dover Beach"

689

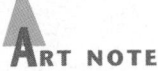

ART NOTE

Sir Luke Fildes, born October 18, 1843, died February 27, 1927, was a fashionable British painter of social scenes and portraits in Victorian England. He began his career in 1863 as a magazine illustrator in London, and illustrated Dickens's last novel, *Edwin Drood.* In the 1870s, he began painting. His most famous works were realistic depictions of social issues. His *Applicants for Admission to a Casual Ward* (1874; Royal Holloway College, London) and *The Doctor* (1891; Tate Gallery, London) were his two most popular works. In 1906, Fildes received a knighthood.

CONNECTIONS ACROSS THE CURRICULUM

ARTS AND HUMANITIES
• Art Criticism, 776
• Art History, 733, 739
• Role of the Artist, 698, 748

MATHEMATICS AND SCIENCES
• Grieving Process, 722
• Mercury Poisoning, 748
• Researching Moors, 812
• Urban Migration, 692

SOCIAL STUDIES
• Aging in the United States, 708
• Census and Religion, 740
• Colonialism, 691
• Darwin and Smith, 692
• English Events, 752
• The English Estate, 792
• Fin de Siècle, 751
• Map Skills, 740
• Mapping Odysseus, 708
• Medieval History, 702
• Research Report, 723
• Role of the Artist, 698
• "The Woman Question," 770
• Victorian Poorhouse, 819

APPLIED ARTS
• A Chapbook, 776
• Weaving, 703

TEACHING THE MULTIPLE INTELLIGENCES

MUSICAL
• Refrain, 706
• Elegiac Lyric, 722
• Setting a Poem to Music, 723

LOGICAL-MATHEMATICAL
• Census and Religion, 740

SPATIAL
• Fin de Siècle, 751
• Mapping Odysseus, 708
• Map Skills, 740
• Place Memories, 795
• Sketch, 775
• Vocabulary Crossword Puzzle, 823
• Weaving, 703

KINESTHETIC
• Comparing Narrators, 819
• Dialogue, 795
• Dramatic Skit, 739
• Poem Role Playing, 728
• Weaving, 703

INTERPERSONAL
• Comparing Narrators, 819
• Elements of Nonverbal Communication, 770
• Friendship, 773
• Ironic Description, 728
• Oral History, 723
• Personal Experiences, 738
• Personal Limitations, 738
• Self-Eulogy, 712

HISTORICAL NOTE

During the reign of Queen Victoria the role of the monarch in England changed drastically. Initially very intrigued by and protective of her political power, Victoria gave increasing control to Albert after their marriage. After Albert died in 1861, Victoria, deeply depressed, retreated into mourning and retirement, surrounding herself with momentos and photographs of her lost husband. Victoria remained absent from both politics and public life until the fiftieth anniversary of her coronation, the Jubilee of 1887. Originally planned as a procession through the London streets to display the restored grandeur of the monarchy and to renew the people's confidence, the Jubilee quickly became something else: an example of the Victorian love of spectacle, a consumer frenzy, and a manufacturer's dream. While the monarchy never regained the political power it held in preceding centuries, it did gain a certain appeal and mystique. Victoria, her image stamped on everything from Jubilee banners to Jubilee commemorative thimbles, became something unique to British history: a living symbol of burgeoning consumer culture. Interested students may read selections of George Grissing's novel about gender roles at that time, *In the Year of Jubilee.*

Queen Victoria of England. *Sir George Hayter, 1838. The Granger Collection, NY*

THE VICTORIAN LEGACY

To understand the world in which we live today, one must go back to the **Victorian Age** (1832–1900), for the titanic forces that have shaped our century emerged during that time. In those years, enormous changes occurred in political and social life in England and in the rest of the world—the scientific and technical innovations of the Industrial Revolution, the emergence of modern nationalism, and the European colonization of much of Africa, the Middle East, and the Far East. The period produced far-reaching new ideas and one of the greatest outpourings of literary production the world has ever seen.

VICTORIA AND ALBERT

The period takes its name from **Queen Victoria** (1819–1901) who ruled England from 1837 to 1901. Her sixty-four-year reign was the longest in British history. When Victoria became queen at the age of eighteen, she was a graceful, self-assured young woman. Throughout her reign, she maintained a sense of dignity and decorum that restored the average person's high opinion of the monarchy after a series of dissolute, ineffectual leaders. (Today, the term *Victorian* is often associated with extreme or hypocritical prudery. However, that fact probably has more to do with middle-class attitudes in Victorian England than with the character of Victoria herself.) In 1840, Victoria married a German prince, Albert of Saxe-Coburg-Gotha, who became not king, but prince consort. Together, Victoria and Albert set a standard of national pride and optimism that influenced their subjects to bring about enormous changes in the world. However, England's political leadership lay not with them but with the prime ministers and the elected members of the two bodies of Parliament, the House of Commons and the House of Lords.

LITERARY EVENTS

► = British Events

► 1850. Tennyson publishes *In Memoriam* and becomes poet laureate

1848. Marx and Engels publish *The Communist Manifesto*

►1847. Charlotte Brontë publishes *Jane Eyre;* Emily Brontë publishes *Wuthering Heights*

►1843. William Wordsworth becomes poet laureate

1830	1835	1840	1845	1850

►1832. First Reform Act extends suffrage to more men

►1833. Abolitionist victory; Britain abolishes slavery within empire

►1834. Poor-Law-Amendment Act extends use of workhouses

►1837. Chartist Movement begins

HISTORICAL EVENTS

►1837. Victoria ascends throne; reigns until 1901

►1840. Victoria marries Prince Albert

►1842–45. Corn Laws repealed

►1844. YMCA founded

►1845. Beginning of Great Potato Famine in Ireland

►1848. Dante Gabrielle Rossetti and friends found Pre-Raphaelite Brotherhood

►1848. Public Health Act improves sanitation, drinking water

►1850. Public Libraries Act establishes libraries

►1851. Great Exhibition held

690 *UNIT NINE / THE VICTORIAN AGE*

THEMATIC CURRENTS

Use the following selections to explore these themes with your students.

DISILLUSIONMENT
- from *In Memoriam,* 712
- "Dover Beach," 740
- "The Darkling Thrush," 751
- "Promises Like Pie-Crust," 772
- "To an Athlete Dying Young," 777

ART
- "The Lady of Shalott," 698
- "Andrea del Sarto," 729
- "In an Artist's Studio," 770
- "The Slave Ship," 810
- Preface to *The Picture of Dorian Gray,* 822

NATURE
- "God's Grandeur," 764
- from *Sing-Song,* 767
- from *The Mill on the Floss,* 781
- "The Night is Darkening," 809

THE GROWTH OF THE BRITISH EMPIRE

During the Victorian Era, England grew to become the most powerful nation on earth, ruler of a vast empire on which, in the words of Prime Minister Benjamin Disraeli, the sun never set. Its dominions included the relatively independent and self-governing countries of Canada, Australia, and New Zealand, as well as imperial colonies in Hong Kong, Singapore, South Africa, Rhodesia (modern Zimbabwe), Kenya, Cyprus, British Guyana, Ceylon, and, the "jewel in the British crown," India (modern India, Pakistan, and Bangladesh).

The origins of **British Imperialism** lay in the defeat, during the Elizabethan Era, of the Spanish Armada, which made England the undisputed master of the seas. During the centuries that followed, England built a large navy and merchant fleet for purposes of trade and colonization. England imported raw materials from overseas, such as cotton from the Americas and silk from China, and exported finished goods made in British factories. By the middle of the eighteenth century, England was the largest exporter and importer, the primary manufacturer, and the wealthiest country in the world.

British dominion over much of the globe led to what most modern people would consider an overweening optimism, smugness, and arrogance among well-to-do English men and women. Many came to believe that it was their country's destiny and duty to bring English values, laws, customs, and religion to poor, benighted "savage races." The British poet **Rudyard Kipling** voiced the prejudices and the uneasiness of many of his countrymen about the costs of the Empire when he wrote,

> Take up the White Man's burden—
> Send forth the best ye breed—
> Go bind your sons to exile
> To serve your captives' need;
> To wait in heavy harness,
> On fluttered folk and wild—
> Your new-caught, sullen peoples,
> Half devil and half child.

▶ 1865. Lewis Carroll publishes *Alice in Wonderland*
▶ 1864. Robert Browning publishes *The Ring and the Book*
▶ 1862. Christina Rossetti publishes *Goblin Market and Other Poems*
▶ 1861. Dickens publishes *Great Expectations*
▶ 1860. George Eliot publishes *The Mill on the Floss* and *Silas Marner*
▶ 1857. Matthew Arnold becomes professor of poetry at Oxford

1855	1860	1865	1870	1875

▶ 1854–55. Britain fights against Russia in Crimean War
▶ 1857. British put down rebellion in India
▶ 1859. Darwin publishes *On the Origin of the Species*
▶ 1860. Florence Nightingale founds nursing school
1861. Beginning of U.S. Civil War

▶ 1867. Suffrage extended to more men
▶ 1869. Debtor's prisons abolished
▶ 1869. John Stuart Mill publishes *On the Subjection of Women*
▶ 1871. Trade Union Act legalizes union organizing

INTRODUCTION **691**

CROSS-CURRICULAR ACTIVITIES

 Social Studies. Have students research the concept of *colonialism.* Students may wish to choose one country that has been colonized by England. How did the British profit from colonization? What were the consequences for the colonized country? They should report on how, when, and why the country threw off British rule, if it did do so, and the contemporary situation in the country.

BIOGRAPHICAL NOTE

Sir Henry Morton Stanley (1841–1904) is famed as an explorer, the rescuer of David Livingstone and Elmin Pasha, and a personification of British Imperialism. It has been suggested that British Imperialism was most effective not in spreading the British political system, religion, and morals, but in spreading its consumer culture; both Stanley's work *In Darkest Africa* and his role as one of the first product endorsers lend this theory some credence. You might ask students to read selections from *In Darkest Africa.* Tell them to note Stanley's treatment of fellow human beings and the numerous product references. Ask them, "To what extent was the rescue of Elmin Pasha a media event?" (You might want to inform them that when Elmin Pasha was "rescued," he was content, was better supplied than Stanley, and seemed surprised to find that he was in need of rescue.)

QUOTABLES

❝Dr. Livingston, I presume?**❞**
—Sir Henry Morton Stanley

LITERARY CURRENTS

Use the following selections to explore these concepts and techniques with your students.

DRAMATIC MONOLOGUE
- "Ulysses," 707
- "My Last Duchess," 724
- "Andrea del Sarto," 729

METAPHOR
- "The Lady of Shallot," 698
- "Dover Beach," 740
- "God's Grandeur," 764
- "In an Artist's Studio," 770
- "Promises Like Pie-Crust," 772

REALISM
- "The Darkling Thrush," 751
- from *The Mill on the Floss*, 781
- from *Wuthering Heights*, 810
- from *Jane Eyre*, 816
- "The Runaway Slave at Pilgrim's Point," 806

Mathematics and Sciences. Have students conduct a study of urban migration in Victorian England. They should determine percentages of population affected and show the shift on a graph. Interested students can prepare maps showing patterns of migration.

Social Studies. Darwin's theory of the evolution of species did not appear out of a vacuum. The idea was on par with much of contemporary Victorian thought. The favored theory of governmental *laissez faire* espoused that the strong would survive and that a vital economy was one in which competition was unchecked, a "survival of the fittest," in a sense. Invite students to compare Darwin's theory of natural selection, as described in *The Origin of Species* (1859), and Adam Smith's theory of the invisible hand, as described in *The Wealth of Nations* (1776), with Victorian ideas about *laissez faire* capitalism.

LITERARY NOTE

In order to give students some idea of the enormous impact the Crystal Palace exhibit had on Victorian society, you may wish to have students read selections of Henry Mayhew and George Cruikshank's novel, *1851,* which parodies this cultural event as much as it explains the transformative effect the Great Exhibition had in bridging the Puritan and modern eras.

Much of the history of the twentieth century has been one of undoing the ugly legacy of European colonialism in the nineteenth century.

THE INDUSTRIAL REVOLUTION AND ITS CONSEQUENCES

The **Industrial Revolution** that gave rise to the modern era began in the late 1700s with the invention of machines for weaving, including the spinning jenny and the power loom. Gradually, a **factory system** emerged in England that supplied much of the rest of the world with finished goods. English textile factories had to be supplied with coal and iron, so mining increased and the canal and railway systems were developed. The coming of factories meant a dramatic shift in the English economy away from agriculture and toward the production of manufactured goods. Millions of people left the land and crowded into factory towns and mill towns. The old landed gentry, the aristocracy of former days, lost power, which shifted almost completely into the hands of factory owners and merchants. England made great progress during this period in the development of the tools and techniques of mass production, which were brilliantly displayed in the **Great Exhibition of 1851**. The exhibition was organized by Prince Albert and housed in a marvel of modern architecture, a **Crystal Palace** of glass and iron. Visitors to the exhibition had a chance to see, firsthand, the machines that were making over the modern world, such as hydraulic presses, locomotives, machine tools, power looms, reapers, and steamboats.

Industrialization in England, perhaps because it occurred there first, was attended by great social evils. Vast wealth was concentrated in a few hands. Most laboring people lived in poverty. Children as young as five years old worked sixteen-hour days in factories and mines. Cities grew beyond their means, and sprawling, vermin-ridden slums appeared. Clean drinking water often could not be found, and epidemics of cholera killed hundreds of thousands of people. Hunger was more common than uncommon. Such conditions bred crime and moral license. They also bred reform.

SOCIAL AND POLITICAL REFORM

The terrible conditions among the working poor in England during the Victorian Age might well have brought about bloody revolution, as it did in France at the end of the preceding

LITERARY EVENTS

► = British Events

►1896. A. E. Housman publishes *A Shropshire Lad*

►1891. Thomas Hardy publishes *Tess of the D'Urbervilles*

1880. Russian Feodor Dostoevsky publishes *The Brothers Karamazov*

1880	1885	1890	1895	1900

►1878. Salvation Army founded

►1879. Zulu war against British in South Africa

►1882. Married Woman's Property Act allows women in England to possess property of their own

►1884. William Morris founds The Socialist League

HISTORICAL EVENTS

►1888. Notorious murders by Jack the Ripper occur

►1901. Death of Queen Victoria

century if not for a long series of social and political reforms aimed at improving those conditions. In 1832, the **First Reform Act** was passed, extending the vote to most middle-class men. In 1833, Britain abolished slavery in all of its colonies and passed a **Factory Act** regulating child labor in factories. In 1834, the **Poor-Law-Amendment Act** applied to all of England a system of workhouses for indigent people, but conditions in the workhouses tended to be miserable, and poverty continued to be a major social problem. In 1842, 1845, and 1846, conservative Prime Minister **Robert Peel,** reacting to the hunger and social unrest at home and to Ireland's **Great Famine** of 1845, pushed through legislation repealing the so-called **Corn Laws** that placed high tariffs on imported grain and kept the price of bread artificially high. Other **Reform Bills** passed in 1867 and 1884–85 extended the vote to almost all English men. In 1869, debtors' prisons were abolished, and nearly universal primary education was instituted. In 1871, the **Trade Union Act** made it legal for laborers to organize to protect their rights. Throughout the Victorian Era, various laws were passed regulating food, drugs, and sanitation. One important force for social change was the **Chartist Movement,** begun in 1837. The Chartists took their name from a document called the **People's Charter,** which called for widespread political reforms, including universal male suffrage and vote by ballot.

RELIGIOUS MOVEMENTS IN VICTORIAN ENGLAND

Much of the character of the Victorian Age can be attributed to the **Evangelical Movement,** which emphasized a Protestant faith in personal salvation through Christ. The Evangelical Movement swept through England, winning much of the population to its vision of a life lived according to a strict moral code. The movement led to an enormous outpouring of philanthropic and charitable work and to the foundation of the **Salvation Army** and the **Young Men's Christian Association,** or **YMCA.**

In contrast to the strict Protestantism of the Evangelicals, the members of the **Oxford Movement,** or **Tractarians,** sought to bring the official English Anglican Church closer in rituals and beliefs to Roman Catholicism. The primary spokesperson for this movement, **John Henry Newman** (1801–1890), later converted to Catholicism, took holy orders, and was elevated to the position of cardinal.

Another religious thinker influential during the Victorian Era was **William Paley,** who lived in the preceding era but whose works struck a chord with Victorians. In his *Natural Theology* (1802), Paley presented the so-called **argument from design.** According to Paley, a person picking up a watch on the street can tell by the complexity and intricacy of its design that it must have had a maker. Similarly, one who observes the complexity and intricacy of nature may conclude that it, as well, had a maker—God.

OTHER CURRENTS OF VICTORIAN THOUGHT

The Victorian Age was a time of vigorous, intense intellectual activity in England. Leading thinkers of the period included the following:

John Stuart Mill (1806–1873), the philosopher and social critic, popularized the **Utilitarianism** of the philosopher **Jeremy Bentham,** arguing that the object of moral action was to bring about "the greatest good for the greatest number" of people. Mill also championed **Liberalism,** arguing that governments had the right to restrict the actions of individuals only when those actions harmed others and that society should use its collective resources to provide for the basic welfare of its members. In his *The Subjection of Women,* Mill argued that women should be treated as equals under the law and provided with opportunities for education.

Charles Darwin. The Granger Collection, NY

Charles Lyell (1797–1875) wrote an influential work, *Principles of Geology,* that showed that geological features on Earth had developed continuously and slowly over immense periods of time. Lyell's **Gradualism** provided an alternative to the **Catastophism** of such nineteenth-century scientists as the French naturalist **George Cuvler.**

Charles Darwin (1809–1882) advanced in his book *On the Origin of Species* the not-entirely-new idea that the many species of animals and plants on the planet had evolved, over time, from common ancestors. The idea had been advanced by Darwin's grandfather, Erasmus, and was separately arrived at by the biologist Alfred Wallace. Darwin's chief contribution to **evolutionary theory** was the mechanism that he provided to explain it. Darwin found his explanation in the writings of **Thomas Malthus** (1766–1834), who argued in his *Essay on the Principle of Population* that populations naturally increase geometrically, while available resources increase only arithmetically. This leads to fierce competition for resources and inevitably to famine, disease, and war. According to Darwin, species changed, or evolved as a result of such competition. In every generation of individuals, there were random variations. Fierce competition for limited resources led to the selective **survival of the fittest**—those creatures best suited to taking advantage of the available resources.

Herbert Spencer (1820–1903) attempted to apply the ideas of Darwin to many areas of human endeavor and thought. Proponents of Spencer's **Social Darwinism** held that in human society, as in nature, survival properly belonged to the fittest—those most able to survive. Social Darwinism was used by many Victorians to justify social inequalities based on race, social or economic class, and gender.

The Social Darwinists championed not only the ideas of Spencer, but also those of the eighteenth-century economist Adam Smith. Smith held that the best government economic policy was to leave the market alone, to follow a *laissez-faire* or "let it be" policy of little or no government intervention. Followers of Mill and other Liberals argued that government did have a proper role in protecting the weak against the strong, the poor against the wealthy. Still more radical thinkers, the Socialists, believed in far-reaching government control and in the abolition of private property in favor of publicly or communally owned lands and businesses. These debates about the proper role of government in public affairs continue into our own time.

Another Victorian-Era debate that has continued into our own time is the one generated by the theory of evolution. In Victorian times, this theory presented for many people a crisis of faith, for it contradicted widely held beliefs, such as the idea expressed by Archbishop Ussher that the world had been created in 4004 BC. Then, as now, many people followed the line of the poet Alfred, Lord Tennyson, who struggled toward a middle path, one that would reconcile his faith with the discoveries of science.

CURRENTS IN VICTORIAN LITERATURE: REALISM AND NATIONALISM

In response to the difficult conditions in many of England's cities during the Victorian Era, a new style of literary expression was born: **Realism.** Realism is the attempt to render in art or literature an accurate portrayal of reality. Although the development of the novel in the eighteenth century, with its detailed descriptions of characters and settings, could be considered Realist, literary historians usually apply the term to works of the late nineteenth century that dealt with the harsher details of ordinary lives.

The Heart of the Empire. Niels Moiler Lund, (1863–1916).
Guildhall Art Gallery, London/Bridgeman Art Library, London

As literacy became more common among the middle class, the popularity of the novel soared to its greatest height. Realistic, detailed descriptions of everyday life, and especially of its darker aspects, appealed to many readers, disillusioned by the "progress" going on around them. Themes in Realist writing included families, religion, and social reform.

Another literary movement founded in the Victorian Age was **Naturalism.** Naturalism is based on the philosophical theory that actions and events are the results, not of human intentions, but of largely uncontrollable external forces. Naturalist writers, like Realists, chose subjects and themes common to the lower and middle classes. They were also attentive to details, striving for accuracy and authenticity in their descriptions. Naturalism had its greatest influence in France and in the United States. However, there are Naturalist elements in the works of the English poet and novelist **Thomas Hardy,** whose characters are typically hapless victims of fate.

The Novel in Victorian England

In the early part of the Victorian Age, there was still a flavor of Romanticism in the novels being written. Works such as **Emily Brontë's** *Wuthering Heights* (1847) and **Charlotte Brontë's** *Jane Eyre* (1847) contained many elements of the passionate and the mysterious and made use of Gothic settings.

Charles Dickens (1812–1870), perhaps the most famous of the Victorian novelists, was wildly popular in his day. Many of his novels were published in serial form in monthly installments or in magazines. This form of publication, and his comic and sentimental descriptions of the lives of people of diverse occupations and social classes, gave Dickens an exceptionally large and

LITERARY NOTE

Many of Thomas Hardy's novels reveal his admiration for Shakespeare. Hardy shares Shakespeare's keen eye for life's tragic elements and his talent for emphasizing the grandeur of passion a character can reach when caught in the web of fate. There are many parallels in the two artists' work, and an excellent, if ambitious, project for a student would be to compare a work of Hardy to a work of Shakespeare. Hardy's *The Mayor of Casterbridge* is similar in characterization, theme, and tragic intensity to Shakespeare's *The Tragedy of King Lear.*

Caricature of Charles Dickens.
Alfred Bryan. The Pierpont Morgan Library, NY.
Gift of Miss Caroline Newtown, 1974.7. © The Pierpont Morgan Library 1995

varied audience. Novels such as *A Christmas Carol* (1843), *David Copperfield* (1850), and *Great Expectations* (1861) are typical of Dickens's fiction in their attacks on social indifference to poverty and injustice, their comic invention, and their call on charity and love to resolve, or at least to alleviate, the troubles of the Victorian Age.

The greatest novels in the Realist tradition produced during the period were those of **George Eliot** (1819–1880), author of *Middlemarch* and *The Mill on the Floss,* and **Thomas Hardy,** author of *Far from the Madding Crowd, Tess of the D'Urbervilles,* and *Jude the Obscure.* Other famous novelists of the Victorian Era include William Makepeace Thackeray, Anthony Trollope, and Samuel Butler.

VICTORIAN POETRY

Even though the Victorian Age could well be called the "Age of the Novel," poetry was not a forgotten literary form. **Alfred, Lord Tennyson** (1809–1892) was the most popular poet of his time. Writing in the style of the Romantics, Tennyson produced long narrative poems, often on themes taken from classical myth or from medieval romance and legend. Gradually, the philosophies of Realism and Naturalism, propelled by reactions to the Industrial Revolution, insinuated their way into the poetry of the day.

The poets influenced by Realism include **Robert Browning** (1812–1889), **Elizabeth Barrett Browning** (1806–1861), and **Matthew Arnold** (1822–1888). In poems such as **"My Last Duchess"** and **"Andrea del Sarto,"** Robert Browning raised the **dramatic monologue** to great heights, making it a superb vehicle for deep psychological probing and character study. Elizabeth Barrett, the other half of one of literature's greatest love affairs, was the more prominent poet at the time of her elopement with Robert Browning in 1846. Her most well-known work is *Sonnets from the Portuguese,* a collection of love sonnets valued for their lyrical beauty, but she also wrote poetry on serious political themes, including **"Runaway Slave."** Arnold's **"Dover Beach"** (1867), partly written during his honeymoon, foreshadowed much of twentieth-century poetry with its ironic pathos, its concern with love as the only remedy for alienation, its use of literary allusion, and its compact, precise, plain statement.

The Victorian Age closed with the dawn of the twentieth century. The Realism of the great literature of that time infuses the modern reader with a sense of what one's everyday life would be like in a time that seems so far away, yet in a sense is very near, for the issues that we grapple with in our time were born in that era.

Echoes:
Victorian England

The general average of mankind . . . have no tastes or wishes strong enough to incline them to do anything unusual, and they consequently do not understand those who have, and class all such with the wild and intemperate whom they are accustomed to look down upon. Now, in addition to this fact which is general, we have only to suppose that a strong movement has set in towards the improvement of morals, and it is evident what we have to expect. . . . much has actually been effected in the way of increased regularity of conduct, and discouragement of excesses; . . . These tendencies of the times cause the public to be more disposed than at most former periods to prescribe general rules of conduct, and endeavor to make everyone conform to the approved standard. . . . Its ideal of character is to be without any marked character, to maim by compression, like a Chinese lady's foot, every part of human nature which stands out prominently.

—John Stuart Mill, *On Liberty*

When I was young, it was not thought proper for young ladies to study very conspicuously; and especially with pen in hand. Young ladies (at least in provincial towns) were expected to sit down in the parlor to sew,—during which reading aloud was permitted,—or to practice their music. . . . Jane Austen herself, the Queen of novelists . . . was compelled by the feelings of her family to cover up her manuscripts with a large piece of muslin work.

—Harriet Martineau, *Autobiography*

HISTORICAL/LITERARY NOTE

The Victorian Period was the age in which advertising as we know it first became an important industry. Many ideals that were important to Victorians can be seen in their advertising. The importance of family, British Imperialism, and Social Darwinism are revealed in period advertisements for products such as Pear's Soap, Eno's Fruit Salts, and even beef bullion. H. G. Wells's novel, *Tono-Bungay,* is an excellent satire of both the Victorian advertising industry and the unregulated "quack medicines" that produced much of this advertising. You might show students examples of Victorian advertisements, and read them some of the satirical advertisements Wells creates. Encourage a discussion on advertising in the Victorian Period and today. What elements of modern advertising stem from the Victorian Period? How has advertising changed? To what extent have our methods of representing the commercial object stayed the same?

ADDITIONAL RESOURCES

READER'S GUIDE
- Selection Worksheet, 9.1

ASSESSMENT PORTFOLIO
- Selection Check Test, 4.9.1
- Selection Test, 4.9.2

ESSENTIAL SKILLS PRACTICE BOOKS
- *Speaking and Listening, 3.2*

AUDIOCASSETTE
- "The Lady of Shalott," Track 16

ENRICHMENT ACTIVITY

 The Role of Art and Artists in Society. Explain to students that during the late nineteenth century a great debate raged over the role of art in human life. The literary critic Matthew Arnold argued that art presents a "criticism of life" and thus serves a moral and social purpose. In contrast, the art critic Walter Pater argued that art exists for its own sake, that its value lies not in moral or social lessons but rather in its beauty or aesthetic value.

During the early twentieth century, many artists accepted the "art for art's sake" position. They believed that artists should live apart from the ordinary world and devote themselves entirely to art. In France, especially, artists adopted "bohemian" lifestyles. They shunned middle-class occupations, habits, and dress. They kept company with other artists in cafés and salons and created the modern conception of artists as a breed apart, concerned only with beauty and not with moral, social, or political affairs.

Have students debate in class the question of the proper relationship of the artist to the rest of the world. Pose the following questions:

1. Should artists devote themselves entirely to art and remain aloof from the world, or should they have ordinary careers and do their artwork on the side? What

(cont.)

PREREADING

"The Lady of Shalott"
"Ulysses"
from *In Memoriam*
by Alfred, Lord Tennyson

ABOUT THE AUTHOR

Alfred, Lord Tennyson (1809–92) was born into a family of twelve children. While still in his teens, he collaborated with two of his brothers on a book of verse that was published in 1827. He attended Cambridge University, where he won a Chancellor's medal for poetry and joined a group of talented undergraduates who called themselves the Apostles. One member of this group, Arthur Hallam, became Tennyson's best friend. In 1833, Hallam died suddenly, sending Tennyson into a deep depression. In the decade that followed, Tennyson fell in love with Emily Sellwood but was unable to marry because of poverty. In 1850 his fortunes changed. In that year, England's poet laureate, William Wordsworth, died, and Tennyson was named to replace him. Tennyson married Emily, and his fame as a poet grew steadily. In 1884 he was made a peer. His work, which often dealt with patriotic themes and subjects from medieval romance, was enormously popular. When the much-loved, legendary poet died, he was buried in Westminster Abbey.

ABOUT THE SELECTIONS

"The Lady of Shalott" tells a story set in the legendary days of King Arthur and his Knights of the Round Table. The city of Camelot, mentioned repeatedly in the poem, was the capital of Arthur's kingdom. Sir Lancelot, also mentioned, was one of Arthur's most capable knights.

Ulysses was the Roman name of Odysseus, a hero from those ancient Greek epic poems attributed to Homer, the *Iliad* and the *Odyssey.* Ulysses fought in the Trojan War and returned to his kingdom, Ithaca. On the decade-long return journey, he saw many strange lands and had many marvelous, heroic adventures. In Tennyson's poem **"Ulysses,"** the aged king Ulysses longs for one last adventure to culminate his career.

In Memoriam is an elegy written by Tennyson over the course of seventeen years, in response to the death of his friend Arthur Hallam. The poem is a moving record of Tennyson's struggle through loss, grief, and doubt toward spiritual renewal.

ENRICHMENT ACTIVITY (CONT.)

might artists gain or lose by being engaged in the world?

2. Which is a better story, one written primarily to teach a lesson or one written primarily to entertain? Which is a better painting, one created to communicate a message or one created simply to be beautiful?

3. Do artists, such as musicians, painters, sculptors, and writers, have a responsibility to support certain moral, social, or political values in their works? Do governments or communities have the right to censor art that does not present ideas or attitudes that most people consider acceptable?

"The Lady of Shalott"

ALFRED, LORD TENNYSON

Part 1

On either side the river lie
Long fields of barley and of rye,
That clothe the wold[1] and meet the sky;
And through the field the road runs by
5   To many-towered Camelot;
And up and down the people go,
Gazing where the lilies blow
Round an island there below,
        The island of Shalott.

10   Willows whiten, aspens quiver,
Little breezes dusk and shiver
Through the wave that runs forever
By the island in the river
        Flowing down to Camelot.
15   Four gray walls, and four gray towers,
Overlook a space of flowers,
And the silent isle imbowers[2]
        The Lady of Shalott.

By the margin, willow-veiled,
20   Slide the heavy barges trailed

---
1. **wold.** Plains
2. **imbowers.** Encloses or shelters

ANSWERS TO GUIDED READING QUESTIONS

❶ The Lady of Shalott lives in the tower.

❷ A "fairy Lady" is some sort of supernatural being. The presence of the fairy Lady indicates that the story is about magical occurrences.

❸ Night and day, the Lady weaves a magic web. She is under a curse that forbids her to look out the window toward Camelot. She doesn't know the exact nature of the curse (i.e., what will happen if she does look toward Camelot).

❹ The Lady sees the world indirectly, viewing its reflection in a mirror. She doesn't look out the window and view the world directly because the curse forbids her to do so.

LITERARY NOTE

Biographical Criticism. "The Lady of Shalott" can be read as an allegory about an important issue in Tennyson's own life. After he became poet laureate in 1850, Tennyson was expected to write works that treated social and political themes, and he had responsibilities that necessarily involved him in the affairs of the country. Tennyson's later works, such as "The Charge of the Light Brigade," tended toward **didacticism**—the teaching of moral lessons related to human affairs such as soldierly duty. "The Lady of Shalott" shows that Tennyson had reservations about such engagement in worldly matters. In the poem, when the artist enters the world her art is destroyed and she dies. On the other hand, the poem shows the life of the unengaged, isolated artist to be unsatisfying, one of shadows and reflections rather than reality. In his own life, Tennyson opted for engaging in the world and for producing art that served the public good, but some critics would argue that he did so at a price, that his later didactic works do not reach the same high artistic level of his earlier, less worldly poetry, of which "The Lady of Shalott" is an example. Refer to *didacticism* in the Handbook of Literary Terms.

❶ What mysterious person lives in the tower on the island of Shalott?

❷ What is a "fairy Lady"? What tells you that you are reading a story about magical occurrences?

❸ What does the Lady do night and day? What curse is on her? Does she know what will happen if she "looks down to Camelot"?

❹ By what means does the Lady see what is happening in the world? Why doesn't she just look out the window and view the world directly?

By slow horses; and unhailed
The shallop[3] flitteth silken-sailed
    Skimming down to Camelot:
But who hath seen her wave her hand?
25   Or at the casement seen her stand?
Or is she known in all the land,
    The Lady of Shalott?

Only reapers, reaping early
In among the bearded barley,
30   Hear a song that echoes cheerly
From the river winding clearly,
    Down to towered Camelot;
And by the moon the reaper weary,
Piling sheaves in uplands airy,
35   Listening, whispers " 'Tis the fairy
    Lady of Shalott."

Part 2

There she weaves by night and day
A magic web with colors gay.
She has heard a whisper say,
40   A curse is on her if she stay
    To look down to Camelot.
She knows not what the curse may be,
And so she weaveth steadily,
And little other care hath she,
45   The Lady of Shalott.

And moving through a mirror clear[4]
That hangs before her all the year,
Shadows of the world appear.
There she sees the highway near
50   Winding down to Camelot;
There the river eddy whirls,
And there the surly village churls,[5]
And the red cloaks of market girls,
    Pass onward from Shalott.

---

3. **shallop.** Open boat
4. **mirror clear.** Weavers often use mirrors to see the progress of their work.
5. **churls.** Peasants

55   Sometimes a troop of damsels glad,
     An abbot on an <u>ambling</u> pad,[6]
     Sometimes a curly shepherd lad,
     Or long-haired page in crimson clad,
         Goes by to towered Camelot;
60   And sometimes through the mirror blue
     The knights come riding two and two:
     She hath no loyal knight and true,
         The Lady of Shalott.

     But in her web she still delights
65   To weave the mirror's magic sights,
     For often through the silent nights
     A funeral, with plumes and lights
         And music, went to Camelot;
     Or when the moon was overhead,
70   Came two young lovers lately wed:
     "I am half sick of shadows," said
         The Lady of Shalott.

         Part 3

     A bowshot from her bower eaves,
     He rode between the barley sheaves,
75   The sun came dazzling through the leaves,
     And flamed upon the brazen greaves[7]
         Of bold Sir Lancelot.
     A red-cross knight forever kneeled
     To a lady in his shield,
80   That sparkled on the yellow field,
         Beside remote Shalott.

     The gemmy bridle glittered free,
     Like to some branch of stars we see
     Hung in the golden Galaxy.
85   The bridle bells rang merrily
         As he rode down to Camelot;

---

6. **pad.** Horse with an easy pace
7. **greaves.** Pieces of armor that protect the lower leg

WORDS FOR EVERYDAY USE:
am • bling (am′bliŋ) *part.,* moving with a smooth, easy gait

❶ *Is there a mate in the Lady's life? How do you know?*

❷ *What causes the Lady to say that she is "half sick of shadows"? What does she see that fills her with yearning?*

❸ *How is Sir Lancelot described? What about him would be attractive to the Lady?*

ANSWERS TO GUIDED READING QUESTIONS

❶ No, the poem says she has no loyal and true knight.

❷ In her mirror, the Lady sees the reflection of two newlyweds. Seeing them fills her with yearning. She seems to wish that she, too, could have a mate and be wed.

❸ He is described as bold and chivalrous. His shield shows a knight kneeling before a lady.

▶ **Teaching note:** Refer students to the entries on *chivalry* and *courtly love* in the Handbook of Literary Terms. Also refer them to Spenser's description of the Red Cross Knight in *The Fœrie Queene,* page 257.

HISTORICAL/LITERARY NOTE

Lancelot is the hero of many medieval romances. For example, he figures prominently in Sir Thomas Malory's *Le Morte d'Arthur.* (See page 167.) The Lady in "The Lady of Shalott" is based on Elaine of Astolat. According to Arthurian legend, Elaine of Astolat fell in love with Lancelot, but her love was not returned. She died of unrequited love and, as she had requested, she was placed in a boat in the Thames and was steered down that river to Camelot.

In the romances, Lancelot is a nearly perfect knight, handsome, brave, strong, courteous, persevering, and devout. However, he has some failings that keep him from being pure enough to achieve the Holy Grail. That feat is accomplished by Galahad, the most perfect of all the knights of medieval legend.

VOCABULARY IN CONTEXT

• He <u>ambled</u> confidently across the factory floor to pick up his first paycheck.

CROSS-CURRICULAR ACTIVITIES

Social Studies. Suggest that students work in a small group to research historical aspects of medieval England. Of special interest might be the role of women. Excellent sources of information on medieval women include the following:

Thiébaux, Marcelle. *The Writings of Medieval Women.* 1994.

Klapisch-Zuber, Christiane, ed. *Silences of the Middle Ages.* Vol. 2. *A History of Women.* Ed. Georges Duby and Michelle Perrot. 1992.

Power, Eileen. *Medieval People.* 1965.

ANSWERS TO GUIDED READING QUESTIONS

❶ Lancelot rides by the tower singing. She wants to see Lancelot. She looks because she is tired of shadows.

❷ Her web flies out and floats wide. Perhaps it flies through the window. Her mirror breaks.

❸ A sense of foreboding or imminent doom is created by words and phrases such as *stormy, straining, pale yellow,* and *waning.*

❶ *What happens just before the Lady looks out? What does she want to see? Why does she look out even though the curse will come upon her if she does?*

❷ *What happens to the Lady's art when she turns her attention to the world?*

❸ *What elements in this description build a sense of foreboding or imminent doom?*

And from his blazoned baldric[8] slung
A mighty silver bugle hung,
And as he rode his armor rung,
90   Beside remote Shalott.

All in the blue unclouded weather
Thick-jeweled shone the saddle leather,
The helmet and the helmet-feather
Burned like one burning flame together,
95   As he rode down to Camelot;
As often through the purple night,
Below the starry clusters bright,
Some bearded meteor, trailing light,
    Moves over still Shalott.

100 His broad clear brow in sunlight glowed;
On burnished hooves his war horse trode;
From underneath his helmet flowed
His coal-black curls as on he rode,
    As he rode down to Camelot.
105 From the bank and from the river
He flashed into the crystal mirror,
"Tirra lirra," by the river
    Sang Sir Lancelot.

She left the web, she left the loom,
110 She made three paces through the room,
She saw the water lily bloom,
She saw the helmet and the plume,
    She looked down to Camelot.
Out flew the web and floated wide;
115 The mirror cracked from side to side;
"The curse is come upon me," cried
    The Lady of Shalott.

Part 4

In the stormy east wind straining,
The pale yellow woods were <u>waning</u>,

---
8. **baldric.** An ornamented belt used to support a sword or bugle

WORDS FOR EVERYDAY USE: **wane** (wān) *vi.,* lose strength

VOCABULARY IN CONTEXT

- The moon has passed full and is now in the <u>waning</u> phase.
- I could tell that he was furious with me when his <u>countenance</u> changed from a smile to a grimace.

The Lady of Shalott. John William Waterhouse. Tate Gallery, London/Art Resource, NY

120   The broad stream in his banks complaining,
        Heavily the low sky raining
              Over towered Camelot;
        Down she came and found a boat
        Beneath a willow left afloat,
125   And round about the prow she wrote
              The Lady of Shalott.

        And down the river's dim expanse
        Like some bold seër[9] in a trance,
        Seeing all his own mischance—
130   With a glassy <u>countenance</u>

---

9. **seër.** Prophet

❶
*What does the
Lady do when she
leaves the tower?*

ART NOTE

Because of its vivid imagery, Tennyson's "The Lady of Shalott" inspired many illustrative paintings. One of the most famous is this work by **John William Waterhouse** (1849–1917). Waterhouse began his career painting in the Classical mode but developed a Romantic style in his mature years. His works were influenced by those of Dante Gabriel Rossetti and other members of the Pre-Raphaelite Brotherhood. The Pre-Raphaelites attempted to restore painting to an imagined purity that existed in the late Middle Ages and early Renaissance. They often treated medieval subjects in a highly Romantic manner tinged with mysticism. Ask students to identify Romantic elements in this painting, such as the three candles blowing in the wind and the wild disarray of the reeds, the trees, and the Lady's hair. Students might notice that two of the three candles are burned out, and the other is flickering. These candles may symbolize the Lady's life force, which is also flickering out. Students might also notice that the right-most scene on the tapestry draped over the boat is the picture of Lancelot as seen in the Lady's mirror.

ANSWER TO GUIDED READING QUESTION

❶ The Lady gets into a boat on which she has written *The Lady of Shalott.*

CROSS-CURRICULAR ACTIVITIES

Weaving
• Suggest that students conduct research into weaving. How does a loom work? How does one weave cloth? How much of the work is done by machines?

• Students may wish to invite a local weaver to demonstrate the process of weaving.

Wᴏʀᴅs ғᴏʀ
Eᴠᴇʀʏᴅᴀʏ Usᴇ: **coun • te • nance** (koun′tə nəns) *n.,* facial expression

ANSWER TO GUIDED READING QUESTION

❶ The crowd was afraid of the Lady. Lancelot remarks that she is beautiful and asks God to bless her. Lancelot is brave and kind-hearted.

Did she look to Camelot.
And at the closing of the day
She loosed the chain, and down she lay;
The broad steam bore her far away,
135   The Lady of Shalott.

Lying, robed in snowy white
That loosely flew to left and right—
The leaves upon her falling light—
Through the noises of the night
140   She floated down to Camelot;
And as the boat-head wound along
The willowy hills and fields among,
They heard her singing her last song,
The Lady of Shalott.

145 Heard a carol, mournful, holy,
Chanted loudly, chanted lowly,
Till her blood was frozen slowly,
And her eyes were darkened wholly,
Turned to towered Camelot.
150 For ere she reached upon the tide
The first house by the waterside,
Singing in her song she died,
The Lady of Shalott.

Under tower and balcony,
155 By garden wall and gallery,
A gleaming shape she floated by,
Dead-pale between the houses high,
Silent into Camelot.
Out upon the wharfs they came,
160 Knight and burgher, lord and dame,
And round the prow they read her name,
The Lady of Shalott.

❶
How does the crowd react on seeing the Lady? How does Sir Lancelot react? What does this tell you about him?

Who is this? and what is here?
And in the lighted palace near
165 Died the sound of royal cheer;
And they crossed themselves for fear,
All the knights at Camelot:

ANALYTIC SCALES FOR RESPONDING IN WRITING

Assign a score from 1 to 25 for each grading criterion below. (For more detailed evaluation, see the evaluation forms for writing, revising, and proofreading, *Assessment Portfolio,* 7.1–7.10.)

1. Critical Essay

• **Content/Unity.** The critical essay presents a sensible interpretation of the symbolism in the poem and a discussion of the role of the artist.

• **Organization/Coherence.** The critical essay presents a clear thesis and adds supporting details in a logical order.

• **Language/Style.** The critical essay uses vivid and precise nouns, verbs, and modifiers.

• **Conventions.** The critical essay avoids errors in spelling, grammar, usage, mechanics, and manuscript form.

(cont.)

> But Lancelot mused a little space;
> He said, "She has a lovely face;
170   God in his mercy lend her grace,
>   The Lady of Shalott." ∎

Responding to the Selection

Do you enjoy stories set in medieval times that involve knights, ladies, and magic? Did you enjoy the story told in "The Lady of Shalott"? What in particular did you like or dislike about it?

Reviewing the Selection

RECALLING

1. Where does the Lady of Shalott spend her time?

2. How does the Lady of Shalott see what is going on in the outside world? How do the arts the Lady practices show her distance from the world?

3. Whom does the Lady see just before going to the window and "looking down to Camelot"?

4. What happens to the Lady when she leaves the tower?

INTERPRETING

➤ 5. Why doesn't the Lady ordinarily interact with people in the outside world?

➤ 6. What art does the Lady practice? What does she portray in her art?

➤ 7. What might have motivated the Lady to look toward Camelot despite the curse that is upon her?

➤ 8. How do the people respond when they see her in the boat?

SYNTHESIZING

9. How do the worlds of the Lady of Shalott and the people outside her window differ?

10. What happens to fulfill the curse on the Lady? What are the immediate consequences? What happens to the mirror? to the Lady's web? What then happens to the Lady herself?

If students do not like medieval tales, suggest that they set their retelling of the poem in a different time period.

ANSWERS FOR REVIEWING THE SELECTION

RECALLING

1. The Lady lives in a tower on an island in the middle of a river.

2. She sees the reflection of life in the mirror on her loom. Her art is a reflection of a reflection which shows how far removed from the world she is.

3. She sees Lancelot.

4. When she leaves the tower, the Lady lies down in a boat and dies.

INTERPRETING

Responses will vary. Possible responses are given.

5. She believes that a curse prohibits her from looking out of her window.

6. The Lady of Shalott weaves. She portrays life outside the tower in her art.

7. The Lady fell in love with Lancelot.

8. The people are afraid and make the sign of the cross.

SYNTHESIZING

Responses will vary. Possible responses are given.

9. The people outside the tower live in an interactive social world, while the Lady of Shalott lives in a private, imaginative world.

10. The Lady leaves her loom and looks out of the window, fulfilling the curse. Her weaving unravels and her mirror breaks. The Lady of Shalott then gets into a boat headed toward Camelot and dies.

ANALYTIC SCALES FOR RESPONDING IN WRITING (CONT.)

2. Romance

• **Content/Unity.** The romance includes the traditional concepts of chivalry and courtly love in a tale inspired by Malory.

• **Organization/Coherence.** The romance presents a sensibly organized narrative.

• **Language/Style.** The romance uses vivid and precise nouns, verbs, and modifiers.

• **Conventions.** The romance avoids errors in spelling, grammar, usage, mechanics, and manuscript form.

► See the evaluation forms for discussion, active listening, and oral communication, *Assessment Portfolio,* 7.11–7.14.

Responses will vary. Possible responses are given.

1. Symbol. The web is the Lady's interpretation of reality. The poem presents a paradox. On one hand, the Lady's art represents reality, but the only reality she experiences is that which she sees in a mirror. As in any reflection in a mirror, she views reality in reverse. On the other hand, when she leaves the tower and her world of imagination for the outside world, she dies.

► **Teaching Note:** Discuss with students the role of the contemporary artist. Do artists have an obligation to become involved with social issues or politics?

2. Refrain. The refrains in "The Lady of Shalott" include "To many-towered Camelot," "The island of Shalott," "Flowing down to Camelot," "The Lady of Shalott," "Skimming down to Camelot," "Down to towered Camelot," "To look down to Camelot," "Winding down to Camelot," "Pass onward from Shalott," "Goes by to towered Camelot," "And music, went to Camelot," "Of bold Sir Lancelot," "Beside remote Shalott," "As he rode down to Camelot," "Moves over still Shalott," "Sang Sir Lancelot," "She looked down to Camelot," "Over towered Camelot," "Did she look to Camelot," "She floated down to Camelot," "Turned to towered Camelot," "Silent into Camelot," and "All the knights at Camelot." The vast majority of the refrains are some variation of going down to Camelot and the Lady of Shalott. The refrains make the poem sound like a song and give a sense of inevitability to the end of the poem. Tennyson uses end rhyme to give this poem a musical quality.

► **Teaching Note:** Ask students to think of songs they know that use refrains. How do the uses of refrains in songs and in "The Lady of Shalott" compare?

3. Foil. The Lady remains shut up in her tower, doing the same thing day after day, and only observes

(cont.)

Understanding Literature (Questions for Discussion)

1. **Symbol.** A **symbol** is a thing that stands for or represents both itself and something else. "The Lady of Shalott" can be read as a simple story about a magical curse and its consequences. However, it also can be read with a symbolic interpretation. One interpretation views the Lady as representative of the artist who necessarily is removed from the world, viewing it in the mirror of his or her imagination. In line with this interpretation, what might the Lady's web stand for? What might the poem be saying about the consequences for an artist of forsaking the world of the imagination for the real world?

2. **Refrain.** A **refrain** is a line or group of lines repeated in a poem or song. What refrains appear in "The Lady of Shalott"? How are these refrains varied throughout the poem? What effect does this use of refrains have on the sound of the poem? What other techniques does Tennyson use in this poem to give it a musical quality?

3. **Foil.** A **foil** is a character whose attributes, or characteristics, contrast with and therefore throw into relief the attributes of another character. What are the differences between the portrayals of the Lady and Sir Lancelot in this poem? What makes them foils for one another? What differences is the poet pointing out between artists and "people of action" or "public people"?

Responding in Writing

1. **Critical Essay.** Write an essay in which you describe a symbolic interpretation of "The Lady of Shalott." In your essay, explain the symbolic significance of the Lady, Sir Lancelot, the mirror, the web, and the death of the Lady when she enters the real world. Do you think that Tennyson implies that artists necessarily must live in a world of the imagination rather than in the real world, or do you think that the poem is a criticism of that idea? Explain your opinion.

2. **Romance.** Review Malory and *Le Morte d'Arthur* on pages 167–177. Then read the entries in the Handbook of Literary Terms on *chivalry, courtly love,* and *romance.* Finally, try your hand at writing a medieval romance tale. You may wish to give one of the traditional motifs of romance literature a twist. For example, you could write about a knight at a tournament who is really a lady in disguise, or you could write about a fair damsel who rescues a knight imprisoned in a tower.

life in the reflection of a mirror. Lancelot travels the countryside having adventures.

The Lady and Lancelot seem to be exact opposites of one another. Stereotypically, artists are thought of as mysterious people who sit alone in a room with their imaginations so that they can create great works of art.

► **Teaching Note:** Encourage students to think of examples of *foils* in contemporary media such as movies and television shows.

Grading scales appear on pages 704 and 705.

READER'S JOURNAL

Suppose that you had very little time in which to live. What would you want to accomplish before you died? Freewrite about this question in your journal.

LANGUAGE SKILLS

Throughout his poem, Tennyson makes use of vivid adjectives and participles. Examples from the first three lines include *idle*, *still*, *barren*, and *aged*. Read the Language Arts Survey, 2.35, "Using Colorful Modifiers." Then read the poem and make a list in your journal of other vivid modifiers that the poet uses.

"Ulysses"[1]

ALFRED, LORD TENNYSON

It little profits that an idle king,
By this still hearth, among these barren crags,
Matched with an aged wife, I mete and dole
Unequal laws[2] unto a savage race,
5   That hoard, and sleep, and feed, and know not me.
    I cannot rest from travel; I will drink
Life to the lees.[3] All times I have enjoyed
Greatly, have suffered greatly, both with those
That loved me, and alone; on shore, and when
10   Through scudding drifts the rainy Hyades[4]
Vexed the dim sea. I am become a name;
For always roaming with a hungry heart
Much have I seen and known—cities of men
And manners, climates, councils, governments,
15   Myself not least, but honored of them all—
And drunk delight of battle with my peers,
Far on the ringing plains of windy Troy,
I am a part of all that I have met;
Yet all experience is an arch wherethrough
20   Gleams that untraveled world whose margin fades
Forever and forever when I move.

---

1. **Ulysses.** Ulysses was a king of Ithaca who fought in the Trojan War. The story of Ulysses is told in Homer's epic poems, the *Iliad* and the *Odyssey*.
2. **mete . . . laws.** Give out rewards and punishments
3. **lees.** Dregs
4. **Through . . . Hyades.** Through driving rain showers which were said to follow the rising of the group of stars known as the Hyades

❶ *What elements in Ulysses's present life are unsatisfying?*

❷ *For what did Ulysses become famous? In other words, what made him "become a name"?*

ADDITIONAL RESOURCES

READER'S GUIDE
- Selection Worksheet, 9.2

ASSESSMENT PORTFOLIO
- Selection Check Test, 4.9.3
- Selection Test, 4.9.4

ESSENTIAL SKILLS PRACTICE BOOKS
- *Language*, 2.35

PREREADING NOTES

READER'S JOURNAL

Suggest that students consider what Ulysses has already done with his life. What other feats might he accomplish before he dies?

LANGUAGE SKILLS

For each word on their lists, students may wish to find one or two similar words in a thesaurus. Have them try substituting words from the thesaurus and discuss how the meaning and tone of the poem are affected.

▶ Additional practice is provided in the *Essential Skills Practice Book: Language*, 2.35.

SUPPORT FOR LEP STUDENTS

A common colloquialism in English is the use of the phrase "to make a name for oneself" to mean "become famous." Tennyson uses a form of this colloquialism in line 11.

ANSWERS TO GUIDED READING QUESTIONS

❶ Ulysses and his wife are getting older, he is dissatisfied with his isolated life as ruler of his people, and his life has none of the danger or adventure he encountered in his travels.

❷ Ulysses became famous for his great journeys.

GOALS/OBJECTIVES

Studying this lesson will enable students to

- empathize with the main character's view of life
- define *dramatic monologue* and *blank verse* and identify these forms in their reading
- describe Alfred, Lord Tennyson's literary accomplishments and explain the historical significance

of his writings
- define *character* and *motivation* and recognize and interpret the motivation of characters they encounter in their reading
- write a thematic comparison essay

The Return of Ulysses. Romare Bearden, 1976. National Museum of American Art/Art Resource, NY

What is the difference between just breathing and really living? What is the "eternal silence" from which "every hour is saved"? What kind of life does he consider unworthy?

❶

25

30

How dull it is to pause, to make an end,
To rust unburnished, not to shine in use!
As though to breathe were life! Life piled on life
Were all too little, and of one to me
Little remains; but every hour is saved
From that eternal silence, something more,
A bringer of new things; and vile it were
For some three suns to store and hoard myself,
And this gray spirit <u>yearning</u> in desire
To follow knowledge like a sinking star,
Beyond the utmost bound of human thought.

This is my son, mine own Telemachus,
To whom I leave the scepter and the isle—
35   Well-loved of me, <u>discerning</u> to fulfill

WORDS FOR EVERYDAY USE:

yearn (yʉrn´) *vi.*, filled with desire
dis • cern • ing (di zʉrn´iŋ) *part.*, showing good judgment

This labor, by slow prudence to make mild
A rugged people, and through soft degrees
Subdue them to the useful and the good.
Most blameless is he, centered in the sphere
40   Of common duties, decent not to fail
In offices of tenderness, and pay
Meet adoration to my household gods,
When I am gone. He works his work, I mine.

     There lies the port, the vessel puffs her sail;
45   There gloom the dark, broad seas. My mariners,
Souls that have toiled, and wrought, and thought with me—
That ever with a frolic welcome took
The thunder and the sunshine, and opposed
Free hearts, free foreheads—you and I are old;
50   Old age hath yet his honor and his toil.
Death closes all; but something ere the end,
Some work of noble note, may yet be done,
Not unbecoming men that strove with Gods.
The lights begin to twinkle from the rocks;
55   The long day wanes; the slow moon climbs; the deep
Moans round with many voices. Come, my friends,
'Tis not too late to seek a newer world.
Push off, and sitting well in order smite
The sounding furrows; for my purpose holds
60   To sail beyond the sunset, and the baths
Of all the western stars, until I die.
It may be that the gulfs will wash us down;
It may be we shall touch the Happy Isles,[5]
And see the great Achilles,[6] whom we knew.
65   Though much is taken, much abides; and though
We are not now that strength which in old days
Moved earth and heaven, that which we are, we are—
One equal temper of heroic hearts,
Made weak by time and fate, but strong in will
70   To strive, to seek, to find, and not to yield. ∎

---

5. **Happy Isles.** Paradise islands of perpetual summer
located in the western ocean according to Greek myth
6. **Achilles.** A Greek warrior in the Trojan War. His
only vulnerable spot was his heel.

❶
What fine qualities does Telemachus have? Does Ulysses have these same qualities?

❷
How does Ulysses feel toward his fellow mariners, now grown old? Does he still believe that he and they can do great things? Why?

VICTORIAN POETRY / "ULYSSES"   709

ANSWERS TO GUIDED READING QUESTIONS

❶ Telemachus is discerning, prudent, honest, caring, and reverent. Ulysses does not have the patience to rule and is much less family-centered than his son.

❷ Ulysses is very fond of his fellow mariners. Though they have all grown old, Ulysses believes that because they once accomplished great things, they may do so again. Ulysses admits that they do not have the strength of their youth, but they have heroic hearts and strong wills.

ANSWERS TO SELECTION CHECK TEST 4.9.3

EX. From what does Ulysses say he cannot rest?
He says that he cannot rest from travel.

1. What experience did Ulysses have in Troy?
He fought in a war, or drank "delight in battle."

2. In this poem is Ulysses young, middle-aged, or old?
He is old.

3. Who will become king after Ulysses?
His son Telemachus will become king.

4. What does Ulysses long to do?
He wants to have one more adventure.

5. Whom does Ulysses think he might see in the Happy Isles?
He might see Achilles.

ADDITIONAL QUESTIONS AND ACTIVITIES

Discuss the following questions with students. What is a hero or a heroic pursuit? Is the modern-day definition of a hero different from that of Ulysses's time, or even Tennyson's time? Rewrite the story told in the poem so that Ulysses embodies modern-day heroic qualities.

VOCABULARY IN CONTEXT

- My sister has been <u>yearning</u> to see the Grand Canyon before she moves to Tokyo.
- The jury was <u>discerning</u> in their refusal to be persuaded by the flimsy evidence presented by the prosecution.

TEACHER'S EDITION   709

Responding to the Selection

Review lines 33–43 of the poem. How do Ulysses and his son Telemachus differ? Which person do you admire more? Which are you more like? Ulysses is an archetype, or model, of the hero. What heroic qualities does he have? What characteristics caused him to live a heroic life? Why is he dissatisfied with his life at home in Ithaca?

Reviewing the Selection

RECALLING

1. How does Ulysses feel about his life at present? What specifics of that life does he relate at the beginning of the poem?

2. What general statements does Ulysses make about himself in lines 6–7? What specific adventures from his past does he recall?

3. To what does Ulysses compare "all experience" in line 19?

4. What is Ulysses's son Telemachus like? How does Ulysses feel toward him?

INTERPRETING

5. In line 5, Ulysses says that the "savage race" of people whom he governs does not know him. What do these people not know?

6. Why is Ulysses, at this point in his life, thinking so much about adventures from his past?

7. Ulysses has traveled more and seen more of the world than most people will in their lifetimes. Is he satisfied with having done that? How do you know?

8. What qualities does Telemachus have that will make him a good king? Ulysses says that "He works his work, I mine." What are the differences between the work that each man is made to do in life?

SYNTHESIZING

9. At the end of the poem, what weaknesses and strengths does Ulysses recognize in himself and in his fellow mariners?

10. Do you think that Ulysses is a hero or an old man still reluctant to give up the pleasures of his youth? What qualities make a person a hero?

Understanding Literature (Questions for Discussion)

1. **Dramatic Monologue.** A **dramatic monologue** is a poem that presents the speech of a single character in a dramatic situation. The technique often is used to explore the psychological state—the thoughts, sensations, and feelings—of characters in times of crises. What crisis is Ulysses facing in this poem? What has he resolved to do?

2. **Character and Motivation.** A **character** is a person who figures in the action of a literary work. **Motivation** is an internal or external force that drives a character to think, speak, or behave in certain ways. The sociologist and psychologist Erik Erikson wrote that in advanced age, people struggle between acceptance and defeat. At the opening of this poem, the character Ulysses speaks in a disillusioned, dispirited tone. In what way would remaining in Ithaca be a defeat for him? What does he refuse to accept? Look at Dylan Thomas's poem "Do Not Go Gentle into That Good Night" on page 876. Would Ulysses understand what Thomas is saying? What motivates Ulysses to leave Ithaca? What shows him still to have a heroic spirit?

3. **Blank Verse. Blank verse** is unrhymed poetry written in iambic pentameter. Many of the great tragic and heroic works in the English language are written in blank verse, including much of Shakespeare's *Macbeth* and all of Milton's *Paradise Lost*. The form is perfect for lofty, heroic poetry. Because it is unrhymed, it sounds more like ordinary speech than poetry often does. However, because it has a regular metrical pattern, it sounds more formal, elevated, or lofty than ordinary speech. In other words, writing in blank verse enables a poet to render realistic characters elevated to a lofty plane. What about the character Ulysses in this poem is realistic? What about him is lofty or heroic? Read aloud a few lines from "The Lady of Shalott." Then read aloud a few lines from "Ulysses." How do the two poems differ in their sound? How can you account for these differences?

Responding in Writing

Thematic Comparison Essay. Read Dylan Thomas's "Do Not Go Gentle into That Good Night" on page 876. Then write an essay in which you analyze Thomas's poem and Tennyson's "Ulysses." In your analyses, explain the central theme of each poem. What are these two poets saying about how we should approach old age and death? You can also compare "Ulysses" with "The Lady of Shalott."

ANALYTIC SCALES FOR RESPONDING IN WRITING

Assign a score from 1 to 25 for each grading criterion below. (For more detailed evaluation, see the evaluation forms for writing, revising, and proofreading, *Assessment Portfolio,* 7.1–7.10.)

Thematic Comparison Essay

• **Content/Unity.** The essay presents a sensible comparison of the themes of each poem.

• **Organization/Coherence.** The essay is clearly organized and clearly distinguishes points of comparison.

• **Language/Style.** The essay uses vivid and precise nouns, verbs, and modifiers

• **Conventions.** The essay avoids errors in spelling, grammar, usage, mechanics, and manuscript form.

ANSWERS FOR UNDERSTANDING LITERATURE

► See the evaluation forms for discussion, active listening, and oral communication, *Assessment Portfolio,* 7.11–7.14.

Responses will vary. Possible responses are given.

1. Dramatic Monologue. Ulysses is facing the end of his life. He has decided that he would rather die at sea in the middle of an adventure than waste away at home.

►**Teaching Note:** Ask students to give a dramatic reading of sections of "Ulysses." You may also want to play a recording of a dramatic monologue such as "Blow, winds, and crack your cheeks. Rage, blow!" from Shakespeare's *King Lear* (Act III, scene ii).

2. Character and Motivation. Ulysses does not want to die quietly in his home. He refuses to accept that his days of exploring and conquest are over. He would agree with Dylan Thomas that "Old age should burn and rave at close of day." He wants to leave Ithaca because he knows that there is still time to make discoveries. He refuses to die quietly.

►**Teaching Note:** Have students discuss how Ulysses's wife might feel about his leaving on another journey. How do they think she feels about getting older?

3. Blank Verse. Ulysses's frustration and anger with getting older are realistic. His refusal to succumb to the inevitable and his determination to go on another journey are heroic. "The Lady of Shalott" is very musical while "Ulysses" reads more like a dramatic speech. "The Lady of Shalott" has end rhymes and refrains. "Ulysses" has blank verse and elevated language.

►**Teaching Note:** Both "The Lady of Shalott" and "Ulysses" deal with serious subjects: the role of the artist and the inevitability of aging and death. Which poetic form do students feel better communicates the seriousness of the poem's theme? Might they be equally effective for their respective purposes?

ADDITIONAL RESOURCES

READER'S GUIDE
• Selection Worksheet, 9.3

ASSESSMENT PORTFOLIO
• Selection Check Test, 4.9.5
• Selection Test, 4.9.6

ESSENTIAL SKILLS PRACTICE BOOKS
• *Language,* 2.152
• *Speaking and Listening,* 3.3
• *Study and Research,* 4.10

ENRICHMENT ACTIVITIES

Suggest that students write either a poem in memory of their own deaths or a prose obituary. What qualities do they possess that are unique and should be mourned? Discuss with students what they learned about themselves in writing this poem.

SUPPORT FOR LEP STUDENTS

In this poem, Tennyson uses archaic word forms that are rarely used in modern speech. For example, *thou* (you), *hast* (have), and *shalt* (shall or will).

ANSWERS TO GUIDED READING QUESTIONS

❶ This person is a slave to darkness. A helmless life would be one without aim (a helm is a steering wheel on a boat); the person would have no control over events.

❷ The speaker compares his heart to a vase filled with cold tears. The vase is in danger of breaking.

❸ At night the speaker is despondent. In the morning, the speaker's will once again comes under control.

READER'S JOURNAL

Have you ever lost someone who was very close to you? Loss of loved ones is an inevitable yet difficult part of life. Almost everyone has to face such loss at some time. What can people do to make themselves feel better in the face of an irretrievable loss? Where and how can one find the courage and spirit to go on? Write about these questions in your journal.

THINKING SKILLS

Read the Language Arts Survey, 4.10, "Analyzing." As you read the excerpts from Tennyson's poem, analyze the stages of the speaker's grief. Notice how his feelings change over time and why.

FROM

In Memoriam

ALFRED, LORD TENNYSON

❶ *What does it mean to be a bondsman to darkness? What would a helmless life be like?*

4

To Sleep I give my powers away;
    My will is bondsman to the dark;
    I sit within a helmless bark,[1]
5 And with my heart I muse and say:

O heart, how fares it with thee now,
    That thou should fail from thy desire,
    Who scarcely darest to inquire,
"What is it makes me beat so low?"

❷ *What object does the speaker describe himself as being? What is in danger of happening to that object?*

10 Something it is which thou hast lost,
    Some pleasure from thine early years.
    Break thou deep vase of chilling tears,
That grief hath shaken into frost!

❸ *How do the speaker's nights differ from his mornings?*

Such clouds of nameless trouble cross
15 All night below the darkened eyes;
    With morning wakes the will, and cries,
"Thou shalt not be the fool of loss."

---

1. **helmless bark.** Unsteered boat

GOALS/OBJECTIVES

Studying this lesson will enable students to

• experience and interpret an elegiac lyric and appreciate a speaker's sense of loss
• describe Alfred, Lord Tennyson's literary accomplishments and explain the historical significance of his writings

• define *elegiac lyric* and identify elegiac lyrics they encounter in future reading
• write an obituary and a dialogue/debate
• recognize and correct clichés and euphemisms

5

I sometimes hold it half a sin
    To put in words the grief I feel;
    For words, like Nature, half reveal
And half conceal the Soul within.

5   But, for the unquiet heart and brain,
        A use in measured language lies;
        The sad mechanic exercise,
    Like dull narcotics, numbing pain.

    In words, like weeds,[2] I'll wrap me o'er,
10   Like coarsest clothes against the cold;
        But that large grief which these enfold
    Is given in outline and no more.

◆   ◆   ◆

26

Still onward winds the dreary way;
    I with it, for I long to prove
    No lapse of moons can <u>canker</u> Love,
Whatever <u>fickle</u> tongues may say.

5   And if that eye which watches guilt
        And goodness, and hath power to see
        Within the green the <u>mouldered</u> tree,
    And towers fallen as soon as built—

    O, if indeed that eye foresee
10   Or see—in Him is no before—
        In more of life true life no more
    And Love the indifference to be,

    Then might I find, ere yet the morn
        Breaks hither over Indian seas,
15   That Shadow waiting with the keys,
    To shroud me from my proper scorn.[3]

---

2. **weeds.** Clothes
3. **eye . . . scorn.** If God, who sees everything, sees that the rest of my life will be as it is now, then let me die tonight so that I won't live to scorn myself as one who could not prove that love can outlast change.

WORDS FOR EVERYDAY USE:
can • ker (kaŋ´kər) *vt.,* infect with corruption
fick • le (fik´əl) *adj.,* unstable in affection, loyalty, interest, etc.
mould • ered or **mold • ered** (mōl´dərd) *adj.,* decayed

PREREADING NOTES

READER'S JOURNAL

Some students may not have experienced the death of someone close to them. Suggest other types of loss such as losing one's home in a fire, experiencing the death of a favorite pet, or moving to another country.

THINKING SKILLS

Suggest that students map out the poem on a separate sheet of paper. As a form of grief is encountered, students can write the line in which the reference occurs and a description of the grief next to the line.

▶ Additional practice is provided in the *Essential Skills Practice Book: Study and Research,* 4.10.

❶
Why does the speaker sometimes think it "half a sin" to try to express his feelings in words? What comfort does writing give him? Is this genuine comfort, or a false covering over of the pain?

❷
What does the speaker long to prove? What claim made by "fickle tongues" does the speaker detest?

ANSWERS TO GUIDED READING QUESTIONS

❶ Words are not sufficient to express the extent of his grief. Working to put his feelings into words seems to numb his pain. The words that help to cover the pain are not a complete relief; they are just an outline.

❷ The speaker longs to prove that a lapse of time will not corrupt love. He detests the idea that his feelings of loss will lessen with time.

VOCABULARY FROM THE SELECTION

canker	moldered
derive	stagnate
diffusive	tumult
fickle	

VOCABULARY IN CONTEXT

- Just one bad apple in a basket can <u>canker</u> the rest of the bushel.
- My <u>fickle</u> dog scurries from one person to the next, hoping for a discarded morsel.
- We had to throw away the <u>moldered</u> quilt we had found in the trunk in the damp basement.

Ask students to look for words that are capitalized in the poem, other than those at the beginning of lines. Why might Tennyson have chosen to capitalize those words? Do their meanings differ when they are capitalized? If so, how?

ANSWERS TO GUIDED READING QUESTIONS

❶ The difference between people and animals is that animals don't have a conscience or feel outrage in the same way that people do. Students may say that loving is an important part of having a full life.

❷ The speaker hears the caroling but is unaffected. The speaker still mourns the death of his friend.

ADDITIONAL QUESTIONS AND ACTIVITIES

Discuss with students the often quoted lines, "'Tis better to have loved and lost/Than never to have loved at all." Why might these lines resonate with some readers more than other lines? Find lines in the poem that seem to speak to you, that resonate with you. Discuss with the class why you chose these lines.

❶ What is the speaker saying about the difference between people and animals? Do you agree with the speaker that it is "better to have loved and lost/Than never to have loved at all"? Why might this be better even though it is so difficult?

❷ How does the speaker respond to the Christmas caroling? Why?

27

I envy not in any moods
    The captive void of noble rage,
    The linnet[4] born within the cage,
That never knew the summer woods;

5   I envy not the beast that takes
    His license in the field of time,
    Unfettered by the sense of crime,
To whom a conscience never wakes;

Nor, what may count itself as blest,
10   The heart that never plighted troth
    But <u>stagnates</u> in the weeds of sloth;
Nor any want-begotten rest.[5]

I hold it true, whate'er befall;
    I feel it, when I sorrow most;
15   'Tis better to have loved and lost
Than never to have loved at all.

28

The time draws near the birth of Christ.[6]
    The moon is hid, the night is still;
    The Christmas bells from hill to hill
Answer each other in the mist.

5   Four voices of four hamlets round,
    From far and near, on mead and moor,
    Swell out and fail, as if a door
Were shut between me and the sound;

Each voice four changes on the wind,
10   That now dilate, and now decrease,

---

4. **linnet.** A type of bird
5. **But . . . rest.** A need or desire has led to complacency.
6. **birth of Christ.** This was the first Christmas after Tennyson's friend Hallam had died.

WORDS FOR EVERYDAY USE:
stag • nate (stag´nāt´) *vi.,* become sluggish

VOCABULARY IN CONTEXT

• Once the dam was built, the formerly swift-moving river <u>stagnated</u>.

Peace and goodwill, goodwill and peace,
    Peace and goodwill, to all mankind.

This year I slept and woke with pain,
    I almost wished no more to wake,
15   And that my hold on life would break
Before I heard those bells again;

But they my troubled spirit rule,
    For they controlled me when a boy;
    They bring me sorrow touched with joy,
20   The merry, merry bells of Yule.

◆ ◆ ◆

48

If these brief lays, of Sorrow born,
    Were taken to be such as closed
    Grave doubts and answers here proposed,
Then these were such as men might scorn.

5   Her[7] care is not to part and prove;
    She takes, when harsher moods remit,
    What slender shade of doubt may flit,
And makes it vassal unto love;

And hence, indeed, she sports with words,
10   But better serves a wholesome law,
    And holds it sin and shame to draw
The deepest measure from the chords;

Nor dare she trust a larger lay,
    But rather loosens from the lip
15   Short swallow-flights of song, that dip
Their wings in tears, and skim away.

◆ ◆ ◆

54

O, yet we trust that somehow good
    Will be the final goal of ill,
    To pangs of nature, sins of will,
Defects of doubt, and taints of blood;

---

7. **Her.** Sorrow's

❶
What conflicting emotions is the speaker feeling? What is the source of his sorrow? of his joy?

❷
What kinds of poetry does the poet reject in the first stanza? What kind of poetry does he say he is unable to write in the third stanza? What kind of poetry can he write?

❸
What trust do people have, according to the speaker?

ANSWERS TO GUIDED READING QUESTIONS

❶ The speaker feels both sorrow and joy. The source of the speaker's sorrow is the death of his friend and possibly the loss of his boyhood innocence. The speaker's joy comes from hearing the bells, which remind him of his happy boyhood.

❷ The poet rejects poems that provide easy answers. He is unable to express deep feelings. He is able to touch only the surface of his feelings in his poetry.

❸ People trust that good will somehow come out of bad events.

QUOTABLES

❝[William] Wordsworth, Tennyson and [Robert] Browning; or, Pure, Ornate, and Grotesque Art in English Poetry.❞

—Walter Bagehot

❶ An example in nature of good
coming out of ill is spring coming out
of winter.

❷ The speaker likens himself to a
crying infant. He has not accepted
the idea that everything happens for
a reason, yet it is still a "dream" for
him.

❸ The speaker finds it ironic that life
is so precious while nature is "careless
of the single life," that is, while
nature has no concern for the
individual soul.

❶
*What event in
nature symbolizes,
for the speaker,
the idea that good
can come of ill?*

❷
*To what does the
speaker liken
himself? Has he
truly accepted
the idea that
everything
happens for a
reason and that
good will come of
ill?*

❸
*In the first stanza
of poem 55, the
speaker says that
something inside
us, the soul, leads
us to have the
wish that all lives
will continue
beyond the grave.
What in the way
that nature treats
life seems,
therefore, ironic
to the speaker?*

5   That nothing walks with aimless feet;
          That not one life shall be destroyed,
          Or cast as rubbish to the void,
       When God hath made the pile complete;

       That not a worm is cloven in vain;
10   That not a moth with vain desire
          Is shriveled in a fruitless fire,
       Or but subserves another's gain.

       Behold, we know not anything;
          I can but trust that good shall fall
15   At last—far off—at last, to all,
       And every winter change to spring.

       So runs my dream; but what am I?
          An infant crying in the night;
          An infant crying for the light,
20   And with no language but a cry.

                        55
       The wish, that of the living whole
          No life may fail beyond the grave,
          <u>Derives</u> it not from what we have
       The likest God within the soul?

5   Are God and Nature then at strife,
          That Nature lends such evil dreams?
          So careful of the type she seems,
       So careless of the single life,

       That I, considering everywhere
10   Her secret meaning in her deeds,
          And finding that of fifty seeds
       She often brings but one to bear,

       I falter where I firmly trod,
          And falling with my weight of cares
15   Upon the great world's altar-stairs
       That slope through darkness up to God,

WORDS FOR   **de • rive** (di rīv´) *vt.*, get from a source
EVERYDAY USE:

VOCABULARY IN CONTEXT

• I <u>derive</u> satisfaction from a job well done.

I stretch lame hands of faith, and grope,
        And gather dust and chaff, and call
        To what I feel is Lord of all,
20   And faintly trust the larger hope.

◆　◆　◆

59

O Sorrow, wilt thou live with me
        No casual mistress, but a wife,
        My bosom friend and half of life;
As I confess it needs must be?

5   O Sorrow, wilt thou rule my blood,
        Be sometimes lovely like a bride,
        And put thy harsher moods aside,
If thou wilt have me wise and good?

My centered passion cannot move,
10   Nor will it lessen from today;
        But I'll have leave at times to play
As with the creature of my love;

And set thee forth, for thou art mine,
        With so much hope for years to come,
15   That, howsoe'er I know thee, some
Could hardly tell what name were thine.

◆　◆　◆

75

I leave thy praises unexpressed
        In verse that brings myself relief,
        And by the measure of my grief
I leave thy greatness to be guessed.

5   What practice howsoe'er expert
        In fitting aptest words to things,
        Or voice the richest-toned that sings,
Hath power to give thee as thou wert?

❶
What faith is the speaker groping toward? What is he learning to trust?

❷
To what is the speaker proposing to wed himself?

❸
What good might come of the speaker's sorrow? What changes might sorrow bring about in him?

❹
Why doesn't the speaker write verse to praise the qualities of his lost friend?

ANSWERS TO GUIDED READING QUESTIONS

❶ The speaker is groping toward faith in the Lord of all. He is learning to trust the larger hope.

❷ The speaker is proposing to wed himself to sorrow.

❸ Sorrow may put her "harsher moods aside," his grief may not be so painful. The speaker may become wise and good.

❹ The speaker is unable to express in words the fine qualities of his friend.

ANSWERS TO GUIDED READING QUESTIONS

❶ The world praises a person's actions; the world is cold to a person's unrealized potential.

❷ The place "somewhere, out of human view" is the afterworld. There the talents of the speaker's dead friend will be known.

LITERARY TECHNIQUE

Image. An image is a word picture—a word or phrase that names something that can be seen, heard, touched, tasted, or smelled. Ask students what images are evoked in lines 9–12 of canto 75. How has the poet's imagery been affected by death? What does a still, dusty place bring to mind? Because the poet is grieving, is he in any sense eternally in a vault or mausoleum of his own creation?

10   I care not in these fading days
        To raise a cry that lasts not long,
        And round thee with the breeze of song
     To stir a little dust of praise.

     Thy leaf has perished in the green,
        And, while we breathe beneath the sun,
15   The world which credits what is done
     Is cold to all that might have been.

     So here shall silence guard thy fame;
        But somewhere, out of human view,
        Whate'er thy hands are set to do
20   Is wrought with <u>tumult</u> of acclaim.

❶ *What does the world praise? To what is the world cold?*

❷ *What is the place "somewhere, out of human view"? What will be known there that is not known now?*

◆ ◆ ◆

WORDS FOR EVERYDAY USE: tu • mult (tōō′mult′) *n.*, commotion; agitation

VOCABULARY IN CONTEXT

• The <u>tumult</u> from the New Year's Eve party next door was more than I could stand or sleep through.

78

Again at Christmas did we weave
   The holly round the Christmas hearth;
   The silent snow possessed the earth,
And calmly fell our Christmas eve.

5   The yule clog[8] sparkled keen with frost,
   No wing of wind the region swept,
   But over all things brooding slept
The quiet sense of something lost.

As in the winters left behind,
10   Again our ancient games had place,
   The mimic picture's[9] breathing grace,
And dance and song and hoodman-blind.[10]

Who showed a token of distress?
   No single tear, no mark of pain—
15   O sorrow, then can sorrow wane?
O grief, can grief be changed to less?

O last regret, regret can die!
   No—mixed with all this mystic frame,
   Her deep relations are the same,
20   But with long use her tears are dry.

♦ ♦ ♦

130

Thy voice is on the rolling air
   I hear thee where the waters run;
   Thou standest in the rising sun,
And in the setting thou art fair.

5   What art thou then? I cannot guess;
   But though I seem in star and flower

---

8. **clog.** Log
9. **mimic picture.** A game in which players pose as a famous statue or painting while others try to guess the source
10. **hoodman-blind.** The blindfolded person in a game of Blindman's Bluff

❶
What joys did the speaker experience at this Christmastime?

❷
Does the speaker really believe that regret can die? What conclusion does he come to on that subject?

❸
In what does the speaker hear and see his departed friend?

ANSWERS TO GUIDED READING QUESTIONS

❶ The speaker enjoyed many of the Christmas foods and events that he used to enjoy before the death of his friend, such as the Yule log, dances, games, and songs.

❷ No. His regret remains deep, but with time the outward display of loss ceases, or runs dry.

❸ The speaker hears his departed friend's voice in the wind and in rivers, and sees him in the rising and setting of the sun.

ANALYTIC SCALES FOR RESPONDING IN WRITING

Assign a score from 1 to 25 for each grading criterion below. (For more detailed evaluation, see the evaluation forms for writing, revising, and proofreading, *Assessment Portfolio,* 7.1–7.10.)

1. Obituary
- **Content/Unity.** The obituary presents a sensible account of the life of the deceased, combining observable fact and personal insights.
- **Organization/Coherence.** The obituary most often will be arranged in chronological order.
- **Language/Style.** The obituary uses vivid and precise nouns, verbs, and modifiers.
- **Conventions.** The obituary avoids errors in spelling, grammar, usage, mechanics, and manuscript form.

2. Dialogue/Debate
- **Content/Unity.** The dialogue presents a sensible discussion of what happens after death.
- **Organization/Coherence.** The dialogue should present the main theory and contrasting theories in a clear and concise manner.
- **Language/Style.** The dialogue uses vivid and precise nouns, verbs, and modifiers.
- **Conventions.** The dialogue avoids errors in spelling, grammar, usage, mechanics, and manuscript form.

ADDITIONAL QUESTIONS AND ACTIVITIES

Discuss with students why Tennyson might have chosen Christmas as a way to mark the passing of time. What ideas was he trying to communicate by referring to that holiday?

Answer. Christmas marks the end of one year and the beginning of the next. Christians also consider the first Christmas as the beginning of a new era on Earth, so the holiday signifies renewal.

❶ The speaker feels that the spirit of his friend is evident in all of nature. The speaker feels that he would always be surrounded by his friend's voice, even if he were to die.

❷ He might be referring to truths having to do with the meaning of life and death. To close with all you have loved and with all that you flow from means to attain unity in the afterlife, presumably in heaven.

ANSWERS TO SELECTION CHECK TEST 4.9.5

EX. About whom was this poem written?
The poem was written about Tennyson's friend, Arthur Hallam.

1. What happened to Tennyson's friend?
He died young.

2. What holiday is mentioned in two of the lyrics in this poem?
Christmas is mentioned in two of the lyrics.

3. According to the poem, what is better than never to have loved at all?
To have loved and lost is better than never to have loved at all.

4. What emotion does the speaker ask to become his wife?
He asks sorrow to become his wife.

5. What does the speaker hear "on the rolling air"?
He hears the voice of his departed friend.

---

❶
In what sense does the speaker still have his friend? How could he not lose his friend even if he lost his own life?

❷
The speaker says that there are truths that cannot be proved. What truths do you think he is referring to? What does it mean to close with all that you have loved and with all that you flow from?

To feel thee some <u>diffusive</u> power,
I do not therefore love thee less.

10   My love involves the love before;
My love is vaster passion now;
Tho' mix'd with God and Nature thou,
I seem to love thee more and more.

15   Far off thou art, but ever nigh;
I have thee still, and I rejoice;
I prosper, circled with thy voice;
I shall not lose thee tho' I die.

131

O living will[11] that shalt endure
When all that seems shall suffer shock,
Rise in the spiritual rock,[12]
Flow through our deeds and make them pure,

5   That we may lift from out of dust
A voice as unto him that hears,
A cry above the conquered years
To one that with us works, and trust,

With faith that comes of self-control,
10   The truths that never can be proved
Until we close with all we loved,
And all we flow from, soul in soul.   ∎

---
11. **living will.** Humankind's moral will
12. **spiritual rock.** Christ

WORDS FOR EVERYDAY USE: **dif • fu • sive** (di fyoo´siv) *adj.*, tending to disperse

---

VOCABULARY IN CONTEXT

• The snake oil salesman's crowd was <u>diffusive</u>, no matter what wondrous cures he effected.

Responding to the Selection

Retrace the development of the speaker's feelings throughout the excerpts. Summarize what he is feeling and thinking in each poem. How do the speaker's feelings evolve over time? At what points were you most moved by the speaker's feelings? Which of the speaker's ideas about love, death, the spirit, and immortality do you agree with? Are there any that you disagree with? Would the conclusions that the speaker comes to be a comfort to you? Why, or why not? Discuss these questions with your classmates.

Reviewing the Selection

RECALLING

1. How does the speaker feel at night and then in the morning, as stated in the last stanza of poem 4?

2. What, according to the first stanza of poem 26, do "fickle tongues" say about love?

3. What famous claim does the speaker make about having loved and lost at the end of poem 27?

4. How did the speaker feel at Christmastime in poem 28? How did he feel at Christmas time in poem 78? How did the responses to Christmas differ?

INTERPRETING

5. Judging from the poem as a whole, would you say that the speaker became "the fool of loss"? Explain.

6. *In Memoriam* was composed over the course of seventeen years. Did the speaker's love die? Did he stop regretting the loss of his friend? Explain.

7. Do you agree with the speaker that it is better to have loved and lost? What did the speaker gain for having had this experience?

8. To what does the speaker attribute the change in his responses to the Christmas season from poem 28 to poem 78?

SYNTHESIZING

9. In poem 59, the speaker expresses the idea that wedding "Sorrow" might well make him wise and good. Considering the conclusion of the poem, do you think that what the speaker predicted came true? Why, or why not?

10. How do the speaker's spiritual ideas develop throughout the poem? To what conclusions does he come, however tentatively, in poems 130 and 131?

RESPONDING TO THE SELECTION

These discussions probably will be most productive in small mixed-ability groups.

ANSWERS FOR REVIEWING THE SELECTION

RECALLING

1. At night the speaker feels despair, as if his life is without aim. In the morning his spirit rallies and he resolves not to have his life destroyed by grief.

2. "Fickle tongues" say that love will become less intense over time. In other words, the speaker will recover from the death of his friend with time.

3. "'Tis better to have loved and lost/Than never to have loved at all."

4. The speaker felt great pain and isolation and wanted to die in poem 28. The speaker was able to join in the festivities during the second Christmas. During the first Christmas, the speaker almost wanted to die, but by the second Christmas he was able to experience some pleasure.

INTERPRETING

Responses will vary. Possible responses are given.

5. Students may notice that the speaker used the term "fool of loss" when he was still very angry and full of despair. Later on, he was better able to deal with his loss.

6. No. His love and grief did not die, but they changed. The speaker realized that he hadn't completely lost his friend; he could still feel his spirit in nature.

7. Students may say that the speaker became wiser and gained a more advanced understanding of life and loss.

8. The speaker still feels loss, but the outward show of his grief has

(cont.)

ANSWERS FOR REVIEWING THE SELECTION (CONT.)

dried out with long use.

SYNTHESIZING

Responses will vary. Possible responses are given.

9. Yes, the speaker has transcended his grief and now has a wiser, more complex view of life.

10. The speaker's spiritual ideas evolve from anger and despair into a more complex concept of the inseparability of nature and the human spirit. One of the speaker's conclusions is that some questions cannot be answered until after death.

► See the evaluation forms for discussion, active listening, and oral communication, *Assessment Portfolio, 7.11–7.14.*

Responses will vary. Possible responses are given.

1. Historical and Biographical Criticism. Initially, the speaker is despondent and feels powerless; he then vows always to suffer the pain of his loss; with time he is less angry and becomes very sad; after a few years, his grief is still very strong, but quieter; and finally, he comes to a higher understanding of death and realizes that his friend is an inextricable part of his memory and of nature. He concludes that sorrow makes people wiser and better (poem 59, line 8). In poem 131, lines 1–8, Tennyson supports the Christian concept of Judgment Day and life after death. All of poem 130 describes Tennyson's feelings of spiritual connection with his dead friend.

►**Teaching Note:** Modern psychologists have determined that there are five stages in the grieving process: denial, anger, bargaining, grief, and acceptance. How are these stages reflected in Tennyson's poem? For additional information, see Kubler-Ross, E. *On Death and Dying.* 1969.

2. Elegiac Lyric. It seems clear that Arthur Hallam was a very good friend, and he was probably quite talented in some way. Hallam died at a young age, before he had "ripened" or matured. It is tragic when a young person dies, because there are so many things he or she was not able to experience, and the death is unexpected and therefore shocking.

►**Teaching Note:** Discuss with students elegiac lyrics with which they may be familiar. Do they know of any songs about someone who has died? You might refer them to "Bonny Barbara Allan" on page 223.

Understanding Literature (Questions for Discussion)

1. **Historical and Biographical Criticism. Criticism** is the act of evaluating or interpreting a work of art or the act of developing general guidelines or principles for such evaluation or interpretation. **Historical criticism** views the work of art as a product of the period in which it was produced. **Biographical criticism** attempts to account for elements of literary works by relating them to events in the lives of their authors. Tennyson was an avid reader of scientific literature and, like other Victorians, struggled deeply with questions about religious faith raised by the writings of scientists like Charles Darwin and Thomas Huxley. The death of his friend Arthur Hallam created a spiritual crisis for Tennyson. He had to face, directly, the question of why loss and pain occur in the world. What stages does his grief go through? What conclusions does he come to about the role played by sorrow in people's lives, about life after death, and about the spiritual bonds of connectedness between people? Explain your answers based on evidence from the poem.

2. **Elegiac Lyric.** An **elegiac lyric** is a musical poem that expresses a speaker's feelings of loss. A eulogy is a speech or writing in praise of a person, event, or thing, especially a person who has recently died. While the speaker of *In Memoriam* does express a profound sense of loss, he disclaims any intention to write a eulogy. He says, in poem 75: "I leave thy praises unexpressed/In verse that brings myself relief,/And by the measure of my grief/I leave thy greatness to be guessed." What kind of person do you think Arthur Hallam was, based on what is said in the poem? What does it mean to say that Hallam "perished in the green"? Why is it particularly tragic for someone to die so young?

Responding in Writing

1. **Obituary.** Choose someone whom you admire who died within the last twenty years. Gather some information about that person. Then write an obituary for that person. Include more than simply important facts from the person's life. Try to include details that will communicate to your readers what was unique or wonderful about the person—details that will help to make that person live in your readers' memories.

2. **Dialogue/Debate.** Create two characters, one who believes in life after death and one who doesn't. Write a dialogue between the two characters in which they debate what happens after death. In the dialogue, express your own opinions about the subject and try to counter common arguments against the position that you hold.

Language Lab

Clichés and Euphemisms. Read the Language Arts Survey, 2.152, "Clichés and Euphemisms." Then rewrite the following sentences, replacing the clichés and euphemisms that you find in them.

1. Arthur Hallam must have been a fine young man.

ANALYTIC SCALES FOR RESPONDING IN WRITING

Grading scales appear on page 719.

2. When Hallam passed away, it broke Tennyson's heart.

3. Tennyson spent seventeen years composing a poem eulogizing the dearly departed.

4. Writing *In Memoriam* helped Tennyson to look on the sunny side of things.

5. Tennyson came to recognize that every cloud has a silver lining and that the passing on of the young Arthur Hallam had deepened his own life, making it more meaningful.

Speaking and Listening Skills

Nonverbal Communication. Read the Language Arts Survey, 3.3, "Elements of Nonverbal Communication." Then describe how each emotion listed below might be communicated though eye contact, facial expressions, gestures, body language, or proximity.

1. grief   3. awe

2. joy   4. fear

PROJECTS

1. **Setting a Poem to Music.** Tennyson's "The Lady of Shalott" is a highly musical poem, one that lends itself quite readily to treatment as a song. Try writing a melody to which "The Lady of Shalott" might be sung. If you play a musical instrument such as the guitar, recorder, flute, or piano, you might compose your melody on that instrument or compose music to accompany the singing of your melody.

2. **Oral History.** As Tennyson's "Ulysses" vividly demonstrates, advanced age does not mean that a person no longer has a great deal to offer. Quite the contrary, elderly people have a lifetime of acquired knowledge and experience, and one can learn much from them. Visit someone at a home for elderly people or seek out an elderly person in your own family, and interview that person to prepare an oral history of his or her life at some specific period in the past. If possible, tape record and transcribe the stories that the person tells you. If you do not have access to a tape recorder, take detailed notes and then write up your notes in the form of a brief report. (See the Language Arts Survey, 4.31, "Informal Note-taking.")

3. **Research Report.** Tennyson memorialized his friend Arthur Hallam by writing *In Memoriam*. With two or three other classmates, prepare a research report on ways in which people around the world memorialize others who have died. You may wish to choose two cultures, such as yours and that of one foreign country, and concentrate on comparing and contrasting memorial rituals in those countries. For example, you might compare and contrast what people do after someone dies in Japan and in the United States.

ANSWERS FOR SPEAKING AND LISTENING SKILLS

Nonverbal Communication
Responses will vary. Possible responses are given.

1. Grief might be signified by crying or covering one's face with one's hands. A person's shoulders would probably be slumped and his or her facial expression might be very sad or vacant.

2. Joy might be shown by a smile, laughter, wide eyes, and a desire for eye contact in order to share the emotion with others. People sometimes clap, shout, or jump up and down when joyful.

3. When people are in awe, their eyes and mouth are usually open and they don't say anything, or they speak only gibberish. Oftentimes people may act awkwardly when they are in awe.

4. Fear often makes people jump back from the object they are afraid of. A person will often have wide eyes and may scream. Sometimes people will fidget and become excitable when fearful.

►Additional practice is provided in the *Essential Skills Practice Book: Speaking and Listening*, 3.3.

PROJECT NOTES

►See the worksheets and evaluation forms for projects, *Assessment Portfolio*, 7.20–7.23.

 1. Setting a Poem to Music. Students may want to set "The Lady of Shalott" to a preexisting melody as a way of experimenting with the rhythm of the poem.

2. Oral History. Students should write down their questions before they interview their subject. However, students should not feel compelled to ask those questions if another more interesting topic presents itself during the interview.

 3. Research Report. Make sure that the two memorial rituals that students compare are contemporaneous.

ANSWERS FOR LANGUAGE LAB

Responses may vary. Possible responses are given.

1. Arthur Hallam was a talented artist and an excellent friend.

2. Tennyson was despondent when Hallam died.

3. Tennyson spent seventeen years composing a poem eulogizing his dead friend.

4. Writing *In Memoriam* helped Tennyson to analyze and understand his grief.

5. Through dealing with his friend's death, Tennyson gained a more complex understanding of love and death, of his relationship to nature, and of his own spirituality.

►Additional practice is provided in the *Essential Skills Practice Book: Language*, 2.152.

ENRICHMENT ACTIVITIES

Encourage students to prepare a brief (one or two pages) speech that reveals an aspect of their personalities or tells about their lives. Students who are comfortable doing so can read their speeches out loud in class. Have other students critique their speeches, noting what the speakers might have unwittingly revealed.

SUPPORT FOR LEP STUDENTS

Discuss with students what different punctuation marks signify in the dramatic monologue. Quotation marks mean that the speaker is using words as words or that he is quoting someone else. Parentheses indicate an aside.

ADDITIONAL VOCABULARY
pretense—claim
avow—promise

PREREADING

VICTORIAN POETRY

"My Last Duchess"
"Andrea del Sarto"
by Robert Browning

ABOUT THE AUTHOR

Robert Browning (1812–1889) grew up in a remarkable household with parents who loved literature and music. Tutored at home, he became one of the most learned men in Europe. While still quite young, he published two volumes of poetry, but neither met with success. He also failed in his first attempt at writing for the stage. His play *Strafford,* produced in 1837, closed after running for only five nights. In subsequent years, he gained some reputation as a writer of verse in which characters speak in their own voices without narrative commentary. In 1846, Robert married Elizabeth Barrett, a poet six years older than he with a far greater reputation than his own. Elizabeth and Robert moved to Italy, partially because of Elizabeth's poor health, but primarily to escape her domineering father. Theirs was one of the great love stories of all time. They had an exceedingly happy marriage and lived in Italy for thirteen years, until Elizabeth's death. Robert then returned to England to teach and write. In his own day, many people considered Browning's poetry to be too unpoetic and obscure. However, in the twentieth century, Browning's reputation has grown enormously. His poetry is modern in its use of realistic speech and its portrayal of the psychological states of characters. His reputation rests primarily on his magnificent **dramatic monologues.**

ABOUT THE SELECTIONS

Browning had a lifelong obsession with Italy and with the Italian Renaissance. In **"My Last Duchess,"** the speaker is a Renaissance-era Italian duke who prattles on, seemingly unaware that he is revealing something horrible about himself. The poem shows Browning's gift for allowing characters to speak in their own voices, inadvertently exposing their innermost conflicts and desires.

The speaker in **"Andrea del Sarto"** is Andrea d'Angelo di Francesca, an Italian Renaissance painter who was called "del Sarto" because his father was a *sarto,* or tailor. Del Sarto gained a reputation for painting works of flawless, faultless perfection. In the poem, del Sarto addresses his wife, Lucrezia del Fede, whose influence was disastrous for his work. This poem has given to our language an immortal phrase, del Sarto's idea that a person's reach (his yearning or desire) should exceed his or her grasp. The painter believes that one should always strive to do more than what one can do well but easily.

GOALS/OBJECTIVES

Studying this lesson will enable students to

- have positive experiences reading dramatic monologues
- describe Browning's literary accomplishments and explain the historical significance of his writings
- define *dramatic monologue* and identify poems that are written as dramatic monologues
- define *metaphor* and *paradox* and recognize and interpret metaphors and paradoxes in a poem
- define *characterization* and *diction* and analyze how characterization and diction are used to give information about a character
- write a dramatic monologue and character sketch
- revise sentences to vary length and structure

READER'S JOURNAL

What would you do if you suspected someone of having committed a horrible crime? Write in your journal a short scene in which someone accidentally reveals to you something horrible that he or she has done. Then, as you read "My Last Duchess," imagine that you are the person to whom the Duke is speaking.

THINKING SKILLS

Read the Language Arts Survey, 4.11 and 4.12, "Generalizing" and "Deducing." Then, as you read the poem, see what conclusions you can draw from the details presented about the relationship between the Duke and the Duchess, and the Duchess's fate.

READER'S JOURNAL

Ask students to determine if there is enough evidence in this poem to report the Duke to the police.

THINKING SKILLS

• Students might imagine that they are prosecuting attorneys investigating the murder of Lucrezia.
• You may want to have students role play an interview between the Duke and police using the information about the Duke and the late Duchess found in the poem.
▶Additional practice is provided in the *Essential Skills Practice Book: Study and Research,* 4.11 and 4.12.

"My Last Duchess"[1]

ROBERT BROWNING

That's my last Duchess painted on the wall,
Looking as if she were alive. I call
That piece a wonder, now: Frà Pandolf's[2] hands
Worked busily a day, and there she stands.
5   Will 't please you sit and look at her? I said
"Frà Pandolf" by design, for never read
Strangers like you that pictured <u>countenance</u>,
The depth and passion of its earnest glance,
But to myself they turned (since none puts by
10   The curtain I have drawn for you, but I)
And seemed as they would ask me, if they durst,
How such a glance came there; so, not the first
Are you to turn and ask thus. Sir, 'twas not
Her husband's presence only, called that spot
15   Of joy into the Duchess' cheek: perhaps
Frà Pandolf chanced to say "Her mantle laps
Over my lady's wrist too much," or "Paint

---

1. **My Last Duchess.** The speaker is Alfonso II, duke of Ferrara, Italy. His wife Lucrezia has died. In the poem he is addressing an agent who is negotiating his next marriage.
2. **Frà Pandolf.** An imaginary painter. *Frà* is short for *Fratello,* Italian for "brother." The painter was a monk.

❶
Whose portrait is the Duke showing to his visitor? What about the portrait causes people to ask questions about it?

ANSWER TO GUIDED READING QUESTION

❶ The Duke is showing his visitor a portrait of the late Duchess. People question the Duchess's lifelike look of passion and joy.

VOCABULARY FROM THE SELECTIONS	
countenance	officious
demur	profusely
munificence	

WORDS FOR EVERYDAY USE: **coun • te • nance** (koun′tə nəns) *n.,* look on a person's face

VOCABULARY IN CONTEXT

• The condemned man had a stoic <u>countenance</u>.

ANSWERS TO GUIDED READING QUESTIONS

❶ The Duke attributes the look to either his own presence or an offhand courteous remark by the artist.

❷ The implication is that the Duchess was a flirt—or worse.

❸ The Duke felt he would be lowering himself if he revealed that her behavior upset him.

❹ The Duke became increasingly jealous because the Duchess gave others the same smile she gave him. That is ominous because he then commanded the cessation of her smiles (and possibly commended her death).

❺ The Duke's choice of words is ominous because they suggest he is already planning on finding another bride, and perhaps, another work of "art."

HISTORICAL NOTE

Neptune is the Roman name for the god of the sea, Poseidon. He was considered a violent and powerful god, and was renowned for his many love affairs.

ANSWERS TO SELECTION CHECK TEST 4.9.7

EX. What does the speaker call the person in the painting?
The speaker calls the person in the painting "my last Duchess."

1. Why do people ask questions about the portrait?
People are drawn to the look on the woman's face.

2. What did the speaker dislike about the Duchess's interactions with other people?
The speaker felt that the Duchess was too friendly and easily pleased by other people.

3. Of what did the speaker believe the Duchess was unappreciative?
The speaker believed the Duchess was unappreciative of being married to him and having his name.

4. What happened to the relationship of the speaker and the Duchess just before she died?
The speaker grew more and more angry and disgusted with her.

5. According to the speaker, what happened to the smiles of the Duchess?
The speaker says that the smiles of the Duchess stopped.

726 TEACHER'S EDITION

---

❶ To what does the Duke attribute the look on the Duchess's face in the portrait?

❷ What is the implication of the Duke's statement that "her looks went everywhere"?

❸ Why did the Duke not tell the Duchess what displeased him about her conduct?

❹ What had happened to the Duke's relationship with his wife before she died? What makes this fact ominous?

❺ What is ominous about the Duke's choice of words here?

Must never hope to reproduce the faint
Half-flush that dies along her throat": such stuff
20 Was courtesy, she thought, and cause enough
For calling up that spot of joy. She had
A heart—how shall I say?—too soon made glad,
Too easily impressed, she liked whate'er
She looked on, and her looks went everywhere.
25 Sir, 'twas all one! My favor at her breast,
The dropping of the daylight in the West,
The bough of cherries some <u>officious</u> fool
Broke in the orchard for her, the white mule
She rode with round the terrace—all and each
30 Would draw from her alike the approving speech,
Or blush, at least. She thanked men—good! but thanked
Somehow—I know not how—as if she ranked
My gift of a nine-hundred-years-old name
With anybody's gift. Who'd stoop to blame
35 This sort of trifling? Even had you skill
In speech—(which I have not)—to make your will
Quite clear to such an one, and say, "Just this
Or that in you disgusts me; here you miss,
Or there exceed the mark"—and if she let
40 Herself be lessoned so, nor plainly set
Her wits to yours, forsooth, and made excuse
—E'en then would be some stooping, and I choose
Never to stoop. Oh sir, she smiled, no doubt,
Whene'er I passed her; but who passed without
45 Much the same smile? This grew; I gave commands;
Then all smiles stopped together. There she stands
As if alive. Will 't please you rise? We'll meet
The company below, then. I repeat,
The Count your master's known <u>munificence</u>
50 Is ample warrant that no just pretense
Of mine for dowry will be disallowed;
Though his fair daughter's self, as I avowed
At starting, is my object. Nay, we'll go
Together down, sir. Notice Neptune, though,
55 Taming a sea horse, thought a rarity,
Which Claus of Innsbruck[3] cast in bronze for me! ∎

---

3. **Claus of Innsbruck.** An imaginary sculptor

WORDS FOR EVERYDAY USE:
of • fi • cious (ə fish´əs) *adj.*, meddlesome
mu • nif • i • cence (myo͞o nif´ə səns) *n.*, generosity

726 UNIT NINE / THE VICTORIAN AGE

VOCABULARY IN CONTEXT

• Todd became <u>officious</u> when the president of the company walked into the room.

• Todd slithered up to Ms. Brahm and said, "The <u>munificence</u> with which you replied to my report was awe-inspiring."

❶ The Duke attributes the look to
either his own presence or an offhand
courteous remark by the artist.

❷ The implication is that the Duchess
was a flirt—or worse.

❸ The Duke felt he would be
lowering himself if he revealed that
her behavior upset him.

❹ The Duke became increasingly
jealous because the Duchess gave
others the same smile she gave him.
That is ominous because he then
commanded the cessation of her
smiles (and possibly commended her
death).

❺ The Duke's choice of words is
ominous because they suggest he is
already planning on finding another
bride, and perhaps, another work of
"art."

HISTORICAL NOTE

Neptune is the Roman name for
the god of the sea, Poseidon. He
was considered a violent and powerful god, and was renowned for
his many love affairs.

ANSWERS TO SELECTION
CHECK TEST 4.9.7

EX. What does the speaker call the
person in the painting?
**The speaker calls the person in
the painting "my last Duchess."**

1. Why do people ask questions
about the portrait?
**People are drawn to the look on
the woman's face.**

2. What did the speaker dislike
about the Duchess's interactions
with other people?
**The speaker felt that the
Duchess was too friendly and
easily pleased by other people.**

3. Of what did the speaker believe
the Duchess was unappreciative?
**The speaker believed the Duchess
was unappreciative of being married to him and having his name.**

4. What happened to the relationship of the speaker and the
Duchess just before she died?
**The speaker grew more and more
angry and disgusted with her.**

5. According to the speaker, what
happened to the smiles of the
Duchess?
**The speaker says that the smiles
of the Duchess stopped.**

❶ To what does the
Duke attribute
the look on the
Duchess's face in
the portrait?

❷ What is the
implication of the
Duke's statement
that "her looks
went
everywhere"?

❸ Why did the Duke
not tell the
Duchess what
displeased him
about her
conduct?

❹ What had
happened to the
Duke's
relationship with
his wife before
she died? What
makes this fact
ominous?

❺ What is ominous
about the Duke's
choice of words
here?

Must never hope to reproduce the faint
Half-flush that dies along her throat": such stuff
20 Was courtesy, she thought, and cause enough
For calling up that spot of joy. She had
A heart—how shall I say?—too soon made glad,
Too easily impressed, she liked whate'er
She looked on, and her looks went everywhere.
25 Sir, 'twas all one! My favor at her breast,
The dropping of the daylight in the West,
The bough of cherries some <u>officious</u> fool
Broke in the orchard for her, the white mule
She rode with round the terrace—all and each
30 Would draw from her alike the approving speech,
Or blush, at least. She thanked men—good! but thanked
Somehow—I know not how—as if she ranked
My gift of a nine-hundred-years-old name
With anybody's gift. Who'd stoop to blame
35 This sort of trifling? Even had you skill
In speech—(which I have not)—to make your will
Quite clear to such an one, and say, "Just this
Or that in you disgusts me; here you miss,
Or there exceed the mark"—and if she let
40 Herself be lessoned so, nor plainly set
Her wits to yours, forsooth, and made excuse
—E'en then would be some stooping, and I choose
Never to stoop. Oh sir, she smiled, no doubt,
Whene'er I passed her; but who passed without
45 Much the same smile? This grew; I gave commands;
Then all smiles stopped together. There she stands
As if alive. Will 't please you rise? We'll meet
The company below, then. I repeat,
The Count your master's known <u>munificence</u>
50 Is ample warrant that no just pretense
Of mine for dowry will be disallowed;
Though his fair daughter's self, as I avowed
At starting, is my object. Nay, we'll go
Together down, sir. Notice Neptune, though,
55 Taming a sea horse, thought a rarity,
Which Claus of Innsbruck[3] cast in bronze for me! ■

---

3. **Claus of Innsbruck.** An imaginary sculptor

WORDS FOR
EVERYDAY USE:

of • fi • cious (ə fish´əs) *adj.*, meddlesome
mu • nif • i • cence (myōō nif´ə səns) *n.*, generosity

VOCABULARY IN CONTEXT

• Todd became <u>officious</u> when the president of the company walked into the room.
• Todd slithered up to Ms. Brahm and said, "The <u>munificence</u> with which you replied to my report
was awe-inspiring."

Responding to the Selection

How do you feel about the Duke after reading this selection? about his "last Duchess"? What do you think happened to the Duchess? Why do you think this?

Reviewing the Selection

RECALLING

1. How does the Duke refer to the person in the portrait in the first line of the poem?

2. What object from his art collection does the Duke mention to his visitor?

3. To what possible causes does the Duke attribute the Duchess's smile in the painting?

4. What did the Duke give to his last Duchess that he considered to be much greater than other people's gifts?

INTERPRETING

5. What can you infer, or conclude, from the way in which the Duke speaks of his former wife?

6. What does the Duke collect besides art?

7. What sort of person was the Duchess? What things did she take joy in? Why was the Duke not happy with her? Was he right in feeling that way?

8. What does the Duke's statement about his "nine-hundred-years-old name" reveal about him? What kind of person is he?

SYNTHESIZING

9. What do you think the Duke intended to do by talking about the Duchess in this way to the emissary?

10. What reasons might the visitor have for not wanting to go through with making marriage arrangements for the Duke? What do you think may have happened to the Duke's former wife?

RESPONDING TO THE SELECTION

Students may wish to discuss their ideas with a partner. Pairs can then present their ideas to a small group.

ANSWERS FOR REVIEWING THE SELECTION

RECALLING

1. The Duke refers to the person in the painting as "my last Duchess."

2. The Duke mentions a statue of Neptune taming a seahorse.

3. He attributes her look to either his own presence or to a courteous remark made by the artist.

4. The Duke considered his marrying her to be a greater gift than anyone else could hope to give her.

INTERPRETING

Responses will vary. Possible responses are given.

5. The Duke despised her and thought of her as a possession.

6. It seems that the Duke collects Duchesses.

7. The late Duchess was a very kindhearted, joyful person. The Duchess found joy in everything. The Duke wanted to be the only thing that made her smile. The Duke was arrogant in feeling that way.

8. The Duke is snobby and self-obsessed. He is a shallow person.

SYNTHESIZING

Responses will vary. Possible responses are given.

9. The Duke may have intended to justify his feelings for his last Duchess and to encourage the emissary to view the Duchess through his own eyes.

10. The visitor may feel worry that much the same thing will happen with a new wife. It seems probable that the Duke killed or ordered the death of his wife.

ANALYTIC SCALES FOR RESPONDING IN WRITING

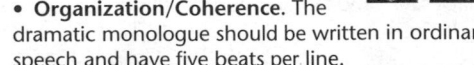

Assign a score from 1 to 25 for each grading criterion below. (For more detailed evaluation, see the evaluation forms for writing, revising, and proofreading, *Assessment Portfolio*, 7.1–7.10.)

Dramatic Monologue

• **Content/Unity.** The dramatic monologue presents a sensible explanation of the reason that the Count's daughter should not marry the Duke.

• **Organization/Coherence.** The dramatic monologue should be written in ordinary speech and have five beats per line.

• **Language/Style.** The dramatic monologue uses vivid and precise nouns, verbs, and modifiers.

• **Conventions.** The dramatic monologue avoids errors in spelling, grammar, usage, mechanics, and manuscript form.

► See the evaluation forms for discussion, active listening, and oral communication, *Assessment Portfolio,* 7.11–7.14.

Responses will vary. Possible responses are given.

1. Dramatic Monologue. The speaker in the poem is the Duke. The Duke is speaking with an agent who is negotiating his next marriage. The Duke shows his visitor the portrait of his late wife. The Duke imagines that the agent wonders why the Duchess has that look on her face. He replies that the look is a result of his presence or of a remark made by the artist. The monologue reveals that the Duke is a self-obsessed, cruel, shallow man.

 ► **Teaching Note:** Some students may find this poem easier to understand if they are able to role play the two parts.

2. Characterization and Irony. Most things brought the Duchess joy: a bough of cherries, a mule, and a sunset. If people were kind to the Duchess, she was kind to them also. The Duchess is a sympathetic character. In trying to present an ugly characterization of his wife, the Duke reveals his own hideous character. The Duke was disgusted by the Duchess's behavior. The Duke is a detestable person.

 ► **Teaching Note:** Discuss *irony* with students. Work together to create your own ironic description of someone or something.

3. Diction. Examples of contractions include *That's, 'twas,* and *who'd.* Examples of exclamations include: "Sir, 'twas all one!" and "good!" Examples of interrupted statements include: "A heart—how shall I say?—too soon made glad" and "but thanked/Somehow—I know not how—as if she ranked/My gift . . ." Examples of words of direct address include: "Will't please you sit and look at her?" and "Will't please you rise?" Examples of questions asked but not meant to be answered include:

(cont.)

Understanding Literature (Questions for Discussion)

1. **Dramatic Monologue.** A **dramatic monologue** is a poem that presents the speech of a single character in a dramatic situation. The speech is one side of an imagined conversation. Who is the speaker in this poem? With whom is he speaking? Why has the visitor come to see the Duke? What does the Duke show his visitor? What question does the Duke imagine coming into his visitor's mind when looking at the painting? What response does the Duke offer to that question? What does the Duke reveal about his personality in the course of the monologue?

2. **Characterization and Irony.** **Characterization** is the use of literary techniques to create a character. **Irony** is a difference between appearance and reality. The Duke provides quite a bit of information about his former wife. He means for these details to provide a negative characterization of her. However, ironically, the details actually present a completely different picture than what the Duke has in mind. What kinds of things brought the Duchess joy? How did she treat people who performed little kindnesses toward her? What sort of character was she? What is ironic in the attempt of the Duke to present an ugly characterization of her? How did the Duke react to the Duchess's kindness and simplicity? What does this reaction reveal about his character?

3. **Diction. Diction,** when applied to writing, refers to word choice. Browning was known for writing poetry that sounded just like ordinary speech. He avoided lofty, sentimental, flowery, "poetic" diction in favor of words and phrases that might be spoken. What examples can you find in the poem of the following elements from ordinary speech: contractions, exclamations, interrupted statements, words of direct address, and questions asked but not meant to be answered?

   What is the significance of the Duke's choice of the word *object* to refer to the woman whom he wants to marry? What other objects does the Duke collect? Why might the Duke's choice of this word horrify his visitor?

Responding in Writing

Dramatic Monologue. Try your hand at writing a dramatic monologue. Imagine that you are the Duke's visitor. You are speaking to the Count, who is anxious to arrange a marriage between his daughter and this rich, powerful Duke. In your monologue, report what you learned during your visit with the Duke and explain why you think the marriage would be inadvisable. Divide your monologue into lines that each have five strong stresses, or beats. Imitate Browning's use of ordinary speech.

"how shall I say?" and "Who'd stoop to blame/This sort of trifling?"

By using the word *object* it is clear that the Duke never considered his wives as equals, or even as human beings. The Duke also collects art. The visitor may realize that the Duke's attitude might relate to the Duchess's death.

► **Teaching Note:** Ask students to think of other words people use that give away their ideas about various issues—referring to women as "girls," for example.

ANALYTIC SCALES FOR RESPONDING IN WRITING
Grading scales appear on page 727.

READER'S JOURNAL

Can you think of a kind of art or music or writing that you dislike because it is so polished and finished, and of another kind that you like because it is ambitious and rough? Write about your response to these pieces of art or music or literature in your journal.

THINKING SKILLS

Read the Language Arts Survey, 4.18 "Reading Actively: Predicting." Then, as you read the poem, make predictions about what the outcome will be of the request that the painter del Sarto makes of his wife at the beginning of the poem.

"Andrea del Sarto"[1]

ROBERT BROWNING

But do not let us quarrel any more,
No, my Lucrezia; bear with me for once:
Sit down and all shall happen as you wish.
You turn your face, but does it bring your heart?
5   I'll work then for your friend's friend, never fear,
Treat his own subject after his own way,
Fix his own time, accept too his own price,
And shut the money into this small hand
When next it takes mine. Will it? tenderly?
10   Oh, I'll content him—but tomorrow, Love!
I often am much wearier than you think,
This evening more than usual, and it seems
As if—forgive now—should you let me sit
Here by the window with your hand in mine
15   And look a half-hour forth on Fiesole,[2]
Both of one mind, as married people use,
Quietly, quietly the evening through,

---

1. **Andrea del Sarto.** Andrea del Sarto was a Florentine painter. Browning draws his information from a biography in Vasari's *The Lives of the Painters.* Del Sarto never fulfilled early signs of promise in his career. Lucrezia, his wife, had great influence on him, and his infatuation with her led to some neglect of his art.
2. **Fiesole.** A hill town overlooking Florence

①
What is the painter agreeing to do? What will he do with the money that he earns? What does he hope for in return?

②
What does the painter want to do this evening?

READER'S JOURNAL

You may want to show students a selection of works by artists with varying styles.

THINKING SKILLS

Students may want to consider the tone in which the request was made and the words that were chosen in order to make their predictions.

▶ Additional practice is provided in the *Essential Skills Practice Book: Study and Research,* 4.18.

ANSWER TO GUIDED READING QUESTION

① The painter will paint a portrait for a friend of Lucrezia's friend. He will give the money to Lucrezia. The painter hopes that Lucrezia will tenderly hold his hand.

② The painter wants to sit for one half hour and look out the window with Lucrezia.

SUPPORT FOR LEP STUDENTS

Explain that del Sarto refers to Lucrezia's love as her "cousin," but he is probably not really her cousin.

IDIOMS

out of hand—with no trouble; carelessly
fair weather—good weather

ADDITIONAL VOCABULARY

quarrel—argue
serpentining—winding
convent—monastery
fetter—bond
strive—try hard
replenish—refill; replace
avail—be effective
illumined—lit
suffice—be enough

❶ The painter is obsessed by his wife's beauty. She does not love him anymore. The line "which everybody looks on and calls his" points to her promiscuous lifestyle.

❷ The painter sees his life as a lesser version of what it might have been had he not moved to Fiesole. He compares his life to a twilight-piece, or something that is at the point just before being extinguished.

LITERARY TECHNIQUE

Image. An image is a word picture—a word or phrase that names something that can be seen, heard, touched, tasted, or smelled. Ask students to list the predominant images in lines 35–49. What do images such as "grayness," twilight," the clinking of the chapel bell, autumn, and a "twilight-piece" seem to suggest? Ask students, "What is coming to an end for del Sarto—his art, his love, his life, his hopes?"

❶
How does the painter feel toward his wife? How does she act toward him? How do you know?

❷
How does the painter characterize his present life? To what does he compare it?

I might get up tomorrow to my work
Cheerful and fresh as ever. Let us try.
20   Tomorrow, how you shall be glad for this!
Your soft hand is a woman of itself,
And mine the man's bared breast she curls inside.
Don't count the time lost, neither; you must serve
For each of the five pictures we require:
25   It saves a model. So! keep looking so—
My serpentining beauty, rounds on rounds![3]
—How could you ever prick those perfect ears,
Even to put the pearl there! oh, so sweet—
My face, my moon, my everybody's moon,
30   Which everybody looks on and calls his,
And, I suppose, is looked on by in turn,
While she looks—no one's: very dear, no less.
You smile? why, there's my picture ready made,
There's what we painters call our harmony!
35   A common grayness silvers[4] everything—
All in a twilight, you and I alike
 —You, at the point of your first pride in me
(That's gone you know)—but I, at every point;
My youth, my hope, my art, being all toned down
40   To yonder sober pleasant Fiesole.
There's the bell clinking from the chapel top;
That length of convent wall across the way
Holds the trees safer, huddled more inside;
The last monk leaves the garden; days decrease,
45   And autumn grows, autumn in everything.
Eh? the whole seems to fall into a shape
As if I saw alike my work and self
And all that I was born to be and do,
A twilight-piece. Love, we are in God's hand.
50   How strange now, looks the life he makes us lead;
So free we seem, so fettered fast we are!
I feel he laid the fetter: let it lie!
This chamber for example—turn your head—
All that's behind us! You don't understand
55   Nor care to understand about my art,
But you can hear at least when people speak:
And that cartoon,[5] the second from the door
—It is the thing, Love! so such things should be—

3. **My . . . rounds.** Hair coiled like a serpent
4. **grayness silvers.** Silver gray was a predominant color in del Sarto's paintings.
5. **cartoon.** Drawing

Behold Madonna!—I am bold to say.
60 I can do with my pencil what I know,
    What I see, what at bottom of my heart
    I wish for, if I ever wish so deep—
    Do easily, too—when I say, perfectly,
    I do not boast, perhaps: yourself are judge,
65 Who listened to the Legate's[6] talk last week,
    And just as much they used to say in France.
    At any rate 'tis easy, all of it!
    No sketches first, no studies, that's long past:
    I do what many dream of, all their lives,
70 —Dream? strive to do, and agonize to do,
    And fail in doing. I could count twenty such
    On twice your fingers, and not leave this town,
    Who strive—you don't know how the others strive
    To paint a little thing like that you smeared
75 Carelessly passing with your robes afloat—
    Yet do much less, so much less, Someone[7] says
    (I know his name, no matter)—so much less!
    Well, less is more, Lucrezia: I am judged.
    There burns a truer light of God in them,
80 In their vexed beating stuffed and stopped-up brain,
    Heart, or whate'er else, than goes on to prompt
    This low-pulsed forthright craftsman's hand of mine.
    Their works drop groundward, but themselves, I know,
    Reach many a time a heaven that's shut to me,
85 Enter and take their place there sure enough,
    Though they come back and cannot tell the world.
    My works are nearer heaven, but I sit here.
    The sudden blood of these men! at a word—
    Praise them, it boils, or blame them, it boils too.
90 I, painting from myself and to myself,
    Know what I do, am unmoved by men's blame
    Or their praise either. Somebody remarks
    Morello's[8] outline there is wrongly traced,
    His hue mistaken; what of that? or else,
95 Rightly traced and well ordered; what of that?
    Speak as they please, what does the mountain care?
    Ah, but a man's reach should exceed his grasp,
    Or what's a heaven for? All is silver-gray
    Placid and perfect with my art: the worse!

---

6. **Legate.** One of the pope's deputies
7. **Someone.** Probably Michelangelo
8. **Morello.** A mountain outside Florence

❶
What is the painter capable of doing?

❷
Del Sarto paints flawlessly, but he feels that there is something lacking in his work. What is lacking that he finds in other painters? What does it mean to say that a person's reach should exceed his or her grasp?

ANSWERS TO GUIDED READING QUESTIONS

❶ The artist is capable of drawing perfectly anything that he wishes.

❷ The artist feels that in other artists' paintings burns a truer light of God, or divine inspiration. This phrase means that a person shouldn't settle for accomplishing those things that are easy.

ADDITIONAL QUESTIONS AND ACTIVITIES

Discuss with students how they think Lucrezia feels about del Sarto's art. How did they form their opinions?

Answer. She is not impressed by del Sarto's art. He painted something that she "smeared/Carelessly" in passing (lines 74–75).

HISTORICAL NOTE

Robert Browning was devoted to his wife, Elizabeth Barrett Browning. Theirs, however, was a more fortunate relationship than that of del Sarto and his wife. After the death of Elizabeth Barrett Browning, Robert Browning responded to criticism of her with the following words.

"How to return your thanks would pass my wits.
Kicking you seems the common lot of ours—
While more appropriate greeting lends you grace!
Spitting from lips once sacrificed by Hers."

That Browning's rejoinder was indignant is understandable, that it was also poetic is remarkable.

Ask students whether they believe the incredible love described in this poem was the result of Browning's own love for his wife.

ANSWERS TO GUIDED READING QUESTIONS

❶ The body of the subject in the painting is depicted imperfectly: the arm is bent or shaped unnaturally. However, the soul of the person is depicted correctly. The viewer can see a personality there. Del Sarto can draw great arms, while Raphael represents great ideas.

❷ Del Sarto wishes that his wife had a mind to match her beautiful body.

❸ Del Sarto blames himself. He says that incentives to create art come from the soul's self. He adds that other great painters didn't have wives to urge them on to creating great works.

ADDITIONAL QUESTIONS AND ACTIVITIES

Discuss with students what they feel is del Sarto's biggest obstacle to artistic success. Why?

Answer. Possible responses include his self-obsession, his interest in his wife, his lack of encouragement from his wife, his laziness or his lack of will, and his overly high expectations.

❶ What does del Sarto mean when he says of Raphael's painting that its body is wrong but its soul is right? In what sense is del Sarto the better painter? In what sense is Raphael the better painter?

❷ What does del Sarto wish his wife had given him?

❸ Does del Sarto blame his wife or himself for his failure to create great work? How do you know?

100 I know both what I want and what might gain,
     And yet how profitless to know, to sigh
     "Had I been two, another and myself,
     Our head would have o'erlooked the world!"⁹ No doubt.
     Yonder's a work now, of that famous youth
105 The Urbinate¹⁰ who died five years ago.
     ('Tis copied, George Vasari sent it me.)
     Well, I can fancy how he did it all,
     Pouring his soul, with kings and popes to see,
     Reaching, that heaven might so replenish him,
110 Above and through his art—for it gives way;
     That arm is wrongly put—and there again—
     A fault to pardon in the drawing's lines,
     Its body, so to speak: its soul is right,
     He means right—that, a child may understand.
115 Still, what an arm! and I could alter it:
     But all the play, the insight and the stretch—
     Out of me, out of me! And wherefore out?
     Had you enjoined them on me, given me soul,
     We might have risen to Rafael, I and you!
120 Nay, Love, you did give all I asked, I think—
     More than I merit, yes, by many times.
     But had you—oh, with the same perfect brow,
     And perfect eyes, and more than perfect mouth,
     And the low voice my soul hears, as a bird
125 The fowler's pipe,¹¹ and follows to the snare—
     Had you, with these the same, but brought a mind!
     Some women do so. Had the mouth there urged
     "God and the glory! never care for gain.
     The present by the future, what is that?
130 Live for fame, side by side with Agnolo!¹²
     Rafael is waiting: up to God, all three!"
     I might have done it for you. So it seems:
     Perhaps not. All is as God overrules.
     Beside, incentives come from the soul's self;
135 The rest avail not. Why do I need you?
     What wife had Rafael, or has Agnolo?
     In this world, who can do a thing, will not;
     And who would do it, cannot, I perceive:
     Yet the will's somewhat—somewhat, too, the power—

---

9. **Had . . . world.** Andrea acknowledges the need for aspiration and dedication combined with the skill he possessed to make a truly great artist.
10. **Urbinate.** Raphael, who was born in Urbino
11. **fowler's pipe.** Hunter's call
12. **Agnolo.** Michelangelo

The Holy Family with the Infant Saint John. Andrea del Sarto, The Metropolitan Museum of Art, Maria DeWitt Jesup Fund, 1922

© 1995 by The Metropolitan Museum of Art

140   And thus we half-men struggle. At the end,
      God, I conclude, compensates, punishes.
      'Tis safer for me, if the award be strict,
      That I am something underrated here.
      Poor this long while, despised, to speak the truth.
145   I dared not, do you know, leave home all day,
      For fear of chancing on the Paris lords.
      The best is when they pass and look aside;
      But they speak sometimes; I must bear it all.
      Well may they speak! That Francis,[13] that first time,

---

13. **Francis.** Andrea was encouraged by King Francis I of France whose court was at Fontainebleau. Andrea supposedly stole funds from Francis which he used to build a house.

❶ Why doesn't del Sarto finish the statement that begins, "had you not grown restless"? What is he thinking about here?

❷ What did the great Michelangelo tell Raphael about del Sarto? Does del Sarto believe that Michelangelo was right?

150   And that long festal year at Fontainebleau!
      I surely then could sometimes leave the ground,
      Put on the glory, Rafael's daily wear,
      In that humane great monarch's golden look—
      One finger in his beard or twisted curl
155   Over his mouth's good mark that made the smile,
      One arm about my shoulder, round my neck,
      The jingle of his gold chain in my ear,
      I painting proudly with his breath on me,
      All his court round him, seeing with his eyes,
160   Such frank French eyes, and such a fire of souls
      Profuse, my hand kept plying by those hearts—
      And, best of all, this, this, this face beyond,
      This in the background, waiting on my work,
      To crown the issue with a last reward!
165   A good time, was it not, my kingly days?
      And had you not grown restless . . . but I know—
      'Tis done and past; 'twas right, my instinct said;
      Too live the life grew, golden and not gray,
      And I'm the weak-eyed bat no sun should tempt
170   Out of the grange whose four walls make his world.
      How could it end in any other way?
      You called me, and I came home to your heart.
      The triumph was—to reach and stay there; since
      I reached it ere the triumph, what is lost?
175   Let my hands frame your face in your hair's gold,
      You beautiful Lucrezia that are mine!
      "Rafael did this, Andrea painted that;
      The Roman's is the better when you pray,
      But still the other's Virgin was his wife—"
180   Men will excuse me. I am glad to judge
      Both pictures in your presence; clearer grows
      My better fortune, I resolve to think.
      For, do you know, Lucrezia, as God lives,
      Said one day Agnolo, his very self,
185   To Rafael . . . I have known it all these years . . .
      (When the young man was flaming out his thoughts
      Upon a palace wall for Rome to see,
      Too lifted up in heart because of it)
      "Friend, there's a certain sorry little scrub
190   Goes up and down our Florence, none cares how,
      Who, were he set to plan and execute
      As you are, pricked on by your popes and kings,
      Would bring the sweat into that brow of yours!"
      To Rafael's—And indeed the arm is wrong.

195 I hardly dare . . . yet, only you to see,
    Give the chalk here—quick, thus the line should go!
    Aye, but the soul! he's Rafael! rub it out!
    Still, all I care for, if he spoke the truth,
    (What he? why, who but Michel Agnolo?)
200 Do you forget already words like those?)
    If really there was such a chance, so lost—
    Is, whether you're—not grateful—but more pleased.
    Well, let me think so. And you smile indeed!
    This hour has been an hour! Another smile?
205 If you would sit thus by me every night
    I should work better, do you comprehend?
    I mean that I should earn more, give you more.
    See, it is settled dusk now; there's a star;
    Morello's gone, the watch-lights show the wall,
210 The cue-owls[14] speak the name we call them by.
    Come from the window, love—come in, at last,
    Inside the melancholy little house
    We built to be so gay with. God is just.
    King Francis may forgive me: oft at nights
215 When I look up from painting, eyes tired out,
    The walls become illumined, brick from brick
    Distinct, instead of mortar, fierce bright gold,
    That gold of his I did cement them with!
    Let us but love each other. Must you go?
220 That Cousin here again? he waits outside?
    Must see you—you—and not with me? Those loans?
    More gaming debts to pay?[15] you smiled for that?
    Well, let smiles buy me! have you more to spend?
    While hand and eye and something of a heart
225 Are left me, work's my ware, and what's it worth?
    I'll pay my fancy. Only let me sit
    The gray remainder of the evening out,
    Idle, you call it, and muse perfectly
    How I could paint, were I but back in France,
230 One picture, just one more—the Virgin's face,
    Not yours this time! I want you at my side
    To hear them—that is, Michel Agnolo—
    Judge all I do and tell you of its worth.
    Will you? Tomorrow, satisfy your friend.
235 I take the subjects for his corridor,

---

14. **Cue-owls.** Owls that make a noise like the Italian word *ciu*

15. **Cousin . . . pay.** Lucrezia's lover had gambling debts that Andrea agreed to cover by painting some pictures.

❶
What does del Sarto implore his wife to do? How might this affect his work? Why?

❷
Who has come to see del Sarto's wife? Why is he there? Why does she want him to do the painting mentioned at the beginning of the poem?

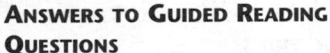

ANSWERS TO GUIDED READING QUESTIONS

❶ Del Sarto wants his wife to sit by him every night while he works. Del Sarto might be able to work better knowing that his wife cared about him and was near him.

❷ A lover has come to see del Sarto's wife. The lover is there to borrow money. Lucrezia wants del Sarto to do the painting to raise money to pay off her lover's gambling debts.

BIBLIOGRAPHICAL NOTE

George Meredith (1828–1909) was known as the author of *The Ordeal of Richard Feverel* (1859) and *The Egoist* (1879). Meredith, however, preferred writing poetry. Meredith's sonnet sequence *Modern Love* shares a common theme with "Andrea del Sarto"— a difficult marriage that causes suffering. Indeed, like Meredith's narrator, Browning's Andrea del Sarto too might have said, "But, oh, the bitter taste her beauty had!"

QUOTABLES

❝'Will you very kindly tell me, Mr. Wilde, in your own words, your viewpoint of George Meredith?'
'George Meredith is a prose Browning, and so is Browning.'
'Thank you. His style?'
'Chaos, illumined by flashes of lightning.'❞

—Oscar Wilde

❶ Del Sarto is attempting to justify spending all of his money on Lucrezia while his parents were living in poverty.

❷ The other artists would outpaint del Sarto because he would still be with Lucrezia. Del Sarto would still be worrying too much about his wife to paint well. Ultimately, del Sarto blames himself for not doing great work.

ANSWERS TO SELECTION CHECK TEST 4.9.9

EX. Who is the speaker in "Andrea del Sarto"?
The speaker is del Sarto.

1. In the poem "Andrea del Sarto," who is Lucrezia?
Lucrezia is Andrea del Sarto's wife.

2. At the opening of the poem, what does Andrea del Sarto say he wants to avoid?
He says he does not want to quarrel.

3. How did Andrea del Sarto earn money?
He was a painter.

4. Why does del Sarto resent the Cousin?
Del Sarto's wife Lucrezia goes out at night with the Cousin and gives him money.

5. What is del Sarto's opinion of his work?
He thinks it is technically excellent but uninspired or soulless.

❶
What is del Sarto attempting to justify here?

❷
Even in heaven, if given one last chance to paint greatly, del Sarto believes that he would be outdone by Leonardo, Raphael, and Michelangelo. Why? What would keep him from having spirit enough to do great work? On whom does the blame ultimately rest for his not doing great work?

Finish the portrait out of hand—there, there,
And throw him in another thing or two
If he <u>demurs</u>; the whole should prove enough
240   To pay for this same Cousin's freak. Beside,
What's better and what's all I care about,
Get you the thirteen scudi[16] for the ruff!
Love, does that please you? Ah, but what does he,
The Cousin! What does he to please you more?

I am grown peaceful as old age tonight.
245   I regret little, I would change still less.
Since there my past life lies, why alter it?
The very wrong to Francis!—it is true
I took his coin, was tempted and complied,
And built this house and sinned, and all is said.
250   My father and my mother died of want.[17]
Well, had I riches of my own? you see
How one gets rich! Let each one bear his lot.
They were born poor, lived poor, and poor they died:
And I have labored somewhat in my time
255   And not been paid <u>profusely</u>. Some good son
Paint my two hundred pictures—let him try!
No doubt, there's something strikes a balance. Yes,
You loved me quite enough, it seems tonight.
This must suffice me here. What would one have?
260   In heaven, perhaps, new chances, one more chance—
Four great walls in the New Jerusalem,
Meted on each side by the angel's reed,
For Leonard,[18] Rafael, Agnolo and me
To cover—the three first without a wife,
265   While I have mine! So—still they overcome
Because there's still Lucrezia—as I choose.

Again the Cousin's whistle! Go my Love.   ∎

---

16. **scudi.** Italian coins
17. **My . . . want.** Vasari claims Andrea stopped supporting his poor parents because of his infatuation for Lucrezia.
18. **Leonard.** Leonardo da Vinci

WORDS FOR
EVERYDAY USE:
de • mur (dē mʉr) *vi.*, hesitate, object
pro • fuse • ly (prō fyōos ′lē) *adv.*, generously; freely

VOCABULARY IN CONTEXT

• Do not <u>demur</u> upon my proposal of marriage.
• I bled <u>profusely</u> when I cut my finger.

Responding to the Selection

What bargain has del Sarto made? What compromise has he made in his art and in his life? Why has he done this? Do you respect him for having done so? Discuss these questions with your classmates.

Reviewing the Selection

RECALLING

1. What has del Sarto's wife asked him to do at the beginning of the poem?

2. What does del Sarto ask his wife to do this evening?

3. What color that covers "everything" does del Sarto mention several times in the poem?

4. Who comes to call at the end of the poem? Why does he come?

INTERPRETING

▶▶ 5. Why have del Sarto and his wife been quarreling at the beginning of the poem? What was their disagreement probably about?

▶▶ 6. How does del Sarto feel toward his wife? How do you know?

▶▶ 7. How does del Sarto describe his house? Why does he describe it in that way?

▶▶ 8. For what purpose does del Sarto's wife need money? Does he know this? Why does he agree, anyway, to do the painting?

SYNTHESIZING

9. Why does del Sarto feel that he could be as great a painter as Raphael or Michelangelo? What keeps him from achieving that goal? What robs him of the spirit to reach beyond his immediate grasp?

10. Del Sarto says near the end of the poem that he regrets little and "would change still less." Do you think that this is so? What does he actually regret? What has he settled for? What has this cost him?

VICTORIAN POETRY / "ANDREA DEL SARTO" **737**

**ANSWERS FOR
UNDERSTANDING LITERATURE**

▶See the evaluation forms for discussion, active listening, and oral communication, *Assessment Portfolio*, 7.11–7.14.

Responses will vary. Possible responses are given.

1. Metaphor. This metaphor compares the waning of the day to the waning of del Sarto's life and talent. His house and his life are gray because he is not living his life as he should. His work is only a shadow of what it should be.
▶**Teaching Note:** Ask students to think of all of the words or ideas that they associate with the color gray.

2. Paradox. The work of the other artists is inspired by great ideas and displays their passion for their work. All of del Sarto's passion is wrapped up in his unfaithful wife.

▶**Teaching Note:** Ask students to think of examples from their own experiences to which the phrase "less is more" might apply.

3. Theme. People should strive to accomplish more than those things easily in reach. Those things in del Sarto's grasp include producing technically perfect, but emotionally bankrupt, art and being an emotional slave to an unfaithful wife. Del Sarto should be reaching for subjects that would inspire him and fill his art with passion. Del Sarto is prevented from reaching beyond his grasp because of both his devotion to a bad marriage and his tendency to make excuses for his lack of inspiration. When an artist reaches beyond his or her grasp to create, that effort is reflected in the work. Great art and a wonderful life can only be accomplished by those who attempt to reach beyond their limitations.
▶**Teaching Note:** Ask students to think about how their own limitations might be preventing them from great works. How might students reach beyond their grasp?

Understanding Literature (Questions for Discussion)

1. **Metaphor.** A **metaphor** is a figure of speech in which one thing is spoken or written about as if it were another. This figure of speech invites the reader to make a comparison between the two things. In this poem, del Sarto describes his "work and self," all that he was "born to be and do" as "a twilight" piece. In other words, his life and his work are both like a painting of a twilight scene, in which "A common grayness silvers everything." What things are being compared in this metaphor? What is del Sarto saying about his life and his work? What makes his house and his life seem gray? In what sense is his work also like the twilight, like grayness, and not like daytime and brightness?

2. **Paradox.** A **paradox** is a contradictory statement, idea, or event. Del Sarto says of other painters in Florence that they are not as skilled as he, that they are able to do less than he can. Then he states a paradox, that "Less is more." In what sense is their work greater than his, even though it is less technically perfect? What is lacking in his work that can be found in theirs, even though it is more crudely made?

3. **Theme.** A **theme** is a central idea in a literary work. One central idea, perhaps the central idea, of this poem is stated in the lines "Ah, but a man's reach should exceed his grasp,/Or what's a heaven for?" What does it mean to have a reach that exceeds your grasp? What is within del Sarto's grasp? For what should he be reaching? What keeps him from doing so? How might reaching beyond one's grasp account for the great works done by human beings? What is Browning saying about the human spirit and its role in creating great art and wonderful lives?

Responding in Writing

Character Sketch. A **character sketch** is a brief piece of writing that presents a character. The character is revealed through details about such matters as appearance, dress, actions, words, attitudes, beliefs, and history. Write a character sketch of Lucrezia, Andrea del Sarto's wife. You can write from the third-person point of view, using a narrator who tells about Lucrezia using such pronouns as *she,* or you can write from the first-person point of view, allowing Lucrezia to speak for herself. Before writing, make a chart in which you note details about Lucrezia. Take what details you can from the poem and invent the rest. Make sure, however, that your details are consistent with the character presented in the poem. How does Lucrezia look? How does she dress? What does she sound like? What habits does she have? What major relationships does she have? How does she feel toward these people? What does she like to do? What are her attitudes, beliefs, and history? Try to answer some or all of these questions in your sketch.

ANALYTIC SCALES FOR RESPONDING IN WRITING

Assign a score from 1 to 25 for each grading criterion below. (For more detailed evaluation, see the evaluation forms for writing, revising, and proofreading, *Assessment Portfolio*, 7.1–7.10.)

Character Sketch

• **Content/Unity.** The character sketch presents a sensible portrayal of elements of Lucrezia's personality and appearance.

• **Organization/Coherence.** The character sketch should recreate Lucrezia's speech and mannerisms in the first person or clearly describe elements of her personality and appearance in the third person.
• **Language/Style.** The character sketch uses vivid and precise nouns, verbs, and modifiers.
• **Conventions.** The character sketch avoids errors in spelling, grammar, usage, mechanics, and manuscript form.

Language Lab

Writing Varied Sentences. Read the Language Arts Survey, 2.55, "Varying Sentence Length and Structure." Then rewrite the following paragraph to vary the length and structure of its sentences.

> Robert Browning wrote "The Pied Piper of Hamlin." It is a famous poem. It tells a marvelous story. The story is often retold in children's books. The story goes like this: A city is plagued with rats. The city fathers are worried. A piper offers to rid the town of rats. The city agrees to pay him. The piper plays. The rats follow him out of the town. The city then refuses to pay the piper. The piper therefore takes revenge. He plays his pipe. The city's children hear the music. They follow him out of town and are not seen or heard of again.

Vocabulary Skills

Base Words and Suffixes. Read the Language Arts Survey, 2.140, "Base Words and Prefixes," and 2.141, "Suffixes." Then underline the base word once and the suffix twice in each of the following words from "Andrea del Sarto." Next look up each suffix in a dictionary and write two additional words that end with the same suffix.

1. cheerful
2. groundward
3. mistaken
4. profitless
5. wrongly

PROJECTS

1. **Dramatic Skit.** Collaborate with one or two other students to write a dramatic scene that presents a confrontation between the Duke in Browning's "My Last Duchess" and his former wife. (This scene will, of course, take place before the time of Browning's poem.) In your scene, portray the characters as they are portrayed in the poem—she is simple, innocent, and kind; he is vain, jealous, possessive, acquisitive, and ruthless. Write parts for each student in your group, including, if your group has three students, a third character such as the "officious fool" mentioned in line 27 of the poem. Rehearse your skit and present it to the rest of the class.

2. **Art History.** As a class, do research on some or all of the following Italian Renaissance painters: Andrea del Sarto, Giotto di Bondone, Michelangelo Buonarroti, Leonardo da Vinci, Raphael (Raffaello Santi), Titian (Tiziano Vecellio), Tintoretto (Jacopo Robusti), and Michelangelo da Caravaggio. Divide into groups. Assign one painter to each group. Research the life and works of these painters. Then present the results of your research in class, combining oral reporting with slides, prints, or pictures from books.

Responses will vary. Possible responses are given.

Robert Browning wrote the famous poem, "The Pied Piper of Hamlin." It is a marvelous story about a city plagued by rats often retold in children's books. A piper offers to rid the town of rats and the worried city fathers agree to pay him. The piper plays. Even though the rats follow him out of town, the town refuses to pay the piper. The piper therefore takes his revenge. He plays his pipe. The city's children hear the music, follow him out of town, and are not seen or heard of again.

FOR MORE PRACTICE

Problem. "Andrea del Sarto" is a poem. "Andrea del Sarto" is by Robert Browning. "Andrea del Sarto" is about an artist. The artist is frustrated in love. He is frustrated in his work. The artist has perfect technical ability. Andrea del Sarto feels he cannot create great art. He blames his devotion to a failed marriage.

Answer. "Andrea del Sarto" is a poem by Robert Browning about an artist who is frustrated in love and in his work. Though he has perfect technical ability, del Sarto feels he cannot create great art because of his devotion to a failed marriage.

► Additional practice is provided in the *Essential Skills Practice Book: Language,* 2.55.

ANSWERS FOR VOCABULARY SKILLS

Responses will vary. Possible responses are given.

1. cheer<u>ful</u>, baleful, mournful
2. ground<u>ward</u>, homeward, toward
3. mistak<u>en</u>, misled, misfire
4. profit<u>less</u>, clueless, hopeless
5. wrong<u>ly</u>, costly, friendly

►Additional practice is provided in the *Essential Skills Practice Book: Language,* 2.140, 2.141.

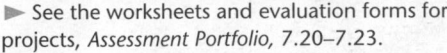

► See the worksheets and evaluation forms for projects, *Assessment Portfolio,* 7.20–7.23.

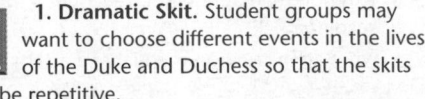 **1. Dramatic Skit.** Student groups may want to choose different events in the lives of the Duke and Duchess so that the skits won't be repetitive.

 2. Art History. Review with students where they might find information on the various artists, including which libraries they might visit.

ENRICHMENT ACTIVITIES

In Victorian times, religion was a very important part of political life. Members of the government were overwhelmingly Anglican. In 1851, Great Britain conducted the only census to ever attempt to determine religious affiliation.

• Have students research the results of that census and analyze how those results affected British politics.
• Students may want to role play a discussion between political opponents about the implications of the census.

SUPPORT FOR LEP STUDENTS

Explain that "straits" (line 3) refers to the Straits of Dover in the English Channel. Have students find Dover and the Aegean on a map of Europe and discuss the similarities.

Suggest that students work with a reading partner. The partners can work together to determine the meaning of unfamiliar words or phrases.

ADDITIONAL VOCABULARY
glimmering—flickering faintly
tranquil—peaceful and calm
blanched—whitened
darkling—dim; obscure

PREREADING

"Dover Beach"
by Matthew Arnold

ABOUT THE AUTHOR

Matthew Arnold (1822–1888) was a multitalented man, a great classics scholar, a distinguished poet and literary critic, and a commentator on education, religion, and culture. The son of the headmaster of Rugby school, he attended Rugby and Oxford. While at Oxford, he received the Newdigate prize for a poem about Oliver Cromwell, leader of England during the Puritan Interregnum. After graduating, Arnold took a government post as inspector of schools, a position that he held for the rest of his working life. In 1853, he published a book entitled *Poems,* which established his reputation as a writer of verse. In 1859, he was appointed foreign assistant commissioner on education and traveled to the continent to observe school systems there. In 1857, he was appointed to the poetry chair at Oxford, a position that he held for ten years. His *New Poems,* containing "Dover Beach," appeared in 1867, but by that time he was devoting his writing primarily to critical essays. He admired the calmness, clarity, and restraint of the great writers of classical Greece and Rome and believed that culture—"the best that has been thought and said in the world"—was the proper antidote for the worries, materialism, and decay of his times. He wrote that literature should be characterized by a "high seriousness" and that poetry should provide a "criticism of life." In 1883 he made a lecture tour in the United States, published as *Discourses in America.*

ABOUT THE SELECTION

No work more typifies the struggle between faith and doubt faced by thinking men and women of the Victorian Age than Matthew Arnold's **"Dover Beach."** Arnold lived in a time when religion was coming under attack from scientific circles and many people were questioning their faith. He felt the loss of his own faith keenly and wrote about it in this famous poem. The poem fully meets Arnold's own criteria for poetry, that it have a "high seriousness" and that it provide a "criticism of life." Many critics have called Arnold's poetry severe and melancholic, and indeed "Dover Beach" is one of the most melancholic poems ever written. However, a close reading of the poem will reveal that Arnold did have some Victorian optimism in him, for the poem offers as a stay against the anarchy and confusion of life the possibility that people can be "true/To one another."

GOALS/OBJECTIVES

Studying this lesson will enable students to

• interpret and appreciate a lyric poem
• describe Matthew Arnold's literary accomplishments and explain the historical significance of his writings
• define *allusion, symbol,* and *extended metaphor* and identify and analyze allusions, symbols, and extended metaphors they encounter in their reading
• write an instruction manual and a setting

READER'S JOURNAL

What scenes or natural sounds make you melancholic? Imagine yourself in such a scene or hearing such a sound. Write about the scene and your feelings about it in your journal.

THINKING SKILLS

Read the Language Arts Survey, 4.7, "Classifying." Then look up the words *sanguine* and *melancholic* in a dictionary. As you read the poem, decide which classification, sanguine or melancholic, fits the speaker of Arnold's poem.

"Dover Beach"

MATTHEW ARNOLD

The sea is calm tonight.
The tide is full, the moon lies fair
Upon the straits—on the French coast the light
Gleams and is gone; the cliffs of England stand,
5   Glimmering and vast, out in the tranquil bay.
Come to the window, sweet is the night air!
Only, from the long line of spray
Where the sea meets the moon-blanched land,
Listen! you hear the grating roar
10 Of pebbles which the waves draw back, and fling,
At their return, up the high <u>strand</u>,
Begin, and cease, and then again begin,
With <u>tremulous</u> cadence slow, and bring
The eternal note of sadness in.

15 Sophocles[1] long ago
Heard it on the Aegean, and it brought
Into his mind the <u>turbid</u> ebb and flow
Of human misery; we
Find also in the sound a thought,
20 Hearing it by this distant northern sea.

---
1. **Sophocles.** Greek playwright (496–406 BC)

❶ What mood is created by the description in lines 1–6? How does this mood change? What word in line 7 signals the change of mood?

❷ What did Sophocles think of when he heard the sound of the waves on the Aegean Sea centuries before?

WORDS FOR EVERYDAY USE:
strand (strand) *n.,* shore
trem • u • lous (trem´yŏŏ ləs) *adj.,* trembling
tur • bid (tur´bid) *adj.,* muddled

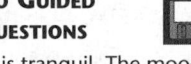

VOCABULARY IN CONTEXT

- My brother and I sat upon the <u>strand</u> and watched the waves roll in.
- The leaves in the willow tree were <u>tremulous</u> in the light breeze.
- Never drink from a <u>turbid</u> stream.

ANSWERS TO GUIDED READING QUESTIONS

❶ The mood is tranquil. The mood changes to one of sadness and melancholy. The word "Only" acts as a signal for a mood change.

❷ Sophocles thought of human misery when he heard the sound of the Aegean Sea.

PREREADING NOTES

READER'S JOURNAL

Students with hearing impairments should analyze the appearance of waves repeatedly hitting the shore.

THINKING SKILLS

Ask students to discuss examples of sanguine and melancholic behavior in order to better recognize the mood of the narrator.

▶ Additional practice is provided in the *Essential Skills Practice Book: Study and Research,* 4.7.

LITERARY TECHNIQUE

Allusion. Arnold alludes to Sophocles's play *Antigone.* Below are some pertinent passages you may wish to read to students:

"Numberless wonders, terrible wonders walk the world but none the match for man—that great wonder crossing the heaving gray sea, . . . on through breakers crashing left and right, holds his steady course, and the oldest of the gods he wears away." (376–382)

"Man the master, ingenious past all measure, past all dreams, the skills within his grasp—he forges on, now to destruction, now again to greatness." (406–409)

"The ruin will never cease . . . like a mounting tide driven on by savage northern gales, surging over the dead black depths rolling up from the bottom dark heaves of sand and the headlands, taking the storm's onslaught full force, roar, and then the low moaning echoes on and on." (659–666)

VOCABULARY FROM THE SELECTION

certitude	tremulous
shingle	turbid
strand	

ANSWERS TO GUIDED READING QUESTIONS

❶ The "Sea of Faith" is shrinking, retreating from its banks.

❷ The speaker asks that he and his love be true to one another, that they love each other. Doing so is necessary because the rest of the world has no joy, love, light, certitude, peace, or help for pain. Their relationship is the only place where they will experience such feelings.

RESPONDING TO THE SELECTION

You may wish to bring a newspaper to class in order to spur discussion of current events.

ANSWERS TO SELECTION CHECK TEST 4.9.11

EX. What body of water does the speaker look out on at the beginning of the poem?
The speaker looks out on the ocean.

1. What causes the "grating roar" that the speaker hears?
The roar is caused by pebbles being flung by the waves.

2. Who heard the eternal note of sadness long ago on the Aegean?
Sophocles heard it.

3. According to the speaker, what was once "at the full" but is now retreating?
The Sea of Faith was once "at the full."

4. Whom does the speaker address in the last stanza of the poem?
He addresses his love.

5. What clashes in the last line of the poem?
Ignorant armies clash by night.

VOCABULARY IN CONTEXT

- It is very painful to sunbathe on a shingle.
- With certitude I raised my hand and strode to the chalkboard to work the arithmetic problem.

---

❶
What, according to the speaker, has happened to the "Sea of Faith"?

❷
What does the speaker ask of his love? Why, according to the speaker, is this necessary?

The Sea of Faith
Was once, too, at the full, and round earth's shore
Lay like the folds of a bright girdle furled.[2]
But now I only hear
25   Its melancholy, long, withdrawing roar,
Retreating, to the breath
Of the night wind, down the vast edges drear
And naked <u>shingles</u> of the world.

Ah, love, let us be true
30   To one another! for the world, which seems
To lie before us like a land of dreams,
So various, so beautiful, so new,
Hath really neither joy, nor love, nor light,
Nor <u>certitude</u>, nor peace, nor help for pain;
35   And we are here as on a darkling plain
Swept with confused alarms of struggle and flight,
Where ignorant armies clash by night. ∎

---

2. **Lay . . . furled.** At high tide, the sea tightly envelopes the land like a girdle.

Responding to the Selection

Do you share the view of the world presented by the speaker in the final stanza of the poem? What evidence do daily events in the news provide that life is a "darkling plain/Swept with confused alarms of struggle and flight,/Where ignorant armies clash by night"? What evidence to the contrary can you find? Discuss these questions with your classmates.

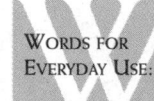

WORDS FOR EVERYDAY USE:
shin • gle (shiŋ´gəl) *n.,* rocky beach
cer • ti • tude (sʉrt´ə tōōd´) *n.,* absolute sureness

ADDITIONAL QUESTIONS AND ACTIVITIES

If students have not read the poems by Tennyson (pages 698, 707, 712) and Robert Browning (pages 724 and 729), suggest that they do so. Ask students to compare the roles that women play in these poems and in "Dover Beach." How do the roles of the women differ from those of the men? Why might that be so?

Reviewing the Selection

RECALLING

1. How does the speaker describe the sea, the tide, the moon, the cliffs, the bay, and the night air in the first few lines of the poem?

2. Whom does the speaker address in this poem? In line 9, to what does the speaker ask this person to listen?

3. What thought did Sophocles have when listening to the sea? What thought, presented in stanza 3, does the speaker have?

4. What does the speaker ask of his love in the last stanza?

INTERPRETING

▶▶ 5. What mood is created by the description of the environment at the beginning of the poem? How does this mood change?

▶▶ 6. What emotions are created in the speaker by what he hears?

▶▶ 7. What does the speaker say has happened to people's faith?

▶▶ 8. Why does the speaker make the request that he makes of his love in the last stanza?

SYNTHESIZING

9. What, according to the speaker, do people expect life to be like in the beginning? What do they actually find?

10. What view of his time does the speaker present in the concluding lines? In what things has the speaker lost faith? What does he need to sustain him?

Understanding Literature (Questions for Discussion)

1. **Allusion.** An **allusion** is a figure of speech in which a reference is made to a person, event, object, or work from history or literature. What allusion does the speaker make in the second stanza of this poem? What is the purpose of this allusion? What idea does the allusion introduce?

2. **Symbol.** A **symbol** is a thing that stands for or represents both itself and something else. Of what is the ebb and flow of the sea a symbol in this poem? What did Sophocles hear in this ebb and flow? What other symbolic significance does the sea have for the speaker? With what does the speaker associate the sea in the third stanza? What has happened to that sea?

VICTORIAN POETRY / "DOVER BEACH" **743**

ANSWERS FOR REVIEWING THE SELECTION

RECALLING

1. The sea is calm, the tide is full, the moon gently shines on the land, the cliffs stand glimmering and vast, the bay is tranquil, and the night air is sweet.

2. The speaker is addressing his love. He asks his love to listen to the grating roar of pebbles that the waves are flinging.

3. Sophocles thought about the cycle of human misery when he heard the sea. The speaker thinks of the shrinking of humanity's faith.

4. The speaker asks that he and his love be true to one another, that they love each other.

INTERPRETING

Responses will vary. Possible responses are given.

5. At the beginning of the poem, the mood is calm and tranquil. The mood of tranquillity soon changes to one of melancholy.

6. The speaker feels sadness and melancholy.

7. People's faith is retreating. People are losing their faith.

8. The speaker knows that only in their relationship can they feel joy, love, certitude, and peace.

SYNTHESIZING

Responses will vary. Possible responses are given.

9. People expect life to be like a land of dreams, various, beautiful, and new. They actually find that life is full of ignorance and strife.

10. The speaker presents his time as one of darkness, confusion, and conflict. The speaker has lost faith in the world and in other people. The speaker needs his relationship with his love to sustain him.

ANSWERS FOR UNDERSTANDING LITERATURE

▶ See the evaluation forms for discussion, active listening, and oral communication, *Assessment Portfolio, 7.11–7.14.*
Responses will vary. Possible responses are given.

1. **Allusion.** The speaker alludes to Sophocles. The purpose of the allusion is to stress that though centuries have passed, the human condition is much the same. (This point is made by Sophocles as well.) The idea of human misery is introduced.

▶**Teaching Note:** Students may benefit from knowing a bit more about Sophocles. See the note on page 741.

2. **Symbol.** The ebb and flow of the sea represent the cycle of life and death. Sophocles heard the ebb and flow of human misery. The speaker also links the retreat of the sea to the diminishing of human faith. The speaker associates the sea with religion, the Sea of Faith, which is retreating.

(cont.)

TEACHER'S EDITION **743**

3. **Extended Metaphor.** An **extended metaphor** is a point-by-point presentation of one thing as though it were another. The description is meant as an implied comparison, inviting the reader to associate the thing being described with something that is quite different from it. To what does the speaker liken life on earth in line 35 of the poem? What might the "confused alarms of struggle and flight" refer to? What are the "ignorant armies"? What does the speaker think of the people of his day, of their ability to understand their lives, and of the activities that they engage in? What view of human life is expressed here?

4. **Theme.** A **theme** is a central idea in a literary work. The speaker in this poem says that the Sea of Faith has receded and describes life as a struggle between ignorant armies on a darkling plain. What one possibility or hope does the speaker place against all this darkness? What do you consider to be the main theme of this poem?

Responding in Writing

1. **Instruction Manual.** Suppose that life came with an instruction manual—a book that gave tips about how to be happy and healthy and prosperous. What do you think such an instruction manual should say? Think about the emphasis that the speaker of "Dover Beach" places on the importance of love. What would your instruction manual say on that subject? How might love for some other person help people face times when, from the rest of the world, there is "neither joy, nor love, nor light,/Nor certitude, nor peace, nor help for pain"? Write about these questions in your journal.

2. **Setting.** The **setting** of a literary work is the time and place in which it occurs, together with all the details used to create a sense of a particular time and place. In "Dover Beach," Arnold uses a seaside setting to create several moods: an opening mood of calmness and tranquility that grows to sadness and, finally at the end of the poem, to melancholy verging on despair. Choose a place that evokes in you a strong emotion. Create a character and place him or her in that setting. Describe elements such as landscape, scenery, light, weather, buildings, and furnishings in such a way as to create a particular emotion in your reader. Choose your words carefully to create an appropriate mood.

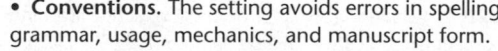

VICTORIAN POETRY

"The Man He Killed"   "The Darkling Thrush"
"Channel Firing"
by Thomas Hardy

ABOUT THE AUTHOR

Thomas Hardy (1840–1928) is perhaps best known as the novelist who wrote such memorable works as *The Return of the Native, The Mayor of Casterbridge, Tess of the D'Urbervilles,* and *Jude the Obscure.* However, Hardy's first love was poetry, and today he is recognized as one of the great forerunners of the modern Realism in verse. Hardy was born in the English west country, the "Wessex" of his novels. Under the influence of his father, a building constructor, he became as a young man apprenticed to a local church architect. Though he showed great talent for architecture, he gave his free time to writing. In 1871, he published his first novel, *Desperate Remedies,* and in 1874, *Far from the Madding Crowd,* which won him much acclaim. Over the coming years, Hardy reached a wide reading public with his novels about characters buffeted by terrible fates. However, he also faced criticism and censorship because of his sympathetic treatment of characters who were driven by circumstances to commit terrible deeds. Financially secure and disgusted with the censorship leveled at his novels, he turned in the later part of his career to his original love, writing poetry. Both Hardy's novels and his poems present a pessimistic view of life, but Hardy himself argued that he was a "meliorist," someone who thinks that the human condition can be improved. His writing about tragic circumstances and lives was intended to arouse human sympathy and compassion by showing people how people come to be as they are. Hardy is buried in the Poet's Corner of Westminster Abbey. His heart, however, is buried in the churchyard at Stinsford in the west country, near Dorchester.

ABOUT THE SELECTIONS

"The Man He Killed" is perhaps the most famous of Hardy's antiwar poems. The poem places an eloquent argument against the inhumanity of war in the mouth of an uneducated speaker of a Wessex **dialect.**

"Channel Firing" again addresses the subject of war and shows Hardy's skill as a **satirist,** one who uses humor, in this case dark humor, to point out human foibles. The poem is remarkable for its combination of humor with high seriousness. It is also remarkable for its visual clarity, which rises to a cinemagraphic climax.

"The Darkling Thrush" demonstrates well Hardy's ability to create a somber **mood** through a few deft strokes of his poetic brush. The poem reflects Hardy's disillusionment with his age and contrasts this disillusionment with a message of hope from a source in nature.

VICTORIAN POETRY **745**

GOALS/OBJECTIVES

Studying this lesson will enable students to

- experience a speaker's feelings toward war death, hope, and nature
- describe the literary significance of Thomas Hardy's writings
- recognize and analyze themes that they encounter in their reading

- write a fable and a fantasy
- explain the concepts of irony, understatement, humor, dialect, concrete universal, metaphor, and simile, and identify and interpret these in poetry
- complete reading comprehension test questions

ENRICHMENT ACTIVITIES

Just before the Victorian Age began, many people believed that state education was the best way to convert the masses to the Church of England and prevent a working class revolution. In his book *Culture and Anarchy* (1896), Matthew Arnold described those people living in the east end of London as "those vast, miserable, unmanageable masses of paupers." Conduct research into the plight of the working class in Victorian England. Write a short report on what it might have been like to be part of that working class. Stage a debate on the role of state education and what students should be taught.

SUPPORT FOR LEP STUDENTS

Explain that Hardy's poems use nonstandard dialect. After students have read the poems, use the activities on dialect and diction, pages 747 and 753.

ADDITIONAL VOCABULARY
ranged—arranged
indifferent—uninteresting; uninterested
dregs—residue; scum
score—scratch lines in
crypt—grave; tomb
canopy—awning (sky)
plume—feathers

PREREADING NOTES

READER'S JOURNAL

Suggest that students consider a particular war in order to help them think about these questions.

THINKING SKILLS

The speaker says that he shot the enemy because he was the speaker's foe. This begs the question because it merely restates the question's premise. The speaker implies that war does not justify killing one's foes, because they might have enlisted carelessly and thus be unprepared to die for a cause.

VOCABULARY FROM THE SELECTIONS

avenge   gaunt
drearisome

ANSWERS TO SELECTION CHECK TEST 4.9.13

EX. Who killed whom?
The speaker of the poem killed an enemy soldier.

1. Where does the speaker imagine meeting the man in stanza 1 of the poem?
He imagines meeting the man in a tavern or inn.

2. What does the speaker imagine that he might have done for the man under other circumstances?
He imagines that he might have bought the man a drink.

3. How was the man killed?
He was shot.

4. What does the speaker imagine that the man might have sold?
He might have sold his traps.

5. According to the speaker, what is "quaint and curious"?
War is "quaint and curious."

READER'S JOURNAL

What are your thoughts about the subject of war? Would you be willing to participate in a war? What might lead you to do so? Write about these questions in your journal.

THINKING SKILLS

Read about begging the question in the Language Arts Survey, 4.14, "Avoiding Faulty Arguments." Then read the poem. What example of begging the question is presented in this poem? Why does the speaker consider it insufficient to say that a killing was just because someone was his foe in a war?

"The Man He Killed"

THOMAS HARDY

❶ What does the speaker imagine that he might have done with the man he killed had they met in other circumstances?

"Had he and I but met
By some old ancient inn,
We should have sat us down to wet
Right many a nipperkin![1]

5   "But ranged as infantry,
And staring face to face,
I shot at him as he at me,
And killed him in his place.

"I shot him dead because—
10   Because he was my foe,
Just so—my foe of course he was;
That's clear enough; although

"He thought he'd 'list,[2] perhaps,
Off-hand like—just as I—
15   Was out of work—had sold his traps—[3]
No other reason why.

❷ Why does shooting the enemy soldier seem curious to the speaker?

"Yes; quaint and curious war is!
You shoot a fellow down
You'd treat if met where any bar is,
20   Or help to half-a-crown."[4]   ■

---
1. **nipperkin.** Half pint of ale
2. **'list.** Enlist
3. **traps.** Traps for hunting
4. **half-a-crown.** English coin

746   UNIT NINE / THE VICTORIAN AGE

ADDITIONAL QUESTIONS AND ACTIVITIES

Have students think about the perception of the working class held by the upper classes and intellectuals in Victorian England.

▶**Teaching Note:** The speaker is an unemployed member of the working class. Discuss how Hardy's characterization of this thoughtful man differs from conventional perception of the working classes held by people like Matthew Arnold.

ANSWERS TO GUIDED READING QUESTIONS

❶ Had the speaker met the man under different circumstances, they probably would have sat and drunk ale together.

❷ Shooting a soldier seems curious to the speaker because in any other situation, he would buy him a drink or loan him money.

Responding to the Selection

How does the speaker feel about what he has done? Does he express great anger, grief, or remorse? How do you feel toward the speaker? toward his action? In what sense has the speaker been simply a pawn?

Reviewing the Selection

RECALLING

1. What does the speaker say he might have done had he met the other man in different circumstances?

2. What does the speaker do at the end of ▶ line 9?

INTERPRETING

▶ 3. What is curious about the fact that in other circumstances the speaker might have helped the other man "to half-a-crown"?

▶ 4. Why do you think the speaker hesitates before making the statement in line 10?

SYNTHESIZING

5. What speculations made in this poem show that the speaker is identifying with the man whom he shot? Why might it be easier to shoot a nameless, unknown enemy than someone who is known?

Understanding Literature (Questions for Discussion)

1. **Dialect.** A **dialect** is a version of a language spoken by the people of a particular place, time, or social group. What nonstandard, dialectical expressions are used in this poem? Why might Hardy have chosen to write this poem in dialect? What does the use of dialect reveal about the speaker? How does the use of dialect help to relate the speaker to the man he killed?

2. **Irony.** **Irony** is a difference between appearance and reality. What was the appearance of the situation between the two men when they met face to face? What was the common reality that they shared? What makes the killing of the other man ironic?

3. **Understatement.** An **understatement** is an ironic expression in which something of importance is emphasized by being spoken of as though it were not important. How does the speaker refer to war at the beginning of the last stanza? What words does he use to describe it? What do these words mean? What are the speaker's feelings about having killed the other man? What makes his description of war an understatement? In what sense might war be considered quaint? In what sense might it be considered curious?

VICTORIAN POETRY / "THE MAN HE KILLED" **747**

ANSWERS FOR UNDERSTANDING LITERATURE (CONT.)

▶ **Teaching Note:** What contemporary nonstandard expressions might one use to make a speaker sound like a regular person?

2. **Irony.** The two men appeared to be enemies, yet they had no quarrel. They were both common men who had enlisted because they were out of work. Neither was fighting for a great cause; they both just needed work.
▶ **Teaching Note:** Discuss with students whether they think that the situation of the speaker is unusual. Do

students think this issue is still relevant today?

3. **Understatement.** The speaker refers to war as "quaint and curious." *Quaint* means "unusual" and *curious* means "strange" or "puzzling." The speaker is perplexed and bemused about killing the other man. Referring to killing a person as unusual and odd rather than tragic or horrifying is an understatement. It is nonetheless unusual and strange to be encouraged to kill other people.

RESPONDING TO THE SELECTION
Suggest that students consider line 17 when discussing these questions.

ANSWERS FOR REVIEWING THE SELECTION

RECALLING
1. In other circumstances, the two might have sat and drunk an ale together.
2. The speaker shoots and kills the soldier.

INTERPRETING
Responses will vary. Possible responses are given.
3. The speaker normally would have been friendly to the man, instead of killing him.
4. The speaker hesitates because he can think of no good reason for killing a human being.

SYNTHESIZING
Responses will vary. A possible response is given.
5. The speaker speculates that they would have been friends in other circumstances and that the soldier enlisted only because he was unemployed. It might be easier to kill a stranger because you wouldn't be familiar with the life you were destroying; the death wouldn't remind you of your own.

ANSWERS FOR UNDERSTANDING LITERATURE
▶ See the evaluation forms for discussion, active listening, and oral communication, *Assessment Portfolio*, 7.11–7.14.
Responses will vary. Possible responses are given.

1. **Dialect.** The speaker uses the phrases "sat us down to wet/Right many a nipperkin," "He thought he'd 'list, perhaps,/Off-hand like—just as I," and "You'd treat if met where any bar is,/Or help to half-a-crown." Hardy may have used dialect to place the speaker in the working class. Hardy may have used dialect to suggest that the speaker and the man he killed were both common people.

(cont.)

READER'S JOURNAL

Remind students of another example in which dead people observe the living in Dickens's *A Christmas Carol* or in Thorton Wilder's *Our Town.*

SPEAKING AND LISTENING SKILLS

Suggest that students read the poem aloud in a small group, with different students assigned to the various voices in the poem.

►Additional practice is provided in the *Essential Skills Practice Book: Speaking and Listening,* 3.6.

ANSWERS TO GUIDED READING QUESTIONS

❶ A corpse resting in the churchyard is the speaker in the beginning of the poem. The explosions of large guns have awakened the dead person.

❷ The speaker thought it was Judgment Day. It is really only shooting practice for the gunners.

CROSS-CURRICULAR ACTIVITIES

Biology. Give background on the phrase "mad as hatters." This phrase described an actual occupational disease encountered by people who made hats in the nineteenth century. Mercury was used in the preparation of felt. Many "hatters" suffered from nerve damage caused by exposure to mercury. You may have some students who could research the mechanisms of mercury poisoning and report to the class. Give them time to prepare so they can report as you begin the lesson.

Arts and Humanities. Consider Tennyson and Arnold's opinions about the role of the artist. Does Hardy share their opinion? Students can write short comparisons of their ideas about the role of the artist. Students may want to stage a debate between Hardyites and Tennysonians or Arnoldites.

READER'S JOURNAL

In your journal, write about a character who is dead. Have the spirit of the character observe living people and comment on their actions or beliefs.

SPEAKING AND LISTENING SKILLS

Read the Language Arts Survey, 3.6, "Discussion." Then, as you read the poem, consider these questions: What prompts the discussion? What topic is being discussed? Who are the participants in the discussion? Who leads the discussion? What opinions do the participants in the discussion express and why?

"Channel Firing"[1]

THOMAS HARDY

❶
Who is speaking at the beginning of the poem? What has awakened this person?

> That night your great guns, unawares,
> Shook all our coffins as we lay,
> And broke the chancel[2] window-squares,
> We thought it was the Judgment-day

5   And sat upright. While <u>drearisome</u>
     Arose the howl of wakened hounds:
     The mouse let fall the altar-crumb,
     The worms drew back into the mounds,

❷
What did the speaker think was happening? What is actually happening?

> The glebe[3] cow drooled. Till God called, "No;
> 10   It's gunnery practice out at sea
> Just as before you went below;
> The world is as it used to be:

     "All nations striving strong to make
     Red war yet redder. Mad as hatters

---

1. **Channel Firing.** In the months preceding World War I, gunnery practice was done in the English Channel.
2. **chancel.** Part of a church near the altar
3. **glebe.** A small field belonging to a church

WORDS FOR EVERYDAY USE: drear • i • some (drir´ē sum) *adj.,* sad

VOCABULARY IN CONTEXT

• The brown stubble and frozen mud of the garden in winter is a <u>drearisome</u> sight.

15   They do no more for Christès[4] sake
        Than you who are helpless in such matters.

        "That this is not the judgment-hour
        For some of them's a blessed thing,
        For if it were they'd have to scour
20   Hell's floor for so much threatening. . . .

        "Ha, ha. It will be warmer when
        I blow the trumpet (if indeed
        I ever do; for you are men,
        And rest eternal sorely need)."

25   So down we lay again. "I wonder,
        Will the world ever saner be,"
        Said one, "than when He sent us under
        In our indifferent century!"

        And many a skeleton shook his head.
30   "Instead of preaching forty year,"
        My neighbor Parson Thirdly said,
        "I wish I had stuck to pipes and beer."

        Again the guns disturbed the hour,
        Roaring their readiness to <u>avenge</u>,
35   As far inland as Stourton Tower,
        And Camelot, and starlit Stonehenge.[5] ■

---

4. **Christès.** The archaic spelling of Christ is meant to suggest a sense of doom, as was common in ballads.
5. **Stourton . . . Stonehenge.** The sound of the guns reached Stourton Tower where King Alfred defeated the Danes in 879, Alfred's court at Camelot, and the prehistoric circle of stones at Stonehenge. The view encompasses much of England both geographically and throughout time.

❶
What does God suggest might happen to the gunners if this were indeed Judgment Day?

❷
What does the parson's comment tell you about how successful he considers his work to have been? Why might the parson feel that he failed?

WORDS FOR EVERYDAY USE: **a • venge** (ə venj´) *vt.*, get revenge for

---

ANSWERS TO GUIDED READING QUESTIONS

❶ If it were Judgment Day, the gunners would be in hell.

❷ The parson wishes he had stuck to drinking and smoking rather than preaching for forty years, because after preaching that one should love thy neighbor, people still prepare for war.

ANSWERS TO SELECTION CHECK TEST 4.9.15

EX. What body of water is referred to in the title of the poem?
The English Channel is referred to in the title.

1. Who sits upright at the beginning of the poem?
Some dead people sit upright.

2. What sound causes them to sit upright?
The sound of guns, or artillery practice, causes them to sit upright.

3. Who speaks to the people who are sitting upright?
God speaks to them.

4. According to the poem, what do men "sorely need"?
They "sorely need" rest.

5. What did the man named Thirdly do for forty years?
He preached.

VOCABULARY IN CONTEXT

• I will <u>avenge</u> my brother's death by bringing his enemy to justice!

ANSWERS FOR REVIEWING THE SELECTION

RECALLING

1. The dead people are awakened by being shaken. They think that Judgment Day has come. Actually the shaking is coming from the explosion of large guns.

2. God assures the dead that it is not Judgment Day; the world is the same as when they died. God wonders if He will ever blow the trumpet to signal Judgment Day. He knows that if He were to blow the trumpet, all people would go to hell, and He doesn't want that.

INTERPRETING

Responses will vary. Possible responses are given.

3. The windows are broken. Dogs howl, mice stop eating, worms retreat into the soil, and cows drool. The mood is a combination of alarm and humor.

(cont.)

RESPONDING TO THE SELECTION

Make sure that students distinguish between the opinions of humanity that God holds and those expressed by the dead people.

ANSWERS FOR UNDERSTANDING LITERATURE

►See the evaluation forms for discussion, active listening, and oral communication, *Assessment Portfolio,* 7.11–7.14.
Responses will vary. Possible responses are given.

1. Setting. The setting of this poem is a church graveyard. The author describes shaking coffins, breaking windows, howling dogs, scurrying mice, retreating worms, and a drooling cow. The mood is darkly humorous.

►**Teaching Note:** Ask students to think about some of the details of setting that Hardy did not dictate. Do students think this poem occurs during the day or night? Why? What are some other setting details that readers might infer?

2. Humor. It is humorous that dead people have been wakened because they mistook gunfire for Judgment Day. God says that humanity is lucky that He hasn't blown his horn, because we are destined for hell, and what people really need is eternal rest. The parson says that he wishes he had stayed with drinking and smoking rather than trying to preach for the last forty years. Underlying all of this humor is the sad state of humanity.

►**Teaching Note:** It is often said that humor is the most difficult type of writing. Is it more difficult to use words to make someone laugh or to cry? Why might that be?

3. Concrete Universal. The author uses the example of gunnery practice at sea. By listing places that cover much of England geographically as well as chronologically, the author universalizes his comments.

►**Teaching Note:** Suggest that students think of other concrete universals they have come across in their reading. How were they used?

Responding to the Selection

> What opinions do the dead people in this poem have of human beings and their preoccupation with warfare? Do you share those opinions? Why, or why not?

Reviewing the Selection

RECALLING

1. What awakens the dead people at the beginning of the poem? What do they think is happening? What is actually happening?

2. Of what does God assure the dead? What reservation does God express about there ever being a Judgment Day? What reason does God give for hesitating on this point?

INTERPRETING

►► 3. What happens to the windows? How do the animals react? What mood is created at the beginning of the poem by these descriptions?

►► 4. How does God feel toward people? What statements show that He is disappointed? What statement shows that He is also understanding?

SYNTHESIZING

5. What events from English history are hinted at in the description at the end of the poem? Why might Hardy have chosen to refer to the whole of England and to the whole of English history in the conclusion of this poem? What perspective is he taking? What comment is he making about nations and their histories?

Understanding Literature (Questions for Discussion)

1. **Setting.** The **setting** of a literary work is the time and place in which it occurs, together with all the details used to create a sense of a particular time and place. What is the setting of this poem? What details of the setting does the author give? What **mood,** or feeling, is created by these details at the beginning of the poem?

2. **Humor.** Psychologists have often pointed out that there is a dark undercurrent to much of what people consider humorous. What elements of this poem are darkly humorous? What humorous comments does God make about Judgment Day and about what men need? What humorous comment does the parson make? What dark reality underlies this humor?

3. **Concrete Universal.** A **concrete universal** is a particular object, person, action, or event that provides an instance or example of a general type. What concrete example does the author give in this poem of people's absurd preoccupation with war? How does the ending of the poem serve to universalize the comments made about that example?

750 *UNIT NINE / THE VICTORIAN AGE*

ANSWERS FOR REVIEWING THE SELECTION (CONT.)

4. God is frustrated that people don't live better lives. He says that men are "mad as hatters"; they don't live a Christian life and would surely go to hell if it were Judgment Day. God shows that He is understanding by saying that people sorely need eternal rest.

SYNTHESIZING

Responses will vary. A possible response is given.

5. Hardy hints at King Alfred's defeat of the Danes in 879, King Arthur's court at Camelot, and Stonehenge. Hardy wants to stress that England has a violent history. He suggests that, while nations may advance in some respects, with regard to war they remain as primitive as ever.

READER'S JOURNAL

Write in your journal about an event that caused in you a sudden change in mood. Describe your initial mood, the event, and the mood that resulted.

READING SKILLS

Read the Language Arts Survey, 4.19, "Reading Charts and Graphs." Then, after you read the poem through once, make a chart of the sensory images that appear in it.

"The Darkling[1] Thrush"

THOMAS HARDY

I leant upon a coppice gate[2]
    When Frost was spectre-gray,
And Winter's dregs made desolate
    The weakening eye of day.
5 The tangled bine-stems[3] scored the sky
    Like strings of broken lyres,[4]
And all mankind that haunted nigh
    Had sought their household fires.

The land's sharp features seemed to be
10   The Century's corpse outleant,[5]
His crypt the cloudy canopy,
    The wind his death-lament.
The ancient pulse of germ and birth
    Was shrunken hard and dry,
15 And every spirit upon earth
    Seemed fervourless[6] as I.

---

1. **Darkling.** In the dark
2. **coppice gate.** Gate leading into a wooded area
3. **tangled bine-stems.** Intertwined stems of shrubs
4. **lyres.** Small stringed instruments like harps
5. **Century's corpse outleant.** The poem was written on Dec. 31, 1900, so the nineteenth century was dead.
6. **fervourless.** Without passion

❶
What does the sharp-featured land symbolize for the speaker?

READER'S JOURNAL

Students should determine how the speaker's mood changes throughout the poem.

READING SKILLS

Students may want to track in their chart the mood of the speaker as it relates to the sensory images used in the poem.

▶Additional practice is provided in the *Essential Skills Practice Book: Study and Research,* 4.19.

SUPPORT FOR LEP STUDENTS

The punch line of the poem, the last stanza, may be difficult for some students to comprehend, as it is one very long sentence. Have students work with a partner to decipher the stanza.

HISTORICAL NOTE

• Discuss with students the term *fin de siècle,* French for "end of the century." *Fin de siècle* refers to a decadent ideal, a "get it all in before the party is over" mentality, such as might be found in the writings of Oscar Wilde or the illustrations of Aubrey Beardsley. *Fin de siècle* thought also manifests itself in an apocalyptic, sometimes self-indulgently hopeless worldview. Discuss how this and other poems that students have read might express a *fin de siècle* mentality. Ask students if they think there will be a reincarnation of *fin de siècle* culture at the end of the present millennium.

• Students may wish to produce a documentary video or multimedia presentation chronicling *fin de siècle* trends in or aspects of modern life.

ANSWER TO GUIDED READING QUESTION

❶ The land symbolizes the body of the dead century laid out on the ground.

ANSWERS TO GUIDED READING QUESTIONS

❶ The speaker hears a thrush. The joyous song of the thrush contrasts with the bleak landscape.

❷ The speaker feels the thrush knows of some hope for the future of which he himself isn't aware.

ADDITIONAL QUESTIONS AND ACTIVITIES

 Have students research the events occurring in the world at the time that Hardy wrote "The Darkling Thrush." Why might Hardy feel so depressed?

ANSWERS TO SELECTION CHECK TEST 4.9.17

EX. On what does the speaker lean?
The speaker leans on a coppice gate.

1. What season is described in the poem?
Winter is described in the poem.

2. How does the speaker feel?
The speaker feels gloomy.

3. Where is the thrush?
The thrush is in a tree overhead.

4. What kind of song comes from the thrush?
A joyful song comes from the thrush.

5. What does the speaker believe the song of the thrush means?
The speaker believes that the song of the thrush means hope.

RESPONDING TO THE SELECTION

Students should look to lines 21-24 for the physical description of the thrush. They should discuss the context of the bleak setting in considering the surprise of the thrush's ecstatic song.

❶
What does the speaker hear? How does this sound contrast with the speaker's environment?

❷
What possibility does the speaker entertain as a result of hearing the thrush's song?

At once a voice arose among
    The bleak twigs overhead
In a full-hearted evensong
    Of joy illimited;
20   An aged thrush, frail, <u>gaunt</u>, and small,
    In blast-beruffled plume,
Had chosen thus to fling his soul
    Upon the growing gloom.

25   So little cause for carolings
    Of such ecstatic sound
Was written on terrestrial things
    Afar or nigh around,
That I could think there trembled through
30   His happy good-night air
Some blessed Hope, whereof he knew
    And I was unaware.　■

WORDS FOR EVERYDAY USE: **gaunt** (gônt) *adj.*, haggard; emaciated

752 *UNIT NINE / THE VICTORIAN AGE*

VOCABULARY IN CONTEXT

• The stray dog looked <u>gaunt</u> and scruffy.

Responding to the Selection

How is the thrush described? What is the thrush's environment like? What makes the thrush's song particularly surprising?

Reviewing the Selection

RECALLING

1. What details of the environment does the speaker describe in stanza 1?

2. To what does the speaker compare the land? How does the speaker describe "every spirit up on earth"?

INTERPRETING

3. At what time of day and in what season of the year is this poem set?

4. How does the speaker feel toward his own time? Why might he feel this way? Does the poem relate, specifically, the reasons for the speaker's feelings?

SYNTHESIZING

5. What does the speaker learn from the thrush? What in the thrush is noble or wonderful? Is the conclusion of the poem optimistic? Why, or why not?

Understanding Literature (Questions for Discussion)

1. **Diction. Diction,** when applied to writing, refers to word choice. In this poem, Hardy uses several archaic, specifically poetic words. These words lend an air of formality and high seriousness to the work. What examples of specifically poetic diction can you find in the poem? What commonplace words might have been used in place of these?

2. **Theme.** A **theme** is a central idea in a literary work. What does the speaker of this poem make of "terrestrial things" both "Afar" and "nigh around"? What two possible references might the word *His* in line 30 have? Whose air might this be? What words in the stanza have connotations of religion? What hope might the speaker be intimating by these references?

3. **Stanza and Slant Rhyme.** A **stanza** is a recurring pattern of grouped lines in a poem. A **slant rhyme** is substitution of assonance or consonance for true rhyme. This poem uses an eight-line stanza, known as an **octave** or **octet.** What is the rhyme scheme of each stanza? Do all the lines end in full rhymes, or do some end with slant rhymes? Which rhymes in the poem seem to you particularly creative?

RECALLING

1. The speaker describes frost, the waning daylight, and shrubs.

2. The speaker compares the land to the corpse of the dead century. "Every spirit up on earth" is passionless.

INTERPRETING

Responses will vary. Possible responses are given.

3. The poem is set at dusk in winter.

4. The speaker feels depressed and hopeless about his time, because the century has ended and he is not optimistic about the path that events are taking. No, the poem doesn't specifically relate the reasons for the speaker's feelings.

SYNTHESIZING

Responses will vary. A possible response is given.

5. The speaker learns that there may be some cause for hope. The thrush is small and weak, yet persists in singing joyfully despite the gloomy setting. Yes, there seems to be so little cause for celebration that the thrush must know something the speaker does not.

ANSWERS FOR UNDERSTANDING LITERATURE

▶ See the evaluation forms for discussion, active listening, and oral communication, *Assessment Portfolio,* 7.11–7.14.

Responses will vary. Possible responses are given.

1. **Diction.** Examples of poetic diction include "tangled bine-stems"; "nigh"; "Century's corpse outleant"; "germ"; "illimited"; "Had chosen thus to fling his soul/ Upon the growing gloom"; and "nigh around." Commonplace words that might be substituted include: "tangled branches"; "near"; "the end of the century"; "seed"; "without limit"; "decided to sing at dusk"; and "nearby."

▶**Teaching Note:** Discuss with students how the tone of this poem might have been different had Hardy used less formal language.

(cont.)

ANSWERS FOR UNDERSTANDING LITERATURE (CONT.)

2. **Theme.** The speaker finds little to celebrate in things "Afar" and "nigh around." *His* might be the thrush or God. The air might be the thrush's song or God's air. The words "carolings," "terrestrial," and "blessed Hope" connote religion. The speaker may be referring to hope for the Second Coming of Christ.

▶**Teaching Note:** You may wish to compare Hardy's thoughts about the end of his century with those of the students about the end of theirs.

3. **Stanza and Slant Rhyme.** The rhyme scheme of each stanza is *ababcdcd.* Some lines do end in slant rhymes. Particularly creative are "outleant" and "death-lament," "overhead" and "illimited," "plume" and "gloom," and "air" and "unaware."

▶**Teaching Note:** Ask students to suggest other words that they think would rhyme better.

(cont.)

ANALYTIC SCALES FOR RESPONDING IN WRITING

Assign a score from 1 to 25 for each grading criterion below. (For more detailed evaluation, see the evaluation forms for writing, revising, and proofreading, *Assessment Portfolio*, 7.1–7.10.)

1. Fable

• **Content/Unity.** The fable presents a sensible discussion of an issue that ends in a moral.

• **Organization/Coherence.** The fable depicts a sensible interchange between two clearly defined characters.

• **Language/Style.** The fable uses vivid and precise nouns, verbs, and modifiers.

• **Conventions.** The fable avoids errors in spelling, grammar, usage, mechanics, and manuscript form.

2. Fantasy

• **Content/Unity.** The fantasy presents a sensible-seeming event with a fantastic twist.

• **Organization/Coherence.** The fantasy contains highly unrealistic elements, but details are organized in a coherent manner.

• **Language/Style.** The fantasy uses vivid and precise nouns, verbs, and modifiers.

• **Conventions.** The fantasy avoids errors in spelling, grammar, usage, mechanics, and manuscript form.

---

4. **Metaphor and Simile.** A **metaphor** is a figure of speech in which one thing is spoken or written about as if it were another. A **simile** is a comparison using *like* or *as*. In metaphors and similes, the writer either makes a comparison or invites the reader to make a comparison between two things. The writer's actual subject is the **tenor** of the metaphor or simile. The thing to which the subject is compared is the **vehicle**. For example, in the sentence "My love is a red, red rose," the tenor is "My love" and the vehicle is the "rose." Identify each of the following as a metaphor or a simile. Then identify the tenor and vehicle of each:

a. Winter's dregs

b. tangled bine-stems . . . /Like strings of broken lyres

c. The weakening eye of day

d. The land's sharp features seemed to be/The Century's corpse

e. His crypt the cloudy canopy

f. The wind his death-lament

g. to fling his soul

h. there trembled through/His happy good-night air/Some blessed Hope

---

Responding in Writing

1. **Fable.** A **fable** is a brief story with animal characters told to express a moral. The animals in fables usually are **personified**, or given human characteristics. Famous writers of fables include Aesop and La Fontaine. Famous examples include "The Tortoise and the Hare" and "The Fox and the Grapes." Write a fable for children using Hardy's human and his thrush as characters. Have the human and the thrush stand for, or represent, differing attitudes toward the world and toward life. The human could represent disappointment, negativity, or disillusionment. The thrush could represent joy and hope. Have the human and the thrush encounter one another in the woods and debate some issue, such as the goodness or badness of winter.

2. **Fantasy.** A **fantasy** is a literary work that contains highly unrealistic elements. Think about the songs of birds and how they differ. Consider, for example, the sounds of owls, ducks, whippoorwills, thrushes, hawks, loons, larks, geese, chickens, and any other birds with which you are familiar. Plan a fantasy story for children in which birds compete in a singing contest. Give the birds a subject to compose their songs about. Think of what words you might put into the mouths of the various birds when they sing. Try to match the words to each bird's unique sound. For example, the chicken might be gossipy, the loon might be loony, and the owl might be spooky or very serious. Also think about what character you might create to judge the singing contest. Possibilities include a personified Mother Nature or some woodland creature such as a fox. Work with a group of other students to write the fantasy. Assign parts to be written by each student. If you wish to do so, put your fantasy together as a children's book, complete with pictures or drawings of the various characters.

ANSWERS FOR UNDERSTANDING LITERATURE (CONT.)

4. Metaphor and Simile

a. metaphor; tenor = winter; vehicle = a glass of liquid

b. simile; tenor = bine-stems; vehicle = the strings of a broken lyre

c. metaphor; tenor = dusk; vehicle = an eye that is losing its sight

d. metaphor; tenor = the land; vehicle = a corpse

e. metaphor; tenor = a crypt; vehicle = cloudy sky

f. metaphor; tenor = the wind; vehicle = his death-lament

g. metaphor; tenor = his soul; vehicle = an object that might be flung

h. metaphor; tenor = hope; vehicle = something that might tremble through a song

Test-taking Skills

Reading Comprehension. Read the Language Arts Survey, 4.43, "Reading Comprehension Questions." Then do the following exercise.

The passage below is followed by questions based on its content. Answer all questions following the passage on the basis of what is *stated* or *implied* in the passage.

The Victorian Era was marked by strong contrasts between prosperity and poverty. During Victoria's long reign (1837–1901), England became the leading manufacturer of exported goods in the world. English factories were the first to be industrialized, and English ships carried goods to every major port around the globe. People flooded into the cities to work in those factories. London grew from a city of a little more than two million to more than six million inhabitants. The wealth brought in by factory work and overseas trade made England the most powerful country on earth. It used its economic wealth to expand its seafaring and military might. Soon England had colonies in every part of the world. For well-to-do English men and women, the Victorian Age was England's finest era. Optimism and natural pride were commonplace. Many English people came to share Rudyard Kipling's racist conviction that it was the destiny of England—the so-called "white man's burden"—to carry English culture and religion to the benighted peoples of the rest of the planet. England ruled its colonies with an iron fist and increased its wealth by imports of luxury goods from those colonies, including spices, cocoa, tea, coffee, figs, wine, porcelain, and cloth.

However, England's prosperity had a price. At home, the disparity between the rich and the poor grew to staggering proportions. In the early part of the Victorian Era, over 70 percent of the population lived in poverty. The government protected wealthy aristocratic landowners by placing high tariffs on imported grains, such as maize, wheat, and rice, known collectively in England as "corn." As a consequence, when crops failed in England, many common people starved. Conditions were hardest for people living in the crowded cities and working in the mills and factories that emerged during the Industrial Revolution. Men, women, and small children, often with very little to eat, worked sixteen-hour days in factories that were unheated and dangerous. Crime and hunger were commonplace. The lives of the poor were brutish, nasty, and short. Poor people were unable to change their conditions because they did not have the right to vote.

Given these conditions, England might well have faced a revolutionary uprising of the poor and middle classes had the government not taken steps to correct the worst excesses of the country's emerging capitalism. The Reform Bill of 1832 extended the right to vote to all men having property worth more than ten pounds annually in rent. A second Reform Bill in 1867 extended that right to all men. In 1846, the Corn Laws were repealed, reducing the tariffs on imported grain.

1. With which of the following statements about Victorian England would the author most likely agree?

   (A) Colonialism was justified by a racist conviction that England had a duty to export its culture to other nations.

   (B) Until 1867, poor people in England did not have the political means to address the terrible conditions under which they lived.

   (C) The poor suffered from high tariffs placed on imported grains.

   (D) The Victorian Age was one of unalloyed prosperity and growth.

2. The author cites as evidence of the wretched conditions of the poor all of the following *except*

   (A) having to work in unheated, dangerous factories.

   (B) having inadequate clothing to wear.

   (C) starvation.

   (D) crowding in the cities.

   (E) the number of people living in poverty.

3. It can be inferred from the author's description of the tariffs on imported corn that

   (A) England imported much of its grain.

   (B) prices paid by ordinary people for food were kept unnaturally high.

   (C) the English use the word *corn* to refer to all grains, such as wheat, barley, millet, maize, and rice.

   (D) food riots broke out in the cities of Manchester and Bristol.

   (E) factory owners provided their workers with very little to eat.

4. Which of the following best summarizes the purpose of the passage?

   (A) To describe the economic conditions of England during the Victorian Age

   (B) To explain the repeal of the Corn Laws

   (C) To explain the origins of British colonialism

   (D) To attack capitalism

   (E) To describe the growth of English power during the Victorian Age

PREREADING

Sonnet 43 ("How do I love thee . . .")
from *Sonnets from the Portuguese*
by Elizabeth Barrett Browning

ABOUT THE AUTHOR

In her own era, **Elizabeth Barrett Browning** (1806–1861) was one of England's most well-known female poets. She is most often associated with the love poetry she wrote for her husband, Robert Browning. However, at the time during which she wrote she was respected as a scholarly poet, and her large body of work raised many moral and political issues. During her early years, Browning received a thorough education. She studied Latin and Greek, philosophy, and literature. As a young child she began to write poetry, and at the age of fourteen she composed an epic poem that her father privately printed. The poet's father, although supportive of his daughter's obvious talent, was overprotective and kept careful watch over Elizabeth. This was especially true when her health began to fail, and she was later confined to her home. She was an invalid living in the family home in London when her literary career began to thrive. At the age of thirty-nine, Elizabeth received her first letter from Robert Browning, an unknown poet who admired her work. She wrote back, and the two began their famous romance, and eventually married. Elizabeth and Robert were supportive of one another in their individual literary careers. However, at the time of Elizabeth's death in 1861, her work was much more popular. Today, her most recognizable pieces come from the book *Sonnets from the Portuguese.* Other important pieces include the lengthy poem "Aurora Leigh" and the ambitious piece "Runaway Slave at Pilgrim's Point."

ABOUT THE SELECTION

Sonnet 43 ("How do I love thee . . .") comes from Browning's book, *Sonnets from the Portuguese,* which is a sequence of forty-five sonnets that Browning wrote to chronicle the stages of her love for her husband Robert. "The Portuguese" was one of Robert's pet names for Elizabeth. Because of the deeply personal nature of the poems, Elizabeth didn't intend for these poems to be published and read by the general public. However, she finally decided to publish the pieces under the title *Sonnets from the Portuguese.* This title was meant to imply that the poems were translations of pieces written in Portuguese, not her original work. The best-known sonnet sequences were written by men, and it was unusual to use the form to tell a love story from the point of view of a woman. Sonnet 43 is by far the most recognizable of any of the poems in the sequence.

ADDITIONAL RESOURCES

READER'S GUIDE
• Selection Worksheet, 9.10

ASSESSMENT PORTFOLIO
• Selection Check Test, 4.9.19
• Selection Test, 4.9.20

ESSENTIAL SKILLS PRACTICE BOOKS
• *Study and Research,* 4.13

ENRICHMENT ACTIVITIES

Suggest that students read other poems from *Sonnets from the Portuguese,* a collection originally intended only for Robert Browning. Discuss the different types of love about which Browning writes. How many types of love can they identify? What are the similarities and differences among them? Have students choose two poems and compare the roles of the speaker and the types of love described. Students can compare their findings in small groups or in expository essays.

SUPPORT FOR LEP STUDENTS

Discuss with students the use of capitalization to signify a divine or otherworldly quality.

GOALS/OBJECTIVES

Studying this lesson will enable students to

• enjoy reading a love sonnet
• describe Elizabeth Barrett Browning's literary accomplishments and explain the historical significance of her writings
• define *repetition* and identify and analyze how it is used in a poem

• define *sonnet* and identify sonnets that they encounter in their reading
• write a question poem and a comparison essay

READER'S JOURNAL

Students may want to think about specific people in their lives and how their feelings for each person differ.

THINKING SKILLS

• Students may wish to research additional literary pairs of their own choosing.

• Discuss with students where they might find information on literary spouses and siblings.

ANSWERS TO GUIDED READING QUESTIONS

❶ The speaker is counting the number of ways in which she loves the subject of the poem.

❷ The speaker's love is very strong and will last even after she dies.

ANSWERS TO SELECTION CHECK TEST 4.9.19

EX. With what question does the poem begin?
The poem begins with the question "How do I love thee?"

1. What does the speaker say that she is going to count?
She is going to count the ways in which she loves the intended recipient of the poetry.

2. According to the speaker, what do some men strive for?
They strive for right.

3. According to the speaker, what do some men turn from?
They turn from praise.

4. With what from her childhood does the speaker love?
She loves with her childhood faith.

5. What will the speaker do after death, if God chooses?
She will love the person better.

READER'S JOURNAL

Freewrite in your journal about what you believe it means to truly love someone. Do you think there are different types of love? What might these different types be, and to what might you compare each type?

THINKING SKILLS

Read the Language Arts Survey, 4.13, "Making Hypotheses." Then think about Elizabeth Barrett and Robert Browning. Based on the information given in this book and in one other source, form a hypothesis about spouses or siblings who simultaneously pursue literary careers. Then read about the following people: Mary and Percy Shelley, Dorothy and William Wordsworth, and Dante Gabriel and Christina Rossetti. Does your hypothesis hold true in these situations? Why or why not?

Sonnet 43

("How do I love thee? . . .")

ELIZABETH BARRETT BROWNING

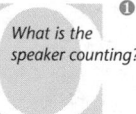

❶ What is the speaker counting?

❷ How strong is the love this speaker feels? How long will it last?

How do I love thee? Let me count the ways.
I love thee to the depth and breadth and height
My soul can reach, when feeling out of sight
For the ends of Being and ideal Grace.
5   I love thee to the level of everyday's
Most quiet need, by sun and candle-light.
I love thee freely, as men strive for Right;
I love thee purely, as they turn from Praise.
I love thee with the passion put to use
10   In my old griefs, and with my childhood's faith.
I love thee with a love I seemed to lose
With my lost saints,—I love thee with the breath,
Smiles, tears, of all my life!—and, if God choose,
I shall but love thee better after death.   ■

Responding to the Selection

> Do you like this poem and the feelings it expresses? Why or why not? Are the feelings expressed here similar to your own feelings about love?

Reviewing the Selection

RECALLING

1. In how many ways does the speaker answer the poem's opening question?

2. In line 6, how does the speaker refer to night and day?

3. How does the speaker love with a "passion put to use/In my old griefs"? Where has she loved before?

4. What does the speaker say about death in the last line of the poem?

INTERPRETING

▶▶ 5. What do the answers to the poem's initial questions have in common with one another?

▶▶ 6. What does the speaker mean by saying that she loves "to the level of every-day's/Most quiet need"? What does this say about the speaker's love and its importance?

▶▶ 7. Why does the speaker refer to "child-hood's faith" and "old griefs"? Explain your answer.

▶▶ 8. How does the last line describe the strength of the speaker's love? For how long and under what circumstances does the speaker expect this love to survive?

SYNTHESIZING

9. How many references to religion do you find in this poem? Why might the speaker be making these references? What is the speaker's attitude toward religion?

10. What type of love is the speaker of this poem proclaiming? Do you think the speaker's feelings are genuine and realistic? Why, or why not?

Assign a score from 1 to 25 for each grading criterion below. (For more detailed evaluation, see the evaluation forms for writing, revising, and proofreading, *Assessment Portfolio*, 7.1–7.10.)

1. Question Poem

• **Content/Unity.** The question poem presents a sensible or satiric description of how the speaker loves.

• **Organization/Coherence.** The question poem gives main points and details in a logical order.

• **Language/Style.** The question poem uses vivid and precise nouns, verbs, and modifiers.

• **Conventions.** The question poem avoids errors in spelling, grammar, usage, mechanics, and manuscript form.

2. Comparison Essay

• **Content/Unity.** The comparison essay presents a sensible opinion regarding the feelings of love expressed in Sonnet 43 and another love poem.

• **Organization/Coherence.** The comparison essay presents reasons for the opinion in a logical manner.

• **Language/Style.** The comparison essay uses vivid and precise nouns, verbs, and modifiers.

• **Conventions.** The comparison essay avoids errors in spelling, grammar, usage, mechanics, and manuscript form.

Understanding Literature (Questions for Discussion)

1. **Repetition.** **Repetition** is the use, again, of a sound, word, phrase, sentence, or other element. Where is repetition used in this poem? How does the repetition emphasize the poem's theme? Does this technique make the poem more effective? Why, or why not?

2. **Sonnet.** A **sonnet** is a fourteen-line poem that follows one of a number of different rhyme schemes. After reading the section on sonnets in the Handbook of Literary Terms, answer the following questions: Is Browning's poem a Shakespearean sonnet, or a Petrarchan sonnet? What is the rhyme scheme of the poem? Does the poem ever deviate from the set rhyme scheme? If yes, what might be the poet's reason for this? In terms of theme and structure, can this sonnet be separated into distinct parts? Explain your answer.

Responding in Writing

1. **Question Poem.** Build a poem from Browning's first line: "How do I love thee? Let me count the ways." Answer this question in your own words, describing the ways in which you love a particular person or thing. You may choose to write a serious poem, in keeping with the style of the original sonnet, or you may choose to put a more light-hearted spin on your poem.

2. **Comparison Essay.** Compare this love poem to any other love poem in this book. Which poem do you feel is stronger? In your opinion, which poem expresses genuine feelings of love? Give reasons for your responses and back up your opinions with details from each poem.

► See the evaluation forms for discussion, active listening, and oral communication, *Assessment Portfolio*, 7.11–7.14.

Responses will vary. Possible responses are given.

1. Repetition. The phrase "I love thee" is used repeatedly and stresses the breadth of the speaker's love for the subject of the poem. Yes, the speaker links the phrase to different kinds of love in order to lend a number of levels of meaning to the phrase.

(cont.)

ANSWERS FOR UNDERSTANDING LITERATURE (CONT.)

►**Teaching Note:** Discuss with students how the poem might read if the repeated phrase were deleted and the poem were rewritten as a list. Is the poem as effective?

 2. Sonnet. Sonnet 43 is a Petrarchan sonnet. The rhyme scheme of the poem is *abbaabba cdcdcd.* "Faith" in line 10 is more of a slant rhyme than an exact rhyme.

Browning may have included a slant rhyme in order to give the reader a focal point. Students might say that the poem cannot be divided into distinct parts because it is a cohesive poem that asks a question in the first half of the first line and then enumerates the answers.

PREREADING

"Pied Beauty"
"God's Grandeur"

by Gerard Manley Hopkins

ABOUT THE AUTHOR

Gerard Manley Hopkins (1844–1889) grew up in a political and poetical family. His father was a poet who had served as the British consul general in Hawaii. Hopkins attended Oxford University and was attracted to the ideas of the Oxford Movement, which attempted to connect the Anglican Church to the tenets and rituals of the early Christian church in response to the increased skepticism of the age. Like John Henry Newman, one of the founders of the Oxford Movement, Hopkins found himself unable to resist the conclusion that the Roman Catholic Church was the true heir of early Christianity, and he converted to Catholicism. In 1868, he joined the Society of Jesus, or Jesuits, and in 1877, he was ordained a priest. He burned the poetry he had written as a youth, considering it unworthy of his high vocation. Some of his superiors did encourage him to resume the writing of poetry, although one of his most ambitious poems, "The Wreck of the Deutschland," about a shipwreck in which five nuns were drowned, was not accepted for publication by the Jesuit periodical to which he submitted it. Very few of Hopkins's poems were published during his lifetime, because few readers could understand their unusual words, highly compressed images, and odd rhythms. Hopkins called his meter **sprung rhythm**, a system in which each line has the same number of stressed syllables but a variable number of unstressed syllables. The lines, therefore, can be of unequal lengths, and the stresses do not fall in a regular pattern; several strong stresses can be placed next to one another. This poetry is among the most beautiful but also among the oddest in the English language. Its conciseness of expression and unconventional use of rhythm have greatly influenced a number of twentieth-century poets.

ABOUT THE SELECTIONS

"**Pied Beauty**" is a celebration of the variety and abundance of nature and of the ultimate source of that variety and abundance. The poem makes extensive use of **alliteration**, or repetition of initial sounds, and is typical of Hopkins's work in its unusual rhythms.

"**God's Grandeur**" is an example of what an extremely original poet can do with a conventional form such as that of the **sonnet**. The poem follows a typical rhyme scheme for an **Italian**, or **Petrarchan**, **sonnet** and makes use of Hopkins's trademark alliteration, unconventional rhythms, and vivid imagery.

VICTORIAN POETRY / *"PIED BEAUTY"* **761**

ENRICHMENT ACTIVITIES

Suggest that students read other poems by Hopkins in order to become more familiar with the concept of sprung rhythm. Have students write a few lines that celebrate nature, using sprung rhythm.

SUPPORT FOR LEP STUDENTS

Students might work with a partner on this poem. Suggest to students that the beauty of Hopkins's poems lies as much in how the words sound when read as in what they mean.

ADDITIONAL VOCABULARY
counter—contrary
charged—energized
tread—step
bleared—blurred; dimmed

VOCABULARY FROM THE SELECTION

dappled   stipple

GOALS/OBJECTIVES

Studying this lesson will enable students to

- experience the speaker's feelings of joy in the variety of wonders in the world
- describe the significance of Gerard Manley Hopkins's writings
- define *sprung rhythm* and identify it in a poem
- use a thesaurus to find synonyms and antonyms
- use evaluating techniques in reading
- define *alliteration, repetition,* and *rhyme* and recognize and analyze them in a poem
- write a persuasive essay

PREREADING NOTES

READER'S JOURNAL

If they are willing, students should share their lists with the class.

RESEARCH SKILLS

Students might try to match the words in the list of synonyms they created with items in the list of dazzling things they created in their reader's journal.

ANSWERS TO GUIDED READING QUESTIONS

❶ The main idea of the poem is to praise God for natural beauty.

❷ God does not change.

ANSWERS TO SELECTION CHECK TEST 4.9.21

EX. What kinds of things does the speaker express thankfulness for in the first line of the poem?
The speaker expresses thankfulness for "dappled things."

1. What are "of couple-colour as a brinded cow"?
Skies are of "couple-colour as a brinded cow."

2. What creatures have "rose-moles all in stipple" upon them?
Trout do.

3. What birds are mentioned in the poem?
Finches are mentioned in the poem.

4. How does the speaker feel toward things that are counter, original, spare, and strange?
The speaker loves these things and is grateful for them.

5. What, according to the speaker, is past change, or unchanging?
God is past change, or unchanging.

READER'S JOURNAL

Make a list in your journal of things that are dazzling to look upon. Try to include in your list as many oddities as you can—the crimson face of a baboon, for example, or the large white polka dots on the giant whale shark.

RESEARCH SKILLS

Read the Language Arts Survey, 4.25, "Using Thesauruses." Look up the word *pied* in a thesaurus. Find as many synonyms and antonyms for the word as you can. List these in your journal. Think about the specific connotations that each word has.

"Pied¹ Beauty"

GERARD MANLEY HOPKINS

❶
What is the main idea of this poem, expressed in the first line?

Glory be to God for <u>dappled</u> things—
    For skies of couple-colour as a brinded² cow;
      For rose-moles all in <u>stipple</u> upon trout that swim;
Fresh-firecoal chestnut-falls,³ finches' wings;
    Landscape plotted and pieced—fold, fallow, and plough;⁴
      And áll trádes, their gear and tackle and trim.

❷
According to the speaker, how does God differ from the world, which is so varied and changeable?

All things counter, original, spare,⁵ strange;
    Whatever is fickle, freckled (who knows how?)
      With swift, slow; sweet, sour; adazzle, dim;
He fathers-forth whose beauty is past change:
              Praise him. ■

5

10

---

1. **Pied.** Marked with blotches of color
2. **brinded.** Brownish orange streaked with gray
3. **Fresh-firecoal chestnut-falls.** Freshly fallen chestnuts, red as coals
4. **fold . . . plough.** The land is colored in patches from the pastures or folds, fallow, unplowed fields, and plowed land.
5. **spare.** Rare

WORDS FOR EVERYDAY USE:
dap • pled (dap´ əld) *adj.,* marked with spots
stip • ple (stip´ əl) *adj.,* flecked

VOCABULARY IN CONTEXT

• The Dalmatian was white <u>dappled</u> with black.
• You can create a <u>stippled</u> look by shaking a paintbrush over your canvas.

Responding to the Selection

Hopkins's "Pied Beauty" is a celebration of the astonishing variety and intricacy in the natural world. What examples does Hopkins give of this variety and intricacy? What examples would you add to his list? What things in the natural world do you think of as unique, peculiar, and amazing?

Reviewing the Selection

RECALLING

1. What things from nature are mentioned in lines 1–5 of the poem?

2. With what request does this poem end?

INTERPRETING

3. What do the things from nature mentioned in lines 1–5 have in common?

4. What particular aspect of God does the speaker want the reader to see as worthy of praise?

SYNTHESIZING

5. How do lines 7–9 extend the idea presented in lines 1–6? What effect does the speaker's list have on the reader? What point is the speaker making about the world? What is the source of all these varied things? How is God different from the world?

Understanding Literature (Questions for Discussion)

1. **Alliteration. Alliteration** is the repetition of initial consonant sounds. What examples of alliteration can you find in this poem? What other repeated sounds can you find?

2. **Sprung Rhythm. Sprung rhythm** is the term coined by Gerard Manley Hopkins to describe the unique metrical forms of his verse. The metrical feet employed by Hopkins include a foot consisting of a single strongly stressed syllable and feet containing a strongly stressed syllable followed by one, two, or three weakly stressed syllables. Try scanning this poem, marking the stressed syllables. At what point in the poem do several strongly stressed syllables appear in a row?

3. **Theme and Paradox.** The **theme** is a central idea in a literary work. A **paradox** is a contradictory statement, idea, or event. What, according to the poem, is the source of the multitudinous variety in the world perceived through our senses? How does this source differ from the world? What paradoxical commentary is the speaker making about God?

VICTORIAN POETRY / "PIED BEAUTY" **763**

ANSWERS FOR UNDERSTANDING LITERATURE (CONT.)

"plotted and pieced—fold, fallow, and plough," "fickle, freckled," "swift, slow; sweet, sour," and "fathers-forth." Another repeated sound occurs in "fickle, freckled."

▶ **Teaching Note:** Discuss with students why alliteration might be used by a writer. Have students read the poem aloud. Did they enjoy reading the alliterative parts of the poem?

2. **Sprung Rhythm.** Line 6 has several strongly stressed

syllables.

▶ **Teaching Note:** Review other forms of rhythm as students discuss how Hopkins's "sprung rhythm" is unique.

3. **Theme and Paradox.** The source of variety in the world is God. God never changes. It is paradoxical that all the great variety of nature was created by a being that never varies.

RESPONDING TO THE SELECTION

Students may wish to refer to back issues of nature magazines for specific examples of oddities in the natural world.

ANSWERS FOR REVIEWING THE SELECTION

RECALLING

1. The following natural things are mentioned in lines 1–5: the sky, a brinded cow, the spots on trout, freshly fallen chestnuts, the wings of finches, and farm fields.

2. The speaker requests that readers praise God.

INTERPRETING

Responses will vary. Possible responses are given.

3. All the items from nature in lines 1–5 are either spotty themselves or create a spotty appearance, such as chestnuts on the ground.

4. The speaker finds particularly praiseworthy the fact that God can create beautiful things in infinite variety, yet be unchanging.

SYNTHESIZING

Responses will vary. A possible response is given.

5. Rather than providing examples of things that are pied, Hopkins provides words to describe the appearance of these things. He allows the reader to come up with her or his own list of things that correspond to each adjective. The world has an endless variety of beautiful things. The source of all of these varied things is God. God does not change.

ANSWERS FOR UNDERSTANDING LITERATURE

▶ See the evaluation forms for discussion, active listening, and oral communication, *Assessment Portfolio, 7.11–7.14.*

Responses will vary. Possible responses are given.

1. **Alliteration.** Examples of alliteration in this poem include: "Glory be to God," "couple-colour," "Fresh-firecoal chestnut-falls, finches' wings,"

(cont.)

TEACHER'S EDITION **763**

PREREADING NOTES

READER'S JOURNAL

Students should think about how recent discoveries about ecology and the environment affect the conclusion of Hopkins's poem.

THINKING SKILLS

• Students should decide whether the passage of almost one hundred years should have any effect on the interpretation of this poem.

• If students were reading this poem one hundred years ago, might they agree with Hopkins's argument?

• Might Hopkins be so optimistic about nature if he were writing the poem today?

ANSWER TO GUIDED READING QUESTION

❶ Nature never runs out.

ANSWERS TO SELECTION CHECK TEST 4.9.23

EX. With what, according to the speaker, is the world charged?
The world is charged with the grandeur of God.

1. The speaker mentions an object that shines when shaken. What is that object?
That object is foil.

2. According to the poem, what oozes when crushed?
Oil oozes when crushed.

3. According to the poem, what do men not now reck, or heed?
They do not reck God's rod.

4. What can feet not now do and why?
They cannot feel, being shod, or covered with shoes.

5. To what is the Holy Ghost compared at the end of the poem?
It is compared to a brooding bird.

READER'S JOURNAL

What effects have humankind's actions had on the natural environment? What has happened as a result of human industry? How resilient is nature? How capable is nature of absorbing the shocks of human actions such as building factories and roads?

THINKING SKILLS

Read the Language Arts Survey, 4.11, "Generalizing." Then, after you read Hopkins's poem, determine what conclusion Hopkins comes to and list the evidence that he presents to support that conclusion.

"God's Grandeur"

GERARD MANLEY HOPKINS

The world is charged with the grandeur of God.
    It will flame out, like shining from shook foil;[1]
    It gathers to a greatness, like the ooze of oil
Crushed.[2] Why do men then now not reck[3] his rod?
5 Generations have trod, have trod, have trod;
    And all is seared with trade; bleared, smeared with toil;
    And wears man's smudge and shares man's smell: the soil
Is bare now, nor can foot feel, being shod.

And for all this, nature is never spent;
10   There lives the dearest freshness deep down things;
And though the last lights off the black West went
    Oh, morning, at the brown brink eastward, springs—
Because the Holy Ghost over the bent
    World broods with warm breast and with ah! bright wings. ∎

❶ *Despite the great age of the world and the many generations that have come and gone, what remains true of nature, according to the speaker?*

---

1. **foil.** Gold foil which glares in the light
2. **ooze . . . Crushed.** Droplets of oil scattered by crushing, gathered back together again. The idea here is that the greatness of God, however diffused in the world, cannot be diminished.
3. **reck.** Reckon with; heed

764 UNIT NINE / THE VICTORIAN AGE

BIOGRAPHICAL NOTE

Students may have difficulty with line 2. Hopkins explained the line in a letter to his friend Robert Bridges. "I mean foil in its sense of leaf or tinsel. . . . Shaken gold foil gives off broad glares like sheet lightning and also, and this is true of nothing else, owing to its zig-zag dints and creasings and network of small many cornered facets, a sort of fork lightning too." (From *Letters of Gerard Manley Hopkins to Robert Bridges.*, Ed. C. C. Abbott. 1955. page 169.)

Responding to the Selection

What abuses of nature are mentioned in Hopkins's poem? What other more contemporary abuses can you add to Hopkins's list? Do you agree with Hopkins that despite these abuses, "There lives the dearest freshness deep down things"?

Reviewing the Selection

RECALLING

1. What, according to line 1, is the world charged with?

2. What, according to line 2 of the poem, happens to the grandeur of God?

3. To what does the speaker compare the grandeur of God in lines 3 and 4?

4. What, according to line 6 of the poem, has happened to all things? What has happened, according to line 8, to the soil and to humankind's connection to it?

INTERPRETING

▶▶ 5. With what force is the word *charge* ordinarily associated? What is Hopkins saying about the relationship of God to the world?

▶▶ 6. Think about line 2 of the poem. According to the speaker, how do you imagine the grandeur of God will show itself?

▶▶ 7. In what way might the grandeur of God be similar to oil that, when diffused by crushing, gathers itself back together into the "greatness" of droplets?

▶▶ 8. Does the speaker believe that humankind's actions have irrevocably destroyed nature? Why, or why not?

SYNTHESIZING

9. What change of mood occurs in lines 9–14 of the poem? What does the speaker believe still exists "deep down"? What example of the resilience, or coming back, of nature does the speaker give in lines 11 and 12?

10. To what does the speaker attribute the resilience of nature? What force broods "over the bent/World"?

ANALYTIC SCALES FOR RESPONDING IN WRITING

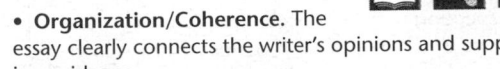

Assign a score from 1 to 25 for each grading criterion below. (For more detailed evaluation, see the evaluation forms for writing, revising, and proofreading, *Assessment Portfolio,* 7.1–7.10.)

Persuasive Essay

• **Content/Unity.** The essay presents a sensible discussion of an opinion on how humanity affects nature, with the intent being to persuade the reader.

• **Organization/Coherence.** The essay clearly connects the writer's opinions and supporting evidence.

• **Language/Style.** The essay uses vivid and precise nouns, verbs, and modifiers.

• **Conventions.** The essay avoids errors in spelling, grammar, usage, mechanics, and manuscript form.

RESPONDING TO THE SELECTION

Students may wish to work with a partner to answer these questions, and then to share their answers with a small group.

ANSWERS FOR REVIEWING THE SELECTION

RECALLING

1. The world is charged with the greatness of God.

2. The grandeur of God makes itself known dramatically.

3. The grandeur of God is like droplets of oil that have been scattered and then pull themselves back together into one pool.

4. All things are dirtied by industry and commerce. The soil is barren and humankind is separated from the earth.

INTERPRETING

Responses will vary. Possible responses are given.

5. The word *charge* is usually associated with electricity. Here it means that God is the motivating force—the energy—in the world.

6. The grandeur of God will flare dramatically, perhaps as lightning.

7. The greatness of God has a unifying force, despite its diffusion over the world. This is much like the tendency of oil droplets to pull together once they have been separated.

8. No. The speaker believes that nature will always endure; "nature is never spent."

SYNTHESIZING

Responses will vary. Possible responses are given.

9. In lines 9–14 the mood of the poem shifts from one that outlines humankind's abuses of nature to one that celebrates nature's freshness, which still exists "deep down." In lines 11 and 12, the speaker says that the continued rising and setting of the sun is an example of nature's resilience.

10. The speaker attributes the resilience of nature to the Holy Ghost, or God, who "broods" "over the bent/World."

►See the evaluation forms for discussion, active listening, and oral communication, *Assessment Portfolio, 7.11–7.14.*

Responses will vary. Possible responses are given.

1. Metaphor. The speaker compares the grandeur of God to electricity in line 1; to fire or a bright flash in line 2; and to droplets of oil that gather together in lines 3 and 4. The grandeur of God brings life to the world, it flashes out all at once, and it is ever present in small amounts. The Holy Ghost is compared to a bird in the last lines of the poem. Both watch carefully over their broods.

►**Teaching Note:** Have students suggest other metaphors that might be used for the Holy Ghost.

2. Sonnet. The grandeur of God is ever present and nature has been overused. The first four lines discuss the grandeur of God. The second four lines describe how the earth has been worn by humanity. The sestet insists that nature is never worn out. Nature will never wear out because God is watching over us. The rhyme scheme is *abbaabba cdcdcd.* The rhyme scheme changes where the octave and sestet break.

►**Teaching Note:** Discuss with students the look of the poem. How has Hopkins chosen to indent the lines of the poem?

3. Symbol. Other symbols of birth include morning and sunrise and a brooding bird. The Holy Spirit is ever present and watches over humanity much like a mother bird watches over her eggs.

►**Teaching Note:** Discuss with students what other symbols for birth or rebirth they have encountered in other poems in this book.

4. Alliteration, Repetition, and Rhyme. Alliteration ties together "grandeur of God," "shining from shook foil," "gathers to a greatness, like the ooze of oil," "reck his rod," "last lights," and "brown brink." The repetition in line 5 is "have trod, have trod, have trod."

(cont.)

Understanding Literature (Questions for Discussion)

1. **Metaphor.** A **metaphor** is a figure of speech in which one thing is spoken or written about as if it were another. This figure of speech invites the reader to make a comparison between two things. To what does the speaker compare the grandeur of God in line 1? in line 2? in lines 3 and 4? What is the speaker saying about God's grandeur in each of these metaphors? To what does the speaker compare the Holy Ghost in the last lines of the poem? What similarity does the Holy Ghost have with a brooding bird (one that incubates its eggs with its warm breast, making it possible for them to break forth in life)?

2. **Sonnet.** A **sonnet** is a fourteen-line poem that follows one of a number of different rhyme schemes. The **Italian** or **Petrarchan** sonnet is divided into two parts: an octave followed by a six-line sestet. What two ideas are presented in the octave of this poem? What description is presented in the first four lines of the octave? What description is presented in the second four lines of the octave? What point is made about nature in the opening of the sestet? To what does the speaker attribute nature's characteristics in the rest of the sestet? What is the rhyme scheme of this sonnet? How does the rhyme scheme help to mirror the division of the poem into parts?

3. **Symbol.** A **symbol** is a thing that stands for or represents both itself and something else. Dawn is a traditional symbol of rebirth. What other references to impending birth are made in the sestet of this poem? What role, according to the speaker, does the Holy Spirit play in the world?

4. **Alliteration, Repetition, and Rhyme.** **Alliteration** is the repetition of initial consonant sounds. **Repetition** is the use, again, of a sound, word, phrase, sentence, or other element. **Rhyme** is the repetition of sounds at the ends of words. **Internal rhyme** is rhyme that occurs within lines. In this poem, Hopkins uses alliteration, repetition, and internal rhyme to tie together key ideas. What words are tied together by alliteration in the poem? What example of repetition appears in line 5? How does this repetition mirror the sense of the line? What internal rhymes are used in lines 6 and 7? What ideas are tied together by these internal rhymes?

Responding in Writing

Persuasive Essay. In a **persuasive essay,** you take a particular point of view and support it with evidence. Hopkins argues in "God's Grandeur," written during the beginnings of the Industrial Revolution, that despite the actions of people, "nature is never spent." Is what Hopkins said still true? Write a persuasive essay on the subject of whether or not humankind has the capability of destroying nature. Is it possible for human actions to exhaust nature? Can you think of counterexamples to Hopkins's claim? Note that the contemporary Harvard zoologist and essayist Stephen Jay Gould has written that while it is possible for humans to bring about ecological disasters, it is presumptuous of us to think that we can destroy nature. Even, he says, if we make the planet uninhabitable for ourselves, nature will endure. Does Gould's comment support Hopkins's claim?

ANSWERS FOR UNDERSTANDING LITERATURE (CONT.)

This repetition mirrors the countless numbers of feet that have trod over the earth. In lines 6 and 7, internal rhymes include *seared, bleared,* and *smeared,* and *wears* and *shares.* All of these rhymes support the idea that the earth has been dirtied by humanity.

►**Teaching Note:** Discuss with students other rhymes Hopkins uses in his poem, specifically end, slant, and exact.

ANALYTIC SCALES FOR RESPONDING IN WRITING

Grading scales appear on page 765.

PREREADING

from *Sing-Song*
"In an Artist's Studio"
by Christina Rossetti

"Promises Like Pie-Crust"
"A Birthday"

ABOUT THE AUTHOR

Christina Rossetti (1830–1894) grew up in a stimulating Anglo-Italian family, the daughter of an exiled Italian poet and politician. In her household, Italian exiles gathered and talked of politics, art, and literature. She and her brothers, Dante and William, wrote poetry and did artwork from childhood on. A deeply religious person, Rossetti became involved in a contemporary movement to restore elements of Catholicism to Anglican religious services. However, her commitment to the Anglican Church was strong enough that she broke off an engagement with one suitor because of his conversion to Catholicism. She later broke off a second relationship because her suitor was insufficiently interested in religion.

Rossetti lived a quiet, thoughtful life, often doing charitable works such as volunteering at a home of the kind that we would today call a "women's shelter." Rossetti's first book of poetry, *Goblin Market and Other Poems*, published in 1862, was an immediate success. The title poem seems, on the surface, to tell a simple children's story, but beneath the simplicity lies a depth of religious symbolism.

Rossetti's brother Dante helped to found a group of writers, artists, and critics known as the Pre-Raphaelite Brotherhood whose purpose was to promote simplicity, naturalness, and expressiveness in art and literature, on the model of artwork done in Italy before the Renaissance. Christina Rossetti's exquisite poetry is often described as Pre-Raphaelite because of its surface simplicity and gracefulness, achieved through a rarely paralleled technical mastery. However, the simplicity of surface in Rossetti's poetry masks a complexity of thought and feeling. Her poems bear reading again and again.

For years, readers and critics tended to dismiss Rossetti because of the sheer variety and magnitude of work by her more famous male contemporaries Tennyson and Browning. However, in recent years her reputation has grown tremendously as readers rediscover the fine artistry of her work. More than any other poet of her age, she exemplifies the common critical observation that a writer must work very hard to make a piece seem simple and easy.

ABOUT THE SELECTIONS

Sing-Song is a collection of Rossetti's children's verse. The selections given here from that volume have all the natural grace of children's rhymes produced by the oral tradition. "**In an Artist's Studio**" shows Rossetti in a realistic, critical vein, commenting on the tendency of male artists to distort their portrayals of women. "**Promises Like Pie-Crust**" and "**A Birthday**" are eloquent, though very different, commentaries on love.

VICTORIAN POETRY **767**

GOALS/OBJECTIVES

Studying this lesson will enable students to

- enjoy the simple beauty of Rossetti's lyric poetry
- describe Rossetti's literary accomplishments and explain the historical significance of her writings
- define *parallelism*, *alliteration*, and *chiasmus* and recognize and analyze them in a poem

- identify participles, gerunds, and infinitives
- write nursery rhymes, art criticism, and comparison and contrast essays
- define *metaphor*, *connotation*, and *symbol*, and recognize and interpret them in a poem

---

READER'S JOURNAL

Students should choose one nursery rhyme from their childhood. They can then use what they have learned about poetry to analyze its rhyme scheme, to identify what kind of rhyme it uses, and to determine the rhyme's meter, and so on.

THINKING SKILLS

Ask students to identify the basis of each comparison and of each contrast. If necessary, explain that some objects mentioned in the poem are not compared or contrasted to anything else.

▶Additional practice is provided in the *Essential Skills Practice Book: Study and Research,* 4.8.

ANSWER TO GUIDED READING QUESTION

❶ We can come to know things that we cannot directly observe by seeing how they react with things we can observe.

ANSWERS TO SELECTION CHECK TEST 4.9.25

EX. According to the poem, what has a rainy sound?
The wind has a rainy sound.

1. What does the speaker wonder about the ships?
She wonders whether they will go down, or sink.

2. According to the speaker, what tumble from their tree?
Apples tumble from their tree.

3. What has no one seen?
No one has seen the wind.

4. What is prettier than boats on the rivers and ships on the seas?
Clouds are prettier than these.

5. What is prettier than bridges on the rivers?
The bow that bridges heaven, the rainbow, is prettier.

READER'S JOURNAL

What children's poems or nursery rhymes do you remember from your childhood? How might exposure to such rhymes in childhood help one to appreciate music and poetry later on?

THINKING SKILLS

Read the Language Arts Survey, 4.8, "Comparing and Contrasting." Then, as you read the verses below from *Sing-Song,* observe the contrasts that the speaker draws between natural and artificial things.

FROM
Sing-Song

CHRISTINA ROSSETTI

The wind has such a rainy sound
   Moaning through the town,
The sea has such a windy sound—
   Will the ships go down?

5 The apples in the orchard
   Tumble from their tree.
Oh, will the ships go down, go down,
   In the windy sea?

♦ ♦ ♦

❶
How can we come to know about things that we cannot directly observe?

Who has seen the wind?
10   Neither I nor you;
But when the leaves hang trembling
   The wind is passing through.

Who has seen the wind?
   Neither you nor I;
15 But when the trees bow down their heads
   The wind is passing by.

♦ ♦ ♦

Boats sail on the rivers,
   And ships sail on the seas;
But clouds that sail across the sky
20   Are prettier far than these.

There are bridges on the rivers,
   As pretty as you please;
But the bow that bridges heaven,
   And overtops the trees,
25 And builds a road from earth to sky,
   Is prettier far than these. ∎

VOCABULARY FROM THE SELECTIONS

dais

halcyon

Responding to the Selection

Memorize the lines from Rossetti's *Sing-Song* and try them out on a young child that you know. Do you consider these lines to be great children's verse? Why, or why not?

Reviewing the Selection

RECALLING

1. What interesting reversal of the roles of wind and water does the speaker make in lines 1 and 3 of the selection?

2. What question does the speaker ask after noting the sounds of the wind and the sea in stanza 1?

3. What evidence of the existence of the wind is spoken of in stanzas 3 and 4?

4. What things are contrasted in stanzas 5 and 6?

INTERPRETING

5. What lesson do stanzas 1 and 2 of the selection teach children about making observations and conclusions?

6. What is ominous about stanzas 1 and 2? How does that ominousness contrast with the sound of the verse?

7. How does the speaker show people's ability to make deductions about unseen things on the basis of what they can see?

8. What point is the speaker making in stanzas 5 and 6 about the relative value of artificial and natural things?

SYNTHESIZING

9. What images, repeated throughout the selection, tie it together and give it unity?

10. How is the speaker's point about deducing the existence of unseen things related to her point about the superiority of nature?

Understanding Literature (Questions for Discussion)

1. **Nursery Rhyme.** A **nursery rhyme** is children's verse. Often nursery rhymes make use of rhyme and of repeated elements, including words, phrases, and images. What repeated words and phrases can you find in this poem?

2. **Chiasmus.** A **chiasmus** is a rhetorical technique in which the order of occurrence of words or phrases is reversed, as in the line "we can weather changes, but we can't change the weather." What examples of chiasmus can you find in this poem?

VICTORIAN POETRY / FROM SING SONG **769**

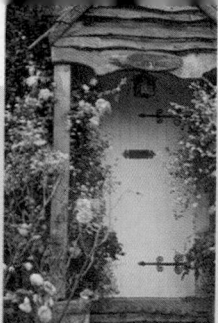

"In an Artist's Studio"

CHRISTINA ROSSETTI

One face looks out from all his canvases,
   One selfsame figure sits or walks or leans:
   We found her hidden just behind those screens,
That mirror gave back all her loveliness.
5   A queen in opal or in ruby dress,
   A nameless girl in freshest summer-greens,
   A saint, an angel—every canvas means
The same one meaning, neither more nor less.
He feeds upon her face by day and night,
10   And she with true kind eyes looks back on him,
Fair as the moon and joyful as the light:
   Not wan with waiting, not with sorrow dim;
Not as she is, but was when hope shone bright;
   Not as she is, but as she fills his dream. ■

❶ *What is not shown in the painter's canvases?*

Responding to the Selection

Does the speaker believe that the painter has represented his subject truly, as she really is? How do you know? What sameness does the speaker find in the expressions on the canvases? What realities does the speaker imagine the painter might have failed to see?

Reviewing the Selection

RECALLING

1. What similarity has the speaker recognized in the painter's canvases?

2. Where, according to the speaker, have "We found her [the model] hidden"?

3. What "gave back all her loveliness"?

4. What verb is used in line 9 to describe the painter's repeated use of this model's face?

INTERPRETING

▶▶ 5. What evidence suggests that the painter used one model many times?

▶▶ 6. What does line 3 mean? What might the line mean if "those screens" is taken to mean the paintings themselves, which screen reality?

▶▶ 7. Shakespeare wrote that drama was a mirror held up to nature. Can the same thing be said of some painting? Explain.

▶▶ 8. What does the verb used in line 9 suggest about the painter?

SYNTHESIZING

9. What does the face depicted on the canvases look like? What is unrealistic about that face appearing, in the same way, over and over again?

10. What might once have been true of the model? What does the painter repeatedly depict?

Understanding Literature (Questions for Discussion)

Metaphor and Connotation. A **metaphor** is a figure of speech in which one thing is spoken or written about as if it were another. A **connotation** is an emotional association or implication attached to an expression. What metaphor is used to describe the painter's relationship toward his model? What are the connotations of the verb used to express this metaphor? What is ominous or ugly about the suggested relationship?

VICTORIAN POETRY / "IN AN ARTIST'S STUDIO" **771**

ANSWERS FOR UNDERSTANDING LITERATURE

▶ See the evaluation forms for discussion, active listening, and oral communication, *Assessment Portfolio,* 7.11–7.14.
Responses will vary. Possible responses are given.
Metaphor and Connotation. The image of eating is used as a metaphor. This metaphor shows the painter

as getting his nourishment and vitality from looking at the subject's face. The image is ugly when one thinks of pigs feeding greedily on slop or of parasites feeding on something rotten, such as a corpse. Perhaps the poet is suggesting that worshiping and idealizing the beloved can consume the beloved's individual identity.

RESPONDING TO THE SELECTION

If students need more direction, suggest that they look at the last line of the poem.

ANSWERS FOR REVIEWING THE SELECTION

RECALLING

1. The same woman appears in all of the artist's paintings.

2. The model is hidden "just behind those screens."

3. The mirror "gave back all her loveliness."

4. The verb *feeds* is used to describe the repeated use of the model's face.

INTERPRETING

Responses will vary. Possible responses are given.

5. Line 1 says that "One face looks out from all his canvases."

6. To understand the model, it is necessary to see beyond how the artist has portrayed her in his paintings. The paintings disguise her true identity.

7. The same thing cannot be said of the paintings in this poem because the artist does not paint his model's nature or essence but his personal and unrealistic vision of her.

8. The use of the word *feeds* suggests that he devours her beauty and is sustained by her, but she is powerless in the relationship.

SYNTHESIZING

Responses will vary. Possible responses are given.

9. The faces that appear in the paintings are young, beautiful, and hopeful. It is unrealistic to suppose that the model will remain unchanged by age or will always be hopeful. These portraits take away most of her personality by reflecting only one small aspect of her identity.

10. At one time the model was apparently in love with the artist. The painter repeatedly depicts how she looked when she loved him then—that is, how she looks in his dreams rather than in reality.

PREREADING NOTES

READER'S JOURNAL

If students cannot think of a real example, suggest that they imagine a situation in which an untrustworthy friend wants to borrow a prized possession.

THINKING SKILLS

Students should consider the words the speaker chooses to turn down her suitor.

▶ Additional practice is provided in the *Essential Skills Practice Book: Study and Research,* 4.3.

ANSWERS TO SELECTION CHECK TEST 4.9.29

EX. In line 1, what does the speaker ask her suitor not to do?
She asks him not to make promises to her.

1. What does the speaker wish to "hold . . . uncast"?
She wants to "hold the die uncast."

2. Who is now cold, and who is warm?
The speaker is cold, and the suitor, or person being addressed, is warm.

3. What is not told because of a fading image?
Their fortune is not told.

4. According to the speaker, what might the suitor do if he did make promises?
He might later grieve for his lost liberty.

5. Of what, according to the speaker, might some people perish?
They might perish of excess.

ANSWERS TO GUIDED READING QUESTIONS

❶ The speaker wants the person addressed not to make any promises.

❷ The speaker wants to remain friends with the person addressed.

READER'S JOURNAL

Have you ever had to deny someone something that he or she wanted of you? How can a person do that with dignity and grace? Write about this question in your journal.

THINKING SKILLS

Read the Language Arts Survey, 4.3, "Strategies for Decision Making." Then, as you read the poem, ask yourself these questions: Why has the speaker decided not to enter into a lifelong union with the person whom she is addressing? Do you consider the reasons that she offers to be sound? Why, or why not?

"Promises Like Pie-Crust"

CHRISTINA ROSSETTI

❶ *What does the speaker want the person addressed not to do?*

> Promise me no promises,
>   So will I not promise you:
> Keep we both our liberties,
>   Never false and never true:
> 5 Let us hold the die uncast,
>   Free to come as free to go:
> For I cannot know your past,
>   And of mine what can you know?
>
> You, so warm, may once have been
> 10   Warmer towards another one:
> I, so cold, may once have seen
>   Sunlight, once have felt the sun:
> Who shall show us if it was
>   Thus indeed in time of old?
> 15 Fades the image from the glass,
>   And the fortune is not told.
>
> If you promised, you might grieve
>   For lost liberty again:
> If I promised, I believe
> 20   I should fret to break the chain.
> Let us be the friends we were,
>   Nothing more but nothing less:
> Many thrive on frugal fare
>   Who would perish of excess. ■

❷ *What sort of relationship does the speaker want to have?*

SUPPORT FOR LEP STUDENTS

Discuss with students the use of the word *promise* in the first two lines of the poem. The word is used both as a noun and as a verb. What other words can students think of that can be used as both nouns and verbs?

ANSWERS FOR UNDERSTANDING LITERATURE

▶ See the evaluation forms for discussion, active listening, and oral communication, *Assessment Portfolio,* 7.11–7.14.

Responses will vary. Possible responses are given.

Metaphor and Symbol. The die uncast shows that the speaker feels that love is a gamble. Warmth and coldness reflect the intensity of feeling or lack thereof for each character. Sunlight and the sun represent

(cont.)

Responding to the Selection

The speaker in this poem says that the image has faded from the glass and "the fortune is not told." She admits that she cannot predict what life would be like with the person whom she is addressing. However, she has her doubts whether such a life would be right for her. Do you consider these to be legitimate concerns? Why, or why not?

Reviewing the Selection

RECALLING

1. What does the speaker ask her suitor not to do in line 1 of the poem?

2. To what in line 5 does the speaker compare making the decision to join with a mate?

3. According to line 6, what will be true of both the speaker and her suitor if they do not unite?

4. Who, according to the poem, is warm, and who is cold?

SYNTHESIZING

9. How are promises like pie-crust? Why does the speaker reject them?

10. What kind of relationship does the speaker want?

INTERPRETING

5. What, according to the speaker, will be the consequence of not making promises to one another?

6. What does the speaker's choice of metaphor in line 5 suggest about her feelings about choosing a mate?

7. Does a romantic union mean that people are not, as a result, "Free to come as free to go"? Why, or why not?

8. What does the speaker suggest about the relationship by her use of the terms *warm* and *cold?*

Understanding Literature (Questions for Discussion)

Metaphor and Symbol. A **metaphor** is a figure of speech in which one thing is spoken or written about as if it were another. A **symbol** is a thing that stands for or represents both itself and something else. What is the significance of the following metaphors and symbols in the poem: the die uncast, warmth and coldness, sunlight and the sun, the fading of the image in the glass, breaking the chain, and frugal fare? How does the crust differ from the whole pie? What does the metaphor of the title suggest about the relationship that the speaker wants?

ANSWERS FOR UNDERSTANDING LITERATURE (CONT.)

warm feelings. The fading image alludes to fortune-telling—an image fading from a crystal ball. Breaking the chain is the wording the speaker uses for getting out of a relationship. Frugal fare is their friendship as opposed to the excess of a love affair. Pie-crust crumbles easily and is less substantial than the rest of the pie. The speaker wants a relationship in which the two will not feel obliged to make promises that probably won't be kept.

▶**Teaching Note:** Discuss with students whether they think that a friendship with the speaker of this poem would be very satisfying. Why, or why not? Do they share the speaker's ideas of friendship? In what ways are their views similar? How are they different?

RESPONDING TO THE SELECTION

Students may find it helpful to consider what qualities they feel are necessary or important in a relationship.

ANSWERS FOR REVIEWING THE SELECTION

RECALLING

1. The speaker asks her suitor not to make her any promises.

2. The speaker compares the decision to rolling dice.

3. If the speaker and suitor do not unite, they will be free to come and go as they please.

4. The suitor is warm and the speaker is cold.

INTERPRETING

Responses will vary. Possible responses are given.

5. If promises are not made, the speaker and suitor will not have to break them.

6. The metaphor in line 5 suggests that the speaker feels that choosing a mate is like gambling.

7. Yes; one has certain responsibilities to the other person in the relationship.

8. The use of the words *warm* and *cold* suggests that the speaker is not particularly interested in her suitor or in any other suitor.

SYNTHESIZING

Responses will vary. Possible responses are given.

9. Promises are like pie-crust in that both are easily broken. The speaker rejects them so that neither she nor her suitor will have to break them.

10. The speaker wants a friendly, not romantic, relationship with her suitor. The speaker seems unwilling to have stronger attachments than friendship because she values honesty and freedom too much to risk compromising them.

PREREADING NOTES

READER'S JOURNAL

Students may want to explain how they felt by making comparisons. They can then liken their comparisons to those of Rossetti.

THINKING SKILLS

Some students may wish to brainstorm qualities of the object to which the speaker compares her heart. They can then decide which qualities apply to the comparison.

ANSWERS TO GUIDED READING QUESTIONS

❶ The speaker compares her heart to a singing bird, an apple tree, and a rainbow shell.

❷ The first birthday is when the speaker was born. The second birthday is when the speaker found love. The speaker's love is important enough to seem like a rebirth.

ANSWERS TO SELECTION CHECK TEST 4.9.31

EX. To what does the speaker compare her heart in the first line of the poem?

She compares it to a singing bird.

1. To what kind of tree does the speaker compare her heart?

She compares it to an apple tree laden with fruit.

2. What "paddles in a halcyon sea"?

A rainbow shell "paddles in a halcyon sea."

3. Why is the speaker's heart so glad?

The speaker's heart is so glad because her love has come to her.

4. According to the speaker, what has a hundred eyes?

Peacocks have a hundred eyes.

5. What birthday is the speaker celebrating?

The speaker is celebrating the birthday of her life.

READER'S JOURNAL

Have you ever felt overwhelming joy? What caused you to feel that way? What things would fulfill you most? make you happiest? In what sense is feeling joy a kind of rebirth? Write about these questions in your journal.

THINKING SKILLS

Read the Language Arts Survey, 4.8, "Comparing and Contrasting." Then, as you read the first stanza of the poem, ask yourself what similarities there are between the speaker's heart and the things to which the heart is compared.

"A Birthday"

CHRISTINA ROSSETTI

❶
To what does the speaker compare her heart?

My heart is like a singing bird
    Whose nest is in a watered shoot;
My heart is like an apple tree
    Whose boughs are bent with thickset fruit;
5 My heart is like a rainbow shell
    That paddles in a <u>halcyon</u> sea;
My heart is gladder than all these
    Because my love is come to me.

Raise me a <u>dais</u> of silk and down;
10   Hang it with vair[1] and purple dyes;[2]
Carve it in doves[3] and pomegranates,[4]
    And peacocks[5] with a hundred eyes;
Work in it gold and silver grapes,
    In leaves and silver fleurs-de-lys;[6]
15 Because the birthday of my life
    Is come, my love is come to me. ∎

❷
In what sense has the speaker had a second birthday? How important is the speaker's love to her?

---

1. **vair.** Gray and white fur used to trim fancy garments
2. **purple dyes.** In former days only royals were allowed to wear cloth-dyed purple.
3. **doves.** Traditional symbols of peace
4. **pomegranates.** Type of fruit
5. **peacocks.** Splendid birds often kept in royal gardens
6. **fleurs-de-lys.** Flowers of the lily, found on coat of arms of the former French royal family

WORDS FOR EVERYDAY USE:

hal • cy • on (hal´sē ən) *adj.,* tranquil, happy

da • is (dā´is *or* dī´is) *n.,* raised platform, as for a seat of honor

---

VOCABULARY IN CONTEXT

• The <u>halcyon</u> days of my childhood were those days I spent playing chess by the lake.
• The speakers were seated at the front of the auditorium on the <u>dais</u>.

Responding to the Selection

Describe in your own words the scene portrayed by the speaker in the first six lines of stanza 2. If you, like this speaker, wished to create a scene perfect for the celebration of a great moment of happiness in your life, what would that scene look like?

Reviewing the Selection

RECALLING

1. To what does the speaker compare her heart in lines 1–2?

2. To what does the speaker compare her heart in lines 3–4?

3. To what does the speaker compare her heart in lines 5–6?

4. What does the speaker say of her heart in lines 7–8?

INTERPRETING

5. What similarities might exist between the things compared in lines 1–2?

6. What similarities might exist between the things compared in lines 3–4?

7. What similarities might exist between the things compared in lines 5–6?

8. How, at the end of the first stanza, does the speaker express that she feels a gladness beyond words?

SYNTHESIZING

9. In what sense has the speaker had a birthday? What has caused the speaker to feel reborn?

10. How would you feel if you were the recipient of this poem? What would it feel like to bring someone else this much joy?

Understanding Literature (Questions for Discussion)

1. **Parallelism. Parallelism** is a literary technique in which a writer emphasizes the equal value or weight of two or more ideas by expressing them in the same grammatical form. What example of parallelism can you find in the first stanza?

2. **Alliteration. Alliteration** is the repetition of initial consonant sounds. Much of the musical effect of this poem is achieved through alliteration. What examples of alliteration can you find in lines 4, 9, 10–12, 13, 14, and 15? What example of repetition of whole words can you find in line 16?

VICTORIAN POETRY / "A BIRTHDAY" **775**

RESPONDING TO THE SELECTION

Students may wish to create a sketch along with a written description of their celebration.

ANSWERS FOR REVIEWING THE SELECTION

RECALLING

1. The speaker compares her heart to a singing bird.

2. The speaker compares her heart to an apple tree.

3. The speaker compares her heart to a rainbow shell.

4. The speaker says that her heart is happier than all of the items compared to it in the previous lines.

INTERPRETING

Responses will vary. Possible responses are given.

5. The speaker's heart may be said to be singing or flying.

6. The speaker's heart may be said to be luxuriant or rich, or the love could be considered successful.

7. The speaker's heart could be said to be tranquil or happy.

8. The speaker's gladness is beyond words because even the three comparisons she made were inadequate to express her feelings.

SYNTHESIZING

Responses will vary. Possible responses are given.

9. The speaker's life has completely changed, so much so that she feels reborn. Perhaps the emotions or qualities associated with childhood birthdays, such as joy and innocence, have been returned to the speaker. The speaker's new love makes the speaker feel reborn.

10. *Responses will vary. Students should give reasons for their answers.*

ANSWERS FOR UNDERSTANDING LITERATURE

▶ See the evaluation forms for discussion, active listening, and oral communication, *Assessment Portfolio, 7.11–7.14. Responses will vary. Possible responses are given.*

1. **Parallelism.** Examples of parallelism in the first stanza are a singing bird, an apple tree, and a rainbow shell.

▶ **Teaching Note:** Have students identify the grammatical form in which the parallel objects are expressed.

2. **Alliteration.** Examples include "boughs are bent"; "dais of silk and down"; purple, pomegranates, and peacocks; "gold and silver grapes"; "leaves and silver fleurs-de-lys"; and "Because the birthday."

▶ **Teaching Note:** The alliteration in this poem is very subtle. Students may find it easier to identify alliteration if they read the poem aloud with a partner.

Responding in Writing

1. **Nursery Rhyme.** Reread the verses from *Sing-Song,* and look up some Mother Goose nursery rhymes in your local library. Then try your hand at writing some nursery rhymes of your own. Here are some idea starters:

   —Write about animals and compare them to humans.
   —Retell, in verse, a familiar children's story such as "Jack and the Beanstalk," but update its characters, setting, events, and action.
   —Write a verse to teach children something such as the days of the week.

2. **Art Criticism.** Choose a famous artist from the past, such as Leonardo da Vinci, Pablo Picasso, John Singer Sargent, or Mary Cassatt, and study his or her depictions of women. Write an essay analyzing those depictions.

3. **Comparison and Contrast.** Write a short critical essay in which you compare and contrast the situations and sentiments expressed in "Promises Like Pie-Crust."

Language Lab

Verbals. Read the Language Arts Survey, 2.16–2.18, on verbals. Then find the participles, gerunds, and infinitives in the following lines from Rossetti's poems.

1. The wind has such a rainy sound
   Moaning through the town,
2. But when the leaves hang trembling
   The wind is passing through.
3. Not wan with waiting, not with sorrow dim;
4. Let us hold the die uncast,
   Free to come as free to go:
5. If I promised, I believe
   I should fret to break the chain.

PROJECT

Chapbook. A **chapbook** is a collection of works from different sources prepared for one's own pleasure or use. Christina Rossetti wrote some of the finest poems in our language on the subject of romantic love. Do some research to identify poems on other kinds of love— love for family members, friends, teachers, mentors; love for one's community, land, or country; love of learning or of art; and so on. Working with other members of your class, design and illustrate an anthology of poems on other kinds of love. You may wish to add works by classmates to the collection.

PREREADING

"To an Athlete Dying Young"
by A. E. Housman

ABOUT THE AUTHOR

Alfred Edward Housman (1859–1936) was a classical scholar and distinguished poet. Although Housman did not put forth a large body of work, his polished, simple style has been influential to a great many other poets.

Housman was born in Worcestershire, near the Shropshire countryside which often appears in his poetry. He attended Oxford University, and although he proved himself to be a brilliant student, he failed his final examination due to personal problems. Housman then went to work as a clerk in the Patent Office and spent ten years there. During this time, he spent evenings at the British Museum reading room studying Latin texts. He wrote articles about his studies and sent them to scholarly journals. Eventually fellow scholars took notice of his work, and in 1892 he was appointed professor of Latin at University College, London. Housman's major scholarly work was an annotated edition of the writings of Manilius. Housman's poetry books are *A Shropshire Lad*, which appeared in 1896, and *Last Poems*, which appeared nearly twenty-five years later. After Housman passed away, his brother published another volume called *More Poems*.

ABOUT THE SELECTION

"To an Athlete Dying Young" appears in Housman's first book, *A Shropshire Lad* (1896). This piece, like his others, is written in a simple style and is pessimistic in tone. The poem reflects Housman's common theme of the transience of youth, beauty, and friendship. The poem harkens back to classical elegies of Greece and Rome, which often dealt with the death of a young athlete or hero.

ADDITIONAL RESOURCES

READER'S GUIDE
- Selection Worksheet, 9.17

ASSESSMENT PORTFOLIO
- Selection Check Test, 4.9.33
- Selection Test, 4.9.34

ESSENTIAL SKILLS PRACTICE BOOKS
- *Study and Research*, 4.10

ENRICHMENT ACTIVITIES

English composer John Nicholson Ireland (1879–1962) wrote a number of short pieces set to poems by Thomas Hardy and A. E. Housman. (Some of these are recorded on the CD *John Ireland: English Songs*, by Rachel Ann Morgan and Tan Crone. EtCetera Records. KTC 1128.) Play a selection for students. Discuss with students why they think the composer chose that particular poem. Students should research other poems set to music and share their findings and the music with the class.

SUPPORT FOR LEP STUDENTS

ADDITIONAL VOCABULARY
threshold—doorway; entry
stiller—quieter
betimes—early; quickly
stopped—blocked
sill—door or window frame
lintel—crosspiece over a door or window

GOALS/OBJECTIVES

Studying this lesson will enable students to

- experience the speaker's feelings toward youth, glory, and death
- define *allusion* and recognize and interpret allusions in a poem
- define *aim* and *tone* and analyze the aim and tone of poems they read
- write a eulogy, a newspaper article, and images of change and victory

"To an Athlete Dying Young"

A. E. HOUSMAN

❶
What takes place in the first stanza? What takes place in the second stanza?

The time you won your town the race
We chaired[1] you through the market-place;
Man and boy stood cheering by,
And home we brought you shoulder-high.

5   Today, the road all runners come,
Shoulder-high we bring you home,
And set you at your threshold down,
Townsman of a stiller town.

❷
According to the speaker, what happens to an athlete's "glory"? Why is this particular athlete "Smart"?

         Smart lad, to slip betimes away
10   From fields where glory does not stay
And early though the laurel grows
It withers quicker than the rose.

         Eyes the shady night has shut
Cannot see the record cut,[2]
15   And silence sounds no worse than cheers
After earth has stopped the ears:

         Now you will not swell the rout
Of lads that wore their honors out,
Runners whom renown outran
20   And the name died before the man.

---
1. **chaired.** Carried you home in victory
2. **cut.** Broken

So set, before its echoes fade
The fleet foot on the sill of shade,
And hold to the low lintel up
The still-defended challenge-cup.

25   And round that early laurelled head
Will flock to gaze the strengthless dead
And find unwithered on its curls
The garland briefer than a girl's. ∎

Responding to the Selection

Do you agree with the sentiment expressed in this poem? How might you add to it? How might you argue with it?

Reviewing the Selection

RECALLING

1. What kind of athlete is featured in this poem? How did the crowd treat the athlete after he won a race?

2. In the third stanza, what does the speaker say about laurel and glory?

3. In the fifth stanza, what does the speaker say will not happen to the athlete who is the subject of this poem?

4. Where is this athlete to set his "fleet foot"? What will the athlete hold up at the doorway? At what will the "strengthless dead" flock to gaze?

INTERPRETING

5. What event is taking place in the second stanza? How is it similar to the event in the first stanza? How is it different?

6. Why does the speaker call the athlete a "Smart lad"? To what is laurel being compared in this stanza?

7. In what way might "the name [die] before the man"?

8. What is the "sill of shade"? Why is the challenge-cup "still-defended," and the garland "unwithered"?

SYNTHESIZING

9. What does the speaker assume would have happened to the athlete had he been able to continue his career?

10. What is the speaker's attitude toward public adoration? What is the speaker's attitude toward death? Do you feel the speaker is accurate?

VICTORIAN POETRY / "TO AN ATHLETE DYING YOUNG"   **779**

ANSWERS FOR REVIEWING THE SELECTION

RECALLING

1. A very successful runner is featured in this poem. The crowd carried him on their shoulders throughout the town.

2. Laurel and glory wither away quickly.

3. The athlete will never have to experience the loss of his fame or his talent.

4. The athlete is to set his "fleet foot" on the "sill of shade" and hold up his trophy at the doorway. The "strengthless dead" will flock to gaze at the athlete.

INTERPRETING

Responses will vary. Possible responses are given.

5. The athlete in his coffin is being carried through the town. In both stanzas, the athlete is carried through the town on the shoulders of townspeople, but in the second stanza the athlete is dead.

6. The speaker calls the athlete a "Smart lad" because he was wise enough to die before his fame slipped away. Laurel refers to the wreath of laurel given in ancient times to heroes, poets, and great athletes. The laurel signifies honor.

7. The fame associated with his name might disappear, or die, before the man himself dies.

8. The "sill of shade" is death. The runner will never run in another race; therefore, he will never again be defeated, nor give reason to have his name tarnished with loss of fame.

SYNTHESIZING

Responses will vary. Possible responses are given.

9. The speaker assumes that the runner eventually would have lost a race.

10. The speaker admires public adoration but knows that it is fickle. The speaker feels that death is a good thing because it ends the continual process of aging and decay.

ANALYTIC SCALES FOR RESPONDING IN WRITING

Assign a score from 1 to 25 for each grading criterion below. (For more detailed evaluation, see the evaluation forms for writing, revising, and proofreading, *Assessment Portfolio*, 7.1–7.10.)

1. Eulogy

• **Content/Unity.** The eulogy celebrates the athlete's achievements and mourns his untimely death.

• **Organization/Coherence.** The eulogy presents main ideas and supporting details in a sensible order.

• **Language/Style.** The eulogy uses vivid and precise nouns, verbs, and modifiers.

• **Conventions.** The eulogy avoids errors in spelling, grammar, usage, mechanics, and manuscript form.

2. Newspaper Articles

• **Content/Unity.** The articles chronicle the rise and fall of the career of a fictitious athlete.

• **Organization/Coherence.** The articles begin with a lead and give details of who, what, when, where, why, and how in a reasonable sequence.

• **Language/Style.** The articles use vivid and precise nouns, verbs, and modifiers.

• **Conventions.** The articles avoid errors in spelling, grammar, usage, mechanics, and manuscript form.

3. Images of Change and Victory

• **Content/Unity.** The images suggest the concepts of change and victory.

• **Organization/Coherence.** The images present a main idea and add supporting details in a sensible order.

• **Language/Style.** The images use vivid and precise nouns, verbs, and modifiers.

• **Conventions.** The images avoid errors in spelling, grammar, usage, mechanics, and manuscript form.

Understanding Literature (Questions for Discussion)

1. **Allusion.** An **allusion** is a figure of speech in which a reference is made to a person, event, object, or work from history or literature. Bearing in mind that Housman was a classical scholar, what allusions can you find in this poem to the practices of ancient Greece and Rome? What do the allusions represent? Do these allusions enhance the poem?

2. **Tone. Tone** is the emotional attitude toward the reader or toward the subject implied by a literary work. Does this poem have a definite tone? If so, what words and phrases create this tone?

Responding in Writing

1. **Eulogy.** Suppose you were asked to write a eulogy for the funeral of the athlete in Housman's poem. Do you share Housman's attitude about life and death, or would you write the eulogy with a completely different attitude? In your own words, tell people about the athlete's accomplishments and about why this person will be missed for having been taken away in the prime of an exciting career. You are provided with only limited information in the poem itself, so use your imagination to fill in the gaps. What do you think this person was like? What might be important qualities to highlight in this athlete's eulogy?

2. **Newspaper Articles.** Create a series of short newspaper or magazine articles that chronicle the career of a fictional athlete. When did this person first gain public attention? How fast did his or her career flourish from that point on? Were there any troublesome incidents that caused the celebrity to temporarily lose public favor? What was the pinnacle of the person's career? How did his or her personal life hold up under public pressure? When did fame begin to fade, and why? Consider each of these questions as you write a series of about four or five brief articles.

3. **Images of Change and Victory.** Housman uses vivid images to illustrate his themes of change and victory. What images come to your own mind when you think about these subjects? Make notes about this in your journal. Then pick three of your favorite images and perfect them. Remember, small, unique details are better than tired, overused images. Think carefully about what these subjects mean to you personally. You may want to share your images with the rest of the class.

ANSWERS FOR UNDERSTANDING LITERATURE

▶ See the evaluation forms for discussion, active listening, and oral communication, *Assessment Portfolio*, 7.11–7.14.

Responses will vary. Possible responses are given.

1. Allusion. Housman alludes to the practice of crowning great athletes with laurel wreaths. The allusions represent a celebration of greatness and a bestowing of fame. Yes, the allusions elevate the subject of the poem to legendary status, rather than chronicling the untimely death of a local boy who won a town footrace.

2. Tone. The tone is disturbingly unemotional for such an emotional topic, so much so that it is debatable whether Housman is being serious or ironic. Words such as *home, town,* and *lad* imply the commonplace, whereas the poem's subject—the death of a young hero—is highly uncommon and even shocking.

PREREADING

VICTORIAN PROSE

from *The Mill on the Floss*
by George Eliot (Mary Ann Evans)

ABOUT THE AUTHOR

Born in the same year as Herman Melville, Walt Whitman, and Queen Victoria, **George Eliot** (1819–1880) was given the name Mary Ann Evans. She grew up in the English countryside and was an avid reader.

When Evans was twenty-one, she moved to Coventry with her father and became involved in literary and intellectual pursuits. She worked on an intellectual journal and did some translation and editorial work. During this time, she met many influential writers and philosophers. One of these people was a literary critic with whom she fell in love and with whom she decided to live, even though he was unable to divorce his wife. This relationship estranged her from her family; her brother Isaac, with whom she had been very close, never spoke to her again. When she began to write fiction later in her life, paying the price for a controversial decision would become a theme in her novels.

In 1857, Evans began to write serial fiction for magazines under the pen name George Eliot. Most people, with the notable exception of Charles Dickens, believed her first book to have been written by a man, perhaps a clergyman, but although she continued to use her masculine pen name, the truth of her identity was soon generally known. After publishing her first novel, *Adam Bede,* at the age of forty, she went on to write seven full-length novels, including *Middlemarch* and *The Mill on the Floss,* which were all well received by the Victorian reading public.

Eliot's novels are generally set in the time period of her own childhood and examine the challenges facing people at that point in history. Often her leading character is a young woman with creativity, imagination, and a desire to be more than society will allow her to be. Eliot was interested in issues related to women's rights, and her characters convey her complex, compelling views on the subject. She presents her characters with accuracy and compassion, calling herself both a scientist and a historian. Critics today consider her to be the greatest English Realist, on equal standing with Leo Tolstoy and Gustave Flaubert.

ABOUT THE SELECTION

The selection is from *The Mill on the Floss,* a novel whose protagonist is Maggie Tulliver, a woman frustrated by the constraints that society places on her. In the opening section of the novel, the protagonist describes an idyllic scene from her childhood. Ironically, the scene is not completely idyllic, for beneath its shining surface lies a dark truth, that the protagonist's brother does not properly respect her. This selection is a subtle, brilliant exposition of the origins of gender inequality in ideas held by children.

ADDITIONAL RESOURCES

READER'S GUIDE
• Selection Worksheet, 9.18

ASSESSMENT PORTFOLIO
• Selection Check Test, 4.9.35
• Selection Test, 4.9.36

ESSENTIAL SKILLS PRACTICE BOOKS
• *Language,* 2.104, 2.105
• *Study and Research,* 4.6

ENRICHMENT ACTIVITIES

In 1856, George Eliot wrote an article titled "Silly Novels by Lady Novelists," in which she attacked many of the novels being written at the time. Encourage students to locate and read this article. Have students discuss the article and determine whether the issue is relevant to contemporary women authors. Students may also want to determine whether it was generally known at the time that George Eliot was a woman. Did readers of "Silly Novels by Lady Novelists" think that the author of the article was a man? How might beliefs about the gender of the article's author affect a reader's interpretation?

GOALS/OBJECTIVES

Studying this lesson will enable students to

• interpret and appreciate a work of Victorian prose
• describe Eliot's literary accomplishments and explain the historical significance of her writings
• define *realism, digression,* and *dramatic irony,* and identify realist works and digressions and dramatic irony that they encounter in their reading

• write a resignation and a setting
• recognize and correct errors in the use of quotation marks

PREREADING NOTES

READER'S JOURNAL

Students may also want to consider social class as a source of discrimination.

THINKING SKILLS

Some students may benefit from a review of the differences between implicit and explicit information before beginning this selection.

SUPPORT FOR LEP STUDENTS

Students may find the last three paragraphs of this selection difficult to read because of Eliot's elevated language. Pair students who have or are likely to have difficulties with more proficient students so that they may decipher this passage together.

ADDITIONAL VOCABULARY

peculiar—singular
radiant—shining
brink—edge
presently—soon
lisping—speak imperfectly
novelty—newness; uniqueness
monotony—dullness; repetitiveness
foliage—leaves
fitful—starting and stopping
furrowed—having ridges
capricious—irregular; unpredictable
hedgerow—bushes serving as a fence

VOCABULARY FROM THE SELECTION

amicable
inextricable

READER'S JOURNAL

Write in your journal about a situation in which you were made to feel inferior. Your experience may have been the result of discrimination based on age, gender, or race.

THINKING SKILLS

Read the Language Arts Survey, 4.6, "Observing." As you read the following selection, note that some of Tom and Maggie's traits are described directly in the text. Others are implied, or hinted at, by what the two characters say and do. As you read the selection, list the traits of each character. Then make inferences—that is, draw conclusions—based on what is implied about each character.

FROM

The Mill on the Floss

GEORGE ELIOT (MARY ANN EVANS)

The next morning Maggie was trotting with her own fishing-rod in one hand and a handle of the basket in the other, stepping always, by a peculiar gift, in the muddiest places, and looking darkly radiant from under her beaver-bonnet because Tom was good to her. She had told Tom, however, that she should like him to put the worms on the hook for her, although she accepted his word when he assured her that worms couldn't feel (it was Tom's private opinion that it didn't much matter if they did). He knew all about worms, and fish, and those things; and what birds were mischievous, and how padlocks opened, and which way the handles of the gates were to be lifted. Maggie thought this sort of knowledge was very wonderful—much more difficult than remembering what was

in the books; and she was rather in awe of Tom's superiority, for he was the only person who called her knowledge "stuff," and did not feel surprised at her cleverness. Tom, indeed, was of opinion that Maggie was a silly little thing; all girls were silly—they couldn't throw a stone so as to hit anything, couldn't do anything with a pocketknife, and were frightened at frogs. Still he was very fond of his sister, and meant always to take care of her, make her his housekeeper, and punish her when she did wrong.

They were on their way to the Round Pool—that wonderful pool, which the floods had made a long while ago: no one knew how deep it was; and it was mysterious, too, that it should be almost a perfect round, framed in with willows and tall

❶
Is Tom really "superior"? What doesn't he sufficiently appreciate in Maggie?

ANSWER TO GUIDED READING QUESTION

❶ Tom is not really superior. Maggie recognizes and admires the knowledge that Tom has, but Tom thinks that Maggie is a "silly little thing" because she can't throw a stone well, use a pocketknife, and she is afraid of frogs. He thinks Maggie's knowledge is useless.

reeds, so that the water was only to be seen when you got close to the brink. The sight of the old favorite spot always heightened Tom's good humour, and he spoke to Maggie in the most <u>amicable</u> whispers, as he opened the precious basket, and prepared their tackle. He threw her line for her, and put the rod into her hand. Maggie thought it probable that the small fish would come to her hook, and the large ones to Tom's. But she had forgotten all about the fish, and was looking dreamily at the glassy water, when Tom said, in a loud whisper, "Look, look, Maggie!" and came running to prevent her from snatching her line away.

Maggie was frightened lest she had been doing something wrong, as usual, but presently Tom drew out her line and brought a large tench bouncing on the grass.

Tom was excited.

"O Magsie! you little duck! Empty the basket."

Maggie was not conscious of unusual merit, but it was enough that Tom called her Magsie, and was pleased with her. There was nothing to mar her delight in the whispers and the dreamy silences, when she listened to the light dipping sounds of the rising fish, and the gentle rustling, as if the willows and the reeds and the water had their happy whisperings also. Maggie thought it would make a very nice heaven to sit by the pool in that way, and never be scolded. She never knew she had a bite till Tom told her; but she liked fishing very much.

It was one of their happy mornings.

They trotted along and sat down together, with no thought that life would ever change much for them: they would only get bigger and not go to school, and it would always be like the holidays; they would always live together and be fond of each other. And the mill with its booming—the great chestnut-tree under which they played at houses—their own little river, the Ripple, where the banks seemed like home, and Tom was always seeing the water-rats, while Maggie gathered the purple plumy tops of the reeds, which she forgot and dropped afterwards—above all, the great Floss, along which they wandered with a sense of travel, to see the rushing springtide, the awful Eagre,[1] come up like a hungry monster, or to see the Great Ash which had once wailed and groaned like a man—these things would always be just the same to them. Tom thought people were at a disadvantage who lived on any other spot of the globe; and Maggie, when she read about Christiana passing "the river over which there is no bridge,"[2] always saw the Floss between the green pastures by the Great Ash.

Life did change for Tom and Maggie; and yet they were not wrong in believing that the thoughts and loves of these first years would always make part of their lives. We could never have loved the earth so well if we had had no childhood in it,— if it were not the earth where the same

❶ *Why is Maggie frightened?*

❷ *Why does Maggie long for a heaven in which she would not be scolded?*

---

1. **Eagre.** A tidal wave in an estuary
2. **Christiana . . . bridge.** Christiana is a character from *Pilgrim's Progress.* She crosses "the river over which there is no bridge" or the river of death.

WORDS FOR EVERYDAY USE: am • i • ca • ble (am´ i kə bəl) *adj.,* friendly

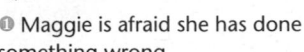

VOCABULARY IN CONTEXT
• One of the things I like best about Mr. Lopez, the librarian, is that he is always <u>amicable</u>, even when I turn in an overdue book.

ANSWERS TO GUIDED READING QUESTIONS

❶ Maggie is afraid she has done something wrong.

❷ Maggie is often scolded for her dreamy ways and she would find it pleasant to be praised rather than scolded.

flowers come up again every spring that we used to gather with our tiny fingers as we sat lisping to ourselves on the grass—the same hips and haws on the autumn hedgerows—the same redbreasts that we used to call "God's birds," because they did no harm to the precious crops. What novelty is worth that sweet monotony where everything is known, and *loved* because it is known?

The wood I walk in on this mild May day, with the young yellow-brown foliage of the oaks between me and the blue sky, the white starflowers and the blue-eyed speedwell and the ground ivy at my feet—what grove of tropic palms, what strange ferns or splendid broad-petalled blossoms, could ever thrill such deep and delicate fibers within me as this home-scene? These familiar flowers, these well-remembered bird-notes, this sky, with its fitful brightness, these furrowed and grassy fields, each with a sort of personality given to it by the capricious hedgerows—such things as these are the mother tongue of our imagination, the language that is laden with all the subtle <u>inextricable</u> associations the fleeting hours of our childhood left behind them. Our delight in the sunshine on the deep-bladed grass to-day, might be no more than the faint perception of wearied souls, if it were not for the sunshine and the grass in the far-off years which still live in us, and transform our perception into love. ∎

Responding to the Selection

Write an editorial for a nineteenth-century English newspaper, defending Maggie's rights against Tom and other males like Tom who lived in that time period. Really try to empathize with Maggie as someone who has many talents that are not recognized or valued by society.

WORDS FOR EVERYDAY USE: **in • ex • tri • ca • ble** (in eks ´tri kə bəl) *adj.*, unable to be disentangled

VOCABULARY IN CONTEXT
• Because of gusty winds, my kite string and that tree branch have become <u>inextricable</u>.

Reviewing the Selection

RECALLING

1. What do Maggie and Tom think of each other, judging by their thoughts and words described in paragraph 1?

2. What happens in paragraphs 2 and 3, and how does each of the children respond?

3. In paragraph 6, what does Maggie think about after she catches the fish?

4. Who is talking in the last two paragraphs of the selection, and what does that person say?

INTERPRETING

5. What is the speaker implying about Tom in the last sentence of paragraph 1?

6. Why might Maggie be "looking dreamily at the glassy water," in paragraph 2?

7. How might the reader feel toward Maggie after reading the last two sentences in paragraph 6 when she describes what she thinks "a very nice heaven" would be?

8. What is the narrator saying about the value to an adult of having experienced nature during childhood?

SYNTHESIZING

9. How does Tom feel toward girls? Which of his comments and actions make this feeling clear? What effect does "Tom's superiority" have on Maggie?

10. Eliot was sympathetic to some of the movements during her lifetime to enlarge opportunities for women. How does what happened to Maggie in this selection explain and express Eliot's opinions about women's struggles for independence?

Understanding Literature (Questions for Discussion)

1. **Realism. Realism** is the attempt to render in art an accurate portrayal of reality. Often Realists write in a reportorial style, describing events and implying the effects of these events on the psychology of characters. What elements in this selection seem to you to be particularly realistic?

2. **Dramatic Irony. Dramatic irony** is when something is known by the reader or audience but unknown to the characters in the work. How does dramatic irony work in this selection? What do we know about Tom that the young Maggie did not understand? What details in the selection give us an unflattering but realistic portrait of Tom? How does this portrait contrast with the professed sweetness of the author's memories?

ANSWERS FOR UNDERSTANDING LITERATURE

► See the evaluation forms for discussion, active listening, and oral communication, *Assessment Portfolio,* 7.11–7.14.

Responses will vary. Possible responses are given.

1. **Realism.** The narrator describes earlier conversations between Tom and Maggie. The Round Pool, the section that describes Maggie and Tom catching the fish, seems particularly realistic.

► **Teaching Note:** Discuss with students how realism can be an important tool in writing social criticism. When an event is portrayed realistically, it seems truthful, yet it is still the author's interpretation. How might a realistic description of the fishing scene differ if told from Tom's point of view?

(cont.)

RECALLING

1. Maggie is in awe of Tom and admires him greatly. Tom thinks that Maggie is silly and feels that he must teach and protect her.

2. Maggie catches a fish. She isn't paying attention, and when Tom grabs her line to pull in her fish, she is frightened that she has done something wrong.

3. While happy that Tom was pleased with her, Maggie realized that she would just as soon sit by the pond as fish in it.

4. The narrator speaks, saying that life changed for Tom and Maggie, but they still were able to love nature because they spent much of their childhood exploring it.

INTERPRETING

Responses will vary. Possible responses are given.

5. She implies that Tom is a sexist. He thinks of women as comprising an inferior class.

6. Maggie is not interested in catching fish and is daydreaming about the mysterious depths.

7. The reader might feel sorry for Maggie, who is continually bossed around and who has come to expect disapproval.

8. Without having experienced nature during childhood, as adults they "could never have loved the earth so well."

SYNTHESIZING

Responses will vary. Possible responses are given.

9. Tom thinks are silly because they "couldn't throw a stone so as to hit anything, couldn't do anything with a pocketknife, and were frightened at frogs." "Tom's superiority" causes Maggie to devalue her own skills and talents and makes her meek.

10. Limits on women's independence have bred the common opinion, shared by Tom, that women are incapable and inferior. Accepting these opinions about themselves is devastating to girls such as Maggie and stunts their individuality.

ANSWERS FOR UNDERSTANDING LITERATURE (CONT.)

2. Dramatic Irony. Maggie and Tom's relationship is ironic in that Tom acts as the authority and believes that Maggie is silly when she is the one doing all of the real thinking. Tom isn't very bright or sympathetic; he doesn't care if the worms are in pain. He thinks that Maggie and all girls are silly. He considers Maggie's seemingly considerable intellect and her knowledge unimportant; he calls it "stuff." Maggie remembers Tom as a heroic figure brimming with knowledge of how the world worked, which was "much more difficult than remembering what was in the books."

▶**Teaching Note:** Discuss with students the following: How does Maggie's perception of her relationship with Tom reflect her feelings about herself and her accomplishments?

3. Digression. Whether the digression contributes or detracts depends on how one views the intent of the first part of the passage. If the first part of the passage was written to describe gender roles and Tom and Maggie's relationship, the latter part of the passage doesn't seem to have a clear purpose other than to show that Maggie has survived her brother's well-meaning oppression. On the other hand, if the passage is intended to illustrate the importance that nature played in Tom's and Maggie's childhood, the second part of the passage is a logical continuation of a theme.

▶**Teaching Note:** Students may benefit from discussing this issue in small groups and then sharing their conclusions with the whole class.

3. Digression. George Eliot prided herself on her philosophical **digressions**, passages in her novels in which she as the narrator appears and gives a philosophical opinion. Do you think the narrator's digression in the last two paragraphs of the selection contributes to or detracts from the piece? Explain.

Responding in Writing

1. **Resignation.** There are at least two denotations to the word *resignation.* One is "reluctant acceptance of the inevitable." The other is "termination of a relationship with an employer or other figure of authority." Write a letter of resignation from Maggie to her brother Tom in which she finally throws off her attitude of "reluctant acceptance of the inevitable" and demands that her brother treat her with respect. Be polite, but assertive, and give specific examples to defend your argument that you are worthy of equal standing with Tom.

2. **Setting.** George Eliot set her realist novels in the time frame of her own childhood. She could have set her novels in any other time and place, but perhaps she felt that she could draw from deeper emotions by bringing her thoughts back to her childhood home. Write a brief dialogue that takes place between two individuals who live in the same time and place as you did when you were a child. Then rewrite the dialogue as though it takes place now or in any other time period. Write a brief analysis of the differences you see between the two pieces and explain your own emotional response to each of the two writing experiences.

Language Lab

Proofreading for Punctuation Errors. Read the Language Arts Survey, 2.104 and 2.105, "Quotation Marks I and II." Revise each of the following sentences to correct errors in the use of quotation marks.

1. George Eliot wrote "The Mill on the Floss" and set her characters and events near a river called the Floss.

2. Maggie said that "she was happy to be allowed to spend time with Tom."

3. At one point in the selection, when Maggie catches a fish, Tom exclaims, "O Magsie"!

4. The narrator says, "What novelty is worth that sweet monotony where everything is known, and loved because it is known"?

5. The narrators believes that "we might not delight in the sunshine on the grass if it weren't for our childhood memories of that grass."

ANSWERS FOR LANGUAGE LAB

1. George Eliot wrote *The Mill on the Floss* and set her characters and events near a river called the Floss.

2. Maggie said that she was "happy to be allowed to spend time with Tom."

3. At one point in the selection, when Maggie catches a fish, Tom exclaims, "O Magsie!"

4. The narrator says, "What novelty is worth that sweet monotony where everything is known, and loved because it is known?"

5. The narrator believes that we might not delight in the sunshine of the grass if it weren't for our childhood memories of that grass.

▶Additional practice is provided in the *Essential Skills Practice Book: Language,* 2.104 and 2.105.

PREREADING

from *Great Expectations*
by Charles Dickens

ABOUT THE AUTHOR

Much of the life of **Charles Dickens** (1812–1870) appeared in fictional form in his literary work. His childhood began happily, but it dramatically changed in his eleventh year when the family moved from Chatham, a port town, to the city of London. Soon after the move, his father was sent to prison for unpaid debts. Young Charles was taken out of school and eventually put to work in a warehouse. The mark that these two experiences left on him was profound. Later in life he became an ardent social critic on behalf of the poor and downtrodden who filled London's streets in the mid-nineteenth century.

Eventually Charles returned to school, but he left again at the age of fifteen to work as a legal clerk and legal reporter. When he was twenty-one, he began contributing stories, many of them humorous, to various newspapers and magazines. His unique writing style and social awareness won him wide popularity. Having found a market and an audience, Dickens began to publish his longer works in serial form or installments. His first novel, *Pickwick Papers,* was published in serial form from 1836 to 1837 and gained him substantial notoriety. Dickens soon became one of the most popular and renowned writers of his day, both in England and the United States. Despite his commercial success, the pain of his childhood haunted him, and many of his novels sympathetically describe the poverty and insecurity of children, clerks, and small merchants struggling on their own in the city.

A Christmas Carol (1843), featuring the character Ebenezer Scrooge, is perhaps Dickens's most well-known work. *A Tale of Two Cities* (1859), a historical novel set in France and England during the French Revolution, is extremely well regarded. Other major works include *Oliver Twist* (1837–1838), *Nicholas Nickleby* (1838–1839), *Bleak House* (1852–1853), and *Hard Times* (1854).

ADDITIONAL RESOURCES

READER'S GUIDE
- Selection Worksheet, 9.19

ASSESSMENT PORTFOLIO
- Selection Check Test, 4.9.37
- Selection Test, 4.9.38

ESSENTIAL SKILLS PRACTICE BOOKS
- *Language*, 2.53
- *Study and Research*, 4.5, 4.27

SUPPORT FOR LEP STUDENTS

Discuss with students Dickens's use of dialect, especially in Joe's speech. Work with students to translate Joe's words into standard English, so that they may better understand the selection. Stress that they are not *correcting* the writing, just translating.

IDIOMS
get the better of—defeat

ADDITIONAL VOCABULARY
hale—healthy
immensely—in a great amount
elevation—height
matronly—dignified; sedate
eloquence—artful speech
consequent—result
abundance—ample amount
ajar—partly open
desolate—barren
solitary—alone
insensible—not capable of feeling
relinquish—give up

GOALS/OBJECTIVES

Studying this lesson will enable students to

- appreciate Dickens's skill as a novelist
- describe Dickens's literary accomplishments and explain the historical significance of his writings
- define *symbol* and *ambiguity* and recognize and analyze symbols and ambiguities that they encounter in their reading
- use remembering and visualizing techniques
- write a memorial plaque and a description that creates a mood
- combine sentences using clauses
- research information in print and nonprint sources

ENRICHMENT ACTIVITIES

Dickens was well known for encouraging many social reforms. One outlet for his ideas was the periodical he created, *Household Words*. Suggest that students research this periodical, determining what authors were published in it, who its intended audience was, what issues it discussed, and what its source of income was (sales, advertising, or donations). Students should discuss their findings with the class. Students may want to think about creating their own magazine to deal with social issues. What issues would they address? How would they attract an audience?

VOCABULARY FROM THE SELECTION

avarice
placid

LITERARY NOTE

Although dedicated to social reform, Dickens was not above satirizing fellow reformers. One of Dickens's most memorable character sketches is that of Mrs. Jellyby, a professional philanthropist. Perhaps what Dickens found objectionable in many philanthropists was their focus on foreign charity. This sentiment is evident in his characterization of Mrs. Jellyby who sacrifices her family's well-being for "Educating the natives of Borrioboola-Gha, on the left bank of the Niger" (*Bleak House*, chapter 4).

ABOUT THE SELECTION

Written at the height of Dickens's literary success, ***Great Expectations*** tells the story of Philip Pirrip, or Pip, from his childhood as an orphan to his adulthood. Pip is raised in the marshlands of Kent by his sister and her husband, a blacksmith to whom the young boy is apprenticed. As a boy he is invited to the decaying mansion of Miss Havisham, a wealthy and eccentric recluse, to entertain Estella, her ward. Pip falls in love with Estella, though she disdains him because of his low social status. When Pip comes of age, a mysterious benefactor provides him with an income large enough to live as a gentleman, and he moves to London. He thinks that the money has come from Miss Havisham, and he views it as a sign of favor which keeps alive his hope of marrying Estella. However, Estella marries an unworthy man who mistreats her, and Pip and Estella are separated for many years. Then the snobbish Pip is appalled to learn that his benefactor is really an escaped convict whom he aided on the marshes one night and who has illegally returned to England from Australia, where he made his fortune. After the convict dies and Pip is injured in an unsuccessful attempt to escape England, Pip leaves England to work in the East. In the selection that follows, he returns to Kent eleven years later, in need of comfort from Joe and his new wife, Biddy, disillusioned about his great expectations and cleansed of the heartlessness to which his ambition to be a gentleman had led him. While roaming the grounds of Miss Havisham's burned-out mansion, Pip sees Estella again, also now much changed from the cold, mercenary beauty Pip knew when they both were young.

from Great Expectations, *Chapter 10*
A Conversation between Pip and Estella

"You must know," said Estella, condescending to me as a brilliant and beautiful woman might, "that I have no heart—if that has anything to do with my memory."

I got through some jargon to the effect that I took the liberty of doubting that. That I knew better. That there could be no such beauty without it. . . .

"I am serious," said Estella, not so much with a frown (for her brow was smooth) as with a darkening of her face; "if we are to be thrown much together, you had better believe it at once. No!" imperiously stopping me as I opened my lips. "I have not bestowed my tenderness anywhere. I have never had any such thing. . . . What is the matter?" asked Estella. "Are you scared again?"

"I should be, if I believed what you said just now," I replied.

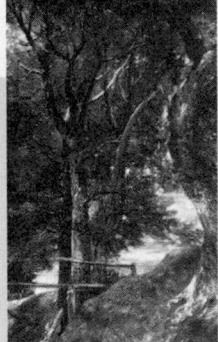

FROM

Great Expectations

CHARLES DICKENS

For eleven years, I had not seen Joe nor Biddy with my bodily eyes though they had both been often before my fancy in the East—when, upon an evening in December, an hour or two after dark, I laid my hand softly on the latch of the old kitchen door. I touched it so softly that I was not heard, and looked in unseen. There, smoking his pipe in the old place by the kitchen firelight, as hale and as strong as ever though a little grey, sat Joe; and there, fenced into the corner with Joe's leg, and sitting on my own little stool looking at the fire, was——I again!

"We giv' him the name of Pip for your sake, dear old chap," said Joe, delighted when I took another stool by the child's side (but I did *not* rumple his hair), "and we hoped he might grow a little bit like you, and we think he do."

I thought so too, and I took him out for a walk next morning, and we talked immensely, understanding one another to perfection. And I took him down to the churchyard, and set him on a certain tombstone there, and he showed me from that elevation which stone was sacred to the memory of Philip Pirrip, late of this Parish, and Also Georgiana, Wife of the Above.

"Biddy," said I, when I talked with her after dinner, as her little girl lay sleeping in her lap, "you must give Pip to me, one of these days; or lend him, at all events."

"No, no," said Biddy, gently. "You must marry."

"So Herbert and Clara say, but I don't think I shall, Biddy. I have so settled down in their home, that it's not at all likely. I am already quite an old bachelor."

Biddy looked down at her child, and put its little hand to her lips, and then put the good matronly hand with which she had touched it, into mine. There was something in the action and in the light pressure of Biddy's wedding-ring, that had a very pretty eloquence in it.

"Dear Pip," said Biddy, "you are sure you don't fret for her?"

"O no—I think not, Biddy."

"Tell me as an old, old friend. Have you quite forgotten her?"

ADDITIONAL QUESTIONS AND ACTIVITIES

You may wish to have students read further from *Great Expectations*. Have them read sections in which Dickens describes the odd lifestyle of Miss Havisham. Inform students that Queen Victoria also led an eccentric life as a widow; she surrounded herself with images of her dead husband and even had a photograph over her bed of her husband after he had died. Ask students to what extent they believe Miss Havisham's character was drawn from that of Queen Victoria.

If Miss Havisham is modeled on Queen Victoria, what is Dickens implying about England's monarch?

❶
Pip claims to have put aside "that poor dream." Has he? Why does he want to revisit the house?

The Dell at Helmingham Park. *John Constable. The Nelson-Atkins Museum of Art*

"My dear Biddy, I have forgotten nothing in my life that ever had a foremost place there, and little that ever had any place there. But that poor dream, as I once used to call it, has all gone by, Biddy, all gone by!"

Nevertheless, I knew while I said those words, that I secretly intended to revisit the site of the old house that evening, alone, for her sake. Yes even so. For Estella's sake.

I had heard of her as leading a most unhappy life, and as being separated from her husband, who had used her with great cruelty, and who had become quite renowned as a compound of pride, avarice, brutality, and meanness. And I had heard of the death of her husband, from an accident consequent on his ill-treatment of a horse. This release had befallen her some two years before; for anything I knew, she was married again.

The early dinner-hour at Joe's, left me abundance of time, without hurrying my talk with Biddy, to walk over to the old spot before dark. But, what with loitering on the way, to look at old objects and to think of old times, the day had quite declined when I came to the place.

There was no house now, no brewery, no building whatever left, but the wall of the old garden. The cleared space had

WORDS FOR EVERYDAY USE:
av • a • rice (avʹə ris) *n.,* greed

VOCABULARY IN CONTEXT
- I'm not surprised my sister wouldn't lend you fifty cents, for she is consumed by <u>avarice</u>.
- The lake on that clear, still summer day was so <u>placid</u> that the boat didn't rock at all.

been enclosed with a rough fence, and, looking over it, I saw that some of the old ivy had struck root anew, and was growing green on low quiet mounds of ruin. A gate in the fence standing ajar, I pushed it open, and went in.

A cold silvery mist had veiled the afternoon and the moon was not yet up to scatter it. But, the stars were shining beyond the mist, and the moon was coming, and the evening was not dark. I could trace out where every part of the old house had been, and where the brewery had been, and where the gates, and where the casks. I had done so, and was looking along the desolate garden-walk, when I beheld a solitary figure in it.

The figure showed itself aware of me, as I advanced. It had been moving towards me, but it stood still. As I drew nearer, I saw it to be the figure of a woman. As I drew nearer yet, it was about to turn away, when it stopped, and let me come up with it. Then, it faltered as if much surprised, and uttered my name, and I cried out:

"Estella!"

"I am greatly changed. I wonder you know me."

The freshness of her beauty was indeed gone, but its indescribable majesty and its indescribable charm remained. Those attractions in it, I had seen before; what I had never seen before, was the saddened softened light of the once proud eyes; what I had never felt before, was the friendly touch of the once insensible hand.

We sat down on a bench that was near, and I said, "After so many years, it is strange that we should thus meet again, Estella, here where our first meeting was! Do you often come back?"

"I have never been here since."

"Nor I."

The moon began to rise, and I thought of the <u>placid</u> look at the white ceiling, which had passed away. The moon began to rise, and I thought of the pressure on my hand when I had spoken the last words he had heard on earth.

Estella was the next to break the silence that ensued between us.

"I have very often hoped and intended to come back, but have been prevented by many circumstances. Poor, poor old place!"

The silvery mist was touched with the first rays of the moonlight, and the same rays touched the tears that dropped from her eyes. Not knowing that I saw them, and setting herself to get the better of them, she said quietly:

"Were you wondering, as you walked along, how it came to be left in this condition?"

"Yes, Estella."

"The ground belongs to me. It is the only possession I have not relinquished. Everything else has gone from me, little by little, but I have kept this. It was the subject of the only determined resistance I made in all the wretched years."

"Is it to be built on?"

"At last it is. I came here to take leave of it before its change. And you," she said, in a voice of touching interest to a wanderer, "you live abroad still?"

"Still."

"And do well, I am sure?"

ANSWER TO GUIDED READING QUESTION

❶ Estella has gotten older and has become humble and friendly. Her cruel husband, unhappy life, and reduced circumstances may have contributed to these changes.

LITERARY/HISTORICAL NOTE

The subject matter of Dickens's *A Christmas Carol,* one of the most famed yuletide tales, was not so much a unique creation but part of a Victorian tradition. Like many novelists, Dickens produced a number of Christmas stories that were sold in special editions before the holiday. Many of Dickens's Christmas stories are collected in *The Christmas Books.* For the most part, these works reach the height of Victorian sentimentality and lack the richness of Dickens's other works. They are, however, interesting documents of how Christmas was rapidly changing in Victorian England from a religious and spiritual holiday to a commercial and sentimental one. In *The Christmas Books* religious overtones are scarce, but gifts, turkeys, and money (and the equation of moral worth with consumerism) abound.

❶
How has Estella changed? What events in her life might have brought about these changes?

WORDS FOR EVERYDAY USE: **plac • id** (plas´id) *adj.,* calm; tranquil

CROSS-CURRICULAR ACTIVITIES

Social Studies. Students may find it surprising that the Havisham complex had its own brewery. Suggest that students research the kinds of buildings and facilities that would be common to an English estate in the mid-nineteenth century.

ANSWERS TO SELECTION CHECK TEST 4.9.37

EX. With whom is Pip still in love after all these years?
Pip is still in love with Estella.

1. What name did Biddy and Joe give to their baby?
They gave their baby the name Pip.

2. What does Pip tell Biddy that he doesn't think he will ever do?
He tells her that he doesn't think he will ever marry.

3. For whose sake does Pip want to visit the old house?
He wants to visit the old house for Estella's sake.

4. How did Estella's husband die?
He died from an accident that occurred as a result of mistreating a horse.

5. From what or whom does Pip see no shadow of parting?
He sees no shadow of parting from her (i.e., Estella).

ANSWERS TO GUIDED READING QUESTIONS

❶ Estella threw away Pip's love for her. She regrets mistreating Pip. She realized during a hard time in her life how valuable Pip's love was.

❷ One reading would be that Pip and Estella go their separate ways. The other reading would be that they stay together. The difference depends on how one interprets the phrase "shadow of another parting." Either they never leave each other again and therefore never part, or they never see each other again and do not experience "another" parting.

"I work pretty hard for a sufficient living, and therefore—Yes, I do well."

"I have often thought of you," said Estella.

"Have you?"

❶
What did Estella throw away? How have her feelings about what she did changed? Why have they changed?

"Of late, very often. There was a long hard time when I kept far from me, the remembrance of what I had thrown away when I was quite ignorant of its worth. But, since my duty has not been incompatible with the admission of that remembrance, I have given it a place in my heart."

"You have always held your place in my heart," I answered. And we were silent again, until she spoke.

"I little thought," said Estella, "that I should take leave of you in taking leave of this spot. I am very glad to do so."

❷
What two possible readings might this ending have? On what do these two readings depend?

"Glad to part again, Estella? To me, parting is a painful thing. To me, the remembrance of our last parting has been ever mournful and painful."

"But you said to me," returned Estella, very earnestly, "'God bless you, God forgive you!' And if you could say that to me then, you will not hesitate to say that to me now—now, when suffering has been stronger than all other teaching, and has taught me to understand what your heart used to be. I have been bent and broken, but—I hope—into a better shape. Be as considerate and good to me as you were, and tell me we are friends."

"We are friends," said I, rising and bending over her, as she rose from the bench.

"And will continue friends apart," said Estella.

I took her hand in mine, and we went out of the ruined place; and, as the morning mists had risen long ago when I first left the forge, so the evening mists were rising now, and in all the broad expanse of tranquil light they showed to me, I saw no shadow of another parting from her. ■

Responding to the Selection

How do you feel about Pip's return to Miss Havisham's estate? Do you feel sympathetic toward Pip? Do you think that you understand what he is feeling? In a small group, compare and explain your feelings.

ADDITIONAL QUESTIONS AND ACTIVITIES

The ending of *Great Expectations* went through a number of revisions. Find out what the original ending was and why Dickens changed it. Which ending do students prefer? Why?

▶ **Teaching Note:** Students should be able to find the answers to these questions in a good Dickens biography or in an annotated text of *Great Expectations,* such as the Oxford UP paperback edition (1994).

RESPONDING TO THE SELECTION

Ask students to find passages in the selection to support their opinions.

Reviewing the Selection

RECALLING

1. Does Biddy think Pip will ever marry? Does Pip expect that he will ever marry? What does Pip tell Biddy about how he feels about the past?

2. Why does Pip visit the site of the old house? Describe the site.

3. What reason does Estella give Pip for her visiting the site of the old house?

4. How does Estella remember the last time she saw Pip? How does Pip remember it?

INTERPRETING

▶▶ 5. What does Pip ask Biddy to lend him? What does he mean by this? Why does Biddy respond to Pip's request by discussing marriage?

▶▶ 6. How does Pip feel on seeing the site of the old house? What evidence supports your interpretation?

▶▶ 7. When they meet unexpectedly at the site of the old house, how do Estella and Pip feel about each other? What does Estella mean when she tells Pip why she decided to visit the site of the old house?

▶▶ 8. Do Estella and Pip reveal their feelings to each other? In what ways does their conversation reveal their feelings?

SYNTHESIZING

9. How does the author use Joe and Biddy to expose the feelings of Pip before he meets Estella?

10. What possible interpretations can be given to the final sentence?

Understanding Literature (Questions for Discussion)

---

1. **Symbol.** A **symbol** is a thing that stands for or represents both itself and something else. Symbols often relate to key themes in a work. What emotions or ideas do you associate with the following objects? What literary themes might be connected to these objects? In the selection, what might the following items symbolize?

   - the graveyard visited by Pip
   - Miss Havisham's destroyed property
   - Estella's name (which is Latin for "star")
   - the moonrise and mists at evening

ANSWERS FOR REVIEWING THE SELECTION (CONT.)

8. Yes; Pip says to Estella that she has always held her place in his heart. Estella tells Pip that she has thought of him often and remembers when she threw away his love, little knowing how valuable it was.

SYNTHESIZING

Responses will vary. Possible responses are given.

9. In conversation with Joe and Biddy, Pip talks about how his feelings for Estella have gone away. Then as an aside, while he thinks about returning to the site of the old house, he admits that he still harbors fond feelings for Estella.

10. The final sentence could mean that they stay together or that they never see each other again.

▶ **Teaching Note:** Ask students which ending they find more realistic. Which ending do they prefer?

ANSWERS FOR REVIEWING THE SELECTION

RECALLING

1. Biddy hopes that Pip may marry, but she is not sure. Pip doesn't expect to marry. Pip tells Biddy that he has never forgotten anything that has happened to him, but realizes that his poor dream of marrying Estella has "gone by."

2. Pip revisits the old house for Estella's sake. There are no buildings left, only a garden wall. A rough fence enclosed the entire area and some ivy was growing over low mounds of ruin.

3. Estella came to visit the site of the old house to say goodbye to it. New buildings will be constructed on the site soon.

4. Estella remembers that even though she had mistreated Pip, he still earnestly said to her, "God bless you, God forgive you." Pip remembers their last meeting as painful.

INTERPRETING

Responses will vary. Possible responses are given.

5. Pip is Biddy to lend him little Pip. Pip wants to have a child of his own. Biddy suggests that marriage is a better way to have children. She may want to make sure that he is over his feelings for Estella.

6. Pip is feeling sentimental. It took him a long time to get to the site because he kept stopping to look at "old objects and think of old times." When he got to the site he was very sad. He saw no buildings, only a fence and ivy growing on the mounds of ruins. Then he saw the stars shining beyond the mist, and the moon came up and the "evening was not dark." Pip regained hope and was able to see the foundations where the buildings had been and was consoled.

7. Estella and Pip are glad to see each other. Because the site will soon have new buildings, she wanted to say goodbye to the way the site used to be.

(cont.)

► See the evaluation forms for discussion, active listening, and oral communication, *Assessment Portfolio*, 7.11–7.14.

Responses will vary. Possible responses are given.

1. Symbol

• A graveyard is commonly associated with sadness. Themes associated with graveyards are death and change. In this selection, the graveyard is where the present Pip forms a special bond with the younger Pip by visiting the graves of his parents.

• Desolation and ruin are associated with Miss Havisham's property. Themes connected to the property are decay and loss. In this selection, the property symbolizes the destruction of a central part of Pip's past.

• Estella's name suggests something bright, cold, and unreachable. The theme associated with her name is unrequited love. In the selection her name represents beauty and inaccessibility.

• The moonrise and mists at evening suggest mysterious happenings. Themes associated with moonrise and mist are romance and inconstancy. In the selection, they set the stage for an unreal, coincidental, romantic meeting between Pip and Estella.

►**Teaching Note:** Discuss with students whether the symbols Dickens uses are conventional or personal.

2. Ambiguity. The passage can be interpreted that Pip and Estella stay together or that they never see each other again. The words "shadow of another parting" are used ambiguously. Yes; he wanted the possibility of a relationship between Pip and Estella to remain open, to let the reader decide for him- or herself.

►**Teaching Note:** Discuss with students why an author might want ambiguity in his or her work. How might an ambiguous ending be more satisfying than an ending that is clear cut? Are there certain types of stories that benefit from an ambiguous ending?

2. Ambiguity. An **ambiguity** is a statement that has a double meaning or a meaning that cannot be clearly resolved. At the end of the selection, Estella says that she and Pip must remain "friends apart," and Pip, the narrator, says, "I saw no shadow of another parting from her." In what different ways can this passage be interpreted? What particular word or words are used ambiguously? Do you think the author intended this ambiguity? If not, which meaning did he intend? If so, what effect might he have wanted the ambiguity to have?

Responding in Writing

1. **Memorial Plaque.** Think back to the place you wrote about in the Reader's Journal. Imagine that it is being commemorated, and that you have been asked to compose the words that will adorn the memorial. Write no more than three sentences or forty words. Before you begin writing, take a moment to reflect on the meaning that this place holds for you and the experiences and feelings that you associate with it.

2. **Description/Mood.** Look back at one of the scenes that Dickens describes in this selection—the ruins of Miss Havisham's estate or the graveyard. Then choose a place of your own to describe. You may use the same one from the Reader's Journal exercise or one of which you have a fresher memory. The important thing is to choose two particular times of day, seasons of the year, or weather conditions to use in your descriptions. Then write two separate paragraphs describing the place in different ways to create different moods.

Language Lab

Combining Sentences. Read the Language Arts Survey, 2.53, "Combining Sentences Using Clauses." Then combine each pair of sentences below into a single sentence by changing one of the pair into a clause.

1. Dickens faced a hard childhood. He struggled to rise above his family's poverty.

2. Pip walked through Miss Havisham's ruined estate. He noticed how it had changed since the days of his youth.

3. At middle age, Dickens had acquired a wide following of readers of his novels. His novels were circulated in magazines and periodicals of the time.

4. Victorian-era London was populated with the rich and the destitute. Both the rich and the destitute filled the city's narrow, dirty streets.

5. Estella saw Pip through the evening mist. She called out his name.

ANSWERS FOR LANGUAGE LAB

Responses will vary. Possible responses are given.

1. Dickens faced a hard childhood, and he struggled to rise above his family's poverty.

2. As Pip walked through Miss Havisham's ruined estate, he noticed how it had changed since the days of his youth.

3. At middle age, Dickens had acquired a wide following of readers of his novels, which were circulated in magazines and periodicals of the time.

4. Victorian-era London was populated with the rich and the destitute, both of whom filled the city's narrow, dirty streets.

5. Estella saw Pip through the evening mist, and she called out his name.

►Additional practice is provided in the *Essential Skills Practice Book: Language,* 2.53.

Research Skills

Further Information. Read the Language Arts Survey, 4.27, "Other Sources of Information." Then complete the following activities.

1. Contact a local or national organization or business to obtain information about traveling to London.

2. Find the name of an expert you could invite to your class to speak about Victorian-era London. On your paper, write the person's name, phone number, area of expertise, and qualifications, and tell how you found this person's name.

3. Use the vertical files at your school library or at a local library to find information on Victorian-era London. If you cannot check out the material, make a photocopy of it.

PROJECTS

1. **Dialogue.** Explore the ambiguity of Dickens's ending. Together with a partner, write one page of dialogue continuing the conversation between Pip and Estella. Decide for yourselves whether the ending will show the two reuniting or going their own ways. You might also choose to have the ending remain ambiguous. Share and discuss your ending with your class.

2. **Place Memories.** Do the members of your family or close friends have memories of a special place? More importantly, could these memories differ? To find out, ask four or five family members or friends to describe the same place to you. Then ask them for a few experiences they can recall having to do with that place. Ask for their memories first, then their experiences, and do this separately with each person so none knows the others' responses. Compare your findings, and prepare a short report on how memories of places are affected by the experiences we associate with them.

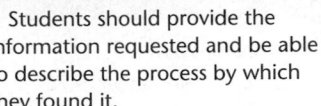

ANSWERS FOR RESEARCH SKILLS

Students should provide the information requested and be able to describe the process by which they found it.

►Ask what difficulties students had and how they solved them.

FOR MORE PRACTICE

Contact a British agency in this country (possibilities include a consulate, a travel agent, an office for tourism, or an airline) for information on historical sites one might visit on a trip to England.

►Additional practice is provided in the *Essential Skills Practice Book: Study and Research,* 4.27.

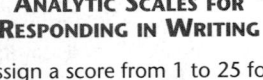

ANALYTIC SCALES FOR RESPONDING IN WRITING

Assign a score from 1 to 25 for each grading criterion below. (For more detailed evaluation, see the evaluation forms for writing, revising, and proofreading, *Assessment Portfolio,* 7.1–7.10.)

1. Memorial Plaque

• **Content/Unity.** The plaque gives emotional and experiential reasons why the place is special.

• **Organization/Coherence.** The plaque presents main ideas and supporting details in a sensible order.

• **Language/Style.** The plaque uses vivid and precise nouns, verbs, and modifiers.

• **Conventions.** The plaque avoids errors in spelling, grammar, usage, mechanics, and manuscript form.

2. Description/Mood

• **Content/Unity.** The descriptions describe the same setting but create two different moods.

• **Organization/Coherence.** The descriptions present main ideas and supporting details in a sensible order.

• **Language/Style.** The descriptions use vivid and precise nouns, verbs, and modifiers.

• **Conventions.** The descriptions avoid errors in spelling, grammar, usage, mechanics, and manuscript form.

PROJECT NOTES

►See the worksheets and evaluation forms for projects, *Assessment Portfolio,* 7.20–7.23.

1. Dialogue. As a way of brainstorming, students may wish to role play the conversation between Pip and Estella, using their extemporaneous exchange as a basis for the final written dialogue.

2. Place Memories

• Students may wish to use a tape recorder when they conduct interviews.

• In preparing their reports, students may want to include a photograph or sketch of the place about which they are writing.

ENRICHMENT ACTIVITIES

One of the contributions Lewis Carroll made to the English language is the word *chortle,* a combination of *snort* and *chuckle.* Students should try to discover a number of words in the English language that are combination, or portmanteau, words. Then in a game-show format, one group can challenge another group to figure out the two words from which their portmanteau originally came. (See the Handbook of Literary Terms, page 1240, for more suggestions of blends or portmanteaus.)

SUPPORT FOR LEP STUDENTS

Stress that much of this selection contains words used to stand for ideas completely different from their customary associations. Students should know that they are not missing anything. The selection is meant to be confusing even for English-proficient students.

ADDITIONAL VOCABULARY

provoking—annoying
anxiety—worry
queer—odd
triumphantly—victoriously
indignantly—with anger at injustice or ingratitude
scornful—angry and disgusted
impenetrable—not solvable; not comprehensible
gimlet—small tool for boring
ingenuity—clever inventiveness
hastily—in a hurry
civil—friendly and polite

PREREADING

VICTORIAN PROSE

from *Through the Looking Glass*
by Lewis Carroll

ABOUT THE AUTHOR

Lewis Carroll was the pen name of Charles Lutwidge Dodgson (1832–1898), the son of an Anglican minister. Like his father, Carroll went to Oxford and was ordained as an Anglican priest. He remained at Christ Church, Oxford, as a mathematics tutor, and he also became a skilled photographer. He is best known today, however, as an author of children's books. His popularity as a children's writer is based on his inventive tales *Alice's Adventures in Wonderland* (1865) and *Through the Looking Glass and What Alice Found There* (1872). Together these books are known as *Alice in Wonderland.*

The first book, *Alice's Adventures in Wonderland,* grew out of tales that Carroll told to a group of children on a boat trip up the Thames River. Alice Liddell, the young daughter of the dean of Carroll's school, pleaded with Carroll to write a story featuring her as the heroine. She wanted him to call these tales "Alice's adventures." He soon created a hand-printed storybook called *Alice's Adventures Underground.* Carroll became convinced the story was publishable, and *Alice's Adventures* soon became one of the most popular works of children's literature in the world. After its publication, Carroll wrote several more books for children as well as some books on mathematics.

ABOUT THE SELECTION

Through the Looking Glass, the sequel to *Alice in Wonderland,* was written in 1871. It continues the adventures of Alice through the make-believe world that Carroll had created, populated with live chessmen, talking insects, and the famous character of Humpty Dumpty. This story, like the first *Alice* book, displays Carroll's creative genius and love of puzzles and riddles. Some of the songs and poems are actual parodies of society, while some are comical bits of nonsense verse. The tales are amazingly intricate and complex, but they are also celebrations of the world of fantasy from which adults, unlike children, are too often separated.

GOALS/OBJECTIVES

Studying this lesson will enable students to

- enjoy a work of fantasy filled with wordplay
- describe Lewis Carroll's literary accomplishments and explain the historical significance of his writings
- use the *Oxford English Dictionary* to research word histories
- define *fantasy* and *riddle* and identify and analyze fantasies and riddles they encounter in their reading
- use classifying techniques
- write a comic strip and a simple rhyme

READER'S JOURNAL

How does our society define "normal"? What, by this standard, is unconventional? In your journal, make a list of people generally thought of as "unconventional," or outside the norm, and then name the quality or attribute that makes them so. In what way do they challenge the concept of "normal"?

THINKING SKILLS

Read the Language Arts Survey, 4.7, "Classifying," and devise a system for classifying the items with strange names that Humpty Dumpty describes to Alice. Avoid obvious categories like "animals." Use your imagination to create categories of your own.

FROM

Through the Looking Glass

LEWIS CARROLL

Humpty Dumpty

HOWEVER, the egg only got larger and larger, and more and more human: when she had come within a few yards of it, she saw that it had eyes and a nose and mouth; and, when she had come close to it, she saw clearly that it was HUMPTY DUMPTY himself. "It ca'n't be anybody else!" she said to herself. "I'm as certain of it, as if his name were written all over his face!"

It might have been written a hundred times, easily, on that enormous face. Humpty Dumpty was sitting, with his legs crossed like a Turk, on the top of a high wall—such a narrow one that Alice quite wondered how he could keep his balance—and, as his eyes were steadily fixed in the opposite direction, and he didn't take the least notice of her, she thought he must be a stuffed figure, after all.

"And how exactly like an egg he is !" she said aloud, standing with her hands ready to catch him, for she was every moment expecting him to fall.

"It's *very* provoking," Humpty Dumpty said after a long silence, looking away from Alice as he spoke, "to be called an egg—*very*!"

"I said you *looked* like an egg, Sir," Alice gently explained. "And some eggs are very pretty, you know," she added, hoping to turn her remark into a sort of compliment.

"Some people," said Humpty Dumpty, looking away from her as usual, "have no more sense than a baby!"

Alice didn't know what to say to this: it wasn't at all like conversation, she thought, as he never said anything to *her*: in fact, his last remark was evidently addressed to a tree—so she stood and softly repeated to herself:—

> *Humpty Dumpty sat on a wall:*
> *Humpty Dumpty had a great fall.*
> *All the King's horses and all the King's men*

❶ *What does Alice say aloud? How does the egg respond?*

❷ *What was strange about Alice's conversation with Humpty Dumpty?*

VICTORIAN PROSE / FROM THROUGH THE LOOKING GLASS **797**

---

❶ Alice finishes Humpty's sentence for him by saying, "To send all his horses and all his men." Humpty accuses Alice of eavesdropping.

❷ Humpty is rude to Alice and insults her. He speaks very condescendingly to her.

LITERARY TECHNIQUE

Satire. Carroll included both satiric and absurd elements in his writing. Students should identify what in this selection is satiric and what is being satirized.

QUOTABLES

❝'What is the use of a book,' thought Alice, 'without pictures or conversations?'❞

—Lewis Carroll

---

❶
How does Alice respond when Humpty Dumpty tells her about what the king has promised? How does he respond to her?

❷
What is Humpty Dumpty's attitude toward Alice? How does he speak to her?

Couldn't put Humpty Dumpty in his place again.

"That last line is much too long for the poetry," she added, almost out loud, forgetting that Humpty Dumpty would hear her.

"Don't stand chattering to yourself like that," Humpty Dumpty said, looking at her for the first time, "but tell me your name and your business."

"My name is Alice, but——"

"It's a stupid name enough!" Humpty Dumpty interrupted impatiently. "What does it mean?"

"*Must* a name mean something?" Alice asked doubtfully.

"Of course it must," Humpty Dumpty said with a short laugh: "*my* name means the shape I am—and a good handsome shape it is, too. With a name like yours, you might be any shape, almost."

"Why do you sit out here all alone?" said Alice, not wishing to begin an argument.

"Why, because there's nobody with me!" cried Humpty Dumpty. "Did you think I didn't know the answer to *that*? Ask another."

"Don't you think you'd be safer down on the ground?" Alice went on, not with any idea of making another riddle, but simply in her good-natured anxiety for the queer creature. "That wall is so *very* narrow !"

"What tremendously easy riddles you ask!" Humpty Dumpty growled out. "Of course I don't think so! Why, if ever I *did* fall off—which there's no chance of—but *if* I did——" Here he pursed up his lips, and looked so solemn and grand that Alice could hardly help laughing. "*If* I *did* fall," he went on, "*the King has promised me*—ah, you may turn pale, if you like! You didn't think I was going to say that, did you? *The*

King has promised me—with his very own mouth—to—to—"

"To send all his horses and all his men," Alice interrupted, rather unwisely.

"Now I declare that's too bad!" Humpty Dumpty cried, breaking into a sudden passion. "You've been listening at doors—and behind trees—and down chimneys—or you couldn't have known it!"

"I haven't, indeed!" Alice said very gently. "It's in a book."

"Ah, well! They may write such things in a *book*," Humpty Dumpty said in a calmer tone. "That's what you call a History of England, that is. Now, take a good look at me! I'm one that has spoken to a King, I am: mayhap you'll never see such another: and, to show you I'm not proud, you may shake hands with me!" And he grinned almost from ear to ear, as he leant forwards (and as nearly as possible fell off the wall in doing so) and offered Alice his hand. She watched him a little anxiously as she took it. "If he smiled much more the ends of his mouth might meet behind," she thought: "And then I don't know *what* would happen to his head! I'm afraid it would come off!"

"Yes, all his horses and all his men," Humpty Dumpty went on. "They'd pick me up again in a minute, *they* would! However, this conversation is going on a little too fast: let's go back to the last remark but one."

"I'm afraid I ca'n't quite remember it," Alice said, very politely.

"In that case we start afresh," said Humpty Dumpty, "and it's my turn to choose a subject——" ("He talks about it just as if it was a game!" thought Alice.) "So here's a question for you. How old did you say you were?"

Alice made a short calculation, and said "Seven years and six months."

**ANSWER TO GUIDED READING
QUESTION**

❶ The question Humpty asked was,
"How old did you say you were?"
even though the subject had not
yet come up. Alice interpreted his
question as a request to know how
old she was rather than as a request
to repeat herself.

**ADDITIONAL QUESTIONS
AND ACTIVITIES**

Ask students if Carroll has
succeeded in believably writing
from the point of view of a child.
To what extent is Humpty's
behavior characteristic of some
adults' behavior to very young
children?

Humpty Dumpty. *From Lewis Carroll's Through the
Looking Glass*

"Wrong!" Humpty Dumpty exclaimed
triumphantly. "You never said a word
like it!"

"I thought you meant 'How old *are*
you?' " Alice explained.

"If I'd meant that, I'd have said it," said
Humpty Dumpty.

Alice didn't want to begin another argument, so she said nothing.

"Seven years and six months!" Humpty
Dumpty repeated thoughtfully. "An
uncomfortable sort of age. Now if you'd

asked *my* advice, I'd have said 'Leave off at
seven' ——but it's too late now."

"I never ask advice about growing,"
Alice said indignantly.

"Too proud?" the other enquired.

Alice felt even more indignant at this
suggestion. "I mean," she said, "that one
ca'n't help growing older."

"*One* ca'n't, perhaps," said Humpty
Dumpty; "but *two* can. With proper assistance, you might have left off at seven."

"What a beautiful belt you've got on!"
Alice suddenly remarked. (They had had
quite enough of the subject of age, she
thought: and, if they really were to take
turns in choosing subjects, it was *her* turn
now.) "At least," she corrected herself on
second thoughts, "a beautiful cravat,[1] I

❶
*How does
Humpty Dumpty
turn a simple
question about
Alice's age into a
trick question?*

---

1. **cravat.** Scarf, necktie, or any article of clothing worn
around the neck

VICTORIAN PROSE / FROM *THROUGH THE LOOKING GLASS*   **799**

ANSWER TO GUIDED READING QUESTION

❶ Humpty received his cravat from the White King and Queen for his un-birthday.

ADDITIONAL QUESTIONS AND ACTIVITIES

Have students choose a character in a nursery rhyme or fairy tale that they would like Alice to meet. Students should write about an encounter between the two characters. What qualities of the character would you emphasize? How might you use that character in a satirical way?

ADDITIONAL QUESTIONS AND ACTIVITIES

Ask students if Humpty Dumpty has anything in common with writers and, in particular, the author of this novel. Point out that Carroll poses riddles to the reader, much like Humpty does to Alice. Humpty shares the writer's freedom to use words as he wills. Also, Carroll and Humpty are both perched precariously on a wall—both are in danger of having their wordplay and riddling alienate a reader or listener. Should the reader be as annoyed with Carroll as Alice is with Humpty? Should the reader admire both Carroll and Humpty's wordplay?

should have said—no, a belt, I mean—I beg your pardon!" she added in dismay, for Humpty Dumpty looked thoroughly offended, and she began to wish she hadn't chosen that subject. "If only I knew," she thought to herself, "which was neck and which was waist!"

Evidently Humpty Dumpty was very angry, though he said nothing for a minute or two. When he *did* speak again, it was in a deep growl.

"It is a—*most—provoking*—thing," he said at last, "when a person doesn't know a cravat from a belt!"

"I know it's very ignorant of me," Alice said, in so humble a tone that Humpty Dumpty relented.

"It's a cravat, child, and a beautiful one, as you say. It's a present from the White King and Queen. There now!"

"Is it really?" said Alice, quite pleased to find that she *had* chosen a good subject after all.

"They gave it me," Humpty Dumpty continued thoughtfully as he crossed one knee over the other and clasped his hands round it, "they gave it me—for an un-birthday present."

"I beg your pardon?" Alice said with a puzzled air.

"I'm not offended," said Humpty Dumpty.

"I mean, what *is* an un-birthday present?"

"A present given when it isn't your birthday, of course."

Alice considered a little. "I like birthday presents best," she said at last.

"You don't know what you're talking about!" cried Humpty Dumpty. "How many days are there in a year?"

❶
On what occasion did Humpty Dumpty receive his cravat? from whom?

"Three hundred and sixty-five," said Alice.

"And how many birthdays have you?"

"One."

"And if you take one from three hundred and sixty-five what remains?"

"Three hundred and sixty-four, of course."

Humpty Dumpty looked doubtful. "I'd rather see that done on paper," he said.

Alice couldn't help smiling as she took out her memorandum-book, and worked the sum for him:

$$
\begin{array}{r}
365 \\
\underline{1} \\
364
\end{array}
$$

Humpty Dumpty took the book and looked at it carefully. "That seems to be done right——" he began.

"You're holding it upside down!" Alice interrupted.

"To be sure I was!" Humpty Dumpty said gaily as she turned it round for him. "I thought it looked a little queer. As I was saying, that *seems* to be done right—though I haven't time to look it over thoroughly just now—and that shows that there are three hundred and sixty-four days when you might get un-birthday presents——"

"Certainly," said Alice.

"And only *one* for birthday presents, you know. There's glory for you!"

"I don't know what you mean by 'glory,' " Alice said.

Humpty Dumpty smiled <u>contemptuously.</u> "Of course you don't—till I tell you. I meant 'there's a nice knock-down argument for you!' "

WORDS FOR EVERYDAY USE: **con • temp • tu • ous • ly** (kən temp´chōō əs lē) *adv.*, scornfully

800   *UNIT NINE / THE VICTORIAN AGE*

VOCABULARY IN CONTEXT

• He spat out <u>contemptuously</u>, "I am not a waiter, I am the maitre d'!"

• I keep my dirty clothes in one compartment of my <u>portmanteau</u>, and my clean clothes in the other.

800   TEACHER'S EDITION

"But 'glory' doesn't mean 'a nice knock-down argument,' " Alice objected.

"When *I* use a word," Humpty Dumpty said, in rather a scornful tone, "it means just what I choose it to mean—neither more nor less."

"The question is," said Alice, "whether you *can* make words mean so many different things."

"The question is," said Humpty Dumpty, "which is to be master——that's all."

Alice was too much puzzled to say anything; so after a minute Humpty Dumpty began again. "They've a temper, some of them—particularly verbs: they're the proudest—adjectives you can do anything with, but not verbs—however, *I* can manage the whole lot of them! Impenetrability! That's what *I* say!"

"Would you tell me please," said Alice, "what that means?"

"Now you talk like a reasonable child," said Humpty Dumpty, looking very much pleased. "I meant by 'impenetrability' that we've had enough of that subject, and it would be just as well if you'd mention what you mean to do next, as I suppose you don't mean to stop here all the rest of your life."

"That's a great deal to make one word mean," Alice said in a thoughtful tone.

"When I make a word do a lot of work like that," said Humpty Dumpty, "I always pay it extra."

"Oh!" said Alice. She was too much puzzled to make any other remark.

"Ah, you should see 'em come round me of a Saturday night," Humpty Dumpty went on, wagging his head gravely from side to side, "for to get their wages, you know."

(Alice didn't venture to ask what he paid them with; and so you see I ca'n't tell *you*.)

"You seem very clever at explaining words, Sir," said Alice. "Would you kindly tell me the meaning of the poem called 'Jabberwocky'?"

"Let's hear it," said Humpty Dumpty. "I can explain all the poems that ever were invented—and a good many that haven't been invented just yet."

This sounded very hopeful, so Alice repeated the first verse:—

> " '*Twas brillig, and the slithy toves*
> *Did gyre and gimble in the wabe:*
> *All mimsy were the borogoves,*
> *And the mome raths outgrabe.*"

"That's enough to begin with," Humpty Dumpty interrupted: "there are plenty of hard words there. '*Brillig*' means four o'clock in the afternoon—the time when you begin *broiling* things for dinner."

"That'll do very well," said Alice: "and '*slithy*'?"

"Well, '*slithy*' means 'lithe and slimy.' 'Lithe' is the same as 'active.' You see it's like a <u>portmanteau</u>— there are two meanings packed up into one word."

"I see it now," Alice remarked thoughtfully: "and what are '*toves*'?"

"Well, '*toves*' are something like badgers—they're something like lizards—and they're something like corkscrews."

"They must be very curious-looking creatures."

WORDS FOR EVERYDAY USE: **port • man • teau** (pôr man´tō´) *n.,* traveling case that opens into two compartments

VICTORIAN PROSE / FROM *THROUGH THE LOOKING GLASS* **801**

❶ *What does Humpty Dumpty say about the meanings of words? What does this say about his character? What does this say about the society in which he lives?*

❷ *What does Alice ask Humpty Dumpty to explain to her? Why does she ask him to do this?*

ANSWERS TO GUIDED READING QUESTIONS

❶ Humpty says that the words he uses mean whatever he wants them to mean. His character is bizarre and difficult to communicate with. The society is probably confusing and somewhat anarchic.

❷ Alice asks Humpty to explain the poem "Jabberwocky." Because the poem is nonsensical and Humpty makes up his own meanings for words, he is the perfect person to interpret the poem.

ADDITIONAL QUESTIONS AND ACTIVITIES

Have students think of other objects or pieces of furniture that might be used to represent certain kinds of words. For example, a sleeper-sofa word might be a word with a hidden meaning. Share these categories and examples of words with the class.

QUOTABLES

❝'Where shall I begin, please your Majesty?' he asked. 'Begin at the beginning,' the King said, gravely, 'and go on till you come to the end: then stop.'❞

—Lewis Carroll

TEACHER'S EDITION **801**

❶ Alice feels she must listen to the poem because Humpty said he created it entirely for her amusement.

❷ Humpty says that Alice's remarks aren't sensible and that they put him out.

❸ Alice found these difficult words in a book.

Additional Questions and Activities

Have students read the poem "Jabberwocky" and, using Humpty Dumpty's interpretation as a model, translate the rest of the poem.

Additional Questions and Activities

Have students briefly review what they learned about the medieval romance. Them have them identify the elements of "Jabberwocky" that seem to come from medieval romance, or works of chivalry.

---

❶ *Why does Alice feel she has to listen to Humpty Dumpty's poem?*

❷ *What does Humpty Dumpty say about Alice's remarks after his verses?*

❸ *Where has Alice heard these difficult words?*

"They are that," said Humpty Dumpty: "also they make their nests under sun-dials—also they live on cheese."

"And what's to 'gyre' and to 'gimble'?"

"To 'gyre' is to go round and round like a gyroscope. To 'gimble' is to make holes like a gimlet."

"And 'the wabe' is the grass-plot round a sundial, I suppose?" said Alice, surprised at her own ingenuity.

"Of course it is. It's called 'wabe' you know, because it goes a long way before it, and a long way behind it——"

"And a long way beyond it on each side," Alice added.

"Exactly so. Well then, 'mimsy' is 'flimsy and miserable' (there's another portmanteau for you). And a 'borogove' is a thin shabby-looking bird with its feathers sticking out all round—something like a live mop."

"And then 'mome raths'?" said Alice. "I'm afraid I'm giving you a great deal of trouble."

"Well, a 'rath' is a sort of green pig: but 'mome' I'm not certain about. I think it's short for 'from home'— meaning that they'd lost their way, you know."

"And what does 'outgrabe' mean?"

"Well, 'outgribing' is something between bellowing and whistling, with a kind of sneeze in the middle: however, you'll hear it done, maybe—down in the wood yonder—and, when you've once heard it, you'll be *quite* content. Who's been repeating all that hard stuff to you?"

"I read it in a book" said Alice. "But I had some poetry repeated to me much easier than that, by— 'Tweedledee, I think it was."

"As to poetry, you know," said Humpty Dumpty, stretching out one of his great hands, "I can repeat poetry as well as other folk, if it comes to that——"

"Oh, it needn't come to that!" Alice hastily said, hoping to keep him from beginning.

"The piece I'm going to repeat," he went on without noticing her remark, "was written entirely for your amusement."

Alice felt that in that case she really *ought* to listen to it; so she sat down, and said "Thank you" rather sadly.

"In winter, when the fields are white,
I sing this song for your delight—

only I don't sing it," he added, as an explanation.

"I see you don't," said Alice.

"If you can *see* whether I'm singing or not, you've sharper eyes than most," Humpty Dumpty remarked severely. Alice was silent.

"In spring, when woods are getting green,
I'll try and tell you what I mean:"

"Thank you very much," said Alice.

"In summer, when the days are long,
Perhaps you'll understand the song:

In autumn, when the leaves are brown,
Take pen and ink, and write it down."

"I will, if I can remember it so long," said Alice.

"You needn't go on making remarks like that," Humpty Dumpty said: "they're not sensible, and they put me out."

"I sent a message to the fish:

I told them 'This is what I wish.'

The little fishes of the sea
They sent an answer back to me.

The little fishes' answer was
'We cannot do it, Sir, because —'"

"I'm afraid I don't quite understand," said Alice.

"It gets easier further on," Humpty Dumpty replied.

"I sent to them again to say
'It will be better to obey.'

The fishes answered, with a grin,
'Why, what a temper you are in!'

I told them once, I told them twice:
They would not listen to advice.

I took a kettle large and new,
Fit for the deed I had to do.

My heart went hop, my heart went thump:
I filled the kettle at the pump.

Then some one came to me and said
'The little fishes are in bed.'

I said to him, I said it plain,
'Then you must wake them up again.'

I said it very loud and clear:
I went and shouted in his ear."

Humpty Dumpty raised his voice almost to a scream as he repeated this verse, and Alice thought, with a shudder, "I wouldn't have been the messenger for *anything*!"

"But he was very stiff and proud:
He said, 'You needn't shout so loud!'

And he was very proud and stiff:
He said 'I'd go and wake them, if—'

I took a corkscrew from the shelf:
I went to wake them up myself.

And when I found the door was locked,
I pulled and pushed and kicked and knocked.

And when I found the door was shut,
I tried to turn the handle, but—"

There was a long pause.
"Is that all?" Alice timidly asked.
"That's all," said Humpty Dumpty. "Good-bye."

This was rather sudden, Alice thought: but, after such a *very* strong hint that she ought to be going, she felt that it would hardly be civil to stay. So she got up, and held out her hand. "Good-bye, till we meet again!" she said as cheerfully as she could.

"I shouldn't know you again if we *did* meet," Humpty Dumpty replied in a discontented tone, giving her one of his fingers to shake: "you're so exactly like other people."

"The face is what one goes by, generally," Alice remarked in a thoughtful tone.

"That's just what I complain of," said Humpty Dumpty. "Your face is the same as everybody has—the two eyes, so——" (marking their places in the air with his thumb) "nose in the middle, mouth under. It's always the same. Now if you had the two eyes on the same side of the nose, for instance—or the mouth at the top—that would be *some* help."

❶
How does Humpty Dumpty let Alice know that she should leave?

❷
What does Humpty Dumpty say about Alice? What does he mean?

❶ Humpty Dumpty tells Alice "Good-bye."

❷ Humpty says that Alice has a face just like everyone else. Her face has two eyes, one nose, and one mouth arranged in the customary way.

ANSWERS TO SELECTION CHECK TEST 4.9.39

EX. On what is Humpty Dumpty sitting?
He is sitting on a wall.

1. Humpty says that it is very provoking to be called what?
He says that it is very provoking to be called an egg.

2. Why does Humpty think that Alice's name is "stupid"?
He thinks that because the name doesn't have a meaning.

3. What has the king promised Humpty should he fall?
The king has promised to send all his horses and all his men.

4. For what does Alice mistake Humpty Dumpty's cravat?
She mistakes it for a belt.

5. What is the title of the poem that Humpty explains to Alice?
The title is "Jabberwocky."

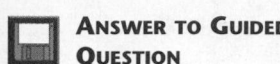

ANSWER TO GUIDED READING QUESTION

❶ Alice doesn't like Humpty Dumpty. He is rude, self-centered, and confusing. The great crash is Humpty Dumpty falling off the wall.

RESPONDING TO THE SELECTION

Ask students to act out their response for the class or for small groups.

ANSWERS FOR REVIEWING THE SELECTION

RECALLING

1. He is sitting cross-legged on top of a high narrow wall.

2. He is wearing a cravat. He received it from the White King and Queen for his un-birthday.

3. Humpty says that he can make words mean anything he likes.

4. He says "Good-bye" to Alice.

INTERPRETING

Responses will vary. Possible responses are given.

5. Humpty says that it is very provoking to be called an egg.

6. Alice can't tell Humpty's neck from his waist because he is shaped like an egg. Humpty is again provoked by this confusion. He becomes much nicer when she admits that she is ignorant.

7. Humpty's distortions of language point to his arrogance and distaste for rules he sees as intended for the small-minded.

8. Humpty likes to be in control of any situation. He dismisses Alice to show his contempt for her.

SYNTHESIZING

Responses will vary. Possible responses are given.

9. Humpty's attitude is scornful. He has no regard for rules and standards. He prefers to make his own rules. His suggestion that Alice choose to stop growing is another example of his distaste for rules.

10. Alice was insulted, and Humpty bewildered rather than helped her. His conversation skills do not enable him to communicate with other persons. Alice's conversation methods show an awareness of the other person's intentions and feelings.

How does Alice feel about Humpty Dumpty? Why does she feel this way? What is the great crash? What has happened to Humpty Dumpty?

"It wouldn't look nice," Alice objected. But Humpty Dumpty only shut his eyes, and said "Wait till you've tried."

Alice waited a minute to see if he would speak again, but, as he never opened his eyes or took any further notice of her, she said "Good-bye!" once more, and, getting no answer to this, she quietly walked way: but she couldn't help saying to herself, as she went, "of all the unsatisfactory——" (she repeated this aloud, as it was a great comfort to have such a long word to say) "of all the unsatisfactory people I *ever* met——" She never finished the sentence, for at this moment a heavy crash shook the forest from end to end. ∎

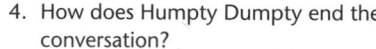

Responding to the Selection

Imagine that you are Alice. How would you react to meeting the character of Humpty Dumpty? Choose a particular exchange from the selection and write your own response as though you were Alice.

Reviewing the Selection

RECALLING

1. What is Humpty Dumpty doing when Alice first encounters him?

2. What is Humpty Dumpty wearing? On what occasion did he receive this item?

3. What does Humpty Dumpty say about words and their meaning?

4. How does Humpty Dumpty end the conversation?

INTERPRETING

5. What is Humpty Dumpty's reaction to Alice's interpretation of his appearance?

6. What is Alice's initial confusion about what Humpty Dumpty is wearing? How does he first react to this confusion, and why does his attitude change?

7. What do Humpty Dumpty's ideas about language say about his character and his attitude toward rules?

8. Why does Humpty Dumpty like to confuse and challenge Alice? Why does he choose to end the conversation abruptly?

SYNTHESIZING

9. What is Humpty Dumpty's attitude as he says "You're so exactly like other people" to Alice? What does this say about Humpty Dumpty's attitude toward rules and standards? What other examples of this attitude exist in the selection?

10. Why does Alice call her meeting with Humpty Dumpty unsatisfactory? What might you say about Humpty Dumpty's conversational skills? What might you say about Alice's?

804   *UNIT NINE / THE VICTORIAN AGE*

ANSWERS FOR LANGUAGE LAB

Responses will vary. Student responses should address each of the five elements of the activity and be clearly written. Praise responses that provide extensive histories, multiple definitions, or multiple related words.

▶Additional practice is available in the *Essential Skills Practice Book: Language,* 2.143 and 2.144.

804   TEACHER'S EDITION

Understanding Literature (Questions for Discussion)

1. **Fantasy.** A **fantasy** is a literary work that contains highly unrealistic elements. However, even a fantasy needs an element of "reality" to make it believable and accessible to the reader. Cite the elements of the Humpty Dumpty story that characterize it as a work of fantasy—and those that are what we would call reality. You may also want to think of a modern example of fantasy and separate its elements of fantasy and reality.

2. **Riddle.** A **riddle** is a word game in which something is described in an unusual way and the reader or listener must figure out what that something is. Humpty Dumpty poses many puzzling questions to Alice. What aim might Humpty Dumpty have in conversing with Alice the way he does? Also, what purpose might Carroll have in creating a character like Humpty Dumpty and bringing him into contact with Alice?

Responding in Writing

1. **Comic Strip.** Choose any inanimate, familiar object and give it human qualities. Change it into a character and give it a name like the transformation of the egg into Humpty Dumpty. Then write a short narrative—in the form of a comic strip—that describes a meeting between you and your object. Focus on the difference between the "real world" that you live in and the imaginary world of your creation.

2. **Simple Rhyme.** Take the story used in your comic strip and convey it in the form of a rhyming poem like the one Humpty Dumpty recites to Alice in the selection. Copy the same meter and rhythm if you wish, and try to use vivid images. Try your hand at some word play and riddles. You may even want to create your own words in the style of Carroll.

Language Lab

Word Origins. Read the Language Arts Survey, 2.143, and 2.144, "Word Origins I and II." Then, using the *Oxford English Dictionary* in your library, look up a word that has a particularly long entry and prepare a short report describing the word's:

1. history—the original form of the word,

2. spelling and pronunciation—how it may have changed through time,

3. archaic forms—forms which are no longer in use,

4. various definitions—if it can be used in more than one way, and

5. "relatives"—other words or uses that are related to it.

ANALYTIC SCALES FOR RESPONDING IN WRITING (CONT.)

fantastic but in some way grounded in reality.
- **Language/Style.** The comic uses vivid and precise nouns, verbs, and modifiers.
- **Conventions.** The comic avoids errors in spelling, grammar, usage, mechanics, and manuscript form.

2. **Simple Rhyme**
- **Content/Unity.** The rhyme communicates the same information as that in the comic strip.

- **Language/Style.** The rhyme uses wordplay, puns, riddles, or made-up words.
- **Conventions.** The rhyme avoids errors in spelling, grammar, usage, mechanics, and manuscript form.

ANSWERS FOR UNDERSTANDING LITERATURE

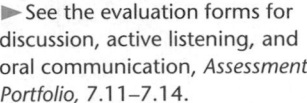

► See the evaluation forms for discussion, active listening, and oral communication, *Assessment Portfolio*, 7.11–7.14.
Responses will vary. Possible responses are given.

1. Fantasy. The most obvious element of fantasy is that Humpty Dumpty is a giant talking egg. His personality is also fantastically absurd. It might be said that the conversation they have, while surreal in parts, is realistic in that it is awkward and unsatisfying.
►**Teaching Note:** Discuss with students why it is important that all fantasies have realistic elements in them.

2. Riddle. Humpty Dumpty wants to confuse Alice and, in doing so, make himself appear superior. Humpty Dumpty's arrogance is an exaggerated version of how many adults treat children. Carroll also emphasizes Alice's good manners and polite behavior in contrast to Humpty Dumpty's rudeness.
►**Teaching Note:** Riddles have been a part of literature for thousands of years. Ask students a famous riddle, the Riddle of the Sphinx, from Sophocles's play *Oedipus Rex:* "What goes on four feet in the morning, two at noon, and in the evening on three?" *Answer.* A person in three stages of life—infancy, maturity, and infirm old age.

ANALYTIC SCALES FOR RESPONDING IN WRITING

Assign a score from 1 to 25 for each grading criterion below. (For more detailed evaluation, see the evaluation forms for writing, revising, and proofreading, *Assessment Portfolio*, 7.1–7.10.)

1. Comic Strip
- **Content/Unity.** The comic depicts an animated object and the student comparing their worlds.
- **Organization/Coherence.** The comic describes a number of differences between worlds, and may describe similarities in a way that is
(cont.)

"Flower in the Crannied Wall"
by Alfred, Lord Tennyson

Flower in the crannied wall,
I pluck you out of the crannies,
I hold you here, root and all, in my hand,
Little flower—but if I could understand
5   What you are, root and all, and all in all,
I should know what God and man is.

"When I Was One-and-Twenty"
by A. E. Housman

When I was one-and-twenty
   I heard a wise man say,
"Give crowns and pounds and guineas[1]
   But not your heart away;
5   Give pearls away and rubies
   But keep your fancy free."
But I was one-and-twenty,
   No use to talk to me.

When I was one-and-twenty
10   I heard him say again,
"The heart out of the bosom
   Was never given in vain;
'Tis paid with sighs a plenty
   And sold for endless rue."
15 And I am two-and-twenty,
   And oh, 'tis true, 'tis true.

"Loveliest of Trees" by A. E. Housman

Loveliest of trees, the cherry now
Is hung with bloom along the bough,
And stands about the woodland ride
Wearing white for Eastertide.

5   Now, of my threescore years and ten,
Twenty will not come again,
And take from seventy springs a score,
It only leaves me fifty more.

---

1. **crowns . . . guineas.** Different units of money

And since to look at things in bloom
10 Fifty springs are little room,
About the woodlands I will go
To see the cherry hung with snow.

"The Runaway Slave at Pilgrim's Point"[2]
by Elizabeth Barrett Browning

I

I stand on the mark beside the shore
   Of the first white pilgrim's bended knee,
Where exile turned to ancestor,
   And God was thanked for liberty.
5   I have run through the night, my skin is dark,
I bend my knee down on this mark:
   I look on the sky and the sea.

II

O pilgrim-souls, I speak to you!
   I see you come proud and slow
10 From the land of the spirits pale as dew
   And round me and round me ye go.
O pilgrims, I have gasped and run
All night long from the whips of one
   Who in your names works sin and woe!

III

15 And thus I thought that I would come
   And kneel here where ye knelt before,
And feel your souls around me hum
   In undertone to the ocean's roar;
And lift my black face, my black hand,
20 Here, in your names, to curse this land
   Ye blessed in freedom's, evermore.

IV

I am black, I am black,
   And yet God made me, they say:
But if He did so, smiling back
25   He must have cast his work away
Under the feet of his white creatures,
With a look of scorn, that the dusky features
   Might be trodden again to clay.

---

2. **Pilgrim's Point.** The Puritans fleeing persecution in England first landed at this point at Plymouth Rock, Massachusetts.

"FLOWER IN THE CRANNIED WALL"

About the Author. A biography of Alfred, Lord Tennyson appears on page 698.

About the Selection. This poem is reminiscent of "In Memoriam" inasmuch as the poet thinks of nature as being inextricably joined with God.

"WHEN I WAS ONE-AND-TWENTY"

"LOVELIEST OF TREES"

About the Author. A biography of A. E. Housman appears on page 777.

About the Selections. Both selections can be linked with "To an Athlete Dying Young" in that they deal with the futility of achievement and the inevitability of death.

ADDITIONAL QUESTIONS AND ACTIVITIES

In 1933, Housman published an essay entitled "The Name and Nature of Poetry." In it he asserts that great poetry is inaccessible to the intellect and reaches "some region deeper than the mind." Ask students whether, according to his own criteria, Housman's poems can be considered great. Why, or why not?

"THE RUNAWAY SLAVE AT PILGRIM'S POINT"

About the Author. A biography of Elizabeth Barrett Browning appears on page 757.

About the Selection. Browning wrote this poem in 1850, just seventeen years after slavery was outlawed in Great Britain and its colonies.

V

30 And yet He has made dark things
　　To be glad and merry as light:
　There's a little dark bird sits and sings,
　　There's a dark stream ripples out of sight,
　And the dark frogs chant in the safe morass,
　And the sweetest stars are made to pass
35 　　O'er the face of the darkest night.

VI

　But *we* who are dark, we are dark!
　　Ah God, we have no stars!
　About our souls in care and cark
　　Our blackness shuts like prison-bars:
40 　The poor souls crouch so far behind
　That never a comfort they can find
　　By reaching through the prison-bars.

VII

　Indeed we live beneath the sky,
　　That great smooth Hand of God stretched out
45 On all his children fatherly,
　　To save them from the dread and doubt
　Which would be if, from this low place,
　All opened straight up to his face
　　Into the grand eternity.

VIII

50 And still God's sunshine and his frost,
　　They make us hot, they make us cold,
　As if we were not black and lost;
　　And the beasts and birds, in wood and fold,
　Do fear and take us for very men:
55 Could the whippoorwill or the cat of the glen
　　Look into my eyes and be bold?

IX

　I am black, I am black!
　　But, once, I laughed in girlish glee,
　For one of my color stood in the track
60 　Where the drivers drove, and looked at me,
　And tender and full was the look he gave—
　Could a slave look *so* at another slave?—
　　I look at the sky and the sea.

X

　And from that hour our spirits grew
65 　As free as if unsold, unbought:
　Oh, strong enough, since we were two,
　　To conquer the world, we thought.
　The drivers drove us day by day;
　We did not mind, we went one way,
70 　And no better a freedom sought.

XI

　In the sunny ground between the canes,[1]
　　He said "I love you" as he passed;
　When the shingle-roof rang sharp with the rains,
　　I heard how he vowed it fast:
75 While others shook he smiled in the hut,
　As he carved me a bowl of the coconut
　　Through the roar of the hurricanes.

XII

　I sang his name instead of a song,
　　Over and over I sang his name,
80 Upward and downward I drew it along
　　My various notes,—the same, the same!
　I sang it low, that the slave-girls near
　Might never guess, from aught they could hear,
　　It was only a name—a name.

XIII

85 I look on the sky and the sea.
　　We were two to love and two to pray:
　Yes, two, O God, who cried to Thee,
　　Though nothing didst Thou say!
　Coldly Thou sat'st behind the sun:
90 And now I cry who am but one,
　　Thou wilt not speak today.

XIV

　We were black, we were black,
　　We had no claim to love and bliss,
　What marvel if each went to wrack?
95 　They wrung my cold hands out of his,
　They dragged him—where? I crawled to touch
　His blood's mark in the dust . . . not much,
　　Ye pilgrim-souls, though plain as *this!*

XV

　Wrong, followed by a deeper wrong!
100 　Mere grief's too good for such as I:
　So the white men brought the shame ere long
　　To strangle the sob of my agony.
　They would not leave me for my dull
　Wet eyes!—it was too merciful
105 　To let me weep pure tears and die.

XVI

　I am black, I am black!
　　I wore a child upon my breast,
　An amulet that hung too slack,
　　And, in my unrest, could not rest:
110 Thus we went moaning, child and mother,
　One to another, one to another,
　　Until all ended for the best.

---

1. **canes.** Sugar canes; these slaves worked on a sugar plantation.

Ask students why Browning might have chosen Pilgrim's Point, or Plymouth Rock, as the setting for this poem. Remind students that Plymouth was founded by pilgrims who fled England seeking religious freedom. What does this juxtaposition of freedom and slavery achieve?

LITERARY TECHNIQUE

A **stanza** is a recurring pattern
of grouped lines in a poem. A
heptastich is a seven-line stanza.
Thirty-six heptastiches, also called
septets, comprise this poem.

**ADDITIONAL QUESTIONS
AND ACTIVITIES**

A **refrain** is a linear group of
lines repeated in a poem or song.
Have students identify the refrains
in the poem and explain how they
illuminate the poem's theme.

XVII

For hark! I will tell you low, low,
    I am black, you see,—
115 And the babe who lay on my bosom so,
      Was far too white, too white for me;
As white as the ladies who scorned to pray
Beside me at church but yesterday,
      Though my tears had washed a place for my
      knee.

XVIII

120 My own, own child! I could not bear
      To look in his face, it was so white;
I covered him up with a kerchief there,
      I covered his face in close and tight:
And he moaned and struggled, as well might be,
125 For the white child wanted his liberty—
      Ha, ha! he wanted the master-right.

XIX

He moaned and beat with his head and feet,
      His little feet that never grew;
He struck them out, as it was meet,
130   Against my heart to break it through:
I might have sung and made him mild,
But I dared not sing to the white faced child
      The only song I knew.

XX

I pulled the kerchief very close:
135   He could not see the sun, I swear,
More, then, alive, than now he does
      From between the roots of the mango . . . where?
I know where. Close! A child and mother
Do wrong to look at one another
140   When one is black and one is fair.

XXI

Why, in that single glance I had
      Of my child's face, . . . I tell you all,
I saw a look that made me mad!
      The *master's* look, that used to fall
145 On my soul like his lash . . . or worse!
And so, to save it from my curse,
      I twisted it round in my shawl.

XXII

And he moaned and trembled from foot to head,
      He shivered from head to foot;
150 Till after a time, he lay instead
      Too suddenly still and mute.
I felt, beside, a stiffening cold:
I dared to lift up just as fold,
      As in lifting a leaf on the mango-fruit.

XXIII

155 But *my* fruit . . . ha, ha!—there, had been
      (I laugh to think on't this hour!)
Your fine white angels (who have seen
      Nearest the secret of God's power)
And plucked my fruit to make them wine,
160 And sucked the soul of that child of mine
      As the hummingbird sucks the soul of
      the flower.

XXIV

Ha, ha, the trick of the angels white!
      They freed the white child's spirit so.
I said not a word, but day and night
165   I carried the body to and fro,
And it lay on my heart like a stone, as chill.
      —The sun may shine out as much as he will:
      I am cold, though it happened a month ago.

XXV

From the white man's house, and the black man's hut,
170   I carried the little body on:
The forest's arms did round us shut,
      And silence through the trees did run:
They asked no question as I went,
They stood too high for astonishment,
175   They could see God sit on his throne.

XXVI

My little body, kerchiefed fast,
      I bore it on through the forest, on;
And when I felt it was tired at last,
      I scooped a hole beneath the moon:
180 Through the forest-tops the angels far,
With a white sharp finger from every star,
      Did point and mock at what was done.

XXVII

Yet when it was all done aright,—
      Earth, 'twixt me and my baby, strewed,—
185 All, changed to black earth,—nothing white,—
      A dark child in the dark!—ensued
Some comfort, and my heart grew young;
I sate down smiling there and sung
      The song I learnt in my maidenhood.

XXVIII

190 And thus we two were reconciled,
      The white child and black mother, thus;
For I sang it soft and wild,
      The same song, more melodious,
Rose from the grave whereon I sate:
195 It was the dead child singing that,
      To join the souls of both of us.

XXIX

I look on the sea and the sky.
    Where the pilgrims' ships first anchored lay
The free sun rideth gloriously,
200   But the pilgrim ghosts have slid away
Through the earliest streaks of the morn:
My face is black, but it glares with a scorn
    Which they dare not meet by day.

XXX

Ha!—in their stead, their hunter sons!
205   Ha, ha! they are on me—they hunt in a ring!
Keep off! I brave you all at once,
    I throw off your eyes like snakes that sting!
You have killed the black eagle at nest, I think:
Did you ever stand still in your triumph, and shrink
210   From the stroke of her wounded wing?

XXXI

(Man, drop that stone you dared to lift!—)
    I wish you who stand there five abreast,
Each, for his own wife's joy and gift,
    A little corpse as safely at rest
215 As mine in the mangoes! Yes, but *she*
May keep live babies on her knee,
    And sing the song she likes the best.

XXXII

I am not mad: I am black.
    I see you staring in my face—
220 I know you staring, shrinking back,
    Ye are born of the Washington-race,
And this land is the free America,
And this mark on my wrist—(I prove what I say)
    Ropes tied me up here to the flogging-place.

XXXIII

225 You think I shrieked then? Not a sound
    I hung, as a gourd hangs in the sun;
I only cursed them all around
    As softly as I might have done
My very own child: from these sands
230 Up to the mountains, lift your hands,
    O slaves, and end what I begun!

XXXIV

Whips, curses; these must answer those!
    For in this union you have set
Two kinds of men in adverse rows,
235   Each loathing each; and all forget
The seven wounds in Christ's body fair,
    While He sees gaping everywhere
Our countless wounds that pay no debt.[1]

XXXV

Our wounds are different. Your white men
240   Are, after all, not gods indeed,
Nor able to make Christs again
    Do good with bleeding. *We* who bleed
(Stand off!) we help not in our loss!
We are too heavy for our cross,
245   And fall and crush you and your seed.

XXXVI

I fall, I swoon! I look at the sky.
    The clouds are breaking on my brain;
I am floated along, as if I should die
    Of liberty's exquisite pain.
250 In the name of the white child waiting for me
In the death-dark where we may kiss and agree,
White men, I leave you all curse-free
    In my broken heart's disdain!

"The Night is Darkening"
by Emily Brontë

The night is darkening round me,
    The wild winds coldly blow;
But a tyrant spell has bound me,
    And I cannot, cannot go.

5 The giant trees are bending
    Their bare boughs weighed with snow;
The storm is fast descending,
    And yet I cannot go.

Clouds beyond clouds above me,
10   Wastes beyond wastes below;
But nothing drear can move me:
    I will not, cannot go.

from *The Subjection of Women*
by John Stuart Mill

The social subordination of women thus stands out an isolated fact in modern social institutions; a solitary breach of what has become their fundamental law; a single relic of an old world of thought and practice exploded in everything else, but retained in the one thing of most universal interest; as if a gigantic dolmen,[2] or a vast temple of Jupiter Olympius, occupied the site of St. Paul's

---

1. **pay no debt.** Jesus' death on the cross was payment for the sins of humanity, according to the Bible.
2. **dolmen.** A neolithic stone monument associated with pagan rites

---

and received daily worship, while the surrounding Christian churches were only resorted to on fasts and festivals. This entire discrepancy between one social fact and all those which accompany it, and the radical opposition between its nature and the progressive movement which is the boast of the modern world, and which has successively swept away everything else of an analogous character, surely affords, to a conscientious observer of human tendencies, serious matter for reflection. It raises a *primâ facie*[1] presumption on the unfavorable side, far outweighing any which custom and usage could in such circumstances create on the favorable; and should at least suffice to make this, like the choice between republicanism and royalty, a balanced question.

"The Slave Ship,"[2] from *Modern Painters*
by John Ruskin

But I think the noblest sea that Turner has ever painted, and, if so, the noblest certainly ever painted by man, is that of "The Slave Ship," the chief Academy picture of the exhibition of 1840. It is a sunset on the Atlantic after prolonged storm; but the storm is partially lulled, and the torn and streaming rain clouds are moving in scarlet lines to lose themselves in the hollow of the night. The whole surface of sea included in the picture is divided into two ridges of enormous swell, not high, nor local, but a low, broad heaving of the whole ocean, like the lifting of its bosom by deep-drawn breath after the torture of the storm. Between these two ridges the fire of the sunset falls along the trough of the sea, dyeing it with an awful but glorious light, the intense and lurid splendor which burns like gold and bathes like blood. Along this fiery path and valley the tossing waves by which the swell of the sea is restlessly divided lift themselves in dark, indefinite, fantastic forms, each casting a faint and ghastly shadow behind it along the illumined foam. They do not rise everywhere, but three or four together in wild groups, fitfully and furiously, as the under-strength of the swell compels or permits them; leaving between them treacherous spaces of level and whirling water, now lighted with green and lamplike fire, now flashing back the gold of the declining sun, now fearfully shed from above with the indistinguishable images of the burning clouds, which fall upon them in flakes of crimson and scarlet and give to the reckless waves the added motion of their own fiery being. Purple and blue, the lurid shadows of the hollow breakers are cast upon the mist of

1. *primâ facie.* First view before further examination
2. **"The Slave Ship."** A painting by Turner, picturing a slave ship at sunset with dead slaves being thrown overboard

night, which gathers cold and low, advancing like the shadow of death upon the guilty ship as it labors amidst the lightning of the sea, its thin masts written upon the sky in lines of blood, girded with condemnation in that fearful hue which signs the sky with horror, and mixes its flaming flood with the sunlight, and, cast far along the desolate heave of the sepulchral waves, incarnadines the multitudinous sea.

I believe, if I were reduced to rest Turner's immortality upon any single work, I should choose this. Its daring conception—ideal in the highest sense of the word—is based on the purest truth, and wrought out with the concentrated knowledge of a life; its color is absolutely perfect, not one false or morbid hue in any part or line, and so modulated that every square inch of canvas is a perfect composition; its drawing as accurate as fearless; the ship buoyant, bending, and full of motion; its tones as true as they are wonderful; and the whole picture dedicated to the most sublime of subjects and impressions—completing thus the perfect system of all truth which we have shown to be formed by Turner's works—the power, majesty, and deathfulness of the open, deep, illimitable Sea.

from *Wuthering Heights*
by Emily Brontë

1801—I have just returned from a visit to my landlord—the solitary neighbor that I shall be troubled with. This is certainly a beautiful country! In all England, I do not believe that I could have fixed on a situation so completely removed from the stir of society. A perfect misanthropist's heaven—and Mr. Heathcliff and I are such a suitable pair to divide the desolation between us. A capital fellow! He little imagined how my heart warmed towards him when I beheld his black eyes withdraw so suspiciously under their brows, as I rode up, and when his fingers sheltered themselves, with a jealous resolution, still further in his waistcoat, as I announced my name.

"Mr. Heathcliff?" I said.

A nod was the answer.

"Mr. Lockwood, your new tenant, sir. I do myself the honor of calling as soon as possible after my arrival, to express the hope that I have not inconvenienced you by my perseverance in soliciting the occupation of Thrushcross Grange: I heard, yesterday, you had had some thoughts—"

"Thrushcross Grange is my own, sir," he interrupted, wincing, "I should not allow any one to inconvenience me, if I could hinder it—walk in!"

The "walk in," was uttered with closed teeth and expressed the sentiment, "Go to the Deuce!" Even the gate over which he leant manifested no sympathizing movement to the words, and I think that circumstance determined me to accept the invitation: I felt interested in a man who seemed more exaggeratedly reserved than myself.

When he saw my horse's breast fairly pushing the barrier, he did pull out his hand to unchain it, and then sullenly preceded me up the causeway, calling, as we entered the court—

"Joseph, take Mr. Lockwood's horse; and bring up some wine."

"Here we have the whole establishment of domestics, I suppose," was the reflection, suggested by this compound order. "No wonder the grass grows up between the flags, and cattle are the only hedgecutters."

Joseph was an elderly, nay, an old man, very old, perhaps, though hale and sinewy.

"The Lord help us!" he soliloquized in an undertone of peevish displeasure, while relieving me of my horse: looking, meantime, in my face so sourly that I charitably conjectured he must have need of divine aid to digest his dinner, and his pious ejaculation had no reference to my unexpected advent.

Wuthering Heights is the name of Mr. Heathcliff's dwelling. "Wuthering" being a significant provincial adjective, descriptive of the atmospheric tumult to which its station is exposed in stormy weather. Pure, bracing ventilation they must have up there, at all times, indeed: one may guess the power of the north wind, blowing over the edge, by the excessive slant of a few stunted firs at the end of the house; and by a range of gaunt thorns all stretching their limbs one way, as if craving alms of the sun. Happily, the architect had foresight to build it strong: the narrow windows are deeply set in the wall, and the corners defended with large jutting stones.

Before passing the threshold, I paused to admire a quantity of grotesque carving lavished over the front, and especially about the principal door, above which, among a wilderness of crumbling griffins and shameless little boys, I detected the date "1500," and the name "Hareton Earnshaw." I would have made a few comments, and requested a short history of the place from the surly owner, but his attitude at the door appeared to demand my speedy entrance, or complete departure, and I had no desire to aggravate his impatience, previous to inspecting the penetralium.

One step brought us into the family sitting-room, without any introductory lobby or passage: they call it here "the house" preeminently. It includes kitchen and parlor, generally, but I believe at Wuthering Heights the kitchen is forced to retreat altogether into another quarter; at least I distinguished a chatter of tongues, and a clatter of culinary utensils deep within; and I observed no signs of roasting, boiling, or baking about the huge fire-place; nor any glitter of copper saucepans and tin cullenders on the walls. One end, indeed, reflected splendidly both light and heat from ranks of immense pewter dishes, interspersed with silver jugs and tankards, towering row after row, in a vast oak dresser, to the very roof. The latter had never been underdrawn: its entire anatomy lay bare to an inquiring eye, except where a frame of wood laden with oatcakes, and clusters of legs of beef, mutton, and ham, concealed it. Above the chimney were sundry villainous old guns, and a couple of horse-pistols, and, by way of ornament, three gaudily-painted canisters disposed along its ledge. The floor was of smooth, white stone; the chairs, high-backed, primitive structures, painted green, one or two heavy black ones lurking in the shade. In an arch under the dresser, reposed a huge, liver-colored bitch pointer surrounded by a swarm of squealing puppies, and other dogs haunted other recesses.

The apartment and furniture would have been nothing extraordinary as belonging to a homely, northern farmer, with a stubborn countenance, and stalwart limbs set out to advantage in knee-breeches and gaiters. Such an individual, seated in his arm-chair, his mug of ale frothing on the round table before him, is to be seen in any circuit of five or six miles among these hills, if you go at the right time, after dinner. But Mr. Heathcliff forms a singular contrast to his abode and style of living. He is a dark-skinned gypsy in aspect, in dress and manners a gentleman, that is, as much a gentleman as many a country squire: rather slovenly, perhaps, yet not looking amiss with his negligence, because he has an erect and handsome figure—and rather morose. Possibly, some people might suspect him of a degree of under-bred pride; I have a sympathetic chord within that tells me it is nothing of the sort: I know, by instinct, his reserve springs from an aversion to showy displays of feeling—to manifestations of mutual kindliness. He'll love and hate, equally under cover, and esteem it a species of impertinence to be loved or hated again—No, I'm running on too fast—I bestow my own attributes over-liberally on him. Mr. Heathcliff may have entirely dissimilar reasons for keeping his hand out of the way when he meets a would-be acquaintance, to those which actuate me. Let me hope my constitution is almost peculiar: my dear mother used to say I should never have a comfortable home, and only last summer I proved myself perfectly unworthy of one.

While enjoying a month of fine weather at the

however, the work is now being looked at with new respect, mainly because of Emily's poetry. Her only novel and greatest artistic achievement, *Wuthering Heights,* appeared two years later along with Charlotte's classic work, *Jane Eyre.* Although Charlotte's work had a much stronger reputation at first, Emily is now considered by many to be the family genius.

About the Selection. *Wuthering Heights* is a passionate and romantic novel set in the bleak moorland countryside of Emily's home district of Yorkshire. Heathcliff is the proprietor of Wuthering Heights, brought there as an orphaned gypsy boy by the previous owner. Throughout the story are many ill-fated romances and marriages involving Heathcliff and Catherine Earnshaw, his childhood companion and later love, and other residents of Wuthering Heights. What was unusual about the book when it first appeared was its structure. We first meet Heathcliff later in life through his tenant, Mr. Lockwood, who calls on his landlord on a stormy evening and unintentionally discovers the tumultuous history of the house. The violence of some of the scenes and unrestrained passion of the characters was disturbing to mid-nineteenth-century readers. Because of this, critics judged the novel harshly. Now, however, it is ranked among the greatest novels of English literature.

LITERARY TECHNIQUE

Many students may have difficulty deciphering Joseph's dialect. Suggest that students read the lines out loud, pronouncing the words phonetically. Students may wish to work with a partner.

sea-coast, I was thrown into the company of a most fascinating creature, a real goddess in my eyes, as long as she took no notice of me. I "never told my love" vocally; still, if looks have language, the merest idiot might have guessed I was over head and ears: she understood me at last, and looked a return—the sweetest of all imaginable looks. And what did I do? I confess it with shame—shrunk icily into myself, like a snail; at every glance retired colder and farther; till, finally, the poor innocent was led to doubt her own senses, and, overwhelmed with confusion at her supposed mistake, persuaded her mamma to decamp.

By this curious turn of disposition I have gained the reputation of deliberate heartlessness, how undeserved, I alone can appreciate.

I took a seat at the end of the hearthstone opposite that towards which my landlord advanced, and filled up an interval of silence by attempting to caress the canine mother, who had left her nursery and was sneaking wolfishly to the back of my legs, her lip curled up, and her white teeth watering for a snatch.

My caress provoked a long, guttural gnarl.

"You'd better let the dog alone," growled Mr. Heathcliff in unison, checking fiercer demonstrations with a punch of his foot. "She's not accustomed to be spoiled—not kept for a pet."

Then, striding to a side-door, he shouted again—
"Joseph!"

Joseph mumbled indistinctly in the depths of the cellar, but gave no intimation of ascending; so his master dived down to him, leaving me *vis-à-vis* the ruffianly bitch and a pair of grim, shaggy sheep dogs, who shared with her a jealous guardianship over all my movements.

Not anxious to come in contact with their fangs, I sat still; but, imagining they would scarcely understand tacit insults, I unfortunately indulged in winking and making faces at the trio, and some turn of my physiognomy so irritated madam, that she suddenly broke into a fury and leapt on my knees. I flung her back, and hastened to interpose the table between us. This proceeding roused the whole hive. Half-a-dozen four-footed fiends, of various sizes and ages, issued from hidden dens to the common centre. I felt my heels and coat-laps peculiar subjects of assault; and, parrying off the larger combatants as effectually as I could with the poker, I was constrained to demand, aloud, assistance from some of the household in re-establishing peace.

Mr. Heathcliff and his man climbed the cellar steps with vexatious phlegm. I don't think they moved one second faster than usual, though the hearth was an absolute tempest of worrying and yelping.

Happily, an inhabitant of the kitchen made more dispatch, a lusty dame, with tucked-up gown, bare arms, and fireflushed cheeks, rushed into the midst of us flourishing a frying-pan; and used that weapon, and her tongue, to such purpose, that the storm subsided magically, and she only remained, heaving like a sea after a high wind, when her master entered on the scene.

"What the devil is the matter?" he asked, eyeing me in a manner that I could ill endure after this inhospitable treatment.

"What the devil, indeed!" I muttered. "The herd of possessed swine could have had no worse spirits in them than those animals of yours, sir. You might as well leave a stranger with a brood of tigers!"

"They won't meddle with persons who touch nothing," he remarked, putting the bottle before me, and restoring the displaced table. "The dogs do right to be vigilant. Take a glass of wine?"

"No, thank you."

"Not bitten, are you?"

"If I had been, I would have set my signet on the biter."

Heathcliff's countenance relaxed into a grin.

"Come, come," he said, "you are flurried, Mr. Lockwood. Here, take a little wine. Guests are so exceedingly rare in this house that I and my dogs, I am willing to own, hardly know how to receive them. Your health, sir!"

I bowed and returned the pledge, beginning to perceive that it would be foolish to sit sulking for the misbehavior of a pack of curs: besides, I felt loath to yield the fellow further amusement, at my expense, since his humor took that turn.

He—probably swayed by prudential considerations of the folly of offending a good tenant—relaxed a little, in the laconic style of chipping off his pronouns and auxiliary verbs, and introduced what he supposed would be a subject of interest to me, a discourse on the advantages and disadvantages of my present place of retirement.

I found him very intelligent on the topics we touched; and, before I went home, I was encouraged so far as to volunteer another visit to-morrow.

He evidently wished no repetition of my intrusion. I shall go, notwithstanding. It is astonishing how sociable I feel myself compared with him.

CHAPTER II

Yesterday afternoon set in misty and cold. I had half a mind to spend it by my study fire, instead of wading through heath and mud to Wuthering Heights.

On coming up from dinner, however (N. B. I dine

between twelve and one o'clock; the housekeeper, a matronly lady taken as a fixture along with the house, could not, or would not comprehend my request that I might be served at five.)—on mounting the stairs with this lazy intention, and stepping into the room, I saw a servant-girl on her knees, surrounded by brushes and coals-cuttles, and raising an infernal dust as she extinguished the flames with heaps of cinders. This spectacle drove me back immediately; I took my hat, and, after a four miles' walk, arrived at Heathcliff's garden gate just in time to escape the first feathery flakes of a snow shower.

On that bleak hill-top the earth was hard with a black frost, and the air made me shiver through every limb. Being unable to remove the chain, I jumped over, and, running up the flagged causeway bordered with straggling gooseberry bushes, knocked vainly for admittance, till my knuckles tingled and the dogs howled.

"Wretched inmates!" I ejaculated, mentally, "you deserve perpetual isolation from your species for your churlish inhospitality. At least, I would not keep my doors barred in the day time. I don't care—I will get in!"

So resolved, I grasped the latch and shook it vehemently. Vinegar-faced Joseph projected his head from a round window of the barn.

"Whet are ye for?" he shouted. "T' maister's dahn i' t'fowld. Goa rahnd by th' end ut' laith,[1] if yah went tuh spake tull him."

"Is there nobody inside to open the door?" I hallooed, responsively.

"They's nobbut t' missis; and shoo'll nut oppen't an ye mak yer flaysome[2] dins till neeght."

"Why? cannot you tell her who I am, eh, Joseph?"

"Nor-ne me! Aw'll hae noa hend wi't," muttered the head vanishing.

The snow began to drive thickly. I seized the handle to essay another trial, when a young man, without coat, and shouldering a pitchfork, appeared in the yard behind. He hailed me to follow him, and, after marching through a washhouse and a paved area containing a coal-shed, pump, and pigeon cote, we at length arrived in the large, warm, cheerful apartment where I was formerly received.

It glowed delightfully in the radiance of an immense fire, compounded of coal, peat, and wood; and near the table, laid for a plentiful evening meal, I was pleased to observe the "missis," an individual whose existence I had never previously suspected.

I bowed and waited, thinking she would bid me take a seat. She looked at me, leaning back in her chair, and

1. **"T' . . . laith."** Joseph's dialect. *T'fowld* means the gold and *laith* is a barn.
2. **fleysome.** Terrible

remained motionless and mute.

"Rough weather!" I remarked. "I'm afraid, Mrs. Heathcliff, the door must bear the consequence of your servants' leisure attendance: I had hard work to make them hear me!"

She never opened her mouth. I stared—she stared also. At any rate, she kept her eyes on me, in a cool, regardless manner, exceedingly embarrassing and disagreeable.

"Sit down," said the young man, gruffly. "He'll be in soon."

I obeyed; and hemmed, and called the villain Juno, who deigned, at this second interview, to move the extreme tip of her tail, in token of owning my acquaintance.

"A beautiful animal!" I commenced again. "Do you intend parting with the little ones, madam?"

"They are not mine," said the amiable hostess more repellingly than Heathcliff himself could have replied.

"Ah, your favorites are among these!" I continued, turning to an obscure cushion full of something like cats.

"A strange choice of favorites," she observed scornfully.

Unluckily, it was a heap of dead rabbits. I hemmed once more, and drew closer to the hearth, repeating my comment on the wildness of the evening.

"You should not have come out," she said, rising and reaching from the chimney-piece two of the painted canisters.

Her position before was sheltered from the light; now, I had a distinct view of her whole figure and countenance. She was slender, and apparently scarcely past girlhood: an admirable form, and the most exquisite little face that I have ever had the pleasure of beholding: small features, very fair; flaxen ringlets, or rather golden, hanging loose on her delicate neck; and eyes—had they been agreeable in expression, they would have been irresistible. Fortunately for my susceptible heart, the only sentiment they evinced hovered between scorn and a kind of desperation, singularly unnatural to be detected there.

The canisters were almost out of her reach; I made a motion to aid her; she turned upon me as a miser might turn if any one attempted to assist him in counting his gold.

"I don't want your help," she snapped, "I can get them for myself."

"I beg your pardon," I hastened to reply.

"Were you asked to tea?" she demanded, tying an apron over her neat black frock, and standing with a spoonful of the leaf poised over the pot.

"I shall be glad to have a cup," I answered.

LITERARY TECHNIQUE

Image and Mood. An **image** is a word or phrase that names something that can be seen, heard, touched, tasted, or smelled. **Mood**, or atmosphere, is the emotion created in the reader by all or part of a literary work. Below are examples of imagery from the selection. What impact do these images have on the reader? How do these images establish a certain mood? How do these images help to characterize the estate of Wuthering Heights?

—the savage barking dogs

—the stormy night

—the front door that is locked throughout the day

Discuss with students other images in *Wuthering Heights* that create suspense. Which do they feel are most effective? Why?

Answers. These images are menacing and mysterious and create a feeling of suspense. These images imply that Wuthering Heights is dangerous and that, unknown to outsiders, something strange is going on there.

Discuss with students how
Lockwood refers to and treats
women in this selection. Given his
misinterpretations of events, people, and relationships, how are we,
as readers, to think of him as a narrator?

LITERARY TECHNIQUE

Point of View. Point of view is
the vantage point from which a
story is told. Choosing a point of
view is an important decision for
a writer. In *Wuthering Heights,*
Lockwood is not the main character, yet we see all the events of the
story through his eyes. Imagine if
the events of the first two chapters
had been told from Heathcliff's
point of view or from the point of
view of another character. Why do
you feel that Brontë chose to tell
the story from Lockwood's point of
view? Discuss with students how
they think the characterization of
Heathcliff would be affected if he
were the narrator.

Answer. Because Lockwood knows
as little about Heathcliff as the
reader does, the reader can discover the mysteries of Wuthering
Heights along with Lockwood. This
adds suspense and interest. If
Heathcliff were the narrator, it
would be difficult to make him
seem mysterious, and there would
be less room for suspense.

"Were you asked?" she repeated.

"No," I said, half smiling. "You are the proper person
to ask me."

She flung the tea back, spoon and all, and resumed her
chair in a pet, her forehead corrugated, and her red
under-lip pushed out, like a child's, ready to cry.

Meanwhile, the young man had slung onto his person
a decidedly shabby upper garment, and, erecting himself
before the blaze, looked down on me from the corner of
his eyes, for all the world as if there were some mortal
feud unavenged between us. I began to doubt whether he
were a servant or not; his dress and speech were both
rude, entirely devoid of the superiority observable in Mr.
and Mrs. Heathcliff; his thick, brown curls were rough
and uncultivated, his whiskers encroached bearishly over
his cheeks, and his hands were embrowned like those of a
common laborer. Still his bearing was free, almost
haughty, and he showed none of a domestic's assiduity in
attending on the lady of the house.

In the absence of clear proofs of his condition, I
deemed it best to abstain from noticing his curious conduct, and, five minutes afterwards, the entrance of
Heathcliff relieved me, in some measure, from my
uncomfortable state.

"You see, sir, I am come according to promise!" I
exclaimed assuming the cheerful; "and I fear I shall be
weather-bound for half an hour, if you can afford me
shelter during that space."

"Half an hour?" he said, shaking the white flakes from
his clothes; "I wonder you should select the thick of a
snow-storm to ramble about in. Do you know that you
run a risk of being lost in the marshes? People familiar
with these moors often miss their road on such evenings,
and, I can tell you, there is no chance of a change at present."

"Perhaps I can get a guide among your lads, and he
might stay at the Grange till morning—could you spare
me one?"

"No, I could not."

"Oh, indeed! Well, then, I must trust to my own
sagacity."

"Umph."

"Are you going to mak th' tea?" demanded he of the
shabby coat, shifting his ferocious gaze from me to the
young lady.

"Is *he* to have any?" she asked, appealing to Heathcliff.

"Get it ready, will you?" was the answer, uttered so
savagely that I started. The tone in which the words
were said revealed a genuine bad nature. I no longer felt
inclined to call Heathcliff a capital fellow.

When the preparations were finished, he invited me
with—

"Now, sir, bring forward your chair." And we all,
including the rustic youth, drew round the table, an aus-
tere silence prevailing while we discussed our meal.

I thought, if I had caused the cloud, it was my duty to
make an effort to dispel it. They could not every day sit
so grim and taciturn, and it was impossible, however
ill-tempered they might be, that the universal scowl they
wore was their every day countenance.

"It is strange," I began in the interval of swallowing
one cup of tea and receiving another, "it is strange how
custom can mould our tastes and ideas; many could not
imagine the existence of happiness in a life of such complete exile from the world as you spend, Mr. Heathcliff;
yet, I'll venture to say, that, surrounded by your family,
and with your amiable lady as the presiding genius over
your home and heart—"

"My amiable lady!" he interrupted, with an almost diabolical sneer on his face. "Where is she—my amiable
lady?"

"Mrs. Heathcliff, your wife, I mean."

"Well, yes—Oh! you would intimate that her spirit has
taken the post of ministering angel, and guards the fortunes of Wuthering Heights, even when her body is
gone. Is that it?"

Perceiving myself in a blunder, I attempted to correct
it. I might have seen there was too great a disparity
between the ages of the parties to make it likely that they
were man and wife. One was about forty, a period of
mental vigour at which men seldom cherish the delusion
of being married for love, by girls: that dream is reserved
for the solace of our declining years. The other did not
look seventeen.

Then it flashed upon me—"The clown at my elbow,
who is drinking his tea out of a basin and eating his
bread with unwashed hands, may be her husband.
Heathcliff, junior, of course. Here is the consequence of
being buried alive: she has thrown herself away upon
that boor, from sheer ignorance that better individuals
existed! A sad pity—I must beware how I cause her to
regret her choice."

The last reflection may seem conceited; it was not. My
neighbor struck me as bordering on repulsive. I knew,
through experience, that I was tolerably attractive.

"Mrs. Heathcliff is my daughter-in-law," said
Heathcliff, corroborating my surmise. He turned, as he
spoke, a peculiar look in her direction, a look of hatred,
unless he has a most perverse set of facial muscles that
will not, like those of other people, interpret the language of his soul.

"Ah, certainly—I see now; you are the favored possessor of the beneficent fairy," I remarked, turning to my
neighbor.

This was worse than before: the youth grew crimson, and clenched his fist with every appearance of a meditated assault. But he seemed to recollect himself, presently, and smothered the storm in a brutal curse, muttered on my behalf, which, however, I took care not to notice.

"Unhappy in your conjectures, sir!" observed my host; "we neither of us have the privilege of owning your good fairy; her mate is dead. I said she was my daughter-in-law, therefore, she must have married my son."

"And this young man is—"

"Not my son, assuredly!"

Heathcliff smiled again, as if it were rather too bold a jest to attribute the paternity of that bear to him.

"My name is Hareton Earnshaw," growled the other; "and I'd counsel you to respect it!"

"I have shown no disrespect," was my reply, laughing internally at the dignity with which he announced himself.

He fixed his eye on me longer than I cared to return the stare, for fear I might be tempted either to box his ears, or render my hilarity audible. I began to feel unmistakably out of place in that pleasant family circle. The dismal spiritual atmosphere overcame, and more than neutralized the glowing physical comforts round me; and I resolved to be cautious how I ventured under those rafters a third time.

The business of eating being concluded, and no one uttering a word of sociable conversation, I approached a window to examine the weather.

A sorrowful sight I saw: dark night coming down prematurely, and sky and hills mingled in one bitter whirl of wind and suffocating snow.

"I don't think it possible for me to get home now, without a guide," I could not help exclaiming. "The roads will be buried already; and, if they were bare, I could scarcely distinguish a foot in advance."

"Hareton, drive those dozen sheep into the barn porch. They'll be covered if left in the fold all night; and put a plank before them," said Heathcliff.

"How must I do?" I continued, with rising irritation.

There was no reply to my question; and, on looking round, I saw only Joseph bringing in a pail of porridge for the dogs, and Mrs. Heathcliff, leaning over the fire, diverting herself with burning a bundle of matches which had fallen from the chimney-piece as she restored the tea-canister to its place.

The former, when he had deposited his burden, took a critical survey of the room, and, in cracked tones, grated out—

"Aw woonder hagh yah can faishion tuh stand thear i' idleness un war, when all on 'em's goan aght! Bud yah're a nowt, and it's noa use talking—yah'll niver mend uh yer ill ways; bud goa raight tuh t' divil, like yer mother afore ye!"

I imagined, for a moment, that this piece of eloquence was addressed to me; and, sufficiently enraged, stepped towards the aged rascal with an intention of kicking him out of the door.

Mrs. Heathcliff, however, checked me by her answer.

"You scandalous old hypocrite!" she replied. "Are you not afraid of being carried away bodily, whenever you mention the devil's name? I warn you to refrain from provoking me, or I'll ask your abduction as a special favor. Stop, look here, Joseph," she continued, taking a long, dark book from a shelf. "I'll show you how far I've progressed in the Black Art—I shall soon be competent to make a clear house of it. The red cow didn't die by chance; and your rheumatism can hardly be reckoned among providential visitations!"

"Oh, wicked, wicked!" gasped the elder, "may the Lord deliver us from evil!"

"No, reprobate! you are a castaway—be off, or I'll hurt you seriously! I'll have you all modeled in wax and clay; and the first who passes the limits I fix, shall—I'll not say what he shall be done to—but, you'll see! Go, I'm looking at you!"

The little witch put a mock malignity into her beautiful eyes, and Joseph, trembling with sincere horror, hurried out praying and ejaculating "wicked" as he went.

I thought her conduct must be prompted by a species of dreary fun; and, now that we were alone, I endeavored to interest her in my distress.

"Mrs. Heathcliff," I said, earnestly, "you must excuse me for troubling you—I presume, because, with that face, I'm sure you cannot help being good-hearted. Do point out some landmarks by which I may know my way home. I have no more idea how to get there than you would have how to get to London!"

"Take the road you came," she answered, ensconcing herself in a chair, with a candle, and the long book open before her. "It is brief advice, but as sound as I can give."

"Then, if you hear of me being discovered dead in a bog, or a pit full of snow, your conscience won't whisper that it is partly your fault?"

"How so? I cannot escort you. They wouldn't let me go to the end of the garden-wall."

"*You!* I should be sorry to ask you to cross the threshold, for my convenience, on such a night," I cried. "I want you to *tell* me my way, not to *show* it; or else to persuade Mr. Heathcliff to give me a guide."

What are your first impressions of Lockwood, Heathcliff, Hareton Earnshaw, and Heathcliff's daughter-in-law? Write one or two sentences about each person.

REVIEWING THE SELECTION

1. What about Heathcliff's home and property is attractive to Lockwood? Initially, how does Lockwood expect he and Heathcliff will get along?

Answers. Lockwood is attracted by the beauty and the remoteness of the location. Lockwood expects that they will have a mutual respect for each other's reserved nature.

2. When do the dogs first attack Lockwood?

Answer. The dogs first attack Lockwood when he is in the sitting room.

3. On Lockwood's second visit to Wuthering Heights, for whom does he mistake the young woman? How does Heathcliff respond to his mistake?

Answers. Lockwood mistakes the young woman for Heathcliff's wife. Heathcliff sneers at Lockwood's mistake.

4. What circumstances keep Lockwood at Wuthering Heights one night?

Answer. A violent snowstorm keeps Lockwood at Wuthering Heights.

5. How is the environment reflective of Lockwood's personality and what Lockwood believes to be Heathcliff's personality?

Answer. The location is remote, quite removed from society, which is how Lockwood likes to think of his and Heathcliff's personalities.

6. Is Lockwood surprised by Heathcliff's reaction to the dog attack? What does Heathcliff's reaction tell the reader about the way in which he deals with people?

Answers. Yes, Lockwood is surprised. Heathcliff does not trust people and prefers not to deal with them at all.

(cont.)

7. How does Heathcliff's daughter-in-law treat Lockwood? What in the text suggests that there is something mysterious about her? *Answers.* Heathcliff's daughter-in-law is extremely rude toward Lockwood. It is not stated why Heathcliff and Hareton Earnshaw hate her so much, or why her husband is dead. She also is not allowed to leave the grounds of the house for some reason.

8. During Lockwood's second visit to Wuthering Heights, what incidents occur that may be construed as strange or unwelcoming? *Answer.* Lockwood is unable to remove the chain on the gate and must climb over. When he knocks on the door of the house, Joseph will not let him in.

9. What might be significant about the continual presence of attack dogs in the novel's opening scene? What aspect of Wuthering Heights might the dogs be emphasizing? *Answers.* The continual presence of the attack dogs sets the tone of the story. The dogs emphasize the menacing, dangerous aspects of Wuthering Heights.

10. How does Lockwood's perception of Heathcliff change throughout the two chapters? Is it beneficial to the reader to see this main character through the eyes of Lockwood? *Answers.* Lockwood initially thinks of Heathcliff as a good-hearted codger. By the end of the second chapter, he considers Heathcliff a villain. Yes; by seeing Heathcliff through Lockwood's eyes, Heathcliff's character becomes mysterious. Readers must guess at Heathcliff's motivation.

"Who? There is himself, Earnshaw, Zillah, Joseph, and I. Which would you have?"

"Are there no boys at the farm?"

"No, those are all."

"Then it follows that I am compelled to stay."

"That you may settle with your host. I have nothing to do with it."

"I hope it will be a lesson to you, to make no more rash journeys on these hills," cried Heathcliff's stern voice from the kitchen entrance. "As to staying here, I don't keep accommodations for visitors; you must share a bed with Hareton, or Joseph, if you do."

"I can sleep on a chair in this room," I replied.

"No, no! A stranger is a stranger, be he rich or poor—it will not suit me to permit any one the range of the place while I am off guard!" said the unmannerly wretch.

With this insult my patience was at an end. I uttered an expression of disgust, and pushed past him into the yard, running against Earnshaw in my haste. It was so dark that I could not see the means of exit, and, as I wandered round, I heard another specimen of their civil behavior amongst each other.

At first, the young man appeared about to befriend me.

"I'll go with him as far as the park," he said.

"You'll go with him to hell!" exclaimed his master, or whatever relation he bore. "And who is to look after the horses, eh?"

"A man's life is of more consequence than one evening's neglect of the horses; somebody must go," murmured Mrs. Heathcliff, more kindly than I expected.

"Not at your command!" retorted Hareton. "If you set store on him, you'd better be quiet."

"Then I hope his ghost will haunt you; and I hope Mr. Heathcliff will never get another tenant, till the Grange is a ruin!" she answered sharply.

"Hearken, hearken, shoo's cursing on em!" muttered Joseph, towards whom I had been steering.

He sat within earshot, milking the cows by the aid of a lantern which I seized unceremoniously, and, calling out that I would send it back on the morrow, rushed to the nearest postern.

"Maister, maister, he's staling t' lantern!" shouted the ancient, pursuing my retreat. "Hey, Gnasher! Hey, dog! Hey, Wolf, holld him, holld him!"

On opening the little door, two hairy monsters flew at my throat, bearing me down and extinguishing the light, while a mingled guffaw, from Heathcliff and Hareton, put the copestone on my rage and humiliation.

Fortunately, the beasts seemed more bent on stretching their paws, and yawning and flourishing their tails,

than devouring me alive; but they would suffer no resurrection, and I was forced to lie till their malignant masters pleased to deliver me: then hatless, and trembling with wrath, I ordered the miscreants to let me out—on their peril to keep me one minute longer—with several incoherent threats of retaliation that, in their indefinite depth of virulency, smacked of King Lear.

The vehemence of my agitation brought on a copious bleeding at the nose, and still Heathcliff laughed, and still I scolded. I don't know what would have concluded the scene had there not been one person at hand rather more rational than myself, and more benevolent than my entertainer. This was Zillah, the stout housewife, who at length issued forth to inquire into the nature of the uproar. She thought that some of them had been laying violent hands on me, and, not daring to attack her master, she turned her vocal artillery against the younger scoundrel.

"Well, Mr. Earnshaw," she cried, "I wonder what you'll have agait next! Are we going to murder folk on our very door-stones? I see this house will never do for me—look at t' poor lad, he's fair choking! Wisht, wisht! you mun't go on so—come in, and I'll cure that. There now, hold ye still."

With these words she suddenly splashed a pint of icy water down my neck, and pulled me into the kitchen. Mr. Heathcliff followed, his accidental merriment expiring quickly in his habitual moroseness.

I was sick exceedingly, and dizzy and faint; and thus compelled, perforce, to accept lodgings under his roof. He told Zillah to give me a glass of brandy, and then passed on to the inner room, while she condoled with me on my sorry predicament, and having obeyed his orders, whereby I was somewhat revived, ushered me to bed.

from *Jane Eyre*
by Charlotte Brontë

There was no possibility of taking a walk that day. We had been wandering, indeed, in the leafless shrubbery an hour in the morning; but since dinner (Mrs. Reed, when there was no company, dined early) the cold winter wind had brought with it clouds so somber, and a rain so penetrating, that further outdoor exercise was now out of the question.

I was glad of it: I never liked long walks, especially on chilly afternoons: dreadful to me was the coming home in the raw twilight, with nipped fingers and toes, and a heart saddened by the chidings of Bessie, the nurse, and humbled by the consciousness of my physical inferiority to Eliza, John, and Georgiana Reed.

The said Eliza, John, and Georgiana were now clustered round their mamma in the drawing-room: she lay reclined on the sofa by the fireside, and with her darlings about her (for the time neither quarreling nor crying) looked perfectly happy. Me, she had dispensed from joining the group; saying, 'She regretted to be under the necessity of keeping me at a distance; but that until she heard from Bessie and could discover by her own observation that I was endeavoring in good earnest to acquire a more sociable and childlike disposition, a more attractive and sprightly manner—something lighter, franker, more natural, as it were—she really must exclude me from privileges intended only for contented, happy, little children.'

'What does Bessie say I have done?' I asked.

'Jane, I don't like cavilers or questioners: besides, there is something truly forbidding in a child taking up her elders in that manner. Be seated somewhere; and until you can speak pleasantly, remain silent.'

A small breakfast-room adjoined the drawing-room. I slipped in there. It contained a bookcase: I soon possessed myself of a volume, taking care that it should be one stored with pictures. I mounted into the window-seat: gathering up my feet, I sat cross-legged like a Turk; and, having drawn the red moreen curtain nearly close, I was shrined in double retirement.

Folds of scarlet drapery shut in my view to the right hand; to the left were the clear panes of glass, protecting, but not separating me from the drear November day. At intervals, while turning over the leaves of my book, I studied the aspect of that winter afternoon. Afar, it offered a pale blank of mist and cloud; near, a scene of wet lawn and storm-beat shrub, with ceaseless rain sweeping away wildly before a long and lamentable blast.

I returned to my book—Bewick's 'History of British Birds': the letterpress thereof I cared little for, generally speaking; and yet there were certain introductory pages that, child as I was, I could not pass quite as a blank. They were those which treat of the haunts of seafowl; of 'the solitary rocks and promontories' by them only inhabited; of the coast of Norway, studded with isles from its southern extremity, the Lindeness, or Naze, to the North Cape—

Where the Northern Ocean, in vast whirls,
Boils round the naked, melancholy isles
Of farthest Thule; and the Atlantic surge
Pours in among the stormy Hebrides.

Nor could I pass unnoticed the suggestion of the bleak shores of Lapland, Siberia, Spitzbergen, Nova Zembla, Iceland, Greenland, with 'the vast sweep of the Arctic Zone, and those forlorn regions of dreary space—that reservoir of frost and snow, where firm fields of ice, the accumulation of centuries of winters, glazed in Alpine heights above heights, surround the pole, and concentre the multiplied rigors of extreme cold.' Of these death-white realms I formed an idea of my own: shadowy, like all the half-comprehended notions that float dim through children's brains, but strangely impressive. The words in these introductory pages connected themselves with the succeeding vignettes, and gave significance to the rock standing up alone in a sea of billow and spray; to the broken boat stranded on a desolate coast; to the cold and ghastly moon glancing through bars of cloud at a wreck just sinking.

I cannot tell what sentiment haunted the quite solitary church yard, with its inscribed headstone; its gate, its two trees, its low horizon, girdled by a broken wall, and its newly-risen crescent, attesting the hour of eventide.

The two ships becalmed on a torpid sea I believed to be marine phantoms.

The fiend pinning down the thief's pack behind him I passed over quickly: it was an object of terror.

So was the black, horned thing seated aloof on a rock, surveying a distant crowd surrounding a gallows.

Each picture told a story; mysterious often to my undeveloped understanding and imperfect feelings, yet ever profoundly interesting: as interesting as the tales Bessie sometimes narrated on winter evenings, when she chanced to be in good humor; and when, having brought her ironing-table to the nursery-hearth, she allowed us to sit about it, and while she got up Mrs. Reed's lace frills, and crimped her night-cap borders, fed our eager attention with passages of love and adventure taken from old fairy tales and older ballads; or (as at a later period I discovered) from the pages of 'Pamela,' and 'Henry, Earl of Moreland.'[1]

With Bewick on my knee, I was then happy: happy at least in my way. I feared nothing but interruption and that came too soon. The breakfast-room door opened.

'Boh! Madame Mope!' cried the voice of John Reed; then he paused: he found the room apparently empty.

'Where the dickens is she?' he continued. 'Lizzy! Georgy! (calling to his sisters) Joan[2] is not here: tell mamma she is run out into the rain—bad animal!'

'It is well I drew the curtain,' thought I; and I wished fervently he might not discover my hiding-place: nor would John Reed have found it out himself; he was not

---

1. **'Pamela,' . . . Moreland.** Samuel Richardson's *Pamela, or Virtue Rewarded* and *The History of Henry, Earl of Moreland* by John Wesley, both well-known novels
2. **Joan.** A nickname for Jane

About the Author. Charlotte Brontë (1816–1855) was a highly independent yet private person. The third of six children, she was brought up by her father and a domineering aunt. Charlotte and her sisters were sent to a private school for the children of clergymen. Poor food and unhealthy living conditions at the school led to the death of the two oldest Brontë children and the near-death of Charlotte and Emily. Charlotte finished her schooling and worked as a teacher and a governess. She disliked both jobs, but as an unmarried woman, she had few options. Her aunt arranged for Charlotte and Emily to open a school. In preparation, Charlotte went to Brussels to study and there met Constantin Héger, for whom she held an unrequited love.

Writing provided Charlotte with an outlet for her talent and emotions. With her brother and sisters, she began writing at an early age. They created an imaginary land based on a set of toy soldiers that their father brought home. Charlotte and her sisters, Emily and Anne, compiled a collection of verses about their fantasy land. This collection was published under the pseudonyms Currer, Ellis, and Acton Bell because writings by women were not taken seriously by critics. The book was not successful, but it sparked Charlotte's desire to write. She turned from her imaginary world to her own life for her subject matter. She is best known for her second novel, *Jane Eyre*, which draws on her experiences at the boarding school and as a governess.

After the death of her brother and sisters, Charlotte found life lonely and empty of her friends and literary circle. A strongly independent woman, she had refused to marry a man she could not respect. However, after turning down three marriage proposals, she wed the curate of her father's church. The marriage contented her, although she felt that as a married woman, little of her time

(cont.)

was her own. Soon after her marriage, she became pregnant and violently ill, and she died before giving birth.

About the Selection. The success of *Jane Eyre* was in part due to its shock value. Romance novels had been merely sentimental stories. *Jane Eyre* speaks of a woman's need for freedom and self-reliance. It is the story of an independent and sensitive woman struggling to find love within the constraints of society. Jane is an orphan who later works as the governess for a man with whom she falls in love. Told in the first person, the opening chapters show Jane as a child and establish the beginnings of the difficult conditions against which she struggles.

LITERARY/BIOGRAPHICAL NOTE

The tone of the Brontë novels may seem exceedingly dark and depressing to some students. Suggest that students research the town of Haworth, where the Brontë family lived. How might that atmosphere have affected the writing of the sisters? Students should work in small groups to prepare a class report on their findings.

quick either of vision or conception; but Eliza just put her head in at the door, and said at once:—'She is in the window-seat, to be sure, Jack.'

And I came out immediately, for I trembled at the idea of being dragged forth by the said Jack.

'What do you want?' I asked, with awkward diffidence.

'Say, "what do you want, Master Reed?"' was the answer. 'I want you to come here;' and seating himself in an arm-chair, he intimated by a gesture that I was to approach and stand before him.

John Reed was a schoolboy of fourteen years old; four years older than I, for I was but ten; large and stout for his age, with a dingy and unwholesome skin; thick lineaments in a spacious visage, heavy limbs and large extremities. He gorged himself habitually at table, which made him bilious, and gave him a dim and bleared eye and flabby cheeks. He ought now to have been at school; but his mamma had taken him home for a month or two, 'on account of his delicate health.' Mr. Miles, the master, affirmed that he would do very well if he had fewer cakes and sweetmeats sent him from home; but the mother's heart turned from an opinion so harsh, and inclined rather to the more refined idea that John's sallowness was owing to over-application and, perhaps, to pining after home.

John had not much affection for his mother and sisters, and an antipathy to me. He bullied and punished me; not two or three times in the week, nor once or twice in the day, but continually: every nerve I had feared him, and every morsel of flesh on my bones shrank when he came near. There were moments when I was bewildered by the terror he inspired, because I had no appeal whatever against either his menaces or his inflictions; the servants did not like to offend their young master by taking my part against him, and Mrs. Reed was blind and deaf on the subject: she never saw him strike or heard him abuse me, though he did both now and then in her very presence; more frequently, however, behind her back.

Habitually obedient to John, I came up to his chair: he spent some three minutes in thrusting out his tongue at me as far as he could without damaging the roots: I knew he would soon strike, and while dreading the blow, I mused on the disgusting and ugly appearance of him who would presently deal it. I wonder if he read that notion in my face; for, all at once, without speaking, he struck suddenly and strongly. I tottered, and regaining my equilibrium retired back a step or two from his chair.

'That is for your impudence in answering mamma a while since,' said he, 'and for your sneaking way of getting behind curtains, and for the look you had in your eyes two minutes since, you rat!'

Accustomed to John Reed's abuse, I never had an idea of replying to it; my care was how to endure the blow which would certainly follow the insult.

'What were you doing behind the curtain?' he asked.

'I was reading.'

'Show the book.'

I returned to the window and fetched it thence.

'You have no business to take our books; you are a dependent, mamma says; you have no money; your father left you none; you ought to beg, and not live here with gentlemen's children like us, and eat the same meals we do, and wear clothes at our mamma's expense. Now, I'll teach you to rummage my book-shelves: for they *are* mine; all the house belongs to me, or will do in a few years. Go and stand by the door, out of the way of the mirror and the windows.'

I did so, not at first aware what was his intention; but when I saw him lift and poise the book and stand in act to hurl it, I instinctively started aside with a cry of alarm: not soon enough, however; the volume was flung, it hit me, and I fell, striking my head against the door and cutting it. The cut bled, the pain was sharp: my terror had passed its climax; other feelings succeeded.

'Wicked and cruel boy!' I said. 'You are like a murderer—you are like a slave-driver—you are like the Roman emperors!'

I had read Goldsmith's 'History of Rome,' and had formed my opinion of Nero, Caligula, etc. Also I had drawn parallels in silence, which I never thought thus to have declared aloud.

'What! what!' he cried. 'Did she say that to me? Did you hear her, Eliza and Georgiana? Won't I tell mamma? but first—'

He ran headlong at me: I felt him grasp my hair and my shoulder: he had closed with a desperate thing. I really saw in him a tyrant: a murderer. I felt a drop or two of blood from my head trickle down my neck, and was sensible of somewhat pungent suffering: these sensations for the time predominated over fear, and I received him in frantic sort. I don't very well know what I did with my hands, but he called me 'Rat! rat!' and bellowed out aloud. Aid was near him: Eliza and Georgiana had run for Mrs. Reed, who was gone upstairs; she now came upon the scene, followed by Bessie and her maid Abbot. We were parted: I heard the words:— 'Dear! dear! What a fury to fly at Master John!'

'Did ever anybody see such a picture of passion!'

Then Mrs. Reed subjoined:—'Take her away to the red-room, and lock her in there.' Four hands were immediately laid upon me, and I was borne upstairs.

CHAPTER II

I resisted all the way: a new thing for me, and a circumstance which greatly strengthened the bad opinion Bessie and Miss Abbot were disposed to entertain of me. The fact is, I was a trifle beside myself; or rather *out* of myself, as the French would say: I was conscious that a moment's mutiny had already rendered me liable to strange penalties, and, like any other rebel slave, I felt resolved, in my desperation, to go all lengths.

'Hold her arms, Miss Abbot: she's like a mad cat.'

'For shame! for shame!' cried the lady's-maid. 'What shocking conduct, Miss Eyre, to strike a young gentleman, your benefactress's son! Your young master.'

'Master! How is he my master? Am I a servant?'

'No; you are less than a servant, for you do nothing for your keep. There, sit down, and think over your wickedness.'

They had got me by this time into the apartment indicated by Mrs. Reed, and had thrust me upon a stool: my impulse was to rise from it like a spring; their two pairs of hands arrested me instantly.

'If you don't sit still, you must be tied down,' said Bessie. 'Miss Abbot, lend me your garters; she would break mine directly.'

Miss Abbot turned to divest a stout leg of the necessary ligature. This preparation for bonds, and the additional ignominy it inferred, took a little of the excitement out of me.

'Don't take them off,' I cried; 'I will not stir.'

In guarantee whereof I attached myself to my seat by my hands.

'Mind you don't,' said Bessie; and when she had ascertained that I was really subsiding, she loosened her hold of me; then she and Miss Abbot stood with folded arms, looking darkly and doubtfully on my face, as incredulous of my sanity.

'She never did so before,' at last said Bessie, turning to the Abigail.

'But it was always in her,' was the reply. 'I've told Missis often my opinion about the child, and Missis agreed with me. She's an underhand little thing: I never saw a girl of her age with so much cover.'[1]

Bessie answered not; but ere long, addressing me, she said:

'You ought to be aware, Miss, that you are under obligations to Mrs. Reed: she keeps you: if she were to turn you off,[2] you would have to go to the poor-house.'

I had nothing to say to these words: they were not new to me: my very first recollections of existence included hints of the same kind. This reproach of my dependence had become a vague sing-song in my ear; very painful and crushing, but only half intelligible. Miss Abbot joined in:—'And you ought not to think yourself on an equality with the Misses Reed and Master Reed, because Missis kindly allows you to be brought up with them. They will have a great deal of money, and you will have none: it is your place to be humble; and to try to make yourself agreeable to them.'

'What we tell you is for your good,' added Bessie, in no harsh voice: 'you should try to be useful and pleasant, then, perhaps, you would have a home here; but if you become passionate and rude, Missis will send you away, I am sure.'

'Besides,' said Miss Abbot, 'God will punish her: He might strike her dead in the midst of her tantrums, and then where would she go? Come, Bessie, we will leave her: I wouldn't have her heart for anything. Say your prayers, Miss Eyre, when you are by yourself; for if you don't repent, something bad might be permitted to come down the chimney, and fetch you away.'

They went, shutting the door, and locking it behind them.

The red-room was a spare chamber, very seldom slept in; I might say never, indeed, unless when a chance influx of visitors at Gateshead Hall rendered it necessary to turn to account all the accommodation it contained: yet it was one of the largest and stateliest chambers in the mansion. A bed supported on massive pillars of mahogany, hung with curtains of deep red damask, stood out like a tabernacle in the center; the two large windows, with their blinds always drawn down, were half shrouded in festoons and falls of similar drapery; the carpet was red; the table at the foot of the bed was covered with a crimson cloth; the walls were a soft fawn colour, with a blush of pink in it; the wardrobe, the toilet-table, the chairs were of darkly-polished old mahogany. Out of these deep surrounding shades rose high, and glared white, the piled-up mattresses and pillows of the bed, spread with a snowy Marseilles[3] counterpane. Scarcely less prominent was an ample, cushioned easy-chair near the head of the bed, also white, with a footstool before it; and looking, as I thought, like a pale throne.

This room was chill, because it seldom had a fire; it was silent, because remote from the nursery and kitchens; solemn, because it was known to be so seldom entered. The housemaid alone came here on Saturdays, to wipe from the mirrors and the furniture a week's quiet dust: and Mrs. Reed herself, at far intervals, visited it to review the contents of a certain secret drawer in the wardrobe, where were stored divers parchments, her

---

1. **cover.** Deceit
2. **turn you off.** Turn you out
3. **Marseilles.** A cotton cloth with raised weave originally made in Marseille

1. Describe Jane's character and appearance. What is her relationship to the other children in the house?

Answer. Jane is small and pale. She has become somewhat of a loner due to repeated punishments. She enjoys sitting and reading and is very imaginative.

2. As the book opens, why is Jane being punished? Why does John Reed decide to punish her? What does he do?

Answers. Jane is punished for being herself, for not being sprightly and attractive. John Reed decides to punish her because she asked Mrs. Reed why she was to be punished. John sticks his tongue out at her, hits her, and throws a book at her.

3. What punishment does Jane receive for her actions against John? Why is the place she is sent so frightening?

Answer. She is shut up in the room in which Mr. Reed died.

4. What is revealed in Chapter II about Jane's situation in the Reed family?

Answer. Jane is actually Mrs. Reed's niece by marriage. When her parents died, Mr. Reed promised to take care of her.

5. How would the Reeds and their servants describe Jane? How does this affect the way she is treated?

Answers. The Reeds and the servants would describe Jane as sullen, ugly, sneaky, and a trouble-maker. Because they see her this way, Jane is often punished for no reason at all.

6. What is Jane's usual reaction to being punished? How is her reaction different when John punishes and attacks her on this day?

Answers. Jane usually receives her punishment without complaint. Jane tells John that he is being unfair and fights back when he tackles her.

(cont.)

---

jewel-casket, and a miniature of her deceased husband; and in those last words lies the secret of the red-room—the spell which kept it so lonely in spite of its grandeur.

Mr. Reed had been dead nine years: it was in this chamber he breathed his last; here he lay in state; hence his coffin was borne by the undertaker's men; and, since that day, a sense of dreary consecration had guarded it from frequent intrusion.

My seat, to which Bessie and the bitter Miss Abbot had left me riveted, was a low ottoman near the marble chimney-piece; the bed rose before me; to my right hand there was the high, dark wardrobe, with subdued, broken reflections varying the gloss of its panels; to my left were the muffled windows; a great looking-glass between them repeated the vacant majesty of the bed and room. I was not quite sure whether they had locked the door; and, when I dared move, I got up, and went to see. Alas! yes: no jail was ever more secure. Returning, I had to cross before the looking-glass; my fascinated glance involuntarily explored the depth it revealed. All looked colder and darker in that visionary hollow than in reality: and the strange little figure there gazing at me, with a white face and arms specking the gloom, and glittering eyes of fear moving where all else was still, had the effect of a real spirit: I thought it like one of the tiny phantoms, half fairy, half imp, Bessie's evening stories represented as coming out of lone, ferny dells in moors, and appearing before the eyes of belated travellers. I returned to my stool.

Superstition was with me at that moment; but it was not yet her hour for complete victory: my blood was still warm; the mood of the revolted slave was still bracing me with its bitter vigor; I had to stem a rapid rush of retrospective thought before I quailed to the dismal present.

All John Reed's violent tyrannies, all his sisters' proud indifference, all his mother's aversion, all the servants' partiality, turned up in my disturbed mind like a dark deposit in a turbid well. Why was I always suffering, always browbeaten, always accused, for ever condemned? Why could I never please? Why was it useless to try to win any one's favor? Eliza, who was headstrong and selfish, was respected. Georgiana, who had a spoiled temper, a very acrid spite, a captious and insolent carriage, was universally indulged. Her beauty, her pink cheeks and golden curls, seemed to give delight to all who looked at her, and to purchase indemnity for every fault. John, no one thwarted, much less punished; though he twisted the necks of the pigeons, killed the little pea-chicks,[1] set the dogs at the sheep, stripped the hothouse vines of their fruit, and broke the buds off the choicest plants in the

---

1. **pea-chicks.** Baby peacocks

---

conservatory: he called his mother 'old girl,' too; sometimes reviled her for her dark skin, similar to his own; bluntly disregarded her wishes; not unfrequently tore and spoiled her silk attire; and he was still 'her own darling.' I dared commit no fault; I strove to fulfill every duty; and I was termed naughty and tiresome, sullen and sneaking, from morning to noon, and from noon to night.

My head still ached and bled with the blow and fall I had received: no one had reproved John for wantonly striking me; and because I had turned against him to avert farther irrational violence, I was loaded with general opprobrium.

'Unjust!—unjust!' said my reason, forced by the agonizing stimulus into precocious though transitory power; and Resolve, equally wrought up, instigated some strange expedient to achieve escape from insupportable oppression—as running away, or, if that could not be effected, never eating or drinking more, and letting myself die.

What a consternation of soul was mine that dreary afternoon! How all my brain was in tumult, and all my heart in insurrection! Yet in what darkness, what dense ignorance, was the mental battle fought! I could not answer the ceaseless inward question—why I thus suffered; now, at the distance of—I will not say how many years, I see it clearly.

I was a discord in Gateshead Hall; I was like nobody there; I had nothing in harmony with Mrs. Reed or her children, or her chosen vassalage. If they did not love me, in fact, as little did I love them. They were not bound to regard with affection a thing that could not sympathize with one amongst them; a heterogeneous thing, opposed to them in temperament, in capacity, in propensities; a useless thing, incapable of serving their interest, or adding to their pleasure; a noxious thing, cherishing the germs of indignation at their treatment, of contempt of their judgment. I know that had I been a sanguine, brilliant, careless, exacting, handsome, romping child—though equally dependent and friendless—Mrs. Reed would have endured my presence more complacently; her children would have entertained for me more of the cordiality of fellow-feeling; the servants would have been less prone to make me the scapegoat of the nursery.

Daylight began to forsake the red-room; it was past four o'clock, and the beclouded afternoon was tending to drear twilight. I heard the rain still beating continuously on the staircase window, and the wind howling in the grove behind the hall; I grew by degrees cold as a stone, and then my courage sank. My habitual mood of humiliation, self-doubt, forlorn depression, fell damp on the embers of my decaying ire. All said I was wicked, and perhaps I might be so: what thought had I been but just conceiving of starving myself to death? That certainly was a crime: and was I fit to die? Or was the vault under the chancel of Gateshead Church an inviting bourn? In such vault I had been told did Mr. Reed lie buried; and led by this thought to recall his idea, I dwelt on it with gathering dread. I could not remember him; but I knew that he was my own uncle—my mother's brother—that he had taken me when a parentless infant to his house; and that in his last moments he had required a promise of Mrs. Reed that she would rear and maintain me as one of her own children. Mrs. Reed probably considered she had kept this promise; and so she had, I dare say, as well as her nature would permit her; but how could she really like an interloper not of her race,[1] and unconnected with her, after her husband's death, by any tie? It must have been most irksome to find herself bound by a hard-wrung pledge to stand in the stead of a parent to a strange child she could not love, and to see an uncongenial alien permanently intruded on her own family group.

A singular notion dawned upon me. I doubted not—never doubted—that if Mr. Reed had been alive he would have treated me kindly; and now, as I sat looking at the white bed and overshadowed walls—occasionally also turning a fascinated eye towards the dimly gleaming mirror—I began to recall what I had heard of dead men, troubled in their graves by the violation of their last wishes, revisiting the earth to punish the perjured and avenge the oppressed; and I thought Mr. Reed's spirit, harassed by the wrongs of his sister's child, might quit its abode—whether in the church vault, or in the unknown world of the departed—and rise before me in this chamber. I wiped my tears and hushed my sobs, fearful lest any sign of violent grief might waken a preternatural voice to comfort me, or elicit from the gloom some haloed face, bending over me with strange pity. This idea, consolatory in theory, I felt would be terrible if realized: with all my might I endeavored to stifle it—I endeavored to be firm. Shaking my hair from my eyes, I lifted my head and tried to look boldly round the dark room. At this moment a light gleamed on the wall. Was it, I asked myself, a ray from the moon penetrating some aperture in the blind? No; moonlight was still, and this stirred; while I gazed, it glided up to the ceiling and quivered over my head. I can now conjecture readily that this streak of light was, in all likelihood, a gleam from a lantern, carried by some one across the lawn: but then,

_____
1. **race.** Family

prepared as my mind was for horror, shaken as my nerves were by agitation, I thought the swift-darting beam was a herald of some coming vision from another world. My heart beat thick, my head grew hot; a sound filled my ears, which I deemed the rushing of wings: something seemed near me; I was oppressed, suffocated: endurance broke down; I rushed to the door and shook the lock in desperate effort. Steps came running along the outer passage; the key turned, Bessie and Abbot entered.

'Miss Eyre, are you ill?' said Bessie.

'What a dreadful noise! it went quite through me!' exclaimed Abbot.

'Take me out! let me go into the nursery!' was my cry.

'What for? Are you hurt? Have you seen something?' again demanded Bessie.

'Oh! I saw a light, and I thought a ghost would come.' I had now got hold of Bessie's hand, and she did not snatch it from me.

'She has screamed out on purpose,' declared Abbot, in some disgust. 'And what a scream! If she had been in great pain one would have excused it, but she only wanted to bring us all here: I know her naughty tricks.'

'What is all this?' demanded another voice, peremptorily; and Mrs. Reed came along the corridor, her cap flying wide, her gown rustling stormily. 'Abbot and Bessie, I believe I gave orders that Jane Eyre should be left in the red-room till I came to her myself.'

'Miss Jane screamed so loud, ma'am,' pleaded Bessie.

'Let her go,' was the only answer. 'Loose Bessie's hand, child: you cannot succeed in getting out by these means, be assured. I abhor artifice, particularly in children; it is my duty to show you that tricks will not answer: you will now stay here an hour longer, and it is only on condition of perfect submission and stillness that I shall liberate you then.'

'Oh aunt, have pity! Forgive me! I cannot endure it— let me be punished some other way! I shall be killed if—'

'Silence! This violence is all most repulsive:' and so, no doubt, she felt it. I was a precocious actress in her eyes: she sincerely looked on me as a compound of virulent passions, mean spirit, and dangerous duplicity.

Bessie and Abbot having retreated, Mrs. Reed, impatient of my now frantic anguish and wild sobs, abruptly thrust me back and locked me in, without farther parley.[2] I heard her sweeping away; and soon after she was gone I suppose I had a species of fit: unconsciousness closed the scene.

_____
2. **parley.** Discussion

ADDITIONAL QUESTIONS AND ACTIVITIES (CONT.)

7. Why did Mrs. Reed choose to send Jane to this particular room? What additional fear does Jane experience while being punished?
Answers. Mrs. Reed knew that being locked in the room would frighten Jane. Jane sees a light and thinks it is a ghost or spirit.

8. How does the information about Jane's situation affect the way the reader feels about Jane's treatment?
Answer. It is surprising to find that Jane and the Reeds are fairly close relatives. This fact makes her treatment all the more despicable.

9. How does Jane try to escape from the unpleasantness of her circumstances? What does her means of escape tell us about her character? Does this means of escape work for her?
Answers. Jane tries to escape from her circumstances by reading and by using her imagination. Her escape methods imply that she is very intelligent and patient. This means of escape offers only temporary relief.

10. Why might this opening scene be important to the book as a whole? What does it reveal about Jane? What questions do you have about her as Chapter II ends? Are you interested in Jane and her plight?
Answers. The opening scene sets the tone for the rest of the novel. Jane has to fight for everything she can get against great odds. How will Jane get out of this awful situation? Will she ever have a happy life? Students might say that they find Jane's plight very interesting.

About the Author. Florence Nightingale (1820–1910) is perhaps the most famous nurse ever. She became a nurse against her parents' wishes and served in the Crimean War. She was later appointed head of the nurses in the military hospitals in Scutari, Turkey. When Nightingale began her work, the mortality rate among injured soldiers was 45 percent, due mostly to fever and infection. She enforced sanitary rules and reduced the death rate to 2 percent.

About the Selection. Just as Florence Nightingale tackled the structure of military hospitals with her revolutionary nursing, here she attacks the institution of marriage by addressing what she believed were flaws in the Victorian concept of marriage.

PREFACE TO *THE PICTURE OF DORIAN GRAY*

About the Author. Oscar Wilde (1854–1900) was best known in Victorian England for his flamboyant personality and for his plays, *The Importance of Being Earnest* and *Lady Windermere's Fan,* and for a novel, *The Picture of Dorian Gray.*

About the Selection. In the book from which the selection is taken, the main character, Dorian, wishes to remain young and handsome while his portrait ages instead. His wish is granted. The novel tells of the dire consequences of this wish.

from *Cassandra* by Florence Nightingale

The intercourse of man and woman—how frivolous, how unworthy it is! Can we call *that* the true vocation of woman—her high career? Look round at the marriages which you know. The true marriage—that noble union, by which a man and woman become together the one perfect being—probably does not exist at present upon earth.

It is not surprising that husbands and wives seem so little part of one another. It is surprising that there is so much love as there is. For there is no food for it. What does it live upon—what nourishes it? Husbands and wives never seem to have anything to say to one another. What do they talk about? Not about any great religious, social, political questions or feelings. They talk about who shall come to dinner, who is to live in this lodge and who in that, about the improvement of the place, or when they shall go to London. If there are children, they form a common subject of some nourishment. But, even then, the case is oftenest thus—the husband is to think of how they are to get on in life; the wife of bringing them up at home.

But any real communion between husband and wife— any descending into the depths of their being, and drawing out thence what they find and comparing it—do we ever dream of such a thing? Yes, we may dream of it during the season of "passion," but we shall not find it afterwards. We even expect it to go off, and lay our account that it will. If the husband has, by chance, gone into the depths of *his* being, and found there anything unorthodox, he, oftenest, conceals it carefully from his wife—he is afraid of "unsettling her opinions."

Preface to *The Picture of Dorian Gray* by Oscar Wilde

The artist is the creator of beautiful things.
To reveal art and conceal the artist is art's aim.
The critic is he who can translate into another manner or a new material his impression of beautiful things.
 The highest, as the lowest, form of criticism is a mode of autobiography.
Those who find ugly meaning in beautiful things are corrupt without being charming. This is a fault.
 Those who find beautiful meanings in beautiful things are the cultivated. For these there is hope.
They are the elect to whom beautiful things mean only Beauty.
 There is no such thing as a moral or an immoral book.
 Books are well written, or badly written. That is all.
The nineteenth-century dislike of Realism is the rage of Caliban[1] seeing his own face in a glass.
 The nineteenth-century dislike of Romanticism is the rage of Caliban not seeing his own face in a glass.
The moral life of man forms part of the subject matter of the artist, but the morality of art consists in the perfect use of an imperfect medium. No artist desires to prove anything. Even things that are true can be proved.
 No artist has ethical sympathies. An ethical sympathy in an artist is an unpardonable mannerism of style.
 No artist is ever morbid. The artist can express everything.
Thought and language are to the artist instruments of an art.
 Vice and Virtue are to the artist materials for an art.
From the point of view of form, the type of all the arts is the art of the musician. From the point of view of feeling, the actor's craft is the type.
 All art is at once surface and symbol.
 Those who go beneath the surface do so at their peril.
 Those who read the symbol do so at their peril.
It is the spectator, and not life, that art really mirrors.
 Diversity of opinion about a work of art shows that the work is new, complex, and vital.
 When critics disagree the artist is in accord with himself. We can forgive a man for making a useful thing as long as he does not admire it. The only excuse for making a useless thing is that one admires it intensely.
 All art is quite useless.

---

1. **Caliban.** Deformed and savage creature in Shakespeare's *The Tempest*

UNIT REVIEW

The Victorian Age

VOCABULARY FROM THE SELECTIONS

ambling, 701
amicable, 783
avarice, 790
avenge, 749
canker, 713
certitude, 742
contemptuously, 800
countenance, 703, 725

dais, 774
dappled, 762
demur, 736
derive, 716
diffusive, 720
discerning, 708
drearisome, 748
fickle, 713
gaunt, 752

halcyon, 774
inextricable, 784
moldered, 713
munificence, 726
officious, 726
placid, 791
portmanteau, 801
profusely, 736
shingle, 742

stagnate, 714
stipple, 762
strand, 741
tremulous, 741
tumult, 718
turbid, 741
wane, 702
yearn, 708

LITERARY TERMS

alliteration, 761, 763, 766, 775
allusion, 743, 780
ambiguity, 794
biographical criticism, 722
blank verse, 711
character, 711
characterization, 728
chiasmus, 769
cliché, 722
concrete universal, 750
connotation, 771
critical essay, 706
dialect, 747
diction, 728, 753
dramatic irony, 785
dramatic monologue, 696, 711, 724, 728

elegiac lyric, 722
euphemism, 722
extended metaphor, 744
fable, 754
fantasy, 754, 805
foil, 706
historical criticism, 722
humor, 750
irony, 728, 747
metaphor, 738, 754, 766, 771, 773
motivation, 711
Naturalism, 695
nursery rhyme, 769, 776
octave, 753
paradox, 738, 763
parallelism, 775
Realism, 694, 785

refrain, 706
repetition, 760, 766
rhyme, 766
riddle, 805
romance, 706
setting, 750, 786
simile, 754
slant rhyme, 753
sonnet, 760, 761, 766
sprung rhythm, 761, 763
stanza, 753
symbol, 706, 743, 766, 773, 793
tenor, 754
theme, 738, 753, 763
tone, 780
understatement, 747
vehicle, 754

VOCABULARY DEVELOPMENT EXERCISE

▶ Give students the following exercise.

Make a crossword puzzle using twenty of the words from the list on page 823. First set up the words in a crossword form. Try to make each word share a letter with each of two other words. Then, beginning at the top left and working your way across each row, number the words consecutively. Next, write definitions of the words to serve as clues. Be sure that your definition matches the form of the word you have used. Finally, number your definitions and label them *across* or *down* to match the words in the puzzle.

▶**Teaching Note:** Bring in a crossword puzzle from a newspaper, magazine, or puzzle book to show students as an example.

ADDITIONAL RESOURCES

ASSESSMENT PORTFOLIO
• Vocabulary Worksheet: Unit 9, 4.9.41
• Study Guide: Unit 9 Test, 4.9.42
• Unit 9 Test, 4.9.43

ESSENTIAL SKILLS PRACTICE BOOKS

Language
• Base Words and Prefixes, 2.140
• Clichés and Euphemisms, 2.152
• Combining Sentences Using Clauses, 2.53
• Quotation Marks I, 2.104
• Quotation Marks II, 2.105
• Suffixes, 2.141
• Varying Sentence Length and Structure, 2.55
• Verbals: Gerunds, 2.17
• Verbals: Infinitives, 2.18
• Verbals: Participles, 2.16
• Word Origins I, 2.143
• Word Origins II, 2.144

Speaking and Listening
• Discussion, 3.6
• Elements of Nonverbal Communication, 3.3
• Elements of Verbal Communication, 3.2   (cont.)

ADDITIONAL RESOURCES (CONT.)

Study and Research
• Analyzing, 4.10
• Avoiding Faulty Arguments, 4.14
• Classifying, 4.7
• Comparing and Contrasting, 4.8
• Deducing, 4.12
• Generalizing, 4.11
• Making Hypotheses, 4.13

• Observing, 4.6
• Other Sources of Information, 4.27
• Reading Actively: Predicting, 4.18
• Reading Charts and Graphs, 4.19
• Reading Comprehension Questions, 4.43
• Remembering and Visualizing, 4.5
• Strategies for Decision Making, 4.3
• Using Thesauruses, 4.25

SYNTHESIS: QUESTIONS FOR WRITING, RESEARCH, OR DISCUSSION

GENRE STUDIES

1. **Realist Fiction.** What examples of Realist fiction appear in this unit? What elements of these fictions make them examples of Realism?

2. **The Dramatic Monologue.** Compare the following dramatic monologues from the unit: "Ulysses," "My Last Duchess," and "Andrea del Sarto." What moment of crisis is presented in each poem? Who is the speaker in each poem? Who is being addressed? What does the speaker reveal about himself through his speech?

3. **Lyric Poetry.** Contrast the styles of Christina Rossetti and Gerard Manley Hopkins. What differences can you find in the rhythms of their poems; in their diction, or word choice; and in their use of figurative language?

THEMATIC STUDIES

3. **Challenges to Conventional Thinking.** The Victorian Age has become synonymous with smug, complacent, conventional thinking. However, many writers of that period challenged accepted ideas. What conventional ideas are challenged in the following selections from the unit: "The Man He Killed," "Channel Firing," and "In an Artist's Studio"? What conventional ideas are challenged in the following pieces from the Selections for Additional Reading: the selection from *The Subjection of Women,* and the Preface to *The Picture of Dorian Gray*?

HISTORICAL AND BIOGRAPHICAL STUDIES

4. **Biographical Elements in Fiction.** Do some research on the lives of George Eliot, Emily Brontë, Charlotte Brontë, and Lewis Carroll. Explain what elements in the selections in this unit can be traced to experiences in the lives of the authors.

LANGUAGE LAB   PROOFREADING FOR OTHER PUNCTUATION ERRORS

When revising and proofreading, you should check carefully for correct use of semicolons, colons, dashes, hyphens, apostrophes, quotation marks, parentheses, brackets, and ellipses. For help in using punctuation marks correctly, see the Language Arts Survey, 2.97–2.106.

EXERCISE A   PROOFREADING A PARAGRAPH FOR CORRECT PUNCTUATION

Proofread the following paragraph for correct punctuation. Rewrite the revised paragraph on your own paper.

EXAMPLE: Christina Rossetti's brother Dante was a painter he was also a poet.
Christina Rossetti's brother Dante was a painter; he was also a poet.

Christina Rossetti 1830-1894 came from a literary family her brother Dante Rossettis poetry is even more well known than is hers. Perhaps Christinas best known work is Goblin Market, a narrative poem. It begins Morning and evening maids heard the goblins cry Come buy our orchard fruits, come buy, come buy . . . The goblins song is alluring, and two sisters their names are Laura and Lizzie have a great adventure because of this. Laura "bowed her head to hear" but Lizzie cried Laura, Laura, you should not peep at goblin men. Laura meets the goblins and eats their fruit but soon after this horrors she can no longer hear their enchanting singing. She loses all of her energy she won't eat or do anything "Till Laura dwindling seemed knocking at Deaths door. . . Then Lizzie. . . . for the first time in her life began to listen and look." The goblins play and dance with her they hug and kiss her they offer her their fruit but she wont eat it. Lizzie has a plan for rescuing her sister however this is not the place to tell about that.

EXERCISE B   PROOFREADING SENTENCES FOR PUNCTUATION ERRORS

Proofread the following sentences for correct punctuation.

EXAMPLE: Icarus flew too close to the sun;
Icarus flew too close to the sun.

1. John Stuart Mill wrote book's on morals and politics On Liberty 1859 Representative Government 1861 The Subjection of Women 1869 and Utilitarianism 1863.

2. Charlotte Brontë's, Emily Brontë's, and Anne Brontë's father, a widower his wife died, was unfortunate enough to outlive all his children.

3. Dickens wrote I never had the courage to go back to the place he refers to the shoe polish factory where my servitude began.

4. The Lady of Shalott, is about a weaver isolated in a tower?

5. Oh father said Eppie what a *pretty* home ours is! I think nobody could be happier than we are. emphasis added

> **LANGUAGE ARTS SURVEY**
>
> *For additional help, see the Language Arts Survey, 2.3–2.11, on nouns and pronouns.*

ANSWERS FOR LANGUAGE LAB

Exercise A

Christina Rossetti (1830–1894) came from a literary family; her brother Dante Rossetti's poetry is even more well known than is hers. Perhaps Christina's best known work is "Goblin Market," a narrative poem. It begins, "Morning and evening maids heard the goblins cry, 'Come buy our orchard fruits, come buy, come buy . . .'" The goblins' song is alluring, and the two sisters—their names are Laura and Lizzie—have a great adventure because of this. Laura "bowed her head to hear," but Lizzie cried, "Laura, Laura, you should not peep at goblin men." Laura meets the goblins and eats their fruit, but soon after this—horrors!—she can no longer hear their enchanting singing. She loses all of her energy; she won't eat or do anything, "Till Laura, dwindling, seemed knocking at Death's door. . . . Then Lizzie . . . for the first time in her life began to listen and look." The goblins play and dance with her; they hug and kiss her; they offer her their fruit, but she won't eat it. Lizzie has a plan for rescuing her sister; however, this is not the place to tell about that.

Exercise B

1. John Stuart Mill wrote books on morals and politics (On Liberty [1859], Representative Government [1861], The Subjection of Women [1869], and Utilitarianism [1863]).

2. Charlotte Brontë's, Emily Brontë's, and Anne Brontë's father, a widower (his wife died), was unfortunate enough to outlive all his children.

3. Dickens wrote, "I never had the courage to go back to the place [he refers to the shoe polish factory] where my servitude began."

4. "The Lady of Shalott" is about a weaver isolated in a tower.

5. "Oh father!" said Eppie, "what a pretty home ours is! I think nobody could be happier than we are." [emphasis added]

UNIT 10 TWENTIETH-CENTURY POETRY
(1900–PRESENT)

The Persistence of Memory. Salvador Dali, 1931. Oil on canvas, 9.5 × 13". The Museum of Modern Art, NY. Given anonymously

GOALS/OBJECTIVES

Studying this unit will enable students to

- interpret and appreciate twentieth-century poetry
- name and describe the accomplishments and significance of some of the main figures of twentieth-century poetry
- explain how repeated warfare affected the poetry of the twentieth century

- describe how English-speaking writers responded to the social and economic upheaval of the twentieth century
- describe some of the themes found particularly in the poetry of women in the twentieth century
- define and identify free verse forms and understand the poetic uses of symbol and metaphor

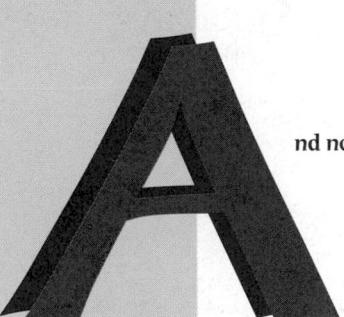

And now for something completely different.

—Monty Python's Flying Circus

827

THE TWENTIETH CENTURY (1900–PRESENT)

At the beginning of the twentieth century, Britain controlled a vast empire and was arguably the wealthiest, most powerful country in the world. During the following decades, Britain lost most of its colonial possessions, fought in two bloody and prolonged world wars, and experienced repeated economic depressions. At times, **William Butler Yeats's** (1865–1939) lines, written in the 1920s, seemed like a prophecy come true:

> Things fall apart; the center cannot hold;
> Mere anarchy is loosed upon the world,
> The blood-dimmed tide is loosed, and everywhere
> The ceremony of innocence is drowned.

THE EDWARDIAN AND GEORGIAN ERAS

Like many Irish writers of the early part of the century, Yeats felt a deep conflict between his nationalism and his loathing for the ambitions of the emerging Irish middle class. During his middle years, Yeats spent considerable time in the homes of the privileged, most notably at the country estate of his friend and fellow author of the **Celtic Twilight**, or **Irish Renaissance, Lady Augusta Gregory** (1852–1932). In these homes he conceived the idea of "the ceremony of innocence," for he admired the cultivation possible among the upper classes, who had leisure to enjoy the arts, literature, and philosophy. Such attitudes came easily in the early years of the twentieth century. When Queen Victoria died in 1901, her son became King Edward VII. The **Edwardian Age**, from 1901 to 1910, was characterized by extravagance among the wealthy and relative ease among the middle and lower classes, who were enjoying near full employment and such amenities as universal education, public libraries, and male suffrage, introduced during the Victorian Age. The **Georgian Age**, named for George V, king from 1910 to 1936, proved to be the last golden moment before the mid-century darkness. Even in that time, many writers were disturbed by inequities between the social classes. Georgian literature dealing with such inequities includes **George Bernard**

LITERARY EVENTS

► = British Events

►1906. Siegfied Sassoon publishes *Poems*
►1905. E. M. Forester (1879–1970) publishes *Where Angels Fear to Tread*

►1914. James Joyce publishes *Dubliners* and *A Portrait of the Artist as a Young Man*
►1913. D. H. Lawrence publishes *Sons and Lovers*
►1912. Joseph Conrad publishes *Twixt Land and Sea*, a collection of stories
►1914. *Pygmalion* by George Bernard Shaw performed at His Majesty's Theater, London

1900	1905	1910

►1901. Queen Victoria dies; Edward VII becomes king

►1910. Edward VII dies; reign of George V begins
►1910. South Africa is established as a dominion within the British Empire

HISTORICAL EVENTS

►1914. World War I begins following the assassination of Franz Ferdinand, Archduke of Austria

828 UNIT TEN / TWENTIETH-CENTURY POETRY

THEMATIC CURRENTS

Use the following selections to explore these themes with your students.

THE MEANING AND POWER OF POETRY
• "Adam's Curse," 844
• "Map of the New World," 905

THE SUFFERING AND LIMITATIONS OF HUMANKIND
• "The Second Coming," 847
• "Preludes," 852
• "Dulce et Decorum Est," 867
• "Do Not Go Gentle into That Good Night," 876

• "Musée des Beaux Arts," 884
• "Not Waving but Drowning," 888
• "Naked Girl and Mirror," 901

Shaw's (1856–1950) play *Pygmalion* and Katherine Mansfield's (1888–1923) brilliant story "The Garden-Party."

WORLD WAR I

In the early years of the century, England was allied with France and Russia, and Austria-Hungary was allied with Germany. In 1914, a Serbian nationalist murdered Archduke Franz Ferdinand, heir to the throne of Austria-Hungary. Austria declared war on Serbia, and Russia entered the war to protect Serbia, another Slavic state. Soon France and Germany entered the conflict, and Germany invaded Belgium, a neutral country that lay in its path toward France. This violation of Belgian neutrality led England into one of the costliest wars in its history.

Battles of the Somme, August 1916

None of the participants in **The Great War**, later called **World War I**, knew at first what lay ahead. In the past, war had been by modern lights relatively benign, even, some thought, glorious. However, modern technology made possible a new kind of warfare. Submarines, battleships, barbed wire, exploding bullets, machine guns, hand grenades, poison gas, and tanks led to carnage on an enormous scale. By the end of the war in 1918, nearly nine million people had died, including almost eight hundred thousand from Britain alone. Many of these casualties resulted from trench warfare, in which both sides dug into foxholes along the Western Front between France and Switzerland. The soldiers remained there for three years in rain-filled, rat-infested trenches, bombarded by heavy artillery and by poison gas. To many who experienced this hell, old slogans about the glories of war seemed not just foolish but demented.

Popperfoto/Archive Photos

▶1925. Virginia Woolf publishes *Mrs. Dalloway*
▶1922. T. S. Eliot publishes *The Wasteland*
▶1921. Siegfied Sassoon publishes *War Poems*
▶1918. *Poems* by Gerard Manley Hopkins published
▶1928. Stephen Spender publishes *Nine Expeditions*
▶1917. T. S. Eliot publishes *Prufrock and Other Observations*
▶1915. Rupert Brooke publishes *The Soldier*
▶1922. James Joyce publishes *Ulysses;* censored in U.S. until 1933

1915	1920	1925

1915 World War I continues; first use of poison gas; Germans sink *Lusitania*
▶1916. Ireland's unsuccessful Easter rebellion
1917. Revolution begins in Russia
1917. United States declares war on Germany
1918. Treaty of Brest-Litovsk ends Russia's participation in war
1919. Treaty of Versailles marks end of World War I
1922. Benito Mussolini becomes dictator of Italy

1923. U.S.S.R. formed
1924. Lenin dies
1925. Hitler writes *Mein Kampf*
1926. Stalin becomes dictator of U.S.S.R.
▶1928. British women are allowed to vote
1929. Great Depression begins in the United States

INTRODUCTION **829**

LITERARY CURRENTS

Use the following selections to explore these concepts and techniques with your students.

SYMBOLISM
• "The Second Coming," 847
• "Snake," 857
• "Thistles," 892
• "Map of the New World," 905
• "Bread," 896

FREE VERSE
• "Snake," 857
• "Thistles," 892

PROSE POEMS
• "Bread," 896

Students can do additional reading to understand the central importance of the Russian Revolution in twentieth-century history. Students might also research the career of Josef Stalin or examine why the Russian Communist experiment had failed by the late twentieth century.

BIOGRAPHICAL NOTE

George Orwell was the son of a minor British civil servant in India. Though he attended the British preparatory school Eton and could have gone on to a university, he opted to enter the civil service. As a police official in Burma he came face to face with the contradictions of British imperialism, an experience that proved radicalizing. He resigned his job and then deliberately sought out the companionship of the poor of London and Paris. Though he fought against Fascism in Spain during its civil war, by the end of that conflict he also found himself battling Communists who had turned on their political opponents. From this turnabout he learned the frightening lesson that Communism and Fascism have common totalitarian elements. His brilliant allegorical exposé of Soviet Communism, *Animal Farm,* appeared in 1945; his last work, *Nineteen Eighty-four,* the anti-utopian depiction of totalitarianism taken to its logical extreme, was published a year before his death in 1950.

QUOTABLES

❝If you want a picture of the future, imagine a boot stamping on a human face—forever.❞

—George Orwell

THE WAR POETS

Rupert Brooke (1887–1915), who died of dysentery and typhoid fever during the war, typified for the English a whole generation of patriotic young men who sacrificed all for their country. His poetry, Georgian in its optimism and nationalistic pride, helped to sustain English spirits during this time when the country lost many of its young people. **Wilfred Owen** (1893–1918) and **Siegfried Sassoon** (1886–1967) depicted in their poetry the other side of war, the carnage and waste that resulted from mechanized killing.

THE RUSSIAN REVOLUTION

Unable to sustain the costs of war, the Russian monarchy toppled in 1917. Czar Nicholas II and his family were executed, and a short-lived democratic government was established. Soon afterward, the **October Revolution** brought **Lenin** (born Vladimir Ilyich Ulanov, 1870–1924) to the head of the first Communist state. This state was founded on the ideas of German economist **Karl Marx** (1818–1883), who did much of his writing while in exile in Britain. Marx theorized that capitalist excesses would lead inevitably to worldwide revolution and to the establishment of worker-run states. These states would eventually evolve into perfect democracies operating for the common good, taking from each "according to his means" and giving to "each according to his needs." In Britain, many idealistic young men and women, such as

George Orwell

poets **Stephen Spender** (1909–) and **W. H. Auden** (1907–1973), flirted with Communism and Socialism but later became disillusioned when they saw the results of the Russian Revolution. Russia under Lenin and his successor **Joseph Stalin** (1879–1953) turned out to be not a worker's paradise but a ruthless dictatorship that suppressed free speech and massacred or imprisoned citizens who voiced opposition to government policies. The English novelist **George Orwell** (1903–1950) at first supported the Russian Revolution and its ideals. However, seeing what became of those ideals, Orwell bitterly critiqued the revolution, writing brilliant attacks on totalitarian dictatorship, including *Animal Farm* and *Nineteen Eighty-four.*

BRITAIN AFTER WORLD WAR I

Socialist Politics and the Labour Party. With most of an entire generation of its young men dead, and deeply in debt because of wartime expenditures, postwar

LITERARY EVENTS

▶1930. W. H. Auden publishes *Poems*

▶1938. Elizabeth Bowen publishes *The Death of the Heart*

▶1936. Dylan Thomas publishes *Twenty-five Poems*

▶1930. Virginia Woolf publishes "A Room of One's Own"; T. S. Eliot publishes "Ash Wednesday"

1930	1935	1940

1933. Nazi party gains control of Reichstag; Adolf Hitler becomes dictator

1936. Edward VIII becomes king and then abdicates

▶1938. British Prime Minister Neville Chamberlain accedes to Hitler's demands of Czechoslovakia

1939. Germany invades Poland, beginning World War II

1941. Germans invade Soviet Union; Japanese bomb Pearl Harbor

1944. D-day—Allied invasion of Normand

HISTORICAL EVENTS

Britain reeled. The period saw economic depression and radical demand for change. Socialism gained ground, supported by labor unions, by working people who felt they deserved more in return for their contributions to the war effort, and by radical members of the intelligentsia. The socialists believed in strong, centralized government as a means for achieving equality among the social classes. In the elections of 1922, the once-weak Labour Party came in second to the Conservatives. In 1924, Labour won, installing the first socialist prime minister. During the rest of the twentieth century, the Conservative and Labour parties vied for power, but for most of the century, socialist ideas held sway. Major businesses were nationalized, and government-run national health care was established.

Demonstration of the unemployed, Tower Hill, 1930

Popperfoto/Archive Photos

The Women's Movement. During this time, women in Britain gained enormous ground. In 1918, after years of protest, including pamphleteering and marching in the streets, women of age thirty and over won the right to vote. In 1928, this right was extended to women who had reached the age of twenty-one, putting British women for the first time on a par with British men. However, the right to vote was but the beginning of a continuing struggle for equal opportunity. Nowhere, perhaps, have the motivating forces for this struggle been more eloquently expressed than in **Virginia Woolf's** (1882–1941) *A Room of One's Own* (1929). In this classic document of the women's movement, Woolf describes the tragic loss that occurs when women are barred from achieving their full potential.

Irish Rebellion. At home, the British faced protest against traditional ideas. In Ireland, they faced armed conflict. Clamor for Irish independence among Catholics had reached a fever pitch at the turn of the century, but famine and migration had kept rebellion in check. After the turn of the century, resentments against English rule blossomed into insurrection. In

►1954. Stephen Spender's collected poems are published

►1953. Samuel Becket introduces the theater of the absurd with his *Waiting for Godot*

►1952. Dylan Thomas writes "Do Not Go Gentle Into That Good Night"

►1949. George Orwell publishes *Nineteen Eighty-four*

►1947. Judith Wright publishes first book of poetry

►1946. Denise Levertov publishes *The Double Image*

►1957. V. S. Naipal publishes *The Mystic Masseur*

►1945. George Orwell publishes *Animal Farm*

1945	1950	1955

1945. May 8, war in Europe ends; U.S. drops two atomic bombs on Japan; August 10, war in Japan ends

1946. United Nations begins its first session

1948. State of Israel established

1949. NATO is formed

1950. First protest against apartheid in South Africa

►1952. Elizabeth II ascends throne

1956. Sputnik I launched by U.S.S.R.

1957. Treaty of Rome establishes the European Common Market

INTRODUCTION **831**

CROSS-CURRICULAR ACTIVITIES

Social Studies. By the mid-1990s, the two sides in the centuries-old feud between Britain and Ireland seemed to have achieved a truce. Students can divide into three groups to research the current status of the conflict among (1) Britain, (2) the nationalists in Ireland who want to see the entire island united, and (3) Unionists in Northern Ireland who want to perpetuate their political connection with Great Britain. Each group should focus on the point of view of one of the parties involved. Group reports should include recommendations for resolving any remaining sources of conflict among the three parties.

HISTORICAL NOTE

The Great Depression in the United States has achieved mythic status in the American consciousness, but few Americans know of its effect on Britain. One index puts the rate of unemployment in that country at 23 percent in 1931, with a smaller overall decrease in production. Britain recovered from the great crash of 1929 much sooner than did the United States. By as early as 1933, production had begun to rise again, and by 1937, it exceeded 1929 levels by 34 percent; unemployment was significantly reduced. By most measures, life for the British working classes was better during the decade of the 1930s than it had been in the 1920s. Overall, however, British exports continued the decline begun earlier in the century.

1916, members of the Irish Republican Brotherhood (later the Irish Republican Army) seized the Dublin Post Office. The Irish rebels knew that they would not be able to resist the British forces that would be mobilized against them, but they were willing to be martyred for their cause. The insurrection was ruthlessly put down, and its leaders were exiled or publicly hanged. Britain's reaction increased Irish nationalism. Much of the literature produced in Ireland during the period, including Lady Augusta Gregory's play *The Rising of the Moon* (see page 48), reflects this national feeling. William Butler Yeats, in his famous poem about the uprising, **"Easter, 1916,"** observed that, "All changed, changed utterly: A terrible beauty is born." In 1922, the British Parliament partitioned Ireland into a northern Protestant section under British control and a southern Irish Free State, of which Yeats became a senator. Fighting between Protestants and Catholics in the north continued throughout much of the century, punctuated by sporadic outbreaks of terrorist violence on both sides.

The British Commonwealth. During the years leading up to World War II, British colonies around the world began clamoring for self-rule. Canada, South Africa, Australia, and New Zealand were already relatively independent, self-governing parts of the empire. In 1926, Parliament officially recognized the autonomy of these countries by passing a resolution naming them as free, equal partners with England in the British Commonwealth of Nations.

Economic Depression. In 1929, a crash at the New York Stock Exchange began a worldwide economic depression already felt keenly in Britain, which was suffering from the costs of World War I, the loss of colonial revenues, and increased global competition for trade. Unemployment soared, fueling Socialist idealism and conservative reaction.

Children sheltering from the Blitz

Popperfoto/Archive Photos

WORLD WAR II

The Great Depression of the 1930s had dramatic consequences for all of Europe. Desperate to improve their economic conditions, Europeans turned to political extremes. In Italy and in Germany, ultranationalist, fascist dictatorships emerged under **Benito Mussolini** (1883–1945) and **Adolf Hitler**

LITERARY EVENTS

► 1966. Margaret Atwood publishes *The Circle Game*

► 1965. Wole Soyinka publishes *The Interlopers*
► 1965. T. S. Eliot dies

1960	1965	1970

1961. Berlin Wall built
1962–1965. Second Vatican Council

1968. Russia invades Czechoslovakia, ending Prague Spring

► 1972. Britain imposes direct rule over Ireland

1964. U.S. escalates undeclared war in Viet Nam

HISTORICAL EVENTS

(1889–1945). In 1938, Hitler invaded Czechoslovakia. Then, in 1939, he entered Poland. This move ignited World War II, pitting Germany and Italy—the Axis powers—against France, England, Russia, and the United States—the Allies. Japan joined the fray by attacking the United States fleet at Pearl Harbor in 1941. For most of the war, Germany occupied France and conducted aerial bombardments of Britain known as the Blitz. In London especially, the British huddled in shelters and subway tunnels under a rain of German V-2 rockets. During this dark time, Prime Minister **Winston Churchill** (1874–1965) kept spirits alive with his famous radio addresses:

Popperfoto/Archive Photos

> You ask, What is our policy? I will say: "It is to wage war, by sea, land and air, with all our might and with all the strength that God can give us: to wage war against a monstrous tyranny, never surpassed in the dark, lamentable catalog of human crime."

Wrens fitting smoke floats on to a plane

Only at war's end was the nature of that "monstrous tyranny" fully known. Before the war, Hitler's National Socialist Party, the Nazis, built nationalist fervor by making scapegoats of subgroups within the European population, particularly Jews, gypsies, homosexuals, and mentally retarded persons. During the war, the Nazis implemented what they called the "final solution" to the "Jewish problem." Millions of Jews and others considered undesirable by the Nazis were put to death in extermination camps.

World War II ended in 1945 when Allied forces invaded Germany and the United States dropped atomic bombs on the Japanese cities of Hiroshima and Nagasaki. Estimates of wartime casualties differ, but about forty million people died in all, including almost nine million in German concentration and extermination camps. For the rest of the century, the world would live in the shadow of nuclear weapons.

1974. Alexander Solzhenitsyn's *Gulag Archipelago* published

►1986. Margaret Atwood publishes *A Handmaiden's Tale*

►1984. Ted Hughes becomes poet laureate of Great Britain

1981. Nadine Gordimer publishes *July's People*

1975	1980	1985

►1973. Great Britain joins European Economic Community
1974. Sears Tower built in Chicago, the world's tallest building (110 stories)

►1979. Margaret Thatcher becomes Prime Minister
1979. Accident at Three-Mile Island nuclear power plant

►1982. Argentina invades Britain's Falkland Islands

1989. Berlin Wall torn down

Winston Churchill's speeches are available on audio recordings. Students can obtain these from area libraries and listen to them in class. To provide the correct ambience for the speeches, darken the room and suggest that students imagine that they are in wartime London, listening to Churchill on the radio at night during an air raid.

ADDITIONAL QUESTIONS AND ACTIVITIES

Students can freewrite in their journals about how American soldiers might have felt when they first reached the sites of the Nazi extermination camps and found thousands of prisoners who had been waiting to die.

QUOTABLES

❝Victory at all costs, victory in spite of all terror, victory however long and hard the road may be; for without victory there is no survival.❞

—Winston Churchill

Queen Elizabeth II making her first Christmas broadcast, 1952

Popperfoto/Archive Photos

POST-WAR BRITAIN

In the years immediately following World War II, Britain's Labour government increased its control over industry and the economy, nationalizing more industries, rationing essential goods, controlling prices, and instituting the sorts of social programs associated with modern "welfare states." Meanwhile, the British economy continued to decline.

On the international scene, Britain lost its empire. India was granted independence in 1947, following successful nonviolent protests led by **Mohandas Gandhi** (1869–1948). Many other former colonies and territories became independent, including Burma, Ceylon (now Sri Lanka), Ghana, Kenya, Nigeria, Rhodesia (now Zimbabwe), Sudan, Trinidad and Tobago, and Uganda.

Immediately following the war, Russia extended its Communist dictatorship over much of Eastern Europe and the Balkan states. Speaking in the United States in 1946, Winston Churchill declared that an **"Iron Curtain"** had fallen across the continent, dividing East and West. Symbolic of the division of Europe was the **Berlin Wall,** which the Communists erected in 1961 to divide Russian-controlled East Berlin from West Berlin. For the next several decades, world politics was dominated by struggles between the Communist states, especially the Soviet Union, and democratic states of Western Europe and North America. Western Europe and the United States formed the **North Atlantic Treaty Organization,** or NATO, in defense against the Communists. England also joined the **Common Market,** or **European Economic Community (EEC),** an organization of Western European states formed to oversee trade between member countries.

In 1953, **Queen Elizabeth II** (1926–) was crowned. The once-powerful English monarchy had been reduced to a largely ceremonial position, but most English men and women continued to support it for the sake of tradition.

The 1960s and 1970s saw a radical revolt among the youth of England, who challenged the values and traditions of their elders. In the early sixties, English rock-and-roll groups such

LITERARY EVENTS

▶1990. Derek Walcott publishes *Omeros*

1990	1995

▶1990. John Major becomes Prime Minister

HISTORICAL EVENTS

as the Beatles and the Rolling Stones became extremely popular, and teenagers around the globe imitated these groups' hairstyles and modes of dress. Throughout the world, the sixties and the seventies were an era of radical experimentation in all the arts, partially fueled by the youth movement.

During the postwar period, modern forms of technologically based entertainment, notably radio, television, and the cinema, came into their own, further increasing the division between lowbrow and highbrow culture that characterized much of the twentieth century.

In 1979, Britain elected its first female prime minister, **Margaret Thatcher** (1925–), a conservative who privatized some British industries and radically cut back social programs. She became Britian's longest-serving prime minister in history. In 1982, under Thatcher, Britain fought a short war with Argentina over control of the Falkland Islands, one of Britain's few remaining colonial possessions. The British lease on Hong Kong expires in 1999. In 1989, the Soviet Union collapsed, and the Berlin Wall came down, signaling the possibility of a future not dominated by East-West tensions. Britain moved toward reducing its isolation by joining with France to build the so-called **Chunnel**, a tunnel beneath the English Channel. In 1993, the last of the European states joined in ratifying the **Maastricht Treaty,** creating a new continent-wide economic entity, the **European Union,** or **EU.** Today, England remains a shadow of its former economic self. However, due to immigration, its population has become more diverse, and with diversity come new possibilities for the future.

Margaret Thatcher, Britain's longest-serving prime minister

Popperfoto/Archive Photos

REALISM

During the late Victorian Era the pressures of modern urban life helped to create a kind of writing known as **Realism** because of its realistic portrayal of life in all its gritty, often disturbing detail. Important late Victorian Realist writers include English novelists **George Eliot**, born Mary Ann Evans (1819–1880), and **Thomas Hardy** (1840–1928) and French novelists **Honoré de Balzac** (1799–1850) and **Émile Zola** (1840–1902). Their writings inspired fine works in the Realist tradition in the early part of the twentieth century. Polish-born **Joseph Conrad** (1857–1924) wrote Realist stories and novels full of psychological probing and dark symbolic undercurrents, including *Lord Jim* (1900) and *Heart of Darkness* (1902). An example of Conrad's fiction, **"The Lagoon,"** can be found on page 967. The early stories of the Irish writer **James Joyce** (1882–1941) were likewise Realist. Other English writers of the early twentieth century who worked in the Realist tradition include **H. G. Wells** (1866–1946), **John Galsworthy** (1867–1933), **Katherine Mansfield** (1888–1923), **E. M. Forster** (1879–1970), and **George Orwell** (1903–1950). The early twentieth century was also the heyday of Realism on the stage. Lady Gregory's *The Rising of the Moon,* on page 48, and George Bernard Shaw's *Pygmalion,* on page 986, are examples.

MODERNISM

Perhaps ironically, Realism contributed to growing discontent with traditional ways of thinking, which in turn helped to create a number of anti-Realist literary and artistic movements collectively referred to as **Modernism.** Modernist art and literature are characterized by several related trends: technicality, primitivism, impersonalism, imagism, aestheticism, and intellectualism.

Three Musicians. Pablo Picasso, 1921. The Museum of Modern Art, NY

Technicality. Modernist art often emphasizes technique and materials over representational content. This trend found perhaps its clearest expression in painting and music. The **Cubist** paintings of **Pablo Picasso** (1881–1973) and **Georges Braque** (1882–1963) represented people, buildings, and everyday objects as abstract arrangements of geometric shapes. Toward the middle of the century, Cubism gave way to **Abstract Expressionism**, which moved further away from representation and toward expression of pure emotion or thought through color, line, and composition. Here, again, Picasso led the way. Other great Abstract Expressionist painters included **Joan Miró** of Spain (1893–1983), **Wassily Kandinsky** of Russia (1866–1940), **Piet Mondrian** of the Netherlands (1872–1944), and U.S.-born **Robert Motherwell** (1915–1991) and **Robert Rauschenberg** (1925–   ). Architects such as **Walter Gropius** (Germany, 1883–1969), **Le Corbusier** (Switzerland, 1887–1965), and **Ludwig Mies Van der Rohe** (Germany, 1886–1969) introduced severely functional buildings viewed as abstract, nondecorated forms, from which evolved the modern skyscraper.

Two Austrian-born musicians, **Arnold Schönberg** (1874–1951) and **Anton Webern** (1883–1945), moved away from traditional tonal music, creating **twelve-tone, atonal** compositions written in no particular key and making extensive use of discordances. **Igor Stravinsky** of Russia (1882–1971) and **Béla Bartók** of Hungary (1881–1945) experimented with alternatives to traditional tonal music, often drawing inspiration from primitive folk sources.

Primitivism. Modernists were attracted to the primitive for two major reasons. First, primitive art and music tended toward abstraction and stylization. Second, Modernists sought in primitive sources a deeper connection to the dark, hidden elements of the human spirit suppressed by Western "civilized" culture. This attraction to the primitive for inspiration owed a debt to the Austrian founder of **psychoanalysis, Sigmund Freud** (1856–1939). Freud proposed that people, in the course of growing up, learn to suppress their primitive, basic impulses, which then find expression in jokes; slips of the tongue; fantasies; wish-fulfilling, symbolic dreams; and works of art (music, dance, theater, painting, sculpture, and literature).

Impersonalism. Modernist literature often deals with subjective feelings in an impersonal, intellectualized style. This contrast between personal subject matter and an impersonal style reflects the alienation of many modern writers—their sense that, more than ever before, people are isolated from one another, crowded together in cities but lacking the interpersonal connections that bound together peasant communities of the past. In Britain, Modernism found expression in different ways in the writings of **James Joyce, Virginia Woolf, D. H. Lawrence** (1885–1930), U.S.-born **T. S. Eliot** (1888–1965), and **Dylan Thomas** (1914–1953).

Major English poets of the period included **Ted Hughes** (1930–) and **Philip Larkin** (1922–1985), members of **The Movement,** a group of poets dedicated to clear, precise, non-Romantic verse in ordinary speech.

Joyce and Woolf experimented with a new kind of fiction writing that used a **stream-of-consciousness** style, attempting to render in prose the subjective flow of thoughts and emotions in a character's mind. Novels such as Virginia Woolf's *Mrs. Dalloway* (1925) and *To the Lighthouse* (1927) and James Joyce's *A Portrait of the Artist as a Young Man* (1914–1915) and *Ulysses* (1922) violated standard fictional conventions by placing the reader inside characters' minds in all their jumbled confusion. Such literature placed high demands on readers and further accentuated the rift between highbrow and lowbrow culture. An example of stream-of-consciousness technique is the excerpt from Joyce's *A Portrait of the Artist as a Young Man* on page 921.

Imagism. American-born **Ezra Pound** (1885–1972) was, perhaps, the primary spokesperson for Modernism in poetry. Pound was initially attracted to **Imagism,** an attempt to free poetry of the speaker's or author's comment about feeling or meaning. A typical Imagist poem presents a single, clear snapshot of a moment of perception. It does not tell the reader how to feel about the picture that is presented. Instead, it presents the picture, or image, and lets it create the emotion in the reader. The author or speaker assumes an "impersonal" stance, not sharing his or her emotions directly, but presenting emotion-creating images. Such impersonality is a hallmark of much Modernist writing. To this day, a major distinction between highbrow literature and lowbrow literature (such as popular romances and mystery stories) is that the latter tends to state feelings directly, while the former tends to present surface details and to let the reader infer what is to be felt about these details. T. S. Eliot, who was born in America but later became an English citizen, coined a term, the *objective correlative,* to describe a group of images that produce a particular emotion in the reader.

Aestheticism. The alienation between high culture and popular culture reflected in Modernism began with the **Aesthetic Movement** at the close of the nineteenth century, the motto of which was "Art for art's sake." **Oscar Wilde's** (1854–1900) preface to *The Picture of Dorian Gray* (1891) expresses this idea in a bold and absolute distinction between the artistic and the useful. The German Nobel Prize winner **Thomas Mann** (1875–1955), in such works as *Buddenbrooks* (1900), *Death in Venice* (1912), and *The Magic Mountain* (1924), wrote about the incompatibility of artistic and utilitarian values and lifestyles. In James Joyce's *A Portrait of the Artist as a Young Man* (1916), the main character, Stephen Dedalus, experiences deep conflicts between his inner artistic nature and the pressures of the practical exterior world.

Intellectualism and Alienation from Popular Culture. The emphasis on technique over representation, on impersonality, and on aestheticism in Modernist art and literature reflects the intellectual revolution of the late nineteenth century. The work of Freud, Marx, **Charles Darwin** (1809–1882), and **Albert Einstein** (1879–1955) forced scholars in every field to rethink the foundations of their disciplines and led to a primary concern with theory *per se.* Art, music, and literature were seen by many as little more than vehicles through which to express ideas about art, music, and literature. Art appreciation became an intellectual task requiring years of training in history and theory. Such ideas fueled a growing separation between artists and the public. Such alienation is expressed powerfully in the writings of Czech **Franz Kafka** (1883–1924) and in the famous painting *The Scream* by Norwegian **Edvard Munch** (1863–1944).

HISTORICAL NOTE

Besides Pound, poets openly espousing Imagism or influenced by it included Conrad Aiken, Richard Aldington, Hilda Doolittle (H. D.), T. S. Eliot, John Gould Fletcher, F. S. Flint, Amy Lowell, Harriet Monroe, Marianne Moore, and Wallace Stevens. The most important Imagist work appeared between 1914 and 1917 in the anthologies *Des Imagistes* and *Some Imagists*, the latter appearing in three separate volumes.

QUOTABLES

❝I have nothing to declare but my genius. ❞

—Oscar Wilde at the New York Customs House

❝History is a nightmare from which I am trying to awake. ❞

—James Joyce

QUOTABLES

❝The only way of expressing emotion in the form of art is by finding an 'objective correlative,' in other words, a set of objects, a situation, a chain of events which shall be the formula of that *particular* emotion; such that when the external facts, which must terminate in sensory experiences, are given, the emotion is immediately evoked. ❞

—T. S. Eliot

• Give students an exercise in impromptu writing and critical thinking. Ask them to answer this question in a ten-minute piece of focused freewriting: Should art be easily accessible to people without extensive education? Each student should give his or her opinion, citing at least two reasons to support the position taken. When the time is up, read some of the papers aloud and discuss the question with the class.

 • The National Endowment for the Arts is a government agency established to distribute public funds to artists to enable them to produce their art. Have students theorize about and then research the rationale for this agency. Ask them to consider the following questions: Should the government directly fund artistic endeavors with public money? If so, should strings be attached to that money? On what bases should such an agency decide to whom money should go and in what amounts?

Robert Frost once compared writing free verse to playing tennis without a net. Have students discuss this point of view, comparing it to Pound's comment that free verse conforms "to the musical phrase, not to the metronome."

QUOTABLES

❝Never trust the artist. Trust the tale.❞

—D. H. Lawrence

REPRESENTATIVE MODERN WRITERS

Eliot's poetry is the prime example of Modernism in literature. The work is detached and impersonal in style but deals with personal, subjective feelings. It tends to be highly intellectual, alluding to other literature and to historical events. Often the symbols used are highly personal. Instead of using traditional symbols, such as a rose for love or the moon for inconstancy, a Modernist poet is likely to present symbols that have personal meaning or associations that must be inferred by the reader. Such use of symbolism was strongly influenced by the **French Symbolist** poets of the nineteenth century, including **Stéphane Mallarmé** (1842–1898), **Arthur Rimbaud** (1854–1891), and **Charles Baudelaire** (1821–1867). Modernist intellectualism, allusiveness, and use of nontraditionally poetic speech owed debts to the Metaphysical poetry of **John Donne** (1572–1631) and to the poetry of **Gerard Manley Hopkins** (1844–1889) published in 1918. In meter as in other areas, Modernist poets made innovations. Conventions of rhythm, rhyme, and stanza form were thrown off in favor of *vers libre,* or **free verse**, that conformed more readily to the stream of the speaker's thought, or, in Pound's famous statement, "to the musical phrase, not to the metronome."

Dylan Thomas and **D. H. Lawrence** represent a different trend in Modernism. Each wrote often in conventional forms but adapted those forms to Modernist purposes. Both writers, influenced by Freud, dealt with basic human impulses, often ones repressed by society. Both made use of personal rather than conventional symbols. Thomas's poetry, in particular, makes great demands on readers because of his often startling and unique symbolism. Despite its difficulty, Thomas's poetry was and still is extremely popular. Thomas had a beautiful speaking voice and popularized his work through public readings. Many people are attracted to his work for its sheer lyrical beauty, aside from any interpretations that they might give to it. Lawrence is known primarily for his novels, notably *Sons and Lovers* (1913), *The Rainbow* (1915), *Women in Love* (1916, published 1920), and *Lady Chatterley's Lover* (1928). These novels challenged the moral sensibilities of many people of the time and were subject to censorship, though by today's standards they are generally considered quite tame. In addition to his novels, Lawrence wrote fine short fiction and poetry, examples of which can be found on pages 31 and 857 of this text.

Echoes:

Twentieth-Century Poetry

• In small groups, students can choose one of the quotes and discuss its meaning in light of the world and time in which they live.

• Students can choose one of these quotes as a springboard for a piece of creative writing such as a story or a poem. Encourage students to explore the ideas these quotes bring to mind before reading the selections from which they come.

"It's certain there's no fine thing
Since Adam's fall but needs much laboring."
—William Butler Yeats,
"Adam's Curse"

Things fall apart; the center cannot hold;
Mere anarchy is loosed upon the world
—William Butler Yeats,
"The Second Coming"

I am moved by fancies that are curled
Around these images, and cling:
The notion of some infinitely gentle
Infinitely suffering thing.
—T. S. Eliot,
"Preludes"

And so, I missed my chance with one of the
lords of life.
And I have something to expiate:
A pettiness.
—D. H. Lawrence,
"Snake"

If in some smothering dreams you too could pace
Behind the wagon that we flung him in . . .
My friend, you would not tell with such high zest
To children ardent for some desperate glory,
The old lie: Dulce et decorum est
Pro patria mori.
—Wilfred Owen,
"Dulce et Decorum Est"

"Imagine a famine. Now imagine a piece of
bread. Both things are real but you happen to be
in the same room with only one of them."
—Margaret Atwood,
"Bread"

INTRODUCTION **839**

ENRICHMENT ACTIVITIES

Students can discuss the advantages and disadvantages of living on a small island and of isolation in general. Ask: What does the desire to go away and live on an island imply about one's view of the world? Could such a desire be temporary? What might cause such a desire?

SUPPORT FOR LEP STUDENTS

Alert students to Yeats's use of repetition. Suggest that this poem will be easier to understand if students look for patterns of repeated ideas such as motion, peacefulness, and hearing.

VOCABULARY FROM THE SELECTIONS

articulate   glade

PREREADING

"The Lake Isle of Innisfree"
"Adam's Curse"
"The Second Coming"

by William Butler Yeats

ABOUT THE AUTHOR

William Butler Yeats (1865–1939) was born near Dublin and grew up there, in London, and in the County Sligo countryside. In Sligo, under the shadow of Ben Bulben Mountain, said by locals to be home to the fairy people known as the Sidhe (She), Yeats imbibed Irish folk tales and legends. He studied painting in Dublin but left school to pursue a literary career. His early poetry drew heavily on traditional legends and myths. As a young man, he fell deeply in love with an actress and Irish revolutionary named Maude Gonne. However, Gonne did not return his affections. His unrequited love for her led to the creation of many of his finest poems. In the late 1890s, Yeats and Lady Augusta Gregory founded the Irish National Theatre, later the Abbey Theatre, and Yeats became its director. For that theater he wrote plays based on Irish themes, some of which used innovative costuming and movement derived from Japanese Nō drama. In 1917, he married Georgie Hyde-Lees and moved into a restored Norman tower called Thoor Ballylee. Yeats had always had a keen interest in spiritualism, and much of the symbolism of his later poetry derives from the "spirit writing" that his wife, Georgie, did in trancelike states. In 1922, Yeats was named a senator of the new Irish Free State (Eire). When he died in January 1939, he left behind a varied, fascinating body of work that reveals him as one of the great poets of the twentieth century.

ABOUT THE SELECTIONS

"The Lake Isle of Innisfree" is one of Yeats's most well-known and well-loved poems. Technically a pastoral verse, it deals with a modern speaker's desire to escape from city life to a life of peace in the countryside.

"Adam's Curse" is an autobiographical poem telling of one small event in the history of Yeats's relationship with Maude Gonne. The poem reveals Yeats's belief that nothing wonderful—poetry, beauty, or love—comes without hard work and sacrifice.

"The Second Coming," published in 1921, shows his mastery of visionary symbolism and of a terse, strong, modern style quite different from that of his dreamy early verse. Written shortly after World War I and the Russian Revolution, the poem prophesies the beginning of a new and frightening cycle of history.

GOALS/OBJECTIVES

Studying this lesson will enable students to

- interpret and appreciate the poetry of William Butler Yeats
- describe W. B. Yeats's literary accomplishments and explain the historical significance of his writings

- define *image* and recognize images within a poem
- define *lyric poetry* and explain why a poem is lyric
- write a critical essay

READER'S JOURNAL

Do you remember someplace special from your childhood, a place you would like to visit again? For Yeats, it was a remote lake, but for someone else it might be a city park or street. Freewrite in your journal about the place you remember.

RESEARCH SKILLS

Read the Language Arts Survey, 4.23, "Using Reference Works." Then look in an atlas or encyclopedia to find a detailed political-physical map of Ireland. Notice both the political divisions and the landscape. Then locate some of the places important to Yeats, specifically County Sligo, Dublin, and, if possible, Innisfree (in Lough [lake] Gill, County Sligo).

"The Lake Isle of Innisfree"[1]

WILLIAM BUTLER YEATS

I will arise and go now, and go to Innisfree,
And a small cabin build there, of clay and wattles[2] made;
Nine bean-rows will I have there, a hive for the honey-bee,
And live alone in the bee-loud <u>glade</u>.

5   And I shall have some peace there, for peace comes dropping slow,
Dropping from the veils of the morning to where the cricket sings;
There midnight's all a glimmer, and noon a purple glow,
And evening full of the linnet's[3] wings.

I will arise and go now, for always night and day
10   I hear lake water lapping with low sounds by the shore;
While I stand on the roadway, or on the pavements gray,
I hear it in the deep heart's core.

❶
What details in the first two stanzas suggest a simple, peaceful, rustic existence?

---

1. **Lake Isle of Innisfree.** Island in County Sligo, Ireland
2. **wattles.** Woven twigs and branches
3. **linnet.** Finch

WORDS FOR
EVERYDAY USE:

    glade (glād) *n.,* open space in a forest

VOCABULARY IN CONTEXT

• Ayesha followed the forest stream through the trees until she came out into a sunny <u>glade</u>.

ANSWER TO GUIDED READING QUESTION

❶ Details that suggest simplicity, peace, and rusticity include the small cabin built of clay and wattles, a garden of beans, a beehive, the sounds of a cricket, and images of natural light by morning, noon, and night.

PREREADING NOTES

READER'S JOURNAL

Students should explain in particular what was special about the place they remember, focusing on any of the five senses that are relevant to their recollections. Ask them which sense evokes the strongest memories of the place they recall and encourage them to explain why.

RESEARCH SKILLS

 Point out to students the general landscape features of Ireland as reflected in the physical map: it has many lakes, bog areas, and ridges cutting across a central highland plain. Discuss how such a landscape would be likely to shape a poet's vision of the world, as opposed to, say, a desert landscape or a tropical jungle.

ADDITIONAL QUESTIONS AND ACTIVITIES

The theme of escape to a rural setting is traditional in poetry. The following are some famous examples: "Well then! I Now Do Plainly See," by Abraham Cowley (1618–1667); "The Choice," by John Pomfret (1667–1702); "Ode on Solitude," by Alexander Pope (1688–1744); "A Cure for the Spleen," by Matthew Green (1696–1737); "The Statesman in Retirement," by William Cowper (1731–1800). Another study of the subject by Yeats—very simple and romantic—is "To an Isle in the Water." Students can look up one of these poems and write a summary to share with the class. Their summaries should indicate any differences in treatment from "The Lake Isle of Innisfree." (Good sources for the eighteenth-century poems are *The Oxford Book of Eighteenth Century Verse* and other period anthologies; the Yeats poem can be found in *The Collected Poems of W. B. Yeats* [New York: Macmillan, 1956].) Students who wish to trace the theme back to one of its oldest sources can read the satire of the Roman poet Horace (65–8 BC) on city versus country life (*Satires* 2:6).

Point out that in describing an ideal place to live, students are making a statement about their needs and desires and their attitude toward humanity. For this reason students may wish to describe more than one spot.

ANSWERS FOR REVIEWING THE SELECTION

RECALLING

1. The speaker plans to rise, go to Innisfree, build a cabin, have a garden and beehive, and live alone.

2. The morning is peaceful, the noon a purple glow, the evening full of the linnet's wings, and midnight all a glimmer.

3. The speaker remembers the sound of lake water lapping on the shore.

4. The speaker evidently lives in an urban environment because he mentions a roadway and gray pavements.

INTERPRETING

Responses will vary. Possible responses are given.

5. The beans and bees seem to represent simplicity and freedom from the cares of making a living.

6. The speaker wants to find a peaceful life alone with only the company of nature.

7. An island is effectively cut off from neighbors.

8. The last stanza implies a contrast between road sounds and lake water lapping on a shore and between the gray pavement of the city and the vivid colors of the island.

SYNTHESIZING

Responses will vary. Possible responses are given.

9. Inasmuch as the desire to "get away from it all" is based on the difficulty of dealing with human society, it is not likely to vary much from century to century.

10. Implicit in the speaker's desire to be alone is the possibility of some disappointment in a particular relationship; otherwise, one might expect he would want some company, however select.

Responding to the Selection

Does Yeats's picture of the island of Innisfree appeal to you, or would you prefer to live in a less secluded, more active place? In your journal, or in class discussion, describe your own ideal spot in which to live.

Reviewing the Selection

RECALLING

1. In the first stanza, what specific plans does the speaker relate?

2. What are the different times of day like on the island?

3. In the third stanza, what memory of Innisfree is strongest when the speaker is not there?

4. Where does the speaker live now? How do you know?

INTERPRETING

5. Does the speaker really want to do farm work, or do the bees and the beans represent something else?

6. What kind of lifestyle does the speaker want to find on Innisfree?

7. Why might it be important for the speaker's retreat to be an island?

8. What contrasts in sights and sounds are described or implied by the last stanza?

SYNTHESIZING

9. Yeats wrote "The Lake Isle of Innisfree" more than one hundred years ago. What relevance does this poem have to life today?

10. Why do you think the speaker wanted to go to Innisfree alone?

ANSWERS TO SELECTION CHECK TEST 4.10.1

EX. Where does the speaker long to go?
He longs to go to Innisfree.

1. What will the speaker build?
The speaker will build a small cabin.

2. Will the speaker live with anyone else?
No, the speaker will live alone.

3. What is unusual about midnight on the Isle of

Innisfree?
Midnight is all a glimmer.

4. What does the speaker hear day and night?
The speaker hears lake water lapping.

5. Where does the speaker now live, in the city or in the country?
The speaker now lives in the city.

Understanding Literature (Questions for Discussion)

1. **Image.** An **image** is a word or phrase that names something that can be seen, heard, touched, tasted, or smelled. Yeats builds his picture of Innisfree with a careful selection of imagery. The second line in the first stanza, for instance, provides a picture of the cabin. What image in that stanza appeals to the sense of hearing? What other auditory images can you find in the poem?

2. **Lyric Poem.** A **lyric poem** is a highly musical verse that expresses the emotions of a speaker. Another way of thinking of a lyric poem is as a song without music. Lyrics depend on rhythm, rhyme, and repeated sounds as well as imagery for their musical quality. Using letters, describe the rhyme scheme of "The Lake Isle of Innisfree." Think of the last word in line 1, *Innisfree*, as *a*. All line-ending words that rhyme with it are also identified as *a*. The last word in line 2 does not rhyme with *Innisfree*, so it becomes *b*. All line-ending words that rhyme with it are also *b*. So the rhyme scheme of the first verse is *abab*. Then look for the sounds of words used musically. For instance, in lines 3 and 4, find the repeated letters *l, b,* and *h,* which are used with open vowel sounds. What mood, or emotional effect, do these sounds create?

Responding in Writing

1. **Travel Brochure.** Choose a place like Yeats's Innisfree that you consider to be both wild and beautiful. Do some research on the place and write a brief travel brochure about it. The brochure should name and describe the place, give directions to it (perhaps with a map), and provide tips on enjoying the place once there.

2. **Critical Essay: Yeats and Thoreau.** Read "Economy," the first chapter of Henry David Thoreau's *Walden.* Imagine one of your friends has also read this and says to you, "I hear that Yeats's 'Lake Isle of Innisfree' was influenced by the first chapter of *Walden,* but I don't see any relationship." Write a short critical piece to convince your friend that such a relationship exists.

"THE LAKE ISLE OF INNISFREE" 843

PREREADING NOTES

READER'S JOURNAL

Observe to students that the goals they discuss may be entirely personal or may focus on changes they wish to see in society at large. To stimulate their thinking, ask them what kind of goals a poet like Yeats probably sets for himself or herself at a young age. What satisfaction might achieving such a goal bring? What disadvantages would pursuing such a goal involve?

THINKING SKILLS

To spark ideas, ask students to consider whether poets apply any of the problem-solving strategies to their difficulties as artists trying to live in a world that often cares little about poetry.

ANSWER TO GUIDED READING QUESTION

❶ Writing poetry takes considerable time and effort, but the end result must seem effortless.

SUPPORT FOR LEP STUDENTS

ADDITIONAL VOCABULARY

pauper—extremely poor person
compound—created through the combining of elements
precedent—example

READER'S JOURNAL

About what do you care enough to work for many years? Think about some goal that you want to accomplish or something that you would like to have happen in the world. Freewrite in your journal about that goal or desire. Tell why it is important to you and what you would be willing to do to achieve it.

THINKING SKILLS

Read the Language Arts Survey, 4.1 and 4.2, "Strategies for Problem Solving I and II." What strategies could you use to achieve the goal that you identified in your Reader's Journal entry? Choose one or more strategies from the survey lessons and explain how you could apply them to achieving your goal.

"Adam's Curse"[1]

WILLIAM BUTLER YEATS

According to the speaker, what paradox does writing poetry involve? ❶

We sat together at one summer's end,
That beautiful mild woman, your close friend,
And you[2] and I, and talked of poetry.
I said: "A line will take us hours maybe;
5   Yet if it does not seem a moment's thought,
Our stitching and unstitching has been naught.
Better go down upon your marrow-bones
And scrub a kitchen pavement, or break stones
Like an old pauper, in all kinds of weather;
10   For to <u>articulate</u> sweet sounds together
Is to work harder than all these, and yet
Be thought an idler by the noisy set
Of bankers, schoolmasters, and clergymen
The martyrs call the world."

15   And thereupon
That beautiful mild woman for whose sake

---

1. **Adam's Curse.** In Genesis, Adam is cursed after the Fall with having to die and with having to live by the sweat of his brow, to work.
2. **you.** This autobiographical poem is addressed to Maude Gonne, the beautiful actress and revolutionary for whom Yeats felt unrequited love during most of his adult life.

WORDS FOR EVERYDAY USE: ar • ti • cu • late (är tik´yōō lāt´) vt., express clearly; join or connect

VOCABULARY IN CONTEXT

• Though Paolo passionately loved Francesca, he was unable to <u>articulate</u> his feelings for her.

There's many a one shall find out all heartache
On finding that her voice is sweet and low
Replied: "To be born woman is to know—
20 Although they do not talk of it at school—
That we must labor to be beautiful."

I said: "It's certain there is no fine thing
Since Adam's fall but needs much laboring.
There have been lovers who thought love should be
25 So much compounded of high courtesy
That they would sigh and quote with learned looks
Precedents out of beautiful old books;
Yet now it seems an idle trade enough."

We sat grown quiet at the name of love;
30 We saw the last embers of daylight die,
And in the trembling blue-green of the sky
A moon, worn as if it had been a shell
Washed by time's waters as they rose and fell
About the stars and broke in days and years.

35 I had a thought for no one's but your ears:
That you were beautiful, and that I strove
To love you in the old high way of love;
That it had all seemed happy, and yet we'd grown
As weary-hearted as that hollow moon. ∎

Responding to the Selection

At what two things has the speaker in this poem worked hard? Judging from the evidence of the poem, at which of these has he been successful? At which has he failed? What makes something worth working hard at, even when there is a chance of failure?

"ADAM'S CURSE" **845**

ANSWER TO GUIDED READING QUESTION

❶ "Much laboring" is needed to create fine things.

(margin) ❶ What, according to the speaker, is required in order to create any "fine thing"?

ANSWERS TO SELECTION CHECK TEST 4.10.3

EX. What curse was placed on Adam?
He was required to work.

1. What subject of discussion does the speaker recall at the beginning of the poem?
The speaker recalls a discussion about poetry.

2. What must seem "a moment's thought" even though it takes a great deal of "stitching and unstitching"?
A line of poetry must seem "a moment's thought."

3. According to the speaker, what is harder work than scrubbing a kitchen floor or breaking stones?
Writing poetry is harder work.

4. According to the "beautiful mild woman," what must women do?
They must labor to be beautiful.

5. The speaker and the person to whom the poem is addressed have grown as "weary-hearted" as what?
They have grown as "weary-hearted as that hollow moon."

RESPONDING TO THE SELECTION

The speaker has worked hard at poetry and at trying to love the woman to whom he speaks. He has been successful at poetry but has failed at love. Students may observe that endeavors where the potential gain from success exceeds the potential loss from failure (endeavors such as art or love) are worth the hard work they require.

ANSWERS FOR REVIEWING THE SELECTION

RECALLING

1. The speaker and two women are holding a conversation at the beginning of the poem.

2. She says that women must labor to be physically beautiful.

3. The speaker introduces the notion of love as an endeavor.

4. The "name of love" causes the people present to grow quiet. He compares the fading daylight to the embers of a fire, the moon to a worn shell, and time to the waters of a sea.

INTERPRETING

Responses will vary. Possible responses are given.

5. Writing poetry is harder than scrubbing a floor or breaking stones. People often think that poets are "idlers" because they do not recognize the work involved in writing poetry.

(cont.)

Reviewing the Selection

1. Who is holding a conversation at the beginning of the poem? What is the subject of that conversation?

2. What comment does the "beautiful mild woman" make in stanza 2?

3. What third subject is introduced by the speaker in stanza 3?

4. What causes the people in this poem to grow quiet? To what does the speaker compare the fading daylight? To what does he compare the moon and time?

5. What is harder than scrubbing a kitchen floor or breaking stones? What do worldly people think of someone who devotes his or her energies to such a task? Why are such people wrong?

6. How is the comment made by the "beautiful mild woman" related to the speaker's initial comments about poetry?

7. How did people in love behave differently in former times? What hard work did they perform?

8. How do the people in the poem feel about the speaker's comments about love? How do you know? How may the description of the daylight and the moon reflect their feelings?

9. To whom does the speaker wish to speak privately at the end of the poem? According to the speaker, how does the conversation that they have been having relate to the two of them? Which person in the poem has labored to be beautiful? Which has labored to love in the old way, "compounded of high courtesy"?

10. What was the curse placed upon Adam? In what sense are the speaker and the person to whom the poem is addressed victims of that curse?

Understanding Literature (Questions for Discussion)

Allusion. An **allusion** is a figure of speech in which a reference is made to a person, event, object, or work from history or literature. In stanza 3, the speaker refers to "high courtesy" and quotations about love from "beautiful old books." The speaker is alluding to romance literature and its ideas of chivalry and courtly love. In that literature, a knight who devoted himself entirely to his beloved, thought only of her welfare, brought her gifts, wrote for her, and did mighty deeds for her was said to have behaved "courteously," or in a manner befitting someone from the court of a king or queen. Read the entries in the Handbook of Literary Terms on *chivalry, courtly love,* and *romance.* How has the speaker acted toward his beloved? What has happened as a result? Why is the speaker sad? The title and lines 22 and 23 of the poem allude to Genesis 3:17–19, which tells of a curse laid on Adam requiring him to work. What three activities described in this poem require work? Do you agree with the poem's view of poetry, beauty, and love?

READER'S JOURNAL

Do you think that life in our time is better or worse than in former times? Is your view of the near- and long-term future positive or negative? In your journal, freewrite about what you think the world will be like in the years to come.

THINKING SKILLS

Read the Language Arts Survey, 4.18, "Reading Actively: Predicting." Then, think about the title of the poem. To Christians, the Second Coming is the time when Jesus is expected to return. Yeats believed that history operated in cycles, each begun by an intervention of the spiritual world in the development of this world. Knowing these things, what do you predict that the poem will be about?

"The Second Coming"

WILLIAM BUTLER YEATS

Turning and turning in the widening gyre[1]
The falcon cannot hear the falconer;[2]
Things fall apart; the center cannot hold;
Mere anarchy is loosed upon the world,
5 The blood-dimmed tide is loosed, and everywhere
The ceremony of innocence is drowned;
The best lack all conviction, while the worst
Are full of passionate intensity.

Surely some revelation is at hand;
10 Surely the Second Coming[3] is at hand.
The Second Coming! Hardly are those words out
When a vast image out of *Spiritus Mundi*[4]
Troubles my sight: somewhere in sands of the desert
A shape with lion body and the head of a man,[5]
15 A gaze blank and pitiless as the sun,
Is moving its slow thighs, while all about it

❶
How does the speaker characterize the times in which he lives?

---

1. **gyre.** Circle or cycle. Yeats believed that history occurred in cycles punctuated by revolutionary events in which the spirit world intersected this world. He called these cycles of history *gyres*, which he pronounced with a hard *g*.
2. **falcon . . . falconer.** The reference is to the sport of falconry, in which a trained falcon is used for hunting. The image suggests violence that is uncontrolled by any authority.

3. **Second Coming.** Many Christian sects believe Jesus will come again to earth at the end of time as we know it. This event is known as the Second Coming.
4. **Spiritus Mundi.** Latin for "the world spirit," Yeats used it as the name for the collective, inherited body of symbols common to all people. The concept is similar to Carl Jung's archetypes of the collective unconscious. See the entries on *Jungian Criticism* and *archetype* in the Handbook of Literary Terms.
5. **lion . . . man.** The Egyptian sphinx

"THE SECOND COMING" **847**

PREREADING NOTES

READER'S JOURNAL

Before students write, discuss with them what the world was like in past times and what it may be like in the future. If students seem extremely negative about the future, point out that at many periods of history people have made dire predictions of the end of the world and other terrible events that never came to be. It is easy to be convinced that the world is on the verge of major upheaval.

THINKING SKILLS

Students may predict that the poem is about the intervention of the spiritual world in the material world.

ANSWER TO GUIDED READING QUESTION

❶ The speaker characterizes the times in which he lives as chaotic, violent, and in the hands of the worst elements.

SUPPORT FOR LEP STUDENTS

ADDITIONAL VOCABULARY
mere—nothing more or other than; only
anarchy—political disorder and violence
conviction—strong belief
indignant—angry; scornful

CROSS-CURRICULAR ACTIVITIES

Social Studies. Students can search current newspapers and news magazines for statements by the media or by political leaders that conditions in their community, town, state, nation, or the world are (a) worsening or (b) improving. They can then make a class collage of the photocopied or clipped references titled *Slouching Toward Bethlehem?*

ANSWER TO GUIDED READING QUESTION

❶ The closing question implies a prophecy of the birth of some horrible beast (instead of Jesus) whose rule will change the world.

CROSS-CURRICULAR ACTIVITIES

Arts and Humanities. Students can create a work of art that shows the Second Coming as conceived by Yeats. The art may be a sculpture (e.g., of the "rough beast"), painting, drawing, or collage (e.g., of the Sphinx "moving its slow thighs" amid a flock of "indignant desert birds"). They can then hold a public reading of the poem and display their completed artwork.

ANSWERS TO SELECTION CHECK TEST 4.10.5

EX. What cannot hear the falconer?
The falcon cannot hear the falconer.

1. According to the speaker, what has been drowned?
The ceremony of innocence has been drowned.

2. According to the speaker, who is "full of passionate intensity"?
The worst people are "full of passionate intensity."

3. According to the speaker, what astonishing event is at hand?
The Second Coming is at hand.

4. What does the speaker envision in the sands of the desert?
The speaker envisions a shape with a lion's body and a man's head.

5. At the end of the poem, what does the speaker suggest is slouching "towards Bethlehem to be born"?
A rough beast is slouching "towards Bethlehem to be born."

Rest on the Flight into Egypt. Luc Olivier Merson, 1874. Courtesy of Museum of Fine Arts, Boston

What prophecy is implied by the speaker's closing question?

Reel shadows of the indignant desert birds.[6]
The darkness drops again; but now I know
That twenty centuries[7] of stony sleep

20   Were vexed to nightmare by a rocking cradle,[8]
And what rough beast, its hour come round at last,
Slouches towards Bethlehem[9] to be born?   ∎

---

6. **Reel . . . birds.** Birds are traditionally associated with omens or predictions. Unscientific peoples often observe their behavior to predict the future. The reeling suggests Yeats's gyres.
7. **twenty centuries.** The two-thousand-year period before the birth of Jesus, thought of by Yeats as the Heroic Age
8. **rocking cradle.** The birth of Jesus
9. **Bethlehem.** The birthplace of Jesus

RESPONDING TO THE SELECTION

Students may observe that the twentieth century was a time of social upheaval, war, massacre, and change on a scale unprecedented in human history. Many people have found appealing the explanation that humanity is approaching the apocalypse, an "end-time" when all civilization will be overturned. Others believe simply that the increase in the population of the world has magnified the scale on which the age-old outrages of humans against humans have taken place.

Responding to the Selection

"The Second Coming" is one of the most famous and most-quoted poems of the twentieth century. Why do you think this is so? In class, discuss your spontaneous reactions to Yeats's vision.

Reviewing the Selection

RECALLING

1. What picture of the state of the world does the speaker draw in stanza 1?

2. What does the opening of stanza 2 predict?

3. What shape does the speaker see in a vision? What does it look like?

4. In the last four lines, what is the meaning of the references to "twenty centuries," "a rocking cradle," and "Bethlehem"?

SYNTHESIZING

9. Yeats used the term *gyre,* which he pronounced with a hard *g,* to refer to the cycles of history. What three cycles of history are referred to in the poem? What event ended the first cycle and started the second? What event does the speaker believe will soon occur to end the second and start the third?

10. The New Testament of the Christian Bible ends with a description of an apocalypse involving fire, earthquakes, and the rule of evil. What question does the speaker ask at the end of the poem? What sort of time does the speaker foresee? How does the speaker's question relate to the idea of a coming apocalypse?

INTERPRETING

5. In stanza 1, what changes and losses particularly trouble the speaker?

6. In lines 12 and 13, what words contradict the speaker's expectation as stated in lines 9 and 10?

7. *Spiritus Mundi* is a Latin term meaning "the world spirit." To Yeats, it meant humankind's collective memory of symbols and dream images. What is the sphinx doing in the speaker's vision? What is the reaction of the birds to this occurrence? What makes this vision ominous?

8. In the final lines, what does the speaker seem to suggest will be the successor to the age begun, two thousand years ago, by the birth of Jesus?

ANSWERS FOR REVIEWING THE SELECTION (CONT.)

cycle and began the second. The birth of some bestial force will end the second and start the third.

10. The speaker asks what kind of beast is going to be born into the world as its ruling force in the next age. The speaker seems to foresee difficult times. The speaker's question suggests that the apocalypse is upon us. Whether the poem predicts a religious or political apocalypse is open to interpretation.

▶ **For Additional Activities:** For other poems relating Yeats's views on the cycles of history, refer students to "Leda and the Swan" and to "The Magi." Yeats believed history to have been divided into a heroic age, which began with the birth to Leda of Helen of Troy, and which was succeeded by a Christian age dating from the birth of Jesus. "The Second Coming" predicts the beginning of a third, apocalyptic age.

ANSWERS FOR REVIEWING THE SELECTION

RECALLING

1. The speaker draws a picture of a world in which everything is falling apart, violence is rampant, innocence is lost, the best people lack convictions, and the worst are full of passion.

2. The opening of stanza 2 refers to the Second Coming (i.e., the return of Jesus to the earth), described in the Bible as occurring after a time of trouble and tribulation.

3. The speaker sees the sphinx. It looks like a lion's body with the head of a man.

4. "Twenty centuries" refers to a period of time before the birth of Jesus and a period of time after the birth of Jesus, a cycle coming around again; "a rocking cradle" and "Bethlehem" refer to the birth of Jesus and therefore possibly indicate that some other similarly major event is going to occur now.

INTERPRETING

Responses will vary. Possible responses are given.

5. The failure of order, the tide of violence, the end of the "ceremony of innocence," the apathy of the best people, and the enthusiasm of the worst are all changes that trouble the speaker.

6. The words *vast image* and *Troubles my sight* suggest that the speaker is not seeing a vision of a returning Jesus.

7. The sphinx is moving its thighs. The birds are indignant. The vision is ominous because it suggests some bestial, monstrous birth.

8. The speaker seems to suggest that an age guided or ruled by some rough beast (a totalitarian government?) will succeed the present age.

SYNTHESIZING

Responses will vary. Possible responses are given.

9. The first cycle is the twenty centuries before the birth of Jesus, the second cycle the period between the birth of Jesus and the present, and the third cycle the time after the Second Coming, whatever form that event takes. The birth of Jesus ended the first

(cont.)

Symbol. 1. Just as the falcon fails to respond to the falconer, the times fail to show any guiding principle at work. The speaker is suggesting that order is no longer an effective force in the world. The decline of order, the "blood-dimmed tide," and anarchy have led to an end of the "ceremony of innocence." Interaction in a peaceful and orderly society depends upon a willingness to suspend cynicism and participate in common, traditional activities, and in that sense society depends upon a "ceremony of innocence." The ceremony has perished, according to the speaker. The best people have no convictions, and the worst people have passionate, intense convictions. 2. The speaker imagines seeing the sphinx. The sphinx is moving. The birds are indignant because the beast is moving, and perhaps because they are outraged at what the movement of the beast portends. The movement of the sphinx might symbolize the imminent birth of a new, even more difficult age. 3. The speaker imagines a beast moving toward Bethlehem to be born. The beast symbolizes the guiding spirit of the world in the next age.

► **Teaching Note:** Students may find the following lines of the poem confusing: "twenty centuries of stony sleep/Were vexed to nightmare by a rocking cradle." One possible interpretation of these lines is that the birth of Jesus was, for the old order, a "nightmare" because that order was thrown into upheaval. (For other poems on this theme, refer students to Yeats's "The Magi" and to Eliot's "The Journey of the Magi.") Another possible interpretation, in keeping with the reference to "its hour come round at last," is that the birth of Jesus prevented the birth of some evil that is now ready to be born.

Understanding Literature (Questions for Discussion)

Symbol. A **symbol** is a thing that stands for or represents both itself and something else. The symbols in "The Second Coming" are mainly visual, and many are beasts.

1. The first symbol in the poem is drawn from the art of falconry, in which a trained falcon is used for hunting. What does the speaker suggest is true about modern times when he says that "The falcon cannot hear the falconer"? What is he saying about what has happened to order in the world? How, according to the speaker, have the decline of order, the "blood-dimmed tide," and anarchy affected the world? In what sense is a society that is peaceful and orderly one in which there is a "ceremony of innocence"? What has happened to that ceremony? What is true, according to the speaker, of the best people in the world today? of the worst?

2. What beast-like shape does the speaker imagine seeing in the desert? What is that shape doing? Why might the birds, circling around, be indignant? (Bear in mind that among many peoples throughout history, birds have often been considered sources of omens about the future.) What might the movement of that shape in the desert symbolize?

3. What beast does the speaker imagine at the end of the poem? What might that beast symbolize?

Responding in Writing

1. **Historical Analysis.** Yeats wrote his poem shortly after a major revolution and war. The poem predicted a coming apocalypse. Write an essay in which you evaluate the accuracy or inaccuracy of Yeats's prediction. In your essay, treat the apocalyptic events that actually did occur in the mid-twentieth century. Then explain whether you believe that the poem is an accurate characterization of the century as a whole, given recent events. Is there more anarchy in the world today? Is there less ceremony? less innocence? Is there reason for feeling more optimistic about the future than Yeats did in the 1920s? Address these questions in the conclusion of your essay.

2. **Titles.** What do the following have in common: *The Widening Gyre, Things Fall Apart, Ceremony of Innocence,* and *Slouching Towards Bethlehem?* All are twentieth-century books whose titles are quotations from Yeats's "The Second Coming." Look back at the poem and choose a phrase or image that you might use as a title in your own writing. Then explain briefly the plot or theme of what you would write—poetry, short story, essay, science fiction, mystery, play—and why this title is appropriate.

ANALYTIC SCALES FOR RESPONDING IN WRITING

Assign a score from 1 to 25 for each grading criterion below. (For more detailed evaluation, see the evaluation forms for writing, revising, and proofreading, *Assessment Portfolio, 7.1–7.10.*)

1. Historical Analysis

• **Content/Unity.** The historical analysis presents a sensible retelling of the historical events of this century and relates them to Yeats's poem.

• **Organization/Coherence.** The historical analysis is clearly organized, offering a clear scheme for comparing history and Yeats's prediction about it.

• **Language/Style.** The historical analysis uses vivid and precise nouns, verbs, and modifiers.

• **Conventions.** The historical analysis avoids errors in spelling, grammar, usage, mechanics, and manuscript form.

(cont.)

Language Lab

Adjectives and Participles. Read the Language Arts Survey, 2.19, "Adjectives and Articles," and 2.16, "Verbals: Participles." Then identify the adjectives and participles in the following lines from Yeats's poem "The Stolen Child."

1. Where dips the rocky highland
2. There lies a leafy island
3. Where flapping herons wake
4. The drowsy water-rats;
5. And of reddest stolen cherries
6. The dim gray sands with light
7. Weaving olden dances
8. And chase the frothy bubbles
9. Where the wandering water gushes
10. We seek for slumbering trout

Applied English/Tech Prep

Résumé Writing. Read about résumé writing in the Language Arts Survey, 5.5, "Types of Business Letters II." Then reread the information about Yeats on page 840. Consult several reference works to learn more about Yeats's life. Based on the information that you gather, write a résumé for W. B. Yeats. Imagine that the year is 1930 and that Yeats is applying for a position as the director of a new theater department at Dublin University.

PROJECT

Nobel Prize Winners. As a class, organize a festival honoring men and women who, like Yeats, won the Nobel Prize for literature. A list of Nobel Prize winners can be found in a standard reference work such as an encyclopedia. By vote, choose ten of these people to be honored at a Nobel Prize festival to be held in your school. Invite parents, teachers, and other students to come to your festival to hear readings from works by Nobel Prize winners. You may also wish to serve refreshments and to prepare exhibits honoring the winners of the prizes. Your exhibits might include pictures of the authors, copies of their works, and posters showing major events and accomplishments in their lives. Publicize your festival by preparing posters, brochures, and public address system announcements. (You may wish to refer to the Language Arts Survey, 5.8, "Writing Promotional and Public Relations Copy.")

ANALYTIC SCALES FOR RESPONDING IN WRITING (CONT.)

2. Titles

• **Content/Unity.** The title explanation offers a reasonable plot or theme for a work based on the chosen line from the poem.

• **Organization/Coherence.** The title explanation is clearly organized, presenting the plot or theme in comprehensible order and giving a coherent reason for the choice of the title.

• **Language/Style.** The title explanation uses vivid and precise nouns, verbs, and modifiers.

• **Conventions.** The title explanation avoids errors in spelling, grammar, usage, mechanics, and manuscript form.

ANSWERS FOR LANGUAGE LAB

1. Adjective: rocky
2. Adjective: leafy
3. Participle: flapping
4. Adjective: drowsy
5. Adjective: reddest; participle: stolen
6. Adjectives: dim, gray
7. Participle: weaving; adjective: olden
8. Adjective: frothy
9. Participle: wandering
10. Participle: slumbering

► For additional practice, see the *Essential Skills Practice Book: Language,* 2.16 and 2.19.

ANSWERS FOR APPLIED ENGLISH/TECH PREP

Responses should follow the résumé form set out in the Language Arts Survey, 5.5, and accurately cite important credentials from Yeats's career.

►For additional practice, see the *Essential Skills Practice Book: Applied English,* 5.5.

PROJECT NOTES

► See the worksheets and evaluation forms for projects, *Assessment Portfolio,* 7.20–7.23.

Nobel Prize Winners

• Students may also perform a play at the festival. Several Nobel Prize winners wrote plays. (Yeats is an example.)

• Encourage students to contribute in ways that most interest them or best suit their skills. Some may find preparing posters or decorating the festival location more exciting than actually performing, while others may thrive on performance.

• Students should strive to make their mix of readings broad enough to include something of interest to everyone who will attend.

ENRICHMENT ACTIVITIES

 To gain a perspective on the full range of Eliot's work, students can read Eliot's book of poems for children, *Old Possum's Book of Practical Cats*, and listen to the soundtrack of the musical based on it, *Cats*. "The Naming of Cats," a poem from this book, appears on page 22.

SUPPORT FOR LEP STUDENTS

Explain that Eliot sometimes uses phrases as sentences that do not have verbs and so are not really complete sentences. Point out that while this type of sentence is frequent in modern poetry, it is not a proper form of sentence to use in schoolwork or in prose in general; it may be confusing to the reader, who will think something is missing.

ADDITIONAL VOCABULARY

insistent—persistent in demands or assertions

resume—begin again

ADDITIONAL QUESTIONS AND ACTIVITIES

 "Preludes" presents urban scenes from shortly after the turn of the century. Students can write a brief essay comparing Eliot's urban imagery with the rustic imagery of Yeats's poem "The Lake Isle of Innisfree" on page 841.

PREREADING

"Preludes"
by T. S. Eliot

ABOUT THE AUTHOR

 Thomas Stearns Eliot (1888–1965) was born and raised in St. Louis, Missouri but lived much of his adult life in England and eventually became an English citizen. Educated at Harvard, the Sorbonne, and Oxford, Eliot steeped himself in philosophy and linguistics. He wrote his first major poems, including "The Love Song of J. Alfred Prufrock" (1910–11), while he was a student in Paris. Eliot's early poems established the major themes of his body of work: the problem of isolation from other people and from God in modern urban life and the search for purpose and meaning. Eliot returned to these themes again and again in poems such as *The Waste Land* (1922), a long narrative poem published as a book; "The Hollow Men" (1927); and "Ash Wednesday" (1930).

Eliot's influence on twentieth-century poetry was tremendous, particularly in the years between the world wars. His poems departed radically from nineteenth-century poetry, not only in theme but in form. Considered one of the inventors of modern poetry, Eliot wrote in **free verse**. Free verse is a flexible form of poetry without regular patterns of rhyme, rhythm, or division into stanzas. It usually has irregular line lengths and, like prose, suits the rhythm and length of the lines to what is being said. In addition to being one of the century's leading poets, Eliot was a distinguished literary critic, editor, and dramatist. In 1948, he was awarded the Nobel Prize in literature.

ABOUT THE SELECTION

"Preludes" (1915) is one of Eliot's early poems. Its drab and seedy images of city life are typical of the view of modern life expressed in Eliot's work. Eliot once explained, "My urban imagery was that of St. Louis, upon which that of Paris and London had been superimposed." The poem is remarkable for finding hope amid the futility and dreariness of modern life.

GOALS/OBJECTIVES

Studying this lesson will enable students to

• feel the speaker's compassion for the subjects of his poem

• describe T. S. Eliot's literary accomplishments and explain the historical significance of his writings

• write a paraphrase of a poem

• define *objective correlative* and recognize Eliot's use of this literary device

• identify semicolons and colons and understand their uses

• write a paraphrase of a poem

READER'S JOURNAL

Imagine a large city between the hours of four and six o'clock in the morning. What are people doing? Where are they going? Is everyone doing the same thing? Assume you are making a film to show life in the city at this time of day. In your journal, write about what the film would show.

LANGUAGE SKILLS

Read the Language Arts Survey, 2.97, "Semicolons," and 2.98, "Colons." Then find places in the poem where the writer has used colons and semicolons. Why is each mark appropriate in its context?

"Preludes"

T. S. ELIOT

I

The winter evening settles down
With smell of steaks in passageways.
Six o'clock.
The burnt-out ends of smoky days.
5   And now a gusty shower wraps
The grimy scraps
Of withered leaves about your feet
And newspapers from vacant lots;
The showers beat
10   On broken blinds and chimney-pots,
And at the corner of the street
A lonely cab-horse steams and stamps.

And then the lighting of the lamps.

II

The morning comes to consciousness
15   Of faint stale smells of beer
From the sawdust-trampled street
With all its muddy feet that press
To early coffee-stands.

How does the last line affect the mood of the first stanza?

PREREADING NOTES

READER'S JOURNAL

• Suggest to students that the key to developing such a film script is to list various occupations that take place at this early hour: baking and other food preparation, newspaper delivery, trash collection, and so on.

• Some students may wish to make a video based on their journal writing.

LANGUAGE SKILLS

Six semicolons are used in the poem, all of them between independent clauses; the semicolon suggests a close relationship between the clauses that a period would not, thus making the reader look for a possible connection in meaning. One colon is used; it indicates that one clause is essentially in apposition to an idea in the preceding clause.

ANSWERS TO SELECTION CHECK TEST 4.10.7

EX. What is the time of day at the beginning of the poem?
The time is six o'clock in the evening.

1. What is being raised by hands "In a thousand furnished rooms"?
Dingy shades are being raised by hands "In a thousand furnished rooms."

2. What does the person in bed hear in the gutters?
The person hears sparrows.

3. What does the person do while "Sitting along the bed's edge"?
The person curls papers from her hair or clasps the yellowed soles of feet in the palms of her hands.

4. The speaker of the poem is moved by the notion of what?
The speaker is moved by the notion of "some infinitely gentle/Infinitely suffering thing."

5. The worlds revolve like what?
They "revolve like ancient women/Gathering fuel in vacant lots."

ANSWER TO GUIDED READING QUESTION

❶ A mood of dreariness, futility, loneliness, and depression is created in the first stanza. Line 12 increases the loneliness of the stanza; line 13 may be seen as one more futile act that sheds light on the grit and grime of the city or as an illumination that softens and improves it. Point out to students that each stanza of the poem moves from some sordid or desperate image to some actual or metaphorical illumination (the lighting of lamps, the raising of window shades, the vision of the street, and the notion of "some infinitely gentle/Infinitely suffering thing").

ANSWERS TO GUIDED READING QUESTIONS

❶ At night the person described in the poem lies upon her back and waits, she dozes, and she watches the night revealing the nightmare or subconscious images of her life in a kind of flickering show on the ceiling.

❷ "His" soul has been stretched across the skies or trampled by feet. This has happened because he has internal-lized or become a part of the city environment and so suffers physically with every sight he sees and sound he hears.

RESPONDING TO THE SELECTION

Suggest that students list the adjective or other word from each line of the poem that is most striking, then review these listed words and ask what cumulative effect they have.

ANSWERS FOR REVIEWING THE SELECTION

RECALLING

1. The speaker describes an urban setting on a rainy evening.

2. In the morning, various "masquerades" take place, such as the raising of shades in many furnished rooms.

3. The night reveals a thousand sordid images.

4. The speaker is moved by fancies associated with "these images" of dismal city life. These fancies involve "some infinitely gentle/ Infinitely suffering thing," perhaps the human soul rising above its circumstances.

INTERPRETING

Responses will vary. Possible responses are given.

5. A mood of dreariness, futility, loneliness, and depression is evoked in the first stanza. This mood is created by images such as the winter evening settling down, day described as being "smoky" and having a burnt-out end like a dead cigarette, and the grimy scraps of withered leaves wrapping around one's feet.

6. The morning is a time in which the masquerades of the day resume.

(cont.)

With the other <u>masquerades</u>
20   That time resumes,
One thinks of all the hands
That are raising dingy shades
In a thousand furnished rooms.

III

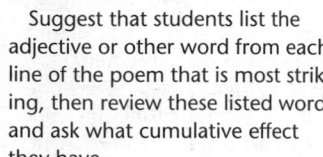

❶ *What happens at night?*

You tossed a blanket from the bed,
25   You lay upon your back, and waited;
You dozed, and watched the night revealing
The thousand <u>sordid</u> images
Of which your soul was <u>constituted</u>;
They flickered against the ceiling.
30   And when all the world came back
And the light crept up between the shutters
And you heard the sparrows in the gutters,
You had such a vision of the street
As the street hardly understands;
35   Sitting along the bed's edge, where
You curled the papers from your hair,
Or clasped the yellow soles of feet
In the palms of both soiled hands.

IV

❷ *What has happened to "His" soul? Why has this happened?*

His soul stretched tight across the skies
40   That fade behind a city block,
Or trampled by insistent feet
At four and five and six o'clock;
And short square fingers stuffing pipes,
And evening newspapers, and eyes
45   Assured of certain certainties,
The conscience of a blackened street
Impatient to assume the world.

I am moved by fancies that are curled
Around these images, and cling:
50   The notion of some infinitely gentle
Infinitely suffering thing.

Wipe your hand across your mouth, and laugh;
The worlds revolve like ancient women
Gathering fuel in vacant lots.

WORDS FOR EVERYDAY USE:

mas • quer • ade (masʹkər ād´) *n.*, ball or party at which masks and fancy costumes or disguises are worn

sor • did (sôrʹdid) *adj.*, dirty; filthy

con • sti • tute (känʹstə tōōt´) *vt.*, make up; be the components or elements of; form; compose

VOCABULARY IN CONTEXT

• As the prom was a <u>masquerade</u>, I was not aware that I was dancing with my sworn enemy.

• The problem with writing about <u>sordid</u> scenes is that one's own writing quickly becomes depressing and grim.

• The fifty states together <u>constitute</u> the United States of America.

Responding to the Selection

Jot down a few words that describe your mood after reading "Preludes." What in this poem creates such a mood?

Reviewing the Selection

RECALLING

1. What setting does the speaker describe in stanza 1?

2. What happens in the morning, according to the speaker?

3. What does the night reveal in stanza 3?

4. What moves the speaker at the end of the poem?

INTERPRETING

5. What mood is evoked in stanza 1? What images are used to create this mood?

6. What is unique about the morning?

7. How does the speaker characterize the soul of the person called "You"?

8. The speaker has a notion of some "Infinitely suffering thing." To what in the poem might this phrase refer? To what might it refer beyond the poem?

SYNTHESIZING

9. Do you think the portrait of the world as portrayed in "Preludes" is an accurate representation of the world today? Is the mood evoked in the poem a prevalent one? Are there times when this is more so than others?

10. Think about other poems you have read. Have any dealt with a similar theme? What effect do other poets feel one's environment has on a person?

Understanding Literature (Questions for Discussion)

1. **Image/Objective Correlative.** An **image** is a word or phrase that names something that can be seen, heard, touched, tasted, or smelled. An **objective correlative** is a group of images that together create a particular emotion in the reader. This term was coined by T. S. Eliot. What images are used in stanza 1 to describe the scene observed by the speaker? What emotion is created by these images?

ANSWERS FOR UNDERSTANDING LITERATURE (CONT.)

and a lonely cab-horse. Emotions of loneliness and depression are evoked by these images.
▶ **Teaching Note:** Point out to students that some of the images in the poem have no symbolic meaning but are intended to create an emotion in the reader.
▶ **Teaching Note:** Haiku has long used objective correlatives. Students can write haiku to better understand the concept. Examples of haiku by Bashō appear on page 681.

2. **Speaker/Tone.** In the first group, the tone is one of weary cynicism; in the second group, one of sensitivity and compassion; in the third group, one of ironic awareness of the inextricable connection in this world of the positive (gathering fuel) and the negative (being ancient and working to gather fuel as the desperately poor do, in vacant lots).

(cont.)

ANSWERS FOR REVIEWING THE SELECTION (CONT.)

7. The soul is described as constituted of a thousand sordid images.

8. The "infinitely suffering thing" may refer to humanity as represented by the humans in the poem, or it may represent the soul stretched tight across the skies. Beyond the poem, the phrase may perhaps refer to the willingness to live; to God (who may be the soul stretched across the sky), to life in general, or to the universe.

SYNTHESIZING

Responses will vary. Possible responses are given.

9. The urban world as portrayed in "Preludes" has not significantly been altered since Eliot wrote this poem. The mood of awareness of this sordidness is probably not prevalent, although arguably the sordidness is. Times of economic depression may make the sordidness more intrusive.

10. Some poets deal only with the internal world of thoughts and feelings; others make a direct connection between thoughts and feelings and the world around them, reading the environment as a representation of the inner world. Students might consider the importance of the natural world to the Romantic poets or Blake's desolate view of urban blight in "London."

ANSWERS FOR UNDERSTANDING LITERATURE

▶ See the evaluation forms for discussion, active listening, and oral communication, *Assessment Portfolio,* 7.11–7.14.

Responses will vary. Possible responses are given.

1. **Image/Objective Correlative.** The speaker mentions the winter evening settling down; the smell of meat; the "smoky" day with a burnt-out end like a dead cigarette; a gusty shower; the grimy scraps of withered leaves wrapping around one's feet, along with newspapers from vacant lots; showers beating on broken blinds;

(cont.)

2. **Speaker/Tone.** The **speaker** is the character who speaks in a poem—the voice assumed by the writer. **Tone** is the emotional attitude toward the reader or toward the subject implied by a literary work. The tone in lines 1–47 of the poem is fairly consistent. It changes in lines 48–51 and shifts again in lines 52–54. What attitude toward the subject does the speaker reveal in each group of lines?

3. **Simile.** A **simile** is a comparison using *like* or *as*. The last stanza contains a simile that compares revolving worlds to ancient women gathering fuel in vacant lots. To understand this simile, first think about the "worlds" that have been described in the poem. How is the activity of the "ancient women" similar to what the city dwellers do? In what ways are they all trying to get by or to survive? Why might the speaker of the poem be moved by their struggles? What might the "infinitely suffering thing" be that the speaker senses within all of these people?

Responding in Writing

1. **Descriptive Writing.** Think of an urban setting that has made an impression on you. Write a description of the scene at a particular time of day. What do you see, hear, feel, and smell at this time of day? In your description, use precise and vivid images to create a particular emotion in your reader.

2. **Paraphrase.** A **paraphrase** is a rewriting of a passage in different words. To appreciate the distance between poetry and prose, write a paraphrase of all or some portion of "Preludes." In your paraphrase, restate the ideas that seem essential. Review your paraphrase. Does the paraphrase help you to gain a better understanding of the poem? What does the paraphrase tell you about the difference between poetry and prose?

PREREADING

"Snake"
by D. H. Lawrence

ABOUT THE AUTHOR

David Herbert Lawrence (1885–1930) led a restless, colorful, controversial life. Born in Nottinghamshire, he was the son of a rough coal miner and a genteel mother. Lawrence's mother longed to have her children rise above their working-class origins, and the young boy identified strongly with his mother. However, as an adult, Lawrence came to appreciate the primitive natural integrity of his father and others of his class as opposed to the smothering conventional aspirations of his mother and other members of the higher social classes. In 1909, Lawrence published his first poems, and in the following year a novel. He taught school for a while but gave this up after meeting Frieda von Richthofen, a German woman whom he married. Lawrence's first major novel, the autobiographical *Sons and Lovers,* was finished shortly thereafter. The novel deals with a boy's attempt to break away from a domineering mother and to establish his own identity. This novel was followed by *The Rainbow,* the first of several of Lawrence's works to be banned in England because of their controversial treatment of human sexuality. Lawrence traveled widely and lived, at different times, in Germany, Italy, Mexico, Australia, and New Mexico. He and his wife Frieda were at the center of the artists' colony in Taos, New Mexico. In addition to his novels, Lawrence wrote poetry, criticism, short stories, and colorful travel sketches. He was also a gifted painter. Lawrence's novel *Lady Chatterley's Lover* became the focus of a legal battle in the United States, ending in a famous victory over censorship. In his mature work, Lawrence championed the primitive, basic instincts of men and women over what he believed to be the artificial, mechanical impositions of contemporary civilized society.

ABOUT THE SELECTION

D. H. Lawrence explored the psychology and subconscious minds of his characters, using intense imagery and symbolism. As a young man, he learned much about poetry by reading English Romantic poets such as Shelley and Wordsworth. He was also strongly influenced by the American Walt Whitman. As a mature poet, he wanted his work to be free of conventional rhythms and phrases and to capture the feeling of the immediate moment. "Snake" was published in the 1923 collection *Birds, Beasts and Flowers,* which contains poems set in many different places around the world. This poem, set in Sicily, shows the speaker's desire to be connected with primitive forces in nature and his opposition to the voices of his "accursed human education."

"SNAKE" 857

ENRICHMENT ACTIVITIES

Students usually find Lawrence's work interesting because it explores many of the challenging issues of relationship to authority, reaction to tradition, and the embracing of vital instincts with which teenagers are often concerned. Lawrence viewed modern "civilized" society with some skepticism. Pose the following questions to students: What are the forces in society that work to uncivilize people? What feelings or experiences, now generally lost, might have been common among our uncivilized ancestors long ago? For a fascinating exploration of what might be learned from so-called "primitive" peoples, refer students to Maybury-Lewis, David. *Millennium: Tribal Wisdom and the Modern World.* 1992. This book is based on a PBS series hosted by Maybury-Lewis, which may be viewed on videotape.

SUPPORT FOR LEP STUDENTS

Explain to students how writers sometimes use italics to indicate the thoughts of characters. Point out line 36 as an example of italics showing internal "voices" in the main character of the poem.

ADDITIONAL VOCABULARY
expiate—make amends or reparations for
pacify—appease, make calm
slackness—looseness

GOALS/OBJECTIVES

Studying this lesson will enable students to

• appreciate the speaker's desire to become connected with primitive, vital natural forces often buried by such "civilizing" forces as education
• describe D. H. Lawrence's literary accomplishments and explain the historical significance of his writings

• define *theme* and compare themes in two literary works
• compose a poem in free verse

PREREADING NOTes

READER'S JOURNAL

Before students begin writing, encourage a class sharing period in which students recount their experiences with wild creatures.

SPEAKING AND LISTENING SKILLS

• Typical nonverbal behaviors used by dogs, for example, include pawing, waiting by a door, bringing a toy, looking plaintively at a box of treats, hanging around an empty food dish, and crowding close to a human to be petted. People communicate with dogs by whistling, clapping hands, snapping fingers, gesturing to a place, or indicating a desired motion such as lying down or sitting. Other animals such as cats and horses that spend a good deal of time in human company also have a large range of communicative behaviors.

• Students may be intrigued by the idea that humans communicate with each other by nonverbal as well as verbal means. Students can brainstorm a list of these behaviors and discuss the purposes of nonverbal communication.

VOCABULARY FROM THE SELECTION

carob	muse
convulse	paltry
fissure	perversity
humility	

READER'S JOURNAL

How do you react to animals that are not house pets? Do you find them scary, revolting, interesting? In your journal, freewrite about your attitudes toward wild animals such as snakes, tigers, rats, and deer. What associations do you have with these creatures? What feelings do they arouse in you?

SPEAKING AND LISTENING SKILLS

Read the Language Arts Survey, 3.3, "Elements of Nonverbal Communication." Think of ways in which people and animals communicate without words. Then make a list of five nonverbal gestures or behaviors that people and animals use to communicate with one another.

"Snake"

D. H. LAWRENCE

A snake came to my water trough
On a hot, hot day, and I in pajamas for the heat,
To drink there.

In the deep, strange-scented shade of the great dark <u>carob</u> tree
5   I came down the steps with my pitcher
And must wait, must stand and wait, for there he was at the trough before me.

He reached down from a <u>fissure</u> in the earth-wall in the gloom
And trailed his yellow-brown slackness soft-bellied down, over the edge of the
     stone trough
And rested his throat upon the stone bottom,
10   And where the water had dripped from the tap, in a small clearness,
He sipped with his straight mouth,
Softly drank through his straight gums, into his slack long body,
Silently.

Someone was before me at my water trough,
15   And I, like a second-comer, waiting.

He lifted his head from his drinking, as cattle do,
And looked at me vaguely, as drinking cattle do,

 WORDS FOR EVERYDAY USE:

car • ob (karˊ əb) *n.,* leguminous tree of the eastern Mediterranean, bearing long, flat, leathery, brown pods with a sweet pulp

fis • sure (fishˊ ər) *n.,* long, narrow, deep cleft or crack

VOCABULARY IN CONTEXT

• The fruit of the <u>carob</u> tree, when dried and made into a powder, serves as a substitute for chocolate.

• In a fairy tale, a young man makes his fortune with a magic stick he finds in a <u>fissure</u> that has opened in the ground during an earthquake.

And flickered his two-forked tongue from his lips, and <u>mused</u> a moment,
And stooped and drank a little more,
20   Being earth-brown, earth-golden from the burning bowels of the earth
On the day of Sicilian July, with Etna smoking.[1]

The voice of my education said to me
He must be killed,
For in Sicily the black black snakes are innocent, the gold are venomous.

25   And voices in me said, If you were a man
You would take a stick and break him now, and finish him off.

But must I confess how I liked him,
How glad I was he had come like a guest in quiet, to drink at my water trough
And depart peaceful, pacified, and thankless
30   Into the burning bowels of this earth?

Was it cowardice, that I dared not kill him?
Was it <u>perversity</u>, that I longed to talk to him?
Was it <u>humility</u>, to feel so honored?
I felt so honored.

35   And yet those voices:
If you were not afraid, you would kill him!

And truly I was afraid, I was most afraid,
But even so, honored still more
That he should seek my hospitality
40   From out the dark door of the secret earth.

He drank enough
And lifted his head, dreamily, as one who has drunken,
And flickered his tongue like a forked night on the air, so black,
Seeming to lick his lips,
45   And looked around like a god, unseeing, into the air,
And slowly turned his head,
And slowly, very slowly, as if thrice adream

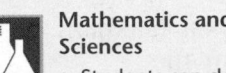

❶ What tells the speaker that he should kill the snake?

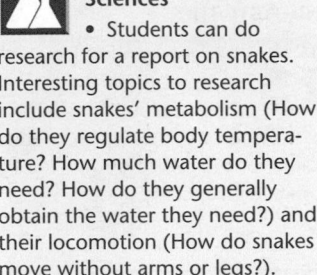

❷ What contradictory feelings does the speaker have about the snake?

---

1. **Etna smoking.** Etna is a volcanic mountain in eastern Sicily.

| **WORDS FOR EVERYDAY USE:** | **muse** (myōōz) *vi.*, think deeply and at length; meditate

per • ver • si • ty (pər vʉr´ sə tē) *n.*, quality or condition of deviating from what is considered | right or good

hu • mil • i • ty (hyōō mil´ ə tē) *n.*, absence of pride or self-assertion |

"SNAKE"   859

VOCABULARY IN CONTEXT

• While he <u>mused</u> on the stars, the philosopher fell into a well.
• They thought they were ready to depart when they had packed the car with six kids and a summer's worth of toys and clothes, but out of sheer <u>perversity</u> the engine would not start.
• "Be instructed by one wiser than the gods," said the old man of the hills. "<u>Humility</u> is a basic requirement for perfection."
• The film was so funny that the audience was <u>convulsed</u> with laughter.
• In some countries, workers earn the <u>paltry</u> sum of a dollar a week.

❶ The speaker decides to act because
he feels horror at the idea that the
snake is going into a hole. This may
make the reader feel sympathy with
the speaker because he did not want
the snake to have to go into the hole,
or irritation with the speaker because
he should have restrained his impulse
and let the snake go into the hole
without interruption.

❷ The speaker regrets his actions and
feels ashamed of his own pettiness.

**ADDITIONAL QUESTIONS
AND ACTIVITIES**

Students can hold an
impromptu debate on
the question, Which is
more important, the "voice of education" or the "voice of the
primitive instinct"?

**ANSWERS TO SELECTION
CHECK TEST 4.10.9**

EX. What came to the speaker's
water trough?
**A snake came to the speaker's
water tough.**

1. Why has the speaker come to
the trough?
**The speaker has come to the
trough to get some water.**

2. Why does the speaker think
that the creature must be killed?
**He recognizes that it is a gold
snake of the venomous variety.**

3. What does the speaker throw
at the snake?
The speaker throws a log.

4. Of what bird does the speaker
think immediately after throwing
something at the creature?
He thinks of the albatross.

5. What word does the speaker
use at the end of the poem to
describe his action?
**He describes his action as a
"pettiness."**

Proceeded to draw his slow length curving round
And climb the broken bank of my wall-face.

50   And as he put his head into that dreadful hole,
And as he slowly drew up, snake-easing his shoulders, and entered further,
A sort of horror, a sort of protest against his withdrawing into that horrid
     black hole,
Deliberately going into the blackness, and slowly drawing himself after,
Overcame me now his back was turned.

55   I looked round, I put down my pitcher,
I picked up a clumsy log
And threw it at the water trough with a clatter.

I think it did not hit him;
But suddenly that part of him that was left behind <u>convulsed</u> in undignified
     haste,
60   Writhed like lightning, and was gone
Into the black hole, the earth-lipped fissure in the wall-front
At which, in the intense still noon, I stared with fascination.

And immediately I regretted it.
I thought how <u>paltry</u>, how vulgar, what a mean act!
65   I despised myself and the voices of my accursed human education.

And I thought of the albatross,[2]
And I wished he would come back, my snake.

For he seemed to me again like a king,
Like a king in exile, uncrowned in the underworld,
70   Now due to be crowned again.

And so, I missed my chance with one of the lords
Of life.
And I have something to expiate:[3]
A pettiness.

❶ *Why does the
speaker decide to
act at this point?
How does this
make you feel
toward the
speaker?*

❷ *How does the
speaker feel
about himself at
the end of the
poem?*

---

2. **albatross.** In Coleridge's "The Rime of the Ancient
Mariner," the mariner kills a friendly sea bird, the albatross, and so brings ghoulish misfortune on himself and
on his shipmates.
3. **expiate.** Get rid of (in myself)

**WORDS FOR
EVERYDAY USE:**

con • vulse (kən vuls ´) *vt.,* shake or disturb violently; agitate
pal • try (pôl ´ trē) *adj.,* practically worthless; trifling; insignificant; contemptible; petty

---

ANALYTIC SCALES FOR RESPONDING IN WRITING

Assign a score from 1 to 25 for each grading criterion
below. (For more detailed evaluation, see the evaluation
forms for writing, revising, and proofreading, *Assessment
Portfolio,* 7.1–7.10.)

Free Verse
• **Content/Unity.** The free verse poem presents a sensible account of a meeting between a human and a wild
animal and a lesson learned as a result of this meeting.

• **Organization/Coherence.** The free verse poem
is clearly organized, presenting a coherent narrative and
a relevant lesson.

• **Language/Style.** The free verse poem uses vivid and
precise nouns, verbs, and modifiers.

• **Conventions.** The free verse poem avoids errors in
spelling, grammar, usage, mechanics, and manuscript
form.

Responding to the Selection

What first, unexamined reaction does the speaker have to the snake? Do you share this feeling toward snakes? How would you react to a snake if you came upon one outdoors?

Reviewing the Selection

RECALLING

1. For what purpose have both the snake and the speaker come out on this hot, hot day?

2. What is the speaker forced to do, according to lines 6 and 15 of the poem?

3. What does the voice of the speaker's education tell him?

4. What contradictory feelings does the speaker find himself having about the snake?

INTERPRETING

5. How does the speaker establish, from the very beginning of the poem, an animal bond between himself and the snake? What need do they both share?

6. What lines at the beginning of the poem show the speaker's irritation toward the snake? Why might the speaker be irritated?

7. What practical reason does the speaker have for thinking he must do something to the snake? What emotional reason also leads him to this thought?

8. What causes the speaker to react physically, finally, to the snake? How is he feeling at that moment? Why?

SYNTHESIZING

9. Why do you think the speaker despises himself after throwing the log? What chance did he miss? What does he have to expiate?

10. To what powerful beings or creatures is the snake compared in this poem? What does the snake symbolize for the speaker?

"SNAKE" 861

RESPONDING TO THE SELECTION

The speaker's first reaction is to think the snake should be killed. Students may recognize that this impulse is part of an unthinking desire to act in an outward way to exert control over an unnerving situation; the real necessity is to exert inward control, remain calm, and assess the circumstances.

ANSWERS FOR REVIEWING THE SELECTION

RECALLING

1. The snake and the speaker have come for water.

2. The speaker must wait for the snake to finish drinking.

3. The voice of his education tells the speaker that if he were a man, he would kill the snake with a stick.

4. The speaker wonders if he is a coward because he does not kill the snake, or eccentric because he wants to talk to the snake, or merely humble because he feels honored at the snake's presence.

INTERPRETING
Responses will vary. Possible responses are given.

5. The speaker acknowledges that the heat affects the snake just as it affects him. They share a need for water.

6. The speaker says, he "must wait, must stand and wait." The speaker is irritated because he wants to get his water and get out of the heat of the day.

7. Conventional wisdom tells the speaker that the snake is venomous. He is also very afraid of the snake.

8. The speaker reacts when the snake returns to a hole in the wall; he feels a horror at the idea that the snake is going into a hole. He does not like the idea that the snake is "deliberately going into the blackness."

SYNTHESIZING
Responses will vary. Possible responses are given.

9. The speaker decides that throwing the log was a paltry, unnecessary act. He missed the chance to honor a creature he considered kingly. He has to expiate his pettiness.

10. The snake is compared to a god, a king, and a lord. It seems to symbolize the power of life.

ANSWERS FOR UNDERSTANDING LITERATURE

► See the evaluation forms for discussion, active listening, and oral communication, *Assessment Portfolio*, 7.11–7.14. *Responses will vary. Possible responses are given.*

1. **Allusion.** Like the mariner, the speaker strikes out at a natural representative of higher forces. Both the speaker and the mariner have to expiate their respective crimes.
► **Teaching Note:** Ask students to compare the relevant passage in Coleridge's poem on page 664, noting that

virtually no motivation is given there for the mariner's act. Suggest that Lawrence was interested in motivation, while Coleridge was not. What does this difference say about Lawrence's art? *Answer.* While Coleridge focused on the moral questions inherent in human action, Lawrence believed the psychological issues involved were equally interesting.

(cont.)

Left sidebar column:

ANSWERS FOR
UNDERSTANDING LITERATURE
(CONT.)

2. Symbol. The snake seems to symbolize the hidden, primitive forces of life that dwell in the dark of the subconscious. The speaker is an educated man who has been taught to distrust the primitive within him. The voices of his human education recognize that his primitive impulses are not always comprehensible or controllable.

▶**Teaching Note:** You may wish to explain to students that snakes have a long history as a symbol of power. In the Judeo-Christian tradition, the snake was the original tempter of the human race and has always represented evil. In earth-religions the snake was typically a symbol of benign, natural power; statues from ancient Crete show women holding writhing snakes, probably a reflection of actual rites performed by priestesses. A similar form of worship occurs among the Hopi of the southwestern United States. Some Protestant sects in the United States also incorporate snake handling in their worship services. In Africa, the python was worshipped; in India, the cobra. The Aztecs of Mexico worshipped a feathered serpent, Quetzalcoatl. Interested students could research the snake as a symbol in world religions and literature and report back to the class.

3. Theme. The speaker believes that people have become prone to paltry, petty acts in rejecting animal powers such as are represented by the snake. The speaker despises his own action because it was unnecessary and ineffectual. Wordsworth spells out his theme by saying, "Little we see in Nature that is ours"; the speaker in Lawrence's poem sees a similar failure of connection between himself and nature as represented by the snake.

(cont.)

ANALYTIC SCALES FOR
RESPONDING IN WRITING

Grading scales appear on page 860.

862   TEACHER'S EDITION

Understanding Literature (Questions for Discussion)

1. **Allusion.** An **allusion** is a figure of speech in which a reference is made to a person, event, object, or work from history or literature. In line 66 of the poem, the speaker says that after throwing the log he "thought of the albatross." This line is an allusion to Samuel Taylor Coleridge's "The Rime of the Ancient Mariner," in which a sailor is punished for killing a noble creature of nature. What similarity exists between the speaker and Coleridge's mariner?

2. **Symbol.** A **symbol** is a thing that stands for of represents both itself and something else. What do you think the snake in this poem symbolizes? Why might the speaker be frightened of his own more primitive nature, his basic animal instincts, and the dark, subterranean recesses of his own spirit? Why might the voices of his human education tell him that these parts of himself should be suppressed?

3. **Theme.** A **theme** is a central idea in a literary work. What does the speaker in this poem think has happened to people as a result of civilizing influences like education? Why does the speaker think that his action was paltry, vulgar, mean, and petty? Read or reread William Wordsworth's "The world is too much with us" on page 611. What similarity in theme can you find in the two poems?

4. **Freudian Criticism. Freudian criticism** draws upon the works of the founder of psychoanalysis, Sigmund Freud, and generally views literary works or the parts thereof as expressions of unconscious desires, as wish fulfillments, or as neurotic sublimations of unresolved conflicts from childhood. Freud believed that children are born with basic, primitive instinctual desires that he called the *id*. As they grow up, according to Freud, children encounter limitations on these desires in the form of rules and codes of behavior enforced by their parents and others. These rules, internalized, become another part of the personality which Freud called the *superego*—what in ordinary speech is called the *conscience*. The desires of the id are suppressed but come out in dreams, fantasies, slips of the tongue, and neurotic behaviors. How do Freud's ideas help to explain Lawrence's poem? With what would he associate Lawrence's "voices of my accursed human education"?

Responding in Writing

Free Verse. Choose an animal with which you have strong emotional associations. Possibilities include sharks, rats, wolves, whales, spiders, deer, bats, eagles, gorillas, and tigers. Do some reading about the habits of your chosen animal. Then write a poem about a character who encounters that animal in the wild and learns a lesson from it. Read the entry on *free verse* in the Handbook of Literary Terms, and write your poem in free verse.

862   UNIT TEN / TWENTIETH-CENTURY POETRY

ANSWERS FOR UNDERSTANDING LITERATURE (CONT.)

▶**Teaching Note:** Mention to students that Wordworth's poem was written in 1806–1807; Lawrence's poem was written in the early 1900s. Ask if students see any change in attitude toward the environment and the natural world today of which Wordsworth and Lawrence would approve.

4. Freudian Criticism. The speaker's impulse to destroy the snake can be identified with the limitations imposed on the id by external rules. Freud would probably identify the snake with the id. He would associate the voices Lawrence hears with the limitations imposed on the id. (Other interpretations are possible: The remorse felt by the speaker could be interpreted as the voice of the superego chastising him for his unnecessary actions.)

PREREADING

"The Soldier"
by Rupert Brooke

ABOUT THE AUTHOR

Of all the young Englishmen who died in World War I, perhaps the most romanticized as a hero was **Rupert Brooke** (1887–1915). Brooke seemed in many respects an ideal young man. Intelligent and athletic, he performed well in his classes and on the cricket and football fields at the Rugby School. He entered King's College, Cambridge, in 1906; made many friends; and was active in university life. He then studied in Europe and traveled to Canada and the South Seas, writing travel articles and publishing a book, *Poems,* in 1911. When war began, Brooke joined the Royal Navy. The sequence of patriotic, idealistic sonnets called *1914* made him famous. On the way to fight in the Gallipoli campaign after a disastrous battle in the North Sea, Brooke contracted blood poisoning and died. He was buried on the Greek island of Skyros. After his death, Winston Churchill wrote an obituary describing Brooke as "all that one would wish England's noblest sons to be."

ABOUT THE SELECTION

World War I—the first "total war"—was so brutal and destructive that it shattered some earlier ideas of war as a heroic occupation for "gentlemen." **"The Soldier,"** like much of Brooke's poetry, written early in the war, presents an idealized view of the war and a stirring heroism. Speaking after the poet's death, Winston Churchill said that the thoughts in Brooke's sonnets "will be shared by many thousands of young men moving resolutely and blithely forward into this, the hardest, the cruelest, and the least rewarded of all the wars that men have fought." Brooke's early death made him a tragic symbol for the English public, even though much of his poetry is joyful. Over the next decade, two volumes of poetry—*1914 and Other Poems* and *Collected Poems*—sold over three hundred thousand copies.

ADDITIONAL RESOURCES

READER'S GUIDE
• Selection Worksheet, 10.6

ASSESSMENT PORTFOLIO
• Selection Check Test, 4.10.11
• Selection Test, 4.10.12

ESSENTIAL SKILLS PRACTICE BOOKS
• *Language,* 2.64
• *Study and Research,* 4.24

ENRICHMENT ACTIVITIES

Students can compare this poem to Wilfred Owen's "Dulce et Decorum Est," which can be found on page 868. In some ways, Owen and Brooke represent opposing viewpoints about war. Owen was intent on stripping war of its glamour; Brooke had accepted what he considered the necessity of war. Students can write an essay in which they contrast the two points of view, weigh them, and explain which viewpoint or mixture of the two they support and why they feel as they do.

SUPPORT FOR LEP STUDENTS

Brooke uses seventeen commas in the fourteen lines of poetry in this selection. Students may have difficulty tracking the sense through these commas. After students have read the poem themselves, develop a paraphrase of it with them to elucidate the purpose of the various clauses and phrases set off by commas.

ADDITIONAL VOCABULARY
roam—travel; wander
shed—discard

GOALS/OBJECTIVES

Studying this lesson will enable students to

• experience the speaker's feelings of love for his country

• describe Rupert Brooke's literary accomplishments and explain the historical significance of his writings

• invert sentences for emphasis

• define *sonnet* and recognize the key features of the sonnet when they encounter one

• write biographical material and an editorial

READER'S JOURNAL

• Tell students that psychological tests have shown that music does make some difficult activities, such as waiting in a dentist's office, more bearable. Music has long been used to build morale; the Scottish Highlanders, for instance, used to march into battle accompanied by drums and wailing bagpipes. In this type of warfare, a prebattle "pep talk," in which a speaker exhorts the troops to bravery using rhetoric often verging on poetry, is traditional in many cultures.

• Students who cannot think of examples of music or poetry affecting their mood should consider the use of music in films. Ask students this: Has the music at the end of a film ever made you feel excited or uplifted? Has a poem ever "sent a thrill down your spine" in a similar way?

SPEAKING AND LISTENING SKILLS

The celebration of the intangible benefits of England and its way of life would have great appeal to the English at a time when they were defending their nation. Students may also notice as a positive factor the attitude that death does not mean waste. Instead, Brooke suggests that he will live on in some form even if he does die.

ANSWERS TO GUIDED READING QUESTIONS

❶ England has borne, shaped, and made the speaker aware; given him flowers to love and places to roam; and provided him with an active body.

❷ The speaker believes that his thoughts will become a part of the "Eternal mind," and so will be given back to people someday.

RESPONDING TO THE SELECTION

Students can consider how they might feel in the speaker's situation. They may also wish to discuss how they feel about the speaker's attitude based on their own feelings about war.

864 TEACHER'S EDITION

READER'S JOURNAL

Can poetry or music influence how people feel as they face danger or undergo pain and hardship? In your journal, freewrite about times in which poetry or music has made you feel happier, calmer, or braver.

SPEAKING AND LISTENING SKILLS

Read the Language Arts Survey, 3.2, "Elements of Verbal Communication." Imagine this poem were given as an inspirational speech. How would this poem have appealed to the English people when they were at war and fearing that their country might be taken over by a foreign power?

"The Soldier"

RUPERT BROOKE

❶
What has England done for this speaker?

❷
What will happen to the happy thoughts given to the speaker by England?

If I should die, think only this of me:
 That there's some corner of a foreign field
That is forever England. There shall be
 In that rich earth a richer dust concealed;
5 A dust whom England bore, shaped, made aware,
 Gave, once, her flowers to love, her ways to roam,
A body of England's, breathing English air,
 Washed by the rivers, blest by suns of home.

And think, this heart, all evil shed away,
10 A pulse in the Eternal mind, no less
 Gives somewhere back the thoughts by England given,
Her sights and sounds; dreams happy as her day;
 And laughter, learnt of friends; and gentleness,
 In hearts at peace, under an English heaven. ∎

ADDITIONAL QUESTIONS AND ACTIVITIES

Women poets of Britain and the United States wrote extensively on World War I. Students can search in anthologies of war poetry for the following poems: "From a Trench," by Maud Anna Bell; "The Recruit," by Isabel Ecclestone Mackay; "At the Movies," by Florence Ripley Mastin; "The Mother," "High Summer," and "After Jutland," by Katharine Tynan; "Letter to an Aviator in France," by Grace Hazard Conkling; and "Captain Guynemer," by Florence Earle Coates.

ANSWERS FOR UNDERSTANDING LITERATURE

▶ See the evaluation forms for discussion, active listening, and oral communication, *Assessment Portfolio,* 7.11–7.14.
Responses will vary. Possible responses are given.

1. Sonnet. "The Soldier" has two stanzas. Stanza 1 has eight lines; stanza 2 has six. The rhyme scheme is *ababcdcd efgefg.*

(cont.)

Responding to the Selection

What is the speaker's general attitude toward his situation? Why does he have this attitude?

Reviewing the Selection

RECALLING

1. Where does the speaker expect to die?

2. How does the speaker feel about England? How do you know?

INTERPRETING

3. What is the "richer dust" buried in the foreign earth? Explain your answer.

4. What does the speaker feel the future holds for him? What will become of the happy thoughts given to him by England?

SYNTHESIZING

5. What is the final mood of this poem? What words and phrases create this mood?

Understanding Literature (Questions for Discussion)

1. **Sonnet.** A **sonnet** is a fourteen-line poem that follows one of a number of different rhyme schemes. Sonnets are also arranged in different stanza forms. In English, many well-known sonnets follow the **Shakespearean** rhyme scheme, but there are many variations. How many stanzas, shown by line breaks, are there in "The Soldier"? How many lines does each stanza have? Using letters, identify the rhyme scheme Brooke used in this sonnet. Consider the last word of line 1, *me,* and all other line-ending words that rhyme with it, as *a.* The last word of line 2 does not rhyme with *me,* so it becomes *b,* and so on. You can see that the first four lines follow the pattern *abab.*

2. **Theme.** A **theme** is a central idea in a literary work. Almost all works of literature, no matter how short, have a unifying theme or statement of the speaker's beliefs or philosophy—what he or she has to say about a specific subject. Longer works, such as a novel, are likely to have several themes. The subject of this poem is England. What is its theme? That is, how does the speaker feel about his subject?

"THE SOLDIER" 865

ANSWERS FOR REVIEWING THE SELECTION

RECALLING

1. The speaker expects to die in a foreign country.

2. The speaker's love for England is expressed in his love for all things English and in his gratitude to the country that bore and shaped him.

INTERPRETING

Responses will vary. Possible responses are given.

3. The richer dust is the speaker's corpse. The speaker claims it is "richer" perhaps because it is English, or perhaps because literally it is organically richer.

4. The speaker expects that he will die on foreign soil, and his happy thoughts will become part of the "Eternal mind."

SYNTHESIZING

Responses will vary.

5. The final mood is upbeat. Words and phrases such as "dreams happy as her day," "laughter, learnt of friends," "gentleness," and "hearts at peace" create this mood.

ANSWERS TO SELECTION CHECK TEST 4.10.11

EX. In the first line, what event does the speaker contemplate? **The speaker contemplates the possibility of his death.**

1. If the speaker dies, what will be true of "some corner of a foreign field"? **The "corner of a foreign field" will be "forever England."**

2. What will be concealed in the rich earth of that place? **A richer dust will be concealed there (i.e., the speaker's body).**

3. What bore that dust, shaped it, and made it aware? **England did.**

4. What does the speaker imagine being shed away after death? **The speaker imagines all evil in his heart being shed away.**

5. Under what does the speaker recall "hearts at peace"? **He recalls "hearts at peace, under an English heaven."**

ANSWERS FOR UNDERSTANDING LITERATURE (CONT.)

▶**Teaching Notes**

• Ask students to determine the rhyme scheme of one of the Shakespearean sonnets on pages 279–283. Ask this: How does it differ from the rhyme scheme Brooke uses? *Answer.* The Shakespearean rhyme scheme differs chiefly in having a final couplet.

• Formal sonnets are defined as much by their meter as by the number of lines and their rhyme. Work with students to mark the stressed syllables of Brooke's poem.

2. Theme. The theme of the poem is love for and duty toward one's country. The soldier expresses his gratitude and obligation to England and his willingness to repay the debt if necessary by dying in a war for his country.

▶**Teaching Note:** For such a short piece, Brooke's poem is thematically very rich. Ask students to identify other themes in the poem. These may include gratitude, purification, eternal life, and the meaning imparted to life by one's environs and by friends.

ANALYTIC SCALES FOR RESPONDING IN WRITING

Assign a score from 1 to 25 for each grading criterion below. (For more detailed evaluation, see the evaluation forms for writing, revising, and proofreading, *Assessment Portfolio*, 7.1–7.10.)

1. Biography
• **Content/Unity.** The biography offers a plausible scenario for Brooke's later life.
• **Organization/Coherence.** The biography presents events in chronological order.
• **Language/Style.** The biography uses vivid and precise nouns, verbs, and modifiers.
• **Conventions.** The biography avoids errors in spelling, grammar, usage, mechanics, and manuscript form.

2. Editorial
• **Content/Unity.** The editorial describes various positive features of the school or town.
• **Organization/Coherence.** The editorial presents a main idea and adds supporting details in a logical order.
• **Language/Style.** The editorial uses vivid and precise nouns, verbs, and modifiers.
• **Conventions.** The editorial avoids errors in spelling, grammar, usage, mechanics, and manuscript form.

ANSWERS FOR RESEARCH SKILLS/VOCABULARY SKILLS

Responses will vary. Possible responses are given.
1. *rich:* abundantly supplied with plant nutrients; of high quality; magnificent or impressive
2. *bore:* gave birth to; carried; supported
3. *air:* mixture of invisible gases that sustain life; atmosphere; demeanor
4. *shed:* cast off; repel; spill
5. *pulse:* sign of life; rhythmic beat; contraction
► For additional practice, see the *Essential Skills Practice Book: Study and Research*, 4.24.

Responding in Writing

1. **Biography.** What if Rupert Brooke had not died during World War I? From what the poem shows about his nature and from what you have read about his early life, write two paragraphs of biography about what he might have done later in life.

2. **Editorial.** Brooke's poem mentions a number of things that made England a special place for him—both physical things such as air and rivers and abstract things such as friendship. For your school paper, write a short editorial describing some things that make your school or town special to you.

Language Lab

Inverted Sentences. Read the Language Arts Survey, 2.64, "Inverting Sentences for Emphasis." Poets frequently use inverted word order for poetic effect, but inversion sometimes makes poetry harder to understand. In each sentence below, underline the word or phrase that is the subject of the sentence. Then rewrite each sentence in normal word order. Drop or add words if you need to do so. (The examples are adapted from Brooke's poetry.)

1. There shall be in that rich earth a richer dust concealed.
2. Forever shall some corner of a foreign field be England.
3. Proud we were.
4. Washed by England's rivers was this body.
5. This heart the thoughts gives back.

Research Skills/Vocabulary Skills

Read the Language Arts Survey, 4.24, "Using Dictionaries." Then look in a dictionary to discover alternative meanings of the italicized words in these phrases from "The Soldier." For each word, first list the meaning used in the poem. Then, in your own words, give at least two other dictionary meanings for the word.

1. *rich* earth
2. whom England *bore*
3. breathing English *air*
4. all evil *shed*
5. a *pulse* in the eternal mind

ANSWERS FOR LANGUAGE LAB

1. a richer dust; A richer dust shall be concealed in that rich earth.
2. some corner; Some corner of a foreign field shall be England forever.
3. we; We were proud.
4. this body; This body was washed by England's rivers.
5. heart; This heart gives back the thoughts.

► Additional practice is provided in the *Essential Skills Practice Book: Language*, 2.64.

"Dulce et Decorum Est"
by Wilfred Owen

ABOUT THE AUTHOR

World War I shaped the lives of several young British soldier-poets. One was **Wilfred Owen** (1893–1918), who was killed in action in France just a week before the Armistice that ended the war (November 11, 1918). Born in Shropshire, he enrolled in the University of London but dropped out because of illness in 1913 and then went to live in France. Working as a tutor, he began to write lyric poetry that was influenced by Keats and Shelley (see Unit 8). In 1915, Owen enlisted in the army and soon was writing angrily about the war and its horrors. In June 1917, suffering from shell shock, he was sent to a hospital in Scotland, where he met the poet Siegfried Sassoon. Both were strongly antiwar, and Sassoon's ideas about poetry also influenced Owen. Though friends tried to find him a staff job behind the lines, Owen went back to France as a platoon commander in August 1918. He won the Military Cross in October and was killed soon afterward.

ABOUT THE SELECTION

Owen's poems, including the selection **"Dulce et Decorum Est,"** were published after his death by the poet Siegfried Sassoon and have become some of the most quoted lines about the cruelty and wastefulness of war. Owen's preface to the volume reads: "Above all, this book is not concerned with/ Poetry, The subject of it is War, and the pity of/ War. The Poetry is in the pity. All a poet can do is warn." *Dulce et decorum est pro patria mori* is a line from the *Odes* of the Roman poet Horace. It means: "It is sweet and proper to die for your country."

"DULCE ET DECORUM EST" **867**

ADDITIONAL RESOURCES

READER'S GUIDE
- Selection Worksheet, 10.7

ASSESSMENT PORTFOLIO
- Selection Check Test, 4.10.13
- Selection Test, 4.10.14

ESSENTIAL SKILLS PRACTICE BOOKS
- *Language*, 2.16–2.17, 2.33

ENRICHMENT ACTIVITIES

To gain perspective on Owen's work and to appreciate the connection between Owen and Siegfried Sassoon, students can read Sassoon's poetry as well. Two of his better-known poems are "Dreamers" and "Base Details."

SUPPORT FOR LEP STUDENTS

Explain the Latin phrase from which the title and the last line of the poem are taken. Point out English words derived from the same roots as the Latin words: *dulcet, decorous, pro* (as in "pro and con"), *patriot,* and *mortal.* Have students look up these English words and their etymologies.

ADDITIONAL VOCABULARY

ecstasy—state of being over-powered by emotion; trance-like state

floundering—struggling awkwardly to move

smothering—suffocating; keeping from getting air

corrupt—changed from a sound condition to an unsound one; spoiled

VOCABULARY FROM THE SELECTION

ardent
gutter

GOALS/OBJECTIVES

Studying this lesson will enable students to

- experience the speaker's disgust and horror at the cruelty of war
- describe Wilfred Owen's literary accomplishments and explain the historical significance of his writings

- define *irony* and *aim* and identify the irony and aim in Owen's poem
- recognize vivid verbs and explain how their use contributes to clear, interesting writing
- compose a piece of descriptive writing

PREREADING NOTES

READER'S JOURNAL

Assign a student to collect a group of quotations on the subject of war from a dictionary of quotations or other readily available source. The student can then read these quotations to the class to stimulate thought before students begin the writing assignment.

LANGUAGE SKILLS

Some of the vivid verbs used include "coughing," "cursed" (line 2); "stumbling" (line 11); "flound'ring" (line 12); "plunges," "guttering" (line 16); and "writhing" (line 19).

ANSWERS TO SELECTION CHECK TEST 4.10.13

EX. What has happened to many of the soldiers' boots?
They have lost them.

1. With what are the soldiers "drunk"?
They are "drunk" with fatigue.

2. Why do the soldiers have to put their "clumsy helmets" on so quickly?
They are being exposed to poison gas.

3. What caused the man to become so sick that he had to be flung into a wagon?
He was gassed.

4. What do people sometimes tell to children "with such high zest"?
They sometimes tell children "The old Lie."

5. What does the Latin sentence "Dulce et decorum est/Pro patria mori" mean?
The sentence means "It is sweet and proper to die for one's country."

READER'S JOURNAL

What are your opinions about war? Do you think it is exciting and heroic or cruel and wasteful? Do your opinions about war depend on the cause for which people are fighting? Freewrite your thoughts in your journal.

LANGUAGE SKILLS

Read the Language Arts Survey, 2.33, "Using Vivid Verbs." Then make a list of the strong verbs Owen uses in the poem. Notice what a clear picture these verbs give of the scene.

"Dulce et Decorum Est"

WILFRED OWEN

Bent double, like old beggars under sacks,
Knock-kneed, coughing like hags, we cursed through sludge,
Till on the haunting flares we turned our backs
And towards our distant rest began to trudge.
5   Men marched asleep. Many had lost their boots
But limped on, blood-shod. All went lame; all blind;
Drunk with fatigue; deaf even to the hoots
Of tired, outstripped Five-Nines[1] that dropped behind.

Gas! Gas! Quick, boys!—An ecstasy of fumbling,
10 Fitting the clumsy helmets just in time;
But someone still was yelling out and stumbling,
And flound'ring like a man in fire or lime . . .
Dim, through the misty panes and thick green light,
As under a green sea, I saw him drowning.

15 In all my dreams, before my helpless sight,
He plunges at me, <u>guttering</u>, choking, drowning.

---

1. **Five-Nines.** Common artillery shells

What do soldiers endure? What descends upon the soldiers?

WORDS FOR
EVERYDAY USE: **gut • ter** (gut´ər) *vi.,* gurgle and sputter

868   UNIT TEN / TWENTIETH-CENTURY POETRY

VOCABULARY IN CONTEXT

• The last thing I saw before all grew black was a face lit by a <u>guttering</u> candle.

ADDITIONAL QUESTIONS AND ACTIVITIES

Students can research the current status of world policies on the use of chemical weapons to answer these questions: When was the last time chemical weapons were used in war? What prevents nations from using chemical weapons? What threatens the current world policy on chemical weapons?

ANSWER TO GUIDED READING QUESTION

❶ The soldiers are forced to slog through sludge and to march long hours beyond the point of exhaustion in order to keep ahead of the shelling; some lose their boots but must continue walking. Poison gas descends upon the soldiers.

If in some smothering dreams you too could pace
Behind the wagon that we flung him in,
And watch the white eyes writhing in his face,
20   His hanging face, like a devil's sick of sin;
If you could hear, at every jolt, the blood
Come gargling from the froth-corrupted lungs,
Obscene as cancer, bitter as the cud
Of vile, incurable sores on innocent tongues,—
25   My friend, you would not tell with such high zest
To children <u>ardent</u> for some desperate glory,
The old Lie: Dulce et decorum est
Pro patria mori.[2]

❶
What is "The old Lie"? What would cause someone not to tell this lie with "such high zest"?

---

2. **Dulce . . . mori.** A Latin phrase from Horace meaning "It is sweet and proper to die for your country."

Responding to the Selection

Imagine that you are one of the soldiers in the poem. Freewrite the thoughts you would have upon arriving home after the experience described here. What would you tell people about what you've been through?

Reviewing the Selection

RECALLING

1. Where are the soldiers in the opening lines going—toward or away from the battle lines? How do you know?

2. What physical hardships do the soldiers face as they march?

3. What is the mood of the men?

4. What do the soldiers do when they realize there is poison gas in the air?

INTERPRETING

▶ 5. What does the scene look like through the transparent window of a gas mask?

▶ 6. How does the gas affect the soldier without a mask?

▶ 7. What do the other soldiers do for the gassed soldier?

▶ 8. To whom do you think Owen is addressing the last lines of the poem?

WORDS FOR EVERYDAY USE: ar • dent (ärd ''nt) *adj.*, intensely enthusiastic or devoted; zealous

"DULCE ET DECORUM EST" **869**

VOCABULARY IN CONTEXT
• Only the most <u>ardent</u> fans braved the rain to watch the soccer match.

RESPONDING TO THE SELECTION

Discuss with students the disjunction between the experience of those at home, who often believe in what Owen calls "the old Lie," and those who have experienced battle. Ask whether a returning soldier might want to avoid talking about his or her experiences. Would those at home want to hear the horrible details? How would a soldier feel if he or she needed or wanted to tell what he or she had seen but no one could bear to hear about it?

ANSWERS FOR REVIEWING THE SELECTION

RECALLING

1. They are going away from the battle lines; they have turned toward their "distant rest."

2. The soldiers have to carry heavy loads; they are sick; they have to march through mud; they are weary nearly to sleep; many have lost their boots; they are virtually lame, blind, and deaf; they are assaulted by poison gas.

3. Their mood is one of pure exhaustion.

4. The soldiers put their helmets or gas masks over their faces.

INTERPRETING

Responses will vary. Possible responses are given.

5. The scene looks like something happening under the sea.

6. The soldier without a mask chokes as if drowning.

7. The soldiers throw him on a wagon to transport him.

8. He may be addressing those left at home.

SYNTHESIZING

Responses will vary. Possible responses are given.

9. The lie is that it is sweet and proper to die for one's country.

10. The poet wants to protect children from falling prey to this lie and seeking glory through war.

ANSWERS FOR UNDERSTANDING LITERATURE

► See the evaluation forms for discussion, active listening, and oral communication, *Assessment Portfolio, 7.11–7.14.*

Responses will vary. Possible responses are given.

1. Irony. The title of the poem is ironic because Owen is deliberately describing a situation that is *not* "sweet and becoming." The imagery is so direct and realistic that it does not allow for much irony. It is only when the entire description of war is contrasted with the glorious image of war in the last lines that the horror becomes ironic.

► **Teaching Note:** A more inclusive definition of irony might be that it is the contradiction of an expectation. Thus we can see irony in the death of Owen only a week before the Armistice: we expect that having survived so much of the war, he would survive through its final week. Ask students to give other examples of situational irony—situations in which expectations are contradicted by the outcome. For instance, it would be ironic to study hard for a test, only to find one had studied the wrong material.

2. Alliteration. The consonant sounds of *b, l, m,* and *d* are the most prominent in these lines. Another example of alliteration can be found in lines 18 and 19: "Behind the *wagon* that *we* flung him in,/And *watch* the *white* eyes *writhing* in his face."

► **Teaching Note:** Mention to students that the difficulty in using alliteration is to do it subtly enough that the alliteration does not distract from the words as conveyors of meaning. Have them read Lewis Carroll's "Jabberwocky" as an example of blatant and ridiculous alliteration.

3. Aim. Owen describes death by gas in all its horror. The reader clearly perceives that there is nothing glamorous or glorious about such a death; it is hideous and painful, accomplishes nothing, and is essentially random. The poem is highly successful.

---

9. What is "The old Lie"?

10. Whom does the poet want to protect from "The old Lie"?

Understanding Literature (Questions for Discussion)

1. **Irony. Irony** is a difference between appearance and reality. For example, it would be ironic if the soldiers in this poem came safely through the battle and then were injured in a car accident on their way back to England. How is the title of the poem ironic? Where else in this poem does Owen describe war ironically?

2. **Alliteration. Alliteration** is the repetition of initial consonant sounds. Though Owen wrote only one published volume of poetry, he influenced other poets by his use of repeated sounds within the line. What consonant sounds are repeated in lines 5–7? Where else does Owen use this technique?

3. **Aim.** A writer's **aim** is the primary purpose that a work is meant to achieve. The purpose of "Dulce et Decorum Est," like that of the works of several of the soldier-poets, was to stop people from seeing war as glorious. What does Owen do to accomplish that purpose? Is he successful?

Responding in Writing

1. **Letter Home.** Imagine you are one of the soldiers in Owen's poem. At the end of the day, you sit down to write a letter home. You decide to include in it some of the incidents in the poem, as well as your own personal reactions to the events of the day.

2. **Descriptive Writing.** Much of the power of Owen's poem comes from the specific physical details he gives, such as the soldiers walking on bloody feet. Imagine yourself in a place where there are many concrete details that you can see, hear, touch, smell, or taste. The place might be, for example, a food market, a gym locker room, or a car dealership. Begin by listing at least one detail for each sense. Then write a descriptive paragraph including vivid, specific details to help your readers experience the place for themselves.

ANALYTIC SCALES FOR RESPONDING IN WRITING

Assign a score from 1 to 25 for each grading criterion below. (For more detailed evaluation, see the evaluation forms for writing, revising, and proofreading, *Assessment Portfolio, 7.1–7.10.*)

1. Letter Home
• **Content/Unity.** The letter offers a plausible account of a soldier's experiences and feelings as addressed to those at home.

• **Organization/Coherence.** The letter is well organized, presenting events in logical and chronological order and relating feelings clearly.

• **Language/Style.** The letter uses vivid and precise nouns, verbs, and modifiers.

• **Conventions.** The letter avoids errors in spelling, grammar, usage, mechanics, and manuscript form.

(cont.)

Language Lab

Verbals: Participles and Gerunds. Read the Language Arts Survey, 2.16, "Verbals: Participles," and 2.17, "Verbals: Gerunds." Much of the strength of Owen's writing lies in his use of strong verbs and verbals. In each of the excerpts below, identify the verbals. If a participle is used as an adjective, identify the noun that it modifies. (Look for both past participles and present participles.) Write *G* after a gerund.

1. Bent double, like old beggars under sacks,/Knock-kneed, coughing like hags, we cursed through sludge . . .

2. Till on the haunting flares we turned our backs . . .

3. An ecstasy of fumbling,/Fitting the clumsy helmets just in time . . .

4. As under a green sea, I saw him drowning.

5. If in some smothering dreams you too could pace/Behind the wagon that we flung him in . . .

PROJECTS

1. **Wartime Technology.** One reason for the horrors and huge casualties of World War I was the introduction of new kinds of weapons and equipment, including machine guns, tanks, modern submarines, and poison gas (as Owen described in his poem). During World War I, airplanes were also used in battle for the first time. With a group of other students, research World War I technology, finding photographs or drawings that illustrate your research. Prepare a presentation on this technology for your class.

2. **Reader's Theater.** Work with other students to write a reader's theater piece that presents the incident described in Owen's poem. Your script should consist mostly of dialogue but may contain a narrator's part as well. Give your soldiers names and write dialogue that might accompany such an incident. Rehearse your script. Then present it to the class as a reading. If you would like to know more about Owen, you might enjoy reading Jon Stallworthy's *Wilfred Owen: a Biography* (Oxford University Press and Chatto and Windus, 1974) and Paul Fussell's *The Great War and Modern Memory* (Oxford University Press, 1975), both prize-winning books.

ANALYTIC SCALES FOR RESPONDING IN WRITING (CONT.)

2. Descriptive Writing

• **Content/Unity.** The descriptive writing offers a description of the sensory experience of the place chosen as a subject.

• **Organization/Coherence.** The descriptive writing is clearly organized, presenting details in an order that can be followed easily through the piece.

• **Language/Style.** The descriptive writing uses vivid and precise nouns, verbs, and modifiers.

• **Conventions.** The descriptive writing avoids errors in spelling, grammar, usage, mechanics, and manuscript form.

ANSWERS FOR LANGUAGE LAB

1. "Bent" (past participle modifying "we"), "coughing" (present participle modifying "we")

2. "Haunting" (present participle modifying "flares")

3. "Fumbling" (G), "fitting" (G)

4. "Drowning" (present participle modifying "him")

5. "Smothering" (present participle modifying "dreams")

FOR MORE PRACTICE

Problem. In all my dreams, before my helpless sight,/He plunges at me, guttering, choking, drowning . . .

Answer. "Guttering, choking, drowning" (present participles modifying "he")

▶For additional practice, see the *Essential Skills Practice Book: Language,* 2.16–2.17.

PROJECT NOTES

▶See the worksheets and evaluation forms for projects, *Assessment Portfolio,* 7.20–7.23.

1. Wartime Technology

• In addition to books, there exist abundant video materials on World War I that can supply information on the technology of the war.

• Mention to students that, considering the nature of Owen's

(cont.)

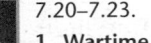

PROJECT NOTES (CONT.)

poem, it would be inappropriate for their presentation to glamorize or glorify the technology used during World War I.

2. Reader's Theater

• Participating students can attempt to use English accents if they feel confident doing so. If the attempt to reproduce accents threatens to make the play silly, advise them to drop the accents and speak as if they were American soldiers.

• Students may want to provide a narrator styled after the chorus in an old play. (They can use as a model the chorus in Marlowe's *The Tragical History of Doctor Faustus,* page 387.) The narrator will then be able to point out the moral given in the last lines of the poem.

READER'S GUIDE
- Selection Worksheet, 10.8

ASSESSMENT PORTFOLIO
- Selection Check Test, 4.10.15
- Selection Test, 4.10.16

ESSENTIAL SKILLS PRACTICE BOOKS
- *Language,* 2.61
- *Study and Research,* 4.18, 4.21, 4.22

ENRICHMENT ACTIVITIES

For a fuller perspective on Spender, students can read his autobiography (cited in "About the Author"), or read his work, *Selected Poems.* Students can then compose a letter to Spender in which they describe their response to his life and accomplishments.

SUPPORT FOR LEP STUDENTS

Several of the phrases in the poem are elliptical and may be difficult for students to understand. "Stripped," for instance, means "took off their clothes to go swimming"; "salt coarse pointing" suggests that the speaker feels the effect of the boys' pointing at him as if it were coarse salt rubbed into a wound or forced into his mouth.

ADDITIONAL VOCABULARY

salt—that which lends a tang or sharpness

coarse—rough; harsh

lithe—bending easily, flexible, supple

ADDITIONAL QUESTIONS AND ACTIVITIES

Students can write a poem from the point of view of one of the "rough children," describing his or her reaction to the speaker as a child.

PREREADING

"Rough"
by Stephen Spender

ABOUT THE AUTHOR

Stephen Spender (1909–) was a leading member of a group of socially conscious British writers of the 1930s. This group took part in "new left" politics and worked for social reform. Born in London, Spender attended University College, Oxford, where he became friends with other writers, including W. H. Auden. While his contemporaries focused on society and its problems, Spender wrote poetry with a more personal and individual voice. Because he was a pacifist, he did not fight in either the Spanish Civil War, as many liberal writers did, or World War II. He was a firefighter in London during the Blitz. By the 1950s, he wrote less poetry and became better known as a critic and lecturer, both in Britain and in the United States. He edited the literary review *Encounter* from 1953 to 1967. *The Creative Element* (1953) is one of Spender's well-known critical works. His autobiography, *World Within World,* was published in 1951 and reissued in 1994.

ABOUT THE SELECTION

Spender is part of the generation of British writers who grew up between the two world wars, during the political upheavals of the 1930s in Europe. His "new poetry" was a bridge between the work of earlier modern poets such as Eliot and that of poets who began to write after World War II. Rapid changes in technology and politics made the interwar years an edgy, uneasy period, as did the worldwide economic depression. Many writers of this period turned to private, personal subjects. **"Rough"** is a highly personal poem in which the speaker deals from an adult perspective with an issue that confronted him in childhood. The poem appears in Spender's *Selected Poems.*

GOALS/OBJECTIVES

Studying this lesson will enable students to

- empathize with the physical and emotional pain the speaker suffered as a child
- describe Stephen Spender's literary accomplishments and explain the historical significance of his writings

- recognize and correct sentence fragments
- define *diction* and *metaphor* and recognize the effect of these devices in poetry
- write a critical analysis
- use a card catalog and a computerized catalog

READER'S JOURNAL

During your childhood, were you ever afraid of a bully? What causes some people to behave in a bullying or taunting manner? What do they get out of acting that way? What causes some young people to be picked on? Are the same qualities that occasionally elicit taunts in childhood ones that lead to success in adulthood? Freewrite about a couple of these questions in your journal.

THINKING SKILLS

Read the Language Arts Survey, 4.18, "Reading Actively." Then read the first line of the poem. From this line, what do you think the poem will be about? If you were going to write a poem that began like this, what would you include in it?

"Rough"

STEPHEN SPENDER

My parents kept me from children who were rough
Who threw words like stones and who wore torn clothes.
Their thighs showed through rags. They ran in the street
And climbed cliffs and stripped by the country streams.

5 I feared more than tigers their muscles like iron
Their jerking hands and their knees tight on my arms.
I feared the salt coarse pointing of those boys
Who copied my lisp behind me on the road.

They were lithe, they sprang out behind hedges
10 Like dogs to bark at my world. They threw mud
While I looked the other way, pretending to smile.
I longed to forgive them, but they never smiled.

❶ From whom was the speaker kept?

❷ What did the speaker long to do? Was he given the opportunity to do so?

Responding to the Selection

What do you feel when you think about the childhood that this speaker experienced? What must his childhood have been like? What feelings do you have with regard to the "children who were rough" described by the speaker? Discuss these questions with your classmates.

"ROUGH"   873

ANSWERS TO SELECTION CHECK TEST 4.10.15

EX. What were the other children's words like?
The other children's words were like stones.

1. The speaker's parents kept him away from whom?
They kept him away from children who were rough.

2. What did the rough children do by country streams?
They stripped by country streams.

3. What did the speaker fear "more than tigers"?
He feared the muscles of the rough children.

4. What did the rough children copy?
They copied the speaker's lisp.

5. What did the speaker long to do?
The speaker longed to forgive the rough children.

ANSWERS FOR REVIEWING THE SELECTION

RECALLING

1. The speaker compares the words to stones.

2. He recalls them taunting him, wearing torn clothes, running in the street, climbing cliffs, and swimming in streams.

3. The speaker recalls having feared the boys' muscles, their hands, their knees, and their pointing.

4. He looks the other way, pretending to smile. He longed to forgive the children.

INTERPRETING

Responses will vary. Possible responses are given.

5. The speaker describes the words as if they created a physical pain, perhaps because as a child he felt them intensely.

6. Running, climbing, and swimming are enjoyable activities. The speaker apparently was not allowed to engage in free-ranging outdoor activities that involved any danger or physical exertion.

7. Evidently the speaker was once pinned down by the bullies; in this situation they would put their knees on his arms.

8. The speaker pretended to smile because he was trying to ingratiate himself with the rough children or to feign nonchalance. He wanted to forgive them because he preferred to be friends with them than to continue to be a victim of their abuse.

SYNTHESIZING

Responses will vary. Possible responses are given.

9. The images of the children as tigers and as being lithe and like dogs suggest a certain admiration on the part of the speaker for the animal vitality and strength of the rough children. The speaker shows that he has not forgotten the pain they caused because he speaks in terms of his remembered fear, and mentions "words like stones," "jerking hands," and their knees on his arms.

10. The speaker seems to have come to terms with his memories of the rough children, perhaps forgiving them for being what they were and for being unable to acknowledge and appreciate him.

Reviewing the Selection

RECALLING

1. What word does the speaker use to describe the children's words in line 2?

2. In stanza 1, in what activities does the speaker recall the rough children engaging?

3. In stanza 2, what does the speaker recall having feared?

4. What does the speaker do while the children are throwing mud? What did he long to do?

INTERPRETING

5. Why would the speaker describe the children's words as he does in line 2? What effect did those words probably have on the speaker?

6. Are these enjoyable activities? What does it tell you about the speaker's situation that he was not allowed to engage in such activities?

7. In what circumstances would knees be "tight on [someone's] arms"? What evidently happened to the speaker during his childhood?

8. Why do you think the speaker pretended to smile? Why did he long to forgive the rough children?

SYNTHESIZING

9. What images in the poem show that the speaker now has some admiration for those rough children? What recalled images and events show that, despite this admiration, the speaker has not forgotten the pain that he felt as a child?

10. Do you think that the speaker has forgiven the rough children? Why or why not? Can one forgive and still not forget?

Understanding Literature (Questions for Discussion)

1. **Diction. Diction,** when applied to writing, refers to word choice. Make a list of the verbs and adjectives in this poem that are associated with the rough children. What do these verbs and adjectives tell about those children? Now make a list of the verbs and verbals associated with the speaker as a child. What do these verbs and verbals tell about the speaker?

2. **Metaphor.** A **metaphor** is a figure of speech in which one thing is spoken or written about as if it were another. With what animals are the rough children in this poem compared? What are these animals like? What do these metaphors say about the rough children? What other words used to describe the rough children describe animal-like qualities? Why might the speaker have wanted to be a little more like those children? In what ways would the speaker not have wanted to be like them?

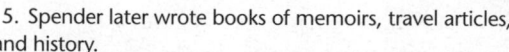

ANSWERS FOR LANGUAGE LAB

Responses will vary. Possible responses are given.

1. In the 1930s, Spender's writing dealt with modern technology, such as airfields and express trains.

2. The young poet became an immediate popular success in a few years.

3. As an older man in the 1960s, Spender wrote sympathetically about student rebellions in Europe and the United States.

4. OK

5. Spender later wrote books of memoirs, travel articles, and history.

► For additional practice, see the *Essential Skills Practice Book: Language,* 2.61.

Responding in Writing

Critical Analysis—Biographical Criticism. Stephen Spender grew up to become a famous poet and literary critic. Why might a person who has been made fun of for his speech become a writer? What qualities must Spender have had as a child that were not appreciated by the "rough children"? Assuming that the speaker is Spender himself, write a short analysis of this poem that tells what Spender's childhood must have been like and how it may have affected the later course of his life.

Language Lab

Sentence Fragments. Read the Language Arts Survey, 2.61, "Correcting Sentence Fragments." Sentence fragments are common in poetry but should generally be avoided in most other kinds of writing. Some of the examples below are fragments; some are not. Rewrite the fragments as complete sentences, adding words as needed. If a sentence is not a fragment, write *OK* by its number.

1. In the 1930s Spender's writing about modern technology, such as airfields and express trains.

2. The young poet an immediate popular success in a few years.

3. As an older man in the 1960s, wrote sympathetically about student rebellions in Europe and the United States.

4. Spender's autobiography, *World Within World,* portrays many other famous writers.

5. Later books of memoirs, travel articles, and history.

Research Skills

Catalog Search. Read the Language Arts Survey, 4.21 and 4.22, "Using Searching Tools" and "Using the Card Catalog." Depending on the cataloging system used in your library, use the card catalog or database to look up works available by Stephen Spender. Compile a selective bibliography that includes a sampling of Spender's poetry, travel writing, and memoirs from all stages of his career.

PROJECTS

Panel Discussion. In class, hold a panel discussion about violence among young people. Consider these questions: What are the causes of violence among the young? What can be done to protect young people from violence? What can be done to eliminate or change its root causes?

ENRICHMENT ACTIVITIES

- Excellent recordings of Dylan Thomas reading his works are available on audiocassette. Assign several students to find a library in the area that has one of Thomas's recordings and borrow it to play during class.
- Dylan Thomas's last, unfinished poem also concerned his father's death. It is tremendously powerful despite its fragmentary state. Students can find it in Thomas, Dylan. *Collected Poems 1934–1952.* New York: New Directions, 1971. pages 200–201.

SUPPORT FOR LEP STUDENTS

Pointing out the structure of the poem may help students to understand it better. The opening stanza serves as an introduction to the theme, and the closing stanza serves as a conclusion and summation. The four stanzas in the center of the poem each give an example of a type of person and then explain why that type does not face death with resignation.

ADDITIONAL VOCABULARY
frail—easily destroyed

PREREADING

"Do Not Go Gentle into That Good Night"
by Dylan Thomas

ABOUT THE AUTHOR

During his lifetime, **Dylan Thomas** (1914–1953) was almost as famous a colorful personality as he was as a poet. He grew up in the industrial city of Swansea, Wales, the son of a schoolteacher. Journals that he kept show him to have had a considerable poetic gift from an early age. He worked briefly as a news reporter, published his first book of poems when he was twenty years old, and then moved to London. Besides writing poetry, Thomas worked for the BBC (British Broadcasting Corporation) and wrote stories and plays, including the play for voices *Under Milk Wood* (1954). His prose memoir *A Child's Christmas in Wales* is a popular classic. Thomas gave many public readings in a rich, Welsh-accented voice that captivated audiences. These readings made him quite popular, even among people who ordinarily did not appreciate poetry. Although Thomas's verse often makes great demands on the reader or listener, most people respond to its passion and to its vivid, charged language, reminiscent of the King James Bible and of Welsh preaching. In person, Thomas was often talkative and witty. However, his alcoholism made a ruin of much of his life, including his marriage to Caitlin Macnamara. Heavy drinking, especially on reading tours, interfered with his writing; his total output of poetry was rather small, and he died before reaching his fortieth birthday.

ABOUT THE SELECTION

Dylan Thomas's poems are rich with imagery and music. Reading his first works, critics thought of him as a wild Romantic. However, it soon became clear that Thomas was a serious craftsman. **"Do Not Go Gentle into That Good Night"** shows Thomas's technical mastery. This poem, written about the death of his father, is an example of the complex French verse form known as the **villanelle**. It may well be the finest example of the form ever produced. It is certainly the most famous.

GOALS/OBJECTIVES

Studying this lesson will enable students to

- empathize with the speaker's feelings about death
- describe Dylan Thomas's literary accomplishments and explain the historical significance of his writings
- define *villanelle* and recognize villanelles they encounter in their reading
- write a reflective essay
- identify and interpret puns in poetry

Suppose that you had the option of living forever. Would you choose to do so? Why, or why not?

SPEAKING AND LISTENING SKILLS

Read the Language Arts Survey, 3.5, "Interpersonal Communication." Then think about family communications. Thomas wrote this poem to his father who was very ill. As you read the poem, consider this question: What message did Thomas want to communicate to his father? What did Thomas want his father to do in the days before death?

"Do Not Go Gentle into That Good Night"

Dylan Thomas

Do not go gentle into that good night,
Old age should burn and rave at close of day;
Rage, rage against the dying of the light.

Though wise men at their end know dark is right,
5 Because their words had forked no lightning they
Do not go gentle into that good night.

Good men, the last wave by, crying how bright
Their frail deeds might have danced in a green bay,
Rage, rage against the dying of the light.

10 Wild men who caught and sang the sun in flight,
And learn, too late, they grieved it on its way,
Do not go gentle into that good night.

Grave men, near death, who see with blinding sight
Blind eyes could blaze like meteors and be gay,
15 Rage, rage against the dying of the light.

And you, my father, there on the sad height,
Curse, bless, me now with your fierce tears, I pray.
Do not go gentle into that good night.
Rage, rage against the dying of the light. ■

❶
What should old age do at "close of day"? What is night in this poem?

❷
Why do even "wise men" not go gentle into that good night?

READER'S JOURNAL

Students should consider both the positive and negative consequences of each option. After writing about these questions students can discuss their ideas on this issue.

SPEAKING AND LISTENING SKILLS

In discussing these questions with students, point out that the "metamessage" of the poem is that Thomas is not resigned to his father's being resigned about death. Ask what this says about Thomas's own attitude toward death—not just toward his father's death, but toward his own.

Answer. Thomas's unwillingness to resign himself to his father's resignation suggests that Thomas still fears and dreads death himself.

ANSWERS TO GUIDED READING QUESTIONS

❶ Old age should "burn and rave at close of day." Night in this poem represents death.

❷ Even "wise men" do not go gentle into death because "their words had forked no lightning," by which Thomas may mean that their wisdom has not yet produced the effect on others that they intended.

ANSWERS TO SELECTION CHECK TEST 4.10.17

EX. What adjective does the speaker repeatedly use to modify the word *night*?

The speaker repeatedly uses the adjective *good*.

1. According to the speaker, what should old age do "at close of day?"

It should burn and rave.

2. According to the speaker, what should people who are nearing death rage against?

They should rage against the dying of the light.

3. Who "caught and sang the sun in flight"?

Wild men "caught and sang the sun in flight."

4. Who sees with blinding sight?

Grave men, near death, see with blinding sight.

5. To whom is the poem addressed?

The poem is addressed to the speaker's father.

Responding to the Selection

Do you agree with the speaker about how someone should confront death? Should a person fight to the end, showing great spirit and determination, or should one meet death with gentleness and resignation? Discuss this question with your classmates.

Reviewing the Selection

RECALLING

1. In line 1 of the poem, what does the speaker urge the dying person to do?

2. What do "wise men at their end" know, according to stanza 2?

3. What regrets do good men, wild men, and grave men have when they near death, according to stanzas 3–5?

4. Where, according to the last stanza of the poem, is the speaker's father?

INTERPRETING

5. To what do the terms "good night," "close of day," and "the dying of the light" all refer? How is the speaker's attitude toward death revealed in the term "good night"? What attitude does the speaker believe that people should adopt when near death?

6. How is the knowledge of wise men, referred to in stanza 2, related to the speaker's calling death "that good night"?

7. Why might the regrets of good men, wild men, and grave men about how they have lived their lives lead them to "rage" at the end of life? How might they want to change their behavior in the last part of life?

8. To what might the term "sad height" in line 16 refer?

SYNTHESIZING

9. The speaker asks his father, in line 17, to curse or bless him. Why might the speaker want his father to give any kind of strong emotional response to him at this time? To what is a curse or a blessing preferable, from the speaker's point of view?

10. Although the speaker calls death a "good night," he nonetheless asks his father to "rage against the dying of the light." Why might the speaker, though accepting death, still want the approach to death to be done without resignation, acceptance, or gentleness?

Understanding Literature (Questions for Discussion)

1. **Villanelle.** A **villanelle** is a nineteen-line French verse form with complex requirements for repetition and rhyme. The first fifteen lines are organized into three-line stanzas, or tercets. The first and last lines of the opening stanza are repeated, alternately, as the last lines of stanzas 2–5 and as the concluding couplet of the last stanza, which is a four-line quatrain. What two lines are repeated throughout Thomas's poem? Does the poem meet the requirements of the villanelle form? To find out the rhyme scheme that a villanelle should follow, study the end rhymes in Thomas's poem. Use the letters *a* and *b* to represent the different rhyming sounds in the poem. Write the poem's rhyme scheme.

2. **Pun.** A **pun** is a play on words, one that wittily exploits a double meaning. What pun appears in line 13 of this poem? What are the two meanings of the word?

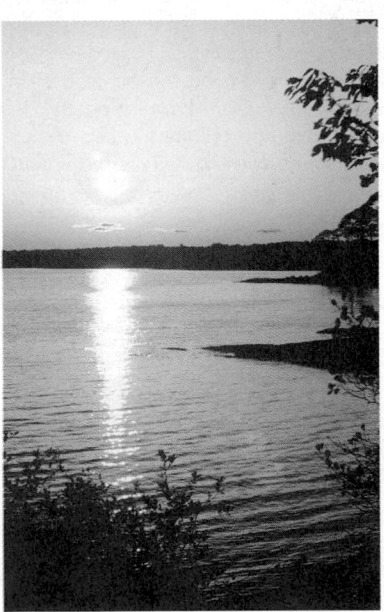

▶ See the evaluation forms for discussion, active listening, and oral communication, *Assessment Portfolio,* 7.11–7.14. *Responses will vary. Possible responses are given.*

1. Villanelle. The two repeated lines in Thomas's poem are "Do not go gentle into that good night," and "Rage, rage against the dying of the light." The poem meets the villanelle requirements. The rhyme scheme is *aba aba aba aba aba abaa.*

▶ **Teaching Note:** Students may be struck by the apparent simplicity of the villanelle; eight of its nineteen lines are shared among the stanzas. If they are assigned the task of writing in the form, however, they may quickly discover that while it is easy to write a villanelle, it is not easy to write a villanelle that is also a great poem.

2. Pun. The pun in line 13 is *grave.* It can be an adjective meaning "sad" or "somber" and a noun referring to a hole in the earth where the dead are buried.

▶ **Teaching Notes:**
• The great punster Shakespeare used the same play on the word *grave* at a critical moment in his tragedy *Romeo and Juliet.* Mercutio has just been stabbed by Tybalt; he realizes he is dying, but continues punning and joking all the same. "Ask for me tomorrow," he tells Romeo, "and you will find me a *grave* man" (Act III, scene i, line 100).
• Ask students to identify other puns in the poem.
Answer. The phrases "good night" and "dying of the light" are also essentially puns; they do not refer only to a common greeting and a common description of twilight, but to death. "Blinding sight" is also a pun referring both to a sight that blinds and (as an oxymoron) to a sight that cannot see.

ENRICHMENT ACTIVITIES

"Poetry makes nothing happen," says Auden, commenting on how little literature affects life. Life, however, has a great influence on literature; and a poet's character and times appear in his verse as in a dark mirror. Students can write a speculative paragraph on what they think Auden and his life were like, based on the Prereading information and on the selections. They can then do research and compare the facts of Auden's personality and biography with their conjectures.

SUPPORT FOR LEP STUDENTS

List Anglicisms students will encounter in Auden's poetry: *pints* for "glasses of beer" and *potter* for "putter."

ADDITIONAL VOCABULARY

figure—person, especially one thought of in a specified way

giddy—feeling dizzy or unsteady

potter—busy oneself in a trifling or aimless way

PREREADING

"Who's Who"
"Musée des Beaux Arts"
by W. H. Auden

ABOUT THE AUTHOR

Wystan Hugh Auden (1907-1973) was considered the leader of the young, politically conscious British poets of the 1930s. As fascism gained ground in Germany and Italy, this group of poets supported left-wing ideas and tried to bring change to British society. At Oxford University, Auden became friends with other writers who achieved fame, including the playwright Christopher Isherwood and the poet Stephen Spender. After spending a year in Germany, Auden returned to England and began teaching. His early poetry soon made him famous. During the 1930s, Auden also wrote dramas, light verse, and political observations, sometimes working with other writers. In 1939, he moved to the United States, where he spent more than thirty years and won the Pulitzer Prize for poetry. He returned to Oxford in 1972. Over time, Auden's style, outlook, and religious beliefs changed, but his social awareness never failed. In the tense Cold War era, he coined the term "Age of Anxiety."

ABOUT THE SELECTIONS

Most of the important themes of Auden's times are represented in his poems. The sonnet **"Who's Who"** reflects his interest in different verse forms as well as his ironic view of worldly fame. Visual arts and music have often inspired modern poets. **"Musée des Beaux Arts"** is a reflection on the sixteenth-century Flemish painting "The Fall of Icarus," by Pieter Brueghel, which is in the collection of the Museum of Fine Arts in Brussels, Belgium. In Greek mythology, Icarus and his father, the architect Daedalus, tried to escape from prison by flying with wings made of wax and feathers. Ignoring his father's warning, Icarus flew too near the sun, which melted his wings, sending him plunging into the sea. Auden uses the poem to comment on suffering and its place in human life.

GOALS/OBJECTIVES

Studying the lesson will enable students to

- empathize with the speaker's attitudes toward fame and with the unnoticed suffering of the world
- describe W. H. Auden's literary accomplishments and explain the historical significance of his writings
- define *sonnet* and *myth* and recognize them when they are encountered in readings
- identify the functions of sentences
- write a character sketch and an elegy

READER'S JOURNAL

If someone were to write your biography in just a few lines, what would you like those lines to include? What one incident, one relationship, or one small detail from your life could give the world a picture of who you are? In your journal, freewrite your ideas about this. Then, based on your freewrite, write a one-paragraph autobiography or self-portrait.

THINKING SKILLS

Read the Language Arts Survey 4.11, "Generalizing." Read the poem. Then write a generalization about the speaker's attitude toward fame and celebrity.

"Who's Who"

W. H. AUDEN

A shilling life[1] will give you all the facts:
How Father beat him, how he ran away,
What were the struggles of his youth, what acts
Made him the greatest figure of his day:
5   Of how he fought, fished, hunted, worked all night,
Though giddy, climbed new mountains; named a sea:
Some of the last researchers even write
Love made him weep his pints like you and me.

    With all his honors on, he sighed for one
10   Who, say astonished critics, lived at home;
Did little jobs about the house with skill
And nothing else; could whistle; would sit still
Or potter round the garden; answered some
Of his long marvellous letters but kept none.

---

1. **shilling life.** A short biography sold in England in Auden's day for a shilling; a shilling was approximately equal in value to a dime.

❶
What sort of life has this person led? Despite fame, for whom does this person "sigh"?

PREREADING NOTES

READER'S JOURNAL

Before students write their one-paragraph autobiography, they can read the entries in a biographical dictionary to see the kinds of details often included in biographical summaries. They should not feel, however, that they have to directly imitate the formal biographies in the dictionary.

THINKING SKILLS

Remind students that Auden himself achieved fame early in life. Discuss with them how this might have colored his attitude toward fame.

ANSWER TO GUIDED READING QUESTION

❶ The subject of the poem has led a life of great activity, struggle, and exploration that has brought him fame. He "sighs for" someone who is a homebody.

ANSWERS TO SELECTION CHECK TEST 4.10.19

EX. From what can one get all the facts about the person's life?
You can get all the facts from "A shilling life."
1. Why did the man run away as a child?
His father beat him.
2. What did the subject of the poem name?
He named a sea.
3. Why did the subject of the poem sometimes weep?
His love was not returned.
4. How was the life of the famous man's love interest different from that of the man?
The love interest lived a quiet, very ordinary life at home.
5. What did the person with whom the man was in love do with his letters?
That person answered some of them but kept none.

VOCABULARY FROM THE SELECTIONS

martyrdom

reverently

QUOTABLES

❝Weep for the lives your wishes never led.❞

—W. H. Auden

RESPONDING TO THE SELECTION

Use a cluster diagram to help students analyze the details in the poem that provide information about each life. For instructions on cluster diagrams, refer students to the Language Arts Survey, 1.17, "Clustering."

ANSWERS FOR REVIEWING THE SELECTION

RECALLING

1. Such a biography would tell you that the subject of the poem was beaten by his father, ran away, struggled as a youth, became a great figure, fought, fished, hunted, worked, climbed new mountains, and named a sea.

2. Two lives are featured in the poem.

3. The critics seem to think the love interest is unworthy of being loved by the great figure.

4. The recipient answers some of them, but does not keep any.

INTERPRETING

Responses will vary. Possible responses are given.

5. The general public probably thinks he has everything he could possibly want and has lived an exciting and fulfilling life.

6. The final lines of each stanza establish their relationship: the first person loves the second passionately, but the second person does not love the first, or at least not passionately.

7. The critics cannot understand how such an accomplished and worldly man could love someone who stayed at home and was content with doing very little.

8. The recipient of the letters respects the sender enough to answer him, but not enough to treasure his letters.

SYNTHESIZING

Responses will vary. Possible responses are given.

9. The poet is contrasting two individuals, one who is famous and applauded but not content, and one who is unknown but is apparently content.

10. The title of the poem refers to the first person described.

882 TEACHER'S EDITION

Responding to the Selection

Of the lives featured in this poem, which would you rather lead? Why does one sound more appealing to you than the other? What details in the poem provide information about each life?

Reviewing the Selection

RECALLING

1. According to the poem, what would a "shilling life" tell you about the main subject of this poem?

2. How many lives are featured in this poem?

3. What do "astonished critics" think about the first person's love interest?

4. What does the recipient of the first person's letters do with the letters?

INTERPRETING

5. How do you think the general public views the first person mentioned in the poem?

6. What establishes the relationship between the people in this poem?

7. Why do critics react the way they do?

8. How does the recipient of the letters feel about the sender of the letters? How do you know?

SYNTHESIZING

9. What is the poet contrasting in this poem?

10. *Who's Who* is a reference book giving short biographies of famous or accomplished people. To which person do you think the title of the poem refers?

Understanding Literature (Questions for Discussion)

1. **Sonnet.** A **sonnet** is a fourteen-line poem that follows one of a number of different rhyme schemes. This sonnet, like many in English, is divided into an octave (the first eight lines) and a sestet (the last six lines). How does Auden use this break between stanzas? How might you summarize the octave? the sestet? How does the rhyme scheme change between the octave and the sestet?

ANSWERS FOR UNDERSTANDING LITERATURE

► See the evaluation forms for discussion, active listening, and oral communication, *Assessment Portfolio,* 7.11–7.14.

Responses will vary. Possible responses are given.

1. **Sonnet.** Auden uses the break between stanzas to switch from recounting the successes of the subject of the poem to describing his failed love for the second person. The octave outlines the success of the first per-

son; the sestet describes the second person in terms that contrast with the first person. The rhyme scheme changes from *ababcdcd* to *efggfe*.

► **Teaching Note:** The sonnet form has been enormously popular over the centuries. Ask students why they think that might be true. Suggest they examine Auden's sonnet for clues. *Answer.* Poets enjoy the opportunity to change subject and sense afforded by the

(cont.)

2. Irony. Irony is a difference between appearance and reality. The use of irony is characteristic of Auden's work, often giving it a wry humor. How is the title of this poem ironic? Of the two people discussed in this poem, who's who in the eyes of the world? Who's who in the eyes of the explorer who is the main subject of the poem? What other examples of irony can you find in the poem?

Responding in Writing

1. **Character Sketch.** Auden tells you only a few facts about the second person in the poem who lived quietly at home. What was this person like? Use your imagination to round out this character in a short character sketch. Supply your reader with facts about this person's age, appearance, voice, background, personality, and daily life.

2. **Personal Letters.** The famous man in this poem wrote "long marvelous letters" to the other person. What do you think makes a letter "marvelous"? Instead of writing a letter, write a short essay that describes what you think makes a letter "marvelous" instead of boring or ordinary.

ANALYTIC SCALES FOR RESPONDING IN WRITING (CONT.)

• **Conventions.** The character sketch avoids errors in spelling, grammar, usage, mechanics, and manuscript form.

2. Personal Letters

• **Content/Unity.** The essay presents precise reasons why a personal letter is marvelous.

• **Organization/Coherence.** The essay offers a clear, orderly rationale for its conclusions.

• **Language/Style.** The essay uses vivid and precise nouns, verbs, and modifiers.

• **Conventions.** The essay avoids errors in spelling, grammar, usage, mechanics, and manuscript form.

ANSWERS FOR UNDERSTANDING LITERATURE (CONT.)

division into octave and sestet. Generally the octave states the problem, issue, or situation, and the sestet resolves it, gives it poignancy, or adds an ironic twist.

2. Irony. The title of the poem is ironic because it refers to a book with collections of supposedly notable people, and yet also poses the question "Who's who?" That is, who's better off—the famous person or the person who is not famous? In the eyes of the world, the former is the important one; in the eyes of the explorer, the latter is the person of true importance. Other examples of irony are the notion that a cheap biography can sum up all the facts about the explorer that are worth knowing, and that although the letters were "marvelous," the recipient did not feel compelled to keep any of them.

►**Teaching Note:** Ask students whether the irony of the final line would have been heightened or lessened if the recipient had never answered any of the sender's letters. *Answer.* The irony may have been lessened. The measured response of answering some letters but not all shows a mild interest that is somehow more poignant and ironic than an utter refusal to reciprocate.

ANALYTIC SCALES FOR RESPONDING IN WRITING

Assign a score from 1 to 25 for each grading criterion below. (For more detailed evaluation, see the evaluation forms for writing, revising, and proofreading, *Assessment Portfolio,* 7.1–7.10.)

1. Character Sketch

• **Content/Unity.** The character sketch presents descriptive facts about the second person in the poem.

• **Organization/Coherence.** The character sketch is clearly organized, and it adds up to a coherent image of the second person.

• **Language/Style.** The character sketch uses vivid and precise nouns, verbs, and modifiers.

(cont.)

TEACHER'S EDITION 883

READER'S JOURNAL

Have you ever seen a painting or photograph that captured your imagination or drew you into its story? What kinds of ideas did it give you? Why do some paintings and photographs appeal to you more than others? Choose a painting or photograph from this textbook that appeals to you. Freewrite your ideas in your journal.

RESEARCH SKILLS

Read the Language Arts Survey 4.22, "Using the Card Catalog," and 4.26, "Computer-Assisted Research." Then use your library's catalog or database to find an art book about sixteenth-century Dutch and Flemish painting. Make a note of (a) biographical information about Brueghel, and (b) the names of at least two of Brueghel's paintings besides *The Fall of Icarus*.

"Musée des Beaux Arts"

W. H. AUDEN

What did the Old Masters understand about suffering? ❶

About suffering they were never wrong,
The Old Masters:[1] how well they understood
Its human position; how it takes place
While someone else is eating or opening a window or just
    walking dully along;
5 How, when the aged are <u>reverently</u>, passionately waiting
For the miraculous birth, there always must be
Children who did not specially want it to happen, skating
On a pond at the edge of the wood:
They never forgot
10 That even the dreadful <u>martyrdom</u> must run its course
Anyhow in a corner, some untidy spot
Where the dogs go on with their doggy life and the
    torturer's horse
Scratches its innocent behind on a tree.

---

1. **Old Masters.** Collective name for great European artists before the eighteenth century

WORDS FOR EVERYDAY USE:

rev • er • ent • ly (rev´ər ənt lē) *adv.*, with respect or awe

mar• tyr • dom (märt´ər dəm) *n.*, death or suffering for a cause

15　　In Brueghel's *Icarus*,[2] for instance: how everything turns away
　　　Quite leisurely from the disaster; the ploughman may
　　　Have heard the splash, the forsaken cry,
　　　But for him it was not an important failure; the sun shone
　　　As it had to on the white legs disappearing into the green
　　　Water; and the expensive delicate ship that must have seen
20　　Something amazing, a boy falling out of the sky,
　　　Had somewhere to get to and sailed calmly on.　　■

---

2. **Brueghel's *Icarus*.** Brueghel was a Flemish painter.
One of his paintings is of the legend of Icarus, who flew
too close to the sun with wings made of wax and fell back
to earth and died.

❶
What was happening as Icarus fell from the sky?

Responding to the Selection

Imagine that you are a bystander in one of the works of art that Auden describes. Freewrite in your journal some of the thoughts that are going on in your head during the moment that is captured in the painting.

Reviewing the Selection

RECALLING

1. According to the poem, what takes place "While someone else is eating or opening a window or just walking dully along"?

2. What event is taking place in lines 5-8?

3. To whom does the "they" refer in line 9?

4. Who witnessed Icarus's fall into the ocean?

INTERPRETING

5. How did the Old Masters depict suffering, according to the poem?

6. Why might young and old people react differently to the same event? How do different reactions add another dimension to the event?

7. What do "they" never forget about how animals and nature behave while humans suffer?

8. How does Brueghel's painting show the reactions to Icarus's fall? Why do you suppose the witnesses reacted the way they did?

 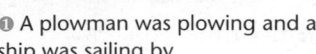

❶ A plowman was plowing and a ship was sailing by.

ANSWERS FOR REVIEWING THE SELECTION

RECALLING

1. Human suffering takes place while these mundane activities are occurring in the vicinity.

2. A miraculous birth is taking place.

3. The line refers to the Old Masters.

4. A plowman and the crew of a ship witnessed Icarus's fall.

INTERPRETING

Responses will vary. Possible responses are given.

5. The Old Masters showed suffering taking place while other irrelevant activities occurred.

6. Children may be less aware of this event or they may be more interested in their own enjoyment. Old people may feel more of a need for a miracle. Seeing different reactions to an event in a painting forces the viewer of the painting to consider the meaning of the event from several perspectives.

7. They never forget that animals go on with their animal lives and that nature proceeds with its senseless, detached rhythms: "the sun [shines]/As it [has] to."

8. Brueghel's painting shows that the reaction to Icarus's fall was one of indifference—the plowman does not think it "an important failure," and the ship "had somewhere to get to and sailed calmly on."

(cont.)

VOCABULARY IN CONTEXT

- The king of Lunonia insisted upon being treated <u>reverently</u> by his subjects.
- Many who make bad choices in life feel compelled to endure their <u>martyrdom</u> rather than act to make changes.

RESPONDING TO THE SELECTION

Remind students about the point of the poem: those present during these great moments have other thoughts and concerns and pay very little attention to the high drama or tragedy taking place.

ANSWERS FOR REVIEWING THE SELECTION (CONT.)

SYNTHESIZING

Responses will vary. Possible responses are given.

9. Auden says that the Old Masters understood that suffering takes place in an essentially indifferent world. People have to deal with their suffering alone because the world is busy about other matters.

10. According to Auden, ordinary everyday events are taking place at the same time amazing events are happening: people are "eating or opening a window or just walking dully along."

ANSWERS FOR UNDERSTANDING LITERATURE

► See the evaluation forms for discussion, active listening, and oral communication, *Assessment Portfolio,* 7.11–7.14.

Responses will vary. Possible responses are given.

1. **Rhyme.** The rhyme scheme is *abcadedbfgfge hhijkkij.*

► **Teaching Notes**

• Students may not realize that lines 4 and 12 run over and are continued as indented lines. Rhyme schemes should reflect the true ends of these lines ("along" and "horse").

• The rhyme scheme, like line length, is obviously very flexible and free. Ask students why Auden bothered to rhyme the poem at all. *Answer.* The rhyme ties the poem together in an unobtrusive way, giving a unity to its free structure.

2. **Theme.** The opening lines say that human suffering goes unnoticed by the world around it. As examples, the poem tells of a martyr being tortured and Icarus falling into the sea. The theme of the poem is that human suffering occurs in a context of general indifference; thus we are essentially alone in our suffering. The theme is elaborated by referring to the Old Masters, who made everyday objects and events the focus of their paintings, while the notable or unusual event occurred in a limited portion of the canvas.

---

9. What does Auden think the Old Masters—the painters of past centuries—understood about suffering? Why, according to the poem, do people have to deal with their suffering alone?

10. According to Auden, what sorts of things are going on in real life when amazing events are taking place?

Understanding Literature (Questions for Discussion)

1. **Rhyme. Rhyme** is the repetition of sounds at the ends of words. Some forms of poetry follow strict schemes in which all lines have a rhyming partner somewhere in the poem; others do not. At first it may seem that "Musée des Beaux Arts" does not rhyme, though it does. Try to figure out the rhyme scheme of the poem.

2. **Theme. Theme** is a central idea in a literary work. What do the opening lines of the poem say about suffering? What examples of this does the poem give? What is the theme of this poem, and how is that theme developed or elaborated?

Responding in Writing

Lyric Poem or Essay. A **lyric poem** is a highly musical verse that expresses the emotions of a speaker. An **essay** is a brief work of nonfiction prose that develops a single main idea. In "Musée des Beaux Arts," Auden draws on his reactions to a painting to express his emotions. Choose a photograph or painting to which you respond emotionally. It can be a dramatic news photograph, a work of fine art, or any other depiction of a scene. Write a short poem or essay in which you describe this photo or painting and the ideas or emotions that you have when you look at it or think about it. If you opt to write a poem, begin by choosing a verse form in which to write. Possibilities include free verse, ballad stanzas, and rhymed couplets. See the definitions of these terms in the Handbook of Literary Terms.

ANALYTIC SCALES FOR RESPONDING IN WRITING

Assign a score from 1 to 25 for each grading criterion below. (For more detailed evaluation, see the evaluation forms for writing, revising, and proofreading, *Assessment Portfolio,* 7.1–7.10.)

Lyric Poem or Essay

• **Content/Unity.** The poem or essay offers a reaction to a photograph or piece of fine art.

• **Organization/Coherence.** The poem or essay pre-

sents the writer's response and adds supporting details in a logical order.

• **Language/Style.** The poem or essay uses vivid and precise nouns, verbs, and modifiers.

• **Conventions.** The poem or essay avoids errors in spelling, grammar, usage, mechanics, and manuscript form.

Language Lab

Building Sentences. Read the Language Arts Survey 2.36, "The Functions of Sentences." Write whether each sentence below is declarative, interrogative, or imperative.

1. About suffering they were never wrong.
2. Were the Old Masters ever wrong about suffering?
3. Consider, for example, Pieter Brueghel's painting of Icarus.
4. Isn't it odd that the ship just sails blithely on?
5. The sailors on that ship must have seen something amazing.

Test-taking Skills/Vocabulary Skills

Synonyms. Read the Language Arts Survey 4.44, "Synonym and Antonym Questions." Then read the underlined words listed below. From the choices listed after each one, choose the one most similar in meaning to the underlined word.

1. reverently—   hopefully, passionately, worshipfully, timidly
2. martyr—   prophet, follower, sufferer, rebel
3. innocent—   calculating, blameless, experienced, unknowing
4. giddy—   friendly, forceful, sick, dizzy
5. astonished—   amazed, fearful, wondering, supportive

PROJECT

Oral History. Auden's "Who's Who" raises interesting issues about the importance (or lack thereof) of fame. It asks us to consider, among other things, whether a simple, quiet life might be more engaging than one of high adventure. Histories are usually written about famous people. However, quite interesting historical writing can be done about people who are not famous, for everyone has interesting stories to tell. Choose an older person whom you know who is not famous and interview that person about his or her early life. Based on your interview, write a short biography of your subject. With your classmates, put together your own "Who's Who" of people who, though not famous, are nonetheless interesting.

ANSWERS FOR LANGUAGE LAB

1. declarative
2. interrogative
3. imperative
4. interrogative
5. declarative

FOR MORE PRACTICE

Problem. I wonder where Daedalus, Icarus's father, is.
Answer. declarative

►For additional practice, see the *Essential Skills Practice Book: Language,* 2.36.

ANSWERS FOR TEST-TAKING SKILLS/VOCABULARY SKILLS

1. worshipfully
2. sufferer
3. blameless
4. dizzy
5. amazed

FOR MORE PRACTICE

Problem. forsaken—abandoned, lost, hopeless, delinquent
Answer. abandoned

►For additional practice, see the *Essential Skills Practice Book: Study and Research,* 4.44.

PROJECT NOTES

►See the worksheets and evaluation forms for projects, *Assessment Portfolio,* 7.20–7.23.

Oral History. Students should prepare interview questions ahead of time, but they should feel free to explore other topics of interest that arise during the interview. For additional information, refer students to the Language Arts Survey, 1.27, "Interviewing." Students might send a copy of the biography they write to the interviewee.

ENRICHMENT ACTIVITIES

• The career of Stevie Smith bears a superficial resemblance to that of the American poet Emily Dickinson. Students can write short comparative biographies of the two writers based on library research.

• Students can read or perform the play *Stevie,* by Hugh Whitemore (published 1977). (Students may want to stage contrasting scenes from *The Belle of Amherst,* a play about Dickinson.)

• Whitemore also wrote the screenplay for the film *Stevie* (1978), starring Glenda Jackson. Students may be interested in obtaining this film from a library or video rental company.

SUPPORT FOR LEP STUDENTS

Explain to students that slant rhyme is rhyme that contrasts word endings that are not quite the same. Point out "moaning" and "drowning" as examples of slant rhyme from Stevie Smith's poem. Many great poets (Yeats is a good example) have exploited slant rhyme in an attempt to move away from strictly rhymed line endings. Point out to students that the pronunciation of slant rhymed words should not be altered to make the words sound more alike.

COLLOQUIALISMS

chap—a man or a boy

PREREADING

"Not Waving but Drowning"
by Stevie Smith

ABOUT THE AUTHOR

Recognition as a poet came late for **Stevie Smith** (1902–1971), whose real name was Florence Margaret Smith. Born in Yorkshire, she lived nearly all her life with an elderly aunt in a London suburb. She led a quiet life, and her wit appeared mainly in her poems and drawings. In 1923 she took a job as a secretary in a publishing firm and kept the same job for thirty years. However, for two brief periods, Stevie Smith was famous. In the 1930s, she became well known for her *Novel on Yellow Paper* (1936) and also had some poems published. Then in the 1960s, after the publication of her collection of poems *Not Waving but Drowning,* Smith became a popular British radio personality and gained new recognition as a contemporary poet. Originality and a strong feminist outlook made her a popular figure in London, where she read and chanted her poems on stage. Smith was given the Gold Medal for Poetry in 1969 by Queen Elizabeth II. After her death, a play and a movie were produced about her career.

ABOUT THE SELECTION

Stevie Smith writes in a conversational style, looking at everyday unhappiness in a wry, unsentimental way. Unlike most of her contemporaries, she did not go to university or become part of any literary group but instead developed her voice on her own. One critic says that she wrote in three voices: little girl, lonely and cynical woman, and skeptical philosopher. The mood changes quickly from solemnity to humor. Stevie Smith's most famous poem, **"Not Waving but Drowning,"** is the title of a collection of poems and drawings published in 1957. The poem itself was written in 1953, and its black humor reflects the poet's deep depression at the time.

GOALS/OBJECTIVES

Studying this lesson will enable students to

• empathize with the drowning man's isolation and helplessness

• describe Stevie Smith's literary accomplishments and explain the historical significance of her writings

• define *figurative language* and *irony* and recognize these devices in a poem

• insert italics and quotation marks as necessary in their writing

• write a monologue or dialogue

"Not Waving but Drowning"

STEVIE SMITH

Nobody heard him, the dead man,
But still he lay moaning:
I was much further out than you thought
And not waving but drowning.

5   Poor chap, he always loved larking[1]
And now he's dead
It must have been too cold for him his heart gave way,
They said.

Oh, no no no, it was too cold always
10   (Still the dead one lay moaning)
I was much too far out all my life
And not waving but drowning. ∎

---
1. **larking.** Kidding around, having fun

❶
What do people say happened to the man?

❷
How does the man respond?

RESPONDING TO THE SELECTION

Students can imagine they are therapists or counselors trying to help the person communicate his problems to family members or friends who are unaware he feels lonely and is in pain.

ANSWERS FOR
REVIEWING THE SELECTION

RECALLING

1. The two voices are a man who has drowned and an unspecified group of others referred to as "they."

2. "They" claim that the man's heart gave way due to the cold while he was having a good time fooling around.

INTERPRETING

Responses will vary. Possible responses are given.

3. The tone of the man is one of pain and self-pity; the word "moaning" suggests this. The tone of the people is one of somewhat callous indifference; the words "poor chap" suggest this.

4. The drowned man explains that he was struggling in the water all alone too far out, not having fun or fooling around, but actually signaling for help.

SYNTHESIZING

Responses will vary.

5. The man may have been too lonely and isolated from others. The "it" might have been his life or his relationships with others.

ANSWERS FOR
UNDERSTANDING LITERATURE

▶ See the evaluation forms for discussion, active listening, and oral communication, *Assessment Portfolio, 7.11–7.14.*

Responses will vary. Possible responses are given.

1. Figurative Language. A person may suffer from depression or isolation after experiencing a loss, for instance, and conceal his or her problem from others until the problem reaches a point where it seems insoluble. A person also might act cheerful out of a desire not to burden others, and so never indicate his or her pain. Others

(cont.)

Responding to the Selection

Who is misunderstood in this poem? How do you think this person is feeling? What might you tell others about how this person is feeling? Freewrite your thoughts about these questions and the poem.

Reviewing the Selection

RECALLING

1. Who are the two voices that speak in this poem?

2. In stanza 2, how do "they" explain what happened?

INTERPRETING

3. What is the tone, or emotional attitude, displayed by both voices in the poem? What words and phrases create this tone?

4. What is the explanation of what happened? Who gives this explanation?

SYNTHESIZING

5. How might this man have been "too far out" all of his life? What might be the "it" that was always too cold?

Understanding Literature (Questions for Discussion)

1. **Figurative Language.** **Figurative language** is language that suggests something more than the literal meanings of the words might be taken to suggest. This man's distress signal was misinterpreted, and he drowned. What are the different ways in which a person might be misunderstood and caused to drown in everyday life? What are the ways in which people's feelings and situations are routinely misinterpreted? What are the ways in which one's surroundings might be "cold"?

2. **Irony.** **Irony** is a difference between appearance and reality. What is ironic about the attitude of the "they" in stanza 2 of the poem? Is the title ironic? How?

ANSWERS FOR UNDERSTANDING LITERATURE (CONT.)

may be too busy or preoccupied to notice, or may underestimate the magnitude of the problems involved. One's surroundings may be "cold" if one feels one does not receive attention, interest, or response from others.

▶**Teaching Note:** The saying "laugh and the world laughs with you, cry and you cry alone" reflects the popular notion that the world pays no attention to suffering. Smith's success lies in finding a new kind of

figurative language, providing a fresh, wry formulation of what could well have been a stale restatement of an old theme.

2. **Irony.** The attitude of the observers referred to as "they" is ironic because they believe the dead man was having fun up to the instant he died; the dead man points out that he was never having fun. The title is ironic; it reflects the drowning man's insistence that he

(cont.)

Responding in Writing

1. **Fable.** Critics have compared Stevie Smith's writing to nursery rhymes and fables (brief stories told to teach). Think of an adult topic for a fable or a simple verse like a nursery rhyme—perhaps something you've often been warned not to do or told you should do—and write your own fable or nursery rhyme.

2. **Monologue/Dialogue.** Pieces like "Not Waving but Drowning" which feature only one or two characters and a single incident can be surprisingly complex and powerful. Many contemporary plays are written as monologues or dialogues. Think of a crisis situation involving one or two actors (for instance, one person on the telephone or two people at a fast-food restaurant). Write a short monologue or dialogue based on the situation and characters you have chosen. Make sure that your piece deals with some conflict or struggle. Use specific details to reveal character. Read your work aloud to make sure that it sounds like real speech.

Language Lab

Proofreading. Read the Language Arts Survey, 2.103, 2.104, and 2.105, "Underlining and Italics" and "Quotation Marks I and II." Revise the sentences below as needed to correct errors in those forms of punctuation. If the punctuation is correct, write *OK*.

1. The heroine of Stevie Smith's first novels, *Novel on Yellow Paper* and "Over the Frontier", is much like the writer herself.

2. Her first book of poetry was called A Good Time Was Had by All.

3. After World War II ended, Stevie began to give public readings of her "poems," sometimes chanting them to the tunes of hymns or "folk songs."

4. Stevie's poem "Thoughts about the Person from Porlock refers to the person who interrupted the poet Coleridge as he was writing his famous poem *Kubla Khan.*

5. The Frog Prince is the best-known poem in Smith's popular 1966 collection of verse.

ADDITIONAL RESOURCES

READER'S GUIDE
• Selection Worksheet, 10.13

ASSESSMENT PORTFOLIO
• Selection Check Test, 4.10.25
• Selection Test, 4.10.26

ESSENTIAL SKILLS PRACTICE BOOKS
• *Language,* 2.32

ENRICHMENT ACTIVITIES

To understand the poem, students need two pieces of information: background on the thistle plant and the outlines of the story of Jason in Greek mythology. They can find pictures of and information about thistles in nature guides, flower identification handbooks, or encyclopedias. The thistle, while beautiful, is a particularly noxious weed, difficult to kill. One of its peculiar characteristics is that after a certain stage of development it can go to seed and reproduce successfully even after it has been mown. The story of Jason's sowing of the dragon's teeth and the warriors that sprang up from the teeth as if they were seed can be found in mythology books.

SUPPORT FOR LEP STUDENTS

Explain to students that for centuries in the Middle Ages the British Isles underwent constant invasion by Vikings, a warlike people who lived in northern Europe and in Iceland. The Vikings were known for their pale, or blond, hair; their Germanic speech is commonly viewed as guttural, that is, as including many sounds produced deep in the throat. In the poem, Hughes imagines that thistles rise up from the bodies of Vikings buried under the ground. This information will allow students to understand many of the references in the poem. For information on dialects, refer students to the Language Arts Survey, 2.150, "Dialects of English."

(cont.)

PREREADING

"Thistles"
by Ted Hughes

ABOUT THE AUTHOR

Ted Hughes (1930–) was born in Mytholmroyd, a milltown in Yorkshire. The experience of growing up in a milltown shaped the unsentimental and often violent view of life that Hughes expresses in his poetry; his dialect, native to the West Riding area of Yorkshire, establishes the vocabulary and tone in his poetry. Another vital influence on Hughes's verse was his early introduction to the poetry of D. H. Lawrence. In 1954, Hughes earned a bachelor's degree at Cambridge, where he read widely in anthropology, mythology, and folklore. While at Cambridge, he met the American poet Sylvia Plath, whom he married in 1956. In 1957, Hughes published his first volume of poetry, *The Hawk in the Rain,* which won immediate critical acclaim. The volume introduced readers to many of the themes characteristic of his work, primarily the violence found in nature and in legend. His second volume, *Lupercal,* was published in 1960. Subsequent volumes include *Wodwo,* a collection of stories, verse, and prose poems; *Crow; Selected Poems: 1957–1967; Season Songs; Cave Birds; Moortown; Under the North Star* (poems for children); and *What Is the Truth?* Considered one of the most individual poetic voices in England since Dylan Thomas, Hughes remarried in 1970 and lives in London. In 1984, he was appointed poet laureate.

ABOUT THE SELECTION

"Thistles" is from the volume *New Selected Poems,* published in 1982. The selection shows many of the elements characteristic of Hughes's work—violence of feeling, vivid and concrete images of nature and animals, direct vocabulary, and surprising meter and rhyme. Also characteristic is the pessimistic, yet vital, point of view toward the human condition.

SUPPORT FOR LEP STUDENTS (CONT.)

ADDITIONAL VOCABULARY

resurrection—rising from the dead, or coming back to life

guttural—characterized by harsh, rasping sounds made in the throat

dialect—form or variety of a spoken language peculiar to a region, community, etc.

GOALS/OBJECTIVES

Studying this lesson will enable students to

• appreciate the fierce tenacity projected by the speaker onto his subject

• define *oxymoron* and *cæsura* and recognize the use of these devices in a poem

• write a free verse poem

"Thistles"

TED HUGHES

Against the rubber tongues of cows and the hoeing hands of men
Thistles spike the summer air
Or crackle open under a blue-black pressure.

5   Every one a revengeful burst
Of resurrection, a grasped fistful
Of splintered weapons and Icelandic frost thrust up

From the underground stain of a decayed Viking.
They are like pale hair and the gutturals of dialects.
Every one manages a plume of blood.

10 Then they grow gray, like men.
Mown down, it is a feud. Their sons appear,
Stiff with weapons, fighting back over the same ground.

❶
According to the poem, what is each thistle?

❷
What happens to the thistles? What appears in their place? What sort of "battle" is taking place?

ANSWERS FOR REVIEWING THE SELECTION

RECALLING

1. The thistles are fighting against "the rubber tongues of cows and the hoeing hands of men."

2. Thistles "spike" it, that is, stab into it, or "crackle open" to disgorge their seed.

3. They reappear like revengeful Vikings with fistfuls of weapons.

4. They "grow gray" like old men.

INTERPRETING

Responses will vary. Possible responses are given.

5. The thistles' opponents are both susceptible to the thistles' prickles.

6. The words "blue-black" suggest a wound of some kind.

7. The image suggests that nature resurrects itself to fight again even when "slain."

8. The sons of the thistles appear to fight back.

SYNTHESIZING

Responses will vary. Possible responses are given.

9. Nature has its powerful renewing energies, which ensure that plants such as the thistle reproduce no matter what humankind does.

10. Neither side really wins in the poem; the battle simply continues. The reader can conclude that the battle will be perpetual.

Responding to the Selection

Imagine that you are the speaker in this poem. In your journal, write your feelings about thistles. Express what you admire about the prickly plant as related in the poem. You may wish to express your feelings in a poem.

Reviewing the Selection

RECALLING

1. What are the thistles fighting against?

2. What do the thistles do in the "summer air"?

3. How do thistles reappear in stanza 2?

4. How do the thistles "grow gray"?

INTERPRETING

5. What do the thistles'"opponents" have in common?

6. What human thing might also be described as crackling "open under a blue-black pressure"?

7. What does this image suggest about the ability of human beings to battle nature?

8. What evidence at the end of the poem suggests the thistles' renewal?

SYNTHESIZING

9. What power do thistles, or nature, have that human beings, or civilization, cannot completely conquer?

10. Which side wins the battle in the poem? What conclusion can the reader or listener draw about the battle?

Understanding Literature (Questions for Discussion)

1. **Image.** An **image** is a word or phrase that names something that can be seen, heard, touched, tasted, or smelled. What concrete images in the poem are particularly powerful and vivid? What emotions or feelings are created by these images?

ANSWERS FOR UNDERSTANDING LITERATURE

Responses will vary. Possible responses are given.

▶ See the evaluation forms for discussion, active listening, and oral communication, *Assessment Portfolio*, 7.11–7.14.

1. **Image.** Vivid images include cow tongues as made of rubber, hands as hoes, fistfuls of splintered weapons, a -flower as a plume of blood, and the thistles going to seed and turning white. Many of the images are violent and reflect a warlike relationship between nature and humans.

▶ **Teaching Note:** Bring to the class a dried or living thistle plant or a photograph so that the students can appreciate the accuracy of Hughes's imagery.

2. **Oxymoron.** The phrase suggests that new life is born out of an impulse to "get back at" those who have killed the previous generation. The phrase reflects the violence inherent in the tone of the poem.

(cont.)

2. **Oxymoron.** An **oxymoron** is a statement that contradicts itself. In the poem, the phrase "a revengeful burst/Of resurrection" is an oxymoron. What does it suggest about new life? How does this oxymoron reflect the tone of the poem?

3. **Cæsura.** A **cæsura** is a major pause in a line of poetry. Writers use cæsuras for effect and to vary the rhythm of the line. Lines 4–7 contain three cæsuras. What effect do they create? How do they alter the rhythm of the stanza? of the poem?

Responding in Writing

Free Verse Poem. Free verse is poetry that avoids use of regular rhyme, rhythm, meter, or division into stanzas. Consider the following lines from the poem:

> Against the rubber tongues of cows and the hoeing hands of men
> Thistles spike the summer air
> Or crackle open under a blue-black pressure.

These lines describe two of the foes against which thistles fight for survival and renewal. Write a free verse poem about renewal from the thistles' point of view. In your poem, use concrete language and images to express the thistles' attitude toward life, death, and renewal.

ANSWERS FOR UNDERSTANDING LITERATURE (CONT.)

▶ **Teaching Note:** Have students create an oxymoron from each of the following words in the poem: "pressure," "weapons," "frost," "feud." *Answers.* Welcoming pressure, tender weapons, boiling frost, cooperative feud.

3. Cæsura. The cæsuras occur after "resurrection," "weapons," and "stain." They make the rhythm mimic the breaking action described in the poem. They slow the rhythm of the stanza and the poem.

▶ **Teaching Note:** Point out that cæsura is effective in verse that follows a regular meter; the pause in sense can be used to work against the flow created by the expected rhythm. Thus the power of Milton's opening to *Paradise Lost:* "Of man's first disobedience, and the fruit/Of that forbidden tree, whose mortal taste . . ." (page 429).

ADDITIONAL RESOURCES

READER'S GUIDE
• Selection Worksheet, 10.14

ASSESSMENT PORTFOLIO
• Selection Check Test, 4.10.27
• Selection Test, 4.10.28

ESSENTIAL SKILLS PRACTICE BOOKS
• *Language,* 2.6–2.9
• *Study and Research,* 4.31

ENRICHMENT ACTIVITIES

• Students can arrange for a visit from a representative of a local organization (such as a branch of Oxfam America) that is working to end world hunger.

• Students can bake a loaf of bread and serve it before giving a reading of the poem.

SUPPORT FOR LEP STUDENTS

Point out that in this selection, each break in the text indicates a shift to another manner of considering the subject, bread. Alert students to the loose connection between the sections of the poem so that they will not be looking for a continuation of thought that is not there. Suggest that students look upon the piece as a connected essay about bread that offers three examples of new ways to look at the subject.

ADDITIONAL VOCABULARY

bloated—swollen

scavenger—one who gathers or collects waste

PREREADING

"Bread"
by Margaret Atwood

ABOUT THE AUTHOR

Although she first became famous as a poet, Canadian writer **Margaret Atwood** (1939–) is also well known for her intense, ironic, and sometimes disturbing novels and stories, such as *Surfacing* (1972), *The Handmaid's Tale* (1986), and *Cat's Eye* (1988). She grew up in Ottawa and Toronto, Ontario, but came to know the Canadian wilderness during summers spent in northern Quebec. She graduated from the University of Toronto and received a master's degree at Radcliffe (Cambridge, MA) in 1962.

Her first book of poetry, *The Circle Game*, won a Governor General's Award in 1966, and she has won many other awards since. Atwood's writing probes varied subjects, including male-female relationships, the Canadian pioneer spirit, the influence of myth, and international human rights. Atwood is also an editor and critic; in a critical study of Canadian literature, she suggested that survival has been the dominant theme in Canadian writing.

ABOUT THE SELECTION

Atwood's poetry is often short, terse, written in everyday language, and filled with sharp or witty observations. Her longer, interconnected poems, like her novels, are rich with symbolism and irony. **"Bread"** is a prose poem taken from *Murder in the Dark*, a 1984 collection of short experimental pieces. Like several other works, including the novel *Bodily Harm* (1981) and the poem "Notes Towards a Poem That Can Never Be Written," this poem reflects her personal concern with human rights abuses and repression everywhere.

GOALS/OBJECTIVES

Studying this lesson will enable students to

• share the speaker's intense feelings of social concern as expressed in the poem

• describe Margaret Atwood's literary accomplishments and explain the historical significance of her writings

• classify pronouns

• define *prose poem* and *tone* and identify each in their reading

• write a personal essay and a play script

READER'S JOURNAL

Think about one thing you had for breakfast or lunch. Now quickly freewrite a spontaneous description of this food, giving your first thoughts and feelings about it as it is set in front of you.

RESEARCH SKILLS

Read the Language Arts Survey, 4.31, "Informal Note-taking." Then consult an anthology of Canadian writing (such as *The New Oxford Book of Canadian Verse in English*, which Atwood edited). In a notebook, compile a rough list of ten Canadian writers of the twentieth century. From this list create a literary map by drawing a map of Canada and locating each writer at a place associated with him or her.

"Bread"

MARGARET ATWOOD

Imagine a piece of bread. You don't have to imagine it, it's right here in the kitchen, on the bread board, in its plastic bag, lying beside the bread knife. The bread knife is an old one you picked up at an auction; it has the word BREAD carved into the wooden handle. You open the bag, pull back the wrapper, cut yourself a slice. You put butter on it, then peanut butter, then honey, and you fold it over. Some of the honey runs out onto your fingers and you lick it off. It takes you about a minute to eat the bread. This bread happens to be brown, but there is also white bread, in the refrigerator, and a heel of rye you got last week, round as a full stomach then, now going mouldy. Occasionally you make bread. You think of it as something relaxing to do with your hands.

♦ ♦ ♦

Imagine a famine. Now imagine a piece of bread. Both of these things are real but you happen to be in the same room with only one of them. Put yourself into a different room, that's what the mind is for. You are now lying on a thin mattress in a hot room. The walls are made of dried earth and your sister, who is younger than you are, is in the room with you. She is starving, her belly is bloated, flies land on her eyes; you brush them off with your hand. You have a cloth too, filthy but damp, and you press it to her lips and forehead. The piece of bread is the bread you've been saving, for days it seems. You are as hungry as she is, but not yet as weak. How long does this take? When will someone come with more bread? You think of going out to see if you might find something that could be eaten, but outside the streets are <u>infested</u> with scavengers and the stink of corpses is everywhere.

❶ What does bread mean to the person in the first paragraph? What does bread mean to the person in the second paragraph?

WORDS FOR EVERYDAY USE: in • fest (in fest ´) vt., overrun in large numbers

READER'S JOURNAL

As an alternative to the activity suggested, give out some kind of simple, staple food (crackers, for example) and have students freewrite on it. Afterward, students can share in class the reactions they have written down.

RESEARCH SKILLS

When the students have drawn their maps, they should write a brief summary describing any geographical patterns they see in it. Do writers tend to cluster, for instance, around Montreal or Toronto? By comparing the maps of other class members, they can see whether their sampling of Canadian writers is indicative of a general trend in location.

ANSWER TO GUIDED READING QUESTION

❶ Bread is something pleasant that is taken for granted by the person in the first paragraph. For the person in the second paragraph, bread is both a link with life and the cause of a terrible moral dilemma.

VOCABULARY FROM THE SELECTION

conjure	subversive
dupe	treacherous
infest	

VOCABULARY IN CONTEXT

• After the math exam, Gilbert dreamed that his bed was <u>infested</u> with real numbers that crawled under his pajamas and made him itch.

❶ When the sister's husband cut himself a slice of bread, blood flowed from the cut.

❷ The yellow bowl held apples and pears. It was in the home. It means food, home, and all the good things the person in prison does not have.

❸ The bread has more meaning for the reader by the last paragraph. The writer claims that the reader will no longer be interested in eating the bread.

ADDITIONAL QUESTIONS
AND ACTIVITIES

Students can write a paragraph in their journals in answer to the speaker's question in the second paragraph: "Should you share the bread or give the whole piece to your sister? Should you eat the piece of bread yourself?" Remind students to explain their reasoning.

ANSWERS TO SELECTION
CHECK TEST 4.10.27

EX. What is the first thing the speaker asks the reader to imagine?

The speaker asks the reader to imagine a piece of bread.

1. What decision does the famine victim have to make?

She has to decide whether to give the bread to her sister, share it with her sister, or eat it herself.

2. What memory does the bread bring back to the prisoner?

It brings back the memory of a yellow bowl.

3. What happened when the husband of the rich sister cut the bread?

When he cut the bread, blood flowed out.

4. What does the speaker say this story is?

The speaker says that it is a "traditional German fairy-tale."

5. Where is the bread in the last section?

It is floating above the kitchen table.

---

❶ What happened as a result of the sister's selfishness?

❷ What did the yellow bowl hold? Where was the yellow bowl? What does it mean to the person in prison?

❸ By the last paragraph, does a loaf of bread hold more meaning for the reader? How does the author show this?

Should you share the bread or give the whole piece to your sister? Should you eat the piece of bread yourself? After all, you have a better chance of living, you're stronger. How long does it take to decide?

◆　◆　◆

Imagine a prison. There is something you know that you have not yet told. Those in control of the prison know that you know. So do those not in control. If you tell, thirty or forty or a hundred of your friends, your comrades, will be caught and will die. If you refuse to tell, tonight will be like last night. They always choose the night. You don't think about the night however, but about the piece of bread they offered you. How long does it take? The piece of bread was brown and fresh and reminded you of sunlight falling across a wooden floor. It reminded you of a bowl, a yellow bowl that was once in your home. It held apples and pears; it stood on a table you can also remember. It's not the hunger or the pain that is killing you but the absence of the yellow bowl. If you could only hold the bowl in your hands, right here, you could withstand anything, you tell yourself. The bread they offered you is <u>subversive</u>, it's <u>treacherous</u>, it does not mean life.

◆　◆　◆

There were once two sisters. One was rich and had no children, the other had five children and was a widow, so poor that she no longer had any food left. She went to her sister and asked her for a mouthful of bread. 'My children are dying,' she said. The rich sister said, 'I do not have enough for myself,' and drove her away from the door. Then the husband of the rich sister came home and wanted to cut himself a piece of bread; but when he made the first cut, out flowed red blood.

Everyone knew what that meant.

This is a traditional German fairy-tale.

◆　◆　◆

The loaf of bread I have <u>conjured</u> for you floats about a foot above your kitchen table. The table is normal, there are no trap doors in it. A blue tea towel floats beneath the bread, and there are no strings attaching the cloth to the bread or the bread to the ceiling or the table to the cloth, you've proved it by passing your hand above and below. You didn't touch the bread though. What stopped you? You don't want to know whether the bread is real or whether it's just a hallucination I've somehow <u>duped</u> you into seeing. There's no doubt that you can see the bread, you can even smell it, it smells like yeast, and it looks solid enough, solid as your own arm. But can you trust it? Can you eat it? You don't want to know, imagine that. ■

WORDS FOR
EVERYDAY USE:

sub • ver • sive (səb vʉr´ siv) *adj.*, with a goal to undermine or corrupt

treach • er • ous (trech´ ər əs) *adj.*, traitorous, disloyal

con • jure (kun´ jər) *vt.*, make appear as by magic

dupe (doop) *vt.*, deceive by trickery

VOCABULARY IN CONTEXT

- The king of Lunonia cracked down harshly on people who insulted his mustache, as well as other elements of the population that he considered dangerous and <u>subversive</u>.
- The <u>treacherous</u> goalie let the soccer ball into the goal without attempting to stop it, and his team lost the championship.
- A truly great poet can <u>conjure</u> a golden world out of a hatful of ordinary words.
- When threatened by the evil genie, the girl <u>duped</u> him into returning to his bottle.

Responding to the Selection

> How do you feel about this poem? Why do you think Atwood chose to write about bread? What thoughts come to your own mind as you think about bread? Record your thoughts in your journal.

Reviewing the Selection

RECALLING

1. What are the setting and events of paragraph 1?

2. How does the scene change in paragraph 2? What happens there?

3. What is the setting of paragraph 3? What is happening there?

4. What does the writer challenge "you"—the reader—to do in the last paragraph?

INTERPRETING

▶▶ 5. What mood, or atmosphere, is Atwood trying to create in paragraph 1? What words and phrases create a picture of abundance?

▶▶ 6. How does Atwood use the bread to link paragraphs 1 and 2 in the reader's mind?

▶▶ 7. What is the significance of the yellow bowl in paragraph 3?

▶▶ 8. By the last paragraph, what has the speaker managed to do to the reader's perception of bread?

SYNTHESIZING

9. How does the speaker manipulate "you"—the reader—throughout the poem?

10. Both the first and final paragraphs are set in an ordinary kitchen. What has happened to the loaf of bread by the final paragraph? How has it changed in the reader's mind?

Understanding Literature (Questions for Discussion)

1. **Prose Poem.** A **prose poem** is a work of prose, usually a short work, that makes such extensive use of poetic language, such as figures of speech and words that echo their sense, that the line between prose and poetry, never a clear one, becomes blurred. Unlike conventional poetry, prose poems are usually written in paragraph form, with no formal rhyme or meter. They still have other characteristics that set them apart from ordinary prose, including the use of rich imagery, metaphor, repetition, and indirect or

"BREAD" **899**

ANSWERS FOR UNDERSTANDING LITERATURE

►See the evaluation forms for discussion, active listening, and oral communication, *Assessment Portfolio*, 7.11–7.14.

Responses will vary. Possible responses are given.

1. Prose Poem. Most of the sensory images in the first paragraph are visual: the word carved into the handle of the knife, the honey running onto your fingers, the brownness of the bread, and the moldy heel of rye in the refrigerator. If "Bread" were written as "pure prose," it would probably be more tightly connected from paragraph to paragraph. If it were written as "pure poetry," it would probably be more lyrical.

►**Teaching Notes**
• To help students contrast the prose poem of Atwood with other poetry, provide them with one of the other poems in this unit, such as Auden's "Musée des Beaux Arts," transcribed in prose-paragraph format.
• The element of lyricism in Atwood's piece is actually rather sparse. Have students take five or six sentences of the work and rewrite them as "pure poetry," trying to increase the lyricism of the sentences through the use of richer imagery, metaphor, repetition, and indirect or implied meanings.

2. Tone. Another way in which the speaker tries to manipulate the reader is by asking direct questions: "How long does this take? When will someone come with more bread? . . . Should you share the bread or give the whole piece to your sister? Should you eat the piece of bread yourself? . . . How long does it take to decide?" The reader has no way of answering these questions.

►**Teaching Note:** Ask students how they feel about the tone of the poem. Is it provocative, irritating, galvanizing, or does it have little effect on them? Would the poem be more or less effective if it had a different tone? Have them offer evidence from the poem in support of statements they make about their reactions.

implied meanings. Look for these characteristics in "Bread." For example, what kind of sensory images can you find in the first paragraph? Discuss how "Bread" might be different if it were written as "pure prose" or "pure poetry."

2. **Tone. Tone** is the emotional attitude toward the reader or toward the subject implied by a literary work. The speaker in "Bread" is teasing or manipulating the reader throughout. One way of doing this is to write in the direct second-person—calling the reader "you." Look through "Bread" to find other ways in which the speaker is challenging or teasing.

Responding in Writing

1. **Personal Essay.** Look back at what you wrote about a specific food in your journal entry for "Reader's Journal." Take the same idea, or think of a different ordinary food or object, and jot down additional thoughts and descriptive details about it. Then organize your notes into a personal essay describing what your relationship is with this food, or what it symbolizes, or what ideas you associate with it.

2. **Play Script.** Read the separate paragraphs or sections of "Bread" as five different scenes in a play. Use Atwood's ideas and words to create a script for this play, describing the setting and characters and creating dialogue. You may want to use Atwood's words as part of a monologue or dialogue or create some new dialogue for each scene.

Language Lab

Pronouns. Read the Language Arts Survey, 2.6, "Personal Pronouns"; 2.7, "Reflexive and Intensive Pronouns"; 2.8, "Demonstrative Pronouns"; and 2.9, "Indefinite Pronouns." Then identify all the pronouns in the following sentences, taken from "Bread." After each pronoun, write *P* (Personal), *R* (Reflexive/Intensive), *D* (Demonstrative), or *I* (Indefinite).

1. You put butter on it, then peanut butter, then honey, and you fold it over.

2. Both of these things are real but you happen to be in the same room with only one of them.

3. How long does this take? When will someone come with more bread?

4. Should you eat the piece of bread yourself?

5. How long does it take to decide?

ANSWERS FOR LANGUAGE LAB

1. You [P]; it [P]; you [P]; it [P]
2. these [D]; you [P]; them [P] (Note that the word *one* is used as a noun.)
3. this [D]; someone [I]
4. you [P]; yourself [R]
5. it [P]

►For additional practice, see the *Essential Skills Practice Book: Language*, 2.6–2.9.

ANALYTIC SCALES FOR RESPONDING IN WRITING

Grading scales appear on page 911.

PREREADING

"Naked Girl and Mirror"
by Judith Wright

ABOUT THE AUTHOR

Judith Wright (1915–) was born in Armidale, Australia. After graduating from the University of Sydney, Wright worked in an advertising agency. Later she was employed as a secretary for the University of Sydney, a clerk in Brisbane, and a statistician. In 1946, Wright published her first volume of poetry, *The Moving Image.* Three years later, Wright began lecturing part-time at various universities in Australia and published her second volume of poetry, *Woman to Man.* Her first two volumes of poetry were followed by *The Gateway; The Two Fires; City Sunrise; The Nature of Love,* a collection of short stories; *Collected Poems 1942–1970;* and *The Double Tree,* an updated selection of Wright's poetry. In addition to poetry, she has written literary criticism, children's books, a biography of the Australian poet Charles Harpur, a book on the Australian short story writer Charles Lawson, and a book on her pioneering grandparents' settlement in Australia. Wright is one of Australia's best-known poets.

ABOUT THE SELECTION

"Naked Girl and Mirror" shows Wright's exploration of the dynamics of human and biological relationships. Characteristic of Wright's work, the exploration into the mysteries of those relationships is progressive and thoroughly modern in idiom. The selection also shows Wright's skill in poetic techniques, such as rhyme and meter, for which she is noted.

ENRICHMENT ACTIVITIES

Students can search anthologies of women's and men's poetry to find other poems about the attitudes of the sexes toward their respective physical forms. They should write a brief summary comparing and contrasting the views expressed in the poems they locate with the attitude expressed by the speaker of "Naked Girl and Mirror."

SUPPORT FOR LEP STUDENTS

Explain to students the basic premise of the poem: a young woman is looking into a mirror and speaking to the image she sees there as if it were someone else.

ADDITIONAL VOCABULARY
tentatively—experimentally
brimming—filling with tears
immoderate—extreme
arrogance—excessive pride or self-centeredness

GOALS/OBJECTIVES

Studying this lesson will enable the student to

- experience the speaker's feelings of ambivalence about her transition into adulthood
- describe Judith Wright's literary accomplishments and explain the historical significance of her writings
- explain the self-revelatory nature of much modern poetry
- define *confessional poetry* and give examples of it

Australia

"Naked Girl and Mirror"

Jᴜᴅɪᴛʜ Wʀɪɢʜᴛ

ANSWERS TO GUIDED READING QUESTIONS

❶ In her childhood, the speaker was not conscious of her body and she was carefree. She now feels trapped in her soft face.

❷ The speaker feels suspicious of and estranged from her body. Her body pleads with her to accept her new body and merge with it completely rather than feel estranged from it.

❸ If a person danced on a bough, it might break, causing injury.

❶
What was the speaker like in her childhood? How has she changed?

❷
How does the speaker feel about her new body? What does her new body plead with her to do?

❸
What might happen to a person who danced on a bough?

This is not I. I had no body once—
only what served my need to laugh and run
and stare at stars and tentatively dance
on the fringe of foam and wave and sand and sun.
5   Eyes loved, hands reached for me, but I was gone
on my own currents, quicksilver, thistledown.
Can I be trapped at last in that soft face?

I stare at you in fear, dark brimming eyes.
Why do you watch me with that immoderate plea—
10 "Look under these curled lashes, recognize
that you were always here; know me—be me."
Smooth once-<u>hermaphrodite</u> shoulders, too tenderly
your long slope runs, above those sudden shy
curves furred with light that spring below your space.

15 No, I have been betrayed. If I had known
that this girl waited between a year and a year,
I'd not have chosen her bough to dance upon.
Betrayed, by that little darkness here, and here
this swelling softness and that frightened stare

Wᴏʀᴅs ꜰᴏʀ Eᴠᴇʀʏᴅᴀʏ Usᴇ: **her • maph • ro • dite** (hər mafʹro dīt´) *adj.,* with both male and female characteristics

VOCABULARY IN CONTEXT
• Some <u>hermaphrodite</u> gods are represented as having characteristics of both sexes.

The Mirror. Thomas Wilmer Dewing, circa 1907. Courtesy of the Freer Gallery of Art, Smithsonian Institution, Washington, DC

20   from eyes I will not answer; shut out here
         from my own self, by its new body's grace—

         for I am betrayed by someone lovely. Yes,
         I see you are lovely, hateful naked girl.
         Your lips in the mirror tremble as I refuse
25   to know or claim you. Let me go—let me be gone.
         You are half of some other who may never come.
         Why should I tend you? You are not my own;
         you seek that other—he will be your home.

         Yet I pity your eyes in the mirror, misted with tears;
30   I lean to your kiss. I must serve you; I will obey.
         Some day we may love. I may miss your going, some day,
         though I shall always resent your dumb and fruitful years.
         Your lovers shall learn better, and bitterly too,
         if their arrogance dares to think I am part of you. ■

❶
How does the speaker view her "self" in relation to her body?

ADDITIONAL QUESTIONS AND ACTIVITIES

Students may want to explore the idea of growth and change in a positive way. They can write in their journals an expressive piece, either poetry or prose, in which they celebrate the growth and change of the body from birth to death.

ANSWERS TO SELECTION CHECK TEST 4.10.29

EX. What was the speaker's body once?
The speaker's body was once only what she needed to laugh and run.

1. How does the speaker describe her motion?
She says she moved like quicksilver or thistledown.

2. How does the speaker stare at her reflection?
She stares at it in fear.

3. What would the speaker not have chosen if she had known that "this girl waited" better?
She would not have chosen that girl's bough to dance upon.

4. Who has betrayed the speaker?
Someone lovely has betrayed the speaker.

5. How does the narrator respond to the eyes misted with tears in the mirror?
The narrator pities the eyes in the mirror.

ANSWERS FOR REVIEWING THE SELECTION

1. The speaker says that the body in the mirror is not she.

2. The speaker fears that her body has grown up.

3. The speaker reads a plea from her body to recognize that body as the speaker's self.

4. Facts that emphasize the shift include once-hermaphrodite shoulders that now have a too tender, long slope and are above "sudden shy curves formed with light."

5. The speaker asks, "Why should I tend you?" and says that this body is not her own.

6. The speaker cites "that little darkness here" (line 18), "this swelling softness" (line 19), "that frightened stare" (line 19), and her new loveliness (lines 22–23).

7. The speaker pities her new body.

8. The speaker decides to accept her new body and says that "someday we may love" and that "I may miss your going, someday."

9. She probably means that this womanly body of the kind that is the object of romantic love is not her essential self and that any future mate should realize that.

10. The speaker seems to feel that her new body is foreign, a usurper, and that her self is now trapped inside it.

Reviewing the Selection

1. What matter-of-fact statement does the speaker make in stanza 1?

2. What does the speaker fear her body has done?

3. What plea does the speaker read in her "dark brimming eyes"?

4. What facts in stanza 2 emphasize the speaker's physical shift from a young girl's body to a young woman's body?

5. What question does the speaker ask of her "new body" in stanza 4?

6. What physical evidence does the speaker give to support her feelings of betrayal?

7. What does the speaker pity in the last stanza?

8. What response does the speaker decide to take toward her "new" body?

9. What does the speaker probably mean in the last two lines of the poem?

10. What sort of relationship between the speaker's "old body" and "new body" is described in this poem? How does that relationship affect the speaker's view of her "self"?

Connections (Questions for Writing or Discussion)

1. Much contemporary poetry, like Judith Wright's "Naked Girl and Mirror," deals with moments of self-revelation or insight, often ones that are psychologically challenging or wrenching. Consider Wright's poem in relation to D. H. Lawrence's "Snake." In each poem, what issue does the speaker confront? What does each speaker learn about himself or herself?

2. Modern so-called **confessional poetry** often deals with the private experiences had by people as they were growing up. What other poem in this unit deals directly with intense experiences from childhood? What personal experiences from childhood are described in each poem?

ANSWERS FOR CONNECTIONS

1. In Wright's poem, the speaker confronts her emerging woman's body, reluctant to let go of her girl's body, which she identifies with her essential self. In Lawrence's poem, the speaker confronts a pettiness in himself that fears the primitive, instinctive natural forces. In the former poem, the speaker learns that her essential self and her body are different things. In the latter poem, the speaker learns that he wishes to get rid of, or expiate, his pettiness.

(cont.)

ANSWERS FOR CONNECTIONS (CONT.)

2. The other poem in the unit that deals directly with intense feelings from childhood is Stephen Spender's "Rough." In "Rough," the speaker describes being teased by rough children during his childhood and longing to be accepted by them. In "Naked Girl and Mirror," the speaker describes carefree times from childhood when she was not at all conscious of even having a body, times when she would "laugh and run/and stare at stares and tentatively dance/on the fringe of foam and wave and sand and sun."

PREREADING

"Map of the New World"
by Derek Walcott

ABOUT THE AUTHOR

The 1992 Nobel Prize for literature went to West Indian poet and playwright **Derek Walcott** (1930–). Born on the island of St. Lucia in the Caribbean, he attended the University of the West Indies in Jamaica, then moved to Trinidad. Walcott began as a painter, then became a writer and teacher. His first book of poems was published in 1948. His work combines the English tradition of lyric poetry with the scenery, attitudes, and sounds of the Caribbean and urban America. Since the 1950s he has lived and taught at universities in Boston and New York but spends part of each year in the West Indies. Walcott has written several book-length poems and numerous plays. *Another Life* (1973) is a saga of a poet's development, written in episodes like scenes in a play. Another of his major works is *Omeros* (1990), an epic poem that takes a new, imaginative look at the epics of the Greek poet Homer.

ABOUT THE SELECTION

Walcott's work dwells on the division between "Englishness" and the black Afro-Caribbean heritage of colonialism. Images and ideas from Homer's *Iliad* and *Odyssey* have long influenced Walcott. They are the background for **"Map of the New World,"** which is an example of a self-referencing poem. It is a poem about the writing of Homer's *Odyssey* that begins by describing its own writing. Its illustration of the act of creation has not been equalled in English since the King James translation of the Book of Genesis. Here, though, the subject is not the creation of the world but the creation by a poet of a world of the imagination.

MULTICULTURAL EXTENSIONS: MODERN POETRY / "MAP OF THE NEW WORLD" 905

ADDITIONAL RESOURCES

READER'S GUIDE
• Selection Worksheet, 10.16

ASSESSMENT PORTFOLIO
• Selection Check Test, 4.10.31
• Selection Test, 4.10.32

ENRICHMENT ACTIVITIES

Walcott has always been fascinated by traditions in poetry—for instance, the tradition of epic poetry. To help students understand the process of adapting traditional materials, have them choose a literary tradition they have studied this year and adapt it to their own voice and time. For instance, they may want to write a heroic horror tale in the tradition of *Beowulf* or a morality play about modern life in the tradition of *Everyman* or a short story in the tradition of Jane Austen's psychologically astute romances.

SUPPORT FOR LEP STUDENTS

Write the line "The ten-years war is finished" on the board to demonstrate how hyphenated adjectives can be formed in English. Ask students to suggest other hyphenated adjectives that might be used to describe a war. Encourage them to be as creative as possible. *Answers.* hope-killing, Widow-making, blood-spilling, heart-piercing, peace-breaking

GOALS/OBJECTIVES

Studying this lesson will enable students to

• feel what it is like to be present at the birth of a great poem
• define *allusion* and give examples of it
• explain the use of allusions to Homer, the *Odyssey,* and the Trojan War in a modern poem

• define *free verse* and contrast it with metrical verse

EX. Where was Derek Walcott born?
Walcott was born in St. Lucia.

1. What begins at the end of the first sentence?
Rain begins at the end of the first sentence.

2. Who or what will lose sight of islands?
A sail will lose sight of islands.

3. What has become a white ashpit?
Troy has become an ashpit.

4. What musical instrument is referred to?
The harp is referred to.

5. At the end of the poem, what antique work of literature is referred to?
The poem refers to the _Odyssey._

ANSWERS TO GUIDED READING QUESTIONS

❶ The sentence in a sense performs the very act that it describes being performed. The words "rain will begin" both _predict_ what will happen at the end of the sentence and _are_ what happens, in the reader's imagination, at the end of the sentence.

❷ _Answers may vary._ Most readers will sense desolation and sadness in these lines.

❸ The man with clouded eyes is the poet Homer. He is beginning to compose the _Odyssey._

MULTICULTURAL EXTENSIONS: MODERN POETRY

St. Lucia

"Map of the New World"

DEREK WALCOTT

❶
In what way does the opening sentence actually carry out, or perform, what it describes?

❷
What feelings are created in you by this description of the ruin of Helen and of Troy?

❸
Who is the man with clouded eyes? What is he doing?

I _Archipelagoes_[1]

At the end of this sentence, rain will begin.
At the rain's edge, a sail.

Slowly the sail will lose sight of islands;
into a mist will go the belief in harbours
5   of an entire race.

The ten-years war is finished.
Helen's hair, a grey cloud.
Troy, a white ashpit
by the drizzling sea.

10   The drizzle tightens like the strings of a harp.
A man with clouded eyes picks up the rain
and plucks the first line of the _Odyssey._[2] ■

---

1. **Archipelagoes.** Seas with many islands in them
2. _Odyssey._ References to Homer's _Odyssey_, an ancient Greek epic poem about the wanderings of Odysseus after the fall of Troy in the Trojan War

Reviewing the Selection

1. What begins at the end of the first sentence?

2. What power does a writer have that is illustrated by the first two lines of the poem? How does Walcott illustrate the act of poetic creation?

3. What scene described in stanza 3 is being left behind by the sailors?

4. At the end of the poem, what else happens as the result of the Trojan War?

5. How is a drizzle similar to the strings of a harp? What mood is created by the last stanza? What is the poem saying about the mood with which Homer begins composing the *Odyssey?*

Connections: (Questions for Writing or Discussion)

1. Modern poetry often makes **allusions,** or references, to the history, literature, art, or thought of the past. To what Roman poet does Owen allude in the title and last lines of "Dulce et Decorum Est"? To what ancient Greek events, people, and literary work does Walcott allude in "Map of the New World"? To what use does the poet, in each case, put these allusions?

2. Modern poetry is often written in **free verse,** verse without a regular pattern of meter of rhyme. What other poems in this unit are in free verse? Why might many modern poets prefer writing in free verse? What limits or constraints are imposed by traditional rhyme metrical stanzas?

1. Rain begins at the end of the first sentence.

2. A writer has the power to bring images into existence in the imagination of readers (or listeners). Walcott demonstrates this power by simultaneously describing the act of creating images and actually creating them.

3. The scene being left by the sailors is the desolation of Troy after that city was destroyed by the Greeks.

4. As a result of the war, the *Odyssey* is composed.

5. Both a drizzle and the strings of a harp appear to be numerous, long, and thin. The last stanza seems sad and tragic. It is with a tragic wisdom that Homer begins to create his great poem.

ANSWERS FOR CONNECTIONS

1. Owen alludes to a line from a poem by Horace. Walcott alludes to the Greeks sailing away from the ruins of Troy, to Helen, to Troy itself, and to "a man with clouded eyes"—Homer. Owen quotes Horace to contradict him. Walcott uses his allusions to demonstrate how, out of events and feelings, a poet shapes his or her work.

2. Poems in the unit that are written in free verse are "The Second Coming," "Preludes," "Snake," "Rough," "Not Waving but Drowning," "Thistles," and "Map of the New World." Many poets prefer writing in free verse because it gives them the freedom to choose precisely the right word, as opposed to a word that merely fits the rhyme scheme or metrical pattern.

► Give students the following exercise.

Write twenty sentences, using in each sentence at least one word from the list on page 908. You may write about changes in literature, the arts, and society that have occurred during the first six decades of the twentieth century, or about the poets and poems you have read in this unit. You should vary the form of the words if necessary to accord with conventional grammar and usage.

ADDITIONAL RESOURCES

ASSESSMENT PORTFOLIO
- Vocabulary Worksheet: Unit 10, 4.10.33
- Study Guide: Unit 10 Test, 4.10.34
- Unit 10 Test, 4.10.35

ESSENTIAL SKILLS PRACTICE BOOKS

Language
- Personal Pronouns, 2.6
- Pronouns, 2.6–2.11
- Transitive and Intransitive Verbs, 2.15
- Verbals: Participles, 2.16
- Verbals: Gerunds, 2.17
- Adjectives and Articles, 2.19
- Using Precise Nouns, 2.32
- Using Vivid Verbs, 2.33
- The Functions of Sentences, 2.36
- Correcting Sentence Fragments, 2.61
- Inverting Sentences for Emphasis, 2.64
- Agreement of Subject and Verb, 2.70
- Pronoun Case, 2.76, 2.77
- Semicolons, 2.97
- Colons, 2.98
- Underlining and Italics, 2.103
- Quotation Marks, 2.104, 2.105
- Proofreading for Spelling Errors, 2.134
- Using Context Clues, 2.138, 2.139

Speaking and Listening
- Elements of Verbal Communication, 3.2
- Elements of Nonverbal Communication, 3.3
- Interpersonal Communication, 3.5

Study and Research
- Strategies for Problem Solving, 4.1, 4.2
(cont.)

908 TEACHER'S EDITION

UNIT REVIEW

Twentieth-Century Poetry

VOCABULARY FROM THE SELECTIONS

ardent, 869	dupe, 898	humility, 859	perversity, 859
articulate, 844	fissure, 858	infest, 897	reverently, 884
carob, 858	glade, 841	martyrdom, 884	sordid, 854
conjure, 898	gutter, 868	masquerade, 854	subversive, 898
constitute, 854	hermaphrodite,	muse, 859	treacherous, 898
convulse, 860	902	paltry, 860	

LITERARY TERMS

Aesthetic Movement, 837	image, 843, 855, 894	simile, 856
aim, 870	irony, 870, 883, 890	sonnet, 865, 882
alliteration, 870	lyric poem, 843	speaker, 856
allusion, 846, 862, 907	metaphor, 874	stream of consciousness, 837
cæsura, 895	Modernism, 835–837	
confessional poetry, 904	objective correlative, 855	symbol, 850, 862
diction, 874	oxymoron, 895	theme, 862, 865, 886
figurative language, 890	prose poem, 899	tone, 856, 900
free verse, 838, 907	pun, 879	villanelle, 876, 879
French Symbolism, 838	Realism, 835	
Freudian criticism, 862	rhyme, 886	

ADDITIONAL RESOURCES (CONT.)

- Memorizing, 4.4
- Observing, 4.6
- Comparing and Contrasting, 4.8
- Generalizing, 4.11
- Reading Actively: Predicting, 4.18
- Using the Card Catalog, 4.22
- Using Reference Works, 4.23
- Using Dictionaries, 4.24

- Computer-assisted Research, 4.26
- Other Sources of Information, 4.27
- Informal Note-taking, 4.31
- Synonym and Antonym Questions, 4.44

Applied English
- Types of Business Letters, 5.5

SYNTHESIS: QUESTIONS FOR WRITING, RESEARCH, OR DISCUSSION

GENRE STUDIES

1. **Free Verse.** Much of the poetry written in the twentieth century has been in free verse. Define free verse and find examples in the unit. Explain what techniques are used in each free verse poem to make the language poetic even though it does not use traditional meters, rhythms, or rhyme schemes.

2. **Confessional Poetry.** A **confessional poem** is one that expresses extremely personal experiences and feelings. In a confessional poem, the speaker generally performs a self-examination or relates private experiences. Much confessional poetry is autobiographical. Which poems in this unit best fit this definition of *confessional poetry* and why?

THEMATIC STUDIES

3. **Irony in Modern Poetry.** The Modern Era has been called the Age of Irony, for many works produced in this century present ironic undercuttings of traditional ideas. What ironies are explored in the following works from the unit?
    "Adam's Curse"
    "Snake"
    "Dulce et Decorum Est"
    "Rough"
    "Who's Who"
    "Not Waving but Drowning"

HISTORICAL AND BIOGRAPHICAL STUDIES

4. **The War Poets.** Contrast the depictions of war in the poems of Wilfred Owen and Rupert Brooke. Refer to the works in this unit and to other works by the two poets.

▶ These prompts are suitable as topics for research papers. Refer to the Language Arts Survey, 4.20–4.34, "Research Skills." To evaluate research papers, see the evaluation forms for writing, revising, and proofreading in the *Assessment Portfolio*, 7.1–7.10.

▶ These prompts can be adapted for use as topics for oral reports or debates. To evaluate these projects, see the evaluation forms in the *Assessment Portfolio*, 7.17–7.19.

ANSWERS FOR LANGUAGE LAB

Exercise A

1. Eliot
   Nobel Prize in literature
2. twentieth-century
3. Military Cross
   World War I
   war
4. Spanish Civil War
   World War II
5. "Musée des Beaux Arts"
   Metropolitan Museum of Art
   Tuesday
   Brueghel
6. "Bread"
   Canadian
   sister
7. Wonder
   I
8. Australia
   Southern Hemisphere
   University of Sydney

Exercise B

William Butler Yeats is one of the great poets of the twentieth century. He was born in Dublin, Ireland, and grew up near London and in the countryside of County Sligo, which he celebrates in his poem "The Lake Isle of Innisfree." Many of his poems and plays have Irish themes. His poem "Easter 1916" is about a revolt of Irish nationalists against the British. The revolt took place in the spring on Easter Monday. The revolt did not succeed, and many of those involved in it were hanged. Yeats knew many of the people who were killed, and the poem remembers the death of Macdonagh, Macbride, and others. Yeats's death in January 1922 was immortalized in a verse by another twentieth-century writer, W. H. Auden, who wrote an occasional poem called "In Memory of W. B. Yeats."

LANGUAGE LAB PROOFREADING FOR CAPITALIZATION ERRORS

Proper nouns are always capitalized. The following chart shows other cases when capitalization is required.

CAPITALIZE	EXAMPLES
Awards	Pulitzer Prize, Nobel Prize in literature
Brand and Trade Names	Levi's, Ritz crackers
Buildings and Structures	Museum of Fine Arts, Stonehenge
Days, Months, Years, and Holidays	Sunday, January, Easter
Directions and Regions	Lake District, the West
Events and Periods	World War I, Age of Reason
Family Relationships (unmodified)	Mother, Aunt Matilda
First Words	Do not tell me war is kind.
Letters	grade of A, high C
Personal Names	Mr. Eliot, William Butler Yeats
Place Names	River Thames, London, Great Britain
Pronoun *I*	I wish I had read "Snake."
Titles of Artworks, Literary Works, and Musical Works	"Not Waving but Drowning," Brueghel's "The Fall of Icarus"

For a more detailed explanation of capitalization rules, see the Language Arts Survey, 2.017–2.133.

EXERCISE A CORRECTING CAPITALIZATION ERRORS

In each of the following sentences decide if the underlined words should be capitalized or not. Write each word correctly along with the rule it follows.

1. T. S. <u>eliot</u> won a <u>nobel prize in literature</u> in 1948.

2. The theme of war is common in <u>Twentieth-Century</u> poetry.

3. Wilfred Owen, who won a <u>military cross</u> in <u>world war I</u>, wrote a stirring poem about attitudes toward <u>War</u>.

> **LANGUAGE ARTS SURVEY**
>
> *For additional help, see the Language Arts Survey, 2.107–2.133, on capitalization.*

4. Because he was a pacifist, Stephen Spender did not fight in the <u>Spanish civil war</u> or in <u>world war II</u>.

5. Auden's poem "<u>musée des beaux arts</u>" inspired me to go to the <u>metropolitan museum of art</u> last <u>tuesday</u> to see some paintings by <u>brueghel</u>.

6. In "<u>bread</u>," Margaret Atwood, a <u>canadian</u> author, says that your <u>Sister</u> is dying of starvation.

7. Atwood talks about many kinds of bread, but she does not mention <u>wonder</u> bread, the kind <u>i</u> eat.

8. Writer Judith Wright hails from <u>australia</u> in the <u>southern hemisphere</u>, and she attended the <u>university of sydney</u>.

EXERCISE B PROOFREADING FOR CAPITALIZATION ERRORS

In the paragraph that follows correct any errors in capitalization.

William butler yeats is one of the great poets of the twentieth Century. He was born in dublin, Ireland, and grew up near London and in the countryside of county sligo, which he celebrates in his poem "The lake isle of innisfree." Many of his poems and plays have irish themes. His poem "easter 1916" is about a revolt of irish nationalists against the british. The Revolt took place in the Spring on Easter monday. the revolt did not succeed, and many of those involved in it were hanged. Yeats knew many of the people who were killed, and the poem remembers the death of Macdonagh, macbride, and others. Yeats's death in january 1922 was immortalized in a verse by another Twentieth-Century writer, W. H. Auden, who wrote an Occasional Poem called "In memory of w. b. Yeats."

UNIT 11 TWENTIETH-CENTURY PROSE
(1900–PRESENT)

Early Morning. *Liubov Sergeievna Popova, 1914.*
Oil on canvas, 27 ³/₄ x 35." The Museum of Modern Art, NY.
The Riklis Collection of McCrory Corporation

GOALS/OBJECTIVES

Studying this unit will enable students to

- interpret and appreciate modern prose
- identify the major literary movements of the twentieth century and the English writers who exemplify them
- describe the stream-of-consciousness technique of writing and identify its major practitioners
- describe political events within England and international events that affected Britain during the twentieth century
- describe how twentieth-century English literature reflects changes in the British class structure, the status of women, and the former colonies

Photograph ©1995 The Museum of Modern Art, NY

LITERARY CURRENTS

Use the following selections to explore these concepts and techniques with your students.

OBJECTIVE CORRELATIVE
- from *A Portrait of the Artist as a Young Man*, 921
- "The Garden-Party," 940
- "The Lagoon," 967

POINT OF VIEW
- "Heat," 972
- "Red Dress—1946," 954

STREAM OF CONSCIOUSNESS
- from *A Portrait of the Artist as a Young Man*, 921

▶**Note:** Lists for "Connections across the Curriculum" and "Teaching the Multiple Intelligences" appear on page 982.

The king died and then the queen died is a story. The king died, and then the queen died of grief is a plot.

—E. M. Forster

913

THEMATIC CURRENTS

Use the following selections to explore these themes with your students.

ALIENATION OF THE INDIVIDUAL
- from *A Portrait of the Artist as a Young Man*, 921
- from *Nineteen Eighty-four*, 931
- "The Lagoon," 967

CLASS STRUGGLE
- from *Nineteen Eighty-four*, 931
- "The Garden-Party," 940
- from *Nectar in a Sieve*, 974

WOMEN IN SOCIETY
- from *A Room of One's Own*, 914
- "The Garden-Party," 940
- "Red Dress—1946," 954
- from *Nectar in a Sieve*, 974

ENRICHMENT ACTIVITIES

Have students write about or discuss the obstacles they believe women faced as artists in Woolf's time and today.

SUPPORT FOR LEP STUDENTS

Students may need help with the conditional verb phrases, formed with *would,* in some of the guided reading questions. Explain that this verb construction indicates a situation that is contrary to fact. Make sure students understand that the whole essay discusses a fictional character. Refer to the Language Arts Survey, 2.69, "Voice and Mood."

IDIOMS

on the sly—secretly

apple of one's eye—one's favorite

ADDITIONAL VOCABULARY

extraordinarily—remarkably, extremely

moon—behave idly

hedge—row of bushes

fancy—imagination

abundantly—amply, more than sufficiently

servile—submissive; lacking self-respect

beguile—spend time leisurely

thwart—prevent

asunder—into separate parts

anguish—severe pain

dilemma—impossible situation

914 TEACHER'S EDITION

PREREADING

from *A Room of One's Own*
by Virginia Woolf

ABOUT THE AUTHOR

Virginia Woolf (1882–1941) was born in London, England, and educated at home by her father, Sir Leslie Stephen. There, young Virginia Stephen made good use of her father's extensive library and met many of the outstanding literary and intellectual figures of the time. After her father's death, Virginia and her sister Vanessa continued to live in Gordon Square, in the Bloomsbury section of London. They hosted gatherings of writers and artists, a circle of Cambridge-educated friends that came to be known as the Bloomsbury Group. In 1912, Virginia married one of these friends, Leonard Woolf, a writer on politics and economics. Five years later, Virginia and Leonard Woolf started Hogarth Press, which became a successful publishing house, printing works by Katherine Mansfield, E. M. Forster, T. S. Eliot, and Virginia Woolf. After Woolf's first two novels, *The Voyage Out* and *Night and Day,* she began to experiment with various elements of fiction, particularly with interior monologues and stream-of-consciousness technique. Her novels include *Jacob's Room, Mrs. Dalloway, To the Lighthouse, Orlando, The Waves,* and *Between the Acts.* Her short stories were published in the collections *Monday or Tuesday* and *A Haunted House.* One of the most distinguished critics of her time, Woolf published numerous essays and works of literary criticism, including *Mr. Bennett and Mrs. Brown, The Common Reader, A Room of One's Own, Flush, Three Guineas, Roger Fry,* and *The Death of the Moth.* In 1953, Leonard Woolf edited and published *A Writer's Diary,* extracts from the diary that Woolf had kept about her work.

ABOUT THE SELECTION

An eloquent and ardent feminist, Virginia Woolf published *A Room of One's Own* (1929), a long essay on the status of women and the difficulties of being a woman artist. Woolf's essay was based on two lectures given at Cambridge University. In the essay, Woolf discussed the Elizabethan Age, the period when Queen Elizabeth I reigned in England (1558–1603). This was a time of extraordinary energy, splendor, and creativity, the age of Marlowe, Jonson, and Shakespeare. In the selection that follows, Woolf considers a dark aspect of the Elizabethan and later periods of English history—the social forces that kept women from exercising their talents. Woolf asks and answers the question, "What if Shakespeare had had an equally talented sister?"

914 UNIT ELEVEN / TWENTIETH-CENTURY PROSE

GOALS/OBJECTIVES

Studying this lesson will enable students to

- empathize with the torment of a creative mind bounded by society
- describe Virginia Woolf's contributions to twentieth-century literature
- define *essay* and identify the writer's purpose, main ideas, and supporting ideas in an essay
- define *character* and identify elements of characterization in literature they read
- write an essay and a brief biography
- rewrite sentences to achieve parallelism
- evaluate hypotheses based on evidence in a text

READER'S JOURNAL

Do you have a talent that you strongly wish to use and develop? Have you been encouraged to develop that talent, or have you been thwarted in your attempts? Think about these questions. Then freewrite about opportunity in your journal.

RESEARCH SKILLS

Read the Language Arts Survey, 4.23, "Using Reference Works." Then use several reference works to find information about the Bloomsbury Group. Identify the members of the group and research their views about literature, art, and politics.

FROM

A Room of One's Own

VIRGINIA WOOLF

Let me imagine, since facts are so hard to come by, what would have happened had Shakespeare had a wonderfully gifted sister, called Judith, let us say. Shakespeare himself went, very probably—his mother was an heiress—to the grammar school, where he may have learnt Latin—Ovid, Virgil and Horace—and the elements of grammar and logic. He was, it is well known, a wild boy who <u>poached</u> rabbits, perhaps shot a deer, and had, rather sooner than he should have done, to marry a woman in the neighborhood, who bore him a child rather quicker than was right. That <u>escapade</u> sent him to seek his fortune in London. He had, it seemed, a taste for the theatre; he began by holding horses at the stage door. Very soon he got work in the theatre, became a successful actor, and lived at the hub of the universe, meeting everybody, knowing everybody, practicing his art on the boards, exercising his wits in the streets, and even getting access to the palace of the queen. Meanwhile his extraordinarily gifted sister, let us suppose, remained at home. She was as adventurous, as imaginative, as <u>agog</u> to see the world as he was. But she was not sent to school. She had no chance of learning grammar and logic, let alone of reading Horace and Virgil. She picked up a book now and then, one of her brother's perhaps, and read a few pages. But then her parents came in and told her to mend the stockings or mind the stew and not moon about with books and papers. They would have spoken sharply but kindly, for they were substantial people who knew the conditions of life for a woman and loved their daughter—

❶ What would Judith's parents have discouraged her from doing? What would Judith have been encouraged to do with her time?

WORDS FOR EVERYDAY USE:
poach (pōch) *vt.,* hunt illegally
es • ca • pade (es′kə pād′) *n.,* reckless adventure
a • gog (ə gäg′) *adj.,* eagerly excited

PREREADING NOTES

READER'S JOURNAL

Students might consider how ideas about gender roles have influenced the advice they've received about pursuing their talents.

RESEARCH SKILLS

Students might work in small groups, with each group member researching one or two members of the Bloomsbury Group.

► Additional practice is provided in the *Essential Skills Practice Book: Study and Research*, 4.23.

ANSWER TO GUIDED READING QUESTION

❶ They would have discouraged her from reading or educating herself. They would have encouraged her to perform household tasks.

VOCABULARY FROM THE SELECTION

agog	guffaw
betrothed	omnibus
escapade	poach

HISTORICAL NOTE

Shakespeare did have two sisters and a daughter named Judith. Little is known about them.

VOCABULARY IN CONTEXT

• Any hunters who <u>poach</u> deer on this land will be arrested.

• The starlet detailed her many wild <u>escapades</u> in her memoirs.

• The children were so <u>agog</u> to visit the amusement park that they got dressed before anyone else was awake.

❶ Judith would not have wanted to marry because she would have felt a need to pursue her gift for writing.

❷ At the theater Judith would have been turned away. People would have laughed at her and demeaned her for thinking she could be an actor.

HISTORICAL NOTE

• Woolf refers to Professor Trevelyan, author of *The History of England* (1926). As she explored Trevelyan's text, Woolf searched in vain for any mention of women in the arts during the sixteenth century. The only entries about women discussed the accepted practice of wife beating and the custom of arranged marriages.

• Point out to students that Aphra Behn was a well-known and extremely popular playwright in the sixteenth century.

indeed, more likely than not she was the apple of her father's eye. Perhaps she scribbled some pages up in an apple loft on the sly, but was careful to hide them or set fire to them. Soon, however, before she was out of her teens, she was to be <u>betrothed</u> to the son of a neighboring wool-stapler. She cried out that marriage was hateful to her, and for that she was severely beaten by her father. Then he ceased to scold her. He begged her instead not to hurt him, not to shame him in this matter of her marriage. He would give her a chain of beads or a fine petticoat, he said; and there were tears in his eyes. How could she disobey him? How could she break his heart? The force of her own gift alone drove her to it. She made up a small parcel of her belongings, let herself down by a rope one summer's night and took the road to London. She was not seventeen. The birds that sang in the hedge were not more musical than she was. She had the quickest fancy, a gift like her brother's, for the tune of words. Like him, she had a taste for the theatre. She stood at the stage door; she wanted to act, she said. Men laughed in her face. The manager—a fat, loose-lipped man—<u>guffawed</u>. He bellowed something about poodles dancing and women acting—no woman, he said, could possibly be an actress. He hinted—you can imagine what. She could get no training in her craft. Could she even seek her dinner in a tavern or roam the streets at midnight? Yet her genius was for fiction and lusted to feed abundantly upon the lives of men and women and the study of their ways. At last—for she was very young, oddly like Shakespeare the poet in

❶ Why would Judith not have wanted to marry the son of the wool-stapler?

❷ What would have happened to Judith at the theater? How would people have reacted to her?

her face, with the same grey eyes and rounded brows—at last Nick Greene the actor-manager took pity on her; she found herself with child by that gentleman and so—who shall measure the heat and violence of the poet's heart when caught and tangled in a woman's body?—killed herself one winter's night and lies buried at some cross-roads where the <u>omnibuses</u> now stop outside the Elephant and Castle.

That, more or less, is how the story would run, I think, if a woman in Shakespeare's day had had Shakespeare's genius. But for my part, I agree with the deceased bishop, if such he was—it is unthinkable that any woman in Shakespeare's day should have had Shakespeare's genius. For genius like Shakespeare's is not born among laboring, uneducated, servile people. It was not born in England among the Saxons and the Britons. It is not born today among the working classes. How, then, could it have been born among women whose work began, according to Professor Trevelyan, almost before they were out of the nursery, who were forced to it by their parents and held to it by all the power of law and custom? Yet genius of a sort must have existed among women as it must have existed among the working classes. Now and again an Emily Brontë or a Robert Burns blazes out and proves its presence. But certainly it never got itself on to paper. When, however, one reads of a witch being ducked, of a woman possessed by devils, of a wise woman selling herbs, or even of a very remarkable man who had a mother, then I think we are on the track of a lost novelist, a suppressed

WORDS FOR
EVERYDAY USE:

be • trothed (bē trô tht´) *adj.,* engaged to be married
guf • faw (gu fô´) *vi.,* let out a short burst of laughter
om • ni • bus (äm´ni bəs) *n.,* bus

VOCABULARY IN CONTEXT

• Did you hear that the bachelor was recently <u>betrothed</u> to an heiress?

• An inappropriate <u>guffaw</u> erupted from the back row of the funeral parlor.

• Because of her fear of flying, the singer toured the country by <u>omnibus</u>.

poet, of some mute and inglorious Jane Austen, some Emily Brontë who dashed her brains out on the moor or mopped and mowed about the highways crazed with the torture that her gift had put her to. Indeed, I would venture to guess that Anon, who wrote so many poems without signing them, was often a woman. It was a woman Edward FitzGerald, I think, suggested who made the ballads and the folk-songs, crooning them to her children, beguiling her spinning with them, or the length of the winter's night.

This may be true or it may be false—who can say?—but what is true in it, so it seemed to me, reviewing the story of Shakespeare's sister as I had made it, is that any woman born with a great gift in the sixteenth century would certainly have gone crazed, shot herself, or ended her days in some lonely cottage outside the village, half witch, half wizard, feared and mocked at. For it needs little skill in psychology to be sure that a highly gifted girl who had tried to use her gift for poetry would have been so thwarted and hindered by other people, so tortured and pulled asunder by her own contrary instincts, that she must have lost her health and sanity to a certainty. No girl could have walked to London and stood at a stage door and forced her way into the presence of actor-managers without doing herself a violence and suffering an anguish which may have been irrational—for chastity may be a fetish invented by certain societies for unknown reasons—but were none the less inevitable. Chastity had then, it has even now, a religious importance in a woman's life, and has so wrapped itself round with nerves and instincts that to cut it free and bring it to the light of day demands courage of the rarest. To have lived a free life in London in the sixteenth century would have meant for a woman who was poet and playwright a nervous stress and dilemma which might well have killed her. Had she survived, whatever she had written would have been twisted and deformed, issuing from a strained and morbid imagination. And undoubtedly, I thought, looking at the shelf where there are no plays by women, her work would have gone unsigned. ∎

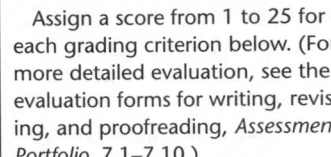

Q What does Woolf suggest about poems signed "anonymous"?

Responding to the Selection

Imagine that you are the fictional gifted sister of Shakespeare. How would it feel to have a talented brother who was given every opportunity to develop his craft and not to have such opportunities yourself? Write a letter to your parents explaining how you want to develop your own talents.

LITERARY TECHNIQUE

Woolf uses an **allusion** to emphasize her point. She speaks of a "mute and inglorious Jane Austen," which recalls "Some mute inglorious Milton" (line 59) from Thomas Gray's "Elegy Written in a Country Churchyard" (page 574). In making such an allusion, Woolf underscores how women have been neglected throughout history; Gray's poem praises the common, unknown *man* but makes no mention of the common, nameless women who lie in the same graveyard.

ANSWERS FOR REVIEWING THE SELECTION

RECALLING

1. She asks them to let her "imagine" that Shakespeare "had a wonderfully gifted sister."

2. He learns Latin, grammar, and logic.

3. Shakespeare begins by holding horses at the stage door, then he works in the theater and becomes an actor.

4. "Anonymous" is the name of the woman poet.

INTERPRETING

Responses will vary. Possible responses are given.

5. Judith is described as "wonderfully gifted," adventurous, imaginative, and as eager to see the world as her brother.

6. Her education consists of quickly reading a few pages from her brother's books.

7. Evidence from Professor Trevelyan's account of the sixteenth-century laws and customs governing women's lives supports Woolf's imagination.

8. Historical evidence of witches, possessed women, herbal healers, and the mothers of "very remarkable" men puts Woolf "on the track" of women's genius.

SYNTHESIZING

Responses will vary. Possible responses are given.

9. Shakespeare's imaginary sister illustrates Woolf's point about the grim obstacles faced by a talented woman in the sixteenth century. She makes Woolf's point clear by providing precise details that are as compelling, real, and universal as the details in any woman's life.

10. Lack of education and financial independence, unequal marriage laws, the custom of "woman's work," and society's limiting view of women's capabilities are reasons for the lack of women writers in the Elizabethan Age. Except for changes in marriage laws and women's legal rights, each reason is still applicable today, although to a lesser degree.

Reviewing the Selection

RECALLING

1. What does the author ask her audience to let her "imagine"?

2. What does William Shakespeare learn in grammar school?

3. What series of jobs gives Shakespeare the opportunity to work his way into theater?

4. What is the name of the woman "who wrote so many poems" during the sixteenth century?

INTERPRETING

5. What qualities does the author give to the imaginary "Judith"?

6. What elements comprise the education of Judith Shakespeare?

7. What evidence supports Woolf's imaginary depiction of Judith's fate?

8. What evidence puts the author "on the track" of women's genius in the sixteenth century?

SYNTHESIZING

9. What purpose does the imaginary sister of Shakespeare serve in the essay? In what way does she make Woolf's point clear?

10. What reasons are presented for the lack of women writers in the Elizabethan Age? Are any of those reasons applicable today? Explain.

Understanding Literature (Questions for Discussion)

1. **Essay.** An **essay** is a brief work of prose nonfiction. Typically, a good essay develops a single idea and is characterized by unity and coherence. What single idea does Woolf present in this excerpt from her long essay? What examples support and develop her main idea?

2. **Character.** A **character** is a person who figures in the action of a literary work. In this essay, Woolf created the character of Judith Shakespeare, an imaginary sister to William Shakespeare. What details about Judith and her life create a compelling and believable portrait?

3. **Aim.** A writer's **aim** is the primary purpose that his or her work is meant to achieve. One aim of *A Room of One's Own* is to illustrate the obstacles faced by women writers in the sixteenth century. From reading the selection, can you tell whether Woolf believed that those obstacles still existed in 1928, the year in which she wrote the essay? Of what significance is the fact that the essay is based on two lectures that Woolf gave at Cambridge University? How might the aim of the essay be different if Woolf were a Cambridge-educated man? What might Woolf have wanted the Cambridge-educated man of her time to understand about social restrictions and their consequences for the development of women's talents?

ANSWERS FOR UNDERSTANDING LITERATURE

▶ See the evaluation forms for discussion, active listening, and oral communication, *Assessment Portfolio*, 7.11–7.14. *Responses will vary. Possible responses are given.*

1. Essay. Woolf's main idea is that talented women in the sixteenth century faced enormous obstacles to practice their craft. Examples of these obstacles are taken from the life of Shakespeare's imaginary sister, Judith: her lack of education, her hateful arranged marriage, her desperate

measure of running away to London to seek the stage, her pregnancy, and her suicide.

▶ **Additional Resources:** *Essential Skills Practice Book: Writing,* 1.31, 1.40.

2. Character. Details of Judith and her life include scribbling pages in an apple loft, disdaining her father's pitiful bribe of a chain of beads or a fine petticoat, her gray eyes and rounded brows, and the mention of the

(cont.)

Responding in Writing

1. **Essay.** Woolf begins her long essay with the question, "But, you may say, we asked you to speak about women and fiction—what has that got to do with a room of one's own?" Think about what freedom to pursue individual interests might mean to the development of a writer, artist, or poet. Then think about the excerpt you have read in light of Woolf's opening question. Write an essay expressing your view of the concept of "a room of one's own."

2. **Biography.** Imagine that you are the biographer of Anonymous. Write about a particularly compelling chapter in her life, such as her decision to write anonymously, the publication of her first poem, or perhaps her risk of public exposure. Use sensory and concrete details in your portrayal.

Language Lab

Achieving Parallelism. Read the Language Arts Survey, 2.57, "Achieving Parallelism." Then rewrite each of the following sentences to make their parts parallel.

1. Virginia Woolf and her sister Vanessa often met with their Bloomsbury friends, many of whom enjoyed discussing political issues and to write essays.

2. To educate women is as important as educating men.

3. Woolf experimented with the form of the novel more than experimentation with the form of the essay.

4. Having a profession guarantees a woman economic independence and to be free intellectually.

5. Having a room of her own and to earn a reasonable income are two necessities for a woman artist, according to Woolf.

Thinking Skills

Hypothesis. Read the Language Arts Survey, 4.13, "Making Hypotheses." Then find statements in the selection that make or support each of the following hypotheses.

1. Hypothesis: In Elizabethan England, women received little or no formal education.

ANSWERS FOR LANGUAGE LAB

1. Virginia Woolf and her sister Vanessa often met with their Bloomsbury friends, many of whom enjoyed discussing political issues and writing essays.

2. Educating women is as important as educating men.

3. Woolf experimented more with the form of the novel than with the form of the essay.

4. Having a profession guarantees a woman economic independence and intellectual freedom.

5. Having a room of her own and earning a reasonable income are two necessities for a woman artist, according to Woolf.

▶Additional practice is provided in the *Essential Skills Practice Book: Language,* 2.57.

ANSWERS FOR UNDERSTANDING LITERATURE (CONT.)

real-life actor-manager Nick Greene.

▶**Teaching Note:** Students can make separate lists of details about Judith's appearance and details about Judith's actions.

3. **Aim.** In her essay, Woolf states that genius "is not born today among the working classes." The implication is that women born among the working classes in 1928 still did not have the advantages of education or financial independence. It is ironic that Woolf was speaking to a highly educated audience about the obstacles, including the lack of education, that faced sixteenth-century women. If Woolf had been a man, perhaps her purpose would have been to celebrate the literary feats of sixteenth-century men such as Shakespeare and Marlowe.

▶**Teaching Note:** Refer students to *feminist criticism* in the Handbook of Literary Terms.

ANSWERS FOR THINKING SKILLS

Responses will vary. Possible responses are given.

1. Judith Shakespeare was not sent to school or given a chance to learn Latin, grammar, or logic.

2. Judith's suicide is evidence of the fate of death. The unknown woman who "mopped and mowed about the highways crazed with the torture of her gift" is evidence of the fate of insanity.

3. Supported by Edward FitzGerald's claim, Woolf declares that it was a woman "who made the ballads and the folk-songs, crooning them to her children."

4. Woolf names no literary genius in Elizabethan England who came from the working classes; she points out that very few literary geniuses—such as Robert Burns and Emily Brontë—ever emerge from the working class.

FOR MORE PRACTICE

Problem. Hypothesis: Women in Elizabethan England were not allowed to become actors.

Answer. The stage manager laughs at Judith's request to act in the theater and declares that no woman can act.

▶Additional practice is provided in the *Essential Skills Practice Book: Study and Research,* 4.13.

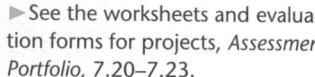

PROJECT NOTES

▶See the worksheets and evaluation forms for projects, *Assessment Portfolio,* 7.20–7.23.

1. Dramatic Monologues. Refer students to Unit 4, The English Renaissance (page 240), for literature from the sixteenth century.

2. Collection of Early Women's Writing. Encourage students to apply Woolf's theory that "Anon . . . was often a woman" to the poems that they find.

2. Hypothesis: To be a talented woman in the sixteenth century meant death or insanity.

3. Hypothesis: Many anonymous sixteenth-century poems were written by women.

4. Hypothesis: Literary genius was not found among the working classes of Elizabethan England.

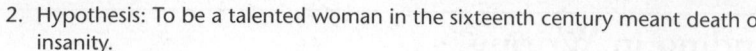

PROJECTS

1. **Dramatic Monologues.** Collaborate with one or two other students to write a dramatic monologue for one of the following characters: an anonymous sixteenth-century poet, the mother of Shakespeare, the imaginary sister of Shakespeare, or a woman poet writing under a male pseudonym. In your monologue, portray the character's experience with as much realistic detail as possible. Rehearse your monologue and present it to the class.

2. **Collection of Early Women's Writing.** As a class, research British women writers of the sixteenth, seventeenth, and eighteenth centuries. Excellent subjects for research include Isabella Whitney, Lady Mary Wroth, Margaret Cavendish, Aphra Behn, Anne Finch, Delarivier Manley, Jane Barker, Lady Mary Wortley Montagu, Eliza Haywood, Sarah Fielding, Mary Wollstonecraft, Mary Hays, Ann Radcliffe, Maria Edgeworth, Dorothy Wordsworth, and Jane Austen. In a small group, investigate the life and work of one of these writers. Present your findings to the class.

920 *UNIT ELEVEN / TWENTIETH-CENTURY PROSE*

ANSWERS TO SELECTION CHECK TEST 4.11.1

EX. The young woman discussed in the selection is the sister of what famous dramatist?
She is Shakespeare's sister.

1. What name does Woolf give to this young woman?
She calls the young woman Judith.

2. Where does the young woman go after leaving her family?
She goes to London.

3. Whom does she tell that she wants to act?
She tells the theater manager that she wants to act.

4. According to Woolf, who was Anon?
Anon was probably a woman.

5. According to Woolf, who probably wrote the ballads and the folk songs?
A woman probably wrote them.

920 TEACHER'S EDITION

PREREADING

from *A Portrait of the Artist as a Young Man*
by James Joyce

ABOUT THE AUTHOR

James Joyce (1882–1941) was born in Dublin, Ireland, and educated at Jesuit schools and at University College, Dublin. In 1902, having rebelled against Catholicism, Irish nationalism, and his family, Joyce left Dublin. He spent the rest of his life in a self-imposed exile, living in Paris, Trieste, Rome, and Zurich, returning to Ireland only for a brief visit. Accompanying him to Trieste in 1904 was Nora Barnacle, an uneducated Dublin chambermaid, whom he eventually married. Supported by Joyce's meager earnings as a clerk and as a teacher of languages, the couple wandered about Europe and had two children. In 1914, Joyce published *Dubliners,* a collection of short stories. The collection was greatly admired by the American poet and critic Ezra Pound, who assisted Joyce throughout the following years. Because of his deteriorating eyesight, Joyce relied on his memory and on the secretarial help of friends in order to work. A perfectionist, Joyce wrote and repeatedly revised his novel *Ulysses* for seven years, from 1914 to 1921. A second large, experimental novel, *Finnegans Wake,* took seventeen years to complete. Both novels incited controversy. They were denounced as obscure, nonsensical, and sometimes even obscene until critics explained Joyce's innovative methods and other writers began imitating his experimental techniques. Joyce is now regarded as one of the twentieth century's greatest writers, known for his revolutionary innovations in prose style, which included the use of stream-of-consciousness technique, frequent allusions, and extensive word play.

ABOUT THE SELECTION

Published in 1916, Joyce's novel **A Portrait of the Artist as a Young Man** is largely autobiographical. The selection portrays the childhood and school days of Stephen Dedalus, an Irish Catholic boy attending a Jesuit school; the novel continues with Dedalus's adolescence and early manhood. Stephen Dedalus later becomes one of the leading characters in *Ulysses.* Throughout *A Portrait of the Artist as a Young Man*, Dedalus's self-awareness as an artist grows, forcing him to reject the world in which he was raised. The novel does not follow a chronological progression but focuses instead on certain experiences that are critical to Dedalus's development as an artist.

FROM *A PORTRAIT OF THE ARTIST AS A YOUNG MAN* **921**

ENRICHMENT ACTIVITIES

Students can discuss why Joyce's stream-of-consciousness works might have been regarded as obscure and nonsensical. Encourage students to share their opinions about the technique and why it is considered a revolution in the art of the novel.

SUPPORT FOR LEP STUDENTS

Explain that the selection does not obviously exhibit the fictional elements of character, setting, and plot. To help students understand this difficult selection, establish the main character, setting, and plot for students before they begin reading. Then pair students with English-proficient students who can help answer questions as they read.

ADDITIONAL VOCABULARY

throng—great number of people gathered together

scrimmage—practice football or rugby game

well-read—having read much

rhetoric—the art of using words effectively

GOALS/OBJECTIVES

Studying this lesson will enable students to

- empathize with the sensitive nature of Stephen in the rough, unkind world
- describe James Joyce's contributions to twentieth-century literature
- define *stream-of-consciousness writing* and identify it as they encounter it in their reading
- differentiate between *image* and *objective correlative* and recognize and interpret images and objective correlatives in literature they read

READER'S JOURNAL

What special words did you use to name things when you were a young child? Did you have a special word for *milk, mother, grandfather, dog*? In your journal, write as many words as you can remember from your childhood vocabulary or from the vocabulary of a child whom you know.

LANGUAGE SKILLS

Read the Language Arts Survey, 2.148, "Register." Then, make a list of words and phrases from the selection that are part of the language register associated with childhood.

FROM

A Portrait of the Artist as a Young Man

JAMES JOYCE

What is the point of view of the opening of the novel? Through whose eyes and ears are these events observed?

Once upon a time and a very good time it was there was a moocow coming down along the road and this moocow that was coming down along the road met a nicens little boy named baby tuckoo. . . .

His father told him that story: his father looked at him through a glass: he had a hairy face.

He was baby tuckoo. The moocow came down the road where Betty Byrne lived: she sold lemon platt.

O, the wild rose blossoms
On the little green place.

He sang that song. That was his song.

O, the green wothe botheth.

When you wet the bed first it is warm then it gets cold. His mother put on the oilsheet. That had the queer smell.

His mother had a nicer smell than his father. She played on the piano the sailor's hornpipe for him to dance. He danced:

Tralala lala
Tralala tralaladdy
Tralala lala
Tralala lala.

Uncle Charles and Dante clapped. They were older than his father and mother but uncle Charles was older than Dante.

Dante had two brushes in her press. The brush with the maroon velvet back was for Michael Davitt[1] and the brush with the green velvet back was for Parnell.[2]

---

1. **Michael Davitt.** Irish nationalist leader (1846–1906)
2. **Charles Stewart Parnell.** Irish nationalist leader (1846–1891)

Dante gave him a cachou[3] every time he brought her a piece of tissue paper.

The Vances lived in number seven. They had a different father and mother. They were Eileen's father and mother. When they were grown up he was going to marry Eileen. He hid under the table. His mother said:

—O, Stephen will apologise.

Dante said:

—O, if not, the eagles will come and pull out his eyes.

> *Pull out his eyes,*
> *Apologise,*
> *Apologise,*
> *Pull out his eyes.*
>
> *Apologise,*
> *Pull out his eyes,*
> *Pull out his eyes,*
> *Apologise.*

◆   ◆   ◆

The wide playgrounds were swarming with boys. All were shouting and the prefects[4] urged them on with strong cries. The evening air was pale and chilly and after every charge and thud of the footballers[5] the greasy leather orb[6] flew like a heavy bird through the grey light. He kept on the fringe of his line, out of sight of his prefect, out of the reach of the rude feet, feigning to run now and then. He felt his body small and weak amid the throng of players and his eyes were weak and watery. Rody Kickham was not like that: he would be captain of the third line all the fellows said.

Rody Kickham was a decent fellow but Nasty Roche was a stink. Rody Kickham had greaves in his number and a hamper in the refectory.[7] Nasty Roche had big hands. He called the Friday pudding

dog-in-the-blanket. And one day he had asked:

—What is your name?

Stephen had answered:

—Stephen Dedalus.

Then Nasty Roche had said:

—What kind of a name is that?

And when Stephen had not been able to answer Nasty Roche had asked:

—What is your father?

Stephen had answered:

—A gentleman.

Then Nasty Roche had asked:

—Is he a magistrate?[8]

He crept about from point to point on the fringe of his line, making little runs now and then. But his hands were bluish with cold. He kept his hands in the side-pockets of his belted grey suit. That was a belt round his pocket. And belt was also to give a fellow a belt. One day a fellow had said to Cantwell:

—I'd give you such a belt in a second.

Cantwell had answered:

—Go and fight your match. Give Cecil Thunder a belt. I'd like to see you. He'd give you a toe in the rump for yourself.

That was not a nice expression. His mother had told him not to speak with the rough boys in the college. Nice mother! The first day in the hall of the castle when she had said goodbye she had put up her veil double to her nose to kiss him: and her nose and eyes were red. But he had pretended not to see that she was going to cry. She was a nice mother but she was not so nice when she cried. And his father had given him two fiveshilling pieces for pocket money. And his father had told

---

3. **cachou.** Lozenge, or perhaps, an onomatopoetic rendering of a sneeze
4. **prefects.** Older students in position of authority
5. **footballers.** Soccer players
6. **orb.** Soccer ball
7. **refectory.** Dining hall
8. **magistrate.** Civil officer

FROM *A PORTRAIT OF THE ARTIST AS A YOUNG MAN* **923**

❶
What aspects of this passage demonstrate a child's understanding?

❷
How does this passage illustrate that even at an early age Stephen is drawn to word play?

him if he wanted anything to write home to him and, whatever he did, never to peach[9] on a fellow. Then at the door of the castle the rector had shaken hands with his father and mother, his soutane[10] fluttering in the breeze, and the car had driven off with his father and mother on it. They had cried to him from the car, waving their hands:

—Goodbye, Stephen, goodbye!

—Goodbye, Stephen, goodbye!

He was caught in the whirl of a scrimmage and, fearful of the flashing eyes and muddy boots, bent down to look through the legs. The fellows were struggling and groaning and their legs were rubbing and kicking and stamping. Then Jack Lawton's yellow boots dodged out the ball and all the other boots and legs ran after. He ran after them a little way and then stopped. It was useless to run on. Soon they would be going home for the holidays. After supper in the studyhall he would change the number pasted up inside his desk from seventyseven to seventysix.

It would be better to be in the studyhall than out there in the cold. The sky was pale and cold but there were lights in the castle. He wondered from which window Hamilton Rowan had thrown his hat on the haha[11] and had there been flowerbeds at that time under the windows. One day when he had been called to the castle the butler had shown him the marks of the soldiers' slugs in the wood of the door and had given him a piece of shortbread that the community ate. It was nice and warm to see the lights in the castle. It was like something in a book. Perhaps Leicester Abbey was like that. And there were nice sentences in Doctor Cornwell's Spelling Book. They were like poetry but they were only sentences to learn the spelling from.

Why does Stephen change the number each day? How does he feel about school? about home?

Wolsey died in Leicester Abbey
Where the abbots buried him.
Canker is a disease of plants,
Cancer one of animals.

It would be nice to lie on the hearthrug before the fire, leaning his head upon his hands, and think on those sentences. He shivered as if he had cold slimy water next his skin. That was mean of Wells to shoulder him into the square ditch because he would not swop his little snuffbox for Wells's seasoned hacking chestnut, the conqueror of forty. How cold and slimy the water had been! A fellow had once seen a big rat jump into the scum. Mother was sitting at the fire with Dante waiting for Brigid to bring in the tea. She had her feet on the fender and her jewelly slippers were so hot and they had such a lovely warm smell! Dante knew a lot of things. She had taught him where the Mozambique Channel was and what was the longest river in America and what was the name of the highest mountain in the moon. Father Arnall knew more than Dante because he was a priest but both his father and uncle Charles said that Dante was a clever woman and a wellread woman. And when Dante made that noise after dinner and then put up her hand to her mouth: that was heartburn.

A voice cried far out on the playground:

—All in!

Then other voices cried from the lower and third lines:

—All in! All in!

The players closed around, flushed and muddy, and he went among them, glad to go in. Rody Kickham held the ball by its greasy lace. A fellow asked him to give it one last: but he walked on without even

---

9. **peach.** Give evidence against
10. **soutane.** Long, loose-fitting vestment, generally black, worn by clergymen
11. **haha.** Fence around a garden

answering the fellow. Simon Moonan told him not to because the prefect was looking. The fellow turned to Simon Moonan and said:

—We all know why you speak. You are McGlade's suck.

Suck was a queer word. The fellow called Simon Moonan that name because Simon Moonan used to tie the prefect's false sleeves behind his back and the prefect used to let on to be angry. But the sound was ugly. Once he had washed his hands in the lavatory of the Wicklow Hotel and his father pulled the stopper up by the chain after and the dirty water went down through the hole in the basin. And when it had all gone down slowly the hole in the basin had made a sound like that: suck. Only louder.

To remember that and the white look of the lavatory made him feel cold and then hot. There were two cocks that you turned and water came out: cold and hot. He felt cold and then a little hot: and he could see the names printed on the cocks. That was a very queer thing.

And the air in the corridor chilled him too. It was queer and wettish. But soon the gas would be lit and in burning it made a light noise like a little song. Always the same: and when the fellows stopped talking in the playroom you could hear it.

It was the hour for sums. Father Arnall wrote a hard sum on the board and then said:

—Now then, who will win? Go ahead, York! Go ahead, Lancaster!

Stephen tried his best but the sum was too hard and he felt confused. The little silk badge with the white rose on it that was pinned on the breast of his jacket began to flutter. He was no good at sums but he tried his best so that York might not lose. Father Arnall's face looked very

black but he was not in a wax: he was laughing. Then Jack Lawton cracked his fingers and Father Arnall looked at his copybook and said:

—Right. Bravo Lancaster! The red rose wins. Come on now, York! Forge ahead!

Jack Lawton looked over from his side. The little silk badge with the red rose on it looked very rich because he had a blue sailor top on. Stephen felt his own face red too, thinking of all the bets about who would get first place in elements, Jack Lawton or he. Some weeks Jack Lawton got the card for first and some weeks he got the card for first. His white silk badge fluttered and fluttered as he worked at the next sum and heard Father Arnall's voice. Then all his eagerness passed away and he felt his face quite cool. He thought his face must be white because it felt so cool. He could not get out the answer for the sum but it did not matter. White roses and red roses: those were beautiful colours to think of. And the cards for first place and second place and third place were beautiful colours too: pink and cream and lavender. Lavender and cream and pink roses were beautiful to think of. Perhaps a wild rose might be like those colours and he remembered the song about the wild rose blossoms on the little green place. But you could not have a green rose. But perhaps somewhere in the world you could.

The bell rang and then the classes began to file out of the rooms and along the corridors towards the refectory. He sat looking at the two prints of butter on his plate but could not eat the damp bread. The tablecloth was damp and limp. But he drank off the hot weak tea which the clumsy scullion,[12] girt with a white apron, poured into his cup. He wondered whether the scullion's apron was damp too or whether all white things were cold and

---

12. **scullion.** Kitchen servant

❶
What aspect of this passage reveals Stephen to be a sensitive boy?

❷
What interests Stephen? What does not interest him? What sorts of associations does he make? What sorts of questions does he ask? How does this passage reveal him to have an artistic bent?

HISTORICAL NOTE

York and Lancaster were the opposing parties in the Wars of the Roses (1455–1485). Members of these two English houses, who fought over the English throne, wore roses to identify their affiliation—white for the House of York and red for the House of Lancaster. At the Battle of Bosworth in 1485, the Lancastrian Henry Tudor defeated the Yorkist Richard III. Henry was proclaimed King Henry IV, and through his marriage to Elizabeth of York, the opposing parties were united.

ADDITIONAL QUESTIONS AND ACTIVITIES

How does the contest at sums mirror the historical contest between York and Lancaster? What mood does this create in the selection?

Answers. Like in the historical contest, Lancaster emerges victorious. It creates a mood of resignation, as if Stephen's failure at sums is already an historical fact. Also, Stephen wears a white rose, one of the images that creates the objective correlative and creates a mood of loneliness and isolation.

ANSWERS TO GUIDED READING QUESTIONS

❶ Stephen is sensitive to the sounds of words. He is also sensitive to the embarrassment and pain of others.

❷ Stephen is interested in colors and beauty and in flowers. He is not interested in school learning. He makes associations with visual images. This shows his artistic tendencies.

❶ He is "sick in his heart" because he feels out of place and homesick.

❷ Stephen is confused because there seems to be no right answer to Wells's question. He does not understand that the other boys are deliberately trying to make him feel bad.

ANSWERS TO SELECTION CHECK TEST 4.11.3

EX. With what famous expression from children's stories does Joyce's novel begin?
It begins with the expression "Once upon a time."

1. What animal is described as "coming down along the road" in the opening paragraph of the selection?
A cow is described as "coming down along the road."

2. Who played the sailor's hornpipe on the piano for the boy to dance?
The boy's mother played it.

3. What game is played by the schoolboys?
They are playing football (soccer).

4. What question does Wells ask Stephen in the playroom, in front of the other boys?
He asks Stephen, "Do you kiss your mother before you go to bed?"

5. What does Stephen imagine being around the universe?
He imagines there being a very thin line around everything.

damp. Nasty Roche and Saurin drank cocoa that their people sent them in tins. They said they could not drink the tea; that it was hogwash. Their fathers were magistrates, the fellows said.

All the boys seemed to him very strange. They had all fathers and mothers and different clothes and voices. He longed to be at home and lay his head on his mother's lap. But he could not: and so he longed for the play and study and prayers to be over and to be in bed.

He drank another cup of hot tea and Fleming said:

—What's up? Have you a pain or what's up with you?

—I don't know, Stephen said.

—Sick in your breadbasket, Fleming said, because your face looks white. It will go away.

—O yes, Stephen said.

But he was not sick there. He thought that he was sick in his heart if you could be sick in that place. Fleming was very decent to ask him. He wanted to cry. He leaned his elbows on the table and shut and opened the flaps of his ears. Then he heard the noise of the refectory every time he opened the flaps of his ears. It made a roar like a train at night. And when he closed the flaps the roar was shut off like a train going into a tunnel. That night at Dalkey the train had roared like that and then, when it went into the tunnel, the roar stopped. He closed his eyes and the train went on, roaring and then stopping; roaring again, stopping. It was nice to hear it roar and stop and then roar out of the tunnel again and then stop.

Then the higher line fellows began to come down along the matting in the middle of the refectory, Paddy Rath and Jimmy Magee and the Spaniard who was allowed to smoke cigars and the little Portuguese who wore the woolly cap. And

❶ Why is Stephen "sick in his heart"?

❷ What might make the boys' teasing Stephen about this subject particularly difficult or confusing to him?

then the lower line tables and the tables of the third line. And every single fellow had a different way of walking.

He sat in a corner of the playroom pretending to watch a game of dominos and once or twice he was able to hear for an instant the little song of the gas. The prefect was at the door with some boys and Simon Moonan was knotting his false sleeves. He was telling them something about Tullabeg.

Then he went away from the door and Wells came over to Stephen and said:

—Tell us, Dedalus, do you kiss your mother before you go to bed?

Stephen answered:

—I do.

Wells turned to the other fellows and said:

—O, I say, here's a fellow says he kisses his mother every night before he goes to bed.

The other fellows stopped their game and turned round, laughing. Stephen blushed under their eyes and said:

—I do not.

Wells said:

—O, I say, here's a fellow says he doesn't kiss his mother before he goes to bed.

They all laughed again. Stephen tried to laugh with them. He felt his whole body hot and confused in a moment. What was the right answer to the question? He had given two and still Wells laughed. But Wells must know the right answer for he was in third of grammar. He tried to think of Wells's mother but he did not dare to raise his eyes to Wells's face. He did not like Wells's face. It was Wells who had shouldered him into the square ditch the day before because he would not swop his little snuffbox for Wells's seasoned hacking chestnut, the conqueror of forty. It was a mean thing to do; all the fellows said it was. And how cold and slimy the water had been! And a fellow had once seen a big rat jump plop into the scum.

The cold slime of the ditch covered his whole body; and, when the bell rang for study and the lines filed out of the play-rooms, he felt the cold air of the corridor and staircase inside his clothes. He still tried to think what was the right answer. Was it right to kiss his mother or wrong to kiss his mother? What did that mean, to kiss? You put your face up like that to say goodnight and then his mother put her face down. That was to kiss. His mother put her lips on his cheek; her lips were soft and they wetted his cheek; and they made a tiny little noise: kiss. Why did people do that with their two faces?

Sitting in the studyhall he opened the lid of his desk and changed the number pasted up inside from seventyseven to seventysix. But the Christmas vacation was very far away: but one time it would come because the earth moved round always.

There was a picture of the earth on the first page of his geography: a big ball in the middle of clouds. Fleming had a box of crayons and one night during free study he had coloured the earth green and the clouds maroon. That was like the two brushes in Dante's press, the brush with the green velvet back for Parnell and the brush with the maroon velvet back for Michael Davitt. But he had not told Fleming to colour them those colours. Fleming had done it himself.

He opened the geography to study the lesson; but he could not learn the names of places in America. Still they were all different places that had those different names. They were all in different countries and the countries were in continents and the continents were in the world and the world was in the universe.

He turned to the flyleaf[13] of the geography and read what he had written there: himself, his name and where he was.

> Stephen Dedalus
> Class of Elements
> Clongowes Wood College
> Sallins
> County Kildare
> Ireland
> Europe
> The World
> The Universe

That was in his writing: and Fleming one night for a cod had written on the opposite page:

> Stephen Dedalus is my name,
> Ireland is my nation.
> Clongowes is my dwellingplace
> And heaven my expectation.

He read the verses backwards but then they were not poetry. Then he read the flyleaf from the bottom to the top till he came to his own name. That was he: and he read down the page again. What was after the universe? Nothing. But was there anything round the universe to show where it stopped before the nothing place began? It could not be a wall but there could be a thin thin line there all round everything. It was very big to think about everything and everywhere. Only God could do that. He tried to think what a big thought that must be but he could think only of God. God was God's name just as his name was Stephen. *Dieu* was the French for God and that was God's name too; and when anyone prayed to God and said *Dieu* then God knew at once that it was a French person that was praying. But though there were different names for

13. **flyleaf.** A blank page at the beginning or end of a book

ANALYTIC SCALES FOR RESPONDING IN WRITING

Assign a score from 1 to 25 for each grading criterion below. (For more detailed evaluation, see the evaluation forms for writing, revising, and proofreading, *Assessment Portfolio,* 7.1–7.10.)

Stream-of-Consciousness Paragraph

• **Content/Unity.** The paragraph presents an image of a person, place, or object that was important to the writer.

• **Organization/Coherence.** The paragraph uses order of association.

• **Language/Style.** The paragraph uses vivid and precise nouns, verbs, and modifiers.

• **Conventions.** The paragraph avoids errors in spelling and manuscript form, but is not restricted by the conventions of grammar, usage, or mechanics.

►Additional practice is provided in the *Essential Skills Practice Book: Writing,* 1.11.

CROSS-CURRICULAR ACTIVITIES

Social Studies. Students can use an atlas to find Stephen's location. Then they can make their own lists of where they are. They should try to make their lists as detailed as possible.

❶ Perhaps Stephen feels confused thinking about things infinite.

❷ Stephen wants to understand politics and cosmology.

RESPONDING TO THE SELECTION

Suggest that students expand on the images and incidents in the selection rather than limiting themselves to recalling them.

ANSWERS FOR REVIEWING THE SELECTION

RECALLING

1. Stephen was called "baby tuckoo."

2. His body feels "small and weak."

3. Father Arnall knows more because he is a priest.

4. He wrote his name, followed by a series of places "where he was," with each place larger than the previous and ending with "The Universe." Stephen wonders what lies beyond the universe and what separates the universe from whatever lies beyond it.

INTERPRETING

Responses will vary. Possible responses are given.

5. Words and phrases such as *moocow, once upon a time,* and *wothe botheth* show infant Stephen's impression of the world.

6. Stephen is not interested in football: he feels that running after the ball would be "useless." He is afraid of the other boys: he feels his body is weak and "all the boys seemed to him very strange." He does not feel comfortable at school: he counts the days till he can leave and thinks frequently of his family.

7. Stephen respects Dante because she knows a lot and has taught him many things. He has fond memories of her from his childhood such as the story of the tissue paper and the cachou. He thinks of her often when he thinks of home.

8. Stephen's questions about the universe show that he is inquisitive and that he is interested in things beyond himself.

(cont.)

God in all the different languages in the world and God understood what all the people who prayed said in their different languages still God remained always the same God and God's real name was God.

It made him very tired to think that way. It made him feel his head very big. He turned over the flyleaf and looked wearily at the green round earth in the middle of the maroon clouds. He wondered which was right, to be for the green or for the maroon, because Dante had ripped the green velvet back off the brush that was for Parnell one day with her scissors and had told him that Parnell was a bad man.[14] He wondered if they were arguing at home about that. That was called politics. There were two sides in it: Dante was on one side and his father and Mr. Casey were on the other side but his mother and uncle Charles were on no side. Every day there was something in the paper about it.

It pained him that he did not know well what politics meant and that he did not know where the universe ended. He felt small and weak. When would he be like the fellows in poetry and rhetoric?[15] They had big voices and big boots and they studied trigonometry. That was very far away. First came the vacation and then the next term and then vacation again and then again another term and then again the vacation. It was like a train going in and out of tunnels and that was like the noise of the boys eating in the refectory when you opened and closed the flaps of the ears. Term, vacation; tunnel, out; noise, stop. How far away it was! It was better to go to bed to sleep. Only prayers in the chapel and then bed. He shivered and yawned. It would be lovely in bed after the sheets got a bit hot. First they were so cold to get into. He shivered to think how cold they were first. But then they got hot and then he could sleep. It was lovely to be tired. He yawned again. Night prayers and then bed: he shivered and wanted to yawn. It would be lovely in a few minutes. He felt a warm glow creeping up from the cold shivering sheets, warmer and warmer till he felt warm all over, ever so warm; ever so warm and yet he shivered a little and still wanted to yawn. ∎

---

14. **bad man.** Parnell, the Irish nationalist leader and supporter of home rule for Ireland, was involved in a scandal that ended his career.

15. **rhetoric.** Speech class

---

❶ *Why does thinking in "that way" make Stephen feel that his head is "very big"?*

❷ *How does this passage reveal Stephen's desire to grow in his understanding of things? What things does he want to understand?*

Responding to the Selection

Imagine that you are young Stephen Dedalus in this selection. Write a letter to your mother, telling her about your experiences at school and explaining what you miss most about home.

ANSWERS FOR REVIEWING THE SELECTION (CONT.)

SYNTHESIZING

Responses will vary. Possible responses are given.

9. Stephen's realities include bullies like Wells, athletes like Rody Kickham, teacher's pets like the prefect's Simon Moonan, and humiliating moments such as being kicked into the ditch or being asked the "kiss" question.

10. Stephen's artistic sensibilities are revealed at an early age when he recognizes the rhymes in "Pull out his eyes" and "apologise" and forms a poem. Later they are revealed in his enjoyment of words in the sentences of his spelling book, his attention to sounds, and his pleasure in the color of cards and roses.

Reviewing the Selection

RECALLING

1. What was Stephen called when he was a very small child?

2. What does the schoolboy Stephen feel his body is like "amid the throng of players"?

3. What reason is given for Father Arnall knowing more than Dante?

4. What did Stephen write on the flyleaf of his geography book? What questions does Stephen have about the universe?

INTERPRETING

5. What words or phrases show the world as little Stephen experiences it?

6. How does Stephen feel toward football (soccer)? toward the other boys? toward school? How do you know?

7. How does Stephen feel about Dante? How do you know?

8. What do Stephen's questions about the universe reveal about him?

SYNTHESIZING

9. What realities are part of Stephen's everyday life at school?

10. What aspects of this selection reveal the young Stephen to have artistic sensibilities?

Understanding Literature (Questions for Discussion)

1. **Stream-of-Consciousness Writing. Stream-of-consciousness writing** is literary work that attempts to render the flow of feelings, thoughts, and impressions within the minds of characters. One characteristic of stream-of-consciousness writing that sets it apart from ordinary narratives is that materials are presented in the order in which they occur in the mind of the protagonist, not necessarily in a logical order. Find passages in the selection that contain such leaps between ideas.

2. **Image/Objective Correlative.** An **image** is a word or phrase that names something that can be seen, heard, touched, tasted, or smelled. An **objective correlative** is a group of images that together create a particular emotion in the reader. What images are used in the selection to describe the feeling of dampness? What is the effect of this group of images on the reader? What do the images convey about Stephen's experience?

ANSWERS FOR UNDERSTANDING LITERATURE

▶See the evaluation forms for discussion, active listening, and oral communication, *Assessment Portfolio*, 7.11–7.14.
Responses will vary. Possible responses are given.

1. Stream-of-Consciousness Writing. Stephen is describing being on the playground. This flows into thoughts of his mother and being left at school. Then his thoughts go back to the scrimmage, the castle, his spelling book, home again, being pushed in the ditch, and again home.

▶**Teaching Note:** Suggest that students consider the descriptive elements and sensory details in the passage that indicate a writer's skill of observation.

2. Image/Objective Correlative. Images of cold, white objects—the oilsheet, lavatory, sink handles, and square ditch—are used throughout to describe the feeling of dampness. The cumulative effect of these images is unpleasant and reminiscent of homesickness and loneliness. They convey that Stephen misses home and feels alone at school.

▶**Teaching Note:** Students can discuss the difference between image and objective correlative by discussing the feelings evoked by a singular image and the cumulative feelings evoked by a series of images.

Responding in Writing

Stream-of-Consciousness Paragraph. Close your eyes and think back to when you were a young child. Try to visualize a place, person, or object that was very important to you—perhaps the bed you slept in or your grandfather's beard or the songs your mother sang. Then write a stream-of-consciousness paragraph while keeping that subject in mind, letting yourself freely associate words, impressions, and reactions to that subject. Write either from the point of view of yourself now, looking back on the subject, or from the point of view of yourself then, actually experiencing the subject.

Language Lab

Correcting Run-ons. Read the Language Arts Survey, 2.62, "Correcting Run-ons." Then revise the sentences below by changing punctuation and capitalization and adding words as necessary.

1. Joyce admired the work of Henrik Ibsen, a Norwegian poet and playwright, Joyce's first publication was an essay, "Ibsen's New Drama."

2. Joyce's *Dubliners* is a brilliant collection of short stories some of these stories are autobiographical.

3. Joyce's books were banned by censors and pirated by publishers these are just two of the reasons why Joyce earned almost nothing from his writing until his last few years.

4. Joyce's hero Stephen Dedalus says, "I will not serve that in which I no longer believe," this statement appears in the novel *A Portrait of the Artist as a Young Man.*

5. Stephen Dedalus appears again later, much older, in another novel by James Joyce, that novel is *Ulysses.*

PROJECTS

1. **Kenning Invention Game.** Sit with your classmates in a circle. Have one person name a common noun—a person, place, or object. Then, going around the circle, have each person invent a compound word to take the place of the common noun.

2. **Children's Book.** As a class, prepare a book of rhymes and songs for young children. Remember to write about objects that children can easily identify. Here are some possible subjects: a moocow, a goodnight kiss, a wide playground, or a roaring train. You may want to prepare illustrations for the cover and interior of your book. When the book is complete, make copies for local elementary schools or day-care centers.

PROJECT NOTES

▶ See the worksheets and evaluation forms for projects, *Assessment Portfolio,* 7.20–7.23.

1. Kenning Invention Game

• Encourage students to brainstorm sensory details about each common noun.

• Students might want to write a children's story using the kennings they invent.

• Students can keep their kennings to themselves and then enact them for the group in a game of charades.

2. Children's Book

Suggest that students spark their thinking by looking at children's books by Dr. Seuss or other writers who create inventive rhymes.

PREREADING

from *Nineteen Eighty-four*
by George Orwell

ABOUT THE AUTHOR

George Orwell (1903–1950) was the pseudonym of Eric Arthur Blair. Orwell was born in India, where his father served in the civil service. He won a scholarship to Eton but was financially unable to continue his education at Oxford or Cambridge. From 1922 to 1927, he worked for the Imperial Police in Burma; the experience provided much of the material for his early work, including the novel *Burmese Days* (1934) and the title work in the essay collection *Shooting an Elephant* (1950). For years Orwell worked at ill-paid jobs. He described his experiences with poverty in *Down and Out in Paris and London* (1933). His experiences in the Spanish Civil War, in which he fought on the Republican side and was wounded, are recounted in *Homage to Catalonia* (1939). An early convert to Socialism, Orwell was angered by the ruthless, authoritarian policies of the Soviet Union under Lenin and Stalin. His two best-known novels, *Animal Farm* (1945) and *Nineteen Eighty-four* (1949), are attacks on Soviet-style totalitarianism. Orwell's other works include *Keep the Aspidistra Flying* (1936), *Coming Up for Air* (1939), and the posthumously published *Collected Essays, Journalism and Letters* (1968).

ABOUT THE SELECTION

The novel ***Nineteen Eighty-four*** is the story of a middle-aged man and a young woman who rebel against the futuristic, totalitarian society in which they live. In this terrifying society, truth is replaced by propaganda, thought and love are punished, individual privacy is impossible, and people are forced to worship the head of the party that controls everything, a figure known as Big Brother. Orwell published his satire against totalitarianism in 1949, the year that the Soviet Union built its first atomic bomb; the satire is mainly directed against the Soviet Union. Big Brother may represent the Soviet leader Joseph Stalin. In the first selection, from Chapter One of the novel, the reader is introduced to the elements of Winston Smith's day-to-day life in the country of Oceania. An account of the structure and etymology of Newspeak, the official language of Oceania, is given in "The Principles of Newspeak," from the Appendix of the novel.

ADDITIONAL RESOURCES

READER'S GUIDE
• Selection Worksheet, 11.3

ASSESSMENT PORTFOLIO
• Selection Check Test, 4.11.5
• Selection Test, 4.11.6

ESSENTIAL SKILLS PRACTICE BOOKS
• *Language*, 2.110, 2.118

ENRICHMENT ACTIVITIES

Students can write about or discuss how living in a totalitarian state would affect their day-to-day lives. Have them draw comparisons between how they live now and how they imagine life in a police state would be.

SUPPORT FOR LEP STUDENTS

Explain that students will encounter many unfamiliar words created by Orwell to satirize propaganda techniques and totalitarianism.

ADDITIONAL VOCABULARY
vile—very disagreeable
conceivable—imaginable
frowsy—untidy; dirty
compromising—exposing to danger
archaic—outdated
tremor—shiver

GOALS/OBJECTIVES

Studying this lesson will enable students to

• experience Winston's feelings of discomfort and fear from a constant state of being under surveillance

• describe George Orwell's political views and explain their effect on his writing

• define *satire* and recognize and interpret satiric elements in literature they read

• define *science fiction* and identify science fiction that they encounter in their reading

• understand propaganda techniques

PREREADING NOTES

READER'S JOURNAL

For an entire day, students can keep a log of every action they perform. At the end of the day, students can comment on their activities and how they felt about tracking themselves.

LANGUAGE SKILLS

Students can also list the buildings and structures named in the selection. Refer students to the Language Arts Survey, 2.110, "Capitalization: Buildings and Structures."

▶ Additional practice is provided in the *Essential Skills Practice Book: Language*, 2.110 and 2.118.

VOCABULARY FROM THE SELECTION

interminable	sordid
magnitude	strident
ramification	tableau
sanguine	truncheon
scrutinize	

ANSWERS TO GUIDED READING QUESTIONS

❶ The message says "Big Brother Is Watching You." The eyes on the picture seem to follow you, giving the impression that you really are being watched.

❷ The telescreen constantly emits noise that cannot be shut off. At this point a "fruity voice" is babbling about pig iron.

READER'S JOURNAL

Have you ever been in a department store where surveillance cameras monitored your actions? What did it feel like to be "watched" by the camera? What would it feel like to have a surveillance camera in your own home, recording every movement that you make? Freewrite about privacy in your journal.

LANGUAGE SKILLS

Read the Language Arts Survey, 2.118, "Capitalization: Organizations and Institutions." Then, as you read the selection, make a list of the organizations and institutions mentioned in it.

FROM

Nineteen Eighty-four

GEORGE ORWELL

CHAPTER 1

❶ What is the message on the poster? How does the design of the picture on the poster add to the effect of the words?

❷ What sound comes from the telescreen?

It was a bright cold day in April, and the clocks were striking thirteen. Winston Smith, his chin nuzzled into his breast in an effort to escape the vile wind, slipped quickly through the glass doors of Victory Mansions, though not quickly enough to prevent a swirl of gritty dust from entering along with him.

The hallway smelt of boiled cabbage and old rag mats. At one end of it a colored poster, too large for indoor display, had been tacked to the wall. It depicted simply an enormous face, more than a meter wide: the face of a man of about forty-five, with a heavy black mustache and ruggedly handsome features. Winston made for the stairs. It was no use trying the lift. Even at the best of times it was seldom working, and at present the electric current was cut off during daylight hours. It was part of the economy drive in preparation for Hate Week. The flat was seven flights up, and Winston, who was thirty-nine, and had a varicose ulcer above his right ankle, went slowly, resting several times on the way. On each landing, opposite the lift shaft, the poster with the enormous face gazed from the wall. It was one of those pictures which are so contrived that the eyes follow you about when you move. BIG BROTHER IS WATCHING YOU, the caption beneath it ran.

Inside the flat a fruity voice was reading out a list of figures which had something to do with the production of pig iron. The voice came from an oblong metal plaque like a dulled mirror which formed part of the surface of the right-hand wall. Winston turned a switch and the voice sank somewhat, though the words were still distinguishable. The instrument (the telescreen, it was called) could be dimmed, but there was no way of shutting it off completely. He moved over to the window: a smallish, frail figure, the meagerness of his body merely emphasized by the blue overalls which were the uniform of the Party. His hair was very fair, his face naturally <u>sanguine</u>, his skin roughened by coarse soap and blunt razor blades and the cold of the winter that had just ended.

Outside, even through the shut window pane, the world looked cold. Down in the street little eddies of wind were whirling dust and torn paper into spirals, and though the sun was shining and the sky a harsh blue, there seemed to be no color in anything except the posters that were plastered everywhere. The black-mustachio'd face gazed down from every commanding corner. There was one on the house front immediately opposite. BIG BROTHER IS WATCHING YOU, the caption said, while the dark eyes looked deep into Winston's own. Down at street level another poster, torn at one corner, flapped fitfully in the wind, alternately covering and uncovering the single word INGSOC.[1] In the far distance a helicopter skimmed down between the roofs, hovered for an instant like a blue-bottle, and darted away again with a curving flight. It was the Police Patrol, snooping into people's windows. The patrols did not matter, however. Only the Thought Police mattered.

Behind Winston's back the voice from the telescreen was still babbling away about pig iron and the overfulfillment of the Ninth Three-Year Plan. The telescreen received and transmitted simultaneously. Any sound that Winston made, above the level of a very low whisper, would be picked up by it; moreover, so long as he remained within the field of vision which the metal plaque commanded, he could be seen as well as heard. There was of course no way of knowing whether you were being watched at any given moment. How often, or on what system, the Thought Police plugged in on any individual wire was guesswork. It was even conceivable that they watched everybody all the time. But at any rate they could plug in your wire whenever they wanted to. You had to live—did live, from habit that became instinct—in the assumption that every sound you made was overheard, and, except in darkness, every movement <u>scrutinized</u>.

Winston kept his back turned to the telescreen. It was safer; though, as he well knew, even a back can be revealing. A kilometer away the Ministry of Truth, his place of work, towered vast and white above the grimy landscape. This, he thought with a sort of vague distaste—this was London, chief city of Airstrip One, itself the third most populous of the provinces of Oceania. He tried to squeeze out some childhood memory that should tell him whether London had always been quite like this. Were there always these vistas of rotting nineteenth-century houses, their sides shored up with balks of timber, their windows patched with cardboard and their roofs with corrugated iron, their crazy garden walls sagging in all directions? And the bombed sites where the plaster dust swirled in the air and the willow herb straggled over the heaps of rubble; and the places where the bombs had cleared a larger path and there had sprung up <u>sordid</u> colonies of wooden

---
1. **INGSOC.** An acronym for "English socialism." INGSOC is the name of the political party that rules Oceania.

❶ How does the telescreen differ from the televisions with which you are familiar?

CROSS-CURRICULAR ACTIVITIES

• **Applied Arts.** Students can discuss modern electronic devices that make possible the kind of surveillance described here. Why are such devices used? By whom?

• **Applied Arts.** Interested students can research and report on how these devices work and their capabilities.

• **Social Studies.** Interested students can research and report on laws protecting privacy, and on the limit of these protections.

• **Arts and Humanities.** Students can draw or paint the view from Winston's window in Victory Mansions. Encourage them to use colors or shading that suggests the scene's mood.

ANSWER TO GUIDED READING QUESTION

❶ The telescreen transmits voices and visual images two ways instead of one. Also, the telescreen cannot be turned off.

VOCABULARY IN CONTEXT

• His complexion became <u>sanguine</u> in extreme cold or heat.
• The meat inspectors <u>scrutinize</u> each piece of meat for any signs of contamination.
• The Red Cross volunteers delivered clean bandages to the refugee camp's <u>sordid</u> medical tent.

HISTORICAL NOTE

In Russia, Stalinistic propaganda of the 1930s and 1940s declared that Stalin's assessment of the arts, science, education, and history was the "true" version. Anyone who dared to disagree was likely to be assassinated or deported to a forced-labor camp.

ANSWERS TO GUIDED READING QUESTIONS

❶ The slogans are "War Is Peace," "Freedom Is Slavery," and "Ignorance Is Strength." The slogans are all paradoxical. They make little sense but promote party ideas that war and ignorance are good things and freedom is a bad thing. All three promote conditions that give the party complete control over people.

❷ The government is divided into four branches: the Ministry of Truth, the Ministry of Peace, the Ministry of Love, and the Ministry of Plenty. The Ministry of Truth is responsible for dispersing approved information which is to be considered truth by the people. The Ministry of Peace is concerned with war. The Ministry of Love maintains law and order, and the Ministry of Plenty is in charge of economics. These names hide a lack of truth, peace, love, and plenty.

dwellings like chicken houses? But it was no use, he could not remember: nothing remained of his childhood except a series of bright-lit tableaux, occurring against no background and mostly unintelligible.

The Ministry of Truth—Minitrue, In Newspeak[2]—was startlingly different from any other object in sight. It was an enormous pyramidal structure of glittering white concrete, soaring up, terrace after terrace, three hundred meters into the air. From where Winston stood it was just possible to read, picked out on its white face in elegant lettering, the three slogans of the Party:

❶
What are the slogans of the party? What do these slogans mean? What does the party stand for?

WAR IS PEACE

FREEDOM IS SLAVERY

IGNORANCE IS STRENGTH

The Ministry of Truth contained, it was said, three thousand rooms above ground level, and corresponding ramifications below. Scattered about London there were just three other buildings of similar appearance and size. So completely did they dwarf the surrounding architecture that from the roof of Victory Mansions you could see all four of them simultaneously. They were the homes of the four Ministries between which the entire apparatus of government was divided: the Ministry of Truth, which concerned itself with news, entertainment, education, and the fine arts; the Ministry of Peace, which concerned itself with war; the Ministry of

❷
How is the government organized? What does each branch do? Why might the branches of the government be named as they are?

2. **Newspeak.** Newspeak is the official language of Oceania.

Love, which maintained law and order; and the Ministry of Plenty, which was responsible for economic affairs. Their names, in Newspeak: Minitrue, Minipax, Miniluv, and Miniplenty.

The Ministry of Love was the really frightening one. There were no windows in it at all. Winston had never been inside the Ministry of Love, nor within half a kilometer of it. It was a place impossible to enter except on official business, and then only by penetrating through a maze of barbed-wire entanglements, steel doors, and hidden machine-gun nests. Even the streets leading up to its outer barriers were roamed by gorilla-faced guards in black uniforms, armed with jointed truncheons.

Winston turned round abruptly. He had set his features into the expression of quiet optimism which it was advisable to wear when facing the telescreen. He crossed the room into the tiny kitchen. By leaving the Ministry at this time of day he had sacrificed his lunch in the canteen, and he was aware that there was no food in the kitchen except a hunk of dark colored bread which had got to be saved for tomorrow's breakfast. He took down from the shelf a bottle of colorless liquid with a plain white label marked VICTORY GIN. It gave off a sickly, oily smell, as of Chinese rice-spirit. Winston poured out nearly a teacupful, nerved himself for a shock, and gulped it down like a dose of medicine.

Instantly his face turned scarlet and the water ran out of his eyes. The stuff was like nitric acid, and moreover, in swallowing it one had the sensation of being hit on the back of the head with a rubber club. The next moment, however, the

WORDS FOR EVERYDAY USE:

tab • leau (tab´lō´) n., dramatic scene
ram • i • fi • ca • tion (ram´ə fi kā´shen) n., branch
trun • cheon (trun´chən) n., short club

934 UNIT ELEVEN / TWENTIETH-CENTURY PROSE

VOCABULARY IN CONTEXT

• The mural's faded tableau depicts a long-forgotten battle.
• Because of the department's many ramifications, most employees only knew those people who worked in their own branch.
• Each police officer's riot gear included a heavy, black truncheon.

photograph ©1995 The Museum of Modern Art, NY

Portrait (Le Portrait). *René Magritte, 1935.*
The Museum of Modern Art, NY.
Gift of Kay Sage Tanguy

burning in his belly died down and the world began to look more cheerful. He took a cigarette from a crumpled packet marked VICTORY CIGARETTES and incautiously held it upright, whereupon the tobacco fell out onto the floor. With the next he was more successful. He went back to the living room and sat down at a small table that stood to the left of the telescreen. From the table drawer he took out a penholder, a bottle of ink, and a thick, quarto-sized blank book with a red back and a marbled cover.

For some reason the telescreen in the living room was in an unusual position. Instead of being placed, as was normal, in the end wall where it could command the whole room, it was in the longer wall, opposite the window. To one side of it there was a shallow alcove in which Winston was now sitting and which, when the flats were built, had probably been intended to hold bookshelves. By sitting in the alcove, and keeping well back, Winston was able to remain outside the range of the telescreen, so far as sight went. He could be heard, of course, but so long as he stayed in his present position he could not be seen. It was partly the unusual geography of the room that had suggested to him the thing that he was now about to do.

But it had also been suggested by the book that he had just taken out of the drawer. It was a peculiarly beautiful book. Its smooth creamy paper, a little yellowed by age, was of a kind that had not been manufactured for at least forty years past. He could guess, however, that the book was much older than that. He had seen it lying in the window of a frowsy little junk shop in a slummy quarter of the town (just what quarter he did not now remember) and had been stricken immediately by an overwhelming desire to possess it. Party members were supposed

❶
What is unusual about the position of Winston's telescreen? What opportunity does this unusual circumstance afford him?

ART NOTE

Belgian artist **René Magritte** (1881–1967) belongs to the Surrealist school of painting. Other Surrealist artists include Salvador Dalí (Spanish), Joan Miró (Spanish), Max Ernst (German), and Jean Arp (French). Although quite different from each other, the Surrealists experimented in individual ways in a common attempt to unite the unconscious—imagination, dreams, and fantasies—with everyday conscious experience. For some artists, this meant transforming their fantasies into a form of reality on canvas. For others, such as Magritte, it meant depicting the irrationality and illogicality of the unconscious: the world of the painting appears realistic and clear but is impossibly undecipherable and self-contradictory.

Although the presentation of objects in a Magritte painting is realistic, the combinations are not. Magritte's strange juxtapositions produce challenging, unsettling effects. The eye staring up from the plate transforms a benign still life into an eerie portrait.

▶**Teaching Note:** Students can discuss whether such artwork would be acceptable in Oceania, and what the painting suggests about performing even the most basic and intimate activities in a totalitarian society.

ANSWER TO GUIDED READING QUESTION

❶ The telescreen in Winston's apartment is so located that he is able to go into an alcove and be out of sight. This allows him the opportunity to engage in unmonitored activities, such as keeping a diary.

ANSWERS TO GUIDED READING QUESTIONS

❶ Winston is about to begin a diary. Such an action would be punishable by death.

❷ Winston feels that writing for the future is useless because if the future were similar to the past, nobody would listen to him, and if the future were different, his situation would be meaningless. This pessimistic attitude might stem from living in a society that condemns individuality and free will and that scorns the notion that an individual can make a difference.

---

not to go into ordinary shops ("dealing on the free market," it was called), but the rule was not strictly kept, because there were various things such as shoelaces and razor blades which it was impossible to get hold of in any other way. He had given a quick glance up and down the street and then had slipped inside and bought the book for two dollars fifty. At the time he was not conscious of wanting it for any particular purpose. He had carried it guiltily home in his brief case. Even with nothing written in it, it was a compromising possession.

The thing that he was about to do was to open a diary. This was not illegal (nothing was illegal, since there were no longer any laws), but if detected it was reasonably certain that it would be punished by death, or at least by twenty-five years in a forced-labor camp. Winston fitted a nib into the penholder and sucked it to get the grease off. The pen was an archaic instrument, seldom used even for signatures, and he had procured one, furtively and with some difficulty, simply because of a feeling that the beautiful creamy paper deserved to be written on with a real nib instead of being scratched with an ink pencil. Actually he was not used to writing by hand. Apart from very short notes, it was usual to dictate everything into the speakwrite, which was of course impossible for his present purpose. He dipped the pen into the ink and then faltered for just a second. A tremor had gone through his bowels. To mark the paper was the decisive act. In small clumsy letters he wrote:

❶ *What is Winston going to do? What are the possible consequences of his actions?*

❷ *What revelation does Winston have about writing for the future? Do you agree with him? Why might Winston have such a pessimistic attitude?*

APRIL 4TH, 1984.

He sat back. A sense of complete helplessness had descended upon him. To begin with, he did not know with any certainty that this *was* 1984. It must be round about that date, since he was fairly sure that his age was thirty-nine, and he believed that he had been born in 1944 or 1945; but it was never possible nowadays to pin down any date within a year or two.

For whom, it suddenly occurred to him to wonder, was he writing this diary? For the future, for the unborn. His mind hovered for a moment round the doubtful date on the page, and then fetched up with a bump against the Newspeak word *doublethink*. For the first time the magnitude of what he had undertaken came home to him. How could you communicate with the future? It was of its nature impossible. Either the future would resemble the present in which case it would not listen to him, or it would be different from it, and his predicament would be meaningless.

For some time he sat gazing stupidly at the paper. The telescreen had changed over to strident military music. It was curious that he seemed not merely to have lost the power of expressing himself, but even to have forgotten what it was that he had originally intended to say. For weeks past he had been making ready for this moment, and it had never crossed his mind that anything would be needed except courage. The actual writing would be easy. All he had to do was to transfer to paper the interminable restless monologue that had been running inside his head, literally for years. ∎

WORDS FOR EVERYDAY USE:

mag • ni • tude (mag′nə tōōd′) *n.,* extent

stri • dent (strīd′′nt) *adj.,* harsh, shrill

in • ter • mi • na • ble (in tʉr′mi nə bəl) *adj.,* without end

---

VOCABULARY IN CONTEXT

- The <u>magnitude</u> of the hurricane's force was woefully underestimated.
- We covered our ears at the sound of the <u>strident</u> whistle.
- Several filmgoers complained that the four-hour documentary seemed <u>interminable</u>.

from "Principles of Newspeak,"
an Appendix to George Orwell's *Nineteen Eighty-four*

Newspeak was the official language of Oceania and had been devised to meet the ideological needs of Ingsoc, or English Socialism. In the year 1984 there was not as yet anyone who used Newspeak as his sole means of communication, either in speech or writing. The leading articles in the *Times* were written in it, but this was a tour de force which could only be carried out by a specialist. It was expected that Newspeak would have finally superseded Oldspeak (or Standard English, as we should call it) by about the year 2050. Meanwhile it gained ground steadily, all Party members tending to use Newspeak words and grammatical constructions more and more in their everyday speech. The version in use in 1984, and embodied in the Ninth and Tenth Editions of the Newspeak dictionary, was a provisional one, and contained many superfluous words and archaic formations which were due to be suppressed later. It is with the final, perfected version, as embodied in the Eleventh Edition of the dictionary, that we are concerned here.

The purpose of Newspeak was not only to provide a medium of expression for the world-view and mental habits proper to the devotees of Ingsoc, but to make all other modes of thought impossible. It was intended that when Newspeak had been adopted once and for all and Oldspeak forgotten, a heretical thought—that is, a thought diverging from the principles of Ingsoc—should be literally unthinkable, at least so far as thought is dependent on words. Its vocabulary was so constructed as to give exact and often very subtle expression to every meaning that a Party member could properly wish to express, while excluding all other meanings and also the possibility of arriving at them by indirect methods. This was done partly by the invention of new words, but chiefly by eliminating undesirable words and by stripping such words as remained of unorthodox meanings, and so far as possible of all secondary meanings whatever. To give a single example. The word *free* still existed in Newspeak, but it could only be used in such statements as "This dog is free from lice" or "This field is free from weeds." It could not be used in its old sense of "politically free" or "intellectually free," since political and intellectual freedom no longer existed even as concepts, and were therefore of necessity nameless. Quite apart from the suppression of definitely heretical words, reduction of vocabulary was regarded as an end in itself, and no word that could be dispensed with was allowed to survive. Newspeak was designed not to extend but to *diminish* the range of thought, and this purpose was indirectly assisted by cutting the choice of words down to a minimum.

RESPONDING TO THE SELECTION

 Students may want to create a code language for writing private entries in their diaries.

ANSWERS FOR REVIEWING THE SELECTION

RECALLING

1. The clocks are striking thirteen.
2. Winston lives in Victory Mansions.
3. "Big Brother Is Watching You" is written on the posters.
4. The government is divided into four Ministries: Truth, Peace, Love, and Plenty.

INTERPRETING

Responses will vary. Possible responses are given.

5. This society runs on military time.
6. The prisonlike quality of Winston's flat is emphasized by the telescreen that monitors Winston's actions and words, thus depriving him of any privacy.
7. He turns his back on "Big Brother" and the telescreen, crowding himself into the tiny alcove to write in the diary.
8. The lack of windows, the maze of barbed wire, steel doors, and "hidden machine-gun nests" support the description.

SYNTHESIZING

Responses will vary. Possible responses are given.

9. The fact that Winston is risking punishment by death or forced labor shows how critical the diary is to his personal survival.
10. The relationship is described as one in which a police state or totalitarian government reduces the human beings, and anything they create through human thought and enterprise, to mere "workers." Such a society would create a hopeless, humorless, thoughtless, apathetic, and diminished individual.

Responding to the Selection

> Imagine that you are Winston Smith in the opening chapter of this novel. You have just entered the date on the first page of your diary. Now write the first paragraph in your diary. Express your feelings toward Big Brother and the party.

Reviewing the Selection

RECALLING

1. What is the time at the beginning of the novel?

2. What is the name of the building in which Winston lives?

3. What caption is written on the posters that are "plastered everywhere"?

4. What four ministries divide up the tasks of the government?

INTERPRETING

5. What organization in the real world uses the same kind of time used in Oceania?

6. What facts emphasize the prisonlike quality of Winston's flat?

7. What action on the part of Winston shows that he does not find comfort in the caption written on the posters?

8. What facts support the description of the Ministry of Love as "the really frightening one"?

SYNTHESIZING

9. What is the significance of Winston Smith's decision to open a diary? What consequences might this action have for him?

10. What sort of relationship between the individual and society is described in this selection? What kind of individual would this kind of society create?

Understanding Literature (Questions for Discussion)

Science Fiction/Dystopia. Science fiction is highly imaginative fiction containing fantastic elements based upon scientific principles, discoveries, or laws. What aspects of this selection make it an example of science fiction? A **dystopia** is an imaginary horrible world, the opposite of a utopia. What specific characteristics make Oceania a dystopia? Science fiction is often written for the purpose of warning us about possible consequences of current trends. About what trends in modern society did Orwell wish to warn us?

ANSWERS FOR UNDERSTANDING LITERATURE

▶ See the evaluation forms for discussion, active listening, and oral communication, *Assessment Portfolio,* 7.11–7.14.

Science Fiction/Dystopia. In Winston's dystopian world, a telescreen informs the Thought Police of what he says and does. The telescreen and the Thought Police are examples of fantastic elements that make this selection an example of science fiction. Oceana is a dystopia because the inhabitants must endure surveillance by the Thought Police, inferior products (coarse soap, blunt razor blades), enforced "economy drives," and substandard living quarters. Orwell warns of the dangers of totalitarian governments and the need to maintain personal freedom.

Responding in Writing

Diary Entry/Science Fiction. Imagine that you are Winston, the protagonist in this novel. Write an entry for your diary describing one of the following events: (a) having someone else discover that you are keeping a diary, (b) encountering a member of a radical underground movement dedicated to overthrowing the party, or (c) being interrogated by officers of the Thought Police.

PROJECTS

1. **Oceania News.** As a class, extend Orwell's critique of totalitarianism by creating the official newspaper published by the Ministry of Truth. Work in groups large enough to cover the official topics: news, entertainment, education, and the fine arts. Write articles and headlines for each of the topics, using language that you think the party in Orwell's novel would approve. Generate a computer or handmade layout of your completed newspaper.

2. **Cold War History.** As a class, do research on the cold war. Form small groups, assigning to each group one of the following figures or developments of the cold war period: Joseph Stalin, Nikita Khrushchev, Harry Truman, Winston Churchill, the Marshall Plan, the Warsaw Pact, Senator Joseph McCarthy, or the Berlin Wall. Then present the results of your research in class, combining oral reporting with slides or photographs from books.

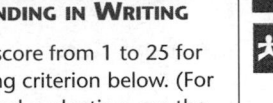

ANALYTIC SCALES FOR RESPONDING IN WRITING

Assign a score from 1 to 25 for each grading criterion below. (For more detailed evaluation, see the evaluation forms for writing, revising, and proofreading, *Assessment Portfolio*, 7.1–7.10.)

Diary Entry/Science Fiction

• **Content/Unity.** The entry presents a description of an event and the writer's reaction to it based on life in a totalitarian society.

• **Organization/Coherence.** The entry presents the events and the writer's feelings in a logical and coherent order.

• **Language/Style.** The entry uses vivid and precise nouns, verbs, and modifiers.

• **Conventions.** The entry avoids errors in spelling, grammar, usage, mechanics, and manuscript form.

PROJECT NOTES

► See the worksheets and evaluation forms for projects, *Assessment Portfolio*, 7.20–7.23.

 1. Oceania News. Instead of printing a newspaper, students might want to present their articles as news reports for the telescreen.

 2. Cold War History. Students might role play figures from the cold war.

 Students can make their presentations in the form of dramatic monologues.

ENRICHMENT ACTIVITIES

Refer students to the historical information about the Georgian Age on page 828. Then have students research the social conditions in England during this period.

SUPPORT FOR LEP STUDENTS

Students who are not as comfortable and familiar with the language might not realize the slightly satiric tone of the portrayal of the upper class. Discuss this aspect of the story with the students.

ADDITIONAL VOCABULARY

kimono—a woman's loose dressing gown

lanky—tall and lean

affected—artificial to impress people

exquisite—very beautiful

alight—come down after flight

frock—a girl's or woman's dress

PREREADING

"The Garden-Party"
by Katherine Mansfield

ABOUT THE AUTHOR

Katherine Mansfield (1888–1923) was born in Wellington, New Zealand. In 1903, she moved to London with her family and stayed to study music at Queen's College. There she met and became friends with D. H. Lawrence and Aldous Huxley, who encouraged her to write. Mansfield returned to New Zealand in 1906, having written numerous poems, sketches, and short stories. Rebellious and ambitious by nature, Mansfield went back to London in 1908 and never returned to New Zealand. Mansfield's first volume of short stories, *In a German Pension*, was published in 1911. One year later, she met the editor and critic John Middleton Murry, whom she married in 1918. Throughout this time, Mansfield experimented with technique, refining her work to achieve a short story that would evoke insights into certain kinds of experiences through patterns of precise imagery and style. She was an ardent admirer of the stories of the Russian writer Anton Chekhov. Her grief over the death of her brother in 1915 seemed to infuse her writing with freshness and greater subtlety. During this time she produced her best stories: "Prelude," "Daughters of the Late Colonel," "At the Bay," and "The Garden-Party." Her collection, *Prelude*, was published in 1918, followed two years later by *Bliss and Other Stories*. By the time of the 1922 publication of *The Garden-Party and Other Stories*, which assured Mansfield's place as a master of the short story, she was already gravely ill with tuberculosis. She died in France in 1923.

ABOUT THE SELECTION

Considered to be one of her best stories, **"The Garden-Party"** was written at a time when Mansfield was looking back at her childhood experiences in New Zealand. One of the events on which Mansfield focused was a garden party given by her mother in the spring of 1907. The basis of her story was a fatal street accident that occurred to a neighbor in the midst of the festivities. The selection shows Mansfield's ability to combine incident, image, symbol, and structure to clarify her protagonist, Laura, and to capture the essential reality of the story.

GOALS/OBJECTIVES

Studying this lesson will enable students to

• empathize with Laura's distress, concern, and discomfort

• describe Katherine Mansfield's contribution to twentieth-century literature and how her writing reflects the social atmosphere of the time

• define *image* and *objective correlative* and determine the emotions such images create in the reader

• define *symbol* and recognize and interpret symbols that they encounter in their reading

• identify base words and suffixes

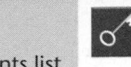

READER'S JOURNAL

Have you had an experience that caused you to look at your own life in a new way? Write about that experience in your journal, telling how you looked at your own life differently and why.

THINKING SKILLS

Read the Language Arts Survey, 4.5, "Remembering and Visualizing." Then create a list of particularly vivid images that describe the setting of the garden party in detail.

"The Garden-Party"

KATHERINE MANSFIELD

And after all the weather was ideal. They could not have had a more perfect day for a garden-party if they had ordered it. Windless, warm, the sky without a cloud. Only the blue was veiled with a haze of light gold, as it is sometimes in early summer. The gardener had been up since dawn, mowing the lawns and sweeping them, until the grass and the dark flat rosettes where the daisy plants had been seemed to shine. As for the roses, you could not help feeling they understood that roses are the only flowers that impress people at garden-parties; the only flowers that everybody is certain of knowing. Hundreds, yes, literally hundreds, had come out in a single night; the green bushes bowed down as though they had been visited by archangels.

Breakfast was not yet over before the men came to put up the <u>marquee</u>.

"Where do you want the marquee put, mother?"

"My dear child, it's no use asking me. I'm determined to leave everything to you children this year. Forget I am your mother. Treat me as an honored guest."

But Meg could not possibly go and supervise the men. She had washed her hair before breakfast, and she sat drinking her coffee in a green turban, with a dark wet curl stamped on each cheek. Jose, the butterfly, always came down in a silk petticoat and a kimono jacket.

"You'll have to go, Laura; you're the artistic one."

Away Laura flew, still holding her piece of bread-and-butter. It's so delicious to have an excuse for eating out of doors, and besides, she loved having to arrange things; she always felt she could do it so much better than anybody else.

Four men in their shirt-sleeves stood grouped together on the garden path. They carried <u>staves</u> covered with rolls of

❶
In what way was the day "ideal"? What was the gardener doing to prepare for the party?

PREREADING NOTES

READER'S JOURNAL

Suggest that students list adjectives and adverbs that reflect how they felt before and after their life-changing experience.

THINKING SKILLS

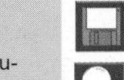

Artistically minded students may wish to paint or sketch a scene from "The Garden-Party."

▶Additional practice is provided in the *Essential Skills Practice Book: Study and Research*, 4.5.

ANSWER TO GUIDED READING QUESTION

❶ The weather and the roses that had opened overnight were "ideal." The gardener was mowing and sweeping the lawns to prepare for the party.

VOCABULARY FROM THE SELECTION

baize	rapturous
enigmatically	sordid
haggard	stave
marquee	veranda

WORDS FOR EVERYDAY USE:

mar • quee (mär kē´) *n.*, tent with open sides
stave (stāv) *n.*, pole

VOCABULARY IN CONTEXT

- When the rain began falling, the garden-party guests took shelter under the <u>marquee</u>.
- After the heavy rain, the <u>staves</u> that supported the tent were stuck in the mud.

canvas, and they had big tool-bags slung on their backs. They looked impressive. Laura wished now that she had not got the bread-and-butter, but there was nowhere to put it, and she couldn't possibly throw it away. She blushed and tried to look severe and even a little bit short-sighted as she came up to them.

❶ Whose voice does Laura imitate when she speaks to the workers? Why does she feel ashamed?

"Good morning," she said, copying her mother's voice. But that sounded so fearfully affected that she was ashamed, and stammered like a little girl, "Oh—er—have you come—is it about the marquee?"

"That's right, miss," said the tallest of the men, a lanky, freckled fellow, and he shifted his tool-bag, knocked back his straw hat and smiled down at her. "That's about it."

His smile was so easy, so friendly that Laura recovered. What nice eyes he had, small, but such a dark blue! And now she looked at the others, they were smiling too. "Cheer up, we won't bite," their smile seemed to say. How very nice workmen were! And what a beautiful morning! she mustn't mention the morning; she must be businesslike. The marquee.

"Well, what about the lily-lawn? Would that do?"

And she pointed to the lily-lawn with the hand that didn't hold the bread-and-butter. They turned, they stared in the direction. A little fat chap thrust out his under-lip, and the tall fellow frowned.

"I don't fancy it," said he. "Not conspicuous enough. You see, with a thing like a marquee," and he turned to Laura in his easy way, "you want to put it somewhere where it'll give you a bang slap in the eye, if you follow me."

Laura's upbringing made her wonder for a moment whether it was quite respectful of a workman to talk to her of bangs slap in the eye. But she did quite follow him.

"A corner of the tennis-court," she suggested. "But the band's going to be in one corner."

"H'm, going to have a band, are you?" said another of the workmen. He was pale. He had a <u>haggard</u> look as his dark eyes scanned the tennis-court. What was he thinking?

"Only a very small band," said Laura gently. Perhaps he wouldn't mind so much if the band was quite small. But the tall fellow interrupted.

"Look here, miss, that's the place. Against those trees. Over there. That'll do fine."

Against the karakas. Then the karaka-trees would be hidden. And they were so lovely, with their broad, gleaming leaves, and their clusters of yellow fruit. They were like trees you imagined growing on a desert island, proud, solitary, lifting their leaves and fruits to the sun in a kind of silent splendor. Must they be hidden by a marquee?

They must. Already the men had shouldered their staves and were making for the place. Only the tall fellow was left. He bent down, pinched a sprig of lavender, put his thumb and forefinger to his nose and snuffed up the smell. When Laura saw that gesture she forgot all about the karakas in her wonder at him caring for things like that—caring for the smell of lavender. How many men that she knew would have done such a thing? Oh, how extraordinarily nice workmen were, she

WORDS FOR EVERYDAY USE:	**hag • gard** (hag′ərd) *adj.*, worn, gaunt

VOCABULARY IN CONTEXT

- The <u>haggard</u> student had stayed up all night cramming for the exam.
- Standing on the <u>veranda</u>, one can see across the vast lawn.
- The <u>baize</u> covering on the card table prevents cards from slipping.

thought. Why couldn't she have workmen for friends rather than the silly boys she danced with and who came to Sunday night supper? She would get on much better with men like these.

It's all the fault, she decided, as the tall fellow drew something on the back of an envelope, something that was to be looped up or left to hang, of these absurd class distinctions. Well, for her part, she didn't feel them. Not a bit, not an atom. . . . And now there came the chock-chock of wooden hammers. Some one whistled, some one sang out, "Are you right there, matey?" "Matey!" The friendliness of it, the—the—Just to prove how happy she was, just to show the tall fellow how at home she felt, and how she despised stupid conventions, Laura took a big bite of her bread-and-butter as she stared at the little drawing. She felt just like a work-girl.

"Laura, Laura, where are you? Telephone, Laura!" a voice cried from the house.

"Coming!" Away she skimmed, over the lawn, up the path, up the steps, across the <u>veranda</u>, and into the porch. In the hall her father and Laurie were brushing their hats ready to go to the office.

"I say, Laura," said Laurie very fast, "you might just give a squiz at my coat before this afternoon. See if it wants pressing."

"I will," said she. Suddenly she couldn't stop herself. She ran at Laurie and gave him a small, quick squeeze. "Oh, I do love parties, don't you?" gasped Laura.

"Ra-ther," said Laurie's warm, boyish voice, and he squeezed his sister too, and gave her a gentle push. "Dash off to the telephone, old girl."

The telephone. "Yes, yes; oh yes. Kitty? Good morning, dear. Come to lunch? Do, dear. Delighted of course. It will only be a very scratch meal—just the sandwich crusts and broken meringue-shells and what's left over. Yes, isn't it a perfect morning? Your white? Oh, I certainly should. One moment—hold the line. Mother's calling." And Laura sat back. "What, mother? Can't hear."

Mrs. Sheridan's voice floated down the stairs. "Tell her to wear that sweet hat she had on last Sunday."

"Mother says you're to wear that *sweet* hat you had on last Sunday. Good. One o'clock. Bye-bye."

Laura put back the receiver, flung her arms over her head, took a deep breath, stretched and let them fall. "Huh," she sighed, and the moment after the sigh she sat up quickly. She was still, listening. All the doors in the house seemed to be open. The house was alive with soft, quick steps and running voices. The green <u>baize</u> door that led to the kitchen regions swung open and shut with a muffled thud. And now there came a long, chuckling absurd sound. It was the heavy piano being moved on its stiff castors. But the air! If you stopped to notice, was the air always like this? Little faint winds were playing chase, in at the tops of the windows, out at the doors. And there were two tiny spots of sun, one on the inkpot, one on a silver photograph frame, playing too. Darling little spots. Especially the one on the inkpot lid. It was quite warm. A warm little silver star. She could have kissed it.

❶
What does Laura discuss with her friend over the phone?

❷
Why does Laura take a big bite of her bread-and-butter?

Words for Everyday Use:

ve • ran • da (və ran´də) *n.*, open porch

baize (bāz) *adj.*, felt-like

---

❶ Laura discusses lunch plans and clothing with her friend.

❷ Laura takes a big bite of her bread-and-butter to prove how comfortable she feels with the workmen and how much she despises the "stupid conventions" of her social class.

LITERARY TECHNIQUE

The difference between appearance and reality is called **irony**, and **dramatic irony** is when something is known by the reader but unknown to the characters. Laura took a bite of the bread-and-butter "just to show the tall fellow how at home she felt" and "felt just like a work-girl" after doing so. Have students discuss how Laura's action and thoughts are an example of dramatic irony.

Answer. Her action and thoughts are ironic because she is not a work-girl; she is watching the workmen work. Although Laura claims she feels free of the "absurd class distinctions," the tall fellow, busily drawing the design for the marquee, is probably unaware of her actions.

Characterization is the use of literary techniques to create a character. One way of creating a character is through the portrayal of a character's behavior, using the actions and speech of the character. Students can discuss what Mrs. Sheridan's actions and speech in the scene about the canna lilies reveal about her character.

ADDITIONAL QUESTIONS AND ACTIVITIES

How does Jose's interaction with the servants contrast with Laura's experience with the workers? What difference in their characters does this reveal?

The front door bell pealed, and there sounded the rustle of Sadie's print skirt on the stairs. A man's voice murmured; Sadie answered, careless, "I'm sure I don't know. Wait. I'll ask Mrs. Sheridan."

"What is it, Sadie?" Laura came into the hall.

"It's the florist, Miss Laura."

It was, indeed. There, just inside the door, stood a wide, shallow tray full of pots of pink lilies. No other kind. Nothing but lilies—canna lilies, big pink flowers, wide open, radiant, almost frighteningly alive on bright crimson stems.

"O-oh, Sadie!" said Laura, and the sound was like a little moan. She crouched down as if to warm herself at that blaze of lilies; she felt they were in her fingers, on her lips, growing in her breast.

"It's some mistake," she said faintly. "Nobody ever ordered so many. Sadie, go and find mother."

But at that moment Mrs. Sheridan joined them.

"It's quite right," she said calmly. "Yes, I ordered them. Aren't they lovely?" She pressed Laura's arm. "I was passing the shop yesterday, and I saw them in the window. And I suddenly thought for once in my life I shall have enough canna lilies. The garden-party will be a good excuse."

"But I thought you said you didn't mean to interfere," said Laura. Sadie had gone. The florist's man was still outside at his van. She put her arm round her mother's neck and gently, very gently, she bit her mother's ear.

"My darling child, you wouldn't like a logical mother, would you? Don't do that. Here's the man."

He carried more lilies still, another whole tray.

"Bank them up, just inside the door, on both sides of the porch, please," said Mrs. Sheridan. "Don't you agree, Laura?"

"Oh, I *do* mother."

In the drawing-room Meg, Jose and good little Hans had at last succeeded in moving the piano.

"Now, if we put this chesterfield against the wall and move everything out of the room except the chairs, don't you think?"

"Quite."

"Hans, move these tables into the smoking-room, and bring a sweeper to take these marks off the carpet and—one moment, Hans—" Jose loved giving orders to the servants, and they loved obeying her. She always made them feel they were taking part in some drama. "Tell mother and Miss Laura to come here at once."

"Very good, Miss Jose."

She turned to Meg. "I want to hear what the piano sounds like, just in case I'm asked to sing this afternoon. Let's try over 'This life is Weary.'"

Pom! Ta-ta-ta *Tee*-ta! The piano burst out so passionately that Jose's face changed. She clasped her hands. She looked mournfully and <u>enigmatically</u> at her mother and Laura as they came in.

This Life is *Wee*-ary,
A Tear—a Sigh.
A Love that *Chan*-ges,
   This Life is *Wee*-ary,
A Tear—a Sigh.
A Love that *Chan*-ges,
And then . . . Good-bye!

 WORDS FOR EVERYDAY USE: en • ig • mat • i • cal • ly (en´ig mat´ik lē) *adv.*, in a perplexed manner

944 UNIT ELEVEN / TWENTIETH-CENTURY PROSE

VOCABULARY IN CONTEXT
- Do you ever wonder why the Mona Lisa smiles so <u>enigmatically</u>?
- The <u>rapturous</u> sounds of the Mozart concerto filled the symphony hall.

But at the word "Good-bye," and although the piano sounded more desperate than ever, her face broke into a brilliant, dreadfully unsympathetic smile.

"Aren't I in good voice, mummy?" she beamed.

> This Life is *Wee*-ary,
> Hope comes to Die.
> A Dream—a *Wa*-kening.

But now Sadie interrupted them. "What is it, Sadie?"

"If you please, m'm, cook says have you got the flags for the sandwiches?"

"The flags for the sandwiches, Sadie?" echoed Mrs. Sheridan dreamily. And the children knew by her face that she hadn't got them. "Let me see." And she said to Sadie firmly, "Tell cook I'll let her have them in ten minutes."

Sadie went.

"Now, Laura," said her mother quickly. "Come with me into the smoking-room. I've got the names somewhere on the back of an envelope. You'll have to write them out for me. Meg, go upstairs this minute and take that wet thing off your head. Jose, run and finish dressing this instant. Do you hear me, children, or shall I have to tell your father when he comes home to-night? And—and, Jose, pacify cook if you do go into the kitchen, will you? I'm terrified of her this morning."

The envelope was found at last behind the dining-room clock, though how it had got there Mrs. Sheridan could not imagine.

"One of you children must have stolen it out of my bag, because I remember vividly—cream cheese and lemon-curd. Have you done that?"

"Yes."

"Egg and—" Mrs. Sheridan held the envelope away from her. "It looks like mice. It can't be mice, can it?"

"Olive, pet," said Laura, looking over her shoulder.

"Yes, of course, olive. What a horrible combination it sounds. Egg and olive."

They were finished at last, and Laura took them off to the kitchen. She found Jose there pacifying the cook, who did not look at all terrifying.

"I have never seen such exquisite sandwiches," said Jose's <u>rapturous</u> voice. "How many kinds did you say there were, cook? Fifteen?"

"Fifteen, Miss Jose."

"Well, cook, I congratulate you."

Cook swept up crusts with the long sandwich knife, and smiled broadly.

"Godber's has come," announced Sadie, issuing out of the pantry. She had seen the man pass the window.

That meant the cream puffs had come. Godber's were famous for their cream puffs. Nobody ever thought of making them at home.

"Bring them in and put them on the table, my girl," ordered cook.

Sadie brought them in and went back to the door. Of course Laura and Jose were far too grown-up to really care about such things. All the same, they couldn't help agreeing that the puffs looked very attractive. Very. Cook began arranging them, shaking off the extra icing sugar.

"Don't they carry one back to all one's parties?" said Laura.

Q

What does Jose do at the end of the song?

WORDS FOR EVERYDAY USE: rap • tur • ous (rap´chər əs) *adj.*, full of pleasure

ANSWER TO GUIDED READING QUESTION

❶ Jose breaks into a huge smile at the end of her song.

ADDITIONAL QUESTIONS AND ACTIVITIES

Mrs. Sheridan's plans for the garden-party are whimsical and unorganized. Ask students to consider why she is able to plan this way. Then students can work in small groups to plan for a party. They should set a budget; decide what is needed for food, decoration, and entertainment; and determine who would do what in order to prepare for the party.

The Idlers. Maurice Prendergast, circa 1916–18, oil on canvas, 21 x 32 in., Louise Jordan Smith Fund, 1949. Maier Museum of Art, Randolph-Macon Woman's College, Lynchburg, VA

❶ *What happened to the man? Why is this incident especially tragic?*

"I suppose they do," said practical Jose, who never liked to be carried back. "They look beautifully light and feathery, I must say."

"Have one each, my dears," said cook in her comfortable voice. "Yer ma won't know."

Oh, impossible. Fancy cream puffs so soon after breakfast. The very idea made one shudder. All the same, two minutes later Jose and Laura were licking their fingers with that absorbed inward look that only comes from whipped cream.

"Let's go into the garden, out by the back way," suggested Laura. "I want to see how the men are getting on with the marquee. They're such awfully nice men."

But the back door was blocked by cook, Sadie, Godber's man and Hans.

Something had happened.

"Tuk-tuk-tuk," clucked cook like an agitated hen. Sadie had her hand clapped to her cheek as though she had toothache. Hans's face was screwed up in the effort to understand. Only Godber's man seemed to be enjoying himself; it was his story.

"What's the matter? What's happened?"

"There's been a horrible accident," said Cook. "A man killed."

"A man killed! Where? How? When?"

But Godber's man wasn't going to have his story snatched from under his very nose.

"Know those little cottages just below here, miss?" Know them? Of course, she knew them. "Well, there's a young chap living there, name of Scott, a carter. His horse shied at a traction-engine, corner of Hawke Street this morning, and he was thrown out on the back of his head. Killed."

"Dead!" Laura stared at Godber's man.

"Dead when they picked him up," said Godber's man with relish. "They were taking the body home as I come up here." And he said to the cook, "He's left a wife and five little ones."

"Jose, come here." Laura caught hold of her sister's sleeve and dragged her through the kitchen to the other side of the green baize door. There she paused and leaned against it. "Jose!" she said, horrified, "however are we going to stop everything?"

"Stop everything, Laura!" cried Jose in astonishment. "What do you mean?"

"Stop the garden-party, of course." Why did Jose pretend?

But Jose was still more amazed. "Stop the garden-party? My dear Laura, don't be so absurd. Of course we can't do anything of the kind. Nobody expects us to. Don't be so extravagant."

"But we can't possibly have a garden-party with a man dead just outside the front gate."

That really was extravagant, for the little cottages were in a lane to themselves at the very bottom of a steep rise that led up to the house. A broad road ran between. True, they were far too near. They were the greatest possible eyesore, and they had no right to be in that neighborhood at all. They were little mean dwellings painted a chocolate brown. In the garden patches there was nothing but cabbage stalks, sick hens and tomato cans. The very smoke coming out of their chimneys was poverty-stricken. Little rags and shreds of smoke, so unlike the great silvery plumes that uncurled from the Sheridans' chimneys. Washerwomen lived in the lane and sweeps and a cobbler, and a man whose house-front was studded all over with minute bird-cages. Children swarmed. When the Sheridans were little they were forbidden to set foot there because of the revolting language and of what they might catch. But since they were grown up, Laura and Laurie on their prowls sometimes walked through. It was disgusting and sordid. They came out with a shudder. But still one must go everywhere; one must see everything. So through they went.

"And just think of what the band would sound like to that poor woman," said Laura.

"Oh, Laura!" Jose began to be seriously annoyed. "If you're going to stop a band playing every time some one has an accident, you'll lead a very strenuous life. I'm every bit as sorry about it as you. I feel just as sympathetic." Her eyes hardened. She looked at her sister just as she used to when they were little and fighting together. "You won't bring a drunken workman back to life by being sentimental," she said softly.

"Drunk! Who said he was drunk?" Laura turned furiously on Jose. She said, just as they had used to say on those occasions, "I'm going straight up to tell mother."

"Do, dear," cooed Jose.

"Mother, can I come into your room?" Laura turned the big glass doorknob.

"Of course, child. Why, what's the matter? What's given you such a color?" And Mrs. Sheridan turned round from her dressing-table. She was trying on a new hat.

"Mother, a man's been killed," began Laura.

"*Not* in the garden?" interrupted her mother.

"No, no!"

❶
What does Laura want to do? How does Jose respond?

❷
How does Laura's mother first react to the news of the man's death?

WORDS FOR EVERYDAY USE: **sor • did** (sôr´did) *adj.*, dirty, wretched

❶ Laura wants to stop the garden-party. Jose responds that it would be "absurd" to cancel the party.

❷ At first, Laura's mother is worried that the man has died in their garden.

ADDITIONAL QUESTIONS AND ACTIVITIES

π • Have students use a comparison and contrast chart to compare and contrast the description of the cottages in the lane to the Sheridan property. Refer them to the Language Arts Survey, 4.8, "Comparing and Contrasting."

• What do Jose's comments about the cause of the workman's death reveal about her beliefs about the working class?

Answer. Jose's assumption that the workman was drunk reveals that she believes the working class is generally unruly.

VOCABULARY IN CONTEXT

• The mayor condemned slum landlords for the sordid living conditions in parts of the city.

❶ Q *What struggle is taking place in Laura's head? What does she finally decide is the best plan?*

❷ Q *What does Laura's mother accuse her of doing?*

"Oh, what a fright you gave me!" Mrs. Sheridan sighed with relief, and took off the big hat and held it on her knees.

"But listen, mother," said Laura. Breathless, half-choking, she told the dreadful story. "Of course, we can't have our party, can we?" she pleaded. "The band and everybody arriving. They'd hear us, mother; they're nearly neighbors!"

To Laura's astonishment her mother behaved just like Jose, it was harder to bear because she seemed amused. She refused to take Laura seriously.

"But, my dear child, use your common sense. It's only by accident we've heard of it. If some one had died there normally— and I can't understand how they keep alive in those poky little holes—we should still be having our party, shouldn't we?"

Laura had to say "yes" to that, but she felt it was all wrong. She sat down on her mother's sofa and pinched the cushion frill.

"Mother, isn't it really terribly heartless of us?" she asked.

"Darling!" Mrs. Sheridan got up and came over to her, carrying the hat. Before Laura could stop her she had popped it on. "My child!" said her mother, "the hat is yours. It's made for you. It's much too young for me. I have never seen you look such a picture. Look at yourself!" And she held up her hand-mirror.

"But, mother," Laura began again. She couldn't look at herself; she turned aside.

This time Mrs. Sheridan lost patience just as Jose had done.

"You are being very absurd, Laura," she said coldly. "People like that don't expect sacrifices from us. And it's not very sympathetic to spoil everybody's enjoyment as you're doing now."

"I don't understand," said Laura, and she walked quickly out of the room into her own bedroom. There, quite by chance, the first thing she saw was this charming girl in the mirror, in her black hat trimmed with gold daisies, and a long black velvet ribbon. Never had she imagined she could look like that. Is mother right? she thought. And now she hoped her mother was right. Am I being extravagant? Perhaps it was extravagant. Just for a moment she had another glimpse of that poor woman and those little children, and the body being carried into the house. But it all seemed blurred, unreal, like a picture in the newspaper. I'll remember it again after the party's over, she decided. And somehow that seemed quite the best plan. . . .

Lunch was over by half-past one. By half-past two they were all ready for the fray. The green-coated band had arrived and was established in a corner of the tennis-court.

"My dear!" trilled Kitty Maitland, "aren't they too like frogs for words? You ought to have arranged them round the pond with the conductor in the middle on a leaf."

Laurie arrived and hailed them on his way to dress. At the sight of him Laura remembered the accident again. She wanted to tell him. If Laurie agreed with the others, then it was bound to be all right. And she followed him into the hall.

"Laurie!"

"Hallo!" He was half-way upstairs, but when he turned round and saw Laura he suddenly puffed out his cheeks and goggled his eyes at her. "My word, Laura; you do look stunning," said Laurie. "What an absolutely topping hat!"

Laura said faintly "Is it?" and smiled up at Laurie, and didn't tell him after all.

Soon after that people began coming in streams. The band struck up; the hired waiters ran from the house to the marquee. Wherever you looked there were couples strolling, bending to the flowers, greeting, moving on over the lawn. They were like bright birds that had alighted in the

Sheridans' garden for this one afternoon, on their way to—where? Ah, what happiness it is to be with people who all are happy, to press hands, press cheeks, smile into eyes.

"Darling Laura, how well you look!"

"What a becoming hat, child!"

"Laura, you look quite Spanish. I've never seen you look so striking."

And Laura, glowing, answered softly, "Have you had tea? Won't you have an ice? The passion-fruit ices really are rather special." She ran to her father and begged him. "Daddy darling, can't the band have something to drink?"

And the perfect afternoon slowly ripened, slowly faded, slowly its petals closed.

"Never a more delightful garden party . . ." "The greatest success . . ." "Quite the most . . ."

Laura helped her mother with the good-byes. They stood side by side in the porch till it was all over.

"All over, all over, thank heaven," said Mrs. Sheridan. "Round up the others, Laura. Let's go and have some fresh coffee. I'm exhausted. Yes, it's been very successful. But oh, these parties, these parties! Why will you children insist on giving parties!" And they all of them sat down in the deserted marquee.

"Have a sandwich, daddy dear. I wrote the flag."

"Thanks." Mr. Sheridan took a bite and the sandwich was gone. He took another. "I suppose you didn't hear of a beastly accident that happened today?" he said.

"My dear," said Mrs. Sheridan, holding up her hand, "we did. It nearly ruined the party. Laura insisted we should put it off."

"Oh, mother!" Laura didn't want to be teased about it.

"It was a horrible affair all the same," said Mr. Sheridan. "The chap was married too. Lived just below in the lane, and leaves a wife and half a dozen kiddies, so they say."

An awkward little silence fell. Mrs. Sheridan fidgeted with her cup. Really, it was very tactless of father . . .

Suddenly she looked up. There on the table were all those sandwiches, cakes, puffs, all uneaten, all going to be wasted. She had one of her brilliant ideas.

"I know," she said. "Let's make up a basket. Let's send that poor creature some of this perfectly good food. At any rate, it will be the greatest treat for the children. Don't you agree? And she's sure to have neighbors calling in and so on. What a point to have it all ready prepared. Laura!" She jumped up. "Get me the big basket out of the stairs cupboard."

"But, mother, do you really think it's a good idea?" said Laura.

Again, how curious, she seemed to be different from them all. To take scraps from their party. Would the poor woman really like that?

"Of course! What's the matter with you to-day? An hour or two ago you were insisting on us being sympathetic, and now—"

Oh, well! Laura ran for the basket. It was filled, it was heaped by her mother.

"Take it yourself, darling," said she. "Run down just as you are. No, wait, take the arum lilies too. People of that class are so impressed by arum lilies."

"The stems will ruin her lace frock," said practical Jose.

So they would. Just in time. "Only the basket, then. And, Laura!"—her mother followed her out of the marquee—"don't on any account—"

"What, mother?"

No, better not put such ideas into the child's head! "Nothing! Run along."

It was just growing dusky as Laura shut their garden gates. A big dog ran by like a

❶ Laura has doubts about delivering the basket because she wonders if the woman would like receiving leftover food.

ADDITIONAL QUESTIONS AND ACTIVITIES

What sort of relationship exists between Laura and Laurie? Why do you think so?

Answers. They are very close. Laura shares her feelings with her brother, expressing her excitement about the party before Laurie leaves for the office. Laura respects his opinion, believing that if "Laurie agreed with the others, then it was bound to be all right."

❶
Why does Laura have doubts about delivering the basket?

ADDITIONAL QUESTIONS AND ACTIVITIES

"Again, how curious, she seemed to be different from them all." How do Laura's ideas on the situation at hand differ from the ideas of the rest of her family? What other examples of Laura's difference appear throughout the story? Why do you think Laura is different?

Answers: Laura, unlike the rest of her family, does not think it a good idea to bring leftover party food to the grieving family. Laura also differs from her family in her treatment of workers, her attitudes toward the poor in general, and mainly in her reaction to the tragic accident. Laura's reaction may be different because she is especially sensitive, or because she has not yet learned all of the expectations and rules of her class.

ADDITIONAL QUESTIONS AND ACTIVITIES

What do you think Mrs. Sheridan was going to say when she began to say "don't on any account"?

Answer. Students might reason that she was going to caution Laura against inviting the family to their house or suggesting that she would bring more food.

ANALYTIC SCALES FOR RESPONDING IN WRITING

Assign a score from 1 to 25 for each grading criterion below. (For more detailed evaluation, see the evaluation forms for writing, revising, and proofreading, *Assessment Portfolio,* 7.1–7.10.)

1. Short Story

• **Content/Unity.** The story presents a character whose life is changed because of a particular experience.

• **Organization/Coherence.** The story uses dialogue, descriptive details, and action to show how the character changes.

• **Language/Style.** The story uses vivid and precise nouns, verbs, and modifiers.

• **Conventions.** The story avoids errors in spelling, grammar, usage, mechanics, and manuscript form.

▶ Additional practice is provided in the *Essential Skills Practice Book: Writing,* 1.9.

2. Invitation

• **Content/Unity.** The invitation presents a formal request to attend a garden-party.

• **Organization/Coherence.** The invitation includes the time, place, and reason for the occasion as well as the name of the hostess.

• **Language/Style.** The invitation uses vivid and precise nouns, verbs, and modifiers.

• **Conventions.** The invitation avoids errors in spelling, grammar, usage, mechanics, and manuscript form.

shadow. The road gleamed white, and down below in the hollow the little cottages were in deep shade. How quiet it seemed after the afternoon. Here she was going down the hill to somewhere where a man lay dead, and she couldn't realize it. Why couldn't she? She stopped a minute. And it seemed to her that kisses, voices, tinkling spoons, laughter, the smell of crushed grass were somehow inside her. She had no room for anything else. How strange! She looked up at the pale sky, and all she thought was, "Yes, it was the most successful party."

Now the broad road was crossed. The lane began, smoky and dark. Women in shawls and men's tweed caps hurried by. Men hung over the palings; the children played in the doorways. A low hum came from the mean little cottages. In some of them there was a flicker of light, and a shadow, crab-like, moved across the window. Laura bent her head and hurried on. She wished now she had put on a coat. How her frock shone! And the big hat with the velvet streamer—if only it was another hat! Were the people looking at her? They must be. It was a mistake to have come; she knew all along it was a mistake. Should she go back even now?

No, too late. This was the house. It must be. A dark knot of people stood outside. Beside the gate an old, old woman with a crutch sat in a chair, watching. She had her feet on a newspaper. The voices stopped as Laura drew near. The group parted. It was as though she was expected, as though they had known she was coming here.

Laura was terribly nervous. Tossing the velvet ribbon over her shoulder, she said to a woman standing by, "Is this Mrs. Scott's house?" and the woman, smiling queerly, said, "It is, my lass."

Oh, to be away from this! She actually said, "Help me, God," as she walked up the

❶ About what does Laura become self-conscious as she walks through the street?

tiny path and knocked. To be away from those staring eyes, or to be covered up in anything, one of those women's shawls even. I'll just leave the basket and go, she decided. I shan't even wait for it to be emptied.

Then the door opened. A little woman in black showed in the gloom.

Laura said, "Are you Mrs. Scott?" But to her horror the woman answered, "Walk in please, miss," and she was shut in the passage.

"No," said Laura, "I don't want to come in. I only want to leave this basket. Mother sent—"

The little woman in the gloomy passage seemed not to have heard her. "Step this way, please, miss," she said in an oily voice, and Laura followed her.

She found herself in a wretched little low kitchen, lighted by a smoky lamp. There was a woman sitting before the fire.

"Em," said the little creature who had let her in. "Em! It's a young lady." She turned to Laura. She said meaningly, "I'm 'er sister, Miss. You'll excuse 'er, won't you?"

"Oh, but of course!" said Laura. "Please, please don't disturb her. I—I only want to leave—"

But at that moment the woman at the fire turned round. Her face, puffed up, red, with swollen eyes and swollen lips, looked terrible. She seemed as though she couldn't understand why Laura was there. What did it mean? Why was this stranger standing in the kitchen with a basket? What was it all about? And the poor face puckered up again.

"All right, my dear," said the other. "I'll thank the young lady."

And again she began, "You'll excuse her, miss, I'm sure," and her face, swollen too, tried an oily smile.

Laura only wanted to get out, to get away. She was back in the passage. The door opened. She walked straight through into the bedroom, where the dead man was lying.

"You'd like a look at 'im, wouldn't you?" said Em's sister, and she brushed past Laura over to the bed. "Don't be afraid, my lass—" and now her voice sounded fond and sly, and fondly she drew down the sheet—" 'e looks a picture. There's nothing to show. Come along, my dear."

Laura came.

There lay a young man, fast asleep—sleeping so soundly, so deeply, that he was far, far away from them both. Oh, so remote, so peaceful. He was dreaming. Never wake him up again. His head was sunk in the pillow, his eyes were closed; they were blind under the closed eyelids. He was given up to his dream. What did garden-parties and baskets and lace frocks matter to him? He was far from all those things. He was wonderful, beautiful. While they were laughing and while the band was playing, this marvel had come to the lane. Happy . . . happy. . . . All is well, said that sleeping face. This is just as it should be. I am content.

But all the same you had to cry, and she couldn't go out of the room without say-ing something to him. Laura gave a loud childish sob.

"Forgive my hat," she said.

And this time she didn't wait for Em's sister. She found her way out of the door, down the path, past all those dark people. At the corner of the lane she met Laurie.

He stepped out of the shadow. "Is that you, Laura?"

"Yes."

"Mother was getting anxious. Was it all right?"

"Yes, quite. Oh, Laurie!" She took his arm, she pressed up against him.

"I say, you're not crying, are you?" asked her brother.

Laura shook her head. She was.

Laurie put his arm round her shoulder. "Don't cry," he said in his warm, loving voice. "Was it awful?"

"No," sobbed Laura. "It was simply marvelous. But, Laurie—" She stopped, she looked at her brother. "Isn't life," she stammered, "isn't life—" But what life was she couldn't explain. No matter. He quite understood.

"*Isn't* it, darling?" said Laurie. ■

What is Laura thinking as she looks at the dead man? What does she say to him?

Responding to the Selection

Imagine that you are Laura in the short story. In your journal, write about your experi- ence at the poverty-stricken home of the laborer's widow and children. Finish the sentence you started to say to your brother Laurie, "*Isn't* life . . . ."

**ANSWERS FOR
REVIEWING THE SELECTION**

RECALLING

1. The weather is described as "ideal."

2. Laura feels that "these absurd class distinctions" do not allow her to have laborers for friends.

3. Laura tries to convince her family to cancel the garden-party.

4. Laura said, "Forgive my hat."

INTERPRETING

Responses will vary. Possible responses are given.

5. Details such as "windless, warm, the sky without a cloud" and "only the blue was veiled with a haze of light gold" prove the description to be accurate.

6. Laura "took a big bite of her bread-and-butter" to show she felt no class distinctions.

7. The mother tries to divert her daughter's attention back to the party by placing the hat on her daughter's head and exclaiming, "My child! The hat is yours."

8. Laura probably feels awkward and out of place and is very aware of the inappropriateness of her hat.

SYNTHESIZING

Responses will vary. Possible responses are given.

9. The realities of poverty, sickness, dirt, hunger, and death enter Laura's life.

10. Perhaps Laura cannot explain that life is a paradoxical combination of beauty and tragedy, wondrousness and injustice, joy and suffering.

**ANSWERS FOR
UNDERSTANDING LITERATURE**

► See the evaluation forms for discussion, active listening, and oral communication, *Assessment Portfolio*, 7.11–7.14.

Responses will vary. Possible responses are given.

1. Image/Objective Correlative. Images such as "fifteen kinds of sandwiches" with "flags" to identify each kind, the "sweet hat" that Laura tells her friend to wear, and the roses which are the "only flowers that impress people at garden-parties" all describe the setting and preparations for the

(cont.)

Reviewing the Selection

RECALLING

1. What word is used to describe the weather on the day of the garden-party?

2. What does Laura feel is the reason why she couldn't have laborers for friends?

3. What does Laura try to convince her family of doing, after they hear of the accident?

4. What did Laura say to the dead man?

INTERPRETING

▶ 5. What details prove that description to be accurate?

▶ 6. What action does Laura take "just to show" that she feels no class distinction between herself and the laborers putting up the marquee?

▶ 7. What action on the part of the mother shows that she is trying to divert her daughter's attention from the accident back to the party?

▶ 8. What is probably the reason that she makes such a comment?

SYNTHESIZING

9. What kinds of realities enter Laura's life because of her experience visiting the widow?

10. What is it about life that Laura cannot explain, but that her brother Laurie understands?

Understanding Literature (Questions for Discussion)

1. **Image/Objective Correlative.** An **image** is a word or phrase that names something that can be seen, heard, touched, tasted, or smelled. An **objective correlative** is a group of images that together create a particular emotion in the reader. What images are used to describe the preparations—the food, clothing, music—for the garden-party? What emotion is created by this group of images? Why?

2. **Symbol.** A **symbol** is a thing that stands for or represents both itself and something else. What is the significance of the hat, which is given to Laura by her mother and which she wears to the widow's home? What does the hat mean to the mother? How does the meaning of the hat change for Laura?

3. **Description.** A **description**, one of the modes of writing, presents a portrayal of a character, an object, or a scene. How is the character of the mother described? What is significant about her "brilliant idea" regarding the leftover food from the garden-party? What does this reveal about her character?

ANSWERS FOR UNDERSTANDING LITERATURE (CONT.)

garden-party. These images create an emotion of distaste because of the overwhelming sense of extravagance and self-indulgence they evoke.

2. Symbol. The significance of the hat is that Laura's mother gave her the hat in order to make her forget about the accident. To the mother, the hat symbolizes the refined world of privilege that should be kept apart from the ugliness of poverty and death. For Laura the hat becomes a symbol of her insensitivity to the plight of

her grieving, less-fortunate neighbors.

►**Teaching Note:** Point out the various compliments Laura receives about the hat at the garden-party. Have students compare Laura's feeling about the hat then to her apology at the widow's cottage.

3. Description. The mother is very concerned with appearances and satisfying her own whims. Her "brilliant idea" makes her seem "generous" and "sympathetic" when, in fact, she is not. The scraps of food are leftovers

(cont.)

Responding in Writing

1. **Short Story.** Katherine Mansfield based this story on an actual experience from her childhood. Think about the experience you wrote about in your Reader's Journal. Use an image, character, or line of dialogue from that experience on which to base a short story in which the protagonist's view of his or her life is changed because of the experience.

2. **Invitation.** Think about the images used to describe the garden-party. What kind of invitation do you think that the mother in the story would have made for the occasion? Create the "ideal" invitation for the garden-party.

Language Lab

Base Words and Suffixes. Read the Language Arts Survey, 2.140, "Base Words and Prefixes," and 2.141, "Suffixes." Then underline the base word once and the suffix twice in each of the following words from "The Garden-Party." Next, look up each suffix in a dictionary and write two additional words that end with the same suffix.

1. enigmatically
2. comfortable
3. sympathetic
4. extravagant
5. tactless

Thinking Skills

Compare and Contrast. Read the Language Arts Survey, 4.8, "Comparing and Contrasting." Make two columns on a piece of paper, one headed *Song* and the other headed *Singers*. To the left of the columns, write *Compare* and under it, *Contrast*. Draw lines across your page starting under each of these two words. List the characteristics of the song "This Life Is Weary" and of the singers who sing it within the boxes of the matrix you have created with these four headings.

PROJECT

Dramatic Skit. Collaborate with one or two other students to write a dramatic scene between Laura and her brother Laurie. The scene will follow the closing of the story and provide the completion to Laura's utterance, "Isn't life . . . ." In your scene, portray the characters as they are in the story, both naive, yet both aware of another world—the world of reality—that exists outside their delicate and artificial world at home.

  PROJECT NOTES

▶See the worksheets and evaluation forms for projects, *Assessment Portfolio*, 7.20–7.23.

Dramatic Skit

• Suggest that students write a scene in which Laura and Laurie walk home or in which the siblings tell their family of the visit.

• Students may want to perform the skits they write.

ANSWERS FOR THINKING SKILLS (CONT.)

to the gathering at the cottage down the lane.

Answer. **Compare:** Many people gathered at garden-party; many people gathered at cottage.

Contrast: People at garden-party are wealthy and carefree; people at cottage are poor and grieving.

▶Additional practice is provided in the *Essential Skills Practice Book: Study and Research*, 4.8.

ANSWERS FOR UNDERSTANDING LITERATURE (CONT.)

from a frivolous party, not food prepared specifically for a wake or visitation. That the mother sees the basket as a way to get rid of food that is otherwise "all going to be wasted" shows her inability to be truly generous of heart and spirit.

▶**Teaching Note:** Students should compare the mother's response to the accident before the party to her response afterward for clues about her character.

▶**Additional Resources:** *Essential Skills Practice Book: Writing*, 1.41 and 1.9.

ANALYTIC SCALES FOR RESPONDING IN WRITING

Grading scales appear on page 950.

ANSWERS FOR LANGUAGE LAB

Responses will vary. Possible responses are given.

1. enigmatically; grammatically, systematically
2. comfortable; reliable, predictable
3. sympathetic; magnetic, angelic
4. extravagant; occupant, defendant
5. tactless; heartless, breathless

▶Additional practice is provided in the *Essential Skills Practice Book: Language*, 2.140 and 2.141.

ANSWERS FOR THINKING SKILLS

Responses will vary. Possible responses are given.

Students' matrixes need to compare and contrast the emotions and meaning of the song lyrics with the emotions and motive of the singers who are singing the song.

	Song	Singers
Compare	mournful tune	mournful appearance
Contrast	about weariness of life	don't know weariness

FOR MORE PRACTICE

Problem. Compare and contrast the gathering at the garden-party

(cont.)

ADDITIONAL RESOURCES

READER'S GUIDE
• Selection Worksheet, 11.5

ASSESSMENT PORTFOLIO
• Selection Check Test, 4.11.9
• Selection Test, 4.11.10

ESSENTIAL SKILLS PRACTICE BOOKS
• *Language,* 2.3, 2.4, 2.20, 2.32, 2.35
• *Study and Research,* 4.7

ENRICHMENT ACTIVITIES

Students can conduct a class interview project in which class members share experiences that helped them shape their self-identity. Students can videotape, tape record, or take notes on the interviews.

SUPPORT FOR LEP STUDENTS

Remind students to use context clues to identify unfamiliar words. For example, students should use the context of sewing to figure out the meaning of *basting, overcasting,* and other unfamiliar words.

ADDITIONAL VOCABULARY

treadle—a pedal used to turn a wheel

embroidered—ornamented with a design in needlework

mimic—imitate

melodramatic—extravagantly emotional

bronchial tubes—branches of the windpipe

bronchitis—disease of the lungs

bobby pin—a small metal hairpin

fluted—a long rounded groove in the shaft of a column; pleated

contempt—scorn

cubicle—any small compartment

Kleenex—trademark for soft tissue paper

paisley—intricate, multicolored pattern

kimono—a dressing gown

PREREADING

"Red Dress—1946"
by Alice Munro

ABOUT THE AUTHOR

Alice Munro (1931–) was born in Wingham, Ontario. After attending the University of Western Ontario, Munro moved to Victoria, British Columbia, where she opened a bookstore. In 1968, Munro published her first collection of short stories, *Dance of the Happy Shades,* which won the Governor General's Literary Award. Three years later, Munro's novel, *Lives of Girls and Women,* won the Canadian Booksellers Award. Her other short story collections include *The Beggar Maid* (originally published in North America as *Who Do You Think You Are?*), *Something I've Been Meaning to Tell You, The Moons of Jupiter and Other Stories, The Progress of Love, Friend of My Youth,* and *Open Secrets.* Munro is considered one of the finest of contemporary short fiction writers and has even been acclaimed as "our Chekhov." Today, Munro lives in Clinton, Ontario, near Lake Huron, where she continues to write.

ABOUT THE SELECTION

"Red Dress—1946" is from Munro's first short story collection, *Dance of the Happy Shades.* Like nearly all of Munro's fiction, this story takes place in semirural southern Ontario, Canada, the landscape of Munro's childhood. The narrator in the selection is a mature woman telling about a pivotal experience, a turning point or epiphany, in her youth. The central character is a precocious and sensitive girl who faces and resolves a crisis of self-doubt and misgivings about the identity that she is expected to take on as she moves into womanhood. It is a story about a time in life when two paths present themselves and one is chosen, though not without misgiving.

GOALS/OBJECTIVES

Studying this lesson will enable students to

• empathize with the main character's feelings of exclusion and social discomfort

• describe Alice Munro's literary accomplishments and her style of writing

• define *characterization* and identify literary tech-

niques used to create characters and analyze their effects

• define *plot* and *conflict* and identify the plot and conflict of stories that they read

• distinguish between common and proper nouns and use proper nouns and proper adjectives correctly

"Red Dress—1946"

ALICE MUNRO

My mother was making me a dress. All through the month of November I would come from school and find her in the kitchen, surrounded by cut-up red velvet and scraps of tissue-paper pattern. She worked at an old treadle machine pushed up against the window to get the light, and also to let her look out, past the stubble fields and bare vegetable garden, to see who went by on the road. There was seldom anybody to see.

The red velvet material was hard to work with, it pulled, and the style my mother had chosen was not easy either. She was not really a good sewer. She liked to make things; that is different. Whenever she could she tried to skip basting and pressing and she took no pride in the fine points of tailoring, the finishing of buttonholes and the overcasting of seams as, for instance, my aunt and my grandmother did. Unlike them she started off with an inspiration, a brave and dazzling idea; from that moment on, her pleasure ran downhill. In the first place she could never find a pattern to suit her. It was no wonder; there were no patterns made to match the ideas that blossomed in her head. She had made me, at various times when I was younger, a flowered <u>organdie</u> dress with a high Victorian neckline edged in scratchy lace, with a poke bonnet to match; a Scottish plaid outfit with a velvet jacket and tam; an embroidered peasant blouse worn with a full red skirt and black laced bodice. I had worn these clothes with <u>docility</u>, even pleasure, in the days when I was unaware of the world's opinion. Now, grown wiser, I wished for dresses like those my friend Lonnie had, bought at Beale's store.

WORDS FOR EVERYDAY USE:

or • gan • dy or or • gan • die (ôr´gən dē) *n.*, sheer fabric

do • cil • i • ty (dō sil´ə tē) *n.*, submissiveness

❶ The young girl fears that Lonnie
will notice her mother. She is sensitive
to Lonnie's criticism because Lonnie is
"a ferocious mimic."

❷ The girl is angry that her mother
talks about her to Lonnie as though
Lonnie were a grown-up and she a
child.

ADDITIONAL QUESTIONS
AND ACTIVITIES

π   Students can use a chart
to compare and contrast
the narrator and Lonnie.
Refer to the Language Arts Survey,
4.8, "Comparing and Contrasting."

I had to try it on. Sometimes Lonnie
came home from school with me and she
would sit on the couch watching. I was
embarrassed by the way my mother crept
around me, her knees creaking, her breath
coming heavily. She muttered to herself.
Around the house she wore no corset or
stockings, she wore wedge-heeled shoes
and ankle socks; her legs were marked with
lumps of blue-green veins. I thought her
squatting position shameless, even obscene;
I tried to keep talking to Lonnie so that her
attention would be taken away from my
mother as much as possible. Lonnie wore
the composed, polite, appreciative expression that was her disguise in the presence
of grownups. She laughed at them and was
a ferocious mimic, and they never knew.

Q❶ *What does the young girl fear that Lonnie will do? About what is she sensitive? Why?*

My mother pulled me about, and
pricked me with pins. She made me turn
around, she made me walk away, she made
me stand still. "What do you think of it,
Lonnie?" she said around the pins in her
mouth.

"It's beautiful," said Lonnie, in her mild,
sincere way. Lonnie's own mother was
dead. She lived with her father who never
noticed her, and this, in my eyes, made
her seem both <u>vulnerable</u> and privileged.

Q❷ *Why does the young girl get angry at her mother?*

"It *will* be, if I can ever manage the fit,"
my mother said. "Ah, well," she said the-
atrically, getting to her feet with a woeful
creaking and sighing, "I doubt if she
appreciates it." She enraged me, talking
like this to Lonnie, as if Lonnie were
grown up and I were still a child. "Stand
still," she said, hauling the pinned and
basted dress over my head. My head was
muffled in velvet, my body exposed, in an
old cotton school slip. I felt like a great

raw lump, clumsy and goose-pimpled. I
wished I was like Lonnie, light-boned,
pale and thin; she had been a Blue Baby.

"Well nobody ever made me a dress
when I was going to high school," my
mother said, "I made my own, or I did
without." I was afraid she was going to
start again on the story of her walking
seven miles to town and finding a job
waiting on tables in a boarding-house, so
that she could go to high school. All the
stories of my mother's life which had once
interested me had begun to seem melodramatic, <u>irrelevant</u>, and tiresome.

"One time I had a dress given to me,"
she said. "It was a cream-coloured cash-
mere wool with royal blue piping down
the front and lovely mother-of-pearl but-
tons, I wonder what ever became of it?"

When we got free Lonnie and I went
upstairs to my room. It was cold, but we
stayed there. We talked about the boys in
our class, going up and down the rows and
saying, "Do you like him? Well, do you
half-like him? Do you *hate* him? Would
you go out with him if he asked you?"
Nobody had asked us. We were thirteen,
and we had been going to high school for
two months. We did questionnaires in
magazines, to find out whether we had
personality and whether we would be popular. We read articles on how to make up
our faces to accentuate our good points
and how to carry on a conversation on the
first date and what to do when a boy tried
to go too far. Also we read articles on
frigidity of the menopause, abortion and
why husbands seek satisfaction away from
home. When we were not doing school
work, we were occupied most of the time

WORDS FOR
EVERYDAY USE:

vul • ner • a • ble (vul´nər ə bəl) *adj.,* open to injury or attack;
easily hurt

ir • rel • e • vant (ir rel´ə vənt) *adj.,* not related to the subject

📖 VOCABULARY IN CONTEXT

- All the cities along the river were <u>vulnerable</u> to enemy invasions.
- Because the environmental study focuses on North America, these rain forest statistics are <u>irrelevant</u>.
- Frequent <u>palpitations</u> could be an indication of a serious heart problem.
- The senator was not amused by the manner in which the comedy team <u>burlesqued</u> his scandalous actions.

with the garnering, passing on and discussing of sexual information. We had made a pact to tell each other everything. But one thing I did not tell was about this dance, the high school Christmas Dance for which my mother was making me a dress. It was that I did not want to go.

At high school I was never comfortable for a minute. I did not know about Lonnie. Before an exam, she got icy hands and <u>palpitations</u>, but I was close to despair at all times. When I was asked a question in class, any simple little question at all, my voice was apt to come out squeaky, or else hoarse and trembling. When I had to go to the blackboard I was sure—even at a time of the month when this could not be true—that I had blood on my skirt. My hands became slippery with sweat when they were required to work the blackboard compass. I could not hit the ball in volleyball; being called upon to perform an action in front of others made all my reflexes come undone. I hated Business Practice because you had to rule pages for an account book, using a straight pen, and when the teacher looked over my shoulder all the delicate lines wobbled and ran together. I hated Science; we perched on stools under harsh lights behind tables of unfamiliar, fragile equipment, and were taught by the principal of the school, a man with a cold, self-relishing voice—he read the Scriptures every morning—and a great talent for inflicting humiliation. I hated English because the boys played bingo at the back of the room while the teacher, a stout, gentle girl, slightly cross-eyed, read Wordsworth at the front. She threatened them, she begged

them, her face red and her voice as unreliable as mine. They offered <u>burlesqued</u> apologies and when she started to read again they took up rapt postures, made swooning faces, crossed their eyes, flung their hands over their hearts. Sometimes she would burst into tears, there was no help for it, she had to run out into the hall. Then the boys made loud mooing noises; our hungry laughter—oh, mine too—pursued her. There was a carnival atmosphere of brutality in the room at such times, scaring weak and suspect people like me.

But what was really going on in the school was not Business Practice and Science and English, there was something else that gave life its urgency and brightness. That old building, with its rock-walled clammy basements and black cloakrooms and pictures of dead royalties and lost explorers, was full of the tension and excitement of sexual competition, and in this, in spite of daydreams of vast successes, I had premonitions of total defeat. Something had to happen, to keep me from that dance.

With December came snow, and I had an idea. Formerly I had considered falling off my bicycle and spraining my ankle and I had tried to manage this, as I rode home along the hard-frozen, deeply rutted country roads. But it was too difficult. However, my throat and bronchial tubes were supposed to be weak; why not expose them? I started getting out of bed at night and opening my window a little. I knelt down and let the wind, sometimes stinging with snow, rush in around my bared throat. I took off my pajama top. I said to myself the words "blue with cold"

WORDS FOR EVERYDAY USE:

pal • pi • ta • tion (pal´pə tā shen) *n.,* rapid heartbeat

bur • lesqued (bər leskd´) *part.,* parody, imitate derisively

"RED DRESS—1946" **957**

❶ The young girl won't tell her friend that she would rather not go to the Christmas Dance because her friend does not share her feelings about the dance.

❷ The girl's primary fear is defeat in the competition for a partner.

❸ She tries to make herself ill so that she won't have to go to the dance.

ADDITIONAL QUESTIONS AND ACTIVITIES

To which teacher does the narrator compare herself? What comparison does she make? How does this comparison relate to the narrator's "premonitions of total defeat"?

Answers. The narrator compares herself to her English teacher whose voice is "as unreliable" as her own. This comparison relates to the narrator's premonitions because the English teacher unsuccessfully tried to make the boys in her class pay attention. In turn, the boys "took up rapt postures, made swooning faces, crossed their eyes, flung their hands over their hearts." The helpless teacher flees the "carnival atmosphere of brutality in the room," an atmosphere that scares the "weak and suspect" narrator.

❶ *What doesn't the young girl want to tell her friend? Why not?*

❷ *What is the girl's primary fear?*

❸ *Why does the girl try to make herself ill?*

ANSWER TO GUIDED READING QUESTION

❶ During the last days of Pompeii, the city was buried in ash and lava. The girl wishes herself there so she will not have to attend the dance.

ADDITIONAL QUESTIONS AND ACTIVITIES

Students can write about something that they felt compelled to do though they did not want to do it. Ask them to consider what they did to try to avoid the situation and how they felt about the situation after they had gone through it.

and as I knelt there, my eyes shut, I pictured my chest and throat turning blue, the cold, greyed blue of veins under the skin. I stayed until I could not stand it any more, and then I took a handful of snow from the windowsill and smeared it all over my chest, before I buttoned my pajamas. It would melt against the flannelette and I would be sleeping in wet clothes, which was supposed to be the worst thing of all. In the morning, the moment I woke up, I cleared my throat, testing for soreness, coughed experimentally, hopefully, touched my forehead to see if I had fever. It was no good. Every morning, including the day of the dance, I rose defeated, and in perfect health.

The day of the dance I did my hair up in steel curlers. I had never done this before, because my hair was naturally curly, but today I wanted the protection of all possible female rituals. I lay on the couch in the kitchen, reading *The Last Days of Pompeii*, and wishing I was there. My mother, never satisfied, was sewing a white lace collar on the dress; she had decided it was too grown-up looking. I watched the hours. It was one of the shortest days of the year. Above the couch, on the wallpaper, were old games of Xs and Os, old drawings and scribblings my brother and I had done when we were sick with bronchitis. I looked at them and longed to be back safe behind the boundaries of childhood.

When I took out the curlers my hair, both naturally and artificially stimulated, sprang out in an <u>exuberant</u> glossy bush. I wet it, I combed it, beat it with the brush and tugged it down along my cheeks. I applied face powder, which stood out

chalkily on my hot face. My mother got out her Ashes of Roses Cologne, which she never used, and let me splash it over my arms. Then she zipped up the dress and turned me around to the mirror. The dress was princess style, very tight in the midriff. I saw how my breasts, in their new stiff brassiere, jutted out surprisingly, with mature authority, under the childish frills of the collar.

"Well I wish I could take a picture," my mother said. "I am really, genuinely proud of that fit. And you might say thank you for it."

"Thank you," I said.

The first thing Lonnie said when I opened the door to her was, "Jesus, what did you do to your hair?"

"I did it up."

"You look like a Zulu. Oh, don't worry. Get me a comb and I'll do the front in a roll. It'll look all right. It'll even make you look older."

I sat in front of the mirror and Lonnie stood behind me, fixing my hair. My mother seemed unable to leave us. I wished she would. She watched the roll take shape and said, "You're a wonder, Lonnie. You should take up hairdressing."

"That's a thought," Lonnie said. She had on a pale blue crepe dress, with a peplum and bow; it was much more grown-up than mine even without the collar. Her hair had come out as sleek as the girl's on the bobby-pin card. I had always thought secretly that Lonnie could not be pretty because she had crooked teeth, but now I saw that crooked teeth or not, her stylish dress and smooth hair made me look a little like a golliwog, stuffed into

❶ *What happened during the last days of Pompeii? Why would the girl wish herself there?*

WORDS FOR EVERYDAY USE: ex•u•ber•ant (eg zoo´bər ənt) *adj.*, full of life

VOCABULARY IN CONTEXT

- After a few minutes of <u>exuberant</u> applause, the singer returned to the stage for an encore.
- You cannot make a rational decision in such a state of <u>delirium</u>.
- The painter's vivid colors and strong brush strokes seem to instill her <u>inanimate</u> subjects with life.
- The exhausted patient spoke <u>languidly</u>.
- The novice reporter felt like a <u>nonentity</u> at the broadcasters' awards banquet.

red velvet, wide-eyed, wild-haired, with a suggestion of <u>delirium</u>.

My mother followed us to the door and called out into the dark, "Au reservoir!" This was a traditional farewell of Lonnie's and mine; it sounded foolish and desolate coming from her, and I was so angry with her for using it that I did not reply. It was only Lonnie who called back cheerfully, encouragingly, "Good night!"

The gymnasium smelled of pine and cedar. Red and green bells of fluted paper hung from the basketball hoops; the high, barred windows were hidden by green boughs. Everybody in the upper grades seemed to have come in couples. Some of the Grade Twelve and Thirteen girls had brought boy friends who had already graduated, who were young businessmen around the town. These young men smoked in the gymnasium, nobody could stop them, they were free. The girls stood beside them, resting their hands casually on male sleeves, their faces bored, aloof and beautiful. I longed to be like that. They behaved as if only they—the older ones—were really at the dance, as if the rest of us, whom they moved among and peered around, were, if not invisible, <u>inanimate</u>; when the first dance was announced—a Paul Jones—they moved out <u>languidly</u>, smiling at each other as if they had been asked to take part in some half-forgotten childish game. Holding hands and shivering, crowding up together, Lonnie and I and the other Grade Nine girls followed.

I didn't dare look at the outer circle as it passed me, for fear I should see some unmannerly hurrying-up. When the music stopped I stayed where I was, and half-raising my eyes I saw a boy named Mason Williams coming reluctantly towards me. Barely touching my waist and my fingers, he began to dance with me. My legs were hollow, my arm trembled from the shoulder, I could not have spoken. This Mason Williams was one of the heroes of the school; he played basketball and hockey and walked the halls with an air of royal sullenness and barbaric contempt. To have to dance with a <u>nonentity</u> like me was as offensive to him as having to memorize Shakespeare. I felt this as keenly as he did, and imagined that he was exchanging looks of dismay with his friends. He steered me, stumbling, to the edge of the floor. He took his hand from my waist and dropped my arm.

"See you," he said. He walked away.

It took me a minute or two to realize what had happened and that he was not coming back. I went and stood by the wall alone. The Physical Education teacher, dancing past energetically in the arms of a Grade Ten boy, gave me an inquisitive look. She was the only teacher in the school who made use of the words social adjustment, and I was afraid that if she had seen, or if she found out, she might make some horribly public attempt to make Mason finish out the dance with me. I myself was not angry or surprised at Mason; I accepted his position, and mine, in the world of school and I saw that what he had done was the realistic thing to do. He was a Natural Hero, not a Student Council type of hero bound for success beyond the school; one of those would have danced with me courteously and

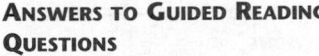
❶ He steers the girl to the edge of the floor, drops her arm, and walks away. He does this because he wants to be with a more popular girl.

❷ The girl wants to be like the older girls, "aloof and beautiful."

❸ Mason dances with her because he is facing her when the music stops and boys in the outer circle stop moving around the girls in the inner circle.

Additional Questions and Activities

What does the description of the dance reveal about the community in which the narrator lives? What does it reveal about the role of women during this time period?

Answers. The fact that grades nine through thirteen attend the same dance reveals that the school population is small. The fact that the boyfriends of the older girls have graduated from the school and remained in the community indicates that most people probably stay in the area. The painful description of the narrator waiting to be chosen by a boy reveals that girls were not encouraged to play active roles in courtship.

❶ *How does Mason Williams end the dance? Why does he do this?*

❷ *What does the girl want to be like?*

❸ *Why does Mason Williams dance with the girl?*

W
Words for Everyday Use:

de • lir • i • um (di lir´ ē əm) *n.*, wild excitement

in • an • i • mate (in an´ə mit) *adj.*, lifeless

lan • guid • ly (laŋ gwid lē) *adv.*, sluggishly; without vigor

non • en • ti • ty (nän en´tə tē) *n.*, person of no importance

"RED DRESS—1946" **959**

❶ A "merry fortune" is a happy future
or bit of luck. Mary's name is
significant because it has the
connotation of cheerfulness and
good luck.

❷ She is questioning why no one has
asked her to dance because it seems
that everyone else, even "Fat girls,
girls with pimples, a poor girl who
didn't own a good dress," is dancing.
She is doing this in the hope that
even she will be asked to dance.
Being left without a partner would
confirm her fear that "there was
something mysterious the matter"
with her.

patronizingly and left me feeling no better off. Still, I hoped not many people had seen. I hated people seeing. I began to bite the skin on my thumb.

When the music stopped I joined the surge of girls to the end of the gymnasium. Pretend it didn't happen, I said to myself. Pretend this is the beginning, now.

The band began to play again. There was movement in the dense crowd at our end of the floor, it thinned rapidly. Boys came over, girls went out to dance. Lonnie went. The girl on the other side of me went. Nobody asked me. I remembered a magazine article Lonnie and I had read, which said *Be gay! Let the boys see your eyes sparkle, let them hear laughter in your voice! Simple, obvious, but how many girls forget!* It was true, I had forgotten. My eyebrows were drawn together with tension, I must look scared and ugly. I took a deep breath and tried to loosen my face. I smiled. But I felt absurd, smiling at no one. And I observed that girls on the dance floor, popular girls, were not smiling; many of them had sleepy, sulky faces and never smiled at all.

Girls were still going out to the floor. Some, despairing, went with each other. But most went with boys. Fat girls, girls with pimples, a poor girl who didn't own a good dress and had to wear a skirt and sweater to the dance; they were claimed, they danced away. Why take them and not me? Why everybody else and not me? I have a red velvet dress, I did my hair in curlers, I used a deodorant and put on cologne. *Pray,* I thought. I couldn't close my eyes but I said over and over again in my mind, *Please, me, please,* and I locked my fingers behind my back in a sign more potent than crossing, the same secret sign Lonnie and I used not to be sent to the blackboard in Math.

It did not work. What I had been afraid of was true. I was going to be left. There

❶
What is a "merry
fortune"? What
significance might
Mary's name
have?

❷
What is the girl
questioning
about herself?
Why is she doing
this?

was something mysterious the matter with me, something that could not be put right like bad breath or overlooked like pimples, and everybody knew it, and I knew it; I had known it all along. But I had not known it for sure, I had hoped to be mistaken. Certainty rose inside me like sickness. I hurried past one or two girls who were also left and went into the girls' washroom. I hid myself in a cubicle.

That was where I stayed. Between dances girls came in and went out quickly. There were plenty of cubicles; nobody noticed that I was not a temporary occupant. During the dances, I listened to the music which I liked but had no part of any more. For I was not going to try any more. I only wanted to hide in here, get out without seeing anybody, get home.

One time after the music started somebody stayed behind. She was taking a long time running the water, washing her hands, combing her hair. She was going to think it funny that I stayed in so long. I had better go out and wash my hands, and maybe while I was washing them she would leave.

It was Mary Fortune. I knew her by name, because she was an officer of the Girls' Athletic Society and she was on the Honour Roll and she was always organizing things. She had something to do with organizing this dance; she had been around to all the classrooms asking for volunteers to do the decorations. She was in Grade Eleven or Twelve.

"Nice and cool in here," she said. "I came in to get cooled off. I get so hot."

She was still combing her hair when I finished my hands. "Do you like the band?" she said.

"It's all right." I didn't really know what to say. I was surprised at her, an older girl, taking this time to talk to me.

"I don't. I can't stand it. I hate dancing when I don't like the band. Listen.

They're so choppy. I'd just as soon not dance as dance to that."

I combed my hair. She leaned against a basin, watching me.

"I don't want to dance and don't particularly want to stay in here. Let's go and have a cigarette."

"Where?"

"Come on, I'll show you."

At the end of the washroom there was a door. It was unlocked and led into a dark closet full of mops and pails. She had me hold the door open, to get the washroom light, until she found the knob of another door. This door opened into darkness.

"I can't turn on the light or somebody might see," she said. "It's the janitor's room." I reflected that athletes always seemed to know more than the rest of us about the school as a building; they knew where things were kept and they were always coming out of unauthorized doors with a bold, <u>preoccupied</u> air. "Watch out where you're going," she said. "Over at the far end there's some stairs. They go up to a closet on the second floor. The door's locked at the top, but there's like a partition between the stairs and the room. So if we sit on the steps, even if by chance someone did come in here, they wouldn't see us."

"Wouldn't they smell smoke?" I said.

"Oh, well. Live dangerously."

There was a high window over the stairs which gave us little light. Mary Fortune had cigarettes and matches in her purse. I had not smoked before except the cigarettes Lonnie and I made ourselves, using papers and tobacco stolen from her father; they came apart in the middle. These were much better.

"The only reason I even came to-night," Mary Fortune said, "is because I am responsible for the decorations and I wanted to see, you know, how it looked once people got in there and everything. Otherwise why bother? I'm not boy-crazy."

In the light from the high window I could see her narrow, scornful face, her dark skin pitted with acne, her teeth pushed together at the front, making her look adult and commanding.

"Most girls are. Haven't you noticed that? The greatest collection of boy-crazy girls you could imagine is right here in this school."

I was grateful for her attention, her company and her cigarette. I said I thought so too.

"Like this afternoon. This afternoon I was trying to get them to hang the bells and junk. They just get up on the ladders and fool around with boys. They don't care if it ever gets decorated. It's just an excuse. That's the only aim they have in life, fooling around with boys. As far as I'm concerned, they're idiots."

We talked about teachers, and things at school. She said she wanted to be a physical education teacher and she would have to go to college for that, but her parents did not have enough money. She said she planned to work her own way through, she wanted to be independent anyway, she would work in the cafeteria and in the summer she would do farm work, like picking tobacco. Listening to her, I felt the <u>acute</u> phase of unhappiness passing. Here was someone who had suffered the same defeat as I had—I saw that—but she was full of energy and self respect. She

❶
What possibility for herself does the girl see in Mary Fortune? In what way has Mary Fortune triumphed despite her "defeat"?

"RED DRESS—1946" **961**

WORDS FOR EVERYDAY USE:

pre • oc • cu • pied (prē äk′yōō pīd) *adj.*, engrossed

a • cute (ə kyōōt′) *adj.*, severe and sharp

HISTORICAL NOTE

Writers use **tag lines** to indicate who is speaking and sometimes the manner in which the speaking is done. In this conversation between the narrator and Mary Fortune, tag lines are used only to indicate who is speaking. Students can discuss why the author might not have included phrases to indicate the manner in which the words are spoken.

VOCABULARY IN CONTEXT

- He must be <u>preoccupied</u> because he hasn't responded to anything I've said.
- An <u>acute</u>, persistent pain on the right side of the body might indicate appendicitis.

ANSWERS TO GUIDED READING QUESTIONS

❶ The girl has decided that she and Lonnie will probably no longer be friends and that she will be friends with Mary instead.

❷ "Bolting" means "moving suddenly" or "fleeing." Raymond's last name might be significant because he might disappear as suddenly as he appeared.

ADDITIONAL QUESTIONS AND ACTIVITIES

Students may discuss whether they think Mary Fortune understood that the narrator's "weak waving motion" indicated that the narrator "didn't know what had happened and also that it was no use waiting" for her.

ANALYTIC SCALES FOR RESPONDING IN WRITING

Assign a score from 1 to 25 for each grading criterion below. (For more detailed evaluation, see the evaluation forms for writing, revising, and proofreading, *Assessment Portfolio*, 7.1–7.10.)

1. Story

• **Content/Unity.** The story presents a character involved in a series of events that build to a suspenseful or highly interesting climax.

• **Organization/Coherence.** The story introduces a central character and a conflict. The conflict is developed through a series of events that build to a climactic scene.

• **Language/Style.** The story uses vivid and precise nouns, verbs, and modifiers.

• **Conventions.** The story avoids errors in spelling, grammar, usage, mechanics, and manuscript form.

(cont.)

---

had thought of other things to do. She would pick tobacco.

We stayed there talking and smoking during the long pause in the music, when, outside, they were having doughnuts and coffee. When the music started again Mary said, "Look, do we have to hang around here any longer? Let's get our coats and go. We can go down to Lee's and have a hot chocolate and talk in comfort, why not?"

We felt our way across the janitor's room, carrying ashes and cigarette butts in our hands. In the closet, we stopped and listened to make sure there was nobody in the washroom. We came back into the light and threw the ashes into the toilet. We had to go out and cut across the dance-floor to the cloak-room, which was beside the outside door.

A dance was just beginning. "Go round the edge of the floor," Mary said. "Nobody'll notice us."

❶ What has the girl decided at this point in the story?

I followed her. I didn't look at anybody. I didn't look for Lonnie. Lonnie was probably not going to be my friend any more, not as much as before anyway. She was what Mary would call boy-crazy.

I found that I was not so frightened, now that I had made up my mind to leave the dance behind. I was not waiting for anybody to choose me. I had my own plans. I did not have to smile or make signs for luck. It did not matter to me. I was on my way to have a hot chocolate, with my friend.

A boy said something to me. He was in my way. I thought he must be telling me that I had dropped something or that I couldn't go that way or that the cloakroom was locked. I didn't understand that he was asking me to dance until he said it over again. It was Raymond Bolting from our class, whom I had never talked to in

❷ What does bolting mean? What significance might Raymond's last name have?

---

my life. He thought I meant yes. He put his hand on my waist and almost without meaning to, I began to dance.

We moved to the middle of the floor. I was dancing. My legs had forgotten to tremble and my hands to sweat. I was dancing with a boy who had asked me. Nobody told him to, he didn't have to, he just asked me. Was it possible, could I believe it, was there nothing the matter with me after all?

I thought that I ought to tell him there was a mistake, that I was just leaving, I was going to have a hot chocolate with my girl friend. But I did not say anything. My face was making certain delicate adjustments, achieving with no effort at all the grave absent-minded look of these who were chosen, those who danced. This was the face that Mary Fortune saw, when she looked out of the cloakroom door, her scarf already around her head. I made a weak waving motion with the hand that lay on the boy's shoulder, indicating that I apologized, that I didn't know what had happened and also that it was no use waiting for me. Then I turned my head away, and when I looked again she was gone.

Raymond Bolting took me home and Harold Simons took Lonnie home. We all walked together as far as Lonnie's corner. The boys were having an argument about a hockey game, which Lonnie and I could not follow. Then we separated into couples and Raymond continued with me the conversation he had been having with Harold. He did not seem to notice that he was now talking to me instead. Once or twice I said, "Well I don't know I didn't see that game," but after a while decided just to say "H'm hmm," and that seemed to be all that was necessary.

One other thing he said was, "I didn't realize you lived such a long ways out." And he sniffled. The cold was making my

962 *UNIT ELEVEN / TWENTIETH-CENTURY PROSE*

ANALYTIC SCALES FOR RESPONDING IN WRITING (CONT.)

2. Plot Diagram

• **Introduction.** Narrator is new to high school.

• **Inciting Incident.** Narrator must attend Christmas Dance.

• **Rising Action.** Narrator attends dance, feels rejected, meets Mary Fortune, decides to leave dance.

• **Crisis or Turning Point.** Raymond Bolting asks her to dance and thinks she says yes.

• **Falling Action.** Narrator chooses to dance with Raymond rather than to leave with Mary.

• **Resolution.** Raymond walks the narrator home.

• **Dénouement.** Narrator sees her mother waiting for her in kitchen, decides she must fulfill her mother's expectations about happiness.

---

nose run a little too, and I worked my fingers through the candy wrappers in my coat pocket until I found a shabby Kleenex. I didn't know whether I ought to offer it to him or not, but he sniffled so loudly that I finally said, "I just have this one Kleenex, it probably isn't even clean, it probably has ink on it. But if I was to tear it in half we'd each have something."

"Thanks," he said. "I sure could use it."

It was a good thing, I thought, that I had done that, for at my gate, when I said, "Well, good night," and after he said, "Oh, yeah. Good night," he leaned towards me and kissed me, briefly, with the air of one who knew his job when he saw it, on the corner of my mouth. Then he turned back to town, never knowing he had been my rescuer, that he had brought me from Mary Fortune's territory into the ordinary world.

I went around the house to the back door, thinking, I have been to a dance and a boy has walked me home and kissed me. It was all true. My life was possible. I went past the kitchen window and I saw my mother. She was sitting with her feet on the open oven door, drinking tea out of a cup without a saucer. She was just sitting and waiting for me to come home and tell her everything that had happened. And I would not do it, I never would. But when I saw the waiting kitchen, and my mother in her faded, fuzzy Paisley kimono, with her sleepy but <u>doggedly</u> expectant face, I understood what a mysterious and <u>oppressive</u> obligation I had, to be happy, and how I had almost failed it, and would be likely to fail it, every time, and she would not know. ∎

❶ In what sense is Raymond the girl's "rescuer"? What is ironic about this, given the preceding description of Raymond?

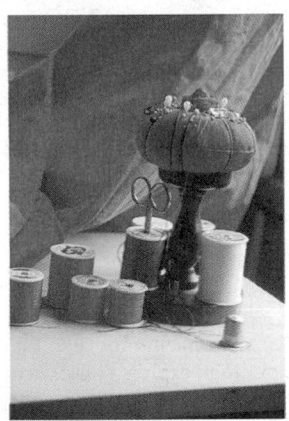

WORDS FOR EVERYDAY USE:

dog • ged • ly (dôg´id lē) adv., persistently

op • pres • sive (ə pres´iv) adj., distressing

❶ Raymond is the girl's "rescuer" because he saves her from the world of defeat to which she had resigned herself. It is ironic because Raymond doesn't seem to listen to the girl or connect with her in the same way Mary Fortune did.

RESPONDING TO THE SELECTION

Students may also want to imagine and write about Mary Fortune's "phase of unhappiness" and how she overcame it.

ANSWERS TO SELECTION CHECK TEST 4.11.9

EX. What does the girl's mother make for her?
She makes a red dress.

1. What is the special event for which the mother is preparing the girl?
The mother is preparing the girl for a dance.

2. Why does the girl try to make herself sick?
She tries to make herself sick so that she will not have to attend the dance.

3. Where does Mary Fortune take the girl?
Mary Fortune takes her to the girls' locker room.

4. What does Mary Fortune suggest to the girl that they do?
She suggests that they leave the dance.

5. What does Raymond Bolting do just after saying, "Good night"?
He kisses the girl on the corner of the mouth.

VOCABULARY IN CONTEXT

• The team of scientists is <u>doggedly</u> pursuing a cure for the disease.
• Even air conditioners seemed useless against the <u>oppressive</u> summer heat.

RECALLING

1. The narrator's mother is making a red velvet dress for her to wear to the Christmas Dance.

2. They made a pact to "tell each other everything."

3. The narrator says that she was "never comfortable for a minute" and was "close to despair at all times."

4. She gives him half of her Kleenex.

INTERPRETING

Responses will vary. Possible responses are given.

5. The narrator's claim is supported by details of previous dresses, for example, a "flowered organdie dress with a high Victorian neckline edged in scratchy lace, with a poke bonnet to match."

6. The narrator probably doesn't tell Lonnie because she senses their difference of opinion regarding attending the dance.

7. The narrator believes that "tension and competition for partners" is what is really going on in school. She has premonitions of "total defeat."

8. She believes she has been "rescued" from the unordinary territory of independent-minded Mary Fortune and brought back to the "ordinary" world of Lonnie and boy-crazy girls. Her "life" now seems possible to her.

SYNTHESIZING

Responses will vary. Possible responses are given.

9. Mary Fortune introduces the narrator to the world of independence and self-respect—a world that does not revolve around other people's opinions. She identifies with Mary Fortune because they have "suffered" the same defeat. However, when the narrator is accidentally pulled back into the "ordinary" world of the dance, she realizes that she wants to be one of the "chosen girls" who won't be left behind or alone. The "weak waving motion" that she makes at Mary and turning her head away so that she doesn't see Mary leave indicate that she has some misgivings about her choice.

(cont.)

Responding to the Selection

Imagine that you are the narrator in this short story. In your journal, write about your "phase of unhappiness." What are your feelings toward the red dress? Why does the dance frighten you? What contradictory feelings do you have during the dance about being accepted, being chosen, and becoming like the other "chosen" girls?

Reviewing the Selection

RECALLING

1. What kind of dress is the narrator's mother making at the beginning of the story? What is the dress for?

2. What pact have the narrator and Lonnie made with each other?

3. On page 957, what two phrases does the narrator use to describe herself and her experience at high school?

4. What does the narrator give to Raymond Bolting while he walks her home?

INTERPRETING

5. What details in the second paragraph support the narrator's claim that "there were no patterns made to match the ideas" in her mother's head?

6. Why might the narrator not want to tell Lonnie that she doesn't want to go to the dance?

7. What does the narrator believe is "really going on" in school? Of what does the narrator have premonitions?

8. From what does the narrator believe she has been "rescued" at the end of the story? Into what world does Raymond bring her back? What now seems possible to her?

SYNTHESIZING

9. What kind of world does Mary Fortune introduce to the narrator? Why does the narrator identify with Mary Fortune but then express relief when returning to the "ordinary world"? What incidents and phrases in the story suggest that the narrator's choice was not made without misgivings?

10. At the end of the story, what does the narrator understand?

ANSWERS FOR REVIEWING THE SELECTION (CONT.)

10. Watching her mother through the window, the narrator understands that she has a "mysterious and oppressive obligation" to happiness; her mother wishes it for her, and the narrator will not tell her otherwise. The narrator understands the expectations and illusions of happiness, but she does not delude herself.

ANALYTIC SCALES FOR RESPONDING IN WRITING

Grading scales appear on page 962.

Understanding Literature (Questions for Discussion)

1. **Narrator/Point of View.** A **narrator** is one who tells a story. **Point of view** is the vantage point from which a story is told. Read the entry on point of view in the Handbook of Literary Terms. In this story, is the narrator omniscient or limited? Is she reliable or unreliable? Is the point of view first person or third person? What thoughts about herself does the narrator reveal? Support your responses with evidence from the selection.

2. **Characterization.** **Characterization** is the use of literary techniques to create a character. For example, a writer might use **direct description** to tell about a character's appearance, habits, dress, background, personality, or motivations. Find an example of direct description in the selection. Explain what the description tells about the character.

3. **Plot/Conflict.** A **plot** is a series of events related to a central conflict. A **conflict** is a struggle between two forces in a literary work. A struggle that takes place between a character and some outside force is called an **external conflict**. A struggle that takes place within a character is called an **internal conflict**. The narrator in this short story experiences both kinds of conflicts. Identify and explain one of the narrator's external conflicts and one of her internal conflicts. What do you think is the central conflict for the narrator? What is the **turning point**, or **crisis**, in the plot that determines the future course of events for the narrator?

Responding in Writing

1. **Story.** A **story**, or narrative, is writing that relates a series of events. Think about a story that you would like to write. Begin by choosing a central character and a conflict, or struggle, that the character is facing. Then brainstorm a list of events to include in your story. Write the climactic scene in your story, the scene in which something of high interest or suspense happens in the plot.

2. **Plot Diagram.** Create a **plot diagram** that shows the plot of the selection. Include the elements of plot named in the following diagram. Begin by copying the diagram onto a piece of paper. Then, beneath each heading on the diagram, describe the events in the story that correspond to that heading.

"RED DRESS—1946" **965**

ANSWERS FOR UNDERSTANDING LITERATURE (CONT.)

3. Plot/Conflict. One of the narrator's external conflicts is having to wear yet another of her mother's creations—the red dress. The narrator struggles internally with her unhappiness. The central conflict is the Christmas Dance. For the narrator, the turning point is purely accidental. It occurs just as she is about to leave the dance with Mary, when Raymond Bolting asks her to dance and thinks that she says yes.

▶ **Teaching Note:** Encourage students to share ideas about the several external and internal conflicts the narrator faces in this story.

ANSWERS FOR LANGUAGE LAB

Responses will vary. Possible responses are given.

1. Germany (noun); German shepherd (adjective)

2. Albert Einstein (noun); Einsteinian theory (adjective)

3. Mars (noun); Martian creatures (adjective)

4. Proust (noun); Proustian analysis (adjective)

5. Queen Elizabeth I (noun); Elizabethan drama (adjective)

FOR MORE PRACTICE

Problem. philosopher

Answer. Socrates (noun); Socratic method (adjective)

▶Additional practice is provided in the *Essential Skills Practice Book: Language,* 2.3 and 2.20.

ANSWERS FOR THINKING SKILLS

Responses will vary. Possible responses are given.

1. homemade, bought at Beale's

2. Grade Ten boy, boyfriends who had graduated, young businessmen

3. popular, unpopular, chosen, left behind, fat girls, girls with pimples, boy-crazy girls, the older ones

4. Lonnie, Mary Fortune

5. narrator's room, world of school, Mary Fortune's territory, ordinary world

▶Additional practice is provided in the *Essential Skills Practice Book: Study and Research,* 4.7.

PROJECT NOTES

▶See the worksheets and evaluation forms for projects, *Assessment Portfolio,* 7.20–7.23.

1. Time Machine. Students should research their topics in a variety of resources, including newspapers, magazines, and radio transcripts.

 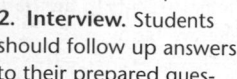

2. Interview. Students should follow up answers to their prepared questions with appropriate impromptu questions.

Language Lab

Proper Nouns and Adjectives. Read the Language Arts Survey, 2.3, "Common and Proper Nouns," and 2.20, "Proper Adjectives." Then form a proper noun and proper adjective for each of the following common nouns.

Example: state; Iowa (noun); *Iowan* magazine (adjective)

1. country
2. scientist
3. planet
4. writer
5. queen

Thinking Skills

Classifying. Read the Language Arts Survey, 4.7, "Classifying." Then, divide each of the following subjects into parts or classes, according to the narrator's observations.

1. dresses
2. boys
3. girls
4. friends
5. world

PROJECTS

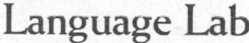

1. **Time Machine.** What was happening in the world in 1946? What was happening in your state, in your town, and in your school? Form seven small groups with each group researching one of the following areas: history and politics, literature and theater, religion and philosophy, visual arts, music, science and technology, and daily life. Create a presentation with posters, magazines and newspapers, videos, tape recordings—whatever will best present your group's area of research into the year 1946.

2. **Interview.** Interview someone who would have been in high school in 1946. Prepare for the interview by listing a number of questions, such as "What did you wear? What kind of haircut did you have? What activities did you participate in? How would you describe your personality in high school? What did you want to do when you got out of school?" Write a short characterization of school life in the 1940s based on the information from the interview.

966   *UNIT ELEVEN / TWENTIETH-CENTURY PROSE*

SELECTIONS FOR ADDITIONAL READING: TWENTIETH-CENTURY PROSE

"The Lagoon"
by Joseph Conrad

The white man, leaning with both arms over the roof of the little house in the stern of the boat, said to the steersman:

"We will pass the night in Arsat's clearing. It is late."

The Malay only grunted, and went on looking fixedly at the river. The white man rested his chin on his crossed arms and gazed at the wake of the boat. At the end of the straight avenue of forests cut by the intense glitter of the river, the sun appeared unclouded and dazzling, poised low over the water that shone smoothly like a band of metal. The forests, somber and dull, stood motionless and silent on each side of the broad stream. At the foot of big, towering trees, trunkless nipa palms rose from the mud of the bank, in bunches of leaves enormous and heavy, that hung unstirring over the brown swirl of eddies. In the stillness of the air every tree, every leaf, every bough, every tendril of creeper and every petal of minute blossoms seemed to have been bewitched into an immobility perfect and final. Nothing moved on the river but the eight paddles that rose flashing regularly, dipped together with a single splash; while the steersman swept right and left with a periodic and sudden flourish of his blade describing a glinting semicircle above his head. The churned-up water frothed alongside with a confused murmur. And the white man's canoe, advancing upstream in the short-lived disturbance of its own making, seemed to enter the portals of a land from which the very memory of motion had forever departed.

The white man, turning his back upon the setting sun, looked along the empty and broad expanse of the sea-reach. For the last three miles of its course the wandering, hesitating river, as if enticed irresistibly by the freedom of an open horizon, flows straight into the sea, flows straight to the east—to the east that harbors both light and darkness. Astern of the boat the repeated call of some bird, a cry discordant and feeble, skipped along over the smooth water and lost itself, before it could reach the other shore, in the breathless silence of the world.

The steersman dug his paddle into the stream, and held hard with stiffened arms, his body thrown forward. The water gurgled aloud; and suddenly the long straight reach seemed to pivot on its center, the forests swung in a semicircle, and the slanting beams of sunset touched the broadside of the canoe with a fiery glow, throwing the slender and distorted shadows of its crew upon the streaked glitter of the river. The white man turned to look ahead. The course of the boat had been altered at right angles to the stream, and the carved dragon head of its prow was pointing now at a gap in the fringing bushes of the bank. It glided through, brushing the overhanging twigs, and disappeared from the river like some slim and amphibious creature leaving the water for its lair in the forests.

The narrow creek was like a ditch: tortuous, fabulously deep; filled with gloom under the thin strip of pure and shining blue of the heaven. Immense trees soared up, invisible behind the festooned draperies of creepers. Here and there, near the glistening blackness of the water, a twisted root of some tall tree showed amongst the tracery of small ferns, black and dull, writhing and motionless, like an arrested snake. The short words of the paddlers reverberated loudly between the thick and somber walls of vegetation. Darkness oozed out from between the trees, through the tangled maze of the creepers, from behind the great fantastic and unstirring leaves, the darkness, mysterious and invincible; the darkness scented and poisonous of impenetrable forests.

The men poled in the shoaling water. The creek broadened, opening out into a wide sweep of a stagnant lagoon. The forests receded from the marshy bank, leaving a level strip of bright green, reedy grass to frame the reflected blueness of the sky. A fleecy pink cloud drifted high above, trailing the delicate coloring of its image under the floating leaves and the silvery blossoms of the lotus. A little house, perched on high piles, appeared black in the distance. Near it, two tall nibong palms, that seemed to have come out of the forests in the background, leaned slightly over the ragged roof, with a suggestion of sad tenderness and care in the droop of their leafy and soaring heads.

The steersman, pointing with his paddle, said, "Arsat is there. I see his canoe fast between the piles."

The polers ran along the sides of the boat glancing over their shoulders at the end of the day's journey. They would have preferred to spend the night somewhere else than on this lagoon of weird aspect and ghostly reputation. Moreover, they disliked Arsat, first as a stranger, and also because he who repairs a ruined house, and dwells in it, proclaims that he is not afraid to live amongst the spirits that haunt the places abandoned by

---

(sidebar content)

"THE LAGOON"

About the Author. Joseph Conrad (1857–1924) was born Józef Teodor Konrad Korzeniowski in Berdichev, Poland. As a young boy, Conrad educated himself by reading in Polish and French. At the age of seventeen, Conrad was orphaned. In 1878, Conrad joined the French Merchant Marine and spent the next twenty years traveling around the world, rising to the rank of captain. It was during his time at sea that Conrad learned English. Conrad published his first novel, *Almayer's Folly,* in 1895. But the 1896 publication of his second novel, *An Outcast of the Islands,* and his marriage convinced Conrad to give up his life at sea. He settled in England, near London, and continued to write, publishing long novels; novellas, including *Heart of Darkness;* and several short stories.

About the Selection. Conrad published **"The Lagoon"** in 1898. The short story includes many of the elements and themes characteristic of Conrad's work: passages rich in description and analysis; tests of human character; and concern with moral questions, isolation, and human psychology.

ADDITIONAL QUESTIONS AND ACTIVITIES

Read aloud part or all of the description of the trip to reach the lagoon. As you read, have students engage in a guided imagery activity, imagining that they are making the trip themselves. Then have students share what they "saw" and felt on their trips to the lagoon.

ADDITIONAL QUESTIONS AND ACTIVITIES

1. What description does the narrator give of Arsat?

Answer. The narrator describes Arsat as "young, powerful, with broad chest and muscular arms." He is dressed only in a sarong and has "big, soft eyes . . . but his voice and demeanor were composed . . . ."

2. Why do the polers dislike Arsat?

Answer. They dislike him because he is "a stranger" and because he has repaired a "ruined house" and lives in it "amongst the spirits that haunt the places abandoned by mankind." The polers are superstitious of such actions and believe that "such a man can disturb the course of fate."

3. What details reveal the seriousness of the woman's illness?

Answer. Details such as "her big eyes, wide open, glittered in the gloom"; her high fever; sunken cheeks; and fixed expression reveal the seriousness of her illness.

Students in small groups can make or find recordings of environmental sounds that they imagine one would hear at the lagoon.

ADDITIONAL QUESTIONS AND ACTIVITIES

Ask students to describe the relationship between Arsat and Tuan. How does Tuan feel toward Arsat? How does Arsat feel about Tuan? Under what circumstances did they become friends?

mankind. Such a man can disturb the course of fate by glances or words; while his familiar ghosts are not easy to propitiate by casual wayfarers upon whom they long to wreak the malice of their human master. White men care not for such things, being unbelievers and in league with the Father of Evil, who leads them unharmed through the invisible dangers of this world. To the warnings of the righteous they oppose an offensive pretense of disbelief. What is there to be done?

So they thought, throwing their weight on the end of their long poles. The big canoe glided on swiftly, noiselessly, and smoothly, toward Arsat's clearing, till, in a great rattling of poles thrown down, and the loud murmurs of "Allah be praised!" it came with a gentle knock against the crooked piles below the house.

The boatmen with uplifted faces shouted discordantly, "Arsat! O Arsat!" Nobody came. The white man began to climb the rude ladder giving access to the bamboo platform before the house. The juragan of the boat said sulkily, "We will cook in the sampan, and sleep on the water."

"Pass my blankets and the basket," said the white man, curtly.

He knelt on the edge of the platform to receive the bundle. Then the boat shoved off, and the white man, standing up, confronted Arsat, who had come out through the low door of his hut. He was a man young, powerful, with broad chest and muscular arms. He had nothing on but his sarong. His head was bare. His big, soft eyes stared eagerly at the white man, but his voice and demeanor were composed as he asked, without any words of greeting:

"Have you medicine, Tuan?"

"No," said the visitor in a startled tone. "No. Why? Is there sickness in the house?"

"Enter and see," replied Arsat, in the same calm manner, and turning short round, passed again through the small doorway. The white man, dropping his bundles, followed.

In the dim light of the dwelling he made out on a couch of bamboos a woman stretched on her back under a broad sheet of red cotton cloth. She lay still, as if dead; but her big eyes, wide open, glittered in the gloom, staring upwards at the slender rafters, motionless and unseeing. She was in a high fever, and evidently unconscious. Her cheeks were sunk slightly, her lips were partly open, and on the young face there was the ominous and fixed expression—the absorbed, contemplating expression of the unconscious who are going to die. The two men stood looking down at her in silence.

"Has she been long ill?" asked the traveler.

"I have not slept for five nights," answered the Malay, in a deliberate tone. "At first she heard voices calling her from the water and struggled against me who held her. But since the sun of today rose she hears nothing—she hears not me. She sees nothing. She sees not me—me!"

He remained silent for a minute, then asked softly:

"Tuan, will she die?"

"I fear so," said the white man, sorrowfully. He had known Arsat years ago, in a far country in times of trouble and danger, when no friendship is to be despised. And since his Malay friend had come unexpectedly to dwell in the hut on the lagoon with a strange woman, he had slept many times there, in his journeys up and down the river. He liked the man who knew how to keep faith in council and how to fight without fear by the side of his white friend. He liked him—not so much perhaps as a man likes his favorite dog—but still he liked him well enough to help and ask no questions, to think sometimes vaguely and hazily in the midst of his own pursuits, about the lonely man and the longhaired woman with audacious face and triumphant eyes, who lived together hidden by the forests—alone and feared.

The white man came out of the hut in time to see the enormous conflagration of sunset put out by the swift and stealthy shadows that, rising like a black and impalpable vapor above the treetops, spread over the heaven, extinguishing the crimson glow of floating clouds and the red brilliance of departing daylight. In a few moments all the stars came out above the intense blackness of the earth and the great lagoon gleaming suddenly with reflected lights resembled an oval patch of night sky flung down into the hopeless and abysmal night of the wilderness. The white man had some supper out of the basket, then collecting a few sticks that lay about the platform, made up a small fire, not for warmth, but for the sake of the smoke, which would keep off the mosquitoes. He wrapped himself in the blankets and sat with his back against the reed wall of the house, smoking thoughtfully.

Arsat came through the doorway with noiseless steps and squatted down by the fire. The white man moved his outstretched legs a little.

"She breathes," said Arsat in a low voice, anticipating the expected question. "She breathes and burns as if with a great fire. She speaks not; she hears not—and burns!"

He paused for a moment, then asked in a quiet, incurious tone:

"Tuan . . . will she die?"

The white man moved his shoulders uneasily and muttered in a hesitating manner:

"If such is her fate."

"No, Tuan," said Arsat, calmly. "If such is my fate. I hear, I see, I wait. I remember. . . . Tuan, do you remember the old days? Do you remember my brother?"

"Yes," said the white man. The Malay rose suddenly and went in. The other, sitting still outside, could hear the voice in the hut. Arsat said: "Hear me! Speak!" His words were succeeded by a complete silence. "O Diamelen!" he cried, suddenly. After that cry there was a deep sigh. Arsat came out and sank down again in his old place.

They sat in silence before the fire. There was no sound within the house, there was no sound near them; but far away on the lagoon they could hear the voices of the boatmen ringing fitful and distinct on the calm water. The fire in the bows of the sampan shone faintly in the distance with a hazy red glow. Then it died out. The voices ceased. The land and the water slept invisible, unstirring and mute. It was as though there had been nothing left in the world but the glitter of stars streaming, ceaseless and vain, through the black stillness of the night.

The white man gazed straight before him into the darkness with wide-open eyes. The fear and fascination, the inspiration and the wonder of death—of death near, unavoidable, and unseen, soothed the unrest of his race and stirred the most indistinct, the most intimate of his thoughts. The ever-ready suspicion of evil, the gnawing suspicion that lurks in our hearts, flowed out into the stillness round him—into the stillness profound and dumb, and made it appear untrustworthy and infamous, like the placid and impenetrable mask of an unjustifiable violence. In that fleeting and powerful disturbance of his being the earth enfolded in the starlight peace became a shadowy country of inhuman strife, a battlefield of phantoms terrible and charming, august or ignoble, struggling ardently for the possession of our helpless hearts. An unquiet and mysterious country of inextinguishable desires and fears.

A plaintive murmur rose in the night; a murmur saddening and startling, as if the great solitudes of surrounding woods had tried to whisper into his ear the wisdom of their immense and lofty indifference. Sounds hesitating and vague floated in the air round him, shaped themselves slowly into words; and at last flowed on gently in a murmuring stream of soft and monotonous sentences. He stirred like a man waking up and changed his position slightly. Arsat, motionless and shadowy, sitting with bowed head under the stars, was speaking in a low and dreamy tone:

". . . for where can we lay down the heaviness of our trouble but in a friend's heart? A man must speak of war and of love. You, Tuan, know what war is, and you have seen me in time of danger seek death as other men seek life! A writing may be lost; a lie may be written; but what the eye has seen is truth and remains in the mind!"

"I remember," said the white man, quietly. Arsat went on with mournful composure:

"Therefore I shall speak to you of love. Speak in the night. Speak before both night and love are gone—and the eye of day looks upon my sorrow and my shame; upon my blackened face; upon my burnt-up heart."

A sigh, short and faint, marked an almost imperceptible pause, and then his words flowed on, without a stir, without a gesture.

"After the time of trouble and war was over and you went away from my country in the pursuit of your desires, which we, men of the islands, cannot understand, I and my brother became again, as we had been before, the sword bearers of the Ruler. You know we were men of family, belonging to a ruling race, and more fit than any to carry on our right shoulder the emblem of power. And in the time of prosperity Si Dendring showed us favor, as we, in time of sorrow, had showed to him the faithfulness of our courage. It was a time of peace. A time of deer hunts and cock fights; of idle talks and foolish squabbles between men whose bellies are full and weapons are rusty. But the sower watched the young rice shoots grow up without fear, and the traders came and went, departed lean and returned fat into the river of peace. They brought news, too. Brought lies and truth mixed together, so that no man knew when to rejoice and when to be sorry. We heard from them about you also. They had seen you here and had seen you there. And I was glad to hear, for I remembered the stirring times, and I always remembered you, Tuan, till the time came when my eyes could see nothing in the past, because they had looked upon the one who is dying there—in the house."

He stopped to exclaim in an intense whisper, "O Mara bahia! O Calamity!" then went on speaking a little louder:

"There's no worse enemy and no better friend than a brother, Tuan, for one brother knows another, and in perfect knowledge is strength for good or evil. I loved my brother. I went to him and told him that I could see nothing but one face, hear nothing but one voice. He told me: 'Open your heart so that she can see what is in it—and wait. Patience is wisdom. Inchi Midah may die or our Ruler may throw off his fear of a woman!' . . . I waited! . . . You remember the lady with the veiled face, Tuan, and the fear of our Ruler before her cunning and temper. And if she wanted her servant, what could I do?

ADDITIONAL QUESTIONS AND ACTIVITIES

What two things does Arsat ask Tuan if he remembers?

Answer. Arsat asks Tuan if he remembers the "old days" and if he remembers his brother.

LITERARY TECHNIQUE

Explain that **personification** is a writing technique in which an idea, animal, or thing is described as if it were a person. Point out the personification of the woods in the following passage: "A plaintive murmur rose in the night; a murmur saddening and startling, as if the great solitudes of surrounding woods had tried to whisper into his ear the wisdom of their immense and lofty indifference." Have students identify other examples of personification in the selection.

ADDITIONAL QUESTIONS AND ACTIVITIES

Arsat says, ". . . for where can we lay down the heaviness of our trouble but in a friend's heart?" Ask students to write about whom they turn to when they are troubled or unhappy. They can also write about a time when they were the friend who received the heavy heart.

ADDITIONAL QUESTIONS AND ACTIVITIES

1. Of whom is Arsat speaking when he says, "I find no warmth in sunlight that does not shine upon her"?

Answer. Arsat is speaking about "the lady with the veiled face" with whom he has fallen in love.

2. While the Ruler and other villagers are fishing at night, what do Arsat and his brother do?

Answer. They steal the woman away from the Ruler.

BIBLIOGRAPHICAL NOTE

Students who are interested in reading more works by Conrad will find a number of critical editions available. Good sources include: *Heart of Darkness.* Ed. Robert Kimbrough. Third ed. 1987. *Lord Jim.* Ed. Thomas C. Moser. 1968. Students also interested in Conrad's life might enjoy Najder, Zdzislaw. *Joseph Conrad: A Chronicle.* 1983.

But I fed the hunger of my heart on short glances and stealthy words. I loitered on the path to the bathhouses in the daytime, and when the sun had fallen behind the forest I crept along the jasmine hedges of the women's courtyard. Unseeing, we spoke to one another through the scent of flowers, through the veil of leaves, through the blades of long grass that stood still before our lips; so great was our prudence, so faint was the murmur of our great longing. The time passed swiftly . . . and there were whispers amongst women—and our enemies watched—my brother was gloomy, and I began to think of killing and of a fierce death. . . . We are of a people who take what they want—like you whites. There is a time when a man should forget loyalty and respect. Might and authority are given to rulers, but to all men is given love and strength and courage. My brother said, 'You shall take her from their midst. We are two who are like one.' And I answered, 'Let it be soon, for I find no warmth in sunlight that does not shine upon her.' Our time came when the Ruler and all the great people went to the mouth of the river to fish by torchlight. There were hundreds of boats, and on the white sand, between the water and the forests, dwellings of leaves were built for the households of the Rajahs. The smoke of cooking fires was like a blue mist of the evening, and many voices rang in it joyfully. While they were making the boats ready to beat up the fish, my brother came to me and said, 'Tonight!' I looked to my weapons, and when the time came our canoe took its place in the circle of boats carrying the torches. The lights blazed on the water, but behind the boats there was darkness. When the shouting began and the excitement made them like mad we dropped out. The water swallowed our fire, and we floated back to the shore that was dark with only here and there the glimmer of embers. We could hear the talk of slave girls amongst the sheds. Then we found a place deserted and silent. We waited there. She came. She came running along the shore, rapid and leaving no trace, like a leaf driven by the wind into the sea. My brother said gloomily, 'Go and take her; carry her into our boat.' I lifted her in my arms. She panted. Her heart was beating against my breast. I said, 'I take you from those people. You came to the cry of my heart, but my arms take you into my boat against the will of the great!' 'It is right,' said my brother. 'We are men who take what we want and can hold it against many. We should have taken her in daylight.' I said, 'Let us be off'; for since she was in my boat I began to think of our Ruler's many men. 'Yes. Let us be off,' said my brother. 'We are cast out and this boat is our country now—and the sea is our refuge.' He lingered with his foot on the shore, and I entreated him to hasten, for I remembered the strokes of her heart against my breast and thought that two men cannot withstand a hundred. We left, paddling downstream close to the bank; and as we passed by the creek where they were fishing, the great shouting had ceased, but the murmur of voices was loud like the humming of insects flying at noonday. The boats floated, clustered together, in the red light of torches, under a black roof of smoke; and men talked of their sport. Men that boasted, and praised, and jeered—men that would have been our friends in the morning, but on that night were already our enemies. We paddled swiftly past. We had no more friends in the country of our birth. She sat in the middle of the canoe with covered face; silent as she is now; unseeing as she is now—and I had no regret at what I was leaving because I could hear her breathing close to me—as I can hear her now."

He paused, listened with his ear turned to the doorway, then shook his head and went on:

"My brother wanted to shout the cry of challenge—one cry only—to let the people know we were freeborn robbers who trusted our arms and the great sea. And again I begged him in the name of our love to be silent.

Could I not hear her breathing close to me? I knew the pursuit would come quick enough. My brother loved me. He dipped his paddle without a splash. He only said, 'There is half a man in you now—the other half is in that woman. I can wait. When you are a whole man again, you will come back with me here to shout defiance. We are sons of the same mother.' I made no answer. All my strength and all my spirit were in my hands that held the paddle—for I longed to be with her in a safe place beyond the reach of men's anger and of women's spite. My love was so great, that I thought it could guide me to a country where death was unknown, if I could only escape from Inchi Midah's fury and from our Ruler's sword. We paddled with haste, breathing through our teeth. The blades bit deep into the smooth water. We passed out of the river; we flew in clear channels amongst the shallows. We skirted the black coast; we skirted the sand beaches where the sea speaks in whispers to the land; and the gleam of white sand flashed back past our boat, so swiftly she ran upon the water. We spoke not. Only once I said, 'Sleep, Diamelen, for soon you may want all your strength.' I heard the sweetness of her voice, but I never turned my head. The sun rose and still we went on. Water fell from my face like rain from a cloud. We flew in the light and heat. I never looked back, but I knew that my brother's eyes, behind me, were looking steadily ahead, for the boat went as straight as a bushman's dart, when it leaves the end of the sumpitan.

There was no better paddler, no better steersman than my brother. Many times, together, we had won races in that canoe. But we never had put out our strength as we did then—then, when for the last time we paddled together! There was no braver or stronger man in our country than my brother. I could not spare the strength to turn my head and look at him, but every moment I heard the hiss of his breath getting louder behind me. Still he did not speak. The sun was high. The heat clung to my back like a flame of fire. My ribs were ready to burst, but I could no longer get enough air into my chest. And then I felt I must cry out with my last breath, 'Let us rest!' . . . 'Good!' he answered; and his voice was firm. He was strong. He was brave. He knew not fear and no fatigue . . . My brother!"

A murmur powerful and gentle, a murmur vast and faint; the murmur of trembling leaves, of stirring boughs, ran through the tangled depths of the forests, ran over the starry smoothness of the lagoon, and the water between the piles lapped the slimy timber once with a sudden splash. A breath of warm air touched the two men's faces and passed on with a mournful sound—a breath loud and short like an uneasy sigh of the dreaming earth.

Arsat went on in an even, low voice.

"We ran our canoe on the white beach of a little bay close to a long tongue of land that seemed to bar our road; a long wooded cape going far into the sea. My brother knew that place. Beyond the cape a river has its entrance, and through the jungle of that land there is a narrow path. We made a fire and cooked rice. Then we lay down to sleep on the soft sand in the shade of our canoe, while she watched. No sooner had I closed my eyes than I heard her cry of alarm. We leaped up. The sun was halfway down the sky already, and coming in sight in the opening of the bay we saw a prau manned by many paddlers. We knew it at once; it was one of our Rajah's praus. They were watching the shore, and saw us. They beat the gong, and turned the head of the prau into the bay. I felt my heart become weak within my breast. Diamelen sat on the sand and covered her face. There was no escape by sea. My brother laughed. He had the gun you had given him, Tuan, before you went away, but there was only a handful of powder. He spoke to me quickly: 'Run with her along the path. I shall keep them back, for they have no firearms, and landing in the face of a man with a gun is certain death for some. Run with her. On the other side of that wood there is a fisherman's house—and a canoe. When I have fired all the shots I will follow. I am a great runner, and before they can come up we shall be gone. I will hold out as long as I

can, for she is but a woman—that can neither run nor fight, but she has your heart in her weak hands.' He dropped behind the canoe. The prau was coming. She and I ran, and as we rushed along the path I heard shots. My brother fired—once—twice—and the booming of the gong ceased. There was silence behind us. That neck of land is narrow. Before I heard my brother fire the third shot I saw the shelving shore, and I saw the water again; the mouth of a broad river. We crossed a grassy glade. We ran down to the water. I saw a low hut above the black mud, and a small canoe hauled up. I heard another shot behind me. I thought, 'That is his last charge.' We rushed down to the canoe; a man came running from the hut, but I leaped on him, and we rolled together in the mud. Then I got up, and he lay still at my feet. I don't know whether I had killed him or not. I and Diamelen pushed the canoe afloat. I heard yells behind me, and I saw my brother run across the glade. Many men were bounding after him. I took her in my arms and threw her into the boat, then leaped in myself. When I looked back I saw that my brother had fallen. He fell and was up again, but the men were closing round him. He shouted, 'I am coming!' The men were close to him. I looked. Many men. Then I looked at her. Tuan, I pushed the canoe! I pushed it into deep water. She was kneeling forward looking at me, and I said, 'Take your paddle,' while I struck the water with mine. Tuan, I heard him cry. I heard him cry my name twice; and I heard voices shouting, 'Kill! Strike!' I never turned back. I heard him calling my name again with a great shriek, as when life is going out together with the voice—and I never turned my head. My own name! . . . My brother! Three times he called—but I was not afraid of life. Was she not there in that canoe? And could I not with her find a country where death is forgotten—where death is unknown!"

The white man sat up. Arsat rose and stood, an indistinct and silent figure above the dying embers of the fire. Over the lagoon a mist drifting and low had crept, erasing slowly the glittering images of the stars. And now a great expanse of white vapor covered the land: it flowed cold and gray in the darkness, eddied in noiseless whirls round the tree trunks and about the platform of the house, which seemed to float upon a restless and impalpable illusion of a sea. Only far away the tops of the trees stood outlined on the twinkle of heaven, like a somber and forbidding shore—a coast deceptive, pitiless and black.

Arsat's voice vibrated loudly in the profound peace.

"I had her there! I had her! To get her I would have faced all mankind. But I had her—and—"

His words went out ringing into the empty distances.

ADDITIONAL QUESTIONS AND ACTIVITIES

1. Why does Diamelen make a "cry of alarm" (page 971)? How does Arsat's brother respond?

Answers. She sees a "prau manned by many paddlers" approaching the shore where she, Arsat, and Arsat's brother are sleeping. Arsat's brother tells him to take Diamelen and run for the fisherman's house and canoe; he plans to fend off the men with his gun and then run back to Arsat in the canoe.

2. What moral dilemma is described in "The Lagoon"? What consequences were suffered because of that dilemma?

Answers. The moral dilemma is the choice that Arsat must make between his brother and Diamelen. If he chooses to help his brother, chances are that both men will die and Diamelen will probably be killed. If Arsat chooses Diamelen, then his brother will die, but Arsat and Diamelen will escape. One of the consequences suffered is the guilt Arsat has lived with and now faces upon remembering his brother's cries for help and his death.

3. What choice did Arsat make (page 971)? What desire influenced his choice?

Answers. Arsat chose Diamelen over his brother. He desired the love of a woman and "peace in my own heart."

4. What is ironic about Arsat's reasoning?

Answer. Arsat chose Diamelen because he desired peace but he has been wracked with guilt since making that decision.

5. What response does Tuan give when Arsat says, "Tuan, I loved my brother" (page 972)?

Answer. Tuan replies, "We all love our brothers."

"Heat"

About the Author. Jean Rhys (1894–1979) was born in Dominica, in the Windward Islands of the West Indies. The daughter of a Creole mother and a Welsh doctor, Rhys lived and went to school in Dominica until the age of sixteen, when she was sent to England to study. Unfortunately, her father died shortly after her arrival in England, and she was left penniless. To support herself, Rhys worked at various jobs, including acting. After her marriage to a Dutch journalist, Rhys moved to Paris, where she met the English novelist Ford Madox Ford. Ford encouraged Rhys in her writing, and in 1927, she published her first book, *The Left Bank and Other Stories.* Her novel *Postures,* published in 1928, was followed by the novels *After Leaving Mr. Mackenzie* and *Voyage in the Dark.* In 1939, she published *Good Morning, Midnight,* and then nearly thirty years passed before she published her enormously successful novel *Wide Sargasso Sea.* Following such a success, her books were reissued, and two new collections of stories were published, *Tigers Are Better Looking* and *Sleep It Off, Lady.* Rhys's unfinished autobiography, *Smile Please,* was published posthumously.

About the Selection. "Heat" is written in the spare and direct style characteristic of Rhys's writing. While much of her writing revolves around the theme of the lonely woman seeking solace in a compassionless, male-dominated world, "Heat" gives a remembered first-person account of Mount Pelée's eruption in 1902. Mount Pelée, located near the city of Saint-Pierre on the island of Martinique, had last erupted in 1856; when it showed signs of erupting again, the signs were not taken seriously by officials. The ensuing volcanic explosion set fire to the island, killing nearly the entire population of Saint-Pierre. A deadly gas, emitted by the volcano, suffocated many of the people.

He paused, and seemed to listen to them dying away very far—beyond help and beyond recall. Then he said quietly:

"Tuan, I loved my brother."

A breath of wind made him shiver. High above his head, high above the silent sea of mist the drooping leaves of the palms rattled together with a mournful and expiring sound. The white man stretched his legs. His chin rested on his chest, and he murmured sadly without lifting his head:

"We all love our brothers."

Arsat burst out with an intense whispering violence:

"What did I care who died? I wanted peace in my own heart."

He seemed to hear a stir in the house—listened— then stepped in noiselessly. The white man stood up. A breeze was coming in fitful puffs. The stars shone paler as if they had retreated into the frozen depths of immense space. After a chill gust of wind there were a few seconds of perfect calm and absolute silence. Then from behind the black and wavy line of the forests a column of golden light shot up into the heavens and spread over the semi-circle of the eastern horizon. The sun had risen. The mist lifted, broke into drifting patches, vanished into thin flying wreaths; and the unveiled lagoon lay, polished and black, in the heavy shadows at the foot of the wall of trees. A white eagle rose over it with a slanting and ponderous flight, reached the clear sunshine and appeared dazzlingly brilliant for a moment, then soaring higher, became a dark and motionless speck before it vanished into the blue as if it had left the earth forever. The white man, standing gazing upwards before the doorway, heard in the hut a confused and broken murmur of distracted words ending with a loud groan. Suddenly Arsat stumbled out with outstretched hands, shivered, and stood still for some time with fixed eyes. Then he said:

"She burns no more."

Before his face the sun showed its edge above the tree-tops rising steadily. The breeze freshened; a great brilliance burst upon the lagoon, sparkled on the rippling water. The forests came out of the clear shadows of the morning, became distinct, as if they had rushed nearer—to stop short in a great stir of leaves, of nodding boughs, of swaying branches. In the merciless sunshine the whisper of unconscious life grew louder, speaking in an incomprehensible voice round the dumb darkness of that human sorrow. Arsat's eyes wandered slowly, then stared at the rising sun.

"I can see nothing," he said half aloud to himself.

"There is nothing," said the white man, moving to the edge of the platform and waving his hand to his boat. A

shout came faintly over the lagoon and the sampan began to glide towards the abode of the friend of ghosts.

"If you want to come with me, I will wait all the morning," said the white man, looking away upon the water.

"No, Tuan," said Arsat, softly. "I shall not eat or sleep in this house, but I must first see my road. Now I can see nothing—see nothing! There is no light and no peace in the world; but there is death—death for many. We are sons of the same mother—and I left him in the midst of enemies; but I am going back now."

He drew a long breath and went on in a dreamy tone:

"In a little while I shall see clear enough to strike—to strike. But she has died, and . . . now . . . darkness."

He flung his arms wide open, let them fall along his body, then stood still with unmoved face and stony eyes, staring at the sun. The white man got down into his canoe. The polers ran smartly along the sides of the boat, looking over their shoulders at the beginning of a weary journey. High in the stern, his head muffled up in white rags, the juragan sat moody, letting his paddle trail in the water. The white man, leaning with both arms over the grass roof of the little cabin, looked back at the shining ripple of the boat's wake. Before the sampan passed out of the lagoon into the creek he lifted his eyes. Arsat had not moved. He stood lonely in the searching sunshine; and he looked beyond the great light of a cloudless day into the darkness of a world of illusions.

"Heat"
by Jean Rhys

Ash had fallen. Perhaps it had fallen the night before or perhaps it was still falling. I can only remember in patches. I was looking at it two feet deep on the flat roof outside my bedroom. The ash and the silence. Nobody talked in the street, nobody talked while we ate, or hardly at all. I know how that they were all frightened. They thought our volcano was going up.

Our volcano was called the boiling lake. That's what it was, a sheet of water that always boiled. From what fires? I thought of it as a mysterious place that few people had ever seen. In the churchyard where we often went—for death was not then a taboo subject—quite near the grave of my little sister, was a large marble headstone. 'Sacred to the memory of Clive—, who lost his life at the boiling lake in Dominica in a heroic attempt to save his guide'. Aged twenty-seven. I remember that too.

He was a young Englishman, a visitor, who had gone exploring with two guides to the boiling lake. As they were standing looking at it one of the guides, who was a

972 *UNIT ELEVEN / TWENTIETH-CENTURY PROSE*

LITERARY TECHNIQUE

Narrator/Point of View. A narrator is one who tells a story. **Point of view** is the vantage point from which a story is told. In this story, written from a first-person point of view, the narrator is someone who witnessed and heard about the eruption of Mount Pelée. Ask students: Does the narrator seem reliable to you? Do her observations seem to be accurate? Why, or why not?

Answers. The narrator appears to be reliable through the detached and objective tone of the writing. In fact, she is unreliable because her story is based on memory, and she admits that she can only remember "in patches." She is insistent, however, at the end of the story that "the English version" of the eruption is inaccurate, "that it wasn't like that at all."

long way ahead, staggered and fell. The other seized hold of the Englishman's hand and said 'Run!' There must have been some local tradition that poisonous gases sometimes came out of the lake. After a few steps the Englishman pulled his hand away and went back and lifted up the man who had fallen. Then he too staggered and they both fell. The surviving guide ran and told what had happened.

In the afternoon two little friends were coming to see us and to my surprise they both arrived carrying large glass bottles. Both the bottles had carefully written labels pasted on: 'Ash collected from the streets of Roseau on May 8th, 1902.' The little boy asked me if I'd like to have his jar, but I refused. I didn't want to touch the ash. I don't remember the rest of the day. I must have gone to bed, for that night my mother woke me and without saying anything, led me to the window. There was a huge black cloud over Martinique. I couldn't ever describe that cloud, so huge and black it was, but I have never forgotten it. There was no moon, no stars, but the edges of the cloud were flame-coloured and in the middle what looked to me like lightning flickered, never stopping. My mother said: 'You will never see anything like this in your life again.' That was all. I must have gone to sleep at the window and been carried to bed.

Next morning we heard what had happened. Was it a blue or a grey day? I only know ash wasn't falling any longer. The Roseau fishermen went out very early, as they did in those days. They met the fishermen from Port de France, who knew. That was how we heard before the cablegrams, the papers and all the rest came flooding in. That was how we heard of Mont Pelée's eruption and the deaths of 40,000 people, and that there was nothing left of St Pierre.

As soon as ships were sailing again between Dominica and Martinique my father went to see the desolation that was left. He brought back a pair of candlesticks, tall heavy brass candlesticks which must have been in a church. The heat had twisted them into an extraordinary shape. He hung them on the wall of the dining-room and I stared at them all through meals, trying to make sense of the shape.

It was after this that the gossip started. That went on for years so I can remember it well. St Pierre, they said, was a very wicked city. It had not only a theatre, but an opera house, which was probably wickeder still. Companies from Paris performed there. But worse than this was the behaviour of the women who were the prettiest in the West Indies. They tied their turbans in a particular way, a sort of language of love that all St Pierre people understood. Tied in one way it meant 'I am in love, I am not free'; tied another way it meant 'You are welcome, I am free'. Even the women who were married, or as good as, tied their kerchiefs in the 'I am free' way. And that wasn't all. The last bishop who had visited the city had taken off his shoes and solemnly shaken them over it. After that, of course, you couldn't wonder.

As I grew older I heard of a book by a man called Lafcadio Hearn who had written about St Pierre as it used to be, about Ti Marie and all the others, but I never found the book and stopped looking for it. However, one day I did discover a pile of old newspapers and magazines, some illustrated: the English version of the eruption. They said nothing about the opera house or the theatre which must have seemed to the English the height of frivolity in a Caribbean island, and very little about the city and its inhabitants. It was nearly all about the one man who had survived. He was a convict imprisoned in an underground cell, so he escaped—the only one out of 40,000. He was now travelling round the music-halls of the world being exhibited. They had taught him a little speech. He must be quite a rich man —what did he do with his money? Would he marry again? His wife and children had been killed in the eruption. . . . I read all this, then I thought but it wasn't like that, it wasn't like that at all.

ADDITIONAL QUESTIONS AND ACTIVITIES

Ask students to think of an event such as a tie-breaking sports play or an accident that they witnessed with other people. After the event was over, what different perspectives did people have of the event? What caused these differences? How does the narrator's conception of the eruption differ from that of the English newspapers? From what different perspectives were they viewing the event?

CROSS-CURRICULAR ACTIVITIES

Social Studies/Sciences. Students can locate Dominica, Roseau, Martinique, Port de France, and Mount Pelée on a map. They can research the causes of volcanoes and determine whether this is a high-risk area for volcanic eruptions.

ENRICHMENT ACTIVITIES

Students can write about or discuss what they know about British colonial rule in India and the Indian struggle for independence. If necessary, students can research the topic.

SUPPORT FOR LEP STUDENTS

Encourage students to use context clues to figure out the meaning of unfamiliar words such as *monsoon, paddy, rupee,* and so on.

IDIOMS
give—absorb pressure or impact

ADDITIONAL VOCABULARY
vigilant—persistently attentive
warily—cautiously
listless—without energy
vessel—container
rivulet—tiny stream
reproach—scold
glimmering—faintly flickering
shrink—turn away from fear
placid—calm
tannery—operation for preparing leather
calamity—disaster
pallid—colorless

PREREADING

from *Nectar in a Sieve*
by Kamala Markandaya

ABOUT THE AUTHOR

Kamala Markandaya (1923–   ) was born and educated in India. In her late thirties she moved to England. She went on to become a prolific British novelist. Her early novels illustrate the political and economic struggles India has faced. She also focuses on the pressures of modernization on traditional Indian society. Some of her titles include *The Silence of Desire* (1960), *Possession* (1963), *A Handful of Rice* (1966), *The Coffer Dams* (1969), and *The Nowhere Man* (1972). Some consider *The Golden Honeycomb* (1977), a book about Indian independence, to be her most ambitious piece.

ABOUT THE SELECTION

This selection comes from Markandaya's first novel, *Nectar in a Sieve*, which tells the story of a woman in a small village in India who, along with her husband, struggles to fulfill the basic needs of her family on a daily basis. This beautiful novel shows how the family changes and adapts when confronted with the challenge of surviving the famine and poverty that gripped India during British colonialism. In the selection you are about to read, the family is picking up the pieces after a devastating natural disaster. Their resources have been depleted by the recent wedding celebration of their daughter Ira, which makes getting on their feet even more difficult. In this excerpt, the character of Kenny appears. Kenny is a supportive and respectful British doctor who lives and works in the community. He encourages the villagers to stand up against Britain's abuses.

GOALS/OBJECTIVES

Studying this lesson will enable students to

- empathize with the narrator's struggle for survival and experience her optimism in the face of adversity
- describe Kamala Markandaya's literary accomplishments and the cultural influences on her writing

- explain the connection between Markandaya's writing and the English literature in this unit
- compare and contrast themes within two or more works of literature

India

FROM

Nectar in a Sieve

KAMALA MARKANDAYA

Nature is like a wild animal that you have trained to work for you. So long as you are vigilant and walk warily with thought and care, so long will it give you its aid; but look away for an instant, be heedless or forgetful, and it has you by the throat.

Ira had been given in marriage in the month of June, which is the <u>propitious</u> season for weddings, and what with the preparing for it, and the listlessness that took hold of me in the first days after her departure, nothing was done to make our hut weatherproof or to secure the land from flooding. That year the monsoon broke early with an evil intensity such as none could remember before.

It rained so hard, so long and so incessantly that the thought of a period of no rain provoked a mild wonder. It was as if nothing had ever been but rain, and the water pitilessly found every hole in the thatched roof to come in, dripping onto the already damp floor. If we had not built on high ground the very walls would have melted in that moisture. I brought out as many pots and pans as I had and we laid them about to catch the drips, but soon there were more leaks than we had vessels. . . . Fortunately, I had laid in a stock of firewood for Ira's wedding, and the few sticks that remained served at least to cook our rice, and while the fire burnt, hissing at the water in the wood, we huddled round trying to get dry. At first the children were cheerful enough—they had not known such things before, and the lakes and rivulets that formed outside gave them endless delight; but Nathan and I watched with heavy hearts while the waters rose and rose and the tender green of the paddy field sank under and was lost.

❶
Why had the family not prepared for monsoon season?

MULTICULTURAL EXTENSIONS

The class struggle described by Kamala Markandaya has parallels in the English literature of the twentieth century. Katherine Mansfield's portrait of the increasing disparity between the lower and upper classes in Georgian England echoes Markandaya's description of the poverty among Indian peasants in British-ruled India. Markandaya and South-African writer Nadine Gordimer both witnessed and wrote about the injustices of colonial rule. Ask students to go to the library and find information about Nadine Gordimer. Suggest that they read some of her short stories, and then compare her themes and ideas with those of Mansfield and Markandaya.

ANSWER TO GUIDED READING QUESTION

❶ Family members had not prepared for the monsoon season because they had been busy with preparations for Ira's wedding.

VOCABULARY FROM THE SELECTION

abate	winnow
gruel	wraithlike
propitious	

VOCABULARY IN CONTEXT

• <u>Propitious</u> wind and water conditions made it a perfect day for a boat race.

ANSWERS TO GUIDED READING QUESTIONS

❶ The older children cried because they realized there was little food, and the younger children cried because they were hungry and uncomfortable.

❷ The storm ruined the narrator's vegetable garden, corn field, and rice paddy. Winds and rain damaged and destroyed huts. Lightning destroyed a tree and killed six people.

CROSS-CURRICULAR ACTIVITIES

Earth Science. Students can create world maps that indicate areas most susceptible to monsoons.

ADDITIONAL QUESTIONS AND ACTIVITIES

Students can discuss other natural disasters they have experienced or learned about through the media. Students may share their personal experiences of loss or rebuilding, or they may discuss relief efforts in such situations. Students may also want to consider how different people react in such situations. Does it become every person for him- or herself or do people pull together?

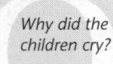

Why did the children cry? ❶

How much damage did the monsoon cause? ❷

"It is a bad season," Nathan said somberly. "The rains have destroyed much of our work; there will be little eating done this year."

At his words, Arjun broke into doleful sobs and his brother, Thambi, followed suit. They were old enough to understand, but the others, who weren't, burst into tears too, for by now they were cramped and out of humour with sitting crouched on the damp floor; and hungry since there was little to eat, for most of the food had gone to make the wedding feast, and the new season's harvesting lay outside ungathered and rotting. I hushed them as best I could, throwing a reproachful glance at my husband for his careless words, but he was unnoticing, sunk in hatred and helplessness.

As night came on—the eighth night of the monsoon—the winds increased, whining and howling around our hut as if seeking to pluck it from the earth. Indoors it was dark—the wick, burning in its shallow saucer of oil, threw only a dim wavering light—but outside the land glimmered, sometimes pale and sometimes vivid, in the flicker of lightning. Towards midnight the storm was at its worst. Lightning kept clawing at the sky almost continuously, thunder shook the earth. I shivered as I looked—for I could not sleep, and even a prayer came with difficulty.

"It cannot last," Nathan said. "The storm will <u>abate</u> by the morning."

Even as he spoke a streak of lightning threw itself down at the earth, there was a tremendous clap of thunder, and when I uncovered my shrinking eyes I saw that

our coconut palm had been struck. That, too, the storm had claimed for its own.

In the morning everything was calm. Even the rain had stopped. After the fury of the night before, an unnatural stillness lay on the land. I went out to see if anything could be saved of the vegetables, but the shoots and vines were battered and broken, torn from their supports and bruised; they did not show much sign of surviving. The corn field was lost. Our paddy field lay beneath a placid lake on which the children were already sailing bits of wood.

Many of our neighbours fared much worse than we had. Several were homeless, and of a group of men who sheltered under a tree when the storm began six had been killed by lightning.

Kali's hut had been completely destroyed in the last final fury of the storm. The roof had been blown away bodily, the mud walls had crumbled.

"At least it stood until the worst was over," said Kali to me, "and by God's grace we were all spared." She looked worn out; in the many years I had known her I had never seen her so deflated. She had come to ask for some palm leaves to thatch the new hut her husband was building; but I could only point to the blackened tree, its head bitten off and hanging by a few fibres from the withered stump.

"We must thatch our roof before the night," I said. "The rains may come again. We need rice too."

Nathan nodded. "We may be able to buy palm leaves in the village—also rice."

He went to the granary in a corner of which the small cloth bundle of our savings

WORDS FOR EVERYDAY USE: **a • bate** (ə bāt´) *vi.,* diminish; terminate

976   *UNIT ELEVEN / TWENTIETH-CENTURY PROSE*

VOCABULARY IN CONTEXT

• Demand for the popular toy <u>abated</u> after the Christmas holiday.

The City Rises. Umberto Boccioni. Oil on canvas, 6′6 1/2″ x 9′10 1/2″
The Museum of Modern Art, NY. Mrs. Simon Guggenheim Fund

ART NOTE

Umberto Boccioni (1882–1916) was an Italian artist important in the Futurist movement, which glorified modern technology. *The City Rises* demonstrates the high-speed motion and machinery of Futurism. Ask students if they feel that the motion in the picture is machinery-based or natural. In what way does it mirror a violent storm? Students might also create depictions of monsoons and destruction. Suggest that they try to capture the motion and energy of the storm in their works of art.

lay buried. It had been heavy once, when we were newly married: now the faded rag in which it was tied was too big and the ends flapped loosely over the knot. Nathan untied it and counted out twelve rupees.

"One will be enough," I said. "Let us go."

"I will take two. We can always put it back."

In the village the storm had left disaster and desolation worse than on our own doorstep. Uprooted trees sprawled their branches in ghastly fashion over streets and houses, flattening them and the bodies of men and women indiscriminately. Sticks and stones lay scattered wildly in angry confusion. The tannery stood, its bricks and cement had held it together despite the raging winds; but the workers' huts, of more flimsy construction, had been demolished. The thatch had been ripped from some, where others stood there was now only a heap of mud with their owners' possessions studding them in a kind of pitiless decoration. The corrugated-iron shacks in which some of the men lived were no more: here and there we could see the iron sheets in unexpected places—suspended from tree tops, or blown and embedded on to the walls of houses still left standing. There was water everywhere, the gutters were overflowing into the streets. Dead dogs, cats and rats cluttered the roadside, or floated starkly on the waters with blown distended bellies.

People were moving about amid this destruction, picking out a rag here, a bundle there, hugging those things that they

ADDITIONAL QUESTIONS AND ACTIVITIES

Ask students to imagine the sound of the "drums of calamity." In class or in a tape recording, students can create their impression of the "grave, throbbing rhythm" of these drums.

ANSWERS TO SELECTION CHECK TEST 4.11.11

EX. According to the narrator, what is like a wild animal?
Nature is like a wild animal.

1. What destroys the crops at the beginning of the selection?
The heavy monsoon rains and subsequent flooding destroy the crops.

2. For what do the people come to Hanuman the shopkeeper?
They come to him for rice.

3. What does Kenny tell Nathan and the narrator that they should not do?
He tells them that they should not remain silent.

3. Why do Nathan and the narrator break down the dams?
They break them down in order to capture fish.

5. What is special about the evening described at the end of the selection?
The family eats a good meal of rice and fish.

---

thought to be theirs, moving haltingly and with a kind of despair about them. People we knew came and spoke to us in low voices, gesturing hopelessly.

"Let us go," I said. "It is no good; we will come back later."

We turned back, the two rupees unspent. Our children came running out to meet us, their faces bright with hope.

"The shops are closed or destroyed," I said. "Go inside. I will get you some <u>gruel</u> presently."

Their faces faded; the two younger ones began crying listlessly from hunger and disappointment. I had no words to comfort them.

At dusk the drums of calamity began; their grave, throbbing rhythm came clearly through the night, throughout the night, each beat, each tattoo, echoing the mighty impotence of our human endeavour. I listened. I could not sleep. In the sound of the drums I understood a vast pervading doom; but in the expectant silences between, my own disaster loomed larger, more consequent and more hurtful.

We ventured out again when the waters had subsided a little, taking with us as before two rupees. This time things were somewhat better; the streets were clear, huts were going up everywhere. My spirits rose.

"To Hanuman first for rice," said Nathan, excited. "The gruel we have been swallowing has been almost plain water these last few days."

I quickened my steps: my stomach began heaving at the thought of food.

Hanuman was standing in the doorway of his shop. He shook his head when he

❶

How are they treated by the two shopkeepers?

saw us. "You have come for rice," he said. "They all come for rice. I have none to sell, only enough for my wife and children."

"And yet you are a merchant who deals in rice?"

"And what if so? Are you not growers of it? Why then do you come to me? If I have rice I do not choose to sell it now; but I have told you, I have none."

"We ask for only a little. We will pay for what we have—see, here is the money."

"No, no rice, but—wait . . . they say Biswas is selling . . . you can try . . ."

To Biswas. "We come for rice. Look, here is our money."

"Two rupees? How much do you think you can buy with two rupees?"

"We thought—"

"Never mind what you thought! Is this not a time of scarcity? Can you buy rice anywhere else? Am I not entitled to charge more for that? Two ollocks I will let you have and that is charity."

"It is very little for two rupees—"

"Take it or leave it. I can get double that sum from the tanners, but because I know you—"

We take it, we give up the silver coins. Now there is nothing left for the thatching, unless we use a rupee or two from the ten that remain in the granary.

I put the rice in my sari, tuck the precious load securely in at the waist. We turn back. On the outskirts of the village there is Kenny. His face is grim and long, his eyes are burning in his pallid face. He sees us and comes up.

"You too are starving, I suppose."

I tap the roll at my waist—the grains give at my touch.

WORDS FOR EVERYDAY USE: gru • el (grōō´əl) *n.,* thin porridge made by cooking grain in water or milk

---

VOCABULARY IN CONTEXT

- The peasant cook made the <u>gruel</u> with oatmeal and goat's milk.
- The workers used forced air to <u>winnow</u> the chaff from the grain.
- In the fog, the person walking by the road has a <u>wraithlike</u> appearance.

"We have a little rice—it will last us until times are better."

"Times are better, times are better," he shouts. "Times will not be better for many months. Meanwhile you will suffer and die, you meek suffering fools. Why do you keep this ghastly silence? Why do you not demand—cry out for help—do something? There is nothing in this country, oh God, there is nothing!"

We shrink from his violence. What can we do—what can he mean? The man is raving. We go on our way.

The paddy was completely destroyed; there would be no rice until the next harvesting. Meanwhile, we lived on what remained of our salted fish, roots and leaves, the fruit of the prickly pear, and on the plantains from our tree. At last the time came for the rice terraces to be drained and got ready for the next sowing. Nathan told me of it with cheer in his voice and I told the children, pleasurably, for the fields were full of fish that would feed us for many a day. Then we waited, spirits lifting, eyes sparkling, bellies painful with anticipation.

At last the day. Nathan went to break the dams and I with him and with me our children, sunken-eyed, noisy as they had not been for many days at the thought of the feast, carrying nets and baskets. First one hole, then another, no bigger than a finger's width, until the water eroded the sides and the outlets grew large enough for two fists to go through. Against them we held our nets, feet firm and braced in the mud while the water rushed away, and the fish came tumbling into them. When the water was all gone, there they were caught in the meshes and among the paddy, shoals of them leaping madly, wet and silver and good to look upon. We gathered them with flying fingers and greedy hearts and bore them away in triumph, with a glow at least as bright as the sun on those shining scales. Then we came and gathered up what remained of the paddy and took it away to thresh and <u>winnow</u>.

Late that night we were still at work, cleaning the fish, hulling the rice, separating the grain from the husk. When we had done, the rice yield was meagre—no more than two measures—all that was left of the year's harvest and the year's labour.

We ate, finding it difficult to believe we did so. The good food lay rich, if uneasy, in our starved bellies. Already the children were looking better, and at the sight of their faces, still pinched but content, a great weight lifted from me. Today we would eat and tomorrow, and for many weeks while the grain lasted. Then there was the fish, cleaned, dried and salted away, and before that was gone we should earn some more money; I would plant more vegetables . . . such dreams, delightful, orderly, satisfying, but of the stuff of dreams, <u>wraithlike</u>. And sleep, such sleep . . . deep and sweet and sound as I had not known for many nights; it claimed me even as I sat amid the rice husks and fish scales and drying salt. ∎

❶ *What does Kenny say about the situation?*

ANSWER TO GUIDED READING QUESTION

❶ Kenny says that the situation will not be better for many months and that people should protest their conditions.

ADDITIONAL QUESTIONS AND ACTIVITIES

What kind of an economy exists in this village? On what does this economy depend?

Answers. An agrarian economy exists in this village. It depends heavily on environmental factors.

ANSWERS FOR REVIEWING THE SELECTION

1. It states that nature "is like a wild animal." Although humans may believe they have tamed it, nature will turn on them as soon as they let down their guard.

2. Nature grabbed this family "by the throat" by damaging their home and virtually destroying their livelihood and basic food sources. Other people in the community lost their homes, their food, and, in some cases, their lives.

3. The family had some money set aside to help them buy food and building materials. They also had the mother's spiritual balance and optimism to sustain them.

4. The two shopkeepers treated them rudely and unfairly. The shopkeepers might have behaved this way because they were exhausted by requests from many villagers and by their own attempts to repair their lives after the storm. In the case of the second shopkeeper, desperation and greed may have also been motivators. The family was finally able to buy a little bit of rice, but the price was outrageously inflated.

5. Kenny was angry that the villagers resigned themselves to their suffering. He told the family to "demand—cry out for help—do something."

ANSWERS FOR CONNECTIONS

1. In "The Garden-Party" the disparities between the classes is seen most vividly through descriptive passages. The author details the excesses of an upper-middle-class family and then contrasts them with the bleak living conditions that exist among the poor laborers who "live far too near" the lavish home. In this selection from *Nectar in a Sieve,* the reader sees only the poverty—inadequate huts with dirt floors—in which the villagers live. In "The Garden-Party" an extravagant afternoon party is given without thought to cost; the family in *Nectar in a Sieve* spends most of its savings to provide their daughter with a proper wedding. Jose and Mrs. Sheridan in "The Garden-Party" both value the party and their social standing above the suffering of others. The shopkeeper Biswas in *Nectar in a Sieve* hardens himself against his neighbors' suffering, insisting that he must maintain his business even in the face of tragedy. In *Nectar in a Sieve* the continual struggle to fulfill basic needs prevents the family from comprehending Kenny's plea to "demand" change. However, this struggle also forges a close bond between neighbors and family, as shown by the "dark knot of people" who stand outside the workman's cottage in "The Garden-Party."

2. Kenny has a different view because he sees the hardships but does not directly experience them. He might also have a different view because he has seen similar conditions and their devastating effects in other places; possibly he has seen the effects of social change in other places as well. Outsiders tend to judge societies by their own standards, and they assume that their values and practices will translate to a different culture. The narrator of "Heat" mourns the loss of Saint-Pierre, whose vibrant sensuality will be forever lost to outsiders. However, outsiders might also be able to see injustices or problems that insiders accept as "normal." In *Nectar in a Sieve,* Kenny, who declares that "there is
(cont.)

Reviewing the Selection

1. What does the opening paragraph state about nature?

2. In what way did nature indeed grab this family "by the throat"? How did other people in the community suffer because of the weather?

3. What resources, both material and spiritual, did the family have upon which to draw?

4. How was the family treated by the two shopkeepers? What might have been the reason for this behavior? What finally happened?

5. Why did Kenny, the community doctor, become angry? What did he tell them to do?

Connections (Questions for Writing or Discussion)

1. Think about classism and the economic disparity between people who have a great deal at their fingertips and people who don't seem to have anything. There are many examples of such disparities in the Unit 11 selections. How is the issue dealt with in "The Garden-Party" and *Nectar in a Sieve?* Is there a point at which people have almost too much in the way of material possessions and lose touch with other aspects of life? How does struggling every day to fulfill basic needs prevent people from fulfilling themselves in other ways? Are there disadvantages to both situations? Think of concrete examples as you prepare your answer.

2. Think about the woman's acceptance of hardships in *Nectar in a Sieve* and about Kenny's anger at this acceptance. Why does Kenny have a different view than the woman? How does an outsider's view of a society differ from that of a member of that society? How does the outsider's view differ from that of the participant in Rhys's story "Heat" on page 972? What kinds of things don't outsiders understand? What perspectives might they have that those closer to a situation might not have? What things are not understood by the outsiders in these two stories? What ideas do the outsiders have that participants do not share?

ANSWERS FOR CONNECTIONS (CONT.)

nothing" in the face of such suffering and acceptance, seems to have no spiritual foundation. The family, however, finds comfort in the possibility of life after such devastation. In "Heat," the insiders attempt to explain the tragedy, while the outsiders concern themselves with the miracle of the sole survivor.

UNIT REVIEW

Twentieth-Century Prose

VOCABULARY FROM THE SELECTIONS

abate, 976	haggard, 942	propitious, 975
acute, 961	inanimate, 959	ramification, 934
agog, 915	interminable, 936	rapturous, 945
baize, 943	irrelevant, 956	sanguine, 933
betrothed, 916	languidly, 959	scrutinize, 933
burlesqued, 957	magnitude, 936	sordid, 933, 947
delirium, 959	marquee, 941	stave, 941
docility, 955	nonentity, 959	strident, 936
doggedly, 963	omnibus, 916	tableau, 934
enigmatically, 944	oppressive, 963	truncheon, 934
escapade, 915	organdy or organdie, 955	veranda, 943
exuberant, 958	palpitation, 957	vulnerable, 956
gruel, 978	poach, 915	winnow, 979
guffaw, 916	preoccupied, 961	wraithlike, 979

LITERARY TERMS

aim, 918	external conflict, 965	plot, 965
character, 918	image, 929, 952	point of view, 965
characterization, 965	internal conflict, 965	science fiction, 938
description, 952	narrator, 965	stream-of-consciousness
dystopia, 938	objective correlative, 929,	writing, 929
essay, 918	952	symbol, 952

VOCABULARY DEVELOPMENT EXERCISE

▶ Give students the following exercise.

Choose twenty words from the list on page 981. For each word, write a sentence that relates to something you've read in this unit. The vocabulary word need not have appeared in the selection to which you refer.

Example.

Shakespeare's sister would have been <u>vulnerable</u> if she had tried to pursue her writing career.

ADDITIONAL RESOURCES

ASSESSMENT PORTFOLIO

- Vocabulary Worksheet: Unit 11, 4.11.13
- Study Guide: Unit 11 Test, 4.11.14
- Unit 11 Test, 4.11.15

ESSENTIAL SKILLS PRACTICE BOOKS

Writing

- Identifying Main Ideas and Supporting Details, 1.31
- Elaboration: Types of Supporting Details, 1.40
- Modes of Writing, 1.9
- Observing, 1.11
- Writing a Thesis Statement and Topic Sentences, 1.41

Language

- Achieving Parallelism, 2.57
- Base Words and Suffixes, 2.140, 2.141
- Compound and Collective Nouns, 2.5
- Concrete and Abstract Nouns, 2.4
- Correcting Errors in Capitalization, 2.107, 2.133
- Correcting Run-ons, 2.62
- Organizations and Institutions, 2.118
- Proper Nouns and Adjectives, 2.3, 2.20
- Sentence Combining, 2.51–2.53
- Using Colorful Modifiers, 2.35
- Using Precise Nouns, 2.32
- Word Origins, 2.143, 2.144

(cont.)

ADDITIONAL RESOURCES (CONT.)

Study and Research

- Classifying, 4.7
- Comparing and Contrasting, 4.8
- Making Hypotheses, 4.13
- Remembering and Visualizing, 4.5

- Understanding Propaganda Techniques, 4.15
- Using Reference Works, 4.23
- Using the Card Catalog, 4.22

► These prompts are suitable as topics for research papers. Refer to the Language Arts Survey, 4.20–4.34, "Research Skills." (To evaluate research papers, see the evaluation forms for writing, revising, and proofreading in the *Assessment Portfolio,* 7.1–7.10.)

► These prompts can be adapted for use as topics for oral reports or debates. (To evaluate these projects, see the evaluation forms in the *Assessment Portfolio,* 7.17–7.19.)

TEACHING THE MULTIPLE INTELLIGENCES

MUSICAL
• Drums of Calamity, 978
• Environmental Recordings, 968

LOGICAL-MATHEMATICAL
• Activity Log, 932
• Adjective and Adverb List, 941
• Comparison and Contrast, 947
• Tracing Stream of Consciousness, 924
• Using Graphing Devices, 956

SPATIAL
• Guided Imagery Activity, 967
• Mapping, 973
• Mapping Monsoons, 976
• Painting a View, 933
• Painting/Sketching a Scene, 941
• Painting/Sketching a Sewing Project, 955
• Set and Costume Design, 948

KINESTHETIC
• Dramatic Monologue, 920
• Dramatic Skit, 953
• Kennings Charades, 930
• Performing Monologues, 917
• Role Play, 939

INTERPERSONAL
• Differences in Impression, 951
• The Woman Artist, 914

SYNTHESIS: QUESTIONS FOR WRITING, RESEARCH, OR DISCUSSION

GENRE STUDIES

1. **Minimalist Writing.** In the first novels that were ever written, it was common for the narrator and/or protagonist to address the reader directly and comment on his or her feelings about the ongoing action of the book. Modern writers tend toward a more impersonal or minimalist style in which the details of the story are often left to speak for themselves without excessive explanation or commentary by the narrator. How do Alice Munro, Jean Rhys, and Katherine Mansfield allow details to speak for themselves in "Red Dress—1946," "Heat," and "The Garden-Party"? What are the most telling, or powerful details in these three stories?

THEMATIC STUDIES

2. **Role of Women.** Look over "The Garden Party," "Red Dress—1946," and the excerpts from *A Room of One's Own* and *Nectar in a Sieve.* How do the women portrayed in each of these selections differ in age and social class, as well as in the culture and period of history in which they were born? In what ways are their lives still similar? Choose three of the pieces listed above and compare the the main characters in this way.

HISTORICAL AND BIOGRAPHICAL STUDIES

3. **Social Commentary.** Many writers in the 20th century have used their writing to make social commentary. The writers in this unit have addressed such issues as education and opportunities of women, the British class system, and totalitarianism. Choose one of these issues and the piece in which it is addressed. Was the writer effective? Why, or why not?

CONNECTIONS ACROSS THE CURRICULUM

ARTS AND HUMANITIES
• Painting a View, 933

SOCIAL STUDIES
• Atlas and Place Lists, 928
• British Colonial Rule, 974
• Class Struggle, 975
• Cold War History, 939
• Geography of "Heat," 973

• Privacy Laws, 933
• Propaganda under Stalin, 937
• Totalitarianism, 931
• Village Economy, 979

APPLIED ARTS AND SCIENCES
• Children's Rhymes, 930
• Collection of Early Women's Writing, 920

• Oceania Telescreen Presentation, 939
• Surveillance Devices, 933
• Videotape Presentation, 960

MATHEMATICS AND SCIENCES
• Geography of "Heat," 973
• Mapping Monsoons, 976

LANGUAGE LAB PROOFREADING FOR SPELLING ERRORS

After checking for other errors in your writing, you should read it through carefully for errors in spelling. If you come across any words that you are not completely sure about, check them in a dictionary.

LANGUAGE ARTS SURVEY

For additional help, see the Language Arts Survey, 2.134–2.136.

EXERCISE A. Using Spelling Rules
In the following sentences, make all the italicized words plural, and add prefixes or suffixes to the underlined words. Use the spelling rules and refer to a dictionary if you are unsure of the correct spelling.

1. The *stitch* in the <u>love</u> (ly) *dress* Mother made were <u>painstaking</u> (ly) done by hand.
2. The *stare* of the *mourner* made Laura blush <u>comfortable</u> (un, ably).
3. One of Woolf's most <u>insight</u> (ful) *essay* is the one about Shakespeare's sister.
4. I have *memory* of the gray *sky* and the <u>pity</u> (ful) *cry* of the dying after the *volcano* erupted.
5. In Orwell's novel, the *life* of *man*, *woman*, and *child* are no longer private. The *person* in the book are like a bunch of *mouse* being watched by a cat who might strike <u>predict</u> (un, ably).

EXERCISE B. Proofreading for Spelling Errors
Read the following paragraph carefully and correct any spelling errors you find. If you are uncertain about any words, refer to a dictionary.

In *A Room of One's Own,* Virginia Woolf discusses the difference in oportunitys availeable to womin and to men. By describeing what the life of Shakespeare's sister would have been like, she shows the kind of education such a woman would have recieved. It would have ben terriblely difficult for her to get any education at all. Most peoples didn't think it was nesisary to edukate girls. This idea was not confined solly to England. In *Nectar in a Sieve,* witch takes place in India, the narator's father teaches her to read, but this was un-common and considered un-wise. Unfortuneatly, lack of access to education and an unsupporteive puplick opinion hindered the writeing careers of many women, and many great women writers may have gone unknown.

ANSWERS FOR LANGUAGE LAB

Exercise A
1. stitches; lovely dresses; painstakingly
2. stares; mourners; uncomfortably
3. insightful; essays
4. memories; skies; pitiful; cries; volcanoes
5. lives; men; women; children; people; mice; unpredictably

Exercise B
In *A Room of One's Own,* Virginia Woolf discusses the difference in opportunities available to women and to men. By describing what the life of Shakespeare's sister would have been like, she shows the kind of education such a woman would have received. It would have been terribly difficult for her to get any education at all. Most people didn't think it was necessary to educate girls. This idea was not confined solely to England. In *Nectar in a Sieve,* which takes place in India, the narrator's father teaches her to read, but this was uncommon and considered unwise. Unfortunately, lack of access to education and an unsupportive public opinion hindered the writing careers of many women, and many great women writers may have gone unknown.

UNIT 12 TWENTIETH-CENTURY DRAMA
(1900–PRESENT)

London Bridge. *André Derain, 1906. Oil on canvas, 26 × 39" (66 × 99.1 cm).*
The Museum of Modern Art, NY. Gift of Mr. and Mrs. Charles Zadok.

GOALS/OBJECTIVES

Studying this unit will enable students to

- enjoy a twentieth-century drama and understand the motifs and themes that differentiate twentieth-century drama from the work of earlier periods

- describe the literary and social significance of George Bernard Shaw's work

- read and understand works of twentieth-century drama

- relate a play to social trends and ideas of its time

- describe elements of drama and identify them in a play

- interpret and evaluate elements of drama as used in a play

Photograph ©1994 The Museum of Modern Art, NY

he play's the thing.

—William Shakespeare

985

ADDITIONAL RESOURCES

READER'S GUIDE
• Selection Worksheet, 12.1

ASSESSMENT PORTFOLIO
• Selection Check Test, 4.12.1
• Selection Test, 4.12.2

ESSENTIAL SKILLS PRACTICE BOOKS
• *Language,* 2.150

ENRICHMENT ACTIVITIES

 Students can read and give a three-minute oral review of a book on gender relations and language. Some possibilities are:

Frank, F. W., P. A. Treichler, et al. *Language, Gender, and Professional Writing: Theoretical Approaches and Guidelines for Non-sexist Usage.* New York: MLA, 1989.

Nilsen, A., et al., eds. *Sexism and Language.* Urbana, IL: NCTE, 1977.

Thorne, B., C. Kramarae, and N. Henley, eds. *Language, Gender and Society.* Rowley, MA: Newbury, 1983.

SUPPORT FOR LEP STUDENTS

Explain to students that Shaw chose not to use an apostrophe to show contractions in his writing. Tell students that the contracted words are pronounced the same way as they usually are, though they may not look the same. Give the following examples of spelling and pronunciation: *Youre, wont (won't), havnt, wasnt, lets, dont, wouldnt.* Observe to students that no matter what Shaw does, they will still be expected to use the usual apostrophes in their own writing.

ADDITIONAL VOCABULARY
oath—vow, promise
subsiding—dying down, lessening
haughtily—arrogantly, disdainfully
detestable—hateful

PREREADING

Pygmalion
by George Bernard Shaw

ABOUT THE AUTHOR

Born in Dublin into a working-class family, **George Bernard Shaw** (1856–1950) confronted poverty throughout his youth. When his parents separated in his teenage years, his mother took him and his two sisters to live in London. There he studied music, art, and literature on his own, interests that were fostered by his mother, who struggled to support the family as a music teacher. Shaw spent his early adulthood trying to become a novelist and failing miserably. Eventually, he took up journalism and began writing book reviews and theater criticism for London periodicals. Not until middle age did he begin writing his own plays, which became more successful than his fiction. At the time, most British plays consisted of fairly simple plots and characters and tended to be overly romantic. Shaw's plays were much more complex. They challenged the social morals and political attitudes of late nineteenth-century England. Since his plays were controversial, they were for a while much more popular in Europe than in England. His great range as a writer enabled him to express his political views in highly effective tragedies and comedies. *Pygmalion* is one of Shaw's finest satires. It combines some of the most humorous scenes in British theater with harsh commentary on the English class system. In 1925, Shaw won the Nobel Prize for literature, perhaps the most prestigious of all literary awards. He kept writing, maintained an active mind, and continued to be a persistent social critic until his death at the age of ninety-four.

ABOUT THE SELECTION

Shaw's *Pygmalion* is a modernization of the Greek mythical tale of the same name, one version of which was told by the Roman poet Ovid in his *Metamorphoses* of AD 15 (page 1057). In the classical myth, a sculptor falls in love with his own creation. In a sense the same thing happens in Shaw's play. Henry Higgins, a speech professor, bets his friend Colonel Pickering that he can turn a lower-class Cockney girl into a woman of high society within six months. The play's wide appeal resulted in a film version in 1938, for which Shaw wrote the screenplay and won an Academy Award. Later, the musical *My Fair Lady* made the story immensely popular. This transformation shows how a classical myth, through the pen of a great author, can become popular entertainment with contemporary relevance.

GOALS/OBJECTIVES

Studying this lesson will enable students to

• enjoy a twentieth-century adaptation of a classical myth

• describe George Bernard Shaw's literary accomplishments and explain the historical significance of his writings

• define *inciting incident, climax,* and *resolution* and discuss the function of each of these in the context of a play

• rewrite sentences to reduce wordiness

• write a critical essay

READER'S JOURNAL

How would you define *independence*? In your journal, list freedoms that you cherish and constraints from which you would like to be free. Then briefly summarize what independence means to you.

LANGUAGE SKILLS

Read the Language Arts Survey, 2.150, "Dialects of English." Then, as you read Act One of *Pygmalion*, note the dialectical differences in the characters' speech and the social consequences of those differences.

Pygmalion

GEORGE BERNARD SHAW

CHARACTERS

Henry Higgins	Mrs. Eynsford Hill
Colonel Pickering	Miss Eynsford Hill
Freddy Eynsford Hill	Mrs. Higgins
Alfred Doolittle	Mrs. Pearce
Bystanders	Parlormaid
Eliza Doolittle	Taximan

ACT ONE

Covent Garden[1] in London at 11.15 p.m. Torrents of heavy summer rain. Cab whistles blowing frantically in all directions. Pedestrians running for shelter into the market and under the portico *of St Paul's Church, where there are already several people, among them a lady and her daughter in evening dress. They are all peering out gloomily at the rain, except one man with his back turned to the rest, who seems wholly preoccupied with a notebook in which he is writing busily.*

The church clock strikes the first quarter.

THE DAUGHTER (*in the space between the central pillars, close to the one on her left*). I'm getting chilled to the bone. What can Freddy be doing all this time? He's been gone twenty minutes.

THE MOTHER (*on her daughter's right*). Not so long. But he ought to have got us a cab by this.

A BYSTANDER (*on the lady's right*). He wont[2] get no cab not until half-past eleven, missus, when they come back after dropping their theatre fares.

---

1. **Covent Garden.** District of London comprised of fruit, vegetable, and flower markets
2. **wont.** Shaw, an advocate of spelling reform, omitted apostrophes in contractions unless the omission was confusing or changed the pronunciation.

WORDS FOR EVERYDAY USE: por • ti • co (pôr´ti kō) *n.*, porch or covered walk in front of a building

VOCABULARY IN CONTEXT

• Many an old southern mansion featured a magnificent portico across its pillared front.

PREREADING NOTES

READER'S JOURNAL

As examples of freedoms students might cherish, mention the right to think freely and to speak freely among their friends; as examples of constraints from which they might like to free themselves, mention financial dependence upon others. Point out that all people are dependent on others to some extent. It is possible to *feel* independent despite being dependent on others in some ways.

LANGUAGE SKILLS

After students have read Act One, ask them the following questions:

1. Whose form of speech in Act One would be considered standard or close to standard English?

2. Whose speech would be considered nonstandard?

3. Which form of speech would be considered standard and which form would be considered nonstandard if Higgins spoke as the flower girl does in the play and she spoke as he does? What does this suggest about the way a standard form of a language is defined?

Answers. 1. Higgins's, Pickering's, the Mother's, Daughter's, and Freddy's speech would be considered standard. 2. The flower girl's speech would be considered nonstandard. 3. The definition of standard and nonstandard would be swapped accordingly. This suggests that the language of the class that has money, status, and power tends to be defined as the standard, no matter what form it takes.

VOCABULARY FROM THE SELECTION

amiable	mendacity
bilious	portico
deprecate	proximity
gumption	repudiate
impertinent	staid
melancholy	

THE MOTHER. But we must have a cab. We cant stand here until half-past eleven. It's too bad.

THE BYSTANDER. Well, it ain't my fault, missus.

THE DAUGHTER. If Freddy had a bit of <u>gumption</u>, he would have got one at the theatre door.

THE MOTHER. What could he have done, poor boy?

THE DAUGHTER. Other people got cabs. Why couldnt he?

(FREDDY *rushes in out of the rain from the Southampton Street side, and comes between them closing a dripping umbrella. He is a young man of twenty, in evening dress, very wet round the ankles.*)

THE DAUGHTER. Well, havnt you got a cab?

FREDDY. Theres not one to be had for love or money.

THE MOTHER. Oh, Freddy, there must be one. You cant have tried.

THE DAUGHTER. It's too tiresome. Do you expect us to go and get one ourselves?

FREDDY. I tell you theyre all engaged. The rain was so sudden: nobody was pre-pared; and everybody had to take a cab. Ive been to Charing Cross one way and nearly to Ludgate Circus the other; and they were all engaged.

THE MOTHER. Did you try Trafalgar Square?

FREDDY. There wasnt one at Trafalgar Square.

What differences in social class are demonstrated in the speech of the flower girl and the other characters introduced so far? What differences in manners are demonstrated by the actions and words of Freddy and the flower girl?

THE DAUGHTER. Did you try?

FREDDY. I tried as far as Charing Cross Station. Did you expect me to walk to Hammersmith?

THE DAUGHTER. You havnt tried at all.

THE MOTHER. You really are very help-less, Freddy. Go again; and dont come back until you have found a cab.

FREDDY. I shall simply get soaked for nothing.

THE DAUGHTER. And what about us? Are we to stay here all night in this draught,[3] with next to nothing on? You selfish pig—

FREDDY. Oh, very well: I'll go, I'll go. (*He opens his umbrella and dashes off Strand-wards, but comes into collision with a flower girl, who is hurrying in for shelter, knocking her basket out of her hands. A blinding flash of lightning, followed instantly by a rattling peal of thunder, orchestrates the incident.*)

THE FLOWER GIRL. Nah then, Freddy: look wh' y' gowin, deah.

FREDDY. Sorry (*he rushes off*).

THE FLOWER GIRL (*picking up her scat-tered flowers and replacing them in the basket*). Theres menners f' yer! Te-oo banches o voylets trod into the mad. (*She sits down on the plinth[4] of the column, sorting her flowers, on the lady's right. She is not at all an attractive person. She is perhaps eighteen, perhaps twenty, hardly older. She wears a little sailor hat of black straw that has long been exposed to the dust and soot of London and has*

---

3. **draught.** British spelling of *draft*
4. **plinth.** The square block at the base of a column or pedestal

WORDS FOR
EVERYDAY USE: **gump • tion** (gump´shən) *n.,* courage, boldness

VOCABULARY IN CONTEXT

• Because of the savagery of critics, writing a play for the public requires considerable <u>gumption</u>.
• Jill accepted Josephine as a roommate because she was the most <u>amiable</u> of all those who inquired about the apartment.

seldom if ever been brushed. Her hair needs washing rather badly: its mousy color can hardly be natural. She wears a shoddy black coat that reaches nearly to her knees and is shaped to her waist. She has a brown skirt with a coarse apron. Her boots are much the worse for wear. She is no doubt as clean as she can afford to be; but compared to the ladies she is very dirty. Her features are no worse than theirs; but their condition leaves something to be desired; and she needs the services of a dentist.)

THE MOTHER. How do you know that my son's name is Freddy, pray?

THE FLOWER GIRL. Ow, eez ye-ooa san, is e? Wal, fewd dan y' de-ooty bawmz a mather should, eed now bettern to spawl a pore gel's flahrzn than ran away athaht pyin. Will ye-oo py me f' them?[5] *(Here, with apologies, this desperate attempt to represent her dialect without a phonetic alphabet must be abandoned as intelligible outside London.)*

THE DAUGHTER. Do nothing of the sort, mother. The idea!

THE MOTHER. Please allow me, Clara. Have you any pennies?

THE DAUGHTER. No. Ive nothing smaller than sixpence.

THE FLOWER GIRL. *(hopefully).* I can give you change for a tanner,[6] kind lady.

THE MOTHER *(to* CLARA*).* Give it to me. *(*CLARA *parts reluctantly.)* Now *(to the girl)* this is for your flowers.

THE FLOWER GIRL. Thank you kindly, lady.

THE DAUGHTER. Make her give you the change. These things are only a penny a bunch.

THE MOTHER. Do hold your tongue, Clara. *(To the girl)* You can keep the change.

THE FLOWER GIRL. Oh, thank you, lady.

THE MOTHER. Now tell me how you know that young gentleman's name.

THE FLOWER GIRL. I didnt.

THE MOTHER. I heard you call him by it. Dont try to deceive me.

THE FLOWER GIRL *(protesting).* Who's trying to deceive you? I called him Freddy or Charlie same as you might yourself if you was talking to a stranger and wished to be pleasant. *(She sits down beside her basket.)*

THE DAUGHTER. Sixpence thrown away! Really, mamma, you might have spared Freddy that. *(She retreats in disgust behind the pillar.)*

(An elderly gentleman of the <u>amiable</u> *military type rushes into the shelter, and closes a dripping umbrella. He is in the same plight as* FREDDY, *very wet about the ankles. He is in evening dress, with a light overcoat. He takes the place left vacant by the daughter's retirement.)*

THE GENTLEMAN. Phew!

THE MOTHER *(to the gentleman).* Oh, sir, is there any sign of its stopping?

THE GENTLEMAN. I'm afraid not. It started worse than ever about two minutes

---

5. **Ow, . . . f' them?** Shaw attempted to spell phonetically the Cockney dialect of London. The passage translates, "Oh, he's your son, is he? Well, if you had done your duty by him as a mother should, he'd know better than to spill a poor girl's flowers and then run away without paying. Will you pay me for them?"

6. **tanner.** British slang for *sixpence* (six pennies)

WORDS FOR EVERYDAY USE: a • mi • a • ble (ā′mē ə bəl) *adj.,* good-natured, friendly

❶
What humorous technique does Shaw use to make the point that upper-class young men, generally, are like Freddy?

❷
How do the Mother and the Daughter differ?

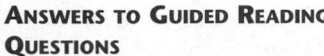

ANSWERS TO GUIDED READING QUESTIONS

❶ When the flower girl uses a general nickname for Freddy's type, accidentally hitting on his real name, the mother assumes the flower girl is actually acquainted with him.

❷ The Mother is generous; the Daughter is stingy.

CROSS-CURRICULAR ACTIVITIES

To better understand Shaw's play and the issues he confronted in it, students should study its social background. They can research and summarize the social situation of London or Great Britain in general before World War I. Good sources of information are histories of Great Britain. Students should look especially for information on the struggle between the classes, the ideas of reformers, and the women's rights movement. The results of researches can be presented in the form of a mini-term paper (two pages) with supporting documentation listed.

ANSWER TO GUIDED READING QUESTION

❶ The flower girl is afraid she will be falsely arrested for soliciting.

ADDITIONAL QUESTIONS AND ACTIVITIES

To become critical readers of Shaw's work, students should bear in mind that he is always attempting to explain something to the audience; as one critic has said, "Mr. Shaw demands, and attempts to supply, a coordination of the essential facts of life into a system." The audience of Shaw's plays is not given a general view of life and then asked to draw their own conclusions about it; they are told what to think about life and society. Says Shaw: "[*Pygmalion*] is so intensely and deliberately didactic, and its subject is esteemed so dry, that I delight in throwing it at the heads of the wiseacres who repeat the parrot cry that art should never be didactic. It goes to prove my contention that art should never be anything else." Ask students what point Shaw is trying to set before the audience in depicting the conflict between the flower girl and the note taker.

Answer. Shaw is protesting police harassment of the lower class and pointing out the continual fear in which the lower class lives.

---

ago. (*He goes to the plinth beside the flower girl; puts up his foot on it; and stoops to turn down his trouser ends.*)

THE MOTHER. Oh dear! (*She retires sadly and joins her daughter.*)

THE FLOWER GIRL (*taking advantage of the military gentleman's proximity to establish friendly relations with him*). If it's worse, it's a sign it's nearly over. So cheer up, Captain; and buy a flower off a poor girl.

THE GENTLEMAN. I'm sorry. I havnt any change.

THE FLOWER GIRL. I can give you change, Captain.

THE GENTLEMAN. For a sovereign? I've nothing less.

THE FLOWER GIRL. Garn! Oh do buy a flower off me, Captain. I can change half-a-crown. Take this for tuppence.[7]

THE GENTLEMAN. Now dont be troublesome: theres a good girl. (*Trying his pockets*) I really havnt any change—Stop: heres three hapence, if thats any use to you. (*He retreats to the other pillar.*)

THE FLOWER GIRL (*disappointed, but thinking three half-pence better than nothing*). Thank you, sir.

THE BYSTANDER (*to the girl*). You be careful: give him a flower for it. Theres a bloke here behind taking down every blessed word youre saying. (*All turn to the man who is taking notes.*)

❶

Of what is the flower girl afraid?

THE FLOWER GIRL (*springing up terrified*). I aint done nothing wrong by speaking to the gentleman. Ive a right to sell flowers if I keep off the kerb.

(*Hysterically*) I'm a respectable girl: so help me, I never spoke to him except to ask him to buy a flower off me.

(*General hubbub, mostly sympathetic to the* FLOWER GIRL, *but deprecating her excessive sensibility. Cries of* Dont start hollerin. Who's hurting you? Nobody's going to touch you. Whats the good of fussing? Steady on. Easy, easy, etc., *come from the elderly staid spectators, who pat her comfortingly. Less patient ones bid her shut her head, or ask her roughly what is wrong with her. A remoter group, not knowing what the matter is, crowd in and increase the noise with question and answer:* What's the row? What she do? Where is he? A tec[8] taking her down. What! him? Yes: him over there: Took money off the gentleman, etc.)

THE FLOWER GIRL (*breaking through them to the* GENTLEMEN, *crying wildly*). Oh, sir, dont let him charge me. You dunno what it means to me. Theyll take away my character and drive me on the streets for speaking to gentlemen. They—

THE NOTE TAKER (*coming forward on her right, the rest crowding after him*). There, there, there, there! who's hurting you, you silly girl? What do you take me for?

THE BYSTANDER. It's all right: he's a gentleman: look at his boots. (*Explaining to the* NOTE TAKER) She thought you was a copper's nark, sir.

THE NOTE TAKER (*with quick interest*). Whats a copper's nark?

---

7. **tuppence.** Alternate spelling of *twopence*
8. **tec.** British slang for detective

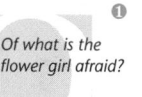

WORDS FOR EVERYDAY USE:

prox • im • i • ty (präks im´ə tē) *n.*, nearness

dep • re • cate (dep´rə kāt´) *vt.*, belittle, disparage

staid (stād) *adj.*, sedate, serious

VOCABULARY IN CONTEXT

- The proximity of the bank where Tex kept his money allowed him to sleep better at night.
- Comments that deprecate the contributions of other group members are counterproductive.
- The jig was so irresistible that even the most staid couple in the hall had to kick off their shoes and dance.
- The seemingly endless series of rainy days contributed to the melancholy I felt when I did not land a part in the play.

THE BYSTANDER (*inapt at definition*). It's a—well, it's a copper's nark, as you might say. What else would you call it? A sort of informer.

THE FLOWER GIRL (*still hysterical*). I take my Bible oath I never said a word—

THE NOTE TAKER (*overbearing but good humored*). Oh, shut up, shut up. Do I look like a policeman?

THE FLOWER GIRL (*far from reassured*). Then what did you take down my words for? How do I know whether you took me down right? You just shew me what youve wrote about me. (*The* NOTE TAKER *opens his book and holds it steadily under her nose, though the pressure of the mob trying to read it over his shoulders would upset a weaker man.*) Whats that? That aint proper writing. I cant read that.

THE NOTE TAKER. I can. (*Reads, reproducing her pronunciation exactly*) "Cheer ap, Keptin; n' baw ya flahr orf a pore gel."

THE FLOWER GIRL (*much distressed*). It's because I called him Captain. I meant no harm. (*To the* GENTLEMAN) Oh, sir, don't let him lay a charge agen me for a word like that. You—

THE GENTLEMAN. Charge! I make no charge. (*To the* NOTE TAKER) Really, sir, if you are a detective, you need not begin protecting me against molestation by young women until I ask you. Anybody could see that the girl meant no harm.

THE BYSTANDERS GENERALLY (*demonstrating against police espionage*). Course they could. What business is it of yours? You mind your own affairs. He wants promotion, he does. Taking down people's words! Girl never said a word to him. What harm if she did? Nice thing a girl cant shelter from the rain without being insulted, etc., etc., etc. (*She is conducted by the more sympathetic demonstrators back to her plinth, where she resumes her seat and struggles with her emotion.*)

THE BYSTANDER. He aint a tec. He's a blooming busybody: thats what he is. I tell you, look at his boots.

THE NOTE TAKER (*turning on him genially*). And how are all your people down at Selsey?

THE BYSTANDER (*suspiciously*). Who told you my people come from Selsey?

THE NOTE TAKER. Never you mind. They did. (*To the girl*) How do you come to be up so far east? You were born in Lisson Grove.

THE FLOWER GIRL (*appalled*). Oh, what harm is there in my leaving Lisson Grove? It wasnt fit for a pig to live in; and I had to pay four-and-six a week. (*In tears*) Oh, boo—hoo—oo—

THE NOTE TAKER. Live where you like; but stop that noise.

THE GENTLEMAN (*to the girl*). Come, come! he cant touch you: you have a right to live where you please.

A SARCASTIC BYSTANDER (*thrusting himself between the* NOTE TAKER *and the* GENTLEMEN). Park Lane, for instance. I'd like to go into the Housing Question with you, I would.

THE FLOWER GIRL (*subsiding into a brooding <u>melancholy</u> over her basket, and*

WORDS FOR EVERYDAY USE: mel • an • chol • y (mel´ən käl´ē) *n.*, state of sadness or depression

LITERARY TECHNIQUE

Motif. A motif is any element that recurs in one or more works of literature or art. Consider the following scene: "It's all right: he's a gentleman," says one of the bystanders of the note taker, "look at his boots." Point out to students that the motif of being a gentleman or a lady runs throughout *Pygmalion.* As they read, students can look for ways in which people are defined as gentlemen or ladies. These defining points include their clothes (as in this case), actions, manners, speech, and the way they are treated by others. On the following pages of dialogue, the note taker is accused several times of not being a gentleman because—despite his appearance—his attitude is not genteel.

ADDITIONAL QUESTIONS AND ACTIVITIES

Ask students to look up the word *didacticism* in the Handbook of Literary Terms. Then ask them to discuss whether or not *Pygmalion* is a didactic play. If some students believe it is, ask them to describe the ways in which it falls into this category. Ask students to discuss art and didacticism. Do they believe art always needs to carry a strong message? Why, or why not?

Answers. Responses will vary. Many students will feel that *Pygmalion* is didactic, due to its strong moral, social, and political messages.

ADDITIONAL QUESTIONS AND ACTIVITIES

 Discuss regional accents with students. Have students suggest words that indicate what region of the United States a person is from. If the class has representatives of different parts of the country, students might be able to perceive among themselves variant pronunciations of the following words: *park, lost, house, Mary, pen, aunt,* and *greasy.* (For more information on American regional dialects, see the article "Dialects of English," in *The American Heritage Dictionary of the English Language* [Boston: Houghton Mifflin].)

ADDITIONAL QUESTIONS AND ACTIVITIES

Ask students:

1. To what extent are differences between the classes a problem in the United States?

2. Are class differences and barriers between the classes as great today in the United States as they were in Great Britain before World War I?

3. Could the dialogue and action detailed in Act One ever take place (with allowances for time and place) in the United States?

Answers. 1. *Responses will vary,* but students should recognize that significant class differences still exist in the United States, especially between the lower classes and the middle and upper classes. 2. Class differences and barriers between the classes in Great Britain at the time in which the play is set were far greater than similar differences and barriers in the United States today. 3. *Responses will vary.* Some students may feel class conflict is not so sharp in the United States; others may feel the types of conflicts depicted in Act One exist in the United States and would allow such a scene to be played out.

Photograph © 1995 Michael Romanos

❝ *So cheer up, captain, and buy a flower off a poor girl.* ❞

992   *UNIT TWELVE / TWENTIETH-CENTURY DRAMA*

talking very low-spiritedly to herself). I'm a good girl, I am.

THE SARCASTIC BYSTANDER (*not attending to her*). Do you know where *I* come from?

THE NOTE TAKER (*promptly*). Hoxton

(*Titterings. Popular interest in the* NOTE TAKER's *performance increases.*)

THE SARCASTIC ONE (*amazed*). Well, who said I didnt? Bly me! You know everything, you do.

THE FLOWER GIRL (*still nursing her sense of injury*). Aint no call to meddle with me, he aint.

THE BYSTANDER (*to her*). Of course he aint. Dont you stand it from him. (*To the* NOTE TAKER) See here: what call have you to know about people what never offered to meddle with you? Wheres your warrant?

SEVERAL BYSTANDERS (*encouraged by this seeming point of law*). Yes: wheres your warrant?

THE FLOWER GIRL. Let him say what he likes. I dont want to have no truck with him.

THE BYSTANDER. You take us for dirt under your feet, dont you? Catch you taking liberties with a gentleman!

THE SARCASTIC BYSTANDER. Yes: tell him where he come from if you want to go fortune-telling.

THE NOTE TAKER. Cheltenham, Harrow, Cambridge, and India.

THE GENTLEMAN. Quite right.

(*Great laughter. Reaction in the* NOTE TAKER's *favor. Exclamations of* He knows all about it. Told him proper. Hear him tell the toff⁹ where he come from? etc.)

THE GENTLEMAN. May I ask, sir, do you do this for your living at a music hall?

THE NOTE TAKER. I've thought of that. Perhaps I shall some day.

(*The rain has stopped; and the persons on the outside of the crowd begin to drop off.*)

THE FLOWER GIRL (*resenting the reaction*). He's no gentleman, he aint, to interfere with a poor girl.

THE DAUGHTER (*out of patience, pushing her way rudely to the front and displacing the* GENTLEMAN, *who politely retires to the other side of the pillar*). What on earth is Freddy doing? I shall get pneumonia if I stay in this draught any longer.

THE NOTE TAKER (*to himself, hastily making a note of her pronunciation of "monia"*). Earlscourt.

THE DAUGHTER (*violently*). Will you please keep your <u>impertinent</u> remarks to yourself.

THE NOTE TAKER. Did I say that out loud? I didnt mean to. I beg your pardon. Your mother's Epsom, unmistakably.

THE MOTHER (*advancing between her daughter and the* NOTE TAKER). How very curious! I was brought up in Largelady Park, near Epsom.

THE NOTE TAKER (*uproariously amused*). Ha! ha! What a devil of a name! Excuse me. (*To the* DAUGHTER) You want a cab, do you?

THE DAUGHTER. Dont dare speak to me.

---

9. **toff.** British slang for a fashionable, upper-class person

WORDS FOR EVERYDAY USE: im • per • ti • nent (im purt″'n ənt) *adj.*, saucy, insolent

PYGMALION, ACT ONE **993**

QUOTABLES

❝There is nothing so bad or so good that you will not find Englishmen doing it; but you will never find an Englishman in the wrong. He does everything on principle. He fights you on patriotic principles; he robs you on business principles; he enslaves you on imperial principles.❞

—George Bernard Shaw

BIOGRAPHICAL NOTE

Shaw was a dedicated member of and instrumental force behind Great Britain's Fabian Society. Founded in 1883–1884, this group of middle-class socialists sought to change their society through "permeation," or education, rather than revolution.

VOCABULARY IN CONTEXT

- Although I would not classify my sister's child as a brat, several of his remarks to me were highly <u>impertinent</u>.

❶ The flower girl says that she has a right to the protection of her reputation just as does a woman of a higher social class and adds that she has enough difficulty making a living without being caused unnecessary trouble.

❷ The note taker's profession and hobby is phonetics.

HISTORICAL NOTE

Shaw believed that the varying dialects of Great Britain were one of the main obstacles to integrating the classes of society. "The reformer England needs today is an energetic phonetic enthusiast: that is why I have made such a one the hero of a popular play. . . . If the play makes the public aware that there are such people as phoneticians, and that they are among the most important people in England at present, it will serve its turn." In recent decades, the advance of nationwide media such as radio and television has made misunderstandings due to dialect less common both in Great Britain and in the United States.

❶
What point does the flower girl make about herself and her rights?

❷
What is the note taker's profession and hobby?

THE MOTHER. Oh please, please, Clara. (*Her daughter <u>repudiates</u> her with an angry shrug and retires haughtily.*) We should be so grateful to you, sir, if you found us a cab. (*The* NOTE TAKER *produces a whistle.*) Oh, thank you. (*She joins her daughter.*)

(*The* NOTE TAKER *blows a piercing blast.*)

THE SARCASTIC BYSTANDER. There! I knowed he was a plainclothes copper.

THE BYSTANDER. That aint a police whistle: thats a sporting whistle.

THE FLOWER GIRL (*still preoccupied with her wounded feelings*). He's no right to take away my character. My character is the same to me as any lady's.

THE NOTE TAKER. I dont know whether youve noticed it; but the rain stopped about two minutes ago.

THE BYSTANDER. So it has. Why didnt you say so before? and us losing our time listening to your silliness! (*He walks off toward the Strand.*)

THE SARCASTIC BYSTANDER. I can tell where you come from. You come from Anwell. Go back there.

THE NOTE TAKER (*helpfully*). Hanwell.

THE SARCASTIC BYSTANDER (*affecting great distinction of speech*). Thenk you, teacher. Haw haw! So long. (*He touches his hat with mock respect and strolls off.*)

THE FLOWER GIRL. Frightening people like that! How would he like it himself?

THE MOTHER. It's quite fine now, Clara. We can walk to a motor bus. Come. (*She gathers her skirts above her ankles and hurries off toward the Strand.*)

THE DAUGHTER. But the cab—(*Her mother is out of hearing.*) Oh, how tiresome! (*She follows angrily.*)

(*All the rest have gone except the* NOTE TAKER, *the* GENTLEMAN, *and the* FLOWER GIRL, *who sits arranging her basket and still pitying herself in murmurs.*)

THE FLOWER GIRL. Poor girl! Hard enough for her to live without being worried and chivied.[10]

THE GENTLEMAN (*returning to his former place on the* NOTE TAKER'S *left*). How do you do it, if I may ask?

THE NOTE TAKER. Simply phonetics. The science of speech. Thats my profession: also my hobby. Happy is the man who can make a living by his hobby! You can spot an Irishman or a Yorkshireman by his brogue. *I* can place any man within six miles. I can place him within two miles in London. Sometimes within two streets.

THE FLOWER GIRL. Ought to be ashamed of himself, unmanly coward!

THE GENTLEMAN. But is there a living in that?

THE NOTE TAKER. Oh yes. Quite a fat one. This is an age of upstarts. Men begin in Kentish Town with £80 a year, and end in Park Lane with a hundred thousand. They want to drop Kentish Town; but they give themselves away every time they open their mouths. Now I can teach them—

THE FLOWER GIRL. Let him mind his own business and leave a poor girl—

---

10. **worrited and chivied.** Worried and troubled

WORDS FOR
EVERYDAY USE:
re • pu • di • ate (ri pyōō′ dē āt′) *vt.,* disown or cast off publicly

VOCABULARY IN CONTEXT

- The candidate hastily <u>repudiated</u> the aides who were caught stuffing ballot boxes with forged votes.
- After a hard morning delivering mail, the last thing the letter carrier needed was to be attacked by Mrs. Gramphone's <u>bilious</u> old cat.
- Although the contractor's name was Speaktruth, he was remarkable for his consistent <u>mendacity</u>.

THE NOTE TAKER (*explosively*). Woman: cease this detestable boohooing instantly; or else seek the shelter of some other place of worship.

THE FLOWER GIRL (*with feeble defiance*). Ive a right to be here if I like, same as you.

THE NOTE TAKER. A woman who utters such depressing and disgusting sounds has no right to be anywhere—no right to live. Remember that you are a human being with a soul and the divine gift of articulate speech: that your native language is the language of Shakespear[11] and Milton and The Bible: and dont sit there crooning like a <u>bilious</u> pigeon.

THE FLOWER GIRL (*quite overwhelmed, looking up at him in mingled wonder and deprecation without daring to raise her head*). Ah-ah-ah-ow-ow-ow-oo!

THE NOTE TAKER (*whipping out his book*). Heavens! what a sound! (*He writes; then holds out the book and reads, reproducing her vowels exactly.*) Ah-ah-ah-ow-ow-ow-oo!

THE FLOWER GIRL (*tickled by the performance, and laughing in spite of herself*). Garn!

THE NOTE TAKER. You see this creature with her kerbstone[12] English: the English that will keep her in the gutter to the end of her days. Well, sir, in three months I could pass that girl off as a duchess at an ambassador's garden party. I could even get her a place as lady's maid or shop assistant, which requires better English. Thats the sort of thing I do for commercial millionaires. And on the profits of it I do genuine scientific work in phonetics, and a little as a poet on Miltonic lines.

THE GENTLEMAN. I am myself a student of Indian dialects; and—

THE NOTE TAKER (*eagerly*). Are you? Do you know Colonel Pickering, the author of Spoken Sanscrit?

THE GENTLEMAN. I am Colonel Pickering. Who are you?

THE NOTE TAKER. Henry Higgins, author of Higgins's Universal Alphabet.

PICKERING. (*with enthusiasm*). I came from India to meet you.

HIGGINS. I was going to India to meet you.

PICKERING. Where do you live?

HIGGINS. 27A Wimpole Street. Come and see me tomorrow.

PICKERING. I'm at the Carlton. Come with me now and lets have a jaw over some supper.

HIGGINS. Right you are.

THE FLOWER GIRL (*to* PICKERING, *as he passes her*). Buy a flower, kind gentleman. I'm short for my lodging.

PICKERING. I really havnt any change. I'm sorry. (*He goes away.*)

HIGGINS (*shocked at the girl's <u>mendacity</u>*). Liar. You said you could change half-a-crown.

THE FLOWER GIRL (*rising in desperation*). You ought to be stuffed with nails, you ought. (*Flinging the basket at his feet*) Take the whole blooming basket for sixpence.

(*The church clock strikes the second quarter.*)

---

11. **Shakespear.** Shaw spelled names phonetically.
12. **kerbstone.** British spelling of *curbstone*

❶
What attitude toward dialectical speech does the note taker have? What does this reveal about him?

❷
What does the note taker claim to be able to do?

WORDS FOR EVERYDAY USE:

bil • ious (bil´yəs) *adj.*, ill-tempered, cranky
men • dac • i • ty (men das´ə tē) *n.*, lying

PYGMALION, ACT ONE **995**

LITERARY NOTE

Hyperbole. Remind students that hyperbole is exaggeration for emphasis. The note taker tells the flower girl that she has "no right to live" because she utters "depressing and disgusting sounds." Such hyperbole is typical of his extravagant and impulsive responses to other characters. Ask students to keep a list as they read and find at least five examples of hyperbole in the play.

ANSWERS TO GUIDED READING QUESTIONS

❶ The note taker claims that the speech of the flower girl is so depressing and disgusting that she has no right to live. This attitude reveals a prejudice against the lower class.

❷ The note taker claims to be able to teach the flower girl to speak so well that she could pass as a duchess at an ambassador's garden party.

ADDITIONAL QUESTIONS AND ACTIVITIES

Students can attempt to interpret the sound represented by the flower girl's "Ah-ah-ah-ow-ow-ow-oo!" Have an "Ah-ow Bee" in which pairs of students try to say the sound more convincingly; after each pair has made an attempt, the class votes on which is better, and the winner advances to the next round. Continue picking winners in this way until a champion is chosen.

ANSWERS TO SELECTION CHECK TEST 4.12.1

EX. Why were people gathering under the portico of St. Paul's Church?

They were trying to avoid the rain.

1. What are the Mother and the Daughter waiting for?

They are waiting for Freddy to get a taxi.

2. Who does Freddy bump into in his haste?

He bumps into a flower girl.

3. What frightens the flower girl?

She is afraid that the man who is recording her words will tell the police.

4. What is the note taker's profession and hobby?

He studies phonetics, or the science of speech.

5. What does Higgins throw into the flower girl's basket?

He throws a handful of money into her basket.

TEACHER'S EDITION **995**

RESPONDING TO THE SELECTION

If students have trouble distinguishing the classes involved in Act One, point out that although the Eynsford Hills are in a social class higher than that of the flower girl, they seem to be lacking in money and are thus slightly lower in standing than Higgins and Pickering. Some of the other bystanders fall in the range between the Eynsford Hill family and the flower girl.

ANSWERS FOR REVIEWING THE SELECTION

RECALLING

1. Freddy and the flower girl meet when Freddy collides with her and knocks over her basket.

2. The flower girl is warned that a man in the crowd is taking notes.

3. The note taker shows that he is able to identify the places they have lived by the way they speak.

4. Higgins gives the flower girl the money to pay for her cab ride.

INTERPRETING

Responses will vary. Possible responses are given.

5. The flower girl is disturbed but does not seem to be surprised at his lack of manners.

6. The flower girl believes that the note taker is an undercover policeman who is going to charge her with a crime.

7. Higgins's ability shows that he is highly intelligent, well educated, and a good observer of details, though not necessarily of larger matters.

8. Both Freddy and Pickering fail to satisfy her desire to make a substantial sale.

SYNTHESIZING

Responses will vary. Possible responses are given.

9. The exchanges of the characters show there was considerable antagonism between the classes in early twentieth-century London.

10. Both Higgins and the flower girl are intelligent to the point of being cunning. Both are self-assertive, though the flower girl is apt to collapse when she feels challenged by someone. Higgins is bold and impatient, while the flower girl is more likely to feel frightened and to sulk when she is wronged.

996 TEACHER'S EDITION

HIGGINS (*hearing in it the voice of God, rebuking him for his pharisaic*[13] *want of charity to the poor girl*). A reminder. (*He raises his hat solemnly; then throws a handful of money into the basket and follows* PICKERING.)

THE FLOWER GIRL (*picking up a half-crown*). Ah-ow-ooh! (*Picking up a couple of florins*) Aaah-ow-ooh! (*Picking up several coins*) Aaaaaah-ow-ooh! (*Picking up a half-sovereign*) Aaaaaaaaaaaah-ow-ooh! ! !

FREDDY (*springing out of a taxicab*). Got one at last. Hallo! (*To the* GIRL) Where are the two ladies that were here?

THE FLOWER GIRL They walked to the bus when the rain stopped.

FREDDY. And left me with a cab on my hands! Damnation!

THE FLOWER GIRL (*with grandeur*). Never mind, young man. *I*'m going home in a taxi. (*She sails off to the cab. The driver puts his hand behind him and holds the door firmly shut against her. Quite understanding his mistrust, she shews him her handful of money.*) Eightpence aint no object to me, Charlie. (*He grins and opens the door.*) Angel Court, Drury Lane, round the corner of Micklejohn's oil shop. Lets see how fast you can make her hop it. (*She gets in and pulls the door to with a slam as the taxicab starts.*)

FREDDY. Well, I'm dashed!

---

13. **pharisaic.** Hypocritical

Responding to the Selection

Judging from the information given on the characters in Act One, how many social classes has Shaw portrayed? Make a chart outlining four or five classes, and place each of the characters in a class. Explain the reasons why you categorized each character as you did.

ANSWERS FOR UNDERSTANDING LITERATURE

▶ See the evaluation forms for discussion, active listening, and oral communication, *Assessment Portfolio,* 7.11–7.14.

Responses will vary. Possible responses are given.

1. Spectacle. Elements of sight described are the portico of St. Paul's Church, the rainfall, and the pedestrians running for shelter. Elements of sound are the falling rain, cab whistles blowing, and the church clock striking the first

quarter. These elements are full of chaotic sound and motion, from which the audience will look for some order or interesting detail to emerge.

▶**Teaching Note:** To give students an idea of how many elements are combined at the beginning of the play, assign different students different roles in reproducing these elements. Some students can mimic the hissing sound of the rain, some the shriek of cab whis-

(cont.)

Reviewing the Selection

RECALLING

1. How do Freddie and the flower girl meet?

2. What warning does the flower girl get from one of the bystanders?

3. What skill does the note taker display to the bystanders?

4. How has the flower girl gotten the money to pay for her cab ride home?

INTERPRETING

5. What is the flower girl's reaction to her "meeting" with Freddie?

6. Why is the flower girl frightened of the note taker?

7. What does Higgins's ability say about his character?

8. In what ways are the flower girl's meetings with Freddie and Colonel Pickering similar?

SYNTHESIZING

9. What do the exchanges between the flower girl and the other characters show about the relationships between the classes in twentieth-century London?

10. What adjectives would you use to describe Higgins and the flower girl? How do their characters differ?

Understanding Literature (Questions for Discussion)

1. **Spectacle.** In drama, the **spectacle** is all the elements that are presented to the senses of the audience, including the lights, setting, costumes, make-up, music, sound effects, and movements of the actors. What elements of sight and sound are described in the stage directions at the very beginning of the play? What about these elements makes them engaging, or dramatic, and therefore appropriate for capturing an audience's interest at the beginning of the play?

2. **Characterization. Characterization** is the use of literary techniques to create a character. Read the entry on *characterization* in the Handbook of Literary Terms. What techniques does Shaw use in this act to characterize the flower girl? What does she look like? How does she dress? act? sound? react to others?

3. **Inciting Incident.** The **inciting incident** is the event that introduces the central conflict. What bet does Higgins make with Pickering? What does Higgins intend to prove? What consequences might result if Higgins were to carry out his plan?

PYGMALION, ACT ONE **997**

Photograph © 1995 Michael Romanos

❝I tell you, it's easy to clean up here. Hot and cold water on tap, just as much as you like, there is. Woolly towels, there is; and a towel horse so hot, it burns your fingers. Soft brushes to scrub yourself, and a wooden bowl of soap smelling like primroses. Now I know why ladies is so clean. Washing's a treat for them. Wish they saw what it is for the like of me!❞

ACT TWO

Next day at 11 A.M. HIGGINS's laboratory in Wimpole Street. It is a room on the first floor, looking on the street, and was meant for the drawing room. The double doors are in the middle of the back wall; and persons entering find in the corner to their right two tall file cabinets at right angles to one another against the walls. In this corner stands a flat writing-table, on which are a phonograph, a laryngoscope,[1] a row of tiny organ pipes with bellows, a set of lamp chimneys for singing flames with burners attached to a gas plug in the wall by an indiarubber tube, several tuning-forks of different sizes, a life-size image of half a human head, shewing in section the vocal organs, and a box containing a supply of wax cylinders for the phonograph.

Further down the room, on the same side, is a fireplace, with a comfortable leather-covered easy-chair at the side of the hearth nearest the door; and a coal-scuttle. There is a clock on the mantel-piece. Between the fireplace and the phonograph table is a stand for newspapers.

On the other side of the central door, to the left of the visitor, is a cabinet of shallow drawers. On it is a telephone and the telephone directory. The corner beyond, and most of the side wall, is occupied by a grand piano, with the keyboard at the end furthest from the door, and a bench for the player extending the full length of the keyboard. On the piano is a dessert dish heaped with fruit and sweets, mostly chocolates.

The middle of the room is clear. Besides the easy-chair, the piano bench, and two chairs at the phonograph table, there is one stray chair. It stands near the fireplace. On the walls, engravings: mostly Piranesis and mezzotint[2] portraits. No paintings.

PICKERING is seated at the table, putting down some cards and a tuning-fork which he has been using. HIGGINS is standing up near him, closing two or three file drawers which are hanging out. He appears in the morning light as a robust, vital, appetizing sort of man of forty or thereabouts, dressed in a professional-looking black frock-coat with a white linen collar and black silk tie. He is of the energetic, scientific type, heartily, even violently interested in everything that can be studied as a scientific subject, and careless about himself and other people, including their feelings. He is, in fact, but for his years and size, rather like a very <u>impetuous</u> baby "taking notice" eagerly and loudly, and requiring almost as much watching to keep him out of unintended mischief. His manner varies from genial bullying when he is in a good humor to stormy petulance when anything goes wrong; but he is so entirely frank and void of malice that he remains likeable even in his least reasonable moments.

HIGGINS (*as he shuts the last drawer*). Well, I think thats the whole show.

PICKERING. It's really amazing. I havnt taken half of it in, you know.

HIGGINS. Would you like to go over any of it again?

PICKERING (*rising and coming to the fireplace, where he plants himself with his back to the fire*). No, thank you; not now. I'm quite done up for this morning.

HIGGINS (*following him, and standing beside him on his left*). Tired of listening to sounds?

---

1. **laryngoscope.** A medical instrument used to examine the larynx
2. **Piranesis and mezzotint.** Piranesi was an Italian artist; mezzotint is a method of engraving on metal.

 WORDS FOR EVERYDAY USE: im • pet • u • ous (im pech´ōō as) *adj.*, acting with little forethought

CROSS-CURRICULAR ACTIVITIES

Arts and Humanities. Students may draw pictures of the set of Act Two according to the stage directions given by Shaw. Those whose drawing skills are minimal can represent the set at least in diagram form; others can represent the set in color as if it were a design for a production of the play. You might ask students to sketch costumes as well.

QUOTABLES

"The worst sin towards our fellow creatures is not to hate them, but to be indifferent to them: That's the essence of inhumanity.**"**

—George Bernard Shaw

VOCABULARY IN CONTEXT

• When the lion was a cub he was <u>impetuous</u>, but as he grew older, he grew cautious.

LITERARY TECHNIQUE

Motif. Remind students that Shaw was keenly aware of the myth of Pygmalion as he wrote. His Professor Higgins is not just a scholar, he is also an artist of sorts. As Higgins takes on the process of transforming Liza, he sees himself as creating a new being out of material that is "of no use to anyone else." References to Higgins as artist or creator appear frequently throughout the play, though some are subtle. In Act Five, for instance, Higgins asks Liza if Freddy can "make anything" of her; clearly this is how he sees his own role. At the beginning of Act Two, Higgins is shown as the professional in his workplace—the artist, so to speak, in his studio. Ask students to remain alert for this motif as they read.

PICKERING. Yes. It's a fearful strain. I rather fancied myself because I can pronounce twenty-four distinct vowel sounds; but your hundred and thirty beat me. I cant hear a bit of difference between most of them.

HIGGINS (*chuckling, and going over to the piano to eat sweets*). Oh, that comes with practice. You hear no difference at first; but you keep on listening, and presently you find theyre all as different as A from B. (MRS. PEARCE *looks in: she is* HIGGINS's *housekeeper.*) Whats the matter?

MRS PEARCE (*hesitating, evidently perplexed*). A young woman wants to see you sir.

HIGGINS. A young woman! What does she want?

MRS PEARCE. Well, sir, she says youll be glad to see her when you know what she's come about. She's quite a common girl, sir. Very common indeed. I should have sent her away, only I thought perhaps you wanted her to talk into your machines. I hope Ive not done wrong; but really you see such queer people sometimes—youll excuse me, I'm sure, sir—

HIGGINS. Oh, thats all right, Mrs Pearce. Has she an interesting accent?

MRS PEARCE. Oh, something dreadful, sir, really. I dont know how you can take an interest in it.

HIGGINS (*to* PICKERING). Lets have her up. Shew her up, Mrs Pearce. (*He rushes across to his working table and picks out a cylinder to use on the phonograph.*)

MRS PEARCE (*only half resigned to it*). Very well, sir. It's for you to say. (*She goes downstairs.*)

HIGGINS. This is rather a bit of luck. I'll shew you how I make records. We'll set her talking; and I'll take it down first in

❶

What do Mrs. Pearce's comments reveal about middle-class attitudes toward the poor?

Bell's visible Speech; then in broad Romic; and then we'll get her on the phonograph so that you can turn her on as often as you like with the written transcript before you.

MRS PEARCE (*returning*). This is the young woman, sir.

(*The* FLOWER GIRL *enters in state. She has a hat with three ostrich feathers, orange, sky-blue, and red. She has a nearly clean apron, and the shoddy coat has been tidied a little. The pathos of this deplorable figure, with its innocent vanity and consequential air, touches* PICKERING, *who has already straightened himself in the presence of* MRS PEARCE. *But as to* HIGGINS, *the only distinction he makes between men and women is that when he is neither bullying nor exclaiming to the heavens against some feather-weight cross,*[3] *he coaxes women as a child coaxes its nurse when it wants to get anything out of her.*)

HIGGINS (*brusquely, recognizing her with unconcealed disappointment, and at once, babylike, making an intolerable grievance of it*). Why, this is the girl I jotted down last night. She's no use: Ive got all the records I want of the Lisson Grove lingo; and I'm not going to waste another cylinder on it. (*To the* GIRL) Be off with you: I dont want you.

THE FLOWER GIRL. Dont you be so saucy. You aint heard what I come for yet. (*To* MRS. PEARCE, *who is waiting at the door for further instructions*) Did you tell him I come in a taxi ?

MRS PEARCE. Nonsense, girl! what do you think a gentleman like Mr Higgins cares what you came in?

THE FLOWER GIRL. Oh, we are proud! He aint above giving lessons, not him: I heard him say so. Well, I aint come here to ask for any compliment; and if my

---

3. **feather-weight cross.** Trivial problem

money's not good enough I can go else-where.

HIGGINS.   Good enough for what?

THE FLOWER GIRL.   Good enough for ye-oo. Now you know, dont you? I'm come to have lessons, I am. And to pay for em too: make no mistake.

HIGGINS (*stupent*).[4] Well!!! (*Recovering his breath with a gasp*) What do you expect me to say to you?

THE FLOWER GIRL.   Well, if you was a gentleman, you might ask me to sit down, I think. Dont I tell you I'm bringing you business?

HIGGINS.   Pickering: shall we ask this baggage to sit down, or shall we throw her out of the window?

THE FLOWER GIRL (*running away in ter-ror to the piano, where she turns at bay*). Ah-ah-oh-ow-ow-ow-oo! (*Wounded and whimpering*) I wont be called a baggage when Ive offered to pay like any lady.

(*Motionless, the two men stare at her from the other side of the room, amazed.*)

PICKERING (*gently*). What is it you want, my girl?

THE FLOWER GIRL.   I want to be a lady in a flower shop stead of selling at the cor-ner of Tottenham Court Road. But they wont take me unless I can talk more gen-teel. He said he could teach me. Well, here I am ready to pay him—not asking any favor—and he treats me as if I was dirt.

MRS PEARCE.   How can you be such a foolish ignorant girl as to think you could afford to pay Mr Higgins?

THE FLOWER GIRL.   Why shouldnt I? I know what lessons cost as well as you do; and I'm ready to pay.

HIGGINS.   How much?

THE FLOWER GIRL (*coming back to him, triumphant*). Now youre talking! I thought youd come off it when you saw a chance of getting back a bit of what you chucked at me last night. (*Confidently*) Youd had a drop in, hadnt you?

HIGGINS (*peremptorily*). Sit down.

THE FLOWER GIRL.   Oh, if youre going to make a compliment of it—

HIGGINS (*thundering at her*). Sit down.

MRS PEARCE (*severely*). Sit down, girl. Do as youre told. (*She places the stray chair near the hearthrug[5] between* HIGGINS *and* PICKERING, *and stands behind it waiting for the girl to sit down.*)

THE FLOWER GIRL.   Ah-ah-ah-ow-ow-oo! (*She stands, half rebellious, half bewildered.*)

PICKERING (*very courteous*). Wont you sit down?

THE FLOWER GIRL/LIZA (*coyly*). Dont mind if I do. (*She sits down.* PICKERING *returns to the hearthrug.*)

HIGGINS.   Whats your name?

THE FLOWER GIRL.   Liza Doolittle.

HIGGINS (*declaiming gravely*).
Eliza, Elizabeth, Betsy and Bess,
They went to the woods to get a bird's nes':

---

4. **stupent.** Astonished
5. **hearthrug.** A rug placed before a fireplace to protect the floor

What actions and comments by the flower girl reveal that she has pride and dignity despite her poverty?

VOCABULARY IN CONTEXT

• "Truly genteel manners," the bag lady told the police officer, "are the outward sign of an inward grace."

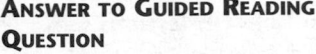
❶ The flower girl is outraged and hurt when she is called baggage and treated as if she were dirt; she wants to raise her standard of living; and she responds only to Pickering's gentility, not to Higgins's and Mrs. Pearce's bullying.

ADDITIONAL QUESTIONS AND ACTIVITIES

• In Great Britain, barri-ers between one class and the next were extremely rigid until well into this century. A person in Liza's situation had few opportunities to work except as a servant. Because she feels she might never raise her standard of living, she is depicted as highly sensitive to any imputa-tion that she is not a good, decent person.

• Students can write an editorial for a newspaper that might have appeared before World War I, in which they call for greater opportu-nities for women of the lower class and suggest means to bring such opportunities.

Discuss with students the point of the rhyme Pickering and Higgins chant about Liza. (*Eliza, Elizabeth, Betsy,* and *Bess* are all names for one girl, who removes only one egg from the nest; the rhyme satirizes those who have names derived as nicknames from *Elizabeth*.) Discuss as well how Pickering's and Higgins's willingness to make fun of Liza's name in her presence reflects their insensitivity to her feelings. Discuss why the men feel it is acceptable to treat her this way.

CROSS-CURRICULAR ACTIVITIES

Mathematics and Sciences

• Students can determine the answer to the following problem: "How much money did Liza offer Professor Higgins, in pre–World War I dollars? How much did she earn a day, in pre–World War I dollars?" Give students the following information about British and American currency values before World War I:

1 crown = 5 shillings

1 shilling = 12 pence

20 shillings = 1 pound

1 pound = $4.86

Answer. Liza offered Higgins one shilling, or one-twentieth of a pound, equal to $4.86 divided by twenty, which is .243 dollars, or about twenty-five cents. She earned a half crown, equal to 2.5 shillings, or thirty pence (2.5 x 12); thirty pence is one-eighth of a pound, and therefore one-eighth of $4.86, or about sixty cents.

• Point out to students that though the dollar had more buying power before World War I, the amount of Liza's daily income still represents a very small sum.

PICKERING.   They found a nest with four eggs in it:

HIGGINS.   They took one apiece, and left three in it. (*They laugh heartily at their own wit.*)

LIZA.   Oh, dont be silly.

MRS PEARCE.   You mustnt speak to the gentleman like that.

LIZA.   Well, why wont he speak sensible to me?

HIGGINS.   Come back to business. How much do you propose to pay me for the lessons?

LIZA.   Oh, I know whats right. A lady friend of mine gets French lessons for eighteenpence an hour from a real French gentleman. Well, you wouldnt have the face to ask me the same for teaching me my own language as you would for French; so I wont give more than a shilling.[6] Take it or leave it.

HIGGINS (*walking up and down the room, rattling his keys and his cash in his pockets*). You know, Pickering, if you consider a shilling, not as a simple shilling, but as a percentage of this girl's income, it works out as fully equivalent to sixty or seventy guineas[7] from a millionaire.

PICKERING.   How so?

HIGGINS.   Figure it out. A millionaire has about £150 a day. She earns about half-a-crown.

LIZA (*haughtily*). Who told you I only—

HIGGINS (*continuing*). She offers me two-fifths of her day's income for a lesson. Two-fifths of a millionaire's income for a day would be somewhere about £60. It's handsome. By George, it's enormous! it's the biggest offer I ever had.

LIZA (*rising, terrified*). Sixty pounds! What are you talking about? I never offered you sixty pounds. Where would I get—

HIGGINS.   Hold your tongue.

LIZA (*weeping*). But I aint got sixty pounds. Oh—

MRS PEARCE.   Dont cry, you silly girl. Sit down. Nobody is going to touch your money.

HIGGINS.   Somebody is going to touch you, with a broomstick, if you dont stop <u>snivelling</u>. Sit down.

LIZA (*obeying slowly*). Ah-ah-ah-ow-oo-o! One would think you was my father.

HIGGINS.   If I decide to teach you, I'll be worse than two fathers to you. Here! (*He offers her his silk handkerchief.*)

LIZA.   Whats this for?

HIGGINS.   To wipe your eyes. To wipe any part of your face that feels moist. Remember: thats your handkerchief; and thats your sleeve. Dont mistake the one for the other if you wish to become a lady in a shop.

(*LIZA, utterly bewildered, stares helplessly at him.*)

MRS PEARCE.   It's no use talking to her like that, Mr Higgins: she doesnt understand you. Besides, youre quite wrong: she

---

6. **shilling.** Former British monetary unit, equal to twelve pence
7. **guineas.** Former British gold coins, equal to twenty-one shillings

WORDS FOR EVERYDAY USE: sniv • el (sniv´əl) *vi.,* whine, cry, and sniffle

VOCABULARY IN CONTEXT

• When the recruit reached Marine boot camp, he discovered to his astonishment that <u>sniveling</u> no longer helped him get what he wanted.

• Although the Puritans of the 1600s are notorious for <u>prudery</u>, in fact some of their customs would seem scandalous to modern Americans.

doesnt do it that way at all. (*She takes the handkerchief.*)

LIZA (*snatching it*). Here! You give me that handkerchief. He give it to me, not to you.

PICKERING (*laughing*). He did. I think it must be regarded as her property, Mrs Pearce.

MRS PEARCE (*resigning herself*). Serve you right, Mr Higgins.

PICKERING. Higgins: I'm interested. What about the ambassador's garden party? I'll say youre the greatest teacher alive if you make that good. I'll bet you all the expenses of the experiment you cant do it. And I'll pay for the lessons.

LIZA. Oh, you are real good. Thank you, Captain.

HIGGINS (*tempted, looking at her*). It's almost irresistible. She's so deliciously low—so horribly dirty—

LIZA (*protesting extremely*). Ah-ah-ah-ah-ow-ow-oo-oo!!! I aint dirty: I washed my face and hands afore I come, I did.

PICKERING. Youre certainly not going to turn her head with flattery, Higgins.

MRS PEARCE (*uneasy*). Oh, dont say that, sir: theres more ways than one of turning a girl's head; and nobody can do it better than Mr Higgins, though he may not always mean it. I do hope, sir, you wont encourage him to do anything foolish.

HIGGINS (*becoming excited as the idea grows on him*). What is life but a series of inspired follies? The difficulty is to find them to do. Never lose a chance: it doesnt come every day. I shall make a duchess of this draggle-tailed guttersnipe.[8]

LIZA (*strongly deprecating this view of her*). Ah-ah-ah-ow-ow-oo!

HIGGINS (*carried away*). Yes: in six months—in three if she has a good ear and a quick tongue—I'll take her anywhere and pass her off as anything. We'll start today: now! this moment! Take her away and clean her, Mrs Pearce. Monkey Brand, if it wont come off any other way. Is there a good fire in the kitchen?

MRS PEARCE (*protesting*). Yes: but—

HIGGINS (*storming on*). Take all her clothes off and burn them. Ring up Whiteley or somebody for new ones. Wrap her up in brown paper til they come.

LIZA. Youre no gentleman, youre not, to talk of such things. I'm a good girl, I am; and I know what the like of you are, I do.

HIGGINS. We want none of your Lisson Grove prudery here, young woman. Youve got to learn to behave like a duchess. Take her away, Mrs Pearce. If she gives you any trouble, wallop her.

LIZA (*springing up and running between* PICKERING *and* MRS. PEARCE *for protection*). No! I'll call the police, I will.

MRS PEARCE. But Ive no place to put her.

HIGGINS. Put her in the dustbin.[9]

LIZA. Ah-ah-ah-ow-ow-oo!

---

8. **draggle-tailed guttersnipe.** A derogatory term referring to a person of the slums
9. **dustbin.** A rubbish container

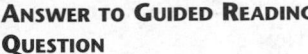

What does Liza think is happening? What does her reaction reveal about her? Why is Higgins's comment ironic?

WORDS FOR EVERYDAY USE:

prud • er • y (prōōd´ər ē) *n.*, condition of being overly modest or proper

---

ANSWER TO GUIDED READING QUESTION

❶ Liza thinks she is going to be called on to do something immoral. Her reaction reveals that she has high moral standards. Higgins's comment that she has to learn to behave like a duchess is undercut by his instruction to Mrs. Pearce to wallop Liza if need be. He does not seem to be in a good position to teach manners, since he does not have very good manners himself.

ADDITIONAL QUESTIONS AND ACTIVITIES

Reread to students Higgins's lines on the nature of life: "What is life but a series of inspired follies? The difficulty is to find them to do. Never lose a chance: it doesn't come every day." Students can write in their journal a list of five "follies" they would like to seize on and do—crazy plans like the notion of "making a duchess" out of Liza.

PICKERING. Oh come, Higgins! be reasonable.

MRS PEARCE (*resolutely*). You must be reasonable, Mr Higgins: really you must. You cant walk over everybody like this.

(HIGGINS, *thus scolded, subsides. The hurricane is succeeded by a* zephyr *of amiable surprise.*)

HIGGINS (*with professional exquisiteness of modulation*). I walk over everybody! My dear Mrs Pearce, my dear Pickering, I never had the slightest intention of walking over anyone. All I propose is that we should be kind to this poor girl. We must help her to prepare and fit herself for her new station in life. If I did not express myself clearly it was because I did not wish to hurt her delicacy, or yours.

(LIZA, *reassured, steals back to her chair.*)

MRS PEARCE (*to* PICKERING). Well, did you ever hear anything like that, sir?

PICKERING (*laughing heartily*). Never, Mrs Pearce: never.

HIGGINS (*patiently*). Whats the matter?

MRS PEARCE. Well, the matter is, sir, that you cant take a girl up like that as if you were picking up a pebble on the beach.

HIGGINS. Why not?

MRS PEARCE. Why not! But you dont know anything about her. What about her parents? She may be married.

LIZA. Garn!

HIGGINS. There! As the girl very properly says, Garn! Married indeed! Dont you know that a woman of that class looks a worn out drudge of fifty a year after she's married?

LIZA. Whood marry me?

HIGGINS (*suddenly resorting to the most thrilling beautiful low tones in his best* elocutionary *style*). By George, Eliza, the streets will be strewn with the bodies of men shooting themselves for your sake before Ive done with you.

MRS PEARCE. Nonsense, sir. You mustnt talk like that to her.

LIZA (*rising and squaring herself determinedly*). I'm going away. He's off his chump, he is. I dont want no balmies[10] teaching me.

HIGGINS (*wounded in his tenderest point by her insensibility to his elocution*). Oh, indeed! I'm mad, am I? Very well, Mrs Pearce: you neednt order the new clothes for her. Throw her out.

LIZA (*whimpering*). Nah-ow. You got no right to touch me.

MRS PEARCE. You see now what comes of being saucy. (*Indicating the door*) This way, please.

LIZA (*almost in tears*). I didn't want no clothes. I wouldnt have taken them. (*She throws away the handkerchief.*) I can buy my own clothes.

HIGGINS (*deftly retrieving the handkerchief and intercepting her on her reluctant way to the door*). Youre an ungrateful wicked girl. This is my return for offering to take you out of the gutter and dress you beautifully and make a lady of you.

---

10. **balmies.** British slang for crazy or foolish people

❶ *What has Higgins actually been doing? How do his former actions contradict his explanations of his intentions?*

WORDS FOR EVERYDAY USE:
zeph • yr (zef´ər) *n.*, mild, gentle breeze
el • o • cu • tion • ar • y (el´ə kyōō´shən er´ē) *adj.*, appropriate for public speaking

VOCABULARY IN CONTEXT

• He built his house in a spot warmed by the sun and fanned by the western zephyrs.
• In the late 1800s, professional speakers toured cities giving elocutionary performances of famous poems.
• After the dancers scratched the gym floor with their tap shoes, they received a severe remonstrance from the principal.
• The captain of the ship resolutely held course through the hurricane and reached the harbor.

MRS PEARCE. Stop, Mr Higgins I wont allow it. It's you that are wicked. Go home to your parents, girl; and tell them to take better care of you.

LIZA. I aint got no parents. They told me I was big enough to earn my own living and turned me out.

MRS PEARCE. Wheres your mother?

LIZA. I aint got no mother. Her that turned me out was my sixth stepmother. But I done without them. And I'm a good girl, I am.

HIGGINS. Very well, then, what on earth is all this fuss about? The girl doesnt belong to anybody—is no use to anybody but me. (*He goes to* MRS PEARCE *and begins coaxing.*) You can adopt her, Mrs Pearce: I'm sure a daughter would be a great amusement to you. Now dont make any more fuss. Take her downstairs; and—

MRS PEARCE. But whats to become of her? Is she to be paid anything? Do be sensible, sir.

HIGGINS. Oh, pay her whatever is necessary: put it down in the housekeeping book. (*Impatiently*) What on earth will she want with money? She'll have her food and her clothes. She'll only drink if you give her money.

LIZA (*turning on him*). Oh you are a brute. It's a lie: nobody ever saw the sign of liquor on me. (*She goes back to her chair and plants herself there defiantly.*)

PICKERING (*in good-humored remonstrance*). Does it occur to you, Higgins, that the girl has some feelings?

HIGGINS (*looking critically at her*). Oh no, I dont think so. Not any feelings that we need bother about. (*Cheerily*) Have you, Eliza?

LIZA. I got my feelings same as anyone else.

HIGGINS (*to* PICKERING, *reflectively*). You see the difficulty?

PICKERING. Eh? What difficulty?

HIGGINS. To get her to talk grammar. The mere pronunciation is easy enough.

LIZA. I dont want to talk grammar. I want to talk like a lady.

MRS PEARCE. Will you please keep to the point, Mr Higgins? I want to know on what terms the girl is to be here. Is she to have any wages? And what is to become of her when youve finished your teaching? You must look ahead a little.

HIGGINS (*impatiently*). Whats to become of her if I leave her in the gutter? Tell me that, Mrs Pearce.

MRS PEARCE. Thats her own business, not yours, Mr Higgins.

HIGGINS. Well, when Ive done with her, we can throw her back into the gutter; and then it will be her own business again; so thats all right.

LIZA. Oh, youve no feeling heart in you: you dont care for nothing but yourself. (*She rises and takes the floor* resolutely.) Here! Ive had enough of this. I'm going. (*Making for the door*) You ought to be ashamed of yourself, you ought.

HIGGINS (*snatching a chocolate cream from the piano, his eyes suddenly beginning to*

❶ *How does Higgins treat Liza? What does his treatment of her reveal about him?*

---

❶ Higgins treats Liza as if she is of no value to anyone and has no feelings worth considering. This attitude reveals that he is self-centered and inconsiderate of others. It is also a reflection of the rigidity of class distinctions.

LITERARY TECHNIQUE

Point of View. Explain to students that point of view is the perspective from which a story is told. In drama, point of view is generally less important than in other forms of fiction. Students can write an account from Liza's point of view of the scene in which Liza first comes to ask for lessons. They should reinterpret Higgins's words and actions as those words and actions would have seemed to Liza, based on her reactions in the play.

twinkle with mischief). Have some chocolates, Eliza.

LIZA (*halting, tempted*). How do I know what might be in them? I've heard of girls being drugged by the like of you.

(HIGGINS *whips out his penknife; cuts a chocolate in two; puts one half into his mouth and bolts it; and offers her the other half.*)

HIGGINS. Pledge of good faith, Eliza. I eat one half: you eat the other. (LIZA *opens her mouth to retort: he pops the half chocolate into it.*) You shall have boxes of them, barrels of them, every day. You shall live on them. Eh?

LIZA (*who has disposed of the chocolate after being nearly choked by it*). I wouldnt have ate it, only I'm too ladylike to take it out of my mouth.

HIGGINS. Listen, Eliza. I think you said you came in a taxi.

LIZA. Well, what if I did? Ive as good a right to take a taxi as anyone else.

HIGGINS. You have, Eliza; and in future you shall have as many taxis as you want. You shall go up and down and round the town in a taxi every day. Think of that, Eliza.

MRS PEARCE. Mr Higgins: youre tempting the girl. It's not right. She should think of the future.

HIGGINS. At her age! Nonsense! Time enough to think of the future when you havnt any future to think of. No, Eliza: do as this lady does: think of other people's futures; but never think of your own. Think of chocolates, and taxis, and gold, and diamonds.

LIZA. No: I dont want no gold and no diamonds. I'm a good girl, I am. (*She sits down again, with an attempt at dignity.*)

HIGGINS. You shall remain so, Eliza, under the care of Mrs Pearce. And you

❶ How does Higgins respond to the suggestion made by Mrs. Pearce and by Pickering that he should explain his plans to Liza so that she can give informed consent to them? Does Higgins's reply meet their objections? Why, or why not?

shall marry an officer in the Guards,[11] with a beautiful moustache: the son of a marquis,[12] who will disinherit him for marrying you, but will relent when he sees your beauty and goodness—

PICKERING. Excuse me, Higgins; but I really must interfere. Mrs Pearce is quite right. If this girl is to put herself in your hands for six months for an experiment in teaching, she must understand thoroughly what she's doing.

HIGGINS. How can she? She's incapable of understanding anything. Besides, do any of us understand what we are doing? If we did, would we ever do it?

PICKERING. Very clever, Higgins; but not sound sense. (*To* ELIZA) Miss Doolittle—

LIZA (*overwhelmed*). Ah-ah-ow-oo!

HIGGINS. There! Thats all youll get out of Eliza. Ah-ah-ow-oo! No use explaining. As a military man you ought to know that. Give her her orders: thats what she wants. Eliza: you are to live here for the next six months, learning how to speak beautifully, like a lady in a florist's shop. If youre good and do whatever youre told, you shall sleep in a proper bedroom, and have lots to eat, and money to buy chocolates and take rides in taxis. If youre naughty and idle you will sleep in the back kitchen among the black beetles, and be walloped by Mrs Pearce with a broomstick. At the end of six months you shall go to Buckingham Palace in a carriage, beautifully dressed. If the King finds out youre not a lady, you will be taken by the police to the Tower of London, where your head will be cut off as a warning to other

---

11. **the Guards.** A highly decorated British military unit
12. **marquis.** A European nobleman, ranked above an earl or count and below a duke

presumptuous flower girls. If you are not found out, you shall have a present of seven-and-sixpence to start life with as a lady in a shop. If you refuse this offer you will be a most ungrateful and wicked girl; and the angels will weep for you. (*To* PICKERING) Now are you satisfied, Pickering? (*To* MRS PEARCE) Can I put it more plainly and fairly, Mrs Pearce?

MRS PEARCE (*patiently*). I think youd better let me speak to the girl properly in private. I dont know that I can take charge of her or consent to the arrangement at all. Of course I know you dont mean her any harm; but when you get what you call interested in people's accents, you never think or care what may happen to them or you. Come with me, Eliza.

HIGGINS. Thats all right. Thank you, Mrs Pearce. Bundle her off to the bath-room.

LIZA (*rising reluctantly and suspiciously*). Youre a great bully, you are. I wont stay here if I dont like. I wont let nobody wallop me. I never asked to go to Bucknam Palace, I didnt. I was never in trouble with the police, not me. I'm a good girl—

MRS PEARCE. Dont answer back, girl. You dont understand the gentleman. Come with me. (*She leads the way to the door, and holds open for* ELIZA.)

LIZA (*as she goes out*). Well, what I say is right. I wont go near the King, not if I'm going to have my head cut off. If I'd known what I was letting myself in for, I wouldnt have come here. I always been a good girl; and I never offered to say a word to him; and I dont owe him nothing; and I dont care; and I wont be put upon; and I have my feelings the same as anyone else—

(MRS PEARCE *shuts the door; and* ELIZA's *plaints are no longer audible.* PICKERING *comes from the hearth to the chair and sits astride it with his arms on the back.*)

PICKERING. Excuse the straight question, Higgins. Are you a man of good character where women are concerned?

HIGGINS (*moodily*). Have you ever met a man of good character where women are concerned?

PICKERING. Yes: very frequently.

HIGGINS (*dogmatically, lifting himself on his hands to the level of the piano, and sitting on it with a bounce*). Well, I havnt. I find that the moment I let a woman make friends with me, she becomes jealous, exacting, suspicious, and a damned nuisance. I find that the moment I let myself make friends with a woman, I become selfish and tyrannical. Women upset everything. When you let them into your life, you find that the woman is driving at one thing and youre driving at another.

PICKERING. At what, for example?

HIGGINS (*coming off the piano restlessly*). Oh, Lord knows! I suppose the woman wants to live her own life; and the man wants to live his; and each tries to drag the other on to the wrong track. One wants to go north and the other south; and the result is that both have to go east, though they both hate the east wind. (*He sits down on the bench at the keyboard.*) So here I am, a confirmed old bachelor, and likely to remain so.

PICKERING (*rising and standing over him gravely*). Come, Higgins! You know what I mean. If I'm to be in this business I shall

---

WORDS FOR EVERYDAY USE:

pre • sump • tu • ous (prē zump´ chō̄ əs) *adj.*, overconfident or arrogant

plaint (plānt) *n.*, complaint or grievance

a • stride (ə strīd´) *adv.*, with legs on either side

dog • mat • i • cal • ly (dôg mat´ ik ə lē) *adv.*, stating an opinion in an arrogant manner

ADDITIONAL QUESTIONS AND ACTIVITIES

Ask the following questions:

1. Why, do you suppose, do women seem to Higgins to become "jealous, exacting, suspicious," and turn into "nuisances" when they become involved with him? How is his statement about women ironic?

2. Why does Higgins become "selfish and tyrannical" when he makes friends with a woman?

3. Why would it be likely that Higgins would believe that women are going in the opposite direction from him?

Answers. 1. Higgins is so impulsive, bullying, self-absorbed, and capricious that he is likely to make a person exacting and suspicious in response. His statement about women is ironic because it is clear to the audience that he is a difficult person to live with and that the characteristics he describes are only a reaction to him. 2. Higgins is almost always self-absorbed and frequently overbearing and pushy; when he makes friends with a woman, he finds himself in a situation in which he can perceive his own personality and sees himself as acting in a selfish and tyrannical manner. 3. Almost anyone dealing with Higgins in a close relationship would have to resist his bullying and coaxing, and so would be perceived by him as "driving at one thing" while he was "driving at another."

VOCABULARY IN CONTEXT

- Donald was <u>presumptuous</u> enough to ask for a raise on his third day on the job.
- The tenants presented the landlord with a list of four hundred and sixty-five <u>plaints</u> about his tenements.
- The logger rode down the rapids <u>astride</u> an enormous fir tree.
- Biff's idea of a discussion was that everyone should listen quietly while he <u>dogmatically</u> asserted his beliefs.

Pickering's scruples may not be clear to students. Ask the following questions to clarify the interchange about Liza between Pickering and Higgins.

1. What does Pickering mean when he says "no advantage is to be taken" of Liza's position?

2. Do you believe Higgins when he says his pupil-teacher relationship with Liza will be "sacred"? Why, or why not?

Answers. 1. Pickering means that Higgins is not to compel or coax Liza into having a romantic relationship with him. 2. Higgins, as Shaw describes him, is not the least malevolent and seems to have little interest in a relationship of any kind with a woman, so his statement about the sacredness of his relationship to Liza can be believed, even if not for the reasons he offers.

ANSWERS TO GUIDED READING QUESTIONS

❶ Mrs. Pearce believes the hat should be disinfected, possibly because it may have lice.

❷ Higgins is not self-aware; if he were, he would know that he is very careless in what he says to others.

▶ **Teaching Note:** The word that "begins with the same letter as bath," which Mrs. Pearce asks Higgins not to use, is *bloody,* a British vulgar curse.

---

feel responsible for that girl. I hope its understood that no advantage is to be taken of her position.

HIGGINS. What! That thing! Sacred, I assure you. (*Rising to explain*) You see, she'll be a pupil; and teaching would be impossible unless pupils were sacred. Ive taught <u>scores</u> of American millionairesses how to speak English: the best looking women in the world. I'm seasoned. They might as well be blocks of wood. *I* might as well be a block of wood. It's—

(MRS PEARCE *opens the door. She has* ELIZA's *hat in her hand.* PICKERING *retires to the easy-chair at the hearth and sits down.*)

HIGGINS (*eagerly*). Well, Mrs Pearce: is it all right?

MRS PEARCE (*at the door*). I just wish to trouble you with a word, if I may, Mr Higgins.

HIGGINS. Yes, certainly. Come in. (*She comes forward.*) Dont burn that, Mrs Pearce. I'll keep it as a curiosity. (*He takes the hat.*)

❶ Why does Mrs. Pearce feel she must put the hat into the oven?

MRS PEARCE. Handle it carefully, sir, please. I had to promise her not to burn it; but I had better put it in the oven for a while.

HIGGINS (*putting it down hastily on the piano*). Oh! thank you. Well, what have you to say to me?

PICKERING. Am I in the way?

❷ Is Higgins very self-aware? How do you know?

MRS PEARCE. Not at all, sir. Mr Higgins: will you please be very particular what you say before the girl?

HIGGINS (*sternly*). Of course. I'm always particular about what I say. Why do you say this to me?

MRS PEARCE (*unmoved*). No, sir: youre not at all particular when youve mislaid anything or when you get a little impatient. Now it doesnt matter before me: I'm used to it. But you really must not swear before the girl.

HIGGINS (*indignantly*). I swear! (*Most emphatically*) I never swear. I detest the habit. What the devil do you mean?

MRS PEARCE (*stolidly*). Thats what I mean, sir. You swear a great deal too much. I dont mind your damning and blasting, and what the devil and where the devil and who the devil—

HIGGINS. Mrs Pearce: this language from your lips! Really!

MRS PEARCE (*not to be put off*).—but there is a certain word I must ask you not to use. The girl has just used it herself because the bath was too hot. It begins with the same letter as bath. She knows no better: she learnt it at her mother's knee. But she must not hear it from your lips.

HIGGINS (*loftily*). I cannot charge myself with having ever uttered it, Mrs Pearce. (*She looks at him* <u>steadfastly</u>. *He adds, hiding an uneasy conscience with a* <u>judicial</u> *air*) Except perhaps in a moment of extreme and justifiable excitement.

MRS PEARCE. Only this morning, sir, you applied it to your boots, to the butter, and to the brown bread.

HIGGINS. Oh, that! Mere alliteration, Mrs Pearce, natural to a poet.

MRS PEARCE. Well, sir, whatever you choose to call it, I beg you not to let the girl hear you repeat it.

WORDS FOR EVERYDAY USE:

score (skôr) *n.,* set of twenty persons or things

stead • fast • ly (sted´fast΄lē) *adv.,* in a firm or established manner

ju • di • cial (jōō dish´əl΄) *adj.,* carefully considering the facts

VOCABULARY IN CONTEXT

- "Three <u>score</u> and ten years" is a common expression signifying a life span.
- The boy tested his morals by <u>steadfastly</u> refusing to steal a single piece of candy.
- The umpire had a <u>judicial</u> manner, but her mask and chest protector did not contribute to a <u>judicial</u> appearance.

HIGGINS. Oh, very well, very well. Is that all?

MRS PEARCE. No, sir. We shall have to be very particular with this girl as to personal cleanliness.

HIGGINS. Certainly. Quite right. Most important.

MRS PEARCE. I mean not to be <u>slovenly</u> about her dress or untidy in leaving things about.

HIGGINS (*going to her solemnly*). Just so. I intended to call your attention to that. (*He passes on to* PICKERING, *who is enjoying the conversation immensely.*) It is these little things that matter, Pickering. Take care of the pence and the pounds will take care of themselves is as true of personal habits as of money. (*He comes to anchor on the hearthrug, with the air of a man in an <u>unassailable</u> position.*)

MRS PEARCE. Yes, sir. Then might I ask you not to come down to breakfast in your dressing-gown, or at any rate not to use it as a napkin to the extent you do, sir. And if you would be so good as not to eat everything off the same plate, and to remember not to put the porridge saucepan out of your hand on the clean tablecloth, it would be a better example to the girl. You know you nearly choked yourself with a fishbone in the jam only last week.

HIGGINS (*routed from the hearthrug and drifting back to the piano*). I may do these things sometimes in absence of mind; but surely I dont do them habitually. (*Angrily*) By the way: my dressing-gown smells most damnably of benzine.

MRS PEARCE. No doubt it does, Mr Higgins. But if you will wipe your fingers—

HIGGINS (*yelling*). Oh very well, very well: I'll wipe them in my hair in future.

MRS PEARCE. I hope youre not offended, Mr Higgins.

HIGGINS (*shocked at finding himself thought capable of an unamiable sentiment*). Not at all, not at all. Youre quite right, Mrs Pearce: I shall be particularly careful before the girl. Is that all?

MRS PEARCE. No, sir. Might she use some of those Japanese dresses you brought from abroad? I really cant put her back into her old things.

HIGGINS. Certainly. Anything you like. Is that all?

MRS PEARCE. Thank you, sir. Thats all. (*She goes out.*)

HIGGINS. You know, Pickering, that woman has the most extraordinary ideas about me. Here I am, a shy, <u>diffident</u> sort of man. Ive never been able to feel really grown-up and tremendous, like other chaps. And yet she's firmly persuaded that I'm an <u>arbitrary</u> overbearing bossing kind of person. I cant account for it.

(MRS PEARCE *returns.*)

MRS PEARCE. If you please, sir, the trouble's beginning already. Theres a dustman[13] downstairs, Alfred Doolittle, wants to see you. He says you have his daughter here.

13. **dustman.** Refuse collector

❶ What does Mrs. Pearce know about Higgins that he doesn't know himself?

❷ What might you be able to predict about Doolittle based on his last name?

PYGMALION, ACT TWO **1009**

CROSS-CURRICULAR ACTIVITIES

Social Studies. Ask students the following questions to clarify differences between British and American culture.

1. List the points of "personal cleanliness" mentioned by Mrs. Pearce and indicate whether they are acceptable behavior in most classes and in most places and social situations in the United States today.

2. What does a comparison of what was acceptable in Shaw's time in Great Britain and what is acceptable today in the United States tell you about what is "normal" or "acceptable" behavior?

Answers. 1. The list of points mentioned by Mrs. Pearce (with a comment about their acceptability in the United States) include the following: being slovenly in dress (casual clothing is more acceptable today than in pre–World War I London); leaving things about (sometimes unacceptable); having breakfast in a dressing-gown (generally acceptable); using a dressing-gown as a napkin (unacceptable); eating everything off the same plate (often perfectly acceptable); and putting the porridge saucepan on the clean tablecloth (unacceptable).

2. "Acceptable" behavior varies from one culture and time to another.

ANSWERS TO GUIDED READING QUESTIONS

❶ Mrs. Pearce knows that Higgins is an overbearing, bossy person.

❷ One might guess that Doolittle is not a hardworking person.

VOCABULARY IN CONTEXT

- The editor soon found to her horror that the historian's research techniques were as <u>slovenly</u> as his greasy tweed jacket.
- People who consider their financial know-how <u>unassailable</u> are frequently the target of con artists.
- Bing was so <u>diffident</u> that I had difficulty maintaining a conversation with him.
- When we realized that the team leader had an <u>arbitrary</u> leadership style, we quickly replaced him with a more productive team member.

PICKERING (*rising*). Phew! I say! (*He retreats to the hearthrug.*)

HIGGINS (*promptly*). Send the blackguard[14] up.

MRS PEARCE. Oh, very well, sir. (*She goes out.*)

PICKERING. He may not be a blackguard, Higgins.

HIGGINS. Nonsense. Of course he's a blackguard.

PICKERING. Whether he is or not, I'm afraid we shall have some trouble with him.

HIGGINS (*confidently*). Oh no: I think not. If theres any trouble he shall have it with me, not I with him. And we are sure to get something interesting out of him.

PICKERING. About the girl?

HIGGINS. No. I mean his dialect.

PICKERING. Oh!

MRS PEARCE (*at the door*). Doolittle, sir. (*She admits* DOOLITTLE *and retires.*)

(ALFRED DOOLITTLE *is an elderly but vigorous dustman, clad in the costume of his profession, including a hat with a back brim covering his neck and shoulders. He has well marked and rather interesting features, and seems equally free from fear and conscience. He has a remarkably expressive voice, the result of a habit of giving vent to his feelings without reserve. His present pose is that of wounded honor and stern resolution.*)

DOOLITTLE (*at the door, uncertain which of the two gentlemen is his man*). Professor Higgins?

HIGGINS Here. Good morning. Sit down.

DOOLITTLE. Morning, Governor. (*He sits down* magisterially.) I come about a very serious matter, Governor.

HIGGINS (*to* PICKERING). Brought up in Hounslow. Mother Welsh, I should think. (DOOLITTLE *opens his mouth, amazed.* HIGGINS *continues.*) What do you want, Doolittle?

DOOLITTLE (*menacingly*). I want my daughter: thats what I want. See?

HIGGINS. Of course you do. Youre her father, arnt you? You dont suppose anyone else wants her, do you? I'm glad to see you have some spark of family feeling left. She's upstairs. Take her away at once.

DOOLITTLE (*rising, fearfully taken aback*). What!

HIGGINS. Take her away. Do you suppose I'm going to keep your daughter for you?

DOOLITTLE (*remonstrating*). Now, now, look here, Governor. Is this reasonable? Is it fairity[15] to take advantage of a man like this? The girl belongs to me. You got her. Where do I come in? (*He sits down again.*)

HIGGINS. Your daughter had the audacity to come to my house and ask me to teach her how to speak properly so that she could get a place in a flower-shop. This gentleman and my housekeeper have been here all the time. (*Bullying him*) How dare you come here and attempt to blackmail me? You sent her here on purpose.

DOOLITTLE (*protesting*). No, Governor.

---

14. **blackguard.** Vulgar person of the lower class
15. **fairity.** Just and honest

WORDS FOR EVERYDAY USE:

mag • is • te • ri • al •ly (maj´is tir´ē əl lē) *adv.*, in a domineering or masterful manner

au • dac • i • ty (ô das´ə tē) *n.*, boldness, insolence

VOCABULARY IN CONTEXT

- When someone coughed before the symphony began, the conductor magisterially stared him into silence.
- The pirate demonstrated his audacity by attacking ships far better armed than his own.
- A favored tactic of organized crime is to extort money from a business in return for a promise not to disrupt it.
- Before beginning his new job plowing snow, Jack took a jaunt to a sunny climate.

HIGGINS. You must have. How else could you possibly know that she is here?

DOOLITTLE. Dont take a man up like that, Governor.

HIGGINS. The police shall take you up. This is a plant—a plot to <u>extort</u> money by threats. I shall telephone for the police. (*He goes resolutely to the telephone and opens the directory.*)

DOOLITTLE. Have I asked you for a brass farthing? I leave it to the gentleman here: have I said a word about money?

HIGGINS (*throwing the book aside and marching down on* DOOLITTLE *with a poser*). What else did you come for?

DOOLITTLE (*sweetly*). Well, what would a man come for? Be human, Governor.

HIGGINS (*disarmed*). Alfred: did you put her up to it?

DOOLITTLE. So help me, Governor, I never did. I take my Bible oath I aint seen the girl these two months past.

HIGGINS. Then how did you know she was here?

DOOLITTLE ("*most musical, most melancholy*"). I'll tell you, Governor, if youll only let me get a word in. I'm willing to tell you. I'm wanting to tell you. I'm waiting to tell you.

HIGGINS. Pickering: this chap has a certain natural gift of rhetoric. Observe the rhythm of his native woodnotes wild.[16] "I'm willing to tell you: I'm wanting to tell you: I'm waiting to tell you." Sentimental rhetoric! thats the Welsh strain in him. It also accounts for his mendacity and dishonesty.

PICKERING. Oh, please, Higgins: I'm west country myself. (*To* DOOLITTLE) How did you know the girl was here if you didnt send her?

DOOLITTLE. It was like this, Governor. The girl took a boy in the taxi to give him a <u>jaunt</u>. Son of her landlady, he is. He hung about on the chance of her giving him another ride home. Well, she sent him back for her luggage when she heard you was willing for her to stop here. I met the boy at the corner of Long Acre and Endell Street.

HIGGINS. Public house. Yes?

DOOLITTLE. The poor man's club, Governor: why shouldnt I?

PICKERING. Do let him tell his story, Higgins.

DOOLITTLE. He told me what was up. And I ask you, what was my feelings and my duty as a father? I says to the boy, "You bring me the luggage," I says—

PICKERING. Why didn't you go for it yourself?

DOOLITTLE. Landlady wouldnt have trusted me with it, Governor. She's that kind of woman: you know. I had to give the boy a penny afore he trusted me with it, the little swine. I brought it to her just to oblige you like, and make myself agreeable. Thats all.

HIGGINS. How much luggage?

DOOLITTLE. Musical instrument, Governor. A few pictures, a trifle of jewelry, and a bird-cage. She said she didn't want

---

16. **rhythm . . . wild.** A reference to the sound of a warbling in the forest

Why has Doolittle come? What does he want?

What does Higgins assume about Doolittle? on what basis? Why does Pickering protest?

PYGMALION, ACT TWO **1011**

---

❶ Doolittle has come for money. He wants some kind of payment from Higgins.

❷ Higgins assumes that Doolittle is dishonest because he is from Wales. Pickering protests because his own background is Welsh.

LITERARY TECHNIQUE

Characterization. Point out to students that Shaw uses interruptions in and responses to Doolittle's account of events to develop our understanding of his character and to advance the plot. Doolittle is interrupted by Higgins first, who identifies the corner of Long Acre and Endell Street as a pub. Next, Pickering interrupts him with a question that results in Doolittle's disclosing that he is not trusted by Liza's landlady. Pickering finally confronts him with the contradiction between his words and his actions, asking him why he brought Liza's luggage if he was intending to rescue her.

ANSWER TO GUIDED READING
QUESTION

❶ Doolittle believes that his daughter
is going to become romantically
involved with Higgins. His actions
reveal he has no objection to that
arrangement as long as he profits
from it, which demonstrates that he
values money more than morality.

ADDITIONAL QUESTIONS
AND ACTIVITIES

The role of Pickering is that of
foil, observer, and occasional
advancer of the plot. Students can
imagine they are Pickering and
write a letter to a friend in India
from his point of view, summarizing the discussion between
Doolittle and Higgins.

❶
*What does
Doolittle think is
occurring? What
do his actions
reveal about him?*

no clothes. What was I to think from that,
Governor? I ask you as a parent what was
I to think?

HIGGINS. So you came to rescue her
from worse than death, eh?

DOOLITTLE (*appreciatively: relieved at
being so well understood*). Just so, Governor.
Thats right.

PICKERING. But why did you bring her
luggage if you intended to take her away?

DOOLITTLE. Have I said a word about
taking her away? Have I now?

HIGGINS (*determinedly*). Youre going to
take her away, double quick. (*He crosses to
the hearth and rings the bell.*)

DOOLITTLE (*rising*). No, Governor.
Dont say that. I'm not the man to stand in
my girl's light. Heres a career opening for
her, as you might say; and—

(MRS PEARCE *opens the door and awaits
orders.*)

HIGGINS. Mrs Pearce: this is Eliza's
father. He has come to take her away.
Give her to him. (*He goes back to the piano,
with an air of washing his hands of the whole
affair.*)

DOOLITTLE. No. This is a misunderstanding. Listen here—

MRS PEARCE. He cant take her away,
Mr Higgins: how can he? You told me to
burn her clothes.

DOOLITTLE. Thats right. I cant carry
the girl through the streets like a blooming monkey, can I? I put it to you.

HIGGINS. You have put it to me that you
want your daughter. Take your daughter. If
she has no clothes go out and buy her some.

DOOLITTLE (*desperate*). Wheres the
clothes she come in? Did I burn them or
did your missus here?

MRS PEARCE. I am the housekeeper, if
you please. I have sent for some clothes
for your girl. When they come you can
take her away. You can wait in the kitchen.
This way, please.

(DOOLITTLE, *much troubled, accompanies her
to the door; then hesitates; finally turns confi-
dentially to* HIGGINS.)

DOOLITTLE. Listen here, Governor.
You and me is men of the world, aint we?

HIGGINS. Oh! Men of the world, are
we? Youd better go, Mrs Pearce.

MRS PEARCE. I think so, indeed, sir.
(*She goes, with dignity.*)

PICKERING. The floor is yours, Mr
Doolittle.

DOOLITTLE (*to* PICKERING). I thank you,
Governor. (*To* HIGGINS, *who takes refuge on
the piano bench, a little overwhelmed by the
proximity of his visitor; for* DOOLITTLE *has a
professional flavour of dust about him.*) Well,
the truth is, Ive taken a sort of fancy to
you, Governor; and if you want the girl,
I'm not so set on having her back home
again but what I might be open to an
arrangement. Regarded in the light of a
young woman, she's a fine handsome girl.
As a daughter she's not worth her keep;
and so I tell you straight. All I ask is my
rights as a father; and youre the last man
alive to expect me to let her go for nothing; for I can see youre one of the straight
sort, Governor. Well, whats a five-pound
note to you? And whats Eliza to me? (*He
returns to his chair and sits down judicially.*)

PICKERING. I think you ought to know,
Doolittle, that Mr Higgins's intentions are
entirely honorable.

DOOLITTLE. Course they are, Governor.
If I thought they wasnt, I'd ask fifty.

HIGGINS (*revolted*). Do you mean to say, you <u>callous</u> rascal, that you would sell your daughter for £50?

DOOLITTLE. Not in a general way I wouldnt; but to oblige a gentleman like you I'd do a good deal, I do assure you.

PICKERING. Have you no morals, man?

DOOLITTLE (*unabashed*). Cant afford them, Governor. Neither could you if you was as poor as me. Not that I mean any harm, you know. But if Liza is going to have a bit out of this, why not me too?

HIGGINS (*troubled*). I dont know what to do, Pickering. There can be no question that as a matter of morals it's a positive crime to give this chap a farthing.[17] And yet I feel a sort of rough justice in his claim.

DOOLITTLE. Thats it, Governor. Thats all I say. A father's heart, as it were.

PICKERING. Well, I know the feeling; but really it seems hardly right—

DOOLITTLE. Dont say that, Governor. Dont look at it that way. What am I, Governors both? I ask you, what am I? I'm one of the undeserving poor: thats what I am. Think of what that means to a man. It means that he's up agen[18] middle class morality all the time. If theres anything going, and I put in for a bit of it, it's always the same story: "Youre undeserving; so you cant have it." But my needs is as great as the most deserving widow's that ever got money out of six different charities in one week for the death of the same husband. I dont need less than a deserving man: I need more. I dont eat less hearty than him; and I drink a lot more. I want a bit of amusement, cause I'm a thinking man. I want cheerfulness and a song and a band when I feel low. Well, they charge me just the same for everything as they charge the deserving. What is middle class morality? Just an excuse for never giving me anything. Therefore, I ask you, as two gentlemen, not to play that game on me. I'm playing straight with you. I aint pretending to be deserving. I'm undeserving; and I mean to go on being undeserving. I like it; and thats the truth. Will you take advantage of a man's nature to do him out of the price of his own daughter what he's brought up and fed and clothed by the sweat of his brow until she's growed big enough to be interesting to you two gentlemen? Is five pounds unreasonable? I put it to you; and I leave it to you.

HIGGINS (*rising, and going over to* PICKERING). Pickering: if we were to take this man in hand for three months, he could choose between a seat in the Cabinet and a popular pulpit in Wales.

PICKERING. What do you say to that, Doolittle?

DOOLITTLE. Not me, Governor, thank you kindly. Ive heard all the preachers and all the prime ministers—for I'm a thinking man and game for politics or religion or social reform same as all the other amusements—and I tell you it's a dog's life any way you look at it. Undeserving poverty is my line. Taking one station in society with

What does Doolittle offer to do? What serious point is Shaw making about morality in this humorous scene?

----

17. **farthing.** Former British coin, equal to one-fourth of a penny
18. **agen.** Against

----

❶ Doolittle suggests that he would raise no objections to his daughter's becoming Higgins's mistress as long as he received fifty pounds himself. Shaw is pointing out that it is easier for well-to-do people to maintain moral standards because their poverty does not compel them to compromise what they think is right.

ADDITIONAL QUESTIONS AND ACTIVITIES

Students can imagine Doolittle is running for public office in the United States and write party platforms describing the proposals he might make for governing the nation and changing society.

VOCABULARY IN CONTEXT

- Even the most <u>callous</u> person in the crowd shed a tear when the little ballerina gave her teacher a bouquet.
- <u>Unabashed</u> by the television cameras, George followed the hypnotist's suggestion, gargling and yodeling wildly.

ANSWER TO GUIDED READING QUESTION

❶ Doolittle argues that the others should not be concerned about his making bad use of the money, because he will spend the money promptly on a drinking spree. He challenges middle-class morality by assuming that a spree is the least harmful use he could make of the money given him.

ADDITIONAL QUESTIONS AND ACTIVITIES

Students can imagine they are advice columnists. Higgins has just written to them to ask whether he should marry Liza. Students can write a one-paragraph response, in view of the situation as it stands in Act Two. Before they begin, they should reread Doolittle's opinion of marriage, as expressed on this page.

---

another, it's—it's—well, it's the only one that has any <u>ginger</u> in it, to my taste.

HIGGINS. I suppose we must give him a fiver.[19]

PICKERING. He'll make a bad use of it, I'm afraid.

DOOLITTLE. Not me, Governor, so help me I wont. Dont you be afraid that I'll save it and spare it and live idle on it. There wont be a penny of it left by Monday: I'll have to go to work same as if I'd never had it. It wont <u>pauperize</u> me, you bet. Just one good spree for myself and the missus, giving pleasure to ourselves and employment to others, and satisfaction to you to think it's not been throwed away. You couldnt spend it better.

HIGGINS (*taking out his pocket book and coming between* DOOLITTLE *and the piano*). This is irresistible. Lets give him ten. (*He offers two notes to the dustman.*)

DOOLITTLE. No, Governor. She wouldnt have the heart to spend ten; and perhaps I shouldnt neither. Ten pounds is a lot of money: it makes a man feel prudent like; and then goodbye to happiness. You give me what I ask you, Governor: not a penny more, and not a penny less.

PICKERING. Why dont you marry that missus of yours? I rather draw the line at encouraging that sort of immorality.

DOOLITTLE. Tell her so, Governor: tell her so. *I'm* willing. It's me that suffers by it. Ive no hold on her. I got to be agreeable to her. I got to give her presents. I got to buy her clothes something sinful. I'm a slave to that woman, Governor, just because I'm not her lawful husband.

❶
What unexpected, unusual argument does Doolittle make? How does he challenge "middle-class morality"?

And she knows it too. Catch her marrying me! Take my advice, Governor: marry Eliza while she's young and dont know no better. If you dont youll be sorry for it after. If you do, she'll be sorry for it after; but better her than you, because youre a man, and she's only a woman and dont know how to be happy anyhow.

HIGGINS. Pickering if we listen to this man another minute, we shall have no convictions left. (*To* DOOLITTLE) Five pounds I think you said.

DOOLITTLE. Thank you kindly, Governor.

HIGGINS. Youre sure you wont take ten?

DOOLITTLE. Not now. Another time, Governor.

HIGGINS (*handing him a five-pound note*). Here you are.

DOOLITTLE. Thank you, Governor. Good morning. (*He hurries to the door, anxious to get away with his booty. When he opens it he is confronted with a dainty and exquisitely clean young Japanese lady in a simple blue cotton kimono printed cunningly with small white jasmine blossoms.* MRS PEARCE *is with her. He gets out of her way deferentially and apologizes.*) Beg pardon, miss.

THE JAPANESE LADY. Garn! Dont you know your own daughter?

DOOLITTLE (*exclaiming* Bly me! it's Eliza!
HIGGINS *simul-* Whats that! This!
PICKERING *taneously*) By Jove!

LIZA. Dont I look silly?

HIGGINS. Silly?

---

19. **fiver.** British slang for a five-pound note

WORDS FOR EVERYDAY USE:

gin • ger (jin´gər) *n.*, liveliness, spirit
pau • per • ize (pô´pər īz´) *vt.*, impoverish

VOCABULARY IN CONTEXT

- "Come on, boys and girls," the band leader said. "Put some <u>ginger</u> in it, or this crowd will fall asleep."
- Tolstoy, insisting upon major changes in society, claimed that charity <u>pauperized</u> the lower class.
- By saving pennies <u>conscientiously</u> for sixty-two years, grandfather was able to retire to Florida.
- I was <u>incensed</u> when the dry cleaners tried to charge me separately for the liner and the shell of my coat.

Mrs Pearce (*at the door*). Now, Mr Higgins, please dont say anything to make the girl conceited about herself.

Higgins (*conscientiously*). Oh! Quite right, Mrs Pearce. (*To* Eliza) Yes: damned silly.

Mrs Pearce. Please, sir.

Higgins (*correcting himself*). I mean extremely silly.

Liza. I should look all right with my hat on. (*She takes up her hat; puts it on; and walks across the room to the fireplace with a fashionable air.*)

Higgins. A new fashion, by George! and it ought to look horrible!

Doolittle (*with fatherly pride*). Well, I never thought she'd clean up as good looking as that, Governor. She's a credit to me, aint she?

Liza. I tell you, it's easy to clean up here. Hot and cold water on tap, just as much as you like, there is. Woolly towels, there is; and a towel horse[20] so hot, it burns your fingers. Soft brushes to scrub yourself, and a wooden bowl of soap smelling like primroses. Now I know why ladies is so clean. Washing's a treat for them. Wish they saw what it is for the like of me!

Higgins. I'm glad the bathroom met with your approval.

Liza. It didnt: not all of it; and I dont care who hears me say it. Mrs Pearce knows.

Higgins. What was wrong, Mrs Pearce?

Mrs. pearce (*blandly*). Oh, nothing, sir. It doesnt matter.

Liza. I had a good mind to break it. I didnt know which way to look. But I hung a towel over it, I did.

Higgins. Over what?

Mrs Pearce. Over the looking-glass, sir.

Higgins. Doolittle: you have brought your daughter up too strictly.

Doolittle. Me! I never brought her up at all, except to give her a lick of a strap now and again. Dont put it on me, Governor. She aint accustomed to it, you see: thats all. But she'll soon pick up your free-and-easy ways.

Liza. I'm a good girl, I am; and I wont pick up no free-and-easy ways.

Higgins. Eliza: if you say again that youre a good girl, your father shall take you home.

Liza. Not him. You dont know my father. All he come here for was to touch you for some money to get drunk on.

Doolittle. Well, what else would I want money for? To put into the plate in church, I suppose. (*She puts out her tongue at him. He is so* <u>incensed</u> *by this that* PICKERING *presently finds it necessary to step between them.*) Dont you give me none of your lip; and dont let me hear you giving this gentleman any of it neither, or youll hear from me about it. See?

Higgins. Have you any further advice to give her before you go, Doolittle? Your blessing, for instance.

---

20. **towel horse.** A metal rack with hot water in it to make towels warm

❶
In what way does Higgins almost immediately violate his promise to Mrs. Pearce?

❷
What does Liza's speech reveal about the plight of poor people in Shaw's day? How does this passage reveal Shaw's compassion?

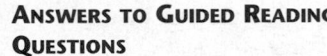

Answers to Guided Reading Questions

❶ Higgins uses inappropriate language.

❷ Shaw points out that the reason the poor in his time were dirty is that they did not have adequate bathing facilities. It seems as if Shaw believes the poor should be provided with these necessities.

Historical Note

Students may find the passage on the looking glass puzzling. Discuss with students how this passage is to be understood. If necessary, explain that in some circles a looking glass was considered a vain and improper furnishing for a house. This explains Higgins's rebuke to Doolittle that he has brought up his daughter too strictly, and Doolittle's rejoinder that Liza will soon pick up such "free-and-easy ways" as regularly consulting in a mirror. A mirror was also an expensive item at one time. In addition, Liza is so modest that she can't bear to see herself in the mirror without clothes on.

ANSWER TO GUIDED READING QUESTION

❶ By insisting that her old acquaintances are no longer her friends, Liza demonstrates that she is vindictive and ready to abandon those whom she once knew. In other words, Liza shows she has faults.

ADDITIONAL QUESTIONS AND ACTIVITIES

Explain to students that people have various ways of manipulating others, including bullying, coaxing, crying, and playing the martyr or victim. One technique commonly used by parents of very small children is to offer a reason to defer a proposed activity in the hopes that the desire for the activity will soon be forgotten. Pickering uses this manipulation strategy when he says to Liza that she should wait to confront her old acquaintances "til we get you something really fashionable." Higgins's actions are frequently directed toward controlling others and making them do as he wishes. Have students list other manipulation strategies used in this act of the play.

ANSWERS TO SELECTION CHECK TEST 4.12.3

EX. Why did Colonel Pickering visit Henry Higgins?
He visited to see Henry's phonetic laboratory.

1. What does the flower girl want from Higgins?
She wants to take lessons from him so that she can sell flowers in a shop.

2. What bet does Pickering make with Higgins?
If Higgins can turn the flower girl into a lady, Pickering will pay all of the expenses.

3. Who comes looking for Liza?
Her father comes to look for her.

4. What does Higgins give to Liza's father?
Higgins gives him a five-pound note.

5. Why does Liza decide to wait to go to Tottenham Court Road?
She decides to wait for her fashionable clothes.

1016 TEACHER'S EDITION

DOOLITTLE. No, Governor: I aint such a mug as to put up my children to all I know myself. Hard enough to hold them in without that. If you want Eliza's mind improved, Governor, you do it yourself with a strap. So long, gentlemen. (*He turns to go.*)

HIGGINS (*impressively*). Stop. Youll come regularly to see your daughter. It's your duty, you know. My brother is a clergyman; and he could help you in your talks with her.

DOOLITTLE (*evasively*). Certainly. I'll come, Governor. Not just this week, because I have a job at a distance. But later on you may depend on me. Afternoon, gentlemen. Afternoon, maam. (*He takes off his hat to* MRS PEARCE, *who* <u>disdains</u> *the salutation and goes out. He winks at* HIGGINS, *thinking him probably a fellow sufferer from* MRS PEARCE's *difficult disposition, and follows her.*)

LIZA. Dont you believe the old liar. He'd as soon you set a bull-dog on him as a clergyman. You wont see him again in a hurry.

HIGGINS. I dont want to, Eliza. Do you?

LIZA. Not me. I dont want never to see him again, I dont. He's a disgrace to me, he is, collecting dust, instead of working at his trade.

PICKERING. What is his trade, Eliza?

LIZA. Taking money out of other people's pockets into his own. His proper trade's a navvy;[21] and he works at it sometimes too—for exercise—and earns good money at it. Aint you going to call me Miss Doolittle any more?

PICKERING. I beg your pardon, Miss Doolittle. It was a slip of the tongue.

❶ What elements in Liza's speech show that Shaw did not sentimentalize even his sympathetic characters?

LIZA. Oh, I dont mind; only it sounded so genteel. I should just like to take a taxi to the corner of Tottenham Court Road and get out there and tell it to wait for me, just to put the girls in their place a bit. I wouldnt speak to them, you know.

PICKERING. Better wait til we get you something really fashionable.

HIGGINS. Besides, you shouldnt cut your old friends now that you have risen in the world. Thats what we call snobbery.

LIZA. You dont call the like of them my friends now, I should hope. Theyve took it out of me often enough with their ridicule when they had the chance; and now I mean to get a bit of my own back. But if I'm to have fashionable clothes, I'll wait. I should like to have some. Mrs Pearce says youre going to give me some to wear in bed at night different to what I wear in the daytime; but it do seem a waste of money when you could get something to shew.[22] Besides, I never could fancy changing into cold things on a winter night.

MRS PEARCE (*coming back*). Now, Eliza. The new things have come for you to try on.

LIZA. Ah-ow-oo-ooh! (*She rushes out.*)

MRS PEARCE (*following her*). Oh, dont rush about like that, girl. (*She shuts the door behind her.*)

HIGGINS. Pickering: we have taken on a stiff job.

PICKERING (*with conviction*). Higgins: we have.

---

21. **navvy.** Common laborer
22. **shew.** Archaic spelling of *show*

W

WORDS FOR EVERYDAY USE:　　**dis • dain** (dis dān´) *vt.,* regard with contempt or scorn

---

VOCABULARY IN CONTEXT

• After the defendant had proved his innocence, he strode out of the court, <u>disdaining</u> to notice his accusers.

RESPONDING TO THE SELECTION

Students may be able to identify gender prejudices by thinking of books, films, or television programs in which the characters behaved offensively because of their prejudices against the opposite gender.

Responding to the Selection

Are any of us immune from gender biases? Do both men and women have prejudices regarding one another's behavior, attitudes, or nature? Think of examples of prejudices that appear in both men and women and write about these in your journal.

Reviewing the Selection

RECALLING

1. Why does Liza come to Higgins for speech lessons?

2. How does Higgins tempt Liza into accepting the lessons and being made into a lady?

3. According to Higgins, what is the basic trouble between men and women?

4. What is the flaw in Doolittle's claim that he wants his daughter back?

INTERPRETING

▶▶ 5. What indicates that Liza is not content with being a simple flower girl?

▶▶ 6. What are Liza's reactions to Higgins's offer? What do her reactions reveal about her?

▶▶ 7. In this scene, which relationship characterizes the conflict Higgins sees between men and women?

▶▶ 8. How is Doolittle's relationship to Higgins similar to that of Liza to Pickering in act one?

SYNTHESIZING

9. Higgins's remark about men and women suggests that there are irreconcilable differences between them. In what way do the actions of Doolittle and Liza support or refute this claim?

10. What attitudes of men of high social standing are revealed in Colonel Pickering's challenge to Higgins?

Understanding Literature (Questions for Discussion)

Satire. Satire is humorous writing or speech intended to point out errors, falsehoods, foibles, or failings. What does the characterization of Higgins reveal about upper-class people and their attitudes toward people of the lower classes? How does the characterization of Mrs. Pearce help to sharpen the portrait of Higgins by providing a contrast, or **foil?** How do Doolittle's speeches satirize the upper and the lower classes?

RECALLING

1. Liza wants to change the way she speaks so that she can obtain a job selling flowers in a shop.

2. Higgins tempts Liza by suggesting that if she learns from him, men will become interested in her and will give her chocolate, taxi rides, and gold and diamonds, and then she shall marry an officer.

3. Higgins believes that men and women want to live different kinds of lives.

4. Although Doolittle claims he wants her back, he repeatedly refuses opportunities to take her.

INTERPRETING

Responses will vary. Possible responses are given.

5. Liza's desire to better her position indicates that she is not content with being a flower girl.

6. Liza responds by saying that she is a good girl, implying that she cannot be bought by material rewards. Her reaction reveals that she cares for herself and has a strong moral sense.

7. The relationship between Liza and Higgins reflects the conflict Higgins sees between the genders.

8. Doolittle is trying to obtain money from Higgins without being accused of impropriety, just as Liza was trying to obtain money from Pickering.

SYNTHESIZING

Responses will vary. Possible responses are given.

9. Their actions demonstrate that Doolittle cares little for his daughter's moral condition; Liza, however, cares a great deal for it. Furthermore, there is little love between father and daughter. Both of these circumstances support Higgins's position.

10. Pickering's challenge reveals that some men of his class believe women are to be treated well, no matter what class they belong to, and that the behavior of men should be up to the highest moral standard.

ANSWERS FOR UNDERSTANDING LITERATURE

▶ See the evaluation forms for discussion, active listening, and oral communication, *Assessment Portfolio,* 7.11–7.14.

Responses will vary. Possible responses are given.

Satire. The characterization of Higgins suggests that upper-class people view people of the lower classes as little better than animals who lack feelings and who should simply be told what to do. The characterization of Mrs. Pearce sharpens that of Higgins. She insists that Liza be made to understand what she is becoming involved in, and her class prejudices do not dehumanize the lower class. Doolittle's speeches satirize the hypocrisy of both classes. He pretends to have high standards only to extort money. He suggests that only the well-off can afford to have moral standards.

Photograph © 1995 Michael Romanos

> *The shallow depression in the west of these islands is likely to move slowly in an easterly direction. There are no indications of any great change in the barometrical situation.*

ACT THREE

It is MRS HIGGINS's *at-home day*. Nobody has yet arrived. Her drawing room, in a flat[1] on Chelsea Embankment, has three windows looking on the river; and the ceiling is not so lofty as it would be in an older house of the same *pretension*. The windows are open, giving access to a balcony with flowers in pots. If you stand with your face to the windows, you have the fireplace on your left and the door in the right-hand wall close to the corner nearest the windows.

MRS HIGGINS *was brought up on Morris[2] and Burne Jones;[3] and her room, which is very unlike her son's room in Wimpole Street, is not crowded with furniture and little tables and nicknacks. In the middle of the room there is a big ottoman;[4] and this, with the carpet, the Morris wall-papers, and the Morris chintz[5] window curtains and brocade covers of the ottoman and its cushions, supply all the ornament, and are much too handsome to be hidden by odds and ends of useless things. A few good oil-paintings from the exhibitions in the Grosvenor Gallery thirty years ago (the Burne Jones, not the Whistler[6] side of them) are on the walls. The only landscape is a Cecil Lawson[7] on the scale of a Rubens.[8] There is a portrait of Mrs Higgins as she was when she defied fashion in her youth in one of the beautiful Rossettian[9] costumes which, when*

caricatured by people who did not understand, led to the absurdities of popular esthetcism in the eighteen-seventies.

In the corner diagonally opposite the door MRS HIGGINS, *now over sixty and long past taking the trouble to dress out of the fashion, sits writing at an elegantly simple writing table with a bell button within reach of her hand. There is a Chippendale[10] chair further back in the room between her and the window nearest her side. At the other side of the room, further forward, is an Elizabethan chair roughly carved in the taste of Inigo Jones.[11] On the same side a piano in a decorated case. The corner between the fireplace and the window is occupied by a divan cushioned in Morris chintz.*

It is between four and five in the afternoon.

The door is opened violently; and HIGGINS *enters with his hat on.*

MRS HIGGINS (*dismayed*). Henry (*scolding him*)! What are you doing here today? It is my at-home day: you promised not to come. (*As he bends to kiss her, she takes his hat off, and presents it to him.*)

HIGGINS. Oh bother! (*He throws the hat down on the table.*)

MRS HIGGINS. Go home at once.

HIGGINS (*kissing her*). I know, mother. I came on purpose.

---

1. **flat.** Apartment or suite of rooms
2. **Morris.** William Morris (1834–1896), English artist and designer
3. **Burne Jones.** Sir Edward Coley Burne-Jones (1833–1898), English painter and designer
4. **ottoman.** Low cushioned seat without back or arms
5. **chintz.** Glazed cotton cloth, often printed with flowers or other colorful patterns
6. **Whistler.** James Abbot McNeill Whistler (1834–1903), U. S. painter and etcher

7. **Cecil Lawson.** English landscape painter (1851–1882)
8. **Rubens.** Peter Paul Rubens (1577–1640), Flemish painter who often painted on very large canvases
9. **Rossettian.** In the style of Dante Gabriel Rossetti (1828–1882), English poet and painter, brother of Christina Rossetti (see page 767)
10. **Chippendale.** Thomas Chippendale (1712–1779), English furniture-maker
11. **Inigo Jones.** English architect and stage designer (1573–1652)

WORDS FOR EVERYDAY USE:

pre • ten • sion (prē ten´shən) *n.*, a showy display of wealth

bro • cade (brō kād´) *n.*, cloth with a raised design woven into it

car • i • ca • ture (kar´i kə chər´) *vt.*, depict in a style involving exaggeration for satirical effect

es • thet • i • cism (es thet´ə siz´əm) *n.*, doctrine that artistic principles should underlie values

---

VOCABULARY IN CONTEXT

- His expensive car perfectly accorded with his vast house and other indications of <u>pretension</u>.
- The weaver produced <u>brocade</u> belts on a small hand loom.
- The employees were unaware that the president of the company was watching them as they <u>caricatured</u> their ineffective manager.
- People who oppose <u>estheticism</u> deny that art is a means to achieving moral good, believing instead that art is an end in itself.

ADDITIONAL QUESTIONS AND ACTIVITIES

Students can write an updated, American version of the description of Mrs. Higgins's drawing room. Before they begin, they should consider what qualities of Mrs. Higgins Shaw was trying to convey by the decor of her drawing room and what contemporary art and furnishings would convey the same impression today.

LITERARY/ART NOTE

Refer students to the decorative pages from Chaucer's *The Canterbury Tales*, illustrated by William Morris, on page 188. A biographical note on William Morris appears on the same page of this *Annotated Teacher's Edition*. Also refer students to the painting by Burne-Jones on page 133. A biographical note on Burne-Jones appears on the same page in this *Annotated Teacher's Edition*.

ANSWERS FOR SELECTION CHECK TEST 4.12.5

EX. Where does Higgins take Liza at the beginning of act III?
He takes her to his mother's at-home day.

1. Who comes to visit?
Mrs. Eynsford Hill, Clara, and Freddy, people Henry recognizes from the portico of St. Paul's Church, come to visit.

2. What does Liza suspect about her aunt's death?
She suspects that the people who stole her hat "done her in," or killed her.

3. For what type of situation does Mrs. Higgins think Liza's language is proper?
She says Liza's language is proper for a canal barge.

4. What problem does Mrs. Higgins foresee?
She foresees the problem of what is to be done with Liza when the experiment is completed.

5. What does Mrs. Higgins exclaim at the end of the scene?
She exclaims, "Oh, men! men!! men!!!"

MRS HIGGINS. But you mustnt. I'm serious, Henry. You offend all my friends: they stop coming whenever they meet you.

HIGGINS. Nonsense! I know I have no small talk; but people dont mind. (*He sits on the settee.*)

MRS HIGGINS. Oh! dont they? Small talk indeed! What about your large talk? Really, dear, you mustnt stay.

HIGGINS. I must. Ive a job for you. A phonetic job.

MRS HIGGINS. No use, dear, I'm sorry; but I cant get round your vowels; and though I like to get pretty postcards in your patent shorthand, I always have to read the copies in ordinary writing you so thoughtfully send me.

HIGGINS. Well, this isnt a phonetic job.

MRS HIGGINS. You said it was.

HIGGINS. Not your part of it. Ive picked up a girl.

MRS HIGGINS. Does that mean that some girl has picked you up?

HIGGINS. Not at all. I dont mean a love affair.

MRS HIGGINS. What a pity!

HIGGINS. Why?

MRS HIGGINS. Well, you never fall in love with anyone under forty-five. When will you discover that there are some rather nice-looking young women about?

HIGGINS. Oh, I cant be bothered with young women. My idea of a lovable woman is something as like you as possible. I shall never get into the way of seriously liking young women: some habits lie too deep to be changed. (*Rising abruptly and walking about, jingling his money and his keys in his trouser pockets*) Besides, theyre all idiots.

MRS HIGGINS. Do you know what you would do if you really loved me, Henry?

❶
Why has Higgins invited Liza to his mother's apartment?

HIGGINS. Oh bother! What? Marry, I suppose?

MRS HIGGINS. No. Stop fidgeting and take your hands out of your pockets. (*With a gesture of despair, he obeys and sits down again.*) Thats a good boy. Now tell me about the girl.

HIGGINS. She's coming to see you.

MRS HIGGINS. I dont remember asking her.

HIGGINS. You didnt. *I* asked her. If youd known her you wouldnt have asked her.

MRS HIGGINS. Indeed! Why?

HIGGINS. Well, it's like this. She's a common flower girl. I picked her off the kerbstone.

MRS HIGGINS. And invited her to my at-home!

HIGGINS (*rising and coming to her to coax her*). Oh, thatll be all right. Ive taught her to speak properly; and she has strict orders as to her behavior. She's to keep to two subjects: the weather and everybody's health—Fine day and How do you do, you know—and not to let herself go on things in general. That will be safe.

MRS HIGGINS. Safe! To talk about our health! about our insides! perhaps about our outsides! How could you be so silly, Henry?

HIGGINS (*impatiently*). Well, she must talk about something. (*He controls himself and sits down again.*) Oh, she'll be all right: dont you fuss. Pickering is in it with me. Ive a sort of bet on that I'll pass her off as a duchess in six months. I started on her some months ago; and she's getting on like a house on fire. I shall win my bet. She has a quick ear; and she's been easier to teach than my middle-class pupils because she's had to learn a complete new language. She talks English almost as you talk French.

LITERARY TECHNIQUE

Foreshadowing is the act of presenting materials that hint at events to occur later in a story. Have students consider what Higgins's comments might foreshadow. Ask students:

1. What is Higgins's idea of a lovable woman?
2. Does Higgins believe he is the kind of person who could become attached to a younger woman?
3. What significance do these remarks have in the play? Do you think they foreshadow Higgins's even-

tually falling in love with Liza, or his being unable to fall in love with Liza?

Answers. 1. Higgins's idea of a lovable woman is someone as much like his mother as possible. 2. Higgins believes he will never seriously like a woman younger than himself. 3. *Responses will vary.* In a way, Higgins's comments foreshadow both of these outcomes: he does grow fond of Liza, but he is unable to view her in romantic terms.

MRS HIGGINS. Thats satisfactory, at all events.

HIGGINS. Well, it is and it isnt.

MRS HIGGINS. What does that mean?

HIGGINS. You see, Ive got her pronunciation all right; but you have to consider not only how a girl pronounces, but what she pronounces; and thats where—

(*They are interrupted by the* PARLORMAID *announcing guests.*)

THE PARLORMAID. Mrs and Miss Eynsford Hill. (*She withdraws.*)

HIGGINS. Oh Lord! (*He rises; snatches his hat from the table; and makes for the door; but before he reaches it his mother introduces him.*)

(MRS *and* MISS EYNSFORD HILL *are the mother and daughter who sheltered from the rain in Covent Garden. The mother is well bred, quiet, and has the habitual anxiety of* straitened *means. The daughter has acquired a gay air of being very much at home in society: the bravado of genteel poverty.*)

MRS EYNSFORD HILL (*to* MRS HIGGINS). How do you do? (*They shake hands.*)

MISS EYNSFORD HILL. How d'you do? (*She shakes.*)

MRS HIGGINS (*introducing*). My son Henry.

MRS EYNSFORD HILL. Your celebrated son! I have so longed to meet you, Professor Higgins.

HIGGINS (*glumly, making no movement in her direction*). Delighted. (*He backs against the piano and bows* brusquely.)

MISS EYNSFORD HILL (*going to him with confident familiarity*). How do you do?

HIGGINS (*staring at her*). Ive seen you before somewhere. I havnt the ghost of a notion where; but Ive heard your voice. (*Drearily*) It doesnt matter. Youd better sit down.

MRS HIGGINS. I'm sorry to say that my celebrated son has no manners. You mustnt mind him.

MISS EYNSFORD HILL (*gaily*). I dont. (*She sits in the Elizabethan chair.*)

MRS EYNSFORD HILL (*a little bewildered*). Not at all. (*She sits on the ottoman between her daughter and* MRS HIGGINS, *who has turned her chair away from the writing-table.*)

HIGGINS. Oh, have I been rude? I didnt mean to be.

(*He goes to the central window, through which, with his back to the company, he contemplates the river and the flowers in Battersea Park on the opposite bank as if they were a frozen desert.*)

(*The* PARLORMAID *returns, ushering in* PICKERING.)

THE PARLORMAID. Colonel Pickering. (*She withdraws.*)

PICKERING. How do you do, Mrs Higgins?

MRS HIGGINS. So glad youve come. Do you know Mrs Eynsford Hill—Miss Eynsford Hill? (*Exchange of bows. The* COLONEL *brings the Chippendale chair a little forward between* MRS HILL *and* MRS HIGGINS, *and sits down.*)

PICKERING. Has Henry told you what weve come for?

❶
What does Higgins's comment foreshadow?

WORDS FOR EVERYDAY USE:

strait • en (strāt´n) *vt.*, subject to privation or deficiency, especially of funds

brusque • ly (brusk´lē) *adv.*, abrupt or curt in manner

VOCABULARY IN CONTEXT

• Although I wanted to go to the concert, I couldn't afford the ticket in my straitened circumstances.
• Though Jill spoke brusquely to me at first, when she found I had really not forgotten her birthday, she changed her tune.

ANSWER TO GUIDED READING QUESTION

❶ According to Higgins, hypocrisy conceals the fact that people are really savages with no genuine knowledge of culture.

ADDITIONAL QUESTIONS AND ACTIVITIES

Students can write the speech Higgins would deliver to the Eynsford Hills if he really did "come out now" and say what he thinks. After volunteers have shared their work with the class, discuss what each character in the scene would probably say if he or she spoke exactly what he or she thought.

HIGGINS (*over his shoulder*). We were interrupted: damn it!

MRS HIGGINS. Oh Henry, Henry, really!

MRS EYNSFORD HILL (*half rising*). Are we in the way?

MRS HIGGINS (*rising and making her sit down again*). No, no. You couldnt have come more fortunately: we want you to meet a friend of ours.

HIGGINS (*turning hopefully*). Yes, by George! We want two or three people. Youll do as well as anybody else.

(*The* PARLORMAID *returns, ushering in* FREDDY.)

THE PARLORMAID. Mr Eynsford Hill.

HIGGINS (*almost audibly, past endurance*). God of Heaven! another of them.

FREDDY (*shaking hands with* MRS HIGGINS). Ahdedo?

MRS HIGGINS. Very good of you to come. (*Introducing*) Colonel Pickering.

FREDDY (*bowing*). Ahdedo?

MRS HIGGINS. I dont think you know my son, Professor Higgins.

FREDDY (*going to* HIGGINS). Ahdedo?

HIGGINS (*looking at him much as if he were a pickpocket*). I'll take my oath Ive met you before somewhere. Where was it?

FREDDY. I dont think so.

HIGGINS (*resignedly*). It dont matter, anyhow. Sit down.

He shakes FREDDY's *hand, and almost slings him on to the ottoman with his face to the windows; then comes round to the other side of it.*

❶ Why does Higgins say hypocrisy is necessary? What social function does it serve?

HIGGINS. Well, here we are, anyhow! (*He sits down on the ottoman next to* MRS EYNSFORD HILL, *on her left.*) And now, what the devil are we going to talk about until Eliza comes?

MRS HIGGINS. Henry: you are the life and soul of the Royal Society's <u>soirées</u>; but really youre rather trying on more commonplace occasions.

HIGGINS. Am I? Very sorry. (*Beaming suddenly*) I suppose I am, you know. (*Uproariously*) Ha, ha!

MISS EYNSFORD HILL (*who considers* HIGGINS *quite eligible matrimonially*). I sympathize. *I* havnt any small talk. If people would only be frank and say what they really think!

HIGGINS (*relapsing into gloom*). Lord forbid!

MRS EYNSFORD HILL (*taking up her daughter's cue*). But why?

HIGGINS. What they think they ought to think is bad enough, Lord knows; but what they really think would break up the whole show. Do you suppose it would be really agreeable if I were to come out now with what *I* really think?

MISS EYNSFORD HILL (*gaily*). Is it so very cynical?

HIGGINS. Cynical! Who the dickens said it was cynical? I mean it wouldnt be decent.

MRS EYNSFORD HILL (*seriously*). Oh! I'm sure you dont mean that, Mr Higgins.

HIGGINS. You see, we're all savages, more or less. We're supposed to be civilized and cultured—to know all about poetry and philosophy and art and science,

---

WORDS FOR EVERYDAY USE: **soi • rée** (swä rā´) *n.*, evening party and so on; but how many of us know even the meanings of these names? (*To* MISS HILL) What do you know of poetry? (*To* MRS HILL) What do you know of science? (*Indicating* FREDDY) What does he know of art or science or anything else? What the devil do you imagine I know of philosophy?

MRS HIGGINS (*warningly*). Or of manners, Henry?

THE PARLORMAID (*opening the door*). Miss Doolittle. (*She withdraws.*)

HIGGINS (*rising hastily and running to* MRS HIGGINS). Here she is, mother. (*He stands on tiptoe and makes signs over his mother's head to* ELIZA *to indicate to her which lady is her hostess.*)

(ELIZA, *who is exquisitely dressed, produces an impression of such remarkable distinction and beauty as she enters that they all rise, quite fluttered. Guided by* HIGGINS's *signals, she comes to* MRS HIGGINS *with studied grace.*)

LIZA (*speaking with* pedantic *correctness of pronunciation and great beauty of tone*). How do you do, Mrs Higgins? (*She gasps slightly in making sure of the H in* HIGGINS, *but is quite successful.*) Mr Higgins told me I might come.

MRS HIGGINS (*cordially*). Quite right: I'm very glad indeed to see you.

PICKERING. How do you do, Miss Doolittle?

LIZA (*shaking hands with him*). Colonel Pickering, is it not?

MRS EYNSFORD HILL. I feel sure we have met before, Miss Doolittle. I remember your eyes.

LIZA. How do you do? (*She sits down on the ottoman gracefully in the place just left vacant by* HIGGINS.)

MRS EYNSFORD HILL (*introducing*). My daughter Clara.

LIZA. How do you do?

CLARA (*impulsively*). How do you do? (*She sits down on the ottoman beside* ELIZA, *devouring her with her eyes.*)

FREDDY (*coming to their side of the ottoman*). Ive certainly had the pleasure.

MRS EYNSFORD HILL (*introducing*). My son Freddy.

LIZA. How do you do?

(FREDDY *bows and sits down in the Elizabethan chair*, infatuated.)

HIGGINS (*suddenly*). By George, yes: it all comes back to me! (*They stare at him.*) Covent Garden! (*Lamentably*) What a damned thing!

MRS HIGGINS. Henry, please! (*He is about to sit on the edge of the table.*) Dont sit on my writing-table: youll break it.

HIGGINS (*sulkily*). Sorry.

(*He goes to the divan, stumbling into the fender and over the fire-irons on his way; extricating himself with muttered* imprecations; *and finishing his disastrous journey by throwing himself so impatiently on the divan that he almost breaks it.* MRS HIGGINS *looks at him, but controls herself and says nothing. A long and painful pause ensues.*)

MRS HIGGINS (*at last, conversationally*). Will it rain, do you think?

LIZA. The shallow depression in the west of these islands is likely to move

❶ **What is the source of Liza's answer? What makes this answer inappropriate and therefore humorous?**

ADDITIONAL QUESTIONS AND ACTIVITIES

Discuss with students who demonstrates better manners when Liza first arrives, Higgins or Liza. Point out that Higgins was raised in an environment with good manners, as his mother demonstrates. Why, then, does he not behave better? What does this say about what manners really reflect?
Answers. Liza demonstrates better manners upon first arriving. Higgins does not use good manners because his personality interferes with his willingness to treat other people considerately. This suggests that manners sometimes do reflect a person's thoughtfulness toward others.

ANSWER TO GUIDED READING QUESTION

❶ Liza seems to have derived this comment from a weather report in a newspaper. The answer is too detailed and technical for the situation.

WORDS FOR EVERYDAY USE:

pe • dan • tic (ped´´nt ik) *adj.*, in a manner stressing minor or trivial points of learning

in • fat • u • at • ed (in fach´o͞ot´id) *adj.*, completely overcome by love

im • pre • ca • tion (im´pri kā´shən) *n.*, obscene language, curse

PYGMALION, ACT THREE **1023**

VOCABULARY IN CONTEXT

- The archaeology professor's wife, a brilliant surgeon, literally fainted with boredom when she was cornered by one of his colleagues at a faculty soirée.
- Deep in his pedantic heart the scientist had one spark of wild enthusiasm left.
- The instant I saw Electra, twenty thousand volts leapt between her eyes and mine, and I was infatuated.
- The alert bank guard suspected the priest was phony when he saw him stub his toe and mutter a string of imprecations.

TEACHER'S EDITION **1023**

• To summarize Liza's grim tale of
her aunt's death, students can
rewrite it as if it were the blurb on
the jacket of a mystery novel.

• How does Liza feel about telling
this story? Does she feel uncomfortable? sad? Does she enjoy
telling it? How does she build up
the story? Why do her listeners
find the story so interesting?

Answers. Liza seems to enjoy telling
this story. She continues to add
dark, interesting details. Her listeners are extremely interested
because they are startled by the
nature of her story and intrigued
by the style in which she tells it. It
is different from any visiting day
conversation they have had.

ADDITIONAL QUESTIONS
AND ACTIVITIES

Students can give examples of
the "new small talk" of their own
generation—that is, words they
use in a special meaning among
people their own age. Before citing
examples, students should read
the Language Arts Survey, 2.147,
"Formal and Informal English."

slowly in an easterly direction. There are
no indications of any great change in the
<u>barometrical</u> situation.

FREDDY. Ha! ha! how awfully funny!

LIZA. What is wrong with that, young
man? I bet I got it right.

FREDDY. Killing!

MRS EYNSFORD HILL. I'm sure I hope it
wont turn cold. Theres so much influenza
about. It runs right through our whole
family regularly every spring.

LIZA (*darkly*). My aunt died of influenza:
so they said.

MRS EYNSFORD HILL (*clicks her tongue
sympathetically*)!!!

LIZA (*in the same tragic tone*). But it's my
belief they done the old woman in.

MRS HIGGINS (*puzzled*). Done her in?

LIZA. Y-e-e-e-es, Lord love you! Why
should she die of influenza? She come
through diphtheria right enough the year
before. I saw her with my own eyes.
Fairly blue with it, she was. They all
thought she was dead; but my father he
kept ladling gin down her throat til she
came to so sudden that she bit the bowl
off the spoon.

MRS EYNSFORD HILL (*startled*). Dear me!

LIZA (*piling up the indictment*). What call
would a woman with that strength in her
have to die of influenza? What become of
her new straw hat that should have come
to me? Somebody pinched it; and what I
say is, them as pinched it done her in.

MRS EYNSFORD HILL. What does doing
her in mean?

HIGGINS. (*hastily*). Oh, thats the new
small talk. To do a person in means to kill
them.

MRS EYNSFORD HILL (*to* ELIZA, *horrified*). You surely dont believe that your
aunt was killed?

LIZA. Do I not! Them she lived with
would have killed her for a hat-pin, let
alone a hat.

MRS EYNSFORD HILL. But it cant have
been right for your father to pour spirits
down her throat like that. It might have
killed her.

LIZA. Not her. Gin was mother's milk to
her. Besides, he'd poured so much down
his own throat that he knew the good of it.

MRS EYNSFORD HILL. Do you mean
that he drank?

LIZA. Drank! My word! Something
chronic.

MRS EYNSFORD HILL. How dreadful
for you!

LIZA. Not a bit. It never did him no
harm what I could see. But then he did not
keep it up regular. (*Cheerfully*) On the
burst, as you might say, from time to time.
And always more agreeable when he had a
drop in. When he was out of work, my
mother used to give him fourpence and
tell him to go out and not come back until
he'd drunk himself cheerful and loving-
like. Theres lots of women has to make
their husbands drunk to make them fit to
live with. (*Now quite at her ease*) You see, it's
like this. If a man has a bit of a conscience,
it always takes him when he's sober; and
then it makes him low-spirited. A drop of

WORDS FOR
EVERYDAY USE: bar • o • met • ri • cal (bar´ə me´trik əl) *adj.,* referring to atmospheric pressure

VOCABULARY IN CONTEXT

• A simple container of properly blown glass can be an accurate <u>barometrical</u> instrument.
• The snob did not just snub Sneezy, he sneered, snidely snickered, <u>sniggered</u> snippily, sniffed and
snuffled snootily, and snarled snappishly at him.
• Freep, the new communications specialist, found the place that would be his bunk for the next
century in the <u>forecastle</u> of the space cruiser.

booze just takes that off and makes him happy. (*To* FREDDY, *who is in convulsions of suppressed laughter*) Here! what are you <u>sniggering</u> at?

FREDDY. The new small talk. You do it so awfully well.

LIZA. If I was doing it proper, what was you laughing at? (*To* HIGGINS) Have I said anything I oughtnt?

MRS HIGGINS (*interposing*). Not at all, Miss Doolittle.

LIZA. Well, thats a mercy, anyhow. (*Expansively*) What I always say is—

HIGGINS (*rising and looking at his watch*). Ahem!

LIZA (*looking round at him; taking the hint; and rising*). Well: I must go. (*They all rise.* FREDDY *goes to the door.*) So pleased to have met you. Goodbye. (*She shakes hands with* MRS HIGGINS.)

MRS HIGGINS. Goodbye.

LIZA. Goodbye, Colonel Pickering.

PICKERING. Goodbye, Miss Doolittle. (*They shake hands.*)

LIZA (*nodding to the others*). Goodbye, all.

FREDDY (*opening the door for her*). Are you walking across the Park, Miss Doolittle? If so—

LIZA. Walk! Not bloody likely. (*Sensation.*) I am going in a taxi. (*She goes out.*)

(PICKERING *gasps and sits down.* FREDDY *goes out on the balcony to catch another glimpse of* ELIZA.)

MRS EYNSFORD HILL (*suffering from shock*). Well, I really cant get used to the new ways.

CLARA (*throwing herself discontentedly into the Elizabethan chair*). Oh, it's all right, mamma, quite right. People will think we never go anywhere or see anybody if you are so old-fashioned.

MRS EYNSFORD HILL. I daresay I am very old-fashioned; but I do hope you wont begin using that expression, Clara. I have got accustomed to hear you talking about men as rotters, and calling everything filthy and beastly; though I do think it horrible and unladylike. But this last is really too much. Don't you think so, Colonel Pickering?

PICKERING. Don't ask me. Ive been away in India for several years; and manners have changed so much that I sometimes dont know whether I'm at a respectable dinnertable or in a ship's <u>forecastle</u>.

CLARA. It's all a matter of habit. Theres no right or wrong in it. Nobody means anything by it. And it's so quaint, and gives such a smart emphasis to things that are not in themselves very witty. I find the new small talk delightful and quite innocent.

MRS EYNSFORD HILL (*rising*). Well, after that, I think it's time for us to go.

(PICKERING *and* HIGGINS *rise.*)

CLARA (*rising*). Oh yes: we have three at-homes to go to still. Goodbye, Mrs. Higgins. Goodbye, Colonel Pickering. Goodbye, Professor Higgins.

HIGGINS (*coming grimly at her from the divan, and accompanying her to the door*). Goodbye. Be sure you try on that small talk at the three at-homes. Dont be nervous about it. Pitch it in strong.

❶ They believe that Liza is speaking a fashionable new form of small talk or slang.

❷ Liza's use of the word *bloody* causes a sensation. Many of Liza's comments are out of place in such a gathering, beginning with her remark that "they done the old woman in," and continuing through her story of her aunt's illness.

ADDITIONAL QUESTIONS AND ACTIVITIES

Ask students to imagine what the conversation would have been like if Liza had not been present. Would it be more or less interesting? Why?

❶ *How have Freddy, Clara, and their mother interpreted Liza's odd comments?*

❷ *What in Liza's response causes a sensation? What comments by her throughout the scene are out of place in a society gathering?*

ADDITIONAL QUESTIONS AND ACTIVITIES

1. How does Freddy feel about Liza?

2. Is Freddy's reaction to Liza based on a real assessment of her personality?

3. Do you think Shaw's depiction of Freddy is intended to be satirical? If so, what is it satirizing?

Answers. 1. Freddy is infatuated with Liza. 2. No; Freddy is in love only with her appearance and what he believes her to be. 3. Shaw seems to be satirizing people's readiness to fall in love with an illusion.

LITERARY NOTE

Some literary critics believe that Shaw paralleled the classical myth of Pygmalion by making Liza pass through three stages: first she was the flower girl (corresponding to the unformed ivory from which the mythic Pygmalion made his statue), then the "triumph" of Higgins's art (corresponding to the statue), and finally a free and independent woman (corresponding to the statue brought to life). Discuss this theory with students. Ask: In what sense is Liza like a statue in this scene? In what sense is she simply her constantly irrepressible, lively self? In what sense is Higgins a sculptor?

Answers. Liza is like a statue only in her attempt to live up to the norm established by her "sculptor," Professor Higgins. When she dips into her own life for material for conversation, she is fresh, original, and lively. Higgins tries to "sculpt" or control Liza, treating her like an inanimate object until she is molded in the shape he wants.

CLARA (*all smiles*). I will. Goodbye. Such nonsense, all this early Victorian prudery!

HIGGINS (*tempting her*). Such damned nonsense!

CLARA. Such bloody nonsense!

MRS EYNSFORD HILL (*convulsively*). Clara!

CLARA. Ha! ha! (*She goes out radiant, conscious of being thoroughly up to date, and is heard descending the stairs in a stream of silvery laughter.*)

FREDDY (*to the heavens at large*). Well, I ask you—(*He gives it up, and comes to* MRS HIGGINS.) Goodbye.

MRS HIGGINS (*shaking hands*). Goodbye. Would you like to meet Miss Doolittle again?

FREDDY (*eagerly*). Yes, I should, most awfully.

MRS HIGGINS. Well, you know my days.

FREDDY. Yes. Thanks awfully. Goodbye. (*He goes out.*)

MRS EYNSFORD HILL. Goodbye, Mr Higgins.

HIGGINS. Goodbye. Goodbye.

MRS EYNSFORD HILL (*to* PICKERING). It's no use. I shall never be able to bring myself to use that word.

PICKERING. Dont. It's not compulsory, you know. Youll get on quite well without it.

MRS EYNSFORD HILL. Only, Clara is so down on me if I am not positively reeking with the latest slang. Goodbye.

PICKERING. Goodbye. (*They shake hands.*)

MRS EYNSFORD HILL (*to* MRS HIGGINS). You mustnt mind Clara. (PICKERING, *catching from her lowered tone that this is not meant for him to hear, discreetly joins* HIGGINS *at the window.*) We're so poor! and she gets so few parties, poor child! She doesnt quite know. (MRS HIGGINS, *seeing that her eyes are moist, takes her hand sympathetically and goes with her to the door.*) But the boy is nice. Dont you think so?

MRS HIGGINS. Oh, quite nice. I shall always be delighted to see him.

MRS EYNSFORD HILL. Thank you, dear. Goodbye. (*She goes out.*)

HIGGINS (*eagerly*). Well? Is Eliza presentable? (*He swoops on his mother and drags her to the ottoman, where she sits down in* ELIZA's *place with her son on her left.*)

(PICKERING *returns to his chair on her right.*)

MRS HIGGINS. You silly boy, of course she's not presentable. She's a triumph of your art and of her dressmaker's; but if you suppose for a moment that she doesnt give herself away in every sentence she utters, you must be perfectly cracked about her.

PICKERING. But dont you think something might be done? I mean something to eliminate the sanguinary[12] element from her conversation.

MRS HIGGINS. Not as long as she is in Henry's hands.

HIGGINS (*aggrieved*). Do you mean that my language is improper?

---

12. **sanguinary.** A reference to Liza's conversational use of the slang term *bloody*

WORDS FOR EVERYDAY USE:

con • vul • sive • ly (kən vul´siv lē) *adv.,* in an agitated manner

VOCABULARY IN CONTEXT

• Any attempt we made to approach the fence made the guard dog lunge <u>convulsively</u> at the wire mesh.

MRS HIGGINS. No, dearest: it would be quite proper—say on a canal barge; but it would not be proper for her at a garden party.

HIGGINS (*deeply injured*). Well I must say—

PICKERING (*interrupting him*). Come, Higgins: you must learn to know yourself. I havnt heard such language as yours since we used to review the volunteers in Hyde Park twenty years ago.

HIGGINS (*sulkily*). Oh, well, if you say so, I suppose I dont always talk like a bishop.

MRS HIGGINS (*quieting* HENRY *with a touch*). Colonel Pickering: will you tell me what is the exact state of things in Wimpole Street?

PICKERING (*cheerfully: as if this completely changed the subject*). Well, I have come to live there with Henry. We work together at my Indian Dialects; and we think it more convenient—

MRS HIGGINS. Quite so. I know all about that: it's an excellent arrangement. But where does this girl live?

HIGGINS. With us, of course. Where should she live?

MRS HIGGINS. But on what terms? Is she a servant? If not, what is she?

PICKERING (*slowly*). I think I know what you mean, Mrs Higgins.

HIGGINS. Well, dash me if *I* do! Ive had to work at the girl every day for months to get her to her present pitch. Besides, she's useful. She knows where my things are, and remembers my appointments and so forth.

MRS HIGGINS. How does your housekeeper get on with her?

HIGGINS. Mrs Pearce? Oh, she's jolly glad to get so much taken off her hands; for before Eliza came, she used to have to find things and remind me of my appointments. But she's got some silly bee in her bonnet about Eliza. She keeps saying "You dont think, sir": doesnt she, Pick?

PICKERING. Yes: thats the formula. "You dont think, sir." Thats the end of every conversation about Eliza.

HIGGINS. As if I ever stop thinking about the girl and her confounded vowels and consonants. I'm worn out, thinking about her, and watching her lips and her teeth and her tongue, not to mention her soul, which is the quaintest of the lot.

MRS HIGGINS. You certainly are a pretty pair of babies, playing with your live doll.

HIGGINS. Playing! The hardest job I ever tackled: make no mistake about that, mother. But you have no idea how frightfully interesting it is to take a human being and change her into a quite different human being by creating a new speech for her. It's filling up the deepest gulf that separates class from class and soul from soul.

PICKERING (*drawing his chair closer to* MRS HIGGINS *and bending over to her eagerly*). Yes: it's enormously interesting. I assure you, Mrs Higgins, we take Eliza very seriously. Every week—every day almost—there is some new change. (*Closer again*) We keep records of every stage—dozens of gramophone disks[13] and photographs—

HIGGINS (*assailing her at the other ear*). Yes, by George: it's the most absorbing experiment I ever tackled. She regularly fills our lives up: doesnt she, Pick?

PICKERING. We're always talking Eliza.

HIGGINS. Teaching Eliza.

PICKERING. Dressing Eliza.

MRS HIGGINS. What!

---

13. **gramophone disks.** Phonograph records

Can a person's social class be changed simply by a change in speech and dress? What is Higgins failing to understand?

ANSWER TO GUIDED READING QUESTION

❶ Learning to blend into a new social class requires more than simply changing speech and dress. Higgins does not seem concerned that he is not giving Liza the knowledge and interests that go along with the class she is supposedly entering.

ADDITIONAL QUESTIONS AND ACTIVITIES

Suggest to students that the basis of personal change is self-awareness. Higgins's character remains constant throughout the play because he never gains any awareness of his own character. "Come, Higgins," says Pickering, "you must learn to know yourself"; yet Higgins never does. Students can write in their journals to explain ways that they can become self-aware and open to personality growth.

LITERARY TECHNIQUE

Students can try reading the simultaneous dialogue of Pickering and Higgins to see what kind of effect it would have on the stage. Ask two volunteers to demonstrate it for the class.

ADDITIONAL QUESTIONS AND ACTIVITIES

Ask students the following questions to explore the material on this page.

1. Why, do you think, are Mrs. Pearce and Mrs. Higgins so sure that Liza's future will be a problem?

2. Why do Higgins and Pickering refuse to face the "problem" of what is to become of Liza when the experiment is over?

Answers. 1. Both Mrs. Pearce and Mrs. Higgins are more perceptive and far-seeing than Higgins and Pickering; they also have an innate sympathy for Liza as a woman.

2. *Responses will vary.* One possible reason is that Higgins and Pickering are enjoying Liza's company so much that they are avoiding the thought that the situation will change.

HIGGINS. Inventing new Elizas.

HIGGINS. *(speaking together)* You know, she has the most extraordinary quickness of ear:

PICKERING. I assure you, my dear Mrs Higgins, that girl

HIGGINS. just like a parrot. Ive tried her with every—

PICKERING. is a genius. She can play the piano quite beautifully.

HIGGINS. possible sort of sound that a human being can make—

PICKERING. We have taken her to classical concerts and to music

HIGGINS. Continental dialects, African dialects, Hottentot

PICKERING. halls; and it's all the same to her: she plays everything

HIGGINS. clicks, things it took me years to get hold of; and

PICKERING. she hears right off when she comes home, whether it's

HIGGINS. she picks them up like a shot, right away, as if she had

PICKERING. Beethoven and Brahms or Lehar and Lionel Monckton;

HIGGINS. been at it all her life.

PICKERING. though six months ago, she'd never as much as touched a piano—

MRS HIGGINS *(putting her fingers in her ears, as they are by this time shouting one another down with an intolerable noise)*. Sh-sh-sh—sh! *(They stop.)*

PICKERING. I beg your pardon. *(He draws his chair back apologetically.)*

HIGGINS. Sorry. When Pickering starts shouting nobody can get a word in edgeways.

MRS HIGGINS. Be quiet, Henry. Colonel Pickering: dont you realize that when Eliza walked into Wimpole Street, something walked in with her?

PICKERING. Her father did. But Henry soon got rid of him.

MRS HIGGINS. It would have been more to the point if her mother had. But as her mother didnt something else did.

PICKERING. But what?

MRS HIGGINS *(unconsciously dating herself by the word)*. A problem.

PICKERING. Oh, I see. The problem of how to pass her off as a lady.

HIGGINS. I'll solve that problem. Ive half solved it already.

MRS HIGGINS. No, you two infinitely stupid male creatures: the problem of what is to be done with her afterwards.

HIGGINS. I dont see anything in that. She can go her own way, with all the advantages I have given her.

MRS HIGGINS. The advantages of that poor woman who was here just now! The manners and habits that disqualify a fine lady from earning her own living without giving her a fine lady's income! Is that what you mean?

PICKERING *(indulgently, being rather bored)*. Oh, that will be all right, Mrs Higgins. *(He rises to go.)*

HIGGINS *(rising also)*. We'll find her some light employment.

PICKERING. She's happy enough. Dont you worry about her. Goodbye. *(He shakes her hands as if he were consoling a frightened child, and makes for the door.)*

ADDITIONAL QUESTIONS AND ACTIVITIES

Point out Pickering's use of paternalistic condescension in dealing with Mrs. Higgins ("He shakes her hands as if he were consoling a frightened child"). Ask students how Mrs. Higgins uses the same technique of condescension in this scene. Give evidence that she also resorts to stereotyping.

Answer. She uses condescension in referring to Higgins and Pickering as "you two infinitely stupid

male creatures" and stereotyping in her final utterance of the act, "Oh, men! men!! men!!!"

HIGGINS. Anyhow, theres no good bothering now. The thing's done. Goodbye, mother. (*He kisses her, and follows* PICKERING.)

PICKERING (*turning for a final consolation*). There are plenty of openings. We'll do whats right. Goodbye.

HIGGINS (*to* PICKERING *as they go out together*). Let's take her to the Shakespear exhibition at Earls Court.

PICKERING. Yes: lets. Her remarks will be delicious.

HIGGINS. She'll mimic all the people for us when we get home.

PICKERING. Ripping.[14] (*Both are heard laughing as they go downstairs.*)

MRS HIGGINS (*rises with an impatient bounce, and returns to her work at the writing-table. She sweeps a litter of disarranged papers out of her way; snatches a sheet of paper from her stationery case; and tries resolutely to write. At the third line she gives it up; flings down her pen; grips the table angrily and exclaims*). Oh, men! men!! men!!!

❶
Why does Mrs. Higgins make this exclamation? What characteristic is she imputing to all men?

---

13. **ripping.** British slang for splendid, excellent

Responding to the Selection

Role play a situation similar to the one presented in this act, but using contemporary characters. That is, invent a character who would be wildly out of place at a party for contemporary teenagers, and do an improvisation showing what might happen if your character came to such a party.

Reviewing the Selection

RECALLING

1. When he arrives at his mother's, what skill does Higgins admit that he lacks?

2. Why does Higgins bring Liza to his mother's for a test?

3. What story does Liza tell to the other guests?

4. What problem does Mrs. Higgins foresee for Higgins's experiment with Liza?

INTERPRETING

5. What does the action of this scene show about Higgins's social skills?

6. Why has Liza's first venture into society failed even though her pronunciation has been correct?

7. How do the guests react to Liza's story, and what do their reactions show about the difference between their background and hers?

8. What do Mrs. Higgins's doubts about her son's experiment reveal about her? How does she differ from her son?

ANSWER TO GUIDED READING QUESTION

❶ Mrs. Higgins is exasperated, presumably because Higgins and Pickering refuse to take seriously her objection that her new speech and habits will disqualify Liza from any way of making a living. She seems to impute to all men this stubborn refusal to listen to common sense.

RESPONDING TO THE SELECTION

Unplanned role playing can quickly lead to stereotyping. Ask students not to rely on stereotypes, but to try to make their characters original individuals.

ANSWERS FOR REVIEWING THE SELECTION

RECALLING

1. Higgins cannot make small talk.

2. Higgins seems to feel that practice at his mother's house will help Liza learn not just how to speak, but what to say.

3. Liza tells a story about her aunt dying of influenza, implying that she was killed by someone.

4. Mrs. Higgins believes that Liza will be given the manners and attitudes of a fine lady without any way of earning the income necessary to live like a fine lady.

INTERPRETING

Responses will vary. Possible responses are given.

5. Higgins's social skills are very poor. He is rude, stubborn, and thoughtless.

6. Liza's choice of topics is inappropriate for the circle of people with whom she is speaking.

7. Mrs. Eynsford Hill is sympathetic and horrified; Freddy and Clara are delighted at Liza's manner of telling the story, and do not seem to object to its subject matter. Their reactions indicate that a situation such as Liza describes is completely foreign to their experience.

8. Mrs. Higgins's objection to her son's experiment reveals that she is more thoughtful and foresightful

(cont.)

than Higgins. She differs from her son in being less impulsive and eager to have her own way.

SYNTHESIZING

Responses will vary. Possible responses are given.

9. Both Higgins's brusque manners and Liza's arrival conflict with the other's intention to make small talk. This reflects the larger conflict in the play between people as they are and people as custom requires them to be.

10. In Act One, Higgins was very much the middle-class professor, conspicuously contrasting with the lower-class people with whom he was dealing. In Act Three, Higgins reveals that he is actually quite out of place in a middle-class setting.

Responses will vary. Possible responses are given.

Dramatic Irony. The audience is aware that Liza is from the lower class, while the Eynsford Hills are not. The humor of the story Liza tells lies in the fact that the Eynsford Hills interpret it in terms of their own background, and imagine Liza experiencing it as a member of the middle class. Freddy's infatuation with Liza is ludicrous because he is ignorant of her background and identity. He thinks the words and phrases she chooses are the new small talk, not realizing that they indicate the social class in which she was raised.

---

9. What, in the scene, conflicts with the guests' "small talk," and what larger contrast or conflict in the play does this reveal?

10. What aspect of Higgins's character shown in this scene contrasts with his character as portrayed in act one?

Understanding Literature (Questions for Discussion)

Dramatic Irony. Irony is a difference between appearance and reality. In **dramatic irony,** something is known by the reader or audience but unknown to the characters. What does the audience know about Liza that the other guests do not know? What makes Liza's telling about her aunt's death humorous? Why is it funny when Freddy becomes infatuated by Liza and her command of "the new small talk"?

Photograph © 1995 Michael Romanos

> “ It's been a long day. The garden party, a dinner party, and the opera! Rather too much of a good thing. But you've won your bet, Higgins. Eliza did the trick, and something to spare, eh? ”

ADDITIONAL RESOURCES

READER'S GUIDE
- Selection Worksheet, 12.4

ASSESSMENT PORTFOLIO
- Selection Check Test, 4.12.7
- Selection Test, 4.12.8

ADDITIONAL QUESTIONS AND ACTIVITIES

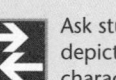 Ask students if the depiction of Shaw's characters shown here matches their own mental pictures of the characters. You might have them discuss the experience of seeing a film or stage version of a novel or play they have read. Is it an exhilarating experience? a disappointing experience? Can it be both?

VOCABULARY FROM THE SELECTION

condescend	pallor
coroneted	perfunctorily
dudgeon	purgatory
millenium	

ANSWERS TO GUIDED READING QUESTIONS

❶ Pickering is learning that Mrs. Pearce becomes upset when people act like slobs and leave their clothing lying around.

❷ The "love letter" turns out to be a bill from a moneylender. Higgins has no room in his life for romance; he is too self-absorbed.

❸ Higgins fails to notice that Liza has brought him his slippers.

ADDITIONAL QUESTIONS AND ACTIVITIES

• Ask students if they notice the mistake of the playwright in the first stage direction of Act Four. *Answer.* In the stage direction, Shaw states that it is a summer night; however, six months have passed since the events of Act One, which (according to the stage direction there) took place during "a heavy summer rain."

• Such errors by authors are not uncommon. A famous error, or perhaps intentional misdirection, by Shakespeare sets Scene iii of Act III of *The Winter's Tale* in a region near the sea in Bohemia. (Bohemia is a landlocked region far from the sea.)

SUPPORT FOR LEP STUDENTS

ADDITIONAL VOCABULARY

flinch—draw back in fear or pain
gorge—stuff; eat a lot
superlatively—better than any other
trivial—unimportant
cant—insincere talk
lavish—spend extravagantly

---

❶ *What is Pickering learning that Higgins has not learned?*

❷ *What is ironic about the actual contents of the letter? What isn't a part of Higgins's life? Why might that be so?*

❸ *What does Higgins fail to notice?*

ACT FOUR

The Wimpole Street laboratory. Midnight. Nobody in the room. The clock on the mantelpiece strikes twelve. The fire is not alight: it is a summer night.

Presently HIGGINS *and* PICKERING *are heard on the stairs.*

HIGGINS (*calling down to* PICKERING). I say, Pick: lock up, will you? I shant be going out again.

PICKERING. Right. Can Mrs Pearce go to bed? We dont want anything more, do we?

HIGGINS. Lord, no!

(ELIZA *opens the door and is seen on the lighted landing in opera cloak, brilliant evening dress, and diamonds, with fan, flowers, and all accessories. She comes to the hearth and switches on the electric lights there. She is tired: her* __pallor__ *contrasts strongly with her dark eyes and hair; and her expression is almost tragic. She takes off her cloak; puts her fan and flowers on the piano; and sits down on the bench, brooding and silent.* HIGGINS, *in evening dress, with overcoat and hat, comes in, carrying a smoking jacket which he has picked up downstairs. He takes off the hat and overcoat; throws them carelessly on the newspaper stand; disposes of his coat in the same way; puts on the smoking jacket; and throws himself wearily into the easy-chair at the hearth.* PICKERING, *similarly attired, comes in. He also takes off his hat and overcoat, and is about to throw them on* HIGGINS's *when he hesitates.*)

PICKERING. I say: Mrs Pearce will row if we leave these things lying about in the drawing room.

HIGGINS. Oh, chuck them over the bannisters into the hall. She'll find them there in the morning and put them away all right. She'll think we were drunk.

PICKERING. We are, slightly. Are there any letters?

HIGGINS. I didnt look. (PICKERING *takes the overcoats and hats and goes downstairs,* HIGGINS *begins half singing half yawning an air from La Fanciulla del Golden West.*[1] *Suddenly he stops and exclaims*) I wonder where the devil my slippers are!

(ELIZA *looks at him darkly; then rises suddenly and leaves the room.*

HIGGINS *yawns again, and resumes his song.* PICKERING *returns, with the contents of the letter-box in his hand.*)

PICKERING. Only circulars, and this __coroneted__ billet-doux[2] for you. (*He throws the circulars into the fender, and posts himself on the hearthrug, with his back to the grate.*)

HIGGINS (*glancing at the billet-doux*). Moneylender. (*He throws the letter after the circulars.*)

(ELIZA *returns with a pair of large down-at-heel slippers. She places them on the carpet before* HIGGINS, *and sits as before without a word.*)

HIGGINS (*yawning again*). Oh Lord! What an evening! What a crew! What a silly tomfoolery! (*He raises his shoe to unlace it, and catches sight of the slippers. He stops unlacing and looks at them as if they had appeared there of their own accord.*) Oh! theyre there, are they?

---

1. **La Fanciulla del Golden West.** An opera by Puccini, *The Girl of the Golden West*
2. **billet-doux.** French term for a love letter (literally a "letter sweet")

WORDS FOR EVERYDAY USE:

pal • lor (pal´ər) *n.*, unnatural paleness
cor • o • net • ed (kôr´ə net´id) *adj.*, with a band of ornamentation

---

VOCABULARY IN CONTEXT

• A few days in the sun after exams will banish your bookish __pallor__.
• The duchess arrived at the ball in a __coroneted__ carriage.
• After Zippy had endured __purgatory__ for five minutes looking through the candy shop window, the door opened and he dashed in.

PICKERING (*stretching himself*). Well, I feel a bit tired. It's been a long day. The garden party, a dinner party, and the opera! Rather too much of a good thing. But youve won your bet, Higgins. Eliza did the trick, and something to spare, eh?

HIGGINS (*fervently*). Thank God it's over!

(ELIZA *flinches violently; but they take no notice of her; and she recovers herself and sits stonily as before.*)

PICKERING. Were you nervous at the garden party? *I* was. Eliza didnt seem a bit nervous.

HIGGINS. Oh, she wasnt nervous. I knew she'd be all right. No: it's the strain of putting the job through all these months that has told on me. It was interesting enough at first, while we were at the phonetics; but after that I got deadly sick of it. If I hadnt backed myself to do it I should have chucked the whole thing up two months ago. It was a silly notion: the whole thing has been a bore.

PICKERING. Oh come! the garden party was frightfully exciting. My heart began beating like anything.

HIGGINS. Yes, for the first three minutes. But when I saw we were going to win hands down, I felt like a bear in a cage, hanging about doing nothing. The dinner was worse: sitting gorging there for over an hour, with nobody but a damned fool of a fashionable woman to talk to! I tell you, Pickering, never again for me. No more artificial duchesses. The whole thing has been simple <u>purgatory</u>.

PICKERING. Youve never been broken in properly to the social routine. (*Strolling over to the piano*) I rather enjoy dipping into it occasionally myself: it makes me feel young again. Anyhow, it was a great success: an immense success. I was quite frightened once or twice because Eliza was doing it so well. You see, lots of the real people cant do it at all: theyre such fools that they think style comes by nature to people in their position; and so they never learn. Theres always something professional about doing a thing superlatively well.

HIGGINS. Yes: thats what drives me mad: the silly people dont know their own silly business. (*Rising*) However, it's over and done with; and now I can go to bed at last without dreading tomorrow.

(ELIZA*'s beauty becomes murderous.*)

PICKERING. I think I shall turn in too. Still, it's been a great occasion: a triumph for you. Goodnight. (*He goes.*)

HIGGINS (*following him*). Goodnight. (*Over his shoulder, at the door*) Put out the lights, Eliza; and tell Mrs Pearce not to make coffee for me in the morning; I'll take tea. (*He goes out.*)

(ELIZA *tries to control herself and feel indifferent as she rises and walks across to the hearth to switch off the lights. By the time she gets there she is on the point of screaming. She sits down in* HIGGINS*'s chair and holds on hard to the arms. Finally she gives way and flings herself furiously on the floor, raging.*)

❶
What interested Higgins? In what did he fail to show interest? What does his failure reveal about his character?

WORDS FOR EVERYDAY USE: pur • ga • to • ry (pur´gə tôr´ē) *n.,* temporary state of suffering or misery

---

❶ Higgins was interested in the phonetic aspects of Liza's transformation, but not the personal aspects. He failed to show interest in Liza as a human being. It shows that he has little compassion or ability to identify with or take interest in others.

LITERARY TECHNIQUE

Aside. Shaw chose not to use a technique students have seen in other works, the aside. Students can write asides for Liza that will express the thoughts and emotions she has as she listens in silence to Pickering and Higgins congratulating themselves on her transformation.

QUOTABLES

❝There are two tragedies in life. One is not to get your heart's desire. The other is to get it.❞

—George Bernard Shaw

HIGGINS (*in despairing wrath outside*).
What the devil have I done with my
slippers? (*He appears at the door.*)

LIZA (*snatching up the slippers, and
hurling them at him one after the other with
all her force*). There are your slippers. And
there. Take your slippers; and may you
never have a day's luck with them!

HIGGINS (*astounded*). What on earth—!
(*He comes to her.*) Whats the matter? Get
up. (*He pulls her up.*) Anything wrong?

LIZA (*breathless*). Nothing wrong—with
you. Ive won your bet for you, havnt I?
Thats enough for you. *I* dont matter, I
suppose.

HIGGINS. You won my bet! You! Presumptuous insect! *I* won it. What did you
throw those slippers at me for?

LIZA. Because I wanted to smash your
face. I'd like to kill you, you selfish brute.
Why didnt you leave me where you
picked me out of—in the gutter? You
thank God it's all over, and that now you
can throw me back again there, do you?
(*She crisps her fingers[3] frantically.*)

HIGGINS (*looking at her in cool wonder*).
The creature is nervous, after all.

LIZA (*gives a suffocated scream of fury, and
instinctively darts her nails at his face*)!!

HIGGINS (*catching her wrists*). Ah! would
you? Claws in, you cat. How dare you
shew your temper to me? Sit down and be
quiet. (*He throws her roughly into the easy-
chair.*)

LIZA (*crushed by superior strength and
weight*). Whats to become of me? Whats
to become of me?

HIGGINS. How the devil do I know
whats to become of you? What does it
matter what becomes of you?

LIZA. You dont care. I know you dont
care. You wouldnt care if I was dead. I'm

❶ *What has Higgins
done wrong?
Why is Liza angry
at him?*

nothing to you—not so much as them
slippers.

HIGGINS (*thundering*). Those slippers.

LIZA (*with bitter submission*). Those
slippers. I didnt think it made any
difference now.

(*A pause.* ELIZA *hopeless and crushed.*
HIGGINS *a little uneasy.*)

HIGGINS (*in his loftiest manner*). Why
have you begun going on like this? May I
ask whether you complain of your treatment here?

LIZA. No.

HIGGINS. Has anybody behaved badly
to you? Colonel Pickering? Mrs Pearce?
Any of the servants?

LIZA. No.

HIGGINS. I presume you dont pretend
that *I* have treated you badly?

LIZA. No.

HIGGINS. I am glad to hear it. (*He
moderates his tone.*) Perhaps youre tired
after the strain of the day. Will you have a
glass of champagne? (*He moves towards the
door.*)

LIZA. No. (*Recollecting her manners*)
Thank you.

HIGGINS (*good-humored again*). This has
been coming on you for some days. I
suppose it was natural for you to be anxious
about the garden party. But thats all over
now. (*He pats her kindly on the shoulder. She
writhes.*) Theres nothing more to worry
about.

LIZA. No. Nothing more for you to
worry about. (*She suddenly rises and gets
away from him by going to the piano bench,*

---

3. **crisps her fingers.** Clenches and unclenches her
hands

where she sits and hides her face.) Oh God! I wish I was dead.

HIGGINS (*staring after her in sincere surprise*). Why? In heaven's name, why? (*Reasonably, going to her*) Listen to me, Eliza. All this irritation is purely subjective.

LIZA. I dont understand. I'm too ignorant.

HIGGINS. It's only imagination. Low spirits and nothing else. Nobody's hurting you. Nothing's wrong. You go to bed like a good girl and sleep it off. Have a little cry and say your prayers: that will make you comfortable.

LIZA. I heard your prayers. "Thank God it's all over!"

HIGGINS (*impatiently*). Well, dont you thank God it's all over? Now you are free and can do what you like.

LIZA (*pulling herself together in desperation*). What am I fit for? What have you left me fit for? Where am I to go? What am I to do? Whats to become of me?

HIGGINS (*enlightened, but not at all impressed*). Oh thats whats worrying you, is it? (*He thrusts his hands into his pockets, and walks about in his usual manner, rattling the contents of his pockets, as if <u>condescending</u> to a trivial subject out of pure kindness.*) I shouldnt bother about it if I were you. I should imagine you wont have much difficulty in settling yourself somewhere or other, though I hadnt quite realized that you were going away. (*She looks quickly at him: he does not look at her, but examines the dessert stand on the piano and decides that he will eat an apple.*) You might marry, you know. (*He bites a large piece out of the apple*

and munches it noisily.) You see, Eliza, all men are not confirmed old bachelors like me and the Colonel. Most men are the marrying sort (poor devils!); and youre not bad-looking: it's quite a pleasure to look at you sometimes—not now, of course, because youre crying and looking as ugly as the very devil; but when youre all right and quite yourself, youre what I should call attractive. That is, to the people in the marrying line, you understand. You go to bed and have a good nice rest; and then get up and look at yourself in the glass; and you wont feel so cheap.

(ELIZA *again looks at him, speechless, and does not stir.*
The look is quite lost on him: he eats his apple with a dreamy expression of happiness, as it is quite a good one.)

HIGGINS (*a genial afterthought occurring to him*). I daresay my mother could find some chap or other who would do very well.

LIZA. We were above that at the corner of Tottenham Court Road.

HIGGINS (*waking up*). What do you mean?

LIZA. I sold flowers. I didn't sell myself. Now youve made a lady of me I'm not fit to sell anything else. I wish youd left me where you found me.

HIGGINS (*slinging the core of the apple decisively into the grate*). Tosh, Eliza. Dont you insult human relations by dragging all this cant about buying and selling into it. You neednt marry the fellow if you dont like him.

LIZA. What else am I to do?

❶
What in this passage reveals Liza's moral superiority?

W **WORDS FOR EVERYDAY USE:** **con • de • scend** (kän´di send´) *vi.*, descend to a less dignified level

---

ANSWER TO GUIDED READING QUESTION

❶ Liza refuses to consider the possibility of a marriage of convenience, equating it with selling herself.

ADDITIONAL QUESTIONS AND ACTIVITIES

Higgins's response to Liza in this scene is anything but romantic. Students can rewrite the discussion between Higgins and Liza (or part of it) as it would be if it were taking place in a popular love story.

LITERARY TECHNIQUE

Myth. A myth is a story that explains objects or events in the natural world as resulting from the action of some supernatural force or entity, most often a god. Considering that Shaw's play is based on Ovid's *Metamorphoses*, you might have students discuss what mystic elements or themes are present in this play. A common character flaw in the hero of Classical Era literature is hubris, or arrogance resulting from excessive pride. Would students describe Higgins's decision to "create" Liza as an act of hubris? Encourage students to note whether or not Higgins falls or suffers as a result of his act of hubris.

VOCABULARY IN CONTEXT
• Jim could tell by the way Peg walked onto the dance floor that she was only <u>condescending</u> to dance with him.

1 It is ironic for Higgins to accuse Liza of a want of feeling, because it is Higgins's, not Liza's, actions that display a want of feeling.

2 Liza is distancing herself from Higgins because she plans to leave. Higgins is surprised because this kind of formality is unusual between them; he may sense that she is distancing herself.

1 *Why is it ironic for Higgins to accuse Liza of a want of feeling?*

HIGGINS. Oh, lots of things. What about your old idea of a florist's shop? Pickering could set you up in one: he's lots of money. (*Chuckling*) He'll have to pay for all those togs you have been wearing today; and that, with the hire of the jewellery, will make a big hole in two hundred pounds. Why, six months ago you would have thought it the <u>millennium</u> to have a flower shop of your own. Come! youll be all right. I must clear off to bed: I'm devilish sleepy. By the way, I came down for something: I forget what it was.

LIZA. Your slippers.

HIGGINS. Oh yes, of course. You shied[4] them at me. (*He picks them up, and is going out when she rises and speaks to him.*)

2 *Why does Liza call him "sir"? Why might Higgins be surprised at this formality?*

LIZA. Before you go, sir—

HIGGINS (*dropping the slippers in his surprise at her calling him Sir*). Eh?

LIZA. Do my clothes belong to me or to Colonel Pickering?

HIGGINS (*coming back into the room as if her question were the very climax of unreason*). What the devil use would they be to Pickering?

LIZA. He might want them for the next girl you pick up to experiment on.

HIGGINS (*shocked and hurt*). Is that the way you feel towards us?

LIZA. I dont want to hear anything more about that. All I want to know is whether anything belongs to me. My own clothes were burnt.

HIGGINS. But what does it matter? Why need you start bothering about that in the middle of the night?

LIZA. I want to know what I may take away with me. I dont want to be accused of stealing.

HIGGINS (*now deeply wounded*). Stealing! You shouldnt have said that, Eliza. That shews a want of feeling.

LIZA. I'm sorry. I'm only a common ignorant girl; and in my station I have to be careful. There cant be any feelings between the like of you and the like of me. Please will you tell me what belongs to me and what doesnt ?

HIGGINS (*very sulky*). You may take the whole damned houseful if you like. Except the jewels. Theyre hired. Will that satisfy you? (*He turns on his heel and is about to go in extreme <u>dudgeon</u>.*)

LIZA (*drinking in his emotion like nectar, and nagging him to provoke a further supply*). Stop, please. (*She takes off her jewels.*) Will you take these to your room and keep them safe? I dont want to run the risk of their being missing.

HIGGINS (*furious*). Hand them over. (*She puts them into his hands.*) If these belonged to me instead of to the jeweller, I'd ram them down your ungrateful throat. (*He <u>perfunctorily</u> thrusts them into his pockets, unconsciously decorating himself with the protruding ends of the chains.*)

LIZA (*taking a ring off*). This ring isnt the jeweller's: it's the one you bought me in Brighton. I dont want it now. (HIGGINS *dashes the ring violently into the fireplace, and turns on her so threateningly that she crouches over the piano with her hands over her face, and exclaims*) Dont you hit me.

---

4. **shied.** Threw or flung sideways

 WORDS FOR EVERYDAY USE:

mil • len • ni • um (mi len´ē əm) *n.,* period of perfection or great prosperity, as in the Golden Age

dudg • eon (duj´ən) *n.,* anger and resentment

per • func • to • ri • ly (pər fuŋk´tə rē lē) *adv.,* in an indifferent or disinterested manner

VOCABULARY IN CONTEXT

- When the <u>millennium</u> comes, the lion and the lamb will be at peace.
- When his favorite television program was dropped from the schedule, Jeb sat down in high <u>dudgeon</u> and wrote a letter to the network.
- Sasha's housecleaning consisted of a dustcloth <u>perfunctorily</u> applied once or twice a week.

HIGGINS. Hit you! You infamous creature, how dare you accuse me of such a thing? It is you who have hit me. You have wounded me to the heart.

LIZA (*thrilling with hidden joy*). I'm glad. Ive got a little of my own back, anyhow.

HIGGINS (*with dignity, in his finest professional style*). You have caused me to lose my temper: a thing that has hardly ever happened to me before. I prefer to say nothing more tonight. I am going to bed.

LIZA (*pertly*). Youd better leave a note for Mrs Pearce about the coffee; for she wont be told by me.

HIGGINS (*formally*). Damn Mrs Pearce; and damn the coffee; and damn you; and damn my own folly in having lavished hard-earned knowledge and the treasure of my regard and intimacy on a heartless guttersnipe. (*He goes out with impressive decorum, and spoils it by slamming the door savagely.*)

(ELIZA *smiles for the first time; expresses her feelings by a wild pantomime in which an imitation of* HIGGINS's *exit is confused with her own triumph; and finally goes down on her knees on the hearthrug to look for the ring.*)

Responding to the Selection

Have you ever thought a change would be for the better but it turned out otherwise? Write about this in your journal, focusing on how the result differed from your expectations, and why you imagined it differently.

RESPONDING TO THE SELECTION

Students who have difficulty identifying such a change can consider those points in life when changes usually occur—moving from one place to another or from one grade in school to another, or adopting a new schedule.

ADDITIONAL QUESTIONS AND ACTIVITIES

Point out to students that in this play Higgins repeatedly threatens Liza with violence. Discuss this with students. Ask students if they think that it was more acceptable for a character in a play in Shaw's time to threaten violence against a woman than it would be in a play written today. In other words, would it be possible today for a character to show such violence and still be considered in any way amiable?

Answers. Judging from the play itself and the context of the instances of threatened physical abuse, it seems to have been considered more forgivable in Shaw's time for a character such as Higgins to threaten violence against a woman than it is today. Anyone who menaced a woman so convincingly that she cowered and protected her face (as in this scene) would today be considered abusive and dangerously disturbed.

ANSWERS FOR SELECTION CHECK TEST 4.12.7

EX. How are Higgins and Pickering dressed?
They are in evening dress.

1. Where had they been that day?
They had been to a garden party, a dinner party, and the opera.

2. What does Liza do when Henry returns to the room?
She throws his slippers at him.

3. Why does Liza wish Higgins had left her where she was?
She thinks she is no longer fit to sell anything but herself.

4. Why does Liza think Pickering might want her to return the clothes he has bought for her?
She thinks he may want them for the next girl they experiment on.

5. What does Liza do with the ring that Henry had given her?
She throws it in the fireplace.

Reviewing the Selection

1. What does Liza do when she, Higgins, and Colonel Pickering return from their social event?

2. What does Higgins look for soon after he enters the room?

3. Has Higgins won his bet with Colonel Pickering? How do you know?

4. What options does Higgins offer Liza for her future?

5. How would you describe Liza's mood at the beginning of the act? How is this mood conveyed?

6. What action illustrates Liza's finally standing up to Higgins and asserting herself?

7. How does Higgins feel about the work he has done with Liza now that the experiment is over?

8. Why do the options that Higgins offers seem distasteful to her?

9. Why is Liza pleased to have hurt Higgins by asking about the clothes and the jewelry?

10. What comments and actions on Higgins's part show that, unknown even to himself, he has grown fond of Liza? How has Liza and Higgins's relationship changed since the beginning of the play? What signifies this change?

Understanding Literature (Questions for Discussion)

Climax. The **climax** is the point of highest interest and suspense in a literary work. What is the climax of this play? What dramatic confrontation occurs to determine the outcome of the relationship between Higgins and Liza?

Photograph © 1995 Michael Romanos

ADDITIONAL RESOURCES

READER'S GUIDE
- Selection Worksheet, 12.5

ASSESSMENT PORTFOLIO
- Selection Check Test, 4.12.9
- Selection Test, 4.12.10

ESSENTIAL SKILLS PRACTICE BOOKS
- *Language*, 2.59

> **❝** *I want a little kindness. I know I'm a common ignorant girl, and you a book-learned gentleman; but I'm not dirt under your feet. What I done . . . what I did was not for the dresses and the taxis: I did it because we were pleasant together and I come—came—to care for you.* **❞**

PYGMALION, ACT FIVE **1039**

ANSWER TO GUIDED READING QUESTION

1 Mrs. Higgins understands that Liza is a person in her own right and not a piece of property.

ADDITIONAL QUESTIONS AND ACTIVITIES

Students can do an improvisation of the telephone conversation between Pickering and the police inspector. They should reread the information about the telephone call given on the first page of Act Five.

SUPPORT FOR LEP STUDENTS

ADDITIONAL VOCABULARY

vehement—forceful
bequest—something left in a will
rogue—scoundrel
contempt—disrespect, scorn

VOCABULARY FROM THE SELECTION

blasphemy	placidly
consort	proffer
impudence	solicitor
incorrigible	spraddle
magnanimous	toady

ACT FIVE

MRS HIGGINS's *drawing room. She is at her writing-table as before. The* PARLORMAID *comes in.*

THE PARLORMAID (*at the door*). Mr Henry, maam, is downstairs with Colonel Pickering.

MRS HIGGINS. Well, shew them up.

THE PARLORMAID. Theyre using the telephone, maam. Telephoning to the police, I think.

MRS HIGGINS. What!

THE PARLORMAID. (*coming further in and lowering her voice*). Mr Henry is in a state, maam. I thought I'd better tell you.

MRS HIGGINS. If you had told me that Mr Henry was not in a state it would have been more surprising. Tell them to come up when theyve finished with the police. I suppose he's lost something.

THE PARLORMAID. Yes, maam (*going*).

MRS HIGGINS. Go upstairs and tell Miss Doolittle that Mr Henry and the Colonel are here. Ask her not to come down til I send for her.

THE PARLORMAID. Yes, maam.

(HIGGINS *bursts in. He is, as the* PARLOR-MAID *has said, in a state.*)

1 *What does Mrs. Higgins understand that her son does not?*

HIGGINS. Look here, mother: heres a confounded thing!

MRS HIGGINS. Yes, dear. Good morning. (*He checks his impatience and kisses her, whilst the* PARLORMAID *goes out.*) What is it?

HIGGINS. Eliza's bolted.

MRS HIGGINS (*calmly continuing her writing*). You must have frightened her.

HIGGINS. Frightened her! nonsense! She was left last night, as usual, to turn out the lights and all that; and instead of going to bed she changed her clothes and

went right off: her bed wasnt slept in. She came in a cab for her things before seven this morning; and that fool Mrs Pearce let her have them without telling me a word about it. What am I to do?

MRS HIGGINS. Do without, I'm afraid, Henry. The girl has a perfect right to leave if she chooses.

HIGGINS (*wandering distractedly across the room*). But I cant find anything. I dont know what appointments Ive got. I'm— (PICKERING *comes in.* MRS HIGGINS *puts down her pen and turns away from the writing-table.*)

PICKERING (*shaking hands*). Good morning, Mrs Higgins. Has Henry told you? (*He sits down on the ottoman.*)

HIGGINS. What does that ass of an inspector say? Have you offered a reward?

MRS HIGGINS (*rising in indignant amazement*). You dont mean to say you have set the police after Eliza.

HIGGINS. Of course. What are the police for? What else could we do? (*He sits in the Elizabethan chair.*)

PICKERING. The inspector made a lot of difficulties. I really think he suspected us of some improper purpose.

MRS HIGGINS. Well, of course he did. What right have you to go to the police and give the girl's name as if she were a thief, or a lost umbrella, or something? Really! (*She sits down again, deeply vexed.*)

HIGGINS. But we want to find her.

PICKERING. We cant let her go like this, you know, Mrs Higgins. What were we to do?

MRS HIGGINS. You have no more sense, either of you, than two children. Why—

(*The* PARLORMAID *comes in and breaks off the conversation.*)

1040 UNIT TWELVE / TWENTIETH-CENTURY DRAMA

ADDITIONAL QUESTIONS AND ACTIVITIES

Explain to students that Shaw's play illustrates one of the contentions of feminist critics of society: that men often objectify women (consider them as things, not people). This is dehumanizing and robs women of their personhood and independence. Discuss how Higgins needs Liza and wants her company, but is incapable of treating her as a human instead of a thing. You may wish to suggest that in

this respect the play echoes the original myth, in which Pygmalion falls in love not with a person, but with a thing that later becomes a person. The myth, in fact, can be seen as an archetypal statement of the objectifying nature of the relationship of men with women.

THE PARLORMAID. Mr Henry: a gentleman wants to see you very particular. He's been sent on from Wimpole Street.

HIGGINS. Oh, bother! I cant see anyone now. Who is it?

THE PARLORMAID. A Mr Doolittle, sir.

PICKERING. Doolittle! Do you mean the dustman?

THE PARLORMAID. Dustman! Oh no, sir: a gentleman.

HIGGINS (*springing up excitedly*). By George, Pick, it's some relative of hers that she's gone to. Somebody we know nothing about. (*To the* PARLORMAID) Send him up, quick.

THE PARLORMAID. Yes, sir. (*She goes.*)

HIGGINS (*eagerly, going to his mother*). Genteel relatives! now we shall hear something. (*He sits down in the Chippendale chair.*)

MRS HIGGINS. Do you know any of her people?

PICKERING. Only her father: the fellow we told you about.

THE PARLORMAID (*announcing*). Mr. Doolittle. (*She withdraws.*)

(DOOLITTLE *enters. He is brilliantly dressed in a new fashionable frock-coat, with white waistcoat and grey trousers. A flower in his buttonhole, a dazzling silk hat, and patent leather shoes complete the effect. He is too concerned with the business he has come on to notice* MRS HIGGINS. *He walks straight to* HIGGINS, *and accosts him with vehement reproach.*)

DOOLITTLE. (*indicating his own person*). See here! Do you see this? You done this.

HIGGINS. Done what, man?

DOOLITTLE. This, I tell you. Look at it. Look at this hat. Look at this coat.

PICKERING. Has Eliza been buying you clothes?

DOOLITTLE. Eliza! not she. Not half. Why would she buy me clothes?

MRS HIGGINS. Good morning, Mr. Doolittle. Wont you sit down?

DOOLITTLE (*taken aback as he becomes conscious that he has forgotten his hostess*). Asking your pardon, maam. (*He approaches her and shakes her <u>proffered</u> hand.*) Thank you. (*He sits down on the ottoman, on* PICKERING's *right.*) I am that full of what has happened to me that I cant think of anything else.

HIGGINS. What the dickens has happened to you?

DOOLITTLE. I shouldnt mind if it had only happened to me: anything might happen to anybody and nobody to blame but Providence, as you might say. But this is something that you done to me: yes, you, Henry Higgins.

HIGGINS. Have you found Eliza? Thats the point.

DOOLITTLE. Have you lost her?

HIGGINS. Yes.

DOOLITTLE. You have all the luck, you have. I aint found her; but she'll find me quick enough now after what you done to me.

MRS HIGGINS. But what has my son done to you, Mr Doolittle?

WORDS FOR EVERYDAY USE:
prof • fer (präf´ər) vt., offer, extend

VOCABULARY IN CONTEXT

- The cabdriver insisted he wanted no tip, but he did take my <u>proffered</u> money.

ADDITIONAL QUESTIONS AND ACTIVITIES

Students can write an essay comparing and contrasting Doolittle's entrance into the middle class with that of Liza. Before writing their essays, students should review the Language Arts Survey, 1.34, "Organizing Ideas: Comparison-and-Contrast Order."

LITERARY NOTE

Despite the fact that Shaw claimed he despised Shakespeare, the two authors share a similar technique—the use of low comic characters to relieve tension. Doolittle, as a proud member of the lower class, a dedicated tavern-goer, and an unwittingly wise orator, bears remarkable resemblance to Shakespearean characters such as Falstaff in *Henry IV,* acts I and II, and the porter in *Macbeth.*

ANSWERS FOR SELECTION CHECK TEST 4.12.9

EX. Why does Higgins call the police?
He calls the police because Liza is missing.

1. Who else is looking for Liza?
Liza's father is looking for her.

2. What does Liza say that Pickering has taught her?
She says Pickering has taught her nice manners and what it feels like to be treated as a lady.

3. Why is Liza's father looking for her?
He wants her to come to his wedding.

4. What excuse does Higgins give for his rudeness toward Liza?
He says it is okay because he treats everybody the same.

5. How does Liza threaten Higgins?
She threatens to advertise in the paper that his duchess was only a flower girl and that she would teach anyone to be a duchess.

ANSWERS TO GUIDED READING QUESTIONS

❶ Doolittle objects to being made a gentleman. He feels he has lost his freedom and his right to ask others for money. (Now that he has money, others request it from him.)

❷ Higgins suggested to Wannafeller that Doolittle was a great moralist. The consequence was that Doolittle gained a large income and became a member of the middle class.

LITERARY TECHNIQUE

Incongruity. Incongruity is the juxtaposition of incompatible things to produce a surprising or humorous effect. Ask students to identify incongruities in the dialogue on this page, or generally in the passage in which Doolittle appears. Examples include Doolittle's appearance versus his claim to be unhappy; Doolittle's lack of morality versus his position as a supposed moralist; Doolittle's "dustman" personality versus his position in the middle class; and the support of the lofty-sounding Moral Reform World League by the ludicrous Pre-digested Cheese Trust.

DOOLITTLE. Done to me! Ruined me. Destroyed my happiness. Tied me up and delivered me into the hands of middle class morality.

HIGGINS (*rising intolerantly and standing over* DOOLITTLE). Youre raving. Youre drunk. Youre mad. I gave you five pounds. After that I had two conversations with you, at half-a-crown an hour. Ive never seen you since.

❶ *To what does Doolittle object? What does he feel he has lost?*

DOOLITTLE. Oh! Drunk! am I? Mad! am I? Tell me this. Did you or did you not write a letter to an old blighter[1] in America that was giving five millions to found Moral Reform Societies all over the world, and that wanted you to invent a universal language for him?

HIGGINS. What! Ezra D. Wannafeller! He's dead. (*He sits down again carelessly.*)

DOOLITTLE. Yes: he's dead; and I'm done for. Now did you or did you not write a letter to him to say that the most original moralist at present in England, to the best of your knowledge, was Alfred Doolittle, a common dustman.

HIGGINS. Oh, after your last visit I remember making some silly joke of the kind.

❷ *What joke did Higgins have at Wannafeller's expense? What were the unexpected consequences of Higgins's joke?*

DOOLITTLE. Ah! You may well call it a silly joke. It put the lid on me right enough. Just give him the chance he wanted to shew that Americans is not like us: that they recognize and respect merit in every class of life, however humble. Them words is in his blooming will, in which, Henry Higgins, thanks to your silly joking, he leaves me a share in his Pre-digested Cheese Trust worth three

thousand a year on condition that I lecture for his Wannafeller Moral Reform World League as often as they ask me up to six times a year.

HIGGINS. The devil he does! Whew! (*Brightening suddenly*) What a lark!

PICKERING. A safe thing for you, Doolittle. They wont ask you twice.

DOOLITTLE. It aint the lecturing I mind. I'll lecture them blue in the face, I will, and not turn a hair. It's making a gentleman of me that I object to. Who asked him to make a gentleman of me? I was happy. I was free. I touched pretty nigh everybody for money when I wanted it, same as I touched you, Henry Higgins. Now I am worrited;[2] tied neck and heels; and everybody touches me for money. It's a fine thing for you, says my <u>solicitor</u>. Is it? says I. You mean it's a good thing for you, I says. When I was a poor man and had a solicitor once when they found a pram in the dust cart, he got me off, and got shut of me and got me shut of him as quick as he could. Same with the doctors: used to shove me out of the hospital before I could hardly stand on my legs, and nothing to pay. Now they finds out that I'm not a healthy man and cant live unless they looks after me twice a day. In the house I'm not let do a hand's turn for myself: somebody else must do it and touch me for it. A year ago I hadnt a relative in the world except two or three that wouldnt speak to me. Now Ive fifty, and not a decent week's wages among the lot

---

1. **old blighter.** British slang for a mean or comtemptible person
2. **worrited.** Worried

WORDS FOR EVERYDAY USE:

so • lic • i • tor (sə lis´it ər) *n.,* lawyer

VOCABULARY IN CONTEXT

• In Great Britain, a lawyer who advises clients and appears for them in lower courts is called a <u>solicitor</u>.

of them. I have to live for others and not for myself: thats middle class morality. You talk of losing Eliza. Dont you be anxious: I bet she's on my doorstep by this: she that could support herself easy by selling flowers if I wasnt respectable. And the next one to touch me will be you, Henry Higgins. I'll have to learn to speak middle class language from you, instead of speaking proper English. Thats where youll come in; and I daresay thats what you done it for.

MRS HIGGINS. But, my dear Mr Doolittle, you need not suffer all this if you are really in earnest. Nobody can force you to accept this bequest. You can repudiate it. Isnt that so, Colonel Pickering?

PICKERING. I believe so.

DOOLITTLE (*softening his manner in deference to her sex*). Thats the tragedy of it, maam. It's easy to say chuck it; but I havnt the nerve. Which of us has? We're all intimidated. Intimidated, maam: thats what we are. What is there for me if I chuck it but the workhouse in my old age? I have to dye my hair already to keep my job as a dustman. If I was one of the deserving poor, and had put by a bit, I could chuck it; but then why should I, acause the deserving poor might as well be millionaires for all the happiness they ever has. They dont know what happiness is. But I, as one of the undeserving poor, have nothing between me and the pauper's uniform but this here blasted three thousand a year that shoves me into the middle class. (Excuse the expression, maam: youd use it yourself if you had my provocation.) Theyve got you every way you turn: it's a choice between the Skilly of the workhouse and the Char Bydis[3] of the middle class; and I havnt the nerve for the workhouse. Intimidated: thats what I am.

Broke. Bought up. Happier men than me will call for my dust, and touch me for their tip; and I'll look on helpless, and envy them. And thats what your son has brought me to. (*He is overcome by emotion.*)

MRS HIGGINS. Well, I'm very glad youre not going to do anything foolish, Mr Doolittle. For this solves the problem of Eliza's future. You can provide for her now.

DOOLITTLE (*with melancholy resignation*). Yes, maam: I'm expected to provide for everyone now, out of three thousand a year.

HIGGINS (*jumping up*). Nonsense! he cant provide for her. He shant provide for her. She doesn't belong to him. I paid him five pounds for her. Doolittle: either youre an honest man or a rogue.

DOOLITTLE (*tolerantly*). A little of both, Henry, like the rest of us: a little of both.

HIGGINS. Well, you took that money for the girl; and you have no right to take her as well.

MRS HIGGINS. Henry: dont be absurd. If you want to know where Eliza is, she is upstairs.

HIGGINS (*amazed*). Upstairs! ! ! Then I shall jolly soon fetch her downstairs. (*He makes resolutely for the door.*)

MRS HIGGINS (*rising and following him*). Be quiet, Henry. Sit down.

HIGGINS. I—

MRS HIGGINS. Sit down, dear; and listen to me.

HIGGINS. Oh very well, very well, very well. (*He throws himself ungraciously on the*

---

3. **Skilly . . . Char Bydis.** A reference to Scylla and Charybdis, a dangerous rock and whirlpool in the waters between Sicily and Italy. They present equal dangers regardless of which course an individual follows.

PYGMALION, ACT FIVE **1043**

❶ *What does Doolittle consider to be "proper English"? Why is it funny that he should describe his speech in that way?*

❷ *What does Higgins still not understand about Liza?*

❸ *How does Doolittle differ from Higgins with regard to cursing? What does this say about him?*

ANSWERS TO GUIDED READING QUESTIONS

❶ Doolittle considers the language of the lower class "proper English." His judgment is humorous because Higgins views middle- and upper-class English as the proper and desirable form of English.

❷ Higgins still views Liza as property.

❸ Doolittle is aware of the effect of his language on others and apologizes for it; Higgins is unaware of the effects of his cursing on others. Doolittle's consciousness suggests that he is more thoughtful toward others than Higgins.

CROSS-CURRICULAR ACTIVITIES

Students can research the situation of retired people in the United States today to learn what percentage live in poverty and what the average income of a retired person is. They should write a statement relating their findings in a general way to the position of Alfred Doolittle.

ANSWERS TO GUIDED READING QUESTIONS

❶ Higgins's disregard for Liza's feelings provoked her to throw the slippers. Higgins doesn't realize how his actions affect other people.

❷ Higgins is furious at the suggestion that he hurt Liza; he prefers to believe that she has wronged him by running away.

ADDITIONAL QUESTIONS AND ACTIVITIES

Students can write a diary account of Liza's thoughts and feelings during the night she spent "partly walking about in a rage, partly trying to throw herself into the river and being afraid to, and partly in the Carlton Hotel."

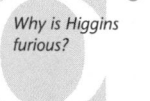

❶ What provocation did Higgins give Liza to throw the slippers? What doesn't he realize about his actions?

❷ Why is Higgins furious?

---

ottoman, with his face towards the windows.) But I think you might have told us this half an hour ago.

MRS HIGGINS. Eliza came to me this morning. She passed the night partly walking about in a rage, partly trying to throw herself into the river and being afraid to, and partly in the Carlton Hotel. She told me of the brutal way you two treated her.

HIGGINS (*bounding up again*). What!

PICKERING (*rising also*). My dear Mrs Higgins, she's been telling you stories. We didnt treat her brutally. We hardly said a word to her; and we parted on particularly good terms. (*Turning on* HIGGINS) Higgins: did you bully her after I went to bed?

HIGGINS. Just the other way about. She threw my slippers in my face. She behaved in the most outrageous way. I never gave her the slightest provocation. The slippers came bang into my face the moment I entered the room—before I had uttered a word. And used perfectly awful language.

PICKERING (*astonished*). But why? What did we do to her?

MRS HIGGINS. I think I know pretty well what you did. The girl is naturally rather affectionate, I think. Isnt she, Mr. Doolittle?

DOOLITTLE. Very tender-hearted, maam. Takes after me.

MRS HIGGINS. Just so. She had become attached to you both. She worked very hard for you, Henry! I dont think you quite realize what anything in the nature of brain work means to a girl like that. Well, it seems that when the great day of trial came, and she did this wonderful thing for you without making a single mistake, you two sat there and never said a word to her, but talked together of how glad you were that it was all over and how

you had been bored with the whole thing. And then you were surprised because she threw your slippers at you! *I* should have thrown the fire-irons[4] at you.

HIGGINS. We said nothing except that we were tired and wanted to go to bed. Did we, Pick?

PICKERING (*shrugging his shoulders*). That was all.

MRS HIGGINS (*ironically*). Quite sure?

PICKERING. Absolutely. Really, that was all.

MRS HIGGINS. You didnt thank her, or pet her, or admire her, or tell her how splendid she'd been.

HIGGINS (*impatiently*). But she knew all about that. We didnt make speeches to her, if thats what you mean.

PICKERING (*conscience stricken*). Perhaps we were a little inconsiderate. Is she very angry?

MRS HIGGINS (*returning to her place at the writing-table*). Well, I'm afraid she wont go back to Wimpole Street, especially now that Mr Doolittle is able to keep up the position you have thrust on her; but she says she is quite willing to meet you on friendly terms and to let bygones be bygones.

HIGGINS (*furious*). Is she, by George? Ho!

MRS HIGGINS. If you promise to behave yourself, Henry, I'll ask her to come down. If not, go home; for you have taken up quite enough of my time.

HIGGINS. Oh, all right. Very well. Pick: you behave yourself. Let us put on our best Sunday manners for this creature that we picked out of the mud. (*He flings himself sulkily into the Elizabethan chair.*)

---

4. **fire-irons.** Metal tools for tending a fireplace

DOOLITTLE (*remonstrating*). Now, now, Henry Higgins! Have some consideration for my feelings as a middle class man.

MRS HIGGINS. Remember your promise, Henry. (*She presses the bell-button on the writing-table.*) Mr. Doolittle: will you be so good as to step out on the balcony for a moment. I dont want Eliza to have the shock of your news until she has made it up with these two gentlemen. Would you mind?

DOOLITTLE. As you wish, lady. Anything to help Henry to keep her off my hands. (*He disappears through the window.*)

(*The* PARLORMAID *answers the bell.* PICKERING *sits down in* DOOLITTLE'*s place.*)

MRS HIGGINS. Ask Miss Doolittle to come down, please.

THE PARLORMAID. Yes, maam. (*She goes out.*)

MRS HIGGINS. Now, Henry: be good.

HIGGINS. I am behaving myself perfectly.

PICKERING. He is doing his best, Mrs Higgins.

(*A pause.* HIGGINS *throws back his head; stretches out his legs; and begins to whistle.*)

MRS HIGGINS. Henry, dearest, you dont look at all nice in that attitude.

HIGGINS (*pulling himself together*). I was not trying to look nice, mother.

MRS HIGGINS. It doesnt matter, dear. I only wanted to make you speak.

HIGGINS. Why?

MRS HIGGINS. Because you cant speak and whistle at the same time.

(HIGGINS *groans. Another very trying pause.*)

HIGGINS (*springing up, out of patience*). Where the devil is that girl? Are we to wait here all day?

(ELIZA *enters, sunny, self-possessed, and giving a staggeringly convincing exhibition of ease of manner. She carries a little workbasket, and is very much at home.* PICKERING *is too much taken aback to rise.*)

LIZA. How do you do, Professor Higgins? Are you quite well?

HIGGINS (*choking*). Am I—(*He can say no more.*)

LIZA. But of course you are: you are never ill. So glad to see you again, Colonel Pickering. (*He rises hastily; and they shake hands.*) Quite chilly this morning, isnt it? (*She sits down on his left. He sits beside her.*)

HIGGINS. Dont you dare try this game on me. I taught it to you; and it doesnt take me in. Get up and come home; and dont be a fool.

(ELIZA *takes a piece of needlework from her basket, and begins to stitch at it, without taking the least notice of this outburst.*)

MRS HIGGINS. Very nicely put, indeed, Henry. No woman could resist such an invitation.

HIGGINS. You let her alone, mother. Let her speak for herself. You will jolly soon see whether she has an idea that I havnt put into her head or a word that I havnt put into her mouth. I tell you I have created this thing out of the squashed cabbage leaves of Covent Garden; and now she pretends to play the fine lady with me.

MRS HIGGINS (*placidly*). Yes, dear; but youll sit down, wont you?

---

① What is Liza doing here? Why does Higgins get angry?

② What is Mrs Higgins saying to her son?

VOCABULARY IN CONTEXT

- Little did the canoeists know that the stream carrying them so <u>placidly</u> along led to a raging waterfall.

(HIGGINS *sits down again, savagely.*)

LIZA (*to* PICKERING, *taking no apparent notice of* HIGGINS, *and working away deftly*). Will you drop me altogether now that the experiment is over, Colonel Pickering?

PICKERING. Oh dont. You mustnt think of it as an experiment. It shocks me, somehow.

LIZA. Oh, I'm only a squashed cabbage leaf—

PICKERING (*impulsively*). No.

LIZA (*continuing quietly*).—but I owe so much to you that I should be very unhappy if you forgot me.

PICKERING. It's very kind of you to say so, Miss Doolittle.

LIZA. It's not because you paid for my dresses. I know you are generous to everybody with money. But it was from you that I learnt really nice manners; and that is what makes one a lady, isnt it? You see it was so very difficult for me with the example of Professor Higgins always before me. I was brought up to be just like him, unable to control myself, and using bad language on the slightest provocation. And I should never have known that ladies and gentlemen didnt behave like that if you hadnt been there.

HIGGINS. Well!!

PICKERING. Oh, thats only his way, you know. He doesnt mean it.

LIZA. Oh, *I* didnt mean it either, when I was a flower girl. It was only my way. But you see I did it; and thats what makes the difference after all.

PICKERING. No doubt. Still, he taught you to speak; and I couldnt have done that, you know.

LIZA (*trivially*). Of course: that is his profession.

① *What wasn't Higgins capable of teaching Liza?*

② *What is the difference between a lady and a flower girl? Why was Pickering so important in Liza's transformation?*

HIGGINS. Damnation!

LIZA (*continuing*). It was just like learning to dance in the fashionable way: there was nothing more than that in it. But do you know what began my real education?

PICKERING. What?

LIZA (*stopping her work for a moment*). Your calling me Miss Doolittle that day when I first came to Wimpole Street. That was the beginning of self-respect for me. (*She resumes her stitching.*) And there were a hundred little things you never noticed because they came naturally to you. Things about standing up and taking off your hat and opening doors—

PICKERING. Oh, that was nothing.

LIZA. Yes: things that shewed you thought and felt about me as if I were something better than a scullery-maid;[5] though of course I know you would have been just the same to a scullery-maid if she had been let into the drawing room. You never took off your boots in the dining room when I was there.

PICKERING. You mustnt mind that. Higgins takes off his boots all over the place.

LIZA. I know. I am not blaming him. It is his way, isn't it? But it made such a difference to me that you didnt do it. You see, really and truly, apart from the things anyone can pick up (the dressing and the proper way of speaking, and so on), the difference between a lady and a flower girl is not how she behaves, but how she's treated. I shall always be a flower girl to Professor Higgins, because he always treats me as a flower girl, and always will; but I know I can be a lady to you, because

---

5. **scullery-maid.** Household help responsible for cleaning pots and pans

you always treat me as a lady, and always will.

MRS HIGGINS. Please dont grind your teeth, Henry.

PICKERING. Well, this is really very nice of you, Miss Doolittle.

LIZA. I should like you to call me Eliza, now, if you would.

PICKERING. Thank you. Eliza, of course.

LIZA. And I should like Professor Higgins to call me Miss Doolittle.

HIGGINS. I'll see you damned first.

MRS HIGGINS. Henry! Henry!

PICKERING (*laughing*). Why dont you slang back at him? Dont stand it. It would do him a lot of good.

LIZA. I cant. I could have done it once; but now I cant go back to it. Last night, when I was wandering about, a girl spoke to me; and I tried to get back into the old way with her; but it was no use. You told me, you know, that when a child is brought to a foreign country, it picks up the language in a few weeks, and forgets its own. Well, I am a child in your country. I have forgotten my own language, and can speak nothing but yours. Thats the real break-off with the corner of Tottenham Court Road. Leaving Wimpole Street finishes it.

PICKERING (*much alarmed*). Oh! but youre coming back to Wimpole Street, arnt you? Youll forgive Higgins?

HIGGINS (*rising*). Forgive! Will she, by George! Let her go. Let her find out how she can get on without us. She will relapse into the gutter in three weeks without me at her elbow.

(DOOLITTLE *appears at the center window. With a look of dignified reproach at* HIGGINS, *he comes slowly and silently to his daughter, who, with her back to the window, is unconscious of his approach.*)

PICKERING. He's <u>incorrigible</u>, Eliza. You wont relapse, will you?

LIZA. No: not now. Never again. I have learnt my lesson. I dont believe I could utter one of the old sounds if I tried. (DOOLITTLE *touches her on her left shoulder. She drops her work losing her self-possession utterly at the spectacle of her father's splendor*) A-a-a-a-a-ah-ow-ooh!

HIGGINS (*with a crow of triumph*). Aha! Just so. A-a-a-a-ahowooh! A-a-a-a-ahowooh! A-a-a-a-ahowooh! Victory! Victory! (*He throws himself on the divan, folding his arms, and* <u>spraddling</u> *arrogantly.*)

DOOLITTLE. Can you blame the girl? Dont look at me like that, Eliza. It aint my fault. Ive come into some money.

LIZA. You must have touched a millionaire this time, dad.

DOOLITTLE. I have. But I'm dressed something special today. I'm going to St George's, Hanover Square. Your stepmother is going to marry me.

LIZA (*angrily*). Youre going to let yourself down to marry that low common woman!

PICKERING (*quietly*). He ought to, Eliza (*To* DOOLITTLE) Why has she changed her mind?

DOOLITTLE (*sadly*). Intimidated, Governor. Intimidated. Middle class morality claims its victim. Wont you put on your

WORDS FOR EVERYDAY USE:

in • cor • ri • gi • ble (in kôr´ə jə bəl) *adj.*, unable to be reformed; unmanageable; unruly

sprad • dle (sprad´əl) *vt.*, sprawl or straddle

 Students can hold a brief debate on the following: "Resolved: That apart from superficial matters such as speech and dress, the difference between a person of one class and a person of another is the way each is treated."

ADDITIONAL QUESTIONS AND ACTIVITIES

Ask students the following interpretive question: Why is Liza attracted to Higgins rather than Pickering, though Pickering treats her better than Higgins?

Answer. Responses will vary. A likely explanation is that Liza is attracted to Higgins because he also needs to be changed. In this sense, Liza is as much a "sculptor" as Higgins is; unfortunately, Higgins is utterly intractable. Liza will eventually realize that her efforts are wasted and will abandon her attempt to elicit a different response from Higgins.

VOCABULARY IN CONTEXT

- I tried to compliment my grandfather on his beautiful woodworking, but the <u>incorrigible</u> old rascal refused to admit the quality of his work.

- The young father soon learned how difficult it is to put a diaper on a <u>spraddling</u> baby.

ADDITIONAL QUESTIONS AND ACTIVITIES

Many couples today write their own wedding vows. Students can imagine they are Doolittle and his bride-to-be and compose vows for their wedding. They should make their vows reflect Doolittle's unique understanding of his situation.

LITERARY TECHNIQUE

Comedy. For centuries, many theatrical comedies produced one or more marriages in its final act. For example, many of Shakespeare's comedies, such as *A Midsummer Night's Dream* and *The Merchant of Venice,* involve young people moving away from childhood and the parental home toward love and marriage. *Pygmalion,* however, ends with an uncomfortable reversal of this convention—a daughter remains single while a father remarries. Ask students why Shaw may have wished to alter the traditional comic ending. Is Shaw's choice of an ending indicative of any changes in twentieth-century literature?

hat, Liza, and come and see me turned off?[6]

LIZA. If the Colonel says I must, I—I'll (*almost sobbing*) I'll demean myself. And get insulted for my pains, like enough.

DOOLITTLE. Dont be afraid: she never comes to words with anyone now, poor woman! respectability has broke all the spirit out of her.

PICKERING (*squeezing* ELIZA'S *elbow gently*). Be kind to them, Eliza. Make the best of it.

LIZA (*forcing a little smile for him through her vexation*). Oh well, just to shew theres no ill feeling. I'll be back in a moment. (*She goes out.*)

DOOLITTLE (*sitting down beside* PICKERING). I feel uncommon nervous about the ceremony, Colonel. I wish youd come and see me through it.

PICKERING. But youve been through it before, man. You were married to Eliza's mother.

DOOLITTLE. Who told you that, Colonel?

PICKERING. Well, nobody told me. But I concluded—naturally—

DOOLITTLE. No: that aint the natural way, Colonel: it's only the middle class way. My way was always the undeserving way. But dont say nothing to Eliza. She dont know: I always had a delicacy about telling her.

PICKERING. Quite right. We'll leave it so, if you dont mind.

DOOLITTLE. And youll come to the church, Colonel, and put me through straight?

PICKERING. With pleasure. As far as a bachelor can.

MRS HIGGINS. May I come, Mr Doolittle? I should be very sorry to miss your wedding.

DOOLITTLE. I should indeed be honored by your condescension, maam; and my poor old woman would take it as a tremendous compliment. She's been very low, thinking of the happy days that are no more.

MRS HIGGINS (*rising*). I'll order the carriage and get ready. (*The men rise, except* HIGGINS) I shant be more than fifteen minutes. (*As she goes to the door* ELIZA *comes in, hatted and buttoning her gloves.*) I'm going to the church to see your father married, Eliza. You had better come in the brougham[7] with me. Colonel Pickering can go on with the bridegroom.

(MRS HIGGINS *goes out.* ELIZA *comes to the middle of the room between the centre window and the ottoman.* PICKERING *joins her.*)

DOOLITTLE. Bridegroom! What a word! It makes a man realize his position, somehow. (*He takes up his hat and goes towards the door.*)

PICKERING. Before I go, Eliza, do forgive him and come back to us.

LIZA. I dont think papa would allow me. Would you, dad?

DOOLITTLE (*sad but* <u>magnanimous</u>). They played you off very cunning, Eliza, them two sportsmen. If it had been only one of them, you could have nailed him. But you see, there was two; and one of

---

6. **turned off.** To be joined in marriage
7. **brougham.** Enclosed four-wheeled carriage

WORDS FOR EVERYDAY USE: **mag • nan • i • mous** (mag nan ´ə məs) *adj.,* gracious and generous

VOCABULARY IN CONTEXT

• The <u>magnanimous</u> forgive and forget most of their enemies; the spiteful cherish each and every one.

them chaperoned the other, as you might say. (*To* PICKERING) It was artful of you, Colonel; but I bear no malice: I should have done the same myself. I been the victim of one woman after another all my life; and I dont grudge you two getting the better of Eliza. I shant interfere. It's time for us to go, Colonel. So long, Henry. See you in St George's, Eliza. (*He goes out.*)

PICKERING   (*coaxing*). Do stay with us, Eliza. (*He follows* DOOLITTLE).

(ELIZA *goes out on the balcony to avoid being alone with* HIGGINS. *He rises and joins her there. She immediately comes back into the room and makes for the door; but he goes along the balcony quickly and gets his back to the door before she reaches it.*)

HIGGINS.   Well, Eliza, youve had a bit of your own back, as you call it. Have you had enough? and are you going to be reasonable? Or do you want any more?

LIZA.   You want me back only to pick up your slippers and put up with your tempers and fetch and carry for you.

HIGGINS.   I havnt said I wanted you back at all.

LIZA.   Oh, indeed. Then what are we talking about?

HIGGINS.   About you, not about me. If you come back I shall treat you just as I have always treated you. I cant change my nature; and I dont intend to change my manners. My manners are exactly the same as Colonel Pickering's.

LIZA.   Thats not true. He treats a flower girl as if she was a duchess.

HIGGINS.   And I treat a duchess as if she was a flower girl.

LIZA.   I see. (*She turns away composedly, and sits on the ottoman, facing the window.*) The same to everybody.

HIGGINS.   Just so.

LIZA.   Like father.

HIGGINS (*grinning, a little taken down*). Without accepting the comparison at all points, Eliza, it's quite true that your father is not a snob, and that he will be quite at home in any station of life to which his eccentric destiny may call him. (*Seriously*) The great secret, Eliza, is not having bad manners or good manners or any other particular sort of manners, but having the same manner for all human souls: in short, behaving as if you were in Heaven, where there are no third-class carriages, and one soul is as good as another.

LIZA.   Amen. You are a born preacher.

HIGGINS   (*irritated*). The question is not whether I treat you rudely, but whether you ever heard me treat anyone else better.

LIZA   (*with sudden sincerity*). I dont care how you treat me. I dont mind your swearing at me. I dont mind a black eye: Ive had one before this. But (*standing up and facing him*) I wont be passed over.

HIGGINS.   Then get out of my way; for I wont stop for you. You talk about me as if I were a motor bus.

LIZA.   So you are a motor bus: all bounce and go, and no consideration for anyone. But I can do without you: dont think I cant.

HIGGINS.   I know you can. I told you you could.

LIZA (*wounded, getting away from him to the other side of the ottoman with her face to the hearth*). I know you did, you brute. You wanted to get rid of me.

HIGGINS.   Liar.

How, according to Higgins, is heaven different from earth?

Higgins makes several important statements in his dialogue. Use the following questions to explore these statements with students:

1. "I cant change my nature," says Higgins. Based on what you have seen of Higgins in the play, do you believe this is true, or just a position he is taking?

2. Do you believe that Higgins is correct when he says that what really matters is not the type of manners one has but that one treats all people the same regardless of their social class?

Answers. 1. Higgins has repeatedly demonstrated a refusal to change his nature. 2. *Responses will vary.* Students may point out that Higgins is half right: what really matters is that one treats all people, regardless of class, with good manners, as Pickering does.

LIZA. Thank you. (*She sits down with dignity.*)

HIGGINS. You never asked yourself, I suppose, whether I could do without you.

LIZA (*earnestly*). Dont you try to get round me. Youll have to do without me.

HIGGINS (*arrogant*). I can do without anybody. I have my own soul: my own spark of divine fire. But (*with sudden humility*) I shall miss you, Eliza. (*He sits down near her on the ottoman.*) I have learnt something from your idiotic notions: I confess that humbly and gratefully. And I have grown accustomed to your voice and appearance. I like them, rather.

LIZA. Well, you have both of them on your gramophone and in your book of photographs. When you feel lonely without me, you can turn the machine on. It's got no feelings to hurt.

HIGGINS. I cant turn your soul on. Leave me those feelings; and you can take away the voice and the face. They are not you.

LIZA. Oh, you are a devil. You can twist the heart in a girl as easy as some could twist her arms to hurt her. Mrs Pearce warned me. Time and again she has wanted to leave you; and you always got round her at the last minute. And you dont care a bit for her. And you dont care a bit for me.

HIGGINS. I care for life, for humanity; and you are a part of it that has come my way and been built into my house. What more can you or anyone ask?

LIZA. I wont care for anybody that doesnt care for me.

HIGGINS. Commercial principles, Eliza. Like (*reproducing her Covent Garden pronunciation with professional exactness*) s'yollin voylets [selling violets], isn't it?

LIZA. Dont sneer at me. It's mean to sneer at me.

HIGGINS. I have never sneered in my life. Sneering doesnt become either the human face or the human soul. I am expressing my righteous contempt for Commercialism. I dont and wont trade in affection. You call me a brute because you couldnt buy a claim on me by fetching my slippers and finding my spectacles. You were a fool: I think a woman fetching a man's slippers is a disgusting sight: did I ever fetch your slippers? I think a good deal more of you for throwing them in my face. No use slaving for me and then saying you want to be cared for: who cares for a slave? If you come back, come back for the sake of good fellowship; for youll get nothing else. Youve had a thousand times as much out of me as I have out of you; and if you dare to set up your little dog's tricks of fetching and carrying slippers against my creation of a Duchess Eliza, I'll slam the door in your silly face.

LIZA. What did you do it for if you didnt care for me?

HIGGINS (*heartily*). Why, because it was my job.

LIZA. You never thought of the trouble it would make for me.

HIGGINS. Would the world ever have been made if its maker had been afraid of making trouble? Making life means making trouble. Theres only one way of escaping trouble; and thats killing things. Cowards, you notice, are always shrieking to have troublesome people killed.

LIZA. I'm no preacher: I dont notice things like that. I notice that you dont notice me.

HIGGINS (*jumping up and walking about intolerantly*). Eliza: youre an idiot. I waste

---

BIOGRAPHICAL NOTES

In the dialogue on this page, Higgins exclaims, "Theres only one way of escaping trouble; and thats killing things. Cowards, you notice, are always shrieking to have troublesome people killed." His "preaching," as Liza calls it, has a larger meaning than that called for in the dialogue.

Shaw was a member of the Fabian Society, a group dedicated to changing British society by per-

meating all levels with its new ideas. When World War I began, Shaw insisted that Britain was as much to blame for hostilities as Germany and its allies—a position that brought him much public censure. In this light, Higgins's statement is typical of the views of the author, who was not afraid to take on trouble in order to improve conditions in society.

---

the treasures of my Miltonic[8] mind by spreading them before you. Once for all, understand that I go my way and do my work without caring twopence what happens to either of us. I am not intimidated, like your father and your stepmother. So you can come back or go to the devil: which you please.

LIZA.   What am I to come back for?

HIGGINS (*bouncing up on his knees on the ottoman and leaning over it to her*). For the fun of it. Thats why I took you on.

LIZA (*with averted face*). And you may throw me out tomorrow if I dont do everything you want me to?

HIGGINS.   Yes; and you may walk out tomorrow if I dont do everything you want me to.

LIZA.   And live with my stepmother?

HIGGINS.   Yes, or sell flowers.

LIZA.   Oh! if I only could go back to my flower basket! I should be independent of both you and father and all the world! Why did you take my independence from me? Why did I give it up? I'm a slave now, for all my fine clothes.

HIGGINS.   Not a bit. I'll adopt you as my daughter and settle money on you if you like. Or would you rather marry Pickering?

LIZA (*looking fiercely round at him*). I wouldnt marry you if you asked me; and youre nearer my age than what he is.

HIGGINS (*gently*). Than he is: not "than what he is."

LIZA (*losing her temper and rising*). I'll talk as I like. Youre not my teacher now.

HIGGINS (*reflectively*). I dont suppose Pickering would, though. He's as confirmed an old bachelor as I am.

LIZA.   Thats not what I want; and dont you think it. Ive always had chaps enough wanting me that way. Freddy Hill writes to me twice and three times a day, sheets and sheets.

HIGGINS (*disagreeably surprised*). Damn his impudence! (*He recoils and finds himself sitting on his heels.*)

LIZA.   He has a right to if he likes, poor lad. And he does love me.

HIGGINS (*getting off the ottoman*). You have no right to encourage him.

LIZA.   Every girl has a right to be loved.

HIGGINS.   What! By fools like that?

LIZA.   Freddy's not a fool. And if he's weak and poor and wants me, may be he'd make me happier than my betters that bully me and dont want me.

HIGGINS.   Can he make anything of you? Thats the point.

LIZA.   Perhaps I could make something of him. But I never thought of us making anything of one another; and you never think of anything else. I only want to be natural.

HIGGINS.   In short, you want me to be as infatuated about you as Freddy? Is that it?

LIZA.   No I dont. Thats not the sort of feeling I want from you. And dont you be too sure of yourself or of me. I could have been a bad girl if I'd liked. Ive seen more of some things than you, for all your

8. **Miltonic.** Like the poet John Milton, that is, brilliant

❶
What does Liza want? What has she wanted from the beginning of act two, when she came to Higgins for lessons?

❷
Why is it important for romantic partners not to try to remake one another?

WORDS FOR EVERYDAY USE:

im • pu • dence (im´pyōō dəns) *n.*, quality of being shamelessly bold or saucy

VOCABULARY IN CONTEXT

• The public finds nothing so unbearable as impudence in a public employee.

---

❶ Liza wants her independence and has wanted it since she first appeared at Higgins's house.

❷ The effort of partners to remake one another is generally bound to fail.

ADDITIONAL QUESTIONS AND ACTIVITIES

Ask these questions to examine more closely the dialogue between Liza and Higgins:

1. Do you believe Liza is operating on a good basis for a relationship when she says, "I wont care for anybody that doesnt care for me"?

2. Why does Higgins call Liza's insistence on receiving something for her affection "commercialism"?

3. Higgins claims that he only created "Duchess Liza" because it was his job. Yet earlier, when Liza told Pickering that she did not owe thanks to Higgins because he was only following his "profession," Higgins was upset. Why does Higgins frequently change his mind and shift ground in this way?

Answers. 1. *Responses will vary.* Students may point out that the insistence upon an equal response from an equal partner is a basic condition of a sound relationship. 2. Higgins views it as akin to "buying and selling" affection. 3. Higgins will say almost anything necessary to keep his opponent off balance or to wheedle or cozen the other into doing what he wants. It is not surprising that this underlying principle frequently leads him into contradictory positions.

Use the table below to explain the various possibilities for Liza's future that are raised and discarded on this and the next two pages.

POSSIBILITY	REASON DISCARDED
Liza could live with her father.	Liza would have to live with her unpleasant stepmother.
Liza could sell flowers for a living.	Liza cannot go back to that life.
Higgins could adopt Liza.	[She ignores this suggestion.]
Liza could marry Pickering.	She implies that Pickering is too old for her.
Liza could marry Freddy.	[This is not discarded by Liza, though Higgins condemns it.]
Liza could have seduced Higgins.	Her moral standards are too high.
Liza could continue living at Higgins's under the same terms that she has been living there.	Liza craves the respect and kindliness that Higgins refuses to give her.
Liza could marry someone of higher social standing than Freddy.	Liza insists that she will at least have independence if she cannot have kindness.
Liza could be an assistant to Professor Nepean.	[Higgins is outraged by this idea, though it is never discarded by Liza.]
Liza could become a teacher of phonetics herself.	[This possibility is never discarded by Liza.]

ANSWER TO GUIDED READING QUESTION

❶ Henry doesn't want to have his "masterpiece thrown away on Freddy." Henry still views Liza as an object and his creation.

---

learning. Girls like me can drag gentlemen down to make love to them easy enough. And they wish each other dead the next minute.

HIGGINS. Of course they do. Then what in thunder are we quarrelling about?

LIZA (*much troubled*). I want a little kindness. I know I'm a common ignorant girl, and you a book-learned gentleman; but I'm not dirt under your feet. What I done (*correcting herself*) what I did was not for the dresses and the taxis: I did it because we were pleasant together and I come—came—to care for you; not to want you to make love to me, and not forgetting the difference between us, but more friendly like.

HIGGINS. Well, of course. Thats just how I feel. And how Pickering feels. Eliza: youre a fool.

LIZA. Thats not a proper answer to give me (*she sinks on the chair at the writing-table in tears*).

HIGGINS. It's all youll get until you stop being a common idiot. If youre going to be a lady, youll have to give up feeling neglected if the men you know dont spend half their time snivelling over you and the other half giving you black eyes. If you cant stand the coldness of my sort of life, and the strain of it, go back to the gutter. Work til you are more a brute than a human being; and then cuddle and squabble and drink til you fall asleep. Oh, it's a fine life, the life of the gutter. It's real: it's warm: it's violent: you can feel it through the thickest skin: you can taste it and smell it without any training or any work. Not like Science and Literature and

❶
Why doesn't Henry want Liza to marry Freddy? What does his statement reveal about the way he views Liza?

Classical Music and Philosophy and Art. You find me cold, unfeeling, selfish, dont you? Very well: be off with you to the sort of people you like. Marry some sentimental hog or other with lots of money, and a thick pair of lips to kiss you with and a thick pair of boots to kick you with. If you cant appreciate what youve got, youd better get what you can appreciate.

LIZA (*desperate*). Oh, you are a cruel tyrant. I cant talk to you: you turn everything against me: I'm always in the wrong. But you know very well all the time that youre nothing but a bully. You know I cant go back to the gutter, as you call it, and that I have no real friends in the world but you and the Colonel. You know well I couldn't bear to live with a low common man after you two; and it's wicked and cruel of you to insult me by pretending I could. You think I must go back to Wimpole Street because I have nowhere else to go but father's. But dont you be too sure that you have me under your feet to be trampled on and talked down. I'll marry Freddy, I will, as soon as he's able to support me.

HIGGINS (*sitting down beside her*). Rubbish! you shall marry an ambassador. You shall marry the Governor-General of India or the Lord-Lieutenant of Ireland, or somebody who wants a deputy-queen. I'm not going to have my masterpiece thrown away on Freddy.

LIZA. You think I like you to say that. But I havent forgot what you said a minute ago; and I wont be coaxed round as if I was a baby or a puppy. If I cant have kindness, I'll have independence.

VOCABULARY IN CONTEXT

- To some people, uttering a negative word about Elvis is <u>blasphemy</u>.
- Though Fritz <u>toadied</u> to her as class president, Carla guessed correctly that he was planning to run against her in the election.
- The flagship of the ill-fated Arctic expedition sank the minute it left the harbor, and its crew was rescued by the <u>consorts</u>.

HIGGINS. Independence? Thats middle class blasphemy. We are all dependent on one another, every soul of us on earth.

LIZA (*rising determinedly*). I'll let you see whether I'm dependent on you. If you can preach, I can teach. I'll go and be a teacher.

HIGGINS. Whatll you teach, in heaven's name?

LIZA. What you taught me. I'll teach phonetics.

HIGGINS. Ha! ha! ha!

LIZA. I'll offer myself as an assistant to Professor Nepean.

HIGGINS (*rising in a fury*). What! That impostor! that humbug! that toadying ignoramus! Teach him my methods! my discoveries! You take one step in his direction and I'll wring your neck. (*He lays hands on her.*) Do you hear?

LIZA (*defiantly non-resistant*). Wring away. What do I care? I knew youd strike me some day. (*He lets her go, stamping with rage at having forgotten himself, and recoils so hastily that he stumbles back into his seat on the ottoman.*) Aha! Now I know how to deal with you. What a fool I was not to think of it before! You cant take away the knowledge you gave me. You said I had a finer ear than you. And I can be civil and kind to people, which is more than you can. Aha! Thats done you, Henry Higgins, it has. Now I dont care that (*snapping her fingers*) for your bullying and your big talk. I'll advertize it in the papers that your duchess is only a flower girl that you taught, and that she'll teach anybody to be a duchess just the same in six months for a thousand guineas. Oh, when I think of myself crawling under your feet and being trampled on and called names, when all the time I had only to lift up my finger to be as good as you, I could just kick myself.

HIGGINS (*wondering at her*). You damned impudent slut, you! But it's better than snivelling; better than fetching slippers and finding spectacles, isn't it? (*Rising*) By George, Eliza, I said I'd make a woman of you; and I have. I like you like this.

LIZA. Yes: you turn round and make up to me now that I'm not afraid of you, and can do without you.

HIGGINS. Of course I do, you little fool. Five minutes ago you were like a millstone round my neck. Now youre a tower of strength: a consort battleship. You and I and Pickering will be three old bachelors together instead of only two men and a silly girl.

(MRS HIGGINS *returns, dressed for the wedding.* ELIZA *instantly becomes cool and elegant.*)

MRS HIGGINS. The carriage is waiting, Eliza. Are you ready?

LIZA. Quite. Is the Professor coming?

MRS HIGGINS. Certainly not. He cant behave himself in church. He makes remarks out loud all the time on the clergyman's pronunciation.

LIZA. Then I shall not see you again, Professor. Goodbye. (*She goes to the door.*)

MRS HIGGINS (*coming to* HIGGINS). Goodbye, dear.

HIGGINS. Goodbye, mother. (*He is about to kiss her, when he recollects something.*) Oh, by the way, Eliza, order a ham and a

---

❶
What idea does Liza propose? Why would she be a better teacher than Henry?

WORDS FOR EVERYDAY USE

WORDS FOR EVERYDAY USE:

blas • phe • my (blas´ fə mē´) *n.*, irreverent or disrespectful remark or action

toad • y (tōd´ ē) *vt.*, flatter in order to gain favor

con • sort (kän´ sôrt´) *n.*, ship that travels with other ships; companion

---

ANSWER TO GUIDED READING QUESTION

❶ Liza proposes to teach phonetics. She has a finer ear and can be civil and kind to people.

ADDITIONAL QUESTIONS AND ACTIVITIES

Students can imagine they are career counselors. Liza Doolittle has come to them to ask them what line of work she should pursue. They should list at least three possible careers for her, giving reasons why each would be appropriate for a person of her background and training.

ADDITIONAL QUESTIONS AND ACTIVITIES

Explain to students that one critic has said of *Pygmalion* that it "fails at the end because its author lost courage." That is, this critic believes that Shaw was unable to bring himself to write an ending that would satisfy the emotional expectations built up over the course of the play. According to these expectations, Liza should be able to change Higgins just as he has changed her, making a continued relationship possible between them. Another critic notes that Shaw did not actually give the play an ending, he simply allowed it to come to a halt. Although *Pygmalion* is perhaps the most popular of all Shaw's plays, when the even more popular musical version was created, the plot was given a new ending in which Professor Higgins and Liza do form a successful romantic bond. Students can discuss their reaction to the end of the play. Ask the following questions:

1. Given the character of Higgins, as Shaw portrays him, is any other ending possible?

2. Is the ending of the play dramatically satisfying? Why, or why not?

Answers. 1. Given Higgins's relentless intractability and incorrigibility, it is unlikely that any other ending would seem credible. If Higgins had given indications that he could change his ways, another ending might be feasible. 2. *Responses will vary.*

Students can write a new ending to the play if they feel it is possible to do so.

ANSWER TO GUIDED READING QUESTION

❶ Higgins thinks that Liza will resume the same role in his household that she has played for the past several months. She seems unlikely to do so.

RESPONDING TO THE SELECTION

Some points students may raise in their discussion are the following: Liza and Doolittle feel the need to conform to the middle-class way of speaking and dressing. Liza feels constrained to do something genteel for a living. Doolittle feels compelled to care for his dependents and relatives.

ANSWERS FOR REVIEWING THE SELECTION

RECALLING

1. Doolittle is dressed like a gentleman, wearing a new coat, trousers, a silk hat, patent leather shoes, and a flower in his buttonhole.

2. Doolittle reacts to his new status with a mixture of regret for his past independence and plaintive resignation.

3. She does not want to be dependent on either her father or Higgins.

4. Higgins says that he treats all people as badly as he treats her, so she should not object.

INTERPRETING

Responses will vary. Possible responses are given.

5. Higgins was indirectly responsible for Doolittle receiving an income from a trust.

6. Doolittle fears he will be forced to go to the workhouse if he does not accept the money offered him.

7. Liza wants Higgins to treat her "more friendly like." While Higgins claims he has always felt "friendly like" toward Liza, he follows this claim by suggesting she return to the gutter, thus revealing that he will never be able to meet her conditions.

8. Higgins is still attempting to treat Liza as a servant he can order

(cont.)

Stilton cheese, will you? And buy me a pair of reindeer gloves, number eights, and a tie to match that new suit of mine, at Eale & Binman's. You can choose the color. (*His cheerful, careless, vigorous voice shows that he is incorrigible.*)

LIZA (*disdainfully*). Buy them yourself. (*She sweeps out.*)

MRS HIGGINS. I'm afraid youve spoiled

What does Higgins think that Liza will do? Will she?

that girl, Henry. But never mind, dear: I'll buy you the tie and gloves.

HIGGINS (*sunnily*). Oh, dont bother. She'll buy em all right enough. Goodbye.

(*They kiss.* MRS HIGGINS *runs out.* HIGGINS, *left alone, rattles his cash in his pocket; chuckles; and disports himself in a highly self-satisfied manner.*) ∎

Responding to the Selection

In this act, both Liza and Doolittle claim that rising out of the lower class has taken away their independence. Ask yourselves what constraints Liza and Doolittle might feel as part of the middle class that they did not feel before.

Reviewing the Selection

RECALLING

1. What does Doolittle look like when he arrives at Mrs. Higgins's?

2. How does Doolittle react to his new status?

3. What relationship does Liza not want to have with Higgins and her father?

4. How does Higgins attempt to justify his bad manners toward Liza?

INTERPRETING

▶ 5. Why does Doolittle blame Higgins for delivering him into the hands of middle-class morality?

▶ 6. What fear keeps Doolittle from renouncing his new station in life?

▶ 7. Under what conditions might Liza have agreed to stay with Higgins? Could Higgins meet those conditions?

▶ 8. How does the relationship between Higgins and Liza differ from their relationship at the close of the previous act?

ANSWERS FOR REVIEWING THE SELECTION (CONT.)

about, but Liza is now resolutely refusing to submit to this treatment.

SYNTHESIZING

Responses will vary. Possible responses are given.

9. Higgins has a high opinion of himself and sets himself apart from other middle-class men and women in his belief that he treats all people with the same lack of consideration. Liza rejects him because she feels

he "passes over" her, that is, treats her without consideration.

10. Liza's decision to set up as a teacher of speaking shows that she now has some resources and the willingness to put them to work. She probably will not buy the tie and gloves for Higgins because of her newfound strength and her bidding Higgins goodbye with the words, "Then I shall not see you again."

9. What opinion does Higgins have of himself? How does he set himself apart from middle-class men and women? Why does Liza reject him?

10. What action or decision on the part of Liza shows that she is quite different from the helpless flower girl who appeared at the beginning of the play? Do you think Liza will buy the tie and gloves for Higgins? Explain your answer.

Understanding Literature (Questions for Discussion)

1. **Resolution.** In a plot, the **resolution** is the point at which the central conflict is ended, or resolved. If this play is viewed as being about Liza's struggle to gain independence, how does the act end, or resolve, that struggle? What idea does Liza hit upon to make herself independent both of Higgins and of her father?

2. **Satire.** Satire is humorous writing or speech intended to point out errors, falsehoods, foibles, or failings. In what ways does Shaw satirize the following in his play?

   —male domination of women

   —"middle-class morality" and the work ethic (through the character of Arthur Doolittle)

   —upper-class attitudes toward the members of the lower classes

   —artificial barriers between the social classes

   —late Victorian prudery

   —fads among young people

Responding in Writing

1. **Epilogue.** An **epilogue** is a concluding section or statement, often one that comments on or draws conclusions from the work as a whole. At the conclusion of *Pygmalion*, Higgins asks Liza to buy him a new tie and a few other things. Although Liza refuses, Higgins seems confident that she will do these things and will return. What evidence in the act indicates that Higgins is wrong? Write a brief prose epilogue for *Pygmalion* in which you tell what happens to each of the main characters after this act and why.

2. **Feminist Criticism.** Shaw, an ardent social reformer, was quite interested in the subject of women's rights. Read the discussion of **feminist criticism** in the entry on **criticism** in the Handbook of Literary Terms. What makes *Pygmalion* a feminist play? What message does Shaw's play deliver about the importance of education in securing equality for women? about the importance of economic opportunity for women? Higgins tells Pickering that it is inevitable that "a man soon wants to go in one way and a woman in

PYGMALION, ACT FIVE **1055**

ANSWERS FOR UNDERSTANDING LITERATURE

▶ See the evaluation forms for discussion, active listening, and oral communication, *Assessment Portfolio,* 7.11–7.14.
Responses will vary. Possible responses are given.

1. Resolution. Act Five resolves Liza's struggle to be independent, because she considers and rejects the various options of dependency open to her (marriage or return to Higgins's or her father's household). Liza speaks of becoming a teacher of speech like Higgins in order to support herself.

2. Satire. Shaw satirizes male domination of women by showing that it is counterproductive and ultimately destructive of the relationship between Higgins and Liza. He uses Doolittle as a running satire on" middle-class morality" by having Doolittle continually flaunt his transgressions of the norms of behavior for the middle class. He satirizes upper-class attitudes toward the members of the lower classes by showing Liza and Alfred Doolittle as equally able to act thoughtfully and intelligently and by characterizing Higgins as perfectly able to be ill-mannered and inconsiderate. The rise of Liza and Alfred Doolittle to the middle class satirizes the artificial distinctions between the classes. Higgins's iconoclastic remarks to the Eynsford Hills in Act Three satirize late Victorian prudery. The fascination of Freddy and Clara with "the new small talk," which exists only in their own imaginations, satirizes fads among young people.

ANALYTIC SCALES FOR RESPONDING IN WRITING

Assign a score from 1 to 25 for each grading criterion below. (For more detailed evaluation, see the evaluation forms for writing, revising, and proofreading, *Assessment Portfolio,* 7.1–7.10.)

1. Epilogue
• **Content/Unity.** The epilogue presents a plausible continuation of the plot of the play.
• **Organization/Coherence.** The epilogue is clearly organized, presenting subsequent events in understandable order.

(cont.)

ANALYTIC SCALES FOR RESPONDING IN WRITING (CONT.)

• **Language/Style.** The epilogue uses vivid and precise nouns, verbs, and modifiers.
• **Conventions.** The epilogue avoids errors in spelling, grammar, usage, mechanics, and manuscript form.

2. Feminist Criticism
• **Content/Unity.** The critical essay offers a sensible discussion of how *Pygmalion* satirizes male domination and promotes women's independence.

• **Organization/Coherence.** The critical essay is clearly organized, presenting views coherently and backing them up with evidence from the play.
• **Language/Style.** The critical essay uses vivid and precise nouns, verbs, and modifiers.
• **Conventions.** The critical essay avoids errors in spelling, grammar, usage, mechanics, and manuscript form.

another." Is this so? What evidence in the play indicates that Liza wants the same thing Higgins wants—her independence? How does Higgins's request of Liza at the end of the play demonstrate that he has not gotten the message that she is his equal, not his creation or his subordinate? In what ways do Mrs. Pearce and Mrs. Higgins attempt to keep Higgins from objectifying Liza and bullying her? Write a critical essay in which you explain how this play satirizes male domination and promotes the ideal of independence and equality for women.

Language Lab

Reducing Wordiness. Read the Language Arts Survey, 2.59, "Reducing Wordiness." Then rewrite the following sentences, eliminating needless words. You may also make other minor revisions, as necessary.

1. It was Colonel Pickering who was the one who challenged Professor Higgins to make a lady out of Liza.

2. Not only the political views, but also the social attitudes of George Bernard Shaw were a cause of conflict with the London of his time.

3. It is in his relationship with his mother that Henry Higgins shows that he is attached to her and tries to avoid attachments to other women.

4. The question of whether or not Doolittle is better off as a middle-class man can be resolved by considering the fact that he has lost his independence.

5. It is Higgins's belief that if it were not for the continuance of his teaching, Liza would end up returning to selling flowers at Covent Garden.

PROJECTS

1. **Comparative Literature: Genre.** Shaw detested the musical theater, considering it trivial and vulgar. During his lifetime, he was offered the opportunity to turn *Pygmalion* into a musical but refused. After he died, however, a musical, *My Fair Lady*, was made of his play. View a videotape of *My Fair Lady* as a class. Then discuss the relative merits of the play and the musical. Was Shaw's play trivialized by making it into a musical? Were its social messages watered down? Does the musical take the same messages to a wider audience? Which do you prefer and why? Debate these issues in class.

2. **Dramatic Performance.** Working in small groups, present short scenes from the play to the rest of the class. Appoint one student in each group to direct the scene and assign roles to the other students. Rehearse your scenes and present them to the class. After each scene, hold a brief discussion of what the scene reveals about the characters.

Responses will vary. Possible responses are given.

1. Colonel Pickering challenged Professor Higgins to make Liza a lady.

2. George Bernard Shaw clashed with both the political views and social attitudes of the London of his time.

3. Henry Higgins is attached to his mother and, for that reason, tries to avoid attachments to other women.

4. Is Doolittle better off as a member of the middle class, considering that he has lost his independence?

5. Higgins believes that without him Liza would soon return to selling flowers at Covent Garden.

FOR MORE PRACTICE

Problem. Although Higgins generated considerable affectionate emotions for Liza, in terms of Colonel Pickering's involvement and participation in a romantic relationship with Liza, there is not much evidence, or even suggestion, of its ever having taken place.

Answer. Though Higgins was in love with Liza, Colonel Pickering was not.

▶ For additional practice, see the *Essential Skills Practice Book: Language,* 2.59.

PROJECT NOTES

 1. **Comparative Literature: Genre.** Use the "Evaluation Form: Debate," in the *Assessment Portfolio,* 7.19.

2. **Dramatic Performance.** You may also let groups choose their own directors. Students might want to invite people from outside the class to watch their performances. Suggest that stu-dents reread the section on drama in Unit 1, pages 44–55, and the Language Arts Survey, 3.8, "Oral Interpretation."

PREREADING

"The Story of Pygmalion" from the *Metamorphoses*

by Ovid, retold by Sara Hyry

ADDITIONAL RESOURCES

READER'S GUIDE
- Selection Worksheet, 12.6

ASSESSMENT PORTFOLIO
- Selection Check Test, 4.12.11
- Selection Test, 4.12.12

ENRICHMENT ACTIVITIES

Ovid's *Metamorphoses* makes entertaining reading and is a tremendous storehouse of Greek and Roman mythology. Students who want to enjoy a fine piece of literature and learn about myths at the same time may read the complete text of Ovid's fascinating poem.

SUPPORT FOR LEP STUDENTS

Though this selection was written thousands of years ago, it has much that students today will find to encourage them in their reading—including a powerful love and a startling transformation.

ADDITIONAL VOCABULARY
vices—evil behavior
disposition—person's nature
crimson—dark red
dubious—doubtful

ABOUT THE AUTHOR

Publius Ovidius Naso (43 BC–AD 17) was born in Sulmo, east of Rome, to a well-to-do family that was able to send him to Athens to finish his education. Originally destined for a law career, he soon turned to poetry and gained some success when his first series of love poems, *Amores,* was written about 15 BC. Ovid's early work showed a casual and witty treatment of love and marriage, and it is as a love poet that he was principally known throughout most of literary history. His fortunes turned drastically in AD 8 when he was banished from Rome by Emperor Augustus for an offense that remains unknown to this day. He was sent to live in Tomis, part of modern-day Romania, then an outpost of the Roman Empire populated by semibarbarous tribes. There Ovid spent the rest of his life, at times depressed and despondent, while his wife back in Rome vainly pleaded his case. The years in exile were still productive, for he continued to write poetry. His interest in amorous subjects decreased, during this time he wrote *Metamorphoses,* which is generally considered to be his greatest work.

ABOUT THE SELECTION

"The Story of Pygmalion" comes from Ovid's *Metamorphoses*. This work, whose title means "changing forms," is a vast compendium of the myths of classical Greece and Rome, many of which deal with miraculous transformations—of Midas's daughter into gold, of Ariadne into a spider, and so on. That Ovid, whose life was subject to the buffeting of change, should have hit upon this subject is not surprising. The Pygmalion myth is an example of both the early and late interests of Ovid, for love is the story's subject, but its theme is transformation.

GOALS/OBJECTIVES

Studying this lesson will enable students to

- enjoy a myth
- give an outline of Ovid's life
- describe the main themes of Ovid's literary works
- recount the myth of Pygmalion as told by Ovid
- compare and contrast Ovid's version of the myth of Pygmalion and Shaw's *Pygmalion*

Italy

"The Story of Pygmalion"

FROM THE *METAMORPHOSES*

PUBLIUS OVIDIUS NASO, RETOLD BY SARA HYRY

MULTICULTURAL EXTENSIONS

Shaw made his debt to classical myth clear in the title he gave his play, *Pygmalion*. It can be argued that, like Liza Doolittle, the "ivory girl" passes through distinct stages—(1) "raw material," (2) a person formed but dependent, then (3) a person independently active. Ovid, however, chose not to deal with some of the issues that interested Shaw, such as the value Liza has as a thinking and feeling human, independent of the expectations and needs of her "creator." In Ovid, presumably, the statue becomes the living version of exactly what her creator wants, whereas in Shaw's play Liza outgrows her creator and moves on in life without him.

ANSWER TO GUIDED READING QUESTION

❶ Pygmalion made a statue of a young woman. He fell in love with his creation.

ANSWERS TO SELECTION CHECK TEST 4.12.11

EX. Did Pygmalion live with others?
No, he lived alone.

1. What beautiful thing does he make?
He makes an ivory statue of a girl.

2. What does Pygmalion love?
He loves his statue.

3. What does Pygmalion ask for in his prayer?
He asks for a wife like his ivory girl.

4. What happens when Pygmalion returns to his statue?
She seems to glow and she begins to move.

5. What does Venus do?
She smiles on the love she has created.

---

❶ What did Pygmalion make? How did he feel about his creation?

Pygmalion the sculptor lived alone. In his loneliness, he carved from a block of snow-white ivory a statue of a girl more beautiful than any who had ever lived. Pygmalion loved his statue so much that it seemed to him nearly alive. He spoke often to the statue and sometimes almost believed that it (or "she", as he preferred to call her) responded. He began to act as if the statue were indeed a real person: he brought her gifts of delicate shells, colorful flowers, pet birds, painted balls, and bits of amber. He dressed her and adorned her with rings, earrings, and ribbons, all of which were very becoming, but it was her own beauty, the beauty that he had given her, that captivated him.

The holiday of Venus, the goddess of love and beauty, came, and the traditional festivities were held. As was customary, Pygmalion made an offering to Venus and humbly presented a petition. He almost asked that his ivory statue be made his wife, but on second thought, he changed his request and asked only for a wife like her. Venus heard his prayer and the true wish behind it and showed her presence in the leaping flame upon the altar.

After offering his prayer, Pygmalion returned to his snow-white statue and, as was his custom, spoke to her and extended her the same kindness he would offer to a person. He gazed at the white loveliness of her cold limbs and imagined what it would be like to see them flush with color. Alas, he thought, that shall never happen. Consider his amazement, then, when he thought he saw her move! He rubbed his eyes and looked again. Her snow-white skin had taken on a lifelike glow. Her stiff ivory limbs began to move fluidly and gracefully. She was alive! Her eyes opened, and she smiled upon him, and from above, Venus smiled upon him too, happy with the love she had created. ∎

ADDITIONAL QUESTIONS AND ACTIVITIES

The myth of Pygmalion, like all myths, has a form in ancient times (Ovid), in modern times (Shaw), and in the future. The examination of the relationship between scientists and the monsters or robots they create is a common one in literature and films. (Mary Wollstonecraft Shelley's *Frankenstein* is a good example in literature; the modern classic *Blade Runner* is a good example among films.) Students can write a science fiction story in which Pygmalion (or Pygmalia) is a scientist who creates an android with whom he (or she) falls in love. In their stories, students should try to deal with one of the issues implicit in the myth: Is getting exactly what we think we want always a good thing? Can the result of our creation ever truly be an independent being? Does the impulse to change or recreate the person one loves interfere with the loving relationship?

Reviewing the Selection

1. What is Pygmalion's profession? What does he make?

2. What feelings does Pygmalion have toward his statue?

3. To whom does Pygmalion pray? What sign does he receive that his prayer has been heard?

4. What prayer does Pygmalion make? What happens as a result of his prayer?

5. What kind of relationship does Pygmalion have with his statue at the end of the story?

Connections (Questions for Writing or Discussion)

1. What similarities are there between the central character of Ovid's story and Henry Higgins in Shaw's *Pygmalion*? In what way is Pygmalion's relationship with his ivory girl similar to Higgins's relationship with Liza?

2. How do the conclusions of the classical story and of Shaw's play differ? What lesson about love does Pygmalion learn in the myth? What lessons about love and pride does Henry Higgins fail to learn? Why is it presumptuous and unforgivable for Higgins to view Liza as his creation? What point is Shaw making about respect as a necessary condition for love?

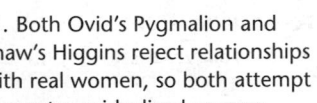

ANSWERS FOR REVIEWING THE SELECTION

1. Pygmalion is a sculptor. He carves an ivory statue.

2. He loves his statue.

3. Pygmalion prays to Venus. A flame leaps upon her altar.

4. Pygmalion prays to have a wife like his ivory girl. His statue comes to life.

5. The statue becomes Pygmalion's wife and the two have a loving relationship.

ANSWERS FOR CONNECTIONS

1. Both Ovid's Pygmalion and Shaw's Higgins reject relationships with real women, so both attempt to create an idealized woman.

2. Unlike Pygmalion, Higgins remains unable to love his "creation." Pygmalion learns to love only what he has created. Higgins fails to learn that his self-absorbed behavior will prevent him from ever having a loving relationship with an equal. Although he gives lip service to the idea, Higgins refuses to acknowledge that Liza is an independent human with needs and desires of her own, and was so before she ever met Higgins; she succeeded in her transformation in large part due to her own effort. Shaw suggests that any relationship not based on mutual respect is bound to be unsatisfactory and one-sided.

VOCABULARY DEVELOPMENT EXERCISE

▶ Give students the following exercise.

Write a dialogue for two people in which you incorporate ten words from the list on page 1060. Then, with a partner, practice both dialogues aloud, paying attention to the correct pronunciation of the new vocabulary words.

ADDITIONAL RESOURCES

ASSESSMENT PORTFOLIO
- Vocabulary Worksheet: Unit 12, 4.12.13
- Study Guide: Unit 12 Test, 4.12.14
- Unit 12 Test, 4.12.15

ESSENTIAL SKILLS PRACTICE BOOKS

Language
- Reducing Wordiness, 2.59
- Dialects of English, 2.150

UNIT REVIEW

Twentieth-Century Drama

VOCABULARY FROM THE SELECTIONS

amiable, 989	disdain, 1016	magisterially, 1010	purgatory, 1033
arbitrary, 1009	dogmatically, 1007	magnanimous, 1048	remonstrance, 1005
astride, 1007	dudgeon, 1036	melancholy, 991	resolutely, 1005
audacity, 1010	elocutionary, 1004	mendacity, 995	repudiate, 994
barometrical, 1024	estheticism, 1019	millennium, 1036	score, 1008
bilious, 995	extort, 1011	pallor, 1032	slovenly, 1009
blasphemy, 1053	forecastle, 1025	pauperize, 1014	snigger, 1025
brocade, 1019	genteel, 1001	pedantic, 1023	snivel, 1002
brusquely, 1021	ginger, 1014	perfunctorily, 1036	soirée, 1022
callous, 1013	gumption, 988	placidly, 1045	solicitor, 1042
caricature, 1019	impertinent, 993	plaint, 1007	spraddle, 1047
condescend, 1035	impetuous, 999	portico, 987	staid, 990
conscientiously, 1015	imprecation, 1023	presumptuous, 1007	steadfastly, 1008
consort, 1053	impudence, 1051	pretension, 1019	straiten, 1021
convulsively, 1026	incensed, 1015	proffer, 1041	toady, 1053
coroneted, 1032	incorrigible, 1047	proximity, 990	unabashed, 1013
deprecate, 990	infatuated, 1023	prudery, 1003	unassailable, 1009
diffident, 1009	jaunt, 1011		zephyr, 1004
	judicial, 1008		

LITERARY TERMS

characterization, 997	inciting incident, 997
climax, 1038	irony, 1030
dramatic irony, 1030	resolution, 1055
epilogue, 1055	satire, 1017, 1055
feminist criticism, 1055	spectacle, 997
foil, 1017	

SYNTHESIS: QUESTIONS FOR WRITING, RESEARCH, OR DISCUSSION

GENRE STUDIES

1. **Dramatic Irony.** Irony is a difference between appearance and reality. Dramatic irony is a type of irony in which something is known by the reader or audience but not known by the characters. Identify instances of dramatic irony in Shaw's *Pygmalion* and in Shakespeare's *Macbeth*. Discuss any similarities between these instances.

2. **Didacticism.** A didactic work is one in which the artistic values of the work are subordinated to the goal of conveying a moral, social, educational, or political message. Is Shaw's play *Pygmalion* a didactic work in this sense? Explain your answer.

3. **Staging in Modern Theater.** Theater changed a great deal between Shakespeare's day and Shaw's day. Discuss some of these changes and their significance by comparing and contrasting the stage directions given in Shakespeare's *Macbeth* and Shaw's *Pygmalion*. You may wish to review the discussion of Elizabethan staging in the Introduction to Unit 5.

THEMATIC STUDIES

4. **Gender.** Shaw's play has much to say about social mores regarding relations between men and women. Compare and contrast the ideas about women's equality expressed in *Pygmalion* with such ideas expressed in one or two of these works: Aemelia Lanyer's "Eve's Apology in Defense of Women," Anne Finch's "The Introduction," Margaret Cavendish's "To All Writing Ladies," or Mary Wollstonecraft's *A Vindication of the Rights of Woman*. In your discussion, point out differences between these speakers' views and techniques and distinguish them from differences between the speakers' respective societies.

HISTORICAL AND BIOGRAPHICAL STUDIES

5. **Social Class.** Compare and contrast the beliefs and attitudes about class distinctions that are presented in Chaucer's "Prologue" to *The Canterbury Tales* and in Shaw's *Pygmalion*. What virtues and vices does each author associate with the aristocracy and the common person?

▶These prompts are suitable as topics for research papers. Refer to the Language Arts Survey, 4.20–4.34, "Research Skills." (To evaluate research papers, see the evaluation forms for writing, revising, and proofreading in the *Assessment Portfolio*, 7.1–7.10.)

▶These prompts can be adapted for use as topics for oral reports or debates. (To evaluate these projects, see the evaluation forms in the *Assessment Portfolio*, 7.17–7.19.)

LANGUAGE LAB   VARIETIES OF ENGLISH

LANGUAGE ARTS SURVEY

For additional help, see the Language Arts Survey, 2.147.

FORMAL AND INFORMAL ENGLISH

English can be both formal and informal. Informal English is distinguished from formal English by the use of nonstandard grammatical structures, colloquialisms, and slang. The following chart will help you determine whether formal or informal English should be used.

FORMAL ENGLISH	INFORMAL ENGLISH
papers and essays	personal notes and letters
some magazine articles	diaries and journals
some nonfiction books	most newspaper and magazine articles
some literary works	some nonfiction and fiction books
public ceremonies	everyday conversation
official speeches	

LANGUAGE ARTS SURVEY

For additional help, see the Language Arts Survey, 2.150.

DIALECTS OF ENGLISH

Dialects are a variety of a language and may be based on social difference or regional difference. The dialect used by the most powerful social class is generally considered the **standard** form of a language; other dialects are considered **nonstandard**. Use of a standard dialect is useful because it is widely understood. Use of nonstandard dialects can make a literary work more lively and add authenticity.

EXERCISE A   REWRITING SENTENCES IN STANDARD ENGLISH

The following sentences from *Pygmalion* are written in Liza's Lisson Grove dialect. Rewrite these sentences in standard English.

EXAMPLE: Nah then, Freddy: look wh' y' gwoin, deah.
          Now then, buddy: look where you're going, dear.

LANGUAGE ARTS SURVEY

For additional help, see the Language Arts Survey, 2.150.

1. Theres menners f' yer! Te-oo banches o voylets trod into the mad.

2. Ow, eez ye-ooa san, is e?

3. Wal, fewd dan y' de-ooty bawmz a mather should, eed now bettern to spawl a pore gel's flahrzn than ran awy athaht pyin.

ANSWERS FOR LANGUAGE LAB

Exercise A

Responses will vary. Possible responses are given.

1. There's manners for you! Two bunches of violets trod into the mud.

2. Oh, so he's your son, is he?

3. Well, if you had done your duty by him as a mother should, he'd know better than to spill a poor girl's flowers and then run away without paying.

4. Will you pay me for them?

5. Show me what you've written about me.

4. Will ye-oo py me f' them?

5. You just show me what youve wrote about me.

EXERCISE B   REWRITING SENTENCES IN STANDARD ENGLISH

The following sentences are from Liza's introduction to her first social setting which was not exactly a success. Change Liza's statements so that they are in standard English and in appropriate language for a formal meeting and conversation.

EXAMPLE: The shallow depression in the west of these islands is likely to move slowly in an easterly direction. There are no indications of any great change in the barometrical situation.

It doesn't seem as though the weather will change soon.

1. But it's my belief they done the old woman in.

2. She come through diphtheria right enough the year before.

3. What become of her new straw hat that should have come to me?

4. Somebody pinched it; and what I say is, them as pinched it done her in.

5. Walk! Not bloody likely.

LANGUAGE ARTS SURVEY

For additional help, see the Language Arts Survey, 2.147 and 2.150.

LANGUAGE ARTS
SURVEY

1065

►Use the Pretest and Post-test for Writing Terminology and Techniques, 3.1.1–3.1.2, in the *Assessment Portfolio.*

►Use the Writing Evaluation Forms, 7.1-7.5, in the *Assessment Portfolio.*

►Use the Study Guide and Test on The Process of Writing, 5.1.1–5.1.2, in the *Assessment Portfolio.*

ESSENTIAL SKILLS:
Writing

INTRODUCTION TO WRITING

Students sometimes think of writing as a mysterious talent that some people are born with and others aren't. That just isn't so. The ability to write is learned through practice and through reading. If you keep writing, as much as you can, as often as you can, eventually you, too, will be one of those mysteriously talented people who can make written words do wonders.

1.1 THE PROCESS OF WRITING

No two people write exactly alike. Some people get everything down on paper quickly and in rough form. Then they rewrite, over and over, until they get it right. Other people work slowly, refining their ideas and expression as they go.

Despite the differences among writers, for purposes of instruction the writing process can be conveniently divided into six stages:

SIX STAGES IN THE PROCESS OF WRITING	
1. **Prewriting**	Choose a topic, audience, purpose, and form. Then gather ideas and organize these in a reasonable way.
2. **Drafting**	Get your ideas down on paper in rough form without worrying about perfecting spelling, grammar, usage, and mechanics.
3. **Peer and Self-Evaluation**	Study your draft by yourself or with one or more of your peers to find ways to improve it.
4. **Revising**	Revise your draft to improve its content, organization, and style.
5. **Proofreading**	Check your revised draft for errors in spelling, grammar, usage, and mechanics (including punctuation and capitalization). Then prepare a final copy in an appropriate manuscript form and proofread again.
6. **Publishing and Presenting**	Share your work with an audience.

▶ ▶ ▶ **A C T I V I T Y 1.1**

Take some time to examine your past experiences as a writer. On a sheet of paper or in your journal, answer the following questions:

1. Do you enjoy writing? Do you think of yourself as a good writer? Are there any writers—famous or not—whose work you admire? What good and bad experiences have you had as a writer? What are your strengths and weaknesses as a writer?

2. What kind of writing do you most enjoy doing? (Consult the list of Forms of Writing on page 1077.) Do you like writing poems, stories, humorous pieces, or reports? Why do you enjoy this kind of writing? What kinds of writing would you like to learn more about? What kinds of writing would you like to master?

3. Many writers are particular about the tools they use. What writing materials do you prefer? Do you like writing in a spiral notebook? on blank pages in a record book? on loose-leaf pages in a ring binder? on a typewriter or computer? with a pencil or a felt-tip pen?

4. When you have written in the past, did you devote a lot of time to prewriting? What sorts of prewriting activities did you do? Which of these activities were most helpful?

5. Are you the kind of writer who works slowly, perfecting each part as you go, or do you prefer to get a lot of material onto the page and then rework it?

6. In what stages of the writing process do you have the most trouble?

7. How do you feel about having other people read or listen to your writing? What can other people, including your classmates and your teacher, do to help you become a better writer?

▶ ▶ ▶ **A C T I V I T Y 1.1**

• *Responses will vary.* This exercise should encourage students to find their strengths and interests in writing and to isolate weak spots that they would like to improve. Remind students that they all have strengths in writing that they should try to discover. Also remind them that there are many different kinds of writing.

• These questions are well suited for discussion in groups of two or three. After small group discussion, discuss question 7 as an entire class.

• Ask students to bring their answers to these questions to their first individual writing conference with you. You may also want to arrange to read these answers before meeting with students.

1.2 KEEPING A WRITER'S JOURNAL

Think of a **writer's journal** as a storehouse of ideas for use in later writing. Keep your journal in a spiral notebook, a loose-leaf binder, a composition book, a scrapbook, or a bound record book of the kind sold in stationery stores. You'll get more out of a journal if you keep it separate from your other notebooks and write in it every day. The following ideas for journal entries will help you to get started.

IDEAS FOR JOURNAL ENTRIES	
The Journal as Diary	Record the observations and experiences from your daily life. Explore your feelings about people and events.
The Journal as Commonplace Book	Record interesting phrases or ideas that you hear from others or that you encounter in your reading.
The Journal as Writer's Lab	Record your ideas for pieces of writing to do in the future. Do freewriting on subjects of interest to you. Try out different kinds of writing, such as monologues, dialogues, song lyrics, concrete poetry, and riddles.

CONTINUED

► ► ► A C T I V I T Y 1.2

• Ask students how they felt about doing the different types of writing. Ask them to develop one of the ideas they wrote about in their journal. If, when given future writing assignments, students suggest they do not know what to write about, have them refer to their journal for ideas.

• For additional tips and ideas for student journals, see the introduction to this *Annotated Teacher's Edition,* page T1.

► ► ► A C T I V I T Y 1.3

• Tell the students whether you would like them to keep a comprehensive portfolio or a selected portfolio. If you choose a selected portfolio, discuss with students the criteria that will be used to evaluate their portfolios, and the criteria they should use when adding work to the portfolio.

• This would be a good time to explain to students how to complete the Comprehensive Portfolio Evaluation Form: Student, 6.4, in the *Assessment Portfolio.* You may also wish to show and explain the Comprehensive Portfolio Evaluation Form: Teacher, 6.5, in the *Assessment Portfolio.*

• Require students to complete the Writing Summary Form, 6.6, in the *Assessment Portfolio,* for each piece of writing they submit. These forms should be kept with the writings in the portfolio.

• If you choose to have students keep selected portfolios, it may be helpful to maintain files in the classroom for the pieces they do not include, in order to minimize loss and damage.

• For additional tips on teaching using portfolios, see the introduction to this *Annotated Teacher's Edition,* page T1.

The Journal as Planner	Write about what you want to do over the next week, month, year, or ten years. Explore your goals and dreams. Think on paper about how to meet your goals. Make lists of activities to help yourself grow.
The Journal as Reader Response Forum	Record your reactions to works that you read for class and on your own. Talk back to the authors, take issue with them, expand on what they say, and explore their ideas

► ► ► A C T I V I T Y 1.2

Begin a journal. For the first week, try your hand at writing each of the different kinds of entries discussed above. Date each entry that you write. Be sure to put your name and address somewhere on the journal so that it can be returned if it gets lost.

1.3 KEEPING A WRITER'S PORTFOLIO

A **writer's portfolio** is a folder in which you store your drafts and finished pieces of writing. Your teacher may ask you to keep a portfolio so that you and she can assess your progress over time. Many teachers believe that a portfolio can show a student's capabilities and progress better than any test or single writing assignment can.

Your teacher may ask you to keep a **comprehensive portfolio**, one that contains all the writing that you do for class, along with evaluation forms for that writing. Another possibility is that you will be asked to keep a **selected portfolio**, one that contains the pieces of writing that you believe to be your best. The items that you choose for a selected portfolio should show the various skills you have developed in your class and the various types of writing that you have done (informative, persuasive, creative, etc.).

When you place writing in your portfolio, remember to keep any earlier notes or drafts attached behind the latest draft. If you do that, then your teacher will be able to see how each piece of writing developed. Your portfolio should also contain any completed evaluation forms that your teacher requests of you.

If you keep a selected portfolio, make sure to save the pieces of writing that you do not include. You or your teacher may want to refer to these pieces later.

From time to time, you and your teacher will evaluate your portfolio. After each of you does a separate evaluation of the portfolio, you will probably have a meeting, or **student-teacher conference**, to discuss your work and to set goals for further development.

► ► ► A C T I V I T Y 1.3

Following your teacher's instructions, begin a writer's portfolio. You may wish to put into this portfolio pieces of writing you've done in the past that you particularly like. You can also put into the portfolio your answers to the questions in Activity 1.1 that follows the Language Arts Survey, 1.1, "The Process of Writing."

1.4 USING COMPUTERS FOR WRITING

Computers aren't essential to good writing. After all, Shakespeare did just fine without one. However, using a personal computer can make many parts of the writing process simpler.

Computer Hardware

Hardware is the actual machinery of a computer. The heart of this machinery is the **central processing unit**, or **CPU**, which carries out the instructions given by the computer user. Connected to the CPU, or sometimes in the same case with it, are various **peripherals**, devices for storing, inputting, and outputting information, or **data.**

COMMON COMPUTER PERIPHERALS	
Storage Devices	• **Floppy diskettes**, or **floppies**, are small, flat media used to store and to transport limited amounts of data, such as individual computer files and programs. • **Hard drives** store large amounts of data on revolving disks. A hard drive can be **internal** (located inside the case with the CPU) or **external** (housed in a separate case and connected to the CPU by a cable). • **Removable media**, like hard drives, store large amounts of data. However, unlike hard drives, they can be inserted and ejected, like floppy disks. Common removable media include CD/ROMs, optical disks, and DAT tapes.
Input Devices	• **Keyboards**, the most common of all input devices, allow you to type numbers, alphabetic characters, and special computer commands. • **Mice** and **trackballs** are devices that are used to point to and select items on a computer monitor. • **Digitizing tablets** allow you to write in longhand and to draw directly onto the computer screen. • **Scanners** allow you to turn pictures or words into computer files that can then be edited or otherwise manipulated. • **Voice recognition devices** allow you to speak commands to the computer. Some will even transcribe, or write, your speech into a computer file that can then be edited.
Output Devices	• **Monitors** are the most common output devices. A monitor is a screen, similar to the ones on televisions, that shows you the work that you are doing on the computer. • **Printers** are machines that create **hard copies**, or printed paper, of the work that you have done on the computer. • **Modems** are devices for communicating, over telephone lines, with other computers.

Computer Software

Software is the set of instructions for making a computer do particular tasks. A particular piece of software is called a **program.** The people who create programs are called **programmers.** The following chart describes common programs used by writers.

SOFTWARE FOR WRITERS	
Operating System	An **operating system,** or **OS,** is a program that tells the computer how to do general tasks—how to create, save, and store files; what to do when specific commands are given; how to print files, and so on.
Application Software	An **application program** enables the user to accomplish a particular kind of task. Common application programs include the following: • **Word-processing programs** allow you to key in words. Most such programs also allow you to revise your writing, to check its spelling, to add special formatting such as boldface or italic letters, and to save and print your work. Many of these programs also allow you to consult a built-in dictionary and/or thesaurus and to check your grammar, usage, capitalization, and punctuation. • **Page-layout programs** allow you to put your writing into columns and boxes and to add graphic elements such as lines, borders, photographs, and illustrations. Such programs are used to produce newsletters, posters, flyers, newspapers, magazines, and books. • **Graphics programs** allow you to create illustrations and to edit photographs. • **Telecommunications programs** allow you to use a **modem** to connect over telephone lines to other computers, to **on-line information services,** or to **computer networks** such as the **Internet.** Other types of programs often used by writers include ones for creating outlines, graphs, charts, indexes, and bibliographies.

Applications of Computers to Writing

Obviously, a computer can be useful simply as a means for getting words onto a page. However, any typewriter can do that. A typewriter also allows you to save separate drafts of your writing as hard copy. Nonetheless, computers offer some advantages that typewriters do not:

• the ability to revise, or edit, your writing easily, simply by moving words, sentences, or paragraphs around on the monitor or disk without having to rekey everything;

• the ability to format your writing in special ways (by adding bold or italic formatting; by specifying the sets of letters, or fonts, to be used; by automating functions such as paragraph, page, and line breaks, and so on);

• the ability to look up definitions, synonyms, and antonyms and to perform, automatically, such editing functions as checking your spelling, grammar, usage, and mechanics;

- the ability to print multiple copies of your work;
- the ability to add photographs and illustrations to your work;
- the ability to use computer-accessed information sources, such as on-line information services and reference materials such as encyclopedias on CD/ROM

Despite these advantages, many writers still prefer to work in longhand or to use typewriters. Like most aspects of writing, the choice of writing instrument is up to you. It depends, of course, not only on your personal preferences, but also on the availability of machines and of instruction on how to use them. Many schools have **writing labs** with computers available to students, and computers are sometimes available in school or public libraries. If you do not have access to a personal computer, check with your teachers and librarians about computers and computer training available to students in your area.

► ► ► **ACTIVITY 1.4a**

Design an ideal computer writing lab for your school. Make a floor plan of the lab. Show how the computers, peripherals, desks, chairs, and other furniture will be arranged. Label each of these items. You may wish to talk to a computer dealer or to look at some computer equipment catalogs to gather information for your plan.

PREWRITING: DEVELOPING A PLAN FOR WRITING

It is theoretically possible to have a wonderful vacation without making any plans beforehand. However, traveling without prior planning usually isn't a good idea. If you make a thorough plan before you go, the trip is more likely to be a success. The same is true of writing. Good writing sometimes results from just being spontaneous and writing whatever comes to mind. However, if you make a plan for writing before you do it, the writing is likely to go more smoothly and to be more fun. A good writing plan begins with the following elements:

ELEMENTS OF A WRITING PLAN	
Topic	The specific subject that you will be writing about
Purpose	The aim, or goal, that you want the piece of writing to accomplish: to express yourself, to create a literary work, to inform, or to persuade
Audience	The person or persons who will read or hear your work
Form	The specific type of writing that you will be doing (for example, a press release or a short story)
Mode	The method of presentation of the ideas in a piece of writing. Common modes, often combined in actual pieces of writing, include narration, dialogue, description, and various kinds of exposition, such as analysis or comparison and contrast.

ESSENTIAL SKILLS: WRITING **1071**

► ► ► **ACTIVITY 1.4a**

Floor plans should be well organized and students should have reasons for including the items they did. After creating their floor plans, students can present their ideas in small groups. Then the group can discuss the benefits of each plan.

► ► ► ACTIVITY 1.4b

The topic the student chooses should be appropriately focused for the form he or she has chosen. Students may begin to develop this piece of writing. As they write, ask them to note if they have decided to change their plans, for example, refocusing their topics or exploring their ideas in a different form.

► ► ► ACTIVITY 1.4b

In your journal, make a plan for a piece of writing that you would like to do in the future. List the topic, purpose, audience, form, and mode of the piece. You may wish to refer to Sections 1.5–1.9 of the Language Arts Survey for information to help you complete this activity.

1.5 CHOOSING AND FOCUSING A TOPIC

Choosing a Topic

"What can I possibly write about?" This is one of the most common questions asked by students. If you find yourself asking this question, don't despair. You are in good company. Most writers occasionally have a difficult time coming up with good ideas for writing. The following tips should help you to find a topic that is interesting and engaging:

TIPS FOR DISCOVERING WRITING TOPICS	
Mine Your Journal	Make a habit of jotting down ideas for writing in your journal. Pretty soon, you will have a store of good ideas to draw from.
Draw on Your Experience	Think about experiences that you have had in the past, from early childhood on. People, places, and events from personal experience make excellent topics for writing. Making a time line of your life might help to jog your memory.
Consult Reference Works and Other Media	Browsing through reference works, looking through the shelves in a library, paging through magazines or newspapers, exploring the contents of informational CD/ROMs—all can help you to find topics worth writing about.
Do Some Freewriting	One interesting way to come up with a writing idea is simply to put your pen to paper and start writing about whatever pops into your mind, without stopping to think about spelling, grammar, usage, and mechanics. Don't force yourself to stick to one subject. Freewriting is one situation in which it's actually good to let your mind wander! Write for five to ten minutes. Then look over your freewriting for topic ideas.
Talk to People	Other people can be excellent resources for writing ideas. Draw on the experiences of the people around you. Ask them about subjects of interest to you and to them.

Focusing a Topic

One way to approach topic selection is first to choose a general topic and then to focus on some part of that topic. Here's an example:

General topic: Popular music

Focused topic 1: Literary references, or allusions, in contemporary popular songs

Focused topic 2: The making of a music video

Just how general your focused topic should be depends on several factors. In most cases, the shorter the piece of writing that you plan to do, the more focused the topic should be. However, the generality of your topic also depends on how much detail you want to include in your piece. Obviously, if you were writing a four-paragraph composition about a topic as general as "popular music," then you wouldn't be able to go into much detail. However, there are times, as when writing for children or for an encyclopedia article, when writing doesn't have to be very detailed and general topics are appropriate.

TECHNIQUES FOR FOCUSING TOPICS	
Analyze the Topic	Break the topic down into its parts. Then think about how the parts relate to one another.
Do a Tree Diagram	Write the topic at the top of a page. Then break it into parts, and break those parts into parts.
Ask Questions	Write questions about the topic beginning with the words *who, what, where, when, why,* and *how.* Decide which answers to these questions are most important for your piece.

Other techniques for focusing topics include freewriting and clustering (see the Language Arts Survey, 1.12, "Freewriting," and 1.17, "Clustering").

►►► ACTIVITIES 1.5

A. Choose a place in your journal to list possible topics for writing. Using the techniques discussed in the lesson above, generate at least ten topics for use in the future. Add to your list of writing topics as ideas occur to you. Keep the list in one place in your journal so that you can easily find and refer to it.

B. Choose one of the general topics below and write three specific, focused topics related to it.

General topics: weather politics
games natural disasters
the future modern art

1.6 CHOOSING A PURPOSE OR AIM

The **purpose,** or **aim,** of a piece of writing is the goal that the writer wishes to accomplish. The study of purpose in writing and speaking is called **rhetoric.**

►►► ACTIVITIES 1.5

A. Suggest that students include some general ideas and some specific ones. Allow ample time for students to try the idea-generating techniques. Students may wish to share their lists with others to generate more ideas. Suggest that students write as much about the ideas as occurs to them.

B. *Responses will vary. Possible responses are given.*

weather: how meteorologists predict the weather, why I like rainy days, the day it snowed in July

games: how to play chess, scoring the winning goal, critique of new video games

the future: personal goals for the next five years, living in a space colony, predictions on the state of the environment in ten years

politics: speech for a school election, my experiences working on a campaign, analysis of a debate between presidential candidates

natural disasters: local effects of the recent hurricane (earthquake, tidal wave, volcanic eruption, etc.), beginnings and development of a tornado, what to do in case of an earthquake

modern art: critique of a modern art exhibit, biography of a modern artist, what I see in (any specific work of art)

Communication is the act of sending and receiving **messages.** Whenever a message is conveyed, there are four elements involved: the **sender** of the message, the **recipient** of the message, the **subject** of the message, and the **code** (the signs or symbols) used to communicate the message. This model of communication is often represented in what is known as the **communication triangle.**

The Communication Triangle

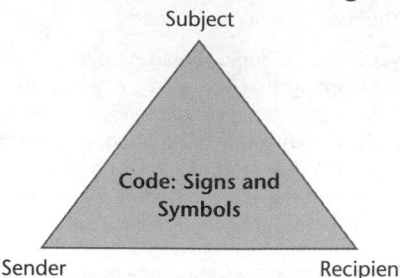

From the time of Aristotle on, teachers of rhetoric have attempted to develop schemes for classifying types of writing and speech. One useful classification method is based on the communications triangle and on the writer's purpose. This method divides pieces of writing into four classes, depending on whether the focus of the writing is on the sender, the recipient, the subject, or the signs and symbols. Notice that each of the four modes involves a different primary purpose.

THE CLASSIFICATION OF WRITING AND SPEECH BY PURPOSE OR AIM			
Type	**Focus is on . . .**	**Purpose is to . . .**	**Examples**
Expressive Writing	the sender (the writer or speaker)	express the feelings of the writer or speaker	journal entry, credo
Informative Writing	the subject	provide information about the subject	accident reports, book report
Persuasive Writing	the recipient (the reader or listener)	move the reader or listener to adopt a point of view or to act in a particular way	campaign speech, public service ad
Literary Writing	the signs or symbols used to communicate the message	create a work of art	lyric poem, short story

Limitations of Classification Systems

A classification system like that shown above is useful for thinking about and discussing writing and speech. However, any such system has its limitations. One limitation is that an actual piece of writing rarely falls neatly and exclusively into one category and rarely serves a single purpose. Consider, for example, William Wordsworth's poem "The world is too much with us," on page 611. Its purpose is literary. The writer obviously thought a great deal on the specific symbols used to communicate his message (that is, he chose his language carefully for artistic purposes) and obviously had in mind the purpose of creating a work of literary art. However, the poem also serves other purposes. It *expresses* the feelings of the speaker, it *informs* the reader about the world that the speaker lived in, and it attempts to *persuade* the reader about the importance of contact with nature.

Purpose and the Writing Process

Thinking about purpose can be useful to you as a writer, despite the limitations discussed above. For example, thinking about purpose can help you to choose what prewriting tasks you undertake. If your major purpose is to inform, then you will probably want to gather facts. If your major purpose is to persuade, you will want to find arguments to support your position and make lists of words and phrases that will appeal to your readers emotionally. Purpose is also a very important consideration during revision. When you evaluate your work prior to revising it, the most important questions to ask yourself are, "Have I accomplished my purpose?" and "If not, how can I change the piece of writing so that it better accomplishes my purpose?"

> ► ► ► **ACTIVITIES 1.6**
>
> **A.** For each communications situation listed below, identify the sender, the recipient, the subject, the code, and the message being sent.
>
> 1. A sailor uses flags to signal to a passing ship that his own ship is in danger.
> 2. A child writes a note to her grandfather, thanking him for a birthday present.
> 3. A space probe sends pictures of the surface of one of Jupiter's moons to a computer terminal at NASA headquarters.
> 4. A political candidate gives a speech on television, urging voters to support her candidacy.
>
> **B.** Identify the primary purpose of each of the following types of writing:
>
> 1. an entry in a diary
> 2. a newspaper editorial supporting a new law
> 3. a short story
> 4. directions for using a modem

1.7 CHOOSING AND ANALYZING AN AUDIENCE

It isn't always possible to know who will read or hear your writing and under what circumstances. However, even when you aren't certain who your audience will be, it's a good idea to write with a specific audience in mind. Thinking about a specific audience—what Robert Graves calls "the reader over your shoulder"—will help you to

- focus your writing;
- choose details, examples, or arguments that your reader will find interesting or convincing;

► ► ► **ACTIVITIES 1.6**

A.

1. sender: sailor
   recipient: sailors on passing ship
   subject: ship in danger
   code: flags (semaphore)
   message: Your ship is in danger.

2. sender: child
   recipient: grandfather
   subject: present
   code: English
   message: Thank you for the present.

3. sender: space probe
   recipient: NASA staff through computer
   subject: one of Jupiter's moons
   code: (digital) computer code
   message: pictures

4. sender: political candidate
   recipient: television viewers
   subject: candidacy
   code: English
   message: Support my candidacy.

B.

1. express feelings or ideas
2. encourage readers to adopt a particular view
3. create a work of art
4. provide information

- decide what information to include or to leave out;
- determine how formal or informal and how complex or simple your language should be.

► ► ► **A C T I V I T Y 1.7**

Rewrite each of the following passages for the audience indicated in parentheses. Discuss with your classmates the kinds of changes you introduced to make the piece appropriate for its new audience.

1. From a technical manual: Avoid immersing the blender in water as this may cause severe damage to the internal mechanism. (Rewrite as a verbal instruction to a friend.)

2. From an encyclopedia article: Yielding to pressure from activists, governments around the globe have in recent years taken legislative steps to reduce the impact on the environment of industrial pollutants. (Rewrite as an explanation to a small child.)

3. From a report made to a city council by the city's Director of Health and Human Services: We estimate that approximately 1,200 homeless people now live in our city, up from 945 last year. On a given night, there are about 800 available beds in the city's licensed homeless shelters. (Rewrite as a paragraph attempting to persuade people to give money to homeless shelters.)

4. From a sports story in a newspaper: After nine scoreless innings, Reds center fielder Manuel Bosco slammed a two-run homer over the left field fence. (Rewrite so that the situation and event would be understandable to someone who is unfamiliar with baseball and baseball jargon.)

1.8 CHOOSING A FORM

One of the most important decisions that a writer makes is about the form that a piece of writing will take. The following chart lists some forms of writing that you might wish to try.

► ► ► **A C T I V I T Y 1.7**

Responses will vary. Possible responses are given.

1. Don't put the blender in water or you'll wreck it.

2. People in a lot of countries have made laws so that big companies won't make the water and air dirty.

3. The number of homeless people in our city has risen dramatically. Today, 1,200 people call the street home; but there are only 800 beds for them in shelters. The shelters need your help. Before you settle into your bed for the night, think of those who don't have a bed to go to and send a donation to Help the Homeless.

4. When the regular part of the game ended with the score zero to zero, the teams continued playing to break the tie. Then Reds player Manuel Bosco had a great hit that allowed his team to score twice.

FORMS OF WRITING

Abstract	Constitution	Graffiti
Acceptance speech	Constructive speech	Grant application
Ad copy	Consumer report	Greeting card
Address to a jury	Contract	Haiku
Adventure	Court decision	Headline
Advice column	Credo	History
Afterword	Critical analysis	Horoscope
Agenda	Curriculum	Human interest story
Allegory	Daydream	Informative essay
Annals	Debate	Instructions
Annotation	Detective story	Insult
Annual report	Dialogue	Interview questions
Apology	Diary	Introduction
Appeal	Diatribe	Invitation
Autobiography	Dictionary entry	Itinerary
Ballad	Directions	Jingle
Ballet	Docudrama	Joke
Bibliography	Dramatic narrative	Journal entry
Billboard	Dream analysis	Keynote address
Biography	Dream report	Lament
Birth announcement	Editorial	Law (statute)
Blank verse	Elegy	Learning log
Book review	Encyclopedia article	Letter of complaint
Brief	Epic	Letter to the editor
Brochure	Epic poem	Libretto
Bulletin board	Epilogue	Limerick
Business letter	Epistolary fiction	Love letter
Business proposal	Epitaph	Lyric poem
Bylaws	Essay	Magazine article
Campaign speech	Eulogy	Manifesto
Captions	Experiment	Manual
Cartoon	Explication	Memorandum
Cause-and-effect essay	Exposé	Memorial plaque
Chant	Fable	Menu
Character sketch	Fabliaux	Minutes
Charter	Family history	Monologue
Cheer	Fantasy	Monument inscription
Children's story	Filmstrip	Movie review
Cinquain	Flyer	Mystery
Classified ad	Foreword	Myth
Comeback speech	Fortune cookie insert	Narrative poem
Comedy	Found poem	Nature guide
Comic strip	Free Verse	News story
Community calendar	Gothic tale	Nomination speech
Concrete poem	Graduation speech	Nonsense rhyme

CONTINUED

Novel	Quatrain	Spenserian)
Novella	Radio play	Specifications
Nursery rhyme	Radio spot	Spell
Obituary	Rap	Sports story
One-act play	Reader's theater production	Storyboard
Oracle	Rebuttal	Stream-of-consciousness
Ottava rima	Recipes	fiction
Packaging copy	Recommendation	Summary
Parable	Referendum question	Summation
Paragraph	Research report	Survey
Paraphrase	Resignation	Sutra
Parody	Restaurant review	Tall tale
Party platform	Résumé	Tanka
Pastoral	Riddle	Technical writing
Persuasive essay	Roast	Terza rima
Petition	Romance	Test
Play	Sales letter	Thank-you note
Police/Accident	Schedule	Theater review
Report	Science fiction	Toast
Political advertisement	Screenplay	Tour guide
Prediction	Sermon	Tragedy
Preface	Short short story	Translation
Press release	Short story	Treaty
Proclamation	Sign	TV spot
Profile	Situation comedy	Villanelle
Prologue	Slide show	Vows
Proposal	Slogan	Want ad
Prose poem	Song lyric	Wanted poster
Protocol	Sonnet (Petrarchan,	Warrant
Public service announcement	Elizabethan, or	Wish list

► ► ► **A C T I V I T Y 1.8**

Students can share their writing with the class or in small groups. They can compare and contrast the originals to their adaptations. They should discuss any difficulties they had in adapting their pieces and how effective they feel their pieces are in the new forms.

► ► ► **A C T I V I T Y 1.8**

One way to become familiar with the possibilities and limitations of forms of writing is to try translating something written in one form into a different form. Choose one of the following possibilities and experiment with it in your journal. Refer to the Handbook of Literary Terms for more information about the forms of writing given below.

1. Rewrite a familiar tall tale, myth, folk tale, or children's tale as a rap poem or song lyric.

2. Choose a short story that you really like and dramatize a scene from it. That is, rewrite the scene using nothing but stage directions or dialogue.

3. Choose an historical account from one of your history textbooks. Rewrite the account as though it were being described as play-by-play action by a sports commentator on television.

1.9 MODES OF WRITING

Another way of classifying types of writing is by **mode.** A mode is a way of presenting ideas, information, and details in a piece of writing. Most pieces of writing combine several different modes, although one usually dominates. The following chart lists some of the most common modes.

COMMON MODES OF WRITING		
Mode	**Explanation**	**Forms in Which This Mode Dominates**
Narration	Presents events, usually in chronological order	Short story News report Process/How-to writing
Dialogue	Presents the speech of characters	Drama Dramatic poem Docudrama
Description	Uses images to present a portrait in words	Imagist poem Tour guide
Exposition	Presents information	(See below)

There are many, many types of exposition. Among the most common are analysis, comparison and contrast, classification, and causal analysis.

An **analysis** breaks a subject down into parts. Then it shows how the parts are related to one another and to the whole. For example, an analysis of a biological organism might break it into digestive, respiratory, excretory, circulatory, and reproductive systems. An analysis of a plot might break it into exposition, inciting incident, rising action, climax, falling action, resolution, and dénouement.

Comparison and contrast writing shows similarities and differences between one or more subjects. For example, a writer might compare the human brain to a digital computer or a dark wood to moral confusion.

Classification divides a group of subjects into groups, or classes, of things with similar characteristics. For example, a writer might divide popular films into comedies, romances, adventure stories, animated children's stories, family classics, and so on.

A **cause and effect analysis** describes a sequence of events in which one or more events cause, or bring about, one or more other events. For example, a cause and effect analysis of the origins of the English Civil War that brought about the execution of Charles I might explain the war as resulting from religious differences between the northern and southern parts of England, power struggles between the landed gentry in rural areas and the merchant class in the cities, and disagreements over taxes between the crown and the House of Commons.

Occasionally, a writer will use one mode almost entirely. For example, a screenplay consists almost entirely of dialogue. However, more commonly, a writer will combine one or more modes, switching between narration, dialogue, description, and exposition to achieve particular purposes within a piece. So, for example, a short story might consist primarily of narration, of presentations of events. However, it will also generally contain descriptions of characters and of the setting as well as dialogue showing what the characters have to say to one another.

• The four short pieces should be about the same topic, and each should be written in a different mode.

• Students may wish to work at combining some or all of their pieces to see how modes can be combined in a piece of writing.

► ► ► **A C T I V I T Y 1.9**

Choose one of the following topics or one of your own. Then write a short piece about the topic in each of the four major modes: narration, description, dialogue, and exposition.

a baseball game	flight
music videos	warfare

PREWRITING: EXPLORING IDEAS ON YOUR OWN

In many traditional cultures around the globe, elderly people are greatly revered because of their knowledge and experience. Every day that you live, you add to what you know and understand. Already, you know enough to fill many, many libraries. This section of the Language Arts Survey will give you some tips about how to draw on your past experience— on what you already know—to find ideas and details for writing.

1.10 RECALLING

Past experience is a superb source of ideas and details for writing. In fact, one of the most common pieces of advice that experienced writers give to young people is, "Write about what you already know." Perhaps you play a musical instrument and know about lessons and practicing and performances. Perhaps you have lived in or visited other places. Perhaps you have had interesting or emotionally significant experiences with friends. The secret to turning such experiences into good writing is **recalling**, or remembering, them vividly. Here are some hints for using recall to come up with writing topics and to generate ideas about these topics:

USING RECALL TO GATHER WRITING IDEAS

1. Choose some time in your life that you want to think about. It might be early child-hood, for example, when you were first learning about the world around you. It might be the time when you started going to a new school or working at a new part-time job.

2. Make a time line of events that occurred during that period. (See the Language Arts Survey, 1.19, for more information on making time lines.)

3. Make a list of questions, problems, opinions, wishes, dreams, or goals that you had during that time.

4. List important things that you learned during that time. How did you grow or change? What brought about this growth or change?

5. Make a list of the important people in your life at that time. What was interesting or engaging or unusual about each of these people? How did they look and dress and talk and behave? What ideas, opinions, attitudes, and habits did they have? What did you learn from them? How did they act toward you and you toward them? Why?

CONTINUED

---

6. Make a list of specific places that you associate with that time. Close your eyes and try to imagine one of these places. Think about what it looked like. What sights, sounds, smells, or tastes come to mind when you think of this place? How did the place make you feel?

7. If you wish to do a piece of imaginative writing, think of past experiences as raw material to be reshaped and transformed. Choose aspects of your past experience and ask yourself questions about them. Begin your questions with the words "What if . . . ?"

What if my little brother's imaginary friend turned out to be real?

What if someone like Aunt Zurletha were president of the United States?

What if the economic circumstances of my family had changed dramatically when I was three or four years old?

After you have come up with a specific person, place, thing, or event from your past to write about, try to recall as many details about it as you can. Use graphic devices such as sensory detail charts, cluster diagrams, character analysis charts, and time lines to generate specific details to use in your writing. (For information about these devices, see the Language Arts Survey, 1.17–1.24.)

> ► ► ► **ACTIVITIES 1.10**
>
> **A.** In your journal, make a time line of your life. On the time line, list major events and the dates when these events occurred.
>
> **B.** Choose one event from your time line and do a cluster chart or freewrite about this event.
>
> **C.** Choose a person from your life who was really important to you or really an interesting character. In your journal, create a character analysis chart describing this person. Describe the person's appearance, expressions, movements, clothing, background, opinions, habits, behaviors, motivations, and relationships.

1.11 OBSERVING

If you get into a habit of writing regularly, you may find that being a writer changes your way of looking at things in general. That's because, for a writer, everything that happens is potential material. Good writers develop their powers of observation. They attend to details in their everyday lives, recording interesting ones in their journals for later use. Of particular importance to good writing is the **telling detail**—one that implies a great deal. Imagine, for example, a description of a house after a fire. A single detail—a half-charred family photograph, for example—could be enough to reveal the terrible loss that has occurred.

Sometimes you may want to make fresh, new observations for a piece of writing. For example, you might want to report on or review an event such as a student council meeting or a school play. When making such observations, remember the questions typically asked by

---

► ► ► **ACTIVITIES 1.10**

A. Students' time lines should be roughly chronological, but they need not give exact dates if they cannot remember them. Suggest that they consider including the first time they did something (went to school, went away to camp, got a job), significant celebrations in which they took part (holidays, weddings, community), and special recognition they have received.

B. Students should use the cluster chart or freewrite to explore varied aspects of the event, or to explore in depth one particular aspect.

C. Students should choose a person they know or knew well.

reporters and answered in news stories: *who? what? where? when? why?* and *how?* Ask yourself these questions as you view the event, and record your answers. Take notes using abbreviations and a modified outline form. (For more information on note-taking, see the Language Arts Survey, 4.31, "Informal Note-taking." Record details of sight, sound, touch, taste, and smell. Be especially careful to record telling details, ones that will be particularly significant to your readers.

▶ ▶ ▶ A C T I V I T I E S **1.11**

For all of these exercises, students should observe carefully and gather as many details as possible.

A. Students should be specific and include details that refer to as many of the senses as possible to describe their place. For information on sensory detail charts, see the Language Arts Survey, 1.18.

B. Students' descriptions should create an image of an object or a piece of clothing and include telling details about its owner. If students are having trouble including details about the person, suggest the following example: "The pen, for once, was not in his mouth, but the ravages of endless hours of nervous chomping had taken their toll."

C. Students should use precise details and vivid images in their description of an animal and its movements. They may find it helpful to use similes in their descriptions. Encourage them to explain the ways in which the tenor and vehicle of the simile are alike.

▶ ▶ ▶ A C T I V I T I E S **1.11**

A. Go to a crowded place—a school cafeteria or a bus stop, for example—and make observations about the place in your journal. Look for interesting, unusual, and telling details. Afterward, make a sensory details chart based on your observations.

B. Choose an object or an article of clothing that belongs to someone you know— something that you associate particularly with that person. Describe it in minute detail. Try to choose details that tell your readers something about the person to whom the object or article of clothing belongs.

C. Choose an animal or insect to observe. Describe its appearance, movements, and, if appropriate, its sounds.

1.12 FREEWRITING

One excellent way to come up with writing ideas or to gather details about a topic is to **freewrite.** When you freewrite, you simply put a pen or pencil to a piece of paper and write whatever comes into your mind without pausing to think about organization, spelling, grammar, usage, mechanics, or manuscript form. Write for one to ten minutes without stopping. If you get stuck, simply repeat the last few words until something new pops into your mind. Here's a sample freewrite done by a student in a writing class:

i dont know what to write about. How can a person just come up with ideas like that, without thinking? Ideas. Like those little light bulbs that appear over the heads of comic strip characters. Or thought bubbles, with those little dots wouldn't it be funny if people in real life had little thought bubbles over their shoulders that showed what they were really thinking? hey, that would make a really funny television comedy program. People are sitting around having dinner and being all polite and everything but there are these thought bubble showing what theyre really thinking. Thinking thinking thinking. I wonder sometimes what my cat is thinking. Do cats think? More than some people, I bet. Gee, I bet the time for this freewrite is just about up. Wonder if we'll be called on to read these things aloud in class. Aloud in class aloud in class aloud in class. You're sitting in class, and suddenly, there's a loud noise. It's coming from outside. What kind of noise? Maybe its a whirring sound, like a flying saucer. Maybe theres a flying saucer landing in the school parking lot and on board are a bunch of teachers from the future, going back in time to see what schools used to be like. No, that wouldn't be a flying saucer that would be a time machine. Time. Wonder if the time is up for this freewrite. I'm stuck again. Gosh, freewriting is a lot like daydreaming on paper. Who would have thought that daydreaming in class would be a good idea?

—Melanie Hernandez

An excellent way to explore what you already know about a topic is to do a **focused freewrite.** A focused freewrite is just like a regular freewrite, except that you begin with one topic and keep bringing yourself back to it whenever your mind wanders to something else.

▶ ▶ ▶ **A CTIVITIES 1.12**

A. Reread the previous freewrite. Make a list of five possible topics for writing based on this freewrite.

B. Choose one of the following topics and do a freewrite in your journal about it for five minutes:

Arcade games	Gifts	Objects found in attics
Bad weather	Heroes	Parties
Being kind to yourself	Jokes that aren't funny	Pet peeves
City life (or country life)	Junk food	Things that live underground
Dating	Losing things	Things to do on a rainy day
	Movies	
	Nightmares	

▶ ▶ ▶ **A CTIVITIES 1.12**

A. *Responses will vary.* Possible topics include a cat's daydreams, aliens arriving at school, what schools were like in the past, time travel, and what people say/what they think.

B. Remind students to write anything that comes to mind and to keep writing for the entire time. After five minutes, have students read what they have written and make a list of five possible writing topics based on their own freewrite.

1.13 QUESTIONING

Asking questions is a superb technique for focusing a writing topic and for gathering ideas. One commonly used technique, previously mentioned, is to ask the so-called **reporting questions:** *who? what? where? when? why?* and *how?* This technique is especially useful when gathering details about events or when planning a narrative such as a news report, a short story, or a narrative poem.

Another questioning technique, especially useful for expressive or literary writing, involves asking questions that begin with the words *what if.* Asking *"What if . . . ?"* questions encourages creative, imaginative thinking. Here are some examples:

EXAMPLES *What if* cars were banned from cities and replaced entirely by elevated monorails? How would cities be different? What use could be made of the spaces now taken up by streets and parking garages? How would the quality of life in cities improve or worsen?

What if some important historical event had had a different outcome? What would have happened, for example, if the South had won the Civil War?

What if all the machines in a house turned on their owner and started playing dangerous tricks?

What if people grew younger instead of older?

What if a worker in a factory discovered that her coworkers were all robots or aliens or conspirators in some wicked undertaking?

A. *Responses will vary.*

Topic: Mountain climbing

Who was the first person to climb Mt. Everest? *Who* was the youngest?

What do you bring with you when you climb a mountain?

Where are the most commonly climbed mountains?

When is the best time to go mountain climbing?

Why do people face the difficulties and at times danger of mountain climbing?

How do people prepare to climb a mountain?

B. *Responses will vary. Possible responses are given.*

What if computers ran the government?

What if the presidents of the United States, Mexico, and France were jazz musicians?

What if the animal shelter were a democracy?

What if your job were to design maps for insects?

What if I wanted to plan an earthquake-proof city?

What if an Aztec civilization were discovered in modern Mexico?

What if humans were an endangered species?

What if a mountain climber broke an arm?

What if the Fourth of July fireworks weren't delivered in time for the holiday?

What if a scuba diver discovered an underwater city?

What if aliens watched a football game? What would they think?

What if a sculpture came to life?

What if a hot air balloon popped?

What if the whales in a marine animal show went on strike?

►**Teaching Note:** Students might choose to explore responses to one of their questions, in either exercise A or B, as a writing topic.

► ► ► A C T I V I T I E S   1 . 1 3

A. Choose one of the following topics. In your journal, write questions about the topic beginning with *who, what, where, when, why,* and *how.*

Computers	Earthquakes	Mountain climbing	Sculpture
Jazz	Mexico	Fireworks	Hot air balloons
Democracy	Endangered	Scuba diving	Whales
Maps	species	Football	

B. Choose four topics from the list above and write *"What if . . . ?"* questions about them.

1.14 ANALYZING

Analyzing is a technique for gathering information about a topic. When you analyze something, you break it down into its parts and then think about how the parts are related. An **analysis chart** lists the parts, describes each, and explains how each is related to the whole.

ANALYSIS OF SHAKESPEARE'S SONNET 29 (PAGE 282)		
Part	**Description**	**Relationship of Part to Whole**
First Quatrain (lines 1–4)	The speaker briefly describes times when he feels bad (when in disgrace, unfortunate, or ill-fated).	Introduces the basic situation of the poem
Second Quatrain (lines 5–8)	The speaker describes, specifically, what he wishes for at such times (to look like someone else, to have friends like someone else, to have someone else's abilities and range of talents ["art" and "scope"]).	Elaborates on the basic situation described in the first quatrain
Third Quatrain (lines 9–12)	The speaker tells how, when he feels this way, he thinks of the person to whom the poem is addressed.	Presents the turning point in the poem—the change in the speaker's feelings
Concluding Couplet (lines 13–14)	The speaker comments that remembering that person's love transforms his state of despair to one of joy, in which he feels more fortunate than kings.	Shows how the basic situation described in the opening eight lines is changed

> > > **A C T I V I T I E S 1.14**

A. Do an analysis chart for Shakespeare's Sonnet 18, on page 280. Follow the model given on page 1084.

B. Choose some activity or process that you enjoy (for example, putting on a play, planning a trip, or setting up a computer). Create an analysis chart describing that process.

C. Choose some organization that you know well (your school, a workplace, or a sports team are some possibilities). Create an analysis chart to describe that organization's structure.

1.15 IMAGINING

Imagining is the process of thinking of things not as they are but as they might be. It is the faculty of imagination that enables writers to create new settings, themes, characters, and plots.

In ancient days, imagining was considered a mysterious, spiritual process. The ancient Greeks explained creativity by saying that sometimes an artist was filled by the spirit of a **Muse**, one of the daughters of Memory and the king of the gods, Zeus. The Muse spoke through the artist, inspiring the creation of poetry, dance, song, comedy, tragedy, history, and so on. In the opening lines of *Paradise Lost,* on page 429, John Milton makes use of this old tradition, calling not upon one of the Greek Muses but rather upon the Christian Holy Spirit to inspire his verse.

Creativity remains today a mysterious process. There is much that we still do not understand about it. However, it is possible to use a few simple techniques, known as **heuristics**, to trigger our imaginations to come up with new, creative ideas for writing.

HEURISTICS FOR IMAGINING

1. Ask questions beginning with the words *what if.* (Example: What if aliens from another world picked up a television broadcast of a football game and based their entire understanding of earth on this broadcast?)

2. Combine previously existing things in a new way. (Example: Create a new character for a story by giving a medieval English king the personality of your younger brother or sister.)

3. Magnify something, making it bigger or more consequential than it is now. (Example: A new cold virus appears that, once caught, does not go away. It spreads rapidly, causing problems over the entire globe.)

4 Simplify something to make it more manageable to write about. (Example: Include in a story a minor character who, like your uncle, is a great teller of funny anecdotes, but make that the single, defining quality of the character.)

5. Make a drawing, sketch, or diagram. (Example: Draw a map of an imaginary island as a setting for a story.)

CONTINUED

> > > **A C T I V I T I E S 1.14**

A.

Part: First Quatrain (lines 1–4)

Description: The speaker wonders whether to describe the subject of the poem as a summer's day and begins to explain why this is not a good comparison.

Relationship of Part to Whole: Poses the initial question that introduces the subject of the poem

Part: Second Quatrain (lines 5–8)

Description: The speaker offers more reasons why the subject and a summer's day are not alike.

Relationship of Part to Whole: Elaborates on the situation described in the first quatrain

Part: Third Quatrain (lines 9–12)

Description: The speaker explains why, ultimately, the two are different.

Relationship of Part to Whole: Presents climax of the contrast between the two subjects

Part: Concluding Couplet (lines 13–14)

Description: The speaker explains what gives long-lasting life to the subject.

Relationship of Part to Whole: Explains the responses to the question posed in the first line

B. *Responses will vary.* Responses should break the process into logical steps and explain what happens at each step and how each step is related to the whole activity.

C. Students' charts should show the different roles in the organization's structure and how each role relates to other roles and to the function of the organization as a whole.

6. Start with something as it is and change it systematically. (Example: Set a story in a school that is like your school except that it is run by the older students, is located in a space colony, has foreign exchange students from other galaxies, and so on.)

7. Project a trend into the future. (Example: Write a poem about a time when there are no more trees or a story about a time when all the powerful political leaders are women.)

8. Work against type. (Example: Write a children's story about a tiger who is a gentle, misunderstood vegetarian.)

► ► ► ACTIVITY 1.15

Choose a technique from the chart above, Heuristics for Imagining, and use it to evoke an idea for a piece of imaginative writing.

1.16 ROLE PLAYING

Role playing involves working with other people, choosing a situation or a setting, taking on characters, and acting out the situation. You can use role playing to generate ideas for writing. Role playing is especially good for developing characters and for exploring controversial issues for pieces of persuasive writing. When you role play, you may wish to tape record or videotape your sessions so that you can consider them more closely later on. Another possibility is to have someone watch your role playing and take notes on it.

► ► ► ACTIVITIES 1.16

A. Working with a partner, role play one of the following situations (or create one of your own to role play):
   • a parent and teen arguing over use of the family car
   • the manager of a nuclear power plant, on her way into work in the morning, confronting a demonstrator outside the plant
   • two fans waiting outside a stage door for a popular musician to appear
   • a couple with very different tastes discussing the movie they will see (or have seen) on an evening out

B. Turn the role playing from Activity A into a short piece of writing (a scene from a play or from a short story).

1.17 CLUSTERING

One excellent way to gather ideas for writing is to make a **cluster chart.** Begin by writing a topic in the middle of a sheet of paper. Circle the topic. Then, in the space outside the circle, write related ideas that come to mind. Circle these, and connect the circles to the center circle by drawing lines. Continue in this manner, writing related ideas, circling them, and connecting them with lines until your page is filled with associated ideas.

► ► ► ACTIVITY 1.15

Students may wish to try all or several of these techniques. They can then choose one of the ideas they have generated to expand into a piece of imaginative writing. The other ideas can be recorded in the writing-ideas section of their journals.

► ► ► ACTIVITIES 1.16

A. Students may wish to switch roles and try the role play a second time to get a different perspective and to explore other ways the incident could take shape.

B. Students should not try to record the role play exactly but rather draw on the ideas and feelings it evoked.

Sample Cluster Chart

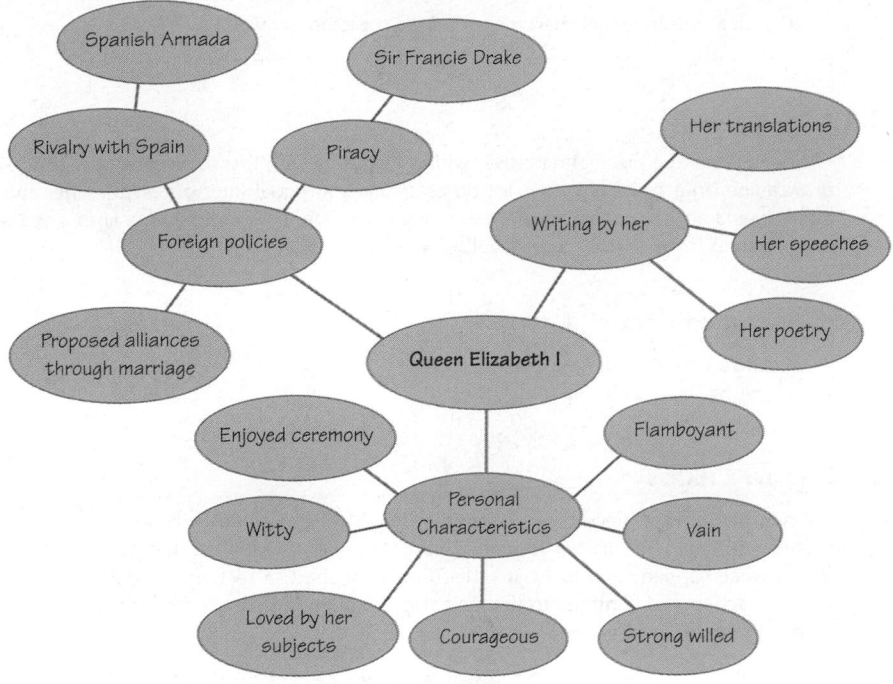

► ► ► **A C T I V I T Y 1.17**

Draw a cluster chart for one of the topics in Activity A, 1.13.

1.18 SENSORY DETAIL CHARTS

A good way to gather details for descriptive writing is to make a **sensory detail chart**. Begin by listing your subject at the top of a page. Beneath the subject, list the five senses: *sight, hearing, touch, taste,* and *smell*. Then, list details about your subject under each heading.

Sample Sensory Detail Chart

DWAYNE'S CAR				
Sight	Hearing	Touch	Taste	Smell
rusted fenders splotchy red paint job	backfiring clattering valves roaring muffler	torn seats	bags from fast-food places on floor empty cola cans	exhaust fumes oil hair tonic

► ► ► **A C T I V I T Y 1.17**

Have students review their charts and make a list of the ideas that they might be interested in using in their writing.

► ► ► **A C T I V I T Y 1.18**

Students should include details from all five senses in their chart. They might try to write a sense cycle essay in which they organize the description of their topic by senses. Refer them to the Language Arts Survey, 1.34, "Organizing Ideas: Classification Order."

► ► ► **A C T I V I T Y 1.19**

As an alternative to making time lines of their own lives, students could make more detailed time lines of the past year of their lives.

► ► ► **A C T I V I T Y 1.20**

Students must choose a process that includes a choice or other variable. Their charts should show how the process proceeds based on all possible decisions.

► ► ► **A C T I V I T Y 1.18**

Create a sensory detail chart for one of the topics in Activity A, 1.13.

1.19 TIME LINES

When planning a piece of narrative writing, you may wish first to make a **time line.** Simply draw a line on a piece of paper, list times or dates at equal intervals on the line, and then insert events at the proper times or dates along the line. (For sample time lines, see the unit introductions throughout this textbook.)

► ► ► **A C T I V I T Y 1.19**

Create a time line for your life.

1.20 FLOW CHARTS

When planning a piece of expository writing that deals with a process or sequence of events, you can often gather ideas and information by creating a flow chart. A flow chart shows what happens and in what order. In a flow chart, a rectangle around a step means "take an action and continue to the next step," a diamond means "make a decision," and a triangle means "stop."

Sample Flow Chart

❶ Get your paycheck

❷ Deposit check at bank

❸ Check balance: is it over $500?

❹ If yes, withdraw $200 for trip

❺ Record balance

❻ Stop

❼ If no, withdraw $50 for trip

❽ Record balance

❾ Stop

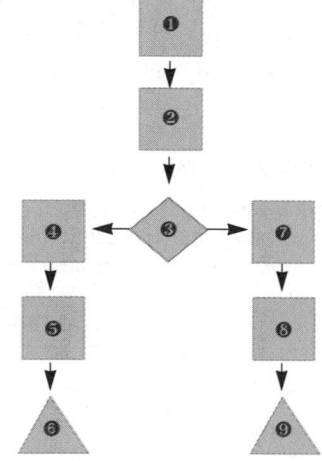

► ► ► **A C T I V I T Y 1.20**

Create a flow chart to describe a process that you go through often.

1.21 STORY MAPS

A **story map** is a chart that shows the elements of a short story. Story maps differ, but most include the following elements: setting, mood, conflict, plot, major characters, and theme.

Sample Story Map

Setting and Mood	Conflict ____✓ internal _____ external
Time _____1990s_____	Student must decide between looking foolish and doing what she believes to be right.
Place ___high school___ in Bronx	**Plot**
Mood ____somber____	Inciting incident ___Student mistakenly submits a copied poem, not one of her own, to school literary magazine; poem wins an award.___
Major characters	Climax ___Student is sitting with proud teacher at awards festival.___
Gelsy Martinez	Resolution ___Student admits in a speech before the student body that she didn't write the poem.___
Ms. Barstow (teacher)	Themes ___Honor, personal integrity, worth, sacrifice___

Story maps may consist of bare outlines of major elements, like the map above, or they may go into detail, describing elements of the setting, traits of the characters, and specific events in the plot.

> ► ► ► A C T I V I T Y **1.21**
>
> Create a story map for a story that you have read.

1.22 PRO AND CON CHARTS

A **pro and con chart** is useful when planning a piece of persuasive writing or when making a decision. At the top of the chart, list a proposition. Common propositions include statements of fact, policy, and value. Beneath the proposition, create two columns, one labeled *Pro* and the other labeled *Con*. In the columns, list arguments or evidence in support of each position on the proposition.

Sample Pro and Con Chart

Proposition: The school should be open on weekends for community events	
Pro	**Con**
—would provide young people with place to go, things to do	—costly
—would improve community relations	—possible insurance risks
	—security personnel needed

► ► ► A C T I V I T Y **1.21**

Students should identify the following elements in their story maps; setting and mood, including time, place, and mood; major characters; plot information, including inciting incident, climax, resolution, and theme; and whether the conflict is internal or external.

After students have practiced creating a story map, they could create a story map for a story they would like to write.

► ► ► **ACTIVITY 1.22**

Students may wish to work together to brainstorm ideas for this chart.

► ► ► **ACTIVITY 1.23**

Charts should break a carnival into parts and explain what the function of each part is and how each part is related to other parts and to the carnival as a whole.

► ► ► **ACTIVITY 1.24**

Students may wish to apply these techniques to one of the topics they generated in any of the previous activities.

► ► ► **ACTIVITY 1.22**

Create a pro and con chart about an important decision faced by students.

1.23 ANALYSIS CHARTS

An **analysis chart** breaks a thing into its parts and then shows how these parts relate to the whole. (See the sample analysis chart in the Language Arts Survey, 1.14.)

► ► ► **ACTIVITY 1.23**

Create an analysis chart to show the parts of a carnival.

1.24 VENN DIAGRAMS

A **Venn diagram** is useful for showing the similarities and differences between two things. It can be used effectively to plan comparison-and-contrast writing. To create such a diagram, draw two intersecting circles and label each with the name of one of your subjects. Then write similarities between the two subjects in the intersection of the two circles. Write differences outside the intersection of the two circles.

Sample Venn Diagram

► ► ► **ACTIVITY 1.24**

Choose two of the graphic techniques above, and use each to develop an idea for a piece of writing.

PREWRITING: USING OUTSIDE SOURCES

1.25 BRAINSTORMING

When you **brainstorm**, you think of as many different ideas as you can, as quickly as you can, without pausing to judge or evaluate the ideas. Brainstorming is to writing what improvisation is to acting. Basically, anything goes. You can brainstorm with a group of other people or by yourself. The main thing to remember is that no idea should be rejected in the brainstorming stage. When you brainstorm with other people or by yourself, the only acceptable response to anyone's idea is, "Great! Any other ideas?"

> ▶ ▶ ▶ **ACTIVITY 1.25**
>
> Choose a subject about which you can brainstorm in a small group for about ten minutes. For example, you might brainstorm about ideas for a story that takes place in a big city hospital. Get a chalkboard or a flip chart and a marker. Have one person record the group's ideas. Try not to interrupt anyone, and try to give everyone a chance to speak.

1.26 DISCUSSION

Discussion, like brainstorming, is a way of sharing ideas with others. In a discussion, members of the discussion group can play different roles. The **group leader** presents the discussion topic, asks questions, elicits responses, mediates between group members, and tries to keep the discussion focused on the topic. The **participants** in the discussion share their thoughts. Participants should attempt to contribute, should listen attentively to others, should respond to other's comments, and should speak calmly and politely. Often groups choose a **secretary** to record the ideas presented in the discussion.

> ▶ ▶ ▶ **ACTIVITY 1.26**
>
> With four other students, conduct a discussion about the uses of writing in modern society. Choose names out of a hat to take on roles of group leader and secretary.

1.27 INTERVIEWING

Another way to gather ideas for writing is to **interview** someone who has some experience or understanding of your subject. You have probably read newspaper articles that contain information taken from interviews. Remember the following tips about interviewing:

- Get permission from the interviewee to print the interview.
- Ask questions that start with the words *who, what, when, where, why,* and *how.*
- Record the interviewee's most important statements word-for-word so that you can quote some of them in your writing.
- Get the correct spelling of the interviewee's name so that you can properly attribute the information you gather to its source.

ESSENTIAL SKILLS: WRITING

> ▶ ▶ ▶ **ACTIVITY 1.25**
>
> Encourage students to listen to the ideas of others; this may spawn other ideas. At the end of the brainstorm, students may wish to copy the ideas that they find most interesting into their writing journal.

> ▶ ▶ ▶ **ACTIVITY 1.26**
>
> • Students should listen to one another, and every student should contribute something to the discussion. The group leader might encourage quieter members of the group to participate by posing a question.
>
> • For additional tips on developing attitudes conducive to group work, see the introduction to this *Annotated Teacher's Edition.*

► ► ► **A C T I V I T Y 1.27**

If students have difficulty finding an expert in their area of interest, they might discuss the idea with teachers, parents, or peers who may know somebody they could contact for an interview; or the student should choose a different interest. Students should set up a convenient time to meet with the expert on their subject and be prepared with questions. Other questions may arise as the interview progresses. Students might send a copy of the article they write with a thank you note to the interviewee.

► ► ► **A C T I V I T Y 1.28**

Students might skim the materials they find to see what kind of information is contained in each. If students begin with a broad topic, they may wish to use these resources to help them narrow it.

► ► ► **A C T I V I T Y 1.29**

Students should talk to a school or community librarian about the resources available locally and about opportunities to draw on other resources. Students should find as many different resources as possible. Then they might create a plan for a particular piece of writing on their subject and determine which of these sources would be most helpful for this purpose.

► ► ► **A C T I V I T Y 1.27**

Choose a subject that interests you and about which someone you know is an expert. For example, if swimming interests you and you know someone who once trained for the Olympics in swimming, you could interview her or him. Record your interview, using either a notepad or a tape recorder. Then write a brief article in which you quote your expert.

1.28 USING PRINT SOURCES

You may want to use print sources to gather information about your subject. Common print sources include books, magazines, newspapers, pamphlets, and reference works. To locate print sources, use your library's card catalog or online catalogs, the *Readers' Guide to Periodical Literature* (for magazines), and print, microfilm, or microfiche indexes to newspapers.

► ► ► **A C T I V I T Y 1.28**

Choose a subject that interests you and that has received some attention in magazines and newspapers in the past few years. Go to your library and find three different kinds of print sources of information about your subject. List the title, author, date, and place of publication for each source. If you do not know how to use the *Readers' Guide to Periodical Literature,* ask the librarian for assistance.

1.29 USING NONPRINT SOURCES

Many students rely exclusively on their own knowledge and on print sources when gathering ideas and information for writing. However, excellent nonprint sources of ideas and information include television and radio programs, films, videos, slides, photographic prints, filmstrips, audiocassette tapes, CD/ROM discs, online computer services, computer bulletin boards, and computer networks. Many of these materials can be found in libraries. CD/ROM discs, including reference works and discs on particular subjects, can be purchased through computer stores or from mail-order catalogs and are sometimes available for free use at computer club and computer lab facilities. For information on other methods of accessing information via computers, contact a computer dealer or knowledgeable faculty member at your school.

► ► ► **A C T I V I T Y 1.29**

Choose a subject of interest to you, such as *primates, sports, music,* or *modern art*. Locate at least three nonprint sources of information on that subject. Make a list of the sources that you found and describe briefly, in writing, the content of each source.

PREWRITING: ORGANIZING YOUR IDEAS

1.30 REVISING YOUR WRITING PLAN

After gathering information for a piece of writing, you should then rethink your original writing plan. Review the topic, purpose, audience, and form you have chosen. Think again about the mode or modes of writing that you want to use. The information that you have gathered may lead you to change parts of your plan. For example, while researching the making of music videos, you might encounter information about the job of a sound engineer and decide to focus on that more narrow topic. The change in topic might in turn lead you to change your intended purpose, audience, form, and primary mode.

> ► ► ► A C T I V I T Y **1.30**
>
> Choose a general subject of interest to you and make plans for two very different pieces of writing related to that subject. In each plan, list a topic, purpose, audience, form, and primary mode.

1.31 IDENTIFYING MAIN IDEAS AND SUPPORTING DETAILS

After gathering information for a piece of writing, the next step is to read through your notes to identify main ideas that you want to express. Then look for supporting details related to these main ideas. If you are doing a short piece of writing, such as a paragraph, you will want to identify a single main idea and several supporting details. If you are doing a longer piece of writing, you may want to begin by creating a **thesis statement** that expresses the major idea that you want to communicate. Then look for several main ideas related to the thesis statement and for details to support each of your main ideas.

> ► ► ► A C T I V I T Y **1.31**
>
> Choose one of the following subjects for a persuasive paragraph:
> - competitive sports for high-school girls;
> - peer counseling for troubled teens;
> - student exchange programs between communities in different parts of the country.
>
> Write a topic sentence to express a main idea about the subject. Then write three supporting details to support your main idea.

1.32 MAKING A ROUGH OUTLINE

One way to sort and organize ideas for a piece of writing is to make a **rough**, or **informal**, **outline**. In such an outline, main ideas are listed in some logical order, and supporting details are listed under the main ideas, preceded by dashes or bullets. Here is a rough outline for a paper about a community program that brings children and seniors together:

Benefits for Children
—Learning from the seniors' stories and experiences
—Feeling appreciated by the seniors

> ► ► ► A C T I V I T Y **1.30**
>
> Students should create an initial writing plan and then use techniques learned in sections 1.5–1.29 to explore their subject. After focusing on and examining their subject, students should be able to come up with other writing plans, even if they are still interested in their initial idea.

> ► ► ► A C T I V I T Y **1.31**
>
> Students should state their main idea clearly and concisely in the topic sentence. The main idea should be a proposition that is specific enough to be judged true or false. Prod students who write vague, diffuse, or overly broad topic sentences to hone their ideas. Check that each of the three supporting details actually pertains to the main idea.

—Learning to have relationships with people outside their age group

—Being cared for by experts who have probably raised children

Benefits for Seniors

—Feeling enlivened by the children's energy and creativity

—Feeling connected to life and to the future

—Feeling appreciated by the children

Possible Problems to be Avoided

—People using the seniors as day-care providers

—Children being frustrated by seniors' physical limitations

—Children experiencing grief if a senior they've become close to dies

—Children dropping out of the program as they get involved in other activities

---

► ► ► **A C T I V I T Y 1.32**

Create a rough outline for a composition or topic of your own choosing.

1.33 MAKING A FORMAL OUTLINE

A **formal outline** uses Roman numerals, letters, and numbers to identify headings and subheadings. The entries on each level should be parallel in grammatical structure and should begin with capital letters. There are two types of formal outline. In a **topic outline**, the entries are words, phrases, or clauses. In a **sentence outline** the entries are complete sentences. The following is a brief sample topic outline:

Elements of Medieval Romance

I. Adventures of knights
   A. Contests
   B. Quests
   C. Battles

II. Codes of conduct
   A. Courtly love
   B. Chivalry
      1. Loyalty
      2. Honesty
      3. Faith
      4. Valor

► ► ► **A C T I V I T Y 1.33**

Choose a subject related to popular culture or the mass media and make a topic outline for a paper on that subject.

1.34 ORGANIZING IDEAS

Writers use outlines to organize their ideas in a logical way. The following chart shows some common ways in which ideas are organized in writing.

► ► ► **A C T I V I T Y 1.32**

Students may wish to use a topic and supporting details generated by one of the previous exercises in this section.

► ► ► **A C T I V I T Y 1.33**

Students should follow proper outline form. Refer them to the Language Arts Survey, 2.119, on capitalization within an outline.

METHODS FOR ORGANIZING IDEAS

Chronological Order	Events are organized in order of their occurrence, often from first to last. Ideas are connected by transitional words and phrases that indicate time or sequence, such as *first, second, finally, next, then, afterward,* and *before.*
Spatial Order	Subjects are organized according to their their positions or locations, often from top to bottom, left to right, front to back, clockwise, or the reverse of any of these. Ideas are connected by transitional words and phrases that indicate position or location, such as *beside, in the middle, next, to the right, on top,* and *in front.*
Degree Order	Ideas are presented in order of degree from most to least or vice versa. For example, they might be presented from most important to least important. Ideas are connected by transitional words and phrases that indicate degree, such as *more, less, most, least, most important,* and *least promising.*
Comparison-and-Contrast Order	Details about two subjects are presented, in one of two ways. In the first method, the characteristics of one subject are presented, followed by the characteristics of a second subject. In the second method, both subjects are compared and contrasted with regard to one characteristic, then with regard to a second characteristic, and so on. Ideas are connected by transitional words and phrases that indicate similarities or differences, such as *likewise, similarly, in contrast, a different kind,* and *another difference.*
Cause-and-Effect Order	One or more causes are presented followed by one or more effects, or one or more effects are presented followed by one or more causes. Ideas are connected by transitional words and phrases that indicate cause and effect, such as *one cause, another effect, as a result, consequently,* and *therefore.*
Classification Order	Subjects are divided into groups, or classes. These groups are then presented, one-by-one, in some reasonable order. Ideas are connected by transitional words and phrases that indicate class membership or the method by which the writer has organized the classes, such as *another group, the first type, one kind,* and *other sorts.*
Part-by-Part Order	Ideas are presented according to no *overall* organizational pattern. However, each idea is connected logically to the one that precedes it and/or to the one that follows it. After chronological order, this is the most common method for organizing ideas in writing. Ideas are connected by any transitional word or phrase that indicates the relationship or connection between the ideas.

► ► ► **A C T I V I T Y 1.34**

Responses will vary. Possible responses are provided.

1. Spatial order would make sense for describing the layout of the park and the relationship between the things in the park.

2. Degree order and order of importance would be an effective way to present a number of reasons.

3. Cause-and-effect order would explain how the events in the accident occurred.

4. Classification order would make sense for most purposes to which the sound, construction, or operation of the instrument is relevant.

5. Chronological order would be best to explain the chain or chains of events leading up to the French Revolution.

► ► ► **A C T I V I T Y 1.35**

Encourage students to write down any ideas that come to mind about their topic. Suggest that this type of draft is like a focused freewrite. Suggest that when writing a discovery draft, unlike when freewriting, it is appropriate to revise wording and organization as ideas occur.

► ► ► **A C T I V I T Y 1.36**

Students can compare this type of draft writing to writing a discovery draft. Writing styles differ, and students may find that they prefer one method of drafting to the other. They may also find that they can use both types effectively for particular forms of writing.

► ► ► **A C T I V I T Y 1.34**

Choose an appropriate method of organization for each of the following pieces of writing and explain why you chose that method.

1. a description of a city park
2. a paragraph presenting reasons for studying a foreign language
3. a report to a police officer about how an automobile accident occurred
4. a composition about types of symphonic instruments
5. a report about the causes of the French Revolution

DRAFTING: APPROACHES TO WRITING A DRAFT

1.35 WRITING A DISCOVERY DRAFT

Once you are finished with your prewriting and are ready to begin your first draft, you can take several approaches. Some writers prefer to begin with a **discovery draft**. When writing a discovery draft, a writer simply gets all of his or her ideas on paper quickly, without worrying about matters such as organization, style, grammar, spelling, and mechanics. Such a draft is very, very rough. It provides the raw material that is later polished, through one or more extensive revisions, to produce the final piece of writing.

► ► ► **A C T I V I T Y 1.35**

Choose one of the following topics, think about the topic for a few minutes, and then write a discovery draft of a paragraph about it. Write quickly, simply putting your ideas down without worrying about creating a polished piece of writing.

Topics: a favorite object or activity from your childhood
a favorite poem, story, play, or novel
a person whom you admire or respect

1.36 WRITING A CAREFUL DRAFT

Some writers like to get everything on paper quickly and then to revise thoroughly. Such writers often do several drafts, each more refined that the one before it. Other writers prefer to work slowly and carefully on the first draft, revising and polishing the piece as they go. Such a **careful draft** is best done based on a thorough outline. You have the choice of whether to write quickly and then revise or to write slowly and revise as you go. Great writing can be produced in either way.

► ► ► **A C T I V I T Y 1.36**

Choose a topic from the list in Activity 1.35, above, and write a careful draft of a paragraph on that topic. Begin by making an outline of your paragraph, listing the main idea and three or four supporting details. Then, draft and revise the topic sentence until you are satisfied with it. Move on to the next sentence and again draft and revise it until you are satisfied. Continue in this manner until your paragraph is completed.

1.37 THE PREWRITING, DRAFTING, AND REVISING CYCLE

Sometimes writing occurs in neatly separated parts—prewriting, drafting, and revising. More commonly, however, writers switch back and forth between the stages. For example, a writer might start by gathering information about a subject, begin drafting based on that information, realize that he or she needs more information, do some more prewriting, and then go back and revise what has already been written before proceeding with the rest of the drafting. The order of the stages is flexible and can be varied to meet the particular problems that you encounter as you do a piece of writing.

DRAFTING: PARAGRAPHS

1.38 PARAGRAPHS WITH TOPIC SENTENCES

A paragraph sometimes contains a **topic sentence** that expresses its main idea. This topic sentence can appear at any place in the paragraph—at the beginning, in the middle, or at the end. In addition to the topic sentence, a paragraph generally contains two or more additional sentences that elaborate on, illustrate, or provide examples of the topic sentence. These sentences are often introduced by transitions that relate them to one another and to the topic sentence. The paragraph may also contain a **clincher sentence** at the end that summarizes or wraps up what has been said in the paragraph. Note the parts in the following paragraph.

Topic Sentence	Mariana's apartment contained far more candles than your average parish church does, perhaps as many as your average candle shop. Every window ledge, mantle, tabletop, and counter was covered with
Supporting Sentences	candles. There were scented candles—candles with ordinary scents like cinnamon, pine, and vanilla, as well as those with exotic scents like jasmine and honeydew melon. There were tapers and cones and tubs in holders of all kinds, from old bottles to crystal candlesticks. My favorites, however, were the figure candles, a peculiar hodgepodge of wax gnomes, elves, sorcerers, dragons, puppies, kittens, moons, stars,
Clincher Sentence	balloons, flowers, fruits, and teddy bears. The candles were largely for display alone, for none had been burned except for a single yellow taper on the night stand beside her bed.

► ► ► **A C T I V I T Y 1.38**

Write a paragraph about one of the following topics or one of your own. Open the paragraph with a topic sentence. Follow that sentence with at least three sentences that present supporting information. End with a clincher sentence that summarizes or wraps up the paragraph.

Possible topics: an interpretation of a poem from this text
                a description of the effect on the viewer of a work of art from this text

► ► ► **A C T I V I T Y 1.38**

The topic sentence should clearly express the main idea. The following sentences should support the topic sentence, and the clincher should summarize the ideas of the paragraph. Students can work in pairs, reviewing each other's work to find extraneous sentences.

1.39 PARAGRAPHS WITHOUT TOPIC SENTENCES

Most paragraphs do not contain topic sentences. In some, the topic sentence is not directly stated but rather implied. For example, the writer might present three sentences, each describing a different kind of pollution in a city, without making a general statement about the city's being polluted. Other paragraphs serve simply as transitions between sections of a composition. Perhaps the most common type of paragraph without a topic sentence is the narrative paragraph that simply presents a sequence of events, one after the other, without a single sentence that summarizes the events. The following is an example of a narrative paragraph without a topic sentence:

> On that bleak hill-top the earth was hard with a black frost, and the air made me shiver through every limb. Being unable to remove the chain, I jumped over, and, running up the flagged causeway bordered with straggling gooseberry bushes, knocked vainly for admittance, till my knuckles tingled and the dogs howled.
>
> —Emily Brontë, *Wuthering Heights*

> ► ► ► **A C T I V I T Y 1.39**
>
> Write a narrative paragraph describing an event that you witnessed. In each sentence, present a description or event. Organize the paragraph in chronological order. Do not include a topic sentence.

1.40 ELABORATION: TYPES OF SUPPORTING DETAILS

If a paragraph presents its main idea in a topic sentence, the rest of the paragraph will elaborate on that main idea by presenting supporting details. Kinds of supporting details often used for **elaboration** include **facts and statistics, sensory details, illustrations and examples, anecdotes,** and **quotations.** A sensory detail is one that appeals to one or more of the five senses (sight, hearing, touch, taste, and smell). An anecdote is a brief story told to make a specific point. In the sample paragraph given in section 1.39, above, the main idea is elaborated using sensory details.

> ► ► ► **A C T I V I T Y 1.40**
>
> For each topic sentence below, tell what kind of supporting information you would use in order to support, or elaborate on, that sentence. Be specific.
>
> 1. The house looked desolate and forlorn, as though no one had cared for it for years.
>
> 2. Often one has to be willing to make mistakes in order to learn how to do something.
>
> 3. Development in the southern part of the state has led to widespread extinctions of wild plants and animals.
>
> 4. Going to a new school for the first time can be quite scary.

> ► ► ► **A C T I V I T Y 1.39**
>
> Students should notice a difference between this paragraph and the paragraph they wrote with a topic sentence.

> ► ► ► **A C T I V I T Y 1.40**
>
> *Responses will vary. Possible responses are given.*
>
> 1. sensory details: peeling paint, broken windows, a creaky door hinge, crumbling porch steps, weeds
>
> 2. anecdote: Benny learned about painting floors the hard way. He carefully and thoroughly painted until he hit the corner. Then he waited for hours while the paint dried so that he could cross the floor to get out the door.
>
> 3. facts and statistics: what species have become extinct, which are endangered, what habitats have been altered
>
> 4. illustrations and examples: Rita was worried about making new friends, meeting new teachers, and finding her classes; Lonny lay awake all night dreading going to his new school the next day.

DRAFTING: COMPOSITIONS

1.41 WRITING A THESIS STATEMENT AND TOPIC SENTENCES

A **thesis statement** expresses the main idea of a composition. In most compositions, the thesis statement appears in the first paragraph; the rest of the paragraph introduces the thesis statement and the composition as a whole using one of many different techniques for writing introductions (See section 1.42 below). Your thesis statement should be brief and to the point. It should show clearly whether your composition is primarily expressive, informative, or persuasive.

After writing a thesis statement, you may wish to write the **topic sentences** for the body paragraphs of your composition. These sentences should present major ideas in support of your thesis. Together, the thesis statement and these topic sentences form the basic skeleton on which the rest of the composition will hang. Once these are written, you need only to write the supporting sentences for the body paragraphs, the rest of your introduction, and your conclusion.

► ► ► A C T I V I T Y 1.41

Choose one of the following general topics, narrow it, and write a thesis statement for an informative or persuasive composition on that topic. Then write three topic sentences for body paragraphs to support the thesis statement.

Possible topics: changes during adolescence
the value of friendships
a current political or social controversy
a school policy

► ► ► A C T I V I T Y 1.41

Students might write the supporting sentences for their topic sentences to fill out the composition. Have students work in pairs to see if their thesis statements have been sufficiently narrowed and if their topic sentences do in fact support their thesis.

1.42 ORGANIZING A COMPOSITION

Every composition should have three parts: an introduction, a body, and a conclusion.

Introduction. The introduction captures the reader's attention and presents the main idea, or thesis, of the composition. You can capture a reader's attention by beginning the composition with one or more of the following openings:

A description (to set the scene)
A paraphrase
A quotation
A statement of opinion
A summary or abstract
An allusion

An anecdote
Background information
Fascinating facts
Questions: *who, what, where, when, why,* and *how*

Body. The body of the composition presents several paragraphs that support the thesis statement. Usually, each paragraph contains a topic sentence that presents a separate main supporting idea. That idea is then elaborated on by the rest of the sentences in the paragraph.

Conclusion. The conclusion of the composition should give your reader a satisfactory sense of an ending. Here are some common techniques for doing that:

Imagine the future
Make a call to action
Make a generalization
Make a prediction
Pose a question

Present a resolution or solution
Present the last event
Restate the thesis
Summarize the main ideas

► ► ► A C T I V I T I E S **1.42**

A. Ask students to explain or discuss how effective the chosen opening technique is. Ask them what other opening techniques might also have been effective. Ask them to begin a paragraph of their own using that opening technique.

B. Ask students to explain or discuss how effective or appropriate the chosen conclusion is. Ask them what other types of conclusions might also have been effective or appropriate. Ask them to imagine using this type of conclusion in a piece of their own writing. In what type of writing would they be most likely to use it? Why?

► ► ► A C T I V I T I E S **1.42**

A. Search for some essays in textbooks, magazines, and essay collections. Find one or two openings that you really like. Bring these to class to present to others in a class discussion. Be prepared to read each opening and to explain what technique the writer used to capture the reader's attention and to tell what the essay is about.

B. Repeat the previous activity, but this time look for interesting or unusual conclusions. Before sharing each conclusion in class, share some background information about the rest of the essay so that your classmates will be able to place the conclusion in context.

REVISING: APPROACHES TO REVISION

1.43 SELF-EVALUATION

After finishing a draft, you will need to **evaluate**, or judge, it to see what changes should be made during revision. Usually, it is a good idea to let a piece of writing sit for a couple of days before reading it for **self-evaluation.** Doing so will help you look at it with a fresh eye. Here is one way to approach self-evaluation:

1. Read the composition through three times, checking first for content, second for organization and coherence, and third for voice and style. Use the following revision checklist:

REVISION CHECKLIST: CONTENT AND UNITY

1. Does the writing achieve its purpose?
2. Are the main ideas related to the thesis statement?
3. Are the main ideas clearly stated and supported by details?

REVISION CHECKLIST: ORGANIZATION AND COHERENCE

1. Are the ideas arranged in a logical order?
2. Do transitions connect ideas to one another both within and between paragraphs?

CONTINUED

REVISION CHECKLIST: VOICE AND STYLE

1. Is the voice—the tone, word choice, and perspective of the writing—authentic? Is it consistent?
2. Is the level of language appropriate to the audience and purpose?
3. Is the mood appropriate to the purpose and form of the writing?

2. Revise your piece by adding, deleting, replacing, or moving material as necessary.

3. Read the piece aloud to check for awkwardness. Revise any awkward passages that you find.

► ► ► ACTIVITY 1.43

Take a piece of writing that you have done previously and revise it using the revision checklist given in this lesson.

1.44 PEER EVALUATION

There are two sets of guidelines for this process, one for the writer and one for the evaluator.

For the Writer

• Tell your evaluator what aspect of your writing worries you. Here are some examples of general concerns you might have:

— **Content.** Do you wonder if your subject is too broad or too narrow? Do you wonder if your emphasis is appropriate?

— **Organization and logic.** Do you wonder if the order you have chosen makes sense? Do you wonder if the writing has unity?

— **Style.** Do you feel you may have used language that is too stilted or too casual? Have you created the mood you intended? Do your transitions work, or are you concerned about coherence?

• Accept the evaluator's comments with grace. If you agree with them, thank the evaluator. If you do not agree, avoid taking criticism personally. Thank the evaluator and ask for further explanation or clarification.

For the Evaluator

• Be focused. You are evaluating content, organization, and style. Ignore mechanics, spelling, and punctuation. These are issues that can be dealt with at the proofreading stage.

• Be positive. Let the writer know what he or she has done right, as well as what you feel could be improved.

► ► ► ACTIVITY 1.43

Students should understand that revision is a part of the writing process. Revision means reseeing. Students should look at their writing with a fresh, critical eye. Self-evaluation, as well as feedback from others, can be very useful in the revision process. All of their writing should be evaluated and revised several times before it is presented or published.

- Students should evaluate their own work first and offer specific concerns to the evaluator. When offering comments, students should remember to point out both things that have been done well and things that could be improved. After a peer evaluation, students should revise their work.

- For additional tips on managing writing teams and developing attitudes conducive to teamwork, see the introduction to this *Annotated Teacher's Edition*.

- Be concrete. Give the writer specific ideas for revision. For example, if you feel the organization needs work, let the writer know what organizational pattern you think might work and how you would arrange the sections of the writing.

- Be diplomatic. Use tactful language and a pleasant tone of voice. There's no need to repeat a criticism more than once or to state it in a way that calls into question the value of the *writer* rather than the problems in the *writing*.

► ► ► A C T I V I T Y 1.44

Choose an assignment that you and one of your peers have both been working on. Exchange papers and take turns evaluating one another's work.

1.45 FOUR TYPES OF REVISION

When you want to mend a pair of jeans, you do one or more of the following four things:

1. **add** a piece of fabric
2. cut off, or **delete** a piece of fabric
3. **replace** a part, such as a broken zipper or a ripped pocket
4. **move** a piece of fabric from one part of the pants to another

These are the same four processes you will use to revise your writing. You will, for example, do the following: **add** supporting details and transitions; **delete** redundant or unrelated details; **replace** clichéd, vague, or dull passages with vivid, original ones; and **move** passages that are out of logical order to their rightful places.

►This exercise is reproduced in the Transparency Set.
Responses will vary. A possible response is given.

Horses should be groomed in the morning. Take the horse out of its stall and secure it by a lead to a post. Then you can groom it. Always begin from the front of the horse so that you don't startle it. If you need to go around the horse, run a hand along its body as you go so that it knows where you are. Remember that a horse needs to be approached gently but with confidence. Use a hard brush first, then a soft one. After brushing the horse, pick up each of its feet to clean it with a pick. While the horse is being groomed, someone can clean and prepare the horse's stall. The stall should be cleaned and filled with fresh hay, and the bins filled with feed and water.

► ► ► A C T I V I T Y 1.45

Revise the following paragraph using the four revision processes. Add, delete, replace, or move materials as necessary to produce a well-written final draft.

You take the horse out of its stall and secure it by a lead to a post. Then you can groom it, using a hard brush first, then a soft one, and picking up each of its feet to clean them with a pick. While the horse is being groomed, someone can clean and prepare the horse's stall. Remember that a horse needs to be approached sweetly, but remember that a horse needs to be approached with confidence. Always go first from the front of the horse so that you don't startle it. While grooming, if you need to go around the horse, run a hand along its body as you go so that it knows what to think and where you are. In the morning, horses should be groomed, their stalls are cleaned and filled with fresh hay, and their bins filled with feed and water.

1.46 MARKING A MANUSCRIPT

Proofreading symbols are handy for marking revisions on your writing because they don't take up as much space as writing out instructions.

1102 *LANGUAGE ARTS SURVEY*

SYMBOL AND EXAMPLE	MEANING OF SYMBOL
The very first time	Delete this material.
french toast	Capitalize this letter.
the vice-President	Lowercase this letter.
cat' cradle	Insert here something that is missing. Write the missing letter(s) or punctuation above the line.
George	Replace this letter or word.
housse	Take out this letter and close up space.
book keeper	Close up space.
gebril	Change the order of these letters.
All the horses (king's)	Move this word to where the arrow points.
end. "Watch out," she yelled.	Begin a new paragraph.
Love conquers all	Put a period here.
Welcome friends.	Put a comma here.
Getthe stopwatch	Put a space here.
Dear Madam	Put a colon here.
She walked he rode.	Put a semicolon here.
name brand products	Put a hyphen here.
cats meow	Put an apostrophe here.
cat's cradle (stet)	Ignore the correction.

PROOFREADING AND PUBLISHING

1.47 PROOFREADING CHECKLIST

After revising your draft, make a clean copy and proofread it for errors in spelling, grammar, usage, and mechanics. Use the following proofreading checklist.

PROOFREADING CHECKLIST	
Spelling	• Are all words, including names, spelled correctly?
Grammar	• Does each verb agree in number with its subject? • Are verb tenses consistent and correct? • Are irregular verbs formed correctly?

CONTINUED

Responses will vary. A sample response with editor's marks follows.

In the classic ~~english~~ family ~~tail~~^tale# *Little Women,* four daughters, endures the hardships of war, at home with ^their~~her~~ brave mother, Meg, Jo, Beth, and Amy are characters ^The always remembered by people who have read this book. Meg, the oldest, ^is~~was~~ quiet, pretty, and responsible. Jo, the narrator, is adventuresome and brave. Beth is kind and cheerful; despite her poor health. Amy is charming, beautiful, and a little bit selfish. ^Each~~All of the~~ girls has her own challenges to face and depends on her sisters and on Marmee, their mother, to help out. Although they ~~don't~~ have no money, and they ~~all~~ worry about their father, who is away at war, the girls have a wonderful life together because they have spirit, humor, and love.

(cont.)

	• Is the referent of each pronoun clear?
	• Does every pronoun agree with its antecedent?
	• Are subject and object forms of pronouns used correctly?
	• Are there any sentence fragments or run-on sentences?
	• Have double negatives been avoided?
Usage	• Have frequently confused words, such as *affect* and *effect*, been used correctly?
Mechanics	• Does every sentence end with an end mark?
	• Are commas, semicolons, hyphens, and dashes used correctly?
	• Do all proper nouns and proper adjectives begin with capital letters?
	• Has proper manuscript form been used?

► ► ► **A C T I V I T Y** **1.47**

Using the Proofreading Checklist, correct the following paragraph:

In the classic american family tail.*Little Women,* four daughters endures the hardships of war at home with her brave mother Meg, Jo, Beth, and Amy are characters always remembered by people who have read this book. Meg, the oldest, was quiet, pretty, and responsible. Jo, the narrator, is adventuresome and brave. Beth is kind and cheerful; despite her poor health. Amy is charming beautiful, and a little bit selfish. All of the girls has her own challenges to face and depends on her sisters and on Marmee, their mother, to help out. Although they don't have no money, and they all worry about their father who is away at war, the girls have a wonderful life together because they have spirit, humor, and love.

1.48 PREPARING YOUR MANUSCRIPT

Once you have proofread your draft, prepare the final manuscript following the guidelines given by your teacher. However, if your teacher prefers, use the following guidelines, which are common:

Guidelines for preparing your manuscript:

1. Type, word process, or write neatly in blue or black ink.
2. Double-space your paper. In other words, leave one blank line between every line of type.
3. Use one side of the paper.
4. Leave one-inch margins on all sides of the text.
5. Indent the first line of each paragraph.
6. In the upper right-hand corner, put your name, class, and date. On every page after the first, include the page number in this heading as follows:

► ► ► **A C T I V I T Y** **1.47** (CONT.)

The revised paragraph reads as follows.

In the classic English family tale, *Little Women,* four daughters at home with their brave mother endure the hardships of war. The characters Meg, Jo, Beth, and Amy are always remembered by people who have read this book. Meg, the oldest, is quiet, pretty, and responsible. Jo, the narrator, is adventuresome and brave. Beth is kind and cheerful, despite her poor health. Amy is charming, beautiful, and a little bit selfish. Each girl has her own challenges to face and depends on her sisters and on Marmee, their mother, to help out. Although they have no money and they worry about their father, who is away at war, the girls have a wonderful life together because they have spirit, humor, and love.

Gloria Ramirez
English 12
May 6, 1999
p. 2

7. Make a cover sheet containing the title of the work, your name, the date, and the class.

After preparing a final manuscript based on these guidelines, proofread it one last time for errors introduced in the typing, word processing, or handwriting.

1.49 PUBLISHING OR PRESENTING YOUR WORK

Some writing is done just for one's self. Journal writing usually falls into that category. However, most writing is meant to be shared with others. There are many, many ways in which to share your work. Here are several ways in which you can publish your writing or present it to others:

- Find a local publication that will accept such work (a school literary magazine, a school newspaper, or a community newspaper are possibilities).

- Submit the work to a regional or national publication. Check a reference work such as *Writer's Market* to find information on types of manuscripts accepted, manuscript form, methods and amounts of payment, and so on.

- Enter the work in a contest. Your teacher may be able to tell you about writing contests for students. You can also find out about such contests by looking for announcements in writer's magazines and literary magazines.

- Read your work aloud to classmates, friends, or family members.

- Obtain permission to read your work aloud over the school's public address system.

- Work with other students to prepare a publication—a brochure, literary magazine, anthology, or newspaper.

- Prepare a poster or bulletin board, perhaps in collaboration with other students, to display your writing.

- Make your own book by typing or word processing the pages and binding them together in some way. Another possibility is to copy your work into a blank book.

- Hold a recital of student writing as a class or school-wide project.

- Share your writing with other students in a small writer's group that meets periodically to discuss one or two students' recent work. (Members of the group should receive the work to be discussed beforehand so they can read it and make notes on it.)

- If the work is dramatic in nature, work with other students to present a performance of it, either as straight drama or as reader's theater. If the work is poetry, fiction, or nonfiction, work with others to present it as an oral interpretation. (One possibility is to pair with another student, exchange pieces, and then coach one another in oral interpretations of the pieces.)

►Use the Pretest and Post-test for Grammar, Usage, Mechanics, and Spelling, 3.2.1–3.2.2, in the *Assessment Portfolio*.

►Use the Tracking Form: Grammar, Usage, Mechanics, and Spelling, 6.2, in the *Assessment Portfolio*.

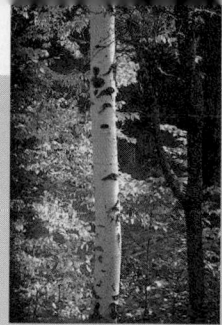

ESSENTIAL SKILLS:
Language

GRAMMAR HANDBOOK

INTRODUCTION TO GRAMMAR

2.1 THE GRAMMAR YOU ALREADY KNOW

Grammar is something you know, even if you have never studied it. Inside the head of every person is a sophisticated device that works, all by itself, to learn how to put words and phrases together grammatically. Even if you don't know an adverb from an aardvark, you know, if you are a speaker of English, that

the little leaf-eating bug

is grammatical and that

the bug little leaf-eating

is not. You can tell that one string of words is grammatical and the other isn't because you have learned, unconsciously, many thousands of rules governing how words can be put together and how they can't.

When you study a grammar textbook, therefore, what you are really learning is not the grammar of the language—for the most part, that's something you already know. What you are learning is terminology for describing what you know so that you can use that terminology when discussing language. Incidentally, as you study textbook grammar, you will also learn a few rules that you never quite learned unconsciously. Remember, however, that most of the grammar is already inside your head. Learning to describe that grammar can therefore be viewed as learning more about yourself and your amazing unconscious abilities.

2.2 THE USES OF GRAMMAR

Why study grammar? After all, no amount of grammar study can match the value of hands-on reading and writing. Grammar is useful, however. It gives you a way to speak about and understand your own writing and that of others. Contrast the following examples:

When the Roman general, sitting at supper with a plate of turnips before him, was solicited by large presents to betray his trust, he asked the messengers whether he that could sup on turnips was a man likely to sell his own country. Upon him who has reduced his sense to obedience, temptation has lost its power; he is able to attend impartially to virtue, and execute her commands without hesitation.

—Samuel Johnson, *The Idler* No. 52

Now what's this? What's the object of all this darkness all over me? They haven't gone and buried me alive while my back was turned, have they? Ah, now would you think they'd do a thing like that! Oh, no, I know what it is. I'm awake. That's it. I've waked up in the middle of the night. Well, isn't that nice. Isn't that simply ideal.

—Dorothy Parker, "The Little Hours"

If you had to describe the difference between these two passages, you would find it useful to have precise grammatical terms at your command. The first sentence in the passage by Johnson is composed of an adverbial clause interrupted by a participial phrase, followed by a sentence with an indirect question containing a subjunctive. The sentences in the passage from Parker's story have few of these devices. They are short, casual, and full of contractions. They consist mostly of simple subjects, verbs, and predicates. You may *sense* the differences in these two styles of writing instinctively, but grammar gives you a way to *understand* and *communicate* those differences.

►Use the Study Guide and Test on The Parts of Speech, 5.2.1–5.2.2, in the *Assessment Portfolio*.

THE PARTS OF SPEECH

2.3 COMMON AND PROPER NOUNS

A **noun** is a word used to refer to a person, place, thing, or idea.

NOUNS	Virginia Woolf, England, stone, beauty

A **common noun** is a name that belongs to (is *common* to) all the persons, places, or things in a group. A **proper noun** refers to a *particular* person, place, or thing and begins with a capital letter.

COMMON NOUNS	woman, state, religion
PROPER NOUNS	Queen Elizabeth I, California, Catholicism

2.4 CONCRETE AND ABSTRACT NOUNS

A **concrete noun** refers to an object that you can perceive by hearing, seeing, smelling, tasting, or touching. An **abstract noun** names a quality, characteristic, or idea.

CONCRETE NOUNS	music, light, smoke, honey, silk
ABSTRACT NOUNS	difficulty, bravery, evil

2.5 Compound and Collective Nouns

A **compound noun** is made up of two or more words used together as a single noun. A **collective noun** refers to a group of similar things.

COMPOUND NOUNS   book review, searchlight, switch-hitter
COLLECTIVE NOUNS   flock, bunch, team, crew, members, House of Commons, Red Sox

2.6 Personal Pronouns

A **pronoun** is a word used as a substitute for a noun. The word a pronoun stands for is called an **antecedent** or **referent**. In the following example, *Homer* is the antecedent of the pronoun *he.*

PRONOUN AND ANTECEDENT   Was **Homer** blind? **He** may have been.

A **personal pronoun** is a pronoun that substitutes for the name of a person or thing. The personal pronouns are *I, me, my, mine, we, us, our, ours, you, your, yours, he, him, his, she, her, hers, it, its, they, them, their,* and *theirs.*

PERSONAL PRONOUNS   **He** believed that the afterlife was one long, happy vacation.
Is that **your** science fiction novel in the transporter room?

2.7 Reflexive and Intensive Pronouns

A **reflexive pronoun** is a pronoun used to show that an action is done to or reflects upon someone or something. An **intensive pronoun** is a pronoun used to emphasize a noun or pronoun already given. The reflexive and intensive pronouns are *myself, ourselves, yourself, yourselves, himself, herself, itself,* and *themselves.*

REFLEXIVE PRONOUN   During the pillow fight, she hit **herself** by accident.
INTENSIVE PRONOUN   Shaw **himself** could not have written such a splendid play.

2.8 Demonstrative Pronouns

A **demonstrative pronoun** is a pronoun used to point out a particular person, place, or thing. The demonstrative pronouns are *this, that, these,* and *those.*

DEMONSTRATIVE PRONOUNS   Do you hear? **That** is the silly jingle stuck in my head.
These are the times that try people's souls.

2.9 INDEFINITE PRONOUNS

An **indefinite** pronoun is a pronoun that points out a person, place, or thing, but not a particular one. Some of the most common indefinite pronouns are *some, someone, somebody, something, any, anyone, anybody, anything, everyone, everybody, everything, other, another, either, neither, all, many, few, each, both, one, none, nobody,* and *nothing*.

INDEFINITE PRONOUNS   The cyclops told his friends that **no one** had hurt him.
Anyone who thinks Marlowe and Jonson wrote novels is mistaken.

2.10 INTERROGATIVE PRONOUNS

An **interrogative pronoun** is a pronoun used in asking a question. The interrogative questions are *who, whose, what, whom,* and *which*.

INTERROGATIVE PRONOUNS   **Who** am I to lecture people about talking too much?
Which is the road that diverged in the yellow wood?

2.11 RELATIVE PRONOUNS

A **relative pronoun** is a pronoun that connects a group of words with an antecedent. The relative pronouns are *that, which, who, whom,* and *whose*.

RELATIVE PRONOUNS   The ship **that** brought Joseph Conrad to Britain was called the *Mavis*.
The woman **whom** Shakespeare married was eight years older than
he was.

2.12 ACTION VERBS

A **verb** is a word that expresses action or a state of being. An **action verb** expresses physical or mental activity.

ACTION VERBS   slip, slink, leap, howl, wonder, fret, fear

2.13 LINKING VERBS

A **linking verb** connects a noun with another noun, pronoun, or adjective that describes it or identifies it. Most linking verbs are forms of the verb *to be*. They include *am, are, is, was,* and *been*. Other words that can be used as linking verbs include *seem, sound, look, stay, feel, remain* and *become*.

LINKING VERBS   Spenser **is** the poet's poet.
Dickens, highly popular in his own time, **remains** a favorite today.

2.14 Auxiliary Verbs

An **auxiliary verb** is a verb that helps to make some form of another verb. Common auxiliary verbs are *can, could, may, might, must, shall, should, will, would,* and forms of the verbs *to be, to have,* and *to do.*

AUXILIARY VERBS	**can** sculpt, **shall have been** applauded, **should** study, **did** believe About the woodlands Joe **will** go, to see the cherry hung with snow. "It **must** be right," said Crabbe. "I've done it from my youth."

2.15 Transitive and Intransitive Verbs

The **direct object** of a verb is a noun or pronoun that names the person or thing upon which the verb acts. Verbs that must have direct objects are **transitive verbs**. Verbs that do not need direct objects are **intransitive verbs**. Some verbs are both transitive and intransitive.

TRANSITIVE VERB	The hero in that Welsh legend **lifted** a rock to use as a shield.
INTRANSITIVE VERB	Hannah More, the English writer of religious pamphlets, **died** in 1833.

2.16 Verbals: Participles

A **participle** is a form of a verb that can be used as an adjective. (See 2.19 for the definition of an adjective.)

PARTICIPLES	**Having endured** two bad marriages, Gissing found love in the last years of his life. The **singing** sailors hoisted the sails. Wordsworth loved the **blossoming** flowers.

2.17 Verbals: Gerunds

A **gerund** is a form of a verb ending in *–ing* that is used as a noun. Be careful not to confuse gerunds with participles, verbal adjectives that end in *–ing.*

GERUNDS	**Wandering** can be liberating. Kirsten's **acting** rapidly improved. He enjoyed **kicking** a football.

2.18 Verbals: Infinitives

An **infinitive** is a form of a verb that can be used as a noun, an adjective, or an adverb. Most infinitives begin with *to.* (See 2.19 and 2.22 for more information about adjectives and adverbs.)

INFINITIVES	**To read** is to travel in realms of gold.
	Tennyson spoke of a desire "**to seek, to strive, to find,** and not **to yield.**"
	Help me **find** my copy of *Jane Eyre*.

2.19 ADJECTIVES AND ARTICLES

An **adjective** is a word used to modify a noun or pronoun. *To modify* means to change the meaning of something. Adjectives change the meaning of nouns or pronouns by answering the questions *What kind? Which one?* or *How many?*

ADJECTIVES	**sentimental** painter, **first** novel, **three** bells

The adjectives *a, an,* and *the* are called **articles.** *A* and *an* are **indefinite articles** because they refer indefinitely to any one of a group. *The* is the **definite article** because it refers to a definite person, place, thing, or idea.

ARTICLES	**a** whirlwind, **an** angel, **the** drawings of William Blake

2.20 PROPER ADJECTIVES

A **proper adjective** is an adjective formed from a proper noun.

PROPER ADJECTIVES	**Homeric** laughter, **Elizabethan** drama, **Kiplingesque** meter

2.21 PREDICATE ADJECTIVES

Every sentence is made up of two parts, a **subject** and a **predicate.** The subject is what or whom the sentence is about. The predicate tells something about the subject's actions or condition.

SUBJECT	**Leigh Hunt** was thrown in jail.
PREDICATE	Shelley practiced **vegetarianism.**

A **predicate adjective** is an adjective that follows a linking verb and modifies the subject of a verb.

PREDICATE ADJECTIVES	Lamb remained **lovable** to the end of his life.
	As a reviewer, Gifford was **savage.**

2.22 ADVERBS

An **adverb** is a word used to modify a verb, an adjective, or another adverb.

ADVERBS	Croker **harshly** attacked the poet.
	Coleridge was once called "an archangel **slightly** damaged."
	He **very** thoroughly combed the old attic, dreaming of finding a lost Mozart operetta.

2.23 ADJECTIVE OR ADVERB?

If you know a word is either an adjective or adverb but are not sure which it is, look at the word it modifies. Adjectives modify nouns and pronouns. Adverbs modify verbs, adjectives, and adverbs.

ADJECTIVES	**rapid** stream, **bare** head, **humorous** parody
ADVERBS	She danced **wildly**, she was **hopelessly** romantic, and she sang **even** more happily than I.

Many, but not all words with *–ly* endings are adverbs. Generally speaking, if you take the *–ly* ending off a word and are left with a noun, the *–ly* word is an adjective. If you are left with an adjective, the *–ly* word is an adverb.

ADJECTIVES	hourly, queenly, motherly, lovely, friendly, costly
ADVERBS	rapidly, barely, humorously, fully,

2.24 PREPOSITIONS

A **preposition** is used to show how a noun or a pronoun, its **object,** is related to some other word in the sentence. Common prepositions are *after, among, at, behind, beside, off, through, until, upon,* and *with.* A preposition introduces a **prepositional phrase.** The following examples show prepositional phrases in sentences.

PREPOSITIONAL PHRASES	Milton and Bunyan both wrote their great Puritan masterpieces **after the Puritan Age.**
	Stevenson's grave is **in Samoa.**

2.25 COORDINATING CONJUNCTIONS

A **conjunction** is a word used to join words or groups of words. A **coordinating conjunction** connects words or groups of words that are used in the same way—nouns with nouns, verbs with verbs, and so on. Thus a coordinating conjunction *coordinates,* or orders the relationship between, two words or groups of words. The main coordinating conjunctions are *and, but, for, nor, or, so,* and *yet.*

COORDINATING CONJUNCTIONS	Gounod **and** Debussy were French composers.
	The old record was scratched **yet** playable.
	Cream rises; **so** does scum.
	She was a friend, **and** I loved her.

2.26 CORRELATIVE CONJUNCTIONS

A **correlative conjunction** is a pair of conjunctions that joins words or groups of words that are used in the same way. Some common correlative conjunctions are *both . . . and; either . . . or; neither . . . nor; not only . . . but also;* and *whether . . . or.*

CORRELATIVE CONJUNCTIONS   William Morris created **both** poetry **and** superb furniture and textiles.

The author of *Alice in Wonderland* may be indexed as **either** *Lewis Carroll* **or** *Charles Dodgson.*

2.27 SUBORDINATING CONJUNCTIONS

A **clause** is a group of words with its own subject and verb.

CLAUSES   **The sun never sets in the east.**

Many great writers supported themselves by editing.

Aphra Behn was the woman **who wrote** *Oronoko,* considered by many to be the first English novel.

A **subordinate clause** is a clause that cannot stand by itself as a complete sentence. It depends on another clause and adds information about that clause. A **subordinating conjunction** connects a subordinate clause to another clause. Some common subordinating conjunctions are *after, as, as well as, because, if, in order that, provided, since, so that, than, that, though, unless, when,* and *why.*

SUBORDINATING CONJUNCTIONS   Did you know **that** Eliot worked in a bank?

If she still wants to marry me, the wedding will take place this June.

2.28 CONJUNCTIVE ADVERBS

A **conjunctive adverb** is a conjunction that both introduces and modifies a clause. Some conjunctive adverbs are *accordingly, furthermore,* and *moreover.*

CONJUNCTIVE ADVERBS   By age fifty he had still failed to publish an article; **accordingly,** his chances of advancement in his profession were slim.

She loved the poor painter; **moreover,** he inspired her to compose still finer music.

2.29 INTERJECTIONS

An **interjection** is a word used to express emotion. It stands apart from the rest of a sentence. Common interjections are *ah, oh, say, well,* and *wow.*

| INTERJECTIONS | **Oh,** can you still see the flag by the dawn's early light? |
| | **Wow!** This girl just finished reading the entire encyclopedia! |

2.30 WORDS AS OTHER PARTS OF SPEECH I

Words often serve as more than one part of speech. A noun, for instance, can become an adjective when it is used to modify another noun.

| NOUNS AS ADJECTIVES | **space** cadet, **rocket** scientist, **brain** surgeon |

Sometimes pronouns can be used as adjectives. Such pronouns show who possesses something and are called *possessive pronouns.*

| PRONOUNS AS ADJECTIVES | **my** stealth, **his** charms, **their** bravado |

2.31 WORDS AS OTHER PARTS OF SPEECH II

A word that is commonly used as a preposition may also be used as an adverb. In such cases, you can tell that such a word is being used as an adverb because it will not have a **prepositional object.** A prepositional object is the noun or pronoun that ends the prepositional phrase.

| PREPOSITION | Turner preferred to paint **outside** his home. |
| ADVERB | Turner preferred to paint **outside.** |

Not only can other parts of speech serve as adjectives and adverbs, but nearly any word can serve as a noun or verb if necessary.

| INTERJECTION AS NOUN | He was gratified by the *ohs* and *ahs* that greeted his new sculpture. |
| INTERJECTION AS VERB | The new musical **wowed** New York. |

USING THE PARTS OF SPEECH IN WRITING

2.32 USING PRECISE NOUNS

When you are writing, choose nouns that tell your reader precisely what you mean. If you use precise nouns, rather than nouns with a vague or general meaning, your writing will sparkle. Avoid using an adjective and a noun, as in *expensive house,* when using a single precise noun, such as *mansion,* will do.

| VAGUE | The **food** reminded him of the **past.** |
| PRECISE | The **graham cracker** reminded him of **kindergarten.** |

▶Use the Study Guide and Test on Using the Parts of Speech in Writing, 5.2.3–5.2.4, in the *Assessment Portfolio.*

Note the precise nouns used in this passage of "A Word with the Wind," by Algernon Charles Swinburne.

> PRECISE NOUNS   Sweet are even the mild low **notes** of wind and sea, but sweeter
> Sounds the song whose choral **wrath** of raging **rhyme**
> Bids the shelving **shoals** keep tune with storm's imperious **meter,**
> Bids the rocks and **reefs** respond in rapturous **chime.**

2.33 USING VIVID VERBS

Like precise nouns, vivid verbs create a picture in the reader's mind. Instead of using a vague, general verb like *walk,* a writer can produce a concrete picture by using a vivid verb such as *hobbled, strolled, meandered, sauntered, marched, tramped, paced, strode, trudged, trekked, hoofed,* or *hiked.* Instead of using an adverb and a verb, as in *ran quickly,* a writer can use a single precise verb such as *sprinted.*

> DULL   Woodcarvers **like** the work of English artist Grinling Gibbons.
> VIVID   Woodcarvers **marvel** at the work of English artist Grinling Gibbons.

Note the vivid verb John Milton chose instead of "sing" in these lines from one of his sonnets:

> O Nightingale, that on yon bloomy spray
> **Warbl'st** at eve, when all the woods are still

2.34 REPLACING LINKING VERBS WITH ACTION VERBS

To give color to your writing, avoid using linking verbs, especially forms of the verb *to be* (*am, are, is, was,* and so on). Instead, use action verbs. Using action verbs will force you to restructure your sentences for greater impact.

> LINKING   Beethoven's *Ninth Symphony* **is** excellent.
> ACTION   Beethoven **soars** beyond limitations in his *Ninth Symphony.*

Note how, in the following passage, the poet Byron has used an action verb to avoid the common expression "she is beautiful."

> ACTION VERB   She **walks** in beauty, like the night
> Of cloudless climes and starry skies.

2.35 USING COLORFUL MODIFIERS

A **modifier** is a word that modifies—that is, changes or explains—the meaning of another word. Adjectives and adverbs are modifiers. Rather than use trite or vague modifiers in your writing, search out adjectives and adverbs that add freshness and meaning. Consider the modifiers Robert Browning chose in these lines from his poem "Meeting at Night":

| COLORFUL MODIFIERS | . . . the **startled little** waves that leap
In **fiery** ringlets from their sleep,
As I gain the cove with **pushing** prow,
And quench its speed i' the **slushy** sand. |

By using precise nouns, vivid action verbs, and colorful modifiers, you can turn bland prose into dynamic reading.

| DULL | Although Alexander Pope was naturally kind, he became mean and spiteful as he grew older. |
| COLORFUL | In the first act of his life, Alexander Pope dealt with everyone amiably; by the closing curtain he had waxed petulant and treacherous. |

► Use the Study Guide and Test on Building Sentences, 5.2.5–5.2.6, in the *Assessment Portfolio*.

BUILDING SENTENCES

2.36 THE FUNCTIONS OF SENTENCES

Sentences are classified according to their functions. They may be **declarative**, **imperative**, **interrogative**, or **exclamatory**. A **declarative sentence** makes a statement and is followed by a period.

| DECLARATIVE SENTENCES | William Hazlitt doted on the word *gusto.*
George Savage Fitzboodle was revealed in time to be none other than the novelist Thackeray. |

An **imperative sentence** gives a command or makes a request. It usually ends with a period but may end with an exclamation point.

| IMPERATIVE SENTENCES | Memorize the sonnet of your choice by tomorrow.
Don't give us that assignment! |

An **interrogative sentence** asks a question. It ends with a question mark.

| INTERROGATIVE SENTENCES | What the dickens are you reading?
You said memorize a sonnet by tomorrow? |

An **exclamatory sentence** expresses a strong feeling about something. It ends with an exclamation point.

| EXCLAMATORY SENTENCES | Help!
I'll never memorize that sonnet by tomorrow!
Victoria proposed to Albert only five days after meeting him! |

2.37 SUBSTANTIVES

A **substantive** is a noun or any other word or group of words that is used as a noun. If a word is used as a subject, direct object, indirect object, object of a preposition, predicate nominative, or objective complement, then it is a substantive. The following are some examples of substantives used as **subjects**, words that name the thing that does the action of the verb.

	SUBSTANTIVES
NOUN	**Marie de France** wrote in French.
PRONOUN	**She** was a lady-in-waiting to Eleanor of Aquitaine, the wife of England's King Henry II.
INFINITIVES	**To entertain** and **to delight** were Marie de France's objectives.
GERUND	**Writing** was Marie de France's great gift.
CLAUSE	**That Marie had talent as a lyricist** is clear.

2.38 SIMPLE SENTENCES: SUB + V

The most basic sentence is one that combines a **substantive** and a verb in the form SUB + V. A substantive is anything used as a noun—a noun, pronoun, gerund, infinitive, or noun clause.

NOUN	**Night** fell.
PRONOUN	**We** were happy then.
GERUND	**Jogging** is good exercise.
INFINITIVE	**To wait** would be disastrous.
NOUN CLAUSE	**When we shall leave** remains uncertain.

2.39 SIMPLE SENTENCES: SUB + AV + SUB

You can build the next kind of basic sentence by adding another substantive as the direct object of an action verb, producing a sentence with the form SUB + AV + SUB. In the following examples, the direct object is boldfaced.

EXAMPLES	Knowledge bursts **bonds.**
	It dashed **hopes.**
	Running confers **health.**
	To know helps **me.**

2.40 SIMPLE SENTENCES: SUB + LV + SUB OR ADJ

Imagine you had a linking verb in your simple sentence instead of an action verb. Your sentence would then follow the pattern SUB + LV + SUB. The second substantive would be a **predicate nominative**, which is a word or group of words that follows a linking verb and refers to the same person or thing as the subject of the verb. In the following examples, the predicate nominative is boldfaced.

EXAMPLES Shakespeare was **an actor.**
That's **politics.**
Seeing is **believing.**
To live is **to struggle.**

Now imagine you made the element after the verb a predicate adjective. (See 2.21 for the definition of a predicate adjective.) Then the sentence pattern would be SUB + LV + ADJ. In the following examples, the predicate adjective is boldfaced.

EXAMPLES Cervantes was **handicapped.**
Griselda felt **powerful.**
Rhyming looks **easy.**
To yearn is **pointless.**

2.41 SIMPLE SENTENCES: SUB + AV + SUB + SUB

Another type of simple sentence can be formed by following the pattern substantive + action verb + substantive + substantive (SUB + AV + SUB + SUB). One of the substantives after the action verb will be a direct object. The other may be an **indirect object.** An indirect object is a noun or pronoun that comes between an action verb and a direct object. It shows *to whom* or *to what* or *for whom* or *for what* the action of the verb is done. In the following examples, the indirect object is boldfaced.

EXAMPLES The ancient mariner told **the wedding guest** his story.
It did **him** good.
Sunning gave **him** a tan.
To surrender costs **you** nothing.

Instead of an indirect object, however, one of the elements may be an **objective complement.** An objective complement is a word or group of words that helps complete the meaning of an action verb by identifying or modifying the direct object. The words *to be* may be inferred as appearing before the objective complement. In the following examples, the objective complement is boldfaced.

EXAMPLES The class elected Mary **president.** (The class elected Mary [to be] president.)
Victoria made Tennyson her **poet laureate.** (Victoria made Tennyson [to be] her poet laureate.)

2.42 INDEPENDENT CLAUSES

An **independent clause** expresses a complete thought and can stand by itself as a sentence. All the examples in 2.38 through 2.41 are also examples of independent clauses.

2.43 COMPOUND SENTENCES

You can expand on a sentence that has only one independent clause by adding another independent clause. You will then have a **compound sentence**—one formed of two or more independent clauses but no subordinate clauses. (See 2.27 for the definition of a subordinate clause.) Related independent clauses can be joined by a semicolon; by a coordinating conjunction such as *and, or, for, nor, but, so,* or *yet* and a comma; or by a semicolon followed by a conjunctive adverb such as *however* or *therefore* and a comma.

COMPOUND SENTENCES	The monkeys chattered; the children laughed.
	Keats died young, **but** his poems will live forever.
	Lancelot was a hero; **however,** he had his faults.

2.44 COMPLEX SENTENCES

You can also expand a sentence that has only one independent clause by adding a subordinate clause. You will then have a **complex sentence**—one formed of an independent clause and at least one subordinate clause. In the following examples the subordinate clauses are boldfaced.

COMPLEX SENTENCES	Waves pounded the shore, **which eroded.**
	Colley Cibber was a playwright **whom Pope disliked.**
	Although he loved Maude, Yeats disapproved of her politics.

2.45 COMPOUND-COMPLEX SENTENCES

If you combine a compound sentence and a complex sentence, you will have a **compound-complex** sentence. This kind of sentence must have two or more independent clauses and at least one subordinate clause. In the following examples the subordinate clauses are boldfaced.

| COMPOUND-COMPLEX SENTENCES | **Although Jean ignored them,** Marisa sang and Liz danced. |
| | The spaceship opened, and Spielberg screamed his head off **when he saw it.** |

EXPANDING SENTENCES

2.46 ADDING MODIFIERS

Simple, compound, complex, and compound-complex sentences can be expanded by adding modifiers such as adjectives and adverbs.

BASIC SENTENCE	The tenor sang.
SENTENCE WITH ADDED MODIFIERS	The **bald** tenor sang **beautifully.**
BASIC SENTENCE	Waves pounded the shore, which eroded.
SENTENCE WITH ADDED MODIFIERS	**Tidal** waves **relentlessly** pounded the shore, which eroded **rapidly.**
BASIC SENTENCE	The spaceship opened, and Spielberg screamed his head off when he saw it.
SENTENCE WITH ADDED MODIFIERS	The **humming** spaceship opened **wide,** and Spielberg **gleefully** screamed his head off when he saw it.

►Use the Study Guide and Test on Expanding Sentences, 5.2.7–5.2.8, in the *Assessment Portfolio.*

ESSENTIAL SKILLS: LANGUAGE

2.47 Adding Prepositional Phrases

Adding a prepositional phrase is another way to expand sentences. The prepositional phrase you add can be an **adjectival phrase** or an **adverbial phrase**. An adjectival phrase modifies a noun or pronoun. An adverbial phrase modifies a verb, an adjective, or an adverb. The following examples are from 2.46, with added prepositional phrases.

WITH ADDED PREPOSITIONAL PHRASES	The bald tenor **in the green tights** sang beautifully.
	Tidal waves **from the earthquake** viciously pounded the shore, which rapidly eroded **to a strip of sand**.
	The humming alien spaceship **on the television** opened wide, and Spielberg gleefully screamed his head off **in the safety of his living room** when he saw it.

Note that expanding sentences can cause problems instead of adding interest and variety. The third sentence, above, is bloated and should be trimmed down.

2.48 Adding Appositives and Appositive Phrases

Still another way to expand sentences is to add an **appositive** or an **appositive phrase**. An appositive is a noun or pronoun placed beside another noun or pronoun to identify or explain it. An appositive phrase is the appositive and its modifiers. The modifiers can be adjectives or adverbs.

BASIC SENTENCE	Sir Walter Scott wrote historical novels.
WITH APPOSITIVES	Sir Walter Scott, an **antiquarian, poet**, and **editor**, wrote historical novels.
WITH APPOSITIVE PHRASES	Sir Walter Scott, an **enthusiastic antiquarian, extremely successful poet**, and **ingenious editor**, wrote historical novels.

2.49 Adding Predicates

A **predicate** is a main verb and any auxiliary verbs, together with any words, phrases, or clauses that modify or complement the verb. You can expand sentences by adding predicates.

BASIC SENTENCE	Shakespeare wrote plays.
WITH ADDED PREDICATE	Shakespeare wrote plays and **acted in theater productions**.

2.50 Adding Subordinate Clauses

Subordinate clauses may also be used to expand the meaning of a sentence.

BASIC SENTENCE	Of all Shelley's friends, Mary Godwin and Leigh Hunt understood him best.
WITH SUBORDINATE CLAUSES	Of all Shelley's friends, Mary Godwin, **who was the daughter of a feminist**, and Leigh Hunt, **who was an outspoken radical**, understood him best.

COMBINING SENTENCES

▶Use the Study Guide and Test on Combining Sentences, 5.2.9–5.2.10, in the *Assessment Portfolio*.

2.51 COMBINING SENTENCES USING SINGLE WORDS

Often you can combine two sentences that deal with the same topic to make your writing briefer and more effective. Rather than repeat information, you take the vital information from one sentence and insert it in the other, either in its original form or slightly altered.

GIVEN SENTENCES	Juno exerted her will. She did so capriciously.
COMBINED SENTENCE	Juno exerted her will **capriciously.**
GIVEN SENTENCES	Thor hammered the board. He hit it hard.
COMBINED SENTENCE	Thor hammered the board **hard.**
GIVEN SENTENCES	The museum would never sell Leonardo's painting. It is priceless.
COMBINED SENTENCE	The museum would never sell Leonardo's **priceless** painting.

2.52 COMBINING SENTENCES USING PHRASES

A second way to combine two sentences that deal with the same topic is to take a prepositional phrase or a participial phrase from one sentence and move it into the other.

GIVEN SENTENCES	She wrote the Great American Novel. She wrote it on the daily commuter train.
COMBINED SENTENCE	She wrote the Great American Novel **on the daily commuter train.**
GIVEN SENTENCES	Milton was praising music. He said sweet compulsion lies in it.
COMBINED SENTENCE	Milton, **praising music,** said that sweet compulsion lies in it.

Sometimes you may need to change a part of the sentence into a prepositional phrase or change a verb into a participle before you can insert the idea into another sentence.

GIVEN SENTENCES	Pollock paints pictures. He often uses spray paint.
COMBINED SENTENCE	Pollock often paints pictures **with spray paint**.
GIVEN SENTENCES	He gulped down the ginger tea. He thought how much he loved the spice.
COMBINED SENTENCE	**Gulping down the ginger tea,** he thought how much he loved the spice.

2.53 COMBINING SENTENCES USING CLAUSES

A third way to combine two sentences that have the same topic is to make one the independent clause and the other the subordinate clause in a combined sentence.

GIVEN SENTENCES	Dogs are wonderful. Dogs can be disgusting.
COMBINED SENTENCE	**Though dogs are wonderful,** they can be disgusting.
GIVEN SENTENCES	Let them dislike me. Let them avoid me.
COMBINED SENTENCE	Let them dislike me, **so long as they avoid me.**

▶ Use the Study Guide and Test on Editing Sentences, 5.2.11–5.2.12, in the *Assessment Portfolio.*

EDITING SENTENCES

2.54 VARYING SENTENCE OPENINGS

Many of the examples in this handbook begin with a subject for the sake of simplicity. When you are writing, however, you will find that *always* beginning with a subject makes for a dull style. You can make your writing more varied and interesting by beginning sentences with adjectives, adverbs, participles—just about any part of speech—as well as with phrases and clauses. You may have to reword your sentences slightly as you vary the sentence openings.

GIVEN SENTENCE	Anyone can be frugal in the country.
EDITED SENTENCE	**In the country,** anyone can be frugal.
GIVEN SENTENCE	The prosecutor rested his case, laughing wildly.
EDITED SENTENCE	**Laughing wildly,** the prosecutor rested his case.
GIVEN SENTENCE	The painter admitted that nature would soon be as good as he was.
EDITED SENTENCE	**Nature,** the painter admitted, would soon be as good as he was.

2.55 VARYING SENTENCE LENGTH AND STRUCTURE

Repeated sentences of the same length and structure soon become monotonous. Use a variety of simple, compound, complex, and compound-complex sentences in your writing.

PASSAGE WITH SIMPLE SENTENCES

Maggie was mortified that she had trouble with math. She found the Latin Grammar book quite soothing. She delighted in new words. She quickly found that there was an English Key at the end. It would make her very wise about Latin. It would not cost much effort. She presently made up her mind to skip the rules in the Syntax. The examples in the Key were so absorbing. The sentences there were so mysterious. They were drawn from an unknown context. They were like the strange horns of beasts. They were like the leaves of unknown plants. It was as if they had been brought from some far-off region. They gave boundless scope to her imagination. They were fascinating. They were in a peculiar tongue of their own. She could learn to interpret it.

PASSAGE WITH VARIED SENTENCE LENGTH AND STRUCTURE

Maggie found the Latin Grammar quite soothing after her mathematical mortification; for she delighted in new words, and quickly found that there was an English Key at the end, which would make her very wise about Latin, at slight expense. She

CONTINUED

presently made up her mind to skip the rules in the Syntax, the examples became so absorbing. These mysterious sentences, snatched from an unknown context—like strange horns of beasts, and leaves of unknown plants, brought from some far-off region—gave boundless scope to her imagination, and were all the more fascinating because they were in a peculiar tongue of their own, which she could learn to interpret.

—George Eliot, *The Mill on the Floss*

2.56 USING THE ACTIVE VOICE

A verb is in the **active voice** when the subject of the verb performs the action. It is in the **passive voice** when the subject of the verb receives the action.

ACTIVE	I **conquered** Mount Everest last Tuesday.
PASSIVE	Mount Everest **was conquered** last Tuesday.

A common characteristic of poor writing is overuse of the passive voice. Keep your verbs in the active voice unless you have a good reason for using the passive voice. In the examples that follow, note how the active verbs make the writing more natural, interesting, and concise.

WITH PASSIVE VERBS	One day a present **was delivered** by ship to George. The present—a new car—**was** from his rich friend. It **was polished** by George until his reflection **could be seen** in it. Then this question **was considered:** Where **could** it **be driven** on the pathless island?
WITH ACTIVE VERBS	One day George's rich friend **sent** him a present by ship—a new car. George **polished** it until he **could see** his reflection in it. Then he **considered** this question: Where **could** he **drive** it on the pathless island?

2.57 ACHIEVING PARALLELISM

A sentence has **parallelism** when it uses the same grammatical forms to express ideas of equal, or parallel, importance. When you edit your sentences during revision, check to be sure that your parallelism is not faulty.

FAULTY	The teacher loved **bookshops** and **to gather a library of first editions.**
PARALLEL	The teacher loved **to visit bookshops** and **to gather a library of first editions.**
FAULTY	Both **having the right light** and **to study a good model** are essential to figure drawing.
PARALLEL	Both **having the right light** and **studying a good model** are essential to figure drawing.
FAULTY	Keats said **the roaring of the wind is my wife** and **the stars through the window pane were his children.**
PARALLEL	Keats said, **"The roaring of the wind is my wife** and **the stars through the window pane are my children."**

ESSENTIAL SKILLS: LANGUAGE **1123**

ESSENTIAL SKILLS: LANGUAGE

TEACHER'S EDITION **1123**

2.58 DELETING REPEATED OR UNNECESSARY IDEAS

When you edit your writing, check carefully for repeated or unnecessary ideas.

SENTENCE WITH REPETITION	He lounged **on the window seat** and called his wife over to sit **on the window seat** beside him.
CORRECTED SENTENCE	He lounged on the window seat and called his wife over to sit beside him.
SENTENCE WITH UNNECESSARY IDEA	He watched the fireworks on Independence Day, **the Fourth of July**.
CORRECTED SENTENCE	He watched the fireworks on Independence Day.

2.59 REDUCING WORDINESS

When you write, use only as many words as you need to express your meaning. While editing, remove words that do not contribute to your meaning and replace complicated or unclear words with ones that are simple and clear.

WORDY	In terms of work produced, I have not accomplished many achievements in the course of this semester's time period.
DIRECT	I have not done much this semester.
WORDY	If you have any interrogatories or inquiries to communicate, please do so via the telecommunication system.
DIRECT	Please call with questions.

Look for ways to reduce the length of your sentences by replacing a clause with a phrase that conveys the same meaning. In some cases, you can even replace a lengthy phrase with a single word.

WORDY	Wolfe, **who was a prolific writer,** believed in putting as much as possible into his books.
DIRECT	Wolfe, **a prolific writer,** believed in putting as much as possible into his books.
WORDY	Fitzgerald believed that **the material that** you leave out of a book is more important than **the material that** you put in it.
DIRECT	Fitzgerald believed that **what** you leave out of a book is more important than **what** you put in.

2.60 CORRECTING SENTENCE STRINGS

Sentence strings are formed of several sentences strung together with conjunctions. Edit sentence strings by breaking them up into separate sentences and subordinate clauses. In the examples that follow, the first passage is a sentence string; the second is a passage broken up into separate sentences and clauses.

STRINGY	Mr. Frank Churchill did not come, and the time proposed drew near, and Mrs. Weston's fears were justified in the arrival of a letter of excuse, and for the present he could not be spared to his "very great mortification and regret, but still he looked forward with the hope of coming to Randalls at no distant period."
REVISED	Mr. Frank Churchill did not come. When the time proposed drew near, Mrs. Weston's fears were justified in the arrival of a letter of excuse. For the present, he could not be spared, to his "very great mortification and regret; but still he looked forward with the hope of coming to Randalls at no distant period."

—Jane Austen, *Emma,* Chapter 18

2.61 CORRECTING SENTENCE FRAGMENTS

A **sentence** should express a complete thought and contain both a subject and a verb. A **sentence fragment** is a phrase or clause that does not express a complete thought but has been punctuated as though it did. You can correct a sentence fragment by changing its punctuation or structure so that it expresses a complete thought.

FRAGMENTED	Someone once said. Life is too short for chess.
CORRECTED	Someone once said, "Life is too short for chess."
FRAGMENTED	The rhinoceros is much sought after. Though it has been called an ugly beast.
CORRECTED	The rhinoceros is much sought after, though it has been called an ugly beast.

In sentences in which the subject will be understood by the reader, the subject can be left unexpressed. Such sentences are not sentence fragments.

SENTENCE WITH IMPLIED, UNEXPRESSED SUBJECT	[You] Call our 800 number today.

2.62 CORRECTING RUN-ONS

A **run-on** is formed of two or more sentences that have been run together as if they were one complete thought. Edit a run-on by making it into two sentences, by adding a comma and a coordinating conjunction, or by adding a semicolon.

RUN-ONS	Einstein theorized the power locked in the atom others built the bomb.
	Einstein theorized the power locked in the atom, others built the bomb.
TWO SENTENCES	Einstein theorized the power locked in the atom. **O**thers built the bomb.
COORDINATED CLAUSES	Einstein theorized the power locked in the atom, **and** others built the bomb.
CLAUSES WITH SEMICOLON	Einstein theorized the power locked in the atom; others built the bomb.

ESSENTIAL SKILLS: LANGUAGE **1125**

2.63 CORRECTING DANGLING OR MISPLACED MODIFIERS

A **dangling modifier** is a modifying phrase or clause that seems to modify a word it is not intended to modify. Sometimes this error occurs because the modifier is too far from the word it is supposed to modify. It is then called a **misplaced modifier**. You can edit dangling and misplaced modifiers by adding a word for the phrase or clause to modify or by rewording the sentence.

DANGLING	She skied into a tree while tying my shoes.
WORDS ADDED	She skied into a tree while I was tying my shoes.
DANGLING	Daring me to follow, the train carried off the fugitive.
REWORDED	The train carried off the fugitive, who dared me to follow.
MISPLACED	Running down the street, the tree fell on Pablo.
REWORDED	As Pablo ran down the street, a tree fell on him.

2.64 INVERTING SENTENCES FOR EMPHASIS

When editing your writing, look for opportunities to add emphasis and clarify your meaning. One way to add emphasis is to **invert** a sentence—to change the usual order of its parts.

REGULAR ORDER	I do not deny the atrocious crime of being correct.
INVERTED ORDER	The atrocious crime of being correct I do not deny.
REGULAR ORDER	There I go, but for the grace of God.
INVERTED ORDER	There, but for the grace of God, go I.

EDITING FOR ERRORS IN VERB TENSE

►Use the Study Guide and Test on Editing for Errors in Verb Tense, 5.2.13–5.2.14, in the *Assessment Portfolio.*

2.65 IMPROPER SHIFTS IN VERB TENSE

When the verbs in a sentence or group of sentences shift from past to present or from present to past without reason, the reader may not be able to follow the intended meaning. Correct the shift by using consistent tenses for all verbs.

WITH TENSE SHIFT	Though he **was** completely blind from the age of forty-four, Milton **writes** three major works in his later life.
CORRECTED	Though he **was** completely blind from the age of forty-four, Milton **wrote** three major works in his later life.

2.66 IRREGULAR VERBS I

Every verb has four **principle parts**: the **base form**, the **present participle**, the **past**, and the **past participle.** All the other verb forms can be made from these parts. As you can see from the table below, the present participle is formed by adding *–ing* to the base form (sometimes dropping an *e*), and the past and past participle are formed by adding *–d* or *–ed* (or sometimes *–t*) to the base form.

BASE FORM	PRESENT PARTICIPLE	PAST	PAST PARTICIPLE
laugh	[is] laughing	laughed	[have] laughed
drudge	[is] drudging	drudged	[have] drudged
requite	[is] requiting	requited	[have] requited

Some verbs, however, form the past and past participle in some other way than by adding *–d* or *–ed* (or sometimes *–t*) to the base form. These verbs are called *irregular verbs.* English has dozens of them. The table below shows just a few examples. If you are in doubt about whether a verb is irregular, look it up in the dictionary; if it is irregular, you will find its principle parts listed.

BASE FORM	PRESENT PARTICIPLE	PAST	PAST PARTICIPLE
be	[is] being	was, were	[have] been
bite	[is] biting	bit	[have] bitten
go	[is] going	went	[have] gone
see	[is] seeing	saw	[have] seen
swim	[is] swimming	swam	[have] swum

2.67 IRREGULAR VERBS II

When using irregular verbs in the so-called perfect tenses (with *has* or *have*), make sure you do not use the past form instead of the past participle.

NONSTANDARD PARTICIPLE	The old familiar faces **have went.**
STANDARD PARTICIPLE	The old familiar faces **have gone.**

Another error to watch for is using the past participle form without a helping verb or mistaking the past participle for the past.

NONSTANDARD	I **been** lost since I was born.
STANDARD	I **have been** lost since I was born.

CONTINUED

| NONSTANDARD | Both Leander and Byron **swum** the Hellespont. |
| STANDARD | Both Leander and Byron **swam** the Hellespont. |

Finally, do not add *–d* or *–ed* or *–t* to the past form of an irregular verb.

| NONSTANDARD | The guard dog **bited** its own tail. |
| STANDARD | The guard dog **bit** its own tail. |

2.68 SPLIT INFINITIVES

In English, the infinitive often takes the form of two words, *to* and the base. In their discussion of this form, the first English grammarians—influenced by their knowledge of Latin, in which the infinitive is a single word—decreed that the infinitive should never be "split" in English. Under this rule, adverbs and other sentence components should not stand between *to* and the base form. However, the normal sentence rhythms of English, and the demands of sense, often call for an infinitive to be split.

STRAINED WORD ORDER	The game wardens remained more than wakeful enough **to fend off busily** the beavers.
NATURAL WORD ORDER	The game wardens remained more than wakeful enough **to busily fend off** the beavers.
STRAINED WORD ORDER	After the fire, Popgunnen's aged mother decided **to forbid flatly** his ironing his own clothes.
NATURAL WORD ORDER	After the fire, Popgunnen's aged mother decided **to flatly forbid** his ironing his own clothes.

In using the infinitive, keep *to* and the base form together where possible, but do not hesitate to separate them where the rhythm or sense of the sentence requires it. (Note that a phrase such as *to be proudly aware* is not a split infinitive; it is an infinitive of the verb *to be* followed by a predicate nominative modified by an adverb.)

| EXAMPLES | **To boldly go** where no human has gone before . . . |
| | He had achieved his highest ambition: **to be utterly contented.** |

Although the rule that infinitives should not be split was based on Latin rather than English, it has been widely accepted. You should be aware that some people may find fault with the use of a split infinitive even in cases where such a use is required by sound and sense. (For more information on the use of split infinitives, see the entry on split infinitives in Fowler's *Modern English Usage.*)

2.69 VOICE AND MOOD

Shifts in **voice** from active to passive can be as confusing as shifts in tense. Check your sentences to be sure voice is consistent. Rewrite and change subjects as necessary.

| WITH VOICE SHIFT | The **critic puzzled over** Christina Rossetti's poem *The Goblin Market,* and then **it was severely censured** by him. |
| CORRECTED | The critic puzzled over Christina Rossetti's poem *The Goblin Market* and then severely censured it. |

In addition to watching for voice shifts, check to be sure your verbs are in the appropriate **mood.** Mood is a characteristic that shows the way in which a verb is used. Each verb has three moods: **indicative, imperative,** and **subjunctive.**

Use a verb in the *indicative mood* to express a fact, an opinion, or a question.

| INDICATIVE MOOD | Before he died, Socrates **asked** Crito to pay his debt to one of the gods. Izaak Walton **believed** that fishing was somewhat like poetry. **Wasn't** it a lie that Washington said, "I cannot tell a lie"? |

Use the *imperative mood* to express a direct command or request.

| IMPERATIVE MOOD | **Be** my friend! Please **help** me get my bearings. |

Use the *subjunctive mood* in the present to express a suggestion or a necessity.

| SUBJUNCTIVE MOOD | Johnson suggested to Boswell that he **be** neither idle nor alone. It is essential that one **know** one knows nothing. |

Use the *past subjunctive* to express a wish or a condition that is not true (contrary to fact).

| PAST SUBJUNCTIVE | I wish I **were** able to read poetry all day. If wishes **were** Harleys, beggars would ride. |

Notice that the singular of most verbs in the subjunctive looks like a plural of a verb in the indicative.

| INDICATIVE PLURAL | They **were** gone in a trice. |
| SUBJUNCTIVE SINGULAR | He wishes he **were** anywhere but in that dentist's office. |

EDITING FOR ERRORS IN SUBJECT/VERB AGREEMENT

2.70 AGREEMENT OF SUBJECT AND VERB

A word that refers to one person or thing is said to be **singular in number.** A word that refers to more than one person or thing is said to be **plural in number.** Most nouns that end in *s* are plural, but most verbs that refer to the present and end in *s* are singular.

▶Use the Study Guide and Test on Editing for Errors in Subject/Verb Agreement, 5.2.15–5.2.16, in the *Assessment Portfolio.*

SINGULAR NOUNS	reptile, wig, pudding
PLURAL NOUNS	reptiles, wigs, puddings
SINGULAR VERBS	surges, wrestles, enchants
PLURAL VERBS	surge, wrestle, enchant

Each verb in a sentence should be singular if its subject is singular and plural if its subject is plural. In other words, a verb must **agree in number** with its subject.

EXAMPLES	In the film, **dinosaurs roar** and **revel.**
	A **pudding enchants** the hungry diner.

The pronouns *I* and *you,* though singular, almost always take forms that look plural. The only exceptions are the forms *I am* and *I was.*

EXAMPLES	**I agree** that technology will not save us.
	Joe, **you claim** Twain was in the Confederate Army.

2.71 AGREEMENT WITH COMPOUND SUBJECTS

A **compound subject** is formed of two or more nouns or pronouns that are joined by a conjunction and have the same verb. A compound subject joined by the conjunction *and* usually takes a plural verb.

EXAMPLE	**Shulamith and Corven are** fine singers.

A compound subject in which the subjects are joined by the conjunction *and* takes a singular verb if the compound subject really names only one person or thing.

EXAMPLE	Her role **model** and favorite **writer is** Virginia Woolf.

A compound subject formed of two singular subjects joined by the conjunctions *or* or *nor* takes a singular verb.

EXAMPLES	Either **Tudor** or **Provincial suits** me fine.
	Neither **Frodo** nor **Samwise is** too bright.

A compound subject formed of a singular subject and a plural subject joined by the conjunctions *or* or *nor* takes a verb that agrees in number with the subject nearer the verb.

EXAMPLES	Either **Sasha** or the **twins are** hiding in that closet.
	Either the **twins** or **Sasha is** hiding in that closet.

2.72 AGREEMENT WITH INDEFINITE PRONOUNS

These indefinite pronouns are singular and take a singular verb: *anybody, anyone, anything, each, either, everybody, everyone, everything, neither, nobody, no one, nothing, one, somebody, someone,* and *something.*

> EXAMPLES   **Anyone** who agrees with Shaw that Homer and Shakespeare are the world's worst writers **has** not read Shaw.
> **Everyone passes** Mr. Framley's courses.

These indefinite pronouns are plural and take a plural verb: *both, few, many,* and *several.*

> EXAMPLES   I know Arnold and Danny, and **both are** ludicrous.
> **Many are** called, but **few are** chosen.

The following indefinite pronouns can be singular or plural: *all, any, most, none,* and *some.*

> EXAMPLES   The situation is hopeless. **All is** lost. (*All* refers to *situation.*)
> The passengers drowned. **All were** lost. (*All* refers to *passengers.*)
> **None** of the cake **was** eaten. **None** of the cakes **were** eaten.

2.73 AGREEMENT IN INVERTED SENTENCES

When you invert sentences for emphasis, make sure you maintain agreement in number between subject and verb.

> EXAMPLES   Hundreds of birds **he saves** from pollution each year.
> A single crust **they have**.

2.74 AGREEMENT WITH *DOESN'T* AND *DON'T*

The contraction *doesn't* (from *does not*) is third-person singular and should be used only with a third-person singular subject. The contraction *don't* (from *do not*) should be used with all other subjects.

> EXAMPLES   **He doesn't** care for abstract art.
> **They don't** have any use for antiques.
> **You don't** need a sweater today.

2.75 OTHER PROBLEMS IN SUBJECT/VERB AGREEMENT

When a sentence begins with *here, there, when,* or *where,* often the subject follows the verb. In editing your writing, use extra care to check that the subject and verb of such sentences agree in number. Remember that the contractions *here's, there's, when's,* and *where's* contain a singular verb (*is*) and should only be used with a singular subject.

EXAMPLES
Here's Johnny!
There are six days until the end of the summer.
When's the movie over?
When are your friends coming over?
Where are your eyebrows?

Also check to be sure a verb in a sentence with a predicate nominative agrees in number with the subject and not with the predicate nominative.

EXAMPLES
Figs are the most tasty fruit.
The most tasty **fruit is** figs.

A collective noun takes a singular verb when the noun refers to the group as a unit, and it takes a plural verb when it refers to the members of the group as individuals.

AS SINGULAR   The family **reads** at meals.
AS PLURAL   The family **argue** among themselves about what to read at meals.

While editing your work, check for nouns that are plural in form but singular in meaning. They should take singular verbs.

EXAMPLES
genetics, mathematics, news, physics

The title of a creative work such as a book or song takes a singular verb, as does a group of words used as a unit.

EXAMPLES
Essays **is** Cowley's finest work.
Dewey, Cheatem, and Howe is a famous law firm.

An expression stating an amount is singular and takes a singular verb when the amount is considered as one unit. It is plural and takes a plural verb when the amount is considered as something with many parts.

AS SINGULAR   **Six candy bars is** a huge dessert for a child of two.
AS PLURAL   **Six candy bars were** in the glove compartment during the heat wave.

A fraction or a percentage is singular when it refers to a singular word and plural when it refers to a plural word.

AS SINGULAR   **One-third** of human **life is** spent in sleep.
AS PLURAL   **One-third** of all your **days are** spent in sleep.
AS SINGULAR   Over **fifty percent** of the **human family is** female.
AS PLURAL   Over **fifty percent** of all **humans are** female.

Expressions of measurement, such as area, length, volume, and weight, are usually singular.

EXAMPLE **Eighty gallons is** a lot of propane to carry up a mountain.

EDITING FOR ERRORS IN PRONOUN USAGE

2.76 PRONOUN CASE I

Case is the form that a noun or a pronoun takes to indicate its use in a sentence. English nouns and pronouns have three cases: **nominative**, **objective**, and **possessive**. The nominative case is used for the subject of a verb or for a predicate nominative. The objective case is used for a direct object, an indirect object, or the object of a preposition. The possessive case is used to show possession. The form of the nominative and objective cases of nouns is the same, and most nouns form possessives by adding an apostrophe and an *s* to the singular and an apostrophe only to the plural. But many pronouns have different forms to show nominative, objective, and possessive cases.

▶Use the Study Guide and Test on Editing Errors in Pronoun Usage, 5.2.17–5.2.18, in the *Assessment Portfolio*.

PERSONAL PRONOUNS		
SINGULAR		
Nominative Case (for subjects or predicate nominatives)	**Objective Case** (for direct objects, indirect objects, and objects of prepositions)	**Possessive Case** (to show possession)
I	me	my, mine
you	you	your, yours
he, she, it	him, her, it	his, her, hers, its
PLURAL		
we	us	our, ours
you	you	your, yours
they	them	their, theirs

To determine which form of the pronoun to use when writing a sentence, first decide whether the pronoun is used as a subject, predicate nominative, as some kind of object, or as a possessive. Doing so will tell you in what case the pronoun should be.

SUBJECT	**She** is much like Shakespeare's Dark Lady.
PREDICATE NOMINATIVE	It is **I** who forbids you.
DIRECT OBJECT	Jake's dithering disturbed **me**.
INDIRECT OBJECT	The teacher forgave **us** our errors.
OBJECT OF PREPOSITION	Between **you** and **me**, I like that person more than I should.

ESSENTIAL SKILLS: LANGUAGE 1133

ESSENTIAL SKILLS: LANGUAGE

Remember that in standard English, prepositions *always* take an object in the objective case. The phrase *between you and I* is nonstandard English.

2.77 PRONOUN CASE II

Use the possessive pronouns *mine, yours, his, hers, its, ours,* and *theirs* just as you use the pronouns in the nominative and objective cases.

AS SUBJECT	His face and **hers** appeared outside the third-story window.
AS PREDICATE NOMINATIVE	This gold is **mine**, all **mine**!
DIRECT OBJECT	First the crowd cheered my Nobel prize, then they cheered **his**.
INDIRECT OBJECT	The judge of pies gave **ours** the blue ribbon.
OBJECT OF PREPOSITION	Best wishes to you and **yours**.

Use the possessive pronouns *my, your, his, her, its, our,* and *their* as adjectives before nouns.

EXAMPLES	If the cats wore pants, **her** feline trousers would be quite shaggy.
	Their insouciance enabled them to penetrate to the depths of the fortress.

As you edit your writing, check the case of nouns and pronouns before a gerund. They should always be in the possessive case.

WITH GERUND	**His jottings** added up to detailed directions to the site of the treasure.

Do not confuse the gerund and the present participle (see 2.16 and 2.17). Compare the example above with the following example, in which no possessive is required before the participle:

WITH PARTICIPLE	We watched the hand **jotting** the directions.

2.78 *WHO* AND *WHOM*

The pronoun *who* is referred to as an **interrogative pronoun** when it is used to form a question. When it is used to introduce a **subordinate clause**, it is referred to as a **relative pronoun.** In both cases, the nominative is *who,* the objective is *whom,* and the possessive is *whose.* As you edit your writing, check these pronouns to see if the form of the pronoun you have used is appropriate for its use in the sentence or subordinate clause in which it appears.

SUBJECT	**Who** goes there?
SUBJECT	The man **who** approached me wore wings.
DIRECT OBJECT	**Whom** did the shark bite?
DIRECT OBJECT	The clown **whom** you saw was named Bumpo.
OBJECT OF PREPOSITION	**To whom** did the sorceress send the dream first?
OBJECT OF PREPOSITION	I do not know **from whom** you get the authority to stop our dancing.

In spoken English, *whom* is gradually being replaced by *who*. In some formal speech, however, and in all writing of standard English except dialogue, the form *whom* should still be used where grammatically correct.

2.79 PRONOUNS WITH APPOSITIVES

When a pronoun is used with an appositive, its form matches its use in the sentence.

SUBJECT	**I, Claudius,** am Emperor of Rome.
PREDICATE NOMINATIVE	The burned-out wrecks in this photo are **we students** after exam week.
INDIRECT OBJECT	Give **us expert hostage negotiators** a chance.
OBJECT OF PREPOSITION	The blame for the revolt fell upon **us peasants.**

2.80 PRONOUNS AS APPOSITIVES

When a pronoun is itself used as an appositive, it should be in the same case as the word to which it refers.

PRONOUN IN APPOSITION TO SUBJECT	Two consummate rhymers, Skelton and **he**, wrote about the death of a sparrow.
PRONOUN IN APPOSITION TO THE OBJECT OF A PREPOSITION	Praising Yeats, T. S. Eliot gave the title of great poet only to Dante, Shakespeare, and **him**.

2.81 PRONOUNS IN COMPARISONS

The ends of sentences that compare people or things are often left unexpressed. Pronouns in such sentences should be in the same case as they would have been if the sentence had been completed.

EXAMPLES	Sforza cared nothing if someone claimed to be braver than **he** [was].
	His prize in composition meant as much to his teacher as [it did] to **him**.

2.82 AGREEMENT OF PRONOUNS AND ANTECEDENTS

Check the pronouns in your writing to be sure they agree in **number, person,** and **gender** with their antecedents. (For a discussion of number, see 2.70.) Person is the form a word takes to indicate the person speaking (the *first person,* corresponding to *I* or *we*), the person spoken to (the *second person,* corresponding to *you*), or the person spoken of or about (the *third person,* corresponding to *he, she, it,* or *they*). Gender is the form a word takes to indicate whether it is *masculine, feminine,* or *neuter* (neither masculine nor feminine).

INCORRECT NUMBER	Pound suggested that the **person** who does not love music cannot write poetry, and **they** should not even attempt it. *CONTINUED*

CORRECT NUMBER	Pound suggested that **people** who do not love music cannot write poetry, and **they** should not even attempt it.
INCORRECT GENDER	**Thomas Shadwell** was poet laureate of England after Dryden, though **she** was not of Dryden's caliber.
CORRECT GENDER	**Thomas Shadwell** was poet laureate of England after Dryden, though **he** was not of Dryden's caliber.

2.83 REFERENCE OF PRONOUNS TO ANTECEDENTS I

As you edit, check each pronoun to be sure that it refers clearly to its antecedent.

CLEAR REFERENCE	**Jack** wandered lonely as a cloud; **he** saw daffodils fluttering and dancing in the breeze.
CLEAR REFERENCES	After the **waves** capsized <u>the</u> <u>schooner</u>, **they** smashed <u>its</u> sides.

Weak reference occurs when a pronoun refers to an antecedent that has not been expressed. If you find a weak reference while editing your writing, either change the pronoun into a noun or give the pronoun a clear antecedent.

WEAK REFERENCE	In the "sport" of bear-baiting, **it** was set upon by several dogs.
PRONOUN CHANGED TO NOUN	In the "sport" of bear-baiting, **a bear** was set upon by several dogs.
WEAK REFERENCE	The rich man had a habit of entering a bookstore and buying **them** all.
PRONOUN GIVEN CLEAR ANTECEDENT	The rich man had a habit of entering a shop full of **books** and buying **them** all.

Ambiguous reference occurs when a pronoun can refer to either of two antecedents. Clarify ambiguous references by rewording the sentence or by replacing the pronouns with a noun.

AMBIGUOUS	After the teacher graduated the student, **he** burst into tears of joy.
CLEAR	After the teacher graduated the student, the **teacher** burst into tears of joy.
CLEAR	After he graduated the student, the **teacher** burst into tears of joy.

2.84 REFERENCE OF PRONOUNS TO ANTECEDENTS II

An **indefinite reference** occurs when the pronouns *you, it,* or *they* have no reference to a specific person or thing. Edit out an indefinite reference by rewording the sentence to explain to whom or what the pronoun refers, or by eliminating the pronoun altogether.

INDEFINITE REFERENCE	**You** can wander through some parts of England even today and see little change from the last century.
PRONOUN ELIMINATED	Some parts of England have changed little from the last century.

CONTINUED

INDEFINITE REFERENCE	On the sign **it** said, "No hunting jabberwocks."
PRONOUN ELIMINATED	The **sign** read, "No hunting jabberwocks."
INDEFINITE REFERENCE	In ancient times **they** believed the four humors or liquids of the body determined a person's character.
PRONOUN REPLACED	In ancient times **medical writers** believed the four humors or liquids of the body determined a person's character.

A **general reference** occurs when a pronoun refers to a general idea implied in the previous clause, rather than to a specific antecedent. Edit general references by replacing the pronoun with a noun or by rewording the sentence.

GENERAL REFERENCE	In England a "public school" is what Americans would call a private school, **which** confuses many readers of English literature.
SENTENCE REWORDED	Many readers of English literature are confused by the term *public school,* which refers to the type of school Americans would call *private.*
GENERAL REFERENCE	Weaving requires a large investment of time. **This** discourages many would-be weavers.
PRONOUN REPLACED AND SENTENCES REWORDED	**The investment of time that weaving requires** discourages many would-be weavers.

EDITING FOR ERRORS IN MODIFIER USAGE

2.85 MODIFIERS WITH ACTION AND LINKING VERBS

When you wish to modify the subject of a linking verb, use an adjective. When you wish to modify an action verb, use an adverb.

LINKING VERB AND ADJECTIVE	He **is** not only **dull** in himself, but the cause of dullness in others.
ACTION VERB AND ADVERB	Consuela **gyrated frenetically** to the crazy dance beat.

Check whether your use of an adjective or adverb is correct by temporarily replacing the verb you have written with the verb *seem.* If the sentence still makes some kind of sense, the original verb is a linking verb and should take an adjective. If the substitution of *seem* produces nonsense, the original verb is an action verb and should take an adverb. You can see how this works by substituting *seem* in each of the examples given above.

SUBSTITUTION MAKES SENSE	He **seems** not only **dull** in himself, but the cause of dullness in others.
SUBSTITUTION MAKES NO SENSE	Consuela **seemed frenetically** to the crazy dance beat.

▶Use the Study Guide and Test on Editing for Errors in Modifier Usage, 5.2.19–5.2.20, in the *Assessment Portfolio.*

2.86 Comparison of Adjectives and Adverbs

Comparison refers to the change in the form of a modifier to show an increase or a decrease in the quality expressed by the modifier. Each modifier has three forms of comparison: **positive**, **comparative**, and **superlative**. Most one-syllable modifiers and some two-syllable modifiers form the comparative and superlative degrees by adding *-er* and *-est*. Other two-syllable modifiers, and all modifiers of more than two syllables, use *more* and *most* to form these degrees.

	POSITIVE	COMPARATIVE	SUPERLATIVE
ADJECTIVES	cute	cuter	cutest
	bonny	bonnier	bonniest
	faithless	more faithless	most faithless
	perfidious	more perfidious	most perfidious
ADVERBS	soon	sooner	soonest
	early	earlier	earliest
	pridefully	more pridefully	most pridefully
	supercilious	more supercilious	most supercilious

To show a decrease in the quality of any modifier, form the comparative and superlative degrees by using *less* and *least.*

EXAMPLES	greedy, less greedy, least greedy
	swiftly, less swiftly, least swiftly

Some modifiers form their comparative and superlative degrees irregularly. Check the dictionary if you are unsure about the comparison of a modifier.

EXAMPLES	good, better, best	well, better, best	bad, worse, worst

Use the comparative degree when comparing two things. Use the superlative degree when comparing more than two things.

COMPARATIVE	Of the two writers Montaigne and Vita Sackville-West, it would be difficult to say which was the **more devoted** gardener.
SUPERLATIVE	Jupiter is the **largest** of the nine planets.

2.87 Illogical and Double Comparisons

As you edit your writing, check sentences for **illogical comparison.** Such comparison occurs when one member of a group is compared with the group of which it is a part. Clarify illogical comparison by including the word *other* or *else* in the sentence.

ILLOGICAL	Grimm loved folk stories more than boys his age.
LOGICAL	Grimm loved folk stories more than **other** boys his age.

Another problem to check for is **double comparison**. This occurs when two comparative forms or two superlative forms are used to modify the same word. Correct double comparison by editing out one of the comparative or superlative forms.

DOUBLE COMPARISON	Let's not put language into the contract that is even **more redundanter** than what we have already.
SINGLE COMPARISON	Let's not put language into the contract that is even **more redundant** than what we have already.

2.88 DOUBLE NEGATIVES

In English a **double negative** is a nonstandard construction in which two negative words are used instead of one. Check your writing to be sure you have not used a negative word such as *no, none, not* (and its contraction, *–n't*), *nothing, barely, hardly,* or *scarcely* with any other negative word. If you find a double negative, change it by deleting one of the negative words.

DOUBLE NEGATIVE	He who does not know himself **cannot hardly** know the world.
SINGLE NEGATIVE	He who does not know himself **cannot** know the world.
SINGLE NEGATIVE	He who does not know himself **can hardly** know the world.
DOUBLE NEGATIVE	Like most writers, Coleridge did**n't** make **no** money.
SINGLE NEGATIVE	Like most writers, Coleridge made **no** money.

2.89 OTHER PROBLEMS WITH MODIFIERS

The demonstrative pronouns *this* and *these* are used to refer to things near the speaker. The pronouns *that* and *those* refer to objects at some distance. Thus you might say, "This apple in my hand is poisonous" if you were referring to an apple you were actually holding, but if you were pointing at an apple in a picture of yourself, you might say, "That apple in my hand is poisonous." The two pairs of pronouns are often used to distinguish between objects or sets of objects.

EXAMPLE	These toes are fine; those toes are broken.

Check your writing to see that your use of *this* and *these,* and *that* and *those* makes sense.

NONSENSICAL	We will play **those** cards in my hand and **these** cards in your hand.
SENSIBLE	We will play **these** cards in my hand and **those** cards in your hand.

The pronoun *them* is a personal pronoun in standard English and should not be substituted for the demonstrative pronoun *those*.

NONSTANDARD	**Them** Three Stooges are the funniest things since the Little Rascals.
STANDARD	**Those** Three Stooges are the funniest things since the Little Rascals.

Modifiers that often give writers trouble are *bad* and *badly*. Check instances of these words in your writing to make sure you have used *bad* as an adjective and *badly* as an adverb. Only the adjective should follow a linking verb such as *feel, hear, see, smell,* or *taste.*

NONSTANDARD	Goldilocks felt **badly** for eating all the bears' porridge.
STANDARD	Goldilocks felt **bad** for eating all the bears' porridge.

Similarly distinguish between *good* and *well*. *Good* is an adjective and should not be used to modify an action verb. *Well,* however, can be used either as an adverb meaning "capably" or "in a satisfactory way," or as an adjective meaning "healthy" or "of a satisfactory condition."

NONSTANDARD	Milton wrote blank verse **good**.
STANDARD	Milton wrote **good** blank verse.
STANDARD	Milton wrote blank verse **well**.
STANDARD	His dimming eyes could not see **well**.
STANDARD	Though blind, he looked **well**.

▶ Use the Study Guide and Test on Editing for Errors in Usage, 5.3.1–5.3.2, in the *Assessment Portfolio*.

USAGE HANDBOOK

The following sections (2.90–2.92) explain some common problems to watch for as you edit your writing.

2.90 USAGE PROBLEMS I

adapt, adopt. *Adapt* means "to make [something] fit a specific use or situation by modifying"; *adopt* means to "take something and make it in some sense one's own."

EXAMPLES	The author of *Troilus and Cressida* **adapted** the story of the Trojan War.
	James Barrie, the playwright who originally told *Peter Pan* to some young friends, later **adopted** two of those youngsters.

affect, effect. If you wish to use a verb meaning "have an effect on," use *affect*. If you wish to use a noun meaning "the result of an action," use *effect*.

VERB	In one of Hardy's short stories, the music of a fiddle **affects** a woman strangely.
NOUN	The wailing of the fiddle had a strange **effect** on her.

As a verb, *effect* means to bring something about despite obstacles.

EXAMPLE	He **effected** the reunion of the twins, who had never known one another.
	The reunion deeply **affected** the two girls.

1140 *LANGUAGE ARTS SURVEY*

2.91 USAGE PROBLEMS II

imply, infer. Most writers accept the following meanings for these words: *imply* means "to express indirectly rather than openly"; *infer* means "to arrive at a conclusion by reasoning from evidence." Although this distinction between *imply* and *infer* has not always been observed, it is a useful one.

> EXAMPLES   His silence **implied** that he consented to her accusations.
> She **inferred** from his silence that he admitted his wrongdoing.

like, as, as if. Although *like* is frequently used to introduce subordinate clauses in informal English, it is considered a preposition, not a conjunction. Do not use it in place of *as* or *as if* in your writing.

> INFORMAL   It looks **like** you were wrong.
> FORMAL   It looks **as if** you were wrong.
> FORMAL   Houses look **like** dollhouses from airplanes.

literally. Most writers limit their use of *literally* to the sense "actually," and avoid using it in the sense "not actually, but in effect, or for all practical purposes." This distinction, though sometimes ignored, is worth observing.

> CLEAR   The opera singer **literally** shattered a crystal glass with her high C.
> CONFUSING   He **literally** turned the house upside-down looking for his keys.

2.92 USAGE PROBLEMS III

of. The preposition *of* should not be used in place of *have* after verbs such as *could, should, would, might, must,* and *ought.*

> NONSTANDARD   I should **of** remembered Ben Franklin's saying that time is money.
> STANDARD   I should **have** remembered Ben Franklin's saying that time is money.
> STANDARD   I should**'ve** remembered Ben Franklin's saying that time is money.

Avoid *off of.*

> NONSTANDARD   The apple fell **off of** William's head.
> STANDARD   The apple fell **off** William's head.

then, than. Use *than* as a conjunction in comparisons. Use *then* as an adverb that tells when something occurred.

> EXAMPLES   Iambic verse is more common **than** amphibrachic.
> First use the iambic, **then** the amphibrachic.

▶Use the Study Guide and Test on Proofreading for Errors in End Marks and Commas, 5.4.1– 5.4.2, in the *Assessment Portfolio.*

MECHANICS HANDBOOK

PROOFREADING FOR ERRORS IN END MARKS AND COMMAS

2.93 END MARKS

An **end mark** signals the end of a sentence. It also shows the purpose of the sentence.

A declarative sentence ends with a **period.** If a declarative sentence already has a period at the end because an abbreviation occurs there, no other end mark is needed. If a declarative sentence ends with a quotation, place the period inside the quotation marks.

DECLARATIVE	The name of his boss was Ebenezer.
WITH ABBREVIATION AT END	He felt as if he were working at Scrooge, Marley, and Co.
WITH QUOTATION AT END	One day his son said, "God bless us every one."

A question ends with a **question mark.** Indirect questions, however, do not require a question mark. If a question ends with an abbreviation, add a question mark after the final period. If a question is quoted, the question mark appears inside the closing quotation marks; if a question contains a quotation, the question mark appears outside the closing quotation marks. Polite questions often end with a period instead of a question mark.

DIRECT QUESTION	Who was Francis Bacon?
ENDING IN ABBREVIATION	Who was Francis Bacon, Esq.?
INDIRECT QUESTION	He asked who Francis Bacon was.
QUOTED QUESTION	He asked, "Who was Francis Bacon?"
QUESTION INCLUDING QUOTATION	Were his exact words "I don't know Francis Bacon"?
POLITE QUESTION	Will you please tell me who Francis Bacon was.

An exclamation ends with an **exclamation point.** If an exclamation is quoted, the exclamation point appears inside the closing quotation marks; if an exclamation contains a quotation, the exclamation point appears outside the closing quotation marks. An imperative sentence may end with a period instead of an exclamation point.

EXCLAMATION	Go! Go finish reading *Tom Jones!*
QUOTED EXCLAMATION	Suzanne groaned, "That book is too long!"
EXCLAMATION CONTAINING QUOTE	I can't believe Suzanne said "I can't read it"!
IMPERATIVE SENTENCE	Let us now begin reading the novel.

2.94 COMMAS I

As you proofread your writing, check to see that you have used commas after certain introductory elements. Such elements include mild exclamations such as *yes, no, oh,* and *well;* participial phrases; two or more prepositional phrases; and adverb clauses.

MILD EXCLAMATION	**Oh,** I thought that painting was a dropcloth.
PARTICIPIAL PHRASE	**Having surfed up to the beach,** Leila soon gathered a crowd with the story of her exploits.
TWO PREPOSITIONAL PHRASES	**Down in the meadow by the old mill stream,** the green grass grows and the katydids dream.
ADVERB CLAUSE	**When he thought of the future,** Famstooper saw nothing but glory for the family name.

A comma is also used to set off an element that interrupts a sentence, such as a parenthetical expression or a word used in direct address.

PARENTHETICAL EXPRESSION	Howey Humhammer has, **however,** heard of her heresy by hearsay.
DIRECT ADDRESS	**Faustine,** have you seen my pet snakes?

2.95 COMMAS II

A **serial comma** is a comma used to separate items in a series, whether the items are words, phrases, or clauses. Some writers omit the last comma when *and, or,* or *nor* joins the last two items in a series, but this construction sometimes makes a sentence unclear.

WORDS	Which time of year did Coleridge call "this dark, hoarse, teeth-chattering month"?
PHRASES	Hobbes claimed that laughter arose from sudden joy in our superiority, from comparison with others who were less fortunate, or from comparison with ourselves when we were less fortunate.
CLAUSES	Patrick Henry noted that Caesar was struck down by Brutus, that Charles the Third was toppled by Cromwell, and that George the Third should profit from their example.

Some paired words may be considered a single item.

PAIRED WORDS	Zimswell fed his prisoner with water, **bread and butter,** and chocolate cake.

If all the items in a series are joined by *and, or,* or *nor,* do not separate them with commas.

EXAMPLE	The waves crashed and lashed and dashed at the imperiled prince.

Two or more adjectives preceding a noun are separated by commas.

EXAMPLE	Swinburne's "sad, bad, glad, mad brother" was the French poet Villon.

Use a comma before *and, but, for, nor, or, so,* and *yet* when they join two independent clauses. The comma may be omitted before *and, but, nor,* and *or* if the clauses are very short and the resulting sentence is still clear in meaning.

LONG CLAUSE	My eyes were the greenest of things blue, and hers were the bluest of things gray.
SHORT CLAUSE	Clarissa sighed but Franz did not hear.

Do not use a comma between two parts of a compound verb or compound predicate.

2.96 COMMAS III

A **nonrestrictive** participial phrase or clause is one that does not restrict or limit the meaning of the substantive to which it refers. You can test a phrase or clause when proofreading your writing by seeing if the main meaning of the sentence is lost if you omit the phrase or clause. If the phrase or clause is indeed nonrestrictive, make sure it is set off by commas.

RESTRICTIVE	The professor **I saw** was the one who could speak five languages
NONRESTRICTIVE	I don't know where he learned the five languages, **which were Finnish, Polynesian, Aboriginal, Latin, and Mohawk.**

Appositives and appositive phrases can be either restrictive or nonrestrictive.

RESTRICTIVE	The book *Anatomy of Melancholy* is surprisingly funny.
NONRESTRICTIVE	*Anatomy of Melancholy*, **a book by Robert Burton,** is surprisingly funny.

PROOFREADING FOR OTHER PUNCTUATION ERRORS

2.97 SEMICOLONS

A **semicolon** is used as punctuation between clauses in several situations. Use a semicolon between closely related independent clauses that are not joined by *and, but, for, nor, or, so,* or *yet.*

EXAMPLE	Fay skipped down the hills of Never; she arrived at the river of Nowhere and crossed over to the hills of Beyond.

Use a semicolon between independent clauses joined by a conjunctive adverb or transitional expression that is followed by a comma.

EXAMPLE	Baba Yaga did not fly about on a broom; however, she was able to move her house on the chicken legs that supported it.

Use a semicolon between linked independent clauses or items in a list if the clauses or items already contain commas.

►Use the Study Guide and Test on Proofreading for Other Punctuation Errors, 5.4.3–5.4.4, in the *Assessment Portfolio.*

INDEPENDENT CLAUSES	He ran, but his running did no good; he shouted, but no one heard; he fell forward face first, but no one helped him up; and at last he awoke.
LIST OF ITEMS WITH COMMAS	McQuirk, the tinker, brought sixty-eight pots, most without handles; forty-one ladles, all with holes; and sixteen cracked shaving mugs.

2.98 COLONS

A **colon** introduces a long statement or quotation or a list of items.

QUOTATION	Goethe's remark about Byron was as follows: "Lord Byron is only great when he acts the poet; as soon as he reflects, he becomes only a child."
LIST	These are some well-known British painters of the 1800s: Varley, Hunt, Constable, Turner, Stubbs, Lawrence, Millais, and Brown.

2.99 DASHES

A **dash** is used to show an abrupt break in thought.

EXAMPLE	The Bird of Time has but a little way To fly—and Lo! the Bird is on the Wing.

Sometimes the dash serves in place of an expression such as *in other words, that is,* or *namely.*

EXAMPLE	The purpose behind the plot was clear—to make Eggbald change his ways.

2.100 HYPHENS

A **hyphen** is used to link words in a compound adjective, adverb, or noun.

EXAMPLES	all-powerful king, eighteenth-century scholar, cross-country race, full-length dress, half-baked idea, quasi-stellar object, self-conscious clown, six-year-old kid, self-restraint, jack-of-all-trades, author-critic, great-grandson

If you have questions about whether you should hyphenate a particular compound word, look it up in the dictionary. If the dictionary offers no information, consider whether the hyphen is needed to make the meaning of the sentence clear.

UNCLEAR	The statue of Balzac was **thought provoking.**
CLEAR	The statue of Balzac was **thought-provoking.**

2.101 PARENTHESES AND BRACKETS

Parentheses are used to enclose an aside or information that is less important than the main information offered in a sentence.

ASIDE	Nagali must recall the spring in Oslo **(at least I think it was Oslo)** when we held that unforgettable family reunion.
LESS IMPORTANT	As you come up the hill, you will see a red house **(the one with the Ford Escort out front, not the one with the Rolls Royce)**; turn in at that drive

Brackets are used to enclose a writer's corrections or comments in someone else's quoted material, and as parentheses within parentheses.

QUOTED MATERIAL	Emerson noted, "A foolish consistency is the hobgoblin **[bogeyman]** of little minds."
PARENTHESES WITHIN PARENTHESES	The essay "Singers on Choppers" (in Claus Anzugell, ed., *Girl Groups* **[Lexford City: Lexford University Press, 1995]**, pp. 63–68) deals with girl-group motorcycle use.

2.102 APOSTROPHES

An **apostrophe** is used to form the possessive of nouns and some—but not all—pronouns. To form the possessive of a singular noun, add an apostrophe and an *s*. If the noun already ends in an *s* sound, has two or more syllables, and would be hard to pronounce with an additional *s*, add only an apostrophe. These rules apply also to hyphenated words, names of organizations, and indefinite pronouns.

WITH ADDED *S*	world**'s** end, Yorick**'s** skull, Grant**'s** tomb, daughter-in-law**'s** husband, everyone**'s** eyeballs, someone else**'s** money, Oxford University**'s** rowing team
WITHOUT ADDED *S*	Achilles' heel, goodness' sake, appearance' sake

To form the possessive of a plural noun, add only an apostrophe if the plural form ends in *s*. If the plural form ends in some other letter, add an apostrophe and an *s*.

ENDING WITH *S*	ten summers' sunshine, two lovers' kisses
ENDING WITHOUT *S*	children**'s** room, women**'s** toolbelts, sheep**'s** bleatings, teeth**'s** sheen

While proofreading, check to see that you have not used an apostrophe to form the plural of a noun. Note also that the possessive pronouns, including *yours, ours, hers,* and *its,* do not have an apostrophe.

INCORRECT PLURAL	Mr. Gleewomp owns six acre's next to the football field.
CORRECT PLURAL	Mr. Gleewomp owns six **acres** next to the football field.

CONTINUED

INCORRECT POSSESSIVE	She swung the hammer and hit the nail on it's head.
CORRECT POSSESSIVE	She swung the hammer and hit the nail on **its** head.

To show joint possession by all people in a group, add 's (or an apostrophe only) to the last word. To show individual possession of similar items by each member of a group, add 's (or an apostrophe only) to each noun in the group.

JOINT POSSESSION	He polished Fregwith, Abercorp, and Steengleen's sailing trophy.
INDIVIDUAL POSSESSION	He retrieved Fregwith's, Abercorp's, and Steengleen's life jacket.

Use an apostrophe to form the possessive of words that refer to time or that indicate amounts in dollars or cents.

EXAMPLES	a hard day's night, a fortnight's journey, a penny's worth of rue

2.103 UNDERLINING AND ITALICS

Italics are a type of slanted printing used to show emphasis. (**Underlining** is used instead of italics in handwritten documents or in forms of printing in which italics are not available.) The following examples show the categories of words that should receive italics (underlining) for emphasis.

WORKS OF ART	Leonardo's *Mona Lisa*, Münch's *The Cry*, Rothko's *Orange Yellow Orange*
BOOKS, PLAYS	Butler's *Erewhon*, Synge's *Riders to the Sea*
FILMS, TELEVISION PROGRAMS, PERIODICALS	*It's a Wonderful Life, Jeopardy The Times, The Liberator*
AIRCRAFT, SHIPS, SPACECRAFT, TRAINS	*Spirit of St. Louis, Titanic, Enterprise, Orient Express*

Italicize the titles of long musical compositions unless they are merely the names of musical forms such as *fantasy, symphony, concerto, sonata,* and *nocturne.* The titles of short pieces such as songs should be placed in quotation marks.

SHORT MUSICAL COMPOSITION	"Another Day Without You"
LONG MUSICAL COMPOSITION	Mozart's *Don Giovanni,* Beethoven's Symphony no. 5

As you proof your writing, check for words used as words, letters used as letters, and words from foreign languages. These should all be in italics (or underlined).

EXAMPLES	The word *cram* is considered offensive in some circles.
	Glickser's mouth dropped open in the shape of an *o.*
	I did not learn that a *faux pas* was a false step, or mistake, until I told someone it was a kind of animal.

2.104 QUOTATION MARKS I

Quotation marks are used to enclose a **direct quotation,** or a person's exact words. They are not used to enclose an **indirect quotation,** which is a reworded version of a person's words. Commas and periods that follow a quotation should be placed inside closing quotation marks; colons and semicolons should be placed outside. Do not, however, use a period to separate a direct quotation from the rest of a sentence.

DIRECT	"Who can refute a sneer?" sneered Paley.
DIRECT WITH PERIOD	In the fourteenth century, William Langland called grammar "that grounde of alle."
DIRECT WITH COMMA	"Grief is a species of idleness," insisted practical Sam Johnson.
DIRECT WITH SEMICOLON	Alice cried, "Curiouser and curiouser!"; for she had seen a sight truly remarkable.
INDIRECT	Walter Pater said that success in life meant to burn always with a hard, gemlike flame.

When writing **dialogue,** a conversation between speakers, begin a new paragraph each time the speaker changes and enclose each speaker's words in quotation marks. When an indication of the speaker, such as *she said,* divides a sentence into two parts, the second part begins with a small letter.

EXAMPLES	Lord Orville, as he well might, laughed but answered, "Yes, a pretty modest-looking girl." "O my Lord!" cried the madman, "she is an angel!" "A *silent* one," returned he.

—Frances Burney, Evelina, Letter 12

2.105 QUOTATION MARKS II

Quotation marks are also used to enclose titles of short works.

PARTS OF BOOKS	"Understanding Literature"
SONGS	"Take Me Out to the Ball Game"
SHORT POEMS	"La Belle Dame Sans Merci"
STORIES	"The Gift of the Magi"
ESSAYS, ARTICLES	"Essay on Milton"

Single quotation marks are used to enclose a quotation within a quotation.

EXAMPLE	The mad scientist murmured, "I think Blake had the right idea when he said, 'Energy is eternal delight.'"

2.106 ELLIPSIS

Ellipsis points are used to indicate an omission in quoted material. Use three ellipsis points (with a space before the first point) if the quoted material that precedes the omission is not a complete sentence; if it is a complete sentence, keep the end mark and add the ellipsis points.

INCOMPLETE SENTENCE BEFORE OMISSION	Congreve asked, "Is there in the world . . . a people more unsteady, more apt to discontent?"
COMPLETE SENTENCE BEFORE OMISSION	"Is there in the world a climate more uncertain than our own? . . . Is there anywhere a people more unsteady, more apt to discontent?"

Ellipsis points are also used in much the same way to show a pause in a written passage.

EXAMPLE   "What the devil . . . oh, it's the minister," said Deewithy.

PROOFREADING FOR ERRORS IN CAPITALIZATION

2.107 ASTRONOMICAL TERMS

Capitalize the names of astronomical bodies.

PLANETS	Saturn, Planet X, Pluto
STARS	Aldebaran, Fomalhaut, Deneb, Beta Centauri
CONSTELLATIONS	Big Dipper, Virgo, Southern Cross

2.108 AWARDS

Capitalize the names of awards and prizes. Some words that go with prize names are not capitalized, however.

EXAMPLES   Pulitzer Prize, Nobel Peace Prize, Nobel Prize in physics, Oscar, Academy Award, National Merit scholarship

2.109 BRAND AND TRADE NAMES

Capitalize the brand names and trademarks of products made by businesses. The dictionary may indicate if a name is trademarked. Do not capitalize the noun following a trade name that indicates what type of product it is.

EXAMPLES   Rayon fiber, Levi's, Frookies

►Use the Study Guide and Test on Proofreading for Errors in Capitalization, 5.4.5–5.4.6, in the *Assessment Portfolio.*

2.110 BUILDINGS AND STRUCTURES

Capitalize the names of important or widely recognized buildings and other structures or monuments. Capitalize the noun following a building, structure, or monument name that indicates its type.

EXAMPLES   Washington Monument, the Sphinx, Stonehenge, the White House, Buckingham Palace, Empire State Building, Golden Gate Bridge

Contrast the absence of capitalization in the following example of a building that is not widely known:

EXAMPLE   I live in the white house down in the hollow.

2.111 DAYS, MONTHS, YEARS, AND HOLIDAYS

Capitalize the names of days, months, and holidays.

DAYS OF THE WEEK   Tuesday, Sunday
MONTHS   September, December
HOLIDAYS   Halloween, Memorial Day

Do not capitalize references to decades or centuries.

EXAMPLES   the fifties, the seventeenth century

2.112 DIRECTIONS AND REGIONS

Capitalize the names of commonly recognized geographical regions.

EXAMPLES   Antarctica, the Pole, the Tropics, Upper Michigan

Do not capitalize words such as *east, west, north,* and *south* when they are used only to indicate direction.

EXAMPLES   Go twelve paces **west** from the rock and dig for treasure.
He went to the **West** during the Gold Rush.

The adjectives *eastern, western, northern,* and *southern* are not capitalized when they are used as temporary designations.

TEMPORARY   southern Pacific Ocean, western Idaho
STANDARD   Northern Hemisphere, Western world

2.113 Events and Periods

Capitalize historical events, special events, and recognized periods of time.

HISTORICAL EVENTS	Boston Tea Party, Gunpowder Plot
HISTORICAL PERIODS	Reconstruction, Reign of Terror, Stone Age
SPECIAL EVENTS	Olympics, Superbowl

2.114 Family Relationships

Capitalize the names of family relationships used as titles unless they are preceded by a modifier.

MODIFIED	My father, your mom, Vanessa's brother
NOT MODIFIED	Hey, Pa, what's for dinner?

If the name of a family relationship precedes a proper name, capitalize it even if it is modified.

EXAMPLES	Uncle Gyro, dear Auntie Em

2.115 First Words

Capitalize the first word in a sentence.

EXAMPLES	The ballot is stronger than the bullet, but the ballet is stronger than either.
	She jests at scars that never felt a wound.

2.116 Interjections

Do not capitalize an interjection such as *oh* unless it begins a sentence or stands alone. Do, however, capitalize the word *O*, which is technically not an interjection but a **vocative**—a word used to call someone.

EXAMPLES	Oh! What are you doing here?
	Oh, I suppose so.
	I can give you . . . oh, about six minutes to get ready.
	Sing to me, O Muse!

2.117 Letters

Capitalize letters used as grades, as musical tones, or as a designation for a person, thing, or location.

EXAMPLES	Gleethwistle's work bought him a big, fat A.
	We listened to a string quartet in G minor by Grieg.

CONTINUED

> If **A** loves **B**, it does not follow that **B** loves **A**.
> How much gas will a Maserati use to travel from point **A** to point **B**, compared to a Honda?

2.118 ORGANIZATIONS AND INSTITUTIONS

Capitalize the names of organizations and institutions, whether they are public, private, athletic, business, or government bodies.

PUBLIC	University of Texas, Textile Workers Union
PRIVATE	Girls Scouts of America, New York Philharmonic
ATHLETIC	New York Giants, Chicago Bulls
BUSINESS	General Foods, Shell Oil
GOVERNMENT	United States Supreme Court, Bureau of the Census

2.119 OUTLINES

Capitalize the first word of each entry in an outline. Most of the index letters that identify parts of the outline are also capitalized. The following example is the first part of an outline for a report on Matthew Arnold; observe that lowercase letters are used as index letters after the Arabic numeral level.

Title: Matthew Arnold as Poet

Thesis statement: Matthew Arnold found less and less impetus to write poetry as he grew older.

I. Background and early life
  A. Family
    1. Mother
    2. Father
    3. Siblings
  B. Education
    1. Rugby School
    2. Oxford University
      a. Newdigate Prize
      b. Second-class honors

II. Employment
  A. Private secretary
  B. School inspector

2.120 PERSONAL NAMES

Capitalize the names of persons and titles of address such as *Mr., Mrs., Ms., Miss, Madame,* or *Monsieur* when used in addressing a person or before a name.

EXAMPLES   **Mrs. Thrale, Harriet Westbrook, Christopher Marlowe, Dr. Johnson**

Check a reference book if you are unsure about the capitalization of *de la, du, van, von,* and other parts of names. Sometimes the part of a name that follows *Mc–* or *Mac–* is capitalized and sometimes it is not.

EXAMPLES   **Madame D'Arblay, Thomas De Quincey, James Macpherson, Charles McCarter**

2.121 PLACE NAMES

Capitalize the names of places, including terms such as *lake, mountain, river,* or *valley,* if it is used as part of a name.

BODIES OF WATER	**Amazon River, River Thames, Firth of Forth**
CITIES AND TOWNS	**Winchester, London, St. Albans**
COUNTIES	**Orange County, Bucks County**
COUNTRIES	**Great Britain, Liberia**
ISLANDS	**Tahiti, Manhattan, Maui**
MOUNTAINS	**Mont Blanc, the Matterhorn**
STATES	**Alaska, Florida**
STREETS AND HIGHWAYS	**Wall Street, Interstate 80**

Do not capitalize generic terms for places without specific modifiers.

EXAMPLES   We drove to **the dump** to watch the bears dine.
The magician was walking down the street and turned into **a building**.

2.122 POETRY

The first word in each line of a poem was capitalized in English until recent times.

EXAMPLE   How I am changed! Alas, how am I grown
      A frightful specter to myself unknown!
          —Lady Mary Wortley Montagu,
          "Saturday: The Small Pox: Flavia"

Most writers in this century, however, have broken with this tradition.

EXAMPLE   One post of Penelope's bed
      was really a living tree,
      and by this sign she knew her mate,
      though time across the sea
      had changed him utterly.
          —Robert Shepherd

2.123 PROPER NOUNS AND ADJECTIVES

Capitalize proper nouns and adjectives.

> EXAMPLES   Hercules, Herculean task
> Russia, Russian dressing

2.124 QUOTATIONS

Capitalize the first word of a sentence in a direct quotation even if it begins within the sentence where it is quoted.

> EXAMPLE   Hemingway said, "The world is a fine place and worth fighting for."

Do not capitalize a quoted fragment that completes the sense of part of the sentence outside the quotation marks.

> EXAMPLE   Creighton remarked that the people who do the most harm are "those who go about doing good."

2.125 SACRED BEINGS AND WRITINGS

Capitalize references to sacred beings or persons, including God, gods, prophets, apostles, and saints. Some adjectives traditionally linked to such beings and persons are sometimes capitalized as well.

> EXAMPLES   the Lord, the Prince of Peace, Jehovah, Allah, Buddhist, the Blessed Virgin

Capitalize the names of sacred writings and parts of such writings.

> EXAMPLES   Bhagavad Gita, the Bible, the Talmud, Quran, Genesis, Revelation

2.126 SCHOOL SUBJECTS, COURSES, GRADES, AND YEARS

Capitalize a school subject when it is also the name of a language or when it is followed by a number indicating that it is the name of a specific course.

> EXAMPLES   Spanish, driver's education, history, math, Algebra II

Expressions such as *tenth grade, twelfth grade, sophomore, junior,* or expressions such as *freshman year, junior year,* are not capitalized unless they are part of the title of an official program.

> EXAMPLES   freshman chemistry, Junior Year Abroad

2.127 THE PRONOUN I

Capitalize the pronoun *I* wherever it appears, except in quoted material where the pronoun is lowercased in the original.

> EXAMPLE   I fall upon the thorns of life; I bleed!
>
> —Percy Bysshe Shelley

2.128 TITLES OF ARTWORKS

Apply **title capitalization** to titles of works of art. In title capitalization, the following are capitalized: the first word, the last word, all nouns, pronouns, adjectives, verbs, adverbs, and subordinating conjunctions. Articles *(a, an, the)* are written lowercased unless they are the first or last word. Some writers also capitalize any preposition over five letters long.

> EXAMPLES   Chagall's *I and the Village,* Rousseau's *Snake Charmer,* Seurat's *Sunday Afternoon on the Island of La Grande Jatte*

2.129 TITLES OF LITERARY WORKS

Apply title capitalization to titles of literary works.

> EXAMPLES   Burns's "To a Mouse," Carlyle's *Sartor Resartus,* Dickens's *Nicholas Nickleby*

2.130 TITLES OF MUSICAL WORKS

Apply title capitalization to titles of musical works.

> EXAMPLES   "I Want to Hold Your Hand," "Jesu, Joy of Man's Desiring," "Auld Lang Syne"

2.131 TITLES OF PERSONS AND OCCUPATIONS

Capitalize official titles of persons when they immediately precede a person's name or when they are used instead of a name in direct address.

> EXAMPLES   President Nelson Mandela, Princess Di, Lord Acton, Pope John Paul II
> "O Captain! My Captain, our fearful trip is done!"

Do not capitalize references to occupations.

> EXAMPLES the **b**utcher, the **b**aker, the **s**oldier, the **s**ailor, the **t**inker, the **t**ailor, the **c**andlestick **m**aker

2.132 UNITS OF TIME

Do not capitalize units of time such as the words *second, minute, hour, day, year, decade, century,* or the names of the seasons.

> EXAMPLES Twenty **c**enturies later, he arrived at Proxima Centauri.
> They were an odd couple: Lady Chuzzleblub was **a**utumn, and Lord Fitzbrain was **s**pring.

2.133 VEHICLES

Capitalize the names of vehicles only if they are trade names.

> EXAMPLES Ford, Cadillac, Corvette, BMW, **s**ports **c**ar, **b**us, **h**ydrofoil, skateboard, shuttle

▶ Use the Study Guide and Test on Proofreading for Spelling Errors, 5.5.1–5.5.2, in the *Assessment Portfolio.*

SPELLING HANDBOOK

2.134 PROOFREADING FOR SPELLING ERRORS

After you have checked your writing for other problems, read it through with an eye open for spelling errors. Even if you have confidence in your spelling, you may make a mistake in keyboarding your work or writing it out by hand. Of course, the difficulty in detecting errors is that you will tend to see the words as you meant to write them, rather than as they really stand on the page. Professional proofreaders have a helpful technique: they read the text backwards word by word. If you come across a word that causes the slightest doubt, check it in the dictionary.

2.135 USING SPELLING RULES I

Many spelling problems arise from a common operation: forming plurals. Form the plurals of most nouns by simply adding *s.*

> EXAMPLES nerd**s**, intellectual**s**, brain**s**, wizard**s**

Some nouns ending in *o* preceded by a consonant have plurals ending in *es,* as do nouns ending in *s, x, z, ch,* or *sh.*

EXAMPLES   Rotten pota**toes** and toma**toes** thrown at singers serve as ve**toes**.
bos**ses**, box**es**, buzz**es**, batch**es**, bash**es**

Form the plurals of most musical terms ending in *o* by adding *s*.

EXAMPLES   During the concer**tos**, he played two so**los** on two pian**os**.

Form the plurals of nouns ending in *y* preceded by a vowel by adding *s*. (The **vowels** are the letters *a, e, i, o, u*. Sometimes the letter *y* also represents a vowel sound.)

EXAMPLES   On Tuesd**ays** I need the k**eys** to let in the b**oys** who carry carb**oys** of water to the turk**eys**.

Form the plurals of nouns ending in *y* preceded by a consonant by changing the *y* to *i* and adding *es*. (The **consonants** are all the letters that are not vowels.)

EXAMPLES   I have several theor**ies** about why there are fl**ies** in the sk**ies**.

The plurals of some nouns are irregular.

EXAMPLES   While driving their ox**en**, the m**en** shuffled their **feet** over the nest of some **mice**.

Form the plural of a compound noun consisting of a noun and a modifier by making the main noun component plural.

EXAMPLES   The mother**s**-in-law showed the passers**by** the fingerprint**s** and told them to call some attorney**s**-at-law.

2.136 USING SPELLING RULES II

Another operation that causes spelling errors is adding **prefixes** or **suffixes** to a word. A prefix is a letter or a group of letters added to the beginning of a word to change its meaning. When adding a prefix to a word, do not change the word itself.

EXAMPLES   super + highway = **super**highway
re + crystallize = **re**crystallize
un + funded = **un**funded

A **suffix** is a letter or group of letters added to the end of a word to change its meaning. The spelling of most words is not changed when the suffix *–ness* or *–ly* is added.

EXAMPLES   high + ness = high**ness**
high + ly = high**ly**

In the case of many words of more than one syllable ending in *y*, however, change the *y* to *i* before adding *–ly* or *ness*.

> EXAMPLES heavy + ly = heav**ily**
> heavy + ness = heav**iness**

In most cases of words ending in a final silent *e*, drop the *e* when adding a suffix beginning with a vowel, and keep the *e* when adding a suffix beginning with a consonant.

> EXAMPLES live + able = liv**able**
> mouse + er = mous**er**
> hate + ful = hat**eful**
> love + less = lov**eless**

VOCABULARY DEVELOPMENT

▶ Use the Tracking Form: Vocabulary Development, 6.3, in the *Assessment Portfolio*.

▶ Use the Study Guide and Test for Vocabulary Development, 5.6.1–5.6.2, in the *Assessment Portfolio*.

2.137 MAKING A PLAN FOR VOCABULARY DEVELOPMENT

You can increase your **vocabulary**—the words you have at your command that empower you in communicating with others—by taking a few simple steps. When you encounter a new word, whether in reading, in speaking with others, in class, or outside school altogether, write it down in a list in your journal. Check the meaning in a dictionary and jot that down, too. Then review your vocabulary list from time to time. This procedure will vastly increase the chances that you will recall the new words you encounter.

2.138 USING CONTEXT CLUES I

Although a dictionary is the best resource to check when you encounter a new word, sometimes a dictionary is not at hand. Even if a dictionary is available, you may prefer not to break the stream of your thought by consulting it. At times like these, you can often deduce the meaning of a word from context clues.

One type of context clue to look for is **restatement.** The author may tell you the meaning of a word you do not know by using different words to express the same idea in another sentence. Consider the following example.

> EXAMPLE Prisons are designed to encourage **recidivism.** By packing criminals together in close quarters where they can share illicit skills and by fostering an atmosphere of hopelessness, prisons guarantee that **offenders will repeat their criminal activities.**

An alert reader will guess from the restatement (printed here in boldface) that *recidivism* means "a tendency to repeat criminal behavior."

A second and related type of context clue is **apposition**. Look for a word or phrase that is specifically intended to clarify or modify the word you do not know.

EXAMPLE   The underlying and uniting theme of Ovid's poem is the **transmogrification, or change of form**, which occurs in various classical myths.

A third related type of context clue is the use of **examples**.

EXAMPLE   Famous **dystopias** include Hell as described by the poet Dante and the dreary urban environs of the film *Blade Runner*.

The examples suggest that *dystopia* means an "imaginary place where people live a miserable existence." (What do you think *utopia* might mean? If unsure, check a dictionary.)

2.139 USING CONTEXT CLUES II

Another context clue is the use of **comparison**. Imagine a reader does not know the meaning of the word *fedora*. The comparison in the following passage will allow him or her to deduce the meaning from the context.

EXAMPLE   A **fedora** lay on the table in the hall. I had no idea whose it was. Could it be Bromergley's? But when I last saw him, he was wearing a **stovepipe**. Was it Thammgudge's? No, I knew he affected a **beret**. Surely the mysterious fedora belonged to the thief.

Comparison indicates that a fedora is a type of hat.

Contrast is a similar type of context clue.

EXAMPLE   Dirk considered Tooten's presence **supererogatory.** Tooten was not of the caliber of Alphitz, who was vital to the project; or Thomlinnkins, without whom nothing could be done; or Bohblinnder, who was indispensable.

Contrast suggests that *supererogatory* means "unnecessary."

2.140 BASE WORDS AND PREFIXES

Building vocabulary is easier if you know the building blocks of words. Many words are formed by adding **prefixes** to a **base**. For example, imagine you come across the word *counterrevolution* and are unfamiliar with it. You do, however, recognize the **base word**, *revolution*. And you know from words such as *counterclockwise* and *countermeasure* that the prefix *counter–* means "against" or "contrary to." You can then quickly deduce that a counterrevolution is a movement in opposition to a revolution. The following table gives further examples.

PREFIX	MEANING	EXAMPLE	MEANING
pseudo–	"false"	pseudoheroic	falsely heroic
ultra–	"extremely"	ultraorganized	highly organized
semi–	"half, partly"	semiopaque	partly opaque
meta–	"more comprehensive"	metalanguage	language used to talk about another language

2.141 SUFFIXES

Like prefixes, **suffixes** can provide valuable clues to words you do not know. The following table lists a few examples.

SUFFIX	MEANING	EXAMPLE	MEANING
–able	"capable of"	tunable	able to be tuned
–fold	"multiplied by"	fourfold	four times as much
–ful	"amount capable of filling"	planetful	amount capable of filling a planet
–less	"not having"	witless	having no wits
–logy	"science of"	zoology	science of living things

2.142 GREEK AND LATIN ROOTS

Although English is primarily a Germanic language, its vocabulary is in large part based on ancient Greek and Latin. Some Greek and Latin words came to English by way of other languages such as French; others were borrowed directly from Greek and Latin sources by scientists, researchers, and writers, who have always looked to Greek and Latin for components to build new words. The word *telephone,* for instance, comes from the Greek root *tele–*, meaning "far away," and *phone,* meaning "voice."

The following table shows some words with **Greek and Latin roots.** Notice that the words formed from Latin roots are more common, though the words formed from Greek roots are nearly identical in meaning.

FROM GREEK	FROM LATIN	MEANING OF GREEK AND LATIN ROOTS
dys-trophy	mal-nutrition	"bad-nourishment"
hypo-thesis	sup-position	"under-put"
peri-phrasis	circum-locution	"around-say"
sym-pathy	com-passion	"with-feel"
dia-phanous	trans-parent	"through-show"
mono-morphic	uni-form	"one-form"
poly-glottal	multi-lingual	"many-tongued"

2.143 WORD ORIGINS I

Knowing how speakers of English form words can help you recognize new words when you see them. **Names of people and places** are a common source of new words. The following table gives several examples.

WORD	ORIGIN
silhouette	From the name of a French official, Étienne de Silhouette, who had a short career in government in 1759. The word was applied to outline portraits cut from paper, since, like Silhouette, they were of fleeting value.
Rube Goldbergian	From the name of an American cartoonist who drew highly complex gadgets to perform simple tasks. The term now means "accomplishing by complex means what could be accomplished very simply."
Delphian	From Delphi, Greece, the location of an oracle that often gave vague or ambiguous answers. The word now means "ambiguous or obscure in meaning."

Another source of new words are **acronyms,** or words formed from the first letter or letters of each of the major parts of a compound term.

EXAMPLES   radar, from "**ra**dio **d**etecting **a**nd **r**anging"; pixel, from "**pic**ture **el**ement"; smog, from **sm**oke and f**og**

Many words are simply **borrowed** from other languages.

EXAMPLES   **ensemble** (French), **sonata** (Italian), **arroyo** (Spanish), **delicatessen** (German), **sauna** (Finnish), **honcho** (Japanese), **yacht** (Dutch), **luau** (Hawaiian), **tomato** (Nahuatl), **potato** (Taino)

2.144 WORD ORIGINS II

New words are also formed by shortening longer words. The word *phone,* short for *telephone,* is one such **clipped form.**

EXAMPLES   **memo** (from *memorandum,* "something that should be remembered"), **limo** (from *limousine*), **cab** (from *cabriolet,* "light carriage"), **bus** (from *omnibus*), **piano** (from *pianoforte*), **stereo** (from *stereophonic receiver*)

New words are often **coined,** or deliberately created to fill a need.

EXAMPLES   **spin doctor,** from the expression "to put a positive spin on something." The term now means an official whose job it is to interpret news in a way that furthers the ends of the group with which he or she is associated.   *CONTINUED*

> **boom box,** a term applied to a portable stereo because of its shape and its ability to project a high volume of sound

Brand names are often taken into the language, even though their owners may struggle to protect their exclusive status.

EXAMPLES   Kleenex, Band-Aid, Xerox

2.145 WORDS FROM OTHER CURRICULAR AREAS I

As you study other subjects besides English, be alert for colorful words that have extended meanings that might be of use in your writing. Keep a list of these words in your journal. The table below gives a few examples of words of this type, as well as sample sentences showing how these words might be used in the study of English.

SUBJECT	WORDS
Arts and Humanities	In the history of the English novel at the beginning of the 1800s, Sir Walter Scott and Jane Austen dance a strange *pas de deux.* English poetry of modern times is generally more **impressionistic** than the poetry before our century. The reader can well imagine some of Frost's dialogues being delivered in an excited **recitative.**
Mathematics	The discussion at the Mermaid veered off on a **tangent** when Will and Kit walked in. The critic defended *The Wasteland* by saying it had become the highest **common denominator** of poetic thought. Two **factors** operated to make Burns's poetry unique: his peasant upbringing and his staunch independence of thought.

2.146 WORDS FROM OTHER CURRICULAR AREAS II

More examples of words from other curricular areas are shown in the table below.

SUBJECT	WORDS
Social Studies	Though blank verse is one of the distinctive verse forms of English, it is not **aboriginal** to the language. My English friend claims that in literature, the **balance of trade** between the United States and Britain is distinctly in Britain's favor.
Science	For my report, I analyzed Wordsworth's "The World Is Too Much with Us" virtually down to the **molecular level.** *CONTINUED*

	The steadily increasing **velocity** at which Byron lived his life contributed to his expulsion from British society. The early English novels are fascinating, yes, but no one can deny that the genre saw a gradual **evolution** to its highest form in George Eliot's work.
Technical Preparatory	The career of Yeats **dovetails** with the culmination of the Irish movement for political independence. The First World War was like a **venturi** that compressed and accelerated the poetic intensity of writers such as Owen and Sassoon. Much of Blake's work reads like a detailed **blueprint** for a poetic edifice he had not lifetime enough to build.

VARIETIES OF ENGLISH

▶ Use the Study Guide and Test on Varieties of English, 5.7.1–5.7.2, in the *Assessment Portfolio*.

2.147 FORMAL AND INFORMAL ENGLISH

Formal English is the kind of English used in writing papers, some magazine articles and nonfiction books, and some literary works. It is spoken at public ceremonies and in official speeches. **Informal English** is the kind of English used in personal notes and letters, in most newspaper and magazine articles, in some nonfiction and fiction books, and in some short stories and plays. It is spoken in everyday conversation.

How do you decide whether to use formal or informal English? You will naturally tend to use informal English, so all you need to bear in mind are those situations (just described) in which formal English may be expected instead.

How do you distinguish formal from informal English? First, informal English allows grammatical constructions that would not be acceptable in formal English. Many of these constructions are described in the Grammar Handbook (where they are labeled "nonstandard"). Second, informal English is enlivened by **colloquialisms.** These are the words and phrases that speakers of a language use naturally in conversation.

EXAMPLES If you don't **get** your paper finished, you'll be **done for**!
Jill **cut in** ahead of me in line.

Third, informal English is often salted with **slang,** a form of speech made up of coined words, words whose meaning has been changed for no known reason, and words used facetiously.

EXAMPLES We decided to **bag it** [stop what we were doing] and **head home**.
Cough up some bread [pay some money].

Informal grammatical constructions, colloquialisms, and slang sometimes have a place even in writing that is otherwise formal. Literary works, for example, may rely on these devices to make dialogue colorful and realistic.

2.148 REGISTER

To understand the concept of **register**, imagine that all the different kinds of usage in a language—both formal and informal—form one large set. A register is a subset of language usage that is used in a particular relationship between people. In talking to a friend, for example, you speak in a register that is casual, warm, and open. In speaking to a little child, you speak in a register that is nonthreatening and simple to understand. In speaking to an official such as a police officer or a government clerk, you speak in a register that is polite but firm—the same register they should use with you. The words you choose, the grammar you employ to say those words, and you tone of voice will change depending on the register in which you are speaking.

Another way to understand register is to think of the meaning of the musical term. In music, *register* means the range of notes a singer or instrument is capable of producing. Your speaking and writing, however, are not limited to one range of usage. You can use any part of a broad scale of usage from a grunt to a complex and formal declaration of your thought.

One hallmark of people who adapt to society is their ability to choose and use the appropriate register for whatever situation they are in. They do not offend strangers by being too familiar or puzzle their friends by being too formal. The same is true of written language. When you write, use language that is appropriate for the context and for your intended reader. Your personal journal will be in a different register from a term paper, and a story you write for a child will be in a different register from a short story you write for your English class.

2.149 TONE AND VOICE

Tone is the quality of a work that shows the attitude of the person writing or supposedly writing it. In Christopher Marlowe's poem "The Passionate Shepherd to His Love," the tone of the speaker is exactly that, passionate. "Come live with me, and be my love," the shepherd implores the nymph. He does not say, "Move your belongings to my place, and consider yourself my spouse," because that tone would be materialistic and practical rather than passionate. On the other hand, Sir Walter Ralegh's poem "The Nymph's Reply to the Shepherd" is written in a tone of detachment and reproof. "A honey tongue, a heart of gall,/ Is fancy's spring but sorrow's fall," says the nymph, coolly implying that the shepherd's promises are empty or deceitful. She does not reply, "How dare you tempt me to run off with you, you wretched liar!" because that tone would be as impassioned as the shepherd's.

In any writing you do, you can adopt a tone appropriate for the message you wish to convey. Your **diction**, or choice of words, determines much of your tone. For instance, when writing a letter to a government official protesting a new regulation, do you want to say, "Your new regulation is utterly unacceptable to the honest citizens of this state," or "The new regulation is unpopular among many of your constituents"? The tone you convey will depend upon your choice.

Voice is the quality of a work that tells you that one person in particular wrote it—not several, and not just anyone. Voice is one feature that makes a work unique. The voice of a work can be difficult to define; it may have to do with the way a writer views people, events, objects, ideas, the passage of time, even life itself. If this treatment of the subject is consistent throughout, despite variations in tone, register, point of view, and so forth, then the writer has **established a voice**, a sense of individuality, in the work.

Voice is difficult to illustrate in a small space. Consider, however, the following passages:

> What in me is dark
> Illumine, what is low raise and support;
> That to the height of this great argument
> I may assert eternal Providence,
> And justify the ways of God to men.
> —Milton, *Paradise Lost*, Book 1, lines 22–25
>
> But at my back I always hear
> Time's wingèd chariot hurrying near;
> And yonder all before us lie
> Deserts of vast eternity.
> —Marvell, "To His Coy Mistress"

Milton's voice, linked to register, is determined by his choice of Latinate words ("illumine," "Providence"); his long sentence, drawn out with subordinate clauses from line to line; and also his belief about what matters: the justification of the ways of his God. Eternity, suggests Milton, is a stage on which Providence reveals itself. Marvell's voice (in this poem, at least) is determined by his shorter units of thought, his simpler vocabulary, and his belief that what matters is what happens now. Eternity, he claims, is a desert.

In your own writing, you should strive to develop your own voice, not to imitate the voices of others. What that voice is, and how it compares to others, are matters no one can decide for you. "To thine own self be true," says Polonius in Shakespeare's *Hamlet*, "and thou canst not then be false to any man." He might well have been speaking about literary voice. Be true to your own voice, and your experience will speak directly to the experience of others.

2.150 DIALECTS OF ENGLISH

Dialects are varieties of a language. Dialects fall into one of two main classes: dialects based on **social differences** (for example, upper class, middle class, and lower class) and dialects based on **regional differences** (in the United States the major regional dialects are northern, southern, midland, and western).

All dialects are equally capable of expressing thought, which is what language is for. Therefore, no dialect is *better* than any other dialect. Some dialects are accepted by social classes that hold power; their dialect is generally considered the **standard** form of a language, and other dialects are considered **nonstandard**. But *standard* does not mean "correct" or "better than others." Knowledge of the standard dialect is useful because it is widely understood, and because in many situations, speaking or writing in the standard dialect will ensure that people focus on *what* you say rather than *how* you say it. They will understand your meaning, without being distracted by your use of an unfamiliar dialect.

Knowledge of nonstandard dialects is also useful to writers. Consider Thomas Hardy's poem "The Man He Killed," which is made more lively and authentic through Hardy's use of dialect words such as *nipperkin,* meaning a half-pint container, and the form *'list,* for the standard *enlist.*

2.151 Jargon and Gobbledygook

Jargon is the specialized vocabulary used by members of a profession. It tends to be incomprehensible to people outside the profession. A plumber may speak of a "hubless fitting" or a "street elbow" (kinds of pipe). A computer programmer may talk of "ram cache" (part of computer memory) or a "shell" (a type of operating software for computers).

Jargon is useful to writers who want to lend authenticity to their description of situations in which jargon would naturally be used. For instance, a novel about fighter pilots on an aircraft carrier would probably be full of aviation jargon. A scriptwriter developing a science fiction film would be sure to work in futuristic jargon about warps in space, energy shields, and tractor beams.

Gobbledygook is unclear, wordy jargon used by bureaucrats or government officials. For instance, instead of saying, "raise taxes," a bureaucrat might say "proactively maximize voluntary revenue income." In requesting six billion dollars for a kind of paper handkerchief for the armed services, a military planner might call the product a "disposable fiber wipeage utensil."

The most famous literary examples of gobbledygook occur in the novel *Nineteen Eighty-four,* by the English writer George Orwell. Gobbledygook is there raised to a standard of its own; called *doublespeak,* it is the officially approved form of communication between the government and the people.

2.152 Clichés and Euphemisms

A **cliché** is an expression that has been used so often it has become colorless and uninteresting.

EXAMPLES	packed in like sardines
	happy as a hog in deep mud
	dog tired
	as the crow flies

The use of clichés instantaneously makes writing dull.

A **euphemism** (from the Greek verb meaning "to speak with good words") is an inoffensive term that substitutes for one considered offensive.

EXAMPLES	waste management (for "garbage removal")
	dearly departed (for "dead")

2.153 CONNOTATION AND DENOTATION

A **denotation** of a word is its dictionary definition. A **connotation** of a word is all the associations that it has in addition to its literal meaning. For example, the denotations of *mud* and *muck* are identical; but *muck* carries a connotation of moral filthiness that makes it a much stronger word than *mud*. Contrast the denotations and connotations of the following examples.

EXAMPLES   dog, hound, cur, mutt, mongrel, canine
nose, beak, honker, proboscis, schnozzle
ma, mom, mother, mater

Writers should be aware of the connotations as well as the denotations of the words they use. You would be remiss to say, "The honcho jabbered for eons about his pet proposition," when what you meant was, "The president spoke for a long time about the proposal he favored."

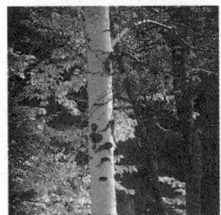

►Use the Pretest and Post-test for Speaking and Listening Terminology and Techniques, 3.3.1–3.3.2, in the *Assessment Portfolio.*

►Use the Communication Evaluation Forms, 7.11-7.14, in the *Assessment Portfolio.*

►Use the Study Guide and Test on Verbal and Nonverbal Communication, 5.8.1–5.8.2, in the *Assessment Portfolio.*

► ► ► **A C T I V I T Y 3.1**

1. Some symbol systems are those used in spoken languages (English, Arabic, Tagalog, Tamil, and so on); American Sign Language; Braille; alphabets (Roman, Hebraic, Cyrillic, and so on); mathematics (arithmetic, algebra, Boolean algebra, geometry, calculus, formal logic, and others); library cataloging systems; dashboard indicators in automobiles; maps, including weather maps; semaphore (flag code); signals used by players, coaches, and officials in sporting events (football, baseball, and so on); hieroglyphics; digital systems such as those used by radio and television transmitters; and computer languages (used by humans to control computers) and computer codes (used by computers to communicate internally and to communicate with each other).

2. *sender:* space probe; *message:* "It looks like this . . ."; *channel:* radio waves; *recipient:* NASA scientists via radio receiver and computer; *feedback:* "Move a little to the left."

(cont.)

ESSENTIAL SKILLS:
Speaking and Listening

3.1 A COMMUNICATION MODEL

When you ask a friend if you can borrow a pencil, you are operating an extremely complex system that no computer can yet operate. Here's the way the system works: A **sender encodes** a **message** using **symbols**. This message is transmitted along some **channel** to a **recipient** who **decodes** it and provides **feedback.** The following chart describes this communication model:

COMMUNICATION MODEL	
Sender	You
Message	"May I borrow a pencil from you?"
Symbols Used	Words in the English language
Channel	Speech
Recipient	Your friend
Feedback	"Sure, I have an extra one."

For complete communication, encoding must be correct, the channel must be clear, and decoding must be correct. So, for example, if a loud stereo were in the room and your friend didn't hear you, the communication would not be complete. You would need to modify the system by adding a tap on your friend's shoulder or perhaps a repetition of the message in a slightly louder voice.

► ► ► **A C T I V I T Y 3.1**

Answer the following questions:

1. What are some different symbol systems used to encode messages? Think of both nonverbal and verbal means of communication. (Hint: Street signs are one common nonverbal means for encoding messages.)

2. A space probe on Mars takes a picture of a crater on Mars and transmits this picture by radio to NASA scientists on Earth. The scientists look at the picture and send a command back to the probe telling it to move a bit to the left and take another picture. Describe the sender, the message, the channel, the recipient, and the feedback in this communication situation.

CONTINUED

3. Using terminology from the preceding communication model, describe what interferes with communication in each of the following examples:

   a. An American tourist in Rome stops a young man on the street to ask directions. The American asks, "Can you tell me how to get to the Forum?" The Italian answers, "Non parlo inglese."

   b. A ship has run into an iceberg and is sinking. Another ship is passing in the distance. A crew member on the first ship attempts to signal the second ship using flags. The people on the second ship can't see the flags because too much fog is in the air.

   c. A student with a stomachache enters class, wearing a grimace. The student's teacher asks, "Would you like to lead the discussion today, Gloria?" Gloria answers, "Sure." However, the teacher looks at the grimace on Gloria's face and concludes that Gloria doesn't really want to lead the discussion. The teacher asks another student to lead the discussion but fails to tell Gloria why he has made this decision.

4. Why is feedback important to good communication? What kind of feedback does an audience give to an actor or to a speaker? How can people in conversation ensure that they have understood one another correctly? How do newspapers receive feedback from their readers?

3.2 ELEMENTS OF VERBAL COMMUNICATION

Communication can be verbal or nonverbal. **Verbal communication** is done by means of words and other sounds uttered by speakers. **Nonverbal communication** is done by other means. The following chart describes the most important elements of verbal communication:

ELEMENTS OF VERBAL COMMUNICATION		
ELEMENT	**DESCRIPTION**	**GUIDELINES FOR SPEAKERS**
Volume	The loudness or softness of the voice	Speak loudly enough to be heard, but not so loudly as to make your audience uncomfortable.
Pitch, or Intonation	The highness or lowness of the voice	Vary your pitch to give your expressions a musical quality and to communicate meaning (for example, a rising pitch at the end of a sentence indicates a question). Avoid using a single pitch, or **monotone.**
Enunciation	The clearness with which syllables are spoken	Slightly exaggerate the clearness of your syllables to ensure that you are understood. Do not drop or clip the ends of words or sentences.

CONTINUED

▶ ▶ ▶ **A C T I V I T Y 3.1** (CONT.)

3. a. Communication fails because the recipient and the sender understand different symbol systems.

   b. Communication fails because the channel (vision) is blocked.

   c. Communication fails because the recipient does not give feedback. The sender cannot tell whether the original message has been correctly interpreted.

4. Feedback enables the sender to tell whether the original message has been correctly interpreted. Feedback thus enables one to check whether communication has been effective and helps future communication. Audiences give feedback in the form of applause, silence, laughter, whispers, gasps, sighs, walking out, ovations, cheers, boos, and other ways. People in conversation can ensure that they have understood one another by repeating the message received and by confirming or amending this feedback. Newspapers receive feedback in the form of letters, telephone calls, and increased or decreased sales and subscriptions.

ELEMENTS OF VERBAL COMMUNICATION

ELEMENT	DESCRIPTION	GUIDELINES FOR SPEAKERS
Pace	The speed with which something is said	Do not speak too slowly or too quickly.
Stress	The emphasis given to syllables, words, or phrases	Use stress to emphasize important ideas. Vary stress along with pitch to avoid monotony.
Tone	The emotional quality of the speech	Suit the tone to the message. Vary the tone appropriately throughout the communication.

In general, when speaking to an audience, follow these guidelines:

USING ELEMENTS OF VERBAL COMMUNICATION IN PUBLIC SPEAKING

1. Make sure that you can be heard and understood by using an appropriate volume and pace.
2. Suit your volume, pitch, pace, stress, and tone to your message.
3. Vary all the verbal elements of your speech to make the presentation more lively, colorful, and interesting.
4. Slightly heighten or exaggerate each of the verbal elements of your speech over the level that you would use in ordinary conversation.

►►► ACTIVITY 3.2

Choose a poem from this textbook to read aloud to your classmates. Make a copy of the poem and mark it to show the following:

1. places where you will increase or decrease your volume;
2. places where you will increase or decrease your pace;
3. words or phrases that you should emphasize by means of volume, pitch, or stress;
4. words or phrases that present enunciation problems for you and that therefore require special attention or practice; and
5. changes in tone or emotion throughout the piece.

Practice reading the selection aloud following the notes that you have made.

3.3 ELEMENTS OF NONVERBAL COMMUNICATION

Face-to-face communication has one major advantage over writing or speaking on the telephone: it enables the communicator to send nonverbal as well as verbal messages. The following chart lists the major elements of nonverbal communication and provides guidelines for using them:

►►► ACTIVITY 3.2

• Ask students why they made some of the decisions they did. Ask them what meaning the elements of verbal communication (slow or fast pace, high or low stress, and tone) normally have. In a large group discussion, ask students how they show particular emotions such as pain, happiness, or worry. Point out that different cultures have different standard ways of showing emotions. Encourage students to tell how their ways of showing emotions differ from or are similar to those of other students in the class.

• Be aware of students who have enunciation problems of which they do not seem to be aware. This might be a good time to encourage them to work on the problem or to refer them to a speech specialist.

ELEMENTS OF NONVERBAL COMMUNICATION

ELEMENT	DESCRIPTION	GUIDELINES FOR SPEAKERS
Eye contact	Looking your audience in the eye	Maintain eye contact to keep your audience engaged in what you are saying.
Facial expressions	Displays of emotion using the face (e.g., smiles, scowls, frowns, etc.)	Match your facial expressions to your message.
Body language	Positions of the body that have meaning to an audience	Match your body language to your message. Maintain good posture.
Gestures	Meaningful motions of the hands and arms	Use gestures sparingly to emphasize points. Match gestures to your message.
Proximity	Distance from the audience	Maintain a comfortable distance, not too close for comfort, but not so far away as to hamper communication.

► ► ► **ACTIVITY 3.3**

Return to the activity that you did for Section 3.2. Mark the poem that you chose to recite to show appropriate facial expressions, gestures, and body language.

3.4 ACTIVE LISTENING

Believe it or not, listening is not a spectator sport. For complete communication to occur, the listener has to participate fully and actively in the process. Here are some ways you can listen actively:

- **Mental Activity.** Listen for main ideas and supporting details. Summarize, predict, question, and interpret as you listen.

- **Note-taking.** If you are listening to a lecture or a long monologue, you may want to take notes in outline form.

- **Questioning and Other Feedback.** As you listen, maintain eye contact. Provide feedback to the speaker by means of gestures, facial expressions, body language, and proximity. In conversation, encourage the speaker and show that you have understood him or her by making statements like "yes," "uh-huh," and "I see." If you think that you may have misunderstood something or if the communication is highly emotional, pause and rephrase what the speaker has said as a means of checking your own understanding. When the speaker has finished a thought and there is a pause in the flow of speech, you can ask questions to clarify or expand upon what the speaker has said.

► ► ► **ACTIVITY 3.3**

Hold a group brainstorming session to help students devise their own notation system for indicating often-used facial expressions, gestures, and body language.

- If students need ideas, hold a group brainstorming session to generate examples of complex processes.
- As an alternative to pairs, you could group students in threes. Assign one student to be the speaker, a second to be the listener, and the third to observe the listener and to make notes on the listener's active listening techniques. They should complete the exercise three times, with each person filling each role. Preliminary to this exercise, you could have them read or review the Language Arts Survey, 4.6, "Observing," and have them prepare observation charts.

► Use the Evaluation Form: Interpersonal Communication, 5.8.3, in the *Assessment Portfolio*.

► ► ► A C T I V I T Y 3.5

At the end of each round, have the speaker name the active listening techniques used by the listener. If the listener used a technique that the speaker did not report, the two can discuss it. After the exercise, hold a group discussion. Ask students to name the communication techniques studied (making eye contact, keeping body stance relaxed and open, giving feedback, mirroring, thinking before speaking, taking a deep breath to control emotions, asking to take a break and continue later). Ask students whether they used all of the techniques. Then ask students to name techniques that they found especially effective and to ask questions about techniques with which they had difficulty.

► ► ► A C T I V I T Y 3.4

Role play a listening session with one of your classmates. First, each of you should make an outline of something relatively complex you would like to explain. Your subject could be something technical, such as the life cycle of a paramecium, or it could be something personal, such as your mixed feelings about your first trip away from home by yourself. Take turns listening to one another, using the techniques described on the previous page.

3.5 INTERPERSONAL COMMUNICATION

Interpersonal communication is communication between individuals. This kind of communication serves a number of important functions:

- Transmission of information
- Establishment of relationships
- Maintenance of relationships
- Personal validation
- Bonding

Here are some ways to use verbal and nonverbal techniques to improve your interpersonal communication:

- Make eye contact and keep your body stance relaxed and open.
- Give feedback by asking questions and by mirroring back what was said.

SPEAKER   I have tons of work to do for that test on Monday.
LISTENER   So, you're anxious about the test. What can you do to get ready for it?

- Think before you speak.
- If you find yourself feeling negative emotions, pause, take a deep breath, and get your emotions under control before continuing the communication. If you cannot get your emotions under control, ask to continue the communication at a later time.

► ► ► A C T I V I T Y 3.5

Role play a conversation with someone about a personal problem. As you speak or listen, apply the techniques of interpersonal communication described in this lesson. Reverse roles after completing one session of interpersonal communication. Note: For this exercise, the problem should be an imaginary one.

3.6 Discussion

Discussion is a means for sharing ideas and information among several people at once. Discussions vary from highly informal chats among friends to highly formal, rule-governed interactions in parliamentary bodies. The following chart describes the roles of group members and important elements of the process followed in a semiformal discussion:

▶ Use the Evaluation Form: Discussion, 5.8.4, in the *Assessment Portfolio.*

DISCUSSION	
Roles	• **Group leader or chairperson.** Keeps the discussion on track when people begin to digress or veer away from the subject, asks questions when the discussion starts to flag, makes sure everyone participates • **Secretary.** Takes notes or records what is said and later prepares a description (**minutes**) of the discussion • **Participants.** Take part in the discussion, listen attentively to others, provide feedback
Process	• **Discussion question.** States the goal or main idea of the discussion and is usually put forward by the group leader. In a formal discussion, the discussion question is called a **proposition**. • **Agenda.** A step-by-step plan for the discussion, usually written and distributed at the beginning of the discussion by the group leader or secretary

▶ ▶ ▶ **ACTIVITY 3.6**

Imagine that you are president of your school's drama club and that the club is going to present a production of George Bernard Shaw's *Pygmalion.* Write an agenda for a meeting of the club in which you will do planning for the production.

3.7 Public Speaking

If you are afraid of speaking in public, you are not alone. Polls consistently show that most people feel extremely anxious when called upon to speak in public. However, by preparing carefully, you can increase your level of comfort about speaking. You may even be able to harness your anxiety and turn it into positive energy that will move your audience.

Types of Speeches. There are three main types of speech. An **impromptu speech** is one given without any preparation. In other words, it is delivered "off the cuff." A **memorized speech** is one that is written out entirely beforehand. The written speech is then committed to memory and recited to the audience. Impromptu speeches suffer from not being prepared in advance. Memorized speeches, on the other hand, tend to sound over-prepared and stilted. That's why most professional speakers prefer the **extemporaneous speech,** in which the speaker delivers a speech based on note cards that have been carefully prepared.

▶ ▶ ▶ **ACTIVITY 3.6**
Responses will vary. Possible responses are given.

AGENDA
I. Introduction
  A. Request additions to agenda
  B. Explain current status of project
    1. Budget
    2. Other?
II. Assign Tasks
  A. Director
  B. Stage manager
  C. Promotions manager
  D. Financial manager
  E. Props manager
  F. Costume manager
  G. Other?
III. Set up casting schedule
IV. Set up performance schedule
V. Plan fund raiser
VI. Adjourn

▶ Use the Evaluation Form: Public Speaking, 5.8.5, in the *Assessment Portfolio.*

ESSENTIAL SKILLS: SPEAKING AND LISTENING

The extemporaneous speech combines the spontaneity of the impromptu speech with the preparedness of the memorized speech.

Writing a Speech. When writing a speech, just as when writing a paper, you should make sure that it has a beginning, a middle, and an end. The **beginning**, or **introduction**, should capture the attention of the audience and present your main topic or idea. The **middle**, or **body**, should develop the main idea. The **end**, or **conclusion**, should be memorable and should give the audience a satisfying sense of an ending. For more information on writing introductions and conclusions, see the Language Arts Survey, 1.42, "Organizing a Composition."

Preparing an Extemporaneous Speech. The following chart describes steps to take when preparing an extemporaneous speech:

STEPS IN PREPARING AN EXTEMPORANEOUS SPEECH
1. Do prewriting.
2. Do research.
3. Prepare note cards.
4. Make a plan for using verbal and nonverbal elements of communication in your speech.
5. Rehearse with your note cards, using a tape recorder, a video recorder, a mirror, or a practice audience.
6. Deliver your speech, attending to both verbal and nonverbal elements of the delivery.

► ► ► **A C T I V I T Y 3.7**

Choose an occasion at which you might be asked to present a speech. Prepare an extemporaneous speech for that occasion, completing steps 1 through 5 in the list above.

3.8 ORAL INTERPRETATION

Oral interpretation is the process of presenting a dramatic reading of a literary work or group of works. The presentation should be sufficiently dramatic to convey to the audience a sense of the particular qualities of the work. The art of oral interpretation is ancient. In fact, people were presenting stories, poems, songs, and other works orally long before these works were written down. Here are the steps you need to follow to prepare an oral interpretation:

1. **Choose a cutting.** The cutting may be a single piece, a selection from a single piece, or several short, related pieces on a single topic or theme. Most commonly, students choose several short pieces or excerpts on a single theme.

► ► ► **A C T I V I T Y 3.7**

• Invite students to deliver their speeches to the class.

• Plan to have students deliver extemporaneous speeches on various noteworthy occasions throughout the school year. The last day before a vacation or major holiday; the first day back from a vacation; the day of an important school event such as a pep rally or homecoming, an awards banquet, or a visit from a dignitary; and anniversaries of major world events such as V-E Day, D-day, and Neil Armstrong's walk on the moon, for example, might be appropriate occasions for students to practice giving speeches. Non-holidays such as Groundhog Day or the first day of spring might be occasions for humorous or light-hearted speeches. Ask them to choose from a list of days that you give them, allow them to select occasions on their own, or assign occasions arbitrarily.

► Use the Evaluation Form: Oral Interpretation, 5.8.6, in the *Assessment Portfolio*.

2. **Write the introduction and any necessary transitions.** The introduction should mention the name of the piece, the author, and, if appropriate, the translator. It should also present the overall topic or theme of the interpretation. Transitions should introduce and connect the parts of the interpretation.

3. **Rehearse, using appropriate variations in volume, pitch, pace, stress, tone, gestures, facial expressions, and body language.** However, avoid movement—that's for drama. If there are different voices (a narrative voice and a character's voice, for example), distinguish them. Try to make your verbal and nonverbal expression mirror what the piece is saying. Practice in front of an audience, a mirror, a video camera, or a tape recorder.

► ► ► **ACTIVITY 3.8**

Choose three short pieces or selections from pieces in this text. All should deal with a single topic or theme (e.g., poems about unrequited love). Copy your pieces onto notebook paper. Write an introduction to your interpretation and transitions between the parts of it. In the introduction, grab your listeners' attention and present your topic or theme. In the transitions, tell the title and author of each piece and make a brief statement connecting the piece to your overall topic or theme. Combine your introduction, your cuttings, and your transitions to make a script. Mark your script to show variations in volume, pitch, pace, stress, tone, gestures, facial expressions, and body language. Memorize your script and rehearse it. Then present it to your classmates.

► ► ► **ACTIVITY 3.8**

The project described is large and complex. Allow students ample time for each step. Encourage them to write out a schedule for completing each task of the project, or prepare a reasonable schedule yourself and distribute it. At various points in the project, students should be required to submit their work-in-progress for a quick review or to submit a brief statement of their progress and their plans for meeting their deadlines. Explain that all of these methods of monitoring are common in the workplace, where managers have the responsibility of ensuring that every individual is making enough progress that the overall project will be completed on time.

▶Use the Pretest and Post-test for Study and Research Skills, 3.4.1–3.4.2, in the *Assessment Portfolio.*

▶Use the Study Guide and Test on Thinking Skills, 5.9.1–5.9.2, in the *Assessment Portfolio.*

ESSENTIAL SKILLS:
Study and Research

THINKING SKILLS

All human beings have a great number of thinking skills and perform astonishing feats of thinking every day, but often people get set in thinking habits and patterns that aren't very efficient. Learning a few simple thinking strategies can improve dramatically anyone's ability to learn, to solve problems, and to make decisions.

4.1 STRATEGIES FOR PROBLEM SOLVING I

All problem solving involves four steps.

Within this **general problem-solving framework,** there are many particular strategies you can use. A guaranteed strategy for solving a problem is called an **algorithm.** A less than sure-fire strategy is called a **heuristic** or, if the strategy is very simple and straightforward, a **rule**

of thumb. For any complex problem you will almost certainly need to use more than one strategy. Try to be creative and flexible: using even a good strategy does not guarantee that you will solve a given problem.

Trial and error. This is the simplest of all problem-solving strategies: make a guess and see if it works. Trial and error is useful when only a few possible solutions seem likely. It can also be useful when there are a great many possibilities and you need to accustom yourself to the problem in order to find a more systematic strategy. As a rule, though, you should not spend very much time using the trial-and-error method.

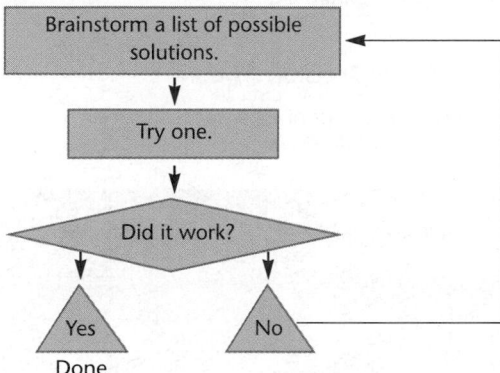

Represent the situation. When you face a problem that is complex or confusing, it can be especially useful to make a visual or physical **representation** of the problem. You might draw a diagram or a picture, or you might construct a model. This technique often helps you to see more clearly important relationships among the parts of the problem.

4.2 STRATEGIES FOR PROBLEM SOLVING II

Means-ends analysis. An **end** is a goal, and **means** are the tools and methods used to achieve the goal. To use this strategy, compare what you know about the current situation and about the situation that will exist when the goal has been reached. Then think of ways to reduce the differences between the two situations.

Divide and conquer. Sometimes it is best to divide the problem into parts and then solve each of the parts separately, one step at a time. If a part is still too difficult to solve immediately, you can apply the same strategy to it. You can work on the parts in a logical sequence.

> PROBLEM   You are writing a story. You have already decided that at the beginning of the story, the main character is an unemployed farm worker in Eastern Europe, and that at the end of the story, he has become a famous movie actor living in Hollywood. How can you get the character to make this change?
>
> *CONTINUED*

ESSENTIAL SKILLS: STUDY AND RESEARCH   **1 1 7 7**

ESSENTIAL SKILLS: STUDY AND RESEARCH

SOLUTION STRATEGY	Break the goal into parts: by the end of the story, the main character must (1) move to Hollywood; (2) become a movie actor; and (3) become famous. Then solve each part separately: (1) Why does he move to Hollywood? (2a) How does he become an actor? (2b) How does he get a role in a movie? (3) How does he become famous?

Work backward. Describe in detail the situation that would exist after you solved the problem. Then think about what would have to happen for that situation to come about. Continue working backward until you get to a situation that you know how to bring about.

4.3 STRATEGIES FOR DECISION MAKING

Pros and cons. Make a list of your options. For each option, list the reasons for choosing it (the **pros**) and the drawbacks of choosing it (the **cons**). Then compare the lists.

PROS AND CONS: POSSIBLE VACATION PLANS			
	Visit Cousins in Colorado	**Visit Cousins in Chicago**	**Washington, D.C.**
Pros	favorite cousins walk in woods mountain climbing skiing	movies comedy shows great museums restaurants	visit president (?) White House, Capitol monuments Smithsonian Museum
Cons	long bus ride expensive travel might be snow haven't been invited	nobody my age there long bus ride expensive travel expensive city	nearby no friends there expensive hotels

Criteria analysis. Make a chart. Down the left side of your chart, list the results you want to achieve. Across the top, list your options. Then, assign points from 1 to 5 to each option, according to how well it will achieve the results you have listed. Add up the points and choose the option with the highest total.

CRITERIA ANALYSIS: ORGANIZATION SYSTEMS			
	Desktop Filing Box	**File Cabinet**	**Boxes under Bed**
1. Convenience	5	4	2
2. Small size	5	1	5
3. Low cost	3	1	5
4. No spare papers, cards, letters	3	3	5
	$\frac{2}{18}$	$\frac{4}{13}$	$\frac{3}{20}$

1178   *LANGUAGE ARTS SURVEY*

4.4 MEMORIZING

Remembering involves two steps. First, you have to save the information in your mind, and then you have to find it when you need it. If you had a contract or a letter you wanted to save, you probably wouldn't just toss it into a large filing cabinet with thousands of other pieces of paper: you'd never be able to find it when you needed it. If you spend a little time thinking about why you are saving it, you can save it in a way that makes it easy to find later. For instance, if the letter was from your grandmother, you might put it in a folder labeled "Letters: Personal," or "Letters from Grandma," or "Grandma: Letters," and then file the folder in alphabetical order. Your mind works in somewhat the same way. The better you understand some idea or piece of information, the easier you can find and then retrieve it from your mental filing system.

Mnemonics. A **mnemonic** is an association that aids memorizing. To use a mnemonic you put together information that you need to remember with information that you can remember easily or that you already know well. The easy-to-remember information helps you remember the information that you pair it with. For instance, you probably learned the alphabet by associating it with an easy-to-remember melody. Mnemonics can use either images or words.

MNEMONICS			
Name of Strategy	**Strategy**	**Information to be Learned**	**Information Easy to Remember**
Embellished Letter	Form an acronym using the first letters of the information to be remembered.	Items in a series, e.g. the colors of the spectrum (red, orange, yellow, green, blue, indigo, violet)	Roy G. Biv
Method of Loci	Imagine a place you knew well (your home, etc.). Form an image of each object to be remembered in a particular spot or room in that place.	Items in a series, e.g., the first ten presidents (Washington, Adams, Jefferson, Adams, Madison, Monroe, Jackson, Van Buren, Harrison, Tyler)	Washington is pitcher, Adams is catcher, Jefferson at first base, etc.
Key Word	Form an image of the items doing something to or with each other.	Associations, e.g., a server at a restaurant must remember that the man in the blue shirt ordered chicken with baked potato.	Bizarre images, e.g., a man is terrified (chicken) of a potato.

Repetition. Merely repeating information over and over is generally a poor way to remember it. If you want to remember something, you should try to become familiar with it and to know it in a variety of ways. However, repetition is an important *part* of memorizing. The more you use or work with some idea or information, the more likely you are to remember how to use it. For instance, you probably know your close friend's phone number without thinking about it, but you probably cannot recall the phone number of a movie theater that you have called only once.

4.5 REMEMBERING AND VISUALIZING

Think of a friend with whom you like to spend time. Can you picture him or her in your mind? Take a moment and try. . . .

Often you will want to visualize a person, scene, or object so you can write about it and describe it accurately and vividly. When trying to remember and visualize, you may find it helpful to use reasoning to remind yourself of details. For instance, when you tried to visualize your friend, you may have thought about articles of clothing that he or she typically wears, places where the two of you have gone together, activities that the two of you have done together, or characteristic facial or verbal expressions that he or she uses.

4.6 OBSERVING

Think of how different would be the observations of Stonehenge made by a geologist, an astronomer, a sculptor, a watercolorist, a graphic designer, a structural engineer, a short story writer, a high school English teacher, etc. In any situation there is an infinite amount of information. It is therefore important that, before you make your observations, you decide what you will look for. If you have a hypothesis you are testing, decide what evidence might be relevant to proving or disproving it. If you want some material on which to base a character sketch, decide beforehand what type or types of character or characters you are interested in. If you are looking for evidence, however, you need to avoid making prejudgments. Be careful that you do not bias your observations by having strong expectations of what you will see.

Usually you will find it helpful to prepare a chart on which to record your observations.

OBSERVATIONS OF PEOPLE WAITING AT BUS STOP

Subject	Appearance, Dress	Attitude Emotions	Expressions	Gestures	Interactions with Others
1					
2					
3					

4.7 CLASSIFYING

To **classify** is to put into classes or categories. Items belong in the same category because they share one or more characteristics. William Wordsworth's poem "I Wandered Lonely as a Cloud" and Percy Shelley's poem "Ode to the West Wind" are classified as Romantic poetry because they have features that characterize Romantic poetry (e.g., importance of the self and individual experience, a sense of nature and the transcendental).

You should have precise definitions of your categories or concepts before you use them for classifying. When you classify, be sure to base your decisions on the particular characteristics that define the class. If you were classifying essays as either persuasive or expository, for example, you would determine for each essay whether its purpose was to explain or to convince, and you would ignore all other features, such as tone or style.

You may find that some of the things you are classifying fit in more than one of your categories. When this occurs, it may be because the categories are imprecisely defined, or because the categories are not parallel. Unit 1 of this book, *Literature and the Language Arts,* presents models of several genres of literature, including poetry, drama, and nonfiction; but sometimes poetry is drama, as, for instance, Shakespeare's *The Tempest;* and sometimes drama is nonfiction, as, for instance, Shakespeare's *Richard II.* The categories poetry, drama, and nonfiction are not parallel, for they fail to refer to parallel features of literary works. Writing is classed as poetry because of its content and language—its special attention to sound and images. Writing is classed as drama because of its form—it includes stage directions and dialogue, for instance. As *The Tempest* shows, writing can have poetic content and language yet be dramatic in form.

The key step in classifying is choosing appropriate categories. Your purposes and needs will partly determine what categories are suitable. For example, if you wanted to compare how Shakespeare's *Macbeth* and Austen's *Pride and Prejudice* treat the theme of pride, you might classify the two works according to literary form—*Macbeth* as drama, *Pride and Prejudice* as novel—and then explain how the works' different treatments of this theme reflect the differences between plays and novels. If you instead wanted to compare how the two works use irony, you might classify the points of your discussion in terms of narrative elements such as characterization, dialogue, plot, and language. As you can see, a classification scheme can provide a natural way of organizing a piece of informative or persuasive writing (see 1.34, "Organizing Ideas").

4.8 COMPARING AND CONTRASTING

To **compare** A **to** B is to describe the similarities between A and B. (To compare A **with** B is to examine A and B in order to describe their similarities and differences.) To **contrast** A **with** B is to describe the differences between A and B. When you compare people or things, you place them in the same category: for instance, King Arthur and Beowulf are comparable characters—they are similar—insofar as they are both legendary heroes. When you contrast people or things, you place them in separate and incompatible categories: for instance, King Arthur and Beowulf are contrasting characters—they are different—in that Arthur is a tragic hero and Beowulf is a warrior hero.

When comparing and contrasting, most often you will want to contrast items that are similar in important respects. In the above example, Arthur and Beowulf are both heroes, but they are different types of heroes. They share a feature that places them in the category "hero," but they share that feature differently and belong in different **subcategories.**

Whenever you compare people or objects, examine carefully the ways in which they exhibit shared features; the ways in which they exhibit these features are likely to differ, and these differences are probably interesting.

The method of comparing and contrasting is a tool that can help you to explain, to define, or to evaluate. In your literature class, you can expect to be asked to compare and contrast periods, authors, works, techniques and devices, or aspects of works. Remember to discuss *both* points of similarity *and* points of difference. (See 1.18, "Sensory Detail Charts"; for tips on organizing a comparison-and-contrast essay, see 1.34, "Organizing Ideas.")

4.9 ESTIMATING AND QUANTIFYING

To support your points in an argument or in a persuasive essay, you need to provide facts, and often the facts you need are numbers or **quantities** (see 1.40, "Elaboration: Types of Supporting Details"). If you claim, for instance, that too many persons are without health insurance, you ought to **quantify** your claim by stating **how many.** The numbers you need may be available in reference works (see 4.23, "Using Reference Works"). If not, a combination of research, general knowledge, and common-sense reasoning can help you **estimate,** or find the approximate quantity. Sometimes you will have only enough knowledge to estimate a **range** within which the actual number probably falls.

PROBLEM	Estimate the number of kindergartners in the United States.
ANSWER	Life expectancy in the United States is approximately 75 years, so an estimate of the number of persons of any given age would be 1/75 of the population. The population of the United States is approximately 320 million. 320 million divided by 75 equals about 4.25 million.
PROBLEM	Estimate the number of kindergarten teachers in the United States.
ANSWER	Suppose there are about 4.25 million kindergartners. A kindergarten class ranges in size from about 12 to 25, and there's one teacher for each class. If we divide the number of students by the number of students per teacher, the result is the number of teachers. Dividing 4.25 million kindergarten students by 12 students per teacher yields a maximum estimate of about 350,000 teachers; dividing 4.25 million by 25 yields a minimum estimate of 170,000 teachers. Thus, the number is estimated to be between 170,000 and 350,000 kindergarten teachers. (Note: this estimates the number who are currently employed.)

4.10 ANALYZING

To **analyze** a thing is to break or divide it in your imagination into its parts and examine the parts and their relations. You can analyze anything in many, many different ways, depending on how you understand its "parts." Suppose, for instance, you were to analyze an automobile. You might analyze it in terms of systems: fuel system, power system, electrical system, cooling system, suspension system, etc. You might analyze it in terms of places: engine compartment, passenger compartment, underside. You might analyze it in terms of individual parts: brake shoes, brake pads, brake lines, brake fluid, fenders, paint, windows, etc. You might analyze it in terms of materials: glass, steel, aluminum, plastic, rubber, petroleum, etc. You might analyze it in terms of how it affects people: costs to individuals, benefits to individuals, costs to society, benefits to society.

To analyze a work of literature, you might look at such parts as words, metaphors, sentence structure, plot, characters, theme, tone, arguments, supporting details, genre, or purpose.

4.11 GENERALIZING

To **generalize** is to make a general or universal claim based on some particular observations. Generalizations are often false because they make claims that are broader than what is strictly justified by the information available. For instance, Chiara has seen swans in parks and zoos and on television, and they have all been white. She could truthfully say, "All the swans I have ever seen are white." This claim is only about what she has actually experienced. She also may be tempted to generalize that "All swans are white," but she would be mistaken to do so; in fact, there are also black swans, even though Chiara has not experienced them.

On the other hand, a generalization is liable to be true when it is based on something more than just observations. Chiara knows that if she drops an egg from the bell tower atop the town hall onto the sidewalk, the egg will break. She knows this even though she has never seen an egg dropped from a bell tower. She knows more than merely what she has observed: she knows *why* eggs break. Forming a general rule based on reasoning—rather than on mere observation—is called **induction.**

4.12 DEDUCING

Deducing or **inferring** is coming to a logical **conclusion** based on some facts, called **premises**. Suppose you know that the Renaissance occurred in England from the late 1400s to the late 1600s (first premise). Later you learn that Shakespeare, the English writer, was born in 1564 (second premise). You can **deduce** that Shakespeare was a Renaissance writer (conclusion). A deduction is **valid** if the conclusion follows from or is forced by the premises; otherwise it is **invalid.** Valid deductions have the important property of preserving truth, which is to say that if you start with true premises and you make valid deductions, then your conclusions will always be true.

> EXAMPLE 1. If a person is able to write in a language, that person must be able to read in that language. 2. Bede wrote in Latin. 3. Therefore, Bede must have been able to read Latin.

Most commonly, a deduction is based on a **conditional** or "If . . . then . . ." statement (although often this statement is tacit). A conditional says that *if* something is true, *then* something else must be true.

In a conditional statement, the part following the *if* is called the **antecedent** (the prefix *ante–* means "before") and the part following the *then* is called the **consequent** (compare *consequence,* meaning "result"). In the example, "a person is able to write in a language" is the antecedent, and "a person must be able to read in that language" is the consequent.

A conditional statement also implies that, if the consequent is false, the antecedent must be false:

> EXAMPLE 1. If a person is able to write in a language, that person must be able to read in that language. 2. Jeffrey cannot read Latin. 3. Therefore, Jeffrey must not be able to write in Latin.

INFERENCES FROM CONDITIONALS	
Facts	**Implications**
Antecedent: true	Consequent: true
Consequent: false	Antecedent: false
Antecedent: false	none*
Consequent: true	none*

*See the Language Arts Survey, 4.14, "Avoiding Faulty Arguments: Fallacies of Affirming the Antecedent and of Denying the Consequent."

4.13 MAKING HYPOTHESES

A **hypothesis** is an educated guess about a cause or an effect. When you make a prediction based on a theory, your prediction is a hypothesis. Also, when you observe something and suggest a possible explanation, your explanation is a hypothesis. A hypothesis always needs to be tested against experience. You can test hypotheses by conducting actual experiments, by examining many relevant examples, or by conducting a **thought experiment**, asking "What if" questions (see 1.13, "Questioning").

Notice that a hypotheses can be disproved by only one counterinstance. However, a hypothesis cannot be proved merely by gathering examples (see 4.11, "Generalizing"). Theories and hypotheses always remain subject to modification in the light of future discoveries.

4.14 AVOIDING FAULTY ARGUMENTS

A **logical fallacy** is a logical mistake. You commit a fallacy when you make an **invalid** inference, one that is not warranted by the facts at hand.

It is important to recognize that while statements based on fallacies are groundless, they still can be true, just as wild guesses can sometimes be correct. As well, not every mistake involves a logical fallacy: errors also result from faulty information, lack of information, carelessness, or other problems. In practice it can be hard to tell when a mistake is a result of faulty logic and when it is a result of something else.

False analogy. An argument by analogy begins by claiming that two things are alike in some way and concludes that they are alike in another way. This type of argument can begin an interesting discussion, but it is not valid and cannot prove what it aims to. To see why it is fallacious, consider that by using this strategy you could "prove" that everything is identical to everything else.

Circularity. A circular argument is one that assumes the truth of the proposition that it is intended to prove. This type of argument is also called **begging the question.** A common type of circular argument merely restates an assumption in different words. Circular arguments can "prove" anything at all, and so are obviously fallacious.

EXAMPLE	"I liked reading this book a lot because I really enjoyed it and thought it was good."
ANALYSIS	The two "reasons" the speaker gives for liking the book are just different ways of saying that the speaker liked the book.

Post hoc (ergo) propter hoc. If one event causes another, the cause always comes before the effect. The *post hoc* fallacy is to assume, simply because one event occurred *after* another, that the first event *caused* the second. This fallacy confuses consequence with sequence, causation with correlation.

EXAMPLE	"As education spending increased in the 1980s, test scores began to decline. Let's cut spending and get our scores back up."
ANALYSIS	The author confuses correlation with causation. No reasoning has been offered to explain why test scores went down. It may or may not have to do with what the money was spent on. In either case, no explanation is offered as to why spending less will result in higher scores.

Fallacies of affirming the antecedent and of denying the consequent. A **conditional** or "If . . . then . . ." statement says that *if* something—the **antecedent**—is true *then* something else—the **consequent**—must be true (see 4.12, "Deducing"). As the chart on page 1184 shows, if the consequent is true, nothing is implied about the antecedent.

EXAMPLE	The more time and effort a person spends studying, the better that person will do in school. What can you conclude about the study habits of someone who does poorly in school?
ANALYSIS	Not much. There are many causes of poor school performance. To infer that the person does not study hard would be fallacious.

As the chart on page 1184 also shows, if the antecedent is false, nothing is implied about the consequent.

EXAMPLE	The more time and effort a person spends studying, the better that person will do in school. What can you conclude about the performance of someone who does not spend much time or effort studying?
ANALYSIS	Again, not much. You can conclude that that person could do better. However, you cannot conclude that that person does poorly. Again, there are many factors in school performance. Perhaps the person performs well without studying because he or she already has learned what is being taught from an interested relative.

Fallacies of composition and decomposition. If a whole has a certain quality, it does not follow that each part of that whole has that quality on its own. To assume that it does is to commit the fallacy of decomposition.

> EXAMPLE "My brother is on our school soccer team; our team is the worst in the state, so my brother is one of the worst soccer players in the state."
>
> ANALYSIS The team might be poor because of the brother, or it may be bad because of the other players. Perhaps they are all average or mediocre players led by a poor coach. The brother may even be one of the best players in the state.

Likewise, it is fallacious to argue that because some parts have a certain quality, whatever they are parts of must also have that quality. This is the fallacy of composition.

> EXAMPLE "Each sentence in my essay is perfect. Therefore, my essay is perfect."
>
> ANALYSIS A good essay is more than just a number of good sentences. The sentences must be organized and related in certain ways. Essays have **holistic** properties—properties that pertain to the whole—such as coherence, unity, order, subordination, and transitions.

Non sequitur. A *non sequitur* is a conclusion that simply does not follow from the reasons given and may have nothing to do with them.

> EXAMPLE "Shakespeare is obviously the greatest playwright that ever lived because he writes about real historical figures, and he has a tremendous vocabulary."
>
> ANALYSIS To say that some person (or thing) is the best is to say that it is better than all of his or her (or its) competitors. In the example, no competitors are mentioned; therefore, the conclusion does not follow.

Ad hominem. An argument that attacks or defends a person instead of the point at issue is known as an *argumentum ad hominem* (literally, "argument to the person"). Whether Tanya Hernandez is a good or bad or a smart or dull person, whether she is a liberal or a conservative or a Communist, or even whether she is honest or dishonest, does not determine the truth of what she says. To see this, consider that since everybody is imperfect in some way, you could use *ad hominem* arguments to "prove" that everything ever said must be false; but since everybody has some good quality, you could also "prove" that everything ever said must be true.

> EXAMPLE "My opponent has a criminal record. Her opinions on this legislation are uninformed and dangerous."
>
> ANALYSIS Nothing that is said here has any bearing on whether the legislation is a good idea. The opponent's opinions have not been attacked directly, let alone disproved.

False dichotomy. To set up a false dichotomy is to assume that there are only two sides to an issue. This type of argument is also called an "either/or" argument. An argument from false dichotomy becomes propagandistic (see 4.15, "Understanding Propaganda Techniques") when it takes a form such as "Anyone who's not for me is against me."

EXAMPLE	"Either you like poetry or you don't."
ANALYSIS	This is a false dichotomy. It assumes that there are only two possibilities, which is false. You may like modern poetry but dislike romantic poetry, or you may like rhythmic poetry and dislike free verse, or you may like good poetry and dislike doggerel.

As always, showing that an argument is faulty shows that the "conclusion" is not proven, but it does not prove that the conclusion is false.

Hasty generalization. To **generalize** is to make a general or universal claim based on some particular observations (see 4.11, "Generalizing"). Generalizations based on too few examples are illegitimate.

EXAMPLE	"I saw an opera once. They're boring."
ANALYSIS	Operas differ greatly from one another. One can't make a conclusion about all opera based on seeing one of them.

Equivocation. An **equivocation** is a statement that is meant to be ambiguous and to mislead because of its ambiguity. Equivocation creates the appearance of a logical connection between the reasons and the conclusion where there is no logical connection, so an argument that equivocates is *ipso facto* a *non sequitur.*

EXAMPLE	"The business of government is business."
ANALYSIS	This clever phrase may appear self-evident, but the appearance belies an equivocation. The term *business* is used in the first instance with the meaning "proper responsibility or concern" and in the second instance with the meaning "commerce and industry."

Vague terms. Most of the time people do not speak as precisely as they could. In particular, people use terms of approval and disapproval in a vague fashion. Very rarely do people specify exactly what they mean by *good, wrong, desirable, harmful,* etc. This practice allows people to agree on practical issues and decisions without first agreeing on every basic issue of politics, morality, and taste. It also affords opportunity for misunderstandings.

EXAMPLE	"I meant no wrong. I regret giving the high-paying cushy job to my sister, and she has resigned."

ANALYSIS Both *meant* and *regret* are vague terms in this example. Is the speaker saying that what she did was not wrong; or that she did not know it was wrong; or that, although she may have known it was wrong, she was not thinking at the time she acted about whether it was wrong? Does the speaker regret the action because she thinks it was morally wrong; or because it was illegal; or because, having been discovered, the action has jeopardized her political career?

4.15 Understanding Propaganda Techniques

You already know that you cannot believe everything you read. How can you decide what is believable? You must rely on your knowledge and your critical-thinking abilities. **Propaganda** is misleading language that tries to lead the reader or listener into a logical mistake by appealing to the emotions. It may work on you if you are not careful to avoid logical fallacies. You can spot the propagandists if you are on your toes *and* if you know what to look for.

Bandwagon. Often, people do not want to feel different from others: they want to feel "hip" and up-to-date; and they don't want to miss out on anything. Propaganda that tries to make people worry about being unique or that appeals to the desire to be part of the crowd is known as **bandwagon appeal.**

EXAMPLE "Everybody's lining up for the big sale starting at nine o'clock. Get down here yourself soon, or you'll never find out what you're missing!"

ANALYSIS Ask yourself, "If I didn't go, would I be missing anything important? If it were important, could I get it somewhere else or at a different time? Won't somebody make more of it if it's so popular? Is it worth it to me to stand in that line behind 'everybody'?" Then tell yourself, "I'm somebody, and I'm not there. I have worthwhile things to do, so it doesn't matter if I never find out what these people are doing."

Transfer. Transfer relies on guilt or honor by association. A television commercial shows a famous athlete using a camera. A billboard shows a famous fashion model wearing a pair of jeans with a prominent label. A newspaper photograph shows a political candidate shaking hands and laughing with a movie star. In each instance, the image has been set up in the hope that your good feeling about someone—the athlete, the model, or the movie star—will **transfer** to or rub off on someone or something else—the camera, the jeans, or the politician. No reasons are even offered: your rationality is bypassed.

False testimonial. A testimonial is a statement endorsing a person, object, or idea. Advertisers and politicians often solicit and pay celebrities to endorse them or their products. When experts offer testimonials without compensation, it is wise to listen.

EXAMPLE "Arnold Muscleman endorses this environmental legislation. It's good for our community."

ANALYSIS Arnold Muscleman may be a famous movie actor and director and a renowned bodybuilder. However, none of this provides a reason to follow his opinion on environmental legislation. If you knew that he was also an environmental biologist, you would have reason to give his opinion some weight.

Loaded words. Different words may refer to the same person or thing while saying different things about that person or thing. (see 2.153, "Connotation and Denotation"). A word may have strongly positive, strongly negative, or relatively neutral connotations. Using words with strong connotations can be a way to sway opinion without offering reasons.

EXAMPLE 1 "Jefferson's program directs tax dollars to provide food and medical care for the needy."

EXAMPLE 2 "Jefferson's program is socialism: it takes from hard-working taxpayers and gives to freeloaders and bums."

ANALYSIS The word *socialism* has strongly negative connotations for many Americans. *Socialism* is a loaded word. The expressions *the needy, hard-working taxpayers, freeloaders* and *bums* are loaded words, too. The first two expressions seem to suggest that these people deserve sympathy, while the second two expressions seem to suggest that these people deserve scorn.

Character assassination. This is a form of *ad hominem* argument that tries to persuade by attacking the opponent's character.

EXAMPLE "That Mr. Heep is a sniveling, conniving, lying sycophant. Don't believe him when he says we need a new wing for the library."

ANALYSIS The library may or may not need a new wing. The need or lack thereof is independent of Mr. Heep's character. The issue depends, instead, on how much space the current library has for books and readers and on how many books and readers there are.

Bias charges. Another form of *ad hominem* argument attacks a speaker's neutrality. Of course, any person who has a personal stake in an issue has a motive to lie or distort the facts in his or her favor. This does not mean that every such person is guilty of distortion. Furthermore, a person who has no personal stake in an issue is not likely to be involved in an argument about it. That a person may be biased is a good reason for scrutinizing what that person says but is not a sufficient reason for ignoring it.

EXAMPLE "Ignore Representative Madison. She opposes this campaign reform law only because this reform would make it harder for incumbents to get re-elected."

ANALYSIS The claim does not give a reason to support the proposed law, nor does it address Madison's reasons (such as they may be) against the law. The argument is not to the point.

▶ Use the Study Guide and Test on Reading Skills, 5.9.3–5.9.4, in the *Assessment Portfolio.*

READING SKILLS

4.16 READING RATES

Depending on your purposes in reading, you may choose among three techniques.

READING RATES		
Technique	Purpose	Tips
Scanning	Finding specific information quickly	Look for key words; look at chapter and part headings.
Skimming	Getting a general idea of the content of a piece	Ask questions; look at introductions; look at chapter and part headings.
Slow and careful reading	Learning and enjoyment	Read actively.

Scanning

Scanning is very quickly looking through a piece of writing to find some particular information that you want. On Monday morning you might scan the newspaper to find out how the Cardinals did on Sunday. You would first scan for the box scores, ignoring the headlines, articles, and advertisements. Once you found the box scores, you would scan for the score you want, ignoring all the other scores.

Scanning is used to find the location of information you want. You will probably want to scan reference works and other works when you are doing research for an essay or project. You will also probably scan reading selections to find answers for written exercises or to find quotations or other support for your opinions.

To scan, pick out a few key words to look for. Capitalized words, such as names, are good words to scan for because capital letters are easily noticed on a page. Glance quickly down each page, one page at a time, looking for those key words. When you find a key word, stop scanning and begin reading carefully to gather the information.

Skimming

Skimming is glancing quickly through a piece of writing to get a general idea of it. Many people use skimming when they have procrastinated and have left themselves insufficient time to do their work. A prudent person such as yourself will avoid such stop-gap measures. When you do research, you will use skimming efficiently to examine books or articles to determine whether they are of potential use or interest to you. You might also use skimming as a technique in previewing your reading (see 4.17, "Previewing Your Reading") or in reviewing your reading before taking a test or planning an essay.

You will skim more effectively if you hold in mind the few questions above you go.

To skim, first find and read the title of the piece and any chapter and section titles until you settle on an answer to the first question. Start reading from the beginning of the piece until you find a general answer to the second question. Then glance at any other headings or other material in distinguishing type to fill out your idea of the author's views and to get an answer to the third question. Last, look rather closely at the first few and the last few paragraphs of each section.

Slow and Careful Reading

When you are reading carefully, you will go more slowly because you will be more thorough. If you come across words you do not know, you will look them up in a dictionary. You will think about the reasons the author gives and the quality of her or his evidence. You will try to imagine what it would be like to know the characters or to be them. You will think of related issues and consider what the author would think about them. You will try to apply the author's ideas to other situations, perhaps situations in your own life. You will ask questions and expect the author to answer them. You will, as some have said, engage in a conversation with the author.

4.17 PREVIEWING YOUR READING

Thinking about what you will read before you begin can help you read more productively. You may ask, "How can I think about what I am going to read if I haven't read it yet?" There are a number of helpful **previewing** activities that will help you once you begin reading *per se.*

PREVIEWING ACTIVITIES

1. **Read** the title.	**Ask:** What is the piece about? What seems to be the author's attitude toward it?
2. **Skim** the first paragraph(s).	**Ask:** What is the main point of the piece?
3. **Skim** the last paragraph(s) (but not if the piece to be read is work of literature).	**Ask:** What is the author's conclusion?
4. **Read** the headings.	**Ask:** What are the main points?
5. **Ask:** Do all the parts seem to fit together? Do I have any unresolved questions?	

4.18 READING ACTIVELY

Reading actively does not mean reading fast, nor does it mean fidgeting in your chair or pacing while you read. Reading actively means thinking about what you are reading. Reading actively is a way to increase reading interest and comprehension.

Responding to Your Reading

Keep your journal next to you as you read and make notes of your initial reactions to what you are reading. Ask yourself these questions after each paragraph or section:

- "In what I've just read, what in particular do I find convincing or unconvincing?"
- "How does what I've just read make me feel? What about it in particular makes me feel that way?"

Feel free to explore your feelings. You may want to wait until after you've finished reading to analyze and evaluate these feelings.

TYPES OF READER RESPONSE QUESTIONS	
Who?	• Questions about characters or persons in the text • Questions about the author
What?	• Questions about objects and events
Where?	• Questions about location
When?	• Questions about sequence • Questions about time period
Why?	• Questions about motivation • Questions about reasoning and evidence
How?	• Questions about possibilities • Questions about actions

Questioning

Asking yourself questions as you read keeps your mind more active and helps you process what you are reading. You can ask questions based on the 5Ws and H: who? what? where? when? why? and how?

When you are reading in this book, you can use the Guided Reading questions and the Responding to the Selection questions in addition to your own questions.

Predicting

As you read, try to guess what will come next. Ask yourself why you think this.

Summarizing

Summarizing is simplifying a statement into a briefer statement of the main points. Summarizing helps you understand what you have read by forcing you to think about what points are important and what are not. Summarizing into your own words also helps you to remember. Be careful to state only the main points and not to inject your own opinions into your summary.

Identifying Main Ideas

In the simplest nonfiction writing, there is one main idea, which is stated clearly in the introduction in a thesis statement and restated in the conclusion. Likewise, the main idea of a paragraph is often stated in a topic sentence. Perhaps most of the writing you see, including some of the most excellent writing, will not be like this. Very often, as with much irony and satire, a main idea is not directly stated at all and must be inferred by the reader.

Identifying Relationships

You can understand better what you are reading if you can discover the writer's plan. Passages that show the writer's ordering scheme—e.g., chronological order or comparison-and-contrast order—provide important clues to interpreting the writer's meaning. More generally, you should pay special attention to any passages that indicate relationships between people, things, or ideas. Make notes of these relationships.

Making Inferences

Making inferences is drawing conclusions and finding implications by putting together facts to figure out something that isn't explicitly stated. Making inferences is an important part of understanding what you read. In nonfiction works, an author will often leave her or his conclusion unstated, so it is up to you to infer (and evaluate, of course) the author's intended conclusion. As well, you can only discover that an author's argument is flawed if you can make an inference that the author overlooked.

Making inferences is also important in reading works of fiction. You often need to make inferences from descriptions and contexts in order to understand the characters' actions and motivations. For instance, if one character says something that contradicts something said earlier by a different character, you need to make inferences to determine what's going on: Is one of them lying, or merely mistaken? Which one? (On drawing conclusions, see 4.12, "Deducing.")

4.19 READING CHARTS AND GRAPHS

Writers use charts and graphs to present ideas and information visually and compactly. The information necessary for reading the chart or graph is given in the title, headings, and other labels surrounding the graphic.

Pie charts. A **pie chart** is used primarily to depict relative proportions or shares in relation to a whole. It shows how different amounts **compare** to each other.

The whole pie represents all of something. In the example on the next page, the pie represents an American football team's total yardage: 6,220 yards. Each piece of the pie represents a portion of that whole. In the example, the portions are yardage from passing and from rushing. The size of the piece represents its share. In the example, rushing has a two-thirds share, twice as much as passing. The pie chart readily shows this relationship visually.

Bar graphs. The length of each bar in a **bar graph** represents an absolute quantity of something. In the graph below, each bar represents the number of syntactical errors of a specific type made by a student on a diagnostic test. Each student's scores are grouped, making it obvious right away how well each student did in relation to each other. Bar graphs show relative quantities, but unlike pie charts they do not depict relation to a whole.

Designers sometimes distort bar graphs in various ways to make them more visually interesting. You should be aware that these design changes often make the graphs' appearance misleading. Read and think carefully before coming to any conclusions.

Key N.P. = noun phrase; AD.P. = adverb phrase; AJ.P. = adjective phrase; V. = verbals

Line graphs. A **line graph** is little more than a bar graph with the bars removed and their top points connected. The line shows a continuous pattern or trend.

RESEARCH SKILLS

▶Use the Study Guide and Test on Research Skills, 5.9.5–5.9.6, in the *Assessment Portfolio.*

Conducting **research** means looking for ideas and information. Research is a combination of detective work, puzzle solving, and learning. When you research, you start with a more or less vague idea of what you want to know or a hypothesis you want to prove. This starts you on a trail. You follow the trail to find some information and then use this information to find other information, and so on.

You probably already know that a library is essentially a storehouse of sources of ideas and information. All this information and all these ideas are linked in a number of different ways. The following sections will teach you some tricks and tools that you can use to navigate these linkages and find the trail to the ideas and information you want.

4.20 THE CLASSIFICATION OF LIBRARY MATERIALS

Each book in a library is assigned a unique number, called a **call number.** The call number is printed on the **spine** (edge) of each book. The numbers serve to classify as well as to help the library keep track of the books.

Libraries commonly use one of two systems for classifying books. Most school and public libraries use the **Dewey Decimal System.** Most college libraries use the **Library of Congress Classification System** (known as the LC system).

THE DEWEY DECIMAL SYSTEM	
Call Numbers	**Subjects[1]**
000–099	Reference and General Works
100–199	Philosophy, Psychology
200–299	Religion
300–399	Social Studies
400–499	Language
500–599	Science, Mathematics
600–699	Technology
700–799	Arts
800–899	Literature
900–999	History, Geography, Biography[2]

1. The Dewey system does not number fiction. Works of fiction are arranged alphabetically by author.
2. Biographies (920s) are arranged alphabetically by subject.

ESSENTIAL SKILLS: STUDY AND RESEARCH

Call Letters	Subjects
A	Reference and General Works
B–BJ	Philosophy, Psychology
BK–BX	Religion
C–DF	History
G	Geography, Autobiography, Recreation
H	Social Sciences
J	Political Science
K	Law
L	Education
M	Music
N	Fine Arts
P	Language, Literature
Q	Science, Mathematics
R	Medicine
S	Agriculture
T	Technology
U	Military Science
V	Naval Science
Z	Bibliography, Library Science

In both systems, the first part of the call number is used to categorize books by subject. Since the call number begins with the subject code, and since books are placed on the shelves in call number order, this means that books on similar subjects can be found next to each other on the shelf. How convenient!

You can see that only general subjects are listed in the charts. Each system has a way to specify further a book's subject. In one Dewey system library, for instance, A. W. Marlow's *The Early American Furnituremaker's Manual* is 684.1 / M. The numbers 600–699 span technology. Within that class, 684 identifies books on furniture making. The subject can be further specified by adding numbers after the decimal point.

For another example, in the LC system, BJ identifies the more specific area of ethics and etiquette within the general area of philosophy, psychology, and religion (B). Further, BJ 1012 identifies the precise topic within that area (here, philosophical ethical theory). There may even be an additional identifying number, beginning with a decimal point, that further narrows the subject.

The second part of the call number is used to distinguish and identify individual books on the same subject. In the Dewey system, the first one to three letters of the author's last name can be added on the line below the subject identifier, as with the *M* in the furniture book. In the LC system, two books might have call numbers of BJ 1012 / .C95 / 1990 and

BJ 1012 / .P24 / 1992, for example. The letter after the decimal is the author's last initial, and the following two digits uniquely identify the author. The last four numbers identify the year of publication.

Locating materials in the library. Besides books, libraries house many types of publications, including magazines, academic and professional journals, newspapers, audio and video recordings, microfiche and microfilm, and government documents. Commonly, each of these types of materials is stored in a distinct place in the library and has its own classification system. For instance, government documents have their own numbering system and their own catalog (see 4.21 and 4.22, "Using Searching Tools" and "Using the Card Catalog"). Recordings also usually have a separate catalog. Many libraries have viewing and listening equipment available for use in the library, and some will allow you to borrow the equipment with your library card.

If you know the call number of the book you want, or if you know the subject classification number (Dewey or LC), you can go to the bookshelves, or **stacks**, and get the book or browse through books nearby. At a large library, look for a sign or notice that lists the locations of the various call numbers. There may be a "map" of the library with the call numbers located on it. These signs are usually posted in the card catalog area, near the circulation (check out and check in) desk, or on the doors to the stacks.

At some libraries, the public is not permitted into the stacks. Here, if you want to look at a book, you must ask a librarian to get it for you by writing its call number on a request slip.

4.21 USING SEARCHING TOOLS

All the books in a library are listed in the library's **catalog.** If your library has one of the many types of computerized catalogs, you will need to learn how to use the particular system it has. At most libraries signs or flyers explain how to use the system, and the computer keys are labeled. There is also usually a "help" button.

Author info.	Read, Herbert Edward, 1892-1968
Title	English Prose Style [New ed.]
Date of pub.	1980
Publisher	Pantheon
LC Call no.	LC PE1421.R35 1952a
ISBN no.	ISBN 0394748980
No. of pages	xvi, 216 p.
Page size, cover material	22 cm., pap
Copyright info.	c1952 Herbert Read, c1980 Benedict Read
Index page nos.	Index p.213-216
Supplementary sections	Hist. Note, App., List of Authors Quoted
Subject	English Language—Style

Generally, you are given a choice of searching by author, title, subject, or key words. See the chart below for tips on searching.

When you search by subject on computer, using the correct subject heads is crucial. Each library chooses the names of the subjects it uses from a special list. Many libraries use the list of subjects published by the Library of Congress, but others use different lists. If you can find nothing on your subject, the library probably uses a different word or phrase than you did to identify your subject. For instance, you will not find any books if you look up "history of marriage" because the library calls that subject "marriage: history." Before you look for books on a subject, check the list to see what wording your library uses. The list will help you find what you want by providing **cross-references**. In the example above, when you looked under "history of marriage" in the subject list, you may have found a note saying: "history of marriage. *See* marriage: history."

When typing your entry, double check your spelling since the computer cannot compensate for spelling errors (however, capitalization does not matter).

Once you get a list of books, you have the choice of getting more ideas and information about specific books in the list, narrowing the list with another search, scrolling up or down to see other titles, or starting over. Use the results of your search to help you search better. For instance, if you turn up a book that seems just what you are looking for, check its key words and subjects, and use those in new searches.

COMPUTERIZED CATALOG SEARCHES		
Search by . . .	**Example**	**Hints**
author	gould, stephen j	Type last name first. Type as much of the name as you know.
title	(the) mismeasure of man	Omit articles such as *a, an,* or *the* at the beginning of titles.
subject	intelligence tests; ability—testing	Use the list of subjects provided by the library.
keywords	darwin; intelligence; craniology	Use related topics if you can't find anything in your subject.

Write down the call numbers of each book you want and head for the shelves (see 4.20, "The Classification of Library Materials: Locating Materials in the Library").

Interlibrary Loan. Your borrowing privileges at your local library may allow you to obtain books and articles from other libraries through an interlibrary loan. In many libraries, the computerized catalog covers the collections of several libraries that participate in a local library network or consortium. The catalog will tell you which library holds the book you want. If your book is in a different library, you will need to fill out a request slip and give it to your librarian. You may wait for one day or for up to a few weeks for your request to be filled.

4.22 USING THE CARD CATALOG

The library's catalog contains basic information about each book in the library. If the library uses a **card catalog,** the information is typed on paper cards. The cards are arranged alphabetically in drawers. For each book there is a **title card,** one **author card** for each author, and at least one **subject card.** All of these cards give the book's title, author, and call number. Hence, you have a variety of ways to find each book; you can search by author, title, or subject (see the Language Arts Survey 4.21, "Using Searching Tools," for tips on how to search).

AN AUTHOR CARD

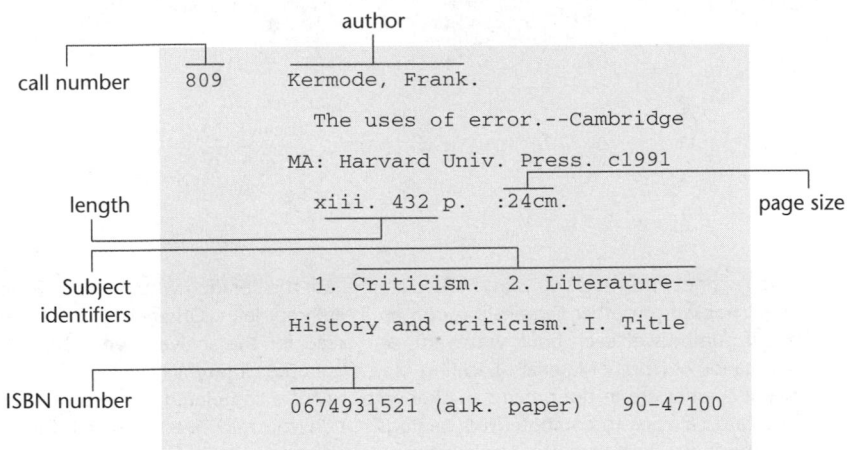

author

call number   809   Kermode, Frank.

       The uses of error.--Cambridge

MA: Harvard Univ. Press. c1991

length   xiii. 432 p. :24cm.   page size

Subject identifiers   1. Criticism. 2. Literature--

History and criticism. I. Title

ISBN number   0674931521 (alk. paper)   90-47100

A TITLE CARD

809   The Uses of Error

Kermode, Frank.

      The uses of error.--Cambridge

MA: Harvard Univ. Press. c1991

     xiii. 432 p. :24cm.

     1. Criticism. 2. Literature--

History and criticism. I. Title

0674931521 (alk. paper)   90-47100

A SUBJECT CARD

```
              CRITICISM
809    Kermode, Frank.
          The uses of error.--Cambridge
       MA: Harvard Univ. Press. c1991
          xiii. 432 p.  :24cm.


          1. Criticism.  2. Literature--
       History and criticism. I. Title


       0674931521 (alk. paper)    90-47100
```

If you cannot find what you want in the catalog, ask the librarian whether your library can get books from other libraries through an interlibrary loan. Otherwise, write down the call numbers of each book you want, and head for the shelves (see 4.20, "The Classification of Library Materials: Locating Materials in the Library").

Many libraries are in the process of changing, or have completed the change, from paper card catalogs to computerized catalogs. Often you may need to search in *both* the computer system—for new books—*and* the card catalog—for older books—to find everything the library has on your topic (see 4.21, "Using Searching Tools").

4.23 USING REFERENCE WORKS

No matter what your interest, the chances are excellent that somebody has written about it. Human beings have been collecting and sharing knowledge for thousands of years. Probably, most of what you want to know can be found in one or more **reference works**, works in which knowledge is compiled and organized for easy access. Some reference works, such as the library catalog and **indexes,** are designed to help you find other works that contain the ideas and information you want. Other reference works contain the ideas and information themselves. For the most part, current reference works cannot be checked out of the library.

Almanacs and **Yearbooks.** An almanac contains statistics and lists of all sorts, such as lists and biographies of important inventors, authors, artists, celebrities, etc.; lists of and statistics about wars, battles, and political figures and events; sports records and achievements; lists of award-winners (e.g., Nobel prize, Pulitzer prize, Oscars); lists of major colleges, museums, and libraries; and statistics and other information about weather and the fifty states. To find information in an almanac, use the index.

Most almanacs also contain a summary of major events that occurred in the previous year. This information is available in more detail in a **yearbook**, which is published separately, like your high school yearbook. Some yearbooks are published by encyclopedia publishers and are shelved with the encyclopedias.

Atlases. An atlas is primarily a collection of maps, but each atlas has its own special focus and contains information in addition to maps. Depending on the focus of the atlas, the maps may show natural features (e.g., mountains, rivers, natural resources), developed features (e.g., roads, bridges, airports), political features (e.g., counties, cities), or other geographic information (e.g., land use, weather, population). An **historical atlas** contains maps depicting places as they used to be and enables you to trace various historical developments. A key feature of many atlases is the **gazetteer,** which is an index listing every item located on the maps.

Encyclopedias. An encyclopedia is meant to provide a survey of knowledge. **General encyclopedias,** such as *World Book, Compton's,* or *Britannica,* contain information on almost every topic imaginable. **Specialized encyclopedias,** such as *The Oxford Companion to English Literature* or *Benet's Readers' Encyclopedia,* contain information on more narrowly defined subjects. Different topics are treated in **articles,** which are arranged alphabetically by topic.

On your first try, you may find nothing on your topic. Don't worry. Most likely, the editors have used a different word or phrase to identify your subject. Use the index to find out which articles cover the information you want. Using the index also ensures that you do not overlook ideas and information when your topic is treated in more than one article. The index of a multivolume encyclopedia is found in one or two separate volumes.

Encyclopedias are excellent first sources, because they provide an outline and overview of just about anything you could want to know about. Since an encyclopedia article is a survey article, you are liable to want more information than it provides. Most encyclopedias supply a list of additional sources of information at the end of each article.

Indexes. An index is an alphabetical directory to published information and ideas. Each index covers a limited range of publications. Many individual periodicals also publish their own indexes from time to time. *The Readers' Guide to Periodical Literature* is a comprehensive index to nearly all of the popular weekly, monthly, and quarterly publications. Many libraries subscribe to the *New York Times Index* because the *New York Times* newspaper covers national and world news. It has been published nearly continuously since 1851 and is available on microfilm. The *Short Story Index* and the *Play Index* list short stories and plays, respectively, that have been published in collected volumes.

Periodicals. Magazines, daily newspapers, specialized newspapers, trade journals, and professional journals are among the publications received by libraries on a regular and **periodic** basis. Because they are published frequently and quickly, periodicals are excellent sources for the latest news and information. On the other hand, information in periodicals is less likely to have been evaluated carefully by experts.

Current issues are usually available in a reading room in the library. Recent issues may be stored beneath or behind the current issue. If the library retains older issues, these are either bound and stored in the stacks or copied onto microfilm or microfiche.

Other reference works. In addition to the above-mentioned works, the reference section of your library probably has collections of quotations (e.g., *Bartlett's Familiar Quotations),* biographies (e.g., *Contemporary Authors, Dictionary of American Biography, Who's Who*), book reviews (e.g., *Book Review Digest*), state and local laws, telephone directories, business directories, guidebooks and manuals, catalogs and admissions information from colleges and universities, and many other materials.

4.24 USING DICTIONARIES

Dictionaries provide much more information about words than just their spellings and definitions.

Immediately following the entry word is the **pronunciation,** usually in parentheses, as in the example here. You can find a complete key to pronunciation symbols by looking in the dictionary table of contents. In some dictionaries, a simplified key for quick reference is at the bottom of each page.

A word's **part-of-speech label** tells the ways in which a word can be used (see the Language Arts Survey 2.3–2.31, "The Parts of Speech"). In the example, the letter *n.* following the pronunciation shows that the word is used as a noun. Later in the entry, the dash followed by *vt.* shows that the word can also be used as a transitive verb. If you glance through a dictionary, you will notice that many words can be used in more than one way.

An **etymology** is a word's history. In most cases, the etymology is summarized in the entry. (When a word is a compound or is a variation on another word, a cross-reference is provided to the entry containing the etymology). In the example, *file* comes from a Middle English (ME) word *file*, which came from an Old English (OE) word *feol*, which may have come from a Dutch (Du) word *vijl*, which may have come from an Indo-European (IE) word, *peik*, meaning "to scratch or prick."

The **definitions** tell the different meanings the word can take. When a word can be used with more than one meaning, the different definitions are numbered. (There are two definitions for *file* in the sample entry.) When a word can be used as different parts of speech, the definitions follow each part-of-speech label. (A definition for *file* used as a transitive verb is provided in the sample.) However, when two words are **homographs**—i.e., have the same spelling but different etymologies and meanings, such as *can* (verb) and *can* (noun)—the words are listed as separate entries. In the sample entry, the superscript *2* after the entry word shows that *file* is a homograph.

Usage notes—such as "slang," "colloquial," or "technical"—describe any nonstandard usages. In the sample, *file* used with the second definition is primarily a British slang word.

If the word were common in any **idiomatic** phrases, these phrases would be defined at the end of the entry. Here, too, would be listed other forms based on the word (none are listed for *file*).

4.25 USING THESAURUSES

A thesaurus is a reference book that groups words with similar meanings. A thesaurus can help you find exact synonyms, related words, and antonyms. It can be useful when you have a word that means almost but not quite what you want, or when you have used a word so many times that it is becoming noticeable and tiresome. You might also enjoy browsing in a thesaurus and contemplating the subtle differences among words in an entry.

There are two types of thesaurus. A dictionary-type thesaurus is organized alphabetically. If the word, you look up is an entry word, related words will be listed beneath it. If it is not an entry word, you should find a cross-reference to an entry word (or else the thesaurus does not recognize your word). Subheadings beneath each entry word identify different meanings or word forms. At the end of the entry is a list of antonyms.

Roget's Thesaurus is organized by idea rather than alphabetically. Pierre Roget tried to devise a system to categorize all existence and ideas. He used his categories as headings, under which he grouped words with similar or related meanings. To this he added an index. To use *Roget's Thesaurus,* look up your word in the index in the back part of the book. Beneath it you will find a number of related words. Choose the related word whose meaning is closest to what you want. (Of course, if the related word *is* the word you want, you're done.) The numbers are not page numbers; they refer to a section and sub-section in the first part of the book.

Roget's Thesaurus may appear complicated at first, but it is an interesting and useful tool once you get used to it.

4.26 COMPUTER-ASSISTED RESEARCH

On-line Research

With a computer and a modem you can connect to a variety of sources of information. If you, your school, or your library subscribes to an on-line service, you probably have access to current news, online encyclopedias, abstracts of periodicals and government documents, homework and studying assistance, online courses, and research services. You may also be able to use the service to connect to the Library of Congress, other libraries and museums, and the Internet, which allows you to connect to universities, libraries, businesses, individuals, and government agencies all around the world. Your school may also be connected to a special education network, such as TENET (Texas Education Network). Find out from your school or public librarian if you can use these services.

CD/ROM and Other Computer Media

A CD/ROM database works just like an on-line database. The difference is that you retrieve the information directly from a CD instead of working through a network. Your library may have a collection of CDs that you can insert into the computer, or the CDs may be changed only by the librarians.

4.27 OTHER SOURCES OF INFORMATION

Vertical files. Besides books and periodicals, libraries collect other sources of information, such as pamphlets, brochures, maps, clippings, photographs, and posters. These items are not cataloged. They are stored in folders in filing cabinets. You can look through the files to see if they include anything on your topic.

Organizations and associations. Local businesses, business groups, religious organizations, environmental groups, political parties and organizations, lobbying groups, charities, volunteer and service organizations, and professional societies are groups of people and/or companies that share interests and concerns. Most are anxious to provide information on topics of concern to them. Since many of these groups strongly advocate a particular point of view, their information is liable to be incomplete or even misleading.

Community institutions such as museums, art galleries, historical societies, orchestras and symphonies, dance troupes, other performing arts groups, and colleges can be good sources of ideas and information on certain topics.

Information about many of these groups is available in the *Encyclopedia of Associations*. You can find names and addresses of local groups in your local telephone listings.

Experts. In your community or in nearby communities, someone may have extensive knowledge of your topic. Anyone who has a love for what he or she does—for work or recreation—will have learned a great deal about it. As well, professionals such as lawyers, doctors, engineers, and college professors have spent several years beyond college studying their specialized subject. Many of these people are glad to have an opportunity to share their knowledge and experience with students and others.

If you don't know anyone who knows about your topic, you can look in the phone book. Better still, ask your teachers, parents, friends, and relatives if they know someone who might help you. Ask your contact if he or she can arrange an interview, or arrange an interview yourself by calling the person directly (see 1.27, "Interviewing").

Before you contact someone for assistance, remind yourself that you are requesting a *favor*. Prepare before approaching people so they do not feel that you are wasting their time. Be as specific as possible about what your project is and what you would like them to do for you. Don't take advantage of others' generosity by asking for too much. You can find out a great deal in fifteen to twenty minutes. Remember to thank the person.

4.28 EVALUATING SOURCES

As you conduct your research, you will soon realize that you cannot read everything that has been written on your topic. You should also remind yourself that you cannot simply believe everything you read. To conduct your research efficiently, you need to evaluate your sources and set priorities among them. Ideally, a source will be . . .

- **Unbiased.** All authors take a personal interest in their subject. However, when an author has a personal stake in what people think about a subject, that author is liable to withhold or distort information. Investigate the author's background to see if she or he is liable to be biased. Using loaded language and overlooking obvious counter-arguments are signs that an author is biased.

- **Authoritative.** An authoritative source is one that is reliable and trustworthy. An author's reputation, especially her or his reputation among others who conduct research in the same field, is a sign of authoritativeness. Likewise, periodicals and publishers acquire reputations for careful and responsible editing and research, or for shoddiness.

- **Timely.** In some subjects the state of knowledge is expanding and changing very rapidly. An astronomy text published last year may already be out of date. In other fields, for instance algebra, older texts may be perfectly adequate. If your interest is historical you will even seek out old and dated works. Consult with your teacher and your librarian to decide how current your sources must be.

- **Available.** Having access to materials across the country and all over the world sounds wonderful. However, when you have an approaching deadline, you may be frustrated to find that the nearest circulating copy of the book you need is two thousand miles away. (In this context, the advantage of getting an early start on your research project becomes starkly clear.) Borrowing through interlibrary loan, tracing a book that is missing, or recalling a book that has been checked out to another person all take time that you may not have. Ask your librarian how long you can expect to wait.

- **At the appropriate level.** You want sources that present useful information in a way you can understand. Materials written for children or "young people" may be so simple as to be uninformative or even misleading. Books written for experts may presume knowledge that you do not have. Struggling with an extremely difficult text is often worth the effort, but if you do so, monitor your time and be sure to keep to your schedule.

4.29 BIBLIOGRAPHIES AND BIBLIOGRAPHY CARDS

Bibliographies. A **bibliography** is a list of sources on some given topic. If you are writing a research paper, your teacher will ask you to include one of the following types of bibliography.

TYPES OF BIBLIOGRAPHY	
Complete Bibliography	A comprehensive list of works on your topic
Works Cited *or* **References**	A list of all the works referred to or quoted in your paper
Works Consulted	A list of every work you learned from in your research, even if you did not directly use or cite these works in your paper

The chart on the following pages provides examples of proper bibliographic form for many different types of materials.

To prepare your bibliography, first arrange your bibliography cards (see page 1210) in alphabetical order. Type or copy the information from each card onto your paper. Follow the form for entries as given in the chart. Set up your pages and type the bibliography as described in the chart on page 1206.

FORMS FOR BIBLIOGRAPHY ENTRIES

A. A book with one author

Percy, Marge. <u>Braided Lives</u>. New York: Summit, 1982.

B. A book with two authors

Note that only the first author's name is inverted.

Woodward, Bob, and Scott Armstrong. <u>The Brethren: Inside the Supreme Court</u>. New York: Simon, 1979.

C. A book with three authors

Note that only the first author's name is inverted.

Hamilton, Alexander, John Jay, and James Madison. <u>The Federalist</u>. 1788. New York: Modern Library, Nd.

D. A book with four or more authors

The abbreviation *et al.* means "and others." Use *et al.* (and others) instead of listing all the authors.

Dewey, John, et al. <u>Creative Intelligence</u>. New York: Holt, 1917.

E. A book with no author given

<u>Literary Market Place: The Directory of the American Book Publishing Industry</u>. 1995 ed. New York: Bowker, 1994.

F. A book with an editor, but no single author

Yeats, W. B., ed. <u>The Oxford Book of Modern Verse</u>. New York: Oxford UP, 1937.

G. A book with two or three editors

Bly, Robert, James Hillman, and Michael Meade, eds. <u>The Rag and Bone Shop of the Heart: Poems for Men</u>. New York: HarperCollins, 1992.

H. A book with four or more editors

The abbreviation *et al.* means "and others." Use *et al.* instead of listing all the authors.

McFarlan, Donald, et al., eds. <u>The Guinness Book of Records 1992</u>. New York: Facts on File, 1991.

I. A book with an author and a translator

Alighieri, Dante. <u>The Divine Comedy</u>. Trans. Henry Wadsworth Longfellow. Boston and New York: Houghton, 1895.

J. A second or later edition of a book

Copi, Irving M. <u>Introduction to Logic</u>. 5th ed. New York: Macmillan, 1978.

K. A book or monograph that is part of a series

Ermarth, Elizabeth Deeds. <u>George Eliot</u>. Twayne's English Authors ser. Boston: Twayne, 1985.

L. A multivolume work
If you use only one volume of a multivolume work, cite only that volume; otherwise cite only the entire work.

The Works of Aphra Behn. Ed. Montagne, Summers, 1915. Vol. 4. New York: Blom, 1967.

The Works of Aphra Behn. Ed. Montagne Summers. 1915. 6 Vols. New York: Blom, 1967.

M. A titled volume with its own title that is part of a multivolume work with a different title

Durant, Will, and Ariel Durant. The Age of Voltaire: A History of Civilization in Western Europe from 1715-1756, with Special Emphasis on The Conflict between Religion and Philosophy. New York: Simon, 1965. Vol. 9 of The Story of Civilization. 11 vols. 1935-75.

N. A republished book or literary work available in several editions
Give the original publication date after the title. Then give complete information, for the edition that you have used.

Twain, Mark [Samuel Clemens]. The Adventures of Tom Sawyer. 1876. New York: Dodd, 1958.

O. A government publication

United States. U.S. Govt. Printing Office. United States Government Printing Office Style Manual. Washington: GPO, 1984.

Parts of Books

A. A poem, short story, essay, or chapter in a collection of works by one author

Vidal, Gore. "The Second American Revolution." United States: Essays: 1952-1992. New York: Random, 1993. 956-79.

B. A poem, short story, essay, or chapter in a collection of works by several authors

Eberle, Nancy. "Dream Houses." Reinventing Home. By Laurie Abraham *et al.* New York: Plume, 1991. 54-58.

C. A novel or play in a collection under one cover

Lorca, Federico García. The House of Bernarda Alba. Three Tragedies. New York: New Directions, 1955. 155-211.

D. An introduction, preface, foreword, or afterword written by the author(s) of a work

Nabokov, Vladimir. Foreword. The Gift. New York: Putnam's, 1963.

E. An introduction, preface, foreword, or afterword written by someone other than the author(s) of a work

Toth, Emily. Introduction. A Vocation and a Voice. By Kate Chopin. New York: Penguin, 1991. vii-xxvi.

F. A reprint of a previously published article or essay

Give complete information for the original publication, followed by "Rpt. in" and complete information for the collection.

```
Sontag, Susan. "Resnais' Muriel." Film Quarterly 17 (1964): 23-27.
    Rpt. in Against Interpretation. New York: Dell, 1966. 232-241.
```

Magazines, Encyclopedias, Reports, Newspapers, and Newsletters

A. An article in a quarterly or monthly magazine

```
Lutz, John. "Beyond Good and Evil." The Writer December 1994:
    9-12.
```

B. An article in a weekly magazine

```
Horowitz, Craig. "The Bronx is Up." New York 21 Nov. 1994:
    54-59.
```

C. A magazine article with no author given

```
"Beowulf Best Dragons in Cyberspace." National Geographic 106.6
    (1994): Np.
```

D. An article in a daily newspaper

```
Savage, David G. "Ruling Boosts Frequent Fliers." Boston Globe
    19 Jan. 1995: 33+.
```

E. An editorial in a newspaper

```
"From Parade to Charade." Editorial. Boston Globe 19 Jan.
    1995: 10.
```

F. An article or story in a journal

Give the volume number, the year, and the page number(s) after the title of the journal.

```
Addison, Catherine. "Once Upon a Time: A Reader-Response to
    Prosody." College English 56.6 (1994): 655-78.
```

G. An article in an encyclopedia, dictionary, or other alphabetically organized reference work

Give the title of the article, the title of the work, and the year.

```
"Hieroglyphics." Dictionary of Literary Themes and Motifs. Ed.
    Jean-Charles Deigneuret. New York: Greenwood, 1988.
```

H. A review

```
Blount, Roy, Jr. "Rustily Vigilant." Rev. of For Keeps: Thirty
    Years at the Movies. By Pauline Kael. New York: Dutton, 1994.
    Atlantic Monthly Dec. 1994: 131-43.
```

I. A report for a pamphlet

Same as for a book.

Media and Other Sources

A. An interview that you have conducted

Sawyer, Dianne. Personal interview. 21 November 1994.

B. A letter that you have received

Bush, Babara. Letter to the author. 11 June 1992.

C. A fax or e-mail communication

Same as for a letter.

D. A thesis or dissertation

Bilow, Scott. "Obligations to Educate." Diss., Cornell U, 1988.

E. A film

The Big Heat. Dir. Fritz Lang. With Glenn Ford and Gloria
   Grahame. Writ. Sidney Boehm. Based on the novel of the same
   title by William P. McGiven. 90 min. Columbia, 1953.

F. A work of visual art

Blake, William. The Ancient Days. British Museum, London.

G. A television or radio program

Give the episode name; the names of the episode's writer, director, producer, or
actors; the series or program title; and any information that you wish to include
about the series's writer, director, or producer. Then give the network, station call letters, city, and date.

"A Dessert Blooming." Writ. Marshall Riggan. Living Wild. Dir.
   Harry L. Gordon. Prod. Peter Argentine. PBS. WTTW, Chicago.
   29 Apr. 1984.

H. A musical composition

Stravinsky, Igor. Le Sacre du Printemps.

I. An audio recording (LP, compact disc, audio-cassette tape)

Davis, Miles "So What." Kind of Blue. LP. Columbia, PC 8163, Nd.

J. A lecture, speech, or address

Give the name of the speaker and the name of the speech. If there is no title, give the
kind of speech—e.g. lecture, introduction, address. Then give the event, place, and date.

Shepherd, Rob. Address. Cape Ann Naturalists Beach Clean-up.
   Essex, MA, 2 Aug. 1995.

MANUSCRIPT FORM FOR BIBLIOGRAPHIES

1. Begin on a new page.

2. Indent one inch from both side margins, one and one-half inches on the left side and one inch on the right side if the report is to be bound.

3. Place your last name and the page number, flush right, half-an-inch from the top of the paper.

4. Drop down another one-half-inch and insert the title "Works Consulted" or "Works Cited." Use uppercase and lowercase letters, and do not underscore.

5. Begin each entry at the left margin. Single space within each entry. Indent run-over lines five spaces from the left margin.

6. Double space between the title and the first entry and between each entry.

Bibliography cards. For each source that you work with, prepare a 3×5 card listing complete bibliographical information. Prepare a card for each possible source you find.

You will need the information on your bibliography cards to prepare your documentation of sources (see 4.33, "Documenting Sources in a Report") for your bibliography, or in case you need to find the book again. Follow the proper form for the type of material, as shown in the chart below, when preparing your cards. Doing so will make preparing the final bibliography easy, and you can be certain that you will not be missing any needed bibliographic information.

INFORMATION TO INCLUDE ON A BIBLIOGRAPHY CARD

Author(s)	Write the complete name(s) of all author(s), editor(s), and translator(s).
Title	Write the complete title, including any subtitle and any series title. If the piece is an article or chapter in a periodical or book, write • the title of the particular piece; • the beginning and ending page numbers; and • the title of the larger work.
Edition	Note "2nd edition," "revised edition," etc.
Publisher	Write exactly as it appears on the title page.
Place and date of publication	For periodicals, write the date as well as the issue and volume numbers. For republished works, write both the original publication date and the date of your edition.
Location and call number	Note where you found the book. If it is in a library collection, write the call number.
Card number	Give each bibliography card that you prepare a number. Write that number in the top right-hand corner of the card and circle it. When you take notes from the source, include this number on each note card so that you will be able to identify the source of the note later on.

①

```
Lord Tennyson, Alfred. Idylls of the
     King. Ed. J. M. Gray.
     New Haven: Yale UP, 1983.

PR        Peabody Institute Library
5558
A1
1983
```

4.30 PARAPHRASING AND SUMMARIZING

Quoting. Words that are **quoted**—borrowed exactly from someone else—should be placed inside quotation marks (on punctuation with quotations, see 2.104 and 2.105; on capitalization with quotations, see 2.124). Use a quotation when you need to prove that someone said something in particular. Avoid quotation for other purposes. In particular, do not quote for the purpose of showing that some esteemed author shares your views.

When you do quote, be sure to provide proper documentation (see 4.33, "Documenting Sources in a Report").

Paraphrasing. Paraphrasing is restating someone else's ideas in your own words. When taking notes, quote directly rather than paraphrase. When you use your note cards to write your paper, you can be sure that you have not inadvertently quoted a source if you have the exact quotations to look at.

Paraphrasing does not relieve you of the obligation to give credit when you use the words or ideas of others (see 4.33, "Documenting Sources in a Report"). Although you do not borrow the words of another when you paraphrase, you do borrow another's ideas, and that borrowing must be acknowledged.

Summarizing. Summarizing a piece of writing is simplifying it into a brief statement of the main points, condensing someone else's ideas into fewer words of your own. When you summarize, you leave out details, even important details.

A summary should tell what the author said. Be careful not to inject your own opinions into your summary. As well, a summary should state only the main points of a piece of writing. Do not include minor or trivial points. Your purposes will determine how much supporting detail to include in your summary and how much to omit.

EXAMPLE

Summary: The *Iliad*

Achaean warriors wage war against the Trojans and rescue Helen, the wife of King Menelaus.

Outlining. An excellent way to summarize nonfiction reading is to outline what you read (see 1.32 and 1.33). Paraphrase the title and headings (if any) in the piece you are summarizing to use as the title and headings of your outline. After each heading, note the main point or points made in the section.

4.31 INFORMAL NOTE-TAKING

Informal note-taking. Take informal notes when you want information for your own use only and when you will not need to quote or document your sources. You would take informal notes when preparing materials to use in studying, for instance, as you watch a film or listen to a lecture.

Informal note-taking is much like outlining (see 1.32, "Making a Rough Outline"). Use important ideas as headings, and write relevant details below.

You will not be able to copy every word, nor is there any need to. Write phrases instead of sentences.

QUOTATION	"James Burbage founded the Blackfriars Theater and shared ownership of the Globe Theater with Shakespeare."
NOTE	James Burbage —founded Blkfrs Th. —part-owner Globe Th. (w/ Shakes.)

You will also want to record information about the event or performance, including the date, time, place, speaker, and title, as applicable.

After you are done taking notes, read them over to ensure that they are legible and meaningful. If you have used idiosyncratic shorthand or abbreviations that you may not later recall, write out your notes more fully.

4.32 FORMAL NOTE-TAKING

Formal note-taking. Take formal notes when you may need to quote or document your sources. When you are keeping formal notes for a research project—for instance, for a debate or a research paper—you should use 4×6 index cards.

PREPARING NOTE CARDS

1. Identify the source at the top right corner of the card. (Use the source numbers from your bibliography cards.)

2. Identify the subject or topic of the note on the top line of the card. (This will make it easier to organize the cards later.)

3. Use a separate card for each fact or quotation. (This will make it easier to organize the cards later.)

4. Write the page number or numbers after the note.

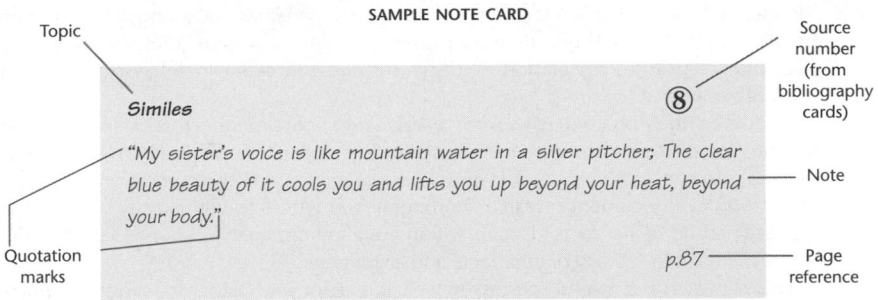

SAMPLE NOTE CARD

Topic

Similes

Source number (from bibliography cards)

⑧

Quotation marks

"My sister's voice is like mountain water in a silver pitcher; The clear blue beauty of it cools you and lifts you up beyond your heat, beyond your body."

Note

p.87

Page reference

Your notes will consist of quotations, paraphrases, and summaries.

FORMAL NOTE-TAKING

Type of Note	When to Use	What to Watch for
Quotation	When the exact wording of a primary source is important to your topic; or When you are providing a definition; or When the wording of a secondary source is particularly elegant, pithy, concise, amusing, etc.	Be sure you exactly copy spelling, capitalization, punctuation, and numbers. Place quotation marks around all direct quotations. Record, when appropriate, explanatory background information about the speaker or the context of a quotation.
Paraphrase	Most of the time	Bear in mind your main purpose, and note only points that are related to your topic. Place quotation marks around any quoted words or phrases.
Summary	When the point in which you are interested does not require the detail of a paraphrase	Reread the source after writing your summary to be sure that you have not altered the meaning.

4.33 DOCUMENTING SOURCES IN A REPORT

Documentation. In your writing, you must indicate to your reader when you are using the words or ideas of others. This is called **documentation.** A note that tells from whom an idea comes is called a **citation** or a **reference.**

Presenting the words or ideas of others as if they were your own is called **plagiarism.** If you use someone else's words or ideas and do not give that person credit, you are guilty of plagiarism—even if you weren't trying to plagiarize.

In most schools plagiarism is punishable by severe penalties, including a failing grade for the project or for the course and possibly even expulsion. Outside of school, plagiarism constitutes a violation of copyright and can result in a lawsuit and great financial expense.

In addition to protecting you from plagiarizing, documenting your sources is an important part of writing. Whether your aim as a writer is to explain or to persuade, your job is to convince your readers. Wouldn't you be more likely to be convinced by an author who can document research thoroughly and who tells you exactly where he or she obtained his or her facts? Documenting your sources enables your reader to judge the reliability and accuracy of your facts and arguments.

Documentation is a helpful courtesy as well. It enables your reader to investigate points you discuss. Finally, documentation is honest. It shows that you recognize and appreciate the contributions to human knowledge made by those who have gone before you.

Parenthetical documentation. Parenthetical documentation is currently the most widely used form of documentation. To use this method to document the source of a quotation or an idea, you place a brief note identifying the source in parentheses immediately after the borrowed material. This type of note is called a **parenthetical citation,** and the act of placing such a note is called **citing a source.**

The first part of a parenthetical citation refers the reader to a source in your list of Works Cited or Works Consulted. Since the reference should make it easy for a reader to find the source in your bibliography, you must cite the work according to how it is listed in the bibliography. The reference to the source should also be as brief as possible. If the source is clearly identified in the text, omit it from the citation and give only the page number.

The second part of the citation refers the reader to a specific page or place within the source. If you are referring to a whole work, do not cite the page numbers since they are already given in the bibliography.

SAMPLE PARENTHETICAL CITATIONS

A. For works listed by title, use an abbreviated title.

"History." _Encyclopedia Britannica: Macropædia_. 1992 ed.

Sample citation

  . . . Historians go through three stages in textual criticism ("History" 615). . . .

B. For works listed by author or editor, use the author's or editor's last name.

Sample bibliographic entry

Brown, Dee. _Bury My Heart at Wounded Knee: An Indian History of the American West_. New York: Holt, 1970.

Sample citation

  . . . "Big Eyes Schurz agreed to the arrest" (Brown 364). . . .

C. When the listed name or title is stated in the text, cite only the page number.

  . . . Brown avers that Big Eyes Schurz agreed to it (364). . . .

CONTINUED

D. For works of multiple volumes, use a colon after the volume number.

Sample bibliographic entry

Pepys, Samuel. *The Diary of Samuel Pepys*. Ed. Robert Latham and William Matthews. 10 vols. Berkeley: University of California Press, 1972.

Sample citation

. . . On the last day of 1665, Pepys took the occasion of the new year to reflect, but not to celebrate (6: 341-2). . . .

E. For works quoted in secondary sources, use the abbreviation "qtd. in."

Sample citation

. . . According to R. Bentley, "reason and the facts outweigh a hundred manuscripts" (qtd. in "History" 615). . . .

F. For classic works that are available in various editions, give the page number from the edition you are using, followed by a semicolon; then identify the section of the work to help people with other editions find the reference.

Sample citation

. . . The scene in <u>Middlemarch</u> between Casaubon and Dorothea (328-31; bk. 5 ch. 48) is a prime example. . . .

G. For classic works of poetry or drama you may omit the page reference completely and cite the section and line numbers.

Sample citation

. . . The king's masquerade the night before the battle (*Henry V* 4.33-229) demonstrates an element common to a number of Shakespeare's plays. . . .

ABBREVIATIONS FOR CITATIONS

pt.	part
bk.	book
ch.	chapter
sec.	section
sc.	scene
par.	paragraph

4.34 FOOTNOTES AND ENDNOTES

The method of documentation described in Section 4.33 is the most used of many accepted systems. The alternatives to parenthetical documentation are footnoting and endnoting.

Footnotes. Instead of putting citations in parentheses within the text, you can place them at the bottom or foot of the page; hence the term **footnote**. With this system, a number or symbol identifies the citation, and a matching number or symbol is placed in the text at the location where the parenthetical citation would otherwise be. Besides their use for documentation, footnotes are also used to supply information useful but extraneous to the immediate purposes of the work. For example, *Literature and the Language Arts* uses numbered footnotes in the literature selections to define obscure words and to provide background information.

Endnotes. Because typists and publishers find it difficult to place notes at the bottom of pages, and because many readers find these notes distracting, many books use **endnotes** instead of footnotes. Endnotes are exactly like footnotes except that they are compiled at the end of a book, a chapter, or an article.

TEST-TAKING SKILLS

OBJECTIVE TESTS

4.35 STRATEGIES FOR TAKING OBJECTIVE TESTS

Your teacher's job is to help you learn. Your teacher may test you periodically to determine how well you have been learning what she or he has taught. Teachers also give tests as additional encouragement to students to learn. All teachers want their students—including you—to do well on their tests, because that shows that they have done their job well.

The way to do well on a classroom test is to study and work with the materials presented to you by your teacher. If you have a text, read it carefully. If your teacher gives lectures or leads discussions, take thorough notes of what is said.

STRATEGIES FOR TAKING OBJECTIVE TESTS

Before the Test
- Get ample sleep the night before the test.
- Eat a nutritious breakfast.
- Study over as long a period of time as possible.
- Review frequently.
- Try to predict questions that may be on the test, and make sure you can answer them.
- Bring *extra* pencils, erasers, and any other required materials.

During the Test
- Determine how much time is allowed for each question. If a question takes too long, guess and/or come back to it if you have time.
- *Read each question carefully.*
- Work quickly but do not rush.
- Write legibly.
- Review all your work before submitting it.

Whenever you are taking a test, skip a question that seems too difficult and go on to the next one. Make a note to return to the unanswered question(s) if you have extra time at the end of the test period.

4.36 TRUE/FALSE QUESTIONS

A true/false question gives you a statement and asks you to decide whether the statement is true or false. If you do not know the answer right away, try to guess.

You probably will not see many true/false tests because scores are too easily influenced by guessing. If you are given a true-false test, watch out for these potential traps:

Negatives and double negatives. The word *not* completely changes the meaning of a sentence. To evaluate a sentence with a negative, see if its opposite makes sense or is plausible. If so, the original must be false.

Quantifiers and qualifiers. Look for words such as *all, sometimes, never,* etc. These words control what a sentence really says.

Excess information. The more information a sentence contains, the more liable it is to be false. Be sure to evaluate all the claims a sentence makes before you judge it.

4.37 MULTIPLE-CHOICE QUESTIONS

Multiple-choice questions are perhaps the most widely used type of test question. A multiple-choice test item asks a question and then gives you a few possible answers from which to choose. Only one is correct; the others are called distracters. You must choose the *best* answer, even if none appears to you to be exactly correct.

If you know the answer from reading the question, look for it. However, some multiple-choice items can be answered only by evaluating all of the choices.

EXAMPLE   Which of the following is NOT a pilgrim from Chaucer's *Canterbury Tales*?
1. the wife of Bath   4. the miller
2. the reeve   5. none of the above
3. the physician

ANSWER TO MULTIPLE-CHOICE QUESTION

3. the physician

4.38 SHORT-ANSWER QUESTIONS

Short-answer questions are common on quizzes and in class discussions. Not surprisingly, a short-answer question calls for a short answer—a word, a phrase, or a sentence.

Most teachers require that all responses to short-answer questions be complete sentences. Your teacher will tell you whether you must provide complete sentences.

EXAMPLE   Who was Ozymandias?
He was an ancient king.

STANDARDIZED TESTS

4.39 STRATEGIES FOR TAKING STANDARDIZED TESTS

The most familiar standardized tests are created by private companies and used by colleges and other organizations to evaluate students as part of the process of granting admissions and scholarships. Standardized tests are also used by states and school districts to assess achievement.

SOME STANDARDIZED TESTS	
Common Abbreviation	**Test**
PSAT/NMSQT	Pre-Scholastic Aptitude Test/National Merit Scholarship Qualifying Test
ACT	American College Testing Program
MAT	Miller Analogies Test
SAT	Scholastic Aptitude Test
ACH	College Board Achievement Tests

These tests are all multiple-choice tests. Items are answered on special sheets that can be read and graded by a computer. You choose your answer by filling in or blackening a bubble. If you take one of these tests, be sure to use the type of pencil or pen specified by the test monitor. Also be sure to fill in bubbles *completely* and *neatly*.

| Not good | Not good: incomplete | Not good: stray marks | Good |

If you do not know the answer, you can at least try to rule out some of the choices and increase your chances.

If a question seems too difficult, remember that your best strategy is to skip it and go on to the next one. You can come back to it if you have extra time at the end of the test period. Blank spaces on your answer sheet will indicate which questions you have not answered. Note that while you can go back to questions within a section, most tests do not allow you to go back to a previous section. Always obey the instructions given to you by the test monitor.

4.40 ANALOGY QUESTIONS

Analogy questions ask you to select a pair of words that bear a particular relationship to each other. Instead of telling you explicitly what relationship you are to form, the test gives you another pair of words as an example.

TOWER: HEIGHT::

    (A) field : crop   (C) length : width   (E) tree : tall

    (B) ditch : depth   (D) car : distance

You can only answer analogy questions by examining *all* the answers. More than one answer may seem correct. Choose the *best* answer.

Do not be misled by irrelevant relationships between the words in the example and words in the choices. Focus on the *relationship between* the two words in the example.

4.41 SENTENCE-COMPLETION QUESTIONS

Sentence-completion questions present you with a sentence that has two words missing. You must select the pair of words that best completes the sentence.

EXAMPLE The completion of the new highway was largely _____ by the press, even though it was a major _____ for the mayor.

    (A) cheered . . . feat   (D) attended . . . expense

    (B) ignored . . . accomplishment   (E) heckled . . . loss

    (C) covered . . . coup

Sentence-completion questions require that you try all the choices to see which words work best in the sentence. You often can eliminate one or two answers right away because they do not fit syntactically or because they make no sense at all. When you come to try the correct answer, you may see a relationship that was not apparent before.

4.42 GRAMMAR, USAGE, AND MECHANICS QUESTIONS

There are at least three common types of grammar, usage, and mechanics questions. All of them present a sentence or paragraph containing underlined and labeled passages. **Error-identification questions** ask you to identify the passage that contains an error. You do not have to tell what type of error it is or correct the error. **Error-correction questions** ask you to correct the error by choosing a passage to replace it.

Example Error-identification Question

Choose the letter that corresponds to any error in the sentence.

Berenice Abbbot <u>began</u> her <u>photographic career</u> <u>as a</u> apprentice
           A   B   C

for Man Ray in the <u>Twenties</u>. <u>No error</u>.
               D   E

(A) (B) (C) (D) (E)

ESSENTIAL SKILLS: STUDY AND RESEARCH

ANSWER TO ANALOGY QUESTION

(B) ditch : depth

ANSWER TO SENTENCE-COMPLETION QUESTION

(B) ignored . . . accomplishment

ANSWER TO ERROR-IDENTIFICATION QUESTION

(C)

ANSWER TO ERROR-CORRECTION QUESTION

(D) wrote

ANSWER TO CONSTRUCTION-SHIFT QUESTION

(B) of the author

Example Error-correction Question

Select the letter of the word or words that should replace the underlined word.

Abbbot <u>writ</u> several books, including *New Guide to Better Photography*.
      1

1. (A) No change   (C) writed   (E) has wrote
    (B) writes   (D) wrote

ANSWERING ERROR-IDENTIFICATION AND ERROR-CORRECTION QUESTIONS

1. Ignore the underlining and proofread the sentence or paragraph carefully.
   • Proofread for errors in grammar, usage, and mechanics.
   • Look especially for agreement—in tense, person, number, and mood.
2. If you do not find the error, look specifically at the underlined passages.
3. Read the whole sentence through before settling on your answer.

Construction-shift questions give you a sentence and ask you to revise it in some specified way.

Example Construction-shift Question

Rewrite the following sentence according to the instruction. Then select the answer that best fits in the revised sentence.

Perhaps the most famous photo of James Joyce is Abbot's photo of the author with his cane and cocked fedora.

Begin with *Abbot's photo*

(A) Joyce, who wore   (C) famous.   (E) fedora, perhaps
(B) of the author   (D) fedora hat

ANSWERING CONSTRUCTION-SHIFT QUESTIONS

• Try to revise the whole sentence as directed.
• Make all necessary changes to avoid errors in grammar and usage.
• Make as few as possible changes in wording.
• Watch for word order and placement of modifiers.

There are usually a few ways in which to revise the sentence. You must find the word or word group that would be in the best possible sentence.

You can practice for all grammar, usage, and mechanics questions by studying the lessons in 2.1–2.133 of this Language Arts Survey, doing the Language Lab activities that follow the selections and units in this textbook, working the activities in the *Essential Skills Practice Book: Language,* and completing your reading and writing assignments conscientiously.

4.43 READING COMPREHENSION QUESTIONS

Reading comprehension questions precede or follow a short piece of writing. The questions address the content of the passage. Many questions will ask you to go beyond the text by making an inference or an interpretation.

STEPS IN ANSWERING READING COMPREHENSION QUESTIONS
1. Read all the questions quickly.
2. Read the passage.
3. Reread the first question carefully.
4. Reread the passage while bearing in mind the first question.
5. Answer the first question.
6. Continue with each subsequent question in the same manner.

To select the correct answer, you will have to try all the choices and select the best available. Be sure that you base your answers only on the passage and not on your own opinions.

4.44 SYNONYM AND ANTONYM QUESTIONS

Synonym and antonym questions give you a word and ask you to select the word that means the same or that means the opposite, respectively. You must select the *best* answer, even if none is exactly correct.

EXAMPLE Write the letter of the word that is most nearly *opposite* in meaning to the word in capital letters.
1. REASON
(A) stupidity   (B) instinct   (C) excuse   (D) error   (E) argument

Synonym and antonym questions require that you try all the choices to see which works best. The choices almost always include both synonyms and antonyms, so make sure that you remember whether you are working on a synonym or an antonym question.

Don't select an answer just because (1) it is similar to the given word in appearance or sound; (2) it shares with the given word a root, prefix, or suffix; or (3) it is a long or unfamiliar-sounding word.

ANSWER TO SYNONYM AND ANTONYM QUESTION

(B) instinct

ESSENTIAL SKILLS: STUDY AND RESEARCH

STRATEGIES FOR TAKING ESSAY TESTS

4.45 ANALYZING AN ESSAY QUESTION

It would appear obvious that you cannot do well on an essay test if you do not understand the essay question. Yet, worried about finishing on time, many students don't take the trouble to make sure they do understand before they begin writing.

After reading the *whole* question carefully, look for key words in the question that indicate what is expected. Underline or circle these words if you are permitted; otherwise, write them on your own note paper. Many questions ask for more than one type of response. Be careful to answer *all* parts of the question.

UNDERSTANDING AN ESSAY QUESTION	
Type of Essay Question	**Tasks of Essay**
analyze (1.14, 1.33, 4.11)	break into parts and describe the parts and their relationships
compare; compare and contrast (1.33, 4.8)	identify and describe similarities and differences
describe; explain (1.33, 4.6)	tell the steps in a process; identify causes and effects
define; describe; identify (4.7)	classify and tell the features of
interpret (4.13)	tell the meaning and significance of
summarize (4.30)	retell very briefly, stating only the main points
argue; prove; show (4.12)	tell and evaluate reasons for believing a statement

4.46 ORGANIZING AN ANSWER TO AN ESSAY QUESTION

In most testing situations, you do not have time to go through the entire writing process. Part of your planning must include allocating your time. Allow time for planning, drafting, and reviewing. If you plan and pace yourself, you will have no reason to worry about running out of time.

Perhaps the most important thing you can do is to plan your essay before you begin writing. The organization of your essay can show your insight, understanding, and originality, even if you do not have time to complete your plan. Make an outline and add notes about points you will make and details, examples, or quotations you can use. Later, if you find yourself running out of time, you would do better to complete the essay by making your main points briefly and without elaboration than to end the essay without a conclusion.

Work hard to write a clear introduction. Your introduction should state your main point or points and present your plan for the essay. As you write each paragraph or section of your essay, check the introduction to see that you are still on track.

You can revise your writing as you go, but watch that you do not use all your time editing an incomplete essay.

4.47 REVIEWING AN ANSWER TO AN ESSAY QUESTION

Before you submit your completed essay, take as much time as you can to review it and apply any polish.

<table>
<tr><td>

QUESTIONS FOR REVIEWING AN ANSWER TO AN ESSAY QUESTION

- Does the essay answer all parts of the question?
- Does the introduction state clearly the main point of the essay?
- Is the conclusion consistent with the main point?
- Does the essay cover all the points in your outline?
- Are there any points that could be made more strongly or clearly?
- Is every word in the essay easily legible?
- Is the essay free of errors in grammar, usage, and mechanics?

</td></tr>
</table>

ESSENTIAL SKILLS: STUDY AND RESEARCH

▶ Use the Pretest and Post-test on Applied English/Tech Prep Skills, 3.5.1–3.5.2, in the *Assessment Portfolio.*

ESSENTIAL SKILLS:
Applied English/Tech Prep

LETTERS AND FORMS

Long after you've written your last high-school essay or college term paper, you'll be using your writing skills in a variety of day-to-day situations. Whether you're corresponding with a loan officer at the bank, writing to a friend across the country, communicating via electronic mail with a co-worker, or penning a thank-you note to a thoughtful aunt, you'll want to take care to ensure that your writing reflects your intentions precisely, conveying your thoughts or feelings or any pertinent information.

Familiarizing yourself with the conventions of letter-writing can help you achieve a positive outcome, particularly when addressing correspondence to individuals or groups who don't know you personally.

5.1 FILLING OUT FORMS AND APPLICATIONS

▶ Use the Study Guide and Test for Letters and Forms, 5.10.1–5.10.2, in the *Assessment Portfolio.*

In our information-based society, forms and applications are ubiquitous. Because they're such efficient mechanisms for collecting data, you can expect to encounter them regularly, in such diverse locations as the doctor's office, the bank, your local dry-cleaning establishment, or a favorite mail-order catalog.

When completing a form or application, you should have two objectives: to provide the information requested and to make a positive impression.

Guidelines for completing forms:
- If possible, obtain an extra copy of the form or application.
- Gather any information you will need to complete the form.
- Read all the directions before you begin to enter your data.
- Be neat. Type or print your responses legibly, in pencil or ink, as directed. Avoid smudges or cross-outs.
- Write "N.A." or "not applicable," rather than leave a space blank, if a section of the form or application does not apply to you.
- Proofread. When you've completed the form, check your spelling, grammar, and punctuation, and review the information you've provided.
- If the form is messy or inaccurate, discard it and complete the extra form or application if you have one.
- When you've completed the form to your satisfaction, submit it to the appropriate person, or mail it to the correct address.

Application for Employment
Brennan's Book Emporium

Position Desired: Sales Clerk

Personal Data

Applicant's Name: Mello Jennifer M.
Last name First Name Middle Initial

Address: 55 Dartmouth St. Brobdingnag Ohio 00703
Street City State Zip

Phone: (586) 555-3250 Date of Birth: 5/10/78

Previous Work Experience

(List last two positions held, beginning with the most recent.)

Employer: Ms. Janice Ingram 17 Howe St., Brobdingnag, Ohio 00703
Name Address

Phone: (586) 555-8020

Employment Period: 1/95–present

Job Title: Tutor

Hours worked: Flexible, 5–10 hrs./wk.

Salary: $5.00/hr.

Description: Help employer's ten-year-old daughter improve her math skills

Reason for leaving: N.A.

Employer: John and Sandra Neils 48 Dart St., Brobdingnag, Ohio 00703
Name Address

Phone: (586) 555-5440

Employment Period: 7/95–9/95

Job Title: Nanny

Hours Worked: 8:30–4:30, Monday–Friday

Salary: $4.50/hr.

Description: Cared for two children, ages 4 and 6, in their home

Reason for Leaving: Returned to school following summer vacation

CONTINUED

Education
(List last school attended.)

Brobdingnag High School	Brobdingnag, OH	9/92–	College prep.	6/96
School Name	*Address*	*Dates Attended*	*Field of Study*	*Date Graduated*

References

Name: Ms. Caroline Sweeney

Relationship to
job applicant: Teacher   Years Acquainted: 2

Address: 14 Howel St., Shalott, Ohio   00702   Phone: (586) 555-1182

Name: Mr. George Humphrey

Relationship to
job applicant: Teacher   Years Acquainted: 2

Address: 7 Main St., Shalott, Ohio   00702   Phone: (586) 555-4725

Signature: *Jennifer M. Mello*   Date: 9/14/95

5.2 THE FORM OF A PERSONAL LETTER

If you check your home mailbox today, you may find it stuffed with bills, magazines, catalogs, and miscellaneous junk mail. Imagine, though, your response if you were to discover a cache of personal letters, cards, and invitations, all addressed to you. A few decades ago, when society relied more heavily on the postal service and less on telecommunications, such a discovery might not have been unusual.

Although we still enjoy receiving personal correspondence, most of us now reach for the telephone—rather than the pen, typewriter, or computer keyboard—when we want to communicate with friends or distant family members. When, however, you sit down to compose a letter, you allow yourself time to develop your thoughts more carefully and express them more deliberately than you would in conversation. Furthermore, written communications, which can be saved and savored time and again, tend to carry more weight than spontaneous comments.

A personal letter may be relatively informal, depending on the writer's relationship with the intended recipient. It will typically include the following:

1. a **return address**, including the writer's address and the date the letter was composed;
2. a **salutation**, or greeting, followed by a comma;
3. the **body**, or text, of the letter;
4. an appropriate **closing**, followed by a comma;
5. a **signature**; and
6. an optional **postscript**, preceded by the abbreviation "P.S."

SAMPLE THANK-YOU LETTER

❶
1430 Hawthorne St.
Lilliput, MO 00117
August 14, 1998

❷ Dear Aunt Rose,

❸   Thank you so much for the great old baseball cap. Where did you ever find it? I'd like to know all the details.
    Over the years you've sent me some wonderful presents, but this gift is a treasure. You know I love memorabilia, and baseball is the only game for me.
    Thanks again, from the bottom of my muddy cleats.

❹   Your appreciative nephew,

                                       Dave
❺

❻   P.S. If you come across any more Brooklyn Dodgers memorabilia, please continue to keep me in mind. (My next birthday is only 360 days away.)

5.3   The Form of a Business Letter

The first rule when writing a business letter is to take nothing for granted. Because your business letters will typically be addressed to strangers or business acquaintances, you can't assume that the individuals receiving them will respond positively to them, or to you, the writer. It's up to you to make a good impression. When composing a business letter, it makes sense to be conservative. If you adhere to widely accepted business conventions, your letter is more likely to be well-received.

Like a typical personal letter, a business letter includes a **return address, salutation, body, closing,** and **signature**. In addition, it includes one more component, called the **inside address**. It will occasionally include a **postscript.** The inside address, located below the heading and above the salutation, will include the name and title of the person to whom you're writing (or a department name, if you're not writing to a specific individual), the name of the company or organization, and its address.

It is important that the salutation and closing of a business letter be respectful and formal. The salutation typically begins with the word "Dear," followed by the courtesy or professional title used in the inside address. "Ms.," "Mr.," "Dr.," "Miss," or "Mrs." are among the appropriate choices. If you aren't writing to a specific person, you can use a salutation such as "Dear Sir or Madam" or "Ladies and Gentlemen." The salutation is followed by a colon.

In a business letter, it isn't advisable to use a creative closing. Acceptable closings include "Very truly yours," "Sincerely," "Sincerely yours," and "Respectfully yours." Note that only the first word of the closing is capitalized.

Sign your name, in either blue or black ink, below the closing. Your full name should be typed below your signature.

Business letters are usually structured in either **block form** or **modified block form**. In **block form** (see 5.4, "Types of Business Letters I"), each of the letter's components—the heading, inside address, salutation, body, closing, and signature—begin at the left margin. Paragraphs are not indented. In **modified block form** (see 5.5, "Types of Business Letters II"), the return address and closing are aligned along an imaginary line located a bit to the right of the center of the page. Paragraphs are indented, typically five spaces from the left margin.

Throughout your letter, try to maintain a courteous, formal tone. Use standard English and avoid slang expressions. Outline your main points before you begin to compose the letter, organizing your thoughts so that your letter will be clear, easy to read, and as brief as possible. Remember to review your grammar, punctuation, and spelling. Your reader will form an impression of you based on what he or she sees on the page.

Guidelines for Writing a Business Letter
- Outline your letter's main points before you begin the writing process.
- Type your letter, if at all possible, and use clean 8$\frac{1}{2}$×11 white or off-white paper. Type on one side of the paper only.
- Select a standard business-letter format, either block form or modified block form.
- Use single-spacing, leaving a blank line between paragraphs.
- Select a standard salutation and closing.
- Stick to the subject, keeping the letter brief and informative.
- Be neat. A sloppy appearance may make your letter less effective.
- Check your grammar, usage, punctuation, capitalization, and spelling.
- Reread your letter. Have you conveyed your main points clearly and effectively? Don't make your reader guess at your intentions.

5.4 TYPES OF BUSINESS LETTERS I

You will come across many opportunities for composing business correspondence. For example, you may want to obtain a schedule of evening classes from a local community college, commend your local fire fighters for their prompt response to an emergency, or inform the telephone company of an error on your bill.

In any of these cases, you might consider making a phone call instead of sending a letter, but a phone call may be less effective. People are often more attentive to written requests than to verbal requests. Moreover, when you write a letter, you can save a copy of your correspondence either electronically (if you've keyed your letter on a computer) or by making a photocopy. Your copy of the letter will then serve as a record of your contact with the individual or group in question.

Letters of commendation are especially welcome. A pat on the back or a verbal "thank you" is nice, but people appreciate it when you go to the extra effort of expressing your thanks in a letter.

SAMPLE LETTER OF REQUEST

14 English Street
Geatland, MA 01970
May 10, 1995

Book Committee
Geatland Public Library
370 Essex Street
Geatland, MA 01970

Ladies and Gentlemen:

While researching a term paper for a recent school assignment, I came across a reference to a book by Lisa Yount entitled *Contemporary Women Scientists.* According to the reference, the book includes biographies of contemporary women who have made significant contributions to modern science.

I had hoped to obtain the book from the library and was disappointed to find that it is not available. Since the book is relatively new, I checked with the librarian to see if it might be on order. He said that it was not.

May I respectfully request that you consider purchasing *Contemporary Women Scientists* for our library? The library includes few books on women scientists, and I believe that this book could introduce young women in our community to positive role models, inspiring some who may never have considered the possibility of pursuing a career in the sciences or encouraging others who, like myself, have already decided to do so.

Sincerely yours,

Zenobia Mafouz

Zenobia Mafouz

5.5 TYPES OF BUSINESS LETTERS II

Perhaps the most important letters you will ever write will be those you address to potential employers. The care you take in preparing these letters will help determine the jobs you'll be hired to fill, and hence the course of your career.

When applying for a job, you commonly submit both a **résumé** and a letter of application, or **cover letter**. Together, these documents should present a brief history of your education, skills, and work experience, highlighting your assets and suggesting how your unique mix of skills and abilities might benefit the organization you hope to join.

The information presented in your résumé and cover letter must be honest and accurate, but you should never minimize or discount the value of your experience. Design your résumé and cover letter in a way that makes the most of what you have to offer, presenting yourself to the reader in a positive light.

While your résumé should be relatively detailed, you will probably want to write it so that it won't require substantial editing each time you apply for a job. The cover letter accompanying your résumé, on the other hand, should address the specific needs of the particular organization to which you are applying.

Guidelines for composing a cover letter:

- Limit your cover letter to a single page.
- State your interest in obtaining a position within the organization, indicating the type of position (or specific job opening) for which you'd like to be considered.
- If you are applying for a specific position, describe how you learned of the job's availability.
- Briefly describe your qualifications.
- Refer to your résumé, enclosed with your letter.
- Mention your interest in scheduling an interview and where and when you may be reached (typically by telephone) to make arrangements.
- Thank the reader for considering your application.

SAMPLE COVER LETTER

423 Rock Ribbon Road
Underhill, OR 00604
June 3, 1998

John Freemont
Managing Editor
The Underhill Examiner
445 Main Street
Underhill, OR 00604

Dear Mr. Freemont:

I recently learned from my high school guidance counselor, Ms. Elizabeth Rowley, that you may be interested in hiring a summer intern to work as an editorial assistant. I would very much like to be considered for that position.

My interest in journalism dates to middle school when I contributed weekly sports bulletins to the school newsletter, *The Burdick Banner*. At West Underhill High, where I am now a junior, I write and edit news articles for *The Chronicle*.

As you can see from my resume, I have computer experience. I am also a proficient typist.

Please call me at 555-8052 if you are interested in arranging an interview. I can usually be reached at that number after 4:00 PM, any weekday.

Thank you for your consideration.

Sincerely,

Consuelo Alvarez

Consuelo Alvarez

Enclosure

The information you include in your résumé may be organized in many different ways. Your guidance counselor or librarian may have a file of sample résumés for you to review. Select a style that looks neat and businesslike. Most résumés list the applicant's **objective** or career goal, **work experience, education, extracurricular activities, skills**, and **references**.

Try to limit your résumé to a single page. It should be typed and printed on high-quality paper, preferably the same paper stock used for your cover letter. Check the quality of the print to make sure it's easy to read.

SAMPLE RÉSUMÉ

Consuelo Alvarez
423 Rock Ribbon Road
Underhill, OR 00604
(995) 555-8052

Objective:

To obtain an entry-level editorial position with a daily newspaper.

Work Experience:

Summer 1994 Editorial Assistant, _Underhill Weekly,_ Underhill, OR

Proofread advertising copy and helped lay out ad pages using layout software running on a personal computer.

9/94–6/96 Clerical Assistant, Office Outlet, Inc., Underhill, OR
Provided part-time, miscellaneous office assistance to the three-person staff of a small retail operation specializing in office supplies.

Education:

West Underhill High School, Class of '96. College Preparatory program
Citation for Excellence in Feature Writing awarded by Journalism Department
Advanced Placement (AP) class in French
Grade-point average: 3.2/4.0

Extracurricular Activities:

Assistant Editor, *The Chronicle*
French Club
Treasurer, Ski Club

References:

Mr. Tyrone Griffith
Owner, Office Outlet, Inc.
Underhill, OR
(995) 555-7594

Ms. Chandra Patel
Editor, *Norwalk Ad Week*
Underhill, OR
(995) 555-9183

WRITING ON THE JOB

In the course of your working life, regardless of whether you choose to become a professional writer, you will have many opportunities to write.

A common complaint heard from employers today is that many employees can't write well enough to communicate with one another or with the clients with whom they interact. Without question, learning to organize your thoughts on paper will serve you well on the job. Sometimes it isn't what you know but how you communicate your knowledge to others, that makes the difference.

5.6 WRITING MEMORANDA

When employees of an organization need to communicate with one another, they often do so via interoffice **memoranda**, or **memos**. A memo may be forwarded from one employee to another or circulated throughout an entire organization, and it can be used to communicate information and ideas on a wide variety of topics. A manager may write a memo to schedule a meeting, to announce changes in an office policy or procedure, or to delegate an assignment, for example.

Today's employees typically compose and type their memos at their computer workstations, forwarding them to one another over a computer network via electronic mail, called "e-mail" for short. Small companies, or those that don't make extensive use of computers, may provide their employees with standard memo forms.

Memos are usually brief but can be used to circulate lengthy reports. Of course, even a short memo must be clear and to the point. Reviewing the memo and proofreading it before photocopying and distributing it or striking that e-mail "send" button can prevent embarrassing errors.

The tone of a memo will depend largely on the memo's topic and the writer's relationship to the person receiving the memo.

Although memos typically communicate work-related information, they also serve a social function. A memo may be circulated regarding an upcoming party for a departing coworker, for example, or serve as an invitation to lunch.

SAMPLE MEMO

Note the "cc" line on the sample form. On the "cc" line, the author includes the name of anyone who will receive a copy of the memo. (The "cc" is an abbreviation for "carbon copy." Today, most companies circulate photocopies or electronic copies of memos rather than carbon copies.)

5.7 TECHNICAL WRITING

If you peruse the Help Wanted section in your Sunday newspaper, you're likely to see many advertisements announcing job openings for technical writers. These ads are typically placed by companies looking for individuals who can write **documentation** to accompany complex products that would be difficult to use without proper explanation and instruction.

The manuals and user guides that technical writers produce help consumers, medical personnel, automobile and aircraft mechanics, and others working with sophisticated equipment. For example, a technical writer may produce documentation to help consumers use a word processing package designed to run on a personal computer or write a manual

Note the "cc" line on the sample form. On the "cc" line, the author includes the name of anyone who will receive a copy of the memo. (The "cc" is an abbreviation for "carbon copy." Today, most companies circulate photocopies or electronic copies of memos rather than carbon copies.)

5.7 TECHNICAL WRITING

If you peruse the Help Wanted section in your Sunday newspaper, you're likely to see many advertisements announcing job openings for technical writers. These ads are typically placed by companies looking for individuals who can write **documentation** to accompany complex products that would be difficult to use without proper explanation and instruction.

The manuals and user guides that technical writers produce help consumers, medical personnel, automobile and aircraft mechanics, and others working with sophisticated equipment. For example, a technical writer may produce documentation to help consumers use a word processing package designed to run on a personal computer or write a manual explaining how to use an electronic data collector to survey a parcel of land.

Nearly every worker, regardless of his or her profession, will eventually be in the position of having to explain a procedure or complex process in writing. A future employer may one day ask you to write a training manual for new employees or to document a procedure that you are familiar with so that others may learn it as well.

If you find yourself in a similar situation, you will benefit by incorporating the basics of good technical writing. Poor documentation can lead to costly, embarrassing, or dangerous mistakes.

Guidelines for documenting technical procedures:

- First, make sure you are very familiar with the procedure you'll be documenting.
- Break the task into a series of short, simple steps.
- Warn the reader of any potentially hazardous steps or materials.
- List any tools or equipment needed to complete the process.
- List each step in the proper sequence.
- Use the second person imperative. Write "Press the enter key," not "The user should press the enter key."
- Keep your vocabulary simple, avoiding unexplained technical jargon.
- If appropriate, incorporate pictures and diagrams.
- Don't leave out any steps or include unnecessary steps.
- Proofread your instructions to make sure they are easy to follow and unambiguous.
- Ask someone who isn't familiar with the operation to follow the directions you have written. If necessary, adjust your instructions based on his or her experience.

Writing documentation can both test just how careful a writer you are and indicate how well you understand the material you are trying to explain. Indeed, you may find that you understand a process better after you have written about it. You won't know how well you have succeeded, though, until your readers try to follow your instructions and you learn whether they have achieved satisfactory results.

Replacing the Strings of the Carcassi Steel-String Guitar

Materials needed:

One set of steel guitar strings (Medium tension silk and steel strings are recommended.)

Steps:

Warning: Never remove more than one string at a time. Doing so could cause warping and thus damage the guitar.

1. Remove the old sixth or low "E" string by twisting the corresponding tuning peg clockwise.

2. Replace the low "E" string by feeding the new string through the sixth hole in the bridge, up the neck of the guitar, and through the corresponding tuning peg hole.

3. Make sure that the new low "E" string is resting in the lowest groove in the nut (the raised white piece) at the top of the guitar neck.

4. Tune the new low "E" string by turning the tuning peg counterclockwise until the string produces the appropriate note when struck.

5. Repeat steps 1 through 4, removing and replacing the rest of the strings, one at a time.

5.8   WRITING PROMOTIONAL AND PUBLIC RELATIONS COPY

Writers of promotional and public relations, or **PR**, copy are practitioners of a delicate art. They must learn to capture a reader's attention and gain his or her sympathy, with the goal of persuading the reader to purchase a product or accept a particular viewpoint. Their task requires proficiency in the craft of writing; an in-depth understanding of their product, organization, or cause; and an ability to empathize with readers and predict their responses.

Promotional and public relations writers are responsible for writing a host of materials, including press releases; radio, television, and newspaper ads; direct mail copy; speeches; news and feature articles; scripts for films, tapes, and slide shows; letters to newspaper and magazine editors; and annual reports. They may work in the service of big corporations or small nonprofit organizations, persuading their audiences to spend their money, make donations, or modify their behavior. They may write fast-food jingles, draft political speeches, or pen slogans for an antismoking campaign.

Writing a good promotional or public relations piece requires research and planning. If the writer's copy isn't grounded in reality, reflecting a product or organization's real merits, it may ultimately fail and spark a negative backlash.

Although you may never work in PR, studying the basic principles of good promotional writing can help make your writing more effective. Like a good promotional writer, you should make a habit of asking yourself one important question: How will my reader react?

SAMPLE PRESS RELEASE

For release: immediately
Contact person: Janice Ingram

Public Relations
Department
(617) 555-7800

Boston, MA, July 10, 1998. Micromind Software, Inc., maker of the world's leading word processing software, Micromind Word, announced today that it will merge with Blueline Business, Inc., maker of Countdown, a popular accounting software package.

Bob Garcia, president of Micromind, made the announcement at a press conference here at the Keynes Convention Center. The announced merger, effective immediately, will strengthen the competitive positions of both Micromind and Blueline, Garcia said. "Together, we will develop the software that will be adopted by the corporate leaders of the twenty-first century," said Garcia. The new company, to be called Micromind Business, Inc., will be the world's leading software vendor.

Garcia will continue to head the firm, while Blueline Business president Louise Antonelli will be named Vice President of Research and Development. Micromind Business will be headquartered in Framingham, MA, presently the home of Micromind Software.

Founded in 1978, Micromind, Software Inc., employs over forty-five hundred workers in twenty-three countries. In addition to Micromind Word, the company offers EasyMail, an electronic mail system, and MicroCalendar, an automated scheduling system.

HANDBOOK OF
Literary Terms

abridgment An **abridgment** is a shortened version of a work. When doing an abridgment, an editor attempts to preserve the most significant elements of the original. See also *abstract, bowdlerize,* and *paraphrase.*

abstract 1. *n.* An **abstract**, *précis,* or **summary** is a brief account of the main ideas or arguments presented in a work. A well-made abstract presents those ideas or arguments in the same order as in the original. Writing an abstract is an excellent way to commit to memory the major ideas of a nonfiction work such as an essay or a chapter in a textbook. See *paraphrase.* 2. *adj.* An **abstract** word or phrase is one that refers to something that cannot be directly perceived by the senses. *Freedom, justice, integrity, dignity,* and *loyalty* are examples of abstract terms. The opposite of *abstract* in this sense is *concrete.* See *concrete.*

absurd See *literature of the absurd.*

accent See *stress.*

acronym An **acronym** is a word created from the first, or initial, letters of a series of words. Examples of acronyms include *scuba,* from the words *self-contained underwater breathing apparatus,* and *radar,* from *radio detecting and ranging.*

acrostic An **acrostic** is a poem organized so that the first or last letters of each line form a word, a phrase, or a regular sequence of letters of the alphabet.

act An **act** is a major division of a drama. The dramas of ancient Rome were generally divided into five acts, as were the plays of Shakespeare and other dramatists of the Elizabethan Age. In modern times, plays are most often divided into three acts, and short plays called "one-acts" are quite common.

action The **action** is the sequence of events that actually occur in a literary work, as opposed to those that occur off-scene or that precede or follow the events in the work itself. A common literary technique, inherited from the classical *epic,* is to begin a work *in medias res,* in the middle of the action, and to fill in the background details later through flashbacks. See *flashback.*

actor An **actor** is one who performs the role of a character in a play. The term is now used both for male and female performers.

adage See *proverb.*

adaptation An **adaptation** is a rewriting of a literary work in another form. In modern times, adaptations for film are often made of successful novels, musicals, and plays. *My Fair Lady* was an adaptation for the musical theater and later for film of George Bernard Shaw's play *Pygmalion.*

aesthetics **Aesthetics** is the philosophical study of beauty. *Aesthetic principles* are guidelines established for the making and judging of works of art. From age to age, accepted aesthetic principles have differed, and these differences have dramatically influenced the nature of works of art produced in those ages. For example, the ancient Greek philosopher Aristotle propounded an aesthetic of *mimesis,* or *imitation,* believing that the proper function of art was to provide an accurate portrayal of life, an idea perhaps best expressed in Shakespeare's description of dramatic art as "a mirror held up to nature." In sharp contrast to such an aesthetic is the idea, derived from the Greek philosopher Plato, that the function of art is to rise above ordinary nature and to embody ideal, or *sublime,* forms of a kind not found in this material world of the ordinary and transient.

In England and the United States, the dominant aesthetics have been the Neoclassical, dating from the eighteenth century; the Romantic, dating from the nineteenth century; and the Realistic and Naturalistic, dating from the late nineteenth and early twentieth centuries.

The Neoclassical aesthetic values order, rationality, and artifice. The Romantic aesthetic values wildness, emotion, imagination, and nature. The Realist aesthetic harkens back to Aristotle and values imitation, but imitation of a modern kind—of the depths as well as the heights of human experience. The Naturalistic aesthetic, like the Realistic, views the purpose of art as the accurate imitation of life, but it also attempts to show how all things, including human actions, thoughts, and feelings, are caused, or determined, by circumstances.

The critic I. A. Richards claimed that a radical shift away from an aesthetic based on beauty to one based on interest occurred in the twentieth century. While beauty, however defined, remains the guiding principle of artistic judgment in low-brow circles—as for example, in popular judgments made about sentimental novels and verses—interest, both intellectual and emotional, has emerged as the primary standard by which professional critics today judge works of art. See *Naturalism*, *Neoclassicism*, *Realism*, and *Romanticism*.

affective fallacy   The **affective fallacy** is the evaluation of works of art based not on their artistic merit but rather on their emotional effects on the reader, viewer, or listener. A person who holds a didactic or utilitarian view of the function of art would not consider this approach a fallacy. See *didacticism* and *Utilitarianism*.

afterword   An **afterword** is a statement made at the end of a work, often an analysis, a summary, or a celebration of the preceding work. See *epilogue*.

Age of Reason   See *Enlightenment* and *Neoclassicism*.

aim   A writer's **aim** is the primary purpose that his or her work is meant to achieve. One commonly used method of classifying writing by aim, proposed by James Kinneavey in *A Theory of Discourse*, describes four major aims: to express oneself (expressive writing), to persuade (persuasive writing), to inform (informative writing), and to create a work of literary art (literary writing).

Alexandrine   An **Alexandrine**, or **iambic hexameter**, is a verse with six iambic feet. The Spenserian stanza used by Edmund Spenser in *The Færie Queene* contained eight pentameter, or five-foot, lines followed by an Alexandrine. See *meter*.

allegory   An **allegory** is a work in which each element *symbolizes*, or represents, something else. In *naive allegory*, of the kind found in *Everyman* or in *The Pilgrim's Progress*, characters, objects, places, and actions are personifications of abstractions such as Good Deeds, Beauty, Vanity, and the journey to the Celestial Kingdom. In more sophisticated allegories, such as Spenser's *The Færie Queene*, the elements of the work make up an *extended metaphor* in which the literal elements are described but their part-by-part interpretation is left up to the reader. In one sense, all literature can be viewed as allegorical in that individual characters, objects, places, and actions are types representing others of their kind. See *concrete universal* and *extended metaphor*.

alliteration   **Alliteration** is the repetition of initial consonant sounds. Some writers use the term as well to describe repeated initial vowel sounds. The following line from Gray's "Elegy Written in a Country Churchyard" contains three examples of alliteration: the repetition of the *pl* sound in *plowman* and *plods*, the repetition of the *h* sound in *homeward* and *his*, and the repetition of the *w* sound in *weary* and *way*.

> The **pl**owman **h**omeward **pl**ods **h**is
> **w**eary **w**ay.

Alliteration was the primary organizing principle of Anglo-Saxon verse. See *Anglo-Saxon verse*.

allusion   An **allusion** is a rhetorical technique in which reference is made to a person, event, object, or work from history or literature. Auden's poem "Musée des Beaux Arts" alludes, or refers, to a painting of the fall of Icarus by Pieter Brueghel.

ambiguity   An **ambiguity** is a statement that has a double meaning or a meaning that cannot be clearly resolved. In English, the word *cleave* is oddly ambiguous, for it can mean either "to cling together" or "to cut apart." Many literary *figures of speech*, including *metaphors, similes, personifications*, and *symbols*, are examples of intentional ambiguity, speaking of one thing when another is intended. The witches' statement to Macbeth that "no man of woman born" can harm him is an example of ambiguity. It can be taken to mean that no man can harm Macbeth, for it is natural to assume that all men are "of woman born."

However, as the play turns out, the statement is actually a reference to Macduff, who was "from his mother's womb untimely ripped," that is, delivered by Cæsarean section and not, therefore, conventionally "born."

amplification   See *elaboration*.

anachronism   An **anachronism** is a reference to something that did not exist at the time being described. Thus a reference to a watch in a modern retelling of an Arthurian romance would be an anachronism because watches had not been invented in the time of King Arthur.

anagram   An **anagram** is a word or a phrase created by rearranging the letters of another word or phrase. The title of Samuel Butler's novel *Erewhon* is an anagram for *nowhere*. See *palindrome*.

analects   **Analects** are collections of passages from the works of one or more authors. A famous example of such a collection is *The Analects* of the Chinese philosopher Confucius.

analogy   An **analogy** is a comparison of two things that are alike in some respects but different in others. In an analogy, the comparison is direct, not implied. A *simile* is a type of analogy. See *simile*.

analysis   **Analysis** is a thinking strategy in which one divides a subject into parts and then examines the relationships among the parts and between individual parts and the whole. An analysis of a short story, for example, might consist of a division of the work into such parts as the exposition, the rising action, the climax, the resolution, and the dénouement, along with an examination of the role played by each of these parts in advancing the plot. An analysis of a line of poetry might consist of a careful examination of its rhythm, its figures of speech, its images, and its meaning or meanings.

anapest   An **anapest** is a poetic foot containing two weakly stressed syllables followed by one strongly stressed syllable, as in the words *unimpressed* and *correlate*. A line of poetry made up of anapests is said to be *anapestic*.

anaphora   An **anaphora**, as that term is used by linguists, is any word or phrase that repeats or refers to something that precedes or follows it. Consider, for example, the opening line of Percy Shelley's "Ode to the West Wind":

> O Wild West Wind, thou breath of
> Autumn's being

In this line, *thou* and *breath of Autumn's being* are both examples of anaphora because they refer back to, or rename, the West Wind. The simplest form of anaphora is repetition of a word or phrase, as in the repetition of the word *Camelot* in Tennyson's "The Lady of Shalott."

anecdote   An **anecdote** is a brief story, usually with a specific point or moral. See *exemplum*.

Anglo-Norman literature   **Anglo-Norman literature** is the literature written in French by the Norman conquerors of England. Anglo-Norman literature, along with literature written in Latin, dominated English literary life for two centuries following the Norman Conquest in 1066. Examples of this literature are the *lais*, or songs, of Marie de France.

Anglo-Saxon   See *Old English*.

Anglo-Saxon Era   The **Anglo-Saxon Era** is the period of English history dating from the Anglo-Saxon invasion of England in the mid-fifth century to the invasion of England by the Normans in 1066. It was during the Anglo-Saxon Era that English literature and the English language were born. See *Old English*.

Anglo-Saxon verse   **Anglo-Saxon verse** is the poetic form used in most Old English poetry. This poetry does not rhyme. It consists of lines that typically have four strong stresses, or beats. In the middle of the line is a pause, or cæsura. Often, the first three stressed words in the line alliterate, or begin with the same sound. An example of Anglo-Saxon verse can be found on page 84.

antagonist   See *character*.

antihero   An **antihero** is a central character who lacks all the qualities traditionally associated with heroes. An antihero may be lacking in beauty, courage, grace, intelligence, or moral scruples. Antiheroes are common figures in modern fiction and drama.

antithesis   **Antithesis** is a rhetorical technique in which words, phrases, or ideas are strongly contrasted, often by means of a repetition of grammatical structure. An example is Pope's description of the ideal critic in "An Essay on Criticism," who is "Still pleased to praise, yet not afraid to blame."

aphorism   An **aphorism** is a short saying or pointed statement. Examples of aphorisms include Tennyson's "Better to have loved and lost/Than never to have loved at all" and Shakespeare's "All the world's a stage." An aphorism that gains currency and is passed from generation to generation is called a *proverb* or *adage*. See *proverb*.

apocrypha **Apocrypha** are works that are doubtful in their origin or authorship. The term was first used to describe works from Biblical times not considered to be divinely inspired. It is now sometimes used to describe works of doubtful authorship. Examples of Shakespearean apocrypha, works attributed to Shakespeare but on questionable evidence, include "A Lover's Complaint" and "The Passionate Pilgrim."

apology An **apology** is a literary defense. Famous examples include Plato's *Apology,* which defends Socrates against the charges of impiety brought against him, and Sir Philip Sidney's "Defense of Poesy," which presents an argument for the value of poetry, claiming that the poet can create a world more beautiful than the real one.

apostrophe An **apostrophe** is a rhetorical technique in which an object or person is directly addressed. Examples include Milton's invocation of the Muse at the beginning of *Paradise Lost* and Percy Shelley's "Ode to the West Wind." See *Muse.*

apposition An **apposition** is a grammatical form in which a thing is renamed, in different words, in a word, phrase, or clause. An example of extended apposition is John of Gaunt's description of his country in Shakespeare's *Richard II:*

> This royal throne of kings, this scepter'd
>   isle,
> This earth of majesty, this seat of Mars,
> This other Eden, demi-paradise,
> This fortress built by Nature for herself
> Against infection and the hand of war,
> This happy breed of men, this little world,
> This precious stone set in a silver sea . . .
> This blessed plot, this earth, this realm, this
>   England.

archaic language **Archaic language** consists of old or obsolete words or phrases such as *smote* for *hit*. Spenser uses intentionally archaic language in *The Færie Queene* to transport his readers back to the days of chivalry and romance.

archetype An **archetype** is an inherited, often unconscious ancestral memory or motif that recurs throughout history and literature. The notion of the archetype derives from the psychology of Carl Jung, who wrote of archetypes as making up humanity's "collective unconscious." The term is often used, more generally, to refer to any element that recurs throughout the literature of the world. Thus the story of the journey, in which someone sets out on a path, experiences adventures, and emerges wiser, may be considered archetypal, for it is found in all cultures and in all times. See *motif.*

argument 1. An **argument** is a summary, in prose, of the plot or meaning of a poem or drama. An example is the introduction to Coleridge's "The Rime of the Ancient Mariner." 2. In nonfiction writing, an **argument** is the case for accepting or rejecting a proposition or course of action.

argumentation **Argumentation**, one of the modes of writing, presents reasons or arguments for accepting a position or for adopting a course of action. See *mode.*

art for art's sake **Art for art's sake** was the rallying cry of a group of nineteenth-century writers, among them Walter Pater, who believed that art should serve the ends of beauty and beauty alone, rather than some political, social, religious, or moral purpose. Other champions of art for art's sake included Oscar Wilde, Andrew Lang, and the American Edgar Allan Poe. The movement influenced other writers, including a young William Butler Yeats.

Arthurian romance **Arthurian romances** are stories of the exploits of the legendary King Arthur and his knights of the Round Table. For more information about these tales, see page 152 and page 167.

article An **article** is a brief work of nonfiction on a specific topic. The term *article* is typically used of encyclopedia entries and short nonfiction works that appear in newspapers and popular magazines. The term is sometimes used as a synonym of *essay,* though the latter term often connotes a more serious, important, or lasting work. See *essay.*

aside An **aside** is a statement made by a character in a play, intended to be heard by the audience but not by other characters on the stage.

assonance **Assonance** is the repetition of vowel sounds in stressed syllables that end with different consonant sounds. An example is the repetition of the long *a* sound in this line from George Crabbe's *The Village:*

The rustic poet praised his native plains.

atmosphere   See *mood.*

autobiography   An **autobiography** is the story of a person's life, written by that person. *The Book of Margery Kempe,* written by a medieval woman, may well be the first full-fledged autobiography in the English language. Some editors and critics distinguish between autobiographies, which focus on personal experiences, and *memoirs,* which focus on public events, though the terms are often used interchangeably.

background information   See *flashback, plot,* and *setting.*

ballad   A **ballad** is a simple narrative poem in four-line stanzas, usually meant to be sung and usually rhyming *abcb. Folk ballads,* composed orally and passed by word of mouth from generation to generation, have enjoyed enormous popularity throughout English literary history, from the Middle Ages to the present. Examples include "Sir Patrick Spens" and "Bonny Barbara Allan." *Literary ballads,* written in imitation of folk ballads, have also been very popular. A famous example of the literary ballad is Coleridge's "The Rime of the Ancient Mariner." The folk ballad stanza usually alternates between lines of four and three feet. Common techniques used in ballads include repeated lines, or *refrains,* and *incremental repetition,* the repetition of lines with slight, often cumulative, changes throughout the poem. See *refrain.*

bibliography   A **bibliography** is a list of works on a given subject or of works consulted by an author. See *List of Works Cited.*

Bildungsroman   A *Bildungsroman* is a novel that tells the story of the growth or development of a person from youth to adulthood. Examples include George Eliot's *The Mill on the Floss,* Charles Dickens's *Great Expectations,* and D. H. Lawrence's *Sons and Lovers.*

biographical criticism   See *criticism.*

biography   A **biography** is the story of a person's life, told by someone other than that person. Perhaps the most famous of all English biographies is James Boswell's *Life of Samuel Johnson, LL. D.*

blank verse   **Blank verse** is unrhymed poetry written in iambic pentameter. An *iambic pentameter* line consists of five *feet,* each containing two syllables, the first weakly stressed and the second strongly stressed. Blank verse was introduced into English in Surrey's translation of Virgil's *Aeneid.* Marlowe and Shakespeare adopted it as the standard medium for their dramatic works. The form was used to great effect by Milton, William Wordsworth, Tennyson, Robert Browning, Arnold, Yeats, and T. S. Eliot, among others. For an example of blank verse, see the selection from Shakespeare's *Richard II* under the heading *apposition.*

blend   A **blend,** or **portmanteau,** is a word created by joining together two previously existing words, such as *smoke* and *fog* for *smog* or *whale* and *horse* for *walrus.* In his poem "Jabberwocky," Lewis Carroll coined *slithy* by joining together, or blending, *lithe* and *slimy.*

Bloomsbury Group   The **Bloomsbury Group** was a circle of English writers and thinkers of the 1920s and 1930s that included Virginia Woolf, John Maynard Keynes, Lytton Strachey, and E. M. Forster.

bowdlerize   To **bowdlerize** a piece of writing is to censor it by deleting material considered offensive. The term comes from the name of Thomas Bowdler, who published a "bowdlerized" edition of Shakespeare's works in the early nineteenth century.

Breton lai   A **Breton lai** is a brief medieval romance of the kind produced in Brittany and later in England in imitation of such works. Breton lais dealt with conventional romance themes such as courtly love. Examples of such works include Marie de France's "Chevrefoil" and the anonymous Middle English poem "Sir Orfeo," a retelling of the Greek myth of Orpheus and Eurydice.

broadside   A **broadside** was a form of short, printed work common in England after the introduction of printing. Broadsides were printed in columns and on one side only. Many early ballads and short political and religious tracts survive in the form of broadsides.

bucolic   A **bucolic** is a fanciful pastoral poem. See *pastoral poem.*

cacophony   **Cacophony** is harsh or unpleasant sound. Writers sometimes intentionally use cacophony for effect, as when Robert Browning began his poem "Soliloquy of the Spanish Cloister" with a growl spelled "Grr . . . ."

cæsura A **cæsura** is a major pause in a line of poetry, as in the following line from Shakespeare's *A Midsummer Night's Dream*:

I know a bank ‖ where the wild thyme blows

Calvinism **Calvinism** is a Protestant theology, based on the teachings of John Calvin, that stresses original sin, the inability of people to exercise free will, the preordination of events by God, and the choice (or election) by God of those who will be saved ("the elect") and those who will be condemned. Puritanism was a Calvinist movement. See *Puritanism*.

canon A **canon** is a group of literary works considered to be authentic or worthy. The term was originally used for Biblical books believed to be divinely inspired. It was later adapted to describe works that can be definitely assigned to a given author (as in *the canonical works of Geoffrey Chaucer*). The term is also used to describe those works in a given literary tradition considered to be classics and thus worthy of inclusion in textbooks, in anthologies, and on the reading lists of courses in schools and universities. In the eighteenth century, there was much debate in France and England concerning whether the canon should include primarily modern or ancient works. In the twentieth century, debates over the canon centered on the inattention given works by non-male, non-European writers. Feminist critics, in particular, noted the tendency of male editors and anthologists to include in their collections works by male writers and to exclude works by female writers. See *feminist criticism* under the entry for *criticism*.

canto A **canto** is a section or part of a long poem. The sections of such long poems as *Beowulf*, Dante's *The Divine Comedy*, and Spenser's *The Fœrie Queene* are called cantos. The word comes from the Latin *cantus*, meaning "song."

caricature In literature, a **caricature** is a piece of writing that exaggerates certain qualities of a character in order to satirize or ridicule that character or type. See *satire*.

carmen figuratum See *concrete poem*.

carpe diem *Carpe diem* is a Latin term meaning "seize the day." The *carpe diem* theme, telling people not to waste time but rather to enjoy themselves while they have a chance, was common in Renaissance English poetry. The following stanza by Robert Herrick is perhaps the most famous expression of this theme in English:

Gather ye rosebuds while ye may,
Old Time is still a-flying;
And this same flower that smiles today,
Tomorrow will be dying.

catalog A **catalog** is a list of people or things. Catalogs are common in epic poetry, as in the catalog of gods in lines 374–505 of Book I of Milton's *Paradise Lost*.

catastrophe The **catastrophe** is a conclusion of a play, particularly of a tragedy, marked by the fall of the central character. In the catastrophe, the central conflict of the play is ended, or resolved. See *plot*.

catharsis The ancient Greek philosopher Aristotle described tragedy as bringing about a **catharsis**, or purging, of the emotions of fear and pity. Debate has raged around the proper interpretation of Aristotle's statement. Some critics take it to mean, simply, that at the end of a tragedy, in the catastrophe or resolution, the emotional equilibrium of the characters is restored. Others take it to mean that viewing a tragedy causes the audience to feel emotions of fear and pity, which are then released at the end of the play, leaving the viewer calm, wiser, and perhaps more thoughtful. The idea that catharsis calms an audience has been contradicted by recent psychological studies that suggest that people tend to imitate enacted feelings and behaviors that they witness. Much of the current debate over violence on television and in films centers on this question of whether enacted violence has a cathartic or an arousing effect on the viewer.

Cavalier poets The **Cavalier poets** were loyal supporters of the English king Charles I, courtiers and soldiers who incidentally wrote lighthearted verse, often on amorous themes. Classified among the Cavalier poets are Sir John Suckling, Richard Lovelace, and Robert Herrick.

Celtic **Celtic** is a term used to refer to the art and culture of the Celts, a people who inhabited ancient Britain and much of Europe. It is also used to refer to the art and culture of descendants of the Celts, including modern Welsh, Cornish, Breton, Irish, Manx, and Scots peoples. The late nineteenth and early twentieth centuries saw in Ireland a Celtic Revival or Celtic Renaissance characterized by the renewed use of the Gaelic language and by an explosion of literary production on Irish themes by authors such as W. B. Yeats, John Millington Synge, and Lady Augusta Gregory.

censorship **Censorship** is the act of examining works to see if they meet predetermined standards of political, social, or moral acceptability. Official censorship is aimed at works that will undermine authority or morals and has often in the past resulted in the suppression of works considered dangerous or licentious. Throughout much of English history, censorship was freely exercised by the church and the state. Milton's *Areopagitica* is an eloquent argument against censorship and in favor of unlicensed printing. Milton's principal argument is that when free expression of ideas is allowed, the truth will prevail, driving out falsehood and error as day drives out night. See *bowdlerize.*

central conflict A **central conflict** is the primary struggle dealt with in the plot of a story or drama. See *conflict* and *plot.*

character A **character** is a person (or sometimes an animal) who figures in the action of a literary work. A *protagonist,* or *main character,* is the central figure in a literary work. An *antagonist* is a character who is pitted against a protagonist. *Major characters* are ones who play significant roles in a work. *Minor characters* are ones who play lesser roles. A *one-dimensional character, flat character,* or *caricature* is one who exhibits a single dominant quality, or *character trait.* A *three-dimensional, full,* or *rounded character* is one who exhibits the complexity of traits associated with actual human beings. A *static character* is one who does not change during the course of the action. A *dynamic character* is one who does change. A *stock character* is one found again and again in different literary works. Examples of stock characters include the braggart soldier of ancient Roman drama, the Virtues and Vices of medieval allegory, and the mad scientist of nineteenth- and twentieth-century science fiction.

characterization **Characterization** is the use of literary techniques to create a character. Writers use three major techniques to create characters: direct description, portrayal of characters' behavior, and representations of characters' internal states. When using direct description, the writer, through a speaker, a narrator, or another character, simply comments on the character, telling the reader about such matters as the character's appearance, habits, dress, background, personality, motivations, and so on. When using portrayal of a character's behavior, the writer presents the actions and speech of the character, allowing the reader to draw his or her own conclusions from what the character says or does. When using representations

of internal states, the writer reveals directly the character's private thoughts and emotions, often by means of what is known as the *internal monologue.* See *character* and *internal monologue.*

chiasmus A **chiasmus** is a rhetorical technique in which the order of occurrence of words or phrases is reversed, as in the line "We can weather changes, but we can't change the weather."

chivalry **Chivalry** was the code of conduct of the medieval knight. The word derives from the French *cheval,* for "horse," indicating the importance of this animal to the knight, who typically traveled and fought on horseback. According to the code of chivalry, a knight was to be a loyal servant to his lord or lady and a perfect exemplar of such virtues as bravery, courage, courtesy, honesty, faith, and gentleness. Medieval romance literature, such as *Sir Gawain and the Green Knight,* typically presents a series of tests (trials or quests) of these knightly virtues. See *romance.*

chronicle A **chronicle** is a record of historical events. The *Anglo-Saxon Chronicle,* begun in the time of King Alfred and covering the period from 60 BC to AD 1154, is one of our major sources of information about the Anglo-Saxon period.

chronological order **Chronological order** is the arrangement of details in order of their occurrence. It is the primary method of organization used in narrative writing. It is also common in nonfiction writing that describes processes, events, and cause-and-effect relationships.

classic A **classic** is a work of literature that is widely held to be one of the greatest creations within a given literary tradition. The question of just what works may be considered classic, and thus the question of what constitutes the *canon,* is a much-debated one. See *canon.*

Classical Era The **Classical Era** is the period in European history that saw the flowering of the ancient Greek and Roman cultures. *Classical literature* is the literature of ancient Greece and Rome from the time of Homer and Hesiod to the fall of the Roman Empire in AD 410.

Classicism **Classicism** is a collection of ideas about literature and about art in general derived from study of works by Greeks and Romans of the *Classical Era.* Definitions of what constitutes the Classical style differ, but most would agree that the Classical aesthetic emphasizes authority, austerity, clarity, conservatism, decorum, imitation, moderation, order, reason, restraint, self-control, simplicity, tradition, and unity. Classicism is most often contrasted with *Romanticism.* See *Classical Era* and *Neoclassicism.*

cliché   A **cliché** is a tired or hackneyed expression such as *quiet as a mouse* or *couch potato.* Most clichés originate as vivid, colorful expressions but soon lose their interest because of overuse. Careful writers and speakers avoid clichés, which are dull and signify lack of originality.

climax   The **climax** is the point of highest interest and suspense in a literary work. The term also is sometimes used to describe the *turning point* of the action in a story or play, the point at which the rising action ends and the falling action begins. See *crisis* and *plot.*

closed couplet   A **closed couplet** is a pair of rhyming lines that present a complete statement.

> True wit is Nature to advantage dressed,
> What oft was thought, but ne'er so well
>   expressed.
> —Alexander Pope, *An Essay on Criticism*

closet drama   A **closet drama** is one that is meant to be read rather than acted. Examples of the form include Milton's *Samson Agonistes,* Percy Shelley's *The Cenci,* and Robert Browning's *Pippa Passes.*

coherence   **Coherence** is the logical arrangement and progression of ideas in a speech or piece of writing. Writers achieve coherence by presenting their ideas in a logical sequence and by using transitions to show how their ideas are connected to one another. See *transition.*

coined words   **Coined words** are ones that are intentionally created, often from the raw materials provided by already existing words and word parts. Examples of recently coined words include *spacewalk* and *quark,* the latter taken from James Joyce's *Finnegans Wake.*

collage   In literature, a **collage** is a work that incorporates or brings together an odd assortment of materials, such as allusions, quotations, bits of song, dialogue, foreign words, mythical or folkloric elements, headlines, and pictures or other graphic devices. Collage is an interesting way to present a portrait of a particular time. In America, John Dos Passos used the technique in sections, called "Newsreels," of his *U.S.A.* trilogy of novels. The technique is used to a lesser degree in much modern poetry and fiction, including James Joyce's *Finnegans Wake* and Ezra Pound's *The Cantos.*

colloquialism   **Colloquialism** is the use of informal language. Much modern poetry is characterized by its use of colloquialism, the language of ordinary speech first championed by William Wordsworth in the Preface to *Lyrical Ballads.*

comedy   Originally a literary work with a happy ending, a **comedy** is any lighthearted or humorous work, especially one prepared for the stage or the screen. Comedy is often contrasted with tragedy, in which the hero meets an unhappy fate. (It is perhaps only a slight exaggeration to say that comedies end with wedding bells and tragedies with funeral bells.) Comedies typically present less-than-exalted characters who display all-too-human limitations, foibles, faults, and misunderstandings. The typical progression of the action in a comedy is from initial order to a humorous misunderstanding or confusion and back to order again. Stock elements of comedy include mistaken identities, word play, satire, and exaggerated characters and events. See *tragedy.*

comedy of manners   The **comedy of manners** is a type of satirical comedy that originated in the Restoration Period and that deals with the conventions and manners of a highly artificial and sophisticated society. Typical subjects dealt with in the comedy of manners include amorous intrigue, fakery, pomposity, and flattery. Examples of the genre include Congreve's *The Way of the World,* Goldsmith's *She Stoops to Conquer,* and Oscar Wilde's *The Importance of Being Earnest.*

comic relief   Writers sometimes insert into a serious work of fiction or drama a humorous scene that is said to provide **comic relief** because it relieves the seriousness or emotional intensity felt by the audience. Paradoxically, a scene introduced for comic relief can sometimes, because of the contrast it provides, increase the perceived intensity or seriousness of the action around it. A famous example of comic relief is the scene of the drunken porter in *Macbeth,* a humorous scene that follows Macbeth's murder of Duncan.

commonplace book   A **commonplace book** is a collection of quotations gleaned from various sources.

comparative literature   **Comparative literature** is the study of relationships among works of literature written at different times, in different places, or in different languages. A study that showed influences of French revolutionary writing on English *Romanticism* would be an example, as would a study that dealt with the motif of the foundling left in a basket floating upon the waters. The latter motif is found in such widely separated stories as the Babylonian *Epic of Gilgamesh,* the story of Moses in the Hebrew Scriptures, and the story of Scyld Scefing told at the beginning of the Old English epic poem *Beowulf.*

complaint   A **complaint** is a lyric poem that deals with loss, regret, unrequited love, or some other negative state experienced by the speaker of the poem. Examples include the Old English poem "The Wife's Lament" and Chaucer's "The Complaint of Chaucer to His Empty Purse."

complication   The **complication** is the part of a plot in which the conflict is developed or built to its high point of intensity. See *plot.*

conceit   A **conceit** is an elaborate or extremely fanciful analogy or metaphor. The conceit was a common element of Renaissance English poetry and of the so-called Metaphysical poetry written by such authors as John Donne. The comparison in Shakespeare's Sonnet 73 of the speaker with nature in the late fall or early winter is an example of conceit, as is Ben Jonson's "Song, to Celia." In Sonnets 18 and 130, Shakespeare mocks the conceits common in poetry of his day.

concrete   A **concrete** word or phrase is one that names or describes something that can be directly perceived by one or more of the five senses. *Rainbow, lark, scorpion,* and *field* are examples of concrete terms. See *abstract* and *concrete universal.*

concrete poem   A **concrete poem** is one printed or written in a shape that suggests its subject matter. An example of the concrete poem, also known as a *shape poem* or *carmen figuratum,* is George Herbert's "Easter Wings."

concrete universal   A **concrete universal** is a particular object, person, action, or event that provides an instance or example of a general type. So, for example, Shakespeare's Macbeth can be seen as a concrete example of a man suffering from extreme guilt and Percy Shelley's statue of Ozymandias can be seen as a concrete example of the general idea that all worldly pomp and pride is eventually reduced to ruin. During the *Neoclassical Age,* writers tended to disparage concrete particulars and to write, instead, in abstract terms. As a result, modern readers sometimes find Neoclassical literature not to their taste. In our time, literary taste tends toward the particular. In the *minimalist style* championed by writers such as Ezra Pound, T. S. Eliot, and Hilda Doolittle, direct statement of abstract ideas and emotions is avoided. Instead, images are presented as concrete examples to arouse abstract ideas and emotions in the reader. So, for example, instead of saying something abstract like "I feel that some terrible, earth-shattering event is about to take place," the later Yeats, who was influenced greatly by Pound, would write,

And what rough beast, its hour come
  round at last,
Slouches towards Bethlehem to be born?
        —W. B. Yeats, "The Second Coming"

The concrete image of the "rough beast" is much more emotionally powerful than the abstract statement. See *abstract, concrete, Neoclassicism,* and *objective correlative.*

confessional poetry   **Confessional poetry** is verse that describes, sometimes with painful explicitness, the private or personal affairs of the writer. Contemporary confessional poets include Allen Ginsberg, Sylvia Plath, Anne Sexton, and Robert Lowell.

conflict   A **conflict** is a struggle between two forces in a literary work. A *plot* involves the introduction, development, and eventual resolution of a conflict. One side of the *central conflict* in a story or drama is usually taken by the *main character.* That character may struggle against another character, against the forces of nature, against society or social norms, against fate, or against some element within himself or herself. A struggle that takes place between a character and some outside force is called an *external conflict.* A struggle that takes place within a character is called an *internal conflict.* Shakespeare's Macbeth experiences external conflicts with Banquo and Macduff. He experiences an internal conflict between his own ambition and his guilt. See *central conflict* and *plot.*

connotation   A **connotation** is an emotional association or implication attached to an expression. For example, the word *inexpensive* has positive emotional associations, whereas the word *cheap* has negative ones, even though the two words both *denote,* or refer to, low cost. Good writers choose their words carefully in order to express appropriate connotations. See *denotation.*

consonance   **Consonance** is the use in stressed syllables of identical final consonants preceded by vowels with different *sounds.* The final lines of Percy Shelley's "Ode to the West Wind" provide an example:

The trumpet of a prophecy! O *Wind*
If Winter comes, can Spring be far *behind?*

convention   A **convention** is an unrealistic element in a literary work that is accepted by readers or viewers because the element is traditional. One of the conventions of fiction, for example, is that it uses the past tense to describe current or present action. Rhyme schemes and organization into stanzas are among the many commonly employed conventions of poetry. Violation of accepted conventions is one of the hallmarks of *avant garde* or *Modernist* literature. See *dramatic convention.*

conventional symbol   See *symbol.*

couplet   A **couplet** is a pair of rhyming lines that expresses a complete thought. These lines from Shakespeare's *Romeo and Juliet* provide an example:

For never was a story of more woe
Than this of Juliet and her Romeo.

A pair of rhyming iambic pentameter lines is called a *heroic couplet.*

courtly love   **Courtly love** is a code of romantic love celebrated in songs and romances of the Medieval Period in France and England. According to this code, the male lover knows himself to be truly in love if he is overcome by extreme, transforming emotion. This emotion, felt for an idealized, venerated woman, leads the smitten man sometimes to depths of despair and sometimes to heights of gentleness, courtesy, and heroism to prove his worth to his lady fair. Courtly love was one of the primary themes of medieval *romance* literature. See *romance.*

crisis   In the plot of a story or a drama, the **crisis** is that point in the development of the conflict at which a decisive event occurs that causes the main character's situation to become better or worse. See *plot.*

critic   A literary **critic** is a person who evaluates or interprets a work of literature. See *criticism.*

critical essay   A **critical essay** is a type of informative or persuasive writing that presents an argument in support of a particular interpretation or evaluation of a work of literature. A well-constructed critical essay presents a clear *thesis,* or main idea, supported by ample evidence from the work or works being considered.

criticism   **Criticism** is the act of evaluating or interpreting a work of art or the act of developing general guidelines or principles for such evaluation or interpretation. Over the centuries, many schools, or philosophies, of criticism have been developed. However, most readers and teachers are eclectic critics, drawing consciously or unconsciously upon various shools of critical thought. Common schools of criticism include the following:

Biographical criticism attempts to account for elements of literary works by relating them to events in the lives of their authors. A reading of Yeats's poem "Adam's Curse" as a reflection on his real-life relationship with actor Maude Gonne would be an example of biographical criticism.

Deconstructionist criticism calls into question the very idea of the meaning or interpretation of a literary work by inviting the reader to reverse the binary, or two-part, relations that structure meaning in the work. For example, a deconstructionist analysis might invite the reader to consider, again, the contrast between natural order and supernatural disorder in *Macbeth.* It might claim that the disorder exemplified by Macbeth and Lady Macbeth's madness is, in fact, in the natural order of things. Such a reading deconstructs the conventional reading of the play, which insists that Shakespeare intended to reveal the awful consequences of an unnatural violation of the moral order of the universe. See *structuralist criticism.*

Didactic criticism evaluates works of art in terms of the moral, ethical, or political messages that they convey. Dismissal of a book as dangerous or obscene would be an example of didactic criticism.

Feminist criticism evaluates and interprets works of art with regard to their portrayal of or influence upon gender roles. Many feminist critics and scholars have been particularly concerned to rescue women writers from the obscurity that male critics, editors, scholars, and teachers may have forced upon them. Other critics have been concerned with pointing out gender bias in literary works, with analyzing variations in literary depictions of males and females, and with understanding the effects of literary works, activities, and movements on cultural norms related to gender. An example of feminist criticism would be an analysis of how women in medieval courtly love and romance literature were idealized and the consequences of that idealization for later Western ideas about femininity and relations between the sexes.

Formal criticism analyzes a work of literature in terms of its genre or type. An explanation of those characteristics of *Paradise Lost* that make it an epic would be an example of formal criticism.

Freudian criticism draws upon the works of the founder of psychoanalysis, Sigmund Freud, and generally views literary works or the parts thereof as expressions of unconscious desires, as wish fulfillments, or as neurotic sublimations of unresolved conflicts from childhood. An example of Freudian criticism would be the interpretation of the ancient Greek Œdipus myth, in which Œdipus unwittingly marries his mother, as an expression of the young male child's competition with his father for his mother's affection.

Historical criticism views the work of art as a product of the period in which it was produced. Examples of historical criticism would be an analysis of the feudal concept of vassalage in Malory's *Le Morte d'Arthur* or a description of the influence of the French and American revolutions on the development of Romanticism in England.

Jungian criticism explores the presence in works of art of *archetypes*—unconscious images, symbols, associations, or concepts presumed to be a common inheritance of all human beings. An analysis of symbols of rebirth in a number of myths or folk tales would be an example of Jungian criticism.

Marxist criticism, based upon the work of the German-born political philosopher Karl Marx, evaluates and interprets works of art with regard to the material economic forces that shape them or with regard to their origins in or depictions of struggle between the social classes. An example of Marxist criticism would be an explanation of the emergence of Neoclassicism in England in terms of desire for order, authority, and control on the part of the privileged classes during the Restoration Era.

Mimetic criticism, which derives from the teachings of Aristotle, views works of art as imitations of nature or of the real world and evaluates them according to the accuracy of those portrayals. Insisting that a character is poorly drawn because he or she is unrealistic is an example of mimetic criticism.

The *New Criticism* championed in the early to mid-twentieth century by such critics as I. A. Richards and Cleanth Brooks insists upon the interpretation and evaluation of literary works based on details found in the works themselves rather than on information gathered from outside the works. It disregards such matters as the life of the author, the period in which the work was written, the literary movement that led to its production, and the emotional effect of the work upon the reader. The New Critics insisted on the importance of close analysis of literary texts and the irreducibility of those texts to generalizations or paraphrases.

Pragmatic or *rhetorical criticism* interprets or evaluates a work of art in terms of its effects on an audience. Many critics have claimed that Milton intended to have his readers identify with Satan as described in the opening books of *Paradise Lost* so that he could then have the reader go through the experience of falling into sin only to be redeemed afterward. This is an example of rhetorical criticism.

Reader-response criticism views the meaning of a text as resulting from a relationship between the text itself and the subjective experiences or consciousness of a reader. According to reader-response theory, a literary text has no meaning *per se.* It is, instead, an occasion for a participatory experience that the reader has. That experience may be meaningful or significant to the reader, but its meaning and significance will depend, in part, on what the reader brings to the text.

Romantic or *expressivist criticism* views a work of art as primarily an expression of the spirit, ideas, beliefs, values, or emotions of its creator. A reading of "Lines Composed a Few Miles above Tintern Abbey" as expressive of the moral posture adopted by William Wordsworth would be an example of expressivist criticism.

Structuralist criticism analyzes works of literature and art in terms of binary, or two-part, relationships or structures. A structuralist analysis of Shakespeare's *Macbeth,* for example, might view the central character as caught between supernatural disorder and the natural order, between reality and illusion.

Textual criticism analyzes the various existing manuscript and printed versions of a work in order to construct an original or definitive text for use by readers.

dactyl A **dactyl** is a poetic foot made up of a strongly stressed syllable followed by two weakly stressed syllables, as in the word *feverish*. A line of poetry made up of dactyls is said to be *dactylic*.

dead metaphor A **dead metaphor** is one that is so familiar that its original metaphorical meaning is rarely thought of when the expression is used. An example would be the word *nightfall,* which describes the coming of darkness as a falling object.

deconstructionist criticism   See *criticism*.

definition   A **definition** is an explanation of the meaning of a word or phrase. A dictionary definition typically consists of two parts: the *genus*, or class to which the thing belongs, and the *differentia*, or differences between the thing and other things of its class. Consider, for example, Samuel Johnson's famous tongue-in-cheek definition of *oats:* "A grain, which in England is generally given to horses, but in Scotland supports the people." In this definition, "grain" is the genus. The rest of the definition presents the differentia.

denotation   The **denotation** is the basic meaning or reference of an expression, excluding its emotional associations, or *connotations*. For example, the words *dirt* and *soil* share a single common denotation. However, *dirt* has negative connotations of uncleanliness, whereas *soil* does not. See *connotation*.

dénouement   See *plot*.

description   A **description**, one of the modes of writing, portrays a character, an object, or a scene. Descriptions make use of *sensory details*—words and phrases that describe how things look, sound, smell, taste, or feel. See *mode*.

dialect   A **dialect** is a version of a language spoken by the people of a particular place, time, or social group. Writers often use dialect, as in Thomas Hardy's "The Man He Killed," to give their works a realistic flavor. In his play *Pygmalion,* George Bernard Shaw satirizes the division of English society along class lines differentiated by the dialects spoken by members of each class. A *regional dialect* is one spoken in a particular place. A *social dialect* is one spoken by members of a particular social group or class.

dialogue   1. **Dialogue** is conversation involving two or more people or characters. Plays are made up of dialogue and stage directions. Fictional works are made up of dialogue, narration, and description. 2. **Dialogue** is also used to describe a type of literary composition in which characters debate or discuss an idea. Many of Plato's philosophical works were presented in the form of dialogues. Dialogues between abstractions such as the body and the soul, or virtue and vice, were common in the poetry of the Middle Ages.

diary   A **diary** is a day-to-day record of a person's activities, experiences, thoughts, and feelings. Perhaps the most famous of all English diaries is that kept by Samuel Pepys. See *journal*.

diction   **Diction**, when applied to writing, refers to word choice. Much of a writer's *style* is determined by his or her diction, the types of words that he or she chooses. Diction can be formal or informal, simple or complex, contemporary or archaic, ordinary or unusual, foreign or native, standard or dialectical, euphemistic or blunt. See *style*.

didactic criticism   See *criticism*.

didactic poem   A **didactic poem** is a verse that has a primary purpose of teaching one or more lessons. Alexander Pope's *An Essay on Criticism* is an example. See *didacticism*.

didacticism   **Didacticism** is the use of works of art to convey moral, social, educational, or political messages. A didactic work is one in which the artistic values of the work are subordinated to the message or meaning. Didacticism was a common element of literature in the Middle Ages and of the *proletarian art* and literature produced in Communist countries in the twentieth century.

dimeter   See *meter*.

dirge   A **dirge** is a funeral song or a poem written in imitation thereof. See Shelley's "A Dirge," page 675.

dominant impression   See *effect*.

drama   A **drama** is a story told through characters played by actors. The script of a drama typically consists of characters' names, *dialogue* spoken by the characters, and *stage directions.* Because it is meant to be performed before an audience, drama can be distinguished from other forms of nonperformance-based literary works by the central role played in it by the *spectacle*—the sensory presentation to the audience, which includes such elements as lighting, costumes, make-up, properties, set pieces, music, sound effects, and the movements and expressions of actors. Another important distinguishing feature of drama is that it is *collaborative.* The interpretation of the work depends not only upon the author and his or her audience, but also upon the director, the actors, and others involved in mounting a production. Two major types of drama are *comedy* and *tragedy.* George Bernard Shaw's *Pygmalion* is an example of the former; Shakespeare's *Macbeth,* of the latter. See *comedy, dialogue, spectacle, stage directions,* and *tragedy*.

dramatic convention   A **dramatic convention** is an unreal element in a drama that is accepted as realistic by the audience because it is traditional. Such conventions include the impersonation of characters by actors, the use of a curtain to open or close an act or a scene, the revelation of a character's thoughts through *asides* and *soliloquies,* and the removal of the so-called *fourth wall* at the front of the stage that allows the audience to see action taking place in an imagined interior. See *convention* and *suspension of disbelief.*

dramatic irony   See *irony.*

dramatic monologue   A **dramatic monologue** is a poem that presents the speech of a single character in a dramatic situation. The speech is one side of an imagined conversation. Robert Browning is often credited with the creation of the dramatic monologue. He popularized the form in such poems as "My Last Duchess" and "Andrea del Sarto." See *soliloquy.*

dramatic poem   A **dramatic poem** is a verse that relies heavily on dramatic elements such as monologue or dialogue. Types of dramatic poetry include the *dramatic monologue* and the *soliloquy.*

dramatis personæ   *Dramatis personæ* are the characters in a literary work. The term is most often used for the characters in a drama.

dream record   A **dream record** is a *diary* or *journal* in which a writer records his or her dreams. See *diary* and *journal.*

dynamic character   See *character.*

dystopia   A **dystopia** is an imaginary horrible world, the opposite of a *utopia.* Dystopias are common in science fiction. Famous examples of dystopias include the societies described in Aldous Huxley's *Brave New World,* H. G. Wells's *The Time Machine,* and George Orwell's *Nineteen Eighty-Four.* See *utopia.*

eclogue   An **eclogue** is a pastoral poem written in imitation of Greek works by Theocritus and Virgil. See *pastoral poem.*

editorial   An **editorial** is a short persuasive piece that appears in a newspaper, magazine, or other periodical.

effect   The **effect** of a literary work is the general impression or emotional impact that it achieves. Some writers and critics, notably Edgar Allan Poe, have insisted that a successful short story or poem is one in which each detail contributes to the overall effect, or *dominant impression,* produced by the piece.

elaboration   **Elaboration,** or **amplification,** is a writing technique in which a subject is introduced and then expanded upon by means of repetition with slight changes, the addition of details, or similar devices.

elegiac lyric   An **elegiac lyric** is a poem that expresses a speaker's feelings of loss. The Anglo-Saxon poem "The Wife's Lament" and William Wordsworth's "She Dwelt among the Untrodden Ways" are examples.

elegy   An **elegy** is a long formal poem about death or loss. Gray's "Elegy Written in a Country Churchyard" and Tennyson's "In Memoriam" are famous examples.

Elizabethan drama   **Elizabethan drama** is the body of plays created during the reign of Queen Elizabeth I of England, from 1558 to 1603. The term is also used to refer to works produced during the reign of James I, which followed that of Elizabeth and lasted until 1625. Famous Elizabethan dramatists included William Shakespeare, Christopher Marlowe, and Ben Jonson.

Elizabethan sonnet   See *sonnet.*

emphasis   **Emphasis** is importance placed on an element in a literary work. Writers achieve emphasis by various means, including repetition, elaboration, stress, restatement in other words, and placement in a strategic position at the beginning or end of a line or a sentence.

end rhyme   **End rhyme** is rhyme that occurs at the ends of lines of verse. See *rhyme.*

end-stopped line   An **end-stopped line** is a line of verse in which both the sense and the grammar are complete at the end of the line. The opposite of an end-stopped line is a *run-on line.* The following lines are end-stopped:

> A little learning is a dangerous thing;
> Drink deep, or taste not the Pierian spring.
> —Alexander Pope, *An Essay on Criticism*

Excessive use of end-stopped lines gives verse an unnatural, halting quality. See *run-on line.*

English sonnet   See *sonnet.*

enjambment   See *run-on line.*

Enlightenment   The **Enlightenment** was an eighteenth-century philosophical movement characterized by belief in reason, the scientific method, and the perfectibility of people and society. Thinkers of the Enlightenment Era, or Age of

Reason, believed that the universe was governed by discoverable, rational principles like the laws of physics discovered by Sir Isaac Newton. By extension, they believed that people could, through application of reason, discover truths relating to the conduct of life or of society. Leading thinkers of the Enlightenment included Diderot, Franklin, Gibbon, Hume, Jefferson, Kant, Montesquieu, Pope, Swift, and Voltaire. See *Neoclassicism.*

epic An **epic** is a long story, often told in verse, involving heroes and gods. Grand in length and scope, an epic provides a portrait of an entire culture, of the legends, beliefs, values, laws, arts, and ways of life of a people. Famous epic poems include Homer's *Iliad* and *Odyssey*, Virgil's *Aeneid*, Dante's *The Divine Comedy*, the anonymous Old English *Beowulf*, and Milton's *Paradise Lost.*

epigram An **epigram** is a short, often witty, saying. Pope's "To err is human, to forgive divine" is an example.

epigraph An **epigraph** is a quotation or motto used at the beginning of the whole or part of a literary work to help establish the work's theme.

epilogue An **epilogue** is a concluding section or statement, often one that comments on or draws conclusions from the work as a whole.

epiphany When applied to literature, the term **epiphany** refers to a moment of sudden insight in which the essence, or nature, of a person, thing, or situation is revealed. The use of the term in this sense was introduced by James Joyce.

episode An **episode** is a complete action within a literary work.

episodic structure **Episodic structure** is the stringing together of loosely related incidents, or episodes. Many medieval romances have an episodic structure. They tell about the loosely related adventures of a knight or group of knights.

epistle An **epistle** is a letter, especially one that is highly formal. Letters in verse are sometimes called epistles.

epistolary fiction **Epistolary fiction** is imaginative prose that tells a story through letters, or epistles. Famous epistolary novels include Samuel Richardson's *Pamela* and his *Clarissa,* written in the mid-1700s.

epitaph An **epitaph** is an inscription or verse written to be used on a tomb or written in commemoration of someone who has died. The epitaph on the grave of William Butler Yeats, written by the poet himself, reads, "Cast a cold eye on life, on death. Horseman, pass by!" The following lines are from an epitaph written by the Elizabethan poet Ben Jonson:

> Underneath this stone doth lie
> As much beauty as could die,
> Which in life did harbor give
> To more virtue than doth live.

epithet An **epithet** is a word or phrase used to describe a characteristic of a person, place, or thing. Homer's description of dawn as "rosy-fingered" is an example.

eponym An **eponym** is a person or character from whose name a word or title is derived, or a name that has become synonymous with some general characteristic or idea. Julius Cæsar is the eponym of the medical term *Cæsarean section.* England's Queen Victoria is the eponym of Victoria Falls. A reference to *Helen of Troy,* used in place of the more general term *beauty,* or a reference to *an Einstein,* in place of a more general term such as *a smart person,* would be an eponym.

essay An **essay** is a brief work of prose nonfiction. The original meaning of essay was "a trial or attempt," and the word retains some of this original force. An essay need not be a complete or exhaustive treatment of a subject but rather a tentative exploration of it. A good essay develops a single idea and is characterized by *unity* and *coherence.* See *coherence* and *unity.*

euphemism A **euphemism** is an indirect word or phrase used in place of a direct statement that might be considered too offensive. The phrase *the dearly departed,* used instead of *the dead person,* is a euphemism.

euphony **Euphony** is pleasing sound. Writers achieve euphony by various means, including repetitions of vowel and consonant sounds, rhyme, and parallelism. See *cacophony.*

exemplum An **exemplum** is a brief story or *anecdote,* common in the Middle Ages, told to illustrate an idea or a moral. Exempla were often inserted into *homilies,* the sermons included as part of the Roman Catholic mass. See *anecdote* and *parable.*

Existentialism **Existentialism** is a twentieth-century philosophical school that postulates the essential absurdity and meaninglessness of life. Existentialist philosophers such as Albert Camus and Jean-Paul Sartre argued that existence, or being, emerges out of nothingness without any essential, or defining, nature. A human being simply finds himself or herself alive and aware without having any essential defining direction. Any choices that a person makes in order to define himself or herself are made freely and therefore absurdly—one may as well make one choice as another. Freedom of the will is therefore seen by the Existentialist as a terrific burden, one causing anguish to the thinking person, who longs for meaningfulness, not absurd choices. Another significant aspect of Existentialism is its insistence on the essential isolation of each individual consciousness and the consequent anguish of people looking for meaningful connection to others. Though many of the essential tenets of Existentialism have been discredited by contemporary philosophers, the school nonetheless exerted tremendous influence on mid-twentieth-century literature in Europe, Great Britain, and the United States. See *literature of the absurd* and *theater of the absurd*.

exposition   **1. Exposition,** one of the modes of writing, presents factual information. See *mode*. **2.** In a plot, the **exposition** is that part of a narrative that provides background information, often about the characters, setting, or conflict. See *plot*.

Expressionism   **Expressionism** is the name given to a twentieth-century movement in literature and art that reacted against Realism in favor of an exaggeration of the elements of the artistic medium itself in an attempt to express ideas or feelings. The use in a play of characters named, simply, Person, Mother, and Character 1 is an example of Expressionism. Modern Expressionist dramatists include Karl Capek, Luigi Pirandello, Elmer Rice, Edward Albee, and to a lesser extent, Tennessee Williams.

extended metaphor   An **extended metaphor** is a point-by-point presentation of one thing as though it were another. The description is meant as an implied comparison, inviting the reader to associate the thing being described with something that is quite different from it. Wyatt's "Whoso List to Hunt" is an example. In the poem, a woman is described as a deer, the pursuit of the woman as poaching, and the woman's mate as Cæsar, the owner of the property on which the poaching might be done.

external conflict   See *conflict*.

eye rhyme   See *sight rhyme*.

fable   A **fable** is a brief story with animal characters told to express a moral. Famous fables include those of Æsop and La Fontaine. George Orwell's *Animal Farm* is an adaptation of the fable form to political satire.

fabliau   A **fabliau** is a brief, humorous tale, often ribald. The form was extremely popular during the Middle Ages. "The Miller's Tale" in Chaucer's *Canterbury Tales* is a famous example. The plural of fabliau is *fabliaux*.

fairy tale   A **fairy tale** is a story that deals with mischievous spirits and other supernatural occurrences, often in medieval settings. The name is generally applied to stories of the kinds collected by Charles Perrault in France and the Brothers Grimm in Germany or told by Hans Christian Andersen of Denmark. "Cinderella," "The White Snake," and "The Little Mermaid" are famous examples.

falling action   See *plot*.

fantasy   A **fantasy** is a literary work that contains highly unrealistic elements. Swift's *Gulliver's Travels* is a fantasy. Fantasy is often contrasted with *science fiction*, in which the unreal elements are given a scientific or pseudo-scientific basis. See *science fiction*.

farce   A **farce** is a type of comedy that depends heavily on so-called low humor and on improbable, exaggerated, extreme situations or characters.

feminist criticism   See *criticism*.

fiction   **Fiction** is prose writing about imagined events or characters. The primary forms of fiction are the *novel* and the *short story*.

figurative language   **Figurative language** is language that suggests something more than the literal meanings of the words might be taken to suggest. See *figures of speech*.

figures of speech   **Figures of speech,** or **tropes,** are expressions that have more than a literal meaning. Hyperbole, metaphor, metonymy, personification, simile, synaesthesia, synecdoche, and understatement are all figures of speech. See *hyperbole, metaphor, metonymy, personification, simile, synaesthesia, synecdoche,* and *understatement*.

first-person point of view   See *point of view*.

flashback   A **flashback** is a section of a literary work that presents an event or series of events

1250   *LANGUAGE ARTS SURVEY*

1250   TEACHER'S EDITION

that occurred earlier than the current time in the work. Writers use flashbacks for many purposes, but most notably to provide *background information*, or exposition. In popular melodramatic works, including modern romance fiction and detective stories, flashbacks are often used to end suspense by revealing key elements of the plot such as a character's true identity or the actual perpetrator of a crime. One common technique is to begin a work with a final event and then to tell the rest of the story as a flashback that explains how that event came about. Another common technique is to begin a story *in medias res* (in the middle of the action) and then to use a flashback to fill in the events that occurred before the opening of the story.

flash fiction   See *short short.*

flat character   See *character.*

foil   A **foil** is a character whose attributes, or characteristics, contrast with and therefore throw into relief the attributes of another character. In Shakespeare's *Hamlet,* for example, Fortinbras, a determined, self-assured person of action, provides a foil for Hamlet, who is plagued with doubts and cannot commit himself to a course of action.

folk ballad   See *ballad.*

folk song   A **folk song** is an anonymous song that is transmitted orally. Examples include the ballad "Bonny Barbara Allan," the sea chantey "Blow the Man Down," the children's song "Row, Row, Row Your Boat," the spiritual "Go Down, Moses," the railroad song "Casey Jones," and the cowboy song "The Streets of Laredo." The term *folk song* is sometimes used for works composed in imitation of true folk songs. Modern composers of songs in the folk tradition include Bob Dylan, Paul Simon, Joan Baez, and the Indigo Girls. See *ballad.*

folk tale   A **folk tale** is a brief story passed by word of mouth from generation to generation. Writers often make use of materials from folk tales. Chaucer's "The Pardoner's Tale," for example, is a retelling of a folk tale, and Yeats's poem "The Stolen Child" is based on Irish folk tales about fairies, called the Sidhe, that steal away children. Famous collections of folk tales include the German *Märchen,* or fairy tales, collected by the Brothers Grimm; Yeats's collection of Irish stories, *Mythologies;* and Zora Neale Hurston's collection of African-American folk tales and other folklore materials, *Their Eyes Were Watching God.* See *fairy tale, folklore,* and *oral tradition.*

folklore   **Folklore** is a body of orally transmitted beliefs, customs, rituals, traditions, songs, verses, or stories. Folk tales, fables, fairy tales, tall tales, nursery rhymes, proverbs, legends, myths, parables, riddles, charms, spells, and ballads are all common kinds of folklore, though each of these can be found, as well, in literary forms made in imitation of works from the *oral tradition.*

foot   In a poem, a **foot** is a unit of rhythm consisting of strongly and weakly stressed syllables. See *meter* and *scansion.* Also see the specific types of feet: *anapest, dactyl, iamb, spondee,* and *trochee.*

foreshadowing   **Foreshadowing** is the act of presenting materials that hint at events to occur later in a story. In Shakespeare's *Macbeth,* the witches' statement that "Fair is foul" and "foul is fair" foreshadows many later events, including Macbeth's confounding of illusion and reality and the several events that occur in the catastrophe of the play that were predicted, but duplicitously, by the witches.

foreword   See *preface.*

formal criticism   See *criticism.*

fourteener   See *meter.*

fourth wall   See *dramatic convention.*

frame tale   A **frame tale** is a story that itself provides a vehicle for the telling of other stories. The *Thousand and One Nights,* Boccaccio's *Decameron,* and Chaucer's *The Canterbury Tales* are frame tales.

free verse   **Free verse,** or *vers libre,* is poetry that avoids use of regular rhyme, rhythm, meter, or division into stanzas. Ted Hughes's "Mooses" and Derek Walcott's "Map of the New World" are examples, though both poems make use of numerous regularities of rhythm. Much of the English and American poetry written in the twentieth century is in free verse.

Freudian criticism   See *criticism.*

full character   See *character.*

genre   A **genre** (zhän′rə) is one of the types or categories into which literary works are divided. Some terms used to name literary genres include *autobiography, biography, comedy, drama, epic, essay, lyric, narrative, novel, pastoral, poetry, short story,* and *tragedy.* Literary works are sometimes classified into genres based on subject matter. Such a classification might describe *detective* stories, mysteries, adventure stories, romances, westerns, and science fiction as different genres of fiction.

gleeman See scop.

Gothic novel A **Gothic novel**, or **Gothic romance**, is a long story containing elements of horror, suspense, mystery, and magic. Gothic novels often contain dark, brooding descriptions of settings and characters. Mary Shelley's Frankenstein and Daphne du Maurier's Rebecca are examples of the form. Emily Brontë's Wuthering Heights contains many Gothic elements.

Gothic romance See Gothic novel.

haiku A **haiku** is a traditional Japanese three-line poem containing five syllables in the first line, seven in the second, and five again in the third. A haiku presents a picture, or image, in order to arouse in the reader a specific emotional and/or spiritual state.

half rhyme See slant rhyme.

heptameter See meter.

heroic couplet See couplet.

heroic epic A **heroic epic** is an epic that has a main purpose of telling the life story of a great hero. Examples of the heroic epic include Homer's Iliad and Odyssey, Virgil's Aeneid, and the Old English poem Beowulf. See epic.

hexameter See meter.

high style See style.

historical criticism See criticism.

hymn A **hymn** is a song or verse of praise, often religious. "Cædmon's Hymn" in praise of God the creator is the earliest known poem written in the English language.

hyperbole A **hyperbole** (hī pur´bə lē) is an exaggeration made for rhetorical effect. Robert Burns uses hyperbole in "To a Red, Red Rose" when he writes,

> And I will love you still, my dear,
>   When all the seas run dry.

iamb An **iamb** is a poetic foot containing one weakly stressed syllable followed by one strongly stressed syllable, as in the words afraid and release. A line of poetry made up of iambs is said to be iambic.

iambic See iamb.

image An **image** is a word picture—a word or phrase that names something that can be seen, heard, touched, tasted, or smelled. The images in a literary work are referred to, collectively, as the work's imagery.

Imagery See image.

in medias res See action and flashback.

inciting incident See plot.

incremental repetition See ballad.

internal conflict See conflict.

internal monologue An **internal monologue** presents the private sensations, thoughts, and emotions of a character. The reader is allowed to step inside the character's mind and overhear what is going on in there. Which characters' internal states can be revealed in a work of fiction depends on the point of view from which the work is told. See point of view.

introduction See preface.

inversion An **inversion** is a poetic technique in which the normal order of words in an utterance is altered. Robert Frost's "Whose woods these are, I think I know" is an inversion of the usual order of expression: "I think I know whose woods these are."

irony **Irony** is a difference between appearance and reality. Types of irony include the following: dramatic irony, in which something is known by the reader or audience but unknown to the characters; verbal irony, in which a statement is made that implies its opposite; and irony of situation, in which an event occurs that violates the expectations of the characters, the reader, or the audience.

irony of situation See irony.

journal A **journal,** like a diary, is a day-to-day record of a person's activities, experiences, thoughts, and feelings. In contrast to diary, the word journal connotes an outward rather than an inward focus. However, the two terms are often used interchangeably. See diary.

Jungian criticism See criticism.

kenning A **kenning** is an imaginative compound used in place of an ordinary noun. Examples of kennings from Old English poetry include whale-road and swan's road for sea and slaughter-wolf for Viking.

limited point of view See narrator and point of view.

List of Works Cited A **List of Works Cited** is a type of bibliography that lists works used or referred to by an author. A standard feature of a research paper, the List of Works Cited appears at the end of the paper and is arranged in alphabetical order.

literary ballad See *ballad.*

literature of the absurd **Literature of the absurd** is literature influenced by Existentialist philosophy, which represents human life as meaningless or absurd because of the supposed lack of essential connection between human beings and the world around them. In brief, the Existentialist philosophers, such as Albert Camus and Jean-Paul Sartre, believed that a person's conscious existence precedes, or comes before, any essential self-definition and that self-definition can occur only as a result of making an absurd, completely free choice to act, think, or believe in certain ways. The literature of the absurd emphasizes the meaninglessness of life and the isolation, or alienation, of individuals. Much of the literature of the absurd is filled with horrors, anguish, random events, and illogical or improbable occurrences. Modern practitioners of the literature of the absurd include the novelists Franz Kafka, Thomas Pynchon, and Kurt Vonnegut, Jr., and the playwrights Eugène Ionesco, Samuel Beckett, Edward Albee, and Harold Pinter. See *Existentialism* and *theater of the absurd.*

low style See *style.*

lyric poem A **lyric poem** is a highly musical verse that expresses the emotions of a speaker. Shakespeare's sonnets and Byron's "She Walks in Beauty" are examples. Lyric poems are often contrasted with narrative poems, which have story telling as their main purpose.

Magical Realism **Magical Realism** is a kind of fiction that is for the most part realistic but that contains elements of fantasy. D. H. Lawrence's "The Rocking-Horse Winner" is an example of Magical Realism.

main character See *character.*

major character See *character.*

Marxist criticism See *criticism.*

metaphor A **metaphor** is a figure of speech in which one thing is spoken or written about as if it were another. This figure of speech invites the reader to make a comparison between the two things. The two "things" involved are the writer's actual subject, the *tenor* of the metaphor, and another thing to which the subject is likened, the *vehicle* of the metaphor. When, in Meditation 17, John Donne writes that "all mankind is of one author and is one volume," he is using two metaphors:

TENOR	VEHICLE
mankind	a volume or book
God	the author of the volume or book

Personifications and similes are types of metaphor. See *dead metaphor, mixed metaphor, personification,* and *simile.*

meter The **meter** of a poem is its rhythmical pattern. English verse is generally described as being made up of rhythmical units called *feet,* as follows:

TYPE OF FOOT	STRESS PATTERN	EXAMPLE
iambic	⌣ /	insist
trochaic	/ ⌣	freedom
anapestic	⌣ ⌣ /	unimpressed
dactylic	/ ⌣ ⌣	feverish
spondaic	/ /	baseball

Some scholars also use the term *pyrrhic* to describe a foot with two weak stresses. Using this term, the word *unbelievable* might be described as consisting of two feet, an anapest followed by a pyrrhic:

$$\text{⌣ ⌣ / } | \text{ ⌣ ⌣}$$
un be liev | a ble

Terms used to describe the number of feet in a line include the following:

monometer for a one-foot line
dimeter for a two-foot line
trimeter for a three-foot line
tetrameter for a four-foot line
pentameter for a five-foot line
hexameter, or *Alexandrine,* for a six-foot line
heptameter for a seven-foot line
octameter for an eight-foot line

A seven-foot line of iambic feet is called a *fourteener.*

A complete description of the meter of a line includes both the term for the type of foot that predominates in the line and the term for the number of feet in the line. The most common

English meters are iambic tetrameter and iambic pentameter. The following are examples of each:

IAMBIC TETRAMETER:

⏑ / ⏑ / ⏑ / ⏑ /
O slow | ly, slow | ly rose | she up

IAMBIC PENTAMETER:

⏑ / ⏑ / ⏑ / ⏑ /
The cur | few tolls | the knell | of part |

⏑ /
ing day,

metonymy   **Metonymy** is the naming of an object associated with a thing in place of the name of the thing itself. Speaking of *the White House* when one means *the administrative or executive branch of the United States government* is an example of metonymy.

Middle English   **Middle English** is the form of the English language that was used from approximately 1100 to 1500. Middle English grew out of Old English and was heavily influenced by the variety of French spoken by the Normans, who conquered England in 1066. Great writers in Middle English included The Pearl Poet and Geoffrey Chaucer.

middle style   See *style.*

mimetic criticism   See *criticism.*

minor character   See *character.*

miracle play   A **miracle play** is a type of medieval drama that tells a story from a saint's life.

mixed metaphor   A **mixed metaphor** is an expression or passage that conflates, or garbles together, two or more metaphors. An example of mixed metaphor would be the sentence "The chariot of the sun screamed across the sky," in which the sun is described, inconsistently, as both a chariot and as something that screams. See *metaphor.*

mode   A **mode** is a form of writing. One common classification system, based on content, divides types of writing into four modes: argumentation, description, exposition, and narration. See *argumentation, description, exposition,* and *narration.*

Modern English   **Modern English** is the form of the English language used from approximately AD 1500 to the present day. Modern English grew out of Middle English. Major influences on the emergence of Modern English include, first, the Renaissance Era revival of Greek and Latin learning, and, second, increased exploration, colonization, and trade. Both led to extensive borrowings from other languages, especially Latin and French.

monometer   See *meter.*

mood   **Mood,** or **atmosphere,** is the emotion created in the reader by part or all of a literary work. A writer creates a mood through judicious use of concrete details.

morality play   A **morality play** is a type of medieval drama in which the characters are abstract caricatures of virtues, vices, and the like. Morality plays are a type of *naive allegory. Everyman* is the most famous example of a morality play. See *allegory.*

motif   A **motif** is any element that recurs in one or more works of literature or art. Examples of common folk tale motifs found in oral traditions throughout the world include grateful animals or the grateful dead, three wishes, the trial or quest, and the magical metamorphosis, or transformation of one thing into another. "Cinderella," "The Ugly Duckling," and the Arthurian "Sword in the Stone" are examples of the transformation motif of the person or creature of humble station who is revealed to be exceptional. Much can be revealed about a literary work by studying the motifs within it. In Shakespeare's *Macbeth,* for example, recurring motifs include ambiguity, disturbances in nature, madness, and blood. At the beginning of the play, the witches, through their double talk, invite Macbeth to violate the moral order. Disturbances in nature, madness, and blood are all consequences of this violation.

motivation   A **motivation** is a force that moves a character to think, feel, or behave in a certain way. In D. H. Lawrence's "The Rocking-Horse Winner," the protagonist, Paul, is motivated by a desire to earn money to make life more pleasant for his mother.

Muse   In ancient Greek and Roman myth, the **Muses**—the nine daughters of Zeus and Mnemosyne, or Memory—were believed to provide the inspiration for the arts and sciences. Calliope was the Muse of epic poetry; Clio, the Muse of history; Erato, the Muse of lyrical poetry; Euterpe, the Muse of music; Melpomene, the Muse of tragedy; Polyhymnia, the Muse of sacred choral poetry; Terpischore, the Muse of choral dance and song; Thalia, the Muse of comedy; and Urania, the Muse of astronomy. The idea of the Muse has often been used by later writers to explain the vagaries and mysteries of literary inspiration. In the opening of *Paradise Lost,* Milton calls upon the Holy Spirit, one of the three members of the Christian Trinity, asking that spirit to be his Muse and to inspire his verse. The connection of the Muses with entertainments and the arts survives in our English words *amusing* and *amusement.*

mystery play A **mystery play** is a type of medieval drama that tells a story from the Bible.

myth A **myth** is a story that explains objects or events in the natural world as resulting from the action of some supernatural force or entity, most often a god. Every early culture around the globe has produced its own myths. A typical example is the Greek myth of the origin of the Narcissus flower. Narcissus was a vain boy who liked to look at his own reflection in pools of water. The punishment for his vanity was to be turned into a flower that grows near water. There he can look at his own reflection for as long as the world lasts. Literature in English often alludes to or makes use of materials from Greek, Roman, Germanic, and Celtic myths. George Bernard Shaw's play *Pygmalion,* for example, is a reworking in modern dress of the Greco-Roman myth of Pygmalion. One version of the myth is told in the Roman poet Ovid's collection of myths known as the *Metamorphoses,* or *Book of Changing Forms.*

narration **Narration,** one of the modes of writing, tells a story. The story is made up of occurrences, or events. See *mode.*

narrative poem A **narrative poem** is a verse that tells a story. The ballad "Sir Patrick Spens" and the epic *Paradise Lost* are both examples of narrative poems. See *ballad* and *epic.*

narrator A **narrator** is one who tells a story. In a drama, the narrator may be a character who introduces, concludes, or comments upon the action of the play. However, dramas typically do not have narrators. Works of fiction, on the other hand, always do, unless they consist entirely of dialogue without *tag lines,* in which case they become no longer fictions but *closet dramas,* ones meant to be read but not performed. The narrator in a work of fiction may be a central or minor character or simply someone who witnessed or heard about the events being related. Writers achieve a wide variety of ends by varying the characteristics of the narrator chosen for a particular work. Of primary importance is the choice of the narrator's *point of view.* Will the narrator be *omniscient,* knowing all things, including the internal workings of the minds of the characters in the story, or will the narrator be *limited* in his or her knowledge? Will the narrator participate in the action of the story or stand outside that action and comment on it? Will the narrator be reliable or unreliable? That is, will the reader be able to trust the narrator's statements? These are all questions that a writer must answer when developing a narrator. See *point of view* and *speaker.*

Naturalism **Naturalism** was a literary movement of the late nineteenth and early twentieth centuries that saw actions and events as resulting inevitably from biological or natural forces or from forces in the environment. Often these forces were beyond the comprehension or control of the characters subjected to them. Taken to its extreme, Naturalism views all events as mechanically determined by external forces, including the decisions made by people. Much of modern fiction, with its emphasis on social conditions leading to particular consequences for characters, is naturalistic in this sense. The novels of Thomas Hardy, which present characters who are victims of fate, are naturalistic in the sense that the characters' destinies are determined. Great writers of fiction informed by the philosophy of Naturalism include Émile Zola, Stephen Crane, Jack London, and Theodore Dreiser.

near rhyme See *slant rhyme.*

Neoclassicism **Neoclassicism** is the term used to describe the revival during the English Enlightenment or Restoration Era of ideals of art and literature derived from the Greek and Roman classics. These ideals included respect for authority and tradition, austerity, clarity, conservatism, decorum, economy, grace, imitation of the natural order, harmony, moderation, proportion, reason, restraint, self-control, simplicity, tradition, wit, and unity. Neoclassical literature was witty and socially astute, but tended toward excessive *didacticism* and an excessive distrust of invention and imagination. Popular forms of Neoclassical writing included the essay, the epistle, the satire, the parody, poems in rhymed couplets, and the earliest novels. As if in response to Pope's dictum that "The proper study of man is man," Neoclassical writers wrote primarily about social life and social interactions. Great English Neoclassical writers included Dryden, Swift, Pope, Behn, Johnson, Boswell, Congreve, Addison, Steele, Defoe, Richardson, Fielding, and Smollett. Romanticism can be seen as a reaction against Neoclassical restraint. See *Classicism,* *didacticism,* and *Romanticism.*

New Criticism   See *criticism.*

nonfiction   **Nonfiction** is writing about real events. Essays, autobiographies, biographies, and news stories are all types of nonfiction. See *prose.*

nonsense verse   A **nonsense verse** is a kind of light verse that contains elements that are silly, absurd, or meaningless. Sometimes, as is the case with Lewis Carroll's "Jabberwocky," the apparent nonsense of the verse gives way to sense upon closer analysis. Carroll's poem turns out not to be nonsense at all, but rather an ingenious retelling, in a mock heroic ballad, of a stock folk tale story, that of a young person who sets off on a quest, slays a terrible beast, and returns home victorious. A purer example of nonsense can be found in the following lines of a famous nursery rhyme:

> As I was going up the stair,
> I met a man who wasn't there.
> He wasn't there again today.
> I wish, I wish he'd go away.

novel   A **novel** is a long work of prose fiction. Often novels have involved plots; many characters, both major and minor; and numerous settings. Among the first extended works of prose fiction in English were Aphra Behn's *Oroonoko,* written in 1688; John Bunyan's *Pilgrim's Progress,* completed in 1684; and Swift's *Gulliver's Travels,* written in 1726. Early novels of note include Defoe's *Robinson Crusoe,* Richardson's *Pamela* and *Clarissa,* Fielding's *Tom Jones,* and Sterne's *Tristram Shandy.* Classic English novels in various genres include Anne Radcliffe's Gothic novel *Mysteries of Udolpho;* Jane Austen's novel of manners *Pride and Prejudice;* Sir Walter Scott's historical novel *Ivanhoe;* and Dickens's *Bildungsroman,* or novel of personal development, *Great Expectations.* Other great British novelists include Emily Brontë, George Eliot, Thomas Hardy, James Joyce, Virginia Woolf, D. H. Lawrence, Henry James, E. M. Forster, Joseph Conrad, Graham Greene, Patrick White, and Doris Lessing.

novella   A **novella** is a short novel.

nursery rhyme   A **nursery rhyme** is a children's verse. Famous English writers of nursery rhymes include Rudyard Kipling and Edward Lear.

objective correlative   An **objective correlative** is a group of images that together create a particular emotion in the reader. The term was coined by T. S. Eliot. See *image.*

occasional verse   An **occasional verse** is one written to celebrate or commemorate some particular event. Auden's "In Memory of W. B. Yeats," written on the death of the great Irish poet, is an example.

octameter   See *meter.*

octave   An **octave** is an eight-line stanza. A Petrarchan sonnet begins with an octave. See *meter* and *sonnet.*

ode   An **ode** is a lofty lyric poem on a serious theme. It may employ alternating stanza patterns, developed from the choral ode of Greek dramatic poetry. These stanza patterns are called the *strophe,* the *antistrophe,* and the *epode.* However, not all odes follow this pattern. Keats's "Ode on a Grecian Urn" is an example of an ode that does not.

off rhyme   See *slant rhyme.*

Old English   Old English, or **Anglo-Saxon,** is the earliest form of the English language. It declined after the Norman invasion of England in 1066. Old English was a highly inflected language, one that used syllables at the ends of words to indicate the words' grammatical functions. It was related to other Germanic languages that gave rise to modern Dutch, German, Icelandic, and Norwegian. For more information on Old English, see page 118.

omniscient point of view   See *narrator* and *point of view.*

one-act   See *act.*

one-dimensional character   See *character.*

onomatopoeia   **Onomatopoeia** is the use of words or phrases that sound like the things to which they refer. Examples of onomatopoeia include words such as *buzz, click,* and *pop.* Poets and other writers often make use of onomatopoeia, as in Tennyson's description of the "murmuring of innumerable bees" in "Come Down, O Maid."

oral tradition   An **oral tradition** is a work, a motif, an idea, or a custom that is passed by word of mouth from generation to generation. Materials transmitted orally may be simplified in the retelling. They also may be sensationalized because of the tendency of retellers to add to or elaborate upon the materials that come down to them. Often, works in an oral tradition contain miraculous or magical elements. Common works found in the oral traditions of peoples around the world include *folk tales, fables, fairy tales, tall tales, nursery rhymes, proverbs, legends, myths, parables, riddles, charms, spells,* and *ballads.* See *folklore.*

ottava rima *Ottava rima* is a stanza form made up of eight iambic pentameter lines rhyming *abababcc.* William Butler Yeats used this form in his poem "Among School Children."

oxymoron An **oxymoron** is a statement that contradicts itself. Words like *bittersweet, tragicomedy,* and *pianoforte* (literally, "soft-loud") are oxymorons that develop a complex meaning from two seemingly contradictory elements. Milton uses an oxymoron in Book I of *Paradise Lost* when he describes the flames of hell as giving no light but rather being "darkness visible."

palindrome A **palindrome** is a word, a phrase, or a sentence that reads the same backward as forward. Examples include the word *radar* and the sentence *Able was I ere I saw Elba,* which describes Napoleon's condition prior to his exile to the island of Elba.

parable A **parable** is a very brief story told to teach a moral lesson. The most famous parables are those such as the parable of the prodigal son told by Christ in the Bible. The medieval *exemplum* was a kind of parable. See *exemplum.*

paradox A **paradox** is a seemingly contradictory statement, idea, or event. All forms of *irony* involve paradox. An *oxymoron* is a paradoxical statement. William Wordsworth's statement that "the child is father to the man" is an example of a paradox that can be resolved, on analysis, into a coherent, noncontradictory idea. Some paradoxes, however, present unresolvable contradictory ideas. An example of such a paradox is the statement, "This sentence is a lie." If the sentence is true, then it is false; if it is false, then it is true. See *irony* and *oxymoron.*

parallelism **Parallelism** is a rhetorical technique in which a writer emphasizes the equal value or weight of two or more ideas by expressing them in the same grammatical form. William Blake uses parallelism in these lines from "The Lamb":

> And I made a rural pen,
> And I stain'd the water clear,
> And I wrote my happy songs
> Every child may joy to hear.

paraphrase A **paraphrase** is a rewriting of a passage in different words. A paraphrase is often distinguished from an *abstract* or *summary* as follows: a summary is shorter than the original, whereas a paraphrase may be as long as or longer than the original. One of the central ideas of the so-called New Criticism was that it is impossible to paraphrase a literary work precisely. Much of the content or meaning of a literary work lies in how it is expressed. Changing the expression therefore inevitably changes the meaning. See *abstract.*

parody A **parody** is a literary work that imitates another work for humorous, often satirical, purposes. The opening lines of Elizabeth Barrett Browning's Sonnet 43,

> How do I love thee? Let me count the
> ways.
> I love thee to the depth and breadth and
> height
> My soul can reach, when feeling out of
> sight
> For the ends of Being and ideal Grace.

have been parodied as follows:

> How do I love thee? Let me count the
> ways.
> Gee, there aren't any. Too bad for you.
> Toodle-loo.

pastoral poem A **pastoral poem**, from the Latin *pastor,* meaning "shepherd," is a verse that relates to idealized rural life. Examples of pastoral poems include the song from the Biblical book Proverbs that begins "The Lord is my shepherd," Marlowe's "The Passionate Shepherd to His Love," and Blake's "The Lamb." Pastoral verse, based on the *Idylls* of Theocritus and the *Eclogues* of Virgil, enjoyed great popularity during the Renaissance Period. Writers of pastoral poems included Spenser, Sidney, and Shakespeare.

pathetic fallacy The **pathetic fallacy** is the tendency to attribute human emotions to nonhuman things, particularly to things in the natural world. The term was coined by the Victorian critic John Ruskin and has often been used to describe the excesses of sentimental verse.

pentameter See *meter.*

periodical A **periodical** is a newspaper, magazine, journal, newsletter, or other publication that is produced on a regular basis.

persona A **persona** consists of the qualities of a person or character that are shown through speech or actions.

personal essay A **personal essay** is a short work of nonfictional prose on a single topic related to the life or interests of the writer. Personal essays are characterized by an intimate and informal style and tone. They often, but not always, are written in the first person. See *essay.*

personal symbol See *symbol.*

personification **Personification** is a figure of speech in which an idea, animal, or thing is described as if it were a person. The speaker of Shelley's "Ode to the West Wind" is using personification when he addresses the wind using the words "thou breath of Autumn's being."

Petrarchan sonnet See *sonnet.*

plagiarism **Plagiarism** is the act of using material gathered from another person or work without crediting the source of the material.

plot A **plot** is a series of events related to a central *conflict,* or struggle. A typical plot involves the introduction of a conflict, its development, and its eventual resolution. Terms used to describe elements of plot include the following:

- The **exposition,** or **introduction,** sets the tone or mood, introduces the characters and the setting, and provides necessary background information.

- The **inciting incident** is the event that introduces the central conflict.

- The **rising action,** or **complication,** develops the conflict to a high point of intensity.

- The **climax** is the high point of interest or suspense in the plot.

- The **crisis,** or **turning point,** often the same event as the climax, is the point in the plot where something decisive happens to determine the future course of events and the eventual working out of the conflict.

- The **falling action** is all of the events that follow the climax.

- The **resolution** is the point at which the central conflict is ended, or resolved.

- The **dénouement** is any material that follows the resolution and that ties up loose ends.

- The **catastrophe,** in tragedy, is the event that marks the ultimate tragic fall of the central character. Often this event is the character's death.

Plots rarely contain all these elements in precisely this order. Elements of exposition may be introduced at any time in the course of a work. A work may begin with a catastrophe and then use flashback to explain it. The exposition or dénouement or even the resolution may be missing. The inciting incident may occur before the beginning of the action actually described in the work. These are but a few of the many possible variations that plots can exhibit. See *conflict.*

poetic license **Poetic license** is the right claimed by writers to change elements of reality to suit the purposes of particular works that they create. Thomas Hardy's use in "Channel Firing" of characters who rise from their graves and talk is an example of poetic license. Such things do not happen in reality, but they are accepted by readers willing to suspend disbelief in order to have imaginary experiences. See *suspension of disbelief.*

point of view **Point of view** is the vantage point from which a story is told. Stories are typically written from a *first-person point of view,* in which the narrator uses words such as *I* and *we,* or from a *third-person point of view,* in which the narrator uses words such as *he, she, it,* and *they* and avoids the use of *I* and *we.* In stories written from a first-person point of view, the narrator may be a participant or witness of the action. In stories told from a third-person point of view, the narrator generally stands outside the action. In some stories, the narrator's point of view is *limited.* In such stories, the narrator can reveal the private, internal thoughts of himself or herself or of a single character. In other stories, the narrator's point of view is *omniscient.* In such stories the narrator can reveal the private, internal thoughts of any character.

portmanteau See *blend.*

poulter's measure **Poulter's measure** is a metrical form that makes use of couplets containing alternating iambic hexameter and iambic heptameter lines. The form is used in Queen Elizabeth I's "Doubt of Future Foes."

pragmatic criticism See *criticism.*

précis See *abstract.*

preface A **preface** is a statement made at the beginning of a literary work, often by way of introduction. The terms *foreword, preface,* and *introduction* are often used interchangeably.

prologue A **prologue** is an introduction to a literary work, often one that sets the scene and introduces the conflict or the main characters. "The Prologue" to Chaucer's *The Canterbury Tales* is an example. In Renaissance times, the use of a prologue spoken by a narrator at the beginning of a drama was quite common.

proscenium stage   See *stage.*

prose   **Prose** is the broad term used to describe all writing that is not drama or poetry, including fiction and nonfiction. Types of prose writing include novels, short stories, essays, and news stories. Most biographies, autobiographies, and letters are written in prose. See *fiction.*

prose poem   A **prose poem** is a work of prose, usually a short work, that makes such extensive use of poetic language, such as figures of speech and words that echo their sense, that the line between prose and poetry, never a clear one, becomes blurred. An example of a prose poem is Margaret Atwood's "Simmering."

prosody   **Prosody,** or **versification,** is the study of the structure of poetry. In particular, prosodists study meter, rhyme, rhythm, and stanza form. See *meter, rhyme, rhythm,* and *stanza.*

protagonist   See *character.*

proverb   A **proverb,** or **adage,** is a traditional saying, such as "You can lead a horse to water, but you can't make it drink" or the title of Shakespeare's play "All's Well That Ends Well."

psalm   A **psalm** is a lyrical hymn of praise, supplication, or thanksgiving. The Biblical hymn, attributed to David, that begins with the line "The Lord is my shepherd," is an example.

pseudonym   A **pseudonym** is a name assumed by a writer. Examples of pseudonyms include *George Eliot,* the pseudonym of Mary Ann Evans, and *Lewis Carroll,* the pseudonym of Charles Dodgson.

psychological fiction   **Psychological fiction** is fiction that emphasizes the interior, subjective experiences of its characters, and especially such fiction when it deals with emotional or mental disturbance or anguish. The selection from Charlotte Brontë's *Jane Eyre* on page 816 is an example.

pun   A **pun** is a play on words, one that wittily exploits a double meaning. The porter scene in Shakespeare's *Macbeth* contains a pun based on an Elizabethan usage. In Elizabethan English, the word *goose* referred both to a type of fowl and to a tailor's pressing iron. Shakespeare has his porter pretend to be the porter of Hell's gate, opening it to let in a tailor guilty of theft: "Who's there? Faith, here's an English tailor come hither for stealing out of a French hose. Come in, tailor. Here you may roast your goose."

Puritanism   **Puritanism** was a Protestant religious movement that emerged in England in the 1500s and later spread to the colonies of New England. The Puritans objected to the wealth, power, authority, and elaborate ritual of the Catholic Church. They professed a desire to "purify" the Church of England by ridding it of Catholic practices. The English Puritans overthrew the monarchy and, under Oliver Cromwell, governed the country during what is known as the Commonwealth, or Puritan Interregnum, from 1642 to 1646. The Puritans are known for their austerity and acceptance of the basic principles of Calvinism, including the ideas of preordination and original sin. Some important English Puritan writers are John Bunyan and John Milton. Important American Puritan writers include Cotton Mather and Jonathan Edwards. See *Calvinism.*

purpose   See *aim.*

pyrrhic   See *meter.*

quatrain   A **quatrain** is a stanza containing four lines.

quintain   A **quintain,** or **quintet,** is a stanza containing five lines.

quintet   See *quintain.*

rap   A **rap** is an improvised rhymed verse that is chanted or sung, often to a musical accompaniment.

reader-response criticism   See *criticism.*

Realism   **Realism** is the attempt to render in art an accurate portrayal of reality. The theory that the purpose of art is to imitate life is at least as old as Aristotle. The eighteenth-century development of the novel, with its attention to details of character, setting, and social life, can be thought of as a step toward increased Realism in writing. However, the term *Realism* is generally applied to literature of the late nineteenth century written in reaction to Romanticism and emphasizing details of ordinary life.

redundancy   **Redundancy** is needless repetition. The phrase *firmly determined* is redundant because the word *determined* already implies firmness.

refrain   A **refrain** is a line or group of lines repeated in a poem or song. Many ballads contain refrains.

regional dialect   See *dialect*.

Renaissance   The **Renaissance** was the period from the fourteenth to the early seventeenth century when Europe was making the transition from the medieval to the modern world. The word *renaissance* means "rebirth." The term refers to the rebirth of interest in ancient Greek and Latin writing that occurred during the period, a rebirth that is known as Humanism. The Renaissance was characterized by a lessening of reliance on authority, by a decline in feudalism and in the universal authority of the church, by increased nationalism, by increasingly active university and city life, by increased opportunities for individual economic attainment and freedom, and by increased belief in the value of this life in and of itself.

repetition   **Repetition** is the use, again, of a sound, word, phrase, sentence, or other element.

resolution   See *plot*.

reversal   A **reversal** is a dramatic change in the direction of events in a drama or narrative, especially a change in the fortunes of the protagonist. See *plot*.

review   A **review** is a written evaluation of a work of art, a performance, or a literary work, especially one that appears in a periodical or on a broadcast news program. Common subjects of reviews include books, films, art exhibitions, restaurants, and performances of all kinds, from rock concerts to ballets.

rhetoric   **Rhetoric** is the study of ways in which speech and writing affect or influence audiences.

rhetorical criticism   See *criticism*.

rhetorical question   A **rhetorical question** is one asked for effect but not meant to be answered because the answer is clear from context, as in Christina Rossetti's lines, "Who has seen the wind?/Neither you nor I."

rhetorical technique   A **rhetorical technique** is an extraordinary but literal use of language to achieve a particular effect on an audience. Common rhetorical techniques include *antithesis, apostrophe, catalog, chiasmus, parallelism, repetition,* and *the rhetorical question*.

rhyme   **Rhyme** is the repetition of sounds at the ends of words. Types of rhyme include *end rhyme* (the use of rhyming words at the ends of lines), *internal rhyme* (the use of rhyming words within lines), *exact rhyme* (in which the rhyming words

end with the same sound or sounds), and *slant rhyme* (in which the rhyming sounds are similar but not identical). An example of exact rhyme is the word pair *moon/June*. Examples of slant rhyme are the word pairs *rave/rove* and *rot/rock*. See *slant rhyme*.

rhythm   **Rhythm** is the pattern of beats or stresses in a line of verse or prose. See *meter*.

riddle   A **riddle** is a word game in which something is described in an unusual way and the reader or listener must figure out what that something is. Riddles are common in folklore and myth throughout the world. Examples include the Anglo-Saxon Riddles collected in *The Exeter Book*.

rising action   See *plot*.

romance   **Romance** is a term used to refer to four types of literature: 1. medieval stories about the adventures and loves of knights; 2. novels and other fictions involving exotic locales and extraordinary or mysterious events and characters; 3. nonrealistic fictions in general; and 4. in popular modern usage, love stories of all kinds. The term originated in the Middle Ages. It was first used to describe stories believed to be based upon Latin originals (stories told by the Romans). It came to be used in Europe and England for stories in prose or poetry about knightly exploits, including those told about such characters as Alexander the Great, Roland, Percival, Tristan and Isolde, and King Arthur and his knights of the Round Table. Because the later medieval romances were for the most part told in prose, the term came to be applied to prose fictions in general, and especially to those that were highly imaginative. In the nineteenth century, the term was commonly used to describe fictional works, such as the novels of Sir Walter Scott, that dealt with adventure in exotic locales. It was used by Nathaniel Hawthorne to describe stories like his *Blithedale Romance* and *House of the Seven Gables* because of their deviations from Realism. Today, the term is quite widely used to refer to love stories, especially popular, sentimental stories of the sort often turned into television movies.

Romantic criticism   See *criticism*.

Romanticism   **Romanticism** was a literary and artistic movement of the eighteenth and nineteenth centuries that placed value on emotion or imagination over reason, the individual over society, nature and wildness over human works, the country over the town, common people over aristocrats, and freedom over control or authority. Major writers of the Romantic Era included William Blake, William Wordsworth, Samuel Taylor Coleridge, Percy Bysshe Shelley, Mary Shelley, and George Gordon, Lord Byron.

rounded character   See *character*.

run-on line   A **run-on line** is a line of verse in which the sense or the grammatical structure does not end with the end of the line but rather is continued on one or more subsequent lines. The following lines from Byron's "She Walks in Beauty" form a single sentence:

> She walks in beauty, like the night
> Of cloudless climes and starry skies;
> And all that's best of dark and bright
> Meet in her aspect and her eyes:
> Thus mellow'd to that tender light
> Which heaven to gaudy day denies.

The act of continuing a statement beyond the end of a line is called *enjambment*. See *end-stopped line*.

satire   **Satire** is humorous writing or speech intended to point out errors, falsehoods, foibles, or failings. It is written for the purpose of reforming human behavior or human institutions. Jonathan Swift's *Gulliver's Travels*, for example, satirizes political and social institutions.

scansion   **Scansion** is the art of analyzing poetry to determine its meter. See *meter*.

scene   A **scene** is a short section of a literary work that presents action that occurs in a single place or at a single time. Long divisions of dramas are often divided into scenes.

science fiction   **Science fiction** is highly imaginative fiction containing fantastic elements based on scientific principles, discoveries, or laws. It is similar to *fantasy* in that it deals with imaginary worlds but differs from fantasy in having a scientific basis. Mary Shelley's *Frankenstein* was an early precursor of modern science fiction. She based her idea of the creation of artificial life on nineteenth-century experiments with so-called animal magnetism, the electrical charges believed by some people in those days to be the force motivating living things and distinguishing them from nonliving things. Arthur C. Clarke's short story "History Lesson," which is set on Venus, is an example of science fiction. George Orwell's *Nineteen Eighty-four* has many science fiction elements. Often science fiction deals with the future, the distant past, or with worlds other than our own such as distant planets, parallel universes, and worlds under the ground or the sea. The genre allows writers to suspend or alter certain elements of reality in order to create fascinating and sometimes instructive alternatives. Important writers of science fiction include H. G. Wells, Jules Verne, Ray Bradbury, Arthur C. Clarke, Isaac Asimov, Ursula K. Le Guin, Robert Heinlein, and Kurt Vonnegut, Jr. See *fantasy*.

scop   An Anglo-Saxon poet or minstrel was known as a **scop**, or **gleeman**. The scop composed verse orally and recited it to the accompaniment of a harp.

sensory detail   See *description*.

sentimentality   **Sentimentality** is an excessive expression of emotion. Much popular literature of the nineteenth and twentieth centuries is characterized by sentimentality.

septet   A **septet** is a stanza with seven lines.

sestet   A **sestet** is a stanza with six lines, such as the second part of a Petrarchan sonnet. See *meter* and *sonnet*.

set   A **set** is a collection of objects on a stage arranged in such a way as to create a scene.

setting   The **setting** of a literary work is the time and place in which it occurs, together with all the details used to create a sense of a particular time and place. Writers create setting by various means. In drama, the setting is often revealed by the stage *set* and the costumes, though it may be revealed through what the characters say about their environs. In fiction, setting is most often revealed by means of description of such elements as landscape, scenery, buildings, furniture, clothing, the weather, and the season. It can also be revealed by how characters talk and behave. In its widest sense, setting includes the general social, political, moral, and psychological conditions in which characters find themselves. See *set*.

Shakespearean sonnet   See *sonnet*.

shape poem   See *concrete poem*.

short short   A **short short**, or **flash fiction**, is an extremely brief short story. This recently recognized genre of the short story is currently enjoying considerable popularity among readers of literary magazines and short story collections published in the United States. Short shorts sometimes take the form of *anecdotes,* or retellings of single incidents. Alternatively, they may attempt to develop an entire plot within the compass of a few paragraphs. Many short shorts are highly poetic and may be considered prose poems. An example of the genre is Margaret Atwood's "Simmering." See *anecdote* and *prose poem.*

sight rhyme   A **sight rhyme**, or **eye rhyme**, is a pair of words, generally at the ends of lines of verse, that are spelled similarly but pronounced differently. This couplet from Shakespeare's *A Midsummer Night's Dream* provides an example:

> Or in the night, imagining some *fear,*
> How easy is a bush suppos'd a *bear!*

simile   A **simile** is a comparison using *like* or *as.* Christina Rossetti's "A Birthday" begins with three similes:

> My heart is like a singing bird
>   Whose nest is in a watered shoot:
> My heart is like an apple tree
>   Whose boughs are bent with thickset fruit;
> My heart is like a rainbow shell
>   That paddles in a halcyon sea.
> My heart is gladder than all these
>   Because my love is come to me.

A simile is a type of *metaphor*, and like any other metaphor, can be analyzed into two parts, the *tenor* (or subject being described), and the *vehicle* (or object being used in the description). In the simile "your locks are like the snow," the tenor is locks of hair and the vehicle is snow. They can be compared because they share some quality, in this case, whiteness. See *metaphor.*

slang   **Slang** is extremely colloquial speech not suitable for formal occasions and usually associated with a particular group of people. An example of slang current among young people in the United States in the 1920s is "the bee's knees," for something uniquely attractive or wonderful. Among young people in the northeastern United States, the word *wicked* is now sometimes used as a slang term meaning "extremely," as in "That song is *wicked* good." Writers sometimes use slang in an attempt to render characters and setting vividly.

slant rhyme   A **slant rhyme, half rhyme, near rhyme,** or **off rhyme** is substitution of assonance or consonance for true rhyme. The pairs *world/boiled* and *bear/bore* are examples. See *assonance, consonance,* and *rhyme.*

social dialect   See *dialect.*

soliloquy   A **soliloquy** is a speech delivered by a lone character that reveals the speaker's thoughts and feelings. Macbeth's "Tomorrow and tomorrow and tomorrow" speech (Act V, scene v) is an example.

sonnet   A **sonnet** is a fourteen-line poem that follows one of a number of different rhyme schemes. The *English, Elizabethan,* or *Shakespearean sonnet* is divided into four parts: three *quatrains* and a final *couplet.* The rhyme scheme of such a sonnet is *abab cdcd efef gg.* The sonnets by Shakespeare in this book are examples. The *Italian* or *Petrarchan sonnet* is divided into two parts: an *octave* and a *sestet.* The rhyme scheme of the octave is *abbaabba.* The rhyme scheme of the sestet can be *cdecde, cdcdcd,* or *cdedce.* Sir Thomas Wyatt's "Whoso List to Hunt" is an example of the Petrarchan sonnet.

sonnet cycle   See *sonnet sequence.*

sonnet sequence   A **sonnet sequence** is a group of related sonnets. Famous sonnet sequences in English include the sonnets of William Shakespeare, Sir Philip Sidney's *Astrophil and Stella,* and Edmund Spenser's *Amoretti.* See *sonnet.*

source   A **source** is a work from which an author takes his or her materials. For example, Shakespeare found the outlines of his story of Macbeth in Ralph Holinshed's *Chronicles.*

speaker   The **speaker** is the character who speaks in, or narrates, a poem—the voice assumed by the writer. The speaker and the writer of a poem are not necessarily the same person. The speaker of Robert Browning's "My Last Duchess," for example, is an Italian duke of the Renaissance Era. The speaker of Thomas Hardy's "Channel Firing" is a dead person. The speakers of the Anglo-Saxon riddles on page 94 are various objects—mead, a shield, and a book.

spectacle   In drama, the **spectacle** is all the elements that are presented to the senses of the audience, including the lights, setting, costumes, make-up, music, sound effects, and movements of the actors.

Spenserian stanza   The **Spenserian stanza,** used by Edmund Spenser in *The Færie Queene,* contains nine lines, the first eight in iambic pentameter and the ninth in iambic hexameter. The rhyme scheme is *ababbcbcc.*

spondee   A **spondee** is a poetic foot containing two strongly stressed syllables, as in the words *compound* and *roughhouse.* Such a foot is said to be *spondaic.*

sprung rhythm   **Sprung rhythm** is the term coined by Gerard Manley Hopkins to describe the unique metrical forms of his verse. Hopkins used a foot consisting of a single stressed syllable and feet containing a stressed syllable followed by one, two, or three weakly stressed syllables. One consequence of Hopkins's use of sprung rhythm was the frequent occurrence in his poetry of several stressed syllables in a row, as in the following line:

> / ˘ / / / / ˘ ˘ ˘
> Summer ends now; now, barbarous in
>
> / ˘ ˘ /   ˘ /
> beauty, the stoks [sheaves] arise

stage   A **stage** is any arena on which the action of a drama is performed. In the Middle Ages, stages often consisted of the beds of wagons, which were wheeled from place to place for performances. From the use of such wagons in innyards, the *thrust stage* developed. This was a platform that extended out into the audience and that was closed at the back. In front of the platform in the first English theaters, such as Shakespeare's Globe Theatre, was an open area, the pit, where common people stood. Around the pit were balconies in imitation of the balconies of inns. The modern *proscenium stage* typically is closed on three sides and open at the front, as though the fourth wall had been removed. Sometimes contemporary plays are performed as *theater in the round,* with the audience seated on all sides of the playing area.

stage directions   **Stage directions** are notes included in a play in addition to the dialogue for the purpose of describing how something should be performed on stage. Stage directions describe setting, lighting, music, sound effects, entrances and exits, properties, and the movements of characters. They are usually printed in italics and enclosed in brackets or parentheses.

stanza   A **stanza** is a recurring pattern of grouped lines in a poem. The following are some types of stanza:

two-line stanza	couplet
three-line stanza	tercet or triplet
four-line stanza	quatrain
five-line stanza	quintain
six-line stanza	sestet
seven-line stanza	heptastich
eight-line stanza	octave

static character   See *character.*

stereotype   A **stereotype** is an uncritically accepted fixed or conventional idea, particularly such an idea held about whole groups of people. A *stereotypical,* or *stock,* character is one who does not deviate from conventional expectations of such a character. Examples of stereotypical characters include the merciless villain, the mad scientist, and the hard-boiled private eye. See *character.*

stock character   See *character* and *stereotype.*

story   A **story,** or **narrative,** is writing or speech that relates a series of events. When these events are causally connected and related to a conflict, they make up a *plot.* See *plot.*

stream-of-consciousness writing   **Stream-of-consciousness writing** is literary work that attempts to render the flow of feelings, thoughts, and impressions within the minds of characters. Modern masters of stream-of-consciousness writing include Virginia Woolf, James Joyce, and William Faulkner. An example of stream-of-consciousness writing is the opening of James Joyce's *A Portrait of the Artist as a Young Man.*

stress   **Stress,** or **accent,** is the level of emphasis given to a syllable. In English *metrics,* the art of rhythm in written and spoken expression, syllables are generally described as being *strongly* or *weakly stressed,* in other words, *accented* or *unaccented.* A strongly stressed or accented syllable receives a strong emphasis. A weakly stressed or unaccented syllable receives a weak one. In the following line on the beauty of Helen of Troy, the strongly stressed or accented syllables are marked with a slash mark (/).

> /   /   /
> Is this the face that launched a
>
> /   /
> thousand ships?

—Christopher Marlowe, *The Tragical History of Doctor Faustus*

structuralist criticism   See *criticism.*

style   **Style** is the manner in which something is said or written. Traditionally, critics and scholars have referred to three levels of style: *high style,* for formal occasions or lofty subjects; *middle style,* for ordinary occasions or subjects; and *low style,* for extremely informal occasions or subjects. A writer's style depends upon many things, including his or her *diction* (the words that the writer chooses), selection of grammatical structures (simple versus complex sentences, for example), and preference for abstract or concrete words. Any recurring feature that distinguishes one writer's work from another can be said to be part of that writer's style. See *abstract* and *fiction*.

subplot   A **subplot** is a subordinate story told in addition to the major story in a work of fiction. Often a subplot mirrors or provides a foil for the primary plot. See *plot* and *story*.

summary   See *abstract*.

suspense   **Suspense** is a feeling of expectation, anxiousness, or curiosity created by questions raised in the mind of a reader or viewer.

suspension of disbelief   **Suspension of disbelief** is the phrase used by Coleridge in his *Biographia Literaria* to describe the act by which the reader willingly sets aside his or her skepticism in order to participate imaginatively in the work being read. A modern adult reader of *Beowulf*, for example, will most likely not believe in dragons. However, he or she may suspend disbelief in dragons and imagine, while reading, what the world would be like if such creatures did exist. The willingness to suspend disbelief, to participate imaginatively in a story being read, is the most important attribute, beyond literacy, that a person can bring to the act of reading.

symbol   A **symbol** is a thing that stands for or represents both itself and something else. Writers use two types of symbols—conventional, and personal or idiosyncratic. A *conventional symbol* is one with traditional, widely recognized associations. Such symbols include doves for peace; laurel wreaths for heroism or poetic excellence; the color green for jealousy; the color purple for royalty; the color red for anger; morning or spring for youth; winter, evening, or night for old age; wind for change or inspiration; rainbows for hope; roses for beauty; the moon for fickleness or inconstancy; roads or paths for the journey through life; woods or darkness for moral or spiritual confusion; thorns for troubles or pain; stars for unchangeableness or constancy; mirrors for vanity or introspection; snakes for evil or duplicity; and owls for wisdom. A *personal* or *idiosyncratic symbol* is one that assumes its secondary meaning because of the special use to which it is put by a writer. Thus in Ted Hughes's poem "Thistles," the thistles become a symbol of a certain toughness or tenacity of the human spirit.

synaesthesia   **Synaesthesia** is a figure of speech that combines in a single expression images related to two or more different senses. William Blake's description in "London" of the "soldier's cry" that "runs in blood down palace walls" is an example of synaesthesia involving the senses of sound and sight.

synecdoche   A **synecdoche** is a figure of speech in which the name of part of something is used in place of the name of the whole or *vice versa*. In the command *"All hands on deck!"* *hands* is a synecdoche in which a part (hands) is used to refer to a whole (people, sailors). Addressing a representative of the country of France as *France* would be a synecdoche in which a whole (France) is used to refer to a part (one French person).

syntax   **Syntax** is the pattern of arrangement of words in a statement. Poets often vary the syntax of ordinary speech or experiment with unusual syntactic arrangements. For example, in "A Refusal to Mourn the Death by Fire of a Child in London," Dylan Thomas begins with a long series of adjectives, delaying until the third line the appearance of the noun that is modified:

> Never until the mankind making,
> Bird, beast, and flower-fathering,
> And all-humbling darkness . . .

See *inversion*.

tag line   A **tag line** is an expression in a work of fiction that indicates who is speaking and sometimes indicates the manner of speaking. Examples include the familiar *she said* as well as more elaborate expressions such as *Raoul retorted angrily*.

tall tale   A **tall tale** is a story, often light-hearted or humorous, that contains highly exaggerated, unrealistic elements. The stories told in Swift's *Gulliver's Travels* are examples.

tenor   See *metaphor*.

tercet   See *triplet*.

terza rima   *Terza rima* is a three-line stanza of the kind used in Dante's *Divine Comedy*, rhyming *aba, bcb, cdc, ded,* and so on. Percy Shelley's "Ode to the West Wind" is written in *terza rima*.

tetrameter   See *meter*.

textual criticism   See *criticism*.

theater (playing area)   See *stage*.

theater in the round   See *stage*.

theater of the absurd   The **theater of the absurd** is a kind of twentieth-century drama that presents illogical, absurd, or unrealistic scenes, characters, events, or juxtapositions in an attempt to convey the essential meaninglessness of human life, although playwrights have often used the form to convey significant moral messages. Practitioners of the theater of the absurd, which grew out of the philosophy of *Existentialism*, include Eugène Ionesco, Samuel Becket, Edward Albee, and Harold Pinter. See *Existentialism* and *literature of the absurd*.

theme A **theme** is a central idea in a literary work. One reading of Wordsworth's "The world is too much with us," for example, would say that the poem's theme is the great spiritual or emotional cost of our modern alienation from the natural world.

thesis A **thesis** is a main idea that is supported in a work of nonfictional prose.

third-person point of view See *point of view*.

three-dimensional character See *character*.

thrust stage See *stage*.

tone **Tone** is the emotional attitude toward the reader or toward the subject implied by a literary work. Examples of the different tones that a work may have include familiar, ironic, playful, sarcastic, serious, and sincere.

tragedy A **tragedy** is a drama (or by extension any work of literature) that tells the story of the fall of a person of high status. Tragedy tends to be serious. It celebrates the courage and dignity of a tragic hero in the face of inevitable doom. Sometimes that doom is made inevitable by a *tragic flaw* in the hero, such as the ambition that brings about the fall of Shakespeare's Macbeth. In the twentieth century, writers have extended the definition of *tragedy* to cover works that deal with the fall of any sympathetic character, despite his or her status.

tragic flaw A **tragic flaw** is a personal weakness that brings about the fall of a character in a tragedy. In Shakespeare's *Romeo and Juliet,* for example, both Romeo and Juliet suffer from the tragic flaw of impetuousness, a flaw to be forgiven, perhaps, by those familiar with young love, but not one that can be forgiven by the fateful stars that govern the fortunes of these two in the play.

transition A **transition** is a word, phrase, sentence, or paragraph used to connect ideas and to show relationships between them. *However, there-*

fore, in addition, and *in contrast* are common transitions. Repeated nouns, synonyms, and pronouns can also serve as transitions. For more information on transitions, see the Language Arts Survey, 1.34, "Organizing Ideas"; 1.38, "Paragraphs with Topic Sentences"; and 1.39, "Paragraphs without Topic Sentences." See *coherence*.

translation **Translation** is the art of rendering speech or writing into another language.

trimeter See *meter*.

triplet A **triplet**, or **tercet,** is a stanza of three lines.

trochee A **trochee** is a poetic foot consisting of a strongly stressed syllable followed by a weakly stressed syllable, as in the word *winter*. A line of poetry made up of trochees is said to be *trochaic*.

trope See *figure of speech*.

turning point See *plot*.

understatement An **understatement** is an ironic expression in which something of importance is emphasized by being spoken of as though it were not important, as in "He's sort of dead, I think."

unity A work has **unity** when its various parts all contribute to creating an integrated whole. An essay with unity, for example, is one in which all the parts help to support the thesis statement, or main idea. See *essay*.

unreliable narrator An **unreliable narrator** is one whom the reader cannot trust. Browning's dramatic monologue "My Last Duchess" employs an unreliable narrator. See *narrator*.

Utilitarianism **Utilitarianism** was a philosophical movement of the nineteenth century associated with Jeremy Bentham and John Stuart Mill in England and with Charles Peirce and William James in the United States. The primary guiding principle of Utilitarianism was that the truth of an idea or the rightness of an action should be judged not according to some abstract or ideal principle, but rather according to its practical consequences. Another tenet of Utilitarianism was that moral and political decisions should be made as a result of considering what course of action would bring about "the greatest good [or happiness] for the greatest number" of people.

utopia A **utopia** is an imaginary, idealized world. The term comes from the title of Sir Thomas More's *Utopia*, which described what

More believed to be an ideal society. More took the word from the Greek roots meaning "no-place." See *dystopia.*

vehicle   See *metaphor.*

verbal irony   See *irony.*

vernacular   The **vernacular** is the speech of the common people. During the Middle Ages, much writing throughout Europe was done in Latin, the official language of the church. Only gradually, during the late Middle Ages and the Renaissance Era, did the vernacular languages of Europe replace Latin for scholarly purposes. The term *vernacular* is often used loosely today to refer to dialogue or to writing in general that uses colloquial, dialectical, or slang expressions.

versification   See *prosody.*

vers libre   See *free verse.*

villanelle   A **villanelle** is a complex and intricate nineteen-line French verse form. The rhyme scheme is *aba aba aba aba abaa.* The first line is repeated as lines 6, 12, and 18. The third line is repeated as lines 9, 15, and 19. The first and third lines appear as a rhymed couplet at the end of the poem. Dylan Thomas's "Do Not Go Gentle into That Good Night" is a villanelle.

Glossary

OF WORDS FOR EVERYDAY USE

A

a • bate (ə bāt´) *vi.*, diminish; terminate

ab • hor • rence (ab hôr´ əns) *n.*, loathing

ab • jure (ab joōr´) *vt.*, renounce; give up publicly

a • bom • i • nate (ə bäm´ə nāt) *vt.*, dislike very much

a • cute (ə kyoōt´) *adj.*, keenly intelligent; severe and sharp

a • dieu (ə dyoō´) *interj.*, goodbye

ad • ver • si • ty (ad vʉr´ sə tē) *n.*, misfortune, trouble

a • gen • cy (ā´jən sē) *n.*, force or power

ag • i • ta • tion (aj´ə tā´shən) *n.*, violent motion

a • gog (ə gäg) *adj.*, eagerly excited

a • gue (ā´ gyoō´) *n.*, fever and chills

am • ble (am´bəl) *vi.*, move with a smooth, easy gait

a • mends (ə mendz´) *n. pl.*, something done to make up for injury, loss, etc., that one has caused

a • mi • a • ble (ā´mē ə bəl) *adj.*, good-natured, friendly

a • mi • a • bly (ā´ mē ə blē) *adv.*, in a pleasant and friendly manner

am • i • ca • ble (am´ i kə bəl) *adj.*, friendly

ar • bi • trar • y (är´bə trer´ē) *adj.*, despotic; dictatorial

ar • dent (ärd ´'nt) *adj.*, intensely enthusiastic or devoted; zealous

ar • du • ous (är´ joō əs) *adj.*, extremely difficult

ar • ti • cu • late (är tik´yoō lāt´) *vt.*, express clearly; join or connect

as • per • i • ty (ə sper´ ə tē) *n.*, harshness

as • pire (ə spīr´) *vi.*, seek to achieve lofty goals

as • sev • er • a • tion (ə sev´ə rā shən) *n.*, act of stating positively; an assertion

a • stride (ə strīd´) *adv.*, with legs on either side

a • sun • der (ə sun´dər) *adv.*, apart; separate

au • dac • i • ty (ô das´ə tē) *n.*, boldness, insolence

aug • ment (ôg ment´) *vt.*, make greater

av • a • rice (av´ə ris) *n.,* greed
a • venge (ə venj´) *vt.,* get revenge for

B

baize (bāz) *n.,* felt-like cloth
bar • o • met • ri • cal (bar´ə me´trik əl) *adj.,* referring to atmospheric pressure
beau • te • ous (byōō´ tē əs) *adj.,* beautiful
be • guile (bē gīl´) *vt.,* mislead by tricking
be • lie (bē lī´) *vt.,* misrepresent
be • tide (bē tīd) *vi.,* happen to
be • trothed (bē trô tht´) *adj.,* engaged to be married
bil • ious (bil´yəs) *adj.,* ill-tempered, cranky
black • guard (blag´ərd) *n.,* scoundrel, villain, low person
blas • phe • my (blas´fə mē´) *n.,* irreverent or dis-respectful remark or action
blight (blīt) *vt.,* destroy, prevent growth
blithe (blī*th*) *adj.,* cheerful; carefree

bro • cade (brō kād´) *n.,* cloth with a raised design woven into it
brook (brōōk) *vt.,* put up with
brusque • ly (brusk´lē) *adv.,* abrupt or curt in manner
bur • lesque (bər lesk´) *vt.,* parody, imitate deri-sively
bur • nish (bʉr´nish) *vt.,* make smooth and shiny by rubbing

C

cai • tiff (kāt´ if) *n.,* mean, cowardly person
ca • jole (kə jōl´) *vt.,* coax with flattery
cal • lous (kal´əs) *adj.,* unfeeling, merciless
can • ker (kaŋ´kər) *vt.,* infect with corruption
ca • price (kə prēs´) *n.,* whim
ca • reer (kə rir´) *vi.,* move at full speed
car • ob (kar´ əb) *n.,* leguminous tree of the east-ern Mediterranean, bearing long, flat, leathery, brown pods with a sweet pulp
cav • ern (kav´ ərn) *n.,* cave
ce • les • tial (sə les´chəl) *adj.,* heavenly, divine
cer • ti • tude (sʉrt´ə tōōd´) *n.,* absolute sureness
chasm (kaz´əm) *n.,* crack in the surface of the earth

chas • tise (chas tīz´) *vt.,* scold or condemn sharply
cir • cum • scribe (sʉr´kəm scrīb) *vt.,* constrict; enclose
cit • a • del (sit´ə del) *n.,* fortress, safe place
cleft (kleft) *vt.,* divided; split
clem • en • cy (klem´ən sē) *n.,* leniency, mercy
clois • ter (klois´tər) *n.,* monastery
come • li • est (kum´lē est) *adj.,* most attractive
come • ly (kum´ lē) *adj.,* attractive
com • pul • sion (kəm pul´ shən) *n.,* coercion, dri-ving force
con • cil • i • ate (kən sil´ē āt´) *vt.,* win over
con • cord (kän´ kôrd) *n.,* agreement
con • de • scend (kän´di send´) *vi.,* descend to a less dignified level
con • fine • less (kən fīn´ləs) *adj.,* limitless
con • found • ed (kən found´əd) *adj.,* confused
con • jure (kun´ jər) *vt.,* make appear as by magic
con • sci • en • tious • ly (kän´shē ən´shəs lē) *adv.,* in an honest or painstaking manner
con • sort (kän´sôrt) *n.,* ship that travels with other ships; companion
con • tem • plate (kän´ təm plāt) *vt.,* think about carefully
con • temp • tu • ous • ly (kən temp´chōō əs lē) *adv.,* scornfully
con • triv • er (kən triv´ər) *n.,* one who plans
con • vulse (kən vuls´) *vt.,* shake or disturb violent-ly; agitate
con • vul • sive • ly (kən vul´siv lē) *adv.,* in an agi-tated manner
copse (käps) *n.,* thicket of small trees or bushes
cor • o • net • ed (kôr´ə net´id) *adj.,* with a band of ornamentation
cor • po • ral (kôr pə rəl) *adj.,* of the body; bodily
cor • po • re • al (kôr pôr´ ē əl) *adj.,* of a bodily or physical nature
corse • let (kôrs´ lit) *n.,* piece of body armor
coun • te • nance (koun´tə nəns) *n.,* facial expres-sion; face or facial features
cov • e • nant (kuv´ə nənt) *n.,* binding agreement
cov • et • ous • ness (kuv´ ət əs nis) *n.,* greed
cun • ning (kun´iŋ) *n.,* skill, cleverness

cyn • i • cal (sin´i kəl) *adj.,* believing that people are insincere or selfish; sarcastic or sneering

D

da • is (dā´is) *n.,* raised platform, as for a seat of honor

dal • li • ance (dal´yəns) *n.,* flirting; toying; trifling

dam • ask (dam´əsk) *vt.,* make a deep pink or rose

dan • dle (dan´dəl) *vt.,* swing up and down

dap • pled (dap´ əld) *adj.,* marked with spots

daunt • less (dônt´ləs) *adj.,* fearless

de • bar (dē bär) *vt.,* keep from some right or privilege; exclude

de • i • ty (dē´ ə tē) *n.,* a god

de • lir • i • um (di lir´ ē əm) *n.,* wild excitement

de • mur (dē mʉr) *vi.,* hesitate, object

dep • re • cate (dep´rə kāt´) *vt.,* belittle, disparage

de • rive (di rīv´) *vt.,* get from a source

de • scry (di skrī´) *vi.,* show clearly

des • o • la • tion (des´ə lā´shən) *n.,* ruin

de • tract (dē trakt) *vt.,* take or draw away

dif • fi • dent (dif´ə dənt) *adj.,* lacking self-confidence, timid

dif • fu • sive (di fyo͞o´ siv) *adj.,* causing diffusion or scattering; tending to disperse

dil • i • gent • ly (dil´ i ə jənt lē) *adv.,* with great care and attention

dirge (dʉrj) *n.,* funeral song

dis • cern • ing (di zʉrn´iŋ) *adj.,* showing good judgment

dis • dain (dis dān´) *vt.,* regard with contempt or scorn

dis • dain • ful (dis dān´ fəl) *adj.,* proud, aloof

dis • po • si • tion (dis´ pə zish´ ən) *n.,* tendency, habit

do • cil • i • ty (dō sil´ə tē) *n.,* submissiveness

doff (dôf) *vt.,* take off, remove

dog • ged • ly (dôg´id lē) *adv.,* persistently

dog • mat • i • cal • ly (dôg mat´ik ə lē´) *adv.,* stating an opinion in an arrogant manner

drear • i • some (drir´ē sum) *adj.,* sad

drudge (druj) *n.,* person who does tedious work

dudg • eon (duj´ən) *n.,* anger and resentment

dupe (do͞op) *vt.,* deceive by trickery

du • ress (do͞o res´) *n.,* constraint by threat

E

ear • nest (ʉr´ nist) *n.,* something given or done as an indication or assurance of what is to come

ec • cle • si • as • ti • cal (e klē´ zē as´ ti kəl) *adj.,* having to do with the church

ef • fi • ca • cious (ef´ i kā´ shəs) *adj.,* effective, producing the desired result

el • o • cu • tion • ar • y (el´ə kyo͞o´shən er´ē) *adj.,* appropriate for public speaking

e • lude (ē lo͞od´) *vt.,* evade, escape

em • bar • go (em bär´gō) *n.,* government order prohibiting the entry or departure of ships

em • i • nent (em´ ə nənt) *adj.,* noteworthy

em • phat • ic (em fat´ ik) *adj.,* forceful, definite

en • cum • ber (en kum´bər) *vt.,* hold back the motion of

en • deav • or (en dev´ər) *vi.,* try, attempt

en • ig • mat • i • cal • ly (en´ig mat´ik lē) *adv.,* in a perplexed manner

en • tail (en tāl) *vt.,* require

en • treat (en trēt´) *vt.,* ask earnestly; beg

ep • i • thet (ep´ə thet´) *n.,* word or phrase used to characterize a person or thing

ep • och (ep´ ək) *n.,* period of time

e • quiv • o • ca • tor (ē kwiv´ə kā´tor) *n.,* one who speaks ambiguously

err (ʉr) *vi.,* be wrong

er • ro • ne • ous (ər rōn´ nē əs) *adj.,* based on error, wrong

es • ca • pade (es´kə pād´) *n.,* reckless adventure

es • thet • i • cism (es thet´ə siz´əm) *n.,* doctrine that artistic principles should underlie values

e • the • re • al (ē thir´ē əl) *adj.,* not earthly; heavenly; celestial

et • y • mol • o • gy (et´ə mäl´ə je) *n.,* origin and development of a word

ex • alt (eg zôlt´) *vt.,* heighten or intensify the action or effect of

ex • hor • ta • tion (eg´ zôr tā´ shən) *n.,* strong urging

ex • tort (eks tôrt´) *vt.,* get something from somebody through threats or violence

ex • trem • i • ties (ek strem´ə tēz) *n.,* outermost parts

ex • u • ber • ant (eg zo͞o´ bər ənt) *adj.,* full of life

F

fast • ness (fast′ nis) *n.*, solid ground
fel • lic • i • ty (fə lis′i tē) *n.*, happiness
fen (fen) *n.*, swamp or bog
fer • vor • less (fʉr′ vər ləs) *adj.*, without passion
fick • le (fik′əl) *adj.*, unstable in affection, loyalty, interest, etc.
fis • sure (fish′ ər) *n.*, long, narrow, deep cleft or crack
flout (flout) *vt.*, show scorn or contempt for
fore • cas • tle (fōk′s′l) *n.*, the crew's quarters in the front of a merchant ship
forged (fôrjd) *adj.*, heated and shaped by pounding
fur • row (fʉr′ō) *n.*, groove made in the earth by a plow
fus • tian (fus′chən) *n.*, coarse cloth

G

gall (gôl) *n.*, bile; bitterness
gaunt (gônt) *adj.*, haggard; emaciated
gen • teel (gen tēl′) *adj.*, elegant, fashionable
gin • ger (jin′gər) *n.*, liveliness, spirit
glade (glād) *n.*, open space in a forest
glis • ter (glis′tər) *vi.*, [archaic var. of *glisten*] shine or sparkle
grav • en (grāv′ ən) *vt.*, engraved
gru • el (grōō′əl) *n.*, thin porridge made by cooking grain in water or milk
guf • faw (gu fô′) *vi.*, let out a short burst of laughter
guile (gīl) *n.*, slyness; deception
gump • tion (gump′shən) *n.*, courage, boldness
gut • ter (gut′ər) *vi.*, gurgle and sputter

H

hacked (hakt) *adj.*, cut rudely, roughly, or irregularly
hag • gard (hag′ərd) *adj.*, worn, gaunt
hal • cy • on (hal′sē ən) *adj.*, tranquil, happy
hale (hāl) *adj.*, strong and healthy
hap • less (hap′lis) *adj.*, unlucky
heath (hēth) *n.*, open wasteland
her • maph • ro • dite (hər maf′ro dīt′) *adj.*, with both male and female characteristics
her • mit • age (hʉr′ mi tij) *n.*, secluded retreat
hith • er • to (hith′ər tōō) *adv.*, until this time
home • ly (hōm′lē) *adj.*, simple, unpretentious
hov • el (huv′əl) *n.*, a shed or hut
hu • mil • i • ty (hyōō mil′ə tē) *n.*, absence of pride or self-assertion

I

ig • no • ble (ig nō′ bəl) *adj.*, dishonorable, mean
ig • no • min • i • ous • ly (ig′nə min′ē əs lē) *adv.*, shamefully; disgracefully
im • pede (im pēd′) *vt.*, obstruct or delay
im • ped • i • ment (im ped′ə mənt) *n.*, obstacle
im • per • ti • nent (im pʉrt′'n ənt) *adj.*, saucy, insolent
im • pet • u • ous (im pech′ōo əs) *adj.*, acting on impulse
im • pi • ous (im′pē əs) *adj.*, lacking respect or dutifulness
im • plic • it • ly (im plis′it lē) *adv.*, doubtlessly
im • po • tent (im′pə tənt) *adj.*, powerless
im • pre • ca • tion (im′pri kā′shən) *n.*, obscene language, curse
im • pu • dence (im′pyōō dəns) *n.*, quality of being shamelessly bold or saucy
in • an • i • mate (in an′ə mit) *adj.*, lifeless
in • censed (in sensd′) *adj.*, very angry, enraged
in • ces • sant (in ses′ənt) *adj.*, never ending
in • cor • ri • gi • ble (in kôr′ə jə bəl) *adj.*, unable to be reformed; unmanageable; unruly
in • dig • na • tion (in′dig nā′ shən) *n.*, anger, scorn
in • ef • fa • ble (in ef′ə bəl) *adj.*, incapable of being expressed or described adequately; inexpressible
in • ex • tri • ca • ble (in eks′tri kə bəl) *adj.*, unable to be disentangled
in • fal • li • bly (in fal′ōō ə blē) *adv.*, unmistakedly
in • fat • u • at • ed (in fach′ōō āt′id) *adj.*, completely overcome by love
in • fest (in fest′) *vt.*, overrun in large numbers
in • gen • ious (in jēn′ yəs) *adj.*, clever, original
in • gen • u • ous (in jen′ yōo əs) *adj.*, artless, naive
in • gra • ti • ate (in grā′shē āt′) *vt.*, bring into favor

in • scru • ta • ble (in skro͞ot′ə bəl) *adj.,* completely obscure or mysterious

in • sin • u • ate (in sin′yo͞o āt′) *vt.,* suggest, imply; work into gradually

in • sip • id (in sip′id) *adj.,* not exciting or interesting

in • so • lence (in′ sə lens) *n.,* disrespect, contempt

in • ter • mi • na • ble (in tʉr′mi nə bəl) *adj.,* without end

in • ter • mit (in′ tər mit′) *vt.,* pause

in • trigue (in trēg′) *vi.,* carry on a secret love affair

ir • rel • e • vant (ir rel′ə vənt) *adj.,* not related to the subject

J

jaunt (jônt) *n.,* short pleasure trip

joc • und (jäk′ənd) *adj.,* cheerful, merry

ju • di • cial (jo͞o dish′əl′) *adj.,* carefully considering the facts

jun • ta (ho͞on′tə) *n.,* council

K

ken (ken) *vt.,* know

kin • dred (kin′ drid) *adj.,* related, similar

L

la • ment (lə ment′) *vt.,* regret

lan • guid • ly (laŋ gwid lē) *adv.,* sluggishly; without vigor

lan • guished (lan′ gwisht) *adj.,* drooping, lacking vitality

lan • yard (lan′yərd) *n.,* cord worn around the neck

len • i • ty (len′ə tē) *n.,* leniency; mildness

lit • er • al (lit′ ər əl) *adj.,* word-for-word; true to the actual or original meaning

loath • some (lōth′ səm) *adj.,* disgusting, detestable

M

mag • is • te • ri • al •ly (maj′is tir′ē əl lē) *adv.,* in a domineering or masterful manner

mag • nan • i • mous (mag nan′ə məs) *adj.,* gracious and generous

mag • ni • tude (mag′nə to͞od′) *n.,* extent

ma • lev • o • lence (mə lev′ə lens) *n.,* malice, spitefulness

man • a • cle (man′ ə kəl) *n.,* handcuff, shackle

mar • quee (mär kē′) *n.,* tent with open sides

mar• tyr • dom (märt′ər dəm) *n.,* death or suffering for a cause

mas • quer • ade (mas′kər ād′) *n.,* ball or party at which masks and fancy costumes or disguises are worn

mead (mēd) *n.,* wine made from honey

me • an • der (mē an′ dər) *vi.,* follow a winding course

mel • an • chol • y (mel′ən käl′ē) *n.,* state of sadness or depression

men • dac • i • ty (men das′ə tē) *n.,* lying

met • a • phy • si • cian (met′ə fə zish′ən) *n.,* one who studies metaphysics, that branch of philosophy that deals with ultimate realities and the nature of being

met • tle (met′l) *n.,* spirit, courage

mil • len • ni • um (mi len′ē əm) *n.,* period of perfection or great prosperity, as in the Golden Age

min • ion (min′ yən) *n.,* favorite

mire (mīr) *n.,* soggy ground

mold • ered (mōl′derd) *adj.,* decayed

moor (mo͝or) *n.,* marshy, open land

mor • tal (môr′təl) *adj.,* deadly

mor • ti • fi • ca • tion (môr′tə fi kā′shən) *n.,* shame, humiliation

mot • ley (mät′lē) *adj.,* multicolored

mul • ti • tu • di • nous (mul′tə to͞o d′ ′nəs) *adj.,* very numerous

mu • nif • i • cence (myo͞o nif′ə səns) *n.,* generosity

muse (myo͞oz) *vi.,* think deeply and at length; meditate

N

na • tiv • i • ty (nə tiv′ ə tē) *n.,* birth

non • en • ti • ty (nän en′tə tē) *n.,* person of no importance

non • pa • reil (nän′pə rel′) *n.,* someone unequaled

O

ob • scure (əb skyo͝or′) *adj.,* faint, undefined

o • di • ous (ō′dē əs) *adj.,* arousing disgust, offensive

of • fi • cious (ə fish´əs) *adj.*, bossy; meddlesome
om • ni • bus (äm´ni bəs) *n.*, bus
om • nip • o • tent (äm nip´ə tənt) *adj.*, having unlimited power
on • slaught (än´ slôt´) *n.*, violent, intense attack
op • pres • sive (ə pres´iv) *adj.*, distressing
or • a • cle (ör´ə kəl) *n.*, person in communication with the gods; person of great knowledge or wisdom
or • gan • dy (ôr´gən dē) *n.*, sheer fabric
or • gan • ic (ôr gan´ ik) *adj.*, inherent, inborn
os • ten • ta • tious (äs´tən tā´shəs) *adj.*, excessively showy
os • ten • ta • tious • ly (äs´ tən tā´ shəs lē) *adv.*, in an excessively showy display

P

pall (pôl) *vt.*, cloak in darkness
pal • lor (pal´ər) *n.*, unnatural paleness
pal • pa • ble (pal´pə bəl) *adj.*, tangible
pal • pi • ta • tion (pal´pə tā shen) *n.*, rapid heartbeat
pal • try (pôl´ trē) *adj.*, practically worthless; trifling; insignificant; contemptible; petty
pan • e • gyr • ic (pan´ə jir´ik) *n.*, high praise
pau • per • ize (pô´pər īz´) *vt.*, impoverish
peak (pēk) *vi.*, become sickly
pe • dan • tic (ped´´nt ik) *adj.*, in a manner stressing minor or trivial points of learning
per • di • tion (pər dish´ən) *n.*, complete and irreparable loss; ruin
per • func • to • ri • ly (pər fuŋk´tə rē lē) *adv.*, in an indifferent or disinterested manner
per • ni • cious (pər nish´əs) *adj.*, causing ruin and death; wicked
per • pen • dic • u • lar (pʉr´pən dik´yoo lər) *adj.*, exactly upright
per • pet • u • al (pər pech´ oo əl) *adj.*, lasting forever
per • son • a • ble (pʉr´sən ə bəl) *adj.*, having a pleasant appearance and personality
per • ver • si • ty (pər vʉr´ sə tē) *n.*, quality or condition of wrongness, wickedness, or corruption
per • vert (pər vʉrt´) *vt.*, distort, misinterpret
pes • ti • lence (pes´tə ləns) *n.*, virulent or infectious disease of epidemic proportions

phan • tas • ma • go • ri • a (fan taz´mə gôr´ē ə) *n.*, rapidly changing series of imagined figures or events
plac • id (plas´id) *adj.*, calm; tranquil
plac • id • ly (plas´id lē) *adv.*, in a tranquil or calm manner
plaint (plānt) *n.*, complaint or grievance
plat • i • tude (plat´ə tood´) *n.*, commonplace quality
poach (pōch) *vt.*, hunt illegally
poll (pôl) *vt.*, cut off
por • ti • co (pôr´ti kō) *n.*, porch or covered walk in front of a building
port • man • teau (pôrt man´tō´) *n.*, traveling case that opens into two compartments
pos • ter • i • ty (päs ter´ ə tē) *n.*, succeeding generations
pos • tern (pōs´tərn) *n.*, private rear entrance
prate (prāt´) *vi.*, chatter
prel • ate (prel´it) *n.*, high-ranking ecclesiastic
pre • oc • cu • pied (prē äk´yoo pīd) *adj.*, engrossed
pre • sump • tu • ous (prē zump´ choo əs) *adj.*, overconfident or arrogant
pre • ten • sion (prē ten´shən) *n.*, a showy display of wealth
pre • vail (prē vāl´) *vi.*, be victorious
prin • ci • pal (prin´ sə pəl) *adj.*, main or chief
pro • bos • cis (prō bäs´is) *n.*, an elephant's trunk; a long, flexible snout
pro • cure (prō´kyoor´) *vt.*, obtain
pro • di • gious (prō dij´əs) *adj.*, amazing, huge
prod • i • gy (präd´ə jē) *n.*, child or other person with talent or genius
prof • fer (präf´ər) *vt.*, offer; extend
pro • found (prō found´) *adj.*, very deep or intense
pro • fuse • ly (prō fyoos´lē) *adv.*, generously; freely
prog • e • ny (präj´ə nē) *n.*, offspring
prom • on • to • ry (präm´ən tôr´ē) *n.*, peak of land that juts into water
pro • pi • tious (prō pish´əs) *adj.*, favorable
pro • voke (prō vōk´) *vt.*, stir up action or feeling
prox • im • i • ty (präks im´ə tē) *n.*, nearness

prud • er • y (pro͞od′ər ē) *n.,* condition of being overly modest or proper

pu • er • ile (pyo͞o′ər il) *adj.,* trivial, silly

pur • ga • to • ry (pʉr′gə tôr′ē) *n.,* temporary state of suffering or misery

pur • vey • or (pər vā ôr′) *n.,* one who supplies or provides

pyre (pīr) *n.,* funeral fire

Q

quell (kwel) *vt.,* put an end to

quill (kwil) *n.,* stiff feather of a bird

quo • rum (kwôr′əm) *n.,* a select group or company

quoth (kwōth) *vt.,* said

R

ram • i • fi • ca • tion (ram′ə fi kā′shen) *n.,* branch

rap • tur • ous (rap′chər əs) *adj.,* full of pleasure

rav • e • nous • ly (rav′ə nəs lē) *adv.,* greedily

re • ca • pit • u • late (rē′ kə pich′ə lāt′) *vi.,* summarize

rec • om • pense (rek′əm pens′) *n.,* repayment; reward

re • course (rē′kôrs′) *n.,* turning to someone for help or protection

re • dress (rē′dres′) *n.,* compensation for wrong done

reg • i • ment (rej′ə ment) *n.,* unit of soldiers

rem • i • nisce (rem′ ə niś) *vi.,* talk about memories

re • mon • strance (ri män′strəns) *n.,* act or instance of protest or complaint

re • mon • strate (ri män′ strāt) *vt.,* say in protest; object

re • morse (rē môrs′) *n.,* pity; compassion

re • pose (ri pōz′) *vt.,* lie quietly; rest

re • pu • di • ate (ri pyo͞o′ dē āt′) *vt.,* disown or cast off publicly

res • o • lute • ly (rez′ə lo͞ot′ lē) *adv.,* with a firm, fixed purpose

re • sound (ri zound′) *vi.,* reverberate, echo

res • pite (res′pit) *n.,* postponement

re • tired (ri tīrd′) *adj.,* withdrawn or apart from; secluded

rev • er • ent • ly (rev′ər ənt lē) *adv.,* with respect or awe

rev • er • ie (rev′ər ē) *n.,* dreaming

S

sanc • ti • tude (saŋk′tə to͝od) *n.,* fact of being sacred or inviolable

san • guine (saŋ′gwin) *adj.,* ruddy

sat • i • rize (sat′ə rīz) *vt.,* attack or ridicule with satire

sa • vor (sā′ vər) *vt.,* enjoy the flavor of

scathe (skāth) *n.,* injury or harm

score (skôr) *n.,* set of twenty persons or things

scorn (skôrn) *vt.,* view with contempt

scourg • er (skʉrj′ər) *n.,* one who scourges, or flogs

scru • ple (scro͞o′pəl) *n.,* qualm about something one feels is wrong

scru • pu • los • i • ty (skro͞o pyo͞o lôs ′i tē) *n.,* moral worry or qualm

scru • pu • lous (skro͞o′ pyə ləs) *adj.,* extremely careful

scru • ti • nize (skro͞ot′′n īz′) *vt.,* examine closely

scur • ril • i • ty (skə ril′ə tē) *n.,* coarseness or indecency of language

se• clud • ed (si klo͞od′ id) *adj.,* hidden from public view

sec • u • lar (sek′yə lər) *adj.,* of the world; not sacred or religious

seem • ly (sēm′lē) *adv.,* proper

sep • ul • cher (sep′əl kər) *n.,* burial vault or tomb

se • rene • ly (sə rēn′lē) *adv.,* peacefully

shin • gle (shiŋ′gəl) *n.,* rocky beach

shun (shun) *vt.,* keep away from; avoid

sig • ni • fy (sig′ nə fī′) *vt.,* show by means of words or a sign

slov • en • ly (sluv′ən lē) *adj.,* careless in appearance, untidy

smite (smīt) *vt.,* inflict a heavy blow

snig • ger (snig′ər) *vi.,* laugh in a derisive manner

sniv • el (sniv′əl) *vi.,* whine, cry, and sniffle

so • ber (sō′bər) *adj.,* serious, grave

soi • rée (swä rā′) *n.,* evening party

so • lic • it (sə lis′it) *vt.,* ask or seek pleadingly

so • lic • i • tor (sə lis′it ər) *n.,* lawyer

so • lic • i • tous (sə lis´ə təs) *adj.*, showing concern

sor • did (sôr´ did) *adj.*, filthy; wretched

spe • cious (spē shəs) *adj.*, seeming sound or logical while not really being so

splayed (splād) *adj.*, spread out

sprad • dle (sprad´əl) *vt.*, sprawl or straddle

stag • nate (stag´nāt´) *vi.*, become sluggish

staid (stād) *adj.*, sedate, serious

stat • ure (stach´ər) *n.*, height

staunch (stônch) *adj.*, strong

staunch • less (stônch´ləs) *adj.*, unstoppable

stave (stāv) *n.*, pole

stead • fast • ly (sted´fast´lē) *adv.*, in a firm or established manner

stealth • y (stel´thē) *adj.*, furtive, sly

stip • ple (stip´əl) *adj.*, flecked

stip • u • late (stip´yōō lāt´) *vt.*, specify conditions of an agreement

strait • en (strāt´n) *vt.*, subject to privation or deficiency, especially of funds

strand (strand) *n.*, shore

strat • a • gem (strat´ə jəm) *n.*, trick or plan

stri • dent (strīd´'nt) *adj.*, harsh, shrill

sub • lime (sə blīm´) *adj.*, noble, majestic

sub • lime • ly (sə blīm´ lē) *adv.*, nobly; majestically

sub • ver • sive (səb vʉr´ siv) *adj.*, with a goal to undermine or corrupt

sul • ly (sul´ē) *vt.*, soil or stain

sun • der (sun´dər) *vt.*, break apart; separate

su • per • flu • i • ty (sōō´pər flōō´ə tē) *n.*, something unnecessary or extra

sur • mise (sər mīz´) *n.*, guessing, imagined actions

swain (swān) *n.*, country youth

T

tab • leau (tab´lō´) *n.*, dramatic scene

taint (tānt) *vi.*, be infected

teem (tēm) *vi.*, bring forth

tem • po • ral (tem´ pə rəl) *adj.*, lasting only for a time, limited; of this world, not spiritual

till • age (til´ij) *n.*, land that is tilled for farming

toad • y (tōd´ ē) *vt.*, flatter in order to gain favor

tract (trakt) *n.*, expanse, area

tran • quil (tran´ kwil) *adj.*, peaceful, calm

trans • gress (trans gres´) *vt.*, overstep or break a law

tran • si • to • ry (tran´sə tôr´ē) *adj.*, temporary

trav • ail (trə vāl´) *n.*, very hard work

treach • er • ous (trech´ ər əs) *adj.*, traitorous, disloyal

treach • er • y (trech´ ər ē) *n.*, betrayal of trust; treason

trem • u • lous (trem´yōō ləs) *adj.*, trembling

tri • fle (trī´fəl) *n.*, something of little value or importance

trib • u • la • tion (trib´ yōō lā´shən) *n.*, deep sorrow, distress; suffering

tri • bute (trib´ yōōt) *n.*, payment made to a ruler as an acknowledgment of subjugation or conquest

trun • cheon (trun´chən) *n.*, a short club

tu • mult (tōō´mult´) *n.*, loud commotion; agitation

tur • bid (tʉr´bid) *adj.*, muddled

U

un • a • bashed (un ə bashd´) *adv.*, without embarrassment

un • as • sail • a • ble (un´ə sāl´ə bəl) *adj.*, undeniable

un • gen • i • al (un jēn´yəl) *adj.*, unpleasant

un • world • ly (un wʉrld´lē) *adj.*, unsophisticated

u • surp (yōō zʉrp´) *vt.*, unlawful seizure of a throne

u • surp • er (yōō sʉrp´ər) *n.*, one who assumes power without right

V

va • grant (vāg´ rənt) *adj.*, nomadic, wandering

vain (vān) *adj.*, empty, worthless

vain • ly (vān´lē) *adv.*, uselessly

van • quish (vaŋ´kwish) *vt.*, conquer or defeat in battle

ven • er • a • tion (ven´ər ā´shən) *n.*, deep respect

venge • ance (ven´jens) *n.*, revenge, retribution

ve • ran • da (və ran´də) *n.*, open porch

vis • age (viz´ ij) *n.*, a face

vi • vac • i • ty (vī vas´ə tē) *n.*, liveliness

vul • ner • a • ble (vul´nər ə bəl) *adj.*, open to injury or attack; easily hurt

W

wan (wän) *adj.,* pale, faint

wane (wān) *vi.,* lose strength

wan • ton (wän´ tən) *adj.,* luxuriant; undisciplined; unmanageable

war • y (wer´ē) *adj.,* cautious

wax (waks) *vi.,* grow gradually larger

whorled (hwôrld) *adj.,* coiled

win • now (win´ō) *vt.,* remove the unusable portion from the grain

with • er (with´ ər) *vi.,* wilt and shrivel

wraith (rāth) *n.,* ghost

wrought (rôt) *adj.,* shaped by hammering or beating; worked

Y

yearn • ing (yʉrn´iŋ) *n.,* deep desire

Z

zeal (zēl) *n.,* passion, fervor

ze • nith (zē´nith) *n.,* the highest point in the sky

zeph • yr (zef´ər) *n.,* mild, gentle breeze

Index of Titles and Authors

Index of Skills

psalm, 296, 1259
pseudonym, 1259
psychological fiction, 1259
pun, 440, 879, 1259
Puritanism, 408–412, 1259
purpose, 58, 60, 61, 80, 422
pyrrhic, 17, 1253, 1259
quatrain, 19, 641, 1259, 1263
quintain, 19, 1259, 1263
quintet, 1259
rap, 1259
reader response, xviii
reader-response criticism, 1246, 1259
Realism, 694–696, 785, 835, 1237, 1250, 1259
Realist Theater, 44
redundancy, 1259
refrain, 706, 1240, 1259
Renaissance, 242–307, 310–405, 1260
repetition, 21, 23, 292, 637, 760, 766, 1240, 1260
resolution, 9, 29, 30, 41, 311, 965, 1055, 1258, 1260
Restoration comedy, 44
reversal, 1260
review, 1260
rhetoric, 63, 1073, 1260
rhetorical criticism, 1246, 1260
rhetorical question, 21, 1260
rhetorical technique, 21, 1260
rhyme, 20, 25, 462, 766, 886, 1248, 1259, 1260, 1262
rhyme scheme, 7, 22, 613
rhythm, 17, 20, 462, 1260
riddle, 94, 98, 805, 1257, 1260
rising action, 29, 30, 311, 965, 1258, 1260
romance, 132, 151, 165, 231, 237, 312, 706, 1245, 1260
Romantic criticism, 1246, 1260
Romanticism, 482, 570–573, 1237, 1243, 1256, 1260
rounded character, 28, 1242
run-on line, 1248, 1261
satire, 26, 204, 231, 470, 479, 511, 563, 565, 1017, 1055, 1241, 1255, 1261
scansion, 1251, 1261
scene, 47, 311, 1261
science fiction, 12, 938, 939, 1250, 1252, 1261
scop, 72, 75, 99, 1252, 1261
script, 46, 1247
sensory detail, 1087, 1098, 1247, 1261
sentimentality, 1261
septet, 1261
sestet, 19, 250, 1261, 1263
set, 46, 47, 1261
setting, 12, 29, 43, 597, 744, 750, 786, 1240, 1261

Shakespearean sonnet, 279, 641, 865, 1261, 1262
shape poem, 1244, 1261
short short, 1251, 1261
short story, 26, 63, 953, 1250
sight rhyme, 1250, 1262
simile, 20, 21, 147, 284, 359, 634, 754, 856, 1237, 1238, 1250, 1254, 1262
slang, 1261
slant rhyme, 20, 488, 753, 1252, 1255, 1256, 1260, 1262
social dialect, 1262
soliloquy, 16, 17, 46, 335, 393, 1248, 1262
sonnet, 16, 248, 253, 279, 297, 305, 606, 613, 641, 760, 761, 766, 865, 882, 1248, 1256, 1258, 1261, 1262
sonnet cycle, 1262
sonnet sequence, 248, 1262
sound effects, 46, 47, 53
source, 260, 1262
speaker, 92, 270, 284, 427, 440, 581, 856, 1255, 1262
spectacle, 46, 47, 55, 63, 1262
Spenserian stanza, 1262
spondee, 17, 1251, 1252
sprung rhythm, 761, 763, 1263
stage, 46, 47, 1259, 1263
stage directions, 46, 48, 55, 1247, 1263
stanza, 6, 11, 18–19, 286, 461, 753, 1259, 1263
static character, 28, 1242, 1263
stereotype, 1263
stock character, 28, 1242, 1263
story, 965, 1263, 1264
storytelling, 4, 87
stream-of-consciousness writing, 837, 921, 929, 930, 1263
stress, 17, 82, 1236, 1263
structuralist criticism, 1245, 1246, 1263
style, 1247, 1252, 1253, 1254
subplot, 1264
summary, 1236, 1257, 1264
suspense, 1264
suspension of disbelief, 599, 1248, 1258, 1264
symbol, 93, 270, 346, 589, 603, 641, 706, 743, 766, 773, 793, 850, 862, 952, 1237, 1245, 1258, 1264
synaesthesia, 21, 1250, 1264
synecdoche, 21, 1250, 1264
syntax, 1264
tag line, 1255, 1264
tall tale, 4, 12, 1257, 1264
tenor, 20, 288, 641, 754, 1253
tercet, 18, 1254, 1263, 1265
terza rima, 1264

tetrameter, 18, 24, 1253, 1264
textual criticism, 1246, 1264
theater, 1264
theater in the round, 46, 1263
theater of the absurd, 1264
theme, 13, 30, 43, 145, 237, 384, 422, 428, 454, 610, 641, 646, 738, 744, 753, 763, 862, 865, 886, 1265
thesis, 385, 537, 1265
third-person point of view, 13, 1258, 1265
three-act play, 47, 1236
three-dimensional character, 28, 1242, 1265
thrust stage, 44, 47, 1263
tone, 272, 519, 780, 900, 1265
tragedy, 44, 312, 320, 394, 403, 1243, 1247, 1251, 1265
tragic flaw, 312, 1265
transition, 1243, 1265
translation, 86, 145, 1265
trimeter, 18, 1253, 1265
triplet, 18, 1263, 1264, 1265
trochee, 17, 1251, 1265
turning point, 29, 311, 359, 965, 1243, 1258, 1265
understatement, 21, 747, 1265
unity, 1249, 1265
unreliable narrator, 1265
Utilitarianism, 693, 1237, 1265
utopia, 1248, 1265
vehicle, 20, 288, 641, 754, 1253, 1262, 1266
verbal irony, 346, 373, 1252
vernacular, 1266
vers libre, 17, 620, 838, 1266
versification, 1258, 1266
villanelle, 876, 879, 1266

Writing

aim, 58, 251, 1073
allegory, 80
analysis, 59, 1079
analysis charts, 12, 1090
analyzing, 149, 712, 1084
anecdote, 548
Anglo-Saxon poem, 115
art criticism, 776
audience, 1071, 1075
autobiography, 184, 641
bill of rights, 489
biography, 866, 919
birth announcement, 178
brainstorming, 1091
careful drafts, 1096
cause-and-effect analysis, 1079
cause-and-effect order, 1095
character sketch, 204, 260, 588, 738, 883
chronological order, 13, 1095
classification, 59, 1079, 1095
cluster charts, 12, 1086

comic strip, 805
comparison and contrast, 59, 346, 776, 1079, 1095
comparison essay, 489, 760
compositions, 1099
computers, 1069
concrete poem, 428
continuation, 604
contract, 394
conversational tone, 610
credo, 527
critical analysis, 875
critical essay, 115, 706, 843
current events poem, 275
debate, 652, 722
degree order, 1095
description, 59, 594, 794
descriptive paragraph, 461
descriptive writing, 98, 165, 359, 856, 870
developing a writing plan, 1071
dialogue, 59, 253, 722, 891
diary entry, 939
dictionary definition, 541
dictionary entries, 145
discovery drafts, 1096
discussion, 1091
drafting, 25, 1066, 1096, 1099
dramatic monologue, 728
dramatic scene, 373
dream record, 87
dream report, 604
editorial, 537, 866
elaboration, 98, 1098
epic, 438
epilogue, 1055
epitaph, 500
essay, 919
essay test strategies, 1222
eulogy, 178, 780
evaluating, 43
exposition, 59
expository essay, 385
expository paragraph, 346
expository writing, 58, 184
expressive writing, 58, 1074
extended definition, 541
fable, 754, 891
fantasy, 754
feminist criticism, 1055
flow charts, 1088
foreshadowing, 260
form, 12, 1071, 1076
formal outlines, 1094
fortune cookie inserts, 221
free verse, 620, 862
free verse poem, 895
freewriting, 13, 1082
Gothic description, 660
headlines, 346
historical analysis, 850
how to, 159
humor, 284

family relationships, capitalization, of, 1151
first words, capitalization of, 1151
formal English, 418, 441, 452, 1062, 1163
functions of sentences, 265, 388, 887, 1116
general reference, 1137
gerunds, 165, 871, 1110
gobbledygook, 1166
good and well, 475, 1140
grammar, 1106
Greek roots, 538, 1160
hyphens, 1145
illogical comparisons, 474, 1138
imperative mood, 1129
imperative sentences, 1116
imply and infer, 566, 1141
improper shifts in verb tense, 306, 621, 1126
indefinite articles, 1111
indefinite pronouns, 900, 1109
indefinite reference, 1136
independent clauses, 1118
indirect objects, 1118
indirect quotations, 1148
infinitives, 1110
informal English, 418, 441, 452, 1062
intensive pronouns, 900, 1108
interjections, 64, 1113
interjections, capitalization of, 1151
interrogative pronouns, 1109, 1134
interrogative sentences, 1116
intransitive verbs, 260, 1110
inverting sentences, 866, 1126
irregular verbs, 306, 1127
italics, 891, 1147
jargon, 1166
Latin roots, 538, 1160
like, as, and as if, 566, 1141
linking verbs, 423, 474, 1109
literally, 1141
misplaced modifiers, 1126
modifier problems, 1139
modifiers, 474, 1115, 1119, 1139
modifiers with action and linking verbs, 1137
mood, 1128
nominative case, 404, 1133
nonrestrictive commas, 1144
nonstandard English, 1062, 1165
nouns, 64, 1107
objective case, 404, 1133
objects, 1112
of and have, 566, 1141
off of, 1141

organizations and institutions, capitalization of, 932, 1152
outlines, capitalization of, 1152
parallelism, 919, 1123
parentheses, 1146
participles, 851, 871, 1110
parts of speech, 64, 138, 145, 1107, 1114
passive voice, 1123
past, 1127
past participles, 1127
periods, 1142
personal names, capitalization of, 1152
personal pronouns, 181, 253, 900, 1108
place names, capitalization of, 1153
poetry, capitalization of, 1153
possessive case, 404, 1133
precise nouns, 95, 893, 955, 1114
predicate adjectives, 1111
predicate nominatives, 1117
predicates, 1111, 1120
prefixes, 739, 953, 1157, 1159
prepositional objects, 1114
prepositional phrases, 58, 1111, 1120
prepositions, 64, 1112
present participles, 1127
pronoun case, 1133
pronoun I, capitalization of, 1155
pronouns, 64, 404, 1108
pronouns as appositives, 1135
pronouns in comparisons, 1135
pronouns with appositives, 1135
proofreading for errors in capitalization, 635, 910, 1149
proofreading for errors in end marks and commas, 786, 1142
proofreading for punctuation errors, 686, 825, 1144
proofreading for spelling errors, 983, 1156
proper adjectives, 966, 1111
proper nouns, 455, 630, 966, 1107
proper nouns and adjectives, capitalization of, 1154
quotation marks, 786, 891, 1148
quotations, capitalization of, 1154
question marks, 1142
reference of pronouns to antecedents, 1136
referents, 1108
reflexive pronouns, 900, 1108
regional dialects, 1165

register, 625, 922, 1164
relative pronouns, 1109, 1134
repeated ideas, 1124
restatement, 1158
run-ons, 80, 238, 461, 637, 930, 1125
sacred beings and writings, capitalization of, 87, 1154
school subjects, courses, grades, and years, capitalization of, 1154
semicolons, 853, 1144
sentence fragments, 238, 489, 875, 1125
sentence strings, 1124
sentences, 238, 1116, 1125
serial commas, 1143
simple sentences, 1117
slang, 1163
social dialects, 1165
spelling rules, 983, 1156
split infinitives, 306, 653, 1128
standard English, 1062, 1165
subjects, 1111, 1117
subjunctive mood, 1129
subordinate clauses, 1113, 1120, 1134
subordinating conjunctions, 1113
substantives, 1117
suffixes, 739, 953, 1157, 1160
that and those, 1139
them and those, 1139
then and than, 566, 1141
this and these, 1139
titles of artworks, capitalization of, 1155
titles of literary works, capitalization of, 222, 1155
titles of musical works, capitalization of, 1155
titles of persons and occupations, capitalization of, 1155
transitive verbs, 260, 1110
underlining, 891, 1147
units of time, capitalization of, 1156
unnecessary ideas, 1124
usage problems, 566, 1140
varieties of English, 1062, 1163
varying sentence length and structure, 739, 1122
varying sentence openings, 1122
vehicles, capitalization of, 1156
verbals, 165, 776, 871, 1110
verbs, 64, 1109
vivid verbs, 95, 500, 893, 1115
vocabulary development, 1158
voice, 519, 648, 1128, 1161
weak reference, 1136
who and whom, 1134
word origins, 143, 805, 1161

wordiness, 25, 210, 1056, 1124
words from other curricular areas, 1162

Speaking and Listening

active listening, 277, 1171
agenda, 1173
body language, 1171
bonding, 1172
channel, 1168
chairperson, 1173
communication model, 1168
choosing a cutting, 1174
discussion, 146, 168, 262, 748, 1173
emotions, 1172
enunciation, 1169
extemporaneous speech, 1173
eye contact, 1171, 1172
facial expressions, 1171
feedback, 1168, 1171, 1172
gestures, 1171
group leader, 1173
impromptu speech, 1173
interpersonal communication, 89, 137, 267, 498, 595, 877, 1172
intonation, 1169
maintenance of relationships, 1172
memorized speech, 1173
mental activity, 1171
message, 1168
minutes, 1173
nonverbal communication, 386, 723, 858, 1169, 1170
note-taking, 1171
oral interpretation, 1174
pace, 1170
participants, 1173
personal validation, 1172
pitch, 1169
preparing a speech, 1174
proximity, 1171
public speaking, 222, 258, 420, 600, 1173
questioning, 1171
recipient, 1168
rehearsing an oral interpretation, 1175
secretary, 1173
sender, 1168
speeches, 1173
stress, 1170
symbols, 1168
tone, 1170
transitions in oral interpretation, 1175
transmission of information, 1172
verbal communication, 321, 386, 699, 864, 1169
volume, 1169

INDEX OF SKILLS **1287**

Index of Fine Art

Art Acknowledgments

1839–1906. Oil on canvas, c. 1895, 65.5 x 81.3 cm. Helen Birch Bartlett Memorial Collection 469; A Scene from the Beggar's Opera. William Hogarth, *circa* 1728–29.Tate Gallery, London/Art Resource, New York 476; Charles II of England. Philippe de Champaigne. Cleveland Museum of Art, Giraudon/Art Resource, New York 478; Queen Anne. Popperfoto, Archive Photo 479; Samuel Pepys's Diary. Masters and Fellows, Magdalene College, Cambridge 480; Great Fire of London, 1666. Museum of London 482; The Lute Player. Orazio Gentileschi, *circa* 1610. © Board of Trustees, National Gallery of Art, Washington, D.C. 494; Great Fire of London, 1666. Museum of London 510; Gulliver Released from the Strings. Gulliver's Travels, illustrated by Arthur Rackham. J. M. Dent & Co., London, courtesy of Wellesley College, Special Collections 515; Portrait of Aphra Behn. Courtesy of the Trustees of the British Museum, Photograph, J. R. Freeman & Co. Ltd. 521; Slave Ship. Joseph Mallord William Turner. Courtesy, the Museum of Fine Arts, Boston. Henry Lillie Pierce Fund 525; Portrait of Samuel Johnson. Wellesley College Library, Special Collections 533; Diagram of Slave Ship. Courtesy Library of Congress, Prints and Reproductions Division, Washington, D.C. 535; Painter's Honeymoon. Frederick Lord Leighton, 1864. Charles H. Bayley Picture and Painting Fund. Courtesy, Museum of Fine Arts, Boston 568; Capture of the Bastille, July 14, 1789. Claude Cholat. The Granger Collection 570; The Meeting of Sir Walter Scott and Robert Burns. C. M. Hardie. The Granger Collection 571; Jane Austen's plaque. Poets' Corner, Courtesy Westminster Abbey. 572; The Village Holiday or Dance of the Peasants. David Teniers, The Younger, ca. 1650. Virginia Museum of Fine Arts, Richmond, VA. The Adolph D. and Wilkins C. Williams Fund 584; The Tyger. William Blake, 1789. Yale Center for British Art, Paul Mellon Collection 593; The Heart of the Empire. Niels Moiler Lund, (1863–1916). Guildhall Art Gallery, London/Bridgeman Art Library, London 596; Housman, Lawrence. Princess Badoura. Illustrated by Edmund Dulac. London, Hodder and Stoughton, [1913]. Wellesley College Library, Special Collections. 601; Sunset with Fishing Boats on Loch Fyne. Joshua Cristall, *circa* 1807. Ashmolean Museum, Oxford 608; Nocturn in Grey and Gold: Chelsea Snow. James McNeill Whistler, 1876. Courtesy of The Fogg Art Museum, Harvard University Art Museums. Bequest—Collection of Maurice Wertheim, Bequest of Grenville L. Winthrop Class of 1906 612; Tintern Abbey on the River Wye. Philip James de Loutherbourg, 1805. Fitzwilliam Museum, Cambridge 615; Portrait of Percy Bysshe Shelley. Wellesley College Library, Special Collections 622; Grecian water jug. *Circa* 510 BC. Courtesy, Museum of Fine Arts, Boston 642, 643; Elenor. Frank Weston Benson, 1907. Charles Henry Hayden Fund. Courtesy, Museum of Fine Arts, Boston 650; Songs of Innocence. William Blake, 1789. Wellesley College Library, Special Collections 685; Fair, quiet and sweet rest. Fildes, Sir Luke, 1844–1927. (detail) Warrington Museum & Art Gallery, Lancs./ Bridgeman Art Library, London 688; Queen Victoria of England. Sir George Hayter, 1838. The Granger Collection 690; Charles Darwin. The Granger Collection 694; The Heart of the Empire. Niels Moiler Lund, (1863–1916). Guildhall Art Gallery, London/ Bridgeman Art Library, London 695; Caricature of Charles Dickens. Alfred Bryan. The Pierpont Morgan Library, New York.

Gift of Miss Caroline Newtown, 1974.7. © The Pierpont Morgan Library 1995 696; The Lady of Shalott. John William Waterhouse. Tate Gallery, London/Art Resource, New York 703; The Return of Ulysses. Romare Bearden, 1976. National Museum of American Art/Art Resource, New York 708; The Holy Family with the Infant Saint John. Andrea del Sarto, The Metropolitan Museum of Art, Maria DeWitt Jesup Fund, 1922 733; Thomas Hardy. Portrait by W. Strang. Wellesley College Library, Special Collections. 745; Charles Dickens. Wellesley College Library, Special Collections. 787; The Dell at Helmingham Park. John Constable. The Nelson-Atkins Museum of Art 790; Humpty Dumpty. From Lewis Carol's Through the Looking Glass. Wellesley College Library, Special Collections 799; London Bridge. André Derain, 1906. The Museum of Modern Art, New York 826; Battles of the Somme, August 1916. Popperfoto/ Archive Photo 829; Demonstration of the unemployed, Tower Hill, 1930. Popperfoto/Archive Photo 831; Children sheltering from the dog fight. Popperfoto/ Archive Photo 832; Wrens fitting smoke floats on to a plane. Popperfoto/Archive Photo 833; Queen Elizabeth II making her first Christmas broadcast, 1952. Popperfoto/Archive Photo 834; Margaret Thatcher. Popperfoto/Archive Photo 835; Three Musicians. Pablo Picasso, 1921. The Museum of Modern Art, New York 836; Portrait of Yeats. City Art Gallery, Manchester 840; Rest on the Flight into Egypt. Luc Olivier Merson, 1874. Courtesy of Museum of Fine Arts, Boston 848; Courtesy of Natalie and Quincy Bent. 881, 883; Viking Ship. Hugan, Popperfoto/Archive Photo 840; The Mirror. Thomas Wilmer Dewing, *circa* 1907. Courtesy of the Freer Gallery of Art, Smithsonian Institution, Washington, D.C. 903; Early Morning. Liubov Popova, The Museum of Modern Art 912; Portrait (Le Portrait). René Magritte, 1935. The Museum of Modern Art, NY. Gift of Kay Sage Tanguy 935; The Idlers. Maurice Prendergast, *circa* 1916–18, oil on canvas, 21 x 32 in., Louise Jordan Smith Fund, 1949. Maier Museum of Art, Randolph-Macon Woman's College, Lynchburg, Virginia 946; The City Rises. Umberto Boccioni, The Museum of Modern Art, New York 977; The Persistence of Memory. Salvador Dali, 1931. The Museum of Modern Art, New York. Given anonymously 994.

Additional Photo and Illustration Credits

Courtesy of Bessann and William Triplett: 267, 268, 415, 458, 459, 529, 590, 632, 922, 1064-65; **Ed Parker:** 250, 257, 261, 266, 286, 316, 412, 425, 429, 442, 451, 457, 491, 501, 511, 528, 542, 574, 582, 589, 599, 605, 631, 638, 698, 740, 757, 761, 777, 830, 852, 857, 863, 872, 876, 880, 888, 892, 896, 901, 914, 921, 940, 986; **Melissa Baker:** 23, 91, 137, 143, 146, 251, 252, 255, 258, 273, 280, 281, 287, 291, 291, 291, 291, 318, 319, 388, 413, 418, 420, 426, 428, 439, 452, 453, 485, 498, 543, 545, 562, 573, 575, 579, 585, 623, 624, 625, 635, 639, 648, 655, 683, 699, 712, 718, 724, 741, 751, 758, 762, 764, 768, 778, 782, 841, 844, 847, 853, 856, 858, 864, 865, 873, 877, 879, 889, 897, 915, 920, 955, 963, 1066, 1106, 1167, 1168, 1176, 1224; **©1995 Michael Romanos:** 992, 1008, 1018, 1031, 1039; **Sol Graphic Design:** 104, 110–111, 140, 322, 347, 336, 360, 374; **Carol O'Malia:** 70, 72, 314; **Anthony O. Constantino:** 1.

Literary Acknowledgments (continued from copyright page)

Harcourt Brace and Company "The Naming of Cats" from *Old Possum's Book of Practical Cats*, copyright 1939 by T. S. Eliot and renewed 1967 by Esme Valerie Eliot, reprinted by permission of Harcourt Brace & Company. Excerpts from *Nineteen Eighty-four* by George Orwell, copyright 1949 by Harcourt Brace & Company and renewed 1977 by Sonia Brownell Orwell, reprinted by permission of the publisher. "Preludes" from *Collected Poems 1909–1962* by T. S. Eliot, copyright 1936 by Harcourt Brace & Company, copyright © 1964, 1963 by T. S. Eliot, reprinted by permission of the publisher. **Harlan Davidson, Inc.** From Petrarch, *Selected Sonnets, Odes, and Letters* edited by Thomas G. Bergin (Crofts Classics Series) pp. 19, 40, 41. Copyright 1966 by Harlan Davidson, Inc. Reprinted by Permission. **HarperCollins Publishers** *The Analects of Confucius,* Arthur Waley, HarperCollins Publishers Limited. "Naked Girl and Mirror" by Judith Wright from her *Collected Poems, 1942–1985* with the permission of HarperCollins Publishers, Inc. EXCERPT from *NECTAR IN A SIEVE* by KAMALA MARKANDAYA. Copyright, 1954, by The John Day Company. Copyright renewed © 1982 by Kamala Markandaya. Reprinted by the permission of HarperCollins Publishers, Inc. ALL LINES from "THISTLES" FROM *WODWO* by TED HUGHES. Copyright © 1961 by Ted Hughes. Reprinted by permission of HarperCollins Publishers, Inc. **Henry Holt and Co., Inc.** "To an Athlete Dying Young," "Loveliest of Trees," and "When I Was One-and-Twenty" from *The Collected Poems of A. E. Housman*. Copyright 1939, 1940 by Henry Holt and Co., Inc. Copyright © 1967 by Robert E. Symons. Reprinted by permission of Henry Holt and Co., Inc. **Louisiana State University Press** Sonnet 77. Reprinted by permission of Louisiana State University Press from *The Poems of Lady Mary Wroth*, edited by Josephine Roberts. Copyright © 1983 by Louisiana State University Press. **Macmillan & Company, Ltd.** *Don Quixote de La Mancha* (excerpts), Miguel de Cervantes Saavedra, Macmillan & Company, Ltd., London, 1957. **McGraw Hill Book Company** Alice Munro, *Red Dress—1946*, McGraw Hill, 1968 **New Directions Publishing Corp.** Stevie Smith: *Collected Poems of Stevie Smith*. Copyright ©1972 by Stevie Smith. Reprinted by permission of New Directions Publishing Corp. "Do not go gentle into that good night." Dylan Thomas: *Poems of Dylan Thomas*. copyright 1945 by The Trustees for the Copyrights on Dylan Thomas, 1952 by Dylan Thomas. Reprinted by permission of New Directions Publishing Corp. "Dulce et Decorum Est." Wilfred Owen: *Collected Poems of Wilfred Owen*. Copyright © 1963 by Chatto & Windus, Ltd. Reprinted by permission of New Directions Publishing Corp. **Penguin Books USA Inc.** Two selections from *The Canterbury Tales* by Geoffrey Chaucer, translated by Nevill Coghill (Penguin Classics 1951, Fourth revised edition, 1977) copyright © Nevill Coghill, 1951, 1958, 1960, 1975, 1977: "The Prologue" (878 lines; pp 19–42) "The Pardoner's Tale" (512 line; pp 268–274) From *A Portrait of the Artist as a Young Man* by James Joyce. Copyright 1916 by B. W. Huebsch, Copyright 1944 by Nora Joyce, Copyright © 1964 by the Estate of James Joyce. Used by permission of Viking Penguin, a division of Penguin Books USA Inc. 4 haiku (pp 63, 68, 82, 87) from *The Narrow Road to the Deep North and Other Travel Sketches* by Bashō, translated by Nobuyuki Yuasa (Penguin Classics, 1966) copyright © Nobuyuki Yuasa, 1966. "The Rocking-Horse Winner, pp. 790–804" by D. H. Lawrence, copyright 1933 by the Estate of D. H. Lawrence, renewed © 1961 by Angelo Ravagli and C. M. Weekley, Executors of the Estate of Frieda Lawrence, from *Complete Short Stories of D. H. Lawrence* by D. H. Lawrence. Used by permission of Viking Penguin, a division of Penguin Books USA Inc. "Snake" by D. H. Lawrence, from *The Complete Poems of D. H. Lawrence* by D. H. Lawrence, Edited by V. de Sola Pinto & F. W. Roberts. Copyright © 1964, 1971 by Angelo Ravagli and C. M. Weekley, Executors of the Estate of Frieda Lawrence Ravagli. Used by permission of Viking Penguin, a division of Penguin Books USA Inc. **Random House, Inc.** "Musee Des Beaux Arts" from *W. H. Auden: Collected Poems* by W. H. Auden, edited by Edward Mendelson Copyright © 1940 and renewed 1968 by W. H. Auden. Reprinted by permission of Random House, Inc. "Rough" from *Selected Poems* by Stephen Spender Copyright © 1934 and renewed 1962 by Stephen Spender. Reprinted by permission of Random House, Inc. "Who's Who" from *W. H. Auden: Collected Poems* by W. H. Auden, edited by Edward Mendelson Copyright © 1937 and renewed 1965 by W. H. Auden. Reprinted by permission of Random House, Inc. **Simon & Schuster, Inc.** "The Lake Isle of Innisfree" and "Adam's Curse." Reprinted with permission of Simon & Schuster, Inc. from *The Poems of W. B. Yeats: A New Edition*, edited by Richard J. Finneran (New York: Macmillan, 1983). "The Man He Killed," "Channel Firing," and "The Darkling Thrush." Reprinted with permission of Simon & Schuster, Inc. from *The Complete Poems of Thomas Hardy*, edited by James Gibson (New York: Macmillan, 1978). "The Second Coming" and "Easter 1916." Reprinted with permission of Simon & Schuster, Inc. from *The Poems of W. B. Yeats: A New Edition*, edited by Richard J. Finneran. Copyright 1924 by Macmillan Publishing Company, renewed 1952 by Bertha Georgie Yeats. **The Society of Authors on behalf of the Estate of Bernard Shaw** *Pygmalion*. © Copyright 1913, 1914, 1916, 1930, 1941, 1944 George Bernard Shaw © Copyright 1957 The Public Trustee as Executor of the Estate of George Bernard Shaw. **Virginia Barber Literary Agency, Inc.** Copyright Alice Munro, 1946 **Wallace Literary Agency, Inc.** "Heat" by Jean Rhys, from *The Collected Short Stories* published W. W. Norton & Company, 1987. Copyright © by Jean Rhys. Use by permission of the Wallace Literary Agency, Inc. **W.W. Norton & Company, Inc.** Reprinted from *Beowulf* translated by E. Talbot Donaldson, with the permission of W. W. Norton & Company, Inc. Copyright © 1966 by W. W. Norton & Company, Inc.

Every effort has been made to trace the ownership of all copyrighted selections found in this book. Omissions brought to our attention will be corrected in subsequent editions.